Contents

1 LOCATION
Town listed alphabetically within county

2 MAP REFERENCE
Map page number followed by a 2-figure National Grid reference (see also page 7)

3 HOTEL NAME
Where the name appears in *italic* type the information that follows has not been confirmed by the establishment for 2010

4 GRADING
Hotels are listed in star rating and merit score order within each location (for full explanation of ratings and awards see page 26)
★ Star rating
% Merit score
◉ Rosette award

5 TYPE OF HOTEL
(see opposite)

6 HOTEL LOGO
If a symbol appears here it represents a hotel group or consortium (See pages 31-37)

7 PICTURE
Optional photograph supplied by establishment

8 ADDRESS AND CONTACT DETAILS

9 DIRECTIONS
Brief details of how to find the hotel

10 DESCRIPTION
Written by the AA inspector at the time of the last visit

11 ROOMS
Number of rooms and prices (see page 6)

12 FACILITIES
Additional facilities including those for children and for leisure activities

13 CONFERENCE
Conference facilities as available (see page 6)

14 NOTES
Additional information (see pages 6-7)

| 1 | GULWORTHY | Map 3 SX47 | 2 |

Horn of Plenty
★★★ 85% ◉◉◉ HOTEL

LOGO

☎ 01822 832528   ▤ 01822 834390
PL19 8JD
e-mail: enquiries@thehornofplenty.co.uk
web: www.thehornofplenty.co.uk
dir: from Tavistock take A390 W for 3m. Right at Gulworthy Cross. In 400yds turn left, hotel in 400yds on right

With stunning views over the Tamar Valley, The Horn of Plenty maintains its reputation as one of Britain's best country-house hotels. The bedrooms are well equipped and have many thoughtful extras with the garden rooms offering impressive levels of comfort and quality. Cuisine here is also impressive and local produce provides interesting and memorable dining.

Rooms 10 (6 annexe) (3 fmly) (4 GF)
S £110-£190; **D** £120-£200 (incl. bkfst)*
Facilities New Year
Conf Class 20 Board 16 Thtr 28 **Parking** 25
Notes Closed 24-26 Dec Civ Wed 80

The
Hotel Guide
2010

AA Lifestyle Guides

43rd edition September 2009.
First published by the Automobile Association as the Hotel and Restaurant Guide, 1967
© AA Media Limited 2009. AA Media Limited retains the copyright in the current edition © 2009 and in all subsequent editions, reprints and amendments to editions. The information contained in this directory is sourced entirely from the AA Media Limited's information resources. All rights reserved. No part of this publication may be reproduced, stored in a retrieval system, or transmitted in any form or by any means - electronic, photocopying, recording or otherwise - unless the written permission of the publishers has been obtained beforehand. This book may not be sold, resold, hired out or otherwise disposed of by way of trade in any form of binding or cover other than that with which it is published, without the prior consent of all relevant publishers. The contents of this publication are believed correct at the time of printing. Nevertheless, the publishers cannot be held responsible for any errors or omissions or for any changes in the details given in this guide or for the consequences of any reliance on the information provided by the same. This does not affect your statutory rights. Assessments of AA inspected establishments are based on the experience of the Hotel and Restaurant Inspectors on the occasion(s) of their visit(s) and therefore descriptions given in this guide necessarily contain an element of subjective opinion which may not reflect or dictate a reader's own opinion on another occasion. See 'AA Star Classification' in the preliminary section for a clear explanation of how, based on our Inspectors' inspection experiences, establishments are graded. If the meal or meals experienced by an Inspector or Inspectors during an inspection fall between award levels the restaurant concerned may be awarded the lower of any award levels considered applicable. AA Media Limited strives to ensure accuracy of the information in this guide at the time of printing. Due to the constantly evolving nature of the subject matter the information is subject to change. AA Media Limited will gratefully receive any advice from our readers of any necessary updated information. Please contact:
Advertising Sales Department: advertisingsales@theAA.com
Editorial Department: lifestyleguides@theAA.com
AA Hotel Scheme Enquiries: 01256 844455

AA Media Limited would like to thank the following photographers, companies and picture libraries for their assistance in the preparation of this book.
Abbreviations for the picture credits are as follows: (t) top; (b) bottom; (l) left; (r) right; (c) centre; (AA) AA World Travel Library.
Front Cover (t) Sheffield Park Hotel; (bl) Gidleigh Park; (br) Fownes Hotel;
Back Cover (l) Verzon House; (c) Swinton Park; (r) Malmaison Hotels.
Every effort has been made to trace the copyright holders, and we apologise in advance for any accidental errors. We would be happy to apply any corrections in the following edition of this publication.

Typeset/Repro: Servis Filmsetting Ltd, Manchester
Printed and bound by Graficas Estella, Spain
This directory is compiled by AA Lifestyle Guides; managed in the Librios Information Management System and generated by the AA establishment database system.

Published by AA Publishing, a trading name of AA Media Limited, whose registered office is Fanum House, Basing View, Basingstoke, Hampshire RG21 4EA.
Registered number 06112600
A CIP catalogue record for this book is available from the British Library
ISBN-13: 978-0-7495-6284-7
A03987

Maps prepared by the Mapping Services Department of AA Publishing.

Maps © AA Media Limited 2009.

 This product includes mapping data licensed from Ordnance Survey® with the permission of the Controller of Her Majesty's Stationery Office. © Crown copyright 2009. All rights reserved. Licence number 100021153.

 Land & Property Services. This is based upon Crown Copyright and is reproduced with the permission of Land & Property Services under delegated authority from the Controller of Her Majesty's Stationery Office.
© Crown copyright and database rights 2009 Licence number 100,363. Permit number 90027

Republic of Ireland mapping based on © Ordnance Survey Ireland/Government of Ireland
Copyright Permit number MP000109

Information on National Parks in England provided by the Countryside Agency (Natural England).
Information on National Parks in Scotland provided by Scottish Natural Heritage.
Information on National Parks in Wales provided by The Countryside Council for Wales.

KEY TO SYMBOLS AND ABBREVIATIONS	
★	Black stars
★	Red stars – indicate AA Inspectors' Choice
◉	AA Rosettes – indicate an AA award for food
	For full explanation of AA ratings and awards
	see page 26
%	Inspector's Merit score (see page 6)
A	Associate Hotels (see this page)
O	Hotel due to open during the currency
	of the guide
U	Star rating not confirmed (see this page)
Fmly	Number of family rooms available
GF	Ground floors rooms available
Smoking	Number of bedrooms allocated for smokers
pri facs	Bedroom with separate private facilities
	(Restaurant with Rooms only)
S	Single room
D	Double room
✳	2009 prices
fr	From
incl. bkfst	Breakfast included in the price
FTV	Freeview
STV	Satellite television
Wi-fi	Wireless network connection
Air con	Air conditioning
⊘	Heated indoor swimming pool
⌁	Outdoor swimming pool
⌁	Heated outdoor swimming pool
♫	Entertainment
Child facilities	Children's facilities (see page 6)
Xmas/New Year	Special programme for Christmas/New Year
♞	Tennis court
⚘	Croquet lawn
⚑	Golf course
CONF	Conference facilities
Thtr	Number of theatre style seats
Class	Number of classroom style seats
Board	Number of boardroom style seats
⊗	No dogs allowed (guide dogs for the
	blind and assist dogs should be allowed)
No children	Children cannot be accommodated
RS	Restricted opening time
Civ Wed	Establishment licensed for civil weddings
	(+ maximum number of guests at ceremony)
LB	Special leisure breaks available
Spa	Hotel has its own spa

TYPES OF HOTEL

The majority of establishments in this guide come under the category of Hotel; other categories are listed below.

TOWN HOUSE HOTEL A small, individual city or town centre property, which provides a high degree of personal service and privacy

COUNTRY HOUSE HOTEL These are quietly located in a rural area

SMALL HOTEL Has fewer than 20 bedrooms and is owner-managed

METRO HOTEL A hotel in an urban location that does not offer an evening meal

BUDGET HOTEL These are usually purpose built modern properties offering inexpensive accommodation. Often located near motorways and in town or city centres

RESTAURANT WITH ROOMS This category of accommodation is now assessed under the AA's Guest Accommodation scheme, therefore, although they continue to have an entry in this guide, we do not include their star rating. Most Restaurants with Rooms have been awarded AA Rosettes for their food and the rooms will meet the required AA standard. For more detailed information about any Restaurant with Rooms please consult The AA Bed and Breakfast Guide or see **theAA.com**

A These are establishments that have not been inspected by the AA but which have been inspected by the national tourist boards in Britain and Northern Ireland. An establishment marked as "Associate" has paid to belong to the AA Associate Hotel Scheme and therefore receives a limited entry in the guide. Descriptions of these hotels can be found on the AA website.*

U A small number of hotels in the guide have this symbol because their star classification was not confirmed at the time of going to press. This may be due to a change of ownership or because the hotel has only recently joined the AA rating scheme.

O These hotels were not open at the time of going to press, but will open in late 2009, or in 2010.

* Check the AA website **theAA.com** for current information and ratings

Merit Score (%)

AA inspectors supplement their reports with an additional quality assessment of everything the hotel provides, including hospitality, based on their findings as a 'mystery guest'. This wider ranging quality assessment results in an overall Merit Score which is shown as a percentage beside the hotel name. When making your selection of hotel accommodation this enables you to see at a glance that a three star hotel with a Merit Score of 79% offers a higher standard overall than one in the same star classification but with a Merit Score of 69%. To gain AA recognition, a hotel must achieve a minimum score of 50%.

AA Awards

Every year the AA presents a range of awards to the finest AA-inspected and rated hotels from England, Scotland, Wales and the Republic of Ireland. The Hotel of the Year is our ultimate accolade and is awarded to those hotels that are recognised as outstanding examples in their field. Often innovative, the winning hotels always set high standards in hotel keeping. The winners for 2009-2010 are listed on pages 8-11.

Rooms

Each entry shows the total number of en suite rooms available (this total will include any annexe rooms). The total number may be followed by a breakdown of the type of rooms available, i.e. the number of annexe rooms; number of family rooms (fmly); number of ground-floor rooms (GF); number of rooms available for smokers.

Bedrooms in an annexe or extension are only noted if they are at least equivalent in quality to those in the main building, but facilities and prices may differ. In some hotels all bedrooms are in an annexe or extension.

Prices

Prices are per room per night and are provided by the hoteliers in good faith. These prices are indications and not firm quotations. ✳ indicates 2009 prices. Perhaps due to the economic climate at the time we were collecting the data for this guide, fewer hotels were willing to tell us their room prices for 2010. Many hotels have introduced special rates so it is worth looking at their websites for the latest information.

Payment

As most hotels now accept credit or debit cards we only indicate if an establishment does not accept any cards for payment. Credit cards may be subject to a surcharge – check when booking if this is how you intend to pay. Not all hotels accept travellers' cheques.

Children

Child facilities may include baby intercom, baby sitting service, playroom, playground, laundry, drying/ironing facilities, cots, high chairs or special meals. In some hotels children can sleep in parents' rooms at no extra cost – check when booking.

If 'No children' is indicated a minimum age may be also given e.g. No children 4yrs would mean no children under 4 years of age would be accepted.

Some hotels, although accepting children, may not have any special facilities for them so it is well worth checking before booking.

Leisure breaks

Some hotels offer special leisure breaks, and these prices may differ from those quoted in this guide and the availability may vary through the year.

Parking

We indicate the number of parking spaces available for guests. This may include covered parking. Please note that some hotels make a charge to use their car park.

Civil Weddings (Civ Wed)

Indicates that the establishment holds a civil wedding licence, and we indicate the number of guests that can be accommodated at the ceremony.

Conference Facilities

We include three types of meeting layouts – Theatre, Classroom and Boardroom style and include the maximum number of delegates for each. The price shown is the maximum 24-hour rate per delegate. Please note that as arrangements vary between a hotel and a business client, VAT may or may not be included in the price quoted in the guide. We also show if Wi-fi connectivity is available, but please check with the hotel that this is suitable for your requirements.

Dogs

Although many hotels allow dogs, they may be excluded from some areas of the hotel and some breeds, particularly those requiring an exceptional licence, may not be acceptable at all. Under the Disability Discrimination Act 1995 access should be allowed for guide dogs and assistance dogs. Please check the hotel's policy when making your booking.

Entertainment (♫)

This indicates that live entertainment should be available at least once a week all year. Some hotels provide live entertainment only in summer or on special occasions – check when booking.

Hotel logos

If an establishment belongs to a hotel group or consortium their logo is included in their entry and these are listed on pages 31-37.

Map references

Each town is given a map reference – the map page number and a two-figure map reference based on the National Grid. For example: **Map 05 SU 48**:

05 refers to the page number of the map section at back of the guide

SU is the National Grid lettered square (representing 100,000sq metres) in which the location will be found

4 is the figure reading across the top or bottom of the map page

8 is the figure reading down at each side of the map page

Restricted service

Some hotels have restricted service (RS) during quieter months, usually during the winter months, and at this time some of the listed facilities will not be available. If your booking is out-of-season, check with the hotel and enquire specifically.

Smoking regulations

If a bedroom has been allocated for smokers, the hotel is obliged to clearly indicate that this is the case. If either the freedom to smoke, or to be in a non-smoking environment is important to you, please check with the hotel when you book.

Spa

For the purposes of this guide the word **Spa** in an entry indicates that the hotel has its own spa which is either managed by themselves or outsourced to an external management company. Facilities will vary but will include a minimum of two treatment rooms. Any specific details are also given, and these are as provided to us by the establishment (i.e. steam room, beauty therapy etc).

ENGLAND

FEVERSHAM ARMS HOTEL & VERBENA SPA
HELMSLEY, NORTH YORKSHIRE

★★★★ 80% ◉◉

Originally a coaching inn once owned by the Earl of Faversham. Today the decor is an eclectic mix of country chic and modern design using warm inviting colours and quality textiles and furnishings. Owner Simon Rhatigan has spent a lifetime in the hospitality industry and it shows; he has made investment not only in the property but in his people too. Guests will receive a genuinely warm welcome and professional service from the dedicated team.

The contemporary, individually designed bedrooms and suites are fabulous, and range from smaller studio doubles through to suites with access to the pool or garden. The sky-lit restaurant offers an award-winning modern British menu that relies heavily on local produce be it game from Yorkshire estates or fish caught in the North Sea.

The new Verbena Spa, linked to the hotel by a glass bridge, is the perfect venue for rejuvinating the mind and body.

LONDON

THE CONNAUGHT HOTEL
LONDON W1

★★★★★ ◉◉◉◉

For over a hundred years this iconic hotel has welcomed guests through its doors, and now, having emerged from a multi-million pound refurbishment, it looks spectacular. Original features have been skilfully restored to blend seamlessly with the luxurious interiors created by leading designers.

The sumptuous suites and elegant bedrooms retain their period grandeur and are elegantly furnished in soft, muted shades, with the finest linen, cashmere blankets and damask drapes; the marble bathrooms have deep tubs, power showers and flat-screen TVs. There's even a personal butler on call 24 hours a day.

There are several eating options, but the award-winning and inspired cuisine of talented head chef Hélène Darroze is outstanding. All the friendly and extremely professional staff will ensure that anyone staying here is made to feel a special and honoured guest.

SCOTLAND

THE GLENEAGLES HOTEL
AUCHTERARDER, PERTH & KINROSS

★★★★★ ❀❀❀❀

World famous Gleneagles is a 5-star resort set in 850 acres of glorious Scottish countryside and probably best known for being home to three championship golf courses and a wide range of exhilarating outdoor pursuits.

Everything here is at the top of its game from the luxury bedrooms and suites through to the choices of restaurants. There are 26 individually designed, sumptuously appointed suites in addition to the 232 luxury bedrooms. Guests are spoilt for choice when it comes to eating – there's Andrew Fairlie's eponymous restaurant, awarded 4 AA Rosettes, Strathearn Restaurant with 2 Rosettes and the smart new Deseo 'Mediterranean Food Market' eaterie. Not to mention the Clubhouse and the many bars. In addition to the golf there's an almost never ending list of leisure activities and country pursuits to enjoy. The ESPA Spa at the hotel has received many accolades, and it's no wonder as once through the doors the calm atmosphere ensures relaxation, and the endless list of the very latest treatments cannot fail to restore the body and soul.

WALES

PENMAENUCHAF HALL HOTEL   WELSH RAREBITS
DOLLGELLAU, GWYNEDD

★★★ ❀❀

Set in the beautiful Snowdonia National Park, Penmaenuchaf Hall is a magnificent Victorian country house surrounded by impeccably presented gardens, just the place to get away from it all. A very warm welcome awaits guests here as Mark Watson and Lorraine Fielding and their staff make every effort to make you feel at ease. The interior retains the grandeur of the age in which it was built with oak-panelled rooms, original fireplaces and Welsh slate floors. Commanding delightful views over the valley to the mountains beyond, the individually designed bedrooms are luxuriously appointed with charming fabrics and furnishings. 21st-century technology is evident too with satellite TV and internet access included.

The elegant conservatory restaurant has a contemporary look and is a delightful place to enjoy the award-winning cuisine, especially when candlelit in the evening.

REPUBLIC OF IRELAND

MOUNT FALCON COUNTRY HOUSE HOTEL
BALLINA, CO. MAYO

★★★★ 81%, ❀❀

In the west of Ireland on the banks of the River Moy is this delightful country house hotel situated in 100 acres of wooded grounds. Substantial refurbishment by the new owners has resulted in a place of real luxury and great charm, offering visitors the chance for total relaxation, with golf courses, horse riding and beaches all nearby.

Fishermen might well beat a path to the door as the hotel has exclusive salmon fishing rights on two miles (both banks) of the river and there's a 3-acre spring fed lake full of rainbow trout.

The bedrooms, ranging from superior, deluxe and suites are superbly appointed and feature high ceilings, antique furniture, marble fireplaces and wooden floors. The award-winning restaurant is located where the old kitchen once was.

VON ESSEN HOTELS

The Von Essen group has grown substantially over the last five years and now has a portfolio of 27 hotels in England, Scotland and Wales. They include stunning properties in amazing locations ranging from grand mansions and castles to small country houses. To guide potential guests, the group has divided their UK establishments into four categories: Classic, Country, Family and Metropolitan.

All the hotels have been awarded two or three AA Rosettes for their cuisine, and twelve have achieved AA red star status making them amongst the very best hotels in the country. Their newest venture is a 70 bedroom, Thames-side hotel in Battersea which will open within the next year. Substantial investment over the years by this group has seen impressive results and anyone staying at a Von Essen hotel will certainly experience a touch of luxury.

Classic

Historic buildings combining elegant tradition with 21st century amenities.

CLIVEDEN, Taplow, Buckinghamshire
SHARROW BAY, Howtown, Cumbria
THE SAMLING, Winderemere, Cumbria
BUCKLAND MANOR, Buckland, Gloucestershire
LOWER SLAUGHTER MANOR, Lower Slaughter, Gloucestershire
THORNBURY CASTLE, Thornbury, Gloucestershire
THE ROYAL CRESCENT, Bath, Somerset
STON EASTON PARK, Ston Easton, Somerset
AMBERLEY CASTLE, Amberley, West Sussex
YNYSHIR HALL, Eglwys Fach, Ceredigion

Country

Country house hotels in beautiful grounds, each with its own character.

SEAHAM HALL HOTEL, Seaham, County Durham
CALLOW HALL, Ashbourne, Derbyshire
LEWTRENCHARD MANOR, Lewdown, Devon
THE GREENWAY, Cheltenham, Gloucestershire
WASHBOURNE COURT HOTEL, Lower Slaughter, Gloucestershire
NEW PARK MANOR, Brockenhurst, Hampshire
CONGHAM HALL, Grimston, Norfolk
HOMEWOOD PARK HOTEL, Hinton Charterhouse, Somerset
MOUNT SOMERSET, Taunton, Somerset
HUNSTRETE HOUSE HOTEL, Hunstrete, Somerset
BISHOPSTROWE HOUSE, Warminster, Wiltshire
DALHOUSIE CASTLE AND AQUEOUS SPA, Edinburgh

Family

Hotels with special facilities for children including Ofsted registered crèches, baby sitting, baby listening and outdoor activities.

FOWEY HALL, Fowey, Cornwall
MOONFLEET MANOR, Weymouth, Dorset
THE ICKWORTH HOTEL & APARTMENTS, Horringer, Suffolk
WOOLLEY GRANGE, Bradford-on-Avon, Wiltshire
THE ELMS HOTEL & RESTAURANT, Abberley, Worcestershire

Metropolitan

HOTEL VERTA, London SW11 *(due to open 2010)*

EXCLUSIVE HOTELS

This is a privately owned group of just four hotels situated in the south of England which maintains the highest standards, and continues to invest in innovative refurbishment programmes. All the hotels are impressive grand houses surrounded by stunning gardens and parkland and may offer golf, fishing, shooting, tennis and spa facilities as ways to relax. As you would expect with these top rated hotels the accommodation is exceptional whether it be in one of the individually designed Suites, Junior Suites or Guest Rooms.

South Lodge Hotel in particular has seen impressive changes with the addition of 40 new bedrooms and new public areas. The Pass, a mini-restaurant within the kitchen itself, is an exciting new eating option at the hotel, and has already been awarded three AA Rosettes.

Superb, award-winning cuisine is to be found at the other hotels in this group too, and anyone staying overnight would be wise to eat in.

Head chef Michael Wignall has made The Latymer restaurant, with 4 AA Rosettes, a true dining destination – dedicated food lovers will certainly appreciate the complexity of his cooking skills. If guests wish to escape the stresses and strains of a hectic lifestyle then Pennyhill Park might just have the answer. Their spa is second to none in offering a state-of-the-art gym and studio; 21 rooms for a myriad of rejuvenating and beauty treatments; and Ozone Ecstasy with no less than eight indoor and outdoor pools.

LAINSTON HOUSE HOTEL, Winchester, Hampshire
PENNYHILL PARK HOTEL & THE SPA, Bagshot, Surrey
SOUTH LODGE HOTEL, Lower Beeding, West Sussex
MANOR HOUSE HOTEL AND GOLF CLUB
Castle Combe, Wiltshire

Family OWNED HOTELS

By **Mark Hayes**

In North Wales, you'll meet a man who used to cook guests lunch in his rugby kit. On the Isle of Skye you'll find someone who came from the other Sky, the broadcaster. And in London you may feel grateful you weren't there 100 years ago, when your knickers could have gone flying out through the roof.

Welcome to the sometimes quirky, often delightful world of the family-run hotel. The best of these establishments treat guests as people rather than punters, try to remember their foibles as well as their names, and generally fuss over them as if they were part of an extended family.

As Andrew Beale of Beales Hotels says, many people would never want to stay in a chain hotel or modern roadside lodge and will seek out individuality and distinctiveness. Such guests develop loyalty to those who've pampered them, and this is proving a godsend in providing repeat custom to help family-run hotels through the recession.

But is there a downside in the form of family feuds, set off by the tension of family members working so closely together? Well, not really. We spoke to hoteliers across Great Britain and Ireland and found that they tend to get on rather well with their family. But then it probably takes a patient sort of person to become a good hotelier – after all, they have to spend every day handling the idiosyncrasies and occasional downright weirdness of their guests.

"I was locked away in the kitchen for 10 years"

Martin Bland needed to be quick on his feet when he played for Moseley, Birmingham's premier rugby club, in his youth. He was also fleet of foot in becoming a hotelier. Within weeks of marrying, he and his wife Janette bought a run-down convalescent home in Llandudno, Conwy, converted it into the St Tudno Hotel and opened for business.

That was at Whitsun, 1972. There was no telephone in the hotel, so they had to use a callbox on the promenade. Neither were there any dining chairs on opening day, but by day two that had been sorted

out and the hotel was full of guests, some of whom returned only two weeks later.

"One of the reasons I married Janette is I thought she was a good cook, and I thought she was going to do all the cooking," Martin jokes, "but it was me. I ended up in the kitchen and I was locked away there for 10 years."

The 18-bedroom hotel offered full board, with lunch at £1.50 extra, and with Martin now playing for Llandudno Rugby Club he would often prepare Saturday lunch in his kit so he could dash off to the match afterwards.

Martin's three daughters have all worked in the hotel, but all now live in London and "realise it's too much hard work" to be hoteliers. Janette, who was awarded an MBE in 1999 for services to tourism, passed away in 2005, and with Martin now 65 his thoughts have started to turn to selling up and retiring.

But in the meantime he enjoys chatting to the guests, having long been allowed out of the kitchen. He checks them all in, then when they're leaving he waits until ▷

Opposite: Kinloch Lodge Hotel, Isle of Skye

Below: St Tudno Hotel & Restaurant, Llandudno

**Above: The Fitzpatrick Scott –
Lennon family**

**Left: Andrew and Edward Beale,
West Lodge Park, Hadley Wood**

Right top: Fitzpatrick Castle, Killiney

until they have looked over the bill
and are about to pay before swooping
downstairs to say goodbye. "I race
everywhere – I'm very fit, I have to be,"
he says, his sports background still in
evidence.

**"If you don't know what you're talking
about you get crucified by the staff"**
Andrew Beale, managing director of
Beales Hotels, is the third generation
of hotelkeepers in his family. His
grandfather, Edward, bought West Lodge
Park in Hadley Wood, Hertfordshire, in
1945 and lived at the hotel.

"Edward never retired, he was the one
who knows everything and can't bear to
give it up, and remained chairman of the
company until he was 85. He died aged
94 still deeply interested in the business
day by day, whereas my father, Trevor,
had 40 years with the firm and on his
65th birthday said, 'That's it, I'm off.'"

Andrew wants to walk a line between
those extremes. "A family business has
more emotion tied up in it than if you
were just turning up for work," he says.
"There's more baggage and history, but
as long as you can get past all of that
then it should and could be an enjoyable

thing to be able to work with family
members."

Andrew is in his 40s and has no
intention of leaving any time soon.
But when he does he has five children
who could take over, as well as a host
of cousins – as long as they follow his
example and get thoroughly trained first.

It's the only way to gain the respect of
the harshest critics – the staff. "If you're
perceived as a shoo-in, daddy's boy or
daddy's girl, they see through that in two
seconds. You either know what you're
talking about or you don't, and if you don't
you get crucified by the staff," he warns.

"It was a huge thing to buy my minority shareholders out of the business"

You may spot Bono, the singer from U2, enjoying a drink at the bar. "We have a lot of celebrity guests living close by," explains Eithne Fitzpatrick Scott-Lennon, owner of Fitzpatrick Castle in the upmarket Dublin suburb of Killiney, overlooking Dublin Bay.

The property now has 113 bedrooms, 11 suites and an array of leisure facilities, but it was "a veritable wreck with no more than 11 rooms" when Eithne's father and mother bought it in the early 1970s. Eithne and her four brothers have all worked there, but four years ago, after her father Paddy's death, Eithne took the decision to buy out her siblings.

"That took a lot of bravery on my part," she says. "It was a huge thing to take on, to refinance and to buy my minority shareholders out of the business."

Thanks to her father's careful succession planning, Eithne's siblings all had their own careers to follow. Two of her brothers have, like her, become hoteliers. John owns the Fitzpatrick Manhattan and the Fitzpatrick Grand Central hotels in New York, while Paul owns The Morgan and The Beacon hotels in Dublin. The other two brothers are builders and developers, whose advice comes in handy when maintaining a building the size of Fitzpatrick Castle.

Eithne and her husband James have four sons and are themselves starting the process of succession planning. One of their offspring, 21-year-old Mark Scott-Lennon, has chosen to do a masters degree in hospitality management so there is at least one potential third-generation hotelier in the family.

"I've said to mum I'll do the flowers, but she won't let me"

Guests often can't tell Vivienne Bess and her sister Hilary Caldwell apart. "We're quite similar to look at and that causes guests some amusement because they don't know who they're talking to," Vivienne explains.

The pair own the 17th century, 32-bedroom Royal Glen Hotel in Sidmouth, Devon. It was home to them both until they were teenagers and before that to their parents, grandparents and great grandmother, the formidable-sounding Grandma Webber, who started off this fourth-generation business in the early 1920s.

Fortuitously for Vivienne and Hilary's marketing efforts the hotel has also been home to Queen Victoria – it's where she spent her first Christmas when she was six months old.

The sisters' mother, Jean, and father, Orson, still help out even though they're in their 80s. "It was their life for so long they can't stay away, which can be ▷

Above: Vivienne Bess and Hilary Caldwell, Royal Glen Hotel, Sidmouth

good and bad. Dad comes in every day to chat to the guests and mum does the flowers. She cuts them from her garden and arranges them in the restaurant – every table has flowers. I've said to mum I'll do the flowers, but she won't let me." Has the strain of working with family ever become too much? "We haven't really had tiffs," Vivienne replies. "I don't think my sister and I have ever had a really bad row. Well, I'm bossy and she's not, you see. With our parents it was quite a tie to tell them to do less and tell dad he wasn't in charge, but we finally got there."

"We get a lot of enjoyment out of it"

Many London-based couples escape the city once they have children, but few get the opportunity to relocate to somewhere as beautiful as Skye. Isabella Macdonald and her husband Tom were doubly lucky – they also got to take over 14-bedroom Kinloch Lodge hotel.

Isabella's parents, Godfrey and Claire Macdonald, had taken on the hotel about 36 years ago. He is High Chief of Clan Donald and was born on Skye; the hotel, originally a shooting lodge, had always been in his family. Claire, meanwhile, spent her time at Kinloch becoming a well-known cookery writer and champion of Scottish food, and her name is still prominent in the hotel's marketing.

Isabella appreciates her luck in taking over seven years ago: "I feel very fortunate that we've picked up the reins on a hotel that already had an internationally recognised brand. But guests' expectations have changed so much over the years that one always has to be thinking ahead and adding special tweaks and being aware of what other hotels are doing. It certainly isn't easy, I can assure anyone that it's not."

Left: Goring Hotel, London

Right: Jeremy Goring

Things are obviously going the right way, with the hotel being promoted to red star status this year, and chef Marcello Tully earning his third AA Rosette for the restaurant.

Tom used to be a reporter for Sky Sports, while Isabella worked in the press office at British Airways. He now looks after the hotel's finances and its alcoholic offerings, while she takes care of "everything else". And they seem to love it. "Obviously it has stresses because we're living within the hotel," Isabella says, "but there's the love, the hospitality side of life, looking after our guests. We're very lucky, we have really wonderful people who come and stay here and we get a lot of enjoyment out of it."

"I'd like to feel that we're still young, a bit of a whippersnapper"

It will be time to celebrate at the Goring Hotel in London as it marks its centenary in 2010 – and time to tell colourful stories about Otto Richard Goring, the German emigrée who built the place on a derelict site near the back gates of Buckingham Palace.

Such as the tale of how his innovative mind came up with the idea of installing a

form of air conditioning. "There was a big fan on the roof and tubes going through the hotel, with an inlet in every ceiling," explains Jeremy Goring, Otto's great-grandson. "If you threw your knickers in the air in passion one night and they got anywhere near this hole in the ceiling they would fly out through the roof."

The system also meant that maids could plug a tube into a hole in the skirting and suck all the dust out of each room. The holes are still there, hidden by brass caps.

Jeremy took over the hotel in 2005 from his father, George, who had run it for 43 years. "I had a one-hour handover with him, he gave me two keys and then went horse riding and boating for three months," Jeremy says. "It was very gutsy of him to draw a line under his reign. I've seen cases where that hasn't happened and I've seen the damage done. You get a mish-mash and conflict."

Jeremy has spent about £20 million in the past five years on refurbishing all 71 of the bedrooms, but he says the best is still to come: "We have 100 years of history, but I'd like to feel that we're not as great as we're going to be – that we're still young, a bit of a whippersnapper." □

What it means to be independent

"It's alien to me some of these hotels where the managers call their guests punters. They barely ever see them. I couldn't do that, it's like a different profession. I get to meet everybody, and I have wonderful guests. That's been the thing over the years that's kept us going and made it enjoyable."
- Martin Bland, St Tudno Hotel & Restaurant, Llandudno

"The difference between a family-run hotel and a group-owned one is most seen in the staff – they're more secure, more nurtured, longer serving and there are probably more of them. I know a lot of group hotels and they're stripped to the bone in staffing – it's just a numbers game, not a customer-care game."
- Andrew Beale, Beales Hotels

"I want guests to feel they're coming into somebody's house. I want them to lie by the fire if that's what they want, to lie on the sofa and read their book. I don't ever want it to be stuffy and formal. We have three lovely big drawing rooms full of family memorabilia, and people love the family feel."
- Isabella Macdonald, Kinloch Lodge, Isle of Skye

"It's a grey old world and everything is becoming homogenised. I think our job as an independent hotel is to rage against that, even when it doesn't make 100 per cent business sense, because people crave something a bit individual."
- Jeremy Goring, The Goring, London SW1

AHH...

Nights spent in luxury five-star resorts, leisurely afternoon teas, aperitifs followed by three-course dinners with wine, room service, cooked breakfasts, weight gain, lack of exercise, sleep deprivation, loneliness.

the life of an AA hotel inspector

By **Fiona Griffiths**

"Everyone thinks this is the dream job, but you're on the road away from family, friends and colleagues for four nights a week, so it's quite a lonely existence. I've been with my partner for 16 years and when I started this job I'd always been at home and it was very hard for him to accept I was going to be away four nights a week," says Giovanna Grossi, AA Hotel Services Group Area Manager.

"Unfortunately you have to eat in this job too – I've had to get a whole new wardrobe because I've put on five stone since I started. I've also got a personal trainer now because as you get older you have to think to yourself 'I've gone up quite a few dress sizes, this isn't healthy'."

But Giovanna isn't complaining. Although she has a degree in accountancy, she grew up working in her father's Italian restaurant in Southport and is driven by a real desire to raise standards in the hospitality industry.

Passion for the industry
"I am absolutely passionate about this industry and I believe to do this job well and for a long period of time you have to be passionate. It's certainly not a 9-5 job – you have to be prepared to order room service at midnight and go and test the leisure facilities at 6am because that necessity is there to fit everything in.

"You also have to love food and be prepared to eat anything, be it offal or food from different cultures."

And eat food we did when I joined Giovanna on one of her undercover inspections – at the Malmaison Charterhouse Square in the City of London.

As always, the staff didn't know Giovanna was coming (she books under another name) and they certainly didn't know I was there to shadow her and find out exactly what goes into producing those shiny new AA hotel and restaurant guides every autumn.

In fact, our identities were kept a secret until after the bill had been settled and we'd checked out the following morning.

The eating begins
The eating began almost straight away, when we headed downstairs to the bar for tea and sandwiches.

Malmaison's funky bar snacks menu didn't offer anything so traditional as a sandwich, but after a brief discussion with a member of staff, Giovanna managed to order exactly what she wanted – a tuna sandwich.

I say 'wanted' but that's not strictly the case. She'd had a large breakfast at the previous inspection hotel – a five-star in the West End – and that three-course dinner was looming ever closer, but it had to be done.

Over tea Giovanna told me more about her week. She'd driven down from her home in Manchester to stay in a four-star in the Midlands on Monday, a three-star ▷

Left: Malmaison Liverpool
Below: Malmaison Aberdeen

Above: Malmaison Belfast
Right: A Malmaison gym

in Norfolk on Tuesday and a five-star in Suffolk on Wednesday.

"The week before I did a two-star and two guest houses. Every week is different. You could be in a coastal B&B one night and a corporate chain hotel the next.

"You have to be a chameleon. The minute you walk through the door of a property you have to start thinking the way a typical person who would stay there would think."

And you might expect Giovanna to look forward most of all to the nights when she's in a swanky five-star hotel – but not so.

"It's a lot harder work staying in a five-star because you don't stop from the minute you arrive – there are so many areas to test. You have to go to the concierge and say things like 'I want to buy this face cream, do you know where I can get it?' or ask the barman 'can you make this particular cocktail?' There are usually leisure facilities so I have to go and have a swim, I have to test the afternoon tea, and I normally have to do a hot meal room service check."

Of course, staying in five-star hotels does have its advantages though.

"You get lots of nice toiletries in the five-stars, so I often take them home and give some to my family".

However, another hazard of the job is that it can take the enjoyment out of going on holiday a little.

"We have a family home in Italy and a lot of my holidays are spent there because I do get fed up with staying in hotels, although I have to say I do love hotels.

"My partner and I like to have a couple of city breaks a year too. Last year we went to Barcelona where we stayed in a five-star, and I have to say we went to a couple of other hotels while we were there and asked to see some bedrooms – it does become a bit of an obsession."

Inspecting the bedrooms

With the sandwiches virtually eaten it was time to go and stake out the Malmaison's bedrooms, beginning with mine and then Giovanna's.

She left no stone – or pillow, duvet or toilet lid – unturned when it came to a thorough housekeeping and comfort check.

All surfaces, including the phone receiver, were tested for dust, the showerhead was scanned for limescale, curtains were moved, beds pulled out, lighting levels measured, TV tuning checked, and even appliances were plugged in and tested to make sure they worked.

Everything was in working order and looked very clean and shiny; the Malmaison's housekeeping inspection was looking rosy.

Giovanna whipped out her laptop and began feeding in the hotel's scores so far – a figure between one and five which relates to the standards expected of a hotel with that equivalent star rating.

She began by marking overall cleanliness, bedrooms and bathrooms, but there would be scores for food and service to add later.

All the while she referred to her "scoring bible" which explains the services and facilities required for each star banding.

As Malmaison is a group of three-star hotels, Giovanna was looking all the time to make sure the hotel met the minimum requirements for a three-star, but on several fronts the hotel's offer actually fell more into the four-star bracket.

"If they wanted to go to four-star they could but they'd have to implement one or two things, like offering a cooked room service breakfast rather than just continental," she explained.

Time for dinner

I was particularly keen to find out how the restaurant would fare under Giovanna's scrutiny, as she'd heard on the grapevine that the hotel was hoping to increase its one AA Rosette to two.

We met in the lounge for pre-dinner drinks (when one of the bar staff impressed Giovanna with his wine knowledge) before being escorted (another brownie point for service) to our table.

My choice of what to eat was governed by Giovanna's need to test the chef's

competence as much as possible. Thus we ordered the chicken livers and the scallops to start with ("both are very easy to overcook and then they're ruined"), followed by rabbit a la moutarde for me and fried skate cheeks for her.

I would've preferred cheese rather than dessert but again Giovanna needed to test something that had been created rather than "just put together on a plate", so I went for the guanaja chocolate fondant, while she tried the fine apple tart.

On this occasion the kitchen team came up trumps, with all three courses meriting two Rosettes (out of a possible five).

"There has to be consistency through the courses," explained Giovanna.

"If the starter and dessert were two Rosettes but the main course was a clear one, well that's the main part of the meal, so I'd have to go with one Rosette.

"What I'm looking at is clarity of flavours, quality of ingredients, seasoning and timing. It is a snapshot but everybody gets the same opportunity and it's about consistency, so if the restaurant is not quite making it this time, they're not consistently making it."

She added: "If I go to a place and think 'wow, I've had a three Rosette meal here' we will get somebody back – or we might even get two people back – because at that level and above you really do need to see consistency."

Post-check-out debrief

There were certainly no complaints at breakfast the next morning either, following a great night's sleep (something Giovanna really cherishes, having experienced more than her fair share of uncomfortable beds). The cooked breakfast was excellent and the cold buffet selection more akin to four-star standard.

Again the service was excellent, too, but Giovanna was convinced it wasn't because she'd been rumbled.

"In London the hotels get a lot of corporate people staying on their own for one night, so they wouldn't know you were there.

The hotel needed to achieve the minimum scores for a three-star in five areas – service and facilities, cleanliness, food, bedrooms and bathrooms – and it had exceeded last year's results across the board.

Giovanna doesn't always have such good news to tell general managers, but it meant she felt relaxed about handing over her business card and asking to see Anthony Thwaites.

We all sat down together and Giovanna talked him through her "customer care journey" – her experience of being a guest from booking over the telephone through to check out – and then we went on a tour to inspect a few more bedrooms.

Anthony was relieved the inspection had gone so well.

"I'm particularly pleased to hear such good comments about service because you can look great and be stylish, but at the end of the day it all comes down to

I WOULD'VE PREFERRED CHEESE RATHER THAN DESSERT BUT AGAIN GIOVANNA NEEDED TO TEST SOMETHING THAT HAD BEEN CREATED RATHER THAN "JUST PUT TOGETHER ON A PLATE"

"I used to work in the Lake District and the hotels are almost next door to each other and everybody knows everybody else's business. They don't get people in suits staying there – more elderly couples and families – so I very quickly learnt to dress a little bit more casual and swap my laptop case for a holdall."

After breakfast it was back up to the room to finish feeding the hotel's scores into the laptop, and a chance for Giovanna to gather her thoughts before the post-check-out debrief with the general manager.

good service," he said.

"As a hotelier it's great to sit down with someone who has very in-depth criteria and get feedback that's spread out right from reservation to check out. Any feedback is a snapshot but you can use it to your advantage and improve for next time."

On that happy note we all went our separate ways – Anthony to congratulate his staff, Giovanna to Kensington for a lunchtime restaurant inspection, and for me, home, to do some writing and not eat again until dinnertime. □

TIME FOR TEA

Reviving the traditional repast

By Julia Hynard

In times of crisis the British instinctively turn to tea, to stimulate and sustain. As gloom and despondency about the economic downturn sets in, more than ever we need the 1930s MGM-style escapist glamour of a Grand Hotel. While sneak-away weekends, lavish lunches or posh frock dinners might be harder to justify financially, what better antidote to tedious belt tightening could there be than a plate of teatime treats lathered with clotted cream in a magnificent hotel setting?

The Ritz, Claridge's and The Dorchester are classics for traditional teatime splendour. Just to sit in the spectacular Palm Court at The Ritz is an experience in itself with all the proper formalities observed (you'll find no jeans and trainers here). Elegant in exclusive Mayfair is Claridge's, where you might be seated in the art deco foyer or the Reading Room restaurant with its suede walls and leather columns. The Promenade is the tea-spot at The Dorchester, running the length of the ground floor, with marble columns topped by gilded Corinthian capitals, and a live pianist adding to the atmosphere of genteel refinement. It's hard to think of a classier venue to celebrate the most special of occasions.

While the hotel tea room might well be on the grand scale, and even a little intimidating, there is something more comfortable, intimate and relaxed about teatime as an occasion, with echoes of the Victorian nursery and some distance from the seriousness of grown-ups' dinner. Smart dress is *de rigueur*, of course, but you can leave the tiara at home.

Tea in a posh hotel speaks of high days and holidays, a respite from the shops, the museums and the galleries in town or the finale to a fine day out in the country. The afternoon ritual provides an affordable taste of the high life and a much needed fillip in times of austerity. Hotels are offering some great bargains at the moment, which are well worth investigating.

Lunch is for wimps

The afternoon tea experience is generally seen as a social event to be enjoyed with family or friends, but the commercial sector has spotted the advantages of a neutral space in impressive surroundings as an ideal place to do business. The working tea is the new business breakfast, often preferred to the lunchtime rendezvous as there is no alcohol involved (although a glass of champagne is often an option and slips down well with a cucumber sandwich). These days, it seems, you can get the carbs to clinch the deal, particularly when the setting is right.

Tea of excellence

One hotel where tea is taken very seriously is the Black Swan in Helmsley, North Yorkshire. Alison Souter had been working at the hotel for 13 years when she was asked to manage the new Tearoom and Patisserie. Friends and colleagues thought she was an ideal choice as she's always been into her specialist teas. Alison's view was that if she was going to take the job on then she was going to do it properly, and signed herself up for a Masterclass Course run by The Tea Guild. The course she did was at Armathwaite Hall in the Lake District. Here Alison learnt all about the history, production and varieties of tea and has become something of an expert.

Alison has put her training to good use at the Black Swan, researching and sourcing teas with great care from eight separate suppliers, and has even had a house tea specially blended for the hotel. It took six months to come up with the final blend, but when staff tasted it the response was unanimous, 'This is the one!'

There are seven teas in the Black Swan blend – the recipe for which is top ▷

secret – but Alison did disclose that it includes a beautiful Ceylon and a first flush Assam. She says they 'sell heaps of it', and that the majority of her customers are looking for a really good quality tea that can also take milk, though when a customer comes in enquiring about a Darjeeling or Pekoe, Alison is in her element and is always 'delighted to talk about tea'.

When I spoke to Alison she had just heard that the Black Swan has achieved an Award of Excellence from The Tea Guild, a rare achievement, with only nine others granted to hotels outside London. Keen to have the skills and expertise imparted by The Tea Guild available more widely in the north (most of the courses are London based), the Black Swan is soon to host its own Guild Masterclass.

Alison emphasises that the tearoom experience amounts to much more than the beverage itself. You could serve the finest cuppa in the county but it won't bring in the customers unless the setting, food and presentation are also up to standard. The Black Swan keeps very busy serving snacks, light lunches, exquisite patisserie, and full afternoon tea on silver-tiered cake stands.

Left: The Black Swan Inn
Right: The Ritz London

The Tea Guild

The Tea Guild was set up by the United Kingdom Tea Council in 1985 and aims to provide recognition to those establishments that meet their exacting standards for serving tea, as measured by their tea inspectors working incognito. Membership is by invitation only, and once obtained remains subject to regular, secret inspection.

The standards demanded by The Tea Guild are judged on wide ranging criteria: hygiene, décor, crockery, staff attitude, efficiency, sugar, variety of tea, cakes and food, milk type, ambience, value for money, and finally on the preparation, service, appearance, temperature and taste of the actual tea.

'Afternoon Tea - Perfect places for afternoon tea' is published by the AA in association with The Tea Guild and The United Kingdom Tea Council*

Tea – A Potted History

◆ Tea first appeared in this country in the mid 17th century and was introduced to the public, strangely enough, by the coffee houses. So popular was tea, and so great its impact on sales of ale and gin in the taverns, that the government lost significant revenue, so tea was taxed from 1676 and coffee houses had to be licensed. Tax on tea rose to an incredible 119%, leading to a flourishing smuggling trade.

◆ In the 17th and 18th centuries the voyages of the enormous East India Company ships bringing tea to Britain could take up to a year and the Company had a monopoly on the trade. When tea was at last freely traded in the 1830s, the ships first back to shore with the latest harvest did the best business, so the fast, narrow tea clippers were born with their tall masts and abundant sails. The Cutty Sark, built in 1869, was last of the tea clippers and is due to re-open to the public in the summer of 2010 following a long period of conservation.

◆ Anna Russell, Duchess of Bedford, is credited with the invention of afternoon tea in the 1840s. She needed a cup of tea and a little something to fill the hungry gap between luncheon and dinner. The duchess so relished this afternoon refreshment that she invited her friends to join her and the fashion for afternoon tea began, with all its associated paraphernalia of tea pots and tea services. □

Top Hotels for Afternoon Tea

England

Buckinghamshire
Hartwell House Hotel, Aylesbury
Danesfield House Hotel & Spa, Marlow
Macdonald Compleat Angler, Marlow
Cliveden Country House Hotel, Taplow

Cheshire
The Chester Grosvenor & Spa, Chester
Crewe Hall, Crewe
Rookery Hall, Nantwich

Cornwall
Headland Hotel, Newquay

Cumbria
Rothay Manor Hotel, Ambleside
Armathwaite Hall, Bassenthwaite
Lakeside Hotel Lake Windermere, Newby Bridge

Devon
Northcote Manor, Burrington
Saunton Sands Hotel, Saunton
Riviera Hotel, Sidmouth
Thurlestone Hotel, Thurlestone

Dorset
Mortons House Hotel, Corfe Castle
Summer Lodge Country House Hotel, Evershot

Gloucestershire
Buckland Manor, Buckland
Mecure Queen's Hotel, Cheltenham
Lords of the Manor, Upper Slaughter

Hampshire
Audleys Wood, Basingstoke
Montagu Arms Hotel, Beaulieu
Rhinefield House Hotel, Brockenhurst
Chewton Glen Hotel & Spa, New Milton
Tylney Hall Hotel, Rotherwick
Lainston House Hotel, Winchester

Hertfordshire
Down Hall Country House Hotel, Bishop's Stortford

Kent
Brandshatch Place Hotel, Brands Hatch
Chilston Park Hotel, Lenham
The Spa Hotel, Royal Tunbridge Wells

London NW1
The Landmark London

London NW4
Hendon Hall Hotel

London SW1
The Capital
The Goring
Jumeirah Carlton Tower Hotel
Mandarin Oriental Hyde Park, London
Rubens at the Palace
Sofitel London St James

London SW7
The Bentley Hotel
Millennium Gloucester Hotel London Kensington

London W1
Athenaeum Hotel & Apartments
Brown's Hotel
The Chesterfield

Mayfair
Claridge's
The Dorchester
Grosvenor House
Hyatt Regency London – The Churchill
Park Plaza Sherlock Holmes Hotel
The Ritz London

London W8
Royal Garden Hotel

London WC1
The Montague on the Gardens

London WC2
Swissôtel The Howard, London

Manchester
The Lowry Hotel

Norfolk
Congham Hall Country House Hotel, Grimston

Northamptonshire
Fawsley Hall, Fawsley

Northumberland
Matfen Hall, Matfen

Oxfordshire
Old Parsonage Hotel, Oxford

Somerset
The Royal Crescent Hotel, Bath
Ston Easton Park, Ston Easton

Suffolk
Hintlesham Hall, Hintlesham

Surrey
Woodlands Park, Stoke d'Abernon
Nutfield Priory Hotel & Spa, Redhill
Oatlands Park Hotel, Weybridge

Sussex, East
The Grand Hotel, Eastbourne

Ashdown Park Hotel and Country Club, Forest Row
Buxted Park Country House Hotel, Uckfield

Sussex, West
Gravetye Manor Hotel, East Grinstead

Tyne & Wear
Jesmond Dene House, Newcastle upon Tyne

Warwickshire
Ettington Park Hotel, Alderminster
Ardencote Manor Hotel, Claverdon

West Midlands
New Hall, Sutton Coldfield

Wiltshire
Manor House Hotel, Castle Combe

Worcestershire
The Elms & Restaurant, Abberley
Barceló The Lygon Arms, Broadway

Yorkshire, North
Black Swan Hotel, Helmsley
Swinton Park, Masham
Crathorne Hall, Yarm

Scotland

City of Edinburgh
The Balmoral
George Hotel
The Howard
Norton House Hotel, Prestonfield
Sheraton Grand Hotel

City of Glasgow
Hotel du Vin at One Devonshire Gardens

Fife
The Old Course Hotel, St Andrews

Wales

Gwynedd
Seiont Manor Hotel, Caernarfon

Monmouthshire
Angel Hotel, Abergavenny

Powys
Gliffaes Country House Hotel, Crickhowell

Channel Islands

Jersey
Château la Chaire, Rozel
L'Horizon Hotel and Spa, St Brelade

Republic of Ireland

Co Clare
Dromoland Castle, Newmarket-in-Fergus

Co Waterford
Waterford Castle, Waterford

*AA Afternoon Tea £9.99. For further information visit **theAA.com**

AA Assessment

In collaboration with VisitBritain, VisitScotland and VisitWales, the AA developed Common Quality Standards for inspecting and rating accommodation. These standards and rating categories are now applied throughout the British Isles.

Any hotel applying for AA recognition receives an unannounced visit from an AA inspector to check standards. The hotels with full entries in this guide have all paid an annual fee for AA inspection, recognition and rating.

AA inspectors pay as a guest for their inspection visit, they do not accept free hospitality of any kind. Although AA inspectors do not stay overnight at Budget Hotels they do carry out regular visits to verify standards and procedures.

A guide to some of the general expectations for each star classification is as follows:

★ One Star

Polite, courteous staff providing a relatively informal yet competent style of service, available during the day and evening to receive guests

- At least one designated eating area open to residents for breakfast
- If dinner is offered it should be on at least five days a week, with last orders no earlier than 6.30pm
- Television in bedroom
- Majority of rooms en suite, bath or shower room available at all times

★★ Two Star

As for one star, plus

- At least one restaurant or dining room open to residents for breakfast (and for dinner at least five days a week)
- Last orders for dinner no earlier than 7pm
- En suite or private bath or shower and WC

★★★ Three Star

- Management and staff smartly and professionally presented and usually uniformed
- A dedicated receptionist on duty at peak times
- At least one restaurant or dining room open to residents and non-residents for breakfast and dinner whenever the hotel is open
- Last orders for dinner no earlier than 8pm
- Remote-control television, direct-dial telephone
- En suite bath or shower and WC.

★★★★ Four Star

- A formal, professional staffing structure with smartly presented, uniformed staff anticipating and responding to your needs or requests. Usually spacious, well-appointed public areas
- Reception staffed 24 hours by well-trained staff
- Express checkout facilities where appropriate
- Porterage available on request
- Night porter available
- At least one restaurant open to residents and non-residents for breakfast and dinner seven days per week, and lunch to be available in a designated eating area
- Last orders for dinner no earlier than 9pm
- En suite bath with fixed overhead shower and WC

★★★★★ Five Star

- Luxurious accommodation and public areas with a range of extra facilities. First time guests shown to their bedroom
- Multilingual service
- Guest accounts well explained and presented
- Porterage offered
- Guests greeted at hotel entrance, full concierge service provided
- At least one restaurant open to residents and non-residents for all meals seven days per week
- Last orders for dinner no earlier than 10pm
- High-quality menu and wine list
- Evening service to turn down the beds. Remote-control television, direct-dial telephone at bedside and desk, a range of luxury toiletries, bath sheets and robes. En suite bathroom incorporating fixed overhead shower and WC

★ Inspectors' Choice

Each year we select the best hotels in each rating. These hotels stand out as the very best in the British Isles, regardless of style. Red Star hotels appear in highlighted panels throughout the guide. Inspectors' Choice Restaurant with Rooms are establishments that have been awarded the highest accommodation rating under the AA Bed & Breakfast scheme.

restaurants in the UK, the AA identifies over 1,900 as the best. The following is an outline of what to expect from restaurants with AA Rosette Awards.

◉ Excellent local restaurants serving food prepared with care, understanding and skill, using good quality ingredients.

◉◉ The best local restaurants, which aim for and achieve higher standards, better consistency and where a greater precision is apparent in the cooking. There will be obvious attention to the selection of quality ingredients.

◉◉◉ Outstanding restaurants that demand recognition well beyond their local area.

◉◉◉◉ Amongst the very best restaurants in the British Isles, where the cooking demands national recognition.

◉◉◉◉◉ The finest restaurants in the British Isles, where the cooking stands comparison with the best in the world.

Additional information

Hints on booking your stay

It's always worth booking as early as possible, particularly for the peak holiday period from the beginning of June to the end of September. Bear in mind that Easter and other public holidays may be busy too and in some parts of Scotland, the ski season is a peak holiday period.

Some hotels will ask for a deposit or full payment in advance, especially for one-night bookings. And some hotels charge half-board (bed, breakfast and dinner) whether you require the meals or not, while others may only accept full-board bookings. Not all hotels will accept advance bookings for bed and breakfast, overnight or short stays. Some will not take reservations from mid week.

Once a booking is confirmed, let the hotel know at once if you are unable to keep your reservation. If the hotel cannot re-let your room you may be liable to pay about two-thirds of the room price (a deposit will count towards this payment). In Britain a legally binding contract is made when you accept an offer of accommodation, either in writing or by telephone, and illness is not accepted as a release from this contract. You are advised to take out insurance against possible cancellation, for example AA Single Trip Insurance (telephone 0800 085 7240).

Booking online

Locating and booking somewhere to stay can be a time-consuming process, but you can search quickly and easily online for a place that best suits your needs. Simply visit theAA.com to search for full details from around 7,000 quality rated hotels and B&Bs in Great Britain and Ireland. Check availability and click on the 'Book it' button.

Prices

The AA encourages the use of the Hotel Industry Voluntary Code of Booking Practice, which aims to ensure that guests know how much they will have to pay and what services and facilities are included, before entering a financially binding agreement. If the price has not previously been confirmed in writing, guests should be given a card stipulating the total obligatory charge when they register at reception.

The Tourism (Sleeping Accommodation Price Display) Order of 1977 compels hotels, travel accommodation, guest houses, farmhouses, inns and self-catering accommodation with four or more letting bedrooms, to display in entrance halls the minimum and maximum price for one or two persons but they may vary without warning.

Facilities for disabled guests

The final stage (Part III) of the Disability Discrimination Act (access to Goods and Services) came into force in October 2004. This means that service providers may have to make permanent adjustments to their premises. For further information, see the government website www.direct.gov.uk/en/DisabledPeople/RightsAndObligations/DisabilityRights/DG_4001068

Please note: AA inspectors are not accredited to make inspections under the National Accessibility Scheme. We indicate in entries if an establishment has ground floor rooms; and if a hotel tells us that they have disabled facilities this is included in the description.

The establishments in this guide should all be aware of their responsibilities under the Act. We recommend that you always telephone in advance to ensure that the establishment you have chosen has appropriate facilities.

Useful Websites

www.holidaycare.org.uk
www.dptac.gov.uk/door-to-door

Licensing Laws

Licensing laws differ in England, Wales, Scotland, the Republic of Ireland, the Isle of Man, the Isles of Scilly and the Channel Islands. Public houses are generally open from mid morning to early afternoon, and from about 6 or 7pm until 11pm, although closing times may be earlier or later and some pubs are open all afternoon. Unless otherwise stated, establishments listed are licensed to serve alcohol. Hotel residents can obtain alcoholic drinks at all times, if the licensee is prepared to serve them. Non-residents eating at the hotel restaurant can have drinks with meals. Children under 14 may be excluded from bars where no food is served. Those under 18 may not purchase or consume alcoholic drinks.

Club licence means that drinks are served to club members only, 48 hours must lapse between joining and ordering.

The Fire Precautions Act does not apply to the Channel Islands, Republic of Ireland, or the Isle of Man, which have their own rules. As far as we are aware, all hotels listed in Great Britain have applied for and not been refused a fire certificate.

For information on Ireland see page 670

Website Addresses

Where website addresses are included they have been supplied and specified by the respective establishment. Such Websites are not under the control of AA Media Limited and as such the AA has no control over them and will not accept any responsibility or liability in respect of any and all matters whatsoever relating to such Websites including access, content, material and functionality. By including the addresses of third party Websites the AA does not intend to solicit business or offer any security to any person in any country, directly or indirectly.

Bank and Public Holidays 2010

New Year's Day	1st January
New Year's Holiday	4th January (Scotland)
Good Friday	2nd April
Easter Monday	5th April
May Day Bank Holiday	3rd May
Spring Bank Holiday	31st May
August Holiday	2nd August (Scotland)
Late Summer Holiday	30th August
St Andrew's Day (Scotland)	30th November
Christmas Day	25th December
Boxing Day	26th December

Hotel Groups Information

Abode	**Abode** A small expanding group currently represented by four hotels in key city centre locations.	www.abodehotels.co.uk
APEX HOTELS	**Apex Hotels** A small group of predominantly four star hotels based primarily in Edinburgh, Dundee and London. Their latest hotels are Waterloo Place, Edinburgh and The Wall in London, opening in late 2009.	0845 365 0000 www.apexhotels.co.uk
Barceló HOTELS & RESORTS	**Barceló** An international group of predominately 4 star hotels in the UK in 2 brands – Barceló Hotels and Barceló Premium Hotels	0870 168 8833 www.barcelo-hotels.co.uk
"bespoke" HOTELS	**Bespoke** A growing group of personally managed three and four star hotels in leisure locations.	0870 423 3550 www.bespokehotels.com
Best Western	**Best Western** Britain's largest consortia group has over 280 independently owned and managed hotels, modern and traditional, in the two, three and four star range. Many have leisure facilities and rosette awards.	08457 737 373 www.bestwestern.co.uk
Best Western PREMIER	**Best Western Premier** These hotels are selected for their beautiful settings, range of facilities and enhanced levels of service. There are currently 7 Best Western Great Britain hotels that have achieved Premier status. These join over 45 Best Western Premier accredited hotels across Europe and Asia.	08457 737 373 www.bestwestern.co.uk
Bewleys Hotels.com	**Bewley's Hotels** Part of the Moran Hotel Group. A privately owned group of high quality, contemporary three star hotels in key locations in the UK and Ireland.	00 353 1 293 5000 www.bewleyshotels.com
Brend Hotels	**Brend** A privately owned group of 11 three and four star hotels in Devon and Cornwall.	01271 344 496 www.brendhotels.co.uk
Campanile	**Campanile** An American owned and French managed company, Campanile has 20 properties in the UK offering modern accommodation in budget hotels.	020 8326 1500 www.envergure.fr
	Choice Choice has four different brands in the UK: Clarion and Quality Hotels are three and four star hotels, Comfort Inns are two and three star hotels, and Sleep Inns are budget hotels.	0800 44 44 44 www.choicehoteleurope.com
CITY INN	**City Inn** A small group of 4 star contemporary hotels located in prime city centre locations	020 7901 1606 www.cityinn.com
CLASSIC BRITISH HOTELS	**Classic British** A consortium of independent hotels at the four star and high-quality three star level, categorised by quality and style, and marketed under the Classic British Hotels hallmark.	0845 070 7090 www.classicbritishhotels.com
corus hotels	**Corus** A small group of 3 star hotels ranging from rural to city centre locations across the UK.	0845 602 6787 www.corushotels.com
CROWNE PLAZA HOTELS & RESORTS	**Crowne Plaza** Four star hotels predominantly found in key city centre locations.	0871 423 4896 www.crowneplaza.co.uk

Hotel Groups Information *continued*

	Days Inn Good quality modern budget hotels with good coverage across the UK.		*0800 028 0400* *www.daysinn.com*
	De Vere Collection A growing group of four and five star hotels with good coverage across the UK.		*0870 111 0516* *www.devere.co.uk*
	Exclusive A small privately owned group of luxury five and four red star hotels, all located in the south of England.		*01276 471 774* *www.exclusivehotels.co.uk*
	Express by Holiday Inn A major international hotel brand with over 100 hotels across the UK and over 60 across Continental Europe.		*0800 43 40 40* *www.hiexpress.co.uk*
	Folio Hotels A collection of three and four star hotels located throughout England and Scotland.		*0870 903 0007* *www.foliohotels.com*
	Forestdale Hotels A privately owned group of 19 three star hotels located across the UK.		*0808 144 9494* *www.forestdale.com*
	Four Pillars Hotels A group of three and four star hotels in the Oxfordshire area.		*0800 374 692* *www.four-pillars.co.uk*
	Gresham Hotels The Gresham Group is an Irish owned and managed company offering quality accommodation in city centre locations.		*00 353 1 8787 966* *www.gresham-hotels.com*
	Handpicked Hotels A group of 14 predominantly four star, high quality country house hotels, with a real emphasis on quality food. Some provide stylish spa facilities		*0845 458 0901* *www.handpicked.co.uk*
	Holiday Inn A major international group with many hotels across the UK.		*0870 400 9670* *www.holiday-inn.co.uk*
	Hotel du Vin A small expanding group of high quality four star hotels, that places a strong emphasis on its destination restaurant concept and appealing menus.		*01962 850676* *www.hotelduvin.com*
	Ibis A growing chain of modern budget hotels with properties across the UK.		*0870 609 0963* *www.ibishotel.com*
	Independents A consortium of independently owned, mainly two, three and four star hotels, across Britain.		*0800 885 544* *www.theindependents.co.uk*
	Innkeeper's Lodge A growing collection of lodges located adjacent to a pub restaurant and featuring comfortable rooms and complimentary breakfast.		*08451 551 551* *www.innkeeperslodge.com*
	Inter-Continental This internationally renowned group has now re-opened the landmark five star Park Lane Hotel after a multi-million pound refurbishment.		*0800 028 9387* *www.ichotelsgroup.com*
	Ireland's Blue Book An association of owner-managed establishments across Ireland.		*00 353 1 676 9914* *www.irelands-blue-book.ie*

Book into AA rated hotels from the comfort of your home. How very accommodating

If you're looking for a hotel or B&B visit theAA.com/travel first. You can book hundreds of AA rated establishments there and then

- All accommodation is rated from one to five stars with detailed listings
- 5% discount available for AA Members at many hotels – look for the Members' 5% off – book it buttons
- Fantastic offers also available on the hotel and B&B homepage

AA Route Planner – guides you through every step of your journey

If you're planning on going on a long journey and need to find a stop over or two on the way, simply go to the AA's new and improved Route Planner. With its new mapping powered by Google™, you just scroll over your route to find available hotels at every step of your journey.

Hotel Groups Information *continued*

Logo	Description	Contact
IRISH COUNTRY HOTELS	**Irish Country Hotels** A collection of over 30 Irish family run hotels, located all across Ireland.	*00 353 1 295 8900 (local)* *0818 281 281* *www.irishcountryhotels.com*
THE DOYLE COLLECTION	**The Doyles Collection** This Irish company has a range of three, four and five star hotels in the UK and the Republic of Ireland.	*00 353 1 607 0070* *www.doylescollection.com*
Lake District Hotels	**Lake District Hotels** A small collection of hotels situated in some of the most beautiful parts of the Lake District countryside and Lakeland towns	*0800 840 1240* *www.lakedistricthotels.net*
LEGACY HOTELS	**Legacy Hotels** A small group of three star hotels growing its coverage across the UK.	*08708 329923* *www.legacy-hotels.co.uk*
Leisureplex	**Leisureplex** A group of 17 two star hotels located in many popular seaside resorts.	*08451 305 666 (Head Office)* *www.alfatravel.co.uk*
MACDONALD HOTELS & RESORTS	**Macdonald** A large group of predominantly four star hotels, both traditional and modern in style and located across the UK. Many hotels enjoy rural settings and state-of-the-art spa facilities	*0870 830 4812* *www.macdonald-hotels.co.uk*
Malmaison	**Malmaison** A growing brand of modern, three star city centre hotels that provide deeply comfortable bedrooms, exciting restaurants and carefullt selected wine lists.	*0845 365 4247* *www.malmaison.com*
MANOR HOUSE HOTELS	**Manor House** Located throughout Ireland, this group offers a selection of independent, high quality country and manor house hotels.	*00 353 1 295 8900 (local)* *0818 281 281* *www.manorhousehotels.com*
Marriott HOTELS & RESORTS	**Marriott** This international brand has four and five star hotels in primary locations. Most are modern and have leisure facilities with a focus on activities such as golf.	*00800 1927 1927* *www.marriott.co.uk*
MAYBOURNE HOTEL GROUP	**Maybourne Hotels** A hotel group representing the prestigious London five star hotels - The Berkeley, Claridge's and The Connaught.	*020 7107 8830 (Head Office)* *www.maybourne.com*
MenziesHotels	**Menzies Hotels** A group of predominately four star hotels in key locations across the UK.	*0870 600 3013* *www.menzies-hotels.co.uk*
Mercure	**Mercure Hotels** A fast growing group with the original hotels in London and Bristol joined by a further 24 throughout the country.	*0870 609 0965* *www.mercure.com*
MILLENNIUM	**Millennium** Part of the Millennium and Copthorne group with 6 high-quality four star hotels, mainly in central London.	*0800 41 47 41* *www.millenniumhotels.com*
MORAN HOTELS	**Moran Hotels** A privately owned group with 4 four star Moran Hotels, and 6 three star Bewley's Hotels. All have strategic locations in the UK and Ireland.	*00 353 1 459 3650* *www.moranhotels.com*
NOVOTEL	**Novotel** Part of French group Accor, Novotel provides mainly modern three star hotels and a new generation of four star hotels in key locations throughout the UK.	*0870 609 0962* *www.novotel.com*

Hotel Groups Information *continued*

	Old English Inns A large collection of former coaching inns that are mainly graded at two and three stars.	0800 917 3085 & 0845 608 6040 www.oldenglishinns.co.uk
OXFORD HOTELS & INNS	**Oxford Hotels and Inns** A large group of 45 hotels with good coverage across the UK, and particularly in Scotland. Each hotel has its own individual style and character.	0871 376 9900 www.oxfordhotelsandinns.com
Park Plaza Hotels & Resorts	**Park Plaza Hotels** A European based group increasing its presence in the UK with quality four star hotels in primary locations.	0800 169 6128 www.parkplaza.com
PEEL HOTELS PLC	**Peel Hotels** A group of mainly three star hotels located across the UK.	0845 601 7335 www.peelhotels.co.uk
PRIDE OF BRITAIN HOTELS	**Pride of Britain** A consortium of privately owned high quality British hotels, often in the country house style, many of which have been awarded red stars and AA Rosettes.	0800 089 3929 www.prideofbritainhotels.com
PRIMA HOTEL GROUP	**Prima Hotels** A small hotel group which currently has 6 four star hotels. Five hotels are in England and one is in Scotland.	www.primahotels.co.uk
PH PRINCIPAL HAYLEY	**Principal** A small group of four star hotels currently represented by 5 hotels situated in prime city centre locations.	0870 242 7474 www.principal-hotels.com
QHOTELS	**QHotels** An expanding hotel group currently with 21 individually styled four star hotels across the UK.	0845 074 0060 www.qhotels.co.uk
Radisson BLU	**Radisson Blu** A recognised international brand increasing its hotels in the UK and Ireland, and offering high-quality four star hotels in key locations. (Formerly known as Radisson SAS).	0800 374 411 www.radisson.com
Radisson EDWARDIAN HOTELS	**Radisson Edwardian** This high-quality London-based group offers mainly four star hotels in key locations throughout the capital.	020 8757 7900 www.radissonedwardian.com
RAMADA HOTEL & RESORT	**Ramada** A large hotel group with many properties throughout the UK in three brands - Ramada Plaza, Ramada and Ramada Hotel & Resort.	0845 2070 100 www.ramadajarvis.co.uk
Red Carnation HOTELS	**Red Carnation** A unique collection of prestigious four and five star central London hotels, providing luxurious surroundings and attentive service.	0845 634 2665 www.redcarnationhotels.com
RELAIS & CHATEAUX	**Relais et Chateaux** An international consortium of rural, privately owned hotels, mainly in the country house style.	00800 2000 0002 www.relaischateaux.com
RENAISSANCE HOTELS	**Renaissance** One of the Marriott brands, Renaissance is a collection of individual hotels offering comfortable guest rooms, quality cuisine and good levels of service.	00800 1927 1927 www.marriott.co.uk

Hotel Groups Information *continued*

RICHARDSON	**Richardson Hotels** A group of 6 three and four star hotels located predominantly in Cornwall and Devon, with one hotel in the Lake District.	www.richardsonhotels.co.uk
RF THE ROCCO FORTE COLLECTION	**Rocco Forte Hotels** A small group of luxury hotels spread across Europe. Owned by Sir Rocco Forte, three hotels in the UK, all situated in major city locations.	0870 458 4040 www.roccofortecollection.com
	Scotland's Hotels of Distinction A consortium of independent Scottish hotels in the three and four star range.	01333 360 888 www.hotels-of-distinction.com
Sheraton HOTELS & RESORTS	**Sheraton** Represented in the UK by a small number of four and five star hotels in London and Scotland.	0800 35 35 35 www.starwoodhotels.com
shire	**Shire** A small group of mostly four star hotels many of which feature spa facilities and well-equipped bedrooms ideal for both the business and leisure guest.	01254 267 444 (Head Office) www.shirehotels.com
	Small Luxury Hotels of the World Part of an international consortium of mainly privately owned hotels, often in the country house style.	00800 5254 8000 www.slh.com
THE CIRCLE	**The Circle** A consortium of independently owned, mainly two and three star hotels, across Britain.	0845 345 1965 www.circle-hotels.co.uk
thistle	**Thistle** A large group of approximately 31 hotels across the UK with a significant number in London.	0870 414 1516 www.thistlehotels.com
TOWER HOTEL GROUP	**Tower Hotel Group** This Irish owned and operated group has quality hotels offering accommodation in convenient locations throughout Ireland.	00353 1 428 2400 www.towerhotelgroup.com
Travelodge	**Travelodge** Good quality, modern, budget accommodation with over 300 properties across the UK and Ireland. Almost every lodge has an adjacent family restaurant, often a Little Chef, Harry Ramsden's or Burger King.	08700 850 950 www.travelodge.co.uk
VENTURE HOTELS	**Venture Hotels** Small group of business and leisure hotels located in the north of England.	www.venturehotels.co.uk
von Essen hotels	**Von Essen** A privately owned collection of country house hotels, all individual in style and offered in 3 main catagories: classic, luxury family and country.	01761 240 121 www.vonessenhotels.co.uk
WELCOMEBREAK	**Welcome Break** Good quality, modern, budget accommodation at motorway services.	01908 299 705 www.welcomebreak.co.uk

England

Beachy Head, East Sussex

BEDFORDSHIRE

ASPLEY GUISE | Map 11 SP93

Best Western Moore Place

★★★ 74% HOTEL

☎ 01908 282000 ▤ 01908 281888
The Square MK17 8DW
e-mail: manager@mooreplace.com
dir: M1 junct 13, take A507 signed Aspley Guise &
Woburn Sands. Hotel on left in village square

This impressive Georgian house, set in delightful gardens
in the village centre, is very conveniently located for the
M1. Bedrooms do vary in size, but consideration has been
given to guest comfort, with many thoughtful extras
provided. There is a wide range of meeting rooms and
private dining options.

Rooms 62 (27 annexe) (16 GF) **Facilities** Xmas New Year
Wi-fi **Conf** Class 24 Board 20 Thtr 40 **Parking** 70
Notes LB RS 27-31 Dec Civ Wed 80

BEDFORD | Map 12 TL04

The Barns Hotel

★★★★ 70% HOTEL

☎ 0844 855 9101 ▤ 01234 273102
Cardington Rd MK44 3SA
e-mail: barns@foliohotels.com
web: www.foliohotels.com/barns
dir: From M1 junct 13, A421, approx 10m to A603 Sandy/
Bedford exit, hotel on right at 2nd rdbt

A tranquil location on the outskirts of Bedford, friendly
staff and well-equipped bedrooms are the main
attractions here. Cosy day rooms and two informal bars
add to the appeal, while large windows in the restaurant
make the most of the view over the river. The original
barn now houses the conference and function suite.

Rooms 49 **Facilities** Free use of local leisure centre (1m)
New Year Wi-fi **Conf** Class 40 Board 40 Thtr 120
Parking 90 **Notes** ⊗ Civ Wed 90

Woodland Manor

★★★ 68% HOTEL

☎ 01234 363281 ▤ 01234 272390
Green Ln, Clapham MK41 6EP
e-mail: reception@woodlandmanorhotel.co.uk
dir: A6 towards Kettering. Clapham 1st village N of town
centre. On entering village 1st right into Green Ln. Hotel
200mtrs on right

Sitting in acres of wooded grounds and gardens, this
secluded Grade II listed, Victorian manor house offers a
warm welcome. The hotel has spacious bedrooms, ample
parking plus meeting rooms that are suitable for a variety
of occasions. Traditional public areas include a cosy bar
and a smart restaurant, where traditional English dishes,
with a hint of French flair, are served.

Rooms 33 **Conf** Class 50 Board 36 Thtr 110

Express by Holiday Inn Bedford

BUDGET HOTEL

☎ 01234 224100 ▤ 01234 224166
Elstow Interchange A6/A421 MK42 9BF
e-mail: bedford@expressholidayinn.co.uk
dir: 1m S of Bedford town centre at Elstow interchange at
junct of A421/A6

A modern hotel ideal for families and business travellers.
Fresh and uncomplicated, the spacious rooms include Sky
TV, power shower and tea and coffee-making facilities.
Continental buffet breakfast is included in the room rate;
other meals may be taken at the nearby family pub or
restaurant. See also the Hotel Groups pages.

Rooms 80 (52 fmly) (20 GF) (4 smoking) **S** £44-£120;
D £44-£120 (incl. bkfst) **Conf** Class 20 Board 20 Thtr 35

Innkeeper's Lodge Bedford

BUDGET HOTEL

☎ 0845 112 6056 ▤ 0845 112 6247
403 Goldington Rd MK41 0DS
web: www.innkeeperslodge.com/bedford
dir: M1 junct 13, A421 to Cambridge/A1. 13m, at rdbt
with A428, left into Goldington Rd. Straight on at next 2
rdbts. Lodge 400yds on left opposite Goldington Green

Innkeeper's Lodge represents an exciting, high value
concept within the budget hotel market. Comfortable
bedrooms provide excellent facilities that include satellite
TV and modem points. Options include family rooms; and
for the corporate guest, cutting edge IT which includes
Wi-fi access. A popular Carvery provides all-day food,
including an extensive, complimentary continental
breakfast. See also the Hotel Groups pages.

Rooms 47 (20 fmly)

Travelodge Bedford

BUDGET HOTEL

☎ 0871 984 6276 ▤ 01234 270908
Saturn Heights, Brickhill Dr MK41 7PH
web: www.travelodge.co.uk
dir: From M1 into Bedford on A421 & A6. Follow A5141 to
Manton Lane

Travelodge offers good quality, good value, budget
accommodation. All offer family rooms sleeping up to four
(two adults, two children) with en suite bathroom/
shower-room, remote-control TV, tea- and coffee-making
facilities and comfortable beds. Food options vary.
Breakfast is at the on-site Bar Café restaurant (if
available) or to take away. See also Hotel Groups pages.

Rooms 51 **S** fr £29; **D** fr £29

Travelodge Bedford Wyboston

BUDGET HOTEL

☎ 0871 984 6010
Black Cat Roundabout MK44 3BE
web: www.travelodge.co.uk
dir: On A1N'bound, at Black Cat rdbt & junct A421

Rooms 40 **S** fr £29; **D** fr £29

DUNSTABLE | Map 11 TL02

Old Palace Lodge

★★★ 81% HOTEL

☎ 01582 662201 ▤ 01582 661848
Church St LU5 4RT
e-mail: reservations@mgmhotels.co.uk
web: www.oldpalacelodge.com
dir: M1 junct 11 take A505. Hotel 2m on right opp Priory
Church

Situated close to the town centre and major road
networks this hotel is steeped in history and has many
original features. The spacious bedrooms are smartly
decorated with co-ordinated fabrics and have many
thoughtful touches. Public rooms include a large lounge
bar with plush sofas and an intimate restaurant.

Rooms 68 (12 fmly) (21 GF) **S** £92-£120; **D** £92-£120
(incl. bkfst)* **Facilities** FTV Full leisure facilities provided
at local fitness centre Xmas New Year Wi-fi **Conf** Class 40
Board 40 Thtr 60 Del from £110 to £130* **Services** Lift
Parking 50 **Notes** LB ⊗ Civ Wed 70

Highwayman

★★ 64% HOTEL

☎ 01582 601122 ▤ 01582 603812
London Rd LU6 3DX
e-mail: 6466@greeneking.co.uk
web: www.oldenglish.co.uk
dir: N'bound: M1 junct 9, A5, 6m on right. S'bound: M1
junct 11, A505, left on A5 towards London. Hotel on left

This hotel continues to prove popular with business
guests, partly due to its convenient location just south of
the town, and for the ample parking space. The
accommodation is comfortable, well equipped and
cheerfully decorated. The public areas include a large
public bar where meals are available.

Rooms 52 (3 fmly) (24 GF) **Facilities** ♫ **Parking** 76
Notes ⊗

Travelodge Dunstable Hockliffe

BUDGET HOTEL

☎ 08719 846 027 🖷 01525 211177
Watling St LU7 9LZ
web: www.travelodge.co.uk
dir: M1 junct 12, A5120 to Toddington. 1st right through Tebworth, right onto A5

Travelodge offers good quality, good value, budget accommodation. All offer family rooms sleeping up to four (two adults, two children) with en suite bathroom/shower-room, remote-control TV, tea- and coffee-making facilities and comfortable beds. Food options vary. Breakfast is at the on-site Bar Café restaurant (if available) or to take away. See also Hotel Groups pages.

Rooms 28 **S** fr £29; **D** fr £29

FLITWICK **Map 11 TL03**

Menzies Flitwick Manor

MenziesHotels

★★★★ 73% ® COUNTRY HOUSE HOTEL

☎ 01525 712242 🖷 01525 718753
Church Rd MK45 1AE
e-mail: flitwick@menzieshotels.co.uk
web: www.menzieshotels.co.uk
dir: M1 junct 12, follow signs for Flitwick, turn left into Church Rd, hotel on left

With its picturesque setting in acres of gardens and parkland, yet only minutes by car from the motorway, this lovely Georgian house combines the best of both worlds, being both accessible and peaceful. Bedrooms are individually decorated and furnished with period pieces; some are air conditioned. Cosy and intimate, the lounge and restaurant help give the hotel a home-from-home feel.

Rooms 18 (1 fmly) (5 GF) (1 smoking) **S** £97-£180; **D** £97-£180* **Facilities** STV 🏊 Putt green 🏌 Xmas New Year Wi-fi **Conf** Class 30 Board 22 Thtr 40 Del from £140 to £210* **Parking** 18 **Notes** Civ Wed 50

LUTON **Map 6 TL02**

Luton Hoo Hotel, Golf and Spa

★★★★★ 86% ®® HOTEL

☎ 01582 734437 🖷 01582 485438
The Mansion House LU1 3TQ
e-mail: reservations@lutonhoo.com
dir: M1 junct 10A, 3rd exit to A1081 towards Harpenden/St Albans. Hotel 2m on left

A luxury hotel with an 18-hole golf course and stunning spa, set in more than 1,000 acres of parkland and gardens that were originally created by the famous landscape designer 'Capability' Brown. Spacious bedrooms combine historic character with modern design - they have well-equipped and stylish bathrooms and most have temperature control, and flat-screen TVs. Suites in the original mansion are particularly impressive.

Sumptuous lounges and three dining options are just a few of the features on offer.

Luton Hoo Hotel, Golf and Spa

Rooms 144 (109 annexe) (50 fmly) (36 GF) **D** £220-£850 (incl. bkfst)* **Facilities** Spa FTV 🕭 🛓 18 🏌 Putt green Fishing 🏊 Gym Angling Bird watching Cycling Snooker ♫ Xmas New Year Wi-fi **Conf** Class 63 Board 45 Thtr 96 **Services** Lift **Parking** 263 **Notes** LB ⊗ Civ Wed 200

Best Western Menzies Strathmore

★★★★ 72% HOTEL

☎ 01582 734199 🖷 01582 402528
Arndale Centre LU1 2TR
e-mail: strathmore@menzieshotels.co.uk
web: www.menzieshotels.co.uk
dir: From M1 junct 10a towards town centre, adjacent to Arndale Centre car park

Situated in the centre of town with adjacent parking, this hotel is convenient for the nearby shopping areas and many guests stay here prior to catching flights at the nearby airport. Bedrooms are comfortable and well equipped with good facilities. Public areas include a spacious lounge bar and an informal brasserie-style restaurant.

Rooms 152 (6 fmly) (21 smoking) **S** £39.90-£135; **D** £49.90-£145 (incl. bkfst)* **Facilities** Spa STV 🕭 supervised Gym Beauty salon Xmas New Year Wi-fi **Conf** Class 120 Board 60 Thtr 250 Del from £85 to £155* **Services** Lift **Parking** 5 **Notes** LB ⊗ Civ Wed 200

Days Hotel Luton

BUDGET HOTEL

☎ 0870 429 9540 🖷 0870 429 9541
Regent St LU1 5FA
e-mail: luton@kewgreen.co.uk
web: www.daysinn.com
dir: M1 junct 10. Follow to junct 10a. 1st left to rdbt. 1st left off rdbt & 1st left again

This modern building offers accommodation in smart, spacious and well-equipped bedrooms, suitable for families and business travellers, and all with en suite bathrooms. Continental breakfast is available and other refreshments may be taken at the nearby family restaurant. See also the Hotel Groups pages.

Rooms 120 (33 fmly) (30 smoking) **S** £49-£115; **D** £49-£115* **Conf** Class 15 Board 20 Thtr 50 Del from £90 to £140*

Travelodge Luton

BUDGET HOTEL

☎ 0871 984 6355 🖷 01582 505249
641 Dunstable Rd LU4 8RQ
dir: M1 junct 11 towards town centre. Lodge on right of dual carriageway, adjacent to Jet petrol station

Travelodge offers good quality, good value, budget accommodation. All offer family rooms sleeping up to four (two adults, two children) with en suite bathroom/shower-room, remote-control TV, tea- and coffee-making facilities and comfortable beds. Food options vary. Breakfast is at the on-site Bar Café restaurant (if available) or to take away. See also the Hotel Groups pages.

Rooms 106 **S** fr £29; **D** fr £29

LUTON AIRPORT **Map 6 TL12**

Express by Holiday Inn London - Luton Airport

BUDGET HOTEL

☎ 0870 444 8920 🖷 0870 444 8930
2 Percival Way LU2 9GP
e-mail: lutonairport@expressbyholidayinn.net
web: www.hiexpress.com/lutonairport
dir: M1 junct 10, follow signs for airport, hotel easily visable, turn right into Percival Way, hotel car park on right

A modern hotel ideal for families and business travellers. Fresh and uncomplicated, the spacious rooms include Sky TV, power shower and tea and coffee-making facilities. Continental buffet breakfast is included in the room rate; other meals may be taken at the nearby family pub or restaurant. See also the Hotel Groups pages.

Rooms 147 (87 fmly) **S** £48.95-£99.95; **D** £48.95-£99.95 (incl. bkfst)* **Conf** Class 30 Board 20 Thtr 60 Del from £99.95 to £130*

Ibis Luton

BUDGET HOTEL

☎ 01582 424488 🖷 01582 455511
Spittlesea Rd LU2 9NH
e-mail: H1040@accor-hotels.com
web: www.ibishotel.com
dir: from M1 junct 10 follow signs to Luton Airport signs. Hotel 600mtrs from airport

Modern, budget hotel offering comfortable accommodation in bright and practical bedrooms. Breakfast is self-service and dinner is available in the restaurant. See also the Hotel Groups pages.

Rooms 98 **Conf** Class 64 Board 80 Thtr 114

MARSTON MORETAINE — Map 11 SP94

Travelodge Bedford Marston Moretaine

BUDGET HOTEL

☎ 0871 984 6011 🖹 01234 766755
Beancroft Road Junction MK43 0PZ
web: www.travelodge.co.uk
dir: on A421, northbound

Travelodge offers good quality, good value, budget accommodation. All offer family rooms sleeping up to four (two adults, two children) with en suite bathroom/shower-room, remote-control TV, tea- and coffee-making facilities and comfortable beds. Food options vary. Breakfast is at the on-site Bar Café restaurant (if available) or to take away. See also Hotel Groups pages.

Rooms 54 **S** fr £29; **D** fr £29

MILTON ERNEST — Map 11 TL05

Queens Head

★★ Ⓐ HOTEL

☎ 01234 822412 🖹 01234 822337
2 Rushden Rd MK44 1RU
e-mail: 6495@greeneking.co.uk
web: www.oldenglish.co.uk
dir: From Beford follow A6 towards Kettering, hotel on left on entering Milton Ernest

Rooms 13 (4 GF) **S** fr £70; **D** fr £80 (incl. bkfst)*
Facilities Wi-fi

SANDY — Map 12 TL14

Holiday Inn Garden Court A1 Sandy - Bedford

★★★ 68% HOTEL

☎ 01767 692220 & 684707 🖹 01767 680452
Girtford Bridge, London Rd SG19 1NA
e-mail: sandysales@holidayinns.co.uk
web: www.holiday-inn.com/sandy-bedford
dir: From M1 junct 13, A421 to Bedford. Take A603 to Sandy. Hotel off A1rdbt

Strategically located on the A1 with easy access from both the M25 and M1, this establishment is the perfect choice for business and leisure travellers alike. Bedrooms are comfortable and well appointed. This property also boasts a conference centre with function rooms for business meetings and special events plus complimentary parking.

Rooms 57 (2 fmly) (17 GF) **S** £49-£105; **D** £49-£105*
Facilities Xmas New Year Wi-fi **Conf** Class 60 Board 35 Thtr 180 Del from £125 to £145* **Parking** 100 **Notes** LB ⊗ Civ Wed 45

TODDINGTON MOTORWAY SERVICE AREA (M1) — Map 11 TL02

Travelodge Toddington (M1 Southbound)

BUDGET HOTEL

☎ 0871 984 6214 🖹 01525 878452
LU5 6HR
web: www.travelodge.co.uk
dir: M1 between juncts 11 & 12

Travelodge offers good quality, good value, budget accommodation. All offer family rooms sleeping up to four (two adults, two children) with en suite bathroom/shower-room, remote-control TV, tea- and coffee-making facilities and comfortable beds. Food options vary. Breakfast is at the on-site Bar Café restaurant (if available) or to take away. See also Hotel Groups pages.

Rooms 66 **S** fr £29; **D** fr £29

WOBURN — Map 11 SP93

The Inn at Woburn

★★★ 81% ◉◉ HOTEL

☎ 01525 290441 🖹 01525 290432
George St MK17 9PX
e-mail: enquiries@theinnatwoburn.com
dir: M1 junct 13, left to Woburn, at Woburn left at T-junct, hotel in village

This inn provides a high standard of accommodation. Bedrooms are divided between the original house, a modern extension and some stunning cottage suites. Public areas include the beamed, club-style Tavistock Bar, a range of meeting rooms and an attractive restaurant with interesting dishes on offer.

Rooms 57 (7 annexe) (4 fmly) (21 GF) **S** £105-£145; **D** £135-£205 **Facilities** ♨ 54 Free access to Woburn Safari Park and Woburn Abbey Xmas **Conf** Class 40 Board 40 Thtr 60 Del from £145 to £165 **Parking** 80 **Notes** LB Civ Wed 60

Bell Hotel & Inn

★★ Ⓐ HOTEL

☎ 01525 290280 🖹 01525 290017
21 Bedford St MK17 9QB
e-mail: bell.woburn@oldenglishinns.co.uk
web: www.oldenglish.co.uk
dir: M1 junct 13/A507 to Woburn Sands. Take 1st left, then next left. At T-junct turn right

Rooms 24 (4 GF) **Facilities** Xmas **Parking** 50 **Notes** ⊗

WYBOSTON — Map 12 TL15

Wyboston Lakes Hotel

★★★ 72% HOTEL

☎ 01480 212625 & 479300 🖹 01480 223000
Wyboston Lakes, Great North Rd MK44 3BA
e-mail: reservations@wybostonlakes.co.uk
dir: Off A1/A428, follow brown Cambridge signs. Wyboston Lakes & hotel on right, marked by flags

Ideally located adjacent to the A1 on the Cambridgeshire/Bedfordshire border, Wyboston Lakes is easily accessible. The hotel is located within an extensive conference and leisure complex that includes a golf course. Bedrooms are tastefully decorated in a contemporary style, and offer a range of amenities to suit both the business and leisure traveller. The dining room overlooks the idyllic lake.

Rooms 103 (39 annexe) (18 fmly) (50 GF) **S** £69-£110; **D** £89-£120 (incl. bkfst)* **Facilities** FTV ⓣ ♨ 18 Fishing Gym Golf driving range Wi-fi **Conf** Class 56 Board 40 Thtr 130 Del from £171 to £207* **Services** Lift **Parking** 200 **Notes** LB ⊗ No children Closed 24 Dec-2 Jan Civ Wed 100

BERKSHIRE

ASCOT — Map 6 SU96

Macdonald Berystede Hotel & Spa

★★★★ 78% ⊛ HOTEL

☎ 0844 879 9104 📄 01344 872301
Bagshot Rd, Sunninghill SL5 9JH
e-mail: general.berystede@macdonald-hotels.co.uk
web: www.macdonald-hotels.co.uk/berystede
dir: A30/B3020 (Windmill Pub). Continue 1.25m to hotel on left just before junct with A330

This impressive Victorian mansion, close to Ascot Racecourse, offers executive bedrooms that are spacious, comfortable and particularly well equipped. Public rooms include a cosy bar and an elegant restaurant in which creative dishes are served. An impressive self-contained conference centre and spa facility appeal to both conference and leisure guests.

Rooms 126 (61 fmly) (33 GF) **S** £80-£150; **D** £90-£160 (incl. bkfst) **Facilities** Spa STV ⚒ ⛱ Gym Leisure complex including thermal & beauty treatment suites Outdoor garden spa Xmas New Year Wi-fi **Conf** Class 220 Board 150 Thtr 330 Del from £160 to £290 **Services** Lift **Parking** 200 **Notes** LB Civ Wed 300

Ramada Plaza The Royal Berkshire

Ⓡ R A M A D A PLAZA

★★★★ 77% COUNTRY HOUSE HOTEL

☎ 01344 623322 📄 01344 627100
London Rd, Sunninghill SL5 0PP
e-mail: sales.royalberkshire@ramadajarvis.co.uk
web: www.ramadajarvis.co.uk/royalberkshire
dir: A30 towards Bagshot, right opposite Wentworth Club onto A329, continue for 2m, hotel entrance on right

Once occupied by the Churchill family, this delightful Queen Anne house is set in 14 acres of attractive gardens on the edge of Ascot. Public areas include a comfortable lounge bar, an attractive restaurant that overlooks the rear gardens and extensive conference facilities. The main house offers smart, well-equipped bedrooms.

Rooms 63 (8 fmly) (8 GF) **Facilities** STV ⚒ ⛱ ⚓ Xmas New Year Wi-fi **Conf** Class 80 Board 60 Thtr 150 **Parking** 150 **Notes** Civ Wed 150

Highclere

★★ 64% METRO HOTEL

☎ 01344 625220 📄 01344 872528
19 Kings Rd, Sunninghill SL5 9AD
e-mail: info@highclerehotel.com
dir: Opposite Sunninghill Post Office

This privately owned establishment is situated in a quiet residential area, close to the racecourse, Windsor and the M3. Modest bedrooms are attractively decorated and well equipped. A cosy bar is available adjacent to the comfortable conservatory lounge. A short dinner menu is available with a number of restaurants within walking distance.

Rooms 11 (1 fmly) (2 GF) **S** £65-£75; **D** £75-£90 (incl. bkfst)* **Facilities** Wi-fi **Conf** Class 15 Thtr 15 **Parking** 11 **Notes** ⊗

BINFIELD — Map 5 SU87

Travelodge Bracknell

BUDGET HOTEL

☎ 0871 984 6015 📄 01344 485940
London Rd RG12 4AA
web: www.travelodge.co.uk
dir: M4 junct 10 (Bracknell) take 1st exit towards Binfield B3408

Travelodge offers good quality, good value, budget accommodation. All offer family rooms sleeping up to four (two adults, two children) with en suite bathroom/ shower-room, remote-control TV, tea- and coffee-making facilities and comfortable beds. Food options vary. Breakfast is at the on-site Bar Café restaurant (if available) or to take away. See also Hotel Groups pages.

Rooms 35 **S** fr £29; **D** fr £29

BRACKNELL — Map 5 SU86

Coppid Beech

★★★★ 75% ⊛ HOTEL

☎ 01344 303333 📄 01344 301200
John Nike Way RG12 8TF
e-mail: sales@coppidbeech.com
web: www.coppidbeech.com
dir: M4 junct 10 take Wokingham/Bracknell onto A329. In 2m take B3408 to Binfield at rdbt. Hotel 200yds on right

This chalet designed hotel offers extensive facilities and includes a ski-slope, ice rink, nightclub, health club and Bier Keller. Bedrooms range from suites to standard rooms - all are impressively equipped. A choice of dining is offered; there's a full bistro menu available in the Keller, and for more formal dining, Rowan's restaurant provides award-winning cuisine.

Rooms 205 (6 fmly) (16 GF) **S** £135-£205; **D** £155-£225 (incl. bkfst) **Facilities** Spa STV ⚒ Gym Ice rink Dry ski slope Snow boarding Freestyle park ♬ New Year Wi-fi **Conf** Class 161 Board 24 Thtr 350 Del from £175 to £250 **Services** Lift Air con **Parking** 350 **Notes** LB Civ Wed 200

Stirrups Country House

★★★ 80% HOTEL

☎ 01344 882284 📄 01344 882300
Maidens Green RG42 6LD
e-mail: reception@stirrupshotel.co.uk
web: www.stirrupshotel.co.uk
dir: 3m N on B3022 towards Windsor

Situated in a peaceful location between Maidenhead, Bracknell and Windsor, this hotel has high standards of comfort in the bedrooms, with some rooms boasting a small sitting room area. There is a popular bar, a restaurant, function rooms and delightful grounds.

Rooms 30 (4 fmly) (2 GF) **Facilities** STV Wi-fi **Conf** Class 50 Board 40 Thtr 100 **Services** Lift **Parking** 100 **Notes** LB Civ Wed 100

Travelodge Bracknell Central

BUDGET HOTEL

☎ 0871 984 6367
London Rd RG12 2UT
dir: Follow signs to town centre on A329 signed Ascot. Lodge approx 50mtrs on left

Travelodge offers good quality, good value, budget accommodation. All offer family rooms sleeping up to four (two adults, two children) with en suite bathroom/ shower-room, remote-control TV, tea- and coffee-making facilities and comfortable beds. Food options vary. Breakfast is at the on-site Bar Café restaurant (if available) or to take away. See also the Hotel Groups pages.

Rooms 102 **S** fr £29; **D** fr £29

COOKHAM DEAN — Map 5 SU88

The Inn on the Green

⊛⊛ RESTAURANT WITH ROOMS

☎ 01628 482638 📄 01628 487474
The Old Cricket Common SL6 9NZ
e-mail: reception@theinnonthegreen.com
dir: In village centre

A traditional English country inn set in rural Berkshire. Bedrooms are spacious and comfortable, with antique furnishings adding to the character. The building retains many traditional features including a wood panelled dining room and Old English bar with log fire. Food is imaginative and noteworthy and can be enjoyed outside in the garden or terrace in warmer months.

Rooms 9

HUNGERFORD Map 5 SU36

Bear

★★★ 80% ◎◎ HOTEL

☎ 01488 682512 🖷 01488 684357
41 Charnham St RG17 0EL
e-mail: info@thebearhotelhungerford.co.uk
web: www.thebearhotelhungerford.co.uk
dir: M4 junct 14, A338 to Hungerford for 3m, left at
T-junct onto A4, hotel on left

Situated five miles south of the M4 this hotel dates back
as far as early 13th century and was once owned by King
Henry VIII. It now has a contemporary feel throughout.
Bedrooms are split between the main house, the
courtyard and Bear Island. The award-winning restaurant
is open for lunch and dinner, and lighter snacks are
available in the bar and lounge. Guests can enjoy a sun
terrace in the summer and log fires in the winter.

Rooms 39 (26 annexe) (2 fmly) (24 GF) **S** £82.50-£150;
D £92.50-£185* **Facilities** FTV Xmas New Year Wi-fi
Conf Class 35 Board 34 Thtr 80 Del from £125 to £165*
Parking 68 **Notes** LB Civ Wed 80

Three Swans

★★★ 70% HOTEL

☎ 01488 682721 🖷 01488 681708
117 High St RG17 0LZ
e-mail: info@threeswans.net
web: www.threeswans.net
dir: M4 junct 14 follow signs to Hungerford. Hotel half
way along High St on left

Centrally located in the bustling market town of
Hungerford this charming former inn, dating back some
700 years, has been renovated in a fresh and airy style.
Visitors will still see the original arch under which the
horse-drawn carriages once passed. There is a wood
panelled bar, a spacious lounge and attractive rear
garden to relax in. The informal restaurant is decorated
with a range of artwork by local artists. Bedrooms are
well appointed and comfortable.

Rooms 25 (10 annexe) (1 fmly) (5 GF) (3 smoking)
Facilities FTV Access to local private gym Xmas New Year
Wi-fi **Conf** Class 40 Board 30 Thtr 55 **Parking** 30

HURLEY Map 5 SU88

Black Boys Inn

◎◎ RESTAURANT WITH ROOMS

☎ 01628 824212
Henley Rd SL6 5NQ
e-mail: info@blackboysinn.co.uk
web: www.blackboysinn.co.uk
dir: 1m W of Hurley on A4130

Just a short drive from Henley, the traditional exterior of
this friendly establishment is a contrast to the smart
modernity within. Popular with locals, the restaurant is
the stage for Simon Bonwick's imaginative cuisine, and
offers a buzzing atmosphere. The well-appointed
bedrooms are situated in converted barns close by.

Rooms 8 (8 annexe)

KNOWL HILL Map 5 SU87

Bird In Hand Country Inn

★★★ 🅰 HOTEL

☎ 01628 826622 & 822781 🖷 01628 826748
Bath Rd RG10 9UP
e-mail: sthebirdinhand@aol.com
web: www.birdinhand.co.uk
dir: On A4 between Maidenhead & Reading

Rooms 15 (1 fmly) (6 GF) **S** £50-£100; **D** £70-£120 (incl.
bkfst) **Facilities** FTV New Year Wi-fi **Conf** Class 30
Board 25 Thtr 50 **Parking** 80 **Notes** LB

MAIDENHEAD Map 6 SU88

Fredrick's Hotel Restaurant Spa

★★★★ ◎◎ HOTEL

☎ 01628 581000 🖷 01628 771054
Shoppenhangers Rd SL6 2PZ
e-mail: reservations@fredricks-hotel.co.uk
web: www.fredricks-hotel.co.uk
dir: M4 junct 8/9 onto A404(M) to Maidenhead West &
Henley. 1st exit 9a to White Waltham. Left into
Shoppenhangers Rd to Maidenhead, hotel on right

Just 30 minutes from London, this delightful hotel
enjoys a peaceful location yet is within easy reach of
the M4 and only 20 minutes' drive from Wentworth and
Sunningdale golf courses. The spacious bedrooms are
comfortably furnished and very well equipped. An
enthusiastic team of staff ensure friendly and efficient
service. The imaginative cuisine is a highlight, as is
the luxurious spa that offers the ultimate in relaxation
and wellbeing.

Rooms 34 (11 GF) **Facilities** Spa ⊘ ⊰ supervised
Gym Rasul suite Oriental steam Dead Sea flotation
room Wi-fi **Conf** Class 80 Board 60 Thtr 120
Services Air con **Parking** 90 **Notes** LB ⊗ Closed 24
Dec-3 Jan Civ Wed 120

Holiday Inn Maidenhead/ Windsor

★★★★ 71% HOTEL

☎ 0870 400 9053 & 01628 506000 🖷 01628 506001
Manor Ln SL6 2RA
e-mail: reservations-maidenhead@ihg.com
web: www.holidayinn.co.uk
dir: A404 towards High Wycombe. Exit at junct 9A. Left at
mini rdbt. Hotel on right

Located close to Maidenhead town centre with transport
links to Windsor and the M4, this well sited hotel is
suitable for both the business and leisure traveller. Public
areas benefit from a spacious lounge bar, brasserie-style
restaurant and extensive conference facilities. The
popular leisure club includes swimming pool and full gym
facilities.

Rooms 197 (23 fmly) (56 GF) (18 smoking) **S** £49-£255;
D £49-£255* **Facilities** STV ⊚ supervised Gym Steam

room Sauna New Year Wi-fi **Conf** Class 200 Board 100 Thtr 400 Del from £99 to £199* **Services** Lift Air con **Parking** 250 **Notes** LB ⊗ Civ Wed 400

Days Inn Membury

BUDGET HOTEL

☎ 01488 72336 🖹 01488 72336
Membury Service Area RG17 7TZ
e-mail: membury.hotel@welcomebreak.co.uk
web: www.welcomebreak.co.uk
dir: M4 between junct 14 & 15

This modern building offers accommodation in smart, spacious and well-equipped bedrooms, suitable for families and business travellers, and all with en suite bathrooms. Continental breakfast is available and other refreshments may be taken at the nearby family restaurant. See also the Hotel Groups pages.

Rooms 38 (32 fmly) (17 GF) **S** £29-£49; **D** £29-£59*
Conf Board 10 Del from £69 to £109*

NEWBURY — Map 5 SU46

See also **Andover (Hampshire)**

INSPECTORS' CHOICE

The Vineyard at Stockcross
★★★★★ ◉◉◉◉ HOTEL

☎ 01635 528770 🖹 01635 528398
Stockcross RG20 8JU
e-mail: general@the-vineyard.co.uk
web: www.the-vineyard.co.uk
dir: from M4 take A34 towards Newbury, exit at 3rd junct for Speen. Right at rdbt then right again at 2nd rdbt.

A haven of style in the Berkshire countryside, this hotel prides itself on a superb art collection, which can be seen throughout the building. Bedrooms come in a variety of styles - many split-level suites that are exceptionally well equipped. Comfortable lounges lead into the stylish restaurant, which serves award-winning, imaginative and precise cooking, complemented by an equally impressive selection of wines from California and around the world. The welcome is warm and sincere, the service professional yet relaxed.

Rooms 49 (15 GF) **Facilities** Spa ⓢ Gym Treatment rooms ♫ Xmas Wi-fi **Conf** Class 50 Board 30 Thtr 100 **Services** Lift Air con **Parking** 100 **Notes** ⊗ Civ Wed 100

Donnington Valley Hotel & Spa
★★★★ 85% ◉◉ HOTEL

☎ 01635 551199 🖹 01635 551123
Old Oxford Rd, Donnington RG14 3AG
e-mail: general@donningtonvalley.co.uk
web: www.donningtonvalley.co.uk
dir: M4 junct 13, take A34 signed Newbury. Take exit signed Donnington/Services, at rdbt take 2nd exit signed Donnington. Left at next rdbt. Hotel 2m on right

In its own grounds complete with an 18-hole golf course, this stylish hotel boasts excellent facilities for both corporate and leisure guests; from the state-of-the-art spa offering excellent treatments, to an extensive range of meeting and function rooms. Air-conditioned bedrooms are stylish, spacious and particularly well equipped with fridges, lap-top safes and internet access. The Wine Press restaurant offers imaginative food complemented by a superb wine list.

Rooms 111 (3 fmly) (36 GF) **Facilities** Spa ⓢ ♨ 18 Putt green Fishing Gym Sauna Aromatherapy Studio Xmas New Year Wi-fi **Conf** Class 60 Board 40 Thtr 140 Del from £180 to £225* **Services** Lift Air con **Parking** 150 **Notes** ⊗ Civ Wed 85

Regency Park Hotel
★★★★ 81% ◉ HOTEL

☎ 01635 871555 🖹 01635 871571
Bowling Green Rd, Thatcham RG18 3RP
e-mail: info.newbury@pedersenhotels.com
web: www.pedersenhotels.com
dir: From Newbury take A4 signed Thatcham & Reading. 2nd rdbt exit signed Cold Ash. Hotel 1m on left

This smart, stylish hotel has benefited from major investment over the last few years and is ideal for both business and leisure guests. Spacious, well-equipped bedrooms include a number of contemporary, tasteful executive rooms. Smart airy public areas include a state-of-the-art spa and leisure club and the Watermark Restaurant offers imaginative, award-winning cuisine.

Rooms 109 (7 fmly) (9 GF) **S** £85-£180; **D** £85-£180*
Facilities Spa ⓢ Gym Xmas New Year Wi-fi **Conf** Class 80 Board 70 Thtr 200 Del from £150 to £195* **Services** Lift **Parking** 160 **Notes** LB ⊗ Civ Wed 100

See advert on page 48

Best Western West Grange
★★★★ 72% HOTEL

☎ 01635 273074 🖹 01635 862351
Cox's Ln, Bath Rd, Midgham RG7 5UP
e-mail: reservations@westgrangehotel.co.uk
dir: A4 Theale, follow signs to Newbury. Hotel on right approx 2m from Woolhampton

This former farmhouse has been turned into a smart and modern hotel that is set in well-managed grounds only a short drive away from Thatcham. Bedrooms offer a quiet and comfortable stay, and guests can relax in the large bar lounge and attractive restaurant. There is also a patio for warmer months.

Rooms 68 (2 fmly) (19 GF) **S** £75-£125; **D** £85-£135*
Facilities STV New Year Wi-fi **Conf** Class 25 Board 30 Thtr 50 **Services** Lift **Parking** 70 **Notes** LB ⊗

Ramada Newbury Elcot Park
★★★★ 71% HOTEL

☎ 01488 658100 & 0844 815 9060 🖹 01488 658288
RG20 8NJ
e-mail: sales.elcotpark@ramadajarvis.co.uk
web: www.ramadajarvis.co.uk/newbury
dir: M4 junct 13, A338 to Hungerford, A4 to Newbury. Hotel 4m from Hungerford

Enjoying a peaceful location yet within easy access to both the A4 and M4, this country-house hotel is set in 16 acres of gardens and woodland. Bedrooms are comfortably appointed and include some located in an adjacent mews. Public areas include the Orangery Restaurant, which enjoys views over the Kennet Valley, a leisure club and a range of conference rooms.

Rooms 73 (17 annexe) (1 fmly) (25 GF) (5 smoking) **Facilities** FTV ⓢ supervised ♨ ♨ Gym Sauna Solarium Steam room Xmas New Year Wi-fi **Conf** Class 45 Board 35 Thtr 110 Del from £99 to £185* **Services** Lift **Parking** 130 **Notes** ⊗ Civ Wed 120

NEWBURY *continued*

Newbury Manor Hotel

★★★ 78% ◉ HOTEL

☎ 01635 528838 📄 01635 523406
London Rd RG14 2BY
e-mail: enquiries@newbury-manor-hotel.co.uk
dir: On A4 between Newbury & Thatcham

A former Georgian watermill, which still features the original millrace, situated beside the River Kennet which flows through the well tended grounds. The character bedrooms that vary in style and size offer many accessories. Guests can dine in the River Bar Restaurant.

Rooms 33 (4 fmly) (11 GF) **S** £75-£120; **D** £75-£120 (incl. bkfst)* **Facilities** STV Fishing ⛳ Xmas New Year Wi-fi **Conf** Class 140 Board 90 Thtr 190 Del from £165 to £215* **Parking** 100 **Notes** LB ⊗ Civ Wed 100

Travelodge Newbury Chieveley (M4)

BUDGET HOTEL

☎ 0871 984 6203 📄 01635 247886
Chieveley, Oxford Rd RG18 9XX
web: www.travelodge.co.uk
dir: On A34, off M4 junct 13

Travelodge offers good quality, good value, budget accommodation. All offer family rooms sleeping up to four (two adults, two children) with en suite bathroom/shower-room, remote-control TV, tea- and coffee-making facilities and comfortable beds. Food options vary. Breakfast is at the on-site Bar Café restaurant (if available) or to take away. See also Hotel Groups pages.

Rooms 126 **S** fr £29; **D** fr £29

Travelodge Newbury Tot Hill

BUDGET HOTEL

☎ 0871 984 6204 📄 01635 278169
Tot Hill Services (A34), Newbury by-pass RG20 9ED
web: www.travelodge.co.uk
dir: Tot Hill Services on A34

Rooms 52 **S** fr £29; **D** fr £29

Holiday Inn Reading West

★★★ 67% HOTEL

☎ 0118 971 4411 📄 0118 971 4442
Bath Rd RG7 5HT
web: www.holidayinn.co.uk
dir: M4 junct 12, follow A4 Theale/Newbury for approx 3.5m. Hotel on left

Located just a moment's drive away from the M4 this hotel is popular with both business and leisure travellers. Bedrooms are comfortable and well equipped with good facilities. Public areas include a lounge bar, restaurant and an intimate courtyard for the summer months. A popular destination for meetings and events.

Rooms 50 (2 fmly) (25 GF) **S** £40-£140; **D** £40-£140* **Facilities** STV Gym New Year Wi-fi **Conf** Class 60 Board 60 Thtr 200 Del from £100 to £185* **Services** Air con **Parking** 150 **Notes** LB ⊗ Civ Wed 160

Elephant at Pangbourne

★★★ 78% ◉ HOTEL

☎ 0118 984 2244 & 07770 268359 📄 0118 976 7346
Church Rd RG8 7AR
e-mail: annica@elephanthotel.co.uk
web: www.elephanthotel.co.uk
dir: A4 Theale/Newbury, right at 2nd rdbt signed Pangbourne. Hotel on left

Centrally located in this bustling village, just a short drive from Reading. Bedrooms are individual in style but identical in the attention to detail, with handcrafted Indian furniture and rich oriental rugs. Guests can enjoy award-winning cuisine in the restaurant or bistro-style dining in the bar area.

Rooms 22 (8 annexe) (2 fmly) (4 GF) **S** £100; **D** £140 (incl. bkfst)* **Facilities** FTV ⛳ Xmas New Year Wi-fi **Conf** Class 40 Board 30 Thtr 60 **Parking** 10 **Notes** ⊗ Civ Wed 60

Forbury Hotel

★★★★★ 81% ◉ HOTEL

☎ 08000 789789 & 0118 958 1234 📄 0118 959 0806
26 The Forbury RG1 3EJ
e-mail: reservations@theforburyhotel.co.uk
dir: Contact hotel for detailed directions

The imposing exterior of this hotel belies the caring approach of the staff who provide helpful service with a smile. The up-to-the-minute bedrooms have very appealing designs and sensory appeal. For film buffs, a

30-seater cinema is also available, complete with refreshments! Cerise is the convivial and stylish venue for enjoying the award-winning cuisine.

Rooms 24 (1 fmly) (1 GF) **Facilities** Xmas New Year Wi-fi **Conf** Class 24 Board 24 Thtr 35 **Services** Lift **Parking** 20 **Notes** ⊗ Civ Wed 50

Crowne Plaza Reading

★★★★ 79% ⊚⊚ HOTEL

☎ 0118 925 9988
Caversham Bridge, Richfield Av RG1 8BD
e-mail: info@cp-reading.co.uk
web: www.crowneplaza.co.uk
dir: A33 to Reading. Follow signs for Caversham & Henley. Take 1st exit at rdbt onto Caversham Rd. Left at rdbt & entrance on right

Located on the banks of the River Thames, this hotel is well positioned for both business and leisure travellers. The air-conditioned bedrooms are smartly appointed and well equipped. Public areas include the stylish Acqua Restaurant, a lounge bar, extensive conference and business facilities and the Revive health club and spa. Secure parking is a real bonus.

Rooms 122 (9 fmly) **S** £65-£185; **D** £65-£185* **Facilities** Spa STV ⓧ Gym Xmas New Year Wi-fi **Conf** Class 110 Board 60 Thtr 200 Del from £179 to £250* **Services** Lift Air con **Parking** 200 **Notes** LB ⊗ Civ Wed 180

Millennium Madejski Hotel Reading

★★★★ 79% ⊚ HOTEL

☎ 0118 925 3500 ▤ 0118 925 3501
Madejski Stadium RG2 0FL
e-mail: sales.reading@millenniumhotels.co.uk
web: www.millenniumhotels.co.uk
dir: M4 junct 11 onto A33, follow signs for Madejski Stadium Complex

A stylish hotel, that features an atrium lobby with specially commissioned water sculpture, is part of the Madejski stadium complex, home to both Reading Football and London Irish Rugby teams. Bedrooms are appointed with spacious workstations and plenty of amenities; there is also a choice of suites and a club floor with its own lounge. The hotel also has a fine dining restaurant.

Rooms 201 (39 fmly) (19 smoking) **Facilities** Spa STV ⓧ supervised Gym Wi-fi **Conf** Class 36 Board 30 Thtr 60 Del from £129 to £299* **Services** Lift Air con **Parking** 250 **Notes** RS Xmas & New Year

Novotel Reading Centre

★★★★ 77% HOTEL

☎ 0118 952 2600 ▤ 0118 952 2610
25b Friar St RG1 1DP
e-mail: h5432@accor.com
web: www.novotel.com
dir: M4 junct 11 or A33 towards Reading, exit on left for Garrard St car park, at rdbt take 3rd exit on Friar St

This attractive and stylish city centre hotel is convenient for Reading's business and shopping centre; it is adjacent to a town centre car park, and has a range of conference facilities and excellent leisure options. The restaurant offers a contemporary style menu and a good wine list too. Bedrooms are comfortable and stylishly designed.

Rooms 178 (15 fmly) **Facilities** STV FTV ⓧ Gym Steam room Wi-fi **Conf** Class 50 Board 36 Thtr 90 **Services** Lift Air con **Parking** 15

Copthorne Hotel Reading

★★★★ 75% HOTEL

☎ 0118 950 0885 ▤ 0118 939 1996
Pingewood RG30 3UN
dir: A33 towards Basingstoke. At Three Mile Cross rdbt right signed Burghfield. After 300mtrs 2nd right, over M4, through lights, hotel on left

Enjoying a secluded and rural setting and yet just a few minutes south of Reading, this modern hotel was built around a man-made lake which is occasionally used for water sport. Bedrooms are generally spacious with good facilities, and most have balconies overlooking the lake and wildlife.

Rooms 81 (23 fmly) **S** £49-£165; **D** £49-£165* **Facilities** STV Gym Watersports Wi-fi **Conf** Class 60 Board 60 Thtr 110 Del from £115 to £185* **Services** Lift **Parking** 250 **Notes** ⊗ Civ Wed 80

Malmaison Reading

★★★ 86% ⊚ HOTEL

☎ 0118 956 2300 ▤ 0118 956 2301
Great Western House, 18-20 Station Rd RG1 1JX
e-mail: reading@malmaison.com
web: www.malmaison.com
dir: Opposite Reading train station

This historic hotel has been transformed to a funky, Malmaison style which reflects its proximity and long-standing relationship with the railway. Public areas feature rail memorabilia and excellent pictures, and include a Café Mal and a meeting room. Bedrooms here have all the amenities a modern executive would expect, plus comfort and quality in abundance. Dining is exciting too, with a menu that features home-grown and local produce accompanied by an impressive wine list.

Rooms 75 (6 fmly) **Facilities** Gym Xmas New Year Wi-fi **Conf** Board 16 **Services** Lift Air con

Best Western Calcot Hotel

★★★ 72% HOTEL

☎ 0118 941 6423 ▤ 0118 945 1223
98 Bath Rd, Calcot RG31 7QN
e-mail: enquiries@calcothotel.net
web: www.calcothotel.co.uk
dir: M4 junct 12 onto A4 towards Reading, hotel in 0.5m on N side of A4

This hotel is conveniently located in a residential area just off the motorway. Bedrooms are well equipped with good business facilities, such as data ports and good workspace. There are attractive public rooms and function suites, and the informal restaurant offers enjoyable food in welcoming surroundings.

Rooms 78 (2 fmly) (6 GF) **Facilities** STV FTV ♫ New Year Wi-fi **Conf** Class 35 Board 35 Thtr 120 Del from £130 to £165 **Parking** 130 **Notes** Closed 25-27 Dec Civ Wed 60

Holiday Inn Reading South

★★★ 70% HOTEL

☎ 0870 400 9067 ▤ 0118 931 1958
Basingstoke Rd RG2 0SL
e-mail: reading@ihg.com
web: www.holidayinn.co.uk
dir: A33 to Reading. 1st rdbt right onto Imperial Way. Hotel on left

This bright hotel provides modern accommodation and the addition of leisure facilities is a bonus at the end of a busy day. Meals are served in Traders restaurant, or snacks are available in the lounge. Callaghans, an Irish style pub offers a relaxing environment with live sports coverage. The business centre offers a good range of conference and meeting rooms.

Rooms 202 (60 fmly) (99 GF) (10 smoking) **S** £45-£155; **D** £45-£155* **Facilities** FTV ⓧ supervised Gym Health & fitness centre Treatment room New Year Wi-fi **Conf** Class 45 Board 50 Thtr 100 Del from £99 to £160 **Services** Air con **Parking** 300 **Notes** LB ⊗ Civ Wed 100

The Wee Waif

Ⓤ

☎ 0118 9440 066 ▤ 0118 9691 525
Old Bath Rd, Charvil RG10 9RJ

Currently the rating for this establishment is not confirmed. This may be due to a change of ownership or because it has only recently joined the AA rating scheme. For further details please see the AA website: theAA.com

Rooms 42

READING *continued*

Comfort Hotel Reading West

[U]

☎ 0118 971 3282 📠 0118 971 4238
Bath Rd, Padworth RG7 5HT
e-mail: info@comfortreading.co.uk
web: www.comfortreading.co.uk
dir: M4 junct 12, A4 (Bath Road) signed Newbury. Hotel approx 2m on left

Currently the rating for this establishment is not confirmed. This may be due to a change of ownership or because it has only recently joined the AA rating scheme. For further details please see the AA website: theAA.com

Rooms 33 (1 fmly) (20 GF) **S** £50-£80; **D** £50-£100 **Facilities** FTV Wi-fi **Conf** Class 50 Board 50 Thtr 120 Del from £90 to £125 **Parking** 40 **Notes** LB ⊗ Civ Wed 100

Ibis Reading Centre

BUDGET HOTEL

☎ 0118 953 3500 📠 0118 953 3501
25A Friar St RG1 1DP
e-mail: H5431@accor.com
web: www.ibishotel.com
dir: Exit A329 into Friar St. Hotel near central train station

Budget Hotel in the main shopping area of Reading with handy NCP parking behind. All rooms are well equipped and comfortable and both dinner and breakfast are available in La Table restaurant. See also the Hotel Groups pages.

Rooms 182 (36 fmly)

Travelodge Reading Central

BUDGET HOTEL

☎ 0871 984 6211 📠 0118 950 3257
Oxford Rd RG1 7LT
web: www.travelodge.co.uk
dir: M4 junct 11, A33 towards Reading, follow signs for A329 (Oxford road)

Travelodge offers good quality, good value, budget accommodation. All offer family rooms sleeping up to four (two adults, two children) with en suite bathroom/shower-room, remote-control TV, tea- and coffee-making facilities and comfortable beds. Food options vary. Breakfast is at the on-site Bar Café restaurant (if available) or to take away. See also Hotel Groups pages.

Rooms 80 **S** fr £29; **D** fr £29

Travelodge Reading (M4 Eastbound)

BUDGET HOTEL

☎ 0871 984 6267 📠 0118 959 2045
Burghfield RG30 3UQ
web: www.travelodge.co.uk
dir: M4 between juncts 11 & 12 eastbound

Rooms 86 **S** fr £29; **D** fr £29 **Conf** Class 20 Board 20 Thtr 20

Travelodge Reading (M4 Westbound)

BUDGET HOTEL

☎ 0871 984 6242 📠 0118 958 2350
Burghfield RG30 3UQ
web: www.travelodge.co.uk
dir: M4 between juncts 11 & 12 westbound

Rooms 100 **S** fr £29; **D** fr £29

Travelodge Reading Oxford Road

BUDGET HOTEL

☎ 0871 984 6357 📠 0118 956 7220
648-654 Oxford Rd RG30 1EH
web: www.travelodge.co.uk
dir: M4 junct 11, follow Reading Town Centre/A33 signs. Then follow A329 signs (through major lights) to dual carriageway. 2nd slip road signed Chatham Street/A329. 1st left signed Pangbourne/A329. At mini rdbt left, remain in right lane. Right at lights onto Oxford Rd. Lodge 1m on right

Rooms 97 (15 fmly) **S** fr £29; **D** fr £29 **Conf** Class 50 Board 40 Thtr 100

Travelodge Reading Whitley

BUDGET HOTEL

☎ 0871 984 6209 📠 0118 975 1303
387 Basingstoke Rd RG2 0JE
web: www.travelodge.co.uk
dir: M4 junct 11, A33 towards Reading, right onto B3031. Lodge 1m on right

Rooms 36 **S** fr £29; **D** fr £29

Copthorne Hotel Slough-Windsor

★★★★ 75% HOTEL

☎ 01753 516222 📠 01753 516237
400 Cippenham Ln SL1 2YE
e-mail: sales.slough@millenniumhotels.co.uk
web: www.millenniumhotels.com
dir: M4 junct 6 & follow A355 to Slough at next rdbt turn left & left again for hotel entrance

Conveniently located for the motorway and for Heathrow Airport, this modern hotel offers visitors a wide range of indoor leisure facilities, and Turner's Grill serves a British menu. Bedrooms provide a useful range of extras including climate control, satellite TV and a trouser press. The hotel offers a discounted entrance fee to some of the attractions in the area.

Rooms 219 (47 fmly) **S** £49-£180; **D** £59-£190*
Facilities STV FTV ✪ Gym Steam room Sauna Wi-fi
Conf Class 160 Board 60 Thtr 250 Del from £140 to £280 **Services** Lift **Parking** 303 **Notes** LB ⊗ Civ Wed 100

The Pinewood Hotel

★★★★ 71% HOTEL

☎ 01753 896400 📠 01753 896500
Wexham Park Ln, George Green SL3 6AP
e-mail: info@pinewoodhotel.co.uk
web: www.bespokehotels.com
dir: A4 N from Slough, A412 towards Uxbridge. Hotel 3m on left

This is a small luxury hotel on the outskirts of Slough. Excellent design is at the forefront throughout, together with good levels of comfort. The Eden brasserie specialises in quality produce, carefully prepared, including dishes cooked on the wood-burning stove. Service is friendly and attentive.

Rooms 49 (16 annexe) (4 fmly) (12 GF) **Facilities** Xmas Wi-fi **Conf** Class 46 Board 40 Thtr 120 **Services** Lift Air con **Parking** 40 **Notes** LB ⊗ Civ Wed 30

Quality Hotel Heathrow

★★★ 73% HOTEL

☎ 01753 684001 🖹 01753 685767
London Rd, Brands Hill SL3 8QB
e-mail: info@qualityheathrow.com
web: www.qualityheathrow.com
dir: M4 junct 5, follow signs for Colnbrook. Hotel approx 250mtrs on right

This stylish, modern hotel is ideally located for Heathrow Airport travellers, and for commercial visitors to Slough. Bedrooms have good facilities, benefit from all-day room service and are smartly furnished. There is a bright and airy open-plan restaurant, bar and lounge. A regular shuttle service, at a small charge, operates for Terminals 1, 2 and 3.

Rooms 128 (23 fmly) (5 GF) **Facilities** STV FTV Gym Wi-fi **Conf** Class 50 Board 40 Thtr 120 Del from £79 to £149* **Services** Lift **Parking** 100 **Notes** ⊗

Holiday Inn Slough-Windsor

★★★ 66% HOTEL

☎ 01753 551551 & 0870 400 7215 🖹 01753 553333
1 Church St, Chalvey SL1 2ND
e-mail: reservations@slough.kewgreen.co.uk
web: www.holidayinn.co.uk
dir: M4 junct 6, take 3rd exit on rdbt onto A355 Tuns Lane. 3rd exit at next rdbt, hotel on right

Located close to the town centre and also to good transport links to Windsor and the M4, this modern hotel is well sited and suitable for business and leisure travellers. Public areas have a bar/lounge area and a brasserie-style restaurant. A good range of meeting and conference rooms is available; secure on-site parking is an additional bonus.

Rooms 150 (64 fmly) (6 GF) (18 smoking) **Facilities** STV Xmas Wi-fi **Conf** Class 12 Board 20 Thtr 40 **Services** Lift **Parking** 150 **Notes** ⊗

Express by Holiday Inn Slough

BUDGET HOTEL

☎ 0844 499 2890 🖹 0844 499 2910
Mill St SL2 5DD
web: www.hiexpress.co.uk
dir: M4 junct 6, A355 signed Slough/Windsor/A332. At Barking Rd 3rd exit into Tuns Lane. Right at Bath Rd, continue into Wellington St. At rdbt 1st exit into William St. Continue into Stoke Rd, right into Mill St

A modern hotel ideal for families and business travellers. Fresh and uncomplicated, the spacious rooms include Sky TV, power shower and tea and coffee-making facilities. Continental buffet breakfast is included in the room rate; other meals may be taken at the nearby family pub or restaurant. See also the Hotel Groups pages.

Rooms 142

Innkeeper's Lodge Slough/Windsor

BUDGET HOTEL

☎ 0845 112 6108 🖹 0845 112 6195
399 London Rd, Langley SL3 8PS
web: www.innkeeperslodge.com/sloughwindsor
dir: M4 junct 5, A4 (London road) towards Slough. Lodge on right

Innkeeper's Lodge represents an exciting, high value concept within the budget hotel market. Comfortable bedrooms provide excellent facilities that include satellite TV and modem points. Options include family rooms; and for the corporate guest, cutting edge IT which includes Wi-fi access. A popular Carvery provides all-day food, including an extensive, complimentary continental breakfast. See also the Hotel Groups pages.

Rooms 57 (15 fmly)

Travelodge Slough

BUDGET HOTEL

☎ 08719 846 253 🖹 0121 521 6026
Landmark Place SL1 1BZ
web: www.travelodge.co.uk
dir: M4 junct 6 towards Slough. Over at rdbt. At 1st lights right towards town centre. At Wellington rdbt right into Windsor Rd (A332). 2nd left into Herschel St

Travelodge offers good quality, good value, budget accommodation. All offer family rooms sleeping up to four (two adults, two children) with en suite bathroom/shower-room, remote-control TV, tea- and coffee-making facilities and comfortable beds. Food options vary. Breakfast is at the on-site Bar Café restaurant (if available) or to take away. See also Hotel Groups pages.

Rooms 156 **S** fr £29; **D** fr £29

The French Horn

★★★ 81% ◎◎ HOTEL

☎ 0118 969 2204 🖹 0118 944 2210
RG4 6TN
e-mail: info@thefrenchhorn.co.uk
dir: From A4 into Sonning, follow B478 through village over bridge, hotel on right, car park on left

This long established Thames-side establishment has a lovely village setting and retains the traditions of classic hotel keeping. The restaurant is a particular attraction and provides attentive service. Bedrooms, including four cottage suites, are spacious and comfortable; many offer stunning views over the river. A private boardroom is available for corporate guests.

Rooms 22 (8 annexe) (4 GF) (4 smoking) **S** £125-£170; **D** £160-£215 (incl. bkfst)* **Facilities** FTV Fishing Wi-fi **Conf** Board 16 **Services** Air con **Parking** 40 **Notes** ⊗ Closed 26-29 Dec

The Swan at Streatley

★★★★ 75% ◎◎ HOTEL

☎ 01491 878800 🖹 01491 872554
High St RG8 9HR
e-mail: sales@swan-at-streatley.co.uk
web: www.swanatstreatley.co.uk
dir: From S right at lights in Streatley, hotel on left before bridge

A stunning location set beside the Thames, ideal for an English summer's day. The bedrooms are well appointed and many enjoy the lovely views. The hotel offers a range of facilities including meeting rooms, and the Magdalen Barge is moored beside the hotel making an unusual, yet perfect meeting venue. A motor launch is available for hire from April to October. The spa includes an indoor heated mineral pool and offers a range of treatments. Cuisine is accomplished and dining here should not be missed.

Rooms 45 (12 GF) **S** £110-£120; **D** £138-£150 (incl. bkfst)* **Facilities** Spa STV 🕓 supervised Fishing ⤴ Gym Electric motor launches for hire Apr-Oct Xmas New Year Wi-fi **Conf** Class 80 Board 60 Thtr 140 Del from £165 to £210* **Parking** 170 **Notes** LB Civ Wed 130

Oakley Court

★★★★ 79% ◎ HOTEL

☎ 01753 609988 & 609900 🖹 01628 637011
Windsor Rd, Water Oakley SL4 5UR
e-mail: reservations@oakleycourt.com
web: www.oakleycourt.com
dir: M4 junct 6, A355, then A332 towards Windsor, right onto A308 towards Maidenhead. Pass racecourse, hotel 2.5m on right

Built in 1859 this splendid Victorian Gothic mansion is enviably situated in extensive grounds that lead down to the Thames. All rooms are spacious, beautifully furnished and many enjoy river views. Extensive public areas include a range of comfortable lounges and the Oakleaf Restaurant. The comprehensive leisure facilities include a 9-hole golf course.

Rooms 118 (109 annexe) (5 fmly) (28 GF) **Facilities** Spa 🕓 ↧ 9 ⚓ ⤴ Gym Boating Sauna Snooker Xmas New Year Wi-fi **Conf** Class 90 Board 50 Thtr 170 **Services** Air con **Parking** 120 **Notes** ⊗ Civ Wed 120

WINDSOR *continued*

Mercure Castle

★★★★ 77% ◉◉ HOTEL

☎ 01753 851577 📄 01753 856930
18 High St SL4 1LJ
e-mail: h6618@accor.com
web: www.mercure-uk.com
dir: M4 junct 6/M25 junct 15 - follow signs to Windsor town centre & castle. Hotel at top of hill by castle opposite Guildhall

This is one of the oldest hotels in Windsor, beginning life as a coaching inn in the 16th century. Located opposite Windsor Castle, it is an ideal base from which to explore the town. Stylish bedrooms are thoughtfully equipped and include four-poster and executive rooms. Public areas are spacious and tastefully decorated.

Rooms 108 (70 annexe) (18 fmly) **S** £80-£310;
D £80-£310* **Facilities** STV Xmas New Year Wi-fi
Conf Class 130 Board 80 Thtr 400 Del from £155 to £295
Services Lift Air con **Parking** 135 **Notes** LB ⊗
Civ Wed 300

Sir Christopher Wren's House Hotel & Spa

★★★★ 76% ◉◉ HOTEL

☎ 01753 861354 & 442400 📄 01753 860172
Thames St SL4 1PX
e-mail: reservations@wrensgroup.com
web: www.sirchristopherwren.co.uk
dir: M4 junct 6, 1st exit from relief road, follow signs to Windsor, 1st major exit on left, turn left at lights

This hotel has an enviable location right on the edge of the River Thames overlooking Eton Bridge. Diners in Strok's, the award-winning restaurant, enjoy the best views. A variety of well-appointed bedrooms are available, including several in the adjacent courtyard rooms. There is also a health and leisure spa, and secure parking is available.

Rooms 95 (38 annexe) (11 fmly) (3 GF) **S** £80-£170;
D £85-£320 **Facilities** Spa FTV Gym Health & beauty club Sauna Xmas New Year Wi-fi **Conf** Class 50 Board 50 Thtr 90 Del from £225 to £260 **Parking** 10 **Notes** LB ⊗ Civ Wed 90

The Harte & Garter Hotel & Spa

folio Hotels

★★★★ 74% HOTEL

☎ 0844 855 9131 📄 01753 830527
High St SL4 1PH
e-mail: harteandgarter@foliohotels.com
web: www.foliohotels.com/harteandgarter
dir: M4 junct 6/ A332 follow town centre signs, hotel opposite front entrance to Windsor Castle

Enjoying an enviable location in the centre of Windsor, this hotel overlooks the magnificent Windsor Castle. Bedrooms are comfortably appointed and interiors blend modern and classic styles well. Public areas include the Tower Brasserie and tea room which also enjoys views of the castle, a new spa facility where guests can unwind, and a range of conference and meeting rooms.

Rooms 79 (40 annexe) (3 GF) **Facilities** Spa FTV Thermal suite & Hydro pool ♫ Xmas New Year Wi-fi **Conf** Class 80 Board 80 Thtr 260 **Services** Lift **Notes** LB ⊗ Civ Wed 180

Royal Adelaide

★★★★ 71% HOTEL

☎ 01753 863916 & 07710 473130 📠 01753 830682
46 Kings Rd SL4 2AG
e-mail: info@theroyaladelaide.com
web: www.theroyaladelaide.com
dir: M4 junct 6, A322 to Windsor. 1st left off rdbt into
Clarence Rd. At 4th lights right into Sheet St and into
Kings Rd. Hotel on right

This attractive Georgian-style hotel enjoys a quiet
location yet is only a short walk from the town centre and
benefiting from off-road parking. Bedrooms vary in size.
Public areas are tastefully appointed and include a range
of meeting rooms, a bar and an elegant restaurant.

Rooms 42 (4 annexe) (6 fmly) (8 GF) (5 smoking)
S fr £69; **D** fr £89 (incl. bkfst)* **Facilities** STV Xmas New
Year Wi-fi **Conf** Class 80 Board 50 Thtr 100
Del from £149* **Services** Air con **Parking** 16 **Notes** LB ⊗
Civ Wed

Christopher Hotel

★★★ 75% HOTEL

☎ 01753 852359 📠 01753 830914
110 High St, Eton SL4 6AN
e-mail: sales@thechristopher.co.uk
web: www.thechristopher.co.uk
dir: M4 junct 5 (Slough E), Colnbrook Datchet Eton
(B470). At rdbt 2nd exit for Datchet. Right at mini rdbt
(Eton), left into Eton Rd (3rd rdbt). Left, hotel on right

This hotel benefits from an ideal location in Eton, being
only a short stroll across the pedestrian bridge from
historic Windsor Castle and the many other attractions
the town has to offer. The hotel has comfortable and
smartly decorated accommodation, and a wide range of
dishes is available in the informal bar and grill. A stylish
room is available for private dining or for meetings.

Rooms 33 (22 annexe) (10 fmly) (22 GF) **S** £98.60–£116;
D £138–£165* **Facilities** FTV Xmas New Year Wi-fi
Conf Board 10 Thtr 30 Del from £178 to £200*
Parking 19 **Notes** LB

Innkeeper's Lodge Old Windsor

BUDGET HOTEL

☎ 0845 112 6104 📠 0845 112 6199
14 Straight Rd, Old Windsor SL4 2RR
web: www.innkeeperslodge.com/oldwindsor
dir: M4 or M25 junct 13 towards Windsor Castle/Old
Windsor on A308 from either direction. Lodge on A308

Innkeeper's Lodge represents an exciting, high value
concept within the budget hotel market. Comfortable
bedrooms provide excellent facilities that include satellite
TV and modem points. Options include family rooms; and
for the corporate guest, cutting edge IT which includes
Wi-fi access. A popular Carvery provides all-day food,
including an extensive, complimentary continental
breakfast. See also the Hotel Groups pages.

Rooms 15 (2 fmly)

Travelodge Windsor Central

BUDGET HOTEL

☎ 0871 984 6331
34 King Edward Court SL4 1TG
web: www.travelodge.co.uk
dir: Within King Edward Court shopping precinct

Travelodge offers good quality, good value, budget
accommodation. All offer family rooms sleeping up to four
(two adults, two children) with en suite bathroom/
shower-room, remote-control TV, tea- and coffee-making
facilities and comfortable beds. Food options vary.
Breakfast is at the on-site Bar Café restaurant (if
available) or to take away. See also Hotel Groups pages.

Rooms 113 **S** fr £29; **D** fr £29

Best Western Reading Moat House

★★★★ 75% HOTEL

☎ 0870 225 0601 📠 0118 935 1646
Mill Ln, Sindlesham RG41 5DF
e-mail: ops.reading@qmh-hotels.com
web: www.bestwestern.co.uk/readingmoathouse
dir: Towards Reading on A329(M), take 1st exit to
Winnersh. Follow Lower Earley Way North. Hotel on left

Located just off the M4 on the outskirts of Reading, this
smart, modern hotel has been sympathetically built

around a 19th-century mill house. Bedrooms are stylish
and have a contemporary feel to them. Spacious public
areas include good conference rooms, a spacious bar and
restaurant, as well as a business centre and a small
fitness area.

Best Western Reading Moat House

Rooms 129 (15 fmly) (22 GF) (10 smoking) **S** £114–£144;
D £114–£144* **Facilities** STV Fishing Gym ♫ Xmas New
Year Wi-fi **Conf** Class 40 Board 40 Thtr 80 **Services** Lift
Air con **Parking** 250 **Notes** LB ⊗ Civ Wed 80

Aztec Hotel & Spa

shire
hotels & spas

★★★★ 80% ⊛ HOTEL

☎ 01454 201090 📠 01454 201593
Aztec West Business Park, Almondsbury BS32 4TS
e-mail: aztec@shirehotels.com
web: www.aztechotelbristol.com
dir: Access via M5 junct 16 & M4

Situated close to Cribbs Causeway shopping centre and
major motorway links, this stylish hotel offers
comfortable, very well-equipped bedrooms. Built in a
Nordic style, public rooms boast log fires and vaulted
ceilings. Leisure facilities include a popular gym and
good size pool. The Quarterjacks restaurant offers relaxed
informal dining with a focus on simply prepared, quality
regional foods.

Rooms 128 (8 fmly) (29 GF) **Facilities** Spa STV Ⓧ Gym
Steam room Sauna Children's splash pool Activity studio
New Year Wi-fi **Conf** Class 120 Board 36 Thtr 200
Services Lift **Parking** 240 **Notes** ⊗ Civ Wed 120

Bristol Marriott Royal Hotel

Marriott
HOTELS & RESORTS

★★★★ 80% ⊛ HOTEL

☎ 0117 925 5100 📠 0117 925 1515
College Green BS1 5TA
e-mail: bristol.royal@marriotthotels.co.uk
web: www.bristolmarriottroyal.co.uk
dir: next to cathedral

A truly stunning hotel located in the centre of the city,
next to the cathedral. Public areas are particularly
impressive with luxurious lounges and a leisure club.
Dining options include the informal Terrace and the really

continued

BRISTOL *continued*

spectacular, restaurant adjacent to the champagne bar. The spacious bedrooms have the benefit of air conditioning, comfortable armchairs and marble bathrooms.

Rooms 242 **Facilities** ⊙ Gym Xmas **Conf** Class 80 Board 84 Thtr 300 **Services** Lift Air con **Parking** 200 **Notes** ⊗ Civ Wed 200

Cadbury House Hotel, Health Club & Spa

★★★★ 78% ⊛⊛ HOTEL

☎ 01934 834343 📠 01934 834390
Frost Hill, Congresbury BS49 5AD
e-mail: info@cadburyhouse.com
web: www.cadburyhouse.com
dir: On B3133, approx 0.25m from A370 at Congresbury

Externally this newly developed hotel presents an interesting blend of old and new, but inside there's contemporary, stylish accommodation with a wide range of facilities, suitable for both business and leisure guests. The bar has a vibrant atmosphere while the restaurant is relaxed and the service friendly. Just a stroll away from the main building is the leisure club and spa featuring a good sized pool, treatment rooms and an air conditioned gym with state-of-the-art equipment.

Rooms 72 (4 fmly) **S** £79-£130; **D** £79-£130
Facilities Spa FTV ⊙ Gym ♫ Xmas New Year Wi-fi
Conf Class 150 Board 60 Thtr 250 Del from £120 to £180
Services Lift Air con **Parking** 350 **Notes** LB ⊗ Civ Wed 130

City Inn Bristol

★★★★ 77% ⊛⊛ HOTEL

CITY INN

☎ 0117 925 1001 📠 0117 907 4116
Temple Way BS1 6BF
e-mail: bristol.reservations@cityinn.com
web: www.cityinn.com
dir: M4 junct 19 onto M32. Continue to end, turn left & follow signs to Temple Meads Station. Through underpass, hotel on right

This hotel was first of the City Inn brand and it enjoys a good central location on Temple Way. Contemporary bedrooms have all benefited from refurbishment, featuring iMac computers, complimentary Wi-fi and enhanced air-conditioning. The popular city café offers a high standard of modern cooking, friendly and attentive

service. Several meeting rooms and limited parking are a further bonus.

Rooms 167 (3 GF) **S** £99-£195; **D** £99-£195*
Facilities STV FTV Gym Xmas New Year Wi-fi
Conf Class 26 Board 28 Thtr 50 Del from £125 to £270*
Services Lift Air con **Parking** 45 **Notes** ⊗ Civ Wed 50

Mercure Holland House Hotel & Spa

★★★★ 77% HOTEL

☎ 0117 968 9900 📠 0117 968 9866
Redcliffe Hill BS1 6SQ
e-mail: h6698@accor.com
web: www.mercure.com
dir: M4 junct 19 towards city centre, follow signs A4 then A370, take A38 Redcliffe Hill. Hotel opposite St Mary Redcliffe Church

This modern hotel, just a ten minute walk from Bristol Temple Meads, has striking, contemporary style throughout, and offers some impressive facilities including a spa, a fitness suite and meeting rooms. The hotel has a green-bicycle service for guests. Bedrooms are stylishly designed with large plasma screen TVs, comfortable beds and free internet access. Dining is offered in the Phoenix Restaurant and bar.

Rooms 275 (44 GF) **S** £69-£280; **D** £79-£380 (incl. bkfst)* **Facilities** Spa FTV ⊙ Gym Free bike rental ♫ Xmas New Year Wi-fi **Conf** Class 150 Board 80 Thtr 240 **Services** Lift Air con **Parking** 144 **Notes** LB Civ Wed 240

Bristol Marriott City Centre

★★★★ 75% HOTEL

☎ 0117 929 4281 📠 0117 927 6377
Lower Castle St BS1 3AD
web: www.bristolmarriottcitycentre.co.uk
dir: M32 follow signs to Broadmead, take slip road to large rdbt, take 3rd exit. Hotel on right

Situated at the foot of the picturesque Castle Park, this mainly business-orientated hotel is well placed for the city centre. Executive and deluxe bedrooms have high speed internet access. In addition to a coffee bar and lounge menu, the Mediterrano Restaurant offers an interesting selection of well-prepared dishes.

Rooms 300 (135 fmly) **Facilities** ⊙ Gym Steam room **Conf** Class 280 Board 40 Thtr 600 **Services** Lift Air con **Notes** ⊗

The Grand by Thistle

thistle

★★★★ 75% HOTEL

☎ 0871 376 9042 📠 0871 376 9142
Broad St BS1 2EL
e-mail: thegrand@thistle.co.uk
web: www.thistle.com/bristol
dir: In city centre pass The Galleries. 3rd right into Broad St

This large hotel is situated in the heart of the city, and benefits from its own secure parking. Bedrooms are well equipped and comfortably appointed, and include a number of Premium Executive rooms. The public areas include leisure and therapy treatment rooms and there is an impressive range of conference and banquet facilities.

Rooms 182 (10 fmly) **Facilities** Spa STV ⊙ supervised Gym Steam room Sauna Solarium Xmas New Year Wi-fi **Conf** Class 250 Board 40 Thtr 600 Del from £130 to £195* **Services** Lift Air con **Parking** 150 **Notes** ⊗ Civ Wed 500

Hotel du Vin Bristol

Hotel du Vin & Bistro

★★★★ 74% ⊛ TOWN HOUSE HOTEL

☎ 0117 925 5577 📠 0117 925 1199
The Sugar House, Narrow Lewins Mead BS1 2NU
e-mail: info.bristol@hotelduvin.com
web: www.hotelduvin.com
dir: From A4 follow city centre signs. After 400yds pass Rupert St NCP on right. Hotel on opposite carriageway

This hotel is part of one of Britain's most innovative and expanding hotel groups that offer high standards of hospitality and accommodation. Housed in a Grade II listed, converted 18th-century sugar refinery, it provides great facilities with a modern, minimalist design. The bedrooms are exceptionally well appointed, and the bistro offers an excellent menu and wine list.

Rooms 40 (10 fmly) **S** £145-£360; **Facilities** STV FTV Xmas New Year Wi-fi **Conf** Class 36 Board 34 Thtr 72 Del from £170 to £205* **Services** Lift **Parking** 28 **Notes** Civ Wed 65

Mercure Brigstow Bristol

★★★★ 74% ◎ HOTEL

☎ 0117 929 1030 📄 0117 929 2030
5-7 Welsh Back BS1 4SP
e-mail: H6548@accor.com
web: www.mercure.com
dir: From the centre follow Baldwin St then right into Queen Charlotte St

In a prime position on the river this handsome purpose-built hotel is designed and finished with care. The shopping centre and theatres are within easy walking distance. The stylish bedrooms are extremely well equipped, including plasma TV screens in the bathrooms. There is an integrated state-of-the-art conference and meeting centre, and a smart restaurant and bar overlooking the harbour. Guests have complimentary use of a squash and health club, plus free internet access.

Rooms 116 **S** £69-£159; **D** £69-£159* **Facilities** STV Gym Free access to nearby gym & squash courts New Year Wi-fi **Conf** Class 25 Board 23 Thtr 70 **Services** Lift Air con **Notes** LB ⊗ Civ Wed 50

The Bristol Hotel

★★★★ 74% HOTEL

☎ 0117 923 0333 📄 0117 923 0300
Prince St BS1 4QF
e-mail: bristol@doylecollection.com
web: www.doylecollection.com
dir: from Temple Meads at 1st rdbt into Victoria St. At Bristol Bridge lights left into Baldwin St, 2nd left into Marsh St, straight ahead

This modern hotel enjoys an excellent location near Bristol's Millennium project. Bedrooms vary in size and are well appointed with a range of facilities. There is a choice of eating options, including a quayside restaurant and adjoining inn. Extensive conference facilities are also available.

Rooms 192 (17 fmly) **Facilities** STV Complimentary use of nearby gym ♬ Xmas New Year Wi-fi **Conf** Class 160 Board 80 Thtr 400 **Services** Lift **Parking** 400 **Notes** ⊗

Ramada Bristol City

★★★★ 74% HOTEL

☎ 0844 845 9100 📄 0117 925 5054
Redcliffe Way BS1 6NJ
e-mail: sales.bristol@ramadajarvis.co.uk
web: www.ramadajarvis.co.uk
dir: 400yds from Temple Meads BR station, before church

This large modern hotel is situated in the heart of the city centre and offers spacious public areas and ample parking. Bedrooms are well equipped for both business and leisure guests. Dining options include a relaxed bar and a unique kiln restaurant where a good selection of freshly prepared dishes is available.

Rooms 201 (4 fmly) (18 smoking) **S** £59-£175; **D** £69-£225 **Facilities** FTV ⌕ supervised Gym Sauna

Steam room New Year Wi-fi **Conf** Class 120 Board 75 Thtr 300 Del from £90 to £155 **Services** Lift Air con **Parking** 150 **Notes** LB ⊗ Civ Wed 250

Holiday Inn Bristol Filton

★★★★ 73% HOTEL

☎ 0870 400 9014 📄 0117 956 9735
Filton Rd, Hambrook BS16 1QX
e-mail: bristol@ihg.com
web: www.holidayinn.co.uk
dir: M4 junct 19/M32 junct 1/A4174 towards Filton & Bristol. Hotel 800yds on left

With easy access of both the M4 and M5 this is, understandably, a popular hotel in particular with business guests. Public areas are spacious and relaxing with a wide choice of comfortable seating options. There are two restaurants - Sampans with a selection of dishes from the Far East, and the more traditional Junction Restaurant. Bedrooms vary in size, but all are well furnished and well equipped. A large car park, leisure facilities and range of conference rooms are all available.

Rooms 211 (40 fmly) (18 GF) (12 smoking) **Facilities** STV ⌕ supervised Fishing Gym Treatment room Xmas New Year Wi-fi **Conf** Class 120 Board 30 Thtr 250 **Services** Lift Air con **Parking** 250 **Notes** ⊗ Civ Wed 150

Grange

★★★★ 71% COUNTRY HOUSE HOTEL

☎ 01454 777333 📄 01454 777447
Northwoods, Winterbourne BS36 1RP
e-mail: sales.grange@ramadajarvis.co.uk
web: www.ramadajarvis.co.uk
dir: A38 towards Filton/Bristol. At rdbt take 1st exit into Bradley Stoke Way, at lights take 1st left into Woodlands Lane, at 2nd rdbt turn left into Tench Lane. After 1m turn left at T-junct, hotel 200yds on left

Situated in 18 acres of attractive grounds, this pleasant hotel is only a short drive from the city centre. Bedrooms are spacious and well equipped; there is a leisure centre and pool and a range of meeting facilities.

Rooms 68 (6 fmly) (22 GF) (6 smoking) **S** £68-£140; **D** £68-£140* **Facilities** Spa STV FTV ⌕ supervised ⌘ Gym Sauna Xmas New Year Wi-fi **Conf** Class 120 Board 134 Thtr 150 Del from £120 to £155 **Parking** 150 **Notes** Civ Wed 150

Novotel Bristol Centre

★★★★ 70% HOTEL

☎ 0117 976 9988 📄 0117 925 5040
Victoria St BS1 6HY
e-mail: H5622@accor.com
web: www.novotel.com
dir: At end of M32 follow signs for Temple Meads station to rdbt. Final exit, hotel immediately on right

This city centre provides smart, contemporary style accommodation. Most of the bedrooms demonstrate the latest Novotel 'Novation' style with unique swivel desk, internet access, air-conditioning and a host of extras. The hotel is convenient for the mainline railway station and also has its own car park.

Rooms 131 (20 fmly) (4 smoking) **S** £59-£149; **D** £59-£149* **Facilities** STV Gym Wi-fi **Conf** Class 70 Board 35 Thtr 210 Del from £130 to £180* **Services** Lift **Parking** 120 **Notes** LB Civ Wed 100

Redwood Hotel & Country Club

★★★★ 70% HOTEL

☎ 01275 393901 📄 01275 392104
Beggar Bush Ln, Failand BS8 3TG
e-mail: info@bespokehotels.com
web: www.bespokehotels.com
dir: M5 junct 19, A369, 3m right at lights. Hotel 1m on left

Situated close to the suspension bridge, this popular hotel offers guests a peaceful location combined with excellent leisure facilities, including a cinema, gym, squash, badminton and tennis courts, plus indoor and outdoor pools. Bedrooms have plenty of amenities and are well suited to the business guest.

Rooms 112 (1 fmly) **Facilities** ⌕ ⌘ ⌘ Gym Squash Cinema Aerobics/Dance studios Badminton courts Xmas New Year Wi-fi **Conf** Class 100 Board 40 Thtr 240 **Parking** 1000 **Notes** ⊗ Civ Wed 200

Berkeley Square

CLASSIC BRITISH HOTELS

★★★ 77% HOTEL

☎ 0117 925 4000 📄 0117 925 2970
15 Berkeley Square, Clifton BS8 1HB
e-mail: berkeley@cliftonhotels.com
web: www.cliftonhotels.com/chg.html
dir: M32 follow Clifton signs. 1st left at lights by Nills Memorial Tower (University) into Berkeley Sq

Set in a pleasant square close to the university, art gallery and Clifton Village, this smart, elegant Georgian hotel has modern, stylishly decorated bedrooms that feature many welcome extras. There is a cosy lounge and stylish restaurant on the ground floor and a smart, contemporary bar in the basement. A small garden is also available at the rear of the hotel.

Rooms 43 (4 GF) **Facilities** Use of local gym & swimming pool **Services** Lift **Parking** 20

BRISTOL *continued*

Arno's Manor

★★★ 74% HOTEL

☎ 0117 971 1461 ▤ 0117 971 5507
470 Bath Rd, Arno's Vale BS4 3HQ
e-mail: arnos.manor@forestdale.com
web: www.arnosmanorhotel.co.uk
dir: From end of M32 follow signs for Bath. Hotel on right of A4 after 2m. Next to ITV West TV studio

Once the home of a wealthy merchant, this historic 18th-century building is now a comfortable hotel and offers spacious, well-appointed bedrooms with plenty of workspace. The lounge was once the chapel and has many original features, while meals are taken in the atmospheric, conservatory-style restaurant.

Rooms 73 (5 fmly) (7 GF) **S** £74-£99; **D** £87-£159 (incl. bkfst)* **Facilities** FTV Xmas New Year Wi-fi **Conf** Class 50 Board 30 Thtr 150 **Services** Lift **Parking** 200 **Notes** ⊗ Civ Wed 100

Holiday Inn Bristol Airport

★★★ 73% HOTEL

☎ 01934 861123 ▤ 01934 861133
A38 Bridgwater Rd, Cowslip Garden BS40 5RB
e-mail: reception@hibristolairport.co.uk
web: www.hibristolairport.co.uk
dir: From Bristol, W on A38. Hotel 3m from Bristol International Airport on right

Situated on the A38 just a short drive from Bristol Airport, this purpose-built hotel provides an ideal stopover for air passengers, but is also well suited for leisure and business guests. Bedrooms are comfortably furnished and include a good range of welcome extras. Dinner and breakfast offer a varied range of dishes and are served in the relaxing 38 Restaurant. There is a small gym, two conference rooms and ample parking.

Rooms 80 (4 fmly) (12 GF) (12 smoking)
S £59.95-£119.95; **D** £59.95-£119.95 **Facilities** STV Gym Wi-fi **Conf** Board 24 Thtr 60 Del from £135 to £145 **Services** Lift Air con **Parking** 120 **Notes** LB ⊗

Best Western Victoria Square

★★ 79% HOTEL

☎ 0117 973 9058 ▤ 0117 970 6929
Victoria Square, Clifton BS8 4EW
e-mail: info@victoriasquarehotel.co.uk
dir: M5 junct 19, follow Clifton signs. Over suspension/ toll bridge, right into Clifton Down Rd. Left into Merchants Rd then into Victoria Square

This welcoming hotel offers high quality, individual bedrooms and bathrooms offering a variety of shapes and sizes. Ideally located, the hotel is just one mile from the city centre and a two-minute stroll from the heart of Clifton village. The atmosphere is relaxed, and guests have a choice of dining options - from lighter meals in

the bar to a range of imaginative dishes in the main restaurant.

Best Western Victoria Square

Rooms 41 (20 annexe) (3 fmly) (3 GF) **S** £59-£95; **D** £79-£125 (incl. bkfst)* **Facilities** FTV Wi-fi **Conf** Class 15 Board 20 Thtr 25 Del from £160 to £175* **Parking** 22 **Notes** LB

Rodney Hotel

★★ 76% ⊛ HOTEL

☎ 0117 973 5422 ▤ 0117 946 7092
4 Rodney Place, Clifton BS8 4HY
e-mail: rodney@cliftonhotels.com
dir: Off Clifton Down Rd

With easy access from the M5, this attractive, listed building in Clifton is conveniently close to the city centre. The individually decorated bedrooms provide a useful range of extra facilities for the business traveller; the public areas include a smart bar and small restaurant offering enjoyable and carefully prepared dishes. A pleasant rear garden provides additional seating in the summer months.

Rooms 31 (1 fmly) (2 GF) **S** £47-£76; **D** £69-£105* **Facilities** STV Wi-fi **Conf** Class 20 Board 20 Thtr 30 **Parking** 10 **Notes** LB Closed 22 Dec-3 Jan RS Sun

Clifton

★★ 75% HOTEL

☎ 0117 973 6882 ▤ 0117 974 1082
St Pauls Rd, Clifton BS8 1LX
e-mail: clifton@cliftonhotels.com
web: www.cliftonhotels.com/clifton
dir: M32 follow Bristol/Clifton signs, along Park St. Left at lights into St Pauls Rd

This popular hotel offers very well equipped bedrooms and relaxed, friendly service. There is a welcoming lounge by the reception, and in summer months drinks and meals can be enjoyed on the terrace. Racks Bar and Restaurant offers an interesting selection of modern dishes in informal surroundings. There is some street parking, but for a small charge, secure garage parking is available.

Rooms 59 (2 fmly) (12 GF) (9 smoking) **S** £37-£77; **D** £58-£86* **Facilities** STV Wi-fi **Services** Lift **Parking** 12 **Notes** LB

Radisson Blu Hotel Bristol *Radisson*

Ⓤ

☎ 01179 349500 ▤ 01179 175518
Broad Qauy BS1 4BY

Opening in Summer 2009, currently the rating for this establishment is not confirmed. This may be due to a change of ownership or because it has only recently joined the AA rating scheme For further details please see the AA website: theAA.com

Rooms 176

The Avon Gorge

Ⓤ

☎ 0117 973 8955 ▤ 0117 923 8125
Sion Hill, Clifton BS8 4LD
e-mail: info@theavongorge.com
dir: From S: M5 junct 19, A369 to Clifton Toll, over suspension bridge, 1st right into Sion Hill. From N: M5 junct 18A, A4 to Bristol, under suspension bridge, follow signs to bridge, exit Sion Hill

Currently the rating for this establishment is not confirmed. This may be due to a change of ownership or because it has only recently joined the AA rating scheme. For further details please see the AA website: theAA.com

Rooms 75 (8 fmly) **S** £69-£99; **D** £79-£135 (incl. bkfst)* **Facilities** STV Xmas New Year Wi-fi **Conf** Class 40 Board 30 Thtr 100 Del from £135 to £165* **Services** Lift **Parking** 25 **Notes** LB Civ Wed 100

Henbury Lodge

Ⓤ

☎ 0117 950 2615 ▤ 0117 950 9532
Station Rd, Henbury BS10 7QQ
e-mail: contactus@henburylodgehotel.com
web: www.henburylodgehotel.com
dir: M5 junct 17/A4018 towards city centre, 3rd rdbt right into Crow Ln. At end turn right, hotel 200mtrs on right

Currently the rating for this establishment is not confirmed. This may be due to a change of ownership or because it has only recently joined the AA rating scheme. For further details please see the AA website: theAA.com

Rooms 20 **Notes** Closed 22 Dec-2 Jan

Express by Holiday Inn Bristol - North

BUDGET HOTEL

☎ 0870 443 0036 🖨 0870 443 0037
New Rd, Bristol Parkway Business Park BS34 8SJ
e-mail: managerbristolnorth@expressholidayinn.co.uk
web: www.hiexpress.com/bristolnorth
dir: M4 junct 19/M32 junct 1. Follow signs for Bristol Parkway Station, right at main rdbt, hotel on left. For access, left at next 2 rdbts onto New Road, hotel entrance 100yds past Bristol & West building

A modern hotel ideal for families and business travellers. Fresh and uncomplicated, the spacious rooms include Sky TV, power shower and tea and coffee-making facilities. Continental buffet breakfast is included in the room rate; other meals may be taken at the nearby family pub or restaurant. See also the Hotel Groups pages.

Rooms 133 (106 fmly) **Conf** Class 20 Board 24 Thtr 30

Travelodge Bristol Central

BUDGET HOTEL

☎ 0871 984 6223 🖨 0117 925 5149
Anchor Rd, Harbourside BS1 5TT
web: www.travelodge.co.uk
dir: on Anchor Road (A4) on left

Travelodge offers good quality, good value, budget accommodation. All offer family rooms sleeping up to four (two adults, two children) with en suite bathroom/shower-room, remote-control TV, tea- and coffee-making facilities and comfortable beds. Food options vary. Breakfast is at the on-site Bar Café restaurant (if available) or to take away. See also Hotel Groups pages.

Rooms 119 **S** fr £29; **D** fr £29

Travelodge Bristol Cribbs Causeway

BUDGET HOTEL

☎ 0871 984 6222 🖨 0117 950 1530
Cribbs Causeway BS10 7TL
web: www.travelodge.co.uk
dir: On A4018, just off M5 junct 17. Behind Lamb & Flag Harvester

Rooms 56 **S** fr £29; **D** fr £29

Innkeeper's Lodge Aylesbury East

BUDGET HOTEL

☎ 0845 112 6094 🖨 0845 112 6209
London Rd HP22 5HP
web: www.innkeeperslodge.com/aylesburyeast
dir: A41, N for 10m, follow Wendover, Dunstable & Tring signs. At top of slip road follow Wendover, Halton & Aston Clinton signs. Into Aston Clinton (London Rd). Lodge on right

Innkeeper's Lodge represents an exciting, high value concept within the budget hotel market. Comfortable bedrooms provide excellent facilities that include satellite TV and modem points. This carefully restored lodge is in a picturesque setting and has its own unique style and quirky character. Food is served all day, and an extensive, complimentary continental breakfast is offered. See also the Hotel Groups pages.

Rooms 11

Hartwell House Hotel, Restaurant & Spa

★★★★ ☺☺☺ HOTEL

☎ 01296 747444 🖨 01296 747450
Oxford Rd HP17 8NR
e-mail: info@hartwell-house.com
web: www.hartwell-house.com
dir: From S: M40 junct 7, A329 to Thame, then A418 towards Aylesbury. After 6m, through Stone, hotel on left. From N: M40 junct 9 for Bicester. A41 to Aylesbury, A418 to Oxford for 2m. Hotel on right

This beautiful, historic house is set in 90 acres of unspoilt parkland. The grand public rooms are truly magnificent, and feature many fine works of art. The service standards are very high, being attentive and traditional without stuffiness. There is an elegant, award-winning restaurant where carefully prepared dishes use the best local produce. Bedrooms are spacious, elegant and very comfortable. Most are in the main house, but some, including suites, are in the nearby, renovated coach house, which also houses an excellent spa.

Rooms 46 (16 annexe) (3 fmly) (10 GF) **S** £160-£200; **D** £185-£360 (incl. bkfst)* **Facilities** Spa STV 🄌 supervised 🏊 🏌 Gym Sauna treatment rooms Steam rooms 🎵 Xmas New Year Wi-fi **Conf** Class 40 Board 40 Thtr 100 Del from £225 to £245* **Services** Lift **Parking** 91 **Notes** LB No children 6yrs RS Xmas/New Year Civ Wed 60

Holiday Inn Aylesbury

★★★ 74% HOTEL

☎ 01296 734000 🖨 01296 392211
Aston Clinton Rd HP22 5AA
e-mail: aylesbury@ihg.com
web: www.holidayinn.co.uk
dir: M25 junct 20, follow A41. Hotel on left on entering Aylesbury

Situated to the south of town, this hotel is conveniently located for local businesses and the town centre. Public areas are extensive including the well-equipped health club and a superb range of meeting rooms. Bedrooms are comfortable and are equipped with a host of extras.

continued

AYLESBURY *continued*

Rooms 139 (45 fmly) (69 GF) (8 smoking) **Facilities** Spa STV ⬚ supervised Gym Steam room, Sauna, Dance studio, Gym New Year Wi-fi **Conf** Class 50 Board 50 Thtr 120 Del from £99 to £165* **Services** Air con **Parking** 160 **Notes** Civ Wed 120

Holiday Inn Garden Court Aylesbury

Ⓤ

☎ 01296 398839 ⓘ 01296 394108
Buckingham Rd, Watermead HP19 0FY
web: www.holidayinn.co.uk
dir: From Aylesbury take A413 towards Buckingham. Hotel on right

Currently the rating for this establishment is not confirmed. This may be due to a change of ownership or because it has only recently joined the AA rating scheme. For further details please see the AA website: theAA.com

Rooms 39

Innkeeper's Lodge Aylesbury South

BUDGET HOTEL

☎ 0845 112 6095 ⓘ 0845 112 6208
40 Main St, Weston Turville HP22 5RW
web: www.innkeeperslodge.com/aylesburysouth
dir: M25 junct 20/A41 towards Hemel Hempstead. Onto A41 towards Aylesbury for 12m to Aston Clinton. Left onto B4544 to Weston Turville. Lodge on left

Innkeeper's Lodge represents an exciting, high value concept within the budget hotel market. Comfortable bedrooms provide excellent facilities that include satellite TV and modem points. Options include family rooms; and for the corporate guest, cutting edge IT includes Wi-fi access. Food is served all day in the adjacent Country Pub. The extensive continental breakfast is complimentary. See also the Hotel Groups pages.

Rooms 16

BEACONSFIELD Map 6 SU99

Innkeeper's Lodge Beaconsfield

BUDGET HOTEL

☎ 0845 112 6096 ⓘ 0845 112 6207
Aylesbury End HP9 1LW
web: www.innkeeperslodge.com/beaconsfield
dir: From M25 junct 16 or M40 junct 2, A355. At rdbt turn left onto A40. Lodge at White Hart on Aylesbury End

Innkeeper's Lodge represents an exciting, high value concept within the budget hotel market. Comfortable bedrooms provide excellent facilities that include satellite TV and modem points. Options include family rooms; and for the corporate guest, cutting edge IT includes Wi-fi access. Food is served all day in the adjacent Country Pub. The extensive continental breakfast is complimentary. See also the Hotel Groups pages.

Rooms 31 (1 fmly) **Conf** Thtr 24

BUCKINGHAM Map 11 SP63

Villiers

★★★★ 74% ◉◉ HOTEL

☎ 01280 822444 ⓘ 01280 822113
3 Castle St MK18 1BS
e-mail: villiers@oxfordshire-hotels.co.uk
web: www.oxfordshire-hotels.co.uk
dir: M1 junct 13 (N) or junct 15 (S) follow signs to Buckingham. Castle St by Old Town Hall

Guests can enjoy a town centre location with a high degree of comfort at this 400-year-old former coaching inn. Relaxing public areas feature flagstone floors, oak panelling and real fires whilst bedrooms are modern, spacious and equipped to a high level. Diners can unwind in the atmospheric bar before taking dinner in the award-winning restaurant.

Rooms 49 (4 fmly) (3 GF) **S** £95-£135; **D** £110-£160 (incl. bkfst)* **Facilities** STV Xmas New Year Wi-fi **Conf** Class 120 Board 80 Thtr 250 Del from £130 to £160* **Services** Lift **Parking** 52 **Notes** LB ⊗ Civ Wed 180

Best Western Buckingham Hotel

★★★ 72% HOTEL

☎ 01280 822622 ⓘ 01280 823074
Buckingham Ring Rd MK18 1RY
e-mail: info@thebuckinghamhotel.co.uk
dir: Follow A421 for Buckingham, take ring road S towards Brackley & Bicester. Hotel on left

A purpose-built hotel, which offers comfortable and spacious rooms with well designed working spaces for business travellers. There are also extensive conference facilities. The open-plan restaurant and bar offer a good range of dishes, and the well-equipped leisure suite is popular with guests.

Rooms 70 (6 fmly) (31 GF) **S** £40-£60; **D** £40-£60 **Facilities** STV ⬚ supervised Gym Xmas New Year Wi-fi **Conf** Class 60 Board 60 Thtr 200 **Parking** 200 **Notes** LB Civ Wed 120

Travelodge Buckingham

BUDGET HOTEL

☎ 0871 984 6087 ⓘ 01280 815 136
A421 Bypass MK18 1SH
web: www.travelodge.co.uk
dir: M1 junct 38/39. Lodge on N'bound & S'bound carriageways of M1

Travelodge offers good quality, good value, budget accommodation. All offer family rooms sleeping up to four (two adults, two children) with en suite bathroom/shower-room, remote-control TV, tea- and coffee-making facilities and comfortable beds. Food options vary. Breakfast is at the on-site Bar Café restaurant (if available) or to take away. See also Hotel Groups pages.

Rooms 40 **S** fr £29; **D** fr £29

BURNHAM Map 6 SU98

Grovefield House Hotel

★★★★ 76% ◉◉ HOTEL

☎ 01628 603131 ⓘ 01628 668078
Taplow Common Rd SL1 8LP
e-mail: info.grovefield@classiclodges.co.uk
web: www.classiclodges.co.uk
dir: From M4 left on A4 towards Maidenhead. Next rdbt turn right under railway bridge. Straight over mini rdbt, garage on right. Continue for 1.5m, hotel on right

Set in its own spacious grounds, the Grovefield is conveniently located near Heathrow Airport as well as the industrial centres of Slough and Maidenhead. Accommodation is spacious and well presented and most rooms have views over the attractive gardens. Public areas include a range of meeting rooms, comfortable bar/lounge area and Hamilton's restaurant.

Rooms 40 (5 fmly) (7 GF) **Facilities** Putt green Fishing ⚓ Xmas New Year **Conf** Class 80 Board 80 Thtr 180 **Services** Lift **Parking** 155 **Notes** Civ Wed 200

Burnham Beeches Hotel

★★★★ 74% ⚜ HOTEL

☎ 0844 736 8603 & 01628 603994 📄 01628 603994
Grove Rd SL1 8DP
e-mail: burnhambeeches@corushotels.com
web: www.corushotels.co.uk/burnhambeeches
dir: M40 junct 2, A355 towards Slough, right at 2nd rdbt, 1st right to Grove Rd

Set in attractive mature grounds on the fringes of woodland, this extended Georgian manor house has spacious, comfortable and well-equipped bedrooms. Public rooms include a cosy lounge/bar offering all-day snacks and an elegant wood-panelled restaurant that serves interesting cuisine; there are also conference facilities, a fitness centre and pool.

Rooms 82 (25 fmly) (9 GF) **S** £99–£200; **D** £109–£200*
Facilities FTV 🕸 🧖 ⛲ Gym Xmas New Year Wi-fi
Conf Class 80 Board 60 Thtr 180 Del from £170 to £260*
Services Lift **Parking** 200 **Notes** LB ⊗ Civ Wed 120

CHENIES Map 6 TQ09

The Bedford Arms Hotel

★★★ 77% ⚜ HOTEL

☎ 01923 283301 📄 01923 284825
WD3 6EQ
e-mail: contact@bedfordarms.co.uk
web: www.bedfordarms.co.uk
dir: M25 junct 18/A404, follow Amersham signs, right after 2.5m & follow signs for hotel

This attractive, 19th-century country inn enjoys a peaceful rural setting. Comfortable bedrooms are decorated in traditional style and feature a range of thoughtful extras. Each room is named after a relation of the Duke of Bedford, whose family has an historic association with the hotel. There are two bars, a lounge and a cosy, wood-panelled restaurant.

Rooms 18 (8 annexe) (2 fmly) (8 GF) **S** £60–£110;
D £95–£140 (incl. bkfst) **Facilities** STV Wi-fi
Conf Class 16 Board 24 Thtr 50 Del from £130 to £170
Parking 60 **Notes** Closed 27 Dec–4 Jan Civ Wed 55

HIGH WYCOMBE Map 5 SU89

Holiday Inn High Wycombe

★★★ 74% HOTEL

☎ 0870 400 9042 📄 01494 439071
Handy Cross HP11 1TL
web: www.holidayinn.co.uk
dir: M40 junct 4, take A4010 towards Aylesbury

A modern, purpose-built hotel, convenient for the motorway networks. Bedrooms are spacious and well-equipped for the business traveller and feature a comprehensive range of extra facilities. Public rooms are particularly stylish, while the Academy offers a full range of meeting and conference services.

Rooms 112 (7 fmly) (10 smoking) **S** £40–£185;
D £40–£185* **Facilities** Wi-fi **Conf** Class 72 Board 50
Thtr 140 Del from £99 to £210* **Services** Air con
Parking 200 **Notes** LB ⊗ Civ Wed 200

Best Western Alexandra

★★★ 70% HOTEL

☎ 01494 463494 📄 01494 463560
Queen Alexandra Rd HP11 2JX
e-mail: reservations@alexandra-hotel.co.uk
web: www.bw-alexandrahotel.co.uk
dir: M40 junct 4, A404 towards town centre, left at bottom of Marlow Hill, 200yds opp hospital

Situated just a five minute walk from the town centre, this popular hotel is ideal for both business and leisure guests. Dinner can be enjoyed in The Terrace restaurant or guests can choose a lighter snack in the lounge bar. The small patio is perfect for relaxing in summer months. Secure parking is an added bonus.

Rooms 29 (1 fmly) (8 GF) **Facilities** Wi-fi **Parking** 20
Notes ⊗ RS 21 Dec–2 Jan Civ Wed 50

Fox Country Inn

★★★ 64% SMALL HOTEL

☎ 01491 639333 📄 01491 639444
Ibstone HP14 3XT
e-mail: info@foxcountryinn.co.uk
dir: M40 junct 5 follow signs to Ibstone, hotel 1.5m on left

This delightful inn benefits from a new conversion to the small family-run hotel. The totally refurbished bedrooms are very well appointed with many added extras, and are designed with comfort in mind. Public areas are modern, and external decking provides further seating in summer months. There is a wide ranging choice of dishes including a Thai menu.

Rooms 18 (3 fmly) (10 GF) **S** £77–£137; **D** £87–£167*
Facilities FTV Xmas New Year Wi-fi **Conf** Class 40
Board 35 Thtr 45 Del from £110 to £195* **Parking** 45
Notes LB ⊗ Civ Wed 100

Ambassador Court

★★★ 63% HOTEL

☎ 01494 461818 📄 01494 461919
145 West Wycombe Rd HP12 3AB
e-mail: ach@fardellhotels.com
web: www.fardellhotels.com/ambassadorcourt
dir: M40 junct 4/A404 to A40 west towards Aylesbury. Hotel 0.5m on left next to petrol station

A small privately owned hotel situated midway between London and Oxford, and handily placed for access to the M40. Bedrooms are pleasantly decorated and equipped with both business and leisure guests in mind. Public rooms are contemporary in style and include a lounge with leather sofas, a cosy bar and Fusions restaurant.

Rooms 18 (2 fmly) (1 GF) **S** £49–£99; **D** £59–£115 (incl. bkfst) **Facilities** FTV Free access to local gym (5 min walk) Xmas Wi-fi **Conf** Class 18 Board 16 Thtr 32
Del from £95 to £145 **Parking** 18 **Notes** LB ⊗

Abbey Lodge

★★ 60% HOTEL

☎ 01494 471013 📄 01494 471015
17 Priory Rd HP13 6SL
e-mail: reservations@abbeylodgehotel.co.uk
dir: M40 junct 4 follow signs to railway station, left into Priory Rd, hotel 300mtrs on right

A comfortable, well-appointed town centre hotel, with attractive, individually decorated rooms offering a good range of amenities including satellite TV and Wi-fi. With its own restaurant and residents' bar, the hotel provides attentive service and a relaxed place to stay for business and leisure guests alike. The parking area is an added bonus.

Rooms 31 (11 GF) **S** £40–£70; **D** £50–£80 (incl. bkfst)*
Facilities STV FTV Wi-fi **Parking** 20 **Notes** LB ⊗

INSPECTORS' CHOICE

Macdonald Compleat Angler

★★★★ ◉◉◉ HOTEL

☎ 0844 879 9128 🗎 01628 486388
Marlow Bridge SL7 1RG
e-mail: compleatangler@macdonald-hotels.co.uk
web: www.macdonald-hotels.co.uk/compleatangler
dir: M4 junct 8/9, A404(M) to rdbt, Bisham exit,1m to
Marlow Bridge, hotel on right

This well-established hotel enjoys an idyllic location
overlooking the River Thames and the delightful Marlow
weir. The bedrooms, which differ in size and style, are all
individually decorated and are equipped with flat screen
TVs, high speed internet and air conditioning. Aubergine (a
sister restaurant to the restaurant of the same name in
Chelsea) now has three AA rosettes and offers modern
French cuisine; Bowaters serves British dishes and has
gained two rosettes. Staff throughout are keen to please
and nothing is too much trouble.

Rooms 64 (6 GF) **S** £99-£250; **D** £99-£250 (incl. bkfst)*
Facilities STV Fishing Fly and course fishing River trips
(Apr-Sep) ♫ Xmas New Year Wi-fi **Conf** Class 65 Board 36
Thtr 150 Del from £190 to £325* **Services** Lift
Parking 100 **Notes** LB Civ Wed 120

Danesfield House Hotel & Spa

★★★★ 85% ◉◉◉◉ HOTEL

☎ 01628 891010 🗎 01628 890408
Henley Rd SL7 2EY
e-mail: reservations@danesfieldhouse.co.uk
web: www.danesfieldhouse.co.uk
dir: 2m from Marlow on A4155 towards Henley

Set in 65 acres of elevated grounds just 45 minutes from
central London and 30 minutes from Heathrow, this hotel
enjoys spectacular views across the River Thames.
Impressive public rooms include the cathedral-like Great
Hall, an impressive spa, and The Orangery for informal
dining. The beautiful Oak Room Restaurant is an ideal
setting to enjoy superb, imaginative fine dining. Some
bedrooms have balconies and stunning views. Nothing is
too much trouble for the team of committed staff.

Rooms 84 (3 fmly) (27 GF) **S** £135-£330; **D** £135-£345
(incl. bkfst) **Facilities** Spa STV ☺ ♨ Putt green ♣ Gym
Jogging trail Steam room Hydrotherapy room Treatment
rooms Xmas New Year Wi-fi **Conf** Class 60 Board 50
Thtr 100 Del from £260 to £315 **Services** Lift
Parking 100 **Notes** LB ⊗ Civ Wed 100

See advert on this page

Crowne Plaza Marlow

★★★★ 80% HOTEL

☎ 0870 444 8940 & 01628 496800 🗎 0870 444 8950
Field House Ln SL7 1GJ
e-mail: enquiries@crowneplazamarlow.co.uk
web: www.crowneplaza.co.uk
dir: A404 exit to Marlow, left at mini rdbt, left into Field
House Lane

This new hotel is not far from the motorway. Public areas
are air-conditioned and include the Agua café and bar
and the Glaze Restaurant. Leisure facilities include an
up-to-the-minute gym and large pool. Bedrooms enjoy
plenty of natural light and have excellent workstations;
clubrooms have European and US power points.

Rooms 168 (47 fmly) (56 GF) (10 smoking) **S** £70-£250;
D £70-£250* **Facilities** Spa STV FTV ☺ ♣ Gym Sauna
Steam room Xmas New Year Wi-fi **Conf** Class 180
Board 30 Thtr 450 Del from £138 to £295* **Services** Lift
Air con **Parking** 300 **Notes** ⊗ Civ Wed 400

See also **Aspley Guise (Bedfordshire)**

Holiday Inn Milton Keynes

★★★ 77% HOTEL

☎ 01908 698541 🗎 01908 698685
500 Saxon Gate West MK9 2HQ
e-mail: reservations-miltonkeynes@ihg.com
web: www.holidayinn.co.uk/miltonkeynes
dir: M1 junct 14. Straight on at 7 rdbts. At 8th (Saxon
South) turn right. Hotel after lights on left

Ideally located to explore central England, with both
Oxford and Cambridge within an hour's drive, and central
London just 40 minutes away by train. The hotel is a
spacious, purpose-built, city-centre property offering a
range of well-appointed bedrooms, conference rooms and
a fully-equipped health club. The Junction restaurant

offers a contemporary dining experience in a relaxing environment.

Rooms 166 (17 fmly) (24 smoking) **D** fr £49 (incl. bkfst)* **Facilities** STV ✈ supervised Gym Sauna Solarium Beauty room ♫ Xmas New Year Wi-fi **Conf** Class 50 Board 50 Thtr 130 Del from £99* **Services** Lift Air con **Parking** 85 **Notes** LB

Mercure Parkside
★★★ 77% HOTEL

☎ 01908 661919 📄 01908 676186
Newport Rd, Woughton on the Green MK6 3LR
e-mail: H6627-gm@accor.com
web: www.mercure-uk.com
dir: M1 junct 14/A509 towards Milton Keynes. 2nd exit on H6 follow signs to Woughton-on-the-Green

Situated in five acres of landscaped grounds in a peaceful village setting, this hotel is only five minutes' drive from the hustle and bustle of the town centre. Bedrooms are divided between executive rooms in the main house and standard rooms in the adjacent coach house. Public rooms include a range of meeting rooms, and Strollers bar. The Lanes Restaurant provides a comfortable venue in which eclectic modern dishes are created with flair and panache.

Rooms 49 (1 fmly) (19 GF) **S** £50-£80; **D** £70-£120 (incl. bkfst)* **Facilities** STV Free entry to health & fitness club (approx 2m) Xmas New Year Wi-fi **Conf** Class 60 Board 50 Thtr 150 **Parking** 75 **Notes** LB Civ Wed 120

Holiday Inn Milton Keynes East
★★★ 75% HOTEL

☎ 01908 613688 & 0870 400 7219 📄 0870 400 7319
London Rd, Newport Pagnell MK16 0JA
e-mail: reservations@miltonkeynes.kewgreen.co.uk
web: www.holidayinn.co.uk
dir: M1 junct 14, A509 (Newport Pagnell), Hotel 0.5m on right

This hotel occupies a surprisingly quiet location within a few minutes drive of the M1. Accommodation is comfortable and smart, and the dining options include 24-hour room service, bar snacks or a three-course meal in the restaurant. A fitness room is available, and there are conference rooms that are ideal for meetings, weddings and dinner functions.

Rooms 53 (12 fmly) (24 GF) **Facilities** STV Gym Limited fitness room Xmas New Year Wi-fi **Conf** Class 80 Board 60 Thtr 200 **Parking** 155 **Notes** ⊗ Civ Wed 200

Novotel Milton Keynes
★★★ 73% HOTEL

☎ 01908 322212 📄 01908 322235
Saxon St, Layburn Court, Heelands MK13 7RA
e-mail: H3272@accor-hotels.com
web: www.novotel.com
dir: M1 junct 14, follow Childsway signs towards city centre. Right into Saxon Way, straight across all rdbts, hotel on left

Contemporary in style, this purpose-built hotel is situated on the outskirts of the town, just a few minutes' drive from the centre and mainline railway station. Bedrooms provide ample workspace and a good range of facilities for the modern traveller, and public rooms include a children's play area and indoor leisure centre.

Rooms 124 (40 fmly) (40 GF) **Facilities** ✈ Gym Steam bath **Conf** Class 75 Board 40 Thtr 120 **Services** Lift **Parking** 130 **Notes** LB Civ Wed 100

Different Drummer
★★ 75% ◉ SMALL HOTEL

☎ 01908 564733 📄 01908 260646
94 High St, Stony Stratford MK11 1AH
e-mail: info@hoteldifferentdrummer.co.uk
web: www.hoteldifferentdrummer.co.uk
dir: In Stony Stratford centre

This attractive hotel located on the high street in historic Stony Stratford extends a genuine welcome to its guests. The oak-panelled restaurant is a popular dining venue and offers an Italian-style menu. Bedrooms are generally spacious and well equipped. There is a contemporary bar that provides a further dining option.

Rooms 23 (4 annexe) (1 fmly) (3 GF) **Facilities** STV Fishing Wi-fi **Conf** Class 40 Board 30 Thtr 40 Del from £150 to £180* **Parking** 10 **Notes** ⊗

Ramada Encore Milton Keynes
Ⓤ

☎ 0870 428 1438 📄 0870 428 1439
312 Midsummer Boulevard MK9 2EA
e-mail: enquiries@encoremiltonkeynes.co.uk

Currently the rating for this establishment is not confirmed. This may be due to a change of ownership or because it has only recently joined the AA rating scheme. For further details please see the AA website: theAA.com

Rooms 159

The Cock Hotel
Ⓤ

☎ 01908 567733 📄 01908 562109
72-74 High St, Stony Stratford MK11 1AH
e-mail: cock.stonystratford@oldenglishinns.co.uk
dir: In village centre

Currently the rating for this establishment is not confirmed. This may be due to a change of ownership or because it has only recently joined the AA rating scheme. For further details please see the AA website: theAA.com

Rooms 31 (13 annexe) **Conf** Class 50 Board 60 Thtr 120

Broughton
BUDGET HOTEL

☎ 01908 667726 📄 01908 604844
Broughton Village MK10 9AA
e-mail: broughtonhotel@greeneking.co.uk
web: www.oldenglish.co.uk
dir: M1 junct 14, at 1st rdbt take A5130 signed Woburn 600yds. Turn right for Broughton village, located on left

This hotel is within easy reach of road networks and offers modern accommodation. Day rooms are dominated by an open-plan lounge bar and the Hungry Horse food concept, which proves particularly popular with young families.

Rooms 30 (2 fmly) (14 GF) **Conf** Class 30 Board 30 Thtr 80

Campanile Milton Keynes
BUDGET HOTEL

☎ 01908 649819 📄 01908 649818
40 Penn Road - off Watling St, Fenny Stratford, Bletchley MK2 2AU
e-mail: miltonkeynes@campanile.com
dir: M1 junct 14, follow A4146 to A5. Southbound on A5. 4th exit at 1st rdbt to Fenny Stratford. Hotel 500yds on left

This modern building offers accommodation in smart, well-equipped bedrooms, all with en suite bathrooms. Refreshments may be taken at the informal bistro. See also the Hotel Groups pages.

Rooms 80 (26 GF) **Conf** Class 30 Board 30 Thtr 40 Del from £100 to £150*

MILTON KEYNES *continued*

Express by Holiday Inn Milton Keynes

BUDGET HOTEL

☎ 01908 681000 📄 01908 609429
Eastlake Park, Tongwell St MK15 0YA
e-mail: miltonkeynes@expressholidayinn.co.uk
web: www.hiexpress.com/exmiltonkeynes
dir: M1 junct 14 follow sign for centre, at Northfields rdbt, straight across dual carriageway (H6) follow signs to Fox Milne 3rd exit V11

A modern hotel ideal for families and business travellers. Fresh and uncomplicated, the spacious rooms include Sky TV, power shower and tea and coffee-making facilities. Continental buffet breakfast is included in the room rate; other meals may be taken at the nearby family pub or restaurant. See also the Hotel Groups pages.

Rooms 178 (96 fmly) (47 GF) **S** £45-£110; **D** £45-£110 (incl. bkfst) **Conf** Class 45 Board 45 Thtr 80 Del from £80 to £140

Innkeeper's Lodge Milton Keynes

BUDGET HOTEL

☎ 0845 112 6057 📄 0845 112 6246
Burchard Crescent, Shenley Church End MK5 6HQ
web: www.innkeeperslodge.com/miltonkeynes
dir: M1 junct 14, A509 towards Milton Keynes. Straight over at rdbt into Childs Way (H6). Over 9 rdbts, at 10th (Knowlhill), right into Watling St (V4). 1st left. Lodge on right

Innkeeper's Lodge represents an exciting, high value concept within the budget hotel market. Comfortable bedrooms provide excellent facilities that include satellite TV and modem points. Options include family rooms; and for the corporate guest, cutting edge IT which includes Wi-fi high speed internet access. A popular Carvery provides all-day food, including an extensive, complimentary continental breakfast. See also the Hotel Groups pages.

Rooms 50 **Conf** Thtr 100

Travelodge Milton Keynes Central

BUDGET HOTEL

☎ 0871 984 6199 📄 01908 241737
109 Grafton Gate MK9 1AL
web: www.travelodge.co.uk
dir: M1 junct 14 to city centre, H6 Childs Ways to junct V6 Grafton Gate, on right after rail station

Travelodge offers good quality, good value, budget accommodation. All offer family rooms sleeping up to four (two adults, two children) with en suite bathroom/shower-room, remote-control TV, tea- and coffee-making facilities and comfortable beds. Food options vary.

Breakfast is at the on-site Bar Café restaurant (if available) or to take away. See also Hotel Groups pages.

Rooms 80 **S** fr £29; **D** fr £29

Travelodge Milton Keynes Old Stratford

BUDGET HOTEL

☎ 0871 984 6001 📄 01908 260802
Old Stratford Roundabout MK19 6AQ
web: www.travelodge.co.uk
dir: On A5 towards Towcester. At rdbt with A508/A422. Lodge on left

Rooms 29 **S** fr £29; **D** fr £29

NEWPORT PAGNELL Map 11 SP84
MOTORWAY SERVICE AREA (M1)

Welcome Lodge Milton Keynes

BUDGET HOTEL

☎ 01908 610878 📄 01908 216539
Newport Pagnell MK16 8DS
e-mail: newport.hotel@welcomebreak.co.uk
web: www.welcomebreak.co.uk
dir: M1 junct 14-15. In service area - follow signs to Barrier Lodge

This modern building offers accommodation in smart, spacious and well-equipped bedrooms, suitable for families and business travellers, and all with en suite bathrooms. Refreshments may be taken at the nearby family restaurant. See also the Hotel Groups pages.

Rooms 90 (54 fmly) **S** £29-£59; **D** £39-£69*
Conf Class 12 Board 16 Thtr 40 Del from £79 to £109*

STOKE POGES Map 6 SU98

Stoke Park

Ⓤ

☎ 01753 717171 📄 01753 717171
Park Rd SL2 4PG
e-mail: info@stokepark.com
dir: M4 junct 6, A355 towards Beaconsfield, B416 Park Rd, Stoke Park 1.25m on right

Currently the rating for this establishment is not confirmed. This may be due to a change of ownership or because it has only recently joined the AA rating scheme. For further details please see the AA website: theAA.com

Rooms 49 (28 annexe) (10 fmly) **S** £180-£285; **D** £180-£1100* **Facilities** Spa STV Ⓒ ⚡ 27 ⛳ Putt green Fishing 🏊 Gym New Year Wi-fi **Conf** Class 30 Board 38 Thtr 80 Del from £299 to £320* **Services** Lift **Parking** 460 **Notes** LB ⊗ Closed 25-26 Dec Civ Wed 120

TAPLOW Map 6 SU98

INSPECTORS' CHOICE

Cliveden Country House Hotel

★★★★★ ◉◉ COUNTRY HOUSE HOTEL

☎ 01628 668561 📄 01628 661837
SL6 0JF
e-mail: reservations@clivedenhouse.co.uk
web: www.vonessenhotels.co.uk
dir: M4 junct 7, A4 towards Maidenhead for 1.5m, onto B476 towards Taplow, 2.5m, hotel on left

This wonderful stately home stands at the top of a gravelled boulevard. Visitors are treated as house-guests and staff recapture the tradition of fine hospitality. Bedrooms have individual quality and style, and reception rooms retain a timeless elegance. Exceptional leisure facilities include cruises along Cliveden Reach and massages in the Pavilion. The Terrace Restaurant with its delightful views has two AA Rosettes. The Rosette award for Waldo's, which offers innovative menus in discreet, luxurious surroundings, is temporarily suspended due to a change of chef; a new award will be in place once our inspectors have completed their assessments of meals cooked by the new kitchen team. See the AA website: theAA.com for up-to-date information. Von Essen Hotels - AA Hotel Group of the Year 2009-10.

Rooms 39 (8 GF) **S** £276-£1989.50; **D** £276-£1689.50 (incl. bkfst)* **Facilities** Spa STV FTV Ⓒ ⚡ 🏊 🏊 Gym Squash Full range of beauty treatments, 3 vintage boats 🚣 Xmas New Year Wi-fi **Conf** Board 40 Thtr 80 Del from £295 to £395 **Services** Lift **Parking** 60 **Notes** Civ Wed 150

Taplow House

★★★★ 74% ◎◎ HOTEL

☎ 01628 670056   📄 01628 773625
Berry Hill SL6 0DA
e-mail: reception@taplowhouse.com
dir: Off A4 onto Berry Hill, hotel 0.5m on right

This elegant Georgian manor is set amid beautiful gardens and has been skilfully restored. Character public rooms are pleasing and include a number of air-conditioned conference rooms and an elegant restaurant. Comfortable bedrooms are individually decorated and furnished to a high standard.

Rooms 32 (8 fmly) (2 GF) **S** £70-£160; **D** £80-£240 (incl. bkfst)* **Facilities** STV FTV ⛳ Xmas New Year Wi-fi **Conf** Class 50 Board 50 Thtr 120 Del from £180 to £285* **Services** Air con **Parking** 100 **Notes** LB Civ Wed 100

WOOBURN COMMON   Map 6 SU98

Chequers Inn

★★★ 75% ◎ HOTEL

☎ 01628 529575   📄 01628 850124
Kiln Ln, Wooburn HP10 0JQ
e-mail: info@chequers-inn.com
web: www.chequers-inn.com
dir: M40 junct 2, A40 through Beaconsfield Old Town towards High Wycombe. 2m from town left into Broad Ln. Inn 2.5m

This 17th-century inn enjoys a peaceful, rural location beside the common. Bedrooms feature stripped-pine furniture, co-ordinated fabrics and an excellent range of extra facilities. The bar, with its massive oak post, beams and flagstone floor, and the restaurant, which overlooks a pretty patio, are very much focal points here.

Rooms 17 (8 GF) **S** £82.50-£99.50; **D** £87.50-£107.50* **Facilities** FTV Wi-fi **Conf** Class 30 Board 20 Thtr 50 **Parking** 60 **Notes** LB ⊗

CAMBRIDGESHIRE

CAMBOURNE   Map 12 TL35

The Cambridge Belfry

★★★★ 82% ◎◎ HOTEL   QHOTELS

☎ 01954 714600   📄 01954 714610
Back St CB3 6BW
e-mail: cambridgebelfry@qhotels.co.uk
web: www.qhotels.co.uk
dir: M11 junct 13 take A428 towards Bedford, follow signs to Cambourne. Exit at Cambourne keeping left. Left at rdbt, hotel on left

This exciting hotel, built beside the water, is located at the gateway to Cambourne Village & Business Park. Contemporary in style throughout, the hotel boasts state-of-the-art leisure facilities, including Reflections Spa offering a range of therapies and treatments, and extensive conference and banqueting rooms. There are two eating options - the award-winning Bridge Restaurant, and the Brooks Brasserie. Original artwork is displayed throughout the hotel.

Rooms 120 (30 GF) **S** £55-£120; **D** £65-£120* **Facilities** Spa ⊗ ⛳ Gym Beauty treatments Xmas New Year Wi-fi **Conf** Class 70 Board 70 Thtr 250 Del from £119 to £189* **Services** Lift **Parking** 200 **Notes** ⊗ Civ Wed 160

CAMBRIDGE   Map 12 TL45

Hotel Felix

★★★★ 82% ◎◎ HOTEL

☎ 01223 277977   📄 01223 277973
Whitehouse Ln CB3 0LX
e-mail: help@hotelfelix.co.uk
web: www.hotelfelix.co.uk
dir: M11 junct 12. From A1 N take A14 turn onto A1307. At 'City of Cambridge' sign left into Whitehouse Ln

A beautiful Victorian mansion set amidst three acres of landscaped gardens, this property was originally built in 1852 for a surgeon from the famous Addenbrookes Hospital. The contemporary-style bedrooms have carefully chosen furniture and many thoughtful touches, whilst public rooms feature an open-plan bar, the adjacent Graffiti restaurant and a small quiet lounge.

Rooms 52 (5 fmly) (26 GF) **Facilities** STV Xmas New Year Wi-fi **Conf** Class 36 Board 34 Thtr 60 **Services** Lift **Parking** 90 **Notes** LB Civ Wed 70

Menzies Cambridge Hotel & Golf Club   MenziesHotels

★★★★ 75% HOTEL

☎ 01954 249988   📄 01954 780010
Bar Hill CB23 8EU
e-mail: cambridge@menzieshotels.co.uk
web: www.menzieshotels.co.uk
dir: M11 N & S to A14 follow signs for Huntingdon. A14 turn off B1050 Bar Hill, hotel 1st exit on rdbt

Ideally situated amidst 200 acres of open countryside, just five miles from the university city of Cambridge. Public rooms include a brasserie restaurant and the popular Gallery Bar. The contemporary-style bedrooms are smartly decorated and equipped with a good range of useful facilities. The hotel also has a leisure club, swimming pool and golf course.

Rooms 136 (35 fmly) (68 GF) (12 smoking) **S** £70-£135; **D** £70-£135* **Facilities** STV ⊗ ↕ 18 ⊕ Putt green Gym Hair & beauty salon Steam room Sauna Xmas New Year Wi-fi **Conf** Class 90 Board 45 Thtr 200 Del from £120 to £160* **Services** Lift **Parking** 200 **Notes** Civ Wed 200

Hotel du Vin Cambridge   Hotel du Vin & Bistro

★★★★ 74% ◎ TOWN HOUSE HOTEL

☎ 01223 227330   📄 01223 227331
15-19 Trumpington St CB2 1QA
e-mail: info.cambridge@hotelduvin.com
web: www.hotelduvin.com
dir: M11 junct 11 Cambridge S, pass Trumpington Park & Ride on left. Hotel 2m on right after double rdbt

This beautiful building, which dates back in part to medieval times, has been transformed to enhance its many quirky architectural features. The bedrooms and suites, some with private terraces, have the company's trademark monsoon showers and Egyptian linen. The French-style bistro has an open-style kitchen and the bar is set in the unusual labyrinth of vaulted cellar rooms. There is also a library, specialist wine tasting room and private dining room.

Rooms 41 (3 annexe) (6 GF) **Facilities** STV Xmas New Year Wi-fi **Conf** Class 18 Board 18 Thtr 30 **Services** Lift Air con **Parking** 24

De Vere University Arms   DE VERE collection

★★★★ 73% HOTEL

☎ 01223 273000   📄 01223 273037
Regent St CB2 1AD
e-mail: dua.sales@devere-hotels.com
web: www.devere.co.uk
dir: M11 junct 11, follow city centre signs for 3m. Right at 2nd mini rdbt, left at lights into Regent St. Hotel 600yds on right

Built in 1834, the University Arms has an enviable position in the very heart of the city, overlooking Parker's Piece. Public rooms include an elegant domed lounge, a

continued

CAMBRIDGE *continued*

smart restaurant, a bar and lounge overlooking the park. Conference and banqueting rooms are extensive, many with oak panelling. Given the hotel's central location parking for guests is a bonus.

Rooms 119 (2 fmly) **S** £69-£210; **D** £85-£265 (incl. bkfst)* **Facilities** STV Complimentary use of local fitness centre Xmas New Year Wi-fi **Conf** Class 150 Board 80 Thtr 300 Del from £125 to £195* **Services** Lift **Parking** 56 **Notes** Civ Wed 250

Crowne Plaza Cambridge

★★★★ 72% HOTEL

☎ 01223 556554 & 0870 400 9180 📄 01223 322374
20 Downing St CB2 3DT
e-mail: britta.weiser@ihg.com
web: www.crowneplaza.co.uk
dir: From M11 take A14. Follow signs for city centre then Grand Arcade car park. Hotel adjacent

Located in the heart of the city, this hotel enjoys an enviable position, with many of the universities and the town centre within easy walking distance. It is located adjacent to the Grand Arcade shopping centre: on site parking, although limited, is a plus. The hotel offers modern accommodation and large open-plan public areas; a fitness room and several conference rooms are also available.

Rooms 198 (30 smoking) **Facilities** STV Gym Sauna New Year Wi-fi **Conf** Class 70 Board 50 Thtr 250 Del from £129 to £220* **Services** Lift Air con **Parking** 50 **Notes** ⊗ Civ Wed 250

Best Western Cambridge Quy Mill Hotel

★★★ 81% ◉ HOTEL

☎ 01223 293383 📄 01223 293770
Church Rd, Stow Cum Quy CB25 9AF
e-mail: cambridgequy@bestwestern.co.uk
web: www.bw-cambridgequymill.co.uk
dir: Exit A14 at junct 35, E of Cambridge, onto B1102 for 50yds. Entrance opposite church

Set in open countryside, this 19th-century former watermill is conveniently situated for access to Cambridge. Bedroom styles differ, yet each room is smartly appointed and brightly decorated; superior, spacious courtyard rooms are noteworthy. Well-designed public areas include several spacious bar/lounges, with a

choice of casual and formal eating areas; service is both friendly and helpful. There is a smart leisure club with state-of-the-art equipment.

Rooms 49 (26 annexe) (2 fmly) (26 GF) **S** £75-£130; **D** £89-£200* **Facilities** STV ⓢ Gym Wi-fi **Conf** Class 30 Board 24 Thtr 80 Del from £130 to £165* **Parking** 90 **Notes** LB ⊗ Closed 24-30 Dec RS 31 Dec Civ Wed 80

Arundel House

★★★ 81% HOTEL

☎ 01223 367701 📄 01223 367721
Chesterton Rd CB4 3AN
e-mail: info@arundelhousehotels.co.uk
web: www.arundelhousehotels.co.uk
dir: City centre on A1303

Overlooking the River Cam and enjoying views over open parkland, this popular and smart hotel was originally a row of townhouses dating from Victorian times. Bedrooms are attractive and have a special character. The smart public areas feature a conservatory for informal snacks, a spacious bar and an elegant restaurant for more serious dining.

Rooms 103 (22 annexe) (7 fmly) (14 GF) **S** £75-£125; **D** £95-£150 (incl. bkfst)* **Facilities** FTV New Year Wi-fi **Conf** Class 34 Board 32 Thtr 50 **Parking** 70 **Notes** LB ⊗ Closed 25-26 Dec

Best Western The Gonville

★★★ 79% HOTEL

☎ 01223 366611 & 221111 📄 01223 315470
Gonville Place CB1 1LY
e-mail: all@gonvillehotel.co.uk
web: www.bw-gonvillehotel.co.uk
dir: M11 junct 11, on A1309 follow city centre signs. At 2nd mini rdbt right into Lensfield Rd, over junct with lights. Hotel 25yds on right

A well established hotel situated on the inner ring road, a short walk across the green from the city centre. The air-conditioned public areas are cheerfully furnished, and include a lounge bar and brasserie; bedrooms are well appointed and appealing, offering a good range of facilities for both corporate and leisure guests.

Rooms 73 (1 fmly) (5 GF) **S** £79-£135; **D** £99-£180* **Facilities** FTV New Year Wi-fi **Conf** Class 100 Board 50 Thtr 200 **Services** Lift **Parking** 80 **Notes** LB RS 24-29 Dec Civ Wed 100

Lensfield

★★★ 78% METRO HOTEL

☎ 01223 355017 📄 01223 312022
53-57 Lensfield Rd CB2 1EN
e-mail: reservations@lensfieldhotel.co.uk
web: www.lensfieldhotel.co.uk
dir: M11 junct 11/12/13, follow signs to city centre, approach hotel via Silver St, Trumpington St, left into Lensfield Rd

Located close to all the city's attractions, this constantly improving hotel provides a range of attractive bedrooms, equipped with thoughtful extras. Comprehensive breakfasts are taken in an elegant dining room and a comfortable bar and cosy foyer lounge are also available.

Rooms 28 (4 fmly) (4 GF) **S** £55-£110; **D** £99-£120 (incl. bkfst)* **Facilities** STV Wi-fi **Parking** 5 **Notes** LB ⊗ Closed last 2 wks in Dec-4 Jan

Royal Cambridge

★★★ 78% HOTEL

☎ 01223 351631 📄 01223 352972
Trumpington St CB2 1PY
e-mail: royal.cambridge@forestdale.com
web: www.theroyalcambridgehotel.co.uk
dir: M11 junct 11, signed city centre. At 1st mini rdbt left into Fen Causeway. Hotel 1st right

This elegant Georgian hotel is situated in the heart of Cambridge. The bedrooms are well equipped and provide great comfort. The stylish restaurant and bar are a popular choice with locals and guests alike. Complimentary parking proves a real benefit in the city centre.

Rooms 57 (5 fmly) (3 GF) **S** £85-£125; **D** £104-£169 (incl. bkfst)* **Facilities** FTV Xmas New Year Wi-fi **Conf** Class 60 Board 40 Thtr 120 **Services** Lift **Parking** 80 **Notes** Civ Wed 100

Holiday Inn Cambridge

★★★ 74% HOTEL

☎ 0870 400 9015 📄 01223 233426
Lakeview, Bridge Rd, Impington CB24 9PH
e-mail: reservations-cambridge@ihg.com
web: www.holidayinn.co.uk
dir: 2.5m N, on N side of rdbt junct A14/B1049

A modern, purpose built hotel conveniently situated just off the A14 junction just a short drive from the city centre. Public areas include a popular bar, the Junction Restaurant and a large open-plan lounge. Bedrooms come in a variety of styles and are suited to the needs of both the business and leisure guest alike.

Rooms 161 (14 fmly) (75 GF) (10 smoking) **S** £75-£175; **D** £75-£195 (incl. bkfst)* **Facilities** Spa STV ⓢ supervised Gym **Conf** Class 40 Board 45 Thtr 20 Del from £99 to £195* **Services** Air con **Parking** 175 **Notes** LB ⊗ Civ Wed 100

Ashley Hotel

★★ 81% METRO HOTEL

☎ 01223 350059 & 319555 📠 01223 350900
74-76 Chesterton Rd CB4 1ER
e-mail: info@arundelhousehotels.co.uk
dir: On city centre ring road

Expect a warm welcome at this delightful Victorian property situated just a short walk from the River Cam. The smartly decorated bedrooms are generally quite spacious and equipped with a good range of useful extras. Breakfast is served at individual tables in the smart lower ground floor dining room.

Rooms 16 (5 fmly) (5 GF) **S** £75-£85; **D** £75-£85 (incl. bkfst)* **Facilities** Wi-fi **Parking** 12 **Notes** ✪ Closed 24-26 Dec

Helen Hotel

★★ 80% METRO HOTEL

☎ 01223 246465 📠 01223 214406
167-169 Hills Rd CB2 2RJ
e-mail: enquiries@helenhotel.co.uk
dir: On A1307, 1.25m from city centre (south side). Cherry-Hinton Rd junct, opposite Homerton College

This extremely well maintained, privately owned hotel is situated close to the city centre and a range of popular eateries. Public areas include a smart lounge bar with plush sofas and a cosy breakfast room. Bedrooms are pleasantly decorated with co-ordinated fabrics and have many thoughtful touches.

Rooms 19 (2 fmly) (2 GF) **Facilities** STV Wi-fi **Parking** 12 **Notes** ✪ Closed Xmas & New Year

Centennial

★★ 71% HOTEL

☎ 01223 314652 📠 01223 315443
63-71 Hills Rd CB2 1PG
e-mail: reception@centennialhotel.co.uk
dir: M11 junct 11 take A1309 to Cambridge. Right onto Brooklands Ave to end. Left, hotel 100yds on right

This friendly hotel is convenient for the railway station and town centre. Well-presented public areas include a welcoming lounge, a relaxing bar and restaurant on the lower-ground level. Bedrooms are generally spacious, well maintained and thoughtfully equipped with a good range of facilities; several rooms are available on the ground floor.

Rooms 39 (1 fmly) (7 GF) **Facilities** Wi-fi **Conf** Class 25 Board 25 Thtr 25 **Parking** 30 **Notes** ✪ Closed 23 Dec-1 Jan

Express by Holiday Inn Cambridge

BUDGET HOTEL

☎ 01223 866800 📠 01223 866857
15/17 Coldhams Park, Norman Way CB1 3LH
e-mail: cambridge@expressholidayinn.co.uk
web: www.expresscambridge.co.uk
dir: B1047 Fen Ditton. Continue for 1m to T-junct, right, at rdbt lleft onto Barnwell Rd & follow to rdbt. Left & follow to Toyota garage, right into Business Park

A modern hotel ideal for families and business travellers. Fresh and uncomplicated, the spacious rooms include Sky TV, power shower and tea and coffee-making facilities. Continental buffet breakfast is included in the room rate; and a choice of light meals are served in the smart restaurant. See also the Hotel Groups pages.

Rooms 100 (8 smoking) **Conf** Class 20 Board 24 Thtr 50 **Del** from £120 to £135

Travelodge Cambridge Central

BUDGET HOTEL

☎ 0871 984 6101
Cambridge Leisure Park, Clifton Way CB1 7DY
web: www.travelodge.co.uk
dir: Off southern inner ring road (East Rd) take Hills Rd towards signs for main railway station. Lodge 0.5m on left

Travelodge offers good quality, good value, budget accommodation. All offer family rooms sleeping up to four (two adults, two children) with en suite bathroom/shower-room, remote-control TV, tea- and coffee-making facilities and comfortable beds. Food options vary. Breakfast is at the on-site Bar Café restaurant (if available) or to take away. See also Hotel Groups pages.

Rooms 120 **S** fr £29; **D** fr £29

Travelodge Cambridge Fourwentways

BUDGET HOTEL

☎ 08719 846 019 📠 01223 839479
Fourwentways CB1 6AP
web: www.travelodge.co.uk
dir: Adjacent to Little Chef at junct of A11 & A1307, 5m S of Cambridge

Rooms 71 **S** fr £29; **D** fr £29

Duxford Lodge

★★★ 75% ◉ HOTEL

☎ 01223 836444   📠 01223 832271
Ickleton Rd CB22 4RT
e-mail: admin@duxfordlodgehotel.co.uk
web: www.duxfordlodgehotel.co.uk
dir: M11 junct 10, onto A505 to Duxford. 1st right at rdbt, hotel 0.75m on left

A warm welcome is assured at this attractive red-brick hotel in the heart of a delightful village. Public areas include a cosy relaxing bar, separate lounge, and an attractive restaurant, where an excellent and imaginative menu is offered. The bedrooms are well appointed, comfortable and smartly furnished.

Rooms 15 (4 annexe) (2 fmly) (4 GF) **S** £78.50-£88.50; **D** £108-£128.50 (incl. bkfst)* **Facilities** FTV Wi-fi **Conf** Class 20 Board 26 Thtr 50 Del from £155* **Parking** 34 **Notes** Closed 25 Dec-2 Jan Civ Wed 50

See advert on page 65

Lamb

★★★ 🅰 HOTEL

☎ 01353 663574   📠 01353 662023
2 Lynn Rd CB7 4EJ
e-mail: lamb.ely@oldenglishinns.co.uk
web: www.oldenglish.co.uk
dir: from A10 into Ely, hotel in town centre

Rooms 31 (6 fmly) **Facilities** Xmas **Conf** Class 40 Board 70 Thtr 100 **Parking** 20

Travelodge Ely

BUDGET HOTEL

☎ 0871 984 6028   📠 01353 668499
Witchford Rd CB6 3NN
web: www.travelodge.co.uk
dir: At rdbt junct of A10 & A142

Travelodge offers good quality, good value, budget accommodation. All offer family rooms sleeping up to four (two adults, two children) with en suite bathroom/shower-room, remote-control TV, tea- and coffee-making facilities and comfortable beds. Food options vary.

Breakfast is at the on-site Bar Café restaurant (if available) or to take away. See also Hotel Groups pages.

Rooms 57 **S** fr £29; **D** fr £29

The Anchor Inn

◉ RESTAURANT WITH ROOMS

☎ 01353 778537   📠 01353 776180
Sutton Gault CB6 2BD
e-mail: anchorinn@popmail.bta.com
dir: 6m W of Ely. Sutton Gault signed off B1381 at S end of Sutton

Located beside the New Bedford River with stunning country views, this 17th-century inn has a wealth of original features enhanced by period furniture. The spacious bedrooms are tastefully appointed and equipped with many thoughtful touches. The friendly team of staff offer helpful and attentive service.

Rooms 4 (2 fmly)

Travelodge Huntingdon Fenstanton

BUDGET HOTEL

☎ 0871 984 6039   📠 01954 230919
PE18 9LP
web: www.travelodge.co.uk
dir: 4m SE of Huntingdon, on A14 E'bound

Travelodge offers good quality, good value, budget accommodation. All offer family rooms sleeping up to four (two adults, two children) with en suite bathroom/shower-room, remote-control TV, tea- and coffee-making facilities and comfortable beds. Food options vary. Breakfast is at the on-site Bar Café restaurant (if available) or to take away. See also Hotel Groups pages.

Rooms 40 **S** fr £29; **D** fr £29

The Old Ferryboat Inn

★★ 🅰 HOTEL

☎ 01480 463227   📠 01480 463245
Back Ln PE27 4TG
e-mail: 8638@greeneking.co.uk
web: www.oldenglish.co.uk

Rooms 7 **Conf** Class 50 Board 35 Thtr 60 **Parking** 70 **Notes** ⊗

Huntingdon Marriott Hotel   ℳarriott
HOTELS & RESORTS

★★★★ 75% HOTEL

☎ 01480 446000   📠 01480 451111
Kingfisher Way, Hinchingbrooke Business Park PE29 6FL
e-mail: mhrs.cbghd.front.office@marriotthotels.com
web: www.huntingdonmarriott.co.uk
dir: on A14, 1m from Huntingdon centre close to Brampton racecourse

With its excellent road links, this modern, purpose-built hotel is a popular venue for conferences and business meetings, and is convenient for Huntingdon, Cambridge and racing at Newmarket. Bedrooms are spacious and offer every modern comfort, including air conditioning. The leisure facilities are also impressive.

Rooms 150 (5 fmly) (45 GF) **Facilities** ◎ supervised Gym Sauna Steam room ♪ Xmas New Year Wi-fi **Conf** Class 150 Board 100 Thtr 300 **Services** Lift Air con **Parking** 200 **Notes** LB Civ Wed 300

The Old Bridge Hotel

★★★ 83% ◉◉ HOTEL

☎ 01480 424300   📠 01480 411017
1 High St PE29 3TQ
e-mail: oldbridge@huntsbridge.co.uk
web: www.huntsbridge.com
dir: From A14 or A1 follow Huntingdon signs. Hotel visible from inner ring road

An imposing 18th-century building situated close to shops and amenities. This charming hotel offers superb accommodation in stylish and individually decorated bedrooms that include many useful extras. Guests can choose from the same menu whether dining in the open-plan terrace, or the more formal restaurant with its bold colour scheme. There is also an excellent business centre. The Old Bridge Hotel is England & the Overall Winner of the AA Wine Award 2010.

Rooms 24 (2 fmly) (2 GF) **S** £95-£130; **D** £130-£195 (incl. bkfst) **Facilities** STV FTV Fishing Private mooring for boats Xmas New Year Wi-fi **Conf** Class 50 Board 30 Thtr 60 Del from £190 to £225 **Services** Air con **Parking** 50 **Notes** LB Civ Wed 100

George
★★★ Ⓐ HOTEL

☎ 01480 432444 🖹 01480 453130
George St PE29 3AB
e-mail: george.huntingdon@oldenglishinns.co.uk
web: www.oldenglish.co.uk
dir: Leave A14 at Huntingdon racecourse exit. Then 3m to junct with ring road. Hotel opposite

Rooms 24 (3 fmly) **S** £60-£80; **D** £80-£120 (incl. bkfst)*
Facilities ♫ Xmas Wi-fi **Conf** Class 60 Board 60 Thtr 80 Del from £105 to £130* **Parking** 55 **Notes** LB
Civ Wed 120

LOLWORTH   Map 12 TL36

Travelodge Cambridge Lolworth

BUDGET HOTEL

☎ 0871 984 6046 🖹 01954 781335
Huntingdon Rd CB3 8DR
web: www.travelodge.co.uk
dir: M11 junct 14, A14 W'bound. Lodge in 3m

Travelodge offers good quality, good value, budget accommodation. All offer family rooms sleeping up to four (two adults, two children) with en suite bathroom/shower-room, remote-control TV, tea- and coffee-making facilities and comfortable beds. Food options vary. Breakfast is at the on-site Bar Café restaurant (if available) or to take away. See also Hotel Groups pages.

Rooms 20 **S** fr £29; **D** fr £29

MARCH   Map 12 TL49

Oliver Cromwell Hotel
★★★ 70% HOTEL

☎ 01354 602890 🖹 01354 602891
High St PE15 9LH
e-mail: belinda@olivercromwellhotel.co.uk
dir: In village centre

This purpose-built hotel is ideally situated for touring the Cambridgeshire countryside, and is within easy reach of Ely and Wisbech. The spacious bedrooms are pleasantly decorated and thoughtfully equipped. Public rooms

include a smart lounge bar and a dining room, as well as conference and banqueting facilities.

Oliver Cromwell Hotel

Rooms 42 **Conf** Class 80 Board 40 Thtr 120

PETERBOROUGH   Map 12 TL19

Peterborough Marriott
Marriott HOTELS & RESORTS
★★★★ 75% HOTEL

☎ 01733 371111 🖹 01733 236725
Peterborough Business Park, Lynchwood PE2 6GB
e-mail: reservations.peterborough@marriotthotels.co.uk
web: www.peterboroughmarriott.co.uk
dir: Opp East of England Showground. From A1 off at Alwalton Showground, Chesterton. Left at T-junct. Hotel on left at next rdbt

This modern hotel is opposite the East of England Showground, and a just few minutes' drive from the heart of the city. Alwalton is famous for being the birthplace of Sir Frederick Henry Royce, one of the founders of the Rolls-Royce company. Air-conditioned bedrooms are spacious and well designed for business use. Public rooms include the Garden Lounge, cocktail bar, Laurels Restaurant and a leisure club.

Rooms 163 (8 fmly) (74 GF) (6 smoking) **Facilities** Spa STV ⓧ Gym Beauty therapist Hairdressing Xmas New Year Wi-fi **Conf** Class 160 Board 45 Thtr 300 Del from £125 to £165 **Services** Air con **Parking** 175 **Notes** Civ Wed 80

Bull
★★★★ 73% HOTEL   PEEL HOTELS PLC

☎ 01733 561364 🖹 01733 557304
Westgate PE1 1RB
e-mail: info@bull-hotel-peterborough.com
web: www.peelhotels.com
dir: Off A1, follow city centre signs. Hotel opp Queensgate shopping centre. Car park on Broadway next to library

This pleasant city-centre hotel offers well-equipped, modern accommodation, which includes several wings of deluxe bedrooms. Public rooms include a popular bar and a brasserie-style restaurant serving a flexible range of dishes, with further informal dining available in the lounge. There is a good range of meeting rooms and conference facilities.

Rooms 118 (3 fmly) (5 GF) **Facilities** STV Xmas New Year Wi-fi **Conf** Class 120 Board 40 Thtr 200 Del from £120 to £145* **Parking** 100 **Notes** ⊗ Civ Wed 200

Bell Inn
★★★ 79% ⊛ HOTEL

☎ 01733 241066 & 242626 🖹 01733 245173
Great North Rd PE7 3RA
e-mail: reception@thebellstilton.co.uk
web: www.thebellstilton.co.uk

(For full entry see Stilton)

Best Western Orton Hall
★★★ 79% ⊛ HOTEL   Best Western

☎ 01733 391111 🖹 01733 231912
Orton Longueville PE2 7DN
e-mail: reception@ortonhall.co.uk
dir: Off A605 E, opposite Orton Mere

An impressive country-house hotel set in 20 acres of woodland on the outskirts of town and with easy access

continued

PETERBOROUGH *continued*

to the A1. The spacious and relaxing public areas include the baronial Great Room and the Orton Suite for banqueting and for meetings, and the oak-panelled, award-winning Huntly Restaurant. The on-site pub, Ramblewood Inn, is an alternative, informal dining option.

Rooms 72 (2 fmly) (15 GF) **S** £50–£140; **D** £50–£190*
Facilities STV ⊗ Gym Sauna Steam room Xmas New Year Wi-fi **Conf** Class 70 Board 60 Thtr 160 **Parking** 200 **Notes** LB Civ Wed 150

Holiday Inn Peterborough West

★★★ 75% HOTEL

☎ 0870 7879 861 & 01733 289988 📠 01733 262737
Thorpe Wood PE3 6SG
e-mail: hipeterborough@qmh-hotels.com
web: www.holidayinn.co.uk
dir: A1(M) junct 17, A1139 towards Peterborough onto Fletton Parkway. Exit at junct 3, 1st exit at rdbt onto Nene Parkway. Exit junct 33 then 1st exit at rdbt Thorpe Wood . Hotel on right

Situated just over two miles from the town centre close to the River Nene, with ample parking and easy access to road networks. The hotel provides air-conditioned accommodation and extensive conference and banqueting facilities together with a modern leisure club.

Rooms 133 (10 fmly) (27 GF) **Facilities** ⊗ supervised Gym Sauna Steam room Beauty salon Dance studio Xmas Wi-fi **Conf** Class 150 Board 100 Thtr 400 **Services** Lift **Parking** 250 **Notes** LB ⊗ Civ Wed 180

Queensgate Hotel

Ⓤ

☎ 01733 562572
5-7 Fletton Av PE2 8AX
e-mail: reservations@thequeensgatehotel.com
dir: In central Peterborough off London Rd on Ketton Ave. Hotel 0.5m from Peterborough Utd Football Stadium

Currently the rating for this establishment is not confirmed. This may be due to a change of ownership or because it has only recently joined the AA rating scheme. For further details please see the AA website: theAA.com

Rooms 40 (2 fmly) (10 GF) **S** £39–£77.50; **D** £49–£87.50 (incl. bkfst) **Facilities** FTV Beauty clinic Xmas New Year Wi-fi **Conf** Class 35 Board 26 Thtr 72 Del from £90 to £130 **Notes** LB ⊗

Travelodge Peterborough Alwalton

BUDGET HOTEL

☎ 0871 984 6250 📠 01733 231109
Great North Rd, Alwalton PE7 3UR
web: www.travelodge.co.uk
dir: on A1, southbound

Travelodge offers good quality, good value, budget accommodation. All offer family rooms sleeping up to four (two adults, two children) with en suite bathroom/shower-room, remote-control TV, tea- and coffee-making facilities and comfortable beds. Food options vary. Breakfast is at the on-site Bar Café restaurant (if available) or to take away. See also Hotel Groups pages.

Rooms 32 **S** fr £29; **D** fr £29

Travelodge Peterborough Central

BUDGET HOTEL

☎ 0871 984 6003
Chapel St PE1 1QF
web: www.travelodge.co.uk
dir: A1139 junct 5. At rdbt take 1st exit onto Boongate (signed city centre), at next rdbt take 2nd exit onto New Rd. Follow signs for Passport Office & Market. Hotel on left

Rooms 79 **S** fr £29; **D** fr £29

Travelodge Peterborough Eye Green

BUDGET HOTEL

☎ 08719 846 303 📠 01733 223199
Crowlands Rd PE6 7SZ
web: www.travelodge.co.uk
dir: At junct of A47 & A1073

Rooms 42 **S** fr £29; **D** fr £29

Olivers Lodge

★★★ 74% HOTEL

☎ 01480 463252 📠 01480 461150
Needingworth Rd PE27 5JP
e-mail: reception@oliverslodge.co.uk
web: www.oliverslodge.co.uk
dir: A14 towards Huntingdon/Cambridge, take B1040 to St Ives. Cross 1st rdbt, left at 2nd then 1st right. Hotel 500mtrs on right

A privately owned hotel situated in a peaceful residential area just a short walk from the town centre. Public rooms include a smart air-conditioned bar, a choice of lounges and a conservatory dining room. The pleasantly decorated bedrooms are equipped with modern facilities and have co-ordinated fabrics.

Rooms 17 (5 annexe) (3 fmly) (5 GF) **Facilities** Wi-fi **Conf** Class 30 Board 25 Thtr 65 **Notes** LB Civ Wed 65

Dolphin

★★★ 68% HOTEL

☎ 01480 466966 📠 01480 495597
London Rd PE27 5EP
e-mail: enquiries@dolphinhotelcambs.co.uk
dir: A14 between Huntingdon & Cambridge onto A1096 towards St Ives. Left at 1st rdbt & immediately right. Hotel on left after 0.5m

This modern hotel sits by delightful water meadows on the banks of the River Ouse. Open-plan public rooms include a choice of bars and a pleasant restaurant offering fine river views. The bedrooms are modern and varied in style; some are in the hotel while others occupy an adjacent wing. All are comfortable and spacious. Conference and function suites are available.

Rooms 67 (37 annexe) (4 fmly) (22 GF) (2 smoking) **S** £80.50–£96.20; **D** £103.20–£122.80 (incl. bkfst)* **Facilities** FTV Fishing Gym **Conf** Class 50 Board 50 Thtr 150 **Parking** 400 **Notes** LB ⊗ RS 24 Dec-2 Jan Civ Wed 60

The George Hotel & Brasserie

★★★ 83% ⑱ HOTEL

☎ 01480 812300 📠 01480 813920
High St, Buckden PE19 5XA
e-mail: mail@thegeorgebuckden.com
web: www.thegeorgebuckden.com
dir: Just off A1 at Buckden, 2m S of A1/A14 interchange

Ideally situated in the heart of this historic town centre and just a short drive from the A1. Public rooms feature a bustling ground-floor brasserie, which offers casual dining throughout the day and evening; there is also an informal lounge bar with an open fire and comfy seating. Bedrooms are stylish, tastefully appointed and thoughtfully equipped.

Rooms 12 (1 fmly) **S** £80–£130; **D** £100–£130 (incl. bkfst)* **Facilities** STV Membership at local leisure centre Xmas **Conf** Class 30 Board 30 Thtr 50 Del from £150 to £180* **Services** Lift **Parking** 25 **Notes** LB Civ Wed 50

STILTON
Map 12 TL18

Bell Inn
★★★ 79% ⊛ HOTEL

☎ 01733 241066 & 242626 🖹 01733 245173
Great North Rd PE7 3RA
e-mail: reception@thebellstilton.co.uk
web: www.thebellstilton.co.uk
dir: A1(M) junct 16, follow Stilton signs. Hotel in village centre

This delightful inn is steeped in history and retains many original features, with imaginative food served in both the character village bar/brasserie and the elegant beamed first floor restaurant; refreshments can be enjoyed in the attractive courtyard and rear gardens when weather permits. Individually designed bedrooms are stylish and equipped to a high standard.

Rooms 22 (3 annexe) (1 fmly) (3 GF) **S** £73.50–£110.50; **D** £100.50–£130.50 (incl. bkfst)* **Facilities** FTV Wi-fi **Conf** Class 46 Board 50 Thtr 130 Del from £132.50* **Parking** 30 **Notes** ⊗ Closed 25 Dec pm RS 26 Dec pm Civ Wed 130

SWAVESEY
Map 12 TL36

Travelodge Cambridge Swavesey

BUDGET HOTEL

☎ 0871 984 6021 🖹 01954 789113
Cambridge Rd CB4 5QR
web: www.travelodge.co.uk
dir: on eastbound carriageway of A14

Travelodge offers good quality, good value, budget accommodation. All offer family rooms sleeping up to four (two adults, two children) with en suite bathroom/ shower-room, remote-control TV, tea- and coffee-making facilities and comfortable beds. Food options vary. Breakfast is at the on-site Bar Café restaurant (if available) or to take away. See also Hotel Groups pages.

Rooms 36 **S** fr £29; **D** fr £29

WISBECH
Map 12 TF40

Crown Lodge
THE INDEPENDENTS
HOTEL ASSOCIATION
★★★ 82% ⊛ HOTEL

☎ 01945 773391 & 772206 🖹 01945 772668
Downham Rd, Outwell PE14 8SE
e-mail: office@thecrownlodgehotel.co.uk
web: www.thecrownlodgehotel.co.uk
dir: On A1122/A1101 approx 5m from Wisbech

Friendly, privately owned hotel situated in a peaceful location on the banks of Well Creek a short drive from Wisbech. The bedrooms are pleasantly decorated, have co-ordinated fabrics and modern facilities. The public areas are very stylish; they include a lounge bar, brasserie restaurant and a large seating area with plush leather sofas.

Rooms 10 (1 fmly) (10 GF) **S** £70–£80; **D** £90–£100 (incl. bkfst)* **Facilities** FTV Squash New Year Wi-fi **Conf** Class 60 Board 40 Thtr 80 **Services** Air con **Parking** 57 **Notes** LB

Elme Hall
★★★ 68% HOTEL

☎ 01945 475566 🖹 01945 475666
Elm High Rd PE14 0DQ
e-mail: elmehallhotel@btconnect.com
web: www.elmehall.co.uk
dir: off A47 onto A1101 towards Wisbech. Hotel on right

An imposing, Georgian-style property conveniently situated on the outskirts of the town centre just off the A47. Individually decorated bedrooms are tastefully furnished with quality reproduction pieces and equipped to a high standard. Public rooms include a choice of attractive lounges, as well as two bars, meeting rooms and a banqueting suite.

Rooms 8 (3 fmly) **S** £58; **D** £78–£245 (incl. bkfst)* **Facilities** FTV ♫ Wi-fi **Conf** Class 200 Board 20 Thtr 350 **Parking** 200 **Notes** Civ Wed 350

CHESHIRE

ALDERLEY EDGE
Map 16 SJ87

Alderley Edge
★★★ 85% ⊛⊛ HOTEL

☎ 01625 583033 🖹 01625 586343
Macclesfield Rd SK9 7BJ
e-mail: sales@alderleyedgehotel.com
web: www.alderleyedgehotel.com
dir: Off A34 in Alderley Edge onto B5087 towards Macclesfield. Hotel 200yds on right

This well-furnished hotel, with its charming grounds, was originally a country house built for one of the region's 'cotton kings'. The bedrooms and suites are attractively furnished, offering excellent quality and comfort. The welcoming bar and adjacent lounge lead into the split-level conservatory restaurant where imaginative, memorable food and friendly, attentive service form highlights of any visit.

Rooms 50 (6 GF) **S** £72.50–£130; **D** £120–£165* **Facilities** STV ♫ Xmas Wi-fi **Conf** Class 40 Board 30 Thtr 120 **Services** Lift **Parking** 90 **Notes** ⊗ Civ Wed 114

Innkeeper's Lodge Alderley Edge

BUDGET HOTEL

☎ 0845 112 6020 🖹 0845 112 6201
5-9 Wilmslow Rd SK9 7NZ
web: www.innkeeperslodge.com/alderleyedge
dir: M56 junct 6, A538 S towards Wilmslow. Right at lights towards Alderley Edge. Lodge on left in Wilmslow Rd just after 2nd rdbt

Innkeeper's Lodge Select represents an exciting, stylish concept within the hotel market. Contemporary style bedrooms provide excellent facilities that include LCD TVs with satellite channels, and modem points. Options

continued

ALDERLEY EDGE *continued*

include spacious family rooms; and for the corporate guest there's Wi-fi access. All-day food is served in a modern country pub & eating house. The extensive continental breakfast is complimentary. See also the Hotel Groups pages.

Rooms 10

Best Western Manor House
★★★ 83% HOTEL

☎ 01270 884000 ▤ 01270 882483
Audley Rd ST7 2QQ
e-mail: mhres@compasshotels.co.uk
web: www.manorhouse-alsager.co.uk
dir: M6 junct 16, A500 towards Stoke. In 0.5m take 1st slip road to Alsager. Left at top. Hotel on left approaching village

Developed around an old farmhouse, the original oak beams are still very much a feature in the hotel bars and restaurant. Modernised and extended over the years, the hotel today is well geared towards the needs of the modern traveller. Some of the main features include a range of conference rooms, a lovely patio garden and an indoor swimming pool.

Rooms 57 (4 fmly) (21 GF) **Facilities** STV Wi-fi **Conf** Class 108 Board 82 Thtr 200 Del from £99 to £145* **Parking** 150 **Notes** RS Sat & Sun Civ Wed 150

De Vere Carden Park
★★★★ 79% HOTEL

DE VERE collection

☎ 01829 731000 ▤ 01829 731599
Carden Park CH3 9DQ
e-mail: reservations.carden@devere-hotels.com
web: www.devere.co.uk
dir: M56 junct 15/M53 Chester. Take A41 for Whitchurch for approx 8m. At Broxton rdbt right onto A534 Wrexham. Hotel 1.5m on left

This impressive Cheshire estate dates back to the 17th century and consists of 750 acres of mature parkland. The hotel offers a choice of dining options along with superb leisure facilities that include golf courses, a fully equipped gym, a swimming pool and popular spa. Spacious, thoughtfully equipped bedrooms have excellent business and in-room entertainment facilities.

Rooms 196 (83 annexe) (24 fmly) (68 GF) **S** £75-£190; **D** £85-£200 (incl. bkfst)* **Facilities** Spa STV supervised 36 Putt green Gym Archery Quadbikes Off-roading Bike/walking trails Laser clay shooting Xmas New Year Wi-fi **Conf** Class 240 Board 125 Thtr 400 Del from £140 to £220* **Services** Lift **Parking** 500 **Notes** LB Civ Wed 375

See also **Puddington**

INSPECTORS' CHOICE

The Chester Grosvenor & Spa
★★★★★ HOTEL

☎ 01244 324024 ▤ 01244 313246
Eastgate CH1 1LT
e-mail: hotel@chestergrosvenor.com
dir: A56 follow signs for city centre hotels. On Eastgate St next to the Eastgate clock

Located within the Roman walls of the city, this Grade II listed, half-timbered building is the essence of Englishness. Furnished with fine fabrics and queen or king-size beds, the suites and bedrooms are of the highest standard, each designed with guest comfort as a priority. The art deco La Brasserie is a bustling venue, and there's also Simon Radley's, the fine-dining restaurant, which offers creative cuisine with flair and style. A luxury spa and small fitness centre are also available. Complimentary undercover parking is available to guests in an adjacent car park.

Rooms 80 (7 fmly) **S** fr £205; **D** £205-£855* **Facilities** Spa Gym New Year Wi-fi **Conf** Class 120 Board 48 Thtr 250 **Services** Lift Air con **Notes** LB Closed 25-26 Dec RS Sun & Mon, 1-20 Jan Civ Wed 250

Doubletree by Hilton Chester
★★★★ 81% HOTEL

☎ 01244 408800 ▤ 01244 320251
Warrington Rd, Hoole Village CH2 3PD
e-mail: enquiries@doubletreechester.com
web: www.hilton.co.uk/chester
dir: M53 junct 12 towards Chester. Hotel 500yds on left

Major investment has transformed this notable 18th-century country house into a must-see destination. Bedrooms, with smart modern bathrooms, are very well equipped and feature a wealth of practical and thoughtful extras. Public areas, furnished in a minimalist style, retain many period features, including a Grade II listed conservatory. The Orchid Restaurant is an ideal setting for both casual and fine dining. A luxury spa is due to open in the autumn of 2009.

Rooms 110 **Conf** Class 140 Board 60 Thtr 300

Rowton Hall Country House Hotel & Spa
★★★★ 81% HOTEL

☎ 01244 335262 ▤ 01244 335464
Whitchurch Rd, Rowton CH3 6AD
e-mail: reception@rowtonhallhotelandspa.co.uk
web: www.rowtonhallhotel.co.uk
dir: M56 junct 12, A56 to Chester. At rdbt left onto A41 towards Whitchurch. Approx 1m, follow hotel signs

This delightful Georgian manor house, set in mature grounds, retains many original features such as a superb carved staircase and several eye-catching fireplaces. Bedrooms vary in style and all have been stylishly fitted and have impressive en suites. Public areas include a smart leisure centre, extensive function facilities and a striking restaurant that serves imaginative dishes.

Rooms 37 (4 fmly) (8 GF) **S** £120-£500; **D** £145-£500* **Facilities** Spa STV FTV Gym Sauna Steam room Xmas New Year Wi-fi **Conf** Class 48 Board 50 Thtr 170 Del from £165 to £225* **Parking** 90 **Notes** LB Civ Wed 120

Crowne Plaza Chester
★★★★ 78% HOTEL

☎ 0870 442 1081 & 01244 899988 ▤ 01244 316118
Trinity St CH1 2BD
e-mail: cpchester@qmh-hotels.com
web: www.crowneplaza.co.uk
dir: M53 junct 12 to A56 onto St Martins Way, under foot bridge, left at lights then 1st right, hotel on right.

Conveniently located in the heart of the city, this modern hotel offers spacious public areas that include the Silks restaurant, leisure club and a range of meeting rooms. Smart air-conditioned bedrooms are comfortably appointed and particularly well equipped. The hotel's own car park is a real bonus.

Crowne Plaza Chester

Rooms 160 (4 fmly) **S** £99–£199; **D** £99–£199 (incl. bkfst)* **Facilities** Spa STV FTV Gym Beauty salon Wi-fi **Conf** Class 250 Board 100 Thtr 600 Del from £125 to £165* **Services** Lift **Parking** 80 **Notes** LB ⊗ Civ Wed 150

Best Western The Queen Hotel

★★★★ 76% HOTEL

☎ 01244 305000   📠 01244 318483
City Rd CH1 3AH
e-mail: queenhotel@feathers.uk.com
web: www.feathers.uk.com
dir: Follow signs for railway station, hotel opposite

This hotel is ideally located opposite the railway station and just a couple minutes' walk from the city. Public areas include a restaurant, small gym, waiting room bar, separate lounge and Roman-themed gardens. Bedrooms are generally spacious and reflect the hotel's Victorian heritage.

Rooms 218 (11 fmly) (12 GF) **S** £59–£250; **D** £79–£400 **Facilities** STV FTV Gym ♬ Xmas New Year Wi-fi **Conf** Class 150 Board 60 Thtr 400 Del from £115 to £165 **Services** Lift **Parking** 150 **Notes** LB ⊗ Civ Wed 400

Ramada Chester

★★★★ 75% HOTEL

☎ 01244 332121 & 0844 815 9001   📠 01244 335287
Whitchurch Rd, Christleton CH3 5QL
e-mail: sales.chester@ramadajarvis.co.uk
web: www.ramadajarvis.co.uk/chester
dir: A41 Whitchurch, hotel on right 200mtrs from A41, 1.3m from city centre

This smart, modern hotel is located just a short drive from the city centre; with extensive meeting and function facilities, a well-equipped leisure club and ample parking, it is a popular conference venue. Bedrooms vary in size and style but all are well equipped for both business and leisure guests. Food is served in the airy restaurant and also in the large open-plan bar lounge.

Rooms 126 (6 fmly) (58 GF) (10 smoking) **Facilities** STV Gym Xmas New Year Wi-fi **Conf** Class 80 Board 60 Thtr 230 **Services** Lift **Parking** 160 **Notes** LB ⊗ Civ Wed 180

CHESTER *continued*

Grosvenor Pulford Hotel & Spa

★★★★ 74% HOTEL

☎ 01244 570560 📠 01244 570809
Wrexham Rd, Pulford CH4 9DG
e-mail: reservations@grosvenorpulfordhotel.co.uk
web: www.grosvenorpulfordhotel.co.uk
dir: M53/A55 at junct signed A483 Chester/Wrexham & North Wales. Left onto B5445, hotel 2m on right

Set in rural surroundings, this modern, stylish hotel features a magnificent spa with a large Roman-style swimming pool. Among the bedrooms available are several executive suites and others containing spiral staircases leading to the bedroom sections. A smart brasserie restaurant and bar provide a wide range of imaginative dishes in a relaxed atmosphere.

Rooms 73 (10 fmly) (21 GF) (6 smoking) **S** £95-£130; **D** £130-£175 (incl. bkfst)* **Facilities** Spa STV FTV 🔄 🏊 Gym Steam room Sauna Xmas New Year Wi-fi **Conf** Class 100 Board 50 Thtr 200 Del from £115 to £145* **Services** Lift **Parking** 200 **Notes** LB Civ Wed 200

Macdonald New Blossoms

★★★★ 71% HOTEL

☎ 01244 323186 & 0844 8799113 📠 01244 346433
St John St CH1 1HL
e-mail: events.blossoms@macdonald-hotels.co.uk
web: www.macdonaldhotels.co.uk/blossoms
dir: M53 junct 12 follow city centre signs for Eastgate, through pedestrian zone, hotel on left

Ideally located to explore the historic city of Chester this is now a modern and contemporary hotel. Bedrooms range from executive to feature four-poster rooms, with many retaining the charm of the original Victorian building. A stylish brasserie restaurant and bar offer an informal dining experience.

Rooms 67 (1 fmly) **S** £59-£164; **D** £59-£174* **Facilities** Xmas New Year Wi-fi **Conf** Class 50 Board 40 Thtr 90 Del from £138 to £238* **Services** Lift **Notes** LB ⊗

See advert on page 71

Best Western Westminster

★★★ 80% HOTEL

☎ 01244 317341 📠 01244 325369
City Rd CH1 3AF
e-mail: westminsterhotel@feathers.uk.com
web: www.feathers.uk.com
dir: A56, 3m to city centre, left signed rail station. Hotel opposite station, on right

Situated close to the railway station and city centre, the Westminster is an old, established hotel. It has an attractive Tudor-style exterior, while bedrooms are brightly decorated with a modern theme. Family rooms are available. There is a choice of bars and lounges, and the dining room serves a good range of dishes.

Rooms 75 (8 fmly) (6 GF) **S** £44-£114; **D** £49-£159* **Facilities** STV Free gym facilities at sister hotel Wi-fi **Conf** Class 60 Board 40 Thtr 150 **Services** Lift **Notes** ⊗ Civ Wed 100

Mill Hotel & Spa Destination

★★★ 79% HOTEL

☎ 01244 350035 📠 01244 345635
Milton St CH1 3NF
e-mail: reservations@millhotel.com
web: www.millhotel.com
dir: M53 junct 12, onto A56, left at 2nd rdbt (A5268), then 1st left , 2nd left

This hotel is a stylish conversion of an old corn mill and enjoys an idyllic canalside location next to the inner ring road and close to the city centre. The bedrooms offer varying styles, and public rooms are spacious and comfortable. There are several dining options and dinner is often served on a large boat that cruises Chester's canal system between courses. A well-equipped leisure centre is also provided.

Rooms 128 (49 annexe) (57 fmly) **S** £73-£93; **D** £91-£112 (incl. bkfst)* **Facilities** Spa STV 🔄 supervised Gym Aerobic studio Hairdresser Sauna Steam room Spa bath Kenesis studio 🎵 Xmas New Year Wi-fi **Conf** Class 27 Board 28 Thtr 40 Del from £125 to £145* **Services** Lift **Parking** 120 **Notes** ⊗

Holiday Inn Chester South

★★★ 73% HOTEL

☎ 0870 400 9019 📠 01244 674100
Wrexham Rd CH4 9DL
e-mail: reservations-chester@ihg.com
web: www.holidayinn.co.uk
dir: Near Wrexham junct on A483, off A55

Located close to the A55 and opposite the Park & Ride for the city centre, this hotel offers spacious and comfortable accommodation. Meals can be taken in the attractive bar or in the restaurant. There is also a well-equipped leisure club for residents, and extensive conference facilities are available.

Rooms 143 (21 fmly) (71 GF) (12 smoking) **D** £49-£190* **Facilities** STV FTV 🔄 supervised Gym Xmas New Year Wi-fi **Conf** Class 70 Board 70 Thtr 80 **Services** Air con **Parking** 150 **Notes** LB ⊗ Civ Wed 50

Curzon

★★ 77% HOTEL

☎ 01244 678581 📠 01244 680866
52/54 Hough Green CH4 8JQ
e-mail: curzon.chester@virgin.net
web: www.curzonhotel.co.uk
dir: At junct of A55/A483 follow sign for Chester, 3rd rdbt, 2nd exit (A5104). Hotel 500yds on right

This smart period property is located in a residential suburb, close to the racecourse and just a short walk from the city centre. Spacious bedrooms are comfortable, well equipped and include family and four-poster rooms. The atmosphere is friendly, and the dinner menu offers a creative choice of freshly prepared dishes.

Rooms 16 (2 fmly) (1 GF) **S** £70-£90; **D** £105-£130 (incl. bkfst) **Facilities** FTV Wi-fi **Parking** 20 **Notes** LB ⊗ Closed 20 Dec-6 Jan

See advert on opposite page

Brookside

★★ 75% HOTEL

☎ 01244 381943 & 390898 🖷 01244 651910
Brook Ln CH2 2AN
e-mail: info@brookside-hotel.co.uk
web: www.brookside-hotel.co.uk
dir: M53 junct 12, A56 towards Chester, then A41. 0.5m
left signed Newton (Plas Newton Ln). 0.5m right into
Brook Ln. Hotel 0.5m on right. Or from Chester inner ring
road follow A5116/Ellesmere Port/Hospital signs (keep in
right lane to take right fork). Immediately left. At mini-
rdbt 2nd right

This hotel is conveniently located in a residential area
just north of the city centre. The attractive public areas
consist of a foyer lounge, a small bar and a split-level
restaurant. The homely bedrooms are thoughtfully
furnished and some feature four-poster beds.

Rooms 26 (9 fmly) (4 GF) **Facilities** Wi-fi **Conf** Class 20
Board 12 **Parking** 20 **Notes** ⊗ Closed 20 Dec-3 Jan

Dene

★★ 75% HOTEL

VENTURE HOTELS

☎ 01244 321165 🖷 01244 350277
95 Hoole Rd CH2 3ND
e-mail: info@denehotel.com
web: www.denehotel.com
dir: M53 junct 12 take A56 for 1m towards Chester. Hotel
1m from M53 next to Alexander Park

This friendly hotel is now part of a small privately owned
group and is located close to both the city centre and
M53. The bedrooms are very well equipped and many are
on ground floor level. Family rooms and interconnecting
rooms are also available. In addition to bar meals, an
interesting choice of dishes is offered in the welcoming
Castra Brasserie, which is also very popular with locals.

Rooms 52 (8 annexe) (5 fmly) (20 GF) **S** £30-£110;
D £35-£125* **Facilities** FTV New Year Wi-fi **Conf** Class 12
Board 16 Thtr 30 Del from £75 to £120 **Parking** 55

See advert on page 71

Comfort Inn Chester

BUDGET HOTEL

Comfort INN

☎ 01244 327542 🖷 01244 344889
74 Hoole Rd, Hoole CH2 3NK
e-mail: info@comfortinnchester.com
dir: M53 junct 12 towards Chester on A56. Hotel opposite
Alexandra Park on right

This former private house has been extended to provide
modern and well-equipped accommodation, including
bedrooms on ground-floor level; some are adapted for
guests with disabilities. The hotel shares the bar and
restaurant facilities of its sister hotel The Dene, which is
located across the road. The M53 and city centre are both
within easy reach. See also the Hotel Groups pages.

Rooms 33 (5 annexe) (2 fmly) (13 GF) **S** £30-£110;
D £35-£120* **Conf** Class 8 Board 15 Thtr 15

See advert on page 71

CHESTER *continued*

Holiday Inn Express at Chester Racecourse

BUDGET HOTEL

☎ 0870 9904065 📠 0870 9904066
The Racecourse, New Crane St CH1 2LY
e-mail: hotel@chester-races.com
web: www.hiexpress.com/exchesterrac
dir: M53, A483/Wrexham. Follow ring road follow signs for A548. Turn right onto New Crane St. Hotel 0.5m on left at racecourse

A modern hotel ideal for families and business travellers. Fresh and uncomplicated, the spacious rooms include Sky TV, power shower and tea and coffee-making facilities. Continental buffet breakfast is included in the room rate; other meals may be taken at the nearby family pub or restaurant. See also the Hotel Groups pages.

Rooms 97 (66 fmly) (4 GF) **S** £69-£90; **D** £69-£90 (incl. bkfst)* **Conf** Class 30 Board 25 Thtr 20 Del from £88.50 to £100*

Innkeeper's Lodge Chester Northeast

BUDGET HOTEL

☎ 0845 112 6021 📠 0845 112 6280
Warrington Rd, Mickle Trafford CH2 4EX
web: www.innkeeperslodge.com/chesternortheast
dir: M53 junct 12, A56 (Warrington road), E towards Mickle Trafford. Lodge on right

Innkeeper's Lodge represents an exciting, high value concept within the budget hotel market. Comfortable bedrooms provide excellent facilities that include satellite TV and modem points. Options include family rooms, and for the corporate guest, cutting edge IT which includes Wi-fi access. A popular Carvery provides all-day food, including an extensive, complimentary continental breakfast. See also the Hotel Groups pages.

Rooms 36 (12 fmly)

Innkeeper's Lodge Chester Southeast

BUDGET HOTEL

☎ 0845 112 6022 📠 0845 112 6279
Whitchurch Rd CH3 6AE
web: www.innkeeperslodge.com/chestersoutheast
dir: M53 junct 12, A56. Left at 1st rdbt onto A41. Left at next rdbt (A41/Whitchurch road). Lodge 0.5m on left

Rooms 14 (3 fmly)

Travelodge Chester Central

BUDGET HOTEL

☎ 0871 984 6363 📠 01244 323408
St John St CH1 1 DD
e-mail: chestercentral@travelodge.co.uk
dir: From A55 take A51 signed Chester. 2.5m. Take A5268 for 0.5m, pass Tourist Information Centre on right. Lodge at lights on right

Travelodge offers good quality, good value, budget accommodation. All offer family rooms sleeping up to four (two adults, two children) with en suite bathroom/shower-room, remote-control TV, tea- and coffee-making facilities and comfortable beds. Food options vary. Breakfast is at the on-site Bar Café restaurant (if available) or to take away. See also Hotel Groups pages.

Rooms 60 **S** fr £29; **D** fr £29

Oddfellows

◎ RESTAURANT WITH ROOMS

☎ 01244 400001
20 Lower Bridge St CH1 1RS
e-mail: reception@oddfellows.biz

Surrounded by designer shops and only a few minutes' walk from the Chester Rows, old-meets-new at this stylish Georgian mansion. The upper ground floor comprises a walled garden with ornamental moat, Arabic tents, a roofed patio, a cocktail bar with an excellent wine selection, a bustling brasserie and an Alice in Wonderland tea room. Fine dining, featuring local produce, is skilfully prepared in a second-floor formal restaurant and a sumptuous 'members' lounge is also available to diners and resident guests. Bedrooms have that wow factor with super beds and every conceivable extra to enhance the guest experience. AA Funky B&B of the Year 2009-10.

Rooms 4

CHILDER THORNTON   Map 15 SJ37

Brook Meadow

★★★ 77% HOTEL   OXFORD HOTELS & INNS

☎ 0151 339 9350 📠 0151 347 4221
Health Ln CH66 7NS
e-mail: reception@brookmeadowhotel.co.uk
web: www.oxfordhotelsandinns.com
dir: M53 junct 5, A41, right onto A550, 2nd right into Heath Ln

This delightful country hotel, set in its own lovely gardens, is within easy reach of Liverpool, Chester and the M53 and M56 motorways. Bedrooms are tastefully decorated and well equipped, and there is a comfortable lounge. The dining room has a conservatory which overlooks the grounds. Two function suites are available.

Rooms 25 (7 fmly) (7 GF) **Facilities** FTV Xmas New Year Wi-fi **Conf** Class 60 Board 60 Thtr 180 **Services** Lift Air con **Parking** 80 **Notes** ⊗ Civ Wed 160

CREWE   Map 15 SJ75

Crewe Hall

★★★★ 77% ◎◎ HOTEL   QHOTELS

☎ 01270 253333 📠 01270 253322
Weston Rd CW1 6UZ
e-mail: crewehall@qhotels.co.uk
web: www.qhotels.co.uk
dir: M6 junct 16 follow A500 to Crewe. Last exit at rdbt onto A5020. 1st exit next rdbt to Crewe. Crewe Hall 150yds on right

Standing in 500 acres of mature grounds, this historic hall dates back to the 17th century. It retains an elaborate interior with Victorian-style architecture. Bedrooms are spacious, well equipped and comfortable with traditionally styled rooms in the main hall and modern suites in the west wing. Guests have a choice of formal dining in the elegant Ranulph restaurant (2 AA Rosettes) or the more relaxed atmosphere of the modern Brasserie (1 AA rosette). The health and beauty spa ensure that it is a popular choice with both corporate and leisure guests.

Rooms 117 (91 annexe) (5 fmly) (35 GF) **S** £67-£252; **D** £77-£262 (incl. bkfst)* **Facilities** Spa STV ③ ⑤ Gym Enclosed events field Wi-fi **Conf** Class 172 Board 96 Thtr 364 Del from £135 to £175* **Services** Lift **Parking** 500 **Notes** LB ⊗ Civ Wed 180

Hunters Lodge

★★★ 80% ⊛ HOTEL

☎ 01270 539100 📄 01270 500553
Sydney Rd, Sydney CW1 5LU
e-mail: info@hunterslodge.co.uk
web: www.hunterslodge.co.uk
dir: M6 junct 16. 1m from Crewe station, off A534

Dating back to the 18th century, this family-run hotel has been extended and modernised. Accommodation, mainly located in adjacent well-equipped bedroom wings, includes family and four-poster rooms. Imaginative dishes are served in the spacious restaurant, and the popular bar also offers a choice of tempting meals. Service throughout is friendly and efficient.

Rooms 57 (4 fmly) (31 GF) (7 smoking) **S** £48-£79; **D** £60-£116 (incl. bkfst) **Facilities** STV Gym Wi-fi **Conf** Class 100 Board 80 Thtr 160 Del from £118.30 to £148.20 **Parking** 240 **Notes** ⊛ RS Sun Civ Wed 130

De Vere Wychwood Park

DE VERE
venues

★★★ 78% HOTEL

☎ 01270 829200 & 829221 📄 01270 829201
CW2 5GP
e-mail: wychwoodsalesteam@deverevenues.co.uk
dir: A531 Keele, left at rdbt onto A531. Hotel on right at next rdbt

Wychwood Park offers light and airy accommodation with a vibrant atmosphere, all packaged in a contemporary style. The restaurant is a modern and comfortable with an open-plan kitchen serving food from its steam, bake and grill menu. The hotel is surrounded by a beautiful PGA European-tour standard golf course with wonderful views of the Cheshire countryside.

Rooms 108 (32 GF) **Facilities** ⚘ 18 Putt green Gym Xmas New Year Wi-fi **Conf** Class 100 Board 80 Thtr 250 **Services** Lift **Parking** 300 **Notes** Civ Wed 120

Ramada Crewe

ⓇRAMADA.

★★★ 73% HOTEL

☎ 01270 504050 📄 01270 504055
Macon Way CW1 6DR
e-mail: info@ramadacrewe.co.uk
dir: From S: M6 junct 16, from N: M6 junct 17. Follow signs for town centre, hotel by McDonalds

This hotel is close to both the local rail station and the M6 and makes an ideal base for accessing the town centre and business park, as well as the Cheshire countryside to the west. A modern, purpose-built hotel with well-appointed and stylish rooms, restaurant, lounge bar and excellent meeting and event facilities. In addition there is an express check in/out facility and Wi-fi access throughout.

Rooms 64 (2 fmly) **S** £68-£105; **D** £85-£145 (incl. bkfst) **Facilities** STV FTV Discounted entry to nearby gym & leisure centre Xmas New Year Wi-fi **Conf** Class 60 Board 50 Thtr 85 Del from £99 to £165 **Services** Lift Air con **Parking** 45 **Notes** LB ⊛

Crewe Arms

★★★ 72% HOTEL

☎ 01270 213204 📄 01270 588615
Nantwich Rd CW2 6DN
e-mail: reservations@crewearmshotel.com
web: www.crewearmshotel.com
dir: M6 junct 6 towards Crewe. At 1st rdbt take 3rd exit, at 2nd rdbt 1st exit. Hotel at end, opposite rail station

Close to Crewe station this popular, busy commercial hotel offers attractive, well-equipped accommodation. Meals are served in the comfortable Carriages lounge bar and the more formal Sophia's Restaurant. There is also a range of conference and meeting rooms.

Rooms 61 (3 fmly) (1 GF) (12 smoking) **S** £39.50-£75; **D** £39.50-£89.50 (incl. bkfst) **Facilities** Xmas New Year Wi-fi **Conf** Class 40 Board 40 Thtr 90 **Parking** 140 **Notes** ⊛ Civ Wed 90

Travelodge Crewe

BUDGET HOTEL

☎ 0871 984 6296 📄 01270 253 518
Crewe Green Rd CW1 2BJ
web: www.travelodge.co.uk
dir: M6 junct 6, A500 to town centre, right onto A534

Travelodge offers good quality, good value, budget accommodation. All offer family rooms sleeping up to four (two adults, two children) with en suite bathroom/shower-room, remote-control TV, tea- and coffee-making facilities and comfortable beds. Food options vary. Breakfast is at the on-site Bar Café restaurant (if available) or to take away. See also Hotel Groups pages.

Rooms 56 **S** fr £29; **D** fr £29

Travelodge Crewe Barthomley

BUDGET HOTEL

☎ 0871 984 6071 📄 01270 883157
Alsager Rd, Barthomley CW2 5PT
web: www.travelodge.co.uk
dir: M6 junct 16, A500 between Nantwich & Stoke-on-Trent

Rooms 42 **S** fr £29; **D** fr £29

DISLEY Map 16 SJ98

Best Western Moorside Grange Hotel & Spa

★★★ 72% HOTEL

☎ 01663 764151 📄 01663 762794
Mudhurst Ln, Higher Disley SK12 2AP
e-mail: sales@moorsidegrangehotel.com
web: www.moorsidegrangehotel.com
dir: Leave A6 at Rams Head, Disley continue along Buxton Old Rd for 1m, turn right onto Mudhurst Lane, hotel on left

Spectacular views of the moors above Higher Disley are one of the attractions of this large complex. The hotel has excellent conference and function facilities, a well-equipped leisure centre and two tennis courts in the extensive grounds. Suites, and bedrooms with four-poster beds, are available.

Rooms 98 (3 fmly) **Facilities** Spa ⓔ supervised ⚖ Gym Squash Xmas New Year Wi-fi **Conf** Class 140 Board 100 Thtr 280 Del from £99 to £145 **Services** Lift **Parking** 250 **Notes** Civ Wed 280

ELLESMERE PORT Map 15 SJ47

Holiday Inn Ellesmere Port/Chester

★★★ 73% HOTEL

☎ 0151 356 8111 📄 0151 356 7181
Centre Island Waterways, Lower Mersey St L65 2AL
web: www.holidayinn.co.uk
dir: At M53 junct 9

Enjoying a waterside location, this modern hotel offers comfortable bedrooms together with attractive public rooms. There is a conference centre and small leisure club.

Rooms 83

HANDFORTH

See Manchester Airport (Greater Manchester)

KNUTSFORD Map 15 SJ77

Cottons Hotel & Spa

shire
hotels & spas

★★★★ 80% HOTEL

☎ 01565 650333 📄 01565 755351
Manchester Rd WA16 0SU
e-mail: cottons@shirehotels.com
web: www.cottonshotel.com
dir: On A50, 1m from M6 junct 19

The superb leisure facilities and quiet location are great attractions at this hotel, which is just a short distance from Manchester Airport. Bedrooms are smartly appointed in various styles, and executive rooms have very good

continued

KNUTSFORD *continued*

working areas. The hotel has spacious lounge areas and an excellent leisure centre.

Rooms 109 (14 fmly) (38 GF) **S** £155-£230; **D** £175-£250* **Facilities** Spa STV 🔵 🧖 Gym Steam room Activity studio for exercise classes Sauna Children's splash pool Xmas New Year Wi-fi **Conf** Class 100 Board 36 Thtr 200 **Services** Lift Air con **Parking** 180 **Notes** LB ⊗ Civ Wed 120

Mere Court Hotel & Conference Centre

★★★★ 78% ⊛ HOTEL

☎ 01565 831000 📠 01565 831001
Warrington Rd, Mere WA16 0RW
e-mail: sales@merecourt.co.uk
web: www.merecourt.co.uk
dir: A50, 1m W of junct with A556, on right

This is a smart and attractive hotel, set in extensive, well-tended gardens. The elegant and spacious bedrooms are all individually styled and offer a host of thoughtful extras. Conference facilities are particularly impressive and there is a large, self contained, conservatory function suite. Dining is available in the fine dining Arboreum Restaurant.

Rooms 34 (24 fmly) (12 GF) **Facilities** STV Wi-fi **Conf** Class 60 Board 35 Thtr 100 **Services** Lift **Parking** 150 **Notes** LB ⊗ Civ Wed 120

See advert on this page

The Longview Hotel & Stuffed Olive Restaurant

★★ 81% HOTEL

☎ 01565 632119 📠 01565 652402
55 Manchester Rd WA16 0LX
e-mail: enquiries@longviewhotel.com
web: www.longviewhotel.com
dir: M6 junct 19 take A556 W towards Chester. Left at lights onto A5033, 1.5m to rdbt then left. Hotel 200yds

This friendly Victorian hotel offers high standards of hospitality and service. Attractive public areas include a cellar bar and foyer lounge area. The restaurant has a traditional feel and offers an imaginative selection of dishes. Bedrooms, some located in a superb renovation of nearby houses, are individually styled and offer a good range of thoughtful amenities, including broadband internet access.

Rooms 32 (19 annexe) (1 fmly) (5 GF) **Facilities** FTV Wi-fi **Parking** 20 **Notes** Closed Xmas

---

Travelodge Knutsford Tabley

BUDGET HOTEL

☎ 0871 984 6153 📠 01565 652187
Chester Rd, Tabley WA16 0PP
web: www.travelodge.co.uk
dir: M6 junct 19, follow signs Manchester Airport signs. Hotel approx 200yds on A556

Travelodge offers good quality, good value, budget accommodation. All offer family rooms sleeping up to four (two adults, two children) with en suite bathroom/shower-room, remote-control TV, tea- and coffee-making facilities and comfortable beds. Food options vary. Breakfast is at the on-site Bar Café restaurant (if available) or to take away. See also Hotel Groups pages.

Rooms 32 **S** fr £29; **D** fr £29

KNUTSFORD MOTORWAY SERVICE AREA (M6)   Map 15 SJ77

Travelodge Knutsford (M6)

BUDGET HOTEL

☎ 0871 984 6151
Moto Service Area, M6 junct 18/19, Off Northwich Rd WA16 0TL
web: www.travelodge.co.uk
dir: Between junct 18 & 19 of M6 northbound

Travelodge offers good quality, good value, budget accommodation. All offer family rooms sleeping up to four (two adults, two children) with en suite bathroom/shower-room, remote-control TV, tea- and coffee-making facilities and comfortable beds. Food options vary. Breakfast is at the on-site Bar Café restaurant (if available) or to take away. See also Hotel Groups pages.

Rooms 54 **S** fr £29; **D** fr £29

LYMM   Map 15 SJ68

The Lymm Hotel

★★★ 73% HOTEL

☎ 01925 752233 📠 01925 756035
Whitbarrow Rd WA13 9AQ
e-mail: general.lymm@macdonald-hotels.co.uk
web: www.macdonaldhotels.co.uk/lymm
dir: M6 junct 20, B5158 to Lymm. Left at junct, 1st right, left at mini-rdbt, into Brookfield Rd, 3rd left into Whitbarrow Rd

In a peaceful residential area, this hotel benefits from both a quiet setting and convenient access to local motorway networks. It offers comfortable bedrooms equipped for both the business and leisure guest. Public areas include an attractive bar and an elegant restaurant. There is also extensive parking.

Rooms 62 (38 annexe) (9 fmly) (11 GF) S £45–£75; D £55–£95* Facilities STV Xmas New Year Wi-fi Conf Class 60 Board 40 Thtr 120 Del from £99 to £140* Parking 75 Notes LB Civ Wed 100

Travelodge Warrington Lymm Services

BUDGET HOTEL

☎ 0871 984 6157 🖷 01925 759341
Lymm Services, Cliffe Ln WA13 0SP
web: www.travelodge.co.uk
dir: A50, intersection of M6 junct 20 & M56 junct 9

Travelodge offers good quality, good value, budget accommodation. All offer family rooms sleeping up to four (two adults, two children) with en suite bathroom/shower-room, remote-control TV, tea- and coffee-making facilities and comfortable beds. Food options vary. Breakfast is at the on-site Bar Café restaurant (if available) or to take away. See also Hotel Groups pages.

Rooms 61 S fr £29; D fr £29

MACCLESFIELD — Map 16 SJ97

Barceló Shrigley Hall Hotel, Golf & Country Club

★★★★ 75% HOTEL

☎ 01625 575757 🖷 01625 573323
Shrigley Park, Pott Shrigley SK10 5SB
e-mail: shrigleyhall@barcelo-hotels.co.uk
web: www.barcelo-hotels.co.uk
dir: Off A523 at Legh Arms towards Pott Shrigley. Hotel 2m on left before village

Originally built in 1825, Shrigley Hall is an impressive hotel set in 262 acres of mature parkland and commands stunning views of the countryside. Features include a championship golf course. There is a wide choice of bedroom size and style. The public areas are spacious, combining traditional and contemporary decor, and include a well-equipped gym.

Rooms 148 (11 fmly) Facilities Spa STV 🏊 supervised ⚓ 18 ⛳ Putt green Fishing Gym Beauty salon Hydro centre ♫ Xmas New Year Wi-fi Conf Class 110 Board 42 Thtr 180 Del from £115* Services Lift Parking 300 Notes Civ Wed 150

Travelodge Macclesfield Adlington

BUDGET HOTEL

☎ 0871 984 6158 🖷 01625 875292
London Road South SK10 4NG
web: www.travelodge.co.uk
dir: on A523

Travelodge offers good quality, good value, budget accommodation. All offer family rooms sleeping up to four (two adults, two children) with en suite bathroom/shower-room, remote-control TV, tea- and coffee-making facilities and comfortable beds. Food options vary. Breakfast is at the on-site Bar Café restaurant (if available) or to take away. See also Hotel Groups pages.

Rooms 32 S fr £29; D fr £29

MIDDLEWICH — Map 15 SJ76

Travelodge Middlewich

BUDGET HOTEL

☎ 0871 984 6163 🖷 01606 738229
CW10 0JB
web: www.travelodge.co.uk
dir: M6 junct 18, A54 westbound

Travelodge offers good quality, good value, budget accommodation. All offer family rooms sleeping up to four (two adults, two children) with en suite bathroom/shower-room, remote-control TV, tea- and coffee-making facilities and comfortable beds. Food options vary. Breakfast is at the on-site Bar Café restaurant (if available) or to take away. See also Hotel Groups pages.

Rooms 32 S fr £29; D fr £29

NANTWICH — Map 15 SJ65

Rookery Hall Hotel and Spa

★★★★ 85% ◉◉ HOTEL

☎ 01270 610016 & 0845 072 7533 🖷 01270 626027
Main Rd, Worleston CW5 6DQ
e-mail: rookeryhall@handpicked.co.uk
web: www.handpicked.co.uk
dir: B5074 off 4th rdbt, on Nantwich by-pass. Hotel 1.5m on right

This fine 19th-century mansion is set in 38 acres of gardens, pasture and parkland. Bedrooms are spacious and appointed to a high standard with wide-screen plasma TVs and DVD players; many rooms have separate walk-in showers as well as deep tubs. Public areas are delightful and retain many original features. There is an extensive, state-of-the art spa and leisure complex.

Rooms 70 (39 annexe) (23 GF) Facilities Spa STV 🏊 Gym Sauna Crystal steam room Hydro therapy pool ♫ Xmas New Year Wi-fi Conf Class 90 Board 46 Thtr 200 Del from £135 to £225 Services Lift Parking 100 Notes ⊗ Civ Wed 140

Best Western Crown Hotel & Restaurant

★★ 71% HOTEL

☎ 01270 625283 🖷 01270 628047
High St CW5 5AS
e-mail: info@crownhotelnantwich.com
web: www.crownhotelnantwich.com
dir: A52 to Nantwich, hotel in town centre

Ideally set in the heart of this historic and delightful market town, The Crown has been offering hospitality for centuries. It has an abundance of original features and the well-equipped bedrooms retain an old world charm. There is also a bar with live entertainment throughout the week and diners can enjoy Italian food in the atmospheric brasserie.

Rooms 18 (2 fmly) (1 smoking) S £78–£80; D £88–£90 Facilities FTV ♫ Wi-fi Conf Class 150 Board 70 Thtr 200 Parking 18 Notes LB Closed 25 Dec Civ Wed 140

PECKFORTON — Map 15 SJ55

Peckforton Castle

★★★ 79% ◉◉ HOTEL

☎ 01829 260930 🖷 01829 261230
Stone House Ln CW6 9TN
e-mail: info@peckfortoncastle.co.uk
web: www.peckfortoncastle.co.uk
dir: A49. At Beeston Castle pub turn right signed Peckforton Castle. Approx 2m, castle entrance on right

Built in the mid 19th century by parliamentarian and landowner Lord John Tollemache and now lovingly cared for by The Naylor Family, this Grade I medieval-styled castle has been sympathetically renovated to provide high standards of comfort without losing original charm and character. Bedrooms and public areas retain any period features, and dining in the 1851 Restaurant is a memorable experience. There is a falconry centre at the castle.

Rooms 38 (6 fmly) (2 GF) Facilities FTV ⛳ Xmas New Year Wi-fi Conf Class 80 Board 34 Thtr 180 Parking 400 Notes LB ⊗ Civ Wed 165

PRESTBURY — Map 16 SJ87

Bridge

★★★ 79% HOTEL

☎ 01625 829326 🖷 01625 827557
The Village SK10 4DQ
e-mail: reception@bridge-hotel.co.uk
web: www.bridge-hotel.co.uk
dir: Off A538 through village. Hotel next to church

Dating in parts from the 17th century, this delightful, stylish hotel stands between the River Bollin and the ancient church. The hotel's bar is the ideal place to relax before enjoying a meal in the Bridge Restaurant. A wide range of bedroom styles is available in both the original building and the modern extension. *continued*

PRESTBURY *continued*

Rooms 23 (1 fmly) (3 GF) **S** £50; **D** £90-£95* **Facilities** ♫ Wi-fi **Conf** Class 56 Board 48 Thtr 100 Del from £125* **Parking** 52 **Notes** LB ❀ Civ Wed 100

PUDDINGTON Map 15 SJ37

Macdonald Craxton Wood
★★★★ 77% ⊛ HOTEL

☎ 0844 879 9038 📄 0151 347 4040
Parkgate Rd, Ledsham CH66 9PB
e-mail: craxton@macdonald-hotels.co.uk
web: www.macdonald-hotels.co.uk
dir: From M6 take M56 towards N Wales, then A5117/A540 to Hoylake. Hotel on left 200yds past lights

Set in extensive grounds, this hotel offers a variety of bedroom styles; the modern rooms are particularly comfortable. The nicely furnished restaurant overlooks the grounds and offers a wide choice of dishes, whilst full leisure facilities and a choice of function suites completes the package.

Rooms 72 (8 fmly) (30 GF) **Facilities** Spa STV ⊙ Gym Xmas New Year **Conf** Class 200 Board 160 Thtr 300 Del from £120 to £160* **Services** Lift **Parking** 220 **Notes** Civ Wed 350

See advert on page 71

RUNCORN Map 15 SJ58

Holiday Inn Runcorn
★★★ 70% HOTEL

☎ 0870 400 9070 📄 01928 714611
Wood Ln, Beechwood WA7 3HA
e-mail: adam.munday@ihg.com
web: www.holidayinn.co.uk
dir: M56 junct 12, left at rdbt, 100yds on left turn into Halton Station Rd under rail bridge, into Wood Ln

This modern hotel offers extensive conference, meeting and leisure facilities. Bedrooms, some upgraded, are well-equipped. The spacious restaurant is open for lunch and dinner and an all-day menu is provided in the lounge and bar. There is also a well-equipped leisure centre, and extensive conference facilities are available.

Rooms 153

Campanile Runcorn
BUDGET HOTEL

☎ 01928 581771 📄 01928 581730
Lowlands Rd WA7 5TP
e-mail: runcorn@campanile.com
dir: M56 junct 12, take A557, then follow signs for Runcorn rail station/Runcorn College

This modern building offers accommodation in smart, well-equipped bedrooms, all with en suite bathrooms. Refreshments may be taken at the informal bistro. See also the Hotel Groups pages.

Rooms 53 (18 GF) **Conf** Class 24 Board 24 Thtr 35

SANDBACH Map 15 SJ76

Innkeeper's Lodge Sandbach
BUDGET HOTEL

☎ 0845 112 6026 📄 0845 112 6275
Brereton Green CW11 1RS
web: www.innkeeperslodge.com/sandbach
dir: M6 junct 17/A534 towards Congleton. Left onto A5022 towards Brereton Green. Left onto A50, 2nd right into Newcastle Road South. Lodge on left

Innkeeper's Lodge represents an exciting, high value concept within the budget hotel market. Comfortable bedrooms provide excellent facilities that include satellite TV and modem points. This carefully restored lodge is in a picturesque setting and has its own unique style and quirky character. Food is served all day, and an extensive, complimentary continental breakfast is offered. See also the Hotel Groups pages.

Rooms 25

SANDIWAY Map 15 SJ67

INSPECTORS' CHOICE

Nunsmere Hall Hotel
★★★★ ⊛⊛ HOTEL

☎ 01606 889100 📄 01606 889055
Tarporley Rd CW8 2ES
e-mail: reception@nunsmere.co.uk
dir: M6 junct 18, A54 to Chester, at x-rds with A49 turn right towards Tarporley, hotel 2m on left

In an idyllic and peaceful setting of well-kept grounds, including a 60-acre lake, this delightful house dates back to 1900. Spacious bedrooms are individually styled, tastefully appointed to a very high standard and thoughtfully equipped. Guests can relax in the elegant lounges, the library or the oak-panelled bar. Dining in the Crystal Restaurant is a highlight and both a traditional carte and a gourmet menu are offered.

Rooms 36 (2 GF) **Facilities** ⊛ Xmas New Year Wi-fi **Conf** Class 24 Board 30 Thtr 50 **Services** Lift **Parking** 80 **Notes** ❀ Civ Wed 120

TARPORLEY Map 15 SJ56

Macdonald Portal
★★★★ 77% ⊛⊛ HOTEL

☎ 0844 879 9082
Cobblers Cross Ln CW6 0DJ
dir: M6 junct 18, A54 towards Middlewich/Winsford. Left onto A49, through Cotebrook. In approx 1m follow signs for hotel

This hotel is located in beautiful rolling countryside and provides a luxury base for both the leisure and business guest. The spacious and well-equipped bedrooms have bathrooms with baths and power showers. Extensive leisure facilities include a superb spa, state-of-the-art fitness equipment, three golf courses and an eye-catching golf academy. The Ranulf Restaurant delivers skilfully prepared, innovative cooking, as well as an excellent breakfast. Staff throughout are very friendly and nothing is too much trouble.

Rooms 83

Willington Hall

★★★ 78% COUNTRY HOUSE HOTEL

☎ 01829 752321 🖺 01829 752596
Willington CW6 0NB
e-mail: enquiries@willingtonhall.co.uk
web: www.willingtonhall.co.uk
dir: 3m NW off unclass road linking A51 & A54, at Clotton
turn off A51 at Bulls Head, then follow signs

Situated in 17 acres of parkland and built in 1829, this
attractively furnished country-house hotel offers spacious
bedrooms, many with views over open countryside.
Service is courteous and friendly, and freshly prepared
meals are offered in the dining room or in the adjacent
bar and drawing room. A smart function suite confirms
the popularity of this hotel as a premier venue for
weddings and conferences.

Rooms 10 (4 fmly) **S** £80; **D** £120-£130 (incl. bkfst)*
Facilities Fishing 🍴 New Year Wi-fi **Conf** Class 80
Board 50 Thtr 160 **Parking** 60 **Notes** LB Closed 25 & 26
Dec Civ Wed 130

The Wild Boar

★★★ 72% HOTEL

☎ 01829 260309 🖺 01829 261081
Whitchurch Rd, Beeston CW6 9NW
e-mail: enquiries@wildboarhotel.co.uk
dir: exit A51(Nantwich/Chester road) at Red Fox pub
lights onto A49 to Whitchurch. Hotel on left at brow of
hill, approx 1.5m

This 17th-century, half-timbered former hunting lodge
has been extended over the years to create a smart,
spacious hotel with comfortable bedrooms and stylish
public areas. Guests can choose between the elegant
Tower Restaurant or the more informal Stables Grill. The
hotel is a popular venue for meetings, functions and
weddings, and offers impressive conference facilities.

Rooms 37 (20 fmly) (11 GF) **Facilities** FTV 🎵 Xmas New
Year Wi-fi **Conf** Class 70 Board 50 Thtr 150 **Parking** 100
Notes LB Civ Wed 100

WARRINGTON   Map 15 SJ68

The Park Royal

★★★★ 77% HOTEL

☎ 01925 730706 🖺 01925 730740
Stretton Rd, Stretton WA4 4NS
e-mail: parkroyalreservations@qhotels.co.uk
web: www.qhotels.co.uk
dir: M56 junct 10, A49 to Warrington, at lights turn right
to Appleton Thorn, hotel 200yds on right

This modern hotel enjoys a peaceful setting, yet is
conveniently located just minutes from the M56. The
bedrooms are modern in style and thoughtfully equipped.
Spacious, stylish public areas include extensive
conference and function facilities, and a comprehensive
leisure centre complete with outdoor tennis courts and an
impressive beauty centre.

Rooms 146 (3 fmly) (34 GF) **S** £74-£84; **D** £155-£165
(incl. bkfst)* **Facilities** Spa STV 🌀 🏊 Gym Dance studio
Xmas New Year Wi-fi **Conf** Class 200 Board 90 Thtr 400
Del from £135 to £175* **Services** Lift **Parking** 400
Notes Civ Wed 300

De Vere Daresbury Park

★★★★ 75% HOTEL

☎ 01925 267331 🖺 01925 265615
Chester Rd, Daresbury WA4 4BB
e-mail: reservations.daresbury@devere-hotels.com
web: www.devere.co.uk
dir: M56 junct 11, take 'Daresbury Park' exit at rdbt. Hotel
100mtrs

Its proximity to the motorway makes this modern,
purpose-built hotel an excellent base for visiting the
cities of Liverpool, Manchester and Chester. Parts of the
hotel have an 'Alice in Wonderland' theme, as its author,
Lewis Caroll was born in nearby village of Daresbury.
There are a number of spacious bedrooms, including 12
well-appointed suites. Public rooms include a bright and
airy foyer serving informal snacks and drinks, a large bar
and restaurant and an indoor leisure centre.

Rooms 189 (12 fmly) (65 GF) **Facilities** Spa STV 🌀
supervised Gym Squash Steam Room Beauty salon Xmas
New Year Wi-fi **Conf** Class 128 Board 80 Thtr 350
Del from £100 to £160* **Services** Lift **Parking** 400
Notes Civ Wed 220

Best Western Fir Grove

★★★ 78% HOTEL

☎ 01925 267471 🖺 01925 601092
Knutsford Old Rd WA4 2LD
e-mail: firgrove@bestwestern.co.uk
web: www.bw-firgrovehotel.co.uk
dir: M6 junct 20, follow signs for A50 to Warrington for
2.4m, before swing bridge over canal, turn right & right
again

Situated in a quiet residential area, this hotel is
convenient for both the town centre and the motorway
network. Comfortable, smart bedrooms, including
spacious executive rooms, offer some excellent extra
facilities such as PlayStations and CD players. Public
areas include a smart lounge/bar, a neatly appointed
restaurant and excellent function and meeting facilities.

Rooms 52 (3 fmly) (20 GF) **Facilities** Xmas New Year
Conf Class 150 Board 50 Thtr 200 **Parking** 100
Notes Civ Wed 200

Holiday Inn Warrington

★★★ 71% HOTEL

☎ 0870 400 9087 🖺 01925 838859
Woolston Grange Av, Woolston WA1 4PX
e-mail: nicola.crowley@ihg.com
web: www.holidayinn.co.uk
dir: M6 junct 21, follow signs for Birchwood

Ideally located within the M62 and M56 interchange, this
hotel provides the ideal base for all areas of the north-
west region for both corporate and leisure guests. Rooms
are spacious and well equipped, and a wide choice of
meals is available in the comfortable restaurant and cosy
bar. Meeting and conference facilities are also available.

Rooms 96 (26 fmly) (9 GF) (7 smoking) **Facilities** STV
Xmas New Year Wi-fi **Conf** Class 10 Board 16 Thtr 30
Services Lift Air con **Parking** 101

Paddington House

★★ 74% HOTEL

☎ 01925 816767 🖺 01925 816651
514 Old Manchester Rd WA1 3TZ
e-mail: hotel@paddingtonhouse.co.uk
web: www.paddingtonhouse.co.uk
dir: 1m from M6 junct 21, off A57, 2m from town centre

This busy, friendly hotel is conveniently situated just over
a mile from the M6. Bedrooms are attractively furnished,
and include four-poster and ground-floor rooms. Guests
can dine in the wood-panelled Padgate Restaurant or in
the cosy bar. Conference and function facilities are
available.

Rooms 37 (9 fmly) (6 GF) **Facilities** FTV New Year Wi-fi
Conf Class 100 Board 40 Thtr 180 Del from £70 to £95*
Services Lift **Parking** 50 **Notes** Civ Wed 150

See advert on page 71

WARRINGTON *continued*

Ramada Encore Warrington

☎ 0844 801 3690 📠 0844 801 3691
Aston Avene, Birchwood Business Park WA3 6ZN
e-mail: gm@encorewarrington.co.uk
dir: M6 junct 21a, follow signs for Birchwood Park on A574

Currently the rating for this establishment is not confirmed. This may be due to a change of ownership or because it has only recently joined the AA rating scheme. For further details please see the AA website: theAA.com

Rooms 103 (16 fmly) (7 GF) **S** £49-£89; **D** £49-£89*
Facilities FTV Wi-fi **Conf** Class 40 Board 12 Thtr 35 Del from £80 to £110* **Services** Lift Air con **Parking** 94 **Notes** LB ⊗

Villaggio

☎ 01925 630106 📠 01925 631377
5-9 Folly Ln WA5 0LZ
dir: M62 junct 9/A49, through 2 rdbts to x-rds. Left at McDonalds, through lights, hotel on left

Currently the rating for this establishment is not confirmed. This may be due to a change of ownership or because it has only recently joined the AA rating scheme. For further details please see the AA website: theAA.com

Rooms 19 (2 fmly) **S** £35-£38.95; **D** £45-£47.95 (incl. bkfst)* **Facilities** FTV Xmas New Year Wi-fi
Conf Class 180 Board 100 Thtr 230 Del from £100 to £130* **Parking** 30

Innkeeper's Lodge Warrington Haydock

BUDGET HOTEL

☎ 0845 112 6028 📠 0845 112 6273
322 Newton Rd, Lowton Village WA3 1HD
web: www.innkeeperslodge.com/warrington
dir: M6 junct 23. 2m from Haydock Racecourse on A580 towards Manchester. After rdbt pass McDonalds, through lights, right for Culcheth, B5207. Right at lights. Lodge opposite

Innkeeper's Lodge represents an exciting, high value concept within the budget hotel market. Comfortable bedrooms provide excellent facilities that include satellite TV and modem points. Options include family rooms; and for the corporate guest, cutting edge IT which includes Wi-fi access. A popular Carvery provides all-day food, including an extensive, complimentary continental breakfast. See also the Hotel Groups pages.

Rooms 58 (18 fmly) **Conf** Thtr 60

Travelodge Warrington

BUDGET HOTEL

☎ 0871 984 6180 📠 01925 639432
Kendrick/Leigh St WA1 1UZ
web: www.travelodge.co.uk
dir: M6 junct 21, A57 towards Liverpool & Widnes to Warrington town centre, through Asda rdbt. Lodge next left at lights

Travelodge offers good quality, good value, budget accommodation. All offer family rooms sleeping up to four (two adults, two children) with en suite bathroom/shower-room, remote-control TV, tea- and coffee-making facilities and comfortable beds. Food options vary. Breakfast is at the on-site Bar Café restaurant (if available) or to take away. See also Hotel Groups pages.

Rooms 63 **S** fr £29; **D** fr £29

The Hillcrest Hotel

★★★ 67% HOTEL

☎ 0844 736 8610 & 0151 424 1616 📠 0151 495 1348
75 Cronton Ln WA8 9AR
e-mail: thehillcrest@corushotels.com
web: www.corushotels.com
dir: M62 junct 6, A5080 towards Cronton for 2m, straight on at lights, hotel 1m on left

This hotel is located within easy reach of the motorway network. All bedrooms are comfortable and well equipped, particularly the executive rooms. Suites with four-poster or canopy beds, and rooms with spa baths are also available. Public areas include extensive conference facilities, Palms restaurant and bar, as well as Nelsons public bar.

Rooms 50 (5 fmly) (4 GF) **S** £35-£79; **D** £35-£79*
Facilities 🎵 Xmas New Year **Conf** Class 80 Board 40 Thtr 140 Del from £80 to £99* **Services** Lift **Parking** 150 **Notes** LB RS Xmas Civ Wed 100

Travelodge Widnes

BUDGET HOTEL

☎ 0871 984 6183 📠 0151 424 8930
Fiddlers Ferry Rd WA8 0HA
web: www.travelodge.co.uk
dir: on A562, 3m S of Widnes

Travelodge offers good quality, good value, budget accommodation. All offer family rooms sleeping up to four (two adults, two children) with en suite bathroom/shower-room, remote-control TV, tea- and coffee-making facilities and comfortable beds. Food options vary. Breakfast is at the on-site Bar Café restaurant (if available) or to take away. See also Hotel Groups pages.

Rooms 52 **S** fr £29; **D** fr £29

See also **Manchester Airport (Greater Manchester)**

De Vere Mottram Hall

DE VERE collection

★★★★ 79% HOTEL

☎ 01625 828135 📠 01625 828950
Wilmslow Rd, Mottram St Andrew, Prestbury SK10 4QT
e-mail: dmh.sales@devere-hotels.com
web: www.devere.co.uk
dir: M6 junct 18 from S, M6 junct 20 from N, M56 junct 6, A538 Prestbury

Set in 272 acres of some of Cheshire's most beautiful parkland, this 18th-century Georgian house is certainly an idyllic retreat. The hotel boasts extensive leisure facilities, including a championship golf course, swimming pool, gym and spa. Bedrooms are well equipped and elegantly furnished, and include a number of four-poster rooms and suites.

Rooms 131 (44 GF) **Facilities** Spa STV ⊛ supervised ♨ 18 ♣ Putt green Gym Squash Children's playground Rugby & football pitch Xmas New Year Wi-fi
Conf Class 120 Board 60 Thtr 180 **Services** Lift **Parking** 300 **Notes** ⊗ Civ Wed 160

Trehellas House Hotel & Restaurant

★★★ 74% ⊛ SMALL HOTEL

☎ 01208 72700 📠 01208 73336
Washaway PL30 3AD
e-mail: enquiries@trehellashouse.co.uk
web: www.trehellashouse.co.uk
dir: Take A389 from Bodmin towards Wadebridge. Hotel on right 0.5m beyond road to Camelford

This 18th-century former posting inn retains many original features and provides comfortable accommodation. Bedrooms are located in both the main house and adjacent coach house - all provide the same high standards. An interesting choice of cuisine, with an emphasis on locally-sourced ingredients, is offered in the impressive slate-floored restaurant.

Rooms 12 (7 annexe) (2 fmly) (5 GF) **S** £40-£75; **D** £50-£160 (incl. bkfst) **Facilities** FTV ⊁ Xmas New Year Wi-fi **Conf** Board 12 Thtr 12 Del from £100 to £150* **Parking** 32 **Notes** LB

Westberry

★★ 78% HOTEL

☎ 01208 72772 📠 01208 72212
Rhind St PL31 2EL
e-mail: westberry@btconnect.com
web: www.westberryhotel.net
dir: On ring road off A30 & A38. St Petroc's Church on right, at mini rdbt turn right. Hotel on right

This popular hotel is conveniently located for both Bodmin town centre and the A30. The bedrooms are attractive and well equipped. A spacious bar lounge and a billiard room are also provided. The restaurant serves a variety of dishes, ranging from bar snacks to a more extensive carte menu.

Rooms 20 (8 annexe) (2 fmly) (6 GF) **S** £48-£68; **D** £58-£78 (incl. bkfst)* **Facilities** STV Full sized snooker table Wi-fi **Conf** Class 80 Board 80 Thtr 100 Del from £78 to £98* **Parking** 30 **Notes** LB

BOSCASTLE — Map 2 SX09

The Wellington Hotel

★★ 81% ⊛ HOTEL

☎ 01840 250202
The Harbour PL35 0AQ
e-mail: info@boscastle-wellington.com
web: www.boscastle-wellington.com
dir: A30/A395 at Davidstowe follow Boscastle signs. B3266 to village. Right into Old Rd

This 16th-century coaching inn has been totally restored to its former glory following the disastrous flood of a few years ago. The Long Bar is popular with visitors and locals alike and features a delightful galleried area. The stylish bedrooms come in varying sizes, including the spacious Tower rooms; all are comfortable and suitably equipped. There is a bar menu, and in the elegant restaurant a daily-changing carte.

Rooms 15 (2 fmly) **S** £40-£47; **D** £80-£134 (incl. bkfst)* **Facilities** FTV ♫ Xmas New Year Wi-fi **Conf** Class 6 Board 24 Thtr 40 Del from £80 to £87* **Parking** 15 **Notes** LB

BUDE — Map 2 SS20

Falcon

★★★ 79% HOTEL

☎ 01288 352005 📠 01288 356359
Breakwater Rd EX23 8SD
e-mail: reception@falconhotel.com
web: www.falconhotel.com
dir: Off A39 into Bude, follow road to Widemouth Bay. Hotel on right over canal bridge

Dating back to 1798, this long-established hotel boasts delightful walled gardens, ideal for afternoon teas. Bedrooms offer high standards of comfort and quality; there is also a four-poster room complete with spa bath. A choice of menus is offered in the elegant restaurant and the friendly bar. The hotel has an impressive function room.

Rooms 29 (7 fmly) **Facilities** STV FTV ♨ New Year Wi-fi **Conf** Class 50 Board 50 Thtr 200 **Services** Lift **Parking** 40 **Notes** ⊗ RS 25 Dec Civ Wed 160

Hartland

★★★ 77% HOTEL

☎ 01288 355661 📠 01288 355664
Hartland Ter EX23 8JY
e-mail: hartlandhotel@aol.com
dir: off A39 to Bude, follow town centre signs. Left into Hartland Terrace opp Boots the chemist. Hotel at seaward end of road

Enjoying a pleasantly quiet yet convenient location, the Hartland has excellent sea views. A popular stay for those wishing to tour the area and also with families, this hotel offers entertainment on many evenings throughout the year. Bedrooms are comfortable and offer a range of sizes. The public areas are smart, and in the dining room a pleasant fixed-price menu is available.

Rooms 28 (2 fmly) **Facilities** ♦ ♫ Xmas **Services** Lift **Parking** 30 **Notes** LB Closed mid Nov-Etr (ex Xmas & New Year) No credit cards

Camelot

★★★ 75% HOTEL

☎ 01288 352361 📠 01288 355470
Downs View EX23 8RE
e-mail: stay@camelot-hotel.co.uk
web: www.camelot-hotel.co.uk
dir: off A39 into town centre, hotel close to golf course

This friendly and welcoming Edwardian property offers a range of facilities including a smart and comfortable conservatory bar and lounge, a games room and Hawkers restaurant, which offers skilful cooking using much local produce. Bedrooms are light and airy, with high standards of housekeeping and maintenance.

Rooms 24 (2 fmly) (7 GF) **Facilities** FTV Games room Wi-fi **Parking** 21 **Notes** LB

Hotel Penarvor

★★ 74% SMALL HOTEL

☎ 01288 352036 📠 01288 355027
Crooklets Beach EX23 8NE
e-mail: hotel.penarvor@boltblue.com
dir: From A39 towards Bude for 1.5m. At 2nd rdbt right, pass shops. Top of hill, left signed Crooklets Beach

Adjacent to the golf course and overlooking Crooklets Beach, this family owned hotel has a relaxed and friendly atmosphere. Bedrooms vary in size but are all equipped to a similar standard. An interesting selection of dishes, using fresh local produce, is available in the restaurant; bar meals are also provided.

Rooms 16 (6 fmly) **Parking** 20 **Notes** LB

Atlantic House

★★ 71% HOTEL

☎ 01288 352451
Summerleaze Crescent EX23 8HJ
e-mail: enq@atlantichousehotel.com
web: www.atlantichousehotel.com
dir: M5 junct 31, follow A30 for approx 24m, then take A386 to Bude

This pleasant hotel has splendid views of the coast and offers a peaceful and relaxing environment. The resident proprietors and staff are friendly and attentive. Bedrooms are comfortable and well appointed, and some rooms have sea views. Cuisine offers freshly prepared and appetising dishes served in the spacious dining room.

continued

BUDE *continued*

Rooms 15 (5 fmly) **S** £34-£88; **D** £68-£88 (incl. bkfst)*
Facilities FTV Xmas New Year Wi-fi **Conf** Class 30
Board 30 Thtr 30 Del from £50 to £100* **Parking** 7
Notes LB ⊗

Tyacks

★★★ 71% HOTEL

☎ 01209 612424 📄 01209 612435
27 Commercial St TR14 8LD
e-mail: booking@tyackshotel.co.uk
dir: W on A30 past A3047 junct & turn off at Camborne
West junct. Left & left again at rdbt, follow town centre
signs. Hotel on left

This 18th-century, former coaching inn has spacious,
well furnished public areas which include a smart lounge
and bar, the popular Coach Bar and a restaurant serving
both fixed-price and carte menus. The comfortable
bedrooms are attractively decorated and well equipped;
two have separate sitting areas.

Rooms 15 (2 fmly) **Facilities** FTV 6x6 Sports'
entertainment screen 🎵 Wi-fi **Conf** Class 35 Board 30
Thtr 30 **Parking** 27

Lanteglos Country House

★★★ 🅰 COUNTRY HOUSE HOTEL

☎ 01840 213551 📄 01840 212372
PL32 9RF
e-mail: enquiries@lantegl1oshotel.co.uk
dir: A39 through Camelford, 0.5m out turn right B3266.
1st left after garage, hotel in 1m

Rooms 13 (6 fmly) **S** £75-£90; **D** £100-£160 (incl. bkfst)*
Facilities STV FTV ⳥ 🎱 Squash Snooker table Wi-fi

Conf Class 30 Board 20 Thtr 50 Del from £145 to £175*
Notes ⊗ Closed Nov-Feb Civ Wed 50

See St Ives

Crantock Bay

★★★ 75% HOTEL

☎ 01637 830229 📄 01637 831111
West Pentire TR8 5SE
e-mail: stay@crantockbayhotel.co.uk
web: www.crantockbayhotel.co.uk
dir: At Newquay A3075 to Redruth. After 500yds right
towards Crantock, follow signs to West Pentire

This family-run hotel has spectacular sea views and a
tradition of friendly and attentive service. With direct
access to the beach from its four acres of grounds, and
its extensive leisure facilities, the hotel is a great place
for families. There are separate lounges, a spacious bar
and enjoyable cuisine is served in the dining room.

Rooms 31 (3 fmly) (9 GF) **S** £63-£110; **D** £126-£220 (incl.
bkfst & dinner)* **Facilities** 🕭 🏊 Putt green ⛳ Gym
Children's games room Xmas New Year Wi-fi Child
facilities **Conf** Class 12 Board 12 Thtr 60 **Parking** 40
Notes LB Closed 2 wks Nov & Jan RS Dec & Feb

See also **Mawnan Smith**

Royal Duchy

★★★★ 79% ◉◉ HOTEL

☎ 01326 313042 📄 01326 319420
Cliff Rd TR11 4NX
e-mail: info@royalduchy.com
web: www.royalduchy.com
dir: On Cliff Rd, along Falmouth seafront

Looking out over the sea and towards Pendennis Castle,
this hotel provides a friendly environment. The
comfortable lounge and cocktail bar are well appointed,
and leisure facilities and meeting rooms are also
available. The restaurant serves carefully prepared dishes
and bedrooms vary in size and aspect, with many rooms
having sea views.

Rooms 43 (6 fmly) (1 GF) **S** £88-£122; **D** £160-£304 (incl.
bkfst)* **Facilities** FTV 🕭 Games room Beauty salon 🎵
Xmas New Year Wi-fi Child facilities **Conf** Class 50
Board 50 Thtr 50 **Services** Lift **Parking** 50 **Notes** LB ⊗
Civ Wed 100

See advert on this page

St Michael's Hotel and Spa

★★★★ 72% @ HOTEL

☎ 01326 312707 🖷 01326 211772
Gyllyngvase Beach, Seafront TR11 4NB
e-mail: info@stmichaelshotel.co.uk
dir: A39 into Falmouth, follow beach signs, at 2nd mini-rdbt into Pennance Rd. Take 2nd left & 2nd left again

Overlooking the bay this hotel is in an excellent position and commands lovely views. It is appointed in a fresh, contemporary style that reflects its location by the sea. The Flying Fish restaurant has a great atmosphere and a buzz. The light and bright bedrooms, some with balconies, are well equipped. There are excellent leisure facilities including a fitness and health club together with the spa offering many treatments; the attractive gardens also provide a place to relax and unwind.

Rooms 61 (8 annexe) (7 fmly) (12 GF) **Facilities** Spa FTV ⓢ Gym Sauna Steam room Aqua-aerobics Fitness Studio Xmas New Year Wi-fi **Conf** Class 150 Board 50 Thtr 200 **Parking** 30 **Notes** ⊗ Civ Wed 80

See advert on this page

The Greenbank

★★★ 80% @ HOTEL

☎ 01326 312440 🖷 01326 211362
Harbourside TR11 2SR
e-mail: reception@greenbank-hotel.co.uk
web: www.greenbank-hotel.co.uk
dir: 500yds past Falmouth Marina on Penryn River

Located by the marina, and with its own private quay dating from the 17th century, this smart hotel has a strong maritime theme throughout. Set at the water's edge, the lounge, restaurant and many bedrooms all benefit from harbour views. The restaurant provides a choice of interesting and enjoyable dishes.

Rooms 59 (6 fmly) **Facilities** FTV Private beach & quay Wi-fi **Conf** Class 90 Board 25 Thtr 90 **Services** Lift **Parking** 68 **Notes** LB ⊗ Civ Wed 90

Best Western Penmere Manor

★★★ 79% @ HOTEL

☎ 01326 211411 & 214525 🖷 01326 317588
Mongleath Rd TR11 4PN
e-mail: reservations@penmere.co.uk
web: www.penmeremanorhotel.co.uk
dir: Turn right off A39 at Hillhead rdbt, over double mini rdbt. After 0.75m left into Mongleath Rd

Set in five acres on the outskirts of town, this Georgian manor house was originally built for a ship's captain.

Now a family owned hotel it provides friendly service and a good range of facilities. Bedrooms vary in size and a located in the manor house and the garden wing. Various menus are available in the bar and the smart, award-winning restaurant. There is a health and beauty centre offering a wide range of treatments and the water in the indoor pool is UV filtered.

Rooms 37 (12 fmly) (13 GF) **S** £62-£72; **D** £124-£186 (incl. bkfst)* **Facilities** FTV ⓢ ⌇ ⌣ Gym Sauna New Year Wi-fi **Conf** Class 20 Board 30 Thtr 60 Del from £117.50 to £144.50* **Parking** 50 **Notes** LB Closed 24-27 Dec Civ Wed 80

Best Western Falmouth Beach Resort Hotel

★★★ 78% HOTEL

☎ 01326 310500 🖷 01326 319147
Gyllyngvase Beach, Seafront TR11 4NA
e-mail: info@falmouthbeachhotel.co.uk
web: www.bw-falmouthbeachhotel.co.uk
dir: A39 to Falmouth, follow seafront signs

Enjoying wonderful views, this popular hotel is situated opposite the beach and within easy walking distance of Falmouth's attractions and port. A friendly atmosphere is maintained and guests have a good choice of leisure, fitness, entertainment and dining options. Bedrooms, many with balconies and sea views, are well equipped and comfortable.

Rooms 120 (20 fmly) (4 GF) **Facilities** Spa FTV ⓢ supervised ⌣ Gym Sauna Steam room Hair & beauty salon ♫ Xmas New Year Wi-fi **Conf** Class 200 Board 250 Thtr 300 Del from £109 to £175* **Services** Lift **Parking** 88 **Notes** Civ Wed 220

See advert on page 85

FALMOUTH *continued*

Green Lawns

THE INDEPENDENTS
HOTEL ASSOCIATION

★★★ 77% HOTEL

☎ 01326 312734 📄 01326 211427
Western Ter TR11 4QJ
e-mail: info@greenlawnshotel.com
web: www.greenlawnshotel.com
dir: On A39

This attractive property enjoys a convenient location close to the town centre and within easy reach of the sea. Spacious public areas include inviting lounges, an elegant restaurant, conference and meeting facilities and a leisure centre. Bedrooms vary in size and style but all are well equipped and comfortable. The friendly service is particularly noteworthy.

Rooms 39 (8 fmly) (11 GF) (2 smoking) **S** £65-£120; **D** £90-£200 (incl. bkfst)* **Facilities** FTV 🖉 🏊 Gym Squash Sauna Steam room Spa bath New Year Wi-fi **Conf** Class 80 Board 100 Thtr 200 Del from £95 to £120* **Parking** 69 **Notes** LB Closed 24-30 Dec Civ Wed 50

Falmouth

RICHARDSON

★★★ 75% ☺ HOTEL

☎ 01326 312671 & 0800 448 8844 📄 01326 319533
Castle Beach TR11 4NZ
e-mail: reservations@falmouthhotel.com
web: www.falmouthhotel.com
dir: Take A30 to Truro then A390 to Falmouth. Follow signs for beaches, hotel on seafront near Pendennis Castle

This spectacular beach-front Victorian property affords wonderful sea views from many of its comfortable bedrooms, some of which have their own balconies. Spacious public areas include a number of inviting lounges, beautiful leafy grounds, a choice of dining options and an impressive range of leisure facilities.

Rooms 69 (17 fmly) **Facilities** Spa STV FTV 🖉 Putt green Gym Beauty salon & Therapeutic rooms Xmas New Year Wi-fi **Conf** Class 150 Board 100 Thtr 250 **Services** Lift **Parking** 120 **Notes** Civ Wed 250

See advert on this page

Penmorvah Manor

★★★ 72% HOTEL

☎ 01326 250277 📄 01326 250509
Budock Water TR11 5ED
e-mail: reception@penmorvah.co.uk
web: www.penmorvah.co.uk
dir: A39 to Hillhead rdbt, take 2nd exit. Right at Falmouth Football Club, through Budock. Hotel opposite Penjerrick Gardens

Situated within two miles of central Falmouth, this extended Victorian manor house is a peaceful hideaway, set in six acres of private woodland and gardens. Penmorvah is well positioned for visiting the local gardens, and offers many garden-tour breaks. Dinner features locally sourced, quality ingredients such as Cornish cheeses, meat, fish and game.

Rooms 27 (1 fmly) (10 GF) **S** £65; **D** £100-£150 (incl. bkfst) **Facilities** Xmas Wi-fi **Conf** Class 100 Board 56 Thtr 250 Del from £100 **Parking** 100 **Notes** LB Closed 31 Dec-31 Jan Civ Wed 120

Hotel Anacapri

★★ 75% HOTEL

☎ 01326 311454 ▤ 01326 311474
Gyllyngvase Rd TR11 4DJ
e-mail: anacapri@btconnect.com
web: www.hotelanacapri.co.uk
dir: A39 (Truro to Falmouth), straight on at lights, straight on at 2 rdbts. 5th right into Gyllyngvase Rd, hotel on right

In an elevated position overlooking Gyllyngvase Beach with views of Falmouth Bay beyond, this family run establishment extends a warm welcome to all. Bedrooms have similar standards of comfort and quality, and the majority have sea views. Public areas include a convivial bar, a lounge and the smart restaurant, where carefully prepared and very enjoyable cuisine is on offer.

Rooms 16 **S** £40-£70; **D** £50-£120 (incl. bkfst)*
Facilities FTV Wi-fi **Parking** 20 **Notes** ⊗ No children 8yrs Closed 13 Dec-10 Jan

Park Grove

★★ 71% HOTEL

☎ 01326 313276 ▤ 01326 211926
Kimberley Park Rd TR11 2DD
e-mail: reception@parkgrovehotel.com
web: www.parkgrovehotel.com
dir: Off A39 at lights by Riders Garage towards harbour. Hotel 400yds on left opposite park

Within walking distance of the town centre, this friendly family-run hotel is situated in a pleasant residential area opposite Kimberley Park. Comfortable accommodation is provided and public areas include a relaxing and stylish lounge and a spacious dining room and bar. Bedrooms are also comfortable and well equipped.

Rooms 17 (6 fmly) (2 GF) **S** £47-£67; **D** £74-£84 (incl. bkfst)* **Facilities** FTV **Parking** 25 **Notes** LB ⊗ Closed Dec-Feb

Broadmead

★★ 69% SMALL HOTEL

☎ 01326 315704 ▤ 01326 311048
66/68 Kimberley Park Rd TR11 2DD
e-mail: frontdesk@broadmead-hotel.co.uk
dir: A39 from Truro to Falmouth, at lights left into Kimberley Park Rd, hotel 200yds on left

Conveniently located, with views across the park and within easy walking distance of the beaches and town centre, this pleasant hotel, has smart and comfortable accommodation. Bedrooms are well equipped and attractively decorated. A choice of lounges is available and, in the dining room, menus offer freshly prepared home-cooked dishes.

Rooms 12 (2 fmly) (2 GF) **S** £30-£40; **D** £60-£80 (incl. bkfst) **Facilities** FTV Wi-fi **Parking** 8 **Notes** LB

Rosslyn

★★ 69% HOTEL

☎ 01326 312699 & 315373 ▤ 01326 312699
110 Kimberley Park Rd TR11 2JJ
e-mail: mail@rosslynhotel.co.uk
web: www.rosslynhotel.co.uk
dir: On A39 towards Falmouth, to Hilend rdbt, turn right and over next mini rdbt. At 2nd mini rdbt left into Trescobeas Rd. Hotel on left past hospital

A relaxed and friendly atmosphere is maintained at this family-run hotel. Situated on the northern edge of Falmouth, the Rosslyn is easily located and is suitable for both business and leisure guests. A comfortable lounge overlooks the well-tended garden, and enjoyable freshly prepared dinners are offered in the restaurant.

Rooms 25 (3 fmly) (6 GF) **S** £25-£35; **D** £50-£70 (incl. bkfst)* **Facilities** FTV Internet access in lounge New Year **Conf** Class 60 Board 20 Del from £40 to £50* **Parking** 22 **Notes** LB

Madeira Hotel

★★ 68% HOTEL

☎ 01326 313531 ▤ 01326 319143
Cliff Rd TR11 4NY
e-mail: madeira.falmouth@alfatravel.co.uk
dir: A39 (Truro to Falmouth), follow tourist signs 'Hotels' to seafront

This popular hotel offers splendid sea views and a pleasant, convenient location, which is close to the town. Extensive sun lounges are popular haunts in which to enjoy the views, while additional facilities include an oak panelled cocktail bar. Bedrooms, many with sea views, are available in a range of sizes.

Rooms 50 (8 fmly) (7 GF) **Facilities** FTV ♫ Xmas New Year **Services** Lift **Parking** 11 **Notes** LB ⊗ Closed Dec-Feb (except Xmas) RS Nov & Mar

Membly Hall

★★ 65% HOTEL

☎ 01326 312869 & 311115 ▤ 01326 211751
Sea Front, Cliff Rd TR11 4NT
e-mail: memblyhallhotel@tiscali.co.uk
dir: A39 to Falmouth. Follow seafront & beaches sign

Located conveniently on the seafront and enjoying splendid views, this family-run hotel offers friendly service. Bedrooms are pleasantly spacious and well equipped. Carefully prepared and enjoyable meals are served in the spacious dining room. Live entertainment is provided on some evenings and there is also a sauna and spa pool.

Rooms 35 (3 fmly) (6 GF) **S** £30-£45; **D** £60-£90 (incl. bkfst)* **Facilities** STV FTV Putt green ⛳ Gym Indoor short bowls Table tennis Pool table ♫ New Year Wi-fi **Conf** Class 130 Board 60 Thtr 150 **Services** Lift **Parking** 30 **Notes** ⊗ Closed Xmas week RS Dec-Jan No credit cards

FOWEY
Map 2 SX15

The Fowey Hotel
★★★★ 71% @ HOTEL

RICHARDSON

☎ 01726 832551   📠 01726 832125
The Esplanade PL23 1HX
e-mail: fowey@richardsonhotels.co.uk
web: www.thefoweyhotel.co.uk
dir: A30 to Okehampton, continue to Bodmin. Then B3269 to Fowey for 1m, on right bend left junct then right into Dagands Rd. Hotel 200mtrs on left

This attractive hotel stands proudly above the estuary, with marvellous views of the river from the public areas and the majority of the bedrooms. High standards are evident throughout, augmented by a relaxed and welcoming atmosphere. There is a spacious bar, elegant restaurant and smart drawing room. Imaginative dinners make good use of quality local ingredients.

Rooms 37 (2 fmly) **S** £108-£228; **D** £108-£228 (incl. bkfst)* **Facilities** Fishing ⅃ Xmas New Year Wi-fi **Conf** Class 60 Board 20 Thtr 100 **Services** Lift **Parking** 18 **Notes** LB

Fowey Hall
★★★ 83% @@ HOTEL

von Essen hotels
a private collection

☎ 01726 833866   📠 01726 834100
Hanson Dr PL23 1ET
e-mail: info@foweyhallhotel.co.uk
web: www.foweyhallhotel.co.uk
dir: In Fowey, over mini rdbt into town centre. Pass school on right, 400mtrs right into Hanson Drive

Built in 1899, this listed mansion looks out on to the English Channel. The imaginatively designed bedrooms offer charm, individuality and sumptuous comfort; the Garden Wing rooms adding a further dimension to staying here. The beautifully appointed public rooms include the wood-panelled dining room where accomplished cuisine is served. Enjoying glorious views, the well-kept grounds

have a covered pool and sunbathing area. Von Essen Hotels - AA Hotel Group of the Year 2009-10.

Rooms 36 (8 annexe) (30 fmly) (6 GF) **Facilities** Spa STV FTV ⓣ ⅃ Table tennis Basketball Trampoline Pool table Xmas New Year Child facilities **Conf** Class 20 Board 20 Thtr 30 Del from £160 to £180* **Parking** 40 **Notes** Civ Wed 120

INSPECTORS' CHOICE

Old Quay House
★★ @@ HOTEL

☎ 01726 833302   📠 01726 833668
28 Fore St PL23 1AQ
e-mail: info@theoldquayhouse.com
dir: M5 junct 31 onto A30 to Bodmin. Then A389 through town, then B3269 to Fowey

Looking out across Fowey's busy waterway, situated at the end of steep and winding streets so typical of Cornwall, this hotel offers very comfortable, stylish bedrooms; some have harbour views. The old quay itself is where guests can either dine or enjoy a drink; the cuisine is accomplished and breakfast is also noteworthy.

Rooms 11 **S** £130-£300; **D** £170-£300 (incl. bkfst)* **Facilities** STV Wi-fi **Notes** LB ⊗ No children 12yrs Civ Wed 100

GOLANT
Map 2 SX15

Cormorant
★★★ 77% @@ HOTEL

☎ 01726 833426   📠 01726 833219
PL23 1LL
e-mail: relax@cormoranthotel.co.uk
web: www.cormoranthotel.co.uk
dir: A390 onto B3269 signed Fowey. In 3m left to Golant, through village to end of road, hotel on right

This hotel focuses on traditional hospitality, attentive service and good food. All the bedrooms enjoy the river view and guests can expect goose and down duvets, flat-screen, digital TVs and free Wi-fi access. Breakfast and

lunch may be taken on the terrace which overlooks the river.

Rooms 14 (4 GF) **S** £80-£200; **D** £110-£235 (incl. bkfst)* **Facilities** FTV ⓣ Xmas New Year Wi-fi **Parking** 14 **Notes** LB ⊗ No children 12yrs

HAYLE
Map 2 SW53

Travelodge Hayle
BUDGET HOTEL

Travelodge

☎ 0871 984 6314
Carwin Roundabout TR27 5DG
web: www.travelodge.co.uk
dir: M5 junct 30, A312. In 2m right onto A244, Hounslow road

Travelodge offers good quality, good value, budget accommodation. All offer family rooms sleeping up to four (two adults, two children) with en suite bathroom/shower-room, remote-control TV, tea- and coffee-making facilities and comfortable beds. Food options vary. Breakfast is at the on-site Bar Café restaurant (if available) or to take away. See also Hotel Groups pages.

Rooms 39 **S** fr £29; **D** fr £29

HELSTON
Map 2 SW62

Gwealdues
★★ 75% HOTEL

☎ 01326 572808   📠 01326 561388
Falmouth Rd TR13 8JX
e-mail: thegwealdueshotel@hotmail.co.uk
web: www.gwealdueshotel.com
dir: Off rdbt on A394. On town outskirts

A family owned and run hotel that is within easy access of the coast and the cathedral city of Truro. The staff are friendly and attentive. The comfortable bedrooms include family rooms. There is a well stocked bar and a traditionally styled restaurant.

Rooms 18 (2 fmly) (1 GF) **S** £50-£55; **D** £70-£80 (incl. bkfst)* **Facilities** FTV Wi-fi **Conf** Class 80 Board 40 Thtr 120 **Parking** 50 **Notes** LB

LAND'S END
Map 2 SW32

The Land's End Hotel
★★★ 64% HOTEL

☎ 01736 871844   📠 01736 871599
TR19 7AA
e-mail: reservations@landsendhotel.co.uk
web: www.landsendhotel.co.uk
dir: From Penzance take A30, follow Land's End signs. After Sennen 1m to Land's End

This famous location provides a very impressive setting for this well-established hotel. Bedrooms, many with stunning views of the Atlantic, are pleasantly decorated and comfortable. A relaxing lounge and attractive bar are provided. The Longships Restaurant, with far reaching sea views, offers fresh local produce, and fish dishes are a speciality.

The Land's End Hotel

Rooms 32 (2 fmly) **Facilities** Free entry Land's End Visitor Centre Xmas New Year **Conf** Class 100 Board 50 Thtr 200 **Parking** 1000 **Notes** Civ Wed 110

LAUNCESTON   Map 3 SX38

See also **Lifton (Devon)**

Eagle House

★★ 74% SMALL HOTEL

☎ 01566 772036 & 774488 🖹 01566 772036
Castle St PL15 8BA
e-mail: eaglehousehotel@aol.com
dir: from Launceston on Holsworthy Rd follow brown hotel signs

Next to the castle, this elegant Georgian house dates back to 1767 and is within walking distance of all the local amienties. Many of the bedrooms have wonderful views over the Cornish countryside. A short carte is served each evening in the restaurant.

Rooms 14 (1 fmly) **Facilities** Wi-fi **Conf** Class 170 Board 170 Thtr 170 **Parking** 80 **Notes** ⊗ Civ Wed 170

LIZARD   Map 2 SW71

Housel Bay

★★★ 67% HOTEL

☎ 01326 290417 & 290917 🖹 01326 290359
Housel Cove TR12 7PG
e-mail: info@houselbay.com
dir: A39 or A394 to Helston, then A3083. At Lizard sign turn left, left at school, down lane to hotel

This long-established hotel has stunning views across the Western Approaches, equally enjoyable from the lounge and many of the bedrooms. Good cuisine is available in the stylish dining room, from where guests might enjoy a stroll to the end of the garden, which leads directly onto the Cornwall coastal path.

Rooms 20 (1 fmly) **Facilities** FTV Xmas New Year **Services** Lift **Parking** 35 **Notes** LB ⊗

LOOE   Map 2 SX25

See also **Portwrinkle**

Trelaske Hotel & Restaurant

★★★ 79% ◉ HOTEL

☎ 01503 262159 🖹 01503 265360
Polperro Rd PL13 2JS
e-mail: info@trelaske.co.uk
dir: B252 signed Looe, over Looe bridge signed Polperro. Follow road for 1.9m, hotel signed off road on right

This small hotel offers comfortable accommodation and professional yet friendly service and award-winning food. Set in its own very well tended grounds and only minutes away from Looe and its attractions.

Rooms 7 (4 annexe) (2 fmly) (2 GF) **S** £65-£70; **D** £95-£105 (incl. bkfst) **Facilities** FTV Mountain bikes for hire Wi-fi **Conf** Class 30 Board 40 Thtr 100 Del from £135 to £140* **Parking** 50

Hannafore Point

THE INDEPENDENTS
HOTEL ASSOCIATION

★★★ 70% HOTEL

☎ 01503 263273 🖹 01503 263272
Marine Dr, West Looe PL13 2DG
e-mail: stay@hannaforepointhotel.com
dir: A38, left onto A385 to Looe. Over bridge turn left. Hotel 0.5m on left

With panoramic coastal views of St George's Island around to Rame Head, this popular hotel provides a warm welcome. The wonderful view is certainly a feature of the spacious restaurant and bar, providing a scenic backdrop for both dinners and breakfasts. Additional facilities include a heated indoor pool and gym.

Rooms 37 (5 fmly) **Facilities** STV ⊛ Gym Spa pool Steam room Sauna ♫ Xmas New Year Wi-fi **Conf** Class 80 Board 40 Thtr 120 Del from £75 to £120 **Services** Lift **Parking** 32 **Notes** Civ Wed 150

See advert on this page

Well House

★★ 85% ◉◉◉ HOTEL

☎ 01579 342001 🖹 01579 343891
St Keyne, Liskeard PL14 4RN
e-mail: enquiries@wellhouse.co.uk
dir: From Liskeard on A38 take B3254 to St Keyne (3m). At church fork left, hotel 0.5m down hill on left

Tucked away in an attractive valley and set in impressive grounds, this hotel enjoys a tranquil setting. Friendly staff provide attentive yet relaxed service which complements the elegant atmosphere of the house. The comfortable lounge offers deep cushioned sofas and an open fire, and the intimate bar has an extensive choice of wines and drinks to choose from. The rosette-awarded cooking is very skilled.

Rooms 9 (1 fmly) (2 GF) **D** £155-£215 (incl. bkfst) **Facilities** FTV ⊰ ⌣ ⤳ Xmas New Year **Conf** Board 20 **Parking** 30 **Notes** LB ⊗ Civ Wed 30

LOOE *continued*

Fieldhead Hotel & Horizons Restaurant

★★ 80% HOTEL

☎ 01503 262689
Portuan Rd, Hannafore PL13 2DR
e-mail: fieldheadhotel@gmail.com
web: www.fieldheadhotel.co.uk
dir: In Looe pass Texaco garage, cross bridge, left to
Hannafore. At Tom Sawyer turn right & right again. Hotel
on left

Overlooking the bay, this engaging hotel has a relaxing
atmosphere. Bedrooms are furnished with care and many
have sea views. Smartly presented public areas include a
convivial bar and restaurant, and outside there is a
palm-filled garden with a secluded patio and swimming
pool. The fixed-price menu changes daily and features
quality local produce.

Rooms 16 (2 fmly) (2 GF) **S** £40-£60; **D** £80-£150 (incl.
bkfst)* **Facilities** FTV ⤡ New Year Wi-fi Child facilities
Parking 15 **Notes** LB Closed 1 day at Xmas

LOSTWITHIEL   Map 2 SX15

Best Western Restormel Lodge

★★★ 73% HOTEL

☎ 01208 872223   📠 01208 873568
Castle Hill PL22 0DD
e-mail: restormellodge@yahoo.co.uk
web: www.restormelhotel.co.uk
dir: on A390 in Lostwithiel

A short drive from the Eden Project, this popular hotel
offers a friendly welcome to all visitors and is ideally
situated for exploring the area. The original building
houses the bar, restaurant and lounges, with original
features adding to the character. Bedrooms are
comfortably furnished, with a number overlooking the
secluded outdoor pool.

Rooms 36 (12 annexe) (2 fmly) (9 GF) **Facilities** FTV ⤡
Xmas New Year Wi-fi **Conf** Class 12 Board 12 Thtr 12
Parking 40 **Notes** LB

Lostwithiel Hotel Golf & Country Club

★★★ 67% HOTEL

☎ 01208 873550   📠 01208 873479
Lower Polscoe PL22 0HQ
e-mail: reception@golf-hotel.co.uk
web: www.golf-hotel.co.uk
dir: Off A38 at Dobwalls onto A390. In Lostwithiel turn
right & hotel signed

This rural hotel is based around its own golf club and
other leisure activities. The main building offers guests a
choice of eating options, including all-day snacks in the
popular Sports Bar. The bedroom accommodation,
designed to incorporate beamed ceilings, has been
developed from old Cornish barns that are set around a
courtyard.

Rooms 27 (2 fmly) (15 GF) (2 smoking) **S** £39-£61;
D £78-£122 (incl. bkfst)* **Facilities** ⤡ ♨ 18 ⛳ Putt
green Fishing Gym Undercover floodlit driving range
Indoor golf simulator Xmas New Year Wi-fi **Conf** Class 40
Board 40 Thtr 120 Del from £75 to £95* **Parking** 120
Notes Civ Wed 120

MARAZION   Map 2 SW53

Mount Haven Hotel & St Michaels Restaurant

★★★ 79% ◉◉ HOTEL

☎ 01736 710249   📠 01736 711658
Turnpike Rd TR17 0DQ
e-mail: reception@mounthaven.co.uk
web: www.mounthaven.co.uk
dir: From A30 towards Penzance. At rdbt take exit for
Helston onto A394. Next rdbt right into Marazion, hotel on
left

A stylish and delightfully located hotel where exceptional
views can be enjoyed - sunrises and sunsets can be
particularly spectacular. Bedrooms, many with balconies,
are comfortably appointed. Fresh seafood and local
produce are simply treated to produce interesting menus
and enjoyable dining. A range of holistic therapies is
available. Service is attentive and friendly creating a
relaxing and enchanting environment throughout.

Rooms 18 (2 fmly) (6 GF) **Facilities** FTV Aromatherapy
Reflexology Massage Reiki Hot rocks Osteopathy Wi-fi
Parking 30 **Notes** LB ⊗ Closed 20 Dec-5 Feb

Marazion

★★ 72% SMALL HOTEL

☎ 01736 710334
The Square TR17 0AP
e-mail: stephanie@marazionhotel.co.uk
web: www.marazionhotel.co.uk
dir: A30 to Penzance, at rdbt follow St Michael's Mount
signs. Hotel on left opposite

Within 50 yards of one of Cornwall's safest beaches, this
family run hotel, offers a relaxed atmosphere with friendly
service. The individually furnished and decorated
bedrooms are comfortable, many with the benefit of
stunning views across to St Michael's Mount. The hotel
incorporates the Cutty Sark public bar and restaurant,
where a wide range of meals is offered to suit all palates
and budgets.

Rooms 10 (3 fmly) **Facilities** Wi-fi **Parking** 20 **Notes** ⊗

MAWGAN PORTH   Map 2 SW86

Bedruthan Steps Hotel

★★★★ 76% ◉ HOTEL

☎ 01637 860555 & 860860   📠 01637 860714
TR8 4BU
e-mail: stay@bedruthan.com
dir: From A39/A30 follow signs to Newquay Airport. Past
airport, right at T-junct to Mawgan Porth. Hotel at top of
hill on left

With stunning views over Mawgan Porth Bay from the
public rooms and the majority of the bedrooms, this is a
child-friendly hotel. Children's clubs for various ages are
provided in addition to children's dining areas and
appropriate meals and times. A homage to architecture of
the 1970s, with a modern, comfortable, contemporary

feel, this hotel also has conference facilities. In the spacious restaurants, an imaginative fixed-price menu is offered; a short carte is available from Tuesdays to Saturdays.

Rooms 101 (60 fmly) (1 GF) **Facilities** Spa ⊕ ⌇ ♨ Gym Jungle tumble ball pool Sauna Steam room Hydro pool Pool table ♫ Xmas New Year Wi-fi Child facilities **Conf** Class 60 Board 40 Thtr 180 Del from £120 to £160* **Services** Lift **Parking** 100 **Notes** ⊗ Closed 23-29 Dec Civ Wed 150

The Scarlet Hotel

[U]

☎ 01637 861800 📠 01637 861225
Tredragon Rd TR8 4DQ
e-mail: stay@scarlethotel.co.uk

Currently the rating for this establishment is not confirmed. This may be due to a change of ownership or because it has only recently joined the AA rating scheme. For further details please see the AA website: theAA.com

Rooms 37 (7 GF) **Facilities** Spa FTV ⊕ ⌇ Dance pavillion Outdoor sauna ♫ Xmas New Year **Conf** Board 16 **Services** Lift **Parking** 37 **Notes** ⊗ No children 16yrs Closed 4 Jan-12 Feb Civ Wed

Budock Vean-The Hotel on the River

★★★★ 79% ☺ COUNTRY HOUSE HOTEL

☎ 01326 252100 & 0800 833927 📠 01326 250892
TR11 5LG
e-mail: relax@budockvean.co.uk
web: www.budockvean.co.uk
dir: From A39 follow tourist signs to Trebah Gardens. 0.5m to hotel

Set in 65 acres of attractive, well-tended grounds, this peaceful hotel offers an impressive range of facilities.

Convenient for visiting the Helford River Estuary and the many local gardens, or simply as a tranquil venue for a leisure break. Bedrooms are spacious and come in a choice of styles; some overlook the grounds and golf course.

Rooms 57 (2 fmly) **S** £65-£123; **D** £130-£246 (incl. bkfst & dinner)* **Facilities** Spa ⊕ ⌇ ≗ 9 ♨ Putt green ♨ Private river boat & foreshore ♫ Xmas New Year Wi-fi **Conf** Class 40 Board 30 Thtr 60 **Services** Lift **Parking** 100 **Notes** LB Closed 3 wks Jan Civ Wed 65

See advert on this page

Meudon

★★★ 85% COUNTRY HOUSE HOTEL

☎ 01326 250541 📠 01326 250543
TR11 5HT
e-mail: wecare@meudon.co.uk
web: www.meudon.co.uk
dir: From Truro A39 towards Falmouth at Hillhead (Anchor & Cannons) rdbt, follow signs to Maenporth Beach. Hotel on left 1m after beach

This charming late Victorian mansion is a relaxing place to stay, with friendly hospitality and attentive service. It sits in impressive nine-acre gardens that lead down to a private beach. The spacious and comfortable bedrooms are situated in a more modern building. The cuisine features the best of local Cornish produce and is served in the conservatory restaurant.

Rooms 29 (2 fmly) (15 GF) **S** £75-£130; **D** £150-£260 (incl. bkfst & dinner) **Facilities** FTV Fishing Private beach Hair salon Yacht for skippered charter Sub-tropical gardens Xmas Wi-fi **Conf** Class 20 Board 15 Thtr 30 Del from £135 to £155 **Services** Lift **Parking** 52 **Notes** LB Closed Jan

Trelawne

★★★ 77% HOTEL

☎ 01326 250226 📠 01326 250909
TR11 5HS
e-mail: info@trelawnehotel.co.uk
web: www.trelawnehotel.co.uk
dir: A39 to Falmouth, right at Hillhead rdbt signed Maenporth. Past beach, up hill and hotel on left

This hotel is surrounded by attractive lawns and gardens, and enjoys superb coastal views. An informal atmosphere prevails, and many guests return year after year. Bedrooms, many with sea views, are of varying sizes, but all are well equipped. Dinner features quality local produce used in imaginative dishes.

Rooms 14 (2 fmly) (4 GF) **S** £45-£65; **D** £86-£110 (incl. bkfst)* **Parking** 20 **Notes** Closed end Nov-mid Feb

Tremarne

★★ 81% HOTEL

☎ 01726 842213 📠 01726 843420
Polkirt PL26 6UY
e-mail: info@tremarne-hotel.co.uk
dir: From A390 at St Austell take B3273 to Mevagissey. Follow Portmellon signs through Mevagissey. At top of Polkirt Hill 1st right into Higherwell Park. Hotel drive facing

A very popular hotel, set in landscaped gardens with a swimming pool, that has superb views across to

continued

MEVAGISSEY *continued*

Mevagissey. The friendliness of Michael, Fitz and the team cannot be bettered. The hotel offers comfortable, individually styled bedrooms that either have views of the sea or the countryside, good service and freshly cooked food from a daily-changing menu.

Rooms 13 (2 fmly) **S** £57-£65; **D** £80-£148 (incl. bkfst)* **Facilities** FTV ⊀ Wi-fi **Parking** 14 **Notes** LB ⊗ No children 6yrs Closed Jan

Trevalsa Court Hotel

Ⓤ

☎ 01726 842468
School Hill, Polstreath PL26 6TH
e-mail: stay@trevalsa-hotel.co.uk
web: www.trevalsa-hotel.co.uk
dir: From St Austell take B3273 to Mevagissey. Pass sign to Pentewan. At top of hill left at x-rds. Hotel signed

Currently the rating for this establishment is not confirmed. This may be due to a change of ownership or because it has only recently joined the AA rating scheme. For further details please see the AA website: theAA.com

Rooms 13 (3 GF) **S** £70-£80; **D** £100-£220 (incl. bkfst)* **Facilities** FTV Wi-fi **Parking** 20 **Notes** Closed Dec & Jan

MOUSEHOLE Map 2 SW42

Old Coastguard Hotel

★★★ 74% ◉◉ HOTEL

☎ 01736 731222 🖹 01736 731720
The Parade TR19 6PR
e-mail: bookings@oldcoastguardhotel.co.uk
web: www.oldcoastguardhotel.co.uk
dir: A30 to Penzance, coast road to Newlyn then Mousehole. 1st building on left on entering village

This truly is a wonderful place to unwind with superb views across Mount's Bay providing a stunning backdrop.

The atmosphere is convivial and relaxing thanks to friendly staff who are keen to help. Bedrooms are bright and stylish, most have sea views and some have balconies. The impressive food features the best of the catch from Newlyn market which can be enjoyed either in the restaurant, or in summer months, alfresco on the terrace.

Rooms 14 (2 fmly) (5 GF) **Facilities** FTV Sub-tropical garden Xmas Wi-fi **Parking** 14 **Notes** LB ⊗ No children 14yrs Closed 25 Dec

The Cornish Range Restaurant with Rooms

◉◉ RESTAURANT WITH ROOMS

☎ 01736 731488
6 Chapel St TR19 6BD
e-mail: info@cornishrange.co.uk
dir: Coast road through Newlyn into Mousehole, along harbour past Ship Inn, sharp right, then left, establishment on right

This is a memorable place to eat and stay. Stylish rooms, with delightful Cornish home-made furnishings, and attentive, friendly service create a relaxing environment. Interesting and accurate cuisine relies heavily on freshly-landed, local fish and shellfish, as well as local meat and poultry, and the freshest fruit and vegetables.

Rooms 3

MULLION Map 2 SW61

Mullion Cove Hotel

★★★ 77% HOTEL

☎ 01326 240328 🖹 01326 240998
TR12 7EP
e-mail: enquiries@mullion-cove.co.uk
dir: A3083 towards The Lizard. Through Mullion towards Mullion Cove. Hotel in approx 1m

Built at the turn of the last century and set high above the working harbour of Mullion, this hotel has spectacular views of the rugged coastline; seaward facing rooms are always popular. The stylish restaurant offers some carefully prepared dishes using local produce; an alternative option is to eat less formally in the bar. After dinner guests might like to relax in one of the elegant lounges.

Rooms 30 (7 fmly) (3 GF) **Facilities** ⊀ Xmas New Year Wi-fi **Services** Lift **Parking** 60 **Notes** LB

Polurrian

★★★ 77% HOTEL

☎ 01326 240421 📠 01326 240083
TR12 7EN
e-mail: relax@polurrianhotel.com
web: www.polurrianhotel.com
dir: A394 to Lizard. Follow signs to the Lizard & Mullion villiage. Hotel on right

With spectacular views across St Mount's Bay, this is a well managed and relaxed hotel where guests are assured of a warm welcome from the friendly team of staff. In addition to the formal eating option, the High Point restaurant offers a more casual approach, open all day and into the evening. The popular leisure club has a good range of equipment. Bedrooms vary in size, and the sea-view rooms are always in demand of course.

Rooms 39 (4 fmly) (8 GF) **S** £61-£87; **D** £122-£208 (incl. bkfst & dinner)* **Facilities** 🕲 ⤳ 🏊 Gym Children's games room & outdoor play area Xmas New Year Wi-fi Child facilities **Conf** Class 25 Board 26 Thtr 50 Del from £95 to £100* **Parking** 100 **Notes** Closed Jan-5 Feb Civ Wed 80

See advert on opposite page

NEWQUAY Map 2 SW86

Headland

★★★★ 77% ⊚ HOTEL

☎ 01637 872211 📠 01637 872212
Fistral Beach TR7 1EW
e-mail: office@headlandhotel.co.uk
web: www.headlandhotel.co.uk
dir: Off A30 onto A392 at Indian Queens, approaching Newquay follow signs for Fistral Beach, hotel adjacent

This Victorian hotel enjoys a stunning location overlooking the sea on three sides - views can be enjoyed from most of the windows. Bedrooms are comfortable and spacious. Grand public areas, with impressive floral displays, include various lounges and in addition to the formal dining room, Sands Brasserie offers a relaxed alternative. Self-catering cottages are available, and guests staying in these can use the hotel facilities.

Rooms 104 (40 fmly) **S** £65-£135; **D** £79-£350 (incl. bkfst)* **Facilities** STV 🕲 ⤳ 🏊 9 🟢 Putt green ⛵ Harry Potter playroom New Year Wi-fi Child facilities **Conf** Class 120 Board 40 Thtr 250 Del from £140 to £195* **Services** Lift **Parking** 400 **Notes** LB Closed 24-27 Dec Civ Wed 250

See advert on this page

Bay Hotel

★★★ 80% HOTEL

☎ 01637 852221 📠 01637 872988
Esplanade Rd, Pentre TR7 1PT
e-mail: thebay@newquay-hotels.co.uk
web: www.newquay-hotels.co.uk
dir: In Newquay 1st exit onto Gannel Rd (signed town centre). At Mount Wise take 1st exit, right onto Esplanade Rd, hotel on left

This popular hotel enjoys a splendid location overlooking the sea and many rooms look out of the water. Bedrooms are comfortable and decorated in soothing colours. The staff are friendly, and off-road parking is available.

Rooms 92 (7 fmly) (6 GF) **S** £35-£55; **D** £70-£110 (incl. bkfst)* **Facilities** Spa STV 🕲 Gym Fitness suite & classes Sauna Steam room 🎵 Xmas New Year Wi-fi **Conf** Class 50 Board 20 Thtr 75 Del from £87.95 to £142.95* **Services** Lift **Parking** 30 **Notes** ⊗ Civ Wed 160

NEWQUAY *continued*

Esplanade Hotel

★★★ 80% HOTEL

☎ 01637 873333 📠 01637 851413
Esplanade Rd, Pentire TR7 1PS
e-mail: info@newquay-hotels.co.uk
web: www.newquay-hotels.co.uk
dir: from A30 take A392 at Indian Queens towards Newquay, follow to rdbt. Left to Pentire, then right to beach

Overlooking the rolling breakers at Fistral Beach, this family-orientated hotel offers a friendly welcome. There is a choice of bedroom sizes; all have modern facilities and the most popular rooms are those that have the stunning sea views. There are a number of bars, a continental-style coffee shop and the more formal Ocean View Restaurant.

Rooms 92 (44 fmly) **Facilities** 🏊 ⌁ Table tennis 🎵 Xmas New Year Child facilities **Conf** Class 180 Board 150 Thtr 300 **Services** Lift **Parking** 40 **Notes** Civ Wed 200

Best Western Hotel Bristol

★★★ 78% HOTEL

☎ 01637 875181 📠 01637 879347
Narrowcliff TR7 2PQ
e-mail: info@hotelbristol.co.uk
web: www.hotelbristol.co.uk
dir: Off A30 onto A392, then onto A3058. Hotel 2.5m on left

This hotel is conveniently situated and many of the bedrooms enjoy fine sea views. Staff are friendly and provide a professional and attentive service. There is a range of comfortable lounges, ideal for relaxing prior to eating in the elegant dining room. There are also leisure and conference facilities.

Best Western Hotel Bristol

Rooms 74 (23 fmly) **S** £60-£90; **D** £109-£138 (incl. bkfst)* **Facilities** STV 🏊 Table tennis New Year Wi-fi Child facilities **Conf** Class 80 Board 20 Thtr 200 Del from £80 to £120* **Services** Lift **Parking** 105 **Notes** LB Closed 23-27 Dec & 4-18 Jan

See advert on this page

Hotel Victoria

★★★ 75% HOTEL

☎ 01637 872255 📠 01637 859295
East St TR7 1DB
e-mail: bookings@hotel-victoria.co.uk
dir: A30 towards Bodmin following signs to Newquay. Hotel next to Newquay's main post office

Standing on the cliffs, overlooking Newquay Bay, this hotel is situated at the centre of this vibrant town. The spacious lounges and bar areas all benefit from glorious views. Varied menus, using the best of local produce, are offered in the restaurant. Bedrooms vary from spacious superior rooms and suites to standard inland-facing rooms. Berties pub, a nightclub and indoor leisure facilities are also available.

Rooms 70 (26 fmly) (18 GF) **Facilities** STV supervised Gym Beauty room Xmas New Year Wi-fi **Conf** Class 130 Board 50 Thtr 200 **Services** Lift Air con **Parking** 50 **Notes** Civ Wed 90

See advert on opposite page

Porth Veor Manor

★★★ 75% HOTEL

☎ 01637 873274 & 839542 📠 01637 879572
Porth Way, Porth TR7 3LW
e-mail: enquiries@porthveormanor.com
web: www.porthveormanor.com
dir: From A3058 at main rdbt onto B3276, hotel 0.5m on left

Overlooking Porth Beach and in a quiet area, this pleasant, professionally run hotel offers a relaxed and friendly atmosphere. Bedrooms are spacious and many have views over the beach. A daily-changing set price menu is served in the dining room.

Rooms 19 (6 fmly) **S** £74-£96; **D** £108-£128 (incl. bkfst)* **Facilities** STV FTV Putt green Xmas New Year Wi-fi **Conf** Class 30 Board 40 Thtr 70 Del from £120 to £164* **Parking** 36 **Notes** LB No children 5yrs

Trebarwith

★★★ 75% HOTEL

☎ 01637 872288 & 0800 387520 📠 01637 875431
Trebarwith Crescent TR7 1BZ
e-mail: trebahotel@aol.com
web: www.trebarwith-hotel.co.uk
dir: From A3058 to Mount Wise Rd. 3rd right down Marcus Hill, across East St into Trebarwith Cres. Hotel at end

With breathtaking views of the rugged coastline and a path leading to the beach, this friendly, family-run hotel is set in its own grounds close to the town centre. The public rooms include a lounge, ballroom, restaurant and cinema. The comfortable bedrooms include four-poster and family rooms, and many benefit from the sea views.

Rooms 41 (8 fmly) (1 GF) **S** £39-£85; **D** £78-£170 (incl. bkfst & dinner)* **Facilities** FTV Fishing Video theatre Games room Surf school Wi-fi **Conf** Thtr 45 Del from £150 to £300* **Parking** 41 **Notes** LB Closed Nov-5 Apr

See advert on this page

NEWQUAY *continued*

Kilbirnie

★★★ 68% HOTEL

☎ 01637 875155 📄 01637 850769
Narrowcliff TR7 2RS
e-mail: info@kilbirniehotel.co.uk
dir: On A392

With delightful views over the open space known as The Barrowfields and beyond to the sea, this privately-run hotel offers an impressive range of facilities. The reception rooms are spacious and comfortable, and during summer months host a programme of entertainment. Bedrooms vary in size and style, and some enjoy fine sea views.

Rooms 66 (6 fmly) (8 GF) **Facilities** 🏊 ⚘ Gym Fitness room Hair salon Xmas New Year Wi-fi **Conf** Class 50 Board 25 Thtr 100 **Services** Lift Air con **Parking** 58 **Notes** ⊗

Hotel California

★★★ 66% HOTEL

☎ 01637 879292 & 872798 📄 01637 875611
Pentire Crescent TR7 1PU
e-mail: info@hotel-california.co.uk
web: www.hotel-california.co.uk
dir: A392 to Newquay, follow signs for Pentire Hotels & Guest Houses

This hotel is tucked away in a delightful location, close to Fistral Beach and adjacent to the River Gannel. Many rooms have views across the river towards the sea, and some have balconies. There is an impressive range of leisure facilities, including indoor and outdoor pools, and ten-pin bowling. Cuisine is enjoyable and menus offer a range of interesting dishes.

Rooms 70 (27 fmly) (13 GF) **Facilities** FTV 🏊 ⚘ Squash 10 pin bowling alley 🎵 Xmas New Year **Conf** Class 100

Board 30 Thtr 100 **Services** Lift **Parking** 66 **Notes** Closed 3 wks Jan Civ Wed 150

See advert on this page

Glendorgal Resort

★★★ 🅰 HOTEL

☎ 01637 874937 & 859981 📄 01637 851341
Lusty Glaze Rd, Porth TR7 3AD
e-mail: info@glendorgal.co.uk
dir: From A30 right onto A392, 2nd rdbt turn right (A3058), at mini rdbt straight on, turn right into Lusty Glaze Rd, follow signs for Glendorgal

Rooms 26 (8 fmly) **S** £55-£100; **D** £100-£185 (incl. bkfst)* **Facilities** FTV 🏊 Gym Steam room Cardiovascular room Sauna Wi-fi **Conf** Class 36 Board 30 Thtr 60 Del from £70 to £145* **Parking** 100 **Notes** Civ Wed 110

Priory Lodge

★★ 72% HOTEL

☎ 01637 874111 📄 01637 851803
30 Mount Wise TR7 2BN
e-mail: fionapocklington@tiscali.co.uk
dir: From lights in town centre onto Berry Rd, right onto B3282 Mount Wise, 0.5m on right

The hotel enjoys a central location close to the town centre, the harbour and the local beaches. Secure parking is available at the hotel along with a range of leisure facilities including a heated pool, sauna, games room and hot tub. Attractively decorated bedrooms vary in size and style with many offering sea views over Towan Beach and Island.

Rooms 28 (6 annexe) (13 fmly) (1 GF) **S** £30-£40; **D** £60-£80 (incl. bkfst)* **Facilities** ⚘ Outdoor hydrotherapy spa bath 🎵 Xmas New Year **Parking** 30 **Notes** ⊗ Closed 11-22 Dec & 4 Jan-early Mar

Eliot

★★ 67% HOTEL

 Leisureplex

☎ 01637 878177 📄 01637 852053
Edgcumbe Av TR7 2NH
e-mail: eliot.newquay@alfatravel.co.uk
dir: A30 onto A392 towards Quintrell Downs. Right at rdbt onto A3058. 4m to Newquay, left at amusements onto Edgcumbe Av. Hotel on left

Located in a quiet residential area just a short walk from the beaches and the varied attractions of the town, this long-established hotel offers comfortable accommodation. Entertainment is provided most nights throughout the season and guests can relax in the spacious public areas.

Rooms 76 (10 fmly) **Facilities** FTV ⚘ Pool table Table tennis 🎵 Xmas New Year **Services** Lift **Parking** 20 **Notes** LB ⊗ Closed Dec-Jan (ex Xmas) RS Nov & Feb-Mar

Sandy Lodge

★★ 67% HOTEL

☎ 01637 872851 📄 01637 872851
6-12 Hilgrove Rd TR7 2QY
e-mail: info@sandylodgehotel.co.uk
dir: Exit Hever Rd onto Hilgrove Rd (by Tesco). Hotel 150yds on left

This friendly, family-run hotel is ideally located for easy access to the seafront and surfing beaches, and is within walking distance of the town centre. Accommodation is comfortable with a choice of family, twin and double rooms. There is a spacious dining room and a choice of lounge areas; nightly entertainment is provided.

Rooms 80 (8 fmly) (12 GF) **S** £36-£42; **D** £72-£84 (incl. bkfst)* **Facilities** 🏊 ⚘ Gym Sauna Spa bath 🎵 Xmas New Year Wi-fi **Conf** Class 40 Board 30 Thtr 100 **Services** Lift **Parking** 50 **Notes** ⊗ Closed 5-23 Jan RS Jan

Hotel California

Pentire Crescent, Newquay TR7 1PU

Tel: 01637 879292

Fax: 01637 875611

Email: reception@hotel-california.co.uk

www.hotel-california.co.uk

Treglos

★★★★ 76% ⊛ COUNTRY HOUSE HOTEL

☎ 01841 520727 🖹 01841 521163
Constantine Bay PL28 8JH
e-mail: stay@tregloshotel.com
web: www.tregloshotel.com
dir: In Constantine Bay. At St Merryn x-rds take B3276 towards Newquay. In 500mtrs right to Constantine Bay, follow brown signs

Owned by the Barlow family for over 40 years, this hotel has a tradition of high standards. The genuine welcome, choice of comfortable lounges, indoor pool and children's play facilities entice guests back year after year. Bedrooms vary in size; those with sea views are always popular. The restaurant continues to provide imaginative menus incorporating seasonal local produce.

Rooms 42 (12 fmly) (1 GF) **S** £79-£113; **D** £158-£226 (incl. bkfst & dinner) **Facilities** Spa FTV ⊗ ♨ 18 Putt green 🏌 Converted boat house for table tennis Infra red treatment cabin 🎵 Wi-fi **Services** Lift **Parking** 58 **Notes** LB Closed 30 Nov-1 Mar

The Metropole

★★★★ 70% ⊛ HOTEL

RICHARDSON

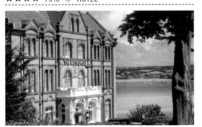

☎ 01841 532486 🖹 01841 532867
Station Rd PL28 8DB
e-mail: info@the-metropole.co.uk
web: www.the-metropole.co.uk
dir: M5/A30 pass Launceston, follow Wadebridge & N Cornwall signs. Take A39, follow Padstow signs

This long-established hotel first opened its doors to guests back in 1904 and there is still an air of the sophistication and elegance of a bygone age. Bedrooms are soundly appointed and well equipped; dining options include the informal Met Café Bar and the main

restaurant, with its enjoyable cuisine and wonderful views over the Camel estuary.

Rooms 58 (3 fmly) (2 GF) **S** £72-£108; **D** £144-£176 (incl. bkfst)* **Facilities** FTV ⊰ Swimming pool open Jul & Aug only Xmas New Year Wi-fi **Conf** Class 20 Board 20 Thtr 40 Del from £99 to £180* **Services** Lift **Parking** 36 **Notes** LB

St Petroc's Hotel and Bistro

★★ 85% ⊛ SMALL HOTEL

☎ 01841 532700 🖹 01841 532942
4 New St PL28 8EA
e-mail: reservations@rickstein.com
dir: A39 onto A389, follow signs to town centre. Follow one-way system, hotel on right on leaving town

One of the oldest buildings in town, this charming establishment is just up the hill from the picturesque harbour. Style, comfort and individuality are all great strengths here, particularly so in the impressively equipped bedrooms. Breakfast, lunch and dinner all reflect a serious approach to cuisine, and the popular restaurant has a relaxed, bistro style. Comfortable lounges, a reading room and lovely gardens complete the picture.

Rooms 14 (4 annexe) (3 fmly) (3 GF) **D** £132.13-£264.26 (incl. bkfst)* **Facilities** FTV Cookery school New Year Wi-fi **Conf** Board 12 **Services** Lift **Parking** 12 **Notes** Closed 1 May & 25-26 Dec RS 24 Dec eve

The Old Ship Hotel

★★ 72% HOTEL

☎ 01841 532357 🖹 01841 533211
Mill Square PL28 8AE
e-mail: stay@oldshiphotel-padstow.co.uk
web: www.oldshiphotel-padstow.co.uk
dir: From M5 take A30 to Bodmin then A389 to Padstow, follow brown tourist signs to car park

This attractive inn is situated in the heart of the old town's quaint and winding streets, just a short walk from the harbour. A warm welcome is assured, accommodation is pleasant and comfortable, and public areas offer plenty of character. Freshly caught fish features on both the bar and restaurant menus. On site parking is a bonus.

Rooms 14 (4 fmly) **S** £36-£51; **D** £72-£102 (incl. bkfst) **Facilities** STV 🎵 Xmas New Year Wi-fi **Parking** 20 **Notes** LB

The Seafood Restaurant

⊛⊛⊛ RESTAURANT WITH ROOMS

☎ 01841 532700 🖹 01841 532942
Riverside PL28 8BY
e-mail: reservations@rickstein.com
dir: Padstow town centre down hill, follow road round sharp bend, on left

Food lovers continue to beat a well-trodden path to this legendary establishment that has benefited from considerable recent investment. Situated on the edge of

the harbour, just a stone's throw from the shops, the Seafood Restaurant offers stylish and comfortable bedrooms that boast numerous thoughtful extras; some have views of the estuary and a couple have stunning private balconies. Service is relaxed and friendly, perfect for that break by the sea; booking is essential for both accommodation and a table in the restaurant.

Rooms 20 (6 annexe) (6 fmly)

Hotel Penzance

★★★ 83% ⊛⊛ HOTEL

☎ 01736 363117 🖹 01736 350970
Britons Hill TR18 3AE
e-mail: enquiries@hotelpenzance.com
web: www.hotelpenzance.com
dir: From A30 pass heliport on right, left at next rdbt for town centre. 3rd right onto Britons Hill. Hotel on right

This Edwardian house has been tastefully redesigned, particularly in the contemporary Bay Restaurant. The focus on style is not only limited to the decor, but is also apparent in the award-winning cuisine that is based upon fresh Cornish produce. Bedrooms have been appointed to modern standards and are particularly well equipped; many have views across Mounts Bay.

Rooms 25 (2 GF) **S** £60-£80; **D** £115-£180 (incl. bkfst)* **Facilities** FTV ⊰ Xmas New Year Wi-fi **Conf** Class 50 Board 25 Thtr 80 **Parking** 14 **Notes** LB

Queens

★★★ 71% HOTEL

☎ 01736 362371 🖹 01736 350033
The Promenade TR18 4HG
e-mail: enquiries@queens-hotel.com
web: www.queens-hotel.com
dir: A30 to Penzance, follow signs for seafront pass harbour and into promenade, hotel 0.5m on right

With views across Mount's Bay towards Newlyn, this impressive Victorian hotel has a long and distinguished history. Comfortable public areas are filled with interesting pictures and artefacts, and in the dining room guests can choose from the daily-changing menu. Bedrooms, many with sea views, vary in style and size.

Rooms 70 (10 fmly) **S** £58-£82; **D** £116-£152 (incl. bkfst)* **Facilities** FTV Yoga weekends Xmas New Year Wi-fi **Conf** Class 200 Board 120 Thtr 200 Del from £75 to £95* **Services** Lift **Parking** 50 **Notes** LB Civ Wed 250

POLPERRO
Map 2 SX25

Talland Bay

★★★ 83% ◉◉ COUNTRY HOUSE HOTEL

☎ 01503 272667
Porthallow PL13 2JB
e-mail: reception@tallandbayhotel.co.uk
web: www.tallandbayhotel.co.uk
dir: signed from x-rds on A387 (Looe to Polperro road)

This hotel has the benefit of a wonderful location, being situated in its own extensive gardens that run down almost to the cliff's edge. The atmosphere is warm and friendly throughout, and some of the bedrooms, available in a number of styles, have sea views and balconies. Accomplished cooking, with an emphasis on carefully prepared local produce, remains a key feature here.

Rooms 23 (3 annexe) (6 GF) **Facilities** ⊰ Putt green ⌁ Xmas New Year **Parking** 23 **Notes** LB

PORT GAVERNE
Map 2 SX08

Port Gaverne

★★ 72% HOTEL

☎ 01208 880244 ▤ 01208 880151
PL29 3SQ
dir: Signed from B3314

In a quiet seaside port half a mile from the old fishing village of Port Isaac, this hotel has a romantic atmosphere, and retaining flagged floors, beamed ceilings and steep stairways. Bedrooms are available in a range of sizes. Local produce features on the restaurant menus, and bar meals always prove popular.

Rooms 14 (4 fmly) **Parking** 30

PORTHLEVEN
Map 2 SW62

Kota Restaurant with Rooms

◉ RESTAURANT WITH ROOMS

☎ 01326 562407 ▤ 01326 562407
Harbour Head TR13 9JA
e-mail: kota@btconnect.com
dir: B3304 from Helston into Porthleven, Kota on harbour head opposite slipway

Overlooking the Harbour Head, this 300-year-old building is the home of Kota Restaurant (Kota being Maori for shellfish). The bedrooms are approached from a granite stairway to the side of the building. The family room is spacious and has the benefit of harbour views, while the smaller, double room is at the rear of the property. The enthusiastic, young owners ensure guests enjoy their stay here and a meal in the restaurant is not to be missed. Breakfast features the best of local produce.

Rooms 2 (2 annexe) (1 fmly)

PORTLOE
Map 2 SW93

Lugger

★★★ 81% ◉ HOTEL

☎ 01872 501322 ▤ 01872 501691
TR2 5RD
e-mail: office@luggerhotel.com
web: www.oxfordhotelsandinns.com
dir: A390 to Truro, B3287 to Tregony, A3078 (St Mawes Rd), left for Veryan, left for Portloe

This delightful hotel enjoys a unique setting adjacent to the slipway of the harbour where fishing boats still come and go. Bedrooms, some in adjacent buildings and cottages, are contemporary in style and well equipped. The sitting room, which reflects the original building's character, has beams and open fireplaces that create a cosy atmosphere. The modern restaurant enjoys superb views, and in warmer months a sun terrace overlooking the harbour proves a popular place.

Rooms 22 (17 annexe) (1 GF) **S** £90-£265; **D** £110-£330 (incl. bkfst)* **Facilities** FTV Xmas New Year Wi-fi **Parking** 26 **Notes** LB ⊗ Civ Wed 50

PORTSCATHO
Map 2 SW83

INSPECTORS' CHOICE

Driftwood

★★★ ◉◉◉ HOTEL

☎ 01872 580644 ▤ 01872 580801
Rosevine TR2 5EW
e-mail: info@driftwoodhotel.co.uk
dir: A390 towards St Mawes. On A3078 turn left to Rosevine at Trewithian

Poised on the cliff side with panoramic views, this contemporary hotel has a peaceful and secluded location. A warm welcome is guaranteed here, where professional standards of service are provided in an effortless and relaxed manner. Cuisine is a feature of any stay with quality local produce used in a sympathetic and highly skilled manner. The extremely comfortable and elegant bedrooms are decorated in soft shades reminiscent of the seashore. There is a sheltered terraced garden that has a large deck with steamer chairs for sunbathing.

Rooms 15 (1 annexe) (3 fmly) (1 GF) **S** £140-£204; **D** £165-£240 (incl. bkfst)* **Facilities** FTV Private beach Treatments on request Wi-fi **Parking** 30 **Notes** ⊗ Closed 7 Dec-5 Feb RS Xmas & New Year

PORTWRINKLE
Map 3 SX35

See also **Looe**

Whitsand Bay Hotel & Golf Club

★★★ 74% ◉ HOTEL

☎ 01503 230276 ▤ 01503 230329
PL11 3BU
e-mail: whitsandbayhotel@btconnect.com
web: www.whitsandbayhotel.co.uk
dir: A38 from Exeter over River Tamar, left at Trerulefoot rdbt onto A374 to Crafthole/Portwrinkle. Follow hotel signs

An imposing Victorian stone building with oak panelling, stained-glass windows and a sweeping staircase. Bedrooms include family rooms and a suite with a balcony, many have superb sea views. Facilities include an 18-hole cliff-top golf course and an indoor swimming pool. The fixed-price menu offers an interesting selection of dishes.

Rooms 32 (7 fmly) **Facilities** ⊛ ⌁ 18 Putt green Gym Games room Lounge with wide screen TV ♫ Xmas **Parking** 60

REDRUTH — Map 2 SW64

Penventon Park

★★★ 79% HOTEL

☎ 01209 203000 📠 01209 203001
TR15 1TE
e-mail: info@penventon.com
web: www.penventon.co.uk
dir: Off A30 at Redruth. Follow signs for Redruth West, hotel 1m S

Set in attractive parkland, this Georgian mansion is ideal for either the business or leisure guest. Bedrooms include twenty Garden Suites. Cuisine offers a wide choice and specialises in British, Cornish, Italian and French dishes. Leisure facilities include a fitness suite and health spa as well as function rooms and bars.

Rooms 64 (3 fmly) (25 GF) **Facilities** Spa ⓢ supervised Gym Leisure spa Masseuse Steam bath Pool table Beautician Solarium 🎵 Xmas New Year Wi-fi **Conf** Class 100 Board 60 Thtr 200 Del from £108* **Parking** 100 **Notes** Civ Wed 150

Crossroads Lodge

THE INDEPENDENTS
HOTEL ASSOCIATION

★★ 64% HOTEL

☎ 01209 820551 📠 01209 820392
Scorrier TR16 5BP
e-mail: crossroads@hotelstruro.com
web: www.hotelstruro.com/crossroads
dir: Turn off A30 onto A3047 towards Scorrier

Situated on an historic stanary site and conveniently located just off the A30, this hotel has a smart appearance. Bedrooms are soundly furnished and include executive and family rooms. Public areas include an attractive dining room, a quiet lounge and a lively bar. Conference, banqueting and business facilities are also available.

Rooms 36 (2 fmly) (8 GF) **S** £52; **D** £72 (incl. bkfst)* **Facilities** Xmas New Year **Conf** Class 80 Board 60 Thtr 150 **Services** Lift **Parking** 140 **Notes** LB Civ Wed 70

RUAN HIGH LANES — Map 2 SW93

Hundred House

★★★ 74% ⓢ COUNTRY HOUSE HOTEL

☎ 01872 501336 📠 01872 501151
TR2 5JR
e-mail: enquiries@hundredhousehotel.co.uk
web: www.hundredhousehotel.co.uk
dir: From B3287 at Tregony, left onto A3078 to St Mawes, hotel 4m on right

This Georgian house is set in attractive gardens and has good access to the Roseland Peninsula, which makes it an ideal base for a relaxing break and for touring the area. Bedrooms are well equipped, and the lounge and bar offer a good level of comfort. Service is attentive as the staff are very much focused on their guests' needs. Both dinner and breakfast offer freshly cooked and appetising dishes.

Rooms 9 (1 GF) **Facilities** FTV 🏊 Xmas Wi-fi **Parking** 15 **Notes** ⊗ No children 14yrs

---

ST AGNES — Map 2 SW75

Rose-in-Vale Country House

★★★ 79% ⓢ COUNTRY HOUSE HOTEL

☎ 01872 552202 📠 01872 552700
Mithian TR5 0QD
e-mail: reception@rose-in-vale-hotel.co.uk
web: www.rose-in-vale-hotel.co.uk
dir: Take A30 S towards Redruth. At Chiverton Cross at rdbt take B3277 signed St Agnes. In 500mtrs turn at tourist info sign for Rose-in-Vale. Into Mithian, right at Miners Arms, down hill. Hotel on left

Peacefully located in a wooded valley this Georgian manor house has a wonderfully relaxed atmosphere and abundant charm. Guests are assured of a warm welcome. Accommodation varies in size and style; several rooms are situated on the ground floor. An imaginative fixed-price menu featuring local produce is served in the spacious restaurant.

Rooms 20 (3 annexe) (2 fmly) (5 GF) **S** £80-£200; **D** £120-£275 (incl. bkfst) **Facilities** FTV ↖ 🏊 Xmas New Year Wi-fi **Conf** Class 50 Board 40 Thtr 75 Del from £145 to £200 **Parking** 52 **Notes** LB No children 12yrs Civ Wed 80

See advert on this page

ST AGNES *continued*

Rosemundy House

★★★ 70% HOTEL

☎ 01872 552101 🖷 01872 554000
Rosemundy Hill TR5 0UF
e-mail: info@rosemundy.co.uk
dir: Off A30 to St Agnes continue for approx 3m. On entering village take 1st right signed Rosemundy, hotel at foot of hill

This elegant Queen Anne house has been carefully restored and extended to provide comfortable bedrooms and spacious, inviting public areas. The hotel is set in well-maintained gardens complete with an outdoor pool available in warmer months. There is a choice of relaxing lounges and a cosy bar.

Rooms 46 (3 fmly) (9 GF) **Facilities** FTV ◝ Putt green ◡ ♫ Xmas New Year **Conf** Board 80 **Parking** 50 **Notes** ⊗ No children 5yrs

Beacon Country House Hotel

★★ 80% COUNTRY HOUSE HOTEL

☎ 01872 552318
Goonvrea Rd TR5 0NW
e-mail: info@beaconhotel.co.uk
web: www.beaconhotel.co.uk
dir: From A30 take B3277 to St Agnes. At rdbt left onto Goonvrea Rd. Hotel 0.75m on right

Set in a quiet and attractive area away from the busy village, this friendly, relaxed hotel has splendid views over the countryside and along the coast to St Ives. Guests are assured of a friendly welcome, and many return for another stay. The bedrooms are comfortable and well equipped, and many benefit from the glorious views.

Rooms 11 (2 GF) **S** £77-£127; **D** £114-£154 (incl. bkfst & dinner)* **Facilities** FTV Wi-fi **Parking** 12 **Notes** LB ⊗ No children 8yrs Closed Dec-Feb

ST AUSTELL   **Map 2 SX05**

The Carlyon Bay Hotel, Spa and Golf Resort

Brend Hotels

★★★★ 77% ⊛ HOTEL

☎ 01726 812304 & 811006 🖷 01726 814938
Sea Rd, Carlyon Bay PL25 3RD
e-mail: reservations@carlyonbay.com
web: www.carlyonbay.com
dir: From St Austell, follow signs for Charlestown. Carlyon Bay signed on left, hotel at end of Sea Rd

Built in the 1920s, this long-established hotel sits on the cliff top in 250 acres of grounds with and include indoor and outdoor pool, a golf course and a newly completed spa. Bedrooms are well maintained, and many have marvellous views across St Austell Bay. A good choice of comfortable lounges is available, whilst facilities for families include kids' clubs and entertainment.

The Carlyon Bay Hotel, Spa and Golf Resort

Rooms 87 (14 fmly) **S** £90-£295; **D** £140-£295*
Facilities Spa FTV ⓢ ◝ ⌁ 18 ⌁ Putt green Gym 9-hole approach course Snooker room ♫ Xmas New Year Wi-fi Child facilities **Services** Lift **Parking** 100 **Notes** LB ⊗ Civ Wed 100

See advert on this page

Porth Avallen

★★★ 77% HOTEL

☎ 01726 812802 🖷 01726 817097
Sea Rd, Carlyon Bay PL25 3SG
e-mail: info@porthavallen.co.uk
web: www.porthavallen.co.uk
dir: A30 onto A391 to St Austell. Right onto A390. Left at lights, follow brown signs, left at rdbt, right into Sea Rd

This traditional hotel boasts panoramic views over the rugged Cornish coastline. It offers smartly appointed public areas and well-presented bedrooms, many with sea views. There is an oak-panelled lounge and conservatory; both are ideal for relaxation. Extensive dining options, including the stylish Reflections Restaurant, invite guests to choose from fixed-price, carte and all-day brasserie menus. The Olive Garden, inspired by the Mediterranean, is a lovely place to eat alfresco.

Porth Avallen

Rooms 28 (3 fmly) (3 GF) **Facilities** FTV Xmas New Year Wi-fi **Conf** Class 100 Board 80 Thtr 160 **Parking** 50 **Notes** ⊗ Civ Wed 160

Pier House

★★★ 72% HOTEL

☎ 01726 67955 📄 01726 69246
Harbour Front, Charlestown PL25 3NJ
e-mail: pierhouse@btconnect.com
dir: Follow A390 to St Austell, at Mt Charles rdbt left down Charlestown Rd

This genuinely friendly hotel boasts a wonderful harbour location. The unspoilt working port has been the setting for many film and television productions. Most bedrooms have sea views, and the hotel's convivial Harbourside Inn is popular with locals and tourists alike. Locally caught fish features on the varied and interesting restaurant menu.

Rooms 28 (2 annexe) (3 fmly) (2 GF) **S** £55-£59; **D** £95-£130 (incl. bkfst)* **Facilities** STV Wi-fi **Parking** 50 **Notes** LB ⊗ Closed 24-25 Dec

Cliff Head

★★★ 70% HOTEL

☎ 01726 812345 📄 01726 815511
Sea Rd, Carlyon Bay PL25 3RB
e-mail: info@cliffheadhotel.com
web: www.cliffheadhotel.com
dir: 2m E off A390

Set in extensive grounds and conveniently located for visiting the Eden Project, this hotel faces south and enjoys views over Carlyon Bay. A choice of lounges is provided, together with a swimming pool and solarium. Expressions restaurant offers a range of menus, which feature an interesting selection of dishes.

Rooms 57 (6 fmly) (11 GF) **Facilities** ⚡ Xmas New Year Wi-fi **Conf** Class 130 Board 70 Thtr 150 **Parking** 60 **Notes** LB ⊗ Civ Wed 120

Boscundle Manor Country House

★★ 82% COUNTRY HOUSE HOTEL

☎ 01726 813557 📄 01726 814997
Tregrehan PL25 3RL
e-mail: stay@boscundlemanor.co.uk
dir: 2m E on A390, 200yds on road signed Tregrehan

Set in beautifully maintained gardens and grounds, this handsome 18th-century stone manor house is a short distance from the Eden Project. Quality and comfort are apparent in the public areas and spacious, well-equipped bedrooms. A choice of eating options is available, with both fine dining and brasserie alternatives. Equally suitable for both leisure and business travellers, Boscundle Manor boasts both indoor and outdoor pools.

Rooms 14 (3 annexe) (4 fmly) (4 GF) **Facilities** ⚡ ⚡ 🏊 Xmas Child facilities **Conf** Class 20 Board 20 Thtr 40 **Parking** 15 **Notes** Closed 2 Jan-13 Feb Civ Wed 60

Travelodge St Austell

BUDGET HOTEL

☎ 0871 984 6160
Trevanion Rd PL25 5DR
web: www.travelodge.co.uk
dir: A391 into St Austell. At Mount Charles rdbt take A390. At next rdbt take B3273

Travelodge offers good quality, good value, budget accommodation. All offer family rooms sleeping up to four (two adults, two children) with en suite bathroom/shower-room, remote-control TV, tea- and coffee-making facilities and comfortable beds. Food options vary. Breakfast is at the on-site Bar Café restaurant (if available) or to take away. See also Hotel Groups pages.

Rooms 67 **S** fr £29; **D** fr £29

ST IVES   Map 2 SW54

Carbis Bay

★★★ 78% ⊛ HOTEL

☎ 01736 795311 📄 01736 797677
Carbis Bay TR26 2NP
e-mail: carbisbayhotel@btconnect.com
web: www.carbisbayhotel.co.uk
dir: A3074, through Lelant. 1m, at Carbis Bay 30yds before lights turn right into Porthrepta Rd to sea & hotel

In a peaceful location with access to its own white-sand beach, this hotel offers comfortable accommodation.

continued

ST IVES *continued*

Attractive public areas feature a smart bar and lounge, and a sun lounge overlooking the sea. Bedrooms, many with fine views, are well equipped. Interesting cuisine and particularly enjoyable breakfasts are offered. A small complex of luxury, self-catering apartments is available.

Carbis Bay

Rooms 40 (16 fmly) **Facilities** ⚲ Fishing Private beach ♫ Xmas New Year **Conf** Class 80 Board 60 Thtr 120 **Parking** 200 **Notes** ⊗ Civ Wed 120

See advert on page 99

Garrack Hotel & Restaurant
★★★ 77% ⊛ HOTEL

☎ 01736 796199 ▤ 01736 798955
Burthallan Ln, Higher Ayr TR26 3AA
e-mail: aa@garrack.com
dir: Exit A30 for St Ives, then from B3311 follow brown signs for Tate Gallery, then brown Garrack signs

Enjoying a peaceful, elevated position with splendid views across the harbour and Porthmeor Beach, the Garrack sits in its own delightful grounds and gardens. Bedrooms are comfortable and many have sea views. Public areas include a small leisure suite, a choice of lounges and an attractive restaurant, where locally sourced ingredients are used in the enjoyable dishes.

Rooms 18 (2 annexe) (2 fmly) **Facilities** FTV ⊛ Gym New Year Wi-fi **Conf** Class 10 Board 10 Thtr 20 **Parking** 30 **Notes** LB

Porthminster
★★★ 77% HOTEL

☎ 01736 795221 ▤ 01736 797043
The Terrrace TR26 2BN
e-mail: reception@porthminster-hotel.co.uk
web: www.porthminster-hotel.co.uk
dir: On A3074

This friendly hotel enjoys an enviable location with spectacular views of St Ives Bay. Extensive leisure facilities, a versatile function suite and a number of lounges are available. The majority of bedrooms are appointed to a very high standard, and many rooms have spectacular sea views; two suites are available.

Rooms 42 (9 fmly) **S** £60-£150; **D** £120-£300 (incl. bkfst)* **Facilities** FTV ⊛ ⚲ ♨ Gym Xmas New Year Wi-fi Child facilities **Conf** Class 20 Board 35 Thtr 130 **Services** Lift **Parking** 43 **Notes** LB Civ Wed 130

See advert on this page

Tregenna Castle Hotel
★★★ 73% HOTEL

☎ 01736 795254 ▤ 01736 796066
TR26 2DE
e-mail: hotel@tregenna-castle.co.uk
web: www.tregenna-castle.co.uk
dir: A30 from Exeter to Penzance, at Lelant take A3074 to St Ives, through Carbis Bay, main entrance signed on left

Sitting at the top of town in beautiful landscaped gardens, this popular hotel boasts spectacular views of St Ives. Many leisure facilities are available, including indoor and outdoor pools, a gym and a sauna. Families

are particularly welcome. Bedrooms are generally spacious. A carte menu or carvery buffet are offered in the restaurant, during the summer months, the Castle Bar and Brasserie provide lighter options, in a less formal atmosphere.

Rooms 81 (12 fmly) (16 GF) **Facilities** Spa ⊛ ⚲ supervised ⚖ 14 ⚲ Putt green ♨ Gym Squash Steam room Badminton court Xmas New Year **Conf** Class 150 Board 30 Thtr 250 **Services** Lift **Parking** 200 **Notes** LB ⊗ Civ Wed 160

Chy-an-Albany
★★★ 70% HOTEL

☎ 01736 796759 ▤ 01736 795584
Albany Ter TR26 2BS
e-mail: info@chyanalbanyhotel.com
dir: From A30 onto A3074 signed St Ives, hotel on left just before junct

Conveniently located, this pleasant hotel enjoys splendid sea views. The comfortable bedrooms come in a variety of sizes; some featuring balconies and sea views. Friendly staff and the relaxing environment mean that guests return on a regular basis. Freshly prepared and appetising cuisine is served in the dining room and a bar menu is also available.

Rooms 39 (11 fmly) **S** £60-£75; **D** £120-£202 (incl. bkfst)* **Facilities** STV ♫ Xmas New Year Wi-fi **Conf** Class 40 Board 30 Thtr 80 **Services** Lift **Parking** 33 **Notes** LB ⊗ Civ Wed 80

Hotel St Eia

★★ 69% HOTEL

☎ 01736 795531 📠 01736 793591
Trelyon Av TR26 2AA
e-mail: info@hotelsteia.co.uk
dir: Off A30 onto A3074, follow signs to St Ives,
approaching town, hotel on right

This smart hotel is conveniently located and enjoys
spectacular views over St Ives, the harbour and
Porthminster Beach. The friendly proprietors provide a
relaxing environment. Bedrooms are comfortable and well
equipped, and some have sea views. The spacious lounge
bar has a well-stocked bar and views can be enjoyed
from the rooftop terrace.

Rooms 18 (3 fmly) (1 GF) **S** £30-£50; **D** £70-£100 (incl.
bkfst)* **Facilities** FTV Wi-fi **Parking** 16 **Notes** ⊗ Closed
Nov-Mar

Cottage Hotel

★★ 68% HOTEL

Leisureplex

☎ 01736 795252 📠 01736 798636
Boskerris Rd, Carbis Bay TR26 2PE
e-mail: cottage.stives@alfatravel.co.uk
dir: From A30 take A3074 to Carbis Bay. Right into
Porthreptor Rd. Just before rail bridge, left through
railway car park into hotel car park

Set in quiet, lush gardens, this pleasant hotel offers
friendly and attentive service. Smart bedrooms are
pleasantly spacious and many rooms enjoy splendid
views. Public areas are varied and include a snooker
room, a comfortable lounge and a spacious dining room
with sea views over the beach and Carbis Bay.

Rooms 80 (7 fmly) (2 GF) **Facilities** FTV ⚞ Snooker ♫
Xmas New Year **Services** Lift **Parking** 20 **Notes** LB ⊗
Closed Dec-Feb (ex Xmas) RS Nov & Mar

Idle Rocks

★★★ 83% ☺☺ HOTEL

RICHARDSON

☎ 01326 270771 📠 01326 270062
Harbour Side TR2 5AN
e-mail: reception@idlerocks.co.uk
web: www.idlerocks.co.uk
dir: Off A390 onto A3078, 14m to St Mawes. Hotel on left

This hotel has splendid sea views overlooking the
attractive fishing port. The lounge and bar also benefit
from the views and in warmer months service is available
on the terrace. Bedrooms are individually styled and
tastefully furnished to a high standard. The daily-
changing menu served in the restaurant features fresh,
local produce in imaginative cuisine.

Rooms 27 (4 annexe) (6 fmly) (2 GF) **D** £116-£295 (incl.
bkfst)* **Facilities** Xmas New Year Wi-fi **Parking** 4

See advert on this page

China Fleet Country Club

★★★ 77% ☺ HOTEL

☎ 01752 854664 & 854661 📠 01752 848456
PL12 6LJ
e-mail: sales@china-fleet.co.uk
web: www.china-fleet.co.uk
dir: A38 towards Plymouth/Saltash. Cross Tamar Bridge,
take slip road before tunnel. Right at lights, 1st left
follow signs, 0.5m

Set in 180 acres of stunning Cornish countryside
overlooking the beautiful Tamar estuary, ideal for access
to Plymouth and the countryside, this hotel offers an
extensive range of leisure facilities including an
impressive golf course. Bedrooms are all located in
annexe buildings; each is equipped with its own kitchen.
There is a range of dining options, and the restaurant
offers interesting and imaginative choices.

China Fleet Country Club

Rooms 40 (21 GF) **Facilities** Spa STV FTV ⊕ supervised ⚓
18 ⛳ Putt green Gym Squash 28-bay floodlit driving
range Health & beauty suite Hairdresser Wi-fi Child
facilities **Conf** Class 80 Board 60 Thtr 300 **Services** Lift
Parking 400 **Notes** ⊗ Civ Wed 300

Travelodge Saltash

BUDGET HOTEL

Travelodge

☎ 0871 984 6051 📠 01752 841079
Callington Rd, Carkeel PL12 6LF
web: www.travelodge.co.uk
dir: on A38 (Saltash bypass), 1m from Tamar Bridge

Travelodge offers good quality, good value, budget
accommodation. All offer family rooms sleeping up to four
(two adults, two children) with en suite bathroom/
shower-room, remote-control TV, tea- and coffee-making
facilities and comfortable beds. Food options vary.
Breakfast is at the on-site Bar Café restaurant (if
available) or to take away. See also Hotel Groups pages.

Rooms 68 **S** fr £29; **D** fr £29 **Conf** Class 15 Board 12
Thtr 25

SCILLY, ISLES OF

BRYHER — Map 2 SV81

INSPECTORS' CHOICE

Hell Bay
★★★ ◎◎ HOTEL

☎ 01720 422947 📠 01720 423004
TR23 0PR
e-mail: contactus@hellbay.co.uk
web: www.hellbay.co.uk
dir: Access by helicopter or boat from Penzance, plane from Bristol, Exeter, Newquay, Southampton, Land's End

Located on the smallest of the inhabited islands of the Scilly Isles on the edge of the Atlantic, this hotel makes a really special destination. The owners have filled the hotel with original works of art by artists who have connections with the islands, and the interior is decorated in cool blues and greens creating an extremely restful environment. The contemporary bedrooms are equally stylish and many have garden access and stunning sea views. Eating here is a delight, and naturally seafood features strongly on the award-winning, daily-changing menus.

Rooms 25 (25 annexe) (3 fmly) (15 GF) **S** £155-£600; **D** £310-£600 (incl. bkfst & dinner)* **Facilities** STV ◆ ↨ 7 Gym Wi-fi **Conf** Class 36 Board 36 Thtr 36 **Notes** LB Closed Nov-Feb

ST MARY'S — Map 2 SV91

Tregarthens
★★★ 74% HOTEL

☎ 01720 422540 📠 01720 422089
Hugh Town TR21 0PP
e-mail: reception@tregarthens-hotel.co.uk
dir: 100yds from quay

Opened in 1848 by Captain Tregarthen this is now a well-established hotel. The impressive public areas provide wonderful views overlooking St Mary's harbour and some of the many islands, including Tresco and Bryher. Bedrooms are well equipped and neatly furnished. Traditional cuisine is served in the restaurant.

Rooms 33 (1 annexe) (5 fmly) **S** £104-£141; **D** £208-£302 (incl. bkfst & dinner)* **Notes** Closed late Oct-mid Mar

TRESCO — Map 2 SV81

INSPECTORS' CHOICE

The Island
★★★ ◎◎ HOTEL

☎ 01720 422883 📠 01720 423008
TR24 0PU
e-mail: islandhotel@tresco.co.uk
web: www.tresco.co.uk/holidays/island_hotel.asp
dir: Helicopter service Penzance to Tresco, hotel on NE of island

This delightful colonial-style hotel enjoys a waterside location in its own attractive gardens. The spacious, comfortable lounges, airy restaurant and many of the bedrooms enjoy stunning sea views. All of the rooms are brightly furnished and many benefit from lounge areas, balconies or terraces. Carefully prepared, imaginative cuisine makes good use of locally caught fish.

Rooms 48 (27 fmly) (2 GF) **S** £135-£412; **D** £260-£720 (incl. bkfst & dinner)* **Facilities** ◆ ◢ Fishing ↨ Boating Table tennis Bowls Boutique Wi-fi **Conf** Class 80 Board 80 Thtr 80 **Notes** LB Closed Nov-Mar Civ Wed 80

TINTAGEL — Map 2 SX08

Atlantic View
★★ 75% SMALL HOTEL

☎ 01840 770221 📠 01840 770995
Treknow PL34 0EJ
e-mail: atlantic-view@eclipse.co.uk
web: www.holidayscornwall.com
dir: B3263 to Tregatta, turn left into Treknow, hotel on road to Trebarwith Strand Beach

Conveniently located for all the attractions of Tintagel, this family-run hotel has a wonderfully relaxed and welcoming atmosphere. Public areas include a bar, comfortable lounge, TV/games room and heated swimming pool. Bedrooms are generally spacious and some have the added advantage of distant sea views.

Rooms 9 (1 fmly) **Facilities** ◆ **Parking** 10 **Notes** LB Closed Nov-Feb RS Mar

TRURO — Map 2 SW84

Alverton Manor
★★★ 81% ◎◎ HOTEL

☎ 01872 276633 📠 01872 222989
Tregolls Rd TR1 1ZQ
e-mail: reception@alvertonmanor.co.uk
web: www.alvertonmanor.co.uk
dir: From Carland Cross, take A39 to Truro

Formerly a convent, this impressive sandstone property stands in six acres of grounds, within walking distance of the city centre. It has a wide range of smart bedrooms, combining comfort with character. Stylish public areas include the library and the former chapel, now a striking function room. An interesting range of dishes, using the very best of local produce (organic whenever possible) is offered in the elegant restaurant.

Rooms 33 (3 GF) **Facilities** ↨ 18 Xmas Wi-fi **Conf** Class 60 Board 40 Thtr 80 **Services** Lift **Parking** 120 **Notes** Closed 28 Dec RS 4 Jan Civ Wed 80

Mannings
★★★ 81% HOTEL

☎ 01872 270345 📠 01872 242453
Lemon St TR1 2QB
e-mail: reception@manningshotels.co.uk
web: www.manningshotels.co.uk
dir: A30 to Carland Cross then Truro. Follow brown signs to hotel in city centre

This popular hotel is located in the heart of Truro and has an engaging blend of traditional and contemporary. Public areas offer a stylish atmosphere with the bar and restaurant proving popular with locals and residents alike. Bedrooms are pleasantly appointed. A wide choice of appetising dishes is available, which feature ethnic, classical and vegetarian as well as daily specials.

Rooms 43 (9 annexe) (4 fmly) (3 GF) **S** £75-£79; **D** £80-£95 (incl. bkfst)* **Facilities** STV Wi-fi **Conf** Class 10 Board 10 Thtr 20 **Parking** 43 **Notes** Closed 25-26 Dec

See advert on opposite page

Brookdale

THE INDEPENDENTS
HOTEL ASSOCIATION

★★★ 64% HOTEL

☎ 01872 273513 📠 01872 272400
Tregolls Rd TR1 1JZ
e-mail: brookdale@hotelstruro.com
web: www.hotelstruro.com
dir: From A30 onto A39, at A390 junct turn right into city centre. Hotel 600mtrs down hill

Pleasantly situated in an elevated position close to the city centre, the Brookdale provides a range of accommodation options; all rooms are pleasantly spacious and well equipped, and some are located in an adjacent annexe. Meals can be served in guests' rooms, or in the restaurant where an interesting selection of dishes is available.

Rooms 30 (2 fmly) (3 GF) **S** fr £65; **D** fr £90 (incl. bkfst)* **Facilities** STV FTV Xmas Wi-fi **Conf** Class 65 Board 30 Thtr 100 Del from £85* **Parking** 30 **Notes** LB

See advert on this page

Carlton

★★ 72% HOTEL

☎ 01872 272450 📠 01872 223938
Falmouth Rd TR1 2HL
e-mail: reception@carltonhotel.co.uk
dir: On A39 straight across 1st & 2nd rdbts onto bypass (Morlaix Ave). At top of sweeping bend/hill turn right at mini rdbt into Falmouth Rd. Hotel 100mtrs on right

This family-run hotel is pleasantly located a short stroll from the city centre. A friendly welcome is assured and both business and leisure guests choose the Carlton on a regular basis. A smart, comfortable lounge is available, along with leisure facilities. A wide selection of home-cooked dishes is offered in the dining room.

Rooms 29 (4 fmly) (4 GF) **Facilities** STV **Conf** Class 24 Board 36 Thtr 60 **Parking** 31 **Notes** Closed 23 Dec-3 Jan

TYWARDREATH
Map 2 SX05

Trenython Manor

★★★ 80% ◉ COUNTRY HOUSE HOTEL

☎ 01726 814797 📠 01726 817030
Castle Dore Rd PL24 2TS
e-mail: trenython@clublacosta.com
web: www.trenython.co.uk
dir: A390/B3269 towards Fowey, after 2m right into Castledore. Hotel 100mtrs on left

Dating from the 1800s, there is something distinctly different about Trenython, an English manor house designed by an Italian architect. Peacefully situated in extensive grounds, public areas have grace and elegance with original features, and many of the bedrooms have wonderful views. The splendour of the panelled restaurant is the venue for contemporary cuisine.

Rooms 23 (3 fmly) **Facilities** Spa STV FTV ⊗ supervised ⌣ Gym Woodland walks Health & beauty centre Pool table Xmas New Year Wi-fi Child facilities **Parking** 50 **Notes** ⊗

INSPECTORS' CHOICE

Nare

★★★★ ◉ COUNTRY HOUSE HOTEL

☎ 01872 501111 📠 01872 501856
Carne Beach TR2 5PF
e-mail: office@narehotel.co.uk
web: www.narehotel.co.uk
dir: From Tregony follow A3078 for approx 1.5m. Left at Veryan sign, through village towards sea & hotel

This delightful hotel offers a relaxed, country-house atmosphere in a spectacular coastal setting. The elegantly designed bedrooms, many with balconies, have fresh flowers, carefully chosen artwork and antiques that contribute to their engaging individuality. The Dining Room has views on three sides and offers guests a daily-changing menu that particularly focuses on the abundant locally caught seafood including Portloe lobster; this is a children-free zone in the evenings (under sevens that is). The Quarterdeck, open for morning coffee through to the supper time is a relaxed place for meeting up, and it's here that children can be served an early evening meal. The leisure facilities are extensive.

Rooms 37 (7 fmly) (7 GF) **S** £135-£250; **D** £246-£460 (incl. bkfst & dinner)* **Facilities** Spa FTV ⊗ ⚲ ♨ ⚜ Gym Health & beauty clinic Hotel sailing boat Shooting Steam room Sauna Xmas New Year Wi-fi **Services** Lift **Parking** 80 **Notes** LB
See advert on this page

The Hotel & Extreme Academy Watergate Bay
★★★ 79% ◉ HOTEL

☎ 01637 860543 📠 01637 860333
TR8 4AA
e-mail: life@watergatebay.co.uk
web: www.watergatebay.co.uk
dir: A30 onto A3059. Follow airport/Watergate Bay signs

With its own private beach, which is home to the 'Extreme Academy' of beach and watersports activities, this hotel boasts a truly a spectacular location. The style here is relaxed with a genuine welcome for all the family. Public areas are stylish and contemporary. Many bedrooms share the breathtaking outlook and a number have balconies. Several dining options are on offer, including the Beach Hut, Brasserie and Jamie Oliver's restaurant, Fifteen Cornwall.

Rooms 66 (16 annexe) (36 fmly) (6 GF) **Facilities** STV ⊗ ⚲ ♨ Surfing Table tennis Billiards Mountain boarding Wave ski-ing Kite surfing Xmas New Year Wi-fi Child facilities **Conf** Class 40 Board 20 Thtr 120 **Services** Lift **Parking** 45 **Notes** Civ Wed 40

ISLES OF SCILLY

See Scilly, Isles of on page 102
See Scilly, Isles of on page 102

CUMBRIA

Lovelady Shield Country House
★★★ 78% ◉◉ COUNTRY HOUSE HOTEL

☎ 01434 381203 & 381305 📠 01434 381515
CA9 3LF
e-mail: enquiries@lovelady.co.uk
dir: 2m E, signed off A689 at junct with B6294

Located in the heart of the Pennines close to England's highest market town, this delightful country house is set in three acres of landscaped gardens. Accommodation is provided in stylish, thoughtfully equipped bedrooms. Carefully prepared meals are served in the elegant dining room and there is a choice of appealing lounges with log fires in the cooler months.

Rooms 10 (1 fmly) **Facilities** Xmas New Year Wi-fi **Conf** Class 12 Board 12 **Parking** 20 **Notes** LB Civ Wed 100

AMBLESIDE   Map 18 NY30
See also **Elterwater**

Waterhead

★★★★ 74% TOWN HOUSE HOTEL

☎ 015394 32566 📠 015394 31255
Lake Rd LA22 0ER
e-mail: waterhead@elhmail.co.uk
web: www.elh.co.uk/hotels/waterhead.htm
dir: A591 into Ambleside, hotel opposite Waterhead Pier

With an enviable location opposite the bay, this well-established hotel offers contemporary and comfortable accommodation with CD/DVD players, plasma screens and internet access. There is a bar with a garden terrace overlooking the lake and a stylish restaurant serving classical cuisine with a modern twist. Staff are very attentive and friendly. Guests can enjoy full use of the Low Wood Hotel leisure facilities nearby.

Rooms 41 (3 fmly) (7 GF) **S** £83-£136; **D** £106-£280 (incl. bkfst)* **Facilities** FTV Free use of leisure facilities at sister hotel (1m) Xmas New Year Wi-fi **Conf** Class 30 Board 26 Thtr 40 Del from £100 to £140* **Parking** 43

Rothay Manor

★★★ 83% ⊛ HOTEL

☎ 015394 33605 📠 015394 33607
Rothay Bridge LA22 0EH
e-mail: hotel@rothaymanor.co.uk
web: www.rothaymanor.co.uk/aa
dir: In Ambleside follow signs for Coniston (A593). Hotel 0.25m SW of Ambleside opposite rugby pitch

A long-established hotel, this attractive listed building built in Regency style, is a short walk from both the town centre and Lake Windermere. Spacious bedrooms, including suites, family rooms and rooms with balconies, are comfortably equipped and furnished to a very high standard. Public areas include a choice of lounges, a spacious restaurant and conference facilities.

Rooms 19 (2 annexe) (7 fmly) (3 GF) **S** £95-£145; **D** £145-£220 (incl. bkfst)* **Facilities** STV Nearby leisure centre free to guests Free fishing permit available Xmas New Year Wi-fi **Conf** Board 18 Thtr 22 Del from £170 to £184.50* **Parking** 45 **Notes** LB ⊗ Closed 3-29 Jan

See advert on this page

Best Western Ambleside Salutation Hotel

★★★ 80% HOTEL

☎ 015394 32244 📠 015394 34157
Lake Rd LA22 9BX
e-mail: ambleside@hotelslakedistrict.com
web: www.hotelslakedistrict.com
dir: A591 to Ambleside, onto one-way system down Wansfell Rd into Compston Rd. Right at lights back into village

A former coaching inn, this hotel lies in the centre of the town. Bedrooms are tastefully appointed and thoughtfully equipped; many boast balconies and fine views. Inviting public areas include an attractive restaurant and a choice of comfortable lounges for relaxing, and for the more energetic there is a swimming pool and small gym.

Rooms 49 (12 annexe) (4 fmly) **S** £53-£147; **D** £106-£174 (incl. bkfst)* **Facilities** Spa STV ⊗ Gym Sauna Steam room Xmas New Year Wi-fi **Conf** Class 36 Board 26 Thtr 80 Del from £117.50 to £139* **Services** Lift **Parking** 50

AMBLESIDE *continued*

Regent

★★★ 80% HOTEL

☎ 015394 32254 📄 015394 31474
Waterhead Bay LA22 0ES
e-mail: info@regentlakes.co.uk
dir: 1m S on A591

This attractive holiday hotel, situated close to Waterhead Bay, offers a warm welcome. Bedrooms come in a variety of styles, including three suites and five bedrooms in the garden wing. There is a modern swimming pool and the restaurant offers a fine dining experience in a contemporary setting.

Rooms 30 (7 fmly) **S** £65-£95; **D** £99-£145 (incl. bkfst)*
Facilities ⓣ New Year Wi-fi **Parking** 39 **Notes** LB Closed 19-27 Dec

Skelwith Bridge

★★★ 75% HOTEL

☎ 015394 32115 📄 015394 34254
Skelwith Bridge LA22 9NJ
e-mail: info@skelwithbridgehotel.co.uk
web: www.skelwithbridgehotel.co.uk
dir: 2.5m W on A593 at junct with B5343 to Langdale

This 17th-century inn is now a well-appointed tourist hotel located at the heart of the Lake District National Park and renowned for its friendly and attentive service. Bedrooms include two rooms with four-poster beds. Spacious public areas include a choice of lounges and bars, and an attractive restaurant overlooking the gardens to the bridge from which the hotel takes its name.

Rooms 28 (6 annexe) (2 fmly) (1 GF) **S** £45-£60; **D** £80-£126 (incl. bkfst)* **Facilities** Xmas New Year **Parking** 60 **Notes** LB

Queens

★★ 69% HOTEL

☎ 015394 32206 📄 015394 32721
Market Place LA22 9BU
e-mail: enquiries@queenshotelambleside.com
web: www.queenshotelambleside.com
dir: A591 to Ambleside, follow town centre signs on one-way system. Take right lane at lights, hotel on right

Situated in the heart of the village, this traditional Lakeland stone-clad hotel offers good tourist facilities. Bedrooms are equipped with both practical and thoughtful extras, and corridors and stairways feature a fine collection of monarchy memorabilia. Public areas include an open-plan bar and lounge area, an intimate restaurant and a themed Cellar Bar with flat-screen TVs for sporting events.

Rooms 26 (4 fmly) **S** £32-£47; **D** £64-£108 (incl. bkfst)*
Facilities STV Xmas New Year Wi-fi **Parking** 6 **Notes** ⊗

The Log House

◉ RESTAURANT WITH ROOMS

☎ 015394 31077
Lake Rd LA22 0DN
e-mail: nicola@loghouse.co.uk
web: www.loghouse.co.uk
dir: On left after Hayes Garden Centre on A591 (Lake Rd)

This charming and historic Norwegian building is located midway between the town centre and the shore of Lake Windermere, just five minutes' walk to each. Guests can enjoy delicious meals in the attractive restaurant, which also has a bar area. There are three comfortable bedrooms, each equipped with thoughtful accessories such as DVD/VCR players, Wi-fi and hairdryers.

Rooms 3

Appleby Manor Country House

★★★★ 76% ◉ COUNTRY HOUSE HOTEL

☎ 017683 51571 📄 017683 52888
Roman Rd CA16 6JB
e-mail: reception@applebymanor.co.uk
web: www.applebymanor.co.uk
dir: M6 junct 40/A66 towards Brough. Take Appleby turn, then immediately right. Continue for 0.5m

This imposing country mansion is set in extensive grounds amid stunning Cumbrian scenery. The Dunbobbin family and their experienced staff ensure a warm welcome and attentive service. The thoughtfully equipped bedrooms vary in style and include the impressive Heelis Suite; some rooms also have patio areas. The bar offers a wide range of malt whiskies and the restaurant serves carefully prepared meals.

Rooms 30 (7 annexe) (9 fmly) (10 GF) **S** £95-£130; **D** £150-£240 (incl. bkfst)* **Facilities** ⓣ Putt green Steam room Table tennis Pool table New Year Wi-fi **Conf** Class 25 Board 28 Thtr 38 Del from £140 to £160* **Parking** 51 **Notes** LB ⊗ Closed 24-26 Dec RS 6-13 Jun Civ Wed 60

Abbey House

★★★ 77% HOTEL

☎ 01229 838282 📄 01229 820403
Abbey Rd LA13 0PA
e-mail: enquiries@abbeyhousehotel.com
dir: A590, follow signs for Furness general hospital/ Furness Abbey. Hotel approx 100yds on left

Set in its own gardens, this smart hotel provides stylish public areas, as well as extensive function and conference facilities. The well-equipped bedrooms vary in style - the more traditional rooms are in the main house and a more contemporary style of accommodation can be found in the extension. Service is friendly and helpful.

Rooms 57 (6 fmly) (2 GF) **Facilities** Xmas Wi-fi **Conf** Class 120 Board 80 Thtr 280 **Services** Lift **Parking** 100 **Notes** LB Civ Wed 120

Clarke's Hotel

★★★ 71% HOTEL

☎ 01229 820303 📄 01229 430954
Rampside LA13 0PX
e-mail: bookings@clarkeshotel.co.uk
dir: A590 to Ulverston then A5087, take coast road for 8m, turn left at rdbt into Rampside

This smart, well-maintained hotel enjoys a peaceful location on the south Cumbrian coast, overlooking Morecambe Bay. The tastefully appointed bedrooms come in a variety of sizes and are thoughtfully equipped particularly for the business guest. Inviting public areas include an open-plan bar and brasserie offering freshly prepared food throughout the day.

Rooms 14 (1 fmly) **Facilities** FTV **Parking** 50

Lisdoonie

★★ 67% HOTEL

☎ 01229 827312 📠 01229 820944
307/309 Abbey Rd LA14 5LF
e-mail: lisdoonie@aol.com
dir: On A590, at 1st set of lights in town (Strawberry pub on left) continue for 100yds, hotel on right

This friendly hotel is conveniently located for access to the centre of the town and is popular with commercial visitors. The comfortable bedrooms are well equipped, and vary in size and style. There are two lounges, one with a bar and restaurant adjacent. There is also a large function suite.

Rooms 12 (2 fmly) (2 smoking) **Facilities** Wi-fi
Conf Class 255 **Parking** 30 **Notes** Closed Xmas & New Year Civ Wed 200

Travelodge Barrow-in-Furness

BUDGET HOTEL

☎ 0871 984 6281 📠 01229 827129
Cockden Villas, Walney Rd LA14 5UG
web: www.travelodge.co.uk
dir: Just off A590, south of Hawcoat

Travelodge offers good quality, good value, budget accommodation. All offer family rooms sleeping up to four (two adults, two children) with en suite bathroom/shower-room, remote-control TV, tea- and coffee-making facilities and comfortable beds. Food options vary. Breakfast is at the on-site Bar Café restaurant (if available) or to take away. See also Hotel Groups pages.

Rooms 59 **S** fr £29; **D** fr £29

BASSENTHWAITE Map 18 NY23

Armathwaite Hall

★★★★ 80% COUNTRY HOUSE HOTEL

☎ 017687 76551 📠 017687 76220
CA12 4RE
e-mail: reservations@armathwaite-hall.com
web: www.armathwaite-hall.com
dir: M6 junct 40/A66 to Keswick rdbt then A591 signed Carlisle. 8m to Castle Inn junct, turn left. Hotel 300yds

Enjoying fine views over Bassenthwaite Lake, this impressive mansion, dating from the 17th century, is peacefully situated amid 400 acres of deer park.

Comfortably furnished bedrooms are complemented by a choice of public rooms featuring splendid wood panelling and roaring log fires in the cooler months.

Rooms 42 (4 fmly) (8 GF) **Facilities** Spa STV 🖲 supervised 🏌 Putt green Fishing ⛴ Gym Archery Beauty salon Clayshooting Quad & mountain bikes Falconry Xmas New Year Wi-fi **Conf** Class 50 Board 60 Thtr 80 **Services** Lift **Parking** 100 **Notes** LB Civ Wed 80

See advert on page 117

Best Western Castle Inn

★★★★ 71% HOTEL

☎ 017687 76401 📠 017687 76604
CA12 4RG
e-mail: gm@castleinncumbria.co.uk
web: www.castleinncumbria.co.uk
dir: A591 to Carlisle, pass Bassenthwaite village on right. Hotel on left of T-junct

Overlooking some of England's highest fells and Bassenthwaite Lake, this fine hotel is ideally situated for exploring Bassenthwaite, Keswick and the Lake District. Newly refurbished accommodation, extensive leisure facilities and friendly service are just some of the strengths here. Ritson's Restaurant and Laker's Lounge offer a range of dishes using locally sourced meats from the Fells.

Rooms 48 (8 fmly) (4 GF) **S** £85-£155; **D** £95-£165 (incl. bkfst)* **Facilities** Spa FTV 🖲 supervised 🏌 Putt green Gym Table tennis Pool table Xmas New Year Wi-fi Child facilities **Conf** Class 108 Board 60 Thtr 200 Del from £120 to £150* **Parking** 120 **Notes** LB ⊗ Civ Wed 180

The Pheasant

★★★ 83% ◉ HOTEL

☎ 017687 76234 📠 017687 76002
CA13 9YE
e-mail: info@the-pheasant.co.uk
web: www.the-pheasant.co.uk
dir: Midway between Keswick & Cockermouth, signed from A66

Enjoying a rural setting, within well-tended gardens, on the western side of Bassenthwaite Lake, this friendly 500-year-old inn is steeped in tradition. The attractive oak-panelled bar has seen few changes over the years and features log fires and a great selection of malt whiskies. The individually decorated bedrooms are stylish and thoughtfully equipped.

Rooms 15 (2 annexe) (2 GF) **S** £83-£88; **D** £156-£206 (incl. bkfst)* **Facilities** New Year Wi-fi **Parking** 40 **Notes** No children 12yrs Closed 25 Dec

Ravenstone

★★ 81% HOTEL

☎ 017687 76240 📠 017687 76733
CA12 4QG
e-mail: andrew@ravenstone-hotel.co.uk
dir: From M6 junct 40 follow A66 W for 17m. At rdbt turn right onto A591, 4m on right

A Victorian country house where a friendly welcome is guaranteed. It has been tastefully extended over the years yet retains many original features. Stylish bedrooms have fine views across to the Lakeland Fells. Day rooms include a spacious lounge, traditional bar and games room. The dining room has pleasant views and local produce is a feature at dinner.

Rooms 19 (1 fmly) **S** £50-£75; **D** £100-£190 (incl. bkfst & dinner)* **Facilities** Xmas New Year Wi-fi **Parking** 30 **Notes** LB ⊗

BORROWDALE Map 18 NY21

See also **Keswick & Rosthwaite**

Lodore Falls Hotel

★★★ 83% HOTEL

☎ 017687 77285 📠 017687 77343
CA12 5UX
e-mail: info@lodorefallshotel.co.uk
web: www.lodorefallshotel.co.uk
dir: M6 junct 40 take A66 to Keswick, then B5289 to Borrowdale. Hotel on left

This impressive hotel has an enviable location overlooking Derwentwater. The bedrooms, many with lake or fell views, are comfortably equipped; family rooms and suites are also available. The dining room, bar and lounge areas were, at the time of inspection, also undergoing refurbishment to a very high standard. One of the treatments in the hotel's Elemis Spa actually makes use of the Lodore Waterfall!

Rooms 69 (11 fmly) **S** £75-£209; **D** £150-£368 (incl. bkfst)* **Facilities** Spa STV FTV 🖲 supervised ☃ 🏌 Fishing Gym Squash Sauna Xmas New Year Wi-fi **Conf** Class 90 Board 45 Thtr 200 Del from £145 to £185* **Services** Lift **Parking** 93 **Notes** LB Civ Wed 130

See advert on page 118

BORROWDALE *continued*

Leathes Head

★★★ 81% ⊛ HOTEL

☎ 017687 77247 & 77650 🖨 017687 77363
CA12 5UY
e-mail: enq@leatheshead.co.uk
web: www.leatheshead.co.uk
dir: 3.5m from Keswick on B5289 (Borrowdale road).
Hotel on left 0.25m before Grange Bridge

Located in the picturesque Borrowdale Valley, this
personally run Edwardian house is a haven of tranquillity.
There are three comfortable lounge areas and an elegant
restaurant serving high quality meals. The well stocked
bar features an extensive wine list, a selection of
whiskies and an amazing range of gins. Bedrooms are
very well equipped with many thoughtful accessories;
most have stunning views.

Rooms 12 (2 fmly) (3 GF) **S** £86-£105; **D** £142-£210 (incl.
bkfst & dinner)* **Facilities** FTV Wi-fi **Parking** 16 **Notes** LB
⊗ No children 15yrs Closed late Nov-mid Feb

Borrowdale Gates Country House

★★★ 79% COUNTRY HOUSE HOTEL

☎ 017687 77204 🖨 017687 77195
CA12 5UQ
e-mail: hotel@borrowdale-gates.com
dir: From A66 follow B5289 for approx 4m. Turn right over
bridge, hotel 0.25m beyond village

This friendly hotel is peacefully located in the Borrowdale
Valley, close to the village but in its own three acres of
wooded grounds. Public rooms include comfortable
lounges and a restaurant with lovely views. Bedrooms vary
in size and style and all have benefited from an upgrade.

Rooms 27 (10 GF) **S** £50-£60; **D** £100-£180 (incl. bkfst)*
Facilities FTV Xmas New Year Wi-fi **Services** Lift
Parking 29 **Notes** Closed 5 Jan-5 Feb Civ Wed 54

See advert on page 118

Borrowdale

★★★ 75% HOTEL

☎ 017687 77224 🖨 017687 77338
CA12 5UY
e-mail: borrowdale@lakedistricthotels.net
dir: 3m from Keswick, on B5289 at S end of Lake
Derwentwater

Situated in the beautiful Borrowdale Valley overlooking
Derwentwater, this traditionally styled hotel guarantees a
friendly welcome. Extensive public areas include a choice
of lounges, traditional dining room, lounge bar and
popular conservatory which serves more informal meals.
Bedrooms vary in style and size including two that are
suitable for less able guests.

Rooms 36 (3 fmly) (3 GF) **S** £90-£112; **D** £180-£224 (incl.
bkfst & dinner) **Facilities** STV FTV Leisure facilities
available at nearby sister hotel Xmas New Year Wi-fi
Conf Class 30 Board 24 Thtr 80 **Parking** 30 **Notes** LB

See advert on page 119

BOWNESS ON WINDERMERE

See Windermere

BRAITHWAITE

The Cottage in the Wood

⊛⊛ RESTAURANT WITH ROOMS

☎ 017687 78409
Whinlatter Pass CA12 5TW
e-mail: relax@thecottageinthewood.co.uk
dir: M6 junct 40 onto A66 W. After Keswick turn off for
Braithwaite via Whinlatter Pass (B5292), located at top
of pass

This charming property sits amid wooded hills with
striking views of Skiddaw, and is in a convenient location
for Keswick. The professional owners provide excellent
hospitality in a relaxed manner and offer a freshly
prepared dinner from a set menu that includes a
vegetarian choice. There is a cosy lounge and a small
bar. The bedrooms are individually decorated, and the
superior rooms include many useful extras.

Rooms 9 (1 fmly)

BRAMPTON
Map 21 NY56

INSPECTORS' CHOICE

Farlam Hall

★★★ ⊛ HOTEL

☎ 016977 46234 🖨 016977 46683
CA8 2NG
e-mail: farlam@relaischateaux.com
web: www.farlamhall.co.uk
dir: On A689 (Brampton to Alston). Hotel 2m on left,
(not in Farlam village)

This delightful family-run country house dates back to
1428. Steeped in history, the hotel is set in beautifully
landscaped Victorian gardens complete with an
ornamental lake and stream. Lovingly restored over
many years, it now provides the highest standards of
comfort and hospitality. Gracious public rooms invite
relaxation, whilst every thought has gone into the
beautiful bedrooms, many of which are simply
stunning.

Rooms 12 (1 annexe) (2 GF) **S** £155-£185;
D £295-£350 (incl. bkfst & dinner) **Facilities** FTV ⊸
New Year Wi-fi **Conf** Class 24 Board 12 Thtr 24
Parking 35 **Notes** LB No children 5yrs Closed 24-30
Dec

BURTON MOTORWAY
SERVICE AREA (M6)
Map 18 SD57

Travelodge Burton (M6 Northbound)

BUDGET HOTEL

☎ 0871 984 6126 🖨 01524 784014
Burton in Kendal LA6 1JF
web: www.travelodge.co.uk
dir: between M6 junct 35/36 northbound

Travelodge offers good quality, good value, budget
accommodation. All offer family rooms sleeping up to four
(two adults, two children) with en suite bathroom/
shower-room, remote-control TV, tea- and coffee-making
facilities and comfortable beds. Food options vary.
Breakfast is at the on-site Bar Café restaurant (if
available) or to take away. See also Hotel Groups pages.

Rooms 47 **S** fr £29; **D** fr £29

BUTTERMERE Map 18 NY11

Bridge

★★★ 79% COUNTRY HOUSE HOTEL

☎ 017687 70252 🖷 017687 70215
CA13 9UZ
e-mail: enquiries@bridge-hotel.com
web: www.bridge-hotel.com
dir: A66 around town centre, off at Braithwaite. Over Newlands Pass. Follow Buttermere signs. Hotel in village

This long standing hotel enjoys a tranquil setting in a dramatic valley close to Buttermere. The bedrooms are tastefully appointed and have stylish bathrooms, and the comfortable public areas include a delightful lounge, attractive dining room and lively bar popular with walkers.

Rooms 21 **S** £62.50-£79; **D** £125-£180 (incl. bkfst & dinner)* **Facilities** Xmas New Year Wi-fi **Conf** Board 10 **Parking** 40 **Notes** ⊗

CARLISLE Map 18 NY35

Crown

★★★ 80% HOTEL

☎ 01228 561888 🖷 01228 561637
Wetheral CA4 8ES
e-mail: info@crownhotelwetheral.co.uk
web: www.crownhotelwetheral.co.uk
dir: M6 junct 42 take B6263 to Wetheral, right at village shop, car park at rear of hotel

Set in the attractive village of Wetheral and with landscaped gardens to the rear, this hotel is well suited to both business and leisure guests. Rooms vary in size and style and include two apartments in an adjacent house ideal for long stays. A choice of dining options is available, with the popular Waltons Bar an informal alternative to the main restaurant.

Crown

Rooms 51 (2 annexe) (10 fmly) (3 GF) **S** £45-£65; **D** £80-£110 (incl. bkfst)* **Facilities** Spa STV supervised Gym Squash Children's splash pool Steam room Beauty facilities Sauna Xmas New Year Wi-fi **Conf** Class 90 Board 50 Thtr 175 Del from £130 to £145* **Parking** 80 **Notes** LB Civ Wed 120

Best Western Cumbria Park

★★★ 73% HOTEL

☎ 01228 522887 🖷 01228 514796
32 Scotland Rd, Stanwix CA3 9DG
e-mail: cumbriaparkhotel@wightcablenorth.net
web: www.cumbriaparkhotel.co.uk
dir: M6 junct 44, A7 towards Carlisle. Hotel on left in 1.5m

Just minutes from the M6, this privately-owned hotel, with its a feature garden, is conveniently placed for the city centre. Well-equipped bedrooms come in a variety of sizes, and several have four-poster beds and whirlpool baths. Functions, conferences and weddings are all well catered for in a wide choice of rooms. Wi-fi is available throughout.

Rooms 47 (3 fmly) (7 GF) (2 smoking) **S** £75-£90; **D** £100-£150 (incl. bkfst)* **Facilities** STV FTV Gym Sauna Steam room Wi-fi **Conf** Class 50 Board 35 Thtr 120 **Services** Lift **Parking** 51 **Notes** ⊗ Closed 25-26 Dec Civ Wed

The Crown & Mitre

★★★ 66% HOTEL

☎ 01228 525491 🖷 01228 514553
4 English St CA3 8HZ
e-mail: info@crownandmitre-hotel-carlisle.com
web: www.crownandmitre-hotel-carlisle.com
dir: A6 to city centre, pass station on left. Right into Blackfriars St. Rear entrance at end

Located in the heart of the city, this Edwardian hotel is close to the cathedral and a few minutes' walk from the castle. Bedrooms vary in size and style, from smart executive rooms to more functional standard rooms. Public rooms include a comfortable lounge area and the lovely bar with its feature stained-glass windows.

The Crown & Mitre

Rooms 95 (20 annexe) (4 fmly) (18 smoking) **S** £50-£75; **D** £70-£120 (incl. bkfst)* **Facilities** Xmas New Year Wi-fi **Conf** Class 250 Board 50 Thtr 400 Del from £100 to £120* **Services** Lift **Parking** 42 **Notes** Civ Wed 100

Ibis Carlisle

BUDGET HOTEL

☎ 01228 518000 🖷 01228 518010
Portlands, Botchergate CA1 1RP
e-mail: H3443@accor-hotels.com
web: www.ibishotels.com
dir: M6 junct 42/43 follow signs for city centre. Hotel on Botchergate

Modern, budget hotel offering comfortable accommodation in bright and practical bedrooms. Breakfast is self-service and dinner is available in the restaurant See also the Hotel Groups pages.

Rooms 102 (17 fmly) (27 smoking)

Travelodge Carlisle Central

BUDGET HOTEL

☎ 0871 984 6374 🖷 01228 521830
Cecil St CA1 1 NL
dir: M6 junct 43, follow A69/Carlisle city centre signs for 1.5m. Turn left before lights at United Reform Church into Cecil St. Lodge 200yds on left

Travelodge offers good quality, good value, budget accommodation. All offer family rooms sleeping up to four (two adults, two children) with en suite bathroom/ shower-room, remote-control TV, tea- and coffee-making facilities and comfortable beds. Food options vary. Breakfast is at the on-site Bar Café restaurant (if available) or to take away. See also the Hotel Groups pages.

Rooms 66 **S** fr £29; **D** fr £29

Travelodge Carlisle Todhills

BUDGET HOTEL

☎ 0871 984 6127 🖷 01228 674335
A74 Southbound, Todhills CA6 4HA
web: www.travelodge.co.uk
dir: S'bound carriageway of A74 (M)

Rooms 40 **S** fr £29; **D** fr £29

CARTMEL — Map 18 SD37

Aynsome Manor

★★ 78% ⊕ COUNTRY HOUSE HOTEL

☎ 015395 36653 📠 015395 36016
LA11 6HH
e-mail: aynsomemanor@btconnect.com
dir: M6 junct 36, A590 signed Barrow-in-Furness towards Cartmel. Left at end of road, hotel before village

Dating back, in part, to the early 16th century, this manor house overlooks the fells and the nearby priory. Spacious bedrooms, including some courtyard rooms, are comfortably furnished. Dinner in the elegant restaurant features local produce whenever possible, and there is a choice of lounges to relax in afterwards.

Rooms 12 (2 annexe) (2 fmly) **S** £85-£95; **D** £145-£168 (incl. dinner) **Facilities** FTV New Year **Parking** 20 **Notes** LB Closed 2-31 Jan RS Sun

L'enclume

⊕ ⊕ ⊕ ⊕ RESTAURANT WITH ROOMS

☎ 015395 36362
Cavendish St LA11 6PZ
e-mail: info@lenclume.co.uk
dir: From A590 turn for Cartmel before Newby Bridge

A delightful 13th-century property in the heart of this delightful village offering 21st-century cooking that is worth travelling for. Simon Rogan cooks imaginative, adventurous food in this stylish restaurant. Individually designed, modern, en suite rooms vary in size and style, and are either in the main property, or dotted about the village, only a few seconds' walk from the restaurant.

Rooms 12 (5 annexe) (3 fmly)

CLEATOR — Map 18 NY01

Ennerdale Country House

★★★ 75% HOTEL

OXFORD
HOTELS & INNS

☎ 01946 813907 📠 01946 815260
CA23 3DT
e-mail: reservations.ennerdale@ohiml.com
web: www.oxfordhotelsandinns.com
dir: M6 junct 40 to A66, A5086 for 12m, hotel on left

This fine Grade II listed building lies on the edge of the village and has landscaped gardens. Impressive bedrooms, including split-level suites and four-poster rooms, are richly furnished, smartly decorated and offer an amazing array of facilities. Attractive public areas include a stylish restaurant and an American themed bar which offers a good range of bar meals.

Rooms 30 (2 fmly) (10 GF) **S** £69-£99; **D** £79-£129 (incl. bkfst) **Facilities** STV Xmas New Year Wi-fi **Conf** Class 60 Board 60 Thtr 160 **Parking** 40 **Notes** LB Civ Wed 160

COCKERMOUTH — Map 18 NY13

The Trout

★★★ 83% HOTEL

☎ 01900 823591 📠 01900 827514
Crown St CA13 0EJ
e-mail: enquiries@trouthotel.co.uk
web: www.trouthotel.co.uk
dir: Next to Wordsworth House

Dating back to 1670, this privately owned hotel has an enviable setting on the banks of the River Derwent. The well-equipped bedrooms, some contained in a wing overlooking the river, are comfortable and mostly spacious. The Terrace Bar and Bistro, serving food all day, has a sheltered patio area. There is also a cosy bar, a choice of lounge areas and an attractive, traditional-style dining room that offers a good choice of set-price dishes.

Rooms 49 (2 annexe) (4 fmly) (15 GF) **S** £99-£119; **D** £119-£190 (incl. bkfst)* **Facilities** STV Fishing Xmas New Year Wi-fi **Conf** Class 20 Board 20 Thtr 25 **Parking** 40 **Notes** LB Civ Wed 60

Shepherds Hotel

★★★ 70% HOTEL

☎ 01900 822673 📠 01900 820129
Lakeland Sheep & Wool Centre, Egremont Rd CA13 0QX
e-mail: reception@shepherdshotel.co.uk
web: www.shepherdshotel.co.uk
dir: At junct of A66 & A5086 S of Cockermouth, entrance off A5086, 200mtrs off rdbt

This hotel is modern in style and offers thoughtfully equipped accommodation. The property also houses the Lakeland Sheep and Wool Centre, with live sheep shows from Easter to mid November. A restaurant serving a wide variety of meals and snacks is open all day.

Rooms 26 (4 fmly) (13 GF) **Facilities** FTV Pool table Small childs play area Wi-fi **Conf** Class 30 Board 30 Thtr 40 **Services** Lift **Parking** 100 **Notes** Closed 25-26 Dec & 4-18 Jan

Travelodge Cockermouth

BUDGET HOTEL

☎ 0871 984 6358 📠 01900 826522
Europe Way CA13 0DP
e-mail: cockermouth@travelodge.co.uk
dir: 1m S of Cockermouth at junct of A5086 & A66

Travelodge offers good quality, good value, budget accommodation. All offer family rooms sleeping up to four (two adults, two children) with en suite bathroom/shower-room, remote-control TV, tea- and coffee-making facilities and comfortable beds. Food options vary. Breakfast is at the on-site Bar Café restaurant (if available) or to take away. See also the Hotel Groups pages.

Rooms 43 **S** fr £29; **D** fr £29

CROOKLANDS — Map 18 SD58

Crooklands

★★★ 76% HOTEL

☎ 015395 67432 📠 015395 67525
LA7 7NW
e-mail: reception@crooklands.com
web: www.crooklands.com
dir: M6 junct 36 onto A65. Left at rdbt. Hotel 1.5m on right past garage

Although only a stone's throw from the M6, this hotel enjoys a peaceful rural location. Housed in a converted

200-year-old farmhouse, the restaurant retains many original features such as the beams and stone walls. Bedrooms are a mix of modern and traditional and vary in size. The hotel is a popular stop-over for both leisure and corporate guests travelling between England and Scotland.

Rooms 30 (3 fmly) (14 GF) **S** £69-£75; **D** £98-£120* **Facilities** New Year Wi-fi **Conf** Class 50 Board 40 Thtr 80 **Services** Lift **Parking** 80 **Notes** ⊗ Closed 24-28 Dec

---

CROSTHWAITE   **Map 18 SD49**

Damson Dene

★★★ 68% HOTEL

☎ 015395 68676   📠 015395 68227
LA8 8JE
e-mail: info@damsondene.co.uk
web: www.bestlakesbreaks.co.uk
dir: M6 junct 36, A590 signed Barrow-in-Furness, 5m right onto A5074. Hotel on right in 5m

A short drive from Lake Windermere, this hotel enjoys a tranquil and scenic setting. Bedrooms include a number with four-poster beds and jacuzzi baths. The spacious restaurant serves a daily-changing menu, with some of the produce coming from the hotel's own kitchen garden. Real fires warm the lounge in the cooler months and leisure facilities are available.

Rooms 40 (3 annexe) (7 fmly) (9 GF) **S** £69-£89; **D** £108-£148 (incl. bkfst) **Facilities** Spa ⊙ Gym Beauty salon Xmas New Year **Conf** Class 60 Board 40 Thtr 140 **Parking** 45 **Notes** LB Civ Wed 120

See advert on this page

ELTERWATER   **Map 18 NY30**

Langdale Hotel & Country Club

★★★ 82% @ HOTEL

☎ 015394 37302   📠 015394 37694
LA22 9JD
e-mail: info@langdale.co.uk
web: www.langdale.co.uk/hotel/index.htm
dir: Into Langdale & hotel part of Langadale Country Estate

Founded on the site of an abandoned 19th-century gunpowder works, this modern hotel is set in 35 acres of woodland and waterways. Comfortable bedrooms, many with spa baths, vary in size. Extensive public areas include a choice of stylish restaurants, conference and leisure facilities and an elegant bar with an interesting selection of snuff. There is also a traditional pub run by the hotel just along the main road.

Rooms 57 (52 annexe) (5 fmly) (25 GF) **Facilities** Spa STV ⊙ supervised ⊋ Gym Steam room Cycle hire Solarium Aerobics studio Health & beauty salon Xmas New Year Wi-fi **Conf** Class 40 Board 35 Thtr 80 **Parking** 65 **Notes** ⊗ Civ Wed 65

New Dungeon Ghyll

★★ 75% HOTEL

☎ 015394 37213   📠 015394 37666
Langdale LA22 9JX
e-mail: enquiries@dungeon-ghyll.com
web: www.dungeon-ghyll.com
dir: From Ambleside follow A593 towards Coniston for 3m, at Skelwith Bridge right onto B5343 towards 'The Langdales'

This friendly hotel enjoys a tranquil, idyllic position at the head of the valley, set among the impressive peaks of Langdale. Bedrooms vary in size and style; the rooms are brightly decorated and smartly furnished. Bar meals are served all day, and dinner can be enjoyed in the restaurant overlooking the landscaped gardens; there is also a cosy lounge/bar.

Rooms 20 (1 fmly) (3 GF) **Facilities** FTV Xmas New Year Wi-fi **Parking** 30

ESKDALE GREEN   **Map 18 NY10**

Bower House Inn

★★ 74% HOTEL

☎ 019467 23244   📠 019467 23308
CA19 1TD
e-mail: Info@bowerhouseinn.co.uk
web: www.bowerhouseinn.co.uk
dir: 4m off A595 0.5m W of Eskdale Green

This former farmhouse enjoys a countryside location with delightful mountain views and offers true peace and relaxation. The traditional bar and formal restaurant, where a good range of dishes is served, reflect the coaching inn origins of the house. The attractive bedrooms are situated in a converted barn, in the original house and in the Garden Cottage.

Rooms 29 (19 annexe) (2 fmly) (9 GF) **Facilities** Xmas New Year Wi-fi **Conf** Class 20 Board 30 Thtr 40 **Parking** 60 **Notes** LB Civ Wed 40

GLENRIDDING · Map 18 NY31

The Inn on the Lake

★★★ 81% ⊛ HOTEL

☎ 017684 82444 📄 017684 82303
Lake Ullswater CA11 0PE
e-mail: info@innonthelakeullswater.co.uk
web: www.innonthelakeullswater.com
dir: M6 junct 40, then A66 to Keswick. At rdbt take A592 to Ullswater Lake. Along lake to Glenridding. Hotel on left on entering village

In a picturesque lakeside setting, this restored Victorian hotel is a popular leisure destination as well as catering for weddings and conferences. Superb views can be enjoyed from the bedrooms and from the garden terrace where afternoon teas are served during warmer months. There is a popular pub in the grounds, and moorings for yachts are available to guests. Sailing tuition can be arranged.

Rooms 47 (6 fmly) (1 GF) **Facilities** ↕ 9 🎱 Putt green Fishing 🏌 Gym Sailing 9 hole pitch & putt Bowls Lake Bathing Xmas New Year Wi-fi **Conf** Class 60 Board 40 Thtr 120 **Services** Lift **Parking** 200 **Notes** LB Civ Wed 100

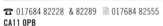

See advert on page 121

Best Western Glenridding Hotel

★★★ 70% HOTEL

☎ 017684 82228 & 82289 📄 017684 82555
CA11 0PB
e-mail: glenridding@bestwestern.co.uk
dir: N'bound M6 junct 36, A591 Windermere then A592, for 14m. S'bound M6 junct 40, A592 for 13m

This friendly hotel benefits from a picturesque location in the village centre, and many rooms have fine views of the lake and fells. Public areas are extensive and include a choice of dining options including Ratchers restaurant and a café. Leisure facilities are available along with a conference room and a garden function room.

Rooms 36 (7 fmly) (8 GF) **Facilities** STV 🏊 Sauna Snooker Table tennis Xmas New Year Wi-fi **Conf** Class 30 Board 24 Thtr 30 **Services** Lift **Parking** 30 **Notes** Civ Wed 120

GRANGE-OVER-SANDS · Map 18 SD47

Netherwood

★★★ 80% HOTEL

☎ 015395 32552 📄 015395 34121
Lindale Rd LA11 6ET
e-mail: enquiries@netherwood-hotel.co.uk
web: www.netherwood-hotel.co.uk
dir: On B5277 before station

This imposing hotel stands in terraced grounds and enjoys fine views of Morecambe Bay. Though a popular conference and wedding venue, good levels of hospitality and service ensure all guests are well looked after. Bedrooms vary in size but all are well furnished and have smart modern bathrooms. Magnificent woodwork is a feature of the public areas.

Rooms 32 (5 fmly) **S** £80-£120; **D** £180-£200 (incl. bkfst) **Facilities** Spa 🏊 supervised 🏌 Gym Beauty salon Steam room Spa bath Sunbed New Year Wi-fi **Conf** Class 40 Board 50 Thtr 150 Del from £140 to £180 **Services** Lift **Parking** 100 **Notes** Civ Wed 180

Cumbria Grand

★★★ 70% HOTEL

☎ 015395 32331 📄 015395 34534
LA11 6EN
e-mail: salescumbria@strathmorehotels.com
dir: M6 junct 36, A590 & follow Grange-over-Sands signs

Set within extensive grounds, this large hotel offers fine views over Morecambe Bay and caters well for a mixed market. Public areas are pure nostalgia, and include a grand dining room and fine ballroom. Good value is provided.

Rooms 122 (10 fmly) (25 GF) **S** £47-£100; **D** £82-£150 (incl. bkfst) **Facilities** STV 🎱 Putt green Snooker & pool table Table tennis Darts ♫ Xmas New Year **Services** Lift **Parking** 75 **Notes** LB

See advert on page 617

Graythwaite Manor

★★★ 68% HOTEL

☎ 015395 32001 & 33755 📄 015395 35549
Fernhill Rd LA11 7JE
e-mail: enquiries@graythwaitemanor.co.uk
dir: B5277 through Grange, Fernhill Rd opposite fire station behind small traffic island, hotel 1st left

This well established hotel is set in beautiful gardens, complete with sub-tropical plants, and offers delightful views out over Morecambe Bay. Public areas include an Orangery, a number of comfortable lounges and an elegant restaurant. The bedrooms, which vary in size, are traditional in style.

Rooms 24 **Facilities** 🏌 Bowling green Xmas **Services** Lift **Parking** 34 **Notes** LB Civ Wed

Hampsfell House

★★ 76% HOTEL

☎ 015395 32567 📄 015395 35995
Hampsfell Rd LA11 6BG
e-mail: enquiries@hampsfellhouse.co.uk
web: www.hampsfellhouse.co.uk
dir: A590 at junct with B5277, signed to Grange-over-Sands. Left at rdbt into Main St, 2nd rdbt right and right at x-rds. Hotel on left

Dating back to 1800, this owner managed hotel is peacefully set in two acres of private grounds yet is just a comfortable walk from the town centre. Bedrooms are smartly decorated and well maintained. There is a cosy bar where guests can relax and enjoy pre-dinner drinks. Comprehensive and imaginative dinners are taken in an attractive dining room.

Rooms 8 (1 fmly) **S** £40-£50; **D** £50-£85 (incl. bkfst)* **Facilities** Xmas New Year Wi-fi **Parking** 20 **Notes** LB

Clare House
★ ⚛ HOTEL

☎ 015395 33026 & 34253 📠 015395 34310
Park Rd LA11 7HQ
e-mail: info@clarehousehotel.co.uk
web: www.clarehousehotel.co.uk
dir: Off A590 onto B5277, through Lindale into Grange, keep left, hotel 0.5m on left past Crown Hill & St Paul's Church

A warm, genuine welcome awaits guests at this delightful, family-run hotel. Situated in its own secluded gardens, it provides a relaxed haven in which to enjoy the panoramic views across Morecambe Bay. Bedrooms and public areas are comfortable and attractively furnished. Skilfully prepared dinners and hearty breakfasts are served in the elegant dining room.

Rooms 18 (4 GF) **S** £83; **D** £166 (incl. bkfst & dinner) **Facilities** Putt green ⛳ Wi-fi **Parking** 18 **Notes** LB ⊗ Closed Nov-22 Mar

---

GRASMERE **Map 18 NY30**

Rothay Garden
★★★★ 80% ⚛⚛ HOTEL

☎ 015394 35334 📠 015394 35723
Broadgate LA22 9RJ
e-mail: stay@rothaygarden.com
web: www.rothaygarden.com
dir: Off A591, opposite Swan Hotel, into Grasmere, 300yds on left

On the edge of the village, and sitting in two acres of riverside gardens, Rothay Garden offers an impressive combination of stylish design and luxurious comfort. Bedrooms include five Loft Suites, each named after one of the fells they overlook; they feature original beams and designer bathrooms with plasma TVs. There is a chic lounge bar and an elegant candlelit conservatory restaurant. The friendly staff provide attentive service.

Rooms 30 (3 fmly) (8 GF) **S** £100-£140; **D** £140-£300 (incl. dinner) **Facilities** FTV Use of local leisure club Xmas New Year Wi-fi **Parking** 38 **Notes** LB No children 5yrs

See advert on this page

Wordsworth
★★★★ 78% ⚛⚛ HOTEL

☎ 015394 35592 📠 015394 35765
LA22 9SW
e-mail: enquiry@thewordsworthhotel.co.uk
web: www.thewordsworthhotel.co.uk
dir: Off A591 centre of village adjacent to St Oswald's Church

Named after the famous poet, this charming hotel is set in two acres of landscaped gardens. Peaceful lounges, furnished with antiques, look out over well-kept lawns and the friendly staff provide professional service. Bedrooms are individually furnished and well equipped. There are comprehensive leisure facilities, and diners have a choice between the popular pub and the more formal Prelude Restaurant.

Rooms 36 (2 fmly) (2 GF) **S** £85-£105; **D** £170-£290 (incl. bkfst & dinner)* **Facilities** ⚛ ⛳ Gym ♫ Xmas New Year Wi-fi **Conf** Class 50 Board 40 Thtr 100 Del from £135 to £167.50* **Services** Lift **Parking** 60 **Notes** LB ⊗ Civ Wed 100

See advert on page 114

GRASMERE *continued*

Best Western Grasmere Red Lion

★★★ 80% HOTEL

☎ 015394 35456 📄 015394 35579
Red Lion Square LA22 9SS
e-mail: reservations@grasmereredlionhotel.co.uk
dir: Off A591, signed Grasmere Village. Hotel in village centre

This modernised and extended 18th-century coaching inn, located in the heart of the village, offers spacious well-equipped rooms and a number of meeting and conference facilities. A range of pub meals complement the more formal Courtyard restaurant. The spacious and comfortable lounge area is ideal for relaxing, and for the more energetic guest there is a pool and gym.

Best Western Grasmere Red Lion

Rooms 47 **S** £53.50-£133.50; **D** £107-£172 (incl. bkfst)*
Facilities STV 🏊 Gym Sauna Steam room Spa bath Xmas New Year Wi-fi **Conf** Class 24 Board 28 Thtr 60
Del from £120.50 to £140.50 **Services** Lift **Notes** LB

See advert on this page

Gold Rill Country House

★★★ 79% COUNTRY HOUSE HOTEL

☎ 015394 35486 📄 015394 35486
Red Bank Rd LA22 9PU
e-mail: reception@gold-rill.com
dir: Turn off A591 into village centre, turn into road opposite St Oswald's Church. Hotel 300yds on left

This popular hotel enjoys a fine location on the edge of the village with spectacular views of the lake and surrounding fells. Attractive bedrooms, some with balconies, are tastefully decorated and many have separate, comfortable seating areas. The hotel boasts a private pier, an outdoor heated pool and a putting green. Public areas include a well-appointed restaurant and choice of lounges.

Rooms 31 (6 annexe) (2 fmly) (11 GF) **S** £63-£92;
D £126-£184 (incl. bkfst & dinner)* **Facilities** STV FTV ⚡
Putt green New Year Wi-fi **Parking** 35 **Notes** LB 🚫 Closed mid Dec-mid Jan (open New Year)

Macdonald Swan

★★★ 77% HOTEL

☎ 0844 879 9120 📠 015394 43432
LA22 9RF
e-mail: sales/oldengland@macdonald-hotels.co.uk
web: www.macdonaldhotels.co.uk
dir: M6 junct 36, A591 towards Kendal, A590 to Keswick through Ambleside. Hotel on right on entering village

Close to Dove Cottage and occupying a prominent position on the edge of the village, this 300-year-old inn is mentioned in Wordsworth's poem 'The Waggoner'. Attractive public areas are spacious and comfortable, and bedrooms are equally stylish with some having CD players. A good range of bar meals is available, while the elegant restaurant offers more formal dining.

Rooms 38 (1 fmly) (28 GF) **Facilities** FTV Xmas New Year Wi-fi **Parking** 45 **Notes** Civ Wed 60

Grasmere

★★ 80% ⊛ HOTEL

☎ 015394 35277 📠 015394 35277
Broadgate LA22 9TA
e-mail: enquiries@grasmerehotel.co.uk
web: www.grasmerehotel.co.uk
dir: From Ambleside take A591 N, 2nd left into Grasmere. Over humpback bridge, past playing field. Hotel on left

Attentive and hospitable service contribute to the atmosphere at this family-run hotel, set in secluded gardens by the River Rothay. There are two inviting lounges (one with residents' bar) and an attractive dining room looking onto the garden. The thoughtfully prepared dinner menu makes good use of fresh ingredients. Pine furniture is featured in most bedrooms, along with welcome personal touches.

Rooms 14 (1 annexe) (2 GF) **Facilities** Full leisure facilities at nearby country club Free fishing permit available Xmas New Year Wi-fi **Parking** 14 **Notes** LB No children 10yrs Closed 3 Jan-early Feb

Oak Bank

★★ 76% HOTEL

☎ 015394 35217 📠 015394 35685
Broadgate LA22 9TA
e-mail: info@lakedistricthotel.co.uk
web: www.lakedistricthotel.co.uk
dir: N'bound: M6 junct 36 onto A591 to Windermere, Ambleside, then Grasmere. S'bound: M6 junct 40 onto A66 to Keswick, A591 to Grasmere

This privately owned and personally run hotel provides well-equipped accommodation, including a bedroom on the ground-floor and a four-poster room. Public areas include a choice of comfortable lounges with welcoming log fires when the weather is cold. There is a pleasant bar and an attractive restaurant with a conservatory extension overlooking the garden.

Rooms 14 (1 GF) **S** £62.50-£105; **D** £85-£165 (incl. bkfst) **Facilities** FTV Corporate membership of leisure facilities at another hotel Xmas New Year Wi-fi **Parking** 14 **Notes** LB Closed 3-28 Jan

See advert on this page

Waterside Hotel

U

☎ 0870 333 9135 📠 0870 333 9235
Keswick Rd LA22 9PR
e-mail: mark@watersidegrasmere.com
dir: M6 junct 36 then A591, past Windermere & Ambleside. Hotel on left on entering Grasmere.

The Waterside Hotel is currently closed for a multi-million pound refurbishment and redevelopment. For further details please see the AA website: theAA.com

Rooms 71 (8 fmly) **S** £50-£112; **D** £59-£120 (incl. bkfst) **Facilities** Fishing Xmas New Year Wi-fi **Conf** Class 60 Board 40 Thtr 110 **Parking** 60 **Notes** LB Civ Wed 120

HAWKSHEAD (NEAR AMBLESIDE) Map 18 SD39

Queen's Head

★★ 75% ® HOTEL

☎ 015394 36271 🖹 015394 36722
Main St LA22 0NS
e-mail: enquiries@queensheadhotel.co.uk
web: www.queensheadhotel.co.uk
dir: M6 junct 36, then A590 to Newby Bridge. Over rdbt, 1st right for 8m into Hawkshead

This 16th-century inn features a wood-panelled bar with low, oak-beamed ceilings and an open log fire. Substantial, carefully prepared meals are served in the bar and in the pretty dining room. The bedrooms, three of which are in an adjacent cottage, are attractively furnished and include some four-poster rooms.

Rooms 13 (2 annexe) (3 fmly) (2 GF) **S** £55-£60; **D** £75-£130 (incl. bkfst)* **Facilities** Xmas New Year Wi-fi **Notes** LB ⊗

See advert on this page

HOWTOWN (NEAR POOLEY BRIDGE) Map 18 NY41

INSPECTORS' CHOICE

Sharrow Bay Country House

★★★ ®® COUNTRY HOUSE HOTEL

☎ 017684 86301 🖹 017684 86349
Sharrow Bay CA10 2LZ
e-mail: info@sharrowbay.co.uk
web: www.vonessenhotels.co.uk
dir: M6 junct 40. From Pooley Bridge right fork by church towards Howtown. Right at x-rds right, follow lakeside road for 2m

Enjoying breathtaking views and an idyllic location on the shores of Lake Ullswater, Sharrow Bay is often described as the first country-house hotel. Individually styled bedrooms, all with a host of thoughtful extras, are situated either in the main house, in delightful buildings in the grounds or at Bank House - an Elizabethan farmhouse complete with lounges and breakfast room. Opulently furnished public areas include a choice of inviting lounges and two elegant dining rooms. Von Essen Hotels - AA Hotel Group of the Year 2009-10.

Rooms 24 (14 annexe) (5 GF) **Facilities** FTV Xmas New Year Wi-fi **Conf** Class 15 Board 20 Thtr 30 **Parking** 35 **Notes** ⊗ No children 10yrs Civ Wed 30

IREBY Map 18 NY23

Overwater Hall

★★★ 82% ®® COUNTRY HOUSE HOTEL

☎ 017687 76566 🖹 017687 76921
CA7 1HH
e-mail: welcome@overwaterhall.co.uk
dir: A591 take turn to Ireby at Castle Inn. Hotel signed after 2m on right.

This privately owned country house dates back to 1811 and is set in lovely gardens surrounded by woodland. The owners have lovingly restored this Georgian property over the last 16 years paying great attention to the authenticity of the original design; guests will receive warm hospitality and attentive service in a relaxed manner. The elegant and well appointed bedrooms include the more spacious Superior Rooms and the Garden Room; all bedrooms have Wi-fi. Creative dishes are served in the traditional-style dining room.

Rooms 11 (2 fmly) (1 GF) **S** £85-£175; **D** £170-£270 (incl. bkfst & dinner)* **Facilities** FTV Xmas New Year Wi-fi **Parking** 20 **Notes** LB Civ Wed 30

KENDAL Map 18 SD59

See also **Crooklands**

Best Western Castle Green Hotel in Kendal

★★★ 83% ®® HOTEL

☎ 01539 734000 🖹 01539 735522
LA9 6RG
e-mail: reception@castlegreen.co.uk
web: www.castlegreen.co.uk
dir: M6 junct 37, A684 towards Kendal. Hotel on right in 5m

This smart, modern hotel enjoys a peaceful location and is conveniently situated for access to both the town

---

centre and the M6. Stylish bedrooms are thoughtfully equipped for both the business and leisure guest. The Greenhouse Restaurant provides imaginative dishes and boasts a theatre kitchen; alternatively Alexander's pub serves food all day. The hotel has a fully equipped business centre and leisure club.

Best Western Castle Green Hotel in Kendal

Rooms 100 (3 fmly) (25 GF) **S** £79-£99; **D** £98-£138 (incl. bkfst)* **Facilities** Spa STV FTV ✪ Gym Steam room Aerobics Yoga Beauty salon ♫ Xmas New Year Wi-fi **Conf** Class 120 Board 100 Thtr 300 Del from £140 to £150* **Services** Lift **Parking** 200 **Notes** LB ⊗ Civ Wed 250

Stonecross Manor

★★★ 74% HOTEL

☎ 01539 733559 🖨 01539 736386
Milnthorpe Rd LA9 5HP
e-mail: info@stonecrossmanor.co.uk
web: www.stonecrossmanor.co.uk
dir: M6 junct 36 onto A590 and follow signs to Windermere, then take exit for Kendal South. Hotel just past 30mph sign on left

Located on the edge of Kendal, this smart hotel offers a good combination of traditional style and modern facilities. Bedrooms are comfortable, well equipped and some feature four-poster beds. Guests can relax in the lounges or bar and enjoy an extensive choice of home

cooked meals in the pleasant restaurant. Facilities also include a swimming pool and spa bath.

Stonecross Manor

Rooms 30 (4 fmly) **S** £77.50-£126.50; **D** £88-£137 (incl. bkfst)* **Facilities** FTV ✪ Xmas New Year Wi-fi **Conf** Class 80 Board 40 Thtr 140 **Services** Lift **Parking** 55 **Notes** LB Civ Wed 130

Riverside Hotel Kendal

★★★ 71% HOTEL

☎ 01539 734861 🖨 01539 734863
Beezon Rd, Stramongate Bridge LA9 6EL
e-mail: info@riversidekendal.co.uk
web: www.bestlakesbreaks.co.uk
dir: M6 junct 36 Sedburgh, Kendal 7m, left at end of Ann St, 1st right onto Beezon Rd, hotel on left

Centrally located in this market town, and enjoying a peaceful riverside location, this 17th-century former tannery provides a suitable base for both business travellers and tourists. The comfortable bedrooms are well equipped, and open-plan day rooms include the attractive restaurant and bar. Conference facilities are available, and the state-of-the-art leisure club has a heated pool, sauna, steam room, solarium and gym.

Rooms 47 (18 fmly) (10 GF) **Facilities** STV ✪ supervised Gym Xmas New Year **Conf** Class 200 Board 90 Thtr 200 **Services** Lift **Parking** 60 **Notes** LB Civ Wed 250

Travelodge Kendal

BUDGET HOTEL

☎ 0871 984 6327 🖨 01539 561018
A591, Prizet LA8 8AA
web: www.travelodge.co.uk
dir: A591 for 5m. Lodge in Prizet just outside Kendal next to BP Garage

Travelodge offers good quality, good value, budget accommodation. All offer family rooms sleeping up to four (two adults, two children) with en suite bathroom/shower-room, remote-control TV, tea- and coffee-making facilities and comfortable beds. Food options vary. Breakfast is at the on-site Bar Café restaurant (if available) or to take away. See also Hotel Groups pages.

Rooms 43 **S** fr £29; **D** fr £29

KESWICK **Map 18 NY22**

Dale Head Hall Lakeside

★★★ 78% ◉ COUNTRY HOUSE HOTEL

☎ 017687 72478
Lake Thirlmere CA12 4TN
e-mail: onthelakeside@daleheadhall.co.uk
web: www.daleheadhall.co.uk
dir: Between Keswick & Grasmere. Off A591 onto private drive

Set in attractive, tranquil grounds on the shores of Lake Thirlmere, this historic lakeside residence dates from the 16th century. Comfortable and inviting public areas include a choice of lounges and a traditionally furnished restaurant featuring a daily-changing menu. Most bedrooms are spacious and have views of the lake or surrounding mountains.

Rooms 12 (1 fmly) (2 GF) **Facilities** STV ⚓ Fishing ⚓ Fishing permit available Boating Xmas New Year Wi-fi **Conf** Class 20 Board 20 Thtr 20 **Parking** 34 **Notes** LB ⊗ Closed 3-30 Jan Civ Wed 50

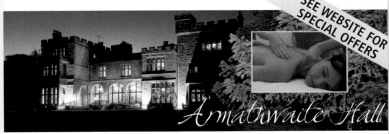

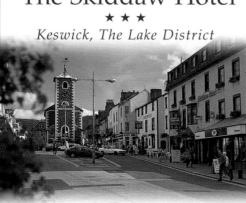

Skiddaw

★★★ 77% HOTEL

☎ 017687 72071 📄 017687 74850
Main St CA12 5BN
e-mail: info@skiddawhotel.co.uk
web: www.skiddawhotel.co.uk
dir: A66 to Keswick, follow town centre signs. Hotel in market square

Occupying a central position overlooking the market square, this hotel provides smartly furnished bedrooms that include several family suites and a room with a four-poster bed. In addition to the restaurant, food is served all day in the bar and in the conservatory bar. There is also a quiet residents' lounge and two conference rooms.

Rooms 43 (7 fmly) (3 smoking) **S** £68-£74; **D** £128-£176 (incl. bkfst)* **Facilities** STV Use of sister hotels leisure facilities (3m away) Xmas New Year Wi-fi **Conf** Class 60 Board 40 Thtr 70 Del from £90 to £180* **Services** Lift **Parking** 35 **Notes** LB Civ Wed 90

See advert on opposite page

Keswick Country House

★★★ 70% HOTEL

☎ 0845 458 4333 📄 01253 754222
Station Rd CA12 4NQ
e-mail: reservations@choice-hotels.co.uk
web: www.thekeswickhotel.co.uk
dir: M6 junct 40/A66 , 1st slip road into Keswick, then follow signs for leisure pool

This impressive Victorian hotel is set amid attractive gardens close to the town centre. Eight superior bedrooms are available in the Station Wing, which is accessed through a conservatory. The attractively appointed main house rooms are modern in style and offer a good range of amenities. Public areas include a well-stocked bar, a spacious and relaxing lounge, and a restaurant serving interesting dinners.

Rooms 74 (6 fmly) (4 GF) **S** £40-£87; **D** £80-£174 (incl. bkfst & dinner)* **Facilities** Putt green 🏊 Leisure facilities close by Xmas New Year Wi-fi **Conf** Class 70 Board 60 Thtr 110 Del from £85 to £125* **Services** Lift **Parking** 70 **Notes** LB ⊗ Civ Wed 100

Swinside Lodge

★★ 85% ⊛⊛ HOTEL

☎ 017687 72948 📄 017687 73312
Grange Rd, Newlands CA12 5UE
e-mail: info@swinsidelodge-hotel.co.uk
web: www.swinsidelodge-hotel.co.uk
dir: A66, left at Portinscale. Follow to Grange for 2m ignoring signs to Swinside & Newlands Valley

Surrounded by fells, this beautifully maintained Georgian property is situated at the foot of Cat Bells and is only a five minute stroll from the shores of Derwentwater. Guests are made to feel genuinely welcome with the friendly proprietors on hand to provide attentive service. The elegantly furnished lounges are an ideal place to relax before dinner. The four-course set dinner menu is

creative, featuring high quality ingredients and beautifully presented dishes.

Rooms 7 (7 fmly) **S** £128; **D** £196-£236 (incl. bkfst & dinner)* **Facilities** New Year Wi-fi **Parking** 12 **Notes** LB ⊗ No children 12yrs

Lairbeck

★★ 82% HOTEL

☎ 017687 73373 📄 0871 661 2552
Vicarage Hill CA12 5QB
e-mail: info@lairbeckhotel-keswick.co.uk
dir: A66 to rdbt with A591. Left then right onto Vicarage Hill, hotel 150yds on right

This fine, impeccably maintained Victorian country house is situated close to the town in peacefully secluded, attractive gardens. There is a welcoming residents' bar and a formal dining room in which a range of freshly prepared dishes are served each day. Bedrooms, which include rooms on ground floor level, are individually styled and well equipped.

Rooms 14 (1 fmly) (2 GF) **S** £52-£60.50; **D** £104-£121 (incl. bkfst)* **Facilities** FTV Wi-fi **Parking** 15 **Notes** LB ⊗ No children 5yrs

Highfield

★★ 81% ⊛⊛ SMALL HOTEL

☎ 017687 72508 📄 017687 80234
The Heads CA12 5ER
e-mail: info@highfieldkeswick.co.uk
web: www.highfieldkeswick.co.uk
dir: M6 junct 40, A66, 2nd exit at rdbt. Left to T-junct, left again. Right at mini-rdbt. Take 4th right

This friendly hotel, close to the centre of town, offers stunning views of Skiddaw, Cats Bells and Derwentwater. Elegant bedrooms, many of them spacious, are

continued

KESWICK *continued*

thoughtfully equipped. Public areas include a choice of comfortable lounges and a traditional restaurant, where imaginative, modern cuisine is served.

Rooms 18 (1 fmly) (2 GF) **S** £75; **D** £140-£170 (incl. bkfst & dinner)* **Facilities** Wi-fi **Parking** 20 **Notes** ⊗ Closed Jan

Lyzzick Hall Country House

★★ 81% ◉ COUNTRY HOUSE HOTEL

☎ 017687 72277 📄 017687 72278
Under Skiddaw CA12 4PY
e-mail: info@lyzzickhall.co.uk
web: www.lyzzickhall.co.uk
dir: M6 junct 40 onto A66 to Keswick. Do not enter town, keep on Keswick by-pass. At rdbt 3rd exit onto A591 to Carlisle. Hotel 1.5m on right

This delightful privately-owned and personally run hotel stands in lovely landscaped gardens in the foothills of Skiddaw and enjoys fabulous views across the valley. Bedrooms are smartly appointed and thoughtfully equipped. Public areas include two spacious lounges, a small bar and an attractive restaurant offering a wide range of international cuisine. Staff are delightful and nothing is too much trouble.

Rooms 31 (1 annexe) (3 fmly) (1 GF) **S** £76-£80; **D** £76-£110 (incl. bkfst & dinner)* **Facilities** ⓢ Wi-fi **Conf** Board 15 **Parking** 40 **Notes** ⊗ Closed 24-26 Dec & mid Jan-mid Feb

KIRKBY LONSDALE   Map 18 SD67

The Whoop Hall

★★ 75% HOTEL

☎ 015242 71284 📄 015242 72154
Burrow with Burrow LA6 2HP
e-mail: info@whoophall.co.uk
dir: on A65 1m SE of Kirkby Lonsdale

This popular inn combines traditional charm with modern facilities, that include a very well-equipped leisure complex. Bedrooms, some with four-poster beds, and some housed in converted barns, are appointed to a smart, stylish standard. A fire warms the bar on chillier days, and an interesting choice of dishes is available in both the bar and galleried restaurant throughout the day and evening.

Rooms 24 (4 fmly) (2 GF) **Facilities** ⓢ supervised Gym Beauty salon Pool table 🎵 Xmas **Conf** Class 72 Board 56 Thtr 169 **Parking** 100 **Notes** LB ⊗ Civ Wed 120

Hipping Hall

◉◉ RESTAURANT WITH ROOMS

☎ 015242 71187 📄 015242 72452
Cowan Bridge LA6 2JJ
e-mail: info@hippinghall.com
dir: M6 junct 36 take A65 through Kirkby Lonsdale towards Skipton. On right after Cowan Bridge

Close to the market town of Kirkby Lonsdale, Hipping Hall offers spacious feature bedrooms, designed in tranquil colours with sumptuous textures and fabrics. Bathrooms use natural stone, slate and limestone and are the perfect place to relax. The sitting room, with large, comfortable sofas, paintings and patterned wallpaper, has a traditional feel. The restaurant is a 15th-century hall with tapestries and a minstrels' gallery that is as impressive as it is intimate.

Rooms 9 (3 annexe)

LOWESWATER   Map 18 NY12

Grange Country House

★★ 69% SMALL HOTEL

☎ 01946 861211 & 861570
CA13 0SU
e-mail: info@thegrange-loweswater.co.uk
dir: Exit A5086 for Mockerkin, through village. After 2m left for Loweswater Lake. Hotel at bottom of hill on left

This delightful country hotel is set in extensive grounds in a quiet valley at the north-western end of Loweswater, and continues to prove popular with guests seeking peace and quiet. It has a friendly and relaxed atmosphere, and the cosy public areas include a small bar, a residents' lounge and an attractive dining room. The bedrooms are well equipped and comfortable, and include four-poster rooms.

Rooms 8 (2 fmly) (1 GF) **S** £50-£60; **D** £88-£120 (incl. bkfst) **Facilities** National Trust boats & fishing Xmas **Conf** Class 25 Board 25 Thtr 25 **Parking** 22 **Notes** RS Jan-Feb No credit cards

NEWBY BRIDGE   Map 18 SD38

Lakeside Hotel Lake Windermere

★★★★ 86% ◉◉ HOTEL

☎ 015395 30001 📄 015395 31699
Lakeside LA12 8AT
e-mail: sales@lakesidehotel.co.uk
web: www.lakesidehotel.co.uk
dir: M6 junct 36, A590 to Barrow, follow signs to Newby Bridge. Right over bridge, hotel 1m on right

This impressive hotel enjoys an enviable location on the southern edge of Lake Windermere and has easy access to the Lakeside & Haverthwaite Steam Railway and ferry terminal. Bedrooms are individually styled and many enjoy delightful lake views. Spacious lounges and a choice of restaurants are available. The state-of-the-art spa is exclusive to residents and provides a range of

treatment suites. Staff throughout are friendly and nothing is too much trouble.

Lakeside Hotel Lake Windermere

Rooms 75 (8 fmly) (8 GF) **S** £120-£390; **D** £140-£425 (incl. bkfst)* **Facilities** Spa STV ⓢ Fishing Gym Private jetty Rowing boats 🎵 Xmas New Year Wi-fi **Conf** Class 50 Board 40 Thtr 100 Del from £140 to £275* **Services** Lift **Parking** 200 **Notes** LB ⊗ Civ Wed 80

Whitewater

★★★ 75% HOTEL

☎ 015395 31133 📄 015395 31881
The Lakeland Village LA12 8PX
e-mail: enquiries@whitewater-hotel.co.uk
web: www.whitewater-hotel.co.uk
dir: M6 junct 36 follow signs for A590 Barrow, 1m through Newby Bridge. Right at sign for Lakeland Village, hotel on left

This tasteful conversion of an old mill on the River Leven is close to the southern end of Lake Windermere. Bedrooms, many with lovely river views, are spacious and comfortable. Public areas include a luxurious, well-equipped spa, squash courts, and a choice of comfortable lounges. The Dolly Blue bar overlooks the river and is a vibrant informal alternative to the fine dining restaurant.

Rooms 35 (10 fmly) (2 GF) **Facilities** Spa STV ⓢ supervised ⚲ Putt green Gym Squash Beauty treatment Table tennis Steam room Golf driving range Xmas New Year Wi-fi **Conf** Class 32 Board 40 Thtr 80 **Services** Lift **Parking** 50 **Notes** LB ⊗ Civ Wed 110

Swan

[U]

☎ 015395 31681   📄 015395 31917
LA12 8NB
e-mail: enquiries@swanhotel.com
web: www.swanhotel.com
dir: M6 junct 36 follow A590 signed Barrow for 16m.
Hotel on right of old 5-arch bridge, at Newby Bridge

Currently the rating for this establishment is not confirmed. This may be due to a change of ownership or because it has only recently joined the AA rating scheme. For further details please see the AA website: theAA.com

Rooms 55 (4 fmly) (14 GF) **Facilities** 🏊 Fishing Gym Steam Room Xmas **Conf** Class 40 Board 40 Thtr 120 **Services** Lift **Parking** 100 **Notes** LB ⊗ Civ Wed 80

See advert on this page

PATTERDALE   Map 18 NY31

Patterdale

★★ 68% HOTEL

☎ 0845 458 4333 & 017684 82231   📄 01253 754222
CA11 0NN
e-mail: reservations@choice-hotels.co.uk
dir: M6 junct 40, A592 towards Ullswater. 10m along Lakeside Rd to Patterdale

Patterdale is a real tourist destination and this hotel makes a good base for those taking part in the many activity pursuits available in this area. The hotel enjoys delightful views of the valley and fells, being located at the southern end of Ullswater. The modern bedrooms vary in style. In busier periods accommodation is let for a minimum period of two nights.

Rooms 57 (16 fmly) (6 GF) **S** £33-£58; **D** £66-£112 (incl. bkfst & dinner)* **Facilities** 🚲 Free bike hire 🎵 Xmas New Year Wi-fi **Services** Lift **Parking** 30 **Notes** LB ⊗

PENRITH   Map 18 NY53
See also **Glenridding and Shap**

North Lakes Hotel & Spa

shire
hotels & spas

★★★★ 79% ⊛ HOTEL

☎ 01768 868111   📄 01768 868291
Ullswater Rd CA11 8QT
e-mail: nlakes@shirehotels.com
web: www.northlakeshotel.com
dir: M6 junct 40 at junct with A66

With a great location, it's no wonder that this modern hotel is perpetually busy. Amenities include a good range of meeting and function rooms and excellent health and leisure facilities including a full spa. Themed public areas have a contemporary, Scandinavian country style and offer plenty of space and comfort. High standards of service are provided by a friendly team of staff.

continued

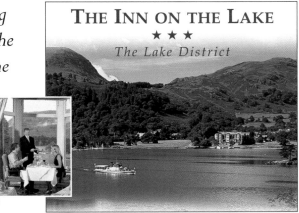

PENRITH *continued*

Rooms 84 (6 fmly) (22 GF) **Facilities** Spa STV 🔲 Gym Children's splash pool Steam room Activity & wellness studios Sauna Xmas New Year Wi-fi **Conf** Class 140 Board 30 Thtr 200 **Services** Lift **Parking** 150 **Notes** ⊗ Civ Wed 200

Temple Sowerby House Hotel & Restaurant

★★★ 86% ◉◉ HOTEL

☎ 017683 61578 📠 017683 61958
CA10 1RZ
e-mail: stay@templesowerby.com
web: www.templesowerby.com

(For full entry see Temple Sowerby)

Westmorland Hotel

★★★ 81% ◉ HOTEL

☎ 015396 24351 📠 015396 24354
Westmorland Place, Orton CA10 3SB
e-mail: reservations@westmorlandhotel.com
web: www.westmorlandhotel.com

(For full entry see Tebay)

George

★★★ 75% HOTEL

☎ 01768 862696 📠 01768 868223
Devonshire St CA11 7SU
e-mail: georgehotel@lakedistricthotels.net
dir: M6 junct 40, 1m to town centre. From A6/A66 to Penrith

This inviting and popular hotel dates back to a time when 'Bonnie' Prince Charlie made a visit. Extended over the years this town centre hotel offers well equipped

bedrooms. The spacious public areas retain a timeless charm and include a choice of lounge areas, popular venues for morning coffees and afternoon teas.

George

Rooms 35 (4 fmly) **Facilities** Xmas New Year Wi-fi **Conf** Class 80 Board 50 Thtr 120 **Parking** 40 **Notes** Civ Wed 120

See advert on this page

Edenhall Country Hotel

★★ 71% HOTEL

☎ 01768 881454 📠 01768 881266
Edenhall CA11 8SX
e-mail: info@edenhallhotel.co.uk
dir: Take A686 from Penrith to Alston. Hotel signed on right in 3m

This hotel has undergone refurbishment but continues to convey a very relaxed atmosphere. Located in a peaceful hamlet yet convenient for the M6, it is popular with both leisure and business guests. Carefully prepared meals are now served in the comfortable lounge bar and in the dining room overlooking the attractive gardens. The friendly staff provide attentive service.

Rooms 18 (1 annexe) (3 fmly) (1 GF) **S** £45-£65.50; **D** £70-£92.50 (incl. bkfst)* **Facilities** STV 🔄 Xmas New Year Wi-fi **Conf** Class 30 Board 30 Thtr 50 **Parking** 60 **Notes** ⊗ Civ Wed 60

Travelodge Penrith

BUDGET HOTEL

☎ 0871 984 6299 📠 01768 866958
Redhills CA11 0DT
web: www.travelodge.co.uk
dir: M6 junct 40, A66. Lodge in 0.25m

Travelodge offers good quality, good value, budget accommodation. All offer family rooms sleeping up to four (two adults, two children) with en suite bathroom/shower-room, remote-control TV, tea- and coffee-making facilities and comfortable beds. Food options vary. Breakfast is at the on-site Bar Café restaurant (if available) or to take away. See also Hotel Groups pages.

Rooms 54 **S** fr £29; **D** fr £29

RAVENGLASS	**Map 18 SD09**

Pennington

★★★ 79% HOTEL

☎ 01229 717222 & 717626
CA18 1SD
dir: In village centre

This hotel has a very relaxed atmosphere throughout and the public areas are open plan with high quality fabrics and artwork. The bedrooms are modern in design and have high spec fixtures and fittings in the bathrooms. Honest cooking, based on local and fine quality ingredients, is offered on the seasonal menus. Staff show exceptional customer awareness by providing very attentive and friendly service.

Rooms 29 (12 annexe) (6 fmly) **Parking** 53

RAVENSTONEDALE — Map 18 NY70

The Fat Lamb

★★ 69% HOTEL

☎ 015396 23242 📄 015396 23285
Crossbank CA17 4LL
e-mail: fatlamb@cumbria.com
dir: On A683, between Kirkby Stephen & Sedbergh

Open fires and solid stone walls feature at this 17th-century inn, set on its own nature reserve. There is a choice of dining options with an extensive menu available in the traditional bar and a more formal dining experience in the restaurant. Bedrooms are bright and cheerful, and include family rooms and easily accessible rooms for guests with limited mobility.

Rooms 12 (4 fmly) (5 GF) **S** £50-£56; **D** £84-£92 (incl. bkfst) **Facilities** Private 5-acre nature reserve Xmas Wi-fi **Conf** Class 30 Board 30 Thtr 60 **Parking** 60 **Notes** LB

ROSTHWAITE — Map 18 NY21

See also **Borrowdale**

Scafell

★★★ 63% HOTEL

☎ 017687 77208 📄 017687 77280
CA12 5XB
e-mail: info@scafell.co.uk
web: www.scafell.co.uk
dir: M6 junct 40 to Keswick on A66. Take B5289 to Rosthwaite

This friendly hotel has long been popular with walkers and enjoys a peaceful location. Bedrooms vary in style from traditional to modern, but are all well equipped and neatly decorated. Public areas include a residents' cocktail bar, lounge and spacious restaurant as well as the popular Riverside Inn pub, offering all-day dining in summer months.

Rooms 23 (2 fmly) (8 GF) **S** £49.95-£87.50; **D** £99.90-£175 (incl. bkfst & dinner)* **Facilities** FTV Guided walks Xmas New Year **Parking** 50 **Notes** LB Civ Wed 75

Royal Oak

★ 72% SMALL HOTEL

☎ 017687 77214 & 77695
CA12 5XB
e-mail: info@royaloakhotel.co.uk
web: www.royaloakhotel.co.uk
dir: 6m S of Keswick on B5289 in centre of Rosthwaite

Set in a village in one of Lakeland's most picturesque valleys, this family-run hotel offers friendly and obliging service. There is a variety of accommodation styles, with particularly impressive rooms being located in a converted barn across the courtyard and backing onto a stream; family rooms are available. The cosy bar is for residents and diners only, and a set home-cooked dinner is served at 7pm.

Rooms 12 (4 annexe) (5 fmly) (4 GF) **S** £35-£58; **D** £72-£96 (incl. bkfst)* **Parking** 15 **Notes** LB Closed 4-21 Jan & 5-28 Dec

SEASCALE — Map 18 NY00

Cumbrian Lodge

RESTAURANT WITH ROOMS

☎ 019467 27309 📄 019467 27158
Gosforth Rd CA20 1JG
e-mail: cumbrianlodge@btconnect.com
web: www.cumbrianlodge.com
dir: Off A595 at Gosforth onto B5344 signed Seascale, 2m on left

A relaxed and friendly atmosphere prevails at this well-run restaurant with rooms, where tasty, well-prepared dinners prove popular locally. The decor and fixtures are modern throughout, and the bedrooms are well-equipped for both business and leisure guests. The thatched garden buildings provide a delightful opportunity for dining alfresco under canvas panels, for up to 12 diners.

Rooms 6 (1 fmly)

SHAP — Map 18 NY51

Best Western Shap Wells

★★★ 74% HOTEL

☎ 01931 716628 📄 01931 716377
CA10 3QU
e-mail: manager@shapwells.com
dir: Between A6 and B6261, 4m S of Shap

This hotel occupies a wonderful secluded position amid trees and waterfalls. Extensive public areas include function and meeting rooms, a well-stocked bar, a choice of lounges and a spacious restaurant. Bedrooms vary in size and style but all are equipped with the expected facilities.

Rooms 98 (7 annexe) (10 fmly) (10 GF) **S** £50-£75; **D** £60-£116 (incl. bkfst) **Facilities** FTV Games room Cardio vascular gym Xmas New Year Wi-fi **Conf** Class 80 Board 40 Thtr 170 Del from £95 **Services** Lift **Parking** 200 **Notes** LB ⊗ Civ Wed 150

SILLOTH — Map 18 NY15

Golf Hotel

★★ 68% HOTEL

☎ 016973 31438 📄 016973 32582
Criffel St CA7 4AB
e-mail: golf.hotel@virgin.net

A friendly welcome waits at this newly refurbished hotel which occupies a prime position in the centre of the historic market town; it is a popular meeting place for the local community. Bedrooms are mostly well proportioned and are comfortably equipped. The lounge bar is a popular venue for dining, with a wide range of dishes on offer.

Rooms 22 (4 fmly) (22 smoking) **S** £35-£50; **D** £70-£90 (incl. bkfst)* **Facilities** Snooker & Games room **Conf** Class 50 Board 30 Thtr 100 **Notes** LB Closed 24-26 Dec

SOUTHWAITE MOTORWAY SERVICE AREA (M6) — Map 18 NY44

Travelodge Carlisle (M6)

BUDGET HOTEL

☎ 0871 984 6128 📄 016974 75354
Broadfield Site CA4 0NT
web: www.travelodge.co.uk
dir: M6, between juncts 41 & 42 S'bound. Access possible from N'bound carriageway

Travelodge offers good quality, good value, budget accommodation. All offer family rooms sleeping up to four (two adults, two children) with en suite bathroom/shower-room, remote-control TV, tea- and coffee-making facilities and comfortable beds. Food options vary. Breakfast is at the on-site Bar Café restaurant (if available) or to take away. See also Hotel Groups pages.

Rooms 53 **S** fr £29; **D** fr £29

TEBAY · Map 18 NY60

Westmorland Hotel

★★★ 81% ⊛ HOTEL

☎ 015396 24351 · 📄 015396 24354
Westmorland Place, Orton CA10 3SB
e-mail: reservations@westmorlandhotel.com
web: www.westmorlandhotel.com
dir: Signed from Westmorland Services between M6
junct 38 & 39 north & southbound

With fine views over rugged moorland, this modern and
friendly hotel is ideal for conferences and meetings.
Bedrooms are spacious and comfortable, with the
executive rooms particularly well equipped. Open-plan
public areas provide a Tyrolean touch and include a split-
level restaurant.

Rooms 51 (5 fmly) (12 GF) **S** £82-£110; **D** £98-£120 (incl.
bkfst)* **Facilities** FTV Xmas New Year Wi-fi **Conf** Class 24
Board 30 Thtr 120 Del from £120 to £127* **Services** Lift
Parking 60 **Notes** LB RS 1 Jan Civ Wed 120

TEMPLE SOWERBY · Map 18 NY62

Temple Sowerby House Hotel & Restaurant

★★★ 86% ⊛⊛ HOTEL

☎ 017683 61578 · 📄 017683 61958
CA10 1RZ
e-mail: stay@templesowerby.com
web: www.templesowerby.com
dir: 7m from M6 junct 40, midway between Penrith &
Appleby, in village centre

The hotel is set in the heart of the Eden Valley, ideal for
exploring the northern Lake District and Pennine Fells.
Bedrooms are comfortable and stylish, most featuring
ultra-modern bathrooms, and there is a choice of
pleasant lounges. The restaurant, with picture windows
overlooking the beautiful walled garden, is a splendid
place to enjoy the award-winning cuisine. Staff
throughout are friendly and keen to please.

Rooms 12 (4 annexe) (2 GF) **S** £90-£120; **D** £120-£175
(incl. bkfst) **Facilities** FTV ⛵ New Year Wi-fi
Conf Class 20 Board 20 Thtr 30 Del from £140 to £160
Parking 15 **Notes** LB ⊗ No children 12yrs Closed 20-29
Dec Civ Wed 40

ULLSWATER

See Glenridding & Patterdale

WATERMILLOCK · Map 18 NY42

Macdonald Leeming House

★★★★ 76% ⊛ HOTEL

☎ 0844 879 9142 · 📄 015394 43432
CA11 0JJ
e-mail: sales/oldengland@macdonald-hotels.co.uk
web: www.macdonald-hotels.co.uk
dir: M6 junct 40, A66 to Keswick. At rdbt A592
(Ullswater). 5m to T-junct, right (A592). Hotel on left in
3m

This hotel enjoys a superb location, being set in 20 acres
of mature wooded gardens in the Lake District National
Park, and overlooking Ullswater and the towering fells.
Many rooms offer views of the lake and the rugged fells
beyond, with more than half having their own balcony.
Public rooms include three sumptuous lounges, a cosy
bar and library.

Rooms 41 (1 fmly) (10 GF) **Facilities** Fishing ⛵ Xmas
New Year **Conf** Class 40 Board 30 Thtr 80 **Parking** 50
Notes Civ Wed 80

Rampsbeck Country House

★★★ ⊛⊛⊛ HOTEL

☎ 017684 86442 · 📄 017684 86688
CA11 0LP
e-mail: enquiries@rampsbeck.co.uk
web: www.rampsbeck.co.uk
dir: M6 junct 40, A592 to Ullswater, at T-junct (with
lake in front) turn right, hotel 1.5m

This fine country house lies in 18 acres of parkland on
the shores of Lake Ullswater, and is furnished with
many period and antique pieces. There are three
delightful lounges, an elegant restaurant and a
traditional bar. Bedrooms come in three grades; the
most spacious rooms are spectacular and overlook the
lake. Service is attentive and the cuisine a real
highlight.

Rooms 19 (1 fmly) (1 GF) **S** £95-£270; **D** £140-£290
(incl. bkfst)* **Facilities** STV FTV Putt green ⛵ Xmas
New Year Wi-fi **Conf** Class 10 Board 15 Thtr 15
Del from £155 to £255* **Parking** 25 **Notes** LB Closed
4-27 Jan Civ Wed 65

WINDERMERE · Map 18 SD49

Gilpin Lodge Country House Hotel & Restaurant

★★★★ ⊛⊛⊛ HOTEL

☎ 015394 88818 · 📄 015394 88058
Crook Rd LA23 3NE
e-mail: hotel@gilpinlodge.co.uk
web: www.gilpinlodge.co.uk
dir: M6 junct 36, take A590/A591 to rdbt north of
Kendal, take B5284, hotel 5m on right

This smart Victorian residence is set amidst delightful
gardens leading to the fells, and is just a short drive
from the lake. The individually designed bedrooms are
stylish and a number benefit from private terraces; all
are spacious and thoughtfully equipped, and each has
a private sitting room. In addition there are luxury
Garden Suites that lead out onto private gardens with
cedar wood hot tubs. The welcoming atmosphere is
notable and the attractive day rooms are perfect for
relaxing, perhaps beside a real fire. Food is placed high
on the agenda here and the new head chef seeks out
the finest, and mostly organic, local produce for his
award-winning modern British menus.

Rooms 20 (6 annexe) (11 GF) **S** £180; **D** £290-£440
(incl. bkfst & dinner)* **Facilities** ⛵ Free membership
at local Leisure Club In-room spa treatment Xmas New
Year Wi-fi **Parking** 40 **Notes** LB ⊗ No children 7yrs

See advert on opposite page

GILPIN

RELAIS & CHATEAUX

★★★★

In the heart of the Lake District, this family run Relais & Châteaux hotel is stylish, warm and comfortable with a touch of home. The cuisine (3 AA rosettes) is modern English with an emphasis on the finest fresh seasonal ingredients (much from within the National Park), beautifully presented without unnecessary fuss.

The sumptuous bedrooms have crisp white linen, luxurious bathrooms, gorgeous fabrics, wonderful upholstery, delicious art, and each of the Garden Suites has its own garden complete with cedarwood hot tub. Relaxed and unhurried, there are no weddings, conferences or children under the age of seven to disturb the peace, just warm smiles, fresh flowers, real fires and friendly, unpretentious service. This is the art of relaxation – perfected.

GILPIN LODGE, CROOK ROAD, NEAR WINDERMERE, THE ENGLISH LAKE DISTRICT, LA23 3NE
WWW.GILPINLODGE.CO.UK   EMAIL: HOTEL@GILPINLODGE.CO.UK   TEL: 015394 88818   FAX: 015394 88058
2 MILES FROM LAKE WINDERMERE, 12 MILES FROM THE M6 (J36), AND ALMOST OPPOSITE WINDERMERE GOLF COURSE.

WINDERMERE *continued*

Holbeck Ghyll Country House

★★★★ ◉◉◉ COUNTRY HOUSE HOTEL

☎ 015394 32375 ◎ 015394 34743
Holbeck Ln LA23 1LU
e-mail: stay@holbeckghyll.com
dir: 3m N of Windermere on A591, right into Holbeck Lane (signed Troutbeck), hotel 0.5m on left

With a peaceful setting in extensive grounds, this beautifully maintained hotel enjoys breathtaking views over Lake Windermere and the Langdale Fells. Public rooms include luxurious, comfortable lounges and two elegant dining rooms, where memorable meals are served. Bedrooms are individually styled, beautifully furnished and many have balconies or patios. Some in an adjacent, more private lodge are less traditional in design and have superb views. The professionalism and attentiveness of the staff is exemplary.

Rooms 33 (19 annexe) (4 fmly) (14 GF) **S** £175-£325; **D** £240-£580 (incl. bkfst & dinner) **Facilities** Spa STV ⛳ Putt green ⤴ Gym Sauna Steam room Treatment rooms Beauty massage Xmas New Year Wi-fi **Conf** Class 25 Board 20 Thtr 45 **Parking** 34 **Notes** LB Civ Wed 65

Macdonald Old England

★★★★ 84% ◉◉ HOTEL

☎ 0844 879 9144 ◎ 015394 43432
Church St, Bowness LA23 3DF
e-mail: sales.oldengland@macdonald-hotels.co.uk
web: www.macdonaldhotels.co.uk
dir: Through Windermere to Bowness, straight across at mini-rdbt . Hotel behind church on right

This hotel stands right on the shore of England's largest lake and boasts superb views. It is currently undergoing a significant refurbishment to upgrade all its accommodation and public areas.

Rooms 106 (3 fmly) (14 GF) **S** £96-£200; **D** £106-£210 (incl. bkfst) **Facilities** Spa STV ⓣ supervised Gym Private jetties Rock sauna Aromatherapy shower Steam room Ice room ♫ Xmas New Year Wi-fi **Conf** Class 60 Board 25 Thtr 100 Del from £150 to £170 **Services** Lift **Parking** 90 **Notes** LB ⊗ Civ Wed 100

Lindeth Howe Country House Hotel & Restaurant

★★★★ 78% ◉◉ COUNTRY HOUSE HOTEL

☎ 015394 45759 ◎ 015394 46368
Lindeth Dr, Longtail Hill LA23 3JF
e-mail: hotel@lindeth-howe.co.uk
web: www.lindeth-howe.co.uk
dir: Turn off A592, 1m S of Bowness onto B5284 (Longtail Hill) signed Kendal & Lancaster, hotel last driveway on right

Historic photographs commemorate the fact that this delightful house was once the family home of Beatrix Potter. Secluded in landscaped grounds, it enjoys views across the valley and Lake Windermere. Public rooms are plentiful and inviting, with the restaurant being the perfect setting for modern country-house cooking. Deluxe and superior bedrooms are spacious and smartly appointed.

Rooms 34 (3 fmly) (2 GF) **S** £65-£85; **D** £180-£250 (incl. bkfst)* **Facilities** STV ⓣ Gym Sauna Fitness room Xmas New Year Wi-fi **Conf** Class 20 Board 18 Thtr 30 Del from £140* **Parking** 50 **Notes** LB ⊗

Storrs Hall

★★★★ 76% ◉◉ HOTEL

☎ 015394 47111 ◎ 015394 47555
Storrs Park LA23 3LG
e-mail: storrshall@elhmail.co.uk
web: www.elh.co.uk/hotels/storrshall
dir: on A592, 2m S of Bowness, on Newby Bridge road

Set in 17 acres of landscaped grounds by the lakeside, this imposing Georgian mansion is delightful. There are numerous lounges to relax in, furnished with fine art and antiques. Individually styled bedrooms are generally spacious and boast impressive bathrooms. Imaginative cuisine is served in the elegant restaurant, which offers fine views across the lawn to the lake and fells beyond.

Rooms 30 **Facilities** FTV Fishing ⤴ Use of nearby sports/beauty facilities Xmas New Year Wi-fi **Conf** Class 35 Board 24 Thtr 50 **Parking** 50 **Notes** LB No children 12yrs Civ Wed 94

Low Wood

★★★★ 75% HOTEL

☎ 015394 33338 & 0845 850 3502 ◎ 015394 34275
LA23 1LP
e-mail: lowwood@elhmail.co.uk
dir: M6 junct 36, follow A590 then A591 to Windermere, then 3m towards Ambleside, hotel on right

Benefiting from a lakeside location, this hotel offers an excellent range of leisure and conference facilities. Bedrooms, many with panoramic lake views, are attractively furnished, and include a number of larger executive rooms and suites. There is a choice of bars, a spacious restaurant and the more informal Café del Lago. The poolside bar offers internet and e-mail access.

Rooms 111 (13 fmly) **S** £79-£150; **D** £96-£264 (incl. bkfst) **Facilities** ⓣ supervised Fishing Gym Squash Water skiing Canoeing Beauty salon Bungy trampoline Wall climbing Marina Xmas New Year Wi-fi **Conf** Class 180 Board 150 Thtr 340 **Services** Lift **Parking** 200 **Notes** LB Civ Wed 300

See advert on opposite page

The Samling
★★★ ◉◉◉ HOTEL

☎ 015394 31922 🖷 015394 30400
Ambleside Rd LA23 1LR
e-mail: info@thesamling.com
web: www.thesamling.com
dir: Turn right off A591, 300mtrs after Low Wood Hotel

This stylish house, built in the late 1700s, is situated in 67 acres of grounds and enjoys an elevated position overlooking Lake Windermere. The spacious, beautifully furnished bedrooms and suites, some in adjacent buildings, are thoughtfully equipped and all have superb bathrooms. Public rooms include a sumptuous drawing room, a small library and an elegant dining room where imaginative, skilfully prepared food is served. Von Essen - AA Hotel Group of the Year 2009-10.

Rooms 11 (6 annexe) (2 GF) **Facilities** STV Xmas New Year **Conf** Board 12 **Parking** 15 **Notes** LB ⊗ Civ Wed 50

Linthwaite House Hotel & Restaurant
★★★ ◉◉ COUNTRY HOUSE HOTEL

☎ 015394 88600 🖷 015394 88601
Crook Rd LA23 3JA
e-mail: stay@linthwaite.com
web: www.linthwaite.com
dir: A591 towards The Lakes for 8m to large rdbt, take 1st exit (B5284), 6m, hotel on left. 1m past Windermere golf club

Linthwaite House is set in 14 acres of hilltop grounds and enjoys stunning views over Lake Windermere. Inviting public rooms include an attractive conservatory and adjoining lounge and an elegant restaurant. Bedrooms, which are individually decorated, combine contemporary furnishings with classical styles; all are thoughtfully equipped and include CD players. Service and hospitality are attentive and friendly.

Rooms 32 (1 fmly) (7 GF) **S** £138-£163; **D** £204-£348 (incl. bkfst & dinner)* **Facilities** STV Putt green Fishing ⬥ Beauty treatments Massage Xmas New Year Wi-fi **Conf** Class 19 Board 25 Thtr 40 Del from £150 to £348* **Parking** 40 **Notes** LB ⊗ Civ Wed 64

Miller Howe
★★★ 86% ◉◉ COUNTRY HOUSE HOTEL

☎ 015394 42536 🖷 015394 45664
Rayrigg Rd LA23 1EY
e-mail: info@millerhowe.com
dir: M6 junct 36 follow A591 past Windermere village, left at rdbt towards Bowness

This long established hotel of much character enjoys a lakeside setting amidst delightful landscaped gardens. The bright and welcoming day rooms include sumptuous lounges, a conservatory and an opulently decorated restaurant. Imaginative dinners make use of fresh, local produce where possible and there is an extensive, well-balanced wine list. Stylish bedrooms, many with fabulous lake views, include well-equipped cottage rooms and a number with whirlpool baths.

Rooms 15 (3 annexe) (1 GF) **S** £90-£150; **D** £180-£300 (incl. bkfst & dinner)* **Facilities** Xmas New Year Wi-fi **Parking** 35 **Notes** LB Civ Wed 75

Fayrer Garden Hotel
★★★ 83% ◉◉ HOTEL

☎ 015394 88195 🖷 015394 45986
Lyth Valley Rd, Bowness-on-Windermere LA23 3JP
e-mail: lakescene@fayrergarden.com
web: www.fayrergarden.com
dir: on A5074, 1m from Bowness Bay

Sitting in lovely landscaped gardens, this elegant hotel enjoys spectacular views over the lake. The comfortably appointed bedrooms come in a variety of styles and sizes, some with bathrooms of a high specification. There is a choice of lounges and a stylish, conservatory restaurant. The attentive, hospitable staff ensure a relaxing stay.

continued

WINDERMERE *continued*

Fayrer Garden Hotel

Rooms 29 (5 annexe) (10 GF) **Facilities** FTV Free membership of leisure club Xmas New Year Wi-fi **Parking** 40 **Notes** LB No children 5yrs Civ Wed 60

Lindeth Fell Country House Hotel

★★★ 83% ⚜ COUNTRY HOUSE HOTEL

☎ 015394 43286 & 44287 📄 015394 47455
Lyth Valley Rd, Bowness-on-Windermere LA23 3JP
e-mail: kennedy@lindethfell.co.uk
web: www.lindethfell.co.uk
dir: 1m S of Bowness on A5074

Enjoying delightful views, this smart Edwardian residence stands in seven acres of glorious, landscaped gardens. Bedrooms, which vary in size and style, are comfortably equipped. Skilfully prepared dinners are served in the spacious dining room that commands fine views. The resident owners and their attentive, friendly staff provide high levels of hospitality and service.

Rooms 14 (2 fmly) (1 GF) **S** £50-£70; **D** £100-£170 (incl. bkfst)* **Facilities** Putt green Fishing ⛵ Bowling Xmas New Year Wi-fi **Conf** Class 12 Board 12 Del from £99.50 to £147* **Parking** 20 **Notes** LB ⊗ Closed 3-29 Jan

Beech Hill

★★★ 81% ⚜⚜ HOTEL

RICHARDSON

☎ 015394 42137 📄 015394 43745
Newby Bridge Rd LA23 3LR
e-mail: reservations@beechhillhotel.co.uk
web: www.beechhillhotel.co.uk
dir: M6 junct 36, A591 to Windermere. Left onto A592 towards Newby Bridge. Hotel 4m from Bowness-on-Windermere

This stylish, terraced hotel is set on high ground leading to the shore of Lake Windermere and has a spacious, open-plan lounge which, like the restaurant, affords splendid views across the lake. Bedrooms come in a range of styles; some have four-poster beds, and all are well equipped. Leisure facilities and a choice of conference rooms complete the package.

Rooms 57 (4 fmly) (4 GF) **S** £69-£89; **D** £118-£228 (incl. bkfst)* **Facilities** FTV ⊗ Fishing ♪ Xmas New Year Wi-fi **Parking** 70 **Notes** LB Civ Wed 130

See advert on this page

Burn How Garden House Hotel

★★★ 80% ⚜ HOTEL

☎ 015394 46226 📄 015394 47000
Back Belsfield Rd, Bowness LA23 3HH
e-mail: info@burnhow.co.uk
web: www.burnhow.co.uk
dir: Exit A591 at Windermere, following signs to Bowness. Pass Lake Piers on right, take 1st left to hotel entrance

Set in its own leafy grounds, this hotel is only a few minutes' walk from both the lake and the town centre. Attractive, spacious rooms, some with four-poster beds, are situated in modern chalets or in an adjacent Victorian house; many have private patios or terraces. Guests can

enjoy creative meals in the stylish dining room, or just relax in the comfortable open-plan lounge areas.

Rooms 28 (28 annexe) (10 fmly) (6 GF) **S** £60-£95; **D** £95-£145 (incl. bkfst) **Facilities** New Year Wi-fi **Parking** 30 **Notes** LB ⊗ Closed 19-27 Dec & 4-11 Jan

Famous Wild Boar Hotel

★★★ 79% HOTEL

☎ 015394 45225 📄 015394 42498
Crook LA23 3NF
e-mail: wildboar@elhmail.co.uk
dir: 2.5m S of Windermere on B5284. From Crook 3.5m, hotel on right

This historic former coaching inn enjoys a peaceful rural location close to Windermere. Public areas include a welcoming lounge, a cosy bar where an extensive range of wines is served by the glass, and a character restaurant serving wholesome food. Bedrooms, some with four-poster beds, vary in style and size.

Rooms 36 (3 fmly) (9 GF) **S** £59-£123; **D** £68-£196 (incl. bkfst)* **Facilities** STV Use of sports/beauty facilities at sister hotel Xmas New Year **Conf** Class 20 Board 26 Thtr 40 Del from £74 to £110* **Parking** 60 **Notes** LB Civ Wed 60

Windermere Manor Hotel

★★★ 78% HOTEL

☎ 01539 445801 ◾ 01539 448397
Rayrigg Rd LA23 1ES
e-mail: windermere@actionforblindpeople.org.uk
dir: A591 towards Ambleside. At mini-rdbt turn left, hotel
1st on left

Set above the shores of Lake Windermere in wooded
landscaped gardens, this former manor house has been
restored to its original splendour. The bedrooms and
suites are smart and well appointed. The attractive
dining room has an unusual barrel-vaulted wooden roof
and serves delicious home cooking. Special facilities for
guide dogs are available.

Rooms 28 (2 fmly) (5 GF) **S** £46-£90; **D** £92-£180 (incl.
bkfst & dinner)* **Facilities** FTV ⊙ supervised Gym ♫
Xmas New Year **Conf** Class 30 Board 15 Thtr 40
Del from £62 to £90* **Services** Lift **Parking** 28 **Notes** LB
Closed 2-22 Jan

The Belsfield Hotel

corus
hotels

★★★ 68% HOTEL

☎ 0844 736 8604 & 015394 42448 ◾ 015394 46397
Kendal Rd, Bowness LA23 3EL
e-mail: belsfield@corushotels.com
web: www.corushotels.com
dir: In Bowness take 1st left after mini-rdbt

This hotel stands in six acres of gardens and has one of
the best locations in the area. Views from public areas
are outstanding. Bedrooms are generally spacious and
well equipped, and come in a variety of styles. Main
meals are taken in the spacious dining room overlooking
the lake.

Rooms 64 (6 fmly) (6 GF) **S** fr £73; **D** fr £125 (incl. bkfst)*
Facilities ⊙ Mini golf - Pitch & Putt 9 holes Xmas New
Year Wi-fi **Conf** Class 60 Board 50 Thtr 130 Del from £135
to £140* **Services** Lift **Parking** 64 **Notes** LB ⊗
Civ Wed 100

Cedar Manor Hotel & Restaurant

★★ 83% ⊛ HOTEL

☎ 015394 43192 & 45970 ◾ 015394 45970
Ambleside Rd LA23 1AX
e-mail: info@cedarmanor.co.uk
dir: From A591 follow signs to Windermere. Hotel on left
just beyond St Mary's Church at bottom of hill

Built in 1854 as a country retreat this lovely old house
enjoys a peaceful location that is within easy walking
distance of the town centre. Bedrooms, some on the
ground floor, are attractive and well equipped, with two
bedrooms in the adjacent coach house. There is a
comfortable lounge bar where guests can relax before
enjoying dinner in the well-appointed dining room.

Cedar Manor Hotel & Restaurant

Rooms 11 (2 annexe) (2 fmly) (3 GF) **S** £63-£75;
D £90-£150 (incl. bkfst)* **Facilities** FTV New Year Wi-fi
Parking 11 **Notes** LB Closed 3-21 Jan

Jerichos at The Waverley

⊛⊛ RESTAURANT WITH ROOMS

☎ 015394 42522 ◾ 015394 88899
College Rd LA23 1BX
e-mail: info@jerichos.co.uk
dir: A591 to Windermere, 2nd left onto Elleray Rd then 1st
right onto College Rd

Dating back to around 1870, this centrally located
property has been lovingly restored by its current owners
over the last twelve years. All the elegantly furnished
bedrooms are en suite and the top floor rooms have views
of the fells. Breakfast is served in the Restaurant Room,
and the comfortable lounge has a real fire to relax by on
chillier days. The chef/proprietor has established a strong
reputation for his creative menus that use the best local
and seasonal produce. The restaurant is always busy so
booking is essential. Wi-fi is available.

Rooms 10 (1 fmly)

The Hideaway at Windermere

⊛ RESTAURANT WITH ROOMS

☎ 015394 43070
Phoenix Way LA23 1DB
e-mail: eatandstay@thehideawayatwindermere.co.uk
web: www.thehideawayatwindermere.co.uk
dir: Exit A591 at Ravensworth B&B, onto Phoenix Way,
The Hideaway 100mtrs on right

Tucked away quietly this beautiful Victorian Lakeland
house is personally run by owners Richard and Lisa.
Delicious food, individually designed bedrooms and warm
hospitality ensure an enjoyable stay. There is a beautifully
appointed lounge looking out to the garden and the
restaurant is split between two light and airy rooms; here
guests will find the emphasis is on fresh, local
ingredients and attentive, yet friendly service. Bedrooms
vary in size and style, with the largest featuring luxury
bathrooms.

Rooms 11 (1 annexe)

Washington Central

★★★ 83% HOTEL

☎ 01900 65772 ◾ 01900 68770
Washington St CA14 3AY
e-mail: kawildwchotel@aol.com
web: www.washingtoncentralhotelworkington.com
dir: M6 junct 40, A66 to Workington. Left at lights, hotel
on right

Enjoying a prominent town centre location, this modern
hotel boasts memorably hospitable staff. The well-
maintained and comfortable bedrooms are equipped with
a range of thoughtful extras. Public areas include
numerous lounges, a spacious bar, Caesars leisure club,
a smart restaurant and a popular coffee shop. The
comprehensive conference facilities are ideal for
meetings and weddings.

Rooms 46 (4 fmly) **S** £85; **D** £125 (incl. bkfst)*
Facilities STV ⊙ supervised Gym Mountain bikes Sauna
Steam room Sunbed New Year Wi-fi **Conf** Class 250
Board 100 Thtr 300 **Services** Lift **Parking** 14 **Notes** LB ⊗
RS 25 Dec Civ Wed 300

Hunday Manor Country House

★★★ 78% COUNTRY HOUSE HOTEL

☎ 01900 61798 ◾ 01900 601202
Hunday, Winscales CA14 4JF
e-mail: info@hunday-manor-hotel.co.uk
dir: A66 onto A595 towards Whitehaven, hotel 3m on
right, signed

Delightfully situated and enjoying distant views of the
Solway Firth, this charming hotel has well-furnished
rooms with lots of extras. The open-plan bar and foyer
lounge boast welcoming open fires, and the attractive
restaurant overlooks the woodland gardens. The provision
of a function suite makes the hotel an excellent wedding
venue.

Rooms 24 (2 fmly) **S** £69-£89; **D** £120-£145 (incl. bkfst)*
Facilities FTV Wi-fi **Conf** Class 200 Board 200 Thtr 200
Del from £100 to £150* **Parking** 50 **Notes** Civ Wed 250

DERBYSHIRE

ALFRETON · Map 16 SK45

Travelodge Alfreton

BUDGET HOTEL

☎ 0871 984 6119 🖷 01773 520040
Old Swanwick Colliery Rd DE55 1HJ
web: www.travelodge.co.uk
dir: 3m from M1 junct 28, at A38 & A61 junct

Travelodge offers good quality, good value, budget accommodation. All offer family rooms sleeping up to four (two adults, two children) with en suite bathroom/shower-room, remote-control TV, tea- and coffee-making facilities and comfortable beds. Food options vary. Breakfast is at the on-site Bar Café restaurant (if available) or to take away. See also Hotel Groups pages.

Rooms 60 **S** fr £29; **D** fr £29

ASHBOURNE · Map 10 SK14

See also **Thorpe**

Callow Hall

★★★ 82% ⍟⍟
COUNTRY HOUSE HOTEL

☎ 01335 300900 🖷 01335 300512
Mappleton Rd DE6 2AA
e-mail: info@callowhall.co.uk
dir: A515 through Ashbourne towards Buxton, left at Bowling Green pub, then 1st right

This delightful, creeper-clad, early Victorian house, set on a 44-acre estate, enjoys views over Bentley Brook and the Dove Valley. The atmosphere is relaxed and welcoming, and some of the spacious bedrooms in the main house have comfortable sitting areas. Public rooms feature high ceilings, ornate plasterwork and antique furniture. There is a good range of dishes offered on both the carte and the fixed-price, daily-changing menus. Von Essen Hotels - AA Hotel Group of the Year 2009-10.

Callow Hall

Rooms 16 (2 fmly) (2 GF) **Facilities** STV Fishing Cycle hire nearby (Tissington Trail) Riding nearby Golf course within 2m Xmas New Year Wi-fi **Conf** Class 25 Board 28 Thtr 30 Del from £155 to £180 **Parking** 21 **Notes** ⍟ Civ Wed

See advert on this page

Travelodge Ashbourne

BUDGET HOTEL

☎ 0871 984 6362 📠 01844 358 681
Carnation Way DE6 1AY
dir: M1 junct 24a, A50 towards Stoke/Derby. At Warren Ln rdbt take 3rd exit onto A50 towards Lockington/Castle Donington/Shardlow. Take A515 towards Ashbourne.

Travelodge offers good quality, good value, budget accommodation. All offer family rooms sleeping up to four (two adults, two children) with en suite bathroom/ shower-room, remote-control TV, tea- and coffee-making facilities and comfortable beds. Food options vary. Breakfast is at the on-site Bar Café restaurant (if available) or to take away. See also the Hotel Groups pages.

Rooms 53 **S** fr £29; **D** fr £29

ASHFORD IN THE WATER   Map 16 SK16

Riverside House

★★★ 88% ◉◉ HOTEL

☎ 01629 814275 📠 01629 812873
Fennel St DE45 1QF
e-mail: riversidehouse@enta.net
dir: Off A6 (Bakewell/Buxton road) 2m from Bakewell, hotel at end of main street

This delightful and welcoming hotel, with outstanding service, is establishing a good reputation for its high quality accommodation and fine dining. In parts dating back to 1630, it enjoys a peaceful location by the River Wye. Individually styled bedrooms are thoughtfully equipped, and the smart public rooms include a bright conservatory, an oak-panelled lounge with inglenook fireplace, a drawing room and two dining rooms.

Rooms 14 (4 GF) **S** £110-£155; **D** £135-£195 (incl. bkfst)* **Facilities** STV ✦ Xmas New Year **Conf** Class 15 Board 15 Thtr 15 **Parking** 40 **Notes** LB ⊗ No children 16yrs Civ Wed 32

BAKEWELL   Map 16 SK26

Rutland Arms

★★★ 70% ◉ HOTEL

☎ 01629 812812 📠 01629 812309
The Square DE45 1BT
e-mail: enquiries@rutlandbakewell.co.uk
dir: M1 junct 28 to Matlock, A6 to Bakewell. Hotel in town centre

This 19th-century hotel lies at the very centre of Bakewell and offers comfortable accommodation. With friendly and welcoming staff, and a newly relaunched restaurant, The Square offering interesting fine dining in elegant surroundings.

Rooms 35 (17 annexe) (2 fmly) (7 GF) **Facilities** New Year Wi-fi **Conf** Class 60 Board 40 Thtr 100 **Parking** 25

Monsal Head Hotel

★★ 82% ◉ HOTEL

☎ 01629 640250 📠 01629 640815
Monsal Head DE45 1NL
e-mail: enquiries@monsalhead.com
web: www.monsalhead.com
dir: A6 from Bakewell to Buxton. After 2m turn into Ashford in the Water, take B6465 for 1m. Hotel on left through public car park entrance

Situated three miles from Bakewell and overlooking the picturesque Monsal Dale in the Peak District National Park, this hotel is full of charm and character. The bedrooms have beautiful views, and public areas include the Ashford Room, a quiet residents' lounge, and Longstone Restaurant. The converted stables bar adjacent to the hotel has an excellent choice of cask ales and lagers.

Rooms 7 (1 fmly) **S** £80-£85; **D** £110-£150 (incl. bkfst & dinner)* **Facilities** Xmas New Year **Conf** Class 30 Board 20 Thtr 50 **Parking** 20 **Notes** LB RS 25 Dec

BARLBOROUGH   Map 16 SK47

Ibis Sheffield South

BUDGET HOTEL

☎ 01246 813222 📠 01246 813444
Tallys End, Chesterfield Rd S43 4TX
e-mail: H3157@accor.com
web: www.ibishotel.com
dir: M1 junct 30. Towards A619, right at rdbt towards Chesterfield. Hotel immediately left

Modern, budget hotel offering comfortable accommodation in bright and practical bedrooms. Breakfast is self-service and dinner is available in the restaurant. See also the Hotel Groups pages.

Rooms 86 (22 fmly) **Conf** Board 18 Thtr 35

BASLOW   Map 16 SK27

INSPECTORS' CHOICE

Fischer's Baslow Hall
★★★ ◉◉◉◉ HOTEL

☎ 01246 583259 📠 01246 583818
Calver Rd DE45 1RR
e-mail: reservations@fischers-baslowhall.co.uk
web: www.fischers-baslowhall.co.uk
dir: On A623 between Baslow & Calver

Located at the end of a chestnut tree-lined drive on the edge of the Chatsworth Estate, in marvellous gardens, this beautiful Derbyshire manor house offers sumptuous accommodation and facilities. Staff provide very friendly and personally attentive service. There are two styles of bedroom available - traditional, individually-themed rooms in the main house and spacious, more contemporary-styled rooms with Italian marble bathrooms in the Garden House. The cuisine is outstanding and will prove the highlight of any stay.

Rooms 11 (5 annexe) (4 GF) **S** £100-£140; **D** £140-£195 (incl. bkfst)* **Facilities** Wi-fi **Conf** Board 16 Thtr 20 **Parking** 40 **Notes** LB ⊗ Closed 25-26 Dec Civ Wed 40

Cavendish

★★★ 86% ◉◉ HOTEL

☎ 01246 582311 📠 01246 582312
DE45 1SP
e-mail: info@cavendish-hotel.net
web: www.cavendish-hotel.net
dir: M1 junct 29/A617 W to Chesterfield & A619 to Baslow. Hotel in village centre, off main road

This stylish property, dating back to the 18th century, is delightfully situated on the outskirts of the Chatsworth Estate. Elegantly appointed bedrooms offer a host of thoughtful amenities, while comfortable public areas are furnished with period pieces and paintings. Guests have a choice of dining in either the informal conservatory Garden Room or the elegant Gallery Restaurant.

continued

BASLOW *continued*

Rooms 24 (3 fmly) (2 GF) **S** £129-£173; **D** £165-£216
Facilities Putt green Fishing Xmas New Year Wi-fi
Conf Class 8 Board 18 Thtr 25 **Parking** 50 **Notes** LB ⊗ RS 25 Dec

---

BELPER   **Map 11 SK34**

Makeney Hall Hotel

★★★★ 73% HOTEL

*f*olio *Hotels*

☎ 0844 855 9111   🖹 01332 842777
Makeney, Milford DE56 0RS
e-mail: makeneyhall@foliohotels.com
web: www.foliohotels.com/makeneyhall
dir: off A6 at Milford, signed Makeney. Hotel 0.25m on left

This restored Victorian mansion stands in six acres of landscaped gardens and grounds above the River Derwent. Bedrooms vary in style and are generally very spacious. They are divided between the main house and the ground floor courtyard. Comfortable public rooms include a lounge, bar and spacious restaurant with views of the gardens.

Rooms 46 (18 annexe) (3 fmly) **Facilities** STV Xmas New Year Wi-fi **Conf** Class 80 Board 50 Thtr 180 **Services** Lift **Parking** 150 **Notes** Civ Wed 180

The Lion Hotel & Restaurant

★★★ 68% HOTEL

☎ 01773 824033   🖹 01773 828393
Bridge St DE56 1AX
e-mail: enquiries@lionhotel.uk.com
web: www.lionhotel.uk.com
dir: 8m NW of Derby, hotel on A6

Situated in the centre of town and on the border of the Peak District, this 18th-century hotel provides an ideal base for exploring the many local attractions. The tastefully decorated bedrooms are well equipped and the public rooms include an attractive restaurant and two cosy bars; a modern function suite also proves popular.

Rooms 22 (3 fmly) **S** £49-£79; **D** £59-£105 (incl. bkfst)*
Facilities STV Xmas New Year Wi-fi **Conf** Class 60 Board 50 Thtr 110 Del from £119 to £149* **Parking** 30 **Notes** LB Civ Wed 90

BREADSALL   **Map 11 SK33**

Marriott Breadsall Priory Hotel & Country Club

Marriott HOTELS & RESORTS

★★★★ 74% ⚘ HOTEL

☎ 01332 832235   🖹 01332 833509
Moor Rd DE7 6DL
web: www.marriottbreadsallpriory.co.uk
dir: A52 to Derby, at Pentagon rdbt 3rd exit towards A61/Chesterfield. At 3rd rdbt take 3rd exit & 1st left into village, left at church into Moor Rd. Hotel 1.5m on left

This extended mansion house is set in 400 acres of parkland and well-tended gardens. The smart bedrooms are mostly contained in the modern wing. There is a vibrant café-bar, a more formal restaurant and a large room-service menu. The extensive leisure facilities, include two golf courses and a swimming pool. Dinner in the Priory Restaurant is a highlight.

Rooms 112 (100 annexe) (40 fmly) **Facilities** Spa ⊛ ✯ 18 ♨ Putt green ⇲ Gym Health, beauty & hair salon Dance studio Xmas New Year Wi-fi **Conf** Class 50 Board 36 Thtr 120 **Services** Lift **Parking** 300 **Notes** ⊗ Civ Wed 100

BUXTON   **Map 16 SK07**

Barceló Buxton Palace Hotel

Barceló HOTELS & RESORTS

★★★★ 72% HOTEL

☎ 01298 22001   🖹 01298 72131
Palace Rd SK17 6AG
e-mail: palace@barcelo-hotels.co.uk
web: www.barcelo-hotels.co.uk
dir: M6 junct 20, follow M56/M60 signs to Stockport then A6 to Buxton, hotel adjacent to railway station

This impressive Victorian hotel is located on the hill overlooking the town. Public areas are traditional and elegant in style, and include chandeliers and decorative ceilings. The bedrooms are spacious and equipped with modern facilities, and The Dovedale Restaurant provides modern British cuisine. Good leisure facilities are available.

Rooms 122 (18 fmly) **Facilities** Spa ⊛ supervised Gym Beauty facilities Xmas New Year Wi-fi **Conf** Class 125 Board 80 Thtr 350 Del from £100* **Services** Lift **Parking** 180 **Notes** Civ Wed 100

Best Western Lee Wood

Best Western

★★★ 79% ⚘ HOTEL

☎ 01298 23002   🖹 01298 23228
The Park SK17 6TQ
e-mail: reservations@leewoodhotel.co.uk
web: www.leewoodhotel.co.uk
dir: From town centre take A5004 NE, hotel 300mtrs beyond Devonshire Royal Hospital

This elegant Georgian hotel offers high standards of comfort and hospitality. Individually furnished bedrooms are generally spacious, with all of the expected modern

conveniences. There is a choice of two comfortable lounges and a conservatory restaurant. The quality cooking, good service and fine hospitality are noteworthy.

Rooms 40 (5 annexe) (4 fmly) **S** £70-£90; **D** £90-£160 (incl. bkfst)* **Facilities** STV FTV New Year Wi-fi **Conf** Class 65 Board 40 Thtr 120 Del from £115 to £150* **Services** Lift **Parking** 50 **Notes** LB Civ Wed 120

Portland Hotel & Park Restaurant

★★ 67% HOTEL

☎ 01298 22462   🖹 01298 27464
32 St John's Rd SK17 6XQ
e-mail: portland.hotel@btinternet.com
dir: on A53 opposite the Pavilion & Gardens

This privately owned and personally run hotel is situated near the famous opera house and the Pavilion Gardens. Facilities include a comfortable lounge and an open-plan bar and restaurant area.

Rooms 22 (3 fmly) **Conf** Class 30 Board 25 Thtr 50 **Parking** 18 **Notes** LB

CASTLETON   **Map 16 SK18**

Innkeeper's Lodge Castleton

BUDGET HOTEL

☎ 0845 112 6046   🖹 0845 112 6256
Castle St S33 8WG
web: www.innkeeperslodge.com/castleton
dir: On A6187, in centre of village

Innkeeper's Lodge represents an exciting, high value concept within the budget hotel market. Comfortable bedrooms provide excellent facilities that include satellite TV and modem points. This carefully restored lodge is in a picturesque setting and has its own unique style and quirky character. Food is served all day, and an extensive, complimentary continental breakfast is offered. See also the Hotel Groups pages.

Rooms 15

Ringwood Hall

★★★ 85% HOTEL

☎ 01246 280077 📠 01246 472241
Brimington S43 1DQ
e-mail: reception@ringwoodhallhotel.com
web: www.ringwoodhallhotel.com
dir: M1 junct 30, A619 to Chesterfield through Staveley.
Hotel on left

This is a splendid Georgian manor house set in 29 acres
of award-winning grounds, between the M1 and
Chesterfield. Modern, comfortable bedrooms complement
the traditional, spacious lounges. The health and fitness
club has a pool, sauna, steam room and fitness suite.

Rooms 70 (6 annexe) (32 fmly) (25 GF) **S** £78-£98;
D £91-£120 (incl. bkfst)* **Facilities** FTV 🕲 Gym Steam
room Sauna Beauty therapy Aqua aerobics Xmas Wi-fi
Conf Class 80 Board 60 Thtr 250 Del from £105 to £126*
Parking 150 **Notes** LB Civ Wed 250

Sandpiper

THE INDEPENDENTS
HOTEL ASSOCIATION

★★★ 67% HOTEL

☎ 01246 450550 📠 01246 452805
Sheffield Rd, Sheepbridge S41 9EH
e-mail: sue@sandpiperhotel.co.uk
web: www.sandpiperhotel.co.uk
dir: M1 junct 29, A617 to Chesterfield then A61 to
Sheffield. 1st exit take Dronfield/Unstone sign. Hotel 0.5m
on left

Conveniently situated for both the A61 and M1 and
providing a good touring base, being just three miles
from Chesterfield, this modern hotel offers comfortable
and well-furnished bedrooms. Public areas are situated
in a separate building across the car park, and include a
cosy bar and open plan restaurant, serving a range of
interesting and popular dishes.

Rooms 46 (8 fmly) (16 GF) **S** £49-£79; **D** £59-£89
Facilities New Year Wi-fi **Conf** Class 35 Board 35
Thtr 100 Del from £99 to £149 **Services** Lift **Parking** 120
Notes LB Civ Wed 90

Legacy Chesterfield

LEGACY
HOTELS

★★★ 64% HOTEL

☎ 0870 832 9907 📠 0870 832 9908
Malkin St S41 7UA
e-mail: res-chesterfield@legacy-hotels.co.uk
web: www.legacy-hotels.co.uk
dir: Hotel on right opposite railway station

This hotel is situated at the gateway of the Peak District
National Park, and is within sight of the famous crooked
spire of St Mary's Church. It makes an ideal base for
exploring the delightful Derbyshire towns of Matlock Bath,
Buxton and Bakewell. The accommodation includes four-
poster rooms, and rooms adapted for wheelchair users.
Public areas include lounge bars, a restaurant and good
leisure facilities.

Rooms 73 (9 fmly) **Facilities** 🕲 supervised Gym Sauna
Steam room Xmas New Year Wi-fi **Conf** Class 60 Board 40
Thtr 200 **Services** Lift **Parking** 100 **Notes** Civ Wed 90

Ibis Chesterfield

BUDGET HOTEL

☎ 01246 221333 📠 01246 221444
Lordsmill St S41 7RW
e-mail: h3160@accor.com
web: www.ibishotel.com
dir: M1 junct 29/A617 to Chesterfield. 2nd exit at 1st
rdbt. Hotel on right at 2nd rdbt

Modern, budget hotel offering comfortable
accommodation in bright and practical bedrooms.
Breakfast is self-service and dinner is available in the
restaurant. See also the Hotel Groups pages.

Rooms 86 (21 fmly) (8 GF) **Conf** Board 20 Thtr 30

Travelodge Chesterfield

BUDGET HOTEL

☎ 0871 984 6129 📠 01246 455411
**Brimmington Rd, Inner Ring Rd, Wittington Moor
S41 9BE**
web: www.travelodge.co.uk
dir: on A61, N of town centre

Travelodge offers good quality, good value, budget
accommodation. All offer family rooms sleeping up to four
(two adults, two children) with en suite bathroom/
shower-room, remote-control TV, tea- and coffee-making
facilities and comfortable beds. Food options vary.
Breakfast is at the on-site Bar Café restaurant (if
available) or to take away. See also Hotel Groups pages.

Rooms 20 **S** fr £29; **D** fr £29

Midland

★★★★ 84% HOTEL

☎ 01332 345894 📠 01332 293522
Midland Rd DE1 2SQ
e-mail: sales@midland-derby.co.uk
web: www.midland-derby.co.uk
dir: opposite rail station

This early Victorian hotel situated opposite Derby Midland
Station provides very comfortable accommodation. The
executive rooms are ideal for business travellers as they

are equipped with writing desks and fax/computer points.
Public rooms include a comfortable lounge and a popular
restaurant. Service is skilled, attentive and friendly. Each
bedroom is equipped with high-speed internet access.
There is also a walled garden and private parking.

Rooms 100 **Facilities** 🎵 Wi-fi **Conf** Class 50 Board 35
Thtr 150 **Services** Lift **Parking** 90 **Notes** ✪ Closed 24-26
Dec & 1 Jan Civ Wed 150

See advert on page 134

Cathedral Quarter

★★★★ 79% ⊛ HOTEL

☎ 01332 546080 & 0115 852 3207 📠 01352 546098
16 St Mary's Gate DE1 3JR
e-mail: stay@cathedralquarterhotel.com
web: www.cathedralquarterhotel.com
dir: Follow brown signs to Cathedral Quarter. Hotel on one
way road

A sympathetic renovation of an elegant Victorian building
has resulted in a vibrant boutique hotel. Many original
features including tiled floors, a magnificent staircase
and stained glass are enhanced by quality minimalist
decor and fine furnishings. Air conditioned bedrooms are
equipped with thoughtful extras and luxurious bathrooms
and the fine dining first floor restaurant is an ideal
setting for a memorable evening. A beauty treatment spa
is also available.

Rooms 38 (6 fmly) (10 GF) **S** £60-£110; **D** £95-£165 (incl.
bkfst)* **Facilities** Spa STV FTV Xmas New Year Wi-fi
Conf Class 60 Board 50 Thtr 100 Del from £135 to £195*
Services Lift **Notes** LB ✪ Civ Wed 100

Marriott Breadsall Priory Hotel & Country Club

Marriott
HOTELS & RESORTS

★★★★ 74% ⊛ HOTEL

☎ 01332 832235 📠 01332 833509
Moor Rd DE7 6DL
web: www.marriottbreadsallpriory.co.uk

(For full entry see Breadsall)

Menzies Mickleover Court

MenziesHotels

★★★★ 74% HOTEL

☎ 01332 521234 📠 01332 521238
Etwall Rd, Mickleover DE3 0XX
e-mail: mickleovercourt@menzieshotels.co.uk
web: www.menzieshotels.co.uk
dir: A50 towards Derby, exit at junct 5. A516 towards
Derby, take exit signed Mickleover

Located close to Derby, this stylish, modern hotel is well
suited to both the conference and leisure markets.
Bedrooms are spacious, well equipped and include some
eye-catching executive rooms and suites. Dining venues
include a modern brasserie or a more traditionally styled
Italian bistro on the third floor. The smartly presented
leisure facilities are amongst the best in the region.

continued

DERBY *continued*

Rooms 99 (20 fmly) (5 smoking) **S** £50-£165;
D £50-£165* **Facilities** STV ⊙ Gym Beauty salon Steam room Xmas New Year Wi-fi **Conf** Class 80 Board 40 Thtr 225 Del from £105 to £165* **Services** Lift Air con **Parking** 270 **Notes** Civ Wed 150

Littleover Lodge

★★★ 73% HOTEL

☎ 01332 510161 ▤ 01332 514010
222 Rykneld Rd, Littleover DE23 4AN
e-mail: enquiries@littleoverlodge.co.uk
web: www.littleoverlodge.co.uk
dir: A38 towards Derby approx 1m on left slip lane signed Littleover/Mickleover/Findon, take 2nd exit off island marked Littleover 0.25m on right

Situated in a rural location this friendly hotel offers modern bedrooms with direct access from the car park. Two styles of dining are available - an informal carvery operation which is very popular locally, and a more formal restaurant which is open for lunch and dinner each day. Service is excellent with long serving staff being particularly friendly.

Littleover Lodge

Rooms 16 (3 fmly) (6 GF) **S** £60-£90; **D** £70-£90 (incl. bkfst)* **Facilities** STV ♫ Xmas New Year Wi-fi **Parking** 75 **Notes** LB Civ Wed 100

See advert on this page

European Inn

★★★ 72% HOTEL

☎ 01332 292000 ▤ 01332 293940
Midland Rd DE1 2SL
e-mail: admin@euro-derby.co.uk
web: www.euro-derby.co.uk
dir: City centre, 200yds from railway station

This is a contemporary hotel, offering quality accommodation with a newly refurbished lounge bar, free Wi-fi and free parking. Situated just a 100 metres from the railway station and a not far from the city centre where there are an abundance of shops and restaurants.

Rooms 88 (18 fmly) **Facilities** Wi-fi **Conf** Class 25 Board 30 Thtr 60 **Services** Lift **Parking** 90 **Notes** ⊛

Legacy Aston Court

★★★ 70% HOTEL

☎ 0870 832 9941 📠 0870 832 9942
Midland Rd DE1 2SL
e-mail: res-astoncourt@legacy-hotels.co.uk
web: www.legacy-hotels.co.uk
dir: M1 junct 25 follow sign to Derby A52. At rdbt follow
signs for city centre S, then for railway station

Situated in the heart of Derby, close to the railway
station, this modernised hotel provides the ideal location
for business and leisure guests. Bedrooms are smartly
furnished and well equipped. The Steaks-n-Stuff
restaurant and lounge bar offer a good range of dishes;
there is also a pool table in bar/lounge area. Spacious
banqueting and meeting facilities plus secure parking
are all available.

Rooms 55 (4 fmly) (6 GF) **S** £40-£90; **D** £50-£110 (incl.
bkfst)* **Facilities** STV Xmas New Year Wi-fi **Conf** Class 90
Board 60 Thtr 250 **Services** Lift **Parking** 80 **Notes** LB ⊗
Civ Wed

International

★★★ 66% HOTEL

☎ 01332 369321 📠 01332 294430
288 Burton Rd DE23 6AD
e-mail: info@international-hotel.co.uk
dir: 0.5m from city centre on A5250

Within easy reach of the city centre, this hotel offers
comfortable, modern public rooms. An extensive range of
dishes is served in the pleasant restaurant. There is a
wide range of bedroom sizes and styles, but each room is
very well equipped; spacious suites are also available.
Parking is a bonus.

Rooms 62 (21 annexe) (4 fmly) (8 GF) (10 smoking)
S £39-£89; **D** £45-£99 (incl. bkfst) **Facilities** STV ♫
Xmas New Year Wi-fi **Conf** Class 40 Board 40 Thtr 100
Del from £90 to £125 **Services** Lift **Parking** 80 **Notes** ⊗
Civ Wed 100

Ramada Encore Derby

Ⓤ

☎ 0844 801 3680 📠 0844 8013681
Locomotive Way, Pride Park DE24 8PU
e-mail: admin@encorederby.co.uk
dir: 10 mins from M1 junct 24/25

Currently the rating for this establishment is not
confirmed. This may be due to a change of ownership or
because it has only recently joined the AA rating scheme.
For further details please see the AA website: theAA.com

Rooms 112 (16 fmly) **S** £55-£65; **D** £65-£75 (incl. bkfst)*
Facilities STV Gym Sauna Wi-fi **Conf** Class 40 Board 20
Thtr 60 Del from £125 to £145* **Services** Lift Air con
Parking 110 **Notes** LB ⊗

Days Hotel Derby

BUDGET HOTEL

☎ 01332 363600 📠 01332 200630
Derbyshire CC Ground, Pentagon Roundabout,
Nottingham Rd DE21 6DA
e-mail: derby@kewgreen.co.uk
web: www.daysinn.com
dir: M1 junct 25, A52 towards Derby. At Pentagon rdbt
take 4th exit, into cricket club

This modern building offers accommodation in smart,
spacious and well-equipped bedrooms, suitable for
families and business travellers, and all with en suite
bathrooms. Continental breakfast is available and other
refreshments may be taken at the nearby family
restaurant. See also the Hotel Groups pages.

Rooms 100 (24 fmly) **Conf** Class 25 Board 18 Thtr 50

Express by Holiday Inn Derby Pride Park

BUDGET HOTEL

☎ 01332 388000 📠 01332 388038
Wheelwright Way, Pride Park DE24 8HX
e-mail: derby@expressholidayinn.co.uk
web: www.hiexpress.com/derby-pridepk
dir: A52 towards Derby, after 7m follow Pride Park signs.
Over 1st 3 rdbts. Right at 4th, left at next. Take 1st left,
hotel on right

A modern hotel ideal for families and business travellers.
Fresh and uncomplicated, the spacious rooms include Sky
TV, power shower and tea and coffee-making facilities.
Continental buffet breakfast is included in the room rate;
other meals may be taken at the nearby family pub or
restaurant. See also the Hotel Groups pages.

Rooms 103 (64 fmly) **Conf** Class 28 Thtr 20

Innkeeper's Lodge Derby

BUDGET HOTEL

☎ 0845 112 6047 📠 0845 112 6255
Nottingham Rd, Chaddesdon DE21 6LZ
web: www.innkeeperslodge.com/derby
dir: M1 junct 25, A52 towards Derby, take exit signed
Spondon & Chaddesden, 4m, at rdbt take exit signed
Chaddesden/A6005, pass Asda store. Lodge 1m on right

Innkeeper's Lodge represents an exciting, high value
concept within the budget hotel market. Comfortable
bedrooms provide excellent facilities that include satellite
TV and modem points. Options include family rooms; and
for the corporate guest, cutting edge IT which includes
Wi-fi access. A popular Carvery provides all-day food,
including an extensive, complimentary continental
breakfast. See also the Hotel Groups pages.

Rooms 29 (2 fmly) **Conf** Thtr 32

Travelodge Derby

BUDGET HOTEL

☎ 0871 984 6072 📠 01332 367255
Kingsway, Rowditch DE22 3NN
web: www.travelodge.co.uk
dir: A38 Derby N, exit at ring road, A5111. Lodge 0.25m
on left

Travelodge offers good quality, good value, budget
accommodation. All offer family rooms sleeping up to four
(two adults, two children) with en suite bathroom/
shower-room, remote-control TV, tea- and coffee-making
facilities and comfortable beds. Food options vary.
Breakfast is at the on-site Bar Café restaurant (if
available) or to take away. See also Hotel Groups pages.

Rooms 40 **S** fr £29; **D** fr £29

DERBY SERVICE AREA (A50) Map 11 SK42

Days Inn Donnington

BUDGET HOTEL

☎ 01332 799666 📠 01332 794166
Welcome Break Services, A50 Westbound DE72 2WA
e-mail: derby.hotel@welcomebreak.co.uk
web: www.welcomebreak.co.uk
dir: M1junct 24/24a, onto A50 towards Stoke/Derby. Hotel
between juncts 1 & 2

This modern building offers accommodation in smart,
spacious and well-equipped bedrooms, suitable for
families and business travellers, and all with en suite
bathrooms. Continental breakfast is available and other
refreshments may be taken at the nearby family
restaurant. See also the Hotel Groups pages.

Rooms 47 (39 fmly) (17 GF) **S** £29-£59; **D** £39-£79*
Conf Class 20 Board 40 Thtr 40 Del from £65 to £105*

GLOSSOP Map 16 SK09

Wind in the Willows

★★ 83% HOTEL

☎ 01457 868001 📠 01457 853354
Derbyshire Level SK13 7PT
e-mail: info@windinthewillows.co.uk
dir: 1m E of Glossop on A57, turn right opp Royal Oak,
hotel 400yds on right

A warm and relaxed atmosphere prevails at this small
and very comfortable hotel. The bedrooms are well
furnished, each offering many thoughtful extras; some
executive rooms are available. Public areas include two
comfortable lounges, a dining room, and a modern
meeting room with views over the extensive grounds.

Rooms 12 **S** fr £88; **D** fr £135 (incl. bkfst)
Facilities Fishing New Year Wi-fi **Conf** Class 12 Board 16
Thtr 40 Del from £145* **Parking** 16 **Notes** LB ⊗ No
children 10yrs

GRINDLEFORD Map 16 SK27

Maynard

★★★ 78% ◎◎ HOTEL

☎ 01433 630321 📠 01433 630445
Main Rd S32 2HE
e-mail: info@themaynard.co.uk
dir: From Sheffield take A625 to Castleton. Left into Grindleford on B6521. On left after Fox House Hotel

This building, dating back over 100 years, is situated in a beautiful and tranquil location yet is within easy reach of Sheffield and the M1. The bedrooms are contemporary in style and offer a wealth of accessories. The Peak District views from the restaurant and garden are stunning.

Rooms 10 (1 fmly) **Facilities** STV ⛳ Wi-fi **Conf** Class 60 Board 40 Thtr 120 **Parking** 70 **Notes** LB Civ Wed 130

HARTINGTON Map 16 SK16

Biggin Hall

★★ 🅰 HOTEL

☎ 01298 84451
SK17 0DH
e-mail: enquiries@bigginhall.co.uk
web: www.bigginhall.co.uk
dir: 0.5m off A515 midway between Ashbourne & Buxton

Rooms 20 (4 fmly) (4 GF) **S** £55-£94; **D** £78-£136 (incl. bkfst & dinner)* **Facilities** ⛳ Xmas New Year Wi-fi **Conf** Class 20 Board 20 Thtr 20 Del from £100 to £145* **Parking** 25 **Notes** LB No children 12yrs Civ Wed 60

HATHERSAGE Map 16 SK28

George Hotel

★★★ 81% ◎◎ HOTEL

☎ 01433 650436 & 0845 456 0581 📠 01433 650099
Main Rd S32 1BB
e-mail: info@george-hotel.net
web: www.george-hotel.net
dir: In village centre on A6187, SW of Sheffield

The George is a relaxing 500-year-old hostelry in the heart of this picturesque town. The beamed bar lounge has great character and traditional comfort, and the restaurant is light, modern and spacious with original artworks. Upstairs the decor is simpler with lots of light hues; the split-level and four-poster rooms are especially appealing. The quality cooking is a key feature of the hotel.

Rooms 22 (2 fmly) (3 GF) **S** £95-£106; **D** £130-£165 (incl. bkfst)* **Facilities** Xmas New Year Wi-fi **Conf** Class 20 Board 36 Thtr 80 **Parking** 40 **Notes** LB ⊗ Civ Wed 50

HIGHAM Map 16 SK35

Santo's Higham Farm Hotel

★★★ 77% ◎ HOTEL

☎ 01773 833812 📠 01773 520525
Main Rd DE55 6EH
e-mail: reception@santoshighamfarm.demon.co.uk
web: www.santoshighamfarm.co.uk
dir: M1 junct 28, A38 towards Derby, then A61 towards Chesterfield. Onto B6013 towards Belper, hotel 300yds on right

With panoramic views across the rolling Amber Valley, this 15th-century crook barn and farmhouse has been expertly restored and extended. There's an Italian wing and an international wing of themed bedrooms of mini suites. Freshly prepared dishes, especially fish, are available in Guiseppe's restaurant. This hotel makes an ideal romantic hideaway.

Rooms 28 (2 fmly) (7 GF) **Facilities** Xmas New Year Wi-fi **Conf** Class 40 Board 34 Thtr 100 **Parking** 100 **Notes** LB ⊗ Civ Wed 100

HOPE Map 16 SK18

Losehill House Hotel & Spa

★★★ 81% ◎ HOTEL

☎ 01433 621219 📠 01433 622501
Edale Rd S33 6RF
e-mail: info@losehillhouse.co.uk
web: www.losehillhouse.co.uk
dir: A6187 into Hope. Take turn opposite church into Edale Rd. 1m, left & follow signs to hotel

Situated down a quiet leafy lane, this hotel occupies a secluded spot in the Peak District National Park. Bedrooms are comfortable and beautifully appointed. The outdoor hot tub, with stunning views over the valley, is a real indulgence; a heated swimming pool, sauna and spa treatments are also on offer. The views from the Orangery Restaurant are a real delight.

Rooms 24 (4 annexe) (4 fmly) (3 GF) **S** £105-£160; **D** £135-£190 (incl. bkfst)* **Facilities** Spa ⊗ Sauna 🎵 Xmas New Year Wi-fi **Conf** Class 20 Board 15 Thtr 30 **Services** Lift **Parking** 20 **Notes** LB ⊗ Civ Wed 100

LONG EATON Map 11 SK43

Ramada Nottingham 🆁 RAMADA

★★★ 71% HOTEL

☎ 0115 946 0000 📠 0115 946 0726
Bostock Ln NG10 4EP
e-mail: sales.nottingham@ramadajarvis.co.uk
web: www.ramadajarvis.co.uk
dir: 0.25m from M1 junct 25

Conveniently located between Nottingham and Derby, this large modern hotel is set just off the M1. Bedrooms are comfortably appointed for both business and leisure guests, and conference facilities are available.

Rooms 101 (10 fmly) (40 GF) (25 smoking) **S** £45-£165; **D** £45-£165 (incl. bkfst)* **Facilities** STV FTV Xmas New Year Wi-fi **Conf** Class 30 Board 20 Thtr 85 Del from £99 to £155 **Parking** 136 **Notes** LB ⊗ Civ Wed 60

Novotel Nottingham East Midlands

★★★ 67% HOTEL

☎ 0115 946 5111 📠 0115 946 5900
Bostock Ln NG10 4EP
e-mail: H0507@accor.com
web: www.novotel.com
dir: M1 junct 25 onto B6002 to Long Eaton. Hotel 400yds on left

In close proximity to the M1, this purpose-built hotel has much to offer. All bedrooms are spacious, have sofa beds and provide exceptional desk space. Public rooms include a bright brasserie, which is open all day and provides extended dining until midnight. There is a comprehensive range of meeting rooms.

Rooms 108 (40 fmly) (20 GF) (8 smoking) **Facilities** ⚡ Wi-fi **Conf** Class 100 Board 100 Thtr 250 **Services** Lift **Parking** 220

MATLOCK Map 16 SK35

The Red House Country Hotel

★★ 85% ⊛ HOTEL

☎ 01629 734854
Old Rd, Darley Dale DE4 2ER
e-mail: enquiries@theredhousecountryhotel.co.uk
web: www.theredhousecountryhotel.co.uk
dir: Off A6 onto Old Rd signed Carriage Museum, 2.5m N of Matlock

A peaceful country hotel set in delightful Victorian gardens. Rich colour schemes are used to excellent effect throughout. The well-equipped bedrooms include three ground floor rooms in the adjacent coach house. A comfortable lounge with delightful rural views is available for refreshments and pre-dinner drinks; service is friendly and attentive.

Rooms 10 (3 annexe) (3 GF) **S** £54-£64; **D** £91-£108 (incl. bkfst)* **Facilities** New Year Wi-fi **Conf** Class 10 Board 10 Thtr 10 **Parking** 12 **Notes** LB ⊗ No children 12yrs Closed 1-14 Jan

Hodgkinsons Hotel & Restaurant

★★ 67% HOTEL

☎ 01629 582170 📠 01629 584891
150 South Pde, Matlock Bath DE4 3NR
e-mail: enquiries@hodgkinsons-hotel.co.uk
dir: On A6 in village centre. On corner of Waterloo Rd & South Parade

This fine Georgian building was renovated in the Victorian era and has many interesting and unusual features. Bedrooms are equipped with fine antique furniture and a wealth of thoughtful extras. The elegant dining room is the setting for imaginative dinners and a comfortable lounge is also available.

Rooms 8 (1 fmly) **S** £40-£85; **D** £90-£140 (incl. bkfst)* **Facilities** Wi-fi **Conf** Class 12 Board 10 Thtr 10 Del from £125 to £145* **Parking** 5 **Notes** LB Closed 24 - 26 Dec

MORLEY Map 11 SK34

The Morley Hayes Hotel

★★★★ 76% ⊛ HOTEL

☎ 01332 780480 📠 01332 781094
Main Rd DE7 6DG
e-mail: hotel@morleyhayes.com
web: www.morleyhayes.com
dir: 4m N of Derby on A608

Located in rolling countryside this modern golfing destination provides extremely comfortable, stylish bedrooms with wide-ranging facilities, plasma TVs, and state-of-the-art bathrooms; the plush suites are particularly eye-catching. Creative cuisine is offered in the Dovecote Restaurant, and both Roosters and the Spikes sports bar provide informal eating options.

Rooms 32 (4 fmly) (15 GF) **S** £125-£250; **D** £145-£266 (incl. bkfst)* **Facilities** STV ⚡ 27 Putt green Golf driving range Wi-fi **Conf** Class 130 Board 122 Thtr 165 **Services** Lift Air con **Parking** 245 **Notes** LB ⊗ Civ Wed 90

RISLEY Map 11 SK43

Risley Hall Hotel & Spa

★★★ 74% ⊛ HOTEL

OXFORD
HOTELS & INNS

☎ 0115 939 9000 & 921 8523 📠 0115 939 7766
Derby Rd DE72 3SS
e-mail: reservations.risleyhall@ohiml.com
web: www.oxfordhotelsandinns.com
dir: M1 junct 25, Sandiacre exit into Bostock Ln. Left at lights, hotel on left in 0.25m

Set in 17 acres of private landscaped grounds and attractive mature gardens, this 11th-century manor house offers a good range of comfortable accommodation and relaxing day rooms. The friendly and attentive service complements the imaginative cuisine in the fine dining restaurant. The spa and beauty treatment rooms prove particularly popular with members and leisure guests alike.

Risley Hall Hotel & Spa

Rooms 35 (8 GF) **Facilities** Spa ⊗ Xmas **Conf** Class 22 Board 20 Thtr 100 **Services** Lift **Notes** LB ⊗ Civ Wed 100

ROWSLEY Map 16 SK26

INSPECTORS' CHOICE

East Lodge Country House

★★★ ⊛⊛ HOTEL

☎ 01629 734474 📠 01629 733949
DE4 2EF
e-mail: info@eastlodge.com
web: www.eastlodge.com
dir: A6, 3m from Bakewell, 5m from Matlock

This hotel enjoys a romantic setting in ten acres of landscaped grounds and gardens. The stylish bedrooms, including three with four-posters, are equipped with many extras such as TVs with DVD players, and most have lovely garden views. The popular restaurant serves much produce sourced from the area, and the conservatory lounge, overlooking the gardens, offers afternoon teas and light meals.

Rooms 12 (2 fmly) (1 GF) **Facilities** STV ⚡ Xmas New Year Wi-fi **Conf** Class 20 Board 22 Thtr 75 **Parking** 40 **Notes** ⊗ No children 7yrs Civ Wed 100

ROWSLEY *continued*

The Peacock at Rowsley
★★★ ◎◎ HOTEL

☎ 01629 733518   🖹 01629 732671
Bakewell Rd DE4 2EB
e-mail: reception@thepeacockatrowsley.com
web: www.thepeacockatrowsley.com
dir: A6, 3m before Bakewell, 6m from Matlock towards
Bakewell

Owned by Lord Manners of Haddon Hall, this hotel
combines stylish contemporary design by India
Mahdavi with original period and antique features.
Bedrooms are individually designed and boast DVD
players, complimentary Wi-fi and smart marble
bathrooms. Two rooms are particularly special - one
with a four-poster and one with an antique bed
originating from Belvoir Castle in Leicestershire.
Imaginative cuisine, using local, seasonal produce, is a
highlight. Guests are warmly welcomed and service is
attentive. Fly fishing is popular in this area and the
hotel has its own fishing rights on seven miles of the
Rivers Wye and Derwent.

Rooms 16 (5 fmly) **S** £75-£95; **D** £145-£230 (incl.
bkfst)* **Facilities** Fishing ⛵ Free use of Woodlands
Fitness Centre Free membership to Bakewell Golf Club
♫ New Year Wi-fi **Conf** Class 8 Board 16 Thtr 16
Del from £170 to £190 **Parking** 25 **Notes** LB No
children 10yrs

SANDIACRE   Map 11 SK43

Holiday Inn Derby/
Nottingham
★★★ 68% HOTEL

☎ 0870 400 9062   🖹 0115 949 0469
Bostocks Ln NG10 5NJ
e-mail: reservations-derby-nottingham@ihg.com
web: www.holidayinn.co.uk
dir: M1 junct 25 follow signs for Sandiacre, hotel on right

This hotel is conveniently located by the M1, ideal for
exploring Derby and Nottingham. The bedrooms are
modern and smart. The newly refurbished restaurant
offers a wide range of dishes for breakfast, lunch and
dinner. The lounge/bar area is a popular meeting place,
with food served all day.

Rooms 92 (31 fmly) (53 GF) (2 smoking) **Facilities** STV
Xmas New Year Wi-fi **Conf** Class 32 Board 30 Thtr 75
Del from £89 to £155 **Services** Air con **Parking** 200
Notes Civ Wed 50

SOUTH NORMANTON   Map 16 SK45

Derbyshire   *PH* PRINCIPAL HAYLEY
Ⓤ

☎ 01773 812000   🖹 01773 813413
Carter Lane East DE55 2EH
e-mail: reservations.derbyshire@principal-hayley.com
dir: M1 junct 28, E on A38 to Mansfield

Currently the rating for this establishment is not
confirmed. This may be due to a change of ownership or
because it has only recently joined the AA rating scheme.
For further details please see the AA website: theAA.com

Rooms 157 (10 fmly) (61 GF) **Facilities** Spa STV ⓢ Gym
Steam room Sauna New Year Wi-fi **Conf** Class 120
Board 25 Thtr 250 **Parking** 220 **Notes** Civ Wed 150

SUDBURY   Map 10 SK13

The Boars Head
★★★ 74% HOTEL

☎ 01283 820344   🖹 01283 820075
Lichfield Rd DE6 5GX
e-mail: enquiries@boars-head-hotel.co.uk
web: www.boars-head-hotel.co.uk
dir: A50 onto A515 towards Lichfield, hotel 1m on right

This popular hotel offers comfortable accommodation in
well-equipped bedrooms. There is a relaxed atmosphere
in the public rooms, which consists of a several bars and
dining options. The beamed lounge bar provides informal
dining thanks to a popular carvery, while the restaurant
and cocktail bar offer a more formal environment.

Rooms 23 (1 annexe) (1 fmly) **Facilities** Xmas
Parking 85 **Notes** LB

See advert under Burton-on-Trent, Staffordshire

SWANWICK

See Alfreton

THORPE (DOVEDALE)   Map 16 SK15

Izaak Walton
★★★ 79% ◎◎ HOTEL

☎ 01335 350555   🖹 01335 350539
Dovedale DE6 2AY
e-mail: reception@izaakwaltonhotel.com
web: www.izaakwaltonhotel.com
dir: A515 onto B5054, to Thorpe, continue straight over
cattle grid & 2 small bridges, 1st right & sharp left

This hotel is peacefully situated, with magnificent views
over the valley of Dovedale to Thorpe Cloud. Many of the
bedrooms have lovely views, and the executive rooms are
particularly spacious. Meals are served in the bar area,
with more formal dining in the Haddon Restaurant. Staff
are friendly and efficient. Fishing on the River Dove can
be arranged.

Rooms 35 (6 fmly) (8 GF) **S** fr £110; **D** fr £145 (incl.
bkfst)* **Facilities** Fishing ⛵ Xmas New Year Wi-fi
Conf Class 40 Board 50 Thtr 50 **Parking** 80
Notes Civ Wed 80

See advert on page 130

DEVON

ASHBURTON — Map 3 SX77

Dartmoor Lodge

★★ 64% HOTEL

☎ 01364 652232 📠 01364 653990
Peartree Cross TQ13 7JW
e-mail: dartmoor.ashburton@newbridgeinns.co.uk
dir: Exit A38 at 2nd exit for Ashburton, right across bridge, left at garage, hotel on right

Nestling on the edge of the Dartmouth National Park and Ashburton, this friendly comfortable hotel provides a perfect base to explore the area. Log fires welcome guests in the beamed bar and restaurant, where locally produced items feature on the extensive menu. Rooms are tastefully furnished and equipped with modern amenities.

Rooms 22 **Conf** Class 36 Board 36 Thtr 90

ASHWATER — Map 3 SX39

INSPECTORS' CHOICE

Blagdon Manor Hotel & Restaurant
★★★ ⑥⑥ HOTEL

☎ 01409 211224 📠 01409 211634
EX21 5DF
e-mail: stay@blagdon.com
web: www.blagdon.com
dir: Take A388 N of Launceston towards Holsworthy. Approx 2m N of Chapman's Well take 2nd right for Ashwater. Next right beside Blagdon Lodge, hotel 0.25m

Located on the borders of Devon and Cornwall within easy reach of the coast, and set in its own beautifully kept yet natural gardens, this small and friendly hotel offers a charming home-from-home atmosphere. The tranquillity of the secluded setting, the character and charm of the house and its unhurried pace ensure calm and relaxation. High levels of service, personal touches and thoughtful extras are all part of a stay here. Steve Morey cooks with passion and his commitment to using only the finest local ingredients speaks volumes.

Rooms 8 **S** fr £85; **D** fr £135 (incl. bkfst)*
Facilities FTV 🏊 Boules Giant chess Wi-fi **Parking** 13
Notes No children 12yrs Closed Jan

AXMINSTER — Map 4 SY29

See also **Colyford**

Fairwater Head Hotel

★★★ 75% ⑥ HOTEL

☎ 01297 678349 📠 01297 678459
Hawkchurch EX13 5TX
e-mail: stay@fairwaterheadhotel.co.uk
web: www.fairwaterheadhotel.co.uk
dir: Off B3165 (Crewkerne to Lyme Regis road). Hotel signed to Hawkchurch

This elegant Edwardian country house provides a perfect location for anyone looking for a peaceful break. Surrounded by extensive gardens and rolling countryside, the setting guarantees relaxation. Bedrooms are located both within the main house and the garden wing; all provide good levels of comfort. Public areas have much appeal and include lounge areas, a bar and an elegant restaurant. Food is a highlight with excellent local produce prepared with care and skill.

Rooms 16 (4 annexe) (8 GF) **S** £75-£100; **D** £95-£120 (incl. bkfst)* **Facilities** Xmas New Year Wi-fi **Conf** Class 25 Board 20 Thtr 35 **Parking** 30 **Notes** LB Closed 1-30 Jan Civ Wed 50

BABBACOMBE

See Torquay

BARNSTAPLE — Map 3 SS53

The Imperial

★★★★ 77% HOTEL

☎ 01271 345861 📠 01271 324448
Taw Vale Pde EX32 8NB
e-mail: info@brend-imperial.co.uk
web: www.brend-imperial.co.uk
dir: M5 junct 27/A361 to Barnstaple. Follow town centre signs, passing Tesco. Straight on at next 2 rdbts. Hotel on right

This smart and attractive hotel is pleasantly located at the centre of Barnstaple and overlooks the river. The staff are friendly and offer attentive service. The comfortable bedrooms are in a range of sizes, some with balconies and many overlooking the river. Afternoon tea is available

in the lounge, and the appetising cuisine is freshly prepared.

Rooms 63 (7 fmly) (4 GF) **S** £87-£185; **D** £97-£185*
Facilities FTV Leisure facilities at sister hotel 🎵 Xmas New Year Wi-fi **Conf** Class 40 Board 30 Thtr 60
Services Lift **Parking** 80 **Notes** LB ⊗

See advert on page 140

Barnstaple Hotel

★★★ 81% HOTEL

☎ 01271 376221 📠 01271 324101
Braunton Rd EX31 1LE
e-mail: info@barnstaplehotel.co.uk
web: www.barnstaplehotel.co.uk
dir: Outskirts of Barnstaple on A361

This well-established hotel enjoys a convenient location on the edge of town. Bedrooms are spacious and well equipped, many with access to a balcony overlooking the outdoor pool and garden. A wide choice is offered from various menus based on local produce, served in the Brasserie Restaurant. There is an extensive range of leisure and conference facilities.

Rooms 60 (4 fmly) (17 GF) **S** £67-£115; **D** £77-£125*
Facilities FTV 🏊 ⅋ Gym Sauna Solarium Snooker room Xmas New Year Wi-fi Child facilities **Conf** Class 100 Board 50 Thtr 250 **Parking** 250 **Notes** LB Civ Wed 150

BARNSTAPLE *continued*

Royal & Fortescue

★★★ 78% HOTEL

☎ 01271 342289 📠 01271 340102
Boutport St EX31 1HG
e-mail: info@royalfortescue.co.uk
web: www.royalfortescue.co.uk
dir: A361 along Barbican Rd signed town centre, turn
right into Queen St & left onto Boutport St, hotel on left

Formerly a coaching inn, this friendly and convivial hotel
is conveniently located in the centre of town. Bedrooms
vary in size and all are decorated and furnished to a
consistently high standard. In addition to the formal
restaurant, guests can take snacks in the popular coffee
shop or dine more informally in The Bank, a bistro and
café bar.

Rooms 49 (4 fmly) (4 GF) **S** £50-£99; **D** £59-£110*
Facilities FTV Leisure facilities available at sister hotel
♫ Xmas New Year Wi-fi **Conf** Class 25 Board 25 Thtr 25
Services Lift **Parking** 40 **Notes** LB

Park

★★★ 74% HOTEL

☎ 01271 372166 📠 01271 323157
Taw Vale EX32 9AE
e-mail: info@parkhotel.co.uk
web: www.parkhotel.co.uk
dir: Opposite Rock Park, 0.5m from town centre

Enjoying views across the park and within easy walking
distance of the town centre, this modern hotel offers a
choice of bedrooms in both the main building and the
Garden Court, just across the car park. Public rooms are
open-plan in style and the friendly staff offer attentive
service in a relaxed atmosphere.

Rooms 40 (17 annexe) (7 fmly) (5 GF) **S** £55-£82;
D £65-£92* **Facilities** FTV Leisure facilities available at
sister hotel Xmas New Year Wi-fi **Conf** Class 50 Board 30
Thtr 80 **Parking** 80 **Notes** LB Civ Wed 100

Cedars Lodge

★★ Ⓐ HOTEL

☎ 01271 371784 📠 01271 325733
Bickington Rd EX31 2HP
e-mail: cedars.barnstaple@oldenglishinns.co.uk
web: www.oldenglish.co.uk
dir: M5 junct 27, A361 signed Tiverton & Barnstaple

Rooms 34 (32 annexe) (6 fmly) (14 GF) **Facilities** Xmas
Conf Class 100 Board 100 Thtr 200 **Parking** 150
Notes LB ☺ Civ Wed 200

Travelodge Barnstaple

BUDGET HOTEL

☎ 0871 984 6345 📠 01271 373907
A39 North Devon Link Rd EX31 3RY
web: www.travelodge.co.uk
dir: Off A39 at Roundswell rdbt take 3rd exit

Travelodge offers good quality, good value, budget
accommodation. All offer family rooms sleeping up to four
(two adults, two children) with en suite bathroom/
shower-room, remote-control TV, tea- and coffee-making
facilities and comfortable beds. Food options vary.
Breakfast is at the on-site Bar Café restaurant (if
available) or to take away. See also Hotel Groups pages.

Rooms 45 **S** fr £29; **D** fr £29

BIDEFORD   Map 3 SS42

Royal

★★★ 74% HOTEL

☎ 01237 472005 📠 01237 478957
Barnstaple St EX39 4AE
e-mail: reservations@royalbideford.co.uk
web: www.royalbideford.co.uk
dir: At eastern end of Bideford Bridge

A quiet and relaxing hotel, the Royal is set near the river
within a five minutes walk of the busy town centre and
quay. The bright, well maintained public areas retain
much of the charm and style of its 16th-century origins,

particularly in the wood-panelled Kingsley Suite. Bedrooms are well equipped and comfortable. The meals at dinner and the lounge snacks are appetising.

Rooms 32 (2 fmly) (2 GF) **S** £65-£109; **D** £79-£109*
Facilities FTV Xmas New Year Wi-fi **Conf** Class 100 Board 100 Thtr 100 **Services** Lift **Parking** 70 **Notes** LB Civ Wed 130

Durrant House

★★★ **A** HOTEL

☎ 01237 472361 📄 01237 421709
Heywood Rd, Northam EX39 3QB
e-mail: info@durranthousehotel.com
dir: A39 to Bideford, over New Torridge Bridge, right at rdbt, hotel 500yds on right

Rooms 125 (25 fmly) (14 GF) **S** £40-£60; **D** £70-£170 (incl. bkfst)* **Facilities** FTV ⌇ Gym Sauna ♫ Xmas New Year Wi-fi **Conf** Class 100 Board 80 Thtr 350 Del from £95 to £105* **Services** Lift **Parking** 200 **Notes** LB Civ Wed 100

Yeoldon Country House

★★ 81% ❀ HOTEL

☎ 01237 474400 📄 01237 476618
Durrant Ln, Northam EX39 2RL
e-mail: yeoldonhouse@aol.com
web: www.yeoldonhousehotel.co.uk
dir: A39 from Barnstaple over River Torridge Bridge. At rdbt right onto A386 towards Northam, then 3rd right into Durrant Lane

In a tranquil location with superb views over attractive grounds and the River Torridge, this is a charming Victorian house. The well-equipped bedrooms are individually decorated and some have balconies with breathtaking views. The public rooms are full of character with many interesting features and artefacts. The daily-changing dinner menu offers imaginative dishes.

Rooms 10 **S** £77.50-£82.50; **D** £120-£135 (incl. bkfst) **Facilities** FTV Wi-fi **Parking** 20 **Notes** LB Closed 24-27 Dec Civ Wed 100

See advert on this page

Henley

★★ 76% SMALL HOTEL

☎ 01548 810240 📄 01548 810240
TQ7 4AR
e-mail: enquiries@thehenleyhotel.co.uk
dir: through Bigbury, past Golf Centre into Bigbury-on-Sea. Hotel on left as road slopes towards shore

Built in Edwardian times and complete with its own private cliff path to a sandy beach, this small hotel boasts stunning views from an elevated position. Family run, it is a perfect choice for guests wishing to escape the hurried pace of life to a peaceful retreat. Personal service, friendly hospitality and food cooked with care using local, fresh produce combine to make this a simple yet special place to stay.

Rooms 6 **Parking** 9 **Notes** No children 12yrs Closed Nov-Mar

The Commodore Hotel

Set in its own grounds nestled in the picturesque village of Instow overlooking the Taw and Torridge estuaries personally owned and managed by The Woolaway Family.

Majority of rooms having private balconies in addition to ground floor luxury rooms with private terraces. Ideally situated for exploring the North Devon and Cornwall coastline.

Telephone: 01271 860347 email: admin@commodore-instow.co.uk

YEOLDON COUNTRY HOUSE HOTEL

Durrant Lane, Northam, Bideford EX39 2RL
Tel: 01237 474400　Fax: 01237 476618
Email: yeoldonhouse@aol.com　Web: www.yeoldonhouse.co.uk

Nestled on the banks of the River Torridge, Yeoldon House is a wonderful place to unwind. The award winning Soyer's Restaurant is open to non-residents for dinner (Monday - Saturday). All rooms are en suite with freeview televisions, wi fi and tea and coffee making facilities.

Resident Proprietors

Available for private parties, exclusive use and licensed for Civil Weddings.

BISHOPSTEIGNTON Map 3 SX97

Cockhaven Manor Hotel

THE INDEPENDENTS
HOTEL ASSOCIATION

★★ 69% HOTEL

☎ 01626 775252 📄 01626 775572
Cockhaven Rd TQ14 9RF
e-mail: cockhaven@btconnect.com
web: www.cockhavenmanor.com
dir: M5/A380 towards Torquay, then A381 towards
Teignmouth. Left at Metro Motors. Hotel 500yds on left

A friendly, family-run inn that dates back to the 16th
century. Bedrooms are well equipped and many enjoy
views across the beautiful Teign estuary. A choice of
dining options is offered, and traditional and interesting
dishes, along with locally caught fish, prove popular.

Rooms 12 (2 fmly) **S** £47-£55; **D** £66-£80 (incl. bkfst)*
Facilities Petanque Wi-fi **Conf** Class 50 Board 30 Thtr 50
Parking 50 **Notes** LB RS 25-26 Dec

BOVEY TRACEY Map 3 SX87

Coombe Cross

★★ 🅰 HOTEL

☎ 01626 832476 📄 01626 835298
Coombe Ln TQ13 9EY
e-mail: info@coombecross.co.uk
web: www.coombecross.co.uk
dir: A38 signed Bovey Tracey & town centre, along High
St, up hill 400yds beyond parish church. Hotel on left

Rooms 23 (3 fmly) (3 GF) **S** £45-£50; **D** £90-£100 (incl.
bkfst)* **Facilities** 🏊 Gym Sauna Xmas New Year Wi-fi
Conf Class 56 Board 70 Thtr 70 **Parking** 18 **Notes** LB
Closed Jan

BRANSCOMBE Map 4 SY18

The Masons Arms

★★ 80% ⊛ HOTEL

☎ 01297 680300 📄 01297 680500
EX12 3DJ
e-mail: reception@masonsarms.co.uk
dir: Off A3052 towards Branscombe, hotel at hill bottom

This delightful, 14th-century village inn is just half a
mile from the sea. The bedrooms in the inn have a
definite period charm, but the thatched annexed cottages
tend to be more spacious and have patios with seating.
In the bar, an extensive selection of dishes, which
includes many local specialities is available, and the
restaurant offers an imaginative range of dishes.

Rooms 21 (14 annexe) (1 fmly) **S** £80-£170; **D** £80-£170
(incl. bkfst)* **Facilities** Xmas New Year Wi-fi **Parking** 43
Notes LB

Bulstone

★★ 64% HOTEL

☎ 01297 680446 📄 01297 680000
High Bulstone EX12 3BL
e-mail: bulstone@aol.com
web: www.childfriendlyhotels.com
dir: A3052, Exeter to Lyme Regis, Branscombe Cross,
follow brown hotel sign

Situated in a peaceful location close to the beautiful east
Devon coast, this family-friendly hotel is ideally placed
for a relaxing break with plenty of attractions within easy
reach. All bedrooms comprise a main bedroom and
separate children's room, each being practically
furnished and equipped. Additional facilities include a
playroom, a snug lounge, and the dining room where
enjoyable home-cooked meals are offered. There is no
charge for children under ten, and children's tea is at
5pm.

Rooms 7 (7 fmly) (4 GF) **D** £90-£110 (incl. bkfst)*
Facilities FTV Xmas New Year Wi-fi Child facilities
Conf Class 25 Board 25 Del from £125 to £150*
Services Air con **Parking** 25 **Notes** LB ⊗

BRIXHAM Map 3 SX95

Quayside

★★★ 73% HOTEL

☎ 01803 855751 📄 01803 882733
41-49 King St TQ5 9TJ
e-mail: reservations@quaysidehotel.co.uk
web: www.quaysidehotel.co.uk
dir: A380, at 2nd rdbt at Kinkerswell towards Brixham on
A3022

With views over the harbour and bay, this hotel was
formerly six cottages. The owners and their team of local
staff provide friendly and attentive service. Public rooms
retain a certain cosiness and intimacy, and include the
lounge, residents' bar and Ernie Lister's public bar.
Freshly landed fish features on menus in the well-
appointed restaurant, and snacks are available in the
public bar.

Rooms 29 (2 fmly) **Facilities** FTV Xmas New Year Wi-fi
Conf Class 18 Board 18 Thtr 25 **Parking** 30

Berry Head

★★★ 72% HOTEL

☎ 01803 853225 ▤ 01803 882084
Berry Head Rd TQ5 9AJ
e-mail: stay@berryheadhotel.com
dir: From marina, 1m, hotel on left

From its stunning cliff-top location, this imposing property that dates back to 1809, has spectacular views across Torbay. Public areas include two comfortable lounges, an outdoor terrace, a swimming pool, together with a bar serving a range of popular dishes. Many of the bedrooms have the benefit of the splendid sea views.

Rooms 32 (7 fmly) **Facilities** STV 🕲 🏊 Petanque Sailing Deep sea fishing Yacht charter 🎵 Xmas New Year Wi-fi **Conf** Class 250 Board 40 Thtr 300 Del from £85 to £125 **Parking** 200 **Notes** Civ Wed 200

See advert on opposite page

BURRINGTON Map 3 SS61
(NEAR PORTSMOUTH ARMS STATION)

INSPECTORS' CHOICE

Northcote Manor

★★★ 🏅🏅 COUNTRY HOUSE HOTEL

☎ 01769 560501 ▤ 01769 560770
EX37 9LZ
e-mail: rest@northcotemanor.co.uk
web: www.northcotemanor.co.uk
dir: Off A377 opposite Portsmouth Arms, into hotel drive. NB. Do not enter Burrington village

A warm and friendly welcome is assured at this beautiful country-house hotel. Built in 1716, the house sits in 20 acres of grounds and woodlands. Guests can enjoy wonderful views over the Taw River Valley whilst relaxing in the delightful environment created by the attentive staff. The elegant restaurant is the highlight of any stay with the finest of local produce used in well-prepared dishes. Bedrooms, including some suites, are individually styled, spacious and well appointed.

Rooms 11 **S** £100-£170; **D** £155-£255 (incl. bkfst)*
Facilities FTV 🕲 🏊 Japanese style water garden Xmas New Year Wi-fi **Conf** Class 50 Board 30 Thtr 80 Del from £155* **Parking** 30 **Notes** LB Civ Wed 100

CHAGFORD Map 3 SX78

INSPECTORS' CHOICE

Gidleigh Park

★★★★ 🏅🏅🏅🏅
COUNTRY HOUSE HOTEL

☎ 01647 432367 ▤ 01647 432574
TQ13 8HH
e-mail: gidleighpark@gidleigh.co.uk
web: www.gidleigh.com
dir: From Chagford, right at Lloyds Bank into Mill St. After 150yds fork right, follow lane 2m to end

Set in 45 acres of lovingly tended grounds this world-renowned hotel retains a timeless charm and a very endearing, homely atmosphere. Individually styled bedrooms are sumptuously furnished; some with separate seating areas, some with balconies and many enjoying panoramic views. The spacious public areas are feature antique furniture, beautiful flower arrangements and magnificent artwork. The award-winning cuisine created by Michael Caines, together with the top quality wine list, will make a stay here a truly memorable experience.

Rooms 24 (3 annexe) (4 fmly) (4 GF) **S** £295-£435; **D** £330-£470 (incl. bkfst) **Facilities** STV FTV 🏊 Putt green Fishing 🏌 Bowls Guided walks Sauna & steam room suite Xmas New Year Wi-fi **Conf** Board 22 Del from £370 to £510 **Parking** 25 **Notes** Civ Wed 54

INSPECTORS' CHOICE

Mill End

★★ 🏅🏅 HOTEL

☎ 01647 432282 ▤ 01647 433106
Dartmoor National Park TQ13 8JN
e-mail: info@millendhotel.com
web: www.millendhotel.com
dir: From A30 at Whiddon Down follow A382 to Moretonhampstead. After 3.5m hump back bridge at Sandy Park, hotel on right by river

In an attractive location, Mill End, an 18th-century working water mill sits by the River Teign that offers six miles of angling. The atmosphere is akin to a family home where guests are encouraged to relax and enjoy the peace and informality. Bedrooms are available in a range of sizes and all are stylishly decorated and thoughtfully equipped. Dining is certainly a highlight of a stay here; the menus offer exciting dishes featuring local produce.

Rooms 14 (3 GF) **S** £90-£160; **D** £90-£220 (incl. bkfst) **Facilities** FTV Fishing 🏌 Xmas New Year Wi-fi **Conf** Class 20 Board 30 Thtr 30 **Parking** 25 **Notes** LB

Three Crowns Hotel

★★ 69% SMALL HOTEL

☎ 01647 433444 ▤ 01647 433117
High St TQ13 8AJ
e-mail: threecrowns@msn.com
web: www.chagford-accom.co.uk
dir: Exit A30 at Whiddon Down. Hotel in town centre opposite church

This 13th-century inn is located in the heart of the village. Exposed beams, mullioned windows and open fires are all part of the charm which is evident throughout. There is a range of bedrooms; all are comfortable and several have four-poster beds. A choice of bars is available along with a pleasant lounge and separate dining room.

Rooms 17 (1 fmly) **Facilities** Pool table in bar Xmas New Year **Conf** Board 150 Thtr 150 **Parking** 20 **Notes** Civ Wed 200

CLOVELLY   Map 3 SS32

Red Lion Hotel
★★ 75% HOTEL

☎ 01237 431237   📠 01237 431044
The Quay EX39 5TF
e-mail: redlion@clovelly.co.uk
web: www.redlion-clovelly.co.uk/redlionindex.html
dir: Exit A39 at Clovelly Cross onto B3237. Pass visitor centre, 1st left by white rails to harbour

'Idyllic' is the only way to describe the harbour-side setting of this charming 18th-century inn, where this famous fishing village forms a spectacular backdrop. Bedrooms are stylish and enjoy delightful views. The inn's relaxed atmosphere is conducive to 'switching off' from the pressures of modern life, even if the harbour comes alive with the activities of the local fishermen during the day.

Rooms 11 (2 fmly) (2 GF) **S** £58.75-£82; **D** £117.50-£134 (incl. bkfst)* **Facilities** Tennis can be arranged Xmas New Year Wi-fi **Parking** 11 **Notes** ⊗ Civ Wed 60

New Inn
★★ 72% HOTEL

☎ 01237 431303   📠 01237 431636
High St EX39 5TQ
e-mail: newinn@clovelly.co.uk
dir: At Clovelly Cross, off A39 onto B3237. Follow down hill for 1.5m. Right at sign 'All vehicles for Clovelly'

Famed for its cobbled descent to the harbour, this fascinating fishing village is a traffic-free zone. Consequently, luggage is conveyed by sledge or donkey to this much-photographed hotel. Carefully renovated bedrooms and public areas are smartly presented with

quality, locally-made furnishings. Meals may be taken in the elegant restaurant or the popular Upalong bar.

Rooms 8 (2 fmly) **S** £49.50-£71.50; **D** £99-£113 (incl. bkfst)* **Facilities** Tennis can be arranged Xmas New Year **Notes** ⊗ Civ Wed 50

COLYFORD   Map 4 SY29

Swallows Eaves
★★ 80% HOTEL

☎ 01297 553184   📠 01297 553574
Swan Hill Rd EX24 6QJ
e-mail: info@swallowseaves.co.uk
web: www.swallowseaves.co.uk
dir: On A3052 between Lyme Regis & Sidmouth, in village centre, opposite post office store

Close to the Devon and Dorset border, this intimate and welcoming hotel is ideally located for exploring this beautiful area. The relaxed atmosphere is matched with attentive service. Comfortable bedrooms come complete with Egyptian cotton bedding and large fluffy towels. Local produce features on the menu which is offered in the stylish Reeds restaurant.

Rooms 8 (1 GF) **S** £56-£65; **D** £80-£124 (incl. bkfst)* **Facilities** FTV Wi-fi **Parking** 10 **Notes** LB ⊗ No children 14yrs

CULLOMPTON   Map 3 ST00

Padbrook Park
★★★ 77% HOTEL

☎ 01884 836100   📠 01884 836101
EX15 1RU
e-mail: info@padbrookpark.co.uk
dir: 1m from M5 junct 28 follow brown signs

This purpose-built hotel is part of a golf and leisure complex located in the Culm Valley, just one mile from the M5. Set in 100 acres of parkland and golf course, Padbrook Park has a friendly, relaxed atmosphere and a contemporary feel. A variety of room types is available, including family, inter-connecting, superior and deluxe rooms.

Rooms 40 (4 fmly) (11 GF) **S** £70-£110; **D** £90-£150 (incl. bkfst)* **Facilities** STV FTV ⅃ 18 Putt green Fishing Gym 3 rink bowling centre Crazy golf ⤳ Xmas New Year Wi-fi **Conf** Class 150 Board 50 Thtr 200 **Services** Lift **Parking** 250 **Notes** LB ⊗ Civ Wed 200

DARTMOUTH   Map 3 SX85

The Dart Marina
★★★★ 79% ◉◉ HOTEL

☎ 01803 832580 & 837120   📠 01803 835040
Sandquay Rd TQ6 9PH
e-mail: reservations@dartmarina.com
web: www.dartmarina.com
dir: A3122 from Totnes to Dartmouth. Follow road which becomes College Way, before Higher Ferry. Hotel sharp left in Sandquay Rd

Boasting a stunning riverside location with its own marina, this is a truly special place to stay. Bedrooms vary in style but all have wonderful views, and some have private balconies to sit and soak up the atmosphere. Stylish public areas take full advantage of the waterside setting with opportunities to dine alfresco. In addition to the Wildfire Bar & Bistro, the River Restaurant is the venue for accomplished cooking.

Rooms 49 (4 annexe) (4 fmly) (4 GF) **S** £95-£155; **D** £130-£195 (incl. bkfst)* **Facilities** Spa ⊙ Gym Canoeing Sailing Xmas New Year Wi-fi **Services** Lift **Parking** 50 **Notes** LB Civ Wed 40

Royal Castle
★★★ 80% HOTEL

☎ 01803 833033   📠 01803 835445
11 The Quay TQ6 9PS
e-mail: enquiry@royalcastle.co.uk
web: www.royalcastle.co.uk
dir: in centre of town, overlooking Inner Harbour

At the edge of the harbour, this imposing 17th-century former coaching inn is filled with charm and character. Bedrooms are well equipped and comfortable; many have harbour views. A choice of quiet seating areas is offered in addition to both the traditional and contemporary bars. A variety of eating options is available, including the main restaurant which features accomplished cuisine and lovely views.

Rooms 25 (3 fmly) **Facilities** ⤳ Xmas New Year Wi-fi **Conf** Class 30 Board 20 Thtr 50 **Parking** 17 **Notes** Civ Wed 80

Stoke Lodge

★★★ 72% HOTEL

☎ 01803 770523 🖨 01803 770851
Stoke Fleming TQ6 0RA
e-mail: mail@stokelodge.co.uk
web: www.stokelodge.co.uk
dir: 2m S A379

This family-run hotel continues to attract returning guests and is set in three acres of gardens and grounds with lovely views across to the sea. A range of leisure facilities is offered including both indoor and outdoor pools, along with a choice of comfortable lounges. Bedrooms are pleasantly appointed. The restaurant offers a choice of menus and an impressive wine list.

Rooms 25 (5 fmly) (7 GF) **S** £66-£75; **D** £92-£130 (incl. bkfst) **Facilities** FTV ⓢ ➘ ☺ Putt green Table tennis Pool & Snooker tables Sauna Xmas New Year Wi-fi **Conf** Class 60 Board 30 Thtr 80 **Parking** 50 **Notes** LB

The New Angel Rooms

RESTAURANT WITH ROOMS

☎ 01803 839425 🖨 01803 839505
51 Victoria Rd TQ6 9RT
e-mail: info@thenewangel.co.uk
dir: In Dartmouth take one-way system, 1st left at NatWest Bank

Just a level stroll from the acclaimed New Angel restaurant, this terrace property offers very comfortable, contemporary accommodation, equipped with numerous extra facilities including a complimentary half bottle of Champagne. Breakfast is a feature, with freshly squeezed orange juice: specials such as eggs Benedict and scrambled eggs with smoked salmon should not be missed.

Rooms 6 (2 fmly)

| DAWLISH | Map 3 SX97 |

Langstone Cliff

THE INDEPENDENTS
HOTEL ASSOCIATION

★★★ 78% HOTEL

☎ 01626 868000 🖨 01626 868006
Dawlish Warren EX7 0NA
e-mail: reception@langstone-hotel.co.uk
web: www.langstone-hotel.co.uk
dir: 1.5m NE off A379 Exeter road to Dawlish Warren

A family owned and run hotel, the Langstone Cliff offers a range of leisure, conference and function facilities. Bedrooms, many with sea views and balconies, are spacious, comfortable and well equipped. There are a number of attractive lounges and a well-stocked bar. Dinner is served, often carvery style, in the restaurant.

Langstone Cliff

Rooms 66 (4 annexe) (52 fmly) (10 GF) **Facilities** STV FTV ⓢ ➘ ☺ Gym Table tennis Golf practice area Hair & beauty salon Ballroom ♫ Xmas New Year Wi-fi Child facilities **Conf** Class 200 Board 80 Thtr 400 **Services** Lift Parking 200 **Notes** Civ Wed 400

| EGGESFORD | Map 3 SS61 |

Fox & Hounds Country Hotel

★★★ 71% ⑱ HOTEL

☎ 01769 580345
EX18 7JZ
e-mail: relax@foxandhoundshotel.co.uk
dir: M5 junct 27, A361 towards Tiverton. Take A396 signped Tiverton/Bickleigh. Then take A3072 to Crediton. Then A377 towards Barnstaple. In 14m pass Eggesford Station, hotel just beyond on left

Situated midway between Exeter and Barnstaple, in the beautiful Taw Valley, this extensively developed hotel was originally a coaching inn dating back to the 1800s. Many of the comfortable, elegant bedrooms have lovely countryside views. Impressive cooking utilises excellent local produce and can be enjoyed in either restaurant or the convivial bar. For fishing enthusiasts, the hotel has direct access to the River Taw, and equipment and tuition can be provided if required.

Rooms 15 (4 fmly) (1 GF) **S** £60-£75; **D** £80-£130 (incl. bkfst)* **Facilities** FTV Fishing Hair & beauty salon Xmas New Year Wi-fi **Conf** Class 60 Board 60 Thtr 100 Del from £95 to £120* **Parking** 100 **Notes** LB Civ Wed 120

| EXETER | Map 3 SX99 |

Mercure Southgate Hotel

★★★★ 74% HOTEL

☎ 01392 412812 🖨 01392 413549
Southernhay East EX1 1QF
e-mail: h6624@accor.com
web: www.mercure-uk.com
dir: M5 junct 30, 3rd exit (Exeter), 2nd left towards city centre, 3rd exit at next rdbt, hotel 2m on right

Centrally located and with excellent parking, The Southgate offers a diverse range of leisure and business facilities. Public areas are pleasantly spacious with comfortable seating in the bar and lounge; there is also a pleasant terrace. A range of bedroom sizes is available and all are well equipped with modern facilities.

Rooms 154 (6 fmly) (23 GF) (8 smoking) **Facilities** FTV ⓢ supervised Gym Sauna Sun shower Spa pool New Year Wi-fi **Conf** Class 70 Board 50 Thtr 150 **Services** Lift Parking 101 **Notes** ⊗ RS Sat/Sun Civ Wed 80

The Rougemont by Thistle

thistle

★★★★ 72% HOTEL

☎ 0871 376 9018 🖨 0871 376 9118
Queen St EX4 3SP
e-mail: exeter@thistle.co.uk
web: www.thistlehotels.com/exeter
dir: M5 junct 30 follow signs to services at 1st rdbt, then 1st left towards city centre. In city centre follow Museum/Central Station signs. Hotel opposite

Centrally located, this elegant hotel is well situated for those visiting the city for business or pleasure. There is a charming, old-fashioned atmosphere here, with traditional hospitality to the fore. All bedrooms offer high levels of comfort with a number of suites also available, a choice of bars is provided - the convivial Drakes Bar and the smart, more formal cocktail bar.

Rooms 98 (2 fmly) **S** £70-£160; **D** £80-£170* **Facilities** STV Wi-fi **Conf** Class 110 Board 70 Thtr 250 Del from £125 to £170* **Services** Lift **Parking** 24 **Notes** LB ⊗ Civ Wed 200

See advert on page 146

Abode Hotel Exeter

aBode

★★★★ 71% ⑱⑱ HOTEL

☎ 01392 319955 🖨 01392 439423
Cathedral Yard EX1 1HD
e-mail: reservationsexeter@abodehotels.co.uk
web: www.abodehotels.co.uk
dir: M5 junct 30 towards A379. Follow city centre signs. Hotel opposite cathedral behind High St

Overlooking the cathedral, this hotel has an exciting contemporary style. Bedrooms are available in a range of comfort styles - all have handcrafted beds and modern facilities with internet access and CD players. The café bar here has an informal style with live music most *continued*

EXETER *continued*

weekends, and there is also a champagne bar. The award-winning Michael Caines Restaurant delivers accomplished cuisine using the finest local produce.

Rooms 53 (4 fmly) **Facilities** Gym Beauty therapy ♫ Xmas New Year Wi-fi **Conf** Class 50 Board 50 Thtr 100 **Services** Lift Air con **Notes** LB ⊗ Civ Wed 50

Buckerell Lodge Hotel

★★★★ 71% HOTEL

☎ 0844 855 9112 ◎ 01392 424333
Topsham Rd EX2 4SQ
e-mail: buckerelllodge@foliohotels.com
web: www.foliohotels.com/buckerelllodge
dir: M5 junct 30 follow city centre signs, hotel 0.5m from Exeter

Although situated outside the city centre, this hotel is easily accessed by car or public transport. Bedrooms, all in modern styles, are comfortable, fairly spacious and generally quiet. Public areas include a popular bar and restaurant and a variety of function rooms. The attractive and extensive gardens are a lovely feature and ideal for alfresco dining during warmer weather.

Rooms 54 (17 GF) **Facilities** STV FTV Wi-fi **Conf** Class 32 Board 35 Thtr 80 **Parking** 60 **Notes** ⊗ Civ Wed 60

Devon

★★★ 75% HOTEL

☎ 01392 259268 ◎ 01392 413142
Exeter Bypass, Matford EX2 8XU
e-mail: info@devonhotel.co.uk
web: www.devonhotel.co.uk
dir: M5 junct 30 follow Marsh Barton Ind Est signs on A379. Hotel on A38 rdbt

Within easy access of the city centre, the M5 and the city's business parks, this smart Georgian hotel offers

modern, comfortable accommodation. The Carriages Bar and Brasserie is popular with guests and locals alike, offering a wide range of dishes as well as a carvery at both lunch and dinner. Service is friendly and attentive, and extensive meeting and business facilities are available.

Devon

Rooms 40 (40 annexe) (3 fmly) (11 GF) **S** £80-£100; **D** £90-£100* **Facilities** FTV Xmas New Year Wi-fi **Conf** Class 80 Board 40 Thtr 150 **Parking** 250 **Notes** LB ⊗ Civ Wed 100

Best Western Lord Haldon Country House

★★★ 73% ⊛ HOTEL

☎ 01392 832483 ◎ 01392 833765
Dunchideock EX6 7YF
e-mail: enquiries@lordhaldonhotel.co.uk
web: www.lordhaldonhotel.co.uk
dir: M5 junct 31, 1st exit off A30, follow signs through Ide to Dunchideock

Set amidst rural tranquillity, this attractive country house goes from strength to strength. Guests are assured of a warm welcome from the professional team of staff and the well-equipped bedrooms are comfortable, many with stunning views. The daily changing menu features skilfully cooked dishes with most of the produce sourced locally.

Best Western Lord Haldon Country House

Rooms 23 (3 fmly) **Facilities** Xmas New Year Wi-fi **Conf** Class 100 Board 40 Thtr 250 **Parking** 120 **Notes** Civ Wed 120

Queens Court

★★★ 73% ⊛ HOTEL

☎ 01392 272709 ◎ 01392 491390
6-8 Bystock Ter EX4 4HY
e-mail: enquiries@queenscourt-hotel.co.uk
web: www.queenscourt-hotel.co.uk
dir: Exit dual carriageway at junct 30 onto B5132 (Topsham Rd) towards city centre. Hotel 200yds from station

Quietly located within walking distance of the city centre, this privately owned hotel is a listed, early Victorian property that provides friendly hospitality. The smart public areas and bedrooms are tastefully furnished in

contemporary style, and the bright and attractive Olive Tree restaurant offers an interesting selection of dishes. Rooms are available for conferences, meetings and other functions. Complimentary parking is available in a public car park directly opposite the hotel entrance.

Rooms 18 (1 fmly) **Facilities** FTV Wi-fi **Conf** Class 30 Board 30 Thtr 60 **Services** Lift **Notes** ⊗ RS 25-30 Dec Civ Wed 60

Barton Cross Hotel & Restaurant

★★★ 71% ⑨ HOTEL

☎ 01392 841245 🖹 01392 841942
Huxham, Stoke Canon EX5 4EJ
e-mail: bartonxhuxham@aol.com
dir: 0.5m off A396 at Stoke Canon, 3m N of Exeter

17th-century charm combined with 21st-century luxury perfectly sums up the appeal of this lovely country hotel. The bedrooms are spacious, tastefully decorated and well maintained. Public areas include the cosy first-floor lounge and the lounge/bar with its warming log fire. The restaurant offers a seasonally changing menu of consistently enjoyable cuisine.

Rooms 9 (2 fmly) (2 GF) (2 smoking) **S** £80-£90; **D** £98-£110 (incl. bkfst) **Facilities** STV FTV Xmas New Year Wi-fi **Conf** Class 20 Board 20 Thtr 20 **Parking** 35 **Notes** LB

See advert on this page

Gipsy Hill Country House Hotel

★★★ 70% HOTEL

☎ 01392 465252 🖹 01392 464302
Gipsy Hill Ln, Monkerton EX1 3RN
e-mail: stay@gipsyhillhotel.co.uk
web: www.gipsyhillhotel.co.uk
dir: M5 junct 29 towards Exeter. Turn right at 1st rdbt and right again at next rdbt. Hotel 0.5m on right

Located on the edge of the city, with easy access to the M5 and the airport, this popular hotel is set in attractive, well-tended gardens and boasts far-reaching country views. The hotel offers a range of conference and function rooms, comfortable bedrooms and modern facilities. An intimate bar and lounge are adjacent to the elegant restaurant.

Rooms 37 (17 annexe) (4 fmly) (12 GF) (1 smoking) **S** £60-£90; **D** £70-£110 (incl. bkfst) **Facilities** FTV Xmas New Year Wi-fi **Conf** Class 80 Board 80 Thtr 300 Del from £95 to £140 **Parking** 60 **Notes** LB ⊗ Civ Wed 130

Great Western

★★ 68% HOTEL

☎ 01392 274039 🖹 01392 425529
St David's Station Approach EX4 4NU
e-mail: bookings@greatwesternhotel.co.uk
dir: M5 junct 30, follow City Centre signs then St Davids Station signs. Hotel on A377 W of city

This long established railway hotel has been providing rest and refreshment for weary travellers for many years. The long tradition of hospitality is still very much in evidence in the convivial bar which is a popular venue with both visitors and locals alike. Bedrooms, in a variety of sizes, are soundly appointed. In addition to the bar menu, guests also have the option of dining in the attractive restaurant.

Rooms 36 (1 fmly) **Conf** Class 12 Board 20 Thtr 35 **Notes** LB

Red House

★★ 64% HOTEL

☎ 01392 256104 🖹 01392 666145
2 Whipton Village Rd EX4 8AR
e-mail: info@redhousehotelexeter.co.uk
dir: M5 junct 30. Left before Middlemoor services, right at rdbt towards Pinhoe & University. 0.75m left to Whipton/University, hotel 1m on right

Located just a mile from the city centre, this family owned establishment has a warm and welcoming atmosphere; the convivial bar is a popular meeting place for visitors and locals alike. Bedrooms are soundly appointed and provide good levels of comfort. An extensive menu is offered either in the bar area or separate restaurant with a carvery operated at lunchtimes.

Rooms 12 (5 fmly) (4 GF) **S** £55; **D** £70 (incl. bkfst)* **Facilities** FTV **Conf** Board 24 Thtr 40 Del from £107 to £120* **Parking** 25 **Notes** LB ⊗

Express by Holiday Inn Exeter, M5 Jct 29

BUDGET HOTEL

☎ 01392 261000 🖹 01392 261061
Guardian Rd EX1 3PE
e-mail: managerexeter@expressholidayinn.co.uk
web: www.expressexeter.com
dir: M5 junct 29, follow signs for Exeter city centre. Hotel on 1st rdbt

A modern hotel ideal for families and business travellers. Fresh and uncomplicated, the spacious rooms include Sky TV, power shower and tea and coffee-making facilities. Continental buffet breakfast is included in the room rate; other meals may be taken at the nearby family pub or restaurant. See also the Hotel Groups pages.

Rooms 149 (94 fmly) (41 GF) (6 smoking) **S** £59-£99.95; **D** fr £99.95 (incl. bkfst) **Conf** Class 20 Board 20 Thtr 30

EXETER *continued*

Innkeeper's Lodge Exeter East

BUDGET HOTEL

☎ 0845 112 6086 📄 0845 112 6217
Clyst St George EX3 0QJ
web: www.innkeeperslodge.com/exetereast
dir: M5 junct 30, A376 towards Clyst St Mary. Right at 1st rdbt onto A376, straight over at 2nd rdbt. Right at 3rd rdbt into Bridge Hill. Lodge on right

Innkeeper's Lodge represents an exciting, high value concept within the budget hotel market. Comfortable bedrooms provide excellent facilities that include satellite TV and modem points. This lodge has a picturesque setting, unique style and quirky character having been carefully restored with traditional and reclaimed local materials. Food is served all day, and an extensive, complimentary continental breakfast is offered. See also the Hotel Groups pages.

Rooms 21 (4 fmly) **Conf** Thtr 20

Travelodge Exeter (M5)

BUDGET HOTEL

☎ 0871 984 6228 📄 01392 410406
Moor Ln, Sandygate EX2 7HF
web: www.travelodge.co.uk
dir: M5 junct 30

Travelodge offers good quality, good value, budget accommodation. All offer family rooms sleeping up to four (two adults, two children) with en suite bathroom/shower-room, remote-control TV, tea- and coffee-making facilities and comfortable beds. Food options vary. Breakfast is at the on-site Bar Café restaurant (if available) or to take away. See also Hotel Groups pages.

Rooms 102 **S** fr £29; **D** fr £29 **Conf** Class 18 Board 25 Thtr 80

Chi Restaurant & Bar with Accommodation

RESTAURANT WITH ROOMS

☎ 01626 890213 📄 01626 891678
Fore St, Kenton EX6 8LD
e-mail: enquiries@chi-restaurant.co.uk
web: www.chi-restaurant.co.uk
dir: 5m S of Exeter. M5 junct 30, A379 towards Dawlish, in Kenton centre

This former pub has been spectacularly transformed into a chic and contemporary bar, allied with a stylish Chinese restaurant. Dishes are beautifully presented with an emphasis on quality produce and authenticity, resulting in a memorable dining experience. Bedrooms are well equipped and all provide good levels of space and comfort, along with modern bathrooms.

Rooms 5 (2 fmly)

EXMOUTH   **Map 3 SY08**

Royal Beacon

★★★ 78% HOTEL

☎ 01395 264886 📄 01395 268890
The Beacon EX8 2AF
e-mail: info@royalbeaconhotel.co.uk
web: www.royalbeaconhotel.co.uk
dir: From M5 take A376 & Marine Way. Follow seafront signs. On Imperial Rd turn left at T-junct then 1st right. Hotel 100yds on left

This elegant Georgian property sits in an elevated position overlooking the town and has fine views of the estuary towards the sea. Bedrooms are individually styled and many have sea views. Public areas include a well stocked bar, a cosy lounge, an impressive function suite, and a choice of restaurants where freshly prepared and enjoyable cuisine is offered.

Rooms 52 (17 annexe) (2 fmly) (8 GF) **S** £65-£100; **D** £105-£120 (incl. bkfst) **Facilities** FTV Xmas New Year Wi-fi **Conf** Class 100 Board 60 Thtr 160 Del from £130 to £150 **Services** Lift **Parking** 28 **Notes** LB ⊗ Civ Wed 160

Manor Hotel

★★ 72% HOTEL

☎ 01395 272549 📄 01395 225519
The Beacon EX8 2AG
e-mail: post@manorexmouth.co.uk
dir: M5 junct 30 take A376 to Exmouth. Hotel 300yds from seafront overlooking Manor Gardens

Conveniently located for easy access to the town centre and with views overlooking the sea, this friendly hotel offers traditional values of hospitality and service, drawing guests back year after year. The well-equipped bedrooms vary in style and size; many have far-reaching views. The fixed price menu offers a varied selection of dishes.

Rooms 39 (3 fmly) **S** £37-£45; **D** £64-£90 (incl. bkfst) **Facilities** Xmas New Year **Conf** Class 60 Board 60 Thtr 100 **Services** Lift **Parking** 15 **Notes** LB ⊗

Cavendish Hotel

★★ 67% HOTEL   *Leisureplex*

☎ 01395 272528 📄 01395 269361
11 Morton Crescent, The Esplanade EX8 1BE
e-mail: cavendish.exmouth@alfatravel.co.uk
dir: Follow seafront signs, hotel in centre of large crescent

Situated on the seafront, this terraced hotel attracts many groups from around the country. With fine views out to sea, the hotel is within walking distance of the town centre. The bedrooms are neatly presented; front-facing rooms are always popular. Entertainment is provided on most evenings during the summer.

Rooms 76 (3 fmly) (19 GF) **Facilities** FTV Snooker ♫ Xmas New Year **Services** Lift **Parking** 25 **Notes** ⊗ Closed Dec-Jan (ex Xmas) RS Nov & Mar

GOODRINGTON

See Paignton

GULWORTHY   **Map 3 SX47**

Horn of Plenty

★★★ 85% ⊕⊕⊕ HOTEL

☎ 01822 832528 📄 01822 834390
PL19 8JD
e-mail: enquiries@thehornofplenty.co.uk
web: www.thehornofplenty.co.uk
dir: From Tavistock take A390 W for 3m. Right at Gulworthy Cross. In 400yds turn left, hotel in 400yds on right

With stunning views over the Tamar Valley, The Horn of Plenty maintains its reputation as one of Britain's best country-house hotels. The bedrooms are well equipped and have many thoughtful extras with the garden rooms offering impressive levels of comfort and quality. Cuisine here is also impressive and local produce provides interesting and memorable dining.

Horn of Plenty

Rooms 10 (6 annexe) (3 fmly) (4 GF) **S** £110-£190;
D £120-£200 (incl. bkfst)* **Facilities** New Year
Conf Class 20 Board 16 Thtr 28 **Parking** 25 **Notes** Closed
24-26 Dec Civ Wed 80

HAYTOR VALE · Map 3 SX77

Rock Inn

★★ 78% ◉ HOTEL

☎ 01364 661305 & 661465 📠 01364 661242
TQ13 9XP
e-mail: inn@rock-inn.co.uk
web: www.rock-inn.co.uk
dir: A38 onto A382 to Bovey Tracey, in 0.5m left onto
B3387 to Haytor

Dating back to the 1750s, this former coaching inn is in a
pretty hamlet on the edge of Dartmoor. Each named after
a Grand National winner, the individually decorated
bedrooms have some nice extra touches. Bars are full of
character, with flagstone floors and old beams and offer
a wide range of dishes, cooked with imagination and
flair.

Rooms 9 (2 fmly) **Facilities** FTV New Year **Parking** 20
Notes ⊗ Closed 25-26 Dec

HOLSWORTHY · Map 3 SS30

Court Barn Country House

★★ 78% COUNTRY HOUSE HOTEL

☎ 01409 271219 📠 01409 271309
Clawton EX22 6PS
e-mail: courtbarnhotel@talk21.com
web: www.hotels-devon.com
dir: 2.5m S of Holsworthy off A388 Tamerton Rd next to
Clawton Church

This engaging, family-run Victorian country house is set
in five acres of attractive grounds, including a 9-hole
putting course and croquet lawn. Comfortable bedrooms
are individually furnished, and there are two relaxing
lounges. A four-course dinner featuring fresh, local
produce is served in the spacious restaurant, and
leisurely breakfasts are taken overlooking the garden.

Rooms 7 (1 fmly) **Facilities** ⌇ Putt green ⛳ Badminton
Xmas New Year **Conf** Board 7 Thtr 25 **Parking** 13
Notes LB Closed 2-10 Jan

HONITON · Map 4 ST10

INSPECTORS' CHOICE

Combe House - Devon
★★★ ◉◉ COUNTRY HOUSE HOTEL

☎ 01404 540400 📠 01404 46004
Gittisham EX14 3AD
e-mail: stay@thishotel.com
web: www.thishotel.com
dir: Off A30 1m S of Honiton, follow Gittisham
Heathpark signs

Standing proudly in an elevated position, this
Elizabethan mansion enjoys uninterrupted views over
acres of its own woodland, meadow and pasture.
Bedrooms are a blend of comfort and quality with
relaxation being the ultimate objective; the Linen Room
suite combines many original features with
contemporary style. A range of atmospheric public
rooms retain all the charm and history of the old house.
Dining is equally impressive - a skilled kitchen brigade
maximises the best of local and home-grown produce,
augmented by excellent wines.

Rooms 16 (1 annexe) (1 fmly) **S** £155-£370;
D £175-£370 (incl. bkfst)* **Facilities** Fishing ⌇ Xmas
New Year Wi-fi **Conf** Class 25 Board 26 Thtr 50
Parking 39 **Notes** LB Closed 14-27 Jan Civ Wed 150

Deer Park Country Hotel

★★★ 72% COUNTRY HOUSE HOTEL

☎ 01404 41266 📠 01404 43958
Weston EX14 3PG
e-mail: admin@deerparkcountryhotel.co.uk
web: www.deerparkcountryhotel.co.uk
dir: M5 junct 28/A373 to Honiton. Right at lights, left to
Heathpark Industrial Estate by BP garage, hotel signed

Peacefully located in 30 acres of wonderful countryside,
this Georgian squire's mansion dates back to 1721. There
is character here in abundance with elegant public rooms
providing ample space for guests to relax and unwind.
Bedrooms are split between the main house and The
Mews, with a variation in size and style. Additional
facilities include outdoor swimming pool, croquet lawn,
tennis courts and fishing on the River Otter.

Rooms 22 (6 annexe) (4 GF) **Facilities** ⌇ ⌇ Putt green
Fishing ⛳ Gym Archery Games room Shooting Snooker
room Xmas New Year **Conf** Class 30 Board 28 Thtr 40
Parking 50 **Notes** Civ Wed 50

Home Farm Hotel & Restaurant
★★ 76% ◉ SMALL HOTEL

☎ 01404 831278 📠 01404 831411
Wilmington EX14 9JR
e-mail: info@thatchedhotel.co.uk
dir: 3m E of Honiton on A35 in village of Wilmington

Set in well-tended gardens, this thatched former
farmhouse is now a comfortable hotel. Many of the
original features have been retained including the
cobbled courtyard. A range of interesting dishes is offered
in the intimate restaurant, with bar meals available at
lunchtime and most evenings except Saturday. Bedrooms,
some with private gardens, are well equipped and
comfortably furnished.

Rooms 12 (5 annexe) (2 fmly) (6 GF) **Facilities** Xmas
Parking 26 **Notes** ⊗

HOPE COVE · Map 3 SX63

Lantern Lodge

★★ 76% HOTEL

☎ 01548 561280 📠 01548 561736
TQ7 3HE
e-mail: lanternlodge@hopecove.wanadoo.co.uk
web: www.lantern-lodge.co.uk
dir: From Kingsbridge on A381 towards Salcombe turn
right. 1st right after passing Hope Cove sign then 1st left
along Grand View Rd

This attractive hotel, close to the South Devon coastal
path, benefits from a friendly team of loyal staff.
Bedrooms are well furnished and some have balconies.
An imaginative range of home cooked meals is available.
There is a choice of lounges and a pretty garden with
putting green. The indoor pool has large doors opening
directly on to the garden.

Rooms 14 (1 fmly) (1 GF) **D** £120-£190 (incl. bkfst &
dinner)* **Facilities** FTV ☃ Putt green Running machine
Sauna Wi-fi **Parking** 15 **Notes** LB ⊗ No children 12yrs
Closed Dec-Feb

HORNS CROSS   Map 3 SS32

The Hoops Inn & Country Hotel
★★★ 71% ◉ HOTEL

☎ 01237 451222 📠 01237 451247
The Hoops EX39 5DL
e-mail: sales@hoopsinn.co.uk
web: www.hoopsinn.co.uk
dir: M5 junct 27 follow Barnstaple signs. A39, by-passing Bideford, towards Bude. Hotel in dip just outside Horns Cross

The Hoops, with its whitewashed walls, thatched roof and real fires, has been welcoming guests for many centuries. Bedrooms offer plenty of character and include a number that have four-poster or half-tester beds. Guests have the private use of a quiet lounge and a pleasant seating area in the delightful rear garden. A fine selection of home-cooked meals can be taken in the bar or restaurant.

Rooms 13 (9 annexe) (1 fmly) (1 GF) **S** £65-£95; **D** £95-£180 (incl. bkfst)* **Facilities** FTV Falconry & Flying Golden Eagle courses Xmas New Year Wi-fi **Conf** Class 25 Board 20 Thtr 35 Del from £95 to £125* **Parking** 101 **Notes** LB

ILFRACOMBE   Map 3 SS54

Darnley
★★ 71% HOTEL

☎ 01271 863955
3 Belmont Rd EX34 8DR
e-mail: darnleyhotel@yahoo.co.uk
web: www.darnleyhotel.co.uk
dir: A361 to Barnstaple & Ilfracombe. Left at Church Hill, 1st left into Belmont Rd. 3rd entrance on left under walled arch

Standing in award-winning, mature gardens, with a wooded path to the High Street and the beach (about a five minute stroll away), this former Victorian gentleman's residence offers friendly, informal service. The individually furnished and decorated bedrooms vary in size. Dinners feature honest home-cooking, with 'old fashioned puddings' always proving popular.

Rooms 10 (2 fmly) (2 GF) **S** £36-£38; **D** £53-£79 (incl. bkfst)* **Facilities** FTV Xmas New Year **Parking** 10

Imperial Hotel
★★ 69% HOTEL   Leisureplex

☎ 01271 862536 📠 01271 862571
Wilder Rd EX34 9AL
e-mail: imperial.ilfracombe@alfatravel.co.uk
dir: opposite Landmark Theatre

This popular hotel is just a short walk from the shops and harbour, overlooking gardens and the sea. Public areas include the spacious sun lounge, where guests can relax and enjoy the excellent views. Comfortable bedrooms are well equipped, with several having the added bonus of sea views.

Rooms 104 (6 fmly) **Facilities** FTV ♫ Xmas New Year **Services** Lift **Parking** 10 **Notes** LB ⊗ Closed Dec-Feb (ex Xmas) RS Mar & Nov

ILSINGTON   Map 3 SX77

Ilsington Country House
★★★ 85% ◉◉
COUNTRY HOUSE HOTEL

☎ 01364 661452 📠 01364 661307
Ilsington Village TQ13 9RR
e-mail: hotel@ilsington.co.uk
web: www.ilsington.co.uk
dir: M5 onto A38 to Plymouth. Exit at Bovey Tracey. 3rd exit from rdbt to 'Ilsington', then 1st right. Hotel in 5m by Post Office

This friendly, family owned hotel, offers tranquillity and far-reaching views from its elevated position on the southern slopes of Dartmoor. The stylish suites and bedrooms, some on the ground floor, are individually furnished. The restaurant provides a stunning backdrop for the innovative, daily changing menus which feature local fish, meat and game.

Ilsington Country House

Rooms 25 (4 fmly) (8 GF) **S** £95-£110; **D** £140-£174 (incl. bkfst)* **Facilities** FTV ⊕ supervised Gym Steam room Sauna Xmas New Year Wi-fi **Conf** Class 60 Board 40 Thtr 150 **Services** Lift **Parking** 100 **Notes** LB

INSTOW   Map 3 SS43

Commodore
★★★ 79% HOTEL

☎ 01271 860347 📠 01271 861233
Marine Pde EX39 4JN
e-mail: admin@commodore-instow.co.uk
web: www.commodore-instow.co.uk
dir: M5 junct 27 follow N Devon link road to Bideford. Right before bridge, hotel in 3m

Maintaining its links with the local maritime and rural communities, The Commodore provides an interesting place to stay. Situated at the mouth of the Tor and Torridge estuaries and overlooking a sandy beach, it offers well equipped bedrooms, many with balconies. The five ground-floor suites are especially suitable for less able visitors. Eating options include the restaurant, the Quarterdeck bar, or the terrace in the warmer months.

Rooms 20 (1 fmly) (5 GF) **S** £79-£100; **D** £130-£190 (incl. bkfst & dinner)* **Facilities** FTV Xmas New Year Wi-fi **Parking** 200 **Notes** LB ⊗ No children 7yrs

See advert on page 141

INSPECTORS' CHOICE

Lewtrenchard Manor
★★★ ◎◎◎ HOTEL

☎ 01566 783256 & 783222 🖷 01566 783332
EX20 4PN
e-mail: info@lewtrenchard.co.uk
web: www.vonessenhotels.co.uk
dir: A30 from Exeter to Plymouth/Tavistock road. At T-junct turn right, then left onto old A30 (Lewdown road). Left in 6m signed Lewtrenchard

This Jacobean mansion was built in the 1600s, with many interesting architectural features, and is surrounded by its own idyllic grounds in a quiet valley close to the northern edge of Dartmoor. Public rooms include a fine gallery, as well as magnificent carvings and oak panelling. Meals can be taken in the dining room where imaginative and carefully prepared dishes are served using the best of Devon produce. Bedrooms are comfortably furnished and spacious. Von Essen Hotels - AA Hotel Group of the Year 2009-10.

Rooms 14 (2 fmly) (3 GF) **S** £105-£190; **D** £135-£220 (incl. bkfst)* **Facilities** Fishing 🛶 Clay pigeon shooting Falconry Beauty therapies Xmas New Year **Conf** Class 40 Board 20 Thtr 50 **Parking** 50 **Notes** Civ Wed 100

Arundell Arms
★★★ 81% ◎◎ HOTEL

☎ 01566 784666 🖷 01566 784494
PL16 0AA
e-mail: reservations@arundellarms.co.uk
dir: 1m off A30, 3m E of Launceston

This former coaching inn, boasting a long history, sits in the heart of a quiet Devon village. It is internationally famous for its country pursuits such as winter shooting and angling. The bedrooms offer individual style and comfort. Public areas are full of character and present a relaxed atmosphere, particularly around the open log fire during colder evenings. Award-winning cuisine is a celebration of local produce.

Rooms 21 (4 GF) **S** fr £95; **D** £170-£230 (incl. bkfst)* **Facilities** STV Fishing Skittle alley Game shooting (in winter) Fly fishing school New Year Wi-fi **Conf** Class 30 Board 40 Thtr 100 Del from £137 to £155* **Parking** 70 **Notes** LB Closed 3 days Xmas Civ Wed 80

See advert on this page

Tinhay Mill Guest House and Restaurant
◎ RESTAURANT WITH ROOMS

☎ 01566 784201 🖷 01566 784201
Tinhay PL16 0AJ
e-mail: tinhay.mill@talk21.com
web: www.tinhaymillrestaurant.co.uk
dir: A30/A388 approach Lifton, establishment at bottom of village on right

The former mill cottages are now a delightful restaurant with rooms of much charm. Beams and open fireplaces set the scene, with everything geared to ensure a relaxed and comfortable stay. Bedrooms are spacious and well equipped, with many thoughtful extras. Cuisine is taken seriously here, using the best of local produce.

Rooms 5

See also **Lynton**

Tors
★★★ 72% ◎ HOTEL

☎ 01598 753236 🖷 01598 752544
EX35 6NA
e-mail: info@torshotellynmouth.co.uk
web: www.torslynmouth.co.uk
dir: Adjacent to A39 on Countisbury Hill just before entering Lynmouth from Minehead

In an elevated position overlooking Lynmouth Bay, this friendly hotel is set in five acres of woodland. The majority of the bedrooms benefit from the superb views, as do the public areas which are generously proportioned and well presented. A fixed-price menu is offered with local, seasonal produce to the fore.

Rooms 31 (6 fmly) **S** £50-£205; **D** £80-£264 (incl. bkfst)* **Facilities** 🏊 Table tennis Pool table Xmas New Year **Conf** Class 40 Board 25 Thtr 60 **Services** Lift **Parking** 40 **Notes** Closed 4-31 Jan RS Oct-Apr Civ Wed 125

LYNMOUTH *continued*

Rising Sun

★★ 74% HOTEL

☎ 01598 753223 📠 01598 753480
Harbourside EX35 6EG
e-mail: reception@risingsunlynmouth.co.uk
web: www.risingsunlynmouth.co.uk
dir: M5 junct 23, A39 to Minehead. Hotel on harbour

This delightful thatched inn, once a smugglers' inn, sits on the harbour front. Popular with locals and hotel guests alike, there is the option of eating in either the convivial bar or the restaurant; a comfortable, quiet lounge is also available. Bedrooms, located in the inn and adjoining cottages, are individually designed and have modern facilities.

Rooms 14 (1 fmly) (1 GF) **Facilities** Xmas

Bath

★★ 69% HOTEL

☎ 01598 752238 📠 01598 753894
Sea Front EX35 6EL
e-mail: info@bathhotellynmouth.co.uk
dir: M5 junct 25, follow A39 to Lynmouth

This well-established, friendly hotel is situated near the harbour and offers lovely views from the attractive, sea-facing bedrooms and is an excellent starting point for scenic walks. There are two lounges and a sun lounge. The restaurant menu is extensive and features daily-changing specials that make good use of fresh produce and local fish.

Rooms 22 (9 fmly) **S** £39-£49; **D** £70-£100 (incl. bkfst)* **Parking** 12 **Notes** Closed Dec & Jan

---

LYNTON Map 3 SS74

See also **Lynmouth**

Lynton Cottage

★★★ 75% ◉◉ HOTEL

☎ 01598 752342 📠 01598 754016
Northwalk EX35 6ED
e-mail: mail@lyntoncottage.co.uk
dir: M5 junct 23 to Bridgwater, then A39 to Minehead & follow signs to Lynton. 1st right after church & right again

Boasting breathtaking views, this wonderfully relaxing and friendly hotel stands some 500 feet above the sea

and makes a peaceful hideaway. Bedrooms are individual in style and size, with the added bonus of the wonderful views; public areas have charm and character in equal measure. Accomplished cuisine is on offer with dishes created with care and skill.

Rooms 16 (1 fmly) (1 GF) **S** £48-£78; **D** £76-£160 (incl. bkfst)* **Facilities** FTV Xmas **Parking** 20 **Notes** Closed 2 Dec-12 Jan

Seawood

★★ 81% SMALL HOTEL

☎ 01598 752272
North Walk EX35 6HJ
e-mail: admin@seawoodhotel.co.uk
dir: Turn right at St Mary's Church in Lynton High St for hotel, 2nd on left

Located on wooded cliffs, some 400ft above the sea, the views from this small and friendly hotel are quite spectacular. Dating back to 1848, there is period charm throughout, with the elegant lounge and dining room both having doors leading to a terrace overlooking Lynmouth Bay. Bedrooms provide comfort and quality with many having the added bonus of sea views. A range of interesting dishes feature on the dinner menu. Wi-fi is available throughout.

Rooms 12 **S** £55; **D** £90-£100 (incl. bkfst)* **Facilities** FTV Xmas Wi-fi **Parking** 12 **Notes** LB No children 12yrs Closed Dec-Feb

Chough's Nest

★★ 76% SMALL HOTEL

☎ 01598 753315
North Walk EX35 6HJ
e-mail: relax@choughsnesthotel.co.uk
web: www.choughsnesthotel.co.uk
dir: On northwalk, just past parish church.

Lying on the south-west coastal path, this charming hotel can claim to have one of the most spectacular views in the area. Bedrooms offer ample comfort and quality, the majority looking out across the sea. The dining room, also sharing the wonderful landscape, is a lovely setting in which to enjoy tasty food and the convivial atmosphere.

Rooms 9 (1 fmly) **S** £42-£58; **D** £84-£116 (incl. bkfst) **Facilities** FTV Wi-fi **Conf** Board 8 **Parking** 10 **Notes** LB ⊗ No children 10yrs Closed 23 Dec-2 Jan

---

MAIDENCOMBE

See Torquay

MARTINHOE Map 3 SS64

Heddon's Gate Hotel

★★ 78% COUNTRY HOUSE HOTEL

☎ 01598 763481
Heddon's Mouth EX31 4PZ
e-mail: hotel@heddonsgate.co.uk
web: www.heddonsgate.co.uk
dir: A39 towards Lynton, left after 4m towards Martinhoe, left towards Hunters Inn, over x-rds, 1st right after Mannacott

Superbly located on the slopes of the Heddon Valley, this hotel is hidden away at the end of a quarter mile private drive. Guests are assured of a warm and friendly welcome, with a complimentary, traditional afternoon tea served daily between 4-5pm. The individually furnished and decorated bedrooms are well equipped, and the majority have superb views. Dinner each evening is described as 'an occasion', and features the best of local produce.

Rooms 10 **Facilities** ⚓ Xmas New Year **Parking** 11 **Notes** LB No children 14yrs

---

MORETONHAMPSTEAD Map 3 SX78

The White Hart Hotel

★★★ 78% ◉ HOTEL

☎ 01647 441340 📠 01647 441341
The Square TQ13 8NF
e-mail: enquiries@whitehartdartmoor.co.uk
dir: A30 towards Oakhampton. At Whiddon Down take A382 for Moretonhampstead

Dating back to the 1700s, this former coaching inn is located on the edge of Dartmoor. A relaxed and friendly atmosphere prevails, with the staff providing attentive service. Comfortable bedrooms have a blend of traditional and contemporary styles with thoughtful extras provided. Dining is in either the brasserie restaurant or more informally in the bar where quality cuisine is served.

Rooms 28 (8 annexe) (6 fmly) (4 GF) (28 smoking) **Facilities** FTV Xmas New Year **Conf** Class 40 Board 40 Thtr 60 **Notes** LB Civ Wed 60

NEWTON ABBOT Map 3 SX87

See also **Ilsington**

Passage House

★★★ 71% HOTEL

☎ 01626 355515 📠 01626 363336
Hackney Ln, Kingsteignton TQ12 3QH
e-mail: hotel@passagehousegroup.co.uk
dir: A380 onto A381, follow racecourse signs

With memorable views of the Teign Estuary, this popular hotel provides spacious, well-equipped bedrooms. An impressive range of leisure and meeting facilities is offered and a conservatory provides a pleasant extension to the bar and lounge. A choice of eating options is available, either in the main restaurant, or the adjacent Passage House Inn for less formal dining.

Rooms 90 (52 annexe) (64 fmly) (26 GF) **Facilities** Spa STV ⓢ supervised Gym Wi-fi **Conf** Class 50 Board 40 Thtr 120 **Services** Lift **Parking** 300 **Notes** ⊗ RS 24-27 Dec Civ Wed 75

Best Western Queens Hotel

★★ 75% METRO HOTEL

☎ 01626 363133 📠 01626 354106
Queen St TQ12 2EZ
e-mail: reservations@queenshotel-southwest.co.uk
dir: A380. At Penn Inn turn right towards town, hotel opposite station

Pleasantly and conveniently located close to the railway station and racecourse, this hotel continues to be a popular venue for both business people and tourists. Bedrooms have are comfortable and spacious. Light snacks and sandwiches are available in the café/bar and lounge.

Rooms 26 (3 fmly) **S** £60-£79; **D** £75-£90 (incl. bkfst)*
Facilities FTV Chargeable gym Wi-fi **Conf** Class 20 Board 20 Thtr 40 **Parking** 6 **Notes** ⊗ RS 24 Dec-2 Jan

---

NEWTON POPPLEFORD Map 3 SY08

Moores Restaurant & Rooms

◉◉ RESTAURANT WITH ROOMS

☎ 01395 568100
6 Greenbank, High St EX10 0EB
e-mail: info.moores@btconnect.com
dir: On A3052 in village centre

Centrally located in the village, this small restaurant offers very comfortable, practically furnished bedrooms. Guests are assured of a friendly welcome and relaxed, efficient service. Good quality, locally sourced ingredients are used to produce imaginative dishes full of natural flavours.

Rooms 3 (2 fmly)

OKEHAMPTON Map 3 SX59

Ashbury

★★ 72% HOTEL

☎ 01837 55453 📠 01837 55468
Higher Maddaford, Southcott EX20 4NL
dir: Off A30 at Sourton Cross onto A386. Left onto A3079 to Bude on A3079 at Fowley Cross. After 1m right to Ashbury. Hotel 0.5m on right

With no less than five courses and a clubhouse with lounge, bar and dining facilities, The Ashbury is a golfer's paradise. The majority of the well-equipped bedrooms are located in the farmhouse and courtyard-style development around the putting green. Guests can enjoy the many on-site leisure facilities or join the activities available at the adjacent sister hotel.

Rooms 184 (79 fmly) (77 GF) **Facilities** ⓢ ♨ 99 🏌 Putt green Fishing Gym Driving range Indoor bowls Ten-pin bowling Outdoor chess Golf simulator New Year **Conf** Thtr 250 Del from £55 to £90* **Parking** 150 **Notes** ⊗

Manor House Hotel

★★ 72% HOTEL

☎ 01837 53053 📠 01837 55027
Fowley Cross EX20 4NA
e-mail: ali@manorhousehotel.co.uk
web: www.manorhousehotel.co.uk
dir: Off A30 at Sourton Cross flyover, right onto A386. Hotel 1.5m on right

Enjoying views to Dartmoor in the distance, this hotel is set within 17 acres of grounds and is located close to the A30. An impressive range of facilities, including golf at the adjacent sister hotel, is available at this friendly establishment, which specialises in short breaks. Bedrooms, many located on the ground floor, are comfortable and well equipped.

Rooms 196 (91 fmly) (90 GF) **Facilities** Spa ⓢ ♨ 99 🏌 Putt green Fishing 🏊 Gym Squash Craft centre Indoor bowls Shooting range Laser clay pigeon shooting Aerobics Xmas New Year **Parking** 200 **Notes** ⊗

White Hart

★★ 71% HOTEL

☎ 01837 52730 & 54514 📠 01837 53979
Fore St EX20 1HD
e-mail: enquiry@thewhitehart-hotel.com
dir: in town centre, adjacent to lights, car park at rear of hotel

Dating back to the 17th century, the White Hart offers modern facilities. Bedrooms are well equipped and spacious and some have four-poster beds. A range of bar meals is offered, or more relaxed dining may be taken in the Courtney Restaurant or Vines pizzeria. Guests can

relax in the lounge or in one of the bars; there is also a traditional skittles and games room.

Rooms 19 (2 fmly) **Facilities** Xmas **Conf** Class 30 Board 40 Thtr 100 **Parking** 20

Travelodge Okehampton Whiddon Down

BUDGET HOTEL

☎ 08719 846 047 📠 01647 231626
Whiddon Down EX20 2QT
web: www.travelodge.co.uk
dir: At Merrymeet rdbt on A30 & A382

Travelodge offers good quality, good value, budget accommodation. All offer family rooms sleeping up to four (two adults, two children) with en suite bathroom/shower-room, remote-control TV, tea- and coffee-making facilities and comfortable beds. Food options vary. Breakfast is at the on-site Bar Café restaurant (if available) or to take away. See also Hotel Groups pages.

Rooms 40 **S** fr £29; **D** fr £29

OTTERY ST MARY Map 3 SY19

Tumbling Weir Hotel

★★ 78% SMALL HOTEL

☎ 01404 812752 📠 01404 812752
Canaan Way EX11 1AQ
e-mail: reception@tumblingweirhotel.com
web: www.tumblingweir-hotel.co.uk
dir: Off A30 take B3177 into Ottery St Mary, hotel signed off Mill St, access through old mill

Quietly located between the River Otter and its millstream and set in well-tended gardens, this family-run hotel offers friendly and attentive service. Bedrooms are equipped with modern comforts. In the dining room, where a selection of carefully prepared dishes makes up the carte menu, beams and subtle lighting help to create an intimate atmosphere.

Rooms 10 (1 fmly) **S** £50-£65; **D** £86-£100 (incl. bkfst) **Facilities** 🏊 Wi-fi **Conf** Class 60 Board 50 Thtr 90 Del from £95 to £105 **Parking** 10 **Notes** LB ⊗ Closed 26 Dec-10 Jan Civ Wed 80

PAIGNTON Map 3 SX86

Redcliffe

★★★ 75% HOTEL

☎ 01803 526397 📠 01803 528030
Marine Dr TQ3 2NL
e-mail: redclfe@aol.com
dir: On seafront at Torquay end of Paignton Green

Set at the water's edge in three acres of well-tended grounds, this popular hotel enjoys uninterrupted views across Tor Bay. Offering a diverse range of facilities including a leisure complex, beauty treatments and lots

continued

PAIGNTON *continued*

of outdoor family activities in the summer. Bedrooms are pleasantly appointed and comfortably furnished, while public areas offer ample space for rest and relaxation.

Rooms 68 (8 fmly) (3 GF) **S** £58-£68; **D** £116-£136 (incl. bkfst) **Facilities** Spa ⏱ supervised ⌇ Putt green Fishing Gym Table tennis Carpet bowls Xmas New Year Wi-fi **Conf** Class 50 Board 50 Thtr 150 Del from £75 to £85* **Services** Lift **Parking** 80 **Notes** LB ⊗ Civ Wed 150

Redcliffe Lodge Hotel

★★ 60% HOTEL

☎ 01803 551394 📠 01803 551394
1 Marine Dr TQ3 2NJ
e-mail: davies.valleyview@tiscali.co.uk
dir: Follow A3022 to Paignton seafront. Hotel is at the end of Marine Drive on the right adjacent to Paignton Green

Handily placed across the road from the seafront, this is an ideal base for visiting the Torbay area. Bedrooms are furnished in traditional style and some have sea views. The dining room has lovely views over the garden to the sea beyond; guests have a choice of lounges and bar.

Rooms 17 (2 fmly) (3 GF) **S** £20-£30; **D** £40-£65 (incl. bkfst) **Facilities** FTV Xmas New Year Wi-fi **Conf** Class 38 Board 30 Thtr 50 Del from £55 to £80 **Parking** 17 **Notes** LB ⊗

See advert on this page

Summerhill

★★ Ⓐ HOTEL

☎ 01803 558101 📠 01803 226106
Braeside Rd TQ4 6BX
e-mail: info@summerhillhotel.co.uk
web: www.summerhillhotel.co.uk
dir: With harbour on left, follow for 600yds

Rooms 25 (8 fmly) (4 GF) **S** £45-£59; **D** £69-£82 (incl. bkfst)* **Facilities** Free membership to nearby leisure centre Wi-fi **Services** Lift **Parking** 40 **Notes** ⊗ No children 4yrs

PLYMOUTH Map 3 SX45

Holiday Inn Plymouth

★★★★ 73% HOTEL

☎ 0870 225 0301 & 01752 63998 📠 01752 673816
Armada Way PL1 2HJ
e-mail: hiplymouth@qmh-hotels.com
web: www.holidayinn.co.uk
dir: Exit A38 at Plymouth city centre & follow signs for Barbican/Hoe. Into Notte St, left into Hoe Approach, right into Citadel Rd. Hotel on right

Overlooking The Hoe and out towards Plymouth Sound, this modern, high-rise hotel offers extensive facilities, including a leisure club and impressive conference and function rooms. Most bedrooms are very spacious and

sea-facing rooms are the most popular. Spectacular, panoramic views of the city can be enjoyed from the restaurant and bar on the top floor.

Holiday Inn Plymouth

Rooms 211 (10 fmly) (12 GF) (21 smoking) **S** fr £69; **D** fr £69* **Facilities** STV ⏱ Gym Beauty salon Dance studio Sauna Steam room Xmas New Year Wi-fi **Conf** Class 260 Board 60 Thtr 425 Del from £95 to £135* **Services** Lift Air con **Parking** 125 **Notes** LB ⊗ Civ Wed 250

Best Western Duke of Cornwall

★★★ 78% ⊛ HOTEL

☎ 01752 275850 & 275855 📠 01752 275854
Millbay Rd PL1 3LG
e-mail: enquiries@thedukeofcornwall.co.uk
web: www.thedukeofcornwall.co.uk
dir: Follow city centre, then Plymouth Pavilions Conference & Leisure Centre signs. Hotel opposite Plymouth Pavilions

A historic landmark, this city centre hotel is conveniently located. The spacious public areas include a popular bar, comfortable lounge and multi-functional ballroom. Bedrooms, many with far reaching views, are individually styled and comfortably appointed. The range of dining options includes meals in the bar, or guests might choose the elegant dining room for a more formal atmosphere.

Best Western Duke of Cornwall

Rooms 71 (6 fmly) (20 smoking) **S** £65-£104; **D** £78-£120 (incl. bkfst) **Facilities** STV FTV Xmas New Year Wi-fi **Conf** Class 125 Board 84 Thtr 300 Del from £160 to £190* **Services** Lift **Parking** 50 **Notes** LB Civ Wed 300

Langdon Court Hotel & Restaurant

★★★ 77% ⊛ HOTEL

☎ 01752 862358 & 07944 483162 ▤ 01752 863428
Langdon, Wendbury PL9 0DY
e-mail: enquiries@langdoncourt.com
web: www.langdoncourt.com
dir: From Elburton follow hotel signs & tourist signs on A379

This magnificent Grade II listed Tudor manor, set in seven acres of lush countryside, has a direct path leading to the beach at Wembury and coastal footpaths. Bedrooms enjoy countryside views while public areas include a stylish bar and brasserie restaurant where the contemporary menu incorporates local produce with excellent seafood.

Rooms 18 (3 fmly) **S** £89-£109; **D** £109-£189 (incl. bkfst) **Facilities** FTV ♫ Xmas New Year Wi-fi **Conf** Class 20 Board 15 Thtr 30 Del from £133 to £153 **Parking** 60 **Notes** LB ⊗ Civ Wed 90

Elfordleigh Hotel Golf Leisure

★★★ 74% HOTEL

☎ 01752 336428 ▤ 01752 344581
Colebrook, Plympton PL7 5EB
e-mail: reception@elfordleigh.co.uk
dir: Leave A38 at city centre exit, at Marsh Mills/ Sainsbury's rdbt take Plympton road. At 4th lights left into Larkham Ln, at end right then left into Crossway. At end left into The Moors, hotel 1m

Located in the beautiful Plym Valley, this well-established hotel is set in attractive wooded countryside. Bedrooms, many with lovely views, are spacious and comfortable. There is an excellent range of leisure facilities including an 18-hole golf course. A choice of dining options is available - a friendly brasserie and the more formal restaurant.

Rooms 34 (2 fmly) (7 GF) **Facilities** Spa STV FTV ⊗ ⅃ 18 ⛳ Putt green Fishing ⌣ Gym Squash Hairdresser Beautician Dance/Aerobics studio 5 aside football pitch (hard) Xmas New Year Wi-fi **Conf** Class 120 Board 50 Thtr 200 Del from £125 to £135* **Services** Lift **Parking** 200 **Notes** Civ Wed 200

Invicta

★★★ 74% HOTEL

☎ 01752 664997 ▤ 01752 664994
11-12 Osborne Place, Lockyer St, The Hoe PL1 2PU
e-mail: info@invictahotel.co.uk
web: www.invictahotel.co.uk
dir: A38 to Plymouth, follow city centre signs, then Hoe Park signs. Hotel opposite park entrance

Just a short stroll from the city centre, this elegant Victorian establishment stands opposite the famous bowling green. The atmosphere is relaxed and friendly and bedrooms are neatly presented, well-equipped and attractively decorated. Eating options include meals in the bar or in the more formal setting of the dining room.

Rooms 23 (6 fmly) (1 GF) **S** £55-£60; **D** £65-£80 (incl. bkfst)* **Facilities** FTV Xmas Wi-fi **Conf** Class 30 Board 45 Thtr 45 Del from £95 to £115* **Parking** 14 **Notes** ⊗

New Continental

★★★ 73% HOTEL

☎ 01752 220782 & 276798 ▤ 01752 227013
Millbay Rd PL1 3LD
e-mail: reservations@newcontinental.co.uk
web: www.newcontinental.co.uk
dir: A38, follow city centre signs for Continental Ferryport. Hotel is before ferryport & next to Plymouth Pavilions Conference Centre

Within easy reach of the city centre and The Hoe, this privately owned hotel continues to offer high standards of service and hospitality. A variety of bedroom sizes and styles is available, all with the same levels of equipment and comfort. The hotel is a popular choice for conferences and functions.

Rooms 99 (20 fmly) **S** £70-£98; **D** £80-£115 (incl. bkfst)* **Facilities** ⊗ supervised Gym Beautician Sauna Steam room Wi-fi **Conf** Class 100 Board 70 Thtr 350 Del from £130 to £145 **Services** Lift **Parking** 100 **Notes** LB ⊗ Closed 24 Dec-2 Jan Civ Wed 140

Novotel Plymouth

★★★ 67% HOTEL

☎ 01752 221422 ▤ 01752 223922
Marsh Mills PL6 8NH
e-mail: h0508@accor.com
web: www.novotel.com
dir: Exit A38 at Marsh Mills, follow Plympton signs, hotel on left

Conveniently located on the outskirts of the city, close to Marsh Mills roundabout, this modern hotel offers good value accommodation. All rooms are spacious and designed with flexibility for family use. Public areas are open-plan with meals available throughout the day in either the Garden Brasserie, the bar, or from room service.

Rooms 100 (17 fmly) (18 GF) **S** £59-£102.95; (incl. bkfst)* **Facilities** STV FTV ⌇ Xmas New Year **Conf** Class 120 Board 100 Thtr 300 Del from £115 to £125* **Services** Lift **Parking** 140 **Notes** LB

Copthorne Hotel Plymouth

☎ 01752 224161 ▤ 01752 670688
Armada Way PL1 1AR
e-mail: sales.plymouth@millenniumhotels.co.uk
web: www.millenniumhotels.co.uk
dir: From M5 follow A38 to Plymouth city centre. Follow ferryport signs over 2 rdbts. Hotel on 1st exit left before 4th rdbt

Currently the rating for this establishment is not confirmed. This may be due to a change of ownership or because it has only recently joined the AA rating scheme For further details please see the AA website: theAA.com

Rooms 135 (29 fmly) **S** £49-£119; **D** £49-£119* **Facilities** STV Gym New Year Wi-fi **Conf** Class 60 Board 60 Thtr 140 Del from £110 to £150* **Services** Lift **Parking** 50 **Notes** LB ⊗ Civ Wed 65

Ibis Hotel Plymouth

BUDGET HOTEL

☎ 01752 601087 ▤ 01752 223213
Marsh Mills, Longbridge Rd, Forder Valley PL6 8LD
e-mail: H2093@accor-hotels.com
web: www.ibishotel.com
dir: A38 to Plymouth, 1st exit after flyover towards Estover, Leigham and Parkway Industrial Est. At rdbt, hotel on 4th exit

Modern, budget hotel offering comfortable accommodation in bright and practical bedrooms. Breakfast is self-service and dinner is available in the restaurant. See also the Hotel Groups pages.

Rooms 52 (26 GF)

PLYMOUTH *continued*

Innkeeper's Lodge Plymouth

BUDGET HOTEL

☎ 0845 112 6087 📠 0845 112 6216
399 Tavistock Rd PL6 7HB
web: www.innkeeperslodge.com/plymouthroborough
dir: From A38 towards Plymouth onto A386 follow airport signs. Lodge on left by airport, opposite B3432 (Plymbridge Rd)

Innkeeper's Lodge represents an exciting, high value concept within the budget hotel market. Comfortable bedrooms provide excellent facilities that include satellite TV and modem points. Options include family rooms; and for the corporate guest, cutting edge IT which includes Wi-fi access. A popular Carvery provides all-day food, including an extensive, complimentary continental breakfast. See also the Hotel Groups pages.

Rooms 40

Innkeeper's Lodge Plymouth (Derriford)

BUDGET HOTEL

☎ 0845 112 6088 📠 0845 112 6215
8-9 Howeson Ln PL6 8BB
web: www.innkeeperslodge.com/plymouth
dir: From A38 towards Plymouth. At junct with A386 north towards airport. At Derriford rdbt (hospital & airport), take 3rd exit into Derriford Rd. Lodge on left

Rooms 75 **Conf** Thtr 30

Travelodge Plymouth

BUDGET HOTEL

☎ 0871 984 6097
Derry's Cross PL1 2SW
web: www.travelodge.co.uk
dir: From A38 take A374 towards town centre, at Charles Cross rdbt left towards us station onto Exeter St, straight over next rdbt onto Royal Pde. Lodge in city centre at Derry's Cross rdbt

Travelodge offers good quality, good value, budget accommodation. All offer family rooms sleeping up to four (two adults, two children) with en suite bathroom/shower-room, remote-control TV, tea- and coffee-making facilities and comfortable beds. Food options vary. Breakfast is at the on-site Bar Café restaurant (if available) or to take away. See also Hotel Groups pages.

Rooms 96 **S** fr £29; **D** fr £29

ROUSDON	Map 4 SY29

Dower House

★★ 72% HOTEL

☎ 01297 21047 📠 01297 24748
Rousdon DT7 3RB
e-mail: info@dhhotel.com
dir: On A3052, 3m W of Lyme Regis

Handily placed a short drive from Lyme Regis and the coast, this fine old Victorian building has an interesting and varied history. The atmosphere is warm and welcoming with all bedrooms offering lots of comfort and character. The friendly bar lounge has doors opening onto a decked area with wonderful views across the rolling countryside. Local produce, including excellent fish, feature on a daily-changing menu, served within the elegant dining room. There is a heated outdoor swimming pool in the grounds.

(2 fmly) (1 GF) **S** £65-£95; **D** £85-£150 (incl. bkfst)*
Facilities ⌁ Xmas New Year Wi-fi **Conf** Class 30 Board 18 Thtr 46 **Parking** 35 **Notes** LB Civ Wed 40

ST MARY CHURCH	

See Torquay

SALCOMBE	Map 3 SX73

See also **Hope Cove**

Thurlestone

★★★★ 81% HOTEL

☎ 01548 560382 📠 01548 561069
TQ7 3NN
e-mail: enquiries@thurlestone.co.uk
web: www.thurlestone.co.uk

(For full entry see Thurlestone)

Soar Mill Cove

★★★★ 79% ◉◉ HOTEL

☎ 01548 561566 📠 01548 561223
Soar Mill Cove, Malborough TQ7 3DS
e-mail: info@soarmillcove.co.uk
web: www.soarmillcove.co.uk
dir: 3m W of town off A381 at Malborough. Follow Soar signs

Situated amid spectacular scenery with dramatic sea views, this hotel is ideal for a relaxing stay. Family-run, with a committed team, keen standards of hospitality and service are upheld. Bedrooms are well equipped and many rooms have private terraces. There are different seating areas where impressive cream teas are served, and for the more active, there's a choice of swimming pools. Local produce and seafood are used to good effect in the restaurant.

Rooms 22 (5 fmly) (21 GF) **S** £105-£195; **D** £130-£220 (incl. bkfst)* **Facilities** FTV ⌁ ⌁ ⌁ Putt green Table tennis Games room ♫ Xmas New Year Wi-fi
Conf Class 50 Board 50 Thtr 100 Del from £150 to £175 **Parking** 30 **Notes** LB Closed 2 Jan-8 Feb Civ Wed 150

Tides Reach

★★★ 82% ◉ HOTEL

☎ 01548 843466 📠 01548 843954
South Sands TQ8 8LJ
e-mail: enquire@tidesreach.com
web: www.tidesreach.com
dir: Off A38 at Buckfastleigh to Totnes. Then A381 to Salcombe, follow signs to South Sands

Superbly situated at the water's edge, this personally run, friendly hotel has splendid views of the estuary and beach. Bedrooms, many with balconies, are spacious and comfortable. In the bar and lounge, attentive service can be enjoyed along with the view, and the Garden Room restaurant serves appetising and accomplished cuisine.

Rooms 35 (7 fmly) **S** £77-£150; **D** £128-£310 (incl. bkfst & dinner)* **Facilities** Spa FTV ⌁ supervised Gym Squash Windsurfing Sailing Kayaking Scuba diving Hair & beauty treatment ♫ Wi-fi **Services** Lift **Parking** 100 **Notes** LB No children 8yrs Closed Dec-early Feb

---

SAMPFORD PEVERELL	Map 3 ST01

Travelodge Tiverton

BUDGET HOTEL

☎ 0871 984 6057 📠 01884 821087
Sampford Peverell Service Area EX16 7HD
web: www.travelodge.co.uk
dir: M5 junct 27

Travelodge offers good quality, good value, budget accommodation. All offer family rooms sleeping up to four (two adults, two children) with en suite bathroom/shower-room, remote-control TV, tea- and coffee-making facilities and comfortable beds. Food options vary. Breakfast is at the on-site Bar Café restaurant (if available) or to take away. See also Hotel Groups pages.

Rooms 40 **S** fr £29; **D** fr £29

SAUNTON Map 3 SS43

Saunton Sands
★★★★ 78% HOTEL

☎ 01271 890212 & 892001 🖷 01271 890145
EX33 1LQ
e-mail: reservations@sauntonsands.com
web: www.sauntonsands.com
dir: Off A361 at Braunton, signed Croyde B3231, hotel 2m
on left

Stunning sea views and direct access to five miles of
sandy beach are just two of the highlights at this popular
hotel. The majority of sea-facing rooms have balconies,
and splendid views can be enjoyed from all of the public
areas, which include comfortable lounges. The Sands
café/bar is a successful innovation and provides an
informal eating option.

Rooms 92 (39 fmly) **S** £90-£129; **D** £170-£364*
Facilities FTV ☜ ⚑ ☺ Putt green Gym Squash OFSTED
registered nursery Snooker room Games room ♫ Xmas
New Year Wi-fi Child facilities **Conf** Class 180 Board 50
Thtr 200 **Services** Lift **Parking** 142 **Notes** LB ⊗
Civ Wed 200

See advert on this page

SIDMOUTH Map 3 SY18

Victoria
★★★★ 83% ⍟ HOTEL

☎ 01395 512651 🖷 01395 579154
The Esplanade EX10 8RY
e-mail: info@victoriahotel.co.uk
web: www.victoriahotel.co.uk
dir: On seafront

This imposing building, with manicured gardens, is
situated overlooking the town. Wonderful sea views can
be enjoyed from many of the comfortable bedrooms and
elegant lounges. With indoor and outdoor leisure, the
hotel caters to a year-round clientele. Carefully prepared
meals are served in the refined atmosphere of the
restaurant, with staff providing a professional and
friendly service.

Rooms 61 (18 fmly) **S** £125-£255; **D** £165-£280*
Facilities FTV ☜ ⚑ ☺ Putt green Sauna Solarium
Snooker room Games room ♫ Xmas New Year Wi-fi Child
facilities **Conf** Thtr 60 **Services** Lift **Parking** 104
Notes LB ⊗

See advert on page 158

Riviera
★★★★ 82% ⍟ HOTEL

☎ 01395 515201 🖷 01395 577775
The Esplanade EX10 8AY
e-mail: enquiries@hotelriviera.co.uk
web: www.hotelriviera.co.uk
dir: M5 junct 30 & follow A3052

Overlooking the sea and close to the town centre, the
Riviera is a fine example of Regency architecture. The
large number of guests that become regular visitors here
are testament to the high standards of service and
hospitality offered. The front-facing bedrooms benefit
from wonderful sea views, and the daily-changing menu
places an emphasis on fresh, local produce.

Rooms 26 (6 fmly) **S** £120-£177; **D** £240-£386 (incl.
bkfst & dinner)* **Facilities** FTV Putt green ♫ Xmas New
Year Wi-fi **Conf** Class 60 Board 30 Thtr 85 **Services** Lift
Air con **Parking** 27 **Notes** LB

See advert on page 159

The most luxurious choice in East Devon

★ ★ ★ ★

The Belmont Hotel
★ ★ ★ ★

Perfectly positioned on Sidmouth's famous esplanade, the Victoria is one of the resort's finest and most picturesque hotels. It's extensive leisure facilities include indoor and outdoor pools, sauna, solarium, spa bath, putting green, tennis court and snooker room. The hotel's resturant has been awarded an AA Rosette for fine cuisine.

The Belmont too commands spectacular views from the famous esplanade. As inviting in January as July, the hotel offers fine cusine and superb service that brings guests back year after year. With the indoor and outdoor leisure facilities of the adjacent Victoria Hotel at your disposal, the Belmont provides the perfect location for your holiday.

Telephone: 01395 512651

Telephone: 01395 512555

www.victoriahotel.co.uk Email: info@victoriahotel.co.uk

www.belmont-hotel.co.uk Email: info@belmont-hotel.co.uk

SIDMOUTH *continued*

Belmont

★★★★ 75% HOTEL

☎ 01395 512555 🖷 01395 579101
The Esplanade EX10 8RX
e-mail: reservations@belmont-hotel.co.uk
web: www.belmont-hotel.co.uk
dir: On seafront

Prominently positioned on the seafront just a few minutes' walk from the town centre, this traditional hotel has a regular following. A choice of comfortable lounges provide ample space for relaxation, and the air-conditioned restaurant has a pianist most evenings. Bedrooms are attractively furnished and many have fine views over the esplanade. Leisure facilities are available at the adjacent sister hotel, The Victoria.

Rooms 50 (4 fmly) (2 GF) **S** £110-£220; **D** £140-£220*
Facilities STV Putt green Leisure facilities available at

sister hotel ♫ Xmas New Year Wi-fi Child facilities **Conf** Thtr 50 **Services** Lift **Parking** 45 **Notes** LB ⊗ Civ Wed 110

See advert on opposite page

Westcliff

★★★ 80% HOTEL

☎ 01395 513252 🖷 01395 578203
Manor Rd EX10 8RU
e-mail: stay@westcliffhotel.co.uk
web: www.westcliffhotel.co.uk
dir: Exit A3052 to Sidmouth then to seafront & esplanade, turn right, hotel directly ahead

This charming hotel is ideally located within walking distance of Sidmouth's elegant promenade and beaches. The spacious lounges and the cocktail bar open onto a terrace which leads to the pool and croquet lawn. Bedrooms, several with balconies and glorious sea views, are spacious and comfortable, whilst the restaurant offers a choice of well-prepared dishes.

Rooms 40 (1 fmly) (5 GF) **S** £60-£120; **D** £65-£260 (incl. bkfst & dinner)* **Facilities** FTV ⊰ Putt green Pool table Table tennis Xmas New Year Wi-fi **Conf** Class 20 Board 15 Thtr 30 Del from £140 to £180* **Services** Lift **Parking** 40 **Notes** Civ Wed 80

Royal Glen

★★★ 73% HOTEL

☎ 01395 513221 & 513456 🖷 01395 514922
Glen Rd EX10 8RW
e-mail: info@royalglenhotel.co.uk
dir: A303 to Honiton, A375 to Sidford, follow seafront signs, right onto esplanade, right at end into Glen Rd

This historic 17th-century, Grade I listed hotel has been owned by the same family for several generations. The

continued

SIDMOUTH *continued*

comfortable bedrooms are furnished in period style. Guests may use the well-maintained gardens and a heated indoor pool, and can enjoy well-prepared food in the dining room.

Rooms 32 (3 fmly) (3 GF) **S** £45-£65; **D** £90-£130 (incl. bkfst)* **Facilities** STV ⓦ **Services** Lift **Parking** 22 **Notes** LB Closed Dec-1 Feb

Bedford

★★★ 72% HOTEL

☎ 01395 513047 & 0797 394 0671 🖷 01395 578563
Esplanade EX10 8NR
e-mail: info@bedfordhotelsidmouth.co.uk
web: www.bedfordhotelsidmouth.co.uk
dir: M5 junct 30/A3052 & to Sidmouth. Hotel at centre of Esplanade

Situated on the seafront, this long established, family-run hotel provides a warm welcome and relaxing atmosphere. Bedrooms are well appointed and many have the added bonus of wonderful sea views. Public areas combine character and comfort with a choice of lounges in which to relax. In addition to the hotel dining room, Pyne's bar and restaurant offers an interesting range of dishes in a convivial environment.

Rooms 37 (1 GF) **Facilities** Xmas **Services** Lift **Parking** 6

Kingswood

★★ 79% HOTEL

☎ 01395 516367 🖷 01395 513185
The Esplanade EX10 8AX
e-mail: kingswood@hotels-sidmouth.co.uk
web: www.hotels-sidmouth.co.uk
dir: Take A375 off A3052 towards seafront. Hotel in centre of Esplanade

Super standards of hospitality are only surpassed by this hotel's prominent position on the esplanade. All bedrooms have modern facilities and some enjoy the stunning sea views. The two lounges offer comfort and space and the attractive dining room serves good traditional cooking.

Rooms 24 (7 fmly) (1 GF) **S** £55-£65; **D** £55-£80 (incl. bkfst & dinner)* **Facilities** Guests receive vouchers for local swimming pool Discounts for local golf course Xmas **Services** Lift **Parking** 17 **Notes** Closed 28 Dec-9 Feb

Royal York & Faulkner

★★ 79% HOTEL

☎ 01395 513043 & 0800 220714 🖷 01395 577472
The Esplanade EX10 8AZ
e-mail: stay@royalyorkhotel.co.uk
web: www.royalyorkhotel.co.uk
dir: M5 junct 30 take A3052, 10m to Sidmouth, hotel in centre of Esplanade

This seafront hotel, owned and run by the same family for over 60 years, maintains its Regency charm and

grandeur. The attractive bedrooms vary in size, and many have balconies and sea views. Public rooms are spacious and traditional dining is offered, alongside Blinis Café-Bar, which is more contemporary in style and offers coffees, lunch and afternoon teas. The spa facilities include a hydrotherapy pool, steam room, sauna and a variety of treatments.

Rooms 70 (2 annexe) (8 fmly) (5 GF) **S** £54.50-£83.50; **D** £109-£188 (incl. bkfst & dinner)* **Facilities** Spa ⓦ Steam cabin Snooker table Sauna ♫ Xmas New Year Wi-fi **Services** Lift **Parking** 20 **Notes** LB Closed Jan

Hotel Elizabeth

★★ 78% HOTEL

☎ 01395 513503 🖷 01395 578000
The Esplanade EX10 8AT
e-mail: elizabeth@hotels-sidmouth.co.uk
web: www.hotels-sidmouth.co.uk
dir: M5 junct 30, then A3052 to Sidmouth. 1st exit on right to Sidmouth, then left onto esplanade

Occupying a prime location on Sidmouth's dignified Esplanade, this elegant hotel attracts many loyal guests who return to enjoy the relaxed atmosphere and attentive service. Bedrooms are both comfortable and smartly appointed; all have sea views and some have balconies. The spacious lounge and sunny patio, with wonderful views across the bay, are perfect places to sit and watch the world go by.

Rooms 28 (3 fmly) (1 GF) **S** £60-£98; **D** £114-£160 (incl. bkfst & dinner)* **Facilities** FTV Xmas **Services** Lift **Parking** 16 **Notes** LB ⊗ Closed 28 Dec-10 Feb

Hunters Moon

★★ 78% HOTEL

☎ 01395 513380 🖷 01395 514270
Sid Rd EX10 9AA
e-mail: huntersmoon.hotel@virgin.net
dir: From Exeter on A3052 to Sidford, right at lights into Sidmouth, 1.5m, at cinema turn left. Hotel in 0.25m

Set amid three acres of attractive and well-tended grounds, this friendly, family-run hotel is peacefully located in a quiet area within walking distance of the town and esplanade. The light and airy bedrooms, some located at ground floor level, are comfortable and well equipped. There is a lounge and a cosy bar. The restaurant provides a choice of imaginative dishes, and weather permitting tea may be taken on the lawn.

Rooms 33 (4 fmly) (11 GF) **S** £77-£79; **D** £126-£146 (incl. bkfst & dinner)* **Facilities** FTV Putt green Xmas Wi-fi **Parking** 33 **Notes** LB No children 3yrs Closed Jan-9 Feb RS Dec & Feb

Mount Pleasant

★★ 78% HOTEL

☎ 01395 514694
Salcombe Rd EX10 8JA
dir: Exit A3052 at Sidford x-rds, in 1.25m turn left into Salcombe Rd, opposite Radway Cinema. Hotel on right after bridge

Quietly located within almost an acre of gardens, this modernised Georgian hotel is minutes from the town centre and seafront. Bedrooms and public areas provide good levels of comfort and high quality furnishings. Guests return on a regular basis, especially to experience the friendly, relaxed atmosphere. The light and airy restaurant that overlooks the pleasant garden, offers a daily-changing menu of imaginative, yet traditional home-cooked dishes.

Rooms 17 (1 fmly) (3 GF) **S** £54-£68; **D** £108-£126 (incl. dinner)* **Facilities** Putt green **Parking** 20 **Notes** ⊗ No children 8yrs Closed Dec-Feb

Devoran

★★ 76% HOTEL

☎ 01395 513151 🖷 01395 579929
Esplanade EX10 8AU
e-mail: devoran@hotels-sidmouth.co.uk
web: www.hotels-sidmouth.co.uk
dir: Turn off B3052 at Bowd Inn, follow Sidmouth sign for approx 2m, turn left onto seafront, hotel 50yds at centre of Esplanade

This long established hotel is located in the heart of Sidmouth's elegant esplanade, and is appointed to high standards throughout. The elegant public rooms have wonderful sea views. Bedrooms are neatly presented, and some have sea facing balconies. Dinner is an enjoyable and civilised occasion with caring staff ensuring a relaxing and pleasant experience.

Rooms 24 (5 fmly) **S** £55-£75; **D** £110-£150 (incl. bkfst & dinner)* **Facilities** FTV **Services** Lift **Parking** 3 **Notes** Closed 30 Oct-10 Mar

The Woodlands Hotel

★★ 72% HOTEL

☎ 01395 513120 🖷 01395 513348
Cotmaton Cross EX10 8HG
e-mail: info@woodlands-hotel.com
web: www.woodlands-hotel.com
dir: follow signs for Sidmouth

Located in the heart of the town and ideally situated for exploring Devon and Dorset, this listed property has numerous character features. There is a spacious bar and a lounge where guests may relax. Freshly prepared dinners can be enjoyed in the smart dining room. Families with children are made very welcome and may dine early.

Rooms 20 (4 fmly) (8 GF) **Facilities** Wi-fi **Parking** 20 **Notes** LB Closed 20 Dec-15 Jan Civ Wed 70

The Salty Monk

◉◉ RESTAURANT WITH ROOMS

☎ 01395 513174
Church St, Sidford EX10 9QP
e-mail: saltymonk@btconnect.com
web: www.saltymonk.co.uk
dir: On A3052 opposite church

Set in the village of Sidford, this attractive property dates from the 16th century. Some of the well-presented bedrooms feature spa baths or special showers, and a ground-floor courtyard room has a king-size water bed. Meals are served in the restaurant, where the two owners both cook. Excellent local produce is used to create thoroughly enjoyable food of a high standard.

Rooms 5

SOURTON Map 3 SX59

Collaven Manor

★★ 78% COUNTRY HOUSE HOTEL

☎ 01837 861522 📠 01837 861614
EX20 4HH
e-mail: collavenmanor@supanet.com
dir: A30 onto A386 to Tavistock, hotel 2m on right

This delightful 15th-century manor house is quietly located in five acres of well-tended grounds. The friendly proprietors provide attentive service and ensure a relaxing environment. Charming public rooms have old oak beams and granite fireplaces, and provide a range of comfortable lounges and a well stocked bar. In the restaurant, a daily-changing menu offers interesting dishes.

Rooms 9 (1 fmly) **Facilities** ⛳ Bowls Child facilities
Conf Class 20 Board 16 Thtr 30 **Parking** 50 **Notes** LB
Civ Wed 50

SOURTON CROSS Map 3 SX59

Travelodge Okehampton Sourton Cross

BUDGET HOTEL

☎ 0871 984 6048 📠 0870 1911548
EX20 4LY
web: www.travelodge.co.uk
dir: S'bound on A30 at junct with A386, 4m W of Okehampton

Travelodge offers good quality, good value, budget accommodation. All offer family rooms sleeping up to four (two adults, two children) with en suite bathroom/shower-room, remote-control TV, tea- and coffee-making facilities and comfortable beds. Food options vary. Breakfast is at the on-site Bar Café restaurant (if available) or to take away. See also Hotel Groups pages.

Rooms 42 **S** fr £29; **D** fr £29

SOUTH BRENT Map 3 SX66

Glazebrook House Hotel

★★ 76% ◉ HOTEL

☎ 01364 73322 📠 01364 72350
TQ10 9JE
e-mail: enquiries@glazebrookhouse.com
web: www.glazebrookhouse.com
dir: Exit A38 at South Brent, follow brown signs to hotel

Enjoying a tranquil and convenient location next to the Dartmoor National Park and set within four acres of gardens, this 18th-century former gentleman's residence offers a friendly welcome and comfortable accommodation. Elegant public areas provide ample space to relax and enjoy the atmosphere, whilst bedrooms are well appointed and include a number with four-poster beds. The dishes on the menus are created from interesting combinations of fresh, locally-sourced produce.

Rooms 10 **S** £50-£55; **D** £80-£125 (incl. bkfst)*
Facilities FTV Xmas New Year Wi-fi **Conf** Class 60
Board 40 Thtr 80 Del from £82.70 to £90* **Parking** 40
Notes LB Closed 2-18 Jan RS 1 wk Aug Civ Wed 80

SOUTH MOLTON Map 3 SS72

The George Hotel

★★ 72% HOTEL

☎ 01769 572514 📠 01769 579218
1 Broad St EX36 3AB
e-mail: info@georgehotelsouthmolton.co.uk
web: www.georgehotelsouthmolton.co.uk
dir: Off A361 at rdbt signed South Molton, 1.5m to centre

Retaining many of its original features, this charming 17th-century hotel is situated in the centre of town. Providing comfortable accommodation, complemented by informal and friendly service to all guests including children, this hotel is an ideal base for touring the area. Regularly changing menus, featuring local produce, are offered in the both the restaurant and the bar, which also serves real ales.

Rooms 9 (2 fmly) **S** £55-£65; **D** £95 (incl. bkfst)*
Facilities FTV ♫ Wi-fi **Conf** Class 30 Board 30 Thtr 100
Del from £85 to £105* **Parking** 12 **Notes** LB ⊗ RS 1st wk
Jan

Stumbles

RESTAURANT WITH ROOMS

☎ 01769 574145 📠 01769 572558
134 East St EX36 3BU
e-mail: info@stumbles.co.uk
dir: M5 junct 27 to South Molton on A361. Establishment in town centre

Located in the centre of this bustling town, Stumbles is a charming place with a friendly and welcoming atmosphere. Bedrooms are individual in style with lots of character and good levels of comfort. A small conservatory area is available for guests. The restaurant is a popular venue for locals and visitors alike, with a varied menu on offer both at lunchtime and in the evenings.

Rooms 10 (4 annexe) (1 fmly)

TAVISTOCK — Map 3 SX47

Bedford

★★★ 75% ◉ HOTEL

☎ 01822 613221 ▤ 01822 618034
1 Plymouth Rd PL19 8BB
e-mail: enquiries@bedford-hotel.co.uk
web: www.bedford-hotel.co.uk
dir: M5 junct 31, A30 (Launceston/Okehampton). Then A386 to Tavistock, follow town centre signs. Hotel opposite church

Built on the site of a Benedictine abbey, this impressive castellated building has been welcoming visitors for over 200 years. Very much a local landmark, the hotel offers comfortable and relaxing public areas, all reflecting charm and character throughout. Bedrooms are traditionally styled with contemporary comforts, whilst the Woburn Restaurant provides a refined setting for enjoyable cuisine.

Rooms 31 (2 fmly) (5 GF) **S** £70; **D** £140-£150 (incl. bkfst) **Facilities** FTV Xmas New Year Child facilities **Conf** Class 100 Board 60 Thtr 160 Del from £110 to £140 **Parking** 45 **Notes** LB Civ Wed 120

TEIGNMOUTH — Map 3 SX97

Cliffden Hotel

★★★ 74% HOTEL

☎ 01626 770052 ▤ 01626 770594
Dawlish Rd, N TQ14 8TE
e-mail: cliffden.hotel@actionforblindpeople.org.uk
dir: M5 junct 31, A380. Then B3192 to Teignmouth. Down hill on Exeter Rd to lights, left to rdbt (station on left). Left & follow Dawlish signs. Up hill. Hotel next right

Whilst this hotel mainly caters for visually impaired guests, their families, friends and guide dogs, its offers a warm welcome to all. Now extended and refurbished, this welcoming establishment is a listed Victorian building set in six acres of delightful gardens overlooking a small valley. Bedrooms are comfortable, very spacious and thoughtfully equipped. There's also leisure facilities and of course special provision for guide dogs.

Rooms 47 (5 fmly) (10 GF) **S** £47-£81; **D** £94-£162 (incl. bkfst & dinner) **Facilities** FTV ⊕ supervised Gym ♫ Xmas New Year **Conf** Class 30 Board 30 Thtr 50 Del from £63 to £90 **Services** Lift **Parking** 25 **Notes** LB Closed 4-23 Jan

THURLESTONE — Map 3 SX64

Thurlestone

★★★★ 81% ◉ HOTEL

☎ 01548 560382 ▤ 01548 561069
TQ7 3NN
e-mail: enquiries@thurlestone.co.uk
web: www.thurlestone.co.uk
dir: A38 take A384 into Totnes, A381 towards Kingsbridge, onto A379 towards Churchstow, onto B3197 turn into lane signed to Thurlestone

This perennially popular hotel has been in the same family-ownership since 1896 and continues to go from strength to strength. A vast range of facilities is available for all the family including indoor and outdoor pools, a golf course and a beauty salon. Bedrooms are equipped to ensure a comfortable stay with many having wonderful views of the South Devon coast. A range of eating options includes the elegant and stylish restaurant with its stunning views.

Rooms 64 (23 fmly) **S** £66-£140; **D** £132-£372 (incl. bkfst)* **Facilities** STV ⊕ ⇃ supervised ♨ 9 ♨ Putt green ♨ Gym Squash Badminton courts Games room Toddler room Snooker room ♫ Xmas New Year Wi-fi Child facilities **Conf** Class 100 Board 40 Thtr 150 Del from £130 to £280* **Services** Lift **Parking** 121 **Notes** LB Closed 1-2 wks Jan Civ Wed 180

TIVERTON — Map 3 SS91

Best Western Tiverton

★★★ 74% HOTEL

☎ 01884 256120 ▤ 01884 258101
Blundells Rd EX16 4DB
e-mail: sales@tivertonhotel.co.uk
web: www.bw-tivertonhotel.co.uk
dir: A396 follow signs for town centre. Right at 2nd rdbt & immediately right into Blundells Rd. Hotel on right

Conveniently situated on the outskirts of the town, with easy access to the M5, this comfortable hotel has a relaxed atmosphere. The spacious bedrooms are well equipped and decorated in a contemporary style. A formal dining option is offered in the Gallery Restaurant, and lighter snacks are served in the bar area. Room service is extensive, as is the range of conference facilities.

Rooms 69 (4 fmly) (30 GF) **Facilities** STV Fishing Xmas New Year Wi-fi **Conf** Class 140 Board 70 Thtr 300 **Services** Lift **Parking** 130 **Notes** LB Civ Wed 200

TORBAY

See under Brixham, Paignton & Torquay

TORQUAY — Map 3 SX96

Barceló Torquay Imperial Hotel

★★★★ 79% HOTEL

☎ 01803 294301 ▤ 01803 298293
Park Hill Rd TQ1 2DG
e-mail: imperialtorquay@barcelo-hotels.co.uk
web: www.barcelo-hotels.co.uk
dir: A380 towards the seafront. Turn left. To harbour, at clocktower turn right. Hotel 300yds on right

This hotel has an enviable location with extensive views of the coastline. Traditional in style, the public areas are elegant and offer a choice of dining options including the Regatta Restaurant, with its stunning views over the bay. Bedrooms are spacious, most with private balconies, and the hotel has an extensive range of indoor and outdoor leisure facilities.

Rooms 152 (14 fmly) **Facilities** Spa STV ⊕ ⇃ supervised ♨ Gym Squash Beauty salon Hairdresser Steam room ♫ Xmas New Year Wi-fi **Conf** Class 200 Board 30 Thtr 350 Del from £100* **Services** Lift **Parking** 140 **Notes** Civ Wed 250

Grand

RICHARDSON

★★★★ 76% ◉ HOTEL

☎ 01803 296677 ▤ 01803 213462
Sea Front TQ2 6NT
e-mail: reservations@grandtorquay.co.uk
web: www.grandtorquay.co.uk
dir: A380 to Torquay. At seafront turn right, then 1st right. Hotel on corner, entrance 1st on left

Within level walking distance of the town, this large Edwardian hotel overlooks the bay and offers modern facilities. Many of the bedrooms, some with balconies, enjoy the best of the views; all are very well equipped. Boaters Bar also benefits from the hotel's stunning position and offers an informal alternative to the Gainsborough Restaurant.

Rooms 132 (32 fmly) (3 GF) **S** £60-£100; **D** £120-£220 (incl. bkfst)* **Facilities** FTV ⊕ ⇃ ♨ Gym Beauty clinic Car valeting ♫ Xmas New Year Wi-fi **Conf** Class 150 Board 60 Thtr 250 Del from £110 to £145 **Services** Lift **Parking** 57 **Notes** LB Civ Wed 250

See advert on opposite page

TORQUAY *continued*

Palace

★★★★ 74% HOTEL

☎ 01803 200200 📄 01803 299899
Babbacombe Rd TQ1 3TG
e-mail: info@palacetorquay.co.uk
web: www.palacetorquay.co.uk
dir: towards harbour, left by clocktower into Babbacombe
Rd, hotel on right after 1m

Set in 25 acres of stunning, beautifully tended wooded
grounds, the Palace offers a tranquil environment.
Suitable for business and leisure, the hotel boasts a huge
range of well-presented indoor and outdoor facilities.
Much of the original charm and grandeur have been
maintained, particularly in the dining room. Many of the
bedrooms enjoy views of the magnificent gardens.

Rooms 141 (7 fmly) **Facilities** 🔲 ⚡ ♨ 9 ⛳ Putt green
⛳ Gym Squash Table tennis Xmas New Year Wi-fi
Conf Class 800 Board 40 Thtr 1000 **Services** Lift
Parking 140 **Notes** LB ⊗

See advert on page 163

Orestone Manor Hotel & Restaurant

★★★ 86% ◉ HOTEL

☎ 01803 328098 📄 01803 328336
Rockhouse Ln, Maidencombe TQ1 4SX
e-mail: info@orestonemanor.com
web: www.orestonemanor.com
dir: A38 onto A380 then B3192

This country-house hotel is located on the fringe of Torbay
and occupies a delightful rural location with distant sea
views. There is a colonial theme throughout the public
areas which creates a charming and comfortable
environment. There are several lounges and a lovely
terrace for drinks and alfresco eating. Bedrooms are
individually styled and spacious; some have balconies.
The cuisine offers an interesting range of dishes based
on local ingredients.

Rooms 12 (3 fmly) (1 GF) **S** £90-£149; **D** £135-£225 (incl.
bkfst) **Facilities** FTV ⚡ Xmas New Year Wi-fi
Conf Class 20 Board 18 Thtr 40 Del from £150 to £215
Parking 40 **Notes** LB Closed 2-26 Jan Civ Wed 70

Best Western Hotel Gleneagles

★★★ 78% HOTEL

☎ 01803 293637 📄 01803 295106
Asheldon Rd, Wellswood TQ1 2QS
e-mail: enquiries@hotel-gleneagles.com
dir: A380 onto A3022 to A379, follow to St Mathias
Church, turn right into Asheldon Rd

From its hillside location, looking out over Anstey's Cove
towards Lyme Bay, this peacefully located hotel is
appointed to an impressive standard. Stylish public areas
combine comfort, flair and quality with ample space in
which to find a quiet spot to unwind. Bedrooms also have
a contemporary feel; many have balconies or patios. The
pool area has a real Riviera feel with elegant Lloyd Loom
sun loungers and palm trees.

Rooms 41 (2 fmly) (5 GF) **Facilities** ⚡ Xmas Wi-fi
Services Lift **Parking** 21 **Notes** LB ⊗

See advert on page 174

Corbyn Head Hotel & Orchid Restaurant

★★★ 77% ◉◉◉ HOTEL

☎ 01803 213611 📄 01803 296152
Torbay Rd, Sea Front TQ2 6RH
e-mail: info@corbynhead.com
web: www.corbynhead.com
dir: Follow signs to Torquay seafront, turn right on
seafront. Hotel on right with green canopies

This hotel occupies a prime position overlooking Torbay,
and offers well-equipped bedrooms, many with sea views
and some with balconies. The staff are friendly and
attentive, and a well-stocked bar and comfortable lounge

are available. Guests can enjoy fine dining in the
award-winning Orchid Restaurant or more traditional
dishes in the Harbour View Restaurant.

Rooms 45 (4 fmly) (9 GF) **Facilities** FTV ⚡ Gym Squash
♫ Xmas New Year Wi-fi **Conf** Class 30 Board 30 Thtr 50
Parking 50

See advert on opposite page

Livermead Cliff

★★★ 71% HOTEL

☎ 01803 299666 📄 01803 294496
Torbay Rd TQ2 6RQ
e-mail: enquiries@livermeadcliff.co.uk
web: www.livermeadcliff.co.uk
dir: A379/A3022 to Torquay, towards seafront, turn right
for Paignton. Hotel 600yds on seaward side

Situated at the water's edge this long-established hotel
offers friendly service. The splendid views can be enjoyed
from the lounge, bar and dining room. Bedrooms, many
with sea views and some with balconies, are comfortable
and well equipped. A range of room size is available.

Rooms 67 (21 fmly) **S** £40-£90; (incl. bkfst & dinner)*
Facilities ⚡ supervised Fishing Use of facilities at sister
hotel ♫ Xmas New Year Wi-fi **Conf** Class 60 Board 40
Thtr 120 Del from £69.50 to £154.50* **Services** Lift
Parking 92 **Notes** LB

See advert on opposite page

TORQUAY *continued*

Livermead House

★★★ 71% HOTEL

☎ 01803 294361 & 294363 📠 01803 200758
Torbay Rd TQ2 6QJ
e-mail: info@livermead.com
web: www.livermead.com
dir: from seafront turn right, follow A379 towards
Paignton & Livermead, hotel opposite Institute Beach

Having a splendid waterfront location, this hotel dates
back to the 1820s and is where Charles Kingsley is said
to have written *The Water Babies*. Bedrooms vary in size
and style, excellent public rooms are popular for private
parties and meetings, and a range of leisure facilities is
provided. Enjoyable cuisine is served in the impressive
restaurant.

Rooms 67 (6 fmly) (2 GF) **Facilities** ⚡ Gym Squash ♫
Xmas **Conf** Class 175 Board 80 Thtr 320 **Services** Lift
Parking 131 **Notes** LB

See advert on this page

Lincombe Hall

★★★ 70% HOTEL

☎ 01803 213361 📠 01803 211485
Meadfoot Rd TQ1 2JX
e-mail: lincombe.hall@lineone.net
web: www.lincombe-hall.co.uk
dir: From harbour into Torwood St, at lights after 100yds,
turn right into Meadfoot Rd. Hotel 200yds on left

With views over Torquay, this hotel is conveniently close
to the town centre and is set in five acres of gardens and
grounds. Facilities include both indoor and outdoor
swimming pools. The tastefully furnished bedrooms vary
in size, and the Sutherland rooms are very spacious.
There are comfortable lounges and Harleys restaurant
offers a comprehensive choice of dishes and wines.

Rooms 44 (19 annexe) (7 fmly) (2 GF) **Facilities** FTV ⚡
⚡ 🏊 Putt green Child's play area Crazy golf Pool table
Table Tennis ♫ Xmas New Year **Conf** Class 30 Board 30
Thtr 30 **Parking** 44

Abbey Lawn

★★★ 66% HOTEL

☎ 01803 299199 & 203181 📠 01803 203181
Scarborough Rd TQ2 5UQ
e-mail: nicky@holdsworthhotels.freeserve.co.uk

Conveniently located for both the seafront and town
centre, this is an ideal base for visiting the attractions of
the 'English Riviera'. Many of the bedrooms, including the
four-poster suite, benefit from lovely sea views. Facilities
include spacious parking, in addition to a health club
with extensive leisure activities and indoor and outdoor
pools. Traditional cuisine is served in elegant restaurant,
and evening entertainment is a regular feature in the
ballroom.

Rooms 57 (3 fmly) **Facilities** 🏊 supervised ⚡ supervised
Gym Steam room ♫ Xmas New Year **Services** Lift
Parking 20 **Notes** ⊗ Closed Jan

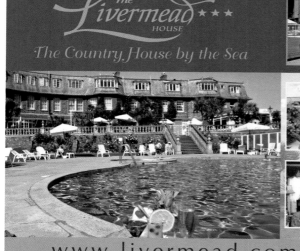

The Grosvenor

★★★ 66% HOTEL

☎ 01803 294373 📠 01803 291032
Belgrave Rd TQ2 5HG
e-mail: enquiries@grosvenorhoteltorquay.co.uk
web: www.grosvenorhoteltorquay.co.uk
dir: Follow signs to seafront, turn left, then 1st left into Belgrave Rd, hotel 1st on left

Offering spacious and attractively furnished bedrooms, this hotel is situated close to the seafront and the main attractions of the bay. Stylish public areas offer high levels of comfort, and guests can choose to dine either in the restaurant, coffee shop or Mima's Italian Restaurant. A range of leisure facilities is available including a gym, a sauna and indoor and outdoor pools.

Rooms 47 (8 fmly) **Facilities** ⊗ ⊀ Gym Mini snooker table Library Hair studio Massage room Beauty therapist ♫ Xmas New Year Wi-fi **Conf** Class 100 Board 40 Thtr 150 **Parking** 50 **Notes** ⊗ Civ Wed 300

Torcroft

★★ 75% HOTEL

☎ 01803 298292 📠 01803 291799
28-30 Croft Rd TQ2 5UE
e-mail: enquiries@torcroft.co.uk
web: www.torcroft.co.uk
dir: A390 onto A3022 to Avenue Rd. Follow seafront signs, turn left, cross lights, up Shedden Hill, 1st left into Croft Rd

This elegant, Grade II listed Victorian property is pleasantly located in a quiet area, a short stroll from the seafront. The delightful garden and patio are very popular with guests, ideal for sunbathing or relaxing with a good book. The comfortable bedrooms, two with balconies, are individually furnished. Pleasant, home-cooked meals are enthusiastically offered and make enjoyable dining.

Rooms 15 (2 fmly) **S** £29-£39; **D** £58-£83 (incl. bkfst)* **Facilities** FTV Wi-fi **Parking** 15 **Notes** ⊗

Hotel Balmoral

★★ 72% HOTEL

☎ 01803 293381 & 299224 📠 01803 299224
Meadfoot Sea Rd TQ1 2LQ
e-mail: thehotelbalmoral@tiscali.co.uk
dir: At harbour turn left at clock tower towards Babbacombe, in 100yds right at lights. Follow to Meadfoot Beach, hotel on right

Situated a short walk from Meadfoot Beach, this friendly, privately-owned and personally run hotel has comfortably appointed bedrooms including family rooms and one on the ground floor. The spacious lounge has views over the well-tended gardens to the sea beyond, whilst the bar is an ideal venue for a drink before enjoying home-cooked dinners in the attractive dining room.

Rooms 24 (4 fmly) (1 GF) **Facilities** Xmas Child facilities **Parking** 18 **Notes** LB

Anchorage Hotel

★★ 69% HOTEL

☎ 01803 326175 📠 01803 316439
Cary Park, Aveland Rd TQ1 3PT
e-mail: enquiries@anchoragehotel.co.uk

Quietly located in a residential area and providing a friendly welcome, this family-run establishment enjoys a great deal of repeat business. Bedrooms offer a range of sizes and all rooms are neatly presented. Evening entertainment is provided regularly in the large and comfortable lounge.

Rooms 56 (5 fmly) (17 GF) **S** £40-£47.50; **D** £80-£95 (incl. bkfst & dinner)* **Facilities** FTV ⊀ ♫ Xmas New Year Wi-fi **Services** Lift **Parking** 26

Elmington Hotel

★★ 69% HOTEL

☎ 01803 605192 📠 01803 690488
St Agnes Ln, Chelston TQ2 6QE
e-mail: mail@elmington.co.uk
web: www.elmington.co.uk
dir: At rear of rail station

Set in sub-tropical gardens with views over the bay, this splendid Victorian villa has been lovingly restored. The comfortable bedrooms are brightly decorated and vary in size and style. There is a spacious lounge, bar and dining room. Diners can choose from a menu of British dishes or an oriental buffet.

Rooms 19 (2 fmly) (1 GF) **S** £28-£34; **D** £36-£70 (incl. bkfst) **Facilities** ⊀ ⊌ Pool table Xmas **Conf** Class 40 Board 30 Thtr 40 **Parking** 22 **Notes** ⊗ Closed Dec-Feb

Frognel Hall

★★ 69% HOTEL

☎ 01803 298339 📠 01803 215115
Higher Woodfield Rd TQ1 2LD
e-mail: enquiries@frognel.co.uk
web: www.frognel.co.uk
dir: Follow signs to seafront, then follow esplanade to harbour, left to Babbacombe, right at lights towards Meadfoot beach, 3rd left, hotel on left

Frognel Hall is a fine old Victorian mansion set in its own landscaped grounds overlooking the town of Torquay and the sea beyond. The hotel is a short walk from the town centre and Meadfoot Beach. Bedrooms are spacious and comfortable many with garden and sea views and Wi-fi is available throughout the hotel.

Rooms 27 (2 annexe) (6 fmly) (6 GF) **S** £29-£35; **D** £55-£94 (incl. bkfst)* **Facilities** FTV ⊌ ♫ Xmas New Year Wi-fi **Conf** Class 30 Board 15 Thtr 50 Del from £60 to £90* **Services** Lift **Parking** 28 **Notes** LB ⊗ Closed Jan (ex New Year)

Albaston House

★★ 68% HOTEL

☎ 01803 296758 📠 01803 209211
27 St Marychurch Rd TQ1 3JF
e-mail: albastonhousehotel@hotmail.com
dir: A380 left at lights then B3199, follow signs for Plainmoor to Westhill Rd. Right at lights. Hotel 0.5m on left

The Albaston is situated close to the town centre and is also convenient for the quieter attractions of Babbacombe. Public areas and bedrooms alike combine comfort and quality. Many guests return time after time to this welcoming, family-run hotel.

Rooms 13 (2 fmly) (3 smoking) **S** £25-£36; **D** £50-£72 (incl. bkfst)* **Facilities** Xmas Wi-fi **Parking** 6 **Notes** LB ⊗

TORQUAY *continued*

The Heritage Hotel

★★ 68% HOTEL

☎ 01803 299332 📠 01803 209191
Seafront, Shedden Hill TQ2 5TY
e-mail: enquiries@heritagehoteltorquay.co.uk
web: www.heritagehoteltorquay.co.uk
dir: A380 to Torquay follow signs to seafront. Hotel on left

In an elevated position overlooking Tor Abbey Sands, this hotel is a short walk from both harbour and shops. Bedrooms are traditionally furnished and come in various sizes; all have sea views except one. There is a variety of eating options based on American food themes. There is a large sun deck for relaxation in summer and also a ground-floor leisure complex.

Rooms 24 (24 fmly) (4 GF) **S** £40-£50; **D** £70-£90 (incl. bkfst) **Facilities** STV ⊗ supervised Gym ♫ Wi-fi **Services** Lift **Parking** 40 **Notes** LB ⊗

Ashley Court

★★ 67% HOTEL

☎ 01803 292417 📠 01803 215035
107 Abbey Rd TQ2 5NP
e-mail: reception@ashleycourt.co.uk
dir: A380 to seafront, left to Shedden Hill to lights, hotel opposite

Located close to the town centre and within easy strolling distance of the seafront, this hotel offers a warm welcome to guests. Bedrooms are pleasantly appointed and some have sea views. The outdoor pool and patio are popular with guests wishing to soak up some sunshine. Live entertainment is provided every night throughout the season.

Rooms 83 (12 fmly) (8 GF) **Facilities** ⅃ Games room ♫ Xmas New Year **Services** Lift **Parking** 51 **Notes** ⊗ Closed 3 Jan-1 Feb

Maycliffe

★★ 67% HOTEL

☎ 01803 294964 📠 01803 201167
St Lukes Road North TQ2 5DP
e-mail: bob.west1@virgin.net
web: www.maycliffehotel.co.uk
dir: Left from Kings Dr, along seafront keep in left lane, at next lights (Belgrave Rd) up Shedden Hill, 2nd right into St Lukes Rd then 1st left

Set in a quiet and elevated position which is convenient for the town centre and attractions, the Maycliffe is a popular venue for leisure breaks. Bedrooms are individually decorated and equipped with modern facilities; there are two rooms on the ground floor suitable for less able guests. There is a quiet lounge for relaxation, whilst in the bar there is a cabaret on some nights during the season.

Rooms 28 (1 fmly) (2 GF) **Facilities** ♫ Xmas **Services** Lift **Parking** 10 **Notes** ⊗ No children 4yrs Closed 2 Jan-12 Feb

Shelley Court

★★ 67% HOTEL

☎ 01803 295642 📠 01803 215793
29 Croft Rd TQ2 5UD
e-mail: shelleycourthotel@hotmail.com
dir: From B3199 up Shedden Hill Rd, 1st left into Croft Rd

This hotel, popular with groups, is located in a pleasant, quiet area that overlooks the town towards Torbay. With a friendly team of staff, many guests return here time and again. Entertainment is provided most evenings in the season. Bedrooms come in a range of sizes and there is a large and comfortable lounge bar.

Rooms 27 (3 fmly) (6 GF) **S** £32-£49; **D** £32-£52.50 (incl. bkfst & dinner) **Facilities** FTV ⅃ Pool table Indoor skittle alley ♫ Xmas New Year **Parking** 20 **Notes** LB Closed 4 Jan-10 Feb

Bute Court

★★ 65% HOTEL

☎ 01803 213408 📠 01803 213429
Belgrave Rd TQ2 5HQ
e-mail: stay@butecourt.co.uk
dir: A3022 into Torquay. Follow signs for seafront

This popular hotel is only a short, level walk from the seafront and resort attractions. It still retains many Victorian features, and the comfortable bedrooms offer modern facilities and many have far reaching views. Public areas include a bar and lounges, while the attractive dining room looks across secluded gardens to the sea. Entertainment is also offered during busier periods.

Rooms 43 (2 fmly) (13 GF) **S** £35-£49; **D** £70-£98 (incl. bkfst & dinner)* **Facilities** ⅃ ♫ Xmas New Year **Services** Lift **Parking** 25

Coppice

★★ 64% HOTEL

☎ 01803 297786 & 211085 📠 01803 211085
Babbacombe Rd TQ1 2QJ
e-mail: reservations@coppicehotel.co.uk
web: www.coppicehotel.co.uk
dir: From harbour left at clock tower. Hotel in 0.75m on left

A friendly, comfortable and well-established hotel, The Coppice is a popular choice and provides a convenient location that is within walking distance of the beaches and shops. In addition to the indoor and outdoor swimming pools, evening entertainment is often provided in the spacious bar. Bedrooms are bright and airy with modern amenities.

Rooms 39 (16 fmly) (22 GF) **S** £30-£45; **D** £60-£90 (incl. bkfst) **Facilities** FTV ⊗ ⅃ Putt green Gym Sauna Boutique spa Pool table Steam room Xmas New Year Wi-fi **Conf** Class 40 Board 40 Thtr 40 **Parking** 35 **Notes** LB ⊗

Regina

★★ 64% HOTEL

Leisureplex

☎ 01803 292904 📠 01803 290270
Victoria Pde TQ1 2BE
e-mail: regina.torquay@alfatravel.co.uk
dir: Into Torquay, follow harbour signs, hotel on outer corner of harbour

This hotel enjoys a pleasant and convenient location right on the harbourside, a short stroll from the town's attractions. Bedrooms, some with harbour views, vary in size. Entertainment is provided on most nights and there is a choice of bars.

Rooms 68 (5 fmly) **Facilities** FTV ♫ Xmas New Year **Services** Lift **Parking** 6 **Notes** LB ⊗ Closed Jan & part Feb RS Nov-Dec (ex Xmas) & Feb-Mar

Kistor Hotel

★★ 61% HOTEL

☎ 01803 293800 📠 01803 212635
Belgrave Rd TQ2 5HF
e-mail: stay@holidaytorquay.com
dir: A380 to Torquay, hotel at junct of Belgrave Rd & promenade

Within a short stroll of Torquay's many amenities and the promenade, the Kistor is conveniently located. Popular with groups, the hotel offers a relaxing and informal base for guests. Most bedrooms have sea views.

Rooms 63 (10 fmly) (4 GF) **Facilities** ⊗ Sauna ♫ Xmas New Year **Services** Lift **Parking** 60 **Notes** ⊗

Red House Hotel

U

☎ 01803 607811 🖹 0871 5289455
Rousdown Rd, Chelston TQ2 6PB
e-mail: stay@redhouse-hotel.co.uk
web: www.redhouse-hotel.co.uk
dir: Towards seafront/Chelston, turn into Avenue Rd, right at 1st lights. Pass shops & church, take next left. Hotel on right

At the time of going to press the rating of this establishment was not confirmed. This may be due to a change of ownership or because it has only recently joined the AA rating scheme. For further details please see the AA website: theAA.com

Rooms 9 (3 fmly) **Facilities** ☜ ↝ Gym Sun shower Beauty room Sauna Xmas New Year **Parking** 9 **Notes** LB

Travelodge Torquay

BUDGET HOTEL

☎ 0871 984 6412
Newton Rd TQ2 5BZ
dir: From M5 junct 31 follow Torquay signs. Pass Torre rail station, filter left into Newton Rd. Follow town centre signs. Lodge on left.

Travelodge offers good quality, good value, budget accommodation. All offer family rooms sleeping up to four (two adults, two children) with en suite bathroom/shower-room, remote-control TV, tea- and coffee-making facilities and comfortable beds. Food options vary. Breakfast is at the on-site Bar Café restaurant (if available) or to take away. See also the Hotel Groups pages.

Rooms 90 **S** fr £29; **D** fr £29

TWO BRIDGES   Map 3 SX67

Two Bridges Hotel

★★★ 77% ◉ HOTEL

☎ 01822 890581 🖹 01822 892306
PL20 6SW
e-mail: enquiries@twobridges.co.uk
web: www.twobridges.co.uk
dir: At junct of B3212 & B3357

This wonderfully relaxing hotel is set in the heart of the Dartmoor National Park, in a beautiful riverside location. Three standards of comfortable rooms provide every modern convenience, and include four-poster rooms. There is a choice of lounges and fine dining is available in the restaurant, where menus feature local game and seasonal produce.

Rooms 33 (2 fmly) (6 GF) **S** £70-£95; **D** £140-£190 (incl. bkfst) **Facilities** STV Fishing Xmas New Year Child facilities **Conf** Class 60 Board 40 Thtr 130 Del from £110 to £140 **Parking** 100 **Notes** LB Civ Wed 130

Prince Hall

★★ 85% ◉◉ COUNTRY HOUSE HOTEL

☎ 01822 890403 🖹 01822 890676
PL20 6SA
e-mail: info@princehall.co.uk
dir: On B3357 1m E of Two Bridges road junct

Charm, peace and relaxed informality pervade at this small hotel, which has a stunning location at the heart of Dartmoor. Bedrooms, each named after a Dartmoor tor, have been equipped with thoughtful extras. The history of this house and its location are reflected throughout the public areas, which are very comfortable. The accomplished cooking is memorable. Dogs are welcomed here as warmly as their owners.

Rooms 8 (1 fmly) **D** £80-£160 (incl. bkfst)* **Facilities** FTV Xmas New Year Wi-fi **Conf** Class 25 Board 20 Del from £120 to £180* **Parking** 12 **Notes** LB No children 10yrs Civ Wed 40

WOODBURY   Map 3 SY08

Woodbury Park Hotel and Golf Club

★★★★ 73% ◉ HOTEL

☎ 01395 233382 🖹 01395 234701
Woodbury Castle EX5 1JJ
e-mail: enquiries@woodburypark.co.uk
web: www.woodburypark.co.uk
dir: M5 junct 30, A376 then A3052 towards Sidmouth, onto B3180, hotel signed

Situated in 500 acres of beautiful and unspoilt countryside, yet within easy reach of Exeter and the M5, this hotel offers smart, well-equipped and immaculately presented accommodation together with a host of sporting and banqueting facilities. There is a choice of golf courses, a Bodyzone beauty centre and enjoyable dining in the Atrium Restaurant.

Rooms 60 (4 annexe) (4 fmly) (19 GF) **S** £95-£120; **D** £130-£150 (incl. bkfst)* **Facilities** Spa STV ☜ ↯ 18 ☜ Putt green Fishing Gym Squash Beauty salon Football pitch Driving range Fitness Studio Xmas New Year Wi-fi **Conf** Class 100 Board 40 Thtr 250 **Services** Lift **Parking** 400 **Notes** LB ⊗ Civ Wed 150

WOODY BAY   Map 3 SS64

Woody Bay Hotel

★★ 75% HOTEL

☎ 01598 763264 & 763563
EX31 4QX
e-mail: info@woodybayhotel.co.uk
dir: Signed off A39 between Blackmoor Gate & Lynton

Popular with walkers, this hotel is perfectly situated to enjoy sweeping views over Woody Bay. Bedrooms vary in style and size, but all boast truly magnificent views across the dense woodland to the sea beyond. The same views accompany the enjoyable dining experience in the restaurant where local fish features prominently in the imaginative menus.

Rooms 7 (1 fmly) **Parking** 7 **Notes** LB ⊗ No children 5yrs Closed Dec-Jan RS Nov-Feb

WOOLACOMBE — Map 3 SS44

Woolacombe Bay
★★★★ 71% HOTEL

☎ 01271 870388 ▤ 01271 870613
South St EX34 7BN
e-mail: woolacombe.bayhotel@btinternet.com
web: www.woolacombebayhotel.com
dir: From A361 take B3343 to Woolacombe. Hotel in centre

This family-friendly hotel is adjacent to the beach and the village centre, and has a welcoming and friendly environment. The public areas are spacious and comfortable, and many of the well-equipped bedrooms have balconies with splendid views over the bay. In addition to the fixed-price menu served in the stylish Doyle's Restaurant, The Bay Brasserie offers an informal alternative.

Rooms 68 (27 fmly) (2 GF) **S** £65-£159; **D** £130-£318 (incl. dinner)* **Facilities** Spa FTV Ⓢ ⚆ ♨ 9 ♨ Gym Squash Creche Paddling pool Table tennis Hairdresser Steam room Snooker Xmas New Year Wi-fi Child facilities **Conf** Class 150 Board 150 Thtr 200 Del from £93 to £165* **Services** Lift **Parking** 150 **Notes** ⊗ Closed 2 Jan-12 Feb Civ Wed 100

Watersmeet
★★★ 88% ⊛ HOTEL

☎ 01271 870333 ▤ 01271 870890
Mortehoe EX34 7EB
e-mail: info@watersmeethotel.co.uk
web: www.watersmeethotel.co.uk
dir: Follow B3343 into Woolacombe, turn right onto esplanade, hotel 0.75m on left

With magnificent views, and steps leading directly to the beach, this popular hotel offers guests attentive service. Bedrooms benefit from these wonderful sea views and some have private balconies. Diners in the attractive

tiered restaurant can admire the beautiful sunsets while enjoying an innovative range of dishes offered on the fixed-price menu.

Rooms 25 (4 fmly) (3 GF) **Facilities** FTV Ⓢ ⚆ ♨ Steam room ♬ Xmas New Year Wi-fi **Conf** Board 20 Thtr 20 **Services** Lift **Parking** 38 **Notes** ⊗ Civ Wed 60

YELVERTON — Map 3 SX56

Moorland Links
★★★ 75% HOTEL

☎ 01822 852245 ▤ 01822 855004
PL20 6DA
e-mail: moorland.links@forestdale.com
web: www.moorlandlinkshotel.co.uk
dir: A38 from Exeter to Plymouth, then A386 towards Tavistock. 5m onto open moorland, hotel 1m on left

Set in nine acres in the Dartmoor National Park, this hotel offers spectacular views from many of the rooms across open moorland and the Tamar Valley. Bedrooms are well equipped and comfortably furnished, and some rooms have open balconies. The stylish restaurant looks out over the oak fringed lawns.

Rooms 44 (4 fmly) (17 GF) **S** £65-£80; **D** £80-£140 (incl. bkfst)* **Facilities** FTV ♨ Xmas New Year Wi-fi **Conf** Class 60 Board 50 Thtr 170 **Parking** 120 **Notes** Civ Wed 80

DORSET

BEAMINSTER — Map 4 ST40

BridgeHouse
★★★ 80% ⊛ HOTEL

☎ 01308 862200 ▤ 01308 863700
3 Prout Bridge DT8 3AY
e-mail: enquiries@bridge-house.co.uk
web: www.bridge-house.co.uk
dir: Off A3066, 100yds from town square

Dating back to the 13th century, this property offers friendly and attentive service. The stylish bedrooms feature Egyptian cotton linens, flat-screen TVs and Wi-fi plus newly fitted bathrooms. There are five types of room to choose from including four-poster and coach house rooms. Smartly presented public areas include the Georgian dining room, cosy bar and adjacent lounge, and a breakfast room together with the Beaminster Brasserie

with its alfresco eating area under a canopy overlooking the attractive walled garden.

Rooms 14 (5 annexe) (1 fmly) (5 GF) **S** £76-£108; **D** £116-£200 (incl. bkfst)* **Facilities** Xmas New Year Wi-fi Child facilities **Conf** Class 14 Board 10 Thtr 24 **Parking** 20 **Notes** LB Civ Wed 50

BLANDFORD FORUM — Map 4 ST80

Crown Hotel
★★★ 73% HOTEL

☎ 01258 456626 ▤ 01258 451084
West St DT11 7AJ
e-mail: crownhotel.blandford@hall-woodhouse.co.uk
dir: 100mtrs from town bridge

Retaining much of its Georgian charm, this former coaching inn provides a friendly welcome allied with efficient service. The well-equipped, stylish bedrooms are furnished to high standards, combining comfort with practicality. Refurbishment has resulted in a makeover for the lounge, restaurant and bar with a successful blend of traditional and contemporary designs. A menu choices have dishes of good quality produce that are served in a relaxed and friendly atmosphere.

Rooms 32 (2 fmly) **Conf** Class 200 Board 60 Thtr 250 **Services** Lift **Parking** 144 **Notes** LB Closed 25-28 Dec Civ Wed 150

BOURNEMOUTH — Map 5 SZ19

See also **Christchurch**

Menzies East Cliff Court   MenziesHotels
★★★★ 80% HOTEL

☎ 01202 554545 ▤ 01202 557456
East Overcliff Dr BH1 3AN
e-mail: eastcliff@menzieshotels.co.uk
web: www.menzieshotels.co.uk
dir: From M3/M27 towards Bournemouth on A338 (leads onto Wessex Way), follow signs to East Cliff, hotel on seafront

Enjoying panoramic views across the bay, this popular hotel offers bedrooms that are modern and contemporary in style, and that have been appointed to a very high standard; many benefit from balconies with sea views. Stylish public areas include a range of inviting lounges, a spacious restaurant and a selection of conference rooms.

Rooms 67 (4 fmly) (2 GF) (5 smoking) **S** £50-£185; **D** £50-£185* **Facilities** STV ♨ Full leisure facilities at adjacent Menzies Carlton Xmas New Year Wi-fi **Conf** Class 80 Board 50 Thtr 200 Del from £99 to £175* **Services** Lift **Parking** 45 **Notes** Civ Wed 250

Bournemouth Highcliff Marriott

★★★★ 78% ◉ HOTEL

☎ 01202 557702 📠 01202 293155
St Michaels Rd, West Cliff BH2 5DU
e-mail: mhrs.bohbm.ays@marriotthotels.co.uk
web: www.bournemouthhighcliffmarriott.co.uk
dir: A338 through Bournemouth. Follow BIC signs to West Cliff Rd. 2nd right into St Michaels Rd. Hotel at end of road on left

Originally built as a row of coastguard cottages, this establishment has expanded over the years into a very elegant and charming hotel. Impeccably maintained throughout, many of the bedrooms have sea views. An excellent range of leisure, business and conference facilities are offered, as well as private dining and banqueting rooms. The hotel also has direct access to the Bournemouth International Centre.

Rooms 160 (19 annexe) (22 fmly) **Facilities** STV FTV 🎣 supervised 🎣 🥅 Putt green ⛳ Gym Beautician Xmas New Year Wi-fi **Conf** Class 180 Board 90 Thtr 350 **Services** Lift Air con **Parking** 92 **Notes** 🐾 Civ Wed 250

Menzies Carlton

MenziesHotels

★★★★ 77% ◉ HOTEL

☎ 01202 552011 📠 01202 299573
East Overcliff BH1 3DN
e-mail: carlton@menzieshotels.co.uk
web: www.menzieshotels.co.uk
dir: From M3/M27, approach Bournemouth on A338 (leads onto Wessex Way), follow signs to the East Cliff, hotel on seafront

Enjoying a prime location on the East Cliff, and with views of the Isle of Wight and Dorset coastline, the Carlton has attractive gardens and pool area. Most of the spacious bedrooms enjoy sea views. Leisure facilities include an indoor and outdoor pool as well as a gym. Guests can enjoy an interesting range of carefully prepared dishes in Frederick's restaurant. The conference and banqueting facilities are varied.

Rooms 76 (17 fmly) (8 GF) (9 smoking) **S** £50-£185; **D** £50-£185* **Facilities** STV 🎣 🥅 Gym Spa pool Hair & beauty salon Xmas New Year Wi-fi **Conf** Class 120 Board 50 Thtr 250 Del from £105 to £175* **Services** Lift **Parking** 87 **Notes** 🐾 Civ Wed 200

De Vere Royal Bath

DE VERE collection

★★★★ 73% HOTEL

☎ 01202 555555 📠 01202 554158
Bath Rd BH1 2EW
e-mail: royalbath@devere-hotels.com
web: www.devere.co.uk
dir: A338, follow signs for pier & beaches. Hotel on seafront before BIC

Overlooking the bay, this well-established seafront hotel is surrounded by beautifully kept gardens. Public rooms, which include lounges, a choice of restaurants and indoor leisure facilities, are of a scale and style befitting the Victorian era in which the hotel was built. Parking space is limited but valet parking, at a charge, is provided.

Rooms 140 (31 fmly) (23 GF) **S** £69-£180; **D** £99-£210 (incl. bkfst) **Facilities** Spa STV 🎣 supervised Gym Beauty salon Hairdressing Xmas New Year Wi-fi **Conf** Class 220 Board 100 Thtr 400 Del from £119 to £210 **Services** Lift **Parking** 70 **Notes** LB 🐾 Civ Wed 400

Norfolk Royale

CLASSIC BRITISH HOTELS

★★★★ 70% HOTEL

☎ 01202 551521 📠 01202 299729
Richmond Hill BH2 6EN
e-mail: clivemoss@englishrosehotels.co.uk
web: www.englishrosehotels.co.uk
dir: A338 into Bournemouth take Richmond Hill exit to A347 Wimborne, turn left at top into Richmond Hill. Hotel on right

Easily recognisable by its wrought iron balconies, this Edwardian hotel is conveniently located for the centre of the town. Most of the bedrooms are contained in a modern wing at the side of the building, overlooking the pretty landscaped gardens. There is a car park at rear of hotel.

Rooms 95 (7 fmly) (9 GF) **S** £129-£139; **D** £159-£219 (incl. bkfst)* **Facilities** STV 🎣 Gym Membership of nearby health club 🎵 Xmas New Year Wi-fi **Conf** Class 50 Board 40 Thtr 150 **Services** Lift **Parking** 95 **Notes** LB 🐾 Civ Wed 150

Hermitage

★★★ 82% ◉ HOTEL

☎ 01202 557363 📠 01202 559173
Exeter Rd BH2 5AH
e-mail: info@hermitage-hotel.co.uk
web: www.hermitage-hotel.co.uk
dir: A338 Ringwood, follow signs for BIC and pier. Hotel directly opposite

Occupying an impressive location overlooking the seafront, at the heart of the town centre, the Hermitage offers friendly and attentive service. The majority of the smart bedrooms are comfortably appointed and all are very well equipped; many rooms have sea views. The wood-panelled lounge provides an elegant and tranquil area, as does the restaurant where well-prepared and interesting dishes are served.

Rooms 74 (11 annexe) (9 fmly) (7 GF) **Facilities** Xmas New Year Wi-fi **Conf** Class 60 Board 60 Thtr 180 **Services** Lift **Parking** 58 **Notes** 🐾

See advert on page 173

BOURNEMOUTH *continued*

Hotel Miramar

★★★ 82% HOTEL

☎ 01202 556581 🖹 01202 291242
East Overcliff Dr, East Cliff BH1 3AL
e-mail: sales@miramar-bournemouth.com
web: www.miramar-bournemouth.com
dir: Wessex Way rdbt turn into St Pauls Rd, right at next rdbt. 3rd exit at next rdbt, 2nd exit at next rdbt into Grove Rd. Hotel car park on right

Conveniently located on the East Cliff, this Edwardian hotel enjoys glorious sea views. The Miramar was a favoured destination of JRR Tolkien, who often stayed here. The friendly staff and a relaxing environment are noteworthy here. The bedrooms are comfortable and well equipped, and there are spacious public areas and a choice of lounges.

Rooms 43 (6 fmly) **S** £46.95-£74.95; **D** £73.90-£189.90 (incl. bkfst & dinner)* **Facilities** FTV 🎵 Xmas New Year Wi-fi **Conf** Class 50 Board 50 Thtr 200 Del from £75 to £130* **Services** Lift **Parking** 80 **Notes** LB Civ Wed 110

Chine Hotel

★★★ 81% ◉ HOTEL

☎ 01202 396234 & 0845 337 1550 🖹 01202 391737
Boscombe Spa Rd BH5 1AX
e-mail: reservations@fjbhotels.co.uk
web: www.fjbhotels.co.uk
dir: Follow BIC signs, A338/Wessex Way to St Pauls rdbt. 1st exit, to next rdbt, 2nd exit signed Eastcliff, Boscombe, Southbourne. Next rdbt, 1st exit into Christchurch Rd. After 2nd lights, right into Boscombe Spa Rd

Benefiting from superb views this popular hotel is set in delightful gardens with private access to the seafront and beach. The excellent range of facilities includes an indoor and outdoor pool, a small leisure centre and a selection of meeting rooms. The spacious bedrooms,

some with balconies, are well appointed and thoughtfully equipped.

Chine Hotel

Rooms 88 (23 annexe) (16 fmly) (8 GF) **S** £45-£105; **D** £90-£210 (incl. bkfst & dinner)* **Facilities** STV 🕲 � supervised Putt green 🏌 Gym Games room Indoor children's play area Xmas New Year Wi-fi **Conf** Class 70 Board 40 Thtr 140 Del from £110 to £140 **Services** Lift **Parking** 55 **Notes** LB ⊗ Civ Wed 120

See advert on opposite page

Langtry Manor - Lovenest of a King

★★★ 81% ◉ HOTEL

☎ 0844 3725 432 🖹 01202 290115
Derby Rd, East Cliff BH1 3QB
e-mail: lillie@langtrymanor.com
web: www.langtrymanor.co.uk
dir: A31/A338, 1st rdbt by rail station turn left. Over next rdbt, 1st left into Knyveton Rd. Hotel opposite

Retaining a stately air, this property was originally built in 1877 by Edward VII for his mistress Lillie Langtry. The individually furnished and decorated bedrooms include several with four-poster beds. Enjoyable cuisine is served in the magnificent dining hall, that displays several large Tudor tapestries. There is an Edwardian banquet on Saturday evenings.

Rooms 20 (8 annexe) (2 fmly) (3 GF) **S** £69-£129; **D** £98-£218 (incl. bkfst)* **Facilities** Free use of local health club 🎵 Xmas New Year **Conf** Class 60 Board 40 Thtr 100 **Parking** 30 **Notes** LB Civ Wed 100

Cumberland

★★★ 81% HOTEL

☎ 01202 290722 🖹 01202 311394
East Overcliff Dr BH1 3AF
e-mail: info@cumberlandbournemouth.co.uk
dir: A35 towards East Cliff & beaches, right onto Holdenhurst Rd, straight over 2 rdbts, left at junct to East Overcliff Drive, hotel on seafront

A purpose built, art deco hotel where many of the bedrooms are appointed in keeping with the hotel's original character. Front-facing bedrooms have balconies with superb sea views. The comfortable public areas are spacious and striking in their design. The Mirabelle Restaurant and Red Door Brasserie offer cuisine prepared from local produce.

Cumberland

Rooms 102 (20 fmly) **S** £39.50-£89; **D** £79-£180 (incl. bkfst)* **Facilities** 🕲 �"" Squash Sauna 🎵 Xmas New Year Wi-fi **Conf** Class 180 Board 40 Thtr 250 Del from £75 to £130* **Services** Lift **Parking** 50 **Notes** LB Civ Wed 100

See advert on page 174

Best Western Connaught Hotel

★★★ 80% ◉ HOTEL

☎ 01202 298020 🖹 01202 298028
West Hill Rd, West Cliff BH2 5PH
e-mail: reception@theconnaught.co.uk
web: www.theconnaught.co.uk
dir: Follow Town Centre West & BIC signs

Conveniently located on the West Cliff, close to the BIC, beaches and town centre, this privately-owned hotel offers well equipped, neatly decorated rooms, some with balconies. The hotel boasts a very well equipped leisure complex with a large pool and gym. Breakfast and dinner offer imaginative dishes made with quality local ingredients.

Rooms 83 (27 annexe) (10 fmly) **S** £40-£80; **D** £60-£120 (incl. bkfst) **Facilities** STV 🕲 supervised Gym Sauna Steam room Spa pool Xmas New Year Wi-fi **Conf** Class 60 Board 35 Thtr 180 Del from £95 to £160 **Services** Lift **Parking** 66 **Notes** LB ⊗ Civ Wed 200

BOURNEMOUTH *continued*

Elstead
★★★ 80% HOTEL

☎ 01202 293071 📠 01202 293827
Knyveton Rd BH1 3QP
e-mail: info@the-elstead.co.uk
web: www.the-elstead.co.uk
dir: A338 Wessex Way to St Pauls rdbt, left & left again

Ideal as a base for both business and leisure travellers, this popular hotel is conveniently located for the town centre, seafront and BIC. An impressive range of facilities is offered, including meeting rooms, an indoor leisure centre and comfortable lounges.

Rooms 50 (15 fmly) **Facilities** 🕒 supervised Gym Steam room Pool & snooker tables Xmas New Year Wi-fi **Conf** Class 60 Board 40 Thtr 80 **Services** Lift **Parking** 40 **Notes** Civ Wed 60

Best Western Hotel Royale
★★★ 78% HOTEL

☎ 01202 554794 📠 01202 299615
16 Gervis Rd BH1 3EQ
e-mail: reservations@thehotelroyale.com
web: www.thehotelroyale.com
dir: M27 junct 1, A31 onto A338 to Bournemouth, follow signs for East Cliff & seafront. Over 2 rdbts into Gervis Rd. Hotel on right

Located on the East Cliff, just a short walk from the seafront and local shops and amenities, this is a privately owned hotel. Public areas are contemporary in style and facilities, and include a small health club and spacious function rooms. Bedrooms are comfortable and well furnished.

Rooms 64 (8 annexe) (22 fmly) (8 GF) **S** £50-£75; **D** £65-£140 (incl. bkfst)* **Facilities** STV FTV 🕒 supervised Gym Xmas New Year Wi-fi **Conf** Class 60 Board 40 Thtr 100 Del from £90 to £130* **Services** Lift **Parking** 80 **Notes** LB ⊗

Trouville
★★★ 78% HOTEL

☎ 01202 552262 📠 01202 293324
Priory Rd BH2 5DH
e-mail: reception@trouvillehotel.com
dir: follow Bournemouth Town Centre West signs, turn off at rdbt signed BIC, West Cliff & Beaches. Take 2nd exit at next rdbt & left at following rdbt, follow road along. Hotel on left towards end of Priory Rd

Located near Bournemouth International Centre, the seafront and the shops, this hotel has the advantage of indoor leisure facilities and a large car park. Bedrooms are generally a good size with comfortable furnishings; there are plenty of family rooms here. The air-conditioned restaurant offers a daily changing menu.

Rooms 76 (17 fmly) (2 GF) **Facilities** 🕒 Gym 🎵 Xmas New Year Wi-fi **Conf** Class 75 Board 40 Thtr 150 **Services** Lift **Parking** 50 **Notes** Civ Wed 100

The Montague Hotel

★★★ 77% HOTEL

☎ 01202 551074 🖹 01202 553948
Durley Road South, West Cliff BH2 5JH
e-mail: enquiries@montaguehotel.co.uk
web: www.montaguehotel.co.uk
dir: A31/A338 to Bournemouth left into Cambridge Rd at Bournemouth West rdbt, take 2nd exit at next rdbt into Durley Chine Rd. Next rdbt take 2nd exit. Hotel on right

With its convenient location a short walk from the attractions of the town centre and beaches, this hotel has a busy leisure trade, especially at weekends. The well-equipped bedrooms are especially attractive with good levels of comfort and useful facilities. Guests can unwind by the outdoor pool or in the relaxing bar. The dinner menu offers an interesting selection of dishes.

Rooms 32 (9 fmly) (10 GF) **S** £40-£83; **D** £55-£98*
Facilities FTV ⚡ Xmas New Year Wi-fi **Conf** Class 12 Board 30 Thtr 60 **Services** Lift **Parking** 22 **Notes** LB ⊗

Queens

★★★ 77% HOTEL

☎ 01202 554415 🖹 01202 294810
Meyrick Rd, East Cliff BH1 3DL
e-mail: reception@queenshotelbournemouth.com
web: www.queenshotelbournemouth.com
dir: M3/M27 onto A338 leading onto Wessex Way. Follow signs to East Cliff

This attractive hotel enjoys a good location near the seafront and is popular for conferences and functions. Public areas include a bar, lounge and a large restaurant.

Leisure facilities include indoor pool and small gym. Bedrooms vary in size and style, many have sea views.

Rooms 109 (44 fmly) **S** £45-£90; **D** £75-£160 (incl. bkfst)* **Facilities** ⚡ Gym Beauty salon Snooker & pool tables ♫ Xmas New Year Wi-fi **Conf** Class 200 Board 100 Thtr 380 Del from £95 to £135* **Services** Lift **Parking** 60 **Notes** LB Civ Wed 120

Royal Exeter

★★★ 77% HOTEL

☎ 01202 438000 🖹 01202 789664
Exeter Rd BH2 5AG
e-mail: enquiries@royalexeterhotel.com
web: www.royalexeterhotel.com
dir: opposite Bournemouth International Centre

Ideally located opposite the Bournemouth International Centre, and convenient for the beach and town centre, this busy hotel caters for both business and leisure guests. Public areas are smart and there's a modern open-plan lounge bar and restaurant together with an exciting adjoining bar complex.

Rooms 54 (13 fmly) (12 smoking) **Facilities** STV Gym ♫ Wi-fi **Conf** Class 40 Board 40 Thtr 100 **Services** Lift **Parking** 50 **Notes** LB ⊗

See advert on this page

Carrington House

★★★ 75% HOTEL

☎ 01202 369988 🖹 01202 292221
31 Knyveton Rd BH1 3QQ
e-mail: carrington.house@forestdale.com
web: www.carringtonhousehotel.co.uk
dir: A338 at St Paul's rdbt, 200mtrs & left into Knyveton Rd. Hotel 400mtrs on right

This hotel occupies a prominent position on a tree-lined avenue and a short walk from the seafront. The bedrooms are comfortable, well equipped and include many purpose-built family rooms. There are two dining options, Mortimers restaurant, and the Kings bar which serves light meals and snacks. Guests can relax in the comfortable lounge areas whilst the leisure complex offers a whole host of activities including a heated swimming pool.

Rooms 145 (42 fmly) (2 GF) **S** £60-£80; **D** £100-£140 (incl. bkfst)* **Facilities** FTV ⚡ Children's play area Xmas New Year Wi-fi **Conf** Class 250 Board 110 Thtr 500 **Services** Lift **Parking** 85 **Notes** Civ Wed 60

BOURNEMOUTH *continued*

Cliffeside

★★★ 75% HOTEL

☎ 01202 555724 📄 01202 314534
East Overcliff Dr BH1 3AQ
e-mail: info@cliffesidebournemouth.co.uk
dir: Off A35/A338 to East Cliff & beaches, right into
Holdenhurst Rd, over next 2 rdbts, at junct left into East
Overcliff Drive, hotel on left on seafront

Benefiting from an elevated position on the seafront and
just a short walk to town, it's no wonder that this friendly
hotel has many returning guests. Bedrooms and public
areas are attractively appointed, many with sea views.
The Atlantic Restaurant offers guests a fixed-price menu.

Rooms 62 (5 fmly) (2 GF) **S** £29.50-£75; **D** £59-£150
(incl. bkfst)* **Facilities** 🕲 ⚡ Squash 🎵 Xmas New Year
Wi-fi **Conf** Class 70 Board 40 Thtr 120 Del from £65 to
£115* **Services** Lift **Parking** 32 **Notes** LB Civ Wed 120

See advert on page 174

Wessex

★★★ 75% HOTEL

☎ 01202 551911 📄 01202 297354
West Cliff Rd BH2 5EU
e-mail: wessex@forestdale.com
web: www.thewessexhotel.co.uk
dir: Follow M27/A35 or A338 from Dorchester & A347 N.
Hotel on West Cliff side of town

Centrally located and handy for the beach, the Wessex is
a popular, relaxing hotel. Bedrooms are well equipped
and comfortable with a range of modern amenities. The
Lulworth restaurant provides a range of appetizing
dishes. The excellent leisure facilities boast both indoor
and outdoor pools, sauna, ample function rooms and an
open-plan bar and lounge.

Rooms 109 (32 fmly) (17 GF) **S** £65-£90; **D** £110-£170
(incl. bkfst)* **Facilities** FTV 🕲 ⚡ Gym Table tennis
Xmas New Year Wi-fi **Conf** Class 150 Board 100 Thtr 400
Services Lift **Parking** 160 **Notes** Civ Wed 200

Hinton Firs

★★★ 74% HOTEL

☎ 01202 555409 📄 01202 299607
Manor Rd, East Cliff BH1 3ET
e-mail: info@hintonfirshotel.co.uk
web: www.hintonfirshotel.co.uk
dir: A338 turn W at St Paul's rdbt, over next 2 rdbts then
fork left to side of church. Hotel on next corner

This hotel is conveniently located on East Cliff, just a
short stroll from the sea. Guests are offered leisure
facilities including indoor pool and sauna. There is also a
spacious lounge, bar and restaurant in which to relax.
The well-appointed bedrooms are light and airy.

Rooms 52 (6 annexe) (12 fmly) (6 GF) **S** £39-£72.50;
D £78-£145 (incl. bkfst & dinner)* **Facilities** STV 🕲 ⚡
Games room 🎵 Xmas New Year Wi-fi **Conf** Class 40
Board 30 Thtr 50 Del from £49.95 to £89.95 **Services** Lift
Parking 40 **Notes** LB ⊗

The Riviera

★★★ 74% HOTEL

☎ 01202 763653 📄 01202 768422
Burnaby Rd, Alum Chine BH4 8JF
e-mail: info@rivierabournemouth.co.uk
web: www.rivierabournemouth.co.uk
dir: A338, follow signs to Alum Chine

The Riviera offers a range of comfortable, well-furnished
bedrooms and bathrooms. Welcoming staff provide
efficient service delivered in a friendly manner. In
addition to a spacious lounge with regular entertainment,
there is an indoor and an outdoor pool, and all just a
short walk from the beach.

Rooms 73 (4 annexe) (25 fmly) (11 GF) **S** £37-£92;
D £74-£184 (incl. bkfst)* **Facilities** FTV 🕲 ⚡ Games
room Sauna Spa bath Treatments available 🎵 Xmas New
Year Wi-fi **Conf** Class 120 Board 50 Thtr 180 Del from £75
to £150* **Services** Lift **Parking** 45 **Notes** LB Civ Wed 160

Suncliff

★★★ 74% HOTEL

☎ 01202 291711 📄 01202 293788
29 East Overcliff Dr BH1 3AG
e-mail: info@suncliffbournemouth.co.uk
dir: A338/A35 towards East Cliff & beaches, right into
Holdenhurst Rd, straight over 2 rdbts, left at junct into
East Overcliff Drive, hotel on seafront

Enjoying splendid views from the East Cliff and catering
mainly for leisure guests, this friendly hotel offers a
range of facilities and services. Bedrooms are well
equipped and comfortable, and many have sea views.
Public areas include a large conservatory, an attractive
bar and pleasant lounges.

Rooms 97 (29 fmly) (14 GF) **S** £29.50-£75; **D** £59-£150
(incl. bkfst)* **Facilities** 🕲 ⚡ Squash 🎵 Xmas New Year
Wi-fi **Conf** Class 70 Board 60 Thtr 100 Del from £65 to
£120* **Services** Lift **Parking** 62 **Notes** LB Civ Wed 80

See advert on page 174

Hotel Piccadilly

★★★ 73% HOTEL

☎ 01202 298024 📄 01202 298235
25 Bath Rd BH1 2NN
e-mail: enquiries@hotelpiccadilly.co.uk
dir: From A338 take 1st exit rdbt, signed East Cliff. 3rd
exit at next rdbt signed Lansdowne, 3rd exit at next rdbt
into Bath Rd

This hotel offers a friendly welcome to guests, many of
whom return on a regular basis, particularly for the
superb ballroom dancing facilities and small break
packages which are a feature here. Bedrooms are smartly
decorated, well maintained and comfortable. Dining in
the attractive restaurant is always popular and dishes
are freshly prepared and appetising.

Rooms 45 (2 fmly) (5 GF) **Facilities** FTV Xmas New Year
Services Lift **Parking** 35 **Notes** ⊗ Civ Wed 150

Durley Dean Hotel

★★★ 72% HOTEL

☎ 0844 855 9103 📠 01202 292815
West Cliff Rd BH2 5HE
e-mail: reservations.durleydean@foliohotels.com
web: www.foliohotels.com/durleydean
dir: In Bournemouth follow signs for Westcliff. Onto Durley Chine Rd South to next rdbt, hotel off 2nd exit on left

Situated close to the seafront on the West Cliff, this modern hotel has recently enjoyed a significant refurbishment. Bedrooms vary in size and style, there is a restaurant, a comfortable bar and several meeting rooms are available. Parking is also a bonus.

Rooms 121 (36 fmly) (6 GF) (121 smoking) **Facilities** FTV ♨ supervised Gym ♫ Xmas New Year Wi-fi **Conf** Class 40 Board 40 Thtr 150 **Services** Lift **Parking** 30 **Notes** LB ⊗

Hotel Collingwood

★★★ 70% HOTEL

☎ 01202 557575 📠 01202 293219
11 Priory Rd, West Cliff BH2 5DF
e-mail: info@hotel-collingwood.co.uk
web: www.hotel-collingwood.co.uk
dir: A338 left at West Cliff sign, over 1st rdbt and left at 2nd rdbt. Hotel 500yds on left

This privately owned and managed hotel is situated close to the BIC. Bedrooms are airy, with the emphasis on comfort. An excellent range of leisure facilities is available and the public areas are spacious and welcoming. Pinks Restaurant offers carefully prepared cuisine and a fixed-price, five-course dinner.

Rooms 53 (16 fmly) (6 GF) **S** £31-£64; **D** £62-£128 (incl. bkfst & dinner)* **Facilities** FTV ♨ Gym Steam room Sauna Games room Snooker room ♫ Xmas New Year Wi-fi **Conf** Class 60 Board 20 Thtr 100 Del from £65 to £135* **Services** Lift **Parking** 55 **Notes** LB

Marsham Court

★★★ 70% HOTEL

☎ 01202 552111 📠 01202 294744
Russell Cotes Rd, East Cliff BH1 3AB
e-mail: reservations@marshamcourt.com
web: www.marshamcourt.com
dir: A338 to Bournemouth East at St Pauls rdbt (ASDA). At next rdbt take 3rd exit into Holdenhurst Rd. At next rdbt take 3rd exit to BIC/Bath Rd. At next rdbt (BP station) take 2nd exit into Grove Rd

This hotel, in a quiet location, is set in attractive gardens with splendid views over the bay; it is a just short stroll from the town, beach and BIC. Bedrooms vary in size but all are comfortably appointed, and some have sea views. The bar and lounge areas lead onto the south facing terrace and outdoor pool. Impressive conference and banqueting facilities are available.

Rooms 87 (15 fmly) **Facilities** FTV ⚲ Pool table ♫ Xmas New Year Wi-fi **Conf** Class 100 Board 80 Thtr 200 **Services** Lift **Parking** 100 **Notes** LB ⊗ Civ Wed 200

Grange

★★★ 68% ❀ HOTEL

☎ 01202 433093 📠 01202 424228
57 Overcliffe Dr, Southbourne BH6 3NL
e-mail: info@grangehotelbournemouth.co.uk
web: www.grangehotelbournemouth.co.uk
dir: A338 Christchurch. Turn off & follow signs to Southbourne

A popular hotel located close to the town centre and convenient for the south coast. Bedrooms are comfortable and well equipped with good facilities; some benefit from balconies with sea views. The large bar is popular with both residents and locals alike. Award-winning cuisine can be experienced in the new Upper Deck restaurant.

Rooms 28 (2 fmly) **S** £38.50-£49; **D** £77-£98 (incl. bkfst) **Facilities** ♫ Xmas New Year Wi-fi **Conf** Thtr 50 **Services** Lift **Parking** 32 **Notes** LB ⊗ Civ Wed 90

Belvedere

★★★ 68% HOTEL

☎ 01202 297556 & 293336 📠 01202 294699
Bath Rd BH1 2EU
e-mail: enquiries@belvedere-hotel.co.uk
web: www.belvedere-hotel.co.uk
dir: From A338 with railway station and Asda on left. At rdbt 1st left then 3rd exit at next 2 rdbts. Hotel on Bath Hill after 4th rdbt

Close to the town centre and the seafront, this friendly, family-run hotel includes a choice of bars, a small indoor leisure club with beauty treatments and an attractive restaurant. There is a range of meeting rooms, which provide an ideal location for conferences or functions.

Rooms 100 (20 fmly) **S** £35-£64; **D** £50-£118 (incl. bkfst) **Facilities** FTV ♨ Gym Sauna ♫ Xmas New Year Wi-fi **Conf** Class 60 Board 50 Thtr 120 Del from £68 to £129* **Services** Lift **Parking** 90 **Notes** LB ⊗

Burley Court

★★★ 66% HOTEL

☎ 01202 552824 & 556704 📠 01202 298514
Bath Rd BH1 2NP
e-mail: info@burleycourthotel.co.uk
dir: leave A338 at St Paul's rdbt, take 3rd exit at next rdbt into Holdenhurst Rd. 3rd exit at next rdbt into Bath Rd, over crossing, 1st left

Located on Bournemouth's West Cliff, this well-established hotel is easily located and convenient for the town and beaches. Bedrooms are pleasantly furnished and decorated in bright colours. A daily-changing menu is served in the spacious dining room.

Rooms 38 (8 fmly) (4 GF) **Facilities** ⚲ Xmas **Conf** Class 15 Board 15 Thtr 30 **Services** Lift **Parking** 35 **Notes** Closed 30 Dec-14 Jan RS 15-31 Jan

Quality Hotel Bournemouth

★★★ 66% HOTEL

☎ 01202 316316 📠 01202 316999
47 Gervis Rd, East Cliff BH1 3DD
e-mail: reservations@qualityhotelbournemouth.com
dir: A338 left at rdbt, right at next rdbt. Take 2nd exit at next rdbt into Meyrick Rd. At next rdbt right into Gervis Rd. Hotel on left

Many years ago this hotel was run by the parents of British comic actor, Tony Hancock, and served as his childhood home. Situated just a short walk from the East Cliff, guests can enjoy the terrace and garden. A lounge menu is available throughout the day. Bedrooms are comfortable and well equipped.

Rooms 53 (9 fmly) **Facilities** FTV Xmas New Year Wi-fi **Conf** Class 100 Board 40 Thtr 120 Del from £80 to £100* **Services** Lift **Parking** 36 **Notes** Civ Wed 100

BOURNEMOUTH *continued*

The Whitehall

★★ 78% HOTEL

☎ 01202 554682 📠 01202 292637
Exeter Park Rd BH2 5AX
e-mail: reservations@thewhitehallhotel.co.uk
web: www.thewhitehallhotel.co.uk
dir: follow BIC signs then turn into Exeter Park Rd off
Exeter Rd

This friendly hotel enjoys an elevated position overlooking
the park and is also close to the town centre and
seafront. The spacious public areas include a choice of
lounges, a cosy bar and a well-presented restaurant. The
well-equipped and inviting bedrooms are spread over
three floors.

Rooms 46 (5 fmly) (3 GF) **Facilities** ♬ Xmas
Conf Class 40 Board 32 Thtr 70 **Services** Lift **Parking** 25

Tower House

★★ 76% HOTEL

☎ 01202 290742 & 299311 📠 01202 553305
West Cliff Gardens BH2 5HP
e-mail: towerhouse.hotel@btconnect.com

A popular family owned and run hotel on the West Cliff.
Owners and their staff are friendly and helpful, rooms are
comfortable and well maintained and it has good off-
road parking.

Rooms 32 (12 fmly) (3 GF) **S** £29-£46; **D** £58-£92 (incl.
bkfst)* **Facilities** FTV Xmas New Year Wi-fi **Services** Lift
Parking 30

Durley Grange

★★ 72% HOTEL

☎ 01202 554473 📠 01202 293774
6 Durley Rd, West Cliff BH2 5JL
e-mail: reservations@durleygrange.com
dir: A338/St Michaels rdbt. Over next rdbt, 1st left into
Sommerville Rd & right into Durley Rd

Located in a quiet area, with parking, the town and
beaches are all in walking distance of this welcoming,
friendly hotel. Bedrooms are brightly decorated,
comfortable and well equipped. There is an indoor pool
and sauna for all-year round use. Enjoyable meals are
served in the smart dining room.

Rooms 52 (8 fmly) (4 GF) **S** £43-£62; **D** £86-£124 (incl.
bkfst)* **Facilities** ⊛ ♬ Xmas New Year **Services** Lift
Parking 35 **Notes** LB ⊛

Bay View Court

★★ 69% HOTEL

☎ 01202 294449 📠 01202 292883
35 East Overcliff Dr BH1 3AH
e-mail: enquiry@bayviewcourt.co.uk
dir: On A338 left at St Paul's rdbt. Over St Swithun's rdbt.
Bear left onto Manor Rd, 1st right, next right

This relaxed and friendly hotel enjoys far-reaching sea
views from many of the public areas and bedrooms.
Bedrooms vary in size and are attractively furnished.
There is a choice of south facing lounges and, for the
more energetic, an indoor swimming pool. Live
entertainment is provided during the evenings.

Rooms 64 (11 fmly) (5 GF) **S** £45-£55; **D** £60-£90 (incl.
bkfst) **Facilities** ⊛ Steam room Snooker room Games
room ♬ Xmas New Year Wi-fi **Conf** Class 85 Board 50
Thtr 170 Del from £55 to £75 **Services** Lift **Parking** 58
Notes LB

Arlington

★★ 68% HOTEL

☎ 01202 552879 & 553012 📠 01202 298317
Exeter Park Rd BH2 5BD
e-mail: enquiries@arlingtonbournemouth.co.uk
dir: follow BIC signs through Priory Rd, onto rdbt and exit
at Royal Exeter Hotel sign.

Well-equipped bedrooms and comfortable
accommodation along with friendly hospitality are offered
at this privately owned and run hotel. Conveniently
located, midway between the square and the pier and
ideally situated for the BIC, the Arlington has direct
access to the Winter Gardens, which are overlooked from
the hotel's lounge and terrace bar.

Rooms 28 (1 annexe) (6 fmly) **Facilities** Xmas
Services Lift **Parking** 21 **Notes** LB ⊛ No children 2yrs
Closed 4-15 Jan

Devon Towers

★★ 68% HOTEL

Leisureplex

☎ 01202 553863 📠 01202 315265
58-62 St Michael's Rd, West Cliff BH2 5ED
e-mail: devontowers.bournemouth@alfatravel.co.uk
dir: A338 into Bournemouth, follow signs for BIC. Left into
St. Michaels Rd at top of hill. Hotel 100mtrs on left

Located in a quiet road within walking distance of the
West Cliff and shops, this hotel appeals to the budget
leisure market. The four-course menus offer plenty of
choice and entertainment is featured most evenings. The
bar and lobby area provide plenty of space for relaxing.

Rooms 62 (6 GF) **Facilities** FTV ♬ Xmas New Year
Services Lift **Parking** 6 **Notes** LB ⊛ Closed Jan-mid Feb
(ex Xmas) RS Nov, mid-end Feb & Mar

Ullswater

★★ 68% HOTEL

☎ 01202 555181 📠 01202 317896
West Cliff Gardens BH2 5HW
e-mail: enquiries@ullswater-hotel.co.uk
web: www.ullswater-hotel.co.uk
dir: In Bournemouth follow signs to West Cliff. Hotel just
off Westcliff Rd

A welcoming family run hotel conveniently located for the
city and the seafront. This popular establishment attracts
a loyal following. The well-equipped bedrooms vary in
size, and the charming lounge bar and dining room are
very smart. Cuisine is hearty and homemade offering a
good choice from the daily-changing menu.

Rooms 42 (8 fmly) (2 GF) **S** £44-£56; **D** £80-£106 (incl.
bkfst) **Facilities** Snooker room Table tennis ♬ Xmas New
Year Wi-fi **Conf** Class 30 Board 24 Thtr 40 Del from £56
to £88 **Services** Lift **Parking** 12 **Notes** LB

Bourne Hall Hotel

★★ 65% HOTEL

☎ 01202 299715 📠 01202 552669
14 Priory Rd, West Cliff BH2 5DN
e-mail: info@bournehall.co.uk
web: www.bournehall.co.uk
dir: M27/A31 from Ringwood into Bournemouth on A338,
Wessex Way. Follow signs to BIC, onto West Cliff. Hotel on
right

This friendly, comfortable hotel is conveniently located
close to the Bournemouth International Centre and the
seafront. Bedrooms are well equipped, some located on
the ground floor and some with sea views. In addition to
the spacious lounge, there are two bars and a meeting
room. A daily-changing menu is served in the dining room.

Rooms 48 (9 fmly) (5 GF) **S** £30-£50; **D** £50-£80 (incl.
bkfst)* **Facilities** STV FTV Free leisure facilities for guests
at Marriott Highcliff Hotel ♬ Xmas New Year Wi-fi
Conf Class 60 Board 40 Thtr 130 Del from £57 to £105
Services Lift **Parking** 35 **Notes** LB

Maemar

Ⓤ

☎ 01202 553167 📠 01202 311919
91-95 Westhill Rd, Westcliff BH2 5PQ
e-mail: enquiries@maemarhotel.co.uk
dir: A31 onto A338 follow Bournemouth signs (approx
8m). At Bournemouth West Rdbt 1st left into Cambridge
Rd. 1st exit at rdbt to Poole Hill. 1st right into West Hill
Rd. Hotel 200yds on left

Currently the rating for this establishment is not
confirmed. This may be due to a change of ownership or
because it has only recently joined the AA rating scheme.
For further details please see the AA website: theAA.com

Rooms 40 (16 fmly) (4 GF) **S** £25-£45; **D** £35-£55 (incl.
bkfst) **Facilities** Xmas New Year Wi-fi **Services** Lift
Notes LB ⊛

Innkeeper's Lodge Bournemouth

BUDGET HOTEL

☎ 0845 112 6085 📠 0845 112 6218
Cooper Dean Roundabout, Castle Lane East BH7 7DP
web: www.innkeeperslodge.com/bournemouth
dir: On A338 & A3060 junct. Follow signs for Royal Bournemouth Hospital. Access via Castle Lane East services

Innkeeper's Lodge represents an exciting, high value concept within the budget hotel market. Comfortable bedrooms provide excellent facilities that include satellite TV and modem points. Options include family rooms; and for the corporate guest, cutting edge IT which includes Wi-fi high speed internet access. A popular Carvery provides all-day food, including an extensive, complimentary continental breakfast. See also the Hotel Groups pages.

Rooms 28 (9 fmly) **Conf** Class 22 Board 18 Thtr 30

Travelodge Bournemouth Central

BUDGET HOTEL

☎ 0871 984 6257
43 Christchurch Rd BH1 3PA
web: www.travelodge.co.uk
dir: Off A35, approaching town centre from Boscombe

Travelodge offers good quality, good value, budget accommodation. All offer family rooms sleeping up to four (two adults, two children) with en suite bathroom/shower-room, remote-control TV, tea- and coffee-making facilities and comfortable beds. Food options vary. Breakfast is at the on-site Bar Café restaurant (if available) or to take away. See also Hotel Groups pages.

Rooms 107 **S** fr £29; **D** fr £29

BRANKSOME

See Poole

BRIDPORT   Map 4 SY49

Haddon House

★★★ 64% HOTEL

☎ 01308 423626 & 425323 📠 01308 427348
West Bay DT6 4EL
e-mail: info@haddonhousehotel.co.uk
dir: At Crown Inn rdbt take B3157 West Bay Rd, hotel 0.5m on right at mini-rdbt

This attractive, creeper-clad Regency-style hotel offers good standards of accommodation and is situated a few minutes' walk from the picturesque harbour and the World Heritage Jurassic Coast. A friendly and relaxed style of service is provided. An extensive range of homemade dishes (including locally caught fish), from lighter bar snacks to main meals, is on offer in the restaurant.

Haddon House

Rooms 12 (2 fmly) (1 GF) **Facilities** FTV Xmas New Year Wi-fi **Conf** Class 20 Board 26 Thtr 40 **Parking** 44 **Notes** ⊗

Bridge House   THE INDEPENDENTS

★★ 76% HOTEL

☎ 01308 423371 📠 01308 459573
115 East St DT6 3LB
e-mail: info@bridgehousebridport.co.uk
dir: Follow signs to town centre from A35 rdbt, hotel 200mtrs on right

A short stroll from the town centre, this 18th-century Grade II listed property offers well-equipped bedrooms that vary in size. In addition to the main lounge, there is a small bar-lounge and a separate breakfast room. An interesting range of home-cooked meals is provided in the newly created wine bar and brasserie.

Rooms 10 (3 fmly) **S** £65-£89; **D** £89-£134 (incl. bkfst) **Facilities** FTV Complimentary membership to leisure park New Year Wi-fi **Conf** Class 20 Board 15 **Parking** 13 **Notes** LB

CHARMOUTH   Map 4 SY39

Fernhill

★★★ 77% HOTEL

☎ 01297 560492 📠 01297 561159
Fernhill DT6 6BX
e-mail: mail@fernhill-hotel.co.uk
dir: A35 onto A3052 to Lyme Regis. Hotel 0.25m on left

A small, friendly hotel on top of the hill in well tended grounds. It boasts an outside pool and treatment rooms, together with comfortable rooms and pleasant public areas. Each bedroom is individually styled and many have views of the Char Valley and beyond. The menus are based on seasonal, locally sourced produce.

Fernhill

Rooms 10 (1 fmly) **Facilities** ⤳ Fishing Holistic treatment centre Air/Massage baths Xmas New Year Wi-fi **Conf** Class 20 Board 24 Thtr 60 **Parking** 30 **Notes** ⊗

CHRISTCHURCH   Map 5 SZ19

Christchurch Harbour Hotel

★★★★ 82% ◉◉ HOTEL

☎ 01202 483434 📠 01202 479004
95 Mudeford BH23 3NT
e-mail: christchurch@harbourhotels.co.uk
web: www.christchurch-harbour-hotel.co.uk
dir: On A35 to Christchurch onto A337 to Highcliffe. Right at rdbt, hotel 1.5m on left

Delightfully situated on the side of Mudeford Quay close to sandy beaches and conveniently located for Bournemouth Airport and the BIC. Now transformed after a multi-million pound refurbishment, the hotel boasts an impressive spa and leisure facility. The bedrooms are particularly well appointed and stylishly finished; many have excellent views and some have balconies. Guests can eat in the Harbour Restaurant, or the waterside Rhodes South - the latest enterprise of Gary Rhodes.

Rooms 64 (7 fmly) (14 GF) **D** £110-£270 (incl. bkfst)* **Facilities** Spa FTV ⓢ Gym Steam room Sauna Exercise classes Hydrotherapy pool ♫ Xmas New Year Wi-fi **Conf** Class 20 Board 24 Thtr 70 Del from £155 to £255* **Services** Lift **Parking** 55 **Notes** Civ Wed 80

CHRISTCHURCH *continued*

Captain's Club Hotel and Spa
★★★★ 80% ◉◉ HOTEL

☎ 01202 475111 🖨 01202 490111
Wick Ferry, Wick Ln BH23 1HU
e-mail: enquiries@captainsclubhotel.com
web: www.captainsclubhotel.com
dir: B3073 to Christchurch. On Fountain rdbt take 5th exit (Sopers Ln) 2nd left (St Margarets Ave) 1st right onto Wick Ln

Situated in the heart of the town on the banks of the River Stour at Christchurch Quay, and only ten minutes from Bournemouth. All bedrooms, including the suites and apartments have views overlooking the river. Guests can relax in the hydrotherapy pool, enjoy a spa treatment or enjoy the cuisine in Tides Restaurant.

Rooms 29 (12 fmly) **S** £125-£169; **D** £149-£199 (incl. bkfst)* **Facilities** Spa FTV Hydro-therapy pool Sauna 🎵 Xmas New Year Wi-fi **Conf** Class 72 Board 64 Thtr 140 Del from £165 to £195* **Services** Lift Air con **Parking** 41 **Notes** LB Civ Wed 80

The Kings
★★★ 81% ◉◉ HOTEL

18 Castle St BH23 1DT
dir: turn off A35 onto Christchurch High St, turn left at rdbt, hotel 20mtrs on left

This newly refurbished small hotel offers guests a luxury stay in the heart of Christchurch. Elegant and sumptuous bedrooms, with huge beds, are equipped with many modern extras such as iPod docking stations and Wi-fi. The luxury bathrooms have huge soft towels, bathrobes and an array of toiletries. The Gary Rhodes Brasserie provides a variety of sharing and tapas style dishes while the cosy bar has an extensive list of tempting cocktails.

Rooms 16 (4 fmly) **Facilities** FTV Xmas New Year Wi-fi **Conf** Class 24 Board 24 Thtr 60 **Services** Lift **Parking** 7 **Notes** LB ⊗

Best Western Waterford Lodge
★★★ 77% HOTEL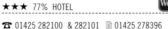

☎ 01425 282100 & 282101 🖨 01425 278396
87 Bure Ln, Friars Cliff BH23 4DN
e-mail: waterfordlodgehotel@yahoo.co.uk
web: www.waterfordlodgehotel.co.uk
dir: A35 onto A337 towards Highcliffe. Turn right from rdbt signed Mudeford. Hotel 0.5m on left

Originally, the West Lodge to Highcliffe Castle and former home of the Dowager Duchess of Waterford, the hotel has been sympathetically extended and tastefully refurbished over the years to provide modern hotel facilities whilst still retaining its character, style and charm. Ideally positioned for easy access to the medieval town of Christchurch and Highcliffe Castle.

Rooms 18 (2 fmly) (3 GF) **S** £75-£105; **D** £100-£160 (incl. bkfst)* **Facilities** STV FTV Xmas New Year Wi-fi **Conf** Class 60 Board 50 Thtr 90 **Parking** 38 **Notes** LB ⊗

CORFE CASTLE Map 4 SY98

Mortons House
★★★ 86% ◉◉ HOTEL

☎ 01929 480988 🖨 01929 480820
49 East St BH20 5EE
e-mail: stay@mortonshouse.co.uk
web: www.mortonshouse.co.uk
dir: on A351 between Wareham & Swanage

Set in delightful gardens and grounds with excellent views of Corfe Castle, this impressive building dates back to Tudor times. The oak-panelled drawing room has a roaring log fire and an interesting range of enjoyable cuisine is available in the well-appointed dining room. Bedrooms, many with views of the castle, are comfortable and well equipped.

Rooms 21 (7 annexe) (2 fmly) (7 GF) **Facilities** Xmas New Year Wi-fi **Conf** Class 45 Board 20 Thtr 45 **Parking** 40 **Notes** LB ⊗ Civ Wed 60

CRANBORNE Map 5 SU01

La Fosse at Cranborne
◉ RESTAURANT WITH ROOMS

☎ 01725 517604
London House, The Square BH21 5PR
e-mail: lafossemail@gmail.com
web: www.la-fosse.com
dir: M27(W) onto A31 to Ringwood, left onto B3081 to Verwood & Cranborne

This charming restaurant with rooms provides a home-from-home atmosphere. Family run by husband and wife team, Mark and Emmanuelle Hartstone, La Fosse provides charming accommodation and wonderful dinners using the best of local produce. On the edge of the New Forest which is ideal for exploring Wiltshire, Dorset and Hampshire. Wi-fi is available.

Rooms 6 (2 fmly)

DORCHESTER Map 4 SY69

Best Western King's Arms
★★★ 74% HOTEL

☎ 01305 265353 🖨 01305 260269
30 High East St DT1 1HF
e-mail: info@kingsarmsdorchester.com
web: www.kingsarmsdorchester.com
dir: In town centre

Previous guests at this 18th-century hotel, set in the very heart of Dorchester, have included Queen Victoria and John Lennon. Built in 1720, many Georgian features still remain, including beams in the cosy bar. Guests can dine in the bar, or in the restaurant which offers a traditional English menu. Bedrooms have suitable facilities, including a number with four-posters.

Rooms 37 (4 fmly) (3 GF) **Facilities** Wi-fi **Conf** Class 60 Board 40 Thtr 100 Del from £155 to £200* **Services** Lift **Parking** 37 **Notes** ⊗ Civ Wed 100

The Wessex Royale
THE INDEPENDENTS
★★★ 70% HOTEL

☎ 01305 262660 🖨 01305 251941
High West St DT1 1UP
e-mail: info@wessex-royale-hotel.com
web: www.wessex-royale-hotel.com
dir: from A35 turn right at rdbt signed town centre. Straight on, hotel at top of hill on left

This centrally situated Georgian townhouse dates from 1756 and successfully combines historic charm with modern comforts. The restaurant is a relaxed location for enjoying innovative food, and the hotel offers the benefit of a smart conservatory ideal for functions. Limited courtyard parking is available.

Rooms 27 (2 annexe) (2 fmly) **Facilities** Wi-fi **Conf** Class 40 Board 40 Thtr 80 **Parking** 12 **Notes** ⊗ Closed 23-30 Dec

EVERSHOT　　　　　　Map 4 ST50

INSPECTORS' CHOICE

Summer Lodge Country House Hotel, Restaurant & Spa

★★★★ ⊛⊛⊛ COUNTRY HOUSE HOTEL

☎ 01935 482000 ≣ 01935 482040
DT2 0JR
e-mail: summer@relaischateaux.com
dir: 1m W of A37 halfway between Dorchester & Yeovil

This picturesque hotel is situated in the heart of Dorset and is the ideal retreat for getting away from it all, and it's worth arriving in time for the excellent afternoon tea. Bedrooms are appointed to a very high standard; each is individually designed with upholstered walls and come with a wealth of luxurious facilities. The delightful public areas include a sumptuous lounge complete with an open fire, and the elegant restaurant where the cuisine continues to be the high point of any stay.

Rooms 24 (14 annexe) (6 fmly) (2 GF) (1 smoking)
S £171-£505; **D** £205-£505 (incl. bkfst) **Facilities** Spa
STV FTV ⊗ ⌇ ⇘ Gym Xmas New Year Wi-fi Child
facilities **Conf** Class 16 Board 16 Thtr 24
Del from £299 to £325 **Services** Air con **Parking** 41
Notes LB Civ Wed 30

LYME REGIS　　　　　　Map 4 SY39

Swallows Eaves

★★ 80% HOTEL

☎ 01297 553184 ≣ 01297 553574
Swan Hill Rd EX24 6QJ
e-mail: info@swallowseaves.co.uk
web: www.swallowseaves.co.uk

(For full entry see Colyford, Devon)

Royal Lion

★★ 71% HOTEL

☎ 01297 445622 ≣ 01297 445859
Broad St DT7 3QF
e-mail: enquiries@royallionhotel.com
web: www.royallionhotel.com
dir: From W on A35, take A3052 or from E take B3165 to
Lyme Regis. Hotel in centre of town, opp The Fossil Shop

This 17th-century, former coaching inn is full of character and charm, and is situated a short walk from the seafront. Bedrooms vary in size; those in the newer wing are more spacious and some have balconies, sea views or a private terrace. In addition to the elegant dining room and guest lounges, a heated pool, jacuzzi, sauna and small gym are available. There is a car park at the rear.

Rooms 33 (14 fmly) (11 GF) **S** £46-£70; **D** £92-£140 (incl.
bkfst)* **Facilities** FTV ⊗ Gym Sauna Jacuzzi Games room
Pool & Snooker tables Table tennis Xmas New Year Wi-fi
Conf Class 20 Board 20 Thtr 50 **Parking** 33 **Notes** LB

MUDEFORD

See Christchurch

POOLE　　　　　　Map 4 SZ09

Harbour Heights

★★★★ 80% ⊛⊛ HOTEL

☎ 01202 707272 & 0845 337 1550 ≣ 01202 708594
73 Haven Rd, Sandbanks BH13 7LW
e-mail: enquiries@fjbhotels.co.uk
web: www.fjbhotels.co.uk
dir: Follow signs for Sandbanks, hotel on left after
Canford Cliffs

The unassuming appearance of this hotel belies a wealth of innovation, quality and style. The very stylish, contemporary bedrooms, many with sea views, combine state-of-the-art facilities with traditional comforts; all have spa baths. The smart public areas include the Harbar brasserie, popular bars and sitting areas where picture windows accentuate panoramic views of Poole Harbour. The sun deck is the perfect setting for watching the cross-channel ferries come and go.

Rooms 38 (2 fmly) **D** £100-£190 (incl. bkfst)*
Facilities STV Spa bath in all rooms Xmas New Year Wi-fi
Conf Class 36 Board 22 Thtr 70 Del from £175 to £195
Services Lift Air con **Parking** 50 **Notes** LB ⊗
Civ Wed 120

See advert on page 173

Hotel du Vin Poole

Hotel du Vin & Bistro

★★★★ 78% ⊛ HOTEL

☎ 01202 758570 ≣ 01202 758571
Thames St BH15 1JN
e-mail: info.poole@hotelduvin.com
web: www.hotelduvin.com
dir: A31 to Poole, follow channel ferry signs. Left at Poole
bridge onto Poole Quay, 1st left into Thames St. Hotel
opposite St James Church

Offering a fresh approach to the well established company style, this property boasts some delightful rooms packed with comfort and all the expected Hotel du Vin features. Situated near the harbour the hotel offers nautically-themed bedrooms and suites that have plasma TVs, DVD players and bathrooms with power showers. The public rooms have been transformed into light and open spaces, and as with the other hotels in this group the bar and restaurant form centre stage.

Rooms 38 (4 GF) **D** £170-£400 (incl. bkfst)*
Facilities STV Xmas New Year Wi-fi **Conf** Class 20
Board 20 Thtr 35 Del from £170 to £210*
Services Air con **Notes** LB Civ Wed 40

POOLE *continued*

Sandbanks

★★★★ 75% ® HOTEL

☎ 01202 707377 & 0845 337 1550 📠 01202 708885
15 Banks Rd, Sandbanks BH13 7PS
e-mail: reservations@fjbhotels.co.uk
web: www.fjbhotels.co.uk
dir: A338 from Bournemouth onto Wessex Way, to
Liverpool Victoria rdbt. Left, then 2nd exit onto B3965.
Hotel on left

Set on the delightful Sandbanks Peninsula, this well
loved hotel has direct access to the blue flag beach and
stunning views across Poole Harbour. Most of the
spacious bedrooms have sea view; some are air
conditioned. There is an extensive range of leisure
facilities, including a state-of-the-art crèche.

Rooms 110 (31 fmly) (4 GF) **S** £75-£155; **D** £150-£310
(incl. bkfst)* **Facilities** Spa STV FTV ⓣ supervised Gym
Sailing Mountain bikes Children's play area Massage
room Watersports academy Xmas New Year Wi-fi Child
facilities **Conf** Class 40 Board 25 Thtr 150 Del from £120
to £150* **Services** Lift **Parking** 120 **Notes** LB ⊗
Civ Wed 70

See advert on page 173

Haven

★★★★ 73% ®® HOTEL

☎ 01202 707333 & 0845 337 1550 📠 01202 708796
Banks Rd, Sandbanks BH13 7QL
e-mail: reservations@fjbhotels.co.uk
web: www.fjbhotels.co.uk
dir: B3965 towards Poole Bay, left onto the Peninsula.
Hotel 1.5m on left next to Swanage Toll Ferry point

Enjoying an enviable location at the water's edge with
views of Poole Bay, this well established hotel was once
the home of radio pioneer, Guglielmo Marconi. A friendly
team of staff provide good levels of customer care.

Bedrooms vary in size and style; many have balconies
and wonderful sea views. Leisure facilities are
noteworthy.

Rooms 78 (4 fmly) **S** £100-£165; **D** £200-£420 (incl.
bkfst)* **Facilities** Spa STV ⓣ ⌁ supervised ⌁ Gym
Dance studio Health & Beauty suite Sauna Steam room
Xmas New Year Wi-fi **Conf** Class 70 Board 50 Thtr 160
Del from £115 to £190* **Services** Lift **Parking** 160
Notes LB ⊗ Civ Wed 100

See advert on page 173

Thistle Poole   thistle

★★★ 79% HOTEL

☎ 0871 376 9032 📠 0871 376 9132
The Quay BH15 1HD
e-mail: poole@thistle.co.uk
web: www.thistlehotels.com/poole
dir: On quay next to Dolphin Marina

Situated on the quayside overlooking the harbour, this
modern hotel is situated close to the ferry terminal and is
also a good base for exploring the beautiful Dorset
countryside. Many of the bedrooms have views of Poole
harbour. There is a restaurant and two bars, plus two
meeting rooms are available.

Rooms 70 (22 GF) **Facilities** Xmas New Year Wi-fi
Conf Class 80 Board 60 Thtr 120 Del from £95 to £180*
Services Lift **Parking** 120 **Notes** Civ Wed 120

Salterns Harbourside

★★★ 70% HOTEL

☎ 01202 707321 📠 01202 707488
38 Salterns Way, Lilliput BH14 8JR
e-mail: reception@salterns-hotel.co.uk
web: www.salterns-hotel.co.uk
dir: In Poole follow B3369 Sandbanks road. 1m at Lilliput
shops turn into Salterns Way by Barclays Bank

Located next to the marina with superb views across to
Brownsea Island, this modernised hotel used to be the
headquarters for the flying boats in WWII and was later a
yacht club. Bedrooms are spacious and some have
private balconies, whilst the busy bar and restaurant
both share harbour views.

Rooms 20 (4 fmly) **S** £75-£125; **D** £85-£135 (incl. bkfst)*
Facilities Wi-fi **Conf** Class 50 Board 30 Thtr 100
Del from £115 to £130* **Parking** 40 **Notes** Civ Wed 120

Arndale Court

★★★ 68% HOTEL

☎ 01202 683746 📠 01202 668838
62/66 Wimborne Rd BH15 2BY
e-mail: info@arndalecourthotel.com
web: www.arndalecourthotel.com
dir: On A349, opp Poole Stadium

Ideally situated for the town centre and ferry terminal,
this is a small, privately owned hotel. Bedrooms are well
equipped, spacious and comfortable. Particularly well
suited to business guests, this hotel has a pleasant
range of stylish public areas and good parking.

Rooms 39 (7 fmly) (14 GF) **S** £65-£80; **D** £80-£105 (incl.
bkfst)* **Facilities** STV FTV Wi-fi **Conf** Class 35 Board 35
Thtr 50 **Parking** 40

Quarterdeck

★★ 71% HOTEL

☎ 01202 740066 📠 01202 736780
2 Sandbanks Rd BH14 8AQ
e-mail: reception@quarterdeckhotel.co.uk
dir: A35 to Civic Centre, hotel next to Poole Park, opposite
police station & Poole Law Courts

A family run hotel adjacent to Poole Park and close to
Poole Harbour and Dorset beaches. Bedrooms are
comfortable and well equipped. Enjoy afternoon tea in the
cosy lounge, a drink in the bar and dinner in the colourful
restaurant. There's a sun terrace perfect for the summer
months.

Rooms 15 (5 GF) **S** £68-£98; **D** £68-£118 (incl. bkfst)
Facilities Wi-fi **Parking** 31 **Notes** LB ⊗

Antelope Inn

★★ Ⓐ HOTEL

☎ 01202 672029 📠 01202 678286
8 High St BH15 1BP
e-mail: 6603@greeneking.co.uk
web: www.oldenglish.co.uk

Rooms 21 (2 fmly) **Facilities** Xmas **Parking** 17 **Notes** LB

Express by Holiday Inn Poole

BUDGET HOTEL

☎ 01202 649222 📠 01202 649666
Walking Field Ln, Seldown Bridge Site BH15 1TJ
e-mail: sales@exhipoole.co.uk
web: www.hiexpress.com/pooleuk
dir: A350 to town centre, pass bus station. Right at next
rdbt, take slip road to left. Hotel next to Dolphin
Swimming Pool

A modern hotel ideal for families and business travellers.
Fresh and uncomplicated, the spacious rooms include Sky
TV, power shower and tea and coffee-making facilities.
Continental buffet breakfast is included in the room rate;

evening meals are available in the spacious café/bar. See also the Hotel Groups pages.

Rooms 85 (42 fmly) (10 GF) (7 smoking)
S £59.95-£115.95; **D** £59.95-£115.95 (incl. bkfst)*
Conf Class 16 Board 18 Thtr 30 Del from £98.95 to £146.95*

ST LEONARDS — Map 5 SU10

St Leonards

★★ 🅰 HOTEL

☎ 01425 471220 📠 01425 480274
Ringwood Rd BH24 2NP
e-mail: 9230@greeneking.co.uk
web: www.oldenglish.co.uk
dir: At end of M27 continue to 1st rdbt. Take slip road on left

Rooms 35 (5 fmly) (15 GF) **Facilities** Xmas
Conf Class 40 Board 40 Thtr 100 **Services** Lift
Parking 50 **Notes** LB Civ Wed 60

SANDBANKS

See Poole

SHAFTESBURY — Map 4 ST82

Best Western Royal Chase

★★★ 71% ⦿ HOTEL

☎ 01747 853355 📠 01747 851969
Royal Chase Roundabout SP7 8DB
e-mail: royalchasehotel@btinternet.com
web: www.theroyalchasehotel.co.uk
dir: A303 to A350 signed Blandford Forum. Avoid town centre, follow road to 3rd rdbt

Equally suitable for both leisure and business guests, this well-known local landmark is situated close to the famous Gold Hill. Both Standard and Crown bedrooms offer good levels of comfort and quality. In addition to the fixed-price menu in the Byzant Restaurant, guests have the option of eating more informally in the convivial bar.

Rooms 33 (13 fmly) (6 GF) **S** £54-£160; **D** £54-£160*
Facilities 🎱 Turkish steam room Wi-fi **Conf** Class 90 Board 50 Thtr 180 Del from £105 to £117.50*
Parking 100 **Notes** LB Civ Wed 76

La Fleur de Lys Restaurant with Rooms

⦿⦿ RESTAURANT WITH ROOMS

☎ 01747 853717 📠 01747 853130
Bleke St SP7 8AW
e-mail: info@lafleurdelys.co.uk
web: www.lafleurdelys.co.uk
dir: 0.25m off junct of A30 with A350 at Shaftesbury towards town centre

Located just a few minutes' walk from the famous Gold Hill, this light and airy restaurant with rooms combines efficient service in a relaxed and friendly atmosphere. Bedrooms, which are suitable for both business and

leisure guests, vary in size but all are well equipped, comfortable and tastefully furnished. A relaxing guest lounge and courtyard are available for afternoon tea or pre-dinner drinks.

Rooms 7 (2 fmly)

SHERBORNE — Map 4 ST61

The Grange at Oborne

★★★ 79% ⦿ HOTEL

☎ 01935 813463 📠 01935 817464
Oborne DT9 4LA
e-mail: reception@thegrange.co.uk
web: www.thegrangeatoborne.co.uk
dir: Exit A30, follow signs through village

Set in beautiful gardens in a quiet hamlet, this 200-year-old, family run, country-house hotel has a wealth of charm and character. It offers friendly hospitality together with attentive service. Bedrooms are comfortable and tastefully appointed. Public areas are elegantly furnished and the popular restaurant offers a good selection of dishes.

Rooms 18 (3 fmly) (5 GF) **S** £90-£120; **D** £109-£150 (incl. bkfst) **Facilities** STV Xmas New Year Wi-fi **Conf** Class 40 Board 30 Thtr 80 Del from £115 to £134 **Parking** 45 **Notes** LB ⊗ Civ Wed 80

Eastbury

★★★ 75% ⦿⦿ HOTEL

☎ 01935 813131 📠 01935 817296
Long St DT9 3BY
e-mail: enquiries@theeastburyhotel.co.uk
web: www.theeastburyhotel.co.uk
dir: From A30 westbound, left into North Rd, then St Swithin's, left at bottom, hotel 800yds on right

Much of the original Georgian charm and elegance is maintained at this smart, comfortable hotel. Just five minutes' stroll from the abbey and close to the town centre, the Eastbury's friendly and attentive staff ensure a relaxed and enjoyable stay. Award-winning cuisine is served in the attractive dining room that overlooks the walled garden.

Rooms 23 (1 fmly) (3 GF) **S** £68; **D** £125-£170 (incl. bkfst)* **Facilities** FTV 🏊 New Year **Conf** Class 40 Board 28 Thtr 80 Del from £121 to £161* **Parking** 30 **Notes** LB ⊗ Civ Wed 80

The Sherborne Hotel

★★ 68% HOTEL

☎ 01935 813191 📠 01935 816493
Horsecastles Ln DT9 6BB
e-mail: info@sherbornehotel.co.uk
dir: At junction of A30 & A352

This hotel is a quiet and attractive grounds, and bedrooms are spacious and well equipped. The open-plan lounge and bar area are comfortable and satellite TV is available. Cuisine offers a good range of choice and the dining room looks out to the garden.

Rooms 60 (24 GF) **S** £49-£59; **D** £59-£69 (incl. bkfst)*
Facilities 🏊 Concessionary swimming rates at leisure centre opposite hotel 🎵 Xmas New Year Wi-fi
Conf Class 35 Board 30 Thtr 80 Del from £70 to £90*
Parking 90 **Notes** ⊗

SWANAGE — Map 5 SZ07

The Pines

★★★ 73% HOTEL

☎ 01929 425211 📠 01929 422075
Burlington Rd BH19 1LT
e-mail: reservations@pineshotel.co.uk
web: www.pineshotel.co.uk
dir: A351 to seafront, left then 2nd right. Hotel at end of road

Enjoying a peaceful location with spectacular views over the cliffs and sea, The Pines is a pleasant place to stay. Many of the comfortable bedrooms have sea views. Guests can take tea in the lounge, enjoy appetising bar snacks in the attractive bar, and interesting and accomplished cuisine in the restaurant.

Rooms 41 (26 fmly) (6 GF) **S** £59-£105; **D** £118-£162 (incl. bkfst)* **Facilities** 🎵 Xmas New Year Wi-fi **Conf** Class 80 Board 80 Thtr 80 Del from £94.20* **Services** Lift **Parking** 60 **Notes** LB

See advert on page 184

SWANAGE *continued*

Purbeck House

★★★ 72% HOTEL

☎ 01929 422872 ▤ 01929 421194
91 High St BH19 2LZ
e-mail: reservations@purbeckhousehotel.co.uk
web: www.purbeckhousehotel.co.uk
dir: A351 to Swanage via Wareham, right into Shore Rd,
into Institute Rd, right into High St

Located close to the town centre, this former convent is
set in well-tended grounds. The attractive bedrooms are
located in the original building and also in an annexe. In
addition to a very pleasant and spacious conservatory,
the smartly presented public areas have some stunning
features, such as painted ceilings, wood panelling and
fine tiled floors.

Rooms 38 (20 annexe) (5 fmly) (10 GF) **S** £44-£64;
D £88-£128 (incl. bkfst) **Facilities** ⍩ New Year Wi-fi
Conf Class 36 Board 25 Thtr 100 **Parking** 50 **Notes** ⊗
Civ Wed 100

Grand

★★★ 70% HOTEL

☎ 01929 423353 ▤ 01929 427068
Burlington Rd BH19 1LU
e-mail: reservations@grandhotelswanage.co.uk
web: www.grandhotelswanage.co.uk

Dating back to 1898, this hotel is located on the Isle of
Purbeck and has spectacular views across Swanage Bay
and Peveril Point. Bedrooms are individually decorated
and well equipped; public rooms offer a number of
choices from relaxing lounges to extensive leisure
facilities. The hotel also has its own private beach.

Rooms 30 (2 fmly) **S** £60-£90; **D** £120-£200 (incl. bkfst)*
Facilities FTV ⍰ supervised Fishing Gym Table tennis
Xmas Wi-fi **Conf** Class 40 Board 40 Thtr 120 **Services** Lift
Parking 15 **Notes** LB Closed 10 days in Jan (dates on
application)

Worgret Manor

★★★ 73% HOTEL

☎ 01929 552957 ▤ 01929 554804
Worgret Rd BH20 6AB
e-mail: admin@worgretmanorhotel.co.uk
web: www.worgretmanorhotel.co.uk
dir: On A352 (Wareham to Wool), 500mtrs from Wareham
rdbt

On the edge of Wareham, with easy access to major
routes, this privately owned Georgian manor house has a
friendly, cheerful atmosphere. The bedrooms come in a
variety of sizes. Public rooms are well presented and
comprise a popular bar, a quiet lounge and an airy
restaurant.

Rooms 12 (1 fmly) (3 GF) **Facilities** Wi-fi **Conf** Class 20
Board 20 Thtr 40 **Parking** 30 **Notes** LB

See Bridport

The Manor

★★ 74% HOTEL

☎ 01308 897616 📄 01308 897704
Beach Rd DT2 9DF
e-mail: themanorhotel@btconnect.com
dir: B3157 to Burton Bradstock, continue to The Bull public house in Swire. Immediately right to West Bexington.

Surrounded by scenic splendour and just a short stroll from the magnificent sweep of Chesil Beach, the atmosphere is relaxed and welcoming with snug lounges and crackling wood fires. Bedrooms are individual in style, many with wonderful sea views and the sound of waves in the background. With an abundance of excellent local produce, dining here, in either the convivial Cellar Bar, or the elegant dining room is recommended.

Rooms 13 (2 fmly) **Facilities** Xmas New Year
Conf Class 40 Board 40 Thtr 40 **Parking** 80
Notes Civ Wed 65

Cromwell House

★★ 75% HOTEL

☎ 01929 400253 & 400332 📄 01929 400566
Lulworth Cove BH20 5RJ
e-mail: catriona@lulworthcove.co.uk
web: www.lulworthcove.co.uk
dir: 200yds beyond end of West Lulworth, left onto high slip road, hotel 100yds on left opposite beach car park

Built in 1881 by the Mayor of Weymouth, specifically as a guest house, this family-run hotel now provides visitors with an ideal base for touring the area and for exploring the beaches and coast. The house enjoys spectacular views across the sea and countryside. Bedrooms, many with sea views, are comfortable and some have been specifically designed for family use.

Rooms 18 (1 annexe) (3 fmly) (2 GF) **S** £40-£60;
D £80-£102 (incl. bkfst)* **Facilities** ‟ Access to Dorset coastal footpath & Jurassic Coast Wi-fi **Parking** 17
Notes LB Closed 22 Dec-3 Jan

Moonfleet Manor

★★★ 75% ®®
COUNTRY HOUSE HOTEL

☎ 01305 786948 📄 01305 774395
Fleet DT3 4ED
e-mail: info@moonfleetmanorhotel.co.uk
web: www.moonfleetmanor.com
dir: A354 to Weymouth, right on B3157 to Bridport. At Chickerell left at mini rdbt to Fleet

This enchanting hideaway, peacefully located at the end of the village of Fleet, enjoys a wonderful sea-facing position. Children are especially welcomed throughout the hotel. Many of the well-equipped bedrooms overlook Chesil Beach and the hotel is furnished with style and panache, particularly in the sumptuous lounges. Accomplished cuisine is served in the beautiful restaurant. Von Essen Hotels - AA Hotel Group of the Year 2009-10.

Rooms 36 (6 annexe) (26 fmly) **S** £144-£290;
D £160-£460 (incl. bkfst & dinner)* **Facilities** STV FTV ⊗ supervised ⌇ ⌇ Squash Children's nursery Xmas Child facilities **Conf** Class 18 Board 26 Thtr 50 **Services** Lift **Parking** 50 **Notes** LB

Hotel Rembrandt

★★★ 74% HOTEL

☎ 01305 764000 📄 01305 764022
12-18 Dorchester Rd DT4 7JU
e-mail: reception@hotelrembrandt.co.uk
web: www.hotelrembrandt.co.uk
dir: 0.75m on left after Manor Rdbt on A354 from Dorchester

Only a short distance from the seafront and the town centre, this hotel is ideal for visiting local attractions. Facilities include indoor leisure, a bar and extensive meeting rooms. The restaurant offers an impressive

carvery and carte menu which proves popular with locals and residents alike.

Rooms 78 (4 fmly) (7 GF) **S** £48-£112.50; **D** £75-£127 (incl. bkfst) **Facilities** STV FTV ⊗ Gym Steam room Sauna Wi-fi **Conf** Class 100 Board 60 Thtr 200 Del from £110 to £125 **Services** Lift **Parking** 80 **Notes** LB ⊗ Civ Wed 100

Best Western Hotel Prince Regent

★★★ 71% HOTEL

☎ 01305 771313 📄 01305 778100
139 The Esplanade DT4 7NR
e-mail: info@princeregentweymouth.co.uk
web: www.princeregentweymouth.co.uk
dir: From A354 follow seafront signs. Left at Jubilee Clock, 25mtrs on seafront

Dating back to 1855, this welcoming resort hotel boasts splendid views over Weymouth Bay from the majority of public rooms and front-facing bedrooms. It is conveniently close to the town centre and harbour, and is opposite the beach. The restaurant offers a choice of menus, and entertainment is regularly provided in the ballroom during the season.

Rooms 70 (12 fmly) (5 GF) **S** £55-£110; **D** £75-£156 (incl. bkfst)* **Facilities** STV Xmas New Year Wi-fi **Conf** Class 150 Board 150 Thtr 180 Del from £89 to £99* **Services** Lift **Parking** 10 **Notes** LB ⊗ Civ Wed 200

Hotel Rex

★★★ 68% HOTEL

☎ 01305 760400 📄 01305 760500
29 The Esplanade DT4 8DN
e-mail: rex@kingshotels.co.uk
web: www.kingshotels.co.uk
dir: On seafront opp Alexandra Gardens

Originally built as the summer residence for the Duke of Clarence, this hotel benefits from its seafront location with stunning views across Weymouth Bay. Bedrooms, including several sea-facing rooms, are well equipped. A wide range of imaginative dishes is served in the popular, vaulted restaurant.

Rooms 31 (2 fmly) (4 smoking) **S** £55-£80; **D** £90-£140 (incl. bkfst) **Facilities** FTV New Year Wi-fi **Conf** Class 30 Board 25 Thtr 40 **Services** Lift **Parking** 10 **Notes** LB ⊗ Closed Xmas

WEYMOUTH *continued*

Crown

★★ 71% HOTEL

☎ 01305 760800 📄 01305 760300
51-53 St Thomas St DT4 8EQ
e-mail: crown@kingshotels.co.uk
web: www.kingshotels.co.uk
dir: From Dorchester, A354 to Weymouth. Follow Back
Water on left & cross 2nd bridge

This popular hotel is conveniently located adjacent to the
old harbour and is ideal for shopping, local attractions
and transportation links, including the ferry. Public areas
include an extensive bar, ballroom and comfortable
residents' lounge on the first floor. Themed events, such
as mock cruises, are a speciality.

Rooms 86 (15 fmly) **S** £52-£57; **D** £98-£108 (incl. bkfst)
Facilities ♫ New Year **Services** Lift **Parking** 14
Notes ⊗ Closed Xmas

Central

★★ 69% HOTEL

☎ 01305 760700 📄 01305 760300
17-19 Maiden St DT4 8BB
e-mail: central@kingshotels.co.uk

Well located for both the town and the beach with off-
road parking, this hotel offers comfortable bedrooms and
friendly staff. It is privately owned and has sister
properties nearby.

Rooms 28 (5 fmly) (4 GF) **S** £40-£55; **D** £60-£90 (incl.
bkfst) **Facilities** ♫ **Services** Lift **Parking** 16 **Notes** LB
⊗ Closed mid Dec-1 Mar

Fairhaven

★★ 68% HOTEL

☎ 01305 760200 📄 01305 760300
37 The Esplanade DT4 8DH
e-mail: fairhaven@kingshotels.co.uk
dir: On right just before Alexandra Gardens

A popular sea facing, family-run hotel which has a
friendly young team of staff. Bedrooms are comfortable
and well maintained, and the hotel boasts two bars, one
with panoramic views of the bay. Entertainment is
provided most nights during the season.

Rooms 82 (23 fmly) (1 GF) **S** £40-£55; **D** £60-£90 (incl.
bkfst) **Facilities** ♫ **Services** Lift **Parking** 16 **Notes** LB
⊗ Closed Nov-1 Mar

Russell

★★ 68% HOTEL

☎ 01305 786059 📄 01305 775723
135-13 The Esplanade DT4 7NG
e-mail: russell@hollybushhotels.co.uk
dir: 500yds from Clock Tower on Esplanade

This hotel offers comfortable and spacious
accommodation, and as it is situated on the seafront
many rooms benefit from magnificent views. With a sister
hotel next door, banqueting facilities in a superb ballroom
are offered. Live music and entertainment are also
provided.

Rooms 93 (23 GF) **S** £39-£79; **D** £55-£100 (incl. bkfst)*
Facilities ♫ Xmas New Year **Services** Lift **Parking** 20
Notes LB ⊗ No children 18yrs

Leam Hotel

Ⓤ

☎ 01305 784127 📄 01305 766538
102-103 The Esplanade DT4 7EB
dir: A35 to Weymouth, hotel on esplanade opposite Jubilee
clock

Currently the rating for this establishment is not
confirmed. This may be due to a change of ownership or
because it has only recently joined the AA rating scheme.
For further details please see the AA website: theAA.com

Rooms 30 (3 fmly) (7 GF) **S** £27-£40; **D** £54-£80 (incl.
bkfst & dinner) **Facilities** ♫ Xmas New Year
Services Lift **Notes** ⊗ No children 14yrs Closed Jan RS 1
Feb

The Heritage Restaurant with Rooms

RESTAURANT WITH ROOMS

☎ 01305 783093 📄 01305 786668
8 East St, Chickerell DT3 4DS
e-mail: mail@the-heritage.co.uk
dir: In village centre

Located just three miles from Weymouth and less than a
mile from the spectacular Chesil Beach, this building
dates back to 1769. Attentive service and a friendly,
caring approach are hallmarks here, with every effort
made to ensure a relaxing stay. Excellent Dorset produce
is featured on the menus that are offered in the elegant
restaurant. After dinner, the comfortable bedrooms await,
each individually styled and well appointed.

Rooms 6 (1 fmly)

WIMBORNE MINSTER | Map 5 SZ06

Kings Head

★★ Ⓐ HOTEL

☎ 01202 880101 📄 01202 881667
The Square BH21 1JG
e-mail: 6474@greeneking.co.uk
web: www.oldenglish.co.uk
dir: From A31 Dorchester take B3073 into Wimborne.
Follow signs to town centre, hotel in square on left

Rooms 27 (1 fmly) **Facilities** Xmas **Conf** Board 20
Thtr 25 **Services** Lift **Parking** 20 **Notes** LB

Les Bouviers Restaurant with Rooms

@@ RESTAURANT WITH ROOMS

☎ 01202 889555 📄 01202 639428
Arrowsmith Rd, Canford Magna BH21 3BD
e-mail: info@lesbouviers.co.uk
web: www.lesbouviers.co.uk
dir: A31 onto A349. In 0.6m turn left. In approx 1m right
onto Arrowsmith Rd. Establishment approx 100yds on
right

A very well patronised restaurant with rooms in a great
location, set in six acres of grounds. Food is a highlight of
any stay here as is the friendly, attentive service.
Bedrooms are extremely well equipped and beds are
supremely comfortable.

Rooms 6 (4 fmly)

CO DURHAM

BARNARD CASTLE
Map 19 NZ01

The Morritt

★★★ 80% HOTEL

☎ 01833 627232 ▤ 01833 627392
Greta Bridge DL12 9SE
e-mail: relax@themorritt.co.uk
web: www.themorritt.co.uk
dir: Turn off A1 (A1(M)) at Scotch Corner onto A66
westbound towards Penrith. Greta Bridge 9m on left

Set off the main road at Greta Bridge, this 17th-century
former coaching house provides comfortable public rooms
full of character. The bar, with its interesting Dickensian
mural, is very much focused on food, but in addition a
fine dining is offered in the oak-panelled restaurant.
Bedrooms come in individual styles and of varying sizes.
The attentive service is noteworthy.

Rooms 27 (6 annexe) (3 fmly) (4 GF) **S** £80-£175;
D £90-£175 (incl. bkfst)* **Facilities** FTV Xmas New Year
Wi-fi **Conf** Class 60 Board 50 Thtr 200 Del from £130*
Parking 40 **Notes** LB Civ Wed 200

Jersey Farm Country Hotel

★★★ 🄰 HOTEL

☎ 01833 638223 ▤ 01833 631988
Darlington Rd DL12 8TA
e-mail: enquiries@jerseyfarm.co.uk
web: www.jerseyfarm.co.uk
dir: On A67 1m E of Barnard Castle

Rooms 22 (11 annexe) (3 fmly) (8 GF) **S** £65-£82;
D £99-£150 (incl. bkfst)* **Facilities** FTV Pool table Xmas
New Year Wi-fi **Conf** Class 80 Board 60 Thtr 200
Parking 150 **Notes** LB Civ Wed

BEAMISH
Map 19 NZ25

Beamish Park

★★★ 80% ◉◉ HOTEL

☎ 01207 230666 ▤ 01207 281260
Beamish Burn Rd, Marley Hill NE16 5EG
e-mail: reception@beamish-park-hotel.co.uk
web: www.beamish-park-hotel.co.uk
dir: A1 junct 63 onto A693 Stanley. Exit rdbt onto A6076,
hotel 2m on right

The Metro Centre, Beamish Museum and south Tyneside
are all within striking distance of this modern hotel, set
in open countryside alongside its own golf course and
floodlit range. Bedrooms are tastefully decorated and well
equipped; some have their own patios. The conservatory
bistro offers an interesting menu using fine ingredients.

Rooms 42 (4 fmly) (27 GF) **S** £75-£150; **D** £85-£175*
Facilities FTV ⚖ 9 Putt green New Year Wi-fi
Conf Class 50 Board 50 Thtr 100 Del from £130 to £180*
Parking 100 **Notes** LB ⊗ Closed 24 Dec-1 Jan
Civ Wed 100

CHESTER-LE-STREET
Map 19 NZ25

Lumley Castle

★★★★ 75% HOTEL

☎ 0191 389 1111 & 0191 389 5854 ▤ 0191 387 1437
Lumley Castle DH3 4NX
e-mail: reservations@lumleycastle.com
dir: A1(M) junct 63, follow Chester-le-Street signs. Follow
signs for Riverside then Lumley Castle

The castle describes itself as 'no ordinary hotel' and has
every justification for doing so. In terms of quality
standards and entertainment, it really is something else.
Deep tones, carefully selected fine silks, fabrics and
atmospheric lighting have been combined to give an
overwhelming feeling of restfulness and relaxation. The
hotel offers large castle rooms and suites plus courtyard
rooms in the converted stable block.

Rooms 74 (48 annexe) (3 fmly) (8 GF) **Facilities** STV FTV
♫ New Year Wi-fi **Conf** Class 65 Board 50 Thtr 150
Services Lift **Parking** 200 **Notes** LB ⊗ Closed 24-26 Dec
& 1 Jan Civ Wed 80

See advert on page 188

Innkeeper's Lodge Durham North

BUDGET HOTEL

☎ 0845 112 6014 ▤ 0845 112 6287
Church Mouse, Great North Rd, Chester Moor DH2 3RJ
web: www.innkeeperslodge.com/durhamnorth
dir: A1(M) junct 63, take A167 S Durham/Chester-Le-
Street. Straight on at 3 rdbts. Lodge on left

Innkeeper's Lodge represents an exciting, high value
concept within the budget hotel market. Comfortable
bedrooms provide excellent facilities that include satellite
TV and modem points. Options include family rooms; and
for the corporate guest, cutting edge IT includes Wi-fi
access. Food is served all day in the adjacent Country
Pub. The extensive continental breakfast is
complimentary. See also the Hotel Groups pages.

Rooms 21 (4 fmly)

CONSETT — Map 19 NZ15

Best Western Derwent Manor

★★★ 73% HOTEL

☎ 01207 592000 📄 01207 502472

Allensford DH8 9BB
e-mail: gm@derwent-manor-hotel.com
web: www.oxfordhotelsandinns.com
dir: On A68

This hotel, built in the style of a manor house, is set in open grounds overlooking the River Derwent. Spacious bedrooms, including a number of suites, are comfortably equipped. A popular wedding venue, there are also extensive conference facilities and an impressive leisure suite. The Grouse & Claret bar serves a wide range of drinks and light meals, and Guinevere's restaurant offers the fine dining option.

Rooms 48 (3 fmly) (26 GF) **Facilities** FTV 🄫 supervised Gym Xmas New Year **Conf** Class 200 Board 60 Thtr 300 **Services** Lift **Parking** 100 **Notes** Civ Wed 300

DARLINGTON — Map 19 NZ21

Headlam Hall

★★★ 85% ⊛ HOTEL

☎ 01325 730238 📄 01325 730790

Headlam, Gainford DL2 3HA
e-mail: admin@headlamhall.co.uk
web: www.headlamhall.co.uk
dir: 2m N of A67 between Piercebridge & Gainford

This impressive Jacobean hall lies in farmland north-east of Piercebridge and has its own 9-hole golf course. The main house retains many historical features, including flagstone floors and a pillared hall. Bedrooms are well proportioned and traditionally styled. A converted coach house contains the more modern rooms, as well as a conference and leisure centre.

Rooms 40 (22 annexe) (4 fmly) (10 GF) **S** £90-£115; **D** £115-£190 (incl. bkfst)* **Facilities** Spa STV 🄫 ♨ 9 ♨ Putt green Fishing ♨ Gym New Year Wi-fi **Conf** Class 40 Board 40 Thtr 120 Del from £135* **Services** Lift **Parking** 80 **Notes** LB Closed 24-26 Dec Civ Wed 150

The Blackwell Grange Hotel

★★★ 78% HOTEL

☎ 0870 609 6121 & 01325 509955 📄 01325 380899
Blackwell Grange DL3 8QH
e-mail: blackwell.grange@forestdale.com
web: www.blackwellgrangehotel.com
dir: On A167, 1.5m from central ring road

This beautiful 17th-century mansion is peacefully situated in nine acres of its own grounds yet is convenient for the motorway network. The pick of the bedrooms are in a courtyard building or the impressive feature rooms in the original house. The Havelock Restaurant offers a range of traditional and continental menus.

Rooms 108 (11 annexe) (3 fmly) (36 GF) **S** £79-£99; **D** £94-£139 (incl. bkfst)* **Facilities** FTV 🄫 Gym Beauty room Xmas **Conf** Class 110 Board 50 Thtr 250 **Services** Lift **Parking** 250 **Notes** Civ Wed 200

Best Western Walworth Castle Hotel

★★★ 75% ⊛ HOTEL

☎ 01325 485470 📄 01325 462257
Walworth DL2 2LY
e-mail: enquiries@walworthcastle.co.uk
web: www.walworthcastle.co.uk
dir: A1(M) junct 58 follow signs to Corbridge. Left at The Dog pub. Hotel on left after 2m

This 12th-century castle is privately owned and has been tastefully converted. Accommodation is offered in a range of styles, including an impressive suite and more compact rooms in an adjoining wing. Dinner can be taken in the fine dining Hansards Restaurant or the more

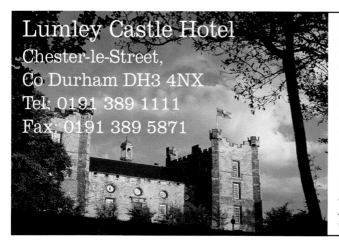

relaxed Farmer's Bar. A popular venue for conferences and weddings.

Rooms 32 (14 annexe) (4 fmly) (8 GF) **S** £85-£180; **D** £110-£245 (incl. bkfst)* **Facilities** 🏊 Xmas New Year Wi-fi **Conf** Board 40 Thtr 120 Del from £115 to £135 **Parking** 100 **Notes** LB ⊗ Civ Wed

Best Western Croft

★★★ 74% HOTEL

☎ 01325 720319 📄 01325 721252
Croft-on-Tees DL2 2ST
e-mail: enquiries@croft-hotel.co.uk
web: www.croft-hotel.co.uk
dir: From Darlington take A167 (Northallerton road). Hotel 3m S

Set in the village of Croft-on-Tees, this hotel offers smart well-equipped accommodation that includes a series of themed bedrooms that reflect different eras and countries around the world. The impressive Raffles Restaurant sports a colonial style and offers an interesting contemporary brasserie menu.

Rooms 20 (2 fmly) **Facilities** STV Gym Sauna Steam room Xmas New Year Wi-fi **Conf** Class 120 Board 50 Thtr 200 **Parking** 60 **Notes** ⊗ Closed 24-25 Dec Civ Wed 150

Hall Garth Hotel, Golf and Country Club

folio Hotels

★★★ 74% HOTEL

☎ 0844 855 9110 📄 01325 310083
Coatham Mundeville DL1 3LU
e-mail: hallgarth@foliohotels.com
web: www.foliohotels.com/hallgarth
dir: A1(M) junct 59, A167 towards Darlington. After 600yds left at top of hill, hotel on right

Peacefully situated in grounds that feature a golf course, this hotel is just a few minutes from the motorway network. The well-equipped bedrooms come in various styles - it's worth asking for one of the trendy, modern rooms. Public rooms include relaxing lounges, a fine-dining restaurant and a separate pub. The extensive leisure and conference facilities are an important focus here.

Rooms 52 (12 annexe) (2 fmly) (1 GF) **Facilities** Spa STV FTV 🔊 supervised 🏊 9 Putt green Gym Steam room Beauty Salon Xmas New Year Wi-fi **Conf** Class 160 Board 80 Thtr 250 **Parking** 150 **Notes** LB Civ Wed 170

Rockliffe Hall

[U]

☎ 01325 722221 📄 01325 285578
Rockliffe Park, Hurworth on Tees DL2 2DU
e-mail: enquiries@rockliffehall.com
dir: A1 N, junct 58, A68 Darlington, B6279 Staindrop Rd, A167 to Hurworth Village. A1 S, A66 Darlington, A167 to Hurworth

At the time of going to press we understood that this hotel would open in the Autumn of 2009, therefore the rating for this establishment has not been confirmed. For further details please see the AA website: theAA.com

Rooms 61 (5 fmly) (17 GF) **D** £230-£700 **Facilities** Spa STV FTV 🔊 🏊 18 Putt green Fishing Gym 🎵 Xmas New Year Wi-fi **Conf** Class 190 Board 40 Thtr 250 Del from £155 to £195 **Services** Lift **Parking** 200 **Notes** LB ⊗ Civ Wed

---

DURHAM   **Map 19 NZ24**

Radisson SAS Durham

★★★★ 77% HOTEL

☎ 0191 372 7200 📄 0191 372 7201
Frankland Ln DH1 5TA
e-mail: reservations.durham@radissonsas.com
dir: A690 signed city centre. 4th rdbt take 1st exit, left at lights to Framwell Gate Waterside, straight on, hotel on left. Follow brown signs from 1st rdbt

Situated on the River Wear this smart hotel is a short walk from the city centre and Durham Castle. The stylish accommodation includes business class rooms and a range of suites; most rooms have views of the cathedral and the old part of the city. Filini Restaurant serves Italian cuisine. The PACE Health Club boasts an indoor pool, steam room, sauna, gym and five treatment rooms, and the impressive conference facilities include a business centre.

Rooms 207 **S** £70-£159; **D** £70-£159* **Facilities** Spa STV 🔊 Gym Sauna Steam room Wi-fi **Conf** Class 200 Board 100 Thtr 450 Del from £130 to £205* **Services** Lift Air con **Parking** 130 **Notes** ⊗ Civ Wed

Durham Marriott Hotel, Royal County

Marriott HOTELS & RESORTS

★★★★ 76% HOTEL

☎ 0191 386 6821 📄 0191 386 0704
Old Elvet DH1 3JN
e-mail: mhrs.xvudm.frontdesk@marriotthotels.com
web: www.durhammarriottroyalcounty.co.uk
dir: From A1(M) junct 62, then A690 to Durham, over 1st rdbt, left at 2nd rdbt left at lights, hotel on left

In a wonderful position on the banks of the River Wear, the hotel's central location makes it ideal for visiting the attractions of this historic city. The building was developed from a series of Jacobean town houses. The bedrooms are tastefully styled. Eating options include the County Restaurant, for formal dining, and the Cruz Restaurant.

Rooms 150 (8 annexe) (10 fmly) (15 GF) (8 smoking) **S** fr £95; **D** fr £95* **Facilities** STV 🔊 supervised Gym Turkish steam room Plunge pool Sanarium Tropical fun shower Wi-fi **Conf** Class 50 Board 50 Thtr 120 Del from £130* **Services** Lift **Parking** 76 **Notes** Civ Wed 70

Ramside Hall

★★★★ 71% HOTEL

☎ 0191 386 5282 📄 0191 386 0399
Carrville DH1 1TD
e-mail: mail@ramsidehallhotel.co.uk
web: www.ramsidehallhotel.co.uk
dir: From A1(M) junct 62, A690 to Sunderland. Straight on at lights. 200mtrs after rail bridge turn right

With its proximity to the motorway and delightful parkland setting, this establishment combines the best of both worlds - convenience and tranquillity. The hotel boasts 27 holes of golf, a choice of lounges, two eating options and two bars. Bedrooms are furnished and decorated to a very high standard and include two very impressive presidential suites.

Rooms 80 (10 fmly) (28 GF) **S** £69-£130; **D** £99-£150 (incl. bkfst)* **Facilities** STV 🏊 27 Putt green Steam room Sauna Golf academy Driving range 🎵 Xmas New Year Wi-fi **Conf** Class 160 Board 40 Thtr 400 Del from £90 to £180 **Services** Lift **Parking** 500 **Notes** LB Civ Wed 400

DURHAM *continued*

Best Western Whitworth Hall Hotel

★★★ 79% COUNTRY HOUSE HOTEL

☎ 01388 811772 🖹 01388 818669
Whitworth Hall Country Park DL16 7QX
e-mail: enquiries@whitworthhall.co.uk
web: www.whitworthhall.co.uk

(For full entry see Spennymoor)

Hallgarth Manor Country Hotel & Restaurant

★★★ 68% HOTEL

☎ 0191 372 1188 🖹 0191 372 1249
Pittington DH6 1AB
e-mail: sales@hallgarthmanorhotel.com
dir: A1(M) junct 62/A690 signed Sunderland. In 0.5m turn right across dual carriageway, follow brown tourist signs to hotel

This traditional 16th-century country house is set in quiet and beautifully maintained grounds just a few miles from Durham. The public areas and the restaurant have been tastefully modernised yet retain many original features. The individually styled bedrooms are all situated on the top two floors of the building. A large function room is available.

Rooms 23 (2 fmly) **S** £70-£90; **D** £90-£150 (incl. bkfst)*
Facilities Xmas New Year Wi-fi **Conf** Class 75 Board 60 Thtr 250 Del from £115 to £150* **Parking** 200 **Notes** LB ⊗ Civ Wed 200

Travelodge Durham

BUDGET HOTEL

☎ 0871 984 6136 🖹 0191 386 5461
Station Rd, Gilesgate DH1 1LJ
web: www.travelodge.co.uk
dir: A1(M) junct 62 onto A690 towards Durham, 1st rdbt, 1st left into Station Rd

Travelodge offers good quality, good value, budget accommodation. All offer family rooms sleeping up to four (two adults, two children) with en suite bathroom/shower-room, remote-control TV, tea- and coffee-making facilities and comfortable beds. Food options vary. Breakfast is at the on-site Bar Café restaurant (if available) or to take away. See also Hotel Groups pages.

Rooms 96 **S** fr £29; **D** fr £29

Best Western Grand

★★★ 75% HOTEL

☎ 01429 266345 🖹 01429 265217
Swainson St TS24 8AA
e-mail: grandhotel@tavistockleisure.com
dir: A689 into town centre. Left onto Victoria Rd, hotel on right.

This hotel retains many original features and the public areas include a grand ballroom, an open-plan lounge bar and the basement restaurant, Italia. The bedrooms are modern in design and have high spec fixtures and fittings. The staff provide attentive and friendly service.

Rooms 47 (1 fmly) (17 smoking) **Facilities** STV FTV Affiliation with local gym ♫ New Year **Conf** Class 200 Board 60 Thtr 250 **Services** Lift **Parking** 50 **Notes** LB ⊗ Civ Wed 200

The Teesdale Hotel

★★ 65% HOTEL

☎ 01833 640264 🖹 01833 640651
Market Place DL12 0QG
e-mail: enquiries@teesdalehotel.co.uk
web: www.teesdalehotel.co.uk
dir: From Barnard Castle take B6278, follow signs for Middleton-in-Teesdale & Highforce. Hotel in town centre

Located in the heart of the popular village, this family-run hotel offers a relaxed and friendly atmosphere. Bedrooms and bathrooms are well equipped and offer a good standard of quality and comfort. Public areas include a residents' lounge on the first floor, a spacious restaurant and a lounge bar which is popular with locals.

Rooms 14 (1 fmly) **S** £30-£45; **D** £70-£80 (incl. bkfst)*
Facilities Xmas Wi-fi **Conf** Class 20 Board 20 Thtr 40 Del from £65 to £80* **Parking** 20 **Notes** LB

Barceló Redworth Hall Hotel

★★★★ 77% COUNTRY HOUSE HOTEL

☎ 01388 770600 🖹 01388 770654
DL5 6NL
e-mail: redworthhall@barcelo-hotels.co.uk
web: www.barcelo-hotels.co.uk
dir: From A1(M) junct 58/A68 signed Corbridge. Follow hotel signs

This imposing Georgian building includes a health club with state-of-the-art equipment and impressive conference facilities making this a popular destination for business travellers. There are several spacious lounges to relax in along with the Conservatory Restaurant. Bedrooms are very comfortable and well equipped.

Rooms 143 (12 fmly) **Facilities** STV ⊛ ♨ ✦ Gym Bodysense Health & Leisure Club ♫ Xmas New Year Wi-fi **Conf** Class 144 Board 90 Thtr 300 Del from £110* **Services** Lift **Parking** 300 **Notes** Civ Wed

INSPECTORS' CHOICE

Rose & Crown
★★ ◉◉ HOTEL

☎ 01833 650213 📠 01833 650828
DL12 9EB
e-mail: hotel@rose-and-crown.co.uk
web: www.rose-and-crown.co.uk
dir: 6m NW from Barnard Castle on B6277

This charming 18th-century country inn is located in the heart of the village, overlooking fine dale scenery. The area is renowned for its walking opportunities and many lovely routes lead from the hotel; a walking guide will be found in each bedroom. The attractively furnished bedrooms, including suites, are split between the main house and the rear courtyard. Guests might like to drink in the cosy bar with its log fire, after returning from a long walk. Good local produce features extensively on the menus that can be enjoyed in the oak-panelled restaurant with its white linen and gleaming silverware, or in the brasserie and bar. Service is both friendly and attentive.

Rooms 12 (5 annexe) (1 fmly) (5 GF) **S** £89; **D** £140-£200 (incl. bkfst)* **Facilities** STV New Year **Parking** 20 **Notes** LB Closed 24-26 Dec

INSPECTORS' CHOICE

Seaham Hall Hotel
★★★★★ ◉◉◉ HOTEL

☎ 0191 516 1400 📠 0191 516 1410
Lord Byron's Walk SR7 7AG
e-mail: info@seaham-hall.co.uk
web: www.seaham-hall.co.uk
dir: From A19 take B1404 to Seaham. At lights straight over level crossing. Hotel approx 0.25m on right

This imposing house was the setting for Lord Byron's marriage to Annabella Milbanke in 1815. Now restored to their opulent glory, the bedrooms, including some stunning suites, offer cutting edge technology, contemporary artwork and a real sense of style. Bathrooms are particularly lavish, with two-person baths a feature. Public rooms are equally impressive. The stunning Oriental Spa, accessed via an underground walkway, offers guests a wide range of treatments plus a Thai brasserie awarded 1 AA Rosette. The much praised cuisine of head chef Kenny Atkinson can be enjoyed in the White Room Restaurant (3 AA Rosettes). Von Essen Hotels - AA Hotel Group of the Year 2009-10.

Rooms 19 (4 GF) **S** £200-£595; **D** £200-£595 (incl. bkfst)* **Facilities** Spa STV FTV 🏊 Gym Xmas New Year Wi-fi **Conf** Class 48 Board 40 Thtr 120 **Services** Lift Air con **Parking** 122 **Notes** LB ⊗ Civ Wed 100

Best Western Hardwick Hall
★★★★ 77% ◉ HOTEL

☎ 01740 620253 📠 01740 622771
TS21 2EH
e-mail: info@hardwickhallhotel.co.uk
dir: off A1(M) junct 60 towards Sedgefield, left at 1st rdbt, hotel 400mtrs on left

Set in extensive parkland, this 18th-century house suits leisure and corporate guests very well. It is a top conference and function venue that offers an impressive meeting and banqueting complex. The bedrooms include a wing of stunning bedrooms to augment those in the original house; all are appointed to the same high standard and many have feature bathrooms and some have stunning views over the lake. Both the modern lounge bar and Cellar Bistro have a relaxed atmosphere.

Rooms 51 (6 fmly) **Facilities** STV FTV **Conf** Board 80 Thtr 700 **Services** Lift **Parking** 200 **Notes** ⊗ Civ Wed 450

Travelodge Sedgefield
BUDGET HOTEL

☎ 0871 984 6174 📠 01740 623399
TS21 2JX
web: www.travelodge.co.uk
dir: On A689, 3m E of A1(M) junct 60

Travelodge offers good quality, good value, budget accommodation. All offer family rooms sleeping up to four (two adults, two children) with en suite bathroom/shower-room, remote-control TV, tea- and coffee-making facilities and comfortable beds. Food options vary. Breakfast is at the on-site Bar Café restaurant (if available) or to take away. See also Hotel Groups pages.

Rooms 40 **S** fr £29; **D** fr £29

Best Western Whitworth Hall Hotel
★★★ 79% COUNTRY HOUSE HOTEL

☎ 01388 811772 📠 01388 818669
Whitworth Hall Country Park DL16 7QX
e-mail: enquiries@whitworthhall.co.uk
web: www.whitworthhall.co.uk
dir: A688 to Spennymoor, then Bishop Auckland. At rdbt right to Middlestone Moor. Left at lights, hotel on right

This hotel, peacefully situated in its own grounds in the centre of the deer park, offers comfortable accommodation. Spacious bedrooms, some with excellent views, offer stylish and elegant decor. Public areas include a choice of restaurants and bars, a bright conservatory and well-equipped function and conference rooms.

Rooms 29 (4 fmly) (17 GF) **Facilities** Fishing Wi-fi **Conf** Class 40 Board 30 Thtr 100 **Parking** 100 **Notes** ⊗ Civ Wed 120

STANLEY
Map 19 NZ15

Beamish Hall Country House Hotel

★★★★ 72% COUNTRY HOUSE HOTEL

☎ 01207 233733 ▤ 01207 299220
Beamish DH9 0YB
e-mail: info@beamish-hall.co.uk
dir: A693 to Stanley. Follow signs for hotel & Beamish Museum. Left at museum entrance. Hotel on left 0.2m after golf club

This hotel is set in 24 acres of impeccably maintained grounds and can trace its history back many centuries. The public areas are elegant and suitably appointed with leather suites and wooden flooring. The beautifully decorated dining room gives that real feeling of grandeur with high ceilings and wonderful views of the gardens. All the bedrooms are stylishly designed and well equipped, and include larger rooms that have jacuzzi baths and separate showers; some of the premier rooms are interconnecting, and there is also a two bedroom apartment with its own kitchen and family room.

Rooms 37 (17 fmly) (4 GF) **Facilities** STV FTV Xmas New Year Wi-fi **Conf** Class 160 Board 160 Thtr 300 Del from £145 to £200* **Services** Lift **Parking** 150 **Notes** ✪ Civ Wed 200

STOCKTON-ON-TEES
Map 19 NZ41

Best Western Parkmore Hotel & Leisure Club

★★★ 79% HOTEL

☎ 01642 786815 ▤ 01642 790485
636 Yarm Rd, Eaglescliffe TS16 0DH
e-mail: enquiries@parkmorehotel.co.uk
dir: Off A19 at Crathorne, follow A67 to Yarm. Through Yarm bear right onto A135 to Stockton. Hotel 1m on left

Set in its own gardens, this smart hotel has grown from its Victorian house origins to provide stylish public areas, as well as extensive leisure and beauty facilities including a hydrotherapy pool and conference facilities. The well-equipped bedrooms include junior suites. The restaurant known as J's@636 boasts a reputation for creativity meals. Service is friendly and obliging.

Rooms 55 (8 fmly) (9 GF) **S** £77-£118; **D** £97-£130*
Facilities Spa STV ⊛ supervised Gym Beauty salon Badminton Aerobics studio Hydrotherapy Xmas New Year Wi-fi **Conf** Class 40 Board 40 Thtr 130 Del from £125 to £129* **Parking** 90 **Notes** LB Civ Wed 130

WEST AUCKLAND
Map 19 NZ12

The Manor House Hotel & Country Club

★★★ 79% HOTEL

☎ 01388 834834 ▤ 01388 833566
The Green DL14 9HW
e-mail: enquiries@manorhousehotelcountydurham.co.uk
web: www.manorhousehotelcountydurham.co.uk
dir: A1(M) junct 58, then A68 to West Auckland. At T-junct turn left, hotel 150yds on right

This historic manor house, dating back to the 14th century, is full of character. Welcoming log fires await guests on cooler evenings. Comfortable bedrooms are individual in style, tastefully furnished and well equipped. The brasserie and Juniper's restaurant both offer an interesting selection of freshly prepared dishes. Well-equipped leisure facilities are available.

Rooms 35 (11 annexe) (6 fmly) (3 GF) **S** £59.50-£79;
D £99-£110 (incl. bkfst)* **Facilities** FTV ⊛ Gym Steam room Sauna Xmas New Year Wi-fi **Conf** Class 80 Board 50 Thtr 100 **Parking** 150 **Notes** LB Civ Wed 120

ESSEX

BASILDON
Map 6 TQ78

Chichester

★★★ 78% HOTEL

☎ 01268 560555 ▤ 01268 560580
Old London Rd, Wickford SS11 8UE
e-mail: reception@chichester-hotel.com
web: www.chichester-hotel.com
dir: Off A129

Set in landscaped gardens and surrounded by farmland, this friendly hotel has been owned and run by the same family for over 25 years. Spacious bedrooms are located around an attractive courtyard, and each is pleasantly decorated and thoughtfully equipped. Public rooms include a cosy lounge bar and a smart restaurant.

Rooms 35 (32 annexe) (6 fmly) (17 GF) **S** £55-£68;
D £55-£68* **Facilities** FTV Wi-fi **Parking** 150 **Notes** ✪

Holiday Inn Basildon

★★★ 70% HOTEL

☎ 0870 400 9003 & 01268 824000 ▤ 01268 530119
Waterfront Walk, Festival Leisure Park SS14 3DG
e-mail: reservations-basildon@ihg.com
web: www.holidayinn.co.uk
dir: From A127 take A176/Basildon Billericay exit. Follow brown signs to Festival Leisure Park

Located at Festival Leisure Park, this hotel is set in its own grounds overlooking a picturesque garden and lake. The air-conditioned bedrooms offer high speed internet access. Ample parking is available for guests attending banqueting events or business meetings. The Festival Leisure Park boasts a wide choice of restaurants, nightclubs and leisure activities.

Rooms 148 (10 fmly) (8 GF) (16 smoking) **S** £39-£135;
D £39-£135 (incl. bkfst)* **Facilities** STV Use of nearby leisure club New Year Wi-fi **Conf** Class 80 Board 80 Thtr 300 Del from £90 to £165* **Services** Lift Air con **Parking** 200 **Notes** LB Civ Wed

Campanile Basildon

BUDGET HOTEL

☎ 01268 530810 ▤ 01268 286710
Pipps Hill, Southend Arterial Rd SS14 3AE
e-mail: basildon@campanile.com
dir: M25 junct 29 Basildon exit, back under A127, then left at rdbt

This modern building offers accommodation in smart, well-equipped bedrooms, all with en suite bathrooms. Refreshments may be taken at the informal bistro. See also the Hotel Groups pages.

Rooms 97 (97 annexe) (8 fmly) (44 GF) **S** £55-£65;
D £55-£65 **Conf** Class 18 Board 24 Thtr 35 Del from £95 to £105

Travelodge Basildon

BUDGET HOTEL

☎ 0871 984 6008 ▤ 01268 186559
Festival Leisure Park, Festival Way SS14 3WB
web: www.travelodge.co.uk
dir: M25 junct 29, A127 follow signs Basildon town centre, onto A176 signed Festival Leisure Park

Travelodge offers good quality, good value, budget accommodation. All offer family rooms sleeping up to four (two adults, two children) with en suite bathroom/

shower-room, remote-control TV, tea- and coffee-making facilities and comfortable beds. Food options vary. Breakfast is at the on-site Bar Café restaurant (if available) or to take away. See also Hotel Groups pages.

Rooms 60 (27 fmly) **S** fr £29; **D** fr £29

BIRCHANGER GREEN MOTORWAY SERVICE AREA (M11)   Map 6 TL52

Days Inn Bishop's Stortford

BUDGET HOTEL

☎ 01279 656477 📠 01279 656590
CM23 5QZ
e-mail: birchanger.hotel@welcomebreak.co.uk
web: www.welcomebreak.co.uk
dir: M11 junct 8

This modern building offers accommodation in smart, spacious and well-equipped bedrooms, suitable for families and business travellers, and all with en suite bathrooms. Continental breakfast is available and other refreshments may be taken at the nearby family restaurant. See also the Hotel Groups pages.

Rooms 60 (57 fmly) **S** £29-£59; **D** £39-£69*

BRAINTREE   Map 7 TL72

White Hart
★★★ 🅰 HOTEL

☎ 01376 321401 📠 01376 552628
Bocking End CM7 9AB
e-mail: whitehart.braintree@greenking.co.uk
web: www.oldenglish.co.uk
dir: Off A120 towards town centre. Hotel at junct B1256 & Bocking Causeway

Rooms 31 (8 fmly) **S** £39-£45; **D** £49-£55 (incl. bkfst)*
Facilities Xmas New Year Wi-fi **Conf** Class 16 Board 24 Thtr 40 Del from £105 to £155* **Parking** 52 **Notes** LB ⊗ Civ Wed 35

BRENTWOOD   Map 6 TQ59

De Rougemont Manor
★★★★ 77% HOTEL

☎ 01277 226418 & 220483 📠 01277 239020
Great Warley St CM13 3JP
e-mail: info@derougemontmanor.co.uk
web: www.derougemontmanor.co.uk
dir: M25 junct 29, A127 to Southend then B186 towards Great Warley

Expect a warm welcome at this family owned and managed hotel, situated on the outskirts of Brentwood just off the M25. The stylish bedrooms are divided between the main hotel and a bedroom wing; each one is tastefully appointed and well equipped. Public rooms include a smart lounge bar, restaurant and a choice of seating areas.

Rooms 79 (10 annexe) (6 fmly) (16 GF) (10 smoking)
S £89-£139; **D** £99-£159 (incl. bkfst)* **Facilities** STV
🏊 Gym 3 acre nature reserve Xmas New Year Wi-fi
Conf Class 120 Board 16 Thtr 200 Del from £130 to £200
Services Lift Air con **Parking** 133 **Notes** ⊗ Civ Wed 90

Marygreen Manor
★★★★ 75% ◎◎ HOTEL

☎ 01277 225252 📠 01277 262809
London Rd CM14 4NR
e-mail: info@marygreenmanor.co.uk
web: www.marygreenmanor.co.uk
dir: M25 junct 28, onto A1023 over 2 sets of lights, hotel on right

A 16th-century house which was built by Robert Wright, who named the house 'Manor of Mary Green' after his young bride. Public rooms exude character and have a wealth of original features that include exposed beams, carved panelling and the impressive Tudors Restaurant. Bedrooms are tastefully decorated and thoughtfully equipped.

Rooms 44 (40 annexe) (35 GF) (9 smoking) **S** £75-£135;
D £90-£155* **Facilities** STV Wi-fi **Conf** Class 20 Board 25 Thtr 50 Del from £165 to £220 **Parking** 100 **Notes** ◎ Civ Wed 60

See advert on this page

Holiday Inn Brentwood
★★★ 77% HOTEL

☎ 0870 400 9012 📠 01277 264264
Brook St CM14 5NF
e-mail: reservations-brentwoodm25@ihg.com
web: www.holidayinn.co.uk
dir: Exit M25 junct 28 (or A12 at M25 interchange). Follow signs to Brentwood/A1023. Hotel 200yds on left

Ideally located just off the M25, this hotel is only 40 minutes from central London and 25 minutes from Stansted Airport, making it the perfect choice for business and leisure travellers alike. The refurbished public areas are smartly appointed; the health and fitness club has an indoor swimming pool.

Rooms 149 (28 fmly) (47 smoking) **Facilities** STV 🏊 Gym New Year Wi-fi **Conf** Class 60 Board 50 Thtr 140
Services Lift Air con **Parking** 276 **Notes** Civ Wed

BRENTWOOD *continued*

Weald Park Hotel, Golf & Country Club

★★★ 71% HOTEL

☎ 01277 375101 ▤ 01277 374888
Coxtie Green Rd, South Weald CM14 5RJ
e-mail: info@wealdpark.net
dir: M25 junct 28 Brentwood, left at 1st lights. Left at T-junct, follow winding road for 1.5m. 2nd right, hotel 1m on right

Expect a warm welcome at this family-run hotel situated in a peaceful rural location yet just a short drive from the M25 and M11. The spacious, tastefully appointed and well-equipped bedrooms are situated in attractive courtyard-style blocks adjacent to the main building. Public rooms include a first-floor function room, a lounge bar, a stylish restaurant and a conservatory.

Rooms 32 (32 annexe) (2 fmly) (25 GF) **Facilities** ⌧ 18 Putt green Wi-fi **Conf** Class 40 Board 20 Thtr 80 **Parking** 180 **Notes** LB ⊗ No children 12yrs

---

CHELMSFORD Map 6 TL70

County Hotel

★★★ 80% ◉ HOTEL

☎ 01245 455700 ▤ 01245 492762
29 Rainsford Rd CM1 2PZ
e-mail: kloftus@countyhotelgroup.co.uk
web: www.countyhotelgroup.co.uk
dir: From town centre, past rail and bus station. Hotel 300yds left beyond lights

This popular hotel is ideally situated within easy walking distance of the railway station, bus depot and town centre. Stylish bedrooms offer spacious comfort and plentiful extras including free Wi-fi. There is a smart restaurant, bar and lounge as well as sunny outdoor terraces for making the most of warm weather. The hotel also has a range of meeting rooms and banqueting facilities.

Rooms 51 (2 fmly) (1 GF) **S** £65-£115; **D** £75-£160* **Facilities** FTV Xmas New Year Wi-fi **Conf** Class 84 Board 64 Thtr 160 Del from £140 to £170* **Services** Lift **Parking** 80 **Notes** ⊗ Closed 27-30 Dec Civ Wed 80

Best Western Atlantic

★★★ 77% HOTEL

☎ 01245 268168 ▤ 01245 268169
New St CM1 1PP
e-mail: info@atlantichotel.co.uk
dir: From Chelmsford rail station, left onto Victoria Rd, left at lights into New St, hotel on right

Ideally situated just a short walk from the railway station with its quick links to London, this modern, purpose-built hotel has contemporary-style bedrooms equipped with modern facilities. The open-plan public areas include the popular New Street Brasserie, a lounge bar and a conservatory.

Rooms 59 (3 fmly) (27 GF) **S** £80-£125; **D** £99-£135 (incl. bkfst)* **Facilities** FTV Gym Complimentary use of facilities at Fitness First ⌐ Wi-fi **Conf** Class 40 Board 10 Thtr 15 **Services** Air con **Parking** 60 **Notes** LB ⊗ Closed 23 Dec-3 Jan

---

Pontlands Park Country Hotel

★★★ 77% HOTEL

☎ 01245 476444 ▤ 01245 478393
West Hanningfield Rd, Great Baddow CM2 8HR
e-mail: sales@pontlandsparkhotel.co.uk
web: www.pontlandsparkhotel.co.uk
dir: A12/A130/A1114 to Chelmsford. 1st exit at rdbt, 1st slip road on left. Left towards Great Baddow, 1st left into West Hanningfield Rd. Hotel 400yds on left

A Victorian country-house hotel situated in a peaceful rural location amidst attractive landscaped grounds. The stylishly furnished bedrooms are generally quite spacious; each is individually decorated and equipped with modern facilities. The elegant public rooms include a tastefully furnished sitting room, a cosy lounge bar, smart conservatory restaurant and an intimate dining room.

Rooms 35 (10 fmly) (11 GF) **Facilities** ⌧ ⌐ Gym Beauty room Wi-fi **Conf** Class 30 Board 30 Thtr 100 **Parking** 100 **Notes** ⊗ Closed 24 Dec-3 Jan (ex 31 Dec) Civ Wed 100

Best Western Ivy Hill

★★★ 75% HOTEL

☎ 01277 353040 & 355111 ▤ 01277 355038
Writtle Rd, Margaretting CM4 0EH
e-mail: sales@ivyhillhotel.co.uk
web: www.heritageleisure.co.uk
dir: A12 junct 14 from London. Hotel on left at top of slip road

A smartly appointed hotel conveniently situated just off the A12. The spacious bedrooms are tastefully decorated, have co-ordinated fabrics and all the usual facilities. Public rooms include a choice of lounges, a cosy bar, a smart conservatory and restaurant, as well as a range of conference and banqueting facilities.

Rooms 33 (5 fmly) (11 GF) **Facilities** FTV Wi-fi **Conf** Class 80 Board 40 Thtr 180 **Parking** 60 **Notes** ⊗ Closed 23-30 Dec Civ Wed 100

Travelodge Chelmsford

BUDGET HOTEL

☎ 0871 984 6379 ▤ 01844 984 6379
Army & Navy, 128-136 Parkway CM2 7PU
dir: M25 junct 28, onto A12 (Brentwood Bypass) 9m. Exit onto slip road, left into Southend Rd. Continue onto Essex Yeomanry Way (A1114). Lodge on right

Travelodge offers good quality, good value, budget accommodation. All offer family rooms sleeping up to four (two adults, two children) with en suite bathroom/shower-room, remote-control TV, tea- and coffee-making facilities and comfortable beds. Food options vary. Breakfast is at the on-site Bar Café restaurant (if available) or to take away. See also the Hotel Groups pages.

Rooms 81 **S** fr £29; **D** fr £29

CLACTON-ON-SEA Map 7 TM11

Esplanade Hotel

★★ 68% HOTEL

☎ 01255 220450 ▤ 01255 221800
27-29 Marine Parade East CO15 1UU
e-mail: mjs@esplanadehoteluk.com
web: www.esplanadehoteluk.com
dir: from A133 to Clacton-on-Sea, follow seafront signs. At seafront turn right. Hotel on right in 50yds

Ideally situated on the seafront overlooking the pier and just a short walk from the town centre. Bedrooms vary in size and style; each one is pleasantly decorated and well equipped; some rooms have lovely sea views. Public rooms include a comfortable lounge bar and Coasters Restaurant.

Rooms 29 (2 fmly) (3 GF) **Facilities** Xmas **Conf** Class 50 Board 50 Thtr 80 **Parking** 13 **Notes** LB ⊗ Civ Wed 85

COGGESHALL Map 7 TL82

White Hart

★★★ 77% ◉ HOTEL

☎ 01376 561654 ▤ 01376 561789
Market End CO6 1NH
e-mail: 6529@greeneking.co.uk
web: www.oldenglish.co.uk
dir: from A12 through Kelvedon & onto B1024 to Coggeshall

A delightful inn situated in the centre of this bustling market town. Bedrooms vary in size and style; each one offers good quality and comfort with extras such as CD players, fruit and mineral water. The heavily beamed public areas include a popular bar serving a varied menu, a large restaurant offering Italian cuisine and a cosy residents' lounge.

Rooms 18 (1 fmly) **Facilities** ⌐ Xmas Child facilities **Conf** Class 10 Board 22 Thtr 30 **Parking** 47

Five Lakes Hotel, Golf, Country Club & Spa

★★★★ 77% HOTEL

☎ 01621 868888 ☐ 01621 869696
Colchester Rd CM9 8HX
e-mail: enquiries@fivelakes.co.uk
web: www.fivelakes.co.uk

(For full entry see Tolleshunt Knights)

Best Western Marks Tey

★★★★ 70% HOTEL

☎ 01206 210001 ☐ 01206 212167
London Rd, Marks Tey CO6 1DU
e-mail: info@marksteyhotel.co.uk
web: www.marksteyhotel.co.uk
dir: Off A12/A120 junct signed Bishops Stortford. At rdbt follow Stanway signs. Follow road over A12, at next rdbt take 1st exit. Hotel on left

A purpose-built hotel situated just off the A12 on the outskirts of Colchester. Public rooms include a brasserie restaurant, a choice of lounges, a bar and a conservatory. Bedrooms come in a variety of styles; each one is smartly furnished and equipped with modern facilities. The hotel also has conference and leisure facilities.

Rooms 110 (57 GF) (22 smoking) **Facilities** ⊞
supervised ⌣ Gym Steam room Beauty treatments Sauna Xmas New Year Wi-fi **Conf** Class 100 Board 60 Thtr 200 **Services** Lift **Parking** 200 **Notes** ⊗ Civ Wed 160

Best Western The Rose & Crown

★★★ 81% ◎◎ HOTEL

☎ 01206 866677 ☐ 01206 866616
East St CO1 2TZ
e-mail: info@rose-and-crown.com
web: www.rose-and-crown.com
dir: From A12 follow Rollerworld signs, hotel by level crossing

This delightful 14th-century coaching inn is situated close to the shops and is full of charm and character. Public areas feature a wealth of exposed beams and timbered walls, and the contemporary East St Grill offers award-winning cuisine. Although the bedrooms vary in size, all are stylishly decorated and equipped with many thoughtful extras suitable for both business and leisure guests. Luxury executive rooms are available.

Rooms 38 (3 fmly) (12 GF) **S** £69-£99; **D** £79-£109 (incl. bkfst)* **Facilities** Wi-fi **Conf** Class 50 Board 45 Thtr 100 Del from £130 to £150 **Services** Lift **Parking** 50 **Notes** ⊗ Civ Wed 80

North Hill

★★★ 81% ◎ HOTEL

☎ 01206 574001 ☐ 01206 562941
51 North Hill CO1 1PY
e-mail: info@northhillhotel.com
dir: Follow signs for town centre. Up North Hill, hotel on left

This hotel is situated in the centre of this historic town. The contemporary open-plan public areas include a small lounge bar and the Green Room restaurant. The smartly appointed bedrooms are modern and well equipped with large flat-screen TVs and many thoughtful touches.

Rooms 13 **S** £59-£79; **D** £79-£99 (incl. bkfst)* **Facilities** FTV Xmas New Year Wi-fi **Notes** ⊗

Best Western Stoke by Nayland Hotel, Golf & Spa

★★★ 78% HOTEL

☎ 01206 262836 ☐ 01206 265840
Keepers Ln, Leavenheath CO6 4PZ
e-mail: sales@stokebynayland.com
web: www.stokebynaylandclub.co.uk
dir: Off A134 at Leavenheath onto B1068, hotel 0.75m on right

This hotel is situated on the edge of Dedham Vale, an Area of Outstanding Natural Beauty, in 300 acres of undulating countryside with lakes and two golf courses. The spacious bedrooms are attractively decorated and equipped with modern facilities, including ISDN lines. Free Wi-fi is available throughout. Public rooms include the Spikes bar, a conservatory, a lounge, a smart restaurant, conference and banqueting suites. The superb Peake Spa and Fitness Centre offers extensive facilities including health and beauty treatments.

Rooms 80 (4 fmly) (26 GF) **S** £59-£132.50;
D £69-£142.50 (incl. bkfst)* **Facilities** Spa STV FTV ⊞
supervised ⌣ 36 Putt green Fishing Gym Squash Driving range Snooker tables Wi-fi **Conf** Class 300 Board 60 Thtr 450 Del from £119 to £139* **Services** Lift **Parking** 335 **Notes** LB ⊗ Civ Wed 200

Holiday Inn Colchester

★★★ 72% HOTEL

☎ 0870 400 9020 ☐ 01206 766577
Abbotts Ln, Eight Ash Green CO6 3QL
web: www.holidayinn.co.uk
dir: Exit A12 at junct with A1124, follow Halstead signs. 0.25m, hotel at rdbt on left

This hotel is situated three miles from Colchester and is ideally located just off the A12 in a quiet village setting. All bedrooms are air-conditioned and have high-speed internet access. Trader's bar and grill offers a relaxed and informal environment; a range of conference rooms can cater for meetings and weddings.

Rooms 109 (25 fmly) (54 GF) **S** £50-£124; **D** £50-£124* **Facilities** Spa STV ⊞ supervised Gym Health club New Year Wi-fi **Conf** Class 60 Board 50 Thtr 120 Del from £99 to £120 **Services** Air con **Parking** 130 **Notes** LB ⊗ Civ Wed 100

George

★★★ 66% HOTEL

☎ 01206 578494 ☐ 01206 761732
116 High St CO1 1TD
dir: In town centre, 200yds from Town Hall

Ideally situated in the centre of town, this 500-year-old establishment has much to offer. The medieval cellar has, preserved behind glass, evidence of the Roman road than once ran through this town. The individually decorated bedrooms are equipped with a range of amenities. There's a popular lounge in which to relax and enjoy good food and real ales. The Bubbles Wine Bar offers an alternative to the traditional lounge.

Rooms 47

DEDHAM — Map 13 TM03

INSPECTORS' CHOICE

Maison Talbooth
★★★ ◎◎ COUNTRY HOUSE HOTEL

☎ 01206 322367 🖷 01206 322752
Stratford Rd CO7 6HN
e-mail: maison@milsomhotels.co.uk
web: www.milsomhotels.com
dir: A12 towards Ipswich, 1st turn signed Dedham,
follow to left bend, turn right. Hotel 1m on right

Warm hospitality and quality service are to be expected
at this Victorian country-house hotel, which is situated
in a peaceful rural location amidst pretty landscaped
grounds overlooking the Stour River Valley. Public areas
include a comfortable drawing room where guests may
take afternoon tea or snacks. Residents are
chauffeured to the popular Le Talbooth Restaurant just
a mile away for dinner. The spacious bedrooms are
individually decorated and tastefully furnished with
lovely co-ordinated fabrics and many thoughtful
touches.

Rooms 12 (1 fmly) (5 GF) **S** £150-£275; **D** £190-£325
(incl. bkfst)* **Facilities** Spa STV ⌖ ♨ ♒ Xmas Wi-fi
Conf Class 20 Board 16 Thtr 30 **Parking** 20 **Notes** LB
⊗ Civ Wed 50

milsoms
★★★ 78% ◎◎ SMALL HOTEL

☎ 01206 322795 🖷 01206 323689
Stratford Rd, Dedham CO7 6HW
e-mail: milsoms@milsomhotels.com
web: www.milsomhotels.com
dir: 6m N of Colchester off A12, follow Stratford St Mary/
Dedham signs. Turn right over A12, hotel on left

Situated in the Dedham Vale, an Area of Outstanding
Natural Beauty, this is the perfect base to explore the
countryside on the Essex/Suffolk border. This
establishment is styled along the lines of a contemporary
'gastro bar' combining good food served in an informal
atmosphere, with stylish and well-appointed
accommodation.

Rooms 15 (3 fmly) (4 GF) **S** £90-£110; **D** £110-£155*
Facilities STV ♫ Xmas Wi-fi **Conf** Board 24 **Parking** 70

EAST HORNDON — Map 6 TQ68

Travelodge Brentwood East Horndon

BUDGET HOTEL

☎ 0871 984 6016 🖷 01277 810819
CM13 3LL
web: www.travelodge.co.uk
dir: M25 junct 29, A127 eastbound. Lodge in 4m

Travelodge offers good quality, good value, budget
accommodation. All offer family rooms sleeping up to four
(two adults, two children) with en suite bathroom/
shower-room, remote-control TV, tea- and coffee-making
facilities and comfortable beds. Food options vary.
Breakfast is at the on-site Bar Café restaurant (if
available) or to take away. See also Hotel Groups pages.

Rooms 45 **S** fr £29; **D** fr £29

FEERING — Map 7 TL82

Travelodge Colchester Feering

BUDGET HOTEL

☎ 0871 984 6029 🖷 01376 572848
A12 London Road Northbound CO5 9EL
web: www.travelodge.co.uk
dir: On N'bound carriageway of A12, 0.5m N of Kelvedon

Travelodge offers good quality, good value, budget
accommodation. All offer family rooms sleeping up to four
(two adults, two children) with en suite bathroom/
shower-room, remote-control TV, tea- and coffee-making
facilities and comfortable beds. Food options vary.
Breakfast is at the on-site Bar Café restaurant (if
available) or to take away. See also Hotel Groups pages.

Rooms 39 **S** fr £29; **D** fr £29

GREAT CHESTERFORD — Map 12 TL54

The Crown House
★★★ 74% ◎ HOTEL

☎ 01799 530515 🖷 01799 530683
CB10 1NY
e-mail: reservations@crownhousehotel.com
web: www.crownhousehotel.com
dir: From N exit M11 at junct 9, from S junct 10, follow
signs for Saffron Walden & then Great Chesterford
(B1383)

This Georgian coaching inn, situated in a peaceful village
close to the M11, has been sympathetically restored and
retains much original character. The bedrooms are well
equipped and individually decorated; some rooms have
delightful four-poster beds. Public rooms include an
attractive lounge bar, an elegant oak-panelled restaurant
and an airy conservatory.

Rooms 22 (14 annexe) (2 fmly) (5 GF) **Facilities** New
Year Wi-fi **Conf** Class 14 Board 12 Thtr 30 Del from £110
to £130 **Parking** 30 **Notes** Closed 27-30 Dec Civ Wed 50

See advert on opposite page

GREAT DUNMOW — Map 6 TL62

Travelodge Stansted Great Dunmow

BUDGET HOTEL

☎ 0871 9846313 🖷 01371 874903
Chelmsford Rd CM6 1LW
web: www.travelodge.co.uk
dir: A120 exit at Dunmow South. 1st exit at rdbt signed
Great Dunmow, then immediately left. Hotel just off
Chelmsford Rd

Travelodge offers good quality, good value, budget
accommodation. All offer family rooms sleeping up to four
(two adults, two children) with en suite bathroom/
shower-room, remote-control TV, tea- and coffee-making

facilities and comfortable beds. Food options vary. Breakfast is at the on-site Bar Café restaurant (if available) or to take away. See also Hotel Groups pages.

Rooms 65 **S** fr £29; **D** fr £29

GREAT YELDHAM   Map 13 TL73

The White Hart

 RESTAURANT WITH ROOMS

☎ 01787 237250   🖻 01787 238044
Poole St CO9 4HJ
e-mail: mjwmason@yahoo.co.uk
dir: On A1017 in village

A large timber framed character building houses the main restaurant and bar areas whilst the bedrooms are located in the converted coach house; all are smartly appointed and well equipped with many thoughtful extras. A comfortable lounge-bar area and beautifully landscaped gardens provide areas for relaxation. Locally sourced produce is used in the main house restaurant, popular with local residents and guests alike.

Rooms 11 (2 fmly)

HALSTEAD   Map 13 TL83

Bull

★★ 🅰 HOTEL

☎ 01787 472144   🖻 01787 472496
Bridge St CO9 1HU
e-mail: bull.halstead@oldenglishinns.co.uk
web: www.oldenglish.co.uk
dir: Off A131 at bottom of hill on High St

Rooms 16 (6 annexe) **Facilities** 🎵 New Year
Conf Class 25 Board 30 Thtr 60 **Parking** 25 **Notes** ⊗
Civ Wed 50

HARLOW   Map 6 TL41

Travelodge Harlow

BUDGET HOTEL

☎ 0871 984 6289   🖻 01279 437 349
Burnt Mill CM20 2JE
web: www.travelodge.co.uk
dir: M11 junct 7, A414, E towards Hertford. Lodge on left

Travelodge offers good quality, good value, budget accommodation. All offer family rooms sleeping up to four (two adults, two children) with en suite bathroom/shower-room, remote-control TV, tea- and coffee-making facilities and comfortable beds. Food options vary. Breakfast is at the on-site Bar Café restaurant (if available) or to take away. See also Hotel Groups pages.

Rooms 90 **S** fr £29; **D** fr £29

Travelodge Harlow North Weald

BUDGET HOTEL

☎ 0871 984 6033   🖻 01992 523276
A414 Eastbound, Tylers Green, North Weald CM16 6BJ
web: www.travelodge.co.uk
dir: M11 junct 7, take A414 towards Chelmsford. Lodge after 2nd rdbt on left

Rooms 61 **S** fr £29; **D** fr £29

HARWICH   Map 13 TM23

The Pier at Harwich

★★★ 82% ◉◉ HOTEL

☎ 01255 241212   🖻 01255 551922
The Quay CO12 3HH
e-mail: pier@milsomhotels.com
web: www.milsomhotels.com
dir: From A12, take A120 to Quay. Hotel opposite lifeboat station

Situated on the quay, overlooking the ports of Harwich and Felixstowe. The bedrooms are tastefully decorated, thoughtfully equipped, and furnished in a contemporary style; many rooms have superb sea views. The public rooms include the informal Ha'Penny Bistro, the first-floor Harbourside Restaurant, a smart lounge bar and a plush residents' lounge.

Rooms 14 (7 annexe) (5 fmly) (1 GF) **S** £80-£95;
D £105-£185 (incl. bkfst)* **Facilities** STV Sea bass fishing Day cruises on yachts Xmas Wi-fi **Conf** Board 16
Parking 10 **Notes** LB ⊗ Civ Wed 50

HARWICH *continued*

Tower Hotel

★★★ 79% HOTEL

☎ 01255 504952 📄 01255 504952
Dovercourt CO12 3PJ
e-mail: reception@tower-hotel-harwich.co.uk
web: www.tower-hotel-harwich.co.uk
dir: Follow main road into Harwich. Past BP garage on left

This hotel is an impressive late 17th-century Italian-style building. There is a wealth of ornamental ceiling cornices, beautiful architraves and an impressive balustrade. Bedrooms, many named after prominent people from Harwich's past, are spacious and furnished to a very high standard. Evening meals and breakfast are served in the decorative dining rooms, and Rigby's bar offers tempting meals and a wide range of refreshments.

Rooms 13 (2 fmly) (2 GF) **S** £40-£65; **D** £55-£85*
Facilities Wi-fi **Conf** Class 30 Board 30 Thtr 30
Parking 30 **Notes** ⊗ Civ Wed 40

Hotel Continental

THE INDEPENDENTS
HOTEL ASSOCIATION

★★ 74% HOTEL

☎ 01255 551298 📄 01255 551698
28/29 Marine Pde, Dovercourt CO12 3RG
e-mail: hotconti@btconnect.com
web: www.hotelcontinental-harwich.co.uk
dir: Exit A120 at Ramsay rdbt onto B1352 to pedestrian crossing & Co-op store on right, right into Fronks Rd, leads to Marine Pde

Privately owned hotel situated on the seafront within easy reach of the ferry terminals and town centre. Bedrooms are pleasantly decorated, well equipped and have many innovative features; some rooms also have lovely sea views. Public rooms include a lounge, popular lounge bar and restaurant.

Rooms 14 (2 fmly) **S** £40-£70; **D** £70-£95* **Facilities** STV FTV Wi-fi **Parking** 4 **Notes** LB ⊗

Cliff

★★ 68% HOTEL

☎ 01255 503345 & 507373 📄 01255 240358
Marine Pde, Dovercourt CO12 3RE
e-mail: reception@cliffhotelharwich.fsnet.co.uk
web: www.thecliffhotelharwich.co.uk
dir: A120 to Parkeston rdbt, take road to Dovercourt, on seafront after Dovercourt town centre

Conveniently situated on the seafront close to the railway station and ferry terminal. Public rooms are smartly appointed and include the Shade Bar, a comfortable lounge, a restaurant and the Marine Bar with views of Dovercourt Bay. The pleasantly decorated bedrooms have co-ordinated soft furnishings and modern facilities; many have sea views.

Rooms 26 (3 fmly) **Facilities** ♫ Wi-fi **Conf** Class 150 Board 40 Thtr 200 Del from £65* **Parking** 50 **Notes** ⊗ RS Xmas & New Year

SOUTHEND-ON-SEA   Map 7 TQ88

Balmoral Hotel

★★★ 78% HOTEL

☎ 01702 342947 📄 01702 337828
34 Valkyrie Rd, Westcliff-on-Sea SS0 8BU
e-mail: enq@balmoralsouthend.com
web: www.balmoralsouthend.com
dir: Off A13

A delightful property situated just a short walk from the main shopping centre, railway station and the seafront. The attractively decorated bedrooms are tastefully furnished and equipped with many thoughtful touches. Public rooms feature a smart open-plan bar/lounge, a conservatory restaurant and a terrace with a large wooden gazebo.

Rooms 34 (4 fmly) (4 GF) **Facilities** Arrangement with nearby health club **Parking** 32

Roslin Beach Hotel

★★★ 77% HOTEL

☎ 01702 586375 📄 01702 586663
Thorpe Esplanade SS1 3BG
e-mail: info@roslinhotel.com
web: www.roslinhotel.com
dir: A127, follow Southend-on-Sea signs. Hotel between Walton Rd & Clieveden Rd on seafront

This friendly hotel is situated at the quiet end of the esplanade, overlooking the beach and sea. The spacious bedrooms are pleasantly decorated and thoughtfully equipped; some rooms have superb sea views. Public rooms include a large lounge bar, the Mulberry Restaurant and a smart conservatory which overlooks the sea.

Rooms 57 (5 fmly) (7 GF) **S** £62-£80; **D** £92-£210 (incl. bkfst)* **Facilities** FTV Xmas New Year Wi-fi **Conf** Class 45 Board 39 Thtr 60 **Parking** 40 **Notes** LB ⊗ Civ Wed 25

Westcliff

★★★ 70% HOTEL

☎ 01702 345247 📄 01702 431814
Westcliff Pde, Westcliff-on-Sea SS0 7QW
e-mail: westcliff@zolahotels.com
dir: M25 junct 29, A127 towards Southend, follow signs for Cliffs Pavillion when approaching town centre

This impressive Grade II listed Victorian building is situated in an elevated position overlooking gardens and cliffs with views to the sea beyond. The spacious bedrooms are tastefully decorated and thoughtfully equipped; many have lovely sea views. Public rooms include a smart conservatory-style restaurant, a spacious lounge and a range of function rooms.

Rooms 55 (2 fmly) **Facilities** FTV ♫ Xmas New Year Wi-fi **Conf** Class 90 Board 64 Thtr 225 **Services** Lift **Notes** ⊗ Civ Wed 120

Camelia

★★★ 🅰 HOTEL

☎ 01702 587917 📄 01702 585704
176-178 Eastern Esplanade, Thorpe Bay SS1 3AA
e-mail: enquiries@cameliahotel.com
web: www.cameliahotel.com
dir: From A13 or A127 follow signs to Southend seafront; on seafront turn left, hotel 1m east of pier

Rooms 28 (8 annexe) (3 fmly) (8 GF) **S** £55-£70; **D** £70-£130 (incl. bkfst) **Facilities** STV New Year Wi-fi **Parking** 100 **Notes** ⊗

Travelodge Southend-on-Sea

BUDGET HOTEL

☎ 0871 984 6247   🖹 01994 232957
Maitland House, Warrior Square, Chichester Rd SS1 2JY
web: www.travelodge.co.uk
dir: In town centre

Travelodge offers good quality, good value, budget accommodation. All offer family rooms sleeping up to four (two adults, two children) with en suite bathroom/shower-room, remote-control TV, tea- and coffee-making facilities and comfortable beds. Food options vary. Breakfast is at the on-site Bar Café restaurant (if available) or to take away. See also Hotel Groups pages.

Rooms 56 **S** fr £29; **D** fr £29

SOUTH WOODHAM FERRERS   Map 7 TQ89

The Oakland Hotel

★★ 68% HOTEL

☎ 01245 322811   🖹 01245 329201
2-6 Reeves Way CM3 5XF
e-mail: info@theoaklandhotel.co.uk
web: www.theoaklandhotel.co.uk
dir: 4m from A130 at Rettendon

Modern purpose-built hotel situated in the centre of this bustling town. Bedrooms are generally quite spacious, and each one is pleasantly decorated and equipped with modern facilities. The public areas include a large sports bar with Sky TV and an open-plan bar/restaurant with a selection of comfy sofas.

Rooms 34 (4 fmly) **S** fr £39.95; **D** £55-£59.50 (incl. bkfst)* **Facilities** ♫ Wi-fi **Conf** Class 20 Board 20 Thtr 30 Del from £65 to £75* **Parking** 4 **Notes** ⊗

STANSTED AIRPORT   Map 6 TL52

See also **see also** Birchanger Green Motorway Service Area (M11)

Radisson Blu Hotel Stansted Airport

★★★★ 75% HOTEL

☎ 01279 661012   🖹 01279 661013
Waltham Close, Stansted Airport CM24 1PP
e-mail: info.stansted@radissonblu.com
web: www.radissonblu.co.uk/hotel-stanstedairport
dir: M11 junct 8 onto A120. Follow London Stansted Airport signs. Hotel linked airport to terminal

This modern glass-fronted hotel, linked to the airport terminal by a covered walkway, is particularly well appointed. Facilities include a wide choice of restaurants, a smart leisure club and spa, extensive conference and meeting rooms, and the much talked about wine tower,

complete with wine angels. Bedrooms follow a contemporary theme and include a host of thoughtful extras.

Rooms 500 (42 fmly) (51 smoking) **S** £89-£135; **D** £89-£145* **Facilities** Spa STV 🖐 Gym Steam room Hair salon ♫ Xmas New Year Wi-fi **Conf** Class 180 Board 36 Thtr 400 Del from £145 to £209* **Services** Lift Air con **Parking** 220 **Notes** ⊗

Best Western Stansted Manor

★★★ 77% HOTEL

☎ 01279 859800   🖹 01279 467245
Birchanger Ln CM23 5ST
e-mail: info@stanstedmanor-hotel.co.uk
web: www.stanstedmanor-hotel.co.uk
dir: M11 junct 8 onto A120 towards Bishop's Stortford. Right at next major rdbt. Hotel on left

Modern, purpose-built hotel conveniently situated just off the M11 very close to London Stansted Airport. The property is reached via a long drive and surrounded by landscaped grounds. Bedrooms feature modern decor, tasteful furnishings and a thoughtful range of extras, including broadband. Open-plan public rooms include a comfortable lobby lounge, a lounge/bar and a conservatory restaurant.

Rooms 70 (8 fmly) (23 GF) (10 smoking) **S** £65-£95; **D** £65-£125 **Facilities** FTV Wi-fi **Conf** Class 16 Board 20 Thtr 35 Del from £125 to £155 **Services** Lift **Parking** 100 **Notes** ⊗ Civ Wed 100

Express by Holiday Inn - Stansted Airport

BUDGET HOTEL

☎ 01279 680015   🖹 01279 680838
Thremhall Av, London Stansted Airport CM24 1PY
e-mail: admin.stansted@kewgreen.co.uk
web: www.hiexpress.com/exstanstedap

A modern hotel ideal for families and business travellers. Fresh and uncomplicated, the spacious rooms include Sky TV, power shower and tea and coffee-making facilities. Continental buffet breakfast is included in the room rate; other meals may be taken at the nearby family pub or restaurant. See also the Hotel Groups pages.

Rooms 254 **Conf** Class 44 Board 44 Thtr 70

STOCK   Map 6 TQ69

Greenwoods Hotel Spa & Retreat

★★★★ 76% HOTEL

☎ 01277 829990   & 829205   🖹 01277 829899
Stock Rd CM4 9BE
e-mail: info@greenwoodshotel.co.uk
dir: A12 junct 16 take B1007 signed Billericay. Hotel on right on entering village

Greenwoods is a beautiful 17th-century, Grade II listed manor house set in extensive landscaped gardens. All bedrooms are tastefully appointed, have a marbled bathroom and a wide range of extras; the premier rooms are equipped with spa baths and antique beds. The spa facilities are impressive and offer the latest beauty treatments, together with saunas, a jacuzzi, steam rooms, a monsoon shower and a 20-metre pool. This stylish hotel could be described as a 'home-from-home'.

Rooms 39 (6 GF) **Facilities** Spa STV 🖐 Gym Steam room Sauna Monsoon shower Xmas New Year Wi-fi **Conf** Class 70 Board 52 Thtr 110 **Services** Lift **Parking** 100 **Notes** ⊗ No children 16yrs Closed 24 & 26 Dec, 1 Jan Civ Wed 110

THAXTED   Map 12 TL63

Swan

★★ 🅰 HOTEL

☎ 01371 830321   🖹 01371 831186
Bullring, Watling St CM6 2PL
e-mail: swan.thaxted@greeneking.co.uk
web: www.oldenglish.co.uk
dir: M11 junct 8, A120 to Great Dunmow, then B184 to Thaxted. Hotel at N end of high street, opposite church

Rooms 19 (6 annexe) (2 fmly) (3 GF) **Facilities** Xmas **Parking** 15

TOLLESHUNT KNIGHTS   Map 7 TL91

Five Lakes Hotel, Golf, Country Club & Spa

★★★★ 77% ☺ HOTEL

☎ 01621 868888   📠 01621 869696
Colchester Rd CM9 8HX
e-mail: enquiries@fivelakes.co.uk
web: www.fivelakes.co.uk
dir: exit A12 at Kelvedon, follow brown signs through Tiptree to hotel

This hotel is set amidst 320 acres of open countryside, featuring two golf courses. The spacious bedrooms are furnished to a high standard and have excellent facilities. The public rooms offer a high degree of comfort and include five bars, two restaurants and a large lounge. The property also boasts extensive leisure facilities.

Rooms 194 (80 annexe) (4 fmly) (40 GF) **Facilities** Spa
🏊 ↯ 36 ⚑ Putt green Gym Squash Steam room Health & Beauty Spa Badminton Aerobics Studio, Hairdresser ♫
Xmas New Year **Conf** Class 700 Board 60 Thtr 2000
Services Lift **Parking** 550 **Notes** ⊗ Civ Wed 250

WALTHAM ABBEY   Map 6 TL30

Waltham Abbey Marriott   **Marriott.**
HOTELS & RESORTS

★★★★ 78% HOTEL

☎ 01992 717170   📠 01992 711841
Old Shire Ln EN9 3LX
web: www.walthamabbeymarriott.co.uk
dir: M25 junct 26

This hotel benefits from convenient access to London and the major road networks. The air-conditioned bedrooms are spacious, tastefully decorated and offer a range of facilities for the modern business traveller. The hotel also provides a range of meeting rooms, a substantial parking area and a well-equipped indoor leisure centre.

Waltham Abbey Marriott

Rooms 162 (16 fmly) (80 GF) **Facilities** ☺ Gym Xmas New Year Wi-fi **Conf** Class 120 Board 50 Thtr 280 **Services** Air con **Parking** 250 **Notes** ⊗ Civ Wed 250

WEST THURROCK   Map 6 TQ57

Ibis London Thurrock

BUDGET HOTEL

☎ 01708 686000   📠 01708 680525
Weston Av RM20 3JQ
e-mail: H2176@accor.com
web: www.ibishotel.com
dir: M25 junct 31 to West Thurrock Services, right at 1st & 2nd rdbts, left at 3rd rdbt. Hotel on right in 500yds

Modern, budget hotel offering comfortable accommodation in bright and practical bedrooms. Breakfast is self-service and dinner is available in the restaurant. See also the Hotel Groups pages.

Rooms 102 (27 GF)

Travelodge Thurrock (M25)   Travelodge

BUDGET HOTEL

☎ 0871 984 6216 & 0800 850950 📠 01708 860971
Moto Service Area, Arterial Rd RM16 3BG
web: www.travelodge.co.uk
dir: M25 junct 30 clockwise; M25 junct 31 anti-clockwise. Off A1306

Travelodge offers good quality, good value, budget accommodation. All offer family rooms sleeping up to four (two adults, two children) with en suite bathroom/shower-room, remote-control TV, tea- and coffee-making facilities and comfortable beds. Food options vary. Breakfast is at the on-site Bar Café restaurant (if available) or to take away. See also Hotel Groups pages.

Rooms 47 **S** fr £29; **D** fr £29

WICKFORD   Map 6 TQ79

Innkeeper's Lodge Basildon/Wickford

BUDGET HOTEL

☎ 0845 112 6055   📠 0845 112 6248
Runwell Rd SS11 7QJ
web: www.innkeeperslodge.com/basildon
dir: A132 to Wickford. At top lights turn left. Lodge 100yds on right

Innkeeper's Lodge represents an exciting, high value concept within the budget hotel market. Comfortable bedrooms provide excellent facilities that include satellite TV and modem points. Options include family rooms; and for the corporate guest, cutting edge IT which includes Wi-fi access. A popular Carvery provides all-day food, including an extensive, complimentary continental breakfast. See also the Hotel Groups pages.

Rooms 24 (6 fmly) **Conf** Thtr 30

WITHAM   Map 7 TL81

Rivenhall

★★★ 77% HOTEL

☎ 01376 516969   📠 01376 513674
Rivenhall End CM8 3HB
e-mail: info@rivenhallhotel.com
web: www.rivenhallhotel.com
dir: M25 junct 28 towards Chelmsford on A12, take exit for Silver End/Great Braxted. At T-junct turn right, then 1st right, hotel directly ahead

This modern hotel is ideally situated just off the main A12 between Chelmsford and Colchester. Bedrooms are pleasantly decorated and equipped with modern facilities. Public rooms include a large restaurant and a comfortable lounge bar; conference and leisure facilities are also available.

Rooms 55 (37 annexe) (6 fmly) (42 GF) **Facilities** STV FTV ☺ Gym Sauna Xmas New Year Wi-fi **Conf** Class 50 Board 50 Thtr 160 **Parking** 150 **Notes** ⊗ Closed 26 Dec RS Xmas Civ Wed 120

GLOUCESTERSHIRE

ALMONDSBURY   Map 4 ST68

Aztec Hotel & Spa

★★★★ 80% ◉ HOTEL

☎ 01454 201090   📄 01454 201593
Aztec West Business Park, Almondsbury BS32 4TS
e-mail: aztec@shirehotels.com
web: www.aztechotelbristol.com

(For full entry see Bristol)

ALVESTON   Map 4 ST68

Alveston House

★★★ 80% ◉ HOTEL

☎ 01454 415050   📄 01454 415425
Davids Ln BS35 2LA
e-mail: info@alvestonhousehotel.co.uk
web: www.alvestonhousehotel.co.uk
dir: M5 junct 14 from N or junct 16 from S, on A38

In a quiet area with easy access to the city and a short drive from both the M4 and M5, this smartly presented hotel provides an impressive combination of good service, friendly hospitality and a relaxed atmosphere. The comfortable bedrooms are well equipped for both business and leisure guests. The restaurant offers carefully prepared fresh food, and the pleasant bar and conservatory area is perfect for enjoying a pre-dinner drink.

Rooms 30 (1 fmly) (6 GF) **S** £75-£105; **D** £99.50-£145 (incl. bkfst) **Facilities** FTV New Year Wi-fi **Conf** Class 48 Board 50 Thtr 85 Del from £135 to £155* **Parking** 75 **Notes** LB Civ Wed 75

ARLINGHAM   Map 4 SO71

The Old Passage Inn

◉◉ RESTAURANT WITH ROOMS

☎ 01452 740547   📄 01452 741871
Passage Rd GL2 7JR
e-mail: oldpassage@ukonline.co.uk
dir: A38 onto B4071 through Arlingham. House by river

Delightfully located on the very edge of the River Severn, this relaxing restaurant with rooms combines high quality food with an air of tranquillity. An outdoor terrace is available in warmer months. The menu offers a wide range of seafood and shellfish dishes including crab, oysters and lobsters from Cornwall kept live in seawater tanks. Bedrooms and bathrooms are decorated in a modern style and include a range of welcome extras such as air conditioning and a well-stocked mini-bar.

Rooms 3

BIBURY   Map 5 SP10

Swan

★★★ 82% ◉ HOTEL   Cotswold Inns & Hotels

☎ 01285 740695   📄 01285 740473
GL7 5NW
e-mail: info@swanhotel.co.uk
web: www.cotswold-inns-hotels.co.uk
dir: 9m S of Burford A40 onto B4425. 6m N of Cirencester A4179 onto B4425

This hotel, built in the 17th century as a coaching inn, is set in peaceful and picturesque surroundings. It provides well-equipped and smartly presented accommodation, including four luxury cottage suites set just outside the main hotel. The elegant public areas are comfortable and have feature fireplaces. There is a choice of dining options to suit all tastes.

Rooms 22 (4 annexe) (1 fmly) **Facilities** Fishing Xmas New Year Wi-fi **Conf** Class 50 Board 32 Thtr 80 **Services** Lift **Parking** 22 **Notes** Civ Wed 110

Bibury Court

★★★ 73% ◉◉ COUNTRY HOUSE HOTEL

☎ 01285 740337 & 741171   📄 01285 740660
GL7 5NT
e-mail: info@biburycourt.com
web: www.biburycourt.com
dir: On B4425, 6m N of Cirencester (A4179). 8m S of Burford (A40), entrance by River Coln

Dating back to Tudor times, this elegant manor is the perfect antidote to the hustle and bustle of the modern world. Public areas have abundant charm and character. Bedrooms are spacious and offer traditional quality with modern comforts. A choice of interesting dishes is available in the conservatory at lunchtime, whereas dinner is served in the more formal restaurant. Staff are friendly and helpful.

Rooms 18 (3 fmly) (1 GF) **S** £79-£135; **D** £160-£240 (incl. bkfst)* **Facilities** FTV Fishing ⚑ Xmas New Year Wi-fi **Conf** Class 12 Board 10 Thtr 30 Del from £190 to £210* **Notes** LB Civ Wed 32

BOURTON-ON-THE-WATER   Map 10 SP12

The Dial House Hotel

★★★ 79% ◉◉ SMALL HOTEL

☎ 01451 822244   📄 01451 810126
The Chestnuts, High St GL54 2AN
e-mail: info@dialhousehotel.com
dir: Off A429, 0.5m to village centre

Located in the main street of this popular Cotswold town, The Dial House has been refurbished to provide high quality and comfort throughout. Bedrooms and bathrooms, in a wide variety of shapes and sizes, are luxuriously decorated and furnished. The building itself dates from 1698 and offers intimate public areas full of character and quality. Dinner, in the delightful award-winning restaurant, utilises the finest produce and should not be missed.

Rooms 13 **S** £110-£210; **D** £120-£220 (incl. bkfst) **Facilities** ⚑ Xmas New Year Wi-fi **Conf** Class 12 Board 12 Thtr 12 Del from £175 to £250 **Parking** 20 **Notes** LB No children 12yrs

Chester House

★★ 79% HOTEL

☎ 01451 820286   📄 01451 820471
Victoria St GL54 2BU
e-mail: info@chesterhousehotel.com
dir: On A429 between Northleach & Stow-on-the-Wold

This hotel occupies a secluded but central location in this delightful Cotswold village. Rooms, some at ground floor level, are situated in the main house and adjoining coach house. The public areas are stylish, light and airy. Breakfast is taken in the main building whereas dinner is served in the attractive restaurant just a few yards away.

Rooms 22 (10 annexe) (8 fmly) (8 GF) **Facilities** Beauty therapist New Year Wi-fi **Parking** 20 **Notes** Closed 7 Jan-1 Feb

Old Manse

★★ 🅰 HOTEL

☎ 01451 820082   📄 01451 810381
Victoria St GL54 2BX
e-mail: 6488@greeneking.co.uk
web: www.oldenglish.co.uk
dir: A429 Bourton turn off, hotel at far end of village high street next to Cotswold Motor Museum.

Rooms 15 (3 annexe) **Facilities** Xmas **Parking** 12 **Notes** LB ⊗

BUCKLAND (NEAR BROADWAY) Map 10 SP03

INSPECTORS' CHOICE

Buckland Manor

★★★ ⊛⊛
COUNTRY HOUSE HOTEL

☎ 01386 852626 📠 01386 853557
WR12 7LY
e-mail: info@bucklandmanor.co.uk
web: www.bucklandmanor.co.uk
dir: Off B4632 (Broadway to Winchcombe road)

A grand 13th-century manor house that is surrounded by well-kept and beautiful gardens that feature a stream and waterfall. Everything at this hotel is geared to encourage rest and relaxation. Spacious bedrooms and public areas are furnished with high quality pieces and decorated in keeping with the style of the manor; crackling log fires warm the wonderful lounges. The elegant dining room, with views over the rolling hills, is the perfect place to enjoy dishes that use high quality local produce. Von Essen Hotels - AA Hotel Group of the Year 2009-10.

Rooms 13 (2 fmly) (4 GF) **S** £275-£480; **D** £285-£490 (incl. bkfst) **Facilities** STV 🏌 Putt green 🏊 Xmas New Year **Parking** 30 **Notes** LB ⊗ No children 12yrs

CHARINGWORTH Map 10 SP13

Charingworth Manor

★★★★ 75% ⊛ COUNTRY HOUSE HOTEL

☎ 01386 593555 📠 01386 593353
Charingworth Manor GL55 6NS
e-mail: gm.charingworthmanor@classiclodges.co.uk
web: www.classiclodges.co.uk

This 14th-century manor house retains many original features including flagstone floors, exposed beams and open fireplaces. The house has a beautiful setting in 50 acres of grounds and has been carefully extended to provide high quality accommodation and a delightful, small leisure spa. Spacious bedrooms are furnished with period pieces and modern amenities.

Charingworth Manor

Rooms 26 (18 annexe) (2 fmly) (12 GF) **Facilities** 🐾 🏊 Gym Xmas New Year **Conf** Class 30 Board 40 Thtr 80 **Parking** 50 **Notes** ⊗ Civ Wed 40

CHELTENHAM Map 10 SO92

Hotel du Vin Cheltenham

★★★★ 80% ⊛ HOTEL

☎ 01242 588450 📠 01242 588455
Parabola Rd GL50 3AQ
e-mail: info@cheltenham.hotelduvin.com
web: www.hotelduvin.com
dir: M5 junct 11, follow signs for city centre. At rdbt opposite Morgan Estate Agents take 2nd left, 200mtrs to Parabola Rd

This hotel, in the Montpellier area of the town, has spacious public areas that are packed with stylish features. The pewter-topped bar has comfortable seating and the spacious restaurant has all characteristic Hotel du Vin trademark design in evidence; alfresco dining is possible on the extensive terrace area. Bedrooms are very comfortable, with Egyptian cotton linen, deep baths and power showers. The spa is the ideal place to relax and unwind. Although parking is limited it is a definite bonus. Service is friendly and attentive.

Rooms 49 (2 fmly) (5 GF) **Facilities** Spa STV Wi-fi **Conf** Class 12 Board 12 Thtr 20 **Services** Lift Air con **Parking** 26 **Notes** LB

The Cheltenham Chase Hotel

★★★★ 79% HOTEL

☎ 01452 519988 & 519980 📠 01452 519977
Shurdington Rd, Brockworth GL3 4PB
e-mail: cheltenham@qhotels.co.uk
web: www.qhotels.co.uk
dir: M5 junct 11a onto A417 Cirencester. 1st exit A46 to Stroud, hotel 500yds on left.

Conveniently positioned for Cheltenham, Gloucester, and the M5, this hotel is set in landscaped grounds with ample parking. Bedrooms are spacious with attractive colour schemes and excellent facilities; executive rooms and suites benefit from air conditioning. Public areas include an open-plan bar/lounge, Hardey's restaurant, extensive meeting and functions rooms and a well-equipped leisure club.

Rooms 122 (19 fmly) (44 GF) **S** £64-£104; **D** £74-£114 (incl. bkfst)* **Facilities** Spa STV FTV 🐾 Gym Steam room Xmas New Year Wi-fi **Conf** Class 150 Board 70 Thtr 400 Del from £130 to £160* **Services** Lift Air con **Parking** 240 **Notes** LB ⊗ Civ Wed 344

Mercure Queen's

★★★★ 76% HOTEL

☎ 0870 400 8107 📠 01242 224145
The Promenade GL50 1NN
e-mail: h6632@accor.com
web: www.mercure-uk.com
dir: Follow town centre signs. Left at Montpellier Walk rdbt. Entrance 500mtrs right

With its spectacular position at the top of the main promenade, this landmark hotel is an ideal base from which to explore the charms of this Regency spa town and also the Cotswolds. Bedrooms are very comfortable and include two beautiful four-poster rooms. Smart public rooms include the popular Gold Cup bar and a choice of dining options.

Rooms 79 (5 smoking) **Facilities** STV Xmas New Year Wi-fi **Conf** Class 60 Board 40 Thtr 100 **Services** Lift Air con **Parking** 80 **Notes** LB ⊗ Civ Wed 100

Barceló Cheltenham Park

★★★★ 72% HOTEL

☎ 01242 222021 📠 01242 254880
Cirencester Rd, Charlton Kings GL53 8EA
e-mail: cheltenhampark@barcelo-hotels.co.uk
web: www.barcelo-hotels.co.uk
dir: On A435, 2m SE of Cheltenham near Lilley Brook Golf Course

Located south of Cheltenham, this attractive Georgian property is set in its own landscaped gardens, adjacent to Lilley Brook Golf Course. All the bedrooms whether premium or standard, are spacious and well equipped for both business and leisure guests. The hotel has an impressive health and leisure club with the latest gym equipment plus a pool, steam room and beauty salon; extensive meeting facilities are available. The Lakeside Restaurant serves carefully prepared cuisine.

Rooms 152 (119 annexe) **Facilities** STV 🐾 supervised Gym Beauty treatment rooms Xmas New Year Wi-fi **Conf** Class 180 Board 110 Thtr 320 Del from £90* **Parking** 170 **Notes** ⊗ Civ Wed 100

Thistle Cheltenham   **thistle**

★★★★ 72% HOTEL

☎ 0871 376 9013 ▤ 0871 376 9113
Gloucester Rd GL51 0TS
e-mail: cheltenham@thistle.co.uk
web: www.thistlehotels.com/cheltenham
dir: M5 junct 11/A40 signed Cheltenham, at 1st rdbt take 2nd exit. Hotel immediately on left

Conveniently located for easy access to the M5, this large hotel offers a good range of dining options in addition to extensive leisure facilities. Bedrooms and bathrooms are well equipped and offer good ease of use for both the business and leisure guest. Ample parking and a range of conference rooms are provided.

Rooms 122 (9 fmly) (40 GF) **Facilities** FTV 🕲 ⏛ Gym Sauna Steam room Xmas New Year Wi-fi **Conf** Class 220 Board 45 Thtr 400 Del from £95 to £160* **Services** Lift Air con **Parking** 300 **Notes** Civ Wed 300

The Greenway

★★★ 86% ⑳⑳
COUNTRY HOUSE HOTEL

☎ 01242 862352 ▤ 01242 862780
Shurdington GL51 4UG
e-mail: info@thegreenway.co.uk
web: www.thegreenway.co.uk
dir: From Cheltenham centre 2.5m S on A46

This hotel, with a wealth of history, is peacefully located in a delightful setting within easy reach of the many attractions of the Cotswolds. The Greenway certainly offers something different. The Manor House bedrooms, now refurbished, are luxuriously appointed - traditional in style yet with plasma TVs and internet access. The tranquil Coach House rooms, in a converted stable block, have direct access to the beautiful grounds. The attractive dining room overlooks the sunken garden and is the venue for exciting food, proudly served by dedicated and attentive staff. Von Essen Hotels - AA Hotel Group of the Year 2009-10.

The Greenway

Rooms 21 (10 annexe) (4 fmly) (4 GF) **S** £100-£425; **D** £100-£425 (incl. bkfst)* **Facilities** FTV 🐦 Clay pigeon shooting Horse riding Mountain biking Beauty treatment Archery Xmas New Year Wi-fi **Conf** Class 18 Board 24 Thtr 42 Del from £145 to £190* **Parking** 50 **Notes** LB Civ Wed 45

George Hotel

★★★ 80% ⑳⑳ HOTEL

☎ 01242 235751 ▤ 01242 224359
St Georges Rd GL50 3DZ
e-mail: hotel@stayatthegeorge.co.uk
web: www.stayatthegeorge.co.uk
dir: M5 junct 11 follow town centre signs. At 2nd lights left into Gloucester Rd, past rail station over mini-rdbt. At lights right into St Georges Rd. Hotel 0.75m on left

A genuinely friendly, privately-owned hotel occupying part of a Regency terrace, just two-minutes walk from the town centre. The contemporary interior is elegant and stylish, and the well-equipped, modern bedrooms offer a relaxing haven; individually designed junior suites and deluxe double rooms are available. Lunch or dinner can be enjoyed in a lively atmosphere of Monty's Brasserie, perhaps followed by an evening in the vibrant and sophisticated cocktail bar which hosts live entertainment on Friday and Saturday evenings.

Rooms 31 (1 GF) **D** £110-£175 (incl. bkfst)*
Facilities STV Complimentary membership of local health club Live entertainment at wknds 🎵 Wi-fi **Conf** Class 18 Board 24 Thtr 30 **Parking** 30 **Notes** LB ⊗ RS 24-26 Dec

The Cheltenham Regency Hotel

★★★ 78% ⑳ HOTEL

☎ 01452 713226 & 0845 194 9867 ▤ 01452 857590
Gloucester Rd, Staverton GL51 0ST
e-mail: info@cheltenhamregency.co.uk
dir: M5 junct 11 onto A40 to Cheltenham. Left at rdbt, hotel 1m on left

Refurbished throughout all areas, this hotel now provides high standards of quality and comfort. The large bedrooms, including several suites, are very well equipped and ideal for both the business and leisure guest. A good selection of carefully prepared dishes is available from either the extensive lounge/bar menu or a more formal offering, utilising high quality produce, can be found in the main restaurant.

Rooms 47 (2 fmly) (16 GF) **S** £65-£85; **D** £90-£190 (incl. bkfst) **Facilities** FTV New Year Wi-fi Child facilities **Conf** Class 90 Board 80 Thtr 170 Del from £115 to £195 **Services** Lift Air con **Parking** 120 **Notes** LB ⊗ Civ Wed 140

Charlton Kings

★★★ 74% SMALL HOTEL

☎ 01242 231061 ▤ 01242 241900
London Rd, Charlton Kings GL52 6UU
e-mail: enquiries@charltonkingshotel.co.uk
dir: Enter Cheltenham from Oxford on A40, 1st on left

Personally run by the resident proprietors, the relatively small size of this hotel enables a good deal of individual guest care and attention. Bedrooms are very well decorated and furnished, and include some welcome extras. Breakfast and dinner, served in the comfortable conservatory-style restaurant, offer a good selection of carefully prepared ingredients. There's a pleasant garden and rear car park.

Rooms 13 (4 GF) **S** £65-£85; **D** £95-£115 (incl. bkfst)* **Facilities** STV Wi-fi **Parking** 15 **Notes** LB

CHELTENHAM *continued*

Royal George

★★★ **A** HOTEL

☎ 01452 862506 📄 01452 862277
Birdlip GL4 8JH
e-mail: royalgeorge.birdlip@greeneking.co.uk
web: www.oldenglish.co.uk
dir: M5 junct 11A take A417 towards Cirencester. At Air
Balloon rdbt take 2nd exit then 1st right into Birdlip,
hotel on right.

Rooms 34 (4 fmly) (12 GF) **Facilities** ♫ Xmas
Conf Class 60 Board 40 Thtr 90 **Notes** LB ⊗ Civ Wed 80

Cotswold Grange

★★ 74% HOTEL

☎ 01242 515119 📄 01242 241537
Pittville Circus Rd GL52 2QH
e-mail: info@cotswoldgrange.co.uk
dir: From town centre, follow Prestbury signs. Right at 1st
rdbt, next rdbt straight over

A delightful building located in a quieter, mainly
residential area of Cheltenham, near Pitville Park and
just a short walk to the town centre. The owners have
made some impressive changes here and offer a relaxed
and welcoming atmosphere; there are now many useful
extras such as Wi-fi in the bedrooms. A range of carefully
cooked and presented dishes is served in the comfortable
restaurant.

Rooms 24 (2 fmly) **S** £49-£70; **D** £65-£90 (incl. bkfst)*
Facilities Wi-fi **Conf** Class 24 Board 28 Thtr 50
Del from £99 to £109* **Parking** 20 **Notes** Closed 25 Dec-1
Jan

Travelodge Cheltenham

BUDGET HOTEL

☎ 0871 984 6202 📄 01242 241 748
Golden Valley Roundabout, Hatherley Ln GL51 6PN
web: www.travelodge.co.uk
dir: M5 junct 11 follow signs for Cheltenham. Lodge at
1st rdbt

Travelodge offers good quality, good value, budget
accommodation. All offer family rooms sleeping up to four
(two adults, two children) with en suite bathroom/
shower-room, remote-control TV, tea- and coffee-making
facilities and comfortable beds. Food options vary.
Breakfast is at the on-site Bar Café restaurant (if
available) or to take away. See also Hotel Groups pages.

Rooms 106 **S** fr £29; **D** fr £29

CHIPPING CAMPDEN Map 10 SP13

INSPECTORS' CHOICE

Cotswold House

★★★★ HOTEL

☎ 01386 840330 📄 01386 840310
The Square GL55 6AN
e-mail: reception@cotswoldhouse.com
web: www.cotswoldhouse.com
dir: A44 take B4081 to Chipping Campden. Right at
T-junct into High St. House in The Square

This is at the cutting edge of hotel-keeping, and guests
will find it easy to relax at this mellow Cotswold stone,
town centre establishment. The individually designed
bedrooms, including some spacious suites, are
impressive and offer a beguiling blend of style, quality
and comfort. The restaurant provides a stunning venue
to sample accomplished and imaginative cuisine, with
local produce at the heart of dishes on offer here.
Alternatively, Hicks Brasserie and bar provides a more
informal dining experience.

Rooms 28 (6 annexe) (1 fmly) (4 GF) **S** £150-£650;
D £150-£650 (incl. bkfst)* **Facilities** STV ⚑ Xmas New
Year Wi-fi **Conf** Class 60 Board 40 Thtr 100
Del from £230 to £330* **Parking** 26 **Notes** LB
Civ Wed 96

Three Ways House

★★★ 81% ⊛ HOTEL

☎ 01386 438429 📄 01386 438118
Mickleton GL55 6SB
e-mail: reception@puddingclub.com
web: www.puddingclub.com
dir: In Mickleton centre, on B4632 (Stratford-upon-Avon
to Broadway road)

Built in 1870, this charming hotel has welcomed guests
for over 100 years and is home to the world famous
Pudding Club, formed in 1985 to promote traditional
English puddings. Individuality is a hallmark here, as
reflected in a number of the bedrooms that have been
styled around to a pudding theme. Public areas are
stylish and include the air-conditioned restaurant,
lounges and meeting rooms.

Rooms 48 (7 fmly) (14 GF) **S** £80-£95; **D** £139-£220 (incl.
bkfst) **Facilities** ♫ Xmas New Year Wi-fi **Conf** Class 40
Board 35 Thtr 100 Del from £145 to £155 **Services** Lift
Parking 37 **Notes** LB Civ Wed 100

Noel Arms

★★★ 75% HOTEL

☎ 01386 840317 📄 01386 841136
High St GL55 6AT
e-mail: reception@noelarmshotel.com
web: www.noelarmshotel.com
dir: Off A44 onto B4081 to Chipping Campden, 1st right
down hill into town. Hotel on right opposite Market Hall

This historic 14th-century hotel has a wealth of character
and charm, and retains some of its original features.
Bedrooms are very individual in style, but all have high
levels of comfort and interesting interior design. Such
distinctiveness is also evident throughout the public
areas, which include the popular bar, conservatory lounge
and attractive restaurant.

Rooms 26 (1 fmly) (6 GF) **Facilities** Xmas New Year Wi-fi
Conf Class 40 Board 40 Thtr 80 **Parking** 26
Notes Civ Wed 100

See advert on opposite page

The Kings

◉ RESTAURANT WITH ROOMS

☎ 01386 840256 & 841056 📠 01386 841598
The Square GL55 6AW
e-mail: info@kingscampden.co.uk
dir: In centre of town square

Located in the centre of a delightful Cotswold town, this establishment effortlessly blends a relaxed and friendly welcome with efficient service. Bedrooms and bathrooms come in a range of shapes and sizes but all are appointed to high levels of quality and comfort. Dining options, whether in the main restaurant or the comfortable bar area, include a tempting menu to suit all tastes from lighter salads and pasta to local meats and fish dishes.

Rooms 19 (5 annexe) (2 fmly)

CIRENCESTER Map 5 SP00

Best Western Stratton House

★★★ 79% HOTEL

☎ 01285 651761 📠 01285 640024
Gloucester Rd GL7 2LE
e-mail: stratton.house@forestdale.com
web: www.strattonhousehotel.co.uk
dir: M4 junct 15, A419 to Cirencester. Hotel on left on A417 or M5 junct 11 to Cheltenham onto B4070 to A417. Hotel on right

This attractive 17th-century manor house is quietly situated about half a mile from the town centre. Bedrooms are well presented, and spacious, stylish premier rooms are available. The comfortable drawing rooms and restaurant have views over well-tended gardens - the perfect place to enjoy pre-dinner drinks on a summer evening.

Rooms 39 (9 GF) **S** £66-£105; **D** £91-£145 (incl. bkfst)* **Facilities** FTV Xmas New Year Wi-fi **Conf** Class 50 Board 30 Thtr 150 **Parking** 100 **Notes** Civ Wed 100

The Crown of Crucis

★★★ 73% HOTEL

☎ 01285 851806 📠 01285 851735
Ampney Crucis GL7 5RS
e-mail: reception@thecrownofcrucis.co.uk
web: www.thecrownofcrucis.co.uk
dir: A417 to Fairford, hotel 2.5m on left

This delightful hotel consists of two buildings; one a 16th-century coaching inn, which now houses the bar and restaurant, and a more modern bedroom block which surrounds a courtyard. Rooms are attractively appointed and offer modern facilities; the restaurant serves a range of imaginative dishes.

Rooms 25 (2 fmly) (13 GF) (4 smoking) **S** £60-£72.50; **D** £80-£99 (incl. bkfst)* **Facilities** FTV Wi-fi **Conf** Class 40 Board 25 Thtr 80 Del from £120 to £140* **Parking** 82 **Notes** RS 25-26 Dec & 1 Jan Civ Wed 90

CIRCENCESTER *continued*

Fleece Hotel

THE INDEPENDENTS
HOTEL ASSOCIATION

★★★ 71% HOTEL

☎ 01285 658507 📠 01285 651017
Market Place GL7 2NZ
e-mail: relax@fleecehotel.co.uk
web: www.fleecehotel.co.uk
dir: A417/A419 Burford road junct, follow signs for town
centre. Right at lights into 'The Waterloo', car park
250yds on left

This old, town centre coaching inn, which dates back to
the Tudor period, retains many original features such as
flagstone-floors and oak beams. Well-equipped bedrooms
vary in size and shape, but all offer good levels of comfort
and have plenty of character. The bar lounge is a popular
venue for morning coffee, and the stylish restaurant
offers a range of dishes in an informal and convivial
atmosphere.

Rooms 28 (3 fmly) (4 GF) **S** £59-£88; **D** £79-£114 (incl.
bkfst)* **Facilities** Xmas New Year Wi-fi **Parking** 10

Corinium Hotel & Restaurant

★★ 🅰 HOTEL

☎ 01285 659711 📠 01285 885807
12 Gloucester St GL7 2DG
e-mail: info@coriniumhotel.co.uk
web: www.coriniumhotel.co.uk
dir: From A417/A419/A429 towards Cirencester. A435 at
rdbt. After 500mtrs turn left at lights, then 1st right, car
park on left

Rooms 15 (2 fmly) (2 GF) **S** £59-£65; **D** £75-£119 (incl.
bkfst)* **Facilities** Wi-fi **Parking** 30 **Notes** LB

Travelodge Cirencester

BUDGET HOTEL

☎ 0871 984 6223 📠 01285 655290
Hare Bushes, Burford Rd GL7 5DS
web: www.travelodge.co.uk
dir: M5 junct 12, A417 to Swindon. Lodge at A417/A429
junct

Travelodge offers good quality, good value, budget
accommodation. All offer family rooms sleeping up to four
(two adults, two children) with en suite bathroom/
shower-room, remote-control TV, tea- and coffee-making
facilities and comfortable beds. Food options vary.
Breakfast is at the on-site Bar Café restaurant (if
available) or to take away. See also Hotel Groups pages.

Rooms 43 **S** fr £29; **D** fr £29

CLEARWELL Map 4 SO50

Tudor Farmhouse Hotel & Restaurant

★★★ 75% ◉◉ HOTEL

☎ 01594 833046 📠 01594 837093
High St GL16 8JS
e-mail: info@tudorfarmhousehotel.co.uk
web: www.tudorfarmhousehotel.co.uk
dir: Off A4136 onto B4228, through Coleford, turn right
into Clearwell, hotel on right just before War Memorial
Cross

Dating from the 13th century, this idyllic former
farmhouse retains a host of original features including
exposed stonework, oak beams, wall panelling and
wonderful inglenook fireplaces. Bedrooms have great
individuality and style and are located either within the
main house or in converted buildings in the grounds.
Creative menus offer quality cuisine, served in the
intimate, candlelit restaurant.

Rooms 20 (15 annexe) (3 fmly) (8 GF) **S** £60-£65;
D £90-£170 (incl. bkfst) **Facilities** STV FTV New Year Wi-fi
Conf Class 20 Board 12 Thtr 30 Del from £90 to £92.50
Parking 30 **Notes** LB Closed 24-27 Dec

Wyndham Arms

★★★ 68% ◉ HOTEL

☎ 01594 833666 📠 01594 836450
GL16 8JT
e-mail: nigel@thewyndhamhotel.co.uk
dir: Off B4228, in village centre on B4231

The history of this charming village inn can be traced
back over 600 years. It has exposed stone-walls, original
beams and an impressive inglenook fireplace in the
friendly bar. Most bedrooms are in a modern extension,
whilst rooms in the main house are more traditional in
style. A range of dishes is offered in the bar or restaurant.

Rooms 18 (12 annexe) (3 fmly) (6 GF) **S** £55-£65;
D £80-£115 (incl. bkfst)* **Facilities** Xmas Wi-fi
Conf Class 30 Board 22 Thtr 56 **Parking** 52 **Notes** LB
Civ Wed 80

CLEVE HILL Map 10 SO92

Rising Sun

★★ 🅰 HOTEL

☎ 01242 676281 📠 01242 673069
GL52 3PX
e-mail: 9210@greeneking.co.uk
web: www.oldenglish.co.uk
dir: On B4632, 4m N of Cheltenham

Rooms 24 (3 fmly) (6 GF) **Facilities** ♫ Xmas New Year
Wi-fi **Parking** 70 **Notes** ⊗

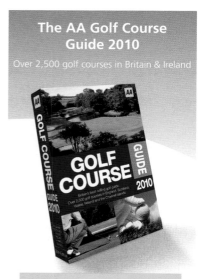

COLEFORD — Map 4 SO51

Speech House

★★★ 66% HOTEL

☎ 01594 822607 ▤ 01594 823658
GL16 7EL
e-mail: info@thespeechhouse.co.uk
dir: M48 junct 2 to Chepstow, A48 to Blakeney, turn left signed Parkend, right, hotel on right

This hotel, dating from the 17th century, is located in the heart of the Forest of Dean, and has plenty of history and character. Bedrooms vary considerably in terms of space, from the larger rooms in the main building to a range of smaller rooms in the adjacent courtyard. The eating options, Verderer's Court and the Freeminer's Restaurant, provide a good selection of carefully prepared ingredients.

Rooms 37 (22 annexe) (3 fmly) (18 GF) S £65-£80;
D £98-£125 (incl. bkfst)* Facilities Xmas New Year Wi-fi
Conf Class 20 Board 20 Thtr 40 Del from £130*
Parking 65 Notes LB Civ Wed

Bells Hotel & The Forest of Dean Golf Club

★★ 71% HOTEL

☎ 01594 832583 ▤ 01594 832584
Lords Hill GL16 8BE
e-mail: enquiries@bells-hotel.co.uk
dir: 0.25m from Coleford. Off B4228

Set in its own grounds, with an 18-hole golf course, this purpose-built establishment offers a range of facilities. Bedrooms vary in style and space, and a number are on the ground floor. There is a small gym, and a comfortable bar and lounge which is available until late. The hotel's club house, just yards away, has a bar with all-day meals and snacks, a restaurant, a games/television room and conference/function rooms.

Bells Hotel & The Forest of Dean Golf Club

Rooms 52 (12 fmly) (35 GF) (3 smoking) Facilities ⚓ 18 ⛳ Putt green Bowling green Short mat bowling room ♫ Xmas New Year Wi-fi Conf Class 250 Board 100 Thtr 350 Del from £75 to £110* Notes Civ Wed 150

COLN ST ALDWYNS — Map 5 SP10

INSPECTORS' CHOICE

New Inn at Coln

★★ ◉◉ HOTEL

☎ 01285 750651 ▤ 01285 750657
GL7 5AN
e-mail: info@thenewinnatcoln.co.uk
web: www.new-inn.co.uk
dir: 8m E of Cirencester, between Bibury & Fairford

This delightful village inn, with origins dating back to the 16th century, has undergone a complete makeover. The stylish, individually designed bedrooms retain original features yet include all the modern amenities such as flat-screen TVs and power showers. The rooms come in a variety of shapes and sizes and display bold, impressive colour schemes. Relaxed and welcoming hospitality mixes easily with efficient service from a dedicated team of staff. Dinner, utilising the best of local produce, is a real treat whether served in the relaxing dining room or, weather permitting, outside on the terrace.

Rooms 13 (5 annexe) (1 fmly) S £60-£160; D £60-£220 (incl. bkfst)* Facilities FTV New Year Wi-fi
Conf Board 10 Del from £80 to £210* Parking 24
Notes LB ⊗

CORSE LAWN — Map 10 SO83

INSPECTORS' CHOICE

Corse Lawn House

★★★ ◉◉ HOTEL

☎ 01452 780771 ▤ 01452 780840
GL19 4LZ
e-mail: enquiries@corselawn.com
web: www.corselawn.com
dir: On B4211 5m SW of Tewkesbury

This gracious Grade II listed Queen Anne house has been home to the Hine family for 31 years. Aided by an enthusiastic and committed team, the family continues to preside over all aspects of the hotel, creating a wonderfully relaxed environment. Bedrooms offer a reassuring mix of comfort and quality. The impressive cuisine is based on excellent produce, much of it locally sourced.

Rooms 19 (2 fmly) (5 GF) S £95-£100; D £150-£170 (incl. bkfst)* Facilities STV ⊗ 🎱 ⛳ Badminton Table tennis New Year Wi-fi Conf Class 30 Board 25 Thtr 50 Parking 62 Notes LB Closed 24-26 Dec Civ Wed 70

See advert on page 214

DUMBLETON — Map 10 SP03

Dumbleton Hall

★★★ 77% HOTEL

☎ 01386 881240 ▤ 01386 882142
WR11 7TS
e-mail: dh@pofr.co.uk
dir: M5 junct 9/A46. 2nd exit at rdbt signed Evesham. Through Beckford for 1m, turn right signed Dumbleton. Hotel at S end of village

Originally constructed in the 16th century, and re-built in the mid-18th century this mansion is set in 19 acres of

continued

DUMBLETON *continued*

landscaped gardens and parkland. Panoramic views of the Vale of Evesham can be seen from every window. Spacious public rooms make this an ideal venue for weddings, conferences or just as a hideaway retreat - its location makes an ideal touring base. The individually designed bedrooms vary in size and layout; one room is adapted for less able guests.

Dumbleton Hall

Rooms 34 (9 fmly) **S** £130; **D** £180-£260 (incl. bkfst) **Facilities** ⚓ Xmas New Year Wi-fi **Conf** Class 60 Board 60 Thtr 100 **Services** Lift **Parking** 60 **Notes** LB Civ Wed 100

FAIRFORD   Map 5 SP10

Bull Hotel

★★ 68% HOTEL

☎ 01285 712535 & 712217 🖹 01285 713782
The Market Place GL7 4AA
e-mail: info@thebullhotelfairford.co.uk
dir: On A417 in market square adjacent to post office

Located in a picturesque Cotswold market town, this family-run inn dates back to the 15th century and still retains much period character and charm. A wide range of meals can be enjoyed in the popular bar or alternatively in the bistro restaurant. Bedrooms are individual in style and a number overlook the square.

Rooms 26 (4 annexe) (4 fmly) (2 GF) **S** £55-£70; **D** £81-£100 (incl. bkfst) **Facilities** FTV Fishing Cycle hire Horse riding New Year Wi-fi **Conf** Class 40 Board 40 Thtr 60 **Parking** 10 **Notes** LB

FALFIELD   Map 4 ST69

Best Western The Gables

★★★ 74% HOTEL

☎ 01454 260502 🖹 01454 261821
Bristol Rd GL12 8DL
e-mail: mail@thegablesbristol.co.uk
web: www.thegablesbristol.co.uk
dir: M5 junct 14 N'bound. Left at end of sliproad. Right onto A38, hotel 300yds on right

Conveniently located, just a few minutes from the motorway this establishment is ideally suited to both business and leisure guests, with easy access to Cheltenham, Gloucester, Bristol and Bath. Bedrooms are spacious and well equipped. Relaxing public areas consist of a light and airy bar and restaurant where meals and all-day snacks are available; a more formal restaurant is open for dinner. There is also a range of meeting rooms.

Rooms 46 (4 fmly) (18 GF) **Facilities** STV Wi-fi **Conf** Class 90 Board 50 Thtr 200 **Parking** 104 **Notes** ⊗ Civ Wed 150

GLOUCESTER   Map 10 SO81

Hatherley Manor

★★★ 80% HOTEL

☎ 01452 730217 🖹 01452 731032
Down Hatherley Ln GL2 9QA
e-mail: reservations@hatherleymanor.com
web: www.hatherleymanor.com
dir: Off A38 into Down Hatherley Lane, signed. Hotel 600yds on left

Within easy striking distance of the M5, Gloucester, Cheltenham and the Cotswolds, this stylish 17th-century manor, set in attractive grounds, remains popular with both business and leisure guests. Bedrooms are well appointed and offer contemporary comforts. A particularly impressive range of meeting and function rooms is available.

Rooms 50 (5 fmly) (18 GF) **S** £64-£245; **D** £64-£255 **Facilities** FTV Xmas New Year Wi-fi **Conf** Class 90 Board 75 Thtr 400 Del from £137 to £157 **Parking** 250 **Notes** LB Civ Wed 300

Ramada Bowden Hall Gloucester

★★★ 80% COUNTRY HOUSE HOTEL

☎ 0844 815 9077 🖹 01452 611885
Bondend Ln, Upton St Leonards GL4 8ED
e-mail: sales.bowdenhall@ramadajarvis.co.uk
web: www.ramadajarvis.co.uk/bowdenhall
dir: A417/A38/Gloucester. At rdbt take 2nd exit. At 2nd lights left onto Abbeymead Ave (becomes Metz Way). 1.5m, 3rd left onto Upton Lane, left into Bondend Rd, then left into Bondend Lane. Hotel at end

Conveniently located, a short distance from the M5, this country hotel is set in delightful grounds and is an ideal venue for weddings, banquets and meetings, or for a quiet country break. Bedrooms are spacious and well appointed and many have lovely views of the grounds. There is a treatment and leisure facility and guests can choose to dine in the restaurant or bar.

Rooms 72 (21 fmly) **S** £65-£300; **D** £75-£350 (incl. bkfst) **Facilities** 🏊 supervised ⬆ 18 ⛳ Gym Trimnasium Beauty therapy wknds New Year Wi-fi **Conf** Class 70 Board 30 Thtr 120 **Parking** 150 **Notes** LB ⊗ Civ Wed 120

Holiday Inn Gloucester-Cheltenham

★★★ 78% HOTEL

☎ 0870 400 9034 🖹 01452 371036
Crest Way, Barnwood GL4 3RX
e-mail: reservations-gloucester@ihg.com
web: www.holidayinn.co.uk
dir: A40 to Gloucester. At rdbt take 2nd exit signed A417/ Cirencester. At next rdbt take 2nd exit then 1st left

This hotel is conveniently located close to the M5, and within easy driving distance of both Gloucester and Cheltenham. Bedrooms vary in size from the larger, well-equipped executive rooms to smaller style standard doubles. A good selection of dining options is available in either the lounge/bar, the relaxing restaurant or via room service. Guests can also enjoy the well-equipped leisure facilities.

Rooms 125 (19 fmly) (62 GF) (6 smoking) **Facilities** Spa STV FTV 🏊 Gym Dance studio Wi-fi **Conf** Class 65 Board 50 Thtr 120 **Services** Air con **Parking** 180 **Notes** ⊗ Civ Wed 120

Hatton Court

★★★ 71% HOTEL

☎ 01452 617412 📠 01452 612945
Upton Hill, Upton St Leonards GL4 8DE
e-mail: res@hatton-court.co.uk
web: www.hatton-court.co.uk
dir: From Gloucester on B4073 Painswick Rd. Hotel at top of hill on right

Built in the style of a 17th-century Cotswold manor house, and set in seven acres of well-kept gardens this hotel is popular with both business and leisure guests. It stands at the top of Upton Hill and commands truly spectacular views of the Severn Valley. Bedrooms are comfortable and tastefully furnished with many extra facilities. The elegant Carringtons Restaurant offers a varied choice of menus, and there is also a traditionally furnished bar and foyer lounge.

Rooms 45 (28 annexe) **S** £55-£120; **D** £55-£120
Facilities STV FTV 🎣 Gym Xmas New Year Wi-fi
Conf Class 30 Board 30 Thtr 60 Del from £119 to £149
Parking 80 **Notes** LB ⊗ No children 7yrs Civ Wed 80

Ramada Gloucester Hotel and Country Club

★★★ 70% HOTEL

☎ 0844 815 9044 📠 01452 307212
Matson Ln, Robinswood Hill GL4 6EA
e-mail: sales.gloucester@ramadajarvis.co.uk
web: www.ramadajarvis.co.uk
dir: A40 towards Gloucester onto A38. 1st exit at 4th rdbt (Painswick Rd). Right onto Matson Lane

Conveniently located close to the M5, this large hotel is set in 240 acres of grounds. Bedrooms are comfortably appointed for both business and leisure guests.

Rooms 97 (7 fmly) (20 GF) **S** £59-£140; **D** £59-£140
Facilities Spa 🔄 supervised ⚓ 18 ⛳ Putt green Gym Squash Dry ski slopes Driving range Xmas New Year Wi-fi
Conf Class 120 Board 60 Thtr 180 Del from £99 to £150
Parking 200 **Notes** LB Civ Wed 140

Travelodge Gloucester

BUDGET HOTEL

☎ 0871 984 6410
St Ann Way GL1 5SF
dir: From A38 take 2nd exit onto Eastern Ave, right into Metz Way (A4302), left into Bruton Way (A430). Leads onto Saint Ann's Way, left & lodge on left

Travelodge offers good quality, good value, budget accommodation. All offer family rooms sleeping up to four (two adults, two children) with en suite bathroom/shower-room, remote-control TV, tea- and coffee-making facilities and comfortable beds. Food options vary. Breakfast is at the on-site Bar Café restaurant (if available) or to take away. See also the Hotel Groups pages.

Rooms 96 **S** fr £29; **D** fr £29

LOWER SLAUGHTER   **Map 10 SP12**

INSPECTORS' CHOICE

Lower Slaughter Manor

★★★ ⚛⚛⚛
COUNTRY HOUSE HOTEL

☎ 01451 820456 📠 01451 822150
GL54 2HP
e-mail: info@lowerslaughterter.co.uk
web: www.lowerslaughter.co.uk
dir: Off A429 signed 'The Slaughters'. Manor 0.5m on right on entering village

There is a timeless elegance about this wonderful manor, which dates back to the 17th century. Its imposing presence makes it very much the centrepiece of this famous Cotswold village. Inside, the levels of comfort and quality are immediately evident, with crackling log fires warming the many sumptuous lounges. The dining room is an elegant creation that suitably complements the excellent cuisine on offer. Spacious and tastefully furnished bedrooms are either in the main building or in the adjacent coach house. Von Essen Hotels - AA Hotel Group of the Year 2009-10.

Rooms 19 (8 annexe) (4 GF) **S** £230-£850;
D £230-£850 (incl. bkfst)* **Facilities** FTV 🍸 🎣 Xmas New Year Wi-fi **Conf** Class 20 Board 22 Thtr 36 **Parking** 30 **Notes** LB ⊗ Civ Wed 70

Washbourne Court

★★★ 88% ⚛⚛ HOTEL

☎ 01451 822143 📠 01451 821045
GL54 2HS
e-mail: info@washbournecourt.co.uk
web: www.vonessenhotels.co.uk
dir: Exit A429 at 'The Slaughters' sign, between Stow-on-the-Wold & Bourton-on-the-Water. Hotel in village centre

Beamed ceilings, log fires and flagstone floors are some of the attractive features of this part 17th-century hotel, set in four acres of immaculate grounds beside the River Eye. The hotel has undergone a stylish, elegant contemporary refurbishment and boasts stunning bedrooms with up-to-the-minute technology and marble bathrooms. Dining, whether in the restaurant or bar is memorable and utilises fine local produce. Von Essen Hotels - AA Hotel Group of the Year 2009-10.

Rooms 30 (9 GF) **S** £135-£225; **D** £135-£350 (incl. bkfst)* **Facilities** FTV Xmas New Year Wi-fi **Conf** Class 40 Board 30 Thtr 70 Del from £170 to £260* **Parking** 40 **Notes** LB Civ Wed 60

MICHAEL WOOD   **Map 4 ST79**
MOTORWAY SERVICE AREA (M5)

Days Inn Michaelwood

BUDGET HOTEL

☎ 01454 261513 📠 01454 269150
Michael Wood Service Area, Lower Wick GL11 6DD
e-mail: michaelwood.hotel@welcomebreak.co.uk
web: www.welcomebreak.co.uk
dir: M5 N'bound between junct 13 & 14

This modern building offers accommodation in smart, spacious and well-equipped bedrooms, suitable for families and business travellers, and all with en suite bathrooms. Continental breakfast is available and other refreshments may be taken at the nearby family restaurant. See also the Hotel Groups pages.

Rooms 38 (34 fmly) **S** £29-£49; **D** £39-£69*
Conf Board 10

MORETON-IN-MARSH — Map 10 SP23

Manor House

★★★★ 75% ⑱⑱ HOTEL

☎ 01608 650501 📠 01608 651481
High St GL56 0LJ
e-mail: info@manorhousehotel.info
web: www.cotswold-inns-hotels.co.uk/manor
dir: Off A429 at south end of town. Take East St off High St, hotel car park 3rd on right

Dating back to the 16th century, this charming Cotswold coaching inn retains much of its original character with stone walls, impressive fireplaces and a relaxed, country-house atmosphere. Bedrooms vary in size and reflect the individuality of the building; all are well equipped and some are particularly opulent. Comfortable public areas include a popular bar, a newly added brasserie and the stylish Mulberry Restaurant where dinner should not be missed.

Rooms 35 (1 annexe) (3 fmly) (1 GF) **Facilities** Xmas New Year Wi-fi **Conf** Class 48 Board 54 Thtr 120 **Services** Lift **Parking** 24 **Notes** Civ Wed 120

Redesdale Arms

★★★ 78% ⑱ HOTEL

☎ 01608 650308 📠 01608 651843
High St GL56 0AW
e-mail: info@redesdalearms.com
dir: On A429, 0.5m from rail station

This fine old inn has played a central role in the town for centuries. Traditional features combine successfully with contemporary comforts; bedrooms are located in the main building and in an annexe. Guests can choose from an imaginative menu in either in the stylish restaurant or the conservatory.

Rooms 24 (16 annexe) (2 fmly) (5 GF) **S** £65-£85; **D** £85-£140 (incl. bkfst)* **Facilities** FTV Xmas New Year Wi-fi **Parking** 14 **Notes** LB ⊗

NAILSWORTH — Map 4 ST89

Egypt Mill

★★ 76% HOTEL

☎ 01453 833449 📠 01453 839919
GL6 0AE
e-mail: reception@egyptmill.com
dir: on A46, midway between Cheltenham & Bath

Millstones and working waterwheels have been incorporated in the innovative design of this 17th-century former corn mill. Well-equipped bedrooms are located in two adjacent buildings and are tastefully furnished. Facilities include the stylish cellar bar and convivial bistro, where accomplished cuisine proves very popular. During summer months the riverside patios and gardens are great places to enjoy a drink.

Rooms 28 (18 annexe) (2 fmly) (2 GF) **Facilities** ↯ Boules pitch Xmas **Conf** Class 80 Board 80 Thtr 100 **Parking** 80 **Notes** LB ⊗ Civ Wed 120

Heavens Above

⑱⑱ RESTAURANT WITH ROOMS

☎ 01453 832615
3 Cossack Square GL6 0DB
e-mail: info@wild-garlic.co.uk
dir: M4 junt 18. A46 towards Stroud. Enter Nailsworth, turn left at rdbt and then an immediate left. Restaurant opposite Britannia Pub

Situated in a quiet corner of this charming Cotswold town, this restaurant with rooms offers a delightful combination of welcoming and relaxed hospitality with high quality cuisine. Bedrooms are located above the restaurant and are spacious and well equipped. A small and friendly team of staff ensure guests are very well looked after throughout their stay.

Rooms 3 (2 fmly)

NEWENT — Map 10 SO72

Three Choirs Vineyards

⑱⑱ RESTAURANT WITH ROOMS

☎ 01531 890223 📠 01531 890877
GL18 1LS
e-mail: info@threechoirs.com
web: www.threechoirs.com
dir: On B4215 N of Newent, follow brown tourist signs

This thriving vineyard continues to go from strength to strength and provides a wonderfully different place to stay. The restaurant, which overlooks the 100-acre estate, enjoys a popular following thanks to well-executed dishes that make good use of local produce. Spacious, high quality bedrooms are equipped with many extras, and each opens on to a private patio area from where wonderful views can be enjoyed.

Rooms 11 (11 annexe) (1 fmly)

OLD SODBURY — Map 4 ST78

Cross Hands

★★ 🅰 HOTEL

☎ 01454 313000 📠 01454 324409
BS37 6RJ
e-mail: 6435@greeneking.co.uk
web: www.crosshandshotel.com
dir: M4 junct 18 signed to Cirencester/Stroud on A46. After 1.5m hotel on left at 1st lights

Rooms 21 (1 fmly) (9 GF) **Facilities** Xmas **Conf** Class 40 Board 50 Thtr 100 **Parking** 120 **Notes** Civ Wed 80

RANGEWORTHY
Map 4 ST68

Rangeworthy Court
★★ 71% HOTEL

☎ 01454 228347 📄 01454 228945
Church Ln, Wotton Rd BS37 7ND
e-mail: reception@rangeworthycourt.com
dir: Signed from B4058. Hotel at end of Church Lane

This welcoming manor house hotel is peacefully located in its own grounds, and is within easy reach of the motorway network. The character bedrooms come in a variety of sizes and there is a choice of comfortable lounges in which to enjoy a drink before dinner. The relaxing restaurant offers a selection of carefully prepared, enjoyable dishes.

Rooms 13 (4 fmly) **S** £82.25; **D** £99.87 (incl. bkfst)*
Facilities FTV ⚡ Wi-fi **Conf** Class 14 Board 16 Thtr 22 Del from £115 to £150* **Parking** 30 **Notes** Closed 24-30 Dec Civ Wed 50

SEVERN VIEW MOTORWAY SERVICE AREA (M48)
Map 4 ST58

Travelodge Bristol Severn View (M48)
BUDGET HOTEL

☎ 0871 984 6052 📄 01454 632482
M48 Motorway, Severn Bridge BS35 4BH
web: www.travelodge.co.uk
dir: M48 junct 1

Travelodge offers good quality, good value, budget accommodation. All offer family rooms sleeping up to four (two adults, two children) with en suite bathroom/shower-room, remote-control TV, tea- and coffee-making facilities and comfortable beds. Food options vary. Breakfast is at the on-site Bar Café restaurant (if available) or to take away. See also Hotel Groups pages.

Rooms 50 **S** fr £29; **D** fr £29

SOUTH CERNEY
Map 5 SU09

Cotswold Water Park Four Pillars Hotel

★★★★ 76% HOTEL

☎ 0800 374692 & 01285 864000 📄 01285 864001
Lake 6 Spine Road East GL7 5FP
e-mail: waterpark@four-pillars.co.uk
web: www.cotswoldwaterpark.co.uk
dir: Off A419, 3m from Cirencester

This impressive hotel has well-appointed bedrooms and suites, conference facilities for up to 800 delegates, a spa with an 11-metre pool, a gym, a hydro pool and treatment rooms. An excellent range of dining options is available. A large car park is provided.

Rooms 219 (29 fmly) (115 GF) **S** £70-£119; **D** £70-£133*
Facilities Spa STV ⚡ Fishing Gym Treatment rooms & therapies Steam room Sauna Xmas New Year Wi-fi **Conf** Class 144 Board 34 Thtr 360 Del from £125 to £185* **Services** Lift **Parking** 200 **Notes** ⊗ Civ Wed 320

STONEHOUSE
Map 4 SO80

Stonehouse Court
★★★ 79% ⊛ HOTEL

☎ 0871 871 3240 & 01453 794 950 📄 0871 871 3241
GL10 3RA
e-mail: info@stonehousecourt.co.uk
dir: M5 junct 13, off A419. Follow signs for Stonehouse, hotel on right 0.25m after 2nd rdbt

Set in six acres of secluded gardens, this Grade II listed manor house dates back to 1601. Bedrooms, including some stylish feature rooms, vary in size and design. Elegant public areas include a lounge, bar and small gym. Guests have the choice of fine dining in Henry's

Restaurant or of choosing lighter, informal eating in the lounge. Extensive conference facilities are available.

Rooms 36 (27 annexe) (2 fmly) (6 GF) **Facilities** ⚡ Gym ♪ Xmas New Year Wi-fi **Conf** Class 75 Board 70 Thtr 150 **Parking** 200 **Notes** LB Civ Wed 150

Travelodge Stonehouse
BUDGET HOTEL

☎ 0871 984 6054 📄 01453 828590
A419, Easington GL10 3SQ
web: www.travelodge.co.uk
dir: M5 junct 13, onto A419

Travelodge offers good quality, good value, budget accommodation. All offer family rooms sleeping up to four (two adults, two children) with en suite bathroom/shower-room, remote-control TV, tea- and coffee-making facilities and comfortable beds. Food options vary. Breakfast is at the on-site Bar Café restaurant (if available) or to take away. See also Hotel Groups pages.

Rooms 40 **S** fr £29; **D** fr £29

STOW-ON-THE-WOLD
Map 10 SP12

Fosse Manor
★★★ 80% ⊛⊛ HOTEL

☎ 01451 830354 📄 01451 832486
GL54 1JX
e-mail: enquiries@fossemanor.co.uk
web: www.fossemanor.co.uk
dir: 1m S on A429, 300yds past junct with A424

Deriving its name from the historic Roman Fosse Way, this popular hotel is ideally situated for exploring the many delights of this picturesque area. Bedrooms, located both in the main building and the adjacent coach house, offer high standards of comfort and quality. Public areas include a small lounge, spacious bar and light and airy restaurant. Classy cuisine is on offer with quality produce used to create imaginative dishes.

Rooms 19 (8 annexe) (3 fmly) (5 GF) **S** £95; **D** £99-£230 (incl. bkfst)* **Facilities** FTV ⚡ Xmas New Year Wi-fi **Conf** Class 20 Board 26 Thtr 60 Del from £125 to £155* **Parking** 30 **Notes** LB ⊗

STOW-ON-THE-WOLD *continued*

Stow Lodge

★★★ 75% SMALL HOTEL

☎ 01451 830485 📄 01451 831671
The Square GL54 1AB
e-mail: enquiries@stowlodge.com
web: www.stowlodge.com
dir: in town centre

Situated in smart grounds, this family-run hotel has direct access to the market square and provides high standards of customer care. Bedrooms are offered both within the main building and in the converted coach house, all of which provide similar standards of homely comfort. Extensive menus and an interesting wine list make for an enjoyable dining experience.

Rooms 21 (10 annexe) (1 fmly) **Parking** 30 **Notes** LB ⊗ No children 5yrs Closed Xmas-end Jan

The Royalist

★★★ 74% ⊛⊛ HOTEL

☎ 01451 830670 & 832412 📄 01451 870048
Digbeth St GL54 1BN
e-mail: stay@theroyalisthotel.com
web: www.theroyalisthotel.com
dir: Off A436

Verified as the oldest inn in England, this charming hotel has a wealth of history and character. Bedrooms and public areas have been stylishly and sympathetically decorated to ensure high levels of comfort at every turn. Some rooms are in an adjoining annexe. There are two eating options: the restaurant offers high-quality cooking and the Eagle and Child provides a more informal alternative.

Rooms 14 (4 annexe) (1 fmly) (2 GF) **S** £55-£110; **D** £80-£160 (incl. bkfst)* **Facilities** FTV Xmas New Year Wi-fi **Parking** 8 **Notes** LB Civ Wed

Old Stocks

★★ 71% SMALL HOTEL

☎ 01451 830666 📄 01451 870014
The Square GL54 1AF
e-mail: aa@oldstockshotel.co.uk
web: www.oldstockshotel.co.uk
dir: Exit A429 to town centre. Hotel facing village green

Overlooking the old market square, this Grade II listed, mellow Cotswold-stone building is a comfortable and friendly base from which to explore this picturesque area. There's lots of character throughout, and the bedrooms offer individuality and charm. Facilities include a guest lounge, restaurant and bar, whilst outside, the patio is a popular summer venue for refreshing drinks and good food.

Rooms 18 (3 annexe) (5 fmly) (4 GF) **S** £35-£55; **D** £70-£130 (incl. bkfst) **Facilities** New Year Wi-fi **Parking** 12 **Notes** LB

STROUD   Map 4 SO80

Burleigh Court

★★★ 79% ⊛⊛ HOTEL

☎ 01453 883804 📄 01453 886870
Burleigh, Minchinhampton GL5 2PF
e-mail: burleighcourt@aol.com
dir: From Stroud A419 towards Cirencester. Right after 2.5m signed Burleigh & Minchinhampton. Left after 500yds signed Burleigh Court. Hotel 300yds on right

Dating back to the 18th century, this former gentleman's manor house is in a secluded yet accessible elevated position with some wonderful countryside views. Public rooms are elegantly styled and include an oak-panelled bar for pre-dinner drinks beside a crackling fire. Combining comfort and quality, no two bedrooms are the same; some are in an adjoining coach house.

Rooms 18 (2 fmly) (3 GF) **S** £85-£105; **D** £130-£190 (incl. bkfst)* **Facilities** ↘ ⚑ New Year Wi-fi **Conf** Class 30 Board 30 Thtr 50 **Parking** 40 **Notes** LB Civ Wed 50

The Bear of Rodborough

COTSWOLD INNS & HOTELS

★★★ 77% HOTEL

☎ 01453 878522 📄 01453 872523
Rodborough Common GL5 5DE
e-mail: info@bearofrodborough.info
web: www.cotswold-inns-hotels.co.uk
dir: M5 junct 13, A419 to Stroud. Follow signs to Rodborough. Up hill, left at top at T-junct. Hotel on right

This popular 17th-century coaching inn is situated high above Stroud within acres of National Trust parkland. Character abounds in the lounges and cocktail bar, and in the Box Tree Restaurant where the cuisine utilises fresh local produce. Bedrooms offer equal measures of comfort and style with plenty of extra touches. There is also a traditional and well-patronised public bar.

Rooms 46 (2 fmly) **Facilities** STV Putt green ⛳ Xmas New Year Wi-fi **Conf** Class 35 Board 30 Thtr 60 **Parking** 70 **Notes** Civ Wed 70

TETBURY   Map 4 ST89

INSPECTORS' CHOICE

Calcot Manor
★★★★ ◎◎ HOTEL

☎ 01666 890391   📠 01666 890394
Calcot GL8 8YJ
e-mail: reception@calcotmanor.co.uk
web: www.calcotmanor.co.uk
dir: 3m West of Tetbury at junct A4135/A46

Cistercian monks built the ancient barns and stables around which this lovely English farmhouse is set. No two rooms are identical, and each is beautifully decorated in a variety of styles and equipped with the contemporary comforts. Sumptuous sitting rooms, with crackling log fires in the winter, look out over immaculate gardens. There are two dining options: the elegant conservatory restaurant and the informal Gumstool Inn. There are also ample function rooms. A superb health and leisure spa includes an indoor pool, high-tech gym, massage tables, complementary therapies and much more. For children, a supervised crèche and 'playzone' are a great attraction.

Rooms 35 (23 annexe) (13 fmly) (17 GF) **S** £207-£247; **D** £230-£430 (incl. bkfst)* **Facilities** Spa STV ⬚ ⬚ ⛳ Gym Clay pigeon shooting Archery Xmas New Year Wi-fi Child facilities **Conf** Class 40 Board 35 Thtr 120 **Parking** 150 **Notes** LB ⊗ Civ Wed 100

Hare & Hounds
★★★ 77% HOTEL

COTSWOLD INNS & HOTELS

☎ 01666 880233 & 881000   📠 01666 880241
Westonbirt GL8 8QL
e-mail: enquiries@hareandhoundshotel.com
web: www.cotswold-inns-hotels.co.uk
dir: 2.5m SW of Tetbury on A433

This popular hotel, set in extensive grounds, is situated close to Westonbirt Arboretum and has remained under the same ownership for over 50 years. Bedrooms are individual in style; those in the main house are more traditional and the stylish cottage rooms are contemporary in design. Public rooms include the informal bar and light, airy lounges - one with a log fire

in colder months. Guests can eat either in the bar or the attractive restaurant.

Hare & Hounds

Rooms 45 (21 annexe) (8 fmly) (13 GF) **Facilities** FTV ⬚ Putt green ⛳ Xmas New Year Wi-fi **Conf** Class 80 Board 40 Thtr 120 **Parking** 85 **Notes** Civ Wed 200

The Priory Inn
★★★ 74% SMALL HOTEL

☎ 01666 502251   📠 01666 503534
London Rd GL8 8JJ
e-mail: info@theprioryinn.co.uk
web: www.theprioryinn.co.uk
dir: on A433 (Cirencester to Tetbury road). Hotel 200yds from Market Square

A warm welcome is assured at this attractive inn where friendly service is a high priority to the team. Public areas and bedrooms have a contemporary style that mixes well with more traditional features, such as an open fireplace in the cosy bar dining room. Cuisine is a highlight of any stay, with locally sourced produce skilfully prepared; an excellent menu choice is available that will suit all tastes.

Rooms 14 (1 fmly) (4 GF) (4 smoking) **Facilities** STV Health & beauty centre 🎵 Xmas New Year Wi-fi Child facilities **Conf** Class 28 Board 28 Thtr 30 **Parking** 35 **Notes** LB ⊗

Snooty Fox
★★★ 74% SMALL HOTEL

☎ 01666 502436   📠 01666 503479
Market Place GL8 8DD
e-mail: res@snooty-fox.co.uk
web: www.snooty-fox.co.uk
dir: In town centre

Centrally situated this 16th-century coaching inn retains original features and is a popular venue for weekend breaks. The relaxed and friendly atmosphere, the high standard of accommodation, and the food offered in the bar and restaurant, are all very good reasons why many guests return here time and again.

Rooms 12 **S** £90-£130; **D** £100-£140 (incl. bkfst)* **Facilities** Xmas New Year **Conf** Class 12 Board 16 Thtr 24 **Notes** LB

Ormond at Tetbury
★★★ 66% HOTEL

☎ 01666 505690   📠 01666 505956
23 Long St GL8 8AA
e-mail: info@theormond.co.uk
dir: Turn off A433 from Cirencester into Long St. Hotel approx 100yds on left

Located on the main street of this charming town, The Ormond provides a choice of individually styled and comfortably furnished bedrooms in a variety of shapes and sizes. The ambience is relaxed and friendly, and guests may chose to dine in either the popular bar area or in the adjoining restaurant. In warmer weather, a range of outdoor seating is available in the courtyard.

Rooms 15 (3 fmly) **Facilities** FTV Xmas New Year Wi-fi Child facilities **Conf** Class 20 Board 20 Thtr 40 **Notes** ⊗

Hunters Hall
★★ Ⓐ SMALL HOTEL

☎ 01453 860393   📠 01453 860707
Kingscote GL8 8XZ
e-mail: huntershall.kingscote@greeneking.co.uk
web: www.oldenglish.co.uk
dir: M4 junct 18, take A46 towards Stroud. In 10m left signed Kingscote, to T-junct, left, hotel 0.5m on left

Rooms 12 (12 annexe) (1 fmly) (8 GF) **Facilities** Pool table Xmas Child facilities **Conf** Class 12 Board 20 Thtr 30 **Parking** 100 **Notes** LB

TEWKESBURY   Map 10 SO83

Bell
★★ Ⓐ HOTEL

☎ 01684 293293   📠 01684 295938
52 Church St GL20 5SA
e-mail: 6408@greeneking.co.uk
web: www.oldenglish.co.uk
dir: M5 junct 9, follow brown tourist signs for Tewkesbury Abbey, hotel directly opposite Abbey

Rooms 24 (1 fmly) (4 GF) **S** £49; **D** £49 (incl. bkfst)* **Facilities** Xmas New Year Wi-fi **Conf** Class 16 Board 24 Thtr 60 **Parking** 20

INSPECTORS' CHOICE

Thornbury Castle
★★★ ◎◎ HOTEL

☎ 01454 281182 📠 01454 416188
Castle St BS35 1HH
e-mail: info@thornburycastle.co.uk
web: www.thornburycastle.co.uk
dir: on A38 N'bound from Bristol take 1st turn to
Thornbury. At end of High St left into Castle St, follow
brown sign, entrance to Castle on left behind St Mary's
Church

Henry VIII ordered the first owner of this castle to be
beheaded! Guests today have the opportunity of
sleeping in historical surroundings fitted out with all
the modern amenities. Most rooms have four-poster or
coronet beds and real fires. Tranquil lounges enjoy
views over the gardens, while elegant, wood-panelled
dining rooms make memorable settings for a leisurely
award-winning meal. Von Essen Hotels - AA Hotel
Group of the Year 2009-10.

Rooms 27 (3 fmly) (4 GF) **Facilities** STV FTV 🏊 Archery
Helicopter ride Clay pigeon shooting Massage
treatment Xmas New Year Wi-fi **Conf** Class 40 Board 30
Thtr 70 **Parking** 50 **Notes** LB Civ Wed 70

Thornbury Golf Lodge
★★ 71% HOTEL

☎ 01454 281144 📠 01454 281177
Bristol Rd BS35 3XL
e-mail: info@thornburygc.co.uk
web: www.thornburygc.co.uk
dir: M5 junct 16, A38 towards Thornbury. At lights
(Berkeley Vale Motors) turn left. Hotel entrance 1m on left

The old farmhouse exterior of Thornbury Golf Lodge
disguises an interior with spacious, well equipped and
comfortable bedrooms. Many have pleasant views over
the centre's two golf courses or towards the Severn
Estuary. Meals are taken in the adjacent clubhouse which
has a full bar and serves a range of hot and cold food all
through the day.

Rooms 11 (7 GF) **Facilities** STV ⚓ 36 Putt green
Conf Class 40 Board 40 Thtr 100 **Parking** 150 **Notes** LB
⊗ No children 5yrs Closed 25 Dec

INSPECTORS' CHOICE

Lords of the Manor
★★★★ ◎◎◎ COUNTRY HOUSE HOTEL

☎ 01451 820243 📠 01451 820696
GL54 2JD
e-mail: enquiries@lordsofthemanor.com
web: www.lordsofthemanor.com
dir: 2m W of A429. Turn off A40 onto A429, take 'The
Slaughters' turn. Through Lower Slaughter for 1m to
Upper Slaughter. Hotel on right

This wonderfully welcoming 17th-century manor house
hotel sits in eight acres of gardens and parkland
surrounded by Cotswold countryside. A relaxed
atmosphere, underpinned by professional and attentive
service is the hallmark here, so that guests are often
reluctant to leave. The hotel has elegant public rooms
that overlook the immaculate lawns, and the
restaurant is the venue for consistently impressive
cuisine. Bedrooms have much character and charm,
combined with the extra touches expected of a hotel of
this stature.

Rooms 26 (4 fmly) (9 GF) **S** £191; **D** £191-£362 (incl.
bkfst)* **Facilities** FTV Fishing 🏊 Xmas New Year Wi-fi
Conf Class 20 Board 20 Thtr 30 Del from £170 to
£210* **Parking** 40 **Notes** LB Civ Wed 50

Wesley House

RESTAURANT WITH ROOMS

☎ 01242 602366 📠 01242 609046
High St GL54 5LJ
e-mail: enquiries@wesleyhouse.co.uk
web: www.wesleyhouse.co.uk
dir: In town centre

This 15th-century, half-timbered property is named after John Wesley, founder of the Methodist Church, who stayed here while preaching in the town. Bedrooms are small but full of character. In the rear dining room, a unique lighting system changes colour to suit the mood required, and to highlight the various floral creations by a world-renowned flower arranger. A glass atrium covers the outside terrace.

Rooms 5

Tortworth Court Four Pillars

★★★★ 74% HOTEL

☎ 0800 374 692 & 01454 263000 📠 01454 263001
Tortworth GL12 8HH
e-mail: tortworth@four-pillars.co.uk
web: www.four-pillars.co.uk/tortworth
dir: M5 junct 14, B4509 towards Wotton. 1st right into Tortworth Rd next right, hotel 0.5m on right

Set within 30 acres of parkland, this Gothic mansion displays original features cleverly combined with contemporary additions. Elegant public rooms include a choice of dining options, one housed within the library, another in the atrium and the third in the orangery. Bedrooms are well equipped, and additional facilities include a host of conference rooms and a leisure centre.

Tortworth Court Four Pillars

Rooms 189 (80 GF) **S** £79-£136; **D** £85-£164*
Facilities Spa FTV Gym Beauty suite Steam room Sauna Xmas New Year Wi-fi **Conf** Class 200 Board 80 Thtr 400 Del from £135 to £189* **Services** Lift **Parking** 350 **Notes** Civ Wed 120

Park

★★ 71% HOTEL

☎ 01454 260550 📠 01454 269255
Whitfield GL12 8DR
e-mail: info@parkhotelfalfield.co.uk
web: www.parkhotelfalfield.co.uk
dir: M5 junct 14, A38, through Falfield. Hotel on left in 0.5m

Not far from the A38 and with easy access to the M5, this family-run hotel offers friendly service. Bedrooms, which vary in size, are located either in the main house or in the cottage annexe, just yards away. There is an informal bar where drinks and bar meals are served, and dinner, featuring homemade dishes, is available in the pleasant restaurant. The garden may be enjoyed during the warmer weather.

Rooms 18 (7 annexe) (2 fmly) (3 GF) **S** £47; **D** £80 (incl. bkfst)* **Facilities** Xmas New Year Wi-fi **Conf** Class 60 Board 40 Thtr 80 **Parking** 80 **Notes** Civ Wed 118

Best Western Cresta Court

★★★ 77% HOTEL

☎ 0161 927 7272 & 927 2601 📠 0161 929 6548
Church St WA14 4DP
e-mail: rooms@cresta-court.co.uk
web: www.cresta-court.co.uk

This modern hotel enjoys a prime location on the A56, close to the station, town centre shops and other amenities. Bedrooms vary in style from spacious four-posters to smaller, traditionally furnished rooms. Public areas include a choice of bars and extensive function and conference facilities.

Rooms 140 (9 fmly) **Facilities** FTV Wi-fi **Conf** Class 200 Board 150 Thtr 350 Del from £120 to £145 **Services** Lift **Parking** 200 **Notes** Civ Wed 300

See advert on this page

Travelodge Manchester Birch (M62 Eastbound)

BUDGET HOTEL

☎ 0871 984 6262 📠 0161 655 3716
M62 Service Area Eastbound OL10 2HQ
web: www.travelodge.co.uk
dir: Between juncts 18 & 19 on M62 E'bound

Travelodge offers good quality, good value, budget accommodation. All offer family rooms sleeping up to four (two adults, two children) with en suite bathroom/

continued

BIRCH MOTORWAY SERVICE AREA *continued*

shower-room, remote-control TV, tea- and coffee-making facilities and comfortable beds. Food options vary. Breakfast is at the on-site Bar Café restaurant (if available) or to take away. See also Hotel Groups pages.

Rooms 55 **S** fr £29; **D** fr £29

Travelodge Manchester North (M62 Westbound)

BUDGET HOTEL

☎ 0871 984 6161   📄 0161 655 6422
M62 Service Area Westbound OL10 2HQ
web: www.travelodge.co.uk
dir: Between juncts 18 & 19 on M62 westbound

Rooms 35 **S** fr £29; **D** fr £29

| **BOLTON** | **Map 15 SD70** |

Holiday Inn Bolton Centre

★★★★ 71% HOTEL

☎ 0870 4420 901 & 01204 879988   📄 01204 879983
1 Higher Bridge St BL1 2EW
e-mail: reservations.hibolton@qmh-hotels.com
web: www.holidayinn.co.uk
dir: M61 junct 3/A666, left at lights (Gordons Ford). Left at next lights, onto Higher Bridge St, hotel on right

Located close to Bolton town centre this modern hotel offers well-equipped accommodation. There is an attractive lounge bar, and dinner and breakfast are available in Hardies Restaurant. There is also a spa and extensive conference facilities.

Rooms 132 (2 fmly) **S** £64-£169; **D** £64-£169 (incl. bkfst)* **Facilities** STV 🟤 supervised Gym Sauna Sunbed Xmas New Year Wi-fi **Conf** Class 125 Board 80 Thtr 340 Del from £99 to £165* **Services** Lift Air con **Parking** 100 **Notes** LB ⊗ Civ Wed 150

Egerton House

★★★ 78% HOTEL

☎ 01204 307171   📄 01204 593030
Blackburn Rd, Egerton BL7 9SB
e-mail: reservation@egertonhouse-hotel.co.uk
web: www.egertonhouse-hotel.co.uk
dir: M61, A666 (Bolton road), pass ASDA on right. Hotel 2m on just passed war memorial on right

Peace and relaxation come as standard at this popular, privately owned hotel, that sits in acres of well-tended woodland gardens. Public rooms are stylishly appointed and have an inviting, relaxing atmosphere. Many of the individually styled, attractive guest bedrooms enjoy delightful garden views. Conferences and meetings are well catered for.

Rooms 29 (7 fmly) **Facilities** FTV Xmas New Year Wi-fi **Conf** Class 90 Board 60 Thtr 150 **Parking** 135 **Notes** ⊗ Civ Wed 140

Mercure Last Drop Village Hotel & Spa

★★★ 75% HOTEL

☎ 01204 591131   📄 01204 304122
Bromley Cross BL7 9PZ
e-mail: h6634@accor.com
web: www.mercure-uk.com
dir: 3m N of Bolton off B5472

A collection of 18th-century farmhouses set on cobbled streets with various shops and a local pub. Extensive self-contained conference rooms, a modern health and beauty spa and breathtaking views of the West Pennine Moors make this a popular choice with both corporate and leisure guests. The bedrooms are well equipped and spacious.

Rooms 128 (10 annexe) (29 fmly) (20 GF) **D** £50-£120 **Facilities** Spa STV 🟤 🟤 supervised Gym Craft shops Thermal suite Rock sauna Steam bath Bio sauna 🎵 Xmas New Year Wi-fi **Conf** Class 300 Board 95 Thtr 700 Del from £99 to £155 **Services** Lift **Parking** 400 **Notes** LB Civ Wed 500

Ramada Bolton

  ⊛ RAMADA

★★★ 74% HOTEL

☎ 01942 814598   📄 01942 816026
Manchester Rd, Blackrod BL6 5RU
e-mail: sales.bolton@ramadajarvis.co.uk
web: www.ramadajarvis.co.uk
dir: M61 junct 6, follow Blackrod A6027 signs. 200yds turn right onto A6 signed Chorley. Hotel 0.5m on right

This modern hotel enjoys easy access to the M61, M62, M60 and M6. Bedrooms are comfortably appointed for both business and leisure guests and there is a well-equipped leisure club.

Rooms 91 (7 fmly) (12 GF) **S** £54-£150; **D** £54-£150* **Facilities** Spa FTV 🟤 supervised Gym Steam room Hairdressing salon Reflexology Beauty treatments Xmas New Year Wi-fi **Conf** Class 100 Board 60 Thtr 300 Del from £99 to £150 **Services** Lift **Parking** 350 **Notes** LB Civ Wed 100

Travelodge Bolton West (M61 Southbound)

BUDGET HOTEL

☎ 0871 984 6334   📄 01204 668585
Bolton West Service Area, Horwich BL6 5UZ
web: www.travelodge.co.uk
dir: Between juncts 6 & 7 of M61

Travelodge offers good quality, good value, budget accommodation. All offer family rooms sleeping up to four (two adults, two children) with en suite bathroom/shower-room, remote-control TV, tea- and coffee-making facilities and comfortable beds. Food options vary. Breakfast is at the on-site Bar Café restaurant (if available) or to take away. See also Hotel Groups pages.

Rooms 32 **S** fr £29; **D** fr £29 **Conf** Class 60 Board 30 Thtr 60

| **BURY** | **Map 15 SD81** |

Travelodge Bury

BUDGET HOTEL

☎ 08719 846 302   📄 0161 796 7547
Little 66, Route 66 Leisure Park, Pilsworth Rd BL9 8RS
web: www.travelodge.co.uk
dir: M66 junct 3, turn left. At rdbt right, 1st right onto Little 66

Travelodge offers good quality, good value, budget accommodation. All offer family rooms sleeping up to four (two adults, two children) with en suite bathroom/shower-room, remote-control TV, tea- and coffee-making facilities and comfortable beds. Food options vary. Breakfast is at the on-site Bar Café restaurant (if available) or to take away. See also Hotel Groups pages.

Rooms 54 **S** fr £29; **D** fr £29

DELPH
Map 16 SD90

Saddleworth

★★★★ 76% COUNTRY HOUSE HOTEL

☎ 01457 871888 📄 01457 871889
Huddersfield Rd OL3 5LX
e-mail: enquiries@thesaddleworthhotel.co.uk
web: www.thesaddleworthhotel.co.uk
dir: A6052 Delph. At White Lion PH left on local road, left after 0.5m onto A62, hotel 0.5m on right

Situated in nine acres of landscaped gardens and woodlands in the Castleshaw Valley, this lovingly restored 17th-century building has stunning views and offers comfort and opulence together with staff who provide delightful customer care. Antique pieces have been acquired from far and wide, and no expense has been spared to provide guests with the latest, modern facilities.

Rooms 13 (5 annexe) (3 fmly) (1 GF) **S** £90–£120; **D** £160–£300 (incl. bkfst)* **Facilities** STV ⚲ Xmas New Year Wi-fi **Conf** Class 40 Board 40 Thtr 70 Del from £170* **Parking** 142 **Notes** ⊗ Civ Wed 250

DIDSBURY
Map 16 SJ89

Travelodge Manchester Didsbury

BUDGET HOTEL

☎ 0871 984 6244 📄 0161 448 0399
Kingsway M20 5PG
web: www.travelodge.co.uk
dir: M60 junct 4, follow A34 towards Didsbury. Lodge at Parswood Leisure Park

Travelodge offers good quality, good value, budget accommodation. All offer family rooms sleeping up to four (two adults, two children) with en suite bathroom/shower-room, remote-control TV, tea- and coffee-making facilities and comfortable beds. Food options vary. Breakfast is at the on-site Bar Café restaurant (if available) or to take away. See also Hotel Groups pages.

Rooms 62 **S** fr £29; **D** fr £29

MANCHESTER
Map 16 SJ89

See also **Manchester Airport & Sale**

The Lowry Hotel

★★★★★ 81% ◉◉ HOTEL

☎ 0161 827 4000 📄 0161 827 4001
50 Dearmans Place, Chapel Wharf, Salford M3 5LH
e-mail: enquiries.lowry@roccofortecollection.com
web: www.roccofortecollection.com
dir: M6 junct 19, A556/M56/A5103 for 4.5m. At rdbt take A57(M) to lights, right onto Water St. Left to New Quay St/Trinity Way. At 1st lights right onto Chapel St for hotel

This modern, contemporary hotel, set beside the River Irwell in the centre of the city, offers spacious bedrooms equipped to meet the needs of business and leisure

---

visitors alike. Many of the rooms look out over the river, as do the sumptuous suites. The River Room restaurant produces good brasserie cooking. Extensive business and function facilities are available, together with a spa to provide extra pampering.

Rooms 165 (7 fmly) **S** £350–£380; **D** £380–£415* **Facilities** Spa STV FTV Gym Swimming facilities available nearby ♫ Xmas New Year Wi-fi **Conf** Class 250 Board 60 Thtr 400 **Services** Lift Air con **Parking** 100 **Notes** LB Civ Wed 400

Radisson Edwardian Hotel Manchester

★★★★★ 🅰 HOTEL

☎ 0161 835 9929 📄 0161 835 9979
Free Trade Hall, Peter St M2 5GP
e-mail: resmanc@radisson.com
dir: From Deansgate, turn onto Peter St at Great Northern building. Hotel 200yds on right.

Rooms 263 (5 fmly) **S** £100–£1500; **D** £100–£1500 **Facilities** Spa ⚲ supervised Gym Xmas Wi-fi **Conf** Class 220 Board 90 Thtr 400 Del from £149 to £295 **Services** Lift Air con **Notes** LB ⊗ Civ Wed 400

The Midland

★★★★ 85% ◉◉ HOTEL

☎ 0161 236 3333 📄 0161 932 4100
Peter St M60 2DS
e-mail: midlandsales@qhotels.co.uk
web: www.qhotels.co.uk
dir: M602 junct 3, follow Manchester Central Convention Complex signs, hotel

This much loved, centrally located, well-established Edwardian-style hotel (Grade II listed) offers stylish, thoughtfully equipped bedrooms that have a contemporary feel. Elegant public areas are equally impressive and facilities include extensive function and meeting rooms. Eating options include the award-winning classical French Restaurant, the Colony Restaurant and the Octogan Lounge.

Rooms 312 (11 fmly) **S** £85–£250; **D** £85–£250* **Facilities** STV ⚲ Gym Squash Hair & beauty salon ♫ Wi-fi **Conf** Class 360 Board 120 Thtr 700 Del from £149 to £229* **Services** Lift Air con **Notes** LB ⊗ Civ Wed 600

City Inn Manchester

★★★★ 80% ◉ HOTEL

☎ 0161 242 1000 📄 0161 242 1001
One Piccadilly Place, 1 Auburn St M1 3DG
e-mail: manchester.reservations@cityinn.com
web: www.cityinn.com
dir: M56/A5103 signed city centre, at rdbt for A57(M) take 2nd exit onto Medlock St (A5103). Right at lights onto Whitworth St (B6469), bear left onto Aytoun St then right onto Auburn St

A large stylish, modern hotel set on the new Piccadilly Place development which is ideally located for both the rail station and the city centre. Spacious, contemporary bedrooms offer city views and boast a wide range of facilities including iMac computers and complimentary Wi-fi. Striking public areas feature modern art and include a range of meeting rooms, a popular bar and city café which offers high quality modern, European cuisine.

Rooms 285 (22 fmly) **S** £99–£225; **D** £99–£225* **Facilities** STV FTV Gym Xmas New Year Wi-fi **Conf** Class 74 Board 70 Thtr 170 Del from £125 to £300* **Services** Lift Air con **Parking** 24 **Notes** ⊗ Civ Wed 120

Marriott Worsley Park Hotel & Country Club

★★★★ 80% ◉ HOTEL

☎ 0161 975 2000 📄 0161 799 6341
Worsley Park, Worsley M28 2QT
e-mail: mangs.salesoffice.northwest@marriotthotels.com
web: www.marriottworsleypark.co.uk
dir: M60 junct 13, over 1st rdbt take A575. Hotel 400yds on left

This smart, modern hotel is set in impressive grounds with a championship golf course. Bedrooms are comfortably appointed and well equipped for both leisure and business guests. Public areas include extensive leisure and conference facilities, and an elegant restaurant offering imaginative cuisine.

Rooms 158 (33 fmly) (49 GF) (6 smoking) **S** £89–£129; **D** £89–£129* **Facilities** Spa STV ⚲ ⛳ 18 Putt green Gym Sauna Fitness suite Steam room Health & beauty salon Aerobics Studio Wi-fi **Conf** Class 150 Board 100 Thtr 250 Del from £139 to £179 **Services** Lift **Parking** 400 **Notes** LB Civ Wed 200

MANCHESTER *continued*

Macdonald Manchester

★★★★ 78% ⊛ HOTEL

☎ 0844 879 9088 & 0161 272 3200 🖨 0870 194 2237
London Rd M1 2PG
e-mail: general.manchester@macdonald-hotels.co.uk
web: www.macdonald-hotels.co.uk
dir: Opposite Piccadilly Station

Ideally situated just a short walk from Piccadilly Station, this converted hotel provides a handy location for both business and leisure travellers. Stylish, modern rooms have plasma TVs and iPod docking stations and the bathrooms offer walk-in power showers and luxury baths. The first-floor restaurant serves skilfully prepared dinners and hearty breakfasts. Staff throughout are cheerful and keen to please.

Rooms 338 (14 fmly) **Facilities** Spa STV Gym Sauna Xmas New Year Wi-fi **Conf** Class 150 Board 80 Thtr 250 **Services** Lift Air con **Parking** 85 **Notes** ⊗ Civ Wed 200

Marriott Manchester Victoria & Albert Hotel

★★★★ 77% HOTEL

☎ 0161 832 1188 🖨 0161 834 2484
Water St M3 4JQ
e-mail: london.regional.reservations@marriott.com
web: www.manchestermarriottvictoriaandalbert.co.uk
dir: M602 to A57 through lights on Regent Rd. Pass Sainsbury's, left at lights onto ring road, right at lights into Water St

This uniquely converted warehouse, with an interior featuring exposed brickwork and iron pillars, is located on the banks of the River Irwell, just a short stroll from the city centre. There are stylish, comfortable and well-equipped bedrooms together with attractive public areas. A large bar lounge leads onto an intimate restaurant, and extensive conference facilities are available.

Rooms 148 (30 fmly) (30 smoking) **Facilities** FTV Complimentary use of Bannatynes Health Club New Year Wi-fi **Conf** Class 120 Board 72 Thtr 250 **Services** Lift Air con **Parking** 100 **Notes** ⊗ Civ Wed 200

Renaissance Manchester

★★★★ 77% HOTEL

☎ 0161 831 6000 🖨 0161 835 3077
Blackfriars St M3 2EQ
e-mail: rhi.manbr.sales@renaissancehotels.com
web: www.renaissancemanchester.co.uk
dir: Follow signs to Deansgate, turn left onto Blackfriars St at 2nd set of lights after Kendals, hotel on right

This smart hotel enjoys a central location just off Deansgate, within easy walking distance of The Arena and the city's many shops and attractions. Stylish, well-equipped bedrooms are extremely comfortable and those on higher floors offer wonderful views. Public areas

include an elegant bar and restaurant and an impressive and smart conference and banqueting suite.

Rooms 203 **Facilities** Complimentary leisure facilities nearby Wi-fi **Conf** Class 300 Board 100 Thtr 400 Del from £139 to £185* **Services** Lift Air con **Parking** 80 **Notes** ⊗ Civ Wed 100

Copthorne Hotel Manchester

★★★★ 76% HOTEL

☎ 0161 873 7321 🖨 0161 877 8112
Clippers Quay, Salford Quays M50 3SN
e-mail: reservations.manchester@millenniumhotels.co.uk
web: www.millenniumhotels.co.uk
dir: From M602 follow signs for Salford Quays & Trafford Park on A5063. Hotel 0.75m on right

This smart hotel enjoys a convenient location on the redeveloped Salford Quays close to Old Trafford, The Lowry Centre and The Imperial War Museum. Bedrooms are comfortably appointed and well equipped for both business and leisure guests. The informal Clippers Restaurant serves a wide range of modern dishes.

Rooms 166 (6 fmly) (23 GF) **S** £56-£152; **D** £56-£152* **Facilities** STV Wi-fi **Conf** Class 80 Board 70 Thtr 160 **Services** Lift **Parking** 120 **Notes** LB ⊗ Civ Wed 160

Abode Manchester

★★★★ 75% ⊛⊛ HOTEL

☎ 0161 247 7744 🖨 0161 247 7747
107 Piccadilly M1 2DB
e-mail: reservationsmanchester@abodehotels.co.uk
web: www.abodehotels.co.uk
dir: M62/M602 follow signs for city centre/Piccadilly

This smart hotel is centrally located in the heart of the city, just moments from the popular Piccadilly area. Spacious public areas include the Michael Caines restaurant where guests can choose from a wonderful carte menu or a grazing selection. There's also a Champagne Bar and a lively café bar. Bedrooms are well equipped and are categorised as Comfortable, Desirable, Enviable and Fabulous on Fifth, all of which come with a wealth of extras.

Rooms 61 **Facilities** Xmas **Conf** Class 20 Board 20 Thtr 50 **Services** Lift

Crowne Plaza Manchester City Centre

★★★★ 75% HOTEL

☎ 0161 828 8600
70 Shudehill M4 4AF
e-mail: enquiries@cpmanchester.com
web: www.crowneplaza.co.uk

This new hotel is situated in the heart of Manchester in the trendy Northern Quarter, with Victoria and Piccadilly Stations and Shudehill Tram & Bus Interchange all within a short walking distance. The bedrooms have either one

or two queen or king sized beds, and there is a club floor with enhanced views and exclusive access to the top floor club lounge; the rooms have LCD TVs, free internet access and contemporary bathrooms with separate bath and shower. Guests have complimentary access to the gym 24 hours a day. Parking is available at the NCP opposite with concessionary rates.

Rooms 228

The Palace

★★★★ 74% HOTEL

☎ 0161 288 1111 🖨 0161 288 2222
Oxford St M60 7HA
e-mail: richard.morrell@principal-hayley.com
web: www.principal-hayley.com
dir: Opposite Manchester Oxford Road rail station

Formerly the offices of the Refuge Life Assurance Company, this impressive neo-Gothic building occupies a central location. There is a vast lobby, spacious open-plan bar lounge and restaurant, and extensive conference and function facilities. Bedrooms vary in size and style but are all spacious and well equipped.

Rooms 275 (59 fmly) **Facilities** STV ♫ Wi-fi **Conf** Class 650 Board 200 Thtr 1000 **Services** Lift **Notes** ⊗ Civ Wed 600

Malmaison Manchester

★★★ 88% ⊛ HOTEL

☎ 0161 278 1000 🖨 0161 278 1002
Piccadilly M1 3AQ
e-mail: manchester@malmaison.com
web: www.malmaison.com
dir: Follow city centre signs, then signs to Piccadilly station. Hotel opposite station, at bottom of station approach

Stylish and chic, Malmaison Manchester offers the very best of contemporary hotel keeping in a relaxed and comfortable environment. Converted from a former warehouse it offers a range of bright meeting rooms, a health spa with gym and treatment rooms, as well as the ever popular bar and French-style brasserie. Air-conditioned suites combine comfort with stunning design. Expect the unusual in some of the rooms, for instance the Cinema Suites have a private screening room with 52" screen with surround-sound.

Rooms 167 **Facilities** STV Gym Xmas New Year Wi-fi **Conf** Class 48 Board 30 Thtr 80 **Services** Lift Air con

Best Western Princess on Portland

★★★ 80% HOTEL

☎ 0844 855 9136 📇 0161 236 4468
101 Portland St M1 6DF
e-mail: reception@princessonportland.co.uk
web: www.princessonportland.co.uk
dir: From Piccadilly Station, along Piccadilly. Left on Portland St, hotel at junct to Princess St

Ideally located in the heart of the city, this former Victorian silk warehouse offers stylish accommodation. The open-plan public areas are contemporary in style and include a split-level brasserie offering an interesting selection of freshly prepared dishes. Smartly presented bedrooms are comfortably furnished and have modern facilities. Staff are friendly and keen to please.

Rooms 85 (7 fmly) **Facilities** FTV New Year Wi-fi **Conf** Class 24 Board 34 Thtr 50 **Services** Lift **Notes** ⊗

Ramada Manchester Piccadilly

★★★ 80% HOTEL

☎ 0161 236 8414 & 0844 815 9024 📇 0161 228 1568
Piccadilly Plaza, Portland St, Piccadilly M1 4PH
e-mail: sales.manchesterpiccadilly@ramadajarvis.co.uk
web: www.ramadajarvis.co.uk/manchester
dir: Opposite Piccadilly Gardens

Situated in the centre of Manchester, this hotel is a prominent landmark. The comfortable, air-conditioned bedrooms are decorated in a modern style and provide a comprehensive range of extra facilities. Public rooms include the contemporary, brasserie-style Arts Restaurant and there's also a popular and spacious bar. With one of the city's largest events rooms plus ten other meeting rooms, this hotel attracts many business clients.

Rooms 280 **Facilities** FTV Wi-fi **Conf** Class 420 Board 30 Thtr 800 Del from £135 to £179* **Services** Lift **Parking** 80 **Notes** Civ Wed 800

Novotel Manchester Centre

★★★ 79% HOTEL

☎ 0161 235 2200 📇 0161 235 2210
21 Dickinson St M1 4LX
e-mail: H3145@accor.com
web: www.novotel.com
dir: From Oxford Street, into Portland Street, left into Dickinson Street. Hotel on right

This smart, modern property enjoys a central location convenient for theatres, shops, China Town, and Manchester's business district. Spacious bedrooms are thoughtfully equipped and brightly decorated. Open-plan, contemporary public areas include an all-day restaurant

and a stylish bar. Extensive conference and meeting facilities are available.

Rooms 164 (15 fmly) (10 smoking) **S** £65-£125; **D** £65-£125* **Facilities** STV FTV Gym Steam room Sauna Aromatherapy Wi-fi **Conf** Class 50 Board 36 Thtr 90 Del from £115 to £165* **Services** Lift Air con **Notes** LB

Best Western Willow Bank

★★★ 78% HOTEL

☎ 0161 224 0461 📇 0161 257 2561
340-342 Wilmslow Rd, Fallowfield M14 6AF
e-mail: gm-willowbank@feathers.uk.com
web: www.feathers.uk.com
dir: M60 junct 5/A5103, turn left on to B5093. Hotel 2.5m on left

This popular hotel is conveniently located three miles from the city centre, close to the universities. Bedrooms vary in size and style but all are appointed to impressively high standards; they are well equipped and many rooms benefit from CD players and PlayStations. Spacious, elegant public areas include a bar, a restaurant and meeting rooms.

Rooms 116 (4 fmly) **Facilities** STV Xmas New Year Wi-fi **Conf** Class 60 Board 70 Thtr 125 **Parking** 100 **Notes** ⊗ Civ Wed 125

Holiday Inn Manchester Central Park

★★★ 77% HOTEL

☎ 0161 277 6910 📇 0161 277 6920
Oldham Rd M40 2ER
e-mail: chris.evans@himanchestercentralpark.com
web: www.holidayinn.co.uk
dir: On A62, 1m from city centre

This is a contemporary hotel located just 10-minute walk from the City of Manchester Stadium (home to Manchester City FC) and just a mile from the city centre. The attractive, spacious and air-conditioned bedrooms are comfortable and well equipped. Meals are served in the modern 888 Restaurant, and function facilities are available.

Rooms 83 (17 GF) (20 smoking) **Facilities** STV Wi-fi **Conf** Class 50 Board 40 Thtr 100 **Services** Lift Air con **Parking** 60 **Notes** LB ⊗

Holiday Inn Manchester - West

★★★ 73% HOTEL

☎ 0161 743 0080 📇 0161 745 8081
Liverpool St M5 4LT
e-mail: info@himanchester-west.co.uk
web: www.himanchester-west.co.uk
dir: M602 junct 3. Left at rdbt, 1st right at lights. Hotel 0.5m on Liverpool St

This refurbished hotel is near many popular Manchester attractions including Old Trafford (home of Manchester United FC), the Imperial War Museum, the Lowry Theatre; the bustling Salford Quays and the GMEX centre. The hotel offers stylish, well-equipped accommodation, a relaxing stylish bar area and the Okra Restaurant where British, European and Asian dishes are served. Extensive conference and banqueting facilities are also available.

Rooms 82 (17 fmly) (14 GF) **Facilities** STV Xmas New Year Wi-fi **Conf** Class 36 Board 28 Thtr 60 Del from £109 to £155* **Services** Lift Air con **Notes** ⊗

Novotel Manchester West

★★★ 72% HOTEL

☎ 0161 799 3535 📇 0161 703 8207
Worsley Brow M28 2YA
e-mail: H0907@accor.com
web: www.novotel.com

(For full entry see Worsley)

Days Hotel Manchester City

★★★ 67% HOTEL

☎ 0161 955 8400 📇 0161 955 8050
Weston Building, Sackville St M1 3BB
e-mail: daysinn@manchester.ac.uk
web: www.daysinn.com
dir: on Sackville St between Whitworth St & Mancunian Way

This modern building offers accommodation in smart, spacious and well-equipped bedrooms, suitable for families and business travellers, and all with en suite bathrooms. Continental breakfast is available and other refreshments may be taken at the nearby family restaurant.

Rooms 117 (2 fmly) **Conf** Class 100 Board 40 Thtr 300 **Services** Lift **Parking** 700 **Notes** Closed 23 Dec-3 Jan

MANCHESTER *continued*

Thistle Manchester

thistle

★★★ 66% HOTEL

☎ 0871 376 9026 📄 0871 376 9126
3/5 Portland St, Piccadilly Gardens M1 6DP
e-mail: manchester@thistle.co.uk
web: www.thistlehotels.com/manchester
dir: M6 junct 19 onto M56, then A5103 signed city centre,
straight on at rdbt, right at 2nd lights, straight at next
lights onto Portland St, hotel on right

The hotel is located close to the Piccadilly Gardens and
five minutes walk from the central and financial districts.
Rooms are compact and well equipped, and the Portland
Bar and Restaurant offers a wide selection of meals,
drinks and wines. There is also an Otrium Leisure Centre,
and conference facilities are available.

continued

Thistle Manchester

Rooms 205 (1 fmly) (29 smoking) **S** £49-£159;
D £49-£159* **Facilities** STV 🎾 supervised Gym Steam
room Sauna Plunge pool New Year Wi-fi **Conf** Class 140
Board 40 Thtr 300 Del from £99 to £199* **Services** Lift
Notes LB ⊗ Civ Wed 220

Chancellors Hotel & Conference Centre

★★★ 64% HOTEL

☎ 0161 9077414
Moseley Rd, Fallowfield M14 6NN

Relax at this hotel, a Grade II listed manor house, set in
five acres of landscaped gardens hidden in the heart of
Fallowfield, well located for the city's shopping, business
and commercial centres. Bedrooms offer modern facilities
and the cuisine is enjoyable. Wi-fi and secure parking are
available.

Rooms 75

Diamond Lodge

★★ 71% HOTEL

☎ 0161 231 0770 📄 0161 231 0660
Hyde Rd, Belle Vue M18 7BA
web: www.diamondlodge.co.uk
dir: On A57 Manchester E, 2.5m W of M60 junct 24,
Manchester orbital

Offering very good value for money, this modern lodge
provides comfortable accommodation near the city
centre, motorway networks and football stadiums. Bright
and airy, open-plan day rooms include a lounge and an
informal dining room where complimentary continental
breakfasts and evening menus are available.

Rooms 85 (13 fmly) **S** £48; **D** £48 (incl. bkfst)*
Parking 90 **Notes** ⊗ Closed 24-26 Dec RS 31 Dec

See advert on this page

Monton House

 VENTURE HOTELS

★★ 67% HOTEL

☎ 0161 789 7811 🖹 0161 787 7609
116-118 Monton Rd, Eccles M30 9HG
e-mail: hotel@montonhousehotel.co.uk
web: www.montonhousehotel.co.uk
dir: M602 junct 2/A576, 2nd left onto B5229 (Half Edge Ln) right onto Monton Rd, pass flats on left, hotel 100yds on right

A modern, purpose-built hotel conveniently situated for the motorway network, airport and city centre. The bedrooms are well equipped, and the brightly furnished restaurant offers an imaginative choice at dinner where dishes provide excellent value for money.

Rooms 60 (2 fmly) (1 GF) **Facilities** FTV New Year Wi-fi **Conf** Class 50 Board 50 Thtr 150 Del from £70 to £95* **Services** Lift **Parking** 100 **Notes** ⊗ Civ Wed 120

See advert on page 71

Campanile Manchester   Campanile

BUDGET HOTEL

☎ 0161 833 1845 🖹 0161 833 1847
55 Ordsall Ln, Regent Rd, Salford M5 4RS
e-mail: manchester@campanile.com
dir: M602 to Manchester, then A57. After large rdbt with Sainsbury's on left, left at next lights. Hotel on right

This modern building offers accommodation in smart, well-equipped bedrooms, all with en suite bathrooms. Refreshments may be taken at the informal bistro. See also the Hotel Groups pages.

Rooms 104 (25 GF) **Conf** Class 40 Board 30 Thtr 50

Express by Holiday Inn - Manchester Salford Quays

 Express by Holiday Inn

BUDGET HOTEL

☎ 0161 868 1000 🖹 0161 868 10 68
Waterfront Quay, Salford Quays M50 3XW
e-mail: dutymanagersalfordquays@expressholidayinn.co.uk
web: www.hiexpress.com/salfordquays

A modern hotel ideal for families and business travellers. Fresh and uncomplicated, the spacious rooms include Sky TV, power shower and tea and coffee-making facilities. Continental buffet breakfast is included in the room rate; other meals may be taken at the nearby family pub or restaurant. See also the Hotel Groups pages.

Rooms 120 **Conf** Class 10 Board 12 Thtr 25

Ibis Hotel Manchester

 ibis HOTEL

BUDGET HOTEL

☎ 0161 272 5000 🖹 0161 272 5010
Charles St, Princess St M1 7DL
e-mail: H3143@accor.com
web: www.ibishotel.com
dir: M62, M602 towards Manchester Centre, follow signs to UMIST (A34)

Modern, budget hotel offering comfortable accommodation in bright and practical bedrooms. Breakfast is self-service and dinner is available in the restaurant. See also the Hotel Groups pages.

Rooms 126 (9 smoking) **S** £59-£95; **D** £59-£95*

Ibis Manchester City Centre

BUDGET HOTEL

☎ 0161 234 0600 🖹 0161 234 0610
96 Portland St M1 4GY
e-mail: H3142@accor.com
web: www.ibishotel.com
dir: In city centre, between Princess St & Oxford St. 10min walk from Piccadilly

Rooms 127 (16 fmly) (7 smoking)

Travelodge Ashton Under Lyne

 Travelodge

BUDGET HOTEL

☎ 0871 984 6284
Lord Sheldon Way OL7 0DN
web: www.travelodge.co.uk
dir: W of M60 junct 23, A635 follow signs for Snipe Retail Park into Lord Sheldon Way. Lodge on left

Travelodge offers good quality, good value, budget accommodation. All offer family rooms sleeping up to four (two adults, two children) with en suite bathroom/shower-room, remote-control TV, tea- and coffee-making facilities and comfortable beds. Food options vary. Breakfast is at the on-site Bar Café restaurant (if available) or to take away. See also Hotel Groups pages.

Rooms 62 **S** fr £29; **D** fr £29

Travelodge Manchester Ancoats

BUDGET HOTEL

☎ 0871 984 6282 🖹 0161 235 8631
22 Great Ancoats St, Ancoats M4 5AZ
web: www.travelodge.co.uk
dir: M60 junct 11, A57, take 5th exit off rdbt. Follow M60/M602 junct 3. Follow signs for A62 to Lodge

Rooms 117 **S** fr £29; **D** fr £29

Travelodge Manchester Central

BUDGET HOTEL

☎ 0871 984 6159 🖹 0161 839 5181
Townbury House, 11 Blackfriars St M3 5AL
web: www.travelodge.co.uk
dir: From city centre N on Deansgate. At junct of Blackfriars St & St Mary Gate, turn left over bridge. Lodge on right

Rooms 181 **S** fr £29; **D** fr £29

Travelodge Manchester Sportcity

BUDGET HOTEL

☎ 0871 984 6293
Hyde Rd, Birch St, West Gorton M12 5NT
web: www.travelodge.co.uk
dir: M60 junct 24, A57 towards city centre for 2m. Lodge on right

Rooms 90 (6 fmly) (28 GF) **S** fr £29; **D** fr £29
Conf Class 50 Board 50 Thtr 100

MANCHESTER *continued*

Travelodge Manchester Trafford Park

BUDGET HOTEL

☎ 0871 984 6338 📠 0161 747 7419
17 Trafford Way, Urmston M17 8DD
web: www.travelodge.co.uk
dir: B5214 Trafford Boulevard towards Trafford Centre. At rdbt take 1st left

Rooms 54 **S** fr £29; **D** fr £29

MANCHESTER AIRPORT	Map 15 SJ88

See also **Altrincham**

Stanneylands

PRIMA HOTEL GROUP

★★★★ 80% ◉◉ HOTEL

☎ 01625 525225 📠 01625 537282
Stanneylands Rd SK9 4EY
e-mail: reservations@stanneylandshotel.co.uk
web: www.stanneylandshotel.co.uk
dir: From M56 at airport turn off, follow signs to Wilmslow. Left into Station Rd, onto Stanneylands Rd. Hotel on right

This traditional hotel offers well-equipped bedrooms and delightful, comfortable day rooms. The cuisine in the restaurant is of a high standard and ranges from traditional favourites to more imaginative contemporary dishes. Staff throughout are friendly and obliging.

Rooms 56 (2 fmly) (10 GF) **Facilities** STV FTV 🎵 Wi-fi **Conf** Class 50 Board 40 Thtr 120 **Services** Lift **Parking** 108 **Notes** ⊗ Civ Wed 100

Manchester Airport Marriott

Marriott HOTELS & RESORTS

★★★★ 80% HOTEL

☎ 0161 904 0301 📠 0161 980 1787
Hale Rd, Hale Barns WA15 8XW
e-mail: london.regional.reservations@marriott.com
web: www.manchesterairportmarriott.co.uk
dir: M56 junct 6, in left lane (Hale, Altrincham). Left at lights, on approach to bridge into right lane. At rdbt 3rd exit into hotel car park

With good airport links and convenient access to the city, this sprawling modern hotel is a popular destination. The hotel offers extensive leisure and business facilities, a choice of eating and drinking options and ample parking.

Bedrooms are situated around courtyards and have a comprehensive range of facilities.

Rooms 215 (22 fmly) (43 GF) (16 smoking) **S** £59-£200; **D** £59-£200* **Facilities** Spa STV 🏊 supervised Gym Wi-fi **Conf** Class 70 Board 50 Thtr 160 Del from £120 to £185* **Services** Lift Air con **Parking** 400 **Notes** LB ⊗ Civ Wed 110

Radisson Blu Hotel Manchester Airport

Radisson BLU

★★★★ 78% HOTEL

☎ 0161 490 5000 📠 0161 490 5100
Chicago Av M90 3RA
e-mail: sales.manchester@radissonblu.com
web: www.radissonblu.co.uk/hotel-manchesterairport
dir: M56 junct 5, follow signs for Terminal 2. At rdbt 2nd left and follow signs for railway station. Hotel next to station

All the airport terminals are quickly accessed by covered, moving walkways from this modern hotel. There is an excellent and well-equipped leisure club complete with indoor pool, and extensive conference and banqueting facilities are available. Air-conditioned bedrooms are thoughtfully equipped and come in a variety of decorative themes. Super views of the runway can be enjoyed in the Phileas Fogg Restaurant that offers creative international cuisine; there's also an all-day brasserie.

Rooms 360 (27 fmly) (23 smoking) **S** £99-£159; **D** £115-£159* **Facilities** 🏊 Gym Health & beauty treatments Wi-fi **Conf** Class 160 Board 60 Thtr 350 Del from £145 to £195* **Services** Lift Air con **Parking** 222 **Notes** LB ⊗ Civ Wed 230

Crowne Plaza Manchester Airport

 CROWNE PLAZA HOTELS & RESORTS

★★★★ 74% HOTEL

☎ 0870 400 9055 📠 0161 436 2340
Ringway Rd M90 3NS
e-mail: reservations-manchesterairport@ihg.com
web: www.crowneplaza.co.uk
dir: M56 junct 5 signed to Manchester Airport. At airport, follow signs to Terminal 1 & 3. Hotel next to Terminal 3. Long stay car park on left

Located close to Terminal 3 this smart, modern hotel offers well equipped, comfortable bedrooms, all with fitted with air conditioning and effective double glazing. A choice of dining styles and bars is available, and the

hotel has spacious leisure facilities and ample on-site parking. Hospitality is friendly with several long-serving staff members who greet regular customers as friends.

Rooms 294 (100 fmly) (51 GF) (25 smoking) **D** £49-£185* **Facilities** STV Gym Saunas Wi-fi **Conf** Class 25 Board 20 Thtr 30 **Services** Lift Air con **Parking** 300 **Notes** LB

Etrop Grange Hotel

 folio Hotels

★★★★ 73% ◉ HOTEL

☎ 0844 855 9118 📠 0161 499 0790
Thorley Ln M90 4EG
e-mail: etrop@foliohotels.com
web: www.foliohotels.com/etropgrange
dir: M56 junct 5 follow signs for Terminal 2, on slip road to rdbt take 1st exit. Immediately left, hotel 400yds

This Georgian country-house style hotel is close to Terminal 2 but one would never know once inside. Stylish, comfortable bedrooms provide modern comforts and good business facilities. Elegant day rooms include the Coach House Restaurant that serves creative dishes. Complimentary chauffeured transport to the airport is available for guests using the airport.

Rooms 64 **Facilities** STV New Year Wi-fi **Conf** Class 35 Board 35 Thtr 80 **Parking** 80 **Notes** LB ⊗ Civ Wed 90

Menzies Pinewood

MenziesHotels

★★★★ 73% HOTEL

☎ 01625 529211 📠 01625 536812
180 Wilmslow Rd, Handforth SK9 3LG
e-mail: pinewood@menzieshotels.co.uk
web: www.menzieshotels.co.uk
dir: M60 junct 3 follow A34 towards Wilmslow at 3rd rdbt turn right onto A555. At end of dual carriageway turn left, hotel on left

Located in Handforth, to the South of Manchester and only four miles from Manchester Airport, this hotel is convenient for airport stopovers and perfectly placed for business and leisure guests. The public areas are spacious and modern, and staff provide high levels of customer service. Bedrooms are modern in design. The gardens are a delight for weddings or special occasion functions.

Rooms 58 (4 fmly) (6 smoking) **S** £49-£125; **D** £49-£135* **Facilities** STV Xmas New Year Wi-fi **Conf** Class 100 Board 60 Thtr 200 Del from £105 to £145* **Services** Lift **Parking** 160 **Notes** ⊗ Civ Wed 130

Bewleys Hotel Manchester Airport

★★★ 77% HOTEL

☎ 0161 498 0333 & 498 1390 ▤ 0161 498 0222
Outwood Ln M90 4HL
e-mail: man@bewleyshotels.com
web: www.bewleyshotels.com
dir: At Manchester Airport. Follow signs to Manchester Airport Terminal 3. Hotel on left on Terminal 3 rdbt

Located adjacent to the airport this modern, stylish hotel provides an ideal stop-off for air travellers and business guests alike. All bedrooms are spacious and well equipped and include a wing of newly built superior rooms. Spacious, open-plan day rooms are stylishly appointed and include a large bar and restaurant along with a good range of meeting and conference facilities.

Rooms 365 (111 fmly) (30 GF) **S** £59-£149; **D** £59-£149
Facilities Wi-fi **Conf** Class 35 Board 18 Thtr 60
Del from £149 **Services** Lift **Parking** 300 **Notes** ⊗

Holiday Inn Manchester Airport

★★★ 74% HOTEL

Holiday Inn Manchester Airport

Rooms 126 (6 fmly) (19 GF) **Facilities** 🏊 Gym Squash Sauna Steam room Squash court Xmas New Year Wi-fi **Conf** Class 150 Board 90 Thtr 300 Del from £99 to £145* **Services** Lift Air con **Parking** 529 **Notes** ⊗ RS 23-31 Dec Civ Wed 300

Travelodge Manchester Airport

BUDGET HOTEL

☎ 0871 984 6181
Runger Ln WA15 8XW
web: www.travelodge.co.uk

Travelodge offers good quality, good value, budget accommodation. All offer family rooms sleeping up to four (two adults, two children) with en suite bathroom/ shower-room, remote-control TV, tea- and coffee-making facilities and comfortable beds. Food options vary. Breakfast is at the on-site Bar Café restaurant (if available) or to take away. See also Hotel Groups pages.

Rooms 201 **S** fr £29; **D** fr £29

OLDHAM **Map 16 SD90**

Best Western Hotel Smokies Park

★★★ 80% HOTEL

☎ 0161 785 5000 ▤ 0161 785 5010
Ashton Rd, Bardsley OL8 3HX
e-mail: sales@smokies.co.uk
web: www.smokies.co.uk
dir: On A627 between Oldham & Ashton-under-Lyne

This modern, stylish hotel offers smart, comfortable bedrooms and suites. A wide range of Italian and English dishes is offered in the Mediterranean-style restaurant and there is a welcoming lounge bar with live entertainment at weekends. There is a small yet well equipped, residents' only fitness centre and extensive function facilities are also available.

Rooms 73 (2 fmly) (22 GF) **S** £56-£86; **D** £62-£102 (incl. bkfst)* **Facilities** STV Gym Xmas New Year Wi-fi **Conf** Class 100 Board 40 Thtr 400 Del from £135 to £155* **Services** Lift **Parking** 120 **Notes** LB ⊗ RS 25 Dec-3 Jan Civ Wed 120

Innkeeper's Lodge Oldham

BUDGET HOTEL

☎ 0845 112 6025 ▤ 0845 112 6276
Burnley Ln, Chadderton OL1 2QS
web: www.innkeeperslodge.com/oldham
dir: M62 junct 20, A627(M) S towards Oldham. At junct with A663 into Burnley Lane. Lodge on left

Innkeeper's Lodge represents an exciting, high value concept within the budget hotel market. Comfortable bedrooms provide excellent facilities that include satellite TV and modem points. Options include family rooms; and for the corporate guest, cutting edge IT which includes Wi-fi access. A popular Carvery provides all-day food, including an extensive, complimentary continental breakfast. See also the Hotel Groups pages.

Rooms 30 **Conf** Thtr 30

Travelodge Oldham

BUDGET HOTEL

☎ 0871 984 6236 ▤ 0161 681 9021
432 Broadway, Chadderton OL9 8AU
web: www.travelodge.co.uk
dir: M60 junct 21, A663 towards Chadderton (or exit M62 follow signs for A627(M) to Oldham, then A663). Lodge 4m on right

Travelodge offers good quality, good value, budget accommodation. All offer family rooms sleeping up to four (two adults, two children) with en suite bathroom/ shower-room, remote-control TV, tea- and coffee-making facilities and comfortable beds. Food options vary. Breakfast is at the on-site Bar Café restaurant (if available) or to take away. See also Hotel Groups pages.

Rooms 50 **S** fr £29; **D** fr £29

Travelodge Oldham Manchester Street

BUDGET HOTEL

☎ 0871 984 6389
Windsor Rd, Manchester St OL8 4AS
e-mail: oldhammanchester@travelodge.co.uk
web: www.travelodge.co.uk
dir: M60 junct 22, follow A62/Oldham signs. Lodge 1m on right

Rooms 102 **S** fr £29; **D** fr £29 **Conf** Class 100 Board 60 Thtr 250

☎ 0870 443 6961 ▤ 01625 531876
Altrincham Rd SK9 4LR
e-mail: himanchester@qmh-hotels.com
web: www.holidayinn.co.uk
dir: M56 junct 6, A538 towards Wilmslow. Approx 1m, over mini rdbt, hotel on left

Just a short distance from Manchester Airport and the M56, this pleasant hotel offers comfortable public areas, modern leisure and meeting facilities. The restaurant provides a wide choice of formal and informal dining. Bedrooms are fully equipped and include air conditioning; 24-hour room service is available.

PRESTWICH — Map 15 SD80

Fairways Lodge & Leisure Club

★★★ 75% HOTEL

☎ 0161 798 8905 ▤ 0161 798 8905
George St, (Off Bury New Road) M25 9WS
e-mail: reservations@fairwayslodge.co.uk
dir: M60 junct 17, A56 for 1.5m, right into George St

This popular hotel is conveniently located within easy reach of the motorway network and is just a short drive from Manchester city centre and Bury. Bedrooms are equipped for both business and leisure guests. Public areas include an extensive leisure club with excellent squash facilities, conference and meeting rooms plus a public bar and restaurant.

Rooms 40 (3 fmly) (20 GF) (10 smoking) **Facilities** STV Gym Squash Dance classes Aerobics Xmas New Year Wi-fi **Conf** Class 60 Board 50 Thtr 150 **Parking** 100 **Notes** Civ Wed 50

ROCHDALE — Map 16 SD81

Mercure Norton Grange Hotel & Spa

Mercure

★★★★ 77% HOTEL

☎ 0870 1942119 ▤ 01706 649313
Manchester Rd, Castleton OL11 2XZ
web: www.mercure-uk.com
dir: M62 junct 20, follow signs for A664 Castleton. Right at next 2 rdbts for hotel 0.5m on left

Standing in nine acres of grounds and mature gardens, this Victorian house provides comfort in elegant surroundings. The well-equipped bedrooms provide a host of extras for both the business and leisure guest. Public areas include the Pickwick bistro and smart Grange Restaurant, both offering a good choice of dishes. There is also an impressive leisure centre.

Rooms 81 (17 fmly) (10 GF) **Facilities** Spa ⓢ Gym Leisure centre Indoor/Outdoor hydrotherapy pool Thermal suite Rock sauna Xmas New Year Wi-fi **Conf** Class 120 Board 70 Thtr 220 **Services** Lift **Parking** 150 **Notes** LB Civ Wed 150

SALE — Map 15 SJ79

Amblehurst Hotel

★★★ 68% HOTEL

☎ 0161 973 8800 ▤ 0161 905 1697
44 Washway Rd M33 7QZ
e-mail: reception@theamblehurst.com
web: www.theamblehurst.com
dir: M60 junct 7 onto A56 (Washway Rd). Hotel 2m

This hotel is located in the centre of Sale which is only a short distance from the centre of Manchester. It offers spacious accommodation and a small function room. Meals are available in the formal dining room or in the popular lounge bar.

Rooms 66 (4 fmly) (21 GF) (14 smoking) **S** £45-£65; **D** £55-£75 (incl. bkfst) **Facilities** FTV ♫ Xmas New Year Wi-fi **Conf** Class 65 Board 30 Thtr 80 Del from £80 to £110 **Services** Lift **Parking** 58 **Notes** ⊗

STOCKPORT — Map 16 SJ89

See also **Manchester Airport**

Bredbury Hall Hotel & Country Club

THE INDEPENDENTS
HOTEL ASSOCIATION

★★★ 77% HOTEL

☎ 0161 430 7421 ▤ 0161 430 5079
Goyt Valley SK6 2DH
e-mail: reservations@bredburyhallhotel.com
dir: M60 junct 25 signed Bredbury, right at lights, left onto Osbourne St, hotel 500mtrs on right

With views over open countryside, this large modern hotel is conveniently located for the M60. The well-equipped bedrooms offer space and comfort and the restaurant serves a very wide range of freshly prepared dishes.

Rooms 150 (2 fmly) (50 GF) **Facilities** STV Fishing Night club (Fri & Sat eve) Casino 36 Stockport ♫ Xmas New Year Wi-fi **Conf** Class 120 Board 60 Thtr 200 **Services** Lift **Parking** 450 **Notes** ⊗ Civ Wed 80

Alma Lodge Hotel

★★★ 75% HOTEL

☎ 0161 483 4431 ▤ 0161 483 1983
149 Buxton Rd SK2 6EL
e-mail: reception@almalodgehotel.com
web: www.almalodgehotel.com
dir: M60 junct 1 at rdbt take 2nd exit under rail viaduct at lights opposite. At Debenhams turn right onto A6. Hotel approx 1.5m on left

A large hotel located on the main road close to the town, offering modern and well-equipped bedrooms. It is family owned and run and serves a good range of quality Italian cooking in Luigi's restaurant. Good function rooms are free internet access are also available.

Rooms 52 (32 annexe) (2 fmly) **S** £45-£67; **D** £75-£85 (incl. bkfst)* **Facilities** FTV Wi-fi **Conf** Class 100 Board 60 Thtr 250 Del from £105 to £126* **Parking** 120 **Notes** ⊗ RS Bank Hols Civ Wed 200

Wycliffe

★★★ 73% HOTEL

☎ 0161 477 5395 ▤ 0161 476 3219
74 Edgeley Rd, Edgeley SK3 9NQ
e-mail: reception@wycliffe-hotel.com
web: www.wycliffe-hotel.com
dir: M60 junct 2 follow A560 for Stockport, at 1st lights turn right, hotel 0.5m on left

This family-run, welcoming hotel provides immaculately maintained and well-equipped bedrooms within main building, and more simply appointed rooms in two houses opposite. There is a well stocked bar and a popular restaurant where the menu has an Italian bias. There is ample, convenient parking.

Rooms 20 (6 annexe) (3 fmly) (2 GF) **S** £50-£67; **D** £70-£75 (incl. bkfst)* **Facilities** FTV Wi-fi **Conf** Class 20 Board 20 Thtr 30 Del from £80 to £100* **Parking** 46 **Notes** ⊗ Closed 25-27 Dec RS BH

Innkeeper's Lodge Stockport

BUDGET HOTEL

☎ 0845 112 6027 📠 0845 112 6274

271 Wellington Rd, North Heaton Chapel SK4 5BP
web: www.innkeeperslodge.com/stockport
dir: M60 junct 1. Follow A5145/Town Centre signs. Left at lights (signed Manchester) into George's Rd. Over rdbt, left at lights, left onto A6/Wellington Road North. Lodge on right

Innkeeper's Lodge represents an exciting, high value concept within the budget hotel market. Comfortable bedrooms provide excellent facilities that include satellite TV and modem points. Options include family rooms; and for the corporate guest, cutting edge IT which includes Wi-fi access. A popular Carvery provides all-day food, including an extensive, complimentary continental breakfast. See also the Hotel Groups pages.

Rooms 22 **Conf** Thtr 80

WIGAN Map 15 SD50

Macdonald Kilhey Court

MACDONALD HOTELS & RESORTS

★★★★ 73% ⚫ HOTEL

☎ 0870 1942122 📠 01257 422401

Chorley Rd, Standish WN1 2XN
e-mail: general.kilheycourt@macdonald-hotels.co.uk
web: www.macdonald-hotels.co.uk/kilheycourt
dir: M6 junct 27, A5209 Standish, over at lights, past church on right, left at T-junct, hotel on right 350yds. M61 junct 6, signed Wigan & Haigh Hall. 3m & right at T-junct. Hotel 0.5 m on right

This hotel is peacefully situated in its own grounds yet conveniently located for the motorway network. The accommodation is comfortable and the rooms are split between the Victorian house and a modern extension. Public areas display many original features and the split-level restaurant has views over the Worthington Lakes. This hotel is a very popular venue for weddings.

Rooms 62 (8 GF) **Facilities** STV ⚫ Gym Aerobics & yoga classes Private fishing arranged Beauty treatments Xmas New Year Wi-fi **Conf** Class 180 Board 60 Thtr 400 **Services** Lift **Parking** 200 **Notes** ⚫ Civ Wed 300

Wrightington Hotel & Country Club

★★★ 80% HOTEL

☎ 01257 425803 📠 01257 425830

Moss Ln, Wrightington WN6 9PB
e-mail: info@wrightingtonhotel.co.uk
dir: M6 junct 27, 0.25m W, hotel on right after church

Situated in open countryside close to the M6, this privately owned hotel offers friendly hospitality. Accommodation is well equipped and spacious, and public areas include an extensive leisure complex complete with hair salon, boutique and sports injury lab. Blazers Restaurant, two bars and air-conditioned banqueting facilities appeal to a broad market.

Rooms 74 (6 fmly) (36 GF) **Facilities** Spa STV FTV ⚫ Gym Squash Hairdressing salon Beauty spa Sports injury clinic New Year Wi-fi **Conf** Class 120 Board 40 Thtr 200 Del from £125 to £150 **Services** Lift **Parking** 240 **Notes** RS 24 Dec-3 Jan Civ Wed 100

The Beeches

RESTAURANT WITH ROOMS

☎ 01257 426432 & 421316 📠 01257 427503

School Ln, Standish WN6 0TD
e-mail: mail@beecheshotel.co.uk
dir: M6 junct 27, A5209 into Standish on School Ln

Located a short drive from M6, this elegant Victorian house has been renovated to provide high standards of comfort. Bedrooms are equipped with practical and homely extras, and public areas include spacious lounges, a popular brasserie, and a self-contained function suite.

Rooms 10 (4 fmly)

WORSLEY Map 15 SD70

Novotel Manchester West

★★★ 72% HOTEL

☎ 0161 799 3535 📠 0161 703 8207

Worsley Brow M28 2YA
e-mail: H0907@accor.com
web: www.novotel.com
dir: Adjacent to M60 junct 13

Well placed for access to the Peak and the Lake District, as well as the City of Manchester, this modern hotel successfully caters for both families and business guests. The spacious bedrooms have sofa beds and a large work area; the hotel boasts an outdoor swimming pool, children's play area, and secure parking.

Rooms 119 (10 fmly) (41 GF) **S** £59-£109; **D** £59-£109* **Facilities** STV ⚫ Gym Wi-fi **Conf** Class 140 Board 25 Thtr 200 Del from £119 to £140* **Services** Lift **Parking** 95 **Notes** Civ Wed 140

HAMPSHIRE

ALDERSHOT Map 5 SU85

Potters International

★★★ 64% HOTEL

☎ 01252 344000 📠 01252 311611

1 Fleet Rd GU11 2ET
e-mail: reservations@pottersinthotel.com
dir: Access via A325 & A321 towards Fleet

This modern hotel is located within easy reach of Aldershot. Extensive air-conditioned public areas include ample lounge areas, a pub and a more formal restaurant; there are also conference rooms and a very good leisure club. Bedrooms, mostly spacious, are well equipped and have been attractively decorated and furnished.

Rooms 103 (9 fmly) (9 GF) **Facilities** STV ⚫ Gym Wi-fi **Conf** Class 250 Board 100 Thtr 400 **Services** Lift **Parking** 120 **Notes** ⚫

ALTON Map 5 SU73

Alton Grange

★★★ 77% ⚫⚫ HOTEL

☎ 01420 86565 📠 01420 541346

London Rd GU34 4EG
e-mail: info@altongrange.co.uk
web: www.altongrange.co.uk
dir: From A31 right at rdbt signed Alton/Holybourne/Bordon B3004. Hotel 300yds on left

A friendly family owned hotel, conveniently located on the outskirts of this market town and set in two acres of lovingly tended gardens. The individually styled bedrooms, including three suites, are all thoughtfully equipped. Diners can choose between the more formal Truffles Restaurant or relaxed Muffins Brasserie. The attractive public areas include a function suite.

Rooms 30 (4 annexe) (4 fmly) (7 GF) **S** £75-£99; **D** £90-£120 (incl. bkfst)* **Facilities** Hot air ballooning Wi-fi **Conf** Class 30 Board 40 Thtr 80 **Parking** 48 **Notes** No children 3yrs Closed 24 Dec-4 Jan Civ Wed 100

Swan Hotel

Ⓤ

☎ 01420 83777 📠 01420 87975

High St GU34 1AT
dir: In town centre

Currently the rating for this establishment is not confirmed. This may be due to a change of ownership or because it has only recently joined the AA rating scheme. For further details please see the AA website: theAA.com

Rooms 36 **Conf** Class 40 Board 60 Thtr 150

ANDOVER
Map 5 SU34

Esseborne Manor
★★★ 79% ® HOTEL

☎ 01264 736444 📄 01264 736725
Hurstbourne Tarrant SP11 0ER
e-mail: info@esseborne-manor.co.uk
web: www.esseborne-manor.co.uk
dir: Halfway between Andover & Newbury on A343, just
1m N of Hurstbourne Tarrant

Set in two acres of well-tended gardens, this attractive
manor house is surrounded by the open countryside of the
North Wessex Downs. Bedrooms are delightfully individual
and are split between the main house, an adjoining
courtyard and separate garden cottage. There's a
wonderfully relaxed atmosphere throughout, and public
rooms combine elegance with comfort.

Rooms 19 (8 annexe) (2 fmly) (6 GF) **S** £90-£130;
D £125-£180 (incl. bkfst)* **Facilities** STV FTV 🎣 🏊 Wi-fi
Conf Class 40 Board 30 Thtr 60 Del from £140 to £150
Parking 50 **Notes** LB Civ Wed 100

Quality Hotel Andover
★★★ 63% HOTEL

☎ 01264 369111 📄 01264 369000
Micheldever Rd SP11 6LA
e-mail: andover@quality-hotels.co.uk
dir: Off A303 at A3093. 1st rdbt take 1st exit, 2nd rdbt
take 1st exit. Turn immediately before Total petrol
station, then left again

Located on the outskirts of the town, this hotel is popular
with business guests. Bedrooms provide useful
accessories; public areas consist of a cosy lounge, a hotel
bar and a traditional style restaurant serving a range of
meals. There is also a large conference suite available
and a pleasant garden with patio seating.

Rooms 49 (36 annexe) (13 GF) **S** £45-£69; **D** £65-£85
(incl. bkfst) **Facilities** Wi-fi **Conf** Class 60 Board 60
Thtr 180 Del from £99 **Parking** 100 **Notes** ✕ Civ Wed 85

Danebury Hotel
Ⓤ

☎ 01264 323332 📄 01264 335440
2 High St SP10 1NX
e-mail: 6441@greeneking.co.uk
dir: In town centre

Currently the rating for this establishment is not
confirmed. This may be due to a change of ownership or
because it has only recently joined the AA rating scheme.
For further details please see the AA website: theAA.com

Rooms 18 **Conf** Class 80 Board 50 Thtr 100

BARTON-ON-SEA
Map 5 SZ29

Pebble Beach
RESTAURANT WITH ROOMS

☎ 01425 627777 📄 01425 610689
Marine Dr BH25 7DZ
e-mail: mail@pebblebeach.uk.com
dir: Follow A35 from Southampton onto A337 to New
Milton, turn left onto Barton Court Av to clifftop

Situated on the cliff top the restaurant at this
establishment boasts stunning views towards The
Needles. Bedrooms and bathrooms, situated above the
restaurant, are well equipped and provide a range of
accessories to enhance guest comfort. A freshly cooked
breakfast is served in the main restaurant.

Rooms 3

BARTON STACEY
Map 5 SU44

Travelodge Barton Stacey
BUDGET HOTEL

☎ 0871 984 6007 📄 01264 720260
SO21 3NP
web: www.travelodge.co.uk
dir: on A303 westbound

Travelodge offers good quality, good value, budget
accommodation. All offer family rooms sleeping up to four
(two adults, two children) with en suite bathroom/
shower-room, remote-control TV, tea- and coffee-making
facilities and comfortable beds. Food options vary.
Breakfast is at the on-site Bar Café restaurant (if
available) or to take away. See also Hotel Groups pages.

Rooms 20 **S** fr £29; **D** fr £29

BASINGSTOKE
Map 5 SU65

See also **Odiham & Stratfield Turgis**

INSPECTORS' CHOICE

Tylney Hall
★★★★ ®® HOTEL

☎ 01256 764881 📄 01256 768141
RG27 9AZ
e-mail: sales@tylneyhall.com
web: www.tylneyhall.com

(For full entry see Rotherwick)

The Hampshire Court Hotel

★★★★ 79% ® HOTEL

☎ 01256 319700 📄 01256 319730
Centre Dr, Chineham RG24 8FY
e-mail: hampshirecourt@qhotels.co.uk
web: www.qhotels.co.uk
dir: Off A33 (Reading road) behind Chineham Shopping
Centre via Great Binfields Rd

This hotel boasts a range of smart, comfortable and
stylish bedrooms, and leisure facilities that are unrivalled
locally. Facilities include indoor and outdoor tennis
courts, two swimming pools, a gym and a number of
treatment rooms.

Rooms 90 (6 fmly) **S** £60-£160; **D** £70-£170 (incl. bkfst)*
Facilities Spa STV 🎣 🏊 Gym Steam room Beauty salon
Sauna Exercise studios Xmas New Year Wi-fi
Conf Class 130 Board 60 Thtr 220 Del from £145 to
£189* **Services** Lift **Parking** 200 **Notes** LB Civ Wed 220

Audleys Wood

★★★★ 77% ®® HOTEL

☎ 01256 817555 📄 01256 817500
Alton Rd RG25 2JT
e-mail: info@audleyswood.com
web: www.audleyswood.com
dir: M3 junct 6. From Basingstoke take A339 towards
Alton, hotel on right

A long sweeping drive leads to what was once a Victorian
hunting lodge. This traditional country-house hotel has
undergone a refurbishment to the majority of its guest
rooms and suites; bedrooms now include flat-screen TVs
and MP3 player connections. Smart and traditional public
areas have log fires, and good food is served in the
contemporary conservatory with a small minstrels'
gallery.

Rooms 72 (23 fmly) (34 GF) **S** £85-£275; **D** £95-£295
(incl. bkfst) **Facilities** STV 🏊 Xmas New Year Wi-fi
Conf Class 80 Board 60 Thtr 200 Del from £145 to £195
Parking 60 **Notes** LB ✕ Civ Wed 100

Barceló Basingstoke Country Hotel

★★★★ 74% HOTEL

☎ 01256 764161 📠 01256 768341
Scures Hill, Nately Scures, Hook RG27 9JS
e-mail: basingstokecountry.mande@barcelo-hotels.co.uk
web: www.barcelo-hotels.co.uk
dir: M3 junct 5, A287 towards Newnham. Left at lights. Hotel 200mtrs on right

This popular hotel is close to Basingstoke and its country location ensures a peaceful stay. Bedrooms are available in a number of styles - all have air conditioning, Wi-fi, in-room safes and hairdryers. Guests have a choice of dining in the formal restaurant, or for lighter meals and snacks there is a relaxed café and a smart bar. Extensive wedding, conference and leisure facilities complete the picture.

Rooms 100 (26 GF) **Facilities** Spa STV 🔄 supervised Gym Sauna Solarium Steam room Dance studio Beauty treatments New Year Wi-fi **Conf** Class 85 Board 80 Thtr 240 Del from £125* **Services** Lift Air con **Parking** 200 **Notes** RS 24 Dec-2 Jan Civ Wed 90

Apollo

★★★★ 73% ☺ HOTEL

☎ 01256 796700 📠 01256 796701
Aldermaston Roundabout RG24 9NU
e-mail: admin@apollohotels.com
web: www.apollohotels.com
dir: M3 junct 6. Follow ring road N, exit A340 (Aldermaston). Hotel on rdbt, 5th exit into Popley Way for access

This modern hotel provides well-equipped accommodation and spacious public areas, appealing to both the leisure and business guest. Facilities include a smartly appointed leisure club, a business centre, along with a good choice of formal and informal eating in two restaurants; Vespers is the fine dining option.

Rooms 125 (32 GF) **Facilities** Spa FTV 🔄 supervised Gym Sauna Steam room Xmas New Year Wi-fi **Conf** Class 196 Board 30 Thtr 255 Del from £150 to £170* **Services** Lift Air con **Parking** 200 **Notes** ⊗ Civ Wed 100

Holiday Inn Basingstoke

★★★ 75% HOTEL

☎ 0870 400 9004 📠 01256 840081
Grove Rd RG21 3EE
e-mail: reservations-basingstoke@ihg.com
web: www.holidayinn.co.uk
dir: On A339 (Alton road) S of Basingstoke

Located conveniently on the southern approach to Basingstoke and close to the M3, this modern, comfortable hotel offers refurbished, well-equipped, air-conditioned bedrooms. There is a busy Conference Academy on site. The staff are friendly throughout the hotel. Free parking is available.

Rooms 86 (1 fmly) (43 GF) (4 smoking) **S** £50-£280; **D** £50-£280 **Facilities** FTV Complimentary passes available at nearby leisure centre Xmas New Year Wi-fi **Conf** Class 70 Board 70 Thtr 140 Del from £89 to £280 **Services** Air con **Parking** 150 **Notes** LB ⊗

Travelodge Basingstoke

BUDGET HOTEL

☎ 0871 984 6009 📠 01256 843566
Stag & Hounds, Winchester Rd RG22 6HN
web: www.travelodge.co.uk
dir: M3 junct 7, A30 towards Basingstoke. Straight on at 1st two rdts, at 3rd rdbt take 1st exit into Winchester Rd. Lodge behind Stag & Hounds Harvester restaurant

Travelodge offers good quality, good value, budget accommodation. All offer family rooms sleeping up to four (two adults, two children) with en suite bathroom/shower-room, remote-control TV, tea- and coffee-making facilities and comfortable beds. Food options vary. Breakfast is at the on-site Bar Café restaurant (if available) or to take away. See also Hotel Groups pages.

Rooms 44 **S** fr £29; **D** fr £29

INSPECTORS' CHOICE

Montagu Arms

★★★ ☺☺ HOTEL

☎ 01590 612324 & 0845 123 5613
📠 01590 612188
Palace Ln SO42 7ZL
e-mail: reservations@montaguarmshotel.co.uk
web: www.montaguarmshotel.co.uk
dir: M27 junct 2, turn left at rdbt, follow signs for Beaulieu. Continue to Dibden Purlieu, then right at rdbt. Hotel on left

Surrounded by the glorious scenery of the New Forest, this lovely hotel, dating back to 1742, manages to achieve the impression of almost total seclusion, though it is within easy reach of the major towns and cities in the area. The uniquely designed bedrooms include some with four-posters. Public rooms include a cosy lounge, an adjoining conservatory and a choice of two dining options, the informal Monty's, or the stylish Terrace Restaurant.

Rooms 22 (3 fmly) **Facilities** FTV 🔄 Complimentary use of spa in Brockenhurst Xmas New Year Wi-fi **Conf** Class 16 Board 26 Thtr 50 **Parking** 86 **Notes** ⊗ Civ Wed 60

See advert on page 228

BEAULIEU *continued*

The Master Builders at Bucklers Hard

★★★ 79% ⚜ HOTEL

☎ 01590 616253 📄 01590 616297
Buckler's Hard SO42 7XB
e-mail: enquiries@themasterbuilders.co.uk
web: www.themasterbuilders.co.uk
dir: M27 junct 2, follow Beaulieu signs. At T-junct left onto B3056, 1st left to Buckler's Hard. Hotel 2m on left before village

A tranquil historic riverside setting creates the backdrop for this newly refurbished property. The main house bedrooms are full of historical features and of individual design, and in addition there are some bedrooms in the newer wing. Public areas include a popular bar and guest lounge, whilst grounds are an ideal location for alfresco dining in the summer months. Award-winning cuisine is served in the stylish dining room.

Rooms 25 (17 annexe) (4 fmly) (8 GF) **S** £100-£140; **D** £140-£180 (incl. bkfst)* **Facilities** FTV Xmas New Year Wi-fi **Conf** Class 30 Board 20 Thtr 40 Del from £148.50 to £178.50* **Parking** 40 **Notes** LB

Beaulieu

★★★ 74% ⚜ HOTEL

☎ 023 8029 3344 📄 023 8029 2729
Beaulieu Rd SO42 7YQ
e-mail: beaulieu@newforesthotels.co.uk
web: www.newforesthotels.co.uk
dir: M27 junct 1/A337 towards Lyndhurst. Left at lights, through Lyndhurst, right onto B3056, continue for 3m

Conveniently located in the heart of the New Forest and close to Beaulieu Road railway station, this popular, small hotel provides an ideal base for exploring this lovely area. Facilities include an indoor swimming pool, an outdoor children's play area and an adjoining pub. A daily changing menu is offered in the restaurant.

Rooms 28 (7 annexe) (6 fmly) (4 GF) **D** £120-£160 (incl. bkfst)* **Facilities** ⊠ Steam room Xmas **Conf** Class 100 Board 160 Thtr 290 Del from £110 to £120* **Services** Lift **Parking** 60 **Notes** LB Civ Wed 205

BOTLEY Map 5 SU51

Macdonald Botley Park, Golf & Country Club

★★★★ 76% ⚜ COUNTRY HOUSE HOTEL

☎ 01489 780 888 & 0870 194 2132 📄 01489 789 242
Winchester Rd, Boorley Green SO32 2UA
e-mail: botleypark@macdonald-hotels.co.uk
web: www.macdonald-hotels.co.uk/botleypark
dir: M27 junct 7, A334 towards Botley. At 1st rdbt left, past M&S store, over at next 5 mini rdbts. At 6th mini rdbt turn right. In 0.5m hotel on left

This modern and spacious hotel sits peacefully in the midst of its own 176-acre parkland golf course. Bedrooms are comfortably appointed with a good range of extras and an extensive range of leisure facilities is on offer. Attractive public areas include a relaxing restaurant and the more informal Swing and Divot Bar.

Rooms 130 (30 fmly) (44 GF) **Facilities** Spa ⊠ ⅃ 18 ⬡ Putt green Gym Squash Dance studio Xmas New Year Wi-fi **Conf** Class 180 Board 100 Thtr 450 **Services** Air con **Parking** 250 **Notes** ⊗ Civ Wed 400

See advert on opposite page

BROCKENHURST — Map 5 SU30

Rhinefield House

Hand PICKED HOTELS

★★★★ 81% ◎◎ HOTEL

☎ 01590 622922 📠 01590 622800
Rhinefield Rd SO42 7QB
e-mail: rhinefieldhouse@handpicked.co.uk
web: www.handpicked.co.uk
dir: A35 towards Christchurch. 3m from Lyndhurst turn left to Rhinefield, 1.5m to hotel

This stunning 19th-century, mock-Elizabethan mansion is set in 40 acres of beautifully landscaped gardens and forest. Bedrooms are spacious and great consideration is given to guest comfort. The elegant and award-winning Armada Restaurant is richly furnished, and features a fireplace carving (nine years in the making) that is worth taking time to admire. If the weather permits, the delightful terrace is just the place for enjoying alfresco eating.

Rooms 50 (10 fmly) (18 GF) **Facilities** STV ⓧ supervised ⌁ ☺ ☙ Gym Hydro-therapy pool Plunge pool Steam room Sauna Treatment room Xmas New Year Wi-fi **Conf** Class 72 Board 56 Thtr 160 Del from £175 to £225* **Services** Lift **Parking** 100 **Notes** ⊗ Civ Wed 110

Careys Manor

★★★★ 79% ◎◎ HOTEL

☎ 01590 623551 & 624467 📠 01590 622799
SO42 7RH
e-mail: stay@careysmanor.com
web: www.careysmanor.com
dir: M27 junct 3, M271, A35 to Lyndhurst. A337 towards Brockenhurst. Hotel on left after 30mph sign

This smart property offers a host of facilities that include an Oriental-style spa and leisure suite with an excellent range of unusual treatments, and three very contrasting restaurants that offer a choice of Thai, French or modern British cuisine. Many of the spacious and well appointed bedrooms have balconies overlooking the gardens. Extensive function and conference facilities are also available.

Rooms 80 (62 annexe) (32 GF) **S** £129-£189; **D** £178-£358 (incl. bkfst)* **Facilities** Spa FTV ⓧ supervised ☙ Gym Steam room Beauty therapists Treatment rooms Hydrotherapy pool Xmas New Year Wi-fi **Conf** Class 70 Board 40 Thtr 120 Del from £172.50 to £224.25* **Services** Lift **Parking** 180 **Notes** LB ⊗ No children 16yrs Civ Wed 100

Balmer Lawn

★★★★ 75% ◎ HOTEL

☎ 01590 623116 📠 01590 623864
Lyndhurst Rd SO42 7ZB
e-mail: info@balmerlawnhotel.com
dir: Just off A337 from Brockenhurst towards Lymington

Situated in the heart of the New Forest, this peacefully located hotel provides comfortable public rooms and a wide range of bedrooms. A selection of carefully prepared and enjoyable dishes is offered in the spacious restaurant. The extensive function and leisure facilities make this popular with both families and conference delegates.

Rooms 54 (10 fmly) **Facilities** FTV ⓧ ⌁ ☺ Gym Squash Indoor leisure suite ♫ Xmas New Year Wi-fi **Conf** Class 76 Board 48 Thtr 150 **Services** Lift **Parking** 100 **Notes** LB Civ Wed 120

See advert on page 230

BROCKENHURST *continued*

Whitley Ridge Hotel

★★★ ◉◉◉ COUNTRY HOUSE HOTEL

☎ 01590 622354 🖹 01590 622856
Beaulieu Rd SO42 7QL
e-mail: info@whitleyridge.co.uk
web: www.whitleyridge.com
dir: At Brockenhurst onto B3055 Beaulieu Road. 1m on left up private road

This charming hotel enjoys a secluded picturesque setting in the heart of the New Forest. The relaxing public areas, delightful grounds, smart and comfortable bedrooms and a team of helpful and attentive staff all contribute to a memorable stay. The cuisine of the well-established Le Poussin restaurant is a highlight at this venue.

Whitley Ridge Hotel

Rooms 18 (2 GF) **S** £113-£142; **D** £125-£275 (incl. bkfst) **Facilities** ◔ Xmas New Year Wi-fi **Conf** Class 20 Board 20 Thtr 35 Del from £170 to £175 **Parking** 6 **Notes** LB Civ Wed 60

New Park Manor

★★★ 83% ◉◉
COUNTRY HOUSE HOTEL

☎ 01590 623467 🖹 01590 622268
Lyndhurst Rd SO42 7QH
e-mail: info@newparkmanorhotel.co.uk
web: www.newparkmanorhotel.co.uk
dir: M27 junct 1, A337 to Lyndhurst & Brockenhurst. Hotel 1.5m on right

Once the favoured hunting lodge of King Charles II, this well presented hotel enjoys a peaceful setting in the New Forest and comes complete with an equestrian centre. The bedrooms are divided between the old house and a purpose-built wing. An impressive spa offers a range of treatments. Von Essen Hotels - AA Hotel Group of the Year 2009-10.

Rooms 24 (6 fmly) **Facilities** Spa STV FTV ◔ ⊰ ⋓ Gym Mountain biking Xmas New Year Wi-fi **Conf** Class 52 Board 60 Thtr 100 **Parking** 70 **Notes** Civ Wed 120

Forest Park

★★★ 73% HOTEL

☎ 01590 622844 🖹 01590 623948
Rhinefield Rd SO42 7ZG
e-mail: forest.park@forestdale.com
web: www.forestparkhotel.co.uk
dir: A337 to Brockenhurst turn into Meerut Rd, follow road through Waters Green. Right at T-junct into Rhinefield Rd

Situated in the heart of the New Forest, this former vicarage and war field hospital is now a hotel which offers a warm and friendly welcome to all its guests. The hotel offers a heated pool, riding, a log cabin sauna and tennis courts. The bedrooms and public areas are comfortable and stylish.

Rooms 38 (2 fmly) (7 GF) **S** £69-£89; **D** £89-£140 (incl. bkfst)* **Facilities** FTV ⊰ ◔ Horse riding stables Sauna Xmas New Year Wi-fi **Conf** Class 20 Board 30 Thtr 50 **Parking** 80 **Notes** Civ Wed 50

Cloud

★★ 83% SMALL HOTEL

☎ 01590 622165 & 622354 🖹 01590 622818
Meerut Rd SO42 7TD
e-mail: enquiries@cloudhotel.co.uk
web: www.cloudhotel.co.uk
dir: M27 junct 1 signed New Forest, A337 through Lyndhurst to Brockenhurst. On entering Brockenhurst 1st right. Hotel 300mtrs

This charming hotel enjoys a peaceful location on the edge of the village. The bedrooms are bright and

comfortable with pine furnishings and smart en suite facilities. Public rooms include a selection of cosy lounges, a delightful rear garden with outdoor seating and a restaurant specialising in home-cooked, wholesome English food.

Rooms 17 (1 fmly) (2 GF) **Facilities** Xmas Wi-fi **Conf** Class 12 Board 12 Thtr 40 **Parking** 20 **Notes** LB No children 8yrs Closed 27 Dec-12 Jan

Watersplash
★★ 63% HOTEL

☎ 01590 622344
The Rise SO42 7ZP
e-mail: bookings@watersplash.co.uk
web: www.watersplash.co.uk
dir: M3 junct 13/M27 junct 1/A337 S through Lyndhurst & Brockenhurst. The Rise on left, hotel on left

This popular, welcoming hotel that dates from Victorian times, has been in the same family for over 40 years. Bedrooms have co-ordinated decor and good facilities. The restaurant overlooks the neatly tended garden and there is also a comfortably furnished lounge, separate bar and an outdoor pool.

Rooms 23 (6 fmly) (3 GF) **Facilities** ₹ Xmas New Year **Conf** Class 20 Board 20 Thtr 80 Del from £95 to £135* **Parking** 29

BROOK (NEAR CADNAM)   Map 5 SU21

Bell Inn
★★★ 83% ◉◉ HOTEL

☎ 023 8081 2214   ▤ 023 8081 3958
SO43 7HE
e-mail: bell@bramshaw.co.uk
web: www.bellinnbramshaw.co.uk
dir: M27 junct 1 onto B3079, hotel 1.5m on right

The inn is part of the Bramshaw Golf Club and has tailored its style to suit this market, but it is also an ideal base for

visiting the New Forest. Bedrooms are comfortable and attractively furnished, and the public areas, particularly the welcoming bar, have a cosy and friendly atmosphere.

Rooms 27 (2 annexe) (1 fmly) (8 GF) **S** £95-£130; **D** £140-£160 (incl. bkfst) **Facilities** FTV ₺ 54 Putt green Xmas New Year Wi-fi **Conf** Class 20 Board 30 Thtr 50 **Parking** 150 **Notes** LB ⊗

BURLEY   Map 5 SU20

Burley Manor
★★★ 75% HOTEL

☎ 01425 403522   ▤ 01425 403227
Ringwood Rd BH24 4BS
e-mail: burley.manor@forestdale.com
web: www.theburleymanorhotel.co.uk
dir: Exit A31at Burley sign, hotel 3m on left

Set in extensive grounds, this 18th-century mansion house enjoys a relaxed ambience and a peaceful setting. Half of the well-equipped, comfortable bedrooms, including several with four-posters, are located in the main house. The remainder, many with balconies, are in the adjacent converted stable block overlooking the outdoor pool. Cosy public rooms benefit from log fires in winter.

Rooms 38 (17 annexe) (2 fmly) (17 GF) **S** £73-£129; **D** £83-£169 (incl. bkfst)* **Facilities** FTV ₹ Horse riding stables Xmas New Year Wi-fi **Conf** Class 24 Board 40 Thtr 70 **Parking** 60 **Notes** Civ Wed 70

Moorhill House
★★★ 71% ◉ COUNTRY HOUSE HOTEL

☎ 01425 403285   ▤ 01425 403715
BH24 4AH
e-mail: moorhill@newforesthotels.co.uk
web: www.newforesthotels.co.uk
dir: M27, A31, follow signs to Burley, through village, up hill, right opposite school & cricket grounds

Situated deep in the heart of the New Forest and formerly a grand gentleman's residence, this charming hotel offers a relaxed and friendly environment. Bedrooms, of varying sizes, are smartly decorated. A range of facilities is provided and guests can relax by walking around the extensive grounds. Both dinner and breakfast offer a choice of interesting and freshly prepared dishes.

Rooms 31 (13 fmly) (3 GF) **Facilities** ⊙ Putt green ⚘ Gym Badminton (Apr-Sep) Xmas New Year Wi-fi **Conf** Class 60 Board 65 Thtr 120 **Parking** 50 **Notes** LB Civ Wed 80

CADNAM   Map 5 SU31

Bartley Lodge
★★★ 75% ◉ HOTEL

☎ 023 8081 2248   ▤ 023 8081 2075
Lyndhurst Rd SO40 2NR
e-mail: bartley@newforesthotels.co.uk
web: www.newforesthotels.co.uk
dir: M27 junct 1 at 1st rdbt 1st exit, at 2nd rdbt 3rd exit onto A337. Hotel sign on left

This 18th-century former hunting lodge is very quietly situated, yet is just minutes from the M27. Bedrooms vary in size but all are well equipped. There is a selection of small lounge areas, a cosy bar and an indoor pool, together with a small fitness suite. The Crystal dining room offers a tempting choice of well prepared dishes.

Rooms 31 (12 fmly) (2 GF) **S** £60-£68; **D** £120-£160 (incl. bkfst)* **Facilities** ⊙ Gym Xmas New Year Wi-fi **Conf** Class 60 Board 60 Thtr 120 Del from £110 to £120* **Parking** 60 **Notes** LB Civ Wed 80

See advert on page 232

DOGMERSFIELD   Map 5 SU75

INSPECTORS' CHOICE

Four Seasons Hotel Hampshire
★★★★★ ◉ HOTEL

☎ 01252 853000   ▤ 01252 853010
Dogmersfield Park, Chalky Ln RG27 8TD
e-mail: reservations.ham@fourseasons.com
dir: M3 junct 5 onto A287 Farnham. After 1.5m left for Dogmersfield, hotel 0.6m on left

This Georgian manor house, set in 500 acres of rolling grounds and English Heritage listed gardens, offers the upmost in luxury and relaxation, just an hour from London. The spacious and stylish bedrooms are particularly well appointed and offer up-to-date technology. Fitness and spa facilities include nearly every conceivable indoor and outdoor activity, in addition to luxurious pampering. An elegant restaurant, a healthy eating spa café and a trendy bar are popular venues.

Rooms 133 (23 GF) **S** £195-£3350; **Facilities** Spa STV ⊙ ᔍ Fishing ⚘ Gym Clay pigeon shooting Bikes Canal boat Falconry Horse riding Jogging trails ♫ Xmas New Year Wi-fi Child facilities **Conf** Class 110 Board 60 Thtr 260 Del from £275* **Services** Lift Air con **Parking** 165 **Notes** Civ Wed 200

Holiday Inn Southampton-Eastleigh M3, Jct 13

★★★ 77% HOTEL

☎ 0870 400 9075 ⓘ 023 8064 3945
Leigh Rd SO50 9PG
e-mail: reservations-eastleigh@ihg.com
web: www.holidayinn.co.uk
dir: M3 junct 13, right at lights, follow signs to Eastleigh, hotel on right

Located close to the M3, this well sited hotel is suitable for both the business and leisure traveller. Public areas benefit from refurbishment, as do some bedrooms. The popular leisure area includes a swimming pool, jacuzzi, and aerobics studio, steam room, sauna and beauty treatments.

Rooms 129 (3 fmly) (27 GF) (12 smoking) **S** fr £48;
D fr £48 (incl. bkfst)* **Facilities** STV ⓢ supervised Gym Xmas New Year Wi-fi **Conf** Class 60 Board 50 Thtr 120 Del from £99 to £160* **Services** Lift Air con **Parking** 120 **Notes** LB ⊗ Civ Wed 100

Ellington Lodge Hotel

★★★ Ⓐ HOTEL

☎ 023 8065 1478 & 8061 3989 ⓘ 023 8065 1479
The Concorde Club SO50 9HQ
e-mail: hotel@theconcordeclub.com
web: www.theconcordeclub.com
dir: M27 junct 5, at rdbt follow Chandlers Ford signs, hotel 500yds on right

Rooms 35 (18 GF) **Facilities** FTV Fishing ♫ Wi-fi
Conf Class 50 Board 40 Thtr 200 Del from £130 to £160 **Services** Lift Air con **Parking** 250 **Notes** No children 18yrs Closed 24-26 Dec

Travelodge Southampton Eastleigh

BUDGET HOTEL

☎ 0871 984 6213 ⓘ 023 8061 6813
Twyford Rd SO50 4LF
web: www.travelodge.co.uk
dir: M3 junct 12, A335 (Eastleigh & Boyatt Wood) to next rdbt, take 2nd exit signed Eastleigh town centre

Travelodge offers good quality, good value, budget accommodation. All offer family rooms sleeping up to four (two adults, two children) with en suite bathroom/shower-room, remote-control TV, tea- and coffee-making facilities and comfortable beds. Food options vary. Breakfast is at the on-site Bar Café restaurant (if available) or to take away. See also Hotel Groups pages.

Rooms 44 **S** fr £29; **D** fr £29

Brookfield

★★★ 79% HOTEL

☎ 01243 373363 ⓘ 01243 376342
Havant Rd PO10 7LF
e-mail: bookings@brookfieldhotel.co.uk
dir: From A27 onto A259 towards Emsworth. Hotel 0.5m on left

This well-established family-run hotel has spacious public areas with popular conference and banqueting facilities. Bedrooms are in a modern style, and comfortably furnished. The popular Hermitage Restaurant offers a seasonally changing menu and an interesting wine list.

Rooms 39 (6 fmly) (16 GF) **S** £80-£108; **D** £90-£128*
Facilities New Year Wi-fi **Conf** Class 50 Board 50 Thtr 100 Del from £120 to £149.95* **Parking** 80 **Notes** LB ⊗ Closed 24-27 Dec Civ Wed 100

Travelodge Chichester Emsworth

BUDGET HOTEL

☎ 0871 984 6024 ⓘ 01243 370877
PO10 7RB
web: www.travelodge.co.uk
dir: On E'bound carriageway of A27, 10m E of Portsmouth. NB access to A27 W'bound is 7m E of Travelodge

Travelodge offers good quality, good value, budget accommodation. All offer family rooms sleeping up to four (two adults, two children) with en suite bathroom/shower-room, remote-control TV, tea- and coffee-making facilities and comfortable beds. Food options vary. Breakfast is at the on-site Bar Café restaurant (if available) or to take away. See also Hotel Groups pages.

Rooms 36 **S** fr £29; **D** fr £29

36 on the Quay

◉◉◉ RESTAURANT WITH ROOMS

☎ 01243 375592 & 372257
47 South St PO10 7EG

Occupying a prime position with far reaching views over the estuary, this 16th-century house is the scene for some accomplished and exciting cuisine. The elegant restaurant occupies centre stage with peaceful pastel shades, local art and crisp napery together with glimpses of the bustling harbour outside. The contemporary bedrooms offer style, comfort and thoughtful extras.

Rooms 5

Solent Hotel & Spa

★★★★ 80% HOTEL

☎ 01489 880000 🖨 01489 880007
Rookery Av, Whiteley PO15 7AJ
e-mail: solent@shirehotels.com
web: www.solenthotel.com
dir: M27 junct 9, hotel on Solent Business Park

Close to the M27 with easy access to Portsmouth, the New Forest and other attractions, this smart, purpose-built hotel enjoys a peaceful location. Bedrooms are spacious and very well appointed and there is a well-equipped spa with health and beauty facilities.

Rooms 111 (9 fmly) (39 GF) **Facilities** Spa STV 🅩 🏊 Gym Steam room Sauna Children's splash pool Activity studio Xmas New Year Wi-fi **Conf** Class 100 Board 80 Thtr 200 **Services** Lift **Parking** 200 **Notes** ⊗ Civ Wed 160

Holiday Inn Fareham-Solent

★★★ 78% HOTEL

☎ 0870 400 9028 🖨 01329 844666
Cartwright Dr, Titchfield PO15 5RJ
e-mail: fareham@ihg.com
web: www.holidayinn.co.uk
dir: M27 junct 9, follow signs for A27. Over Segensworth rdbt 1.5m, left at next rdbt

This hotel is well positioned and attracts both the business and leisure markets. Bedrooms are spacious and smart, and stylish public areas include a number of conference rooms. Beauty treatments are available in the leisure area which has a swimming pool, aerobics studio and gym.

Rooms 124 (4 fmly) (72 GF) (9 smoking) **S** £210; **D** £210 **Facilities** 🅩 supervised Gym Sauna Treatment rooms Wi-fi **Conf** Class 64 Board 45 Thtr 140 **Services** Air con **Notes** LB ⊗ Civ Wed 60

Lysses House

★★★ 72% ◉ HOTEL

☎ 01329 822622 🖨 01329 822762
51 High St PO16 7BQ
e-mail: lysses@lysses.co.uk
web: www.lysses.co.uk
dir: M27 junct 11 follow signs for Farnham,stay in left lane. At rdbt 3rd exit into East St & follow into High St. Hotel at top on right

This attractive Georgian hotel is situated on the edge of the town in a quiet location and provides spacious and well-equipped accommodation. There are conference facilities, and a lounge bar serving a range of snacks together with the Richmond Restaurant that offers accomplished and imaginative cuisine.

Rooms 21 (7 GF) **S** £60.20-£85.65; **D** £87.60-£107.20 (incl. bkfst)* **Facilities** FTV Wi-fi **Conf** Class 42 Board 28 Thtr 95 **Services** Lift **Parking** 30 **Notes** ⊗ Closed 25 Dec-1 Jan RS 24 Dec & BHs Civ Wed 100

Red Lion Hotel

Ⓤ

☎ 01329 822640 🖨 01329 823579
East St PO16 0BP
e-mail: redlion.fareham@oldenglishinns.co.uk

Currently the rating for this establishment is not confirmed. This may be due to a change of ownership or because it has only recently joined the AA rating scheme. For further details please see the AA website: theAA.com

Rooms 46 **Conf** Class 60 Board 40 Thtr 100

Aviator

★★★★ 72% HOTEL

☎ 01252 555890 🖨 01252 555899
Farnborough Rd GU14 6EL
e-mail: enquiries@aviatorfarnborough.co.uk
web: www.aviatorfarnborough.co.uk
dir: A325 to Aldershot, continue for 3m, hotel on right

A striking, newly built property with a modern, sleek interior overlooking Farnborough airfield and located close to the main transport networks. This hotel is suitable for both the business and leisure travellers. The bedrooms have are well designed and provide complimentary Wi-fi. Both the Brasserie and the Deli source local ingredients for their menus.

Rooms 169 **Facilities** STV Gym Exercise studio Wi-fi **Conf** Class 30 Board 40 Thtr 90 **Services** Lift Air con **Parking** 169 **Notes** ⊗

Holiday Inn Farnborough

★★★ 79% HOTEL

☎ 0870 400 9029 & 01252 894300 🖨 01252 523166
Lynchford Rd GU14 6AZ
e-mail: reservations-farnborough@ihg.com
web: www.holidayinn.co.uk
dir: M3 junct 4, follow A325 through Farnborough towards Aldershot. Hotel on left at The Queen's rdbt

This hotel occupies a perfect location for events in Aldershot and Farnborough with ample parking on site and easy access to the M3. Modern bedrooms provide good comfort levels, and internet access is provided throughout. Leisure facilities comprise a swimming pool, gym and beauty treatment rooms. Smart meeting rooms are also available.

Rooms 142 (31 fmly) (35 GF) (7 smoking) **S** £40-£159; **D** £50-£169 (incl. bkfst)* **Facilities** STV 🅩 supervised Sauna Steam room Beauty room ♫ Xmas New Year Wi-fi **Conf** Class 80 Board 60 Thtr 180 Del from £89 to £175* **Services** Air con **Parking** 170 **Notes** Civ Wed 180

Falcon

★★★ 70% HOTEL

☎ 01252 545378 🖨 01252 522539
68 Farnborough Rd GU14 6TH
e-mail: hotel@falconfarnborough.com
dir: A325 off M3, pass Farnborough Gate Retail Park. Left at next rdbt & straight at next 2 rdbts. Hotel on left at junct of aircraft esplanade & A325

This hotel is conveniently situated close to the M3, opposite Farnborough Airport and only a 20-minute drive from the market town of Farnham. Stylish public areas including Landings Restaurant have undergone a major refurbishment, and at the time of our inspection was underway in the bedrooms and bathrooms. Enjoyable restaurant meals are all freshly prepared to order. The staff are helpful and professional.

Rooms 29 (2 fmly) (3 GF) **S** £59-£109; **D** £69-£119 (incl. bkfst) **Facilities** STV FTV Wi-fi **Parking** 20 **Notes** ⊗ Closed 24 Dec-2 Jan

Lismoyne

★★★ 72% HOTEL

☎ 01252 628555 🖨 01252 811761
Church Rd GU51 4NE
e-mail: info@lismoynehotel.com
web: www.lismoynehotel.com
dir: M3 junct 4a. B3013, over railway bridge to town centre. Through lights, take 4th right. Hotel 0.25m on left

Set in extensive grounds, this attractive hotel is located close to the town centre. Public rooms include a comfortable lounge and pleasant bar with a conservatory overlooking the garden, and a traditional restaurant. Accommodation is divided between the bedrooms in the original building and those in the modern extension; styles vary but all rooms are well equipped.

Rooms 62 (3 fmly) (19 GF) **Facilities** STV Gym Xmas New Year Wi-fi **Conf** Class 92 Board 80 Thtr 170 **Parking** 150 **Notes** LB ⊗ Civ Wed 170

FLEET *continued*

Innkeeper's Lodge Fleet

BUDGET HOTEL

☎ 0845 112 6101 📠 0845 112 6197
Cove Rd GU51 2SH
web: www.innkeeperslodge.com/fleet
dir: M3 junct 4a, south on A327 towards Fleet. Right at
1st rdbt (continue on A327). Lodge at next rdbt at A3013
& B3014 junct.

Innkeeper's Lodge represent an exciting, high value
concept within the budget hotel market. Comfortable
bedrooms provide excellent facilities that include satellite
TV and modem points. Options include spacious family
rooms; and for the corporate guest, cutting edge IT is
provided with Wi-fi access. All-day food is provided in the
adjacent pub restaurant. The extensive continental
breakfast is complimentary. See also the Hotel Groups
pages.

Rooms 40

**FLEET MOTORWAY SERVICE
AREA (M3)**   Map 5 SU75

Days Inn Fleet

BUDGET HOTEL

☎ 01252 815587 📠 01252 815587
Fleet Services GU51 1AA
e-mail: fleet.hotel@welcomebreak.co.uk
web: www.welcomebreak.co.uk
dir: Between junct 4a & 5 southbound on M3

This modern building offers accommodation in smart,
spacious and well-equipped bedrooms, suitable for
families and business travellers, and all with en suite
bathrooms. Continental breakfast is available and other
refreshments may be taken at the nearby family
restaurant. See also the Hotel Groups pages.

Rooms 58 (46 fmly) **S** £39-£69; **D** £49-£79*

FOUR MARKS   Map 5 SU63

Travelodge Alton Four Marks

BUDGET HOTEL

☎ 0871 984 6002 📠 01420 562659
156 Winchester Rd GU34 5HZ
web: www.travelodge.co.uk
dir: 5m S of Alton on A31 N'bound

Travelodge offers good quality, good value, budget
accommodation. All offer family rooms sleeping up to four
(two adults, two children) with en suite bathroom/
shower-room, remote-control TV, tea- and coffee-making
facilities and comfortable beds. Food options vary.
Breakfast is at the on-site Bar Café restaurant (if
available) or to take away. See also Hotel Groups pages.

Rooms 50 **S** fr £29; **D** fr £29

HARTLEY WINTNEY   Map 5 SU75

The Elvetham Hotel
★★★ 79% HOTEL

☎ 01252 844871 📠 01252 844161
RG27 8AR
e-mail: enq@theelvetham.co.uk
web: www.theelvetham.co.uk
dir: M3 junct 4A W, junct 5 E (or M4 junct 11, A33,
B3011). Hotel signed from A323 between Hartley Wintney
& Fleet

A spectacular 19th-century mansion set in 35 acres of
grounds with an arboretum. All bedrooms are individually
styled and many have views of the manicured gardens. A
popular venue for weddings and conferences, the hotel
lends itself to team building events and outdoor pursuits.

Rooms 70 (29 annexe) (7 GF) **S** £60-£110; **D** £95-£135*
Facilities STV ॐ Putt green ✌ Gym Badminton Boules
Volleyball New Year Wi-fi **Conf** Class 80 Board 48
Thtr 110 **Parking** 200 **Notes** Closed 24-27 Civ Wed 200

HAVANT   Map 5 SU70

The Bear Hotel
Ⓤ

☎ 023 9284 6501 📠 023 9247 0551
15-17 East St PO9 1AA
e-mail: 9110@greeneking.co.uk

Currently the rating for this establishment is not
confirmed. This may be due to a change of ownership or
because it has only recently joined the AA rating scheme.
For further details please see the AA website: theAA.com

Rooms 42 **Conf** Class 40 Board 40 Thtr 100

HOOK   Map 5 SU75

Raven Hotel
Ⓤ

☎ 01256 762541 📠 01256 768677
Station Rd RG27 9HS
e-mail: raven.hook@newbridgeinns.co.uk

Currently the rating for this establishment is not
confirmed. This may be due to a change of ownership or
because it has only recently joined the AA rating scheme.
For further details please see the AA website: theAA.com

Rooms 38 **Conf** Class 60 Board 70 Thtr 100

ISLE OF WIGHT

See Wight, Isle of

LIPHOOK   Map 5 SU83

Old Thorns Hotel Golf & Country Estate
★★★ 82% HOTEL

☎ 01428 724555 📠 01428 725036
Griggs Green GU30 7PE
e-mail: sales@oldthorns.com
dir: Griggs Green exit off A3 hotel 0.5m off exit

This hotel is peacefully located in 400 acres of rolling
countryside with a championship golf course, and has
easy access to the A3. Bedrooms and bathrooms are
stylish in design and offer high levels of comfort and
space. Leisure facilities are extensive, and the Greenview
Restaurant, overlooking the 9th and 18th greens, offers
all day dining.

Rooms 83 (2 fmly) (14 GF) **Facilities** Spa STV FTV ⊙
supervised ⅃ 18 ⓈPutt green Gym Xmas New Year Wi-fi
Conf Class 100 Board 30 Thtr 250 **Parking** 100 **Notes** LB
Civ Wed 250

Travelodge Liphook

BUDGET HOTEL

☎ 0871 984 6044 📠 01428 727619
GU30 7TT
web: www.travelodge.co.uk
dir: From A3 southbound, pass 1st turn for Liphook &
Shell petrol station. Take Griggs Green turn, over bridge
to N'bound carriageway. Then on A3, 0.5m into Liphook
services

Travelodge offers good quality, good value, budget
accommodation. All offer family rooms sleeping up to four
(two adults, two children) with en suite bathroom/
shower-room, remote-control TV, tea- and coffee-making
facilities and comfortable beds. Food options vary.
Breakfast is at the on-site Bar Café restaurant (if
available) or to take away. See also Hotel Groups pages.

Rooms 40 **S** fr £29; **D** fr £29

LYMINGTON Map 5 SZ39

Macdonald Elmers Court Hotel & Resort

★★★ 82% HOTEL

☎ 0844 879 9060 🖨 01590 679780
South Baddesley Rd SO41 5ZB
e-mail: elmerscourt@macdonald-hotels.co.uk
web: www.macdonaldhotels.co.uk
dir: M27 junct 1, through Lyndhurst, Brockenhurst & Lymington, hotel 200yds right after Lymington ferry terminal

Originally known as The Elms, this Tudor manor house dates back to the 1820s. Ideally located at the edge of the New Forest and overlooking The Solent with views towards the Isle of Wight, the hotel offers suites and self-catering accommodation in the grounds, along with a host of leisure facilities.

Rooms 42 (42 annexe) (8 fmly) (22 GF) **S** £57-£245; **D** £67-£255 (incl. bkfst)* **Facilities** Spa ⊗ ⋋ supervised ⛲ Putt green ⛳ Gym Squash Steam room Aerobics classes Sauna Table tennis ♫ Xmas New Year Wi-fi **Conf** Class 40 Board 40 Thtr 100 **Parking** 100 **Notes** LB ⊗ Civ Wed 100

Passford House

★★★ 82% HOTEL

☎ 01590 682398 🖨 01590 683494
Mount Pleasant Ln SO41 8LS
e-mail: sales@passfordhousehotel.co.uk
web: www.passfordhousehotel.co.uk
dir: From A337 at Lymington over 2 mini rdbts. 1st right at Tollhouse pub, then after 1m right into Mount Pleasant Lane

A peaceful hotel set in attractive grounds on the edge of town. Bedrooms vary in size but all are comfortably furnished and well equipped. Extensive public areas include lounges, a smartly appointed restaurant and bar plus leisure facilities. The friendly and well-motivated staff provide attentive service.

Rooms 51 (2 annexe) (10 GF) **S** £60-£110; **D** £120-£250 (incl. bkfst)* **Facilities** ⊗ ⋋ Putt green ⛳ Gym Petanque Table tennis Pool table Xmas New Year **Conf** Class 30 Board 30 Thtr 80 **Parking** 100 **Notes** LB No children 8yrs Civ Wed 40

Stanwell House

★★★ 80% ⊛ HOTEL

☎ 01590 677123 🖨 01590 677756
14-15 High St SO41 9AA
e-mail: enquiries@stanwellhouse.com
dir: M27 junct 1, follow signs to Lyndhurst into Lymington centre & High Street

A privately owned Georgian house situated on the wide high street only a few minutes from the marina and a short drive from the New Forest. Styling itself as a boutique hotel the bedrooms are individually designed; there are Terrace rooms with garden access, four-poster rooms, and Georgian rooms in the older part of the building. The four suites include two with their own roof terrace. Dining options include the informal bistro and the intimate Seafood Restaurant. Service is friendly and attentive. A meeting room is available for hire.

Rooms 27 (3 fmly) (4 GF) **S** £99-£135; **D** £135-£195 (incl. bkfst)* **Facilities** FTV Xmas New Year Wi-fi **Conf** Class 25 Board 20 Thtr 70 Del from £120 to £140* **Notes** LB Civ Wed 70

LYNDHURST — Map 5 SU30

Bell Inn

★★★ 83% ◎◎ HOTEL

☎ 023 8081 2214 🖹 023 8081 3958
SO43 7HE
e-mail: bell@bramshaw.co.uk
web: www.bellinnbramshaw.co.uk

(For full entry see Brook (Near Cadnam))

Best Western Forest Lodge

★★★ 79% ◎◎ HOTEL

☎ 023 8028 3677 🖹 023 8028 2940
Pikes Hill, Romsey Rd SO43 7AS
e-mail: forest@newforesthotels.co.uk
web: www.newforesthotels.co.uk
dir: M27 junct 1, A337 towards Lyndhurst. In village, with police station & courts on right, take 1st right into Pikes Hill

Situated on the edge of Lyndhurst, this hotel is set well back from the main road. The smart, contemporary bedrooms include four-poster rooms and family rooms; children are very welcome here and parents will find that the hotel offers many child-friendly facilities. The eating options are the Forest Restaurant and the fine-dining Glasshouse Restaurant. There is an indoor swimming pool and Nordic sauna.

Rooms 28 (7 fmly) (6 GF) **D** £120-£160 (incl. bkfst)*
Facilities FTV ☆ Xmas New Year Wi-fi **Conf** Class 70 Board 60 Thtr 120 Del from £110 to £120* **Parking** 50
Notes LB Civ Wed 60

Best Western Crown

★★★ 75% HOTEL

☎ 023 8028 2922 🖹 023 8028 2751
High St SO43 7NF
e-mail: reception@crownhotel-lyndhurst.co.uk
web: www.crownhotel-lyndhurst.co.uk
dir: In centre of village, opposite church

The Crown, with its stone mullioned windows, panelled rooms and elegant period decor evokes the style of an Edwardian country house. Bedrooms are generally a good size and offer a useful range of facilities. Public areas have style and comfort and include a choice of function

and meeting rooms. The pleasant garden and terrace are havens of peace and tranquillity.

Rooms 38 (8 fmly) **S** £49-£72.50; **D** £80-£145 (incl. bkfst)* **Facilities** FTV Xmas New Year Wi-fi **Conf** Class 30 Board 45 Thtr 70 Del from £130 to £140* **Services** Lift **Parking** 60 **Notes** LB Civ Wed 70

Lyndhurst Park

★★★ 73% HOTEL

☎ 023 8028 3923 🖹 023 8028 3019
High St SO43 7NL
e-mail: lyndhurst.park@forestdale.com
web: www.lyndhurstparkhotel.co.uk
dir: M27 junct 1-3 to A35 to Lyndhurst. Hotel at bottom of High St

Although it is just by the High Street, this hotel is afforded seclusion and tranquillity from the town due to its five acres of mature grounds. The comfortable bedrooms include home-from-home touches. The bar offers a stylish setting for a snack whilst the oak-panelled Tudor restaurant provides a more formal dining venue.

Rooms 59 (3 fmly) **S** £69-£94; **D** £90-£149 (incl. bkfst)* **Facilities** FTV ☆ 🌊 Sauna Xmas New Year Wi-fi **Conf** Class 120 Board 85 Thtr 300 **Services** Lift **Parking** 100 **Notes** Civ Wed 120

Penny Farthing Hotel

★★ 80% METRO HOTEL

☎ 023 8028 4422 🖹 023 8028 4488
Romsey Rd SO43 7AA
e-mail: stay@pennyfarthinghotel.co.uk
dir: In Lyndhurst, hotel on left opposite old thatched cottage

This friendly, well-appointed establishment on the edge of town is suitable for business or for exploring the New Forest area. The attractive bedrooms are well-equipped, with some located in an adjacent cottage. There is a spacious breakfast room, a comfortable lounge bar and a bicycle store.

Rooms 20 (4 annexe) (1 fmly) (1 GF) **Facilities** FTV Wi-fi **Parking** 26 **Notes** ⊗ Closed Xmas week & New Year

Ormonde House

★★ 75% HOTEL

☎ 023 8028 2806 🖹 023 8028 2004
Southampton Rd SO43 7BT
e-mail: enquiries@ormondehouse.co.uk
web: www.ormondehouse.co.uk
dir: 800yds E of Lyndhurst on A35 to Southampton

Set back from the main road on the edge of Lyndhurst, this welcoming hotel combines an efficient mix of relaxed hospitality and attentive service. Bedrooms, including some on the ground floor, are well furnished and

equipped. Larger suites with kitchen facilities are also available. Home-cooked dinners feature a range of carefully presented fresh ingredients.

Rooms 25 (6 annexe) (1 fmly) (8 GF) **S** £46-£53; **D** £84-£136 (incl. bkfst)* **Facilities** New Year Wi-fi **Parking** 26 **Notes** LB Closed Xmas week

Knightwood Lodge

★★ 67% SMALL HOTEL THE INDEPENDENTS HOTEL ASSOCIATION

☎ 023 8028 2502 🖹 023 8028 3730
Southampton Rd SO43 7BU
e-mail: jackie4r@aol.com
web: www.knightwoodlodge.co.uk
dir: M27 junct 1, A337 to Lyndhurst. Left at lights in village onto A35 towards Southampton. Hotel 0.25m on left

This friendly, family-run hotel is situated on the outskirts of Lyndhurst. Comfortable bedrooms are modern in style and well equipped with many useful extras. The hotel offers an excellent range of facilities including a swimming pool, a jacuzzi and a small gym area. Two separate cottages are available for families or larger groups, and dogs are also welcome to accompany their owners in these units.

Rooms 18 (4 annexe) (2 fmly) (3 GF) **S** £35-£50; **D** £70-£100 (incl. bkfst)* **Facilities** FTV ☆ Gym Steam room Sauna Spa bath **Parking** 15 **Notes** LB

Parkhill

[U]

☎ 023 8028 2944
Beaulieu Rd SO43 7FZ
e-mail: info@lepoussin.co.uk
dir: Off A35 onto B3056 towards Beaulieu, hotel 1m on left

At the time of going to press we were informed that the multi-million pound rebuild of Parkhill is nearing completion. The meticulously restored country house situated deep in the New Forest is due to open in the autumn of 2009; the hotel will have new interior designs by David Collins. There will be 30 bedrooms and a number of guest lounges, whilst dining options in the two restaurants will include award-winning chef/director Alex Aitken's signature dining room showcasing his unique dishes of wild forest produce, and a more informal 'scullery'. A luxury spa with gym will be situated within the landscaped grounds. Please see the AA website: theAA.com for up-to-date information.

Rooms 30 **Conf** Class 20 Board 16 Thtr 30

Travelodge Stoney Cross Lyndhurst

BUDGET HOTEL

☎ 0871 984 6200 📠 023 8081 1544
A31 Westbound SO43 7GN
web: www.travelodge.co.uk
dir: M27 W'bound becomes A31. Lodge on left after Rufus Stone sign

Travelodge offers good quality, good value, budget accommodation. All offer family rooms sleeping up to four (two adults, two children) with en suite bathroom/shower-room, remote-control TV, tea- and coffee-making facilities and comfortable beds. Food options vary. Breakfast is at the on-site Bar Café restaurant (if available) or to take away. See also Hotel Groups pages.

Rooms 32 **S** fr £29; **D** fr £29

MILFORD ON SEA   Map 5 SZ29

Westover Hall

★★★ 88% ◉◉ COUNTRY HOUSE HOTEL

☎ 01590 643044 📠 01590 644490
Park Ln SO41 0PT
e-mail: info@westoverhallhotel.com
dir: M3 & M27 W onto A337 to Lymington, follow signs to Milford on Sea onto B3058, hotel outside village centre towards cliff

Just a few moments' walk from the beach and boasting uninterrupted views across Christchurch Bay to the Isle of Wight in the distance, this late-Victorian mansion offers a relaxed, informal and friendly atmosphere together with efficient standards of hospitality and service. Bedrooms do vary in size and aspect, but all have been decorated with flair and style. Architectural delights include dramatic stained-glass windows, extensive oak panelling and a galleried entrance hall. The cuisine is prepared with much care and attention to detail.

Rooms 15 (3 annexe) (2 fmly) (2 GF) **S** fr £145; **D** fr £290 (incl. bkfst & dinner) **Facilities** Xmas New Year Wi-fi **Conf** Class 14 Board 18 Thtr 35 Del from £195 to £220 **Parking** 50 **Notes** LB Civ Wed 50

See advert on page 235

South Lawn

★★★ 63% HOTEL

 OXFORD
HOTELS & INNS

☎ 01590 643911 📠 01590 645843
Lymington Rd SO41 0RF
e-mail: reservations.southlawn@ohiml.com
web: www.oxfordhotelsandinns.com
dir: M27 junct 1, take A337 to Lymington, follow signs for Christchurch, after 3m turn left on B3058 signed Milford on Sea, hotel 1m on right

Close to the coast and enjoying a quiet location, this pleasant hotel is set in well tended and spacious grounds this hotel is a comfortable place to stay. Bedrooms are spacious and well appointed. Guests can relax or take afternoon tea in the lounge; the restaurant menu offers a good range of choice. Staff are friendly and attentive.

Rooms 24 (3 fmly) (3 GF) **S** £65-£95; **D** £94-£156 (incl. bkfst & dinner)* **Facilities** Xmas New Year Wi-fi **Conf** Class 40 Board 30 Thtr 100 Del from £115 to £130* **Parking** 60 **Notes** LB ⊗ Civ Wed 120

NEW ALRESFORD   Map 5 SU53

Swan

★★ 67% HOTEL

☎ 01962 732302 & 734427 📠 01962 735274
11 West St SO24 9AD
e-mail: swanhotel@btinternet.com
web: www.swanhotelalresford.com
dir: Off A31 onto B3047

This former coaching inn dates back to the 18th century and remains a busy and popular destination for travellers and locals alike. Bedrooms are situated in both the main building and the more modern wing. The lounge bar and adjacent restaurant are open all day; for more traditional dining there is another restaurant which overlooks the busy village street.

Rooms 23 (12 annexe) (3 fmly) (5 GF) **S** £45-£55; **D** £75-£85 (incl. bkfst)* **Facilities** New Year Wi-fi **Conf** Class 60 Board 40 Thtr 90 Del from £75 to £100* **Parking** 25 **Notes** RS 25 Dec

See advert on this page

NEW MILTON — Map 5 SZ29

INSPECTORS' CHOICE

Chewton Glen Hotel & Spa
★★★★★ @@@ HOTEL

☎ 01425 275341 📄 01425 272310
Christchurch Rd BH25 5QS
e-mail: reservations@chewtonglen.com
web: www.chewtonglen.com
dir: A35 from Lyndhurst for 10m, left at staggered junct. Follow tourist sign for hotel through Walkford, take 2nd left

This outstanding hotel has been at the forefront of British hotel-keeping for many years. Once past the wrought iron entrance gates, guests are transported into a world of luxury. Log fires and afternoon tea are part of the tradition here, and lounges enjoy fine views over sweeping croquet lawns. Most bedrooms are very spacious, with private patios or balconies. Dining is a treat, and the extensive wine lists are essential reading for the enthusiast. The spa and leisure facilities are among the best in the country.

Rooms 58 (9 GF) **S** £313-£1244; **D** £313-£1244*
Facilities Spa FTV ☜ ⤳ ↕ 9 ⚒ Putt green ⤳ Gym Hydrotherapy spa Dance studio Cycling & jogging trail Clay shooting Archery ♫ Xmas New Year Wi-fi **Conf** Class 70 Board 40 Thtr 150 **Services** Air con **Parking** 100 **Notes** LB ⊗ Civ Wed 140

ODIHAM — Map 5 SU75

George
★★★ 72% HOTEL

☎ 01256 702081 📄 01256 704213
High St RG29 1LP
e-mail: reception@georgehotelodiham.com
web: www.georgehotelodiham.com
dir: M3 junct 5 follow Alton & Odiham signs. Through North Warnborough into Odiham left at top of hill, hotel on left

The George is over 450 years old and is a fine example of an old English inn. Bedrooms come in a number of styles; the older part of the property has beams and period features, whilst newer rooms have a contemporary feel. Guests can dine in the all-day bistro or the popular restaurant.

Rooms 28 (9 annexe) (1 fmly) (6 GF) (4 smoking)
S £65-£95; **D** £85-£130 (incl. bkfst)* **Facilities** FTV Wi-fi **Conf** Class 10 Board 26 Thtr 30 **Parking** 20 **Notes** LB Closed 24-26 Dec

PETERSFIELD — Map 5 SU72

Langrish House
★★★ 75% @@ HOTEL

☎ 01730 266941 📄 01730 260543
Langrish GU32 1RN
e-mail: frontdesk@langrishhouse.co.uk
web: www.langrishhouse.co.uk
dir: A3 onto A272 towards Winchester. Hotel signed, 2.5m on left

Langrish House has been in the same family for seven generations. It is located in an extremely peaceful area just a few minutes drive from Petersfield, halfway between Guildford and Portsmouth. Bedrooms are comfortable and well equipped with stunning views across the gardens to the hills. Guests can eat in the intimate Frederick's Restaurant with views over the lawn, or in the Old Vaults which have an interesting history dating back to 1644. The hotel is licensed for civil ceremonies and various themed events take place throughout the year.

Rooms 13 (1 fmly) (3 GF) **S** £80-£100; **D** £116-£170 (incl. bkfst)* **Facilities** ⤳ Xmas New Year Wi-fi **Conf** Class 18 Board 25 Thtr 60 **Parking** 80 **Notes** LB Closed 2 weeks in Jan Civ Wed 60

PORTSMOUTH & SOUTHSEA — Map 5 SU60

Portsmouth Marriott Hotel Marriott HOTELS & RESORTS
★★★★ 77% HOTEL

☎ 0870 400 7285 📄 0870 400 7385
Southampton Rd PO6 4SH
web: www.portsmouthmarriott.co.uk
dir: M27 junct 12, keep left , hotel on left

Close to the motorway and ferry port, this hotel is well suited to the business trade. The comfortable and well laid-out bedrooms provide a comprehensive range of facilities including up-to-date workstations. The leisure club offers a pool, a gym, and a health and beauty salon.

Rooms 174 (77 fmly) **Facilities** ☜ supervised Gym Exercise studio, Beauty salon Xmas **Conf** Class 180 Board 30 Thtr 350 **Services** Lift Air con **Parking** 250 **Notes** Civ Wed 100

Holiday Inn Portsmouth Holiday Inn HOTELS · RESORTS
★★★ 78% HOTEL

☎ 0870 400 9065 📄 023 9275 6715
Pembroke Rd PO1 2TA
e-mail: portsmouth@ihg.com
web: www.holidayinn.co.uk
dir: M275 into city centre, follow signs for seafront. Hotel on right after Kings Rd rdbt

This hotel occupies a great location close to Portsmouth seafront and near the Gunwharf Quays Shopping Centre. Restricted, complimentary parking is available on a first-come-first-served-basis at the hotel. Accommodation is comfortable and very well maintained; some rooms have magnificent sea views. On-site facilities include a swimming pool, fitness room, and a stylish restaurant; meeting rooms are available.

Rooms 165 (12 fmly) (6 GF) (13 smoking) **S** £80-£190; **D** £80-£190 (incl. bkfst)* **Facilities** FTV ☜ supervised Gym Health club Steam room Sauna Xmas New Year Wi-fi **Conf** Class 70 Board 60 Thtr 160 Del from £99 to £180* **Services** Lift Air con **Parking** 66 **Notes** LB ⊗ Civ Wed 160

Queen's

★★★ 77% HOTEL

☎ 023 9282 2466 📠 023 9282 1901
Clarence Pde, Southsea PO5 3LJ
e-mail: queenshotelports@aol.com
web: www.queenshotelportsmouth.com
dir: M27 junct 12 onto M275. Follow Southsea seafront signs, hotel on seafront. From A3, follow south to Portsmouth, take A27, follow signs to seafront

This hotel occupies a prominent position, only a couple of minutes from the seafront and Southsea's centre; the restaurant and many of the bedrooms have stunning sea views. Accommodation offers comfort and thoughtful accessories throughout. Enjoyable dinners and substantial breakfasts are available in the grand restaurant overlooking the well maintained gardens.

Rooms 72 (6 fmly) **Facilities** STV 🎵 Xmas New Year Wi-fi **Conf** Class 80 Board 60 Thtr 150 **Services** Lift **Parking** 60 **Notes** LB ⊗ Civ Wed 150

Westfield Hall

★★★ 74% HOTEL

☎ 023 9282 6971 📠 023 9287 0200
65 Festing Rd, Southsea PO4 0NQ
e-mail: enquiries@whhotel.info
web: www.whhotel.info
dir: From M275 follow Southsea seafront signs. Left onto Clarence Esplanade on South Parade Pier, left onto St Helens Parade, hotel 150yds

This hotel is situated in a quiet side road close to the seafront and town centre. The accommodation is split between two identical houses and all rooms are smartly appointed and well equipped. Public rooms are

attractively decorated and include three lounges, a bar and a restaurant.

Rooms 26 (11 annexe) (12 fmly) (6 GF) **S** £50-£59; **D** £68-£120 (incl. bkfst)* **Facilities** STV FTV Wi-fi **Parking** 16 **Notes** ⊗

Best Western Royal Beach

★★★ 73% HOTEL

☎ 023 9273 1281 📠 023 9281 7572
South Pde, Southsea PO4 0RN
e-mail: enquiries@royalbeachhotel.co.uk
web: www.royalbeachhotel.co.uk
dir: M27 to M275, follow signs to seafront. Hotel on seafront

This former Victorian seafront hotel is a smart and comfortable venue suitable for leisure and business guests alike. Bedrooms and public areas are well presented and generally spacious, and the smart Coast Bar is an ideal venue for a relaxing drink.

Rooms 124 (18 fmly) (47 smoking) **S** £60-£95; **D** £80-£125 (incl. bkfst) **Facilities** STV Xmas New Year Wi-fi **Conf** Class 180 Board 40 Thtr 280 Del from £124.95 **Services** Lift **Parking** 50 **Notes** LB

Seacrest

★★ 72% HOTEL

☎ 023 9273 3192 📠 023 9283 2523
11/12 South Pde, Southsea PO5 2JB
e-mail: office@seacresthotel.co.uk
dir: From M27/M275 follow signs for seafront, Pyramids & Sea Life Centre. Hotel opposite Rock Gardens & Pyramids

In a premier seafront location, this smart hotel provides the ideal base for exploring the town. Bedrooms, many benefiting from sea views, are decorated to a high standard with good facilities. Guests can relax in either the south-facing lounge, furnished with large leather sofas, or the adjacent bar; there is also a cosy dining room popular with residents.

Rooms 28 (3 fmly) (4 GF) **S** £49-£69; **D** £65-£89 (incl. bkfst) **Facilities** STV FTV Wi-fi **Services** Lift **Parking** 12 **Notes** LB

Express by Holiday Inn Portsmouth Gunwharf Quays

BUDGET HOTEL

☎ 023 9289 4240 📠 023 9289 4241
Gunwharf Quays PO1 3FD
e-mail: portsmouth@kewgreen.co.uk
web: www.hiexpress.com/exportsmouth

A modern hotel ideal for families and business travellers. Fresh and uncomplicated, the spacious rooms include Sky TV, power shower and tea and coffee-making facilities. Continental buffet breakfast is included in the room rate; other meals may be taken at the nearby family pub or restaurant. See also the Hotel Groups pages.

Rooms 130 **Conf** Board 24 Thtr 50

The Farmhouse

BUDGET HOTEL

☎ 023 9265 0510 📠 023 9269 3458
Burrfields Rd PO3 5HH
e-mail: farmhouse.portsmouth@greenekinginns.co.uk
web: www.farmhouseinnlodge.com
dir: A3(M)/M27 onto A27. Take Southsea exit, follow A2030. 3rd lights right into Burrfields Road. Hotel 2nd car park on left

Located on the eastern fringe of the city, this purpose-built hotel is conveniently located for all major routes. The spacious, modern bedrooms are well equipped and include ground floor and family rooms. The Farmhouse Hungry Horse Pub offers a wide range of eating options, and there is an ActionZone adventure area.

Rooms 74 (6 fmly) (33 GF) **Conf** Class 64 Board 40 Thtr 150

PORTSMOUTH & SOUTHSEA *continued*

Ibis Portsmouth Centre

BUDGET HOTEL

☎ 023 9264 0000 📠 023 9264 1000
Winston Churchill Av PO1 2LX
e-mail: h1461@accor.com
web: www.ibishotel.com
dir: M27 junct 12 onto M275. Follow signs for city centre, Sealife Centre & Guildhall. Right at rdbt into Winston Churchill Ave

Modern, budget hotel offering comfortable accommodation in bright and practical bedrooms. Breakfast is self-service and dinner is available in the restaurant. See also the Hotel Groups pages.

Rooms 144 **Conf** Class 20 Board 20 Thtr 30

Innkeeper's Lodge Portsmouth

BUDGET HOTEL

☎ 0845 112 6105 📠 0845 112 6198
Copnor Rd, Hilsea PO3 5HS
web: www.innkeeperslodge.com/portsmouth
dir: A27 onto A2030. Right at lights, over 3 rdbts into Norway Rd. Hotel on A288 (Copnor Rd) at junct with Norway Rd

Innkeeper's Lodge represents an exciting, high value concept within the budget hotel market. Comfortable bedrooms provide excellent facilities that include satellite TV and modem points. Options include family rooms; and for the corporate guest, cutting edge IT which includes Wi-fi access. A popular Carvery provides all-day food, including an extensive, complimentary continental breakfast. See also the Hotel Groups pages.

Rooms 33 (5 fmly)

Travelodge Portsmouth

BUDGET HOTEL

☎ 0871 984 6170 📠 023 9263 9121
Kingston Crescent, North End PO2 8AB
web: www.travelodge.co.uk
dir: M27, M275 towards north end of town centre & Continental Ferries. At Rudmore rdbt 2nd exit into Kingston Crescent. Lodge on right

Travelodge offers good quality, good value, budget accommodation. All offer family rooms sleeping up to four (two adults, two children) with en suite bathroom/shower-room, remote-control TV, tea- and coffee-making facilities and comfortable beds. Food options vary. Breakfast is at the on-site Bar Café restaurant (if available) or to take away. See also Hotel Groups pages.

Rooms 108 **S** fr £29; **D** fr £29

Tyrrells Ford Country House

★★★ 71% SMALL HOTEL

☎ 01425 672646 📠 01425 672262
Avon BH23 7BH
e-mail: info@tyrrellsford.co.uk
web: www.tyrrellsford.co.uk
dir: from A31 to Ringwood take B3347. Hotel 3m S on left

Set in the New Forest, this delightful family-run hotel has much to offer. Most bedrooms have views over the open country. Diners may eat in the formal restaurant, or sample the wide range of bar meals; all dishes are prepared using fresh local produce. The Gallery Lounge offers guests a peaceful area in which to relax.

Rooms 14 **Conf** Class 20 Board 20 Thtr 40 **Parking** 100
Notes LB ⊗ Civ Wed 60

Travelodge Ringwood

BUDGET HOTEL

☎ 0871 984 6237 📠 01425 475941
St Leonards BH24 2NR
web: www.travelodge.co.uk
dir: Off A31 eastbound

Travelodge offers good quality, good value, budget accommodation. All offer family rooms sleeping up to four (two adults, two children) with en suite bathroom/shower-room, remote-control TV, tea- and coffee-making facilities and comfortable beds. Food options vary. Breakfast is at the on-site Bar Café restaurant (if available) or to take away. See also Hotel Groups pages.

Rooms 31 (23 fmly) **S** fr £29; **D** fr £29

Potters Heron Hotel

★★★ 75% HOTEL

☎ 023 8027 7800 📠 023 8025 1359
Winchester Rd, Ampfield SO51 9ZF
e-mail: thepottersheron@pebblehotels.com
dir: M3 junct 12 follow Chandler's Ford signs. 2nd exit at 3rd rdbt follow Ampfield signs, over x-rds. Hotel on left in 1m

This distinctive thatched hotel retains many of its original features. In a convenient location with access to Winchester, Southampton and the M3, this establishment has modern accommodation and stylish, spacious public areas. Most of the bedrooms have their own balcony or terrace. The pub and restaurant both offer an interesting range of dishes that will suit a variety of tastes.

Rooms 54 (1 fmly) (29 GF) **S** £65-£85; **D** £65-£110*
Facilities STV FTV Xmas New Year Wi-fi **Conf** Class 40 Board 30 Thtr 100 Del from £120 to £150 **Services** Lift **Parking** 120 **Notes** LB ⊗ Civ Wed 100

INSPECTORS' CHOICE

Tylney Hall

★★★★ ⊛⊛ HOTEL

☎ 01256 764881 📠 01256 768141
RG27 9AZ
e-mail: sales@tylneyhall.com
web: www.tylneyhall.com
dir: M3 junct 5, A287 to Basingstoke, over junct with A30, over railway bridge, towards Newnham. Right at Newnham Green. Hotel 1m on left

A grand Victorian country house set in 66 acres of beautiful parkland. The hotel offers high standards of comfort in relaxed yet elegant surroundings, featuring magnificently restored water gardens, originally laid out by the famous gardener, Gertrude Jekyll. Spacious public rooms include the Wedgwood drawing room and panelled Oak Room, which are filled with stunning flower arrangements and warmed by log fires. The spacious bedrooms are traditionally furnished and offer a high degree of comfort.

Rooms 112 (77 annexe) (1 fmly) (21 GF) **S** £155-£450;
D £205-£500 (incl. bkfst)* **Facilities** Spa STV ⊗ ⟲ ⟳ ⟳
⟳ Gym Clay pigeon shooting Archery Falconry Balloon rides Laser shooting ♫ Xmas New Year Wi-fi
Conf Class 70 Board 40 Thtr 120 **Parking** 120
Notes LB ⊗ Civ Wed 100

Innkeeper's Lodge Portsmouth North

BUDGET HOTEL

☎ 0845 112 6106 📠 0845 112 6197
Whichers Gate Rd PO9 6BB
web: www.innkeeperslodge.com/portsmouthnorth
dir: A3(M) junct 2. Right at rdbt onto B2149 towards Rowland's Castle. 2m, turn left onto B2148 (Whichers Gate Road). Lodge on left

Innkeeper's Lodge represent an exciting, high value concept within the budget hotel market. Comfortable bedrooms provide excellent facilities that include satellite TV and modem points. Options include spacious family rooms; and for the corporate guest, cutting edge IT is provided with Wi-fi access. All-day food is provided in the adjacent pub restaurant. The extensive continental breakfast is complimentary. See also the Hotel Groups pages.

Rooms 21 (3 fmly)

SHEDFIELD
Map 5 SU51

Marriott Meon Valley Hotel & Country Club

★★★★ 76% ◉ HOTEL

☎ 01329 833455 ≣ 01329 834411
Sandy Ln SO32 2HQ
web: www.marriottmeonvalley.co.uk
dir: M27 junct 7 take A334 towards Wickham & Botley. Sandy Ln on left 2m from Botley

This modern, smartly appointed hotel and country club has extensive indoor and outdoor leisure facilities, including two golf courses. Bedrooms are spacious and well equipped, and guests have a choice of eating and drinking options. It is ideally suited for easy access to both Portsmouth and Southampton.

Rooms 113 (43 fmly) (29 GF) (10 smoking) **S** £85-£165; **D** £95-£175 (incl. bkfst) **Facilities** Spa FTV ⊙ ⚡ 27 ⚡ Putt green Gym Cardio-vascular aerobics Health & beauty salon Xmas New Year Wi-fi **Conf** Class 50 Board 32 Thtr 100 Del from £130 to £165* **Services** Lift **Parking** 360 **Notes** ⊗ Civ Wed 90

SOUTHAMPTON
Map 5 SU41

See also **Botley & Woodlands**

De Vere Grand Harbour
DE VERE collection

★★★★ 77% HOTEL

☎ 023 8063 3033 ≣ 023 8063 3066
West Quay Rd SO15 1AG
e-mail: grandharbour@devere-hotels.com
web: www.devere.co.uk
dir: M27 junct 3 follow Waterfront signs. Keep in left lane of dual carrriageway, then follow Heritage & Waterfront signs onto West Quay Road

Enjoying views of the harbour, this hotel stands alongside the medieval town walls and close to the West Quay centre. The modern design is impressive, with leisure facilities located in the dramatic glass pyramid. The spacious bedrooms are well appointed and thoughtfully equipped. For dining, guests can choose between two bars as well as fine dining within Allertons Restaurant and a more informal style within No 5 Brasserie.

Rooms 173 (22 fmly) **Facilities** Spa ⊙ Gym Beauty suite Xmas New Year **Conf** Class 200 Board 150 Thtr 500 **Services** Lift **Parking** 190 **Notes** LB ⊗ Civ Wed 310

Legacy Botleigh Grange

★★★★ 75% ◉ HOTEL

☎ 0870 832 9950 ≣ 01489 788535
Hedge End SO30 2GA
e-mail: res-botleighgrange@legacy-hotels.co.uk
web: www.legacy-hotels.co.uk
dir: M27 junct 7, A334 to Botley, hotel 0.5m on left

This impressive mansion, situated close to the M27, displays good quality throughout. The bedrooms are spacious with a good range of facilities. Public areas include a large conference room and a pleasant terrace with views overlooking the gardens and lake. The restaurant offers interesting menus using fresh, local produce.

Rooms 56 (8 fmly) **S** £65-£145; **D** £71-£165 (incl. bkfst)* **Facilities** Spa STV ⊙ Putt green Fishing Gym Relaxation room Steam room Sauna Xmas New Year Wi-fi **Conf** Class 175 Board 60 Thtr 500 Del from £130 to £165* **Services** Lift **Parking** 200 **Notes** LB ⊗ Civ Wed 180

Holiday Inn Express Southampton - M27, Jct 7
Express

★★★ HOTEL

☎ 023 8060 6060 & 8060 6040 ≣ 023 8060 6050
Botley Rd, West End SO30 3XH
e-mail: reservations@expressbyholidayinn.uk.net
web: www.hiexpress.com/exsouthampton
dir: M27 junct 7, follow brown signs to The Rose Bowl. Hotel 1m from junct 7 at entrance to The Rose Bowl

This hotel, adjacent to the Rose Bowl, is conveniently located for Southampton Airport and Docks and has ample parking. There is an air-conditioned restaurant serving conference lunches and evening meals, a fully licensed bar and lounge area with a 42" plasma TV and Sky Sports. The hotel offers high speed internet access in all bedrooms and meeting rooms, plus Wi-fi in the public areas. Use of leisure facilities are available at the adjacent Esporta Leisure Centre.

Rooms 176 (39 fmly) (38 GF) (9 smoking) **S** £49-£99; **D** £49-£99 (incl. bkfst) **Facilities** STV Use of leisure facilities at adjacent Esporta Leisure Centre Wi-fi **Conf** Class 26 Board 20 Thtr 52 Del from £99 to £149 **Services** Lift **Parking** 176 **Notes** LB

Chilworth Manor
CLASSIC BRITISH HOTELS

★★★ 77% HOTEL

☎ 023 8076 7333 ≣ 023 8070 1743
SO16 7PT
e-mail: sales@chilworth-manor.co.uk
web: www.chilworth-manor.co.uk
dir: 1m from M3/M27 junct on A27 (Romsey road) N from Southampton. Pass Chilworth Arms on left, in 200mtrs turn left at Southampton Science Park sign. Hotel immediately right

Set in 12 acres of delightful grounds, this attractive Edwardian manor house is conveniently located for Southampton and also the New Forest, now designated a National Park. Bedrooms are located in both the main house and an adjoining wing. The hotel is particularly popular as both a conference and a wedding venue.

Rooms 95 (6 fmly) (23 GF) **S** £60-£140; **D** £70-£150* **Facilities** Spa STV FTV ⊙ supervised ⚡ ⚡ Gym Trim trail walking Giant chess Petanque New Year Wi-fi **Conf** Class 50 Board 50 Thtr 130 Del from £140 to £165* **Services** Lift **Parking** 200 **Notes** LB Civ Wed 105

Novotel Southampton

★★★ 74% HOTEL

☎ 023 8033 0550 ≣ 023 8022 2158
1 West Quay Rd SO15 1RA
e-mail: H1073@accor.com
web: www.novotel.com
dir: M27 junct 3, follow city centre/A33 signs. In 1m take right lane for West Quay & Dock Gates 4-10. Hotel entrance on left. Turn at lights by McDonalds, left at rdbt, hotel straight ahead

Modern purpose-built hotel situated close to the city centre, railway station, ferry terminal and major road networks. The brightly decorated bedrooms are ideal for families and business guests; four rooms have facilities for the less mobile. The open-plan public areas include the Garden Brasserie, a bar and a leisure complex.

Rooms 121 (50 fmly) (9 smoking) **Facilities** STV FTV ⊙ Gym New Year Wi-fi **Conf** Class 300 Board 150 Thtr 450 **Services** Lift **Parking** 300 **Notes** LB Civ Wed 150

SOUTHAMPTON *continued*

Highfield House Hotel

★★★ 71% METRO HOTEL

☎ 0844 855 9125 🖹 023 8058 1914
Highfield Ln, Portswood SO17 1AQ
e-mail: gm.highfieldhouse@foliohotels.com
web: www.foliohotels.com/highfield
dir: M27 junct 5, A335 to city centre, at 5th lights follow
signs for Portswood/University, hotel on right after
Shaftesbury Ave

Located in a leafy suburb of Southampton, a short drive
to the city centre, well positioned for both business and
leisure travellers. The smartly appointed bedrooms are
well equipped and feature a number of accessories to
enhance guest comfort. Public areas include the lounge,
breakfast room and a number of meeting rooms. Staff are
happy to recommend a nearby restaurant.

Rooms 71 (8 fmly) (10 GF) **Facilities** STV FTV Wi-fi
Conf Class 40 Board 24 Thtr 150 **Parking** 55 **Notes** ⊗

Southampton Park

★★★ 71% HOTEL

☎ 023 8034 3343 🖹 023 8033 2538
Cumberland Place SO15 2WY
e-mail: southampton.park@forestdale.com
web: www.southamptonparkhotel.com
dir: At north end of Inner Ring Road, opposite Watts Park
& Civic Centre

This modern hotel, in the heart of the city, provides well-
equipped, smartly appointed and comfortable bedrooms.
It boasts a well equipped spa with all modern facilities
and a beauty salon for those who wish to pamper
themselves. The public areas are spacious and include
the popular MJ's Brasserie. Parking is available in a
multi-storey behind the hotel.

Rooms 72 (10 fmly) **S** £55-£85; **D** £80-£140 (incl. bkfst)*
Facilities Spa FTV ⓣ supervised Gym New Year Wi-fi
Conf Class 60 Board 50 Thtr 150 **Services** Lift
Notes Closed 25 & 26 Dec nights

Holiday Inn Southampton

★★★ 70% HOTEL

☎ 0870 400 9073 🖹 023 8063 4769
Herbert Walker Av SO15 1HJ
e-mail: southamptonhi@ihg.com
web: www.holidayinn.co.uk
dir: M27 junct 3 follow 'Dockgate 1-10 & Southampton
Waterfront' signs. Hotel adjacent to Dock Gate 8

Convenient for both the port and town centre, this modern
hotel is popular with both business and leisure guests.
The well-equipped bedrooms are comfortably furnished.
Public areas include an informal lounge bar and a
contemporary restaurant offering an extensive range of
popular dishes. Conference and leisure facilities are also
available.

Rooms 130 (6 fmly) (15 smoking) **Facilities** ⓣ
supervised Gym New Year Wi-fi **Conf** Class 75 Board 60
Thtr 180 **Services** Lift Air con **Parking** 140 **Notes** ⊗
Civ Wed

Elizabeth House

★★ 76% HOTEL

☎ 023 8022 4327 🖹 023 8022 4327
42-44 The Avenue SO17 1XP
e-mail: mail@elizabethhousehotel.com
web: www.elizabethhousehotel.com
dir: On A33, hotel on left after Southampton Common,
before main lights

This hotel is conveniently situated close to the city centre,
so provides an ideal base for both business and leisure
guests. The bedrooms are well equipped and are
attractively furnished with comfort in mind. There is also
a cosy and atmospheric bistro in the cellar where evening
meals are served.

Rooms 27 (7 annexe) (9 fmly) (8 GF) **S** £55-£64.50;
D £65-£77.50 (incl. bkfst)* **Facilities** FTV Wi-fi
Conf Class 24 Board 24 Thtr 40 Del from £99 to £101*
Parking 31

Ibis Southampton Centre

BUDGET HOTEL

☎ 023 8063 4463 🖹 023 8022 3273
West Quay Rd, Western Esplanade SO15 1RA
e-mail: H1039@accor.com
web: www.ibishotel.com
dir: M27 junct 3/M271. Left to city centre (A35), follow
Old Town Waterfront until 4th lights, left, then left again,
hotel opposite station

Modern, budget hotel offering comfortable
accommodation in bright and practical bedrooms.
Breakfast is self-service and dinner is available in the
restaurant. See also the Hotel Groups pages.

Rooms 93 (9 smoking) **Conf** Class 50 Board 40 Thtr 80

Travelodge Southampton

BUDGET HOTEL

☎ 0871 984 6212 🖹 023 8033 4569
Lodge Rd SO14 6QR
web: www.travelodge.co.uk
dir: M3 junct 14, A33 to Southampton, on left after 6th
lights

Travelodge offers good quality, good value, budget
accommodation. All offer family rooms sleeping up to four
(two adults, two children) with en suite bathroom/
shower-room, remote-control TV, tea- and coffee-making
facilities and comfortable beds. Food options vary.
Breakfast is at the on-site Bar Café restaurant (if
available) or to take away. See also Hotel Groups pages.

Rooms 59 **S** fr £29; **D** fr £29

SOUTHSEA

See Portsmouth & Southsea

STOCKBRIDGE Map 5 SU33

Grosvenor Hotel

Ⓤ

☎ 01264 810606 🖹 01264 810747
23 High St SO20 6EU
e-mail: 9180@greeneking.co.uk

Currently the rating for this establishment is not
confirmed. This may be due to a change of ownership or
because it has only recently joined the AA rating scheme.
For further details please see the AA website: theAA.com

Rooms 26 (12 annexe) **Conf** Class 50 Board 35 Thtr 100

SUTTON SCOTNEY Map 5 SU43

Norton Park

★★★★ 76% HOTEL

☎ 0845 0740055 & 01962 763000 🖹 01962 760860
SO21 3NB
e-mail: nortonpark@qhotels.co.uk
web: www.qhotels.co.uk
dir: From all directions follow A303/A34 intersection then
signs to Sutton Scotney. Hotel on Micheldever Station Rd
(old A30) 1m from Sutton Scotney

Set in 54 acres of beautiful parkland in the heart of
Hampshire, Norton Park offers both business and leisure
guests a great range of amenities. Dating from the 16th
century, this hotel is now complemented by extensive
buildings housing the bedrooms, and public areas which
include a superb leisure club and numerous conference
facilities. Ample parking is available.

Rooms 185 (11 fmly) (80 GF) **Facilities** Spa ⓣ
supervised 🏊 Gym Steam room Sauna Experience shower
Ice fountain Xmas New Year Wi-fi **Conf** Class 250
Board 80 Thtr 340 Del from £90 to £195 **Services** Lift
Parking 220 **Notes** Civ Wed 340

Travelodge Sutton Scotney
(A34 Northbound)

BUDGET HOTEL

☎ 0871 984 6217 🖹 01962 761096
SO21 3JY
web: www.travelodge.co.uk
dir: on A34 northbound

Travelodge offers good quality, good value, budget
accommodation. All offer family rooms sleeping up to four
(two adults, two children) with en suite bathroom/
shower-room, remote-control TV, tea- and coffee-making
facilities and comfortable beds. Food options vary.
Breakfast is at the on-site Bar Café restaurant (if
available) or to take away. See also Hotel Groups pages.

Rooms 31 **S** fr £29; **D** fr £29

Travelodge Sutton Scotney (A34 Southbound)

BUDGET HOTEL

☎ 0871 984 6217 📠 01962 761096
SO21 3JY
web: www.travelodge.co.uk
dir: on A34 southbound

Rooms 40 **S** fr £29; **D** fr £29

SWAY Map 5 SZ29

Sway Manor Restaurant & Hotel

★★★ 75% HOTEL

☎ 01590 682754 📠 01590 682955
Station Rd SO41 6BA
e-mail: info@swaymanor.com
web: www.swaymanor.com
dir: Exit B3055 (Brockenhurst/New Milton road) into village centre

Built at the turn of the 20th century, this attractive mansion is set in its own grounds, and conveniently located in the village centre. Bedrooms are well appointed and generously equipped; most have views over the gardens and pool. The bar and conservatory restaurant, both with views over the gardens, are popular with locals.

Rooms 15 (3 fmly) **S** £63.50-£69.50; **D** £127-£139 (incl. bkfst)* **Facilities** ⚄ 🎵 Xmas New Year Wi-fi **Conf** Class 20 Board 15 Del from £86.50 to £92.50* **Services** Lift **Parking** 40 **Notes** LB Civ Wed 80

WICKHAM Map 5 SU51

Old House Hotel & Restaurant

★★★ 77% ◉◉ HOTEL

☎ 01329 833049 📠 01329 833672
The Square PO17 5JG
e-mail: enquiries@oldhousehotel.co.uk
web: www.oldhousehotel.co.uk
dir: M27 junct 10, N on A32 for 2m towards Alton

This hotel, a Grade II listed building, occupies a convenient location in the heart of historic Wickham, which is not far from Portsmouth and Southampton. Bedrooms and bathrooms are smartly co-ordinated, and include stylish Garden Suites that look out on the delightful garden. The public areas have much character and charm and the service is attentive and friendly. The award-winning cuisine utilises seasonal, local produce.

Rooms 12 (4 annexe) (2 fmly) (4 GF) **D** £90-£165 (incl. bkfst)* **Facilities** STV FTV Xmas New Year Wi-fi **Conf** Board 14 Del from £200* **Parking** 8 **Notes** LB ⊗ Civ Wed 70

WINCHESTER Map 5 SU42

Lainston House

★★★★ ◉◉◉ HOTEL

☎ 01962 776088 📠 01962 776672
Sparsholt SO21 2LT
e-mail: enquiries@lainstonhouse.com
web: www.exclusivehotels.co.uk
dir: 2m NW off B3049 towards Stockbridge

This graceful example of a William and Mary House enjoys a countryside location amidst mature grounds and gardens. Staff provide good levels of courtesy and care with a polished, professional service. Bedrooms are tastefully appointed and include some spectacular spacious rooms with stylish handmade beds and stunning bathrooms. Public rooms include a cocktail bar built entirely from a single cedar and stocked with an impressive range of rare drinks and cigars. Exclusive Hotels - AA Small Hotel Group of the Year 2009-10.

Rooms 50 (6 fmly) (18 GF) **S** £125; **D** £125-£360* **Facilities** ⚄ Fishing 🏌 Gym Archery Clay pigeon shooting Cycling Hot air ballooning Walking 🎵 Xmas New Year Wi-fi **Conf** Class 80 Board 40 Thtr 166 Del from £200 to £295* **Parking** 200 **Notes** Civ Wed 200

The Winchester Hotel

★★★★ 76% ◉ HOTEL

☎ 01962 709988 📠 01962 840862
Worthy Ln SO23 7AB
e-mail: pauleaves@pedersenhotels.com
web: www.pedersenhotels.com/winchester
dir: A33 then A3047, hotel 1m on right

This hotel is just a few minutes' walk from the city centre, is very smartly appointed throughout, and includes a great leisure centre. The staff are extremely friendly and helpful, and award-winning food is served in the contemporary Hutton's Brasserie.

Rooms 98 (2 fmly) (8 GF) **S** £40-£145; **D** £40-£200* **Facilities** FTV ⚄ supervised Gym Sauna Steam room Spa bath Xmas New Year Wi-fi **Conf** Class 100 Board 40 Thtr 200 Del from £130 to £150* **Services** Lift Air con **Parking** 60 **Notes** LB ⊗ Civ Wed 180

WINCHESTER *continued*

Hotel du Vin Winchester

★★★★ 75% @@ TOWN HOUSE HOTEL

☎ 01962 841414 ≣ 01962 842458
Southgate St SO23 9EF
e-mail: info@winchester.hotelduvin.com
web: www.hotelduvin.com
dir: M3 junct 11 towards Winchester, follow signs. Hotel in approx 2m on left just past cinema

Continuing to set excellent standards, this inviting hotel is best known for its high profile bistro. The individually designed bedrooms have all the Hotel du Vin signature touches including fine Egyptian cotton linen, power showers and Wi-fi. The bistro serves imaginative yet simply cooked dishes from a seasonal, daily-changing menu.

Rooms 24 (4 annexe) (4 GF) **S** £140-£225; **D** £140-£225*
Facilities STV Xmas New Year Wi-fi **Conf** Class 30 Board 20 Thtr 40 Del from £205* **Parking** 35 **Notes** LB Civ Wed 60

Mercure Wessex

★★★★ 70% HOTEL

☎ 01962 861611 ≣ 01962 841503
Paternoster Row SO23 9LQ
web: www.mercure-uk.com
dir: M3, follow signs for town centre, at rdbt by King Alfred's statue past Guildhall, next left, hotel on right

Occupying an enviable location in the centre of this historic city and adjacent to the spectacular cathedral, this hotel is quietly situated on a side street. Inside, the atmosphere is restful and welcoming, with public areas and some bedrooms enjoying unrivalled views of the hotel's centuries-old neighbour.

Rooms 94 (6 fmly) **Facilities** STV Gym Xmas New Year Wi-fi **Conf** Class 60 Board 60 Thtr 100 **Services** Lift **Parking** 60 **Notes** Civ Wed 100

The Winchester Royal

★★★ 77% @ HOTEL

☎ 01962 840840 ≣ 01962 841582
Saint Peter St SO23 8BS
e-mail: winchester.royal@forestdale.com
web: www.thewinchesterroyalhotel.co.uk
dir: M3 junct 9 to Winnall Trading Estate. Follow to city centre, cross river, left, 1st right. Onto one-way system, take 2nd right. Hotel immediately on right

Situated in the heart of the former capital of England, a warm welcome awaits at this friendly hotel, which in parts, dates back to the 16th century. The bedrooms may vary in style but they are all comfortable and well equipped; the modern annexe rooms overlook the attractive well-tended gardens. The conservatory restaurant makes a very pleasant setting for enjoyable meals.

Rooms 75 (56 annexe) (1 fmly) (27 GF) **S** £85-£110; **D** £105-£150 (incl. bkfst)* **Facilities** FTV Xmas New Year Wi-fi **Conf** Class 50 Board 50 Thtr 120 **Parking** 50 **Notes** Civ Wed 100

Marwell

★★★ 73% HOTEL

☎ 01962 777681 ≣ 01962 777160
Thompsons Ln, Colden Common, Marwell SO21 1JY
e-mail: info@marwellhotel.co.uk
web: www.marwellhotel.co.uk
dir: B3354 through Twyford. 1st exit at rdbt continue on B3354, then left onto B2177 signed Bishop Waltham. Turn left into Thomsons Ln after 1m, hotel on left

Taking its theme from the adjacent zoo, this unusual hotel is based on the famous TreeTops safari lodge in Kenya. The well equipped bedrooms, split between four lodges, reflect with a hint of safari style, while the smart public areas include an airy lobby bar and an 'Out of Africa' themed restaurant. There is also a selection of meeting and leisure facilities.

Rooms 66 (10 fmly) (36 GF) **S** £75-£119; **D** £85-£134 (incl. bkfst)* **Facilities** STV FTV ✎ supervised ⅃ 18 Gym Sauna New Year Wi-fi **Conf** Class 60 Board 60 Thtr 175 Del from £135 to £160* **Parking** 120 **Notes** LB ⊗ Civ Wed 150

YATELEY | Map 5 SU86

Casa dei Cesari Restaurant & Hotel

★★★ 71% HOTEL

☎ 01252 873275 ≣ 01252 870614
Handford Ln GU46 6BT
e-mail: reservations@casadeicesari.co.uk
dir: M3 junct 4a, follow signs for town centre. Hotel signed

This delightful hotel where a warm welcome is guaranteed is ideally located for transport networks. It

boasts rooms with quality and comfort, and the Italian-themed restaurant, which is very popular locally, serves an extensive traditional menu.

Rooms 63 (2 fmly) (15 GF) (33 smoking) **Facilities** Xmas New Year Wi-fi **Conf** Class 60 Board 60 Thtr 150 **Services** Lift **Parking** 80 **Notes** ⊗ Civ Wed 150

HEREFORDSHIRE

HEREFORD | Map 10 SO54

See also **Leominster**

Castle House

★★★ 87% @@@ HOTEL

☎ 01432 356321 ≣ 01432 365909
Castle St HR1 2NW
e-mail: info@castlehse.co.uk
web: www.castlehse.co.uk
dir: Follow signs to City Centre East. At junct of Commercial Rd & Union St follow hotel signs

Enjoying a prime city centre location and with a terraced garden leading to the castle moat, this delightful Grade II listed Georgian mansion is the epitome of elegance and sophistication. The character bedrooms are equipped with every luxury to ensure a memorable stay and are complemented perfectly by the well-proportioned and restful lounge and bar, together with the elegant topiary-themed restaurant where award-winning modern British cuisine is served.

Rooms 15 (1 GF) **Facilities** FTV Free membership at local spa Xmas New Year Wi-fi **Services** Lift **Parking** 12 **Notes** LB ⊗

See advert on opposite page

Belmont Lodge & Golf

★★★ 74% HOTEL

☎ 01432 352666 ≣ 01432 358090
Belmont HR2 9SA
e-mail: info@belmont-hereford.co.uk
web: www.belmont-hereford.co.uk
dir: From Hereford towards Abergavenny on A465. Pass Tesco on right, straight on at rdbt. 0.25m turn right into Ruckhall Ln (signed Belmont Golf Course). Hotel on right in 0.5m

This impressive complex, surrounded by its own golf course, commands delightful views over the River Wye and the countryside, and is less than a ten minute drive from the city centre. Bedrooms, in a modern lodge, are comfortable and well equipped, while the smart restaurant and bar, in the main house, offer an excellent choice of food.

Rooms 30 (4 fmly) (15 GF) **S** £65-£75; **D** £59-£69* **Facilities** ᠘ 18 ᠑ Putt green Fishing ᠓ Games room with pool table Xmas **Conf** Class 25 Board 25 Thtr 50 **Parking** 150 **Notes** LB ⊗

Three Counties Hotel

★★★ 73% HOTEL

☎ 01432 299955 ▤ 01432 275114
Belmont Rd HR2 7BP
e-mail: enquiries@threecountieshotel.co.uk
web: www.threecountieshotel.co.uk
dir: On A465 Abergavenny Rd

Just a mile west of the city centre, this large, privately owned, modern complex has well-equipped, spacious bedrooms; many are located in separate single-storey buildings around the extensive car park. There is a spacious, comfortable lounge, a traditional bar and an attractive restaurant.

Rooms 60 (32 annexe) (4 fmly) (46 GF) **S** £65.50-£80; **D** £75.50-£92.50 (incl. bkfst)* **Facilities** STV Wi-fi **Conf** Class 200 Board 120 Thtr 450 Del from £95 to £105* **Parking** 250 **Notes** LB Civ Wed 250

See advert on page 246

Travelodge Hereford

BUDGET HOTEL

☎ 08719 846 343 ▤ 01432 351819
Pomana Place HR4 0EF
web: www.travelodge.co.uk
dir: A438, left onto Grimmer Rd, then left onto Pomana Place

Travelodge offers good quality, good value, budget accommodation. All offer family rooms sleeping up to four (two adults, two children) with en suite bathroom/shower-room, remote-control TV, tea- and coffee-making facilities and comfortable beds. Food options vary. Breakfast is at the on-site Bar Café restaurant (if available) or to take away. See also Hotel Groups pages.

Rooms 52 **S** fr £29; **D** fr £29

Travelodge Hereford Grafton

BUDGET HOTEL

☎ 0871 984 6422 ▤ 01432 354312
Grafton, Ross Rd HR2 8ED
dir: Off A49, S of Hereford

Rooms 38 **S** fr £29; **D** fr £29

HORWICH Map 15 SD61

De Vere Whites

★★★★ 76% HOTEL

DE VERE venues

☎ 01204 667788 ▤ 01204 673721
De Havilland Way BL6 6SF
e-mail: whites@devere-hotels.com
web: www.devere.co.uk
dir: M61 junct 6. 3rd right from slip road rdbt onto A6027 Mansell Way. Follow visitors car park A for hotel

Fully integrated within the Reebok Stadium, home of Bolton Wanderers FC, this modern hotel is a popular venue for business and conferences. Bedrooms are contemporary in style and equipped with a range of extras; many offer views of the pitch. The hotel has two eating options - a fine dining restaurant and informal brasserie. It also boasts a fully equipped indoor leisure centre and spacious bar/lounge area.

Rooms 125 (1 fmly) **Facilities** ᠑ supervised Gym Steam room Beauty salon Xmas New Year **Conf** Class 1080 Board 72 Thtr 1500 **Services** Lift **Parking** 2750 **Notes** LB ⊗ Civ Wed 1000

KINGTON — Map 9 SO25

Burton

★★★ 74% HOTEL

☎ 01544 230323 ▤ 01544 239023
Mill St HR5 3BQ
e-mail: info@burtonhotel.co.uk
web: www.burtonhotel.co.uk
dir: At A44/A411rdbt junct take road signed Town Centre

Situated in the town centre, this friendly, privately-owned hotel offers spacious, pleasantly proportioned and well-equipped bedrooms. Smartly presented public areas include a lounge bar, leisure facilities including a swimming pool, and an attractive restaurant where carefully prepared cuisine can be enjoyed. There are function and meeting facilities available in a purpose-built, modern wing.

Rooms 16 (5 fmly) **S** £50-£60; **D** £89-£120 (incl. bkfst)* **Facilities** Spa FTV ⓣ supervised Gym Steam room Therapy rooms Xmas New Year Wi-fi **Conf** Class 100 Board 20 Thtr 150 Del from £70 to £85* **Services** Lift **Parking** 50 **Notes** LB Civ Wed 120

LEDBURY — Map 10 SO73

Verzon House

★★★ 82% ◉◉ HOTEL

☎ 01531 670381 ▤ 01531 670830
Hereford Rd, Trumpet HR8 2PZ
e-mail: info@verzonhouse.com
web: www.verzonhouse.com
dir: M5 junct 8/M50 junct 2, follow signs for Hereford A438. Hotel on right

Dating back to 1790 this elegant establishment stands in extensive gardens with far-reaching views over the Malvern Hills. Bedrooms are very well appointed and spacious; one has a four-poster bed. Stylish public areas include the popular bar and brasserie restaurant where a range of well-executed dishes can be enjoyed.

Rooms 8 **Facilities** Wi-fi **Conf** Class 15 Board 24 Thtr 50 **Parking** 70 **Notes** LB ⊗ No children 8yrs Closed 3-14 Jan

Feathers

★★★ 80% ◉ HOTEL

☎ 01531 635266 ▤ 01531 638955
High St HR8 1DS
e-mail: mary@feathers-ledbury.co.uk
web: www.feathers-ledbury.co.uk
dir: S from Worcester on A449, E from Hereford on A438, N from Gloucester on A417. Hotel in town centre

A wealth of authentic features can be found at this historic timber-framed hotel, set in the middle of town. The comfortably equipped bedrooms are tastefully decorated; new additions are Eve's Cottage in the hotel grounds and Lanark House, a two-bedroom apartment that is ideal for families. Well-prepared meals can be taken in Fuggles Brasserie with its adjoining bar, and breakfast is served in Quills Restaurant.

Rooms 22 (3 annexe) (2 fmly) **S** fr £87.50; **D** £130-£225 (incl. bkfst)* **Facilities** STV ⓣ Gym Steam room New Year Wi-fi **Conf** Class 80 Board 40 Thtr 140 **Parking** 30 **Notes** Civ Wed 100

Best Western Talbot

★★★ 75% HOTEL

☎ 01568 616347   📠 01568 614880
West St HR6 8EP
e-mail: talbot@bestwestern.co.uk
dir: From A49, A44 or A4112, hotel in centre of town

This charming former coaching inn is located in the town centre and offers an ideal base from which to explore this delightful area. Public areas feature original beams and antique furniture, and include an atmospheric bar and elegant restaurant. Bedrooms vary in size but all are comfortably furnished and equipped. Facilities are available for private functions and conferences.

Rooms 28 (3 fmly) **Conf** Class 25 Board 30 Thtr 130 **Parking** 26 **Notes** LB

Wilton Court Hotel

★★★ 81% ●● HOTEL

☎ 01989 562569   📠 01989 768460
Wilton Ln HR9 6AQ
e-mail: info@wiltoncourthotel.com
web: www.wiltoncourthotel.com
dir: M50 junct 4 onto A40 towards Monmouth at 3rd rdbt turn left signed Ross-on-Wye then take 1st right, hotel on right

Dating back to the 16th century, this hotel has great charm and a wealth of character. Standing on the banks of the River Wye and just a short walk from the town centre, there is a genuinely relaxed, friendly and unhurried atmosphere here. Bedrooms are tastefully furnished and well equipped, while public areas include a comfortable lounge, traditional bar and pleasant restaurant with a conservatory extension overlooking the garden. High standards of food, using fresh locally-sourced ingredients, are offered.

Rooms 10 (1 fmly) **S** £80-£135; **D** £105-£155 (incl. bkfst)* **Facilities** FTV Fishing 🏌 Boule Xmas New Year Wi-fi **Conf** Class 25 Board 25 Thtr 40 Del from £120 to £145* **Parking** 24 **Notes** LB Civ Wed 50

Chase

CLASSIC BRITISH HOTELS

★★★ 80% ● HOTEL

☎ 01989 763161   & 760644   📠 01989 768330
Gloucester Rd HR9 5LH
e-mail: res@chasehotel.co.uk
web: www.chasehotel.co.uk
dir: M50 junct 4, 1st left exit towards rdbt, left at rdbt towards A40. Right at 2nd rdbt towards town centre, hotel 0.5m on left

This attractive Georgian mansion sits in its own landscaped grounds and is only a short walk from the town centre. Bedrooms, including two four-poster rooms, vary in size and character; all rooms are appointed to impressive standards. There is also a light and spacious bar, and also Harry's restaurant which offers an excellent selection of enjoyable dishes.

Rooms 36 (1 fmly) **S** £90-£195; **D** £110-£195 (incl. bkfst)* **Facilities** STV New Year Wi-fi **Conf** Class 100 Board 80 Thtr 300 Del from £110 to £145* **Parking** 150 **Notes** LB ⊗ Closed 24-27 Dec Civ Wed 300

Pengethley Manor

★★★ 77% HOTEL

☎ 01989 730211   📠 01989 730238
Pengethley Park HR9 6LL
e-mail: reservations@pengethleymanor.co.uk
web: www.pengethleymanor.co.uk
dir: 4m N on A49 (Hereford road), from Ross-on-Wye

This fine Georgian mansion is set in extensive grounds with glorious views and two successful vineyards that produce over 1,000 bottles a year. The bedrooms are tastefully appointed and come in a wide variety of styles; all are well equipped. The elegant public rooms are furnished in a style that is in keeping with the house's character. Dinner provides a range of enjoyable options and is served in the spacious restaurant.

Rooms 25 (14 annexe) (3 fmly) (4 GF) **Facilities** 🏹 ⅃ 9 🏌 Golf improvement course Xmas New Year Wi-fi **Conf** Class 25 Board 28 Thtr 70 **Parking** 70 **Notes** LB Civ Wed 90

Glewstone Court

★★★ 73% ● COUNTRY HOUSE HOTEL

☎ 01989 770367   📠 01989 770282
Glewstone HR9 6AW
e-mail: glewstone@aol.com
web: www.glewstonecourt.com
dir: From Ross-on-Wye Market Place take A40/A49 Monmouth/Hereford, over Wilton Bridge to rdbt, turn left onto A40 to Monmouth, after 1m turn right for Glewstone

This charming hotel enjoys an elevated position with views over Ross-on-Wye, and is set in well-tended gardens. Informal service is delivered with great enthusiasm by Bill Reeve-Tucker, whilst the kitchen is the domain of Christine Reeve-Tucker who offers an extensive menu of well executed dishes. Bedrooms come in a variety of sizes and are tastefully furnished and well equipped.

Rooms 8 (2 fmly) **S** £80-£95; **D** £120-£140 (incl. bkfst) **Facilities** 🏌 New Year Wi-fi **Conf** Board 12 Thtr 18 Del from £120 to £170* **Parking** 25 **Notes** LB Closed 25-27 Dec Civ Wed 65

Pencraig Court Country House Hotel

★★★ 70% COUNTRY HOUSE HOTEL

☎ 01989 770306   📠 01989 770040
Pencraig HR9 6HR
e-mail: info@pencraig-court.co.uk
web: www.pencraig-court.co.uk
dir: Off A40, into Pencraig 4m S of Ross-on-Wye

This Georgian mansion commands impressive views of the River Wye to Ross-on-Wye beyond. Guests can be assured of a relaxing stay and the proprietors are on hand to ensure personal attention and service. The bedrooms have a traditional feel and include one room with a four-poster bed. The country-house atmosphere is carried through in the lounges and the elegant restaurant.

Rooms 11 (1 fmly) **S** £49-£75; **D** £89-£106 (incl. bkfst)* **Facilities** 🏌 Wi-fi **Conf** Class 10 Board 10 Thtr 20 Del from £120 to £130* **Parking** 20 **Notes** LB RS 24-27 Dec

ROSS-ON-WYE *continued*

The Royal

★★★ ⚠ HOTEL

☎ 01989 565105 📄 01989 768058
Palace Pound HR9 5HZ
e-mail: 6504@greeneking.co.uk
web: www.oldenglish.co.uk
dir: At end of M50 take A40 signed 'Monmouth'. At 3rd
rdbt, left to Ross-on-Wye, over bridge, take road signed
'The Royal Hotel' after left bend

Rooms 42 (1 fmly) **S** £19.95-£70; **D** £39.90-£145 (incl.
bkfst)* **Facilities** STV Xmas New Year Wi-fi **Conf** Class 20
Board 28 Thtr 85 **Parking** 38 **Notes** LB ⊗ Civ Wed 75

Chasedale

★★ 72% SMALL HOTEL

☎ 01989 562423 & 565801 📄 01989 567900
Walford Rd HR9 5PQ
e-mail: chasedale@supanet.com
web: www.chasedale.co.uk
dir: From town centre, S on B4234, hotel 0.5m on left

This large, mid-Victorian property is situated on the
south-west outskirts of the town. Privately owned and
personally run, it provides spacious, well-proportioned
public areas and extensive grounds. The accommodation
is well equipped and includes ground floor and family
rooms, whilst the restaurant offers a wide selection of
wholesome food.

Rooms 10 (2 fmly) (1 GF) **S** £42-£45; **D** £84-£90 (incl.
bkfst) **Facilities** Xmas Wi-fi **Conf** Class 30 Board 25
Thtr 40 **Parking** 14 **Notes** LB

King's Head

★★ 72% HOTEL

☎ 01989 763174 📄 01989 769578
8 High St HR9 5HL
e-mail: enquiries@kingshead.co.uk
web: www.kingshead.co.uk
dir: in town centre, turn right past Royal Hotel

This establishment dates back to the 14th century and
has a wealth of charm and character. Bedrooms are well
equipped and include both four-poster and family rooms.
The restaurant doubles as a coffee shop during the day
and is a popular venue with locals. There is also a very
pleasant bar and comfortable lounge.

Rooms 15 (1 fmly) (2 smoking) **S** £45-£53.50;
D £90-£100 (incl. bkfst)* **Facilities** Wi-fi **Parking** 13
Notes LB

The Bridge at Wilton

◎◎ RESTAURANT WITH ROOMS

☎ 01989 562655 📄 01989 567652
Wilton HR9 6AA
e-mail: info@bridge-house-hotel.com
web: www.bridge-house-hotel.com
dir: Off junct A40 & A49 into Ross-on-Wye, 300yds on left

Built about 1740, this elegant house is just a stroll
across the bridge from delightful Ross-on-Wye. Standards
here are impressive and bedrooms offer ample space,
comfort and genuine quality. Period features in the public
areas add to the stylish ambience, and the gardens run
down to the river. The restaurant serves accomplished
cuisine.

Rooms 9

Orles Barn

RESTAURANT WITH ROOMS

☎ 01989 562155 📄 01989 768470
Wilton HR9 6AE
e-mail: reservations@orles-barn.co.uk
web: www.orles-barn.co.uk
dir: A49/A40 rdbt outside Ross-on-Wye, take slip road
between petrol station & A40 to Monmouth. 100yds on
left

Kelly and Richard Bailey offer a warm welcome to all
guests at their property that dates from the 14th and
17th centuries when it was a farmhouse and barn. The
bedrooms are comfortable, and public areas include a
smart cosy lounge with a bar plus a spacious restaurant.
Here, dinners and Sunday lunches are served from a
balanced menu of fresh local and seasonal ingredients.
Breakfast provides some quality local items and a good
start to the day.

Rooms 8 (1 fmly)

BALDOCK Map 12 TL23

Travelodge Baldock
Hinxworth

BUDGET HOTEL

☎ 0871 984 6005 📄 01462 835329
Great North Rd, Hinxworth SG7 5EX
web: www.travelodge.co.uk
dir: on A1, southbound

Travelodge offers good quality, good value, budget
accommodation. All offer family rooms sleeping up to four
(two adults, two children) with en suite bathroom/
shower-room, remote-control TV, tea- and coffee-making
facilities and comfortable beds. Food options vary.
Breakfast is at the on-site Bar Café restaurant (if
available) or to take away. See also Hotel Groups pages.

Rooms 40 **S** fr £29; **D** fr £29

BISHOP'S STORTFORD Map 6 TL42

Down Hall Country House

★★★★ 76% ◎◎ HOTEL

☎ 01279 731441 📄 01279 730416
Hatfield Heath CM22 7AS
e-mail: reservations@downhall.co.uk
web: www.downhall.co.uk
dir: A1060, at Hatfield Heath keep left. Turn right into
lane opposite Hunters Meet restaurant & left at end,
follow sign

Imposing country-house hotel set amidst 100 acres of
mature grounds in a peaceful location just a short drive
from Stansted Airport. Bedrooms are generally quite
spacious; each one is pleasantly decorated, tastefully
furnished and equipped with modern facilities. Public
rooms include a choice of restaurants, a cocktail bar, two
lounges and leisure facilities.

Rooms 99 (20 GF) (10 smoking) **S** £74-£125;
D £109-£155* **Facilities** ⊗ ♨ ⚓ Giant chess Whirlpool
Sauna Snooker room Gym equipment Xmas New Year Wi-fi
Conf Class 140 Board 68 Thtr 200 **Services** Lift
Parking 150 **Notes** LB Civ Wed 120

Great Hallingbury Manor

★★★★ 71% ◉◉ HOTEL

☎ 01279 506475 📠 01279 505523
Great Hallingbury CM22 7TJ
e-mail: ludo@greathallingburymanor.com
dir: M11 junct 8, B1256 towards Great Dunmow signed Takeley. Right at Esso Petrol Station into Tile Kiln Rd signed Great & Little Hallingbury. Under bridge at sharp left bend, hotel 500yds on left

Located in a peaceful village yet conveniently located for road networks and Stansted Airport. A traditional property now brought up-to-date with modern amenities and with guest comfort in mind. The stylish public areas are comfortable and well appointed with original artwork on display. Many eco-sensitive initiatives have been successfully implemented at the hotel. Anton Edlemans' award-winning cuisine can be enjoyed at this 'destination' restaurant.

Rooms 46 (16 annexe) (4 fmly) (20 GF) **S** £30-£120; **D** £85-£180 (incl. bkfst) **Facilities** FTV 🎵 Xmas New Year Wi-fi **Conf** Class 40 Board 30 Thtr 70 Del from £145 to £180 **Parking** 90 **Notes** LB Civ Wed 200

Days Hotel London Stansted

BUDGET HOTEL

☎ 01279 213900 📠 01279 213901
M11 Motorway, Junction 8, Old Dunmow Rd CM23 5QZ
dir: Adjacent to M11 junct 8

This modern building offers accommodation in smart, spacious and well-equipped bedrooms, suitable for families and business travellers, and all with en suite bathrooms. There is an attractive lounge area and a dining room where breakfast is served and other refreshments may be taken. See also the Hotel Groups pages.

Rooms 77 (16 fmly) (16 GF) (8 smoking) **S** £39-£69; **D** £39-£69* **Conf** Class 26 Board 26 Thtr 40 Del from £99 to £149*

BOREHAMWOOD   Map 6 TQ19

Holiday Inn London - Elstree

★★★★ 71% HOTEL

☎ 0870 443 1271 & 020 8214 9988 📠 020 8207 6817
Barnet Bypass WD6 5PU
e-mail: hielstree@qmh-hotels.com
web: www.holidayinn.co.uk
dir: M25 junct 23, take A1 S towards London. After 2m take B5135 towards Borehamwood. Hotel at 1st rdbt

Ideally located for motorway links and easy travel into the city, this hotel boasts excellent conference and event facilities, secure parking and leisure and beauty treatment options. A range of bedroom sizes is available; all are well equipped and have air conditioning. Dining is available in either the restaurant, which offers both carvery and carte choices, or in the bar serving a range of dishes.

Rooms 135 (5 fmly) (25 GF) (8 smoking) **S** £57.50-£150; **D** £57.50-£150* **Facilities** STV 🏊 Gym Steam room Beauty salon Wi-fi **Conf** Class 150 Board 60 Thtr 400 Del from £125 to £165 **Services** Lift Air con **Parking** 350 **Notes** LB ⊗ Civ Wed 250

Ibis London Elstree Borehamwood

BUDGET HOTEL

☎ 020 8736 2600 📠 020 8736 2610
Elstree Way WD6 1JY
e-mail: H6186@accor.com
dir: M25 junct 23 then A1 exit at Borehamwood, follow A5135 Elstree Way

Modern, budget hotel offering comfortable accommodation in bright and practical bedrooms. Breakfast is self-service and dinner is available in the restaurant. See also the Hotel Groups pages.

Rooms 122 (16 fmly) (16 GF) **S** £45-£55; **D** £45-£55*

Innkeeper's Lodge London Borehamwood

BUDGET HOTEL

☎ 0845 112 6120 📠 0845 112 6183
Studio Way WD6 5JY
web: www.innkeeperslodge.com/borehamwood
dir: M25 junct 23/A1(M) signed to London. Follow signs to Borehamwood after double rdbt turn into Studio Way

Innkeeper's Lodge represents an exciting, high value concept within the budget hotel market. Comfortable bedrooms provide excellent facilities that include satellite TV and modem points. Options include family rooms; and for the corporate guest, cutting edge IT which includes Wi-fi access. A popular Carvery provides all-day food, including an extensive, complimentary continental breakfast. See also the Hotel Groups pages.

Rooms 55 (8 fmly) **Conf** Thtr 36

Travelodge Borehamwood

BUDGET HOTEL

☎ 0871 984 6346
Elstree Way WD6 1SD
dir: M25 junct 23, A1 (Barnet Bypass) towards Borehamwood. 2m. Left onto A5135. At rdbt 2nd exit onto A5135 (Elstree Way). Keep right & into Rowley Ln

Travelodge offers good quality, good value, budget accommodation. All offer family rooms sleeping up to four (two adults, two children) with en suite bathroom/shower-room, remote-control TV, tea- and coffee-making facilities and comfortable beds. Food options vary. Breakfast is at the on-site Bar Café restaurant (if available) or to take away. See also the Hotel Groups pages.

Rooms 96 **S** fr £29; **D** fr £29

CHESHUNT   Map 6 TL30

Cheshunt Marriott

Marriott HOTELS & RESORTS

★★★★ 76% HOTEL

☎ 01992 451245 📠 01992 440120
Halfhide Ln, Turnford EN10 6NG
web: www.cheshuntmarriott.co.uk
dir: Exit A10 at Broxbourne, right and right again at rdbt, hotel on right at next rdbt.

This popular suburban hotel has an attractive courtyard garden, overlooked by many of the guest bedrooms. All rooms are spacious and air conditioned. Public areas include a small, unsupervised leisure facility, along with the busy Washington Bar and Restaurant.

Rooms 143 (37 fmly) (39 GF) **Facilities** STV 🏊 Gym Xmas New Year Wi-fi **Conf** Class 72 Board 56 Thtr 150 **Services** Lift Air con **Parking** 200 **Notes** ⊗ Civ Wed 120

CHESHUNT *continued*

Travelodge Cheshunt

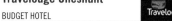

BUDGET HOTEL

☎ 08719 846 349
Park Plaza EN8 8DY
web: www.travelodge.co.uk
dir: M25 junct 25, A10 N'bound towards Cheshunt/
Waltham Cross. Hotel 500mtrs from junct on east side

Travelodge offers good quality, good value, budget
accommodation. All offer family rooms sleeping up to four
(two adults, two children) with en suite bathroom/
shower-room, remote-control TV, tea- and coffee-making
facilities and comfortable beds. Food options vary.
Breakfast is at the on-site Bar Café restaurant (if
available) or to take away. See also Hotel Groups pages.

Rooms 100 **S** fr £29; **D** fr £29

| **ELSTREE** | **Map 6 TQ19** |

Corus hotel Elstree

★★★ 74% HOTEL

☎ 020 8953 8227 & 0844 736 8602 📄 020 8207 3668
Barnet Ln WD6 3RE
e-mail: elstree@corushotels.com
web: www.corushotels.com
dir: M1 junct 5, A41 to Harrow, left onto A411 into Elstree.
Through x-rds into Barnet Ln, hotel on right

Sitting in ten acres of landscaped gardens this hotel is
full of charm and character, with a Tudor-style façade
and interiors of a traditional design. The oak-panelled
bar, with two large fireplaces, and the stately Cavendish
restaurant enjoy wonderful views over the gardens and
the city beyond.

Rooms 49 (36 annexe) (4 fmly) (13 GF) **Facilities** STV FTV
Wi-fi **Conf** Class 35 Board 35 Thtr 80 Del from £150 to
£180* **Parking** 100 **Notes** ⊗ Civ Wed 90

| **HARPENDEN** | **Map 6 TL11** |

Harpenden House Hotel

folio Hotels

★★★★ 72% HOTEL

☎ 0870 609 6170 📄 01582 769858
18 Southdown Rd AL5 1PE
e-mail: harpendenhouse@foliohotels.com
web: www.foliohotels.com/harpendenhouse
dir: M1 junct 10 left at rdbt. Next rdbt right onto A1081 to
Harpenden. Over 2 mini rdbts, through town centre. Next
rdbt left, hotel 200yds on left

This attractive Grade II listed Georgian building overlooks
East Common. The hotel gardens are particularly
attractive and the public areas are stylishly decorated,
including the restaurant that has an impressively
decorated ceiling. Some of the bedrooms and a large

suite are located in the original house but most of the
accommodation is in the annexe.

Rooms 76 (59 annexe) (13 fmly) (2 GF)
Facilities Complimentary use of local leisure centre Wi-fi
Conf Class 60 Board 60 Thtr 150 **Parking** 80 **Notes** ⊗
RS wknds & BHs Civ Wed 120

| **HATFIELD** | **Map 6 TL20** |

Beales

★★★★ 80% ⊛⊛ HOTEL

☎ 01707 288500 📄 01707 256282
Comet Way AL10 9NG
e-mail: hatfield@bealeshotels.co.uk
web: www.bealeshotels.co.uk
dir: On A1001 opposite Galleria Shopping Mall - follow
signs for Galleria

This hotel is a stunning contemporary property. Within
easy access of the M25, its striking exterior incorporates
giant glass panels and cedar wood slats. Bedrooms have
luxurious beds, flat-screen TVs and smart bathrooms.
Public areas include a small bar and attractive
restaurant, which opens throughout the day. The hotel is
fully air-conditioned and free wired broadband is
available in bedrooms, conference and banqueting rooms.

Rooms 53 (3 fmly) (21 GF) **Facilities** STV FTV Use of
nearby leisure club Xmas New Year Wi-fi **Conf** Class 124
Board 64 Thtr 300 **Services** Lift Air con **Parking** 126
Notes ⊗ RS 27-30 Dec Civ Wed 300

Bush Hall

★★★ 77% ⊛⊛ HOTEL

☎ 01707 271251 📄 01707 272289
Mill Green AL9 5NT
e-mail: enquiries@bush-hall.com
dir: A1(M) junct 4, 2nd left at rdbt onto A414 signed
Hertford & Welwyn Garden City. Left at rdbt, take A1000.
Hotel on left

Standing in delightful grounds with a river running
through it, this hotel boasts extensive facilities. Outdoor
enthusiasts can enjoy a range of activities including go-
karting and clay pigeon shooting. Bedrooms and public
areas are comfortable and tastefully decorated. Kipling's
restaurant continues to offer a wide range freshly
prepared dishes using quality produce; service is both
professional and friendly.

Rooms 25 (2 fmly) (8 GF) **S** £60-£80; **D** £90-£100*
Facilities Clay pigeon shooting Archery Wi-fi
Conf Class 70 Board 50 Thtr 150 **Parking** 100 **Notes** ⊗
Closed 24 Dec-3 Jan Civ Wed 160

Ramada Hatfield

⊛ RAMADA

★★★ 75% HOTEL

☎ 01707 265411 📄 01707 264019
301 St Albans Road West AL10 9RH
e-mail: sales.hatfield@ramadajarvis.co.uk
web: www.ramadajarvis.co.uk
dir: A1(M) junct 3, take 2nd exit at rdbt signed Hatfield.
Hotel on left

Conveniently located close to the A1(M) with good links to
London, this large hotel is a themed, Grade II listed art
deco building and retains many of its original 1930s
features. Spacious bedrooms are comfortably appointed
in a modern style and very well equipped. Public areas
include a substantial range of conference rooms, a small
gym and the popular Arts Bar & Grill.

Rooms 128 (4 fmly) (53 GF) (12 smoking) **Facilities** Wi-fi
Conf Class 100 Board 60 Thtr 120 **Parking** 150
Notes RS between Xmas & New Year Civ Wed 140

Travelodge Hatfield Central

BUDGET HOTEL

☎ 0871 984 6316 📠 01707 266331
Comet Way AL10 0XR
web: www.travelodge.co.uk
dir: A1001 to 1st rdbt, right signed Hatfield Business Park, left at Porsche dealership, hotel signed

Travelodge offers good quality, good value, budget accommodation. All offer family rooms sleeping up to four (two adults, two children) with en suite bathroom/shower-room, remote-control TV, tea- and coffee-making facilities and comfortable beds. Food options vary. Breakfast is at the on-site Bar Café restaurant (if available) or to take away. See also Hotel Groups pages.

Rooms 120 **S** fr £29; **D** fr £29

HEMEL HEMPSTEAD Map 6 TL00

The Bobsleigh Hotel

★★★ 77% ◉ HOTEL

☎ 0844 879 9033 📠 01442 832471
Hempstead Rd, Bovingdon HP3 0DS
e-mail: bobsleigh@macdonald-hotels.co.uk
web: www.macdonald-hotels.co.uk
dir: M1 junct 8, A414 signed Hemel Hempstead. At Plough Rdbt follow railway station signs. Pass rail station on left, straight on at rdbt, under 2 bridges. Left onto B4505 (Box Lane) signed Chesham. Hotel 1.5m on left

Located just outside the town, the hotel enjoys a pleasant rural setting, yet is within easy reach of local transport links and the motorway network. Bedrooms vary in size; all are modern in style. There is an open-plan lobby, a bar area and an attractive dining room with views over the garden.

Rooms 47 (15 annexe) (8 fmly) (29 GF) **S** £38-£100; **D** £38-£120* **Facilities** STV Xmas New Year Wi-fi **Conf** Class 50 Board 40 Thtr 150 Del from £100 to £160 **Parking** 60 **Notes** LB Civ Wed 100

Holiday Inn Hemel Hempstead

★★★ 75% HOTEL

☎ 0870 400 9041 📠 01442 211283
Breakspear Way HP2 4UA
e-mail: reservations-hemelhempsteadml@ihg.com
web: www.holidayinn.co.uk
dir: M1 junct 8, over rdbt, 1st left after BP garage

A modern, purpose-built hotel that is convenient for the motorway networks. Bedrooms are spacious and well suited to the business traveller. Executive rooms and public areas are particularly well styled. Other facilities include a leisure club and a range of meeting rooms.

Rooms 144 (38 fmly) (42 GF) (14 smoking) **Facilities** Spa ⊙ supervised Gym Beauty treaments & physiotherapy by appointment **Conf** Class 22 Board 30 Thtr 80 **Services** Lift Air con **Parking** 200 **Notes** ⊗ Civ Wed 60

Ramada Hemel Hempstead
 RAMADA
★★★ 75% HOTEL

☎ 01582 792105 📠 01582 792001
Hemel Hempstead Rd, Redbourn AL3 7AF
e-mail: sales.hemel@ramadajarvis.co.uk
web: www.ramadajarvis.co.uk
dir: M1 junct 9 follow Hemel Hempstead & St Albans signs for 3m, straight across 2 rdbts onto B487 signed Hemel Hempstead. Hotel on right

With easy access to both the M1 and M25 motorways, this well presented hotel is set in six acres of landscaped gardens. Bedrooms are comfortably appointed for both business and leisure guests.

Rooms 137 (4 fmly) (67 GF) **S** £59-£149; **D** £59-£149* **Facilities** Xmas Wi-fi **Conf** Class 50 Board 40 Thtr 100 Del from £99 to £155* **Services** Lift **Parking** 150 **Notes** Civ Wed 100

Best Western The Watermill
★★★ 74% HOTEL

☎ 01442 349955 📠 01442 866130
London Rd, Bourne End HP1 2RJ
e-mail: info@hotelwatermill.co.uk
web: www.hotelwatermill.co.uk
dir: From M25 & M1 follow signs to Aylesbury on A41, then A4251 to Bourne End. Hotel 0.25m on right

In the heart of the county this modern hotel has been built around an old flour mill on the banks of the River Bulbourne with water meadows adjacent. The thoughtfully equipped, contemporary bedrooms are located in three annexes situated around the complex. A good range of air-conditioned conference and meeting rooms complement the lounge bar and restaurant.

Rooms 71 (67 annexe) (9 fmly) (35 GF) (8 smoking) **S** £59-£85; **D** £59-£110 (incl. bkfst) **Facilities** STV Fishing Xmas Wi-fi **Conf** Class 60 Board 50 Thtr 100 **Parking** 100 **Notes** LB ⊗ Civ Wed 90

Express by Holiday Inn Hemel Hempstead
 Express
BUDGET HOTEL

☎ 0870 4585485 📠 0870 4585488
Stationers Place, Apsley Lock HP3 9RH
e-mail: hemel@expressholidayinn.co.uk
web: www.hiexpress.com/hemelhempstead
dir: M25 junct 20, Kings Langley, hotel on right after 3rd rdbt

A modern hotel ideal for families and business travellers. Fresh and uncomplicated, the spacious rooms include Sky TV, power shower and tea and coffee-making facilities. Continental buffet breakfast is included in the room rate; other meals may be taken at the nearby family pub or restaurant. See also the Hotel Groups pages.

Rooms 116 **S** £49-£109; **D** £49-£109 (incl. bkfst)* **Conf** Class 18 Board 18 Thtr 40 Del from £115 to £135*

Travelodge Hemel Hempstead

BUDGET HOTEL

☎ 08719 846 036 📠 01442 266887
Wolsey House, Wolsey Rd HP2 4SS
web: www.travelodge.co.uk
dir: M1 junct 8 into city centre, 5th rdbt turn back towards M1, take 1st left

Travelodge offers good quality, good value, budget accommodation. All offer family rooms sleeping up to four (two adults, two children) with en suite bathroom/shower-room, remote-control TV, tea- and coffee-making facilities and comfortable beds. Food options vary. Breakfast is at the on-site Bar Café restaurant (if available) or to take away. See also Hotel Groups pages.

Rooms 53 **S** fr £29; **D** fr £29

HERTFORD Map 6 TL31

White Horse
★★★ 68% HOTEL

☎ 01992 586791 📠 01992 550809
Hertingfordbury Rd, Hertingfordbury SG14 2LB
e-mail: bgray@aquriushotels.co.uk
dir: From A10 follow A414 signs. From Hertford under rail bridge, over rdbt, left at next rdbt, hotel 300yds on right

The Georgian façade of this former coaching inn belies a much older interior with oak beams dating back from 400 years. However, this comfortable establishment has undergone a total refurbishment and now offers modern facilities. Many of the spacious bedrooms overlook the picturesque gardens. Public rooms include a beamed bar with its open fireplace and a spacious conservatory restaurant.

Rooms 42 **Conf** Class 22 Board 26 Thtr 60

HITCHIN — Map 12 TL12

Redcoats Farmhouse Hotel

★★★ 71% @ SMALL HOTEL

☎ 01438 729500 ▤ 01438 723322
Redcoats Green SG4 7JR
e-mail: sales@redcoats.co.uk
web: www.redcoats.co.uk
dir: A602 to Wymondley. Turn left to Redcoats Green. At top of hill straight over at junct

This delightful 15th-century property is situated in four acres of landscaped grounds only a short drive from the A1(M). Bedrooms in the main house and courtyard annexe are well appointed and spacious. Breakfast and dinner are served in the conservatory which overlooks the garden, and a series of intimate dining rooms is also available.

Rooms 13 (9 annexe) (1 fmly) (9 GF) **Facilities** FTV
New Year Wi-fi **Conf** Board 15 Thtr 30 **Parking** 50
Notes Closed BH & Xmas-7Jan Civ Wed 75

Sun

★★ A HOTEL

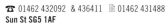

☎ 01462 432092 & 436411 ▤ 01462 431488
Sun St SG5 1AF
e-mail: sun.hitchin@greeneking.co.uk
web: www.oldenglish.co.uk

Rooms 32 (6 GF) **Conf** Thtr 100 **Parking** 24 **Notes** LB ⊗
Civ Wed 100

Travelodge Stevenage Little Wymondley

BUDGET HOTEL

☎ 0871 984 6420 ▤ 01844 358681
Blakemore End Rd, Little Wymondley SG4 7JJ
dir: A1(M) junct 8, 2nd exit onto Stevenage Rd to Little Wymondley, through village. At mini rdbt turn left onto Blakemore Rd. Lodge 200mtrs on left

Travelodge offers good quality, good value, budget accommodation. All offer family rooms sleeping up to four (two adults, two children) with en suite bathroom/shower-room, remote-control TV, tea- and coffee-making facilities and comfortable beds. Food options vary. Breakfast is at the on-site Bar Café restaurant (if available) or to take away. See also the Hotel Groups pages.

Rooms 69 **S** fr £29; **D** fr £29 **Conf** Class 80 Board 60
Thtr 250

LONDON COLNEY — Map 6 TL10

Innkeeper's Lodge St Albans

BUDGET HOTEL

☎ 0845 112 6058 ▤ 0845 112 6245
1 Barnet Rd AL2 1BL
web: www.innkeeperslodge.com/stalbans
dir: M25 junct 22 (keep in left lane), A1081at rdbt 1st left & straight over to next rdbt. Lodge 500yds on right

Innkeeper's Lodge represents an exciting, high value concept within the budget hotel market. Comfortable bedrooms provide excellent facilities that include satellite TV and modem points. This carefully restored lodge is in a picturesque setting and has its own unique style and quirky character. Food is served all day, and an extensive, complimentary continental breakfast is offered. See also the Hotel Groups pages.

Rooms 13

POTTERS BAR — Map 6 TL20

Ponsbourne Park Hotel

★★★★ 76% @@ HOTEL

☎ 01707 876191 & 879277 ▤ 01707 875190
Newgate Street Village SG13 8QT
e-mail: reservations@ponsbournepark.co.uk
web: www.ponsbournepark.com
dir: M25 junct 25, Newgate Street Village

Set within 200 acres of quiet parkland, this 17th-century country house offers contemporary accommodation and public rooms, along with a flexible range of leisure and conference facilities. Smart modern bedrooms are located in the main house and adjacent annexe; each room is well equipped, but typically main house rooms are more spacious. The fine dining restaurant is supplemented by a bistro.

Rooms 51 (28 annexe) (8 fmly) (10 GF) **Facilities** STV
9 Gym New Year Wi-fi **Conf** Class 40 Board 40
Thtr 100 Del from £120 to £150* **Parking** 125 **Notes** ⊗
Civ Wed 92

RICKMANSWORTH — Map 6 TQ09

See also **Chenies, Buckinghamshire**

The Grove

★★★★★ 89% HOTEL

☎ 01923 807807 ▤ 01923 221008
Chandler's Cross WD3 4TG
e-mail: info@thegrove.co.uk
web: www.thegrove.co.uk
dir: From M25 follow A411 signs towards Watford. Hotel entrance on right. From M1 follow brown hotel signs

Set amid 300 acres of rolling countryside, much of which is golf course, the hotel combines its historic characteristics with cutting-edge, modern design. The spacious bedrooms feature the latest in temperature control, flat-screen TVs and lighting technology; many have balconies. Suites in the original mansion are particularly stunning. Championship golf, a world-class spa and three dining options are just a few of the treasures to sample here. The hotel also has extensive crèche facilities. The cuisine previously won 3 AA Rosettes but this award is temporarily suspended as there has been a change of chef. An award will be in place once our inspectors have completed their assessments of meals cooked by the new kitchen team. For up-to-date information please see the AA website: theAA.com

Rooms 227 (32 fmly) (35 GF) **Facilities** Spa STV FTV
supervised 18 Putt green Gym Kids' club Beach Walking & cycling trails Giant chess Orchid house Xmas New Year Wi-fi Child facilities **Conf** Class 300 Board 78 Thtr 450 Del from £260 to £413* **Services** Lift Air con **Parking** 400 **Notes** LB ⊗ Civ Wed 450

Long Island

★★ **A** HOTEL

☎ 01923 779466 📠 01923 896248
2 Victoria Close WD3 4EQ
e-mail: office@longisland.fsbusiness.co.uk
web: www.oldenglish.co.uk
dir: M25 junct 18 onto A404, 1.5m. Turn left at rdbt onto Nightingale Rd, 1st left

Rooms 50 (3 fmly) (12 GF) **Facilities** ♫ **Parking** 120 **Notes** ⊗

| ST ALBANS | Map 6 TL10 |

Sopwell House

★★★★ 78% ⊛ HOTEL

☎ 01727 864477 📠 01727 844741
Cottonmill Ln, Sopwell AL1 2HQ
e-mail: enquiries@sopwellhouse.co.uk
web: www.sopwellhouse.co.uk
dir: M25 junct 22, A1081 St Albans. At lights left into Mile House Ln, over mini-rdbt into Cottonmill Ln

This imposing Georgian house retains an exclusive ambience. Bedrooms vary in style and include a number of self-contained cottages within the Sopwell Mews. Meeting and function rooms are housed in a separate section, and leisure and spa facilities are particularly impressive. Dining options include the brasserie and the fine-dining Magnolia restaurant.

Rooms 129 (16 annexe) (12 fmly) (11 GF) **Facilities** Spa ⊛ Gym Hairdressing salon ♫ Xmas New Year **Conf** Class 220 Board 120 Thtr 400 **Services** Lift **Parking** 350 **Notes** LB ⊗ Civ Wed 250

St Michael's Manor

★★★★ 77% ⊛⊛ HOTEL

☎ 01727 864444 📠 01727 848909
Fishpool St AL3 4RY
e-mail: reservations@stmichaelsmanor.com
dir: From St Albans Abbey follow Fishpool Street towards St Michael's village. Hotel 0.5m on left

Hidden from the street, adjacent to listed buildings, mills and ancient inns, this hotel, with a history dating back 500 years, is set in six acres of beautiful landscaped grounds. Inside there is a real sense of luxury, the high standard of decor and attentive service is complemented by award-winning food; the elegant restaurant overlooks the gardens and lake. The bedrooms are individually styled and have satellite TVs, DVDs and free internet access.

Rooms 30 (8 annexe) (3 fmly) (4 GF) (6 smoking)
S £145-£240; **D** £180-£345 (incl. bkfst)* **Facilities** STV FTV ⊌ Licenced fishing in season Guided tours New Year Wi-fi **Conf** Class 20 Board 24 Thtr 30 Del from £225 to £310* **Parking** 75 **Notes** LB ⊗ Civ Wed

Thistle St Albans

thistle

★★★★ 77% HOTEL

☎ 0871 376 9034 📠 0871 376 9134
Watford Rd AL2 3DS
e-mail: stalbans@thistle.co.uk
web: www.thistlehotels.com/stalbans
dir: M1 junct 6/M25 junct 21a, follow St. Albans signs, A405. Hotel 0.5m

Conveniently located for access to both the M1 and M25, this Victorian hotel lies within its own grounds and has secure parking. Bedrooms are neatly appointed in a traditional style. Public areas include a choice of restaurants, The Noke or the more informal Oak and Avocado, and there is also a small modern leisure club.

Rooms 111 (2 fmly) (56 GF) (15 smoking) **Facilities** ⊛ supervised Gym Sauna Steam room Xmas New Year Wi-fi **Conf** Class 30 Board 30 Thtr 300 Del from £119 to £155* **Parking** 150 **Notes** ⊗ Civ Wed 100

Holiday Inn Luton South

Holiday Inn
HOTELS · RESORTS

★★★ 75% HOTEL

☎ 0870 4431 781 & 01582 449988 📠 01582 449041
London Rd, Markyate AL3 8HH
e-mail: hiluton@qmh-hotels.com
web: www.holidayinn.co.uk
dir: M1 junct 9 N towards Dunstable/Whipsnade, hotel 1m on right

Situated a short drive from the M1 and Luton Airport, this hotel has a pleasant setting with country views. There is a health and fitness club and a good range of air-conditioned conference and meeting facilities. The contemporary bedrooms are well appointed and have a good range of facilities.

Rooms 140 (12 fmly) (44 GF) **D** £49-£150* **Facilities** ⊛ Gym Sauna Beauty salon Steam room Studio with classes Wi-fi **Conf** Class 90 Board 50 Thtr 200 Del from £110 to £150 **Services** Lift **Parking** 260 **Notes** LB ⊗ Civ Wed 150

ST ALBANS *continued*

Quality Hotel St Albans

★★★ 71% HOTEL

☎ 01727 857858 📄 01727 855666
232-236 London Rd AL1 1JQ
e-mail: st.albans@quality-hotels.net
dir: M25 junct 22 follow A1081 to St Albans, after 2.5m hotel on left, before overhead bridge

This smartly presented property is conveniently situated close to the major road networks and the railway station. The contemporary style bedrooms have co-ordinated fabrics and a good range of useful facilities. Public rooms include an open-plan lounge bar and brasserie restaurant. A leisure complex has been created, along with air-conditioned meeting rooms.

Rooms 81 (7 fmly) (14 GF) (6 smoking) **S** £45-£95; **D** £55-£120* **Facilities** STV 🏊 supervised Gym Saunarium Sunbed Beauty treatments Wi-fi **Conf** Class 40 Board 50 Thtr 220 Del from £90 to £130* **Services** Lift **Parking** 80 **Notes** LB ⊗

Ardmore House

★★★ 68% HOTEL

☎ 01727 859313 📄 01727 859313
54 Lemsford Rd AL1 3PR
e-mail: info@ardmorehousehotel.co.uk
web: www.ardmorehousehotel.co.uk
dir: A1081 signed St Albans, over 3 sets of lights & 2 mini rdbts. Right at 3rd mini rdbt, across 2 sets of lights. Hotel on right after 800yds

Located in immaculate surroundings close to the town centre and cathedral, this extended Edwardian house and annexe has been carefully renovated, providing a range of facilities much appreciated by a loyal commercial clientele. The practically furnished bedrooms offer a good range of facilities and the extensive public areas include a spacious conservatory dining room.

Rooms 40 (4 annexe) (5 fmly) (5 GF) **S** £68; **D** £81-£135 (incl. bkfst)* **Facilities** STV Wi-fi **Conf** Class 17 Board 18 Thtr 130 **Parking** 40 **Notes** LB ⊗ Civ Wed 150

SAWBRIDGEWORTH	Map 6 TL41

Manor of Groves Hotel, Golf & Country Club

★★★ 77% HOTEL

☎ 01279 600777 & 0870 410 8833 📄 01279 600374
High Wych CM21 0JU
e-mail: info@manorofgroves.co.uk
web: www.manorofgroves.com
dir: A1184 to Sawbridgeworth, left to High Wych, right at village green & hotel 200yds left

Delightful Georgian manor house set in 150 acres of secluded grounds and gardens, with its own 18-hole championship golf course and superb leisure facilities. Public rooms include an imposing open-plan glass atrium that features a bar, lounge area and modern restaurant. The spacious bedrooms are smartly decorated and equipped with modern facilities.

Rooms 80 (2 fmly) (17 GF) **S** £80-£125; **D** £95-£150 (incl. bkfst) **Facilities** Spa STV 🏊 supervised ⛳ 18 Putt green Gym Dance studio Beauty salon Sauna Steam rooms Xmas New Year Wi-fi **Conf** Class 250 Board 50 Thtr 500 Del from £129 to £169* **Services** Lift **Parking** 350 **Notes** LB ⊗ RS 24 Dec-2 Jan Civ Wed 300

See advert on this page

SOUTH MIMMS SERVICE AREA (M25) — Map 6 TL20

Days Inn South Mimms
BUDGET HOTEL

☎ 01707 665440 📄 01707 660189
Bignells Corner EN6 3QQ
e-mail: south.mimms@welcomebreak.co.uk
web: www.welcomebreak.co.uk
dir: M25 junct 23, at rdbt follow signs

This modern building offers accommodation in smart, spacious and well-equipped bedrooms, suitable for families and business travellers, and all with en suite bathrooms. Continental breakfast is available and other refreshments may be taken at the nearby family restaurant. See also the Hotel Groups pages.

Rooms 74 (55 fmly) **S** £29-£49; **D** £39-£69*
Conf Board 10 Del from £79 to £109*

STEVENAGE — Map 12 TL22

Novotel Stevenage
★★★ 77% HOTEL

☎ 01438 346100 📄 01438 723872
Knebworth Park SG1 2AX
e-mail: H0992@accor.com
web: www.novotel.com
dir: A1(M) junct 7, at entrance to Knebworth Park

Ideally situated just off the A1(M) is this purpose built hotel, which is a popular business and conference venue. Bedrooms are pleasantly decorated and equipped with a good range of useful extras. Public rooms include a large open plan lounge bar serving a range of snacks, and a smartly appointed restaurant.

Rooms 101 (20 fmly) (30 GF) (8 smoking) **Facilities** STV ➷ Use of local health club New Year Wi-fi **Conf** Class 80 Board 70 Thtr 150 **Services** Lift **Parking** 120 **Notes** Civ Wed 120

Best Western Roebuck Inn
★★★ 71% HOTEL

☎ 01438 365445 📄 01438 741308
London Rd, Broadwater SG2 8DS
e-mail: hotel@roebuckinn.com
dir: A1(M) junct 7, right towards Stevenage. At 2nd rdbt take 2nd exit signed Roebuck-London/Knebworth/B197. Hotel in 1.5m

Suitable for both the business and leisure traveller, this hotel provides spacious contemporary accommodation in well-equipped bedrooms. The older part of the building, where there is a restaurant and a cosy public bar with log fire and real ales, dates back to the 15th century.

Rooms 26 (8 fmly) (13 GF) **S** £55-£79; **D** £65-£109 **Facilities** STV FTV Xmas New Year Wi-fi **Conf** Class 20 Board 30 Thtr 50 Del from £100 to £150 **Parking** 50 **Notes** ⊗

Holiday Inn Stevenage

Ⓤ

☎ 01438 722727 & 346060 📄 01438 727752
St George's Way SG1 1HS
e-mail: reservations@histevenage.com
dir: A602, across 1st rdbt, 1st exit at 2nd rdbt, 2nd eixt at next rdbt along St George's Way. Hotel 300yds on right

Currently the rating for this establishment is not confirmed. This may be due to a change of ownership or because it has only recently joined the AA rating scheme. For further details please see the AA website: theAA.com

Rooms 140 (8 fmly) **S** £49-£144; **D** £49-£144*
Facilities STV FTV Gym Xmas New Year Wi-fi
Conf Class 180 Board 190 Thtr 350 Del from £110 to £155* **Services** Lift Air con **Notes** LB Civ Wed 300

Ibis Stevenage Centre
BUDGET HOTEL

☎ 01438 779955 📄 01438 741880
Danestrete SG1 1EJ
e-mail: H2794@accor.com
web: www.ibishotel.com
dir: In town centre adjacent to Tesco & Westgate multi storey car park

Modern, budget hotel offering comfortable accommodation in bright and practical bedrooms. Breakfast is self-service and dinner is available in the restaurant. See also the Hotel Groups pages.

Rooms 98 (10 smoking)

TRING — Map 6 SP91

Pendley Manor
★★★★ 76% ◉ HOTEL

☎ 01442 891891 📄 01442 890687
Cow Ln HP23 5QY
e-mail: info@pendley-manor.co.uk
web: www.pendley-manor.co.uk
dir: M25 junct 20, A41 (Tring exit). At rdbt follow Berkhamsted/London signs. 1st left signed Tring Station & Pendley Manor

This impressive Victorian mansion is set in extensive and mature landscaped grounds where peacocks roam. The spacious bedrooms are situated in both the manor house and the wing, and offer a useful range of facilities. Public areas include a cosy bar, a conservatory lounge and an intimate restaurant as well as a leisure centre.

Rooms 73 (17 fmly) (17 GF) **S** £100-£140; **D** £110-£150 (incl. bkfst)* **Facilities** Spa ➷ ♨ ♨ Gym Steam room Dance Studio Beauty spa Sauna Snooker room New Year Wi-fi **Conf** Class 80 Board 80 Thtr 250 Del from £180 to £230* **Services** Lift **Parking** 150 **Notes** LB ⊗ Civ Wed 160

The Rose & Crown Hotel
★★★ 70% HOTEL

☎ 01442 824071 📄 01442 890735
High St HP23 5AH
e-mail: salesrose-crown@pendley-manor.co.uk
dir: Off A41 between Aylesbury & Hempstead, hotel in town centre

This Tudor-style manor house in the centre of town, offers a great deal of charm. Bedrooms vary in size and style but all are generally well equipped. The restaurant and bar form the centre of the hotel and are popular with locals and residents alike.

Rooms 27 (3 fmly) **Facilities** Full indoor leisure facilities available at sister hotel **Conf** Class 30 Board 30 Thtr 80 **Parking** 60 **Notes** ⊗ Civ Wed 100

WARE — Map 6 TL31

Marriott Hanbury Manor Hotel & Country Club
★★★★★ 79% ◉◉ COUNTRY HOUSE HOTEL

☎ 01920 487722 & 0870 400 7222 📄 01920 487692
SG12 0SD
e-mail: mhrs.stngs.guestrelations@marriotthotels.com
web: www.marriotthanburymanor.co.uk
dir: M25 junct 25, take A10 north for 12m, then A1170 exit, right at rdbt, hotel on left

Set in 200 acres of landscaped grounds, this impressive Jacobean-style mansion boasts an enviable range of leisure facilities, including an excellent health club and championship golf course. Bedrooms are traditionally and comfortably furnished in the country-house style and have lovely marbled bathrooms. There are a number of food and drink options, including the renowned Zodiac and Oakes restaurants.

Rooms 161 (27 annexe) (3 GF) **D** £99-£400 (incl. bkfst)* **Facilities** Spa STV ⓒ supervised ⚐ 18 ⛳ Putt green ♨ Gym Health & beauty treatments Aerobics Yoga Dance class Xmas New Year Wi-fi **Conf** Class 76 Board 36 Thtr 120 Del from £199 to £279* **Services** Lift **Parking** 200 **Notes** LB Civ Wed 120

WARE *continued*

Roebuck

★★★ 74% HOTEL

☎ 01920 409955 📠 01920 468016
Baldock St SG12 9DR
e-mail: roebuck@forestdale.com
web: www.theroebuckhotel.co.uk
dir: A10 onto B1001, left at rdbt, 1st left behind fire station

The Roebuck is a comfortable and friendly hotel situated close to the old market town of Ware, it is also within easy reach of Stansted Airport, Cambridge and Hertford. The hotel has spacious bedrooms, a comfortable lounge, bar and conservatory restaurant. There is also a range of air-conditioned meeting rooms.

Rooms 47 (1 fmly) (16 GF) **S** £57-£77; **D** £77-£119 (incl. bkfst)* **Facilities** FTV Wi-fi **Conf** Class 75 Board 60 Thtr 200 **Services** Lift **Parking** 64 **Notes** Civ Wed 80

Feathers Inn

Ⓤ

☎ 01920 462606 📠 01920 469994
Wadesmill SG12 0TN
e-mail: feathers.wadesmill@newbridgeinns.co.uk

Currently the rating for this establishment is not confirmed. This may be due to a change of ownership or because it has only recently joined the AA rating scheme. For further details please see the AA website: theAA.com

Rooms 31

WATFORD Map 6 TQ19

Ramada Watford

Ⓡ RAMADA.

★★★ 78% HOTEL

☎ 0844 815 9056 📠 020 8950 7809
A41, Watford Bypass WD25 8JH
e-mail: sales.watford@ramadajarvis.co.uk
web: www.ramadajarvis.co.uk/watford
dir: M1 junct 5, A41 S to London. Straight on at island, hotel 1m on left

This large, modern hotel is conveniently located close to both the M1 and M25 and is a popular venue for conferences. Bedroom options include stylish studio rooms with leather easy chairs; all bedrooms are well equipped and comfortably appointed for both business and leisure guests. A good choice of meals is served in the contemporary Arts Restaurant and Bar.

Rooms 218 (6 fmly) (80 GF) (10 smoking) **Facilities** Spa FTV 🏊 Gym Steam room Sauna 🎵 New Year Wi-fi **Conf** Class 120 Board 60 Thtr 200 Del from £99 to £180 **Parking** 250 **Notes** Civ Wed 180

Best Western White House

★★★ 73% HOTEL

☎ 01923 237316 📠 01923 233109
Upton Rd WD18 0JF
e-mail: info@whitehousehotel.co.uk
web: www.whitehousehotel.co.uk
dir: From main Watford centre ring road into Exchange Rd, Upton Rd left turn off, hotel on left

This popular commercial hotel is situated within easy walking distance to the town centre. Bedrooms are pleasantly decorated and offer a good range of facilities that include interactive TV with internet. The public areas are open plan in style; they include a comfortable lounge/bar, cosy snug and an attractive conservatory restaurant with a sunny open terrace for summer dining. Functions suites are also available.

Rooms 57 (8 GF) **S** £52-£95; **D** £65-£115* **Facilities** STV FTV Wi-fi **Conf** Class 80 Board 50 Thtr 200 Del from £115 to £145* **Services** Lift **Parking** 50 **Notes** LB ⊗ RS 25 Dec-2 Jan Civ Wed 120

Park Inn Watford

Ⓤ

☎ 01923 429988 & 429900 📠 01923 221175
30-40 St Albans Rd WD17 1RN
e-mail: reservations.watford@rezidorparkinn.com
web: www.watford.parkinn.co.uk
dir: On A412 between Town Hall and Watford Junction Station

Currently the rating for this establishment is not confirmed. This may be due to a change of ownership or because it has only recently joined the AA rating scheme. For further details please see the AA website: theAA.com

Rooms 100 (6 fmly) **S** £40-£165; **D** £40-£165* **Facilities** STV FTV Gym Xmas New Year Wi-fi Child facilities **Conf** Class 140 Board 70 Thtr 200 Del from £90 to £250* **Services** Lift Air con **Parking** 118 **Notes** Civ Wed 100

Express by Holiday Inn London - Watford Junction

BUDGET HOTEL

☎ 0871 423 4876
19 Bridle Path WD17 1UE
e-mail: info@express-watford.com

A modern hotel ideal for families and business travellers. Fresh and uncomplicated, the spacious rooms include Sky TV, power shower and tea and coffee-making facilities. Continental buffet breakfast is included in the room rate; other meals may be taken at the nearby family pub or restaurant. See also the Hotel Groups pages.

Conf Class Board Thtr

Travelodge Watford Central

BUDGET HOTEL

☎ 0871 984 6320 📠 01923 213502
23-25 Market Steet WD18 0PA
web: www.travelodge.co.uk
dir: A4008 towards town centre. In 1m take left slip lane to bypass 1st rdbt. At next rdbt take 2nd exit towards town centre. Bear left onto ring road. Hotel on right in 0.5m

Travelodge offers good quality, good value, budget accommodation. All offer family rooms sleeping up to four (two adults, two children) with en suite bathroom/shower-room, remote-control TV, tea- and coffee-making facilities and comfortable beds. Food options vary. Breakfast is at the on-site Bar Café restaurant (if available) or to take away. See also Hotel Groups pages.

Rooms 93 **S** fr £29; **D** fr £29

WELWYN GARDEN CITY Map 6 TL21

Tewin Bury Farm Hotel

★★★★ 74% ⊛ HOTEL

☎ 01438 717793 📠 01438 840440
Hertford Road (B1000) AL6 0JB
e-mail: reservations@tewinbury.co.uk
dir: From N: A1(M) junct 6, 1st exit signed A1000, at next rdbt 1st exit towards Digswell. 0.1m straight on at rdbt. 1m (on B100) Hotel on left.

Situated not far from the A1(M) and within easy reach of Stevenage and Knebworth House, this delightful country-house hotel is part of a thriving farm. Stylish, well-equipped bedrooms of varying sizes are perfectly suited for both leisure and business guests. An award-winning restaurant and meeting rooms are all part of this family-run establishment.

Rooms 39 (30 annexe) (6 fmly) (26 GF) **S** £120-£140; **D** £135-£155 (incl. bkfst)* **Facilities** STV FTV Fishing Cycling New Year Wi-fi **Conf** Class 180 Board 40 Thtr 500 Del from £165 to £210* **Services** Lift **Parking** 400 **Notes** LB ⊗ Civ Wed 150

Best Western Homestead Court Hotel

★★★ 74% HOTEL

☎ 01707 324336 📄 01707 326447
Homestead Ln AL7 4LX
e-mail: enquiries@homesteadcourt.co.uk
web: www.bw-homesteadcourt.co.uk
dir: Off A1000, left at lights at Bushall Hotel. Right at rdbt into Howlands, 2nd left at Hollybush public house into Hollybush Lane. 2nd right at War Memorial into Homestead Lane

A friendly hotel ideally situated less than two miles from the city centre in a tranquil location adjacent to parkland. The property boasts stylish, brightly decorated public areas that include a smart lounge bar and a large restaurant. Bedrooms are pleasantly appointed and equipped with modern facilities. Conference rooms are also available.

Rooms 67 (8 annexe) (6 fmly) (2 GF) (2 smoking) **S** £55-£85; **D** £69-£95* **Facilities** STV Wi-fi **Conf** Class 60 Board 60 Thtr 200 Del from £125 to £145* **Services** Lift **Parking** 70 **Notes** ⊗ Civ Wed 110

KENT

ASHFORD Map 7 TR04

INSPECTORS' CHOICE

Eastwell Manor
★★★★ ⊛⊛ HOTEL

☎ 01233 213000 📄 01233 635530
Eastwell Park, Boughton Lees TN25 4HR
e-mail: enquiries@eastwellmanor.co.uk
dir: On A251, 200yds on left when entering Boughton Aluph

Set in 62 acres of landscaped grounds, this lovely hotel dates back to the Norman Conquest and boasts a number of interesting features, including carved wood-panelled rooms and huge baronial stone fireplaces. Accommodation is divided between the manor house and the courtyard mews cottages. The luxury Pavilion Spa in the grounds has an all-day brasserie, whilst fine dining in the main restaurant is a highlight of any stay.

Rooms 62 (39 annexe) (2 fmly) **Facilities** Spa STV ⓢ ⚄ ♨ 9 ♨ Putt green ⚜ Gym Boules Xmas New Year Wi-fi **Conf** Class 60 Board 48 Thtr 200 **Services** Lift **Parking** 200 **Notes** LB ⊗ Civ Wed 250

Ashford International Hotel

★★★★ 81% HOTEL

☎ 01233 219988 📄 01233 647743
Simone Weil Av TN24 8UX
e-mail: ashford@qhotels.co.uk
web: www.qhotels.co.uk
dir: M20 junct 9, 3rd exit for Ashford/Canterbury. Left at 1st rdbt, hotel 200mtrs on left

Situated just off the M20 and with easy links to the Eurotunnel, Eurostar and ferry terminals, this hotel has been stunningly appointed. The slick, stylishly presented bedrooms are equipped with the latest amenities. Public areas include the spacious Horizons Wine Bar and Restaurant serving a competitively priced menu, and Quench Sports Bar for relaxing drinks. The Reflections leisure club boasts a pool, fully-equipped gym, spa facilities and treatment rooms.

Rooms 179 (29 fmly) **Facilities** Spa ⓢ Gym Aroma steam room Rock sauna Feature shower Ice fountain Xmas New Year Wi-fi **Conf** Class 160 Board 26 Thtr 400 Del from £119 to £165* **Services** Lift Air con **Parking** 400 **Notes** Civ Wed 150

Holiday Inn Ashford-Central

★★★ 79% HOTEL

☎ 0870 400 9001 📄 01233 643176
Canterbury Rd TN24 8QQ
e-mail: reservations-ashford@ihg.com
web: www.holidayinn.co.uk
dir: A28, at 2nd lights turn left. Hotel approx 90mtrs

Ideally situated within easy reach of Eurostar and Eurotunnel terminals and a short drive to historic Canterbury, this popular hotel offers stylish facilities for both business and leisure travellers. Comfortable, well-equipped bedrooms vary in size and include spacious family rooms with modern sofa beds. Public areas include a casual restaurant, lounges, bar and attractive garden area.

Rooms 103 (40 fmly) (50 GF) (12 smoking) **Facilities** STV Xmas Wi-fi **Conf** Class 64 Board 40 Thtr 120 **Parking** 120 **Notes** ⊗ Civ Wed 130

Holiday Inn Ashford-North A20

★★★ 78% HOTEL

☎ 01233 713333 📄 01233 712082
Maidstone Rd, Hothfield TN26 1AR
e-mail: reception.ashford@hiashford.com
web: www.holidayinn.co.uk
dir: M20 junct 9, at rdbt take 3rd exit signed Ashford. Canterbury. At next rdbt 4th exit signed Lenham. Straight on at next rdbt. Hotel approx 3.5m on left just after Esso petrol station

This hotel is ideally situated to meet the needs of business and leisure travellers. It enjoys a rural outlook whilst occupying a convenient location for travel via the Eurostar terminal at Ashford, the channel port of Dover and the M20. There's a small bar, gym and restaurant with a 'local pub' in the grounds. Ample free parking is available.

Rooms 92 (5 fmly) (20 GF) (9 smoking) **Facilities** Gym Wi-fi **Conf** Class 28 Board 32 Thtr 125 Del from £105 to £135* **Services** Lift Air con **Parking** 140 **Notes** ⊗ Civ Wed 60

Travelodge Ashford

BUDGET HOTEL

☎ 0871 984 6004 📄 01233 622676
Eureka Leisure Park TN25 4BN
web: www.travelodge.co.uk
dir: M20 junct 9, take 1st exit on left

Travelodge offers good quality, good value, budget accommodation. All offer family rooms sleeping up to four (two adults, two children) with en suite bathroom/shower-room, remote-control TV, tea- and coffee-making facilities and comfortable beds. Food options vary. Breakfast is at the on-site Bar Café restaurant (if available) or to take away. See also Hotel Groups pages.

Rooms 112 **S** fr £29; **D** fr £29

BRANDS HATCH — Map 6 TQ56

Thistle Brands Hatch — thistle

★★★★ 80% HOTEL

☎ 0871 376 9008 ▤ 0871 376 9108
DA3 8PE
e-mail: brandshatch@thistle.co.uk
web: www.thistlehotels.com/brandshatch
dir: Follow Brands Hatch signs, hotel on left of racing circuit entrance

Ideally situated overlooking Brands Hatch race track and close to the major road networks (M20/M25). The open-plan public areas include a choice of bars, large lounge and a restaurant. Bedrooms are stylishly appointed and well equipped for both leisure and business guests. Extensive meeting rooms and Otium leisure facilities are also available.

Rooms 121 (5 fmly) (60 GF) (10 smoking) **Facilities** Spa
🅢 Gym New Year Wi-fi **Conf** Class 120 Board 60 Thtr 270 Del from £125 to £175* **Parking** 200 **Notes** Civ Wed 100

Brandshatch Place Hotel & Spa — Hand PICKED HOTELS

★★★★ 79% ◉◉ HOTEL

☎ 01474 875000 ▤ 01474 879652
Brands Hatch Rd, Fawkham DA3 8NQ
e-mail: brandshatchplace@handpicked.co.uk
web: www.handpicked.co.uk
dir: M25 junct 3/A20 West Kingsdown. Left at paddock entrance/Fawkham Green sign. 3rd left signed Fawkham Rd. Hotel 500mtrs on right

This charming 18th-century Georgian country house close to the famous racing circuit offers stylish and elegant rooms. Bedrooms are appointed to a very high standard, offering impressive facilities and excellent levels of comfort and quality. The hotel also features an excellent and comprehensive leisure club with substantial crèche facilities.

Rooms 38 (12 annexe) (1 fmly) (6 GF) **Facilities** Spa STV
🅢 ♨ Gym Squash Xmas New Year Wi-fi **Conf** Class 60 Board 50 Thtr 160 **Services** Lift **Parking** 100 **Notes** ⊗ Civ Wed 110

BROADSTAIRS

See advert on this page

CANTERBURY — Map 7 TR15

Abode Canterbury — aBode

★★★★ 79% ◉◉ HOTEL

☎ 01227 766266 & 826678 ▤ 01227 784874
High St CT1 2RX
e-mail: reservationscanterbury@abodehotels.co.uk
web: www.abodehotels.co.uk
dir: M2 junct 7. Follow Canterbury signs onto ringroad. At Wincheap rdbt turn into city. Left into Rosemary Ln, into Stour St. Hotel at end

Dating back to the 12th century this hotel reflects the Abode Hotels' lifestyle concept. Fine dining is offered in the Michael Caines Restaurant, and there is also a Champagne bar, as well as more informal dining in the Tavern. Bedrooms are individually decorated, and have comfortable beds and an impressive range of facilities.

Rooms 72 (3 fmly) **Facilities** FTV Gym & treatment room Xmas New Year Wi-fi **Conf** Class 60 Board 45 Thtr 130 Del from £155 to £175* **Services** Lift Air con **Parking** 22 **Notes** ⊗ Civ Wed 80

Best Western Abbots Barton

★★★ 87% HOTEL

☎ 01227 760341 📄 01227 785442
New Dover Rd CT1 3DU
e-mail: sales@abbotsbartonhotel.com
dir: A2 onto A2050 at bridge, S of Canterbury. Hotel 0.75m past Old Gate Inn on left

Delightful property with a country-house hotel feel set amid two acres of pretty landscaped gardens close to the city centre and major road networks. The spacious accommodation includes a range of stylish lounges, a smart bar and the Fountain Restaurant, which serves imaginative food. Conference and banqueting facilities are also available.

Rooms 50 (2 fmly) (6 GF) **S** £60–£120; **D** £70–£190
Facilities Xmas New Year Wi-fi **Conf** Class 80 Board 60 Thtr 150 Del from £120 to £185 **Services** Lift Air con **Parking** 80 **Notes** LB Civ Wed 100

Chaucer

★★★ 71% HOTEL

☎ 01227 464427 & 453779 📄 01227 450397
Ivy Ln CT1 1TU
e-mail: res.chaucer@crerarmgmt.com
dir: Towards city on A2, exit at Harbledown. Right at 5th rdbt, then 1st left

This historic hotel is located just a short walk from Canterbury Cathedral and the city centre. Retaining much of its original character it offers well-appointed, comfortable bedrooms and modern amenities including Wi-fi. Public areas include the popular Pilgrims lounge/bar and more formal Restaurant 63.

Rooms 42 **Facilities** STV Xmas New Year Wi-fi
Conf Class 50 Board 50 Thtr 100 **Parking** 42 **Notes** LB ⊗ Civ Wed 100

Victoria

★★★ 70% HOTEL

☎ 01227 459333 📄 01227 781552
59 London Rd CT2 8JY
e-mail: info@thevictoriahotel.co.uk
dir: M2/A2 onto A2052, on entering city hotel on left off 1st rdbt

Well situated on the outskirts of the city centre yet just a short walk from the shops and within sight of the cathedral. Bedrooms vary in size; each one is pleasantly decorated and has a good range of useful facilities such as free Wi-fi. Public areas include a stylish bar/lounge, sunny conservatory and a carvery restaurant. Spacious parking is available.

Rooms 33 (3 fmly) (10 GF) **Facilities** Xmas Wi-fi
Conf Class 20 Board 20 Thtr 20 **Parking** 70 **Notes** LB ⊗

Canterbury Cathedral Lodge

★★★ Ⓐ METRO HOTEL

☎ 01227 865350 📄 01227 865388
The Precincts CT1 2EH
e-mail: stay@canterbury-cathedral.org
web: www.canterburycathedrallodge.org/
dir: Within grounds of cathedral

Rooms 35 (6 annexe) (1 fmly) (13 GF) **S** £60–£89;
D £65–£99 (incl. bkfst)* **Facilities** Wi-fi **Conf** Class 95 Board 40 Thtr 250 Del from £135 to £149* **Services** Lift **Parking** 15 **Notes** ⊗ RS Xmas

Express by Holiday Inn Canterbury

BUDGET HOTEL

☎ 01227 865000 📄 01227 865100
A2 Dover Rd, Upper Harbledown CT2 9HX
e-mail: canterbury@exbhi.co.uk
web: www.expressbyholidayinncanterbury.co.uk
dir: On A2, 4m from city centre. Hotel accessed via Texaco petrol station at Upper Harbledown

A modern hotel ideal for families and business travellers. Fresh and uncomplicated, the spacious rooms include Sky TV, power shower and tea and coffee-making facilities. Continental buffet breakfast is included in the room rate; other meals may be taken at the nearby family pub or restaurant. See also the Hotel Groups pages.

Rooms 89 (38 GF) **S** £55–£129; **D** £55–£129 (incl. bkfst)*
Conf Class 20 Board 10 Thtr 36

Innkeeper's Lodge Canterbury

BUDGET HOTEL

☎ 0845 112 6099
162 New Dover Rd CT1 3EL
web: www.innkeeperslodge.com/canterbury
dir: M2 junct 7, A2 towards Canterbury/Dover. Take exit for OBridge, right at end of sliproad, then right again. Right at road end & follow A2050/Canterbury signs. Lodge 1m on left

Innkeeper's Lodge represents an exciting, high value concept within the budget hotel market. Comfortable bedrooms provide excellent facilities that include satellite TV and modem points. This carefully restored lodge is in a picturesque setting and has its own unique style and quirky character. Food is served all day, and an extensive, complimentary continental breakfast is offered. See also the Hotel Groups pages.

Rooms 9 (1 fmly)

CANTERBURY *continued*

Travelodge Canterbury Dunkirk

BUDGET HOTEL

☎ 0871 984 6023 📠 01227 752781
Gate Service Area, Dunkirk ME13 9LN
web: www.travelodge.co.uk
dir: W on A2. Lodge 1m from M2 junct 7. Or S'bound on A2, 1st left after Little Chef signed Upper Harbledown. 1st right over bridge, leads to W'bound carriageway . Lodge behind Little Chef & garage

Travelodge offers good quality, good value, budget accommodation. All offer family rooms sleeping up to four (two adults, two children) with en suite bathroom/shower-room, remote-control TV, tea- and coffee-making facilities and comfortable beds. Food options vary. Breakfast is at the on-site Bar Café restaurant (if available) or to take away. See also Hotel Groups pages.

Rooms 40 **S** fr £29; **D** fr £29

Travelodge Margate Westwood

BUDGET HOTEL

☎ 0871 984 6341 📠 01843 861 796
Unit 53 Westwood Cross, Margate Rd, Broadstairs CT10 2BF
e-mail: margatewestwood@travelodge.co.uk
dir: From A299 into Herne Bay. At St Nicolas-at-Wade rdbt 3rd exit onto A299 (signed Ramsgate). At Monkton rdbt 2nd exit onto A253. Continue onto Canterbury Rd West, into Cliffsend. At rdbt 1st exit into Haine Rd. Approx 1m, lodge on right

Rooms 48 **S** fr £29; **D** fr £29

CHATHAM　Map 7 TQ76

Bridgewood Manor Hotel

★★★★ 72% HOTEL

☎ 01634 201333 📠 01634 201330
Bridgewood Roundabout, Walderslade Woods ME5 9AX
e-mail: bridgewoodmanor@qhotels.co.uk
web: www.qhotels.co.uk
dir: Adjacent to Bridgewood rdbt on A229. Take 3rd exit signed Walderslade & Lordswood. Hotel 50mtrs on left

A modern, purpose-built hotel situated on the outskirts of Rochester. Bedrooms are pleasantly decorated, comfortably furnished and equipped with many thoughtful touches. The hotel has an excellent range of leisure and conference facilities. Guests can dine in the informal Terrace Bistro or experience fine dining in the more formal Squires restaurant, where the service is both attentive and friendly.

Rooms 100 (12 fmly) (26 GF) **S** £65-£105; **D** £65-£125 (incl. bkfst)* **Facilities** Spa STV ⓣ supervised ♨ Gym Beauty treatments Xmas New Year Wi-fi **Conf** Class 110 Board 80 Thtr 200 Del from £99 to £145* **Services** Lift **Parking** 170 **Notes** LB Civ Wed 130

Holiday Inn Rochester-Chatham

★★★ 77% HOTEL

☎ 0870 400 9006 & 07736 746229 📠 01322 625584
Maidstone Rd ME5 9SF
e-mail: adrienne.reader@ihg.com
web: www.holidayinn.co.uk
dir: M2 junct 3 or M20 junct 6, then A229 for Chatham

A modern, well-equipped hotel close to Rochester, Canterbury and the historic Chatham Dockyards. Bedrooms, including family rooms, are comfortable and spacious; all have air conditioning and broadband access. Public facilities include a lounge, bar and modern restaurant. There is a gym, indoor pool, sauna, spa and an impressive self-contained conference centre.

Rooms 149 (29 fmly) (53 GF) (16 smoking) **S** £60-£129; **D** £60-£129* **Facilities** STV ⓣ supervised Gym Steam room Sauna Pilates & beauty evenings Wi-fi **Conf** Class 45 Board 45 Thtr 100 Del from £110 to £145* **Services** Lift Air con **Parking** 200 **Notes** Civ Wed 100

Ramada Encore Chatham

Ⓤ

☎ 0844 801 0313 📠 0844 801 0314
Western Av, Chatham Historic Dockyard ME4 4NT
e-mail: operations@encorechatham.co.uk
dir: Follow signs for Chatham Historic Dockyard

Currently the rating for this establishment is not confirmed. This may be due to a change of ownership or because it has only recently joined the AA rating scheme. For further details please see the AA website: theAA.com

Rooms 90 (14 fmly) (8 smoking) **Facilities** STV FTV Wi-fi **Conf** Class 12 Board 12 Thtr 20 **Services** Lift Air con **Parking** 60 **Notes** ⊗

DARTFORD　Map 6 TQ57

Rowhill Grange Hotel & Utopia Spa

★★★★ 82% ◉◉◉ HOTEL

☎ 01322 615136 📠 01322 615137
DA2 7QH
e-mail: admin@rowhillgrange.co.uk
web: www.rowhillgrange.co.uk
dir: M25 junct 3 take B2173 to Swanley, then B258 to Hextable

Set within nine acres of mature woodland this hotel enjoys a tranquil setting, yet is accessible to road networks. Bedrooms are stylishly and individually decorated; many have four-poster or sleigh beds. There is a smart, conservatory restaurant offering memorable, seasonal dishes, and also a more informal brasserie. The elegant lounge is popular for afternoon teas. The leisure and conference facilities are impressive.

Rooms 38 (8 annexe) (4 fmly) (3 GF) **S** £175-£260; **D** £200-£370 (incl. bkfst)* **Facilities** Spa STV FTV ⓣ ♨ Gym Beauty treatment Hair salon Aerobic studio Japanese Therapy pool Xmas New Year Wi-fi **Conf** Class 64 Board 34 Thtr 160 **Services** Lift **Parking** 150 **Notes** LB ⊗ Civ Wed 150

Campanile Dartford

BUDGET HOTEL

☎ 01322 278925 📠 01322 278948
1 Clipper Boulevard West, Crossways Business Park DA2 6QN
e-mail: dartford@campanile.com
dir: Follow signs for Ferry Terminal from Dartford Bridge

This modern building offers accommodation in smart, well-equipped bedrooms, all with en suite bathrooms. Refreshments may be taken at the informal bistro. See also the Hotel Groups pages.

Rooms 125 (14 fmly) **Conf** Class 30 Board 30 Thtr 40 Del from £110 to £135

Express by Holiday Inn Dartford Bridge

BUDGET HOTEL

☎ 01322 290333 📄 01322 290444
Dartford Bridge, University Way DA1 5PA
e-mail: gm.dartford@expressholidayinn.co.uk
web: www.hiexpress.com/dartfordbridge
dir: A206 to Erith. Hotel off University Way via signed sliproad

A modern hotel ideal for families and business travellers. Fresh and uncomplicated, the spacious rooms include Sky TV, power shower and tea and coffee-making facilities. Continental buffet breakfast is included in the room rate; other meals may be taken at the nearby family pub or restaurant. See also the Hotel Groups pages.

Rooms 126 (34 fmly) **Conf** Board 25 Thtr 35

Travelodge Dartford

BUDGET HOTEL

☎ 0871 984 6025 📄 01322 387854
Charles St, Greenhithe DA9 9AP
web: www.travelodge.co.uk
dir: M25 junct 1a, take A206 towards Gravesend

Travelodge offers good quality, good value, budget accommodation. All offer family rooms sleeping up to four (two adults, two children) with en suite bathroom/shower-room, remote-control TV, tea- and coffee-making facilities and comfortable beds. Food options vary. Breakfast is at the on-site Bar Café restaurant (if available) or to take away. See also Hotel Groups pages.

Rooms 65 **S** fr £29; **D** fr £29

DEAL Map 7 TR35

Dunkerleys Hotel & Restaurant

★★★ 80% ◉◉ HOTEL

☎ 01304 375016 📄 01304 380187
19 Beach St CT14 7AH
e-mail: ddunkerley@btconnect.com
web: www.dunkerleys.co.uk
dir: From M20 or M2 follow signs for A258 Deal. Hotel close to Pier

This hotel is centrally located and on the seafront. Bedrooms are furnished to a high standard with a good range of amenities. The restaurant and bar offer a comfortable and attractive environment in which to relax and to enjoy the cuisine that makes the best use of local ingredients. Service throughout is friendly and attentive.

Rooms 16 (2 fmly) **S** £70-£90; **D** £100-£130 (incl. bkfst)
Facilities STV FTV Xmas Wi-fi **Notes** LB ⊗ RS Sun eve & Mon

---

DOVER Map 7 TR34

Wallett's Court Country House Hotel & Spa

★★★★ 74% ◉◉ HOTEL

☎ 01304 852424 & 0800 035 1628 📄 01304 853430
West Cliffe, St Margarets-at-Cliffe CT15 6EW
e-mail: wc@wallettscourt.com
web: www.wallettscourt.com
dir: From Dover take A258 towards Deal. 1st right to St Margarets-at-Cliffe & West Cliffe, 1m on right opposite West Cliffe church

A lovely Jacobean manor situated in a peaceful location on the outskirts of town. Bedrooms in the original house are traditionally furnished whereas the rooms in the courtyard buildings are more modern; all are equipped to a high standard. Public rooms include a smart bar, a lounge and a restaurant that utilises local organic produce. An impressive spa facility is housed in converted barn buildings in the grounds.

Rooms 16 (13 annexe) (2 fmly) (7 GF) **S** £109-£139; **D** £129-£199 (incl. bkfst) **Facilities** Spa FTV ⊗ ⊗ Putt green ⊛ Gym Treatment suite Aromatherapy massage Golf pitching range Beauty therapy New Year Wi-fi **Conf** Class 25 Board 16 Thtr 25 Del from £149 to £169 **Parking** 30 **Notes** LB Closed 24-26 Dec

Ramada Hotel Dover

◈RAMADA

★★★★ 74% HOTEL

☎ 01304 821230 📄 01304 825576
Singledge Ln, Whitfield CT16 3EL
e-mail: reservations@ramadadover.co.uk
web: www.ramadadover.co.uk
dir: From M20 follow signs to A2 towards Canterbury. Turn right after Whitfield rdbt. From A2 towards Dover, turn left before Whitfield rdbt

A modern purpose-built hotel situated in a quiet location between Dover and Canterbury, close to the ferry port and

---

seaside. The open-plan public areas are contemporary in style and include a lounge, a bar and Bleriot's Restaurant. The stylish bedrooms are simply decorated with co-ordinated soft furnishings and many thoughtful extras.

Rooms 68 (68 GF) **S** £64-£129; **D** £64-£129*
Facilities STV Gym Xmas New Year Wi-fi **Conf** Thtr 400 **Services** Air con **Parking** 110 **Notes** ⊗ Civ Wed

White Cliffs

★★★ 75% ◉ HOTEL

☎ 01304 852229 & 852400 📄 01304 851880
High St, St Margaret's-at-Cliffe CT15 6AT
e-mail: mail@thewhitecliffs.com
dir: Opposite church in village centre

This fresh-looking traditional weather boarded inn has a contemporary feel although still retaining much of its traditional character. Comfortably appointed bedrooms, divided between the main house and The Mews, boast luxurious beds and well co-ordinated furnishings. Public areas are sympathetically styled highlighting the relaxed beach atmosphere. A mini spa is also available.

Rooms 15 (9 annexe) (2 fmly) (4 GF) **S** £59-£79; **D** £89-£129 (incl. bkfst) **Facilities** FTV Xmas New Year Wi-fi Child facilities **Conf** Class 20 Board 14 Thtr 20 Del from £129 to £149 **Parking** 20 **Notes** LB

Best Western Churchill Hotel and Health Club

★★★ 72% HOTEL

☎ 01304 203633 📄 01304 216320
Dover Waterfront CT17 9BP
e-mail: enquiries@churchill-hotel.com
web: www.bw-churchillhotel.co.uk
dir: A20 follow Hoverport signs, left onto seafront, hotel in 800yds

Attractive terraced waterfront hotel overlooking the harbour that offers a wide range of facilities including

continued

DOVER *continued*

meeting rooms, health club, hairdresser and beauty treatments. Some of the tastefully decorated bedrooms have balconies, some have broadband access and many of the rooms have superb sea views. Public rooms include a large, open-plan lounge bar and a smart bistro restaurant.

Rooms 80 (5 fmly) **S** £63-£82; **D** £68-£100* **Facilities** STV Gym Health club Hair & beauty salons Xmas New Year Wi-fi **Conf** Class 60 Board 50 Thtr 110 Del from £90 to £100* **Services** Lift **Parking** 32 **Notes** ⊗ Civ Wed 100

The Marquis at Alkham

⍟⍟ RESTAURANT WITH ROOMS

☎ 01304 873410 📠 01304 873418
Alkham Valley Rd, Alkham CT15 7DF
e-mail: info@themarquisatalkham.co.uk
web: www.themarquisatalkham.co.uk
dir: From Dover take A256, at rdbt 1st exit onto London Rd, then left onto Alkham Rd, then Alkham Valley Rd. 1.5m after sharp bend

Located between Dover and Folkestone, this modern, contemporary restaurant with rooms offers luxury accommodation with modern features - flat-screen TVs, Wi-fi, power showers and bath robes to name but a few. All bedrooms are individually designed and stylish with fantastic views of the Kent Downs. The award-winning restaurant, open for lunch and dinner, serves modern British cuisine. Continental and a choice of cooked breakfasts are offered.

Rooms 5 (1 fmly)

| FAVERSHAM | Map 7 TR06 |

Travelodge Canterbury Whitstable

BUDGET HOTEL

☎ 0871 984 6022 📠 01227 281135
Thanet Way ME13 9EL
web: www.travelodge.co.uk
dir: M2 junct 7, A299 to Ramsgate. Lodge 4m on left

Travelodge offers good quality, good value, budget accommodation. All offer family rooms sleeping up to four (two adults, two children) with en suite bathroom/shower-room, remote-control TV, tea- and coffee-making facilities and comfortable beds. Food options vary. Breakfast is at the on-site Bar Café restaurant (if available) or to take away. See also Hotel Groups pages.

Rooms 40 **S** fr £29; **D** fr £29

| FOLKESTONE | Map 7 TR23 |

The Burlington

★★★ 77% HOTEL

☎ 01303 255301 📠 01303 251301
Earls Av CT20 2HR
e-mail: info@theburlingtonhotel.com
dir: M20 junct 13. At rdbt 3rd exit signed A20/Folkstone. At next rdbt 2nd exit into Cherry Garden Lane. To lights, take middle lane into Beachborough Rd, under bridge, left into Shorncliffe Rd. 5th right signed Hythe & Hastings. Hotel at end on right

Situated close to the beach in a peaceful side road just a short walk from the town centre. The public rooms include a choice of lounges, the Bay Tree restaurant and a large cocktail bar. Bedrooms are pleasantly decorated and equipped with modern facilities; some rooms have superb sea views.

Rooms 50 (6 fmly) (5 GF) **S** £28-£68; **D** £33-£108* **Facilities** FTV Putt green Xmas New Year Wi-fi **Conf** Class 100 Board 80 Thtr 240 **Services** Lift **Parking** 20 **Notes** LB Civ Wed 100

Best Western Clifton

★★★ 75% HOTEL

☎ 01303 851231 📠 01303 223949
The Leas CT20 2EB
e-mail: reservations@thecliftonhotel.com
dir: M20 junct 13, 0.25m W of town centre on A259

This privately-owned Victorian-style hotel occupies a prime location, looking out across the English Channel. The bedrooms are comfortably appointed and most have views of the sea. Public areas include a traditionally furnished lounge, a popular bar serving a good range of beers and several well-appointed conference rooms.

Rooms 80 (5 fmly) **Facilities** STV FTV Games room Xmas New Year Wi-fi **Conf** Class 36 Board 32 Thtr 80 Del from £95 to £125* **Services** Lift **Notes** ⊗

The Southcliff

★★ 69% HOTEL

☎ 01303 850075 📠 01303 850070
22-26 The Leas CT20 2DY
e-mail: sales@thesouthcliff.co.uk
web: www.thesouthcliff.co.uk
dir: M20 junct 13, follow signs for The Leas. Left at rdbt onto Sandgate Rd, right at Blockbusters, right at end of road, hotel on right

Perched atop the south cliff with a bird's eye view of the sea this historical Victorian hotel is perfectly located for the Folkstone channel crossings and is only minutes from the town centre. The bedrooms are spacious and airy with some boasting balconies and sea views. Enjoy dinner in the spacious restaurant or contemporary on-site bistro. Parking is available by arrangement.

The Southcliff

Rooms 68 (2 fmly) (5 smoking) **S** £27.50-£69.50; **D** £45-£89.50 **Facilities** STV ♫ Xmas New Year Wi-fi **Conf** Class 120 Board 50 Thtr 200 Del from £55 to £75* **Services** Lift **Parking** 24 **Notes** LB ⊗

| GILLINGHAM | Map 7 TQ76 |

Travelodge Medway (M2)

BUDGET HOTEL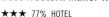

☎ 0871 984 6198 📠 01634 263187
Medway Motorway Service Area, Rainham ME8 8PQ
web: www.travelodge.co.uk
dir: between juncts 4 & 5 of M2 westbound

Travelodge offers good quality, good value, budget accommodation. All offer family rooms sleeping up to four (two adults, two children) with en suite bathroom/shower-room, remote-control TV, tea- and coffee-making facilities and comfortable beds. Food options vary. Breakfast is at the on-site Bar Café restaurant (if available) or to take away. See also Hotel Groups pages.

Rooms 58 **S** fr £29; **D** fr £29

| GRAVESEND | Map 6 TQ67 |

Best Western Manor Hotel

★★★ 77% HOTEL

☎ 01474 353100 📠 01474 354978
Hever Court Rd DA12 5UQ
e-mail: manor@bestwestern.co.uk
web: www.bw-manorhotel.co.uk
dir: At junct of A2 Gravesend East exit

Situated close to the major road networks with links to Dover, Channel Tunnel and Bluewater shopping village. The attractively decorated bedrooms are generally quite spacious and each one is equipped with many useful facilities. Public rooms include a bar and a smart restaurant as well as an impressive health club.

Rooms 59 (3 fmly) (20 GF) **Facilities** STV ⏰ supervised Gym Fitness centre Steam room Sauna New Year Wi-fi **Conf** Class 100 Board 25 Thtr 200 Del from £125 to £145* **Parking** 100 **Notes** ⊗ Closed 24-26 & 31 Dec

Hadlow Manor

★★★ 77% HOTEL

☎ 01732 851442 🖹 01732 851875
Goose Green TN11 0JH
e-mail: hotel@hadlowmanor.co.uk
dir: On A26 (Maidstone to Tonbridge road). 1m E of Hadlow

This is a friendly, independently owned country-house hotel, ideally situated between Maidstone and Tonbridge. Traditionally styled bedrooms are spacious and attractively furnished with many amenities. Public areas include a sunny restaurant, bar and lounge. The gardens are delightful and there's a seated area ideal for relaxation in warmer weather. Meeting and banqueting facilities are available.

Rooms 29 (2 fmly) (8 GF) **S** £54-£85; **D** £54-£85*
Facilities STV New Year Wi-fi **Conf** Class 90 Board 103 Thtr 200 **Parking** 120 **Notes** ❀ Civ Wed 200

Ramada Maidstone

RAMADA
HOTEL & RESORT

★★★ 77% HOTEL

☎ 01622 631163 & 0844 815 9045 🖹 01622 735290
Ashford Rd ME17 1RE
e-mail: sales.maidstone@ramadajarvis.co.uk
web: www.ramadajarvis.co.uk
dir: M20 junct 8, follow Leeds Castle signs, at 3rd rdbt turn right

A large, purpose-built hotel that is conveniently close to the M20, Channel Tunnel and Leeds Castle. Public areas include an attractive contemporary bar, restaurant and comfortable lounge. Bedrooms are stylishly decorated and furnished, with modern amenities such as flat-screen TVs, internet and movie channels.

Rooms 126 (4 fmly) **S** £59-£129; **D** £59-£129*
Facilities Spa STV ❂ supervised ⚑ Putt green Fishing ⚑ Gym Pitch & putt Jogging track Steam room Sauna Table tennis ♫ Xmas New Year Wi-fi **Conf** Class 220 Board 60 Thtr 650 Del from £99 to £150* **Services** Lift **Parking** 500 **Notes** LB ❀ Civ Wed 150

Mercure Hythe Imperial

Mercure

★★★★ 74% HOTEL

☎ 01303 267441 🖹 01303 264610
Princes Pde CT21 6AE
e-mail: h6862@accor.com
web: www.mercure-uk.com
dir: M20, junct 11 onto A261. In Hythe follow Folkestone signs. Right into Twiss Rd to hotel

This impressive seafront hotel is enhanced by impressive grounds including a 13-hole golf course, tennis court and extensive gardens. Bedrooms are varied in style but all offer modern facilities, and many enjoy stunning sea views. The elegant restaurant, bar and lounges are traditional in style and retain many original features. The leisure club includes a gym, a squash court, an indoor pool, and the spa offers a range of luxury treatments.

Rooms 100 (6 fmly) (6 GF) **S** £75-£145; **D** £75-£145
Facilities Spa STV ❂ ⚑ 13 ⚑ Putt green Gym Squash Xmas New Year Wi-fi **Conf** Class 120 Board 80 Thtr 220 Del from £115 to £185* **Services** Lift **Parking** 207 **Notes** LB Civ Wed 120

Best Western Stade Court

Best Western

Ⓤ

☎ 01303 268263 🖹 01303 261803
West Pde CT21 6DT
e-mail: stadecourt@bestwestern.co.uk
dir: M20 junct 11 follow signs for Hythe town centre. Follow brown tourist sign for hotel

Currently the rating for this establishment is not confirmed. This may be due to a change of ownership or because it has only recently joined the AA rating scheme. For further details please see the AA website: theAA.com

Rooms 42 (5 fmly) (10 smoking) **S** £40-£75; **D** £55-£115 (incl. bkfst)* **Facilities** FTV Fishing ♫ Xmas New Year Wi-fi **Conf** Class 20 Board 30 Thtr 40 Del from £99 to £125 **Services** Lift **Parking** 11 **Notes** LB Civ Wed 60

The Fayreness

★★★ 79% HOTEL

☎ 01843 868641 & 861103 🖹 01843 608750
Marine Dr CT10 3LG
e-mail: info@fayreness.co.uk
web: www.fayreness.co.uk
dir: A28 onto B2051 which becomes B2052. Pass Holy Trinity Church on right and '19th Hole' public house. Next left, down Kingsgate Ave, hotel at end on left

Situated on the cliff top overlooking the English Channel, just a few steps from a sandy beach and adjacent to the North Foreland Golf Club. The spacious bedrooms are tastefully furnished with many thoughtful touches including free Wi-fi; some rooms have stunning sea views. Public rooms include a large open-plan lounge/bar, a function room, dining room and conservatory restaurant.

Rooms 29 (3 fmly) (5 GF) (4 smoking) **S** £57.50-£157; **D** £73.50-£167 (incl. bkfst)* **Facilities** STV New Year Wi-fi **Conf** Class 28 Board 36 Thtr 50 Del from £80 to £150* **Parking** 70 **Notes** LB Civ Wed 80

See advert on page 258

INSPECTORS' CHOICE

Chilston Park

HandPICKED

★★★★ ◉◉ HOTEL

☎ 01622 859803 🖹 01622 858588
Sandway ME17 2BE
e-mail: chilstonpark@handpicked.co.uk
web: www.handpickedhotels.co.uk
dir: From A20 turn off to Lenham, turn right onto High St, pass station on right, 1st left, over x-roads, hotel 0.25m on left

This elegant Grade I listed country house is set in 23 acres of immaculately landscaped gardens and parkland. An impressive collection of original paintings and antiques creates a unique environment. The sunken Venetian-style restaurant serves modern British food with French influences. Bedrooms are individual in design, some have four-poster beds and many have garden views.

Rooms 53 (23 annexe) (2 fmly) (3 GF) **S** £70-£225; **D** £80-£235* **Facilities** STV FTV Fishing ⚑ Xmas New Year Wi-fi **Conf** Class 60 Board 50 Thtr 100 Del from £110 to £160* **Services** Lift **Parking** 100 **Notes** LB ❀ Civ Wed 90

MAIDSTONE — Map 7 TQ75

Tudor Park, a Marriott Hotel & Country Club

Marriott HOTELS & RESORTS

★★★★ 79% HOTEL

☎ 01622 734334 & 632004 📠 01622 735360
Ashford Rd, Bearsted ME14 4NQ
e-mail: mhrs.tdmgs.salesadmin@marriotthotels.com
web: www.marriotttudorpark.co.uk
dir: M20 junct 8 to Lenham. Right at rdbt towards
Bearsted and Maidstone on A20. Hotel 1m on left

Located on the outskirts of Maidstone in a wooded valley
below Leeds Castle, this fine country hotel is set amidst
220 acres of parkland. Spacious bedrooms provide good
levels of comfort and a comprehensive range of extras.
Facilities include a championship golf course, a fully
equipped gym and two dining options.

Rooms 120 (48 fmly) (60 GF) (8 smoking) Facilities Spa
🕲 ♨ 18 ⚑ Putt green Gym Driving range Beauty salon
Steam room Xmas New Year Wi-fi Conf Class 100
Board 60 Thtr 250 Services Lift Parking 250 Notes ⊗
Civ Wed 160

Best Western Russell

Best Western

★★★ 75% HOTEL

☎ 01622 692221 📠 01622 762084
136 Boxley Rd ME14 2AE
e-mail: res@therussellhotel.com
web: www.therussellhotel.com
dir: M20 junct 7, A249 Maidstone. At 2nd rdbt take 2nd
exit to Boxley. Left at 3rd rdbt, hotel on left at top of hill

Since its days as a Carmelite convent, this Victorian
building has been extended and modernised. Set in
attractive grounds and offering a range of function
rooms, the hotel is a popular venue for weddings and
conferences. The well-maintained bedrooms are
contemporary in style and equipped with modern
facilities.

Rooms 42 (4 fmly) Facilities STV Free use of facilities at
David Lloyd Health & Fitness Centre Xmas New Year Wi-fi
Conf Class 100 Board 70 Thtr 300 Parking 100 Notes ⊗
Civ Wed 250

Grange Moor

★★★ 72% HOTEL

☎ 01622 677623 📠 01622 678246
St Michael's Rd ME16 8BS
e-mail: reservations@grangemoor.co.uk
dir: From town centre towards A26 (Tonbridge road). Hotel
0.25m on left, just after church

Expect a warm welcome at this friendly, privately owned
hotel, which is ideally situated, within easy walking
distance of the town centre. The smartly decorated
bedrooms have co-ordinated soft fabrics and many
thoughtful touches. Public areas include a popular bar, a
cosy restaurant and a small residents' lounge.

Rooms 50 (12 annexe) (5 fmly) (12 GF) (9 smoking)
S £52-£55; D £60-£69 (incl. bkfst)* Facilities FTV Wi-fi
Conf Class 60 Board 40 Thtr 100 Parking 60 Notes LB ⊗
Closed 24-30 Dec Civ Wed 80

Innkeeper's Lodge Maidstone

BUDGET HOTEL

☎ 0845 112 6103 📠 0845 112 6200
Sandling Rd ME14 2RF
web: www.innkeeperslodge.com/maidstone
dir: M20 junct 6, A229 towards Maidstone. Left at 3rd
rdbt into Station Road, left into Sandling Road. Lodge on
left

Innkeeper's Lodge represents an exciting, high value
concept within the budget hotel market. Comfortable
bedrooms provide excellent facilities that include satellite
TV and modem points. This carefully restored lodge is in a
picturesque setting and has its own unique style and
quirky character. Food is served all day, and an extensive,
complimentary continental breakfast is offered. See also
the Hotel Groups pages.

Rooms 12 (1 fmly)

MARGATE — Map 7 TR37

Smiths Court

★★★ 🅰 HOTEL

☎ 01843 222310 📠 01843 222312
Eastern Esplanade, Cliftonville CT9 2HL
e-mail: info@smithscourt.co.uk
dir: From clocktower on seafront take left fork on A28 for
approx 1m. Hotel on right Eastern Esplanade at junct with
Godwin Rd.

Rooms 43 (10 fmly) (4 GF) Facilities FTV Gym 🎵 New
Year Wi-fi Conf Class 50 Board 80 Thtr 80 Services Lift
Parking 15 Notes Civ Wed 80

RAMSGATE — Map 7 TR36

Pegwell Bay

★★★ 77% HOTEL

☎ 01843 599590 📠 01843 599591
81 Pegwell Rd, Pegwell Village CT11 0NJ
e-mail: reception@pegwellbayhotel.co.uk
dir: A28 to Ramsgate. Follow directions to Pegwell.
Continue on Chiltern Lane, hotel on left

Boasting stunning views over The Channel, this historic
cliff-top hotel makes an ideal location for guests either
on business or for leisure. Spacious, comfortable
bedrooms are well equipped and include Wi-fi. A modern
lounge, majestic dining room and traditional pub offer a
variety of options for eating and for relaxation.

Rooms 42 (1 fmly) (6 GF) Facilities FTV Xmas New Year
Wi-fi Conf Class 65 Board 65 Thtr 100 Services Lift
Notes ⊗ Civ Wed 70

The Oak Hotel

★★ 84% HOTEL

☎ 01843 583686 & 581582 📠 01843 581606
66 Harbour Pde CT11 8LN
e-mail: reception@oakhotel.co.uk
dir: Follow road around harbour & turn right into Harbour
Pde

Located within easy reach of the railway station, ferry
terminal and the town centre's shops, this stylish hotel
enjoys spectacular views of the marina and harbour. The
comfortable bedrooms are attractively presented and very
well equipped. The Atlantis fish restaurant, Caffe Roma
and the contemporary bar offer a variety of dining
options.

Rooms 34 (9 fmly) S £50; D £67.50-£100 (incl. bkfst)*
Facilities Wi-fi Conf Class 60 Board 50 Thtr 100
Notes LB ⊗

Royal Harbour

★★ 80% METRO HOTEL

☎ 01843 591514 📠 01843 570443
10-11 Nelson Crescent CT11 9JF
e-mail: info@royalharbourhotel.co.uk
dir: A253 to Ramsgate. Follow signs to seafront. At Churchill Tavern, 1st left into Nelson Crescent

This hotel is made up of adjoining Georgian Grade II listed townhouses that date back to 1799, and occupy a prime position in the town's well known historic garden crescent. Many of the bedrooms boast magnificent views over the 'Royal Harbour', the yacht marina and the English Channel. The atmosphere is relaxed, the service is attentive and the breakfast is superb.

Rooms 19 (3 fmly) (1 GF) **S** £79-£99; **D** £99-£199 (incl. bkfst)* **Facilities** FTV Wi-fi **Parking** 4

Express by Holiday Inn Kent International Airport-Minster

BUDGET HOTEL

☎ 020 8554 9933 📠 020 8554 1898
Tothill St CT12 4AU
e-mail: reservations@express-kia.co.uk
web: www.hiexpress.co.uk
dir: A299 Minster, Ramsgate

A modern hotel ideal for families and business travellers. Fresh and uncomplicated, the spacious rooms include Sky TV, power shower and tea and coffee-making facilities. Continental buffet breakfast is included in the room rate; other meals may be taken at the nearby family pub or restaurant. See also the Hotel Groups pages.

Rooms 105 (62 fmly) (33 GF) (17 smoking)
S £39.95-£79.95; **D** £39.95-£79.95 (incl. bkfst)
Conf Class 30 Board 20 Thtr 40 Del from £55 to £300

The Bell

★★★ Ⓐ HOTEL

☎ 01304 613388 📠 01304 615308
The Quay CT13 9EF
e-mail: reservations@bellhotelsandwich.co.uk
web: www.bellhotelsandwich.co.uk
dir: In town centre (Quay side)

Rooms 34 (4 fmly) **S** £90-£210; **D** £108-£210 (incl. bkfst)* **Facilities** FTV Xmas New Year Wi-fi **Conf** Class 80 Board 50 Thtr 150 Del from £140 to £180* **Parking** 7
Notes LB Civ Wed 80

Best Western Donnington Manor

★★★ 79% HOTEL

☎ 01732 462681 📠 01732 458116
London Rd, Dunton Green TN13 2TD
e-mail: fdesk@donningtonmanorhotel.co.uk
web: www.bw-donningtonmanor.co.uk
dir: M25 junct 4, follow signs for Bromley/Orpington to rdbt. Left onto A224 (Dunton Green), left at 2nd rdbt. Left at Rose & Crown, hotel 300yds on right

An extended 15th-century manor house situated on the outskirts of Sevenoaks. Public rooms in the original part of the building have a wealth of character; they include an attractive oak-beamed restaurant, a comfortable lounge and a cosy bar. The purpose-built bedrooms are smartly decorated and well equipped. The hotel also has leisure facilities.

Rooms 59 (2 fmly) (16 GF) **S** £70-£95; **D** £75-£95 (incl. bkfst)* **Facilities** STV 🏊 Gym Saunas Xmas New Year Wi-fi **Conf** Class 70 Board 50 Thtr 180 Del from £110 to £145* **Services** Lift Air con **Parking** 120 **Notes** LB ⊗ Civ Wed 130

Hempstead House Country Hotel

★★★ 86% ◉ HOTEL

☎ 01795 428020 📠 01795 436362
London Rd, Bapchild ME9 9PP
e-mail: info@hempsteadhouse.co.uk
web: www.hempsteadhouse.co.uk
dir: 1.5m from town centre on A2 towards Canterbury

Expect a warm welcome at this charming detached Victorian property, situated amidst four acres of mature landscaped gardens. Bedrooms are attractively decorated with lovely co-ordinated fabrics, tastefully furnished and equipped with many thoughtful touches. Public rooms feature a choice of elegant lounges as well as a superb conservatory dining room. In summer guests can eat on the terraces. The brand new spa and fitness suite, AquaManda, is now open.

Rooms 34 (7 fmly) (1 GF) **Facilities** Spa STV FTV 🏊 🛥 Gym Fitness studio Steam room Sauna Hydrotherapy pool Xmas New Year Wi-fi **Conf** Class 150 Board 100 Thtr 150 **Services** Lift **Parking** 100 **Notes** Civ Wed 150

Little Silver Country Hotel

★★★ 78% HOTEL

☎ 01233 850321 & 0845 166 2516 📠 01233 850647
Ashford Rd, St Michael's TN30 6SP
e-mail: enquiries@little-silver.co.uk
web: www.little-silver.co.uk
dir: M20 junct 8, A274 signed Tenterden

Located just outside the charming town of Tenterden and within easy reach of many local Kentish attractions, this charming hotel is ideal for leisure and business guests as well as being a popular wedding venue. Bedrooms are spaciously appointed and well equipped; many boast spa baths. There is a spacious lounge, small bar and the modern restaurant overlooks beautifully tended gardens.

Rooms 16 (2 fmly) (6 GF) **S** £60-£75; **D** £95-£195 (incl. bkfst)* **Facilities** STV FTV Xmas Wi-fi **Conf** Class 50 Board 25 Thtr 75 **Parking** 70 **Notes** LB ⊗ Civ Wed 120

TENTERDEN *continued*

London Beach Country Hotel, Spa & Golf Club

★★★ 75% HOTEL

☎ 01580 766279 📠 01580 763884
Ashford Rd TN30 6HX
e-mail: enquiries@londonbeach.com
web: www.londonbeach.com
dir: M20 junct 9, A28 follow signs to Tenterden (10m). Hotel on right 1m before Tenterden.

A modern purpose-built hotel situated in mature grounds on the outskirts of Tenterden. The spacious bedrooms are smartly decorated, have co-ordinated soft furnishings and most rooms have balconies with superb views over the golf course. The open-plan public rooms feature a brasserie-style restaurant, where a good choice of dishes is served.

Rooms 26 (2 fmly) (3 smoking) **S** fr £75; **D** fr £115 (incl. bkfst)* **Facilities** Spa ⚲ 🏌 9 Putt green Fishing Driving range Health club Xmas New Year Wi-fi **Conf** Class 75 Board 40 Thtr 100 Del from £135* **Services** Lift **Parking** 100 **Notes** LB ⊗ Civ Wed 100

TONBRIDGE — Map 6 TQ54

Best Western Rose & Crown

★★★ 72% HOTEL

☎ 01732 357966 📠 01732 357194
125 High St TN9 1DD
e-mail: rose.crown@bestwestern.co.uk
dir: M25 junct 5, A21 to Hastings. At 2nd junct take B245 through Hildenborough. Continue to Tonbridge. At 1st lights right, straight on at next set. Hotel on left

A 15th-century coaching inn situated in the heart of this bustling town centre, the hotel still retains much of its original character such as oak beams and Jacobean panelling. Bedrooms are stylishly decorated, spacious and well presented; amenities include Wi-fi access. A

choice of traditional restaurant or comfortable bar is available for dining. The attractive coffee lounge provides a cosy option for impromptu meetings.

Rooms 56 (2 fmly) (10 GF) **Facilities** STV Xmas New Year Wi-fi **Conf** Class 60 Board 60 Thtr 125 **Parking** 47 **Notes** ⊗ Civ Wed 40

The Langley

★★★ 59% HOTEL

☎ 01732 353311 📠 01732 771471
18-20 London Rd TN10 3DA
e-mail: thelangley@btconnect.com
dir: from Tonbridge towards Hildenborough N, hotel on Tonbridge/Hildenborough border

Privately owned hotel located just a short drive from the centre of Tonbridge and ideally situated for business and leisure guests alike. Bedrooms are generally quite spacious; each one is pleasantly decorated and equipped with modern facilities. The restaurant offers a varied menu of carefully prepared fresh produce.

Rooms 39 (3 fmly) (8 GF) **Facilities** Xmas New Year **Conf** Class 50 Board 40 Thtr 150 **Services** Lift **Parking** 60 **Notes** ⊗ Civ Wed 150

TUNBRIDGE WELLS (ROYAL) — Map 6 TQ53

Brew House

★★★★ 77% HOTEL

☎ 01892 520587 & 552591 📠 01892 534979
1 Warwick Park TN2 5TA
e-mail: frontoffice@brewhousehotel.com
web: www.brewhousehotel.com
dir: A267, 1st left onto Warwick Park, hotel immediately on left

Located adjacent to The Pantiles and a short walk from the historic town centre with its interesting boutiques, restaurants & bars. Built in the 18th-century and now renovated in a contemporary style, this hotel offers accommodation of the highest quality including impressive state-of-the-art bathrooms and hi-tech amenities. The popular, modern restaurant, brasserie and bar has mood lighting and chic furnishings creating a relaxed atmosphere.

Rooms 10 **D** £120-£175 (incl. bkfst)* **Facilities** STV 🎵 Xmas New Year Wi-fi **Conf** Thtr 120 **Services** Lift Air con **Parking** 8 **Notes** LB ⊗

See advert on opposite page

The Spa

★★★★ 77% HOTEL

☎ 01892 520331 📠 01892 510575
Mount Ephraim TN4 8XJ
e-mail: reservations@spahotel.co.uk
web: www.spahotel.co.uk
dir: Off A21 to A26, follow signs to A264 East Grinstead, hotel on right

Set in 14 acres of beautifully tended grounds, this imposing 18th-century mansion has undergone an impressive refurbishment programme. Spacious, modern bedrooms are stylishly decorated and thoughtfully equipped. The public rooms include the award-winning Chandelier Restaurant, a champagne bar and the new Orangery which complements the traditional lounge. There are extensive meeting and health club facilities, and The Spa offers treatment rooms and is licensed for civil wedding ceremonies.

Rooms 70 (4 fmly) (1 GF) **S** £105-£115; **D** £150-£190* **Facilities** Spa STV ⚲ 🏊 🦢 Gym 🎵 Xmas New Year Wi-fi **Conf** Class 90 Board 90 Thtr 300 **Services** Lift **Parking** 150 **Notes** LB ⊗ Civ Wed 150

Hotel du Vin Tunbridge Wells

★★★★ 75% TOWN HOUSE HOTEL

☎ 01892 526455 📠 01892 512044
Crescent Rd TN1 2LY
e-mail: reception.tunbridgewells@hotelduvin.com
web: www.hotelduvin.com
dir: Follow town centre to main junct of Mount Pleasant Road & Crescent Road/Church Road. Hotel 150yds on right just past Phillips House

This impressive Grade II listed building dates from 1762, and as a princess, Queen Victoria often stayed here. The spacious bedrooms are available in a range of sizes, beautifully and individually appointed, and equipped with a host of thoughtful extras. Public rooms include a bistro-style restaurant, two elegant lounges and a small bar.

Rooms 34 **D** £125-£230* **Facilities** STV Boules court in garden Wi-fi **Conf** Class 30 Board 25 Thtr 40 Del from £165 to £205* **Services** Lift **Parking** 30 **Notes** LB Civ Wed 84

Ramada Tunbridge Wells

★★★★ 74% HOTEL

☎ 01892 823567 🖷 01892 823931
8 Tonbridge Rd, Pembury TN2 4QL
e-mail: sales.tunwells@ramadajarvis.co.uk
web: www.ramadatunbridgewells.co.uk
dir: From M25 junct 5 follow A21 S. Turn left at 1st rdbt signed Pembury Hospital. Hotel on left, 400yds past hospital

Built in the style of a traditional Kentish oast house, this well presented hotel is conveniently located just off the A21 with easy access to the M25. Bedrooms are comfortably appointed for both business and leisure guests. Public areas include a leisure club and a range of meeting rooms.

Rooms 84 (8 fmly) (40 GF) **Facilities** 🕙 Steam room Sauna Xmas New Year Wi-fi **Conf** Class 150 Board 107 Thtr 390 **Parking** 200 **Notes** LB Civ Wed 70

Russell Hotel

★★ 64% METRO HOTEL

☎ 01892 544833 🖷 01892 515846
80 London Rd TN1 1DZ
e-mail: sales@russell-hotel.com
web: www.russell-hotel.com
dir: At junct A26/A264 uphill onto A26, hotel on right

This detached Victorian property is situated just a short walk from the centre of town. The generously proportioned bedrooms in the main house are pleasantly decorated and well equipped. In addition, there are several smartly appointed self-contained suites in an adjacent building. The public rooms include a lounge and cosy bar.

Rooms 25 (5 annexe) (5 fmly) (1 GF) **Facilities** Wi-fi **Conf** Class 10 Board 10 Thtr 10 **Parking** 15 **Notes** ⊗

Innkeeper's Lodge Tunbridge Wells

BUDGET HOTEL

☎ 0845 112 6109 🖷 0845 112 6194
21 London Rd, Southborough TN4 0QB
web: www.innkeeperslodge.com/tunbridgewells
dir: M25, A21, A26 (Tonbridge/Southborough). Lodge in Southborough on A26, opposite cricket green

Innkeeper's Lodge Select represents an exciting, stylish concept within the hotel market. Contemporary style bedrooms provide excellent facilities that include LCD TVs with satellite channels, and modem points. Options include spacious family rooms; and for the corporate guest there's Wi-fi access. All-day food is served in a modern country pub & eating house. The extensive continental breakfast is complimentary. See also the Hotel Groups pages.

Rooms 14 (3 fmly)

Travelodge Tunbridge Wells

BUDGET HOTEL

☎ 0871 984 6381 🖷 01892 521569
Mount Ephraim TN4 8BU
e-mail: tunbridgewells@travelodge.co.uk
dir: From A26 follow Tunbridge Wells onto A264. At T-junct left, next right, left onto Mount Ephriam

Travelodge offers good quality, good value, budget accommodation. All offer family rooms sleeping up to four (two adults, two children) with en suite bathroom/shower-room, remote-control TV, tea- and coffee-making facilities and comfortable beds. Food options vary. Breakfast is at the on-site Bar Café restaurant (if available) or to take away. See also the Hotel Groups pages.

Rooms 86 **S** fr £29; **D** fr £29 **Conf** Class 100 Board 50 Thtr 100

WESTERHAM   Map 6 TQ45

Kings Arms Hotel

Ⓤ

☎ 01959 562990 🖷 01959 561240
Market Square TN16 1AN
e-mail: kingsarms.westerham@oldenglishinns.co.uk

Currently the rating for this establishment is not confirmed. This may be due to a change of ownership or because it has only recently joined the AA rating scheme. For further details please see the AA website: theAA.com

Rooms 16 **Conf** Class 30 Board 30 Thtr 60

WROTHAM
Map 6 TQ65

Holiday Inn Maidstone Sevenoaks

★★★ 73% HOTEL

☎ 0870 400 9054 & 01732 781510 ☐ 01732 885850
London Rd, Wrotham Heath TN15 7RS
e-mail: reservations-maidstone@ihg.com
web: www.holidayinn.co.uk
dir: M26 junct 2A onto A20. Hotel on left

This purpose-built hotel is located within easy reach of the world famous Brands Hatch racing circuit as well as historic Leeds and Hever castles. Rooms are very spacious, comfortably furnished with many accessories. A fully equipped leisure centre, bar, restaurant and lounges are also available as well as a selection of modern meeting rooms.

Rooms 105 (16 fmly) (6 GF) (10 smoking) **Facilities** STV ⊙ supervised Gym Steam room Sauna New Year Wi-fi **Conf** Class 35 Board 30 Thtr 70 **Services** Air con **Parking** 120 **Notes** Civ Wed 60

LANCASHIRE

ACCRINGTON
Map 18 SD72

Mercure Dunkenhalgh Hotel & Spa

★★★★ 72% ⊛ HOTEL

☎ 01254 398021 ☐ 01254 872230
Blackburn Rd, Clayton-le-Moors BB5 5JP
e-mail: H6617@accor.com
web: www.mercure-uk.com
dir: M65 junct 7, left at rdbt, left at lights, hotel 100yds on left

Set in delightfully tended grounds yet a stones' throw from the M65, this fine mansion has conference and banqueting facilities that attract the wedding and corporate markets. The state-of-the-art thermal suite allows guests to relax and take life easy. Bedrooms come in a variety of styles, sizes and standards; some outside the main hotel building.

Rooms 175 (119 annexe) (36 fmly) (43 GF) (9 smoking) **Facilities** Spa STV ⊙ Gym Thermal suite Aerobics studio Xmas New Year Wi-fi **Conf** Class 200 Board 100 Thtr 400 **Services** Lift **Parking** 400 **Notes** ⊗ Civ Wed 300

Sparth House Hotel

★★★ 77% SMALL HOTEL

☎ 01254 872263 ☐ 01254 872263
Whalley Rd, Clayton Le Moors BB5 5RP
e-mail: mail.sparth@btinternet.com
web: www.sparthhousehotel.co.uk
dir: A6185 to Clitheroe along Dunkenhalgh Way, right at lights onto A678, left at next lights, A680 to Whalley. Hotel on left after 2 sets of lights

This 18th-century listed building sits in three acres of well-tended gardens. Bedrooms offer a choice of styles from the cosy modern rooms ideal for business guests, to the spacious classical rooms - including one with furnishings from one of the great cruise liners. Public rooms feature a panelled restaurant and plush lounge bar.

Rooms 16 (3 fmly) **S** £68-£95; **D** £89-£110 (incl. bkfst)* **Facilities** FTV **Conf** Class 50 Board 40 Thtr 160 **Parking** 50 **Notes** ⊗ Civ Wed

BARTON
Map 18 SD53

Barton Grange

★★★★ 77% HOTEL

☎ 01772 862551 ☐ 01772 861267
Garstang Rd PR3 5AA
e-mail: stay@bartongrangehotel.com
web: www.bartongrangehotel.co.uk
dir: M6 junct 32, follow Garstang (A6) signs for 2.5m. Hotel on right

Situated close to the M6, this modern, stylish hotel benefits from extensive public areas that include leisure facilities with a swimming pool, sauna and gym. Comfortable, well-appointed bedrooms include executive rooms and family rooms, as well as attractive accommodation in an adjacent cottage. The unique Walled Garden Bistro offers all-day eating.

Rooms 51 (8 annexe) (4 fmly) (4 GF) **S** £65-£95; **D** £75-£115 **Facilities** STV ⊙ Gym Xmas New Year Wi-fi **Conf** Class 100 Board 80 Thtr 300 Del from £99 to £150 **Services** Lift **Parking** 250 **Notes** LB ⊗ Civ Wed 300

BLACKBURN
Map 18 SD62

See also **Langho**

Millstone at Mellor

shire
hotels & spas

★★ 85% ⊛⊛ HOTEL

☎ 01254 813333 ☐ 01254 812628
Church Ln, Mellor BB2 7JR
e-mail: info@millstonehotel.co.uk
web: www.millstonehotel.co.uk
dir: 3m NW off A59

Once a coaching inn, the Millstone is situated in a village just outside the town. The hotel provides a very high standard of accommodation, professional and friendly service and good food. Bedrooms, some in an adjacent house, are comfortable and generally spacious, and all are very well equipped. A room for less able guests is also available.

Rooms 23 (6 annexe) (5 fmly) (8 GF) **S** £109-£124; **D** £124-£155 (incl. bkfst)* **Facilities** STV New Year Wi-fi **Parking** 40 **Notes** LB ⊗ Civ Wed 60

BLACKPOOL
Map 18 SD33

De Vere Herons' Reach

DE VERE
collection

★★★★ 75% HOTEL

☎ 01253 838866 ☐ 01253 798800
East Park Dr FY3 8LL
e-mail: reservations.herons@devere-hotels.com
web: www.devere.co.uk
dir: A583. At 4th lights turn right into South Park Dr for 0.25m, right at mini-rdbt onto East Park Dr, hotel 0.25m on right

Set in over 200 acres of grounds, this hotel is popular with both business and leisure guests. The Pleasure Beach is a few minutes' walk from the hotel, and the Lake District and the Trough of Bowland are just an hour away. Extensive indoor and outdoor leisure facilities include an 18-hole championship golf course. Bedrooms include a number of suites and smart, well-appointed clubrooms.

Rooms 172 (51 fmly) (20 GF) **Facilities** Spa STV ⊙ ♨ 18 ⅏ Putt green Gym Squash Aerobic studio Beauty room Spinning studio Xmas New Year Wi-fi **Conf** Class 250 Board 70 Thtr 650 **Services** Lift **Parking** 500 **Notes** ⊗ Civ Wed 650

Barceló Blackpool Imperial Hotel

Barceló

★★★★ 74% HOTEL

☎ 01253 623971 ☐ 01253 751784
North Promenade FY1 2HB
e-mail: imperialblackpool@barcelo-hotels.co.uk
web: www.barcelo-hotels.co.uk
dir: M55 junct 2, take A583 North Shore, follow signs to North Promenade. Hotel on seafront, north of tower

Enjoying a prime seafront location, this grand Victorian hotel offers smartly appointed, well-equipped bedrooms and spacious, elegant public areas. Facilities include a smart leisure club; a comfortable lounge, the No.10 bar and an attractive split-level restaurant that overlooks the seafront. Conferences and functions are extremely well catered for.

Rooms 180 (16 fmly) **Facilities** Spa STV 🐾 supervised supervised Gym Xmas New Year Wi-fi **Conf** Class 280 Board 70 Thtr 600 Del from £100* **Services** Lift **Parking** 150 **Notes** Civ Wed 200

Big Blue Hotel
★★★★ 72% HOTEL

☎ 0845 367 3333 & 01253 400045 📠 01253 400046
Ocean Boulevard FY4 1ND
e-mail: reservations@bigbluehotel.com
dir: M6 junct 32 onto M55. Follow tourist signs for Pleasure Beach. Hotel on Pleasure Beach near south rail station

This stylish hotel is ideally located adjacent to the Pleasure Beach, boasting excellent family facilities. A large proportion of family suites offer separate children's rooms furnished with bunk beds, each with their own individual TV screens. Spacious executive rooms boast seating areas with flat-screen TVs and DVD players. Public areas include a smart bar and brasserie, a range of meeting facilities and a residents' gym.

Rooms 157 (84 fmly) (37 GF) (4 smoking) **Facilities** Gym Xmas New Year Wi-fi **Conf** Class 25 Board 30 Thtr 55 **Services** Lift Air con **Parking** 250 **Notes** ✖ Civ Wed 100

Best Western Carlton
★★★ 76% HOTEL

☎ 01253 628966 📠 01253 752587
282-286 North Promenade FY1 2EZ
e-mail: mail@carltonhotelblackpool.co.uk
web: www.bw-carltonhotel.co.uk
dir: M6 junct 32/M55 follow signs for North Shore. Between Blackpool Tower & Gynn Sq

Enjoying a prime seafront location, this hotel offers bedrooms that are brightly appointed and modern in style. Public areas include an open-plan dining room and lounge bar, and a spacious additional bar where lunches are served. Functions are well catered for and ample parking is available.

Rooms 58 **S** £40-£75; **D** £60-£120 (incl. bkfst) **Facilities** STV Xmas New Year Wi-fi **Conf** Class 40 Board 40 Thtr 90 Del from £85 to £140 **Services** Lift **Parking** 43 **Notes** LB ✖ Civ Wed 80

Carousel
★★★ 75% HOTEL

☎ 01253 402642 📠 01253 341100
663-671 New South Prom FY4 1RN
e-mail: carousel.reservations@sleepwellhotels.com
web: www.sleepwellhotels.com
dir: from M55 follow signs to airport, pass airport to lights. Turn right, hotel 100yds on right

This friendly seafront hotel, close to the Pleasure Beach, offers smart, contemporary accommodation. Bedrooms are comfortably appointed and have a modern, stylish feel to them. An airy restaurant and a spacious bar/lounge both overlook the Promenade. The hotel has good conference/meeting facilities and its own car park.

Rooms 92 (7 fmly) **Facilities** STV 🎵 Xmas New Year Wi-fi **Conf** Class 30 Board 40 Thtr 100 **Services** Lift **Parking** 46 **Notes** LB ✖ Civ Wed 150

Chequers Plaza Hotel
★★★ 🅰 HOTEL

☎ 01253 356431 & 0800 027 3107 📠 01253 500076
24-26 Queens Promenade FY2 9RN
e-mail: enquiries@chequersplaza.com
web: www.chequersplaza.com
dir: Towards Blackpool Promenade, 1m past North Pier, on corner of Empress Drive/Queens promenade

Rooms 48 (7 fmly) **S** £35-£45; **D** £45-£70 (incl. bkfst)* **Facilities** FTV Free use of leisure facilities at Hilton Hotel 🎵 Xmas New Year Wi-fi **Conf** Class 90 Board 60 Thtr 40 Del from £75 to £105* **Services** Lift **Parking** 21 **Notes** ✖

Viking
★★ 75% HOTEL

☎ 0845 458 4222 📠 01253 754222
479 South Promenade FY4 1AY
e-mail: reservations@choice-hotels.co.uk
dir: M55 junct 3, follow Pleasure Beach signs

Located close to the centre of the South Promenade, this establishment offers well equipped accommodation and a warm welcome. Meals are served in the attractive sea view restaurant and entertainment is available in the renowned 'Talk of the Coast' night club. Leisure facilities at sister hotels are also available free of charge.

Rooms 101 (10 GF) (25 smoking) **S** £26-£69; **D** £52-£138 (incl. bkfst & dinner)* **Facilities** Cabaret club 🎵 Xmas New Year **Services** Lift **Parking** 50 **Notes** LB ✖ No children

Claremont
★★ 74% HOTEL

☎ 0845 458 4222 📠 01253 754222
270 North Promenade FY1 1SA
e-mail: reservations@choice-hotels.co.uk
dir: M55 junct 3 follow sign for promenade. Hotel beyond North Pier

Conveniently situated this is a popular family holiday hotel. The bedrooms are bright and attractively decorated. The extensive public areas include a spacious air-conditioned restaurant which offers a good choice of dishes. There is a well equipped, supervised children's play room, and entertainment is provided during the season.

Rooms 143 (50 fmly) **S** £28-£60; **D** £58-£120 (incl. bkfst & dinner)* **Facilities** 🐾 Gym 🎵 Xmas New Year **Conf** Class 300 Board 75 Thtr 530 Del from £74 to £96* **Services** Lift **Parking** 40 **Notes** LB ✖

Cliffs
★★ 74% HOTEL

☎ 0845 458 4222 & 01253 595559 📠 01253 754222
Queens Promenade FY2 9SG
e-mail: reservations@choice-hotels.co.uk
dir: M55 junct 3, follow Promenade signs. Hotel just after rdbt

This large, privately owned and extremely popular hotel is within easy reach of the town centre. The bedrooms, including spacious family rooms, vary in size. Public areas offer an all-day coffee shop, a smart restaurant and a family room where children are entertained.

Rooms 163 (53 fmly) **S** £30-£65; **D** £60-£130 (incl. bkfst & dinner)* **Facilities** 🐾 supervised Gym Beauty treatments 🎵 Xmas New Year **Conf** Class 210 Board 50 Thtr 475 Del from £74 to £96* **Services** Lift **Parking** 30 **Notes** LB ✖

Hotel Sheraton
★★ 71% HOTEL

☎ 01253 352723 📠 01253 595499
54-62 Queens Promenade FY2 9RP
e-mail: email@hotelsheraton.co.uk
web: www.hotelsheraton.co.uk
dir: 1m N from Blackpool Tower towards Fleetwood

This family-owned and run hotel is situated at the quieter, northern end of the promenade. Public areas include a choice of spacious lounges with sea views, a large function suite where popular dancing and cabaret evenings are held, and a heated indoor swimming pool. The smartly appointed bedrooms come in a range of sizes and styles.

Rooms 104 (45 fmly) (15 smoking) **Facilities** 🐾 Table tennis Darts 🎵 Xmas New Year **Conf** Class 100 Board 150 Thtr 200 **Services** Lift **Parking** 20 **Notes** ✖

BLACKPOOL *continued*

Headlands

★★ 68% HOTEL

☎ 01253 341179 📄 01253 342657
611-613 South Promenade FY4 1NJ
e-mail: headlands@blackpool.net
dir: M55 & filter left, right at rdbt to Promenade, turn
right. Hotel 0.5m on right

This friendly, family owned hotel stands on the South
Promenade, close to the Pleasure Beach and many of the
town's major attractions. Bedrooms are traditionally
furnished, many enjoying sea views. There is a choice of
lounges and live entertainment is provided regularly.
Home cooked food is served in the panelled dining room.

Rooms 41 (10 fmly) **S** £39.95-£49.50; **D** £79-£99 (incl.
bkfst)* **Facilities** Darts Games room Pool Snooker ♫
Xmas New Year Child facilities **Services** Lift **Parking** 46
Notes LB Closed 2-15 Jan

Belgrave Madison

★★ 67% HOTEL

☎ 01253 351570 📄 01253 500698
270-274 Queens Promenade FY2 9HD
e-mail: belgravemadison@yahoo.co.uk
dir: From M55 follow signs for Tower/Promenade, turn
right onto Promenade. Hotel 2.5m N of tower

This family-run hotel enjoys a seafront location at the
quieter end of town. Thoughtfully equipped bedrooms vary
in size and include family and four-poster rooms.
Spacious public areas include a choice of lounges with
views over the promenade, a bar lounge where guests can
enjoy live entertainment and a bright restaurant.

Rooms 43 (10 fmly) (2 GF) **S** £26-£36; **D** £52-£74 (incl.
bkfst)* **Facilities** ♫ Xmas New Year Wi-fi **Services** Lift
Parking 28 **Notes** LB ⊗

Lyndene

★★ 🅰 HOTEL

☎ 01253 346779 📄 01253 346466
303/315 Promenade FY1 6AN
e-mail: enquiries@lyndenehotel.com

Rooms 140 (60 fmly) (12 GF) (140 smoking) **S** £24-£120;
D £36-£124 (incl. bkfst & dinner)* **Facilities** FTV ♫
Xmas New Year **Services** Lift **Parking** 70 **Notes** LB ⊗ No
children 5yrs

Travelodge Blackpool Central

BUDGET HOTEL

☎ 0871 984 6425 📄 01253 623944
Talbot Square FY1 1ND
dir: M55 junct 4, follow signs for A583 Blackpool North
Shore, approx 4m to seafront. Lodge on right opposite
North Pier entrance

Travelodge offers good quality, good value, budget
accommodation. All offer family rooms sleeping up to
four (two adults, two children) with en suite bathroom/
shower-room, remote-control TV, tea- and coffee-making
facilities and comfortable beds. Food options vary.
Breakfast is at the on-site Bar Café restaurant (if
available) or to take away. See also the Hotel Groups
pages.

Rooms 90 **S** fr £29; **D** fr £29

Travelodge Blackpool South Promenade

BUDGET HOTEL

☎ 0871 984 6191 📄 01253 405876
Balmoral Rd, South Shore FY4 1HP
dir: M6 junct 32 onto M55, follow signs for Blackpool,
South Shore (via Blackpool Airport). Follow brown tourist
signs to Pleasure Beach. Lodge 100yds from Pleasure
Beach on left

Rooms 79 **S** fr £29; **D** fr £29

Travelodge Blackpool South Shore

BUDGET HOTEL

☎ 0871 984 6351 📄 01253 400785
Seasiders Way FY1 6JJ
dir: At end of M55 follow South Shore/Town Centre signs.
Lodge on right adjacent to Blackpool FC stadium

Rooms 124 **S** fr £29; **D** fr £29

BURNLEY   Map 18 SD83

Oaks

★★★ 80% HOTEL

CLASSIC
BRITISH HOTELS

☎ 01282 414141 📄 01282 433401
Colne Rd, Reedley BB10 2LF
e-mail: oaks@lavenderhotels.co.uk
dir: 2m N, off A682

A wealthy coffee merchant's house back in the Victorian
era, this hotel offers traditional public areas and modern,
well-equipped bedrooms that come in a variety of styles
and sizes. A well-equipped leisure club is available on
site. The delightfully peaceful and attractive location
together with the impressive function facilities make this

a popular wedding venue. The staff throughout provide
excellent levels of hospitality.

Rooms 52 (22 fmly) (14 GF) **S** £65-£106; **D** £74-£113
(incl. bkfst)* **Facilities** STV ⊛ supervised Gym Xmas
New Year Wi-fi **Conf** Class 100 Board 60 Thtr 150
Del from £125 to £145* **Parking** 100 **Notes** Civ Wed 150

Rosehill House

★★★ 78% HOTEL

☎ 01282 453931 📄 01282 455628
Rosehill Av BB11 2PW
e-mail: rhhotel@provider.co.uk
dir: 0.5m S of town centre, off A682

This fine Grade II listed building stands its own leafy
grounds in a quiet area of town. The hotel features
original and beautifully ornate ceilings and mosaic
flooring. The boutique-style bedrooms are tastefully
finished and comfortably equipped; the two loft
conversions and the former coach house offer spacious
yet more traditional-style accommodation.

Rooms 34 (3 fmly) (4 GF) **Facilities** STV Snooker room
Wi-fi **Conf** Class 30 Board 30 Thtr 50 **Parking** 52
Notes ⊗ Civ Wed 90

Travelodge Burnley

BUDGET HOTEL

☎ 08719 846 125 📄 01282 416039
Cavalry Barracks, Barracks Rd BB11 4AS
web: www.travelodge.co.uk
dir: at junct of A671 & A679

Travelodge offers good quality, good value, budget
accommodation. All offer family rooms sleeping up to four
(two adults, two children) with en suite bathroom/
shower-room, remote-control TV, tea- and coffee-making
facilities and comfortable beds. Food options vary.
Breakfast is at the on-site Bar Café restaurant (if
available) or to take away. See also Hotel Groups pages.

Rooms 32 **S** fr £29; **D** fr £29

CHARNOCK RICHARD   Map 15 SD51
MOTORWAY SERVICE AREA (M6)

Welcome Lodge Charnock Richard

BUDGET HOTEL

☎ 01257 791746 📄 01257 793596
Welcome Break Service Area PR7 5LR
e-mail: charnockhotel@welcomebreak.co.uk
web: www.welcomebreak.co.uk
dir: Between junct 27 & 28 of M6 N'bound. 500yds from
Camelot Theme Park via Mill Lane

This modern building offers accommodation in smart,
spacious and well-equipped bedrooms, suitable for

families and business travellers, and all with en suite bathrooms. Continental breakfast is available and other refreshments may be taken at the nearby family restaurant. See also the Hotel Groups pages.

Rooms 100 (68 fmly) (32 GF) **S** £29-£59; **D** £39-£69*
Conf Class 16 Board 24 Thtr 40 Del from £69 to £99*

CHORLEY Map 15 SD51

Best Western Park Hall
★★★ 74% HOTEL

☎ 01257 455000 🖷 01257 451838
Park Hall Rd, Charnock Richard PR7 5LP
e-mail: conference@parkhall-hotel.co.uk
web: www.parkhall-hotel.co.uk
dir: Between Preston & Wigan, signed from M6 junct 27 N'bound & junct 28 S'bound, or from M61 junct 8

The popular Camelot Theme Park is just a short stroll across the grounds from this hotel, which focuses on the leisure and corporate/conference markets. Conveniently located for the motorway network, this idyllic country retreat is shared between the main hotel and The Village, a series of chalet bungalows. The Cadbury and Bassett rooms with special themed furnishings prove a real hit with children.

Rooms 140 (84 annexe) (52 fmly) (84 GF) **Facilities** Spa
🏊 supervised Gym Steam room Sauna Solarium Dance studio Xmas New Year Wi-fi **Conf** Class 240 Board 70 Thtr 700 **Services** Lift **Parking** 2600 **Notes** LB ⊗ Civ Wed 200

Travelodge Preston Chorley
BUDGET HOTEL

☎ 08719 846 172 🖷 01772 311963
Preston Rd, Clayton-le-Woods PR6 7JB
web: www.travelodge.co.uk
dir: M6 junct 28, B5256 for 2m. Through lights, straight on at 2 rdbts. At 3rd rdbt Lodge 200yds on left behind Halfway House Pub. Or from M61 junct 8, A6 N to Preston Rd. Lodge in 3m

Travelodge offers good quality, good value, budget accommodation. All offer family rooms sleeping up to four (two adults, two children) with en suite bathroom/ shower-room, remote-control TV, tea- and coffee-making facilities and comfortable beds. Food options vary. Breakfast is at the on-site Bar Café restaurant (if available) or to take away. See also Hotel Groups pages.

Rooms 40 **S** fr £29; **D** fr £29

CLITHEROE Map 18 SD74

Eaves Hall Country Hotel
★★★ 77% HOTEL

☎ 01200 425271 🖷 01200 425131
Eaves Hall Ln, West Bradford BB7 3JG
e-mail: reservations@eaveshall.co.uk
web: www.eaveshall.co.uk
dir: A59 onto Pimlico link. Take 3rd left towards Waddington. At T-junct turn left, hotel 1st on right

A country-house hotel set in 13 acres of landscaped gardens with its own crown bowling green, tennis courts and pitch & putt among other activities. Eaves Hall offers the perfect place to relax and 'get away from it all'. Bedrooms are spacious and well equipped. Jonathan's Restaurant, with lovely views over the grounds, is the setting for meals, and the hotel is a popular venue for weddings.

Rooms 34 (7 fmly) **S** £40-£70; **D** £65-£180 (incl. bkfst)*
Facilities ♨ 9 🏊 Putt green Fishing ⛳ Snooker table
Pitch & putt Bowling green Xmas New Year Wi-fi
Conf Class 90 Board 50 Thtr 100 Del from £108 to £180
Services Lift **Parking** 70 **Notes** LB Civ Wed 100

Shireburn Arms
★★★ 74% HOTEL

☎ 01254 826518 🖷 01254 826208
Whalley Rd, Hurst Green BB7 9QJ
e-mail: sales@shireburnarmshotel.com
web: www.shireburnarmshotel.com
dir: A59 to Clitheroe, left at lights to Ribchester, follow Hurst Green signs. Hotel on B6243 at entrance to Hurst Green village

This long established, family-owned hotel dates back to the 17th century and enjoys panoramic views over the Ribble Valley. Rooms are individually designed and thoughtfully equipped. The lounge bar offers a selection of real ales, and the spacious restaurant, opening onto an attractive patio and garden, offers home-cooked food.

Rooms 22 (3 fmly) **S** £50-£70; **D** £80-£130 (incl. bkfst)
Facilities STV FTV Xmas Wi-fi Child facilities
Conf Class 50 Board 50 Thtr 100 Del from £110
Parking 71 **Notes** Civ Wed 100

Old Post House
★★ Ⓐ HOTEL

☎ 01200 422025 🖷 01200 423059
44-48 King St BB7 2EU
e-mail: rooms@posthousehotel.co.uk
dir: A59 follow signs to Clitheroe. Through Castle St, left into King St, hotel on right

Rooms 11 (4 fmly) **Facilities** FTV Wi-fi **Conf** Class 14 Board 18 Thtr 30 Del from £75 to £90 **Parking** 10 **Notes** ⊗

DARWEN Map 15 SD62

Travelodge Blackburn M65
BUDGET HOTEL

☎ 08719 846 122 🖷 01254 776058
Darwen Motorway Services BB3 0AT
web: www.travelodge.co.uk
dir: Just off M65 junct 4 towards Blackburn, follow signs for Darwen Service area

Travelodge offers good quality, good value, budget accommodation. All offer family rooms sleeping up to four (two adults, two children) with en suite bathroom/ shower-room, remote-control TV, tea- and coffee-making facilities and comfortable beds. Food options vary. Breakfast is at the on-site Bar Café restaurant (if available) or to take away. See also Hotel Groups pages.

Rooms 48 (45 fmly) **S** fr £29; **D** fr £29

FORTON MOTORWAY SERVICE AREA (M6) Map 18 SD55

Travelodge Lancaster (M6)
BUDGET HOTEL

☎ 08719 846 152 🖷 01524 791703
White Carr Ln, Bay Horse LA2 9DU
web: www.travelodge.co.uk
dir: M6, between juncts 32 & 33

Travelodge offers good quality, good value, budget accommodation. All offer family rooms sleeping up to four (two adults, two children) with en suite bathroom/ shower-room, remote-control TV, tea- and coffee-making facilities and comfortable beds. Food options vary. Breakfast is at the on-site Bar Café restaurant (if available) or to take away. See also Hotel Groups pages.

Rooms 53 **S** fr £29; **D** fr £29

GARSTANG
Map 18 SD44

Best Western Garstang Country Hotel & Golf Centre

★★★ 77% HOTEL

☎ 01995 600100 🖷 01995 600950
Garstang Rd, Bowgreave PR3 1YE
e-mail: reception@ghgc.co.uk
web: www.garstanghotelandgolf.com
dir: M6 junct 32 take 1st right after Rogers Esso garage on A6 onto B6430. 1m, hotel on left

This smart, purpose-built hotel enjoys a peaceful location alongside its own 18-hole golf course. Comfortable and spacious bedrooms are well equipped for both business and leisure guests, whilst inviting public areas include a restaurant and a choice of bars - one serving food.

Rooms 32 (16 GF) **S** £50-£70; **D** £60-£100 (incl. bkfst)*
Facilities STV FTV ♨ 18 Putt green Golf driving range Xmas New Year Wi-fi **Conf** Class 100 Board 80 Thtr 200 **Services** Lift **Parking** 172 **Notes** LB ⊗ Civ Wed 200

Pickerings Country House Hotel

★★★ 75% HOTEL

☎ 01995 600999 🖷 01995 602100
Garstang Rd, Catterall PR3 0HD
e-mail: info@pickerings-hotel.co.uk
dir: On B6430, S of Garstang

An 18th-century country house, in large immaculately kept gardens, that has been sympathetically renovated to provide good standards of comfort and extensive facilities. Some bedrooms are very spacious, and all are equipped with a range of practical and thoughtful extras. Public areas include a choice of lounges, and well-equipped function rooms are also available.

Rooms 12 (1 fmly) **S** £50-£80; **D** £80-£120*
Facilities FTV Childrens' play area Xmas New Year Wi-fi **Conf** Class 90 Board 40 Thtr 150 Del from £100 to £150*
Parking 51 **Notes** LB ⊗ Civ Wed 150

GISBURN
Map 18 SD84

Stirk House

★★★ 71% HOTEL

☎ 01200 445581 🖷 01200 445581
BB7 4LJ
e-mail: reservations@stirkhouse.co.uk
dir: W of village, on A59. Hotel 0.5m on left

This delightful historic hotel enjoys a peaceful location in its own grounds, amid rolling countryside. Extensive public areas include excellent conference and banqueting facilities, a leisure centre and an elegant restaurant. The stylish bedrooms and suites vary in size and style but all are comfortable and well equipped. Hospitality is warm and friendly, and service attentive.

Rooms 30 (10 annexe) (2 fmly) (12 GF) **S** £55-£98; **D** £110-£150 (incl. bkfst)* **Facilities** STV ⊗ supervised ♨ Gym Aromatherapy Personal training Kick boxing Xmas New Year Wi-fi **Conf** Class 150 Board 45 Thtr 200 **Parking** 400 **Notes** LB Civ Wed 200

LANCASTER
Map 18 SD46

Lancaster House

★★★★ 76% ⚜ HOTEL

☎ 01524 844822 🖷 01524 844766
Green Ln, Ellel LA1 4GJ
e-mail: lancaster@elhmail.co.uk
web: www.elh.co.uk/hotels/lancaster
dir: M6 junct 33 N towards Lancaster. Through Galgate, into Green Ln. Hotel before university on right

This modern hotel enjoys a rural setting south of the city and close to the university. The attractive open-plan reception and lounge boast a roaring log fire in colder months. Bedrooms are spacious, and include 19 rooms that are particularly well equipped for business guests. There are leisure facilities with a hot tub and a function suite.

Rooms 99 (29 fmly) (44 GF) **Facilities** Spa STV ⊗ supervised Gym Beauty salon Xmas New Year Wi-fi **Conf** Class 60 Board 48 Thtr 200 **Parking** 120 **Notes** LB Civ Wed 100

Holiday Inn Lancaster

★★★ 78% HOTEL

☎ 01524 541313 & 0870 400 9047 🖷 01524 841265
Waterside Park, Caton Rd LA1 3RA
e-mail: reservations-lancaster@ihg.com
web: www.holidayinn.co.uk
dir: M6 junct 34 towards Lancaster. Hotel 1st on right

Close to the M6 and the historic city of Lancaster, this modern hotel caters well for business and leisure guests, including families. The ground floor is open plan, with an informal atmosphere in the lounge-bar and Traders restaurant. The Spirit Health Club features a 15-metre pool, sauna, steam room, beauty treatment rooms and a well-equipped gym.

Rooms 156 (72 fmly) (25 GF) (8 smoking) **Facilities** STV ⊗ supervised Gym Fitness classes Xmas New Year Wi-fi **Conf** Class 60 Board 60 Thtr 120 **Services** Lift Air con **Parking** 200

Best Western Royal Kings Arms

★★★ 72% HOTEL

☎ 01524 32451 🖷 01524 841698
Market St LA1 1HP
e-mail: reservations.lancaster@ohiml.com
web: www.oxfordhotelsandinns.com
dir: M6 junct 33, follow A6 to city centre, turn 1st left, after Market Hotel. Hotel at lights before Lancaster Castle

A distinctive period building located in the town centre, close to the castle. Bedrooms are comfortable and suitable for both business and leisure guests. Public areas include a small lounge on the ground floor and The Castle Bar and Brasserie Restaurant on the first floor. The hotel also has a private car park.

Rooms 55 (14 fmly) **Facilities** Xmas **Conf** Class 60 Board 40 Thtr 100 **Services** Lift **Parking** 26 **Notes** Civ Wed 100

LANGHO — Map 18 SD73

Northcote
★★★★ 80% ®®® SMALL HOTEL

☎ 01254 240555 📄 01254 246568
Northcote Rd BB6 8BE
e-mail: reservations@northcote.com
web: www.northcote.com
dir: M6 junct 31, 9m to Northcote. Follow Clitheroe (A59) signs, Hotel on left before rdbt

This is a gastronomic haven where guests return to sample the delights of its famous kitchen. Excellent cooking includes Lancashire's finest fare, and fruit and herbs from the hotel's own beautifully laid out organic gardens. Drinks can be enjoyed in the comfortable, elegantly furnished lounges and bar. The stylish bedrooms have been individually furnished and thoughtfully equipped.

Rooms 14 (2 fmly) (4 GF) **S** £170-£210; **D** £200-£250 (incl. bkfst)* **Facilities** STV FTV 🏊 Wi-fi **Conf** Class 10 Board 20 Thtr 36 **Parking** 50 **Notes** LB ⊗ Closed 25 Dec Civ Wed 40

Mytton Fold Hotel and Golf Complex
★★★ 🅰 HOTEL

☎ 01254 240662 & 245392 📄 01254 248119
Whalley Rd BB6 8AB
e-mail: reception@myttonfold.co.uk
web: www.myttonfold.co.uk
dir: At large rdbt on A59, follow signs for Whalley, exit onto Whalley New Road. Hotel on right

Rooms 28 (3 fmly) (3 GF) **S** £55-£73; **D** £89-£106 (incl. bkfst)* **Facilities** STV ⚑ 18 Putt green Wi-fi **Conf** Class 60 Board 40 Thtr 290 Del from £87 to £98* **Parking** 300 **Notes** LB ⊗ RS 24-26 Dec & 1 Jan Civ Wed 150

The Avenue Hotel & Restaurant
★★ 79% HOTEL

☎ 01254 244811 📄 01254 244812
Brockhall Village BB6 8AY
e-mail: info@theavenuehotel.co.uk
dir: Exit A59 by Northcote Manor, follow for 1m. Right then 1st left into Brockhall Village

The Avenue offers a modern and relaxed atmosphere throughout. The bedrooms are especially stylish being very well equipped and delightfully furnished. A wide range of dishes is available in the café bar/restaurant, and good conference facilities are on offer.

Rooms 21 (9 fmly) (11 GF) **Facilities** STV New Year **Conf** Class 30 Board 40 Thtr 50 Del from £80 to £90* **Parking** 30 **Notes** ⊗ Closed 24-25 Dec

LEYLAND — Map 15 SD52

Best Western Premier Leyland
★★★★ 77% HOTEL

☎ 01772 422922 📄 01772 622282
Leyland Way PR25 4JX
e-mail: leylandhotel@feathers.uk.com
web: www.feathers.uk.com
dir: M6 junct 28 turn left at end of slip road, hotel 100mtrs on left

This purpose-built hotel enjoys a convenient location, just off the M6, within easy reach of Preston and Blackpool. Spacious public areas include extensive conference and banqueting facilities as well as a smart leisure club.

Rooms 93 (4 fmly) (31 GF) **S** £60-£150; **D** £70-£160 (incl. bkfst)* **Facilities** STV FTV 🏊 supervised Gym Xmas New Year Wi-fi **Conf** Class 250 Board 250 Thtr 500 Del from £120 to £160* **Parking** 150 **Notes** LB Civ Wed 200

Farington Lodge
🅄

☎ 01772 421321 📄 01772 455388
Stanifield Ln, Farington PR25 4QR
e-mail: info.farington@classiclodges.co.uk
web: www.classiclodges.co.uk
dir: Left at rdbt at end of M6 & left at next rdbt. Entrance 1m on right after lights

Currently the rating for this establishment is not confirmed. This may be due to a change of ownership or because it has only recently joined the AA rating scheme For further details please see the AA website: theAA.com

Rooms 27 (3 fmly) (6 GF) **S** £65-£105; **D** £75-£145* **Facilities** STV Xmas Wi-fi **Conf** Class 80 Board 60 Thtr 180 Del from £135 to £146* **Parking** 90 **Notes** ⊗ Civ Wed 150

LOWER BARTLE — Map 18 SD43

Bartle Hall
★★★ 75% HOTEL

☎ 01772 690506 📄 01772 690841
Lea Ln PR4 0HA
e-mail: recp@bartlehall.co.uk
dir: M6 junct 32 onto Tom Benson Way, follow signs for Woodplumpton

Ideally situated between Preston and Blackpool, Bartle Hall is within easy access of the M6 and the Lake District. Set in its own extensive grounds the hotel offers comfortable, well-equipped and renovated accommodation. The restaurant cuisine uses local produce and there is a large comfortable bar and lounge. There are also extensive conference facilities, and this hotel is a popular wedding venue.

Rooms 14 (1 annexe) (3 fmly) (1 GF) **S** £75-£140; **D** £105-£180 (incl. bkfst) **Facilities** FTV New Year Wi-fi **Conf** Class 50 Board 40 Thtr 200 Del from £105 to £150 **Parking** 150 **Notes** LB ⊗ Closed 25-26 Dec Civ Wed 130

LYTHAM ST ANNES — Map 18 SD32

Clifton Arms Hotel
★★★★ 79% ® HOTEL

☎ 01253 739898 📄 01253 730657
West Beach, Lytham FY8 5QJ
e-mail: welcome@cliftonarms-lytham.com
web: www.cliftonarms-lytham.com
dir: On A584 along seafront

This well established hotel occupies a prime position overlooking Lytham Green and the Ribble estuary beyond. Bedrooms vary in size and are appointed to a high standard; front-facing rooms are particularly spacious and enjoy splendid views. There is an elegant restaurant, a stylish open-plan lounge and cocktail bar as well as function and conference facilities.

Rooms 48 (2 fmly) **S** £70-£130; **D** £125-£185 (incl. bkfst)* **Facilities** STV FTV Xmas New Year Wi-fi **Conf** Class 100 Board 60 Thtr 200 Del from £155* **Services** Lift **Parking** 50 **Notes** LB ⊗ Civ Wed 100

Bedford
★★★ 79% HOTEL

☎ 01253 724636 📄 01253 729244
307-313 Clifton Drive South FY8 1HN
e-mail: reservations@bedford-hotel.com
web: www.bedford-hotel.com
dir: From M55 follow signs for airport to last lights. Left through 2 sets of lights. Hotel 300yds on left

This popular family-run hotel is close to the town centre and the seafront. Bedrooms vary in size and style and include superior and club class rooms. The newer bedrooms are particularly elegant and tastefully appointed. Spacious public areas include a choice of lounges, a coffee shop, fitness facilities and an impressive function suite.

Rooms 45 (6 GF) **Facilities** STV FTV Gym Hydrotherapy spa bath Xmas New Year Wi-fi **Conf** Class 140 Board 60 Thtr 200 **Services** Lift **Parking** 25 **Notes** LB ⊗ Civ Wed 200

LYTHAM ST ANNES *continued*

Best Western Glendower Hotel

★★★ 77% HOTEL

☎ 01253 723241 ▤ 01253 640069
North Promenade FY8 2NQ
e-mail: recp@theglendowerhotel.co.uk
web: www.theglendowerhotel.co.uk
dir: M55 follow airport signs. Left at Promenade to St
Annes. Hotel 500yds from pier

Located on the seafront and with easy access to the town
centre, this popular, friendly hotel offers comfortably
furnished, well-equipped accommodation. Bedrooms vary
in size and style, and include four-poster rooms and very
popular family suites. Public areas feature a choice of
smart, comfortable lounges, a bright, modern leisure club
and function facilities.

Rooms 60 (17 fmly) **Facilities** FTV ☜ supervised Gym
Children's playroom Snooker Xmas New Year Wi-fi
Conf Class 120 Board 50 Thtr 150 Del from £95 to £155
Services Lift **Parking** 45 **Notes** ⊗ Civ Wed 150

Chadwick

THE INDEPENDENTS
HOTEL ASSOCIATION

★★★ 77% HOTEL

☎ 01253 720061 ▤ 01253 714455
South Promenade FY8 1NP
e-mail: info@thechadwickhotel.com
web: www.thechadwickhotel.com
dir: M6 junct 32 take M55 to Blackpool then A5230 to
South Shore. Follow signs for St Annes, hotel on
promenade south end

This popular, comfortable and traditional hotel enjoys a
seafront location. Bedrooms vary in size and style, but all
are very thoughtfully equipped; those at the front boast
panoramic sea views. Public rooms are spacious and
comfortably furnished and the smart bar is stocked with

some 200 malt whiskies. The hotel has a well-equipped,
air-conditioned gym and indoor pool.

Rooms 75 (28 fmly) (13 GF) **S** £55-£65; **D** £85-£107 (incl.
bkfst) **Facilities** FTV ☜ Gym Turkish bath Games room
Soft play adventure area Sauna Solarium ♫ Xmas New
Year Wi-fi Child facilities **Conf** Class 24 Board 28 Thtr 72
Del from £89.50 to £109.50 **Services** Lift **Parking** 40
Notes LB ⊗

See advert on this page

Dalmeny Hotel

★★★ 77% HOTEL

☎ 01253 712236 ▤ 01253 724447
19-33 South Promenade FY8 1LX
e-mail: reservations@dalmenyhotel.co.uk
web: www.dalmenyhotel.co.uk

With a superb seafront location and extensive facilities
including comfortable lounges, leisure centre, beauty and
hair salons centre. There are three
restaurants: the Patio Restaurant, The Carvery and the
contemporary, split level Atrium Restaurant. Children are
well catered for; spacious bedrooms, many with sea
views, include family rooms.

Rooms 125 (68 fmly) (11 GF) **S** £77.50-£115; **D** £98-£184
(incl. bkfst)* **Facilities** Spa FTV ☜ Gym Squash Beauty
salon Aerobics centre ♫ New Year Wi-fi Child facilities
Conf Class 80 Board 50 Thtr 150 **Services** Lift
Parking 120 **Notes** LB ⊗ Closed 24-26 Dec

MORECAMBE Map 18 SD46

Clarendon

★★★ 68% HOTEL

☎ 01524 410180 ▤ 01524 421616
76 Marine Road West, West End Promenade LA4 4EP
e-mail: clarendon@mitchellshotels.co.uk
dir: M6 junct 34 follow Morecambe signs. At rdbt (with
'The Shrimp' on corner) 1st exit to Westgate, follow to
seafront. Right at lights, hotel 3rd block

This traditional seafront hotel offers views over
Morecambe Bay, modern facilities and convenient
parking. An extensive fish and grill menu is offered in the
contemporary Waterfront Restaurant and guests can relax
in the comfortable lounge bar. Davy Jones Locker in the
basement has a more traditional pub atmosphere and
offers cask ales and regular live entertainment.

Rooms 29 (4 fmly) **S** £60; **D** £60-£90 (incl. bkfst)*
Facilities Xmas New Year Wi-fi **Conf** Class 40 Board 40
Thtr 90 **Services** Lift **Parking** 22 **Notes** Civ Wed 60

Hotel Prospect

★ 75% HOTEL

☎ 01524 417819 ▤ 01524 417819
363 Marine Road East LA4 5AQ
e-mail: peter@hotel-prospect.fsnet.co.uk

Situated on the promenade, this friendly, family-run
establishment has panoramic views over the bay to the
Lakeland mountains. Bedrooms are comfortably
proportioned and thoughtfully furnished, and the bright
dining room extends into a small lounge area which has a
well-stocked bar and overlooks the sea.

Rooms 13 (4 fmly) (2 GF) **S** £22-£23; **D** £44-£46 (incl.
bkfst)* **Facilities** Xmas **Parking** 14 **Notes** LB

ORMSKIRK — Map 15 SD40

West Tower Country House

★★★ 82% HOTEL

☎ 01695 423328 📠 01695 420704
Mill Ln, Aughton L39 7HJ
e-mail: info@westtower.com
web: www.westtower.co.uk

An impressive former country residence set in its own attractive grounds with views over the Mersey Estuary. The hotel offers spacious, luxury, contemporary style accommodation in annexes close to the main building. An extensive range of dishes is served in the restaurant that overlooks the grounds or in the attractive cellar style Café West. Also a popular venue for meetings and weddings.

Rooms 12 (12 annexe) (7 GF) **Facilities** FTV Xmas Wi-fi **Conf** Class 100 Board 50 Thtr 150 **Parking** 100 **Notes** ✪ Civ Wed 110

PRESTON — Map 18 SD52

See also **Garstang**

Barton Grange

★★★★ 77% HOTEL

☎ 01772 862551 📠 01772 861267
Garstang Rd PR3 5AA
e-mail: stay@bartongrangehotel.com
web: www.bartongrangehotel.co.uk

(For full entry see Barton)

Preston Marriott Hotel

Marriott HOTELS & RESORTS

★★★★ 76% HOTEL

☎ 01772 864087 📠 01772 861728
Garstang Rd, Broughton PR3 5JB
e-mail: reservations.preston@marriotthotels.co.uk
web: www.prestonmarriott.co.uk
dir: M6 junct 32 onto M55 junct 1, follow A6 towards Garstang. Hotel 0.5m on right

Exuding a country-club atmosphere this stylish hotel enjoys good links to both the city centre and motorway network. There are two dining options and the extensive leisure facilities ensure that there is plenty to do. The bedrooms are smartly decorated and equipped with a comprehensive range of extras.

Rooms 149 (40 fmly) (63 GF) **Facilities** STV 🏊 supervised Gym Steam room Beauty salon Hairdressing New Year Wi-fi **Conf** Class 100 Board 70 Thtr 220 **Services** Lift Air con **Parking** 250 **Notes** ✪ Civ Wed 180

Pines

★★★ 80% ⚜ HOTEL

☎ 01772 338551 📠 01772 629002
570 Preston Rd, Clayton-Le-Woods PR6 7ED
e-mail: mail@thepineshotel.co.uk
dir: From A6 towards Preston/Whittle-le-Woods. Approx 2.5m, hotel on right

This unique and stylish hotel sits in four acres of mature grounds just a short drive from the motorway network. Elegant bedrooms are individually designed and offer high levels of comfort and facilities. Day rooms include a smart bar and Haworth's restaurant, while extensive function rooms make this hotel a popular venue for weddings.

Rooms 35 (2 fmly) (14 GF) **Facilities** STV FTV 🎵 New Year Wi-fi **Conf** Class 250 Board 100 Thtr 400 Del from £96 to £115* **Parking** 120 **Notes** ✪ Civ Wed 250

PRESTON *continued*

Macdonald Tickled Trout

★★★ 75% HOTEL

☎ 0870 1942120 📠 01772 877463
Preston New Rd, Samlesbury PR5 0UJ
e-mail: tickledtrout@macdonald-hotels.co.uk
web: www.macdonald-hotels.co.uk
dir: M6 junct 31. Off A59 towards Preston

On the banks of the River Ribble, this hotel is conveniently located for the motorway, making it a popular venue for both business and leisure guests. Smartly appointed bedrooms are all tastefully decorated and equipped with a thoughtful range of extras. The hotel boasts a stylish wing of meeting rooms.

Rooms 102 (6 fmly) **Facilities** Fishing ♪ Xmas
Conf Class 60 Board 50 Thtr 120 **Services** Lift
Parking 240 **Notes** LB Civ Wed 100

See advert on page 275

Holiday Inn Preston

★★★ 74% HOTEL

☎ 0870 400 9066 & 01772 567000 📠 01772 201923
Ringway PR1 3AU
e-mail: reservations@hipreston.com
web: www.hipreston.com
dir: M6 junct 31, A59 follow signs for town centre. Right at T-junct, hotel on left

This modern hotel enjoys a prime town centre location and is fully air-conditioned. The bedrooms have high speed internet access, and Wi-fi is available in the bar lounge. The stylish public areas include a smart restaurant and adjacent bar, offering an all-day lounge menu. The Meetings & Training Centre provides a good venue for business needs.

Rooms 133 (8 fmly) **S** £60-£110; **D** £60-£110 (incl. bkfst)* **Facilities** STV Gym Wi-fi **Conf** Class 50 Board 30 Thtr 90 Del from £89 to £135* **Services** Lift Air con **Parking** 50 **Notes** LB ⊗

Haighton Manor Country House

★★ 71% HOTEL

☎ 01772 663170 📠 01772 663171
Haighton Green Ln, Haighton PR2 5SQ
e-mail: info@haightonmanor.com
web: www.haightonmanor.com
dir: Off A6 onto Durton Rd, or from M6 junct 32 right at rdbt & right onto Durton Rd. Right at end into Haighton Green Lane. Hotel 2m on left

Located in sleepy, rolling countryside just ten minutes east of the city, this impressive hotel is ideally situated for both the business and leisure guest. External appearances are deceptive, for once inside, this 17th-century manor house has very modern bedrooms and stylishly fashioned day rooms providing a wonderful fusion of traditional and modern. Wide-ranging creative menus can be sampled in the candlelit restaurant. This hotel is a popular wedding venue.

Rooms 8 (2 fmly) **Facilities** STV ♪ Xmas New Year
Conf Class 80 Board 80 Thtr 100 **Parking** 70 **Notes** LB ⊗ Civ Wed 200

Ibis Preston North

BUDGET HOTEL

☎ 01772 861800 📠 01772 861900
Garstang Rd, Broughton PR3 5JE
e-mail: H3162@accor.com
web: www.ibishotel.com
dir: M6 junct 32, then M55 junct 1. Left lane onto A6. Left at slip road, left again at mini-rdbt. 2nd turn, hotel on right past pub

Modern, budget hotel offering comfortable accommodation in bright and practical bedrooms. Breakfast is self-service, food is available all day and a full dinner menu is available in the restaurant. See also the Hotel Groups pages.

Rooms 82 (27 fmly) (16 GF) (12 smoking) **S** £47-£51;
D £47-£51* **Conf** Class 20 Board 20 Thtr 30

Travelodge Preston Central

BUDGET HOTEL

☎ 08719 846 150
Preston Farmers Office, New Hall Ln PR1 5JX
web: www.travelodge.co.uk
dir: M6 junct 31. Follow signs for Preston. Lodge on right

Travelodge offers good quality, good value, budget accommodation. All offer family rooms sleeping up to four (two adults, two children) with en suite bathroom/shower-room, remote-control TV, tea- and coffee-making facilities and comfortable beds. Food options vary. Breakfast is at the on-site Bar Café restaurant (if available) or to take away. See also Hotel Groups pages.

Rooms 72 **S** fr £29; **D** fr £29

ST ANNES

See Lytham St Annes

WREA GREEN Map 18 SD33

Villa Country House

★★★ 75% HOTEL

☎ 01772 684347 📠 01772 687647
Moss Side Ln PR4 2PE
e-mail: info@the-villahotel.co.uk
dir: M55 junct 3 follow signs to Kirkham at Wrea Green follow signs to Lytham

This 19th-century residence stands in a peaceful location close to the village of Wrea Green. There are extensive bars and a good range of quality food is served either in the bar or the many-roomed restaurant. The modern, air-conditioned bedrooms are very well designed. The staff are friendly and helpful.

Rooms 25 (1 fmly) (10 GF) **S** £75-£110; **D** £90-£130 (incl. bkfst) **Facilities** STV New Year Wi-fi **Conf** Class 15 Board 14 Thtr 60 Del from £90 to £140 **Services** Lift **Parking** 75 **Notes** LB Civ Wed 60

LEICESTERSHIRE

ASHBY-DE-LA-ZOUCH Map 11 SK31

Royal

★★★ 68% HOTEL

☎ 01530 412833 📠 01530 564548
Station Rd LE65 2GP
e-mail: theroyalhotel@email.com
web: www.royalhotelashby.co.uk
dir: A42 junct 12, 3m hotel on right

Charming 18th-century property situated in the centre of the historic town centre. The property has a wealth of original features including high ceilings, sweeping staircases and impressive chandeliers. Bedrooms are pleasantly decorated and equipped with modern facilities. Public rooms include the Castle Room Restaurant, a large lounge bar and function rooms.

Rooms 34 (5 fmly) **S** £47.50-£75; **D** £60-£90 (incl. bkfst)* **Facilities** Xmas New Year Wi-fi **Conf** Class 26 Board 26 Thtr 70 Del from £75 to £125* **Parking** 95 **Notes** LB Civ Wed 65

The Queen's Head

◎◎ RESTAURANT WITH ROOMS

☎ 01530 222359 📠 01530 224680
2 Long St LE12 9TP
e-mail: enquiries@thequeenshead.org
web: www.thequeenshead.org
dir: From Loughborough turn left onto B5324, 3m into Belton

This well furnished establishment is found in the village centre and has public rooms with a modern feel. The individually designed bedrooms feature crisp white linen, fluffy duvets and pillows, 19-inch LCD TVs with Freeview and DVD players. The restaurant has earned a well deserved reputation for its award-winning cuisine; the menus are based on the freshest, locally sourced produce quality.

Rooms 6 (2 fmly)

See East Midlands Airport

Hermitage Park

★★★ 73% HOTEL

☎ 01530 814814 📠 01530 814202
Whitwick Rd LE67 3FA
e-mail: hotel@hermitageparkhotel.co.uk
dir: A511 to outskirts of Coalville. Follow brown tourist signs around bypass. Into Coalville at Morrisons supermarket. Hotel on left

Relaxed and friendly environment throughout this modern building which sits within easy access of major road networks. Bedrooms are contemporary and well equipped; a number of ground floor rooms are available. Open plan public areas include a lounge bar and informal dining area.

Rooms 28 (5 fmly) (14 GF) **S** £50-£81.50; **D** £55-£89 (incl. bkfst)* **Facilities** STV ♫ Xmas New Year Wi-fi **Conf** Class 30 Board 30 Thtr 50 Del from £128* **Parking** 40 **Notes** LB ⊗ Civ Wed 100

Best Western Premier Yew Lodge Hotel & Spa

★★★★ 80% ◎ HOTEL

☎ 01509 672518 📠 01509 674730
Packington Hill DE74 2DF
e-mail: info@yewlodgehotel.co.uk
web: www.yewlodgehotel.co.uk
dir: M1 junct 24. Follow signs to Loughborough & Kegworth on A6. On entering village, 1st right, after 400yds hotel on right

This smart, family-owned hotel is close to both the motorway and airport, yet is peacefully located. Modern, stylish bedrooms and public areas are thoughtfully appointed and smartly presented. The restaurant serves interesting dishes, while lounge service and extensive conference facilities are available. A very well equipped spa and leisure centre complete the picture.

Rooms 100 (22 fmly) **Facilities** Spa STV ♨ Gym Beauty therapy suite Foot spas Steam room Sauna Xmas New Year Wi-fi **Conf** Class 150 Board 84 Thtr 330 **Services** Lift **Parking** 180 **Notes** Civ Wed 260

The Priest House

★★★★ 78% ◎◎ HOTEL

☎ 01332 810649 📠 01332 811141
Kings Mills, Castle Donington DE74 2RR
e-mail: enquiries@priesthouse.co.uk
web: www.handpicked.co.uk
dir: M1 junct 24, onto A50, take 1st slip road signed Castle Donington. Right at lights, hotel in 2m

A historic hotel peacefully situated in a picturesque riverside setting. Public areas include a fine dining restaurant, a modern brasserie and conference rooms. Bedrooms are situated in both the main building and converted cottages, and the executive rooms feature state-of-the-art technology.

Rooms 42 (18 annexe) (5 fmly) (16 GF) **S** £65-£105; **D** £85-£135 (incl. bkfst)* **Facilities** STV FTV Fishing Xmas New Year Wi-fi **Conf** Class 40 Board 40 Thtr 120 Del from £135 to £195* **Parking** 200 **Notes** LB ⊗ Civ Wed 100

Thistle East Midlands Airport thistle

★★★★ 75% HOTEL

☎ 0871 376 9015 📠 0871 376 9115
DE74 2SH
e-mail: eastmidlandsairport@thistle.co.uk
web: www.thistle.com/eastmidlandsairport
dir: On A453, at entrance to East Midlands Airport

This large, well-presented hotel is conveniently located next to East Midlands Airport with easy access to the M1. Accommodation is generally spacious. Substantial public areas include the popular Lord Byron bar, a comprehensive range of meeting rooms and an Otium health and leisure club.

Rooms 164 (11 fmly) (82 GF) (6 smoking) **Facilities** STV ♨ supervised Gym Sauna Steam room Spa bath Xmas New Year Wi-fi **Conf** Class 150 Board 54 Thtr 250 Del from £95 to £190* **Services** Air con **Parking** 350 **Notes** Civ Wed 250

Donington Manor

★★★ 78% ◎ HOTEL

☎ 01332 810253 📠 01332 850330
High St DE74 2PP
e-mail: enquiries@doningtonmanorhotel.co.uk
dir: 1m into village on B5430, left at lights

Near the village centre, this refined Georgian building offers high standards of hospitality and a professional service. Many of the original architectural features have been preserved; the elegant dining room is particularly appealing. Bedrooms are individually designed, and the newer suites are especially comfortable and well equipped.

Rooms 33 (6 annexe) (8 fmly) (4 GF) **S** £59-£104; **D** £69-£114 (incl. bkfst)* **Facilities** STV New Year Wi-fi **Conf** Class 60 Board 40 Thtr 120 Del from £120 to £135* **Parking** 40 **Notes** RS 24-30 Dec Civ Wed 100

Express by Holiday Inn East Midlands Airport

BUDGET HOTEL

☎ 01509 678000 📠 01509 670954
Hunter Rd, Pegasus Business Park DE74 2TQ
e-mail: ema@expressholidayinn.co.uk
web: www.hiexpress.com/emidlandsapt
dir: Follow East Midlands Airport signs, right into Pegasus Business Park, hotel on left

A modern hotel ideal for families and business travellers. Fresh and uncomplicated, the spacious rooms include Sky TV, power shower and tea and coffee-making facilities. Continental buffet breakfast is included in the room rate; other meals may be taken at the nearby family pub or restaurant. See also the Hotel Groups pages.

Rooms 90 (55 fmly) **Conf** Class 26 Board 20 Thtr 40

EAST MIDLANDS AIRPORT *continued*

Travelodge East Midlands Airport

BUDGET HOTEL

☎ 0871 984 6073 📄 01509 673494
DE74 2TN
web: www.travelodge.co.uk
dir: M1 junct 23a follow signs for A453

Travelodge offers good quality, good value, budget accommodation. All offer family rooms sleeping up to four (two adults, two children) with en suite bathroom/shower-room, remote-control TV, tea- and coffee-making facilities and comfortable beds. Food options vary. Breakfast is at the on-site Bar Café restaurant (if available) or to take away. See also Hotel Groups pages.

Rooms 80 **S** fr £29; **D** fr £29

GRIMSTON

Best Western Leicester North

★★★ 71% HOTEL

☎ 01664 823212 📄 01664 823371
A46 Fosse Way, Station Rd, Upper Broughton LE14 3BH
e-mail: info@lnhotel.co.uk
dir: A46 towards Grantham. Hotel at junct for Upper Broughton & Willoughby

Very conveniently located right next to the Fosse Way (A46), this hotel offers well equipped and smart bedrooms. There is a small restaurant and bar area as well as very large conferencing facilities. Ample parking is a bonus. This makes an ideal base for visits to Nottingham, Leicester, Loughborough and Belvoir Castle.

Rooms 75 **S** £70-£110; **D** £80-£120* **Facilities** STV FTV Wi-fi **Conf** Class 100 Board 100 Thtr 300 **Parking** 200 **Notes** ⊗

HINCKLEY Map 11 SP49

Sketchley Grange

★★★★ 80% ⊛⊛ HOTEL

☎ 01455 251133 📄 01455 631384
Sketchley Ln, Burbage LE10 3HU
e-mail: info@sketchleygrange.co.uk
web: www.sketchleygrange.co.uk
dir: SE of town, off A5/M69 junct 1, take B4109 to Hinckley. Left at 2nd rdbt. 1st right onto Sketchley Lane

Close to motorway connections, this hotel is peacefully set in its own grounds, and enjoys open country views. Extensive leisure facilities include a stylish health and leisure spa with a crèche. Modern meeting facilities, a choice of bars, and two dining options, together with comfortable bedrooms furnished with many extras, make this a special hotel.

Rooms 52 (9 fmly) (1 GF) **Facilities** Spa ③ supervised Gym Steam room Hairdressing Crèche ♫ Wi-fi **Conf** Class 150 Thtr 300 **Services** Lift **Parking** 200 **Notes** Civ Wed 300

See advert on this page

Barceló Hinckley Island Hotel

★★★★ 76% HOTEL

☎ 01455 631122 📄 01455 634536
Watling Street (A5) LE10 3JA
e-mail: hinckleyisland@barcelo-hotels.co.uk
web: www.barcelo-hotels.co.uk
dir: On A5, S of junct 1 on M69

A large, constantly improving hotel offering good facilities for both leisure and business guests. Bedrooms are well equipped, with the Club Floors providing high levels of comfort and workspace. A choice of dining styles is available in the Brasserie or Conservatory restaurants and the Triumph Bar is a must for motor cycle enthusiasts. The modern leisure club also offers a range of spa treatments.

Rooms 362 (14 GF) **Facilities** STV ③ supervised Gym Steam room Wi-fi **Conf** Class 240 Board 40 Thtr 400 Del from £99* **Services** Lift Air con **Parking** 600 **Notes** ⊗ Civ Wed 350

KEGWORTH

See East Midlands Airport

The Ideal Venue for Business or Pleasure

Sketchley Grange Hotel
Sketchley Lane • Burbage • Hinckley • Leics LE10 3HU
Telephone 01455 251133 • Fax 01455 631384
email: reservations@sketchleygrange.co.uk
www.sketchleygrange.co.uk

Sketchley Grange is a privately owned Country House Hotel, ideally located in a rural setting just minutes from the Midlands motorway network. The Hotel boasts elegantly furnished bedrooms including four poster rooms and luxurious suites. The award winning Willow Restaurant creates the perfect setting for the appreciation of fine cuisine. For something a little different the Terrace Bistro & Bar provides the perfect environment for you to relax and unwind whilst enjoying a mouth watering menu in a contemporary style bar. An array of conference suites and function rooms cater for weddings, banquets, conferences and private parties, with Romans Health and Leisure Club with its award winning swimming pool is the ideal sanctuary to workout relax and unwind.

See also **Rothley**

LEICESTER Map 11 SK50

Leicester Marriott

★★★★ 79% HOTEL

☎ 0116 282 0100 📄 0116 282 0101
Smith Way, Grove Park, Enderby LE19 1SW
web: www.leicestermarriott.co.uk
dir: M1 junct 21/A563 signed Leicester. At rdbt take 1st left onto A563. Into right lane, at 2nd slip road turn right. At rdbt take last exit, hotel straight ahead

This purpose-built hotel offers stylish bedrooms, some of which are executive rooms with access to the executive lounge. There is a popular brasserie, cocktail bar, atrium lounge, indoor heated pool, gym, sauna and steam room. 18 meeting rooms provide conference facilities for up to 500 delegates and parking is extensive.

Rooms 227 (91 fmly) **Facilities** STV 🐾 supervised Gym Wi-fi **Conf** Class 180 Board 52 Thtr 500 **Services** Lift Air con **Parking** 280 **Notes** LB ⊗ Civ Wed 300

Hotel Maiyango

★★★★ 78% ◉ SMALL HOTEL

☎ 0116 251 8898 📄 0116 242 1339
13-21 St Nicholas Place LE1 4LD
e-mail: reservations@maiyango.com
dir: B4114 (Narborough Rd) to city centre, right onto A47 (Hinkley Rd), keep right into St Nicholas Place

A boutique hotel offering a warm welcome and professional service. Access to the public areas is via a discreet foyer adjacent to an Eastern themed restaurant under same ownership, where imaginative food is sure to be a memorable experience. Spacious bedrooms, decorated in minimalist style are enhanced by quality modern art, fine furnishings and superb bathrooms.

Rooms 14 **S** £145-£185; **D** £145-£185 (incl. bkfst) **Facilities** FTV ♫ Xmas New Year Wi-fi **Conf** Class 50 Board 30 Thtr 70 Del from £185 to £225 **Services** Lift Air con **Notes** LB ⊗

Belmont Hotel

★★★ 80% HOTEL

☎ 0116 254 4773 📄 0116 247 0804
De Montfort St LE1 7GR
e-mail: info@belmonthotel.co.uk
web: www.belmonthotel.co.uk
dir: from A6 take 1st right after rail station. Hotel 200yds on left

This well established hotel, under the same family ownership, has been welcoming guests for over 70 years. It is conveniently situated within easy walking distance of the railway station and city centre though it sits in a quiet leafy residential area. Extensive public rooms are smartly appointed and include the informal Bowie's Bistro, Jamie's Bar with its relaxed atmosphere, and the more formal Cherry Restaurant.

Rooms 77 (7 fmly) (9 GF) (10 smoking) **Facilities** FTV Gym Wi-fi **Conf** Class 75 Board 65 Thtr 175 **Services** Lift **Parking** 75 **Notes** LB Closed 25-26 Dec Civ Wed 150

Ramada Leicester

® RAMADA.

★★★ 80% HOTEL

☎ 0116 255 5599 📄 0116 254 4736
Granby St LE1 6ES
e-mail: sales.leicester@ramadajarvis.co.uk
web: www.ramadajarvis.co.uk
dir: A5460 into city. Follow Leicester Central Station signs. Granby Street is left off St. Georges Way, A594

This Grade II listed Victorian hotel is set in the heart of the commercial and shopping centre. Although bedrooms vary in size, all offer modern amenities and comfort; there is a popular restaurant and ample private parking.

Rooms 104 (1 fmly) (8 smoking) **Facilities** Xmas New Year **Conf** Class 200 Board 35 Thtr 450 Del from £120 to £150* **Services** Lift **Parking** 120 **Notes** Civ Wed 120

Holiday Inn Leicester

★★★ 77% HOTEL

☎ 0871 942 9048 📄 0116 251 3169
St Nicholas Circle LE1 5LX
web: www.holidayinn.co.uk
dir: From S: M1 junct 21 follow A5460 towards city centre. In approx 3m follow Castle Gardens signs. Hotel at next rdbt. From N: M1 junct 22, A50 to city centre. Onto Vaughan Way then follow signs for A47(avoid underpass). Hotel at rdbt

This purpose-built city centre hotel offers impressive accommodation suitable for both business and leisure guests. The smartly appointed bar and restaurant are open throughout the day and there is a well-equipped leisure club. Overnight guests are offered free parking at the adjacent multi-storey car park.

Rooms 188 (12 smoking) **S** £59-£250; **D** £59-£250* **Facilities** 🐾 supervised Gym Wi-fi **Conf** Class 100 Thtr 250 Del from £110 to £175* **Services** Lift Air con **Notes** LB Civ Wed 200

Regency

★★★ 71% HOTEL

☎ 0116 270 9634 📄 0116 270 1375
360 London Rd LE2 2PL
e-mail: info@the-regency-hotel.com
dir: On A6, 1.5m from city centre

This friendly hotel is located on the edge of town and provides smart accommodation, suitable for both business and leisure guests. Dining options include a cosy conservatory brasserie and a formal restaurant. A relaxing lounge bar is also available, along with good banqueting and conference facilities. Bedrooms come in a variety of styles and sizes and include some spacious and stylish rooms.

Rooms 32 (2 fmly) (5 smoking) **S** fr £49; **D** fr £67 (incl. bkfst)* **Facilities** STV ♫ Xmas New Year Wi-fi **Conf** Class 40 Board 30 Thtr 50 Del from £92* **Parking** 32 **Notes** ⊗ Civ Wed 140

LEICESTER *continued*

Campanile Leicester

BUDGET HOTEL

☎ 0116 261 6600 ▤ 0116 261 6601
St Matthew's Way, 1 Bedford Street North LE1 3JE
e-mail: leicester@campanile.com
dir: A5460. Right at end of road, left at rdbt on A594.
Follow Vaughan Way, Burleys Way then St. Matthews Way.
Hotel on left

This modern building offers accommodation in smart,
well-equipped bedrooms, all with en suite bathrooms.
Refreshments may be taken at the informal bistro. See
also the Hotel Groups pages.

Rooms 93 **S** £49.95-£56.95; **D** £49.95-£56.95*
Conf Class 30 Board 30 Thtr 40

Days Inn Leicester Central

BUDGET HOTEL

☎ 0116 251 0666 & 0870 033 9633 ▤ 0870 033 9634
14-17 Abbey St LE1 3TE
e-mail: reception.leicester.central@daysinn.co.uk
web: www.daysinn.com

This modern building offers accommodation in smart,
spacious and well-equipped bedrooms, suitable for
families and business travellers, and all with en suite
bathrooms. Continental breakfast is available and other
refreshments may be taken at the nearby family
restaurant. See also the Hotel Groups pages.

Rooms 73 **Conf** Class 100 Board 40 Thtr 150

Express by Holiday Inn Leicester - Walkers

BUDGET HOTEL

☎ 0116 249 4590 ▤ 0116 249 4591
Filbert Way, Raw Dykes Rd LE2 7FQ
e-mail: info@exhileicester.co.uk
web: www.hiexpress.com/leicesterwalke

A modern hotel ideal for families and business travellers.
Fresh and uncomplicated, the spacious rooms include Sky
TV, power shower and tea and coffee-making facilities.
Continental buffet breakfast is included in the room rate;
other meals may be taken at the nearby family pub or
restaurant. See also the Hotel Groups pages.

Rooms 110 **Conf** Class 40 Board 35 Thtr 70

Ibis Leicester

BUDGET HOTEL

☎ 0116 248 7200 ▤ 0116 262 0880
St Georges Way, Constitution Hill LE1 1PL
e-mail: H3061@accor.com
web: www.ibishotel.com
dir: From M1/M69 junct 21, follow town centre signs,
central ring road (A594)/railway station, hotel opposite
Leicester Mercury

Modern, budget hotel offering comfortable
accommodation in bright and practical bedrooms.
Breakfast is self-service and dinner is available in the
restaurant. See also the Hotel Groups pages.

Rooms 94 (15 fmly) **S** £52-£57; **D** £52-£57*

Innkeeper's Lodge Leicester

BUDGET HOTEL

☎ 0845 112 6048 ▤ 0845 112 6254
Hinckley Rd LE3 3PG
web: www.innkeeperslodge.com/leicester
dir: M1(M69) junct 21, A5460 towards Leicester. Left
towards ring road, right at rdbt onto A563. Left at A47
rdbt towards Hinckley. Through lights (B5380 junct).
Lodge on right

Innkeeper's Lodge represents an exciting, high value
concept within the budget hotel market. Comfortable
bedrooms provide excellent facilities that include satellite
TV and modem points. Options include family rooms; and
for the corporate guest, cutting edge IT includes Wi-fi
access. Food is served all day in the adjacent Country
Pub. The extensive continental breakfast is
complimentary. See also the Hotel Groups pages.

Rooms 31

Travelodge Leicester Central

BUDGET HOTEL

☎ 0871 984 6235 ▤ 0116 251 0560
Vaughan Way LE1 4NN
web: www.travelodge.co.uk
dir: M1/M69 interchange (junct 21), follow signs for city
centre (A5460) signs, approx 4m at main lights right
(A47) onto St Agustine Rd. Then St Nicholas Circle (follow
signs for Shires Shopping Centre). Then High St. 1st exit
into Highcross St. Lodge 0.2m on left

Travelodge offers good quality, good value, budget
accommodation. All offer family rooms sleeping up to four
(two adults, two children) with en suite bathroom/
shower-room, remote-control TV, tea- and coffee-making
facilities and comfortable beds. Food options vary.
Breakfast is at the on-site Bar Café restaurant (if
available) or to take away. See also Hotel Groups pages.

Rooms 95 **S** fr £29; **D** fr £29

LEICESTER FOREST MOTORWAY SERVICE AREA (M1)   **Map 11 SK5**

Days Inn Leicester Forest East

BUDGET HOTEL

☎ 0116 239 0534 ▤ 0116 239 0546
Leicester Forest East, Junction 21 M1 LE3 3GB
e-mail: leicester.hotel@welcomebreak.co.uk
web: www.welcomebreak.co.uk
dir: On M1 northbound between junct 21 & 21A

This modern building offers accommodation in smart,
spacious and well-equipped bedrooms, suitable for
families and business travellers, and all with en suite
bathrooms. Continental breakfast is available, and other
refreshments may be taken at the nearby family
restaurant. See also the Hotel Groups pages.

Rooms 92 (71 fmly) **S** £29-£59; **D** £39-£79*
Conf Board 10 Del from £69 to £99*

LOUGHBOROUGH   **Map 11 SK51**

Quorn Country Hotel

★★★★ 76% HOTEL

☎ 01509 415050 & 415061 ▤ 01509 415557
Charnwood House, 66 Leicester Rd LE12 8BB
e-mail: reservations@quorncountryhotel.co.uk
web: www.quorncountryhotel.co.uk

(For full entry see Quorn)

LUTTERWORTH   **Map 11 SP58**

Travelodge Lutterworth

BUDGET HOTEL

☎ 0871 984 6182
Mill Farm LE17 4BP
web: www.travelodge.co.uk

Travelodge offers good quality, good value, budget
accommodation. All offer family rooms sleeping up to four
(two adults, two children) with en suite bathroom/
shower-room, remote-control TV, tea- and coffee-making
facilities and comfortable beds. Food options vary.
Breakfast is at the on-site Bar Café restaurant (if
available) or to take away. See also Hotel Groups pages.

Rooms 40 **S** fr £29; **D** fr £29

MARKET HARBOROUGH Map 11 SP78

Best Western Three Swans

★★★ 78% HOTEL

☎ 01858 466644 📠 01858 433101
21 High St LE16 7NJ
e-mail: sales@threeswans.co.uk
web: www.bw-threeswanshotel.co.uk
dir: M1 junct 20 take A304 to Market Harborough.
Through town centre on A6 from Leicester, hotel on right

Public areas in this former coaching inn include an
elegant fine dining restaurant and cocktail bar, a smart
foyer lounge and popular public bar areas. Bedroom
styles and sizes vary, but are very well appointed and
equipped. Those in the wing are particularly impressive,
offering high quality and spacious accommodation.

Rooms 61 (48 annexe) (8 fmly) (20 GF) **S** £71.50-£88.50;
D £88-£110 (incl. bkfst) **Facilities** STV Xmas New Year
Wi-fi **Conf** Class 90 Board 50 Thtr 250 Del from £135 to
£150 **Services** Lift **Parking** 100 **Notes** LB Civ Wed 140

MARKFIELD Map 11 SK40

Field Head

★★★ 🅰 HOTEL

☎ 01530 245454 📠 01530 243740
Markfield Ln LE6 9PS
e-mail: 9160@greeneking.co.uk
web: www.oldenglish.co.uk
dir: M1 junct 22, towards Leicester. At rdbt turn left, then
right

Rooms 28 (1 fmly) (13 GF) **S** £40-£80; **D** £50-£120 (incl.
bkfst) **Facilities** FTV 🎵 Xmas New Year Wi-fi
Conf Class 30 Board 36 Thtr 60 Del from £100 to £150
Parking 65 **Notes** LB Civ Wed 50

Travelodge Leicester Markfield

BUDGET HOTEL

☎ 0871 984 6254 📠 01530 244580
**Moto Service Area, A50/ M1 Interchange, Littleshaw Ln
LE67 9PP**
web: www.travelodge.co.uk
dir: M1 junct 22, at rdbt junct of A50 & A511

Travelodge offers good quality, good value, budget
accommodation. All offer family rooms sleeping up to four
(two adults, two children) with en suite bathroom/
shower-room, remote-control TV, tea- and coffee-making
facilities and comfortable beds. Food options vary.
Breakfast is at the on-site Bar Café restaurant (if
available) or to take away. See also Hotel Groups pages.

Rooms 60 **S** fr £29; **D** fr £29

MEDBOURNE Map 11 SP89

The Horse & Trumpet

◉◉ RESTAURANT WITH ROOMS

☎ 01858 565000 📠 01858 565551
Old Green LE16 8DX
e-mail: info@horseandtrumpet.com
dir: In village centre, opposite church

Tucked away behind the village bowling green, this
carefully restored and re-thatched former farmhouse and
pub now offers fine dining and quality accommodation.
The golden stone three-storey building hosts three dining
rooms, in which chef Gary Maganani and his team
provides imaginative food from high quality produce;
service is both professional and friendly. The smartly
appointed bedrooms are located to the rear of the
building in a barn conversion; attractively furnished and
thoughtfully equipped for modern travellers.

Rooms 4 (4 annexe)

MELTON MOWBRAY Map 11 SK71

INSPECTORS' CHOICE

Stapleford Park

★★★★ ◉◉ COUNTRY HOUSE HOTEL

☎ 01572 787000 📠 01572 787651
Stapleford LE14 2EF
e-mail: reservations@stapleford.co.uk
web: www.staplefordpark.com
dir: 1m SW of B676, 4m E of Melton Mowbray & 9m W
of Colsterworth

This stunning mansion, dating back to the 14th century,
sits in over 500 acres of beautiful grounds. Spacious,
sumptuous public rooms include a choice of lounges
and an elegant restaurant; an additional brasserie-style
restaurant is located in the golf complex. The hotel also
boasts a spa with health and beauty treatments and
gym, plus horse-riding and many other country pursuits.
Bedrooms are individually styled and furnished to a
high standard. Attentive service is delivered with a
relaxed yet professional style. Dinner, in the impressive
dining room, is a highlight of any stay.

Rooms 55 (7 annexe) (10 fmly) **Facilities** Spa STV FTV
🅎 🎣 Putt green Fishing 🔧 Gym Archery Croquet
Falconry Horse riding Petanque Shooting Billiards Xmas
New Year Wi-fi **Conf** Class 140 Board 80 Thtr 200
Services Lift **Parking** 120 **Notes** LB Civ Wed 150

Sysonby Knoll

★★★ 77% HOTEL

☎ 01664 563563 📠 01664 410364
Asfordby Rd LE13 0HP
e-mail: reception@sysonby.com
web: www.sysonby.com
dir: 0.5m from town centre beside A6006

This well-established hotel is on the edge of town and set
in attractive gardens. A friendly and relaxed atmosphere
prevails and the many returning guests have become
friends. Bedrooms, including superior rooms in the
annexe, are generally spacious and thoughtfully
equipped. There is a choice of lounges, a cosy bar, and a
smart a restaurant that offers carefully prepared meals.

Rooms 30 (7 annexe) (1 fmly) (7 GF) **S** £69-£93;
D £85-£115 (incl. bkfst)* **Facilities** FTV Fishing 🔧 Wi-fi
Conf Class 25 Board 34 Thtr 50 Del from £110*
Parking 48 **Notes** LB Closed 25 Dec-1 Jan

See advert on page 282

MELTON MOWBRAY *continued*

Quorn Lodge

★★★ 71% HOTEL

☎ 01664 566660 📠 01664 480660
46 Asfordby Rd LE13 0HR
e-mail: quornlodge@aol.com
dir: From town centre take A6006. Hotel 300yds from
junct of A606/A607 on right

Centrally located, this smart privately owned and
managed hotel offers a comfortable and welcoming
atmosphere. Bedrooms are individually decorated and
thoughtfully designed. The public rooms consist of a
bright restaurant overlooking the garden, a cosy lounge
bar and a modern function suite. High standards are
maintained throughout and parking is a bonus.

Rooms 19 (2 fmly) (3 GF) **S** £66-£69; **D** £70-£85 (incl.
bkfst)* **Facilities** STV Wi-fi **Conf** Class 70 Board 80
Thtr 100 **Parking** 38 **Notes** LB ⊗ Civ Wed 80

Scalford Hall

★★★ 🅰 HOTEL

☎ 0845 400 1403 📠 01664 444487
Scalford Rd LE14 4UB
e-mail: sales@scalfordhall.co.uk
dir: A6006 towards Melton Mowbray. Left at 2nd lights
into Scalford Rd, hotel 3m on left

Rooms 88 (21 annexe) (6 fmly) (19 GF) **S** £65-£100;
D £75-£125 (incl. bkfst)* **Facilities** FTV Putt green ♨
Gym New Year Wi-fi **Conf** Class 36 Board 40 Thtr 150
Del from £125 to £165* **Parking** 120 **Notes** LB
Civ Wed 100

Kilworth House

★★★★ 84% ⑳⑳ HOTEL

☎ 01858 880058 📠 01858 880349
Lutterworth Rd LE17 6JE
e-mail: info@kilworthhouse.co.uk
web: www.kilworthhouse.co.uk
dir: A4304 towards Market Harborough, after Walcote,
hotel 1.5m on right

A restored Victorian country house located in 38 acres of
private grounds offering state-of-the-art conference
rooms. The gracious public areas feature many period
pieces and original art works. The bedrooms are very
comfortable and well equipped, and the large Orangery is
now used for informal dining, while the opulent
Wordsworth Restaurant has a more formal air.

Rooms 44 (2 fmly) (13 GF) **S** £140-£215; **D** £140-£215*
Facilities FTV Fishing ♨ Gym Beauty therapy rooms
Xmas Wi-fi **Conf** Class 30 Board 30 Thtr 80 **Services** Lift
Parking 140 **Notes** ⊗ Civ Wed 130

QUORN — Map 11 SK51

Quorn Country Hotel

★★★★ 76% HOTEL

☎ 01509 415050 & 415061 📄 01509 415557
Charnwood House, 66 Leicester Rd LE12 8BB
e-mail: reservations@quorncountryhotel.co.uk
web: www.quorncountryhotel.co.uk
dir: M1 junct 23 onto A512 into Loughborough. Follow A6 signs. At 1st rdbt towards Quorn, through lights, hotel 500yds from 2nd rdbt

Professional service is one of the key strengths of this pleasing hotel, which sits beside the river in four acres of landscaped gardens and grounds. The smart modern conference centre and function suites are popular for both corporate functions and weddings. Public rooms include a smart comfortable lounge and bar, whilst guests have the choice of two dining options: the formal Shires restaurant and the informal conservatory-style Orangery.

Rooms 36 (2 fmly) (9 GF) **Facilities** STV Fishing New Year Wi-fi **Conf** Class 162 Board 40 Thtr 300 Del from £140 to £175* **Services** Lift **Parking** 100 **Notes** ⊗ Civ Wed 200

ROTHLEY — Map 11 SK51

Rothley Court
★★★ Ⓐ HOTEL

☎ 0116 237 4141 📄 0116 237 4483
Westfield Ln LE7 7LG
e-mail: 6501@greeneking.co.uk
web: www.oldenglish.co.uk
dir: On B5328

Rooms 30 (18 annexe) (3 fmly) (6 GF) **Facilities** Xmas **Conf** Class 35 Board 35 Thtr 100 Del from £140 to £175* **Parking** 100 **Notes** ⊗ Civ Wed 85

SIBSON — Map 11 SK30

Millers
★★ Ⓐ HOTEL

☎ 01827 880223 📄 01827 880990
Twycross Rd CV13 6LB
e-mail: 6483@greeneking.co.uk
web: www.oldenglish.co.uk
dir: A5 onto A444 towards Burton. Hotel 3m on right.

Rooms 35 (3 fmly) (15 GF) **Facilities** ♫ **Conf** Class 24 Board 35 Thtr 50 **Parking** 90 **Notes** ⊗ Civ Wed 80

SUTTON IN THE ELMS — Map 11 SP59

Mill on the Soar

BUDGET HOTEL

☎ 01455 282419 📄 01455 285937
Coventry Rd LE9 6QA
e-mail: 1968@greeneking.co.uk
web: www.oldenglish.co.uk
dir: M1 junct 21, follow signs for Narborough. After 3m hotel on left.

This is a popular inn, set in grounds with two rivers and a lake, that caters especially well for family dining. The open-plan bar offers meals and snacks throughout the day, and is divided into family and adults-only areas; for the summer months, there is also an attractive patio. Practical bedrooms are housed in a lodge-style annexe in the grounds.

Rooms 25 (5 annexe) (19 fmly) (13 GF) **Conf** Class 25 Board 25 Thtr 50

THRUSSINGTON — Map 11 SK61

Travelodge Leicester Thrussington

BUDGET HOTEL

☎ 0871 984 6083 📄 0870 1911584
LE7 4TF
web: www.travelodge.co.uk
dir: On A46, southbound

Travelodge offers good quality, good value, budget accommodation. All offer family rooms sleeping up to four (two adults, two children) with en suite bathroom/shower-room, remote-control TV, tea- and coffee-making facilities and comfortable beds. Food options vary. Breakfast is at the on-site Bar Café restaurant (if available) or to take away. See also Hotel Groups pages.

Rooms 32 **S** fr £29; **D** fr £29

ULLESTHORPE — Map 11 SP58

Best Western Ullesthorpe Court Hotel & Golf Club

★★★★ 76% HOTEL

☎ 01455 209023 📄 01455 202537
Frolesworth Rd LE17 5BZ
e-mail: bookings@ullesthorpecourt.co.uk
web: www.bw-ullesthorpecourt.co.uk
dir: M1 junct 20 towards Lutterworth. Follow brown tourist signs

Complete with its own golf club, this impressively equipped hotel is within easy reach of the motorway network, NEC and Birmingham airport. Public areas include both formal and informal eating options and extensive conference and leisure facilities. Spacious bedrooms are thoughtfully equipped for both the business and leisure guests, and a four-poster room is available.

Rooms 72 (3 fmly) (16 GF) **S** £60-£133; **D** £60-£133* **Facilities** Spa STV ⌖ supervised ⚓ 18 ⛳ Putt green Gym Beauty room Steam room Sauna Snooker room New Year Wi-fi **Conf** Class 48 Board 30 Thtr 80 Del from £120 to £145* **Services** Lift **Parking** 280 **Notes** LB ⊗ RS 25 & 26 Dec Civ Wed 120

LINCOLNSHIRE

ALFORD — Map 17 TF47

Half Moon Hotel & Restaurant
★★★ Ⓐ

☎ 01507 463477 📄 01507 462916
25-28 West St LN13 9DG
e-mail: halfmoonalford25@aol.com
dir: Exit A16 at Ulceby, at rdbt take A1104 into Alford, 3m. Hotel opposite The Manor House

Rooms 16 (2 annexe) (2 fmly) (4 GF) **S** £50-£60; **D** £80 (incl. bkfst)* **Facilities** Wi-fi **Conf** Class 50 Board 50 Thtr 60 Del from £85 to £115* **Parking** 16 **Notes** LB ⊗ Civ Wed 60

BELTON · Map 11 SK93

De Vere Belton Woods

DE VERE collection

★★★★ 75% HOTEL

☎ 01476 593200 ▤ 01476 574547
NG32 2LN
e-mail: belton.woods@devere-hotels.com
web: www.devere.co.uk
dir: A1 to Gonerby Moor Services. B1174 towards Great Gonerby. At top of hill turn left towards Manthorpe/Belton. At T-junct turn left onto A607. Hotel 0.25m on left

Beautifully located amidst 475 acres of picturesque countryside, this is a destination venue for lovers of sport, especially golf, as well as a relaxing executive retreat for seminars. Comfortable and well-equipped accommodation complements the elegant and spacious public areas, which provide a good choice of drinking and dining options.

Rooms 136 (136 fmly) (68 GF) **Facilities** Spa ⟐
supervised ☇ 45 ⟐ Putt green Fishing ⟐ Gym Squash Outdoor activity centre (quad biking, laser shooting etc) Xmas New Year Wi-fi **Conf** Class 180 Board 80 Thtr 245 **Services** Lift **Parking** 350 **Notes** ⊗ Civ Wed 80

BOSTON · Map 12 TF34

Boston West

★★★ 71% HOTEL

☎ 01205 292969 & 290670 ▤ 01205 290725
Hubberts Bridge PE20 3QX
e-mail: info@bostonwesthotel.co.uk
dir: A1121 signed Boston, hotel on left after speed camera

A modern, purpose-built hotel situated in a rural location on the outskirts of town. The smartly appointed bedrooms are spacious and thoughtfully equipped; some rooms have balconies with stunning countryside views. Public rooms include a restaurant and a large open-plan lounge bar which overlooks the golf course.

Rooms 24 (5 fmly) (12 GF) **S** £54.50-£70; **D** £54.50-£70 **Facilities** FTV ☇ 18 Putt green Driving range New Year Wi-fi **Conf** Class 60 Board 40 Thtr 80 **Services** Lift **Parking** 24 **Notes** LB ⊗ Civ Wed 110

Poacher's Country Hotel

★★ 72% HOTEL

☎ 01205 290310 ▤ 01205 290254
Swineshead Rd, Kirton Holme PE20 1SQ
e-mail: poachers@kirtonholme.wandoo.co.uk
dir: A17 Bicker Bar, turn at rdbt onto A52, hotel 2m

A delightful hotel with modern and nicely furnished bedrooms. A very wide range of well prepared dishes is on offer. Expect attentive and friendly service.

Rooms 16 (2 fmly) (7 GF) **S** £35-£37.50; **D** £49.50-£55 (incl. bkfst) **Facilities** FTV Xmas New Year Wi-fi **Conf** Class 100 Board 40 Thtr 150 **Parking** 60 **Notes** LB Civ Wed 150

CLEETHORPES · Map 17 TA30

Kingsway

★★★ 77% ⊛ HOTEL

☎ 01472 601122 ▤ 0871 236 0671
Kingsway DN35 0AE
e-mail: reception@kingsway-hotel.com
web: www.kingsway-hotel.com
dir: Exit A180 at Grimsby, to Cleethorpes seafront. Hotel at Kingsway & Queen Parade junct (A1098)

This seafront hotel has been in the same family for four generations and continues to provide traditional comfort and friendly service. The lounges are comfortable and good food is served in the pleasant dining room. The bedrooms are bright and nicely furnished - most are comfortably proportioned.

Rooms 49 **S** £75-£88; **D** £92-£105 (incl. bkfst)*
Facilities STV Wi-fi **Conf** Board 18 Thtr 22 **Services** Lift **Parking** 50 **Notes** ⊗ No children 5yrs Closed 25-26 Dec

Dovedale Hotel & Restaurant

★★ 72% HOTEL

☎ 01472 692988 ▤ 01472 692992
14 Albert Rd DN35 8LX
web: www.dovedalehotel.com
dir: In town centre. Off A1098 (Alexandra Rd)

This hotel stands in a quite side road just off the seafront. The bedrooms offer good all round comforts, and there is a modern bar and lounge. The menu offers a wide choice of dishes that are served in delightful restaurant. Service is both friendly and attentive.

Rooms 22 (9 fmly) (4 GF) **Facilities** FTV Wi-fi **Parking** 12 **Notes** LB

COLSTERWORTH · Map 11 SK92

Travelodge Grantham Colsterworth

Travelodge

BUDGET HOTEL

☎ 08719 846 075 ▤ 01476 860680
Moto Service Area A1 NG35 5JR
web: www.travelodge.co.uk
dir: A1 & A151 Colsterworth rdbt, 8m S of Grantham

Travelodge offers good quality, good value, budget accommodation. All offer family rooms sleeping up to four (two adults, two children) with en suite bathroom/shower-room, remote-control TV, tea- and coffee-making facilities and comfortable beds. Food options vary. Breakfast is at the on-site Bar Café restaurant (if available) or to take away. See also Hotel Groups pages.

Rooms 31 **S** fr £29; **D** fr £29

GAINSBOROUGH · Map 17 SK88

Hickman Hill

★★ 63% HOTEL

☎ 01427 613639 ▤ 01427 677591
Cox's Hill DN21 1HH
e-mail: info@hickmanhill.co.uk
web: www.hickmanhill.co.uk
dir: Right off B1433 after rail bridge, hotel up hill 100mtrs on right

Dating back to 1795, and once a school, this establishment became a hotel over 25 years ago; it retains many original features. The stylish and spacious bedrooms are named after the school's head teachers. The two-acre gardens are ideal for relaxing in after the stressful day. The restaurant is in the old school hall and offers tasty home-made dishes that use many locally sourced ingredients.

Rooms 9 (1 fmly) (1 GF) **S** £80-£95; **D** £95-£130 (incl. bkfst) **Facilities** FTV Wi-fi **Conf** Class 40 Board 30 Thtr 60 **Parking** 25 **Notes** ⊗

GRANTHAM · Map 11 SK93

Ramada Grantham

Ⓡ RAMADA.

★★★★ 74% HOTEL

☎ 01476 593000 ▤ 01476 592592
Swingbridge Rd NG31 7XT
e-mail: info@ramadagrantham.co.uk
dir: Exit A1 at Grantham/Melton Mowbray junct onto A607. From N: 1st exit at mini rdbt, hotel on right. From S: at rdbt 2nd exit. Next left at T-junct. At mini rdbt 2nd exit. Hotel on right

A modern, purpose-built hotel ideally placed for touring the local area. Bedrooms are spacious, smartly decorated and equipped with modern facilities. Public rooms include a large open-plan lounge/bar area with comfortable seating and an intimate restaurant as well as conference and banqueting facilities. The property also has smart leisure facilities.

Rooms 89 (44 GF) (10 smoking) **S** £50-£99; **D** £55-£105* **Facilities** STV ⟐ Gym Steam room Sauna Xmas New Year Wi-fi **Conf** Class 90 Board 60 Thtr 200 Del from £120 to £142* **Parking** 102 **Notes** ⊗ Civ Wed 200

Best Western Kings

★★★ 73% HOTEL

☎ 01476 590800 ▤ 01476 577072
North Pde NG31 8AU
e-mail: kings@bestwestern.co.uk
web: www.bw-kingshotel.co.uk
dir: S on A1, 1st exit to Grantham. Through Great Gonerby, 2m on left

A friendly atmosphere exists at this extended Georgian house. Modern bedrooms are attractively decorated and furnished, and suitably equipped to meet the needs of corporate and leisure guests. Dining options include the formal Victorian restaurant and the popular Orangery, which also operates as an informal coffee shop and breakfast room; a lounge bar and a comfortable open-plan foyer lounge are also available.

Rooms 21 (3 fmly) (3 GF) **S** £58.50-£84; **D** £68.50-£94 (incl. bkfst)* **Facilities** STV New Year Wi-fi **Conf** Class 50 Board 40 Thtr 90 Del from £91.50 to £107.50* **Parking** 40 **Notes** LB Closed 25-26 Dec RS 24 Dec

Travelodge Grantham (A1)

BUDGET HOTEL

☎ 0871 984 6077 ▤ 01476 577500
Grantham Service Area, Grantham North, Gonerby Moor NG32 2AB
web: www.travelodge.co.uk
dir: At Moto service area on A1, 4m N of Grantham

Travelodge offers good quality, good value, budget accommodation. All offer family rooms sleeping up to four (two adults, two children) with en suite bathroom/shower-room, remote-control TV, tea- and coffee-making facilities and comfortable beds. Food options vary. Breakfast is at the on-site Bar Café restaurant (if available) or to take away. See also Hotel Groups pages.

Rooms 40 **S** fr £29; **D** fr £29

Millfields

★★★ Ⓐ HOTEL

☎ 01472 356068 ▤ 01472 250286
53 Bargate DN34 5AD
e-mail: info@millfieldshotel.co.uk
web: www.millfieldshotel.co.uk
dir: A180, right at KFC rdbt then left at next rdbt. Right at 2nd lights & right onto Bargate, hotel 0.5m on left after Wheatsheaf pub

Rooms 27 (4 annexe) (7 fmly) (13 GF) **S** fr £60; **D** £75-£150 (incl. bkfst)* **Facilities** FTV Gym Squash Sauna Steam room Hairdresser Beauty salon Aromatherapist Wi-fi **Conf** Class 25 Board 25 Thtr 50 Del from £125* **Parking** 75 **Notes** LB Civ Wed 50

St James Hotel

Ⓤ

☎ 01472 359 771 ▤ 01472 241427
St James's Square DN31 1EP
e-mail: gm.stjames@corushotels.com
dir: From Scunthorpe on A180 to Grimsby, at 3rd rdbt right into Victoria St. Right at 2nd lights into Frederick Ward Way. Left in 800yds. Hotel on right

Currently the rating for this establishment is not confirmed. This may be due to a change of ownership or because it has only recently joined the AA rating scheme. For further details please see the AA website: theAA.com

Rooms 124 (6 fmly) **Facilities** Xmas **Conf** Class 20 Board 35 Thtr 70 **Services** Lift **Parking** 70

Best Western Admiral Rodney

★★★ 71% HOTEL

☎ 01507 523131 ▤ 01507 523104
North St LN9 5DX
e-mail: reception@admiralrodney.com
web: www.admiralrodney.com
dir: Off A153 (Louth to Horncastle)

Once a coaching inn and enjoying a prime location in the town centre, this smart hotel offers a high standard of accommodation. Bedrooms are well appointed and thoughtfully equipped for both business and leisure guests. Public areas include the Rodney Bar ideal for enjoying a drink, a range of meeting and conference rooms plus a conservatory-style restaurant and adjoining lounge.

Rooms 31 (3 fmly) (7 GF) **S** £65-£85; **D** £90-£110 (incl. bkfst)* **Facilities** Xmas New Year Wi-fi **Conf** Class 60 Board 50 Thtr 140 **Services** Lift **Parking** 60 **Notes** LB ⊗

Legacy Oaklands

★★★ 71% HOTEL

☎ 0870 832 9909 ▤ 0870 832 9910
Barton St DN37 7LF
e-mail: res-oaklands@legacy-hotel.co.uk
web: www.legacy-hotels.co.uk
dir: A18 to rdbt, straight over, hotel 75yds on right

Built in the 19th century, the main house still retains much of the elegance of an English mansion. The hotel is set in five acres of parkland and lawns. The garden restaurant serves traditional English cuisine. Modern, comfortable bedrooms complement the traditional, spacious lounges now used for conferences, meetings and other special occasions.

Rooms 45 (3 fmly) (10 GF) **Facilities** STV Xmas New Year Wi-fi **Conf** Class 60 Board 40 Thtr 200 **Parking** 110 **Notes** LB Civ Wed

Best Western Bentley Hotel & Leisure Club

★★★ 85% HOTEL

☎ 01522 878000 ▤ 01522 878001
Newark Rd, South Hykeham LN6 9NH
e-mail: infothebentleyhotel@btconnect.com
web: www.thebentleyhotel.uk.com
dir: From A1 take A46 E towards Lincoln for 10m. Over 1st rdbt on Lincoln Bypass to hotel 50yds on left

This modern hotel is on a ring road, so it is conveniently located for all local attractions. Attractive bedrooms, most with air conditioning are well equipped and spacious. The hotel has a leisure suite with gym and large pool (with a hoist for the less able). Extensive conference facilities are available.

Rooms 80 (5 fmly) (26 GF) **S** £90-£115; **D** £105-£140 (incl. bkfst) **Facilities** Spa STV ⓢ Gym Beauty salon Steam room Sauna New Year Wi-fi **Conf** Class 150 Board 30 Thtr 300 **Services** Lift Air con **Parking** 170 **Notes** LB ⊗ Civ Wed 120

LINCOLN *continued*

Branston Hall

★★★ 75% ◎◎ COUNTRY HOUSE HOTEL

☎ 01522 793305 ▤ 01522 790734
Branston Park, Branston LN4 1PD
e-mail: info@branstonhall.com
web: www.branstonhall.com
dir: on B1188

Dating back to 1885 this country house sits in 88 acres of beautiful grounds complete with a lake. There is an elegant restaurant, a spacious bar and a beautiful lounge in addition to impressive conference and leisure facilities. Individually styled bedrooms vary in size and include several with four-poster beds. The hotel is a popular wedding venue.

Rooms 50 (7 annexe) (3 fmly) (4 GF) **Facilities** Spa ◌ Gym Jogging circuit Xmas New Year Wi-fi **Conf** Class 54 Board 40 Thtr 200 **Services** Lift **Parking** 100 **Notes** LB ⊗ Civ Wed 160

The Lincoln

★★★ 74% HOTEL

☎ 01522 520348 ▤ 01522 510780
Eastgate LN2 1PN
e-mail: reservations@thelincolnhotel.com
web: www.thelincolnhotel.com
dir: Adjacent to cathedral

This privately owned modern hotel enjoys superb uninterrupted views of Lincoln Cathedral. There are ruins of the Roman wall and Eastgate in the grounds. Bedrooms are contemporary with up-to-the-minute facilities. An airy restaurant and bar, plus a comfortable lounge are provided. There are substantial conference and meeting facilities.

The Lincoln

Rooms 72 (4 fmly) (8 GF) **S** £70-£105; **D** £80-£115 (incl. bkfst)* **Facilities** FTV Wi-fi **Conf** Class 50 Board 40 Thtr 120 Del from £100 to £165 **Services** Lift **Parking** 120 **Notes** LB ⊗ Civ Wed 150

Holiday Inn Lincoln

★★★ 73% HOTEL

☎ 01522 544244 ▤ 01522 560805
Brayford Wharf North LN1 1YW
e-mail: reservations@lincoln.kewgreen.co.uk
web: www.holidayinn.co.uk
dir: A46 onto A57 to Lincoln Central. Left at lights, right, next right onto Lucy Tower St. Right onto Brayford Wharf North. Hotel on right

In a wonderful, central location at Brayford Marina, this hotel is ideally placed for exploring the historic city of Lincoln. All air-conditioned bedrooms are well equipped with a work desk, data point and many modern extras, and have either a view of the waterfront or the cathedral and castle.

Rooms 97 (32 fmly) (9 GF) **Facilities** Gym Wi-fi **Conf** Class 15 Board 18 Thtr 30 **Services** Lift Air con **Parking** 100 **Notes** LB

Washingborough Hall

★★★ 72% ◎ HOTEL

☎ 01522 790340 ▤ 01522 792936
Church Hill, Washingborough LN4 1BE
e-mail: enquiries@washingboroughhall.com
dir: B1190 into Washingborough. Right at rdbt, hotel 500yds on left

This Georgian manor stands on the edge of the quiet village of Washingborough and is set in attractive gardens. Public rooms are pleasantly furnished and comfortable, while the restaurant offers interesting menus. Bedrooms are individually designed and most

have views out over the grounds to the countryside beyond.

Rooms 12 (3 fmly) **S** £70-£85; **D** £100-£130 (incl. bkfst) **Facilities** FTV ⌘ Bicycles for hire New Year Wi-fi Child facilities **Conf** Class 25 Board 25 Thtr 50 Del from £137.50 to £160 **Parking** 50 **Notes** LB Civ Wed 48

The White Hart

★★★ 68% HOTEL

☎ 01522 526222 & 563293 ▤ 01522 531798
Bailgate LN1 3AR
e-mail: info@whitehart-lincoln.co.uk
web: www.whitehart-lincoln.co.uk
dir: turn off A46 onto B1226, through Newport Arch. Hotel 0.5m on left as road bends left

Lying in the shadow of Lincoln's magnificent cathedral, this hotel is perfectly positioned for exploring the shops and sights of this medieval city. The attractive bedrooms are furnished and decorated in a traditional style and many have views of the cathedral. Given the hotel's central location, parking is a real benefit.

Rooms 50 **Facilities** FTV Xmas New Year Wi-fi **Conf** Class 80 Board 103 Thtr 160 **Services** Lift **Parking** 50 **Notes** Civ Wed 120

Castle

★★ 80% HOTEL

☎ 01522 538801 ▤ 01522 575457
Westgate LN1 3AS
e-mail: info@castlehotel.net
web: www.castlehotel.net
dir: Follow signs for Historic Lincoln. Hotel at NE corner of castle

Located in the heart of historic Lincoln, this privately owned and run hotel has been carefully restored to offer comfortable, attractive, well-appointed accommodation. Bedrooms are thoughtfully equipped, particularly the deluxe rooms and the spacious Lincoln Suite. Specialising in traditional fayre, Knights Restaurant has an interesting medieval theme.

Rooms 19 (3 annexe) (5 GF) **Facilities** Wi-fi **Conf** Class 40 Board 30 Thtr 20 **Parking** 20 **Notes** LB No children 8yrs RS 25-26 Dec evening

Tower Hotel

★★ 71% HOTEL

☎ 01522 529999 📠 01522 560596
38 Westgate LN1 3BD
e-mail: tower.hotel@btclick.com
dir: From A46 follow signs to Lincoln N then to Bailgate area. Through arch, 2nd left

This hotel faces the Norman castle wall and is in a very convenient location for the city. The relaxed and friendly atmosphere is very noticeable here. There's a modern conservatory bar and a stylish restaurant where contemporary dishes are available throughout the day.

Rooms 15 (1 fmly) **S** £65; **D** £90-£100 (incl. bkfst)*
Facilities STV Wi-fi **Conf** Class 24 Board 16 Thtr 24
Parking 4 **Notes** LB Closed 24-27 Dec & 1 Jan

Express by Holiday Inn Lincoln City Centre

BUDGET HOTEL

☎ 0871 423 4876
Ruston Way, Brayford Park LN6 7DQ
e-mail: gm@expresslincoln.co.uk

A modern hotel ideal for families and business travellers. Fresh and uncomplicated, the spacious rooms include Sky TV, power shower and tea and coffee-making facilities. Continental buffet breakfast is included in the room rate; other meals may be taken at the nearby family pub or restaurant. See also the Hotel Groups pages.

Rooms 118

Ibis Lincoln

BUDGET HOTEL

☎ 01522 698333 📠 01522 698444
Runcorn Rd (A46), off Whisby Rd LN6 3QZ
e-mail: H3161@accor-hotels.com
web: www.ibishotel.com
dir: Off A46 ring road onto Whisby Rd. 1st turning on left

Enjoying a convenient location, adjacent to the A46 on the edge of the city, this modern purpose-built hotel offers well-equipped en suite bedrooms, suitable for both leisure and business guests. The open-plan public rooms are light and contemporary in style. See also the Hotel Groups pages.

Rooms 86 (19 fmly) (8 GF) **S** £39-£60; **D** £39-£60
Conf Class 12 Board 20 Thtr 35

Travelodge Lincoln Thorpe on the Hill

BUDGET HOTEL

☎ 0871 984 6084 📠 01522 697213
Thorpe on the Hill LN6 9AJ
web: www.travelodge.co.uk
dir: On A46 (Newark/Lincoln rdbt), 9m SW of Lincoln

Travelodge offers good quality, good value, budget accommodation. All offer family rooms sleeping up to four (two adults, two children) with en suite bathroom/shower-room, remote-control TV, tea- and coffee-making facilities and comfortable beds. Food options vary. Breakfast is at the on-site Bar Café restaurant (if available) or to take away. See also Hotel Groups pages.

Rooms 52 **S** fr £29; **D** fr £29

The Old Bakery

 RESTAURANT WITH ROOMS

☎ 01522 576057
26/28 Burton Rd LN1 3LB
e-mail: enquiries@theold-bakery.co.uk
dir: Exit A46 at Lincoln North follow signs for cathedral. 3rd exit at 1st rdbt, 1st exit at next rdbt

Situated close to the castle at the top of the town, this converted bakery offers well-equipped bedrooms and a delightful dining operation. The cooking is international and uses much local produce. Expect good friendly service from a dedicated staff.

Rooms 4 (1 fmly)

LONG SUTTON Map 12 TF42

Travelodge King's Lynn Long Sutton

BUDGET HOTEL

☎ 0871 984 6082 📠 01406 362230
Wisbech Rd PE12 9AG
web: www.travelodge.co.uk
dir: on rdbt junct of A17 & A1101

Travelodge offers good quality, good value, budget accommodation. All offer family rooms sleeping up to four (two adults, two children) with en suite bathroom/shower-room, remote-control TV, tea- and coffee-making facilities and comfortable beds. Food options vary. Breakfast is at the on-site Bar Café restaurant (if available) or to take away. See also Hotel Groups pages.

Rooms 40 **S** fr £29; **D** fr £29

LOUTH Map 17 TF38

Brackenborough Hotel

★★★ 86% HOTEL

☎ 01507 609169 📠 01507 609413
Cordeaux Corner, Brackenborough LN11 0SZ
e-mail: arlidgard@oakridgehotels.co.uk
web: www.oakridgehotels.co.uk
dir: Off A16 2m N of Louth

Set amid well-tended gardens and patios, this hotel offers attractive bedrooms, each individually decorated with co-ordinated furnishings and many extras. Tippler's Retreat lounge bar offers informal dining; the more formal Signature Restaurant provides dishes using the best of local produce including fish from Grimsby. Wi-fi is available.

Rooms 24 (2 fmly) (6 GF) **S** £82-£119; **D** £97-£154 (incl. bkfst)* **Facilities** FTV 𝄞 Xmas New Year Wi-fi
Conf Class 40 Board 30 Thtr 70 **Services** Air con
Parking 91 **Notes** LB ⊗ Civ Wed 80

Best Western Kenwick Park

★★★ 79% HOTEL

☎ 01507 608806 📠 01507 608027
Kenwick Park Estate LN11 8NR
e-mail: enquiries@kenwick-park.co.uk
web: www.kenwick-park.co.uk
dir: A16 from Grimsby, then A157 Mablethorpe/Manby Rd. Hotel 400mtrs down hill on right

This elegant Georgian house is situated on the 320-acre Kenwick Park estate, overlooking its own golf course. Bedrooms are spacious, comfortable and provide modern facilities. Public areas include a restaurant and a conservatory bar that overlook the grounds. There is also an extensive leisure centre and state-of-the-art conference and banqueting facilities.

Rooms 34 (5 annexe) (10 fmly) **Facilities** Spa ⊙ supervised ⚐ 18 ⚑ Putt green Gym Squash Health & beauty centre Xmas New Year Wi-fi **Conf** Class 40 Board 90 Thtr 250 **Parking** 100 **Notes** LB Civ Wed 200

MARSTON
Map 11 SK84

The Olde Barn
★★★ 75% HOTEL

☎ 01400 250909 📠 01400 250130
Toll Bar Rd NG32 2HT
e-mail: reservations@theoldebarnhotel.co.uk
dir: From A1 N: left to Marston next to petrol station. From
A1 S: 1st right after Gonerby rdbt signed Marston

Located in the countryside one mile from the A1, this
sympathetically renovated and extended former period
barn provides a range of thoughtfully furnished
bedrooms, ideal for both business and leisure customers.
Imaginative food is offered in an attractive beamed
restaurant and extensive leisure facilities include a
swimming pool, sauna, steam room and a well-equipped
gym.

Rooms 103 (11 fmly) (51 GF) (6 smoking) **S** £49-£59;
D £49-£79 **Facilities** STV ⊛ Gym Xmas New Year Wi-fi
Conf Class 180 Board 100 Thtr 300 Del from £125 to
£145 **Services** Lift **Parking** 280 **Notes** Civ Wed 250

SCUNTHORPE
Map 17 SE81

Forest Pines Hotel & Golf Resort

★★★★ 79% ⊛ HOTEL

☎ 01652 650770 📠 01652 650495
Ermine St, Broughton DN20 0AQ
e-mail: forestpines@qhotels.co.uk
web: www.qhotels.co.uk
dir: 200yds from M180 junct 4, on Brigg-Scunthorpe rdbt

This smart hotel provides a comprehensive range of
leisure facilities. Extensive conference rooms, a modern
health and beauty spa, and a championship golf course
ensure that it is a popular choice with both corporate and
leisure guests. The well-equipped bedrooms are modern,
spacious, and appointed to a good standard. Extensive
public areas include a choice of dining options, with fine
dining available in The Eighteen57 fish restaurant, and
more informal eating in the Grill Bar.

Rooms 188 (66 fmly) (67 GF) **Facilities** Spa STV FTV ⊛
supervised ⅃ 27 Putt green Gym Mountain bikes Jogging
track Xmas New Year Wi-fi **Conf** Class 170 Board 96
Thtr 370 Del from £139 to £199* **Services** Lift
Parking 300 **Notes** Civ Wed 250

Wortley House
★★★ 74% HOTEL

☎ 01724 842223 📠 01724 280646
Rowland Rd DN16 1SU
e-mail: reception@wortleyhousehotel.co.uk
web: www.wortleyhousehotel.co.uk
dir: M180 junct 3, A18. Follow Grimsby/airport signs. 2nd
left into Brumby Wood Ln, over rdbt into Rowland Rd

A friendly hotel with good facilities for conferences,
meetings, banquets and other functions. Bedrooms offer
modern comfort and good facilities. An extensive range of
dishes is available in both the formal restaurant and the
more relaxed bar.

Rooms 45 (4 annexe) (5 fmly) (4 GF) **S** £50-£60;
D £50-£80 (incl. bkfst) **Facilities** FTV Xmas New Year
Wi-fi **Conf** Class 250 Board 50 Thtr 300 **Parking** 100
Notes LB Civ Wed 250

Travelodge Scunthorpe

BUDGET HOTEL

☎ 0871 984 6286 📠 01724 289 391
Doncaster Rd, Gunness DN15 8TE
web: www.travelodge.co.uk
dir: M18 junct 5, take M180 towards Scunthorpe. 1st exit
signed Scunthorpe. In 1.5 m take 3rd exit at traffic island.
Lodge on right

Travelodge offers good quality, good value, budget
accommodation. All offer family rooms sleeping up to four
(two adults, two children) with en suite bathroom/
shower-room, remote-control TV, tea- and coffee-making
facilities and comfortable beds. Food options vary.
Breakfast is at the on-site Bar Café restaurant (if
available) or to take away. See also Hotel Groups pages.

Rooms 40 **S** fr £29; **D** fr £29

SKEGNESS
Map 17 TF56

Best Western Vine

★★★ 68% HOTEL

☎ 01754 763018 & 610611 📠 01754 769845
Vine Rd, Seacroft PE25 3DB
e-mail: info@thevinehotel.com
dir: A52 to Skegness, S towards Gibraltar Point, turn right
on to Drummond Rd, 0.5m turn right into Vine Rd

Reputedly the second oldest building in Skegness, this
traditional style hotel offers two character bars that serve
excellent local beers. Freshly prepared dishes are served
in both the bar and the restaurant; service is both friendly
and helpful. The smartly decorated bedrooms are well
equipped and comfortably appointed.

Rooms 25 (3 fmly) **Facilities** FTV Xmas New Year Wi-fi
Conf Class 25 Board 30 Thtr 100 **Parking** 50
Notes Civ Wed 100

Crown
★★★ 66% HOTEL

☎ 01754 610760 📠 01754 610847
Drummond Rd PE25 3AB
e-mail: enquiries@crownhotel.biz
dir: On entering town follow Gibraltar Point Nature
Reserve signs

The Crown is ideally situated just a short walk from the
seafront and town centre, close to Seacroft Golf Course
and the bird sanctuary. Homely bedrooms are attractively
decorated and thoughtfully equipped. Public areas
include a spacious bar offering a wide selection of
dishes, a formal restaurant, residents' TV lounge and
indoor pool; ample parking is provided.

Rooms 29 (4 fmly) **Facilities** ⊛ Wi-fi **Conf** Class 60
Board 60 Thtr 100 **Services** Lift **Parking** 52 **Notes** LB ⊗
Civ Wed 120

See advert on opposite page

North Shore Hotel & Golf Course
★★ 72% HOTEL

☎ 01754 763298 📠 01754 761902
North Shore Rd PE25 1DN
e-mail: info@northshorehotel.co.uk
dir: 1m N of town centre on A52, turn right into North
Shore Rd (opposite Fenland laundry)

This hotel enjoys an enviable position on the beachfront,
adjacent to its own championship golf course and only
ten minutes from the town centre. Spacious public areas
include a terrace bar serving informal meals and real
ales, a formal restaurant and impressive function rooms.
Bedrooms are smartly decorated and thoughtfully
equipped.

Rooms 36 (3 annexe) (4 fmly) **S** £40-£66; **D** £62-£90
(incl. bkfst)* **Facilities** ⅃ 18 Putt green Xmas New Year
Wi-fi **Conf** Class 60 Board 60 Thtr 220 **Parking** 200
Notes LB ⊗ Civ Wed 180

SLEAFORD Map 12 TF04

Carre Arms Hotel & Conference Centre

★★★ 68% SMALL HOTEL

☎ 01529 303156 📠 01529 303139
1 Mareham Ln NG34 7JP
e-mail: enquiries@carrearmshotel.co.uk
web: www.carrearmshotel.co.uk
dir: Take A153 to Sleaford, hotel on right at level crossing

This friendly, family run hotel is located close to the station and offers suitably appointed accommodation. Public areas include a smart brasserie and two spacious bars where a good selection of meals is offered. There is also a conservatory and a former stable that houses the spacious function room.

Rooms 13 (2 fmly) **S** £55-£65; **D** £75-£85 (incl. bkfst)*
Facilities Wi-fi **Conf** Class 70 Board 40 Thtr 120
Del from £75* **Parking** 80 **Notes** ⊗

The Lincolnshire Oak

THE INDEPENDENTS
★★★ 68% HOTEL

☎ 01529 413807 📠 01529 413710
East Rd NG34 7EH
e-mail: reception@lincolnshire-oak.co.uk
web: www.lincolnshire-oak.co.uk
dir: From A17 (by-pass) exit on A153 into Sleaford. Hotel 0.75m on left

Located on the edge of the town in well-tended grounds, this hotel has a relaxed and friendly atmosphere. A comfortable open-plan lounge bar is complemented by a cosy restaurant that looks out onto the rear garden. There are also several meeting rooms. Bedroom styles differ, but all rooms are well furnished and suitably equipped; the superior rooms, as expected, are more comfortably appointed.

Rooms 17 **S** £67-£87.75; **D** £88.50-£103.50 (incl. bkfst)*
Facilities FTV Wi-fi **Conf** Class 70 Board 50 Thtr 140
Parking 80 **Notes** LB ⊗ Civ Wed 90

Travelodge Sleaford

BUDGET HOTEL

☎ 0871 984 6104 📠 01529 414752
Holdingham NG34 8PN
web: www.travelodge.co.uk
dir: On A15 towards Lincoln, just off Holdingham rdbt at A15 & A17 junct, 1m N of Sleaford

Travelodge offers good quality, good value, budget accommodation. All offer family rooms sleeping up to four (two adults, two children) with en suite bathroom/shower-room, remote-control TV, tea- and coffee-making facilities and comfortable beds. Food options vary. Breakfast is at the on-site Bar Café restaurant (if available) or to take away. See also Hotel Groups pages.

Rooms 40 **S** fr £29; **D** fr £29

SOUTH WITHAM — Map 11 SK91

Travelodge Grantham South Witham

BUDGET HOTEL

☎ 0871 984 6076 📠 01572 767 586
New Fox NG33 5LN
web: www.travelodge.co.uk
dir: on A1, northbound

Travelodge offers good quality, good value, budget accommodation. All offer family rooms sleeping up to four (two adults, two children) with en suite bathroom/shower-room, remote-control TV, tea- and coffee-making facilities and comfortable beds. Food options vary. Breakfast is at the on-site Bar Café restaurant (if available) or to take away. See also Hotel Groups pages.

Rooms 32 **S** fr £29; **D** fr £29

SPALDING — Map 12 TF22

Travelodge Spalding

BUDGET HOTEL

☎ 0871 9846383 📠 01775 711810
Springfields Outlet Centre, Camel Gate PE12 6EU
e-mail: spalding.mgr@travelodge.co.uk
dir: From A1 take A52 towards Boston then take A17. Then follow brown signs to Springfields Outlet Centre on A16 (Spalding Bypass)

Travelodge offers good quality, good value, budget accommodation. All offer family rooms sleeping up to four (two adults, two children) with en suite bathroom/shower-room, remote-control TV, tea- and coffee-making facilities and comfortable beds. Food options vary. Breakfast is at the on-site Bar Café restaurant (if available) or to take away. See also Hotel Groups pages.

Rooms 43 **S** fr £29; **D** fr £29

STALLINGBOROUGH — Map 17 TA11

Stallingborough Grange Hotel

★★★ 72% HOTEL

☎ 01469 561302 📠 01469 561338
Riby Rd DN41 8BU
e-mail: grange.hot@virgin.net
web: www.stallingborough-grange.com
dir: From A180 follow Stallingborough Interchange signs. Through village. From rdbt follow A1173/Caistor signs. Hotel 1m on left just past windmill

This 18th-century country house has been tastefully extended to provide spacious and well-equipped bedrooms, particularly in the executive wing. A family-run hotel that is popular with locals who enjoy the wide range of food offered in either the bar or the restaurant.

Rooms 41 (6 fmly) (9 GF) **S** £90–£110; **D** £105–£125 (incl. bkfst)* **Facilities** STV FTV Wi-fi **Conf** Class 40 Board 28 Thtr 60 **Parking** 100 **Notes** ⊗ Civ Wed 65

STAMFORD — Map 11 TF00

The George of Stamford

★★★ 86% ◉ HOTEL

☎ 01780 750750 & 750700 (res) 📠 01780 750701
71 St Martins PE9 2LB
e-mail: reservations@georgehotelofstamford.com
web: www.georgehotelofstamford.com
dir: A1, 15m N of Peterborough onto B1081, hotel 1m on left

Steeped in hundreds of years of history, this delightful coaching inn provides spacious public areas that include a choice of dining options, inviting lounges, a business centre and a range of quality shops. A highlight is afternoon tea, taken in the colourful courtyard when weather permits. Bedrooms are stylishly appointed and range from traditional to contemporary in design.

Rooms 47 (24 fmly) **S** £93–£98; **D** £132.50–£254 (incl. bkfst)* **Facilities** STV ⬥ Complimentary membership to local gym Xmas New Year Wi-fi **Conf** Class 25 Board 25 Thtr 50 Del from £145 to £175* **Parking** 110 **Notes** LB Civ Wed 50

Crown

★★★ 77% HOTEL

☎ 01780 763136 📠 01780 756111
All Saints Place PE9 2AG
e-mail: reservations@thecrownhotelstamford.co.uk
web: www.thecrownhotelstamford.co.uk
dir: Off A1 onto A43, through town to Red Lion Sq, hotel behind All Saints Church

This small, privately owned hotel where hospitality is spontaneous and sincere, is ideally situated in the town centre. Unpretentious British food is served in the modern dining areas and the spacious bar is popular with locals. Bedrooms are appointed to a very high standard being quite contemporary in style and very well equipped; some have four-poster beds. Additional 'superior' rooms are located in a renovated Georgian town house just a short walk up the street.

Rooms 26 (9 annexe) (1 fmly) (1 GF) **S** fr £90; **D** £110–£150 (incl. bkfst) **Facilities** STV Use of local health/gym club Wi-fi **Conf** Class 12 Board 12 Thtr 20 Del from £140 to £180 **Parking** 21 **Notes** LB ⊗

Garden House Hotel

★★★ 72% HOTEL

☎ 01780 763359 📠 01780 763339
High St, St Martins PE9 2LP
e-mail: enquiries@gardenhousehotel.com
web: www.gardenhousehotel.com
dir: A1 to South Stamford, B1081, signed Stamford & Burghley House. Hotel on left on entering town

Situated within a few minutes' walk of the town centre, this transformed 18th-century town house provides pleasant accommodation. Bedroom styles vary; all are well equipped and comfortably furnished. Public rooms include a charming lounge bar, conservatory restaurant and a smart breakfast room. Service is attentive and friendly throughout.

Rooms 20 (2 fmly) (4 GF) **S** fr £65; **D** £95-£100 (incl. bkfst)* **Facilities** STV Xmas New Year Wi-fi **Conf** Class 20 Board 20 Thtr 40 Del from £130* **Parking** 22 **Notes** LB Closed 26-30 Dec RS 1-12 Jan Civ Wed 60

Candlesticks
RESTAURANT WITH ROOMS

☎ 01780 764033 📠 01780 756071
1 Church Ln PE9 2JU
e-mail: info@candlestickshotel.co.uk
dir: On B1081 High Street St Martins. Church Ln opposite St Martin Church

A 17th-century property situated in a quite lane in the oldest part of Stamford just a short walk from the centre of town. The bedrooms are pleasantly decorated and equipped with a good range of useful extras. Public rooms feature Candlesticks restaurant, a small lounge and a cosy bar.

Rooms 8

The Grange & Links
★★★ 73% ⊛ HOTEL

☎ 01507 441334 📠 01507 443033
Sea Ln, Sandilands LN12 2RA
e-mail: grangeandlinkshotel@btconnect.com
web: www.grangeandlinkshotel.co.uk
dir: A1111 to Sutton-on-Sea, follow signs to Sandilands

This friendly, family-run hotel sits in five acres of grounds, close to both the beach and its own 18-hole links golf course. Bedrooms are pleasantly appointed and are well equipped for both business and leisure guests. Public rooms include ample lounge areas, a formal restaurant and a traditional bar, serving a wide range of meals and snacks.

Rooms 23 (10 fmly) (3 GF) **S** £64.50; **D** £84 (incl. bkfst)* **Facilities** ⌁ 18 ⬁ Putt green ⬆ Gym Xmas New Year **Conf** Class 200 Board 100 Thtr 200 Del from £75 to £87* **Parking** 60 **Notes** LB Civ Wed 150

INSPECTORS' CHOICE

Winteringham Fields
⊛⊛ RESTAURANT WITH ROOMS

☎ 01724 733096 📠 01724 733898
DN15 9PF
e-mail: wintfields@aol.com
dir: In village centre at x-rds

This highly regarded restaurant with rooms, located deep in the countryside in Winteringham village, is six miles west of the Humber Bridge. Public rooms and bedrooms, some of which are housed in renovated barns and cottages, are delightfully cosseting. Award-winning food is available in the restaurant.

Rooms 10 (6 annexe)

Petwood
★★★ 74% HOTEL

☎ 01526 352411 📠 01526 353473
Stixwould Rd LN10 6QG
e-mail: reception@petwood.co.uk
web: www.petwood.co.uk
dir: From Sleaford take A153 (signed Skegness). At Tattershall turn left on B1192. Hotel is signed from village

This lovely Edwardian house, set in 30 acres of gardens and woodlands, is adjacent to Woodhall Golf Course. Built in 1905, the house was used by 617 Squadron, the famous Dambusters, as an officers' mess during World War II. Bedrooms and public areas are spacious and comfortable, and retain many original features. Weddings and conferences are well catered for in modern facilities.

Rooms 53 (3 GF) **S** fr £95; **D** fr £145 (incl. bkfst)* **Facilities** Putt green ⬆ ♫ Xmas New Year Wi-fi **Conf** Class 100 Board 50 Thtr 250 Del from £110 to £125* **Services** Lift **Parking** 140 **Notes** LB Civ Wed 200

Woodhall Spa
★★★ 71% HOTEL

☎ 01526 353231 📠 01526 352797
The Broadway LN10 6ST
e-mail: reception@woodhallspahotel.co.uk
web: www.woodhallspahotel.co.uk
dir: In village centre, 500tmrs from golf course

This family owned hotel is located in the centre of town, close to local shops and golf courses. Modern bedrooms are equipped for both business and leisure guests. Public areas include a bar and a formal restaurant where a good range of dishes to suit all tastes is offered. Conference and meeting facilities are also available.

Rooms 25 (2 fmly) (2 GF) **S** £70-£115; **D** £95-£125 (incl. bkfst)* **Facilities** FTV Xmas Wi-fi **Conf** Class 40 Board 40 Thtr 100 **Services** Lift **Parking** 30 **Notes** LB ⊗ Civ Wed 86

Golf Hotel
★★★ 63% HOTEL

☎ 01526 353535 📠 01526 353096
The Broadway LN10 6SG
e-mail: reception@thegolf-hotel.com
web: www.thegolf-hotel.com
dir: From Lincoln take B1189 to Metheringham onto B1191 towards Woodhall Spa. Hotel on left in approx 500yds from rdbt

Located near the centre of the village, this traditional hotel is ideally situated to explore the Lincolnshire countryside and coast. The adjacent golf course makes this a popular venue for golfers, and the hotel's hydrotherapy suite uses the original spa water supplies. Bedrooms vary in size.

Rooms 50 (2 fmly) (8 GF) (3 smoking) **Facilities** Spa FTV Xmas New Year Wi-fi **Conf** Class 50 Board 50 Thtr 150 Del from £95 to £100* **Services** Lift **Parking** 100 **Notes** Civ Wed 150

London

The London Eye

Index of London Hotels

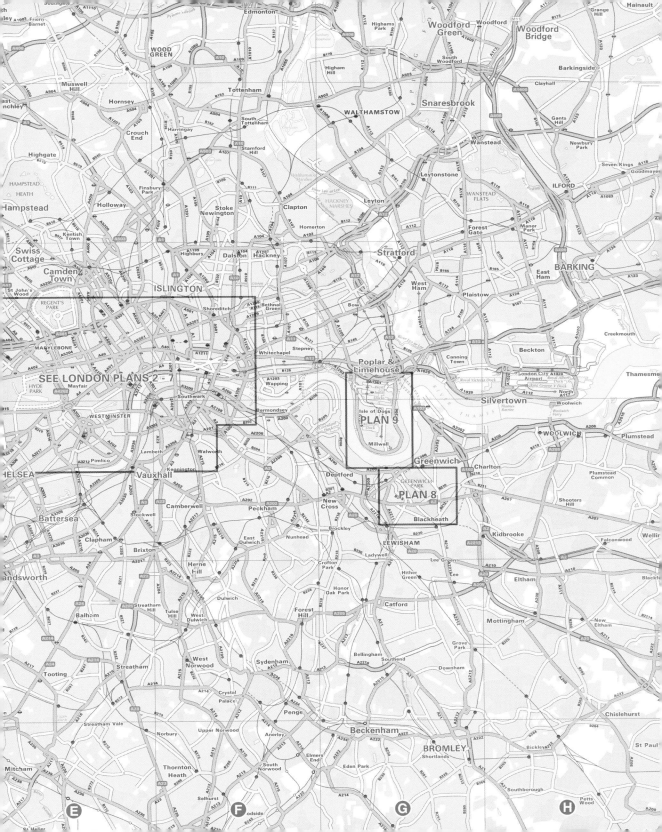

London Plan 4

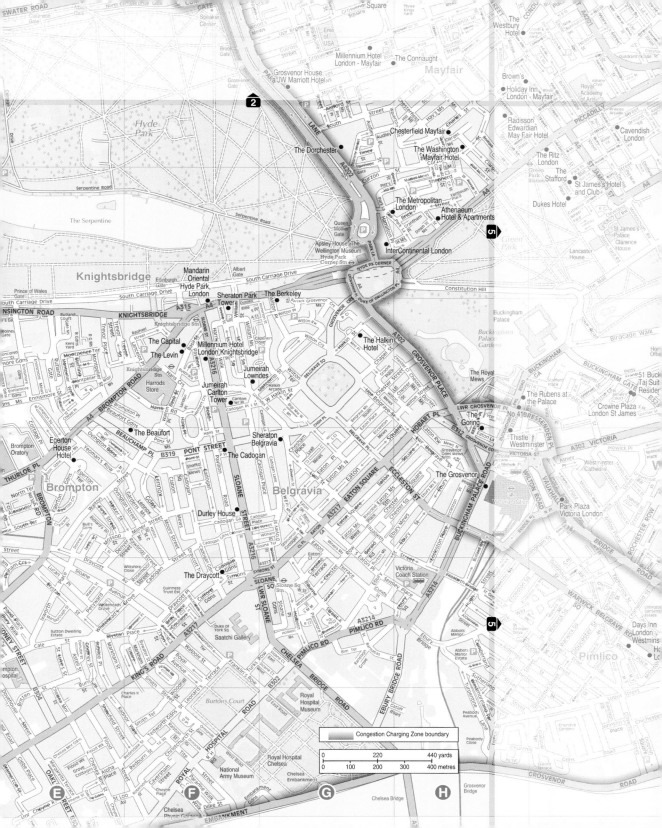

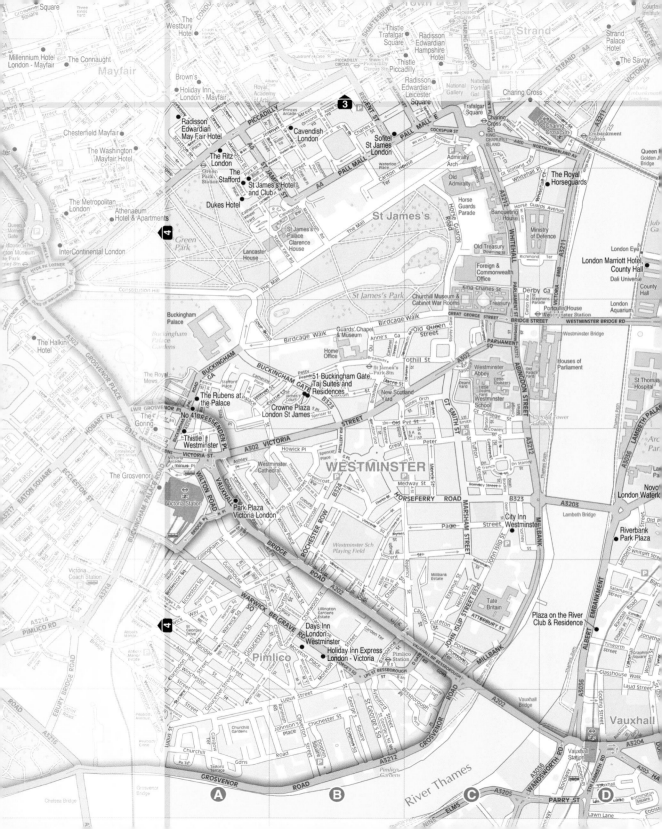

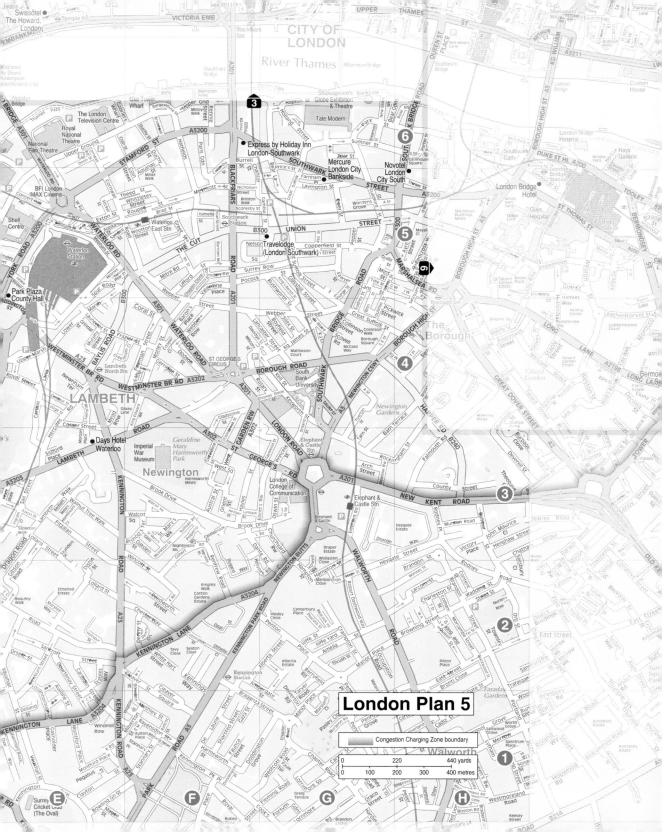

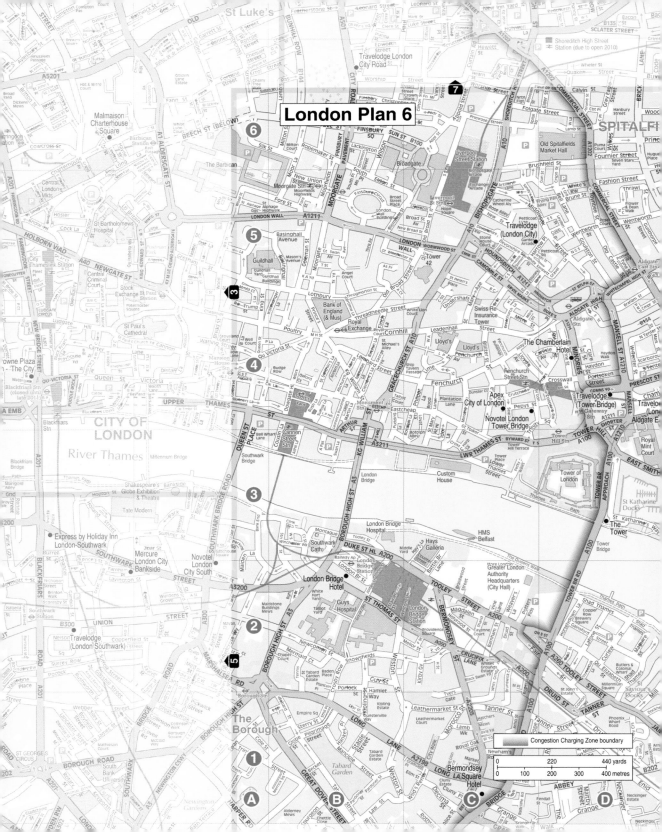

London Plan 6

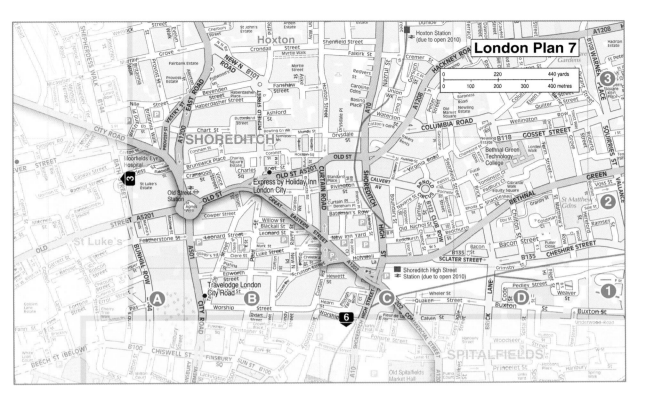

London Plan 7

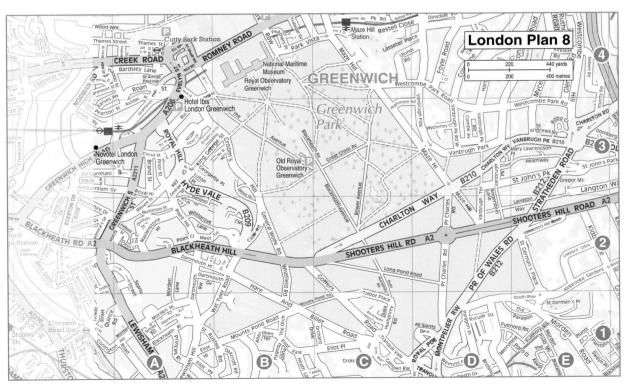

London Plan 8

LONDON

LONDON

Greater London Plans 1-9, pages 298-310. (Small scale maps 6 & 7 at back of book.) Hotels are listed below in postal district order, commencing East, then North, South and West, with a brief indication of the area covered. Detailed plans 2-9 show the locations of AA-appointed hotels within the Central London postal districts. If you do not know the postal district of the hotel you want, please refer to the index preceding the street plans for the entry and map pages.

E1 STEPNEY AND EAST OF THE TOWER OF LONDON

See also LONDON plan 1 G4

The Tower

★★★★ 75% HOTEL PLAN 6 D3

☎ 0870 333 9106 📠 0870 333 9206
St Katherine's Way E1W 1LD
e-mail: tower@guoman.com
dir: Follow signs for Tower Bridge, turn left into St. Katharine's Way. Car park under hotel via control barrier

This extensive modern hotel enjoys superb views over the Thames, Tower Bridge and St Katherine's Docks. Public areas include several lounges, a modern, contemporary bar and a choice of restaurants. Bedrooms are traditionally furnished and include a selection of impressive suites.

Rooms 801 (34 fmly) (90 smoking) **Facilities** Gym Xmas New Year Wi-fi **Conf** Class 350 Board 65 Thtr 500 **Services** Lift Air con **Parking** 200 **Notes** ⊗ Civ Wed 500

Crowne Plaza Hotel London - Shoreditch

★★★★ 71% HOTEL

☎ 020 7613 9800 📠 020 7613 9811
100 Shoreditch High St E1 6JQ
e-mail: info@cplondon.com
web: www.crowneplaza.co.uk

This hotel is located in London's fashionable east end, close to the financial district and many attractions. It is contemporary in style and rooms are well appointed and tastefully decorated; air conditioning and the mini bar are just two of the many amenities available. Dinner and breakfast are served in the rooftop restaurant which commands fantastic views.

Rooms 196

Express by Holiday Inn London - Limehouse

BUDGET HOTEL

☎ 020 7791 3850 📠 020 7791 3851
469-475 The Highway E1W 3HN
e-mail: jcniclas@exhi-limehouse.co.uk
web: www.hiexpress.com/limehouse

A modern hotel ideal for families and business travellers. Fresh and uncomplicated, the spacious rooms include Sky TV, power shower and tea and coffee-making facilities. Continental buffet breakfast is included in the room rate; other meals may be taken at the nearby family pub or restaurant. See also the Hotel Groups pages.

Rooms 150 **Conf** Class 26 Board 25 Thtr 60

Travelodge London Aldgate East

BUDGET HOTEL PLAN 6 D4

☎ 0871 984 6406 📠 020 7481 3914
6 - 13 Chamber St E1 8BL
e-mail: londonaldgate@travelodge.co.uk
dir: From A11 & A13, at large junct follow signs towards The Tower of London, left into Lehman St, 3rd left into Chamber St. Lodge on left

Travelodge offers good quality, good value, budget accommodation. All offer family rooms sleeping up to four (two adults, two children) with en suite bathroom/shower-room, remote-control TV, tea- and coffee-making facilities and comfortable beds. Food options vary. Breakfast is at the on-site Bar Café restaurant (if available) or to take away. See also the Hotel Groups pages.

Rooms 69 **S** fr £29; **D** fr £29

Travelodge London Liverpool Street

BUDGET HOTEL PLAN 6 C5

☎ 08719 846 190 📠 020 7626 1105
1 Harrow Place E1 7DB
web: www.travelodge.co.uk
dir: Exit Liverpool Street Station onto Bishopsgate, cross road, turn right, after Orange Mobile Phone Store left down Devonshire Row. Lodge 400yds

Rooms 142 **S** fr £29; **D** fr £29

Travelodge London Tower Bridge

BUDGET HOTEL PLAN 6 D4

☎ 0871 984 6388 📠 020 7680 9166
Lloyds Court Business Centre, 1 Goodmans Yard E1 8AT
dir: From Whitechapel High St, follow signs to Tower Bridge, into Mansell St. Lodge near to Minories car park on A1210

Rooms 190 **S** fr £29; **D** fr £29

E4 CHINGFORD   Map 6 TQ39

Ridgeway

★★ 57% SMALL HOTEL

☎ 020 8529 1964 📠 020 8524 9130
115/117 The Ridgeway, North Chingford E4 6QU
e-mail: reception@ridgewayhotel.com
dir: M25 junct 26, Sewardstone Rd; or M25 junct 25, A10 (Great Cambridge Rd)

The Ridgeway is within easy reach of the North Circular and the M25 and can cater for meetings and functions. Bedrooms vary in size and style, including a four-poster room, and public areas include a smart dining room, lounge bar and an attractive garden.

Rooms 20 (2 fmly) (4 GF) **Facilities** FTV Wi-fi **Conf** Class 40 Board 20 Thtr 30 **Parking** 9

Express by Holiday Inn London Chingford

BUDGET HOTEL

☎ 0870 444 2789 📠 0870 444 2790
5 Walthamstow Av, Chingford E4 8ST
e-mail: dgmchingford@expressholidayinn.co.uk
web: www.hiexpress.com/lonchingford
dir: on A406 (North Circular) at Crooked Billet rdbt, adjacent to A112 (Chingford-Walthamstow)

A modern hotel ideal for families and business travellers. Fresh and uncomplicated, the spacious rooms include Sky TV, power shower and tea and coffee-making facilities. Continental buffet breakfast is included in the room rate; other meals may be taken at the nearby family pub or restaurant. See also the Hotel Groups pages.

Rooms 102 (65 fmly) **Conf** Class 10 Board 16 Thtr 20

E11 SNARESBROOK

See LONDON plan 1 G5

Innkeeper's Lodge London Snaresbrook

BUDGET HOTEL

☎ 0845 112 6122 📠 0845 112 6181
73 Hollybush Hill, Snaresbrook E11 1PE
web: www.innkeeperslodge.com/snaresbrook
dir: M11 junct 4 onto A406. Left, at rdbt take A12 (The City). Left (Wanstead). Right at lights (High Street). Continue over lights to junct with Hollybush Hill. Lodge on right

Innkeeper's Lodge represents an exciting, high value concept within the budget hotel market. Comfortable bedrooms provide excellent facilities that include satellite TV and modem points. Options include family rooms; and for the corporate guest, cutting edge IT which includes Wi-fi access. A popular Carvery provides all-day food, including an extensive, complimentary continental breakfast. See also the Hotel Groups pages.

Rooms 24

E14 CANARY WHARF & LIMEHOUSE

See also LONDON plan 1 G3

INSPECTORS' CHOICE

Four Seasons Hotel Canary Wharf
★★★★★ ⊚⊚ HOTEL PLAN 9 A6

☎ 020 7510 1999 📄 020 7510 1998
Westferry Circus, Canary Wharf E14 8RS
e-mail: res.canarywharf@fourseasons.com
web: www.fourseasons.com/canarywharf
dir: From A13 follow signs to Canary Wharf, Isle of Dogs and Westferry Circus. Hotel off 3rd exit of Westferry Circus rdbt

With superb views over the London skyline, this stylish modern hotel enjoys a delightful riverside location. Spacious contemporary bedrooms are particularly thoughtfully equipped. Public areas include the Italian Quadrato Bar and Restaurant, an impressive business centre and a gym. Guests also have complimentary use of the impressive Holmes Place health club and spa. Welcoming staff provide exemplary levels of service and hospitality.

Rooms 142 (20 smoking) **S** £287.50–£310.50;
Facilities Spa STV FTV ⊙ supervised ⩍ Gym Fitness centre ♬ Xmas New Year Wi-fi **Conf** Class 120 Board 56 Thtr 200 **Services** Lift Air con **Parking** 54
Notes LB Civ Wed 200

London Marriott West India Quay

Marriott
HOTELS & RESORTS

★★★★★ 78% HOTEL PLAN 9 B6

☎ 020 7093 1000 📄 020 7093 1001
22 Hertsmere Rd, Canary Wharf E14 4ED
web: www.londonmarriottwestindiaquay.co.uk
dir: Exit Aspen Way at Hertsmere Road. Hotel opposite, adjacent to Canary Wharf

This spectacular skyscraper with curved glass façade is located at the heart of the docklands, adjacent to Canary Wharf and overlooking the water. The hotel is modern, but not pretentiously trendy; eye-catching floral displays add warmth to the public areas. Bedrooms, many of which overlook the quay, provide every modern convenience, including broadband and air-conditioning. Curve Restaurant offers good quality cooking focusing on fresh fish.

Rooms 301 (22 fmly) **S** fr £99; **D** fr £99* **Facilities** STV Gym Wi-fi **Conf** Class 132 Board 27 Thtr 290 **Services** Lift Air con **Notes** ⊗ Civ Wed 290

Ibis London Docklands
BUDGET HOTEL PLAN 9 D6

ibis
HOTEL

☎ 020 7517 1100 📄 020 7987 5916
1 Baffin Way E14 9PE
e-mail: H2177@accor.com
web: www.ibishotel.com
dir: from Tower Bridge follow City Airport and Royal Docks signs,exit for 'Isle of Dogs'. Hotel on 1st left opposite McDonalds

Modern, budget hotel offering comfortable accommodation in bright and practical bedrooms. Breakfast is self-service and dinner is available in the restaurant. See also the Hotel Groups pages.

Rooms 87

Travelodge London Docklands

Travelodge

BUDGET HOTEL

☎ 0871 984 6192 📄 020 7515 9178
Coriander Av, East India Dock Rd E14 2AA
web: www.travelodge.co.uk
dir: On A13 at East India Dock Rd

Travelodge offers good quality, good value, budget accommodation. All offer family rooms sleeping up to four (two adults, two children) with en suite bathroom/shower-room, remote-control TV, tea- and coffee-making facilities and comfortable beds. Food options vary. Breakfast is at the on-site Bar Café restaurant (if available) or to take away. See also Hotel Groups pages.

Rooms 232 **S** fr £29; **D** fr £29

E15 STRATFORD

See LONDON plan 1 G4

Express by Holiday Inn London - Stratford

Express
by Holiday Inn

BUDGET HOTEL

☎ 0870 240 5708 & 020 8536 8000 📄 020 8536 8036
196 High St, Stratford E15 2PD
e-mail: reservations@express-holidayinn.com
web: www.hiexpress.com/londonstratfrd
dir: A12, hotel 1.5m on High St towards town centre

A modern hotel ideal for families and business travellers. Fresh and uncomplicated, the spacious rooms include Sky TV, power shower and tea and coffee-making facilities. Continental buffet breakfast is included in the room rate; other meals may be taken at the nearby family pub or restaurant. See also the Hotel Groups pages.

Rooms 114 (62 fmly) (19 smoking) **S** £69-£159; **D** £69-£159 (incl. bkfst)* **Conf** Class 16 Board 24 Thtr 25 Del from £135 to £149

Ibis London Stratford
BUDGET HOTEL

ibis
HOTEL

☎ 020 8536 3700 📄 020 8519 5161
1A Romford Rd, Stratford E15 4LJ
e-mail: h3099@accor.com
web: www.ibishotel.com

Modern, budget hotel offering comfortable accommodation in bright and practical bedrooms. Breakfast is self-service and dinner is available in the restaurant. See also the Hotel Groups pages.

Rooms 108 (15 fmly)

See LONDON plan 1 H3/H4

Crowne Plaza London - Docklands

★★★★ 74% HOTEL

☎ 0870 990 9692 📠 0870 990 9693
Royal Victoria Dock, Western Gateway E16 1AL
e-mail: sales@crowneplazadocklands.co.uk
web: www.crowneplaza.docklands.co.uk
dir: A1020 towards Excel. Follow signs for Excel West. Hotel on left 400mtrs before Excel

Ideally located for the ExCel exhibition centre, Canary Wharf and London City airport, this unique, contemporary hotel overlooking Royal Victoria Dock, offers accommodation suitable for both the leisure and business travellers. Rooms are spacious and equipped with all modern facilities. The hotel houses a busy bar, a contemporary restaurant and health and fitness facilities with an indoor pool, Jacuzzi and sauna.

Rooms 210 (12 fmly) (42 smoking) **Facilities** STV 🖥 supervised Gym Beauty treatments Sauna Steam room Xmas New Year Wi-fi **Conf** Class 140 Board 62 Thtr 275 Del from £225 to £360* **Services** Lift Air con **Parking** 75 **Notes** ⊗ Civ Wed 275

Novotel London ExCel

★★★★ 72% HOTEL

☎ 020 7540 9700 & 0870 850 4560 📠 020 7540 9710
7 Western Gateway, Royal Victoria Docks E16 1AA
e-mail: H3656@accor.com
web: www.novotel.com
dir: M25 junct 30. A13 towards 'City', exit at Canning Town. Follow signs to 'ExCel West'. Hotel adjacent

This hotel is situated adjacent to the ExCel exhibition centre and overlooks the Royal Victoria Dock. Design throughout the hotel is contemporary and stylish. Public rooms include a range of meeting rooms, a modern coffee station, indoor leisure facilities and a smart bar and restaurant, both with a terrace overlooking the dock. Bedrooms feature modern decor, a bathroom with separate bath and shower, and an extensive range of extras.

Rooms 257 (211 fmly) **Facilities** STV FTV Gym Steam room Relaxation room with massage bed Wi-fi **Conf** Class 55 Board 30 Thtr 70 **Services** Lift Air con **Parking** 160 **Notes** Civ Wed 50

Ramada Hotel & Suites London Docklands

 RAMADA

★★★★ 71% HOTEL

☎ 0870 111 8779 & 020 7540 4820 📠 0870 111 8789
Excel 2 Festoon Way, Royal Victoria Dock E16 1RH
e-mail: reservations@ramadadocklands.co.uk
dir: Follow signs to Excel East & London City Airport. Over Connaught Bridge then immediate left at rdbt

This hotel benefits from a stunning waterfront location and is close to the events venue, ExCel, the O2 Arena, Canary Wharf and London City Airport. The accommodation comprises a mix of spacious bedrooms and suites. The relaxed public areas consist of a modern restaurant and informal lounge area. Parking, a fitness room and meeting rooms are available on site.

Rooms 224 (71 fmly) (50 smoking) **Facilities** FTV Gym Xmas Wi-fi **Conf** Class 20 Board 25 Thtr 30 **Services** Lift Air con **Parking** 60 **Notes** Civ Wed 120

Express by Holiday Inn London Royal Docks

BUDGET HOTEL

☎ 020 7540 4040 📠 020 7540 4050
1 Silvertown Way, Silvertown E16 1EA
e-mail: info@exhi-royaldocks.co.uk
web: www.hiexpress.com/londonroyal
dir: From A13 take A1011 towards Silvertown, City Airport & Excel. Hotel on left

A modern hotel ideal for families and business travellers. Fresh and uncomplicated, the spacious rooms include Sky TV, power shower and tea and coffee-making facilities. Continental buffet breakfast is included in the room rate; other meals may be taken at the nearby family pub or restaurant. See also the Hotel Groups pages.

Rooms 136 (48 fmly) **Conf** Class 30 Board 30 Thtr 80

Ibis London ExCel

ibis

BUDGET HOTEL

☎ 020 7055 2300 📠 020 7055 2310
9 Western Gateway, Royal Victoria Docks E16 1AB
e-mail: H3655@accor.com
web: www.ibishotel.com
dir: M25 then A13 to London, City Airport, ExCel East

Modern, budget hotel offering comfortable accommodation in bright and practical bedrooms. Breakfast is self-service and dinner is available in the restaurant See also the Hotel Groups pages.

Rooms 278 (64 fmly)

Travelodge London City Airport

BUDGET HOTEL

☎ 0871 984 6290 📠 020 7474 2671
Hartman Rd, Silvertown E16 2BZ
web: www.travelodge.co.uk
dir: Follow signs for London City Airport

Travelodge offers good quality, good value, budget accommodation. All offer family rooms sleeping up to four (two adults, two children) with en suite bathroom/shower-room, remote-control TV, tea- and coffee-making facilities and comfortable beds. Food options vary. Breakfast is at the on-site Bar Café restaurant (if available) or to take away. See also Hotel Groups pages.

Rooms 157 **S** fr £29; **D** fr £29

Malmaison Charterhouse Square

★★★ 86% ◎◎ HOTEL PLAN 3 G4

☎ 020 7012 3700 📠 020 7012 3702
18-21 Charterhouse Square, Clerkenwell EC1M 6AH
e-mail: london@malmaison.com
web: www.malmaison.com
dir: Exit Barbican Station turn left, take 1st left

Situated in a leafy and peaceful square, Malmaison Charterhouse maintains the same focus on quality service and food as the other hotels in the group. The bedrooms, stylishly decorated in calming tones, have all the expected facilities including power showers, CD players and free internet access. The brasserie and bar at the hotel's centre has a buzzing atmosphere and offers traditional French cuisine.

Rooms 97 (5 GF) **S** £270; **D** £287* **Facilities** STV Gym Wi-fi **Conf** Board 16 Thtr 30 **Services** Lift Air con **Notes** LB

Thistle City Barbican

thistle

★★★ 77% HOTEL PLAN 3 G5

☎ 0871 376 9004 📠 0871 376 9104
Central St, Clerkenwell EC1V 8DS
e-mail: citybarbican@thistle.co.uk
web: www.thistlehotels.com/citybarbican
dir: From Kings Cross E, follow Pentonville Rd, right into Goswell Rd. At lights left into Lever St. Hotel at junct of Lever St & Central St

Situated on the edge of The City, this modern hotel offers a complimentary shuttle bus to Barbican, Liverpool Street and Moorgate tube stations at peak times. Bedrooms are well equipped and include some smart executive and superior rooms; public areas include a bar, a coffee shop and restaurant along with a smart Otium leisure club.

Rooms 463 (166 annexe) (13 fmly) **Facilities** Spa STV FTV 🖥 supervised Gym Sauna Steam room Xmas New Year Wi-fi **Conf** Class 75 Board 35 Thtr 175 Del from £175 to £416* **Services** Lift **Parking** 10 **Notes** LB ⊗

EC1 CITY OF LONDON *continued*

Express by Holiday Inn London City

BUDGET HOTEL PLAN 7 B2

☎ 020 7300 4300 📠 020 7300 4400
275 Old St EC1V 9LN
e-mail: reservations@expressbyholidayinn-london.co.uk
web: www.hiexpress.com/londoncityex
dir: At City Rd rdbt turn left, hotel on left, next to fire station

A modern hotel ideal for families and business travellers. Fresh and uncomplicated, the spacious rooms include Sky TV, power shower and tea and coffee-making facilities. Continental buffet breakfast is included in the room rate; other meals may be taken at the nearby family pub or restaurant. See also the Hotel Groups pages.

Rooms 224 (132 fmly) **Conf** Class 32 Board 32 Thtr 70

Travelodge London City Road

BUDGET HOTEL PLAN 7 B1

☎ 0871 984 6333
1-23 City Rd EC1Y 1AE
web: www.travelodge.co.uk
dir: At junct of City Rd & Tabernacle St, approx 450yds from Old Street (Northern Line) underground station

Travelodge offers good quality, good value, budget accommodation. All offer family rooms sleeping up to four (two adults, two children) with en suite bathroom/shower-room, remote-control TV, tea- and coffee-making facilities and comfortable beds. Food options vary. Breakfast is at the on-site Bar Café restaurant (if available) or to take away. See also Hotel Groups pages.

Rooms 392 **S** fr £29; **D** fr £29

EC3 CHEAPSIDE

Apex City of London

★★★★ 81% @@ HOTEL PLAN 6 C4

☎ 0845 365 0000 & 020 7702 2020 📠 020 7702 2217
No 1 Seething Ln EC3N 4AX
e-mail: london.reservations@apexhotels.co.uk
web: www.apexhotels.co.uk
dir: Opposite Tower of London

Situated close to Tower Bridge, this is one of the city's luxury hotels. Set at the heart of the business district, the Apex is also ideal for leisure travellers. Bedrooms are of a high standard and include walk-in power showers. The gym has the most up-to-date equipment, and there is a sauna room. Dining in Addendum Restaurant is a highlight and a less formal brasserie/bar is also available.

Rooms 179 (5 GF) (6 smoking) **S** £224-£305; **D** £224-£305* **Facilities** STV Gym Xmas Wi-fi **Conf** Class 36 Board 30 Thtr 80 **Services** Lift Air con **Notes** LB @

The Chamberlain

★★★★ 70% HOTEL PLAN 6 D4

☎ 020 7680 1500 📠 020 7702 2500
130-135 Minories EC3N 1NU
e-mail: thechamberlain@fullers.co.uk
web: www.thechamberlainhotel.com
dir: M25 junct 30, A13 W towards London. Follow into Aldgate, left after bus station. Hotel halfway down Minories

This smart hotel is ideally situated for the City, Tower Bridge, plus both Aldgate and Tower Gateway tube stations. Impressive bedrooms are stylish, well-equipped and comfortable, and the modern bathrooms are fitted with TVs to watch while you soak in the bath. Informal day rooms include a popular pub, a lounge and an attractive split-level dining room.

Rooms 64 **S** £95-£230; **D** £125-£230* **Facilities** STV Wi-fi **Conf** Class 20 Board 22 Thtr 50 Del from £150 to £285* **Services** Lift Air con **Notes** LB @ Closed 24-28 Dec

Novotel London Tower Bridge

★★★ 78% HOTEL PLAN 6 C4

☎ 020 7265 6000 & 7265 6026 📠 020 7265 6060
10 Pepys St EC3N 2NR
e-mail: H3107@accor.com
web: www.novotel.com

Located near the Tower of London, this smart hotel is convenient for Docklands, the City, Heathrow and London City airports. Air-conditioned bedrooms are spacious, modern, and offer a great range of facilities. There is a smart bar and restaurant, a small gym, children's play area and extensive meeting and conference facilities.

Rooms 203 (54 fmly) (22 smoking) **Facilities** STV FTV Gym Steam room Sauna Xmas Wi-fi **Conf** Class 56 Board 25 Thtr 100 **Services** Lift Air con

EC4

Crowne Plaza London - The City

★★★★ 77% @@ HOTEL PLAN 3 F2

☎ 0870 4009190 📠 020 7438 8080
19 New Bridge St EC4V 6DB
e-mail: loncy.info@ihg.com
web: www.crowneplaza.co.uk
dir: Opposite Blackfriars station

This hotel has a 1919 façade, but is modern and bright inside; it is situated close to the north bank of the River Thames and also to Blackfriar's station. Bedrooms are modern and well equipped. There is a small gym and valet parking is available. Bookings for dinner are required.

Rooms 203 (60 fmly) (8 smoking) **Facilities** STV Gym Sauna 🎵 Xmas New Year Wi-fi **Conf** Class 100 Board 50 Thtr 160 Del from £320 to £480* **Services** Lift Air con **Notes** @ Civ Wed 150

N3 FINCHLEY, GOLDERS GREEN

Express by Holiday Inn London Golders Green North

BUDGET HOTEL PLAN 1 D5

☎ 0870 770 4059 📠 020 7433 6667
58 Regents Park Rd N3 3JN
web: www.hiexpress.co.uk

A modern hotel ideal for families and business travellers. Fresh and uncomplicated, the spacious rooms include Sky TV, power shower and tea and coffee-making facilities. Continental buffet breakfast is included in the room rate; other meals may be taken at the nearby family pub or restaurant. See also the Hotel Groups pages.

Rooms 83

N14 SOUTHGATE — Map 6 TQ29

Innkeeper's Lodge Southgate

BUDGET HOTEL

☎ 0845 112 6123 📠 0845 112 6180
22 The Green, Southgate N14 6EN
web: www.innkeeperslodge.com/southgate
dir: M25 junct 24, A111, 3m to rdbt with A1004. Right into High Street. Lodge at next rdbt

Innkeeper's Lodge represents an exciting, high value concept within the budget hotel market. Comfortable bedrooms provide excellent facilities that include satellite TV and modem points. Options include family rooms; and for the corporate guest, cutting edge IT includes Wi-fi access. Food is served all day in the adjacent Country Pub. The extensive continental breakfast is complimentary. See also the Hotel Groups pages.

Rooms 19 (5 fmly) **Conf** Thtr 30

See LONDON SECTION plan 1 E4

INSPECTORS' CHOICE

The Landmark London
★★★★★ ◉◉ HOTEL PLAN 2 F4

☎ 020 7631 8000 ▤ 020 7631 8080
222 Marylebone Rd NW1 6JQ
e-mail: reservations@thelandmark.co.uk
web: www.landmarklondon.co.uk
dir: Adjacent to Marylebone Station

Once one of the last truly grand railway hotels, The Landmark boasts a number of stunning features, the most spectacular being the naturally lit central atrium forming the focal point. When it comes to eating and drinking there are a number of choices, including the Cellars bar for cocktails and upmarket bar meals, or the Mirror Bar. The Winter Garden restaurant has the centre stage in the atrium and is a great place to watch the world go by. The air-conditioned bedrooms are luxurious and have large, stylish bathrooms.

Rooms 299 (60 fmly) (50 smoking) **Facilities** Spa STV ◔ Gym Beauty treatments & massages ♫ Xmas Wi-fi **Conf** Class 224 Board 50 Thtr 380 **Services** Lift Air con **Parking** 80 **Notes** LB ⊗ Civ Wed 300

Dorset Square Hotel
★★★★ 80% ◉ TOWN HOUSE HOTEL PLAN 2 F4

☎ 020 7723 7874 ▤ 020 7724 3328
39-40 Dorset Square NW1 6QN
e-mail: reservations@dorsetsquare.co.uk
dir: M40 onto A40 (Euston Rd). Left lane off flyover. Turn left onto Gloucester Place. Hotel 1st left

This delightfully restored Regency townhouse enjoys a prime location close to Hyde Park, Regents Park and all of central London's attractions. Stylish bedrooms are individually themed and extremely well equipped for both business and leisure guests. Elegant public areas include the popular Potting Shed Restaurant and Bar as well as an inviting sumptuous lounge. Service is personalised and attentive.

Rooms 37 (2 fmly) (4 GF) **S** £120-£150; **D** £140-£280* **Facilities** STV ♫ Xmas New Year Wi-fi **Conf** Class 20 Board 10 Thtr 12 **Services** Lift Air con **Notes** ⊗ RS Sat & Sun lunch, Sun dinner & BH's Civ Wed 40

Meliá White House
★★★★ 80% HOTEL PLAN 3 A5

☎ 020 7391 3000 ▤ 020 7388 0091
Albany St, Regents Park NW1 3UP
e-mail: melia.white.house@solmelia.com
dir: Opposite Gt Portland St underground station

Owned by the Spanish Sol company, this impressive art deco property is located opposite Great Portland Street tube station. Spacious public areas offer a high degree of comfort and include an elegant cocktail bar, a fine dining restaurant and a more informal brasserie. Stylish

bedrooms come in a variety of sizes, but all offer high levels of comfort and are thoughtfully equipped.

Rooms 581 (7 fmly) (61 smoking) **S** £80-£280; **D** £80-£280 **Facilities** STV FTV Gym ♫ Xmas New Year Wi-fi **Conf** Class 80 Board 60 Thtr 140 **Services** Lift Air con **Parking** 7 **Notes** ⊗ Civ Wed 140

Thistle Euston   thistle
★★★★ 75% HOTEL PLAN 3 B6

☎ 0871 376 9017 ▤ 0871 376 9117
Cardington St NW1 2LP
e-mail: euston@thistle.co.uk
web: www.thistlehotels.com/euston
dir: From M40 continue to end of A40, follow Marylebone Rd, take Euston Rd to Melton St into Cardington St.

This smart, modern hotel is ideally located a short walk from Euston Station. Spacious public areas include a spacious bar/lounge, extensive meeting and function rooms and a bright basement restaurant. Bedrooms include a large number of deluxe and executive rooms that are spacious, comfortable and well equipped. The hotel also boasts limited on-site parking.

Rooms 362 (18 fmly) (42 GF) **S** £89-£200; **D** £99-£210* **Facilities** STV FTV Wi-fi **Conf** Class 45 Board 35 Thtr 90 Del from £190 to £330* **Services** Lift Air con **Parking** 21 **Notes** LB ⊗

Novotel London St Pancras
★★★★ 73% ◉ HOTEL PLAN 3 C5

☎ 020 7666 9000 & 7666 9010 ▤ 020 7766 9001
100-110 Euston Rd NW1 2AJ
e-mail: H5309@accor.com
web: www.novotel.com
dir: Between St Pancras & Euston stations

This hotel enjoys a central location adjacent to the British Library and close to some of London's main transport hubs. The style is modern and contemporary throughout. Bedrooms vary in size but are all very well equipped and many have views over the city. Open-plan public areas include a leisure suite and extensive conference facilities including the Shaw Theatre.

Rooms 312 (29 fmly) (25 smoking) **S** £89-£280; **D** £89-£280* **Facilities** Gym Steam room Sauna Xmas Wi-fi **Conf** Class 220 Board 80 Thtr 446 Del from £202 to £282* **Services** Lift Air con **Notes** LB ⊗

NW1 REGENT'S PARK *continued*

Holiday Inn London Camden Lock

★★★★ 68% HOTEL

☎ 020 7485 4343 📠 020 7485 4344
30 Jamestown Rd, Camden Lock NW1 7BY
e-mail: info@holidayinncamden.co.uk
web: www.holidayinn.co.uk
dir: From Camden Town tube station take left fork. Jamestown Rd 2nd on left

In the heart of Camden this smart modern hotel has rooms which overlook the Camden Lock. Bedrooms are spacious and well equipped, whilst the light and airy, first-floor restaurant offers innovative Mediterranean dishes. A small but well-equipped gym is located on the ground floor, as is a good selection of meeting rooms.

Rooms 130 (40 fmly) (35 smoking) **Facilities** STV Gym Xmas New Year Wi-fi **Conf** Class 60 Board 36 Thtr 180 Del from £182 to £300* **Services** Lift Air con **Notes** ✪ Civ Wed 150

Ibis London Euston St Pancras

BUDGET HOTEL PLAN 3 B5

☎ 020 7388 7777 📠 020 7388 0001
3 Cardington St NW1 2LW
e-mail: H0921@accor-hotels.com
web: www.ibishotel.com
dir: From Euston Rd or station, right to Melton St leading to Cardington St

Modern, budget hotel offering comfortable accommodation in bright and practical bedrooms. Breakfast is self-service and dinner is available in the restaurant. See also the Hotel Groups pages.

Rooms 380 **S** £75-£130; **D** £75-£130* **Conf** Class 40 Board 40 Thtr 100

Travelodge London Euston

BUDGET HOTEL PLAN 3 B5

☎ 0871 984 6332 📠 020 7383 7881
1-11 Grafton Way NW1 1DJ
dir: Adjacent to Euston rail station

Travelodge offers good quality, good value, budget accommodation. All offer family rooms sleeping up to four (two adults, two children) with en suite bathroom/shower-room, remote-control TV, tea- and coffee-making facilities and comfortable beds. Food options vary. Breakfast is at the on-site Bar Café restaurant (if available) or to take away. See also the Hotel Groups pages.

Rooms 150 **S** fr £29; **D** fr £29

Travelodge London Marylebone

BUDGET HOTEL PLAN 2 E4

☎ 0871 984 6311 & 020 7723 8569
Harewood Row NW1 6SE
web: www.travelodge.co.uk
dir: M40/A40, over Paddington flyover onto Marylebone Rd, left into Lison Green, 1st left into Harewood Row

Rooms 92 **S** fr £29; **D** fr £29

NW2 BRENT CROSS & CRICKLEWOOD

See LONDON plan 1 D5

Crown Moran

★★★★ 76% HOTEL

☎ 020 8452 4175 📠 020 8452 0952
142-152 Cricklewood Broadway, Cricklewood NW2 3ED
e-mail: crownres@moranhotels.com
web: www.crownmoranhotel.co.uk
dir: M1 junct 1 follow signs onto North Circular (W) A406. Junct with A5 (Staples Corner). At rdbt take 1st exit onto A5 to Cricklewood

This striking hotel is connected by an impressive glass atrium to the popular Crown Pub. Features include excellent function and conference facilities, a leisure club, a choice of stylish lounges and bars and a contemporary restaurant. The air-conditioned bedrooms are appointed to a high standard and include a number of trendy suites.

Rooms 116 (8 fmly) (20 GF) **S** £99-£170; **D** £99-£190 (incl. bkfst) **Facilities** Gym ♫ New Year Wi-fi **Conf** Class 200 Board 80 Thtr 300 Del from £170 to £190 **Services** Lift Air con **Parking** 41 **Notes** LB ✪ Closed 24-26 Dec Civ Wed 300

Holiday Inn London - Brent Cross

★★★ 77% HOTEL PLAN 1 D5

☎ 0870 400 9112 & 020 8967 6359 📠 020 8967 6372
Tilling Rd, Brent Cross NW2 1LP
web: www.holidayinn.co.uk
dir: At M1 junct 1. At rdbt after bridge left into Tilling Rd

Ideally located beside the M1 on the A406 North Circular, just a few minutes' walk from Brent Cross Shopping Centre and four miles from Wembley Stadium. The hotel offers well-appointed bedrooms with air conditioning and

high-speed internet access; Wi-fi is available in the public areas. Conference rooms and a contemporary restaurant are available, plus there is ample parking.

Rooms 154 (87 fmly) (16 smoking) **Facilities** STV New Year Wi-fi **Conf** Class 40 Board 32 Thtr 80 **Services** Lift Air con **Parking** 150 **Notes** ✪

NW3 HAMPSTEAD AND SWISS COTTAGE

See LONDON plan 1 E4/E5

London Marriott Hotel Regents Park

★★★★ 75% HOTEL

☎ 0870 400 7240 📠 0870 400 7340
128 King Henry's Rd NW3 3ST
e-mail: london.regional.reservations@marriott.com
web: www.londonmarriottregentspark.co.uk
dir: 200yds off Finchley Rd on A41

Situated in a quieter part of town and close to the tube station, this hotel offers guests comfortably appointed, air-conditioned accommodation; all rooms boast balconies and are particularly well equipped to meet the needs of today's business traveller. The open-plan ground floor is spacious and airy and includes a well-equipped leisure centre with indoor pool. Secure parking is a bonus.

Rooms 304 (148 fmly) **S** £99-£195; **D** £99-£205 **Facilities** STV ⊗ supervised Gym Hair & Beauty salon Steam room Wi-fi **Conf** Class 150 Board 120 Thtr 300 Del from £174 to £325 **Services** Lift Air con **Parking** 110 **Notes** ✪ Civ Wed 300

Express by Holiday Inn London - Swiss Cottage

BUDGET HOTEL

☎ 020 7433 6666 📠 020 7433 6667
152-156 Finchley Rd NW3 5HD
e-mail: reservations@expressbyholidayinnsc.com
web: www.hiexpress.com/lonswisscott

A modern hotel ideal for families and business travellers. Fresh and uncomplicated, the spacious rooms include Sky TV, power shower and tea and coffee-making facilities. Continental buffet breakfast is included in the room rate; other meals may be taken at the nearby family pub or restaurant. See also the Hotel Groups pages.

Rooms 79 **Conf** Class 12 Board 12 Thtr 25

NW4 HENDON

See LONDON plan 1 D5

Hendon Hall

★★★★ 75% ⊕ HOTEL

☎ 020 8203 3341 📠 020 8457 2502
Ashley Ln, Hendon NW4 1HF
e-mail: info@hendonhall.com
dir: M1 junct 2 follow A406. Right at lights onto Parson St, right onto Ashley Ln. Hotel on right

This smart property was mentioned in the Domesday Book and was originally known as Hendon Manor. Now it is a stylish hotel boasting smart, well-equipped, comfortable bedrooms with luxury toiletries, free Wi-fi and well-appointed en suites. Public areas include meeting and conference facilities, a contemporary cocktail bar and a richly decorated restaurant that opens onto a garden terrace. Staff are friendly and attentive.

Rooms 57 **S** £85-£95; **D** £105-£165 (incl. bkfst) **Facilities** Xmas New Year Wi-fi **Conf** Class 130 Board 76 Thtr 350 Del from £165 to £205 **Services** Lift Air con **Parking** 70 **Notes** LB ⊗ Civ Wed 120

NW6 MAIDA VALE

See LONDON plan 1 D6

London Marriott Maida Vale

★★★★ 77% HOTEL PLAN 2 B6

☎ 020 7543 6000 📠 020 7543 2100
Plaza Pde, Maida Vale NW6 5RP
e-mail: reservations.london.england.maidavale@marriotthotels.com
web: www.londonmarriottmaidavale.co.uk
dir: From M1 take A5 S'bound for 3m. Hotel on left. From Marble Arch take A5 N'bound. Hotel on right

This smart, modern hotel is conveniently located just north of central London. Air-conditioned bedrooms are tastefully decorated and provide a range of extras. The hotel also boasts extensive function facilities as well as a smart indoor leisure centre which has a swimming pool, gym and health and beauty salon.

Rooms 237 (40 fmly) (10 smoking) **Facilities** STV ⊗ Gym Hair & beauty salon including treatment rooms Exercise studio & classes Xmas Wi-fi **Conf** Class 70 Board 30 Thtr 200 **Services** Lift Air con **Parking** 28 **Notes** ⊗ Civ Wed 100

NW10 WILLESDEN

See LONDON plan 1 D4

Travelodge Wembley

BUDGET HOTEL

☎ 020 8963 9143 📠 020 8963 1754
North Circular Rd NW10 7UG
web: www.travelodge.co.uk
dir: A40/A406 N, keep left, 1st slip road on left

Travelodge offers good quality, good value, budget accommodation. All offer family rooms sleeping up to four (two adults, two children) with en suite bathroom/shower-room, remote-control TV, tea- and coffee-making facilities and comfortable beds. Food options vary. Breakfast is at the on-site Bar Café restaurant (if available) or to take away. See also Hotel Groups pages.

Rooms 176 (19 fmly) **S** fr £29; **D** fr £29 **Conf** Class 20 Board 28 Thtr 50

SE1 SOUTHWARK AND WATERLOO

London Marriott Hotel County Hall

★★★★★ 88% ⊕ HOTEL PLAN 5 D5

☎ 020 7928 5200 📠 020 7928 5300
Westminster Bridge Rd, County Hall SE1 7PB
e-mail: sales.countyhall@marriott.com
web: www.londonmarriottcountyhall.co.uk
dir: On Thames South Bank, between Westminster Bridge & London Eye

This impressive building, appointed to a very high standard, enjoys an enviable position on the south bank of the Thames, adjacent to the London Eye. Public areas have a traditional elegance and the crescent-shaped restaurant offers fine views of Westminster. All bedrooms are smartly laid out and thoughtfully equipped with the business traveller in mind.

Rooms 200 (58 fmly) **S** fr £165; **D** fr £165 **Facilities** Spa STV ⊗ Gym Sauna Steam room Pilates Dance studio 🎵 Xmas New Year Wi-fi **Conf** Class 40 Board 30 Thtr 80 Del from £270 **Services** Lift Air con **Parking** 70 **Notes** LB ⊗ Civ Wed 80

Plaza on the River - Club & Residence

★★★★★ 83% TOWN HOUSE HOTEL PLAN 5 D2

☎ 020 7769 2525 📠 020 7769 2524
18 Albert Embankment SE1 7TJ
e-mail: jjacobsen@plazaontheriver.co.uk
dir: From Houses of Parliament turn onto Millbank, at rdbt left onto Lambeth Bridge. At rdbt 3rd exit onto Albert Embankment

This is a superb modern townhouse overlooking London from the south bank of the Thames, with outstanding views of the capital's landmarks. The bedrooms are large and many are full suites with state-of-the-art technology and kitchen facilities; all are decorated in an elegant modern style. Service includes a full range of in-room dining options; additionally, the bar and restaurant in the adjacent Park Plaza are available to guests.

Rooms 65 **S** £136.85-£316.25; **D** £136.85-£316.25* **Facilities** STV FTV Gym Xmas New Year Wi-fi **Conf** Thtr 650 **Services** Lift Air con **Parking** 69 **Notes** Civ Wed 600

Park Plaza County Hall

★★★★ 79% HOTEL PLAN 5 E5

☎ 020 7021 1800 📠 020 7021 1801
1 Addington St SE1 7RY
e-mail: ppchsales@pphe.com
web: www.parkplazacountyhall.com
dir: From Houses of Parliament cross Westminster Bridge (A302). At rdbt turn left. 1st right into Addington St. Hotel on left

Located just south of Westminster Bridge near Waterloo international rail station, this contemporary design-led, air-conditioned establishment features studios and suites, most with kitchenettes and seating areas with a flat-screen TV. There are six meeting rooms, an executive lounge, a restaurant and bar plus a fully-equipped gym with sauna and steam room. Wi-fi is available.

Rooms 398 (303 fmly) **Facilities** STV Gym Sauna Steam room Beauty therapy room Xmas New Year Wi-fi **Conf** Class 60 Board 40 Thtr 100 **Services** Lift Air con **Parking** 3 **Notes** ⊗

SE1 SOUTHWARK AND WATERLOO *continued*

Riverbank Park Plaza

★★★★ 77% ◉ HOTEL PLAN 5 D3

☎ 020 7958 8000 📄 020 7769 2400
Albert Embankment SE1 7SP
e-mail: rppres@pphe.com
web: www.riverbankparkplaza.com
dir: From Houses of Parliament turn onto Millbank, at rdbt left onto Lambeth Bridge. At rdbt take 3rd exit onto Albert Embankment

This hotel features eye-catching, contemporary design coupled with a host of up-to-date facilities and a high level of comfort. Facilities include Wi-fi, high tech conference rooms and a gym. Parking is available. The hotel also has its own pier and offers a river taxi service to the City and Canary Wharf.

Rooms 394 **S** £79.35-£228.85; **D** £79.35-£228.85*
Facilities Gym ♫ Wi-fi **Conf** Class 405 Board 40 Thtr 530
Services Lift Air con **Parking** 124 **Notes** ⊗ Civ Wed 150

London Bridge Hotel

★★★★ 77% HOTEL PLAN 6 B2

☎ 020 7855 2200 📄 020 7855 2233
8-18 London Bridge St SE1 9SG
e-mail: sales@londonbridgehotel.com
web: www.londonbridgehotel.com
dir: Access through London Bridge Station (bus/taxi yard), into London Bridge St (one-way). Hotel on left, 50yds from station

This elegant, independently owned hotel enjoys a prime location on the edge of the city, adjacent to London Bridge station. Smartly appointed, well-equipped bedrooms include a number of spacious deluxe rooms and suites. Compact yet sophisticated public areas

include a selection of meeting rooms and a well-equipped gym. The eating options are Georgetown for Malaysian cuisine, Londinium offering modern British food, and the Borough Bar with an all-day menu. Free Wi-fi is available.

London Bridge Hotel

Rooms 138 (12 fmly) (10 smoking) **Facilities** STV FTV Gym Wi-fi **Conf** Class 36 Board 36 Thtr 80 **Services** Lift Air con **Notes** ⊗

Mercure London City Bankside

★★★★ 73% HOTEL PLAN 5 G5

☎ 020 7902 0800 📄 020 7902 0810
71-79 Southwark St SE1 0JA
e-mail: H2814@accor.com
web: www.mercure-uk.com
dir: A200 to London Bridge. Left into Southwark St.

This smart, contemporary hotel forms part of the rejuvenation of the South Bank. With the City of London just over the river and a number of tourist attractions within easy reach, the hotel is well located for business and leisure visitors alike. Facilities include spacious air-cooled bedrooms, a modern bar and the stylish Loft Restaurant.

Rooms 144 (15 fmly) (5 GF) (6 smoking) **S** £109-£255;
D £119-£295 (incl. bkfst & dinner)* **Facilities** STV Gym ♫ Wi-fi **Conf** Class 40 Board 30 Thtr 60 **Services** Lift Air con **Parking** 6 **Notes** LB

Novotel London City South

★★★★ 73% HOTEL PLAN 5 H5

☎ 020 7089 0400 📄 020 7089 0410
Southwark Bridge Rd SE1 9HH
e-mail: H3269@accor.com
web: www.novotel.com
dir: At junct at Thrale St, off Southwark St

Conveniently located for both business and leisure guests, with The City just across the Thames; other major attractions are also easily accessible. The hotel is contemporary in design with smart, modern bedrooms and spacious public rooms. There is a gym, sauna and steam room on the 6th floor, and limited parking is available at the rear of the hotel.

Rooms 182 (139 fmly) (9 smoking) **S** £250-£340;
D £270-£340 **Facilities** STV FTV Gym Steam room Sauna Wi-fi **Conf** Class 40 Board 35 Thtr 100 **Services** Lift Air con **Parking** 80

Bermondsey Square Hotel

★★★ 80% HOTEL PLAN 6 C1

☎ 0870 111 2525 📄 0870 111 2526
Bermondsey Square, Tower Bridge Rd, Southward SE1 3UN
e-mail: gm@bermondseysquarehotel.co.uk
dir: From London Bridge Station exit towards Guys Hospital, left into St Thomas St, 200mtrs then right into Bermondsey St, 400mtrs cross Abbey St into Bermondsey Square

This establishment offers a perfect haven for a variety of visitors including local residents, leisure and business guests. Alfie's provides a buzzing environment and a great range of freshly prepared food. A members and residents' club is available on the first floor providing a more exclusive area in which to relax and unwind. Accommodation is extremely stylish and comfortable with a range of individually designed, luxurious, rooftop rooms that have stunning views of London. Health and beauty treatments are available.

Rooms 79 (10 fmly) **S** £99-£179; **D** £99-£299*
Facilities Spa STV FTV Access to local gym Xmas New Year Wi-fi **Conf** Class 48 Board 40 Thtr 77 **Services** Lift Air con **Notes** LB Civ Wed 80

Novotel London Waterloo

★★★ 79% HOTEL PLAN 5 D3

☎ 020 7793 1010 📄 020 7793 0202
113 Lambeth Rd SE1 7LS
e-mail: h1785@accor.com
web: www.novotel.com
dir: Opposite Houses of Parliament on S bank of River Thames, off Lambeth Bridge, opposite Lambeth Palace

This hotel has an excellent location with Lambeth Palace, the Houses of Parliament and Waterloo Station all within a short walk. Bedrooms are spacious and air conditioned; a number of rooms have been designed for less able guests. The open-plan public areas include the Garden Brasserie, the Flag and Whistle Pub and a children's play area.

Rooms 187 (80 fmly) (10 smoking) **S** £89-£210; **D** £89-£230* **Facilities** STV Gym Steam room Fitness room Wi-fi **Conf** Class 24 Board 24 Thtr 40 **Services** Lift Parking 40 **Notes** LB

Days Hotel London Waterloo

BUDGET HOTEL PLAN 5 E3

☎ 020 7922 1331 📄 020 7922 1441
54 Kennington Rd SE1 7BJ
e-mail: waterloores@khl.uk.com
web: www.daysinn.com
dir: On corner of Kennington Rd & Lambeth Rd. Opposite Imperial War Museum

This modern building offers accommodation in smart, spacious and well-equipped bedrooms, suitable for families and business travellers, and all with en suite bathrooms. Continental breakfast is available and other refreshments may be taken at the nearby family restaurant. See also the Hotel Groups pages.

Rooms 162 (15 fmly) (13 GF) **S** £79-£149; **D** £79-£149

Express by Holiday Inn London - Southwark

BUDGET HOTEL PLAN 5 F6

☎ 020 7401 2525 📄 020 7401 3322
103-109 Southwark St SE1 0JQ
e-mail: stay@expresssouthwark.co.uk
web: www.hiexpress.com/lon-southwark
dir: A20 onto A2 to city centre towards Elephant & Castle. Right before Blackfriars Bridge at 1st large lights junct

A modern hotel ideal for families and business travellers. Fresh and uncomplicated, the spacious rooms include Sky TV, power shower and tea and coffee-making facilities. Continental buffet breakfast is included in the room rate; other meals may be taken at the nearby family pub or restaurant. See also the Hotel Groups pages.

Rooms 88 (10 fmly) **Conf** Board 12

Travelodge London Southwark

BUDGET HOTEL PLAN 5 G5

☎ 0871 984 6352 📄 020 7261 9644
202-206 Union St SE1 0LH
dir: Near Southwark tube station

Travelodge offers good quality, good value, budget accommodation. All offer family rooms sleeping up to four (two adults, two children) with en suite bathroom/shower-room, remote-control TV, tea- and coffee-making facilities and comfortable beds. Food options vary. Breakfast is at the on-site Bar Café restaurant (if available) or to take away. See also the Hotel Groups pages.

Rooms 202 **S** fr £29; **D** fr £29

SE10 GREENWICH

See also LONDON plan 1 G3

Novotel London Greenwich

★★★★ 72% HOTEL PLAN 8 A3

☎ 020 8312 6800 📄 020 8312 6810
173-185 Greenwich High Rd SE10 8JA
e-mail: H3476@accor.com
web: www.novotel.com
dir: Adjacent to Greenwich Station

This purpose-built hotel is conveniently located for rail and DLR stations, as well as major attractions such as the Royal Maritime Museum and the Royal Observatory. Air-conditioned bedrooms are spacious and equipped with a host of extras, and public areas include a small gym, contemporary lounge bar and restaurant.

Rooms 151 (34 fmly) **Facilities** STV FTV Gym Steam room Wi-fi **Conf** Class 40 Board 32 Thtr 92 **Services** Lift Air con Parking 30 **Notes** LB

Express by Holiday Inn London - Greenwich

BUDGET HOTEL

☎ 020 8269 5000 📄 020 8269 5069
162 Bugsby Park SE10 0DQ
e-mail: greenwich@expressholidayinn.co.uk
web: www.hiexpress.com/greenwicha102m

A modern hotel ideal for families and business travellers. Fresh and uncomplicated, the spacious rooms include Sky TV, power shower and tea and coffee-making facilities. Continental buffet breakfast is included in the room rate; other meals may be taken at the nearby family pub or restaurant. See also the Hotel Groups pages.

Rooms 162 **Conf** Class 55 Board 35 Thtr 80

Ibis London Greenwich

BUDGET HOTEL PLAN 8 A4

☎ 020 8305 1177 📄 020 8858 7139
30 Stockwell St, Greenwich SE10 9JN
e-mail: H0975@accor.com
web: www.ibishotel.com
dir: From Waterloo Bridge, Elephant & Castle, A2 to Greenwich

Modern, budget hotel offering comfortable accommodation in bright and practical bedrooms. Breakfast is self-service and dinner is available in the restaurant. See also the Hotel Groups pages.

Rooms 82 (10 fmly) (12 GF)

SW1 WESTMINSTER

INSPECTORS' CHOICE

The Berkeley

★★★★★ 😊😊😊😊😊
HOTEL PLAN 4 G4

MAYBOURNE HOTEL GROUP

☎ 020 7235 6000 📄 020 7235 4330
Wilton Place, Knightsbridge SW1X 7RL
e-mail: info@the-berkeley.co.uk
dir: 300mtrs from Hyde Park Corner along Knightsbridge

This stylish hotel, just off Knightsbridge, boasts an excellent range of bedrooms; each furnished with care and a host of thoughtful extras. Newer rooms feature trendy, spacious glass and marble bathrooms and some of the private suites have their own roof terrace. The striking Blue Bar enhances the reception rooms, all adorned with magnificent flower arrangements. The health spa offers a range of treatment rooms and includes a stunning open-air, roof-top pool. Two renowned, award-winning restaurants provide a complete contrast of styles - a modern upscale New York style café, the Boxwood with 2 AA Rosettes, and the stunning French cuisine at Marcus Wareing at The Berkeley with 5 AA Rosettes. Marcus Wareing is the winner of the AA Chefs' Chef Award for 2010.

Rooms 214 **Facilities** Spa STV FTV 🏊 supervised Gym Beauty/therapy treatments Wi-fi **Conf** Class 80 Board 52 Thtr 250 **Services** Lift Air con **Parking** 50 **Notes** ⊗ Civ Wed 160

SW1 WESTMINSTER *continued*

Mandarin Oriental Hyde Park, London

★★★★★ @@@@ HOTEL PLAN 4 F4

☎ 020 7235 2000 📠 020 7235 2001
66 Knightsbridge SW1X 7LA
e-mail: molon-reservations@mohg.com
web: www.mandarinoriental.com/london
dir: With Harrods on right, hotel 0.5m on left opp
Harvey Nichols

Situated in fashionable Knightsbridge and overlooking
Hyde Park, this iconic venue is a popular destination
for highfliers, celebrities and the young and
fashionable. Bedrooms, many with park views, are
appointed to the highest standards with luxurious
features such as the finest Irish linen and goose down
pillows. Guests have a choice of dining options, from
the brasserie-style, all-day dining Park Restaurant to
the chic, award-winning Foliage Restaurant. The
Mandarin Bar also serves light snacks and cocktails.
The stylish spa is a destination in its own right and
offers a range of innovative treatments.

Rooms 198 **Facilities** Spa STV Gym Sanarium Steam
room Vitality pool Zen colour therapy areas 🎵 Xmas
New Year Wi-fi **Conf** Class 120 Board 60 Thtr 250
Del from £75 to £95* **Services** Lift Air con **Notes** ⊗
Civ Wed 250

The Halkin Hotel

★★★★★ @@@ TOWN HOUSE HOTEL PLAN 4 G4

☎ 020 7333 1000 📠 020 7333 1100
Halkin St, Belgravia SW1X 7DJ
e-mail: res@halkin.como.bz
dir: Between Belgrave Sq & Grosvenor Place. Via
Chapel St into Headfort Place, left into Halkin St

This smart, contemporary hotel has an enviable and
peaceful position just a short stroll from both Hyde
Park and the designer shops of Knightsbridge. Service
is attentive, friendly and very personalised. The stylish
bedrooms and suites are equipped to the highest
standard with marble bathrooms and every conceivable
extra. Each floor is discreetly designed following the
themes of earth, wind, fire, water and the universe.
Public areas include an airy bar lounge and the
famous, award-winning Thai restaurant, Nahm.

Rooms 41 **S** £250-£1500; **D** £250-£1500 **Facilities** STV
FTV Gym Complimentary use of gym & spa at sister
hotel Wi-fi **Conf** Class 20 Board 26 Thtr 40
Services Lift Air con **Notes** LB ⊗

The Goring

★★★★★ @@ HOTEL PLAN 4 H3

☎ 020 7396 9000 📠 020 7834 4393
Beeston Place, Grosvenor Gardens SW1W 0JW
e-mail: reception@thegoring.com
web: www.thegoring.com
dir: Off Lower Grosvenor Place, just prior to Royal Mews

This icon of British hospitality for over 100 years is
centrally located and within walking distance of the
Royal Parks and principal shopping areas. Spacious
bedrooms and suites, some contemporary in style with
state-of-the-art technology and others more classically
furnished; all boast high levels of comfort and quality.
Elegant day rooms include the Garden Bar and the
drawing room, both popular for afternoon tea and
cocktails. The stylish airy restaurant offers a popular
menu of contemporary British cuisine and delightful
private dining rooms are available. Guests will
experience a personalised service from the attentive
and friendly team.

Rooms 71 (9 fmly) **S** £228.85-£379.50;
D £320.85-£448.50* **Facilities** STV Free membership of
nearby health club 🎵 Xmas New Year Wi-fi
Conf Class 30 Board 25 Thtr 50 **Services** Lift Air con
Parking 16 **Notes** LB ⊗ Civ Wed 50

Jumeirah Carlton Tower
★★★★★ @@ HOTEL PLAN 4 F4

☎ 020 7235 1234   🖷 020 7235 9129
Cadogan Place SW1X 9PY
e-mail: jctinfo@jumeirah.com
web: www.jumeirahcarltontower.com
dir: A4 towards Knightsbridge, right onto Sloane St.
Hotel on left before Cadogan Place

This impressive hotel enjoys an enviable position in the heart of Knightsbridge, overlooking Cadogan Gardens. The stunningly designed bedrooms, including a number of suites, vary in size and style and many have wonderful city views. Leisure facilities include a glass-roofed swimming pool, a well-equipped gym and a number of treatment rooms. The renowned Rib Room provides excellent dining, together with the other options of the Club Room, the Chinoiserie and the Champagne Lounge.

Rooms 220 (59 fmly) (70 smoking) **S** £199-£7000;
D £199-£7000* **Facilities** Spa STV FTV ☜ supervised
♨ Gym Golf simulator (50 courses) ♬ Xmas New Year
Wi-fi **Conf** Class 250 Board 30 Thtr 400 **Services** Lift
Air con **Parking** 170 **Notes** ⊗ Civ Wed 320

The Stafford
★★★★★ @@ HOTEL PLAN 5 A5

☎ 020 7493 0111   🖷 020 7493 7121
16-18 St James's Place SW1A 1NJ
e-mail: information@thestaffordhotel.co.uk
web: www.thestaffordhotel.co.uk
dir: Off Pall Mall into St James's St. 2nd left into St
James's Place

Tucked away in a quiet corner of St James's, this classically styled boutique hotel retains an air of understated luxury. The American Bar is a fabulous venue in its own right, festooned with an eccentric array of celebrity photos, caps and ties. Afternoon tea is a long established tradition here. From the pristine, tastefully decorated and air-conditioned bedrooms, to the highly professional, yet friendly service, this exclusive hotel maintains the highest standards. 26 stunning mews suites are available.

Rooms 105 (26 annexe) (8 GF) (2 smoking)
Facilities STV Gym Use of fitness club nearby Xmas
Wi-fi **Conf** Class 20 Board 24 Thtr 60 **Services** Lift
Air con **Notes** ⊗ Civ Wed 44

No 41
★★★★★

Red Carnation HOTELS

TOWN HOUSE HOTEL PLAN 5 A4

☎ 020 7300 0041   🖷 020 7300 0141
41 Buckingham Palace Rd SW1W 0PS
e-mail: book41@rchmail.com
web: www.41hotel.com
dir: Opp Buckingham Palace Mews entrance

Small, intimate and very private, this stunning town house is located opposite the Royal Mews. Decorated in stylish black and white, bedrooms successfully combine comfort with state-of-the-art technology. The large lounge is the focal point; food and drinks are available as are magazines and newspapers from around the world plus internet access. Attentive personal service and a host of thoughtful extra touches make No 41 really special.

Rooms 30 (2 fmly) (1 smoking) **S** £345; **D** £345*
Facilities STV Local health club Beauty treatments
Xmas New Year Wi-fi **Conf** Board 10 **Services** Lift
Air con

SW1 WESTMINSTER *continued*

51 Buckingham Gate, Taj Suites and Residences

★★★★★ 89% TOWN HOUSE HOTEL PLAN 5 B4

☎ 020 7769 7766 📠 020 7828 5909
SW1E 6AF
e-mail: info@51-buckinghamgate.co.uk
dir: From Buckingham Palace onto Buckingham Gate, 100mtrs, hotel on right

This all-suites hotel is a favourite with those who desire a quiet, sophisticated environment. Each of the suites has its own butler on hand plus a kitchen, and most have large lounge areas furnished in a contemporary style with modern accessories. There are one, two, three and four bedroom suites to choose from. The spa specialises in Sodashi treatments and also has a well-equipped gym.

Rooms 86 (86 fmly) (4 GF) **D** £235-£385* **Facilities** Spa STV Gym Sauna Steam room Solarium Xmas New Year Wi-fi **Conf** Class 90 Board 60 Thtr 180 Del from £225 to £300* **Services** Lift Air con **Notes** LB ⊗ Civ Wed 150

Sheraton Park Tower

★★★★★ 88% ◉◉◉ HOTEL PLAN 4 F4

☎ 020 7235 8050 📠 020 7235 8231
101 Knightsbridge SW1X 7RN
e-mail: 00412.central.london.reservations@sheraton.com
web: www.luxurycollection.com/parktowerlondon
dir: Next to Harvey Nichols

Superbly located for some of London's most fashionable stores, the Park Tower offers stunning views over the city. Bedrooms combine a high degree of comfort with up-to-date decor and a super range of extras; the suites are particularly impressive. The hotel offers the intimate Knightsbridge lounge, the more formal Piano Bar and extensive conference and banqueting facilities. Restaurant One-O-One is renowned for its seafood.

Rooms 280 (280 fmly) **Facilities** Gym Fitness room ♫ **Conf** Class 60 Board 26 Thtr 120 **Services** Lift Air con **Parking** 67

St James's Hotel and Club

★★★★★ 85% ◉◉ TOWN HOUSE HOTEL
PLAN 5 A5

☎ 020 7316 1600 📠 020 7316 1602
7-8 Park Place SW1A 1LP
e-mail: info@stjameshotelandclub.com
web: www.stjameshotelandclub.com
dir: On A4 near Picadilly Circus & St James's St

Dating back to 1857 this elegant property with its distinctive neo-Gothic exterior is discreetly set in the heart of St James. Extensive refurbishment has resulted in impressive decor from interior designer Anne Maria Jagdfeld. Air-conditioned bedrooms are appointed to a very high standard and feature luxurious beds and a range of modern facilities. Stylish open-plan public areas offer a smart bar/lounge and the Andaman Restaurant serves precise modern cuisine.

Rooms 60 (8 fmly) (15 GF) **S** £199-£345; **D** £199-£425* **Facilities** ♫ Wi-fi **Conf** Class 30 Board 25 Thtr 40 Del from £335* **Services** Lift Air con **Notes** LB ⊗ Civ Wed

Dukes

★★★★★ 82% HOTEL PLAN 5 A5

☎ 020 7491 4840 📠 020 7493 1264
35 St James's Place SW1A 1NY
e-mail: bookings@dukeshotel.com
dir: From Pall Mall turn into St James's St. 2nd left into St James's Place. Hotel in courtyard on left

Discreetly tucked away in St James's, Dukes is steeped in history and is over 100 years old. Its style is understated with smart, well-equipped bedrooms and public areas. Facilities include a gym, marble steam room and body-care treatments. The intimate street-facing restaurant offers diners a good selection of British dishes. A smart lounge and a sophisticated and buzzing cocktail bar add to guests' enjoyment, and Martinis are a must!

Rooms 90 (4 GF) **S** £178.25-£380; **D** £201.25-£419.75* **Facilities** STV FTV Gym Steam room Health club Xmas New Year Wi-fi **Conf** Class 30 Board 30 Thtr 80 **Services** Lift Air con **Notes** ⊗ Civ Wed 60

Sofitel London St James

★★★★★ 81% ◉
HOTEL PLAN 5 B6

☎ 020 7747 2200 📠 020 7747 2210
6 Waterloo Place SW1Y 4AN
e-mail: H3144@sofitel.com
dir: 3 mins walk from Piccadilly Circus and Trafalgar Square

Located in the exclusive area of St James's, this Grade II listed, former bank is convenient for most of the city's attractions, theatres and the financial district. The modern bedrooms are equipped to a high standard and feature luxurious beds, whilst more traditional public

areas, including the Brasserie Roux and the Rose Lounge, provide a taste of classical charm.

Rooms 186 (98 fmly) (34 smoking) **S** £180-£1400; **D** £180-£1400 **Facilities** Spa STV Gym Nail lounge Hamam Hydrotherapy bath Turkish steam bath Fitness suite ♫ Xmas New Year Wi-fi **Conf** Class 110 Board 50 Thtr 180 **Services** Lift Air con **Notes** LB Civ Wed 140

See advert on opposite page and page 331

The Royal Horseguards

★★★★★ 81% HOTEL PLAN 5 D5 GUOMAN HOTELS

☎ 0871 376 9033 📠 0871 376 9133
2 Whitehall Court SW1A 2EJ
e-mail: royalhorseguards@thistle.co.uk
web: www.theroyalhorseguards.com
dir: Trafalgar Sq to Whitehall, left to Whitehall Pl & turn right

This majestic looking hotel in the heart of Whitehall sits beside the Thames and enjoys unrivalled views of the London Eye and the city skyline. Bedrooms, appointed to a high standard, are well equipped and some of the luxurious bathrooms are finished in marble. Impressive public areas and outstanding meeting facilities are also available.

Rooms 280 (7 fmly) (10 smoking) **Facilities** STV Gym ♫ Xmas New Year **Conf** Class 180 Board 84 Thtr 240 **Services** Lift Air con **Notes** ⊗ Civ Wed 228

The Rubens at the Palace

Red Carnation HOTELS

★★★★ 85% ◉ HOTEL PLAN 5 A4

☎ 020 7834 6600 📠 020 7233 6037
39 Buckingham Palace Rd SW1W 0PS
e-mail: bookrb@rchmail.com
web: www.rubenshotel.com
dir: Opposite Royal Mews, 100mtrs from Buckingham Palace

This hotel enjoys an enviable location next to Buckingham Palace. Stylish, air-conditioned bedrooms include the pinstripe-walled Saville Row rooms, which follow a tailoring theme, and the opulent Royal rooms, named after different monarchs. Public rooms include the Library fine dining restaurant and a comfortable stylish cocktail bar and lounge. The team here pride themselves on their warmth and friendliness.

Rooms 161 (13 fmly) (14 smoking) **S** £249; **D** £259* **Facilities** STV Health club & beauty treatment available nearby ♫ Xmas New Year Wi-fi **Conf** Class 40 Board 30 Thtr 90 **Services** Lift Air con **Notes** Civ Wed 80

Cavendish London

★★★★ 81% HOTEL PLAN 5 B6

☎ 020 7930 2111 📄 020 7839 2125
81 Jermyn St SW1Y 6JF
e-mail: info@thecavendishlondon.com
web: www.thecavendishlondon.com
dir: From Piccadilly, (pass The Ritz), 1st right into Dukes
St before Fortnum & Mason

This smart, stylish hotel enjoys an enviable location in
the prestigious St James's area, just a short walk from
Green Park and Piccadilly. Bedrooms have a fresh,
contemporary feel, and there are a number of spacious
executive rooms, studios and suites. Elegant public areas
include a spacious first-floor lounge, the popular David
Britton at The Cavendish Restaurant and well-appointed
conference and function facilities.

Rooms 230 (12 fmly) **Facilities** STV Wi-fi **Conf** Class 50
Board 40 Thtr 80 **Services** Lift Air con **Parking** 50
Notes LB ⊗

Sheraton Belgravia

★★★★ 81% HOTEL PLAN 4 G3 Sheraton

☎ 020 7235 6040 📄 020 7259 6243
20 Chesham Place SW1X 8HQ
e-mail: reservations.sheratonbelgravia@sheraton.com
dir: A4 (Brompton Rd) into central London. After
Brompton Oratory right into Beauchamp Pl. Follow into
Pont St, cross Sloane St & hotel on corner

This smart, boutique-style hotel offers a real home-from-
home experience with a friendly team on hand. Quiet and
very well equipped bedrooms include a number of
spacious executive rooms and suites. Bijou public areas
include a stylish lounge where all-day snacks are
available, and a restaurant offering a more formal eating
option.

Rooms 89 (16 fmly) **S** £169-£319; **D** £169-£339*
Facilities Complimentary fitness facilities available
locally ♫ Wi-fi Child facilities **Conf** Class 14 Board 20
Thtr 35 **Services** Lift Air con **Notes** LB

City Inn Westminster

★★★★ 80% HOTEL PLAN 5 C3 CITY INN

☎ 020 7630 1000 📄 020 7233 7575
30 John Islip St SW1P 4DD
e-mail: westminster.res@cityinn.com
web: www.cityinn.com
dir: From Millbank into Horseferry Rd. 2nd left into John
Islip St. Hotel on left approx 200mtrs

The group's flagship hotel is set in the heart of
Westminster close to the River Thames and the Houses of
Parliament. Spacious, contemporary, air-conditioned
bedrooms boast a wide range of facilities including iMac
computers and complimentary Wi-fi. Striking public areas
feature regularly changing modern art; and include a
range of meeting rooms and the popular cocktail bar, the
Millbank Lounge. The hotel's restaurant, City Café Art
Street Terrace offers the option of alfresco dining in
warmer months.

Rooms 460 (7 fmly) **S** £109-£295; **D** £109-£295*
Facilities STV FTV Gym Xmas New Year Wi-fi
Conf Class 70 Board 80 Thtr 180 Del from £195 to £395*
Services Lift Air con **Parking** 35 Notes ⊗ Civ Wed 130

Park Plaza Victoria London

★★★★ 80% HOTEL PLAN 5 A3 Park Plaza
Hotels & Resorts

☎ 020 7769 9999 & 7769 9800 📄 020 7769 9998
239 Vauxhall Bridge Rd SW1V 1EQ
e-mail: info@victoriaparkplaza.com
web: www.parkplaza.com
dir: Turn right out of Victoria Station

This smart modern hotel close to Victoria station is well
located for all of central London's major attractions.
Air-conditioned bedrooms are tastefully appointed and
thoughtfully equipped for both business and leisure
guests. Airy, stylish public areas include an elegant bar
and restaurant, a popular coffee bar and extensive
conference facilities complete with a business centre.

Rooms 299 **Facilities** Spa STV FTV Gym Sauna Steam
room Xmas Wi-fi **Conf** Class 240 Board 45 Thtr 550
Services Lift Air con **Parking** 36 **Notes** ⊗ Civ Wed 500

Crowne Plaza London St James

★★★★ 79% ◉ HOTEL PLAN 5 B4

☎ 020 7834 6655 ▤ 020 7630 7587
Buckingham Gate SW1E 6AF
e-mail: sales@cplonsj.co.uk
web: www.crowneplaza.co.uk
dir: Facing Buckingham Palace, left to Buckingham Gate. After 100mtrs hotel on right

Enjoying a prestigious location, this elegant Victorian hotel is a few minutes' walk from Buckingham Palace. Air-conditioned bedrooms are smartly appointed and superbly equipped. Public areas include a choice of three restaurants (Bank, Bistro 52 and Quilon), two bars, conference and business facilities and a fitness club with Sodashi Spa. Service is attentive and friendly.

Rooms 342 **S** £295; **D** £500* **Facilities** Spa Gym Steam room Sauna Solarium ♫ Xmas New Year Wi-fi **Conf** Class 90 Board 60 Thtr 180 **Services** Lift Air con **Notes** LB ⊗ Civ Wed 150

Durley House

★★★★ 76% TOWN HOUSE HOTEL PLAN 4 F3

☎ 020 7235 5537 ▤ 020 7259 6977
115 Sloane St SW1X 9PF
e-mail: info@durleyhouse.com

A hotel of distinction situated on ever popular Sloane Street that leads to all the top branded shops; it is also close to London's fashionable areas for dining and entertainment. The hotel offers a range of fully serviced suites, some with two bedrooms and kitchens, and 24-hour room service is also available. The attentive service provided by the staff demonstrates a high degree of professionalism.

Rooms 11 **Facilities** ⌛ Wi-fi **Conf** Class 12 Board 12 Thtr 12 **Services** Lift **Notes** LB ⊗

Millennium Hotel London Knightsbridge

★★★★ 73% ◉ HOTEL PLAN 4 F4

☎ 020 7235 4377 ▤ 020 7235 3705
17 Sloane St, Knightsbridge SW1X 9NU
e-mail: reservations.knightsbridge@millenniumhotels.co.uk
web: www.millenniumhotels.co.uk
dir: From Knightsbridge tube station towards Sloane St. Hotel 70mtrs on right

This fashionable hotel boasts an enviable location in Knightsbridge's chic shopping district. Air-conditioned, thoughtfully equipped bedrooms are complemented by a popular lobby lounge and MU Restaurant and Lounge

where the cuisine is French with Asian influences. Valet parking is available if pre-booked.

Rooms 222 (41 fmly) (38 smoking) **S** £140-£320; **D** £160-£350* **Facilities** STV FTV New Year Wi-fi **Conf** Class 80 Board 50 Thtr 120 Del from £264 to £370* **Services** Lift Air con **Parking** 10 **Notes** LB ⊗ Civ Wed 100

Cadogan

★★★★ 73% HOTEL PLAN 4 F3

☎ 020 7235 7141 ▤ 020 7245 0994
75 Sloane St SW1X 9SG
e-mail: amoza@cadogan.com
dir: A4 towards Knightsbridge, right at lights after Harrods on Sloane St.

This smart hotel, once home to Lillie Langtry, enjoys a prime Knightsbridge location overlooking Cadogan Gardens; Sloane Square, Harrods and Harvey Nichols are just a stone's throw away. Bedrooms and suites vary in size and style but all are stylishly appointed and attractively furnished. Public rooms include the beautifully panelled drawing room, a stylish bar and restaurant.

Rooms 60 (1 fmly) **Facilities** STV FTV ⌛ Gym Xmas Wi-fi **Conf** Class 30 Board 37 Thtr 38 **Services** Lift Air con **Notes** ⊗ Civ Wed 70

Thistle Westminster   thistle

★★★★ 71% HOTEL PLAN 5 A3

☎ 0871 376 9039 ▤ 0871 376 9139
49 Buckingham Palace Rd SW1W 0QT
e-mail: westminster@thistle.co.uk
web: www.thistlehotels.com/westminster
dir: Opposite Buckingham Palace Mews

A purpose built hotel situated in the heart of London's political landmarks and close to Buckingham Palace. The spacious bedrooms come in a variety of styles; each one is smartly decorated and well equipped. Public rooms include a large lounge, a bar, a brasserie and a range of meeting rooms.

Rooms 134 (66 fmly) **Facilities** STV FTV Wi-fi **Conf** Class 70 Board 45 Thtr 170 **Services** Lift **Parking** 7 **Notes** ⊗

Jumeirah Lowndes

Ⓤ PLAN 4 F4

☎ 020 7823 1234 ▤ 020 7235 1154
21 Lowndes St SW1X 9ES
e-mail: jlhinfo@jumeirah.com
dir: M4 onto A4 into London. Left from Brompton Rd to Sloane St. Left into Pont St, Lowndes St next left. Hotel on right

This hotel is a smart modern townhouse set in the Belgravia area of Knightsbridge. Public areas are limited in scale but include Mimosa, an all-day bar and restaurant with an outside terrace overlooking the leafy side street. The bedrooms vary in size, but all have a very modern style and have high spec facilities such as air-conditioning and iPod speakers. Guests can also enjoy the extensive facilities at the nearby Jumeirah Carlton Hotel. For further details please see the AA website: theAA.com

Rooms 87 **Facilities** STV Use of facilities at Jumeirah Carlton Tower Hotel Wi-fi **Conf** Class 12 Board 18 Thtr 25 **Services** Lift Air con **Notes** ⊗

The Grosvenor

Ⓤ PLAN 4 H3

☎ 0870 333 9120 ▤ 0870 333 9220
101 Buckingham Palace Rd SW1W 0SJ
e-mail: victoria@thistle.co.uk
web: www.thistlehotels.com/victoria
dir: Adjacent to Victoria Station

Currently the rating for this establishment is not confirmed. This may be due to a change of ownership or because it has only recently joined the AA rating scheme. For further details please see the AA website: theAA.com

Rooms 357 (8 fmly) **Facilities** Wi-fi **Conf** Class 80 Board 60 Thtr 200 **Services** Lift **Notes** LB

Days Inn London Westminster

BUDGET HOTEL PLAN 5 B2

☎ 020 7828 8661 & 7802 0507 📄 020 7821 0525
80-86 Belgrave Rd SW1V 2BJ
e-mail: info@daysinn-westminster.co.uk
web: www.daysinn.com
dir: From Victoria Station take Vauxhall Bridge Rd. Turn right on Wilton Rd, after 2nd lights left, hotel on right

This modern building offers accommodation in smart, spacious and well-equipped bedrooms, suitable for families and business travellers, and all with en suite bathrooms. Continental breakfast is available and other refreshments may be taken at the nearby family restaurant. See also the Hotel Groups pages.

Rooms 81 (15 fmly) (10 GF)

Holiday Inn Express London - Victoria

BUDGET HOTEL PLAN 5 B2

☎ 020 7630 8888 📄 020 7828 0441
106-110 Belgrave Rd, Victoria SW1V 2BJ
e-mail: info@hiexpressvictoria.co.uk
web: www.hiexpress.com/londonvictoria
dir: 600mtrs from Pimlico Underground

A modern hotel ideal for families and business travellers. Fresh and uncomplicated, the spacious rooms include Sky TV, power shower and tea and coffee-making facilities. Continental buffet breakfast is included in the room rate; other meals may be taken at the nearby family pub or restaurant. See also the Hotel Groups pages.

Rooms 52 (9 fmly) (4 GF) (15 smoking) **S** £99-£165; **D** £109-£165 (incl. bkfst)

SW3 CHELSEA, BROMPTON

The Capital
★★★★★ ⚫⚫⚫⚫
TOWN HOUSE HOTEL PLAN 4 F4

☎ 020 7589 5171 📄 020 7225 0011
Basil St, Knightsbridge SW3 1AT
e-mail: reservations@capitalhotel.co.uk
web: www.capitalhotel.co.uk
dir: 20yds from Harrods

Personal service is assured at this small, family-owned hotel set in the heart of Knightsbridge. Beautifully designed bedrooms come in a number of styles, but all rooms feature antique furniture, a marble bathroom and a thoughtful range of extras. Dinner is a highlight of any visit; Eric Chavot and his committed brigade continue to cook to a consistently high standard. Cocktails are a speciality in the delightful, stylish bar, whilst afternoon tea in the elegant, bijou lounge is a must.

Rooms 49 **S** £200-£230; **D** £280-£455* **Facilities** STV Wi-fi **Conf** Board 24 Thtr 30 **Services** Lift Air con **Parking** 21 **Notes** ⊗

Egerton House

★★★★★ 83% TOWN HOUSE HOTEL PLAN 4 E3

☎ 020 7589 2412 📄 020 7584 6540
17 Egerton Ter, Knightsbridge SW3 2BX
e-mail: bookeg@rchmail.com
web: www.egertonhousehotel.com
dir: Just off Brompton Rd, between Harrods and Victoria & Albert Museum, opposite Brompton Oratory

This delightful town house enjoys a prestigious Knightsbridge location, a short walk from Harrods and close to the Victoria & Albert Museum. Air-conditioned

---

bedrooms and public rooms are appointed to the highest standards, with luxurious furnishings and quality antique pieces; an exceptional range of facilities include iPods, safes, mini bars and flat-screen TVs. Staff offer the highest levels of personalised, attentive service.

Rooms 28 (5 fmly) (2 GF) (1 smoking) **S** £255-£275; **D** £255-£495* **Facilities** STV Xmas New Year Wi-fi **Conf** Class 12 Board 10 Thtr 14 **Services** Lift Air con

The Draycott

★★★★★ 78% TOWN HOUSE HOTEL PLAN 4 F2

☎ 020 7730 6466 📄 020 7730 0236
26 Cadogan Gardens SW3 2RP
e-mail: reservations@draycotthotel.com
web: www.draycotthotel.com
dir: From Sloane Sq station towards Peter Jones, keep to left. At Kings Rd take 1st right into Cadogan Gdns, 2nd right, hotel on left

Enjoying a prime location just yards from Sloane Square, this town house provides an ideal base in one of the most fashionable areas of London. Many regular guests regard this as their London residence and staff pride themselves on their hospitality. Beautifully appointed bedrooms include a number of very spacious suites and all are equipped to a high standard. Attractive day rooms, furnished with antique and period pieces, include a choice of lounges, one with access to a lovely sheltered garden.

Rooms 35 (9 fmly) (2 GF) (4 smoking)
S £155.25-£178.25; **D** £253-£362.25* **Facilities** STV Beauty treatments Massage Wi-fi **Conf** Class 12 Board 12 Thtr 20 **Services** Lift Air con

SW3 CHELSEA, BROMPTON *continued*

INSPECTORS' CHOICE

The Levin
★★★★ TOWN HOUSE HOTEL PLAN 4 F4

☎ 020 7589 6286 ▤ 020 7823 7826
28 Basil St, Knightsbridge SW3 1AS
e-mail: reservations@thelevin.co.uk
web: www.thelevinhotel.co.uk
dir: 20yds from Harrods

This sophisticated town house is the sister property to the adjacent Capital Hotel and enjoys a prime location on the doorstep of Knightsbridge's stylish department and designer stores. Bedrooms and en suites offer stylish elegance alongside a host of up-to-date modern comforts; extra touches include champagne bars and state-of-the-art audio-visual systems. Guests can enjoy all-day dining in the stylish, popular, lower ground floor Metro Restaurant.

Rooms 12 **D** £205-£435 (incl. bkfst)* **Facilities** STV Wi-fi **Conf** Board 24 Thtr 30 **Services** Lift Air con **Parking** 11 **Notes** LB ✪

The Beaufort
★★★★ 76% TOWN HOUSE HOTEL PLAN 4 F3

☎ 020 7584 5252 ▤ 020 7589 2834
33 Beaufort Gardens SW3 1PP
e-mail: reservations@thebeaufort.co.uk
web: www.thebeaufort.co.uk
dir: 100yds past Harrods on left of Brompton Rd

This friendly, attractive town house enjoys a peaceful location in a tree-lined cul-de-sac just a few minutes' walk from Knightsbridge. Air-conditioned bedrooms are thoughtfully furnished and equipped with CD players, movie channel access, safes and free Wi-fi. Guests are offered complimentary drinks and afternoon cream tea

with homemade scones and clotted cream. A good continental breakfast is served in guests' own rooms.

Rooms 29 (3 GF) **Facilities** STV Wi-fi **Conf** Thtr 10 **Services** Lift Air con **Notes** ✪

SW5 EARL'S COURT

London Marriott Kensington
★★★★ 82% HOTEL PLAN 4 B3

Marriott.
HOTELS & RESORTS

☎ 020 7973 1000 ▤ 020 7370 1685
Cromwell Rd SW5 0TH
e-mail: kensington.marriott@marriotthotels.com
web: www.londonmarriottkensington.co.uk
dir: On A4, opposite Cromwell Rd Hospital

This stylish contemporary hotel features a stunning glass exterior and a seven-storey atrium lobby. Fully air conditioned throughout, the hotel has elegant design combined with a great range of facilities, including indoor leisure, a range of conference rooms and parking. Smart bedrooms offer a host of extras including the very latest communications technology.

Rooms 216 (39 fmly) **Facilities** STV FTV ⊛ Gym Wi-fi **Conf** Class 80 Board 60 Thtr 150 **Services** Lift Air con **Parking** 20 **Notes** ✪

Cranley
★★★★ 79% TOWN HOUSE HOTEL PLAN 4 C2

☎ 020 7373 0123 ▤ 020 7373 9497
10 Bina Gardens, South Kensington SW5 0LA
e-mail: info@thecranley.com
web: www.franklynhotels.com/cranley
dir: Gloucester Rd towards Old Brompton Rd. 3rd right after station into Hereford Sq, then 3rd left into Bina Gardens

This period building, in the heart of South Kensington, is well located for fashionable shops and restaurants, with an NCP nearby. Small elegant public areas are furnished with quality pieces of artwork. Individually styled bedrooms are very well designed; all rooms have modern facilities with safes, internet access and mini bars; many rooms boast feature beds.

Rooms 38 (5 GF) **Facilities** STV Wi-fi **Conf** Board 12 **Services** Lift Air con **Notes** ✪

Twenty Nevern Square
★★★★ 70% TOWN HOUSE HOTEL PLAN 4 A2

☎ 020 7565 9555 & 7370 4934 ▤ 020 7565 9444
20 Nevern Square, Earls Court SW5 9PD
e-mail: hotel@twentynevernsquare.co.uk
web: www.twentynevernsquare.co.uk
dir: From station take Warwick Rd exit, right, 2nd right into Nevern Sq. Hotel 30yds on right

This smart boutique-style town house hotel is discreetly located in Nevern Square and is ideally situated for both Earls Court and Olympia. The stylish bedrooms, which vary in shape and size, are appointed to a high standard and are well equipped. Public areas include a delightful lounge and Café Twenty where breakfast and light meals are served.

Rooms 20 (3 GF) **Facilities** FTV Wi-fi **Services** Lift **Parking** 4 **Notes** ✪

See advert on opposite page

K + K Hotel George
★★★ 85% HOTEL PLAN 4 A2

☎ 020 7598 8700 & 7598 8707 ▤ 020 7370 2285
1-15 Templeton Place, Earl's Court SW5 9NB
e-mail: hotelgeorge@kkhotels.co.uk
web: www.kkhotels.com/george
dir: A3220 Earls Court Rd, right onto Trebovir Rd, right onto Templeton Place

This smart hotel enjoys a central location, just a few minutes' walk from Earls Court and with easy access to London's central attractions. Smart public areas include a bar/bistro, an executive lounge and meeting facilities and a stylish restaurant that overlooks the attractive rear garden. Bedrooms are particularly well equipped with a host of useful extras including free, high-speed internet access.

Rooms 154 (38 fmly) (8 GF) (28 smoking)
S £125-£224.25; **D** £145-£253 (incl. bkfst)*
Facilities STV FTV Gym Wellness area with exercise machines Sauna Wi-fi **Conf** Class 14 Board 18 Thtr 35 Del from £170 to £250* **Services** Lift Air con **Parking** 20 **Notes** LB

Twenty Nevern Square

TWENTY NEVERN SQUARE

A distinctive, unique and elegantly stylish hotel that overlooks a tranquil garden square, providing a luxurious haven for travellers on business or pleasure . . .

"The difference is in the detail . . ."

For reservations or a brochure please contact us on
+44 (0) 2075659555 or visit www.twentynevernsquare.co.uk
20 Nevern Square, London, SW5 9PD
A PART OF THE MAYFLOWER COLLECTION:
www.themayflowercollection.com

SW5 EARL'S COURT *continued*

Best Western Burns Hotel

★★★ 70% METRO HOTEL PLAN 4 B2

☎ 020 7373 3151 📠 020 7370 4090
18-26 Barkston Gardens, Kensington SW5 0EN
e-mail: burnshotel@vienna-group.co.uk
dir: Off A4, right to Earls Court Rd (A3220), 2nd left

This friendly Victorian hotel overlooks a leafy garden in a quiet residential area not far from the Earls Court exhibition centre and tube station. Bedrooms are attractively appointed, with modern facilities; beds have duvets. Public areas, although not extensive, are stylish.

Rooms 105 (10 fmly) **Services** Lift **Notes** ⊗

SW6 FULHAM

See also LONDON plan 1 D2/3 & E3

Millennium & Copthorne Hotels at Chelsea FC

★★★★ 76% HOTEL

☎ 020 7565 1400 📠 020 7565 1450
Stamford Bridge, Fulham Rd SW6 1HS
e-mail: reservations@chelseafc.com
web: www.millenniumhotels.co.uk
dir: 4 mins walk from Fulham Broadway tube station

A unique destination in a fashionable area of the city. Situated at Chelsea's famous Stamford Bridge football club the accommodation offered here is very up-to-the-minute. Bedroom facilities include flat-screen LCD TVs, video on demand, broadband, Wi-fi and good sized desk space; larger Club rooms have additional features. For eating there's a brasserie, the Bridge Bar and sports bar, and for corporate guests a flexible arrangement of meeting and event rooms is available.

Rooms 275 (64 fmly) **S** £74.75-£247; **D** £74.75-£247*
Facilities Spa STV FTV ⓢ Gym Health club Treatments Xmas New Year Wi-fi **Conf** Class 600 Board 30 Thtr 950 Del from £159 to £300* **Services** Lift Air con **Parking** 360 **Notes** LB ⊗ Civ Wed 50

Ibis London Earls Court

★★★ 71% HOTEL PLAN 4 A1

☎ 020 7610 0880 📠 020 7381 0215
47 Lillie Rd SW6 1UD
e-mail: h5623@accor.com
web: www.ibishotel.com
dir: From Hammersmith flyover towards London, keep in right lane, right at Kings pub on Talgarth Rd to join North End Rd. At mini-rdbt turn right. Hotel on left

Situated opposite the Earls Court Exhibition Centre, this large, modern hotel is popular with business and leisure guests. Bedrooms are comfortable and well equipped. There is a café bar open all day and a restaurant that serves evening meals. There are also extensive conference facilities and an underground car park.

Rooms 504 (20 fmly) **Facilities** Health club & gym nearby Wi-fi **Conf** Class 750 Board 25 Thtr 1200 **Services** Lift **Parking** 130

Travelodge Fulham

BUDGET HOTEL

☎ 0871 9846429 📠 01844 358681
290-302 North End Rd, Fulham SW6 1NQ
dir: M25 junct 15 onto M4. 9m, then onto A4 (Great West Rd) for 1m. At rdbt take 2nd exit, 1m then right onto B317 (North End Rd). 0.6m. Lodge on right.

Travelodge offers good quality, good value, budget accommodation. All offer family rooms sleeping up to four (two adults, two children) with en suite bathroom/shower-room, remote-control TV, tea- and coffee-making facilities and comfortable beds. Food options vary. Breakfast is at the on-site Bar Café restaurant (if available) or to take away. See also Hotel Groups pages.

Rooms 74 **S** fr £29; **D** fr £29

SW7 SOUTH KENSINGTON

The Bentley

★★★★★ 83% HOTEL PLAN 4 C2

☎ 020 7244 5555 📠 020 7244 5566
27-33 Harrington Gardens SW7 4JX
e-mail: info@thebentley-hotel.com
web: www.thebentley-hotel.com
dir: S of A4 into Knightsbridge at junct with Gloucester Rd, right, 2nd right turn, hotel on left just after mini-rdbt

This hotel, discreetly located in the heart of Kensington, features lavish opulence throughout the public areas. Spacious air-conditioned bedrooms are equally luxurious, and the marble clad bathrooms have jacuzzi baths and walk-in showers. Public areas include the Peridot where breakfast, lunch and dinner are served, and the luxuriously furnished cocktail bar, Malachite. Stylish rooms are available to hire for private dining or for holding meetings.

Rooms 64 **Facilities** Spa Gym Traditional Turkish Hamam ⓣ Xmas New Year Wi-fi **Conf** Class 60 Board 50 Thtr 70 **Services** Lift Air con **Notes** ⊗ Civ Wed 80

The Kensington Hotel

★★★★ 82% HOTEL PLAN 4 D2

☎ 020 7589 6300 📠 020 7581 1492
109-113 Queensgate, South Kensington SW7 5LR
e-mail: kensington@doylecollection.com
web: www.doylecollection.com
dir: From A4 take Cromwell Rd, turn right at V&A Museum onto Queensgate, hotel at end on left

This beautiful building is in an excellent location and has smartly appointed public areas that include an open-plan lobby/bar, Copplestones restaurant with adjoining library lounge and the lively Kavanagh's bar. Bedrooms vary in size and are well equipped.

Rooms 174 (174 annexe) (10 fmly) **Facilities** Local health club at discounted rate ⓣ Xmas Child facilities **Conf** Class 45 Board 40 Thtr 90 **Services** Lift Air con **Notes** ⊗

Millennium Gloucester Hotel London Kensington

★★★★ 77% HOTEL PLAN 4 C2

☎ 020 7373 6030 📠 020 7373 0409
4-18 Harrington Gardens SW7 4LH
e-mail: reservations.gloucester@millenniumhotels.co.uk
web: www.millenniumhotels.co.uk
dir: Opposite Gloucester Rd underground station

This spacious, stylish hotel is centrally located, close to The Victoria & Albert Museum and Gloucester Road tube station. Air-conditioned bedrooms are furnished in a variety of contemporary styles and Clubrooms benefit from a dedicated club lounge with complimentary breakfast and snacks. A wide range of eating options includes Singaporean and Mediterranean cuisine.

Rooms 610 (6 fmly) (66 smoking) **Facilities** STV Gym Wi-fi **Conf** Class 300 Board 40 Thtr 500 **Services** Lift Air con **Parking** 110 **Notes** ⊗ Civ Wed 500

Harrington Hall

★★★★ 74% HOTEL PLAN 4 C2

☎ 020 7396 9696 📠 020 7396 9090
5-25 Harrington Gardens SW7 4JW
e-mail: book.london@nh-hotels.com
web: www.nh-hotels.com
dir: 2 mins walk from Gloucester Road underground station

This splendid period property is centrally located just a stone's throw from Gloucester Road tube station and is convenient for visiting the museums and for shopping in Knightsbridge. Spacious bedrooms are smartly appointed and boast a host of extra touches. The public areas include extensive meeting facilities, a lounge bar and a restaurant.

Rooms 200 **Facilities** STV FTV Gym Xmas New Year Wi-fi **Conf** Class 100 Board 50 Thtr 240 **Services** Lift Air con **Notes** ⊗ Civ Wed 200

Millennium Bailey's Hotel London Kensington

★★★★ 73% HOTEL PLAN 4 C3

☎ 020 7373 6000 📠 020 7370 3760
140 Gloucester Rd SW7 4QH
e-mail: reservations.baileys@millenniumhotels.co.uk
web: www.millenniumhotels.co.uk
dir: A4, turn right at Cromwell Hospital into Knaresborough Place, follow to Courtfield Rd to corner of Gloucester Rd, hotel opposite underground station

This elegant hotel has a town house feel and enjoys a prime location. Air-conditioned bedrooms are smartly appointed and thoughtfully equipped, particularly the club rooms which benefit from DVD players. Public areas include a stylish contemporary restaurant and bar. Guests may also use the facilities at the adjacent, larger sister hotel.

Rooms 211 (20 smoking) **Facilities** STV Gym Wi-fi **Conf** Class 12 Board 12 Thtr 12 **Services** Lift Air con **Parking** 110 **Notes** ✷

Radisson Edwardian Vanderbilt

★★★★ 🅰 HOTEL PLAN 4 C3

☎ 020 7761 9000 📠 020 7761 9001
68-86 Cromwell Rd SW7 5BT
e-mail: resvand@radisson.com
dir: A4 into central London on Cromwell Rd. Hotel on left at junct of Gloucester Rd & Cromwell Rd

Rooms 215 (18 fmly) (28 GF) **Facilities** Fitness room Wi-fi **Conf** Class 56 Board 40 Thtr 100 **Services** Lift Air con **Notes** ✷ No children 16 yrs

Crowne Plaza London-Kensington

★★★★ 🅰 HOTEL PLAN 4 C3

☎ 020 7373 2222 📠 020 7373 0559
100 Cromwell Rd SW7 4ER
web: www.holidayinn.co.uk
dir: Opp Gloucester Road tube station. From M4 follow Central London signs

Rooms 162

Best Western The Cromwell

★★★ 78% METRO HOTEL PLAN 4 C2

☎ 020 7244 1720 📠 020 7373 3706
110-112 Cromwell Rd, Kensington SW7 4ES
e-mail: reception@thecromwell.com
dir: M4/A4 towards London, pass Cromwell Hospital, hotel in 0.5m

Just minutes away from the tube station and within easy access of all main tourist attractions, this hotel offers comfortable, modern accommodation. Fully air

conditioned and with free Wi-fi this is an ideal location for both leisure and business guests. Amenities include an on-site meeting room, and secure parking is available nearby.

Rooms 85 (4 fmly) (11 GF) **S** £74-£294; **D** £79-£299*
Facilities STV Fitness room Wi-fi **Conf** Board 8
Services Lift Air con **Notes** ✷

Holiday Inn London - Kensington Forum

🔁 PLAN 4 C3

☎ 0870 400 9100 📠 020 7373 1448
97 Cromwell Rd SW7 4DN
e-mail: hikensingtonforum@ihg.com
web: www.holidayinn.co.uk
dir: From S Circular onto N Circular at Chiswick Flyover. Onto A4 Cromwell Rd as far as Gloucester Rd

Currently the rating for this establishment is not confirmed. This may be due to a change of ownership or because it has only recently joined the AA rating scheme For further details please see the AA website: theAA.com

Rooms 906 (26 fmly) (106 smoking) **D** £90-£250*
Facilities STV FTV Gym Fitness room Xmas New Year Wi-fi **Conf** Class 150 Board 35 Thtr 300 **Services** Lift Air con **Parking** 76 **Notes** LB ✷

SW10 WEST BROMPTON

See LONDON plan 1 D/E3

Wyndham Grand London Chelsea Harbour

★★★★★ 83% @ HOTEL

☎ 020 7823 3000 📠 020 7351 6525
Chelsea Harbour SW10 0XG
e-mail: wyndhamlondon@wyndham.com
web: www.wyndham.com
dir: A4 to Earls Court Rd S towards river. Right into Kings Rd, left down Lots Rd. Chelsea Harbour in front

Against the picturesque backdrop of Chelsea Harbour's small marina, this modern hotel offers spacious, comfortable accommodation. All rooms are suites, which are superbly equipped; many enjoy splendid views of the marina. In addition, there are also several luxurious penthouse suites. Public areas include a modern bar and restaurant, excellent leisure facilities and extensive meeting and function rooms.

Rooms 158 (39 fmly) (46 smoking) **Facilities** Spa STV 🅢 Gym 🎵 Xmas New Year Wi-fi **Conf** Class 500 Board 200 Thtr 800 **Services** Lift Air con **Parking** 2000 **Notes** Civ Wed 800

SW11 BATTERSEA

See LONDON plan 1 E3

Travelodge London Battersea

BUDGET HOTEL

☎ 0871 984 6189 📠 020 7978 5898
200 York Rd, Battersea SW11 3SA
web: www.travelodge.co.uk
dir: From Wandsworth Bridge southern rdbt, take A3205 (York Rd) towards Battersea. Lodge 0.5m on left

Travelodge offers good quality, good value, budget accommodation. All offer family rooms sleeping up to four (two adults, two children) with en suite bathroom/shower-room, remote-control TV, tea- and coffee-making facilities and comfortable beds. Food options vary. Breakfast is at the on-site Bar Café restaurant (if available) or to take away. See also Hotel Groups pages.

Rooms 121 **S** fr £29; **D** fr £29

Hotel Verta

○

☎ 020 7978 0875
6 Heliport House, 38 Lombard Rd, Battersea SW11 3RP

This Hotel is due to open in 2010; for up-to-date information please see the AA website: theAA.com. Von Essen Hotels - AA Hotel Group of the Year 2009-10.

Rooms 70

SW15 PUTNEY

See LONDON plan 1 D2/3

Best Western Lodge

★★★ 75% METRO HOTEL

☎ 020 8874 1598 📠 020 8874 0910
52 -54 Upper Richmond Rd, Putney SW15 2RN
e-mail: res@thelodgehotellondon.com
dir: M25 junct 10/A3 towards central London. A219 to Putney, right to Upper Richmond, left at lights after 0.5m

This friendly hotel is conveniently located for East Putney tube station. Public areas include a bar/lounge with satellite TV and conference and banqueting facilities. A buffet breakfast is served in the garden conservatory. Thoughtfully equipped, comfortable bedrooms include a selection of executive rooms and suites. Parking for residents is an asset.

Rooms 64 (12 fmly) (15 GF) (12 smoking) **S** £85-£150; **D** £95-£160* **Facilities** STV FTV Wi-fi **Conf** Class 40 Board 30 Thtr 90 Del from £140 to £180* **Parking** 35 **Notes** LB Civ Wed 100

SW19 WIMBLEDON

See LONDON plan 1 D2

Cannizaro House

★★★★ 77% ☺☺ COUNTRY HOUSE HOTEL

☎ 020 8879 1464 📠 020 8879 7338
West Side, Wimbledon Common SW19 4UE
e-mail: info@cannizarohouse.com
dir: From A3 follow A219 signed Wimbledon into Parkside, right onto Cannizaro Rd, sharp right onto Westside Common

This unique, elegant 18th-century house has a long tradition of hosting the rich and famous of London society. A few miles from the city centre, the landscaped grounds provide a peaceful escape and a country-house ambience; fine art, murals and stunning fireplaces feature throughout. Spacious bedrooms are individually furnished and equipped to a high standard. The award-winning restaurant menus proudly herald locally sourced, organic ingredients.

Rooms 46 (10 fmly) (5 GF) **S** £99–£395; **D** £99–£395 (incl. bkfst)* **Facilities** STV ⛵ Xmas New Year Wi-fi
Conf Class 50 Board 40 Thtr 120 Del from £199 to £350*
Services Lift **Parking** 95 **Notes** LB Civ Wed 100

Express by Holiday Inn London Wimbledon-South

BUDGET HOTEL

☎ 020 8545 7300 📠 020 8545 7301
Miller's Meadhouse, 200 High St, Colliers Wood SW19 2BH
e-mail: info@exhiwimbledon.co.uk
web: www.hiexpress.com/wimbledonso
dir: M25/A3 signed central London, then A238, past Wimbledon for 3.2m. Hotel on left opposite large office block

A modern hotel ideal for families and business travellers. Fresh and uncomplicated, the spacious rooms include Sky TV, power shower and tea and coffee-making facilities. Continental buffet breakfast is included in the room rate; other meals may be taken at the nearby family pub or restaurant. See also the Hotel Groups pages.

Rooms 83 (60 fmly) **Conf** Class 16 Board 22 Thtr 40

W1 WEST END

INSPECTORS' CHOICE

The Connaught

★★★★★ ☺☺☺ MAYBOURNE HOTEL GROUP
HOTEL PLAN 2 G1

☎ 020 7499 7070 📠 020 7495 3262
Carlos Place W1K 2AL
e-mail: info@the-connaught.co.uk
dir: Between Grosvenor Sq and Berkeley Sq in Mayfair

This iconic hotel has emerged from a multi-million pound restoration and is now truly spectacular. There's stunning interior design, sumptuous day rooms, and stylish bedrooms with state-of-the-art facilities which include marble en suites with deep tubs, TV screens and power showers. Butlers are available at the touch of a button and guests are pampered by friendly, attentive staff offering intuitive service. A choice of bars and restaurants is available; the award-winning cuisine of Hélène Darroze is imaginative, inspired and truly memorable. The Connaught is the AA Hotel of the Year for London 2009-10.

Rooms 123 (17 smoking) **Facilities** STV FTV Gym Fitness studio Health club facilities at sister hotels Wi-fi **Conf** Board 18 **Services** Lift Air con **Notes** ⊗ Civ Wed 20

INSPECTORS' CHOICE

Brown's

★★★★★ ☺☺☺ HOTEL PLAN 3 A1 THE ROCCO FORTE COLLECTION

☎ 020 7493 6020 📠 020 7493 9381
Albemarle St, Mayfair W1S 4BP
e-mail: reservations.browns@roccofortecollection.com
web: www.roccofortecollection.com
dir: A short walk from Green Park, Bond St & Piccadilly

Brown's is a London hospitality icon that retains much charm by the successful balance of the traditional and the contemporary. Bedrooms are luxurious, furnished to the highest standard and come with all the modern comforts expected of such a grand Mayfair hotel. The hotel has 29 suites including two Royal Suites and two Presidential Suites. The elegant, yet informal, Albemarle restaurant (the oldest hotel restaurant in London) serves a traditional selection of popular dishes that are created with great skill; the lounges prove popular venues for afternoon tea.

Rooms 117 (12 smoking) **D** £230-£740* **Facilities** Spa STV Gym ♬ Xmas New Year Wi-fi **Conf** Class 30 Board 30 Thtr 70 **Services** Lift Air con **Notes** ⊗ Civ Wed 70

INSPECTORS' CHOICE

Claridge's

★★★★★ ⓐⓐⓐ
HOTEL PLAN 2 H2

MAYBOURNE HOTEL GROUP

☎ 020 7629 8860 📄 020 7499 2210
Brook St W1A 2JQ
e-mail: info@claridges.co.uk
dir: 1st turn after Green Park underground station to Berkeley Sq & 4th exit into Davies St. 3rd right into Brook St

Once renowned as the resort of kings and princes, Claridge's today continues to set the standards by which other hotels are judged. The sumptuous, air-conditioned bedrooms are elegantly themed to reflect the Victorian or art deco architecture of the building. Gordon Ramsay at Claridge's is now established as one of London's most popular dining venues, while the stylish cocktail bar is a hit with residents and non-residents alike. Service throughout is punctilious and thoroughly professional.

Rooms 203 (144 fmly) **Facilities** Spa STV Gym Beauty & health treatments Use of sister hotel's swimming pool ♫ Xmas New Year Wi-fi **Conf** Class 130 Board 60 Thtr 250 **Services** Lift Air con **Notes** ⊗ Civ Wed 200

INSPECTORS' CHOICE

The Dorchester

★★★★★ ⓐⓐ HOTEL PLAN 4 G6

☎ 020 7629 8888 📄 020 7629 8080
Park Ln W1K 1QA
e-mail: info@thedorchester.com
dir: Halfway along Park Ln between Hyde Park Corner & Marble Arch

One of London's finest. The Dorchester remains one of the best-loved hotels in the country and always delivers. The spacious bedrooms and suites are beautifully appointed and feature fabulous marble bathrooms. Leading off from the foyer, The Promenade is the perfect setting for afternoon tea or drinks. In the evening guests can relax to the sound of live jazz, whilst enjoying a cocktail in the stylish bar. Dining options include the sophisticated Chinese restaurant China Tang (2 AA Rosettes); Restaurant Alain Ducasse from the world renowned French chef of the same name (3 AA Rosettes), and of course The Grill (2 AA Rosettes).

Rooms 250 **Facilities** Spa STV FTV Gym Steam rooms ♫ Xmas New Year Wi-fi **Conf** Class 300 Board 42 Thtr 500 **Services** Lift Air con **Notes** ⊗ Civ Wed 500

INSPECTORS' CHOICE

The Ritz London

★★★★★ ⓐⓐ HOTEL PLAN 5 A6

☎ 020 7493 8181 📄 020 7493 2687
150 Piccadilly W1J 9BR
e-mail: enquire@theritzlondon.com
web: www.theritzlondon.com
dir: From Hyde Park Corner E on Piccadilly. Hotel on right after Green Park

This renowned, stylish hotel offers guests the ultimate in sophistication whilst still managing to retain all of its former historical glory. Bedrooms and suites are exquisitely furnished in Louis XVI style, with fine marble bathrooms and every imaginable comfort. Elegant reception rooms include the Palm Court with its legendary afternoon teas, the beautiful fashionable Rivoli Bar and the sumptuous Ritz Restaurant, complete with gold chandeliers and extraordinary trompe-l'oeil decoration.

Rooms 137 (44 fmly) (27 smoking) **S** £293.75-£405.38; **D** £317.25-£522.88* **Facilities** STV Gym Treatment room Hairdressing Fitness centre The Ritz Club Casino ♫ Xmas New Year **Conf** Class 40 Board 30 Thtr 60 **Services** Lift Air con **Parking** 10 **Notes** ⊗ Civ Wed 60

W1 WEST END *continued*

Athenaeum Hotel & Apartments

★★★★★ ⚙ HOTEL PLAN 4 H5

☎ 020 7499 3464 📠 020 7493 1860
116 Piccadilly W1J 7BJ
e-mail: info@athenaeumhotel.com
web: www.athenaeumhotel.com
dir: On Piccadilly, overlooking Green Park

With a discreet address in Mayfair, this well-loved hotel offers bedrooms appointed to the highest standard; several boast views over Green Park. The delightful bar has an excellent stock of whiskies which complements the stunning Garden Lounge and stylish restaurant. A row of Edwardian townhouses adjacent to the hotel offers a range of spacious and well-appointed apartments. There is an extensive range of beauty treatments available along with conference and meeting facilities.

Rooms 157 (8 smoking) **D** £150-£710 **Facilities** STV Gym Steam rooms Sauna Hairdressing salon Xmas New Year Wi-fi **Conf** Class 35 Board 36 Thtr 55 **Services** Lift Air con **Notes** LB ⊗ Civ Wed 80

Hyatt Regency London - The Churchill

★★★★★ 84% ⚙⚙⚙ HOTEL PLAN 2 F2

☎ 020 7486 5800 📠 020 7486 1255
30 Portman Square W1H 7BH
e-mail: london.churchill@hyatt.com
dir: From Marble Arch rdbt, follow signs for Oxford Circus onto Oxford St. Left turn after 2nd lights onto Portman St. Hotel on left

This smart hotel enjoys a central location overlooking Portman Square. Excellent conference, hairdressing and beauty facilities plus a fitness room make this the ideal choice for both corporate and leisure guests. The Montagu

restaurant offers contemporary dining within the hotel, plus the option to sit at the Chef's Table.

Rooms 444 (87 smoking) **S** £213-£437; **D** £213-£437* **Facilities** STV FTV 💆 Gym Jogging track ♫ Xmas New Year Wi-fi **Conf** Class 160 Board 68 Thtr 250 Del from £319 to £550* **Services** Lift Air con **Parking** 48 **Notes** ⊗ Civ Wed 250

The Langham, London

★★★★★ 84% ⚙⚙⚙ HOTEL PLAN 2 H4

☎ 020 7636 1000 📠 020 7323 2340
Portland Place W1B 1JA
e-mail: lon.info@langhamhotels.com
dir: N of Regent St, left opposite All Soul's Church

This hotel has now undergone a multi-million pound refurbishment and has a new grand entrance which leads into restored interior elegance. Dating back to 1865 the building now displays a contemporary, luxurious style. Situated on Regent Street it is ideally located for both theatreland and the principal shopping areas. Bedrooms are delightfully appointed and many have excellent views. The Landau restaurant and Artesian bar offer high standards of service, delivered by a friendly team. There is also an extensive health club complete with a 16-metre pool.

Rooms 382 (5 fmly) (15 smoking) **S** £234.18-£476.48; **D** £234.18-£476.48* **Facilities** Spa STV 🐾 Gym Health club and spa facilities Sauna Steam room ♫ Xmas New Year Wi-fi **Conf** Class 200 Board 80 Thtr 300 **Services** Lift Air con **Notes** LB ⊗ Civ Wed 280

InterContinental London Park Lane

INTER·CONTINENTAL
HOTELS AND RESORTS

★★★★★ 83% ⚙⚙⚙ HOTEL PLAN 4 G5

☎ 020 7409 3131 📠 020 7493 3476
1 Hamilton Place, Hyde Park Corner W1J 7QY
e-mail: london@interconti.com
dir: at Hyde Park Corner, on corner of Park Lane and Piccadilly

A well-known and well-loved landmark on Hyde Park Corner, this hotel boasts elegant guest rooms and

spectacular suites, including the split level loft style London Suite and a stunning Club InterContinental lounge. A choice of restaurants includes the superb Theo Randall. Public areas also include a chic urban spa run in partnership with Elemis and a contemporary event space with a ballroom and 12 meeting rooms.

Rooms 447 **Facilities** Spa Gym ♫ Xmas New Year Wi-fi **Conf** Class 340 Board 62 Thtr 750 **Services** Lift Air con **Parking** 100 **Notes** ⊗ Civ Wed 750

London Marriott Hotel Park Lane

Marriott
HOTELS & RESORTS

★★★★★ 83% HOTEL PLAN 2 F2

☎ 020 7493 7000 📠 020 7493 8333
140 Park Ln W1K 7AA
e-mail: mhrs.parklane@marriotthotels.com
dir: From Hyde Park Corner left on Park Ln onto A4202, 0.8m. At Marble Arch onto Park Ln. Take 1st left onto North Row. Hotel on left

This modern and stylish hotel is situated in a prominent position in the heart of central London. Bedrooms are superbly appointed and air conditioned. Public rooms include a popular lounge/bar, and there are excellent leisure facilities and an executive lounge.

Rooms 157 (31 smoking) **D** £199-£365* **Facilities** STV 🐾 Gym Steam room Xmas New Year Wi-fi **Conf** Class 33 Board 42 Thtr 72 Del from £55 to £85* **Services** Lift Air con **Notes** ⊗

Metropolitan London

★★★★★ 82% ⚙⚙ HOTEL PLAN 4 G5

☎ 020 7447 1000 📠 020 7447 1100
Old Park Ln W1K 1LB
e-mail: res.lon@metropolitan.como.bz
dir: On corner of Old Park Ln and Hertford St, within 200mtrs from Hyde Park corner

Overlooking Hyde Park this hotel is located within easy reach of the fashionable stores of Knightsbridge and Mayfair. The hotel's contemporary style allows freedom and space to relax. Understated luxury is the key here with bedrooms enjoying great natural light. There is also a Shambhala Spa, steam room and fully equipped gym. For those seeking a culinary experience, Nobu offers innovative Japanese cuisine with an upbeat atmosphere.

Rooms 150 **Facilities** Spa STV FTV Gym Treatments Steam rooms Wi-fi **Conf** Board 30 Thtr 40 **Services** Lift Air con **Parking** 15 **Notes** Civ Wed 30

The Westbury

★★★★★ 82% ◎◎ HOTEL PLAN 3 A2

☎ 020 7629 7755 📄 020 7495 1163
Bond St W1S 2YF
e-mail: reservations@westburymayfair.com
dir: from Oxford Circus S down Regent St, right onto
Conduit St, hotel at junct of Conduit St & Bond St

A well-known favourite with an international clientele,
The Westbury is located at the heart of London's finest
shopping district and provides a calm atmosphere away
from the hubbub. The standards of accommodation are
high throughout. Reception rooms offer a good choice for
both relaxing and eating and include the stylish Polo Bar
and the smart, contemporary Artisan restaurant.

Rooms 249 (86 fmly) (7 GF) **Facilities** STV FTV Gym
Fitness centre Steam room Sauna Xmas New Year Wi-fi
Conf Class 65 Board 35 Thtr 100 **Services** Lift Air con
Notes ⊗ Civ Wed 80

Grosvenor House, A JW Marriott Hotel

GROSVENOR HOUSE
A JW MARRIOTT HOTEL
LONDON

★★★★★ 80% HOTEL PLAN 2 G1

☎ 020 7499 6363 & 7399 8400 📄 020 7493 3341
Park Ln W1K 7TN
e-mail: grosvenor.house@marriotthotels.com
web: www.londongrosvenorhouse.co.uk
dir: Centrally located on Park Ln, between Hyde Park
Corner & Oxford St

This quintessentially British hotel, overlooking Hyde Park
has completed an extensive restoration. Grosvenor House
promises approachable luxury and epitomises the fine
hotel culture of London. The property boasts the largest
ballroom in Europe, and now has a French-style brasserie,
Bord'deaux, and a Champagne Bar. The Park Room is the
perfect setting for afternoon tea. The new spa, fitness
and pool area are due to open in late 2010.

Rooms 494 (111 smoking) **Facilities** STV Gym Health &
Fitness centre Xmas New Year Wi-fi **Conf** Class 800
Board 140 Thtr 1500 **Services** Lift Air con **Parking** 70
Notes ⊗ Civ Wed 1500

Radisson Edwardian May Fair Hotel

Radisson
EDWARDIAN
HOTELS

★★★★★ 🅰 HOTEL PLAN 5 A6

☎ 020 7629 7777 📄 020 7629 1459
Stratton St W1J 8LL
e-mail: mayfair@interconti.com
dir: from Hyde Park Corner or Piccadilly left onto Stratton
Street, hotel on left

Rooms 289 (14 fmly) **Facilities** Spa Gym ♫ Xmas Wi-fi
Conf Class 108 Board 60 Thtr 292 **Services** Lift Air con
Notes ⊗ No children 16 yrs Civ Wed 250

Chesterfield Mayfair

Red
Carnation
HOTELS

★★★★ 84% ◎ HOTEL PLAN 4 H6

☎ 020 7491 2622 📄 020 7491 4793
35 Charles St, Mayfair W1J 5EB
e-mail: bookch@rchmail.com
web: www.chesterfieldmayfair.com
dir: Hyde Park Corner along Piccadilly, left into Half Moon
St. At end left & 1st right into Queens St, then right into
Charles St

Quiet elegance and an atmosphere of exclusivity
characterise this stylish Mayfair hotel where attentive,
friendly service is a highlight. Bedrooms have been
decorated in a variety of contemporary styles, some with
fabric walls; all are thoughtfully equipped and boast
marble-clad bathrooms. Air conditioned throughout.

Rooms 107 (7 fmly) (10 smoking) **S** £155-£328;
D £189-£805 **Facilities** STV ♫ Xmas Wi-fi **Conf** Class 45
Board 45 Thtr 100 Del from £275 to £350 **Services** Lift
Air con **Notes** LB Civ Wed 120

London Marriott Hotel Marble Arch

Marriott
HOTELS & RESORTS

★★★★ 84% HOTEL PLAN 2 F3

☎ 020 7723 1277 📄 020 7402 0666
134 George St W1H 5DN
e-mail: salesadmin.marblearch@marriotthotels.co.uk
web: www.londonmarriottmarblearch.co.uk
dir: From Marble Arch turn into Edgware Rd, then 4th
right into George St. Left into Dorset St for entrance

Situated just off the Edgware Road and close to the
Oxford Street shops, this friendly hotel offers smart, well-
equipped, air-conditioned bedrooms. Public areas are
stylish, and include a smart indoor leisure club and an
Italian themed restaurant. Secure underground parking is
available.

Rooms 240 (100 fmly) **Facilities** STV ⓒ supervised Gym
Sun beds Xmas Wi-fi **Conf** Class 75 Board 80 Thtr 150
Services Lift Air con **Parking** 83 **Notes** ⊗

London Marriott Hotel Grosvenor Square

Marriott
HOTELS & RESORTS

★★★★ 83% ◎◎ HOTEL PLAN 2 G2

☎ 020 7493 1232 📄 020 7514 1528
Grosvenor Square W1K 6JP
e-mail: philip.hyland@marriotthotels.com
web: www.londonmarriottgrosvenorsquare.co.uk
dir: M4 E to Cromwell Rd through Knightsbridge to Hyde
Park Corner. Park Lane right at Brook Gate onto Upper
Brook St to Grosvenor Sq

Situated adjacent to Grosvenor Square in the heart of
Mayfair, this hotel boasts convenient access to the city,
West End and some of London's most exclusive shops.
Bedrooms and public areas are furnished and decorated
to a high standard and retain the traditional elegance for
which the area is known. The hotel's eating options are the
Maze Grill (2 AA Rosettes), and Gordon Ramsay's Maze
(4 AA Rosettes) with impressive cooking by Jason Atherton.

Rooms 237 (26 fmly) **S** fr £169; **D** fr £209* **Facilities** Gym
Exercise & fitness centre Xmas Wi-fi **Conf** Class 500
Board 120 Thtr 900 **Services** Lift Air con **Parking** 80
Notes ⊗ Civ Wed 600

The Mandeville Hotel

★★★★ 83% ◎ HOTEL PLAN 2 G3

☎ 020 7935 5599 📄 020 7935 9588
Mandeville Place W1U 2BE
e-mail: sales@mandeville.co.uk
web: www.mandeville.co.uk
dir: 3 mins walk from Bond St tube station

This is a stylish and attractive boutique style hotel with a
very contemporary feel. Bedrooms have state-of-the-art
TVs and large very comfortable beds, all are air-
conditioned. One of the suites has a patio with views over
London. The cocktail bar is a popular attraction.

Rooms 142 **Facilities** STV FTV Xmas New Year Wi-fi
Conf Board 20 Thtr 40 **Services** Lift Air con **Notes** ⊗

Millennium Hotel London Mayfair

MILLENNIUM
HOTELS AND RESORTS
MILLENNIUM HOTELS
COPTHORNE HOTELS

★★★★ 80% ◎◎ HOTEL PLAN 2 G1

☎ 020 7629 9400 📄 020 7629 7736
Grosvenor Square W1K 2HP
e-mail: reservations@millenniumhotels.co.uk
web: www.millenniumhotels.co.uk
dir: S side of Grosvenor Square

This hotel benefits from a prestigious location in the
heart of Mayfair, close to Bond Street. Smart bedrooms
are generally spacious and club-floor rooms have use of
their own lounge with complimentary refreshments. A
choice of bars and dining options are available along
with conference facilities and a fitness room.

Rooms 336 **S** £145-£520; **D** £145-£520* **Facilities** STV
Gym Fitness suite ♫ Xmas New Year Wi-fi
Conf Class 250 Board 70 Thtr 500 Del from £295 to
£658* **Services** Lift Air con **Notes** LB ⊗ Civ Wed 250

W1 WEST END *continued*

The Marylebone Hotel

★★★★ 79% HOTEL PLAN 2 G3

☎ 020 7486 6600 📠 020 7935 2463
47 Welbeck St W1G 8DN
e-mail: marylebone@doylecollection.com
web: www.doylecollection.com/marylebone
dir: From Portland Place into New Cavendish St. Welbeck St last turn on left

This well kept hotel enjoys a central location just a five minute walk from Oxford Street and fashionable Bond Street. Bedrooms vary in space and style and include a number of penthouse apartments with balconies. Public areas include an excellent leisure club with a good-sized swimming pool, extensive conference facilities and a spacious lounge, bar and restaurant.

Rooms 257 (20 fmly) (35 smoking) **S** £110-£390; **D** £120-£400 **Facilities** STV FTV ⓢ Gym Sauna Steam room Dance studio Spinning room Wi-fi **Conf** Class 48 Board 38 Thtr 70 Del from £210 to £350* **Services** Lift Air con **Notes** LB ⊗

The Washington Mayfair Hotel

★★★★ 77% HOTEL PLAN 4 H6

☎ 020 7499 7000 📠 020 7495 6172
5-7 Curzon St, Mayfair W1J 5HE
e-mail: sales@washington-mayfair.co.uk
web: www.washington-mayfair.co.uk
dir: From Green Park station take Piccadilly exit & turn right. 4th street on right into Curzon Street

Situated in the heart of Mayfair, this stylish independently owned hotel offers a very high standard of accommodation. Personalised, friendly service is noteworthy. Bedrooms are attractively furnished and provide high levels of comfort. The hotel is also a popular venue for afternoon tea and refreshments, served in the marbled and wood-panelled lounge.

Rooms 171 **S** £150-£700; **D** £150-£700 **Facilities** Gym Xmas New Year Wi-fi **Conf** Class 40 Board 36 Thtr 110 Del from £270 to £450 **Services** Lift Air con **Notes** LB ⊗

Park Plaza Sherlock Holmes

★★★★ 76% HOTEL PLAN 2 F4

☎ 020 7486 6161 📠 020 7958 5211
108 Baker St W1U 6LJ
e-mail: info@sherlockholmeshotel.com
web: www.sherlockholmeshotel.com
dir: from Marylebone Flyover onto Marylebone Rd. At Baker St turn right for hotel on left

Chic and modern, this boutique-style hotel is near a number of London underground lines and rail stations. Public rooms include a popular bar, sited just inside the main entrance, and Sherlock's Grill, where the mesquite-wood burning stove is a feature of the cooking. The hotel also features an indoor health suite and a relaxing lounge.

Rooms 119 (20 fmly) **Facilities** STV Gym ♫ Xmas Wi-fi **Conf** Class 50 Board 30 Thtr 80 **Services** Lift Air con **Notes** ⊗ Civ Wed 70

Thistle Marble Arch

★★★★ 76% HOTEL PLAN 2 F2

☎ 0871 971 1753 & 020 7629 8040 📠 0871 376 9127
Bryanston St W1A 4UR
e-mail: marblearch@thistle.co.uk
web: www.thistlehotels.com/marblearch
dir: From Marble Arch monument down Oxford St. 1st left onto Portman St, 1st left onto Bryanston St. Hotel entrance on left

This centrally located hotel, adjacent to a car park, is ideal for the attractions of Oxford Street and Knightsbridge. The spacious bedrooms come in a range of size and price options, but all are very well equipped and have air conditioning. The public areas include a fast food service, Co-Motion, and a more leisurely carvery restaurant, which also offers a carte menu. There is also a gym, a range of meeting rooms and an executive lounge.

Rooms 692 (60 fmly) (97 smoking) **Facilities** STV FTV Gym ♫ Xmas New Year Wi-fi **Conf** Class 180 Board 94 Thtr 380 Del from £170 to £200* **Services** Lift Air con **Notes** ⊗

The Cumberland

★★★★ 75% ⊛ HOTEL PLAN 2 F2

☎ 0870 333 9280 📠 0870 333 9281
Great Cumberland Place W1A 4RF
e-mail: enquiries@thecumberland.co.uk
dir: Behind Marble Arch monument, at top of Park Lane & Oxford St

This landmark hotel, occupying a prime position at Marble Arch, has a striking, airy lobby that is the focal point. A choice of bars, two Gary Rhodes restaurants (one with 3 AA Rosettes and the other with 1 Rosette) and extensive conference and meeting facilities are just some of what's on offer here. Bedrooms have a stylish contemporary feel and boast an excellent range of facilities.

Rooms 1019 (119 annexe) (8 fmly) (9 GF) (100 smoking) **Facilities** Gym ♫ Xmas New Year Wi-fi **Conf** Class 170 Board 85 Thtr 350 **Services** Lift Air con **Notes** LB ⊗ Civ Wed 300

Holiday Inn London - Regents Park

★★★★ 72% HOTEL PLAN 3 A4

☎ 0870 400 9111 & 020 7387 2806 📠 020 7387 2806
Carburton St, Regents Park W1W 5EE
e-mail: lawder.smith@ihg.com
web: www.holidayinn.co.uk
dir: From E: from King's Cross, A50, left into Bolsover St before Gt Portland Rd tube station. From W: A40 onto A501(Regent's Pk Station on right). Left onto Albany St & 1st right to cross Euston Rd. Pass Gt Portland St tube station to Bolsover St. Hotel on left

Ideally located and with the benefit of an adjacent public car park, this popular modern hotel provides a range of comfortable bedrooms equipped for both business and leisure guests. The attractive Junction Restaurant is the setting for brasserie-style eating and a comprehensive buffet breakfast provides a good start to the day. The hotel also provides excellent conference facilities within The Academy Centre.

Rooms 332 (2 fmly) (28 smoking) **Facilities** STV Wi-fi **Conf** Class 180 Board 50 Thtr 350 **Services** Lift Air con **Parking** 65

Radisson Blu Portman

★★★★ 72% HOTEL PLAN 2 F3

☎ 020 7208 6000 📠 020 7208 6001
22 Portman Square W1H 7BG
e-mail: reservations.london@radissonblu.com
web: www.radissonblu.com
dir: 100mtrs N of Oxford St; 300mtrs E of Edgware Rd

This smart, popular hotel enjoys a prime location a short stroll from Oxford Street and close to all the city's major attractions. The spacious, well-equipped bedrooms are themed ranging from Oriental through to classical and contemporary Italian decor. Public areas include extensive conference facilities, a bar and the modern European Portman Restaurant.

Rooms 272 (93 fmly) (14 smoking) **Facilities** FTV ⓢ Gym Xmas Wi-fi **Conf** Class 280 Board 70 Thtr 600 **Services** Lift Air con **Parking** 400 **Notes** ⊗ Civ Wed 500

Holiday Inn London - Mayfair

★★★★ 71% HOTEL PLAN 3 A1

☎ 0870 400 9110 📠 020 7629 2827
3 Berkeley St W1J 8NE
e-mail: himayfair-reservations@ihg.com
web: www.holidayinn.co.uk
dir: At corner of Berkeley St & Piccadilly

Located in the heart of Mayfair and just minutes from Green Park tube station, this busy hotel has the benefit of well-proportioned, attractive bedrooms and elegant public areas. Options for dining include the graceful Nightingales Restaurant or choices from a substantial snack menu in the lounge bar.

Rooms 194 (63 fmly) (24 smoking) **S** £99–£385; **D** £99–£385 **Facilities** STV Xmas New Year Wi-fi **Conf** Class 32 Board 30 Thtr 65 **Services** Lift Air con **Parking** 18 **Notes** LB ⊗

Radisson Edwardian Berkshire

★★★★ 🅰 HOTEL PLAN 2 H2

☎ 020 7629 7474 📠 020 7629 8156
350 Oxford St W1N 0BY
e-mail: resberk@radisson.com
dir: opposite Bond St underground. Entrance on Marylebone Lane

Rooms 147 (10 fmly) **Facilities** Wi-fi **Conf** Class 16 Board 16 Thtr 40 **Services** Lift Air con **Notes** ⊗ No children

Radisson Edwardian Grafton Hotel

★★★★ 🅰 HOTEL PLAN 3 B4

☎ 020 7388 4131 📠 020 7387 7394
130 Tottenham Court Rd W1T 5AY
e-mail: resgraf@radisson.com
dir: from Euston Rd onto Tottenham Court Rd. Past Warren St underground station

Rooms 330 (23 fmly) **Facilities** Fitness room. Xmas Wi-fi **Conf** Class 50 Board 30 Thtr 100 **Services** Lift Air con **Notes** ⊗ No children 16yrs

Best Western Mostyn Hotel

★★★ 77% ⊛⊛⊛ HOTEL PLAN 2 F2

☎ 020 7935 2361 📠 020 7487 2759
4 Bryanston St W1H 7BY
e-mail: info@mostynhotel.co.uk
web: www.bw-mostynhotel.co.uk
dir: A40(M) Marylebone Rd, close to Marble Arch and Bond St underground

The Mostyn enjoys an enviable location, just behind Oxford Street, in the heart of the West End. Originally built as a residence for Lady Black, a lady-in-waiting at the court of George II, the hotel retains many original features. Well-equipped, modern bedrooms have air conditioning, and public rooms include a stylish open-plan lounge and cocktail bar. The stunning restaurant, Texture, delivers impressive, modern cooking.

Rooms 121 (15 fmly) (9 GF) **S** £110–£155; **D** £125–£185 **Facilities** Gym Wi-fi **Conf** Class 70 Board 50 Thtr 130 Del from £225 to £285 **Services** Lift Air con **Parking** 400 **Notes** ⊗

See advert on this page

Thistle Piccadilly

thistle

★★★ 77% METRO HOTEL PLAN 3 C1

☎ 0871 376 9031 📠 0871 376 9131
39 Coventry St W1D 6BZ
e-mail: piccadilly@thistle.co.uk
web: www.thistlehotels.com/piccadilly
dir: From Kings Cross follow signs for West End & Piccadilly

This popular hotel is centrally located between Leicester Square and Piccadilly Circus, ideal for all of the West End's attractions. Bedrooms vary in size and style but all are well equipped; deluxe and stylish executive rooms boast air-conditioning. Public areas include a cosy bar/lounge where snacks are available and a smart breakfast room. Numerous restaurants are located within walking distance.

Rooms 92 (3 fmly) (24 smoking) **S** £100–£250; **D** £110–£260* **Facilities** STV FTV Wi-fi **Services** Lift Air con **Notes** LB ⊗

Holiday Inn London – Oxford Circus

★★★ 75% HOTEL PLAN 2 H3

☎ 020 7935 4442 📠 020 7487 3782
57 - 59 Welbeck St W1M 8HS
e-mail: dmelrose@holidayinnoxfordcircus.com
web: www.holidayinn.co.uk
dir: From M1, North Circular Rd, A41. Down Finchley Rd & Baker St to Portman Sq. Left on Wigmore St, left into Queen Anne St. Left into Wellbeck St

This Edwardian property enjoys a prime location only a few minutes walk from Oxford Street and close to all of London's major theatres, shops and attractions. Bedrooms are particularly well equipped and include a number of spacious executive and junior suites. Public areas include a split-level bar, restaurant and mini-gym.

Rooms 164 (18 fmly) (25 smoking) **S** £79–£190; **D** £99–£290 **Facilities** STV Gym Wi-fi **Conf** Class 45 Board 32 Thtr 75 Del from £175 to £255 **Services** Lift Air con **Notes** LB ⊗

W1 WEST END *continued*

Radisson Edwardian Sussex

★★★ **A** HOTEL PLAN 2 G2

☎ 020 7408 0130 🖹 020 7493 2070
19-25 Granville Place W1H 6PA
e-mail: ressuss@radisson.com
dir: off Oxford St. Turn left to Portman St. Then right into Granville Place

Rooms 101 (12 fmly) **Facilities** Gym Wi-fi **Conf** Board 10 **Services** Lift Air con **Notes** ⊗

The Montcalm-Hotel Nikko London

U PLAN 2 F2

☎ 020 7402 4288 🖹 020 7724 9180
Great Cumberland Place W1H 7TW
e-mail: reservations@montcalm.co.uk
dir: 2 mins' walk N from Marble Arch station

Currently the rating for this establishment is not confirmed. This may be due to a change of ownership or because it has only recently joined the AA rating scheme For further details please see the AA website: theAA.com

Rooms 120 (4 fmly) **Facilities** Wi-fi **Conf** Class 40 Board 36 Thtr 80 **Services** Lift Air con **Parking** 10 **Notes** LB ⊗

W2 BAYSWATER, PADDINGTON

Lancaster London

★★★★ 81% ◉ HOTEL PLAN 2 D2

☎ 020 7262 6737 🖹 020 7724 3191
Lancaster Ter W2 2TY
e-mail: book@royallancaster.com
web: www.royallancaster.com
dir: Adjacent to Lancaster Gate underground station

Formerly the Royal Lancaster, this large hotel offers a wide range of facilities. There are a wide variety of room types; higher floors have excellent city views and the suites are most impressive. The hotel also offers two different award-winning dining venues - the contemporary Island Restaurant & Bar, and Nipa restaurant with authentic Thai cuisine. There are

extensive conference and banqueting facilities, a 24-hour business centre and secure parking.

Rooms 416 (11 fmly) **S** £113.85-£356.50;
D £113.85-£356.50* **Facilities** STV Xmas New Year Wi-fi Child facilities **Conf** Class 600 Board 40 Thtr 1400 Del from £209 to £276* **Services** Lift Air con **Parking** 65 **Notes** LB ⊗

Royal Park

★★★★ 78% TOWN HOUSE HOTEL PLAN 2 D2

☎ 020 7479 6600 🖹 020 7479 6601
3 Westbourne Ter, Lancaster Gate, Hyde Park W2 3UL
e-mail: growlands@theroyalpark.com
dir: From Lancaster Gate tube station on Bayswater Rd turn right onto Lancaster Terrace, onto Sussex Gardens then left onto Westbourne Terrace

This Grade II listed town house enjoys a central location a stone's throw from Hyde Park and a short walk from Marble Arch, Oxford Street and Park Lane. Bedrooms, which include four-poster suites, are all beautifully appointed and boast handmade mattresses with crisp luxury linens, safes, mini-bars and internet access. Limited off-street parking is available.

Rooms 48 (5 GF) **Facilities** STV FTV Xmas New Year Wi-fi **Conf** Board 10 **Services** Lift Air con **Parking** 10 **Notes** ⊗

Novotel London Paddington

★★★★ 77% HOTEL PLAN 2 C3

☎ 020 7266 6000 🖹 020 7266 6010
3 Kingdom St, Paddington W2 6BD
e-mail: h6455@accor.com
dir: Easy access from Westway A40 & Bishops Bridge Rd A4206

Located in the Paddington Central area, this hotel is easily accessible by road, and is only a few minutes walk from Paddington Station. Ideal for business or leisure guests. The facilities include the Elements Restaurant, a bar, conference facilities, a swimming pool, sauna, plus steam and fitness rooms. An NCP car park is a 5-minute walk away.

Rooms 206 (24 fmly) **Facilities** STV 🏊 Gym Steam room Sauna Wi-fi **Conf** Class 70 Board 40 Thtr 150 **Services** Lift

Ramada Hyde Park

★★★★ 74% HOTEL PLAN 2 B1

☎ 0844 815 9048 🖹 020 7229 2623
150 Bayswater Rd W2 4RT
e-mail: sales.hydepark@ramadajarvis.co.uk
web: www.ramadajarvis.co.uk
dir: From Hammersmith flyover left into Warwick Rd. At Kensington High St turn right, to Kensington Church St, left to T-junct, right into Bayswater Rd. Hotel 0.25m

This large hotel overlooks Kensington Gardens and Hyde Park and is ideal for the West End, Oxford Street and Paddington. Modern air-conditioned bedrooms are

comfortably appointed for both business and leisure guests. Public areas include the Arts Restaurant and a range of meeting rooms. Limited parking is available.

Rooms 213 (10 GF) **Facilities** STV FTV Wi-fi **Conf** Class 50 Board 30 Thtr 100 **Services** Lift Air con **Parking** 39 **Notes** ⊗

Thistle Hyde Park

★★★★ 74% HOTEL PLAN 2 C1

☎ 0871 376 9022 🖹 0871 376 9122
90-92 Lancaster Gate W2 3NR
e-mail: hydepark@thistle.co.uk
web: www.thistlehotels.com/hydepark
dir: From Marble Arch rdbt take A404/Bayswater Rd

Delightful building ideally situated overlooking Hyde Park and just a short walk from Kensington Gardens. The stylish public areas include a piano bar, a lounge and a smart restaurant. Bedrooms are tastefully appointed and equipped with many thoughtful touches; some rooms have views of the park.

Rooms 54 (12 fmly) **S** £75-£305; **Facilities** STV FTV Wi-fi **Conf** Class 20 Board 20 Thtr 30 Del from £175 to £405* **Services** Lift Air con **Parking** 20 **Notes** LB ⊗

Hotel Indigo

★★★★ 72% HOTEL PLAN 2 D2

☎ 020 7706 4444 🖹 020 7706 1100
16 London St, Paddington W2 1HL
e-mail: maloclm@lth-hotels.com

This smart new hotel is located within a stone's throw of Paddington Station. Contemporary and stylish, bedrooms are equipped with all modern extras; they boast high quality comfy beds ensuring a great night's sleep and en suites with power showers and quality toiletries. Delightful public areas include a restaurant, bar and a coffee shop offering delicious cakes.

Rooms 64 **Facilities** STV FTV Gym Wi-fi **Services** Lift Air con **Notes** ⊗

Best Western Delmere

★★ 71% METRO HOTEL PLAN 2 D2

☎ 020 7706 3344 🖹 020 7262 1863
130 Sussex Gardens, Hyde Park W2 1UB
e-mail: reservations@delmerehotel.co.uk
dir: M25 take A40 to London, exit at Paddington. Along Westbourne Terrace into Sussex Gdns

This friendly, privately owned hotel is situated within walking distance of Paddington Station, Hyde Park and Marble Arch. The smartly presented bedrooms are extremely well equipped and include some ground floor rooms. A small bar, a comfortable, elegant lounge and an Italian-style restaurant complete the picture.

Rooms 36 (7 GF) **Facilities** STV Wi-fi **Services** Lift **Parking** 2 **Notes** ⊗

Mitre House

★★ 65% METRO HOTEL PLAN 2 D2

☎ 020 7723 8040 ▤ 020 7402 0990
178-184 Sussex Gardens, Hyde Park W2 1TU
e-mail: reservations@mitrehousehotel.com
web: www.mitrehousehotel.com
dir: Parallel to Bayswater Rd & one block from
Paddington Station

This family-run hotel continues to offers a warm welcome
and attentive service. It is ideally located, close to
Paddington station and near the West End and major
attractions. Bedrooms include a number of family suites
and there is a lounge bar. Limited parking is available.

Rooms 69 (7 fmly) (7 GF) (69 smoking) **S** £80; **D** £90
(incl. bkfst)* **Facilities** STV Wi-fi **Services** Lift **Parking** 20
Notes ⊗

Thistle Kensington Gardens

 thistle

Ⓤ PLAN 2 C1

☎ 0871 376 9024 ▤ 0871 376 9024
104 Bayswater Rd W2 3HL
e-mail: kensingtongardens@thistle.co.uk
web: www.thistlehotels.com/kensingtongardens

Currently the rating for this establishment is not
confirmed. This may be due to a change of ownership or
because it has only recently joined the AA rating scheme.
For further details please see the AA website: theAA.com

Rooms 174 (13 fmly) (11 smoking) **Facilities** STV FTV
Wi-fi **Conf** Class 30 Board 30 Thtr 45 Del from £153 to
£377* **Services** Lift Air con **Parking** 108 **Notes** ⊗
Civ Wed 100

Corus hotel Hyde Park

 corus hotels

Ⓤ PLAN 2 D2

☎ 0844 736 8601 ▤ 020 7724 8666
1-7 Lancaster Gate W2 3LG
e-mail: londonhydepark@corushotels.com
web: www.corushotels.com
dir: 200yds from Lancaster Gate underground. 0.25m
from Paddington Station

Centrally located adjacent to Hyde Park and a short walk
from Marble Arch, this smart hotel is a great base to tour
the city. The bedrooms, including a number of spacious
executive rooms and suites, are fitted out with modern
colour schemes and a useful range of facilities; some
have air conditioning. Open-plan public areas include a
popular restaurant and bar. For further details please see
the AA website: theAA.com

Rooms 390 (10 fmly) (12 GF) (26 smoking) **S** £89-£240;
D £99-£260 **Facilities** FTV Wi-fi **Conf** Class 40 Board 36
Thtr 90 Del from £140 to £200* **Services** Lift Air con
Notes LB ⊗

Days Inn London Hyde Park

 DAYS INN

BUDGET HOTEL PLAN 2 D2

☎ 020 7723 2939 ▤ 020 7723 6225
148/152 Sussex Gardens W2 1UD
e-mail: reservations@daysinnhydepark.com
web: www.daysinn.com
dir: On N side of Hyde Park. 2 min walk from Paddington
Station

This modern building offers accommodation in smart,
spacious and well-equipped bedrooms, suitable for
families and business travellers, and all with en suite
bathrooms. Continental breakfast is available and other
refreshments may be taken at the nearby family
restaurant. See also the Hotel Groups pages.

Rooms 57 (5 fmly) (11 GF) **S** £65-£95; **D** £85-£110 (incl.
bkfst)*

W3 ACTON

See LONDON plan 1 C3/4

Ramada Encore London West

★★★ 74% HOTEL

☎ 0870 0667 123 ▤ 0870 0667 144
4 Portal Way, Gypsy Corner, A40 Western Av W3 6RT
e-mail: reservations@encorelondonwest.co.uk
web: www.encorelondonwest.co.uk

Conveniently situated on the A40 this modern, purpose
built, glass fronted hotel is ideal for visitors to London.
Air-conditioned bedrooms offer smartly appointed modern
accommodation with en suite power shower rooms. Open-
plan public areas include a popular Asian and European
restaurant, Wok Around the World, and a 2go café and
sandwich bar. Secure parking and a range of meeting
rooms complete the picture.

Rooms 150 (35 fmly) (15 smoking) **S** £69.95-£159.95;
D £69.95-£159.95* **Facilities** STV FTV Wi-fi
Conf Class 28 Board 26 Thtr 50 Del from £129 to £159
Services Lift Air con **Parking** 72 **Notes** LB ⊗

Express by Holiday Inn London - Park Royal

 Express by Holiday Inn

BUDGET HOTEL

☎ 020 8896 4460 ▤ 020 8896 4461
Victoria Rd, Acton W3 6UB
e-mail: info@exhiparkroyal.co.uk
web: www.hiexpress.co.uk
dir: A4000 Victorian Rd towards North Acton. 1st right
onto Portal Way. Left Wales Farm Rd, left Victoria Rd,
hotel 100mtrs on right

A modern hotel ideal for families and business travellers.
Fresh and uncomplicated, the spacious rooms include Sky
TV, power shower and tea and coffee-making facilities.
Continental buffet breakfast is included in the room rate;
other meals may be taken at the nearby family pub or
restaurant. See also the Hotel Groups pages.

Rooms 104 (35 fmly) **S** fr £49; **D** fr £49 (incl. bkfst)*
Conf Class 30 Board 30 Thtr 50

Travelodge London Park Royal

 Travelodge

BUDGET HOTEL

☎ 0871 984 6195 ▤ 020 8752 1134
A40 Western Ave, Acton W3 0TE
web: www.travelodge.co.uk
dir: Off A40 (Western Ave) eastbound

Travelodge offers good quality, good value, budget
accommodation. All offer family rooms sleeping up to four
(two adults, two children) with en suite bathroom/
shower-room, remote-control TV, tea- and coffee-making
facilities and comfortable beds. Food options vary.
Breakfast is at the on-site Bar Café restaurant (if
available) or to take away. See also Hotel Groups pages.

Rooms 64 **S** fr £29; **D** fr £29

W4 CHISWICK

See LONDON plan 1 C3

Chiswick Moran
★★★★ 79% HOTEL

☎ 020 8996 5200   📠 020 8996 5201
626 Chiswick High Rd W4 5RY
e-mail: chiswickres@moranhotels.com
web: www.chiswickmoranhotel.co.uk
dir: 200yds from M4 junct 2

This stylish, modern hotel is conveniently located for Heathrow and central London, with Gunnersby tube station just a few minutes walk away. Airy, spacious public areas include a modern restaurant, a popular bar and excellent meeting facilities. Fully air-conditioned bedrooms are stylish and extremely well appointed with broadband, laptop safes and flat-screen TVs. All boast spacious, modern bathrooms, many with walk-in rain showers.

Rooms 122 (6 fmly) (7 smoking) **D** £79-£230 (incl. bkfst)* **Facilities** STV Gym Wi-fi **Conf** Class 45 Board 40 Thtr 90 Del from £199 to £250* **Services** Lift Air con **Parking** 40 **Notes** LB ⊗ Civ Wed 80

W5 EALING

See LONDON SECTION plan 1 C4

Crowne Plaza London-Ealing
★★★★ 74% HOTEL PLAN 1 C4

☎ 0870 400 9114 & 020 8233 3200   📠 020 8233 3201
Western Av, Hanger Ln, Ealing W5 1HG
e-mail: info@cp-londonealing.co.uk
web: www.cp-londonealing.co.uk
dir: A40 from Central London towards M40. Exit at Ealing & North Circular A406 sign. At rdbt take 2nd exit signed A40. Hotel on left

Now refurbished to a high standard, this hotel occupies a prime position on the A40 and North Circular at Hangar Lane; Wembley Stadium is easily accessible. Modern, well-equipped, air-conditioned and sound-proofed bedrooms offer good facilities. There is a smart gym, a steam room together with meeting facilities and the West 5 Brasserie. On-site parking is available.

Rooms 131 (17 GF) (15 smoking) **S** £80-£235; **D** £130-£295* **Facilities** FTV Gym Steam room Xmas New Year Wi-fi **Conf** Class 48 Board 35 Thtr 80 Del from £165 to £250* **Services** Lift Air con **Parking** 85 **Notes** LB ⊗ Civ Wed 80

Ramada London Ealing

★★★ 79% HOTEL

☎ 0844 815 9035   📠 020 8992 7082
Ealing Common W5 3HN
e-mail: sales.ealing@ramadajarvis.co.uk
web: www.ramadajarvis.co.uk
dir: At junct of North Circular A406 & Uxbridge Road, A4020

This large modern, comfortable hotel is conveniently located a few minutes walk from Ealing Common underground and easy access to the M40. Bedrooms, which vary in size, are comfortably appointed for both business and leisure guests. There is substantial parking, a spacious Arts Restaurant and a range of meeting rooms.

Rooms 189 (3 fmly) **S** £209; **D** £244 (incl. bkfst)* **Facilities** FTV Xmas New Year Wi-fi **Conf** Class 110 Board 80 Thtr 200 Del from £135 to £195* **Services** Lift Air con **Parking** 150 **Notes** LB ⊗ Civ Wed 200

W6 HAMMERSMITH

See LONDON plan 1 D3

Novotel London West

★★★★ 71% HOTEL

☎ 020 8741 1555   📠 020 8741 2120
1 Shortlands W6 8DR
e-mail: H0737@accor.com
web: www.novotellondonwest.co.uk
dir: M4 (A4) & A316 junct at Hogarth rdbt. Along Great West Rd, left for Hammersmith before flyover. On Hammersmith Bridge Rd to rdbt, take 5th exit. 1st left into Shortlands, 1st left to hotel main entrance

A Hammersmith landmark, this substantial hotel is a popular base for both business and leisure travellers. Spacious, air-conditioned bedrooms have a good range of extras and many have additional beds, making them suitable for families. The hotel also has its own car park, business centre and shop, and boasts one of the largest convention centres in Europe.

Rooms 630 (148 fmly) **Facilities** STV Gym Wi-fi **Conf** Class 700 Board 200 Thtr 1700 **Services** Lift Air con **Parking** 240 **Notes** Civ Wed 1400

Express by Holiday Inn London - Hammersmith

BUDGET HOTEL

☎ 020 8746 5100   📠 020 8746 5199
120 -124 King St W6 0QU
e-mail: gsm.hammersmith@expressholidayinn.co.uk
web: www.hiexpress.com/hammersmith
dir: M4/A4 junct 1 to Hammersmith Broadway. 2nd left to A315 towards Chiswick (King St). Hotel on right

A modern hotel ideal for families and business travellers. Fresh and uncomplicated, the spacious rooms include Sky TV, power shower and tea and coffee-making facilities.

Continental buffet breakfast is included in the room rate; other meals may be taken at the nearby family pub or restaurant. See also the Hotel Groups pages.

Rooms 135 (49 fmly) **Conf** Class 18 Board 20 Thtr 35

W8 KENSINGTON

INSPECTORS' CHOICE

Royal Garden Hotel
★★★★★ ⊛⊛⊛ HOTEL PLAN 4 B5

☎ 020 7937 8000   📠 020 7361 1991
2-24 Kensington High St W8 4PT
e-mail: sales@royalgardenhotel.co.uk
web: www.royalgardenhotel.co.uk
dir: Next to Kensington Palace

This well-known landmark hotel is just a short walk from the Royal Albert Hall. Bedrooms are of contemporary design, equipped with many up-to-date facilities; many are spacious and offer super views over Kensington Gardens. The contemporary Min Jiang is the exciting Chinese restaurant on the top floor that has professional and attentive service. The authentic Chinese cuisine impresses with a number of dishes from Sichuan Provence and also the signature dish of Beijing Duck cooked in the traditional way over apple wood.

Rooms 396 (19 fmly) **S** £171.35-£240.35; **D** £205.85-£274.85* **Facilities** Spa STV Gym Health & fitness centre Xmas New Year Wi-fi **Conf** Class 260 Board 80 Thtr 550 **Services** Lift Air con **Notes** LB ⊗ Civ Wed 400

Milestone Hotel

★★★★★

HOTEL PLAN 4 B4

☎ 020 7917 1000 📠 020 7917 1010
1 Kensington Court W8 5DL
e-mail: bookms@rchmail.com
web: www.milestonehotel.com
dir: From Warwick Rd right into Kensington High St.
Hotel 400yds past Kensington underground

This delightful town house enjoys a wonderful location opposite Kensington Palace and is near the elegant shops. Individually themed bedrooms include a selection of stunning suites that are equipped with every conceivable extra. Public areas include the luxurious Park Lounge where afternoon tea is served, a delightful panelled bar, a sumptuous restaurant and a small gym and resistance pool.

Rooms 63 (3 fmly) (2 GF) (5 smoking) **S** £275-£311;
Facilities STV FTV ⌨ Gym Health club ♫ Xmas New
Year Wi-fi **Conf** Class 20 Board 20 Thtr 50 **Services** Lift
Air con **Parking** 1 **Notes** Civ Wed 30

Copthorne Tara Hotel London Kensington

★★★★ 75% HOTEL PLAN 4 B4

☎ 020 7937 7211 & 7872 2000 📠 020 7937 7100
Scarsdale Place, Wrights Ln W8 5SR
e-mail: reservations.tara@millenniumhotels.co.uk
web: www.millenniumhotels.com/tara
dir: Off Kensington High Street down Wright's Ln

This expansive hotel that is ideally placed for the stylish shops and also the tube station. Smart public areas include a trendy coffee shop, a gym, a stylish brasserie and bar plus extensive conference facilities. Bedrooms include several well-equipped rooms for less mobile guests, in addition to a number of Connoisseur rooms that have the use of a club lounge with its many complimentary facilities.

Rooms 833 (3 fmly) (68 smoking) **D** £75-£225
Facilities STV Gym Beauty & well-being room Xmas New
Year Wi-fi **Conf** Class 160 Board 90 Thtr 280 **Services** Lift
Air con **Parking** 101 **Notes** LB ⊗ Civ Wed 280

See LONDON plan 1 B3

K West Hotel & Spa

★★★★ 80% HOTEL PLAN 1 D3

☎ 020 8008 6600 📠 020 8008 6650
Richmond Way W14 0AX
e-mail: info@k-west.co.uk
web: www.k-west.co.uk
dir: From A40/M take Shepherd's Bush Exit. Holland Park
rdbt 3rd exit. Take 1st left & left again. Hotel straight
ahead

This stylish, contemporary hotel is conveniently located for Notting Hill, the exhibition halls and the BBC; Bond Street is only a 10-minute tube journey away. Funky, minimalist public areas include a trendy lobby bar and mezzanine style restaurant, and free internet access is available. Spacious bedrooms and suites are extremely well appointed and offer luxurious bedding and a host of thoughtful extras such as CD and DVD players. Wi-fi is available throughout. The spa offers a comprehensive range of health, beauty and relaxation treatments.

Rooms 220 (31 GF) (44 smoking) **Facilities** Spa STV FTV
Gym ♫ Xmas New Year Wi-fi **Conf** Class 20 Board 25
Thtr 50 **Services** Lift Air con **Parking** 100 **Notes** ⊗

Express by Holiday Inn London - Earl's Court

BUDGET HOTEL PLAN 4 A1

☎ 020 7384 5151 📠 020 7384 5152
295 North End Rd W14 9NS
e-mail: info@exhiearlscourt.co.uk
web: www.hiexpress.com/lonearlscourt

A modern hotel ideal for families and business travellers. Fresh and uncomplicated, the spacious rooms include Sky TV, power shower and tea and coffee-making facilities. Continental buffet breakfast is included in the room rate; other meals may be taken at the nearby family pub or restaurant. See also the Hotel Groups pages.

Rooms 100 (65 fmly) **Conf** Class 12 Board 12 Thtr 50

Renaissance Chancery Court

★★★★★ 86% ◉◉◉

HOTEL PLAN 3 D3

☎ 020 7829 9888 📠 020 7829 9889
252 High Holborn WC1V 7EN
e-mail: rhi.loncc.sales.cord@renaissancehotels.com
web: www.renaissancechancerycourt.co.uk
dir: A4 along Piccadilly onto Shaftesbury Av. Into High
Holborn, hotel on right

This is a grand place with splendid public areas, decorated from top to bottom in rare marble. Craftsmen have meticulously restored the sweeping staircases, archways and stately rooms of the 1914 building. The result is a spacious, relaxed hotel offering everything from stylish, luxuriously appointed bedrooms to a health club and state-of-the-art meeting rooms. The sophisticated Pearl Restaurant & Bar offers an impressive standard of cooking.

Rooms 356 (68 fmly) (14 smoking) **S** £188-£394;
D £188-£394* **Facilities** Spa Gym **Conf** Class 234
Board 120 Thtr 435 **Services** Lift Air con **Notes** ⊗
Civ Wed 301

WC1 BLOOMSBURY, HOLBORN *continued*

The Montague on the Gardens

★★★★ 84% HOTEL PLAN 3 C4

☎ 020 7637 1001 ▤ 020 7637 2516
15 Montague St, Bloomsbury WC1B 5BJ
e-mail: bookmt@rchmail.com
web: www.montaguehotel.com
dir: Just off Russell Square, adjacent to British Museum

This stylish hotel is situated right next to the British Museum. A special feature is the alfresco terrace overlooking a delightful garden. Other public rooms include the Blue Door Bistro and Chef's Table, a bar, a lounge and a conservatory where traditional afternoon teas are served. The bedrooms are beautifully appointed and range from split-level suites to more compact rooms.

Rooms 100 (10 fmly) (19 GF) (5 smoking) **S** £135-£215; **D** £155-£235* **Facilities** STV Gym ♫ Xmas New Year Wi-fi Child facilities **Conf** Class 50 Board 50 Thtr 120 Del from £195 to £295* **Services** Lift Air con **Notes** LB Civ Wed 90

The Bloomsbury Hotel

★★★★ 80% HOTEL PLAN 3 C3

☎ 020 7347 1000 ▤ 020 7347 1001
16-22 Great Russell St WC1B 3NN
e-mail: gtrussellstreet@doylecollection.com
web: www.doylecollection.com
dir: A40 onto A400, Gower St then south to Bedford Sq. Turn right, then 1st left to end of road

On the doorstep of Covent Garden, Oxford Street and the West End, this impressive building, designed by the renowned British architect Sir Edwin Lutyens in the 1930s, retains many original features. Bedrooms are attractively appointed and benefit from an excellent range of facilities. Public areas include a grand reception lounge, an elegant bar and restaurant plus extensive conference facilities.

Rooms 153 (1 fmly) **S** £95-£285; **D** £95-£285* **Facilities** STV Xmas Wi-fi **Conf** Class 180 Board 60 Thtr 300 Del from £305 to £455* **Services** Lift Air con **Notes** LB Civ Wed 200

Hotel Russell

★★★★ 74% HOTEL PLAN 3 C4

☎ 020 7837 6470 ▤ 020 7837 2857
Russell Square WC1B 5BE
e-mail: russell.reservations@principal-hayley.com
web: www.principal-hotels.com
dir: From A501 into Woburn Place. Hotel 500mtrs on left

This landmark Grade II, Victorian hotel is located on Russell Square, within walking distance of the West End and theatre district. Many bedrooms are stylish and state-of-the-art in design, and others are more traditional. Spacious public areas include the impressive

foyer with a restored mosaic floor, a choice of lounges and an elegant restaurant.

Rooms 373 **Facilities** STV FTV Wi-fi **Conf** Class 200 Board 75 Thtr 450 **Services** Lift Air con **Notes** Civ Wed 300

Holiday Inn Kings Cross/ Bloomsbury

★★★★ 71% HOTEL PLAN 3 E5

☎ 020 7833 3900 ▤ 020 7917 6163
1 Kings Cross Rd WC1X 9HX
e-mail: sales@holidayinnlondon.com
web: www.holidayinn.co.uk
dir: 0.5m from Kings Cross Station on corner of King Cross Rd & Calthorpe St

Conveniently located for Kings Cross station and The City, this modern hotel offers smart, spacious air-conditioned accommodation with a wide range of facilities. There are versatile meeting rooms, a bar, a well-equipped fitness centre and a choice of restaurants including one serving Indian cuisine.

Rooms 405 (163 fmly) (126 smoking) **Facilities** STV FTV ⚙ Gym **Conf** Class 120 Board 30 Thtr 220 **Services** Lift Air con **Parking** 15 **Notes** LB

Holiday Inn London Bloomsbury

★★★★ 71% HOTEL PLAN 3 C4

☎ 0870 400 9222 ▤ 020 7837 5374
Coram St WC1N 1HT
e-mail: bloomsbury@ihg.com
web: www.holidayinn.co.uk
dir: off Upper Woburn Place near Russell Sq

Centrally located, this modern and stylish hotel is within easy reach of many of London's tourist attractions and close to St Pancras International Rail Station. The bedrooms boast a pillow menu, air-conditioning and high-speed internet access. The Junction restaurant offers a modern menu whilst Callaghans is a traditional Irish pub featuring the best of Irish beers. The meeting rooms can cater for many different events.

Rooms 311 (30 fmly) (16 smoking) **Facilities** Wi-fi **Conf** Class 180 Board 80 Thtr 300 **Services** Lift Air con **Notes** Civ Wed 50

Radisson Edwardian Bloomsbury Street Hotel

★★★★ ⓐ HOTEL PLAN 3 C3

☎ 020 7636 5601 ▤ 020 7636 0532
Bloomsbury St WC1B 3QD
e-mail: resmarl@radisson.com
dir: Pass Oxford St, down New Oxford St into Bloomsbury St

Rooms 174 (3 fmly) (5 smoking) **Facilities** Xmas Wi-fi **Conf** Class 150 Board 60 Thtr 300 Del from £270 to £350* **Services** Lift Air con **Notes** No children 16 yrs

Radisson Edwardian Kenilworth

★★★★ ⓐ HOTEL PLAN 3 C3

☎ 020 7637 3477 ▤ 020 636 0532
Great Russell St WC1B 3LB
e-mail: reskeni@radisson.com
dir: from New Oxford St into Bloomsbury St, then Great Russell St

Rooms 186 (15 fmly) **Facilities** Fitness room Xmas Wi-fi **Conf** Class 50 Board 35 Thtr 120 **Services** Lift Air con **Notes** No children 16 yrs

The Kingsley by Thistle

thistle

★★★ 73% HOTEL PLAN 3 C3

☎ 0871 376 9006 ▤ 0871 376 9106
Bloomsbury Way WC1A 2SD
e-mail: thekingsley@thistle.co.uk
dir: A40(M) to A501 (Marylebone Rd), take sliproad before underpass to Holburn. Into Gower St, Bloomsbury St (A400). Left into Oxford St & onto Bloomsbury Way

Well situated for theatregoers, this hotel enjoys a convenient central location. The well-equipped rooms are generally spacious with good quality fabrics and furnishings, with both family rooms and executive suites available. The ground-floor bar and lounge areas are well appointed. There is a public car park nearby.

Rooms 129 **S** £109-£209; **D** £119-£229* **Facilities** STV FTV Wi-fi **Conf** Class 50 Board 30 Thtr 120 Del from £200 to £275* **Services** Lift Air con **Notes** LB

Bedford

★★★ 66% HOTEL PLAN 3 D4

☎ 020 7636 7822 & 7692 3620 ▤ 020 7837 4653
83-93 Southampton Row WC1B 4HD
e-mail: info@imperialhotels.co.uk
web: www.imperialhotels.co.uk

Just off Russell Square, this intimate hotel is ideal for visits to the British Museum and Covent Garden. The bedrooms are well equipped with all the expected facilities including modem points if requested. The ground floor has a lounge, a bar and restaurant plus there's a delightful secret rear garden. An underground car park is a bonus.

Rooms 184 (1 fmly) **S** £76; **D** £103 (incl. bkfst)*
Facilities FTV Xmas New Year Wi-fi **Conf** Board 12
Services Lift **Parking** 50 **Notes** ⊗

Travelodge London Farringdon

BUDGET HOTEL PLAN 3 E6

☎ 08719 846 274 📠 020 7837 3776
10-42 Kings Cross Rd WC1X 9QN
web: www.travelodge.co.uk
dir: Between King's Cross & Farringdon stations. Exit King's Cross station into Pentonville Rd. Right into King's Cross Rd (A201). Hotel 0.25m on left

Travelodge offers good quality, good value, budget accommodation. All offer family rooms sleeping up to four (two adults, two children) with en suite bathroom/shower-room, remote-control TV, tea- and coffee-making facilities and comfortable beds. Food options vary. Breakfast is at the on-site Bar Café restaurant (if available) or to take away. See also Hotel Groups pages.

Rooms 219 (18 fmly) **S** fr £29; **D** fr £29 **Conf** Class 18 Board 30 Thtr 50

Travelodge London Kings Cross

BUDGET HOTEL PLAN 3 D6

☎ 0871 984 6256 📠 020 7278 7396
Willing House, Grays Inn Rd, Kings Cross WC1X 8BH
web: www.travelodge.co.uk
dir: 200yds from entrance to Kings Cross Station & Thames Link

Rooms 140 **S** fr £29; **D** fr £29

Travelodge London Kings Cross Royal Scot

BUDGET HOTEL PLAN 3 E5

☎ 0871 984 6272 📠 020 7833 0798
100 Kings Cross Rd WC1X 9DT
web: www.travelodge.co.uk
dir: Exit King's Cross Station into Pentonville Rd. Right into King's Cross Rd (A201) Lodge on left

Rooms 408 (22 fmly) **S** fr £29; **D** fr £29 **Conf** Class 60 Board 50 Thtr 170

WC2 SOHO, STRAND

INSPECTORS' CHOICE

One Aldwych
★★★★★ ⊛ HOTEL PLAN 3 D2

☎ 020 7300 1000 & 7300 0500 📠 020 7300 1001
1 Aldwych WC2B 4RH
e-mail: reservations@onealdwych.com
web: www.onealdwych.com
dir: At Aldwych & The Strand junct, opposite Waterloo Bridge

Although well established for some years now, One Aldwych continues to be highly considered for its blend of chic design and consistent high standards. Bedrooms vary in size, but all are stylish, very well equipped and have excellent beds with giant pillows and high quality bedding. There are a host of facilities - two fine restaurants, Axis (2 AA Rosettes) with a separate entrance and open-plan Indigo (1 AA rosette), a health club with underwater music in the therapeutic pool, the Lobby Bar and also a private screening room.

Rooms 105 (18 fmly) (36 smoking) **D** £225-£449*
Facilities Spa STV ⊗ Gym Sauna Steam & Treatment rooms Xmas New Year Wi-fi **Conf** Board 40 Thtr 60
Services Lift Air con **Notes** ⊗ Civ Wed 60

Swissôtel The Howard, London
★★★★★ 83% ⊛⊛ HOTEL PLAN 3 E2

☎ 020 7836 3555 📠 020 7379 4547
Temple Place WC2R 2PR
e-mail: london@swissotel.com
web: www.swissotel.com/london
dir: From E turn off Aldwych, keep left of church (in centre of road). Turn left into Surrey St. Hotel at end

This smart hotel enjoys wonderful views across London's historic skyline from its riverside location, and the Eurostar terminal, Covent Garden and Theatreland are all within easy reach. The air-conditioned bedrooms offer a host of extra facilities. The restaurant, now called 12 Temple Place, has changed its focus and offers a modern British menu of regional and seasonal produce. The bar opens out onto a delightful garden where alfresco dining is possible when the weather permits.

Rooms 189 (43 smoking) **S** £138-£310.50;
D £138-£310.50* **Facilities** STV Complimentary use of nearby health club ♬ Xmas New Year Wi-fi **Conf** Class 60 Board 60 Thtr 120 Del from £290.50 to £499*
Services Lift Air con **Parking** 30 **Notes** LB ⊗ Civ Wed 120

Radisson Edwardian Hampshire Hotel

★★★★★ Ⓐ HOTEL PLAN 3 C1

☎ 020 7839 9399 📠 020 7930 8122
31 Leicester Square WC2H 7LH
e-mail: reshamp@radisson.com
dir: from Charing Cross Rd turn into Cranbourn St at Leicester Sq. Left at end, hotel at bottom of square

Rooms 124 (5 fmly) **Facilities** Gym Fitness room Wi-fi **Conf** Class 48 Board 35 Thtr 100 **Services** Lift Air con **Notes** ⊗ No children 16 yrs

Charing Cross

★★★★ 76% ⊛ HOTEL PLAN 3 C1

☎ 0871 376 9012 📠 0870 333 9205
The Strand WC2N 5HX
e-mail: charingcross@guoman.co.uk
web: www.guoman.com
dir: E along The Strand towards Trafalgar Square, right into station forecourt

This centrally located and historic landmark hotel provides a friendly welcome. Spacious in design, the original grand architecture blends nicely with the modern style of interior appointments, particularly in the bedrooms and bathrooms. There is a choice of dining options including the relaxed Terrace on the Strand which has splendid views of London especially at night.

Rooms 239 (83 annexe) (12 fmly) (8 smoking) **Facilities** STV ♬ Xmas New Year Wi-fi **Conf** Class 96 Board 46 Thtr 140 **Services** Lift Air con **Notes** LB Civ Wed 140

Radisson Edwardian Mountbatten

★★★★ Ⓐ HOTEL PLAN 3 C2

☎ 020 7836 4300 📠 020 7240 3540
Monmouth St, Seven Dials, Covent Garden WC2H 9HD
e-mail: resmoun@radisson.com
dir: off Shaftesbury Av, on corner of Seven Dials rdbt

Rooms 151 **Facilities** FTV Fitness room Xmas New Year Wi-fi **Conf** Class 45 Board 32 Thtr 90 **Services** Lift Air con **Notes** ⊗

The Royal Trafalgar by Thistle   thistle
★★★ 77% HOTEL PLAN 3 C2

☎ 0871 376 9037 📠 0871 376 9137
Whitcomb St WC2H 7HG
e-mail: theroyaltrafalgar@thistle.co.uk
web: www.thistlehotels.com/tralalgarsquare
dir: 100mtrs from Trafalgar Sq adjacent to Sainsbury Wing of National Gallery

Quietly located, this handily placed hotel is just a short walk from Trafalgar Square and theatreland. Bedrooms

continued

WC2 SOHO, STRAND *continued*

offer good levels of comfort with a variety of standards available. Dining options include the Squares Restaurant offering a wide selection, or alternatively, light meals can be taken in the Gravity Lounge and Bar.

Rooms 108 (16 fmly) (12 smoking) **Facilities** STV FTV Wi-fi **Services** Lift Air con **Notes** ⊗

Strand Palace

★★★ 74% HOTEL PLAN 3 D2

☎ 020 7836 8080 & 020 7497 4100 📄 020 7836 2077
372 The Strand WC2R 0JJ
e-mail: reservations@strandpalacehotel.co.uk
dir: From Trafalgar Square, on A4 to Charing Cross, 350mtrs, hotel on left.

At the heart of Theatreland, this vast hotel is proud of its friendly and efficient staff. The bedrooms vary in style and include bright Club rooms with enhanced facilities. The extensive public areas include shops, a popular cocktail bar and there is the Strand Carvery and Johnson's Brasserie as eating options.

Rooms 786 **S** £75-£175; **D** £95-£195 (incl. bkfst)*
Facilities STV Xmas New Year Wi-fi **Conf** Class 90 Board 40 Thtr 180 Del from £166 to £265* **Services** Lift **Notes** ⊗

Radisson Edwardian Leicester Square

★★★ 🅰 HOTEL PLAN 3 C1

☎ 020 7930 8641 & 020 7451 0227 📄 020 7451 0191
3-6 Saint Martins St WC2H 7HL
e-mail: reshamp@radisson.com
dir: from Whitcomb Street left into Panton Street. Saint Martins Street off Leicester Square

Rooms 58 **Facilities** Gym **Services** Lift **Notes** ⊗

The Savoy

Ⓤ PLAN 3 D1

☎ 020 7836 4343 📄 020 7240 6040
Strand WC2R 0EU
e-mail: savoy@fairmont.com
dir: Halfway along The Strand between Trafalgar Sq & Aldwych

The Savoy Hotel has been at the fore of the London hotel scene since it opened in 1889. Now taken over by the Fairmont Group, the hotel has benefited from some loving restoration with much of the its art deco heritage kept intact. The 233 bedrooms, including 72 suites, vary in style and size, and many overlook the Thames. The famous River Restaurant, Savoy Grill and American Bar remain as well loved dining destinations, and the Thames

Foyer is well known for its theatre and afternoon teas. As we went to press we understood that the hotel would open at the end of 2009. For up-to-date information please see the AA website: theAA.com

Travelodge London Covent Garden

BUDGET HOTEL PLAN 3 D2

☎ 0871 984 6245 📄 01376 572 724
10 Drury Ln, High Holborn WC2B 5RE
web: www.travelodge.co.uk
dir: On High Holborn off Drury Lane

Travelodge offers good quality, good value, budget accommodation. All offer family rooms sleeping up to four (two adults, two children) with en suite bathroom/shower-room, remote-control TV, tea- and coffee-making facilities and comfortable beds. Food options vary. Breakfast is at the on-site Bar Café restaurant (if available) or to take away. See also Hotel Groups pages.

Rooms 392 (4 fmly) **S** fr £29; **D** fr £29 **Conf** Class 40 Board 30 Thtr 100

LONDON GATEWAY MOTORWAY SERVICE AREA (M1)	Map 6 TQ19

Days Hotel London North

★★★ 67% HOTEL

☎ 020 8906 7000 📄 020 8906 7011
Welcome Break Service Area NW7 3HU
e-mail: lgw.hotel@welcomebreak.co.uk
web: www.welcomebreak.co.uk
dir: On M1 between junct 2/4 northbound & southbound

This modern building offers accommodation in smart, spacious and well-equipped bedrooms, suitable for families and business travellers, and all with en suite bathrooms. Continental breakfast is available and other refreshments may be taken at the nearby family restaurant.

Rooms 200 (190 fmly) (80 GF) **S** £29-£59; **D** £39-£79*
Facilities FTV Wi-fi **Conf** Class 30 Board 50 Thtr 70 Del from £75 to £125* **Services** Lift Air con **Parking** 160 **Notes** LB Civ Wed 80

LONDON, GREATER

BARKING

See LONDON SECTION plan 1 H4

Ibis London Barking

BUDGET HOTEL

☎ 020 8477 4100 📄 020 8477 4101
Highbridge Rd IG11 7BA
e-mail: H2042@accor.com
web: www.ibishotel.com
dir: exit Barking from A406 or A13

Modern, budget hotel offering comfortable accommodation in bright and practical bedrooms. Breakfast is self-service and dinner is available in the restaurant. See also the Hotel Groups pages.

Rooms 86 (26 GF) (9 smoking)

Travelodge London Barking

BUDGET HOTEL

☎ 0871 984 6416 📄 0208 507 7171
Pionaworks, 4 Arboretum Place IG11 7RX
dir: Exit A13 at junct with A123 towards Barking, left at 1st lights. From A406 (S) take A124, follow town centre signs

Travelodge offers good quality, good value, budget accommodation. All offer family rooms sleeping up to four (two adults, two children) with en suite bathroom/shower-room, remote-control TV, tea- and coffee-making facilities and comfortable beds. Food options vary. Breakfast is at the on-site Bar Café restaurant (if available) or to take away. See also the Hotel Groups pages.

Rooms 66 **S** fr £29; **D** fr £29

BARNET	Map 6 TQ29

Savoro Restaurant with Rooms

◎ RESTAURANT WITH ROOMS

☎ 020 8449 9888 📄 020 8449 7444
206 High St EN5 5SZ
e-mail: savoro@savoro.co.uk
web: www.savoro.co.uk
dir: M25 junct 23 on A1000 in crescent behind Hadley Green Jaguar Garage

Set back from the main high street, the traditional frontage of this establishment belies the stylishly modern bedrooms and well designed bathrooms within. The award-winning restaurant is an additional bonus.

Rooms 11 (2 fmly)

BECKENHAM

BECKENHAM

See LONDON SECTION plan 1 G1

Innkeeper's Lodge London Beckenham

BUDGET HOTEL

☎ 0845 112 6126 📠 0845 112 6184
422 Upper Elmers End Rd BR3 3HQ
web: www.innkeeperslodge.com/beckenham
dir: From M25 junct 6 Croydon, A22 towards Croydon, then A232 for Shirley. At West Wickham take A214. Lodge opposite Eden Park Station

Innkeeper's Lodge represents an exciting, high value concept within the budget hotel market. Comfortable bedrooms provide excellent facilities that include satellite TV and modem points. Options include family rooms; and for the corporate guest, cutting edge IT which includes Wi-fi access. A popular Carvery provides all-day food, including an extensive, complimentary continental breakfast. See also the Hotel Groups pages.

Rooms 24 (1 fmly)

BEXLEY   Map 6 TQ47

Bexleyheath Marriott Hotel

★★★★ 75% HOTEL

☎ 020 8298 1000 📠 020 8298 1234
1 Broadway DA6 7JZ
e-mail: bexleyheath@marriotthotels.co.uk
web: www.bexleyheathmarriott.co.uk
dir: M25 junct 2/A2 towards London. Exit at Black Prince junct onto A220, signed Bexleyheath. Left at 2nd lights into hotel

Well positioned for access to major road networks, this large, modern hotel offers spacious, air-conditioned bedrooms with a comprehensive range of extra facilities. Planters Bar is a popular venue for pre-dinner drinks and offers guests a choice of lighter dining, whilst a more formal restaurant is also available. The hotel boasts a well-equipped leisure centre and undercover parking.

Rooms 142 (16 fmly) (26 GF) **D** £85-£129 (incl. bkfst)* **Facilities** STV 🔄 supervised Gym Steam room Health beauty treatment Xmas New Year Wi-fi **Conf** Class 120 Board 34 Thtr 250 Del from £138 to £150* **Services** Lift Air con **Parking** 77 **Notes** ⊗ Civ Wed 60

Holiday Inn London - Bexley

★★★ 75% HOTEL

☎ 0870 400 9006 & 01322 625513 📠 01322 526113
Black Prince Interchange, Southwold Rd DA5 1ND
e-mail: bexley@ihg.com
web: www.holidayinn.co.uk
dir: M25 junct 2, A2 towards London. Exit at Black Prince interchange (signed Bexley, Bexleyheath, A220, A223). Hotel on left

This hotel is within easy access of London and the Kent countryside; only 10 minutes from the famous Bluewater Shopping Centre and 15 minutes from Brands Hatch motor racing circuit. All bedrooms are air conditioned; suites are available. The hotel has a range of meeting rooms.

Rooms 107 (11 fmly) (33 GF) (16 smoking) **Facilities** New Year Wi-fi **Conf** Class 42 Board 50 Thtr 120 **Services** Lift Air con **Parking** 200 **Notes** Civ Wed 80

BRENTFORD

See LONDON plan 1 C3

Holiday Inn London Brentford Lock

★★★★ 75% HOTEL

☎ 020 8232 2000 📠 020 8232 2001
High St TW8 8JZ
e-mail: info@holidayinnbrentford.co.uk
web: www.holidayinn.co.uk
dir: M4 junct 2 onto A4. At rdbt take 4th exit onto A315, hotel on right

This smart, modern hotel is located beside the Grand Union Canal in the heart of Brentford. Central London, the major motorway networks and Heathrow Airport are all within easy reach. Stylish bedrooms are thoughtfully equipped and contemporary public areas include a bar/lounge, restaurant, conference and function facilities. There is a spacious underground car park.

Rooms 134 (30 fmly) (30 smoking) **Facilities** Wi-fi **Conf** Class 200 Board 120 Thtr 700 **Services** Lift Air con **Parking** 60 **Notes** ⊗ Civ Wed 180

Travelodge London Kew Bridge

BUDGET HOTEL

☎ 0871 984 6040 📠 020 8758 1190
North Rd, High St TW8 0BD
web: www.travelodge.co.uk
dir: M4 junct 2 at Chiswick rdbt take right exit towards Kew. At lights right into Kew Bridge Rd. Lodge 400yds on right

Travelodge offers good quality, good value, budget accommodation. All offer family rooms sleeping up to four (two adults, two children) with en suite bathroom/

shower-room, remote-control TV, tea- and coffee-making facilities and comfortable beds. Food options vary. Breakfast is at the on-site Bar Café restaurant (if available) or to take away. See also Hotel Groups pages.

Rooms 111 **S** fr £29; **D** fr £29

BROMLEY

See LONDON SECTION plan 1 G1

Best Western Bromley Court

★★★ 77% HOTEL

☎ 020 8461 8600 📠 020 8460 0899
Bromley Hill BR1 4JD
e-mail: enquiries@bromleycourthotel.co.uk
web: www.bw-bromleycourthotel.co.uk
dir: N of town centre, off A21. Private drive opposite Volkswagen garage on Bromley Hill

Set amid three acres of grounds, this smart hotel enjoys a peaceful location, in a residential area on the outskirts of town. Well maintained bedrooms are smartly appointed and thoughtfully equipped. The contemporary-style restaurant offers a good choice of meals in comfortable surroundings. Extensive facilities include a leisure club and a good range of meeting rooms.

Rooms 114 (4 fmly) **S** £95-£110; **D** £99-£120 (incl. bkfst)* **Facilities** STV Gym Steam room Spa pool Wi-fi **Conf** Class 80 Board 45 Thtr 150 Del from £140 to £150 **Services** Lift Air con **Parking** 100 **Notes** ⊗ Civ Wed 65

CHESSINGTON   Map 6 TQ16

Holiday Inn London - Chessington

★★★★ 71% HOTEL

☎ 01372 734600 📠 01372 734600
Leatherhead Rd KT9 2NE
e-mail: enquiries@holidayinnchessington.co.uk
web: www.holidayinnchessington.co.uk
dir: Follow signs for Chessington World of Adventures. Hotel at North Car Park entrance

In a convenient location just off the M25 (junction 9), two miles from the A3 and just 12 miles from London, this hotel is, of course, ideal for those visiting Chessington World of Adventures and the zoo. The bedrooms are safari-themed and include family rooms with a separate sleeping area for children with their own TV. The Merula Bar and lounge is a great place to relax, and guests can

continued

CHESSINGTON *continued*

eat in the Langata brasserie. The leisure facilities are extensive and there's ample parking.

Holiday Inn London - Chessington

Rooms 150 (56 fmly) (10 smoking) **S** £59-£217; **D** £59-£217 (incl. bkfst) **Facilities** Spa STV FTV ⓣ Gym Sauna Steam room Beauty salon Xmas New Year Wi-fi Child facilities **Conf** Class 150 Board 70 Thtr 300 Del from £145 to £215 **Services** Lift Air con **Parking** 120 **Notes** Civ Wed 100

| CROYDON | Map 6 TQ36 |

Coulsdon Manor

★★★★ 73% HOTEL OXFORD HOTELS & INNS

☎ 020 8668 0414 📄 020 8668 3118
Coulsdon Court Rd, Coulsdon CR5 2LL
e-mail: reservations.coulsdon@ohiml.com
web: www.oxfordhotelsandinns.com
dir: M23/25 junct 7, A23 for 2.5m, B2030 for 1m, left onto Coulsdon Rd, then 0.5m to hotel

This delightful Victorian manor house is peacefully set amidst 140 acres of landscaped parkland, complete with its own professional 18-hole golf course. Bedrooms are spacious and comfortable, whilst public areas include a choice of lounges and an elegant restaurant serving carefully prepared, imaginative food.

Rooms 35 (4 fmly) **S** £40-£110; **D** £60-£138 (incl. bkfst)* **Facilities** STV FTV ♨ 18 ⛳ Putt green Gym Squash Aerobic studio Steam room Sauna Xmas New Year Wi-fi **Conf** Class 90 Board 70 Thtr 180 Del from £120 to £175* **Services** Lift **Parking** 200 **Notes** LB ⊗ Civ Wed 60

South Park Hotel

★★★ 74% HOTEL

☎ 020 8688 5644 📄 020 8760 0861
3-5 South Park Hill Rd, South Croydon CR2 7DY
e-mail: reception@southparkhotel.co.uk
web: www.southparkhotel.co.uk
dir: follow A235 to town centre. At Coombe Rd lights turn right (A212) towards Addington, 0.5m to rdbt take 3rd exit into South Park Hill Rd, hotel on left

This intimate hotel has easy access to rail and road networks with some off-street parking available. Attractively decorated bedrooms vary in size and offer a good range of in-room facilities. Public areas consist of a bar and lounge with large sofas and an informal dining area where meals are served.

Rooms 30 (2 fmly) (9 GF) **Facilities** FTV Wi-fi **Conf** Class 50 Board 30 Thtr 60 **Parking** 15 **Notes** ⊗

Selsdon Park Hotel & Golf Club

Ⓤ

☎ 020 8657 8811 📄 020 8651 6171
Addington Rd, Sanderstead CR2 8YA
dir: 3m SE of Croydon, off A2022

Currently the rating for this establishment is not confirmed. This may be due to a change of ownership or because it has only recently joined the AA rating scheme. For further details please see the AA website: theAA.com

Rooms 199 (19 fmly) (33 GF) **Facilities** Spa STV ⓣ supervised ⛲ supervised ♨ 18 ⛳ Putt green ⛳ Gym Squash Xmas New Year Wi-fi **Services** Lift **Parking** 300 **Notes** ⊗ Civ Wed 350

Express by Holiday Inn London - Croydon

BUDGET HOTEL

☎ 020 8253 1200 📄 020 8253 1201
1 Priddys Yard, Off Frith Rd CR0 1TS
e-mail: admin@exhicroydon.com
web: www.hiexpress.com/london-croydon

A modern hotel ideal for families and business travellers. Fresh and uncomplicated, the spacious rooms include Sky TV, power shower and tea and coffee-making facilities. Continental buffet breakfast is included in the room rate; other meals may be taken at the nearby family pub or restaurant. See also the Hotel Groups pages.

Rooms 156 **Conf** Class 30 Board 30 Thtr 60

Innkeeper's Lodge Croydon South

BUDGET HOTEL

☎ 0845 112 6118 📄 0845 112 6185
415 Brighton Rd CR2 6EJ
web: www.innkeeperslodge.com/croydon
dir: M23 junct 7/A23 or M25 junct 6/A22. At Purley take A235 Brighton road, N towards South Croydon, for 1m. Lodge on right

Innkeeper's Lodge represents an exciting, high value concept within the budget hotel market. Comfortable bedrooms provide excellent facilities that include satellite TV and modem points. Options include family rooms; and for the corporate guest, cutting edge IT which includes Wi-fi access. A popular Carvery provides all-day food, including an extensive, complimentary continental breakfast. See also the Hotel Groups pages.

Rooms 30 (5 fmly)

Travelodge Croydon Central

BUDGET HOTEL

☎ 0871 984 6318 📄 020 8686 7808
Norfolk House, Wellesley Rd CR0 1LH
web: www.travelodge.co.uk
dir: A212 signed Central Croydon. Croydon Underpass. Lodge on right

Travelodge offers good quality, good value, budget accommodation. All offer family rooms sleeping up to four (two adults, two children) with en suite bathroom/shower-room, remote-control TV, tea- and coffee-making facilities and comfortable beds. Food options vary. Breakfast is at the on-site Bar Café restaurant (if available) or to take away. See also Hotel Groups pages.

Rooms 147 **S** fr £29; **D** fr £29

| ENFIELD | Map 6 TQ39 |

Royal Chace

★★★★ 77% ◉ HOTEL

☎ 020 8884 8181 📄 020 8884 8150
The Ridgeway EN2 8AR
e-mail: reservations@royalchacehotel.co.uk
dir: M25 junct 24 take A1005 towards Enfield. Hotel 3m on right

This professionally run, privately owned hotel enjoys a peaceful location with open fields to the rear. Public rooms are smartly appointed; the first-floor Chace Brasserie is particularly appealing with its warm colour schemes and friendly service. Bedrooms are well presented and thoughtfully equipped.

Rooms 92 (5 fmly) (32 GF) **S** £95-£115; **D** £110-£130 (incl. bkfst)* **Facilities** FTV ⛲ Gym New Year Wi-fi **Conf** Class 100 Board 40 Thtr 250 Del from £120 to £155 **Parking** 200 **Notes** LB ⊗ Closed 24-30 Dec RS Lunchtime/Sun eve Civ Wed 220

Comfort Hotel Enfield

★★★ 72% HOTEL

☎ 020 8366 3511 📄 020 8366 2432
52 Rowantree Rd EN2 8PW
e-mail: admin@comfortenfield.co.uk
web: www.comfortenfield.co.uk
dir: M25 junct 24 follow signs for A1005 towards Enfield.
Hospital on left, across mini-rdbt, 3rd left onto Bycullah
Rd, 2nd left into Rowantree Rd

This hotel is situated in a quiet residential area, close to
the centre of Enfield. Comfortable accommodation is
provided in the thoughtfully equipped bedrooms, which
include ground floor and family rooms. Public areas
include a cosy bar and lounge, conference and function
rooms and the smart Etruscan Restaurant.

Rooms 34 (34 annexe) (3 fmly) **S** £45-£99; **D** £55-£109
(incl. bkfst) **Facilities** FTV Wi-fi **Conf** Class 25 Board 25
Thtr 65 Del from £90 to £135 **Parking** 17 **Notes** LB ⊗
Civ Wed 65

FELTHAM

See LONDON plan 1 A2

Travelodge Feltham

BUDGET HOTEL

☎ 0871 984 6319 📄 020 8890 0664
Res Centre, High St TW13 4EX
web: www.travelodge.co.uk
dir: A308 Staines. Right at Shears junct onto A244
Cadbury Rd, A244 onto Feltham High St

Travelodge offers good quality, good value, budget
accommodation. All offer family rooms sleeping up to four
(two adults, two children) with en suite bathroom/
shower-room, remote-control TV, tea- and coffee-making
facilities and comfortable beds. Food options vary.
Breakfast is at the on-site Bar Café restaurant (if
available) or to take away. See also Hotel Groups pages.

Rooms 115 **S** fr £29; **D** fr £29

HADLEY WOOD   Map 6 TQ29

West Lodge Park

★★★★ 80% ◉◉ HOTEL

☎ 020 8216 3900 & 8216 3903 📄 020 8216 3937
Cockfosters Rd EN4 0PY
e-mail: westlodgepark@bealeshotels.co.uk
web: www.bealeshotels.co.uk
dir: On A111, 1m S of M25 junct 24

A stylish country house set in stunning parkland and
gardens, yet only 12 miles from central London and a few
miles from the M25. Bedrooms are individually decorated
in traditional style and offer excellent in-room facilities.
Annexe rooms feature air-conditioning and have access
to an outdoor patio area. Public rooms include the award-
winning Cedar Restaurant, cosy bar area and separate
lounge.

Rooms 59 (13 annexe) (1 fmly) (11 GF) **S** £90-£160;
D £140-£230* **Facilities** STV Putt green ⛳ Free use of
nearby leisure club ♫ New Year Wi-fi **Conf** Class 30
Board 30 Thtr 64 Del from £199 to £225* **Services** Lift
Parking 200 **Notes** LB ⊗ Civ Wed 72

HAMPTON COURT

See LONDON SECTION plan 1 B1

The Carlton Mitre

★★★★ 72% HOTEL

☎ 020 8979 9988 & 8783 3505 📄 020 8979 9777
Hampton Court Rd KT8 9BN
e-mail: mitre@carltonhotels.co.uk
dir: M3 junct 1 follow signs to Sunbury & Hampton Court
Palace. At Hampton Court Palace rdbt right, hotel on right

This hotel, dating back in parts to 1655, enjoys an
enviable setting on the banks of the River Thames
opposite Hampton Court Palace. The riverside restaurant
and Edge bar/brasserie command wonderful views as
well as spacious terraces for alfresco dining. Bedrooms
are spacious and elegant with excellent facilities. Parking
is limited.

Rooms 36 (2 fmly) **S** £135-£185; **D** £135-£185 (incl.
bkfst)* **Facilities** STV FTV Xmas New Year Wi-fi
Conf Class 60 Board 40 Thtr 120 Del from £185 to £220*
Services Lift Air con **Parking** 13 **Notes** LB ⊗
Civ Wed 100

Liongate

★★ 68% HOTEL

☎ 020 8977 8121 📄 020 8943 4029
Hampton Court Rd KT8 9DD
e-mail: lionres@dhillonhotels.co.uk
dir: M25 junct 12/M3 towards London. M3 junct 1, A308
at mini-rdbt turn left. Hotel opposite Hampton Court
Palace gates

Dating back to 1721 this hotel enjoys a wonderful
location opposite the Lion Gate entrance to Hampton
Court and beside the gate into Bushy Park. Despite the
hotel's age the bedrooms have a contemporary style. The
public bar, restaurant and lounge area are open-plan and
designed in a chic style that creates a bright and
spacious atmosphere.

Rooms 32 (18 annexe) (2 fmly) (12 GF) **Facilities** Xmas
Conf Class 50 Board 35 Thtr 60 **Parking** 30 **Notes** LB ⊗
Civ Wed 50

HARROW

See LONDON SECTION plan 1 B5

The Harrow Hotel

★★★ 74% HOTEL

☎ 020 8427 3435 📄 020 8861 1370
12-22 Pinner Rd HA1 4HZ
e-mail: info@harrowhotel.co.uk
web: www.harrowhotel.co.uk
dir: Off rdbt on A404 at junct with A312

This privately owned hotel offers a great variety of
accommodation to suit all needs. At the top of the range
are the air-conditioned executive rooms and suites which
have hi-tech facilities including MD/CD, interactive TV
and multiple phone lines. Public areas include a bar,
conservatory lounge, meeting rooms and a smart
restaurant.

Rooms 79 (4 fmly) (17 GF) **Conf** Class 60 Board 60
Thtr 160 **Services** Lift **Parking** 70 **Notes** RS Xmas
Civ Wed 80

See advert on page 346

HARROW *continued*

Best Western Cumberland

★★★ 72% METRO HOTEL

☎ 020 8863 4111 📠 020 8861 5668
1 St Johns Rd HA1 2EF
e-mail: reservations@cumberlandhotel.co.uk
web: www.cumberlandhotel.co.uk
dir: On reaching Harrow using Station or Sheepcote Rd, turn onto Gayton Rd, then Lyon Rd which becomes St Johns Rd

Situated within walking distance of the town centre, this hotel is ideally located for all local attractions and amenities. Bedrooms provide good levels of comfort and are practically equipped to meet the requirements of all travellers. Impressive public areas include a restaurant and bar, both serving a good variety of fresh food.

Rooms 84 (53 annexe) (5 fmly) (15 GF) (23 smoking) **S** £45-£80.50; **D** £55-£96* **Facilities** FTV Gym Sauna Xmas New Year Wi-fi **Conf** Class 70 Board 62 Thtr 130 **Parking** 67 **Notes** ⊗ Civ Wed 150

Crescent

★★ 60% METRO HOTEL

☎ 020 8863 5491
58-62 Welldon Crescent, Harrow HA1 1QR
e-mail: Jivraj@crsnthtl.demon.co.uk
web: www.crsnthtl.demon.co.uk
dir: A312 onto Headstone Rd, 2nd right onto Hindes Rd,1st night

This family-run hotel is in a quiet residential area in the heart of Harrow. The comfortable accommodation is well equipped with thoughtful extras. The public areas include a cosy lounge and an attractive breakfast room that looks over a large garden.

Rooms 21 (2 fmly) **Notes** ⊗ Closed Xmas

Comfort Hotel Harrow

Ⓤ

☎ 020 8427 2899 📠 020 8863 2314
Northwick Park Rd HA1 2NT
e-mail: info@comfortharrow.com
web: www.comforthotel.com
dir: Off A4006 signed to Kenton, take 1st left, hotel 250yds on right

Currently the rating for this establishment is not confirmed. This may be due to a change of ownership or because it has only recently joined the AA rating scheme. For further details please see the AA website: theAA.com

Rooms 73 (20 annexe) (13 fmly) (16 GF) (67 smoking) **S** £39-£89; **D** £39-£99* **Facilities** STV Xmas New Year Wi-fi **Conf** Class 80 Board 60 Thtr 180 **Del** from £99 to £120* **Parking** 50 **Notes** ⊗ Civ Wed 150

See LONDON plan 1 B6

Grim's Dyke

★★★ 78% ⊛⊛ HOTEL

☎ 020 8385 3100 📠 020 8954 4560
Old Redding HA3 6SH
e-mail: reservations@grimsdyke.com
web: www.grimsdyke.com
dir: A410 onto A409 north towards Bushey, at top of hill at lights turn left into Old Redding

Once home to Sir William Gilbert, this Grade II mansion contains many references to well-known Gilbert and Sullivan productions. The house is set in over 40 acres of beautiful parkland and gardens. Rooms in the main house are elegant and traditional, while those in the adjacent lodge are aimed more at the business guest.

Rooms 46 (37 annexe) (4 fmly) (17 GF) **S** £85-£350; **D** £95-£350 (incl. bkfst) **Facilities** STV ⅛ Gilbert & Sullivan opera dinner Murder mystery evenings ♫ Xmas New Year Wi-fi **Conf** Class 60 Board 32 Thtr 90 **Del** from £140 to £160 **Parking** 97 **Notes** LB RS 24-27 Dec Civ Wed 90

See also **Slough (Berkshire) & Staines (Surrey)**

See LONDON SECTION plan 1 A/B3

Sheraton Skyline

★★★★ 79% ⊛ HOTEL

☎ 020 8564 3300 & 8759 2535 📠 020 8750 9154
Bath Rd UB3 5BP
dir: M4 junct 4 for Heathrow, follow Terminal 1,2 & 3 signs. Before airport entrance take slip road to left for 0.25m signed A4/Central London

Within easy reach of all terminals this hotel offers well appointed bedrooms featuring air conditioning. Bedrooms

provide excellent levels of quality and comfort. The extensive, contemporary public areas are light and spacious, and include a wide range of eating and drinking options, function rooms, club lounge and a gym.

Rooms 350 (58 fmly) (27 smoking) **S** fr £247.48; **D** fr £247.48* **Facilities** STV FTV ☜ supervised Gym Fitness centre Xmas New Year Wi-fi **Conf** Class 325 Board 100 Thtr 500 **Services** Lift Air con **Parking** 327 **Notes** LB Civ Wed 360

Crowne Plaza London - Heathrow

★★★★ 78% HOTEL

☎ 0870 400 9140 📄 01895 445122
Stockley Rd UB7 9NA
e-mail: reservations.cplhr@ichotelsgroup.com
web: www.crowneplaza.co.uk
dir: M4 junct 4 follow signs to Uxbridge on A408, hotel 400yds on left

This smart hotel is conveniently located for access to Heathrow Airport and the motorway network. Excellent facilities include versatile conference and meeting rooms, a spa and leisure complex. Guests have the choice of two bars, both serving food plus two restaurants. Air-conditioned bedrooms are furnished and decorated to a high standard and feature a comprehensive range of extra facilities.

Rooms 463 (203 fmly) (38 GF) (20 smoking)
Facilities STV ☜ supervised ⚓ 9 Putt green Gym Steam room Sauna Wi-fi **Conf** Class 120 Board 75 Thtr 200 Del from £150 to £195* **Services** Lift Air con **Parking** 800 **Notes** ⊗

London Heathrow Marriott

Marriott
HOTELS & RESORTS

★★★★ 76% HOTEL

☎ 020 8990 1100 & 8990 1119 📄 020 8990 1110
Bath Rd UB3 5AN
e-mail: mhrs.lhrhr.ays@marriott.com
web: www.londonheathrowmarriott.co.uk
dir: M4 junct 4, follow signs for Heathrow Terminals 1, 2 & 3. Left at rdbt onto A4 towards central London. Hotel 0.5m on left

This smart, modern hotel, with its striking design, meets all the expectations of a successful airport hotel. The light and airy atrium offers several eating and drinking options, each with a different theme. Spacious bedrooms are appointed to a good standard with an excellent range of facilities, and there is a leisure club and business centre.

Rooms 393 (143 fmly) (30 smoking) **S** £90.85-£205.85; **D** £90.85-£205.85* **Facilities** STV ☜ supervised Gym Steam room Sauna Spa pool Xmas Wi-fi **Conf** Class 300 Board 65 Thtr 480 Del from £165 to £230* **Services** Lift Air con **Parking** 220 **Notes** LB ⊗ Civ Wed 440

Heathrow/Windsor Marriott

Marriott
HOTELS & RESORTS

★★★★ 75% HOTEL

☎ 01753 544244 📄 01753 540240
Ditton Rd, Langley SL3 8PT
e-mail: mhrs.lhrsl.conferenceandevents@marriotthotels.com
web: www.heathrowwindsormarriott.co.uk
dir: M4 junct 5, follow 'Langley' signs, left at lights into Ditton Rd

Ideally located for access to Heathrow and the M4, this smart hotel offers a wide range of facilities. There is a well-appointed leisure centre, extensive conference facilities, a bar offering 24-hour snacks and light meals, and a restaurant with a wide ranging cuisine. Spacious bedrooms are well equipped for both leisure and business guests.

Rooms 382 (120 fmly) (96 GF) **Facilities** STV ☜ supervised ⚓ Gym Wi-fi **Conf** Class 220 Board 42 Thtr 400 Del from £140 to £210* **Services** Lift Air con **Parking** 550 **Notes** ⊗ Civ Wed 300

Renaissance London Heathrow Hotel

★★★★ 74% HOTEL

☎ 020 8897 6363 📄 020 8897 1113
Bath Rd TW6 2AQ
e-mail: rhi.lhrbr.guest.services@renaissancehotels.com
web: www.renaissancelondonheathrow.co.uk
dir: M4 junct 4 follow spur road towards airport, then 2nd left. At rdbt take 2nd exit signed 'Renaissance Hotel'. Hotel next to Customs House

Located right on the perimeter of the airport, this hotel commands superb views over the runways. The smart bedrooms are fully soundproofed and equipped with air conditioning - each is well suited to meet the needs of today's business travellers. The hotel boasts extensive conference facilities, and is a very popular venue for air travellers and conference organisers.

Rooms 649 (59 GF) (40 smoking) **S** £80-£175; **D** £80-£175 (incl. bkfst) **Facilities** Gym Steam room Fitness studio Massage treatment Personal trainer Solarium Xmas Wi-fi **Conf** Class 300 Board 80 Thtr 450 Del from £159 to £179 **Services** Lift Air con **Parking** 700 **Notes** ⊗ Civ Wed 150

Novotel London Heathrow

NOVOTEL

★★★★ 72% HOTEL

☎ 01895 431431 📄 01895 431221
Cherry Ln UB7 9HB
e-mail: H1551-gm@accor.com
web: www.novotel.com
dir: M4 junct 4, follow Uxbridge signs on A408. Keep left, take 2nd exit off traffic island into Cherry Ln signed West Drayton. Hotel on left

Conveniently located for Heathrow Airport and the motorway network, this modern hotel provides comfortable accommodation. The large, airy indoor atrium creates a sense of space to the public areas, which include an all-day restaurant and bar, meeting rooms, fitness centre and swimming pool. Ample secure parking is available.

Rooms 178 (178 fmly) (10 GF) **S** £65-£155; **D** £65-£155* **Facilities** STV ☜ Gym Wi-fi **Conf** Class 100 Board 90 Thtr 250 Del from £150 to £185* **Services** Lift Air con **Parking** 100 **Notes** LB

Ramada London Heathrow

★★★★ 72% HOTEL

☎ 0844 815 9041 📄 020 8897 7014
Bath Rd, Cranford TW5 9QE
e-mail: sales.lhr@ramadajarvis.co.uk
dir: M4 junct 3 follow signs to Heathrow Terminals 1, 2 & 3. Hotel on right of A4 Bath Rd

This well presented hotel is conveniently situated just three miles from Heathrow Airport. Bedrooms are located in a smart new block and all are well appointed for both business and leisure guests; each has a flat-screen TV with multi-channel choice, climate control and good lighting. Arts Bar and Brasserie lead from a contemporary open-plan reception area. Chargeable car park on site.

Rooms 200 (14 fmly) (45 GF) **D** £59-£159 (incl. bkfst)* **Facilities** FTV Wi-fi **Conf** Class 30 Board 40 Thtr 100 **Services** Lift Air con **Parking** 60 **Notes** LB ⊗ Civ Wed 65

Holiday Inn London - Heathrow

Holiday Inn
HOTELS · RESORTS

★★★★ 71% HOTEL

☎ 020 8990 0000 📄 020 8564 7744
Bath Rd, Corner Sipson Way UB7 0DP
web: www.holidayinn.co.uk
dir: Exit airport via main tunnel, at end left towards A4/Other Routes, follow signs for A4. At main lights (hotel visable) turn right, 1st left into Sipson Way

A newly built property close to the terminals and with a frequent bus service to the airport. Public areas include a large brasserie-style restaurant and bar plus shop, mini gym and parking. Bedrooms are spacious and air conditioned, with facilities to suit the business traveller; there are a number of executive rooms available.

Rooms 230

HEATHROW AIRPORT (LONDON) *continued*

Radisson Edwardian Heathrow

★★★★ 🅐 HOTEL

☎ 020 8759 6311   📠 020 8759 4559
Bath Rd UB3 5AW
e-mail: resreh@radisson.com

Rooms 459 (83 GF) **Facilities** Gym Massage Hairdressing
Xmas Wi-fi **Conf** Class 300 Board 60 Thtr 700
Services Lift Air con **Parking** 550 **Notes** ⊗ Civ Wed 368

Holiday Inn London Heathrow Ariel

★★★ 77% HOTEL

☎ 0870 400 9040   📠 020 8564 9265
118 Bath Rd UB3 5AJ
e-mail: reservations-heathrow@ihg.com
web: www.holidayinn.co.uk
dir: M4 junct 4, take Spur Rd to Heathrow Airport, 1st left
onto A4 Bath Rd, through 3 sets of lights. Hotel on left

Located close to Heathrow Airport with good public
transport links to all terminals, this well sited hotel is
suitable for both the business and leisure traveller. Public
areas benefit from a spacious lounge bar area, brasserie-
style restaurant and extensive conference facilities.
Ample secure parking is an additional plus.

Rooms 184 (18 smoking) **Facilities** STV Xmas Wi-fi
Conf Class 35 Board 25 Thtr 50 **Services** Lift Air con
Parking 100 **Notes** ⊗

Thistle London Heathrow

thistle

★★★ 74% HOTEL

☎ 0871 376 9021   📠 0871 376 9121
Bath Rd, Longford UB7 0EQ
e-mail: londonheathrow@thistle.co.uk
web: www.thistlehotels.com/londonheathrow
dir: M25 junct 14 signed Terminal 4 & Cargo Area. Right
at 1st rdbt signed Heathrow. Left at lights onto A3044
signed Colnbrook & Longford

Located adjacent to the airport and with the benefit of
secure parking and regular coach transfers, this long
established hotel provides a range of well equipped
bedrooms for both the business and leisure guest.
Imaginative food is available in an attractive restaurant
and comprehensive breakfasts are served in a separate
first-floor dining room.

Rooms 264 (3 fmly) (132 GF) **S** £46.20-£172.50;
D fr £261* **Facilities** STV FTV Use of nearby health club
Xmas New Year Wi-fi **Conf** Class 300 Board 25 Thtr 700
Del from £109 to £198* **Services** Air con **Parking** 450
Notes LB Civ Wed 500

Comfort Hotel Heathrow

★★★ 71% HOTEL

☎ 020 8573 6162   📠 020 8848 1057
Shepiston Ln UB3 1LP
e-mail: info@comfortheathrow.com
web: www.comfortheathrow.com
dir: M4 junct 4, follow directions to Hayes & Shepiston
Lane, hotel approx 1m, next to fire station

This hotel is located a short drive from the airport, and
guests may prefer its quieter position. There is a frequent
bus service, which runs to and from the hotel throughout
the day. Bedrooms are thoughtfully equipped and many
benefit from air conditioning.

Rooms 184 (7 fmly) (50 GF) (18 smoking) **Facilities** STV
FTV Gym Wi-fi **Conf** Class 72 Board 90 Thtr 150
Del from £99 to £135 **Services** Lift **Parking** 120 **Notes** ⊗
Civ Wed 90

The Master Robert Hotel

★★ 69% HOTEL

☎ 020 8570 6261   📠 020 8569 4016
366 Great West Rd TW5 0BD
e-mail: stay@masterrobert.co.uk
web: www.masterrobert.co.uk
dir: M4 junct 3 take A312 & follow Airport signs. At 1st
rdbt take 1st exit, 100yds straight onto 2nd rdbt, turn
left. Hotel on left by 2nd lights

A well-known landmark on the Great West Road, this
hotel is conveniently located near Heathrow and the
area's business community. Bedrooms are set in motel-
style buildings behind the main hotel; most are spacious
with good facilities. There is residents' lounge bar, a
restaurant and a popular pub.

Rooms 96 (96 annexe) (22 fmly) (40 GF) (25 smoking)
Facilities STV FTV Local health club nearby Wi-fi
Conf Class 60 Board 40 Thtr 150 **Parking** 200 **Notes** ⊗
Civ Wed 80

Days Hotel Hounslow

☎ 020 8538 1230   📠 020 8570 5053
8-10 Lampton Rd TW3 1JL
e-mail: gm@dhhounslow.com
dir: A4 (Bath Rd), then A3006 follow onto Lampton Rd
(A3005)

Currently the rating for this establishment is not
confirmed. This may be due to a change of ownership or
because it has only recently joined the AA rating scheme.
For further details please see the AA website: theAA.com

Rooms 96 (11 fmly) (4 GF) **Facilities** FTV 🎵 Xmas New
Year Wi-fi **Conf** Class 50 Board 60 Thtr 100 **Services** Lift
Air con **Parking** 20 **Notes** LB ⊗

Holiday Inn London Heathrow M4 Jct 4

Ⓤ

☎ 0870 400 8595   📠 020 8897 8659
Sipson Rd UB7 0JU
e-mail: reservations-heathrowm4@ihg.com
web: www.holidayinn.co.uk
dir: M4 junct 4, keep left, take 1st left into Holloway Lane,
left at mini rdbt then left

Currently the rating for this establishment is not
confirmed. This may be due to a change of ownership or
because it has only recently joined the AA rating scheme.
For further details please see the AA website: theAA.com

Rooms 617 (25 smoking) **Facilities** STV Xmas New Year
Conf Class 60 Board 35 Thtr 130 **Services** Lift Air con
Parking 450 **Notes** LB ⊗ No children 16yrs

Ibis London Heathrow Airport

BUDGET HOTEL

☎ 020 8759 4888   📠 020 8564 7894
112/114 Bath Rd UB3 5AL
e-mail: H0794@accor.com
web: www.ibishotel.com
dir: Follow Heathrow Terminals 1, 2 & 3 signs, then onto
spur road, exit at sign for A4/Central London. Hotel 0.5m
on left

Modern, budget hotel offering comfortable
accommodation in bright and practical bedrooms.
Breakfast is self-service and dinner is available in the
restaurant. See also the Hotel Groups pages.

Rooms 351 (24 fmly) (39 GF) **S** £42-£62; **D** £42-£62*
Conf Class 16 Board 16 Thtr 20 **Del** from £82 to £102*

Travelodge Heathrow Central

BUDGET HOTEL

☎ 0871 984 6249   📠 020 8897 6600
Hertz House, 700 Bath Rd TW5 9SW
dir: From M4 junct 3. At rdbt 4th exit onto Parkway
(A312). At rdbt 3rd exit onto Bath Rd (A4). Lodge on left

Travelodge offers good quality, good value, budget
accommodation. All offer family rooms sleeping up to
four (two adults, two children) with en suite bathroom/
shower-room, remote-control TV, tea- and coffee-making
facilities and comfortable beds. Food options vary.
Breakfast is at the on-site Bar Café restaurant (if
available) or to take away. See also the Hotel Groups
pages.

Rooms 307 **S** fr £29; **D** fr £29

Travelodge Heathrow Terminal 5

BUDGET HOTEL

☎ 0871 984 6353
Calder Way, Horton Rd SL3 0AT
e-mail: heathrow5@travelodge.co.uk
dir: M25 junct 14, A3113 signed Poyle/Datchet (Horton Rd). In 200mtrs right into Calder Way at Poyle 14 sign. 1st right after 50mtrs

Rooms 297 **S** fr £29; **D** fr £29

HESTON MOTORWAY SERVICE AREA (M4)

See LONDON SECTION plan 1 B3

Travelodge Heathrow Heston (M4 Eastbound)

BUDGET HOTEL

☎ 0871 984 6037 📄 020 8580 2028
Phoenix Way TW5 9NB
web: www.travelodge.co.uk
dir: Between M4 juncts 2 & 3, accessed from eastbound & westbound carriageways

Travelodge offers good quality, good value, budget accommodation. All offer family rooms sleeping up to four (two adults, two children) with en suite bathroom/ shower-room, remote-control TV, tea- and coffee-making facilities and comfortable beds. Food options vary. Breakfast is at the on-site Bar Café restaurant (if available) or to take away. See also Hotel Groups pages.

Rooms 66 **S** fr £29; **D** fr £29

Travelodge Heathrow Heston (M4 Westbound)

BUDGET HOTEL

☎ 0871 984 6261 📄 020 8580 2006
Cranford Ln TW5 9NB
web: www.travelodge.co.uk
dir: M4 junct 2 & 3 accessed eastbound & westbound

Rooms 145 **S** fr £29; **D** fr £29

ILFORD

See LONDON SECTION plan 1 H5

Express by Holiday Inn London Newbury Park

BUDGET HOTEL

☎ 020 8709 2200 📄 020 8554 6232
713 Eastern Av IG2 7RH
web: www.hiexpress.com/londongantshil
dir: On A12

A modern hotel ideal for families and business travellers. Fresh and uncomplicated, the spacious rooms include Sky TV, power shower and tea and coffee-making facilities.

Continental buffet breakfast is included in the room rate; other meals may be taken at the nearby family pub or restaurant. See also the Hotel Groups pages.

Rooms 126 **S** £60-£180; **D** £60-£180 (incl. bkfst)
Conf Class 50 Board 50 Thtr 200 Del from £130 to £200

Travelodge London Ilford

BUDGET HOTEL

☎ 0871 984 6194 📄 020 8553 2920
Clements Rd IG1 1BA
web: www.travelodge.co.uk
dir: M25 junct 28, A12 to Hackney. At A406, left onto A118 for Ilford/Romford, left before cinema complex

Travelodge offers good quality, good value, budget accommodation. All offer family rooms sleeping up to four (two adults, two children) with en suite bathroom/ shower-room, remote-control TV, tea- and coffee-making facilities and comfortable beds. Food options vary. Breakfast is at the on-site Bar Café restaurant (if available) or to take away. See also Hotel Groups pages.

Rooms 91 **S** fr £29; **D** fr £29

Travelodge London Ilford Gants Hill

BUDGET HOTEL

☎ 0871 984 6193 📄 020 8551 1712
Beehive Ln, Gants Hill IG4 5DR
web: www.travelodge.co.uk
dir: Off A12 on B192, adjacent to Beehive Harvester Restaurant

Rooms 32 **S** fr £29; **D** fr £29

KINGSTON UPON THAMES

See LONDON SECTION plan 1 C1

Travelodge Kingston upon Thames Central

BUDGET HOTEL

☎ 08719 848484 📄 01844 381658
International House, Wheatfield Way KT1 2PD
dir: M3 junct 1, A308 for approx 6m.Left onto A307, 0.6 m then right onto Old London Rd. Lodge on right

Travelodge offers good quality, good value, budget accommodation. All offer family rooms sleeping up to four (two adults, two children) with en suite bathroom/ shower-room, remote-control TV, tea- and coffee-making facilities and comfortable beds. Food options vary. Breakfast is at the on-site Bar Café restaurant (if available) or to take away. See also the Hotel Groups pages.

Rooms 102 **S** fr £29; **D** fr £29

Travelodge London Kingston upon Thames

BUDGET HOTEL

☎ 0871 984 6241 📄 020 8546 5904
21-23 London Rd KT2 6ND
web: www.travelodge.co.uk
dir: Vehicle access to Old London Rd t via Queen Elizabeth Rd/London Rd. Lodge behind The Rotunda

Rooms 72 **S** fr £29; **D** fr £29

MORDEN

See LONDON SECTION plan 1 D1

Travelodge Wimbledon Morden

BUDGET HOTEL

☎ 0871 984 6196 📄 020 8640 8227
Epsom Rd SM4 5PH
web: www.travelodge.co.uk
dir: On A24

Travelodge offers good quality, good value, budget accommodation. All offer family rooms sleeping up to four (two adults, two children) with en suite bathroom/ shower-room, remote-control TV, tea- and coffee-making facilities and comfortable beds. Food options vary. Breakfast is at the on-site Bar Café restaurant (if available) or to take away. See also Hotel Groups pages.

Rooms 56 **S** fr £29; **D** fr £29

NORTHOLT

See LONDON SECTION plan 1 B4

Innkeeper's Lodge London Northolt

BUDGET HOTEL

☎ 0845 112 6121 📄 0845 112 6182
Mandeville Rd UB5 4LU
web: www.innkeeperslodge.com/northolt
dir: M40 junct 1, A40 for 6m. Left onto A312 rdbt. Lodge on right just after Northolt underground station

Innkeeper's Lodge represent an exciting, high value concept within the budget hotel market. Comfortable bedrooms provide excellent facilities that include satellite TV and modem points. Options include spacious family rooms; and for the corporate guest, cutting edge IT is provided with Wi-fi access. All-day food is provided in the adjacent pub restaurant. The extensive continental breakfast is complimentary. See also the Hotel Groups pages.

Rooms 21

PINNER

See LONDON SECTION plan 1 A5

Tudor Lodge
★★★ 70% HOTEL

☎ 020 8429 0585   📠 020 8429 0117
50 Field End Rd, Eastcote HA5 2QN
e-mail: tudorlodge@meridianleisure.com
web: www.meridianleisure.com
dir: Off A40 at Target rdbt onto A312 to Harrow. Left at Northolt Station to Eastcote

This friendly hotel, set in its own grounds, is convenient for Heathrow Airport and many local golf courses. Bedrooms vary in style and size but all are well equipped, with some suitable for families. A good range of bar snacks is offered as an alternative to the main restaurant.

Rooms 46 (22 annexe) (9 fmly) (17 GF) **S** fr £60;
D fr £69* **Facilities** FTV Discounted day rates at local gym Xmas Wi-fi **Conf** Class 20 Board 26 Thtr 60
Parking 30 **Notes** ❸ Civ Wed 25

See advert on this page

RAINHAM Map 6 TQ58

Manor Hotel & Restaurant
★★★ 77% HOTEL

☎ 01708 555586   📠 01708 630055
Berwick Pond Rd RM13 9EL
e-mail: info@themanoressex.co.uk
web: www.themanoressex.co.uk
dir: M25 junct 30/31, A13, 1st exit signed Wennington, right, at main lights right onto Upminster Rd North, left into Berwick Pond Rd

Located in the countryside the former Berwick Manor has been lovingly restored, and today offers well-appointed, contemporary accommodation. The rooms are equipped with a good range of amenities including complimentary Wi-fi. Lunch and dinner are served in the attractive restaurant whilst alfresco dining is possible on the terrace. Two function suites provide ideal venues for a variety of events.

Rooms 15 (1 fmly) **S** £90-£110; **D** £99-£110 (incl. bkfst)*
Facilities STV Xmas New Year Wi-fi **Conf** Class 60 Board 40 Thtr 100 **Services** Lift **Parking** 60 **Notes** LB ❸ Civ Wed 60

RICHMOND (UPON THAMES)

See LONDON SECTION plan 1 C2

The Petersham Hotel
★★★★ 78% ❀❀ HOTEL

☎ 020 8940 7471   📠 020 8939 1098
Nightingale Ln TW10 6UZ
e-mail: enq@petershamhotel.co.uk
web: www.petershamhotel.co.uk
dir: From Richmond Bridge rdbt (A316) follow Ham & Petersham signs. Hotel in Nightingale Ln on left off Petersham Rd

Managed by the same family for over 25 years, this attractive hotel is located on a hill overlooking water meadows and a sweep of the River Thames. Bedrooms and suites are comfortably furnished, whilst public areas combine elegance and some fine architectural features. High quality produce features in dishes offered in the restaurant that looks out over the Thames below.

Rooms 60 (6 fmly) (3 GF) **S** £95-£135; **D** £150-£235 (incl. bkfst)* **Facilities** STV FTV Xmas New Year Wi-fi **Conf** Board 25 Thtr 35 Del from £235 to £290*
Services Lift **Parking** 60 **Notes** LB ❸ Civ Wed 40

The Richmond Gate Hotel

folio Hotels

★★★★ 74% ◉◉ HOTEL

☎ 0844 855 9121 📄 020 8332 0354
152-158 Richmond Hill TW10 6RP
e-mail: richmondgate@foliohotels.com
web: www.foliohotels.com/richmondgate
dir: from Richmond to top of Richmond Hill. Hotel on left opposite Star & Garter home at Richmond Gate exit

This stylish Georgian hotel sits at the top of Richmond Hill, opposite the gates to Richmond Park and has a real country house feel to it. Bedrooms are equipped to a very high standard and include luxury doubles and spacious suites. Dinner in the Park Restaurant features bold, contemporary cooking and is the highlight of any visit. A smart leisure club and spa facilities complete the picture.

Rooms 68 **Facilities** STV ⌖ supervised Gym Health & beauty salon Steam room Sauna Wi-fi **Conf** Class 25 Board 28 Thtr 90 **Services** Air con **Parking** 150 **Notes** ⊗ Civ Wed 70

The Richmond Hill Hotel

folio Hotels

★★★★ 73% ◉ HOTEL

☎ 0844 855 9122 📄 020 8940 5424
Richmond Hill TW10 6RW
e-mail: richmondhill@foliohotels.com
web: www.foliohotels.com/richmondhill
dir: A316 for Richmond, hotel at top of Richmond Hill

This attractive Georgian manor is situated on Richmond Hill, enjoying elevated views over the Thames. The town and the park are within walking distance. Bedrooms vary in size and style, all are comfortable and of modern design. There is a stylish, well-designed health club which is shared with sister hotel, the Richmond Gate.

Rooms 149 (1 fmly) (15 GF) **Facilities** Spa STV ⌖ Gym Steam room Health & beauty suite Sauna New Year Wi-fi **Conf** Class 80 Board 50 Thtr 180 **Services** Lift **Parking** 150 **Notes** LB ⊗ Civ Wed 182

Bingham

★★★ 81% ◉◉◉ TOWN HOUSE HOTEL

☎ 020 8940 0902 📄 020 8948 8737
61-63 Petersham Rd TW10 6UT
e-mail: info@thebingham.co.uk
web: www.thebingham.co.uk
dir: on A307

This Georgian building, dating back to 1740, overlooks the River Thames and is within easy reach of the town centre, Kew Gardens and Hampton Court. The contemporary bedrooms feature bespoke art deco style furniture and up-to-the-minute facilities such as Wi-fi, a digital music library, flat-screen TVs and 'rain dance' showers. Public rooms have views of the pretty garden and river. Guests can choose from a selection of meals from light snacks to two or three-course dinners.

Rooms 15 (2 fmly) **Facilities** In room treatments ♫ Wi-fi **Conf** Class 30 Board 20 Thtr 50 **Services** Air con **Notes** LB ⊗ Civ Wed 60

ROMFORD Map 6 TQ58

Travelodge Romford Central

BUDGET HOTEL

☎ 0871 984 6255 📄 01708 766867
St Edwards Way, Market Place RM1 1XJ
web: www.travelodge.co.uk
dir: From A125 signed Romford. At rdbt 1st exit onto St Edwards Way (A118) signed Gidea Park/Brentwood/A12. Hotel on left

Travelodge offers good quality, good value, budget accommodation. All offer family rooms sleeping up to four (two adults, two children) with en suite bathroom/shower-room, remote-control TV, tea- and coffee-making facilities and comfortable beds. Food options vary. Breakfast is at the on-site Bar Café restaurant (if available) or to take away. See also Hotel Groups pages.

Rooms 80 **S** fr £29; **D** fr £29

RUISLIP

See LONDON SECTION plan 1 A5

Barn Hotel

★★★ 78% ◉◉ HOTEL

☎ 01895 636057 📄 01895 638379
West End Rd HA4 6JB
e-mail: info@thebarnhotel.co.uk
web: www.thebarnhotel.co.uk
dir: From A40 take A4180 (Polish War Memorial) exit to Ruislip. 2m to hotel entrance off a mini-rdbt before Ruislip underground station

Once a farm, with parts dating back to the 17th century, this impressive property sits in three acres of gardens. Bedrooms vary in style, from contemporary to traditional

continued

RUISLIP *continued*

with oak-beams; all are comfortable and well appointed. The public areas provide a high level of quality and luxury.

Rooms 73 (3 fmly) (33 GF) (20 smoking) **S** £85-£150; **D** £95-£180 (incl. bkfst) **Facilities** FTV Xmas New Year Wi-fi **Conf** Class 50 Board 30 Thtr 80 Del from £165 to 210 **Parking** 42 **Notes** ⊗ Civ Wed 74

See advert on page 351

SOUTH RUISLIP

See LONDON SECTION plan 1 A/B5

Days Hotel London South Ruislip

BUDGET HOTEL PLAN 1 A5

☎ 020 8845 8400 ◳ 020 8845 5500
Long Dr, Station Approach HA4 0HG
e-mail: sales@daysinnheathrow.com
web: www.daysinn.com
dir: Exit A40 at Polish War Memorial, follow signs to Ruislip and South Ruislip

This modern building offers accommodation in smart, spacious and well-equipped bedrooms, suitable for families and business travellers, and all with en suite bathrooms. Continental breakfast is available and other refreshments may be taken at the nearby family restaurant. See also the Hotel Groups pages.

Rooms 78 (8 fmly) (7 GF) (21 smoking) **S** fr £89; **D** fr £89* **Conf** Class 40 Board 30 Thtr 60 Del from £140*

SUTTON — Map 6 TQ26

Holiday Inn London - Sutton

★★★ 75% HOTEL

☎ 020 8234 1100 & 8234 1104 ◳ 020 8770 1539
Gibson Rd SM1 2RF
e-mail: sales-sutton@ichhotelsgroup.com
web: www.holidayinn.co.uk
dir: M25 junct 8, A217, then B2230. Pass rail station, follow one-way system in right lane. At lights, right then immediately left, left again into Gibson Rd

Well located for many famous attractions and events such as Chessington World of Adventure, Wimbledon Tennis Tournament and Epsom Racecourse. This hotel offers air-conditioned bedrooms ranging from standard to executive, a variety of conference rooms, and leisure facilities with a swimming pool.

Rooms 115 (39 fmly) (15 smoking) **S** £49-£119; **D** £49-£119 (incl. bkfst)* **Facilities** Spa STV ◳ Gym Xmas New Year Wi-fi **Conf** Class 100 Board 70 Thtr 180 **Services** Lift Air con **Parking** 100 **Notes** ⊗ Civ Wed 140

TOLWORTH — Map 6 TQ16

Travelodge Chessington Tolworth

BUDGET HOTEL

☎ 0871 984 6210
Tolworth Tower KT6 7EL
web: www.travelodge.co.uk
dir: Exit A3 at Tolworth junct. At rdbt take 2nd exit signed London (A3). Immediate left onto Ewell Rd. Lodge on left

Travelodge offers good quality, good value, budget accommodation. All offer family rooms sleeping up to four (two adults, two children) with en suite bathroom/shower-room, remote-control TV, tea- and coffee-making facilities and comfortable beds. Food options vary. Breakfast is at the on-site Bar Café restaurant (if available) or to take away. See also Hotel Groups pages.

Rooms 132 **S** fr £29; **D** fr £29

TWICKENHAM

See LONDON SECTION plan 1 C2

London Marriott Hotel Twickenham

Marriott
HOTELS & RESORTS

★★★★ 79% HOTEL

☎ 020 8891 8200 ◳ 020 8891 8201
198 Whitton Rd TW2 7BA
e-mail: lynn.greybe@marriotthotels.com
dir: A316, at rdbt make slight dogleg into Rugby Road. Hotel on left

This new purpose-built hotel occupies an area of the South Stand of the Twickenham Rugby Club Stadium. The bedrooms have the latest Marriott innovations including flat-screen LCD TVs and state-of-the-art technology; six suites even overlook the pitch. There is a popular Twenty Two South restaurant, the Side Step sports bar and a café lounge. Guests can use the health club and there's a wide range of meeting rooms and conference facilities. Hampton Court Palace, Kew Gardens and the River Thames are all close by. Parking is available.

Rooms 156 (76 fmly) **S** £105-£145; **D** £105-£145* **Facilities** STV ◳ supervised Gym Xmas New Year Wi-fi **Conf** Class 1000 Board 1000 Thtr 1000 **Services** Lift Air con **Parking** 150 **Notes** ⊗

UXBRIDGE

Travelodge Uxbridge Central

BUDGET HOTEL

☎ 0871 984 6373
Colham House, Bakers Rd UB8 1RG
dir: M40 junct 1, A40/A4020. Follow signs for Uxbridge Town Centre/Underground Station, right into Park Rd then right into Bakers Rd. Lodge on left opposite undergound station

Travelodge offers good quality, good value, budget accommodation. All offer family rooms sleeping up to four (two adults, two children) with en suite bathroom/shower-room, remote-control TV, tea- and coffee-making facilities and comfortable beds. Food options vary. Breakfast is at the on-site Bar Café restaurant (if available) or to take away. See also the Hotel Groups pages.

Rooms 121 **S** fr £29; **D** fr £29

WEMBLEY

See LONDON SECTION plan 1 C5

Quality Hotel, Wembley

★★★ 71% HOTEL

☎ 020 8733 9000 ◳ 020 8733 9001
Empire Way HA9 0NH
e-mail: sales@hotels-wembley.com
dir: M1 junct 6 onto A406, right onto A404. Right onto Empire Way, after rdbt at lights. Hotel on right

Conveniently situated within walking distance of both the Arena and conference centres this modern hotel offers smart, comfortable, spacious bedrooms; many are air conditioned. All rooms offer an excellent range of amenities. Air-conditioned public areas include a large restaurant serving a wide range of contemporary dishes.

Rooms 165 (70 fmly) (3 GF) (76 smoking) **S** £120-£149; **D** £130-£169 (incl. bkfst)* **Facilities** STV FTV Wi-fi **Conf** Class 90 Board 90 Thtr 120 Del from £140 **Services** Lift Air con **Parking** 65 **Notes** ⊗

Ibis London Wembley

BUDGET HOTEL

☎ 0870 220 6581 ◳ 020 8453 5110
Southway HA9 6BA
e-mail: H3141@accor.com
web: www.ibishotel.com
dir: From Hanger Lane on A40, take A406 north, exit at Wembley. A404 to lights junct with Wembley Hill Road, turn right then 1st right into Southway. Hotel 75mtrs on left

Modern, budget hotel offering comfortable accommodation in bright and practical bedrooms. Breakfast is self-service and dinner is available in the restaurant. See also the Hotel Groups pages.

Rooms 210 (44 fmly) **S** £35-£80; **D** £35-£80*

WEST DRAYTON

Hotels are listed under Heathrow Airport

WOODFORD BRIDGE

See LONDON plan 1 H6

Menzies Prince Regent MenziesHotels

★★★★ 72% HOTEL

☎ 020 8505 9966 📄 020 8506 0807
Manor Rd IG8 8AE
e-mail: princeregent@menzieshotels.co.uk
web: www.menzieshotels.co.uk
dir: M25 junct 26, to Loughton and Chigwell, hotel on Manor Rd

Situated on the edge of Woodford Bridge and Chigwell, this hotel with delightful rear gardens, offers easy access into London as well as the M11 and M25. There is a good range of spacious, well-equipped bedrooms. Extensive conference and banqueting facilities are particularly well appointed, and are well suited to weddings and business events.

Rooms 61 (4 fmly) (15 GF) (10 smoking) **S** £65-£125; **D** £65-£125* **Facilities** STV Xmas New Year Wi-fi **Conf** Class 150 Board 80 Thtr 350 Del from £110 to £170* **Services** Lift **Parking** 225 **Notes** Civ Wed 350

WOODFORD GREEN

See LONDON SECTION plan 1 G6

Innkeeper's Lodge Chigwell

BUDGET HOTEL

☎ 0845 112 6117 📄 0845 112 6186
735 Chigwell Rd IG8 8AS
web: www.innkeeperslodge.com/chigwell
dir: M25 junct 26, A121 towards Loughton. Left at mini rdt onto A1168 (signed Chigwell) to junct with A113. Turn right, lodge 2m on left

Innkeeper's Lodge represents an exciting, high value concept within the budget hotel market. Comfortable bedrooms provide excellent facilities that include satellite TV and modem points. Options include family rooms; and for the corporate guest, cutting edge IT includes Wi-fi access. Food is served all day in the adjacent Country Pub. The extensive continental breakfast is complimentary. See also the Hotel Groups pages.

Rooms 34

MERSEYSIDE

BEBINGTON Map 15 SJ38

Travelodge Wirral Eastham

BUDGET HOTEL

☎ 0871 984 6184 📄 0151 327 2489
New Chester Rd CH62 9AQ
web: www.travelodge.co.uk
dir: Just off M53 junct 5. Lodge on A41 N'bound

Travelodge offers good quality, good value, budget accommodation. All offer family rooms sleeping up to four (two adults, two children) with en suite bathroom/shower-room, remote-control TV, tea- and coffee-making facilities and comfortable beds. Food options vary. Breakfast is at the on-site Bar Café restaurant (if available) or to take away. See also Hotel Groups pages.

Rooms 30 **S** fr £29; **D** fr £29

BIRKENHEAD Map 15 SJ38

RiverHill

★★★ 80% HOTEL

☎ 0151 653 3773 📄 0151 653 7162
Talbot Rd, Prenton CH43 2HJ
e-mail: reception@theriverhill.co.uk
dir: M53 junct 3, A552. Left onto B5151 at lights, hotel 0.5m on right

Pretty lawns and gardens provide the setting for this friendly, privately owned hotel, which is conveniently situated about a mile from the M53. Attractively furnished, well-equipped bedrooms include ground floor, family, and four-poster rooms. Business meetings and weddings can be catered for. A wide choice of dishes is available in the restaurant which overlooks the garden.

Rooms 15 (1 fmly) **Facilities** STV FTV Free use of local leisure facilities Wi-fi **Conf** Class 30 Board 50 Thtr 50 **Parking** 32 **Notes** ⊗ Civ Wed 40

See advert on this page

FORMBY · Map 15 SD30

Formby Hall Golf Resort & Spa

☎ 01704 875699 📠 01704 832134
Southport Old Rd L37 0AB
e-mail: salesmanager@formbyhallgolfresort.co.uk
web: www.formbyhallgolfresort.co.uk
dir: A565 to 2nd rdbt, follow brown signs

Currently the rating for this establishment is not confirmed. This may be due to a change of ownership or because it has only recently joined the AA rating scheme. For further details please see the AA website: theAA.com

Rooms 62 (10 fmly) (29 GF) **Facilities** Spa STV FTV 🕲 🟍 18 Putt green Gym Kinesis studio Driving range Short ball area Xmas New Year Wi-fi **Conf** Class 60 Board 40 Thtr 300 **Services** Lift Air con **Parking** 457 **Notes** LB ⊗ Civ Wed 100

HAYDOCK · Map 15 SJ59

Thistle Haydock **thistle**

★★★★ 76% HOTEL

☎ 0871 376 9044 📠 0871 376 9144
Penny Ln WA11 9SG
e-mail: haydock@thistle.co.uk
web: www.thistle.com/haydock
dir: M6 junct 23, follow Racecourse signs (A49) towards Ashton-in-Makerfield, 1st left, after bridge 1st turn

A smart, purpose-built hotel which offers an excellent standard of thoughtfully equipped accommodation. It is conveniently situated between Liverpool and Manchester, just off the M6. The wide range of leisure and meeting facilities prove popular with guests.

Rooms 137 (10 fmly) (65 GF) (8 smoking) **Facilities** STV 🕲 supervised Gym Children's play area Sauna Steam room Wi-fi **Conf** Class 140 Board 40 Thtr 300 Del from £120 to £190* **Parking** 210 **Notes** Civ Wed 220

Travelodge Haydock St Helens

Travelodge

BUDGET HOTEL

☎ 0871 984 6145 📠 01942 272067
Piele Rd WA11 0JZ
web: www.travelodge.co.uk
dir: M6 junct 23, A580 towards Liverpool. Lodge in 1m

Travelodge offers good quality, good value, budget accommodation. All offer family rooms sleeping up to four (two adults, two children) with en suite bathroom/shower-room, remote-control TV, tea- and coffee-making facilities and comfortable beds. Food options vary. Breakfast is at the on-site Bar Café restaurant (if available) or to take away. See also Hotel Groups pages.

Rooms 62 **S** fr £29; **D** fr £29

KNOWSLEY · Map 15 SJ49

Suites Hotel Knowsley

★★★★ 73% HOTEL

☎ 0151 549 2222 📠 0151 549 1116
Ribblers Ln L34 9HA
e-mail: enquiries@suiteshotelgroup.com
web: www.suiteshotelgroup.com
dir: M57 junct 4, at x-rds of A580, East Lancashire Rd

Located a close to the M54, this hotel is just a 10-minute drive from Liverpool's city centre. It offers superior, well-equipped accommodation and there is a choice of lounges plus Handley's Restaurant. Guests have the use of the impressive leisure centre, and there are extensive conference facilities.

Rooms 101 (39 fmly) (20 GF) (10 smoking) **S** £85-£133; **D** £90-£143 (incl. bkfst)* **Facilities** STV 🕲 supervised Gym Xmas New Year Wi-fi **Conf** Class 60 Board 50 Thtr 240 Del from £112 to £142* **Services** Lift Air con **Parking** 200 **Notes** LB ⊗ Civ Wed 140

LIVERPOOL · Map 15 SJ39

Crowne Plaza Liverpool - John Lennon Airport

★★★★ 79% HOTEL

☎ 0151 494 5000 📠 0151 494 5050
Speke Aerodrome L24 8QD
e-mail: reservations@liverpool.kewgreen.co.uk
web: www.crowneplaza.co.uk
dir: M62 junct 6, take Knowsley Expressway towards Speke. At end of Expressway right onto A561 towards Liverpool. Approx 4m, hotel on left just after Estuary Commerce Park

Previously Liverpool Airport's building where fans gathered in the 1960s to see The Beatles, this hotel is now Grade II listed. It has a distinctive look, reflected in its art deco architecture and interior design. The spacious bedrooms are fully air-conditioned and feature a comprehensive range of facilities. Feature rooms include the Presidential Suite in the base of the old control tower.

Rooms 164 (50 fmly) (46 GF) **Facilities** STV 🕲 🟍 supervised 🏊 Gym Squash Xmas New Year Wi-fi **Conf** Class 120 Board 80 Thtr 280 **Services** Lift Air con **Notes** ⊗ Civ Wed 280

Hope Street Hotel

★★★★ 78% ⊛⊛ HOTEL

☎ 0151 709 3000 📠 0151 709 2454
40 Hope St L1 9DA
e-mail: sleep@hopestreethotel.co.uk
dir: Follow Cathedral & University signs on entering city

This stylish property is located within easy walking distance of the city's cathedrals, theatres, major shops and attractions. Stylish bedrooms and suites are appointed with flat-screen TVs, DVD players, internet access and comfy beds with Egyptian cotton sheets; the en suites boast rain showers and deep tubs. The London Carriage Works Restaurant specialises in local, seasonal produce and the adjacent lounge bar offers lighter, all-day dining and wonderful cocktails.

Rooms 89 (15 fmly) (5 GF) **D** £99-£350* **Facilities** STV Gym Massage & beauty rooms 🎵 New Year Wi-fi **Conf** Class 40 Board 30 Thtr 60 Del from £170 to £190* **Services** Lift Air con **Notes** LB Civ Wed 50

Crowne Plaza Liverpool

★★★★ 78% HOTEL

☎ 0151 243 8000 📠 0151 243 8008
St Nicholas Place, Princes Dock, Pier Head L3 1QW
web: www.crowneplaza.co.uk

Situated right on the waterfront, yet still within striking distance of the city centre this hotel offers comprehensive leisure and meeting facilities, whether taking a snack in the spacious lounge or using the business centre. Contemporary in style with superb quality, this hotel offers a welcome to business or leisure guests alike.

Rooms 159 **Facilities** Spa STV FTV 🕲 Gym Sauna Steam room New Year Wi-fi **Conf** Class 340 Board 30 Thtr 500 **Services** Lift Air con **Parking** 150 **Notes** ⊗ Civ Wed 500

Thornton Hall Hotel and Spa

★★★★ 77% ⊛⊛ HOTEL

☎ 0151 336 3938 📠 0151 336 7864
Neston Rd CH63 1JF
e-mail: reservations@thorntonhallhotel.com
web: www.thorntonhallhotel.com

(For full entry see Thornton Hough)

Liverpool Marriott Hotel City Centre

★★★★ 77% HOTEL

☎ 0151 476 8000 📠 0151 474 5000
1 Queen Square L1 1RH
e-mail: liverpool.city@marriotthotels.com
web: www.liverpoolmarriottcitycentre.co.uk
dir: End of M62 follow city centre signs, A5047, Edge Lane. From city centre follow signs for Queens Square parking

An impressive modern hotel located in the heart of the city. The elegant public rooms include a ground-floor café bar, and a cocktail bar and stylish Oliver's Restaurant on the first floor. The hotel also boasts a well-equipped, indoor leisure health club with pool. Bedrooms are stylishly appointed and benefit from a host of extra facilities.

Rooms 146 (29 fmly) (21 smoking) **Facilities** ⓣ Gym Boxercise Aqua aerobics Body sculpture Xmas New Year Wi-fi **Conf** Class 90 Board 30 Thtr 300 **Services** Lift Air con **Parking** 137 **Notes** ⊗ Civ Wed 150

Atlantic Tower by Thistle

thistle

★★★★ 71% HOTEL

☎ 0871 376 9025 📠 0871 376 9125
Chapel St L3 9RE
e-mail: atlantictower@thistle.co.uk
web: www.thistle.com/atlantic_tower
dir: M6 onto M62 follow signs for Albert Dock, turn right at Liver Building. Stay in lane marked Chapel St, hotel on left

Designed with the shape of a ship's prow, this notable hotel commands a prominent position overlooking Pier Head and the Liver Building. Recent years has seen bedroom refurbishment and there's now a choice of junior suites, executive and standard rooms, and although many are compact, all are of good quality and benefit from full air conditioning. Public areas include a choice of lounges and The Vu Bar which adjoins an attractive patio garden with superb river views.

Rooms 225 (24 smoking) **S** £65-£175; **D** £65-£175*
Facilities STV FTV Wi-fi **Conf** Class 40 Board 30 Thtr 120 Del from £130 to £170* **Services** Lift Air con **Parking** 50 **Notes** LB Civ Wed 120

Malmaison Liverpool

★★★ 82% ⊛ HOTEL

☎ 0151 229 5000 📠 0151 229 5025
7 William Jessop Way, Princes Dock L3 1QZ
e-mail: liverpool@malmaison.com
dir: A5080 follow signs for Pier Head/Southport/Bootle. Into Baln St to rdbt, 1st exit at rdbt, immediately left onto William Jessop Way

Malmaison Liverpool is a purpose built hotel with cutting edge and contemporary style, a strong brand standard of this company. 'Mal' Liverpool has a stunning location, alongside the river and docks, and in the heart of the city's regeneration. Bedrooms are stylish and comfortable and are provided with lots of extra facilities. The public areas are packed with fun and style, and there is a number of meeting rooms as well as private dining available here, including a chef's table.

Rooms 130 **Facilities** Gym Wi-fi **Conf** Class 28 Board 18 Thtr 50 **Services** Lift Air con

Best Western Alicia

Best Western

★★★ 77% HOTEL

☎ 0151 727 4411 📠 0151 727 6752
3 Aigburth Dr, Sefton Park L17 3AA
e-mail: aliciahotel@feathers.uk.com
web: www.feathers.uk.com
dir: From end of M62 take A5058 to Sefton Park, then left, follow park around

This stylish and friendly hotel overlooks Sefton Park and is just a few minutes' drive from both the city centre and John Lennon Airport. Bedrooms are well equipped and comfortable. Day rooms include a striking modern restaurant and bar. Extensive, stylish function facilities make this a popular wedding venue.

Rooms 41 (8 fmly) **Facilities** STV Xmas New Year Wi-fi **Conf** Class 80 Board 40 Thtr 120 **Services** Lift **Parking** 40 **Notes** LB ⊗ Civ Wed 120

Staybridge Suites Liverpool

ⓤ

☎ 0871 423 4876 📠 0151 703 9710
21 Keel Wharf L3 4FN

Currently the rating for this establishment is not confirmed. This may be due to a change of ownership or because it has only recently joined the AA rating scheme. For further details please see the AA website: theAA.com

Rooms 132

Campanile Liverpool

Campanile

BUDGET HOTEL

☎ 0151 709 8104 📠 0151 709 8725
Chaloner St, Queens Dock L3 4AJ
e-mail: liverpool@campanile.com
dir: Follow tourist signs marked Albert Dock. Hotel on waterfront

This modern building offers accommodation in smart, well-equipped bedrooms, all with en suite bathrooms. Refreshments may be taken at the informal bistro. See also the Hotel Groups pages.

Rooms 100 (4 fmly) (33 GF) **S** £59-£80; **D** £59-£80*
Conf Class 18 Board 24 Thtr 35

Express by Holiday Inn Liverpool - Knowsley

BUDGET HOTEL

☎ 0151 549 2700 📠 0151 549 2800
Ribblers Ln, Knowsley L34 9HA
e-mail: liverpool@exhi.co.uk
web: www.hiexpress.com/lpool-knowsley
dir: M57 junct 4, last exit off rdbt, then 1st left. Hotel on left

A modern hotel ideal for families and business travellers. Fresh and uncomplicated, the spacious rooms include Sky TV, power shower and tea and coffee-making facilities. Continental buffet breakfast is included in the room rate; other meals may be taken at the nearby family pub or restaurant. See also the Hotel Groups pages.

Rooms 86 (62 fmly)

Ibis Liverpool City Centre

BUDGET HOTEL

☎ 0151 706 9800 📠 0151 706 9810
27 Wapping L1 8LY
e-mail: H3140@accor-hotels.com
web: www.ibishotel.com
dir: From M62 follow Albert Dock signs. Opposite Dock entrance

Modern, budget hotel offering comfortable accommodation in bright and practical bedrooms. Breakfast is self-service and dinner is available in the restaurant. See also the Hotel Groups pages.

Rooms 127 (15 fmly) (23 GF) **S** £41.30-£125; **D** £41.30-£125*

LIVERPOOL *continued*

Innkeeper's Lodge Liverpool North

BUDGET HOTEL

☎ 0845 112 6023 📠 0845 112 6278
502 Queen's Dr, Stoneycroft L13 0AS
web: www.innkeeperslodge.com/liverpoolnorth
dir: End of M62, A5080. Under flyover, signed Bootle. At A57 lights, straight on into Queen's Dr

Innkeeper's Lodge represents an exciting, high value concept within the budget hotel market. Comfortable bedrooms provide excellent facilities that include satellite TV and modem points. Options include family rooms; and for the corporate guest, cutting edge IT which includes Wi-fi access. A popular Carvery provides all-day food, including an extensive, complimentary continental breakfast. See also the Hotel Groups pages.

Rooms 21 (6 fmly)

Innkeeper's Lodge Liverpool South (Airport)

BUDGET HOTEL

☎ 0845 112 6024 📠 0845 112 6277
531 Aigburth Rd L19 9DN
web: www.innkeeperslodge.com/liverpoolsouth
dir: M62 junct 6 or M57 junct 1, A5300, follow Liverpool (S)/Airport signs. A562. A561 through Garston. Lodge on right

Innkeeper's Lodge represents an exciting, high value concept within the budget hotel market. Comfortable bedrooms provide excellent facilities that include satellite TV and modem points. Options include family rooms; and for the corporate guest, cutting edge IT which includes Wi-fi access. A popular Carvery provides all-day food, including an extensive, complimentary continental breakfast. See also the Hotel Groups pages.

Rooms 32 (6 fmly) **Conf** Thtr 12

Travelodge Liverpool Central

BUDGET HOTEL

☎ 0871 984 6156 📠 0151 227 5838
25 Haymarket L1 6ER
web: www.travelodge.co.uk
dir: In city centre near Liverpool Lime Street Station. Adjacent to entrance to Birkenhead Tunnel

Travelodge offers good quality, good value, budget accommodation. All offer family rooms sleeping up to four (two adults, two children) with en suite bathroom/shower-room, remote-control TV, tea- and coffee-making facilities and comfortable beds. Food options vary. Breakfast is at the on-site Bar Café restaurant (if available) or to take away. See also Hotel Groups pages.

Rooms 105 **S** fr £29; **D** fr £29

Travelodge Liverpool Docks

BUDGET HOTEL

☎ 0871 984 6030 📠 0151 707 7769
Brunswick Dock, Sefton St L3 4BH
web: www.travelodge.co.uk
dir: Follow signs to City Centre & Docks, pass by Albert Docks on right, right at lights. Royal Navy HQ 1m on right. Lodge adjacent

Rooms 31 **S** fr £29; **D** fr £29

MORETON Map 15 SJ28

Leasowe Castle

★★★ 77% HOTEL

☎ 0151 606 9191 📠 0151 678 5551
Leasowe Rd CH46 3RF
e-mail: reservations@leasowecastle.com
web: www.leasowecastle.com
dir: M53 junct 1, 1st exit from rdbt onto A551. Hotel 0.75m on right

Located adjacent to Leasowe Golf Course and within easy reach of Liverpool, Chester and all of the Wirral's attractions, this historic hotel dates back to 1592. Bedrooms are smartly appointed and well equipped, many enjoying ocean views. Public areas retain many original features. Weddings and functions are well catered for.

Rooms 47 (3 fmly) **S** £55-£95; **D** £65-£175 (incl. bkfst)* **Facilities** FTV Gym Water sports Sea Fishing Sailing Health club Xmas New Year Wi-fi **Conf** Class 200 Board 80 Thtr 400 Del from £99 to £125* **Services** Lift Parking 200 **Notes** LB ⊗ Civ Wed 250

NEWTON-LE-WILLOWS Map 15 SJ59

Holiday Inn

★★★ 77% HOTEL

☎ 0870 400 9039 📠 01942 718419
Lodge Ln, Newton Le Willows WA12 0JG
e-mail: haydock@ihg.com
web: www.holidayinn.co.uk
dir: M6 junct 23, A49 to Ashton-in-Makerfield. Hotel 0.25m on right by racecourse

This hotel has an ideal location adjacent to Haydock Racecourse and within easy reach of most north-west cities and attractions. A variety of bedrooms is available and public areas include extensive meeting and conference facilities, a smart Spirit health and leisure club and a spacious bar and restaurant.

Rooms 136 (12 fmly) (23 GF) (38 smoking) **Facilities** STV ☜ Gym Xmas New Year **Conf** Class 70 Board 60 Thtr 180 **Services** Lift Air con **Parking** 204 **Notes** Civ Wed 120

SOUTHPORT Map 15 SD31

Vincent

★★★★ 82% ◉ TOWN HOUSE HOTEL

☎ 01704 883800 📠 01704 883830
98 Lord St PR8 1JR
dir: M58 junct 3, follow signs to Ormskirk & Southport. Hotel on Lord St

This stylish, boutique property occupies a prime location on Southport's famous boulevard. Bedrooms, some with views of the beach, are appointed to a high standard with oversized beds, extremely well stock mini-bars and stylish en suites with deep tubs. Public areas include a trendy cocktail bar, an all-day dining concept. Friendly staff offer personalised service.

Rooms 60 **D** £85-£140 (incl. bkfst)* **Facilities** STV FTV Gym Wi-fi **Conf** Class 96 Board 50 Thtr 196 **Services** Lift Air con **Parking** 20 **Notes** LB ⊗ Civ Wed 150

Scarisbrick

★★★ 77% HOTEL

☎ 01704 543000 📠 01704 533335
Lord St PR8 1NZ
e-mail: info@scarisbrickhotel.com
web: www.scarisbrickhotel.co.uk
dir: From S: M6, M58 to Ormskirk then Southport. From N: A59 from Preston, well signed

Centrally located on Southport's famous Lord Street, this privately owned hotel offers a high standard of attractively furnished, thoughtfully equipped accommodation. A wide range of eating options is available, from the bistro style of Maloney's Kitchen to the more formal Knightsbridge restaurant. Extensive leisure and conference facilities are also available.

Rooms 88 (5 fmly) (7 smoking) **S** £30-£85; **D** £60-£125 (incl. bkfst)* **Facilities** STV ☜ Gym Use of private leisure centre Beauty & aromatherapy studio ♫ Xmas New Year Wi-fi **Conf** Class 100 Board 80 Thtr 200 Del from £85 to £115 **Services** Lift **Parking** 68 **Notes** LB ⊗ Civ Wed 170

Best Western Royal Clifton Hotel & Spa

★★★ 74% HOTEL

☎ 01704 533771 📠 01704 500657
Promenade PR8 1RB
e-mail: sales@royalclifton.co.uk
dir: Adjacent to Marine Lake

This grand, traditional hotel benefits from a prime location on the promenade. Bedrooms range in size and style, but all are comfortable and thoughtfully equipped. Public areas include the lively Bar C, the elegant Pavilion Restaurant and a modern, well-equipped leisure club. Extensive conference and banqueting facilities make this hotel a popular function venue.

Best Western Royal Clifton Hotel & Spa

Rooms 120 (23 fmly) (6 GF) **Facilities** Spa STV ⓧ supervised Gym Hair & beauty Steam room Aromatherapy ♫ Xmas New Year Wi-fi **Conf** Class 100 Board 65 Thtr 250 Del from £95 to £125* **Services** Lift **Parking** 60 **Notes** ⊗ Civ Wed 150

Cambridge House

★★ 81% HOTEL

☎ 01704 538372 📠 01704 547183
4 Cambridge Rd PR9 9NG
e-mail: info@cambridgehouse.co.uk
dir: A565 N from town centre, over 2 rdbts

This delightful house is in a peaceful location close to Hesketh Park, a short drive from Lord Street. The spacious, individually styled bedrooms, including a luxurious honeymoon suite, are furnished to a very high standard. Stylish public areas include a lounge, a cosy bar and a dining room. Service is attentive.

Rooms 16 (2 fmly) (2 GF) **S** £55-£70; **D** £78-£118 (incl. bkfst) **Facilities** Wi-fi **Conf** Class 30 Thtr 30 **Parking** 20 **Notes** LB

Balmoral Lodge

★★ 74% HOTEL

☎ 01704 544298 📠 01704 501224
41 Queens Rd PR9 9EX
e-mail: balmorallg@aol.com
dir: On edge of town on A565 (Preston road). E at rdbt at North Lord St, left at lights, hotel 200yds on left

Situated in a quiet residential area this popular, friendly hotel is ideally situated just 50 yards from the Lord Street. Accommodation is comfortably equipped and family rooms are available. In addition to the restaurant which offers freshly prepared dishes, there is a choice of lounges including a comfortable lounge bar.

Rooms 15 (4 annexe) (3 fmly) (4 GF) **S** £35-£45; **D** £70-£90 (incl. bkfst)* **Facilities** STV FTV Wi-fi **Conf** Class 30 Board 30 Thtr 30 Del from £50 to £80* **Parking** 12 **Notes** LB

THORNTON HOUGH   Map 15 SJ38

Thornton Hall Hotel and Spa

★★★★ 77% ◉◉ HOTEL

☎ 0151 336 3938 📠 0151 336 7864
Neston Rd CH63 1JF
e-mail: reservations@thorntonhallhotel.com
web: www.thorntonhallhotel.com
dir: M53 junct 4, B5151/Neston onto B5136 to Thornton Hough (signed)

Dating back to the mid 1800s, this country-house hotel has been carefully extended and restored. Public areas include an impressive leisure spa boasting excellent facilities, a choice of restaurants and a spacious bar. Bedrooms vary in style and include feature rooms in the main house and more contemporary rooms in the garden wing. Delightful grounds and gardens, and impressive function facilities make this a popular wedding venue.

Rooms 63 (6 fmly) (28 GF) **Facilities** Spa ⓧ ♨ Gym Beauty spa & clinic Hairdressing salon Wi-fi **Conf** Class 225 Board 80 Thtr 650 Del from £123 to £158* **Parking** 250 **Notes** ⊗ Closed 1 Jan Civ Wed 500

WALLASEY   Map 15 SJ29

Grove House

★★★ 79% HOTEL

☎ 0151 639 3947 & 0151 630 4558 📠 0151 639 0028
Grove Rd CH45 3HF
e-mail: reception@thegrovehouse.co.uk
dir: M53 junct 1, A554 (Wallasey New Brighton), right after church onto Harrison Drive, left after Windsors Garage onto Grove Rd

Pretty lawns and gardens provide the setting for this friendly hotel, conveniently situated about a mile from the M53. Attractively furnished, well-equipped bedrooms include family and four-poster rooms. Business meetings and weddings can be catered for. A wide choice of dishes is available in the restaurant that overlooks the garden.

Rooms 14 (7 fmly) **S** £69.50; **D** £79.50-£115.10* **Facilities** FTV Wi-fi **Conf** Class 30 Board 50 Thtr 50 Del from £108.90 to £126.90* **Parking** 28 **Notes** LB ⊗ RS Bank holidays Civ Wed 50

See advert on this page

NORFOLK

ACLE — Map 13 TG41

Travelodge Great Yarmouth Acle

BUDGET HOTEL

☎ 0871 984 6032 ▤ 01493 751970
NR13 3BE
web: www.travelodge.co.uk
dir: At junct of A47, A1064 & Acle bypass. E of Acle on A47

Travelodge offers good quality, good value, budget accommodation. All offer family rooms sleeping up to four (two adults, two children) with en suite bathroom/shower-room, remote-control TV, tea- and coffee-making facilities and comfortable beds. Food options vary. Breakfast is at the on-site Bar Café restaurant (if available) or to take away. See also Hotel Groups pages.

Rooms 59 **S** fr £29; **D** fr £29

ALBURGH — Map 13 TM28

The Dove Restaurant with Rooms

◎◎ RESTAURANT WITH ROOMS

☎ 01986 788315 ▤ 01986 788315
Holbrook Hill IP20 0EP
e-mail: thedovenorfolk@freeola.com
dir: Between Harleston & Bungay at junct A143 & B1062

A warm welcome awaits at this restaurant with rooms. Bedrooms are pleasantly decorated, furnished with pine pieces and have modern facilities. Public rooms include a lounge area with a small bar, and a smart restaurant with well-spaced tables.

Rooms 2 (1 fmly)

ATTLEBOROUGH — Map 13 TM09

Sherbourne House

◎ RESTAURANT WITH ROOMS

☎ 01953 454363
8 Norwich Rd NR17 2JX
e-mail: stay@sherbourne-house.co.uk
web: www.sherbourne-house.co.uk
dir: Off B1077

Expect a warm welcome from the caring hosts at this delightful 17th-century property situated just a short walk from the centre of a historic market town. Public rooms include a choice of lounges, a sunny conservatory/lounge bar and a restaurant that serves dishes based on the highest quality, locally sourced produce. The individually decorated bedrooms are smartly appointed and have many thoughtful touches.

Rooms 8 (1 fmly)

BARNHAM BROOM — Map 13 TG00

Barnham Broom Hotel, Golf & Restaurant

★★★ 83% ◎◎ HOTEL

☎ 01603 759393 ▤ 01603 758224
NR9 4DD
e-mail: amortimer@barnham-broom.co.uk
web: www.barnham-broom.co.uk
dir: A11/A47 towards Swaffham, follow brown tourist signs

Situated in a peaceful rural location just a short drive from Norwich, this hotel offers contemporary style bedrooms that are tastefully furnished and thoughtfully equipped. The Sports Bar serves a range of snacks and meals throughout the day, or guests can choose from the carte menu in Flints Restaurant. There also are extensive leisure, conference and banqueting facilities.

Rooms 52 (7 fmly) (22 GF) **Facilities** STV ⊕ supervised ⅃ 36 ⌕ Putt green Gym Squash Sauna Steam room Personal trainers Xmas New Year Wi-fi **Conf** Class 100 Board 80 Thtr 250 **Parking** 150 **Notes** LB Civ Wed 200

BLAKENEY
Map 13 TG04

Morston Hall
★★★ ◉◉◉ HOTEL

☎ 01263 741041 📄 01263 740419
Morston, Holt NR25 7AA
e-mail: reception@morstonhall.com
web: www.morstonhall.com
dir: 1m W of Blakeney on A149 (King's Lynn to Cromer road)

This delightful 17th-century country-house hotel enjoys a tranquil setting amid well-tended gardens. The comfortable public rooms offer a choice of attractive lounges and a sunny conservatory, while the elegant dining room is the perfect setting to enjoy Galton Blackiston's award-winning cuisine. The spacious bedrooms are individually decorated and stylishly furnished with modern opulence.

Rooms 13 (6 annexe) (7 GF) **Facilities** STV New Year Wi-fi **Parking** 40 **Notes** Closed Jan-2 Feb & 2 days Xmas

The Blakeney
★★★ 82% ◉ HOTEL

☎ 01263 740797 📄 01263 740795
The Quay NR25 7NE
e-mail: reception@blakeney-hotel.co.uk
web: www.blakeney-hotel.co.uk
dir: Off A149 (coast road) 8m W of Sheringham

A traditional, privately owned hotel situated on the quayside with superb views across the estuary and the salt marshes to Blakeney Point. Public rooms feature an elegant restaurant, ground-floor lounge, a bar and a first-floor sun lounge overlooking the harbour. Bedrooms are smartly decorated and equipped with modern facilities; some enjoy the lovely sea views.

Rooms 64 (16 annexe) (20 fmly) (18 GF) **S** £82-£138; **D** £164-£300 (incl. bkfst & dinner)* **Facilities** FTV ⊗ Gym Billiards Snooker Table tennis Sauna Steam room Spa bath Xmas New Year Wi-fi **Conf** Class 100 Board 100 Thtr 150 **Services** Lift **Parking** 60 **Notes** LB

Blakeney Manor
★★ 76% HOTEL

☎ 01263 740376 📄 01263 741116
The Quay NR25 7ND
e-mail: reception@blakeneymanor.co.uk
web: www.blakeneymanor.co.uk
dir: Exit A149 at Blakeney towards Blakeney Quay. Hotel at end of quay between Mariner's Hill & Friary Hills

An attractive Norfolk flint building overlooking Blakeney Marshes close to the town centre and quayside. The bedrooms are located in flint-faced barns in a courtyard adjacent to the main building. The spacious public rooms include a choice of lounges, a conservatory, a popular bar and a large restaurant offering an interesting choice of dishes.

Rooms 35 (28 annexe) (26 GF) **Facilities** Xmas New Year Wi-fi **Parking** 40 **Notes** No children 14yrs

The Pheasant
★★ 76% HOTEL

☎ 01263 588382 📄 01263 588101
Coast Rd, Kelling NR25 7EG
e-mail: enquiries@pheasanthotelnorfolk.co.uk
dir: On A149 (coast road) mid-way between Sheringham & Blakeney

A popular hotel ideally situated on the main coast road just a short drive from the bustling town of Holt. Bedrooms are split between the main house and a modern wing of spacious rooms to the rear of the property. Public rooms include a busy lounge bar, a residents' lounge and a large restaurant.

Rooms 30 (1 fmly) (24 GF) **S** £52-£62; **D** £104-£114 (incl. bkfst)* **Facilities** Xmas New Year Wi-fi **Conf** Class 50 Board 50 Thtr 80 Del from £75 to £99* **Parking** 80 **Notes** LB

BRANCASTER STAITHE
Map 13 TF74

White Horse
★★★ 79% ◉◉ HOTEL

☎ 01485 210262 📄 01485 210930
PE31 8BY
e-mail: reception@whitehorsebrancaster.co.uk
web: www.whitehorsebrancaster.co.uk
dir: On A149 (coast road) midway between Hunstanton & Wells-next-the-Sea

A charming hotel situated on the north Norfolk coast with contemporary bedrooms in two wings, some featuring an interesting cobbled fascia. Each room is attractively decorated and thoughtfully equipped. There is a large bar and a lounge area leading through to the conservatory restaurant, with stunning tidal marshland views across to Scolt Head Island.

Rooms 15 (8 annexe) (4 fmly) (8 GF) **S** £50-£108; **D** £100-£156 (incl. bkfst)* **Facilities** Xmas New Year Wi-fi **Parking** 60 **Notes** LB

BURNHAM MARKET — Map 13 TF84

Hoste Arms

★★★ 87% ◉◉ HOTEL

☎ 01328 738777 🖨 01328 730103
The Green PE31 8HD
e-mail: reception@hostearms.co.uk
web: www.hostearms.co.uk
dir: Signed on B1155, 5m W of Wells-next-the-Sea

A stylish, privately-owned inn situated in the heart of a bustling village close to the north Norfolk coast. The extensive public rooms feature a range of dining areas that include a conservatory with plush furniture, a sunny patio and a traditional pub. The tastefully furnished and thoughtfully equipped bedrooms are generally very spacious and offer a high degree of comfort.

Rooms 35 (7 GF) **S** £104-£190; **D** £128-£225 (incl. bkfst)* **Facilities** STV Xmas New Year Wi-fi **Conf** Board 16 Thtr 25 **Services** Air con **Parking** 45

See advert on this page

CROMER — Map 13 TG24

Elderton Lodge Hotel & Langtry Restaurant

★★★ 87% ◉◉ HOTEL

☎ 01263 833547 🖨 01263 834673
Gunton Park NR11 8TZ
e-mail: enquiries@eldertonlodge.co.uk
web: www.eldertonlodge.co.uk
dir: At North Walsham take A149 towards Cromer, hotel 3m on left, just before Thorpe Market

Ideally placed for touring the north Norfolk coastline, this delightful former shooting lodge is set amidst six acres of mature gardens adjacent to Gunton Hall estate. The individually decorated bedrooms are tastefully furnished and thoughtfully equipped. Public rooms include a smart lounge bar, an elegant restaurant and a sunny conservatory breakfast room.

Elderton Lodge Hotel & Langtry Restaurant

Rooms 11 (2 fmly) (2 GF) **S** £75; **D** £100-£120 (incl. bkfst)* **Facilities** Xmas New Year Wi-fi **Parking** 50 **Notes** LB Civ Wed 55

Sea Marge

★★★ 86% ◉ HOTEL

☎ 01263 579579 🖨 01263 579524
16 High St, Overstrand NR27 0AB
e-mail: info@mackenziehotels.com
dir: A140 from Norwich then A149 to Cromer, B1159 to Overstrand. Hotel in village centre

An elegant Grade II listed Edwardian mansion perched on the clifftop amidst pretty landscaped gardens which lead down to the beach. Bedrooms are tastefully decorated and thoughtfully equipped; many have superb sea views. Public rooms offer a wide choice of areas in which to relax, including Frazer's restaurant and a smart lounge bar.

Rooms 25 (6 annexe) (6 fmly) (2 GF) **S** fr £91; **D** fr £142 (incl. bkfst)* **Facilities** ⤴ Xmas New Year Wi-fi **Conf** Class 55 Board 30 Thtr 70 Del from £112.95* **Services** Lift **Parking** 50 **Notes** LB

The Cliftonville

★★★ 74% HOTEL

☎ 01263 512543 🖨 01263 515700
NR27 9AS
e-mail: reservations@cliftonvillehotel.co.uk
web: www.cliftonvillehotel.co.uk
dir: From A149 (coast road), 500yds from town centre, N'bound on clifftop by sunken gardens

An imposing Edwardian hotel situated on the main coast road with stunning views of the sea. Public rooms feature a magnificent staircase, minstrels' gallery, coffee shop, lounge bar, a further residents' lounge, Boltons Bistro and an additional restaurant. The pleasantly decorated bedrooms are generally quite spacious and have lovely sea views.

Rooms 30 (5 fmly) **S** £55-£72; **D** £110-£144 (incl. bkfst)* **Facilities** Xmas New Year Wi-fi **Conf** Class 100 Board 60 Thtr 150 Del from £90 to £150* **Services** Lift **Parking** 21 **Notes** LB

Red Lion

★★ 78% HOTEL

☎ 01263 514964 📠 01263 512834
Brook St NR27 9HD
e-mail: enquiries@yeolderedlionhotel.co.uk
web: www.yeolderedlionhotel.co.uk
dir: from town centre 1st left after church

A Victorian property situated in an elevated position overlooking the beach and the sea. The smartly appointed public areas include a billiard room, lounge bar, a popular restaurant, a sunny conservatory and a first-floor residents' lounge with superb sea views. The spacious bedrooms are tastefully decorated, with co-ordinated soft furnishings and many thoughtful touches.

Rooms 12 (1 fmly) **Facilities** Discount for local leisure centre **Conf** Class 50 Board 60 Thtr 100 **Parking** 12 **Notes** LB ⊗ Closed 25 Dec

Hotel de Paris

Leisureplex

★★ 69% HOTEL

☎ 01263 513141 📠 01263 515217
High St NR27 9HG
e-mail: deparis.cromer@alfatravel.co.uk
dir: enter Cromer on A140 (Norwich road). Left at lights onto Mount St. At 2nd lights right into Prince of Wales Rd. 2nd right into New St leading into High St

An imposing, traditional-style resort hotel, situated in a prominent position overlooking the pier and beach. The bedrooms are pleasantly decorated and equipped with a good range of useful extras; many rooms have lovely sea views. The spacious public areas include a large lounge bar, restaurant, games room and a further lounge.

Rooms 56 (5 fmly) **Facilities** FTV Games room ♫ Xmas New Year **Services** Lift **Parking** 14 **Notes** LB ⊗ Closed Dec-Feb (except Xmas) RS Mar & Nov

DEREHAM Map 13 TF91

George

★★ 76% HOTEL

☎ 01362 696801 📠 01362 695711
Swaffham Rd NR19 2AZ
web: www.lottiesrestaurant.co.uk
dir: From A47 follow Dereham signs. In High St to memorial, hotel on left

Delightful old inn situated in the heart of this bustling market town and ideally placed for touring Norfolk. The spacious bedrooms are pleasantly decorated, furnished with pine pieces and have many thoughtful touches. Public rooms include a smart restaurant, a stylish lounge with leather sofas, a conservatory dining room and a large lounge bar.

Rooms 8 (2 fmly) **Facilities** New Year **Parking** 50 **Notes** ⊗ Closed 26 Dec Civ Wed 50

DISS Map 13 TM18

Scole Inn

★★★ 67% HOTEL

OXFORD
HOTELS & INNS

☎ 01379 740481 📠 01379 740762
Ipswich Rd, Scole IP21 4DR
e-mail: manager.scoleinn@ohiml.com
web: www.oxfordhotelsandinns.com
dir: A140, Diss rdbt signed Scole, left at T-junct, hotel on left

A charming 17th-century inn situated in the heart of the village where King Charles II and highwayman John Belcher are said to have stayed. Bedrooms come in a variety of styles; each one is pleasantly decorated and well equipped. The hotel retains a wealth of original features such as exposed brickwork, huge open fires and a superb carved wooden staircase. The public areas include a bar, restaurant and lounge bar.

Rooms 23 (12 annexe) (1 fmly) (7 GF) **Facilities** ♫ Xmas Wi-fi **Conf** Class 26 Board 35 Thtr 45 **Parking** 60 **Notes** LB Civ Wed 50

DOWNHAM MARKET Map 12 TF60

Castle

★★ 78% HOTEL

☎ 01366 384311 📠 01366 384311
High St PE38 9HF
e-mail: howards@castle-hotel.com
dir: M11 take A10 for Ely into Downham Market. Hotel opp lights on corner of High St

This popular coaching inn is situated close to the centre of town and has been welcoming guests for over 300 years. Well maintained public areas include a cosy lounge bar and two smartly appointed restaurants. Inviting bedrooms, some with four-poster beds, are attractively decorated, thoughtfully equipped, and have bright, modern decor.

Rooms 12 **Facilities** Xmas **Conf** Class 30 Board 40 Thtr 60 **Parking** 26 **Notes** LB

FRITTON Map 13 TG40

Caldecott Hall Golf & Leisure

★★★ 78% HOTEL

☎ 01493 488488 📠 01493 488561
Caldecott Hall, Beccles Rd NR31 9EY
e-mail: hotel@caldecotthall.co.uk
web: www.caldecotthall.co.uk
dir: On A143 (Beccles to Great Yarmouth road), 4m from Great Yarmouth

Ideally situated in its own attractive, landscaped grounds that has a golf course, fishing lakes and the Redwings horse sanctuary. The individually decorated bedrooms are spacious, and equipped with many thoughtful touches.

Public rooms include a smart sitting room, a lounge bar, restaurant, clubhouse and smart leisure complex.

Rooms 8 (3 fmly) **Facilities** FTV ⊛ supervised ⚐ 36 Putt green Gym Driving range **Conf** Class 80 Board 20 Thtr 100 **Parking** 100 **Notes** ⊗ Civ Wed 150

GREAT BIRCHAM Map 13 TF73

Kings Head

★★★ 86% ⊛ HOTEL

☎ 01485 578265 📠 01485 578635
PE31 6RJ
e-mail: welcome@the-kings-head-bircham.co.uk
web: www.the-kings-head-bircham.co.uk
dir: From King's Lynn take A149 towards Fakenham. After Hillington, turn left onto B1153, to Great Bircham

This inn is situated in a peaceful village location close to the north Norfolk coastline. The spacious, individually decorated bedrooms are tastefully appointed with superb co-ordinated furnishings and many thoughtful touches. The contemporary, public rooms include a brasserie restaurant, a relaxing lounge, a smart bar and a private dining room.

Rooms 12 (2 fmly) **Facilities** Xmas Wi-fi **Conf** Class 16 Board 20 Thtr 30 **Parking** 25 **Notes** Civ Wed 130

GREAT YARMOUTH Map 13 TG50

Imperial

THE INDEPENDENTS
HOTEL ASSOCIATION

★★★★ 71% ⊛ HOTEL

☎ 01493 842000 📠 01493 852229
North Dr NR30 1EQ
e-mail: reservations@imperialhotel.co.uk
web: www.imperialhotel.co.uk
dir: Follow signs to seafront, turn left. Hotel opposite tennis courts

This friendly, family-run hotel is situated at the quieter end of the seafront within easy walking distance of the town centre. Bedrooms are attractively decorated with co-ordinated soft furnishings and many thoughtful touches; most rooms have superb sea views. Public areas include the smart Savoie Lounge Bar and the Rambouillet Restaurant.

Rooms 39 (4 fmly) **S** £60-£90; **D** £70-£120 (incl. bkfst) **Facilities** FTV New Year Wi-fi **Conf** Class 40 Board 30 Thtr 140 Del from £80 to £140 **Services** Lift **Parking** 50 **Notes** LB Civ Wed 140

GREAT YARMOUTH *continued*

Comfort Hotel Great Yarmouth

★★★ 75% HOTEL

☎ 01493 855070 & 850044 📠 01493 853798
Albert Square NR30 3JH
e-mail: sales@comfortgreatyarmouth.co.uk
web: www.comfortgreatyarmouth.co.uk
dir: from seafront left at Wellington Pier into Kimberley
Terrace. Left into Albert Square, hotel on left

A large hotel situated in the quieter end of town, just off
the seafront and within easy walking distance of the town
centre. The pleasantly decorated, well-equipped
bedrooms are generally quite spacious and include Wi-fi.
Public rooms include a comfortable lounge, a bar and
smart brasserie-style-restaurant. The hotel has an
outdoor swimming pool.

Rooms 50 (6 fmly) (3 GF) (12 smoking) **Facilities** STV ᠀
Xmas New Year Wi-fi **Conf** Class 50 Board 30 Thtr 120
Parking 19 **Notes** LB ⊗ Civ Wed 120

Furzedown

★★★ 73% HOTEL

☎ 01493 844138 📠 01493 844138
19-20 North Dr NR30 4EW
e-mail: paul@furzedownhotel.co.uk
web: www.furzedownhotel.co.uk
dir: At end of A47 or A12, towards seafront, left, hotel
opposite Waterways

Expect a warm welcome at this family-run hotel situated
at the northern end of the seafront overlooking the town's
Venetian Waterways. Bedrooms are pleasantly decorated
and thoughtfully equipped; many rooms have superb sea
views. The stylish public areas include a comfortable
lounge bar, a smartly appointed restaurant and a cosy TV
room.

Rooms 20 (11 fmly) **S** £52-£62; **D** £72-£84 (incl. bkfst)*
Facilities FTV New Year Wi-fi **Conf** Class 80 Board 40
Thtr 75 Del from £74 to £94 **Parking** 30

Burlington Palm Hotel

★★★ 67% HOTEL

☎ 01493 844568 & 842095 📠 01493 331848
11 North Dr NR30 1EG
e-mail: enquiries@burlington-hotel.co.uk
web: www.burlington-hotel.co.uk
dir: A12 to seafront, left at Britannia Pier. Hotel near
tennis courts

This privately owned hotel is situated at the quiet end of
the resort, overlooking the sea. Bedrooms come in a
variety of sizes and styles; they are pleasantly decorated
and well equipped, and many have lovely sea views. The
spacious public rooms include a range of seating areas,
a choice of dining rooms, two bars and a heated indoor
swimming pool.

Rooms 70 (9 fmly) (1 GF) **Facilities** ᠀ Turkish steam
room Xmas Wi-fi **Conf** Class 60 Board 30 Thtr 120
Services Lift **Parking** 70 **Notes** LB ⊗ Closed Jan-Feb
RS Dec-Feb

See advert on page 359

The Arden Court Hotel

★★ 76% HOTEL

☎ 01493 855310 📠 01493 843413
93-94 North Denes Rd NR30 4LW
e-mail: info@ardencourt-hotel.co.uk.
web: www.ardencourt-hotel.co.uk
dir: At seafront left along North Drive. At boating lake left
along Beaconsfield Rd. At mini rdbt right into North Denes
Rd

Friendly, family-run hotel situated in a residential area
just a short walk from the seafront. The individually
decorated bedrooms are smartly furnished and equipped
with a good range of useful extras. Public rooms are
attractively presented; they include a smart lounge bar
and a restaurant serving an interesting choice of dishes.

Rooms 14 (5 fmly) (2 GF) **Facilities** Xmas **Parking** 10
Notes LB ⊗

New Beach Hotel

★★ 69% HOTEL

Leisureplex

☎ 01493 332300 📠 01493 331880
67 Marine Pde NR30 2EJ
e-mail: newbeach.gtyarmouth@alfatravel.co.uk
dir: Follow signs to seafront. Hotel facing Britannia Pier

This Victorian building is centrally located on the
seafront, overlooking Britannia Pier and the sandy beach.
Bedrooms are pleasantly decorated and equipped with
modern facilities; many have lovely sea views. Dinner is
taken in the restaurant which doubles as the ballroom,
and guests can also relax in the bar or sunny lounge.

Rooms 75 (3 fmly) **Facilities** FTV ♫ Xmas New Year
Services Lift **Notes** LB ⊗ Closed Dec-Feb (except Xmas)
RS Nov & Mar

Travelodge Great Yarmouth

BUDGET HOTEL

☎ 0871 984 6366 📠 01493 659012
Sidegate Ln, Beacon Park Gorleston NR31 7RA
e-mail: greatyarmouth@travelodge.co.uk
dir: From Norwich on A47 signed Great Yarmouth. Lodge
on A12, 3.5m S of Great Yarmouth

Travelodge offers good quality, good value, budget
accommodation. All offer family rooms sleeping up to
four (two adults, two children) with en suite bathroom/
shower-room, remote-control TV, tea- and coffee-making
facilities and comfortable beds. Food options vary.
Breakfast is at the on-site Bar Café restaurant (if
available) or to take away. See also the Hotel Groups
pages.

Rooms 52 **S** fr £29; **D** fr £29

Andover House

◉ RESTAURANT WITH ROOMS

☎ 01493 843490 📠 01493 852546
28-30 Camperdown NR30 3JB
e-mail: info@andoverhouse.co.uk
web: www.andoverhouse.co.uk
dir: Opposite Wellington Pier, turn onto Shadingfield
Close, right onto Kimberley Terrace, follow onto
Camperdown. Property on left

This lovely Victorian house has been totally transformed
by the current owners, following a complete internal
renovation. The property features a series of contemporary
spaces that include a large open-plan lounge bar, a
brasserie-style restaurant, a cosy lounge and a smart sun
terrace. Bedrooms are tastefully appointed with
co-ordinated soft furnishings and have many thoughtful
touches.

Rooms 20

GRIMSTON — Map 12 TF72

INSPECTORS' CHOICE

Congham Hall Country House Hotel

★★★ ◉◉ COUNTRY HOUSE HOTEL

☎ 01485 600250 📠 01485 601191
Lynn Rd PE32 1AH
e-mail: info@conghamhallhotel.co.uk
web: www.conghamhallhotel.co.uk
dir: At A149/A148 junct, NE of King's Lynn, take A148 towards Fakenham for 100yds. Right to Grimston, hotel 2.5m on left

Elegant 18th-century Georgian manor set amid 30 acres of mature landscaped grounds and surrounded by parkland. The inviting public rooms provide a range of tastefully furnished areas in which to sit and relax. Imaginative cuisine is served in the Orangery Restaurant which has an intimate atmosphere and panoramic views of the gardens. The bedrooms, tastefully furnished with period pieces, have modern facilities and many thoughtful touches. Von Essen Hotels - AA Hotel Group of the Year 2009-10.

Rooms 14 (1 GF) **Facilities** ⚐ Putt green ⚑ Xmas New Year Wi-fi **Conf** Class 12 Board 28 Thtr 50 Del from £180 to £190* **Parking** 50 **Notes** ⊗ Civ Wed 100

HEACHAM — Map 12 TF63

Heacham Manor Hotel

[U]

☎ 01485 536030 & 579800 📠 01485 533815
Hunstanton Rd PE36 5BB
e-mail: info@heacham-manor.co.uk
dir: On A149 between Heacham & Hunstanton. Near Hunstanton rdbt with water tower

At the time of going to press the rating for this establishment was not confirmed. This may be due to a change of ownership or because it has only recently joined the AA rating scheme. For further details please see the AA website: theAA.com

Rooms 45 (32 annexe) (10 fmly) (12 GF) **S** £85-£205; **D** £95-£215 (incl. bkfst)* **Facilities** FTV ⚓ 18 Swimming pools & leisure facilities available at sister resort Xmas New Year Wi-fi **Conf** Class 35 Board 20 Thtr 40 Del from £95 to £145* **Parking** 55 **Notes** LB ⊗

See advert on page 365

HETHERSETT — Map 13 TG10

Park Farm

★★★ 82% ◉ HOTEL

☎ 01603 810264 📠 01603 812104
NR9 3DL
e-mail: enq@parkfarm-hotel.co.uk
web: www.parkfarm-hotel.co.uk
dir: 5m S of Norwich, off A11 on B1172

An elegant Georgian farmhouse set in landscaped grounds surrounded by open countryside. The property has been owned and run by the Gowing family since 1958. Bedrooms are pleasantly decorated and tastefully furnished; some rooms have patio doors with a sun terrace. Public rooms include a stylish conservatory, a lounge bar, a smart restaurant and superb leisure facilities.

Rooms 53 (50 annexe) (15 fmly) (26 GF) **Facilities** ⚐ supervised Gym Beauty salon Hairdressing Xmas New Year Wi-fi **Conf** Class 50 Board 50 Thtr 120 **Parking** 150 **Notes** LB ⊗ Civ Wed 100

See advert on page 367

HOLKHAM
Map 13 TF84

The Victoria at Holkham

★★ 83% ◉◉ SMALL HOTEL

☎ 01328 711008 📠 01328 711009
Park Rd NR23 1RG
e-mail: victoria@holkham.co.uk
web: www.victoriaatholkham.co.uk
dir: A149, 2m W of Wells-next-the-Sea

A Grade II listed property, built from local flint, is ideally situated on the north Norfolk coast road and forms part of the Holkham Estate. Decor is very much influenced by the local landscape: the stylish bedrooms are individually decorated and tastefully furnished with pieces specially made for the hotel in India. The brasserie-style restaurant serves an interesting choice of dishes.

Rooms 10 (1 annexe) (2 fmly) (1 GF) **Facilities** Fishing Shooting on Holkham Estate, Bird watching reserve nearby Xmas Child facilities **Conf** Class 40 Board 30 Thtr 12 **Parking** 30 **Notes** LB ⊗ Civ Wed 70

HOLT
Map 13 TG03

The Lawns Wine Bar

◉ RESTAURANT WITH ROOMS

☎ 01263 713390
26 Station Rd NR25 6BS
e-mail: mail@lawnsatholt.co.uk
dir: A148 (Cromer road). 0.25m from Holt rdbt, turn left, 400yds along Station Rd

A superb Georgian house situated in the centre of this delightful north Norfolk market town. The open-plan public areas include a large wine bar with plush sofas, a conservatory and a smart restaurant. The spacious bedrooms are tastefully appointed with co-ordinated soft furnishings and have many thoughtful touches.

Rooms 8

HORNING
Map 13 TG31

Innkeeper's Lodge Norfolk Broads - Horning

BUDGET HOTEL

☎ 0845 112 6060
The Swan Inn, Lower St NR12 8AA
dir: From A47 (Norwich ring road) take A1151 to Wroxham. Cross Wroxham Bridge, 2nd right signed Horning (A1062). On entering Horning, hotel on right

Innkeeper's Lodge represents an exciting, high value concept within the budget hotel market. Comfortable bedrooms provide excellent facilities that include satellite TV and modem points. This carefully restored lodge is in a picturesque setting and has its own unique style and quirky character. Food is served all day, and an extensive, complimentary continental breakfast is offered. See also the Hotel Groups pages.

Rooms 8

HUNSTANTON
Map 12 TF64

Best Western Le Strange Arms

★★★ 82% HOTEL

☎ 01485 534411 📠 01485 534724
Golf Course Rd, Old Hunstanton PE36 6JJ
e-mail: reception@lestrangearms.co.uk
dir: Off A149 1m N of Hunstanton. Left at sharp right bend by pitch & putt course

An impressive hotel with superb views from the wide lawns down to the sandy beach and across The Wash. Bedrooms in the main house have period furnishings whereas the rooms in the wing are more contemporary in style. Public rooms include a comfortable lounge bar and a conference and banqueting suite, plus a choice of dining options - Le Strange Restaurant and the Ancient Mariner.

Rooms 36 (2 fmly) **S** £65-£103.50; **D** £105-£152.50 (incl. bkfst)* **Facilities** STV Xmas New Year Wi-fi **Conf** Class 150 Board 50 Thtr 180 **Services** Lift **Parking** 80 **Notes** LB Civ Wed 70

Caley Hall

★★★ 82% HOTEL

☎ 01485 533486 📠 01485 533348
Old Hunstanton Rd PE36 6HH
e-mail: mail@caleyhallhotel.co.uk
web: www.caleyhallhotel.co.uk
dir: 1m from Hunstanton, on A149

Situated within easy walking distance of the seafront. The tastefully decorated bedrooms are in a series of converted outbuildings; each is smartly furnished and thoughtfully equipped. Public rooms feature a large open-plan lounge/bar with plush leather seating, and a restaurant offering an interesting choice of dishes.

Rooms 40 (20 fmly) (30 GF) **S** £50-£200; **D** £70-£200 (incl. bkfst)* **Facilities** STV Wi-fi Child facilities **Parking** 50 **Notes** LB Closed 18 Dec-20 Jan

The Neptune Restaurant with Rooms

◉◉◉ RESTAURANT WITH ROOMS

☎ 01485 532122
85 Old Hunstanton Rd, Old Hunstanton PE36 6HZ
e-mail: reservations@theneptune.co.uk
web: www.theneptune.co.uk
dir: On A149, past Hunstanton, 200mtrs on left after post office

This charming 18th-century coaching inn, now a restaurant with rooms, is ideally situated for touring the Norfolk coast. The smartly appointed bedrooms are brightly finished with co-ordinated fabrics and handmade New England furniture. Public rooms feature white clapboard walls, polished dark wood floors, fresh flowers and Lloyd Loom furniture. The food is very much a draw here with the carefully prepared, award-winning cuisine utilising excellent local produce, from oysters and mussels from Thornham to quinces grown on a neighbouring farm.

Rooms 7

KING'S LYNN   **Map 12 TF62**

INSPECTORS' CHOICE

Congham Hall Country House Hotel

★★★ ◉◉ COUNTRY HOUSE HOTEL

☎ 01485 600250   🖹 01485 601191
Lynn Rd PE32 1AH
e-mail: info@conghamhallhotel.co.uk
web: www.conghamhallhotel.co.uk

(For full entry see Grimston)

Bank House

★★★ 83% ◉ HOTEL

☎ 01553 660492
King's Staithe Square PE30 1RD
e-mail: info@thebankhouse.co.uk
dir: Towards quay, follow to end, through floodgates, hotel on right

This Grade II listed, 18th-century town house is situated on the quay side in the heart of King's Lynn's historical quarter. Bedrooms are individually decorated and have high quality fabrics and furnishings along with a range of useful facilities. Public rooms include the Counting House coffee shop, a wine bar and brasserie restaurant, as well as a residents' lounge.

Rooms 11 (5 fmly) **S** £80-£90; **D** £100-£120 (incl. bkfst)*
Facilities FTV Xmas New Year Wi-fi **Conf** Class 20 Board 15 **Parking** 1 **Notes** LB ⊗

Best Western Knights Hill

★★★ 78% HOTEL

☎ 01553 675566   🖹 01553 675568
Knights Hill Village, South Wootton PE30 3HQ
e-mail: reception@knightshill.co.uk
dir: At junct A148 & A149

This hotel village complex is set on a 16th-century site on the outskirts of town. The smartly decorated, well-equipped bedrooms are situated in extensions of the original hunting lodge. Public areas have a wealth of historic charm; they include the Garden Restaurant and the Farmers Arms pub. The hotel also has conference and leisure facilities, including Imagine Spa.

Rooms 79 (12 annexe) (1 fmly) (38 GF) **Facilities** Spa STV ③ ◞ ◞ Gym Xmas New Year Wi-fi **Conf** Class 150 Board 30 Thtr 200 **Parking** 350 **Notes** ⊗ Civ Wed 90

KING'S LYNN *continued*

Stuart House

★★★ 70% HOTEL

☎ 01553 772169 📠 01553 774788
35 Goodwins Rd PE30 5QX
e-mail: reception@stuarthousehotel.co.uk
web: www.stuarthousehotel.co.uk
dir: At A47/A10/A149 rdbt follow signs to town centre.
Under Southgate Arch, right into Guanock Terrace, right
into Goodwins Rd

Small privately-owned hotel situated in a peaceful
residential area just a short walk from the town centre.
Bedrooms come in a variety of styles and sizes; all are
pleasantly decorated and thoughtfully equipped. There is
a choice of dining options with informal dining in the bar
and a daily-changing menu in the elegant restaurant.

Rooms 18 (2 fmly) **S** £75; **D** £89-£150 (incl. bkfst)
Facilities 🎵 Wi-fi **Conf** Class 30 Board 20 Thtr 50
Parking 30 **Notes** LB ⊗ RS 25-26 Dec & 1 Jan
Civ Wed 60

Grange

★★ 68% HOTEL

☎ 01553 673777 & 671222 📠 01553 673777
Willow Park, South Wootton Ln PE30 3BP
e-mail: info@thegrangehotelkingslynn.co.uk
dir: A148 towards King's Lynn for 1.5m. At lights left into
Wootton Rd, 400yds on right into South Wootton Ln. Hotel
1st on left

Expect a warm welcome at this Edwardian house which is
situated in a quiet residential area in its own grounds.
Public rooms include a smart lounge bar and a cosy
restaurant. The spacious bedrooms are pleasantly
decorated and equipped with many thoughtful touches;
some are located in an adjacent wing.

Rooms 9 (4 annexe) (2 fmly) (4 GF) **Facilities** Xmas
Conf Class 15 Board 12 Thtr 20 **Parking** 15

MUNDESLEY Map 13 TG33

Manor

★★ 69% HOTEL

☎ 01263 720309 📠 01263 721731
7 Beach Rd NR11 8BG
e-mail: reservations@manorhotelnorfolk.com
dir: B1150 (Norwich to North Walsham) then follow
coastal route & Mundesley signs

Set in the quite rural town of Mundesley close to the
beach and shops. The public areas include two bars, a
choice of lounges, a residents' dining room and a smart
seafood restaurant overlooking the sea. Bedrooms are
pleasantly decorated and thoughtfully equipped; most
rooms have superb sea views.

Rooms 26 (4 annexe) (1 GF) **Facilities** ⌁ 🎵 Xmas New
Year Wi-fi **Conf** Class 40 Board 48 Thtr 80 **Parking** 30
Notes ⊗

NORTH WALSHAM Map 13 TG23

INSPECTORS' CHOICE

Beechwood

★★★ ◉◉ HOTEL

☎ 01692 403231 📠 01692 407284
Cromer Rd NR28 0HD
e-mail: info@beechwood-hotel.co.uk
web: www.beechwood-hotel.co.uk
dir: B1150 from Norwich. At North Walsham left at 1st
lights, then right at next

Expect a warm welcome at this elegant 18th-century
house, situated just a short walk from the town centre.
The individually styled bedrooms are tastefully
furnished with well-chosen antique pieces, attractive
co-ordinated soft fabrics and many thoughtful touches.
The spacious public areas include a lounge bar with
plush furnishings, a further lounge and a smartly
appointed restaurant.

Rooms 17 (4 GF) **S** fr £75; **D** £90-£160 (incl. bkfst)
Facilities FTV ⌁ New Year Wi-fi **Conf** Class 20
Board 20 Thtr 20 Del from £130 **Parking** 20 **Notes** LB
No children 10yrs

NORWICH Map 13 TG20

Marriott Sprowston Manor Hotel & Country Club

Marriott HOTELS & RESORTS

★★★★ 81% ◉◉ HOTEL

☎ 01603 410871 📠 01603 423911
Sprowston Park, Wroxham Rd, Sprowston NR7 8RP
e-mail: mhrs.nwigs.frontdesk@marriotthotels.com
web: www.marriottsprowstonmanor.co.uk
dir: From A11/A47, 2m NE on A115 (Wroxham road).
Follow signs to Sprowston Park

Surrounded by open parkland, this imposing property is
set in attractively landscaped grounds and is just a short
drive from the city centre. Bedrooms are spacious and
feature a variety of decorative styles. The hotel also has
extensive conference, banqueting and leisure facilities.
Other public rooms include an array of seating areas and
the elegant Manor Restaurant.

Marriott Sprowston Manor Hotel & Country Club

Rooms 94 (3 fmly) (5 GF) (8 smoking) **S** £120-£145;
D £130-£155 (incl. bkfst)* **Facilities** Spa FTV ⊛
supervised ⌁ 18 Putt green Gym Xmas New Year Wi-fi
Conf Class 50 Board 50 Thtr 500 Del from £140 to £195
Services Lift **Parking** 150 **Notes** LB Civ Wed 300

St Giles House

★☆★★ 81% ◉◉ HOTEL

☎ 01603 275180 📠 0845 299 1905
41-45 St Giles St NR2 1JR
e-mail: info@stgileshousehotel.com
web: www.stgileshousehotel.com
dir: A11 into central Norwich. Left at rdbt (Chapelfield
Shopping Centre). 3rd exit at next rdbt. Left onto St Giles
St. Hotel on left

A stylish 19th-century, Grade II listed building situated in
the heart of the city. The property has a wealth of
magnificent original features such as wood-panelling,
ornamental plasterwork and marble floors. Public areas
include an open-plan lounge bar/restaurant, a smart
lounge with plush sofas and a Parisian style terrace. The
spacious, contemporary bedrooms are individually
designed and have many thoughtful touches.

Rooms 24 **S** £120-£210; **D** £130-£220 (incl. bkfst)
Facilities Spa FTV Xmas New Year Wi-fi **Conf** Class 20
Board 24 Thtr 45 Del from £160 **Services** Lift **Parking** 23
Notes LB ⊗ Civ Wed 60

De Vere Dunston Hall

DE VERE collection

★★★★ 78% ◉ HOTEL

☎ 01508 470444 📠 01508 471499
Ipswich Rd NR14 8PQ
e-mail: dhreception@devere-hotels.com
web: www.devere.co.uk
dir: from A47 take A140 (Ipswich road). 0.25m, hotel on left

Imposing Grade II listed building set amidst 170 acres of
landscaped grounds just a short drive from the city centre.
The spacious bedrooms are smartly decorated, tastefully
furnished and equipped to a high standard. The
attractively appointed public rooms offer a wide choice of
areas in which to relax, and the hotel also boasts a superb
range of leisure facilities including an 18-hole PGA golf
course, floodlit tennis courts and a football pitch.

Rooms 169 (16 fmly) (16 GF) **Facilities** Spa ⊛ ⌁ 18 Putt
green Gym Floodlit driving range Xmas New Year Wi-fi
Conf Class 140 Board 80 Thtr 300 **Services** Lift
Parking 500 **Notes** ⊗ Civ Wed 90

The Maids Head Hotel

★★★★ 75% ⑧ HOTEL

☎ 0844 855 9120 📠 01603 613688
Tombland NR3 1LB
e-mail: maidshead@foliohotels.com
web: www.foliohotels.com/maidshead
dir: follow city centre signs past Norwich Castle. 3rd turn after castle into Upper King St. Hotel opposite cathedral

Imposing 13th-century building situated close to the impressive Norman cathedral, the Anglian TV studios and within easy walking distance of the city centre. The bedrooms are pleasantly decorated and thoughtfully equipped; some rooms have original oak beams. The spacious public rooms include a Jacobean bar, a range of seating areas and the Courtyard Restaurant.

Rooms 84 (10 fmly) **Facilities** Treatment room Xmas New Year Wi-fi **Conf** Class 30 Board 50 Thtr 180 **Services** Lift **Parking** 70 **Notes** ❀ Civ Wed 100

Holiday Inn Norwich-North

★★★★ 71% HOTEL

☎ 01603 410544 📠 01603 487701
Cromer Rd NR6 6JA
e-mail: frontoffice@hinorwich.com
web: www.hinorwich.com
dir: A140 signed for Cromer, turn right at lights signed 'Airport Passengers'. Hotel on right

A modern, purpose-built hotel situated to the north of Norwich at the airport. Bedrooms are smartly decorated, equipped with modern facilities and have a good range of useful extras. Public areas include a large open-plan lounge bar and restaurant, as well as meeting rooms, a banqueting suite and leisure facilities.

Rooms 121 (8 fmly) (34 GF) (4 smoking) **Facilities** ☼ Gym ♫ Wi-fi **Conf** Class 200 Board 50 Thtr 500 **Services** Lift Air con **Parking** 200 **Notes** ❀ Civ Wed 500

Best Western Annesley House

★★★ 85% ⑧⑧ HOTEL

☎ 01603 624553 📠 01603 621577
6 Newmarket Rd NR2 2LA
e-mail: annesleyhouse@bestwestern.co.uk
dir: On A11, 0.5m before city centre

Delightful Georgian property set in three acres of landscaped gardens close to the city centre. Bedrooms are split between three separate houses, two of which are linked by a glass walkway. Each one is attractively decorated, tastefully furnished and thoughtfully equipped. Public rooms include a comfortable lounge/bar and a smart conservatory restaurant which overlooks the gardens.

Rooms 26 (8 annexe) (1 fmly) (7 GF) **S** £50-£90; **D** £70-£120* **Facilities** Wi-fi **Conf** Board 16 Thtr 16 Del from £130* **Parking** 25 **Notes** LB ❀ Closed 24 Dec-2 Jan

Barnham Broom Hotel, Golf & Restaurant

★★★ 83% ⑧⑧ HOTEL

☎ 01603 759393 📠 01603 758224
NR9 4DD
e-mail: amortimer@barnham-broom.co.uk
web: www.barnham-broom.co.uk

(For full entry see Barnham Broom)

Beeches Hotel & Victorian Gardens

THE INDEPENDENTS

★★★ 81% HOTEL

☎ 01603 621167 📠 01603 620151
2-6 Earlham Rd NR2 3DB
e-mail: reception@beeches.co.uk
web: www.mjbhotels.com
dir: W of city centre on B1108, next to St Johns Cathedral, off inner ring road

Ideally situated just a short walk from the city centre, and set amidst landscaped grounds that include a lovely sunken Victorian garden. The bedrooms are in five separate buildings; each one is tastefully decorated and equipped with many thoughtful touches. Public rooms include a smart lounge bar, a bistro-style restaurant and a residents' lounge.

Rooms 43 (20 GF) **Facilities** Xmas Wi-fi **Parking** 50 **Notes** ❀ No children 12yrs

Holiday Inn Norwich City

★★★ 80% HOTEL

☎ 0870 890 1000 📠 0870 890 1111
Carrow Rd NR1 1HU
e-mail: info.norwich@kewgreen.co.uk
web: www.holidayinn.co.uk
dir: A11 turn right to A47 signed Football Ground. Hotel at Norwich City Football Club

A modern, purpose-built hotel situated adjacent to Norwich City Football Club and within easy walking distance of the railway station and city centre. The contemporary style, open-plan public areas include a lounge bar and a brasserie restaurant. The bedrooms are stylish and suitably equipped for both leisure and business guests; many of the rooms overlook the pitch.

Rooms 150 **S** £60-£110; **D** £70-£125* **Facilities** STV Gym Xmas Wi-fi **Conf** Class 25 Board 16 Thtr 30 **Services** Lift Air con **Parking** 57 **Notes** LB ❀

NORWICH *continued*

Ramada Norwich

®RAMADA.

★★★ 78% HOTEL

☎ 01603 787260 📄 01603 400466
121-131 Boundary Rd NR3 2BA
e-mail: gm.norwich@ramadajarvis.co.uk
web: www.ramadajarvis.co.uk
dir: Approx 2m from airport on A140 (Norwich ring road)

A purpose-built hotel conveniently situated on the outer ring road close to the city centre. Bedrooms are pleasantly decorated and equipped with a good range of useful facilities. Public rooms include a large open-plan lounge bar and a smart restaurant. Meeting rooms as well as banqueting suites and leisure facilities are available.

Rooms 107 (8 fmly) (22 GF) (5 smoking) **Facilities** ⌨ Gym Xmas **Conf** Class 150 Board 80 Thtr 300 **Parking** 230 **Notes** ⊗ Civ Wed 400

Holiday Inn Norwich

★★★ 74% HOTEL

☎ 0870 400 9060 & 0800 405060 📄 01603 506400
Ipswich Rd NR4 6EP
e-mail: reservations-norwich@ihg.com
web: www.holidayinn.co.uk
dir: A47 (Great Yarmouth) then A140 (Norwich). 1m, hotel on right

A modern, purpose-built hotel situated just off the A140 which is a short drive from the city centre. Public areas include a popular bar, the Junction Restaurant and a large open-plan lounge. Bedrooms come in a variety of styles and are suited to the needs of both the business and leisure guest alike.

Rooms 119 (41 fmly) (39 GF) (10 smoking) **S** £49-£165; **D** £49-£165 (incl. bkfst)* **Facilities** FTV ⌨ supervised Gym Sauna Steam room Xmas New Year Wi-fi **Conf** Class 48 Board 40 Thtr 150 Del from £95 to £180* **Services** Air con **Parking** 250 **Notes** ⊗ Civ Wed 120

Best Western George Hotel

Best Western

★★★ 72% ◉ HOTEL

☎ 01603 617841 📄 01603 663708
10 Arlington Ln, Newmarket Rd NR2 2DA
e-mail: reservations@georgehotel.co.uk
web: www.arlingtonhotelgroup.co.uk
dir: From A11 follow city centre signs. Newmarket Rd towards centre. Hotel on left

Within just 10 minutes' walk of the town centre, this friendly, family-run hotel is well placed for guests wishing to explore the many sights of this historic city. The hotel occupies three adjacent buildings; the restaurant, bar and most bedrooms are located in the main building, while the adjacent cottages have been converted into comfortable and modern guest bedrooms.

Best Western George Hotel

Rooms 43 (5 annexe) (4 fmly) (19 GF) **S** £45-£78; **D** £65-£98 (incl. bkfst) **Facilities** Beauty therapist Holistic treatments Xmas New Year **Conf** Class 30 Board 30 Thtr 70 Del from £99 to £120 **Parking** 40 **Notes** LB ⊗

INSPECTORS' CHOICE

The Old Rectory
★★ ◉◉ SMALL HOTEL

☎ 01603 700772 📄 01603 300772
103 Yarmouth Rd, Thorpe St Andrew NR7 0HF
e-mail: enquiries@oldrectorynorwich.com
web: www.oldrectorynorwich.com
dir: From A47 southern bypass onto A1042 towards Norwich N & E. Left at mini rdbt onto A1242. After 0.3m through lights. Hotel 100mtrs on right

This delightful Grade II listed Georgian property is ideally located in a peaceful area overlooking the River Yare, just a few minutes' drive from the city centre. Spacious bedrooms are individually designed with carefully chosen soft fabrics, plush furniture and many thoughtful touches; many of the rooms overlook the swimming pool and landscaped gardens. Accomplished cooking is offered via an interesting daily-changing menu, which features skilfully prepared local produce.

Rooms 8 (3 annexe) **S** £85-£115; **D** £115-£145 (incl. bkfst)* **Facilities** FTV ⌨ Wi-fi **Conf** Class 18 Board 16 Thtr 25 Del from £143 to £153* **Parking** 15 **Notes** LB ⊗ Closed 23 Dec-3 Jan

---

Stower Grange

★★ 85% ◉ HOTEL

☎ 01603 860210 📄 01603 860464
School Rd, Drayton NR8 6EF
e-mail: enquiries@stowergrange.co.uk
web: www.stowergrange.co.uk
dir: Norwich ring road N to Asda supermarket. Take A1067 (Fakenham road) at Drayton, right at lights into School Rd. Hotel 150yds on right

Expect a warm welcome at this 17th-century, ivy-clad property situated in a peaceful residential area close to the city centre and airport. The individually decorated bedrooms are generally quite spacious; each one is tastefully furnished and equipped with many thoughtful touches. Public rooms include a smart open-plan lounge bar and an elegant restaurant.

Rooms 11 (1 fmly) **S** fr £75; **D** £95-£150 (incl. bkfst)* **Facilities** ⌂ New Year Wi-fi **Conf** Class 45 Board 30 Thtr 100 Del from £135* **Parking** 40 **Notes** Civ Wed 100

Express by Holiday Inn Norwich

Express by Holiday Inn

BUDGET HOTEL

☎ 01603 780010 📄 01603 780011
Drayton High Rd, Hellesdon NR6 5DU
e-mail: gm@exhinorwich.co.uk
web: www.hiexpress.com/norwich
dir: At junct of A140 (ring road) & A1067 to Fakenham, follow brown tourist signs

A modern hotel ideal for families and business travellers. Fresh and uncomplicated, the spacious rooms include Sky TV, power shower and tea and coffee-making facilities. Continental buffet breakfast is included in the room rate; other meals may be taken at the nearby family pub or restaurant. See also the Hotel Groups pages.

Rooms 78 (45 fmly) (14 GF) (14 smoking) **S** £49.95-£79.95; **D** £49.95-£84.95 (incl. bkfst)*

Travelodge Norwich Central

BUDGET HOTEL

☎ 0871 984 6297 📠 01603 768262
Queens road NR1 2AA
web: www.travelodge.co.uk
dir: A11 towards city centre. Right at rdbt. Lodge on left

Travelodge offers good quality, good value, budget accommodation. All offer family rooms sleeping up to four (two adults, two children) with en suite bathroom/shower-room, remote-control TV, tea- and coffee-making facilities and comfortable beds. Food options vary. Breakfast is at the on-site Bar Café restaurant (if available) or to take away. See also Hotel Groups pages.

Rooms 104 **S** fr £29; **D** fr £29

Travelodge Norwich Cringleford

BUDGET HOTEL

☎ 0871 984 6205 📠 0870 191 1704
Thickthorn Service Area, Norwich Southern Bypass NR9 3AU
web: www.travelodge.co.uk
dir: At junct of A11 & A47

Rooms 62 **S** fr £29; **D** fr £29

REEPHAM · Map 13 TG12

Old Brewery House

★★ 72% HOTEL

OXFORD
HOTELS & INNS

☎ 01603 870881 📠 01603 870969
Market Place NR10 4JJ
e-mail: reservations.oldbreweryhouse@ohiml.com
web: www.oxfordhotelsandinns.com
dir: A1067, right at Bawdeswell onto B1145 into Reepham, hotel on left in Market Place

This Grade II listed Georgian building is situated in the heart of this bustling town centre. Public areas include a cosy lounge, a bar, a conservatory and a smart restaurant. Bedrooms come in a variety of styles; each one is pleasantly decorated and equipped with a good range of facilities.

Rooms 23 (2 fmly) (7 GF) **Facilities** ⓧ Gym Squash Xmas **Conf** Class 80 Board 30 Thtr 200 **Parking** 40 **Notes** LB Civ Wed 45

SHERINGHAM · Map 13 TG14

Dales Country House Hotel

★★★★ 83% ⊛⊛ HOTEL

☎ 01263 824555 📠 01263 822647
Lodge Hill, Upper Sheringham NR26 8TJ
e-mail: dales@mackenziehotels.com
dir: on B1157 1m S of Sheringham, from A148 take turn at entrance to Sheringham Park, 0.5m, hotel on left

Superb Grade II listed building situated in extensive landscaped grounds on the edge of Sheringham Park. The attractive public rooms are full of original character; they include a choice of lounges as well as an intimate restaurant and a cosy lounge bar. The spacious bedrooms are individually decorated, with co-ordinated soft furnishings and many thoughtful touches.

Rooms 21 (5 GF) **Facilities** ⓧ ⓨ Giant garden games - chess & Jenga Xmas New Year Wi-fi **Conf** Class 20 Board 27 Thtr 40 **Services** Lift **Parking** 50 **Notes** LB ⓧ No children 14yrs

Roman Camp Inn

★★★ 78% SMALL HOTEL

☎ 01263 838291 📠 01263 837071
Holt Rd, Aylmerton NR11 8QD
e-mail: enquiries@romancampinn.co.uk
web: www.romancampinn.co.uk
dir: On A148 between Sheringham and Cromer, approx 1.5m from Cromer

A smartly presented hotel ideally placed for touring the north Norfolk coastline. The property provides spacious, pleasantly decorated bedrooms with a good range of useful facilities. Public rooms include a smart conservatory-style restaurant, a comfortable open-plan lounge/bar and a dining area.

Rooms 15 (1 fmly) (10 GF) **S** £56-£70; **D** £92-£120 (incl. bkfst) **Facilities** FTV **Conf** Class 12 Board 16 Thtr 25 **Parking** 50 **Notes** LB ⓧ Closed 25-26 Dec

See advert on page 358

Beaumaris

★★ 79% HOTEL

☎ 01263 822370 📠 01263 821421
South St NR26 8LL
e-mail: beauhotel@aol.com
web: www.thebeaumarishotel.co.uk
dir: Turn off A148, turn left at rdbt, 1st right over railway bridge, 1st left by church, 1st left into South St

Situated in a peaceful side road just a short walk from the beach, town centre and golf course. This friendly hotel has been owned and run by the same family for over 60 years and continues to provide comfortable, thoughtfully equipped accommodation throughout. Public rooms feature a smart dining room, a cosy bar and two quiet lounges.

Rooms 21 (5 fmly) (2 GF) **S** £50-£60; **D** £100-£120 (incl. bkfst) **Parking** 25 **Notes** LB ⓧ Closed mid Dec-1 Mar

SWAFFHAM · Map 13 TF80

Best Western George Hotel

★★★ 74% ⊛ HOTEL

☎ 01760 721238 📠 01760 725333
Station Rd PE37 7LJ
e-mail: georgehotel@bestwestern.co.uk
web: www.arlingtonhotelgroup.co.uk
dir: Exit A47 signed Swaffham. Hotel opposite St Peter & St Paul church

A Georgian hotel situated in the heart of this bustling market town, which is ideally placed for touring north Norfolk. Bedrooms vary in size and style; each one is pleasantly decorated and well equipped. Public rooms include a cosy restaurant, a lounge and a busy bar where a range of drinks and snacks is available.

Rooms 29 (1 fmly) **S** £55-£75; **D** £70-£95 (incl. bkfst)* **Facilities** FTV New Year Wi-fi **Conf** Class 70 Board 70 Thtr 150 Del from £95 to £125* **Parking** 100

THETFORD · Map 13 TL88

Bell

★★★ 🅰 HOTEL

☎ 01842 754455 📠 01842 755552
King St IP24 2AZ
e-mail: bell.thetford@oldenglishinns.co.uk
web: www.oldenglish.co.uk
dir: From S exit A11. 2m to lights. Right onto A134. 100yds left into Bridge St. 150yds over bridge

Rooms 46 (1 fmly) **Facilities** Xmas **Conf** Class 45 Board 40 Thtr 70 **Parking** 55 **Notes** LB

THORNHAM · Map 12 TF74

Lifeboat Inn

★★ 78% ⊛ HOTEL

☎ 01485 512236 📠 01485 512323
Ship Ln PE36 6LT
e-mail: reception@lifeboatinn.co.uk
web: www.lifeboatinn.co.uk
dir: Follow A149 from Hunstanton for approx 6m. 1st left after Thornham sign

This popular 16th-century smugglers' alehouse enjoys superb views across open meadows to Thornham Harbour. The tastefully decorated bedrooms are furnished with

continued

THORNHAM *continued*

pine pieces and have many thoughtful touches. The public rooms have a wealth of character and feature open fireplaces, exposed brickwork and oak beams.

Rooms 13 (3 fmly) (1 GF) **Facilities** FTV Xmas New Year Wi-fi **Conf** Class 30 Board 30 Thtr 50 **Parking** 120

THURSFORD   Map 13 TF93

The Old Forge Seafood Restaurant

◉ RESTAURANT WITH ROOMS

☎ 01328 878345
Seafood Restaurant, Fakenham Rd NR21 0BD
e-mail: sarah.goldspink@btconnect.com
dir: On A148 (Fakenham to Holt road), next to garage at Thursford

Expect a warm welcome at this delightful relaxed restaurant with rooms. The open-plan public areas include a lounge bar area with comfy sofas, and a intimate restaurant with pine tables. Bedrooms are pleasantly decorated and equipped with a good range of useful facilities.

Rooms 2

TITCHWELL   Map 13 TF74

Titchwell Manor

★★★ 86% ◉◉ HOTEL

☎ 01485 210221   📄 01485 210104
PE31 8BB
e-mail: margaret@titchwellmanor.com
web: www.titchwellmanor.com
dir: On A149 (coast road) between Brancaster & Thornham

Friendly family-run hotel ideally placed for touring the north Norfolk coastline. The tastefully appointed bedrooms are very comfortable; some in the adjacent annexe offer ground floor access. Smart public rooms include a lounge area, relaxed informal bar and a delightful conservatory restaurant, overlooking the walled garden. Imaginative menus feature quality local produce and fresh fish.

Rooms 26 (18 annexe) (4 fmly) (16 GF) **D** £110-£250 (incl. bkfst) **Facilities** Xmas New Year **Conf** Class 25 Board 25 Thtr 25 **Parking** 50 **Notes** LB Civ Wed 80

Briarfields

★★★ 75% HOTEL

☎ 01485 210742   📄 01485 210933
Main St PE31 8BB
e-mail: briarfields@norfolk-hotels.co.uk
web: www.norfolk-hotels.co.uk
dir: A149 (coast road) towards Wells-next-the-Sea, Titchwell 7m from Hunstanton. Hotel on left into village

Situated close to Titchwell Reserve on the north Norfolk coast, this hotel has evolved from a collection of

---

sympathetically converted barns and farm buildings. The open-plan public rooms include a choice of lounges with plush sofas and a large brasserie-style restaurant with great views over the marshes. The contemporary bedrooms have a good range of thoughtful extras.

Rooms 22 (18 annexe) (4 fmly) (13 GF) **S** £60-£85; **D** £90-£120 (incl. bkfst) **Facilities** Xmas New Year Wi-fi Child facilities **Conf** Class 80 Board 24 Thtr 120 Del from £90 to £110 **Parking** 75 **Notes** LB

WATTON   Map 13 TF90

Broom Hall Country Hotel

★★★ 🅰 HOTEL

☎ 01953 882125   📄 01953 885325
Richmond Rd, Saham Toney IP25 7EX
e-mail: enquiries@broomhallhotel.co.uk
web: www.broomhallhotel.co.uk
dir: Leave A11 at Thetford onto A1075 to Watton (12m), B1108 towards Swaffham, in 0.5m at rdbt turn right to Saham Toney, hotel 0.5m on left

Rooms 15 (5 annexe) (3 fmly) (5 GF) **S** £65-£105; **D** £85-£165 (incl. bkfst) **Facilities** 🅀 Massage Wi-fi **Conf** Class 30 Board 22 Thtr 80 Del from £110 to £130 **Parking** 30 **Notes** LB Closed 24 Dec-4 Jan Civ Wed 70

WROXHAM   Map 13 TG31

Hotel Wroxham

★★ 71% HOTEL

☎ 01603 782061   📄 01603 784279
The Bridge NR12 8AJ
e-mail: reservations@hotelwroxham.co.uk
web: www.arlingtonhotelgroup.co.uk
dir: From Norwich, A1151 signed Wroxham & The Broads for approx 7m. Over bridge at Wroxham take 1st right, & sharp right again. Hotel car park on right

Perfectly placed for touring the Norfolk Broads this hotel is in the heart of this bustling town centre. The bedrooms are pleasantly decorated and well equipped; some rooms have balconies with lovely views of the busy waterways. The open-plan public rooms include the lively riverside bar, a lounge, a large sun terrace and a smart restaurant.

Rooms 18 **Facilities** Fishing Boating facilities (by arrangement) Xmas New Year Wi-fi **Conf** Class 50 Board 20 Thtr 200 Del from £75 to £85 **Parking** 45 **Notes** 🐾 Civ Wed 40

NORTHAMPTONSHIRE

AYNHO   Map 11 SP53

Cartwright Hotel

★★★ 82% HOTEL

☎ 01869 811885   📄 01869 812809
1-5 Croughton Rd OX17 3BE
e-mail: cartwright@oxfordshire-hotels.co.uk
dir: M40 junct 10, A43 then B4100 to Aynho

Ideally located to explore tourist destinations near Banbury and Oxford plus the Silverstone race track and Blenheim Palace. After an extensive refurbishment, this hotel features individually designed bedrooms which range from double to executive and premiere standards with flat-screen digital TV and complimentary Wi-fi. Secure parking is available.

Rooms 21 (12 annexe) (2 fmly) (12 GF) **S** £90-£155; **D** £99-£155 (incl. bkfst)* **Facilities** STV FTV Xmas New Year Wi-fi **Conf** Class 40 Board 20 Thtr 60 Del from £135 to £160* **Parking** 15 **Notes** LB 🐾 RS 25 Dec eve

---

CASTLE ASHBY   Map 11 SP85

Falcon

★★ 🅰 HOTEL

☎ 01604 696200   📄 01604 696673
NN7 1LF
e-mail: falcon.castleashby@oldenglishinns.co.uk
web: www.oldenglish.co.uk
dir: off A428

Rooms 16 (11 annexe) (1 fmly) **Facilities** Xmas **Conf** Class 30 Board 25 Thtr 50 **Parking** 75 **Notes** Civ Wed 60

CORBY   Map 11 SP88

Holiday Inn Corby-Kettering A43

★★★ 72% HOTEL

☎ 01536 401020   📄 01536 400767
Geddington Rd NN18 8ET
e-mail: samanthawhitelock@hicorby.com
web: www.hicorby.com
dir: M1 junct 19, A14 towards Kettering. Exit at junct 7 towards Corby. Follow Stamford & Corby East, A43. At end of road left through Geddington. After Eurohub rdbt turn left at next lights

Situated just one hour from three major airports and close to major motorway networks this establishment proves a good destination for both the business and leisure traveller. The comfortable bedrooms are well equipped and include free Wi-fi. The facilities include a 15-metre pool, steam room, sauna and fully equipped gym.

continued

Holiday Inn Corby-Kettering A43

Rooms 105 (9 GF) **D** £49.50-£189* **Facilities** Spa STV FTV 🏊 Gym Sauna Steam room Xmas New Year Wi-fi **Conf** Class 70 Board 44 Thtr 250 Del from £99 to £169* **Services** Lift Air con **Parking** 250 **Notes** LB Civ Wed 200

CRICK — Map 11 SP57

Holiday Inn Rugby/ Northampton

★★★ 70% HOTEL

☎ 0870 400 9059 & 0800 405060 🖷 01788 823 8955 **NN6 7XR** **e-mail:** rugbyhi@ihg.com **web:** www.holidayinn.co.uk **dir:** 0.5m from M1 junct 18

Situated in pleasant surroundings, located just off the M1, this modern hotel offers well-equipped and comfortable bedrooms. Public areas include the popular Traders restaurant and a comfortable lounge where an all-day menu is available. The Spirit Health Club provides indoor swimming and a good fitness facility.

Rooms 90 (19 fmly) (42 GF) (12 smoking) **Facilities** STV 🏊 Gym New Year Wi-fi **Conf** Class 90 Board 64 Thtr 170 Del from £99 to £160* **Services** Lift Air con **Parking** 250 **Notes** Civ Wed

Ibis Rugby East

BUDGET HOTEL

☎ 01788 824331 🖷 01788 824332 **Parklands NN6 7EX** **e-mail:** H3588@accor-hotels.com **web:** www.ibishotel.com **dir:** M1 junct 18, follow Daventry/Rugby A5 signs. At rdbt 3rd exit signed DIRFT East. Hotel on right

Modern, budget hotel offering comfortable accommodation in bright and practical bedrooms. Breakfast is self-service and dinner is available in the café restaurant. See also the Hotel Groups pages.

Rooms 111 (47 fmly) (12 GF) **Conf** Class 25 Board 25 Thtr 40

DAVENTRY — Map 11 SP56

INSPECTORS' CHOICE

Fawsley Hall

★★★★ ❀❀❀ HOTEL

☎ 01327 892000 🖷 01327 892001 **Fawsley NN11 3BA** **e-mail:** reservations@fawsleyhall.com **web:** www.fawsleyhall.com **dir:** A361 (Daventry), follow for 12m. Turn right, signed Fawsley Hall

Dating back to the 15th century, this delightful hotel is peacefully located in beautiful gardens designed by 'Capability' Brown. Spacious, individually designed bedrooms and stylish public areas are beautifully furnished with antique and period pieces. Afternoon tea is served in the impressive Great Hall. Dinner is available in the fine-dining Equilibrium Restaurant while a more relaxed style is found in Bess's Brasserie. The new Grayshot Spa features an ozone pool, treatment rooms and fitness studio.

Rooms 58 (14 annexe) (2 GF) **S** fr £170; **D** £170-£475 (incl. bkfst)* **Facilities** Spa STV 🏊 🧖 🏊 Gym Health & beauty treatment rooms Fitness studio 29-seat cinema Xmas New Year Wi-fi **Conf** Class 64 Board 40 Thtr 120 **Parking** 140 **Notes** LB Civ Wed 120

Barceló Daventry Hotel

★★★★ 72% HOTEL

☎ 01327 307000 🖷 01327 706313 **Sedgemoor Way NN11 0SG** **e-mail:** daventry@barcelo-hotels.co.uk **web:** www.barcelo-hotels.co.uk **dir:** M1 junct 16/A45 to Daventry, at 1st rdbt turn right to Kilsby/M1(N). Hotel on right in 1m

This modern, striking hotel overlooking Drayton Water boasts spacious public areas that include a good range of banqueting, meeting and leisure facilities. It is a popular venue for conferences. Bedrooms are suitable for both business and leisure guests.

Rooms 155 (17 fmly) **Facilities** STV 🏊 supervised Gym Steam room Health & beauty salon Xmas New Year Wi-fi **Conf** Class 200 Board 100 Thtr 600 Del from £99* **Services** Lift **Parking** 350 **Notes** Civ Wed 280

HELLIDON — Map 11 SP55

Hellidon Lakes Golf & Spa Hotel

★★★★ 70% HOTEL

☎ 01327 262550 🖷 01327 262559 **NN11 6GG** **e-mail:** hellidonlakes@qhotels.co.uk **web:** www.qhotels.co.uk **dir:** Off A361 between Daventry & Banbury, signed

Some 220 acres of beautiful countryside, which include 27 holes of golf and 12 lakes, combine to form a rather spectacular backdrop to this impressive hotel. Bedroom styles vary, from ultra smart, modern rooms through to those in the original wing that offer superb views. There is an extensive range of facilities available from meeting rooms to a swimming pool, gym and ten-pin bowling. Golfers of all levels can try some of the world's most challenging courses on the indoor golf simulator.

Rooms 110 (5 fmly) **S** £109-£145; **D** £130-£151 (incl. bkfst)* **Facilities** Spa STV 🏊 ⚲ 27 ⛳ Putt green Fishing 🎣 Gym Beauty therapist Indoor smart golf 10-pin bowling Steam room Coarse fishing lake Xmas New Year Wi-fi **Conf** Class 150 Board 80 Thtr 300 **Services** Lift **Parking** 200 **Notes** LB Civ Wed 220

KETTERING — Map 11 SP87

Kettering Park Hotel & Spa

shire hotels & spas

★★★★ 80% ❀ HOTEL

☎ 01536 416666 🖷 01536 416171 **Kettering Parkway NN15 6XT** **e-mail:** kpark@shirehotels.com **web:** www.ketteringparkhotel.com **dir:** Off A14 junct 9 (M1 to A1 link road), hotel in Kettering Venture Park

Expect a warm welcome at this stylish hotel situated just off the A14. The spacious, smartly decorated bedrooms are well equipped and meticulously maintained. Guests can choose from classical or contemporary dishes in the restaurant and lighter meals are served in the bar. The extensive leisure facilities are impressive.

Rooms 119 (29 fmly) (35 GF) **Facilities** STV 🏊 Gym Steam room Sauna Children's splash pool Activity studio New Year Wi-fi **Conf** Class 120 Board 40 Thtr 260 **Services** Lift Air con **Parking** 200 **Notes** ❌ Civ Wed 120

KETTERING *continued*

Rushton Hall Hotel and Spa

★★★★ 76% ◉◉ COUNTRY HOUSE HOTEL

☎ 01536 713001 📠 01536 713010
NN14 1RR
e-mail: enquiries@rushtonhall.com
web: www.rushtonhall.com
dir: A14 junct 7. A43 to Corby then A6003 to Rushton turn after bridge

An elegant country house hotel set amidst 30 acres of parkland and surrounded by open countryside. The stylish public rooms include a library, a superb open-plan lounge bar with a magnificent vaulted ceiling and plush sofas, and an oak-panelled dining hall. The tastefully appointed bedrooms have co-ordinated fabrics and many thoughtful touches.

Rooms 44 (5 fmly) (3 GF) **S** £150-£350; **D** £150-£350 (incl. bkfst)* **Facilities** Spa FTV ③ ⚘ ⚘ Gym Billiard table Sauna Steam room Wi-fi **Conf** Class 250 Board 40 Thtr 250 **Services** Lift **Parking** 140 **Notes** ⊗ Civ Wed 160

See advert on this page

Travelodge Kettering

BUDGET HOTEL

☎ 0871 984 6081
A14 (Westbound) NN14 1RW
web: www.travelodge.co.uk
dir: M6 junct 1 or M1 junct 19, take A14, 0.5m past A43 junct

Travelodge offers good quality, good value, budget accommodation. All offer family rooms sleeping up to four (two adults, two children) with en suite bathroom/ shower-room, remote-control TV, tea- and coffee-making facilities and comfortable beds. Food options vary. Breakfast is at the on-site Bar Café restaurant (if available) or to take away. See also Hotel Groups pages.

Rooms 40 **S** fr £29; **D** fr £29

NORTHAMPTON Map 11 SP76

Northampton Marriott Hotel

★★★★ 73% HOTEL

☎ 01604 768700 📠 01604 769011
Eagle Dr NN4 7HW
e-mail: mhrs.ormnh.salesadmin@marriotthotels.com
web: www.northamptonmarriott.co.uk
dir: M1 junct 15, follow signs to Delapre Golf Course, hotel on right

Located on the outskirts of town, close to major road networks, this modern hotel caters to a cross section of guests. A self-contained management centre makes this a popular conference venue, and its spacious and well designed bedrooms will suit business travellers particularly well. This makes a good base for exploring all the attractions the area has to offer.

Rooms 120 (10 fmly) (52 GF) (10 smoking) **Facilities** STV ③ supervised Gym Steam room Beauty treatment room Solarium Sauna Xmas New Year Wi-fi **Conf** Class 72 Board 30 Thtr 250 Del from £130 to £155* **Services** Air con **Parking** 200 **Notes** ⊗ Civ Wed 180

Holiday Inn Northampton

★★★ 73% HOTEL

☎ 01604 622777 & 0870 400 7214 📠 0870 400 7314
Bedford Rd NN4 7YF
e-mail: reservations@northampton.kewgreen.co.uk
web: www.holidayinn.co.uk
dir: M1 junct 15 onto A508 towards Northampton. Follow A45 towards Wellingborough for 2m then A428 towards Bedford, hotel on left

With its convenient location on the eastern edge of town and easy access to transport links, this modern hotel is particularly popular with business travellers. Accommodation is spacious, smartly appointed, and includes a good range of accessories. The contemporary open-plan public areas help to create an informal atmosphere, and the staff are genuinely friendly.

Rooms 104 (3 fmly) (26 GF) **D** £50-£140 (incl. bkfst)* **Facilities** STV Gym Xmas New Year Wi-fi **Conf** Class 30 Board 35 Thtr 70 **Services** Lift Air con **Parking** 125 **Notes** LB ⊗ Civ Wed 40

Best Western Lime Trees

★★★ 71% HOTEL

☎ 01604 632188 📄 01604 233012
8 Langham Place, Barrack Rd NN2 6AA
e-mail: info@limetreeshotel.co.uk
web: www.limetreeshotel.co.uk
dir: from city centre 0.5m N on A508 towards Market
Harborough, near racecourse & cathedral

This well presented hotel is popular with business
travellers during the week and leisure guests at the
weekend. Service is both efficient and friendly. Bedrooms
are comfortable and in addition to all the usual facilities,
many offer air conditioning. Notable features include an
internal courtyard and a row of charming mews houses
that have been converted into bedrooms.

Rooms 28 (8 annexe) (4 fmly) (5 GF) **Facilities** FTV Xmas
New Year Wi-fi **Conf** Class 50 Board 45 Thtr 140
Services Air con **Parking** 25 **Notes** Civ Wed 140

Campanile Northampton

Campanile

★★★ 67% HOTEL

☎ 01604 662599 📄 01604 622598
Cheaney Dr, Grange Park NN4 5FB
e-mail: northampton@campanile.com
dir: M1 junction 15 onto A508 towards Northampton. 2nd
exit at first roundabout and 2nd exit at second
roundabout into Grange Park.

This modern building offers accommodation in smart,
well-equipped bedrooms, all with en suite bathrooms.
Refreshments may be taken at the informal bistro.

Rooms 87 (18 fmly) **S** £55-£69; **D** £55-£69*
Facilities STV FTV Xmas New Year Wi-fi **Conf** Class 60
Board 60 Thtr 150 Del from £115 to £135* **Services** Lift
Air con **Parking** 100 **Notes** LB

Holiday Inn

★★★ 64% HOTEL

☎ 01327 349022 📄 01327 349017
High St, Flore NN7 4LP
e-mail: sarah.potter@kewgreen.co.uk
web: www.holidayinn.co.uk
dir: M1 junct 16, follow signs for Daventry. Hotel approx
1.5m on right

Located just minutes away from the M1, this hotel offers
a comfortable stay for both the business traveller and
leisure guest. Bedrooms are equipped with high speed
internet. There is a small gym facility on site.

Rooms 53 (9 fmly) (42 GF) (5 smoking) **Facilities** STV FTV
Gym Xmas New Year Wi-fi **Conf** Class 50 Board 40
Thtr 150 **Services** Air con **Parking** 150 **Notes** LB
Civ Wed 120

Express by Holiday Inn Northampton M1 Jct 15

BUDGET HOTEL

☎ 01604 432800 📄 01604 432832
Loake Close, Grange Park NN4 5EZ
e-mail: northampton@expressholidayinn.co.uk
web: www.hiexpress.com/exnorthampton
dir: Just off M1 junct 15, follow signs for Grange Park

A modern hotel ideal for families and business travellers.
Fresh and uncomplicated, the spacious rooms include Sky
TV, power shower and tea and coffee-making facilities.
Continental buffet breakfast is included in the room rate;
other meals may be taken at the nearby family pub or
restaurant. See also the Hotel Groups pages.

Rooms 126 **Conf** Class 28 Board 28 Thtr 70

Ibis Northampton Centre

BUDGET HOTEL

☎ 01604 608900 📄 01604 608910
Sol Central, Marefair NN1 1SR
e-mail: H3657@accor-hotels.com
web: www.ibishotel.com
dir: M1 junct 15/15a & city centre towards railway station

Modern, budget hotel offering comfortable
accommodation in bright and practical bedrooms.
Breakfast is self-service and dinner is available in the
restaurant. See also the Hotel Groups pages.

Rooms 151 (14 fmly)

Innkeeper's Lodge Northampton East

BUDGET HOTEL

☎ 0845 112 6049 📄 0845 112 6253
Talavera Way, Round Spinney NN3 8RN
web: www.innkeeperslodge.com/northamptoneast
dir: M1 junct 15, A508, A45 towards Northampton. Left
onto A43 (signed Kettering). Lodge at 2nd rdbt

Innkeeper's Lodge represents an exciting, high value
concept within the budget hotel market. Comfortable
bedrooms provide excellent facilities that include satellite
TV and modem points. Options include family rooms; and
for the corporate guest, cutting edge IT which includes
Wi-fi access. A popular Carvery provides all-day food,
including an extensive, complimentary continental
breakfast. See also the Hotel Groups pages.

Rooms 31 **Conf** Thtr 40

Innkeeper's Lodge Northampton M1 Jct 15

BUDGET HOTEL

☎ 0845 112 6050 📄 0845 112 6252
London Rd, Wootton NN4 0TG
web: www.innkeeperslodge.com/northamptonsouth
dir: M1 junct 15 take A508, towards Northampton. Pass
under flyover, exit left immediately & turn right at rdbt
into London Rd. Lodge on right.

Innkeeper's Lodge represents an exciting, high value
concept within the budget hotel market. Comfortable
bedrooms provide excellent facilities that include satellite
TV and modem points. Options include family rooms; and
for the corporate guest, cutting edge IT which includes
Wi-fi access. A popular Carvery provides all-day food,
including an extensive, complimentary continental
breakfast. See also the Hotel Groups pages.

Rooms 51 (21 fmly) **Conf** Thtr 100

Travelodge Northampton Upton Way

BUDGET HOTEL

☎ 0871 984 6089 📄 01604 758395
Upton Way NN5 4EG
web: www.travelodge.co.uk
dir: M1 junct 15a, A43 signed Northampton. Approx 2m
take A45 towards Coventry. Lodge opp Sixfields Stadium

Travelodge offers good quality, good value, budget
accommodation. All offer family rooms sleeping up to four
(two adults, two children) with en suite bathroom/
shower-room, remote-control TV, tea- and coffee-making
facilities and comfortable beds. Food options vary.
Breakfast is at the on-site Bar Café restaurant (if
available) or to take away. See also Hotel Groups pages.

Rooms 62 **S** fr £29; **D** fr £29

RUSHDEN — Map 11 SP96

Travelodge Wellingborough Rushden

BUDGET HOTEL

☎ 0871 984 6115 ▤ 01933 57008
Saunders Lodge NN10 6AP
web: www.travelodge.co.uk
dir: on A45, eastbound

Travelodge offers good quality, good value, budget accommodation. All offer family rooms sleeping up to four (two adults, two children) with en suite bathroom/ shower-room, remote-control TV, tea- and coffee-making facilities and comfortable beds. Food options vary. Breakfast is at the on-site Bar Café restaurant (if available) or to take away. See also Hotel Groups pages.

Rooms 40 **S** fr £29; **D** fr £29

THRAPSTON — Map 11 SP97

Travelodge Kettering Thrapston

BUDGET HOTEL

☎ 0871 984 6111 ▤ 01832 735199
Thrapston Bypass NN14 4UR
web: www.travelodge.co.uk
dir: On A14 (A1/M1 link road) 12m Eof Kettering

Travelodge offers good quality, good value, budget accommodation. All offer family rooms sleeping up to four (two adults, two children) with en suite bathroom/ shower-room, remote-control TV, tea- and coffee-making facilities and comfortable beds. Food options vary. Breakfast is at the on-site Bar Café restaurant (if available) or to take away. See also Hotel Groups pages.

Rooms 40 **S** fr £29; **D** fr £29

TOWCESTER — Map 11 SP64

Saracens Head

★★ Ⓐ HOTEL

☎ 01327 350414 ▤ 01327 359879
219 Watling St NN12 7BX
e-mail: saracenshead.towcester@greeneking.co.uk
web: www.oldenglish.co.uk
dir: A5 to Towcester. Follow signs into town centre

Rooms 21 (3 fmly) **Facilities** ♫ Xmas **Conf** Class 50 Board 50 Thtr 80 **Parking** 20 **Notes** LB ⊗ RS 25 Dec Civ Wed 90

Travelodge Towcester Silverstone

BUDGET HOTEL

☎ 0871 984 6112 ▤ 01327 359105
NN12 6TQ
web: www.travelodge.co.uk
dir: M1 junct 15a, A43 follow Oxford signs. After 5m straight over 1st rdbt. 3rd exit at next rdbt. Lodge behind McDonalds restaurant

Travelodge offers good quality, good value, budget accommodation. All offer family rooms sleeping up to four (two adults, two children) with en suite bathroom/ shower-room, remote-control TV, tea- and coffee-making facilities and comfortable beds. Food options vary. Breakfast is at the on-site Bar Café restaurant (if available) or to take away. See also Hotel Groups pages.

Rooms 55 **S** fr £29; **D** fr £29

WELLINGBOROUGH — Map 11 SP86

The Hind

★★ 64% HOTEL

☎ 01933 222827 ▤ 01933 441921
Sheep St NN8 1BY
e-mail: enquiries@thehind.co.uk
dir: on A509 in town centre

Dating back to Jacobean times, this centrally located hotel provides a good base for business and leisure guests visiting the town. A good choice of dishes is available in the restaurant; alternatively the all-day coffee shop offers light snacks. Bedrooms come in a variety of styles, mostly of spacious dimensions.

Rooms 34 (2 fmly) (5 GF) **Facilities** Pool table **Conf** Class 40 Board 40 Thtr 70 **Parking** 17 **Notes** RS 24 Dec-2 Jan Civ Wed 70

Ibis Wellingborough

BUDGET HOTEL

☎ 01933 228333 ▤ 01933 228444
Enstone Court NN8 2DR
e-mail: H3164@accor-hotels.com
web: www.ibishotel.com
dir: At junct of A45 & A509 towards Kettering, SW outskirts of Wellingborough

Modern, budget hotel offering comfortable accommodation in bright and practical bedrooms. Breakfast is self-service and dinner is available in the restaurant. See also the Hotel Groups pages.

Rooms 78 (20 fmly) (2 GF)

WHITTLEBURY — Map 11 SP64

Whittlebury Hall

★★★★ 81% ◉◉ HOTEL

☎ 01327 857857 ▤ 01327 857987
NN12 8QH
e-mail: sales@whittleburyhall.co.uk
web: www.whittleburyhall.co.uk
dir: A43/A413 towards Buckingham, through Whittlebury, turn for hotel on right (signed)

A purpose-built, Georgian-style country house hotel with excellent spa and leisure facilities and pedestrian access to the Silverstone circuit. Grand public areas include F1 car racing memorabilia and the accommodation includes some lavishly appointed suites. Food is a strength, with a choice of various dining options. Particularly noteworthy are the afternoon teas in the spacious, comfortable lounge and the fine dining in Murrays Restaurant.

Rooms 211 (3 fmly) (13 smoking) **S** £135-£155; **D** £160-£180 (incl. bkfst)* **Facilities** Spa FTV ⓩ Gym Beauty treatments Relaxation room Hair studio Heat & Ice experience Leisure club Xmas New Year Wi-fi **Conf** Class 175 Board 40 Thtr 500 **Services** Lift **Parking** 450 **Notes** LB ⊗

NORTHUMBERLAND

ALNWICK — Map 21 NU11

See also **Embleton**

White Swan

★★★ 80% HOTEL

☎ 01665 602109 ▤ 01665 510400
Bondgate Within NE66 1TD
e-mail: info.whiteswan@classiclodges.co.uk
web: www.classiclodges.co.uk
dir: from A1 follow town centre signs. Hotel in town centre near Bondgate Tower

Situated in the heart of the historic town, this charming 300-year-old coaching inn still retains many authentic period features. The Olympic Suite Dining Room, with its original oak panelling and stained glass windows, salvaged from the *SS Olympic* (sister ship of the ill fated *Titanic*) blends well with the modern Hardy's bistro. All the bedrooms are stylishly appointed and well equipped.

Rooms 56 (5 fmly) (11 GF) **Facilities** Xmas New Year Wi-fi **Conf** Class 50 Board 40 Thtr 150 **Parking** 25 **Notes** LB ⊗ Civ Wed 150

| BAMBURGH | Map 21 NU13 |

Waren House

★★★ 79% COUNTRY HOUSE HOTEL

☎ 01668 214581 ☰ 01668 214484
Waren Mill NE70 7EE
e-mail: enquiries@warenhousehotel.co.uk
web: www.warenhousehotel.co.uk
dir: 2m E of A1 turn onto B1342 to Waren Mill, at T-junct turn right, hotel 100yds on right

This delightful Georgian mansion is set in six acres of woodland and offers a welcoming atmosphere and views of the coast. The individually themed bedrooms and suites include many with large bathrooms. Good, home-cooked food is served in the elegant dining room. A comfortable lounge and library are also available.

Rooms 13 (1 GF) **S** £95-£160; **D** £125-£250 (incl. bkfst) **Facilities** FTV Xmas New Year Wi-fi **Conf** Class 16 Board 16 **Parking** 20 **Notes** No children 14yrs

Victoria

★★ 80% HOTEL

☎ 01668 214431 ☰ 01668 214404
Front St NE69 7BP
e-mail: enquiries@thevictoriahotelbamburgh.co.uk
web: www.thevictoriahotelbamburgh.co.uk
dir: Off A1, N of Alnwick onto B1342, near Belford & follow signs to Bamburgh. Hotel in town centre

Overlooking the village green, this hotel offers an interesting blend of traditional and modern. Public areas, including the residents and diners' bar lounge, are relaxing venues throughout the day and evening, while the brasserie, with its conservatory roof, provides a more

contemporary dinner menu. Bedrooms come in a variety of styles and sizes.

Rooms 36 (2 fmly) (2 GF) **S** £40-£70; **D** £80-£200 (incl. bkfst)* **Facilities** FTV Xmas New Year Wi-fi **Conf** Class 30 Board 20 Thtr 50 Del from £80 to £120 **Parking** 18 **Notes** LB Closed 3-8 Jan Civ Wed 50

The Lord Crewe

★★ 78% HOTEL

☎ 01668 214243 & 214613 ☰ 01668 214273
Front St NE69 7BL
e-mail: enquiries@lordcrewe.co.uk
dir: Just below castle

Located in the heart of the village in the shadow of impressive Bamburgh Castle, this hotel has been developed from an old inn. Public areas include a choice of lounges, a cosy bar and a smart modern restaurant. Bedrooms vary in size, but all offer good levels of comfort and are well equipped.

Rooms 17 **S** £55-£65; **D** £70-£130 (incl. bkfst)* **Facilities** FTV **Parking** 20 **Notes** ⊗ No children 5yrs Closed Dec & Jan

| BELFORD | Map 21 NU13 |

Blue Bell

★★★ 64% HOTEL

☎ 01668 213543 ☰ 01668 213787
Market Place NE70 7NE
e-mail: enquiries@bluebellhotel.com
web: www.bluebellhotel.com
dir: In village centre

Formerly a coaching inn, this popular and long established hotel is located in the village square. It offers a choice of superior and standard bedrooms all in classical style. Well-prepared meals can be enjoyed in the restaurant and in addition to the bar there is a comfortable lounge in which to relax.

Rooms 28 (11 annexe) (4 fmly) (13 GF) **S** £45-£65; **D** £90-£140 (incl. bkfst) **Facilities** Xmas New Year Wi-fi **Conf** Class 40 Board 30 Thtr 80 **Parking** 16 **Notes** LB ⊗ Civ Wed 100

Purdy Lodge

★★ 74% HOTEL

☎ 01668 213000 ☰ 01668 213131
Adderstone Services NE70 7JU
e-mail: stay@purdylodge.co.uk
web: www.purdylodge.co.uk
dir: A1 onto B1341 then immediately left

Situated off the A1, this family-owned lodge provides newly modernised bedrooms that look out over the fields

towards Bamburgh Castle. Food is readily available in the attractive restaurant, the new Café One, and the lounge bar. This is a great stop off hotel with a friendly welcome guaranteed.

Rooms 20 (4 fmly) (10 GF) **S** £52.95-£74.95; **D** £52.95-£74.95* **Facilities** FTV Xmas New Year Wi-fi **Parking** 60 **Notes** LB

| BERWICK-UPON-TWEED | Map 21 NT95 |

Queens Head

★★★ 73% SMALL HOTEL

☎ 01289 307852 ☰ 01289 307858
Sandgate TD15 1EP
e-mail: info@queensheadberwick.co.uk
dir: A1 towards centre & town hall, along High St. Turn right at bottom to Hide Hill. Hotel next to cinema

This small hotel is situated in the town centre, close to the old walls of this former garrison town. Bedrooms have now been refurbished; many thoughtful extras are provided as standard. Dining remains a strong aspect with a carte menu that offers an impressive choice of tasty, freshly prepared dishes served in the comfortable lounge or dining room.

Rooms 11 (2 fmly) **Facilities** FTV Wi-fi **Notes** ⊗

Marshall Meadows Country House

★★★ 70% COUNTRY HOUSE HOTEL

☎ 01289 331133 ☰ 01289 331438
TD15 1UT
e-mail: gm.marshallmeadows@classiclodges.co.uk
web: www.classiclodges.co.uk
dir: signed directly off A1, 300yds from Scottish border

This stylish Georgian mansion is set in wooded grounds flanked by farmland and has convenient access from the A1. A popular venue for weddings and conferences, it offers comfortable and well-equipped bedrooms. Public rooms include a cosy bar, a relaxing lounge and a two-tier restaurant which serves imaginative dishes.

Rooms 19 (1 fmly) **Facilities** ⚓ Xmas New Year **Conf** Class 120 Board 40 Thtr 200 **Parking** 87 **Notes** LB Civ Wed 200

BERWICK-UPON-TWEED *continued*

Travelodge Berwick-upon-Tweed

BUDGET HOTEL

☎ 0871 984 6279 📄 01289 306555
Loaning Meadow, North Rd TD15 1UQ
web: www.travelodge.co.uk
dir: From A1 to rdbt with A1167

Travelodge offers good quality, good value, budget accommodation. All offer family rooms sleeping up to four (two adults, two children) with en suite bathroom/shower-room, remote-control TV, tea- and coffee-making facilities and comfortable beds. Food options vary. Breakfast is at the on-site Bar Café restaurant (if available) or to take away. See also Hotel Groups pages.

Rooms 40 **S** fr £29; **D** fr £29

CORNHILL-ON-TWEED   **Map 21 NT83**

Tillmouth Park Country House

★★★ 86% ⚫ COUNTRY HOUSE HOTEL

☎ 01890 882255 📄 01890 882540
TD12 4UU
e-mail: reception@tillmouthpark.f9.co.uk
web: www.tillmouthpark.co.uk
dir: Off A1(M) at East Ord rdbt at Berwick-upon-Tweed. Take A698 to Cornhill and Coldstream. Hotel 9m on left

An imposing mansion set in landscaped grounds by the River Till. Gracious public rooms include a stunning galleried lounge with a drawing room adjacent. The quiet, elegant dining room overlooks the gardens, whilst lunches and early dinners are available in the bistro. Bedrooms retain much traditional character and include several magnificent master rooms.

Rooms 14 (2 annexe) (4 smoking) **S** £70-£189; **D** £142-£205 (incl. bkfst)* **Facilities** FTV 🎣 Game shooting Fishing New Year Wi-fi **Conf** Class 20 Board 20 Thtr 50 Del from £160* **Parking** 50 **Notes** Closed 3 Jan-1 Apr Civ Wed 50

CRAMLINGTON   **Map 21 NZ27**

Innkeeper's Lodge Cramlington

BUDGET HOTEL

☎ 0845 112 6013 📄 0845 112 6288
Blagdon Ln NE23 8AU
web: www.innkeeperslodge.com/cramlington
dir: A1 onto A19. At rdbt, left onto A1068. Lodge at junct of Blagdon Ln & Fisher Ln

Innkeeper's Lodge represents an exciting, high value concept within the budget hotel market. Comfortable bedrooms provide excellent facilities that include satellite TV and modem points. Options include family rooms; and for the corporate guest, cutting edge IT includes Wi-fi access. Food is served all day in the adjacent Country Pub. The extensive continental breakfast is complimentary. See also the Hotel Groups pages.

Rooms 18

EMBLETON   **Map 21 NU22**

Dunstanburgh Castle Hotel

★★ 78% HOTEL

☎ 01665 576111 📄 01665 576203
NE66 3UN
e-mail: stay@dunstanburghcastlehotel.co.uk
web: www.dunstanburghcastlehotel.co.uk
dir: From A1, take B1340 to Denwick past Rennington & Masons Arms. Take next right signed Embleton

The focal point of the village, this friendly, family-run hotel has a dining room and grill room that offer different menus, plus a cosy bar and two lounges. In addition to the main bedrooms, a barn conversion houses three stunning suites, each with a lounge and gallery bedroom above.

Rooms 20 (4 fmly) **S** £41.50-£55.50; **D** £83-£125 (incl. bkfst)* **Parking** 16 **Notes** LB Closed Dec-Jan

---

HEDDON-ON-THE-WALL   **Map 21 NZ16**

Close House

★★★★ 75% HOTEL

☎ 01661 852255 📄 01661 853322
NE15 0HT
e-mail: reservations@closehouse.co.uk
web: www.closehouse.co.uk
dir: A1 N, A69 W. Follow B6528 at junct turn left, hotel signed

Dating back to 1779, this is a magnificent country house set in 300 acres of woodland and parkland in the secluded and beautiful Tyne Valley. It is just 20 minutes from Newcastle city centre that has good national and international transport links. The hotel provides accommodation designed to make a stay relaxing and special. All the bedrooms are equipped with high-tech mod cons. There is a magnificent restaurant and bar, and 24-hour room service is also available. There is an 18-hole golf course in the grounds.

Rooms 19 **S** £117.50-£140; **D** £175-£220 (incl. bkfst)* **Facilities** STV ⚓ 18 Putt green Driving range Xmas New Year Wi-fi **Conf** Class 30 Board 30 Thtr 140 Del from £150 to £170* **Parking** 87 **Notes** LB Civ Wed 100

HEXHAM   **Map 21 NY96**

Langley Castle

★★★★ 82% ⚫⚫ HOTEL

☎ 01434 688888 📄 01434 684019
Langley on Tyne NE47 5LU
e-mail: manager@langleycastle.com
web: www.langleycastle.com
dir: From A69 S on A686 for 2m. Hotel on right

Langley is a magnificent 14th-century fortified castle, with its own chapel, set in ten acres of parkland. There is an award-winning restaurant, a comfortable drawing room and a cosy bar. Bedrooms are furnished with period pieces and most feature window seats. Restored buildings in the grounds have been converted into very stylish Castle View bedrooms.

Rooms 27 (18 annexe) (8 fmly) (9 GF) **S** £112.50-£199.50; **D** £139-£269 (incl. bkfst)* **Facilities** STV Xmas Wi-fi **Conf** Class 60 Board 40 Thtr 120 Del from £175 to £199* **Parking** 70 **Notes** LB ⊗ Civ Wed 120

De Vere Slaley Hall

DE VERE collection

★★★★ 80% ⊛ HOTEL

☎ 01434 673350 🖹 01434 673962
Slaley NE47 0BX
e-mail: slaley.hall@devere-hotels.com
web: www.devere.co.uk
dir: A1 from S to A68 link road follow signs for Slaley Hall

One thousand acres of Northumbrian forest and parkland, two championship golf courses and indoor leisure facilities can all be found here. Spacious bedrooms are fully air conditioned, equipped with a range of extras and the deluxe rooms offer excellent standards. Public rooms include a number of lounges and dining options of the fine-dining Dukes Grill, informal Claret Jug and impressive main restaurant overlooking the golf course.

Rooms 142 (18 fmly) (37 GF) **Facilities** Spa ⊗ supervised ⌗ 36 Putt green Gym Quad bikes Archery Clay pigeon shooting 4x4 driving Xmas New Year Wi-fi **Conf** Class 220 Board 150 Thtr 300 Del from £120 to £190 **Services** Lift Air con **Parking** 500 **Notes** Civ Wed 250

Best Western Beaumont

Best Western

★★★ 78% HOTEL

☎ 01434 602331 🖹 01434 606184
Beaumont St NE46 3LT
e-mail: reservations@beaumonthotel.eclipse.co.uk
dir: A69 towards town centre

In a region steeped in history, this family-run hotel is located in the centre of this popular town, overlooking the park and 7th-century abbey. The hotel has now been refurbished and has two bars, a comfortable reception lounge and a first-floor restaurant. Bedrooms are a mix of traditional and contemporary; the new South Wing rooms are spacious with a more contemporary feel and have 37" flat-screen TVs.

Rooms 35 (3 fmly) **S** £80-£100; **D** £110-£130 (incl. bkfst) **Facilities** FTV Wi-fi **Conf** Class 60 Board 40 Thtr 100 Del from £100 to £130 **Services** Lift **Parking** 16 **Notes** LB ⊗ Closed 25-26 Dec

The County Hotel & Restaurant

★★ 68% SMALL HOTEL

☎ 01434 603601 🖹 01434 603601
Priestpopple NE46 1PS
e-mail: reception@thecountyhexham.co.uk
dir: off A69, follow signs for General Hospital. Hotel at top of hill

The resident owners of this establishment, located in the centre of this popular market town, provide their guests

with a caring and personal service. Bedrooms are comfortably equipped. The eating options are the County Restaurant and Bottles bistro - both offer an interesting selection of freshly prepared dishes that utilise local produce.

Rooms 7 (1 fmly) **Facilities** Wi-fi **Notes** ⊗

LONGHORSLEY Map 21 NZ19

Macdonald Linden Hall, Golf & Country Club

MACDONALD HOTELS & RESORTS

★★★★ 82% ⊛⊛ HOTEL

☎ 01670 500000 🖹 01670 500001
NE65 8XF
e-mail: enquiries@macdonald.hotels.co.uk
web: www.macdonaldhotels.co.uk
dir: N'bound on A1 take A697 towards Coldstream. Hotel 1m N of Longhorsley

This impressive Georgian mansion lies in 400 acres of parkland and offers extensive indoor and outdoor leisure facilities including a golf course. The Dobson Restaurant provides a fine dining experience, or guests can eat in the more informal Linden Tree pub. The good-sized bedrooms have a restrained modern style. The team of staff are enthusiastic and professional.

Rooms 50 (3 fmly) (16 GF) **Facilities** Spa STV FTV ⊗ supervised ⌗ 18 ⌗ Putt green ⌗ Gym Steam room Sauna Xmas New Year Wi-fi **Conf** Class 100 Board 30 Thtr 300 Del from £129 to £145 **Services** Lift **Parking** 300 **Notes** Civ Wed 120

MATFEN Map 21 NZ07

Matfen Hall

PRIMA HOTEL GROUP

★★★★ 81% ⊛⊛ HOTEL

☎ 01661 886500 & 855708 🖹 01661 886055
NE20 0RH
e-mail: info@matfenhall.com
web: www.matfenhall.com
dir: Off A69 to B6318. Hotel just before village

This fine mansion lies in landscaped parkland overlooking its own golf course. Bedrooms are a blend of contemporary and traditional, but all are very comfortable and well equipped. Impressive public rooms include a splendid drawing room and the elegant Library and Print Room Restaurant, as well as a conservatory bar and very stylish spa, leisure and conference facilities.

Rooms 53 (11 fmly) **S** £125; **D** £185-£275 (incl. bkfst)* **Facilities** Spa STV FTV ⊗ supervised ⌗ 27 Putt green Gym Sauna Steam room Salt grotto Ice fountain Aerobics Driving range Golf academy Xmas Wi-fi **Conf** Class 46 Board 40 Thtr 120 **Services** Lift **Parking** 150 **Notes** LB Civ Wed 120

See advert on page 459

OTTERBURN Map 21 NY89

The Otterburn Tower Hotel

★★★ 75% HOTEL

☎ 01830 520620 🖹 01830 521504
NE19 1NT
e-mail: info@otterburntower.com
web: www.otterburntower.com
dir: in village, on A696 (Newcastle to Edinburgh road)

Built by the cousin of William the Conqueror, this mansion is set in its own wooded grounds. The hotel is steeped in history, and Sir Walter Scott stayed here in 1812. Bedrooms come in a variety of sizes and some have huge ornamental fireplaces; though furnished in period style, they are equipped with all modern amenities. The restaurant features 16th-century oak panelling.

Rooms 18 (2 fmly) (2 GF) **Facilities** Fishing ⌗ Clay target shooting Xmas New Year Wi-fi Child facilities **Conf** Class 60 Board 60 Thtr 120 **Parking** 70 **Notes** LB Civ Wed 150

Percy Arms

★★ 71% HOTEL

☎ 01830 520261 🖹 01830 520567
NE19 1NR
e-mail: percyarmshotel@yahoo.co.uk
dir: In village centre on A696

This former coaching inn lies in the centre of the village, with good access to the Northumberland countryside. The welcoming public areas boast real fires in the cooler months. A very good range of dishes is offered in either the restaurant or cosy bar/bistro. Bedrooms are cheerfully decorated and thoughtfully equipped.

Rooms 27 (2 fmly) (3 GF) **Facilities** FTV Fishing ⌗ Xmas New Year Wi-fi **Conf** Class 40 Board 50 Thtr 70 **Parking** 74 **Notes** LB Civ Wed 80

SEAHOUSES

Map 21 NU23

Olde Ship

★★ 84% SMALL HOTEL

☎ 01665 720200 📠 01665 721383
NE68 7RD
e-mail: theoldeship@seahouses.co.uk
dir: lower end of main street above harbour

Under the same ownership since 1910, this friendly hotel overlooks the harbour. Lovingly maintained, its sense of history is evident by the amount of nautical memorabilia on display. Public areas include a character bar, cosy snug, restaurant and guests' lounge with snooker area. The individual bedrooms are smartly presented. Two separate buildings contain executive apartments, all with sea views.

Rooms 18 (6 annexe) (3 GF) **Facilities** FTV **Parking** 18
Notes ⊗ No children 10yrs Closed Dec-Jan

Beach House

★★ 78% HOTEL

☎ 01665 720337 📠 01665 720921
Sea Front NE68 7SR
e-mail: enquiries@beachhousehotel.co.uk
web: www.beachhousehotel.co.uk
dir: Follow signs from A1 between Alnwick & Berwick

Enjoying a seafront location and views of the Farne Islands, this family-run hotel offers a relaxed and friendly atmosphere. Bedrooms come in a variety of sizes, but all are bright and airy. Dinner makes use of fresh produce and breakfast features local specialities. There is a well-stocked bar and comfortable lounge.

Rooms 27 (5 fmly) (4 GF) **S** £40-£56; **D** £90-£151.50
(incl. bkfst)* **Facilities** Xmas New Year **Conf** Thtr 50
Parking 20 **Notes** ⊗ No children 4yrs

NOTTINGHAMSHIRE

BARNBY MOOR

Map 16 SK68

Ye Olde Bell Hotel & Restaurant

★★★★ 72% HOTEL

☎ 01777 705121 📠 01777 860424
DN22 8QS
e-mail: enquiries@yeoldebell-hotel.co.uk
web: www.yeoldebell-hotel.co.uk
dir: A1(M) south near junct 34, exit Barnby Moor or A1(M) north exit A620 Retford. Hotel on A638 between Retford & Bawtry

A 17th-century coaching inn situated in the rural village of Barnby Moor near Retford. Over the last year the current owners have totally refurbished the property to a very high standard. Public rooms have a wealth of original character such as traditional log fires, ornate plaster work and wood panelling. The tastefully appointed bedrooms have superb co-ordinated soft furnishings and many thoughtful touches.

Rooms 49 (5 fmly) **S** £90; **D** £125-£225 (incl. bkfst)
Facilities FTV Xmas New Year Wi-fi **Conf** Class 100
Board 50 Thtr 250 Del from £110 to £140 **Parking** 200
Notes LB ⊗ Civ Wed 250

BLYTH

Map 16 SK68

Best Western Charnwood

★★★ 82% HOTEL

☎ 01909 591610 📠 01909 591429
Sheffield Rd S81 8HF
e-mail: reception@thecharnwood.com
web: www.thecharnwoodhotel.com
dir: A614 into Blyth, right past church onto A634 (Sheffield road). Hotel 0.5m on right past humpback bridge

In peaceful rural setting surrounded by attractive gardens with lovely views, this hotel offers a range of carefully

prepared meals and snacks in either the formal restaurant, or the comfortable lounge bar. Bedrooms are comfortably furnished and attractively decorated. Service is friendly and attentive.

Rooms 45 (14 GF) **Facilities** STV FTV New Year Wi-fi
Conf Class 60 Board 45 Thtr 140 Del from £100 to £135*
Services Lift **Parking** 165 **Notes** ⊗ Civ Wed 110

Travelodge Blyth (A1(M))

BUDGET HOTEL

☎ 0871 984 6123 📠 01909 591831
Hilltop Roundabout S81 8HG
web: www.travelodge.co.uk
dir: at junct of A1(M) & A614

Travelodge offers good quality, good value, budget accommodation. All offer family rooms sleeping up to four (two adults, two children) with en suite bathroom/shower-room, remote-control TV, tea- and coffee-making facilities and comfortable beds. Food options vary. Breakfast is at the on-site Bar Café restaurant (if available) or to take away. See also Hotel Groups pages.

Rooms 39 **S** fr £29; **D** fr £29

LANGAR

Map 11 SK73

Langar Hall

★★★ 81% ⊛⊛ HOTEL

☎ 01949 860559 📠 01949 861045
NG13 9HG
e-mail: info@langarhall.co.uk
web: www.langarhall.com
dir: Via Bingham from A52 or Cropwell Bishop from A46, both signed. Hotel behind church

This delightful hotel enjoys a picturesque rural location, yet is only a short drive from Nottingham. Individually styled bedrooms are furnished with fine period pieces and benefit from some thoughtful extras. There is a choice of lounges, warmed by real fires, and a snug little bar. Imaginative food is served in a dining room and the garden conservatory provides a lighter menu.

Rooms 12 (1 fmly) (1 GF) **S** £85-£125; **D** £95-£210 (incl. bkfst)* **Facilities** FTV Fishing ⚓ Xmas New Year Wi-fi
Conf Class 16 Board 12 Thtr 16 Del from £170 to £185*
Parking 20 **Notes** Civ Wed 50

MANSFIELD — Map 16 SK56

Pine Lodge

★★ 70% SMALL HOTEL

☎ 01623 622308 📠 01623 656819
281-283 Nottingham Rd NG18 4SE
e-mail: enquiries@pinelodge-hotel.co.uk
web: www.pinelodge-hotel.co.uk
dir: On A60 (Nottingham to Mansfield road), hotel 1m S of Mansfield

Located on the edge of Mansfield, this hotel offers welcoming and personal service to its guests - many return time and again. The public rooms include a comfortable lounge bar, a cosy restaurant and a choice of meeting and function rooms. Bedrooms are thoughtfully equipped and are carefully maintained; a suite is available.

Rooms 20 (2 fmly) **S** £30-£60; **D** £65-£70 (incl. bkfst)*
Facilities STV FTV Wi-fi **Conf** Class 30 Board 35 Thtr 50 Del from £67.50 to £97.50* **Parking** 40 **Notes** ⊗ Closed 25-26 Dec

Travelodge Mansfield

BUDGET HOTEL

☎ 0871 984 6140 📠 01623 552919
Lakeside Point, Mansfield Rd, Sutton in Ashfield NG17 4NU
web: www.travelodge.co.uk
dir: M1 junct 28, A38 towards Mansfield. Approx 3m

Travelodge offers good quality, good value, budget accommodation. All offer family rooms sleeping up to four (two adults, two children) with en suite bathroom/shower-room, remote-control TV, tea- and coffee-making facilities and comfortable beds. Food options vary. Breakfast is at the on-site Bar Café restaurant (if available) or to take away. See also Hotel Groups pages.

Rooms 51 **S** fr £29; **D** fr £29

MARKHAM MOOR — Map 17 SK77

Travelodge Retford Markham Moor

BUDGET HOTEL

☎ 0871 984 6098 📠 01777 838091
DN22 0QU
web: www.travelodge.co.uk
dir: On A1 at junct with A57, 14m N of Newark-on-Trent

Travelodge offers good quality, good value, budget accommodation. All offer family rooms sleeping up to four (two adults, two children) with en suite bathroom/shower-room, remote-control TV, tea- and coffee-making facilities and comfortable beds. Food options vary. Breakfast is at the on-site Bar Café restaurant (if available) or to take away. See also Hotel Groups pages.

Rooms 40 **S** fr £29; **D** fr £29

NEWARK-ON-TRENT — Map 17 SK75

The Grange Hotel

★★★ 82% ⊛ HOTEL

☎ 01636 703399 📠 01636 702328
73 London Rd NG24 1RZ
e-mail: info@grangenewark.co.uk
web: www.grangenewark.co.uk
dir: From A1 follow signs to Balderton, hotel opposite Polish War Graves

Expect a warm welcome at this family-run hotel, situated just a short walk from the town. Bedrooms are attractively decorated with co-ordinated soft furnishings and equipped with many thoughtful extras. Public rooms include the Potters Bar, a residents' lounge and the Cutlers Restaurant, where enjoyable cuisine is presented. In the summer guests can enjoy the delightful terrace gardens.

Rooms 19 (9 annexe) (1 fmly) **S** £79-£110; **D** £110-£155 (incl. bkfst) **Facilities** Wi-fi **Parking** 17 **Notes** LB ⊗ Closed 24 Dec-3 Jan

NORTH MUSKHAM — Map 17 SK75

Travelodge Newark North Muskham

BUDGET HOTEL

☎ 0871 984 6088 📠 01636 703635
NG23 6HT
web: www.travelodge.co.uk
dir: Approx 4m N of Newark on A1 S'bound

Travelodge offers good quality, good value, budget accommodation. All offer family rooms sleeping up to four (two adults, two children) with en suite bathroom/shower-room, remote-control TV, tea- and coffee-making facilities and comfortable beds. Food options vary. Breakfast is at the on-site Bar Café restaurant (if available) or to take away. See also Hotel Groups pages.

Rooms 30 **S** fr £29; **D** fr £29

NOTTINGHAM — Map 11 SK53

See also Langar

Hart's

★★★★ 82% ⊛⊛ HOTEL

☎ 0115 988 1900 📠 0115 947 7600
Standard Hill, Park Row NG1 6FN
e-mail: reception@hartshotel.co.uk
web: www.hartsnottingham.co.uk
dir: At junct of Park Row & Ropewalk, close to city centre

This outstanding modern building stands on the site of the ramparts of the medieval castle, overlooking the city. Many of the bedrooms enjoy splendid views. Rooms are well appointed and stylish, while the Park Bar is the focal point of the public areas; service is professional and caring. Fine dining is offered at nearby Hart's Restaurant. Secure parking and private gardens are an added bonus.

Rooms 32 (1 fmly) (7 GF) **Facilities** STV FTV Gym Small unsupervised exercise room Xmas New Year Wi-fi **Conf** Class 75 Board 30 Thtr 100 Del from £175* **Services** Lift **Parking** 19 **Notes** Civ Wed 100

Nottingham Belfry

★★★★ 81% HOTEL

☎ 0115 973 9393 📠 0115 973 9494
Mellor's Way, Off Woodhouse Way NG8 6PY
e-mail: nottinghambelfry@qhotels.co.uk
web: www.qhotels.co.uk
dir: A610 towards Nottingham. A6002 to Stapleford/Strelley. 0.75m, last exit of rdbt, hotel on right.

Set conveniently close to the motorway links, yet not far from the city centre attractions, this modern hotel has a stylish and impressive interior. Bedrooms and bathrooms are spaciously appointed and very comfortable. There are two restaurants and two bars that offer interesting and satisfying cuisine. Staff are friendly and helpful.

Rooms 120 (20 fmly) (36 GF) **S** £45-£99; **D** £55-£119*
Facilities Spa STV FTV ⊗ Gym Steam room Treatment rooms Aerobic studio Xmas New Year Wi-fi **Conf** Class 360 Board 60 Thtr 700 Del from £110 to £189* **Services** Lift **Parking** 250 **Notes** LB ⊗ Civ Wed 150

NOTTINGHAM *continued*

Lace Market

★★★★ 75% ◉◉ TOWN HOUSE HOTEL

☎ 0115 852 3232 🖩 0115 852 3223
29-31 High Pavement NG1 1HE
e-mail: stay@lacemarkethotel.co.uk
web: www.lacemarkethotel.co.uk
dir: Follow tourist signs for Galleries of Justice. Hotel opposite

This smart town house, a conversion of two Georgian houses, is located in the trendy Lace Market area of the city. Smart public areas, including the stylish and very popular Merchants Restaurant and Saints Bar, are complemented by the 'Cock and Hoop', a traditional pub offering real ales and fine wines. Accommodation is stylish and contemporary and includes spacious superior rooms and split-level suites; are all thoughtfully equipped with a host of extras including CD players and mini bars.

Rooms 42 **S** £79-£119; **D** £99-£169 (incl. bkfst)*
Facilities Complimentary use of nearby health club, including indoor pool. Wi-fi **Conf** Class 35 Board 20 Thtr 35 Del from £165 to £195* **Services** Lift **Notes** LB Civ Wed 60

Colwick Hall Hotel

★★★★ 73% HOTEL

☎ 0115 950 0566 & 0870 755 7756 🖩 0115 924 3797
Colwick Park, Racecourse Rd NG2 4BH
e-mail: reservations@colwickhallhotel.com
web: www.colwickhallhotel.com
dir: From Nottingham Forest FC, left into Radcliffe Rd (A6520), left at Lady Bay Bridge, at lights right into Meadow Ln, at rdbt 4th exit onto A612 (Daleside Rd) signed Southwell, at rdbt 2nd exit into Daleside Rd

This splendid palladian Georgian mansion sits in 60 acres of well established gardens and parkland, conveniently located for the adjacent racecourse and just two miles from the city centre. Character Grade II listed day rooms, which include the Georgetown Restaurant (specialising in colonial Malaysian cuisine) are complemented by some splendidly appointed accommodation. The superior bedrooms are luxurious and particularly spacious.

Rooms 16 (4 fmly) **D** £59-£200 (incl. bkfst)*
Facilities FTV Xmas New Year Wi-fi **Conf** Class 300 Board 200 Thtr 700 Del from £130 to £180* **Parking** 120
Notes ⊗ Civ Wed 350

Park Plaza Nottingham

★★★★ 72% HOTEL

☎ 0115 947 7200 🖩 0115 947 7300
41 Maid Marian Way NG1 6GD
e-mail: info@parkplazanottingham.com
web: www.parkplaza.com
dir: A6200 Derby Rd onto Wollaton St. 2nd exit onto Maid Marian Way. Hotel on left

This ultra modern hotel is located in the centre of the city within walking distance of retail, commercial and tourist attractions. Bedrooms are spacious and comfortable, with many extras, including laptop safes, high-speed telephone lines and air conditioning. Service is discreetly attentive in the foyer lounge and the Chino Latino restaurant, where Pan Asian cooking is a feature.

Rooms 178 (10 fmly) (37 smoking) **Facilities** STV FTV Gym Complimentary fitness suite Wi-fi **Conf** Class 100 Board 54 Thtr 200 **Services** Lift Air con **Notes** ⊗

Crowne Plaza Nottingham

★★★★ 71% HOTEL

☎ 0115 936 9988 & 0870 787 5161 🖩 0115 947 5667
Wollaton St NG1 5RH
e-mail: cpnottingham@qmh-hotels.com
web: www.crowneplaza.co.uk
dir: Follow city centre signs on A6200 to Canning Circus. Down hill & straight ahead at bottom lights

Located in the heart of the city centre this is a large, purpose-built hotel. Spacious public areas uniquely centre on a tree-lined avenue and include a popular bar and extensive meeting rooms. Air-conditioned bedrooms, which vary in size, include flat-screen TVs. The hotel also has a leisure club and extensive parking.

Rooms 210 **Facilities** STV ⓢ Gym Beautician Hairdresser Dance studio Treatment rooms Xmas New Year Wi-fi **Conf** Class 300 Board 40 Thtr 400 Del from £125 to £175* **Services** Lift Air con **Parking** 600 **Notes** ⊗ Civ Wed 400

Holiday Inn Nottingham

★★★ 79% HOTEL

☎ 0115 993 5000 🖩 0115 993 4000
Castle Marina Park NG7 1GX
e-mail: holidayinn.nottingham@btconnect.com
web: www.nottingham.holiday-inn.com
dir: Between A6005 (Castle Boulevard) & A453 (Queens Drive) at Castle Marina

This hotel, suited for both business and leisure guests, is located at the Castle Marina in the city centre. The bedrooms are contemporary and smart. The restaurant, Eaton's Brasserie, offers a tempting selection of freshly prepared dishes. There is an air conditioned mini-gym and ample free on-site parking. Guests will receive a warm welcome.

Rooms 128 (43 fmly) (15 GF) (19 smoking) **S** £70-£170; **D** £70-£170 (incl. bkfst)* **Facilities** STV Gym Wi-fi **Conf** Class 16 Board 24 Thtr 50 Del from £128 to £150* **Services** Lift **Parking** 115

Best Western Westminster

★★★ 74% HOTEL

☎ 0115 955 5000 🖩 0115 955 5005
312 Mansfield Rd, Carrington NG5 2EF
e-mail: mail@westminster-hotel.co.uk
web: www.westminster-hotel.co.uk
dir: On A60, 1m N of town centre

This smart hotel is conveniently located close to the city centre, and offers well-appointed accommodation, suitably equipped for both business and leisure guests. The spacious superior rooms are particularly impressive. Public areas include a lounge, bar restaurant and range of meeting and function rooms. There is a complimentary internet booth in reception, and Wi-fi access is available. On site, CCTV monitored parking.

Rooms 73 (24 fmly) (9 GF) **Facilities** FTV Wi-fi **Conf** Class 30 Board 30 Thtr 60 **Services** Lift **Parking** 66 **Notes** ⊗ Closed 27 Dec-2 Jan

Best Western Bestwood Lodge

★★★ 71% HOTEL

☎ 0115 920 3011 📠 0115 964 9678
Bestwood Country Park, Arnold NG5 8NE
e-mail: bestwoodlodge@btconnect.com
web: www.bw-bestwoodlodge.co.uk
dir: 3m N off A60. Left at lights into Oxclose Ln, right at next lights into Queens Bower Rd. 1st right. Keep right at fork in road

Set in 700 acres of parkland this Victorian building, once a hunting lodge, has stunning architecture that includes Gothic features and high vaulted ceilings. Bedrooms include all modern comforts, suitable for both business and leisure guests, and the popular restaurant serves an extensive menu.

Rooms 39 (5 fmly) **Facilities** 🏊 Guided walks Xmas Wi-fi **Conf** Class 65 Board 50 Thtr 200 **Parking** 120 **Notes** RS 25 Dec & 1 Jan Civ Wed 80

See advert on this page

Rutland Square Hotel

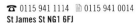

★★★ 70% HOTEL

☎ 0115 941 1114 📠 0115 941 0014
St James St NG1 6FJ
e-mail: rutland.square@forestdale.com
web: www.rutlandsquarehotel.co.uk
dir: Follow signs to castle. Hotel on right 50yds beyond castle

The enviable location in the heart of the city adjacent to the castle makes this hotel a popular choice with both leisure and business travellers. The hotel is modern and comfortable with excellent business facilities. Bedrooms offer a host of thoughtful extras to guests and the penthouse has its own jacuzzi. The contemporary Woods Restaurant offers a full range of dining options.

Rooms 87 (3 fmly) **S** £65-£79; **D** £80-£130 (incl. bkfst)* **Facilities** FTV Discounted day passes to nearby gym Xmas Wi-fi **Conf** Class 70 Board 45 Thtr 200 **Services** Lift **Parking** 30

Nottingham Gateway

★★★ 67% HOTEL

☎ 0115 979 4949 📠 0115 979 4744
Nuthall Rd, Cinderhill NG8 6AZ
e-mail: sales@nottinghamgatewayhotel.co.uk
web: www.nottinghamgatewayhotel.co.uk
dir: M1 junct 26, A610, hotel on 3rd rdbt on left

Located approximately three miles from the city centre, and with easy access to the M1. This modern hotel provides spacious public areas, with a popular restaurant and lounge bar, and the contemporary accommodation is suitably well equipped. Ample parking is a bonus.

Rooms 108 (18 fmly) (10 smoking) **S** £49-£85; **D** £49-£90 (incl. bkfst) **Facilities** STV FTV Xmas New Year Wi-fi **Conf** Class 150 Board 60 Thtr 250 Del from £90 to £140 **Services** Lift **Parking** 250 **Notes** LB Civ Wed 250

NOTTINGHAM *continued*

Swans Hotel & Restaurant

★★★ 67% HOTEL

☎ 0115 981 4042 📠 0115 945 5745
84-90 Radcliffe Rd, West Bridgford NG2 5HH
e-mail: enquiries@swanshotel.co.uk
web: www.swanshotel.co.uk
dir: From A60 or A52, hotel on A6011 close to Trent Bridge

This privately owned hotel is located on the outskirts of the city, conveniently placed for the various sporting stadiums. Bedrooms vary in size, but are all equipped to meet the needs of both business and leisure visitors. An interesting range of dishes is served in either the cosy bar or, more formally, in the restaurant.

Rooms 30 (3 fmly) (1 GF) **S** £35-£58; **D** £45-£65 (incl. bkfst)* **Facilities** STV FTV Wi-fi **Conf** Class 10 Board 24 Thtr 50 Del from £75 to £97* **Services** Lift **Parking** 26 **Notes** ⊗ Closed 24-28 Dec

The Strathdon

★★ 68% HOTEL

☎ 0115 941 8501 📠 0115 948 3725
Derby Rd NG1 5FT
e-mail: info@strathdon-hotel-nottingham.com
web: www.strathdon-hotel-nottingham.com
dir: Follow city centre signs. Enter one-way system into Wollaton Street, keep right and next right to hotel

This city-centre hotel has modern facilities and is very convenient for all city attractions. A popular themed bar has a large-screen TV and serves an extensive range of popular fresh food, while more formal dining is available in Bobbins Restaurant on certain evenings.

Rooms 68 (4 fmly) (16 smoking) **Facilities** STV Wi-fi **Conf** Class 60 Board 40 Thtr 150 **Services** Lift **Parking** 4 **Notes** Civ Wed 65

Express by Holiday Inn Nottingham City Centre

BUDGET HOTEL

☎ 0115 941 9931 📠 0115 941 5764
Chapel Quarter, Maid Marion Way NG1 6JQ
e-mail: nottingham@kewgreen.co.uk
web: www.hiexpress.com/exnottinghamcc

A modern hotel ideal for families and business travellers. Fresh and uncomplicated, the spacious rooms include Sky

TV, power shower and tea and coffee-making facilities. Continental buffet breakfast is included in the room rate; other meals may be taken at the nearby family pub or restaurant. See also the Hotel Groups pages.

Rooms 120 **Conf** Class 16 Board 40 Thtr 40

Innkeeper's Lodge Nottingham

BUDGET HOTEL

☎ 0845 112 6051 📠 0845 112 6251
Derby Rd, Wollaton Vale NG8 2NR
web: www.innkeeperslodge.com/nottingham
dir: M1 junct 25, take A52 to Nottingham. At 3rd rdbt, left into Wollaton Vale, right across central reservation into car park

Innkeeper's Lodge represents an exciting, high value concept within the budget hotel market. Comfortable bedrooms provide excellent facilities that include satellite TV and modem points. Options include family rooms; and for the corporate guest, cutting edge IT which includes Wi-fi access. A popular Carvery provides all-day food, including an extensive, complimentary continental breakfast. See also the Hotel Groups pages.

Rooms 34 (14 fmly) **Conf** Thtr 80

Travelodge Nottingham Central

BUDGET HOTEL

☎ 0871 984 6280 📠 0115 941 4610
New City House, Maid Marion Way NG1 6DD
web: www.travelodge.co.uk

Travelodge offers good quality, good value, budget accommodation. All offer family rooms sleeping up to four (two adults, two children) with en suite bathroom/shower-room, remote-control TV, tea- and coffee-making facilities and comfortable beds. Food options vary. Breakfast is at the on-site Bar Café restaurant (if available) or to take away. See also Hotel Groups pages.

Rooms 114 **S** fr £29; **D** fr £29

Travelodge Nottingham Riverside

BUDGET HOTEL

☎ 0871 984 6092 📠 0115 986 0467
Riverside Retail Park NG2 1RT
web: www.travelodge.co.uk
dir: M1 junct 24, A453. Right at 2nd rdbt signed Nottingham City Centre. Lodge on Riverside Retail Park on left

Rooms 85 **S** fr £29; **D** fr £29

Restaurant Sat Bains with Rooms

◉◉◉◉◉ RESTAURANT WITH ROOMS

☎ 0115 986 6566 📠 0115 986 0343
Trentside, Lenton Ln NG7 2SA
e-mail: info@restaurantsatbains.net
dir: M1 junct 24 take A453 Nottingham S. Over River Trent in central lane to rdbt. Left then left again towards river. Establishment on left after bend

This charming restaurant with rooms, a stylish conversion of Victorian farm buildings, is situated on the river and close to the industrial area of Nottingham. The bedrooms create a warmth and magic by using quality soft furnishings and antique and period furniture; suites and four-poster rooms are available. Public areas are chic and cosy, and the delightful restaurant complements the outstanding cuisine on offer.

Rooms 8 (4 annexe)

Cockliffe Country House

◉ RESTAURANT WITH ROOMS

☎ 0115 968 0179 📠 0115 968 0623
Burntstump Country Park, Burntstump Hill, Arnold NG5 8PQ
e-mail: enquiries@cockliffehouse.co.uk

Expect a warm welcome at this delightful property situated in a peaceful rural location amidst neat landscaped grounds, close to Sherwood Forest. Public areas include a smart breakfast room, a tastefully appointed restaurant and a cosy lounge bar. The individually decorated bedrooms have co-ordinated soft furnishings and many thoughtful touches.

Rooms 11 (4 annexe)

Best Western West Retford

★★★ 74% HOTEL

☎ 01777 706333 📠 01777 709951
24 North Rd DN22 7XG
e-mail: reservations@westretfordhotel.co.uk
web: www.westretfordhotel.co.uk
dir: From A1 take A620 to Ranby/Retford. Left at rdbt into North Rd (A638). Hotel on right

Stylishly appointed throughout, and set in very attractive gardens close to the town centre, this 18th-century manor house offers a good range of well-equipped meeting facilities. The spacious, well-laid out bedrooms and suites are located in separate buildings and all offer modern facilities and comforts.

Rooms 63 (32 GF) **S** £65-£97; **D** £70-£104 (incl. bkfst) **Facilities** FTV Xmas New Year Wi-fi **Conf** Class 80 Board 40 Thtr 150 **Parking** 150 **Notes** LB Civ Wed 150

SOUTHWELL — Map 17 SK65

Saracens Head

★★★ 73% HOTEL

☎ 01636 812701 📠 01636 815408
Market Place NG25 0HE
e-mail: info@saracensheadhotel.net
web: www.saracensheadhotel.net
dir: from A1 to Newark turn off & follow B6386 for
approx 7m

This half-timbered inn, rich in history, is set in the centre
of town and close to the Minster. There is a relaxing
atmosphere within the sumptuous public areas, which
include a small bar, a comfortable lounge and a fine
dining restaurant. Bedroom styles vary - all are
appealing, comfortable and well equipped.

Rooms 27 (2 fmly) **Facilities** FTV Xmas New Year Wi-fi
Conf Class 60 Board 40 Thtr 80 **Parking** 102 **Notes** LB ⊗
Civ Wed 70

TROWELL MOTORWAY SERVICE AREA (M1) — Map 11 SK43

Travelodge Nottingham Trowell (M1)

BUDGET HOTEL

☎ 0871 984 6093 📠 0115 944 7815
NG9 3PL
web: www.travelodge.co.uk
dir: M1 junct 25/26 northbound

Travelodge offers good quality, good value, budget
accommodation. All offer family rooms sleeping up to four
(two adults, two children) with en suite bathroom/
shower-room, remote-control TV, tea- and coffee-making
facilities and comfortable beds. Food options vary.
Breakfast is at the on-site Bar Café restaurant (if
available) or to take away. See also Hotel Groups pages.

Rooms 35 **S** fr £29; **D** fr £29

WORKSOP — Map 16 SK57

Clumber Park

★★★ 79% HOTEL

☎ 01623 835333 📠 01623 835525
Clumber Park S80 3PA
e-mail: reservations@clumberparkhotel.com
dir: M1 junct 30/31 follow signs to A57 & A1. From A1
take A614 towards Nottingham. Hotel 2m on left

Beside the A614, this hotel is situated in open
countryside, edging on to Sherwood Forest and Clumber
Park. Bedrooms are comfortably furnished and well
equipped and public areas include a choice of formal and
informal eating options. Dukes Tavern is lively and
casual, while the restaurant offers a more traditional
style of service.

Rooms 73 (5 fmly) (15 GF) **S** £90–£110; **D** £120–£140*
Facilities Spa FTV ③ Gym Sauna Steam room Xmas New
Year Wi-fi **Conf** Class 90 Board 40 Thtr 250 **Parking** 100
Notes Civ Wed 100

Best Western Lion

★★★ 78% HOTEL

☎ 01909 477925 📠 01909 479038
112 Bridge St S80 1HT
e-mail: reception@thelionworksop.co.uk
web: www.thelionworksop.co.uk
dir: A57 to town centre, turn right at Sainsburys, follow to
Norfolk Arms, turn left

This former coaching inn lies on the edge of the main
shopping precinct, with a car park to the rear. It has been
extended to offer modern accommodation that includes
excellent executive rooms. A wide range of interesting
dishes is offered in both the restaurant and bar.

Rooms 46 (3 fmly) (7 GF) **S** £55–£85; **D** £65–£115 (incl.
bkfst)* **Facilities** STV FTV Xmas New Year Wi-fi
Conf Class 80 Board 70 Thtr 160 Del from £88 to £145*
Services Lift **Parking** 50 **Notes** LB Civ Wed 150

Travelodge Worksop

BUDGET HOTEL

☎ 0871 984 6185 📠 0870 191 1684
St Anne's Dr, Dukeries Dr S80 3QD
web: www.travelodge.co.uk
dir: on rdbt junct of A619 & A57

Travelodge offers good quality, good value, budget
accommodation. All offer family rooms sleeping up to four
(two adults, two children) with en suite bathroom/
shower-room, remote-control TV, tea- and coffee-making
facilities and comfortable beds. Food options vary.
Breakfast is at the on-site Bar Café restaurant (if
available) or to take away. See also Hotel Groups pages.

Rooms 40 **S** fr £29; **D** fr £29

OXFORDSHIRE

ABINGDON — Map 5 SU49

Abingdon Four Pillars Hotel

★★★ 78% HOTEL

☎ 0800 374 692 & 01235 553456 📠 01235 554117
Marcham Rd OX14 1TZ
e-mail: abingdon@four-pillars.co.uk
web: www.four-pillars.co.uk/abingdon
dir: A34 at junct with A415, in Abingdon, turn right at
rdbt, hotel on right

On the outskirts of Abingdon, this busy commercial hotel
is well located for access to major roads. The bedrooms
are comfortable and well equipped with extras such as
safes and trouser presses. All day refreshments are
offered in the stylish lounge and conservatory.

Rooms 63 (3 fmly) (32 GF) **S** £60–£115; **D** £70–£145*
Facilities FTV Xmas New Year Wi-fi **Conf** Class 80
Board 40 Thtr 140 Del from £130 to £169* **Parking** 85
Notes LB ⊗ Civ Wed 100

Upper Reaches

★★★ 75% HOTEL

☎ 01235 522536 & 462140 📠 01235 555682
Thames St OX14 3JA
e-mail: reservations@upperreaches-abingdon.co.uk
web: www.upperreaches-abingdon.co.uk
dir: On A415 in Abingdon follow signs for Dorchester, turn
left just before bridge over Thames

Built from Abingdon Abbey's old corn mill, the hotel
enjoys an attractive location. It offers well-appointed
rooms, individually styled and with a wide range of
amenities. The aptly named Millrace Restaurant is
situated in the ancient mill house and still features a
working wheel and has views of the river flowing beneath.

Rooms 31 (5 GF) **Facilities** FTV Fishing Xmas New Year
Wi-fi **Parking** 60 **Notes** ⊗

ABINGDON *continued*

Crown & Thistle

★★ 64% HOTEL

☎ 01235 522556 📠 01235 553281
18 Bridge St OX14 3HS
e-mail: reception@crownandthistle.com
dir: Follow A415 towards Dorchester into town centre

A cosy hotel situated at edge of historical market town and a stone's throw from the Thames. There is a variety of bar and lounge areas and a maze of bright, airy corridors linking individually-styled bedrooms. The spacious reception leads to an outdoor courtyard for alfresco drinks and snacks. The Gallery Restaurant and bar provides a pleasant atmosphere with satisfying cuisine served by friendly, efficient staff.

Rooms 19 (3 fmly) **Facilities** Pool table Xmas
Conf Class 8 Board 12 Thtr 12 **Parking** 35 **Notes** ⊗

Dog House

★★ 🅰 HOTEL

☎ 01865 390830 📠 01865 390860
Faringdon Rd, Frilford Heath OX13 6QJ
e-mail: doghouse.frilford@oldenglishinns.co.uk
web: www.oldenglish.co.uk

Rooms 20 (2 fmly) (4 GF) **Facilities** Xmas **Conf** Class 15
Board 12 Thtr 30 **Parking** 40

ADDERBURY   Map 11 SP43

Red Lion

★★ 🅰 HOTEL

☎ 01295 810269 📠 01295 811906
The Green, Oxford Rd OX17 3LU
e-mail: 6496@greeneking.co.uk
web: www.oldenglish.co.uk
dir: M40 junct 11 into Banbury, take A4260 towards Bodicote into Adderbury, hotel on left

Rooms 12 (1 GF) **Facilities** FTV Xmas New Year Wi-fi
Conf Class 16 Board 15 Thtr 20 **Parking** 20 **Notes** ⊗

BANBURY   Map 11 SP44

Best Western Wroxton House

★★★ 80% ◉ HOTEL

☎ 01295 730777 📠 01295 730800
Wroxton St Mary OX15 6QB
e-mail: reservations@wroxtonhousehotel.com
dir: M40 junct 11, take A422 signed Banbury & Wroxton. Approx 3m, hotel on right on entering Wroxton

Dating in parts from 1649, this partially thatched hotel is set just off the main road. Bedrooms, either been created from cottages or are situated in a contemporary wing, are comfortable and well equipped with Wi-fi and LCD TVs.

The public areas are open plan and the low-beamed Inglenook Restaurant has a peaceful atmosphere for dining.

Rooms 32 (3 annexe) (6 fmly) (8 GF) **S** £54-£78;
D £58-£87* **Facilities** FTV Xmas New Year Wi-fi
Conf Class 30 Board 30 Thtr 60 Del from £119 to £130*
Parking 60 **Notes** LB Civ Wed 60

Mercure Whately Hall

★★★ 77% HOTEL

☎ 01295 253261
Banbury Cross OX16 0AN
e-mail: h6633@accor.com
web: www.mercure-uk.com
dir: M40 junct 11, straight over 2 rdbts, left at 3rd, 0.25m to Banbury Cross, hotel on right

Dating back to 1677, this historic inn boasts many original features such as stone passages, priests' holes and a fine wooden staircase. Spacious public areas include the oak-panelled restaurant, which overlooks the attractive well-tended gardens, a choice of lounges and a traditional bar. Smartly appointed bedrooms vary in size and style but all are thoughtfully equipped.

Rooms 69 (4 fmly) (2 GF) (5 smoking) **Facilities** FTV
Xmas New Year Wi-fi **Conf** Class 40 Board 60 Thtr 150
Services Lift **Parking** 52 **Notes** Civ Wed 150

Cromwell Lodge Hotel

★★ 🅰 HOTEL

☎ 01295 259781 📠 01295 276619
9-11 North Bar OX16 0TB
e-mail: 6434@greeneking.co.uk
web: www.oldenglish.co.uk
dir: M40 junct 11 towards Banbury, through 3 sets of lights, hotel on left just before Banbury Cross

Rooms 23 (1 fmly) (3 GF) **Facilities** Xmas **Conf** Class 30
Board 20 Thtr 30 **Parking** 20

Express by Holiday Inn Banbury M40, Jct 11

BUDGET HOTEL

☎ 01295 234567 📠 01295 234568
Ermont Way, Stroud Park OX16 4TJ
e-mail: reception@exhibanbury.co.uk
web: www.hiexpress.co.uk

A modern hotel ideal for families and business travellers. Fresh and uncomplicated, the spacious rooms include Sky TV, power shower and tea and coffee-making facilities. Continental buffet breakfast is included in the room rate; other meals may be taken at the nearby family pub or restaurant. See also the Hotel Groups pages.

Rooms 120 **Conf** Class Board Thtr

BICESTER   Map 11 SP52

Bignell Park Hotel & Oaks Restaurant

★★★ 75% ◉ HOTEL   THE INDEPENDENTS

☎ 01869 326550 & 0870 042 1024 📠 01869 322729
Chesterton OX26 1UE
e-mail: enq@bignellparkhotel.co.uk
dir: M40 junct 9/A41 to Bicester, over 1st & 2nd rdbts, left at mini-rdbt, follow signs to Witney A4095. Hotel 0.5m

This pleasant property is situated in the peaceful village of Chesterton, just a short drive from Bicester Village Retail Outlet, the M40 and Oxford. Public rooms feature a superb oak-beamed restaurant, a smart bar and a comfortable lounge with plush sofas. Bedrooms are smartly decorated, well maintained and equipped with modern facilities.

Rooms 23 (4 fmly) (9 GF) **Facilities** FTV Xmas New Year
Wi-fi **Conf** Class 16 Board 60 Thtr 100 Del from £140 to
£160* **Parking** 40 **Notes** ⊗ Civ Wed 60

Travelodge Bicester Cherwell Valley (M40)

BUDGET HOTEL

☎ 0871 984 6012 📠 01869 346390
Moto Service Area, Northampton Rd, Ardley OX27 7RD
web: www.travelodge.co.uk
dir: M40 junct 10

Travelodge offers good quality, good value, budget accommodation. All offer family rooms sleeping up to four (two adults, two children) with en suite bathroom/ shower-room, remote-control TV, tea- and coffee-making facilities and comfortable beds. Food options vary. Breakfast is at the on-site Bar Café restaurant (if available) or to take away. See also Hotel Groups pages.

Rooms 133 **S** fr £29; **D** fr £29 **Conf** Class 20 Board 20
Thtr 40

BLETCHINGDON

BLETCHINGDON
Map 11 SP51

The Oxfordshire Inn

★★ 61% HOTEL

☎ 01869 351444 🗎 01869 351555
Heathfield Village OX5 3DX
e-mail: staff@oxfordshireinn.co.uk
web: www.oxfordshireinn.co.uk
dir: M40 junct 9, A34 towards Oxford, then A4027 towards Bletchingdon. Hotel signed 0.7m on right

A converted farmhouse with additional outbuildings that is located close to major motorway networks. Accommodation is set around an open courtyard, and includes suites that have four-poster beds. There is a spacious bar and restaurant.

Rooms 28 (4 fmly) (15 GF) **S** £49-£97; **D** £59-£104 (incl. bkfst) **Facilities** Putt green Golf driving range Xmas New Year Wi-fi **Conf** Class 80 Board 30 Thtr 140 **Parking** 50 **Notes** LB

BURFORD
Map 5 SP21

The Lamb Inn

★★★ 81% ⊛⊛ SMALL HOTEL

☎ 01993 823155 🗎 01993 822228
Sheep St OX18 4LR
e-mail: info@lambinn-burford.co.uk
web: www.cotswold-inns-hotels.co.uk
dir: A40 into Burford, downhill,1st left into Sheep St, hotel last on right

This enchanting old inn is just a short walk from the centre of this delightful Cotswold village. An abundance of character and charm is found inside with a cosy lounge and log fire, and in intimate bar with flagged floors. An elegant restaurant offers locally sourced produce in carefully prepared dishes. Bedrooms, some with original features, are comfortable and well appointed.

Rooms 17 (1 fmly) (4 GF) **Facilities** Xmas New Year Wi-fi

The Bay Tree Hotel

★★★ 79% ⊛ HOTEL

☎ 01993 822791 🗎 01993 823008
Sheep St OX18 4LW
e-mail: info@baytreehotel.info
web: www.cotswold-inns-hotels.co.uk/bay-tree
dir: A40 or A361 to Burford. From High St turn into Sheep St, next to old market square. Hotel on right

The modern decorative style combines seamlessly with features from this delightful inn's long history. Bedrooms are tastefully furnished and some have four-poster and half-tester beds. Public areas consist of a character bar, a sophisticated airy restaurant, a selection of meeting rooms and an attractive walled garden.

Rooms 21 (13 annexe) (2 fmly) **Facilities** 🏊 Xmas New Year Wi-fi **Conf** Class 12 Board 25 Thtr 40 **Parking** 50 **Notes** Civ Wed 60

Cotswold Gateway

★★★ 70% HOTEL

☎ 01993 822695 🗎 01993 823600
Cheltenham Rd OX18 4HX
e-mail: cotswoldgateway@btconnect.com
dir: Hotel on rdbt at A40 Oxford/Cheltenham at junct with A361

Ideally located for both business and leisure guests, this hotel prominently situated on the A40 and yet only a short walk away from Burford. Bedrooms are comfortable and well appointed with many guest comforts. Dinners have an extensive choice of popular dishes and the option of eating in the character bar, the coffee shop or brasserie style restaurant.

Rooms 20 (5 annexe) (2 fmly) (4 GF) **S** £65-£85; **D** £85-£140 (incl. bkfst)* **Facilities** FTV New Year Wi-fi **Parking** 30 **Notes** Closed 25-26 Dec

The Inn For All Seasons

THE INDEPENDENTS
HOTEL ASSOCIATION

★★ 75% HOTEL

☎ 01451 844324 🗎 01451 844375
The Barringtons OX18 4TN
e-mail: sharp@innforallseasons.com
web: www.innforallseasons.com
dir: 3m W of Burford on A40 towards Cheltenham

This 16th-century coaching inn is conveniently located near Burford. Bedrooms are comfortable, and public areas retain much period charm with original fireplaces and oak beams still remaining. A good selection of bar meals is available at lunchtime, while the evening menu includes an appetising selection of fresh fish.

Rooms 10 (1 annexe) (2 fmly) (1 GF) **S** £35-£68; **D** £50-£95 (incl. bkfst)* **Facilities** Xmas New Year Wi-fi **Conf** Class 30 Board 30 Thtr 25 Del from £125 to £155* **Parking** 62 **Notes** LB

Travelodge Burford Cotswolds

BUDGET HOTEL

☎ 0871 984 6018 🗎 01993 822699
Bury Barn OX18 4JF
web: www.travelodge.co.uk
dir: On rdbt junct of A40 & A361 midway between Cheltenham & Oxford

Travelodge offers good quality, good value, budget accommodation. All offer family rooms sleeping up to four (two adults, two children) with en suite bathroom/shower-room, remote-control TV, tea- and coffee-making facilities and comfortable beds. Food options vary. Breakfast is at the on-site Bar Café restaurant (if available) or to take away. See also Hotel Groups pages.

Rooms 40 **S** fr £29; **D** fr £29

BURFORD *continued*

The Angel at Burford

◉◉ RESTAURANT WITH ROOMS

☎ 01993 822714 📠 01993 822069
14 Witney St OX18 4SN
e-mail: paul@theangelatburford.co.uk
web: www.theangelatburford.co.uk
dir: Off A40 at Burford rdbt, down hill, 1st right onto
Swan Ln, 1st left to Pytts Ln, left at end onto Witney St

A coaching inn in the 16th century, this establishment is
situated in the centre of Burford, the Gateway to The
Cotswolds. Three attractively decorated en suite
bedrooms offer plentiful accessories and share a cosy
residents' lounge. The award-winning restaurant is open
for lunch and dinner. The peaceful courtyard and walled
garden are perfect for relaxing in the summer.

Rooms 3

| DEDDINGTON | Map 11 SP43 |

Deddington Arms

★★★ 78% ◉ HOTEL

☎ 01869 338364 📠 01869 337010
Horsefair OX15 0SH
e-mail: deddarms@oxfordshire-hotels.co.uk
web: www.oxfordshire-hotels.co.uk
dir: From S: M40 junct 10/A43. 1st rdbt left to Aynho
(B4100) & left to Deddington (B4031). From N: M40
junct 11 to hospital & Adderbury on A4260, then to
Deddington

This charming and friendly old inn is conveniently located
off the Market Square. The well-equipped bedrooms are
comfortably appointed and situated either in the main
building or a purpose-built courtyard wing. The bar is full
of character, and the delightful restaurant enjoys a well-
deserved local following.

Rooms 27 (4 fmly) (10 GF) (2 smoking) **S** £90-£99;
D £99-£110 (incl. bkfst)* **Facilities** STV Xmas New Year
Wi-fi **Conf** Class 20 Board 25 Thtr 40 **Parking** 36
Notes LB ⊗

| DORCHESTER (ON THAMES) | Map 5 SU59 |

White Hart

★★★ 71% ◉ HOTEL

☎ 01865 340074 📠 01865 341082
High St OX10 7HN
e-mail: whitehart@oxfordshire-hotels.co.uk
web: www.oxfordshire-hotels.co.uk
dir: M40 junct 6, take B4009 through Watlington &
Benson to A4074. Follow signs to Dorchester. Hotel on
right

Period charm and character are plentiful throughout this
17th-century coaching inn, which is situated in the heart
of a picturesque village. The spacious bedrooms are
individually decorated and thoughtfully equipped. Public
rooms include a cosy bar, a choice of lounges and an
atmospheric restaurant, complete with vaulted timber
ceiling.

Rooms 26 (4 annexe) (2 fmly) (9 GF) **Facilities** Xmas
Wi-fi **Conf** Class 20 Board 18 Thtr 30 Del from £100 to
£130 **Parking** 36

George

★★ 67% HOTEL

☎ 01865 340404 📠 01865 341620
25 High St OX10 7HH
e-mail: thegeorgehotel@fsmail.net
dir: M40 junct 6 onto B4009 through Watlington &
Benson. Take A4074 at BP petrol station, follow
Dorchester signs. Hotel on left

Full of character and charm, this quintessential coaching
inn stands beside Dorchester Abbey and dates back to
the 15th century. The bedrooms are decorated in keeping
with the style of the building, and are divided between
the main house and the courtyard. Meals can be taken
either in the lively, atmospheric bar or in the intimate
restaurant.

Rooms 17 (8 annexe) (1 fmly) (6 GF) **Conf** Class 20
Board 24 Thtr 40 **Parking** 50 **Notes** ⊗

| FARINGDON | Map 5 SU29 |

Best Western Sudbury House Hotel & Conference Centre

★★★ 75% ◉ HOTEL

☎ 01367 241272 📠 01367 242346
London St SN7 8AA
e-mail: stay@sudburyhouse.co.uk
web: www.sudburyhouse.co.uk
dir: Off A420, signed Folly Hill

Situated on the edge of the Cotswolds and set in nine
acres of pleasant grounds, this hotel offers spacious and
well-equipped bedrooms that are attractively decorated
in warm colours. Dining options include the comfortable
restaurant for a good selection of carefully presented
dishes, and the bar for lighter options. A comprehensive
room service menu is also available.

Rooms 49 (2 fmly) (10 GF) (2 smoking) **Facilities** STV ⦿
Gym Badminton Boules New Year Wi-fi **Conf** Class 30
Board 34 Thtr 100 **Services** Lift **Parking** 100
Notes Civ Wed 160

See advert on opposite page

| GORING | Map 5 SU68 |

The Miller of Mansfield

◉ RESTAURANT WITH ROOMS

☎ 01491 872829 📠 01491 873100
High St RG8 9AW
e-mail: reservations@millerofmansfield.com
web: www.millerofmansfield.com

The frontage of this former coaching inn hides sumptuous
rooms with a distinctive and individual style, an award-
winning restaurant that serves appealing dishes using
locally sourced ingredients and a comfortable bar, which
serves real ales, fine wines, afternoon tea and a bar
menu for a quick bite.

Rooms 13 (2 fmly)

GREAT MILTON — Map 5 SP60

INSPECTORS' CHOICE

Le Manoir Aux Quat' Saisons
★★★★★ ☺☺☺☺☺ HOTEL

☎ 01844 278881 📄 01844 278847
Church Rd OX44 7PD
e-mail: lemanoir@blanc.co.uk
web: www.manoir.com
dir: From A329 2nd right to Great Milton Manor, hotel 200yds on right

Even though Le Manoir is now very much part of the British scene, its iconic chef patron, Raymond Blanc, still fizzes with new ideas and projects. His first loves are his kitchen and his garden and the vital link between them. The fascinating grounds feature a Japanese tea garden and two acres of vegetables and herbs that supply the kitchen with an almost never ending supply of top notch produce. Even the car park has a stunning artichoke sculpture. The kitchen is the epicentre, with outstanding cooking highlighting freshness and seasonality. Bedrooms in this idyllic 'grand house on a small scale' are either in the main house or around an outside courtyard. All offer the highest levels of comfort and quality, have magnificent marble bathrooms and are equipped with a host of thoughtful extra touches. Raymond Blanc has been awarded the AA's Lifetime Achievement Award 2009-10.

Rooms 32 (23 annexe) **Facilities** STV FTV 🏊 Cookery school Water Gardens Bikes Spa treatment Xmas New Year Wi-fi **Conf** Board 20 Thtr 24 **Parking** 60 **Notes** ⊗ Civ Wed 50

HENLEY-ON-THAMES — Map 5 SU78

Hotel du Vin Henley-on-Thames
★★★★ 76% ☺☺ TOWN HOUSE HOTEL

☎ 01491 848400 📄 01491 848401
New St RG9 2BP
e-mail: info@henley.hotelduvin.com
web: www.hotelduvin.com
dir: M4 junct 8/9 signed High Wycombe, take 2nd exit and onto A404 in 2m. A4130 into Henley, over bridge, through lights, up Hart St, right onto Bell St, right onto New St, hotel on right

Situated just 50 yards from the water's edge, this hotel retains the character and much of the architecture of the former brewery. Food, and naturally wine, take on a strong focus here and guests will find an interesting mix of dishes to choose from; there are three private dining rooms where the fermentation room and old malt house used to be; alfresco dining is popular when the weather permits. Bedrooms provide comfort, style and a good range of facilities including power showers. Parking is available and there is a drop-off point in the courtyard.

Rooms 43 (4 fmly) (4 GF) **Facilities** STV Use of local spa & gym Xmas New Year Wi-fi **Conf** Class 20 Board 36 Thtr 30 **Services** Air con **Parking** 36 **Notes** LB Civ Wed 60

KINGHAM — Map 10 SP22

Mill House Hotel & Restaurant
★★★ 81% ☺☺ HOTEL

☎ 01608 658188 📄 01608 658492
OX7 6UH
e-mail: stay@millhousehotel.co.uk
web: www.millhousehotel.co.uk
dir: Off A44 onto B4450. Hotel indicated by tourist sign

This Cotswold-stone, former mill house has been carefully converted into a comfortable and attractive hotel. It is set in well-kept grounds bordered by its own trout stream. Bedrooms are comfortable and provide thoughtfully equipped accommodation. There is a peaceful lounge and bar, plus an atmospheric restaurant where the imaginative, skilfully cooked dishes are a highlight of any stay.

Rooms 23 (2 annexe) (1 fmly) (7 GF) **S** £65-£75; **D** £80-£120 (incl. bkfst) **Facilities** STV FTV Fishing 🎣 Xmas New Year Wi-fi **Conf** Class 24 Board 24 Thtr 70 **Parking** 62 **Notes** LB Civ Wed 100

KIRTLINGTON | Map 11 SP41

Dashwood Hotel and Restaurant

★★★ 81% HOTEL

☎ 01869 352707 📄 01869 351432
South Green, Heyford Rd OX5 3HJ
e-mail: info@thedashwood.co.uk
web: www.thedashwood.co.uk
dir: M40 junct 10, S on B430 signed Middleton Stoney.
After lights in Middleton Stoney, right onto A4095 signed
Kirtlington. In village, hotel approx 800mtrs on right just
before sharp bend

This former inn in the centre of the village provides
striking, modern bedrooms with LCD flat-screen TVs,
broadband and tailor-made oak furniture. The
sophisticated bar and restaurant have a wealth of period
features and look onto the open-plan kitchen where well-
sourced seasonal produce is used to prepare modern
cuisine.

Rooms 12 (7 annexe) (1 fmly) (3 GF) **S** £90-£130;
D £115-£160 (incl. bkfst)* **Facilities** Xmas **Parking** 27
Notes LB ⊗ Closed New Year

MIDDLETON STONEY | Map 11 SP52

Best Western Jersey Arms

★★ 74% HOTEL

☎ 01869 343234 📄 01869 343565
OX25 4AD
e-mail: jerseyarms@bestwestern.co.uk
web: www.jerseyarms.co.uk
dir: 3m from A34, on B430, 10m N of Oxford, between
junct 9 & 10 of M40

With a history dating back to the 13th century, the Jersey
Arms combines old-fashioned charm with contemporary
style and elegance. The individually designed bedrooms
are well equipped and comfortable. The lounge has an
open fire, and the smart and spacious restaurant
provides a calm atmosphere in which to enjoy the hotel's
popular cuisine.

Rooms 20 (14 annexe) (3 fmly) (9 GF) **S** £79-£85;
D £95-£125 (incl. bkfst)* **Facilities** FTV Xmas New Year
Wi-fi **Conf** Class 20 Board 20 Thtr 20 Del from £110 to
£145 **Parking** 55 **Notes** LB ⊗

MILTON COMMON | Map 5 SP60

The Oxford Belfry

★★★★ 76% HOTEL

☎ 01844 279381 📄 01844 279624
OX9 2JW
e-mail: oxfordbelfry@qhotels.co.uk
web: www.qhotels.co.uk
dir: M40 junct 7 onto A329 to Thame. Left onto A40, hotel
300yds on right

This modern hotel has a relatively rural location and
enjoys lovely views of the countryside to the rear. The

hotel is built around two very attractive courtyards and
has a number of lounges and conference rooms, as well
as indoor leisure facilities and outdoor tennis courts.
Bedrooms are large and feature a range of extras.

Rooms 154 (20 fmly) (66 GF) **S** £59-£180; **D** £69-£190
(incl. bkfst) **Facilities** Spa STV ⊛ ⊛ ⊛ Gym Steam room
Sauna Aerobics studio Xmas New Year Wi-fi
Conf Class 180 Board 100 Thtr 450 Del from £130 to
£215 **Services** Lift **Parking** 350 **Notes** LB Civ Wed 300

OXFORD | Map 5 SP50

INSPECTORS' CHOICE

Le Manoir Aux Quat' Saisons

★★★★★ ⊛⊛⊛⊛⊛ HOTEL

☎ 01844 278881 📄 01844 278847
Church Rd OX44 7PD
e-mail: lemanoir@blanc.co.uk
web: www.manoir.com

(For full entry see Great Milton)

Macdonald Randolph

★★★★★ 81% ⊛⊛ HOTEL

☎ 01865 256400 📄 01865 792133
Beaumont St OX1 2LN
e-mail: randolph@macdonald-hotels.co.uk
web: www.macdonaldhotels.co.uk
dir: M40 junct 8, A40 towards Oxford. Follow city centre
signs, leading to St Giles, hotel on right

Superbly located near the city centre, The Randolph
boasts impressive neo-Gothic architecture and tasteful
decor. The spacious and traditional restaurant, complete
with picture windows, is an ideal place to watch the
world go by while enjoying freshly prepared, modern
dishes. Bedrooms include a mix of classical and
contemporary wing rooms, which have been appointed to
a high standard. Parking is a real bonus.

Rooms 151 **Facilities** Spa STV Gym Treatment rooms
Thermal suite Mini gym ♫ Xmas New Year Wi-fi
Conf Class 130 Board 60 Thtr 300 **Services** Lift
Parking 60 **Notes** Civ Wed 120

The Old Bank Hotel

★★★★ 79% ⊛ TOWN HOUSE HOTEL

☎ 01865 799599 📄 01865 799598
92-94 High St OX1 4BN
e-mail: info@oldbank-hotel.co.uk
web: www.oldbank-hotel.co.uk
dir: From Magdalen Bridge into High St, hotel 50yds on
left

Located close to the city centre and the colleges, this
former bank benefits from an excellent location. An
eclectic collection of modern pictures and photographs,
many by well-known artists, are on display. Bedrooms are
smart with excellent business facilities plus the benefit of
air conditioning. Public areas include the vibrant all-day
Quod Bar and Restaurant. The hotel also has its own car
park - a definite advantage in this busy city.

Rooms 42 (10 fmly) (1 GF) **S** £125-£210; **D** £135-£250*
Facilities STV Discounts with various leisure facilities ♫
Wi-fi **Conf** Class 30 Board 40 Thtr 50 Del from £220 to
£260* **Services** Lift Air con **Parking** 60 **Notes** LB ⊗

See advert on opposite page

Barceló Oxford Hotel

★★★★ 76% HOTEL

☎ 01865 489988 📄 01865 489952
Godstow Rd, Wolvercote Roundabout OX2 8AL
e-mail: oxford@barcelo-hotels.co.uk
web: www.barcelo-hotels.co.uk
dir: Adjacent to A34/A40, 2m from city centre

Conveniently located on the northern edge of the city
centre, this purpose-built hotel offers bedrooms that are
bright, modern and well equipped. Guests can eat in the
Medio Restaurant or try the Cappuccino Lounge menu.
There is the option to eat alfresco on the Patio Terrace
when the weather is fine. The hotel offers impressive
conference, business and leisure facilities.

Rooms 168 (11 fmly) (89 GF) **Facilities** Spa STV ⊛
supervised Gym Squash Steam room Beauty treatments
New Year Wi-fi **Conf** Class 130 Board 110 Thtr 320
Del from £100* **Parking** 250 **Notes** Civ Wed 250

Old Parsonage

★★★★ 75% ◉ TOWN HOUSE HOTEL

☎ 01865 310210 📄 01865 311262
1 Banbury Rd OX2 6NN
e-mail: info@oldparsonage-hotel.co.uk
web: www.oldparsonage-hotel.co.uk
dir: From Oxford ring road to city centre via Summertown. Hotel last building on right next to St Giles Church before city centre

Dating back in parts to the 16th century, this stylish hotel offers great character and charm and is conveniently located at the northern edge of the city centre. Bedrooms are attractively styled and particularly well appointed. The focal point of the operation is the busy all-day bar and restaurant; the small garden areas and terraces prove popular in summer months.

Rooms 30 (4 fmly) (10 GF) **S** £125-£190; **D** £175-£260*
Facilities FTV Beauty treatments Free use of nearby leisure facilities, punt & house bikes 🎯 Xmas Wi-fi
Conf Class 8 Board 12 Thtr 20 Del from £200 to £250*
Services Air con **Parking** 14 **Notes** LB Civ Wed 20

See advert on this page

Cotswold Lodge

★★★★ 75% HOTEL

☎ 01865 512121 📄 01865 512490
66a Banbury Rd OX2 6JP
e-mail: info@cotswoldlodgehotel.co.uk
web: www.cotswoldlodgehotel.co.uk
dir: Off A40 Oxford ring road onto A4165 (Banbury road) signed city centre & Summertown. Hotel 2m on left

This Victorian property is located close to the centre of Oxford and offers smart, comfortable accommodation. Stylish bedrooms and suites are attractively presented and some have balconies. The public areas have an elegant country-house feel. The hotel is popular with business guests and caters for conferences and banquets.

Rooms 49 (14 GF) **Facilities** STV New Year Wi-fi
Conf Class 45 Board 40 Thtr 100 **Parking** 40 **Notes** ⊗

OXFORD *continued*

Oxford Thames Four Pillars Hotel

★★★★ 74% HOTEL

☎ 0800 374 692 & 01865 334444 🖹 01865 334400
Henley Rd, Sandford-on-Thames OX4 4GX
e-mail: thames@four-pillars.co.uk
web: www.four-pillars.co.uk/thames
dir: M40 junct 8 towards Oxford, follow ring road. Left at
rdbt towards Cowley. At rdbt with lights turn left to
Littlemore, hotel approx 1m on right

The main house of this hotel is built from local, yellow
stone. The spacious and traditional River Restaurant has
superb views of the hotel's own boat, moored on the river.
The gardens can be enjoyed from the patios or balconies
in the newer bedroom wings. Public rooms include a
beamed bar and lounge area with minstrels' gallery.

Rooms 62 (1 fmly) (28 GF) **S** £90-£185; **D** £120-£215*
Facilities STV 🕲 ♨ Gym Steam room Sauna Xmas New
Year Wi-fi **Conf** Class 80 Board 40 Thtr 150 Del from £145
to £195* **Parking** 120 **Notes** LB ⊗ Civ Wed 120

Oxford Spires Four Pillars Hotel

★★★★ 71% HOTEL

☎ 0800 374 692 & 01865 324324 🖹 01865 324325
Abingdon Rd OX1 4PS
e-mail: spires@four-pillars.co.uk
web: www.four-pillars.co.uk/spires
dir: M40 junct 8 towards Oxford. Left towards Cowley. At
3rd rdbt follow city centre signs. Hotel 1m

This purpose-built hotel is surrounded by extensive
parkland, yet is only a short walk from the city centre.
Bedrooms are attractively furnished, well equipped and
include several apartments. Public areas include a

spacious restaurant, open-plan bar/lounge, leisure club
and extensive conference facilities.

Rooms 160 (14 fmly) (50 GF) **S** £69-£165; **D** £69-£165*
Facilities STV 🕲 Gym Beauty Steam room Sauna Xmas
New Year Wi-fi **Conf** Class 96 Board 76 Thtr 266
Del from £130 to £195* **Services** Lift **Parking** 95
Notes LB ⊗ Civ Wed 140

Malmaison Oxford

★★★ 85% ⏱ HOTEL

☎ 01865 268400 🖹 01865 268402
3 Oxford Castle, New Rd OX1 1AY
web: www.malmaison.com
dir: M40 junct 9, A34 N to Botley interchange. Follow city
centre & rail station signs. At rail station straight ahead
to 2nd lights. Turn right, at next lights left into Park End
St. Straight on at next lights, hotel 2nd left

Once the city's prison, this is definitely a hotel with a
difference. Many of the rooms are actually converted from
the old cells. Not to worry though there have been many
improvements since the previous occupants left!
Exceedingly comfortable beds and luxury bathrooms are
just two of the changes. The hotel has a popular brasserie
with quality and value much in evidence. A small amount
of parking space is available.

Rooms 94 (5 GF) **Facilities** STV Gym Xmas New Year Wi-fi
Services Lift **Parking** 20 **Notes** Civ Wed 80

Mercure Eastgate

★★★ 83% ⏱ HOTEL

☎ 0870 400 8201 & 01865 248332 🖹 01865 791681
73 High St OX1 4BE
e-mail: h6668-sb@accor.com
web: www.mercure-uk.com
dir: A40 follow signs to Headington & Oxford city centre,
over Magdalen Bridge, stay in left lane, through lights,
left into Merton St, entrance to car park on left

Just a short stroll from the city centre, this hotel, as its
name suggests, occupies the site of the city's medieval
East Gate and boasts its own car park. Bedrooms are
appointed and equipped to a high standard. Stylish
public areas include the all-day Town House Brasserie
and Bar.

Rooms 63 (3 fmly) **Conf** Board 16 **Services** Lift Air con
Parking 40 **Notes** LB ⊗

Holiday Inn Oxford

★★★ 79% HOTEL

☎ 0870 400 9086 🖹 01865 888321
Peartree Roundabout, Woodstock Rd OX2 8JD
e-mail: reservations-oxford@ihg.com
web: www.holidayinn.co.uk
dir: A34 Peartree Interchange signed Oxford & Services.
Hotel within service area

Located at The Peartree Roundabout, this purpose-built,
modern hotel is ideal for business and leisure guests
visiting Oxford. Bedrooms are spacious, well equipped
and have air cooling. There is a smart bar and restaurant
plus as a well-equipped gym and large swimming pool.
There are meeting facilities and ample free parking.

Rooms 154 (25 fmly) (23 GF) (14 smoking) **D** £72-£159*
Facilities Spa STV 🕲 supervised Gym Wi-fi **Conf** Class 65
Board 65 Thtr 150 Del from £99 to £150* **Services** Lift
Air con **Notes** LB ⊗ Civ Wed 120

Weston Manor

★★★ 78% ⏱⏱ HOTEL

☎ 01869 350621 🖹 01869 350901
OX25 3QL
e-mail: reception@westonmanor.co.uk
web: www.westonmanor.co.uk

(For full entry see Weston-on-the-Green)

Westwood Country Hotel

★★★ 78% HOTEL

☎ 01865 735408 🖹 01865 736536
Hinksey Hill, Boars Hill OX1 5BG
e-mail: reservations@westwoodhotel.co.uk
web: www.westwoodhotel.co.uk
dir: Off Oxford ring road at Hinksey Hill junct towards
Boars Hill & Wootton. At top of hill road bends to left.
Hotel on right

This Edwardian country-house hotel is prominently set in
terraced landscaped grounds and is within easy reach of
the city centre by car. The hotel is modern in style with
very comfortable, well-equipped and tastefully decorated
bedrooms. Public areas include a contemporary bar, a

cosy lounge and a restaurant overlooking the pretty garden.

Rooms 20 (5 fmly) (7 GF) **S** £65-£110; **D** £95-£135 (incl. bkfst) **Facilities** FTV Arrangement with local health club, golf club & riding school Xmas New Year Wi-fi **Conf** Class 36 Board 35 Thtr 60 Del from £130 to £160* **Parking** 50 **Notes** Civ Wed 200

Hawkwell House

★★★ 74% ⊛ HOTEL

☎ 01865 749988 ▤ 01865 748525
Church Way, Iffley Village OX4 4DZ
e-mail: reservations@hawkwellhouse.co.uk
web: www.bespokehotels.com
dir: A34 follow signs to Cowley. At Littlemore rdbt take A4158 exit onto Iffley Rd. After lights turn left to Iffley

Set in a peaceful residential location, Hawkwell House is just a few minutes' drive from the Oxford ring road. The spacious rooms are modern, attractively decorated and well equipped. Public areas are tastefully appointed and the conservatory-style restaurant offers an interesting choice of dishes. The hotel also has a range of conference and function facilities.

Rooms 66 (10 fmly) (4 GF) **Facilities** FTV Xmas New Year Wi-fi **Conf** Class 100 Board 80 Thtr 200 **Services** Lift **Parking** 120 **Notes** ⊗ Civ Wed 150

Best Western Linton Lodge

★★★ 74% HOTEL

☎ 01865 553461 ▤ 01865 553691
11-13 Linton Rd OX2 6UJ
e-mail: sales@lintonlodge.com
web: www.lintonlodge.com
dir: Towards city centre on Banbury Rd. In 0.5m right into Linton Rd. Hotel opposite St Andrews Church

Located in a residential area, this hotel is within walking distance of the city centre. Bedrooms are modern, well equipped and comfortable. The oak-panelled Linton's Restaurant serves both set and carte menus, and the Dragon Bar, overlooking the extensive lawned gardens, is the ideal place to relax and have a drink.

Rooms 70 (2 fmly) (14 GF) **S** £65-£95; **D** £75-£150 **Facilities** FTV ⍩ Wi-fi **Conf** Class 50 Board 40 Thtr 120 Del from £100 to £155* **Services** Lift **Parking** 40 **Notes** LB ⊗ Civ Wed 120

Manor House

★★ 68% METRO HOTEL

☎ 01865 727627 ▤ 01865 200478
250 Iffley Rd OX4 1SE
dir: On A4158, 1m from city centre

This family run establishment is easily accessible from the city centre and all major road links. The hotel provides informal but friendly and attentive service. The comfortably furnished bedrooms are well equipped. The hotel has a bar but there is a selection of restaurants and popular pubs within easy walking distance. Limited private parking is available.

Rooms 8 (2 fmly) **S** £69-£99; **D** £69-£99 (incl. bkfst)* **Parking** 6 **Notes** ⊗ Closed 20 Dec-20 Jan

Victoria

★★ 61% METRO HOTEL

☎ 01865 724536 ▤ 01865 794909
180 Abingdon Rd OX1 4RA
e-mail: info@victoriahotelox.com
web: www.victoriahotelox.com
dir: from M40/A40 take eastern bypass & A4144 into city

Located within easy reach of Oxford city centre and the motorway networks, this metro hotel offers comfortable bedrooms, well maintained and furnished to a high standard. A conservatory bar with large flat-screen TV is an ideal place to relax.

Rooms 20 (5 annexe) (2 fmly) (6 GF) **Facilities** Xmas Wi-fi **Parking** 20 **Notes** ⊗

The Balkan Lodge Hotel

★★ 60% METRO HOTEL

☎ 01865 244524 ▤ 01865 251090
315 Iffley Rd OX4 4AG
e-mail: balkanlodge@aol.co.uk
web: www.hometown.aol.com/balkanlodge
dir: from M40/A40 take eastern bypass, into city on A4158

Conveniently located for the city centre and the ring road, this family operated metro hotel offers a comfortable stay. Bedrooms are attractive and well equipped. Public areas include a lounge and bar. A large, secure private car park is located to the rear of the building.

Rooms 13 **Facilities** Wi-fi **Notes** LB ⊗

Bath Place

★★ 57% METRO HOTEL

☎ 01865 791812 ▤ 01865 791834
4-5 Bath Place, Holywell St OX1 3SU
e-mail: info@bathplace.co.uk
dir: On S side of Holywell St (parallel to High St)

The hotel has been created from a group of 17th-century cottages originally built by Flemish weavers who were permitted to settle outside the city walls. This lovely hotel

is very much at the heart of the city today and offers individually designed bedrooms, including some with four-posters.

Rooms 15 (3 fmly) (4 GF) **S** £75-£105; **D** £95-£145 (incl. bkfst)* **Facilities** FTV Wi-fi **Parking** 15 **Notes** LB

Express by Holiday Inn Oxford-Kassam Stadium

BUDGET HOTEL

☎ 01865 780888 ▤ 01865 780999
Grenoble Rd OX4 4XP
e-mail: reservations@expressoxford.com
web: www.hiexpress.com/oxfrdkassam
dir: M40 junct 8 onto A40 for 4m. Left at McDonald's onto A4142. After 3.5m left onto A4074, take 1st exit signed Science Park & Kassam Stadium

A modern hotel ideal for families and business travellers. Fresh and uncomplicated, the spacious rooms include Sky TVs, power showers and tea and coffee-making facilities. A continental buffet breakfast is included in the room rate; other meals may be taken at the nearby family pub or restaurant. See also the Hotel Groups pages.

Rooms 162 (131 fmly) **Conf** Class 18 Board 28 Thtr 30

Travelodge Oxford Peartree

BUDGET HOTEL

☎ 0871 984 6096 ▤ 01865 513474
Peartree Roundabout, Woodstock Rd OX2 8JZ
web: www.travelodge.co.uk
dir: at junct of A34 & A44

Travelodge offers good quality, good value, budget accommodation. All offer family rooms sleeping up to four (two adults, two children) with en suite bathroom/ shower-room, remote-control TV, tea- and coffee-making facilities and comfortable beds. Food options vary. Breakfast is at the on-site Bar Café restaurant (if available) or to take away. See also Hotel Groups pages.

Rooms 197 **S** fr £29; **D** fr £29 **Conf** Class 150 Board 60 Thtr 300

Travelodge Oxford Wheatley

BUDGET HOTEL

☎ 0871 984 6206 ▤ 01865 875905
London Rd, Wheatley OX33 1JH
web: www.travelodge.co.uk
dir: On A22, just off Boship Farm rdbt at junct of A267 & A271

Rooms 36 **S** fr £29; **D** fr £29

OXFORD MOTORWAY SERVICE AREA (M40)
Map 5 SP60

Days Inn Oxford

BUDGET HOTEL

☎ 01865 877000 ▤ 01865 877016
M40 junction 8A, Waterstock OX33 1LJ
e-mail: oxford.hotel@welcomebreak.co.uk
web: www.welcomebreak.co.uk
dir: M40 junct 8a, at Welcome Break service area

This modern building offers accommodation in smart, spacious and well-equipped bedrooms, suitable for families and business travellers, and all with en suite bathrooms. Continental breakfast is available and other refreshments may be taken at the nearby family restaurant. See also the Hotel Groups pages.

Rooms 59 (56 fmly) **S** £29-£49; **D** £39-£69* **Conf** Board 8 Del from £79 to £109*

STEEPLE ASTON
Map 11 SP42

The Holt Hotel
★★★ 70% HOTEL

☎ 01869 340259 ▤ 01869 340865
Oxford Rd OX25 5QQ
e-mail: info@holthotel.co.uk
web: www.holthotel.co.uk
dir: At junct of B4030 & A4260

This attractive former coaching inn has given hospitality to many over the centuries, not least to Claude Duval, a notorious 17th-century highwayman. Today guests are offered well-equipped, modern bedrooms and attractive public areas, which include a relaxing bar, restaurant and a well-appointed lounge. A selection of meeting rooms is available.

Rooms 86 (19 fmly) **Facilities** Xmas New Year Wi-fi **Conf** Class 70 Board 44 Thtr 140 **Parking** 200 **Notes** Civ Wed 100

THAME
Map 5 SP70

Travelodge Thame

BUDGET HOTEL

☎ 0871 984 6215 ▤ 01844 218740
OX9 3AX
web: www.travelodge.co.uk
dir: M40 junct 7 or junct 8a signed Wheatley, follow signs for Thame/Aylesbury & Long Crendon. Left at rdbt junct of A418 & B4011 to Long Crendon. Lodge on right behind Esso service station

Travelodge offers good quality, good value, budget accommodation. All offer family rooms sleeping up to four (two adults, two children) with en suite bathroom/shower-room, remote-control TV, tea- and coffee-making facilities and comfortable beds. Food options vary. Breakfast is at the on-site Bar Café restaurant (if available) or to take away. See also Hotel Groups pages.

Rooms 51 **S** fr £29; **D** fr £29

WALLINGFORD
Map 5 SU68

The Springs Hotel & Golf Club
★★★ 80% ⊛ HOTEL

☎ 01491 836687 ▤ 01491 836877
Wallingford Rd, North Stoke OX10 6BE
e-mail: info@thespringshotel.com
web: www.thespringshotel.com
dir: Off A4074 (Oxford-Reading road) onto B4009 (Goring). Hotel approx 1m on right

Set on its own 18-hole, par 72 golf course, this Victorian mansion has a timeless and peaceful atmosphere. The generously equipped, individually styled bedrooms vary in size but many are spacious. Some bedrooms overlook the pool and grounds while others have views of the spring-fed lake as does the elegant restaurant. There is also a comfortable lounge, with original features, to relax in.

Rooms 32 (4 fmly) (8 GF) **Facilities** FTV ⌖ ⚓ 18 Putt green Fishing 🚣 Clay pigeon shooting nearby Horse riding ♫ Xmas New Year Wi-fi **Conf** Class 16 Board 26 Thtr 60 Del from £155 to £165* **Parking** 150 **Notes** Civ Wed 150

The George
★★★ 77% HOTEL

PEEL HOTELS PLC

☎ 01491 836665 ▤ 01491 825359
High St OX10 0BS
e-mail: info@george-hotel-wallingford.com
web: www.peelhotel.com
dir: E side of A329 on N entry to town

Old world charm and modern facilities merge seamlessly in this former coaching inn. Bedrooms in the main house have character in abundance. Those in the wing have a more contemporary style, but all are well equipped and attractively decorated. Diners can choose between the restaurant and bistro, or relax in the cosy bar.

Rooms 39 (1 fmly) (9 GF) **S** £70-£125; **D** £90-£152* **Facilities** STV Xmas New Year Wi-fi **Conf** Class 60 Board 50 Thtr 150 Del from £125 to £145* **Parking** 60 **Notes** LB ⊗ Civ Wed 100

Shillingford Bridge
★★★ 74% HOTEL

☎ 01865 858567 ▤ 01865 858636
Shillingford OX10 8LZ
e-mail: shillingford.bridge@forestdale.com
web: www.shillingfordbridgehotel.com
dir: M4 junct 10, A329 through Wallingford towards Thame, then B4009 through Watlington. Right on A4074 at Benson, then left at Shillingford rdbt (unclass road) Wallingford Road

This hotel enjoys a superb position right on the banks of the River Thames, and benefits from private moorings and has a waterside open-air swimming pool. Public areas are stylish with a contemporary feel and have large picture windows making the best use of the view. Bedrooms are well equipped and furnished with guest comfort in mind.

Rooms 40 (8 annexe) (6 fmly) (9 GF) **S** £70-£95; **D** £102-£154 (incl. bkfst)* **Facilities** FTV ⌖ supervised Fishing Table tennis ♫ Xmas New Year Wi-fi **Conf** Class 40 Board 36 Thtr 80 **Parking** 100 **Notes** Civ Wed 150

WESTON-ON-THE-GREEN   Map 11 SP51

Weston Manor

★★★ 78% ◎◎ HOTEL

☎ 01869 350621   ▤ 01869 350901
OX25 3QL
e-mail: reception@westonmanor.co.uk
web: www.westonmanor.co.uk
dir: M40 junct 9, exit A34 to Oxford then 1st exit on left signed Weston-on-Green/Middleton Stony B4030. Right at mini rdbt, hotel 400yds on left

Character, charm and sophistication blend effortlessly in this friendly hotel set in well-tended grounds. Bedrooms are well equipped and are located in the main house, coach house or a cottage annexe. Award-winning food can be enjoyed in the impressive vaulted restaurant, complete with original oak panelling and minstrels' gallery; other public areas include an atmospheric foyer lounge, a bar and meeting facilities.

Rooms 35 (20 annexe) (5 fmly) (6 GF) **S** £70–£115; **D** £87.50–£127.50 (incl. bkfst)* **Facilities** FTV ⚲ ⛳ New Year Wi-fi **Conf** Class 30 Board 40 Thtr 80 Del from £140 to £175* **Parking** 100 **Notes** LB ⊗ Civ Wed 100

WITNEY   Map 5 SP31

Witney Four Pillars Hotel

★★★★ 73% HOTEL

☎ 0800 374692 & 01993 779777   ▤ 01993 703467
Ducklington Ln OX28 4TJ
e-mail: witney@four-pillars.co.uk
web: www.four-pillars.co.uk/witney
dir: M40 junct 9, A34 to A40, exit A415 Witney/Abingdon. Hotel on left, 2nd exit for Witney

This attractive modern hotel is close to Oxford and Burford and offers spacious, well-equipped bedrooms. The cosy Spinners Bar has comfortable seating areas and the popular Weavers Restaurant offers a good range of dishes. Other amenities include extensive function and leisure facilities, complete with indoor swimming pool.

Rooms 87 (14 fmly) (18 GF) **S** £50–£140; **D** £50–£140* **Facilities** FTV ⓢ Gym Steam room Sauna Xmas New Year Wi-fi **Conf** Class 76 Board 44 Thtr 180 Del from £99 to £179* **Parking** 170 **Notes** ⊗ Civ Wed 120

WOODSTOCK   Map 11 SP41

Macdonald Bear

★★★★ 76% ◎◎ HOTEL   ▣ MACDONALD
HOTELS & RESORTS

☎ 0844 879 9143   ▤ 01993 813380
Park St OX20 1SZ
e-mail: gm.bear@macdonaldhotels.co.uk
web: www.macdonaldhotels.co.uk
dir: M40 junct 9 follow signs for Oxford & Blenheim Palace. A44 to town centre hotel on left

With its ivy-clad façade, oak beams and open fireplaces, this 13th-century coaching inn exudes charm and cosiness. The bedrooms are decorated in a modern style that remains in keeping with the historic character of the building. Public rooms include a variety of function rooms, an intimate bar area and an attractive restaurant where attentive service and good food are offered.

Rooms 54 (18 annexe) (1 fmly) (8 GF) **Facilities** STV Xmas New Year Wi-fi **Conf** Class 12 Board 24 Thtr 40 **Parking** 40

Feathers

★★★ 83% ◎◎ HOTEL

☎ 01993 812291   ▤ 01993 813158
Market St OX20 1SX
e-mail: enquiries@feathers.co.uk
dir: From A44 (Oxford to Woodstock), 1st left after lights. Hotel on left

This intimate and unique hotel enjoys a town centre location with easy access to nearby Blenheim Palace. Public areas are elegant and full of traditional character from the cosy drawing room to the atmospheric restaurant. Individually styled bedrooms are appointed to a high standard and are furnished with attractive period and reproduction furniture.

Rooms 20 (5 annexe) (4 fmly) (2 GF) **S** £109–£219; **D** £169–£279 (incl. bkfst) **Facilities** FTV 1 suite has steam room Xmas New Year Wi-fi **Conf** Class 20 Board 30 Thtr 20 **Notes** LB

Kings Arms

★★★ 78% HOTEL

☎ 01993 813636   ▤ 01993 813737
19 Market St OX20 1SU
e-mail: stay@kingshotelwoodstock.co.uk
web: www.kings-hotel-woodstock.co.uk
dir: In town centre, on corner of Market St & A44

This appealing and contemporary hotel is situated in the centre of town just a short walk from Blenheim Palace. Public areas include an attractive bistro-style restaurant and a smart bar. Bedrooms and bathrooms are comfortably furnished and equipped, and appointed to a high standard.

Rooms 15 **S** £75–£100; **D** £140–£150 (incl. bkfst) **Facilities** FTV Xmas New Year Wi-fi **Notes** LB ⊗ No children 12yrs

RUTLAND

GREETHAM   Map 11 SK91

Greetham Valley

★★★ 74% HOTEL

☎ 01780 460444   ▤ 01780 460623
Wood Ln LE15 7NP
e-mail: info@gvgc.co.uk
web: www.greethamvalley.co.uk
dir: A1/B668. Left towards Greetham, Cottesmore & Oakham. Left at x-rds after 0.5m, follow brown signs to golf club entrance

Spacious bedrooms with storage facilities designed for golfers, offer high levels of comfort and many have superb views over the two 18-hole golf courses. Meals are taken in the clubhouse restaurants with a choice of informal or more formal styles. A beauty suite and extensive conference facilities are ideal for both large and small groups.

Rooms 35 (17 GF) **S** £52.50–£81; **D** £60.50–£89 (incl. bkfst)* **Facilities** FTV ⚿ 36 Putt green Fishing 4x4 Off road course Archery centre Bowls green New Year Wi-fi **Conf** Class 150 Thtr 200 **Services** Lift **Parking** 300 **Notes** LB ⊗ Civ Wed 200

MORCOTT — Map 11 SK90

Travelodge Uppingham Morcott

BUDGET HOTEL

☎ 0871 984 6113 📠 01572 747719
Uppingham LE15 9DL
web: www.travelodge.co.uk
dir: on A47, eastbound

Travelodge offers good quality, good value, budget accommodation. All offer family rooms sleeping up to four (two adults, two children) with en suite bathroom/shower-room, remote-control TV, tea- and coffee-making facilities and comfortable beds. Food options vary. Breakfast is at the on-site Bar Café restaurant (if available) or to take away. See also Hotel Groups pages.

Rooms 40 **S** fr £29; **D** fr £29

NORMANTON — Map 11 SK90

Best Western Normanton Park

★★★ 73% HOTEL

☎ 01780 720315 📠 01780 721086
Oakham LE15 8RP
e-mail: info@normantonpark.co.uk
web: www.normantonpark.com
dir: From A1 follow A606 towards Oakham, 5m. Turn left, 1.5m. Hotel on right

This delightful hotel, on Rutland Water's south shore, is appointed to a high standard and there are two dining styles available including an extensive Chinese menu. Bedrooms are well furnished and there are ample public rooms for guests to relax in.

Rooms 30 (7 annexe) (6 fmly) (11 GF) **S** fr £80; **D** £100-£270 (incl. bkfst)* **Facilities** FTV Xmas New Year Wi-fi **Conf** Class 60 Board 80 Thtr 200 Del from £125 to £145* **Parking** 100 **Notes** LB Civ Wed 100

OAKHAM — Map 11 SK80

Hambleton Hall

★★★★ ◉◉◉◉
COUNTRY HOUSE HOTEL

☎ 01572 756991 📠 01572 724721
Hambleton LE15 8TH
e-mail: hotel@hambletonhall.com
web: www.hambletonhall.com
dir: 3m E off A606

Established over 25 years ago by Tim and Stefa Hart this delightful country house enjoys tranquil and spectacular views over Rutland Water. The beautifully manicured grounds are a delight to walk in. The bedrooms in the main house are stylish, individually decorated and equipped with a range of thoughtful extras. A two-bedroom folly, with its own sitting and breakfast room, is only a short walk away. Day rooms include a cosy bar and a sumptuous drawing room, both featuring open fires. The elegant restaurant serves skilfully prepared, award-winning cuisine with menus highlighting locally sourced, seasonal produce - some grown in the hotel's own grounds.

Rooms 17 (2 annexe) **S** £175-£205; **D** £205-£600 (incl. bkfst)* **Facilities** STV ≈ ◡ ◡ Private access to lake Xmas New Year **Conf** Board 24 Thtr 40 Del from £270 to £300* **Services** Lift **Parking** 40 **Notes** LB Civ Wed 64

Barnsdale Lodge

★★★ 78% ◉ HOTEL

☎ 01572 724678 📠 01572 724961
The Avenue, Rutland Water, North Shore LE15 8AH
e-mail: enquiries@barnsdalelodge.co.uk
web: www.barnsdalelodge.co.uk
dir: Off A1 onto A606. Hotel 5m on right, 2m E of Oakham

A popular and interesting hotel converted from a farmstead overlooking Rutland Water. The public areas are dominated by a very successful food operation with a good range of appealing meals on offer for either formal or informal dining. Bedrooms are comfortably appointed with excellent beds enhanced by contemporary soft furnishings and thoughtful extras.

Rooms 44 (2 fmly) (15 GF) **S** £80-£90; **D** £90-£145 (incl. bkfst) **Facilities** FTV Fishing ◡ Archery Beauty treatments Golf Shooting Xmas New Year **Conf** Class 120 Board 76 Thtr 330 Del from £112.50 **Parking** 200 **Notes** LB Civ Wed 160

Nick's Restaurant at Lord Nelson's House

◉◉ RESTAURANT WITH ROOMS

☎ 01572 723199
11 Market Place LE15 6HR
e-mail: simon@nicksrestaurant.co.uk
web: www.nicksrestaurant.co.uk
dir: A1(M) onto A606, after 2nd rdbt, Market Place on right

Tucked away in the corner of the market square, this restaurant with rooms offers fine dining and four individually appointed bedrooms with a range of antiques and knick-knacks. Service is attentive and helpful, and the food a delight, offering a selection of carefully crafted dishes using the best of quality seasonal produce.

Rooms 4

UPPINGHAM — Map 11 SP89

The Lake Isle

@@ RESTAURANT WITH ROOMS

☎ 01572 822951 📄 01572 824400
16 High Street East LE15 9PZ
e-mail: info@lakeisle.co.uk
web: www.lakeisle.co.uk
dir: From A47, turn left at 2nd lights, 100yds on right

This attractive, townhouse centres round a delightful restaurant and small elegant bar. There is also an inviting first-floor guest lounge, and the bedrooms are extremely well appointed and thoughtfully equipped; spacious split-level cottage suites situated in a quiet courtyard are also available. The imaginative cooking and an extremely impressive wine list are highlights.

Rooms 11 (2 annexe) (1 fmly)

SHROPSHIRE

ALVELEY — Map 10 SO78

Mill Hotel & Restaurant

★★★★ 78% HOTEL

☎ 01746 780437 📄 01746 780850
WV15 6HL
e-mail: info@themill-hotel.co.uk
web: www.themill-hotel.co.uk
dir: Midway between Kidderminster & Bridgnorth, turn off A442 signed Enville & Turley Green

Built around a 17th-century water mill, with the original water wheel still on display, this extended and renovated hotel is set in eight acres of landscaped grounds. Bedrooms are pleasant, well equipped and include some superior rooms, which have sitting areas. There are also some rooms with four-poster beds. The restaurant provides carefully prepared dishes and there are extensive wedding and function facilities.

Rooms 41 (5 fmly) **S** £80-£88; **D** £90-£150 (incl. bkfst)*
Facilities STV Gym Xmas New Year Wi-fi **Conf** Class 180 Board 80 Thtr 250 **Services** Lift **Parking** 212 **Notes** LB ⊗ Civ Wed 140

BRIDGNORTH — Map 10 SO79

INSPECTORS' CHOICE

Old Vicarage Hotel

★★★ @@@ SMALL HOTEL

☎ 01746 716497 📄 01746 716552
Worfield WV15 5JZ
e-mail: admin@the-old-vicarage.demon.co.uk
web: www.oldvicarageworfield.com
dir: Off A454, approx 3.5m NE of Bridgnorth, 5m S of Telford's southern business area. Follow brown signs

This delightful property is set in acres of wooded farmland in a quiet and peaceful area of Shropshire. Service is friendly and helpful, and customer care is one the many strengths of this charming small hotel. The well-equipped bedrooms are individually appointed, and thoughtfully and luxuriously furnished. The lounge and conservatory are the perfect places to enjoy a pre-dinner drink or the complimentary afternoon tea. The restaurant is a joy, serving award-winning modern British cuisine in elegant surroundings.

Rooms 14 (4 annexe) (1 fmly) (2 GF) **S** £80-£110; **D** £130-£170 (incl. bkfst) **Facilities** FTV ⬛ New Year Wi-fi **Conf** Class 40 Board 30 Thtr 60 **Parking** 30 **Notes** LB Civ Wed 60

CHURCH STRETTON — Map 15 SO49

Longmynd Hotel

★★★ 73% HOTEL

☎ 01694 722244 📄 01694 722718
Cunnery Rd SY6 6AG
e-mail: info@longmynd.co.uk
web: www.longmynd.co.uk
dir: A49 into town centre on Sandford Ave, left at Lloyds TSB, over mini-rdbt, 1st right into Cunnery Rd, hotel at top of hill on left

Built in 1901 as a spa, this family-run hotel overlooks this country town, and the views from many of the rooms and public areas are breathtaking. The attractive wooded grounds include a unique wood sculpture trail. Bedrooms, with smart modern bathrooms, are comfortable and well equipped; suites are available. Facilities include a choice

of relaxing lounges. An ethical approach to climatic issues is observed, and a warm welcome is assured.

Rooms 50 (6 fmly) **S** £50-£65; **D** £100-£130 (incl. bkfst)*
Facilities ⬛ Putt green Pitch and putt Sauna Xmas New Year Wi-fi **Conf** Class 50 Board 40 Thtr 100 **Services** Lift **Parking** 100 **Notes** LB Civ Wed 100

HADNALL — Map 15 SJ52

Saracens at Hadnall

@ RESTAURANT WITH ROOMS

☎ 01939 210877 📄 01939 210877
Shrewsbury Rd SY4 4AG
e-mail: reception@saracensathadnall.co.uk
web: www.saracensathadnall.co.uk
dir: M54 onto A5, at junct of A5/A49 take A49 towards Whitchurch. Follow A49 to Hadnall, diagonally opposite church

This Georgian Grade II listed former farmhouse and village pub has been tastefully converted into a very smart restaurant-with-rooms, without any loss of its original charm and character. The bedrooms are thoughtfully equipped and include a family room. Skilfully prepared meals are served in either the elegant dining room or the adjacent conservatory where the glass-topped well is a feature.

Rooms 5 (1 fmly)

LLANFAIR WATERDINE — Map 9 SO27

The Waterdine

@@ RESTAURANT WITH ROOMS

☎ 01547 528214
LD7 1TU
e-mail: info@waterdine.com
dir: Off B4355 into village, last property on left before church

Standing in pretty, mature gardens in an Area of Outstanding Natural Beauty, which includes part of Offa's Dyke, this former 16th-century drovers' inn retains much of its original character. Bedrooms are filled with a wealth of thoughtful extras and have modern bathrooms. Public areas include a cosy lounge bar and an elegant restaurant, the setting for imaginative dinners that use quality, seasonal local produce.

Rooms 3

LUDLOW · Map 10 SO57

Overton Grange Hotel and Restaurant

★★★ 86% ◉◉ HOTEL

☎ 01584 873500 & 0845 476 1000 📄 01584 873524
Old Hereford Rd SY8 4AD
e-mail: info@overtongrangehotel.com
web: www.overtongrangehotel.com
dir: Off A49 at B4361 to Ludlow. Hotel 200yds on left

This is a traditional country-house hotel with stylish, comfortable bedrooms, and high standards of guest care. Food is an important part of what the hotel has to offer and the restaurant serves classically based, French-style cuisine using locally sourced produce where possible. Meeting and conference rooms are available.

Rooms 14 **Facilities** ⊗ Xmas New Year Wi-fi
Conf Class 50 Board 30 Thtr 100 **Parking** 45 **Notes** ⊗ No children 7yrs Civ Wed 70

Fishmore Hall

★★★ 85% ◉◉ SMALL HOTEL

☎ 01584 875148 📄 01584 877907
Fishmore Rd SY8 3DP
e-mail: reception@fishmorehall.co.uk
web: www.fishmorehall.co.uk
dir: A49 onto Henley Rd. 1st right, Weyman Rd, at bottom of hill right onto Fishmore Rd

Located in a rural area within easy reach of town centre, this Palladian styled Georgian house has been sympathetically renovated and extended to provide high standards of comfort and facilities. A contemporary styled interior highlights the many retained period features and public areas include a comfortable lounge and restaurant, the setting for imaginative cooking.

Rooms 15 (1 GF) **S** £100-£210; **D** £140-£250 (incl. bkfst) **Facilities** FTV 🧖 Beauty treatments Massage Xmas New Year Wi-fi **Conf** Class 20 Board 30 Thtr 40 **Services** Lift **Parking** 48 **Notes** LB Civ Wed 80

Dinham Hall

★★★ 80% ◉ HOTEL

☎ 01584 876464 📄 01584 876019
By The Castle SY8 1EJ
e-mail: info@dinhamhall.com
dir: In town centre, opposite castle

Built in 1792, this lovely old house stands in attractive gardens immediately opposite Ludlow Castle. It has a well-deserved reputation for warm hospitality. Well-equipped bedrooms include two in a converted cottage and some with four-poster beds. The comfortable public rooms are elegantly appointed.

Rooms 13 (2 annexe) (2 fmly) (2 GF) **S** £85-£140; **D** £140-£240 (incl. bkfst)* **Facilities** Xmas New Year **Conf** Class 20 Board 26 Thtr 40 Del from £134.50 to £155* **Parking** 16 **Notes** LB Civ Wed 40

Feathers

★★★ 80% ◉ HOTEL

☎ 01584 875261 📄 01584 876030
The Bull Ring SY8 1AA
e-mail: feathers.ludlow@btconnect.com
web: www.feathersatludlow.co.uk
dir: From A49 follow town centre signs to centre. Hotel on left

Famous for the carved woodwork outside and in, this picturesque 17th-century hotel is one of the town's best known landmarks and is in an excellent location. Bedrooms are traditional in style and décor. Public areas have retained much of the traditional charm; the first-floor lounge is particularly stunning.

Rooms 40 (3 fmly) **S** £75-£85; **D** £95-£130 (incl. bkfst)* **Facilities** STV FTV Xmas New Year Wi-fi **Conf** Class 40 Board 40 Thtr 80 Del from £120 to £140* **Services** Lift **Parking** 33 **Notes** LB Civ Wed 50

Cliffe

★★ 76% SMALL HOTEL

☎ 01584 872063 📄 01584 873991
Dinham SY8 2JE
e-mail: thecliffehotel@hotmail.com
web: www.thecliffehotel.co.uk
dir: In town centre turn left at castle gates to Dinham, follow over bridge. Take right fork, hotel 200yds on left

Built in the 19th century and standing in extensive grounds and gardens, this privately owned and personally run hotel is quietly located close to the castle and the river. It provides well-equipped accommodation, and facilities include a lounge bar, a pleasant restaurant and a patio overlooking the garden.

Rooms 9 (2 fmly) **S** £50-£60; **D** £60-£80 (incl. bkfst) **Facilities** Wi-fi **Parking** 22 **Notes** LB

Travelodge Ludlow

BUDGET HOTEL

☎ 0871 984 6347 📄 01584 879098
Foldgate Ln SY8 1LS
web: www.travelodge.co.uk
dir: A49. At rdbt 1st exit Sheet Rd, left onto Foldgate Ln. Lodge on right

Travelodge offers good quality, good value, budget accommodation. All offer family rooms sleeping up to four (two adults, two children) with en suite bathroom/shower-room, remote-control TV, tea- and coffee-making facilities and comfortable beds. Food options vary. Breakfast is at the on-site Bar Café restaurant (if available) or to take away. See also Hotel Groups pages.

Rooms 41 **S** fr £29; **D** fr £29

Travelodge Ludlow Woofferton

BUDGET HOTEL

☎ 0871 984 6086 📄 01584 711695
Woofferton SY8 4AL
web: www.travelodge.co.uk
dir: on A49 at junct A456 & B4362

Rooms 32 **S** fr £29; **D** fr £29

The Clive Bar & Restaurant with Rooms

◉◉ RESTAURANT WITH ROOMS

☎ 01584 856565 & 856665 📄 01584 856661
Bromfield SY8 2JR
e-mail: info@theclive.co.uk
web: www.theclive.co.uk
dir: 2m N of Ludlow on A49 in village of Bromfield

The Clive is just two miles from the busy town of Ludlow and is a convenient base for visiting the local attractions or for business. The bedrooms are spacious and very well equipped, and some are suitable for families. Meals are available in the well-known Clive Restaurant or the Cookhouse café bar. A small meeting room is also available.

Rooms 15 (15 annexe) (9 fmly)

MARKET DRAYTON · Map 15 SJ63

Goldstone Hall

★★★ 83% ◉◉ HOTEL

☎ 01630 661202 📄 01630 661585
Goldstone TF9 2NA
e-mail: enquiries@goldstonehall.com
dir: 4m S of Market Drayton off A529 signed Goldstone Hall Hotel. 4m N of Newport signed from A41

Situated in extensive grounds, this sympathetically refurbished period property is a family-run hotel. It provides traditionally furnished, well-equipped accommodation with outstanding en suite bathrooms and lots of thoughtful extras. Public rooms are extensive and include a choice of lounges, a snooker room and a conservatory. The hotel has a well deserved reputation for good food that utilises home-grown produce. A warm welcome is assured.

Rooms 12 (2 GF) **S** £87.50-£105; **D** £130-£162 (incl. bkfst)* **Facilities** STV FTV Snooker table New Year Wi-fi **Conf** Class 30 Board 30 Thtr 50 **Parking** 60 **Notes** LB ⊗ Civ Wed 96

Ternhill Farm House & The Cottage Restaurant
⊚ RESTAURANT WITH ROOMS

☎ 01630 638984 ▤ 01630 638752
Ternhill TF9 3PX
e-mail: info@ternhillfarm.co.uk
web: www.ternhillfarm.co.uk
dir: On junct A53 & A41, archway off A53

The elegant Grade II listed Georgian farmhouse stands in a large pleasant garden and has been modernised to provide quality accommodation. There is a choice of comfortable lounges, and the Cottage Restaurant features imaginative dishes using local produce. Secure parking is an additional benefit.

Rooms 5 (2 fmly)

Raven
★★★ 78% ⊚⊚ HOTEL

☎ 01952 727251 ▤ 01952 728416
Barrow St TF13 6EN
e-mail: enquiry@ravenhotel.com
web: www.ravenhotel.com
dir: M54 junct 4 or 5, take A442 S, then A4169 to Much Wenlock

This town centre hotel is spread across several historic buildings with a 17th-century coaching inn at its centre.

Accommodation is well furnished and equipped to offer modern comfort, with some ground floor rooms. Public areas feature an interesting collection of prints and memorabilia connected with the modern-day Olympic Games - an idea which was, interestingly, born in Much Wenlock.

Rooms 15 (7 annexe) **Facilities** Beauty salon **Conf** Board 16 Thtr 16 **Parking** 30 **Notes** ⊗

Gaskell Arms
★★★ 74% SMALL HOTEL

☎ 01952 727212 ▤ 01952 728505
Bourton Rd TF13 6AQ
e-mail: maxine@gaskellarms.co.uk
web: www.gaskellarms.co.uk
dir: M6 junct 10A onto M54, exit at junct 4, follow signs for Ironbridge/Much Wenlock & A4169

This 17th-century former coaching inn has exposed beams and log fires in the public areas, and much original charm and character is retained throughout. In addition to the lounge bar and restaurant, offering a wide range of meals and snacks, there is a small bar which is popular with locals. Well-equipped bedrooms, some located within stylishly renovated stables, provide good standards of comfort.

Rooms 16 (3 fmly) (5 GF) **S** £75-£85; **D** £95-£120 (incl. bkfst)* **Facilities** FTV **Parking** 40 **Notes** LB ⊗

Hundred House Hotel
★★ 84% ⊚⊚ HOTEL

☎ 01952 580240 ▤ 01952 580260
Bridgnorth Rd TF11 9EE
e-mail: reservations@hundredhouse.co.uk
web: www.hundredhouse.co.uk
dir: between Telford & Bridgnorth on A442. In town centre

Primarily Georgian, but with parts dating back to the 14th century, this friendly family owned and run hotel offers individually styled, well-equipped bedrooms which have period furniture and attractive soft furnishings. Public areas include cosy bars and intimate dining areas where memorable meals are served. There is an attractive conference centre in the old barn.

Rooms 10 (4 fmly) **Facilities** Xmas New Year Wi-fi **Conf** Class 30 Board 32 Thtr 80 **Parking** 45 **Notes** LB Closed 25 & 26 Dec nights RS Sun evenings Civ Wed

Wynnstay
★★★★ 80% ⊚⊚ HOTEL   **CLASSIC** BRITISH HOTELS

☎ 01691 655261 ▤ 01691 670606
Church St SY11 2SZ
e-mail: info@wynnstayhotel.com
web: www.wynnstayhotel.com
dir: B4083 to town, fork left at Honda Garage, right at lights. Hotel opposite church

This Georgian property was once a coaching inn and posting house and surrounds a unique 200-year-old Crown Bowling Green. Elegant public areas include a health, leisure and beauty centre, which is housed in a former coach house. Well-equipped bedrooms are individually styled and decorated and include several suites, four-poster rooms and a self-catering apartment.

continued

OSWESTRY *continued*

The Four Seasons Restaurant has a well deserved reputation for its food, and the adjacent Wilsons café/bar is a stylish informal alternative.

Rooms 34 (5 fmly) **S** £65-£85; **D** £95-£111*
Facilities Spa FTV 🍸 Gym Crown bowling green Beauty suite New Year Wi-fi **Conf** Class 150 Board 50 Thtr 290 **Parking** 80 **Notes** ⊗ Civ Wed 90

See advert on page 397

Lion Quays Waterside Resort

★★★★ 78% HOTEL

☎ 01691 684300 📠 01691 684313
Moreton, Weston Rhyn SY11 3EN
e-mail: reservations@lionquays.co.uk
dir: On A483 3m north of Oswestry

This resort is situated beside the Llangollen Canal and is in a convenient location for visiting Chester to the north and the Snowdonia region to the west. The comfortable bedrooms have views over the countryside or the magnificent grounds and gardens. Guests can dine either in the Waterside Bar or the newly created Country Club which offers the use of a stunning 25-metre swimming pool, a modern gym plus spa facilities. Extensive conference and meeting facilities are also available.

Rooms 82 (3 fmly) (24 GF) (5 smoking) **S** £50-£90; **D** £80-£110 (incl. bkfst)* **Facilities** Spa STV 🍸 supervised 🏊 Gym Xmas New Year Wi-fi **Conf** Class 200 Board 150 Thtr 600 Del from £100 to £130* **Services** Lift Air con **Parking** 250 **Notes** LB Civ Wed 600

Pen-y-Dyffryn Country Hotel

★★★ 82% ⊛⊛ HOTEL

☎ 01691 653700 📠 01978 211004
Rhydycroesau SY10 7JD
e-mail: stay@peny.co.uk
web: www.peny.co.uk
dir: A5 into town centre. Follow signs to Llansilin on B4580, hotel 3m W of Oswestry before Rhydycroesau

Peacefully situated in five acres of grounds, this charming old house dates back to around 1840, when it was built as a rectory. The tastefully appointed public rooms have real fires during cold weather, and the accommodation includes several mini-cottages, each with its own patio. This hotel attracts many guests for its food and attentive, friendly service.

Rooms 12 (4 annexe) (1 fmly) (1 GF) **S** £85-£86; **D** £56-£82 (incl. bkfst)* **Facilities** STV Guided walks Xmas New Year Wi-fi **Parking** 18 **Notes** LB No children 3yrs Closed 18 Dec-19 Jan

Sebastian's Hotel & Restaurant

★★ 85% ⊛⊛ SMALL HOTEL

☎ 01691 655444 📠 01691 653452
45 Willow St SY11 1AQ
e-mail: sebastians.rest@virgin.net
web: www.sebastians-hotel.co.uk
dir: Follow town centre signs. Take road towards Selattyn & Llansilin for 300yds into Willow St, hotel on left

A privately owned and personally run hotel and restaurant dating back to 1640 which has a wealth of charm and character enhanced by original features. The popular bistro-style restaurant offers skilfully prepared dishes. The well-equipped bedrooms, including four in a separate building, are tastefully appointed in a style befitting the property's character.

Rooms 6 (4 annexe) (6 fmly) (2 GF) **S** fr £65; **D** fr £75 **Facilities** Wi-fi **Parking** 7 **Notes** ⊗

Travelodge Oswestry

BUDGET HOTEL

☎ 08719 846 389 📠 0870 191 1596
Mile End Service Area SY11 4JA
web: www.travelodge.co.uk
dir: at junct of A5 & A483

Travelodge offers good quality, good value, budget accommodation. All offer family rooms sleeping up to four (two adults, two children) with en suite bathroom/shower-room, remote-control TV, tea- and coffee-making facilities and comfortable beds. Food options vary. Breakfast is at the on-site Bar Café restaurant (if available) or to take away. See also Hotel Groups pages.

Rooms 40 **S** fr £29; **D** fr £29

SHIFNAL Map 10 SJ70

Park House

★★★★ 76% ⊛ HOTEL

☎ 01952 460128 📠 01952 461658
Park St TF11 9BA
e-mail: reception@parkhousehotel.net
dir: M54 junct 4 follow A464 (Wolverhampton road) for approx 2m, under railway bridge, hotel 100yds on left

This hotel was created from what were originally two country houses of very different architectural styles. Located on the edge of the historic market town, it offers

---

guests easy access to motorway networks, a choice of banqueting and meeting rooms, plus leisure facilities. Butlers Bar and Restaurant is the setting for imaginative food. Service is friendly and attentive.

Rooms 54 (16 annexe) (4 fmly) (8 GF) (4 smoking) **S** £60-£100; **D** £85-£120 (incl. bkfst)* **Facilities** STV FTV 🍸 Gym Steam room Sauna Beauty room Xmas New Year Wi-fi **Conf** Class 80 Board 40 Thtr 160 Del from £132.50 to £150* **Services** Lift **Parking** 90 **Notes** LB Civ Wed 200

Haughton Hall

★★★ 71% HOTEL

☎ 01952 468300 📠 01952 468313
Haughton Ln TF11 8HG
e-mail: reservations@haughtonhall.com
dir: M54 junct 4 take A464 into Shifnal. Turn left into Haughton Lane, hotel 600yds on left

This listed building dates back to 1718 and stands in open parkland close to the town. It is well geared for the conference trade and also has a 9-hole par 4 golf course, fishing lake and fine leisure club. Comfortable public rooms are available and the dinner menu is extensive. Bedrooms are comfortable and well equipped.

Rooms 36 (6 annexe) (5 fmly) (3 GF) **Facilities** FTV 🍸 supervised ⚓ 9 🏊 Fishing Gym Steam room Therapy room Solarium Xmas New Year Wi-fi **Conf** Class 60 Board 25 Thtr 120 **Parking** 60 **Notes** LB ⊗ Civ Wed 120

SHREWSBURY Map 15 SJ41

See also **Church Stretton**

Mercure Albrighton Hall Hotel & Spa

★★★★ 78% ⊛⊛ HOTEL

☎ 01939 291000 📠 01939 291123
Albrighton SY4 3AG
e-mail: H6629@accor.com
web: www.mercure-uk.com
dir: From S: M6 junct 10a to M54 to end. From N: M6 junct 12 to M5 then M54. Follow signs Harlescott & Ellesmere to A528

Dating back to 1630, this former ancestral home is set in 15 acres of attractive gardens. Rooms are generally spacious and the stable rooms are particularly popular. Elegant public rooms have rich oak panelling and there is a modern, well-equipped health and fitness centre.

continued

Rooms 87 (16 annexe) (6 fmly) (21 GF) **Facilities** Spa STV ⊛ ⤴ Gym Squash Beauty treatment rooms Thermal suite Relax room Spray tan Aerobics Xmas New Year Wi-fi **Conf** Class 150 Board 80 Thtr 300 **Services** Lift **Parking** 200 **Notes** Civ Wed 250

Albright Hussey Manor Hotel & Restaurant

★★★★ 73% ⊛ HOTEL

☎ 01939 290571 & 290523 📄 01939 291143
Ellesmere Rd SY4 3AF
e-mail: info@albrighthussey.co.uk
web: www.albrighthussey.co.uk
dir: 2.5m N of Shrewsbury on A528, follow signs for Ellesmere

First mentioned in the Domesday Book, this enchanting medieval manor house is complete with a moat. Bedrooms are situated in either the sumptuously appointed main house or in the more modern wing. The intimate restaurant displays an abundance of original features and there is also a comfortable cocktail bar and lounge.

Rooms 26 (4 fmly) (8 GF) **S** £79-£130; **D** £95-£190 (incl. bkfst)* **Facilities** ⤴ Xmas New Year Wi-fi **Conf** Class 180 Board 80 Thtr 250 **Parking** 100 **Notes** LB Civ Wed 180

Rowton Castle Hotel

★★★ 88% ⊛ HOTEL

☎ 01743 884044 📄 01743 884949
Halfway House SY5 9EP
e-mail: post@rowtoncastle.com
web: www.rowtoncastle.com
dir: from A5 near Shrewsbury take A458 to Welshpool. Hotel 4m on right

Standing in 17 acres of grounds where a castle has stood for nearly 800 years, this Grade II listed building dates in parts back to 1696. Many original features remain, including the oak panelling in the restaurant and a magnificent carved oak fireplace. Most bedrooms are spacious and all have modern facilities; some have four-poster beds. The hotel has a well deserved reputation for its food and is understandably a popular venue for weddings.

Rooms 19 (3 fmly) **Facilities** ⤴ Wi-fi **Conf** Class 30 Board 30 Thtr 80 **Parking** 100 **Notes** ⊗ Civ Wed 110

Prince Rupert

★★★ 82% HOTEL

☎ 01743 499955 📄 01743 357306
Butcher Row SY1 1UQ
e-mail: post@prince-rupert-hotel.co.uk
web: www.prince-rupert-hotel.co.uk
dir: Follow town centre signs, over English Bridge & Wyle Cop Hill. Right into Fish St, 200yds

Parts of this popular town centre hotel date back to medieval times and many bedrooms have exposed beams and other original features. Luxury suites, family rooms and rooms with four-poster beds are all available. As an alternative to the main Royalist Restaurant, diners have two less formal options - La Trattoria for authentic Italian dishes and Chambers, a popular brasserie. The Camellias Tea Rooms are adjacent. The hotel's valet parking service is also commendable.

Rooms 70 (4 fmly) **S** £69; **D** £99-£175 (incl. bkfst) **Facilities** FTV Gym Weight training room Steam shower Sauna Snooker room Xmas New Year Wi-fi **Conf** Class 80 Board 40 Thtr 120 Del from £110 to £130* **Services** Lift **Parking** 70 **Notes** LB ⊗

See advert on page 400

Mytton & Mermaid

★★★ 77% ⊛⊛ HOTEL

☎ 01743 761220 📄 01743 761292
Atcham SY5 6QG
e-mail: admin@myttonandmermaid.co.uk
web: www.myttonandmermaid.co.uk
dir: From Shrewsbury over old bridge in Atcham. Hotel opposite main entrance to Attingham Park

Convenient for Shrewsbury, this ivy-clad former coaching inn enjoys a pleasant location beside the River Severn. Some bedrooms, including family suites, are in a converted stable block adjacent to the hotel. There is a large lounge bar, a comfortable lounge, and a brasserie

---

that has gained a well-deserved local reputation for the quality of its food.

Rooms 18 (7 annexe) (1 fmly) **S** £85-£95; **D** £110-£175 (incl. bkfst)* **Facilities** Fishing ♫ New Year Wi-fi **Conf** Class 24 Board 28 Thtr 70 Del from £150 to £170* **Parking** 50 **Notes** LB ⊗ Closed 25 Dec Civ Wed 80

Lord Hill

★★★ 75% HOTEL

☎ 01743 232601 📄 01743 369734
Abbey Foregate SY2 6AX
e-mail: reception@thelordhill.co.uk
web: www.thelordhill.co.uk
dir: From M54 take A5, at 1st rdbt left then 2nd rdbt take 4th exit into London Rd. At next rdbt (Lord Hill Column) take 3rd exit, hotel 300yds on left

This pleasant, attractively appointed hotel is located close to the town centre. Most of the modern bedrooms are set in a separate purpose-built property, but those in the main building include one with a four-poster, as well as full suites. Public areas include a conservatory restaurant and spacious function suites.

Rooms 36 (24 annexe) (2 fmly) (8 GF) **Facilities** FTV Beauty treatments Wi-fi **Conf** Class 180 Board 180 Thtr 250 **Parking** 110 **Notes** Civ Wed 70

The Lion

★★★ 70% HOTEL

☎ 01743 353107 📄 01743 352744
Wyle Cop SY1 1UY
e-mail: info@thelionhotelshrewsbury.com
dir: From S cross English Bridge, fork right, hotel at hill top on left. From N follow Castle St into Dogpole, hotel ahead

A 14th-century coaching inn, located in the heart of the town centre, boasts Charles Dickens as a previous guest. Bedrooms come in a variety of sizes, those at the rear being quieter. Public areas include the magnificent Adam Ballroom with oak beams and an original fireplace. Sam Haywards restaurant serves locally sourced ingredients in the homemade food.

Rooms 59 (3 fmly) **S** £76; **D** £94 (incl. bkfst)* **Facilities** Xmas New Year Wi-fi **Conf** Class 80 Board 60 Thtr 200 Del from £95 to £125* **Services** Lift **Parking** 59 **Notes** LB ⊗ Civ Wed 200

SHREWSBURY *continued*

Abbots Mead Hotel

★★ 71% METRO HOTEL

☎ 01743 235281 📄 01743 369133
9 St Julian's Friars SY1 1XL
e-mail: res@abbotsmeadhotel.co.uk
dir: Entering town from south 2nd left after English Bridge

This well maintained Georgian town house is located in a quiet cul-de-sac, near the English Bridge and close to both the River Severn and town centre with its many restaurants. Bedrooms are compact, neatly decorated and well equipped. Two lounges are available in addition to an attractive dining room, the setting for breakfasts and dinner parties, by arrangement.

Rooms 16 (2 fmly) **S** £50-£60; **D** £65-£75 (incl. bkfst)*
Facilities Wi-fi **Parking** 10 **Notes** Closed Few days over Xmas

Travelodge Shrewsbury Battlefield

BUDGET HOTEL

☎ 0871 984 6120 📄 01743 465754
A49/A53 Roundabout, Battlefield SY4 3EQ
web: www.travelodge.co.uk

Travelodge offers good quality, good value, budget accommodation. All offer family rooms sleeping up to four (two adults, two children) with en suite bathroom/shower-room, remote-control TV, tea- and coffee-making facilities and comfortable beds. Food options vary. Breakfast is at the on-site Bar Café restaurant (if available) or to take away. See also Hotel Groups pages.

Rooms 41 **S** fr £29; **D** fr £29

Travelodge Shrewsbury Bayston Hill

BUDGET HOTEL

☎ 0871 984 6103 📄 01743 874256
Bayston Hill Services SY3 0DA
web: www.travelodge.co.uk
dir: At junct of A5 & A49

Rooms 40 **S** fr £29; **D** fr £29

Telford Hotel & Golf Resort

★★★★ 75% HOTEL

☎ 01952 429977 📄 01952 586602
Great Hay Dr, Sutton Heights TF7 4DT
e-mail: telford@qhotels.co.uk
web: www.qhotels.co.uk
dir: M54 junct 4, A442. Follow signs for Telford Golf Club

Set on the edge of Telford with panoramic views of the famous Ironbridge Gorge, this hotel offers excellent standards. Smart bedrooms are complemented by spacious public areas, large conference facilities, a spa with treatment rooms, a golf course and a driving range. Ample parking is available.

Rooms 114 (8 fmly) (50 GF) **S** £75-£165; **D** £95-£185 (incl. bkfst)* **Facilities** Spa STV ⑤ ⌁ 18 Putt green Gym Xmas New Year Wi-fi **Conf** Class 220 Board 100 Thtr 350 Del from £119 to £165* **Services** Lift **Parking** 200 **Notes** LB Civ Wed 250

Best Western Valley

★★★ 81% ◎◎ HOTEL

☎ 01952 432247 📄 01952 432308
TF8 7DW
e-mail: info@thevalleyhotel.co.uk
dir: M6, M54 junct 6 onto A5223 to Ironbridge

This privately owned hotel is situated in attractive
gardens, close to the famous Iron Bridge. It was once the
home of the Maws family who manufactured ceramic
tiles, and fine examples of their craft are found
throughout the house. Bedrooms vary in size and are split
between the main house and a mews development;
imaginative meals are served in the attractive Chez
Maws restaurant.

Rooms 44 (3 fmly) (6 GF) **Facilities** FTV Wi-fi
Conf Class 80 Board 60 Thtr 150 Del from £130 to £160*
Services Lift **Parking** 80 **Notes** LB ⊗ Closed 24 Dec-2
Jan RS 25 Dec Civ Wed 150

Hadley Park House

★★★ 78% ◎ HOTEL

☎ 01952 677269 📄 01952 676938
Hadley Park TF1 6QJ
e-mail: info@hadleypark.co.uk
dir: Off Hadley Park Island off A442 to Whitchurch

Located in Telford, but close to Ironbridge this elegant
Georgian mansion is situated in three acres of its own
grounds. Bedrooms are spacious and well equipped.
There is a comfortable bar and lounge and meals are
served in the attractive conservatory-style restaurant.

Rooms 12 (3 fmly) **Facilities** FTV New Year Wi-fi
Conf Class 40 Board 30 Thtr 80 **Parking** 40 **Notes** LB ⊗
Closed 26 Dec & 1 Jan Civ Wed 80

Holiday Inn Telford/ Ironbridge

★★★ 75% HOTEL

☎ 01952 527000 📄 01952 291949
St Quentin Gate TF3 4EH
e-mail: holidayinn.telford@virgin.net
web: www.holidayinn.co.uk
dir: From N: M6 junct 11. From S: M6 junct 10A, take
M54. Exit at junct 4, follow Telford International Centre
signs. Hotel adjacent

This large, modern, purpose built hotel is located close to
the International Exhibition Centre and is convenient for
the town centre and M54. Well-equipped accommodation
includes executive bedrooms. Public areas are attractively
designed and include a business centre and leisure club.

Rooms 150 (72 fmly) (48 GF) (4 smoking) **S** £70-£145;
D £70-£145* **Facilities** Spa STV ⓥ Gym Sauna Steam
room Wi-fi **Conf** Class 120 Board 80 Thtr 250
Del from £95 to £145* **Services** Lift Air con **Parking** 296
Notes LB Civ Wed 250

Buckatree Hall

★★★ 70% HOTEL

☎ 01952 641821 📄 01952 247540
The Wrekin, Wellington TF6 5AL
dir: M54 junct 7, turn left. At T-junct turn left, hotel
0.25m on left

The name Buckatree means 'the well where deer drink'.
Little wonder then that the hotel started life as a hunting
lodge. The extensive wooded estates on the slopes of the
Wrekin make for a peaceful retreat for guests as well as
providing a scenic wedding venue. Bedrooms are
furnished and decorated in a traditional style and some
have balconies.

Rooms 62 (5 fmly) (15 GF) **Facilities** STV Xmas New Year
Wi-fi **Conf** Class 110 Board 48 Thtr 180 **Services** Lift
Parking 85 **Notes** LB Civ Wed 180

TELFORD *continued*

Travelodge Telford Shawbirch

BUDGET HOTEL

☎ 0871 984 6110 📠 01952 246534
Whitchurch Dr, Shawbirch TF1 3QA
web: www.travelodge.co.uk
dir: M54 junct 6, follow Whitchurch signs to Shawbirch rdbt. Lodge on A5223 at A442 & B4394 junct.

Travelodge offers good quality, good value, budget accommodation. All offer family rooms sleeping up to four (two adults, two children) with en suite bathroom/shower-room, remote-control TV, tea- and coffee-making facilities and comfortable beds. Food options vary. Breakfast is at the on-site Bar Café restaurant (if available) or to take away. See also Hotel Groups pages.

Rooms 40 **S** fr £29; **D** fr £29

TELFORD SERVICE AREA (M54)   Map 10 SJ70

Days Inn Telford

BUDGET HOTEL

☎ 01952 238400 📠 01952 238410
Telford Services, Priorslee Rd TF11 8TG
e-mail: telford.hotel@welcomebreak.co.uk
web: www.welcomebreak.co.uk
dir: M54 junct 4

This modern building offers accommodation in smart, spacious and well-equipped bedrooms, suitable for families and business travellers, and all with en suite bathrooms. Continental breakfast is available, and other refreshments may be taken at the nearby family restaurant. See also the Hotel Groups pages.

Rooms 48 (45 fmly) (21 GF) **S** £29-£59; **D** £39-£79*
Conf Board 8 Del from £79 to £169*

WESTON-UNDER-REDCASTLE   Map 15 SJ52

Hawkstone Park Hotel

Ⓤ

☎ 01948 841700 📠 01939 200335
SY4 5UY
e-mail: enquiries@hawkstone.co.uk
dir: 1m E of A49 between Shrewsbury & Whitchurch

Currently the rating for this establishment is not confirmed. This may be due to a change of ownership or because it has only recently joined the AA rating scheme. For further details please see the AA website: theAA.com

Rooms 67 (19 annexe) (2 fmly) (26 GF) **S** £49-£119; **D** £69-£129 (incl. bkfst)* **Facilities** STV ⚓ 42 Putt green ⚓ Xmas New Year **Conf** Class 90 Board 50 Thtr 200 Del from £95 to £130* **Parking** 200 **Notes** LB Civ Wed 200

WHITCHURCH   Map 15 SJ54

Macdonald Hill Valley

★★★★ 76% HOTEL

☎ 0844 879 9000 📠 01948 667373
Tarporley Rd SY13 4JH
e-mail: general.hillvalley@macdonald-hotels.co.uk
web: www.macdonald-hotels.co.uk/hillvalley
dir: 2nd exit off A41 towards Whitchurch

Located in rural surroundings on the town's outskirts, this modern hotel is surrounded by two golf courses and very well equipped leisure spa is also available. Spacious bedrooms, with country views, are furnished in minimalist style and public areas include a choice of bar lounges and extensive conference facilities.

Rooms 80 (27 GF) **S** £70-£143; **D** £80-£153 (incl. bkfst)* **Facilities** Spa STV ⚓ ⚓ 18 Putt green Gym Xmas New Year Wi-fi **Conf** Class 150 Board 150 Thtr 300 Del from £120 to £155* **Services** Lift **Parking** 300 **Notes** LB ⚓ Civ Wed 300

Dodington Lodge

★★★ 72% SMALL HOTEL

☎ 01948 662539 📠 01948 667992
Dodington SY13 1EN
e-mail: info@dodingtonlodge.co.uk
web: www.dodingtonlodge.co.uk
dir: From S on A41/A49 towards Whitchurch, hotel on left

This privately owned hotel is conveniently situated close to the centre of the town, within easy reach of Chester and North Wales. Bedrooms are tastefully decorated and well equipped, and guests will find a welcoming atmosphere in the lounge bar. A choice of eating options is offered - from a light snack to a full meal. The function suite is a popular choice for weddings and meetings.

Rooms 10 (2 fmly) **S** £59.50-£74.50; **D** £69.50-£84.50 (incl. bkfst) **Facilities** Wi-fi **Conf** Class 40 Board 25 Thtr 60 Del from £85 to £100 **Parking** 45 **Notes** LB ⚓

SOMERSET

BATH   Map 4 ST76

See also **Colerne (Wiltshire) & Hinton Charterhouse**

Macdonald Bath Spa

★★★★★ 84% ⚓⚓ HOTEL

☎ 0844 879 9106 & 01225 444424 📠 01225 444006
Sydney Rd BA2 6JF
e-mail: sales.bathspa@macdonald-hotels.co.uk
web: www.macdonaldhotels.co.uk/bathspa
dir: A4, left onto A36 at 1st lights. Right at lights after pedestrian crossing left into Sydney Place. Hotel 200yds on right

A delightful Georgian mansion set amidst seven acres of pretty landscaped grounds, just a short walk from the many and varied delights of the city centre. A timeless elegance pervades the gracious public areas and bedrooms. Facilities include a popular leisure club, a choice of dining options and a number of meeting rooms.

Rooms 129 (3 fmly) (17 GF) **S** £115-£250; **D** £130-£298 (incl. bkfst) **Facilities** Spa STV ⚓ supervised ⚓ Gym Beauty treatment Thermal suite Outdoor hydro pool Whirlpool Xmas New Year Wi-fi **Conf** Class 100 Board 50 Thtr 130 Del from £160 to £295 **Services** Lift **Parking** 160 **Notes** LB Civ Wed 130

The Royal Crescent

★★★★★ 84% ◉◉ HOTEL

☎ 01225 823333 📠 01225 339401
16 Royal Crescent BA1 2LS
e-mail: info@royalcrescent.co.uk
web: www.vonessenhotels.co.uk
dir: From A4, right at lights. 2nd left onto Bennett St. Continue into The Circus, 2nd exit onto Brock St

John Wood's masterpiece of fine Georgian architecture provides the setting for this elegant hotel in the centre of the world famous Royal Crescent. Spacious, air-conditioned bedrooms are individually designed and furnished with antiques. Delightful central grounds lead to a second house, which is home to further rooms, the award-winning Dower House restaurant and the Bath House which offers therapies and treatments. Von Essen Hotels - AA Hotel Group of the Year 2009-10.

Rooms 45 (8 fmly) (7 GF) **Facilities** Spa STV FTV ⊞ ⛵ Gym 1920s river launch Xmas New Year Wi-fi **Conf** Class 25 Board 24 Thtr 50 **Services** Lift Air con **Parking** 27 **Notes** Civ Wed 50

INSPECTORS' CHOICE

The Bath Priory Hotel, Restaurant & Spa

★★★★ ◉◉◉ HOTEL

☎ 01225 331922 📠 01225 448276
Weston Rd BA1 2XT
e-mail: mail@thebathpriory.co.uk
web: www.thebathpriory.co.uk
dir: Adjacent to Victoria Park

Set in delightful walled gardens, this attractive Georgian house provides peace and tranquillity, within easy reach of the city. After extensive refurbishment, the stylish new restaurant operation is now overseen by Michael Caines and offers memorable, classic dishes. An extensive display of paintings and fine art adorn the sumptuously furnished day rooms, whilst bedrooms are equally stylishly and boast beautifully appointed en suites. A new Garden Spa is under construction.

The Bath Priory Hotel, Restaurant & Spa

Rooms 31 (2 fmly) (1 GF) **S** £185-£250; **D** £260-£410 (incl. bkfst)* **Facilities** Spa STV ⊞ ⛵ Gym Xmas New Year Wi-fi **Conf** Class 25 Board 25 Thtr 32 Del from £265 to £295* **Parking** 40 **Notes** ⊗ Civ Wed 80

BATH *continued*

Barceló Combe Grove Manor

★★★★ 73% ◉◉
COUNTRY HOUSE HOTEL

☎ 01225 834644 📠 01225 834961
Brassknocker Hill, Monkton Combe BA2 7HS
e-mail: combegrovemanor@barcelo-hotels.co.uk
web: www.barcelo-hotels.co.uk
dir: Exit A36 at Limpley Stoke onto Brassknocker Hill.
Hotel 0.5m up hill on left

Set in over 80 acres of gardens, this Georgian mansion
commands stunning views over Limpley Stoke Valley.
Most bedrooms are in the Garden Lodge, a short walk
from the main house. The superb range of indoor and
outdoor leisure facilities includes a beauty clinic with
holistic therapies, golf, tennis and two pools.

Rooms 42 (33 annexe) (5 fmly) (8 GF) **Facilities** Spa STV
🏊 supervised ⚲ ⚓ 5 🅟 Putt green ⛳ Gym Squash
Driving range Xmas New Year Wi-fi **Conf** Class 60
Board 30 Thtr 90 Del from £115* **Parking** 400 **Notes** ⊗
Civ Wed 50

INSPECTORS' CHOICE

Queensberry

★★★ ◉◉ HOTEL

☎ 01225 447928 📠 01225 446065
Russel St BA1 2QF
e-mail: reservations@thequeensberry.co.uk
web: www.thequeensberry.co.uk
dir: 100mtrs from the Assembly Rooms

This charming family-run hotel, situated in a quiet
residential street near the city centre, consists of four
delightful townhouses. The spacious bedrooms offer
deep armchairs, marble bathrooms and a range of
modern comforts. Sumptuously furnished sitting rooms
add to The Queensberry's appeal and allow access to
the very attractive and peaceful walled gardens. The
Olive Tree is a stylish restaurant that combines
Georgian opulence with contemporary simplicity.
Innovative menus are based on best quality ingredients
and competent cooking. Valet parking proves a useful
service.

Rooms 29 (2 fmly) (2 GF) **S** £115-£170; **D** £120-£425*
Facilities FTV Wi-fi **Conf** Class 12 Board 25 Thtr 35
Del from £215 to £260* **Services** Lift **Parking** 9
Notes ⊗

Best Western The Cliffe

★★★ 84% ◉ HOTEL

☎ 01225 723226 📠 01225 723871
Cliffe Dr, Crowe Hill, Limpley Stoke BA2 7FY
e-mail: cliffe@bestwestern.co.uk
dir: A36 S from Bath onto B3108 at lights left towards
Bradford-on-Avon, 0.5m. Right before bridge through
village, hotel on right

With stunning countryside views, this attractive country
house is just a short drive from the City of Bath.
Bedrooms vary in size and style but are well equipped;
several are particularly spacious and a number of rooms
are on the ground floor. The restaurant overlooks the well-
tended garden and offers a tempting selection of
carefully prepared dishes. Wi-fi is available throughout.

Rooms 11 (3 annexe) (2 fmly) (4 GF) **S** £85-£120;
D £130-£200 (incl. bkfst)* **Facilities** ⚲ Xmas New Year
Wi-fi **Conf** Class 15 Board 10 Thtr 20 Del from £120 to
£150* **Parking** 20 **Notes** LB

Dukes

★★★ 82% ◉◉ SMALL HOTEL

☎ 01225 787960 🖹 01225 787961
Great Pulteney St BA2 4DN
e-mail: info@dukesbath.co.uk
web: www.dukesbath.co.uk
dir: A46 to Bath, at rdbt right on A4. 4th set of lights turn left (A36), then right onto Great Pulteney St. Hotel on left

A fine elegant, Grade I listed Georgian building, just a few minutes' walk from Pulteney Bridge. The well-equipped bedrooms, which differ in size and style, provide plenty of comfort and have flat-screen TVs; suites and ground-floor rooms are available. Staff are particularly friendly and attentive and contribute to an engaging and welcoming atmosphere. There is a courtyard terrace, leading from the lounge/bar, where guests can enjoy an aperitif or lunch during the summer months. The Cavendish restaurant offers a very creative and interesting menu in a relaxed, light and airy environment.

Rooms 17 (5 fmly) (2 GF) **S** £99-£140; **D** £131-£232 (incl. bkfst)* **Facilities** FTV Xmas New Year Wi-fi **Conf** Board 20 Thtr 35 Del from £145 to £165* **Notes** LB

Haringtons

★★★ 79% SMALL HOTEL

☎ 01225 461728 & 445883 🖹 01225 444804
8-10 Queen St BA1 1HE
e-mail: post@haringtonshotel.co.uk
web: www.haringtonshotel.co.uk
dir: A4 to George St & turn into Milsom St. 1st right into Quiet St & 1st left into Queen St

Dating back to the 18th century, this hotel is situated in the heart of the city and provides all the expected modern facilities and comforts. The café-bistro is light and airy and is open throughout the day for light meals and refreshments. A warm welcome is assured from the proprietors and staff, making this a delightful place to stay.

Rooms 13 (3 fmly) **Facilities** STV FTV Xmas Wi-fi **Conf** Class 10 Board 12 Thtr 18 **Parking** 11 **Notes** ⊗

Bailbrook House Hotel

★★★ 78% HOTEL

☎ 01225 855100 🖹 01225 855200
Eveleigh Av, London Road West BA1 7JD
e-mail: bailbrook@hilwoodresorts.com
web: www.bailbrookhouse.co.uk
dir: M4 junct 18/A46, at bottom of long hill take slip road to city centre. At rdbt take 1st exit, London Rd. Hotel 200mtrs on left

Located in its own grounds, just a short drive or bus ride from the city centre, this establishment is made up of a historic main house with annexe buildings where the bedrooms, restaurant and bar are situated. It is suited to both business and leisure guests; extensive conference facilities are available. There is a first-floor bar, and a ground-floor restaurant where freshly made dishes may be enjoyed.

Rooms 78 (78 annexe) (2 fmly) (26 GF) **S** £60-£158; **D** £70-£158* **Facilities** FTV 🏊 Gym Sauna Wi-fi **Conf** Class 72 Board 40 Thtr 160 Del from £130 to £178* **Parking** 120 **Notes** ⊗ Civ Wed 120

Mercure Francis

★★★ 73% HOTEL

☎ 01225 424105 & 338970 🖹 01225 319715
Queen Square BA1 2HH
e-mail: h6636@accor.com
web: www.mercure.com
dir: M4 junct 18/A46 to Bath junct. 3rd exit onto A4, right into George St, left into Gay St into Queen Sq. Hotel on left

Overlooking Queen Square in the centre of the city, this elegant Georgian hotel is situated within walking distance of Bath's many attractions. Public rooms provide a variety of environments where guests can eat, drink and relax - from the informal café-bar to the traditional lounge and more formal restaurant. Bedrooms have air conditioning.

Rooms 95 (17 fmly) (5 smoking) **Facilities** Xmas New Year Wi-fi **Conf** Class 40 Board 30 Thtr 80 **Services** Lift **Parking** 40 **Notes** LB Civ Wed 100

Best Western Abbey Hotel

★★★ 72% HOTEL

☎ 0845 130 2556 & 01225 461603 🖹 0870 950 2443
North Pde BA1 1LF
e-mail: ahres@compasshotels.co.uk
dir: Close to the Abbey in city centre

Originally built for a wealthy merchant in the 1740s and forming part of a handsome Georgian terrace, this welcoming hotel is situated in the heart of the city. The thoughtfully equipped bedrooms vary in size and style. Public areas include a smart lounge bar and although the restaurant is available, many guests take dinner in the lounge or choose from extensive room service menu.

Rooms 60 (4 fmly) (2 GF) **S** £75-£105; **D** £99-£141* **Facilities** FTV Wi-fi **Services** Lift **Notes** ⊗

Pratt's

★★★ 72% HOTEL

☎ 01225 460441 🖹 01225 448807
South Pde BA2 4AB
e-mail: pratts@forestdale.com
web: www.prattshotel.co.uk
dir: A46 into city centre. Left at 1st lights (Curfew Pub), right at next lights. 2nd exit at next rdbt, right at lights, left at next lights, 1st left into South Pde

Built in 1743 this popular Georgian hotel still has many original features and is centrally placed for exploring Bath. The bedrooms, each with their own individual character and style, offer great comfort. The lounge has original open fireplaces and offers a relaxing venue for afternoon tea.

Rooms 46 (2 fmly) **S** £70-£100; **D** £90-£155 (incl. bkfst)* **Facilities** FTV Xmas New Year Wi-fi **Conf** Class 12 Board 20 Thtr 50 **Services** Lift

Carfax

★★★ Ⓐ HOTEL

☎ 01225 462089 🖹 01225 443257
13-15 Great Pulteney St BA2 4BS
e-mail: reservations@carfaxhotel.co.uk
dir: A36 onto Great Pulteney St

Rooms 30 (5 fmly) (4 GF) **S** £75-£85; **D** £105-£160 (incl. bkfst)* **Facilities** STV FTV Wi-fi Child facilities **Conf** Class 18 Board 12 Thtr 30 Del from £96 to £150* **Services** Lift **Parking** 13 **Notes** LB ⊗

BATH *continued*

Old Malt House

★★ 74% HOTEL

☎ 01761 470106 ▤ 01761 472726
Radford, Timsbury BA2 0QF
e-mail: hotel@oldmalthouse.co.uk
dir: A367 towards Radstock for 1m, pass Park & Ride, right onto B3115 towards Tunley & Timsbury. At sharp bend straight ahead & hotel 2nd left, 50mtrs from junct

Dating back to 1835, this building was originally the malt house for the Radford Brewery. Just six miles from Bath, this small and welcoming family-run hotel is an ideal base for exploring many places of interest. Bedrooms are individual in style but all have lovely countryside views. In addition to the convivial bar/lounge, the patio is also a popular venue for drinks before enjoying some good, honest home-cooking in the restaurant.

Rooms 11 (1 fmly) (2 GF) **S** £60; **D** £75-£90 (incl. bkfst)*
Parking 20 **Notes** ⊗ Closed Xmas & New Year

Wentworth House Hotel

★★ 68% HOTEL

☎ 01225 339193 ▤ 01225 310460
106 Bloomfield Rd BA2 2AP
e-mail: stay@wentworthhouse.co.uk
web: www.wentworthhouse.co.uk
dir: A36 towards Bristol at railway arches, hotel on right

This hotel is located on the outskirts of Bath yet is within walking distance of the city. Bedrooms vary in size and style; ground-floor rooms have their own conservatory seating area, some have four-posters and one has superb city views. The dinner menu features authentic home-cooked Indian dishes. There is a garden, which has a pool to enjoy in fine weather.

Rooms 19 (2 fmly) **S** £50-£85; **D** £65-£135 (incl. bkfst)
Facilities STV FTV ⤏ Xmas Wi-fi **Conf** Class 40 Board 35 Del from £115 to £135 **Parking** 19 **Notes** ⊗ No children 7yrs

Express by Holiday Inn Bath

BUDGET HOTEL

☎ 0870 444 2792 ▤ 0870 444 2793
Lower Bristol Rd, Brougham Hayes BA2 3QU
e-mail: bath@ebhi.fsnet.co.uk
web: www.hiexpress.co.uk/bath
dir: from A4, right into Bathwick St, over rdbt onto Pulteney Rd. Into Claverton St, straight over at next rdbt (Lower Bristol Rd). Hotel opposite Sainsburys

A modern hotel ideal for families and business travellers. Fresh and uncomplicated, the spacious rooms include Sky TV, power shower and tea and coffee-making facilities. Continental buffet breakfast is included in the room rate; other meals may be taken at the nearby family pub or restaurant. See also the Hotel Groups pages.

Rooms 126 (75 fmly) (31 GF) **Conf** Class 10 Board 20 Thtr 30

Travelodge Bath Central

BUDGET HOTEL

☎ 0871 984 6219 ▤ 01225 442061
York Buildings, George St BA1 2EB
web: www.travelodge.co.uk
dir: At corner of George St (A4) & Broad St

Travelodge offers good quality, good value, budget accommodation. All offer family rooms sleeping up to four (two adults, two children) with en suite bathroom/shower-room, remote-control TV, tea- and coffee-making facilities and comfortable beds. Food options vary. Breakfast is at the on-site Bar Café restaurant (if available) or to take away. See also Hotel Groups pages.

Rooms 66 **S** fr £29; **D** fr £29

Travelodge Bath Waterside

BUDGET HOTEL

☎ 0871 984 6407 ▤ 01225 428149
Rossiter Rd, Widcombe Basin BA2 4JP
e-mail: bathwaterside@travelodge.co.uk
dir: Follow signs to city centre, at 3rd lights left onto A36 (Bathwick St) keep right, follow Puttney Rd, keep left under rail bridge, then keep right in one-way system. Double back onto Rossiter Rd. Lodge on left

Rooms 53 **S** fr £29; **D** fr £29 **Conf** Class 70 Board 60 Thtr 120

BECKINGTON — Map 4 ST85

Woolpack Inn

★★ Ⓐ SMALL HOTEL

☎ 01373 831244 ▤ 01373 831223
BA12 6SP
web: www.oldenglish.co.uk
dir: On A36

Rooms 12 **Facilities** Xmas **Conf** Class 20 Board 20 Thtr 30 **Parking** 16 **Notes** No children 5yrs

Travelodge Beckington

BUDGET HOTEL

☎ 0871 984 6220 ▤ 01373 830251
BA11 6SF
web: www.travelodge.co.uk
dir: At junct of A36 & A361

Travelodge offers good quality, good value, budget accommodation. All offer family rooms sleeping up to four (two adults, two children) with en suite bathroom/shower-room, remote-control TV, tea- and coffee-making facilities and comfortable beds. Food options vary. Breakfast is at the on-site Bar Café restaurant (if available) or to take away. See also Hotel Groups pages.

Rooms 40 **S** fr £29; **D** fr £29

BRENT KNOLL — Map 4 ST35

Brent Knoll Lodge & Fox & Goose Inn

★★ 76% HOTEL

☎ 01278 760008 ▤ 01278 769236
Bristol Rd TA9 4HH
e-mail: reception@brentknolllodge.com
web: www.brentknolllodge.com
dir: On A38 approx 500mtrs N of M5 junct 22

This establishment is conveniently located just a few minutes drive from the M5 and is next door to the Fox and Goose Inn which offers a wide range of beverages and freshly prepared dishes. An American-style diner has now been added, providing something that is distinctly different. Bedrooms, some located at ground-floor level, are well equipped and spacious.

Rooms 14 (3 fmly) (7 GF) **S** £60-£70; **D** £70-£90*
Facilities FTV Xmas Wi-fi **Conf** Class 32 Board 20 Thtr 32 Del from £99 to £115* **Services** Lift Air con **Parking** 60 **Notes** LB

BRIDGWATER — Map 4 ST23

See also **Holford**

Walnut Tree
★★★ 75% ⊛ HOTEL

☎ 01278 662255 ▤ 01278 663946
North Petherton TA6 6QA
e-mail: reservations@walnuttreehotel.com
web: www.walnuttreehotel.com
dir: M5 junct 24 centre of North Petherton

Popular with both business and leisure guests, this 18th-century former coaching inn is conveniently located within easy reach of the M5. The spacious and smartly decorated bedrooms are well furnished to ensure a comfortable and relaxing stay. An extensive selection of dishes is offered in either the restaurant, or the more informal setting of the bistro.

Rooms 30 (3 fmly) (3 GF) **S** £80-£120; **D** £90-£150 (incl. bkfst)* **Facilities** FTV Xmas New Year Wi-fi **Conf** Class 60 Board 50 Thtr 100 Del from £155 to £195* **Parking** 70 **Notes** LB ⊗ Civ Wed 100

Apple Tree
★★ 72% HOTEL

☎ 01278 733238 ▤ 01278 732693
Keenthorne TA5 1HZ
e-mail: reservations@appletreehotel.com
web: www.appletreehotel.com

(For full entry see Nether Stowey)

Travelodge Bridgwater (M5)
BUDGET HOTEL   Travelodge

☎ 0871 984 6243 ▤ 01278 450 432
Huntsworth Business Park TA6 6TS
web: www.travelodge.co.uk
dir: M5 junct 24 A38 towards Bridgwater. Follow signs for Services. Lodge in Service Area

Travelodge offers good quality, good value, budget accommodation. All offer family rooms sleeping up to four (two adults, two children) with en suite bathroom/shower-room, remote-control TV, tea- and coffee-making facilities and comfortable beds. Food options vary. Breakfast is at the on-site Bar Café restaurant (if available) or to take away. See also Hotel Groups pages.

Rooms 29 **S** fr £29; **D** fr £29

CASTLE CARY — Map 4 ST63

The George
★★ 65% HOTEL

☎ 01963 350761 ▤ 01963 350035
Market Place BA7 7AH
e-mail: castlecarygeorge.aol.co.uk
dir: A303 onto A371. Signed Castle Cary, 2m on left

This 15th-century coaching inn provides well-equipped bedrooms that are generally spacious. Most rooms are at the back of the house, enjoying a quiet aspect, and some are on the ground floor; one is suitable for less able guests. Diners can choose to eat in the more formal dining room, or in one of the two cosy bars.

Rooms 17 (5 annexe) (1 fmly) (5 GF) **S** £59.50-£62.50; **D** £79.50-£95 (incl. bkfst) **Facilities** Xmas New Year Wi-fi **Conf** Class 40 Board 20 Thtr 50 Del from £109 to £200 **Parking** 7 **Notes** LB

CHARD — Map 4 ST30

Lordleaze
★★★ 75% HOTEL

☎ 01460 61066 ▤ 01460 66468
Henderson Dr, Forton Rd TA20 2HW
e-mail: info@lordleazehotel.co.uk
web: www.lordleazehotel.co.uk
dir: From Chard take A358, at St Mary's Church turn left to Forton & Winsham on B3162. Follow signs to hotel

Conveniently and quietly located, this hotel is close to the Devon, Dorset and Somerset borders, and only minutes from Chard. All bedrooms are well equipped and comfortable. The friendly lounge bar has a wood-burning stove and serves tempting bar meals. The conservatory restaurant offers more formal dining.

Rooms 25 (2 fmly) (7 GF) **S** £70-£75; **D** £105-£110 (incl. bkfst)* **Facilities** FTV Xmas New Year Wi-fi **Conf** Class 60 Board 40 Thtr 180 Del from £115 to £125* **Parking** 55 **Notes** LB Civ Wed 100

DUNSTER — Map 3 SS94

The Luttrell Arms Hotel
★★★ 73% HOTEL

☎ 01643 821555 ▤ 01643 821567
High St TA24 6SG
e-mail: info@luttrellarms.fsnet.co.uk
web: www.luttrellarms.co.uk/main.htm
dir: A39/A396 S toward Tiverton. Hotel on left opposite Yarn Market

Occupying an enviable position on the high street, this 15th-century hotel looks up towards the town's famous castle. Beautifully renovated and decorated, high levels of comfort can be found throughout. Some of the spacious bedrooms have four-poster beds. The warm and friendly staff provide attentive service in a relaxed atmosphere.

Rooms 28 (3 fmly) **S** £70-£102; **D** £104-£140 (incl. bkfst)* **Facilities** Exmoor safaris Historic tours Walking tours New Year **Conf** Class 20 Board 20 Thtr 35 **Notes** LB

Yarn Market Hotel
★★★ ⓐ HOTEL

☎ 01643 821425 ▤ 01643 821475
25-33 High St TA24 6SF
e-mail: yarnmarket.hotel@virgin.net
web: www.yarnmarkethotel.co.uk
dir: M5 junct 23, follow A39. Hotel in village centre

Rooms 20 (5 annexe) (3 fmly) **S** £55-£75; **D** £80-£120 (incl. bkfst)* **Facilities** Xmas New Year Wi-fi **Conf** Class 30 Board 25 Thtr 60 Del from £90 to £100* **Parking** 4 **Notes** LB

See advert on page 408

EXFORD Map 3 SS83

Crown

★★★ 75% ☺☺ HOTEL

☎ 01643 831554 📠 01643 831665
TA24 7PP
e-mail: info@crownhotelexmoor.co.uk
web: www.crownhotelexmoor.co.uk
dir: M5 junct 25, follow Taunton signs. Take A358 from Taunton, then B3224 via Wheddon Cross to Exford

Guest comfort is certainly the hallmark here at this family-run hotel. Afternoon tea is served in the lounge beside a roaring fire, and tempting menus of modern English fare are offered in the cosy bar and award-winning restaurant - all part of the charm of this delightful 17th-century coaching inn. Bedrooms retain a traditional style yet offer a range of modern comforts and facilities, many with views of this pretty moorland village.

Crown

Rooms 17 (3 fmly) **S** £70; **D** £110-£140 (incl. bkfst)*
Facilities Xmas New Year Wi-fi **Conf** Board 15 Del from £115 to £150* **Parking** 30 **Notes** LB

GLASTONBURY Map 4 ST53

Travelodge Glastonbury

BUDGET HOTEL

☎ 0871 984 6339
A39 Wirral Park BA6 9XE
web: www.travelodge.co.uk
dir: M5 junct 23, A39 signed Glastonbury. 10m. At rdbt take 2nd exit. At next rdbt take 1st exit. At 3rd rdbt take 1st exit. Hotel on right

Travelodge offers good quality, good value, budget accommodation. All offer family rooms sleeping up to four (two adults, two children) with en suite bathroom/shower-room, remote-control TV, tea- and coffee-making facilities and comfortable beds. Food options vary. Breakfast is at the on-site Bar Café restaurant (if available) or to take away. See also Hotel Groups pages.

Rooms 48 **S** fr £29; **D** fr £29

GORDANO SERVICE AREA (M5) Map 4 ST57

Days Inn Bristol West

BUDGET HOTEL

☎ 01275 373709 & 373624 📠 01275 374104
BS20 7XJ
e-mail: gordano.hotel@welcomebreak.co.uk
web: www.welcomebreak.co.uk
dir: M5 junct 19, follow signs for Gordano Services

This modern building offers accommodation in smart, spacious and well-equipped bedrooms, suitable for families and business travellers, and all with en suite bathrooms. Continental breakfast is available and other refreshments may be taken at the nearby family restaurant. See also the Hotel Groups pages.

Rooms 60 (52 fmly) (29 GF) **S** £39-£59; **D** £49-£69*
Conf Board 10 Del from £79 to £109*

HIGHBRIDGE Map 4 ST34

Sundowner

★★ 68% SMALL HOTEL

☎ 01278 784766 📠 01278 794133
74 Main Rd, West Huntspill TA9 3QU
e-mail: runnalls@msn.com
dir: From M5 junct 23, 3m N on A38

Friendly service and an informal atmosphere are just two of the highlights of this small hotel. The open-plan lounge/bar is a comfortable, homely area in which to relax after a busy day exploring the area or working in the locality. An extensive menu, featuring freshly cooked, imaginative dishes, is offered in the popular restaurant.

Rooms 8 (1 fmly) **S** £50-£55; **D** £65-£70 (incl. bkfst)*
Facilities Wi-fi **Parking** 18 **Notes** Closed 26-31 Dec & 1 Jan RS 25 Dec

Laburnum House Lodge

★★ Ⓐ HOTEL

☎ 01278 781830 🖷 01278 781612
Sloway Ln, West Huntspill TA9 3RJ
e-mail: laburnumhh@aol.com
web: www.laburnumhh.co.uk
dir: M5 junct 22. W on A38 approx 5m, right at Crossways Inn. 300yds & left into Sloway Ln, 300yds to hotel

Rooms 68 (15 fmly) (68 GF) **S** £48-£58; **D** £68-£84 (incl. bkfst)* **Facilities** 🐟 🚣 Fishing Gym Shooting Water-ski park Go karting Skittles Xmas New Year Wi-fi
Conf Class 60 Board 40 Thtr 100 Del from £72 to £96
Parking 100 **Notes** LB Civ Wed 100

HINTON CHARTERHOUSE   Map 4 ST75

Homewood Park

★★★ 86% ◉◉ HOTEL

☎ 01225 723731 🖷 01225 723820
BA2 7TB
e-mail: info@homewoodpark.co.uk
web: www.homewoodpark.co.uk
dir: 6m SE of Bath on A36, turn left at 2nd sign for Freshford

Homewood Park, an unassuming yet stylish Georgian house set in delightful grounds, offers relaxed surroundings and maintains high standards of quality and comfort throughout. Bedrooms, all individually decorated, include thoughtful extras to ensure a comfortable stay. The hotel has a reputation for excellent cuisine - offering an imaginative interpretation of classical dishes. Von Essen Hotels - AA Hotel Group of the Year 2009-10.

Rooms 19 (3 fmly) (2 GF) **Facilities** FTV ₹ 🚣 🛥 Xmas New Year Wi-fi **Conf** Class 30 Board 25 Thtr 40 **Parking** 30 **Notes** LB Civ Wed 50

HOLFORD   Map 4 ST14

Combe House

★★★ 75% ◉ HOTEL

☎ 01278 741382 & 741213 🖷 01278 741322
TA5 1RZ
e-mail: enquiries@combehouse.co.uk
web: www.combehouse.co.uk
dir: From A39 W left in Holford then left at T-junct. Left at fork, 0.25m to Holford Combe

Located in a peaceful wooded valley with four acres of tranquil gardens to explore, the atmosphere here is relaxed and welcoming. The individually styled bedrooms have lots of comfort - all are designed for a cosseted and pampered stay. Public areas have equal charm with traditional features interwoven with contemporary style. Food comes highly recommended with a dedicated kitchen team producing accomplished, seasonal dishes.

Rooms 18 (1 annexe) (3 fmly) (2 GF) **S** £65-£90; **D** £85-£140 (incl. bkfst)* **Facilities** 🐟 🛥 Sauna Small gym Beauty therapy treatments Xmas New Year Wi-fi **Conf** Class 30 Board 20 Thtr 30 Del from £150 to £175 **Parking** 36 **Notes** LB Civ Wed 130

HUNSTRETE   Map 4 ST66

Hunstrete House

★★★ 82% ◉◉
COUNTRY HOUSE HOTEL

☎ 01761 490490 🖷 01761 490732
BS39 4NS
e-mail: info@hunstretehouse.co.uk
web: www.hunstretehouse.co.uk
dir: from Bath take A4 to Bristol. At Globe Inn rdbt 2nd left onto A368 to Wells. 1m after Marksbury turn right for Hunstrete. Hotel next left

This delightful Georgian house enjoys a stunning setting in 92 acres of deer park and woodland on the edge of the Mendip Hills. Elegant bedrooms in the main building and coach house are both spacious and comfortable. Public areas feature antiques, paintings and fine china. The restaurant enjoys a well-deserved reputation for its fine cuisine that utilises much home-grown produce. Von Essen Hotels - AA Hotel Group of the Year 2009-10.

Rooms 25 (2 fmly) (8 GF) **Facilities** ₹ 🚣 🛥 Xmas New Year Wi-fi **Conf** Class 40 Board 30 Thtr 50 **Parking** 50 **Notes** Civ Wed 50

ILMINSTER   Map 4 ST31

Best Western Shrubbery

★★★ 78% HOTEL

☎ 01460 52108 🖷 01460 53660
TA19 9AR
e-mail: stuart@shrubberyhotel.com
web: www.shrubberyhotel.com
dir: 0.5m from A303 towards Ilminster town centre

Set in attractive terraced gardens, the Shrubbery is a well established hotel in this small town. Bedrooms are well equipped and bright, and include three ground-floor rooms and impressive executive rooms. Bar meals or full meals are available in the bar, lounges and restaurant. Additional facilities include a range of function rooms.

Rooms 21 (3 fmly) (3 GF) **S** £60-£100; **D** £80-£140 (incl. bkfst)* **Facilities** STV ₹ New Year Wi-fi **Conf** Class 100 Board 60 Thtr 200 Del from £110 to £140* **Parking** 70 **Notes** LB Closed 24-26 Dec Civ Wed 200

Travelodge Ilminster

BUDGET HOTEL

☎ 0871 984 6229 🖷 01460 53748
Southfields Roundabout, Horton Cross TA19 9PT
web: www.travelodge.co.uk
dir: on A303/A358 at junct with Ilminster bypass

Travelodge offers good quality, good value, budget accommodation. All offer family rooms sleeping up to four (two adults, two children) with en suite bathroom/shower-room, remote-control TV, tea- and coffee-making facilities and comfortable beds. Food options vary. Breakfast is at the on-site Bar Café restaurant (if available) or to take away. See also Hotel Groups pages.

Rooms 52 **S** fr £29; **D** fr £29

MARTOCK   Map 4 ST41

The Hollies

★★★ 79% HOTEL

☎ 01935 822232 🖷 01935 822249
Bower Hinton TA12 6LG
e-mail: info@thehollieshotel.com
web: www.thehollieshotel.co.uk
dir: On B3165 S of town centre off A303, take Bower Hinton slip road & follow hotel signs

Within easy access of the A303, this popular establishment offers spacious, well-equipped bedrooms that are located to the rear of the property in a purpose-built wing and include both suites and mini-suites. The bar and restaurant are housed in an attractive 17th-century farmhouse; bar meals are available in addition to the interesting main menu.

Rooms 44 (44 annexe) (2 fmly) (30 GF) **S** £90-£120; **D** £100-£140 (incl. bkfst)* **Facilities** STV FTV Wi-fi **Conf** Class 80 Board 60 Thtr 150 Del from £150 to £175* **Parking** 80 **Notes** LB ⊗ RS Xmas & New Year Civ Wed 250

MARTOCK *continued*

Ash House Country Hotel

★★★ 75% COUNTRY HOUSE HOTEL

☎ 01935 822036 & 823126 ▤ 01935 822992
41 Main St, Ash TA12 6PB
e-mail: reception@ashhousecountryhotel.co.uk
dir: Off A303 at Tintinhull Forts junct, left at top of slip
road. 0.5m into Ash, on right opposite Ash recreation
ground

Set in its own grounds, the host and hostess personally
make guests feel welcome at this Georgian, family-run
hotel. Bedrooms are equipped with a considerable
number of extras. There is a choice of two lounge areas,
and dinner, featuring fresh local produce, is served in
either the traditionally styled formal restaurant or the
relaxed environment of the conservatory which overlooks
the gardens.

Rooms 9 (2 fmly) **Facilities** STV Wi-fi **Conf** Class 30
Board 20 Thtr 50 **Parking** 35 **Notes** LB ⊗ Closed 24-26
& 31 Dec & 1 Jan Civ Wed 60

MIDSOMER NORTON	Map 4 ST65

Best Western Centurion

★★★ 78% HOTEL

☎ 01761 417711 & 412214 ▤ 01761 418357
Charlton Ln BA3 4BD
e-mail: enquiries@centurionhotel.co.uk
web: www.centurionhotel.com
dir: Off A367, 10m S of Bath

This privately owned, purpose-built hotel incorporates the
adjacent Fosse Way Country Club with its 9-hole golf
course and extensive leisure amenities. Bedrooms, some
at ground floor level, are well equipped. Public areas
include a choice of bars, an attractive lounge and a range
of meeting/function rooms. The restaurant is stylish, light
and airy with large windows overlooking the rear garden
and grounds.

Rooms 44 (4 fmly) (18 GF) **Facilities** FTV ⊗ ♨ 9 Putt
green Gym Sun bed New Year Wi-fi **Conf** Class 70
Board 50 Thtr 180 **Parking** 100 **Notes** ⊗ Closed 24-27
Dec Civ Wed 100

The Moody Goose at The Old Priory

★★★ 77% ⊛⊛ SMALL HOTEL

☎ 01761 416784 & 410846 ▤ 01761 417851
Church Square BA3 2HX
e-mail: info@theoldpriory.co.uk
web: www.theoldpriory.co.uk
dir: A362 for 1m left to High Street to lights, turn right to
small rdbt by St John's Church, turn right. Hotel ahead

Dating back to the 12th century, this establishment has
been sensitively restored, maintaining some original
features and plenty of historic charm and character.
Bedrooms, one with a four-poster, are individually styled
and furnished and all are equipped with useful extras.
The intimate, open-plan restaurant serves innovative,
carefully prepared dishes made from local produce
(whenever possible). There are two cosy lounges, where
log fires burn during cooler months.

Rooms 6 (1 fmly) **S** £85-£95; **D** £110-£145 (incl. bkfst)*
Facilities Wi-fi **Conf** Class 6 Board 12 Thtr 12
Del from £170 to £200* **Parking** 14 **Notes** ⊗ Closed 25
Dec & 1 Jan RS Sun evening

MINEHEAD	Map 3 SS94

Best Western Northfield

★★★ 74% HOTEL

☎ 01643 705155 & 0845 1302678 ▤ 01643 707715
Northfield Rd TA24 5PU
e-mail: reservations@northfield-hotel.co.uk
web: www.northfield-hotel.co.uk
dir: M5 junct 23, follow A38 to Bridgwater then A39 to
Minehead

Located conveniently close to the town centre and the
seafront, this hotel is set in delightfully maintained
gardens and has a loyal following. A range of comfortable
sitting rooms and leisure facilities, including an indoor,
heated pool is provided. A fixed-price menu is served
every evening in the oak-panelled dining room. The
attractively co-ordinated bedrooms vary in size and are
equipped to a good standard.

Rooms 30 (7 fmly) (4 GF) (6 smoking) **Facilities** STV FTV
⊗ Putt green Gym Steam room Xmas New Year Wi-fi
Conf Class 45 Board 30 Thtr 70 **Services** Lift **Parking** 34

Alcombe House

★★ 85% HOTEL

☎ 01643 705130 ▤ 01643 705130
Bircham Rd, Alcombe TA24 6BG
e-mail: alcombe.house@virgin.net
web: www.alcombehouse.co.uk
dir: On A39 on outskirts of Minehead opposite West
Somerset Community College

Located midway between Minehead and Dunster on the
coastal fringe of Exmoor National Park, this Grade II
listed, Georgian hotel offers a delightful combination of
efficient service and genuine hospitality delivered by the
very welcoming resident proprietors. Public areas include
a comfortable lounge and a candlelit dining room where a
range of carefully prepared dishes is offered from a daily-
changing menu.

Rooms 7 **S** £44; **D** £68 (incl. bkfst)* **Facilities** Xmas
Parking 9 **Notes** No children 15yrs Closed 8 Nov-18 Mar

Channel House

★★ 84% SMALL HOTEL

☎ 01643 703229 ▤ 01643 708925
Church Path TA24 5QG
e-mail: channel.house@virgin.net
dir: From A39 right at rdbt to seafront, then left onto
promenade. 1st right, 1st left to Blenheim Gdns and 1st
right into Northfield Rd

This family-run hotel offers relaxing surroundings, yet is
only a short walk from the town centre. The South West
coastal path starts from the hotel's two-acre gardens.
Many of the exceptionally well-equipped bedrooms benefit
from wonderful views. Imaginative menus are created
from the best local produce. The hotel is totally non-
smoking.

Rooms 8 **S** £66-£80; **D** £102-£130 (incl. bkfst)*
Services Air con **Parking** 10 **Notes** ⊗ No children 15yrs
Closed 29 Dec-15 Feb

See advert on opposite page

NETHER STOWEY — Map 4 ST13

Apple Tree

★★ 72% HOTEL

☎ 01278 733238 📄 01278 732693
Keenthorne TA5 1HZ
e-mail: reservations@appletreehotel.com
web: www.appletreehotel.com
dir: From Bridgwater follow A39 towards Minehead. Hotel on left 2m past Cannington

Parts of this cottage-style property, conveniently located for the coast and the M5, date back some 340 years. Bedrooms, which vary in character and style, are suited to both leisure and corporate guests; some are in a single storey annexe adjacent to the main building. Public areas include an attractive conservatory restaurant, a bar and a library lounge. The friendly owners and their staff make every effort to guarantee an enjoyable stay.

Rooms 15 (2 fmly) (5 GF) **Facilities** FTV Wi-fi
Conf Class 12 Board 14 Thtr 25 **Parking** 30 **Notes** ⊗

PODIMORE — Map 4 ST52

Travelodge Yeovil Podimore

BUDGET HOTEL
Travelodge

☎ 0871 984 6059 📄 01935 840074
BA22 8JG
web: www.travelodge.co.uk
dir: on A303, near junct with A37

Travelodge offers good quality, good value, budget accommodation. All offer family rooms sleeping up to four (two adults, two children) with en suite bathroom/shower-room, remote-control TV, tea- and coffee-making facilities and comfortable beds. Food options vary. Breakfast is at the on-site Bar Café restaurant (if available) or to take away. See also Hotel Groups pages.

Rooms 49 **S** fr £29; **D** fr £29

PORLOCK — Map 3 SS84

INSPECTORS' CHOICE

The Oaks

★★★ 🏵 HOTEL

☎ 01643 862265 📄 01643 863131
TA24 8ES
e-mail: info@oakshotel.co.uk
dir: From E of A39, enter village (road narrows to single track) then follow hotel sign. From W: down Porlock Hill, through village, hotel sign on right

A relaxing atmosphere is found at this charming Edwardian house, located near to the setting of R D Blackmore's novel *Lorna Doone*. Quietly located and set in attractive grounds, the hotel enjoys elevated views across the village towards the sea. Bedrooms are thoughtfully furnished and comfortable, and the public rooms include a charming bar and a peaceful drawing room. In the dining room, guests can choose from the daily-changing menu, which features fresh, quality local produce.

Rooms 8 **S** £127.50; **D** £195 (incl. dinner)*
Facilities FTV Xmas New Year Wi-fi **Parking** 12
Notes LB ⊗ No children 8yrs Closed Nov-Mar (ex Xmas & New Year)

SEDGEMOOR MOTORWAY SERVICE AREA (M5) — Map 4 ST35

Days Inn Sedgemoor

BUDGET HOTEL

☎ 01934 750831 📄 01934 750808
Sedgemoor BS24 0JL
e-mail: sedgemoor.hotel@welcomebreak.co.uk
web: www.welcomebreak.co.uk
dir: M5 northbound junct 21/22

This modern building offers accommodation in smart, spacious and well-equipped bedrooms, suitable for families and business travellers, and all with en suite bathrooms. Continental breakfast is available and other refreshments may be taken at the nearby family restaurant. See also the Hotel Groups pages.

Rooms 40 (39 fmly) (19 GF) **S** £39-£49; **D** £39-£69*

SHEPTON MALLET Map 4 ST64

INSPECTORS' CHOICE

Charlton House Hotel & Restaurant
★★★★ ◎◎ COUNTRY HOUSE HOTEL

☎ 01749 342008 🖷 01749 346362
Charlton Rd BA4 4PR
e-mail: enquiry@charltonhouse.com
web: www.charltonhouse.com
dir: On A361 towards Frome, 1m from town centre

The design at this delightful hotel is modelled on Mulberry fabrics and furnishings and the bedrooms are decorated in imaginative and individual style. Monty's Spa has hydrotherapy pools and treatment rooms for the ultimate pampering experience. The smart, spacious conservatory-style restaurant and easy lounges overlook the manicured lawns, and quality cooking utilises produce from the owner's Sharpham Park estate.

Rooms 25 (4 annexe) (1 fmly) **S** £147-£246; **D** £180-£465 (incl. bkfst)* **Facilities** Spa FTV 🕸 🎿 🥤 Gym Archery Clay pigeon shooting Ballooning Xmas New Year Wi-fi **Conf** Class 60 Board 40 Thtr 100 Del from £199 to £249* **Parking** 72 **Notes** LB Civ Wed 100

STON EASTON Map 4 ST65

INSPECTORS' CHOICE

Ston Easton Park
★★★★ ◎◎
COUNTRY HOUSE HOTEL

☎ 01761 241631 🖷 01761 241377
BA3 4DF
e-mail: info@stoneaston.co.uk
web: www.stoneaston.co.uk
dir: On A37

This outstanding Palladian mansion lies in extensive parklands that were landscaped by Humphrey Repton. The architecture and decorative features are stunning and the Saloon is considered to be one of Somerset's finest rooms. The helpful and attentive team provide a very efficient service, and good, award-winning cuisine is on offer. The public areas, bedrooms and bathrooms are all appointed to a very high standard. Von Essen Hotels - AA Hotel Group of the Year 2009-10.

Rooms 22 (3 annexe) (2 fmly) **S** £145-£320; **D** £175-£475 (incl. bkfst)* **Facilities** STV 🎿 Fishing 🥤 Archery Clay pigeon shooting Quad bikes Hot air balloon Xmas New Year Wi-fi **Conf** Class 60 Board 30 Thtr 100 Del from £212 to £247* **Parking** 120 **Notes** LB Civ Wed 100

STREET Map 4 ST43

Wessex
Ⓤ

☎ 01458 443383 🖷 01458 446589
High St BA16 0EF
e-mail: info@wessexhotel.com
dir: from A303, onto B3151 to Somerton. Then 7m, pass lights by Millfield School. Left at mini-rdbt

Currently the rating for this establishment is not confirmed. This may be due to a change of ownership or because it has only recently joined the AA rating scheme. For further details please see the AA website: theAA.com

Rooms 50 (4 fmly) **Facilities** FTV Xmas New Year Wi-fi **Conf** Class 120 Board 80 Thtr 400 **Services** Lift **Parking** 70 **Notes** LB ⊗ Closed 27-29 Dec & 2-6 Jan Civ Wed 200

TAUNTON Map 4 ST22

The Mount Somerset
★★★ 77% ◎◎ HOTEL

☎ 01823 442500 🖷 01823 442900
Lower Henlade TA3 5NB
e-mail: info@mountsomersethotel.co.uk
web: www.vonessenhotels.co.uk
dir: M5 junct 25, A358 towards Chard/Ilminster, at Henlade right into Stoke Rd, left at T-junct at end, then right into drive

From its elevated and rural position, this impressive Regency house has wonderful views over Taunton Vale. Some of the well-appointed bedrooms have feature bathrooms, and the elegant public rooms are stylish with an intimate atmosphere. In addition to the daily-changing, fixed-price menu, a carefully selected seasonal carte is available in the restaurant. Von Essen Hotels - AA Hotel Group of the Year 2009-10.

Rooms 11 (1 fmly) **S** £110-£150; **D** £125-£280 (incl. bkfst)* **Facilities** 🥤 Beauty treatments Xmas New Year Wi-fi **Conf** Class 30 Board 20 Thtr 60 Del from £195 to £205* **Services** Lift **Parking** 100 **Notes** Civ Wed 60

Rumwell Manor
★★★ 75% HOTEL

☎ 01823 461902 🖷 01823 254861
Rumwell TA4 1EL
e-mail: reception@rumwellmanor.co.uk
dir: On A38 on right Rumwell Inn

In a countryside location, surrounded by lovingly tended gardens, Rumwell Manor has easy access to Taunton and the M5. Bedrooms vary in style, with those in the main house offering greater space and more character. A selection of freshly prepared dishes is served in the restaurant. In addition to the cosy bar and adjacent lounge, several meeting and conference rooms are available.

Rooms 20 (10 annexe) (7 fmly) (6 GF) (4 smoking) **Facilities** Xmas New Year Wi-fi **Conf** Class 24 Board 26 Thtr 40 Del from £129.50 to £145* **Parking** 71 **Notes** LB Civ Wed 50

Farthings Country House Hotel and Restaurant

★★★ 73% ◉ SMALL HOTEL

☎ 01823 480664 & 0785 668 8128 🖹 01823 481118
Village Rd, Hatch Beauchamp TA3 6SG
e-mail: info@farthingshotel.co.uk
web: www.farthingshotel.co.uk
dir: From A358, between Taunton & Ilminster turn into Hatch Beauchamp for hotel in village centre

This delightful hotel, set in its own extensive gardens in a peaceful village location, offers comfortable accommodation, combined with all the character and charm of a building dating back over 200 years. The calm atmosphere makes this a great place to relax and unwind. Dinner service is attentive, and menus feature best quality local ingredients prepared and presented with care.

Rooms 12 (2 fmly) (3 GF) **S** £69-£155; **D** £79-£195 (incl. bkfst)* **Facilities** FTV ⚓ Xmas New Year Wi-fi **Conf** Class 15 Board 16 Thtr 50 **Parking** 25 **Notes** LB Civ Wed 200

Holiday Inn Taunton M5 Jct 25

★★★ 72% HOTEL

☎ 0870 400 9080 & 01823 281600 🖹 01823 332266
Deane Gate Av TA1 2UA
web: www.holidayinn.co.uk
dir: Adjacent to M5 junct 25, hotel behind Murco garage

Handily located close to the M5, this is a popular choice for both business and leisure travellers. Open-plan public areas have a light and airy feel with extensive leisure facilities also provided. Bedrooms, including executive rooms, are well equipped and contemporary in style. A choice of menus with daily specials is served in the relaxed atmosphere of the restaurant.

Rooms 99 (68 fmly) (48 GF) (8 smoking) **D** £80-£140 (incl. bkfst)* **Facilities** ⊕ Gym Xmas New Year Wi-fi **Conf** Class 100 Board 30 Thtr 280 Del from £100 to £184 **Services** Lift Air con **Parking** 300 **Notes** LB ⊗ Civ Wed 200

Corner House Hotel

★★★ 68% HOTEL

☎ 01823 284683 🖹 01823 323464
Park St TA1 4DQ
e-mail: res@corner-house.co.uk
web: www.corner-house.co.uk
dir: 0.3m from town centre. Hotel on junct of Park St & A38 Wellington Rd

The unusual Victorian façade of the Corner House, with its turrets and stained glass windows, belies a wealth of innovation, quality and style to be found inside. The contemporary bedrooms are equipped with state-of-the-art facilities but also offer traditional comforts, and the smart public areas include the Bistro 4DQ - a relaxed place to eat. Informality and exceptional value-for-money are the hallmarks here.

Rooms 44 (9 annexe) (8 fmly) (5 GF) **S** £69; **D** £75-£85* **Facilities** Wi-fi **Conf** Class 30 Board 28 Thtr 50 Del from £99.50 to £132.50* **Parking** 30 **Notes** ⊗

Salisbury House

★★ 78% HOTEL

☎ 01823 272083 🖹 01823 365978
14 Billetfield TA1 3NN
e-mail: res@salisburyhousehotel.co.uk
web: www.salisburyhousehotel.co.uk

Centrally and conveniently located, this elegant establishment dates back to the 1850s and retains many original features such as stained-glass windows and a wonderful oak staircase. Bedrooms provide impressive levels of comfort and quality with well-equipped, modern bathrooms. Public areas reflect the same high standards that are a hallmark throughout this hotel.

Rooms 17 (4 fmly) (6 GF) **S** £65-£105; **D** £80-£125 (incl. bkfst) **Facilities** Wi-fi **Parking** 17 **Notes** ⊗

Express by Holiday Inn Taunton, M5 Jct 25

BUDGET HOTEL

☎ 01823 624000 🖹 01823 624024
Blackbrook Business Park, Blackbrook Park Av TA1 2PX
e-mail: managertaunton@expressholidayinn.co.uk
web: www.hiexpress.com/taunton
dir: M5 junct 25. Follow signs for Blackbrook Business Park. 100yds on right

A modern hotel ideal for families and business travellers. Fresh and uncomplicated, the spacious rooms include Sky TV, power shower and tea and coffee-making facilities. Continental buffet breakfast is included in the room rate; other meals may be taken at the nearby family pub or restaurant. See also the Hotel Groups pages.

Rooms 92 (55 fmly) (22 GF) (8 smoking) **S** £39-£94.95; **D** £39-£94.95 (incl. bkfst)* **Conf** Class 24 Board 16 Thtr 30 Del from £89.95 to £125

Travelodge Taunton

BUDGET HOTEL

☎ 0871 984 6056 🖹 01823 444704
Riverside Retail Park, Hankridge Farm TA1 2LR
web: www.travelodge.co.uk
dir: M5 junct 25, follow Taunton signs. Right at 1st rdbt, right at 2nd rdbt. Lodge 100yds on right

Travelodge offers good quality, good value, budget accommodation. All offer family rooms sleeping up to four (two adults, two children) with en suite bathroom/ shower-room, remote-control TV, tea- and coffee-making facilities and comfortable beds. Food options vary. Breakfast is at the on-site Bar Café restaurant (if available) or to take away. See also Hotel Groups pages.

Rooms 64 **S** fr £29; **D** fr £29

WELLINGTON Map 3 ST12

The Cleve Hotel & Country Club

★★★ 68% HOTEL

☎ 01823 662033 🖹 01823 660874
Mantle St TA21 8SN
e-mail: reception@clevehotel.com
web: www.clevehotel.com
dir: M5 junct 26 follow signs to Wellington. Left before Total petrol station

This hotel was originally built as a gentleman's country residence in the Victorian era and from its elevated and quiet location affords lovely views of the Blackdown Hills. The atmosphere is relaxed and guests can enjoy Mediterranean influenced cuisine in the stylish restaurant. Extensive leisure facilities are available, including a heated indoor pool, a well-equipped gym, sauna and snooker table.

Rooms 20 (5 fmly) (3 GF) **S** £70-£90; **D** £85-£105.50 (incl. bkfst)* **Facilities** FTV ⊗ Gym Steam room Sauna Fitness studio Xmas Wi-fi **Conf** Class 130 Board 70 Thtr 300 **Parking** 100 **Notes** LB Civ Wed 200

Best Western Swan

★★★ 85% ◉◉ HOTEL

☎ 01749 836300   🖷 01749 836301
Sadler St BA5 2RX
e-mail: info@swanhotelwells.co.uk
dir: A39, A371, on entering Wells follow signs for Hotels & Deliveries. Hotel on right opposite cathedral

Situated in the shadow of Wells Cathedral, this privately owned hotel enjoys a truly stunning location and extends a genuinely friendly welcome. Full of character and with a rich history, the hotel has been restored and extended to provide high levels of quality and comfort. Guests can choose between the larger, period bedrooms in the main building or the more contemporary coach house rooms. Dinner in the oak-panelled restaurant should not be missed.

Rooms 50 (4 fmly) (4 GF) **D** £134-£170 (incl. bkfst)*
Facilities FTV Xmas New Year Wi-fi **Conf** Class 45 Board 40 Thtr 120 **Parking** 30 **Notes** LB ⊗ Civ Wed 90

White Hart

THE INDEPENDENTS
HOTEL ASSOCIATION

★★ 77% HOTEL

☎ 01749 672056   🖷 01749 671074
Sadler St BA5 2EH
e-mail: info@whitehart-wells.co.uk
web: www.whitehart-wells.co.uk
dir: Sadler St at start of one-way system. Hotel opposite cathedral

A former coaching inn dating back to the 15th century, this hotel offers comfortable, modern accommodation. Some bedrooms are in an adjoining former stable block

and some are at ground floor level. Public areas include a guest lounge, a bar and a popular restaurant that serves a good choice of fish, meat, vegetarian dishes and daily specials.

Rooms 15 (3 fmly) (2 GF) **S** £77.50-£85;
D £87.50-£107.50 (incl. bkfst)* **Facilities** Xmas New Year Wi-fi **Conf** Class 50 Board 35 Thtr 150 **Parking** 17 **Notes** Civ Wed 100

Coxley Vineyard

★★ 72% HOTEL

☎ 01749 670285   🖷 01749 679708
Coxley BA5 1RQ
e-mail: max@orofino.freeserve.co.uk
dir: A39 from Wells signed Coxley. Village halfway between Wells & Glastonbury. Hotel off main road at end of village

This privately owned and personally run hotel was built on the site of an old cider farm. It was later part of a commercial vineyard and some of the vines are still in evidence. It provides well equipped, modern bedrooms; most are situated on the ground floor. There is a comfortable bar and a spacious restaurant with an impressive lantern ceiling. The hotel is a popular venue for conferences and other functions.

Rooms 9 (5 fmly) (8 GF) **S** £60-£70; **D** £65-£89.50 (incl. bkfst)* **Facilities** ⚑ Xmas Wi-fi **Conf** Class 50 Board 40 Thtr 90 Del from £70 to £80* **Parking** 50 **Notes** LB

Ancient Gate House

★★ 67% HOTEL

☎ 01749 672029   🖷 01749 670319
20 Sadler St BA5 2SE
e-mail: info@ancientgatehouse.co.uk
dir: 1st hotel on left on cathedral green

Guests are treated to good old-fashioned hospitality in a friendly informal atmosphere at this charming hotel. Bedrooms, many with unrivalled cathedral views and four-poster beds, are well equipped and furnished in keeping with the age and character of the building. The Rugantino Restaurant remains popular, offering typically Italian specialities and traditional English dishes.

Rooms 8 **S** fr £70; **D** fr £80 (incl. bkfst)* **Facilities** Xmas New Year Wi-fi **Notes** LB Closed 27-29 Dec

Walnut Tree

★★ 81% ◉ HOTEL

☎ 01935 851292   🖷 01935 852119
Fore St BA22 7QW
e-mail: info@thewalnuttreehotel.com
web: www.thewalnuttreehotel.com
dir: From Yeovil take A303 towards Salisbury, pass Fleet Air Arm Museum turn right to West Camel. Hotel on right

This small hotel, where friendliness and personal service are high on the agenda, has the atmosphere of a village inn. The focus here is the imaginative cuisine offered in either the bar or the more formal dining room. The bar is traditional with oak beams and exposed brickwork. The modern bedrooms are well maintained.

Rooms 13 (6 GF) **S** £79; **D** £98-£135 (incl. bkfst)*
Facilities FTV New Year Wi-fi **Parking** 40 **Notes** ⊗ Closed 25-26 Dec & 1 Jan

See advert on page 404

The Royal Hotel

★★★ 74% HOTEL

☎ 01934 423100   🖷 01934 415135
1 South Pde BS23 1JP
e-mail: reservations@royalhotelweston.com
web: www.royalhotelweston.com
dir: M5 junct 21, follow signs to seafront. Hotel next to Winter Gardens Pavillion

The Royal, which opened in 1810, was the first hotel in Weston and occupies a prime seafront position. It is a grand building and many of the bedrooms, including some with sea views, are spacious and comfortable. A number of newly completed family apartments are also available. Public areas include a choice of bars and a refurbished restaurant which offers a range of dishes to meet all tastes. Entertainment is provided during the season.

Rooms 40 (3 annexe) (5 fmly) **S** £69-£79; **D** £99-£140 (incl. bkfst) **Facilities** Beauty room ♬ Wi-fi **Conf** Class 100 Board 60 Thtr 200 Del from £110 to £125 **Services** Lift **Parking** 152 **Notes** LB ⊗ Civ Wed 200

Beachlands

★★★ 71% HOTEL

☎ 01934 621401 🖷 01934 621966
17 Uphill Road North BS23 4NG
e-mail: info@beachlandshotel.com
web: www.beachlandshotel.com
dir: M5 junct 21, follow signs for hospital. At hospital rdbt follow signs for beach, hotel 300yds before beach

This popular hotel is very close to the 18-hole links course and a short walk from the seafront. Elegant public areas include a bar, a choice of lounges and a bright dining room. Bedrooms vary slightly in size, but all are well equipped for both the business and leisure guest. There is the added bonus of a 10-metre indoor pool and sauna.

Rooms 21 (6 fmly) (11 GF) **S** £65-£100; **D** £80-£133.95 (incl. bkfst)* **Facilities** ⊘ New Year Wi-fi **Conf** Class 20 Board 30 Thtr 60 Del from £90 to £110 **Parking** 28 **Notes** LB ⊗ Closed 23 Dec-2 Jan Civ Wed 110

Lauriston Hotel

★★★ 70% HOTEL

☎ 01934 620758 🖷 01934 621154
6-12 Knightstone Rd, N BS23 2AN
e-mail: lauriston.hotel@actionforblindpeople.org.uk
dir: 1st right after Winter Gardens, hotel entrance opposite Cabot public house

A friendly welcome is assured at this pleasant hotel, located right on the seafront, just a few minutes' stroll from the pier. The hotel extends a warm welcome to everyone but caters especially for visually impaired people, their family, friends and guide dogs. There are comfortable and well-appointed bedrooms; special facilities for the guide dogs are, of course, available.

Rooms 37 (2 fmly) (8 GF) **S** £40-£59; **D** £80-£118 (incl. bkfst & dinner)* **Facilities** ♬ Xmas New Year **Conf** Class 12 Board 10 Thtr 18 Del from £56 to £75* **Services** Lift **Parking** 16 **Notes** LB Closed 4-30 Jan

New Birchfield

★★ 69% HOTEL

☎ 01934 621839 & 621829 🖷 01934 626474
8-9 Manilla Crescent BS23 2BS
e-mail: newbirchfieldhotel@aol.com
dir: M5 junct 21/22. Hotel on seafront at N end of town

This establishment, popular with coach parties, is located just over the road from the beach. Bedrooms are individually sized and styled; some have sea views and some are located on the ground floor. There is a first-floor lounge and the dining room has large picture windows to make the most of the pleasant views. There is daily entertainment after dinner.

Rooms 30 (4 fmly) (4 GF) **S** £40-£42; **D** £76-£84 (incl. bkfst)* **Facilities** ♬ Xmas New Year **Services** Lift **Parking** 10 **Notes** LB Closed Jan

New Ocean

★★ 68% HOTEL

☎ 01934 621839 & 621829 🖷 01934 626474
Madeira Cove BS23 2BS
e-mail: newoceanhotel@aol.com
web: www.newoceanhotel.co.uk
dir: M5 junct 21/22 follow signs for Seafront North

Ideally positioned on the seafront, opposite the Marine Lake, several bedrooms at this family-run hotel enjoy pleasant views over Weston Bay. In the downstairs restaurant, dinner offers traditional home cooking using fresh ingredients. The smart public areas include a well-furnished bar and lounge, where entertainment is regularly provided.

Rooms 53 (2 fmly) **S** £40-£42; **D** £76-£84 (incl. bkfst) **Facilities** ♬ Xmas New Year Wi-fi **Services** Lift **Parking** 6 **Notes** LB RS Jan

Anchor Head

★★ 64% HOTEL **Leisureplex**

☎ 01934 620880 🖷 01934 621767
19 Claremont Crescent, Birnbeck Rd BS23 2EE
e-mail: anchor.weston@alfatravel.co.uk
dir: M5 junct 21/A370 to seafront, right towards north end of resort past Grand Pier towards Brimbeck Pier. Hotel at end of terrace on left

Enjoying a very pleasant location with views across the bay, the Anchor Head offers a varied choice of comfortable lounges and a relaxing outdoor patio area. Bedrooms and bathrooms are traditionally furnished and include several ground-floor rooms. Dinner and breakfast are served in the spacious dining room that also benefits from sea views.

Rooms 52 (1 fmly) (5 GF) **Facilities** FTV ♬ Xmas New Year **Services** Lift **Notes** LB ⊗ Closed Dec-Feb (except Xmas) RS Mar & Nov

WINCANTON Map 4 ST72

Holbrook House

★★★ 79% ⊛⊛ COUNTRY HOUSE HOTEL

☎ 01963 824466 & 828844 🖷 01963 32681
Holbrook BA9 8BS
e-mail: enquiries@holbrookhouse.co.uk
web: www.holbrookhouse.co.uk
dir: From A303 at Wincanton left onto A371 towards Castle Cary & Shepton Mallet

This handsome country house offers a unique blend of quality and comfort combined with a friendly atmosphere. Set in 17 acres of peaceful gardens and wooded grounds, Holbrook House makes a perfect retreat. The restaurant provides a selection of innovative dishes prepared with enthusiasm and served by a team of caring staff.

Rooms 21 (5 annexe) (2 fmly) (5 GF) **D** £140-£250 (incl. bkfst) **Facilities** Spa FTV ⊘ ⊠ ⤳ Gym Beauty treatment Exercise classes Sauna Steam room Fitness suite ♬ Xmas New Year Wi-fi **Conf** Class 50 Board 55 Thtr 200 **Parking** 100 **Notes** LB Civ Wed 150

YATTON Map 4 ST46

Bridge Inn

BUDGET HOTEL

☎ 01934 839100 & 839101 🖷 01934 839149
North End Rd BS49 4AU
e-mail: bridge.yatton@newbridgeinns.co.uk
web: www.oldenglish.co.uk
dir: M5 junct 20, take B3133 to Yatton. Take 1st left at rdbt, 1st left at 2nd rdbt. Hotel 2.5m on right

This establishment offers spacious, well-equipped bedrooms, and the bar/restaurant serves a variety of dishes throughout the day in a relaxed and informal environment. Breakfast is a self-service buffet plus a full English breakfast served at the table. There is also a play zone area for children.

Rooms 41 (4 fmly) (20 GF) **Conf** Class 30 Board 50 Thtr 100

YEOVIL · Map 4 ST51

See also **Martock**

Lanes

★★★ 80% ◎◎ HOTEL

☎ 01935 862555 ▤ 01935 864260
West Coker BA22 9AJ
e-mail: stay@laneshotel.net
web: www.laneshotel.net
dir: 2m W of Yeovil on A30 in centre of West Coker

This splendid building, once a rectory, has a cleverly
designed, contemporary extension. Guests are assured of
a relaxed and friendly stay. The stylish, modern bedrooms,
with their superb bathrooms, are equipped with many
extras. The brasserie-style restaurant offers an
imaginative range of dishes, using local produce
whenever possible. There is also a luxury jacuzzi, sauna
and small gym.

Rooms 27 (17 annexe) (3 fmly) (8 GF) **S** £90;
D £110-£150 (incl. bkfst)* **Facilities** FTV ⚑ Gym 🎵
Xmas New Year Wi-fi **Conf** Class 40 Board 20 Thtr 60
Del from £135* **Services** Lift **Parking** 40 **Notes** LB ⊗

The Yeovil Court Hotel & Restaurant

★★★ 78% ◎◎ HOTEL

☎ 01935 863746 ▤ 01935 863990
West Coker Rd BA20 2HE
e-mail: unwind@yeovilhotel.com
web: www.yeovilcourthotel.com
dir: 2.5m W of town centre on A30

This comfortable, family-run hotel offers a very relaxed
and caring atmosphere. Bedrooms are well equipped and
neatly presented; some are located in an adjacent
building. Public areas consist of a smart lounge, a
popular bar and an attractive restaurant. Menus combine
an interesting selection that includes lighter options and
dishes suited to special occasion dining.

The Yeovil Court Hotel & Restaurant

Rooms 30 (12 annexe) (3 fmly) (11 GF) **S** £55-£82;
D £75-£140 (incl. bkfst)* **Facilities** FTV Wi-fi
Conf Class 18 Board 22 Thtr 50 Del from £110 to £160
Parking 65 **Notes** LB RS Sat lunch, 25 Dec eve & 26 Dec

Manor

★★★ 🅰 HOTEL

☎ 01935 423116 ▤ 01935 706607
Hendford BA20 1TG
e-mail: manor.yeovil@oldenglishinns.co.uk
web: www.oldenglish.co.uk
dir: A303 onto A3088 to Yeovil. Over River Yeo, 2nd exit at
rdbt immediately left into Hendford.

Rooms 41 (1 fmly) (10 GF) **Conf** Class 50 Board 45
Thtr 150 **Parking** 60 **Notes** LB ⊗ Civ Wed 60

INSPECTORS' CHOICE

Little Barwick House
◎◎◎ RESTAURANT WITH ROOMS

☎ 01935 423902 ▤ 01935 420908
Barwick Village BA22 9TD
e-mail: littlebarwick@hotmail.com
dir: From Yeovil A37 towards Dorchester, left at 1st
rdbt, 1st left, 0.25m on left

Situated in a quiet hamlet in three and half acres of
gardens and grounds, this listed Georgian dower house
is an ideal retreat for those seeking peaceful
surroundings and good food. Just one of the highlights
of a stay here is a meal in the restaurant, where good
use is made of local ingredients. Each of the bedrooms
has its own character, and a range of thoughtful extras
such as fresh flowers, bottled water and magazines.

Rooms 6

STAFFORDSHIRE

BARTON-UNDER-NEEDWOOD · Map 10 SK11

Travelodge Burton (A38 Northbound)

BUDGET HOTEL

☎ 0871 984 6069 ▤ 01283 716343
DE13 8EG
web: www.travelodge.co.uk
dir: on A38, northbound

Travelodge offers good quality, good value, budget
accommodation. All offer family rooms sleeping up to four
(two adults, two children) with en suite bathroom/
shower-room, remote-control TV, tea- and coffee-making
facilities and comfortable beds. Food options vary.
Breakfast is at the on-site Bar Café restaurant (if
available) or to take away. See also Hotel Groups pages.

Rooms 20 **S** fr £29; **D** fr £29

Travelodge Burton (A38 Southbound)

BUDGET HOTEL

☎ 0871 984 6068 ▤ 01283 716784
Rykneld St DE13 8EH
web: www.travelodge.co.uk
dir: on A38, southbound

Rooms 40 **S** fr £29; **D** fr £29

BURTON UPON TRENT · Map 10 SK22

Three Queens

★★★ 81% ◎ HOTEL

☎ 01283 523800 & 0845 230 1332 ▤ 01283 523823
One Bridge St DE14 1SY
e-mail: hotel@threequeenshotel.co.uk
web: www.threequeenshotel.co.uk
dir: On A511 in Burton upon Trent at junct of Bridge St &
High St. Town side of Old River Bridge

Located in the centre of the town close to the river, this
smartly presented hotel provides an appealing, high
quality base from which to tour the area. Bedrooms come
in a mix of styles that include spacious duplex suites and
executive rooms located in the original Jacobean heart of
the building. Smart day rooms include the medieval
styled Grill Restaurant, a modern bar and a contemporary
breakfast room. A warm welcome is assured from the
professional staff.

Rooms 38 (7 smoking) **S** £55-£90; **D** £65-£130 (incl.
bkfst)* **Facilities** STV FTV Xmas New Year Wi-fi
Conf Class 40 Board 30 Thtr 60 Del from £99.50 to
£129.50* **Services** Lift Air con **Parking** 40 **Notes** LB ⊗

Newton Park

 RAMADA.

★★★ 79% COUNTRY HOUSE HOTEL

☎ 01283 703568 📄 01283 709235
Newton Solney DE15 0SS
e-mail: sales.newtonpark@ramadajarvis.co.uk
web: www.ramadajarvis.co.uk
dir: On B5008 past Repton to Newton Solney. Hotel on left

Set in well tended gardens, this country-house hotel is a popular venue for conferences and meetings. Bedrooms are comfortably appointed for both business and leisure guests.

Rooms 50 (5 fmly) (7 GF) (2 smoking) **Facilities** FTV Xmas New Year Wi-fi **Conf** Class 70 Board 60 Thtr 100 Del from £120 to £165* **Services** Lift **Parking** 120 **Notes** Civ Wed 100

Riverside

★★ 🅰 HOTEL

☎ 01283 511234 📄 01283 511441
Riverside Dr, Branston DE14 3EP
e-mail: riverside.branston@oldenglishinns.co.uk
web: www.oldenglish.co.uk
dir: on A5121 follow signs for Branston, over small humped-backed bridge, right into Warren Ln. 2nd left into Riverside Dr

Rooms 22 (10 GF) **Facilities** Fishing Xmas **Conf** Class 60 Board 30 Thtr 120 **Parking** 200 **Notes** Civ Wed 120

Express by Holiday Inn Burton upon Trent

BUDGET HOTEL

☎ 01283 504300 📄 01283 504301
2nd Av, Centrum 100 DE14 2WF
e-mail: info@exhiburton.co.uk
web: www.hiexpress.com/burton-n-trent
dir: From A38 Branston exit take A5121 signed Town Centre. At McDonalds rdbt, turn left into 2nd Avenue. Hotel on left

A modern hotel ideal for families and business travellers. Fresh and uncomplicated, the spacious rooms include Sky TV, power shower and tea and coffee-making facilities. Continental buffet breakfast is included in the room rate; other meals may be taken at the nearby family pub or restaurant. See also the Hotel Groups pages.

Rooms 82 (47 fmly) **Conf** Class 30 Board 30 Thtr 65

LEEK

Map 16 SJ95

Three Horseshoes Inn & Country Hotel

★★★ 75% ◉ HOTEL

☎ 01538 300296 📄 01538 300320
Buxton Rd, Blackshaw Moor ST13 8TW
e-mail: enquires@threeshoesinn.co.uk
web: www.threeshoesinn.co.uk
dir: 2m N of Leek on A53

This traditional, family-owned hostelry provides stylish, individually designed, modern bedrooms, including several four-poster rooms. The smart brasserie, with an open kitchen and countryside views, offers modern English and Thai dishes, and there is also a pub and carvery; the award-winning gardens and grounds are ideal for alfresco dining. The staff are attentive and friendly.

Rooms 26 (2 fmly) (10 GF) **Facilities** FTV **Conf** Class 50 Board 25 Thtr 60 **Services** Lift **Parking** 80 **Notes** ⊗ Closed 24 Dec-1 Jan Civ Wed 120

LICHFIELD — Map 10 SK10

INSPECTORS' CHOICE

Swinfen Hall
★★★★ ◉◉ HOTEL

☎ 01543 481494 📄 01543 480341
Swinfen WS14 9RE
e-mail: info@swinfenhallhotel.co.uk
web: www.swinfenhallhotel.co.uk
dir: Set back from A38, 2.5m outside Lichfield, towards Birmingham

Dating from 1757, this lavishly decorated mansion has been painstakingly restored by the present owners. Set in 100 acres of parkland which includes a deer park. Public rooms are particularly stylish, with intricately carved ceilings and impressive oil portraits. Bedrooms on the first floor boast period features and tall sash windows; those on the second floor (the former servants' quarters) are smaller and more contemporary by comparison. Service within the award-winning restaurant is both professional and attentive.

Rooms 17 (5 fmly) **S** £135-£275; **D** £160-£295 (incl. bkfst)* **Facilities** STV ♨ Fishing ⛵ New Year Wi-fi **Conf** Class 50 Board 120 Thtr 96 Del from £160 to £180* **Parking** 80 **Notes** ⊗ Civ Wed 120

Best Western The George
★★★ 77% HOTEL

☎ 01543 414822 📄 01543 415817
12-14 Bird St WS13 6PR
e-mail: mail@thegeorgelichfield.co.uk
web: www.thegeorgelichfield.co.uk
dir: From Bowling Green Island on A461 take Lichfield exit. Left at next island into Swan Rd, as road bears left, turn right into Bird St for hotel car park

Situated in the city centre, this privately owned hotel provides good quality, well-equipped accommodation which includes a room with a four-poster bed. Facilities here include a large ballroom, plus several other rooms for meetings and functions.

Rooms 45 (5 fmly) **S** £45-£156; **D** £64-£156 (incl. bkfst) **Facilities** FTV Gym Wi-fi **Conf** Class 60 Board 40 Thtr 110 Del from £110 to £145 **Services** Lift **Parking** 45 **Notes** ⊗ Civ Wed 110

Innkeeper's Lodge Lichfield
BUDGET HOTEL

☎ 0845 112 6074 📄 0845 112 6232
Stafford Rd WS13 8JB
web: www.innkeeperslodge.com/lichfield
dir: M6 junct 15, A50 towards Burton. A38 south for Lichfield, exit at Streethay onto A5192 to A51(Stafford Rd). From M42 junct 10, A5 towards Tamworth. A51 north through Lichfield.

Innkeeper's Lodge represents an exciting, high value concept within the budget hotel market. Comfortable bedrooms provide excellent facilities that include satellite TV and modem points. This carefully restored lodge is in a picturesque setting and has its own unique style and quirky character. Food is served all day, and an extensive, complimentary continental breakfast is offered. See also the Hotel Groups pages.

Rooms 10 (2 fmly)

NEWCASTLE-UNDER-LYME — Map 10 SJ84

Holiday Inn Stoke-on-Trent
★★★ 74% HOTEL

☎ 01782 557000 & 557018 📄 01782 557022
Clayton Rd, Clayton ST5 4DL
e-mail: stoke@ihg.com
web: www.holidayinn.co.uk
dir: Just off M6 junct 15. Follow Clayton Rd signs towards Newcastle-under-Lyme. Hotel 200yds on left

Stylish and contemporary, this modern hotel is well located just minutes from the motorway. Bedrooms are comfortable and boast an excellent range of facilities. Guests have the use of the leisure club.

Rooms 118 (12 fmly) (8 smoking) **Facilities** STV ⓢ supervised Gym Xmas New Year Wi-fi **Conf** Class 30 Board 22 Thtr 70 **Services** Air con **Parking** 150 **Notes** ⊗

PATTINGHAM — Map 10 SO89

Patshull Park Hotel Golf & Country Club
★★★ 77% HOTEL

☎ 01902 700100 📄 01902 700874
Patshull Park WV6 7HR
e-mail: sales@patshull-park.co.uk
web: www.patshull-park.co.uk
dir: 1.5m W of Pattingham, at church take Patshull Rd, hotel 1.5m on right

Dating from the 1730s and sitting in 280 acres of parkland, with good golf and fishing, this comfortably appointed hotel has a range of modern leisure and conference facilities. Public rooms include a lounge bar, Earl's Brasserie and the Lakeside Restaurant with delightful views over the lake. Bedrooms are well appointed and thoughtfully equipped; most have good views of either the golf course or lake.

Rooms 49 (15 fmly) (16 GF) **Facilities** STV ⓢ ♨ 18 Putt green Fishing Gym Beauty therapist Cardio suite New Year Wi-fi **Conf** Class 75 Board 44 Thtr 160 Del from £139 to £145* **Parking** 200 **Notes** RS 24-26 Dec Civ Wed 100

See advert on page 401

RUGELEY — Map 10 SK01

Travelodge Rugeley
BUDGET HOTEL

☎ 0871 984 6102 📠 01889 570096
Western Springs Rd WS15 2AS
web: www.travelodge.co.uk
dir: M6 junct 11 (Cannock N'bound) or junct 13/14
S'bound, take A460 through Cannock to Rugeley. Hotel on
A51 in Rugeley centre

Travelodge offers good quality, good value, budget
accommodation. All offer family rooms sleeping up to four
(two adults, two children) with en suite bathroom/
shower-room, remote-control TV, tea- and coffee-making
facilities and comfortable beds. Food options vary.
Breakfast is at the on-site Bar Café restaurant (if
available) or to take away. See also Hotel Groups pages.

Rooms 32 **S** fr £29; **D** fr £29

STAFFORD — Map 10 SJ92

The Moat House
★★★★ 85% ⚛⚛ HOTEL

☎ 01785 712217 📠 01785 715344
Lower Penkridge Rd, Acton Trussell ST17 0RJ
e-mail: info@moathouse.co.uk
web: www.moathouse.co.uk
dir: M6 junct 13 onto A449 through Acton Trussell. Hotel
on right on exiting village

This 17th-century timbered building, with an idyllic
canal-side setting, has been skilfully extended. Bedrooms
are stylishly furnished, well equipped and comfortable.
The bar offers a range of snacks and the restaurant
boasts a popular fine dining option where the head chef
displays his skills using top quality produce.

Rooms 41 (4 fmly) (15 GF) **S** £130; **D** £150 (incl. bkfst)*
Facilities New Year Wi-fi **Conf** Class 60 Board 50
Thtr 200 **Services** Lift **Parking** 200 **Notes** LB ⊗ Closed
25 Dec Civ Wed 150

The Swan
★★★ 78% HOTEL

☎ 01785 258142 📠 01785 223372
46 Greengate St ST16 2JA
e-mail: info@theswanstafford.co.uk
dir: From north on A34, access via Mill Street in town
centre. From south on A449

This former coaching inn located in the town centre offers
spacious, modern public areas that include a popular
brasserie, a choice of elegant bars, a coffee shop and
conference facilities. Individually styled bedrooms, many
with original period features, are tastefully appointed and
include two four-poster suites. Executive rooms are air
conditioned.

Rooms 31 (3 fmly) **S** £80; **D** £100 (incl. bkfst)*
Facilities FTV Wi-fi **Services** Lift **Parking** 40 **Notes** LB ⊗
Closed 25 Dec

Abbey
★★ 74% HOTEL

THE INDEPENDENTS
HOTEL ASSOCIATION

☎ 01785 258531 📠 01785 246875
65-68 Lichfield Rd ST17 4LW
web: www.abbeyhotelstafford.co.uk
dir: M6 junct 13 towards Stafford. Right at Esso garage,
to mini-rdbt, follow Silkmore Lane to 2nd rdbt. Hotel
0.25m on right

This friendly privately owned and personally run hotel
provides well-equipped accommodation and is
particularly popular with commercial visitors. Family and
ground floor rooms are both available. Facilities here
include a choice of lounges and the spacious car park
proves a real benefit to guests in this area of the city.

Rooms 17 (3 fmly) **S** £49-£65; **D** £60-£75 (incl. bkfst)*
Facilities FTV Wi-fi **Parking** 21 **Notes** ⊗ Closed
22 Dec-7 Jan

Travelodge Stafford Central
BUDGET HOTEL

☎ 0871 984 6361 📠 01785 248589
Hough Retail Park, Lichfield Rd ST17 4ER
dir: M6 junct 13, A449, follow Stafford signs. 3m to one-
way system. Take A34, follow to right at Queensway. Left
into Litchfield Rd. Or from M6 junct 14, A5013, follow
Stafford signs. At rdbt 2nd exit onto A34/Greyfriars,
through 2 rdbts. Left into Litchfield Rd

Travelodge offers good quality, good value, budget
accommodation. All offer family rooms sleeping up to
four (two adults, two children) with en suite bathroom/
shower-room, remote-control TV, tea- and coffee-making
facilities and comfortable beds. Food options vary.
Breakfast is at the on-site Bar Café restaurant (if
available) or to take away. See also the Hotel Groups
pages.

Rooms 62 **S** fr £29; **D** fr £29

STAFFORD MOTORWAY SERVICE AREA (M6) — Map 10 SJ82

Travelodge Stafford (M6)
BUDGET HOTEL

☎ 0871 984 6105 📠 01785 816107
Moto Service Area, Eccleshall Rd ST15 0EU
web: www.travelodge.co.uk
dir: Between M6 juncts 14 & 15 northbound only

Travelodge offers good quality, good value, budget
accommodation. All offer family rooms sleeping up to four
(two adults, two children) with en suite bathroom/
shower-room, remote-control TV, tea- and coffee-making
facilities and comfortable beds. Food options vary.
Breakfast is at the on-site Bar Café restaurant (if
available) or to take away. See also Hotel Groups pages.

Rooms 62 **S** fr £29; **D** fr £29

STOKE-ON-TRENT   Map 10 SJ84

Best Western Stoke-on-Trent Moat House

★★★★ 74% HOTEL

☎ 0870 225 4601 & 01782 206101 📠 01782 206101
Etruria Hall, Festival Way, Etruria ST1 5BQ
e-mail: reservations.stoke@qmh-hotels.com
web: www.bestwestern.co.uk/content/hotel-details-
leisure.aspx/hotel/83862
dir: M6/A500. A53 Festival Park. Keep in left lane exit,
take first slip road on left. Left at island, hotel opposite at
next island

A large, modern hotel located in Stoke's Festival Park,
that adjoins Etruria Hall, the former home of Josiah
Wedgwood. The bedrooms are spacious and well equipped
and include family rooms, suites and executive rooms.
Public areas include a spacious lounge bar and
restaurant as well as a business centre, extensive
conference facilities and a leisure club.

Rooms 147 (63 fmly) (22 smoking) **S** £49-£129;
D £59-£129* **Facilities** ⊙ supervised Gym Beauty salon
Sauna Steam room Solarium Dance studio Xmas New
Year Wi-fi **Conf** Class 400 Board 40 Thtr 550 Del from £99
to £150* **Services** Lift Air con **Parking** 350 **Notes** LB ⊗
Civ Wed 80

Best Western Manor House

★★★ 83% HOTEL

☎ 01270 884000 📠 01270 882483
Audley Rd ST7 2QQ
e-mail: mhres@compasshotels.co.uk
web: www.manorhouse-alsager.co.uk

(For full entry see Alsager, Cheshire)

Manor at Hanchurch

★★★ 80% ⊛⊛ HOTEL

☎ 01782 643030 & 07703 744479 📠 01782 714840
Newcastle Rd, Hanchurch ST4 8SD
e-mail: info@hanchurchmanor.co.uk
dir: A519, follow through lights & under M6 bridge. Hotel
immediately on right

Dating back to the 19th century the manor was designed
by Sir Charles Barry, the architect noted for his rebuilding
work on the Houses of Parliament, and is set in secluded
grounds with mature shrubs and trees. Bedrooms are very
smartly presented and thoughtfully equipped to suit both
the business and leisure guest. Carefully prepared meals
are served in the elegant, fine-dining restaurant. The
grandeur of the house and beauty of the grounds make
this a very popular venue for weddings.

Rooms 7 (1 fmly) **Facilities** FTV Fishing ♫ Xmas New
Year Wi-fi **Conf** Class 24 Board 12 Thtr 30 **Parking** 36
Notes LB ⊗ No children 12yrs RS Sun & Mon night
Civ Wed 40

Quality Hotel Stoke

★★★ 70% HOTEL

☎ 01782 202361 📠 01782 286464
66 Trinity St, Hanley ST1 5NB
e-mail: enquiries@qualityhotelsstoke.co.uk
dir: M6 junct 15(S)/16(N) then A500 to city centre &
Festival Park. A53 to Leek, keep in left lane, 3rd exit at
rdbt for Hanley/City Centre/Cultural Quarter. Hotel on left
at top of hill

This large city centre hotel provides a range of bedrooms
and extensive public areas including a choice of popular
bars. A well lit spacious car park and modern leisure
facilities are additional benefits.

Rooms 136 (8 annexe) (54 fmly) (5 GF) (15 smoking)
S £40-£120; **D** £60-£140 (incl. bkfst) **Facilities** STV ⊙
supervised Gym Children's games room mid Jul-early Sep
New Year Wi-fi **Conf** Class 125 Board 60 Thtr 300
Del from £90 to £125 **Services** Lift **Parking** 150 **Notes** LB
Civ Wed 250

Haydon House

★★★ 67% ⊛ HOTEL

☎ 01782 711311 & 753690 📠 01782 717470
Haydon St, Basford ST4 6JD
e-mail: enquiries@haydon-house-hotel.co.uk
dir: A500/A53 (Hanley/Newcastle), turn left at rdbt, 2nd
left at brow of hill, into Haydon St. Hotel on left

A Victorian property, within easy reach of Newcastle-
under-Lyme. The public rooms are furnished in a style
befitting the age and character of the house. Bedrooms
are also furnished in traditional style and several rooms
are located in a separate house across the road. The hotel
is popular with local businesses and organisations.

Rooms 17 (1 fmly) **S** £50-£65; **D** £60-£75 (incl. bkfst)*
Conf Class 30 Board 30 Thtr 80 **Parking** 52
Notes Civ Wed 80

Express by Holiday Inn Stoke-on-Trent

BUDGET HOTEL

☎ 01782 377000 📠 01782 377037
Sir Stanley Matthews Way, Trentham Lakes ST4 4EG
e-mail: stokeontrent@expressholidayinn.co.uk
web: www.hiexpress.co.uk/stoke-on-trent
dir: M6 junct 15, follow signs for Uttoxeter/Derby which
leads to A50. Hotel adjacent to Britannia Stadium

A modern hotel ideal for families and business travellers.
Fresh and uncomplicated, the spacious rooms include Sky
TV, power shower and tea and coffee-making facilities.
Continental buffet breakfast is included in the room rate;
other meals may be taken at the nearby family pub or
restaurant. See also the Hotel Groups pages.

Rooms 123 (73 fmly) **Conf** Class 16 Board 18 Thtr 35

Innkeeper's Lodge Stoke-on-Trent

BUDGET HOTEL

☎ 0845 112 6074 📠 0845 112 6229
Longton Rd ST4 8BU
web: www.innkeeperslodge.com/stokeontrent
dir: M6 junct 15, A500 to slip road for A34 towards Stone.
At rdbt take left onto A5035. Lodge 0.5m on right

Innkeeper's Lodge represents an exciting, high value
concept within the budget hotel market. Comfortable
bedrooms provide excellent facilities that include satellite
TV and modem points. Options include family rooms; and
for the corporate guest, cutting edge IT which includes
Wi-fi access. A popular Carvery provides all-day food,
including an extensive, complimentary continental
breakfast. See also the Hotel Groups pages.

Rooms 30 (8 fmly)

Weathervane

BUDGET HOTEL

☎ 01782 388799 🖹 01782 388804
Lysander Rd ST3 7WA
e-mail: 5305@greenking.co.uk
web: www.oldenglish.co.uk

A few minutes from A50 and convenient for both the city and industrial areas, this popular, modern pub and restaurant, under the 'Hungry Horse' brand, provides hearty, well-cooked food at reasonable prices. Adjacent bedrooms are furnished for both commercial and leisure customers.

Rooms 39 (8 fmly) (18 GF) **Conf** Class 20 Board 20 Thtr 20

STONE   Map 10 SJ93

Crown

★★★ 74% HOTEL

☎ 01785 813535 🖹 01785 815942
38 High St ST15 8AS
e-mail: info@stonehotels.co.uk
dir: M6 junct 14, A34 N to Stone. M6 junct 15, A34 S to Stone

A former coaching inn in the town centre where staff are helpful and friendly. The hotel has a glass domed restaurant that offers a choice of menus, and the front lounge is delightfully furnished. Bedrooms, some located in a separate building, are well equipped and comfortable.

Rooms 32 (16 annexe) (2 fmly) (8 GF) **S** £39.50-£69.50; **D** £49.50-£109.50 **Facilities** STV FTV ♫ New Year **Conf** Class 80 Board 60 Thtr 150 **Parking** 40 **Notes** ✪ Civ Wed 100

Stone House

★★★ 71% HOTEL

OXFORD
HOTELS & INNS

☎ 01785 815531 🖹 01785 814764
Stafford Rd ST15 0BQ
e-mail: reservations.stone@ohiml.com
web: www.oxfordhotelsandinns.com
dir: M6 junct 14 (N) or junct 15 (S). Hotel on A34

This former country house, set in attractive grounds, is located within easy reach of the M6. Attractive comfortable bedrooms and tastefully appointed public areas together with leisure and conference facilities make the hotel popular with both corporate and leisure guests. A light menu is offered in the bar and lounge areas, or guests can choose to dine in the stylish restaurant.

Rooms 50 (1 fmly) (15 GF) **S** £55-£84; **D** £60-£91 (incl. bkfst)* **Facilities** ⊗ supervised Gym New Year **Conf** Class 50 Board 40 Thtr 150 Del from £97.50 to £125* **Parking** 100 **Notes** LB ✪ Civ Wed 60

TALKE   Map 15 SJ85

Travelodge Stoke Talke

BUDGET HOTEL

☎ 0871 984 6106 🖹 01782 777000
Newcastle Rd ST7 1UP
web: www.travelodge.co.uk
dir: at junct of A34 & A500

Travelodge offers good quality, good value, budget accommodation. All offer family rooms sleeping up to four (two adults, two children) with en suite bathroom/shower-room, remote-control TV, tea- and coffee-making facilities and comfortable beds. Breakfast is at the on-site Bar Café restaurant (if available) or to take away. See also Hotel Groups pages.

Rooms 63 **S** fr £29; **D** fr £29 **Conf** Class 25 Board 32 Thtr 50

TAMWORTH   Map 10 SK20

Drayton Court Hotel

★★ 81% HOTEL

☎ 01827 285805 🖹 01827 284842
65 Coleshill St, Fazeley B78 3RG
e-mail: draytoncthotel@yahoo.co.uk
web: www.draytoncourthotel.co.uk
dir: M42 junct 9, A446 to Lichfield, at next rdbt right onto A4091. 2m, Drayton Manor Theme Park on left. Hotel on right

Conveniently located close to the M42, this lovingly restored hotel offers bedrooms that are elegant and have been thoughtfully equipped to suit both business and leisure guests. Beds are particularly comfortable, and one room has a four-poster. Public areas include a panelled bar, a relaxing lounge and an attractive restaurant.

Rooms 19 (3 fmly) **S** £62.50-£78; **D** £88-£108 (incl. bkfst)* **Facilities** Wi-fi **Conf** Board 12 **Parking** 23 **Notes** ✪ Closed 22 Dec-1 Jan

Travelodge Tamworth (M42)

BUDGET HOTEL

☎ 0871 984 6109 & 0800 850950 🖹 01827 260145
Moto Service Area, Green Ln B77 5PS
web: www.travelodge.co.uk
dir: M42 junct 10, follow signs for Services

Travelodge offers good quality, good value, budget accommodation. All offer family rooms sleeping up to four (two adults, two children) with en suite bathroom/shower-room, remote-control TV, tea- and coffee-making facilities and comfortable beds. Food options vary. Breakfast is at the on-site Bar Café restaurant (if available) or to take away. See also Hotel Groups pages.

Rooms 63 **S** fr £29; **D** fr £29

UTTOXETER   Map 10 SK03

Travelodge Uttoxeter

BUDGET HOTEL

☎ 0871 984 6114 🖹 01889 562043
Ashbourne Rd ST14 5AA
web: www.travelodge.co.uk
dir: At junct of A50 & B5030 on outskirts of Uttoxeter, 7m S of Alton Towers Theme Park

Travelodge offers good quality, good value, budget accommodation. All offer family rooms sleeping up to four (two adults, two children) with en suite bathroom/shower-room, remote-control TV, tea- and coffee-making facilities and comfortable beds. Food options vary. Breakfast is at the on-site Bar Café restaurant (if available) or to take away. See also Hotel Groups pages.

Rooms 32 **S** fr £29; **D** fr £29

SUFFOLK

ALDEBURGH　　Map 13 TM45

Wentworth

★★★ 88% ◉◉ HOTEL

☎ 01728 452312 ▤ 01728 454343
Wentworth Rd IP15 5BD
e-mail: stay@wentworth-aldeburgh.co.uk
web: www.wentworth-aldeburgh.com
dir: Off A12 onto A1094, 6m to Aldeburgh, with church on left, left at bottom of hill

A delightful privately owned hotel overlooking the beach. The attractive, well-maintained public rooms include three stylish lounges as well as a cocktail bar and elegant restaurant. Bedrooms are smartly decorated with co-ordinated fabrics and have many thoughtful touches; some rooms have superb sea views. Several very spacious Mediterranean-style rooms are located across the road.

Rooms 35 (7 annexe) (5 GF) **S** £58–£100; **D** £98–£232 (incl. bkfst)* **Facilities** FTV Xmas New Year Wi-fi **Conf** Class 12 Board 12 Thtr 15 Del from £95 to £115 **Parking** 30 **Notes** LB

The Brudenell

★★★ 87% ◉◉ HOTEL

☎ 01728 452071 ▤ 01728 454082
The Parade IP15 5BU
e-mail: info@brudenellhotel.co.uk
web: www.brudenellhotel.co.uk
dir: A12/A1094, on reaching town, turn right at junct into High St. Hotel on seafront adjoining Fort Green car park

Situated at the far end of the town centre just a step away from the beach, this hotel has a contemporary appearance, enhanced by subtle lighting and quality soft furnishings. Many of the bedrooms have superb sea views; they include deluxe rooms with king-sized beds and superior rooms suitable for families. The informal restaurant showcases skilfully prepared dishes that use fresh, seasonal produce especially local fish, seafood and game.

Rooms 42 (15 fmly) **S** £64–£115; **D** £114–£238 (incl. bkfst)* **Facilities** Xmas New Year Wi-fi **Services** Lift **Parking** 16 **Notes** LB

Best Western White Lion

★★★ 82% ◉ HOTEL

☎ 01728 452720 ▤ 01728 452986
Market Cross Place IP15 5BJ
e-mail: info@whitelion.co.uk
web: www.whitelion.co.uk
dir: A12 onto A1094, follow signs to Aldeburgh at junct on left. Hotel on right

A popular 15th-century hotel situated at the quiet end of town overlooking the sea. Bedrooms are pleasantly decorated and thoughtfully equipped, many rooms have lovely sea views. Public areas include two lounges and an elegant restaurant, where locally-caught fish and seafood are served. There is also a modern brasserie.

Rooms 38 (1 fmly) **S** £68–£99.50; **D** £110–£214 (incl. bkfst)* **Facilities** STV Xmas New Year Wi-fi **Conf** Class 50 Board 50 Thtr 120 **Parking** 15 **Notes** LB Civ Wed 100

BARTON MILLS　　Map 12 TL77

Travelodge Barton Mills

BUDGET HOTEL

☎ 0871 984 6006 ▤ 01638 717675
Fiveways IP28 6AE
web: www.travelodge.co.uk
dir: on A11 at Fiveways rdbt

Travelodge offers good quality, good value, budget accommodation. All offer family rooms sleeping up to four (two adults, two children) with en suite bathroom/shower-room, remote-control TV, tea- and coffee-making facilities and comfortable beds. Food options vary. Breakfast is at the on-site Bar Café restaurant (if available) or to take away. See also Hotel Groups pages.

Rooms 62 **S** fr £29; **D** fr £29

BECCLES　　Map 13 TM48

Waveney House

★★★ 78% HOTEL

☎ 01502 712270 ▤ 01502 470370
Puddingmoor NR34 9PL
e-mail: enquiries@waveneyhousehotel.co.uk
web: www.waveneyhousehotel.co.uk
dir: From A146 turn right onto Common Lane North, left into Pound Rd, bear left into Ravensmere, right onto Smallgate, right onto Old Market & continue to Puddingmoor

An exceptionally well presented, privately owned hotel situated by the River Waveney on the edge of this busy little market town. The stylish public rooms include a smart lounge bar and a contemporary-style restaurant with views over the river. The spacious bedrooms are attractively decorated with co-ordinated fabrics and have many thoughtful touches.

Rooms 12 (3 fmly) **Facilities** Xmas New Year Wi-fi **Conf** Class 100 Board 50 Thtr 160 **Parking** 45 **Notes** ⊗ Civ Wed 80

BILDESTON   Map 13 TL94

Bildeston Crown

★★★ ◎◎◎ HOTEL

☎ 01449 740510 📠 01449 741843
104 High St IP7 7EB
e-mail: hayley@thebildestoncrown.co.uk
web: www.thebildestoncrown.co.uk
dir: A12 junct 31, turn right onto B1070 & follow signs to Hadleigh. At T-junct turn left onto A1141, then immediately right onto B1115. Hotel 0.5m

Charming inn situated in a peaceful village close to the historic town of Lavenham. Public areas feature beams, exposed brickwork and oak floors, with contemporary style decor; they include a choice of bars, a lounge and a restaurant. The tastefully decorated bedrooms have lovely co-ordinated fabrics and modern facilities that include a Yamaha music system and LCD TVs. Food here is the real focus and draw; guests can expect fresh, high-quality local produce and accomplished technical skills in both modern and classic dishes.

Rooms 13 **S** £80–£150; **D** £150–£250 (incl. bkfst)*
Facilities STV FTV Xmas New Year Wi-fi **Conf** Class 25 Board 16 Thtr 40 Del from £135 to £175* **Services** Lift **Parking** 30 **Notes** Civ Wed 50

BUNGAY   Map 13 TM38

Kings Head

★★ 60% HOTEL

☎ 01986 893583
2 Market Place NR35 1AW
e-mail: info@kingsheadhotel.biz
web: www.kingsheadhotel.biz
dir: A143 to town centre

This 18th-century coaching inn is situated in the heart of town, amid a range of antique shops. The spacious bedrooms are furnished with pine pieces and have a good range of useful extras; one room has a superb four-poster bed. Public rooms include a restaurant, the Duke of Wellington lounge bar and Oddfellows bar.

Rooms 13 (1 fmly) (4 smoking) **Conf** Class 50 Board 50 Thtr 100 **Parking** 29

BURY ST EDMUNDS   Map 13 TL86

Angel

★★★★ 80% ◎◎ TOWN HOUSE HOTEL

☎ 01284 714000 📠 01284 714001
Angel Hill IP33 1LT
e-mail: staying@theangel.co.uk
web: www.theangel.co.uk
dir: From A134, left at rdbt into Northgate St. Continue to lights, right into Mustow St, left into Angel Hill. Hotel on right

An impressive building situated just a short walk from the town centre. One of the Angel's more notable guests over the last 400 years was Charles Dickens who is reputed to have written part of the *Pickwick Papers* whilst in residence. The hotel offers a range of individually designed bedrooms that includes a selection of four-poster rooms and a suite.

Rooms 75 (7 fmly) (15 GF) **D** £90–£150 (incl. bkfst)*
Facilities FTV Xmas New Year Wi-fi **Conf** Class 20 Board 30 Thtr 90 **Services** Lift **Parking** 20 **Notes** LB Civ Wed 80

Ravenwood Hall

★★★ 88% ◎◎ COUNTRY HOUSE HOTEL

☎ 01359 270345 📠 01359 270788
Rougham IP30 9JA
e-mail: enquiries@ravenwoodhall.co.uk
web: www.ravenwoodhall.co.uk
dir: 3m E off A14, junct 45. Hotel on left

Delightful 15th-century property set in seven acres of woodland and landscaped gardens. The building has many original features including carved timbers and inglenook fireplaces. The spacious bedrooms are attractively decorated, tastefully furnished with well-chosen pieces and equipped with many thoughtful touches. Public rooms include an elegant restaurant and a smart lounge bar with an open fire.

Rooms 14 (7 annexe) (5 GF) **Facilities** ⤳ ⤴ Shooting fishing & horse riding can be arranged Xmas New Year Wi-fi **Conf** Class 80 Board 40 Thtr 130 **Parking** 150 **Notes** Civ Wed 130

Best Western Priory

★★★ 82% ◎◎ HOTEL

☎ 01284 766181 📠 01284 767604
Mildenhall Rd IP32 6EH
e-mail: reservations@prioryhotel.co.uk
web: www.prioryhotel.co.uk
dir: From A14 take Bury St Edmunds W slip road. Follow signs to Brandon. At mini-rdbt turn right. Hotel 0.5m on left

An 18th-century Grade II listed building set in landscaped grounds on the outskirts of town. The attractively decorated, tastefully furnished and thoughtfully equipped bedrooms are split between the main house and garden wings, which have their own sun terraces. Public rooms feature a smart restaurant, a conservatory dining room and a lounge bar.

Rooms 39 (30 annexe) (1 fmly) (30 GF) **Facilities** FTV Xmas New Year Wi-fi **Conf** Class 20 Board 20 Thtr 40 **Parking** 60 **Notes** Civ Wed 50

BURY ST EDMUNDS *continued*

Suffolk Hotel Golf & Leisure Club

★★★ 77% HOTEL

☎ 01284 706777 📄 01284 754767
Fornham St Genevieve IP28 6JQ
e-mail: sales.suffolkgolf@ohiml.com
web: www.oxfordhotelsandinns.com
dir: A14 junct 42 & follow B1106 & through Fornham All
Saints towards Thetford. Hotel 0.75m on right

Situated on the outskirts of this historic town just a few
minutes from the A14. The modern, well equipped
bedrooms are suitable for both business and leisure
guests alike; some rooms have superb countryside views.
Public rooms include a smart lounge bar and an intimate
restaurant. The hotel has an 18-hole golf course, gym,
heated indoor pool and spa facilities.

Rooms 40 (3 fmly) (15 GF) **Facilities** 🕲 🏊 18 Putt green
Gym Xmas New Year Wi-fi **Conf** Class 60 Board 60
Thtr 100 **Services** Lift **Parking** 100 **Notes** 🕲 Civ Wed

Grange

★★★ 72% COUNTRY HOUSE HOTEL

☎ 01359 231260 📄 01359 231387
Barton Rd, Thurston IP31 3PQ
e-mail: info@thegrangehotel.uk.com
web: www.thegrangehotel.uk.com
dir: A14 junct 45 towards Gt Barton, right at T-junct. At
x-rds left into Barton Rd to Thurston. At rdbt, left after
0.5m, hotel on right

A Tudor-style country-house hotel situated on the
outskirts of town. The individually decorated bedrooms
have co-ordinated fabrics and many thoughtful touches;
some rooms have nice views of the gardens. Public areas
include a smart lounge bar, two private dining rooms, the
Garden Restaurant and banqueting facilities.

Rooms 18 (5 annexe) (1 fmly) (3 GF) **S** £79.50;
D £100-£125 (incl. bkfst)* **Facilities** FTV Xmas New Year
Wi-fi **Conf** Class 40 Board 30 Thtr 135 Del from £1400*
Parking 100 **Notes** LB Civ Wed 150

DUNWICH Map 13 TM47

The Ship Inn

★★ 76% SMALL HOTEL

☎ 01728 648219
St James St IP17 3DT
e-mail: graeme@agellushotels.co.uk
dir: From N: A12, exit at Blythburgh onto B1125, then left
to village. Inn at end of road. From S: A12, turn right to
Westleton. Follow signs for Dunwich

A delightful inn situated in the heart of this quiet village,
surrounded by nature reserves and heathland just a short
walk from the beach. Public rooms feature a smart lounge
bar with an open fire and real ales on tap. The
comfortable bedrooms are traditionally furnished; some
rooms have lovely views across the sea or marshes.

Rooms 20

EYE Map 13 TM17

Cornwallis

★★★★ 73% 🏵 HOTEL

☎ 01379 870326 📄 01379 870326
Rectory Rd, Brome IP23 8AJ
e-mail: reservations.cornwallis@ohiml.com
web: www.oxfordhotelsandinns.com

Situated just off the A140 at the end of a tree lined lane,
this charming property has a wealth of original character
such as exposed beams, open fireplaces and wood
carvings. Public rooms include a large bar, a lounge, a
conservatory and a fine-dining restaurant. Bedrooms are
tastefully appointed and well equipped.

Rooms 16 (5 annexe) (1 fmly) (3 GF) **Facilities** Xmas
New Year Wi-fi **Conf** Class 70 Board 30 Thtr 50
Parking 100 **Notes** LB 🕲 Civ Wed 80

FELIXSTOWE Map 13 TM33

The Brook Hotel

★★★ 77% HOTEL

☎ 01394 278441 📄 01394 670422
Orwell Rd IP11 7PF
e-mail: welcome@brookhotel.com

A modern, well furnished hotel ideally situated in a
residential area close to the town centre and the sea.
Public areas include a lounge bar, a large open-plan
restaurant with a bar area and a residents' lounge.
Bedrooms are generally quite spacious; each one is
pleasantly decorated and equipped with modern
facilities.

Rooms 25 (5 fmly) (3 GF) **Facilities** 🎵 Xmas New Year
Conf Class 60 Board 60 Thtr 100 **Parking** 20 **Notes** LB 🕲
Civ Wed 150

Waverley

★★ 76% HOTEL

☎ 01394 282811 📄 01394 670185
2 Wolsey Gardens IP11 7DF
e-mail: enquiries@waverleyhotel.net

A small privately owned hotel situated in an elevated
position just a short walk from the town centre. Bedrooms
are pleasantly decorated and equipped with a good range
of useful extras; many rooms have superb sea views.
Public areas include a smart lounge bar and the Woolsey
Restaurant where an interesting choice of homemade
dishes is available.

Rooms 19 (4 fmly) **Facilities** Xmas New Year **Parking** 20
Notes LB Civ Wed 60

Marlborough

★★ 72% HOTEL

☎ 01394 285621 📄 01394 670724
Sea Front IP11 2BJ
e-mail: hsm@marlborough-hotel-felix.com
web: www.marlborough-hotel-felix.com
dir: From A14 follow 'Docks' signs. Over Dock rdbt,
railway crossing and lights. Left at T-junct. Hotel 400mtrs
on left

Situated on the seafront, overlooking the beach and just
a short stroll from the pier and town centre. This
traditional resort hotel offers a good range of facilities
including the smart Rattan Restaurant, Flying Boat Bar
and L'Aperitif lounge. The pleasantly decorated bedrooms
come in a variety of styles; some have lovely sea views.

Rooms 48 (1 fmly) **S** £56; **D** £70 (incl. bkfst)*
Facilities STV FTV Pool table Xmas New Year Wi-fi
Conf Class 60 Board 40 Thtr 80 Del from £79*
Services Lift **Parking** 16 **Notes** LB 🕲

HAVERHILL — Map 12 TL64

Days Inn Haverhill

BUDGET HOTEL

☎ 0870 4233088 & 01440 716950 ◾ 01440 716951
Phoenix Road & Bumpstead Rd, Haverhill Business Park CB9 7AE
e-mail: reservations@daysinnhaverhill.co.uk
web: www.daysinn.com
dir: A1017 Haverhill bypass. Hotel on 5th rdbt.

This modern building offers accommodation in smart, spacious and well-equipped bedrooms, suitable for families and business travellers, and all with en suite bathrooms. Continental breakfast is available and other refreshments may be taken at the nearby family restaurant. See also the Hotel Groups pages.

Rooms 80 (8 fmly) (14 GF) **S** £49.50-£88.50;
D £59.50-£98.50 (incl. bkfst)* **Conf** Class 28 Board 24
Thtr 60 Del from £116.50 to £122.50*

HINTLESHAM — Map 13 TM04

INSPECTORS' CHOICE

Hintlesham Hall
★★★★ ◎◎ HOTEL

☎ 01473 652334 ◾ 01473 652463
George St IP8 3NS
e-mail: reservations@hintleshamhall.com
web: www.hintleshamhall.com
dir: 4m W of Ipswich on A1071 to Hadleigh & Sudbury

Hospitality and service are key features at this imposing Grade I listed country-house hotel, situated in 175 acres of grounds and landscaped gardens. Individually decorated bedrooms offer a high degree of comfort; each one is tastefully furnished and equipped with many thoughtful touches. The spacious public rooms include a series of comfortable lounges and an elegant restaurant, which serves fine classical cuisine. Wi-fi is available throughout.

Rooms 33 (10 GF) **Facilities** ≈ ⌘ 18 ≋ Putt green ≋
Gym Health & Beauty services Clay pigeon shooting ♫
Xmas **Conf** Class 50 Board 32 Thtr 80 **Parking** 60
Notes LB RS Sat Civ Wed 110

HORRINGER — Map 13 TL86

The Ickworth Hotel & Apartments

★★★★ 72% ◎◎ COUNTRY HOUSE HOTEL

☎ 01284 735350 ◾ 01284 736300
IP29 5QE
e-mail: info@ickworthhotel.co.uk
web: www.ickworthhotel.co.uk
dir: A14 exit for Bury St Edmunds, follow brown signs for Ickworth House, 4th exit at rdbt, cross staggered x-rds. Then onto T-junct, right into village, almost immediately right into Ickworth Estate

Gifted to the National Trust in 1956 this stunning property is in part a luxurious hotel that combines the glorious design and atmosphere of the past with a reputation for making children very welcome. The staff are friendly and easy going, there is a children's play area, crèche, horses and bikes to ride, and wonderful 'Capability' Brown gardens to roam in. Plus tennis, swimming, beauty treatments and two dining rooms. Von Essen Hotels - AA Hotel Group of the Year 2009-10.

Rooms 39 (12 annexe) (35 fmly) (4 GF) **Facilities** Spa STV
FTV ⌘ ≋ ≋ Children's crèche Massage Manicures
Adventure playground Vineyard Xmas New Year Wi-fi
Child facilities **Conf** Class 30 Board 20 Thtr 35
Services Lift **Parking** 40 **Notes** Civ Wed 40

IPSWICH — Map 13 TM14

Salthouse Harbour

★★★★ 80% ◎◎ TOWN HOUSE HOTEL

☎ 01473 226789 ◾ 01473 226927
No 1 Neptune Quay IP4 1AX
e-mail: staying@salthouseharbour.co.uk
dir: From A16 junct 56 follow signs for town centre, then Salthouse signs

Situated just a short walk from the town centre, overlooking Neptune Marina. This hotel offers accommodation that is a clever mix of contemporary style and original features. Spacious bedrooms provide luxurious comfort with good facilities. Two air conditioned suites with stunning views are available. Award-winning food is served in the busy ground-floor brasserie.

Rooms 70 (6 fmly) **S** £80-£150; **D** £90-£220*
Facilities STV Xmas New Year Wi-fi **Services** Lift
Parking 30

Best Western Claydon Country House

★★★ 81% ◎ HOTEL

☎ 01473 830382 ◾ 01473 832476
16-18 Ipswich Rd, Claydon IP6 0AR
e-mail: reception@hotelsipswich.com
dir: From A14, NW of Ipswich. After 4m take Great Blakenham Rd, B1113 to Claydon, hotel on left

A delightful hotel situated just off the A14, within easy driving distance of the town centre. The pleasantly decorated bedrooms are thoughtfully equipped and one room has a lovely four-poster bed. An interesting choice of freshly prepared dishes is available in the smart restaurant, and guests have the use of a relaxing lounge bar.

Rooms 36 (5 fmly) (13 GF) **S** £49-£89; **D** £69-£129
Facilities STV Xmas New Year Wi-fi **Conf** Class 60
Board 55 Thtr 120 **Services** Air con **Parking** 85 **Notes** LB
⊗ Civ Wed 100

Best Western The Gatehouse

★★★ 75% ◎ HOTEL

☎ 01473 741897 ◾ 01473 744236
799 Old Norwich Rd IP1 6LH
dir: A14 junct 53 take A1156 Ipswich left at lights onto Norwich road, hotel on left

A Regency-style property set amidst three acres of landscaped grounds, on the outskirts of town in a quiet road just a short drive from the A14. The spacious bedrooms have co-ordinated soft furnishings and many thoughtful touches. Public rooms include a smart lounge bar, an intimate restaurant and a cosy drawing room with plush leather sofas.

Rooms 15 (4 annexe) (3 fmly) (5 GF) **Facilities** STV Wi-fi
Conf Class 20 Board 16 Thtr 25 **Parking** 25 **Notes** LB ⊗

IPSWICH *continued*

Holiday Inn Ipswich

★★★ 74% HOTEL

☎ 0870 400 9045 ▤ 01473 680412
London Rd IP2 0UA
e-mail: reservations-ipswich@ichotelsgroup.com
web: www.holidayinn.co.uk
dir: From A14 & A12 junct take A1214 to West Ipswich.
Over 1st rdbt. Hotel on left on A1071

A modern, purpose built hotel conveniently situated just
off the A12/A14 junction to the west of the town centre.
Public areas include a popular bar, the Junction
Restaurant and a large open-plan lounge. Bedrooms
come in a variety of styles and are suited to the needs of
both the business and leisure guest alike.

Rooms 108 (40 fmly) (48 GF) (7 smoking) **Facilities** STV
FTV ☜ supervised Gym Sauna Xmas New Year Wi-fi
Conf Class 50 Board 40 Thtr 120 Del from £89 to £130*
Services Lift Air con **Parking** 200 **Notes** Civ Wed 80

Novotel Ipswich Centre

★★★ 73% HOTEL

☎ 01473 232400 ▤ 01473 232414
Greyfriars Rd IP1 1UP
e-mail: h0995@accor.com
web: www.novotel.com
dir: from A14 towards Felixstowe. Left onto A137, follow
for 2m into town centre. Hotel on double rdbt by Stoke
Bridge

A modern, red brick hotel perfectly placed in the centre of
town close to shops, bars and restaurants. The open-plan
public areas include a Mediterranean-style restaurant
and a bar with a small games area. The bedrooms are
smartly appointed and have many thoughtful touches;
three rooms are suitable for less mobile guests.

Rooms 101 (8 fmly) **Facilities** Gym Pool table Sauna
Xmas New Year Wi-fi **Conf** Class 75 Board 45 Thtr 180
Services Lift Air con **Parking** 53 **Notes** LB Civ Wed 75

Holiday Inn Ipswich - Orwell

★★★ 71% HOTEL

☎ 01473 272244 ▤ 01473 272484
3 The Havens, Ransomes Europark IP3 9SJ
web: www.holidayinn.co.uk
dir: E on A14, over Orwell Bridge take next slip road
signed Ransomes Europark (remain in right lane). Hotel
accessed via 2nd exit off rdbt

A modern, purpose-built hotel ideally situated close to the
major road networks. The open-plan public areas include
a smart lobby with comfortable seating, a smart lounge
bar and a brasserie-style restaurant. Bedrooms come in a

variety of styles; each one is pleasantly decorated and
equipped with modern facilities.

Rooms 60 (2 fmly) (30 GF) (16 smoking) **Facilities** STV
Gym Xmas New Year Wi-fi **Conf** Class 70 Board 55
Thtr 160 **Services** Lift **Parking** 100 **Notes** ⊗ Civ Wed 110

Travelodge Ipswich Capel St Mary

BUDGET HOTEL

☎ 0871 984 6042 ▤ 0870 1911542
Capel St Mary IP9 2JP
web: www.travelodge.co.uk
dir: M11 junct 8, at rdbt onto A120, through 8 rdts. Road
becomes A12, right into Pound Ln, turn right back onto
A12. Lodge 5m S of Ipswich

Travelodge offers good quality, good value, budget
accommodation. All offer family rooms sleeping up to four
(two adults, two children) with en suite bathroom/
shower-room, remote-control TV, tea- and coffee-making
facilities and comfortable beds. Food options vary.
Breakfast is at the on-site Bar Café restaurant (if
available) or to take away. See also Hotel Groups pages.

Rooms 32 **S** fr £29; **D** fr £29

Milsoms Kesgrave Hall

★★★ 85% ⊛ HOTEL

☎ 01473 333741 ▤ 01473 617614
Hall Rd IP5 2PU
e-mail: reception@kesgravehall.com
web: www.kesgravehall.com
dir: A12 N of Ipswich, left at Ipswich/Woodbridge rdbt
onto B1214. Right after 0.5m into Hall Rd. Hotel 200yds
on left

A superb 18th-century, Grade II listed Georgian mansion
set amidst 38 acres of mature grounds. Appointed in a
contemporary style, the large open-plan public areas
include a smart bar, a lounge with plush sofas, and a
restaurant where guests can watch the chefs in action.
Bedrooms are tastefully appointed and thoughtfully
equipped.

Rooms 23 (8 annexe) (4 fmly) (8 GF) **S** £90-£165;
D £110-£195* **Facilities** STV ♫ Xmas Wi-fi
Conf Board 24 **Parking** 100 **Notes** LB

The Swan

★★★★ 82% ⊛⊛ HOTEL

☎ 01787 247477 ▤ 01787 248286
High St CO10 9QA
e-mail: info@theswanatlavenham.co.uk
web: www.theswanatlavenham.co.uk
dir: From Bury St Edmunds take A134 (S), then A1141 to
Lavenham

A delightful collection of listed buildings dating back to
the 14th century, lovingly restored to retain their original
charm. Public rooms include comfortable lounge areas, a
charming rustic bar, an informal brasserie and a fine-
dining restaurant. Bedrooms are tastefully furnished and
equipped with many thoughtful touches. The friendly
staff are helpful, attentive and offer professional service.

Rooms 45 (11 fmly) (13 GF) **S** £75-£85; **D** £160-£280
(incl. bkfst)* **Facilities** STV FTV Xmas New Year Wi-fi
Conf Class 36 Board 30 Thtr 50 Del from £145 to £165*
Parking 62 **Notes** LB Civ Wed 100

Lavenham Great House 'Restaurant With Rooms'

⊛⊛ RESTAURANT WITH ROOMS

☎ 01787 247431 ▤ 01787 248007
Market Place CO10 9QZ
e-mail: info@greathouse.co.uk
web: www.greathouse.co.uk
dir: Off A1141 onto Market Ln, behind cross on Market
Place

The 18th-century front on Market Place conceals a
15th-century timber-framed building that houses a
restaurant with rooms. The Great House remains a pocket
of France offering high-quality rural cuisine served by
French staff. The spacious bedrooms are individually
decorated and thoughtfully equipped with many useful
extras; some rooms have a separate lounge area.

Rooms 5 (1 fmly)

The Angel

RESTAURANT WITH ROOMS

☎ 01787 247388 📠 01787 248344
Market Place CO10 9QZ
e-mail: angel@maypolehotels.com
web: www.maypolehotels.com
dir: From A14 take Bury E & Sudbury turn onto A143. After 4m take A1141 to Lavenham. Off High Street

A delightful 15th-century inn overlooking the market place in the heart of this historic medieval town. The Angel is well known for its cuisine and offers an imaginative menu based on fresh ingredients. Public rooms include a residents' lounge and open-plan bar/dining area. Bedrooms are tastefully furnished, attractively decorated and thoughtfully equipped.

Rooms 8 (1 fmly)

LONG MELFORD **Map 13 TL84**

The Black Lion

★★★ 81% ⑳ HOTEL

☎ 01787 312356 📠 01787 374557
Church Walk, The Green CO10 9DN
e-mail: enquiries@blacklionhotel.net
web: www.blacklionhotel.net
dir: At junct of A134 & A1092

This charming 15th-century hotel is situated on the edge of this bustling town overlooking the green. Bedrooms are generally spacious and each is attractively decorated, tastefully furnished and equipped with useful extras. An interesting range of dishes is served in the lounge bar or guests may choose to dine from the same innovative menu in the more formal restaurant.

Rooms 10 (1 fmly) **S** £99.50-£132.50; **D** £153-£199 (incl. bkfst)* **Facilities** Xmas New Year Wi-fi **Conf** Class 28 Board 28 Thtr 50 **Parking** 10 **Notes** LB Civ Wed 50

The Bull

★★★ 🅰 HOTEL

☎ 01787 378494 📠 01787 880307
Hall St CO10 9JG
e-mail: bull.longmelford@greeneking.co.uk
web: www.oldenglish.co.uk
dir: 3m N of Sudbury on A134

Rooms 25 (4 fmly) **Facilities** Xmas **Conf** Class 40 Board 30 Thtr 100 **Parking** 35 **Notes** LB ⊗ Civ Wed 100

LOWESTOFT **Map 13 TM59**

Hotel Victoria

★★★ 83% ⑳ HOTEL

☎ 01502 574433 📠 01502 501529
Kirkley Cliff NR33 0BZ
e-mail: info@thehotelvictoria.co.uk
dir: A12 to seafront on one-way system signed A12 Ipswich. Hotel on seafront just beyond thatched cottage

Attractive Victorian building situated on the esplanade overlooking the sea and has direct access to the beach. Bedrooms are pleasantly decorated and thoughtfully equipped; many rooms have sea views. Public rooms include modern conference and banqueting facilities, a choice of lounges, a comfortable bar and a restaurant, which overlooks the pretty garden.

Rooms 24 (4 fmly) **Facilities** Xmas New Year Wi-fi **Conf** Class 150 Board 50 Thtr 200 **Services** Lift **Parking** 45 **Notes** ⊗ Civ Wed 200

Ivy House Country Hotel

★★★ 82% ⑳⑳ HOTEL

☎ 01502 501353 & 588144 📠 01502 501539
Ivy Ln, Beccles Rd, Oulton Broad NR33 8HY
e-mail: aa@ivyhousecountryhotel.co.uk
web: www.ivyhousecountryhotel.co.uk
dir: On A146 SW of Oulton Broad turn into Ivy Ln beside Esso petrol station. Over railway bridge, follow private drive

Peacefully located, family-run hotel set in three acres of mature landscaped grounds just a short walk from Oulton Broad. Public rooms include an 18th-century thatched

barn restaurant where an interesting choice of dishes is served. The attractively decorated bedrooms are housed in garden wings, and many have lovely views of the grounds to the countryside beyond.

Ivy House Country Hotel

Rooms 20 (20 annexe) (1 fmly) (17 GF) **S** £99-£119; **D** £135-£170 (incl. bkfst)* **Fàcilities** FTV Wi-fi **Conf** Board 22 Thtr 55 Del from £145 to £165* **Parking** 50 **Notes** LB Closed 23 Dec-6 Jan Civ Wed 80

Travelodge Lowestoft

BUDGET HOTEL

☎ 0871 984 6408 📠 01502 733165
Leisure Way NR32 4TZ
dir: A1117 into Lowestoft, at rdbt 2nd exit into Bentley Dr. At next rdbt 2nd exit into Leisure Way. Lodge behind Harvester pub

Travelodge offers good quality, good value, budget accommodation. All offer family rooms sleeping up to four (two adults, two children) with en suite bathroom/shower-room, remote-control TV, tea- and coffee-making facilities and comfortable beds. Food options vary. Breakfast is at the on-site Bar Café restaurant (if available) or to take away. See also the Hotel Groups pages.

Rooms 47 **S** fr £29; **D** fr £29

MILDENHALL — Map 12 TL77

The Olde Bull Inn

★★★ 80% ⚜ HOTEL

☎ 01638 711001 📠 01638 712003
The Street, Barton Mills IP28 6AA
e-mail: bookings@bullinn-bartonmills.com
dir: Off A11 between Newmarket & Mildenhall, signed
Barton Mills. Hotel by Five Ways rdbt

This delightful 16th-century coaching inn has been
lovingly refurbished by the present owners. Public rooms
offer a choice of bars, a brasserie-style restaurant and a
further lounge area. The contemporary bedrooms are
tastefully appointed with co-ordinated soft furnishings
and many thoughtful touches.

Rooms 14 (2 annexe) (2 fmly) (2 GF) **S** £75-£95;
D £85-£115 (incl. bkfst)* **Facilities** STV FTV Wi-fi
Conf Class 20 Board 20 Thtr 30 **Parking** 60 **Notes** LB ⊗
RS 25 Dec

See advert on opposite page

Riverside Hotel, Bar and Restaurant

★★★ 73% HOTEL

☎ 01638 717274 📠 01638 715997
Mill St IP28 7DP
e-mail: reservations.riverside@ohiml.com
web: www.oxfordhotelsandinns.com
dir: M11 junct 9 onto A11, at Fiveways rdbt take A1101
signed Milenhall, straight over rdbt, left onto High St for
0.5m onto Mill St, hotel on left before bridge

An 18th-century, red brick building situated in the heart
of this charming town on the banks of the River Lark.
Public rooms include a smart restaurant, which overlooks
the river and the attractive gardens at the rear. The
smartly decorated bedrooms have co-ordinated soft
furnishings and many thoughtful touches.

Rooms 22 (6 annexe) (3 fmly) (4 GF) **Facilities** Xmas
New Year Wi-fi **Conf** Class 50 Board 30 Thtr 120
Services Lift **Parking** 35 **Notes** Civ Wed 100

NEEDHAM MARKET — Map 13 TM05

Travelodge Ipswich Beacon Hill

BUDGET HOTEL

☎ 0871 984 6041 📠 01449 721640
Beacon Hill IP6 8LP
web: www.travelodge.co.uk
dir: From Ipswich westbound on A14. Exit at junction with
A140 (Norwich Rd). Lodge off rdbt in Service Area

Travelodge offers good quality, good value, budget
accommodation. All offer family rooms sleeping up to four
(two adults, two children) with en suite bathroom/
shower-room, remote-control TV, tea- and coffee-making
facilities and comfortable beds. Food options vary.
Breakfast is at the on-site Bar Café restaurant (if
available) or to take away. See also Hotel Groups pages.

Rooms 40 **S** fr £29; **D** fr £29

NEWMARKET — Map 12 TL66

Bedford Lodge Hotel

★★★★ 81% ⚜⚜ HOTEL

☎ 01638 663175 📠 01638 667391
Bury Rd CB8 7BX
e-mail: info@bedfordlodgehotel.co.uk
web: www.bedfordlodgehotel.co.uk
dir: From town centre take A1304 towards Bury St
Edmunds, hotel 0.5m on left

Imposing 18th-century Georgian hunting lodge set in
three acres of secluded landscaped gardens. Public
rooms feature the elegant Orangery restaurant, a smart
lounge bar and a small lounge. The hotel also features
superb leisure facilities and self-contained conference
and banqueting suites. Contemporary bedrooms have a
light, airy feel, and each is tastefully furnished and well
equipped.

Rooms 55 (3 fmly) (16 GF) (3 smoking) **S** £120-£330;
D £137-£341 (incl. bkfst) **Facilities** FTV ⓢ Gym Steam
room Sauna Xmas New Year Wi-fi **Conf** Class 80 Board 60
Thtr 200 Del from £163 to £205 **Services** Lift
Parking 120 **Notes** LB ⊗ RS Sat lunch Civ Wed 150

Rutland Arms

★★★ 79% ⚜ HOTEL — OXFORD HOTELS & INNS

☎ 01638 664251 📠 01638 666298
High St CB8 8NB
e-mail: reservations.rutlandarms@ohiml.com
web: www.oxfordhotelsandinns.com
dir: A14 junct 37 onto A142, or M11 junct 9 onto A11 then
A1304 - follow signs for town centre

Expect a warm welcome at this 16th-century former
coaching inn situated in the heart of town. The property is
built around a cobbled courtyard and still retains many of
its original features. Public rooms include a large lounge
bar and Carriages, a contemporary restaurant and wine
bar. Bedrooms are smartly appointed and well equipped.

Rooms 46 (1 fmly) **Facilities** Wi-fi **Conf** Class 40
Board 30 Thtr 70 **Parking** 40 **Notes** LB ⊗

Best Western Heath Court

★★★ 78% HOTEL

☎ 01638 667171 📠 01638 666533
Moulton Rd CB8 8DY
e-mail: quality@heathcourthotel.com
dir: Leave A14 at Newmarket & Ely exit onto A142. Follow
town centre signs over mini rdbt. At clocktower left into
Moulton Rd

Modern red-brick hotel situated close to Newmarket
Heath and perfectly placed for the town centre. Public
rooms include a choice of dining options - informal meals
can be taken in the lounge bar or a modern carte menu is
offered in the restaurant. The smartly presented

bedrooms are mostly spacious and some have air conditioning.

Rooms 41 (2 fmly) **Facilities** STV New Year Wi-fi **Conf** Class 50 Board 40 Thtr 130 Del from £85 to £145* **Services** Lift **Parking** 60 **Notes** Civ Wed 80

Cadogan

★★★ 73% SMALL HOTEL

☎ 01638 663814 & 07776 258688 📠 01638 561480
Fordham Rd CB8 7AA
e-mail: kgreed@btinternet.com
dir: A142 to Newmarket. Over 2 rdbts signed Town Centre. Continue on A142 for 1.5m. At 30mph limit hotel 500mtrs on left

This small, friendly, family run hotel is situated just a short walk from the town centre within easy reach of Newmarket racecourse. Public rooms include an open-plan lounge bar with plush seating and a smart dining room. The bedrooms are pleasantly decorated with co-ordinated fabrics and have a good range of facilities.

Rooms 12 (2 fmly) (1 GF) **S** £65-£95; **D** £90-£155 (incl. bkfst) **Facilities** FTV Wi-fi **Parking** 18 **Notes** ⊗ Closed 24 Dec-2 Jan

---

| ORFORD | Map 13 TM45 |

The Crown & Castle

★★★ 85% ⊛⊛ HOTEL

☎ 01394 450205
IP12 2LJ
e-mail: info@crownandcastle.co.uk
web: www.crownandcastle.co.uk
dir: Turn right from B1084 on entering village, towards castle

Delightful inn situated adjacent to the Norman castle keep. Contemporary style bedrooms are spilt between the main house and the garden wing; the latter are more spacious and have patios with access to the garden. The restaurant has an informal atmosphere with polished tables and local artwork; the menu features quality, locally sourced produce.

Rooms 19 (12 annexe) (1 fmly) (11 GF) **S** £92-£164; **D** £115-£205 (incl. bkfst)* **Facilities** Xmas New Year Wi-fi **Conf** Board 10 **Parking** 20 **Notes** LB No children 4yrs Closed 4-7 Jan

---

| SOUTHWOLD | Map 13 TM57 |

Swan

★★★ 81% ⊛⊛ HOTEL

☎ 01502 722186 📠 01502 724800
Market Place IP18 6EG
e-mail: swan.hotel@adnams.co.uk
dir: A1095 to Southwold. Hotel in town centre. Parking via archway to left of building

A charming 17th-century coaching inn situated in the heart of this bustling town centre overlooking the market place. Public rooms feature an elegant restaurant, a comfortable drawing room, a cosy bar and a lounge where guests can enjoy afternoon tea. The spacious bedrooms are attractively decorated, tastefully furnished and thoughtfully equipped.

Rooms 42 (17 annexe) (17 GF) **Facilities** Xmas New Year **Conf** Class 24 Board 12 Thtr 40 **Services** Lift **Parking** 35 **Notes** LB Civ Wed 40

SOUTHWOLD *continued*

The Crown

★★ 85% ® HOTEL

☎ 01502 722275 📠 01502 727263
90 High St IP18 6DP
e-mail: crown.hotel@adnams.co.uk
dir: A12 onto A1095 to Southwold. Hotel on left in High Street

Delightful old posting inn situated in the heart of this bustling town. The property combines a pub, wine bar and restaurant with superb accommodation. The tastefully decorated bedrooms have attractive co-ordinated soft furnishings and many thoughtful touches. Public rooms feature an elegant lounge and a back room bar serving traditional Adnams ales.

Rooms 14 (2 fmly) **Facilities** Xmas New Year **Conf** Board 8 **Parking** 23 **Notes** LB ⊗

Blyth

★★ 85% SMALL HOTEL

☎ 01502 722632 & 0845 348 6867
Station Rd IP18 6AY
e-mail: reception@blythhotel.com

Expect a warm welcome at this delightful family run hotel which is situated just a short walk from the town centre. The spacious public rooms include a smart residents' lounge, an open-plan bar and a large restaurant. Bedrooms are tastefully appointed with co-ordinated fabrics and have many thoughtful touches.

Rooms 13 **S** £65-£75; **D** £95-£115 (incl. bkfst)* **Facilities** FTV Xmas New Year Wi-fi **Conf** Class 20 Board 12 Thtr 20 Del from £90 to £150* **Parking** 8 **Notes** LB

Sutherland House

®® RESTAURANT WITH ROOMS

☎ 01502 724544
56 High St IP18 6DN
e-mail: enquiries@sutherlandhouse.co.uk
web: www.sutherlandhouse.co.uk
dir: A1095 into Southwold, on High St on left after Victoria St

A delightful 16th-century house situated in the heart of the bustling town centre with a wealth of character; there are oak beams, exposed brickwork, open fireplaces and two superb ornate plasterwork ceilings. The stylish bedrooms are tastefully decorated, have co-ordinated fabrics and many thoughtful touches. Public rooms feature a large open-plan contemporary restaurant with plush furniture.

Rooms 4 (1 fmly)

STOKE-BY-NAYLAND — Map 13 TL93

Crown

★★★ 83% ®® SMALL HOTEL

☎ 01206 262001 & 262346 📠 01206 264026
CO6 4SE
e-mail: reservations@crowninn.net
web: www.crowninn.net
dir: Stoke-by-Nayland signed from A12 & A134. Hotel in village off B1068 towards Higham

Situated in a picturesque village this establishment has an award-winning restaurant which has a reputation for making everyone feel welcome. It offers quietly located, individually decorated rooms that look out over the countryside. Ground floor rooms, including three with a terrace, are of a contemporary design while upstairs rooms are in a country-house style; each room has Wi-fi, DVDs and luxury toiletries.

Rooms 11 (1 fmly) (8 GF) **S** £70-£185; **D** £70-£185 (incl. bkfst)* **Facilities** FTV New Year Wi-fi **Conf** Board 10 **Parking** 49 **Notes** LB ⊗

STOWMARKET — Map 13 TM05

Cedars

THE INDEPENDENTS
HOTEL ASSOCIATION

★★★ 72% HOTEL

☎ 01449 612668 📠 01449 674704
Needham Rd IP14 2AJ
e-mail: info@cedarshotel.co.uk
dir: A14 junct 15, A1120 towards Stowmarket. At junct with A1113 turn right. Hotel on right

Expect a friendly welcome at this privately owned hotel, which is situated just off the A14 within easy reach of the town centre. Public rooms are full of charm and character with features such as exposed beams and open fireplaces. Bedrooms are pleasantly decorated and thoughtfully equipped with modern facilities.

Rooms 25 (3 fmly) (9 GF) **S** fr £65; **D** fr £72 (incl. bkfst)* **Facilities** Wi-fi **Conf** Class 60 Board 40 Thtr 150 **Parking** 75 **Notes** LB Closed 25 Dec-1 Jan

Travelodge Ipswich Stowmarket

BUDGET HOTEL

☎ 0871 984 6043 📠 01449 615347
IP14 3PY
web: www.travelodge.co.uk
dir: on A14 westbound

Travelodge offers good quality, good value, modern accommodation. Ideal for families, the spacious en suite bedrooms include remote-control TV, tea and coffee-making facilities and comfortable beds. Meals can be taken at the nearby family restaurant. See also the Hotel Groups pages.

Rooms 40 **S** fr £29; **D** fr £29

SUDBURY

The Case Restaurant with Rooms

RESTAURANT WITH ROOMS

☎ 01787 210483 📠 01787 211725
Further St, Assington CO10 5LD
e-mail: restaurant@thecaserestaurantwithrooms.co.uk
dir: Exit A12 at Colchester and take A134 to Sudbury. 7m from Colchester on left

Now completely refurbished, The Case Restaurant with Rooms offers exceptional dining in comfortable surroundings, along with luxurious accommodation in bedrooms that all enjoy independent access. Some bathrooms come complete with corner Jacuzzi, while internet access comes as standard. In the restaurant, local produce is used in all dishes, and fresh bread and desserts are made every day.

Rooms 7 (2 fmly)

THORPENESS
Map 13 TM45

Thorpeness Hotel
★★★ 78% HOTEL

☎ 01728 452176 📠 01728 453868
Lakeside Av IP16 4NH
e-mail: info@thorpeness.co.uk
web: www.thorpeness.co.uk
dir: A1094 towards Aldeburgh, then coast road north for 2m

Ideally situated in an unspoilt, tranquil setting close to Aldeburgh and Snape Maltings. The extensive public rooms include a choice of lounges, a restaurant, a smart bar, a snooker room and clubhouse. The spacious bedrooms are pleasantly decorated, tastefully furnished and equipped with modern facilities. An 18-hole golf course and tennis courts are also available.

Rooms 36 (36 annexe) (10 fmly) (10 GF) **S** £80-£111; **D** £90-£152 (incl. bkfst)* **Facilities** ≵ 18 🏊 Putt green Fishing Cycle hire Rowing boat hire Birdwatching Xmas New Year Wi-fi **Conf** Class 30 Board 24 Thtr 130 Del from £110 to £160* **Parking** 80 **Notes** LB Civ Wed 130

WESTLETON
Map 13 TM46

Westleton Crown
★★★ 78% ◉◉ HOTEL

☎ 01728 648777 📠 01728 648239
The Street IP17 3AD
e-mail: reception@westletoncrown.co.uk
web: www.westletoncrown.co.uk
dir: A12 N, turn right for Westleton just after Yoxford. Hotel opposite on entering Westleton

Charming coaching inn situated in a peaceful village location just a few minutes from the A12. Public rooms include a smart, award-winning restaurant, comfortable lounge, and busy bar with exposed beams and open fireplaces. The stylish bedrooms are tastefully decorated and equipped with many thoughtful little extras.

Rooms 25 (3 annexe) (3 fmly) (8 GF) **S** £95-£115; **D** £115-£180 (incl. bkfst)* **Facilities** Xmas New Year Wi-fi **Conf** Class 40 Board 30 Thtr 60 **Parking** 45 **Notes** Closed 25 Dec

WOODBRIDGE
Map 13 TM24

Seckford Hall
★★★ 81% ◉◉ HOTEL

☎ 01394 385678 📠 01394 380610
IP13 6NU
e-mail: reception@seckford.co.uk
web: www.seckford.co.uk
dir: Signed on A12. (NB do not follow signs for town centre)

An elegant Tudor manor house set amid landscaped grounds just off the A12. It is reputed that Queen Elizabeth I visited this property, and it retains much of its original character. Public rooms include a superb panelled lounge, a cosy bar and an intimate restaurant. The spacious bedrooms are attractively decorated, tastefully furnished and thoughtfully equipped.

Rooms 32 (10 annexe) (4 fmly) (7 GF) **S** fr £80; **D** £120-£210* **Facilities** 🕐 ≵ 18 Putt green Fishing Gym Beauty salon New Year Wi-fi **Conf** Class 46 Board 40 Thtr 100 Del from £166 to £199* **Parking** 100 **Notes** LB Closed 25 Dec Civ Wed 120

Best Western Ufford Park Hotel Golf & Spa

★★★ 78% HOTEL

☎ 01394 383555 📠 0844 4773727
Yarmouth Rd, Ufford IP12 1QW
e-mail: mail@uffordpark.co.uk
web: www.uffordpark.co.uk
dir: A12 N to A1152, in Melton left at lights, follow B1438, hotel 1m on right

A modern hotel set in open countryside boasting superb leisure facilities including a challenging golf course. The spacious public rooms provide a wide choice of areas in which to relax and include a busy lounge bar, a carvery restaurant and the Vista Restaurant. Bedrooms are smartly appointed and pleasantly decorated, each thoughtfully equipped; many rooms overlook the golf course.

Rooms 87 (20 fmly) (32 GF) **S** £90-£120; **D** £110-£170 (incl. bkfst)* **Facilities** Spa FTV 🕐 supervised ≵ 18 Putt green Fishing 🏊 Gym Golf Academy with PGA tuition 2 storey floodlit driving range Dance Studio Xmas New Year Wi-fi **Conf** Class 120 Board 120 Thtr 300 Del from £99 to £116* **Services** Lift **Parking** 250 **Notes** LB Civ Wed 120

YAXLEY
Map 13 TM17

The Auberge
◉◉ RESTAURANT WITH ROOMS

☎ 01379 783604 📠 01379 788486
Ipswich Rd IP23 8BZ
e-mail: aubmail@the-auberge.co.uk
web: www.the-auberge.co.uk
dir: On A140 between Norwich & Ipswich at B1117 x-rds with Eye & Thornham Parva

A warm welcome awaits at this charming 15th-century property, which has been lovingly converted by the present owners into a smart restaurant with rooms. The public areas have a wealth of character, such as exposed brickwork and beams. The spacious bedrooms are tastefully appointed and have many thoughtful touches.

Rooms 11 (7 annexe) (2 fmly)

YOXFORD
Map 13 TM36

Satis House
★★★ 86% ◉◉ COUNTRY HOUSE HOTEL

☎ 01728 668418 📠 01728 668640
IP17 3EX
e-mail: enquiries@satishouse.co.uk
web: www.satishouse.co.uk
dir: Off A12 between Ipswich & Lowestoft. 9m E Aldeburgh & Snape

Expect a warm welcome from the caring hosts at this delightful 18th-century, Grade II listed property set in three acres of parkland. The stylish public areas have a really relaxed atmosphere; they include a choice of dining rooms, a smart bar and a cosy lounge. The individually decorated bedrooms are tastefully appointed and thoughtfully equipped.

Rooms 9 (2 annexe) (1 fmly) (2 GF) **Facilities** STV FTV Xmas New Year **Conf** Class 40 Board 20 Thtr 40 **Parking** 30 **Notes** Closed 2-18 Jan Civ Wed 50

SURREY

BAGSHOT — Map 6 SU96

INSPECTORS' CHOICE

Pennyhill Park Hotel & The Spa

★★★★★ @@@@ COUNTRY HOUSE HOTEL

☎ 01276 471774 📠 01276 473217
London Rd GU19 5EU
e-mail: enquiries@pennyhillpark.co.uk
web: www.exclusivehotels.co.uk
dir: M3 junct 3, follow signs to Camberley. On A30 between Bagshot & Camberley

This delightful country-house hotel set in 120-acre grounds provides every modern comfort. The stylish bedrooms are individually designed and have impressive bathrooms. The award-winning Latymer Restaurant is among the range of dining options and there is a choice of lounges and bars. Leisure facilities include a jogging trail, a golf course and a state-of-the-art spa with a thermal sequencing experience, ozone treated swimming and hydrotherapy pools along with a comprehensive range of therapies and treatments. Exclusive Hotels - AA Small Hotel Group of the Year 2009-10.

Rooms 123 (97 annexe) (6 fmly) (26 GF)
D £295-£1250* **Facilities** Spa STV ⊗ ⤸ ↕ 9 ⤸
Fishing ⤸ Gym Archery Clay shooting Plunge pool
Turkish steam room Rugby/football pitch ♫ Xmas New
Year Wi-fi **Conf** Class 80 Board 60 Thtr 160
Del from £320 to £395* **Services** Lift **Parking** 500
Notes LB Civ Wed 140

CAMBERLEY — Map 6 SU86
See also **Yateley (Hampshire)**

Macdonald Frimley Hall Hotel & Spa

★★★★ 78% @@ HOTEL

☎ 0844 879 9110 📠 01276 670362
Lime Av GU15 2BG
e-mail: sales.frimleyhall@macdonald-hotels.co.uk
web: www.macdonaldhotels.co.uk/frimleyhall
dir: M3 junct 3, A321 follow Bagshot signs. Through lights, left onto A30 signed Camberley & Basingstoke. To rdbt, 2nd exit onto A325, take 5th right

The epitome of classic English elegance this ivy-clad Victorian manor house is set in two acres of immaculate grounds in the heart of Surrey. The bedrooms and public areas are smart and have a modern decorative theme. The hotel boasts an impressive health club and spa with treatment rooms, a fully equipped gym and heated indoor swimming pool.

Rooms 98 (15 fmly) **S** £94-£225; **Facilities** Spa STV ⊗
Gym Beauty treatment rooms Technogym Sauna Steam
room Relaxation Xmas New Year Wi-fi **Conf** Class 100
Board 60 Thtr 250 Del from £195 to £320 **Parking** 150
Notes LB Civ Wed 220

Lakeside International
★★★ 70% HOTEL

☎ 01252 838000 📠 01252 837857
Wharf Rd, Frimley Green GU16 6JR
e-mail: info@lakesideinthotel.com
dir: Off A321 at mini-rdbt turn into Wharf Rd. Lakeside complex on right

This hotel, geared towards the business market, enjoys a lakeside location with noteworthy views. Bedrooms are modern, comfortable and with a range of facilities. Public areas are spacious and include a residents' lounge, bar and games room, a smart restaurant and an established health and leisure club.

Rooms 98 (1 fmly) (31 GF) **Facilities** ⊗ Gym Squash
Wi-fi **Conf** Class 100 Board 40 Thtr 120 **Services** Lift
Parking 250 **Notes** ⊗ Civ Wed 100

The Ely

[U]

☎ 01252 860444 📠 01252 878265
London Road (A30), Blackwater GU17 9LJ
e-mail: ely.yateley@newbridgeinns.co.uk
dir: M3 junct 4A, A327 towards Yateley. Right onto A30

Currently the rating for this establishment is not confirmed. This may be due to a change of ownership or because it has only recently joined the AA rating scheme. For further details please see the AA website: theAA.com

Rooms 35

Travelodge Camberley

BUDGET HOTEL

☎ 0871 984 6315 📠 01276 82839
507-537 London Rd GU15 3UR
web: www.travelodge.co.uk
dir: M3 junct 4, A331 (signed Camberley/Wokingham/
Reading). At lights continue onto A331. Right, then at
rdbt take A30 signed Staines/London. Right. After 1st
lights right into Yorktown Way for lodge

Travelodge offers good quality, good value, budget accommodation. All offer family rooms sleeping up to four (two adults, two children) with en suite bathroom/ shower-room, remote-control TV, tea- and coffee-making facilities and comfortable beds. Food options vary. Breakfast is at the on-site Bar Café restaurant (if available) or to take away. See also Hotel Groups pages.

Rooms 66 **S** fr £29; **D** fr £29

CATERHAM — Map 6 TQ35

Travelodge Caterham Whyteleafe

BUDGET HOTEL

☎ 0871 984 6317 📠 01883 627581
431 Godstone Rd, Whyteleafe CR3 0BF
web: www.travelodge.co.uk
dir: A22 towards London. Straight over at rdbt to
Whyteleafe, 1m. Right across carriageway to car park

Travelodge offers good quality, good value, budget accommodation. All offer family rooms sleeping up to four (two adults, two children) with en suite bathroom/ shower-room, remote-control TV, tea- and coffee-making facilities and comfortable beds. Food options vary. Breakfast is at the on-site Bar Café restaurant (if available) or to take away. See also Hotel Groups pages.

Rooms 60 **S** fr £29; **D** fr £29

CHURT — Map 5 SU83

Best Western Frensham Pond Hotel

★★★ 76% HOTEL

☎ 01252 795161 📠 01252 792631
Bacon Ln GU10 2QB
e-mail: info@frenshampondhotel.co.uk
web: www.frenshampondhotel.co.uk
dir: A3 onto A287. 4m left at 'Beware Horses' sign. Hotel 0.25m

This 15th-century house occupies a superb location on the edge of Frensham Pond. The bedrooms are mainly spacious, and the superior executive garden annexe rooms have their own patio, air conditioning and flat-screen TVs. The contemporary bar and lounge offers a range of snacks, and the leisure club has good facilities.

Rooms 51 (12 annexe) (14 fmly) (27 GF) **S** £65-£125; **D** £65-£185 (incl. bkfst)* **Facilities** STV ⊗ supervised Gym Squash Steam room Sauna Xmas New Year Wi-fi **Conf** Class 45 Board 40 Thtr 120 Del from £99 to £145* **Parking** 120 **Notes** LB ⊗ Civ Wed 130

DORKING — Map 6 TQ14

Mercure Burford Bridge

★★★★ 74% ⊛⊛ HOTEL

☎ 01306 884561 📠 01306 880386
Burford Bridge, Box Hill RH5 6BX
e-mail: h6635@accor.com
web: www.mercure-uk.com
dir: M25 junct 9/A245 towards Dorking. Hotel within 5m on A24

Steeped in history, this hotel was reputedly where Lord Nelson and Lady Hamilton met for the last time, and it is said that the landscape around the hotel has inspired many poets. The hotel has a contemporary feel throughout. The grounds, running down to the River Mole, are extensive, and there are good transport links to major centres, including London. The elegant Emlyn Restaurant offers a modern award-winning menu.

Rooms 57 (22 fmly) (3 GF) **Facilities** ⊗ ♬ Xmas New Year Wi-fi **Conf** Class 80 Board 60 Thtr 120 **Parking** 130 **Notes** LB ⊗ Civ Wed 200

Gatton Manor Hotel & Golf Club

★★★ 79% HOTEL

☎ 01306 627555 📠 01306 627713
Standon Ln RH5 5PQ
e-mail: info@gattonmanor.co.uk
web: www.gattonmanor.co.uk

(For full entry see Ockley)

Mercure White Horse

★★★ 66% HOTEL

☎ 0870 400 8282 📠 01306 887241
High St RH4 1BE
web: www.mercure-uk.com
dir: M25 junct 9, A24 S towards Dorking. Hotel in town centre

The hotel was first established as an inn in 1750, although parts of the building date back as far as the 15th century. Its town centre location and Dickensian charm have long made this a popular destination for travellers. There's beamed ceilings, open fires and four-poster beds; more contemporary rooms can be found in the garden wing.

Rooms 78 (41 annexe) (2 fmly) (5 GF) **Facilities** Xmas **Conf** Class 30 Board 30 Thtr 50 **Parking** 73

Travelodge Dorking

BUDGET HOTEL

☎ 0871 984 6026 📠 01306 741673
Reigate Rd RH4 1QB
web: www.travelodge.co.uk
dir: 0.5m E of Dorking, on A25

Travelodge offers good quality, good value, budget accommodation. All offer family rooms sleeping up to four (two adults, two children) with en suite bathroom/shower-room, remote-control TV, tea- and coffee-making facilities and comfortable beds. Food options vary. Breakfast is at the on-site Bar Café restaurant (if available) or to take away. See also Hotel Groups pages.

Rooms 55 **S** fr £29; **D** fr £29

EAST HORSLEY — Map 6 TQ05

Ramada Guildford/Leatherhead

Ⓡ RAMADA

★★★ 80% HOTEL

☎ 01483 280500 📠 01483 284222
Guildford Rd KT24 6TB
e-mail: sales.guildford@ramadajarvis.co.uk
web: www.ramadajarvis.co.uk
dir: A25 towards Leatherhead & Dorking. Pass West Horsley, hotel 0.5m on left

With easy access to the M25 the hotel's 19th-century oak beamed exterior conceals a wide range of modern facilities. Bedrooms are comfortably appointed for both business and leisure guests.

Rooms 87 (11 fmly) (20 GF) **Facilities** FTV Xmas New Year Wi-fi **Conf** Class 70 Board 66 Thtr 170 **Services** Lift **Parking** 110 **Notes** Civ Wed 120

EGHAM — Map 6 TQ07

Great Fosters

★★★★ 80% ⊛⊛ HOTEL

☎ 01784 433822 📠 01784 472455
Stroude Rd TW20 9UR
e-mail: enquiries@greatfosters.co.uk
web: www.greatfosters.co.uk
dir: From A30 (Bagshot to Staines), right at lights by Wheatsheaf pub into Christchurch Rd. Straight on at rdbt (pass 2 shop parades on right). Left at lights into Stroude Rd. Hotel 0.75m on right

This Grade I listed mansion dates back to the 16th century. The main house rooms are very much in keeping with the house's original style but are, of course, up-to-date with modern amenities. The stables and cloisters provide particularly stylish and luxurious accommodation. Public areas include a cosy bar and the award-winning Oak Room Restaurant, as well as a host of meeting and event facilities. Alfresco dining, overlooking the well manicured grounds, in the summer months is a must. Please note that from Friday to Sunday the room rate includes breakfast.

Rooms 44 (22 annexe) (1 fmly) (13 GF) **S** £125-£155; **D** £195-£425* **Facilities** STV ⊗ ⊗ ⊗ Xmas New Year Wi-fi **Conf** Class 72 Board 50 Thtr 150 Del from £275 to £325* **Parking** 200 **Notes** LB ⊗ Civ Wed 180

Runnymede Hotel & Spa

★★★★ 78% HOTEL

☎ 01784 436171 📠 01784 436340
Windsor Rd TW20 0AG
e-mail: info@runnymedehotel.com
web: www.runnymedehotel.com
dir: M25 junct 13, onto A308 towards Windsor

Enjoying a peaceful location beside the River Thames, this large modern hotel, with its excellent range of facilities, balances both leisure and corporate business well. The extensive function suites, together with spacious lounges and stylish, well laid out bedrooms are impressive. Superb spa facilities are available, and the good food and beverage venues offer wonderful river views.

Rooms 180 (19 fmly) **Facilities** Spa STV ⊗ ⊗ ⊗ Gym Dance studio Children's play area River boat hire Treatment suite ♬ New Year Wi-fi **Conf** Class 250 Board 76 Thtr 300 **Services** Lift Air con **Parking** 280 **Notes** LB ⊗ RS Sat lunch/Sun dinner Civ Wed 140

See advert on page 52

EPSOM
Map 6 TQ26

Chalk Lane Hotel
★★★ 78% HOTEL

☎ 01372 721179 🖺 01372 727878
Chalk Ln, Woodcote End KT18 7BB
e-mail: smcgregor@chalklanehotel.com
web: www.chalklanehotel.com
dir: M25 junct 9 onto A24 to Epsom. Right at lights by BP garage. Left into Avenue Rd, right into Worple Rd. Left at T-junct & hotel on right

This delightful, privately owned hotel enjoys a peaceful location just a ten minute walk from Epsom Racecourse. Stylish bedrooms are generally spacious and all are appointed to a high standard. Public areas are attractively furnished and include a choice of lounges, an excellent range of function and meeting facilities. A smartly appointed restaurant offers imaginative, accomplished cuisine.

Rooms 22 (1 fmly) **Facilities** FTV Wi-fi **Conf** Class 40 Board 30 Thtr 140 **Parking** 60

Express by Holiday Inn London - Epsom Downs
BUDGET HOTEL

☎ 0871 423 4876
Langley Vale Rd KT18 5LG
e-mail: epsom@expressbyholidayinn.net

A modern hotel ideal for families and business travellers. Fresh and uncomplicated, the spacious rooms include Sky TV, power shower and tea and coffee-making facilities. Continental buffet breakfast is included in the room rate; other meals may be taken at the nearby family pub or restaurant. See also the Hotel Groups pages.

Rooms 120

EWELL
Map 6 TQ26

Nonsuch Park Hotel
★★ 64% SMALL HOTEL

☎ 020 8393 0771 🖺 020 8393 1415
355-357 London Rd KT17 2DE
e-mail: reservations@nonsuchparkhotel.com
web: www.nonsuchparkhotel.com
dir: A240 onto A24 (London Rd) for 0.75m

This comfortable accommodation stands opposite Nonsuch Park. The attractive bedrooms have good facilities, and the public areas include a small bar area and a lounge-dining room overlooking the rear patio.

Rooms 11 (2 fmly) (4 GF) **Parking** 11 **Notes** ✖ Closed 2-3 wks Xmas

FARNHAM
Map 5 SU84

Best Western Frensham Pond Hotel

★★★ 76% HOTEL

☎ 01252 795161 🖺 01252 792631
Bacon Ln GU10 2QB
e-mail: info@frenshampondhotel.co.uk
web: www.frenshampondhotel.co.uk

(For full entry see Churt)

Mercure Bush

★★★ 75% HOTEL

☎ 0870 400 8225 & 01252 715237 🖺 01252 733530
The Borough GU9 7NN
e-mail: H6621@accor.com
web: www.mercure-uk.com
dir: M3 junct 4, A31, follow town centre signs. At East Street lights turn left, hotel on right

Dating back to the 17th century, this extended coaching inn is attractively presented and has a courtyard and a lawned garden. The bedrooms are well appointed, with quality fabrics and good facilities. The public areas include the panelled Oak Lounge, a smart cocktail bar and a conference facility in an adjoining building.

Rooms 83 (3 fmly) (22 GF) (5 smoking) **Facilities** STV New Year Wi-fi **Conf** Class 80 Board 30 Thtr 140 **Parking** 70 **Notes** Civ Wed 90

FRIMLEY
Map 5 SU85

Innkeeper's Lodge Camberley Frimley
BUDGET HOTEL

☎ 0845 112 6098 🖺 0845 112 6205
114 Portsmouth Rd GU15 1HS
web: www.innkeeperslodge.com/frimley
dir: M3 junct 4, A331 then left onto A325 (Portsmouth road). Straight on at 2 rdbts. Lodge approx 1m on left

Innkeeper's Lodge represents an exciting, high value concept within the budget hotel market. Comfortable bedrooms provide excellent facilities that include satellite TV and modem points. Options include family rooms; and for the corporate guest, cutting edge IT which includes Wi-fi access. A popular Carvery provides all-day food, including an extensive, complimentary continental breakfast. See also the Hotel Groups pages.

Rooms 43 (2 fmly) **Conf** Thtr 30

GODALMING
Map 6 SU94

Innkeeper's Lodge Godalming

BUDGET HOTEL

☎ 0845 112 6102 🖺 0845 112 6201
Ockford Rd GU7 1RH
web: www.innkeeperslodge.com/Godalming
dir: M25 junct 10 south towards Guildford on A3. Left at Milford junct, at rdbt take A283. Left towards Godalming on A3100, into Ockford Road. Lodge on right just after rail bridge

Innkeeper's Lodge Select represents an exciting, stylish concept within the hotel market. Contemporary style bedrooms provide excellent facilities that include LCD TVs with satellite channels, and modem points. Options include spacious family rooms; and for the corporate guest there's Wi-fi access. All-day food is served in a modern country pub & eating house. The extensive continental breakfast is complimentary. See also the Hotel Groups pages.

Rooms 14

GUILDFORD
Map 6 SU94

Holiday Inn Guildford

★★★ 79% HOTEL

☎ 0870 400 9036 🖺 01483 457256
Egerton Rd GU2 7XZ
e-mail: reservations-guildford@ihg.com
web: www.holidayinn.co.uk
dir: A3 to Guildford. Exit at sign for Research Park/Onslow Village. 3rd exit at 1st rdbt, 2nd exit at 2nd rdbt

This hotel is in a convenient location just off the A3 and within a 25 minute-drive of the M25. Public areas are stylish, and on-site facilities include a swimming pool and gym. The accommodation is spacious and comfortable and caters well for both the business and leisure markets. A number of well-equipped meeting rooms is available. Ample complimentary parking is available.

Rooms 168 (52 fmly) (66 GF) (9 smoking) **S** £65-£260; **D** £65-£260 **Facilities** Spa STV ③ Gym Fitness studio Beauty treatments Wi-fi **Conf** Class 100 Board 60 Thtr 180 Del from £99 to £355 **Services** Air con **Parking** 230 **Notes** LB ✖ Civ Wed 180

Travelodge Guildford

BUDGET HOTEL

☎ 0871 984 6295   📄 01483 450174
Woodbridge Rd, Woodbridge Meadows GU1 1BD
web: www.travelodge.co.uk
dir: A322 onto A25 (Middleton Rd). Right onto A25 to Woodbridge Meadows, then right

Travelodge offers good quality, good value, budget accommodation. All offer family rooms sleeping up to four (two adults, two children) with en suite bathroom/shower-room, remote-control TV, tea- and coffee-making facilities and comfortable beds. Food options vary. Breakfast is at the on-site Bar Café restaurant (if available) or to take away. See also Hotel Groups pages.

Rooms 152 **S** fr £29; **D** fr £29

HASLEMERE   Map 6 SU93

Lythe Hill Hotel and Spa

★★★★ 76% ◉◉ HOTEL

☎ 01428 651251   📄 01428 644131
Petworth Rd GU27 3BQ
e-mail: lythe@lythehill.co.uk
web: www.lythehill.co.uk
dir: Left from High St onto B2131. Hotel 1.25m on right

This privately owned hotel sits in 30 acres of attractive parkland with lakes, complete with roaming geese. The hotel has been described as a hamlet of character buildings, each furnished in a style that complements the age of the property; the oldest one dating back to 1475. Cuisine in the adjacent 'Auberge de France' offers interesting, quality dishes, whilst breakfast is served in the hotel dining room. The bedrooms are split between a number of 15th-century buildings and vary in size. The stylish spa includes a 16-metre swimming pool.

Rooms 41 (8 fmly) (18 GF) **Facilities** Spa FTV ⊛ ♨ Fishing ⚑ Gym Boules ♬ Xmas New Year Wi-fi **Conf** Class 40 Board 30 Thtr 128 **Parking** 200 **Notes** Civ Wed 128

HINDHEAD   Map 6 SU83

Devils Punch Bowl Hotel

★★ 71% HOTEL

☎ 01428 606565   📄 01428 605713
London Rd GU26 6AG
e-mail: hotel@punchbowlhotels.co.uk
web: www.punchbowlhotels.co.uk
dir: Hotel on A3 north of Hindhead lights, opposite Devils Punch Bowl site

This establishment occupies a great location on the main road in Hindhead which has excellent links for Guildford, Petersfield, the M25 and Portsmouth. The accommodation is comfortable with a range of double, twins and family rooms. Substantial evening meals are served in the traditionally styled bar area and a very good breakfast is available in the restaurant. Good sized meeting, banqueting and wedding reception facilities available.

Rooms 32 (4 fmly) (10 GF) **S** £74.45; **D** £81.40 (incl. bkfst) **Facilities** Xmas New Year Wi-fi **Conf** Class 40 Board 40 Thtr 85 **Parking** 52 **Notes** LB ⊗ Civ Wed 85

HORLEY

Hotels are listed under Gatwick Airport (Sussex, West)

LEATHERHEAD   Map 6 TQ15

Bookham Grange

★★ 65% HOTEL

☎ 01372 452742 & 459899   📄 01372 450080
Little Bookham Common, Bookham KT23 3HS
e-mail: bookhamgrange@easynet.co.uk
web: www.bookham-grange.co.uk
dir: off A246 at Bookham High St onto Church Rd, 1st right after Bookham railway station

This smart property enjoys a tranquil setting yet is only a short drive from Leatherhead, Guildford and Epsom, with good access to the M25 and London's major airports. Bedrooms are generally spacious and all are smartly appointed. Public areas include a lounge, bar and restaurant as well as conference and meeting facilities. Weddings are well catered for.

Rooms 27 (3 fmly) **Facilities** Xmas New Year Wi-fi **Conf** Class 30 Board 24 Thtr 80 **Parking** 60 **Notes** ⊗ Civ Wed 100

Travelodge Leatherhead

BUDGET HOTEL

☎ 0871 984 6154   📄 01372 386577
The Swan Centre, High St KT22 8AA
web: www.travelodge.co.uk
dir: Follow town centre signs, from one-way system into High St. Lodge ajacent to Swan Shopping Centre

Travelodge offers good quality, good value, budget accommodation. All offer family rooms sleeping up to four (two adults, two children) with en suite bathroom/shower-room, remote-control TV, tea- and coffee-making facilities and comfortable beds. Food options vary. Breakfast is at the on-site Bar Café restaurant (if available) or to take away. See also Hotel Groups pages.

Rooms 91 **S** fr £29; **D** fr £29

OCKLEY   Map 6 TQ14

Gatton Manor Hotel & Golf Club

★★★ 79% HOTEL

☎ 01306 627555   📄 01306 627713
Standon Ln RH5 5PQ
e-mail: info@gattonmanor.co.uk
web: www.gattonmanor.co.uk
dir: Off A29 at Ockley turn into Cat Hill Lane, left into Standon Ln, follow signs for approx 1m

Gatton Manor enjoys a peaceful setting in private grounds. It is a popular golf and country club, with an 18-hole professional course and offers a range of comfortable, modern bedrooms. The public areas include the main club bar and restaurant. Conference facilities are also available.

Rooms 18 (2 fmly) **S** £85-£130; **D** £99-£140 (incl. bkfst)* **Facilities** STV ⚑ 18 Putt green Fishing Gym New Year Wi-fi **Conf** Class 22 Board 30 Thtr 80 **Parking** 250 **Notes** LB ⊗ Closed 25 Dec Civ Wed 90

OTTERSHAW — Map 6 TQ06

Foxhills Resort & Spa

★★★★ 79% HOTEL

☎ 01932 872050 & 704500 📠 01932 874762
Stonehill Rd KT16 0EL
e-mail: reservations@foxhills.co.uk
web: www.foxhills.co.uk
dir: M25, A320 to Woking. 2nd rdbt last exit into
Chobham Rd. Right into Foxhills Rd, left into Stonehill Rd

This 19th-century mansion hotel enjoys a peaceful setting
in extensive grounds, not far from the M25 and Heathrow.
Spacious well-appointed bedrooms are provided in a
choice of annexes that are situated a short walk from the
main house. Golf, tennis, three pools and impressive
indoor leisure facilities are on offer. There is a superb spa
offering a range of treatments and therapies plus a
health club with all the latest fitness equipment. The
eating options are the Manor Restaurant, in the former
music room, and the Summerhouse Brasserie overlooking
one of the pools.

Rooms 70 (7 fmly) (39 GF) S £120-£190; D £120-£300*
Facilities Spa STV FTV 🏊 ⚲ ⚑ 45 🏌 Putt green ⛳ Gym
Squash Children's adventure playground Country pursuits
Off-road course Hairdressers 🎵 Xmas New Year Wi-fi
Child facilities Conf Class 52 Board 56 Thtr 100
Del from £220 to £290* Services Lift Parking 500
Notes LB ⊗ Civ Wed 75

REDHILL — Map 6 TQ25

Nutfield Priory

*Hand*PICKED

★★★★ 80% ⊛⊛ HOTEL

☎ 01737 824400 & 0845 072 7485 📠 01737 824410
Nutfield RH1 4EL
e-mail: nutfieldpriory@handpicked.co.uk
web: www.handpicked.co.uk/nutfield
dir: M25 junct 6, follow Redhill signs via Godstone on
A25. Hotel 1m on left after Nutfield Village. Or M25
junct 8 follow A25 through Reigate, Redhill & Godstone.
Hotel on right 1.5m after railway bridge

This Victorian country house dates back to 1872 and is
set in 40 acres of grounds with stunning views over the
Surrey countryside. Bedrooms are individually decorated
and equipped with an excellent range of facilities. Public

areas include the impressive grand hall, Cloisters
Restaurant, the library, and a cosy lounge bar area.

Rooms 60 (4 fmly) Facilities Spa STV 🏊 Gym Squash
Steam room Beauty therapy Aerobic & Step classes
Saunas Wi-fi Conf Class 45 Board 40 Thtr 80
Services Lift Air con Parking 130 Notes ⊗ Civ Wed 80

Innkeeper's Lodge Redhill (Gatwick)

BUDGET HOTEL

☎ 0845 112 6107 📠 0845 112 6196
2 Redstone Hill RH1 4BL
web: www.innkeeperslodge.com/redhillgatwick
dir: M25 junct 6 or 8, follow signs for Redhill (A25). At
railway station, left towards Godstone, lodge on right

Innkeeper's Lodge represents an exciting, high value
concept within the budget hotel market. Comfortable
bedrooms provide excellent facilities that include satellite
TV and modem points. Options include family rooms; and
for the corporate guest, cutting edge IT which includes
Wi-fi access. A popular Carvery provides all-day food,
including an extensive, complimentary continental
breakfast. See also the Hotel Groups pages.

Rooms 37 (8 fmly) Conf Thtr 20

REIGATE — Map 6 TQ25

Best Western Reigate Manor

Best Western

★★★ 73% HOTEL

☎ 01737 240125 📠 01737 223883
Reigate Hill RH2 9PF
e-mail: hotel@reigatemanor.co.uk
web: www.reigatemanor.co.uk
dir: On A217, 1m S of junct 8 on M25

On the slopes of Reigate Hill, the hotel is ideally located
for access to the town and for motorway links. A range of
public rooms is provided along with a variety of function
rooms. Bedrooms are either traditional in style in the old
house or of contemporary design in the wing.

Rooms 50 (1 fmly) S £98; D £110 (incl. bkfst)*
Facilities STV Wi-fi Conf Class 80 Board 50 Thtr 200
Parking 130 Notes ⊗ Civ Wed 200

SEALE — Map 6 SU84

Ramada Farnham

⊗ RAMADA

★★★ 80% HOTEL

☎ 01252 782345 📠 01252 783113
Hog's Back GU10 1EX
e-mail: sales.farnham@ramadajarvis.co.uk
web: www.ramadajarvis.co.uk
dir: A31, 1st exit onto Hog's Back towards Guildford. Take
next slip road signed Seale/Tongham/Runford. Hotel on
left past service station

Set high on the Hog's Back Ridge in well-presented
grounds, this large hotel is a popular venue for both

conferences and meetings. Bedrooms are comfortably
appointed for both business and leisure guests. Public
areas include a range of meeting rooms and the
Sebastian Coe health club.

Rooms 96 (6 fmly) (27 GF) Facilities Spa STV 🏊 Gym
Whirlpool Sauna Steam room Weights room Fitness studio
Xmas New Year Wi-fi Conf Class 188 Board 160 Thtr 420
Parking 150 Notes ⊗ Civ Wed 140

SHEPPERTON

Holiday Inn London - Shepperton

★★★★ 70% HOTEL

☎ 0870 225 8701 & 01932 899900 📠 01932 245231
Felix Ln TW17 8NP
e-mail: hishepperton@qmh-hotels.com
web: www.holidayinn.co.uk
dir: M3 junct 1, B375 to Lower Sunbury, 5th exit Green St,
right at T-junct. Felix Ln 1.5m on left

This hotel has a range of modern, well-equipped leisure
and conference facilities. Its hidden, tranquil location
also makes it ideal for a family break. The spacious
bedrooms are pleasantly appointed and have air
conditioning. The restaurant offers a carte menu, and the
bar provides an alternative dining venue.

Rooms 185 (11 fmly) (37 GF) (9 smoking) Facilities STV
🏊 Gym Beauty salon Sauna Wi-fi Conf Class 60 Board 40
Thtr 120 Del from £115 to £180* Services Lift Air con
Parking 160 Notes ⊗ Civ Wed 80

STAINES
Map 6 TQ07

Mercure Thames Lodge

★★★ 72% HOTEL

☎ 01784 464433 📠 01784 454858
Thames St TW18 4SJ
e-mail: h6620-re@accor.com
web: www.mercure-uk.com
dir: M25 junct 13. Follow A30/town centre signs (bus station on right). Hotel straight ahead

Located on the banks of the River Thames in a bustling town, this hotel is well positioned for both business and leisure travellers. Meals are served in the Riverside Restaurant, and snacks are available in the spacious lounge/bar; weather permitting the terrace provides a good place for a drink on a summer evening. Onsite parking is an additional bonus.

Rooms 79 (17 fmly) (23 GF) **S** £70-£160; **D** £80-£170* **Facilities** STV Riverside restaurant & tea gardens with riverside frontage moorings New Year Wi-fi **Conf** Class 40 Board 40 Thtr 50 Del from £145 to £160* **Parking** 40 **Notes** LB

Travelodge Staines

BUDGET HOTEL

☎ 0871 984 6246 📠 01784 491 026
Hale St, Two Rivers Retail Park TW18 4UW
web: www.travelodge.co.uk
dir: M25 junct 13, B376 signed Wraysbury. At next rdt left signed B376 Staines. 1m. At 1st lights left into Two Rivers Retail Park. Lodge on left

Travelodge offers good quality, good value, budget accommodation. All offer family rooms sleeping up to four (two adults, two children) with en suite bathroom/shower-room, remote-control TV, tea- and coffee-making facilities and comfortable beds. Food options vary. Breakfast is at the on-site Bar Café restaurant (if available) or to take away. See also Hotel Groups pages.

Rooms 49 **S** fr £29; **D** fr £29

STOKE D'ABERNON
Map 6 TQ15

Woodlands Park

★★★★ 80% ☺ HOTEL

☎ 01372 843933 📠 01372 842704
Woodlands Ln KT11 3QB
e-mail: woodlandspark@handpicked.co.uk
web: www.handpicked.co.uk
dir: A3 exit at Cobham. Through town centre & Stoke D'Abernon, left at garden centre into Woodlands Lane, hotel 0.5m on right

Originally built for the Bryant family, of the matchmaker firm Bryant & May, this lovely Victorian mansion enjoys an attractive parkland setting in ten and a half acres of Surrey countryside. Bedrooms in the wing are contemporary in style while those in the main house are more traditionally decorated. The hotel boasts two dining options, Benson's Brasserie and the Oak Room Restaurant.

Rooms 57 (4 fmly) **Facilities** ♨ ⚒ Xmas New Year Wi-fi **Conf** Class 20 Board 50 Thtr 150 **Services** Lift **Parking** 150 **Notes** ⊗ Civ Wed 200

SUNBURY

See LONDON plan 1 A1

Travelodge Sunbury M3

BUDGET HOTEL

☎ 0871 984 6356
Hanworth Rd TW16 5DJ
web: www.travelodge.co.uk
dir: M3 junct 1, 5th exit onto A308 (Staines Road East). Take 1st left. Turn right onto Hanworth Rd. Hotel on right

Travelodge offers good quality, good value, budget accommodation. All offer family rooms sleeping up to four (two adults, two children) with en suite bathroom/shower-room, remote-control TV, tea- and coffee-making facilities and comfortable beds. Food options vary. Breakfast is at the on-site Bar Café restaurant (if available) or to take away. See also Hotel Groups pages.

Rooms 131 **S** fr £29; **D** fr £29

WALTON-ON-THAMES

See LONDON SECTION plan 1 A1

Innkeeper's Lodge Walton-on-Thames

BUDGET HOTEL

☎ 0845 112 6110 📠 0845 112 6193
Ashley Park Rd KT12 1JP
web: www.innkeeperslodge.com/waltononthames
dir: From A245 onto B365 towards Walton, pass 2 rdbts. Left at 3rd rdbt cross rail bridge, turn right. Lodge opposite station

Innkeeper's Lodge represent an exciting, high value concept within the budget hotel market. Comfortable bedrooms provide excellent facilities that include satellite TV and modem points. Options include spacious family rooms; and for the corporate guest, cutting edge IT is provided with Wi-fi access. All-day food is provided in the adjacent pub restaurant. The extensive continental breakfast is complimentary. See also the Hotel Groups pages.

Rooms 32 (6 fmly)

WEYBRIDGE
Map 6 TQ06

See LONDON SECTION plan 1 A1

Oatlands Park

★★★★ 74% HOTEL

☎ 01932 847242 📠 01932 842252
146 Oatlands Dr KT13 9HB
e-mail: info@oatlandsparkhotel.com
web: www.oatlandsparkhotel.com
dir: through Weybridge High Street onto Monument Hill mini rdbt. Left into Oatlands Drive. Hotel 500yds on left

Once a palace for Henry VIII, this impressive building sits in extensive grounds encompassing tennis courts, a gym and a 9-hole golf course. The spacious lounge and bar create a wonderful first impression with tall marble pillars and plush comfortable seating. Most of the bedrooms are very spacious, and all are well equipped.

Rooms 144 (24 fmly) (39 GF) (8 smoking) **Facilities** STV ♨ 9 ⚒ Putt green ⚒ Gym Jogging course Fitness suite Wi-fi **Conf** Class 150 Board 80 Thtr 300 **Services** Lift Air con **Parking** 144 **Notes** LB Civ Wed 220

WEYBRIDGE *continued*

The Ship

★★★ 77% HOTEL

☎ 01932 848364 📄 01932 857153
Monument Green KT13 8BQ
e-mail: reservations@desboroughhotels.com
dir: M25 junct 11, at 3rd rdbt left into High St. Hotel 300yds on left

A former coaching inn retaining much period charm that is now a spacious and comfortable hotel. Bedrooms, some overlooking a delightful courtyard, are spacious and cheerfully decorated. Public areas include a lounge and cocktail bar, restaurant and a popular pub. The high street location and private parking are a bonus.

Rooms 76 (2 fmly) **Facilities** Wi-fi **Conf** Class 70 Board 60 Thtr 180 **Services** Lift **Parking** 65

Innkeeper's Lodge Weybridge

BUDGET HOTEL

☎ 0845 112 6111 📄 0845 112 6192
25 Oatlands Chase KT13 9RW
web: www.innkeeperslodge.com/weybridge
dir: M25 junct 11, A317 towards Weybridge, at 3rd rdbt take A3050, left 1m. Right into Oatlands Chase, lodge on left

Innkeeper's Lodge represents an exciting, high value concept within the budget hotel market. Comfortable bedrooms provide excellent facilities that include satellite TV and modem points. This carefully restored lodge is in a picturesque setting and has its own unique style and quirky character. Food is served all day, and an extensive, complimentary continental breakfast is offered. See also the Hotel Groups pages.

Rooms 19

Holiday Inn Woking

★★★ 78% HOTEL

☎ 01483 221000 📄 01483 221021
Victoria St GU21 8EW
e-mail: reservations@wokingholiday-inn.com
web: www.hiwoking.co.uk
dir: A320 to Woking. After last rdbt to town centre take left slip road off dual carriageway. Hotel on left

Situated in a convenient town centre location with parking facilities and only ten minutes from Woking main line train station. Public areas are stylish and comfortable; dining options include bar snacks, a substantial restaurant meal or choices from room service. Bedrooms and bathrooms are generally spacious and offer good levels of comfort.

Rooms 161 (30 fmly) (17 smoking) **Facilities** STV FTV Gym Wi-fi **Conf** Class 40 Board 40 Thtr 50 Del from £160 to £220 **Services** Lift Air con **Parking** 50 **Notes** ⊗ Civ Wed 60

Innkeeper's Lodge Woking

BUDGET HOTEL

☎ 0845 112 6112 📄 0845 112 6191
Chobham Rd, Horsell GU21 4AL
web: www.innkeeperslodge.com/woking
dir: A320 to Woking. Pass 3 rdbts, after 4th at lights turn right into Chobham Rd, over rdbt, Lodge on left. (Car park entrance in Bromhall Rd)

Innkeeper's Lodge represent an exciting, high value concept within the budget hotel market. Comfortable bedrooms provide excellent facilities that include satellite TV and modem points. Options include spacious family rooms; and for the corporate guest, cutting edge IT is provided with Wi-fi access. All-day food is provided in the adjacent pub restaurant. The extensive continental breakfast is complimentary. See also the Hotel Groups pages.

Rooms 34

Deans Place

★★★ 82% ⚜ HOTEL

☎ 01323 870248 📄 01323 870918
Seaford Rd BN26 5TW
e-mail: mail@deansplacehotel.co.uk
web: www.deansplacehotel.co.uk
dir: Off A27, signed Alfriston & Drusillas Zoo Park. Continue south through village

Situated on the southern fringe of the village, this friendly hotel is set in attractive gardens. Bedrooms vary in size and are well appointed with good facilities. A wide range of food is offered including an extensive bar menu and a fine dining option in Harcourt's Restaurant.

Rooms 36 (4 fmly) (8 GF) **S** £80-£90; **D** £120-£170 (incl. bkfst) **Facilities** STV FTV ⚲ Putt green ⛳ Boules Xmas New Year Wi-fi **Conf** Class 100 Board 60 Thtr 200 **Parking** 100 **Notes** LB Civ Wed 150

Star Inn

★★★ 70% HOTEL

☎ 01323 870495 🖹 01323 870922
BN26 5TA
e-mail: bookings@thestaralfriston.co.uk
dir: 2m off A27, at Drusillas rdbt follow Alfriston signs.
Hotel on right in centre of High St

Built in the 13th century and reputedly one of the country's oldest inns, this charming establishment is ideally situated for walking the South Down or exploring the Sussex coast. Bedrooms, including two feature rooms and mini suite, are traditionally decorated but with comfortable, modern facilities. Public areas include cosy lounges with open log fires, a bar and a popular restaurant serving a wide choice of dishes using mainly local produce. Guests can also enjoy luxury spa treatments by appointment.

Rooms 37 (1 fmly) (11 GF) **S** £70-£80; **D** £110-£125 (incl. bkfst)* **Facilities** Xmas New Year Wi-fi **Conf** Class 60 Board 76 Thtr 120 Del from £110 to £135* **Parking** 35 **Notes** Civ Wed

---

BATTLE	**Map 7 TQ71**

Powder Mills

★★★ 79% ◉ HOTEL

☎ 01424 775511 🖹 01424 774540
Powdermill Ln TN33 0SP
e-mail: powdc@aol.com
web: www.powdermillshotel.com
dir: M25 junct 5, A21 towards Hastings. At St Johns Cross take A2100 to Battle. Pass Abbey on right, 1st right into Powdermills Ln. 1m, hotel on right

A delightful 18th-century country-house hotel set amidst 150 acres of landscaped grounds with lakes and woodland. The individually decorated bedrooms are tastefully furnished and thoughtfully equipped; some rooms have sun terraces with lovely views over the lake. Public rooms include a cosy lounge bar, music room, drawing room, library, restaurant and conservatory.

Rooms 40 (10 annexe) (5 GF) **S** £87.50-£115; **D** £140-£350 (incl. bkfst)* **Facilities** ↖ ⚒ Fishing Jogging trails Woodland walks Clay pigeon shooting Xmas New Year Wi-fi **Conf** Class 50 Board 16 Thtr 250 Del from £135 to £145* **Parking** 101 **Notes** LB Civ Wed 100

Brickwall Hotel

★★★ 75% HOTEL

☎ 01424 870253 & 870339 🖹 01424 870785
The Green, Sedlescombe TN33 0QA
e-mail: info@brickwallhotel.com
web: www.brickwallhotel.com
dir: Off A21 on B2244 at top of Sedlescombe Green

This is a well-maintained Tudor house, which is situated in the heart of this pretty village and overlooks the green. The spacious public rooms feature a lovely wood-panelled restaurant with a wealth of oak beams, a choice of lounges and a smart bar. Bedrooms are pleasantly decorated and some have garden views.

Rooms 25 (2 fmly) (17 GF) **S** £50-£75; **D** £85-£115 (incl. bkfst)* **Facilities** STV ↖ Xmas New Year Wi-fi **Conf** Class 40 Board 30 Thtr 30 **Parking** 40 **Notes** LB ⊗

BEXHILL	**Map 6 TQ70**

Cooden Beach Hotel

★★★ 80% HOTEL

☎ 01424 842281 🖹 01424 846142
Cooden Beach TN39 4TT
e-mail: jk@thecoodenbeachhotel.co.uk
web: www.thecoodenbeachhotel.co.uk
dir: A259 towards Cooden. Signed at rdbt in Little Common Village. Hotel at end of road

This privately owned hotel is situated in two acres of private gardens that have direct access to the beach. With a train station within walking distance the location is perfectly suited for both business and leisure guests. Bedrooms are comfortably appointed, and public areas include a spacious restaurant, lounge, bar and leisure centre with swimming pool.

Rooms 41 (8 annexe) (10 fmly) (4 GF) **Facilities** FTV ⊗ Gym Sauna Steam room ♫ Xmas New Year Wi-fi **Conf** Class 40 Board 40 Thtr 120 **Parking** 60 **Notes** Civ Wed 120

BRIGHTON & HOVE	**Map 6 TQ30**

Thistle Brighton

★★★★ 80% HOTEL   thistle

☎ 01273 206700 🖹 0870 333 9229
King's Rd BN1 2GS
e-mail: Brighton@Thistle.co.uk
web: www.thistlehotels.com/brighton
dir: A23 to seafront. At rdbt turn right, hotel 200yds on right

Situated overlooking the sea and within easy reach of the town's many attractions this hotel is built around an atrium and offers air-conditioned rooms including luxury suites. The restaurant provides stunning sea views, and a comfortable, spacious lounge and bar offer a full range of drinks, light refreshments and meals. The Otium Health & Fitness club provides pool, sauna, and gym facilities plus health and beauty treatments.

Rooms 210 (29 fmly) (6 smoking) **Facilities** ⊗ supervised Sauna Solarium Xmas New Year Wi-fi **Conf** Class 180 Board 120 Thtr 300 Del from £135 to £290* **Services** Lift Air con **Parking** 68 **Notes** Civ Wed 300

Hotel du Vin Brighton

★★★★ 76% ◉ TOWN HOUSE HOTEL   Hotel du Vin & Bistro

☎ 01273 718588 🖹 01273 718599
2-6 Ship St BN1 1AD
e-mail: info@brighton.hotelduvin.com
web: www.hotelduvin.com
dir: From A23 follow seafront/city centre signs. Right at seafront, right into Middle St. Follow to end bear right into Ship St. Hotel on right

This tastefully converted mock-Tudor building occupies a convenient location in a quiet side street close to the seafront. The individually designed bedrooms have a wine theme, and all are comprehensively equipped. Public areas offer a spacious split-level bar, an atmospheric and locally popular restaurant, plus useful private dining and meeting facilities.

Rooms 49 (4 GF) **Facilities** STV Xmas New Year Wi-fi **Conf** Board 60 Thtr 80 **Services** Air con **Notes** Civ Wed 80

BRIGHTON & HOVE *continued*

Drakes

★★★★ 74% ◉◉ SMALL HOTEL

☎ 01273 696934 📠 01273 684805
43-44 Marine Pde, N BN2 1PE
e-mail: info@drakesofbrighton.com
dir: From A23 at Brighton Pier rdbt. Left into Marine Pde towards marina. Hotel on left before lights (ornate water feature at front)

This independently owned double fronted Georgian townhouse is in a great location on the seafront and within walking distance of the pier and town centre. The interior design is stunning throughout and all bedrooms offer a touch of luxury - Egyptian cotton linen, goose and duckdown duvets and pillows and velvet throws plus LCD satellite TV, DVD/CD players and Wi-fi; some rooms have free standing baths in front of large picture windows affording spectacular sea views, others have wet rooms. Dinner and breakfast can be enjoyed in the basement restaurant with an intimate yet relaxed atmosphere with staff offering friendly service.

Rooms 20 **Conf** Class 18 Board 12 Thtr 18

Barceló Brighton Old Ship Hotel

★★★★ 73% HOTEL

☎ 01273 329001 📠 01273 820718
King's Rd BN1 1NR
e-mail: oldship@barcelo-hotels.co.uk
web: www.barcelo-hotels.co.uk
dir: A23 to seafront, right at rdbt along Kings Rd. Hotel 200yds on right

This historic hotel enjoys a stunning seafront location and offers guests elegant surroundings to relax in. Bedrooms are well designed, with modern facilities ensuring comfort. Many original features have been retained, including the newly renovated Paganini Ballroom. Facilities include a sleek bar, alfresco dining and a variety of conference rooms.

Rooms 152 **Facilities** STV Xmas New Year Wi-fi
Conf Class 100 Board 35 Thtr 250 Del from £110*
Services Lift **Parking** 40 **Notes** Civ Wed 150

Holiday Inn Brighton - Seafront

Holiday Inn
HOTELS · RESORTS

★★★★ 71% HOTEL

☎ 01273 828250 📠 01273 775877
137 Kings Rd BN1 2JF
web: www.holidayinn.co.uk
dir: M25 junct 7 to M23 southbound, A23 to town centre, follow signs to seafront, hotel on A259 opp West Pier

Overlooking the seafront and within walking distance to the town centre, restaurants and pier, this spacious hotel offers modern amenities for leisure and business guests. The bedrooms are spacious and well equipped, and the executive rooms have additional facilities. Public areas include spacious lounges, sports bar and a modern

restaurant with an outdoor terrace. A range of meeting rooms is also available.

Rooms 131 (23 fmly) **S** £89-£250; **D** £89-£350 (incl. bkfst)* **Facilities** STV Xmas New Year Wi-fi
Conf Class 200 Board 50 Thtr 450 Del from £99 to £250*
Services Lift Air con **Parking** 64 **Notes** LB Civ Wed 400

Lansdowne Place

★★★★ 71% HOTEL

☎ 01273 736266 📠 01273 729802
Lansdowne Place BN3 1HQ
e-mail: reservations@lansdowneplace.co.uk
web: www.lansdowneplace.co.uk
dir: A23 to seafront. Right at Brighton Pier, along seafront, right at Lansdowne Place

Following a £2 million refurbishment this establishment, now known as a boutique hotel, proves a very stylish choice. The bright and spacious bedrooms, many with sea views, include plasma screen TVs and walk-in showers; suites are also available. The hotel offers a full range of beauty treatments and therapies in its state-of-the-art spa, and for the energetic there is a well-equipped gym. Weddings and meetings are catered for.

Rooms 84 **Facilities** Spa Gym Wi-fi **Conf** Class 217 Board 206 Thtr 340 **Services** Lift **Parking** 14 **Notes** LB ⊗ Civ Wed 200

Imperial

★★★ 77% HOTEL

☎ 01273 777320 📠 01273 777310
First Av BN3 2GU
e-mail: info@imperial-hove.com
web: www.imperial-hove.com
dir: M23 to Brighton seafront, right at rdbt to Hove. 1.5m to First Ave, turn right

Located within minutes of the seafront, this Regency property is constantly being improved and upgraded. A good range of conference suites complement the

comfortable public rooms, which include a lounge, a smart bar area and an attractive restaurant. Bedrooms are generally of comfortable proportions, well appointed and with a good range of facilities.

Rooms 76 (2 fmly) (6 smoking) **Facilities** Xmas Wi-fi
Conf Class 30 Board 34 Thtr 110 **Services** Lift **Notes** LB ⊗

Best Western Princes Marine

Best Western

★★★ 75% HOTEL

☎ 01273 207660 📠 01273 325913
153 Kingsway BN3 4GR
e-mail: princesmarine@bestwestern.co.uk
dir: right at Brighton Pier, follow seafront for 2m. Hotel 200yds from King Alfred leisure centre

This friendly hotel enjoys a seafront location and offers spacious, comfortable bedrooms equipped with a good range of facilities including free Wi-fi. There is a stylish restaurant, modern bar and selection of roof-top meeting rooms with sea views. Limited parking is available at the rear.

Rooms 48 (4 fmly) **Facilities** Xmas **Conf** Class 40 Board 40 Thtr 80 **Services** Lift **Parking** 30 **Notes** LB

Ramada Brighton

⊛RAMADA

★★★ 75% HOTEL

☎ 0844 815 9061 📠 01273 821752
149 Kings Rd BN1 2PP
e-mail: sales.brighton@ramadajarvis.co.uk
web: www.ramadajarvis.co.uk/brighton
dir: A23 follow signs for seafront. Right at Brighton Pier rdbt. Hotel on right, just after West Pier

This Regency-style hotel enjoys a prime seafront location on Kings Road. Bedrooms are comfortably appointed for both business and leisure guests. Public areas include the Arts Bar and Restaurant and a range of meeting rooms. Limited parking is available.

Rooms 117 (52 annexe) (2 fmly) **S** £55-£170;
D £65-£270* **Facilities** Xmas New Year Wi-fi
Conf Class 160 Board 185 Thtr 455 Del from £95 to £210* **Services** Lift **Parking** 41 **Notes** LB ⊗ Civ Wed 60

Best Western Brighton Hotel

★★★ 71% HOTEL

☎ 01273 820555 📠 01273 821555
143/145 King's Rd BN1 2PQ
e-mail: info@thebrightonhotel.com
web: www.thebrightonhotel.com
dir: M23 onto A23 to pier. Right at rdbt, hotel just past West Pier

This friendly hotel is well placed in a prime seafront location that is close to the historic West Pier. All bedrooms are of a contemporary style, spaciously appointed and well equipped. Lounge, bar and restaurant are sunny, bright and comfortable with great views of the sea. Parking facilities, though limited, are a real bonus in this area of town.

Rooms 55 (6 fmly) **Facilities** FTV Xmas New Year Wi-fi
Conf Class 25 Board 30 Thtr 30 Del from £155 to £165*
Services Lift **Parking** 10 **Notes** ⊗ Civ Wed 70

The Courtlands Hotel & Conference Centre

★★★ 67% HOTEL

THE COURTLANDS
HOTEL AND CONFERENCE CENTRE

☎ 01273 731055 📠 01273 328295
15-27 The Drive BN3 3JE
e-mail: info@courtlandshotel.com
dir: At junct of A23/ A27. Take 1st exit to Hove, 2nd exit at rdbt, right at 1st junct. Left at shops. Straight on at junct. Hotel on left

This hotel is located on a tree-lined avenue within walking distance of the seafront and has its own small car park. The bedrooms come in a variety of styles and include executive rooms and suites. Guests have the use of a comfortable lounge, a light and spacious restaurant. Service is both friendly and attentive.

Rooms 67 (7 annexe) (8 fmly) **S** £42-£98; **D** £62-£125
Facilities FTV ⊗ Xmas New Year Wi-fi **Conf** Class 20
Board 30 Thtr 60 Del from £75 to £85 **Services** Lift
Parking 30 **Notes** ⊗

Preston Park Hotel

★★★ 64% HOTEL

☎ 01273 507853 📠 01273 540039
216 Preston Rd BN1 6UU
e-mail: manager@prestonparkhotel.co.uk
dir: On A23 towards town centre

This hotel enjoys a convenient roadside location on the outskirts of Brighton. Bedrooms are modern in style and well provisioned for both the leisure and business guest. Freshly prepared meals are offered in the spacious Sussex Bar (open 24 hours to residents) and in the more intimate and relaxing restaurant. Guests can enjoy a drink on the patio in summer.

Rooms 33 (4 fmly) **Facilities** ⊗ supervised Gym Xmas
Conf Class 60 Board 60 Thtr 100 **Parking** 60
Notes Civ Wed 150

De Vere Grand, Brighton

DE VERE
collection

Ⓤ

☎ 01273 224300 📠 01273 224321
King's Rd BN1 2FW
e-mail: reservations@grandbrighton.co.uk
web: www.devere.co.uk
dir: On A259, seafront road between piers, adjacent to Brighton Centre

Currently the rating for this establishment is not confirmed. This may be due to a change of ownership or because it has only recently joined the AA rating scheme. For further details please see the AA website: theAA.com

Rooms 200 (60 fmly) **Facilities** STV Gym In room
therapies Xmas New Year Wi-fi **Conf** Class 420 Board 50
Thtr 700 **Services** Lift **Parking** 50 **Notes** Civ Wed 800

Radisson Blu Hotel, Brighton

Radisson

Ⓤ

☎ 01273 766700 📠 01273 766707
Royal Steine BN1 1NP
e-mail: info.brighton@radissonblu.com
dir: A23 to city centre, hotel 0.2m past Royal Pavillion adjacent to Brighton Pier

Currently the rating for this establishment is not confirmed. This may be due to a change of ownership or because it has only recently joined the AA rating scheme. For further details please see the AA website: theAA.com

Rooms 59 **Conf** Class 30 Board 20 Thtr 40

Innkeeper's Lodge Brighton

BUDGET HOTEL

☎ 0845 112 6097 📠 0845 112 6260
London Rd, Patcham BN1 8YQ
web: www.innkeeperslodge.com/brighton
dir: A23 at junct with A27 remain on A23. Straight on at next rdbt. Lodge on left

Innkeeper's Lodge represent an exciting, high value concept within the budget hotel market. Comfortable bedrooms provide excellent facilities that include satellite TV and modem points. Options include spacious family rooms; and for the corporate guest, cutting edge IT is provided with Wi-fi access. All-day food is provided in the adjacent pub restaurant. The extensive continental breakfast is complimentary. See also the Hotel Groups pages.

Rooms 17 **Conf** Thtr 30

Travelodge Brighton

Travelodge

BUDGET HOTEL

☎ 0871 984 6017 📠 01273 554917
Preston Rd BN1 6AU
web: www.travelodge.co.uk
dir: South on A23, follow signs for town centre. Lodge on right

Travelodge offers good quality, good value, budget accommodation. All offer family rooms sleeping up to four (two adults, two children) with en suite bathroom/shower-room, remote-control TV, tea- and coffee-making facilities and comfortable beds. Food options vary. Breakfast is at the on-site Bar Café restaurant (if available) or to take away. See also Hotel Groups pages.

Rooms 94 **S** fr £29; **D** fr £29

Travelodge Brighton Seafront

BUDGET HOTEL

☎ 0871 984 6405
West St BN1 2RQ
e-mail: brightonseafront@travelodge.co.uk
dir: A23 towards Brighton seafront, then A259 towards Worthing. Follow right lane for 200yds, right into West St. Lodge on left (NCP car park in Russell St behind lodge)

Rooms 159 **S** fr £29;

EASTBOURNE
Map 6 TV69

The Grand Hotel
★★★★★ 83% @@ HOTEL

☎ 01323 412345 📠 01323 412233
King Edward's Pde BN21 4EQ
e-mail: reservations@grandeastbourne.com
web: www.grandeastbourne.com
dir: On seafront W of Eastbourne, 1m from railway station

This famous Victorian hotel offers high standards of service and hospitality. The extensive public rooms feature a magnificent Great Hall, with marble columns and high ceilings, where guests can relax and enjoy afternoon tea. The spacious bedrooms provide high levels of comfort and some rooms have balconies with stunning sea views. There is a choice of restaurants and bars as well as superb leisure facilities.

Rooms 152 (20 fmly) (4 GF) **S** £160-£505; **D** £190-£535 (incl. bkfst)* **Facilities** Spa STV 🅥 supervised ⚡ Putt green Gym Hairdressing Beauty therapy ♫ Xmas New Year Child facilities **Conf** Class 200 Board 40 Thtr 350 Del from £230 to £268* **Services** Lift **Parking** 80 **Notes** LB Civ Wed 300

Waterside
★★★ 81% HOTEL

☎ 01323 646566 📠 01323 416857
11-12 Royal Pde BN22 7AR

This stylish small hotel is conveniently located a stone's throw from the popular beach and pier, and a moment's walk from the town centre. Bedrooms, individually designed with original contemporary artwork, are smartly appointed and well equipped with many thoughtful extras; some have sea views. Public areas include a bar/lounge and restaurant areas providing comfortable seating in well designed surroundings.

Rooms 20

Hydro
★★★ 80% HOTEL

☎ 01323 720643 📠 01323 641167
Mount Rd BN20 7HZ
e-mail: Sales@hydrohotel.com
dir: from pier/seafront, right along Grand Parade. At Grand Hotel follow Hydro Hotel sign. Up South Cliff 200yds

This well-managed and popular hotel enjoys an elevated position with views of attractive gardens and the sea beyond. The spacious bedrooms are attractive and well equipped. In addition to the comfortable lounges, guests also have access to fitness facilities and a hairdressing salon. Service is both professional and efficient throughout.

Rooms 84 (3 fmly) (3 GF) **Facilities** ⚡ Putt green 🏊 Beauty room Hair salon 3/4 size snooker table Xmas New Year Wi-fi **Conf** Class 90 Board 40 Thtr 140 **Services** Lift **Parking** 40 **Notes** RS 24-28 & 30-31 Dec Civ Wed 120

Best Western Lansdowne
★★★ 78% HOTEL

☎ 01323 725174 📠 01323 739721
King Edward's Pde BN21 4EE
e-mail: reception@lansdowne-hotel.co.uk
web: www.bw-lansdownehotel.co.uk
dir: At W end of seafront opposite Western Lawns

Enjoying an enviable position at the quieter end of the parade, this hotel overlooks the Western Lawns and Wish Tower, and is just a few minutes' walk from many of the town's attractions. Public rooms include a variety of lounges, a range of meeting rooms and games rooms. Bedrooms are attractively decorated and many offer sea views. The hotel has a wheelchair lift near the front entrance that operates between the pavement to one of the ground-floor rooms.

Rooms 102 (10 fmly) (16 smoking) **S** £53-£79; **D** £99-£174 (incl. bkfst) **Facilities** STV FTV Table tennis Pool table Xmas New Year Wi-fi **Conf** Class 40 Board 40 Thtr 80 Del from £85 to £130 **Services** Lift **Parking** 22 **Notes** LB Civ Wed 80

See advert on this page

Devonshire Park

★★★ 77% HOTEL

☎ 01323 728144 📠 01323 419734
27-29 Carlisle Rd BN21 4JR
e-mail: info@devonshire-park-hotel.co.uk
web: www.devonshire-park-hotel.co.uk
dir: Follow signs to seafront, exit at Wish Tower. Hotel
opposite Congress Theatre

A handsome family-run hotel handily placed for the
seafront and theatres. Attractively furnished rooms are
spacious and comfortable; many boast king-sized beds
and all are equipped with Wi-fi and satellite TV. Guests
can relax in the well presented lounges, the cosy bar or,
when the weather's fine, on the garden terrace.

Rooms 35 (8 GF) **S** £45-£75; **D** £80-£150 (incl. bkfst)
Facilities STV Xmas Wi-fi **Services** Lift **Parking** 25
Notes LB ⊗ No children 12yrs

Best Western York House

★★★ 76% HOTEL

☎ 01323 412918 📠 01323 646238
14-22 Royal Pde BN22 7AP
e-mail: info@yorkhousehotel.co.uk
dir: A27 to Eastbourne. On seafront 0.25m E of pier

With a prime location on the seafront many rooms enjoy
wonderful panoramic views. Bedrooms vary in size but all
are bright, spacious and attractively furnished. The
public areas include a contemporary bar, lounge, library
and sunny outdoor terrace overlooking the sea. There is
also an indoor swimming pool.

Rooms 87 (13 fmly) (5 GF) (13 smoking) **Facilities** FTV ⓒ
♫ Xmas New Year Wi-fi **Conf** Class 40 Board 24 Thtr 100
Del from £86 to £150* **Services** Lift **Notes** Civ Wed 50

Langham

★★★ 75% ⓦ HOTEL

☎ 01323 731451 📠 01323 646623
Royal Pde BN22 7AH
web: www.langhamhotel.co.uk
dir: Follow seafront signs. Hotel 0.5m E of pier

This popular hotel is situated in a prominent position
with superb views of the sea and pier. Bedrooms are
pleasantly decorated and equipped with modern
facilities. Superior rooms, some with four-poster beds
are stylish and offer sea views. The spacious public rooms

include the Grand Parade bar, a lounge and a fine dining
conservatory restaurant.

Rooms 83 (2 fmly) **Facilities** ♫ Xmas New Year Wi-fi
Conf Class 40 Board 30 Thtr 80 Del from £90 to £99*
Services Lift **Parking** 5 **Notes** ⊗ Civ Wed 140

Chatsworth

★★★ 75% HOTEL

☎ 01323 411016 📠 01323 643270
Grand Pde BN21 3YR
e-mail: stay@chatsworth-hotel.com
web: www.chatsworth-hotel.com
dir: M23 then A27 to Polegate. A2270 into Eastbourne,
follow seafront signs. Hotel near pier

Within minutes of the town centre and pier, this attractive
Edwardian hotel is located on the seafront. The public
areas consist of the Chatsworth Bar, a cosy lounge and
the Devonshire Restaurant. Bedrooms, many with sea
views, are traditional in style and have a range of
facilities. Service is friendly and helpful throughout.

Rooms 47 (2 fmly) **S** £55-£65; **D** £100-£130 (incl. bkfst)
Facilities STV ♫ Xmas New Year Wi-fi **Conf** Class 60
Board 40 Thtr 100 Del from £105 to £145 **Services** Lift
Notes LB Civ Wed 140

New Wilmington

★★★ 73% HOTEL

☎ 01323 721219 📠 01323 746255
25 Compton St BN21 4DU
e-mail: info@new-wilmington-hotel.co.uk
web: www.new-wilmington-hotel.co.uk
dir: A22 to Eastbourne seafront. Right along promenade
to Wish Tower. Right, then left at end of road, hotel 2nd
on left

This friendly, family-run hotel is conveniently located
close to the seafront, the Congress Theatre and Winter
Gardens. Public rooms are well presented and include a
cosy bar, a small comfortable lounge and a spacious
restaurant. Bedrooms are comfortably appointed and
tastefully decorated; family and superior bedrooms are
available.

Rooms 40 (14 fmly) (3 GF) **S** £44-£55; **D** £78-£98 (incl.
bkfst)* **Facilities** STV ♫ Xmas New Year Wi-fi
Conf Class 20 Board 20 Thtr 40 **Services** Lift **Parking** 3
Notes LB Closed 3 Jan-mid Feb

Albany Lions Hotel

★★★ 70% HOTEL

☎ 01323 722788 📠 01323 419373
Grand Pde BN21 4DJ
e-mail: reception@albanylionshotel.com
dir: From town centre follow Seafront/Pier signs

This hotel, close to the bandstand, has a seafront
location that is within walking distance of the main town
shopping. A carvery dinner is served in the restaurant,
which has great sea views from most tables, and a
relaxing drink or afternoon tea can be enjoyed in the sun
lounge.

Rooms 61 (5 fmly) **S** £50-£60; **D** £90-£120 (incl. bkfst)
Facilities STV ♫ Xmas New Year Wi-fi **Conf** Class 60
Board 40 Thtr 120 Del from £95 to £120 **Services** Lift
Notes LB ⊗

Claremont Lions

★★★ 70% HOTEL

☎ 01323 731417 📠 01323 720413
Grand Pde BN21 3YL
e-mail: reception@claremontlionshotel.com
dir: A27 E to Eastbourne. Follow seafront signs, hotel
opposite pier

Located directly opposite the beautiful Carpet Gardens,
the seafront and pier this majestic hotel offers spacious
bedrooms that are comfortably furnished; all have fridges
and many have sea views. Public areas including the
elegant dining room are attractively presented and
comfortable. Ground floor rooms are well equipped for
less able guests.

Rooms 67 (2 fmly) (4 GF) **S** £50-£60; **D** £90-£120 (incl.
bkfst) **Facilities** STV ♫ Xmas New Year **Conf** Class 50
Board 40 Thtr 100 Del from £95 to £120 **Services** Lift
Parking 6 **Notes** LB ⊗ Closed 2 Jan-28 Feb

Courtlands

★★★ 70% HOTEL

☎ 01323 723737 📠 01323 732902
3-5 Wilmington Gardens BN21 4JN
e-mail: bookings@courtlandseastbourne.com
dir: Exit Grand Parade at Carlisle Rd

Situated opposite the Congress Theatre, this hotel is just
a short walk from both the seafront and Devonshire Park.
Bedrooms are comfortably furnished and pleasantly
decorated. Public areas are smartly appointed and
include a cosy bar, a separate lounge and an attractive
dining room.

Rooms 46 (4 fmly) (3 GF) **S** £50-£69; **D** £100-£140 (incl.
bkfst & dinner)* **Facilities** STV FTV ⓢ ♫ Xmas New Year
Conf Class 60 Board 60 Thtr 60 Del from £75 to £150*
Services Lift **Parking** 36 **Notes** LB Civ Wed 100

EASTBOURNE *continued*

Mansion Lions Hotel

★★★ 70% HOTEL

☎ 01323 727411 📄 01323 720665
Grand Pde BN21 3YS
e-mail: reception@mansionlionshotel.com
dir: From town centre follow Seafront/Pier signs. Hotel on seafront

Directly overlooking the beach, this Victorian hotel is only two minutes' walk from the magnificent pier, the shopping centre and bandstand. The well-equipped bedrooms are spacious, comfortably furnished and some have sea views. An enjoyable four-course evening meal and a filling breakfast are served in the stylish Hartington Restaurant. There is an attractive lounge, and a pretty garden can be found at the back of the hotel.

Rooms 106 (6 fmly) (4 GF) **S** £50-£60; **D** £90-£120 (incl. bkfst) **Facilities** STV ♬ Xmas New Year Wi-fi **Conf** Class 80 Board 40 Thtr 150 Del from £95 to £120 **Services** Lift **Notes** LB ⊗ Closed Jan-Feb Civ Wed 150

Oban

★★ 78% HOTEL

☎ 01323 731581 📄 01323 721994
King Edwards Pde BN21 4DS
e-mail: info@oban-hotel.co.uk
web: www.oban-hotel.co.uk
dir: opposite Wish Tower on seafront

Situated on the seafront overlooking the Wish Tower this privately owned hotel provides a friendly welcome. Bedrooms vary in size and are pleasantly decorated. Public areas include a smartly decorated, large, open-plan lounge bar area with a small terrace. Enjoyable meals are served in the lower ground-floor dining room.

Rooms 31 (2 fmly) (4 GF) **Facilities** ♬ Xmas **Services** Lift **Notes** LB

Queens Hotel

★★ 72% HOTEL

☎ 01323 722822 📄 01323 731056
Marine Pde BN21 3DY
e-mail: queens.eastbourne@alfatravel.co.uk
dir: Follow signs for seafront, hotel opposite pier

Popular with tour groups, this long-established hotel enjoys a central, prominent seafront location overlooking the pier. Spacious public areas include a choice of lounges, and regular entertainment is also provided. Bedrooms are suitably appointed and equipped.

Rooms 122 (5 fmly) **Facilities** FTV Snooker ♬ Xmas New Year **Services** Lift **Parking** 50 **Notes** LB ⊗ Closed Jan (ex New Year) RS Nov, Feb-Mar

Congress

★★ 71% HOTEL

☎ 01323 732118 📄 01323 720016
31-41 Carlisle Rd BN21 4JS
e-mail: reservations@congresshotel.co.uk
web: www.congresshotel.co.uk
dir: From Eastbourne seafront W towards Beachy Head. Right at Wishtower into Wilmington Sq, cross Compton St, hotel on left

An attractive Victorian property ideally located close to the seafront, Wish Tower and Congress Theatre. The bedrooms are bright and spacious. Family rooms are available plus facilities for less able guests. Entertainment is provided in a large dining room that has a dance floor and bar.

Rooms 61 (6 fmly) (8 GF) **S** £33-£47; **D** £66-£94 (incl. bkfst) **Facilities** Games room ♬ Xmas New Year Wi-fi **Services** Lift **Parking** 12 **Notes** LB RS Jan-Feb

Palm Court

★★ 69% HOTEL

☎ 01323 725811 📄 01323 430236
15 Burlington Place BN21 4AR
e-mail: thepalmcourt@btconnect.com
dir: From pier, W along seafront, Burlington Place 5th right

This family-run hotel is ideally situated close to the seafront and local theatres. The well appointed public areas include the lounge, spacious bar and stylish restaurant. Bedrooms vary in size but all offer plenty of handy accessories, comfortable furnishings and bright modern bathrooms. Good mobility facilities are provided.

Rooms 38 (5 GF) **S** £30-£45; **D** £60-£90 (incl. bkfst) **Facilities** Xmas New Year Wi-fi **Services** Lift **Notes** LB ⊗

Alexandra

★★ 68% HOTEL

☎ 01323 720131 📄 01323 417769
King Edwards Pde BN21 4DR
e-mail: alexandrahotel@mistral.co.uk
web: http://alexandrahotel.eastbourne.biz/
dir: On seafront at junct of Carlisle Road & King Edward Parade

Located at the west end of the town, opposite the Wishing Tower, this hotel boasts panoramic views of the sea from many rooms. Bedrooms vary in size but are comfortable

with good facilities for guests. A warm welcome is guaranteed at this long-standing, family run establishment.

Rooms 38 (2 fmly) (3 GF) **S** £32-£45; **D** £64-£104 (incl. bkfst)* **Facilities** ♬ Xmas New Year **Services** Lift **Notes** ⊗ Closed Jan & Feb RS Mar

West Rocks

★★ 65% HOTEL

☎ 01323 725217 📄 01323 720421
Grand Pde BN21 4DL
e-mail: westrockshotel@btinternet.com
dir: West end of seafront

Ideally located near to the pier and bandstand, this hotel is only a short walk from the town centre. Bedrooms vary in size, with many offering stunning sea views. Guests have the choice of two comfortable lounges and a bar.

Rooms 47 (8 fmly) (6 GF) **Facilities** ♬ Xmas **Conf** Class 12 Board 12 Thtr 20 **Services** Lift **Notes** LB ⊗ Closed 3 Jan -20 Feb

Afton

★★ 62% HOTEL

☎ 01323 733162 📄 01323 645720
2-8 Cavendish Place BN21 3EJ
e-mail: info@aftonhotel.com
dir: From A22, A27 or A259, follow seafront signs. Hotel by pier

This friendly family run hotel is ideally located in the centre of town, opposite the pier and close to the shopping centre. Bedrooms vary in size but are all comfortable and well co-ordinated. The spacious restaurant serves traditional home cooking. A full programme of entertainment is provided.

Rooms 56 (4 fmly) (4 GF) **S** £35-£40; **D** £70-£85 (incl. bkfst)* **Facilities** ♬ Xmas New Year Wi-fi **Conf** Class 50 Board 50 Thtr 100 Del from £100 to £150* **Services** Lift **Notes** LB

Savoy Court

★★ 61% HOTEL

☎ 01323 723132 📄 01323 737902
11-15 Cavendish Place BN21 3EJ
e-mail: info@savoycourthotel.co.uk
web: www.savoycourthotel.co.uk
dir: M25 junct 6, A22 to Eastbourne. Hotel 50mtrs from pier

Located close to the pier and within easy walking distance of the beaches and open-air bandstand this hotel is under new ownership. Bedrooms are pleasantly decorated and furnished and public areas include a cosy lounge and spacious bar/lounge for relaxing at the end of the day.

continued

Savoy Court

Rooms 29 (3 fmly) (5 GF) **S** £30-£55; **D** £58-£108 (incl. bkfst)* **Facilities** Xmas New Year Wi-fi **Conf** Class 20 Board 10 Thtr 30 Del from £50 to £120 **Services** Lift **Notes** LB ⊗

Eastbourne Riviera Hotel

[U]
- -
☎ 01323 430302 & 07852 301852 📠 01323 430436
26 Marine Pde BN22 7AY
e-mail: eastbourneriviera@yahoo.com
web: www.eastbourneriviera.co.uk
dir: A22 to Eastbourne, 100mtrs east of the Victorian pier

Currently the rating for this establishment is not confirmed. This may be due to a change of ownership or because it has only recently joined the AA rating scheme. For further details please see the AA website: theAA.com

Rooms 37 (8 fmly) **S** £30-£50; **D** £60-£110 (incl. bkfst)* **Facilities** FTV 🎵 Xmas New Year Wi-fi **Conf** Class 20 Board 20 Thtr 30 Del from £45 to £90 **Services** Lift **Notes** LB Civ Wed 200

Innkeeper's Lodge Eastbourne

BUDGET HOTEL
- -
☎ 0845 112 6100 📠 0845 112 6203
Highfield Park, Willingdon Drove BN23 8AL
web: www.innkeeperslodge.com/eastbourne
dir: From A22 onto Shinewater rdbt. Take 3rd exit into Willingdon Drove. Right at next rdbt into Highfield Park. Lodge on right

Innkeeper's Lodge represents an exciting, high value concept within the budget hotel market. Comfortable bedrooms provide excellent facilities that include satellite TV and modem points. Options include family rooms; and for the corporate guest, cutting edge IT which includes Wi-fi access. A popular Carvery provides all-day food, including an extensive, complimentary continental breakfast. See also the Hotel Groups pages.

Rooms 42

Travelodge Eastbourne

BUDGET HOTEL
- -
☎ 0871 984 6354
Marine Pde BN22 7AY
web: www.travelodge.co.uk
dir: A259 along Royal Parade into Marine Parade. Lodge 400yds from pier

Travelodge offers good quality, good value, budget accommodation. All offer family rooms sleeping up to four (two adults, two children) with en suite bathroom/shower-room, remote-control TV, tea- and coffee-making facilities and comfortable beds. Food options vary. Breakfast is at the on-site Bar Café restaurant (if available) or to take away. See also Hotel Groups pages.

Rooms 90 **S** fr £29; **D** fr £29

| FOREST ROW | Map 6 TQ43 |

INSPECTORS' CHOICE

Ashdown Park Hotel and Country Club
★★★★ ⑳⑳ HOTEL

☎ 01342 824988 📠 01342 826206
Wych Cross RH18 5JR
e-mail: reservations@ashdownpark.com
web: www.ashdownpark.com
dir: A264 to East Grinstead, then A22 to Eastbourne. 2m S of Forest Row at Wych Cross lights. Left to Hartfield, hotel on right 0.75m

Situated in 186 acres of landscaped gardens and parkland, this impressive country house enjoys a peaceful countryside setting in the heart of the Ashdown Forest. Bedrooms are individually styled and decorated. Public rooms include a chapel, now converted to a conference room, extensive indoor and outdoor leisure facilities, including three drawing rooms, a cocktail bar and the award-winning Anderida Restaurant plus an 18-hole, par 3 golf course and driving range.

Rooms 106 (16 GF) **S** £160-£390; **D** £190-£420 (incl. bkfst)* **Facilities** Spa STV ⊛ ⚓ 18 🏊 Putt green ⛳ Gym Beauty salon Aerobics studio Treatment rooms Mountain bike hire Steam room 🎵 Xmas New Year Wi-fi **Conf** Class 80 Board 40 Thtr 170 Del from £280 to £450* **Parking** 200 **Notes** LB ⊗ Civ Wed 150

The Roebuck

[U]
- -
☎ 01342 823811 📠 01342 824790
Wych Cross RH18 5JL
e-mail: 6499@greeneking.co.uk

Currently the rating for this establishment is not confirmed. This may be due to a change of ownership or because it has only recently joined the AA rating scheme. For further details please see the AA website: theAA.com

Rooms 30 **Conf** Class 50 Board 50 Thtr 80

| HAILSHAM | Map 6 TQ50 |

Boship Farm
★★★ 74% HOTEL
- -

☎ 01323 844826 & 442600 📠 01323 843945
Lower Dicker BN27 4AT
e-mail: info@boshipfarmhotel.co.uk
dir: On A22. At A267 & 271 junct (Boship rdbt)

Dating back to 1652, a lovely old farmhouse forms the hub of this hotel, which is set in 17 acres of well-tended grounds. Guests have the use of an all-weather tennis court, an outdoor pool and a croquet lawn. Bedrooms are smartly appointed and well equipped; most have views across open fields and countryside.

Rooms 47 (3 fmly) (21 GF) **Facilities** ⚓ 🏊 ⛳ Gym Badminton Sauna Steam room Xmas New Year **Conf** Class 40 Board 46 Thtr 175 **Parking** 110 **Notes** LB Civ Wed 140

The Olde Forge Hotel & Restaurant
★★ 76% HOTEL
- -
☎ 01323 842893 📠 01323 842893
Magham Down BN27 1PN
e-mail: theoldeforgehotel@tesco.net
web: www.theoldeforgehotel.co.uk
dir: Off Boship rdbt on A271 to Bexhill & Herstmonceux. Hotel 3m on left

In the heart of the countryside, this family-run hotel offers a friendly welcome and an informal atmosphere. The bedrooms are attractively decorated with thoughtful extras. The restaurant, with its timbered beams and log fires, was a forge in the 16th century; today it has a good local reputation for both its cuisine and service.

Rooms 7 **S** £48; **D** £85-£95 (incl. bkfst)* **Facilities** Wi-fi **Parking** 11 **Notes** LB

HAILSHAM *continued*

Travelodge Hellingly Eastbourne

BUDGET HOTEL

☎ 0871 984 6035 📠 01323 844556
Boship Roundabout, Hellingly BN27 4DT
web: www.travelodge.co.uk
dir: On A22 at Boship rdbt

Travelodge offers good quality, good value, budget accommodation. All offer family rooms sleeping up to four (two adults, two children) with en suite bathroom/ shower-room, remote-control TV, tea- and coffee-making facilities and comfortable beds. Food options vary. Breakfast is at the on-site Bar Café restaurant (if available) or to take away. See also Hotel Groups pages.

Rooms 58 **S** fr £29; **D** fr £29

HALLAND	Map 6 TQ41

Halland Forge

★★ 64% HOTEL

☎ 01825 840456 📠 01825 840773
BN8 6PW
e-mail: info@hallandforgehotel.co.uk
dir: on A22 at junct with B2192, 4.5m S of Uckfield

Conveniently located, this hotel offers comfortable annexed accommodation with parking spaces directly outside the bedrooms. Public areas include a spacious lounge bar, attractive outdoor seating (weather permitting) and an informal restaurant serving generous portions at dinner. An attractively presented room is available for private dining, special occasions or for meetings by prior arrangement.

Rooms 20 (20 annexe) (2 fmly) (8 GF) **Conf** Class 20 Board 26 Thtr 45 **Parking** 70 **Notes** ⊗

HASTINGS & ST LEONARDS	Map 7 TQ80

Best Western Royal Victoria

★★★ 74% HOTEL

☎ 01424 445544 📠 01424 721995
Marina, St Leonards-on-Sea TN38 0BD
e-mail: reception@royalvichotel.co.uk
web: www.royalvichotel.co.uk
dir: on A259 (seafront road) 1m W of Hastings pier

This imposing 18th-century property is situated in a prominent position overlooking the sea. A superb marble staircase leads up from the lobby to the main public areas on the first floor which has panoramic views of the sea. The spacious bedrooms are pleasantly decorated and well equipped, and include duplex and family suites.

Rooms 50 (15 fmly) **Facilities** Xmas **Conf** Class 40 Board 40 Thtr 100 **Services** Lift **Parking** 6 **Notes** LB Civ Wed 50

The Chatsworth Hotel

★★★ 72% ⊛ HOTEL

☎ 01424 720188 📠 01424 445865
Carlisle Pde TN34 1JG
e-mail: info@chatsworthhotel.com
dir: A21 to town centre. At seafront turn right before next lights

Enjoying a central position on the seafront, close to the pier, this hotel is a short walk from the old town and within easy reach of the county's many attractions. Bedrooms are smartly decorated, equipped with a range of extras and many rooms enjoy splendid sea views. Guests can also enjoy an exciting Indian meal in the contemporary restaurant.

Rooms 52 (5 fmly) **Facilities** Xmas New Year Wi-fi **Conf** Class 20 Board 20 Thtr 40 **Services** Lift **Parking** 8 **Notes** LB ⊗

High Beech

★★★ 67% HOTEL

☎ 01424 851383 📠 01424 854265
Eisenhower Dr, Battle Rd, St Leonards-on-Sea TN37 7BS
e-mail: highbeech@barbox.net
dir: Off A2100 into Washington Ave from Battle Rd

A privately owned hotel situated between the historic towns of Hastings and Battle in a woodland setting. The generously proportioned bedrooms are pleasantly decorated and thoughtfully equipped. Public rooms include the Mountbatten Bar, which also doubles as the lounge area, and the elegant Wedgwood Restaurant where an interesting and varied menu is served.

Rooms 17 (4 fmly) **Facilities** New Year Wi-fi **Conf** Class 100 Board 50 Thtr 200 **Parking** 70 **Notes** LB ⊗ Civ Wed 55

Travelodge Hastings

BUDGET HOTEL

☎ 0871 984 6310 📠 01424 437277
Bohemia Rd TN34 1ET
web: www.travelodge.co.uk
dir: A21 into Hastings. Police HQ & Courts on left. Lodge next left before ambulance HQ

Travelodge offers good quality, good value, budget accommodation. All offer family rooms sleeping up to four (two adults, two children) with en suite bathroom/ shower-room, remote-control TV, tea- and coffee-making facilities and comfortable beds. Food options vary. Breakfast is at the on-site Bar Café restaurant (if available) or to take away. See also Hotel Groups pages.

Rooms 50 (8 fmly) **S** fr £29; **D** fr £29 **Conf** Class 150 Board 120 Thtr 250

HOVE

See Brighton & Hove

LEWES	Map 6 TQ41

Shelleys Hotel

★★★★ 71% HOTEL

☎ 01273 472361 & 483403 📠 01273 483152
136 High St BN7 1XS
e-mail: reservations@shelleys-hotel-lewes.com
dir: A23 to Brighton onto A27 to Lewes. At 1st rdbt left for town centre, after x-rds hotel on left

Originally a coaching inn dating from the 16th century, this charming establishment is the perfect base for exploring the South Downs and a relaxing venue when shopping in nearby Brighton. All rooms are comfortably furnished in a traditional style and equipped with modern amenities such as Wi-fi. As well as a cosy bar and lounge, a fine dining restaurant is available, and homemade cream teas in the stunning garden are a speciality.

Rooms 19 (1 fmly) **S** £125-£150; **D** £165-£305 (incl. bkfst)* **Facilities** STV ⤷ Xmas New Year Wi-fi **Conf** Class 20 Board 25 Thtr 60 Del from £200 to £275* **Parking** 20 **Notes** LB Civ Wed 60

NEWICK · Map 6 TQ42

INSPECTORS' CHOICE

Newick Park Hotel & Country Estate
★★★ ◉◉◉ HOTEL

☎ 01825 723633 ▤ 01825 723969
BN8 4SB
e-mail: bookings@newickpark.co.uk
web: www.newickpark.co.uk
dir: Exit A272 at Newick Green, 1m, pass church & pub. Turn left, hotel 0.25m on right

Delightful Grade II listed Georgian country house set amid 250 acres of Sussex parkland and landscaped gardens. The spacious, individually decorated bedrooms are tastefully furnished, thoughtfully equipped and have superb views of the grounds; many rooms have huge American king-size beds. The comfortable public rooms include a study, a sitting room, lounge bar and an elegant restaurant.

Rooms 16 (3 annexe) (5 fmly) (1 GF) **S** £125; **D** £165-£285 (incl. bkfst)* **Facilities** FTV ⌇ ⌣ Fishing ⌣ Badminton Clay pigeon shooting Helicopter rides Quad biking Tank driving Xmas Wi-fi **Conf** Class 40 Board 40 Thtr 80 Del from £216.45 to £240* **Parking** 52 **Notes** Civ Wed 100

See advert on this page

PEASMARSH · Map 7 TQ82

Best Western Flackley Ash
★★★ 78% HOTEL

☎ 01797 230651 ▤ 01797 230510
TN31 6YH
e-mail: enquiries@flackleyashhotel.co.uk
web: www.flackleyashhotel.co.uk
dir: Exit A21 onto A268 to Newenden, next left A268 to Rye. Hotel on left on entering Peasmarsh

Five acres of beautifully kept grounds make a lovely setting for this elegant Georgian country house. The hotel is superbly situated for exploring the many local attractions, including the ancient Cinque Port of Rye. Stylishly decorated bedrooms are comfortable and boast many thoughtful touches. A sunny conservatory dining room, luxurious beauty spa and a swimming pool are available.

Rooms 45 (5 fmly) (19 GF) (10 smoking) **S** £85-£100; **D** £120-£160 (incl. bkfst) **Facilities** Spa STV ⌕ supervised Putt green ⌣ Gym Beauty salon Steam room Saunas Xmas New Year Wi-fi **Conf** Class 60 Board 40 Thtr 100 **Parking** 80 **Notes** Civ Wed 100

ROTTINGDEAN · Map 6 TQ30

White Horse Hotel
Ⓤ

☎ 01273 300301 ▤ 01273 308716
Marine Dr BN2 7HR
e-mail: 5308@greeneking.co.uk

Currently the rating for this establishment is not confirmed. This may be due to a change of ownership or because it has only recently joined the AA rating scheme. For further details please see the AA website: theAA.com

Rooms 18 **Conf** Board 25 Thtr 50

RYE · Map 7 TQ92

George in Rye
★★★★ 77% ◉ HOTEL

☎ 01797 222114 ▤ 01797 224065
98 High St TN31 7JT
e-mail: stay@thegeorgeinrye.com
dir: M20 junct 10, then A2070 to Brenzett then A259 to Rye

This attractive 16th-century property, situated in the heart of historic Rye, has been sympathetically styled to retain many original features including a stunning Georgian ballroom complete with a minstrels' gallery. The bedrooms are stylishly appointed and filled with an abundance of thoughtful touches. Contemporary public areas include a bar, lounge and dining room and an excellent alfresco area for summer dining.

Rooms 24 (3 GF) **S** £95-£125; **D** £125-£225 (incl. bkfst)* **Facilities** FTV Xmas New Year Wi-fi **Conf** Class 65 Board 40 Thtr 100 Del from £185* **Notes** LB ⊗ Civ Wed 100

RYE *continued*

Mermaid Inn

★★★ 79% ◉ HOTEL

☎ 01797 223065 & 223788 ▤ 01797 225069
Mermaid St TN31 7EY
e-mail: info@mermaidinn.com
web: www.mermaidinn.com
dir: A259, follow signs to town centre, then into Mermaid St

Situated near the top of a cobbled side street, this famous smugglers' inn is steeped in history. The charming interior has many architectural features such as attractive stone work. The bedrooms vary in size and style but all are tastefully furnished. Delightful public rooms include a choice of lounges, cosy bar and smart restaurant.

Rooms 31 (5 fmly) **S** £75; **D** £150-£220 (incl. bkfst)*
Facilities Xmas New Year Wi-fi **Conf** Class 40 Board 30 Thtr 50 **Parking** 25 **Notes** LB ⊗

The Hope Anchor

★★★ 75% SMALL HOTEL

☎ 01797 222216 ▤ 01797 223796
Watchbell St TN31 7HA
e-mail: info@thehopeanchor.co.uk
web: www.thehopeanchor.co.uk
dir: From A268, Quayside, turn right into Wish Ward, up Mermaid St, right into West St, right into Watchbell St, hotel at end

This historic inn sits high above the town with enviable views out over the harbour and Romney Marsh, and is accessible via delightful cobbled streets. A relaxed and friendly atmosphere prevails within the cosy public rooms, while the attractively furnished bedrooms are well equipped and many enjoy good views over the marshes.

Rooms 16 (2 fmly) (1 GF) **S** £65-£140; **D** £85-£160 (incl. bkfst)* **Facilities** FTV Xmas New Year Wi-fi **Conf** Class 30 Board 20 Thtr 40 Del from £160 to £200 **Parking** 12 **Notes** LB

Rye Lodge

★★★ 75% HOTEL

☎ 01797 223838 ▤ 01797 223585
Hilders Cliff TN31 7LD
e-mail: info@ryelodge.co.uk
web: www.ryelodge.co.uk
dir: One-way system in Rye, follow signs for town centre, through Landgate arch, hotel 100yds on right

Standing in an elevated position, Rye Lodge has panoramic views across Romney Marshes and the Rother Estuary. Traditionally styled bedrooms come in a variety of sizes; they are attractively decorated and thoughtfully equipped. Public rooms feature indoor leisure facilities and the Terrace Room Restaurant where home-made dishes are offered. Lunch and afternoon tea are served on the flower-filled outdoor terrace in warmer months.

Rooms 18 (5 GF) **S** £75-£125; **D** £110-£220 (incl. bkfst) **Facilities** STV ⊗ Aromatherapy Steam cabinet Sauna Exercise machines Xmas New Year Wi-fi **Parking** 20 **Notes** LB

White Vine House

RESTAURANT WITH ROOMS

☎ 01797 224748
24 High St TN31 7JF
e-mail: info@whitevinehouse.co.uk
dir: In centre of High Street

Situated in the heart of the ancient Cinque Port town of Rye, this property's origins go back to the 13th century. The cellar is the oldest part, but the current building dates from 1560, and boasts an impressive Georgian frontage. The original timber framework is visible in many areas, and certainly adds to the house's sense of history. The bedrooms have period furniture along with luxury bath or shower rooms; one bedroom has an antique four-poster.

Rooms 7 (1 fmly)

ST LEONARDS-ON-SEA

See Hastings & St Leonards

TICEHURST   Map 6 TQ63

Dale Hill Hotel & Golf Club

★★★★ 82% ◉ HOTEL

☎ 01580 200112 ▤ 01580 201249
TN5 7DQ
e-mail: info@dalehill.co.uk
web: www.dalehill.co.uk
dir: M25 junct 5/A21. 5m after Lamberhurst turn right at lights onto B2087 to Flimwell. Hotel 1m on left

This modern hotel is situated just a short drive from the village. Extensive public rooms include a lounge bar, a conservatory brasserie, a formal restaurant and the Spike Bar, which is mainly frequented by golf club members and has a lively atmosphere. The hotel also has two superb 18-hole golf courses, a swimming pool and gym.

Rooms 35 (8 fmly) (23 GF) **S** £80-£90; **D** £90-£130 (incl. bkfst)* **Facilities** STV ⊗ ♨ 36 Putt green Gym Covered driving range Pool table Xmas New Year Wi-fi **Conf** Class 50 Board 50 Thtr 120 Del from £130 to £150* **Services** Lift **Parking** 220 **Notes** LB ⊗ Civ Wed 150

UCKFIELD   Map 6 TQ42

Buxted Park Country House Hotel

★★★★ 84% ◉◉ HOTEL

☎ 01825 733333 ▤ 01825 732 990
Buxted TN22 4AY
e-mail: buxtedpark@handpicked.co.uk
web: www.handpicked.co.uk
dir: From A26 (Uckfield bypass) take A272 signed Buxted. Through lights, hotel 1m on right

An attractive Grade II listed Georgian mansion dating back to the 17th century. The property is set amidst 300 acres of beautiful countryside and landscaped gardens. The stylish, thoughtfully equipped bedrooms are split between the main house and the modern Garden Wing. An interesting choice of dishes is served in the restaurant.

Rooms 44 (6 fmly) (16 GF) **Facilities** FTV Putt green Fishing ✈ Gym Fishing Mountain biking Orienteering Xmas New Year Wi-fi **Conf** Class 80 Board 60 Thtr 180 **Services** Lift **Parking** 150 **Notes** LB ⊗ Civ Wed 130

INSPECTORS' CHOICE

Horsted Place
★★★ ⊛ HOTEL

☎ 01825 750581 📠 01825 750459
Little Horsted TN22 5TS
e-mail: hotel@horstedplace.co.uk
dir: 2m S on A26 towards Lewes

This 17th-century property is one of Britain's finest examples of Gothic revivalist architecture. It is situated in extensive landscaped grounds, with a tennis court and croquet lawn, and is adjacent to the East Sussex National Golf Club. The spacious bedrooms are attractively decorated, tastefully furnished and equipped with many thoughtful touches such as flowers and books. Most rooms also have a separate sitting area.

Rooms 20 (3 annexe) (5 fmly) (2 GF) **S** £140-£350; **D** £140-£350 (incl. bkfst)* **Facilities** STV ⅃ 36 ⊛ 🏊 Free use of gym & pool at nearby hotel ♫ Xmas New Year Wi-fi **Conf** Class 50 Board 40 Thtr 80 Del from £170* **Services** Lift **Parking** 32 **Notes** LB ⊗ No children 7yrs Civ Wed 100

WILMINGTON   Map 6 TQ50

Crossways
⊛⊛ RESTAURANT WITH ROOMS

☎ 01323 482455 📠 01323 487811
Lewes Rd BN26 5SG
e-mail: stay@crosswayshotel.co.uk
web: www.crosswayshotel.co.uk
dir: On A27 between Lewes & Polegate, 2m E of Alfriston rdbt

Amidst stunning gardens and attractively tended grounds sits this well-established, popular restaurant. The well-presented bedrooms are tastefully decorated and provide an abundance of thoughtful amenities including free Wi-fi. Guest comfort is paramount and naturally warm hospitality ensures guests often return.

Rooms 7

SUSSEX, WEST

AMBERLEY   Map 6 TQ01

INSPECTORS' CHOICE

Amberley Castle
★★★★ ⊛⊛⊛
COUNTRY HOUSE HOTEL

☎ 01798 831992 📠 01798 831998
BN18 9LT
e-mail: info@amberleycastle.co.uk
web: www.amberleycastle.co.uk
dir: On B2139, off A29 between Bury & Storrington

This delightful castle idyllically set in the Sussex countryside boasts 900 years of history. The battlements, complete with a mighty portcullis (one of the few in Europe that still works) enclose the hotel. Beyond these walls are acres of stunning parkland that feature formal gardens, Koi ponds and Mistletoe Lodge, a thatched tree house accessed by a rope bridge. Here, from May to September, it is possible to dine on a special seasonal menu for two. In a more formal setting guests can enjoy award-winning cuisine in the magnificent Queen's Room - pre-booking is essential. Named after Sussex castles each of the sumptuously furnished bedrooms and suites is unique in design; some have four-poster beds. All have whirlpool baths and have lots of little luxuries such as fruit, biscuits and chocolates. Von Essen Hotels - AA Hotel Group of the Year 2009-10.

Rooms 19 (5 annexe) (6 GF) **D** £190-£520 (incl. bkfst)* **Facilities** ⊛ Putt green ⊛ Xmas New Year **Conf** Class 25 Board 30 Thtr 50 Del from £340 to £450* **Parking** 40 **Notes** ⊗ No children 12yrs Civ Wed 110

ARUNDEL   Map 6 TQ00

White Swan
★★★ 79% HOTEL

☎ 01903 882677 📠 01903 884154
16 Chichester Rd BN18 0AD
e-mail: thewhiteswan.arundel@pebblehotels.com
dir: off A27, 0.5m W

This hotel has undergone a complete refurbishment resulting in very comfortable and stylish guest accommodation. There is a character bar, lounge and restaurant, and an informal service is provided by the friendly team. Substantial snacks and meals are can be ordered throughout the day and evening. Complimentary Wi-fi is available throughout the public areas.

Rooms 20 (6 GF) **Facilities** FTV Wi-fi **Conf** Class 50 Board 40 Thtr 130 **Parking** 110 **Notes** LB ⊗ Civ Wed 80

Norfolk Arms
★★★ 75% HOTEL

☎ 01903 882101 📠 01903 884275
High St BN18 9AB
e-mail: norfolk.arms@forestdale.com
web: www.norfolkarmshotel.com
dir: On High St in city centre

Built by the 10th Duke of Norfolk, this Georgian coaching inn enjoys a superb setting beneath the battlements of Arundel Castle. Bedrooms vary in sizes and character - all are comfortable and well equipped. Public areas include two bars serving real ales, comfortable lounges with roaring log fires, a traditional restaurant and a range of meeting and function rooms.

Rooms 33 (13 annexe) (4 fmly) (8 GF) **S** £70-£89; **D** £90-£125 (incl. bkfst)* **Facilities** FTV Xmas New Year Wi-fi **Conf** Class 36 Board 40 Thtr 100 **Parking** 34 **Notes** Civ Wed 60

Comfort Inn
★★ 67% HOTEL

☎ 01903 840840 📠 01903 849849
Crossbush BN17 7QQ
e-mail: reservations@comfortinnarundel.co.uk
dir: A27/A284, 1st right into services

This modern, purpose-built hotel provides a good base for exploring the nearby historic town. Good access to local road networks and a range of meeting rooms, all air-conditioned, also make this an ideal venue for business guests. Bedrooms are spacious, smartly decorated and well equipped.

Rooms 53 (4 fmly) (25 GF) (12 smoking) **S** £55-£65; **D** £55-£75 (incl. bkfst)* **Facilities** STV FTV Xmas New Year Wi-fi **Conf** Class 30 Board 30 Thtr 30 **Parking** 53

ARUNDEL *continued*

Innkeeper's Lodge Arundel Chichester (Fontwell Park)

BUDGET HOTEL

☎ 0845 112 6093 📄 0845 112 6210
Fontwell Park Racecourse, Fontwell BN18 0SY
web: www.innkeeperslodge.com/arundelchichester
dir: Lodge at Fontwell Park Racecourse on A27/A29 rdbt between Chichester & Arundel

Innkeeper's Lodge represents an exciting, high value concept within the budget hotel market. Comfortable bedrooms provide excellent facilities that include satellite TV and modem points. Options include family rooms; and for the corporate guest, cutting edge IT includes Wi-fi access. Food is served all day in the adjacent Country Pub. The extensive continental breakfast is complimentary. See also the Hotel Groups pages.

Rooms 40

The Townhouse

RESTAURANT WITH ROOMS

☎ 01903 883847
65 High St BN18 9AJ
e-mail: enquiries@thetownhouse.co.uk
web: www.thetownhouse.co.uk
dir: Follow A27 to Arundel, onto High Street, establishment on left at top of hill

This is an elegant, Grade II-listed Regency building overlooking Arundel Castle, just a short walk from the shops and centre of the town. Bedrooms and public areas retain the unspoilt characteristics of the building. The ceiling in the dining room is particularly spectacular and comes all the way from 16th-century Florence. The owners can be justifiably proud of the enterprise they took on just a short years ago.

Rooms 4

BOGNOR REGIS Map 6 SZ99

The Russell Hotel

★★★ 77% HOTEL

☎ 01243 871300 📄 01243 871301
King's Pde PO21 2QP
e-mail: russell.hotel@actionforblindpeople.org.uk
dir: A27 follow signs for town centre, hotel on seafront

Situated in a pleasant location close to the seafront, the Russell Hotel offers large and well-appointed bedrooms; some are fully accessible and many have sea views. This hotel also caters for visually impaired people, their families, friends and their guide dogs, as well as offering a warm welcome to business and leisure guests. There are of course special facilities for the guide dogs. Leisure facilities are also available.

Rooms 40 **D** £84-£164 (incl. bkfst & dinner)*
Facilities FTV 🏊 supervised Gym 🎵 Xmas New Year
Conf Class 40 Board 20 Thtr 50 Del from £58 to £90*
Services Lift **Parking** 6 **Notes** LB Closed Jan

Beachcroft

★★★ 72% HOTEL

Best Western

☎ 01243 827142 📄 01243 863500
Clyde Rd, Felpham Village PO22 7AH
e-mail: reservations@beachcroft-hotel.co.uk
web: www.beachcroft-hotel.co.uk
dir: From A259 between Chichester & Littlehampton at Felpham, follow village signs, hotel signed

This popular hotel overlooks a secluded part of the seafront. Bedrooms are bright and spacious, and leisure facilities include a heated indoor swimming pool and treatment rooms. Diners may choose from the varied choice of the traditional restaurant menus or the more informal cosy bar.

Rooms 35 (4 fmly) (6 GF) **S** £53.10-£85.80;
D £70.20-£106.70 (incl. bkfst)* **Facilities** FTV 🏊 Xmas New Year Wi-fi **Conf** Class 30 Board 30 Thtr 60 Del from £84.95* **Parking** 27 **Notes** ⊗

Royal Norfolk

★★★ 71% HOTEL

☎ 01243 826222 📄 01243 826325
The Esplanade PO21 2LH
e-mail: accommodation@royalnorfolkhotel.com
web: www.royalnorfolkhotel.com
dir: From A259 follow Longford Rd through lights to Canada Grove to T-junct. Right, take 2nd exit at rdbt. Hotel on right

On the Esplanade, but set back behind lawns and gardens, this fine-looking hotel has been welcoming guests since Regency times. Today the traditionally furnished bedrooms, four with four-poster beds, are well provided with all the modern comforts. Public areas offer sea views from the elegant restaurant and comfortable lobby lounge.

Rooms 43 (4 fmly) **S** £45-£65; **D** £90-£120 (incl. bkfst)*
Facilities 🎵 Xmas New Year Wi-fi **Conf** Class 140 Board 140 Thtr 140 Del from £75 to £90* **Services** Lift **Parking** 60 **Notes** LB

The Inglenook

★★★ 64% SMALL HOTEL

☎ 01243 262495 & 265411 📄 01243 262668
255 Pagham Rd, Nyetimber PO21 3QB
e-mail: reception@the-inglenook.com
dir: A27 to Vinnetrow Road left at Walnut Tree, 2.5m on right

This 16th-century inn retains much of its original character, including exposed beams throughout. Bedrooms are individually decorated and vary in size. There is a cosy lounge, a well-kept garden and a bar that offers a popular evening menu and convivial atmosphere. The restaurant, overlooking the garden, also serves enjoyable cuisine.

Rooms 18 (1 fmly) (2 GF) **S** £50-£75; **D** £70-£200 (incl. bkfst)* **Facilities** FTV Xmas New Year Wi-fi **Conf** Class 50 Board 50 Thtr 100 Del from £90* **Parking** 35 **Notes** LB Civ Wed 80

The Royal

★ ◪ SMALL HOTEL

☎ 01243 864665 📠 01243 863175
The Esplanade PO21 1SZ
e-mail: david@royalhotelbognor.co.uk
dir: Opposite Bognor Pier, 300yds from town centre

Rooms 22 (3 fmly) **Facilities** Xmas New Year
Conf Class 30 Board 30 Thtr 60 **Services** Lift

BOSHAM   Map 5 SU80

The Millstream Hotel & Restaurant

★★★ 83% ◉◉ HOTEL

☎ 01243 573234 📠 01243 573459
Bosham Ln PO18 8HL
e-mail: info@millstream-hotel.co.uk
web: www.millstream-hotel.co.uk
dir: 4m W of Chichester on A259, left at Bosham rdbt.
After 0.5m right at T-junct signed to church & quay. Hotel
0.5m on right

Lying in the idyllic village of Bosham, this attractive hotel
provides comfortable, well-equipped and tastefully
decorated bedrooms. Many guests regularly return here
for the relaxed atmosphere created by the notably
efficient and friendly staff. Public rooms include a
cocktail bar that opens onto the garden, and a pleasant
restaurant where varied and freshly prepared cuisine can
be enjoyed.

Rooms 35 (2 annexe) (2 fmly) (9 GF) **S** £83-£93;
D £142-£162 (incl. bkfst)* **Facilities** FTV Painting &
Bridge breaks ♫ Xmas New Year Wi-fi **Conf** Class 20
Board 20 Thtr 45 Del from £125 to £150* **Parking** 44
Notes LB ⊗ Civ Wed 92

CHICHESTER   Map 5 SU80

The Goodwood Park Hotel

★★★★ 77% ◉◉ HOTEL

☎ 01243 775537 📠 01243 520120
PO18 0QB
e-mail: reservations@thegoodwoodparkhotel.co.uk
web: www.thegoodwoodparkhotel.co.uk

(For full entry see Goodwood)

Crouchers Country Hotel & Restaurant

★★★ 81% ◉◉ HOTEL

☎ 01243 784995 📠 01243 539797
Birdham Rd PO20 7EH
e-mail: crouchers@btconnect.com
dir: From A27 Chichester bypass onto A286 towards West
Wittering, 2m, hotel on left between Chichester Marina &
Dell Quay

This friendly, family-run hotel, situated in open
countryside, is just a short drive from the harbour. The
comfortable and well-equipped bedrooms include some in
a separate barn and coach house, and the open-plan
public areas have pleasant views.

Rooms 26 (23 annexe) (2 fmly) (15 GF) **S** £75-£115;
D £105-£150 (incl. bkfst)* **Facilities** STV FTV Xmas New
Year Wi-fi **Conf** Class 80 Board 50 Thtr 80 Del from £110
to £120 **Parking** 80 **Notes** LB

INSPECTORS' CHOICE

West Stoke House

◉◉◉ RESTAURANT WITH ROOMS

☎ 01243 575226 📠 01243 574655
Downs Rd, West Stoke PO18 9BN
e-mail: info@weststokehouse.co.uk
dir: 3m NW of Chichester. Off B286 to West Stoke, next
to St Andrew's Church

This fine country house, part Georgian and part
medieval, with over five acres of lawns and gardens,
lies on the edge of the South Downs. The large
uncluttered bedrooms have smart modern bathrooms
and great country views. The restaurant provides very
good cooking in a relaxed atmosphere. Public rooms
have a light-filled elegance and are adorned with an
eclectic mix of period furniture and contemporary art.

Rooms 8 (1 fmly)

CLIMPING   Map 6 SU90

INSPECTORS' CHOICE

Bailiffscourt Hotel & Spa

★★★ ◉◉ HOTEL

☎ 01903 723511 📠 01903 723107
Climping St BN17 5RW
e-mail: bailiffscourt@hshotels.co.uk
web: www.hshotels.co.uk
dir: A259, follow Climping Beach signs. Hotel 0.5m on
right

This delightful moated 'medieval manor' dating back
only to the 1920s has the appearance of having been in
existence for centuries. It was built for Lord Moyne, a
member of the Guinness family, who wanted to create
an ancient manor house. It became a hotel just over 60
years ago and sits in 30 acres of delightful parkland
that leads to the beach. Bedrooms vary from
atmospheric feature rooms with log fires, oak beams
and four-poster beds to spacious, stylish and
contemporary rooms located in the grounds. The
Tapestry Restaurant serves award-winning classic
European cuisine, and in summer the Courtyard is the
place for informal light lunches and afternoon tea.
Superb facilities are to be found in the health spa.

Rooms 39 (30 annexe) (25 fmly) (16 GF) **S** £200-£485;
D £215-£545 (incl. bkfst)* **Facilities** Spa STV FTV ⊛
supervised ⟍ supervised ⬗ ⬗ Gym Sauna Steam
room Dance/fitness studio Yoga/Pilates/gym inductions
Xmas New Year Wi-fi **Conf** Class 20 Board 26 Thtr 40
Parking 100 **Notes** LB Civ Wed 60

COPTHORNE

See Gatwick Airport

CRAWLEY

See Gatwick Airport

CUCKFIELD — Map 6 TQ32

INSPECTORS' CHOICE

Ockenden Manor
★★★ ◉◉◉ HOTEL

☎ 01444 416111 🖹 01444 415549
Ockenden Ln RH17 5LD
e-mail: reservations@ockenden-manor.com
web: www.hshotels.co.uk
dir: A23 towards Brighton. 4.5m left onto B2115
towards Haywards Heath. Cuckfield 3m. Ockendon Lane
off High St. Hotel at end

This charming 16th-century property enjoys fine views
of the South Downs. The individually designed
bedrooms and suites offer high standards of
accommodation, some with unique historic features.
Public rooms, retaining much original character,
include an elegant sitting room with all the elements
for a relaxing afternoon in front of the fire. Imaginative,
noteworthy cuisine is a highlight to any stay. The
beautiful rooms and lovely garden make Ockenden a
popular wedding venue. A spa is planned for 2010.

Rooms 22 (4 fmly) (4 GF) **S** £108-£195; **D** £179-£367
(incl. bkfst)* **Facilities** STV FTV ✈ Xmas New Year
Wi-fi **Conf** Class 20 Board 26 Thtr 50 Del from £175 to
£260 **Parking** 43 **Notes** LB Civ Wed 75

EAST GRINSTEAD — Map 6 TQ33

Felbridge Hotel & Spa
★★★★ 86% ◉◉ HOTEL

CLASSIC BRITISH HOTELS

☎ 01342 337700 🖹 01342 337715
London Rd RH19 2BH
e-mail: info@felbridgehotel.co.uk
dir: From W exit M23 junct 10, follow signs to A22. From
N, exit M25 junct 6. Hotel on A22 at Felbridge

This luxurious hotel is within easy of the M25 and Gatwick
as well as Eastbourne and the glorious south coast. All

bedrooms are beautifully styled and offer a wealth of
amenities. Diners can choose from the Bay Tree Brasserie,
Anise Fine Dining Restaurant or contemporary QUBE Bar.
Facilities include a selection of modern meeting rooms,
the luxurious Chakra Spa and swimming pool.

Rooms 120 (16 fmly) (53 GF) (9 smoking) **S** £79-£290;
D £79-£290* **Facilities** Spa STV FTV ◎ supervised Gym
Sauna Steam room Hairdresser Xmas New Year Wi-fi
Conf Class 120 Board 100 Thtr 500 Del from £140 to
£350 **Services** Air con **Parking** 300 **Notes** LB ⊗
Civ Wed 150

INSPECTORS' CHOICE

Gravetye Manor
★★★ ◉◉◉ HOTEL

☎ 01342 810567 🖹 01342 810080
RH19 4LJ
e-mail: info@gravetyemanor.co.uk
web: www.gravetyemanor.co.uk
dir: B2028 to Haywards Heath. 1m after Turners Hill
fork left towards Sharpthorne, immediate 1st left into
Vowels Lane

This beautiful Elizabethan mansion was built in 1598
and enjoys a tranquil setting. It was one of the first
country-house hotels and remains a shining example in
its class. There are several day rooms, each with oak
panelling, fresh flowers and open fires that combine to
create a relaxing atmosphere. Bedrooms are decorated
in traditional English style, furnished with antiques
and with many thoughtful extras. The cuisine is
excellent and makes full use of home grown fruit and
vegetables. Guests should take time to explore the
outstanding gardens.

Rooms 18 **S** £110-£180; **D** £170-£345* **Facilities** STV
Fishing ✈ Wi-fi **Conf** Board 12 Del from £280 to £350*
Parking 35 **Notes** ⊗ No children 7yrs RS 25 Dec
Civ Wed 45

FIVE OAKS — Map 6 TQ02

Travelodge Billingshurst Five Oaks

BUDGET HOTEL

☎ 0871 984 6013 🖹 01403 782711
Staines St RH14 9AE
web: www.travelodge.co.uk
dir: on A29 N'bound, 1m N of Billingshurst

Travelodge offers good quality, good value, budget
accommodation. All offer family rooms sleeping up to four
(two adults, two children) with en suite bathroom/
shower-room, remote-control TV, tea- and coffee-making
facilities and comfortable beds. Food options vary.
Breakfast is at the on-site Bar Café restaurant (if
available) or to take away. See also Hotel Groups pages.

Rooms 26 **S** fr £29; **D** fr £29

FONTWELL — Map 6 SU90

Travelodge Arundel Fontwell

BUDGET HOTEL

☎ 0871 984 6014 🖹 01243 543973
BN18 0SB
web: www.travelodge.co.uk
dir: On A27, 5m N of Bognor Regis

Travelodge offers good quality, good value, budget
accommodation. All offer family rooms sleeping up to four
(two adults, two children) with en suite bathroom/
shower-room, remote-control TV, tea- and coffee-making
facilities and comfortable beds. Food options vary.
Breakfast is at the on-site Bar Café restaurant (if
available) or to take away. See also Hotel Groups pages.

Rooms 62 **S** fr £29; **D** fr £29

GATWICK AIRPORT (LONDON) Map 6 TQ24

See also **Dorking & Reigate (Surrey)**, **East Grinstead (Sussex, West)**

INSPECTORS' CHOICE

Langshott Manor
★★★★ ◎◎ COUNTRY HOUSE HOTEL

☎ 01293 786680 🖹 01293 783905
Langshott Ln RH6 9LN
e-mail: admin@langshottmanor.com
dir: From A23 take Ladbroke Rd, off Chequers rdbt to Langshott, after 0.75m hotel on right

Charming timber-framed Tudor house set amidst beautifully landscaped grounds on the outskirts of town. The stylish public areas feature a choice of inviting lounges with polished oak panelling, exposed beams and log fires. The individually decorated bedrooms combine the most up-to-date comforts with flair, individuality and traditional elegance. The Mulberry restaurant overlooks a picturesque pond and offers an imaginative menu.

Rooms 22 (8 annexe) (2 fmly) (8 GF) **S** £130-£150; **D** £150-£320 (incl. bkfst)* **Facilities** STV FTV ⇘ Xmas New Year Wi-fi **Conf** Class 20 Board 22 Thtr 40 Del from £215 to £250* **Parking** 25 **Notes** LB ⊗ Civ Wed 60

Sofitel London Gatwick
★★★★ 80% ◎ HOTEL   SOFITEL

☎ 01293 567070 & 555000 🖹 01293 567739
North Terminal RH6 0PH
e-mail: h6204-re@accor.com
dir: M23 junct 9, follow to 2nd rdbt. Hotel large white building straight ahead

One of the closest hotels to the airport, this modern, purpose-built hotel is located only minutes from the terminals. Bedrooms are contemporary and all are air-

conditioned. Guests have a choice of eating options including a French-style café, brasserie and oriental restaurant.

Rooms 518 (19 fmly) **Facilities** Gym Wi-fi **Conf** Class 150 Board 90 Thtr 300 Del from £145 to £160 **Services** Lift Air con **Parking** 200 **Notes** ⊗

Ramada London Gatwick   ®RAMADA
★★★★ 75% HOTEL

☎ 01293 561186 🖹 01293 561169
Tinsley Lane South, Three Bridges RH10 8XH
e-mail: sales.londongatwick@ramadajarvis.co.uk
web: www.ramadajarvis.co.uk
dir: M23 junct 10, A2011 to Crawley. Hotel at 1st rdbt on left

This modern, purpose-built hotel is just four miles from the airport with easy access to the M23. Spacious bedrooms are comfortably appointed and well equipped including some family rooms. Air-conditioned public areas include a brightly appointed Arts restaurant, first-floor conference centre and Sebastian Coe health club.

Rooms 151 (31 fmly) **Facilities** STV Gym Beauty salon Hairdresser New Year Wi-fi **Conf** Class 80 Board 40 Thtr 210 Del from £135 to £165 **Services** Lift Air con **Parking** 150 **Notes** ⊗ Closed 24-25 Dec Civ Wed 150

Menzies Chequers   MenziesHotels
★★★★ 74% HOTEL

☎ 01293 766750 🖹 01293 820625
Brighton Rd RH6 8PH
e-mail: chequers@menzieshotels.co.uk
web: www.menzieshotels.co.uk
dir: M23 junct 9, A23 towards Redhill. At 'Longbridge' rdbt take 3rd exit signed Horley/A23. 1m to Sainsburys/Shell rdbt. Take 1st exit, hotel on right

A popular hotel located close to the town centre and also convenient for Gatwick Airport; original parts of the building date back to the 1750s. Bedrooms are comfortable and well equipped with good facilities. Dining areas include the contemporary restaurant and the traditional Chequers pub. Secure parking is available.

Rooms 104 (10 fmly) (46 GF) (6 smoking) **S** £58-£119; **D** £58-£119* **Facilities** STV Xmas New Year Wi-fi **Conf** Class 25 Board 32 Thtr 70 Del from £95 to £135* **Services** Lift **Parking** 140 **Notes** ⊗

Copthorne Hotel and Resort Effingham Park London Gatwick   MILLENNIUM
★★★★ 72% HOTEL

☎ 01342 714994 🖹 01342 716039
West Park Rd RH10 3EU
e-mail: sales.effingham@millenniumhotels.co.uk
web: www.millenniumhotels.co.uk
dir: M23 junct 10, A264 towards East Grinstead. Over rdbt, at 2nd rdbt left onto B2028. Effingham Park on right

A former stately home, set in 40 acres of grounds, this hotel is popular for conference and weekend functions. The main restaurant is an open-plan brasserie serving modern continental cuisine, and snacks are also available in the bar. Bedrooms are spacious and well equipped. Facilities include a golf course and a leisure club.

Rooms 122 (7 fmly) (20 GF) **S** £65-£125; **D** £65-£125* **Facilities** STV ♦ 9 ♨ Putt green Gym Aerobic & Dance studios Xmas New Year Wi-fi **Conf** Class 450 Board 250 Thtr 900 Del from £138 to £185* **Services** Lift **Parking** 500 **Notes** LB ⊗ Civ Wed 600

Copthorne Hotel London Gatwick   MILLENNIUM
★★★★ 71% HOTEL

☎ 01342 348800 & 348888 🖹 01342 348833
Copthorne Way RH10 3PG
e-mail: sales.gatwick@millenniumhotels.co.uk
web: www.millenniumhotels.co.uk
dir: On A264, 2m E of A264/B2036 rdbt

Situated in a tranquil position, the Copthorne is set in 100 acres of wooded, landscaped gardens containing jogging tracks, a putting green and a petanque pit. The sprawling building is built around a 16th-century farmhouse and has comfortable bedrooms; many are air conditioned. There are three dining options, ranging from the informal bar or carvery to the more formal Lion d'Or.

Rooms 227 (10 fmly) **S** £66-£135; **D** £66-£135* **Facilities** STV ♦ ♨ Gym Squash Aerobic studio Wi-fi **Conf** Class 60 Board 40 Thtr 135 Del from £125 to £190* **Services** Lift **Parking** 300 **Notes** LB ⊗ Civ Wed 100

Crowne Plaza Hotel Gatwick-Crawley   CROWNE PLAZA
★★★★ 71% HOTEL

☎ 01293 608608 🖹 01293 515913
Langley Dr RH11 7SX
e-mail: info@cpgatwick.co.uk
web: www.cpgatwick.co.uk
dir: M23 junct 10, 3rd exit at rdbt & 3rd exit at next rdbt. At lights take 3rd exit at rdbt

Ideally located for Gatwick Airport, this contemporary hotel offers comfortable and well-furnished rooms suitable for both the leisure and business travellers. Elite

continued

GATWICK AIRPORT (LONDON) *continued*

Health and Fitness Centre is a relaxing leisure centre, which houses a stunning indoor swimming pool. Cube Restaurant & Bar offers a relaxed dining experience and the Gallery Sports Bar, an informal alternative. The hotel also has extensive conference facilities.

Rooms 288 (12 fmly) (43 smoking) **Facilities** STV FTV ☺ supervised Gym Saunas Steam room Bubble spa Wi-fi **Conf** Class 110 Board 40 Thtr 230 Del from £129 to £179* **Services** Lift Air con **Parking** 200 **Notes** ⊗ Civ Wed 150

Stanhill Court

★★★ 85% ☺☺ HOTEL

☎ 01293 862166 🖶 01293 862773
Stanhill Rd, Charlwood RH6 0EP
e-mail: enquiries@stanhillcourthotel.co.uk
web: www.stanhillcourthotel.co.uk
dir: N of Charlwood towards Newdigate

This hotel dates back to 1881 and enjoys a secluded location in 35 acres of well-tended grounds with views over the Downs. Bedrooms are individually furnished and decorated, and many have four-poster beds. Public areas include a library, a bright Spanish-style bar and a traditional wood-panelled restaurant. Extensive and varied function facilities make this a popular wedding venue.

Rooms 34 (3 fmly) (1 GF) **Facilities** Putt green Fishing **Conf** Class 120 Board 66 Thtr 300 **Parking** 110 **Notes** LB Civ Wed 220

Best Western Gatwick Moat House

★★★ 80% HOTEL

☎ 0870 443 1671 & 01293 899988 🖶 01293 899904
Longbridge Roundabout RH6 0AB
e-mail: gatwick@qmh-hotels.com
web: www.bestwestern.co.uk/content/hotel-details-leisure.aspx/hotel/83860
dir: M23 junct 9, follow signs for North Terminal, take 4th exit at rdbt signed A23/Redhill. At 1st rdbt take 1st exit then 1st left

Ideally situated for both terminals, this hotel provides a shuttle service to the airport plus secure undercover parking. Modern conference facilities and a spacious break-out area are provided. The smart bedrooms have air conditioning and a contemporary feel; some family suites can sleep up to seven guests.

Best Western Gatwick Moat House

Rooms 125 (20 fmly) **Facilities** Xmas New Year Wi-fi **Conf** Class 20 Board 18 Thtr 40 **Services** Lift Air con **Parking** 138 **Notes** ⊗

Holiday Inn Gatwick Airport

★★★ 78% HOTEL

☎ 0870 400 9030 & 01293 787648 🖶 01293 771054
Povey Cross Rd RH6 0BA
web: www.holidayinn.co.uk
dir: M23 junct 9, follow Gatwick, then Reigate signs. Hotel on left after 3rd rdbt

Situated close to the airport, this modern hotel provides air conditioned smart accommodation with facilities suiting both the business and leisure guest. There is a restaurant and bar, and a variety of conference rooms plus a supporting business centre. Park and Fly stays are popular.

Rooms 216 (13 fmly) (37 GF) (22 smoking) **Facilities** STV Wi-fi **Conf** Class 70 Board 50 Thtr 150 **Services** Lift Air con **Parking** 600

Gatwick Worth Hotel

★★★ 73% HOTEL

☎ 01293 884806 🖶 01293 882444
Crabbet Park, Turners Hill Rd, Worth RH10 4ST
e-mail: reception@gatwickworthhotel.co.uk
web: www.gatwickworthhotel.co.uk
dir: M23 junct 10, left to A264. At 1st rdbt take last exit. 1st left, 1st right at T-junct, hotel next right

This purpose-built hotel is ideally placed for access to Gatwick Airport. The bedrooms are spacious and suitably appointed with good facilities. Public areas consist of a light and airy bar area and a brasserie-style restaurant offering good value meals. Guests have use of the superb leisure club next door.

Rooms 118 (24 fmly) (56 GF) **Facilities** Wi-fi **Conf** Class 110 Board 100 Thtr 360 **Parking** 150 **Notes** ⊗ Civ Wed 70

Express by Holiday Inn Gatwick - Crawley

BUDGET HOTEL

☎ 01293 529991 🖶 01293 525529
Haslett Av, The Squareabout RH10 1UA
e-mail: ebhi-crawley@btconnect.com
web: www.hiexpress.com/crawleyuk

A modern hotel ideal for families and business travellers. Fresh and uncomplicated, the spacious rooms include Sky TV, power shower and tea and coffee-making facilities. Continental buffet breakfast is included in the room rate; other meals may be taken at the nearby family pub or restaurant. See also the Hotel Groups pages.

Rooms 74 (55 fmly) **Conf** Class 12 Board 16 Thtr 35

Ibis London Gatwick Airport

BUDGET HOTEL

☎ 01293 590300 🖶 01293 590310
London Rd, County Oak RH10 9GY
e-mail: H1889@accor.com
web: www.ibishotel.com
dir: M23 junct 10, A2011 towards Crawley. Onto A23 left towards Crawley/Brighton. Hotel on left

Modern, budget hotel offering comfortable accommodation in bright and practical bedrooms. Breakfast is self-service and dinner is available in the restaurant. See also the Hotel Groups pages.

Rooms 141 **D** £49-£75*

Travelodge Gatwick Airport

BUDGET HOTEL

☎ 0871 984 6031 🖶 01293 535369
Church Rd, Lowfield Heath RH11 0PQ
web: www.travelodge.co.uk
dir: M23 junct 10, A264 follow Crawley signs. At 1st rdbt take A264 for Langley Green. At 2nd rdbt take 4th exit (A23/Gatwick). Through 3 lights, straight on at 3rd rdbt. At 4th rdbt follow Lowfield Heath & Charlwood signs. Lodge at mini rdbt

Travelodge offers good quality, good value, budget accommodation. All offer family rooms sleeping up to four (two adults, two children) with en suite bathroom/shower-room, remote-control TV, tea- and coffee-making facilities and comfortable beds. Food options vary. Breakfast is at the on-site Bar Café restaurant (if available) or to take away. See also Hotel Groups pages.

Rooms 185 **S** fr £29; **D** fr £29 **Conf** Class 25 Board 25 Thtr 60

GOODWOOD Map 6 SU81

The Goodwood Park Hotel

★★★★ 77% ◎◎ HOTEL

☎ 01243 775537 📄 01243 520120
P018 0QB
e-mail: reservations@thegoodwoodparkhotel.co.uk
web: www.thegoodwoodparkhotel.co.uk
dir: off A285, 3m NE of Chichester

Set in the middle of the 12,000-acre Goodwood Estate, this attractive hotel boasts extensive indoor and outdoor leisure facilities, along with a range of meeting rooms plus conference and banqueting facilities. Bedrooms are furnished to a consistently high standard. Public rooms include the Richmond Restaurant and a smart cocktail bar which reflects the motor-racing heritage at Goodwood.

Rooms 94 **Facilities** Spa ◑ 💁 Putt green Gym Golf driving range Sauna Steam room Fitness studio Xmas New Year Wi-fi **Conf** Class 60 Board 50 Thtr 150 **Parking** 350 **Notes** LB ⊗ Civ Wed 120

HAYWARDS HEATH Map 6 TQ32

Best Western The Birch Hotel

★★★ 74% HOTEL

☎ 01444 451565 📄 01444 440109
Lewes Rd RH17 7SF
e-mail: info@birchhotel.co.uk
dir: On A272 opposite Princess Royal Hospital & behind Shell Garage

Originally the home of an eminent Harley Street surgeon, this attractive Victorian property has been extended to combine modern facilities with the charm of its original period. Public rooms include the conservatory-style Pavilion Restaurant, along with an open-plan lounge and brasserie-style bar serving a range of light meals.

Rooms 51 (3 fmly) (12 GF) **Facilities** STV Wi-fi **Conf** Class 30 Board 26 Thtr 60 Del from £95 to £155* **Parking** 60 **Notes** Civ Wed 60

HICKSTEAD Map 6 TQ22

Hickstead

★★★ 79% COUNTRY HOUSE HOTEL

☎ 01444 248023 📄 01444 245280
Jobs Ln, Bolney RH17 5NZ
e-mail: info.hickstead@classiclodges.co.uk
web: www.classiclodges.co.uk
dir: M23 south, take A2300 exit (Burgess Hill), 1st left, next right, hotel 100yds on left

This hotel is located in seven acres of grounds not far from the main London to Brighton road. Now refurbished, the smart bedrooms have satellite TV, free Wi-fi and power showers. Guests can choose to eat in the Oak Tree Bistro or in the Grange Bar. The indoor leisure centre is very popular. The hotel is close to a business park and within easy striking distance of the south coast.

Rooms 52 (5 fmly) (26 GF) **Facilities** STV Xmas New Year Wi-fi **Conf** Class 60 Board 55 Thtr 150 Del from £130 to £145* **Parking** 100 **Notes** ⊗ Civ Wed 80

Travelodge Hickstead

BUDGET HOTEL

☎ 0871 984 6038 📄 01444 881377
Jobs Ln RH17 5NX
web: www.travelodge.co.uk
dir: On A23 southbound

Travelodge offers good quality, good value, budget accommodation. All offer family rooms sleeping up to four (two adults, two children) with en suite bathroom/shower-room, remote-control TV, tea- and coffee-making facilities and comfortable beds. Food options vary. Breakfast is at the on-site Bar Café restaurant (if available) or to take away. See also Hotel Groups pages.

Rooms 55 **S** fr £29; **D** fr £29

LOWER BEEDING Map 6 TQ22

South Lodge

★★★★★ 89% ◎◎◎
COUNTRY HOUSE HOTEL

☎ 01403 891711 📄 01403 891766
Brighton Rd RH13 6PS
e-mail: enquiries@southlodgehotel.co.uk
web: www.exclusivehotels.co.uk
dir: On A23 left onto B2110. Turn right through Handcross to A281 junct. Turn left, hotel on right

This impeccably presented 19th-century lodge with stunning views of the rolling South Downs is an ideal retreat. Both the restaurants in this hotel have been awarded three AA Rosettes. There is the traditional and elegant Camellia Restaurant that offers memorable, seasonal dishes, and the exciting new addition which forms a mini-restaurant in the kitchen itself - The Pass is an innovative take on the chef's table concept. The elegant lounge is popular for afternoon teas. Bedrooms are individually designed with character and quality throughout. The conference facilities are impressive. Exclusive Hotels - AA Small Hotel Group of the Year 2009-10.

Rooms 89 (11 fmly) (19 GF) **D** £125-£620* **Facilities** STV ⅃ 36 💁 Putt green 🤸 Gym Mountain biking Xmas New Year Wi-fi **Conf** Class 60 Board 50 Thtr 160 Del from £240 to £340* **Services** Lift **Parking** 200 **Notes** LB ⊗ Civ Wed 120

MIDHURST Map 6 SU82

Spread Eagle Hotel and Spa

★★★ 79% ◎◎ HOTEL

☎ 01730 816911 📄 01730 815668
South St GU29 9NH
e-mail: spreadeagle@hshotels.co.uk
web: www.hshotels.co.uk/spread/spreadeagle-main.htm
dir: M25 junct 10, A3 to Milford, take A286 to Midhurst. Hotel adjacent to market square

Offering accommodation since 1430, this historic property is full of character, evident in its sloping floors and inglenook fireplaces. Individually styled bedrooms provide modern comforts; those in the main house have oak panelling and include some spacious feature rooms. The hotel also boasts a well-equipped spa and offers noteworthy food in the oak beamed restaurant.

Rooms 39 (4 annexe) (8 GF) **S** £80-£495; **D** £100-£495 (incl. bkfst)* **Facilities** Spa STV FTV ◑ Gym Health & beauty treatment rooms Steam room Sauna Fitness trainer Xmas New Year Wi-fi **Conf** Class 40 Board 34 Thtr 80 Del from £135 to £280* **Parking** 75 **Notes** LB Civ Wed 120

RUSPER · Map 6 TQ23

Ghyll Manor

★★★ 85% ◎◎ COUNTRY HOUSE HOTEL

☎ 0845 345 3426 📠 01293 871419
High St RH12 4PX
e-mail: ghyllmanor@csma.uk.com
web: www.ghyllmanor.co.uk
dir: A24 onto A264. Turn off at Faygate, follow signs for Rusper, 2m to village

Located in the quiet village of Rusper, this traditional mansion house is set in 45 acres of idyllic, peaceful grounds. Accommodation is in either the main house or a range of courtyard-style cottages. A pre-dinner drink can be taken beside the fire, followed by an imaginative meal in the charming restaurant.

Rooms 29 (21 annexe) (1 fmly) (19 GF) **Facilities** STV FTV ॐ Gym Xmas New Year Wi-fi **Conf** Class 50 Board 45 Thtr 120 Del from £140 to £190* **Parking** 100 **Notes** Civ Wed 80

RUSTINGTON · Map 6 TQ00

Travelodge Littlehampton Rustington

BUDGET HOTEL

☎ 0871 984 6045 📠 01903 733150
Worthing Rd BN17 6LZ
web: www.travelodge.co.uk
dir: On A259, 1m E of Littlehampton

Travelodge offers good quality, good value, budget accommodation. All offer family rooms sleeping up to four (two adults, two children) with en suite bathroom/shower-room, remote-control TV, tea- and coffee-making facilities and comfortable beds. Food options vary. Breakfast is at the on-site Bar Café restaurant (if available) or to take away. See also Hotel Groups pages.

Rooms 36 **S** fr £29; **D** fr £29

STAPLEFORD · Map 5 SZ89

The Crab & Lobster

◎ RESTAURANT WITH ROOMS

☎ 01243 641233
Mill Ln PO20 7NB
e-mail: enquiries@crab-lobster.co.uk
dir: A27 onto B2145 Selsey. Take 1st left after garage at Sidlesham onto Rookery Ln. Follow road to Crab and Lobster

Hidden away on the south coast near Pagham Harbour and only a short drive from Chichester is the stylish Crab & Lobster. Bedrooms are superbly appointed, and bathrooms are a feature with luxury toiletries and powerful 'raindrop' showers. Guests can enjoy lunch or dinner in the smart restaurant where the menu offers a range of locally caught fresh fish amongst other regionally-sourced, seasonal produce.

Rooms 4

STEYNING · Map 6 TQ11

Best Western Old Tollgate Restaurant & Hotel

★★★ 73% HOTEL

☎ 01903 879494 📠 01903 813399
The Street, Bramber BN44 3WE
e-mail: info@oldtollgatehotel.com
web: www.bw-oldtollgatehotel.com
dir: From A283 at Steyning rdbt to Bramber. Hotel 200yds on right

As its name suggests, this well-presented hotel is built on the site of the old toll house. The spacious bedrooms are smartly designed and are furnished to a high standard; eight rooms are air conditioned and have smart power showers. Open for both lunch and dinner, the popular carvery-style restaurant offers an extensive choice of dishes.

Rooms 38 (29 annexe) (5 fmly) (14 GF) **S** £65-£120; **D** £75-£150 (incl. bkfst)* **Facilities** STV New Year Wi-fi **Conf** Class 32 Board 26 Thtr 50 **Services** Lift **Parking** 60 **Notes** LB ⊗ Civ Wed 70

TURNERS HILL · Map 6 TQ33

Alexander House Hotel & Utopia Spa

★★★★ ◎◎ HOTEL

☎ 01342 714914 📠 01342 717328
East St RH10 4QD
e-mail: info@alexanderhouse.co.uk
web: www.alexanderhouse.co.uk
dir: 6m from M23 junct 10, on B2110 between Turners Hill & East Grinstead

Set in 175 acres of parkland and landscaped gardens, this delightful country house hotel dates back to the 17th century. Most of the bedrooms are very spacious and all have luxurious bathrooms; the rooms in the most recent wing are particularly stunning. There are two options for dining - the formal Alexander's which has been awarded AA Rosettes, or the lively Reflections which is set around an open courtyard, ideal for alfresco eating. The Utopia Spa has a state-of-the-art pool and gym, as well as specialised treatments.

Rooms 38 (12 fmly) (1 GF) **S** £165-£500; **D** £195-£500 (incl. bkfst)* **Facilities** Spa STV ③ ॐ ॐ Gym Clay Shooting Archery Mountain bikes Pony trekking Xmas New Year Wi-fi **Conf** Class 70 Board 40 Thtr 150 Del from £270 to £375* **Services** Lift **Parking** 100 **Notes** LB ⊗ No children 7yrs Civ Wed 60

WEST CHILTINGTON · Map 6 TQ01

Best Western Roundabout

★★★ 75% HOTEL

☎ 01798 813838 📠 01798 812962
Monkmead Ln RH20 2PF
e-mail: roundabouthotelltd@btinternet.com
web: www.bw-roundabouthotel.co.uk
dir: A24 onto A283, right at mini rdbt in Storrington, left at hill top. Left after 1m

Enjoying a lovely peaceful setting, surrounded by gardens, this well-established hotel is located deep in the Sussex countryside; mock Tudor in style it has plenty of character. The comfortably furnished bedrooms are well equipped, and public areas offer a spacious lounge, bar and terrace. A variety of dishes to suit all tastes can be enjoyed in the restaurant.

Rooms 25 (6 annexe) (4 fmly) (5 GF) **Facilities** Xmas Wi-fi **Conf** Class 20 Board 26 Thtr 60 **Parking** 46 **Notes** LB ⊗ No children 3yrs Civ Wed 49

WORTHING
Map 6 TQ10

Ardington
★★★ 80% HOTEL

☎ 01903 230451 ▤ 01903 526526
Steyne Gardens BN11 3DZ
e-mail: reservations@ardingtonhotel.co.uk
web: www.ardingtonhotel.co.uk
dir: A27 to Lancing, then to seafront. Follow signs for Worthing. Left at 1st church into Steyne Gardens

Overlooking Steyne Gardens adjacent to the seafront, this popular hotel offers well-appointed bedrooms with a good range of facilities. There's a stylishly modern lounge/bar with ample seating, where a light menu is available throughout the day. The popular restaurant offers local seafood and a choice of modern dishes. Wi-fi is available in lounge/bar.

Rooms 45 (4 fmly) (12 GF) **S** £55-£75; **D** £75-£150 (incl. bkfst) **Facilities** STV FTV Wi-fi **Conf** Class 60 Board 35 Thtr 140 **Notes** LB Closed 25 Dec-4 Jan

Beach
★★★ 74% HOTEL

☎ 01903 234001 ▤ 01903 234567
Marine Pde BN11 3QJ
e-mail: info@thebeachhotel.co.uk
web: www.thebeachhotel.co.uk
dir: W of town centre, approx 0.3m from pier

With an impressive 1930s façade this well-established hotel is extremely popular with both leisure and business guests. Bedrooms, some with sea views and balconies, are comfortable and well equipped. Spacious public areas incorporate a busy restaurant serving a range of popular dishes. Secure parking is available.

Rooms 79 (8 fmly) **S** £58-£67; **D** £95-£108 (incl. bkfst) **Facilities** Wi-fi **Conf** Class 60 Board 60 Thtr 90 Del from £95 to £100* **Services** Lift **Parking** 55 **Notes** LB ⊗

Findon Manor
★★★ 71% HOTEL

☎ 01903 872733 ▤ 01903 877473
High St, Findon BN14 0TA
e-mail: hotel@findonmanor.com
dir: 500yds off A24 between Worthing & Horsham. At sign for Findon follow signs to Findon Manor into village

Located in the centre of the village, Findon Manor was built as a rectory and has a beamed lounge which doubles as the reception area. Bedrooms, several with four-poster beds, are attractively decorated in a traditional style. The cosy bar offers a very good range of bar food, and is popular with locals, while the restaurant overlooks a garden and offers modern and traditional dishes.

Rooms 11 (2 GF) **Facilities** ⚓ Boule Xmas New Year Wi-fi **Conf** Class 18 Board 25 Thtr 50 **Parking** 25 **Notes** ⊗ RS 24-30 Dec Civ Wed 60

See advert on this page

Kingsway
★★ 74% HOTEL

☎ 01903 237542 ▤ 01903 204173
Marine Pde BN11 3QQ
e-mail: kingsway-hotel@btconnect.com
dir: A27 to Worthing seafront follow signs 'Hotel West'. Hotel 0.75m west of pier

Ideally located on the seafront and close to the town centre, this family-owned property extends a warm welcome to guests. Bedrooms vary in size, and some are very spacious with impressive sea views. Comfortable public areas include two modern lounges, a bright, stylish bar and well appointed restaurant.

Rooms 36 (7 annexe) (4 fmly) (3 GF) **S** £40-£79; **D** £60-£122 (incl. bkfst) **Facilities** FTV Xmas Wi-fi **Conf** Class 25 Board 25 Thtr 50 Del from £90 to £130 **Services** Lift **Parking** 9

Cavendish
THE INDEPENDENTS
HOTEL ASSOCIATION
★★ 61% HOTEL

☎ 01903 236767 ▤ 01903 823840
115 Marine Pde BN11 3QG
e-mail: reservations@cavendishworthing.co.uk
web: www.cavendishworthing.co.uk
dir: On seafront, 600yds W of pier

This popular, family-run hotel enjoys a prominent seafront location. Bedrooms are well equipped and soundly decorated. Guests have an extensive choice of meal options, with a varied bar menu, and carte and daily menus offered in the restaurant. Limited parking is available at the rear of the hotel.

Rooms 17 (4 fmly) (1 GF) (6 smoking) **S** £45-£49; **D** £69.50-£85 (incl. bkfst)* **Facilities** STV Wi-fi **Services** Air con **Parking** 5

WORTHING *continued*

Travelodge Worthing Seafront

BUDGET HOTEL

☎ 0871 984 6409 📠 01903 205385
86-95 Marine Pde, N BN11 3QD
dir: From A27 & A24 follow Worthing seafront signs.
Lodge 0.5m W of pier

Travelodge offers good quality, good value, budget
accommodation. All offer family rooms sleeping up to
four (two adults, two children) with en suite bathroom/
shower-room, remote-control TV, tea- and coffee-making
facilities and comfortable beds. Food options vary.
Breakfast is at the on-site Bar Café restaurant (if
available) or to take away. See also the Hotel Groups
pages.

Rooms 90 **S** fr £29; **D** fr £29 **Conf** Class 50 Board 50
Thtr 100

TYNE & WEAR

GATESHEAD Map 21 NZ26

See also **Beamish (Co Durham) & Whickham**

Newcastle Marriott Hotel MetroCentre

Marriott
HOTELS & RESORTS

★★★★ 78% HOTEL

☎ 0191 493 2233 📠 0191 493 2030
MetroCentre NE11 9XF
e-mail: reservations.newcastle.england.metrocentre@
marriotthotels.co.uk
web: www.newcastlemarriottmetrocentre.co.uk
dir: From N exit A1 at MetroCentre exit, take 'Other
Routes'. From S exit A1 at MetroCentre exit, turn right

Set just off the A1 and on the doorstep of the popular
Metro shopping centre, this stylish purpose-built hotel
provides modern amenities including a leisure centre,
conference facilities and an informal stylish restaurant
offering a range of dining styles. All bedrooms are smartly
laid out and thoughtfully equipped to suit both the
business traveller and the leisure guest.

Rooms 150 (147 fmly) (5 smoking) **Facilities** Spa STV 🐾
Gym Health & beauty clinic Dance studio Hairdresser
Spinning studio Wi-fi **Conf** Class 172 Board 48 Thtr 400
Del from £130 to £160* **Services** Lift Air con **Parking** 300
Notes ⊗ Civ Wed 100

Eslington Villa

★★★ 78% HOTEL

☎ 0191 487 6017 & 420 0666 📠 0191 420 0667
8 Station Rd, Low Fell NE9 6DR
e-mail: home@eslingtonvilla.co.uk
dir: From A1(M) exit for Team Valley Trading Estate. Right
at 2nd rdbt along Eastern Av. Left at car show room, hotel
100yds on left

Set in a residential area, this smart hotel combines a
bright, contemporary atmosphere with the period style of
a fine Victorian villa. The overall ambience is relaxed and
inviting. Chunky sofas grace the cocktail lounge, while
tempting dishes can be enjoyed in either the classical
dining room or modern conservatory overlooking the Team
Valley.

Rooms 17 (2 fmly) (3 GF) **S** £69.50-£79.50;
D £89.50-£94.50 (incl. bkfst)* **Facilities** FTV Wi-fi
Conf Class 30 Board 25 Thtr 36 Del from £125 to £135
Parking 28 **Notes** LB ⊗ Closed 25-26 Dec RS Sun/BHs

Travelodge Gateshead

BUDGET HOTEL

☎ 08719 846 283
Clasper Way, Swalwell NE16 3BE
web: www.travelodge.co.uk
dir: Follow signs for A694/695, then A1114 (Metro
Centre). Lodge 0.25m, opposite TGI Friday's

Travelodge offers good quality, good value, budget
accommodation. All offer family rooms sleeping up to four
(two adults, two children) with en suite bathroom/
shower-room, remote-control TV, tea- and coffee-making
facilities and comfortable beds. Food options vary.
Breakfast is at the on-site Bar Café restaurant (if
available) or to take away. See also Hotel Groups pages.

Rooms 60 **S** fr £29; **D** fr £29

HOUGHTON-LE-SPRING Map 19 NZ34

Chilton Country Pub & Hotel

★★ 74% HOTEL

☎ 0191 385 2694 📠 0191 385 6762
Black Boy Rd, Chilton Moor, Fencehouses DH4 6LX
e-mail: reception@chiltoncountrypub.co.uk
dir: A1(M) junct 62, onto A690 to Sunderland. Left at
Rainton Bridge & Fencehouses sign, cross rdbt, 1st left

This country pub and hotel has been extended from the
original farm cottages. Bedrooms are modern and
comfortable and some rooms are particularly spacious.
This hotel is popular for weddings and functions; there is
also a well stocked bar, and a wide range of dishes is
served in the Orangery and restaurant.

Rooms 25 (7 fmly) (11 GF) **S** £45-£60; **D** £55-£70 (incl.
bkfst) **Facilities** STV Horse riding 🐎 Xmas **Conf** Class 50
Board 30 Thtr 60 Del from £88 to £110 **Parking** 100
Notes LB ⊗

See advert on page 187

NEWCASTLE UPON TYNE Map 21 NZ26

See also **Seaton Burn & Whickham**

INSPECTORS' CHOICE

Jesmond Dene House

★★★★ HOTEL

☎ 0191 212 3000 📠 0191 212 3001
Jesmond Dene Rd NE2 2EY
e-mail: info@jesmonddenehouse.co.uk
web: www.jesmonddenehouse.co.uk
dir: A167 N to A184. Right, then right again along
Jesmond Dene Rd, hotel on left

This grand house, overlooking the wooded valley of
Jesmond Dene, yet just five minutes from the centre of
town, has been sympathetically converted into a
stylish, contemporary hotel destination. Bedrooms are
beautifully designed and boast sumptuous beds with
Egyptian cotton linen, CD and DVD players, well-
stocked mini bars, broadband and safes. Equally eye-
catching bathrooms with under floor heating are
equipped with high quality bespoke amenities.
Innovative cooking is a highlight.

Rooms 40 (8 annexe) (1 fmly) (4 GF) **S** fr £165;
D £175-£450* **Facilities** Xmas New Year Wi-fi
Conf Class 80 Board 44 Thtr 125 **Services** Lift
Parking 64 **Notes** LB ⊗ Civ Wed 80

Vermont

★★★★ 81% HOTEL

☎ 0191 233 1010 📠 0191 233 1234
Castle Garth NE1 1RQ
e-mail: info@vermont-hotel.co.uk
web: www.vermont-hotel.com
dir: City centre by high level bridge & castle keep

Adjacent to the castle and close to the buzzing quayside
area, this imposing hotel enjoys fine views of the Tyne
Bridge. Thoughtfully equipped bedrooms offer a variety of

styles, including grand suites. The elegant reception lounge and adjoining bar invite relaxation, while the Bridge Restaurant is the focus for dining.

Rooms 101 (12 fmly) **S** £100–£190; **D** £100–£190*
Facilities STV FTV Gym Xmas New Year Wi-fi
Conf Class 60 Board 30 Thtr 200 Del from £135 to £190*
Services Lift **Parking** 100 **Notes** Civ Wed 120

Hotel du Vin Newcastle
★★★★ 79% ⊛ TOWN HOUSE HOTEL

☎ 0191 229 2200 📄 0191 229 2201
Allan House, City Rd NE1 2AP
e-mail: ikelk@malmaison.com
dir: A1 junct 65 slip road to A184 Gateshead/Newcastle, Quayside to City Road

The former maintenance depot of the Tyne Tees Shipping Company this is a landmark building on the Tyne. It has now been transformed into a modern and stylish hotel. Bedrooms are well equipped and deeply comfortable with all the Hotel du Vin trademark items such as Egyptian cotton sheets, plasma TVs, DVD players, monsoon showers etc. Guests can dine in the bistro or alfresco if the weather allows in the courtyard.

Rooms 42 (6 GF) **D** £79–£160* **Facilities** STV Wi-fi
Conf Board 20 Thtr 26 Del from £175 to £225*
Services Lift Air con **Parking** 10 **Notes** LB Civ Wed 40

Newcastle Marriott Hotel MetroCentre
Marriott HOTELS & RESORTS
★★★★ 78% HOTEL

☎ 0191 493 2233 📄 0191 493 2030
MetroCentre NE11 9XF
e-mail: reservations.newcastle.england.metrocentre@ marriotthotels.co.uk
web: www.newcastlemarriottmetrocentre.co.uk

(For full entry see Gateshead)

Newcastle Marriott Hotel Gosforth Park
Marriott HOTELS & RESORTS
★★★★ 77% HOTEL

☎ 0191 236 4111 📄 0191 236 8192
High Gosforth Park, Gosforth NE3 5HN
web: www.newcastlemarriottgosforthpark.co.uk
dir: Onto A1056 to Killingworth & Wideopen. 3rd exit to Gosforth Park, hotel ahead

Set within its own grounds, this modern hotel offers extensive conference and banqueting facilities, along with indoor and outdoor leisure. There is a choice of dining in the more formal Plate Restaurant or the relaxed Chat's lounge bar. Many of the air-conditioned bedrooms have views over the park. The hotel is conveniently located for the by-pass, airport and racecourse.

Rooms 178 (17 smoking) **Facilities** Spa STV ◉ supervised ⌂ Gym Squash Jogging trail ♫ New Year Wi-fi **Conf** Class 280 Board 60 Thtr 800 Del from £135 to £145* **Services** Lift Air con **Parking** 340 **Notes** RS Xmas & New Year Civ Wed 300

Copthorne Hotel Newcastle
MILLENNIUM
★★★★ 71% HOTEL

☎ 0191 222 0333 📄 0191 230 1111
The Close, Quayside NE1 3RT
e-mail: sales.newcastle@millenniumhotels.co.uk
web: www.millenniumhotels.co.uk
dir: Follow signs to Newcastle city centre. Take B1600 Quayside exit, hotel on right

Set on the banks of the River Tyne close to the city centre, this stylish purpose-built hotel provides modern amenities including a leisure centre, conference facilities and a choice of restaurants for dinner. Bedrooms overlook the river, and there is a floor of 'Connoisseur' rooms that have their own dedicated exclusive lounge and business support services.

Rooms 156 (4 fmly) **S** £95–£220; **D** £95–£220*
Facilities Spa STV ◉ supervised Gym Steam room Solarium Fitness studio Xmas New Year Wi-fi
Conf Class 90 Board 60 Thtr 220 Del from £145 to £195*
Services Lift **Parking** 180 **Notes** ⊗ Civ Wed 150

Malmaison Newcastle
Malmaison
★★★ 88% ⊛ HOTEL

☎ 0191 245 5000 📄 0191 245 4545
Quayside NE1 3DX
e-mail: newcastle@malmaison.com
dir: Follow signs for city centre, then for Quayside/Law Courts. Hotel 100yds past Law Courts

Overlooking the river and the Millennium Bridge, the hotel has a prime position in the very popular re-developed quayside district. Bedrooms have striking decor, CD/DVD players, mini-bars and a number of individual touches. Food and drink are an integral part of the operation here, with a stylish brasserie-style restaurant and café bar, plus the Café Mal, a deli-style café next door to the main entrance.

Rooms 122 (10 fmly) **D** £79–£160* **Facilities** Spa STV Gym Wi-fi **Conf** Board 18 Thtr 30 Del from £160 to £175*
Services Lift Air con **Parking** 50 **Notes** LB

NEWCASTLE UPON TYNE *continued*

Eslington Villa

★★★ 78% ❀ HOTEL

☎ 0191 487 6017 & 420 0666 📄 0191 420 0667
8 Station Rd, Low Fell NE9 6DR
e-mail: home@eslingtonvilla.co.uk

(For full entry see Gateshead)

County Hotel by Thistle

thistle

★★★ 78% HOTEL

☎ 0871 376 9029 📄 0871 376 9129
Neville St NE1 5DF
e-mail: newcastle@thistle.co.uk
web: www.thistlehotels.com/newcastle
dir: A1 onto A184 cross Redheugh Bridge turn right at
2nd lights, turn right after cathedral, left at pedestrian
zone

A 19th-century listed building, the hotel enjoys a central
location opposite the city's Central Station, which also
has links to the Metro system. Bedrooms are comfortably
appointed for both business and leisure guests. Limited
free parking is available.

Rooms 114 **S** £55-£147; **D** £65-£199 (incl. bkfst)*
Facilities Complimentary use of nearby gym New Year
Wi-fi **Conf** Class 100 Board 100 Thtr 250 Del from £125
to £165* **Services** Lift **Parking** 19 **Notes** LB ⊗
Civ Wed 100

Holiday Inn Newcastle upon Tyne

Holiday Inn
HOTELS · RESORTS

★★★ 78% HOTEL

☎ 0870 787 3291 & 0191 201 9988 📄 0191 236 8091
Great North Rd, Seaton Burn NE13 6BP
e-mail: hinewcastle@qmh-hotels.com
web: www.holidayinn.co.uk
dir: A1/A19, 6m N of Newcastle. A190/Tyne Tunnel exit
A1. Follow brown Holiday Inn signs

This modern hotel is set in 16 acres and is convenient for
Newcastle International Airport, Tyne Tunnel and the
North Sea Ferry Terminal. Each bedroom is fully equipped
with all necessary facilities, and executive rooms are
available. The Convivium Restaurant serves breakfast
and dinner, and the Mercury Bar offers a snack menu
from 11 to 11. A leisure club is available, and there are
plenty of activities for children.

Holiday Inn Newcastle upon Tyne

Rooms 154 (56 fmly) (72 GF) **S** £50-£170; **D** £50-£170
Facilities STV 🏊 supervised Gym Cardiovascular &
weights room Sauna Beauty salon ♫ Xmas New Year
Wi-fi **Conf** Class 150 Board 60 Thtr 400 Del from £99 to
£142 **Services** Air con **Parking** 350 **Notes** LB ⊗
Civ Wed 300

George Washington Golf & Country Club

★★★ 75% HOTEL

☎ 0191 402 9988 📄 0191 415 1166
Stone Cellar Rd, High Usworth NE37 1PH
e-mail: reservations@georgewashington.co.uk
web: www.georgewashington.co.uk

(For full entry see Washington)

Best Western New Kent Hotel

Best Western

★★★ 73% HOTEL

☎ 0191 281 7711 📄 0191 281 3369
127 Osborne Rd NE2 2TB
e-mail: newkenthotel@hotmail.com
web: www.newkenthotel.com
dir: Beside B1600, opposite St Georges Church

This popular business hotel offers relaxed service and
typical Geordie hospitality. The bright modern bedrooms
are well equipped and the modern bar is an ideal meeting
place. A range of generous, good value dishes is served in
the restaurant, which doubles as a wedding venue.

Rooms 32 (4 fmly) **S** £52.50-£69.50; **D** £89.50 (incl.
bkfst)* **Facilities** STV FTV Xmas New Year Wi-fi
Conf Class 30 Board 40 Thtr 60 **Parking** 22 **Notes** LB
Civ Wed 90

The Caledonian Hotel, Newcastle

PEEL HOTELS PLC

★★★ 70% HOTEL

☎ 0191 281 7881 📄 0191 281 6241
64 Osborne Rd, Jesmond NE2 2AT
e-mail: info@caledonian-hotel-newcastle.com
web: www.peelhotel.com
dir: From A1 follow signs to Newcastle City, cross Tyne
Bridge to Tynemouth. Left at lights at Osborne Rd, hotel
on right

This hotel is located in the Jesmond area of the
city. Bedrooms are comfortable and well equipped many
have been modernised and refurbished. Public areas
include the trendy Billabong Bar and Bistro, which serves
food all day, and the terrace where a cosmopolitan
atmosphere prevails. Alfresco dining is now available.

Rooms 91 (6 fmly) (7 GF) (15 smoking) **S** £79-£99;
D £84-£110 (incl. bkfst)* **Facilities** Xmas New Year Wi-fi
Conf Class 50 Board 50 Thtr 100 Del from £120 to £145*
Services Lift **Parking** 35 **Notes** LB ⊗ Civ Wed 70

Kenilworth Hotel

★★ 71% SMALL HOTEL

☎ 0191 281 8111 & 281 9111 📄 0191 281 9476
44 Osborne Rd, Jesmond NE2 2AL
e-mail: info@thekenilworthhotel.co.uk
web: www.thekenilworthhotel.co.uk
dir: A1058 signed Tynemouth for 1m. Left at lights onto
Osborne Road, hotel 0.5m on right

This hotel has now been refurbished and the public areas
feature wooden floors and leather furniture, and include a
modern bar area. The smart bedrooms have satellite TVs,
DVD players, beverage trays and hairdryers. The main
attraction is El Castano, the Spanish tapas restaurant,
where the extensive menu features carefully prepared
dishes using produce that is sourced both locally and
directly from Spain.

Rooms 11 (3 fmly) **S** £40-£60; **D** £60-£85 (incl. bkfst)*
Facilities FTV Access to leisure centre 1.5km away Xmas
New Year Wi-fi **Conf** Class 60 Board 60 Thtr 80
Parking 10 **Notes** LB

Cairn

★★ 68% HOTEL

☎ 0191 281 1358 🖹 0191 281 9031
97/103 Osborne Rd, Jesmond NE2 2TJ
e-mail: info@cairnnewcastle.com

A smart modern reception hall welcomes guests to this commercial hotel in the village suburb of Jesmond. Bedrooms are well equipped. There is a lively bar and a bright, colourful restaurant. The hotel benefits from limited parking to the rear of the property.

Rooms 50 (2 fmly) **S** £39–£65; **D** £60–£95 (incl. bkfst)
Facilities Wi-fi **Conf** Class 110 Board 100 Thtr 150
Del from £60 to £120* **Parking** 12 **Notes** LB

Express by Holiday Inn Newcastle City Centre

BUDGET HOTEL

☎ 0870 4281488 🖹 0870 4281477
Waterloo Square, St James Boulevard NE1 4DN
e-mail: gm.newcastle@expressholidayinn.co.uk
web: www.hiexpress.com/newcastlectyct

A modern hotel ideal for families and business travellers. Fresh and uncomplicated, the spacious rooms include Sky TV, power shower and tea and coffee-making facilities. Continental buffet breakfast is included in the room rate; other meals may be taken at the nearby family pub or restaurant. See also the Hotel Groups pages.

Rooms 130 (50 fmly) **S** £60–£95; **D** £60–£95
Conf Class 15 Board 16 Thtr 30

Innkeeper's Newcastle/ Gosforth

BUDGET HOTEL

☎ 0845 112 6016 🖹 0845 112 6285
Vintage Inns, Falcons Nest, Rotary Way NE3 5EH
web: www.innkeeperslodge.com/newcastlegosforth
dir: A1 to Newcastle upon Tyne, take A1056 signed Wideopen & Killingworth. At rdbt take 2nd exit onto A1056. At Gosforth Park rdbt take 1st exit. Lodge 300yds on left

Innkeeper's Lodge represents an exciting, high value concept within the budget hotel market. Comfortable bedrooms provide excellent facilities that include satellite TV and modem points. Options include family rooms; and for the corporate guest, cutting edge IT includes Wi-fi access. Food is served all day in the adjacent Country Pub. The extensive continental breakfast is complimentary. See also the Hotel Groups pages.

Rooms 53 **Conf** Thtr 25

Travelodge Newcastle Central

BUDGET HOTEL

☎ 08719 846 6164 🖹 0191 261 7105
Forster St NE1 2NH
web: www.travelodge.co.uk
dir: From A1 or A194(M) to city centre, over Tyne Bridge, right into Melbourne St, right into Forster St

Travelodge offers good quality, good value, budget accommodation. All offer family rooms sleeping up to four (two adults, two children) with en suite bathroom/shower-room, remote-control TV, tea- and coffee-making facilities and comfortable beds. Food options vary. Breakfast is at the on-site Bar Café restaurant (if available) or to take away. See also Hotel Groups pages.

Rooms 203 **S** fr £29; **D** fr £29

Travelodge Newcastle Silverlink

BUDGET HOTEL

☎ 0871 984 6399
Silverlink Park, Coast Rd NE28 9HP
e-mail: newcastlesilver@travelodge.co.uk
dir: At rdbt junct of A19 & A1058 (coast road) on N side of Tyne Tunnel follow signs for Silverlinks Park. In park, lodge off 1st exit of 1st rdbt

Rooms 126 **S** fr £29; **D** fr £29 **Conf** Class 200 Board 24 Thtr 400

NEWCASTLE UPON TYNE AIRPORT Map 21 NZ17

Novotel Newcastle Airport

★★★ 78% HOTEL

☎ 0191 214 0303 🖹 0191 214 0633
Ponteland Rd, Kenton NE3 3HZ
e-mail: H1118@accor-hotels.com
web: www.novotel.com
dir: off A1(M) airport junct onto A696, take Kingston Park exit

This modern well-proportioned hotel lies just off the bypass and is within easy reach of the airport and city centre and has secure parking. Bedrooms are spacious with a range of extras and boast modern new bathrooms. The new concept "Elements" restaurant offers a flexible dining option and is open until late. There is a contemporary style lounge bar and also a small leisure centre for the more energetic guests.

Rooms 126 (36 fmly) **Facilities** ⓢ Gym Wi-fi
Conf Class 90 Board 40 Thtr 200 **Services** Lift
Parking 260 **Notes** Civ Wed 200

Innkeeper's Lodge Newcastle (Airport)

BUDGET HOTEL

☎ 0845 112 6015 🖹 0845 112 6286
Kenton Bank NE3 3TY
web: www.innkeeperslodge.com/newcastle
dir: From A1(M), exit A696/B6918. At 1st rdbt, take B6918 (Kingston Park), 2nd rdbt turn right. Lodge on left

Innkeeper's Lodge represents an exciting, high value concept within the budget hotel market. Comfortable bedrooms provide excellent facilities that include satellite TV and modem points. Options include family rooms; and for the corporate guest, cutting edge IT which includes Wi-fi access. A popular Carvery provides all-day food, including an extensive, complimentary continental breakfast. See also the Hotel Groups pages.

Rooms 30 **Conf** Thtr 30

SEATON BURN **Map 21 NZ27**

Travelodge Newcastle Seaton Burn

BUDGET HOTEL

☎ 0871 984 6166 🖹 0191 217 0107
Front St NE13 6ED
web: www.travelodge.co.uk
dir: A1 exit for Tyne Tunnel (A19). Lodge at 1st rdbt

Travelodge offers good quality, good value, budget accommodation. All offer family rooms sleeping up to four (two adults, two children) with en suite bathroom/shower-room, remote-control TV, tea- and coffee-making facilities and comfortable beds. Food options vary. Breakfast is at the on-site Bar Café restaurant (if available) or to take away. See also Hotel Groups pages.

Rooms 40 **S** fr £29; **D** fr £29

SOUTH SHIELDS **Map 21 NZ36**

Best Western Sea

★★★ 74% HOTEL

☎ 0191 427 0999 🖹 0191 454 0500
Sea Rd NE33 2LD
e-mail: info@seahotel.co.uk
dir: A1(M), past Washington Services onto A194. Then A183 through town centre along Ocean Road. Hotel on seafront

Dating from the 1930s this long-established business hotel overlooks the boating lake and the Tyne estuary. Bedrooms are generally spacious and well equipped and include five annexe rooms with wheelchair access. A range of generously portioned meals are served in both the bar and restaurant.

Rooms 37 (5 annexe) (5 fmly) (5 GF) **S** £64.50–£66;
D £77.50–£79 (incl. bkfst)* **Facilities** STV New Year Wi-fi
Conf Class 100 Board 50 Thtr 200 **Parking** 70
Notes RS 26 Dec

SUNDERLAND — Map 19 NZ35

Sunderland Marriott

★★★★ 75% HOTEL

☎ 0191 529 2041 ▤ 0191 529 4227
Queen's Pde, Seaburn SR6 8DB
e-mail: mhrs.nclsl.frontoffice@marriotthotels.com
web: www.sunderlandmarriott.co.uk
dir: A19, A184 (Boldon/Sunderland North), then 3m. At rdbt turn left, then right. At rdbt turn left, follow to coast. Turn right, hotel on right

Comfortable and spacious accommodation, some with fabulous views of the North Sea and vast expanses of sandy beach, is provided in this seafront hotel. Public rooms are bright and modern and a number of meeting rooms are available. The hotel is conveniently located for access to the local visitor attractions.

Rooms 82 (6 fmly) **Facilities** STV ⊕ Gym Xmas New Year Wi-fi **Conf** Class 120 Board 70 Thtr 300 Del from £130 to £160* **Services** Lift **Parking** 110 **Notes** ⊗ Civ Wed 80

Best Western Roker

★★★ 75% HOTEL

☎ 0191 567 1786 & 567 8221 ▤ 0191 510 0289
Roker Ter, Roker SR6 9ND
e-mail: info@rokerhotel.co.uk

This modern hotel offers stunning views of the coastline. Well-equipped bedrooms come in a variety of sizes, and several have feature bathrooms. Functions, conferences and weddings are all well catered for in the function suite. A choice of dining options is available including Restaurant Italia and Restaurant China, as well as an impressive range of bar meals in the R-bar.

Rooms 43 (8 fmly) (3 GF) **S** £55-£80; **D** £65-£135 (incl. bkfst) **Facilities** STV FTV Gym ♫ Wi-fi **Conf** Class 150 Board 100 Thtr 300 Del from £110 to £140 **Services** Lift Air con **Parking** 150 **Notes** LB ⊗ Civ Wed 350

Travelodge Sunderland Central

BUDGET HOTEL

☎ 0871 984 6050 ▤ 0191 514 3453
Low Row SR1 3PT
web: www.travelodge.co.uk
dir: S'bound: A1(M) junct 65, A1231 towards city centre. Follow Empire Theatre signs. Lodge opposite university. N'bound: A1(M) junct 62, A690, follow city centre signs onto A1231. Lodge on right by lights

Travelodge offers good quality, good value, budget accommodation. All offer family rooms sleeping up to four (two adults, two children) with en suite bathroom/shower-room, remote-control TV, tea- and coffee-making facilities and comfortable beds. Food options vary. Breakfast is at the on-site Bar Café restaurant (if available) or to take away. See also Hotel Groups pages.

Rooms 62 (53 fmly) **S** fr £29; **D** fr £29

TYNEMOUTH — Map 21 NZ36

Grand

★★★ 77% HOTEL

☎ 0191 293 6666 ▤ 0191 293 6665
Grand Pde NE30 4ER
e-mail: info20@grandhotel-uk.com
web: www.grandhotel-uk.com
dir: A1058 for Tynemouth. At coast rdbt turn right. Hotel on right approx 0.5m

This grand Victorian building offers stunning views of the coast. Bedrooms come in a variety of styles and are well equipped, tastefully decorated and have impressive bathrooms. In addition to the restaurant there are two bars; the elegant and imposing staircase is a focal point and much photographed at weddings held here.

Rooms 45 (5 annexe) (11 fmly) (10 smoking) **S** £75-£175; **D** £85-£175 (incl. bkfst)* **Facilities** STV ♫ Xmas New Year Wi-fi **Conf** Class 40 Board 40 Thtr 130 **Services** Lift **Parking** 16 **Notes** ⊗ RS Sun evening Civ Wed 120

WARDLEY — Map 21 NZ36

Travelodge Newcastle Whitemare Pool

BUDGET HOTEL

☎ 0871 984 6165 ▤ 0191 469 5718
Wardley, Whitemare Pool NE10 8YB
web: www.travelodge.co.uk
dir: From N & W follow A1 S, take A184 through Gateshead to Sunderland & South Shields. 4m E of Gateshead take A194 to South Shields

Travelodge offers good quality, good value, budget accommodation. All offer family rooms sleeping up to four (two adults, two children) with en suite bathroom/shower-room, remote-control TV, tea- and coffee-making facilities and comfortable beds. Food options vary. Breakfast is at the on-site Bar Café restaurant (if available) or to take away. See also Hotel Groups pages.

Rooms 71 **S** fr £29; **D** fr £29

WASHINGTON — Map 19 NZ35

George Washington Golf & Country Club

★★★ 75% HOTEL

☎ 0191 402 9988 ▤ 0191 415 1166
Stone Cellar Rd, High Usworth NE37 1PH
e-mail: reservations@georgewashington.co.uk
web: www.georgewashington.co.uk
dir: A1(M) junct 65 onto A194(M). Take A195 signed Washington North. Take last exit from rdbt for Washington then right at mini-rdbt. Hotel 0.5m on right

Popular with business and leisure guests, this purpose-built hotel boasts two golf courses and a driving range. Bedrooms are stylish and modern, generally spacious and comfortably equipped. Public areas include extensive conference facilities, a business centre and fitness club.

Rooms 103 (9 fmly) (41 GF) (6 smoking) **Facilities** STV FTV ⊕ supervised ⏃ 18 Putt green Gym Squash Golf driving range Pool table Beauty salon Xmas Wi-fi **Conf** Class 80 Board 80 Thtr 200 Del from £110 to £130* **Parking** 180 **Notes** ⊗ Civ Wed 180

Holiday Inn Washington

★★★ 73% HOTEL

☎ 0870 400 9084 📠 0191 415 3371
Emerson District 5 NE37 1LB
e-mail: washington@ihg.com
web: www.holidayinn.co.uk
dir: Just off A1(M) junct 64. Left at rdbt, hotel on left

This is an ideally located hotel, just off the A1(M), and centrally located between historic Durham, Sunderland and Newcastle's city centre. It is a well established hotel noted for its friendly staff. Bedrooms are air conditioned and executive rooms are available. Traders Restaurant and the lounge bar area serve food. The hotel has a 'Kids Stay and Eat Free' offer.

Rooms 136 (6 GF) (6 smoking) **S** £59-£135; **D** £59-£135 (incl. bkfst)* **Facilities** STV Discounted leisure facilities at nearby club Xmas New Year Wi-fi **Conf** Class 60 Board 50 Thtr 100 **Services** Lift Air con **Parking** 200 **Notes** LB Civ Wed 150

Campanile Washington
BUDGET HOTEL

☎ 0191 416 5010 📠 0191 416 5023
Emerson Rd, District 5 NE37 1LE
e-mail: washington@campanile.com
dir: A1(M) junct 64, A195 to Washington, 1st left at rdbt into Emerson Road. Hotel 800yds on left

This modern building offers accommodation in smart, well-equipped bedrooms, all with en suite bathrooms. Refreshments may be taken at the informal bistro. See also the Hotel Groups pages.

Rooms 79 (79 annexe) (1 fmly) (28 GF) **Conf** Class 15 Board 25 Thtr 40

Travelodge Washington A1 Northbound

BUDGET HOTEL

☎ 0871 984 6270
Motorway Service Area, Portobello DH3 2SJ
web: www.travelodge.co.uk
dir: On northbound carriageway of A1(M

Travelodge offers good quality, good value, budget accommodation. All offer family rooms sleeping up to four (two adults, two children) with en suite bathroom/shower-room, remote-control TV, tea- and coffee-making facilities and comfortable beds. Food options vary. Breakfast is at the on-site Bar Café restaurant (if available) or to take away. See also Hotel Groups pages.

Rooms 31 **S** fr £29; **D** fr £29

Travelodge Washington A1 Southbound
BUDGET HOTEL

☎ 0871 984 6271
Portobello DH3 2SJ
web: www.travelodge.co.uk
dir: On S'bound carriageway of A1(M)

Rooms 36 **S** fr £29; **D** fr £29

Gibside
★★★ 71% HOTEL

☎ 0191 488 9292 📠 0191 488 8000
Front St NE16 4JG
e-mail: reception@gibside-hotel.co.uk
web: www.gibside-hotel.co.uk
dir: Off A1(M) towards Whickham on B6317, onto Front St, 2m on right

Conveniently located in the village centre, this hotel is close to the Newcastle by-pass and its elevated position affords views over the Tyne Valley. Bedrooms come in two styles, classical and contemporary. Public rooms include the Egyptian-themed Sphinx bar and a more formal restaurant. Secure garage parking is available.

Rooms 45 (2 fmly) (13 GF) **S** £55-£75; **D** £66-£85* **Facilities** FTV Golf Academy at The Beamish Park ♫ New Year Wi-fi **Conf** Class 50 Board 50 Thtr 100 Del from £90 to £110* **Services** Lift **Parking** 28 **Notes** LB

Best Western Salford Hall
★★★ 80% ⊛ HOTEL

☎ 01386 871300 & 0800 212671 📠 01386 871301
WR11 5UT
e-mail: reception@salfordhall.co.uk
web: www.salfordhall.co.uk
dir: From A46 follow Salford Priors, Abbot's Salford & Harvington signs . Hotel 1.5m on left

Built in 1470 as a retreat for the Abbot of Evesham, this impressive building retains many original features. Bedrooms have their own individual character and most have a view of the attractive gardens. Oak-panelling, period tapestries, open fires and fresh flowers grace the public areas. Eating is available in the Stanford Room, once a chapel, and also in the conservatory setting of Minstrels Bistro.

Rooms 33 (19 annexe) (4 GF) **Facilities** STV ♨ Xmas New Year Wi-fi **Conf** Class 35 Board 25 Thtr 50 **Parking** 51 **Notes** LB ⊗ Closed 24-30 Dec Civ Wed 80

Kings Court
★★★ 71% HOTEL

☎ 01789 763111 📠 01789 400242
Kings Coughton B49 5QQ
e-mail: info@kingscourthotel.co.uk
web: www.kingscourthotel.co.uk
dir: 1m N on A435

This privately owned hotel dates back to Tudor times and the bedrooms in the original house have oak beams. Most guests are accommodated in the well-appointed modern wings. The bar and restaurant offer very good cooking on interesting menus. The hotel is licensed to hold civil ceremonies and the pretty garden is ideal for summer weddings.

Rooms 39 (35 annexe) (3 fmly) (21 GF) (26 smoking) **S** £30-£68; **D** £49-£90 (incl. bkfst)* **Facilities** STV Wi-fi **Conf** Class 60 Board 40 Thtr 100 Del from £80 to £104* **Parking** 120 **Notes** LB Closed 24-30 Dec Civ Wed 100

ALCESTER *continued*

Travelodge Stratford Alcester

BUDGET HOTEL

☎ 0871 984 6107 📄 01789 765749
A435 Birmingham Rd, Oversley Mill Roundabout B49 6PQ
web: www.travelodge.co.uk
dir: At junct of A46 & A435, 8m W of Stratford-upon-Avon

Travelodge offers good quality, good value, budget accommodation. All offer family rooms sleeping up to four (two adults, two children) with en suite bathroom/shower-room, remote-control TV, tea- and coffee-making facilities and comfortable beds. Food options vary. Breakfast is at the on-site Bar Café restaurant (if available) or to take away. See also Hotel Groups pages.

Rooms 66 **S** fr £29; **D** fr £29

ALDERMINSTER Map 10 SP24

INSPECTORS' CHOICE

Ettington Park

★★★★ ⚜⚜ HOTEL

☎ 01789 450123 & 0845 072 7454
📄 01789 450472
CV37 8BU
e-mail: ettingtonpark@handpicked.co.uk
web: www.handpicked.co.uk
dir: Off A3400, 5m S of Stratford, just outside Alderminster

Set in 40-acre grounds in the picturesque Stour Valley, Ettington Park offers the best of both worlds - the peace of the countryside and easy access to main roads and motorway networks. Bedrooms are spacious and individually decorated; views include the delightful grounds and gardens, or the historic chapel. Luxurious day rooms extend to the period drawing room, the oak-panelled dining room with inlays of family crests, a range of contemporary meeting rooms and indoor leisure centre.

Rooms 48 (20 annexe) (5 fmly) (10 GF) **Facilities** STV
🏊 ⚓ Fishing 🎯 Clay pigeon shooting Archery Sauna Steam room Xmas New Year Wi-fi **Conf** Class 48 Board 48 Thtr 90 Del from £165 to £210 **Services** Lift **Parking** 100 **Notes** ⊗ Civ Wed 96

ANSTY Map 11 SP48

Macdonald Ansty Hall

★★★★ 76% HOTEL

☎ 0844 879 9031 📄 024 7660 2155
Main Rd CV7 9HZ
e-mail: ansty@macdonald-hotels.co.uk
web: www.macdonald-hotels.co.uk/anstyhall
dir: M6 junct 2 onto B4065 signed Ansty. Hotel 1.5m on left

Dating back to 1678, this Grade II listed Georgian house is set in eight acres of attractive grounds and woodland. The hotel enjoys a central yet tranquil location. Spacious bedrooms feature a traditional decorative style and a range of extras. Rooms are divided between the main house and the newer annexe.

Rooms 62 (39 annexe) (4 fmly) (22 GF) **Facilities** STV Xmas New Year Wi-fi **Conf** Class 60 Board 60 Thtr 150 Del from £130 to £180 **Services** Lift **Parking** 150 **Notes** Civ Wed 100

ATHERSTONE Map 10 SP39

Chapel House Restaurant With Rooms

⚜ RESTAURANT WITH ROOMS

☎ 01827 718949 📄 01827 717702
Friar's Gate CV9 1EY
e-mail: info@chapelhouse.eu
web: www.chapelhouse.eu
dir: A5 to town centre, right onto Church St. Right onto Sheepy Rd & left onto Friar's Gate

Sitting next to the church this 18th-century town house offers excellent hospitality and service while the cooking, using much local produce, is very notable. Bedrooms are well equipped and lounges are extensive; there is also a delightful walled garden for guests to use.

Rooms 12

BARFORD Map 10 SP26

The Glebe at Barford

★★★ 72% HOTEL

☎ 01926 624218 📄 01926 624625
Church St CV35 8BS
e-mail: sales@glebehotel.co.uk
dir: M40 junct 15/A429 (Stow). At mini island turn left, hotel 500mtrs on right

The giant Lebanese cedar tree in front of this hotel was ancient even in 1820, when the original rectory was built. Public rooms within the house include a lounge bar and the aptly named Cedars Conservatory Restaurant which offers interesting cuisine. Individually appointed bedrooms are tastefully decorated in soft pastel fabrics, with coronet, tented ceiling or four-poster style beds.

Rooms 39 (3 fmly) (4 GF) **Facilities** 🏋 Gym Beauty salon Xmas **Services** Lift **Parking** 60 **Notes** LB Civ Wed 70

BRANDON Map 11 SP47

Mercure Brandon Hall Hotel & Spa

★★★ 77% HOTEL

☎ 024 7654 6000 📄 024 7654 4909
Main St CV8 3FW
e-mail: h6625@accor.com
web: www.mercure-uk.com
dir: A45 towards Coventry S. After Peugeot-Citroen garage on left, at island take 5th exit to M1 South/London (back onto A45). After 200yds, immediately after Texaco garage, left into Brandon Ln, hotel after 2.5m

An impressive tree lined avenue leads to this 17th-century property which sits in 17 acres of grounds. The hotel provides a peaceful and friendly sanctuary away from the hustle and bustle. The bedrooms provide comfortable facilities and a good range of extras for guest comfort. There is a Spa Naturel with health, beauty and fitness facilities in a separate building with ample parking.

Rooms 120 (30 annexe) (50 GF) (8 smoking)
D £55-£155* **Facilities** Spa STV 🏋 Gym New Year Wi-fi **Conf** Thtr 250 **Services** Lift **Parking** 200 **Notes** LB ⊗ Civ Wed 150

CLAVERDON   Map 10 SP16

Ardencote Manor Hotel, Country Club & Spa

★★★★ 77% ◉◉ HOTEL

☎ 01926 843111 ▤ 01926 842646
The Cumsey, Lye Green Rd, Claverdon CV35 8LT
e-mail: hotel@ardencote.com
web: www.ardencote.com
dir: In Claverdon centre follow Shrewley signs off A4189. Hotel 0.5m on right

Originally built as a gentleman's residence around 1860, this hotel is set in 83 acres of landscaped grounds. Public rooms include a choice of lounge areas, a cocktail bar and conservatory breakfast room. Main meals are served in the Lodge, a separate building with a light contemporary style, which sits beside a small lake. An extensive range of leisure and conference facilities is provided and bedrooms are smartly decorated and tastefully furnished.

Rooms 110 (10 fmly) (30 GF) **S** £80-£150; **D** £80-£165 (incl. bkfst) **Facilities** Spa STV ☜ ⚡ ♨ 9 ⚑ Putt green ⛳ Gym Squash Sauna Steam room Outdoor heated whirlpool Fitness classes Xmas New Year Wi-fi Child facilities **Conf** Class 70 Board 50 Thtr 175 Del from £135 to £180* **Services** Lift Air con **Parking** 200 **Notes** LB ⊗ Civ Wed 150

See advert on page 472

COLESHILL   Map 10 SP28

Grimstock Country House

★★★ 71% COUNTRY HOUSE HOTEL

☎ 01675 462121 & 462161 ▤ 01675 467646
Gilson Rd, Gilson B46 1LJ
e-mail: enquiries@grimstockhotel.co.uk
web: www.grimstockhotel.co.uk
dir: Off A446 at rdbt onto B4117 to Gilson, hotel 100yds on right

This privately owned hotel is convenient for Birmingham International Airport and the NEC, and benefits from a peaceful rural setting. Bedrooms are spacious and comfortable. Public rooms include two restaurants, a wood-panelled bar, good conference facilities and a gym featuring the latest cardiovascular equipment.

Rooms 44 (1 fmly) (13 GF) **S** £65-£95; **D** £75-£125 (incl. bkfst) **Facilities** STV Gym Xmas New Year Wi-fi **Conf** Class 60 Board 50 Thtr 100 Del from £125 to £140 **Parking** 100 **Notes** LB Civ Wed 100

Coleshill Hotel

★★ ⒶHOTEL

☎ 01675 465527 ▤ 01675 464013
152 High St B46 3BG
e-mail: 9130@greeneking.co.uk
web: www.oldenglish.co.uk
dir: M6 junct 4. After 2nd island turn right onto Coventry road. Hotel on left approx 100yds after mini rdbt

Rooms 23 (8 annexe) (3 fmly) (3 GF) **Facilities** ♫ Xmas **Conf** Class 50 Board 40 Thtr 100 **Parking** 30 **Notes** LB

Innkeeper's Lodge Birmingham Coleshill (NEC)

BUDGET HOTEL

☎ 0845 112 6063 ▤ 0845 112 6240
High St B46 3BL
web: www.innkeeperslodge.com/birminghamcoleshill
dir: M6 junct 4, A446 N signed M42 North/Lichfield. At 2nd rdbt right onto B4114 towards Coleshill. Right onto High St

Innkeeper's Lodge represents an exciting, high value concept within the budget hotel market. Comfortable bedrooms provide excellent facilities that include satellite TV and modem points. Options include family rooms; and for the corporate guest, cutting edge IT which includes Wi-fi high speed internet access. A popular Carvery provides all-day food, including an extensive, complimentary continental breakfast. See also the Hotel Groups pages.

Rooms 33 **Conf** Thtr 56

CORLEY MOTORWAY SERVICE AREA (M6)   Map 10 SP38

Days Inn Corley - NEC (M6)

BUDGET HOTEL

☎ 01676 543800 & 540111 ▤ 01676 540128
Junction 3-4, M6 North, Corley CV7 8NR
e-mail: corley.hotel@welcomebreak.co.uk
dir: On M6 between juncts 3 & 4 N'bound

This modern building offers accommodation in smart, spacious and well-equipped bedrooms, suitable for families and business travellers, and all with en suite bathrooms. Continental breakfast is available and other refreshments may be taken at the nearby family restaurant. See also the Hotel Groups pages.

Rooms 50 (13 fmly) (24 GF) (44 smoking) **S** £29-£59; **D** £39-£69*

DUNCHURCH   Map 11 SP47

Travelodge Rugby Dunchurch

BUDGET HOTEL

☎ 0871 984 6099 ▤ 01788 521538
London Rd, Thurlaston CV23 9LG
web: www.travelodge.co.uk
dir: 4m S of Rugby, on A45, westbound

Travelodge offers good quality, good value, budget accommodation. All offer family rooms sleeping up to four (two adults, two children) with en suite bathroom/ shower-room, remote-control TV, tea- and coffee-making facilities and comfortable beds. Food options vary. Breakfast is at the on-site Bar Café restaurant (if available) or to take away. See also Hotel Groups pages.

Rooms 40 **S** fr £29; **D** fr £29

KENILWORTH   Map 10 SP27

Chesford Grange

★★★★ 80% HOTEL

☎ 01926 859331 ▤ 01926 859272
Chesford Bridge CV8 2LD
e-mail: chesfordgrangereservations@qhotels.co.uk
web: www.qhotels.co.uk
dir: 0.5m SE of junct A46/A452. At rdbt turn right signed Leamington Spa, follow signs to hotel

This much-extended hotel set in 17 acres of private grounds is well situated for Birmingham International Airport, the NEC and major routes. Bedrooms range from traditional style to contemporary rooms featuring state-of-the-art technology. Public areas include a leisure club and extensive conference and banqueting facilities.

Rooms 209 (20 fmly) (43 GF) **S** £85-£140; **D** £95-£150 (incl. bkfst) **Facilities** Spa STV ☜ supervised Gym Steam room Solarium Xmas New Year Wi-fi **Conf** Class 350 Board 50 Thtr 710 Del from £145 to £219 **Services** Lift **Parking** 650 **Notes** LB Civ Wed 700

KENILWORTH *continued*

Best Western Peacock

★★★ 78% HOTEL

☎ 01926 851156 & 864500 ▤ 01926 864644
149 Warwick Rd CV8 1HY
e-mail: reservations@peacockhotel.com
dir: A46/A452 signed Kenilworth. Hotel 0.25m on right after St John's Church

Conveniently located for the town centre, the Peacock offers a peaceful retreat, and service is delivered in a very professional manner by friendly staff. The accommodation is attractive, and vibrant colour schemes run throughout the pleasant public rooms; there are two dining options: the Malabar Room offering modern European dining, and the Coconut Lagoon serving southern Indian dishes.

Rooms 29 (6 annexe) (5 fmly) (10 GF) **Facilities** Xmas Wi-fi **Conf** Class 24 Board 28 Thtr 60 **Parking** 30 **Notes** LB ⊗ Civ Wed 70

LEA MARSTON	**Map 10 SP29**

Lea Marston Hotel

★★★★ 72% ⊛ HOTEL

☎ 01675 470468 & 471305 ▤ 01675 470871
Haunch Ln B76 0BY
e-mail: info@leamarstonhotel.co.uk
web: www.leamarstonhotel.co.uk
dir: M42 junct 9, A4097 to Kingsbury. Hotel signed 1.5m on right

Excellent access to the motorway network and a good range of sports facilities make this hotel a popular choice

for conferences and leisure breaks. Bedrooms are mostly set around an attractive quadrangle and are generously equipped. Diners can choose between the popular Sportsman's Lounge Bar and the elegant Adderley Restaurant.

Rooms 88 (4 fmly) (49 GF) (88 smoking) **Facilities** STV ⊛ ₤ 9 ♨ Putt green Gym Golf driving range Golf simulator Beauty salon Xmas New Year Wi-fi **Conf** Class 50 Board 30 Thtr 140 **Services** Lift **Parking** 220 **Notes** ⊗ Civ Wed 100

LEAMINGTON SPA (ROYAL)	**Map 10 SP36**

INSPECTORS' CHOICE

Mallory Court

★★★ ⊛⊛⊛ HOTEL

☎ 01926 330214 ▤ 01926 451714
Harbury Ln, Bishop's Tachbrook CV33 9QB
e-mail: reception@mallory.co.uk
web: www.mallory.co.uk
dir: M40 junct 13 N'bound left, left again towards Bishops Tachbrook, right onto Harbury Ln after 0.5m. M40 junct 14 S'bound A452 to Leamington, at 2nd rdbt left onto Harbury Ln

With its tranquil rural setting, this elegant Lutyens-style country house is an idyllic retreat. Set in ten acres of landscaped gardens with immaculate lawns and orchard. Relaxation is easy in the two sumptuous lounges, drawing room or conservatory. Dining is a treat in either the elegant restaurant or the brasserie. Simon Haigh heads up a team of expert chefs producing dishes that continue to delight. Bedrooms in the main house are luxuriously decorated and most have wonderful views. Those in the Knights Suite are more contemporary and have their own access via a smart conference and banqueting facility.

Rooms 30 (11 annexe) (2 fmly) (4 GF) **S** £125-£350; **D** £149-£425 (incl. bkfst) **Facilities** STV ₹ ♨ ♨ Use of nearby club facilities Xmas New Year Wi-fi **Conf** Class 160 Board 50 Thtr 200 Del from £159 to £240 **Services** Lift **Parking** 100 **Notes** LB ⊗ Civ Wed 160

Angel

★★★ 75% HOTEL

☎ 01926 881296 ▤ 01926 313853
143 Regent St CV32 4NZ
e-mail: angelhotel143@hotmail.com
web: www.angelhotelleamington.co.uk
dir: In town centre at junct of Regent St & Holly Walk

This centrally located hotel is divided in two parts - the original inn and a more modern extension. Public rooms include a comfortable foyer lounge area, a smart restaurant and an informal bar. Bedrooms are individual in style, and, whether modern or traditional, all have the expected facilities.

Rooms 48 (3 fmly) (3 GF) **Facilities** Xmas **Conf** Class 40 Board 40 Thtr 70 **Services** Lift **Parking** 38 **Notes** LB

Best Western Falstaff

★★★ 72% HOTEL

☎ 01926 312044 ▤ 01926 450574
16-20 Warwick New Rd CV32 5JQ
e-mail: sales@falstaffhotel.com
web: www.falstaffhotel.com
dir: M40 junct 13 or 14, follow Leamington Spa signs. Over 4 rdbts, under bridge. Left into Princes Dr, right at mini-rdbt

Bedrooms at this hotel come in a variety of sizes and styles and are well equipped, with many thoughtful extras. Snacks can be taken in the relaxing lounge bar, and an interesting selection of English and continental dishes is offered in the restaurant; 24-hour room service is also available. Conference and banqueting facilities are extensive.

Rooms 63 (2 fmly) (16 GF) **S** £50-£95; **D** £60-£105 (incl. bkfst) **Facilities** FTV Arrangement with local health club Xmas New Year Wi-fi **Conf** Class 30 Board 30 Thtr 70 Del from £90 to £145 **Parking** 50 **Notes** LB Civ Wed 50

See advert on opposite page

Holiday Inn Leamington Spa - Warwick

★★★ 66% HOTEL

☎ 01926 425522 & 0870 400 7212 📠 01926 881322
Olympus Av CV34 6RJ
e-mail: reservations@leamington.kewgreen.co.uk
web: www.holidayinn.com/leamingtonspa
dir: M40 junct 13/14, follow signs for Leamington & A452. Hotel on right immediately afterwards

Situated in pleasant surroundings, this modern hotel offers well-equipped and comfortable bedrooms. Public areas include Spa's restaurant and a combined bar and lounge where a menu is available throughout the day. The bedrooms are modern with all the expected facilities; executive club level rooms and suites are available.

Rooms 91 (15 fmly) (14 GF) **Facilities** Gym Xmas New Year Wi-fi **Conf** Class 40 Board 40 Thtr 80 Del from £110 to £160* **Services** Lift **Parking** 130

Travelodge Leamington Spa

BUDGET HOTEL

☎ 0871 984 6239 📠 01926 432 473
The Parade CV32 4AT
web: www.travelodge.co.uk
dir: A425 follow town centre signs. Lodge off B4087

Travelodge offers good quality, good value, budget accommodation. All offer family rooms sleeping up to four (two adults, two children) with en suite bathroom/shower-room, remote-control TV, tea- and coffee-making facilities and comfortable beds. Food options vary. Breakfast is at the on-site Bar Café restaurant (if available) or to take away. See also Hotel Groups pages.

Rooms 54 **S** fr £29; **D** fr £29

NUNEATON   **Map 11 SP39**

Best Western Weston Hall

★★★ 68% HOTEL

☎ 024 7631 2989 📠 024 7664 0846
Weston Ln, Bulkington CV12 9RU
e-mail: info@westonhallhotel.co.uk
dir: M6 junct 2 follow B4065 through Ansty. Left in Shilton, follow Nuneaton signs out of Bulkington, turn into Weston Ln at 30mph sign

This Grade II listed hotel, whose origins date back to the reign of Elizabeth I, sits within seven acres of peaceful grounds. The original three-gabled building retains many original features, such as the carved wooden fireplace in the library. Friendly service is provided; and the bedrooms, that vary in size, are thoughtfully equipped.

Rooms 40 (1 fmly) (14 GF) **Facilities** FTV ⚓ New Year Wi-fi **Conf** Class 100 Board 60 Thtr 200 **Parking** 300 **Notes** LB Civ Wed 200

Days Inn Nuneaton

BUDGET HOTEL

☎ 024 7635 7370 & 0870 428 0928 📠 0870 428 0929
St David's Way, Bermuda Park CV10 7SD
e-mail: reservations@daysinnnuneaton.co.uk
web: www.daysinn.com
dir: M6 junct 3 onto A444 Nuneaton. 1m, left onto Bermuda Park. At rdbt right onto St David's Way, hotel on right

This modern building offers accommodation in smart, spacious and well-equipped bedrooms, suitable for families and business travellers, and all with en suite bathrooms. Continental breakfast is available and other refreshments may be taken at the nearby family restaurant. See also the Hotel Groups pages.

Rooms 101 (4 fmly) (10 GF) **Conf** Class 20 Board 24 Thtr 40 Del from £70 to £105*

Travelodge Nuneaton

BUDGET HOTEL

☎ 0871 984 6094 📠 0870 1911594
St Nicholas Park Dr CV11 6EN
web: www.travelodge.co.uk
dir: On A47

Travelodge offers good quality, good value, budget accommodation. All offer family rooms sleeping up to four (two adults, two children) with en suite bathroom/shower-room, remote-control TV, tea- and coffee-making facilities and comfortable beds. Food options vary. Breakfast is at the on-site Bar Café restaurant (if available) or to take away. See also Hotel Groups pages.

Rooms 28 **S** fr £29; **D** fr £29

NUNEATON *continued*

Travelodge Nuneaton Bedworth

BUDGET HOTEL

☎ 0871 984 6062 ▤ 024 7638 2541
Bedworth CV10 7DA
web: www.travelodge.co.uk
dir: on A444

Rooms 40 **S** fr £29; **D** fr £29

| RUGBY | Map 11 SP57 |

Brownsover Hall Hotel

★★★ 78% HOTEL

☎ 0844 855 9123 ▤ 01788 535367
Brownsover Ln, Old Brownsover CV21 1HU
e-mail: brownsover@foliohotels.com
web: www.foliohotels.com/brownsoverhall
dir: M6 junct 1, A426 to Rugby. After 0.5m at rdbt follow Brownsover signs, right into Brownover Rd, right again into Brownsover Ln. Hotel 250yds on left

A Grade II listed, Victorian Gothic hall designed by Sir Gilbert Scott, set in seven acres of wooded parkland. Bedrooms vary in size and style, including spacious and contemporary rooms in the converted stable block. The former chapel makes a stylish restaurant, and for a less formal meal or a relaxing drink, the Whittle Bar is popular.

Rooms 47 (20 annexe) (3 fmly) **Facilities** Free use of Virgin Active gym nearby Xmas New Year Wi-fi **Conf** Class 36 Board 40 Thtr 70 **Parking** 100 **Notes** LB ⊗ Civ Wed 56

Golden Lion Hotel

★★★ 72% HOTEL

☎ 01788 833577 & 832265 ▤ 01788 832878
Easenhall CV23 0JA
e-mail: reception@goldenlionhotel.org
web: www.goldenlionhotel.org
dir: A426 Avon Mill rdbt turn to Newbold-upon-Avon B4112, approx 2m left at Harborough Parva sign & follow brown tourist signs, opposite agricultural showroom, then 1m to Easenhall

This friendly, family-run, 16th-century inn is situated between Rugby and Coventry, and is convenient for access to the M6. Bedrooms, some of which are within a smart extension, are equipped with both practical and

homely items; one features a stunning Chinese bed. The beamed bar and restaurant retain many original features and a warm welcome is assured.

Rooms 20 (2 fmly) (6 GF) **S** £50-£75; **D** £60-£85 (incl. bkfst) **Facilities** FTV New Year Wi-fi **Conf** Class 30 Board 24 Thtr 80 Del from £120 to £135 **Parking** 80 **Notes** LB ⊗ Civ Wed 100

Innkeeper's Lodge Rugby

BUDGET HOTEL

☎ 0845 1126073 ▤ 0845 112 6230
The Green, Dunchurch CV22 6NJ
web: www.innkeeperslodge.com/rugbysouth
dir: M1 junct 17/M45/A45. Follow signs for Dunchurch B4429. Lodge in village centre on x-rds of A426 & B4429

Innkeeper's Lodge represents an exciting, high value concept within the budget hotel market. Comfortable bedrooms provide excellent facilities that include satellite TV and modem points. This carefully restored lodge is in a picturesque setting and has its own unique style and quirky character. Food is served all day, and an extensive, complimentary continental breakfast is offered. See also the Hotel Groups pages.

Rooms 16 (2 fmly) **Conf** Thtr 30

| STRATFORD-UPON-AVON | Map 10 SP25 |

INSPECTORS' CHOICE

Ettington Park

★★★★ ◉◉ HOTEL

☎ 01789 450123 & 0845 072 7454
▤ 01789 450472
CV37 8BU
e-mail: ettingtonpark@handpicked.co.uk
web: www.handpicked.co.uk

(For full entry see Alderminster)

Menzies Welcombe Hotel Spa & Golf Club

MenziesHotels

★★★★ 85% ◉◉ HOTEL

☎ 01789 295252 ▤ 01789 414666
Warwick Rd CV37 0NR
e-mail: welcombe@menzieshotels.co.uk
web: www.menzieshotels.co.uk
dir: M40 junct 15, A46 towards Stratford-upon-Avon, at rdbt follow signs for A439. Hotel 3m on right

This Jacobean manor house is set in 157 acres of landscaped parkland. Public rooms are impressive, especially the lounge with its wood panelling and ornate marble fireplace, and the gentleman's club-style bar. Bedrooms in the original building are the stylish and gracefully proportioned; those in the garden wing are comfortable and thoughtfully equipped. The spa development incorporates advanced, luxurious facilities and treatments.

Rooms 78 (12 fmly) (11 GF) (6 smoking) **S** £85-£185; **D** £85-£185* **Facilities** Spa STV ⊕ ᒻ 18 ৯ Putt green Gym Xmas New Year Wi-fi **Conf** Class 75 Board 40 Thtr 200 Del from £130 to £195* **Parking** 200 **Notes** ⊗ Civ Wed 120

Macdonald Alveston Manor

MACDONALD HOTELS & RESORTS

★★★★ 79% ◉ HOTEL

☎ 0844 879 9138 ▤ 01789 414095
Clopton Bridge CV37 7HP
e-mail: sales.alvestonmanor@macdonald-hotels.co.uk
web: www.macdonald-hotels.co.uk
dir: On rdbt south of Clopton Bridge

A striking red-brick and timbered façade, well-tended grounds, and a giant cedar tree all contribute to the charm of this well-established hotel, just five minutes from Stratford. The bedrooms vary in size and character - the coach house conversion offers an impressive mix of full and junior suites. The superb leisure complex offers a 20-metre swimming pool, steam room, sauna, a high-tech gym and a host of beauty treatments.

Rooms 113 (8 fmly) (45 GF) **S** £64-£185; **D** £74-£195* **Facilities** Spa FTV ⊕ supervised Gym Techno-gym Beauty treatments New Year Wi-fi **Conf** Class 80 Board 40 Thtr 140 Del from £150 to £200* **Services** Air con **Parking** 150 **Notes** LB Civ Wed 110

The Stratford

★★★★ 79% ® HOTEL

☎ 01789 271000 & 271007 📠 01789 271001
Arden St CV37 6QQ
e-mail: thestratfordreservations@qhotels.co.uk
web: www.qhotels.co.uk
dir: A439 into Stratford. In town follow A3400/
Birmingham, at lights left into Arden St, hotel 150yds on right

Situated adjacent to the hospital, this eye-catching modern hotel with its red-brick façade is within walking distance of the town centre. The hotel offers modern, well-equipped and spacious bedrooms. The open-plan public areas include a comfortable lounge, a small, atmospheric bar and a spacious restaurant with exposed beams.

Rooms 102 (7 fmly) (14 GF) **S** £74-£149; **D** £84-£159 (incl. bkfst)* **Facilities** STV Gym Xmas New Year Wi-fi **Conf** Class 66 Board 54 Thtr 132 Del from £120 to £170 **Services** Lift Air con **Parking** 102 **Notes** LB ⊗ Civ Wed 132

Barceló Billesley Manor Hotel

★★★★ 77% ®® HOTEL

☎ 01789 279955 📠 01789 764145
Billesley, Alcester B49 6NF
e-mail: billesleymanor@barcelo-hotels.co.uk
web: www.barcelo-hotels.co.uk
dir: A46 towards Evesham. Over 3 rdbts, right for Billesley after 2m

This 16th-century manor is set in peaceful grounds and parkland with a delightful yew topiary garden and fountain. The spacious bedrooms and suites, most in traditional country-house style, are thoughtfully designed and well equipped. Conference facilities and some of the bedrooms are found in the cedar barns. Public areas retain many original features, such as oak panelling, fireplaces and exposed stone.

Rooms 72 (29 annexe) (5 GF) **Facilities** Spa ⊙ supervised ⊆ ⊌ Gym Steam room Beauty treatments Yoga studio Xmas New Year **Conf** Class 60 Board 50 Thtr 100 Del from £125* **Parking** 100 **Notes** Civ Wed 75

Stratford Manor

★★★★ 77% HOTEL

☎ 01789 731173 📠 01789 731131
Warwick Rd CV37 0PY
e-mail: stratfordmanor@qhotels.co.uk
web: www.qhotels.co.uk
dir: M40 junct 15, A46 signed Stratford. At 1st rdbt take A439 signed Stratford Town Centre. Hotel in 1m on left. Or from Stratford centre take A439 signed Warwick & M40. Hotel in 3m on right

Just outside Stratford, this hotel is set against a rural backdrop with lovely gardens and ample parking. Public areas include a stylish lounge bar and a contemporary restaurant. Service is both professional and helpful. Bedrooms are smartly appointed, spacious and have generously sized beds and a range of useful facilities. The leisure centre boasts a large indoor pool.

Rooms 104 (8 fmly) (24 GF) **Facilities** ⊙ ⊆ Gym Sauna Steam room Xmas New Year Wi-fi **Conf** Class 200 Board 100 Thtr 350 **Services** Lift **Parking** 250 **Notes** Civ Wed 250

Mercure Shakespeare

★★★★ 72% ® HOTEL

☎ 01789 294997 📠 01789 415411
Chapel St CV37 6ER
e-mail: h6630@accor.com
web: www.mercure-uk.com
dir: M40 junct 15. Follow signs for Stratford town centre on A439. Follow one-way system onto Bridge St. Left at rdbt, hotel 200yds on left opp HSBC bank

Dating back to the early 17th century, The Shakespeare is one of the oldest hotels in this historic town. The hotel name represents one of the earliest exploitations of Stratford as the birthplace of one of the world's leading playwrights. With exposed beams and open fires, the public rooms retain an ambience reminiscent of this era. Bedrooms are appointed to a good standard and remain in keeping with the style of the property.

Rooms 74 (11 annexe) (3 GF) (3 smoking) **S** £60-£150; **D** £60-£200 (incl. bkfst)* **Facilities** Xmas New Year Wi-fi **Conf** Class 60 Board 40 Thtr 80 Del from £120 to £160 **Services** Lift **Parking** 34 **Notes** LB Civ Wed 100

Legacy Falcon

★★★★ 71% ® HOTEL

☎ 0870 832 9905 📠 0870 832 9906
Chapel St CV37 6HA
e-mail: res-falcon@legacy-hotels.co.uk
web: www.legacy-hotels.co.uk
dir: M40 junct 15, follow signs to town centre, turn into Chapel St, 2nd right into Scholars Ln, right again into hotel car park

Situated in the heart of the town just a short walk from all the Shakespeare properties. The hotel dates back to 1500, and in the 17th century an extra storey was added.

Bedrooms provide contemporary accommodation and the public areas are cosy. Service is provided by a friendly team. The restaurant provides good quality cuisine using fresh, local ingredients.

Rooms 83 (11 annexe) (6 fmly) (3 GF) **S** £60-£120; **D** £70-£160 (incl. bkfst) **Facilities** STV Xmas New Year Wi-fi **Conf** Class 80 Board 50 Thtr 150 Del from £135 to £165 **Services** Lift **Parking** 122 **Notes** LB Civ Wed 150

Holiday Inn Stratford-upon-Avon

★★★★ 71% HOTEL

☎ 0870 225 4701 & 01789 279988 📠 01789 298589
Bridgefoot CV37 6YR
e-mail: histratford@qmh-hotels.com
web: www.holidayinn.co.uk
dir: A439 to Stratford-upon-Avon. On entering town road bears left, hotel 200mtrs on left

This large modern hotel sits beside the River Avon in landscaped grounds and has ample parking. Bedrooms have a light contemporary feel and are equipped with a good range of facilities that include air-conditioning and Wi-fi. Day rooms include a terrace lounge and bar, a carvery restaurant and the Club Moativation health and fitness facility that proves popular with both corporate and leisure guests.

Rooms 259 (8 fmly) **S** £60-£145; **D** £60-£145* **Facilities** ⊙ supervised Gym Sauna Beauty Salon Xmas New Year Wi-fi **Conf** Class 340 Board 42 Thtr 550 Del from £120 to £190 **Services** Lift Air con **Parking** 350 **Notes** LB ⊗

STRATFORD-UPON-AVON *continued*

Macdonald Swan's Nest

 MACDONALD HOTELS & RESORTS

★★★★ 71% HOTEL

☎ 0844 879 9140 ▤ 01789 414547
Bridgefoot CV37 7LT
e-mail: sales.swansnest@macdonald-hotels.co.uk
web: www.macdonald-hotels.co.uk/swansnest
dir: A439 towards Stratford, follow one-way system, turn
left (A3400) over bridge, hotel on right

Dating back to the 17th century, this hotel is said to be
one of the earliest brick-built houses in Stratford. It
occupies a prime position on the banks of the River Avon
and is ideally situated for exploring the town. Bedrooms
and bathrooms are appointed to a high standard with
some thoughtful guest extras provided.

Rooms 68 (2 fmly) (25 GF) **S** £59-£130; **D** £75-£150*
Facilities FTV Use of facilities at Alveston Manor New
Year Wi-fi **Conf** Class 100 Board 60 Thtr 150
Del from £120 to £150* **Parking** 80 **Notes** LB
Civ Wed 150

Thistle Stratford-upon-Avon   thistle

★★★ 81% HOTEL

☎ 0871 376 9035 ▤ 0871 376 9135
Waterside CV37 6BA
e-mail: stratforduponavon@thistle.co.uk
web: www.thistlehotels.com/stratforduponavon
dir: M40 junct 15, A46 to Stratford-upon-Avon, take 1st
exit at rdbt towards town centre, A439.

The hotel is located just a very short walk from the town
centre, sitting directly opposite the world famous
Shakespeare and Swan theatres and is fronted by award-
winning gardens. Service throughout the day rooms is
both friendly and professional, offering separate bar and
lounge areas, with the dining room providing interesting
menu selections. Bedrooms are well equipped and
comfortably appointed.

Rooms 63 (3 fmly) (3 GF) **Facilities** STV Xmas New Year
Wi-fi **Conf** Class 24 Board 30 Thtr 50 **Parking** 55
Notes Civ Wed 60

Best Western Salford Hall

 Best Western

★★★ 80% ◉ HOTEL

☎ 01386 871300 & 0800 212671 ▤ 01386 871301
WR11 5UT
e-mail: reception@salfordhall.co.uk
web: www.salfordhall.co.uk

(For full entry see Abbot's Salford)

Best Western Grosvenor House

 Best Western

★★★ 78% HOTEL

☎ 01789 269213 ▤ 01789 266087
Warwick Rd CV37 6YT
e-mail: info@bwgh.co.uk
web: www.bwgh.co.uk
dir: M40 junct 15, follow Stratford signs to A439 Warwick
Rd. Hotel 7m, on one-way system

This hotel is a short distance from the town centre and
many of the historic attractions. Bedroom styles and sizes
vary, and the friendly staff offer an efficient service.
Refreshments are served in the lounge all day, and room
service is available. The Garden Room restaurant offers a
choice of dishes from set priced and carte menus.

Rooms 73 (16 fmly) (25 GF) **S** £59-£140; **D** £59-£140
Facilities STV FTV Xmas New Year Wi-fi **Conf** Class 45
Board 50 Thtr 100 Del from £99 to £160 **Parking** 46
Notes LB ⊗ Civ Wed 70

Charlecote Pheasant Hotel   *folio* Hotels

★★★ 78% HOTEL

☎ 0844 855 9126 ▤ 01789 470222
Charlecote CV35 9EW
e-mail: charlecote@foliohotels.com
web: www.foliohotels.com/charlcotepheasant
dir: M40 junct 15, A429 towards Cirencester through
Barford. In 2m right into Charlecote, hotel opposite
Charlecote Park

Located just outside Stratford, this hotel is set in
extensive grounds and is a popular conference venue.
Various bedroom styles are available within the annexe
wings, ranging from standard rooms to executive suites.
The main building houses the restaurant and a lounge
bar area.

Rooms 70 (39 fmly) **Facilities** FTV ⚲ ♨ Children's play
area Xmas New Year Wi-fi **Conf** Class 70 Board 40
Thtr 160 **Parking** 100 **Notes** LB Civ Wed 176

The New Inn Hotel & Restaurant

★★ Ⓐ

☎ 01789 293402 ▤ 01789 292716
Clifford Chambers CV37 8HR
e-mail: thenewinn65@aol.com
web: www.thenewinnhotel.co.uk
dir: A3400 onto B4632, 500yds on left

Rooms 13 (2 fmly) (3 GF) **Facilities** ♫ New Year Wi-fi
Parking 40 **Notes** ⊗ Closed 23-28 Dec

Travelodge Stratford-upon-Avon

 Travelodge

BUDGET HOTEL

☎ 0871 984 6414 ▤ 01789 205709
Birmingham Rd CV37 0HS
dir: M40 junct 15, A46 for approx 6m, at Park & Ride rdbt
take 1st exit into A3400/Birmingham Rd for 0.6m. Lodge
on right of Hamlet Way

Travelodge offers good quality, good value, budget
accommodation. All offer family rooms sleeping up to four
(two adults, two children) with en suite bathroom/shower-
room, remote-control TV, tea- and coffee-making facilities
and comfortable beds. Food options vary. Breakfast is at
the on-site Bar Café restaurant (if available) or to take
away. See also the Hotel Groups pages.

Rooms 91 **S** fr £29; **D** fr £29

STUDLEY   Map 10 SP06

Best Western Studley Castle

 Best Western

★★★ 72% HOTEL

☎ 01527 853111 & 855200 ▤ 01527 855000
Castle Rd B80 7AJ
e-mail: bookings@studleycastle.com
dir: A435 S into Studley, left at castle sign, hotel 1m on
right

This hotel has a delightful parkland location close to
Stratford. Specialising in providing meeting room venues,
the hotel has an impressive range of public areas. The
restaurant also offers a relaxing environment and lovely
views across the countryside. Bedrooms are available in a
range of sizes and all are well equipped.

Rooms 57 (2 fmly) **Facilities** STV Gym Xmas New Year
Wi-fi **Conf** Class 66 Board 20 Thtr 150 Del from £110 to
£165* **Services** Lift **Parking** 150 **Notes** LB Civ Wed 150

See advert on opposite page

THURLASTON   Map 11 SP47

Draycote

★★★ 68% ◉ HOTEL

☎ 01788 521800 ▤ 01788 521695
London Rd CV23 9LF
e-mail: mail@draycotehotel.co.uk
web: www.draycotehotel.co.uk
dir: M1 junct 17 onto M45/A45. Hotel 500mtrs on left

Located in the picturesque Warwickshire countryside and
within easy reach of motorway networks, this hotel offers
modern, comfortable and well-equipped accommodation
with a relaxed and friendly welcome. The hotel has a
challenging golf course.

Rooms 49 (24 fmly) (24 GF) **Facilities** STV ⚲ 18 Putt
green Gym Gold driving range Chipping green New Year
Wi-fi **Conf** Class 78 Board 72 Thtr 250 **Parking** 150
Notes LB ⊗ Civ Wed 180

See advert on opposite page

See also **Honiley & Leamington Spa (Royal)**

Chesford Grange

★★★★ 80% HOTEL

☎ 01926 859331 📄 01926 859272
Chesford Bridge CV8 2LD
e-mail: chesfordgrangereservations@qhotels.co.uk
web: www.qhotels.co.uk

(For full entry see Kenilworth)

Ardencote Manor Hotel, Country Club & Spa

★★★★ 77% ◉◉ HOTEL

☎ 01926 843111 📄 01926 842646
The Cumsey, Lye Green Rd, Claverdon CV35 8LT
e-mail: hotel@ardencote.com
web: www.ardencote.com

(For full entry see Claverdon)

Express by Holiday Inn Warwick

BUDGET HOTEL

☎ 01926 483000 📄 01926 483033
Stratford Rd CV34 6TW
e-mail: warwick@expressbyholidayinn.co.uk
web: www.hiexpress.com/warwickuk
dir: M40 junct 15, follow signs A429 to Warwick. Take 1st right

A modern hotel ideal for families and business travellers. Fresh and uncomplicated, the spacious rooms include Sky TV, power shower and tea and coffee-making facilities. Continental buffet breakfast is included in the room rate; other meals may be taken at the nearby family pub or restaurant. See also the Hotel Groups pages.

Rooms 138 (59 fmly) (36 GF) (19 smoking) **S** £39-£99.95; **D** £49-£99.95 (incl. bkfst)* **Conf** Class 18 Board 20 Thtr 40

WARWICK MOTORWAY SERVICE AREA (M40)   Map 10 SP35

Days Inn Warwick North

BUDGET HOTEL

☎ 01926 651681   📠 01926 651634
Warwick Services, M40 Northbound Junction 12-13, Banbury Rd CV35 0AA
e-mail: warwick.north.hotel@welcomebreak.co.uk
web: www.welcomebreak.co.uk
dir: M40 northbound between junct 12 & 13

This modern building offers accommodation in smart, spacious and well-equipped bedrooms, suitable for families and business travellers, and all with en suite bathrooms. Continental breakfast is available and other refreshments may be taken at the nearby family restaurant. See also the Hotel Groups pages.

Rooms 54 (45 fmly) **S** £29-£59; **D** £39-£69*
Conf Board 30 Del from £79 to £109*

Days Inn Warwick South

BUDGET HOTEL

☎ 01926 650168   📠 01926 651601
Warwick Services, M40 Southbound, Banbury Rd CV35 0AA
e-mail: warwick.south.hotel@welcomebreak.co.uk
web: www.welcomebreak.co.uk
dir: M40 southbound between junct 14 & 12

Rooms 40 (38 fmly) **S** £29-£59; **D** £39-£69*

WELLESBOURNE   Map 10 SP25

Barceló Walton Hall

★★★★ 79% ⚜⚜ HOTEL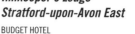

☎ 01789 842424   📠 01789 470418
Walton CV35 9HU
e-mail: waltonhall.mande@barcelo-hotels.co.uk
dir: A429 through Bradford towards Wellsbourne, right after watermill, follow signs to hotel

Sitting in 65 acres of beautiful countryside, this hotel is just 10 minutes from the M40. It has a fascinating history, with parts dating back to the 1500s. The property has been appointed in a style that combines both traditional and modern design. The individually designed bedrooms, many with stunning views over the lake and garden, have plasma screen TVs, DVD players and lap top-sized safes. Premium rooms and suites are available. The award-winning Moncreiffe Restaurant is situated in the hall and has views over the lovely gardens.

Rooms 56 (19 annexe) (11 GF) **Facilities** Spa STV FTV ☜ supervised ⛳ Gym Dance studio Beauty salon Xmas New Year Wi-fi **Conf** Class 60 Board 36 Thtr 240 Del from £125* **Services** Air con **Parking** 240 **Notes** ⊛ Civ Wed 240

Innkeeper's Lodge Stratford-upon-Avon East

BUDGET HOTEL

☎ 0845 112 6075   📠 0845 112 6228
Warwick Rd CV35 9LX
web: www.innkeeperslodge.com/stratford
dir: M40 junct 15 S onto A429 towards Wellesbourne. Turn left at rdbt onto B4086. Lodge 300yds on right

Innkeeper's Lodge represents an exciting, high value concept within the budget hotel market. Comfortable bedrooms provide excellent facilities that include satellite TV and modem points. This carefully restored lodge is in a picturesque setting and has its own unique style and quirky character. Food is served all day, and an extensive, complimentary continental breakfast is offered. See also the Hotel Groups pages.

Rooms 9

WROXALL   Map 10 SP27

Wroxall Abbey Estate
★★★ 78% HOTEL

☎ 01926 484470 📠 01926 485206
Birmingham Rd CV35 7NB
e-mail: info@wroxall.com
dir: Between Solihull & Warwick on A4141

Situated in 27 acres of open parkland, yet only 10 miles from the NEC and Birmingham International Airport, this hotel is a magnificent Victorian mansion. Some of the individually designed bedrooms have traditional décor but there are some modern loft rooms as well; some rooms have four-posters. Sonnets Restaurant, with its impressive fireplace and oak panelling, makes the ideal setting for fine dining.

Rooms 70 (22 annexe) (10 GF) **D** £79-£399*
Facilities Spa STV 🅣 🐟 Fishing Gym Ten pin bowling Walks/jogging trail 🎵 Xmas New Year Wi-fi
Conf Class 80 Board 60 Thtr 160 **Services** Lift
Parking 200 **Notes** LB ⊗ No children 12yrs Civ Wed 200

WEST MIDLANDS

BALSALL COMMON   Map 10 SP27

Nailcote Hall
★★★★ 76% ⊛ HOTEL   CLASSIC BRITISH HOTELS

☎ 024 7646 6174 📠 024 7647 0720
Nailcote Ln, Berkswell CV7 7DE
e-mail: info@nailcotehall.co.uk
web: www.nailcotehall.co.uk
dir: On B4101

This 17th-century house, set in 15 acres of grounds, boasts a 9-hole championship golf course and Roman bath-style swimming pool amongst its many facilities. Rooms are spacious and elegantly furnished. The eating options are the fine dining restaurant where smart casual dress is required, or in The Piano Bar for informal meals.

Rooms 40 (19 annexe) (2 fmly) (15 GF) **Facilities** STV 🅣 supervised 👣 9 🏌 Putt green 🏌 Gym Beauty room 🎵 Xmas New Year Wi-fi **Conf** Class 80 Board 44 Thtr 140 **Services** Lift **Parking** 200 **Notes** ⊗ Civ Wed 120

Haigs
★★★ 72% HOTEL

☎ 01676 533004 📠 01676 535132
Kenilworth Rd CV7 7EL
e-mail: info@haigshotel.co.uk
dir: A45 towards Coventry, at Stonebridge Island turn right, 4m S of M42 junct 6

Conveniently located just five miles from Birmingham Airport and twelve miles from Stratford-upon-Avon. This hotel offers a comfortable stay at a small family run operation. Enjoyable meals can be taken in Mckees Brasserie.

Rooms 23 (2 fmly) (5 GF) **Facilities** Xmas New Year Wi-fi **Conf** Board 20 Thtr 25 **Parking** 23 **Notes** ⊗ Civ Wed 60

BIRMINGHAM   Map 10 SP08

See also **Bromsgrove (Worcestershire), Lea Marston (Warwickshire), Oldbury & Sutton Coldfield**

Birmingham Marriott Hotel   **Marriott** HOTELS & RESORTS
★★★★ 80% ⊛ HOTEL

☎ 0121 452 1144 📠 0121 456 3442
12 Hagley Rd, Five Ways B16 8SJ
e-mail: pascal.demarchi@marriotthotels.com
web: www.birminghammarriott.co.uk
dir: Leebank Middleway to Five Ways rdbt, 1st left then right. Follow signs for hotel

Situated in the suburb of Edgbaston, this Edwardian hotel is a prominent landmark on the outskirts of the city centre. Air-conditioned bedrooms are decorated in a comfortable, modern style and provide a comprehensive range of extra facilities. Public rooms include the contemporary, brasserie-style West 12 Bar and Restaurant.

Rooms 104 **Facilities** Spa STV 🅣 Gym Steam room Wi-fi **Conf** Board 35 Thtr 80 **Services** Lift Air con **Parking** 50 **Notes** LB ⊗ Civ Wed 60

Hotel du Vin Birmingham   Hotel du Vin & Bistro
★★★★ 78% ⊛ TOWN HOUSE HOTEL

☎ 0121 200 0600 📠 0121 236 0889
25 Church St B3 2NR
e-mail: info@birmingham.hotelduvin.com
web: www.hotelduvin.com
dir: M6 junct 6/A38(M) to city centre, over flyover. Keep left & exit at St Chads Circus signed Jewellery Quarter. At lights & rdbt take 1st exit, follow signs for Colmore Row, opposite cathedral. Right into Church St, across Barwick St. Hotel on right

The former Birmingham Eye Hospital has become a chic and sophisticated hotel. The stylish, high-ceilinged rooms, all with a wine theme, are luxuriously appointed and feature stunning bathrooms, sumptuous duvets and Egyptian cotton sheets. The Bistro offers relaxed dining and a top-notch wine list, while other attractions include a champagne bar, a wine boutique and a health club.

Rooms 66 **Facilities** Spa STV Gym Treatment rooms Steam room Sauna Xmas New Year Wi-fi **Conf** Class 40 Board 40 Thtr 84 **Services** Lift Air con **Notes** LB Civ Wed 84

Macdonald Burlington   MACDONALD HOTELS & RESORTS
★★★★ 77% HOTEL

☎ 0844 879 9019 & 0121 643 9191 📠 0121 628 5005
Burlington Arcade, 126 New St B2 4JQ
e-mail: events.burlington@macdonald-hotels.co.uk
web: www.macdonaldhotels.co.uk/burlington
dir: M6 junct 6, follow signs for city centre, then take A38

The Burlington's original Victorian grandeur - the marble and iron staircases and the high ceilings - blend seamlessly with modern facilities. Bedrooms are equipped to a good standard and public areas include a stylish bar and coffee lounge. The Berlioz Restaurant specialises in innovative dishes using fresh produce.

Rooms 112 (6 fmly) **Facilities** STV New Year Wi-fi **Conf** Class 175 Board 60 Thtr 400 **Services** Lift **Notes** ⊗ Closed 24-26 Dec Civ Wed 400

City Inn Birmingham   CITY INN
★★★★ 76% ⊛ HOTEL

☎ 0845 838 1255 & 0121 643 1003 📠 0121 643 1005
1 Brunswick Square, Brindley Place B1 2HW
e-mail: birmingham.reservations@cityinn.com
web: www.cityinn.com
dir: M6 junct 6/A38M follow signs for A456. Right into Sheepcote St, hotel straight ahead

This large modern hotel is conveniently situated close to the heart of the city in the popular Brindley Place. Modern and contemporary in style, air-conditioned bedrooms are comfortable and well laid out, feature iMac computers, TV with Sky channels and free Wi-fi. Public areas include a range of meeting rooms, the City Café and the hotel's restaurant which offers modern cuisine.

Rooms 238 **S** £99-£225; **D** £99-£225* **Facilities** STV FTV Gym Xmas New Year Wi-fi **Conf** Class 50 Board 50 Thtr 100 Del from £125 to £300* **Services** Lift Air con **Parking** 24 **Notes** ⊗ Civ Wed 100

BIRMINGHAM *continued*

Novotel Birmingham Centre

★★★★ 70% HOTEL

☎ 0121 643 2000 📠 0121 643 9786
70 Broad St B1 2HT
e-mail: h1077@accor.com
web: www.novotel.com
dir: A38/A456, hotel on right beyond International
Convention Centre

This large, modern, purpose-built hotel benefits from an
excellent city centre location, with the bonus of secure
parking. Bedrooms are spacious, modern and well
equipped especially for business users; four rooms have
facilities for less able guests. Public areas include the
Garden Brasserie, function rooms and a fitness room.

Rooms 148 (148 fmly) (11 smoking) **S** £75-£185;
D £75-£185* **Facilities** Gym Fitness room Cardio-
vascular equipment Sauna Spa bath Wi-fi **Conf** Class 120
Board 90 Thtr 300 Del from £130 to £250* **Services** Lift
Air con **Parking** 53 **Notes** LB

Copthorne Hotel Birmingham

★★★★ 68% HOTEL

☎ 0121 200 2727 📠 0121 200 1197
Paradise Circus B3 3HJ
e-mail: reservations.birmingham@millenniumhotels.
co.uk
web: www.millenniumhotels.co.uk
dir: M6 junct 6, city centre A38(M). After Queensway
Tunnel emerge left, follow International Convention
Centre signs. At Paradise Circus island follow right lane.
Hotel in centre

This hotel is one of the few establishments in the city
that benefits from its own car park. Bedrooms are
spacious and come in a choice of styles, all with excellent

facilities. Guests can enjoy a variety of dining options,
including the contemporary menu in Goldies Brasserie.

Rooms 212 **S** £67-£137; **D** £74-£144 (incl. bkfst)*
Facilities STV Gym Xmas New Year Wi-fi **Conf** Class 120
Board 30 Thtr 200 Del from £120 to £180* **Services** Lift
Parking 78 **Notes** ⊗ Civ Wed 150

Best Western Westley

★★★ 82% HOTEL

☎ 0121 706 4312 📠 0121 706 2824
80-90 Westley Rd, Acocks Green B27 7UJ
e-mail: reservations@westley-hotel.co.uk
dir: A41 signed Birmingham on Solihull by-pass, continue
to Acocks Green. At rdbt, 2nd exit B4146 Westley Rd.
Hotel 200yds on left

Situated in the city suburbs and conveniently located for
the N.E.C. and the airport, this friendly hotel provides
well-equipped, smartly presented bedrooms. In addition
to the main restaurant, there is also a lively bar and
brasserie together with a large function room.

Rooms 37 (11 annexe) (1 fmly) (3 GF) **S** £85-£130;
D £95-£150 (incl. bkfst) **Facilities** STV ♬ New Year Wi-fi
Conf Class 80 Board 50 Thtr 200 Del from £140 to £150
Parking 150 **Notes** LB ⊗ Civ Wed 200

Malmaison Birmingham

★★★ 80% HOTEL

☎ 0121 246 5000 📠 0121 246 5002
1 Wharfside St, The Mailbox B1 1RD
e-mail: birmingham@malmaison.com
web: www.malmaison.com
dir: M6 junct 6, follow A38 towards Birmingham. Hotel
within The Mailbox, signed from A38

The 'Mailbox' development, of which this stylish and
contemporary hotel is a part, incorporates the very best in

fashionable shopping, an array of restaurants and ample
parking. Air-conditioned bedrooms are stylishly decorated
and feature comprehensive facilities. Public rooms
include a contemporary bar and brasserie which prove a
hit with guests and locals alike. Gymtonic and a Petit Spa
are also available, offering rejuvenating treatments.

Rooms 189 **Facilities** Gym Wi-fi **Conf** Class 40 Board 24
Thtr 50 **Services** Lift Air con **Notes** LB

Menzies Strathallan

★★★ 80% HOTEL

☎ 0121 455 9777 📠 0121 454 9432
225 Hagley Rd, Edgbaston B16 9RY
e-mail: strathallan@menzieshotels.co.uk
web: www.menzies-hotels.co.uk
dir: From A38 follow signs for ICC onto Broad St, towards
Five Ways island, take underpass to Hagley Rd. Hotel 1m

Located just a few minutes from the city's central
attractions and with the benefit of excellent parking, this
hotel provides a range of comfortable and well-equipped
bedrooms. A modern lounge bar and contemporary
restaurant offer a good range of dining options.

Rooms 135 **S** £39-£135; **D** £49-£145* **Facilities** STV FTV
Xmas New Year Wi-fi **Conf** Class 90 Board 50 Thtr 170
Del from £105 to £145* **Services** Lift **Parking** 120
Notes ⊗ Civ Wed 40

Holiday Inn Birmingham City

★★★ 78% HOTEL

☎ 0870 400 9008 📠 0121 631 2528
Smallbrook Queensway B5 4EW
e-mail: reservations-birminghamcity@ihg.com
web: www.holidayinn.co.uk
dir: M6 junct 6, A38(M) to city centre, keep left after flyover & two underpasses. 2nd left into Suffolk Place. 1st right into St Jude's Passage

This is a large hotel in the city centre with parking close by. Facilities include extensive meeting rooms and a business centre. The lounge bar with a roof terrace is a popular meeting place. The Carvery restaurant offers lunch and dinner; 24-hour room service is also available.

Rooms 248 (8 fmly) (25 smoking) **S** £45-£189; **D** £50-£199* **Facilities** STV FTV Xmas New Year Wi-fi **Conf** Class 300 Board 150 Thtr 630 Del from £99 to £189* **Services** Lift Air con **Parking** 10 **Notes** LB Civ Wed 630

The Royal Angus by Thistle

thistle

★★★ 78% HOTEL

☎ 0871 376 9005 📠 0871 376 9105
St Chads, Queensway B4 6HY
e-mail: birminghamcity@thistle.co.uk
web: www.thistle.com/birminghamcity
dir: From M6 junct 6 onto Aston Expressway towards city centre, after 1m exit A38 signed Jewellery Quarter. Hotel on left

This hotel benefits from a central location and is convenient for both the motorway network and extensive parking facilities. Bedrooms range in size and style with executive rooms providing air conditioning and a host of thoughtful extras. A modern comfortable lounge bar links to a terrace.

Rooms 133 (3 fmly) **S** £49-£159; **D** £59-£169* **Facilities** STV Xmas New Year Wi-fi **Conf** Class 90 Board 35 Thtr 180 Del from £132 to £179* **Services** Lift **Notes** LB ✪ Civ Wed 170

Edgbaston Palace

★★★ 71% HOTEL

☎ 0121 452 1577 📠 0121 455 7933
198-200 Hagley Rd, Edgbaston B16 9PQ
e-mail: enquiries@edgbastonpalacehotel.com
dir: M5 junct 3 north then A456 for 4.3m. Hotel on right

Dating back to the 19th century, this Grade II listed Victorian property has been refurbished. Bedrooms are modern, well appointed and offer good comfort levels. The hospitality is warm, personal and refreshing. Supervised children under 18 are welcome.

Rooms 48 (21 annexe) (3 fmly) (16 GF) **Facilities** FTV Wi-fi **Conf** Class 70 Board 60 Thtr 200 **Parking** 70 **Notes** ✪

Holiday Inn Birmingham M6 Jct 7

★★★ 70% HOTEL

☎ 0870 400 9009 & 0121 357 7303 📠 0121 357 7503
Chapel Ln, Great Barr B43 7BG
web: www.holidayinn.co.uk
dir: M6 junct 7, A34 signed Walsall. Hotel 200yds on right across carriageway in Chapel Ln

Situated in pleasant surroundings, this modern hotel offers well-equipped and comfortable bedrooms. Public areas include the popular Traders restaurant and a comfortable lounge where a menu is available to guests all day. There is also 24-hour room service; a courtyard patio and a garden.

Rooms 190 (45 fmly) (67 GF) (12 smoking) **Facilities** STV ✪ supervised Gym Xmas New Year Wi-fi **Conf** Class 75 Board 50 Thtr 160 **Services** Air con **Parking** 250 **Notes** Civ Wed 100

Great Barr Hotel & Conference Centre

★★★ 66% HOTEL

☎ 0121 357 1141 📠 0121 357 7557
Pear Tree Dr, Newton Rd, Great Barr B43 6HS
e-mail: sales@thegreatbarrhotel.com
web: www.thegreatbarrhotel.com
dir: M6 junct 7, at Scott Arms x-rds right towards West Bromwich (A4010) Newton Rd. Hotel 1m on right

This busy hotel, situated in a leafy residential area, is particularly popular with business clients; after a major refurbishment the hotel has excellent, state-of-the-art training and seminar facilities. There is a traditional oak-panelled bar and formal restaurant. The refit has extended to many of the bedrooms too; all are appointed to a good standard and have the expected amenities.

Rooms 105 (6 fmly) **Facilities** STV Xmas Wi-fi **Conf** Class 90 Board 60 Thtr 200 **Parking** 200 **Notes** LB ✪ RS BH (Restaurant may close) Civ Wed 200

Woodlands

★★ 60% METRO HOTEL

☎ 0121 420 2341 📠 0121 429 3935
379-381 Hagley Rd, Edgbaston B17 8DL
e-mail: hotel@woodlands2000.freeserve.co.uk
web: www.thewoodlandshotel.co.uk
dir: Follow sign to city centre along A456 (Hagley Rd) for 3.5m. Hotel on left where Sandon Rd meets Hagley Rd

Ideally located for major links to the west of city, this modern hotel provides a range of thoughtfully furnished bedrooms; some are suitable for families. Public areas are both comfortable and spacious, and the large car park is a real benefit.

Rooms 20 (4 fmly) **S** £45-£55; **D** £60-£70 (incl. bkfst)* **Facilities** FTV Wi-fi **Parking** 20 **Notes** ✪ Civ Wed 100

Comfort Inn Birmingham

Ⓤ

☎ 0121 643 1134 📠 0121 643 3209
Station St B5 4DY
e-mail: enquiries@thecomfortinnbirmingham.co.uk
dir: M6 junct 6, A38(M) towards city centre. Take Queensway Ring Road, Holloway Head to Smallbridge Queensway. Left into Hill St, 2nd right into Station St

Currently the rating for this establishment is not confirmed. This may be due to a change of ownership or because it has only recently joined the AA rating scheme. For further details please see the AA website: theAA.com

Rooms 40 (3 fmly) (10 smoking) **S** £49-£89; **D** £49-£99* **Facilities** Wi-fi **Conf** Class 25 Board 25 Thtr 45 **Services** Lift **Notes** LB ✪

Crowne Plaza Birmingham City

Ⓤ

☎ 0870 400 9150 📠 0121 224 5119
Central Square B1 1HH
e-mail: enquiries@cpbhamcity.com
web: www.crowneplaza.co.uk
dir: A38, follow city centre signs. After 2nd tunnel (Suffolk Queensway) into left slip road, follow signs for New St Station & The Mailbox. Hotel adjacent to The Mailbox

Currently the rating for this establishment is not confirmed. This may be due to a change of ownership or

continued

BIRMINGHAM *continued*

because it has only recently joined the AA rating scheme. For further details please see the AA website: theAA.com

Rooms 312 (242 fmly) **Facilities** Gym New Year Wi-fi **Conf** Class 150 Board 40 Thtr 300 Del from £150 to £225 **Services** Lift Air con **Notes** Civ Wed 300

Campanile Birmingham

BUDGET HOTEL

☎ 0121 359 3330   📠 0121 359 1223
Chester St, Aston B6 4BE
e-mail: birmingham@campanile.com
dir: next to rdbt at junct of A4540/A38

This modern building offers accommodation in smart, well-equipped bedrooms, all with en suite bathrooms. Refreshments may be taken at the informal bistro. See also the Hotel Groups pages.

Rooms 109 (3 fmly) **Conf** Class 100 Board 100 Thtr 250

Express by Holiday Inn Birmingham

BUDGET HOTEL

☎ 0121 747 6633   📠 0121 747 6644
1200 Chester Rd, Castle Bromwich B35 7AF
e-mail: castlebromwich@holidayinnexpress.co.uk
web: www.hiexpress.com/birminghamex
dir: M6 junct 5/6/A38 for Tyburn, right into Chester Rd, follow Park signs

A modern hotel ideal for families and business travellers. Fresh and uncomplicated, the spacious rooms include Sky TV, power shower and tea and coffee-making facilities. Continental buffet breakfast is included in the room rate; other meals may be taken at the nearby family pub or restaurant. See also the Hotel Groups pages.

Rooms 110 (21 fmly) (12 GF) **Conf** Class 16 Board 16 Thtr 20

Express by Holiday Inn Birmingham City Centre

BUDGET HOTEL

☎ 0845 1126151   📠 0121 200 1910
65 Lionel St B3 1JE
e-mail: enquiries@hiexpressbirminghamcitycentre.co.uk
web: www.hiexpress.com/exb'minghamc
dir: A38 to City Centre until Paradise Circus, take 4th exit on Queensway, 1st left into Lionel St, hotel on right

Rooms 120 **S** £55-£120; **D** £55-£120 (incl. bkfst)*
Conf Class 16 Board 16 Thtr 30 Del from £95 to £195*

Ibis Birmingham Bordesley Circus

BUDGET HOTEL

☎ 0121 506 2600   📠 0121 506 2610
1 Bordesley Park Rd, Bordesley B10 0PD
e-mail: H2178@accor.com
web: www.ibishotel.com

Modern, budget hotel offering comfortable accommodation in bright and practical bedrooms. Breakfast is self-service and dinner is available in the restaurant. See also the Hotel Groups pages.

Rooms 87 (16 GF) (8 smoking)

Ibis Birmingham City Centre

BUDGET HOTEL

☎ 0121 622 6010   📠 0121 622 6020
Arcadian Centre, Ladywell Walk B5 4ST
e-mail: h1459@accor-hotels.com
web: www.ibishotel.com
dir: From motorways follow city centre signs. Then follow Bullring or Indoor Market signs. Hotel adjacent to market

Rooms 159 (5 fmly) **D** £50-£95* **Conf** Class 60 Board 50 Thtr 120 Del from £85 to £115*

Ibis Birmingham Holloway Circus

BUDGET HOTEL

☎ 0121 622 4925   📠 0121 622 4195
55 Irving St B1 1DH
e-mail: H2092@accor.com
web: www.ibishotel.com
dir: From M6 take A38/City Centre, left after 2nd tunnel. Right at rdbt, 4th left (Sutton St) into Irving St. Hotel on left

Rooms 51 (26 GF) (7 smoking) **S** £40-£75; **D** £40-£75*

Innkeeper's Lodge Birmingham West (Quinton)

BUDGET HOTEL

☎ 0845 112 6066   📠 0845 112 6237
563 Hagley Road West, Quinton B32 1HP
web: www.innkeeperslodge.com/birminghamwest
dir: M5 junct 3, A456 east towards Birmingham. Lodge on opposite side of dual carriageway, cross short distance from rdbt

Innkeeper's Lodge represents an exciting, high value concept within the budget hotel market. Comfortable bedrooms provide excellent facilities that include satellite TV and modem points. Options include family rooms; and for the corporate guest, cutting edge IT which includes Wi-fi access. A popular Carvery provides all-day food, including an extensive, complimentary continental breakfast. See also the Hotel Groups pages.

Rooms 24 (9 fmly) **Conf** Thtr 40

Travelodge Birmingham Central

BUDGET HOTEL

☎ 0871 984 6064   📠 0121 644 5251
230 Broad St B15 1AY
web: www.travelodge.co.uk
dir: M6 junct 6, A38(M) for Birmingham Central. Under tunnel (St. Chad's Queensway) then follow Great Charles Queensway. 2nd exit onto A456/Kidderminster. Lodge on left just past O'Neils

Travelodge offers good quality, good value, budget accommodation. All offer family rooms sleeping up to four (two adults, two children) with en suite bathroom/ shower-room, remote-control TV, tea- and coffee-making facilities and comfortable beds. Food options vary. Breakfast is at the on-site Bar Café restaurant (if available) or to take away. See also the Hotel Groups pages.

Rooms 136 **S** fr £29; **D** fr £29

Travelodge Birmingham Central Broadway Plaza

BUDGET HOTEL

☎ 0871 984 6325   📠 0121 455 8733
Broadway Plaza, 220 Ladywood, Middleway B16 8LP
web: www.travelodge.co.uk
dir: A38(M) Birmingham Central. Stay in 2nd lane approx 2m. Follow signs for city centre

Rooms 74 **S** fr £29; **D** fr £29

Travelodge Birmingham Central Newhall Street

BUDGET HOTEL

☎ 0871 984 6377 📠 0121 236 3961
Charlotte St, off Newhall St B3 1PW
dir: A41 to rdbt junct with A4540. Right into Birstol St (A38) onto Royal Mail St. Exit into Navigation St, into Suffolk St Queensway, continue into Paradise Circus Queensway. At rdbt take 4th exit onto Parade (A457), left into Charlotte St

Rooms 100 **S** fr £29; **D** fr £29

Travelodge Birmingham Fort Dunlop

BUDGET HOTEL

☎ 0871 984 6312 📠 0121 747 9958
Fort Parkway, Erdington B24 9FD
web: www.travelodge.co.uk

Rooms 100 **S** fr £29; **D** fr £29

Travelodge Birmingham Maypole

BUDGET HOTEL

☎ 0871 984 6304 📠 0121 430 7565
Maypole Ln B14 5JF
web: www.travelodge.co.uk
dir: A435 (Alcester road) towards city centre. Lodge at 3rd rdbt on corner of Alcester Rd & Maypole Lane

Rooms 60 **S** fr £29; **D** fr £29

Travelodge Birmingham Yardley

BUDGET HOTEL

☎ 0871 984 6065 📠 0121 764 5882
A45 Coventry Rd, Acocks Green, Yardley B26 1DS
web: www.travelodge.co.uk
dir: M42 junct 6, A45. Lodge approx 5m

Rooms 64 **S** fr £29; **D** fr £29

 **BIRMINGHAM AIRPORT** Map 10 SP08

Novotel Birmingham Airport

★★★ 77% HOTEL

☎ 0121 782 7000 & 782 4111 📠 0121 782 0445
B26 3QL
e-mail: H1158@accor.com
web: www.novotel.com
dir: M42 junct 6/A45 to Birmingham, signed to airport. Hotel opposite main terminal

This large, purpose-built hotel is located opposite the main passenger terminal. Bedrooms are spacious, modern in style and well equipped, including Playstations to keep the children busy. Several rooms have facilities for less able guests. The Garden Brasserie is open from noon until midnight; the bar is open 24 hours and a full room service is available.

Rooms 195 (36 fmly) (20 smoking) **Facilities** STV Wi-fi **Conf** Class 20 Board 22 Thtr 35 **Services** Lift **Notes** LB

Holiday Inn Birmingham Airport

★★★ 73% HOTEL

☎ 0870 400 9007 📠 0121 782 2476
Coventry Rd B26 3QW
web: www.hiairport.co.uk
dir: From M1, M6, M40 take M42. Exit at junct 6, take A45 towards Birmingham. Hotel in 2m on right

This hotel, close to the NEC and Birmingham Airport, offers a range of well-equipped, comfortable bedrooms. Guests can enjoy a snack in the bar or a more substantial meal in the restaurant. It has a range of event and meeting rooms, providing great flexibility to the corporate guest. Limited parking available is available. New leisure centre under construction.

Rooms 141

BIRMINGHAM (NATIONAL EXHIBITION CENTRE) Map 10 SP18

Nailcote Hall

★★★★ 76% ⓔ HOTEL

☎ 024 7646 6174 📠 024 7647 0720
Nailcote Ln, Berkswell CV7 7DE
e-mail: info@nailcotehall.co.uk
web: www.nailcotehall.co.uk

(For full entry see Balsall Common)

Crowne Plaza Birmingham NEC

★★★★ 75% HOTEL

☎ 0870 400 9160 📠 0121 781 4321
National Exhibition Centre, Pendigo Way B40 1PS
e-mail: necroomsales@ihg.com
web: www.crowneplaza.com
dir: M42 junct 6, follow signs for NEC, take 2nd exit on left, South Way for hotel entrance 50mtrs on right

On the doorstep of the NEC and overlooking Pendigo Lake, this hotel has contemporary design and offers well-equipped bedrooms with air conditioning. Rooms have ample working space and high-speed internet access (for an additional charge). Eating options include the modern Pendigo Restaurant overlooking the lake, the bar and 24-hour room service.

Rooms 242 (12 fmly) (15 smoking) **S** £69-£240; **D** £69-£240 **Facilities** STV Gym Sauna Wi-fi **Conf** Class 140 Board 56 Thtr 200 Del from £99 to £190 **Services** Lift Air con **Parking** 348 **Notes** ⊗ Civ Wed 160

Best Western Premier Moor Hall Hotel & Spa

★★★★ 74% HOTEL

☎ 0121 308 3751 📠 0121 308 8974
Moor Hall Dr, Four Oaks B75 6LN
e-mail: mail@moorhallhotel.co.uk
web: www.moorhallhotel.co.uk

(For full entry see Sutton Coldfield)

Haigs

★★★ 72% HOTEL

☎ 01676 533004 📠 01676 535132
Kenilworth Rd CV7 7EL
e-mail: info@haigshotel.co.uk

(For full entry see Balsall Common)

Arden Hotel & Leisure Club

★★★ 70% HOTEL

☎ 01675 443221 📠 01675 445604
Coventry Rd, Bickenhill B92 0EH
e-mail: enquiries@ardenhotel.co.uk
dir: M42 junct 6/A45 towards Birmingham. Hotel 0.25m on right, just off Birmingham International railway island

This smart hotel neighbouring the NEC offers modern rooms and well-equipped leisure facilities. After dinner in the formal restaurant, the place to relax is the spacious lounge area. A buffet breakfast is served in the bright and airy Meeting Place.

Rooms 216 (6 fmly) (6 GF) **Facilities** Spa ⓢ supervised Gym Sports therapy Beautician ⬆ Xmas New Year Wi-fi **Conf** Class 40 Board 60 Thtr 200 **Services** Lift **Parking** 300 **Notes** RS 25-28 Dec Civ Wed 100

Heath Lodge

★★ 63% HOTEL

☎ 0121 779 2218 📠 0121 770 5648
117 Coleshill Rd, Marston Green B37 7HT
e-mail: reception@heathlodgehotel.freeserve.co.uk
dir: 1m N of NEC or Birmingham International Airport & station. From M6 take A446, then A452 junct 4

This privately owned and personally run hotel is ideally located for visitors to the NEC and Birmingham Airport. Hospitality and service standards are high and while some bedrooms are compact, all are well equipped and comfortable. Public areas include a bar and a lounge, and a dining room that overlooks the pretty garden.

Rooms 17 (1 fmly) (1 GF) **Facilities** Child facilities **Conf** Class 16 Board 14 Thtr 20 **Parking** 24 **Notes** LB Closed 25-26 Dec & 1 Jan

CASTLE BROMWICH — Map 10 SP18

Innkeeper's Lodge Birmingham Castle Bromwich

BUDGET HOTEL

☎ 0845 112 6076
Chester Rd B36 0AG
web: www.innkeeperslodge.com
dir: A452 signed Leamington. Right into Parkfield Drive then right into Beechcroft Rd. Left at rdbt into Chester Rd, B4118. Lodge on right

Innkeeper's Lodge represents an exciting, high value concept within the budget hotel market. Comfortable bedrooms provide excellent facilities that include satellite TV and modem points. Options include family rooms; and for the corporate guest, cutting edge IT which includes Wi-fi high speed internet access. A popular Carvery provides all-day food, including an extensive, complimentary continental breakfast. See also the Hotel Groups pages.

Rooms 30

COVENTRY — Map 10 SP37

See also **Brandon & Nuneaton (Warwickshire), Meriden (West Midlands)**

Holiday Inn Coventry

★★★ 80% HOTEL

☎ 0870 400 9021 📠 024 7658 7404
Hinckley Rd CV2 2HP
e-mail: reservations-coventrym6@ihg.com
web: www.holidayinn.co.uk
dir: M6 junct 2. Hotel on A4600

Situated close to the city centre & major motorway networks, this hotel offers comfortable & modern accommodation. Facilities include the Spirit leisure suite, Traders Restaurant, spacious lounges where food is served all day & extensive conference services.

Rooms 158

Novotel Coventry

★★★ 72% HOTEL

☎ 024 7636 5000 📠 024 7636 2422
Wilsons Ln CV6 6HL
e-mail: h0506@accor-hotels.com
web: www.novotel.com
dir: M6 junct 3. Follow signs for B4113 towards Longford & Bedworth. 3rd exit on large rdbt

A modern hotel convenient for Birmingham, Coventry and the motorway network, offering spacious, well-equipped accommodation. The bright brasserie has extended dining hours, and alternatively there is an extensive room-service menu. Family rooms and a play area make this a child-friendly hotel, and there is also a selection of meeting rooms.

Rooms 98 (33 fmly) (25 GF) (8 smoking) **Facilities** STV Wi-fi **Conf** Class 100 Board 40 Thtr 200 Del from £105 to £145 **Services** Lift **Parking** 120 **Notes** Civ Wed 50

Brooklands Grange Hotel & Restaurant

★★★ 70% HOTEL

☎ 024 7660 1601 📠 024 7660 1277
Holyhead Rd CV5 8HX
e-mail: info@brooklands-grange.co.uk
web: www.brooklands-grange.co.uk
dir: exit A45 at city centre rdbt. At next rdbt take A4114. Hotel 100yds on left

Behind the Jacobean façade of Brooklands Grange is a well run modern and comfortable business hotel. Well-appointed bedrooms are thoughtfully equipped and a smartly appointed four-poster bedroom is available. Contemporary, well-flavoured dishes are on offer

Rooms 31 (3 fmly) (11 GF) **Conf** Class 10 Board 14 Thtr 20 **Parking** 52 **Notes** LB Closed 26-28 Dec & 1-2 Jan RS 24 Dec-2 Jan

The Chace

★★★ 68% HOTEL

☎ 0844 736 8607 📠 024 7630 1816
London Rd, Toll Bar End CV3 4EQ
e-mail: chacehotel@corushotels.com
web: www.corushotels.com
dir: A45 or A46 follow to Toll Bar Roundabout/Coventry Airport, take B4116 to Willenhall, over mini-rdbt, hotel on left

A former doctor's mansion, the main building retains many of its original Victorian features, including public rooms with high ceilings, stained glass windows, oak panelling and an impressive staircase; there is also a patio and well-kept gardens. Bedroom styles and sizes vary; most are attractively appointed, bright and modern.

Rooms 66 (23 fmly) (24 GF) (2 smoking) **S** £35-£105; **D** £45-£115* **Facilities** ⚓ Nearby leisure centre New Year Wi-fi **Conf** Class 50 Board 30 Thtr 70 Del from £90 to £155* **Parking** 120 **Notes** LB ⊗ RS Xmas period Civ Wed 70

Holiday Inn Coventry South

★★★ 67% HOTEL

☎ 024 7630 1585 & 0870 400 7216 📠 0870 400 7216
London Rd, Ryton on Dunsmore CV8 3DY
e-mail: reservations@coventrykewgreen.co.uk
web: www.holidayinn.co.uk
dir: M6 junct 2, A46 towards Warwick, then A45/London at Coventry Airport

Located just minutes from the historical centre of Coventry and less than a mile from Coventry International Airport. This hotel offers spacious public areas and comfortable bedrooms, each with high speed internet access. The Brasserie Restaurant serves a range of international dishes.

Rooms 51 (15 fmly) (27 GF) (6 smoking) **Facilities** STV Gym New Year Wi-fi **Conf** Class 100 Board 60 Thtr 300 **Parking** 150 **Notes** ⊗ Civ Wed 280

Quality Hotel

★★★ 64% HOTEL

☎ 024 7640 3835 📠 024 7640 3081
Birmingham Rd, Allesley CV5 9BA
e-mail: enquiries@qualityhotelcoventry.co.uk
dir: A45 onto A4114 towards Allesley. Follow brown signs for hotel

Conveniently situated on the A45 close to Birmingham Airport and the National Exhibition Centre. The bedrooms offer good comfort and space for both the business traveller or a leisure guest. There is a sauna and steam room on site.

Rooms 80 (1 fmly) (21 GF) (27 smoking) **Facilities** FTV Sauna Steam room Xmas New Year Wi-fi **Conf** Class 40 Board 30 Thtr 120 Del from £105 to £125* **Parking** 150 **Notes** Civ Wed 75

Campanile Coventry

BUDGET HOTEL

☎ 024 7662 2311 📠 024 7660 2362
4 Wigston Rd, Walsgrave CV2 2SD
e-mail: coventry@campanile.com
dir: M6 exit 2, at 2nd rdbt turn right

This modern building offers accommodation in smart, well-equipped bedrooms, all with en suite bathrooms. Refreshments may be taken at the informal bistro. See also the Hotel Groups pages.

Rooms 47 **S** £46-£59; **D** £46-£59* **Conf** Class 18 Board 24 Thtr 35 Del from £80 to £95*

Ibis Coventry Centre

BUDGET HOTEL

☎ 024 7625 0500 🖷 024 7655 3548
Mile Ln, St John's Ringway CV1 2LN
e-mail: H2793@accor.com
web: www.ibishotel.com
dir: A45 to Coventry, then A4114 signed Jaguar Assembly Plant. At inner ring road towards ring road S. Off exit 5 for Mile Lane

Modern, budget hotel offering comfortable accommodation in bright and practical bedrooms. Breakfast is self-service and dinner is available in the restaurant. See also the Hotel Groups pages.

Rooms 89 (25 fmly) (25 GF)

Ibis Coventry South Whitley

BUDGET HOTEL

☎ 024 7663 9922 🖷 024 7630 6898
Abbey Rd, Whitley CV3 4BJ
e-mail: H2094@accor-hotels.com
web: www.ibishotel.com
dir: Signed from A46/A423 rdbt. Take A423 towards A45. Follow signs for Esporta Health Club and Jaguar Engineering Plant

Rooms 51 (25 GF) (7 smoking) **S** £42-£62; **D** £42-£62*
Conf Class 20 Board 16 Thtr 20

Innkeeper's Lodge Coventry

BUDGET HOTEL

☎ 0845 112 6068 🖷 0845 112 6235
Brinklow Rd, Binley CV3 2DS
web: www.innkeeperslodge.com/coventry
dir: M6 junct 2, A46 towards Coventry. At junct with A428 turn right. Pass 3 rdbts. Right into Brinklow Rd. Lodge on right

Innkeeper's Lodge represents an exciting, high value concept within the budget hotel market. Comfortable bedrooms provide excellent facilities that include satellite TV and modem points. Options include family rooms; and for the corporate guest, cutting edge IT which includes Wi-fi access. A popular Carvery provides all-day food, including an extensive, complimentary continental breakfast. See also the Hotel Groups pages.

Rooms 40 **Conf** Thtr 42

Innkeeper's Lodge Meriden/Solihull (NEC)

BUDGET HOTEL

☎ 0845 112 6072 🖷 0845 112 6231
Main Rd, Meriden CV7 7NN
web: www.innkeeperslodge.com/Meriden
dir: M42 junct 6, A45 towards Coventry. Left just before Little Chef, signed Meriden. Right at T-junct. Over A45, left at rdbt, straight over next rdt into Main Rd. Lodge on left.

Innkeeper's Lodge represents an exciting, high value concept within the budget hotel market. Comfortable bedrooms provide excellent facilities that include satellite TV and modem points. This carefully restored lodge is in a picturesque setting and has its own unique style and quirky character. Food is served all day, and an extensive, complimentary continental breakfast is offered.

Rooms 13 (4 fmly)

Travelodge Coventry

BUDGET HOTEL

☎ 0871 984 6385
Broadgate CV1 1LZ
dir: From ring road exit at junct 9, follow West Orchards Car Park signs, leads to shopping centre car park. Lodge adjacent to car park entrance

Travelodge offers good quality, good value, budget accommodation. All offer family rooms sleeping up to four (two adults, two children) with en suite bathroom/shower-room, remote-control TV, tea- and coffee-making facilities and comfortable beds. Food options vary. Breakfast is at the on-site Bar Café restaurant (if available) or to take away. See also the Hotel Groups pages.

S fr £29; **D** fr £29 **Conf** Class 160 Board 60 Thtr 600

The Forest

◉◉ ⊛ RESTAURANT WITH ROOMS

☎ 01564 772120 🖷 01564 732680
25 Station Rd B93 8JA
e-mail: info@forest-hotel.com
web: www.forest-hotel.com
dir: In town centre near station

The well-established and very individual establishment is well placed for routes to Birmingham, Stratford-upon-Avon and Warwick. Rooms are very well equipped with modern facilities, and imaginative food is served in the bars and intimate restaurant. A warm welcome is assured.

Rooms 12

Copthorne Hotel Merry Hill - Dudley

★★★★ 73% HOTEL

☎ 01384 482882 🖷 01384 482773
The Waterfront, Level St, Brierley Hill DY5 1UR
e-mail: reservations.merryhill@millenniumhotels.co.uk
web: www.copthornehotels.co.uk
dir: Follow signs for Merry Hill Centre

The hotel enjoys a waterfront aspect and is close to the Merry Hill shopping mall. Polished marble floors, rich fabrics and striking interior design are all in evidence in the stylish public areas. Bedrooms are spacious and some have Connoisseur status, which includes the use of a private lounge. A modern leisure centre with pool occupies the lower level.

Rooms 138 (14 fmly) **Facilities** STV ⊛ supervised Gym Aerobics Beauty/massage therapists Steam room Sauna Dance studio New Year Wi-fi **Conf** Class 240 Board 60 Thtr 570 Del from £10 to £199* **Services** Lift **Parking** 100 **Notes** ⊗ Civ Wed 400

DUDLEY *continued*

Travelodge Birmingham Dudley

BUDGET HOTEL

☎ 0871 984 6063 ▤ 0870 191 1563
Dudley Rd, Brierley Hill DY5 1LQ
web: www.travelodge.co.uk
dir: 3m W of Dudley, on A461

Travelodge offers good quality, good value, budget accommodation. All offer family rooms sleeping up to four (two adults, two children) with en suite bathroom/ shower-room, remote-control TV, tea- and coffee-making facilities and comfortable beds. Food options vary. Breakfast is at the on-site Bar Café restaurant (if available) or to take away. See also Hotel Groups pages.

Rooms 32 **S** fr £29; **D** fr £29

FRANKLEY (M5) Map 10 SO98

Travelodge Birmingham Frankley

BUDGET HOTEL

☎ 0871 984 6067 ▤ 0121 501 2880
Illey Ln, Frankley Motorway Service Area, Frankley B32 4AR
web: www.travelodge.co.uk
dir: On s'bound carriageway between juncts 3 & 4 of M5

Travelodge offers good quality, good value, budget accommodation. All offer family rooms sleeping up to four (two adults, two children) with en suite bathroom/ shower-room, remote-control TV, tea- and coffee-making facilities and comfortable beds. Food options vary. Breakfast is at the on-site Bar Café restaurant (if available) or to take away. See also Hotel Groups pages.

Rooms 62 **S** fr £29; **D** fr £29

HILTON PARK MOTORWAY SERVICE AREA (M6) Map 10 SJ90

Travelodge Birmingham Hilton Park (M6 Southbound)

BUDGET HOTEL

☎ 0871 984 6066 ▤ 01922 701967
Hilton Park Services (M6), Essington WV11 2AT
web: www.travelodge.co.uk
dir: M6, between juncts 10a & 11 S'bound

Travelodge offers good quality, good value, budget accommodation. All offer family rooms sleeping up to four (two adults, two children) with en suite bathroom/ shower-room, remote-control TV, tea- and coffee-making facilities and comfortable beds. Food options vary. Breakfast is at the on-site Bar Café restaurant (if available) or to take away. See also Hotel Groups pages.

Rooms 63 **S** fr £29; **D** fr £29

HOCKLEY HEATH Map 10 SP17

Nuthurst Grange Country House & Restaurant

★★★ 87% ◉◉ HOTEL

☎ 01564 783972 ▤ 01564 783919
Nuthurst Grange Ln B94 5NL
e-mail: info@nuthurst-grange.co.uk
web: www.nuthurst-grange.co.uk
dir: off A3400, 0.5m south of Hockley Heath. Turn at sign into Nuthurst Grange Lane

A stunning avenue drive is the approach to this country-house hotel, set amid several acres of well-tended gardens and mature grounds with views over rolling countryside. The spacious bedrooms and bathrooms offer considerable luxury and comfort, and public areas include restful lounges, meeting rooms and a sunny restaurant. The kitchen brigade produces highly imaginative British and French cuisine, complemented by very attentive, professional restaurant service.

Rooms 19 (19 fmly) (2 GF) **Facilities** STV FTV ⬥ Wi-fi **Conf** Class 50 Board 45 Thtr 100 **Parking** 80 **Notes** LB ⊗ Civ Wed 100

KINGSWINFORD Map 10 SO88

Innkeeper's Lodge Dudley Kingswinford

BUDGET HOTEL

☎ 0845 112 6069 ▤ 0845 112 6234
Swindon Rd DY6 9XA
web: www.innkeeperslodge.com/kingswinford
dir: M5 junct 2, A4123 towards Dudley. Pass 5 rdbts, onto A461, then A459 onto A4101. Through Kingswinford to Summerhill. Lodge on right at 2nd lights

Innkeeper's Lodge represent an exciting, high value concept within the budget hotel market. Comfortable bedrooms provide excellent facilities that include satellite TV and modem points. Options include spacious family rooms; and for the corporate guest, cutting edge IT is provided with Wi-fi access. All-day food is provided in the adjacent pub restaurant. The extensive continental breakfast is complimentary. See also the Hotel Groups pages.

Rooms 22 (11 fmly)

KNOWLE Map 10 SP17

Innkeeper's Lodge Knowle/ Solihull

BUDGET HOTEL

☎ 0845 112 6070 ▤ 0845 112 6233
Warwick Rd, Knowle B93 0EE
web: www.innkeeperslodge.com/knowle
dir: M42 junct 5, A4141, S towards Knowle. 2m, through Knowle. Lodge on right, adjacent to Grand Union Canal

Innkeeper's Lodge represents an exciting, high value concept within the budget hotel market. Comfortable bedrooms provide excellent facilities that include satellite TV and modem points. This carefully restored lodge is in a picturesque setting and has its own unique style and quirky character. Food is served all day, and an extensive, complimentary continental breakfast is offered. See also the Hotel Groups pages.

Rooms 12 (1 fmly) **Conf** Thtr 20

MERIDEN Map 10 SP28

Marriott Forest of Arden Hotel & Country Club

★★★★ 79% COUNTRY HOUSE HOTEL

☎ 01676 522335 ▤ 01676 523711
Maxstoke Ln CV7 7HR
web: www.marriottforestofarden.co.uk
dir: M42 junct 6 onto A45 towards Coventry, over Stonebridge flyover. After 0.75m left into Shepherds Ln. Hotel 1.5m on left

The ancient oaks, rolling hills and natural lakes of the 10,000 acre Forest of Arden estate provide an idyllic backdrop for this modern hotel and country club. The hotel boasts an excellent range of leisure facilities and is regarded as one of the finest golfing destinations in the UK. Bedrooms provide every modern convenience and a full range of facilities.

Rooms 214 (65 GF) (5 smoking) **Facilities** Spa ⬥ supervised ⬥ 18 ⬥ Putt green Fishing ⬥ Gym Floodlit golf academy Health & beauty salon Xmas New Year Wi-fi **Conf** Class 180 Board 40 Thtr 300 **Services** Lift Air con **Parking** 300 **Notes** ⊗ Civ Wed 160

Manor

★★★ 82% ⊛ HOTEL

☎ 01676 522735 🖹 01676 522186
Main Rd CV7 7NH
e-mail: reservations@manorhotelmeriden.co.uk
web: www.manorhotelmeriden.co.uk
dir: M42 junct 6, A45 towards Coventry then A452 signed Leamington. At rdbt take B4102 signed Meriden, hotel on left

A sympathetically extended Georgian manor in the heart of a sleepy village is just a few minutes away from the M6, M42 and National Exhibition Centre. The Regency Restaurant offers modern dishes, while the Triumph Buttery serves lighter meals and snacks. The bedrooms are smart and well equipped.

Rooms 110 (20 GF) **S** £70-£140; **D** £80-£180 (incl. bkfst)* **Facilities** Wi-fi **Conf** Class 150 Board 60 Thtr 250 Del from £100 to £160* **Services** Lift **Parking** 200 **Notes** LB RS 24 Dec-2 Jan Civ Wed 150

OLDBURY Map 10 SO98

Express by Holiday Inn Birmingham Oldbury M5

BUDGET HOTEL

☎ 0121 511 0000 🖹 0121 511 0051
Birchley Park B69 2BD
e-mail: oldbury@expressholidayinn.co.uk
web: www.hiexpress.com/bhx-oldbury
dir: off M5 junct 2, behind Total Garage on Wolverhampton Rd

A modern hotel ideal for families and business travellers. Fresh and uncomplicated, the spacious rooms include Sky TV, power shower and tea and coffee-making facilities. Continental buffet breakfast is included in the room rate; other meals may be taken at the nearby family pub or restaurant. See also the Hotel Groups pages.

Rooms 109 (55 fmly) (16 GF) **Conf** Class 20 Board 25 Thtr 30

Travelodge Birmingham Oldbury

BUDGET HOTEL

☎ 0871 984 6095 🖹 0121 552 2967
Wolverhampton Rd B69 2BH
web: www.travelodge.co.uk
dir: M5 junct 2 take A4123 (Wolverhampton Rd) N towards Dudley

Travelodge offers good quality, good value, budget accommodation. All offer family rooms sleeping up to four (two adults, two children) with en suite bathroom/shower-room, remote-control TV, tea- and coffee-making facilities and comfortable beds. Food options vary. Breakfast is at the on-site Bar Café restaurant (if available) or to take away. See also Hotel Groups pages.

Rooms 33 **S** fr £29; **D** fr £29

SOLIHULL Map 10 SP17
See also **Dorridge**

Holiday Inn Solihull

★★★★ 77% HOTEL

☎ 0870 2255 401 🖹 0121 711 2696
61 Homer Rd B91 3QD
e-mail: hisolihull@qmh-hotels.com
web: www.holidayinn.co.uk
dir: M42 junct 5 follow signs to town centre, left at St Alphege Church into Church Hill Rd, continue to rdbt, hotel on right

Conveniently located for access to the NEC and motorway network, this modern hotel proves to be equally popular with both corporate and leisure guests. Bedrooms have been appointed to a smart contemporary standard, offering the benefits of air conditioning as standard. Public areas include the Club Moativation health and fitness club.

Rooms 120 (8 fmly) **Facilities** ⚫ supervised Gym Sauna Steam room Dance studio Xmas Wi-fi **Conf** Class 100 Board 100 Thtr 200 **Services** Lift Air con **Parking** 162 **Notes** Civ Wed 60

Ramada Solihull/ Birmingham

RAMADA

★★★ 77% HOTEL

☎ 0121 711 2121 & 0844 815 9011 🖹 0121 711 3374
The Square B91 3RF
e-mail: sales.solihull@ramadajarvis.co.uk
web: www.ramadajarvis.co.uk/solihull
dir: M42 junct 5, A41 towards Solihull. 1st left on slip road. Right at island, left at 2 sets of lights. Hotel 600yds on right

Within a few minutes walk of the central attractions, this modern hotel provides a range of well-equipped bedrooms, with Studio rooms being particularly attractive. Extensive conference facilities are available and public areas include Arts Restaurant, overlooking one of the world's oldest bowling greens, and cosy bars dating from the 16th century.

Rooms 145 (14 fmly) (36 GF) (7 smoking) **Facilities** FTV Crown Green bowling Xmas New Year Wi-fi **Conf** Class 186 Board 289 Thtr 568 Del from £99 to £155* **Services** Lift **Parking** 180 **Notes** Civ Wed 120

Corus

★★★ 68% HOTEL

☎ 0844 736 8605 & 0121 745 0400 🖹 0121 733 3801
Stratford Rd, Shirley B90 4EB
e-mail: solihull@corushotels.com
web:
dir: M42 junct 4 onto A34 for Shirley, cross 1st 3 rdbts, then double back along dual carriageway, hotel on left

A large, friendly hotel attracting both corporate and leisure guests. It is ideally located within a few minutes of the major transportation links and benefits from its own extensive leisure centre that includes a lagoon pool, sauna and gym.

Rooms 111 (11 fmly) (13 GF) **S** £49-£109; **D** £49-£189 **Facilities** ⚫ Gym Steam room Plunge pool Sauna ♫ Xmas New Year Wi-fi **Conf** Class 80 Board 60 Thtr 180 Del from £69 to £189 **Services** Lift **Parking** 275 **Notes** LB RS Xmas Civ Wed 150

St Johns Hotel

Ⓤ

☎ 0121 711 3000 🖹 0121 705 6629
651 Warwick Rd B91 1AT
dir: M42 junct 5, follow Solihull centre signs. 2nd left at rdbt (Warwick Rd). Straight over 3rd set of lights. (Barley Mow pub on left on approaching large rdbt). Straight ahead, hotel on right

Currently the rating for this establishment is not confirmed. This may be due to a change of ownership or because it has only recently joined the AA rating scheme For further details please see the AA website: theAA.com

Rooms 180 (15 fmly) **Facilities** STV ⚫ Gym Xmas New Year Wi-fi **Conf** Class 350 Board 60 Thtr 850 **Services** Lift Air con **Parking** 300 **Notes** Civ Wed 700

SUTTON COLDFIELD — Map 10 SP19

New Hall

 HandPICKED

★★★★ 77% ◎◎ HOTEL

☎ 0121 378 2442 📠 0121 378 4637
Walmley Rd B76 1QX
e-mail: newhall@handpicked.co.uk
dir: M42 junct 9, A4097, 2m to rdbt, take 2nd exit signed Walmley. Take 2nd exit from next 5 rdbts follow Sutton Coldfield signs. At 6th rdbt take 3rd exit follow Sutton Coldfield signs. Hotel on left

Situated in 26 acres of beautiful grounds this hotel is reputed to be the oldest inhabited, moated house in the country. The house's medieval charm and character combine well with 21st-century guest facilities. Executive and luxury suites are available. Public areas, with their fine panelling and mullioned stained-glass windows include the magnificent Great Chamber.

Rooms 60 (14 fmly) (25 GF) **S** £85-£235; **D** £95-£245 (incl. bkfst)* **Facilities** Spa STV FTV ➰ supervised ♨ 9 ♨ Fishing ♨ Gym Xmas New Year Wi-fi **Conf** Class 75 Board 35 Thtr 150 **Parking** 80 **Notes** LB ⊗ Civ Wed 60

Best Western Premier Moor Hall Hotel & Spa

Best Western PREMIER

★★★★ 74% HOTEL

☎ 0121 308 3751 📠 0121 308 8974
Moor Hall Dr, Four Oaks B75 6LN
e-mail: mail@moorhallhotel.co.uk
web: www.moorhallhotel.co.uk
dir: From A38 take A453 towards Sutton Coldfield, right at lights into Weeford Rd. Hotel 150yds on left

Although only a short distance from the city centre this hotel enjoys a peaceful setting, overlooking extensive grounds and an adjacent golf course. Bedrooms are well equipped and executive rooms are particularly spacious. Public rooms include the formal Oak Room Restaurant, and the informal Country Kitchen, which offers carvery and blackboard specials. The hotel also offers a well-equipped spa with pool, sauna, steam room, jacuzzi and treatment rooms.

Rooms 82 (5 fmly) (33 GF) **S** £54-£150; **D** £84-£170 (incl. bkfst) **Facilities** Spa FTV ➰ Gym Aerobics studio Sauna Steam room 3 treatment rooms Wi-fi **Conf** Class 120 Board 45 Thtr 250 Del from £139 to £190* **Services** Lift **Parking** 170 **Notes** LB ⊗ Civ Wed 180

See advert on page 474

Ramada Birmingham, Sutton Coldfield

 RAMADA
HOTEL & RESORT

★★★ 73% HOTEL

☎ 0121 351 3111 📠 0844 815 9022
Penns Ln, Walmley B76 1LH
e-mail: sales.birmingham@ramadajarvis.co.uk
web: www.ramadajarvis.co.uk
dir: A5127 towards Sutton Coldfield for 2m, through lights, 4th right into Penns Lane. Hotel 1m on right follow brown tourist signs

Conveniently located for both M42 and M6 this large hotel is set in private grounds overlooking a lake. Bedrooms are comfortably appointed for both business and leisure guests. Public areas include the Club Restaurant and bar, a leisure club and extensive conference facilities.

Rooms 170 (13 annexe) (20 fmly) (20 GF) (7 smoking) **Facilities** Spa ➰ supervised Fishing Gym Squash Hairdressing salon Xmas New Year Wi-fi **Conf** Class 200 Board 40 Thtr 500 **Services** Lift **Parking** 500 **Notes** Civ Wed 150

Innkeeper's Lodge Birmingham Sheldon (NEC)

BUDGET HOTEL

☎ 0845 112 6064 📠 0845 112 6239
2225 Coventry Rd, Sheldon B26 3EH
web: www.innkeeperslodge.com/birminghamsouth
dir: M42 junct 6/A45 towards Birmingham for 2m. Lodge on left. (Less than 3m from Birmingham International Airport)

Innkeeper's Lodge represents an exciting, high value concept within the budget hotel market. Comfortable bedrooms provide excellent facilities that include satellite TV and modem points. Options include family rooms; and for the corporate guest, cutting edge IT which includes Wi-fi access. A popular Carvery provides all-day food, including an extensive, complimentary continental breakfast. See also the Hotel Groups pages.

Rooms 85 (4 fmly) **Conf** Thtr 40

Innkeeper's Lodge Birmingham Sutton Coldfield

BUDGET HOTEL

☎ 0845 112 6065 📠 0845 112 6238
Chester Rd, Streetley B73 6SP
web: www.innkeeperslodge.com/birminghameast
dir: M6 junct 7 to A34 S'bound, left onto A4041. At 4th rdbt right onto A452 (Chester road), lodge less 1m on right

Innkeeper's Lodge represents an exciting, high value concept within the budget hotel market. Comfortable bedrooms provide excellent facilities that include satellite TV and modem points. Options include family rooms; and for the corporate guest, cutting edge IT which includes

Wi-fi access. A popular Carvery provides all-day food, including an extensive, complimentary continental breakfast. See also the Hotel Groups pages.

Rooms 66 (5 fmly) **Conf** Thtr 25

Travelodge Birmingham Sutton Coldfield

 Travelodge

BUDGET HOTEL

☎ 0871 984 6108 📠 0121 355 0017
Boldmere Rd B73 5UP
web: www.travelodge.co.uk
dir: M6 junct 6 S'bound or junct 5 N'bound. Lodge on A4142 between A452 & A453

Travelodge offers good quality, good value, budget accommodation. All offer family rooms sleeping up to four (two adults, two children) with en suite bathroom/shower-room, remote-control TV, tea- and coffee-making facilities and comfortable beds. Food options vary. Breakfast is at the on-site Bar Café restaurant (if available) or to take away. See also Hotel Groups pages.

Rooms 32 **S** fr £29; **D** fr £29

WALSALL — Map 10 SP09

Fairlawns Hotel & Spa

 CLASSIC
BRITISH HOTELS

★★★ 85% ◎◎ HOTEL

☎ 01922 455122 📠 01922 743148
178 Little Aston Rd WS9 0NU
e-mail: reception@fairlawns.co.uk
web: www.fairlawns.co.uk
dir: Off A452 towards Aldridge at x-roads with A454. Hotel 600yds on right

In a rural location with immaculate landscaped grounds, this constantly improving hotel offers a wide range of facilities and modern, comfortable bedrooms. Family rooms, one with a four-poster bed, and suites are also available. The Fairlawns Restaurant serves a wide range of award-winning seasonal dishes. The extensive comprehensively equipped leisure complex is mainly for adult use as there is restricted availability to young people.

Rooms 59 (8 fmly) (1 GF) (6 smoking) **S** £75-£165; **D** £85-£245 (incl. bkfst) **Facilities** Spa STV FTV ➰ supervised ♨ ♨ Gym Dance studio Beauty salon Bathing suite Floatation suite Sauna Aromatherapy room New Year Wi-fi **Conf** Class 40 Board 30 Thtr 80 Del from £145 to £195* **Services** Lift **Parking** 150 **Notes** LB RS 24 Dec-2 Jan Civ Wed 100

Menzies Baron's Court

MenziesHotels

★★★ 78% HOTEL

☎ 01543 452020 🖩 01543 361276
Walsall Rd, Walsall Wood WS9 9AH
e-mail: baronscourt@menzieshotels.co.uk
web: www.menzieshotels.co.uk
dir: M6 junct 7, A34 towards Walsall, then A4148 (ring road), at rdbt right onto A461 towards Lichfield, hotel 3m on right

This hotel prides itself on warm hospitality and is conveniently situated for business guests visiting this area. The lounge, bar and restaurant are modern and thoughtfully designed. Additional features include a small leisure complex and conference facilities.

Rooms 94 (7 fmly) (9 smoking) **S** £49-£99; **D** £49-£99*
Facilities STV ⌖ Gym Sauna Steam room Xmas New Year Wi-fi **Conf** Class 80 Board 40 Thtr 200 Del from £99 to £130* **Services** Lift **Parking** 120 **Notes** Civ Wed 200

Beverley

★★★ 67% HOTEL

☎ 01922 622999 🖩 01922 724187
58 Lichfield Rd WS4 2DJ
e-mail: info@beverley-hotel.com
dir: 1m N of Walsall town centre on A461 to Lichfield

This privately owned hotel dates back to 1880. Bedrooms are comfortably appointed, and the tastefully decorated public areas include a spacious bar combined with a conservatory. The restaurant offers guests a choice of carefully prepared, appetising dishes.

Rooms 40 (2 fmly) (4 GF) **Facilities** New Year **Conf** Class 30 Board 30 Thtr 60 **Parking** 68 **Notes** ⊗ RS 24 Dec-2 Jan Civ Wed 58

Express by Holiday Inn Walsall M6 Jct 10

BUDGET HOTEL

☎ 01922 705250 🖩 01922 705260
Tempus Ten, Tempus Dr WS2 8TJ
web: www.hiexpress.co.uk

A modern hotel ideal for families and business travellers. Fresh and uncomplicated, the spacious rooms include Sky TV, power shower and tea and coffee-making facilities. Continental buffet breakfast is included in the room rate; other meals may be taken at the nearby family pub or restaurant. See also the Hotel Groups pages.

Rooms 120

Travelodge Birmingham Walsall

BUDGET HOTEL

☎ 0871 984 6323 🖩 01922 631 734
Birmingham Rd WS5 3AB
web: www.travelodge.co.uk
dir: M6 junct 7, A34 N to Walsall. Lodge 2m on left

Travelodge offers good quality, good value, budget accommodation. All offer family rooms sleeping up to four (two adults, two children) with en suite bathroom/shower-room, remote-control TV, tea- and coffee-making facilities and comfortable beds. Food options vary. Breakfast is at the on-site Bar Café restaurant (if available) or to take away. See also Hotel Groups pages.

Rooms 96 (3 fmly) (4 GF) **S** fr £29; **D** fr £29 **Conf** Class 30 Board 30 Thtr 60

WOLVERHAMPTON · · · · · · · · · · · Map 10 SO99

See also **Pattingham (Staffordshire)**

Novotel Wolverhampton

★★★ 75% HOTEL

☎ 01902 871100 🖩 01902 870054
Union St WV1 3JN
e-mail: H1188@accor.com
web: www.novotel.com
dir: 6m from M6 junct 10. A454 to Wolverhampton. Hotel on main ring road

This large, modern, purpose-built hotel stands close to the town centre. It provides spacious, smartly presented and well-equipped bedrooms, all of which contain convertible bed settees for family occupancy. In addition to the open-plan lounge and bar area, there is an attractive brasserie-style restaurant, which overlooks an attractive patio garden.

Rooms 132 (9 fmly) (15 smoking) **S** £50-£130; **D** £50-£130* **Facilities** STV Wi-fi **Conf** Class 100 Board 80 Thtr 200 Del from £99 to £145* **Services** Lift **Parking** 120 **Notes** LB RS 23 Dec-4 Jan Civ Wed 200

Best Western Connaught

★★★ 72% HOTEL

☎ 01902 424433 🖩 01902 710353
Tettenhall Rd WV1 4SW
e-mail: info@theconnaughthotel.net
dir: A41 junct 3, 1st exit at rdbt. Follow signs for Tettenhall. In Tettenhall Rd, hotel on left

This hotel is located a short walk from the city centre and the railway station, with convenient access to the motorway networks. Bedrooms provide modern comfort with a contemporary decor. Wi-fi is available throughout the hotel. Swags Restaurant and Terrace Bar offer a traditional and European cuisine. There are seven air-conditioned conference and banqueting suites.

Rooms 90 (3 fmly) (3 GF) **Facilities** STV FTV Xmas New Year Wi-fi **Conf** Class 100 Board 60 Thtr 300 Del from £99 to £135* **Services** Lift **Parking** 120 **Notes** ⊗ Civ Wed 300

Holiday Inn Wolverhampton

★★★ 68% HOTEL

☎ 01902 390004 🖩 01902 714364
Dunstall Park WV6 0PE
e-mail: holidayinn@wolverhampton-racecourse.com
web: www.holidayinn.co.uk
dir: Off A449, 1.5m from city centre. Follow brown sign for Dunstall Park

Set within Wolverhampton Racecourse, Britain's first floodlit racecourse with afternoon and evening meetings throughout the year. This modern hotel provides a range of well-equipped bedrooms and an open-plan public area with bar, lounge and brasserie-style restaurant.

Rooms 54 (18 fmly) **Facilities** STV Wi-fi **Services** Lift **Parking** 1500

Travelodge Wolverhampton Central

BUDGET HOTEL

☎ 0871 984 6221 🖩 0190 242 6130
Bankfield House, Waterloo Rd WV1 4QL
dir: M6 junct 10, A454, at 3rd rdbt 2nd exit into Ring Rd Saint Georges, follow A4150, right into Ring Rd Saint Johns. At rdbt 2nd exit into Ring Rd Saint Andrews

Travelodge offers good quality, good value, budget accommodation. All offer family rooms sleeping up to four (two adults, two children) with en suite bathroom/shower-room, remote-control TV, tea- and coffee-making facilities and comfortable beds. Food options vary. Breakfast is at the on-site Bar Café restaurant (if available) or to take away. See also the Hotel Groups pages.

Rooms 99 **S** fr £29; **D** fr £29

WIGHT, ISLE OF

COWES · · · · · · · · · · · · · · · · · Map 5 SZ49

Best Western New Holmwood

★★★ 70% HOTEL

☎ 01983 292508 🖩 01983 295020
Queens Rd, Egypt Point PO31 8BW
e-mail: reception@newholmwoodhotel.co.uk
dir: from A3020 at Northwood Garage lights, left & follow to rdbt. 1st left then sharp right into Baring Rd, 4th left into Egypt Hill. At bottom turn right, hotel on right

Just by the Esplanade, this hotel has an enviable outlook. Bedrooms are comfortable and very well equipped, and the light and airy, glass-fronted restaurant looks out to sea and serves a range of interesting meals. The sun terrace is delightful in the summer and there is a small pool area.

Rooms 26 (1 fmly) (9 GF) **Facilities** STV ⌖ Xmas New Year Wi-fi **Conf** Class 60 Board 50 Thtr 120 **Parking** 20

See advert on page 484

FRESHWATER *continued*

FRESHWATER
Map 5 SZ38

Farringford

★★★ 76% @ HOTEL

☎ 01983 752500 📄 01983 756515
Bedbury Ln PO40 9PE
e-mail: enquiries@farringford.co.uk
web: www.farringford.co.uk
dir: A3054, left to Norton Green down Pixlie Hill. Left to Freshwater Bay. At bay turn right into Bedbury Lane, hotel on left

Upon seeing Farringford, Alfred Lord Tennyson is said to have remarked "we will go no further, this must be our home" and so it was for some forty years. Some 150 years later, the hotel provides bedrooms ranging in style and size, from large rooms in the main house to adjoining chalet-style rooms. The atmosphere is relaxed, and dinner features fresh local produce.

Farringford

Rooms 18 (4 annexe) (5 fmly) (4 GF) **Facilities** ₹ ♨ 9 ⚘
Putt green ♨ Beauty treatment room Bowling Green ♫
Conf Class 50 Board 50 Thtr 120 **Parking** 55
Notes Closed Nov-Mar Civ Wed 130

Travelodge Newport Isle of Wight

BUDGET HOTEL

☎ 0871 984 6348 📄 01983 532026
Lugley St PO30 5HE
e-mail: newportiow@travelodge.co.uk
dir: Enter Newport on A3020 (Medina Way), exit slip road signed Quay/Town Centre. At mini rdbt (Lidl) into Holyrood St. 2nd right into Lugley St. Lodge 100yds on left

Travelodge offers good quality, good value, budget accommodation. All offer family rooms sleeping up to four (two adults, two children) with en suite bathroom/shower-room, remote-control TV, tea- and coffee-making facilities and comfortable beds. Food options vary. Breakfast is at the on-site Bar Café restaurant (if available) or to take away. See also the Hotel Groups pages.

Rooms 64 **S** fr £29; **D** fr £29

Map 5 SZ59

Lakeside Park

★★★★ 74% HOTEL

☎ 01983 882266 🗈 01983 883380
High St PO33 4LJ
e-mail: reception@lakesideparkhotel.com
web: www.lakesideparkhotel.com
dir: A3054 towards Newport. Hotel on left after crossing Wotton Bridge

This newly completed hotel has picturesque views of the tidal lake and surrounding countryside. Bedrooms are well appointed with modern amenities, stylish design with guest comfort in mind. Public areas feature a comfortable open-plan bar and lounge with dining options from the two restaurants showcase the best of island produce. Sizable conference and banqueting facilities are available whilst the leisure area includes an indoor pool and spa therapy.

Rooms 44 (2 fmly) (16 GF) **Facilities** Spa FTV🖎 Steam room Relaxation room Sauna Xmas New Year Wi-fi **Conf** Class 60 Board 40 Thtr 150 **Services** Lift Air con **Parking** 140 **Notes** ⊛ Civ Wed 120

Yelf's

★★★ 74% HOTEL

☎ 01983 564062 🗈 01983 563937
Union St PO33 2LG
e-mail: manager@yelfshotel.com
web: www.yelfshotel.com
dir: From Ryde Esplanade turn into Union Street. Hotel on right

This former coaching inn has smart public areas including a busy bar, a separate lounge and an attractive dining room. Bedrooms are comfortably furnished and well equipped; some are located in an adjoining wing and some in an annexe. A conservatory lounge bar and stylish terrace are ideal for relaxing.

Rooms 40 (9 annexe) (5 fmly) (3 GF) (6 smoking) **S** £79-£84; **D** £94-£99 (incl. bkfst) **Facilities** STV Spa & treatments available at nearby sister hotel Wi-fi **Conf** Class 30 Board 50 Thtr 100 **Services** Lift **Parking** 23 **Notes** LB Civ Wed 100

Appley Manor

★★ 71% HOTEL

☎ 01983 564777 🗈 01983 564704
Appley Rd PO33 1PH
e-mail: appleymanor@lineone.net
web: www.appley-manor.co.uk
dir: A3055 onto B3330. Hotel 0.25m on left

A Victorian manor house located only five minutes from the town and set in peaceful surroundings. The spacious bedrooms are well furnished and decorated. Dinner can be taken in the popular adjoining Manor Inn.

Rooms 12 (2 fmly) **Conf** Class 40 Board 30 Thtr 40 **Parking** 60 **Notes** ⊛

Ryde Castle

☎ 01983 563755 🗈 01983 566906
The Esplanade PO33 1JA
e-mail: 6506@greeneking.co.uk

Currently the rating for this establishment is not confirmed. This may be due to a change of ownership or because it has only recently joined the AA rating scheme. For further details please see the AA website: theAA.com

Rooms 18 **Conf** Class 80 Board 50 Thtr 200

Map 5 SZ58

Melville Hall Hotel & Utopia Spa

★★★ 79% HOTEL

☎ 01983 400500 & 406526 🗈 01983 407093
Melville St PO36 9DH
e-mail: enquiries@melvillehall.co.uk
dir: Exit A3055, hotel 30yds on left (5 minute walk from train station)

Situated in the quiet semi-rural outskirts of Sandown, a few minutes walk from the seafront, cliff walks and shops. There is a leisure suite, with both indoor and outdoor pool, and beauty treatment rooms are available. Bedrooms offer a good range of accessories and many have jacuzzi baths.

Rooms 30 (3 fmly) (4 GF) **Facilities** Spa STV🖎 🎿 Putt green Xmas New Year Wi-fi **Parking** 20 **Notes** LB ⊛

The Wight Montrene

★★ 72% HOTEL

☎ 01983 403722 🗈 01983 405553
11 Avenue Rd PO36 8BN
e-mail: enquiries@wighthotel.co.uk
web: www.wighthotel.co.uk
dir: 100yds after mini-rdbt between High St & Avenue Rd

A family hotel, set in secluded grounds, that is only a short walk from Sandown's beach and high street shops. Bedrooms provide comfort and are either on the ground or first floor. Guests can relax in the heated swimming pool and enjoy the spa facility; there's also evening entertainment in the bar. The dinner menu changes nightly, and a plentiful breakfast is served in the colourful dining room.

Rooms 41 (18 fmly) (21 GF) **S** £30-£48; **D** £60-£90 (incl. bkfst)* **Facilities** Spa🖎 Gym Spa, Steam room, Sauna, Solarium, Table tennis, Full size snooker table 🎵 Xmas New Year Wi-fi **Conf** Thtr 80 **Parking** 40

See advert on opposite page

Sandringham

★★ 71% HOTEL

☎ 01983 406655 🗈 01983 404395
Esplanade PO36 8AH
e-mail: info@sandringhamhotel.co.uk

With a prime seafront location and splendid views, this is one of the largest hotels on the island. Comfortable public areas include a spacious lounge and a heated indoor swimming pool and jacuzzi. Bedrooms vary in size and many sea-facing rooms have a balcony. Regular entertainment is provided in the ballroom.

Rooms 110 (39 fmly) (6 GF) **Facilities** 🖎 🎵 Xmas **Services** Lift **Parking** 82 **Notes** ⊛

SANDOWN continued

Bayshore

Leisureplex

★★ 69% HOTEL

☎ 01983 403154 📄 01983 406574
12-16 Pier St PO36 8JX
e-mail: bayshore.sandown@alfatravel.co.uk
dir: From Broadway into Melville St, signed to Tourist Information Office. Across High St, bear right opposite pier. Hotel on right

This large hotel is located on the seafront opposite the pier and offers extensive public rooms where live entertainment is provided in season. The bedrooms are well equipped and staff very friendly and helpful.

Rooms 80 (18 fmly) (2 GF) **Facilities** FTV ♫ Xmas New Year **Services** Lift **Notes** ⊗ Closed Dec-Feb (except Xmas) RS Mar & Nov

Riviera

★★ 68% HOTEL

☎ 01983 402518 📄 01983 406532
2 Royal St PO36 8LP
e-mail: enquiries@rivierahotel.org.uk
web: www.rivierahotel.org.uk
dir: Top of Sandown High St, turning past main Post Office

Guests return year after year to this friendly and welcoming family-run hotel. It is located near to the High Street and just a short stroll from the beach, pier and shops. Bedrooms, including several at ground floor level, are very well furnished and comfortably equipped. Enjoyable home-cooked meals are served in the spacious dining room.

Rooms 43 (6 fmly) (11 GF) **Facilities** ♫ Xmas New Year **Parking** 30

SEAVIEW Map 5 SZ69

The Seaview

★★★ 82% ◉◉ HOTEL

☎ 01983 612711 📄 01983 613729
High St PO34 5EX
e-mail: reception@seaviewhotel.co.uk
dir: From B3330 (Ryde-Seaview road), turn left via Puckpool along seafront

A relaxed and charming hotel in a quiet location just a short stroll from the seafront. The contemporary bedrooms, including the Seafront Modern rooms, are designer led in their fittings and furnishings - crisp white linen, intimate lighting, flat-screen TVs, DVD/CD players set the style. The same menu can be enjoyed in the traditional Victorian dining room or the Sunshine Conservatory restaurant.

Rooms 28 (20 fmly) (4 GF) **D** £120-£199 (incl. bkfst)*
Facilities FTV Beauty therapy New Year Wi-fi
Conf Class 50 Board 30 Del from £150 to £200*
Services Lift **Parking** 9 **Notes** ⊗ Closed 21-26 Dec

Priory Bay

★★★ 79% ◉ HOTEL

☎ 01983 613146 📄 01983 616539
Priory Dr PO34 5BU
e-mail: enquiries@priorybay.co.uk
web: www.priorybay.co.uk
dir: B3330 towards Seaview, through Nettlestone. (NB do not follow Seaview turn, but continue 0.5m to hotel sign)

This peacefully located hotel has much to offer and comes complete with its own stretch of private beach and 6-hole golf course. Bedrooms are a wonderful mix of styles, all of which provide much comfort and character. Public areas are equally impressive with a choice of enticing lounges to relax and unwind. The kitchen creates interesting and imaginative dishes, using the excellent island produce as much as possible.

Rooms 22 (4 annexe) (6 fmly) (2 GF) **S** £70-£225;
D £110-£270 (incl. bkfst)* **Facilities** ↘ ⌿ 6 ◉ ᛋ Private beach Xmas New Year Wi-fi **Conf** Class 60 Board 40 Thtr 80 Del from £110 to £195* **Parking** 100 **Notes** LB Civ Wed 100

SHANKLIN Map 5 SZ58

Luccombe Hall

★★★ 78% HOTEL

☎ 01983 869000 📄 01983 863082
8 Luccombe Rd PO37 6RL
e-mail: enquiries@luccombehall.co.uk
dir: Take A3055 to Shanklin, through old village then 1st left into Priory Rd, left into Popham Rd, 1st right into Luccombe Rd. Hotel on left

Appropriately described as 'the view with the hotel', this property was originally built in 1870 as a summer home for the Bishop of Portsmouth. Enjoying an impressive cliff-top location, the hotel benefits from wonderful sea views, delightful gardens and direct access to the beach. Well-equipped bedrooms are comfortably furnished and there is a range of leisure facilities.

Rooms 29 (15 fmly) (7 GF) **S** £40-£70; **D** £80-£190 (incl. bkfst)* **Facilities** STV ⌖ ↖ Putt green Gym Squash Games room Treatment room Sauna Xmas New Year Wi-fi **Parking** 20 **Notes** LB ⊗

Channel View

★★★ 77% HOTEL

☎ 01983 862309 📄 01983 868400
Hope Rd PO37 6EH
e-mail: enquiries@channelviewhotel.co.uk
web: www.channelviewhotel.co.uk
dir: Exit A3055 at Esplanade & Beach sign. Hotel 250mtrs on left

With an elevated cliff-top location overlooking Shanklin Bay, several rooms at this hotel enjoy pleasant views and all are very well decorated and furnished. The hotel is family run, and guests can enjoy efficient service, regular evening entertainment, a heated indoor swimming pool and holistic therapy.

Rooms 56 (15 fmly) **S** £32-£49; **D** £64-£98 (incl. bkfst)*
Facilities ⌖ Holistic therapies Aromatherapy ♫
Services Lift **Parking** 22 **Notes** LB Closed Jan-Feb

Cliff Hall

★★ 74% HOTEL

☎ 01983 862828
16 Crescent Rd PO37 6DJ
e-mail: cliffhallhotel@btconnect.com
web: www.cliffhallhotel.co.uk
dir: A3055/A3056 to Shanklin. Right at lake, down Lake
Hill, left at Clarendon Rd, hotel at top of hill

A privately owned hotel situated close to the beach lift
and town centre. The pleasantly decorated bedrooms are
generally quite spacious and have all the usual facilities;
many rooms also have stunning sea views. Public areas
include a lounge, bar, restaurant, coffee shop and a
superb terrace with an outdoor swimming pool.

Rooms 26 (16 fmly) (9 GF) **S** £36-£55; **D** £72-£110 (incl.
bkfst & dinner)* **Facilities** ⚡ Full sized snooker table
Xmas New Year **Parking** 30 **Notes** LB ⊗ Closed Jan/Feb

Malton House

★★ 65% HOTEL

☎ 01983 865007 ▤ 01983 865576
8 Park Rd PO37 6AY
e-mail: couvoussis@maltonhouse.freeserve.co.uk
web: www.maltonhouse.co.uk
dir: Up hill from Hope Rd lights then 3rd left

A well-kept Victorian hotel set in its own gardens in a
quiet area, conveniently located for cliff-top walks and
the public lift down to the promenade. The bedrooms are
comfortable and public areas include a small lounge, a
separate bar and a dining room where traditional
homemade meals are served.

Rooms 13 (3 fmly) (2 GF) **S** £34-£36; **D** £60-£64 (incl.
bkfst)* **Parking** 12 **Notes** LB ⊗ No children 3 yrs Closed
Nov-Jan

VENTNOR	Map 5 SZ57

The Royal Hotel

★★★★ 76% ⚘⚘ HOTEL

☎ 01983 852186 ▤ 01983 855395
Belgrave Rd PO38 1JJ
e-mail: enquiries@royalhoteliow.co.uk
web: www.royalhoteliow.co.uk
dir: A3055 into Ventnor follow one-way system, after
lights left into Belgrave Rd. Hotel on right

This smart hotel enjoys a central yet peaceful location in
its own gardens, complete with an outdoor pool.

Spacious, elegant public areas include a bright
conservatory, bar and lounge. Bedrooms, appointed to a
high standard, vary in size and style. Staff are friendly
and efficient, particularly in the smart restaurant, where
modern British cuisine is offered.

Rooms 54 (8 fmly) **S** £105-£138; **D** £170-£270 (incl.
bkfst)* **Facilities** ⚡ Xmas New Year Wi-fi **Conf** Class 40
Board 24 Thtr 100 Del from £110 to £200* **Services** Lift
Parking 50 **Notes** LB ⊗ Closed 1st 2 wks Jan
Civ Wed 150

Best Western Ventnor Towers

★★★ 73% HOTEL

☎ 01983 852277 ▤ 01983 855536
54 Madeira Rd PO38 1QT
e-mail: reservations@ventnortowers.com
web: www.ventnortowers.com
dir: From E, 1st left off A3055 just before pelican crossing

This mid-Victorian hotel, set in spacious grounds from
where a path leads down to the shore, is high above the
bay and enjoys splendid sea views. Many potted plants
and fresh flowers grace the day rooms, which include two
lounges and a spacious bar. Bedrooms include two four-
poster rooms and some that have their own balconies.

Rooms 25 (4 fmly) (6 GF) **Facilities** ⚡ ⚑ Putt green
Conf Class 60 Board 44 Thtr 100 **Parking** 20 **Notes** LB
Closed 24-26 Dec

Eversley

★★★ 70% HOTEL

☎ 01983 852244 & 852462 ▤ 01983 856534
Park Av PO38 1LB
e-mail: eversleyhotel@yahoo.co.uk
web: www.eversleyhotel.com
dir: on A3055 W of Ventnor, next to Ventnor Park

Located west of Ventnor, this hotel enjoys a quiet location
and has some rooms with garden and pool views. The
spacious restaurant is sometimes used for local
functions, and there is a bar, television room, lounge
area, a card room as well as a jacuzzi and gym. Bedrooms
are generally a good size.

Rooms 30 (8 fmly) (2 GF) **Facilities** ⚡ Gym Pool table
Xmas **Conf** Class 40 Board 20 **Parking** 23 **Notes** Closed
30 Nov-22 Dec & 2 Jan-8 Feb

Wellington

★★★ Ⓐ HOTEL

☎ 01983 856600 ▤ 01983 856611
Belgrave Rd PO38 1JH
e-mail: enquiries@thewellingtonhotel.net
web: www.thewellingtonhotel.net

Rooms 28 (5 fmly) (7 GF) (14 smoking) **S** £80-£95;
D £110-£135 (incl. bkfst)* **Facilities** STV Xmas New Year
Wi-fi **Conf** Class 28 Board 28 Thtr 28 **Parking** 10
Notes LB ⊗ Civ Wed 60

Burlington Hotel

★★ 69% HOTEL

☎ 01983 852113 ▤ 01983 857462
Bellevue Rd PO38 1DB
e-mail: info@burlingtonhotel.uk.com
dir: In one way system turn left at lights. Up hill, take 2nd
right & immediate right into Bellevue Rd. Hotel 100mtrs
on left.

Eight of the attractively decorated bedrooms at this
establishment benefit from balconies, and the three
ground floor rooms have French doors that lead onto the
garden. There is a cosy bar, a comfortable lounge and a
dining room where home-made bread rolls accompany
the five-course dinners. Service is friendly and attentive.

Rooms 24 (12 fmly) (3 GF) **Facilities** ⚡ Wi-fi **Parking** 20
Notes ⊗ No children 3yrs Closed Dec-Etr

INSPECTORS' CHOICE

The Hambrough
⚘⚘⚘ RESTAURANT WITH ROOMS

☎ 01983 856333 ▤ 01983 857260
Hambrough Rd PO38 1SQ
e-mail: info@thehambrough.com

A Victorian villa set on the hillside above Ventnor and
with memorable views out to sea. It has a modern,
stylish interior with well-equipped and comfortable
bedrooms. The team's passion for food is clearly
evident in the superb cuisine served in the minimalist
decor of the restaurant.

Rooms 7

YARMOUTH — Map 5 SZ38

INSPECTORS' CHOICE

George Hotel
★★★ ◉◉ HOTEL

☎ 01983 760331 🖨 01983 760425
Quay St PO41 0PE
e-mail: res@thegeorge.co.uk
dir: Between castle & pier

This delightful 17th-century hotel enjoys a wonderful location at the water's edge, adjacent to the castle and the quay. Public areas include a bright brasserie where organic and local produce are utilised, a cosy bar and an inviting lounge. Individually styled bedrooms, with many thoughtful extras, are beautifully appointed; some benefit from spacious balconies. The hotel's motor yacht is available for hire by guests.

Rooms 19 (1 GF) **S** £100-£162.50; **D** £190-£267.50 (incl. bkfst)* **Facilities** STV Sailing from Yarmouth Mountain biking Xmas New Year **Conf** Class 20 Board 20 Thtr 40 **Notes** ⊗ No children 10yrs

WILTSHIRE

AMESBURY — Map 5 SU14

Travelodge Amesbury Stonehenge

BUDGET HOTEL

☎ 0871 984 6218 🖨 01980 625273
Countess Services SP4 7AS
web: www.travelodge.co.uk
dir: At junct of A345 & A303 E'bound, 7m N of Salisbury

Travelodge offers good quality, good value, modern accommodation. Ideal for families, the spacious en suite bedrooms include remote-control TV, tea and coffee-making facilities and comfortable beds. Meals can be taken at the nearby family restaurant. See also the Hotel Groups pages.

Rooms 69 **S** fr £29; **D** fr £29

BRADFORD-ON-AVON — Map 4 ST86

Woolley Grange
★★★ 82% ◉◉ HOTEL

von Essen hotels
a private collection

☎ 01225 864705 🖨 01225 864059
Woolley Green BA15 1TX
e-mail: info@woolleygrangehotel.co.uk
web: www.woolleygrangehotel.co.uk
dir: A4 onto B3109. Bradford Leigh, left at x-roads, hotel 0.5m on right at Woolley Green

This splendid Cotswold manor house is set in beautiful countryside. Children are made especially welcome; there is a trained nanny on duty in the nursery. Bedrooms and public areas are charmingly furnished and decorated in true country-house style, with many thoughtful touches and luxurious extras. The hotel offers a varied and well-balanced menu selection, including ingredients from the hotel's own garden. Von Essen Hotels - AA Hotel Group of the Year 2009-10.

Rooms 26 (14 annexe) (20 fmly) (3 GF) **S** £145-£200; **D** £200-£510 (incl. bkfst & dinner)* **Facilities** FTV ⟋ 🏊 Beauty treatments Football Table tennis Trampoline Boules Cricket Xmas New Year Wi-fi Child facilities **Conf** Class 12 Board 22 Thtr 35 Del from £155 to £165* **Parking** 40 **Notes** LB Civ Wed 30

Widbrook Grange
★★★ 74% ◉ COUNTRY HOUSE HOTEL

☎ 01225 864750 & 863173 🖨 01225 862890
Trowbridge Rd, Widbrook BA15 1UH
e-mail: stay@widbrookgrange.com
dir: 1m SE from Bradford on A363, hotel diagonally opposite Bradford Marina & Arabian Stud

This former farmhouse, built as a model farm in the 18th century, has been carefully renovated to provide modern comforts, suitable for both business and leisure guests. Some bedrooms are in the main house, but most are in adjacent converted buildings, and these rooms have their own courtyard entrance and many are located on the ground floor. The lounges offer a good level of comfort. The friendly staff provide a personal and relaxed service.

Rooms 20 (15 annexe) (6 fmly) (13 GF) **S** £95; **D** £125-£135 (incl. bkfst) **Facilities** ⊕ Gym Children's weekend play room New Year Wi-fi Child facilities **Conf** Class 35 Board 25 Thtr 50 **Parking** 50 **Notes** LB ⊗ Closed 24-30 Dec Civ Wed 50

Old Manor
★★ 69% HOTEL

☎ 01225 777393 🖨 01225 765443
Trowle Common BA14 9BL
e-mail: romanticbeds@oldmanorhotel.com
dir: On A363 between Bradford-on-Avon & Trowbridge

This hotel stands in its own grounds and has been developed from farm buildings that retain much character and charm, and is filled with antiques. Bedrooms are mostly located in annexes and are individually styled; some having four-poster beds. The lounge and restaurant are open-plan and the atmosphere is relaxed.

Rooms 19 (15 annexe) (4 fmly) (15 GF) **Facilities** Wi-fi **Conf** Class 40 Board 30 Thtr 70 **Parking** 60 **Notes** LB

CALNE — Map 4 ST97

Lansdowne
★★★ 66% HOTEL

☎ 01249 812488 🖨 01249 815323
The Strand SN11 0EH
e-mail: reservations@lansdownestrand.co.uk
dir: From Chippenham A4 signed Calne. Straight over at both rdbts, hotel in town centre

Situated in a picturesque market town, The Lansdowne was originally built in the 16th century as a coaching inn, and it still retains much of the charm and character of that era. Bedrooms are spacious and furnished in a traditional style. Guests can enjoy dinner in the pleasant bistro, in either of the bar areas, or choose from a varied room-service menu. An outdoor courtyard seating area is also available.

Rooms 26 (2 fmly) **S** £50-£60; **D** £70-£90 (incl. bkfst)* **Facilities** STV FTV Wi-fi **Conf** Class 60 Board 50 Thtr 60 Del from £95 to £110 **Parking** 15 **Notes** ⊗ RS 25 Dec

Bowood Hotel, Spa and Golf Resort

☎ 01249 822228 📠 01249 822218
Derry Hill SN11 9PQ
e-mail: resort@bowood.org
web: www.bowood.org
dir: M4 junct 17, 2.5m W of Calne off A4

Currently the rating for this establishment is not confirmed. This may be due to a change of ownership or because it has only recently joined the AA rating scheme. For further details please see the AA website: theAA.com

Rooms 43 (2 fmly) (10 GF) **S** £220-£390; **D** £220-£390 (incl. bkfst & dinner)* **Facilities** Spa FTV ⓈⓉ 𝑙 18 Putt green 🛳 Gym Adventure playground New Year Wi-fi **Conf** Class 140 Board 85 Thtr 240 **Services** Lift Air con **Parking** 200 **Notes** LB ⊗ Civ Wed 60

CASTLE COMBE Map 4 ST87

Manor House Hotel and Golf Club

★★★★ ⑳⑳⑳ COUNTRY HOUSE HOTEL

☎ 01249 782206 📠 01249 782159
SN14 7HR
e-mail: enquiries@manorhouse.co.uk
web: www.exclusivehotels.co.uk
dir: M4 junct 17 follow Chippenham signs onto A420 Bristol, then right onto B4039. Through village, right after bridge

This delightful hotel is situated in a secluded valley adjacent to a picturesque village, where there have been no new buildings for 300 years. There are 365 acres of grounds to enjoy, complete with an Italian garden and an 18-hole golf course. Bedrooms, some in the main house and some in a row of stone cottages, have been superbly furnished, and public rooms include a number of cosy lounges with roaring fires. Service is a pleasing blend of professionalism and friendliness. The award-winning food utilises top quality local produce. Exclusive Hotels - AA Small Hotel Group of the Year 2009-10.

Rooms 48 (26 annexe) (8 fmly) (12 GF) **S** £150-£600; **D** £180-£600 (incl. bkfst)* **Facilities** STV 𝑙 18 🛳 Putt green Fishing 🛳 Jogging track Hot air ballooning Xmas New Year Wi-fi **Conf** Class 70 Board 30 Thtr 100 Del from £200 to £360* **Parking** 100 **Notes** LB Civ Wed 110

CHIPPENHAM Map 4 ST97

Best Western Angel Hotel

★★★ 80% HOTEL

☎ 01249 652615 📠 01249 443210
Market Place SN15 3HD
e-mail: reception@angelhotelchippenham.co.uk
web: www.angelhotelchippenham.co.uk
dir: Follow tourist signs for Bowood House. Under railway arch, follow 'Borough Parade Parking' signs. Hotel next to car park

These impressive buildings combine to make a smart and comfortable hotel. The well-equipped bedrooms vary from those in the main house where character is the key, to the smart executive-style, courtyard rooms. The lounge and restaurant are bright and modern, and offer an imaginative carte and an all-day menu.

Rooms 50 (35 annexe) (3 fmly) (12 GF) **Facilities** STV FTV Ⓢ Gym Wi-fi **Conf** Class 50 Board 50 Thtr 100 **Parking** 50

Stanton Manor Hotel

★★★ 79% ⑳ HOTEL

☎ 01666 837552 & 0870 890 02880 📠 01666 837022
SN14 6DQ
e-mail: reception@stantonmanor.co.uk
web: www.stantonmanor.co.uk

(For full entry see Stanton St Quintin)

COLERNE Map 4 ST87

Lucknam Park

★★★★★ ⑳⑳⑳
COUNTRY HOUSE HOTEL

☎ 01225 742777 📠 01225 743536
SN14 8AZ
e-mail: reservations@lucknampark.co.uk
web: www.lucknampark.co.uk
dir: M4 junct 17, A350 towards Chippenham, then A420 towards Bristol for 3m. At Ford left to Colerne, 3m, right at x-rds, entrance on right

Guests on arrival at this Palladian mansion may well experience a sense of the theatrical as they drive along a magnificent mile-long avenue of beech and lime trees. Surrounded by 500 acres of parkland and beautiful gardens, this fine hotel offers a wealth of choices ranging from enjoying pampering treatments to taking vigorous exercise. Elegant bedrooms and suites are split between the main building and adjacent courtyard. Dining options range from the informal Pavilion Restaurant, to the formal, and very accomplished, main restaurant.

Rooms 41 (18 annexe) (16 GF) **S** £280-£950; **D** £280-£950* **Facilities** Spa STV FTV Ⓢ 🛳 🛳 Gym Cross country course Mountain bikes Equestrian centre Steam room Sauna 🎵 Xmas New Year Wi-fi Child facilities **Conf** Class 24 Board 24 Thtr 60 Del from £295* **Parking** 70 **Notes** LB ⊗ Civ Wed 110

See advert on page 403

Cricklade Hotel

★★★ 77% HOTEL

☎ 01793 750751 📄 01793 751767
Common Hill SN6 6HA
e-mail: reception@crickladehotel.co.uk
web: www.crickladehotel.co.uk
dir: Off A419 onto B4040. Turn left at clock tower. Right at rdbt. Hotel 0.5m up hill on left

A haven of peace and tranquillity with spectacular views, this hotel is set in over 30 acres of beautiful countryside. Bedrooms vary in size and style with a choice of rooms in the main building and courtyard rooms - all offer high levels of comfort and quality. Public areas include an elegant lounge, dining room and a Victorian-style conservatory that runs the full length of the building. Extensive leisure facilities include a 9-hole golf course, an indoor pool and a gym.

Rooms 46 (21 annexe) (1 fmly) (5 GF) **S** £90-£100; **D** £110-£130 (incl. bkfst)* **Facilities** STV FTV ③ ♨ 9 ♨ ⚘ Gym Aromatherapy Beautician New Year Wi-fi **Conf** Class 60 Board 30 Thtr 80 **Parking** 100 **Notes** LB ⊗ No children 14yrs Closed 25-26 Dec Civ Wed 120

Bear

★★★ 77% HOTEL

☎ 01380 722444 📄 01380 722450
Market Place SN10 1HS
e-mail: info@thebearhotel.net
web: www.thebearhotel.net
dir: In town centre, follow Market Place signs

Situated in the market place of this small Wiltshire town, this hotel has a strong local following. The bedrooms and bathrooms are appointed to a high standard, and include a 20-inch, flat-screen TVs and writing desks, but lots of the original charm still remains. The attractive lounge

includes a quiet area for enjoying afternoon tea. For dinner guests can choose either the very popular homemade pizza parlour or the Master Lambton Restaurant.

Rooms 25 (5 fmly) **S** £80-£85; **D** £105 (incl. bkfst)*
Facilities ♫ Wi-fi **Conf** Class 60 Board 60 Thtr 100
Services Lift **Parking** 14 **Notes** ⊗ Closed 25-26 Dec Civ Wed 100

Travelodge Devizes

BUDGET HOTEL

☎ 0871 984 6410
London Rd SN10 2HL
dir: Off A361, N of Devizes

Travelodge offers good quality, good value, budget accommodation. All offer family rooms sleeping up to four (two adults, two children) with en suite bathroom/shower-room, remote-control TV, tea- and coffee-making facilities and comfortable beds. Food options vary. Breakfast is at the on-site Bar Café restaurant (if available) or to take away. See also Hotel Groups pages.

Rooms 53 **S** fr £29; **D** fr £29

Jesmonds of Highworth

◉◉ RESTAURANT WITH ROOMS

☎ 01793 762364 📄 01793 861201
Jesmond House SN6 7HJ
e-mail: info@jesmondsofhighworth.com
web: www.jesmondsofhighworth.com
dir: A419 onto B4019 to Highworth, left at lights, establishment on left

Jesmonds offers high quality bedrooms and bathrooms in addition to a contemporary restaurant providing memorable cuisine. The young team of staff offer an effortless mix of professional service delivered in a relaxed and welcoming manner. In addition to a comfortable bar and separate lounge, guests are encouraged to enjoy the pleasant Zen-inspired rear garden. Head Chef William Guthrie and his team skilfully utilise high quality produce in an interesting combination of textures and flavours.

Rooms 10 (2 fmly)

Bath Arms at Longleat

★★★ 75% ◉ HOTEL

☎ 01985 844308 & 07770 268359 📄 01985 845187
Longleat Estate BA12 7LY
e-mail: sara@batharms.co.uk
web: www.batharms.co.uk
dir: A36 Warminster. At Cotley Hill rdbt 2nd exit (Longleat), Cleyhill rdbt 1st exit. Through Hitchcombe Bottom, right at x-rds. Hotel at the Green

Set in a quintessential English village, The Bath Arms is a stylish and quirky boutique hotel in the heart of the Longleat Estate. The bedrooms are individual in their striking designs and some have a touch of appealing eccentricity about them. Good British cuisine, either home-grown, or sourced locally, is on offer. Guests can relax at The Hip Bath, a holistic treatment room using 100% organic products.

Rooms 15 (6 annexe) (4 fmly) (6 GF) **S** £70-£169.50; **D** £80-£209 (incl. bkfst)* **Facilities** FTV Treatment room Xmas New Year Wi-fi **Conf** Class 22 Board 22 Thtr 40 Del from £135.50 to £172.50* **Parking** 10 **Notes** ⊗

Travelodge Chippenham Leigh Delamere

BUDGET HOTEL

☎ 0871 984 6264 📄 01666 837112
SN14 6LB
web: www.travelodge.co.uk
dir: M4, between juncts 17 & 18

Travelodge offers good quality, good value, budget accommodation. All offer family rooms sleeping up to four (two adults, two children) with en suite bathroom/shower-room, remote-control TV, tea- and coffee-making facilities and comfortable beds. Food options vary. Breakfast is at the on-site Bar Café restaurant (if available) or to take away. See also Hotel Groups pages.

Rooms 70 **S** fr £29; **D** fr £29

Travelodge Chippenham Leigh Delamere M4 Westbound

BUDGET HOTEL

☎ 0871 984 6227 📄 01666 838529
Service Area SN14 6LB
web: www.travelodge.co.uk
dir: Between juncts 17 & 18 of M4

Rooms 31 **S** fr £29; **D** fr £29

MALMESBURY
Map 4 ST98

INSPECTORS' CHOICE

Whatley Manor
★★★★★ ◎◎◎◎ HOTEL

☎ 01666 822888 ▤ 01666 826120
Easton Grey SN16 0RB
e-mail: reservations@whatleymanor.com
web: www.whatleymanor.com
dir: M4 junct 17, follow signs to Malmesbury, continue over 2 rdbts. Follow B4040 & signs for Sherston, hotel 2m on left

Sitting in 12 acres of beautiful countryside, this impressive country house provides the most luxurious surroundings. Spacious bedrooms, most with views over the attractive gardens, are individually decorated with splendid features. Several eating options are available: Le Mazot, a Swiss-style brasserie, The Dining Room that serves classical French cuisine with a contemporary twist, plus the Kitchen Garden Terrace for alfresco breakfasts, lunches and dinners. The old Loggia Barn is ideal for wedding ceremonies, and the Aquarius Spa is magnificent.

Rooms 23 (4 GF) **D** £295-£855 (incl. bkfst)*
Facilities Spa STV Fishing Gym Cinema Hydro pool Xmas New Year Wi-fi **Conf** Class 20 Board 25 Thtr 60 Del from £265 to £335* **Services** Lift **Parking** 100 **Notes** LB No children 12yrs Civ Wed 120

Old Bell
★★★ 80% ◎◎ HOTEL

☎ 01666 822344 ▤ 01666 825145
Abbey Row SN16 0BW
e-mail: info@oldbellhotel.com
web: www.oldbellhotel.com
dir: M4 junct 17, follow A429 north. Left at 1st rdbt. Left at T-junct. Hotel next to Abbey

Dating back to 1220, the Old Bell is reputed to be the oldest purpose-built hotel in England. Bedrooms vary in size and style; those in the main house tend to be more spacious and are traditionally furnished with antiques, while the newer bedrooms of the coach house have a contemporary feel. Guests have a choice of comfortable sitting areas and dining options including the main restaurant where the award-winning cuisine is based on high quality ingredients.

Rooms 33 (15 annexe) (7 GF) **S** £90; **D** £110-£235 (incl. bkfst)* **Facilities** FTV Xmas New Year Wi-fi **Conf** Class 32 Board 32 Thtr 60 **Parking** 33 **Notes** LB Civ Wed 80

Best Western Mayfield House
★★★ 72% ◎ HOTEL

☎ 01666 577409 ▤ 01666 577977
Crudwell SN16 9EW
e-mail: reception@mayfieldhousehotel.co.uk
web: www.mayfieldhousehotel.co.uk
dir: M4 junct 17, A429 to Cirencester. 3m N of Malmesbury on left in Crudwell

This popular hotel is in an ideal location for exploring many of the nearby attractions in Wiltshire and The Cotswolds. Bedrooms come in a range of shapes and sizes, and include some on the ground-floor in a cottage adjacent to the main hotel. In addition to outdoor seating, guests can relax with a drink in the comfortable lounge area where orders are taken for the carefully prepared dinner to follow.

Best Western Mayfield House

Rooms 28 (8 annexe) (4 fmly) (8 GF) **S** £50-£75; **D** £80-£138 (incl. bkfst)* **Facilities** FTV Xmas New Year Wi-fi **Conf** Class 30 Board 25 Thtr 40 Del from £99 to £135* **Parking** 50 **Notes** LB

MARLBOROUGH
Map 5 SU16

Ivy House
★★★ 64% HOTEL

☎ 01672 515333 ▤ 01672 515338
43 High St SN8 1HJ
e-mail: enquiries@ivyhousemarlborough.co.uk
web: www.ivyhousemarlborough.co.uk
dir: In town centre

Situated in the delightful high street of this historic market town, this Grade II listed Georgian hotel is run by friendly and attentive staff. The bedrooms are spacious, comfortable and very well equipped. Cuisine in Scott's Restaurant is enjoyable and features fresh local produce. In warmer months guests can dine alfresco in the pleasant courtyard.

Rooms 28 (3 fmly) (8 GF) **Facilities** Wi-fi **Conf** Class 30 Board 30 Thtr 60 **Parking** 35 **Notes** ⊗

See advert on this page

MARLBOROUGH *continued*

The Castle & Ball

★★★ Ⓐ HOTEL

☎ 01672 515201 🖷 01672 515895
High St SN8 1LZ
web: www.oldenglish.co.uk
dir: A338 and A4 to Marlborough

Rooms 35 (1 annexe) (5 fmly) **Facilities** Xmas New Year Wi-fi **Conf** Class 30 Board 30 Thtr 45 **Parking** 48

MELKSHAM   Map 4 ST96

Beechfield House

★★★ 79% ⏺ HOTEL

☎ 01225 703700 🖷 01225 790118
Beanacre SN12 7PU
e-mail: reception@beechfieldhouse.co.uk
web: www.beechfieldhouse.co.uk
dir: 1m N via A350

This is a charming, privately owned hotel set within eight acres of beautiful grounds that has its own arboretum. Bedrooms are individual styled and include four-poster rooms, and ground floor rooms in the coach house. Relaxing public areas are comfortably furnished and there is a beauty salon with a range of pampering treatments available. At dinner there is a very good selection of carefully prepared dishes with an emphasis on seasonal and local produce.

Rooms 24 (6 fmly) (4 GF) **S** fr £95; **D** fr £125 (incl. bkfst) **Facilities** FTV ⚲ 🏓 Table tennis Beauty treatment room Xmas Wi-fi **Conf** Class 60 Board 45 Thtr 100 Del from £132.50 **Parking** 50 **Notes** LB Civ Wed 70

Shaw Country

★★ 76% SMALL HOTEL

☎ 01225 702836 & 790321 🖷 01225 790275
Bath Rd, Shaw SN12 8EF
e-mail: info@shawcountryhotel.com
web: www.shawcountryhotel.com
dir: 1m from Melksham, 9m from Bath on A365

Located within easy reach of both Bath and the M4, this relaxed and friendly hotel sits in its own gardens and

includes a patio area ideal for enjoying a drink during the summer months. The house boasts some very well-appointed bedrooms, a comfortable lounge and bar, and the Mulberry Restaurant, where a wide selection of innovative dishes make up both carte and set menus. A spacious function room is a useful addition.

Rooms 13 (2 fmly) **S** £61-£80; **D** £85-£105 (incl. bkfst) **Facilities** FTV Wi-fi **Conf** Class 40 Board 20 Thtr 60 **Parking** 30 **Notes** LB RS 26-27 Dec & 1 Jan Civ Wed 90

PURTON   Map 5 SU08

The Pear Tree at Purton

★★★ 80% ⏺⏺ HOTEL

☎ 01793 772100 🖷 01793 772369
Church End SN5 4ED
e-mail: stay@peartreepurton.co.uk
dir: M4 junct 16 follow signs to Purton, at Spar shop turn right. Hotel 0.25m on left

A charming 15th-century, former vicarage set amidst extensive landscaped gardens in a peaceful location in the Vale of the White Horse and near the Saxon village of Purton. The resident proprietors and staff provide efficient, dedicated service and friendly hospitality. The spacious bedrooms are individually decorated and have a good range of thoughtful extras such as fresh fruit, sherry and shortbread. Top quality fresh ingredients feature on the award-winning menus.

Rooms 17 (2 fmly) (6 GF) **S** £115-£160; **D** £115-£160 (incl. bkfst) **Facilities** STV 🎲 Outdoor giant chess Vineyard Wi-fi **Conf** Class 30 Board 30 Thtr 70 Del from £165 to £178 **Parking** 60 **Notes** LB Closed 26-30 Dec Civ Wed 50

ROWDE   Map 4 ST96

The George & Dragon

⏺⏺ RESTAURANT WITH ROOMS

☎ 01380 723053
High St SN10 2PN
e-mail: thegandd@tiscali.co.uk
dir: 1.5m from Devizes on A350 towards Chippenham

This is a traditional inn dating back to the 14th century when it was a meeting house. Exposed beams, wooden floors, antique rugs and open fires create a warm atmosphere in the bar and restaurant. Bedrooms and bathrooms are very well decorated and equipped with some welcome extras. Dining in the bar or restaurant should not be missed, as local produce and fresh fish deliveries from Cornwall are offered from the daily-changing blackboard menu.

Rooms 3 (1 fmly)

SALISBURY   Map 5 SU12

Legacy Rose & Crown

★★★★ 71% HOTEL

☎ 0870 832 9946 🖷 0870 832 9947
Harnham Rd, Harnham SP2 8JQ
e-mail: res-roseandcrown@legacy-hotels.co.uk
web: www.legacy-hotels.co.uk
dir: A338 towards Harnham, then Harnham Rd, hotel on right

This 13th-century coaching inn, situated beside the river, enjoys picturesque views of Salisbury Cathedral, especially from the Pavilion Restaurant which provides a good range of dishes. Many original features are still retained in the heavy oak-beamed bars. All bedrooms and bathrooms are beautifully appointed. Excellent conference and banqueting facilities are available.

Rooms 28 (5 fmly) (2 GF) **Facilities** STV FTV Fishing Xmas New Year Wi-fi **Conf** Class 30 Board 26 Thtr 90 **Parking** 60 **Notes** LB ⊗ Civ Wed 110

Mercure White Hart

★★★ 82% HOTEL

☎ 0870 400 8125 & 01722 327476 🖷 01722 412761
St John St SP1 2SD
e-mail: H6616@accor.com
web: www.mercure-uk.com
dir: M3 junct 7/8, A303 to A343 for Salisbury then A30. Follow city centre signs on ring road, into Exeter St, leading into St. John St. Car park at rear

There has been a hotel on this site since the 16th century. Bedrooms vary - some are contemporary and some are decorated in more traditional style, but all boast a comprehensive range of facilities. The bar and lounge areas are popular with guests and locals alike for morning coffees and afternoon teas.

Rooms 68 (6 fmly) (3 smoking) **Facilities** STV Xmas New Year Wi-fi **Conf** Class 40 Board 40 Thtr 100 **Parking** 60 **Notes** Civ Wed 100

Milford Hall

★★★ 81% ⏺ HOTEL

☎ 01722 417411 & 424116 🖷 01722 419444
206 Castle St SP1 3TE
e-mail: reception@milfordhallhotel.com
web: www.milfordhallhotel.com
dir: Near junct of Castle Street, A36 (ring road) & A345 (Amesbury road)

This hotel offers high standards of accommodation and is within easy walking distance of the city centre. There are two categories of bedroom - traditional rooms in the original Georgian house, and spacious, modern rooms in a purpose-built extension; all are extremely well equipped. Meals are served in the smart brasserie where a varied choice of dishes is provided.

Rooms 35 (1 fmly) (20 GF) **S** £90-£135; **D** £110-£175*
Facilities STV Free facilities at local health clubs New Year Wi-fi **Conf** Class 90 Board 60 Thtr 160 **Parking** 60
Notes LB ⊗ Civ Wed 120

Holiday Inn Salisbury - Stonehenge

★★★ 81% HOTEL

☎ 0845 241 3535 🖷 0845 241 3536
Midsummer Place, Solstice Park SP4 7SQ
e-mail: reservations@hisalisbury-stonehenge.co.uk
web: www.holidayinn.co.uk
dir: Exit A303 follow signs into Solstice Park. Hotel clearly visible from A303, next to service area

This hotel of striking modern design is located on the A303 very close to Stonehenge. All rooms have been appointed to the highest standards with unique headboards, air conditioning and broadband connection included in the generous amenities. Fluffy towels and powerful showers are provided in the modern bathrooms. The Solstice Bar and Grill is open from 7am-11pm offering a range of delicious snacks and meals.

Rooms 103 (1 fmly) (8 GF) **Facilities** FTV Wi-fi
Conf Class 12 Board 16 Thtr 20 **Del** from £130 to £180*
Services Lift Air con **Notes** ⊗

Best Western Red Lion

★★★ 77% ⊛ HOTEL

☎ 01722 323334 🖷 01722 325756
Milford St SP1 2AN
e-mail: reception@the-redlion.co.uk
web: www.the-redlion.co.uk
dir: in city centre close to Guildhall Square

This 750-year-old hotel is full of character, with individually designed bedrooms that combine contemporary comforts with historic features; one room has a medieval fireplace dating back to 1220. The distinctive public areas include a bar, lounge and the elegant Vine Restaurant that serves an interesting mix of modern and traditional dishes.

Rooms 51 (1 fmly) **Facilities** Xmas New Year Wi-fi
Conf Class 50 Board 40 Thtr 100 **Services** Lift **Notes** LB
⊗ Civ Wed 80

Grasmere House Hotel

★★★ 68% HOTEL

☎ 01722 338388 🖷 01722 333710
Harnham Rd SP2 8JN
e-mail: info@grasmerehotel.com
web: www.grasmerehotel.com
dir: On A3094 on S side of Salisbury next to All Saints Church in Harnham

This popular hotel, dating from 1896, has gardens that overlook the water meadows and the cathedral. The attractive bedrooms vary in size, some offer excellent quality and comfort, and some rooms are specially equipped for less mobile guests. In summer there is the option of dining on the pleasant outdoor terrace.

Rooms 38 (31 annexe) (16 fmly) (9 GF)
S £82.50-£125.50; **D** £110.50-£165.50 (incl. bkfst)
Facilities STV FTV Fishing ⚓ Xmas New Year Wi-fi
Conf Class 45 Board 45 Thtr 110 **Del** from £132.50 to £165.50 **Parking** 64 **Notes** LB Civ Wed 120

STANTON ST QUINTIN Map 4 ST97

Stanton Manor Hotel

★★★ 79% ⊛ HOTEL

☎ 01666 837552 & 0870 890 02880 🖷 01666 837022
SN14 6DQ
e-mail: reception@stantonmanor.co.uk
web: www.stantonmanor.co.uk
dir: M4 junct 17 onto A429 Malmesbury/Cirencester, within 200yds turn 1st left signed Stanton St Quintin, entrance to hotel on left just after church

Set in five acres of lovely gardens that includes a short golf course, this charming manor house, mentioned in the Domesday Book, has easy access to the M4. Public areas are a delight offering both character and comfort. The restaurant offers a short carte of imaginative dishes and an interesting wine selection.

Rooms 23 (4 fmly) (7 GF) **S** £115-£185; **D** £145-£215 (incl. bkfst)* **Facilities** ↕ 9 Putt green ⚓ Xmas New Year Wi-fi Child facilities **Conf** Class 40 Board 32 Thtr 80 **Del** from £145 to £195* **Parking** 60 **Notes** LB Civ Wed 120

SWINDON Map 5 SU18
See also **Wootton Bassett**

Swindon Marriott Hotel

★★★★ 76% HOTEL

☎ 01793 512121 🖷 01723 513114
Pipers Way SN3 1SH
e-mail: mhrs.swidt.frontdesk@marriotthotels.com
web: www.swindonmarriott.co.uk
dir: M4 junct 15, follow A419, then A4259 to Coate rdbt & B4006 signed 'Old Town'

With convenient access to the motorway, this hotel is a good venue for meetings, and an ideal base from which to explore Wiltshire and the Cotswolds. The hotel offers a good range of public rooms, including a well-equipped leisure centre, Chats café bar and the informal, brasserie-style Mediterrano restaurant.

Rooms 156 (42 fmly) **Facilities** Spa ⚐ ⚒ Gym Aerobics studio Hairdresser Health & beauty salon Sauna Spa bath Steam room Wi-fi **Conf** Class 100 Board 40 Thtr 280 **Services** Lift Air con **Parking** 300 **Notes** ⊗ Civ Wed 280

Best Western Premier Blunsdon House

★★★★ 74% HOTEL

☎ 01793 721701 🖷 01793 721056
Blunsdon SN26 7AS
e-mail: info@blunsdonhouse.co.uk
web: www.blunsdonhouse.co.uk
dir: 200yds off A419

Located just to the north of Swindon, Blunsdon House is set in 30 acres of well-kept grounds, and offers extensive leisure facilities and spacious day rooms. The hotel has a choice of eating and drinking options in three bars and two restaurant; the lively and informal Christopher's, and Nichols for fine dining. Bedrooms are comfortably furnished, and include family rooms with bunk beds and the contemporary spacious Pavilion rooms.

Rooms 116 (15 fmly) (27 GF) **S** £79-£144; **D** £84-£149 (incl. bkfst) **Facilities** Spa STV FTV ⚐ ↕ 9 ⚒ Putt green Gym Squash Beauty therapy Woodland walk Xmas New Year Wi-fi Child facilities **Conf** Class 200 Board 55 Thtr 300 **Del** from £125 to £174 **Services** Lift **Parking** 300 **Notes** LB ⊗ Civ Wed 200

SWINDON *continued*

Menzies Swindon

MenziesHotels

★★★★ 72% ⊛ HOTEL

☎ 01793 528282 📄 01793 541283
Fleming Way SN1 1TN
e-mail: swindon@menzieshotels.co.uk
web: www.menzieshotels.co.uk
dir: M4 junct 15/16, follow town centre signs

This modern hotel is conveniently located in the centre of the town with the added advantage of nearby parking. The bedrooms and bathrooms are well equipped with plenty of useful extras. Dining areas include the popular Havanah bar and award-winning cuisine in the brasserie where an exciting selection of dishes is provided. There are also various conference and event facilities available.

Rooms 95 (2 fmly) **S** £60-£140; **D** £60-£140*
Facilities STV Xmas New Year Wi-fi **Conf** Class 80
Board 60 Thtr 200 Del from £99 to £145* **Services** Lift
Notes ⊗ Civ Wed 200

The Pear Tree at Purton

★★★ 80% ⊛⊛ HOTEL

☎ 01793 772100 📄 01793 772369
Church End SN5 4ED
e-mail: stay@peartreepurton.co.uk

(For full entry see Purton)

Cricklade Hotel

★★★ 77% HOTEL

☎ 01793 750751 📄 01793 751767
Common Hill SN6 6HA
e-mail: reception@crickladehotel.co.uk
web: www.crickladehotel.co.uk

(For full entry see Cricklade)

Chiseldon House

★★★ 75% ⊛⊛ HOTEL

☎ 01793 741010 & 07770 853883 📄 01793 741059
New Rd, Chiseldon SN4 0NE
e-mail: info@chiseldonhousehotel.co.uk
web: www.chiseldonhousehotel.co.uk
dir: M4 junct 15/A346 signed Marlborough. After 0.5m turn right onto B4500 for 0.25m, hotel on right

Conveniently located for the M4, Chiseldon House offers a quiet location and a relaxed ambience. Bedrooms include a number of larger rooms but all styles are comfortably furnished. Guests are welcome to enjoy the pleasant garden with outdoor seating. A selection of carefully prepared dishes utilising high quality produce is available in the comfortable restaurant.

Rooms 21 (8 fmly) **S** £60-£90; **D** £80-£110 (incl. bkfst)
Facilities STV Xmas New Year Wi-fi **Conf** Class 60
Board 25 Thtr 35 **Parking** 80 **Notes** LB ⊗ Civ Wed 120

Stanton House

★★★ 75% HOTEL

☎ 0870 084 1388 📄 01793 861857
The Avenue, Stanton Fitzwarren SN6 7SD
e-mail: reception@stantonhouse.co.uk
dir: off A419 onto A361 towards Highworth, then turn left towards Stanton Fitzwarren about 600yds past business park, hotel on left

Extensive grounds and superb gardens surround this Cotswold-stone manor house. Smart, well-maintained bedrooms have been equipped with modern comforts. Public areas include a games room, lounge, bar, conference facilities and an informal restaurant specialising in English and Japanese cuisine; the Mt Fuji Restaurant serves authentic Japanese food in Japanese surroundings. The friendly, multi-lingual staff create a relaxing atmosphere for their guests.

Rooms 82 (31 GF) (10 smoking) **Facilities** STV Xmas New
Year Wi-fi **Conf** Class 70 Board 40 Thtr 110
Del from £105* **Services** Lift **Parking** 110 **Notes** ⊗
Civ Wed 110

Holiday Inn Swindon

★★★ 74% HOTEL

☎ 01793 817000 & 0874 400 9079 📄 01793 512887
Marlborough Rd SN3 6AQ
e-mail: swindon@ihg.com
web: www.holidayinn.co.uk
dir: M4 junct 15, A419 towards Swindon. Take A4259 for 1m. Hotel on right behind Sun Inn

With convenient access to both the M4 and Swindon's centre, this hotel provides an ideal base for business and leisure guests. Bedrooms are well decorated and provide a good range of useful extras. Guests can enjoy the facilities of The Spirit Health and Fitness Club and then relax in the comfortable bar. A good selection of dishes is available whether by way of room service, lounge snacks or the welcoming, informal restaurant.

Rooms 99 (25 fmly) (48 GF) (9 smoking) **S** £69-£121;
D £90-£146* **Facilities** STV FTV ⊗ supervised Gym Wi-fi
Conf Class 30 Board 30 Thtr 60 Del from £125 to £145
Services Air con **Parking** 120 **Notes** LB ⊗ Civ Wed 40

Marsh Farm

★★★ 73% HOTEL

☎ 01793 848044 & 842800 📄 01793 851528
Coped Hall SN4 8ER
e-mail: info@marshfarmhotel.co.uk
web: www.marshfarmhotel.co.uk
dir: M4 junct 16 onto A3102, straight on at 1st rdbt, right at 2nd rdbt. Hotel 200yds on left

The well-appointed bedrooms at this hotel are situated in annexes around the original farmhouse, which is set in its own grounds less than two miles from the M4. An extensive range of dishes is offered in The Glasshouse Restaurant, a light and airy conservatory.

Rooms 50 (39 annexe) (1 fmly) (16 GF) **S** £63-£105;
D £73-£135 (incl. bkfst)* **Facilities** STV Putt green Use of nearby leisure centre New Year Wi-fi **Conf** Class 60
Board 50 Thtr 120 Del from £135 to £155* **Parking** 120
Notes LB ⊗ Closed 26-30 Dec RS 25 Dec Civ Wed 100

Liddington

★★★ 71% HOTEL

☎ 01793 791000 📄 01793 791502
Foxhill SN4 0DZ
e-mail: enq@liddingtonhotel.co.uk
dir: A419 Swindon. Take slip road signed Swindon & Aldbourne (B4192). At rdbt 4th exit, past Liddington, over M4, next left signed Baydon. 0.5m pass back over M4, hotel on left

The Liddington is peacefully located yet is within easy reach of Swindon and the M4. Set in its own grounds, the hotel is very popular for business guests and has a wide range of conference rooms and facilities. The vast majority of bedrooms are for single use. The range of dining options includes a lounge bar area and a large restaurant.

Rooms 198 (64 GF) **Facilities** STV ⊋ Putt green ⊌ Gym
Wi-fi **Conf** Class 22 Board 80 Thtr 320 **Services** Lift
Parking 320 **Notes** ⊗ Closed 23 Dec-4 Jan

Campanile Swindon

Campanile

BUDGET HOTEL

☎ 01793 514777 📠 01793 514570
Delta Business Park, Great Western Way SN5 7XG
e-mail: swindon@campanile.com
web: www.campanile-swindon.co.uk
dir: M4 junction 16, A3102 towards Swindon. After 2nd
rdbt, 2nd exit onto Welton Rd (Delta Business Park), 1st
left

This modern building offers accommodation in smart,
well-equipped bedrooms, all with en suite bathrooms.
Refreshments may be taken at the informal bistro. See
also the Hotel Groups pages.

Rooms 120 (6 fmly) (22 GF) **S** £46.95-£120;
D £46.95-£120* **Conf** Class 40 Board 40 Thtr 70
Del from £100*

Express by Holiday Inn Swindon City Centre

BUDGET HOTEL

☎ 0870 444 3758 📠 0870 444 3759
Bridge St SN1 5BT
e-mail: info@exhiswindon.co.uk
web: www.hiexpress.com/exhiswindon

A modern hotel ideal for families and business travellers.
Fresh and uncomplicated, the spacious rooms include Sky
TV, power shower and tea and coffee-making facilities.
Continental buffet breakfast is included in the room rate;
other meals may be taken at the nearby family pub or
restaurant. See also the Hotel Groups pages.

Rooms 134 **Conf** Class 30 Board 24 Thtr 50

Express by Holiday Inn Swindon West, M4 Jct 16

BUDGET HOTEL

☎ 01793 818800 📠 01793 818888
Frankland Rd, Blagrove SN5 8UD
e-mail: swindon@expressholidayinn.co.uk
web: www.hiexpress.com/swindonwest
dir: M4 junct 16, follow signs for town centre (A3102),1st
left after rdbt

Rooms 121 (85 fmly) (10 GF) (10 smoking) **Conf** Class 30
Board 27 Thtr 56

Travelodge Swindon Central

Travelodge

BUDGET HOTEL

☎ 0871 984 6328
Princes Way, Princes St SN1 2SF
web: www.travelodge.co.uk
dir: Follow signs for town centre, then Civic Centre. From
Fleming Way turn into Princes St, hotel 200yds on left

Travelodge offers good quality, good value, budget
accommodation. All offer family rooms sleeping up to four
(two adults, two children) with en suite bathroom/
shower-room, remote-control TV, tea- and coffee-making
facilities and comfortable beds. Food options vary.
Breakfast is at the on-site Bar Café restaurant (if
available) or to take away. See also Hotel Groups pages.

Rooms 81 **S** fr £29; **D** fr £29

Fieldways Hotel & Health Club

★★ 67% SMALL HOTEL

☎ 01225 768336 📠 01225 753649
Hilperton Rd BA14 7JP
e-mail: fieldwayshotel@yahoo.co.uk
dir: A631 from Trowbridge towards Melksham,
Chippenham, Devizes. Hotel last property on left

Originally part of a Victorian mansion this hotel is quietly
set in well-kept grounds and provides a pleasant
combination of spacious, comfortably furnished
bedrooms. There are two splendid wood-panelled dining
rooms, one of which is impressively finished in oak, pine,
rosewood and mahogany. The indoor leisure facilities
include a gym, a pool and treatment rooms; 'Top to Toe'
days are especially popular.

Rooms 13 (5 annexe) (2 fmly) (2 GF) **S** £60-£80;
D £80-£90 (incl. bkfst)* **Facilities** Spa ☜ Gym Range of
beauty treatments/massage Specialists in pampering
days **Conf** Class 40 Board 20 Thtr 40 Del from £100 to
£150* **Parking** 70 **Notes** LB

Bishopstrow House

★★★★ 77% ⑧⑧ HOTEL

☎ 01985 212312 📠 01985 216769
BA12 9HH
e-mail: info@bishopstrow.co.uk
web: www.vonessenhotels.co.uk
dir: A303, A36, B3414, hotel 2m on right

This is a fine example of a Georgian country home,
situated in 27 acres of grounds. Public areas are
traditional in style and feature antiques and open fires.
Most bedrooms offer DVD players. A spa, a tennis court
and several country walks ensure there is something for
all guests. The restaurant serves top quality,
contemporary cuisine. Von Essen Hotels - AA Hotel Group
of the Year 2009-10.

Rooms 32 (2 annexe) (2 fmly) (7 GF) **Facilities** Spa ☜ ☝
🏊 Fishing ⚓ Gym Clay pigeon shooting Archery Cycling
Xmas New Year Wi-fi **Conf** Class 32 Board 36 Thtr 65
Parking 100 **Notes** LB Civ Wed 65

Travelodge Warminster

Travelodge

BUDGET HOTEL

☎ 0871 984 6058 📠 01985 214380
A36 Bath Rd BA12 7RU
web: www.travelodge.co.uk
dir: at junct of A350 & A36

Travelodge offers good quality, good value, budget
accommodation. All offer family rooms sleeping up to four
(two adults, two children) with en suite bathroom/
shower-room, remote-control TV, tea- and coffee-making
facilities and comfortable beds. Food options vary.
Breakfast is at the on-site Bar Café restaurant (if
available) or to take away. See also Hotel Groups pages.

Rooms 53 **S** fr £29; **D** fr £29

The Cedar

★★★ 71% HOTEL

☎ 01373 822753 📠 01373 858423
Warminster Rd BA13 3PR
e-mail: info@cedarhotel-wiltshire.co.uk
dir: on A350, 0.5m S of town towards Warminster

This 18th-century hotel is an ideal base for exploring
Bath and the surrounding area and is popular with both
leisure and corporate guests. The bedrooms are attractive
and well equipped; some are located at ground-floor level
in an annexe. An interesting selection of meals is
available in both the lounge bar and conservatory, and
the Regency Restaurant is the venue for more formal
dining.

Rooms 20 (12 annexe) (4 fmly) (10 GF) **S** £65-£70;
D £78-£88 (incl. bkfst)* **Facilities** FTV Xmas New Year
Wi-fi **Conf** Class 20 Board 25 Thtr 35 Del from £60 to
£150* **Parking** 30 **Notes** LB

WHITLEY — Map 4 ST86

The Pear Tree Inn

◉◉ RESTAURANT WITH ROOMS

☎ 01225 709131 🗎 01225 702276
Maypole Group, Top Ln SN12 8QX
e-mail: peartreeinn@maypolehotels.com

This inn provides luxurious bedrooms, some in an adjoining annexe at ground floor level, and some in the main building. The restaurant draws visitors from a wide area to experience the interesting menu, the rustic atmosphere and the friendliness of the hosts.

Rooms 8 (4 annexe) (2 fmly)

WOOTTON BASSETT — Map 5 SU08

Best Western The Wiltshire

★★★ 78% HOTEL

☎ 01793 849999 🗎 01793 849988
SN4 7PB
e-mail: reception@the-wiltshire.co.uk
dir: M4 junct 16 follow Wootton Bassett signs. Hotel 1m S of Wootton Bassett on left of A3102 towards Lyneham

Overlooking rolling countryside and set on a parkland golf course, this hotel offers contemporary bedrooms that include purpose-designed disabled access rooms. The air-conditioned restaurant and bar open onto a large patio which overlooks the 18th green, and there are splendid leisure facilities including a techno-gym and 18-metre swimming pool.

Rooms 58 (29 GF) **S** £75; **D** £85 (incl. bkfst)*
Facilities FTV ⓣ ⚓ 27 Putt green Gym Sauna Steam room Wi-fi **Conf** Class 120 Board 30 Thtr 250 Del from £125*
Services Lift **Parking** 250 **Notes** LB ⊗ Closed 24-25 Dec Civ Wed 80

WORCESTERSHIRE

ABBERLEY — Map 10 SO76

The Elms Hotel & Restaurant

★★★ 88% ◉◉ HOTEL

☎ 01299 896666 🗎 01299 896804
Stockton Rd WR6 6AT
e-mail: info@theelmshotel.co.uk
web: www.theelmshotel.co.uk
dir: On A443, 2m beyond Great Witley

This imposing Queen Anne mansion set in delightful grounds dates back to 1710 and offers a sophisticated yet relaxed atmosphere throughout. The spacious public rooms and generously proportioned bedrooms offer elegance and charm. The hotel is particularly well geared for families, with a host of child friendly facilities and features including a crèche, a play area and wonderful high teas. Imaginative cooking is served in the elegant restaurant. Von Essen Hotels - AA Hotel Group of the Year 2009-10.

Rooms 23 (6 annexe) (1 fmly) (3 GF) **D** £215-£495 (incl. bkfst & dinner)* **Facilities** Spa FTV ⓣ ⚓ ⚑ Gym Xmas New Year Wi-fi **Conf** Class 30 Board 30 Thtr 70 Del from £175 to £205* **Parking** 100 **Notes** Civ Wed 70

BEWDLEY — Map 10 SO77

Ramada Hotel Kidderminster

RAMADA
HOTEL & RESORT

★★★ 79% HOTEL

☎ 01299 406400 🗎 01299 400921
Habberley Rd DY12 1LA
e-mail: sales.kidderminster@ramadajarvis.co.uk
web: www.ramadajarvis.co.uk
dir: A456 towards Kidderminster to ring road, follow signs to Bewdley. Pass Safari Park then exit A456/Town Centre, take sharp right after 200yds onto B4190, hotel 400yds on right

Located within 16 acres of landscaped grounds, this Victorian house has been sympathetically renovated and extended to provide good standards of comfort and facilities. A wide range of well equipped bedrooms include both family and executive rooms. There is an on-site Sebastian Coe Health Club that guests are welcome to use.

Rooms 44 (3 fmly) (18 GF) (3 smoking) **S** £64-£150; **D** £64-£150 (incl. bkfst) **Facilities** STV ⓣ supervised ⚑ Gym Beauty & hair salon Dance studio Steam room Sauna Sun bed New Year Wi-fi **Conf** Class 120 Board 60 Thtr 350 Del from £99 to £160 **Parking** 150 **Notes** LB ⊗ Civ Wed 250

BROADWAY — Map 10 SP03

See also **Buckland (Gloucestershire)**

Barceló The Lygon Arms

Barceló
HOTELS & RESORTS

★★★★ 80% ◉◉ HOTEL

☎ 01386 852255 🗎 01386 854470
High St WR12 7DU
e-mail: thelygonarms@barcelo-hotels.co.uk
web: www.barcelo-hotels.co.uk
dir: From Evesham take A44 signed Oxford, 5m. Follow Broadway signs. Hotel on left

A hotel with a wealth of historic charm and character, the Lygon Arms dates back to the 16th century. There is a choice of restaurants, a stylish cosy bar, an array of lounges and a smart spa and leisure club. Bedrooms vary in size and style, but all are thoughtfully equipped and include a number of stylish contemporary rooms as well as a cottage in the grounds.

Rooms 77 (9 GF) **Facilities** Spa STV ⓣ ⚑ Gym Beauty treatments Xmas New Year Wi-fi **Conf** Class 46 Board 30 Thtr 80 Del from £145* **Parking** 200 **Notes** Civ Wed 80

Dormy House

★★★★ 77% ◉◉ HOTEL

☎ 01386 852711 🗎 01386 858636
Willersey Hill WR12 7LF
e-mail: reservations@dormyhouse.co.uk.
web: www.dormyhouse.co.uk
dir: 2m E off A44, top of Fish Hill, turn for Saintbury/Picnic area. After 0.5m left, hotel on left

A converted 17th-century farmhouse set in extensive grounds and with stunning views over Broadway. Some rooms are in an annexe at ground-floor level, some have a contemporary style. The best traditions are retained - customer care, real fires, comfortable sofas and afternoon teas. Dinner features an interesting choice of dishes created by a skilled kitchen brigade.

Rooms 45 (20 annexe) (8 fmly) (21 GF) **Facilities** STV Putt green ⚑ Gym Nature & jogging trail Sauna Steam room Xmas New Year Wi-fi **Conf** Class 100 Board 25 Thtr 170 **Parking** 90 **Notes** ⊗ Closed 25-28 Dec Civ Wed 170

Broadway

★★★ 77% HOTEL

Cotswold
Inns & Hotels

☎ 01386 852401 📄 01386 853879
The Green, High St WR12 7AA
e-mail: info@broadwayhotel.info
web: www.cotswold-inns-hotels.co.uk
dir: Follow signs to Evesham, then Broadway

A half-timbered Cotswold-stone property, built in the 15th century as a retreat for the Abbots of Pershore. The hotel combines modern, attractive decor with original charm and character. Bedrooms are tastefully furnished and well equipped while public rooms include a relaxing lounge, cosy bar and charming restaurant; alfresco all-day dining in summer months proves popular.

Rooms 19 (1 fmly) (3 GF) **Facilities** Xmas New Year Wi-fi
Conf Board 12 Thtr 20 **Parking** 20 **Notes** Civ Wed 50

Russell's

◉◉ RESTAURANT WITH ROOMS

☎ 01386 853555 📄 01386 853555
20 High St WR12 7DT
e-mail: info@russellsofbroadway.com
dir: Opposite village green

Situated in the centre of a picturesque Cotswold village this restaurant with rooms is a great base for exploring local attractions. Bedrooms, each with their own character, boast superb quality, air conditioning and a wide range of extras for guests. Cuisine is a real draw here with freshly-prepared, local produce skilfully utilised.

Rooms 7 (3 annexe) (4 fmly)

BROMSGROVE **Map 10 SO97**

Holiday Inn Birmingham - Bromsgrove

Holiday Inn
HOTELS · RESORTS

★★★★ 73% HOTEL

☎ 01527 576600 & 0871 942 9142 📄 01527 878981
Kidderminster Rd B61 9AB
e-mail: info@hi-birminghambromsgrove.co.uk
dir: From S: M5 junct 5, A38 to Bromsgrove 2m. At rdbt left, B4091,1.5m. Left at 2nd rdbt A448. Hotel 0.5m on left. From N: M5 junct 4, A38/Bromsgrove for 2m. Through lights, straight on at rdbt. Right at next rdbt onto A448. Hotel 0.5m on left

Public areas in this striking building have a Mediterranean theme with white-washed walls, a courtyard garden and plenty of natural light. Bedrooms are in a variety of styles; some are more compact than others but all offer an excellent working environment for the business guest. Leisure facilities include a steam room, sauna, pool and gym.

Rooms 110 (11 fmly) (31 GF) **Facilities** Spa STV ◉ supervised Gym Beauty salon 2 treatment rooms Sauna Steam room Spa bath Wi-fi **Conf** Class 120 Board 50 Thtr 220 **Services** Lift Air con **Parking** 250 **Notes** ⊗ Civ Wed 180

Ladybird Hotel

★★★ 78% HOTEL

☎ 01527 889900 📄 01527 889949
2 Finstall Rd, Aston Fields B60 2DZ
e-mail: info@ladybirdhotel.co.uk
web: www.ladybirdhotel.co.uk
dir: Enter Bromsgrove on A38, follow signs for Aston Fields (B4184)

Located on the town's outskirts, this attractive modern hotel is an extension of the popular Ladybird Inn, popular for its range of quality pub food. Bedrooms are very well equipped for both business and leisure guests and Rosado's Italian Restaurant is the perfect setting for an intimate dinner.

Rooms 43 (9 fmly) (14 GF) **S** £46-£100; **D** £60-£110 (incl. bkfst)* **Facilities** STV Wi-fi **Conf** Class 25 Board 30 Thtr 40 **Services** Lift **Parking** 60 **Notes** LB ⊗

Innkeeper's Lodge Bromsgrove

Innkeeper's
Lodge

BUDGET HOTEL

☎ 0845 112 6067 📄 0845 112 6236
462 Birmingham Rd, Marlbrook B61 0HR
web: www.innkeeperslodge.com/bromsgrove
dir: M5 junct 4 or M42 junct 1 w'bound only (restricted junction). Lodge on A38 (Birmingham road).

Innkeeper's Lodge represents an exciting, high value concept within the budget hotel market. Comfortable bedrooms provide excellent facilities that include satellite TV and modem points. Options include family rooms; and for the corporate guest, cutting edge IT which includes Wi-fi access. A popular Carvery provides all-day food, including an extensive, complimentary continental breakfast. See also the Hotel Groups pages.

Rooms 29 (3 fmly) **Conf** Thtr 25

CHADDESLEY CORBETT **Map 10 SO87**

INSPECTORS' CHOICE

Brockencote Hall Country House

★★★ ◉◉ HOTEL

☎ 01562 777876 📄 01562 777872
DY10 4PY
e-mail: info@brockencotehall.com
web: www.brockencotehall.com
dir: 0.5m W, off A448, opposite St Cassians Church

Glorious countryside extends all around this magnificent mansion, and grazing sheep can be seen from the conservatory. Not surprisingly, relaxation comes high on the list of priorities here. Despite its very English location the hotel's owner actually hails from Alsace and the atmosphere is very much that of a provincial French château. The chef too is French (from Paris) and the chandeliered dining room is a popular venue for the accomplished modern French cuisine.

Rooms 17 (2 fmly) (5 GF) **S** £96-£140; **D** £120-£190 (incl. bkfst)* **Facilities** FTV ◉ Fishing ◉ Reflexology Aromatherapy Massage Facials Xmas New Year Wi-fi **Conf** Class 20 Board 20 Thtr 30 Del from £175 to £190* **Services** Lift **Parking** 45 **Notes** LB ⊗ Closed 1-18 Jan Civ Wed 70

DROITWICH — Map 10 SO86

Express by Holiday Inn Droitwich M5 Jct 5

BUDGET HOTEL

☎ 0870 442 5658   ▤ 0870 442 5659
Worcester Rd, Wychbold WR9 7PA
e-mail: dgmdroitwich@expressholidayinn.co.uk
web: www.hiexpress.com/droitwichm5j
dir: M5 junct 5, at rdbt take A38 towards Bromsgrove. Hotel 300yds on left next to MacDonalds

A modern hotel ideal for families and business travellers. Fresh and uncomplicated, the spacious rooms include Sky TV, power shower and tea and coffee-making facilities. Continental buffet breakfast is included in the room rate; other meals may be taken at the nearby family pub or restaurant. See also the Hotel Groups pages.

Rooms 94 (44 fmly) **Conf** Class 18 Board 20 Thtr 40

Travelodge Droitwich

BUDGET HOTEL

☎ 0871 984 6074   ▤ 01527 861807
Rashwood Hill WR9 0BJ
web: www.travelodge.co.uk
dir: 0.5m W of M5 junct 5 on A38

Travelodge offers good quality, good value, budget accommodation. All offer family rooms sleeping up to four (two adults, two children) with en suite bathroom/shower-room, remote-control TV, tea- and coffee-making facilities and comfortable beds. Food options vary. Breakfast is at the on-site Bar Café restaurant (if available) or to take away. See also Hotel Groups pages.

Rooms 32 **S** fr £29; **D** fr £29

EVESHAM — Map 10 SP04

Northwick Hotel

★★★ 82% ◉ HOTEL

☎ 01386 40322   ▤ 01386 41070
Waterside WR11 1BT
e-mail: enquiries@northwickhotel.co.uk
dir: Off A46 onto A44 over lights, right at next lights onto B4035. Past hospital, hotel on right opposite river

Located close to the centre of the town, this hotel overlooks River Avon and its adjacent park. Bedrooms are traditional in style and feature broadband access; one room has been adapted for disabled access. Public areas offer a choice of drinking options, meeting rooms and a restaurant.

Rooms 29 (4 fmly) (1 GF) **S** £81-£87; **D** £115-£118 (incl. bkfst)* **Facilities** STV FTV New Year Wi-fi **Conf** Class 150 Board 80 Thtr 240 **Parking** 110 **Notes** LB ⊗ Closed 25-28 Dec Civ Wed 70

See advert on this page

The Evesham

★★★ 79% ◉ HOTEL

☎ 01386 765566 & 0800 716969 (Res)
▤ 01386 765443
Coopers Ln, Off Waterside WR11 1DA
e-mail: reception@eveshamhotel.com
web: www.eveshamhotel.com
dir: Coopers Lane is off road by River Avon

Dating from 1540 and set in extensive grounds, this delightful hotel has well-equipped accommodation that includes a selection of quirkily themed rooms - Alice in Wonderland, Egyptian, and Aquarium (which has a tropical fish tank in the bathroom). A reputation for food is well deserved, with a particularly strong choice for vegetarians. Children are welcome and toys are always available.

Rooms 40 (1 annexe) (3 fmly) (11 GF) **S** £73-£87; **D** £120-£123 (incl. bkfst) **Facilities** FTV ◔ Putt green ⛳ New Year Wi-fi Child facilities **Conf** Class 12 Board 12 Thtr 12 **Parking** 50 **Notes** LB Closed 25-26 Dec

Dumbleton Hall

★★★ 77% HOTEL

☎ 01386 881240   ▤ 01386 882142
WR11 7TS
e-mail: dh@pofr.co.uk

(For full entry see Dumbleton, Gloucestershire)

Travelodge Hartlebury

BUDGET HOTEL

☎ 0871 984 6079 📄 01299 251774
Shorthill Nurseries DY13 9SH
web: www.travelodge.co.uk
dir: A449, southbound

Travelodge offers good quality, good value, budget accommodation. All offer family rooms sleeping up to four (two adults, two children) with en suite bathroom/shower-room, remote-control TV, tea- and coffee-making facilities and comfortable beds. Food options vary. Breakfast is at the on-site Bar Café restaurant (if available) or to take away. See also Hotel Groups pages.

Rooms 32 **S** fr £29; **D** fr £29

Stone Manor

★★★★ 78% HOTEL

CLASSIC
BRITISH HOTELS

☎ 01562 777555 📄 01562 777834
Stone DY10 4PJ
e-mail: enquiries@stonemanorhotel.co.uk
web: www.stonemanorhotel.co.uk
dir: 2.5m from Kidderminster on A448, on right

This converted, much extended former manor house stands in 25 acres of impressive grounds and gardens. The well-equipped accommodation includes rooms with four-poster beds and luxuriously appointed annexe bedrooms. Quality furnishing and decor styles throughout the public areas highlight the intrinsic charm of the interior; the hotel is a popular venue for wedding receptions.

Rooms 57 (5 annexe) (7 GF) **Facilities** STV ⌖ ♨ ⛲ Pool table Complimentary use of local leisure centre **Conf** Class 48 Board 60 Thtr 150 Del from £135 to £185* **Parking** 400 **Notes** ⊗ Civ Wed 150

Gainsborough House

★★★ 80% HOTEL

☎ 01562 820041 📄 01562 66179
Bewdley Hill DY11 6BS
e-mail: reservations@gainsboroughhousehotel.com
web: www.gainsboroughhousehotel.com
dir: Follow A456 to Kidderminster (West Midlands Safari Park), pass hospital, hotel 500yds on left

This listed Georgian hotel provides a wide range of thoughtfully furnished bedrooms with smart modern bathrooms. The contemporary decor and furnishing style throughout the public areas highlights the many retained period features. A large function suite and several meeting rooms are also available.

Rooms 42 (16 fmly) (12 GF) **S** £55-£75; **D** £75-£95 (incl. bkfst)* **Facilities** STV FTV Xmas New Year Wi-fi **Conf** Board 60 Thtr 250 Del from £95 to £120* **Services** Air con **Parking** 90 **Notes** LB ⊗ Civ Wed 250

The Granary Hotel & Restaurant

★★★ 78% ◉◉ HOTEL

☎ 01562 777535 📄 01562 777722
Heath Ln, Shenstone DY10 4BS
e-mail: info@granary-hotel.co.uk
web: www.granary-hotel.co.uk
dir: On A450 between Stourbridge & Worcester, 1m from Kidderminster

This modern hotel offers spacious, well-equipped accommodation with many rooms enjoying views towards Great Witley and the Amberley Hills. Public areas include a cocktail lounge and an attractive modern restaurant featuring locally sourced produce, cooked with flair and imagination. There are also extensive conference facilities and the hotel is popular as a wedding venue.

Rooms 18 (1 fmly) (18 GF) **S** £75-£90; **D** £90-£140 (incl. bkfst)* **Facilities** FTV Wi-fi **Conf** Class 80 Board 70 Thtr 200 **Parking** 96 **Notes** LB Closed 24-26 Dec Civ Wed 120

The Cottage in the Wood Hotel

★★★ 85% ◉◉ HOTEL

☎ 01684 588860 📄 01684 560662
Holywell Rd, Malvern Wells WR14 4LG
e-mail: reception@cottageinthewood.co.uk
web: www.cottageinthewood.co.uk
dir: 3m S of Great Malvern off A449, 500yds N of B4209, on opposite side of road

Sitting high up on a wooded hillside, this delightful, family-run hotel boasts lovely views over the Severn Valley. The bedrooms are divided between the main house, Beech Cottage and the Pinnacles. The public areas are very stylishly decorated, and imaginative food is

served in an elegant dining room, overlooking the immaculate grounds.

The Cottage in the Wood Hotel

Rooms 30 (23 annexe) (9 GF) **S** £79-£112; **D** £99-£185 (incl. bkfst)* **Facilities** Direct access to Malvern Hills Xmas New Year Wi-fi **Conf** Board 14 Thtr 20 **Parking** 40

Colwall Park Hotel, Bar & Restaurant

★★★ 81% ◉◉ HOTEL

☎ 01684 540000 📄 01684 540847
Walwyn Rd, Colwall WR13 6QG
e-mail: hotel@colwall.com
web: www.colwall.co.uk
dir: Between Malvern & Ledbury in centre of Colwall on B4218

Standing in extensive gardens, this hotel was purpose built in the early 20th century to serve the local racetrack. Today the proprietors and loyal staff provide high levels of hospitality and service. The Seasons Restaurant has a well-deserved reputation for its cuisine. Bedrooms are tastefully appointed and public areas help to create a fine country-house atmosphere.

Rooms 22 (1 fmly) **S** £79; **D** £99-£150 (incl. bkfst)* **Facilities** FTV ⛲ Boules Xmas New Year Wi-fi **Conf** Class 80 Board 50 Thtr 150 **Parking** 40 **Notes** LB ⊗

MALVERN *continued*

Cotford Hotel & L'Amuse Bouche Restaurant

★★★ 79% ◉ HOTEL

☎ 01684 572427 ▤ 01684 572952
51 Graham Rd WR14 2HU
e-mail: reservations@cotfordhotel.co.uk
web: www.cotfordhotel.co.uk
dir: From Worcester follow signs to Malvern on A449. Left into Graham Rd signed town centre, hotel on right

This delightful house, built in 1851, reputedly for the Bishop of Worcester, stands in attractive garden with stunning views of The Malverns. Rooms have been authentically renovated, retaining many of the original features, and other all the expected comforts. Food, service and hospitality are all major strengths.

Rooms 15 (3 fmly) (1 GF) **S** £65-£79; **D** £99-£115 (incl. bkfst) **Facilities** STV ⏂ Wi-fi **Conf** Class 26 Board 12 Thtr 26 Del from £132 to £146 **Parking** 15 **Notes** LB

The Malvern Hills Hotel

★★★ 77% HOTEL

☎ 01684 540690 ▤ 01684 540327
Wynds Point WR13 6DW
e-mail: malhilhotl@aol.com
web: www.malvernhillshotel.co.uk
dir: 4m S, at junct of A449 with B4232

This 19th-century hostelry is situated to the west of Malvern, opposite the British Camp, which was fortified and occupied by the Ancient Britons. The bedrooms are well equipped and benefit from smart modern bathrooms. Public areas include a choice of bars, retaining original features, modern conference facilities and an attractive restaurant.

Rooms 14 (1 fmly) (2 GF) **S** £55-£70; **D** £95-£125 (incl. bkfst)* **Facilities** FTV Xmas New Year Wi-fi **Conf** Class 24 Board 30 Thtr 40 Del from £130 to £160* **Parking** 45 **Notes** LB

Best Western Foley Arms

★★★ 73% HOTEL

☎ 01684 573397 ▤ 01684 569665
14 Worcester Rd WR14 4QS
e-mail: reservations@foleyarmshotel.com
web: www.foleyarmshotel.co.uk
dir: M5 junct 8 N (or junct 7 S) or M50 junct 1 to Great Malvern on A449

Situated in the centre of town and with spectacular views of the Severn Valley, this hotel is reputed to be the oldest hotel in Malvern. The bedrooms are comfortable and tastefully decorated with period furnishings and modern facilities. Public areas include the Terrace Restaurant, a popular bar and a choice of comfortable lounges.

Rooms 28 (2 fmly) **Facilities** STV FTV Xmas New Year Wi-fi **Conf** Class 40 Board 45 Thtr 150 Del from £125 to £145* **Parking** 60 **Notes** Civ Wed 100

Holdfast Cottage

★★ 82% ◉ HOTEL

☎ 01684 310288 ▤ 01684 311117
Marlbank Rd, Welland WR13 6NA
e-mail: enquiries@holdfast-cottage.co.uk
web: www.holdfast-cottage.co.uk
dir: M50 junct 1 signed Upton Three Counties A38, turn onto A4104 through to Welland

At the base of the Malvern Hills this delightful wisteria-covered hotel sits in attractive manicured grounds. Charming public areas include an intimate bar, a log fire enhanced lounge and an elegant dining room. Bedrooms vary in size but all are comfortable and well appointed. Fresh local and seasonal produce are the basis for the cuisine.

Rooms 8 (1 fmly) **S** £55; **D** £75-£98 (incl. bkfst)* **Facilities** ⏂ Xmas New Year **Conf** Class 30 Board 30 **Parking** 15 **Notes** LB Civ Wed 35

Mount Pleasant

★★ 71% HOTEL

☎ 01684 561837 ▤ 01684 569968
Belle Vue Ter WR14 4PZ
e-mail: reception@mountpleasanthotel.co.uk
web: www.mountpleasanthotel.co.uk
dir: On A449, in town central by x-rds opp Priory church

An attractive Georgian house in the town centre that occupies an elevated position and overlooks Priory Church and the picturesque Severn Valley. The bedrooms are spacious, and there is a smart bar and brasserie where guests can enjoy a full meal or just a drink or a snack. In warmer months the small terrace on the lawn makes a delightful place to relax.

Rooms 14 (1 fmly) **S** £45-£68; **D** £60-£98 (incl. bkfst)* **Facilities** FTV Hair salon ♬ Xmas New Year Wi-fi **Conf** Class 40 Board 50 Thtr 90 **Parking** 20 **Notes** LB ⊗

REDDITCH **Map 10 SP06**

Best Western Abbey Hotel Golf & Country Club

★★★★ 77% HOTEL

☎ 01527 406600 ▤ 01527 406514
Hither Green Ln, Dagnell End Rd, Bordesley B98 9BE
e-mail: info@theabbeyhotel.co.uk
web: www.theabbeyhotel.co.uk
dir: M42 junct 2, A441 to Redditch. End of carriageway turn left (A441), Dagnell End Rd on left. Hotel 600yds on right

With convenient access to the motorway and a proximity to local attractions, this modern hotel is popular with both business and leisure travellers. Bedrooms are well equipped and attractively decorated; the executive corner rooms are especially spacious. Facilities include an 18-hole golf course, pro shop, large indoor pool and extensive conference facilities.

Rooms 100 (20 fmly) (23 GF) **Facilities** STV ⏂ ⏂ 18 Putt green Fishing Gym Beauty salon Golf driving range Xmas New Year Wi-fi **Conf** Class 60 Board 30 Thtr 170 **Services** Lift **Parking** 200 **Notes** LB ⊗ Civ Wed 100

Express by Holiday Inn Redditch

BUDGET HOTEL

☎ 01527 584658 📄 01527 597905
Hewell Rd, Enfield B97 6AE
e-mail: reservations@express.gb.com
web: www.hiexpress.com/redditch
dir: M42 junct 2/A441 follow signs to rail station. Before station turn right into Hewell Rd, 1st left into Gloucester Close

A modern hotel ideal for families and business travellers. Fresh and uncomplicated, the spacious rooms include Sky TV, power shower and tea and coffee-making facilities. Continental buffet breakfast is included in the room rate; other meals may be taken at the nearby family pub or restaurant. See also the Hotel Groups pages.

Rooms 100 (4 fmly) (10 GF) (15 smoking) **S** £49-£99; **D** £49-£99 (incl. bkfst) **Conf** Class 26 Board 20 Thtr 50

Campanile Redditch

BUDGET HOTEL

☎ 01527 510710 📄 01527 517269
Far Moor Ln, Winyates Green B98 0SD
e-mail: redditch@campanile.com
dir: A435 towards Redditch, then A4023 to Redditch & Bromsgrove

This modern building offers accommodation in smart, well-equipped bedrooms, all with en suite bathrooms. Refreshments may be taken at the informal bistro. See also the Hotel Groups pages.

Rooms 46 (46 annexe) (20 GF) **Conf** Class 15 Board 15 Thtr 25 Del from £95 to £120*

Travelodge Redditch

BUDGET HOTEL

☎ 0871 984 6344
Meadlow Farm, Dagnell End Rd B98 9BJ
web: www.travelodge.co.uk
dir: A441, left on B4101 Beoley, left again onto Dagnell End Rd

Travelodge offers good quality, good value, budget accommodation. All offer family rooms sleeping up to four (two adults, two children) with en suite bathroom/ shower-room, remote-control TV, tea- and coffee-making facilities and comfortable beds. Food options vary.

Breakfast is at the on-site Bar Café restaurant (if available) or to take away. See also Hotel Groups pages.

Rooms 42 **S** fr £29; **D** fr £29

STOURPORT-ON-SEVERN — Map 10 SO87

Menzies Stourport Manor — MenziesHotels

★★★★ 75% HOTEL

☎ 01299 289955 📄 01299 878520
35 Hartlebury Rd DY13 9JA
e-mail: stourport@menzieshotels.co.uk
web: www.menzieshotels.co.uk
dir: M5 junct 6, A449 towards Kidderminster, B4193 towards Stourport. Hotel on right

Once the home of Prime Minister Sir Stanley Baldwin, this much extended country house is set in attractive grounds. A number of bedrooms and suites are located in the original building, although the majority are in a more modern, purpose-built section. Spacious public areas include a range of lounges, a popular restaurant, a leisure club and conference facilities.

Rooms 68 (17 fmly) (31 GF) (10 smoking) **S** £59-£130; **D** £59-£130* **Facilities** STV 🏊 ⚓ Putt green Gym Squash Xmas New Year Wi-fi **Conf** Class 110 Board 40 Thtr 350 Del from £105 to £150* **Parking** 300 **Notes** Civ Wed 300

TENBURY WELLS — Map 10 SO56

Cadmore Lodge Hotel & Country Club

★★ 74% ⚘ HOTEL

☎ 01584 810044 📄 01584 810044
Berrington Green, St Michaels WR15 8TQ
e-mail: reception.cadmore@cadmorelodge.com
web: www.cadmorelodge.com
dir: Off A4112 (Leominster-Tenbury Wells road), follow sign on left for Berrington

Cadmore Lodge is situated in an idyllic rural location overlooking a private lake. The 70-acre private estate features a 9-hole golf course and two fishing lakes. The traditionally styled bedrooms have modern amenities, and a large function room with lake views is popular for weddings and special occasions. The hotel is earning itself a well deserved reputation for its food.

Rooms 15 (1 fmly) **S** £45-£60; **D** £70-£130 (incl. bkfst) **Facilities** 🏌 ⚓ 9 Fishing Gym Bowling green Steam room Nature reserve Xmas New Year **Conf** Class 40 Board 20 Thtr 100 **Parking** 100 **Notes** LB ❌ Civ Wed 160

UPTON UPON SEVERN — Map 10 SO84

White Lion

★★★ 71% ⚘ HOTEL

☎ 01684 592551 📄 01684 593333
21 High St WR8 0HJ
e-mail: reservations@whitelionhotel.biz
dir: A422, A38 towards Tewkesbury. In 8m take B4104, after 1m cross bridge, turn left to hotel, past bend on left

Famed for being the inn depicted in Henry Fielding's novel *Tom Jones*, this 16th-century hotel is a reminder of 'Old England' with features such as exposed beams and wall timbers still remaining. The quality furnishing and the decor throughout enhance its character; the bedrooms are smart and include one four-poster room.

Rooms 13 (2 annexe) (2 fmly) (2 GF) **S** £70-£75; **D** £99-£145 (incl. bkfst)* **Facilities** FTV Wi-fi **Conf** Class 12 Board 12 Thtr 24 Del from £90 to £100 **Parking** 14 **Notes** LB Closed 1 Jan RS 25 Dec

---

WORCESTER — Map 10 SO85

Pear Tree Inn & Country Hotel

★★★ 77% HOTEL

☎ 01905 756565 📄 01905 756777
Smite WR3 8SY
e-mail: info@thepeartree.co.uk
dir: M5 junct 6 take A4538 towards Droitwich. In 300yds 1st right into small country lane, over canal bridge, up hill, hotel on left

Located close to M5 in pretty landscaped grounds, this traditional English inn and country hotel has spacious, air-conditioned bedrooms with attractive colour schemes and good facilities. Four suites are available. Guests can enjoy good food and a drink in relaxed surroundings; there is an excellent range of conference and function rooms.

Rooms 24 (2 fmly) (12 GF) **S** £50-£100; **D** £70-£120* **Facilities** Fishing Wi-fi **Conf** Class 150 Board 40 Thtr 250 **Services** Lift Air con **Parking** 200 **Notes** ❌ Closed 25-26 Dec Civ Wed 120

WORCESTER *continued*

Fownes

★★★ 67% HOTEL

☎ 01905 613151 📄 01905 23742
City Walls Rd WR1 2AP
e-mail: reservations@fowneshotel.co.uk
web: www.fownesgroup.co.uk
dir: M5 junct 7 take A44 for Worcester city centre. Turn
right at 4th set of lights into City Walls Rd

On the Birmingham Canal and located close to the city
centre this former Victorian glove factory has been
converted into a modern hotel with well proportioned
bedrooms. Snacks are available in the lounge bar and the
King's Restaurant offers an interesting carte menu.
Conference and meeting facilities are available.

Rooms 61 (3 fmly) (10 GF) **S** £75.50-£115;
D £89.50-£175 (incl. bkfst)* **Facilities** Xmas New Year
Wi-fi **Conf** Class 50 Board 50 Thtr 100 **Services** Lift
Parking 82 **Notes** LB Civ Wed 80

Ye Olde Talbot

★★ Ⓐ HOTEL

☎ 01905 23573 📄 01905 612760
Friar St WR1 2NA
e-mail: 9250@greeneking.co.uk
web: www.oldenglish.co.uk

Rooms 29 (6 fmly) (6 GF) **S** £45-£55; **D** £70-£90 (incl.
bkfst)* **Facilities** FTV Xmas New Year Wi-fi **Notes** LB ⊗

Travelodge Worcester

BUDGET HOTEL

☎ 0871 984 6277
Cathedral Plaza, 3 High St WR1 2QS
web: www.travelodge.co.uk
dir: M5 junct 7 (A44). Follow signs to city centre. Lodge
opp cathedral. Entrance in Cathedral Plaza shopping
mall

Travelodge offers good quality, good value, budget
accommodation. All offer family rooms sleeping up to four
(two adults, two children) with en suite bathroom/
shower-room, remote-control TV, tea- and coffee-making
facilities and comfortable beds. Food options vary.
Breakfast is at the on-site Bar Café restaurant (if
available) or to take away. See also Hotel Groups pages.

Rooms 92 **S** fr £29; **D** fr £29

YORKSHIRE, EAST RIDING OF

BEVERLEY — Map 17 TA03

Tickton Grange

★★★ 82% ◎◎ HOTEL

☎ 01964 543666 📄 01964 542556
Tickton HU17 9SH
e-mail: info@ticktongrange.co.uk
dir: 3m NE on A1035

A charming Georgian country house situated in four acres
of private grounds and attractive gardens. Bedrooms are
individual, and decorated to a high specification. Pre-
dinner drinks may be enjoyed in the comfortable library
lounge, prior to enjoying fine, modern British cooking in
the restaurant. The hotel has excellent facilities for both
weddings and business conferences.

Rooms 20 (3 annexe) (2 fmly) (4 GF) **S** £82.50-£92.50;
D £105-£125 (incl. bkfst)* **Facilities** STV FTV Wi-fi
Conf Class 100 Board 80 Thtr 200 Del from £135.25*
Parking 90 **Notes** ⊗ RS 25-29 Dec Civ Wed 200

Best Western Lairgate Hotel

★★★ 72% HOTEL

☎ 01482 882141 📄 01482 861067
30/32 Lairgate HU17 8EP
dir: A63 towards town centre. Hotel 220yds on left - follow
one-way system

Located just off the market square, this pleasing
Georgian hotel has been appointed to offer stylish
accommodation. Bedrooms are elegant and well
equipped, and public rooms include a comfortable
lounge, a lounge bar, and restaurant with a popular sun
terrace.

Rooms 30 (1 fmly) (8 GF) **Facilities** FTV New Year Wi-fi
Conf Class 20 Board 20 Thtr 20 **Parking** 18 **Notes** ⊗
Closed 26 Dec & 1 Jan RS 25 Dec Civ Wed 70

BRANDESBURTON — Map 17 TA14

Burton Lodge

★★ 72% HOTEL

☎ 01964 542847 📄 01964 544771
YO25 8RU
e-mail: enquiries@burton-lodge.co.uk
dir: 7m from Beverley off A165, at Hainsworth Park Golf
Club

A tennis court, sports play area and extensive lawns are
features of this friendly hotel, which is situated in two
acres of grounds adjoining a golf course. The modern
bedrooms look out either onto the golf course or the
countryside; there is a comfortable lounge with a small
bar and a spacious restaurant that offers tasty home
cooking.

Rooms 9 (2 annexe) (3 fmly) (2 GF) **Facilities** ↓ 18 ⌣
Putt green Pitch and putt **Conf** Class 20 **Parking** 15
Notes LB Closed 25-26 Dec

BRIDLINGTON — Map 17 TA16

Expanse

★★★ 75% HOTEL

☎ 01262 675347 📄 01262 604928
North Marine Dr YO15 2LS
e-mail: reservations@expanse.co.uk
web: www.expanse.co.uk
dir: follow North Beach signs, pass under railway arch for
North Marine Drive. Hotel at bottom of hill

This traditional seaside hotel overlooks the bay and has
been in the same family's ownership for many years.
Service is relaxed and friendly and the modern bedrooms
are well equipped. Comfortable public areas include a
conference suite, a choice of bars and an inviting lounge.

Rooms 47 (5 fmly) (27 smoking) **Facilities** ♫ Xmas New
Year Wi-fi **Conf** Class 50 Board 50 Thtr 180 **Services** Lift
Parking 23 **Notes** LB ⊗ Civ Wed

See advert on opposite page

The Expanse Hotel

A haven of peace and comfort overlooking the Beach and Flamborough Head Heritage Coast, where the beach and cliff walks beckon. The Expanse is a place to relax, with a feel all of its own – built to capture those unique views, where friendly old world courtesy and modern facilities combine for a special break.

North Marine Drive · Bridlington · YO15 2LS
Tel 01262 675347
Fax 01262 604928

DRIFFIELD (GREAT) Map 17 TA05

Best Western Bell

★★★ 78% HOTEL

☎ 01377 256661 📠 01377 253228
46 Market Place YO25 6AN
e-mail: bell@bestwestern.co.uk
web: www.bw-bellhotel.co.uk
dir: From A164, right at lights. Car park 50yds on left behind black railings

This 250-year-old hotel incorporates the old corn exchange and the old town hall. It is furnished with antique and period pieces, and contains many items of local historical interest. The bedrooms vary in size, but all offer modern facilities and some have their own sitting rooms. The hotel has a relaxed and very friendly atmosphere. There is a spa and gym providing a very good range of facilities and treatments.

Rooms 16 (3 GF) **S** £76-£85; **D** £100-£112 (incl. bkfst)*
Facilities Spa FTV ⚑ Gym Squash Masseur Hairdressing Chiropody Snooker ♫ New Year Wi-fi **Conf** Class 100 Board 40 Thtr 150 **Services** Lift **Parking** 18 **Notes** ⊗ No children 16yrs Closed 25 Dec & 1 Jan RS 24 & 26 Dec Civ Wed 70

FLAMBOROUGH Map 17 TA27

North Star

★★ 75% SMALL HOTEL

☎ 01262 850379 📠 01262 850379
North Marine Dr YO15 1BL
web: www.thenorthstarhotel.co.uk
dir: B1229 or B1255 to Flamborough. Follow signs for North Landing along North Marine Dr. Hotel 100yds from sea

Standing close to the North Landing of Flamborough Head, this family-run hotel overlooks delightful countryside. It provides excellent accommodation and caring hospitality. A good range of fresh local food, especially fish, is available in both the bar and the dining room.

Rooms 7 **Parking** 30 **Notes** ⊗ Closed Xmas & 2 wks Nov

KINGSTON UPON HULL Map 17 TA02

Portland

★★★★ 71% HOTEL

☎ 01482 326462 📠 01482 213460
Paragon St HU1 3JP
e-mail: info@portland-hotel.co.uk
web: www.portland-hull.com
dir: M62 junct 38 onto A63, to 1st main rdbt. Left at 2nd lights, over x-rds. Right at next junct onto Carr Ln, follow one-way system

A modern hotel situated next to the City Hall providing a good range of accommodation. Most of the public rooms are on the first floor and Wi-fi is available. The Bay Tree Café, at street level, is open during the day and evening. Staff are friendly and helpful and take care of car parking for hotel guests.

Rooms 126 (4 fmly) **S** £65-£160; **D** £65-£160*
Facilities STV FTV Complimentary use of nearby health & fitness centre Xmas New Year Wi-fi **Conf** Class 100 Board 50 Thtr 220 Del from £125 to £165* **Services** Lift **Notes** Civ Wed 100

Best Western Willerby Manor

★★★ 82% ◉◉ HOTEL

☎ 01482 652616 📠 01482 653901
Well Ln HU10 6ER
e-mail: willerbymanor@bestwestern.co.uk
web: www.willerbymanor.co.uk

(For full entry see Willerby)

Holiday Inn Hull Marina

★★★ 79% HOTEL

☎ 0870 400 9043 & 01482 386300 📠 01482 386325
The Marina, Castle St HU1 2BX
e-mail: reservations-hull@ihg.com
web: www.holidayinn.com
dir: M62 junct 38, A63 to Hull. Follow Marina & Ice Arena signs. Hotel on left next to Ice Arena

Situated overlooking the marina just off the A63. The well-equipped accommodation includes executive rooms. Public areas are attractively designed and include meeting rooms and a leisure club. The Junction

restaurant serves contemporary cuisine, and guests can eat alfresco on the patio if weather permits.

Rooms 100 (10 fmly) **Facilities** STV ⚑ supervised Gym New Year Wi-fi **Conf** Class 70 Board 50 Thtr 120 **Services** Lift Air con **Parking** 151 **Notes** ⊗ Civ Wed 120

Campanile Hull

BUDGET HOTEL

☎ 01482 325530 📠 01482 587538
Beverley Rd, Freetown Way (City Centre) HU2 9AN
e-mail: hull@campanile.com
dir: M62 junct 38, A63 to Hull, pass Humber Bridge on right. Over flyover, follow railway station signs onto A1079. Hotel at bottom of Ferensway

This modern building offers accommodation in smart, well-equipped bedrooms, all with en suite bathrooms. Refreshments may be taken at the informal bistro. See also the Hotel Groups pages.

Rooms 47 (47 annexe) **S** £49-£60; **D** £49-£60*
Conf Class 15 Board 15 Thtr 25 Del from £70 to £95

Holiday Inn Express Hull City Centre

BUDGET HOTEL

☎ 01482 485700 📠 01482 485701
80 Ferensway HU2 8LN
e-mail: hull@foremusthotels.co.uk
dir: A63 to Hull, follow signs for train station. Pass hotel, 2nd left into St Stephens multi-storey car park. Hotel entrance linked to level 2 of car park

A modern hotel ideal for families and business travellers. Fresh and uncomplicated, the spacious rooms include Sky TV, power shower and tea and coffee-making facilities. Continental buffet breakfast is included in the room rate; other meals may be taken at the nearby family pub or restaurant. See also the Hotel Groups pages.

Rooms 128 **S** fr £49; **D** fr £49 (incl. bkfst)* **Conf** Class 36 Board 32 Thtr 55 Del from £94

Ibis Hull

BUDGET HOTEL

☎ 01482 387500 📠 01482 385510
Osborne St HU1 2NL
e-mail: h3479-gm@accor-hotels.com
web: www.ibishotel.com
dir: M62/A63 straight across at rdbt, follow signs for Princes Quay onto Myton St. Hotel on corner of Osborne St & Ferensway

Modern, budget hotel offering comfortable accommodation in bright and practical bedrooms. Breakfast is self-service and dinner is available in the restaurant. See also the Hotel Groups pages.

Rooms 106 (19 GF)

| **POCKLINGTON** | **Map 17 SE84** |

Feathers

★★ 67% HOTEL

☎ 01759 303155 📠 01759 304382
56 Market Place YO42 2AH
e-mail: info@thefeathers-hotel.co.uk
dir: from York, B1246 signed Pocklington. Hotel just off A1079

This busy, traditional inn provides comfortable, well-equipped and spacious accommodation. Public areas are smartly presented. Enjoyable meals are served in the bar and the conservatory restaurant; the wide choice of dishes makes excellent use of local and seasonal produce.

Rooms 16 (10 annexe) (1 fmly) (10 GF) **Facilities** 🎵 **Conf** Class 40 Board 30 Thtr 80 **Parking** 30 **Notes** ⊗

| **SOUTH CAVE** | **Map 17 SE93** |

Cave Castle Hotel & Country Club

★★★ 71% HOTEL

☎ 01430 422245 📠 01430 421118
Church Hill HU15 2EU
web: www.cavecastlehotel.com
dir: In village, 1m past school. Hotel on bend on right

This beautiful Victorian manor retains original turrets, stone features and much charm together with modern comforts and style. It stands in 150 acres of meadow and parkland that provide a peaceful location. Bedrooms offer a careful mix of traditional and contemporary styles. Public areas include a well-equipped leisure complex and pool.

Rooms 70 (14 GF) **Facilities** ⓣ supervised ⚓ 18 Putt green Gym Wi-fi **Conf** Class 150 Board 100 Thtr 250 **Services** Lift **Parking** 100 **Notes** ⊗ Civ Wed

---

Travelodge Hull South Cave

BUDGET HOTEL

☎ 0871 984 6147 📠 01430 424455
Beacon Service Area HU15 1RZ
web: www.travelodge.co.uk
dir: M62 junct 38, A63 eastbound towards Hull. Lodge in 0.5m

Travelodge offers good quality, good value, budget accommodation. All offer family rooms sleeping up to four (two adults, two children) with en suite bathroom/shower-room, remote-control TV, tea- and coffee-making facilities and comfortable beds. Food options vary. Breakfast is at the on-site Bar Café restaurant (if available) or to take away. See also Hotel Groups pages.

Rooms 40 **S** fr £29; **D** fr £29

| **WILLERBY** | **Map 17 TA03** |

Best Western Willerby Manor

★★★ 82% ◉◉ HOTEL

☎ 01482 652616 📠 01482 653901
Well Ln HU10 6ER
e-mail: willerbymanor@bestwestern.co.uk
web: www.willerbymanor.co.uk
dir: off A63, signed Humber Bridge. Right at rdbt by Waitrose. At next rdbt hotel signed

Set in a quiet residential area, amid well-tended gardens, this hotel was originally a private mansion; it has now been thoughtfully extended to provide very comfortable bedrooms, equipped with many useful extras. There are extensive leisure facilities and a choice of eating options of various styles, including the smart Icon Restaurant.

Rooms 63 (6 fmly) (20 GF) (3 smoking) **S** £65-£98; **D** £106-£126 (incl. bkfst)* **Facilities** STV FTV ⓣ supervised ⚓ Gym Steam room Beauty therapist Aerobic classes New Year Wi-fi **Conf** Class 200 Board 100 Thtr 500 **Parking** 300 **Notes** LB ⊗ Closed 24-26 Dec RS 1st wk Jan, 2 wks Aug & BH Civ Wed 150

Ramada Hull

®RAMADA

★★★ 75% HOTEL

☎ 0844 815 9037 📠 01482 655848
Main St HU10 6EA
e-mail: sales.hull@ramadajarvis.co.uk
web: www.ramadajarvis.co.uk
dir: A164 to Beverley signed Willerby Shopping Park. Left at rdbt into Grange Park Lane, hotel at end

Situated between Hull and Beverley, this large hotel is set in 12 acres of landscaped gardens. Bedrooms are comfortably appointed for both business and leisure guests. There are extensive conference facilities, and The Seb Coe Leisure Club has a hair and beauty centre.

Rooms 100 (8 fmly) (15 GF) (5 smoking) **S** £49-£140; **D** £49-£140* **Facilities** FTV ⓣ supervised Gym Steam room Sauna New Year Wi-fi **Conf** Class 250 Board 80 Thtr 550 Del from £99 to £155* **Services** Lift **Parking** 600 **Notes** LB ⊗ Civ Wed 120

Innkeeper's Lodge Hull

BUDGET HOTEL

☎ 0845 112 6036 📠 0845 112 6266
Beverley Rd HU10 6NT
web: www.innkeeperslodge.com/hull
dir: M62/A63, exit at Humber Bridge follow signs for A164 north for Beverley. Lodge 3m on left opposite Willerby Shopping Park

Innkeeper's Lodge represents an exciting, high value concept within the budget hotel market. Comfortable bedrooms provide excellent facilities that include satellite TV and modem points. Options include family rooms; and for the corporate guest, cutting edge IT which includes Wi-fi access. A popular Carvery provides all-day food, including an extensive, complimentary continental breakfast. See also the Hotel Groups pages.

Rooms 32 (12 fmly)

| **YORKSHIRE, NORTH** |

| **ALDWARK** | **Map 19 SE46** |

Aldwark Manor Golf & Spa Hotel

★★★★ 73% HOTEL

☎ 01347 838146 📠 01347 838867
YO61 1UF
e-mail: aldwarkmanor@qhotels.co.uk
web: www.qhotels.co.uk
dir: A1/A59 towards Green Hammerton, then B6265 Little Ouseburn. Follow signs for Aldwark Bridge/Manor. A19 through Linton-on-Ouse

Mature parkland forms the impressive backdrop for this rambling 19th-century mansion, with the River Ure flowing gently through the hotel's own 18-hole golf course. Bedrooms vary; the main-house rooms are traditional and those in the extension are modern in design. Impressive conference and banqueting facilities and a stylish, very well equipped leisure club are available.

Rooms 54 (6 fmly) **Facilities** Spa STV ⓣ ⚓ 18 Putt green Gym Health & beauty Xmas New Year Wi-fi **Conf** Class 100 Board 80 Thtr 240 Del from £130 to £150* **Services** Lift **Parking** 150 **Notes** ⊗ Civ Wed 140

ASKRIGG — Map 18 SD99

White Rose

★★ 72% SMALL HOTEL

☎ 01969 650515 📄 01969 650176
Main St DL8 3HG
e-mail: stay@thewhiterosehotelaskrigg.co.uk
dir: M6 or A1onto A684. Follow signs to Askrigg, hotel in centre of village

This family-run hotel dates from the 19th century, and is situated in the heart of Askrigg which was the fictional town of Darrowby in the BBC's *All Creatures Great and Small* series. The friendliness of the staff is noteworthy. The accommodation is tastefully decorated and comfortably furnished, and home cooked food is served in the conservatory overlooking the beer garden.

Rooms 12 **S** £45; **D** £70-£80 (incl. bkfst)* **Facilities** New Year **Parking** 20 **Notes** LB Closed 24-25 Dec

---

AUSTWICK — Map 18 SD76

The Austwick Traddock

★★ 84% ◉ SMALL HOTEL

☎ 015242 51224 📄 015242 51796
LA2 8BY
e-mail: info@austwicktraddock.co.uk
dir: Off A65 into village centre, 3m NW of Settle

Situated within the Yorkshire Dales National Park and in a peaceful village environment, this Georgian country house with well-tended gardens offers a haven of calm. There are two comfortable lounges, with real fires and fine furnishings, as well as a cosy bar and an elegant dining room serving good food. Bedrooms are all individually styled with many homely touches.

Rooms 12 (1 fmly) (1 GF) **S** £85-£95; **D** £90-£175 (incl. bkfst)* **Facilities** Xmas New Year Wi-fi **Conf** Board 16 Del from £150 to £189* **Parking** 20 **Notes** LB

AYSGARTH

George & Dragon

◉ RESTAURANT WITH ROOMS

☎ 01969 663358 📄 01969 668773
DL8 3AD
e-mail: info@georgeanddragonaysgarth.co.uk
dir: A684, on main road in village

This 17th-century coaching inn offers spacious, comfortably appointed rooms. Popular with walkers, the cosy bar has a real fire and a good selection of local beers. The beamed restaurant serves hearty breakfasts and interesting meals using fresh local produce. Service is very friendly and attentive.

Rooms 7 (2 fmly)

BAINBRIDGE — Map 18 SD99

Rose & Crown

★★ 67% HOTEL

☎ 01969 650225 📄 01969 650735
DL8 3EE
e-mail: info@theprideofwensleydale.com
dir: on A684 between Hawes & Leyburn

This traditional coaching inn, overlooking the village green, is full of character. Bedrooms are appropriately furnished and comfortably equipped. There are two well-stocked bars, one very popular with locals, both offering an interesting range of dishes. Finer dining is served in the restaurant, and a cosy residents' lounge is also provided.

Rooms 12 (1 fmly) **Conf** Class 30 Board 30 **Parking** 65

BILBROUGH — Map 16 SE54

Travelodge York Tadcaster

BUDGET HOTEL

☎ 0871 984 6186 📄 0870 191 1685
Tadcaster LS24 8EG
web: www.travelodge.co.uk
dir: On A64 eastbound

Travelodge offers good quality, good value, budget accommodation. All offer family rooms sleeping up to four (two adults, two children) with en suite bathroom/shower-room, remote-control TV, tea- and coffee-making facilities and comfortable beds. Food options vary. Breakfast is at the on-site Bar Café restaurant (if available) or to take away. See also Hotel Groups pages.

Rooms 62 **S** fr £29; **D** fr £29

BOLTON ABBEY — Map 19 SE05

INSPECTORS' CHOICE

The Devonshire Arms Country House Hotel & Spa

★★★★ ◉◉◉ HOTEL

☎ 01756 710441 & 718111 📄 01756 710564
BD23 6AJ
e-mail: res@thedevonshirehotels.co.uk
web: www.devonshirehotels.co.uk
dir: On B6160, 250yds N of junct with A59

With stunning views of the Wharfedale countryside this beautiful hotel, owned by the Duke and Duchess of Devonshire, dates back to the 17th century. Bedrooms are elegantly furnished; those in the old part of the house are particularly spacious and have four-posters and fine antiques. The sitting rooms are delightfully cosy with log fires, and the dedicated staff deliver service with a blend of friendliness and professionalism. The Burlington Restaurant offers award-winning, highly accomplished cuisine, while the Brasserie provides a lighter alternative.

Rooms 40 (1 fmly) (17 GF) **S** £186-£342; **D** £245-£420 (incl. bkfst) **Facilities** Spa STV ⊗ supervised ♨ Fishing 🐟 Gym Classic cars Falconry Laser pigeon shooting Fly fishing Cricket Xmas New Year Wi-fi **Conf** Class 80 Board 30 Thtr 90 **Parking** 150 **Notes** LB Civ Wed 90

BOROUGHBRIDGE — Map 19 SE36

Best Western Crown

★★★ 75% HOTEL

☎ 01423 322328 📄 01423 324512
Horsefair YO51 9LB
e-mail: sales@crownboroughbridge.co.uk
web: www.crownboroughbridge.co.uk
dir: A1(M) junct 48. Hotel 1m towards town centre at T-junct

Situated in the centre of town but convenient for the A1, The Crown provides a full leisure complex, conference rooms and a secure car park. Bedrooms are well appointed. A wide range of well-prepared dishes can be enjoyed in both the restaurant and bar.

Rooms 37 (3 fmly) (2 GF) **Facilities** ⊗ supervised Gym Xmas **Conf** Class 80 Board 80 Thtr 150 **Services** Lift **Parking** 60 **Notes** LB ⊗ Civ Wed 120

BURNSALL — Map 19 SE06

Red Lion Hotel & Manor House

★★ 75% ◉ HOTEL

☎ 01756 720204 ▤ 01756 720292
By the Bridge BD23 6BU
e-mail: redlion@daelnet.co.uk
web: www.redlion.co.uk
dir: On B6160 between Grassington and Bolton Abbey

This delightful 16th-century Dales' inn stands adjacent to a five-arch bridge over the scenic River Wharfe. Stylish, comfortable bedrooms are individually decorated and well equipped. Public areas include a tasteful lounge and a traditional oak-panelled bar. The elegant restaurant makes good use of fresh local ingredients, and breakfasts are memorable. Guests are free to fish in the hotel's own stretch of water.

Rooms 25 (15 annexe) (5 fmly) (4 GF) **S** fr £60; **D** £80-£152.50 (incl. bkfst)* **Facilities** FTV Fishing Xmas New Year Wi-fi **Conf** Class 50 Board 25 Thtr 60 Del from £198* **Parking** 80 **Notes** LB Civ Wed 125

Devonshire Fell

RESTAURANT WITH ROOMS

☎ 01756 729000 ▤ 01756 729009
BD23 6BT
e-mail: manager@devonshirefell.co.uk
web: www.devonshirefell.co.uk
dir: On B6160, 6m from Bolton Abbey rdbt A59 junct

Located on the edge of the attractive village of Burnsall, this establishment offers comfortable, well-equipped accommodation in a relaxing atmosphere. There is an extensive menu featuring local produce, and meals can be taken either in the bar area or the more formal restaurant. A function room with views over the valley is also available.

Rooms 12 (2 fmly)

BYLAND ABBEY — Map 19 SE57

The Abbey Inn

◉ RESTAURANT WITH ROOMS

☎ 01347 868204 ▤ 01347 868678
YO61 4BD
e-mail: paul.tatham@english-heritage.org.uk
web: www.bylandabbeyinn.com

There is an abundance of history, charm and character at this romantic inn located at the foot of the Hambleton Hills and opposite the ruins of Byland Abbey. Delicious meals are prepared using high quality, local ingredients and served in the candlelit dining rooms. There are three delightfully furnished bedrooms, each with generously sized en suite bathrooms.

Rooms 3

CRATHORNE — Map 19 NZ40

INSPECTORS' CHOICE

Crathorne Hall

★★★★ ◉◉ HOTEL

☎ 01642 700398 ▤ 01642 700814
TS15 0AR
e-mail: crathornehall@handpicked.co.uk
web: www.handpicked.co.uk
dir: Off A19, take slip road signed Teesside Airport & Kirklevington, then right signed Crathorne to hotel

This splendid Edwardian hall sits in its own landscaped grounds and enjoys fine views of the Leven Valley and rolling Cleveland Hills. Both the impressively equipped bedrooms and the delightful public areas offer sumptuous levels of comfort, with elegant antique furnishings that complement the hotel's architectural style. The elegant Leven Restaurant is a traditional setting for fine dining; there's also the Drawing Room and Nancy Tennant Lounge for lighter food options. Weather permitting, alfresco eating is available on the terrace, and a luxury hamper can be provided for guests venturing further afield. Conference and banqueting facilities are available.

Rooms 37 (4 fmly) **Facilities** ✤ Jogging track Clay pigeon shooting Xmas Wi-fi **Conf** Class 75 Board 60 Thtr 120 **Services** Lift **Parking** 88 **Notes** ⊗ Civ Wed 90

EASINGTON — Map 19 NZ71

Grinkle Park

★★★ 81% ◉ HOTEL

☎ 01287 640515 ▤ 01287 641278
TS13 4UB
e-mail: info.grinklepark@classiclodges.co.uk
web: www.classiclodges.co.uk
dir: Take A171 from Guisborough towards Whitby. Hotel signed on left

A baronial hall built in 1880 situated between the North Yorkshire Moors and the coast, and surrounded by 35 acres of parkland and gardens where peacocks roam. It retains many original features including fine wood panelling, and the bedrooms are individually designed. The comfortable lounge and bar have welcoming log fires. The Camelia Room is ideal for smaller weddings and private dining.

Rooms 20 (1 fmly) **Facilities** ⦵ ✤ Xmas New Year Wi-fi **Conf** Class 80 Board 40 Thtr 120 **Parking** 150 **Notes** ⊗ Civ Wed 150

EASINGWOLD — Map 19 SE56

George

THE CIRCLE

★★ 75% SMALL HOTEL

☎ 01347 821698 ▤ 01347 823448
Market Place YO61 3AD
e-mail: info@the-george-hotel.co.uk
web: www.the-george-hotel.co.uk
dir: Off A19 midway between York & Thirsk, in Market Place

A friendly welcome awaits at this former coaching inn that faces the Georgian market square. Bedrooms are very comfortably furnished and well equipped, and the mews homes have their own external access. An extensive range of well-produced food is available both in the bar and restaurant. There are two comfortable lounges and complimentary use of a local fitness centre.

Rooms 15 (2 fmly) (6 GF) **S** £75-£85; **D** £80-£110 (incl. bkfst)* **Facilities** STV Complimentry use of local fitness centre New Year Wi-fi **Conf** Board 12 Del from £100 to £150* **Parking** 10 **Notes** LB ⊗

ESCRICK Map 16 SE64

Parsonage Country House

★★★ 78% ⚜ COUNTRY HOUSE HOTEL

☎ 01904 728111 ▤ 01904 728151
York Rd YO19 6LF
e-mail: reservations@parsonagehotel.co.uk
web: www.parsonagehotel.co.uk
dir: A64 onto A19 Selby. Follow to Escrick. Hotel by St Helens Church

This 19th-century, former parsonage, has been carefully restored and extended to provide delightful accommodation, set in well-tended gardens. Bedrooms are smartly appointed and well equipped both for business and leisure guests. Spacious public areas include an elegant restaurant, excellent meeting and conference facilities and a choice of attractive lounges.

Rooms 50 (13 annexe) (4 fmly) (9 GF) (8 smoking)
S £85-£140; **D** £99-£140 (incl. bkfst)* **Facilities** STV Putt green Xmas New Year Wi-fi **Conf** Class 80 Board 50 Thtr 180 Del from £135 to £140* **Services** Lift **Parking** 100 **Notes** LB ⊗ Civ Wed 150

See advert on page 527

GUISBOROUGH Map 19 NZ61

Macdonald Gisborough Hall

★★★★ 80% ⚜ HOTEL

☎ 0844 879 9149 ▤ 01287 610844
Whitby Ln TS14 6PT
e-mail: general.gisboroughhall@macdonald-hotels.co.uk
web: www.macdonald-hotels.co.uk
dir: A171, follow signs for Whitby to Waterfall rdbt then 3rd exit into Whitby Lane, hotel 500yds on right

Dating back to the mid-19th century, this elegant establishment provides a pleasing combination of original features and modern facilities. Bedrooms, including four-poster and family rooms, are richly furnished, while there is a choice of welcoming lounges with log fires. Imaginative fare is served in Tockett's restaurant.

Rooms 71 (2 fmly) (12 GF) **S** £83-£172; **D** £93-£182 (incl. bkfst)* **Facilities** STV ⭤ Beauty treatment rooms Xmas New Year Wi-fi **Conf** Class 150 Board 32 Thtr 400 Del from £130 to £175* **Services** Lift **Parking** 180 **Notes** LB Closed 2-6 Jan Civ Wed 250

HACKNESS Map 17 SE99

Hackness Grange Country House

★★★ 73% HOTEL

☎ 01723 882345 & 374374 ▤ 01723 882391
North York National Park YO13 0JW
e-mail: admin@englishrosehotels.co.uk
dir: A64 to Scarborough, then A171 to Whitby & Scalby. Follow Hackness & Forge Valley National Park signs, through Hackness, hotel on left

Close to Scarborough, and set in the North Yorkshire Moors National Park, Hackness Grange is surrounded by well-tended gardens. Comfortable bedrooms have views of the open countryside; those in the cottages are ideally suited to families, and the courtyard rooms include facilities for the less able. Lounges and the restaurant are spacious and relaxing.

Rooms 33 (21 annexe) (5 fmly) (8 GF) **S** £49.50-£89; **D** £89-£150 (incl. bkfst)* **Facilities** ⊛ ⭤ Putt green Xmas New Year **Conf** Board 14 Thtr 20 Del from £105 to £175* **Parking** 60 **Notes** LB ⊗

HAROME

See Helmsley

HARROGATE Map 19 SE35

See also **Knaresborough**

INSPECTORS' CHOICE

Rudding Park Hotel & Golf
★★★★ ⚜⚜ HOTEL

☎ 01423 871350 ▤ 01423 872286
Rudding Park, Follifoot HG3 1JH
e-mail: reservations@ruddingpark.com
web: www.ruddingpark.co.uk
dir: From A61 at rdbt with A658 take York exit, follow signs to Rudding Park

In the heart of 200-year-old landscaped parkland, this modern hotel is elegant and stylish. Bedrooms, including two luxurious suites, are very smartly presented and thoughtfully equipped. Carefully prepared meals and Yorkshire tapas are served in the Clocktower, with its striking, contemporary decor. The stylish bar leads to the conservatory with a generous terrace for alfresco dining. The grandeur of the mansion house and the grounds make this a very popular venue for weddings. There is an adjoining 18-hole, par 72 golf course and an 18-bay floodlit, covered driving range; this hotel also provides extensive facilities for corporate activities.

Rooms 49 (19 GF) **S** £165-£375; **D** £195-£375 (incl. bkfst)* **Facilities** STV ⭤ 18 Putt green Driving range Jogging trail Membership of local gym Xmas New Year Wi-fi **Conf** Class 150 Board 40 Thtr 300 Del from £215 to £445* **Services** Lift **Parking** 150 **Notes** LB Civ Wed 300

Hotel du Vin Harrogate

★★★★ 81% ⚜⚜ TOWN HOUSE HOTEL

☎ 01423 856800 ▤ 01423 856801
Prospect Place HG1 1LB
e-mail: info@harrogate.hotelduvin.com
web: www.hotelduvin.com
dir: A1(M) junct 47, A59 to Harrogate, follow town centre signs to Prince of Wales rdbt, 3rd exit, remain in right lane. Right at lights into Albert St, right into Prospect Place

This town house was created from eight Georgian-style properties and overlooks The Stray. The spacious, open-plan lobby has seating, a bar and the reception desk. Hidden downstairs is a cosy snug cellar. The French-influenced bistro offers high quality cooking and a great choice of wines. Bedrooms face front and back, and are smart and modern, with excellent 'deluge' showers.

Rooms 51 (4 GF) **Facilities** STV FTV Xmas New Year Wi-fi **Conf** Board 20 Thtr 50 **Services** Lift **Parking** 30 **Notes** LB Civ Wed 90

Barceló Harrogate Majestic Hotel

★★★★ 75% HOTEL

☎ 01423 700300 📄 01423 502283
Ripon Rd HG1 2HU
e-mail: majestic@barcelo-hotels.co.uk
web: www.barcelo-hotels.co.uk
dir: From M1 onto A1(M) at Wetherby. Take A661 to Harrogate. Hotel in town centre adjacent to Royal Hall

Popular for conferences and functions, this grand Victorian hotel is set in 12 acres of landscaped grounds that is within walking distance of the town centre. It benefits from spacious public areas, and the comfortable bedrooms, including some spacious suites, come in a variety of sizes.

Rooms 174 (8 fmly) **Facilities** Spa STV ⊛ supervised ⊛ Gym Golf practice net Xmas New Year Wi-fi **Conf** Class 260 Board 70 Thtr 500 Del from £99* **Services** Lift **Parking** 250 **Notes** Civ Wed 200

Holiday Inn Harrogate

★★★★ 72% HOTEL

☎ 0870 4431 761 📄 01423 524435
Kings Rd HG1 1XX
e-mail: gm.hiharrogate@qmh-hotels.com
web: www.holidayinn.co.uk
dir: A1 to A59. Hotel adjoins International Conference Centre

Situated just a short walk from the town centre, this impressive hotel lies adjacent to the Harrogate International Conference Centre. Bedrooms are stylishly furnished. Extensive conference facilities and a business centre are provided. Public areas include the first-floor restaurant and ground floor lounge bar. Nearby private parking is a bonus.

Rooms 214 (7 fmly) **Facilities** Gym Wi-fi **Conf** Class 150 Board 100 Thtr 300 **Services** Lift **Parking** 160 **Notes** LB

Best Western Cedar Court

★★★★ 70% HOTEL

☎ 01423 858585 & 858595 (res) 📄 01423 504950
Queens Buildings, Park Pde HG1 5AH
e-mail: cedarcourt@bestwestern.co.uk
web: www.cedarcourthotels.co.uk
dir: From A1(M) follow signs to Harrogate on A661 past Sainsburys. At rdbt left onto A6040. Hotel right after church

This Grade II listed building was Harrogate's first hotel and enjoys a peaceful location in landscaped grounds, close to the town centre. It provides spacious, well-equipped accommodation. Public areas include a brasserie-style restaurant, a small gym and an open-plan lounge and bar. Functions and conferences are particularly well catered for.

Rooms 100 (8 fmly) (7 GF) **S** £89-£149; **D** £89-£149 (incl. bkfst) **Facilities** FTV Gym Xmas New Year Wi-fi **Conf** Class 300 Board 240 Thtr 650 Del from £119 to £159 **Services** Lift **Parking** 150 **Notes** LB ⊗ Civ Wed 150

HARROGATE *continued*

The Boar's Head Hotel

★★★ 83% ◉◉ HOTEL

☎ 01423 771888 📄 01423 771509
Ripley Castle Estate HG3 3AY
e-mail: reservations@boarsheadripley.co.uk
dir: On A61 (Harrogate to Ripon road). Hotel in town centre

Part of the Ripley Castle estate, this delightful and popular hotel is renowned for its warm hospitality and as a dining destination. Bedrooms offer many comforts, and the luxurious day rooms feature works of art from the nearby castle. The banqueting suites in the castle are very impressive.

Rooms 25 (6 annexe) (2 fmly) **S** £105-£125; **D** £125-£150 (incl. bkfst)* **Facilities** ⚲ Fishing Clay pigeon shooting Tennis Fishing 🎵 Xmas New Year Wi-fi **Conf** Class 80 Board 150 Thtr 150 Del from £155* **Parking** 50 **Notes** LB Civ Wed 120

Number 28 (formerly Studley Hotel)

★★★ 78% ◉ HOTEL

☎ 01423 560425 📄 01423 530967
Swan Rd HG1 2SE
e-mail: info@studleyhotel.co.uk
web: www.studleyhotel.co.uk
dir: Adjacent to Valley Gardens, opposite Mercer Gallery

This friendly, well-established hotel, close to the town centre and Valley Gardens, is well known for its Orchid Restaurant, which provides a dynamic and authentic approach to Pacific Rim and Asian cuisine. Bedrooms are modern and come in a variety of styles and sizes, whilst the stylish bar lounge provides guests with an excellent place for relaxing.

Rooms 31 (1 fmly) **Facilities** Free use of local Health & Spa Club Wi-fi **Conf** Class 15 Board 12 Thtr 15 **Services** Lift **Parking** 15 **Notes** ⊗ Closed 23-30 Dec

Old Swan

★★★ 78% HOTEL

☎ 01423 500055 📄 01423 501154
Swan Rd HG1 2SR
e-mail: gm.oldswan@macdonald-hotels.co.uk
dir: From A1, A59 Ripon, left Empress rdbt, stay on left, right Prince of Wales rdbt. Straight across lights & turn left into Swan Rd

In the heart of Harrogate and within walking distance of the Harrogate International Centre and Valley Gardens, this hotel is famed as being Agatha Christie's hiding place during her disappearance in 1926. The bedrooms are stylishly furnished, and the public areas include the Library Restaurant, the Wedgwood Room and the lounge bar. Extensive conference and banqueting facilities are available.

Rooms 136 **S** £49-£108; **D** £67-£148* **Facilities** STV ⚲ Xmas New Year Wi-fi **Conf** Class 130 Board 100 Thtr 450 Del from £135 to £165* **Services** Lift **Parking** 175 **Notes** LB ⊗ Civ Wed 300

Ascot House Hotel

★★★ 75% HOTEL

☎ 01423 531005 📄 01423 503523
53 Kings Rd HG1 5HJ
e-mail: admin@ascothouse.com
dir: Follow Town Centre/Conference/Exhibition Centre signs into Kings Rd, hotel on left after park

This friendly privately owned and family run hotel provides well-equipped accommodation, rooms vary in style and size and include a four-poster room. Public areas include a choice of the cosy lounge or pleasant bar as well as the impressive function room and the attractive restaurant overlooking the gardens.

Rooms 18 (2 fmly) (4 GF) **S** £67-£77; **D** £97-£131 (incl. bkfst)* **Facilities** Xmas New Year Wi-fi **Conf** Class 36 Board 36 Thtr 80 **Parking** 18 **Notes** Civ Wed 86

The Yorkshire Hotel

folio Hotels

★★★ 75% HOTEL

☎ 0844 855 9114 📄 01423 500082
Prospect Place HG1 1LA
e-mail: gm.yorkshire@foliohotels.com
web: www.foliohotels.com/yorkshire
dir: A1 junct 24/A59 to town centre, right at Betty's Tea Rooms

Ideally situated in the heart of this beautiful spa town, The Yorkshire was transformed from a typical Victorian property to one that is fresh and contemporary, yet retains all the elegance of its original era. The refurbishment also included the stylish Hg1 Bar & Brasserie, very popular with both guests and local residents, that serves meals and light bites throughout the day.

Rooms 80 (1 fmly) **Facilities** FTV Xmas New Year Wi-fi **Conf** Class 60 Board 45 Thtr 120 **Services** Lift **Parking** 33 **Notes** ⊗ Civ Wed 100

Cairn

★★★ Ⓐ HOTEL

☎ 01423 504005 📄 01423 500056
Ripon Rd HG1 2JD
e-mail: salescairn@strathmorehotels.com

Rooms 135 (6 fmly) **Facilities** STV Gym 🎵 Xmas New Year Wi-fi **Conf** Class 200 Board 100 Thtr 400 **Services** Lift **Parking** 200 **Notes** LB ⊗ Civ Wed 300

See advert on page 617

Kimberley

Ⓤ

☎ 01423 505613 & 0800 783 7642 📄 01423 530276
11-19 Kings Rd HG1 5JY
dir: Follow signs for Harrogate International Centre or Kings Rd. Hotel 150yds N of centre

Currently the rating for this establishment is not confirmed. This may be due to a change of ownership or because it has only recently joined the AA rating scheme. For further details please see the AA website: theAA.com

Rooms 48

Innkeeper's Lodge Harrogate West

BUDGET HOTEL

☎ 0845 112 6034 🗎 0845 112 6268
Otley Rd, Beckwith Knowle HG3 1PR
web: www.innkeeperslodge.com/harrogatewest
dir: A1(M) junct 47, A59 for Harrogate. Over 2 rdbts, at 3rd take B6162 (Otley Road). Lodge on left opposite church

Innkeeper's Lodge Select represents an exciting, stylish concept within the hotel market. Contemporary style bedrooms provide excellent facilities that include LCD TVs with satellite channels, and modem points. Options include spacious family rooms; and for the corporate guest there's Wi-fi access. All-day food is served in a modern country pub & eating house. The extensive continental breakfast is complimentary. See also the Hotel Groups pages.

Rooms 13 (2 fmly)

Travelodge Harrogate

BUDGET HOTEL

☎ 0871 984 6238 🗎 01423 562734
The Ginnel, Off Parliament St HG1 2RB
web: www.travelodge.co.uk
dir: Follow signs for town centre. Lodge behind Royal Baths Assembly Rooms, just off Parliament St. Accessed off The Ginnel

Travelodge offers good quality, good value, budget accommodation. All offer family rooms sleeping up to four (two adults, two children) with en suite bathroom/shower-room, remote-control TV, tea- and coffee-making facilities and comfortable beds. Food options vary. Breakfast is at the on-site Bar Café restaurant (if available) or to take away. See also Hotel Groups pages.

Rooms 46 **S** fr £29; **D** fr £29

HAWES   Map 18 SD88

Simonstone Hall

★★ 78% HOTEL

☎ 01969 667255 🗎 01969 667741
Simonstone DL8 3LY
e-mail: email@simonstonehall.demon.co.uk
web: www.simonstonehall.co.uk
dir: 1.5m N on road signed to Muker and Buttertubs

This former hunting lodge provides professional, friendly service and a relaxed atmosphere. There is an inviting drawing room, stylish fine dining restaurant, a bar and conservatory. The generally spacious bedrooms are elegantly finished to reflect the style of the house, and many offer spectacular views of the countryside.

Rooms 18 (10 fmly) (2 GF) **S** £95-£100; **D** £105-£155 (incl. bkfst)* **Facilities** Xmas Wi-fi **Conf** Class 20 Board 20 Thtr 50 **Parking** 40 **Notes** Civ Wed 72

HELMSLEY   Map 19 SE68

HOTEL OF THE YEAR

Feversham Arms Hotel & Verbena Spa

★★★★ 80% ◎◎ HOTEL

☎ 01439 770766 🗎 01439 770346
1 High St YO62 5AG
e-mail: info@fevershamarmshotel.com
web: www.fevershamarmshotel.com
dir: A168 (signed Thirsk) from A1 then A170 or A64 (signed York) from A1 to York North, then B1363 to Helmsley. Hotel 125mtrs from Market Place

This long established hotel lies just round the corner from the main square, and under its caring ownership proves to be a refined operation, yet without airs and graces. There are several lounge areas and a high-ceilinged conservatory restaurant where good local ingredients are prepared with skill and minimal fuss. The bedrooms, including four poolside suites, have their own individual character and decor.
AA Hotel of the Year for England 2009-10.

Rooms 33 (9 fmly) (8 GF) **Facilities** Spa STV FTV ⚡ Sauna Saunarium Spa opening Oct 2008 Xmas New Year Wi-fi **Conf** Class 20 Board 24 Thtr 35 **Services** Lift **Parking** 50 **Notes** LB Civ Wed 50

Black Swan Hotel

★★★★ 78% HOTEL

☎ 01439 770466 🗎 01439 770174
Market Place YO62 5BJ
e-mail: enquiries@blackswan-helmsley.co.uk
web: www.blackswan-helmsley.co.uk
dir: A1 junct 49, A168, A170 east, hotel 14m from Thirsk

People have been visiting this establishment for over 200 years and it has become a landmark that dominates the market square. The hotel is renowned for its hospitality and friendliness; many of the staff are long-serving and dedicated. The bedrooms are stylish and include a junior suite and feature rooms. The hotel has a Tearoom and Patisserie that is open daily. The AA Rosette award for the restaurant cuisine is currently suspended due to a change of chef.

Rooms 45 (4 fmly) **Facilities** STV ⚡ Use of leisure & spa facilities at nearby sister hotel Xmas New Year Wi-fi **Conf** Class 30 Board 26 Thtr 50 Del from £145 to £165 **Parking** 50 **Notes** Civ Wed 130

HOVINGHAM   Map 19 SE67

Worsley Arms

★★★ 72% HOTEL

☎ 01653 628234 🗎 01653 628130
High St YO62 4LA
e-mail: worsleyarms@aol.com
dir: A64, signed York, towards Malton. At dual carriageway left to Hovingham. At Slingsby left, then 2m

Overlooking the village green, this hotel has relaxing and attractive lounges with welcoming open fires. Bedrooms are also comfortable and several are contained in cottages across the green. The restaurant provides interesting quality cooking, with less formal dining in the Cricketers' Bar and Bistro to the rear.

Rooms 20 (8 annexe) (2 fmly) (4 GF) **S** £65-£85; **D** £90-£140 (incl. bkfst) **Facilities** FTV ⚡ Shooting Xmas New Year **Conf** Class 40 Board 20 Thtr 40 Del from £150 to £170 **Parking** 25 **Notes** LB Civ Wed 100

KNARESBOROUGH — Map 19 SE35

Innkeeper's Lodge Harrogate East

BUDGET HOTEL

☎ 0845 112 6033 🖨 0845 112 6269
Wetherby Rd, Plompton HG5 8LY
web: www.innkeeperslodge.com/harrogateeast
dir: A1(M) junct 47, A59 for Harrogate.Then A658 over 2 rdbts. At 3rd rdbtright onto A661 (Wetherby Rd). Lodge on left

Innkeeper's Lodge represents an exciting, high value concept within the budget hotel market. Comfortable bedrooms provide excellent facilities that include satellite TV and modem points. This carefully restored lodge is in a picturesque setting and has its own unique style and quirky character. Food is served all day, and an extensive, complimentary continental breakfast is offered. See also the Hotel Groups pages.

Rooms 10 **Conf** Thtr 25

General Tarleton Inn

⊛⊛ RESTAURANT WITH ROOMS

☎ 01423 340284 🖨 01423 340288
Boroughbridge Rd, Ferrensby HG5 0PZ
e-mail: gfi@generaltarleton.co.uk
dir: A1(M) junct 48 at Boroughbridge, take A6055 to Knaresborough. 4m on right

Food is a real feature here with skilfully prepared meals served in the restaurant, traditional bar and modern conservatory. Accommodation is provided in brightly decorated and airy rooms, and the bathrooms are thoughtfully equipped. Enjoying a country location, yet close to the A1(M), the inn remains popular with both business and leisure guests.

Rooms 14

LASTINGHAM — Map 19 SE79

Lastingham Grange

★★★ 80% HOTEL

☎ 01751 417345 & 417402 🖨 01751 417358
Y062 6TH
e-mail: reservations@lastinghamgrange.com
dir: From A170 follow signs for Appleton-le-Moors, continue into Lastingham, pass church on left & turn right then left up hill. Hotel on right

A warm welcome and sincere hospitality have been the hallmarks of this hotel for over 50 years. Antique furniture is plentiful, and the lounge and the dining room both look out onto the terrace and sunken rose garden below. There is a large play area for older children and the moorland views are breathtaking.

Rooms 12 (2 fmly) **S** £100-£125; **D** £180-£210 (incl. bkfst)* **Facilities** 🧸 Large adventure playground Wi-fi **Parking** 30 **Notes** LB Closed Dec-Feb

LEEMING BAR — Map 19 SE28

Lodge at Leeming Bar

★★ 71% HOTEL

☎ 01677 422122 🖨 01677 424507
The Great North Rd DL8 1DT
e-mail: thelodgeatleemingbar@btinternet.com
dir: Off A1 at Bedale/Northallerton A684 junct. Follow signs for Leeming Bar/Services & Motel

Conveniently located just off the A1, this hotel offers bedrooms that vary in style, but all are well equipped for business and leisure guests; some feature flat-screen TVs and air conditioning. Meals are served in the bar and Old Market Square Restaurant. A meeting room is also available, and there is ample parking as well as a shop and café on site.

Rooms 39 **Notes** Closed 25-26 Dec

The White Rose

★★ 65% HOTEL

☎ 01677 422707 🖨 01677 425123
Bedale Rd DL7 9AY
e-mail: reception@whiterosehotel.co.uk
dir: A1 onto A684, left towards Northallerton. Hotel 0.25m on left

Conveniently located just minutes from the A1, this commercial hotel offers pleasant, well-equipped

bedrooms situated in a modern block to the rear. Good-value meals are offered in either the traditional bar or attractive dining room.

Rooms 18 (2 fmly) (1 GF) **Facilities** STV 🎵 Wi-fi **Parking** 50

LEYBURN — Map 19 SE19

Golden Lion Hotel & Restaurant

Ⓤ

☎ 01969 622161
Market Place DL8 5AS
web: www.thegoldenlion.co.uk
dir: on A684 in market square

Currently the rating for this establishment is not confirmed. This may be due to a change of ownership or because it has only recently joined the AA rating scheme. For further details please see the AA website: theAA.com

Rooms 13 (4 fmly) **Facilities** FTV Xmas New Year **Conf** Board 30 Thtr 40 **Services** Lift **Notes** LB

LUMBY — Map 16 SE43

Quality Hotel Leeds Selby

★★★ 63% HOTEL

☎ 01977 682761 🖨 01977 685462
A1/A63 Junction LS25 5LF
e-mail: enquiries@hotels-leeds-selby.com
dir: A1(M) junct 42/A63 signed Selby, hotel on A63 on left

A modern hotel situated in extensive grounds near the A1/A63 junction. Attractive day rooms include the Woodlands Restaurant and the Leisure Club includes outdoor tennis and golf. Service, includes an all-day lounge menu and 24-hour room service.

Rooms 97 (18 fmly) (40 GF) **Facilities** STV 🏊 🏌 Putt green Gym Xmas New Year Wi-fi **Conf** Class 100 Board 80 Thtr 160 **Parking** 250 **Notes** LB Civ Wed 120

MALTON — Map 19 SE77

Burythorpe House Hotel

★★★ 82% ⊛ COUNTRY HOUSE HOTEL

☎ 01653 658200 🖨 01653 658204
Burythorpe Y017 9LB
e-mail: reception@burythorpehousehotel.com
dir: 4m S of Malton & 4m from A64 (York to Scarborough road

A delightful country house offering a relaxed atmosphere combined with attentive service. The individually styled and furnished bedrooms feature beautifully presented beds, high quality accessories such as flat-screen TVs and all have lovely outlooks; some rooms are really stunning. Public areas include a spacious comfortable lounge. Delicious, skilfully prepared meals using fresh, local ingredients are served in the oak-panelled dining room.

Rooms 13 (1 GF) **S** £82.50-£125; **D** £105-£190 (incl. bkfst)* **Facilities** FTV ⓒ 🌊 🌱 Gym Xmas New Year Wi-fi **Conf** Class 40 Board 24 Thtr 50 **Notes** ⊗ Civ Wed 60

Talbot

★★ 64% HOTEL

☎ 01653 693355 & 01723 374374 📠 01653 698165
Yorkersgate YO17 7AJ
e-mail: sales@englishrosehotels.co.uk
dir: Off A64 towards Malton. Hotel on right

Situated close to the centre of town this long-established, creeper-covered hotel looks out towards the River Derwent and open countryside. Bedroom sizes vary, but all are comfortable. The public rooms are traditional and elegantly furnished, and include a bar plus a separate lounge.

Rooms 31 (3 fmly) **S** £39.50-£65; **D** £70-£130 (incl. bkfst)* **Facilities** Xmas New Year **Conf** Board 20 Thtr 50 Del from £70 to £125* **Parking** 30 **Notes** LB ⊗

MARKINGTON Map 19 SE26

Hob Green

★★★ 82% COUNTRY HOUSE HOTEL

☎ 01423 770031 📠 01423 771589
HG3 3PJ
e-mail: info@hobgreen.com
web: www.hobgreen.com
dir: From A61, 4m N of Harrogate, left at Wormald Green, follow hotel signs

This hospitable country house is set in delightful gardens amidst rolling countryside midway between Harrogate and Ripon. The inviting lounges boast open fires in season and there is an elegant restaurant with a small private dining room. The individual bedrooms are very comfortable and come with a host of thoughtful extras.

Rooms 12 (1 fmly) **S** £95-£115; **D** £115-£135 (incl. bkfst)* **Facilities** 🌱 Xmas New Year **Conf** Class 10 Board 10 Thtr 15 **Parking** 40 **Notes** LB Civ Wed 35

See advert on page 509

MASHAM Map 19 SE28

INSPECTORS' CHOICE

Swinton Park

★★★★ ◉◉◉ HOTEL

☎ 01765 680900 📠 01765 680901
HG4 4JH
e-mail: enquiries@swintonpark.com
web: www.swintonpark.com
dir: A1 onto B6267/8 to Masham. Follow signs through town centre & turn right into Swinton Terrace. 1m past golf course, over bridge, up hill. Hotel on right

Although extended during the Victorian and Edwardian eras, the original part of this welcoming castle dates from the 17th century. Bedrooms are luxuriously furnished and come with a host of thoughtful extras. Samuel's restaurant (built for the current owner's great-great-great grandfather) is very elegant and serves imaginative dishes using local produce, much being sourced from the Swinton estate itself.

Rooms 30 (5 fmly) **S** £160-£350; **D** £160-£350 (incl. bkfst)* **Facilities** Spa FTV ⚡ 9 Putt green Fishing 🌱 Gym Shooting Falconry Pony trekking Cookery school Off-road driving Spa Xmas New Year Wi-fi Child facilities **Conf** Class 60 Board 40 Thtr 120 Del from £205 to £230* **Services** Lift **Parking** 50 **Notes** LB Civ Wed 120

The Kings Head

★★ 69% HOTEL

☎ 01765 689295 📠 01765 689070
Market Place HG4 4EF
e-mail: kings.head.6395@thespiritgroup.com
dir: from A1 take B6267/8 to Masham, follow Market Place signs

This historic hotel, with its uneven floors, beamed bars and attractive window boxes, looks out over the large market square. Guests have the option of choosing either the elegant bedrooms in the main building or the more contemporary ones at the rear of the property; all rooms

---

are thoughtfully equipped. Public areas are traditional in style and include a popular bar and smartly appointed restaurant.

Rooms 27 (15 annexe) (4 fmly) (10 GF) **Facilities** FTV Wi-fi **Conf** Class 24 Board 30 Thtr 54 **Parking** 3 **Notes** LB ⊗

MIDDLESBROUGH Map 19 NZ41

Thistle Middlesbrough   thistle

★★★★ 73% HOTEL

☎ 0871 376 9028 📠 0871 376 9128
Fry St TS1 1JH
e-mail: middlesbrough@thistle.co.uk
web: www.thistlehotels.com/middlesbrough
dir: A19 onto A66 signed Middlesbrough. A66 after Zetland car park. 3rd exit at 1st rdbt, 2nd exit at 2nd rdbt

The staff here are committed to guest care and nothing is too much trouble. Located close to the town centre and football ground this establishment offers bedrooms of varying sizes, that are well furnished and comfortably equipped. The contemporary first-floor CoMotion café bar leads into the open-plan Gengis restaurant featuring an interesting range of globally inspired dishes. Guests have full use of the hotel's Otium health club.

Rooms 132 (8 fmly) **S** £65-£75; **D** £65-£85 (incl. bkfst)* **Facilities** STV FTV ⓒ Gym Beautician Steam room Sauna New Year Wi-fi **Conf** Class 144 Board 100 Thtr 400 Del from £110 to £130* **Services** Lift **Parking** 66 **Notes** LB Civ Wed 400

Best Western Middlesbrough

★★★ 72% HOTEL

☎ 01642 817638 📠 01642 821219
335 Marton Rd TS4 2PA
e-mail: info@thehighfieldhotel.co.uk
dir: From A66 onto A172 to Stokesley, right at rdbt, straight on at mini rdbt. Left at next mini rdbt, hotel 150yds on right

A modernised, small hotel in the residential suburbs offering comfortable and practical bedrooms. Informal dining is very popular in the Tavistock Italia restaurant where guests will find that is service is very friendly.

Rooms 32 (2 fmly) (9 GF) **S** £45-£99; **D** £55-£124 (incl. bkfst)* **Facilities** Xmas New Year Wi-fi **Conf** Class 15 Board 15 Thtr 45 Del from £115 to £135* **Notes** ⊗

MIDDLESBOROUGH *continued*

Travelodge Middlesbrough

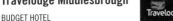

BUDGET HOTEL

☎ 0871 984 6375 📄 01642 252104
Newport Rd TS1 1JE
dir: From A19 take A66 signed Middlesbrough. At rdbt take exit signed Canon Park/Newport Rd. Lodge 0.5m on right at rear of Aldi superstore

Travelodge offers good quality, good value, budget accommodation. All offer family rooms sleeping up to four (two adults, two children) with en suite bathroom/shower-room, remote-control TV, tea- and coffee-making facilities and comfortable beds. Food options vary. Breakfast is at the on-site Bar Café restaurant (if available) or to take away. See also the Hotel Groups pages.

Rooms 55 **S** fr £29; **D** fr £29

MONK FRYSTON	Map 16 SE52

Monk Fryston Hall

★★★ 81% COUNTRY HOUSE HOTEL

☎ 01977 682369 📄 01977 683544
LS25 5DU
e-mail: reception@monkfrystonhallhotel.co.uk
web: www.monkfrystonhallhotel.co.uk
dir: A1(M) junct 42/A63 towards Selby. Monk Fryston 2m, hotel on left

This delightful 16th-century mansion house enjoys a peaceful location in 30 acres of grounds, yet is only minutes' drive from the A1. Many original features have been retained and the public rooms are furnished with antique and period pieces. Bedrooms are individually styled and thoughtfully equipped for both business and leisure guests.

Rooms 29 (2 fmly) (5 GF) **S** £75-£105; **D** £110-£175 (incl. bkfst) **Facilities** STV 🏌 Xmas New Year Wi-fi **Conf** Class 30 Board 25 Thtr 70 **Parking** 80 **Notes** LB Civ Wed 72

NORTHALLERTON	Map 19 SE39

Solberge Hall

★★★ 71% HOTEL

☎ 01609 779191 📄 01609 780472
Newby Wiske DL7 9ER
e-mail: reservations@solbergehall.co.uk
web: www.solbergehall.co.uk
dir: Exit A1 at Leeming Bar, follow A684, turn right at x-rds, hotel in 2m on right

This Grade II listed Georgian country house is set in parkland and award-winning gardens, and commands panoramic views over open countryside. Spacious

---

bedrooms, some with four-poster beds, vary in style. Public areas include a comfortable lounge bar and an elegant drawing room. The restaurant offers an interesting range of carefully prepared dishes.

Rooms 24 (7 fmly) (5 GF) **S** £50-£105; **D** £95-£150 (incl. bkfst) **Facilities** STV 🏌 Clay Pigeon Shooting (charges apply) Walks Xmas **Conf** Class 60 Board 50 Thtr 250 Del from £124.50 to £134.50* **Parking** 100 **Notes** LB Civ Wed 100

Three Tuns

RESTAURANT WITH ROOMS

☎ 01609 883301 📄 01609 883988
9 South End, Osmotherley DL6 3BN
e-mail: enquiries@threetunsrestaurant.co.uk
dir: NE of Northallerton. Off A19 into Osmotherley

Situated in the popular village of Osmotherley, the Three Tuns is full of character. Bedrooms, set above the bar and also in an adjoining building, vary in size but are stylishly furnished in pine and equipped to meet the needs of tourists and business travellers alike. The restaurant offers an imaginative menu of wholesome, modern British dishes.

Rooms 7 (4 annexe) (1 fmly)

PICKERING	Map 19 SE78

The White Swan Inn

★★★ 80% ◉ HOTEL

☎ 01751 472288 📄 01751 475554
Market Place YO18 7AA
e-mail: welcome@white-swan.co.uk
web: www.white-swan.co.uk
dir: In town, between church & steam railway station

This 16th-century coaching inn offers well-equipped, comfortable bedrooms, including suites, either of a more traditional style in the main building or modern rooms in the annexe. Service is friendly and attentive. Good food is served in the attractive restaurant, in the cosy bar and

---

the lounge, where a log fire burns in cooler months. A comprehensive wine list focuses on many fine vintages. A private dining room is also available.

Rooms 21 (9 annexe) (3 fmly) (8 GF) **D** £145-£250 (incl. bkfst)* **Facilities** FTV Xmas New Year Wi-fi **Conf** Class 18 Board 25 Thtr 35 **Parking** 45 **Notes** LB Civ Wed 40

Best Western Forest & Vale

★★★ 80% HOTEL

☎ 01751 472722 📄 01751 472972
Malton Rd YO18 7DL
e-mail: forestvale@bestwestern.co.uk
dir: On A169 towards York at rdbt on outskirts of Pickering

This lovely 18th-century hotel is an excellent base from which to explore the North Yorkshire Moors, one of England's most beautiful areas. A dedicated approach to upgrading means that the hotel is particularly well maintained, inside and out. Bedrooms vary in size and include some spacious 'superior' rooms, including one with a four-poster bed.

Rooms 22 (5 annexe) (7 fmly) (5 GF) **S** £82-£135; **D** £82-£135* **Facilities** FTV Wi-fi **Conf** Class 50 Board 30 Thtr 120 Del from £146* **Parking** 70 **Notes** LB ❀ Closed 24-26 Dec Civ Wed 90

Fox & Hounds Country Inn

★★ 78% ◉ HOTEL

☎ 01751 431577 📄 01751 432791
Main St, Sinnington YO62 6SQ
e-mail: foxhoundsinn@easynet.co.uk
web: www.thefoxandhoundsinn.co.uk
dir: 3m W of Pickering, off A170, between Pickering & Helmsley

This attractive inn lies in the quiet village of Sinnington just off the main road. The smartly maintained, yet traditional public areas are cosy and inviting. The menu offers a good selection of freshly cooked, modern British dishes and is available in the restaurant or informally in the bar. Bedrooms and bathrooms are well equipped and offer a good standard of quality and comfort. Service throughout is friendly and attentive.

Rooms 10 (4 GF) **S** £49-£69; **D** £70-£160 (incl. bkfst)* **Facilities** New Year **Parking** 40 **Notes** Closed 25-26 Dec

Old Manse

★★ 75% HOTEL

☎ 01751 476484 📠 01751 477124
19 Middleton Rd YO18 8AL
e-mail: info@oldmansepickering.com
web: www.oldmansepickering.co.uk
dir: A169, left at rdbt, through lights, 1st right into Potter Hill. Follow road to left. From A170 left at 'local traffic only' sign

A peacefully located house standing in mature grounds close to the town centre. It offers a combined dining room and lounge area and comfortable bedrooms that are also well equipped. Expect good hospitality from the resident owners.

Rooms 10 (2 fmly) (2 GF) **D** £79-£95 (incl. bkfst)*
Facilities New Year Wi-fi **Conf** Class 12 Board 10 Thtr 20
Del from £125 to £150* **Parking** 12 **Notes** LB
Closed 24-27 Dec

| PICKHILL | Map 19 SE38 |

Nags Head Country Inn

★★ 75% ⊛ HOTEL

☎ 01845 567391 & 567570 📠 01845 567212
YO7 4JG
e-mail: reservations@nagsheadpickhill.co.uk
web: www.nagsheadpickhill.co.uk
dir: 4m SE of Leeming Bar, 1.25m E of A1

Convenient for the A1, this 200-year-old country inn offers superb hospitality and an extensive range of food either in the bar or the attractive Library Restaurant. The bars, offering a wide range of handpicked wines, are full of character and feature country sports memorabilia. Bedrooms are well equipped and appointed to a high standard.

Rooms 14 (6 annexe) (1 fmly) (3 GF) **S** £60-£75;
D £80-£102.50 (incl. bkfst)* **Facilities** FTV Putt green ⛳
Quoits pitch Petanque New Year Wi-fi **Conf** Class 18
Board 18 Thtr 36 **Parking** 50 **Notes** LB Closed 25 Dec

| RAVENSCAR | Map 19 NZ90 |

Raven Hall Country House

★★★ 74% HOTEL

☎ 01723 870353 📠 01723 870072
YO13 0ET
e-mail: enquiries@ravenhall.co.uk
web: www.ravenhall.co.uk
dir: A171 towards Whitby. At Cloughton turn right onto unclassified road to Ravenscar

This impressive cliff top mansion enjoys breathtaking views over Robin Hood's Bay. Extensive well-kept grounds include tennis courts, putting green, swimming pools and historic battlements. The bedrooms vary in size but all are comfortably equipped, many offer panoramic views.

There are also eight new environmentally-friendly Finnish lodges that have been furnished to a high standard.

Rooms 52 (20 fmly) (5 GF) **S** £40-£75; **D** £80-£150 (incl. bkfst)* **Facilities** ⊕ ⅃ 9 ⛳ Putt green ⛳ Gym Archery Bowls Table tennis Xmas New Year **Conf** Class 80 Board 40 Thtr 100 Del from £110 to £140 **Services** Lift **Parking** 200 **Notes** LB Civ Wed 100

| RICHMOND | Map 19 NZ10 |

Frenchgate Restaurant and Hotel

★★★ 78% ⊛ SMALL HOTEL

☎ 01748 822087
59-61 Frenchgate DL10 7AE
e-mail: info@thefrenchgate.co.uk
web: www.thefrenchgate.co.uk
dir: A1 into Richmond, on A6108 past war memorial on left at lights. 1st left into Lile Close for hotel car park

A friendly welcome is offered at this elegant Georgian townhouse that sits on a quiet cobbled street. Now
continued

FRENCHGATE
RESTAURANT
&
HOTEL

The Frenchgate Restaurant & Hotel is the result of the remodelling of a delightful Georgian gentleman's residence that dates back to the mid 18th century. We are located in the heart of old Frenchgate, one of Richmond's quietest and most beautiful cobbled streets, a short walk from the famous market place, Norman castle, Georgian theatre and many delights of Richmond.

Stylish dining, stunning, newly refurbished, individual guest bedrooms, private parties, weddings, gardens, fully licensed with some of the finest food, service and hospitality around!

Dinner 7.00pm - 9.30pm Lunch 12.00pm - 2.30pm

Teas, coffees - All day

59-61 FRENCHGATE • RICHMOND • N. YORKSHIRE • DL10 7AE

T +44(0)1748 822087 W www.thefrenchgate.co.uk

E info@thefrenchgate.co.uk

RICHMOND *continued*

extensively refurbished, the hotel offers individually designed and stylishly furnished bedrooms, of varying sizes, that feature superb bath or shower rooms; bespoke beds with super mattresses, flat-screen LCD TVs, and music systems are just some of the new innovations. A beautiful four-poster room is available. Carefully cooked, contemporary dishes are served in the elegant restaurant that displays works by local artists.

Rooms 9 (1 fmly) (1 GF) **S** £88-£138; **D** £118-£250 (incl. bkfst)* **Facilities** FTV Xmas New Year Wi-fi **Conf** Class 20 Board 20 Thtr 20 Del from £135 to £145* **Parking** 12 **Notes** LB ⊗ Civ Wed 60

See advert on page 515

RIPON Map 19 SE37

Best Western Ripon Spa

★★★ 79% HOTEL

☎ 01765 602172 📄 01765 690770
Park St HG4 2BU
e-mail: spahotel@bronco.co.uk
web: www.bw-riponspa.com
dir: From A61 to Ripon, follow Fountains Abbey signs. Hotel on left after hospital. Or from A1(M) junct 48, B6265 to Ripon, straight on at 2 rdbts. Right at lights towards city centre. Left at hill top. Left at Give Way sign. Hotel on left

This privately owned hotel is set in extensive and attractive gardens just a short walk from the city centre. The bedrooms are well equipped to meet the needs of leisure and business travellers alike, while the comfortable lounges are complemented by the convivial atmosphere of the Turf Bar.

Rooms 40 (5 fmly) (4 GF) **Facilities** STV ⅃ Free use of nearby gym Xmas New Year Wi-fi **Conf** Class 35 Board 40 Thtr 150 **Services** Lift **Parking** 60 **Notes** LB Civ Wed 150

ROBIN HOOD'S BAY Map 19 NZ90

Bramblewick

RESTAURANT WITH ROOMS

☎ 01947 880960 & 880339 📄 01947 880960
2 King St YO22 4SH
e-mail: bramblewick@btinternet.com
web: www.bramblewick.org
dir: A171 onto B1447 to rdbt, straight over & down steep hill into 'Old Village', establishment at bottom on left

Only yards from the lifeboat slipway and the beach, this building dates from the 17th century. Modern en suite bedrooms have great charm with low beams, and below on the ground floor is a popular daytime café that changes in the evening to offer intimate candlelight dinners. Parking is at Bank Top, a five-minute walk from the old village; cars can stop briefly in the old village to drop off or pick up passengers.

Rooms 3

SALTBURN-BY-THE-SEA Map 19 NZ62

Rushpool Hall Hotel

★★★ 73% HOTEL

☎ 01287 624111 📄 01287 625255
Saltburn Ln TS12 1HD
e-mail: enquiries@rushpoolhallhotel.co.uk
web: www.rushpoolhallhotel.co.uk
dir: A174 Redcar & Whitby, straight over 5 rdbts, at 6th rdbt take 3rd exit for Skelton, left at next 2 rdbts, hotel 0.5m on left

A grand Victorian mansion located in its own grounds and woodlands. Stylish, elegant bedrooms are well equipped and spacious; many enjoy excellent sea views. The interesting public rooms are full of charm and character, and roaring fires welcome guests in cooler months. The hotel boasts an excellent reputation as a wedding venue thanks to its superb location and experienced event management.

Rooms 21 (3 smoking) **S** £65-£90; **D** £135-£165 (incl. bkfst)* **Facilities** STV FTV Fishing ⅃ Bird watching Walking Jogging track Wi-fi Child facilities **Conf** Class 75 Board 60 Thtr 100 Del from £75 to £110* **Parking** 120 **Notes** ⊗ Civ Wed 110

Hunley Hall Golf Club & Hotel

Ⓤ

☎ 01287 676216 📄 01287 678250
Ings Ln, Brotton TS12 2QQ
e-mail: reservations@hunleyhall.co.uk
dir: From A174 bypass left at rdbt with monument, left at T-junct, pass church, turn right. 50yds right, through housing estate, hotel approx 0.5m

Currently the rating for this establishment is not confirmed. This may be due to a change of ownership or because it has only recently joined the AA rating scheme. For further details please see the AA website: theAA.com

Rooms 28 (2 fmly) (18 GF) **Facilities** FTV ⅃ 27 Putt green New Year **Conf** Class 32 Board 28 Thtr 50 **Parking** 100 **Notes** LB ⊗

SCARBOROUGH Map 17 TA08

Crown Spa

★★★★ 75% HOTEL

☎ 01723 357400 📄 01723 357404
Esplanade YO11 2AG
e-mail: info@crownspahotel.com
web: www.crownspahotel.com
dir: On A64 follow town centre signs to lights opposite railway station, turn right over Valley Bridge, 1st left, right into Belmont Rd to cliff top

This well known hotel has an enviable position overlooking the harbour and South Bay and most of the front-facing bedrooms have excellent views. All the bedrooms, including suites, have a modern appearance and have the latest amenities including feature bathrooms. An extensive range of treatments is available in the outstanding spa.

Rooms 115 (7 fmly) **S** £52-£90; **D** £62-£140* **Facilities** Spa FTV ⓢ Gym Fitness classes Massage Sauna Steam room Beauty treatments Xmas New Year Wi-fi **Conf** Class 110 Board 100 Thtr 200 Del from £135 to £210* **Services** Lift **Parking** 10 **Notes** LB ⊗ Civ Wed 160

See advert on opposite page

Best Western Ox Pasture Hall Country Hotel

★★★ 80% ⊛ HOTEL

☎ 01723 365295 📄 01723 355156
Lady Edith's Dr, Raincliffe Woods YO12 5TD
e-mail: oxpasturehall@btconnect.com
web: www.oxpasturehall.com
dir: A171, left onto Lady Edith's Drive, 1.5m, hotel on right

This charming country hotel is set in the North Riding Forest Park and has a very friendly atmosphere. Bedrooms (split between the main house, townhouse and the delightful courtyard) are stylish, comfortable and well equipped. Public areas include a split-level bar, quiet lounge and an attractive restaurant. There is also an extensive banqueting area licensed for civil weddings.

Rooms 22 (1 fmly) (14 GF) **Facilities** Xmas New Year Wi-fi **Conf** Class 75 Board 50 Thtr 150 **Parking** 100 **Notes** LB Civ Wed 100

See advert on page 518

The Crescent

★★★ 77% HOTEL

☎ 01723 360929 📄 01723 354126
2 Belvoir Ter YO11 2PP
e-mail: reception@thecrescenthotel.com
web: www.thecrescenthotel.com
dir: From A64 towards railway station, follow signs to Brunswick Pavilion. At lights turn into hotel entrance

This smart Grade II listed building is a short distance from the town centre. The comfortable accommodation is comprehensively equipped, and there are spacious bars and lounges. There is a choice of dining areas and bars: Reflections, the elegant restaurant, serves both a carte and set-price menus. A separate carvery, Cooney's, offers a less formal option. Service is caring and attentive.

Rooms 22 **Facilities** Wi-fi **Conf** Class 25 Board 25 Thtr 30 **Services** Lift **Notes** ⊗ No children 6yrs Closed 25-26 Dec

Wrea Head Country Hotel

★★★ 77% HOTEL

☎ 01723 378211 & 374374 📄 01723 371780
Barmoor Ln, Scalby YO13 0PB
e-mail: wreahead@englishrosehotels.co.uk
dir: A171 from Scarborough towards Whitby, hotel sign on left, turn into Barmoor Ln, through ford. Hotel entrance immediately left

This elegant country house is situated in 14 acres of grounds and gardens. Bedrooms are individually furnished and decorated; many have fine views. Public rooms include a conservatory, the oak-panelled lounge with inglenook fireplace and a beautiful library lounge that is full of books and games.

Rooms 20 (2 fmly) (1 GF) **S** £49.50-£90; **D** £90-£200 (incl. bkfst)* **Facilities** Putt green ⛳ Xmas New Year Wi-fi **Conf** Class 16 Board 20 Thtr 40 Del from £95 to £155* **Parking** 50 **Notes** LB ⊗ Civ Wed 50

See advert on page 519

Beiderbecke's Hotel

★★★ 74% HOTEL

☎ 01723 365766 📄 01723 367433
1-3 The Crescent YO11 2PW
e-mail: info@beiderbeckes.com
dir: In town centre, 200mtrs from railway station

Situated in a Georgian crescent this hotel is close to all the main attractions. Bedrooms are very smart, well equipped and offer plenty of space and comfort. Some rooms have views over the town to the sea. Marmalade's, the restaurant, offers international cuisine with a modern twist and hosts live music acts at weekends, including the resident jazz band.

Rooms 27 (1 fmly) **S** £80-£130; **D** £120-£170 (incl. bkfst)* **Facilities** STV ♫ Xmas New Year Wi-fi **Conf** Class 35 Board 28 Thtr 35 Del from £120 to £160 **Services** Lift **Parking** 18 **Notes** ⊗

SCARBOROUGH *continued*

Palm Court

★★★ 74% HOTEL

☎ 01723 368161 📠 01723 371547
St Nicholas Cliff YO11 2ES
e-mail: info@palmcourt-scarborough.co.uk
dir: Follow signs for town centre & town hall, hotel before
town hall on right

The public rooms are spacious and comfortable at this
modern, town centre hotel. Traditional cooking is provided
in the attractive restaurant and staff are friendly and
helpful. Bedrooms are quite delightfully furnished and
are also well equipped. Extra facilities include a
swimming pool and free, covered parking.

Rooms 40 (7 fmly) **S** £50-£58; **D** £95-£120 (incl. bkfst)*
Facilities 🕲 Xmas New Year Wi-fi **Conf** Class 100
Board 60 Thtr 180 Del from £95 to £115* **Services** Lift
Parking 40 **Notes** ⊗

See advert on page 521

East Ayton Lodge Country House

★★★ 73% HOTEL

☎ 01723 864227 📠 01723 862680
Moor Ln, Forge Valley YO13 9EW
e-mail: ealodgehtl@cix.co.uk
dir: 400yds off A170

Set in three acres of grounds close to the River Derwent
and discreetly situated in a quiet lane on the edge of the
forest, this hotel is constructed around two cottages, the
original buildings on the site. Bedrooms are well
equipped and those on the courtyard are particularly
spacious; public rooms include a large conservatory. A
good range of food is available.

Rooms 27 (14 annexe) (5 fmly) (7 GF) **S** £50-£60;
D £59-£95 (incl. bkfst) **Facilities** Xmas New Year
Conf Board 30 Thtr 50 **Parking** 70 **Notes** LB

Royal

★★★ 73% HOTEL

☎ 01723 364333 & 374374 📠 01723 371780
St Nicholas St YO11 2HE
e-mail: sales@englishrosehotels.co.uk
web: www.englishrosehotels.co.uk
dir: A64 into town. Follow town centre/South Bay signs.
Hotel opposite town hall

This smart hotel enjoys a central location. Bedrooms are
neatly appointed and offer a variety of styles from
contemporary to traditional and include some suites.
Public areas are elegant and include well-equipped
conference and banqueting facilities, a leisure suite and
the popular and modern Cafe Bliss where light snacks
are served all day.

Rooms 118 (14 fmly) **S** £49.50-£89; **D** £90-£180 (incl.
bkfst)* **Facilities** 🕲 supervised Gym Beauty treatments
Steam room Sauna 🎵 Xmas New Year Wi-fi
Conf Class 125 Board 75 Thtr 300 Del from £95 to £175*
Services Lift **Notes** LB ⊗ Civ Wed 150

See advert on opposite page

Ambassador

★★★ 70% HOTEL

☎ 01723 362841 📠 01723 366166
Centre of the Esplanade YO11 2AY
e-mail: ask@ambassadorhotelscarborough.co.uk
web: www.ambassadorhotelscarborough.co.uk
dir: A64, right at 1st small rdbt opposite B&Q, right at
next small rdbt, immediate left down Avenue Victoria to
Cliff Top

Standing on the South Cliff with excellent views over the
bay, this friendly hotel has undergone extensive
refurbishment and offers well-equipped bedrooms, some
of which are executive rooms. An indoor swimming pool,
sauna and solarium are also available. Entertainment is
provided during the summer season.

Rooms 59 (10 fmly) (1 GF) **S** £39-£98; **D** £59-£150 (incl.
bkfst)* **Facilities** FTV 🕲 Sauna Spa bath 🎵 Xmas New
Year Wi-fi **Conf** Class 60 Board 40 Thtr 100 Del from £55
to £130* **Services** Lift Air con **Notes** LB Civ Wed 120

See advert on page 521

Built in 1881, this elegant Country House Hotel is set in acres of private grounds on the edge of the North Yorkshire Moors, offering truly breathtaking views across the Yorkshire countryside.

Wrea Head provides the perfect retreat, where you can choose to make your break as active, or relaxing, as you like.

As well as the 20 individually styled bedrooms guests will also enjoy the Four Seasons Restaurant, Cocktail Lounge, Library and the wood panelled halls.

Barmoor Lane, Scalby, Scarborough, North Yorkshire YO13 0PB

Telephone: 01723 374 374
Email: sales@englishrosehotels.co.uk

WREA HEAD
Country House Hotel
Scalby

www.ENGLISH ROSE HOTELS.co.uk

THE
ROYAL
HOTEL
Scarborough

WiFi

The Royal dates from the 1830s, and its grand imposing architecture, still bears the hallmarks of the Regency period.

Situated in an enviable location in the centre of the town and overlooking South Bay, The Royal is the only choice for those visiting the town, whether your trip is for business or for pleasure.

All 118 of the hotel's well appointed, en suite bedrooms have been stylishly designed and thoughtfully equipped and many enjoy spectacular sea views.

St. Nicholas Street, Scarborough, North Yorkshire YO11 2HE

Telephone: 01723 364 333
Email: sales@englishrosehotels.co.uk

www.ENGLISH ROSE HOTELS.co.uk

Set overlooking Scarborough's vast North Bay the ever-popular Clifton Hotel has always been a firm favourite with our guests for many years.

Offering some of the most amazing, uninterrupted sea views in Scarborough and situated only a short distance from many of the town's attractions, The Clifton makes the perfect base when visiting the Yorkshire Coast.

Queen's Parade, Scarborough, North Yorkshire YO12 7HX

Telephone: 01723 375 691
Email: sales@englishrosehotels.co.uk

THE
CLIFTON
HOTEL
Scarborough

www.ENGLISH ROSE HOTELS.co.uk

SCARBOROUGH *continued*

Esplanade

★★★ 68% HOTEL

☎ 01723 360382 📠 01723 376137
Belmont Rd YO11 2AA
e-mail: enquiries@theesplanade.co.uk
dir: From town centre over Valley Bridge, left then immediately right onto Belmont Rd, hotel 100mtrs on right

This large hotel enjoys a superb position overlooking South Bay and the harbour. Both the terrace, leading from the lounge bar, and the restaurant, with its striking oriel window, benefit from magnificent views. Bedrooms are comfortably furnished and are well equipped. Touring groups are also well catered for.

Rooms 73 (9 fmly) **S** £30-£55; **D** £60-£106 (incl. bkfst)*
Facilities Xmas New Year **Conf** Class 100 Board 40 Thtr 140 Del from £60 to £80* **Services** Lift **Parking** 15 **Notes** LB Closed 2 Jan-9 Feb RS 9 Feb-1 Mar

Brooklands

★★★ 66% HOTEL

☎ 01723 376576 📠 01723 341093
Esplanade Gardens, South Cliff YO11 2AW
e-mail: info@brooklands-scarborough.co.uk
dir: From A64 York, left at B&Q rdbt, right at next mini-rdbt, 1st left onto Victoria Ave, at end turn left then 2nd left

Located on the South Cliff, overlooking the Esplanade Gardens and very close to the seafront, this contemporary hotel has benefited from full refurbishment. There is a friendly team of staff and a range of stylish lounge areas, a games room and spacious restaurant. Entertainment is provided most evenings in the lower-ground floor bar.

Rooms 63 (13 fmly) (2 GF) **S** £30-£55; **D** £60-£110 (incl. bkfst)* **Facilities** ♫ Xmas New Year Wi-fi **Conf** Class 90 Board 40 **Services** Lift **Notes** LB

The Mount

★★ 75% HOTEL

☎ 01723 375850 📠 01723 375850
Cliff Bridge Ter, Saint Nicholas Cliff YO11 2HA
e-mail: info@mounthotel.com

Standing in a superb, elevated position and enjoying magnificent views of the South Bay, this elegant Regency hotel is operated to high standards. The richly furnished and comfortable public rooms are inviting, and the well-equipped bedrooms have been attractively decorated. The spacious deluxe rooms are mini-suites.

Rooms 50 (5 fmly) **Facilities** Xmas **Services** Lift **Notes** Closed Jan-mid Mar

See advert on opposite page

Clifton

★★ 74% HOTEL

☎ 01723 375691 & 374374 📠 01723 364203
Queens Pde, North Cliff YO12 7HX
e-mail: clifton@englishrosehotels.co.uk
dir: On entering town centre, follow signs for North Bay

Standing in an impressive location with commanding fine views over the bay, this large holiday hotel is convenient for Peasholm Park and other local leisure attractions; tour groups are especially well catered for. Bedrooms are pleasant, and entertainment is provided in the spacious public rooms during the high season.

Rooms 71 (11 fmly) **S** £40-£70; **D** £80-£125 (incl. bkfst)* **Facilities** ♫ Xmas New Year **Conf** Class 50 Board 50 Thtr 120 Del from £80 to £115* **Services** Lift **Parking** 45 **Notes** LB ☻

See advert on page 519

Park Manor

★★ 72% HOTEL

☎ 01723 372090 📠 01723 500480
Northstead Manor Dr YO12 6BB
e-mail: info@parkmanor.co.uk
web: www.parkmanor.co.uk
dir: Off A165, next to Peasholm Park

Enjoying a peaceful residential setting with sea views, this smartly presented, friendly hotel provides the seaside tourist with a wide range of facilities. Bedrooms vary in size and style but all are smartly furnished and well equipped. There is a spacious lounge, smart restaurant, games room and indoor pool plus a steam room for relaxation.

Rooms 42 (6 fmly) **S** £38-£46; **D** £76-£102 (incl. bkfst)* **Facilities** ☻ Pool table Spa bath Steam room Table tennis Xmas New Year Wi-fi **Conf** Class 20 Board 20 Thtr 30 Del from £60 to £80* **Services** Lift **Parking** 20 **Notes** LB ☻ No children 3yrs

Red Lea

★★ 72% HOTEL

☎ 01723 362431 📠 01723 371230
Prince of Wales Ter YO11 2AJ
e-mail: redlea@globalnet.co.uk
web: www.redleahotel.co.uk
dir: follow South Cliff signs. Prince of Wales Terrace is off Esplanade opposite cliff lift

This friendly, family-run hotel is situated close to the cliff lift. Bedrooms are well equipped and comfortably furnished, and many at the front have picturesque views of the coast. There are two large lounges and a spacious dining room in which good-value, traditional food is served.

Rooms 67 (7 fmly) (2 GF) **Facilities** FTV ☻ Gym Xmas New Year **Conf** Class 25 Board 25 Thtr 40 **Services** Lift **Notes** LB ☻

The Cumberland

Leisureplex

★★ 68% HOTEL

☎ 01723 361826 📠 01723 500081
Belmont Rd YO11 2AB
e-mail: cumberland.scarborough@alfatravel.co.uk
dir: From A64, turn right onto B1437, left at A165 towards town centre. Right into Ramshill Rd, right into Belmont Rd

On the South Cliff, convenient for the Spa Complex, beach and town centre shops, this hotel offers comfortably appointed bedrooms; each floor can be accessed by lift. Entertainment is provided most evenings and the meals are carefully cooked.

Rooms 81 (6 fmly) **S** £38-£43; **D** £60-£72 (incl. bkfst)* **Facilities** FTV ♫ Xmas New Year **Services** Lift **Notes** LB ☻ Closed Jan RS Nov-Dec & Feb

SCARBOROUGH *continued*

Delmont

★★ 64% HOTEL

☎ 01723 364500 📄 01723 363554
18/19 Blenheim Ter YO12 7HE
e-mail: enquiries@delmonthotel.co.uk
dir: Follow signs to North Bay. At seafront to top of cliff. Hotel near castle

Popular with groups, a friendly welcome is found at this hotel on the North Bay. Bedrooms are comfortable, and many have sea views. There are two lounges, a bar and a spacious dining room in which good-value, traditional food is served along with entertainment on most evenings.

Rooms 51 (18 fmly) (5 GF) **S** £46-£56; **D** £46-£56 (incl. bkfst & dinner) **Facilities** Games Room Pool table 🎵 Xmas New Year **Services** Lift **Parking** 2

SCOTCH CORNER (NEAR RICHMOND)
Map 19 NZ20

Travelodge Scotch Corner (A1)

BUDGET HOTEL

☎ 0871 984 6173 📄 0870 1911675
Skeeby DL10 5EQ
web: www.travelodge.co.uk
dir: Off rdbt at junct of A1 & A66, S'bound

Travelodge offers good quality, good value, budget accommodation. All offer family rooms sleeping up to four (two adults, two children) with en suite bathroom/shower-room, remote-control TV, tea- and coffee-making facilities and comfortable beds. Food options vary. Breakfast is at the on-site Bar Café restaurant (if available) or to take away. See also Hotel Groups pages.

Rooms 50 **S** fr £29; **D** fr £29

Travelodge Scotch Corner Skeeby

BUDGET HOTEL

☎ 0871 984 6176 📄 01325 377616
Middleton Tyas Ln DL10 6PQ
web: www.travelodge.co.uk
dir: On A1 N'bound, 0.5m S of Scotch Corner

Rooms 40 **S** fr £29; **D** fr £29

SKIPTON
Map 18 SD95

The Coniston

★★★ 81% HOTEL

☎ 01756 748080 📄 01756 749487
Coniston Cold BD23 4EB
e-mail: info@theconistonhotel.com
dir: on A65, 6m NW of Skipton

Privately owned and situated on a 1,400 acre estate centred around a beautiful 24-acre lake, this hotel offers guests many exciting outdoor activities. The modern bedrooms are comfortable and most have king-size beds. Macleod's Bar and the main restaurant serve all-day meals, and fine dining is available in the evening from both carte and fixed-price menus. Staff are very friendly and nothing is too much trouble.

Rooms 50 (13 fmly) (25 GF) **Facilities** Fishing Clay pigeon shooting Falconry Off-road Land Rover driving Xmas New Year Wi-fi **Conf** Class 80 Board 50 Thtr 200 **Parking** 120 **Notes** Civ Wed 100

Rendezvous

CLASSIC BRITISH HOTELS

★★★ 77% HOTEL

☎ 01756 700100 📄 01756 700107
Keighley Rd BD23 2TA
e-mail: admin@rendezvous-skipton.com
dir: On A6131 (Keighley road) S from town centre

Located beside the canal just outside the town, the hotel has the advantage of plenty of parking and a leisure club with pool and gym. Bedrooms are well equipped and spacious, and have delightful views over the rolling countryside. There are extensive conference facilities. This hotel makes an ideal base for touring The Dales.

Rooms 79 (10 fmly) (12 GF) **Facilities** 🏊 supervised Gym Xmas New Year Wi-fi **Conf** Class 200 Board 120 Thtr 500 **Services** Lift **Parking** 120 **Notes** LB ⊗ Civ Wed 400

Herriots Hotel

★★★ 75% HOTEL

☎ 01756 792781 📄 01756 793967
Broughton Rd BD23 1RT
e-mail: info@herriotsforleisure.co.uk
web: www.herriotsforleisure.co.uk
dir: 2m off A59 at entrance to town & 50yds from railway station

Close to the centre of the market town, this friendly hotel offers tastefully decorated bedrooms that are well equipped. The open-plan brasserie is a relaxing place and offers a varied and interesting menu; meals and snacks are also available in the bar. The extension includes modern bedrooms and a stylish conservatory lounge.

Rooms 23 (3 fmly) **S** £55-£79; **D** £75-£110 (incl. bkfst)* **Facilities** Private access onto Leeds Liverpool canal Xmas New Year Wi-fi **Conf** Class 50 Board 52 Thtr 100 Del from £130 to £145* **Services** Lift **Parking** 26 **Notes** LB ⊗ Civ Wed 80

Travelodge Skipton

BUDGET HOTEL

☎ 08719 846 177 📄 0870 1911676
Gargrave Rd BD23 1UD
web: www.travelodge.co.uk
dir: At junct of A65 & A59

Travelodge offers good quality, good value, budget accommodation. All offer family rooms sleeping up to four (two adults, two children) with en suite bathroom/shower-room, remote-control TV, tea- and coffee-making facilities and comfortable beds. Food options vary. Breakfast is at the on-site Bar Café restaurant (if available) or to take away. See also Hotel Groups pages.

Rooms 32 **S** fr £29; **D** fr £29

WEST WITTON Map 19 SE08

Wensleydale Heifer
★★ 82% ◉◉ HOTEL

☎ 01969 622322 & 622725 📄 01969 624183
Main St DL8 4LS
e-mail: info@wensleydaleheifer.co.uk
web: www.wensleydaleheifer.co.uk
dir: A1 to Leeming Bar junct, A684 towards Bedale for approx 10m to Leyburn, then towards Hawes 3.5m to West Witton

Describing itself as a boutique hotel, this 17th-century coaching inn has been transformed in recent years. The bedrooms (a four-poster room and junior suite included) are each designed with a unique and interesting theme - for example, Chocolate, Malt Whisky, James Herriott and Shooter. Food is very much the focus at the Wensleydale Heifer whether it be in the informal fish bar or the contemporary style restaurant. The kitchen prides itself on sourcing the freshest fish and locally reared meats.

Rooms 9 (3 fmly) **S** £70-£90; **D** £110-£140 (incl. bkfst)* **Facilities** Xmas New Year **Parking** 40

WHITBY Map 19 NZ81

Dunsley Hall
★★★ 81% ◉ COUNTRY HOUSE HOTEL

☎ 01947 893437 📄 01947 893505
Dunsley YO21 3TL
e-mail: reception@dunsleyhall.com
web: www.dunsleyhall.com
dir: 3m N of Whitby, signed off A171

Friendly service is found at this fine country mansion set in a quiet hamlet with coastal views north of Whitby. The house has Gothic overtones and boasts fine woodwork and panelling, no more so than in the magnificent lounge. Two lovely dining rooms offer imaginative dishes and there is also a cosy bar.

Rooms 26 (2 fmly) (2 GF) **S** £95-£120; **D** fr £149 (incl. bkfst)* **Facilities** ⛳ Putt green Xmas New Year **Conf** Class 50 Board 40 Thtr 95 **Parking** 30 **Notes** LB ⊗ Civ Wed 100

Cliffemount
★★★ 80% SMALL HOTEL

☎ 01947 840103 📄 01947 841025
Bank Top Ln, Runswick Bay TS13 5HU
e-mail: info@cliffemounthotel.co.uk
dir: Exit A174, 8m N of Whitby, 1m to end

Overlooking Runswick Bay this property is newly refurbished and offers a relaxed and romantic atmosphere with open fires and individual, carefully designed bedrooms; some have a private balcony overlooking the bay. Dining is recommended; the food is modern British in style and uses locally sourced fresh seafood and game from nearby estates.

Rooms 20 (4 fmly) (5 GF) **S** £60-£75; **D** £110-£160 (incl. bkfst)* **Facilities** FTV Xmas New Year Wi-fi **Parking** 25 **Notes** LB

Saxonville
★★★ 77% HOTEL

☎ 01947 602631 📄 01947 820523
Ladysmith Av, Argyle Rd YO21 3HX
e-mail: newtons@saxonville.co.uk
web: www.saxonville.co.uk
dir: A174 to North Promenade. Turn inland at large four-towered building visible on West Cliff, into Argyle Rd, then 1st right

The friendly service is noteworthy at this long-established holiday hotel. Well maintained throughout it offers comfortable bedrooms and inviting public areas that include a well-proportioned restaurant where quality dinners are served.

Rooms 23 (2 fmly) (1 GF) **S** £64-£69; **D** £128-£158 (incl. bkfst)* **Conf** Class 40 Board 40 Thtr 100 Del from £99* **Parking** 20 **Notes** ⊗ Closed Dec-Jan RS Feb-Mar & Nov

---

Estbek House
◉◉ RESTAURANT WITH ROOMS

☎ 01947 893424 📄 01947 893625
East Row, Sandsend YO21 3SU
e-mail: info@estbekhouse.co.uk
dir: On Cleveland Way, within Sandsend, next to East Beck

A speciality seafood restaurant on the first floor is the focus of this listed building in a small coastal village north west of Whitby. Below is a small bar and breakfast room, while up above are four individually presented bedrooms offering luxury and comfort.

Rooms 4

The White Horse & Griffin
◉ RESTAURANT WITH ROOMS

☎ 01947 825026 & 604857 📄 01947 604857
Church St YO22 4BH
e-mail: info@whitehorseandgriffin.co.uk
web: www.whitehorseandgriffin.co.uk
dir: From town centre E across Bridge St bridge, 2nd left, 50mtrs on right next to Whitby

This historic inn, now a restaurant with rooms, is as quaint as the cobbled side street in which it lies. Cooking is good with the emphasis on fresh fish. The bedrooms, some reached by steep staircases, retain a rustic charm but are well equipped and include CD players.

Rooms 20 (10 annexe) (1 fmly)

YARM
Map 19 NZ41

INSPECTORS' CHOICE

Judges Country House Hotel
★★★ ◉◉◉ HOTEL

☎ 01642 789000 🖷 01642 782878
Kirklevington Hall TS15 9LW
e-mail: enquiries@judgeshotel.co.uk
web: www.judgeshotel.co.uk
dir: 1.5m from A19. At A67 junct, follow Yarm road, hotel on left

Formerly a lodging for local circuit judges, this gracious mansion lies in landscaped grounds through which a stream runs. Stylish bedrooms are individually decorated and come with 101 extras, including a pet goldfish! The Conservatory restaurant serves award-winning cuisine, and the genuinely caring and attentive service is equally memorable.

Rooms 21 (3 fmly) (5 GF) **S** £142–£155; **D** £175–£185* **Facilities** STV 🏊 Gym Boating 4x4 hire Mountain bikes Nature trails Shooting Horse riding Xmas New Year Wi-fi **Conf** Class 120 Board 80 Thtr 200 **Parking** 102 **Notes** LB ❀ Civ Wed 200

YORK
Map 16 SE65

See also **Aldwark & Escrick**

INSPECTORS' CHOICE

Middlethorpe Hall & Spa
★★★★ ◉◉ HOTEL

☎ 01904 641241 🖷 01904 620176
Bishopthorpe Rd, Middlethorpe YO23 2GB
e-mail: info@middlethorpe.com
dir: A1/A64 follow York West (A1036) signs, then Bishopthorpe, Middlethorpe racecourse signs

This fine house, dating from the reign of William and Mary, sits in acres of beautifully landscaped gardens. The bedrooms vary in size but all are comfortably furnished; some are located in the main house, and others are in a cottage and converted courtyard stables. Public areas include a small spa and a stately drawing room where afternoon tea is quite an event. The delightful panelled restaurant is a perfect setting for enjoying the imaginative cuisine.

Rooms 29 (19 annexe) (2 fmly) (10 GF) **S** £130–£160; **D** £190–£260 (incl. bkfst)* **Facilities** Spa FTV 🌀 🏊 Gym Health & Beauty spa Xmas New Year Wi-fi **Conf** Class 30 Board 25 Thtr 56 Del from £150 to £190* **Services** Lift **Parking** 71 **Notes** LB No children 6yrs RS 25 & 31 Dec Civ Wed 56

Hotel du Vin York
★★★★ 81% ◉ HOTEL

☎ 01904 557350 🖷 01904 557351
89 The Mount YO24 1AX
e-mail: info.york@hotelduvin.com
web: www.hotelduvin.com
dir: A1036 towards city centre, 6m. Hotel on right through lights.

This Hotel du Vin makes an unrestrained statement of luxury and quality that will cosset even the most discerning guest. Bedrooms are decadent in design and the bathrooms have huge monsoon showers and 'feature' baths. Dinner in the bistro provides a memorable highlight thanks to exciting menus and a superb wine list. Staff throughout are naturally friendly, nothing is too much trouble.

Rooms 44 (3 fmly) (14 GF) **Facilities** STV FTV Wi-fi **Conf** Class 8 Board 22 Thtr 22 **Services** Lift Air con **Parking** 18

Best Western Dean Court
★★★★ 77% ◉◉ HOTEL

☎ 01904 625082 🖷 01904 620305
Duncombe Place YO1 7EF
e-mail: info@deancourt-york.co.uk
web: www.deancourt-york.co.uk
dir: City centre opposite York Minster

This smart hotel enjoys a central location overlooking The Minster, and guests will find the service is particularly friendly and efficient. Bedrooms are stylishly appointed and vary in size. Public areas are elegant in a contemporary style and include the popular D.C.H. restaurant which enjoys wonderful views of the cathedral, and The Court café-bistro and bar where a more informal, all-day menu is offered. Valet parking is available.

Rooms 37 (4 fmly) **S** £95–£135; **D** £120–£225 (incl. bkfst)* **Facilities** FTV Xmas New Year Wi-fi **Conf** Class 12 Board 32 Thtr 50 **Services** Lift **Parking** 30 **Notes** LB ❀ Civ Wed 80

The Grange

★★★★ 77% ◉◉ HOTEL

☎ 01904 644744 📄 01904 612453
1 Clifton YO30 6AA
e-mail: info@grangehotel.co.uk
web: www.grangehotel.co.uk
dir: On A19 York/Thirsk road, approx 500yds from city centre

This bustling Regency town house is just a few minutes' walk from the centre of York. A professional service is efficiently delivered by caring staff in a very friendly and helpful manner. Public rooms are comfortable and have been stylishly furnished; these include two dining options, the popular and informal Cellar Bar, and main hotel restaurant The Ivy Brasserie, which offers fine dining in a lavishly decorated environment. The individually designed bedrooms are comfortably appointed and have been thoughtfully equipped.

Rooms 36 (6 GF) **S** £117-£188; **D** £160-£225 (incl. bkfst) **Facilities** STV FTV Use of nearby health club Xmas New Year Wi-fi **Conf** Class 24 Board 24 Thtr 50 Del from £156.50 to £173.95 **Parking** 26 **Notes** LB Civ Wed 90

York Marriott

Marriott.
HOTELS & RESORTS

★★★★ 76% HOTEL

☎ 01904 701000 📄 01904 702308
Tadcaster Rd YO24 1QQ
e-mail: mhrs.qqyyk.pa@marriotthotels.com
web: www.yorkmarriott.co.uk
dir: From A64 at York 'West' onto A1036, follow signs to city centre. Approx 1.5m, hotel on right after church and lights

Overlooking the racecourse and Knavesmire Parkland, the hotel offers modern accommodation, including family rooms, all with comfort cooling. Within the hotel, guests enjoy the use of extensive leisure facilities including indoor pool, putting green and tennis court. For those wishing to explore the historic and cultural attractions, the city is less than a mile away.

Rooms 151 (14 fmly) (27 GF) (10 smoking) **Facilities** Spa STV ⓢ ⓢ Putt green Gym Beauty treatment New Year Wi-fi **Conf** Class 90 Board 40 Thtr 190 **Services** Lift Air con **Parking** 160 **Notes** ⊗ Civ Wed 140

See advert on this page

Royal York Hotel & Events Centre

RH PRINCIPAL HAYLEY

★★★★ 74% HOTEL

☎ 01904 653681 📄 01904 623503
Station Rd YO24 1AA
e-mail: royalyork.reservations@principal-hayley.com
web: www.principal-hayley.com
dir: Adjacent to railway station

Situated in three acres of landscaped grounds in the very heart of the city, this Victorian railway hotel has views over the city and York Minster. Contemporary bedrooms are divided between those in the main hotel and the air-conditioned garden mews. There is also a leisure complex and state-of-the-art conference centre.

Rooms 167 (8 fmly) **Facilities** ⓢ supervised Gym Steam room Xmas New Year Wi-fi **Conf** Class 250 Board 80 Thtr 410 **Services** Lift **Parking** 80 **Notes** ⊗ Civ Wed 160

YORK *continued*

Fairfield Manor

®RAMADA.

★★★★ 72% COUNTRY HOUSE HOTEL

☎ 01904 670222 📄 01904 670311
Shipton Rd, Skelton YO30 1XW
e-mail: sales.york@ramadajarvis.co.uk
web: www.ramadajarvis.co.uk
dir: Turn off A1237 onto A19, hotel 0.5m on left

This stylish Georgian mansion stands in six acres of
private grounds on the outskirts of the city. The
contemporary bedrooms, styled in reds or blues, have
broadband access and flat-screen TVs; some rooms have
garden and courtyard views. The suites have either four-
poster or king-size beds and a separate seating area.
Kilby's Restaurant serves bistro food, and 24-hour room
service is available. There are good conference facilities.

Rooms 89 (20 fmly) (24 GF) **Facilities** Xmas New Year
Wi-fi **Conf** Class 72 Board 60 Thtr 180 **Services** Lift
Parking 130 **Notes** Civ Wed 150

Marmadukes

★★★ 80% SMALL HOTEL

☎ 0845 460 9010 📄 01904 636196
St Peters Grove, Bootham YO30 6AQ
e-mail: mail@marmadukeshotel.co.uk
web: www.marmadukeshotel.co.uk
dir: On A19 (Thirsk road) 600mtrs from Bootham Bar City
Gates, opposite St Peters School

Situated on a quiet road just a short, flat walk from the
Minster, this elegant Victorian house offers very stylish
bedrooms furnished with antiques; the Loft Suite is more
contemporary and has its own lounge and sauna. Drinks
are served in the lounge bar, or can be enjoyed in the
lawned Roman garden with its relaxation suite. Dinner
can be taken at Harvilles Restaurant in the city centre -
complimentary travel is provided.

Rooms 21 (2 GF) **S** £65; **D** £100-£250 (incl. bkfst)*
Facilities FTV Gym Sauna Plunge shower Wi-fi **Parking** 14
Notes ⊗ No children 12yrs

Best Western Monkbar

★★★ 79% HOTEL

☎ 01904 638086 📄 01904 629195
Monkbar YO31 7JA
e-mail: sales@monkbarhotel.co.uk
dir: A64 onto A1079 to city, turn right at city walls, take
middle lane at lights. Hotel on right

This smart hotel enjoys a prominent position adjacent to
the city walls, and just a few minutes' walk from the
cathedral. Individually styled bedrooms are well equipped
for both business and leisure guests. Spacious public
areas include comfortable lounges, an American-style
bar, an airy restaurant and impressive meeting and
training facilities.

Rooms 99 (8 fmly) (2 GF) **S** £95-£125; **D** £105-£175 (incl.
bkfst)* **Facilities** STV FTV Xmas New Year Wi-fi Child
facilities **Conf** Class 80 Board 50 Thtr 140 Del from £130
to £175* **Services** Lift **Parking** 66 **Notes** LB Civ Wed 80

Holiday Inn York

Holiday Inn
HOTELS · RESORTS

★★★ 79% HOTEL

☎ 0870 400 9085 📄 01904 702804
Tadcaster Rd YO24 1QF
e-mail: reservations-york@ihg.com
web: www.holidayinn.co.uk
dir: From A1(M) take A64 towards York. In 7m take A106
to York. Straight over at rdbt to city centre. Hotel 0.5m on
right

Located in a suburban area close to the city centre and
overlooking York race course, this modern hotel caters
equally well for business and leisure guests. Public areas
include the spacious family friendly Junction Restaurant,
lounge bar and the Cedar Tree Terrace. Seven function
rooms are also available for meetings and social events.

Rooms 142 **S** fr £69; **D** fr £79 (incl. bkfst)* **Facilities** STV
FTV Xmas New Year Wi-fi **Conf** Class 45 Board 55
Thtr 100 **Services** Lift Air con **Parking** 200 **Notes** LB

Novotel York Centre

★★★ 79% HOTEL

☎ 01904 611660 📄 01904 610925
Fishergate YO10 4FD
e-mail: H0949@accor.com
web: www.novotel.com
dir: A19 north to city centre, hotel set back on left

Set just outside the ancient city walls, this modern,
family-friendly hotel is conveniently located for visitors to
the city. Bedrooms feature bathrooms with a separate
toilet room, plus excellent desk space and sofa beds. Four
rooms are equipped for less able guests. The hotel's
facilities include indoor and outdoor children's play areas
and an indoor pool.

Rooms 124 (124 fmly) (5 smoking) **Facilities** STV ⊗
Xmas New Year Wi-fi **Conf** Class 100 Board 120 Thtr 220
Del from £119 to £169* **Services** Lift **Parking** 140

Churchill

★★★ 78% ◉ HOTEL

☎ 01904 644456 📄 01904 663322
65 Bootham YO30 7DQ
e-mail: info@churchillhotel.com
dir: On A19 (Bootham), W from York Minster, hotel 250yds
on right

A late Georgian manor house set in its own grounds, just
a short walk from the Minster and other attractions.
Period features and interesting artefacts relating to
Winston Churchill are incorporated into smart
contemporary design and up-to-date technology. Public
areas include the Piano Bar & Restaurant, where
innovative menus feature high quality, local produce.

Rooms 32 (4 fmly) (5 GF) **S** £59-£110; **D** £69-£110
Facilities ♫ Xmas New Year Wi-fi **Conf** Class 50
Board 30 Thtr 100 Del from £100 to £154 **Services** Lift
Parking 40 **Notes** LB Civ Wed 70

Parsonage Country House

★★★ 78% ◉ COUNTRY HOUSE HOTEL

☎ 01904 728111 📄 01904 728151
York Rd YO19 6LF
e-mail: reservations@parsonagehotel.co.uk
web: www.parsonagehotel.co.uk

(For full entry see Escrick)

See advert on this page

Best Western Kilima Hotel

★★★ 78% HOTEL

☎ 01904 625787 📄 01904 612083
129 Holgate Rd YO24 4AZ
e-mail: sales@kilima.co.uk
web: www.kilima.co.uk
dir: On A59, on W outskirts

This establishment, a former rectory, is conveniently situated within easy walking distance of the city centre. There is a relaxed and friendly atmosphere with professional, friendly staff providing attentive service. Bedrooms are comfortable and well equipped. There is an indoor pool, a fitness centre and a Turkish steam room.

Rooms 26 (2 fmly) (10 GF) **Facilities** FTV ⊗ Gym Leisure complex Steam room Fitness Suite Xmas New Year Wi-fi **Conf** Board 14 **Parking** 26 **Notes** ⊗

Mount Royale

★★★ 74% ◉ HOTEL

☎ 01904 628856 📄 01904 611171
The Mount YO24 1GU
e-mail: reservations@mountroyale.co.uk
web: www.mountroyale.co.uk
dir: W on A1036, 0.5m after racecourse. Hotel on right after lights

This friendly hotel, a William IV listed building, offers comfortable bedrooms in a variety of styles, several leading onto the delightful gardens. Public rooms include a lounge, a meeting room and a cosy bar; the hotel has an outdoor pool, a sauna and a hot tub plus a beauty therapist. There is a separate restaurant called One 19 The Mount and a cocktail lounge overlooking the gardens (all meals and drinks can be charged to room accounts).

Rooms 24 (3 fmly) (6 GF) **S** £85-£135; **D** £99-£210 (incl. bkfst) **Facilities** Spa FTV ⊀ supervised Beauty treatment centre Sauna Steam room ♫ Xmas New Year Wi-fi **Conf** Board 25 Thtr 35 **Parking** 27 **Notes** LB

See advert on this page

YORK *continued*

Best Western York Pavilion

★★★ 74% HOTEL

☎ 01904 622099 🖹 01904 626939
45 Main St, Fulford YO10 4PJ
e-mail: reservations@yorkpavilionhotel.com
web: www.yorkpavilionhotel.com
dir: Exit A64 (York ring road) at A19 junct towards York.
Hotel 0.5m on right opposite Pavilion Court

An attractive Georgian hotel situated in its own grounds.
All the bedrooms are individually designed to a high
specification; some are in the old house and some in the
converted stables set around a garden terrace. There is a
comfortable lounge, a conference centre and an inviting
brasserie-style restaurant with a regularly changing
menu.

Rooms 57 (4 fmly) (11 GF) **Facilities** Xmas New Year
Wi-fi **Conf** Class 60 Board 45 Thtr 150 **Parking** 40
Notes ⊗ Civ Wed 80

Burn Hall Hotel and Conference Centre

★★★ 72% HOTEL

☎ 01347 825400 🖹 01347 838878
Tollerton Rd, Huby YO61 1JB
e-mail: enquiries@burn-hall.co.uk
web: www.burn-hall.co.uk
dir: A19 signed Huby, hotel 0.5m on left

Now completely refurbished this Victorian mansion house
is set in eight acres of parkland. Bedrooms vary in size
and style, from smart executive rooms to more functional
standard rooms. Extensive conference and meeting
facilities are available.

Rooms 95 (9 fmly) (30 GF) **S** £42-£102; **D** £42-£102
Facilities FTV ⌣ Gym Xmas New Year Wi-fi **Conf** Class 70
Board 40 Thtr 250 Del from £98 to £112* **Services** Lift
Parking 150 **Notes** LB Civ Wed 250

Minster Hotel

★★★ 70% HOTEL

☎ 01904 621267 🖹 01904 654719
60 Bootham YO30 7BZ
e-mail: info@yorkminsterhotel.co.uk
web: www.yorkminsterhotel.co.uk
dir: from A1237 (York outer ring road) exit A19 N into city
centre. Hotel on right 150yds from Bootham Bar

Within easy walking distance of the Minster and the city
centre, this careful conversion of two large Victorian
houses provides stylish, comfortable and well-equipped
bedrooms. There is a cosy bar and a bistro serving
imaginative dishes; conference facilities are also
available along with secure parking.

Rooms 34 (3 annexe) (10 fmly) (7 GF) **Facilities** STV
Xmas New Year Wi-fi **Conf** Class 45 Board 30 Thtr 65
Services Lift **Parking** 30 **Notes** LB ⊗

Beechwood Close Hotel

★★ 75% HOTEL

☎ 01904 658378
19 Shipton Rd, Clifton YO30 5RE
e-mail: info@beechwood-close-co.uk
dir: From York ring road at A19/Thirsk rdbt take A19
towards city centre. 1m, hotel on right just after 30mph
signs

Just one mile north of the city this smartly presented
hotel is conveniently located for both business and leisure
guests. The ground floor areas have now been refurbished
and there is a well stocked bar and lounge. A wide choice
of meals is offered in the stylish, airy restaurant which
looks out onto the attractive rear gardens.

Rooms 14 **Conf** Class 20 Board 30 Thtr 50

Knavesmire Manor

★★ 74% SMALL HOTEL

☎ 01904 702941 🖹 01904 709274
302 Tadcaster Rd YO24 1HE
e-mail: enquire@knavesmire.co.uk
dir: A1036 into city centre. Hotel on right, overlooking
racecourse

Commanding superb views across York's famous
racecourse, this former manor house offers comfortable,
well-equipped bedrooms, either in the main house or the
garden rooms to the rear. Comfortable day rooms are
stylishly furnished, whilst the heated indoor pool provides
a popular addition.

Rooms 20 (9 annexe) (3 fmly) **S** £55-£89; **D** £69-£95
(incl. bkfst) **Facilities** ⌕ New Year Wi-fi **Conf** Class 36
Board 30 Thtr 40 Del from £99 to £119 **Services** Lift
Parking 28 **Notes** LB Closed 23-27 Dec Civ Wed 60

Lady Anne Middleton's Hotel

★★ 69% HOTEL

☎ 01904 611570 🖹 01904 613043
Skeldergate YO1 6DS
e-mail: bookings@ladyannes.co.uk
web: www.ladyannes.co.uk
dir: From A64 (Leeds) A1036 towards city centre. Right at
City Walls lights, keep left, 1st left before bridge, then 1st
left into Cromwell Rd. Hotel on right

This hotel has been created from several listed buildings
and is very well located in the centre of York. Bedrooms
are comfortably equipped. Among its amenities is a bar-
lounge and a dining room where a satisfying range of
food is served. An extensive fitness club is also available
along with private parking.

Rooms 54 (17 annexe) (5 fmly) (12 GF) **S** £67-£72;
D £92-£98 (incl. bkfst)* **Facilities** ⌕ Gym Fitness centre
Wi-fi **Conf** Class 30 Board 30 Thtr 100 Del from £95 to
£135* **Parking** 40 **Notes** ⊗ Closed 24-29 Dec

Express by Holiday Inn York - East

BUDGET HOTEL

☎ 01904 438660 🖹 01904 438560
Malton Rd YO32 9TE
e-mail: ebhi-york-east@btconnect.com
web: www.hiexpress.com/york-east
dir: From A64 take A1036 towards York centre. Hotel on
left behind The Hopgrove Toby Carvery

A modern hotel ideal for families and business travellers.
Fresh and uncomplicated, the spacious rooms include Sky
TV, power shower and tea and coffee-making facilities.
Continental buffet breakfast is included in the room rate;
other meals may be taken at the nearby family pub or
restaurant. See also the Hotel Groups pages.

Rooms 49 (20 fmly) (21 GF) **D** £59.95-£150 (incl. bkfst)*

Innkeeper's Lodge York

BUDGET HOTEL

☎ 0845 112 6042 🖹 0845 112 6260
Hull Rd YO10 3LF
web: www.innkeeperslodge.com/york
dir: A1079 (Hull road) towards York, over next rdbt. Lodge
on left

Innkeeper's Lodge represent an exciting, high value
concept within the budget hotel market. Comfortable
bedrooms provide excellent facilities that include satellite
TV and modem points. Options include spacious family
rooms; and for the corporate guest, cutting edge IT is
provided with Wi-fi access. All-day food is provided in the
adjacent pub restaurant. The extensive continental
breakfast is complimentary. See also the Hotel Groups
pages.

Rooms 40 **Conf** Thtr 15

Travelodge York Central

BUDGET HOTEL

☎ 0871 984 6187 🖹 01904 652171
90 Piccadilly YO1 9NX
web: www.travelodge.co.uk
dir: A1(M) follow A64, 3rd exit for A19 & York

Travelodge offers good quality, good value, budget
accommodation. All offer family rooms sleeping up to four
(two adults, two children) with en suite bathroom/
shower-room, remote-control TV, tea- and coffee-making
facilities and comfortable beds. Food options vary.
Breakfast is at the on-site Bar Café restaurant (if
available) or to take away. See also Hotel Groups pages.

Rooms 93 **S** fr £29; **D** fr £29

YORKSHIRE, SOUTH

BARNSLEY — Map 16 SE30

Tankersley Manor

★★★★ 77% HOTEL

☎ 01226 744700 📠 01226 745405
Church Ln S75 3DQ
e-mail: tankersleymanor@qhotels.co.uk
web: www.qhotels.co.uk

(For full entry see Tankersley)

Brooklands Hotel

★★★★ ⓐ HOTEL

☎ 01226 299571 & 329182 📠 01226 249465
Barnsley Rd, Dodworth S75 3JT
e-mail: enquiries@brooklandshotel.com
dir: A628 onto B6449 to Dodworth, 1st right at mini rdbt

Rooms 77 (5 fmly) **Facilities** STV ⓒ Gym Health club
Xmas New Year Wi-fi **Conf** Class 200 Board 90 Thtr 420
Services Lift **Parking** 200 **Notes** LB ⊗ Civ Wed 200

Best Western Ardsley House Hotel

★★★ 79% HOTEL

☎ 01226 309955 📠 01226 205374
Doncaster Rd, Ardsley S71 5EH
e-mail: ardsley.house@forestdale.com
web: www.ardsleyhousehotel.co.uk
dir: on A635, 0.75m from Stairfoot rdbt

This late 18th-century building has retained many of its
original Georgian features. Bedrooms are both
comfortable and well equipped. The excellent leisure
facilities including a gym, pool and beauty salon. The
Allendale restaurant with views of the nearby woodlands
offers an extensive menu.

Rooms 75 (12 fmly) (14 GF) **Facilities** Spa ⓒ supervised
Gym Beauty spa 3 treatment rooms ♫ Xmas New Year
Wi-fi **Conf** Class 250 Board 40 Thtr 350 **Parking** 200
Notes LB Civ Wed 250

Travelodge Barnsley

BUDGET HOTEL

☎ 0871 984 6121 📠 01226 298799
School St S70 3PE
web: www.travelodge.co.uk
dir: At Stairfoot rdbt junct of A633 & A635

Travelodge offers good quality, good value, budget
accommodation. All offer family rooms sleeping up to four
(two adults, two children) with en suite bathroom/
shower-room, remote-control TV, tea- and coffee-making
facilities and comfortable beds. Food options vary.
Breakfast is at the on-site Bar Café restaurant (if
available) or to take away. See also Hotel Groups pages.

Rooms 32 **S** fr £29; **D** fr £29

CARCROFT — Map 16 SE50

Travelodge Doncaster

BUDGET HOTEL

☎ 0871 984 6131 📠 0870 1911631
Great North Rd DN6 9LF
web: www.travelodge.co.uk
dir: on A1 northbound

Travelodge offers good quality, good value, budget
accommodation. All offer family rooms sleeping up to four
(two adults, two children) with en suite bathroom/
shower-room, remote-control TV, tea- and coffee-making
facilities and comfortable beds. Food options vary.
Breakfast is at the on-site Bar Café restaurant (if
available) or to take away. See also Hotel Groups pages.

Rooms 40 **S** fr £29; **D** fr £29

DONCASTER — Map 16 SE50

Best Western Premier Mount Pleasant

★★★★ 79% ⓐ HOTEL

☎ 01302 868696 & 868219 📠 01302 865130
Great North Rd DN11 0HW
e-mail: reception@mountpleasant.co.uk
web: www.mountpleasant.co.uk

(For full entry see Rossington)

Holiday Inn Doncaster A1(M) Jct 36

★★★ 77% HOTEL

☎ 0870 442 8761 & 01302 799988 📠 01302 310197
High Rd, Warmsworth DN4 9UX
e-mail: hidoncaster@qmh-hotels.com
web: www.holidayinn.co.uk
dir: 200mtrs W of A1(M) junct 36

This hotel is situated in the grounds of the 17th-century
Warmsworth Hall; the hall as been splendidly restored
and is now the conference centre. All the bedrooms are
very well appointed, and include rooms designed for
disabled guests. The informal and relaxing restaurant
provides a wide range of dishes.

Holiday Inn Doncaster A1(M) Jct 36

Rooms 102 (6 fmly) (22 GF) **Facilities** STV ⓒ supervised
Gym Beautician Steam room Xmas New Year Wi-fi
Conf Class 250 Board 100 Thtr 250 **Services** Lift
Parking 250 **Notes** ⊗ Civ Wed 250

Regent

★★★ 74% HOTEL

☎ 01302 364180 & 381960 📠 01302 322331
Regent Square DN1 2DS
e-mail: reservations@theregenthotel.co.uk
web: www.theregenthotel.co.uk
dir: on corner of A630 & A638, 1m from racecourse

This town centre hotel overlooks a delightful small
square. Public rooms include the modern bar and
delightful restaurant, where an interesting range of
dishes is offered. Service is friendly and attentive. Modern
bedrooms have been furnished in a contemporary style
and offer high levels of comfort.

Rooms 53 (6 fmly) (8 GF) **Facilities** FTV ♫ Wi-fi
Conf Class 50 Board 40 Thtr 125 **Services** Lift
Parking 20 **Notes** Closed 25 Dec & 1 Jan RS BH
Civ Wed 120

Danum

★★★ 70% HOTEL

☎ 01302 342261 📠 01302 329034
High St DN1 1DN
e-mail: info@danumhotel.com
dir: M18 junct 3, A6182 to Doncaster. Over rdbt, right at
next. Right at 'give way' sign, left at mini rdbt, hotel
ahead

Situated in the centre of the town, this Edwardian hotel
offers well equipped conference rooms together with
comfortable bedrooms. A contemporary lounge area
provides modern dining and especially negotiated rates
at a local leisure centre are offered.

Rooms 64 (5 fmly) (12 smoking) **Facilities** STV FTV
Special rates at Cannons Health Club ♫ Xmas New Year
Wi-fi **Conf** Class 160 Board 100 Thtr 350 Del from £80 to
£110 **Services** Lift **Parking** 36 **Notes** RS 26-30 Dec
Civ Wed 250

DONCASTER *continued*

Grand St Leger

★★★ 66% HOTEL

☎ 01302 364111 📠 01302 329865
Bennetthorpe DN2 6AX
e-mail: sales@grandstleger.com
web: www.grandstleger.com
dir: Follow Doncaster Racecourse signs. At racecourse rdbt hotel on corner

This friendly hotel is located next to the racecourse and is only ten minutes' walk from the town centre. There is a cheerful bar-lounge and a pleasant restaurant offering an extensive choice of dishes. The bedrooms are comfortable and thoughtfully equipped, including Wi-fi access.

Rooms 20 **Facilities** FTV Wi-fi **Conf** Class 50 Board 30 Thtr 80 Del from £100 to £150* **Parking** 28 **Notes** ⊗ RS 25 Dec Civ Wed 60

Ramada Encore Doncaster Airport

ⓤ

☎ 0844 801 1020 📠 0844 801 1021
Robin Hood Airport DN9 3RH
e-mail: rm@encoredoncaster.co.uk
dir: M180 junct 1, follow signs for airport

Currently the rating for this establishment is not confirmed. This may be due to a change of ownership or because it has only recently joined the AA rating scheme. For further details please see the AA website: theAA.com

Rooms 102 (36 fmly) (3 GF) (9 smoking) **S** £50-£125; **D** £50-£125* **Facilities** FTV Wi-fi **Conf** Class 20 Board 20 Thtr 40 Del from £95 to £105* **Services** Lift Air con **Parking** 144 **Notes** ⊗

Campanile Doncaster

BUDGET HOTEL

☎ 01302 370770 📠 01302 370813
Doncaster Leisure Park, Bawtry Rd DN4 7PD
e-mail: doncaster@campanile.com
dir: Follow signs to Doncaster Leisure Centre, left at rdbt before Dome complex

This modern building offers accommodation in smart, well-equipped bedrooms, all with en suite bathrooms. Refreshments may be taken at the informal bistro. See also the Hotel Groups pages.

Rooms 50 **Conf** Class 15 Board 15 Thtr 25

Express by Holiday Inn Doncaster

BUDGET HOTEL

☎ 0870 890 9988 & 01302 314100 📠 0870 890 9989
Catesby Business Park, First Point DN4 5JH
e-mail: doncaster@expressbyholidayinn.net
web: www.hiexpress.com/doncaster
dir: M18 junct 3/A6182, left at 1st rdbt onto Woodfield Way, straight over next rdbt, hotel on left

A modern hotel ideal for families and business travellers. Fresh and uncomplicated, the spacious rooms include Sky TV, power shower and tea and coffee-making facilities. Continental buffet breakfast is included in the room rate; other meals may be taken at the nearby family pub or restaurant. See also the Hotel Groups pages.

Rooms 94 (63 fmly) (16 GF) (20 smoking)
S £49.95-£89.95; **D** £49.95-£89.95 (incl. bkfst)
Conf Class 16 Board 20 Thtr 40 Del from £79 to £105

Innkeeper's Lodge Doncaster

BUDGET HOTEL

☎ 0845 112 6032 📠 0845 112 6270
Bawtry Rd, Bessacarr DN4 7BS
web: www.innkeeperslodge.com/doncaster
dir: M18 junct 3, A6182 towards Doncaster. A18 signed Thorne. A638, pass racecourse. Lodge 1.5m

Innkeeper's Lodge represents an exciting, high value concept within the budget hotel market. Comfortable bedrooms provide excellent facilities that include satellite TV and modem points. Options include family rooms; and for the corporate guest, cutting edge IT which includes Wi-fi high speed internet access. A popular Carvery provides all-day food, including an extensive, complimentary continental breakfast. See also the Hotel Groups pages.

Rooms 25 **Conf** Thtr 40

Travelodge Doncaster (M18/M180)

BUDGET HOTEL

☎ 0871 984 6132 📠 01302 845469
DN8 5GS
web: www.travelodge.co.uk
dir: M18 junct 5/M180

Travelodge offers good quality, good value, budget accommodation. All offer family rooms sleeping up to four (two adults, two children) with en suite bathroom/shower-room, remote-control TV, tea- and coffee-making facilities and comfortable beds. Food options vary. Breakfast is at the on-site Bar Café restaurant (if available) or to take away. See also Hotel Groups pages.

Rooms 41 **S** fr £29; **D** fr £29

MEXBOROUGH Map 16 SE40

Best Western Pastures

★★★ 75% HOTEL

☎ 01709 577707 📠 01709 577795
Pastures Rd S64 0JJ
e-mail: info@pastureshotel.co.uk
web: www.pastureshotel.co.uk
dir: 0.5m from town centre on A6023, left by ATS Tyres, signed Denaby Ings & Cadeby. Hotel on right

This private hotel has a modern, purpose-built block of bedrooms and a separate lodge where food is served. It is in a rural setting beside a working canal with view of Conisbro Castle in the distance, and is convenient for Doncaster or the Dearne Valley with its nature reserves and leisure centre. Compact bedrooms are quiet, comfortable and equipped with many modern facilities.

Rooms 60 (5 fmly) (28 GF) **S** £65-£120; **D** £70-£120 (incl. bkfst)* **Facilities** STV Xmas New Year Wi-fi **Conf** Class 170 Board 100 Thtr 250 **Services** Lift **Parking** 179 **Notes** LB ⊗ Civ Wed 200

ROSSINGTON — Map 16 SK69

Best Western Premier Mount Pleasant

★★★★ 79% ⊛ HOTEL

☎ 01302 868696 & 868219 📠 01302 865130
Great North Rd DN11 0HW
e-mail: reception@mountpleasant.co.uk
web: www.mountpleasant.co.uk
dir: On A638 (Great North Road) between Bawtry & Doncaster

This charming 18th-century house stands in 100 acres of wooded parkland between Doncaster and Bawtry near Robin Hood Airport. The spacious public areas that include cosy lounges and an elegant restaurant have been designed for maximum comfort. The spacious bedrooms are beautifully furnished and individual in design; some rooms have four-poster beds, half-tester beds or sledge beds - one even has a five poster!

Rooms 56 (12 fmly) (28 GF) **S** £63-£165; **D** £81-£184.50 (incl. bkfst) **Facilities** STV Beauty salon Wi-fi **Conf** Class 70 Board 70 Thtr 200 Del from £145 to £170 **Services** Lift **Parking** 140 **Notes** LB ⊗ Closed 25 Dec RS 24 Dec Civ Wed 180

ROTHERHAM — Map 16 SK49

Hellaby Hall

PRIMA HOTEL GROUP

★★★★ 71% HOTEL

☎ 01709 702701 📠 01709 700979
Old Hellaby Ln, Hellaby S66 8SN
e-mail: reservations@hellabyhallhotel.co.uk
web: www.hellabyhallhotel.co.uk
dir: 0.5m off M18 junct 1, onto A631 towards Maltby. Hotel in Hellaby. (NB do not use postcode for sat nav)

This 17th-century house was built to a Flemish design with high, beamed ceilings, staircases which lead off to private meeting rooms and a series of oak-panelled lounges. Bedrooms are elegant and well equipped, and guests can dine in the formal Attic Restaurant. There are extensive leisure facilities and conference areas, and the hotel holds a licence for civil weddings.

Rooms 90 (2 fmly) (17 GF) **Facilities** Spa STV FTV ⊛ Gym Beauty room Exercise studio Xmas New Year Wi-fi **Conf** Class 300 Board 150 Thtr 500 **Services** Lift **Parking** 250 **Notes** Civ Wed 200

Best Western Elton

★★★ 78% HOTEL

☎ 01709 545681 📠 01709 549100
Main St, Bramley S66 2SF
e-mail: bestwestern.eltonhotel@btinternet.com
web: www.bw-eltonhotel.co.uk
dir: M18 junct 1 follow A631 Rotherham signs, turn right to Ravenfield, hotel at end of Bramley, follow brown signs

Within easy reach of the M18, this welcoming, stone-built hotel is set in well-tended gardens. The Elton offers good, modern accommodation, with larger rooms in the extension that are particularly comfortable and well equipped. A civil licence is held for wedding ceremonies, and conference rooms are available.

Rooms 29 (16 annexe) (4 fmly) (11 GF) **S** £37-£65.50; **D** £42-£98* **Facilities** FTV Wi-fi **Conf** Class 24 Board 26 Thtr 55 Del from £110 to £120* **Parking** 48 **Notes** LB Civ Wed 48

Holiday Inn Rotherham-Sheffield M1, Jct 33

★★★ 78% HOTEL

☎ 01709 830630 📠 01709 786005
West Bawtry Rd S60 4NA
web: www.holidayinn.co.uk
dir: M1 junct 33, follow Rotherham signs. At rdbt take 1st exit. Hotel on right

Stylish and contemporary, this hotel is well located just five minutes from the motorway. Bedrooms are spacious and boast an excellent range of facilities. Guests have the use of the leisure club with its large swimming pool, spa bath and steam room.

Rooms 104

Best Western Consort Hotel

★★★ 77% HOTEL

☎ 01709 530022 📠 01709 531529
Brampton Rd, Thurcroft S66 9JA
e-mail: info@consorthotel.com
web: www.consorthotel.com
dir: M18 junct 1, right towards Bawtry on A631. 250yds to rdbt, then 200yds turn left then 1.5m to x-rds, hotel opposite

Bedrooms at this modern, friendly hotel are comfortable, attractive and air conditioned, and include ten superior rooms. A wide range of dishes is served in the open-plan bar and restaurant, and there is a comfortable foyer lounge. There are good conference and function facilities, and entertainment evenings are often hosted here.

Rooms 27 (2 fmly) (9 GF) **S** £57.50-£93.50; **D** £65.50-£103.50 (incl. bkfst) **Facilities** FTV ♬ Wi-fi **Conf** Class 120 Board 50 Thtr 350 Del from £100 to £125 **Services** Air con **Parking** 90 **Notes** LB ⊗ Civ Wed 300

Carlton Park

★★★ 77% HOTEL

☎ 01709 849955 📠 01709 368960
102/104 Moorgate Rd S60 2BG
e-mail: reservations@carltonparkhotel.com
web: www.carltonparkhotel.com
dir: M1 junct 33, onto A631, then A618. Hotel 800yds past hospital

This modern hotel is situated in a pleasant residential area of the town, close to the District General Hospital, yet within minutes of the M1. Bedrooms and bathrooms offer very modern facilities; three have separate sitting rooms. The restaurant and bar provide a lively atmosphere and there is a pool and leisure centre.

Rooms 80 (14 fmly) (16 GF) (7 smoking) **S** £38-£72; **D** £48-£92* **Facilities** STV ⊛ Gym ♬ Xmas New Year Wi-fi **Conf** Class 160 Board 60 Thtr 250 Del from £95 to £130* **Services** Lift **Parking** 120 **Notes** ⊗ Civ Wed 150

Restover Lodge

★★ 67% HOTEL

☎ 01709 700255 📠 01709 545169
Hellaby Industrial Estate, Lowton Way, off Denby Way S66 8RY
e-mail: rotherham@envergure.co.uk
dir: M18 junct 1. Follow signs for Maltby. Left at lights, 2nd on left

This modern building offers accommodation in smart, well equipped bedrooms. Refreshments may be taken at the informal restaurant or bar.

Rooms 50 (12 fmly) **Facilities** Xmas Wi-fi **Conf** Class 35 Board 30 Thtr 40 **Parking** 40

Ibis Rotherham

BUDGET HOTEL

☎ 01709 730333 📠 01709 730444
Moorhead Way, Bramley S66 1YY
e-mail: H3163@accor-hotels.com
web: www.ibishotel.com
dir: M18 junct 1, left at rdbt, left at 1st lights. Hotel adjacent to supermarket

Modern, budget hotel offering comfortable accommodation in bright and practical bedrooms. Breakfast is self-service and dinner is available in the restaurant. See also the Hotel Groups pages.

Rooms 86 (22 fmly) **Conf** Class 30 Board 30 Thtr 40

SHEFFIELD Map 16 SK49

Sheffield Park

★★★★ 77% ⊛ HOTEL

☎ 0114 282 9988 📠 0114 237 8140
Chesterfield Road South S8 8BW
e-mail: info.sheffield@pedersenhotels.com
web: www.pedersenhotels.com/sheffieldparkhotel
dir: From N: M1 junct 33, A630 Sheffield. A61
Chesterfield. After Graves Tennis Centre follow A6/
Chesterfield/M1 South signs. Hotel 200yds on left. From
S: M1 junct 29, A617 Chesterfield. Follow A61/Sheffield
signs. After City of Sheffield boundary, double back at
rdbt, hotel on left

A large modern hotel located on the ring road. The
bedrooms are spacious and well equipped and include
family rooms, suites and executive rooms. Other facilities
include a leisure club, meeting rooms and ample secure
parking.

Rooms 95 (20 GF) **S** £60-£140; **D** £60-£140 (incl. bkfst)
Facilities STV FTV ⟲ Gym Steam room Sauna Xmas New
Year Wi-fi **Conf** Class 200 Board 80 Thtr 500
Del from £100 to £155 **Services** Lift **Parking** 260
Notes LB ⊗ Civ Wed 300

Mercure St Paul's Hotel & Spa

★★★★ 77% HOTEL

☎ 0870 122 6585 📠 0870 122 6586
119 Norfolk St S1 2JE
e-mail: h6628@accor.com
web: www.mercure-uk.com
dir: M1 junct 33, 4th exit at rdbt, left at 1st lights, right
at 2nd in front of Crucible Theatre

This modern, luxury hotel enjoys a central location close
to key attractions in the city. Open-plan public areas are
situated in a steel and glass atrium and include a
popular Champagne bar, the Yard Restaurant and Zucca,
an Italian Bistro. Bedrooms are superbly presented and
richly furnished. The Vital health and beauty treatment
centre provides a fabulous thermal suite.

Rooms 163 (40 fmly) **Facilities** Spa ⟲ Sauna Steam
room Snail shower Ice fountain Fitness classes Xmas New
Year Wi-fi **Conf** Class 400 Board 30 Thtr 600
Del from £130 to £195* **Services** Lift Air con **Notes** ⊗
Civ Wed 350

Holiday Inn Sheffield

★★★★ 🅰 HOTEL

☎ 0114 252 6511 📠 0114 272 4519
Victoria Station Rd S4 7YE
web: www.holidayinn.co.uk
dir: M1 junct 33, follow signs to city centre, then A57
Glossop. Hotel on left after 2.5m

In a quiet and peaceful location at the end of a private
drive this Grade II listed building is within walking
distance of Ponds Forge, The Crucible and Lyceum
Theatres. The tastefully decorated bedrooms include
executive rooms and suites. Fine dining is available in
Cunningham's Restaurant, and drinks and snacks in the
Grand Lounge Bar. Guests have free use of the health
suite (open 24 hours) which includes a fully-equipped
gym and saunas.

Rooms 107 (43 fmly) (19 smoking) **Facilities** STV FTV
Gym Xmas New Year Wi-fi **Conf** Class 200 Board 45
Thtr 400 **Services** Lift **Parking** 240 **Notes** LB Civ Wed 250

Whitley Hall

★★★ 85% ⊛⊛ HOTEL

CLASSIC
BRITISH HOTELS

☎ 0114 245 4444 & 246 0456 📠 0114 245 5414
Elliott Ln, Grenoside S35 8NR
e-mail: reservations@whitleyhall.com
web: www.whitleyhall.com
dir: A61 past football ground, then 2m, right just before
Norfolk Arms, left at bottom of hill. Hotel on left

This 16th-century house stands in 20 acres of
landscaped grounds and gardens. Public rooms are full
of character and interesting architectural features, and
command the best views of the gardens. The individually
styled bedrooms are furnished in keeping with the country
house setting, as are the oak-panelled restaurant and
bar.

Rooms 31 (1 annexe) (2 fmly) (5 GF) **Facilities** STV FTV
Wi-fi **Conf** Class 50 Board 34 Thtr 70 Del from £145 to
£165* **Services** Lift **Parking** 100 **Notes** ⊗ Civ Wed 100

Staindrop Lodge

★★★ 80% ⊛ HOTEL

☎ 0114 284 3111 📠 0114 284 3110
Lane End, Chapeltown S35 3UH
e-mail: info@staindroplodge.co.uk
dir: M1 junct 35, take A629 for 1m, straight over 1st rdbt,
right at 2nd rdbt, hotel approx 0.5m on right

This hotel, bar and brasserie offers smart modern public
areas and accommodation. An art deco theme continues
throughout the open-plan public rooms and the
comfortably appointed, spacious bedrooms. Service is
relaxed and friendly, and all-day menus are available.

Rooms 37 (5 annexe) (6 fmly) (3 GF) **Facilities** STV Wi-fi
Conf Class 60 Board 40 Thtr 80 **Services** Air con
Parking 80 **Notes** LB ⊗ Civ Wed 80

Best Western Mosborough Hall

★★★ 80% HOTEL

☎ 0114 248 4353 📠 0114 247 9759
High St, Mosborough S20 5EA
e-mail: hotel@mosboroughhall.co.uk
web: www.mosboroughhall.co.uk
dir: M1 junct 30, A6135 towards Sheffield. Follow
Eckington/Mosborough signs 2m. Sharp bend at top of
hill, hotel on right

This 16th-century, Grade II listed manor house is set in
gardens not far from the M1 and is convenient for the city
centre. The bedrooms offer very high quality and good
amenities; some are very spacious. There is a galleried
bar and conservatory lounge, and freshly prepared dishes
are served in the traditional style dining room.

Rooms 43 (4 fmly) (16 GF) **S** £49-£89; **D** £49-£89*
Facilities FTV Spa & beauty treatments Xmas New Year
Wi-fi **Conf** Class 125 Board 70 Thtr 300 Del from £99 to
£149* **Parking** 100 **Notes** LB ⊗ Civ Wed 250

Novotel Sheffield

★★★ 79% HOTEL

☎ 0114 278 1781 📠 0114 278 7744
50 Arundel Gate S1 2PR
e-mail: h1348-re@accor.com
web: www.novotel.com
dir: Between Registry Office & Crucible/Lyceum Theatres,
follow signs to Town Hall/Theatres & Hallam University

In the heart of the city centre, this new generation Novotel
has stylish public areas including a very modern
restaurant, indoor swimming pool and a range of meeting
rooms. Spacious bedrooms are suitable for family
occupation, and the Novation rooms are ideal for
business users.

Rooms 144 (136 fmly) **S** £69-£119; **D** £69-£119*
Facilities STV FTV ⟲ Local gym facilities free for
residents use Xmas New Year Wi-fi **Conf** Class 180
Board 100 Thtr 220 Del from £125 to £165 **Services** Lift
Air con **Parking** 60 **Notes** Civ Wed 180

Best Western Cutlers Hotel

★★★ 72% HOTEL

☎ 0114 273 9939 📠 0114 276 8332
Theatreland George St S1 2PF
e-mail: enquiries@cutlershotel.co.uk
dir: M1 junction 33. At Park Sq follow signs to City Centre
& Theatres. At top of Commercial St, left into Arundel
Gate. Into right lane, at lights right into Norfolk St 2nd
right into George St. Hotel 50mtrs on left

Situated right in the heart of the city, near the theatres
and only minutes away from the rail station. Public areas
include a lower ground floor bistro, and room service is
available if required. Discounted overnight parking is
provided in the nearby public car park.

Rooms 45 (2 fmly) **S** £50-£80; **D** £65-£110 (incl. bkfst)
Facilities STV FTV Xmas New Year Wi-fi **Conf** Class 20
Board 25 Thtr 80 Del from £95 to £130 **Services** Lift
Notes LB ⊗ Civ Wed 60

Garrison

★★★ 72% HOTEL

☎ 0114 249 9555 📠 0114 249 1900
Hillsborough Barracks, Penistone Rd S6 2GB
e-mail: garrisonhotel@btconnect.com

This unique hotel as been created from the former
Hillsborough barracks and retains some of the original
features. Bedrooms are modern and well equipped and a
wide range of food is available in the main building. The
adjacent Supertram provides easy access to the city.

Rooms 43 (2 fmly) **D** £62-£69 (incl. bkfst)* **Facilities** FTV
Wi-fi **Conf** Class 30 Board 30 Thtr 30 Del from £92.10 to
£108.05* **Services** Lift **Parking** 60 **Notes** ⊗ Closed
24-28 Dec & 1 Jan Civ Wed 120

Kenwood Hall

U

☎ 0114 258 3811 📠 0114 255 4744
Kenwood Rd S7 1NQ
dir: A61(Barnsley ring road) into St Mary's Rd. Straight
over rdbt, left into London Rd, right at lights. 2nd exit at
2nd rdbt, hotel ahead

Currently the rating for this establishment is not
confirmed. This may be due to a change of ownership or
because it has only recently joined the AA rating scheme.
For further details please see the AA website: theAA.com

Rooms 114 (8 fmly) **S** £79-£159; **D** £79-£159 (incl.
bkfst)* **Facilities** STV ⊙ Fishing Gym Steam room Sauna
New Year Wi-fi **Conf** Class 100 Board 60 Thtr 250
Del from £119 to £189* **Services** Lift **Parking** 150
Notes LB Civ Wed 260

Ibis Sheffield

BUDGET HOTEL

☎ 0114 241 9600 📠 0114 241 9610
Shude Hill S1 2AR
e-mail: H2891@accor.com
web: www.ibishotel.com
dir: M1 junct 33, follow signs to Sheffield City
Centre(A630/A57), at rdbt take 5th exit, signed Ponds
Forge, for hotel

Modern, budget hotel offering comfortable
accommodation in bright and practical bedrooms.
Breakfast is self-service and dinner is available in the
restaurant. See also the Hotel Groups pages.

Rooms 95 (15 fmly) (3 GF) (8 smoking) **S** £37.80-£70;
D £37.80-£70

Innkeeper's Lodge Sheffield South

BUDGET HOTEL

☎ 0845 112 6041 📠 0845 112 6261
Hathersage Rd, Longshaw S11 7TY
web: www.innkeeperslodge.com/sheffieldsouth
dir: M1 junct 33 towards Sheffield City Centre rail station.
Past station towards A625. 5m. Right onto A6187
(Hathersage Rd). Lodge on right.

Innkeeper's Lodge represents an exciting, high value
concept within the budget hotel market. Comfortable
bedrooms provide excellent facilities that include satellite
TV and modem points. This carefully restored lodge is in a
picturesque setting and has its own unique style and
quirky character. Food is served all day, and an extensive,
complimentary continental breakfast is offered. See also
the Hotel Groups pages.

Rooms 10 (2 fmly)

Travelodge Sheffield Central

BUDGET HOTEL

☎ 0871 984 6305 📠 01142 723584
1 Broad Street West S1 2BG
web: www.travelodge.co.uk
dir: A57 Park Square rdbt, 2nd exit onto Broad St

Travelodge offers good quality, good value, budget
accommodation. All offer family rooms sleeping up to four
(two adults, two children) with en suite bathroom/
shower-room, remote-control TV, tea- and coffee-making
facilities and comfortable beds. Food options vary.
Breakfast is at the on-site Bar Café restaurant (if
available) or to take away. See also Hotel Groups pages.

Rooms 114 **S** fr £29; **D** fr £29

Travelodge Sheffield Richmond

BUDGET HOTEL

☎ 0871 984 6175 📠 0114 253 0935
340 Prince of Wales Rd S2 1FF
web: www.travelodge.co.uk
dir: M1 junct 33, A630 towards city centre. Take exit for
ring road & services. Lodge 3m from M1

Rooms 68 **S** fr £29; **D** fr £29 **Conf** Board 20 Thtr 30

TANKERSLEY   Map 16 SK39

Tankersley Manor

★★★★ 77% HOTEL

☎ 01226 744700 📠 01226 745405
Church Ln S75 3DQ
e-mail: tankersleymanor@qhotels.co.uk
web: www.qhotels.co.uk
dir: M1 junct 36 take A61 (Sheffield road). Hotel 0.5m on
left

High on the moors with views over the countryside, this
17th-century residence is well located for major cities,
tourist attractions and motorway links. Where
appropriate, bedrooms retain original features such as
exposed beams or Yorkshire-stone window sills. The hotel
has its own traditional country pub, complete with old
beams and open fires, alongside the more formal
restaurant and bar. A well-equipped leisure centre is also
available.

Rooms 99 (2 fmly) (16 GF) **S** £55-£135; **D** £65-£145 (incl.
bkfst)* **Facilities** Spa STV ⊙ Gym Swimming lessons
Beauty treatments Xmas New Year Wi-fi **Conf** Class 200
Board 100 Thtr 400 **Services** Lift **Parking** 200 **Notes** LB
Civ Wed 95

TODWICK — Map 16 SK48

Red Lion

★★★ A HOTEL

☎ 01909 771654 📠 01909 773704
Worksop Rd S26 1DJ
e-mail: 7933@greeneking.co.uk
web: www.oldenglish.co.uk
dir: On A57, 1m from M1 junct 31 towards Worksop

Rooms 27 (1 fmly) (14 GF) **Facilities** Xmas
Conf Class 30 Board 25 Thtr 25 **Parking** 80 **Notes** LB ✦

WOODALL MOTORWAY SERVICE AREA (M1) — Map 16 SK48

Days Inn Sheffield

BUDGET HOTEL

☎ 0114 248 7992 📠 0114 248 5634
Woodall Service Area S26 7XR
e-mail: woodall.hotel@welcomebreak.co.uk
web: www.welcomebreak.co.uk
dir: M1 southbound, at Woodall Services, between juncts 30 & 31

This modern building offers accommodation in smart, spacious and well-equipped bedrooms, suitable for families and business travellers, and all with en suite bathrooms. Continental breakfast is available and other refreshments may be taken at the nearby family restaurant. See also the Hotel Groups pages.

Rooms 38 (32 fmly) **S** £29-£59; **D** £39-£69*
Conf Board 10 **Del** from £65 to £95*

YORKSHIRE, WEST

BINGLEY — Map 19 SE13

Ramada Bradford/Leeds   ⓦ RAMADA.

★★★ 74% HOTEL

☎ 01274 567123 & 0844 815 9004 📠 01274 551331
Bradford Rd BD16 1TU
e-mail: sales.bradford@ramadajarvis.co.uk
web: www.ramadajarvis.co.uk
dir: From M62 junct 26 onto M606, at rdbt follow signs for A650 Skipton/Keighley, hotel 2m from Shipley.

This large hotel is set in private landscaped grounds with views over the Aire Valley. Bedrooms, split between various wings, are neatly appointed for both business and leisure guests. Public areas include the Arts Restaurant, the Club Bar and a substantial conference centre. Extensive parking is available.

Rooms 103 (14 fmly) (2 GF) **Facilities** STV FTV Fishing Gym Xmas New Year Wi-fi **Conf** Class 328 Board 246 Thtr 560 **Services** Lift **Parking** 300 **Notes** Civ Wed 300

Five Rise Locks Hotel & Restaurant

★★ 72% SMALL HOTEL

☎ 01274 565296 📠 01274 568828
Beck Ln BD16 4DD
e-mail: info@five-rise-locks.co.uk
dir: Off Main St onto Park Rd, 0.5m left onto Beck Ln

A warm welcome and comfortable accommodation await you at this impressive Victorian building. Bedrooms are of a good size and feature homely extras. The restaurant offers imaginative dishes and the bright breakfast room overlooks open countryside.

Rooms 9 (2 GF) **S** £60-£65; **D** £85-£105 (incl. bkfst)*
Facilities FTV Wi-fi **Conf** Class 16 Board 18 Thtr 25 **Del** from £100 to £125* **Parking** 20

BRADFORD — Map 19 SE13

See also **Gomersal & Shipley**

Cedar Court

★★★★ 71% HOTEL

☎ 01274 406606 & 0845 409 0426 📠 01274 406600
Mayo Av, Off Rooley Ln BD5 8HZ
e-mail: sales@cedarcourtbradford.co.uk
dir: M62 junct 26/M606. At end turn right at lights then 1st left to hotel car park

This purpose built, modern hotel is conveniently located just off the motorway and close to the city centre and the airport. The hotel boasts extensive function and conference facilities, a well-equipped leisure club and an elegant restaurant. Bedrooms are comfortably appointed for both business and leisure guests.

Rooms 131 (7 fmly) (23 GF) (10 smoking) **S** £70-£135; **D** £70-£135 **Facilities** STV FTV ⊕ Gym Steam room New Year Wi-fi **Conf** Class 300 Board 100 Thtr 800 **Del** from £99 to £145 **Services** Lift **Parking** 350 **Notes** LB ✦ Civ Wed 500

Midland Hotel

★★★ 79% HOTEL

PEEL HOTELS PLC

☎ 01274 735735 📠 01274 720003
Forster Square BD1 4HU
e-mail: info@midland-hotel-bradford.com
web: www.midland-hotel-bradford.com
dir: M62 junct 26/M606, left opp ASDA, left at rdbt onto A650. Through 2 rdbts & 2 lights. Follow A6181/Haworth signs. Up hill, next left into Manor Row. Hotel 400mtrs

Ideally situated in the heart of the city, this grand Victorian hotel provides modern, very well equipped accommodation and comfortable, spacious day rooms. Ample parking is available in what used to be the city's railway station, and a Victorian walkway linking the hotel to the old platform can still be used today.

Rooms 90 (4 fmly) (14 smoking) **Facilities** ♫ Xmas New Year Wi-fi **Conf** Class 150 Board 100 Thtr 450 **Del** from £115 to £165 **Services** Lift **Parking** 50 **Notes** Civ Wed 400

Best Western Guide Post Hotel

★★★ 74% HOTEL

Best Western

☎ 0845 409 1362 📠 01274 671085
Common Rd, Low Moor BD12 0ST
e-mail: sue.barnes@guideposthotel.net
web: www.guideposthotel.net
dir: From M606 rdbt take 2nd exit (Little Chef on right). At next rdbt take 1st exit (Cleckheaton Rd). 0.5m, turn right at bollard into Common Rd

Situated south of the city, this hotel offers attractively styled, modern, comfortable bedrooms. The restaurant offers an extensive range of food using fresh, local produce; lighter snack meals are served in the bar. There is also a choice of well-equipped meeting and function rooms. There is disabled access to the hotel, restaurant and one function room.

Best Western Guide Post Hotel

Rooms 42 (8 fmly) (13 GF) (8 smoking) **S** £50-£94; **D** £59-£105 **Facilities** STV FTV Complimentary use of nearby swimming & gym facilities Wi-fi **Conf** Class 80 Board 60 Thtr 120 Del from £119 to £129 **Parking** 100 **Notes** LB Civ Wed 120

Campanile Bradford

Campanile

★★★ 70% HOTEL

☎ 01274 683683
6 Roydsdale Way, Euroway Estate BD4 6SA
e-mail: bradford@campanile.com
web: www.campanile.com
dir: M62 junct 26 onto M606. Exit Euroway Estate East onto Merrydale Rd, right onto Roydsdale Way

This modern building offers accommodation in smart, well-equipped bedrooms, all with en suite bathrooms. Refreshments may be taken at the informal bistro.

Rooms 130 (37 fmly) (22 GF) **S** £52.95-£69.95; **D** £52.95-£69.95* **Facilities** STV FTV Wi-fi **Conf** Class 100 Board 100 Thtr 300 Del from £95 to £114* **Services** Lift **Parking** 200 **Notes** LB

BRIGHOUSE   **Map 16 SE12**

Holiday Inn Leeds-Brighouse

★★★ 80% HOTEL

☎ 0870 400 9013   🖹 01484 400068
Clifton Village HD6 4HW
e-mail: brighouse@ihg.com
web: www.holidayinn.co.uk
dir: M62 junct 25, A644 signed Brighouse. Remain in right lane, 1st right, hotel at next left

A modern hotel built from traditional Yorkshire stone, and easily accessible from the M62. The bedrooms are spacious and include executive rooms. Other facilities include a leisure club, meeting rooms and ample parking.

Rooms 94 (14 fmly) (43 GF) **Facilities** STV 🕾 supervised Gym Xmas New Year Wi-fi **Conf** Class 120 Board 50 Thtr 200 **Services** Air con **Parking** 197 **Notes** LB ⊗ Civ Wed 200

CLECKHEATON   **Map 19 SE12**

The Whitcliffe

★★★ 71% HOTEL

☎ 0845 833 5362   🖹 01274 870376
Prospect Rd BD19 3HD
e-mail: info@thewhitcliffehotel.co.uk
web: www.thewhitcliffehotel.co.uk
dir: M62 junct 26, A638 to Dewsbury, over 1st lights, right into Mount St, to T-junct, right then 1st left

This popular and conveniently located commercial hotel offers comfortably equipped bedrooms. Spacious public areas provide a variety of amenities, including several meeting rooms, an attractive bar, and Flickers Brasserie.

Rooms 41 (6 annexe) (3 fmly) (7 GF) **S** £45-£69; **D** £60-£74 (incl. bkfst)* **Facilities** FTV 🎵 Wi-fi **Conf** Class 60 Board 40 Thtr 120 **Parking** 150 **Notes** ⊗ Civ Wed 80

DEWSBURY   **Map 16 SE22**

Healds Hall

THE INDEPENDENTS
HOTEL ASSOCIATION

★★★ 74% ◉ HOTEL

☎ 01924 409112   🖹 01924 401895
Leeds Rd, Liversedge WF15 6JA
e-mail: enquire@healdshall.co.uk
web: www.healdshall.co.uk
dir: On A62 between Leeds & Huddersfield. 50yds on left after lights at Swan Pub

This 18th-century house, in the heart of West Yorkshire, provides comfortable and well-equipped accommodation and excellent hospitality. The hotel has earned a good local reputation for the quality of its food and offers a choice of casual or more formal dining styles, from a wide range of dishes on the various menus.

Rooms 24 (3 fmly) (3 GF) **S** £55-£75; **D** £75-£95 (incl. bkfst)* **Facilities** Wi-fi **Conf** Class 60 Board 80 Thtr 100 Del from £80 to £110* **Parking** 90 **Notes** LB ⊗ Closed 1 Jan & BH Mon Civ Wed 100

Heath Cottage Hotel & Restaurant

★★★ 72% HOTEL

☎ 01924 465399   🖹 01924 459405
Wakefield Rd WF12 8ET
e-mail: info@heathcottage.co.uk
dir: M1 junct 40/A638 for 2.5m towards Dewsbury. Hotel before lights, opposite Earlsheaton Cemetery

Standing in an acre of grounds, Heath Cottage is just two and a half miles from the M1. The service is friendly and professional. All the bedrooms are modern and well appointed, and some are in a converted stable building. The lounge bar and restaurant are air conditioned. Extensive parking is available.

Rooms 28 (6 annexe) (3 fmly) (3 GF) **S** £39-£59; **D** £49.50-£99 (incl. bkfst)* **Facilities** Wi-fi **Conf** Class 56 Board 32 Thtr 100 Del from £79 to £99* **Parking** 60 **Notes** RS 23-27Dec Civ Wed 100

FERRYBRIDGE SERVICE AREA (M62/A1)　Map 16 SE42

Travelodge Pontefract Ferrybridge (M62/A1)

BUDGET HOTEL

☎ 0871 984 6251　📄 01977 622509
WF11 0AF
web: www.travelodge.co.uk
dir: M62 junct 33

Travelodge offers good quality, good value, budget accommodation. All offer family rooms sleeping up to four (two adults, two children) with en suite bathroom/shower-room, remote-control TV, tea- and coffee-making facilities and comfortable beds. Food options vary. Breakfast is at the on-site Bar Café restaurant (if available) or to take away. See also Hotel Groups pages.

Rooms 35 **S** fr £29; **D** fr £29

GARFORTH　Map 16 SE43

Best Western Milford Hotel

★★★ 81% HOTEL

☎ 01977 681800　📄 01977 681245
A1 Great North Rd, Peckfield LS25 5LQ
e-mail: enquiries@mlh.co.uk
web: www.mlh.co.uk
dir: On A63, 1.5m W of A1(M) junct 42 & 4.5m E of M1 junct 46

This friendly, family owned and run hotel is conveniently situated on the A1, and provides very comfortable, modern accommodation. The air-conditioned bedrooms are particularly spacious and well equipped, and ten boutique-style superior rooms are now available. Public areas include a relaxing lounge area and the contemporary Watermill Restaurant and lounge bar which has a working waterwheel.

Rooms 46 (13 GF) (6 smoking) **S** £46.40-£80; **D** £46.40-£80* **Facilities** STV FTV Xmas New Year Wi-fi **Conf** Class 35 Board 30 Thtr 60 Del from £99 to £135* **Services** Air con **Parking** 80 **Notes** LB

Holiday Inn Leeds Garforth

★★★ 81% HOTEL

☎ 0113 286 6556　📄 0113 286 8326
Wakefield Rd LS25 1LH
e-mail: reservations@hileedsgarforth.com
web: www.holidayinn.co.uk
dir: At junct of A63/A642. Hotel opposite rdbt

Located just outside Leeds, this hotel has excellent access to the M1 and M62 making it an ideal base for exploring the area. Well-equipped accommodation includes executive bedrooms. Public areas are attractively designed and include meeting rooms and leisure club. Aioli's Restaurant serves contemporary cuisine.

Rooms 144 (30 fmly) (35 GF) (15 smoking) **Facilities** FTV ⌾ supervised Gym New Year Wi-fi **Conf** Class 120 Board 50 Thtr 350 Del from £99 to £145* **Services** Air con **Parking** 250 **Notes** Civ Wed 140

GOMERSAL　Map 19 SE22

Gomersal Park

★★★ 78% HOTEL

☎ 01274 869386　📄 01274 861042
Moor Ln BD19 4LJ
e-mail: enquiries@gomersalparkhotel.com
web: www.gomersalparkhotel.com
dir: A62 to Huddersfield. At junct with A65, by Greyhound Pub right, after 1m take 1st right after Oakwell Hall

Constructed around a 19th-century house, this stylish, modern hotel enjoys a peaceful location and pleasant grounds. Deep sofas ensure comfort in the open-plan lounge and imaginative meals are served in the popular Brasserie 101. The well-equipped bedrooms provide high quality and comfort. Extensive public areas include a well-equipped leisure complex and pool, and a wide variety of air-conditioned conference rooms.

Rooms 100 (3 fmly) (32 GF) **Facilities** ⌾ supervised Gym Wi-fi **Conf** Class 130 Board 60 Thtr 250 Del from £90 to £140* **Services** Lift **Parking** 150 **Notes** Civ Wed 200

HALIFAX　Map 19 SE02

Holdsworth House

★★★ 85% ⚛⚛ HOTEL

☎ 01422 240024　📄 01422 245174
Holdsworth HX2 9TG
e-mail: info@holdsworthhouse.co.uk
web: www.holdsworthhouse.co.uk
dir: from town centre take A629 (Keighley road). Right at garage up Shay Ln after 1.5m. Hotel on right after 1m

This delightful 17th-century Jacobean manor house, set in well tended gardens, offers individually decorated, thoughtfully equipped bedrooms. Public rooms, adorned with beautiful paintings and antique pieces, include a choice of inviting lounges and superb conference and function facilities. Dinner provides the highlight of any stay and is served in the elegant restaurant by friendly, attentive staff.

Rooms 40 (2 fmly) (15 GF) **Facilities** STV New Year Wi-fi **Conf** Class 75 Board 50 Thtr 150 **Parking** 60 **Notes** LB Civ Wed 120

The White Swan Hotel

★★★ 74% HOTEL

☎ 01422 355541　📄 01422 357311
Princess St HX1 1TS
e-mail: info@whiteswanhalifax.com
dir: Adjacent to Town Hall

A well established hotel noted for its friendly staff. Located in the heart of the town it offers comfortable, well-equipped bedrooms plus conference and function facilities. The lounge area is ideal for relaxing, and for the more energetic guest there is a small fitness room.

Rooms 41 **S** £40; **D** £55-£65 (incl. bkfst)* **Facilities** STV Gym New Year Wi-fi **Conf** Class 35 Board 35 Thtr 80 **Services** Lift **Parking** 9 **Notes** LB

Imperial Crown Hotel

★★★ 63% HOTEL

☎ 0844 736 8608 ⬚ 01422 349866
42/46 Horton St HX1 1QE
e-mail: imperialcrown@corushotels.com
web: www.corushotels.com
dir: opposite railway station & Eureka Children's Museum

This friendly hotel enjoys a central location and, in addition to the main accommodation, there are ten contemporary rooms in a building opposite. The Wallis Simpson Restaurant and Bar feature interesting memorabilia and extensive conference and banqueting facilities are available.

Rooms 56 (15 annexe) (4 fmly) (6 smoking) **S** fr £45; **D** fr £55* **Facilities** Use of nearby leisure club Wi-fi **Conf** Class 120 Board 70 Thtr 150 Del from £99* **Parking** 60 **Notes** LB ✺ RS Xmas Civ Wed 150

Travelodge Halifax

BUDGET HOTEL

☎ 0871 984 6144 ⬚ 01422 362669
Dean Clough Park HX3 5AY
web: www.travelodge.co.uk
dir: M62 junct 24, A629, follow signs for town centre, then brown tourist signs for Dean Clough Mills

Travelodge offers good quality, good value, budget accommodation. All offer family rooms sleeping up to four (two adults, two children) with en suite bathroom/shower-room, remote-control TV, tea- and coffee-making facilities and comfortable beds. Food options vary. Breakfast is at the on-site Bar Café restaurant (if available) or to take away. See also Hotel Groups pages.

Rooms 51 **S** fr £29; **D** fr £29

HARTSHEAD MOOR MOTORWAY SERVICE AREA (M62) Map 19 SE12

Days Inn Bradford

BUDGET HOTEL

☎ 01274 851706 ⬚ 01274 855169
Hartshead Moor Service Area, Clifton HD6 4JX
e-mail: hartshead.hotel@welcomebreak.co.uk
web: www.welcomebreak.co.uk
dir: M62 between junct 25 and 26

This modern building offers accommodation in smart, spacious and well-equipped bedrooms, suitable for families and business travellers, and all with en suite bathrooms. Continental breakfast is available and other refreshments may be taken at the nearby family restaurant. See also the Hotel Groups pages.

Rooms 38 (33 fmly) **S** £39-£59; **D** £39-£69* **Conf** Board 10 Del from £65 to £95*

HAWORTH Map 19 SE03

Old White Lion

★★ 71% HOTEL

☎ 01535 642313 ⬚ 01535 646222
Main St BD22 8DU
e-mail: enquiries@oldwhitelionhotel.com
web: www.oldwhitelionhotel.com
dir: from A629 onto B6142, hotel 0.5m past Haworth Station, at top of cobbled main street adjoining Tourist Information Centre

Prominently situated at the top of an old cobbled street in a very popular village, this hotel is steeped in history. There is a small oak-panelled residents' lounge and a choice of cosy bars, serving a range of meals. More formal dining is available in the popular restaurant. Comfortably furnished bedrooms are well equipped and vary in size and style.

Rooms 15 (3 fmly) **S** £63-£73; **D** £87.50-£97.50 (incl. bkfst) **Facilities** STV Xmas New Year Wi-fi **Conf** Class 20 Board 38 Thtr 90 **Parking** 10 **Notes** LB ✺

Weavers Restaurant with Rooms

◉ RESTAURANT WITH ROOMS

☎ 01535 643822 ⬚ 01535 644832
13/17 West Ln BD22 8DU
e-mail: weaversltd@btconnect.com
dir: In village centre. Pass Brontë Weaving Shed on right, 100yds left to Parsonage car park

Centrally located on the cobbled main street, this family-owned restaurant with rooms provides well-equipped, stylish and comfortable accommodation. Each of the three rooms is en suite and has many thoughtful extras. The kitchen serves both modern and traditional dishes with flair and creativity.

Rooms 3

HEBDEN BRIDGE Map 19 SD92

Moyles

◉ RESTAURANT WITH ROOMS

☎ 01422 845272 ⬚ 01422 847663
6 - 10 New Rd HX7 8AD
e-mail: enquire@moyles.com
dir: A646 to Hebden Bridge, hotel opposite marina

Centrally located in the charming town of Hebden Bridge, this Victorian building as been modernised to offer a high standard of contemporary accommodation. Fresh, local produce features on the imaginative menus served in the bar and in the restaurant. There's a relaxing ambience throughout.

Rooms 12 (6 fmly)

HUDDERSFIELD Map 16 SE11

Cedar Court

★★★★ 71% HOTEL

☎ 01422 375431 ⬚ 01422 314050
Ainley Top HD3 3RH
e-mail: huddersfield@cedarcourthotels.co.uk
web: www.cedarcourthotels.co.uk
dir: 500yds from M62 junct 24

Sitting adjacent to the M62, this hotel is an ideal location for business travellers and for those touring the West Yorkshire area. Bedrooms are comfortably appointed; there is a busy lounge with snacks available all day, as well as a modern restaurant and a fully equipped leisure centre. In addition the hotel has extensive meeting and banqueting facilities.

Rooms 114 (6 fmly) (10 GF) **Facilities** STV FTV ⌲ supervised Gym Steam room Wi-fi **Conf** Class 150 Board 100 Thtr 500 **Services** Lift **Parking** 250 **Notes** Civ Wed 400

Bagden Hall

★★★ 74% HOTEL

☎ 01484 865330 ⬚ 01484 861001
Wakefield Rd, Scissett HD8 9LE
e-mail: info@bagdenhallhotel.co.uk
web: www.bagdenhallhotel.co.uk
dir: on A636, between Scissett & Denby Dale

This elegant mansion house with wonderful views over the valley boasts its own nine-hole golf course. Comfortable bedrooms include classical feature rooms in the main house and contemporary rooms in a separate building. Guests can dine in the all-day Mediterranean bistro or the more formal elegant restaurant. An airy, stylish conference suite and beautiful grounds make this a popular wedding destination.

Rooms 36 (3 fmly) (15 GF) **Facilities** STV ⌗ 9 Putt green Wi-fi **Conf** Class 120 Board 50 Thtr 180 **Parking** 96 **Notes** ✺ RS 25-26 Dec Civ Wed 150

HUDDERSFIELD *continued*

Pennine Manor

★★★ 74% HOTEL

☎ 01484 642368 📄 01484 642866
Nettleton Hill Rd, Scapegoat Hill HD7 4NH
e-mail: penninemanor@thedeckersgroup.com
dir: M62 junct 24, signed Rochdale (A640)/Outlane
Village, left after Commercial pub, hotel signed

Set high in The Pennines, this attractive stone-built hotel
enjoys magnificent panoramic views. Bedrooms are
thoughtfully equipped and have benefited from a stylish
contemporary refurbishment. There is a popular bar with
log burning stove and a cosy atmosphere, offering a good
selection of snacks and meals. The restaurant and
meeting rooms enjoy fine views over the valley. Free Wi-fi
is available.

Rooms 30 (4 fmly) (15 GF) **S** £40-£65; **D** £45-£85 (incl.
bkfst)* **Facilities** STV Wi-fi **Conf** Class 56 Board 40
Thtr 132 **Parking** 115 **Notes** LB ⊗ Civ Wed 100

The Old Golf House Hotel

★★★ 68% HOTEL

☎ 0844 736 8609 & 01422 379311 📄 01422 372694
New Hey Rd, Outlane HD3 3YP
e-mail: oldgolfhouse@corushotels.com
web: www.corushotels.com
dir: M62 junct 23 (eastbound only), or junct 24. Follow
A640 to Rochdale. Hotel on A640

Situated close to the M62, this traditionally styled hotel
offers well-equipped bedrooms. A wide choice of dishes is
offered in the restaurant, and lighter meals are available
in the lounge bar. The hotel, with lovely grounds, is a
popular venue for weddings.

Rooms 52 (4 fmly) (19 GF) (10 smoking) **S** £79-£89;
D £79-£89* **Facilities** STV Putt green Mini golf Xmas New
Year Wi-fi **Conf** Class 35 Board 30 Thtr 70 Del from £90
to £110* **Parking** 100 **Notes** LB RS 25 Dec Civ Wed 100

Travelodge Huddersfield Mirfield

BUDGET HOTEL

☎ 0871 984 6146 📄 01924 489921
Leeds Rd, Mirfield WF14 0BY
web: www.travelodge.co.uk
dir: M62 junct 25, follow A62 across 2 rdbts. Lodge on
right

Travelodge offers good quality, good value, budget
accommodation. All offer family rooms sleeping up to four
(two adults, two children) with en suite bathroom/
shower-room, remote-control TV, tea- and coffee-making
facilities and comfortable beds. Food options vary.
Breakfast is at the on-site Bar Café restaurant (if
available) or to take away. See also Hotel Groups pages.

Rooms 27 **S** fr £29; **D** fr £29

Weavers Shed Restaurant with Rooms

◉◉ RESTAURANT WITH ROOMS

☎ 01484 654284 📄 01484 650980
86-88 Knowl Rd, Golcar HD7 4AN
e-mail: info@weaversshed.co.uk
web: www.weaversshed.co.uk
dir: 3m W of Huddersfield. A62 onto B6111 to Milnsbridge
& Scar Ln to Golcar, right onto Knowl Rd, signed Colne
Valley Museum

This converted house has spacious bedrooms named
after local textile mills; all are extremely well equipped.
An inviting bar-lounge leads into the well known
restaurant where fresh produce, much from the
establishment's own gardens, forms the basis of
excellent meals.

Rooms 5

ILKLEY　　　　　　　　　　　Map 19 SE14

Best Western Rombalds Hotel & Restaurant

★★★ 83% ◉ HOTEL

☎ 01943 603201 📄 01943 816586
11 West View, Wells Rd LS29 9JG
e-mail: reception@rombalds.demon.co.uk
web: www.rombalds.co.uk
dir: A65 from Leeds. Left at 3rd main lights, follow Ilkley
Moor signs. Right at HSBC Bank onto Wells Rd. Hotel
600yds on left

This elegantly furnished Georgian townhouse is located in
a peaceful terrace between the town and the moors.
Delightful day rooms include a choice of comfortable
lounges and an attractive restaurant that provides a
relaxed venue in which to sample the skilfully prepared,
imaginative meals. The bedrooms are tastefully
furnished, well equipped and include several spacious
suites.

Rooms 15 (2 fmly) **Facilities** STV Xmas Wi-fi
Conf Class 40 Board 25 Thtr 70 Del from £115 to £130*
Parking 28 **Notes** Closed 28 Dec-2 Jan Civ Wed 70

The Craiglands

★★★ 68% HOTEL

☎ 01943 430001 & 886450 📄 01943 430002
Cowpasture Rd LS29 8RQ
e-mail: reservations@craiglands.co.uk
web: www.craiglands.co.uk
dir: A65 into Ilkley. Left at T-junct. Past rail station, fork
right into Cowpasture Rd. Hotel opposite school

This grand Victorian hotel is ideally situated close to the
town centre. Spacious public areas and a good range of
services are ideal for business or leisure. Extensive
conference facilities are available along with an elegant
restaurant and traditionally styled bar and lounge.
Bedrooms, varying in size and style, are comfortably
furnished and well equipped.

Rooms 61 (6 fmly) **Facilities** STV Xmas New Year Wi-fi
Conf Class 200 Board 100 Thtr 500 **Services** Lift
Parking 200 **Notes** LB ⊗ Civ Wed 500

Innkeeper's Lodge Ilkley

BUDGET HOTEL

☎ 0845 112 6037 📄 0845 112 6265
Hangingstone Rd LS29 8BT
web: www.innkeeperslodge.com/ilkley
dir: A65 onto B6382 towards Ilkley. Pass Ilkley Station,
right into Cowpasture Rd, leads into Hangingstone Rd.
Lodge 0.5m on left

Innkeeper's Lodge represents an exciting, high value
concept within the budget hotel market. Comfortable
bedrooms provide excellent facilities that include satellite
TV and modem points. This carefully restored lodge is in a
picturesque setting and has its own unique style and
quirky character. Food is served all day, and an extensive,
complimentary continental breakfast is offered. See also
the Hotel Groups pages.

Rooms 14 (2 fmly) **Conf** Thtr 24

KEIGHLEY — Map 19 SE04

Dalesgate
★★ 70% HOTEL

☎ 01535 664930 ⧉ 01535 611253
406 Skipton Rd, Utley BD20 6HP
e-mail: stephen.e.atha@btinternet.com
dir: In town centre follow A629 over rdbt onto B6265.
Right after 0.75m into St. John's Rd. 1st right into hotel
car park

Originally the residence of a local chapel minister, this
modern, well-established hotel provides well-equipped,
comfortable bedrooms. It also boasts a cosy bar and
pleasant restaurant, serving an imaginative range of
dishes. A large car park is provided to the rear.

Rooms 20 (2 fmly) (3 GF) **S** £40-£45; **D** £60-£65 (incl.
bkfst)* **Parking** 25 **Notes** RS 22 Dec-4 Jan

Innkeeper's Lodge Keighley

BUDGET HOTEL

☎ 0845 112 6038 ⧉ 0845 112 6264
Bradford Rd BD21 4BB
web: www.innkeeperslodge.com/keighley
dir: M606 onto A6177, at next rdbt A641(city centre).
Follow A650 towards Bingley & Keighley. Lodge on 2nd
rdbt

Innkeeper's Lodge represents an exciting, high value
concept within the budget hotel market. Comfortable
bedrooms provide excellent facilities that include satellite
TV and modem points. Options include family rooms; and
for the corporate guest, cutting edge IT which includes
Wi-fi access. A popular Carvery provides all-day food,
including an extensive, complimentary continental
breakfast. See also the Hotel Groups pages.

Rooms 43 **Conf** Thtr 24

KIRKBURTON — Map 16 SE11

Innkeeper's Lodge Huddersfield

BUDGET HOTEL

☎ 0845 112 6035 ⧉ 0845 112 6267
36a Penistone Rd HD8 0PQ
web: www.innkeeperslodge.com/huddersfield
dir: M62 junct 24, A629 east towards Huddersfield. Onto
A62 (ring road), left onto A629 towards Wakefield. In
Kirkburton, lodge on right

Innkeeper's Lodge represents an exciting, high value
concept within the budget hotel market. Comfortable
bedrooms provide excellent facilities that include satellite
TV and modem points. Options include family rooms; and
for the corporate guest, cutting edge IT includes Wi-fi
access. Food is served all day in the adjacent Country
Pub. The extensive continental breakfast is
complimentary. See also the Hotel Groups pages.

Rooms 23 (3 fmly) **Conf** Board 20 Thtr 30

LEEDS — Map 19 SE23

See also **Gomersal & Shipley**

Thorpe Park Hotel & Spa

★★★★ 83% ◉ HOTEL

☎ 0113 264 1000 ⧉ 0113 264 1010
Century Way, Thorpe Park LS15 8ZB
e-mail: thorpepark@shirehotels.com
web: www.thorpeparkhotel.com
dir: M1 junct 46, follow signs off rdbt for Thorpe Park

Conveniently close to the M1, this hotel offers bedrooms
that are modern in both style and facilities. The terrace
and courtyard offer all-day casual dining and
refreshments, and the restaurant features a
Mediterranean-themed menu. There is also a state-of-
the-art spa and leisure facility.

Rooms 111 (3 fmly) (25 GF) **S** £100-£160; **D** £150-£180*
Facilities Spa STV ⊙ Gym Activity studio Steam room
Sauna New Year Wi-fi **Conf** Class 100 Board 50 Thtr 200
Del from £155 to £185* **Services** Lift Air con **Parking** 200
Notes LB ⊗ Civ Wed 150

De Vere Oulton Hall

★★★★ 82% ◉◉ HOTEL

☎ 0113 282 1000 ⧉ 0113 282 8066
Rothwell Ln, Oulton LS26 8HN
e-mail: oulton.hall@devere-hotels.com
web: www.devere.co.uk
dir: 2m from M62 junct 30, follow Rothwell signs, then
'Oulton 1m' sign. 1st exit at next 2 rdbts. Hotel on left. Or
1m from M1 junct 44, follow Castleford & Pontefract
signs on A639

Surrounded by the beautiful Yorkshire Dales, yet only 15
minutes from the city centre, this elegant 19th-century
house offers the best of both worlds. Impressive features
include stylish, opulent day rooms and delightful formal
gardens, which have been restored to their original
design. The hotel boasts a choice of dining options,
extensive leisure facilities and golfers can book
preferential tee times at the adjacent golf club.

Rooms 152 **Facilities** ⊙ ↥ 27 ⛳ Gym 9 treatment rooms
Beauty therapy Aerobics Xmas New Year **Conf** Class 150
Board 40 Thtr 350 **Services** Lift Air con **Parking** 260
Notes LB ⊗ Civ Wed 200

The Queens
★★★★ 80% HOTEL

☎ 0113 243 1323 ⧉ 0113 243 5315
City Square LS1 1PJ
e-mail: queensreservations@qhotels.co.uk
web: www.qhotels.co.uk
dir: M621, M1 & M62 follow signs for city centre & train
station, along Neville St towards City Square. Pass under
railway bridge & at lights take left into slip road in front
of hotel

A legacy from the golden age of railways and located in
the heart of the city, overlooking City Square. This grand
Victorian hotel retains much of its original splendour.
Public rooms include the spacious lounge bar, a range of
conference and function rooms along with the grand
Ballroom. Bedrooms vary in size but all are very well
equipped, and there is a choice of suites available.

Rooms 217 (26 fmly) **S** £79-£165; **D** £89-£175
Facilities STV Gym Xmas New Year Wi-fi **Conf** Class 255
Board 80 Thtr 600 Del from £145 to £195 **Services** Lift
Air con **Parking** 80 **Notes** LB Civ Wed 600

LEEDS *continued*

Radisson Blu Leeds

★★★★ 74% HOTEL

☎ 0113 236 6000 🖹 0113 236 6100
No 1 The Light, The Headrow LS1 8TL
e-mail: info.leeds@radissonblu.com
web: www.radissonblu.co.uk
dir: follow city centre 'loop' towards The Headrow/Light
Complex. Hotel on Cockeridge St off The Headrow

Situated in the shopping complex known as 'The Light',
the hotel occupies a converted building that was formerly
the headquarters of the Leeds Permanent Building
Society. Three styles of bedrooms are available but all
have air conditioning and excellent business facilities.
The lobby bar area serves substantial meals and is ideal
for relaxation. Public parking is available, contact the
hotel for details.

Rooms 147 **Facilities** STV Access to Esporta Health Club
♫ Xmas New Year Wi-fi **Conf** Class 28 Board 24 Thtr 60
Services Lift Air con **Notes** LB ⊗ Civ Wed 60

Leeds Marriott Hotel

★★★★ 73% HOTEL

☎ 0113 236 6366 🖹 0113 236 6367
4 Trevelyan Square, Boar Ln LS1 6ET
e-mail: london.regional.reservations@marriott.com
web: www.leedsmarriott.co.uk
dir: M621/M1 junct 3. Follow signs for city centre on
A653. Stay in right lane. Energis building on left, right,
follow signs to hotel

With a charming courtyard setting in the heart of the city,
this modern, elegant hotel provides the perfect base for
shopping and sightseeing. Air-conditioned bedrooms are
tastefully decorated and offer good workspace. Public
areas include a leisure club, an informal bar, lobby
lounge area and a choice of restaurants including
Georgetown which offers Colonial Malaysian cuisine.
Valet parking available.

Rooms 244 (29 fmly) (10 smoking) **S** £159; **D** £169 (incl.
bkfst)* **Facilities** STV ⊗ supervised Gym Sauna Steam
Room Wi-fi **Conf** Class 144 Board 80 Thtr 300
Del from £129 to £169* **Services** Lift Air con **Notes** ⊗
Civ Wed 300

Park Plaza Leeds

Park Plaza
Hotels & Resorts

★★★★ 73% HOTEL

☎ 0113 380 4000 🖹 0113 380 4100
Boar Ln LS1 5NS
e-mail: pplinfo@parkplazahotels.co.uk
web: www.parkplaza.com
dir: Follow signs for city centre

Chic, stylish, ultra modern, city-centre hotel located just
opposite City Square. Chino Latino, located on the first
floor, is a fusion Far East and modern Japanese
restaurant with a Latino bar. Stylish, air-conditioned
bedrooms are spacious and have a range of modern
facilities, including high-speed internet connection.

Rooms 185 **Facilities** STV Gym Wi-fi **Conf** Class 70
Board 40 Thtr 160 **Services** Lift Air con
Notes Civ Wed 120

The Met

★★★★ 72% HOTEL

☎ 0113 245 0841 🖹 0113 242 5156
King St LS1 2HQ
e-mail: metropole.sales@principal-hotels.com
web: www.principal-hotels.com
dir: from M1, M62 & M621 follow city centre signs. A65
into Wellington St. At 1st traffic island right into King St,
hotel on right

Said to be the best example of this type of building in the
city, this splendid terracotta-fronted hotel is centrally
located and convenient for the railway station. All
bedrooms are appointed to suit the business traveller,
with hi-speed internet access and a working area. The
Restaurant and the Tempest Bar make convenient dining
options. There are impressive conference and banqueting
facilities. Some parking space is available.

Rooms 120 **Conf** Class 100 Board 80 Thtr 250
Services Lift **Parking** 40 **Notes** LB ⊗ RS 24 Dec-1 Jan
Civ Wed 200

Crowne Plaza Hotel Leeds

CROWNE PLAZA
HOTELS & RESORTS

★★★★ 71% HOTEL

☎ 0870 400 9170 🖹 0113 244 0460
Wellington St LS1 4DL
e-mail: sales.cpleeds@ihg.com
web: www.crowneplaza.co.uk
dir: from M1 follow signs to city centre. Left at City Sq
into Wellington St

With easy accessibility of the motorway and city centre,
this modern hotel is an ideal choice for the business
traveller. Bedrooms are all of a good size with excellent
facilities including air conditioning. There's a good sized
pool and large gym - both are well worth a visit.

Rooms 135 (38 fmly) **Facilities** Spa STV ⊗ Gym Xmas
New Year Wi-fi **Conf** Class 80 Board 60 Thtr 180
Services Lift Air con **Parking** 120 **Notes** Civ Wed 180

Malmaison Hotel

Malmaison

★★★ 82% ⊛ HOTEL

☎ 0113 398 1000 🖹 0113 398 1002
1 Swinegate LS1 4AG
e-mail: leeds@malmaison.com
web: www.malmaison.com
dir: M621/M1 junct 3, follow city centre signs. At KPMG
building, right into Sovereign Street. Hotel at end on right

Close to the waterfront, this stylish property offers
striking bedrooms with CD players and air conditioning.
The popular bar and brasserie feature vaulted ceilings,
intimate lighting and offer a choice of a full three-course
meal or a substantial snack. Service is both willing and
friendly. A small fitness centre and impressive meeting
rooms complete the package.

Rooms 100 (4 fmly) **S** £79-£135; **D** £79-£170*
Facilities STV Gym Xmas New Year Wi-fi **Conf** Class 20
Board 24 Thtr 45 Del from £145 to £185* **Services** Lift
Air con **Notes** LB

Best Western Milford Hotel

Best
Western

★★★ 81% HOTEL

☎ 01977 681800 🖹 01977 681245
A1 Great North Rd, Peckfield LS25 5LQ
e-mail: enquiries@mlh.co.uk
web: www.mlh.co.uk

(For full entry see Garforth)

Novotel Leeds Centre

NOVOTEL

★★★ 81% HOTEL

☎ 0113 242 6446 🖹 0113 242 6445
4 Whitehall, Whitehall Quay LS1 4HR
e-mail: H3270@accor.com
web: www.novotel.com
dir: M621 junct 3, follow signs to rail station. Into Aire St
& left at lights

With a minimalist style, this contemporary hotel provides a
quality, value-for-money experience close to the city centre.
Spacious, climate-controlled bedrooms are provided, whilst
public areas offer deep leather sofas and an eye-catching
water feature in reception. Light snacks are provided in the
airy bar, and the restaurant doubles as a bistro. Staff are
committed to guest care and nothing is too much trouble.

Rooms 195 (50 fmly) **Facilities** Gym Playstation in rooms
Play area Steam room Xmas **Conf** Class 50 Board 50
Thtr 100 **Services** Lift Air con **Parking** 140
Notes Civ Wed 70

Chevin Country Park Hotel & Spa

★★★ 74% ⊛ HOTEL

☎ 01943 467818 🖹 01943 850335
Yorkgate LS21 3NU
e-mail: chevin@crerarhotels.com

(For full entry see Otley)

Bewleys Hotel Leeds

★★★ 73% HOTEL

☎ 0113 234 2340 📠 0113 234 2349
City Walk, Sweet St LS11 9AT
e-mail: leeds@bewleyshotels.com
web: www.bewleyshotels.com
dir: M621 junct 3, at 2nd lights left into Sweet St then right & right again

Located on the edge of the city centre, this hotel has the added advantage of secure underground parking. Bedrooms are spacious and comfortable with an extensive room service menu. Downstairs, the light and airy bar lounge leads into a brasserie where a wide selection of popular dishes is offered. High quality meeting rooms are also available.

Rooms 334 (99 fmly) **Facilities** Wi-fi **Conf** Class 36 Board 18 **Services** Lift **Parking** 160 **Notes** LB ✪ Closed 24-26 Dec

The Cosmopolitan Hotel

★★★ 72% HOTEL

PEEL HOTELS PLC

☎ 0113 243 6454 📠 0113 243 4241
2 Lower Briggate LS1 4AE
e-mail: info@goldenlion-hotel-leeds.com
web: www.thegoldenlion-leeds.co.uk
dir: M621 junct 3. Keep in right lane. Follow until road splits into 4 lanes. Keep right & right at lights. (ASDA House on left). Left at lights. Over bridge, turn left, hotel opposite. Parking 150mtrs further on

This smartly presented, Victorian building is located on the south side of the city. The well-equipped bedrooms offer a choice of standard or executive grades. Staff are friendly and helpful ensuring a warm and welcoming atmosphere. Free overnight parking is provided in the adjacent 24-hour car park.

Rooms 89 (5 fmly) **S** £59-£110; **D** £69-£135*
Facilities STV FTV Xmas Wi-fi **Conf** Class 45 Board 40 Thtr 120 Del from £110 to £145* **Services** Lift

Ramada Leeds Parkway

★★★ 72% HOTEL

☎ 0844 815 9020 📠 0113 267 4410
Otley Rd LS16 8AG
e-mail: sales.leeds@ramadajarvis.co.uk
web: www.ramadajarvis.co.uk
dir: From A1 take A58 towards Leeds, then right onto A6120. At A660 turn right towards Airport/Skipton. Hotel 2m on right

This large hotel is situated next to Golden Acre Park and Nature Reserve. The interior is a blend of 1930s glamour and modern décor. Bedrooms are comfortably appointed for both business and leisure guests; most rooms have balconies and there are two with four-posters. Contemporary cuisine is available in the Arts Brasserie.

Rooms 118 (2 fmly) (21 GF) **Facilities** STV FTV ⊗ supervised ⌗ Gym Hair & Beauty salon Xmas New Year Wi-fi **Conf** Class 120 Board 40 Thtr 300 **Services** Lift **Parking** 250 **Notes** ✪ Civ Wed 200

Ramada Leeds North

★★★ 66% HOTEL

☎ 0113 273 2323 & 0844 815 9108 📠 0113 232 3222
Mill Green View, Ring Rd, Seacroft LS14 5QF
e-mail: sales.leedsnorth@ramadajarvis.co.uk
web: www.ramadajarvis.co.uk
dir: M1 junct 46 towards Leeds/Airport. Follow A6120 over several rdbts to Crossgates. Hotel 1m on right - double back at next rdbt

Located on the outskirts of the city, this modern hotel is within easy reach of the city centre and major motorway networks. Bedrooms vary in size and style but are all comfortably appointed for both business and leisure guests. Events and meeting facilities are available with ample parking proving a bonus.

Rooms 102 (22 fmly) (21 GF) **S** £30-£145; **D** £30-£145*
Facilities STV FTV Xmas New Year Wi-fi **Conf** Class 200 Board 40 Thtr 340 **Services** Lift **Parking** 150 **Notes** LB Civ Wed 250

Express by Holiday Inn Leeds - Armouries

BUDGET HOTEL

☎ 0870 890 0455 📠 0870 890 0456
Armouries Dr LS10 1LT
e-mail: leeds@expressbyholidayinn.net
web: www.hiexpress.com/leeds

A modern hotel ideal for families and business travellers. Fresh and uncomplicated, the spacious rooms include Sky TV, power shower and tea and coffee-making facilities. Continental buffet breakfast is included in the room rate; other meals may be taken at the nearby family pub or restaurant. See also the Hotel Groups pages.

Rooms 130 (60 fmly) (40 smoking) **S** £49-£79; **D** £49-£79 (incl. bkfst) **Conf** Class 18 Board 20 Thtr 30 Del from £99 to £110*

Express by Holiday Inn Leeds City Centre

BUDGET HOTEL

☎ 0113 242 6200 📠 0113 242 6300
Cavendish St LS3 1LY
e-mail: res.leeds@expressholidayinn.co.uk
web: www.hiexpress.com/leedscityctr
dir: M621 junct 2, A643 to city centre. At large rdbt 3rd exit signed A58(M). 1st left onto A65. Right after pedestrian crossing & right again

Rooms 112 (28 fmly) **Conf** Class 15 Board 20 Thtr 35 Del from £115*

Ibis Leeds Centre

BUDGET HOTEL

☎ 0113 220 4100 📠 0113 220 4110
Marlborough St LS1 4PB
e-mail: H3652@accor.com
web: www.ibishotel.com
dir: From M1 junct 43 or M62 junct 2 take A643 & follow city centre signs. Left on slip road opposite Yorkshire Post. Hotel opposite

Modern, budget hotel offering comfortable accommodation in bright and practical bedrooms. Breakfast is self-service and dinner is available in the restaurant See also the Hotel Groups pages.

Rooms 168 (14 fmly)

Innkeeper's Lodge Leeds East

BUDGET HOTEL

☎ 0845 112 6039 📠 0845 112 6263
Aberford Rd, Oulton LS26 8EJ
web: www.innkeeperslodge.com/leedseast
dir: M62 junct 29, E towards Pontefract. Exit at junct 30, A642 signed Rothwell. Lodge opposite at 1st rdbt

Innkeeper's Lodge represents an exciting, high value concept within the budget hotel market. Comfortable bedrooms provide excellent facilities that include satellite TV and modem points. Options include family rooms; and for the corporate guest, cutting edge IT which includes Wi-fi access. A popular Carvery provides all-day food, including an extensive, complimentary continental breakfast. See also the Hotel Groups pages.

Rooms 77 **Conf** Thtr 40

LEEDS *continued*

Innkeeper's Lodge Leeds South

BUDGET HOTEL

☎ 0845 112 6040 📠 0845 112 6262
Bruntcliffe Rd, Morley LS27 0LY
web: www.innkeeperslodge.com/leedssouth
dir: M62/M621 junct 27 take A650 towards Morley. Lodge on junct of A650 & A643

Rooms 32 (5 fmly)

Travelodge Leeds Central

BUDGET HOTEL

☎ 0871 984 6275 📠 0113 246 0076
Blaydes Court, Blaydes Yard, off Swinegate LS1 4AD
web: www.travelodge.co.uk
dir: M62 at M621 to city centre, right before Hilton Hotel into Sovereign St

Travelodge offers good quality, good value, budget accommodation. All offer family rooms sleeping up to four (two adults, two children) with en suite bathroom/shower-room, remote-control TV, tea- and coffee-making facilities and comfortable beds. Food options vary. Breakfast is at the on-site Bar Café restaurant (if available) or to take away. See also Hotel Groups pages.

Rooms 100 **S** fr £29; **D** fr £29

Travelodge Leeds Central Vicar Lane

BUDGET HOTEL

☎ 0871 984 6337 📠 0113 244 5040
97-107 Vicar Ln LS1 6PJ
e-mail: leedsvicarlane@travelodge.co.uk
dir: In city centre follow loop road. Exit at junct 8, right onto Merrion St, right at bottom Lodge 100mtrs on right

Rooms 127 **S** fr £29; **D** fr £29

Travelodge Leeds Colton

BUDGET HOTEL

☎ 0871 984 6155 📠 0113 264 8839
Stile Hill Way, Colton LS15 9JA
web: www.travelodge.co.uk
dir: M1 junct 46

Rooms 61 **S** fr £29; **D** fr £29

Holiday Inn Leeds - Bradford

★★★★ 71% HOTEL

☎ 0113 285 4646 & 0870 400 7218 📠 0113 285 9329
The Pastures, Tong Ln BD4 0RP
e-mail: reception@leeds.kewgreen.co.uk
web: www.holidayinn.co.uk
dir: A650 towards Bradford. 3rd exit at rdbt towards Gildersome, 1st left into Tong Lane, hotel 0.5m on right

Situated on the outskirts of Leeds and Bradford in the ancient village of Tong, surrounded by beautifully countryside, and with the convenience of being just minutes from the M62. The Courtyard Restaurant offers a range of international cuisine. A fitness suite with cardiovascular equipment is available.

Rooms 53 (29 fmly) (11 GF) (12 smoking) **S** £39-£120; **D** £39-£120 **Facilities** Gym Xmas New Year Wi-fi **Conf** Class 150 Board 50 Thtr 220 Del from £70 to £150 **Services** Lift **Parking** 220 **Notes** LB ✿ Civ Wed 220

Travelodge Leeds Bradford Airport

BUDGET HOTEL

☎ 0871 984 6248 📠 0113 250 6842
White House Ln LS19 7TZ
web: www.travelodge.co.uk
dir: On A658

Travelodge offers good quality, good value, budget accommodation. All offer family rooms sleeping up to four (two adults, two children) with en suite bathroom/shower-room, remote-control TV, tea- and coffee-making facilities and comfortable beds. Food options vary. Breakfast is at the on-site Bar Café restaurant (if available) or to take away. See also Hotel Groups pages.

Rooms 48 (45 fmly) (23 GF) **S** fr £29; **D** fr £29

The Olive Branch Restaurant with Rooms

RESTAURANT WITH ROOMS

☎ 01484 844487
Manchester Rd HD7 6LU
e-mail: mail@olivebranch.uk.com
web: www.olivebranch.uk.com
dir: 1m NE of Marsden on A62

The Olive Branch, once a roadside inn, was developed into a popular restaurant with three comfortable bedrooms. The menu features the best of seasonal produce cooked with flair and enthusiasm. The surrounding countryside has many historic attractions and pleasant walking.

Rooms 3

Chevin Country Park Hotel & Spa

★★★ 74% ◉ HOTEL

☎ 01943 467818 📠 01943 850335
Yorkgate LS21 3NU
e-mail: chevin@crerarhotels.com
dir: From Leeds/Bradford Airport rdbt take A658 N, towards Harrogate, for 0.75m to 1st lights. Turn left, then 2nd left onto 'Yorkgate'. Hotel 0.5m on left

This hotel, peacefully situated in its own woodland yet conveniently located for major road links and the airport, offers comfortable accommodation. Rooms are split between the original main log building and chalet-style accommodation, situated in the extensive grounds. Public areas are spacious and well equipped. The Lakeside Restaurant provides views over the small lake and good leisure facilities are also available.

Rooms 49 (30 annexe) (7 fmly) (45 GF) **S** £70-£120; **D** £90-£140 (incl. bkfst) **Facilities** FTV ◉ ♨ Fishing Gym Xmas New Year Wi-fi **Conf** Class 90 Board 50 Thtr 120 Del from £135 to £155* **Parking** 100 **Notes** LB Civ Wed 100

Wentbridge House

★★★★ 75% ◉◉ HOTEL

☎ 01977 620444 📠 01977 620148
Wentbridge WF8 3JJ
e-mail: info@wentbridgehouse.co.uk
web: www.wentbridgehouse.co.uk
dir: 0.5m off A1 & 4m S of M62 junct 33 onto A1 south

This well-established hotel sits in 20 acres of landscaped gardens, offering spacious, well-equipped bedrooms and a choice of dining styles. Service in the Fleur de Lys restaurant is polished and friendly, and a varied menu offers a good choice of interesting dishes. The Brasserie has a more relaxed style of modern dining.

Rooms 41 (4 annexe) (4 GF) **S** £100–£180; **D** £130–£210 (incl. bkfst)* **Facilities** FTV Xmas New Year Wi-fi **Conf** Class 100 Board 60 Thtr 130 Del from £110 to £150* **Services** Lift **Parking** 100 **Notes** LB ⊗ Closed 25 Dec–evening only Civ Wed 130

Best Western Rogerthorpe Manor

★★★ 76% HOTEL

☎ 01977 643839 ⁂ 01977 641571
Thorpe Ln, Badsworth WF9 1AB
e-mail: ops@rogerthorpemanor.co.uk
dir: A639 from Pontefract to Badsworth. Follow B6474 through Thorpe Audlin, hotel on left at end of village

This Jacobean manor house is situated in extensive grounds and lovely gardens, within easy access of road networks. Bedrooms vary between the old house with their inherent charm, and the more modern rooms in the extensions. A choice of dining styles, real ales, civil weddings, modern conference facilities and ample parking are all offered.

Rooms 22 (4 fmly) (4 smoking) **S** £90; **D** £110–£130 (incl. bkfst)* **Facilities** STV Wi-fi **Conf** Class 80 Board 50 Thtr 250 Del from £129.95 to £149.95* **Services** Air con **Parking** 150 **Notes** LB ⊗ Civ Wed 200

PUDSEY   Map 19 SE23

Innkeeper's Lodge Leeds Calverley

BUDGET HOTEL

☎ 0845 1126 043
Calverley Ln, Calverley LS28 5QQ
dir: M621 junct, A6110 signed Ring Road. 3m, through 5 rdbts & onto A647. At next rdbt onto A6120 signed Ring Road. 1.1m left onto Calverley Lne (B6156). Lodge on right at Calverley Arms Vintage Inn

Innkeeper's Lodge represents an exciting, high value concept within the budget hotel market. Comfortable bedrooms provide excellent facilities that include satellite TV and modem points. This carefully restored lodge is in a picturesque setting and has its own unique style and quirky character. Food is served all day, and an extensive, complimentary continental breakfast is offered. See also the Hotel Groups pages.

Rooms 14

SHIPLEY   Map 19 SE13

Marriott Hollins Hall Hotel & Country Club

Marriott HOTELS & RESORTS

★★★★ 78% ⊛ HOTEL

☎ 01274 530053 ⁂ 01274 534251
Hollins Hill, Baildon BD17 7QW
e-mail: mhrs.lbags.eventorganiser@marriotthotels.com
web: www.marriotthollinshall.co.uk
dir: from A650 follow signs to Salt Mill. At lights in Shipley take A6038. Hotel 3m on left

The hotel is located close to Leeds and Bradford and is easily accessible from motorway networks. Built in the 19th-century, this Elizabethan-style building is set within 200 acres of grounds and offers extensive leisure facilities, including a golf course and gym. Bedrooms are attractively decorated and have a range of additional facilities.

Rooms 122 (50 fmly) (25 GF) **Facilities** ⊙ supervised ↕ 18 Putt green ⚓ Gym Crèche Dance studio Swimming lessons Xmas **Conf** Class 90 Board 80 Thtr 200 **Services** Lift **Parking** 260 **Notes** ⊗ Civ Wed 70

Ibis Bradford Shipley

BUDGET HOTEL

☎ 01274 589333 ⁂ 01274 589444
Quayside, Salts Mill Rd BD18 3ST
e-mail: H3158@accor.com
web: www.ibishotel.com
dir: Follow tourist signs for Salts Mill. Follow A650 signs through & out of Bradford for approx 5m to Shipley

Modern, budget hotel offering comfortable accommodation in bright and practical bedrooms. Breakfast is self-service, food is available all day and a full dinner menu is available in the restaurant. See also the Hotel Groups pages.

Rooms 78 (20 fmly) (22 GF) **S** £47–£55; **D** £47–£55* **Conf** Class 16 Board 18 Thtr 20 Del from £70 to £120*

THORNBURY

Travelodge Bradford

BUDGET HOTEL

☎ 0871 984 6124 ⁂ 01274 665436
1 Mid Point, Dick Ln BD3 7AY
web: www.travelodge.co.uk
dir: M62 junct 26 (M606), take A6177 towards Leeds, A647. Lodge 2m on left

Travelodge offers good quality, good value, budget accommodation. All offer family rooms sleeping up to four (two adults, two children) with en suite bathroom/shower-room, remote-control TV, tea- and coffee-making facilities and comfortable beds. Food options vary. Breakfast is at the on-site Bar Café restaurant (if available) or to take away. See also Hotel Groups pages.

Rooms 48 **S** fr £29; **D** fr £29

WAKEFIELD   Map 16 SE32

Cedar Court

★★★★ 72% HOTEL

☎ 01924 276310 ⁂ 01924 280221
Denby Dale Rd WF4 3QZ
e-mail: sales@cedarcourthotels.co.uk
web: www.cedarcourthotels.co.uk
dir: Adjacent to M1 junct 39

This hotel enjoys a convenient location just off the M1. Traditionally styled bedrooms offer a good range of facilities while open-plan public areas include a busy bar and restaurant operation. Conferences and functions are extremely well catered for.

Rooms 149 (2 fmly) (74 GF) **Facilities** ⊙ supervised Gym Xmas New Year Wi-fi **Conf** Class 140 Board 80 Thtr 400 **Services** Lift Air con **Parking** 350 **Notes** Civ Wed 250

Waterton Park

CLASSIC BRITISH HOTELS

★★★★ 72% HOTEL

☎ 01924 257911 & 249800 ⁂ 01924 259686
Walton Hall, The Balk, Walton WF2 6PW
e-mail: info@watertonparkhotel.co.uk
web: www.watertonparkhotel.co.uk
dir: 3m SE off B6378. Exit M1 junct 39 towards Wakefield. At 3rd rdbt right for Crofton. At 2nd lights right

This Georgian mansion, built on an island in the centre of a 26-acre lake is in an idyllic setting. The main house contains many feature bedrooms, and the annexe houses more spacious rooms, all equally well equipped with modern facilities; most of the rooms have views over the lake or the 18-hole golf course. The delightful beamed restaurant, two bars and leisure club are located in the old hall, and there is a licence for civil weddings.

Rooms 65 (43 annexe) (5 fmly) (23 GF) **S** fr £80; **D** fr £110 (incl. bkfst)* **Facilities** STV ⊙ supervised Fishing Gym Steam room Sauna Xmas New Year Wi-fi **Conf** Class 80 Board 80 Thtr 150 Del from £145* **Services** Lift **Parking** 200 **Notes** LB ⊗ Civ Wed 130

WAKEFIELD *continued*

Best Western Hotel St Pierre

★★★ 75% HOTEL

☎ 01924 255596 📠 01924 252746
Barnsley Rd, Newmillerdam WF2 6QG
e-mail: enq@hotelstpierre.co.uk
dir: M1 junct 39, A636 to Wakefield, right at 2nd rdbt into
Asdale Rd to lights. Right onto A61 towards Barnsley.
Hotel just after lake on left

This well-furnished hotel lies south of Wakefield, close to
Newmillerdam. The interior of the modern building has
comfortable and thoughtfully equipped bedrooms and
smart public rooms. Meals are served in the Pierre's
Restaurant, and there is a good selection of conference
rooms.

Rooms 54 (3 fmly) (4 GF) **S** £59-£89; **D** £64-£94 (incl.
bkfst)* **Facilities** STV Xmas New Year Wi-fi **Conf** Class 60
Board 60 Thtr 120 Del from £95 to £110* **Services** Lift
Parking 70 **Notes** LB ⊗ Civ Wed 120

Holiday Inn Leeds - Wakefield

★★★ 73% HOTEL

☎ 0870 400 9082 📠 01924 230684
Queen's Dr, Ossett WF5 9BE
e-mail: wakefield@ichotelsgroup.com
web: www.holidayinn.co.uk
dir: M1 junct 40 follow signs for Wakefield. Hotel on right
in 200yds

Situated close to major motorway networks, this modern
hotel offers well-equipped and comfortable bedrooms.
Public areas include the popular Traders restaurant and
a comfortable lounge where a menu is available
throughout the day. Conference facilities are also
available.

Rooms 104 (32 fmly) (35 GF) (9 smoking) **Facilities** STV
Xmas New Year Wi-fi **Conf** Class 80 Board 80 Thtr 160
Services Lift Air con **Parking** 105 **Notes** Civ Wed 160

Campanile Wakefield

Campanile

BUDGET HOTEL

☎ 01924 201054 📠 01924 290976
Monckton Rd WF2 7AL
e-mail: wakefield@campanile.com
dir: M1 junct 39, A636, 1m towards Wakefield, left into
Monckton Rd, hotel on left

This modern building offers accommodation in smart,
well-equipped bedrooms, all with en suite bathrooms.
Refreshments may be taken at the informal bistro. See
also the Hotel Groups pages.

Rooms 76 (76 annexe) (4 fmly) (25 GF) **S** £42-£46;
D £42-£46* **Conf** Class 15 Board 15 Thtr 25 Del from £59
to £99*

Days Hotel Leeds / Wakefield

BUDGET HOTEL

☎ 01924 274200 & 0800 0280 400 📠 01924 274246
Fryers Way, Silkwood Park, Ossett WF5 9TJ
e-mail: wakefield@kewgreen.co.uk
web: www.daysinn.com
dir: M1 junct 40, follow signs to Wakefield, hotel 400yds
on left

This modern building offers accommodation in smart,
spacious and well-equipped bedrooms, suitable for
families and business travellers, and all with en suite
bathrooms. Continental breakfast is available and other
refreshments may be taken at the nearby family
restaurant. See also the Hotel Groups pages.

Rooms 100 (27 fmly) (20 GF) **Conf** Class 18 Board 22
Thtr 40

Travelodge Wakefield

BUDGET HOTEL

☎ 0871 984 6368 📠 01924 200833
Lower Warrengate WF1 1SA
dir: M1 junct 39, A636 signed Wakefield. Approx 2.5m,
follow City Centre signs. Straight on at 4 rdbts, at 5th
rdbt 2nd exit signed City Centre/B6444. At 2nd lights turn
left. Next right into Sun Ln. Lodge at end

Travelodge offers good quality, good value, budget
accommodation. All offer family rooms sleeping up to
four (two adults, two children) with en suite bathroom/
shower-room, remote-control TV, tea- and coffee-making

facilities and comfortable beds. Food options vary.
Breakfast is at the on-site Bar Café restaurant (if
available) or to take away. See also the Hotel Groups
pages.

Rooms 56 **S** fr £29; **D** fr £29

WETHERBY	**Map 16 SE44**

INSPECTORS' CHOICE

Wood Hall

*Hand*PICKED

★★★★ ◉◉ COUNTRY HOUSE HOTEL

☎ 01937 587271 📠 01937 584353
Trip Ln, Linton LS22 4JA
e-mail: woodhall@handpicked.co.uk
web: www.handpicked.co.uk
dir: from Wetherby take Harrogate road N (A661) for
0.5m, left to Sicklinghall & Linton. Cross bridge, left to
Linton & Wood Hall. Turn right opposite Windmill Inn,
1.25m to hotel

A long sweeping drive leads to this delightful Georgian
house situated in 100 acres of parkland. Spacious
bedrooms are appointed to an impressive standard and
feature comprehensive facilities, including large
plasma screen TVs. Public rooms reflect the same
elegance and include a smart drawing room and dining
room, both with fantastic views. A state-of-the-art
Technogym is available.

Rooms 44 (30 annexe) (5 fmly) **S** £115-£195;
D £125-£205 (incl. bkfst)* **Facilities** Spa ◉
supervised Fishing Gym Beauty spa 2 treatment rooms
Xmas New Year Wi-fi **Conf** Class 70 Board 40 Thtr 100
Del from £140 to £185* **Services** Lift **Parking** 200
Notes LB ⊗ Civ Wed 100

The Bridge Hotel

★★★★ 75% HOTEL

☎ 01937 580115 📠 01937 580556
Walshford LS22 5HS
e-mail: info@bridgewetherby.co.uk
web: www.bridgewetherby.co.uk
dir: From N exit A1(M) at junct 47 (York) or S junct 46
(Wetherby Race Centre), 1st left Walshford, follow brown
tourist signs

A very conveniently located hotel close to the A1 with
spacious public areas and a good range of services make
this an ideal venue for business or leisure. The stylish
bedrooms are comfortable and well equipped. The Bridge

offers a choice of bars and a large open-plan restaurant. Conference and banqueting suites are also available.

Rooms 30 (2 fmly) (10 GF) **S** £65-£85; **D** £85-£130 (incl. bkfst) **Facilities** FTV Gym Xmas New Year Wi-fi **Conf** Class 50 Board 50 Thtr 150 Del from £110 to £135* **Parking** 150 **Notes** LB Civ Wed

---

Ramada Wetherby

★★★ 72% HOTEL

☎ 0844 815 9067 📠 01937 580062
Leeds Rd LS22 5HE
e-mail: sales.wetherby@ramadajarvis.o.uk
web: www.ramadajarvis.co.uk
dir: A1/A659, then follow A168. Hotel on rdbt

Set in the countryside, just a few minutes from the town centre and conveniently located for the A58 and A1, this large hotel is particularly popular with business guests and features extensive conference facilities. Bedrooms are modern, well equipped and comfortable. Public areas include a spacious bar area/coffee lounge and large restaurant.

Rooms 103 (2 fmly) (51 GF) (11 smoking) **S** £80-£161; **D** £80-£161 (incl. bkfst)* **Facilities** Xmas New Year Wi-fi **Conf** Class 50 Board 50 Thtr 150 Del from £110 to £160* **Services** Lift **Parking** 170 **Notes** LB ⊗ Civ Wed 150

WOOLLEY EDGE MOTORWAY SERVICE AREA (M1)	Map 16 SE31

Travelodge Wakefield Woolley Edge (M1 North)

BUDGET HOTEL

☎ 0871 984 6263 📠 01924 830609
M1 Service Area, West Bretton WF4 4LQ
web: www.travelodge.co.uk
dir: M1 between juncts 38 & 39, adjacent to service area

Travelodge offers good quality, good value, budget accommodation. All offer family rooms sleeping up to four (two adults, two children) with en suite bathroom/shower-room, remote-control TV, tea- and coffee-making facilities and comfortable beds. Food options vary. Breakfast is at the on-site Bar Café restaurant (if available) or to take away. See also Hotel Groups pages.

Rooms 32 **S** fr £29; **D** fr £29

Travelodge Wakefield Woolley Edge (M1 South)

BUDGET HOTEL

☎ 0871 984 6179 📠 01924 830174
Moto Service Area, J39-38 M1 Southbound, West Bretton WF4 4LQ
web: www.travelodge.co.uk
dir: M1 junct 38/39. Lodge accessed from both N'bound & S'bound carriageways

Rooms 41 **S** fr £29; **D** fr £29

CHANNEL ISLANDS
ALDERNEY

ALDERNEY

Braye Beach

★★★★ 71% HOTEL

☎ 01481 824300 📠 01481 824301
Braye St GY9 3XT
e-mail: reception@brayebeach.com
web: www.brayebeach.com
dir: Follow coast road from airport

Situated just a stone's throw from Braye's harbour and beach, this hotel provides comfortable yet stylish accommodation where many guest rooms have sea views; all bedrooms are well appointed and generously equipped. Public rooms include the popular bar and lounge, spacious terrace for the summer months and even a cinema. The well-appointed restaurant offers a varied seasonal menu often showcasing locally caught fish. Private dining can be catered for in the vaulted wine cellar.

Rooms 27 (2 fmly) **S** £70-£120; **D** £120-£160 (incl. bkfst)* **Facilities** FTV Cinema Xmas New Year Wi-fi **Conf** Class 12 Board 16 Thtr 19 Del from £115 to £165* **Services** Lift **Notes** LB ⊗ Civ Wed 80

GUERNSEY
CASTEL Map 24

La Grande Mare Hotel Golf & Country Club

★★★★ 71% ⓢ HOTEL

☎ 01481 256576 📠 01481 256532
The Coast Rd, Vazon Bay GY5 7LL
e-mail: reservations@lagrandemare.com
web: www.lgm.guernsey.net
dir: From airport turn right. At Coast Rd turn right again

Set in 110 acres of private grounds, this hotel is located next to a sandy bay, incorporates an 18-hole golf course and has a health suite. Bedrooms range from spacious studios to deluxe suites, and feature handcrafted furniture and impressive decor. The health suite features a 40ft swimming pool that has dedicated children's swimming times.

Rooms 24 (13 fmly) (5 GF) **Facilities** ⓢ supervised ⊸ ♨ 18 ⚐ Putt green Fishing Gym ♫ Xmas New Year Wi-fi Child facilities **Conf** Class 21 Board 22 Thtr 48 **Services** Lift **Parking** 200 **Notes** LB ⊗

Cobo Bay

★★★ 82% ⓢⓢ HOTEL

☎ 01481 257102 📠 01481 254542
Coast Rd, Cobo GY5 7HB
e-mail: reservations@cobobayhotel.com
web: www.cobobayhotel.com
dir: From airport turn right, follow road to W coast at L'Eree. Turn right onto coast road for 3m to Cobo Bay. Hotel on right

A popular hotel situated on the seafront overlooking Cobo Bay. The well-equipped bedrooms are pleasantly decorated; many of the front rooms have balconies and there is a secluded sun terrace to the rear. Public rooms include the Chesterfield Bar with its leather sofas and armchairs and a welcoming restaurant with stunning views of the bay.

Rooms 34 (4 fmly) **S** £49-£89; **D** £59-£140 (incl. bkfst)* **Facilities** Spa STV Gym Exercise machines Sauna Wi-fi **Conf** Class 30 Board 20 Thtr 50 Del from £75 to £99* **Services** Lift **Parking** 60 **Notes** LB ⊗ Closed Jan-Feb

See advert on page 546

CASTEL *continued*

Hotel Hougue du Pommier

★★★ 70% HOTEL

☎ 01481 256531 📄 01481 256260
Hougue du Pommier Rd GY5 7FQ
e-mail: hotel@houguedupommier.guernsey.net
dir: Turn inland from Cobo (coast road). Left at 1st junct.
Hotel 50yds on right

Retaining much of its 18th-century character and charm,
the hotel combines modern comforts with friendly yet
efficient service. Bedrooms vary in size and standard, and
include exceptionally well-appointed and spacious deluxe
rooms. In addition to the restaurant an informal eating
option is available in the beamed bar that features an
open fire, and offers a spit-roast menu.

Rooms 40 (5 annexe) (5 fmly) (13 GF) **S** £52.50-£83;
D £90-£130 (incl. bkfst)* **Facilities** ᚖ ᚖ Beauty salon
Xmas New Year Wi-fi **Parking** 60 **Notes** LB

See advert on this page

FERMAIN BAY — Map 24

Le Chalet

★★★ 74% HOTEL

☎ 01481 235716 📄 01481 235718
GY4 6SD
e-mail: stay@lechaletguernsey.com
web: www.lechaletguernsey.com

A popular hotel that sits in a wooded valley within
walking distance of Fermain Bay, ideal for those seeking
a peaceful and quiet stay. Bedrooms vary in size and
style; each one is pleasantly decorated and equipped with
many thoughtful touches. Public areas include a panelled
lounge, a bar area, a spacious restaurant and a stunning
sun terrace adjoining the small indoor leisure facility.

Rooms 38 (4 fmly) **S** £44-£60; **D** £80-£120 (incl. bkfst)*
Facilities ᚖ Xmas New Year Wi-fi **Parking** 30 **Notes** LB ⊗

FOREST — Map 24

Le Chene

★★ 72% HOTEL

☎ 01481 235566 📄 01481 239456
Forest Rd GY8 0AH
e-mail: info@lechene.co.uk
web: www.lechene.co.uk
dir: Between airport & St Peter Port. From airport left to St
Peter Port. Hotel on right after 1st lights

This Victorian manor house is well located for guests
wishing to explore Guernsey's spectacular south coast.
The building has been skilfully extended to house a range
of well-equipped, modern bedrooms. There is a swimming
pool, a cosy cellar bar and a varied range of enjoyable
freshly cooked dishes at dinner.

Rooms 26 (2 fmly) (1 GF) (1 smoking) **S** £30-£48;
D £50-£106 (incl. bkfst)* **Facilities** ᚖ Library Xmas New
Year Wi-fi **Parking** 20 **Notes** LB ⊗

ST MARTIN — Map 24

La Barbarie

★★★ 80% ◉ HOTEL

☎ 01481 235217 📄 01481 235208
Saints Rd, Saints Bay GY4 6ES
e-mail: reservations@labarbariehotel.com
web: www.labarbariehotel.com

This former priory dates back to the 17th century and
retains much charm and style. Staff provide a very
friendly and attentive environment, and the modern
facilities offer guests a relaxing stay. Excellent choices
and fresh local ingredients form the basis of the
interesting menus in the attractive restaurant and bar.

Rooms 22 (3 fmly) (8 GF) **S** £57-£74; **D** £74-£108 (incl.
bkfst)* **Facilities** ᚖ Wi-fi **Parking** 50 **Notes** LB ⊗
Closed 2 Nov-13 Mar

ST MARTIN *continued*

Hotel Jerbourg

★★★ 78% HOTEL

☎ 01481 238826 🖥 01481 238238
Jerbourg Point GY4 6BJ
e-mail: stay@hoteljerbourg.com
dir: from airport turn left to St Martin village, right onto
filter road, straight on at lights, hotel at end of road on
right

This hotel boasts excellent sea views from its cliff-top
location. Public areas are smartly appointed and include
an extensive bar/lounge and bright conservatory-style
restaurant. In addition to the fairly extensive carte, a
daily-changing menu is available. Bedrooms are well
presented and comfortable, and the luxury bay rooms are
generally more spacious.

Rooms 32 (4 fmly) (5 GF) **S** £42-£62; **D** £82-£117 (incl.
bkfst)* **Facilities** STV ⚘ Xmas New Year Wi-fi
Parking 50 **Notes** LB ⊗ Closed 5 Jan-3 Mar

La Trelade

★★★ 78% HOTEL

☎ 01481 235454 🖥 01481 237855
Forest Rd GY4 6UB
e-mail: reservations@latreladehotel.co.uk
web: www.latreladehotel.co.uk
dir: 3m from St Peter Port, 1m from airport

This hotel offers a stylish and versatile range of public
areas and an impressive leisure suite. Located close to
the airport, La Trelade is an ideal base from which to
explore the island, and is equally suitable for business
guests. Bedrooms and bathrooms are tastefully decorated
and equipped to high standards with modern comforts.

Rooms 45 (3 fmly) **S** £66-£80; **D** £92-£120 (incl. bkfst)*
Facilities STV FTV ⌗ Gym Xmas New Year Wi-fi
Conf Class 48 Board 40 Thtr 120 Del from £80*
Services Lift **Parking** 80 **Notes** LB ⊗

Saints Bay Hotel

★★★ 77% HOTEL

☎ 01481 238888 🖥 01481 235558
Icart Rd GY4 6JG
e-mail: info@saintsbayhotel.com
dir: From St Martin village take Saints Rd onto Icart Rd

Ideally situated in an elevated position near Icart Point
headland and above the fishing harbour at Saints Bay,
this hotel has superb views. The spacious public rooms
include a smart lounge bar, a first-floor lounge and a
smart conservatory restaurant that overlooks the
swimming pool. Bedrooms are pleasantly decorated and
thoughtfully equipped.

Rooms 35 (2 fmly) (13 GF) **S** £39-£63.80; **D** £58-£107.60
(incl. bkfst)* **Facilities** ⚘ Wi-fi **Parking** 15 **Notes** LB ⊗

La Villette Hotel & Leisure Suite

★★★ 75% HOTEL

☎ 01481 235292 🖥 01481 237699
GY4 6QG
e-mail: reservations@lavillettehotel.co.uk
dir: Turn left from airport. Follow road past La Trelade
Hotel. Take next right, hotel on left

Set in spacious grounds, this peacefully located, family-
run hotel has a friendly atmosphere. The well-equipped
bedrooms are spacious and comfortable. Live music is a
regular feature in the large bar, while in the separate
restaurant a fixed-price menu is provided. Residents have
use of the excellent indoor leisure facilities.

Rooms 35 (3 fmly) (14 GF) **S** £44-£50.50; **D** £76-£89
(incl. bkfst)* **Facilities** STV ⌔ supervised ⚘ Gym Steam
room Leisure suite Beauty salon Hairdresser Petanque
Xmas New Year Wi-fi **Conf** Board 40 Thtr 80 **Services** Lift
Parking 50 **Notes** ⊗

Hotel La Michele

80% HOTEL

☎ 01481 238065 🖥 01481 239492
Les Hubits GY4 6NB
e-mail: info@lamichelehotel.com
dir: Approx 1.5m from St Peter Port

Expect a warm welcome from the caring hosts at this
friendly family-run hotel, which is situated in a peaceful

location. Bedrooms are particularly well equipped; each
one is pleasantly decorated and has co-ordinated fabrics.
Public areas include a conservatory and a cosy bar, and
guests can relax in the well-tended gardens or around the
pool.

Rooms 16 (3 fmly) (6 GF) **S** £44-£65; **D** £88-£130 (incl.
bkfst & dinner)* **Facilities** ⚘ **Parking** 16 **Notes** ⊗ No
children 10yrs Closed Nov-Mar

| ST PETER PORT | Map 24 |

Old Government House Hotel & Spa

Red Carnation HOTELS

★★★★ 80% ◉◉ HOTEL

☎ 01481 724921 🖥 01481 724429
St Ann's Place GY1 2NU
e-mail: ogh@theoghhotel.com
web: www.theoghhotel.com
dir: At junct of St Julian's Ave & College St

The affectionately known OGH is one of the island's
leading hotels. Located in the heart of St Peter Port, it is
the perfect base to explore Guernsey and the other islands
of the Bailiwick. Bedrooms vary in size but are
comfortable and offer high quality accommodation. There
is an indulgent health club and spa, and the eating
options are the OGH Brasserie, and award-winning
Governor's that offer local produce with a French twist.

Rooms 59 (6 fmly) **S** £135; **D** £150 (incl. bkfst)*
Facilities Spa STV ⚘ Gym Steam room Sauna Spa baths
Aerobics studio Xmas New Year Wi-fi **Conf** Class 180
Board 90 Thtr 300 **Services** Lift **Parking** 20 **Notes** LB

Fermain Valley

★★★★ 78% HOTEL

☎ 01481 235666 & 0800 316 0314 🖷 01481 235413
Fermain Ln GY1 1ZZ
e-mail: info@fermainvalley.com
dir: Turn left from airport, follow Forest Rd, turn right
onto Le Route de Sausmarez

This hotel occupies an amazing location high above
Fermain Bay with far reaching views out to sea. There are
lovely walks along the cliff or down the lanes from the
hotel. The delightfully furnished bedrooms, some with
balconies, have views of the sea, the valley or the well
tended gardens. The leisure facilities include a pool, a
sauna and a private cinema. Informal and fine dining
options are available in the Brasserie, on the terrace and
in the Valley Restaurant. The well trained staff provide a
warm and friendly service.

Rooms 45 (13 annexe) (1 fmly) (6 GF) **S** £110-£200;
D £120-£220 (incl. bkfst)* **Facilities** STV FTV ⊠ Cinema
Sauna Xmas New Year Wi-fi **Conf** Class 60 Board 40
Thtr 80 **Services** Lift **Parking** 40 **Notes** LB ⊗

The Duke of Richmond

★★★ 79% HOTEL

☎ 01481 726221 🖷 01481 728945
Cambridge Park GY1 1UY
e-mail: manager@dukeofrichmond.com
web: www.dukeofrichmond.com
dir: On corner of Cambridge Park & L'Hyvreuse Ave,
opposite leisure centre

Peacefully located in a mainly residential area
overlooking Cambridge Park, this hotel has comfortable,
well-appointed bedrooms that vary in size. Public areas
include a spacious lounge, a terrace and the unique
Sausmarez Bar, with its nautical theme. The smartly

uniformed team of staff provide professional standards
of service.

Rooms 75 (16 fmly) **S** £65-£87.50; **D** £95-£115 (incl.
bkfst)* **Facilities** STV ⌇ Leisure centre close to hotel
Xmas New Year Wi-fi **Conf** Class 50 Board 36 Thtr 150
Del from £100 to £122.50* **Services** Lift **Parking** 6
Notes LB ⊗

St Pierre Park

★★★ 79% HOTEL

☎ 01481 728282 🖷 01481 712041
Rohais GY1 1FD
e-mail: reservations@stpierrepark.co.uk
dir: 10 mins from airport. From harbour straight over
rdbt, up hill through 3 sets of lights. Right at filter,
continue to lights. Straight ahead, hotel 100mtrs on left

Peacefully located on the outskirts of town amidst 45
acres of grounds featuring a 9-hole golf course. Most of
the bedrooms overlook the pleasant gardens and have
either a balcony or a terrace. Public areas include a
choice of restaurants and a lounge bar that opens onto a
spacious terrace with an elegant water feature.

Rooms 131 (5 fmly) (20 GF) **S** £99-£155; **D** £132-£195
(incl. bkfst)* **Facilities** Spa STV ⊠ ↥ 9 ☷ Putt green ⌘
Gym Bird watching Children's playground Crazy golf
Xmas New Year Wi-fi **Conf** Class 120 Board 70 Thtr 200
Del from £125 to £199* **Services** Lift **Parking** 150
Notes LB ⊗

Best Western Hotel de Havelet

★★★ 78% HOTEL

☎ 01481 722199 🖷 01481 714057
Havelet GY1 1BA
e-mail: havelet@sarniahotels.com
web: www.havelet.sarniahotels.com
dir: from airport follow signs for St Peter Port through St.
Martins. At bottom of 'Val de Terres' hill turn left into
Havelet

This extended Georgian hotel looks over the harbour to
Castle Cornet. Many of the well-equipped bedrooms are
set around a pretty colonial-style courtyard. Day rooms in
the original building have period elegance; the restaurant
and bar are on the other side of the car park in converted
stables.

Rooms 34 (4 fmly) (8 GF) (17 smoking) **S** £50-£120;
D £90-£150 (incl. bkfst)* **Facilities** ⊠ Sauna Steam
room Xmas New Year Wi-fi **Conf** Class 24 Board 26
Thtr 40 Del from £120 to £160* **Parking** 40 **Notes** LB ⊗

Les Rocquettes

★★★ 78% HOTEL

☎ 01481 722146 🖷 01481 714543
Les Gravees GY1 1RN
e-mail: rocquettes@sarniahotels.com
dir: From ferry terminal take 2nd exit at rdbt, through 5
sets of lights. After 5th lights continue straight into Les
Gravees. Hotel on right opposite church.

This late 18th-century country mansion is in a good
location close to St Peter Port and Beau Sejour. Guests
can eat in Oaks restaurant and bar. Bedrooms come in
three grades - Deluxe, Superior and Standard, but all
have plenty of useful facilities. The hotel has attractive
lounge areas on three levels; there is a health suite with
a gym and swimming pool with an integrated children's
pool.

Rooms 51 (5 fmly) **S** £65-£100; **D** £84-£140 (incl. bkfst)*
Facilities ⊠ supervised Gym Treatment rooms ♫ Xmas
New Year Wi-fi **Conf** Class 60 Board 60 Thtr 100
Del from £100 to £160* **Services** Lift **Parking** 60
Notes LB ⊗

ST PETER PORT *continued*

Best Western Moores

★★★ 73% HOTEL

☎ 01481 724452 📠 01481 714037
Pollet GY1 1WH
e-mail: moores@sarniahotels.com
dir: left at airport, follow signs to St Peter Port. Fort Road to seafront, straight on, turn left before rdbt, to hotel

An elegant granite town house situated in the heart of St Peter Port amidst the shops and amenities. Public rooms feature a smart conservatory restaurant which leads out onto a first-floor terrace for alfresco dining; there is also a choice of lounges and bars as well as a patisserie. Bedrooms are pleasantly decorated and thoughtfully equipped.

Rooms 49 (3 annexe) (8 fmly) (10 smoking) **S** £65-£120; **D** £90-£144 (incl. bkfst)* **Facilities** Gym Sauna Solarium Xmas New Year Wi-fi **Conf** Class 20 Board 18 Thtr 40 Del from £110 to £150* **Services** Lift **Notes** LB ⊗

Duke of Normandie

★★ 74% HOTEL

☎ 01481 721431 📠 01481 711763
Lefebvre St GY1 2JP
e-mail: dukeofnormandie@cwgsy.net
web: www.dukeofnormandie.com
dir: From harbour rdbt St Julians Ave, 3rd left into Anns Place, continue to right, up hill, then left into Lefebvre St, archway entrance on right

An 18th-century hotel situated close to the high street and just a short stroll from the harbour. Bedrooms vary in style and include some that have their own access from the courtyard. Public areas feature a smart brasserie, a contemporary lounge/lobby area and a busy bar with beams and an open fireplace.

Rooms 37 (17 annexe) (8 GF) **Facilities** STV Xmas Wi-fi **Conf** Class 30 Board 20 Thtr 40 Del from £73 to £80.50* **Parking** 15 **Notes** ⊗

ST SAVIOUR

Farmhouse Hotel

★★★★ 80% ◉ SMALL HOTEL

☎ 01481 264181 📠 01481 266272
Route Des Bas Courtils GY7 9YF
e-mail: enquiries@thefarmhouse.gg
web: www.thefarmhouse.gg
dir: From airport, left to 1st lights . Left then left again around runway perimeter. After 1m left at x-rds. Hotel 100mtrs on right

This hotel provides spacious accommodation with amazingly comfortable beds and state-of-the-art bathrooms with under-floor heating. Guests can choose from various stylish dining options including alfresco eating in the warmer months. The outdoor swimming pool is available to guests in the summer and there are lots of countryside walks to enjoy.

Rooms 14 (7 fmly) **S** £110-£200; **D** £140-£250 (incl. bkfst) **Facilities** STV ⌇ ♫ Xmas New Year Wi-fi **Conf** Class 130 Board 30 Thtr 150 Del from £130 to £150 **Services** Air con **Parking** 80 **Notes** LB ⊗

See advert on page 547

VALE | Map 24

Peninsula

★★★ 74% HOTEL

☎ 01481 248400 📠 01481 248706
Les Dicqs GY6 8JP
e-mail: peninsula@guernsey.net
dir: Coast Rd, Grand Havre Bay

Adjacent to the sandy beach and set in five acres of grounds, this modern hotel provides comfortable accommodation. Bedrooms have an additional sofa bed to suit families and good workspace for the business traveller. Both fixed-price and carte menus are served in the restaurant, or guests can eat informally in the bar.

Rooms 99 (99 fmly) (25 GF) (20 smoking) **S** £67.50-£86; **D** £105-£142 (incl. bkfst)* **Facilities** STV ⌇ Putt green Petanque Children's playground Xmas New Year Wi-fi **Conf** Class 140 Board 105 Thtr 250 Del from £109.50 to £128* **Services** Lift **Parking** 120 **Notes** LB ⊗ Closed Jan

---

HERM

HERM | Map 24

White House

★★★ 74% ◉ HOTEL

☎ 01481 722159 📠 01481 710066
GY1 3HR
e-mail: hotel@herm-island.com
web: www.herm-island.com
dir: close to harbour

Enjoying a unique island setting, this attractive hotel is just 20 minutes from Guernsey by sea. Set in well-tended gardens, the hotel offers neatly decorated bedrooms, located in either the main house or adjacent cottages; the majority of rooms have sea views. Guests can relax in one of several lounges, enjoy a drink in one of two bars and choose from two dining options.

White House

Rooms 40 (23 annexe) (23 fmly) (7 GF) **S** £85-£130; **D** £170-£260 (incl. bkfst & dinner)* **Facilities** ⌇ ⊜ ⊌ Fishing trips Yacht & motor boat charters Wi-fi **Conf** Board 10 **Notes** ⊗ Closed Nov-Mar

---

JERSEY

GOREY | Map 24

Old Court House

★★★ 74% HOTEL

☎ 01534 854444 📠 01534 853587
JE3 9FS
e-mail: ochhotel@itl.net
web: www.ochhoteljersey.com

Situated on the east of the island, a short walk from the beach, this long established hotel continues to have a loyal following for its relaxed atmosphere and friendly staff. Bedrooms are of similar standard throughout and some have balconies overlooking the gardens. Spacious public areas include a comfortable, quiet lounge, a restaurant, and a large bar with a dance floor.

Rooms 58 (4 fmly) (9 GF) **S** £50-£69; **D** £100-£151 (incl. bkfst)* **Facilities** STV ⌇ ♫ **Services** Lift **Parking** 40 **Notes** LB Closed Nov-Mar

The Moorings Hotel & Restaurant

★★★ 73% HOTEL

☎ 01534 853633 ᤀ 01534 857618
Gorey Pier JE3 6EW
e-mail: reservations@themooringshotel.com
web: www.themooringshotel.com
dir: At foot of Mont Orgueil Castle

Enjoying an enviable position by the harbour, the heart of this hotel is the restaurant where a selection of menus offers an extensive choice of dishes. Other public areas include a bar, coffee shop and a comfortable first-floor residents' lounge. Bedrooms at the front have a fine view of the harbour; three have access to a balcony. A small sun terrace at the back of the hotel is available to guests.

Rooms 15 **S** £56-£72; **D** £112-£144 (incl. bkfst)*
Facilities STV Xmas New Year Wi-fi **Conf** Class 20
Board 20 Thtr 20 Del from £165 to £195* **Notes** LB ⊗

Dolphin Hotel and Restaurant

★★ 68% HOTEL

☎ 01534 853370 ᤀ 01534 855343
Gorey Pier JE3 6EW
e-mail: dolphinhotel@jerseymail.co.uk
dir: At foot of Mont Orgueil Castle

Located on the main harbour at Gorey, many bedrooms at this popular hotel enjoy views over the sea and beaches. The relaxed and friendly style is apparent from the moment of arrival, and the busy restaurant and bar are popular with locals and tourists alike. Outdoor seating is available in season, and fresh fish and seafood are included on the menu.

Rooms 16 **S** £40-£51.50; **D** £80-£103 (incl. bkfst)*
Facilities STV Xmas New Year **Conf** Class 20 Board 20
Thtr 20 Del from £145 to £175* **Notes** LB ⊗

Maison Gorey

★★ 67% HOTEL

☎ 01534 857775 & 07797 736059 ᤀ 01534 857779
Gorey Village Main Rd JE3 9EP
e-mail: maisongorey@jerseymail.co.uk
dir: Next to Jersey Pottery

Located in the middle of Gorey this small, relaxing hotel provides well-equipped bedrooms and bathrooms. In addition to a spacious bar, a small TV lounge is available for guests. Some off-street parking is available in front of the hotel.

Rooms 26 (26 annexe) (2 fmly) **S** £30-£40; **D** £65-£80
(incl. bkfst) **Facilities** FTV ♬ Xmas New Year Wi-fi
Parking 6 **Notes** LB ⊗ No children 5yrs

GROUVILLE Map 24

Beausite

★★★ 71% HOTEL

☎ 01534 857577 ᤀ 01534 857211
Les Rue des Pres, Grouville Bay JE3 9DJ
e-mail: beausite@jerseymail.co.uk
web: www.southernhotels.com
dir: Opposite Royal Jersey Golf Course

This hotel is situated on the south-east side of the island; a short distance from the picturesque harbour at Gorey. With parts dating back to 1636, the public rooms retain original character and charm; bedrooms are generally spacious and modern in design. The indoor swimming pool, fitness room, saunas and spa bath are an added bonus.

Rooms 75 (5 fmly) (18 GF) **S** £49-£94.50; **D** £82-£126
(incl. bkfst)* **Facilities** STV ⊘ Gym Wi-fi **Parking** 60
Notes LB Closed Nov-Mar

Lavender Villa

★★ 65% HOTEL

☎ 01534 854937 ᤀ 01534 856147
La Rue A Don JE3 9DX
e-mail: lavendervilla@jerseymail.co.uk
dir: Close to Royal Jersey Golf course, 1m from Gorey

A small hotel where the guests receive friendly and personal attention from the resident proprietors and their welcoming team of staff. Bedrooms come in a variety of shapes and sizes but all are comfortable and well equipped. The bar and guest lounge are the ideal places to enjoy a drink before choosing from a range of carefully prepared dishes served in the cosy restaurant.

Rooms 21 (2 fmly) (6 GF) **S** £32-£44; **D** £64-£88 (incl. bkfst)* **Facilities** ↘ ♬ **Parking** 22 **Notes** LB ⊗ Closed Dec-Feb

ROZEL Map 24

INSPECTORS' CHOICE

Château la Chaire

★★★ ◉◉ HOTEL

☎ 01534 863354 ᤀ 01534 865137
Rozel Bay JE3 6AJ
e-mail: res@chateau-la-chaire.co.uk
web: www.chateau-la-chaire.co.uk
dir: from St Helier on B38 turn left in village by Rozel Bay Inn, hotel 100yds on right

Built as a gentleman's residence in 1843, Château la Chaire is a haven of peace and tranquillity, set within a secluded wooded valley. Picturesque Rozel Harbour is within easy walking distance and the house is surrounded by terraced gardens. There is a wonderful atmosphere here and the helpful staff deliver high standards of guest care. Imaginative menus, making the best use of local produce, are served in the oak-panelled dining room. Bedrooms styles and sizes are varied - all are beautifully appointed and include many nice touches such as flowers and mineral water.

Rooms 14 (2 fmly) (1 GF) **S** £85-£135; **D** £95-£295
(incl. bkfst)* **Facilities** STV Xmas New Year Wi-fi
Conf Class 20 Board 20 Thtr 20 Del from £133 to
£188* **Parking** 30 **Notes** LB ⊗ No children 7yrs
Civ Wed 60

ST AUBIN   Map 24

Somerville

★★★★ 77% ◎◎ HOTEL

☎ 01534 741226 ▤ 01534 746621
Mont du Boulevard JE3 8AD
e-mail: somerville@dolanhotels.com
web: www.dolanhotels.com
dir: from village, follow harbour into Mont du Boulevard

Enjoying spectacular views of St Aubin's Bay, this friendly hotel is very popular. Bedrooms vary in style and a number of superior rooms offer higher levels of luxury. Public areas are smartly presented and include a spacious bar-lounge and elegant dining room; both take full advantage of the hotel's enviable views. An outdoor swimming pool is available in summer months.

Rooms 56 (4 GF) **S** £65-£145; **D** £109-£219 (incl. bkfst)* **Facilities** STV ⇥ ♫ Xmas New Year Wi-fi **Conf** Class 33 Board 36 Thtr 55 Del from £110 to £125* **Services** Lift **Parking** 26 **Notes** ⊗ No children 4yrs Civ Wed 40

See advert on opposite page

Hotel La Tour

★★★ 77% HOTEL

☎ 01534 743770 ▤ 01534 747143
La Rue du Crocquet JE3 8BZ
e-mail: enquiries@hotellatour.com
web: www.hotellatour.com
dir: On High St behind church (street parallel to seafront)

This elevated hotel has been furnished in contemporary style yet retains much historic character. Public rooms are light and airy, and bedrooms are individually designed. At dinner guests are offered a choice of dining at the sister hotel or a local restaurant where all meals and drinks can be charged direct to their hotel account. Complimentary transport is included to both restaurants and can also be arranged for travel to and from the airport.

Rooms 30 (6 fmly) **Facilities** Indoor/outdoor swimming pool at sister hotel. Personal trainer on request Xmas New Year Wi-fi **Parking** 15 **Notes** LB ⊗

ST BRELADE   Map 24

INSPECTORS' CHOICE

The Atlantic
★★★★ ◎◎◎ HOTEL

☎ 01534 744101 ▤ 01534 744102
Le Mont de la Pulente JE3 8HE
e-mail: info@theatlantichotel.com
web: www.theatlantichotel.com
dir: from Petit Port turn right into Rue de la Sergente & right again, hotel signed

Adjoining the manicured fairways of La Moye championship golf course, this hotel enjoys a peaceful setting with breathtaking views over St Ouen's Bay. Stylish bedrooms look out over the course or the sea, and offer a blend of high quality and reassuring comfort. An air of understated luxury is apparent throughout, and the attentive service achieves the perfect balance of friendliness and professionalism. The Ocean restaurant offers sophisticated, modern surroundings in which to enjoy some highly accomplished cooking.

The Atlantic

Rooms 50 (8 GF) **S** £125-£200; **D** £150-£350 (incl. bkfst)* **Facilities** STV ⊚ ⇥ ⅋ Gym ♫ Xmas New Year Wi-fi **Conf** Class 40 Board 20 Thtr 60 Del from £200 to £250* **Services** Lift **Parking** 60 **Notes** LB ⊗ Closed 3 Jan-4 Feb Civ Wed 80

L'Horizon Hotel and Spa

★★★★ 84% ◎◎ HOTEL

☎ 01534 743101 ▤ 01534 746269
St Brelade's Bay JE3 8EF
e-mail: lhorizon@handpicked.co.uk
web: www.handpicked.co.uk/lhorizon
dir: 3m from airport. From airport right at rdbt towards St Brelades & Red Houses. Through Red Houses, hotel 300mtrs on right in centre of bay

The combination of a truly wonderful setting on the golden sands of St Brelade's Bay, a relaxed atmosphere and excellent facilities prove a winning formula here. Bedrooms are stylish and have a real contemporary feel, all with plasma TVs and a host of extras; many have balconies or terraces and superb sea views. Spacious public areas include a spa and leisure club, a choice of dining options and relaxing lounges.

Rooms 106 (1 fmly) (15 GF) **S** £55-£145; **D** £110-£250 (incl. bkfst)* **Facilities** Spa STV ⊚ Gym Treatment rooms Windsurfing Water skiing ♫ Xmas New Year Wi-fi **Conf** Class 100 Board 50 Thtr 250 Del from £160 to £250* **Services** Lift **Parking** 125 **Notes** LB ⊗ Civ Wed 250

St Brelade's Bay Hotel

★★★★ 78% HOTEL

☎ 01534 746141 ▤ 01534 747278
JE3 8EF
e-mail: info@stbreladesbayhotel.com
web: www.stbreladesbayhotel.com
dir: SW corner of island

This family hotel overlooking the bay has many loyal guests and dedicated members of staff. The attractive tiered grounds, with easy access to the beach, are ablaze with colour in summer. There is an extensive range of indoor and outdoor recreational facilities including a choice of pools. Most bedrooms have king-size beds, many have inter-connecting children's rooms; there are stunning penthouse suites too. The tariff includes morning and afternoon tea.

Rooms 81 (50 fmly) **S** £88-£137; **D** £140-£344 (incl. bkfst)* **Facilities** STV ⇥ supervised ⅏ Putt green ⅋ Gym Petanque Mini-gym Games room Table tennis ♫ Wi-fi Child facilities **Conf** Board 12 Thtr 20 **Services** Lift **Parking** 60 **Notes** ⊗ Closed 3 Nov-4 Apr

Hotel La Place

★★★★ 73% ⚛ HOTEL

☎ 01534 744261 🖺 01534 745164
Route du Coin, La Haule JE3 8BT
e-mail: reservations@hotellaplacejersey.com
dir: Off main St Helier/St Aubin coast road at La Haule
Manor (B25). Up hill, 2nd left (to Red Houses), 1st right.
Hotel 100mtrs on right

Developed around a 17th-century farmhouse and well
placed for exploration of the island. Attentive, friendly
service is the ethos here. A range of bedroom types is
provided, some having private patios and direct access to
the pool area. The cocktail bar is popular for pre-dinner
drinks and a traditional lounge has a log fire in colder
months. An interesting menu is offered.

Rooms 42 (1 fmly) (10 GF) **Facilities** ⚲ Discount at Les
Ormes Country Club, including golf, gym & indoor tennis
Xmas Wi-fi **Conf** Class 40 Board 40 Thtr 100 **Parking** 100
Notes Civ Wed 100

Golden Sands

★★★ 78% HOTEL

☎ 01534 741241 🖺 01534 499366
St Brelade's Bay JE3 8EF
e-mail: goldensands@dolanhotels.com
web: www.dolanhotels.com
dir: Follow St Brelade's Bay signs. Hotel on coast side of
road

With direct access to the beach, this popular hotel
overlooks the wonderful sandy expanse of St Brelade's
Bay. Many of the comfortable bedrooms are sea facing
with balconies where guests can relax and breathe in the
fresh air. Public areas include a lounge, bar and
restaurant, all of which enjoy bay views.

Golden Sands

Rooms 62 (9 fmly) **S** £45-£244; **D** £72-£271 (incl. bkfst)*
Facilities STV Children's play room ♫ Wi-fi **Services** Lift
Notes ⊗ Closed Nov-mid Apr

See advert on this page

Beau Rivage

★★★ 77% HOTEL

☎ 01534 745983 🖺 01534 747127
St Brelade's Bay JE3 8EF
e-mail: beau@jerseyweb.demon.co.uk
web: www.jersey.co.uk/hotels/beau
dir: Sea side of coast road in centre of St Brelade's Bay,
1.5m S of airport

With direct access to one of Jersey's most popular
beaches, residents and non-residents alike are welcome
to this hotel's bar and terrace. All of the well-equipped
bedrooms are now suites, most have wonderful sea views,
and some have the bonus of balconies. Residents have a
choice of lounges, plus a sun deck exclusively for their
use. A range of dishes, featuring English and Continental
cuisine, is available from a selection of menus in either
the bar or the main bistro restaurant.

Rooms 22 (12 fmly) (22 smoking) **D** £50-£155*
Facilities STV Games room ♫ Wi-fi **Services** Lift
Parking 16 **Notes** LB ⊗ RS Nov-Mar Civ Wed 80

Hotel Miramar

★★ 72% HOTEL

☎ 01534 743831 🖺 01534 745009
Mont Gras d'Eau JE3 8ED
e-mail: miramarjsy@localdial.com
dir: From airport take B36 at lights, turn left onto A13,
1st right into Mont Gras d'Eau

A friendly welcome awaits at this family-run hotel set in
delightful sheltered gardens, overlooking the beautiful
bay. Accommodation is comfortable with well appointed
bedrooms; some are on the ground floor, and there are
two on the lower ground with their own terrace
overlooking the outdoor heated pool. The restaurant offers
a varied set menu.

Rooms 38 (2 fmly) (14 GF) **S** £32-£49.90; **D** £64-£99.80
(incl. bkfst)* **Facilities** ⚲ **Parking** 30 **Notes** Closed Oct-
mid Apr

ST CLEMENT — Map 24

Pontac House

★★★ 75% HOTEL

☎ 01534 857771 📠 01534 857031
St Clements Bay JE2 6SE
e-mail: info@pontachouse.com
web: www.pontachouse.com
dir: 10 mins from St Helier

Overlooking the sandy beach of St Clement's Bay, this hotel is located on the south eastern corner of Jersey. Many guests return on a regular basis to experience the friendly, relaxed style of service. The bedrooms, most with splendid views, are comfortable and well equipped. Varied menus, featuring local seafood, are on offer each evening.

Rooms 27 (1 fmly) (5 GF) **S** £33.50-£52.50; **D** £67-£105 (incl. bkfst)* **Facilities** ﹡ Wi-fi **Parking** 35 **Notes** LB Closed 18 Dec-7 Feb

ST HELIER — Map 24

INSPECTORS' CHOICE

The Club Hotel & Spa

★★★★ ◉◉◉◉ HOTEL

☎ 01534 876500 📠 01534 720371
Green St JE2 4UH
e-mail: reservations@theclubjersey.com
web: www.theclubjersey.com
dir: 5 mins walk from main shopping centre

This swish, town-house hotel is conveniently located close to the centre of town and features stylish, contemporary decor throughout. All the guest rooms and suites include power showers and state-of-the-art technology including wide-screen LCD TV, DVD and CD systems. The choice of restaurants includes Bohemia, a sophisticated eating option that continues to offer very highly accomplished cooking. For relaxation there is an elegant spa with a luxurious range of treatments.

Rooms 46 (4 fmly) (4 GF) (5 smoking) **S** £130-£215; **D** £130-£215 (incl. bkfst)* **Facilities** Spa STV FTV ﹡ Sauna Steam room Salt cabin Hydrothermal bench Rasul room New Year Wi-fi **Conf** Class 35 Board 32 Thtr 50 Del from £169 to £195* **Services** Lift Air con **Parking** 30 **Notes** LB ⊗ Closed 24-30 Dec Civ Wed 50

Royal Yacht

★★★★ 82% ◉◉ HOTEL

☎ 01534 720511 📠 01534 767729
The Weighbridge JE2 3NF
e-mail: reception@theroyalyacht.com
dir: in town centre, opposite marina & harbour

Overlooking the marina and steam clock, the Royal Yacht is thought to be the oldest established hotel on the island. Very much a 21st century hotel, it has state-of-the-art technology in all the bedrooms and the two penthouse suites. There is a range of impressive dining options to suit all tastes with Sirocco's Restaurant offering high quality local produce. In addition to a choice of bars and conference facilities guests can enjoy the luxury spa with an indoor pool and gym.

Rooms 110 **S** £125-£205; **D** £125-£205 (incl. bkfst)* **Facilities** Spa STV ⊙ Gym ♫ Xmas New Year Wi-fi **Conf** Class 150 Board 40 Thtr 280 Del from £149 to £210* **Services** Lift Air con **Notes** LB ⊗ Civ Wed 250

Radisson Blu Waterfront Hotel, Jersey

★★★★ 80% ⊛ HOTEL

☎ 01534 671100 & 671173 📠 01534 671101
The Waterfront, La Rue de L'Etau JE2 4HE
web: www.radissonblu.com/hotel-jersey
dir: Follow signs to town centre, just before harbour take 3rd exit at rdbt, continue to hotel

Most of the bedrooms at this purpose-built hotel have fabulous views of the coastline. There is a popular brasserie, cocktail bar, lounges, indoor heated pool, gym, sauna and steam room. A wide range of meeting rooms provides conference facilities for delegates; parking is extensive.

Rooms 195 **Facilities** Spa STV ⊗ supervised Gym 🎵 Xmas New Year Wi-fi **Conf** Class 184 Board 30 Thtr 416 **Services** Lift Air con **Parking** 95 **Notes** LB ⊗ Civ Wed 280

Grand, Jersey

★★★★ 79% ⊛⊛⊛ HOTEL

☎ 01534 722301 📠 01534 737815
The Esplanade JE4 8WD
e-mail: adowling@hilwoodresorts.com

A local landmark, the Grand Hotel has pleasant views across St Aubin's Bay to the front and the bustling streets of St Helier to the rear. Having undergone a multi-million pound transformation the hotel is elegant and contemporary in design, with a real touch of grandeur. The air conditioned bedrooms, including six suites, come in a variety of designs, but all have luxurious beds, ottomans and LCD TVs. The spacious public areas, many looking out onto the bay, include the very popular Champagne Bar, the modern Brasserie Victorias, and the impressive and intimate Tassili fine-dining restaurant. There is a large terrace for alfresco eating, and the spa offers an indoor pool, gym and treatment rooms.

Rooms 123 (53 fmly) (6 GF) **Facilities** STV ⊗ supervised Gym 🎵 Xmas Wi-fi **Conf** Class 193 Board 112 Thtr 356 **Services** Lift Air con **Parking** 27 **Notes** ⊗ Civ Wed

Pomme d'Or

★★★★ 77% ⊛⊛ HOTEL

☎ 01534 880110 📠 01534 737781
Liberation Square JE1 3UF
e-mail: enquiries@pommedorhotel.com
dir: opposite harbour

This historic hotel overlooks Liberation Square and the marina and offers comfortably furnished, well-equipped bedrooms. Popular with the business fraternity, a range of conference facilities and meeting rooms are available. Dining options include the traditional fine dining in the Petite Pomme, the smart carvery restaurant and the informal coffee shop.

Rooms 143 (3 fmly) **S** £99-£200; **D** £99-£200 (incl. bkfst)* **Facilities** STV Use of Aquadome at Merton Hotel. Xmas New Year Wi-fi **Conf** Class 100 Board 50 Thtr 220 **Services** Lift Air con **Notes** ⊗

Hotel Savoy

★★★★ 72% ⊛ HOTEL

☎ 01534 727521 📠 01534 727521
37 Rouge Bouillon JE2 3ZA
e-mail: info@thesavoy.biz
web: www.thesavoy.biz

This family-run hotel sits peacefully in its own grounds, just a short walk from the main shopping area in St Helier. A 19th-century manor house, this hotel offers spacious, comfortable accommodation and smart public rooms. The Montana Restaurant serves carefully prepared, imaginative cuisine.

Rooms 53 (9 GF) (45 smoking) **S** £67.50-£112.50; **D** £90-£150 (incl. bkfst)* **Facilities** STV ⊗ Gym 🎵 Wi-fi **Conf** Class 70 Board 12 Thtr 120 **Services** Lift **Parking** 45 **Notes** ⊗ Closed 21 Dec-5 Jan

Best Western Royal

★★★ 78% ⊛ HOTEL

☎ 01534 726521 & 873006 📠 01534 811046
David Place JE2 4TD
e-mail: enquiries@royalhoteljersey.com
web: www.royalhoteljersey.com
dir: follow signs for Ring Rd, pass Queen Victoria rdbt keep left, left at lights, left into Piersons Rd. Follow one-way system to Cheapside, Rouge Bouillon, at A14 turn to Midvale Rd, hotel on left

This long established hotel is located in the centre of town and is within walking distance of the business district and shops. Seasons Restaurant offers a modern approach to dining, and the adjoining bar provides a relaxed venue for residents and locals alike. The bedrooms are individually styled. Extensive conference facilities are available.

Rooms 88 (39 fmly) **Facilities** Gym Xmas New Year Wi-fi **Conf** Class 120 Board 80 Thtr 300 **Services** Lift **Parking** 15 **Notes** LB ⊗ Civ Wed 30

Hotel Revere

★★★ 71% HOTEL

☎ 01534 611111 📠 01534 611116
Kensington Place JE2 3PA
e-mail: reservations@revere.co.uk
web: www.revere.co.uk
dir: From Esplanade turn left after De Vere Grand Hotel

Situated on the west side of the town and convenient for the centre and harbour side, this hotel dates back to the 17th century and retains many period features. The style here is engagingly different, and bedrooms are individually decorated. There are three dining options and a small sun terrace.

Rooms 56 (2 fmly) (3 GF) **Facilities** STV ⊗ 🎵 Xmas New Year Wi-fi **Notes** ⊗ Civ Wed 50

Apollo

★★★ 70% HOTEL

☎ 01534 725441 📠 01534 722120
St Saviours Rd JE2 4GJ
e-mail: reservations@huggler.com
web: www.huggler.com
dir: On St Saviours Rd at junct with La Motte St

Centrally located, this popular hotel has a relaxed, informal atmosphere. Bedrooms are comfortably furnished and include useful extras. Many guests return regularly to enjoy the variety of leisure facilities including an outdoor pool with water slide and indoor pool with separate jacuzzi. The separate cocktail bar is an ideal place for a pre-dinner drink.

Rooms 85 (5 fmly) **S** £59-£142; **D** £59-£142 (incl. bkfst)* **Facilities** FTV ⊗ supervised ⊗ supervised Gym Xmas New Year Wi-fi **Conf** Class 100 Board 80 Thtr 150 Del from £89 to £149* **Services** Lift **Parking** 40 **Notes** LB ⊗

ST HELIER *continued*

Millbrook House

★★ 74% HOTEL

☎ 01534 733036 🖹 01534 724317
Rue De Trachy, Millbrook JE2 3JN
e-mail: millbrook.house@jerseymail.co.uk
web: www.millbrookhousehotel.com
dir: 1.5m W of town off A1

Peacefully located within its own grounds, this small, personally run hotel offers a friendly welcome and relaxing ambience. Bedrooms and bathrooms vary in size, and many have pleasant, countryside views. In addition to outdoor seating in the warmer months, guests can relax in the library, maybe with a drink before dinner.

Rooms 24 (2 fmly) (5 GF) **S** £35-£44; **D** £70-£88 (incl. bkfst)* **Services** Lift **Parking** 20 **Notes** ⊗ Closed 1 Oct-13 May

Sarum

★★ 64% METRO HOTEL

☎ 01534 731340 🖹 01534 758163
19/21 New St Johns Rd JE2 3LD
e-mail: sarum@jerseyweb.demon.co.uk
dir: On NW edge of St Helier, 0.5m from town centre

This hotel, just 600yds from the beach, offers self-catering bedrooms and a number of suites. The friendly staff provide a warm welcome, and there is a spacious recreational lounge with pool tables, plasma-screen TV and internet access. A garden and outdoor pool are also available. Local restaurants are just a short walk away, and bar snacks are available throughout the day.

Rooms 52 (5 annexe) (6 fmly) (2 GF) (52 smoking) **S** £34-£56; **D** £47-£86* **Facilities** STV ⌁ Wi-fi **Services** Lift **Parking** 10 **Notes** LB ⊗ RS Oct-Mar

---

ST LAWRENCE Map 24

Hotel Cristina

★★★ 78% ⊛ HOTEL

☎ 01534 758024 🖹 01534 758028
Mont Feland JE3 1JA
e-mail: cristina@dolanhotels.com
web: www.dolanhotels.com
dir: A10 to Mont Feland Exit, hotel on left

This hotel offers smartly styled and comfortable bedrooms. Public areas reflect a contemporary style that makes this a refreshingly different hotel, with a modern restaurant serving a range of fresh produce in a bistro atmosphere. The terrace is adorned with flowers and is a popular place for soaking up the sun.

Rooms 63 (3 fmly) **S** £33.50-£162; **D** £53-£240 (incl. bkfst)* **Facilities** STV ⌁ ♫ Wi-fi **Parking** 60 **Notes** ⊗ Closed Nov-Mar Civ Wed 30

See advert on page 553

ST MARY Map 24

West View

★★ 69% HOTEL

☎ 01534 481643 🖹 01534 483283
La Grande Rue JE3 3BD
e-mail: westview@jerseymail.co.uk
web: www.westviewhoteljersey.com
dir: at junct of B33 & C103

Located in the quiet parish of St Mary, this welcoming hotel is close to the delightful walks and cycle routes of the north coast. Bedrooms here are well equipped especially the larger, superior rooms. Entertainment is provided in the lounge bar during the summer months, when guests can also enjoy a swim in the heated outdoor pool.

Rooms 42 (3 fmly) (18 GF) **S** £33.25-£46.25; **D** £59.50-£92.50 (incl. bkfst)* **Facilities** ⌁ Wi-fi **Parking** 38 **Notes** ⊗ Closed Nov-Apr

ST PETER Map 24

Greenhills Country Hotel

★★★★ 74% ⊛ COUNTRY HOUSE HOTEL

☎ 01534 481042 🖹 01534 485322
Mont de L'Ecole JE3 7EL
e-mail: reserve@greenhillshotel.co.uk
dir: From A1 signed St Peter's Valley (A11), in 4m right onto E112

Centrally located on the island and very close to The Living Legends display, this relaxing country house hotel has a lovely atmosphere and a delightful garden that surrounds it. Bedrooms extend from the main building around the courtyard; all are comfortable and well equipped. A varied menu, based on fresh local produce, is served in the spacious restaurant.

Rooms 31 (2 fmly) (9 GF) **S** £57.50-£82.50; **D** £115-£165 (incl. bkfst)* **Facilities** STV FTV ⌁ Wi-fi **Conf** Class 12 Board 16 Thtr 20 Del from £95 to £120* **Parking** 40 **Notes** LB ⊗ Closed mid Dec-early Feb Civ Wed 40

ST SAVIOUR — Map 24

INSPECTORS' CHOICE

Longueville Manor
★★★★★ ◉◉◉ HOTEL

☎ 01534 725501 📠 01534 731613
JE2 7WF
e-mail: info@longuevillemanor.com
web: www.longuevillemanor.com
dir: A3 E from St Helier towards Gorey. Hotel 1m on left

Dating back to the 13th century, there is something very special about Longueville Manor, which is why so many guests return. It is set in 17 acres of grounds including woodland walks, a spectacular rose garden and a lake. Bedrooms have great style and individuality boasting fresh flowers, fine embroidered bed linen and a host of extras. The committed team of staff create a welcoming atmosphere and every effort is made to ensure a memorable stay. The accomplished cuisine is also a highlight.

Rooms 30 (1 annexe) (7 GF) (6 smoking) **S** £185-£380; **D** £210-£600 (incl. bkfst)* **Facilities** STV ⬦ ⬦ ⬦ Xmas New Year Wi-fi **Conf** Class 30 Board 30 Thtr 45 Del from £245* **Services** Lift **Parking** 40 **Notes** LB Civ Wed 40

TRINITY — Map 24

Water's Edge
★★★ 78% ◉◉ HOTEL

☎ 01534 862777 📠 01534 863645
Bouley Bay JE3 5AS
e-mail: mail@watersedgehotel.co.je
web: www.watersedgehotel.co.je

Set in the tranquil surroundings of Bouley Bay on Jersey's north coast, this hotel is exactly as its name conveys and offers breathtaking views. The bedrooms offer high standards of quality and comfort. Dining options include the relaxed atmosphere of the adjoining Black Dog bar or the more formal award-winning restaurant.

Rooms 50 (3 fmly) **Facilities** ⬦ ♪ **Conf** Class 25 Board 20 Thtr 30 **Services** Lift **Parking** 20 **Notes** LB ⊗ Closed mid Oct-mid Apr Civ Wed 80

ISLE OF MAN

DOUGLAS — Map 24 SC37

Sefton
★★★★ 78% ◉◉ HOTEL

☎ 01624 645500 📠 01624 676004
Harris Promenade IM1 2RW
e-mail: info@seftonhotel.co.im
web: www.seftonhotel.co.im
dir: 500yds from Ferry Dock on promenade

This Victorian hotel, extended over the years offers comfortably furnished bedrooms; many are spacious. Some have balconies overlooking the atrium water garden, while others enjoy sweeping views across the bay. A choice of comfortable lounges is available and freshly prepared dishes are served in the informal Gallery Restaurant.

Rooms 96 (3 fmly) **Facilities** ⬦ Gym Cycle hire, Steam room, Library ♪ New Year Wi-fi **Conf** Class 30 Board 50 Thtr 150 Del from £170 to £200* **Services** Lift **Parking** 36 **Notes** ⊗

Mount Murray Hotel and Country Club
★★★★ 75% HOTEL

☎ 01624 661111 📠 01624 611116
Santon IM4 2HT
e-mail: manager@mountmurray.com
web: www.mountmurray.com
dir: 4m from Douglas towards airport. Hotel signed at Santon

This large, modern hotel and country club offers a wide range of sporting and leisure facilities, and a superb health and beauty salon. The attractively appointed public areas give a choice of bars and eating options. The spacious bedrooms are well equipped and many enjoy fine views over the 200-acre grounds and golf course. There is a very large conference suite.

Rooms 100 (4 fmly) (27 GF) (8 smoking) **S** £59-£89; **D** £82-£99 (incl. bkfst)* **Facilities** STV ⬦ ⬦ 18 Putt green Gym Squash Driving range Xmas New Year Wi-fi **Conf** Class 200 Board 100 Thtr 300 **Services** Lift **Parking** 400 **Notes** LB ⊗

PORT ERIN — Map 24 SC16

Falcon's Nest
★★ 67% HOTEL

☎ 01624 834077 📠 01624 835370
The Promenade IM9 6AF
e-mail: falconsnest@enterprise.net
web: www.falconsnesthotel.co.uk
dir: follow coast road, S from airport or ferry. Hotel on seafront, immediately after steam railway station

Situated overlooking the bay and harbour, this Victorian hotel offers generally spacious bedrooms. There is a choice of bars, one of which attracts many locals. Meals can be taken in the lounge bar, the conservatory or in the attractively decorated main restaurant.

Rooms 35 (9 fmly) (15 smoking) **S** £35-£42.50; **D** £70-£85 (incl. bkfst) **Facilities** FTV Xmas New Year Wi-fi **Conf** Class 50 Board 50 Thtr 50 Del from £80 to £100* **Parking** 30

Scotland

Kilchurn Castle, Loch Awe

ABERDEEN   Map 23 NJ90

See also **Aberdeen Airport**

Doubletree by Hilton Aberdeen

★★★★ 78% HOTEL

☎ 01224 633339 & 380000 📄 01224 638833
Beach Boulevard AB24 5EF
e-mail: sales.doubletreeaberdeen@hilton.com
web: www.hilton.co.uk/aberdeencity
dir: from A90 follow signs for city centre, then for beach.
On Beach Blvd, left at lights, hotel on right

This modern, purpose-built hotel lies close to the
seafront. Bedrooms come in two different styles - the
retro-style Classics and spacious Premiers. In addition
the Platinum Club offers a unique experience of 44
superb high-spec bedrooms that have their own reception
bar, lounge and dinner and breakfast room. The
restaurant and striking Atrium bar are housed in the
main building.

Rooms 168 (44 annexe) (8 fmly) (22 GF) (41 smoking)
S £65-£200; **D** £65-£200 **Facilities** Spa STV ✪ Gym
Steam room Treatment room Sauna Solarium Fitness
Studio New Year Wi-fi **Conf** Class 80 Board 50 Thtr 150
Del from £130 to £185 **Services** Lift **Parking** 172

Norwood Hall

★★★★ 75% ⚜ HOTEL

☎ 01224 868951 📄 01224 869868
Garthdee Rd, Cults AB15 9FX
e-mail: info@norwood-hall.co.uk
web: www.norwood-hall.co.uk
dir: off A90, at 1st rdbt cross Bridge of Dee, left at rdbt
onto Garthdee Rd (B&Q & Sainsburys on left) continue to
hotel sign

This imposing Victorian mansion has retained many of its
features, most notably the fine oak staircase, stained
glass and ornately decorated walls and ceilings.
Accommodation comes in three different styles -
individually designed bedrooms in the main house, a
wing of spacious superior rooms and an older wing of
modern but less spacious rooms. The extensive grounds
ensure the hotel is popular as a wedding venue.

Rooms 36 (6 GF) **S** £185-£225; **D** £205-£245 (incl.
bkfst)* **Facilities** STV Xmas New Year Wi-fi
Conf Class 100 Board 70 Thtr 200 **Services** Lift
Parking 100 **Notes** LB ⊗ Civ Wed 150

Copthorne Hotel Aberdeen

★★★★ 75% HOTEL

☎ 01224 630404 📄 01224 640573
122 Huntly St AB10 1SU
e-mail: reservations.aberdeen@millenniumhotels.co.uk
web: www.millenniumhotels.co.uk/aberdeen
dir: West end of city centre, off Union St, up Rose St, hotel
0.25m on right on corner with Huntly St

Situated just outside of the city centre, this hotel offers
friendly, attentive service. The smart bedrooms are well
proportioned and guests will appreciate the added quality
of the Connoisseur rooms. Mac's bar provides a relaxed

atmosphere in which to enjoy a drink or to dine informally,
whilst Poachers Restaurant offers a slightly more formal
dining experience.

Rooms 89 (15 fmly) **S** £57-£208; **D** £65-£216
Facilities STV New Year Wi-fi **Conf** Class 100 Board 70
Thtr 200 Del from £150 to £250 **Services** Lift **Parking** 15
Notes LB RS 24-26 Dec Civ Wed 180

Holiday Inn Aberdeen West

★★★★ 74% HOTEL

☎ 01224 270300 📄 01224 270323
Westhill Dr, Westhill AB32 6TT
e-mail: info@hiaberdeenwest.co.uk
web: www.holidayinn.co.uk
dir: On A944 in Westhill

In a good location at the west side of the city, this modern
hotel caters well for the needs of both business and
leisure guests. The nicely appointed bedrooms and
bathrooms have a contemporary feel. Luigi's restaurant
serves modern Italian food, and the popular lounge offers
more informal dining. There is a separate pub operation
with wide-screen TVs showing a range of sporting events.

Rooms 86 (30 fmly) (6 smoking) **Facilities** STV Gym
Beautician services Wi-fi **Conf** Class 150 Board 80
Thtr 300 **Services** Lift Air con **Parking** 90 **Notes** LB
Civ Wed 250

Maryculter House Hotel

★★★★ 73% ® HOTEL

☎ 01224 732124 📠 01224 733510
South Deeside Rd, Maryculter AB12 5GB
e-mail: info@maryculterhousehotel.com
web: www.maryculterhousehotel.com
dir: Off A90 on S side of Aberdeen, onto B9077. Hotel 8m on right, 0.5m beyond Lower Deeside Caravan Park

Set in grounds on the banks of the River Dee, this charming Scottish mansion dates back to medieval times and is now a popular wedding and conference venue. Exposed stonework and open fires feature in the oldest parts, which house the cocktail bar and Priory Restaurant. Lunch and breakfast are taken overlooking the river; bedrooms are equipped with business travellers in mind.

Rooms 40 (1 fmly) (16 GF) **S** £90-£155; **D** £135-£165 (incl. bkfst) **Facilities** STV FTV Fishing Clay pigeon shooting Archery Xmas New Year **Conf** Class 100 Board 50 Thtr 220 Del from £140 to £150 **Parking** 150 **Notes** LB ® Civ Wed 150

Mercure Ardoe House Hotel & Spa

Mercure

★★★★ 73% HOTEL

☎ 01224 860600 📠 01224 861283
South Deeside Rd, Blairs AB12 5YP
e-mail: h6626@accor.com
web: www.mercure-uk.com
dir: 4m W of city off B9077

From its elevated position on the banks of the River Dee, this 19th-century baronial-style mansion commands excellent countryside views. Beautifully decorated, thoughtfully equipped bedrooms are located in the main house, and in the more modern extension. Public rooms include a spa and leisure club, a cosy lounge and cocktail bar and impressive function facilities.

Rooms 109 **D** £80-£225 (incl. bkfst)* **Facilities** Spa STV ⊗ ⊗ Gym Aerobics studio Xmas New Year Wi-fi **Conf** Class 200 Board 150 Thtr 600 Del from £155 to £280 **Services** Lift **Parking** 220 **Notes** LB ® Civ Wed 250

The Caledonian by Thistle

thistle

★★★★ 71% HOTEL

☎ 0870 333 9151 📠 0870 333 9251
10-14 Union Ter AB10 1WE
e-mail: aberdeencaledonian@thistle.co.uk
web: www.thistlehotels.com/aberdeencaledonian
dir: Follow signs to city centre & Union St. Turn into Union Terrace. Hotel on left

Centrally located just off Union Street and overlooking Union Terrace Gardens this traditional hotel offers comfortable and well-appointed bedrooms, and public areas in keeping with the age of the building. The upbeat Café Bar Caley serves informal food, but for a more formal dining experience there's the Restaurant on the Terrace. A small car park is available to the rear.

Rooms 80 (1 fmly) **Facilities** STV Wi-fi **Conf** Class 50 Board 30 Thtr 80 Del from £100 to £195* **Services** Lift **Parking** 22 **Notes** ® Civ Wed 40

Malmaison Aberdeen

★★★ 86% ®® HOTEL

☎ 01224 327370 📠 01224 327371
49-53 Queens Rd AB15 4YP
e-mail: info.aberdeen@malmaison.com
dir: A90, 3rd exit onto Queens Rd at 3rd rdbt, hotel on right

Popular with business travellers and as a function venue, this well-established hotel lies east of the city centre. Public areas include a reception lounge and an intimate restaurant; however the extensive bar menu remains a preferred choice for many regulars. There are two styles of accommodation, with the superior rooms being particularly comfortable and well equipped.

Rooms 80 (33 GF) **S** £95-£375; **D** £95-£375* **Facilities** Spa STV Gym New Year Wi-fi **Conf** Board 12 **Services** Lift **Parking** 45 **Notes** LB

Atholl

★★★ 81% HOTEL

☎ 01224 323505 📠 01224 321555
54 Kings Gate AB15 4YN
e-mail: info@atholl-aberdeen.co.uk
web: www.atholl-aberdeen.com
dir: In West End 400yds from Anderson Drive (A90)

High levels of hospitality and guest care are found at this hotel which is set in the suburbs within easy reach of central amenities and the ring road. The modern bedrooms include free broadband. Guests can choose between the restaurant and bar to enjoy the great value lunch and dinner menus.

Rooms 34 (1 fmly) **S** £60-£105; **D** £80-£150 (incl. bkfst)* **Conf** Class 25 Board 25 Thtr 60 **Parking** 60 **Notes** LB ® Closed 1 Jan

The Mariner Hotel

★★★ 79% ® HOTEL

☎ 01224 588901 📠 01224 571621
349 Great Western Rd AB10 6NW
e-mail: info@themarinerhotel.co.uk
dir: E off Anderson Drive (A90) at Great Western Rd. Hotel on right on corner of Gray St

This well maintained, family operated hotel is located west of the city centre. The smart, spacious bedrooms are well equipped and particularly comfortable, with executive suites available. The public rooms are restricted to the lounge bar, which is food driven, and the Atlantis Restaurant that showcases the region's wide choice of excellent seafood and meats.

Rooms 25 (8 annexe) (4 GF) **S** £55-£100; **D** £85-£130 (incl. bkfst)* **Facilities** STV New Year Wi-fi **Parking** 51 **Notes** ®

ABERDEEN *continued*

Thistle Aberdeen Altens

thistle

★★★ 78% HOTEL

☎ 0871 376 9002 📄 0871 376 9102
Souter Head Rd, Altens AB12 3LF
e-mail: aberdeenaltens@thistle.co.uk
web: www.thistle.com/aberdeenaltens
dir: A90 onto A956 signed Aberdeen Harbour. Hotel just off rdbt

Popular with oil industry personnel, this large purpose-built hotel lies in the Altens area, south east of the city. It's worth asking for one of the executive bedrooms that provide excellent space. Guests can eat in the restaurant, brasserie or the bar.

Rooms 216 (7 fmly) (39 GF) (2 smoking) **S** £50-£195; **D** £50-£195* **Facilities** STV 🏊 Gym Sauna Steam room Solarium Aerobic studio New Year Wi-fi **Conf** Class 144 Board 30 Thtr 400 **Services** Lift **Parking** 300 **Notes** LB Civ Wed 150

The Craighaar

★★★ 77% HOTEL

☎ 01224 712275 📄 01224 716362
Waterton Rd, Bucksburn AB21 9HS
e-mail: info@craighaar.co.uk
dir: From A96 (Airport/Inverness) onto A947, hotel signed

Conveniently located for the airport, this welcoming hotel is a popular base for business people and tourists alike. Guests can make use of a quiet library lounge, and enjoy meals in the bar or restaurant. All bedrooms are well equipped, plus there is a wing of duplex suites that provide additional comfort.

Rooms 55 (6 fmly) (18 GF) (6 smoking) **S** £109; **D** £129 (incl. bkfst) **Facilities** STV FTV Wi-fi **Conf** Class 33 Board 30 Thtr 90 **Parking** 80 **Notes** LB ⊗ Closed 26 Dec Civ Wed 40

Holiday Inn Aberdeen-Bridge of Don

★★★ 74% HOTEL

☎ 0870 400 9046 📄 01224 823923
Claymore Dr, Bridge of Don AB23 8BL
web: www.holidayinn.co.uk

Situated three miles north of the city and adjoining the Exhibition and Conference Centre, this purpose-built hotel caters well for the business traveller and for guests on a leisure break. Bedrooms are well presented and offer a good range of amenities. Public areas are open-plan with flat-screen TVs in the bar area. At the time of going to press we were informed that this hotel will close for redevelopment in early 2010. Please see the AA website (the.AA.com) for up-to-date information.

Rooms 123

Express by Holiday Inn Aberdeen City Centre

BUDGET HOTEL

☎ 01224 623500 📄 01224 623523
Chapel St AB10 1SQ
e-mail: info@hieaberdeen.co.uk
web: www.hiexpress.com/exaberdeencc
dir: In west end of city, just off Union Street

A modern hotel ideal for families and business travellers. Fresh and uncomplicated, the spacious rooms include Sky TV, power shower and tea and coffee-making facilities. Continental buffet breakfast is included in the room rate; other meals may be taken at the nearby family pub or restaurant. See also the Hotel Groups pages.

Rooms 155 (102 fmly) (30 smoking) **S** £49-£149; **D** £49-£149 (incl. bkfst)* **Conf** Class 18 Board 16 Thtr 35

Express by Holiday Inn Aberdeen-Exhibition Centre

BUDGET HOTEL

☎ 0871 423 4876
Parkway East, Bridge of Don AB23 8AJ
e-mail: info@hieaberdeenexhibitioncentre.co.uk

Rooms 155 **Conf** Board 18 Thtr 35

Travelodge Aberdeen Bucksburn

BUDGET HOTEL

☎ 0871 984 6118 📄 01224 715609
Inverurie Rd, Bucksburn AB21 9BB
web: www.travelodge.co.uk
dir: West of A96 & A947 junct, towards Inverurie

Travelodge offers good quality, good value, budget accommodation. All offer family rooms sleeping up to four (two adults, two children) with en suite bathroom/shower-room, remote-control TV, tea- and coffee-making

facilities and comfortable beds. Food options vary. Breakfast is at the on-site Bar Café restaurant (if available) or to take away. See also Hotel Groups pages.

Rooms 48 **S** fr £29; **D** fr £29

Travelodge Aberdeen Central

BUDGET HOTEL

☎ 0871 984 6117 📄 01224 584587
9 Bridge St AB11 6JL
web: www.travelodge.co.uk
dir: Into city on A90. Lodge at junct of Union St & Bridge St

Rooms 97 **S** fr £29; **D** fr £29

ABERDEEN AIRPORT   Map 23 NJ81

Thistle Aberdeen Airport

thistle

★★★★ 79% HOTEL

☎ 0871 376 9001 📄 0871 376 9101
Aberdeen Airport, Argyll Rd AB21 0AF
e-mail: aberdeenairport@thistle.co.uk
web: www.thistle.com/aberdeenairport
dir: Adjacent to Aberdeen Airport

Ideally located at the entrance to the airport this hotel offers ample parking plus a courtesy bus service to the terminal. This is a well presented establishment that benefits from good-sized bedrooms and comfortable public areas. Just Gym offers a good variety of exercise equipment.

Rooms 147 (3 fmly) (74 GF) (18 smoking) **S** £65-£195; **D** £75-£205 (incl. bkfst)* **Facilities** STV Gym Wi-fi **Conf** Class 350 Board 100 Thtr 600 Del from £135 to £165* **Parking** 300 **Notes** LB ⊗

Aberdeen Marriott Hotel

Marriott
HOTELS & RESORTS

★★★★ 74% HOTEL

☎ 01224 770011 📄 01224 722347
Overton Circle, Dyce AB21 7AZ
e-mail: reservations.scotland@marriotthotels.com
web: www.aberdeenmarriott.co.uk
dir: follow A96 to Bucksburn, right at rdbt onto A947. Hotel in 2m at 2nd rdbt

Close to the airport and conveniently located for the business district, this purpose-built hotel is a popular conference venue. The well-proportioned bedrooms come with many thoughtful extras. Public areas include an informal bar and lounge, a split-level restaurant and a leisure centre that can be accessed directly from a number of bedrooms.

Rooms 155 (81 fmly) (61 GF) (10 smoking) **Facilities** STV 🏊 supervised Gym Saunas (male & female) Solarium New Year Wi-fi **Conf** Class 200 Board 60 Thtr 400 Del from £190 to £240* **Services** Air con **Parking** 180 **Notes** ⊗ Civ Wed 90

Menzies Dyce Aberdeen Airport

MenziesHotels

★★★ 74% HOTEL

☎ 01224 723101 📠 01224 773883
Farburn Ter, Dyce AB21 7DW
e-mail: dyce@menzieshotels.co.uk
dir: A96/A947 airport E after 1m turn left at lights. Hotel in 250yds

Benefiting from a refurbishment throughout this hotel is transformed. Spacious, well-equipped bedrooms cater well for the needs of the modern traveller. Public areas are welcoming and comfortable. Secure parking and Wi-fi are also provided.

Rooms 198 (198 annexe) (3 fmly) (107 GF) (54 smoking)
S £60–£180; **D** £60–£180* **Facilities** STV Xmas New Year Wi-fi **Conf** Class 160 Board 120 Thtr 400 Del from £120 to £165* **Parking** 150 **Notes** Civ Wed 220

Travelodge Aberdeen Airport

Travelodge

BUDGET HOTEL

☎ 0871 984 6309 📠 01224 772968
Burnside Dr, off Riverside Dr, Dyce AB21 0HW
web: www.travelodge.co.uk
dir: From Aberdeen A96 towards Inverness, right at rdbt onto A947, at 2nd rdbt right then 2nd right

Travelodge offers good quality, good value, budget accommodation. All offer family rooms sleeping up to four (two adults, two children) with en suite bathroom/shower-room, remote-control TV, tea- and coffee-making facilities and comfortable beds. Food options vary. Breakfast is at the on-site Bar Café restaurant (if available) or to take away. See also Hotel Groups pages.

Rooms 40 **S** fr £29; **D** fr £29

ABERDEENSHIRE

ABOYNE
Map 23 NO59

Huntly Arms

OXFORD
HOTELS & INNS

★★★ 68% HOTEL

☎ 01339 886101 📠 01339 886804
Charlestown Rd AB34 5HS
e-mail: generalmanager.huntlyarms@ohiml.com
web: www.oxfordhotelsandinns.com
dir: On A93 from Ballater to Aberdeen

This popular hotel, originally built in 1432, is among the oldest coaching inns in Scotland and enjoys a prominent position in the charming village of Aboyne. The bedrooms are thoughtfully equipped and brightly decorated, and the day rooms extend to a traditionally-styled dining room and a cosy bar. A warm welcome is assured from the friendly staff.

Rooms 49 (4 fmly) **Facilities** ♫ Xmas New Year **Conf** Class 70 Board 70 Thtr 120 **Parking** 10 **Notes** LB ⊗

BALLATER
Map 23 NO39

INSPECTORS' CHOICE

Darroch Learg

★★★ ◉◉◉ SMALL HOTEL

☎ 013397 55443 📠 013397 55252
Braemar Rd AB35 5UX
e-mail: enquiries@darrochlearg.co.uk
web: www.darrochlearg.co.uk
dir: on A93, W of Ballater

Set high above the road in extensive wooded grounds, this long-established hotel offers superb views over the hills and countryside of Royal Deeside. Nigel and Fiona Franks are caring and attentive hosts who improve their hotel every year. Bedrooms, some with four-poster beds, are individually styled, bright and spacious. Food is a highlight of any visit, whether it is a freshly prepared breakfast or the fine cuisine served in the delightful conservatory restaurant.

Rooms 17 (5 annexe) (1 GF) **S** £130–£190;
D £210–£310 (incl. bkfst & dinner) **Facilities** New Year **Conf** Board 12 Thtr 25 Del from £155 to £220 **Parking** 25 **Notes** LB Closed Xmas & Jan (ex New Year)

Loch Kinord

★★★ 80% ◉ HOTEL

☎ 013398 85229 📠 013398 87007
Ballater Rd, Dinnet AB35 5JY
e-mail: stay@kinord.com
dir: Between Aboyne & Ballater, on A93, in village of Dinnet

Family-run, this roadside hotel is well located for leisure and sporting pursuits. It has lots of character and a friendly atmosphere. There are two bars, one outside and a cosy one inside, plus a dining room with a bold colour scheme. Bedrooms are stylish and have smart bathrooms.

Rooms 20 (3 fmly) (4 GF) **Facilities** Pool table Xmas Child facilities **Conf** Class 30 Board 30 Thtr 40 **Parking** 20 **Notes** LB Civ Wed 50

Cambus O'May

★★★ 🅰 HOTEL

☎ 013397 55428 📠 013397 55428
AB35 5SE
e-mail: mckechnie@cambusomay.freeserve.co.uk
web: www.cambusomayhotel.co.uk
dir: A93 from Ballater, 4m towards Aberdeen, hotel on left

Rooms 12 (1 fmly) **S** £45–£48; **D** £90–£106 (incl. bkfst) **Parking** 12 **Notes** LB No credit cards

The Green Inn

◉◉ RESTAURANT WITH ROOMS

☎ 013397 55701
9 Victoria Rd AB35 5QQ
e-mail: info@green-inn.com
web: www.green-inn.com
dir: In village centre

A former temperance hotel, the Green Inn enjoys a central location in the pretty village of Ballater. Bedrooms are all of a high standard and attractively presented. The restaurant has a strong reputation for its fine cuisine, which can be enjoyed in the stylish conservatory restaurant. Breakfast is equally enjoyable and not to be missed. Genuine hospitality from the enthusiastic proprietors is a real feature of any stay.

Rooms 3

The Auld Kirk

◉ RESTAURANT WITH ROOMS

☎ 01339 755762 & 07918 698000 📠 0700 6037 559
Braemar Rd AB35 5RQ
e-mail: info@theauldkirk.com
dir: From A93 Braemar, on right just before town centre

A Victorian Scottish Free Church building that is now a contemporary restaurant with rooms boasting newly refurbished and well-appointed bedrooms and bathrooms. Many original features of this kirk have been restored and incorporated in the design. The Spirit Restaurant with its high ceilings and tall windows provides a wonderful setting to enjoy the award-winning, seasonal food. There is a stylish bar with a good selection of malts and a terrace for alfresco eating when the weather permits.

Rooms 7 (1 fmly)

BANCHORY   Map 23 NO69

Banchory Lodge

★★★ 81% ◉ COUNTRY HOUSE HOTEL

☎ 01330 822625 & 822681 📄 01330 825019
AB31 5HS
e-mail: enquiries@banchorylodge.co.uk
web: www.banchorylodge.co.uk
dir: off A93, 13m W of Aberdeen, hotel off Dee St

This hotel enjoys a scenic setting in grounds by the River Dee. Inviting public areas include a choice of lounges, a cosy bar and a restaurant with views of the river. Bedrooms come in two distinct styles; those in the original part of the house contrasting with the newer wing rooms, which are particularly spacious.

Rooms 22 (10 fmly) (3 smoking) **S** £90-£120; **D** £130-£150 (incl. bkfst)* **Facilities** Fishing Children's play area Xmas New Year Child facilities **Conf** Class 30 Board 28 Thtr 90 Del from £140* **Parking** 50 **Notes** LB Civ Wed 150

Best Western Burnett Arms

★★★ 64% SMALL HOTEL

☎ 01330 824944 📄 01330 825553
25 High St AB31 5TD
e-mail: theburnett@btconnect.com
dir: Town centre on N side of A93

This popular hotel is located in the heart of the town centre and gives easy access to the many attractions of Royal Deeside. Public areas include a choice of eating and drinking options, with food served in the restaurant, bar and foyer lounge. Bedrooms are thoughtfully equipped and comfortably modern.

Rooms 18 (1 fmly) **S** £69-£79; **D** £94-£98 (incl. bkfst) **Facilities** STV FTV Xmas New Year Wi-fi **Conf** Class 50 Board 50 Thtr 100 Del from £96 to £106 **Parking** 23 **Notes** Civ Wed 100

See advert on page 560

HUNTLY   Map 23 NJ53

Gordon Arms Hotel

★★ 64% HOTEL

☎ 01466 792288 📄 01466 794556
The Square AB54 8AF
e-mail: reception@gordonarms.demon.co.uk
dir: off A96 (Aberdeen to Inverness road) at Huntly. Hotel immediately on left after entering town square

This friendly, family-run hotel is located in the town square and offers a good selection of tasty, well-portioned dishes served in the bar, and also in the restaurant at weekends or midweek by appointment. Bedrooms come in a variety of sizes, but all have a good range of accessories.

Rooms 13 (3 fmly) **Facilities** FTV ♬ **Conf** Class 80 Board 60 Thtr 160 **Notes** LB

INVERURIE   Map 23 NJ72

Macdonald Pittodrie House

MACDONALD
HOTELS & RESORTS

★★★★ 74% HOTEL

☎ 0870 1942111 & 01467 681744 📄 01467 681648
Chapel of Garioch, Pitcaple AB51 5HS
e-mail: pittodrie@macdonald-hotels.co.uk
web: www.macdonald-hotels.com/pittodrie
dir: From A96 towards Inverness, pass Inverurie under bridge with lights. Turn left & follow signs

Set in extensive grounds this house dates from the 15th century and retains many of its historic features. Public rooms include a gracious drawing room, restaurant, and a cosy bar boasting an impressive selection of whiskies. The well-proportioned bedrooms are found in both the original house and in the extension that was designed to match the existing building.

Rooms 27 (3 fmly) **Facilities** STV Clay pigeon shooting Quad biking Outdoor activities Xmas New Year Wi-fi **Conf** Class 75 Board 50 Thtr 150 **Parking** 200 **Notes** Civ Wed 120

KILDRUMMY   Map 23 NJ41

Kildrummy Castle Hotel

★★★★ 🅰 COUNTRY HOUSE HOTEL

☎ 019755 71288 📄 019755 71345
AB33 8RA
e-mail: kildrummy@btconnect.com
web: www.kildrummycastlehotel.co.uk
dir: Off A97 (Huntly to Ballater road)

Rooms 16 (2 fmly) **S** £95-£120; **D** £169-£213 (incl. bkfst)* **Facilities** Fishing Xmas New Year Wi-fi **Conf** Board 18 Del from £165* **Parking** 25 **Notes** LB Closed 3-24 Jan

NEWBURGH   Map 23 NJ92

Udny Arms

★★★ 70% HOTEL   OXFORD
HOTELS & INNS

☎ 01358 789444 📄 01358 789012
Main St AB41 6BL
e-mail: generalmanager.udnyarms@ohiml.com
web: www.oxfordhotelsandinns.com
dir: A90 N, 8m N of Aberdeen turn right to Newburgh (A975), hotel in village centre

Overlooking the picture postcard scenery of the Ythan Estuary and the Newburgh links golf course this hotel offers friendly service in relaxed and comfortable surroundings. The well equipped and nicely presented bedrooms have flat screen TVs. The split-level restaurant looks out onto the golf course.

Rooms 30 (1 fmly) **Facilities** Xmas New Year Wi-fi **Conf** Class 100 Board 60 Thtr 60 Del from £115 to £185 **Parking** 70 **Notes** Civ Wed 115

Meldrum House Hotel Golf & Country Estate

★★★ 85% ⊛ COUNTRY HOUSE HOTEL

☎ 01651 872294   🖷 01651 872464
AB51 0AE
e-mail: enquiries@meldrumhouse.co.uk
dir: 11m from Aberdeen on the A947 Aberdeen to Banff road

Set in 350 acres of wooded parkland this imposing baronial country mansion has a golf course as its centrepiece. Tastefully restored to highlight its original character it provides a peaceful retreat. Bedrooms are massive, and like the public rooms, transport guests back to a bygone era, but at the same time provide stylish modern amenities including smart bathrooms.

Rooms 22 (13 annexe) (1 fmly) (1 GF) **S** £65-£140; **D** £80-£180 (incl. bkfst)* **Facilities** FTV ⌁ 18 Putt green ⚑ Xmas New Year Wi-fi **Conf** Class 20 Board 30 Thtr 80 Del from £125 to £145* **Parking** 45 **Notes** LB Civ Wed 70

Buchan Braes Hotel

★★★★ 75% ⊛ HOTEL

☎ 01779 871471   🖷 01779 871472
Boddam AB42 3AR
e-mail: info@buchanbraes.co.uk
dir: From Aberdeen take A90 , follow Fraserburgh/Peterhead signs. Right at Toll of Birness. 1st right in Stirling signed Boddam. 50mtrs, 1st right

A contemporary hotel located in Boddam that is an excellent base for exploring the attractions of this wonderful part of Scotland. There is an open-plan lounge for drinks and snacks and the Grill Room with an open

kitchen that offers a weekly changing, seasonal menu of locally sourced produce. All the bedrooms, including three suites, have 32" flat-screen TVs with satellite channels, king-sized beds and free Wi-fi.

Rooms 47 (1 fmly) (27 GF) **S** £95-£110; **D** £105-£120 (incl. bkfst)* **Facilities** FTV Xmas New Year Wi-fi **Conf** Class 100 Board 80 Thtr 250 **Services** Lift **Parking** 40 **Notes** ⊗ Civ Wed 220

Palace

★★★ 80% HOTEL

☎ 01779 474821   🖷 01779 476119
Prince St AB42 1PL
e-mail: info@palacehotel.co.uk
web: www.palacehotel.co.uk
dir: A90 from Aberdeen, follow signs to Peterhead, on entering town turn into Prince St, then right into main car park

This town centre hotel is popular with business travellers and for social events. Bedrooms come in two styles, with the executive rooms being particularly smart and spacious. Public areas include a themed bar, an informal diner reached via a spiral staircase, and a brasserie restaurant and cocktail bar.

Rooms 64 (2 fmly) (14 GF) **S** £70-£80; **D** £80-£90 (incl. bkfst)* **Facilities** Pool table Snooker room ♫ Xmas New Year Wi-fi **Conf** Class 120 Board 50 Thtr 250 Del from £130 to £150* **Services** Lift **Parking** 50 **Notes** Civ Wed 280

Carnoustie Golf Hotel & Spa

★★★★ 76% ⊛ HOTEL   OXFORD HOTELS & INNS

☎ 01241 411999 & 411978   🖷 01241 411998
The Links DD7 7JE
e-mail: reservations.carnoustie@ohiml.com
web: www.oxfordhotelsandinns.com
dir: Adjacent to Carnoustie Golf Links

This fine hotel enjoys an enviable location and is adjacent to the 1st and 18th green of the famous Championship Course of Carnoustie. All bedrooms are spacious and attractively presented; most overlook the magnificent course and enjoy breathtaking coastal views. Fine dining

can be enjoyed in the restaurant with more informal meals served in the comfortable bar.

Rooms 85 (11 fmly) **S** £63.50-£389.50; **D** £69-£395 (incl. bkfst)* **Facilities** Spa FTV ⓢ Putt green Gym Xmas New Year Wi-fi **Conf** Class 200 Board 100 Thtr 350 Del from £89 to £189* **Services** Lift Air con **Parking** 100 **Notes** LB ⊗ Civ Wed 325

INSPECTORS' CHOICE

Castleton House

★★★ ⊛⊛ COUNTRY HOUSE HOTEL

☎ 01307 840340   🖷 01307 840506
Castleton of Eassie DD8 1SJ
e-mail: hotel@castletonglamis.co.uk
web: www.castletonglamis.co.uk
dir: On A94 midway between Forfar & Coupar Angus, 3m W of Glamis

Set in its own grounds and with a moat, this impressive Victorian house has a relaxed and friendly atmosphere. Accommodation is provided in individually designed, spacious bedrooms. Personal service from the enthusiastic proprietors is noteworthy and many guests return time and again. Accomplished cooking, utilising the best local produce, is served in the conservatory restaurant.

Rooms 6 (2 fmly) **Facilities** FTV Putt green ⚑ Xmas Wi-fi **Conf** Class 20 Board 20 Thtr 30 **Parking** 50 **Notes** Civ Wed 50

Gordon's

⊛⊛ RESTAURANT WITH ROOMS

☎ 01241 830364   🖷 01241 830364
Main St DD11 5RN
e-mail: gordonsrest@aol.com
dir: Off A92, follow signs for Inverkeilor

It's worth a detour off the main road to this family-run restaurant with rooms set in the centre of the village. It has earned AA Rosettes for its dinners, though the excellent breakfasts are equally memorable. A huge fire dominates the restaurant on cooler evenings and there is a small lounge with limited seating. The attractive bedrooms are tastefully decorated and thoughtfully equipped, the larger two being furnished in pine.

Rooms 5 (1 annexe)

ARGYLL & BUTE

ARDUAINE Map 20 NM71

Loch Melfort
★★★ 78% ◎◎ HOTEL

☎ 01852 200233 ▤ 01852 200214
PA34 4XG
e-mail: reception@lochmelfort.co.uk
web: www.lochmelfort.co.uk
dir: on A816, midway between Oban & Lochgilphead

Enjoying one of the finest locations on the West Coast, this popular, family-run hotel has outstanding views across Asknish Bay towards the Islands of Jura, Scarba and Shuna. Accommodation is provided in either the balconied rooms of the Cedar wing or the more traditional rooms in the main hotel. Dining options include the main restaurant offering stunning views or the more informal bistro.

Rooms 25 (20 annexe) (2 fmly) (10 GF) **D** £180-£250 (incl. bkfst & dinner)* **Facilities** 4 moorings Beauty treatments ♫ Xmas New Year Wi-fi Child facilities **Conf** Class 40 Board 20 Thtr 50 Del from £100 to £200* **Parking** 50 **Notes** Closed 12 Jan-2 Feb Civ Wed 100

CAMPBELTOWN Map 20 NR72

White Hart
★★ 65% HOTEL

OXFORD
HOTELS & INNS

☎ 01586 552440 ▤ 01586 554972
Main St PA28 6AN
e-mail: whitehearthotel@ohiml.com
web: www.oxfordhotelsandinns.com
dir: From Glasgow A82, A83 follow signs to Campbeltown. 1m, right at Main St/Longrow junct. Hotel 100mtrs

Located in the heart of the town just a few minutes walk from the harbour, this hotel offers good value-for-money accommodation. For dinner there is a good choice with a menu backed up by an array of specials. The friendly bar is popular with locals and residents alike; entertainment, such as quizzes, takes place during on week nights.

Rooms 19 (2 fmly) **Facilities** STV ♫ Xmas New Year Wi-fi **Conf** Class 32 Board 12 Thtr 32 **Notes** LB

CONNEL Map 20 NM93

Falls of Lora
★★★ 77% HOTEL

☎ 01631 710483 ▤ 01631 710694
PA37 1PB
e-mail: enquiries@fallsoflora.com
web: www.fallsoflora.com
dir: From Glasgow take A82, A85. Hotel 0.5m past Connel sign

Personally run and welcoming, this long-established and thriving holiday hotel enjoys inspiring views over Loch Etive. The spacious ground floor takes in a comfortable, traditional lounge and a cocktail bar with over a hundred whiskies and an open log fire. Guests can eat in the popular, informal bistro, which is open all day. Bedrooms come in a variety of styles, ranging from the cosy standard rooms to high quality luxury rooms.

Rooms 30 (4 fmly) (4 GF) (30 smoking) **S** £47.50-£59.50; **D** £55-£139 (incl. bkfst)* **Facilities** Wi-fi Child facilities **Conf** Class 20 Board 15 Thtr 45 **Parking** 40 **Notes** LB Closed mid Dec & Jan

See advert on page 568

DUNOON Map 20 NS17

Selborne
★★ 75% HOTEL

Leisureplex

☎ 01369 702761 ▤ 01369 704032
Clyde St, West Bay PA23 7HU
e-mail: selborne.dunoon@alfatravel.co.uk
dir: From Caledonian MacBrayne pier. Past castle, left into Jane St, right into Clyde St

This holiday hotel is situated overlooking the West Bay and provides unrestricted views of the Clyde Estuary towards the Isles of Cumbrae. Tour groups are especially well catered for in this good-value establishment, which offers entertainment most nights. Bedrooms are comfortable and many have sea views.

Rooms 98 (6 fmly) (14 GF) **Facilities** FTV Pool table Table tennis ♫ Xmas New Year **Services** Lift **Parking** 30 **Notes** LB ⊗ Closed Dec-Feb (ex Xmas) RS Nov & Mar

ERISKA Map 20 NM94

INSPECTORS' CHOICE

Isle of Eriska
★★★★★ ◎◎◎
COUNTRY HOUSE HOTEL

☎ 01631 720371 ▤ 01631 720531
Eriska PA37 1SD
e-mail: office@eriska-hotel.co.uk
dir: Exit A85 at Connel, onto A828, follow for 4m, then follow hotel signs from N of Benderloch

Situated on its own private island with delightful beaches and walking trails, this hotel offers a tranquil, personal setting for total relaxation. Spacious bedrooms, some now refurbished, are comfortable and boast some fine antique pieces. Local seafood, meats and game feature prominently on the award-winning menu, as do vegetables and herbs grown in the hotel's kitchen garden. Leisure facilities include an indoor swimming pool, gym, spa treatment rooms and a small golf course.

Rooms 23 (2 GF) **Facilities** Spa FTV ③ supervised ↓ 9 ❀ Putt green Fishing ⤴ Gym Sauna Steam room Skeet shooting Nature trails Xmas New Year Wi-fi **Conf** Class 30 Board 30 Thtr 30 Del from £200 to £400* **Parking** 40 **Notes** Closed Jan Civ Wed 50

HELENSBURGH Map 20 NS28

Innkeeper's Lodge
Helensburgh

BUDGET HOTEL

☎ 0845 112 6005 ▤ 0845 112 6295
112-17 West Clyde St G84 8ES
web: www.innkeeperslodge.com/helensburgh
dir: M8 junct 30, M898. Over Erskine Bridge take exit for Crianlarich onto A82 to Dumbarton. At junct with A814, left, at rdbt follow Helensburgh signs. 10m, Lodge on right near pier

Innkeeper's Lodge represents an exciting, high value concept within the budget hotel market. Comfortable bedrooms provide excellent facilities that include satellite TV and modem points. Options include family rooms; and for the corporate guest, cutting edge IT includes Wi-fi access. Food is served all day in the adjacent Country Pub. The extensive continental breakfast is complimentary. See also the Hotel Groups pages.

Rooms 44 **Conf** Thtr 200

KILCHRENAN — Map 20 NN02

The Ardanaiseig

★★★ 86% ◉◉ COUNTRY HOUSE HOTEL

☎ 01866 833333 🖹 01866 833222
by Loch Awe PA35 1HE
e-mail: ardanaiseig@clara.net
dir: From A85 at Taynuilt onto B845 to Kilchrenan. Left in front of pub (road very narrow) signed 'Ardanaiseig Hotel' & 'No Through Road'. Continue for 3m

Set amid lovely gardens and breathtaking scenery beside the shore of Loch Awe, this peaceful country-house hotel was built in a Scottish baronial style in 1834. Many fine pieces of furniture are evident in the bedrooms and charming day rooms, which include a drawing room, a library bar and an elegant dining room. Dinner provides the highlight of any visit with skilfully cooked dishes making excellent use of local, seasonal produce.

Rooms 18 (4 fmly) (5 GF) **S** £64-£137; **D** £128-£274 (incl. bkfst) **Facilities** FTV Fishing ⛵ Boating Clay pigeon shooting Bikes for hire Xmas New Year Wi-fi **Parking** 20 **Notes** Closed 2 Jan-1 Feb Civ Wed 50

Taychreggan

★★★ 85% ◉◉
COUNTRY HOUSE HOTEL

☎ 01866 833211 & 833366 🖹 01866 833244
PA35 1HQ
e-mail: info@taychregganhotel.co.uk
dir: W from Crianlarich on A85 to Taynuilt, S for 7m on B845 (single track) to Kilchrenan

Surrounded by stunning Highland scenery this stylish and superbly presented hotel, once a drover's cottage, enjoys an idyllic setting in 40 acres of wooded grounds on the shores of Loch Awe. Now refurbished the hotel has a smart bar with adjacent courtyard Orangerie and a choice of quiet lounges with deep, luxurious sofas. A well earned reputation has been achieved by the kitchen for the skilfully prepared dinners that showcase the local and seasonal Scottish larder. Families, and also dogs and their owners, are welcome.

Rooms 18 **S** £85-£167; **D** £110-£274 (incl. bkfst)*
Facilities FTV Fishing ⛵ Clay pigeon shooting Falconry Archery Air rifle range Mock deer stalk New Year Wi-fi **Conf** Class 15 Board 20 **Parking** 40 **Notes** Closed 25-26 Dec & 3 Jan-10 Feb Civ Wed 60

LOCHGILPHEAD — Map 20 NR88

Cairnbaan

★★★ 77% ◉ HOTEL

☎ 01546 603668 🖹 01546 606045
Crinan Canal, Cairnbaan PA31 8SJ
e-mail: info@cairnbaan.com
web: www.cairnbaan.com
dir: 2m N, A816 from Lochgilphead, hotel off B841

Located on the Crinan Canal, this small hotel offers relaxed hospitality in a delightful setting. Bedrooms are thoughtfully equipped, generally spacious and benefit from stylish decor. Fresh seafood is a real feature in both the formal restaurant and the comfortable bar area. Alfresco dining is popular in the warmer months.

Rooms 12 **Facilities** Xmas **Conf** Class 100 Board 80 Thtr 160 **Parking** 53 **Notes** Civ Wed 120

LUSS — Map 20 NS39

The Lodge on Loch Lomond

★★★★ 74% ◉◉ HOTEL

☎ 01436 860201 🖹 01436 860203
G83 8PA
e-mail: res@loch-lomond.co.uk
web: www.loch-lomond.co.uk
dir: off A82, follow sign for hotel

This hotel is idyllically set on the shores of Loch Lomond. Public areas consist of an open-plan, split-level bar and fine dining restaurant overlooking the loch. The pine-finished bedrooms also enjoy the views and are comfortable, spacious and well equipped; all have saunas and some have DVDs and internet access. There is a stunning state-of-the-art leisure suite.

Rooms 47 (17 annexe) (20 fmly) (13 GF) **Facilities** Spa STV FTV 🏊 Fishing Boating Xmas New Year Wi-fi **Conf** Class 80 Board 60 Thtr 150 **Parking** 120 **Notes** Civ Wed 100

OBAN — Map 20 NM93

Manor House

★★★ 82% ◉ HOTEL

☎ 01631 562087 🖹 01631 563053
Gallanach Rd PA34 4LS
e-mail: info@manorhouseoban.com
web: www.manorhouseoban.com
dir: follow MacBrayne Ferries signs, pass ferry entrance for hotel on right

Handy for the ferry terminal and with views of the bay and harbour, this elegant Georgian residence was built in 1780 as the dower house for the family of the Duke of Argyll. Comfortable and attractive public rooms invite relaxation, whilst most of the well-equipped bedrooms are furnished with period pieces.

Rooms 11 (1 GF) **Facilities** New Year Wi-fi **Parking** 20 **Notes** No children 12yrs Closed 25-26 Dec Civ Wed 30

Falls of Lora

★★★ 77% HOTEL

☎ 01631 710483 🖹 01631 710694
PA37 1PB
e-mail: enquiries@fallsoflora.com
web: www.fallsoflora.com

(For full entry see Connel & advert on page 568)

The Oban Caledonian Hotel

★★★ 75% HOTEL

☎ 0844 855 9135 🖹 01631 562998
Station Square PA34 5RT
e-mail: gm.caledonian@foliohotels.com
web: www.foliohotels.com/caledonian
dir: at head of main pier, close to rail terminal

This Victorian hotel, overlooking the bay, has an enviable location close to the ferry terminal and parking, as well as Oban's many attractions. Public areas are modern and stylish and include a smart restaurant, spacious lounges and an informal dining option in Café Caledonian. Attractive bedrooms come in a number of different styles and grades, some with comfortable seating areas, feature bathrooms and fine sea views.

Rooms 59 (6 fmly) **Facilities** Xmas New Year Wi-fi **Conf** Class 90 Board 50 Thtr 100 **Services** Lift **Notes** Civ Wed 100

OBAN *continued*

Royal
★★★ 73% HOTEL

☎ 01631 563021 📠 01631 562811
Argyll Sqaure PA34 4BE
e-mail: salesroyaloban@strathmorehotels.com
dir: A82 from Glasgow towards Loch Lomond & Crianlarich then A85 (pass Loch Awe) to Oban

Well situated in the heart of Oban, just minutes from the ferry terminal and with all the shops on its doorstep, this hotel really is central. The comfortable and well presented bedrooms differ in size, and all public areas are smart.

Rooms 91 (5 fmly) **Facilities** ♫ Xmas New Year Wi-fi **Conf** Class 60 Board 30 Thtr 140 **Services** Lift **Parking** 25

See advert on page 617

PORT APPIN   Map 20 NM94

INSPECTORS' CHOICE

Airds
★★★★ ◉◉◉ SMALL HOTEL

☎ 01631 730236 📠 01631 730535
PA38 4DF
e-mail: airds@airds-hotel.com
web: www.airds-hotel.com
dir: from A828 (Oban to Fort William road), turn at Appin signed Port Appin. Hotel 2.5m on left

The views are stunning from this small, luxury hotel on the shores of Loch Linnhe and where the staff are delightful and nothing is too much trouble. The well-equipped bedrooms provide style and luxury whilst many bathrooms are furnished in marble and have power showers. Expertly prepared dishes, utilising the finest of ingredients, are served in the elegant dining room. Comfortable lounges with deep sofas and roaring fires provide the ideal retreat for relaxation. A real get-away-from-it-all experience.

Rooms 11 (3 fmly) (2 GF) **S** £180-£370; **D** £245-£435 (incl. bkfst & dinner)* **Facilities** FTV Putt green ⚉ Xmas New Year Wi-fi **Conf** Class 16 Board 16 Thtr 16 **Parking** 20 **Notes** RS Nov-Jan Civ Wed 40

Pierhouse
★★★ 74% SMALL HOTEL

☎ 01631 730302 & 730622 📠 01631 730400
PA38 4DE
e-mail: reservations@pierhousehotel.co.uk
web: www.pierhousehotel.co.uk
dir: A828 from Ballachulish to Oban. In Appin right at Port Appin & Lismore ferry sign. After 2.5m left after post office, hotel at end of road by pier

Originally the residence of the Pier Master, with parts of the building dating back to the 19th century, this hotel is located on the shores of Loch Linnhe with picture-postcard views to the islands of Lismore and Mull. The beautifully appointed, individually designed bedrooms have Wi-fi access and include Arran Aromatics toiletries. The hotel has a Finnish sauna, and also offers a range of treatments.

Rooms 12 (3 fmly) (6 GF) **S** £70-£100; **D** £100-£160 (incl. bkfst) **Facilities** FTV ⚉ Aromatherapy Massage Sauna New Year Wi-fi **Conf** Class 20 Board 20 Thtr 20 Del from £125 to £150 **Parking** 20 **Notes** Closed 25-26 Dec Civ Wed 70

STRACHUR Map 20 NN00

Creggans Inn

★★★ 79% ⊛ HOTEL

☎ 01369 860279 📄 01369 860637
PA27 8BX
e-mail: info@creggans-inn.co.uk
web: www.creggans-inn.co.uk
dir: A82 from Glasgow, at Tarbet take A83 towards
Cairndow, left onto A815 to Strachur

Benefiting from a super location on the shores of Loch
Fyne, this well established family-run hotel caters well for
both the leisure and corporate market. Many of the
bedrooms are generous in size and are enhanced with
picture postcard views onto the loch. During the cooler
months open log fires are lit in the bar lounge and
restaurant. Wi-fi is available throughout.

Rooms 14 (2 fmly) **S** £75-£115; **D** £100-£180 (incl. bkfst)
Facilities New Year Wi-fi **Conf** Del from £120 to £160
Parking 16 **Notes** LB Civ Wed 80

TARBERT LOCH FYNE Map 20 NR86

Stonefield Castle

★★★★ 73% ⊛ HOTEL

OXFORD
HOTELS & INNS

☎ 01880 820836 📄 01880 820929
PA29 6YJ
e-mail: reservations.stonefieldcastle.@ohiml.com
web: www.oxfordhotelsandinns.com
dir: From Glasgow take M8 towards Erskine Bridge, follow
signs for Loch Lomond on A82. From Arrochar follow signs
for A83 through Inveraray & Lochgilphead, hotel on left
2m before Tarbert

This fine baronial castle commands a superb lochside
setting amidst beautiful woodland gardens renowned for
their rhododendrons - visit in late spring to see them at
their best. Elegant public rooms are a feature, and the
picture-window restaurant offers unrivalled views across
Loch Fyne. Bedrooms are split between the main house
and a purpose-built wing.

Rooms 32 (2 fmly) (10 GF) **S** £55-£140; **D** £65-£180 (incl.
bkfst)* **Facilities** Xmas New Year Wi-fi **Conf** Class 40
Board 50 Thtr 120 Del from £135 to £195 **Services** Lift
Parking 50 **Notes** LB Civ Wed 100

TIGHNABRUAICH Map 20 NR97

INSPECTORS' CHOICE

An Lochan

★★★ ⊛⊛ SMALL HOTEL

☎ 01700 811239 📄 01700 811300
Shore Rd PA21 2BE
e-mail: info@anlochan.co.uk
web: www.anlochan.co.uk
dir: From Strachur on A886 right onto A8003 to
Tighnabruaich. Hotel on right at bottom of hill

This outstanding family-run hotel provides high levels
of personal care from the proprietors and their locally
recruited staff. Set just yards from the loch shore,
stunning views are guaranteed from many rooms,
including the elegant Crustacean Restaurant, and the
more informal Deck Restaurant. Seafood and game,
sourced on the doorstep, feature strongly on the menus.
Guest can expect to find Egyptian cotton sheets, fluffy
towels and locally produced toiletries in the
individually-styled, luxuriously appointed bedrooms.

Rooms 11 **Facilities** Sailing Fishing Windsurfing Riding
New Year Wi-fi **Conf** Class 20 Board 10 **Parking** 20
Notes Closed 4 days Xmas Civ Wed 40

CLACKMANNANSHIRE

DOLLAR
Map 21 NS99

Castle Campbell Hotel

★★★ 77% SMALL HOTEL

☎ 01259 742519 ▨ 01259 743742
11 Bridge St FK14 7DE
e-mail: bookings@castle-campbell.co.uk
web: www.castle-campbell.co.uk
dir: On A91 (Stirling to St Andrews road), in centre of
Dollar, by bridge overlooking Dollar Burn & Clock Tower

Built in 1822 as a coaching inn this small hotel offers
comfortable & welcoming public areas. Food is served in
both the stylish restaurant or the relaxed bar. Bedrooms
are comfortable with many thoughtful extras provided as
standard. Easy striking distance for Edinburgh, Glasgow,
Perth & Gleneagles is just a few miles away.

Rooms 9 (1 fmly) **S** £67.50; **D** £105 (incl. bkfst)*
Facilities Wi-fi **Conf** Class 40 Board 30 Thtr 80 **Notes** LB
Civ Wed 80

DUMFRIES & GALLOWAY

AUCHENCAIRN
Map 21 NX75

Balcary Bay

★★★ 86% ◉◉ HOTEL

☎ 01556 640217 & 640311 ▨ 01556 640272
DG7 1QZ
e-mail: reservations@balcary-bay-hotel.co.uk
web: www.balcary-bay-hotel.co.uk
dir: On A711 between Dalbeattie & Kirkcudbright, hotel
2m from village

Taking its name from the bay on which it lies, this hotel
has lawns running down to the shore. The larger
bedrooms enjoy stunning views over the bay, whilst
others overlook the gardens. Comfortable public areas
invite relaxation. Imaginative dishes feature at dinner,
accompanied by a good wine list.

Rooms 20 (1 fmly) (3 GF) **S** £70-£72; **D** £126-£156 (incl.
bkfst) **Facilities** FTV **Parking** 50 **Notes** LB Closed 1st Sun
Dec-1st Fri Feb

CARRUTHERSTOWN
Map 21 NY17

Best Western Hetland Hall

★★★ 70% HOTEL

☎ 01387 840201 ▨ 01387 840211
DG1 4JX
e-mail: info@hetlandhallhotel.co.uk
web: www.hetlandhallhotel.co.uk
dir: midway between Annan & Dumfries on A75

An imposing country house, Hetland Hall lies in 18-acres
of parkland with lovely views of the Solway Firth looking
out towards the mountains of the Lake District. It is
popular for weddings and conferences and its menus,
available in both bar and the Copper Beech restaurant,
also draw praise. Bedrooms come in contrasting styles
and sizes.

Rooms 32 (14 annexe) (5 fmly) (1 GF) **S** £49-£80;
D £49-£95 (incl. bkfst)* **Facilities** Putt green Gym
Mini pitch & putt Xmas New Year Child facilities
Conf Class 100 Board 100 Thtr 200 Del from £75 to
£110* **Parking** 60 **Notes** LB Civ Wed 150

Best Western Station

★★★ 79% HOTEL

☎ 01387 254316 📠 01387 250388
49 Lovers Walk DG1 1LT
e-mail: info@stationhotel.co.uk
web: www.stationhotel.co.uk
dir: A75, follow signs to Dumfries town centre, hotel opp railway station

This hotel, sympathetically modernised in harmony with its fine Victorian features, offers well-equipped bedrooms. The Courtyard Bistro offers a popular menu in an informal atmosphere during the evening. In addition good value meals are also served in the lounge bar and conservatory during the day.

Rooms 32 (2 fmly) **Facilities** Use of local gym Xmas
Conf Class 35 Board 30 Thtr 60 **Services** Lift **Parking** 34
Notes LB Civ Wed 60

Cairndale Hotel & Leisure Club

★★★ 78% HOTEL

☎ 01387 254111 📠 01387 240288
English St DG1 2DF
e-mail: sales@cairndalehotel.co.uk
web: www.cairndalehotel.co.uk
dir: From S on M6 take A75 to Dumfries, left at 1st rdbt, cross rail bridge to lights, hotel 1st building on left

Within walking distance of the town centre, this hotel provides a wide range of amenities, including leisure facilities and an impressive conference and entertainment centre. Bedrooms range from stylish suites to cosy singles. There's a choice of eating options in the evening. The Reivers Restaurant is smartly modern with food to match.

Cairndale Hotel & Leisure Club

Rooms 91 (22 fmly) (5 GF) **Facilities** 🕲 supervised Gym Steam room Sauna 🎵 Xmas New Year Wi-fi
Conf Class 150 Board 50 Thtr 300 **Services** Lift
Parking 100 **Notes** Civ Wed 200

Travelodge Dumfries

BUDGET HOTEL

☎ 0871 984 6134 📠 01387 750658
Annan Rd, Collin DG1 3SE
web: www.travelodge.co.uk
dir: 2m E of Dumfries, on A75

Travelodge offers good quality, good value, budget accommodation. All offer family rooms sleeping up to four (two adults, two children) with en suite bathroom/shower-room, remote-control TV, tea- and coffee-making facilities and comfortable beds. Food options vary.

continued

DUMFRIES *continued*

Breakfast is at the on-site Bar Café restaurant (if available) or to take away. See also Hotel Groups pages.

Rooms 40 **S** fr £29; **D** fr £29

GATEHOUSE OF FLEET — Map 20 NX55

Cally Palace

★★★★ 74% ⚜ COUNTRY HOUSE HOTEL

☎ 01557 814341 📄 01557 814522
DG7 2DL
e-mail: info@callypalace.co.uk
web: www.callypalace.co.uk
dir: M6 & A74, signed A75 Dumfries then Stranraer. At Gatehouse-of-Fleet turn right onto B727, left at Cally

A resort hotel with extensive leisure facilities, this grand 18th-century building is set in 500 acres of forest and parkland that incorporates its own golf course. Bedrooms are spacious and well equipped, whilst public rooms retain a quiet elegance. The short dinner menu focuses on freshly prepared dishes. A pianist plays most nights and the wearing of jacket and tie is obligatory.

Rooms 55 (7 fmly) **S** £101-£107; **D** £96-£114 (incl. bkfst & dinner)* **Facilities** ⓒ ♨ 18 🏌 Putt green Fishing 🚣 Gym Table tennis Practice fairway Xmas New Year Wi-fi **Conf** Class 40 Board 25 Thtr 40 **Services** Lift **Parking** 100 **Notes** LB ⊗ Closed Jan-early Feb

See advert on page 571

GRETNA SERVICE AREA (A74(M)) — Map 21 NY36

Days Inn Gretna Green

BUDGET HOTEL

☎ 01461 337566 📄 01461 337823
Welcome Break Service Area DG16 5HQ
e-mail: gretna.hotel@welcomebreak.co.uk
web: www.welcomebreak.co.uk
dir: between junct 21/22 on M74 - accessible from both N'bound & S'bound carriageway

This modern building offers accommodation in smart, spacious and well-equipped bedrooms suitable for families and business travellers, and all with en suite bathrooms. Continental breakfast is available and other refreshments may be taken at the nearby family restaurant. See also the Hotel Groups pages.

Rooms 64 (54 fmly) (64 GF) (20 smoking) **S** £39-£69; **D** £39-£79*

GRETNA (WITH GRETNA GREEN) — Map 21 NY36

Smiths at Gretna Green

★★★★ 74% ⚜ HOTEL

☎ 01461 337007 📄 01461 336000
Gretna Green DG16 5EA
e-mail: info@smithsgretnagreen.com
web: www.smithsgretnagreen.com
dir: From M74 junct 22 follow signs to Old Blacksmith's Shop. Hotel opposite

Located next to the World Famous Old Blacksmith's Shop Centre just off the motorway linking Scotland and England. The bedrooms offer a spacious environment, complete with flat-screen TVs, DVD players and broadband. Family rooms feature a separate children's area with bunk beds, each with its own TV. Three suites and a penthouse apartment are also available. Open-plan contemporary day rooms lead to the brasserie restaurant; impressive conference and banqueting facilities are provided.

Rooms 50 (8 fmly) **S** £110-£252; **D** £156-£480 (incl. bkfst) **Facilities** STV FTV New Year Wi-fi **Conf** Class 100 Board 40 Thtr 250 Del from £125 to £175 **Services** Lift Air con **Parking** 115 **Notes** LB Civ Wed 150

Gretna Chase

★★★ 75% HOTEL   THE INDEPENDENTS
HOTEL ASSOCIATION

☎ 01461 337517 📄 01461 337766
DG16 5JB
e-mail: enquiries@gretnachase.co.uk
dir: Off M74 onto B7076, left at top of slip road, hotel 400yds on right

With its colourful landscaped gardens, this hotel is a favourite venue for wedding parties. Bedrooms range from the comfortable, traditional, standard rooms to the impressively spacious superior and honeymoon rooms; all are well equipped. There is a foyer lounge, a spacious dining room that can accommodate functions, and a popular lounge bar serving food.

Rooms 19 (9 fmly) **S** £64.95-£150; **D** £99-£250 (incl. bkfst)* **Conf** Class 30 Board 20 Thtr 50 Del from £125 to £175* **Parking** 40 **Notes** LB ⊗

Garden House

★★★ 73% HOTEL

☎ 01461 337621 📄 01461 337692
Sarkfoot Rd DG16 5EP
e-mail: info@gardenhouse.co.uk
web: www.gardenhouse.co.uk
dir: just off M6 junct 45

This purpose-built modern hotel lies on the edge of the village. With a focus on weddings its landscaped gardens provide an ideal setting, while inside corridor walls are adorned with photographs portraying that 'special day'. Accommodation is well presented including bedrooms that overlook the Japanese water gardens.

Rooms 38 (11 fmly) (14 GF) **Facilities** ⓒ supervised 🎵 Xmas New Year **Conf** Class 80 Board 40 Thtr 150 **Services** Lift **Parking** 105 **Notes** ⊗ Civ Wed 150

KIRKBEAN — Map 21 NX95

INSPECTORS' CHOICE

Cavens

★★ ⚜ COUNTRY HOUSE HOTEL

☎ 01387 880234 📄 01387 880467
DG2 8AA
e-mail: enquiries@cavens.com
web: www.cavens.com
dir: on entering Kirkbean on A710, hotel signed

Set in parkland gardens, Cavens encapsulates all the virtues of an intimate country-house hotel. Quality is the keynote, and the proprietors spared no effort in completing a fine renovation of the house. Bedrooms are delightfully individual and very comfortably equipped, and a choice of lounges invites peaceful relaxation. A set dinner offers the best of local and home-made produce.

Rooms 5 (1 GF) **S** £80-£150; **D** £80-£240 (incl. bkfst)* **Facilities** 🚣 Shooting Fishing Horse riding New Year **Conf** Class 20 Board 20 Thtr 20 **Parking** 12 **Notes** LB No children 12yrs Closed Jan Civ Wed 100

Best Western Selkirk Arms

★★★ 77% HOTEL

☎ 01557 330402 📠 01557 331639
Old High St DG6 4JG
e-mail: reception@selkirkarmshotel.co.uk
web: www.selkirkarmshotel.co.uk
dir: On A71, 5m S of A75.

The Selkirk Arms is aptly named, as it was originally the hostelry where Robert Burns wrote the Selkirk Grace. It is now a smart and stylish hotel set in secluded gardens just off the town centre. Inviting public areas include the attractive Artistas restaurant, bistro, air conditioned lounge bar and the Burns lounge.

Rooms 17 (3 annexe) (2 fmly) (1 GF) **S** £79; **D** £98-£110 (incl. bkfst)* **Facilities** STV FTV New Year Wi-fi **Conf** Class 30 Board 30 Thtr 50 **Parking** 10 **Notes** LB Closed 24-26 Dec

Arden House Hotel

★★ 69% HOTEL

☎ 01557 330544 📠 01557 330742
Tongland Rd DG6 4UU
dir: Off A57, 4m W of Castle Douglas onto A711. Follow Kirkcudbright, over Telford Bridge. Hotel 400mtrs on left

Set well back from the main road in extensive grounds on the northeast side of town, this spotlessly maintained hotel offers attractive bedrooms, a lounge bar and adjoining conservatory serving a range of popular dishes, which are also available in the dining room. It boasts an impressive function suite in its grounds.

Rooms 9 (7 fmly) (5 smoking) **S** fr £55; **D** £75-£80 (incl. bkfst)* **Conf** Class 175 Thtr 175 **Parking** 70 **Notes** LB No credit cards

Dryfesdale Country House

★★★★ 75% HOTEL

☎ 01576 202427 📠 01576 204187
Dryfebridge DG11 2SF
e-mail: reception@dryfesdalehotel.co.uk
web: www.dryfesdalehotel.co.uk
dir: From M74 junct 17 follow Lockerbie North signs, 3rd left at 1st rdbt, 1st exit left at 2nd rdbt, hotel 200yds

Conveniently situated for the M74, yet discreetly screened from it, this friendly hotel provides attentive service. Bedrooms, some with access to patio areas, vary in size and style; all offer good levels of comfort and are well equipped. Creative, good value dinners make use of local produce and are served in the airy restaurant that overlooks the manicured gardens and rolling countryside.

Rooms 28 (5 fmly) (19 GF) **Facilities** STV FTV Putt green 🏌 Clay pigeon shooting Fishing 🎵 Xmas New Year Wi-fi **Conf** Class 100 Board 100 Thtr 150 Del from £100 to £125 **Parking** 60 **Notes** Civ Wed 150

Kings Arms Hotel

★★ 78% HOTEL

☎ 01576 202410 📠 01576 202410
High St DG11 2JL
e-mail: reception@kingsarmshotel.co.uk
web: www.kingsarmshotel.co.uk
dir: A74(M), 0.5m into town centre, hotel opposite town hall

Dating from the 17th century this former inn lies in the town centre. Now a family-run hotel, it provides attractive well-equipped bedrooms with Wi-fi access. At lunch a menu ranging from snacks to full meals is served in both the two cosy bars and the restaurant at dinner.

Rooms 13 (2 fmly) **S** £47.50; **D** £80 (incl. bkfst)* **Facilities** FTV Xmas New Year Wi-fi **Conf** Class 40 Board 30 Thtr 80 **Parking** 8

Ravenshill House

★★ 71% HOTEL

☎ 01576 202882
12 Dumfries Rd DG11 2EF
e-mail: aaenquiries@ravenshillhotellockerbie.co.uk
web: www.ravenshillhotellockerbie.co.uk
dir: from A74(M) Lockerbie junct onto A709. Hotel 0.5m on right

Set in spacious gardens on the fringe of the town, this friendly, family-run hotel offers cheerful service and good value, home-cooked meals. Bedrooms are generally spacious and comfortably equipped, including an ideal two-room family unit.

Rooms 8 (2 fmly) **S** £50-£65; **D** £75-£85 (incl. bkfst)* **Facilities** FTV **Conf** Class 20 Board 12 Thtr 30 **Parking** 35 **Notes** LB Closed 1-3 Jan

Best Western Moffat House

★★★ 73% HOTEL

☎ 01683 220039 📠 01683 221288
High St DG10 9HL
e-mail: reception@moffathouse.co.uk
dir: M74 junct 15 into town centre

This fine Adam mansion, in its own neatly tended gardens, is set back from the main road in the centre of this popular country town. Inviting public areas include a quiet sun lounge to the rear, a comfortable lounge bar serving tasty meals and an attractive restaurant for the more formal occasion. Bedrooms present a mix of classical and modern styles.

Rooms 21 (4 fmly) (4 GF) **S** £49-£79; **D** £69-£99 (incl. bkfst) **Facilities** STV Xmas New Year Wi-fi **Conf** Class 80 Board 50 Thtr 100 Del from £99 to £119 **Parking** 30 **Notes** Civ Wed 150

INSPECTORS' CHOICE

Kirroughtree House

★★★ ◉◉ HOTEL

☎ 01671 402141 📠 01671 402425
Minnigaff DG8 6AN
e-mail: info@kirroughtreehouse.co.uk
web: www.kirroughtreehouse.co.uk
dir: From A75 take A712, entrance to hotel 300yds on left

This imposing mansion enjoys a peaceful location in eight acres of landscaped gardens near Galloway Forest Park. It is said that Robert Burns sat on the staircase at Kirroughtree and recited his poems. The inviting day rooms comprise a choice of lounges, and two elegant dining rooms where guests can enjoy the delightful cuisine which is firmly based on top quality, locally sourced ingredients. Well-proportioned, individually styled bedrooms include some suites and mini-suites and many rooms enjoy fine views. Service is very friendly and attentive.

Rooms 17 **S** £105-£115; **D** £180-£250 (incl. bkfst)* **Facilities** 🛁 ⛳ 9 hole pitch and putt Xmas New Year Wi-fi **Conf** Class 20 Board 20 Thtr 30 Del from £160 to £170* **Services** Lift **Parking** 50 **Notes** LB No children 10yrs Closed 2 Jan-mid Feb

NEWTON STEWART *continued*

Bruce Hotel

★★★ 71% HOTEL

☎ 01671 402294 📄 01671 402294
88 Queen St DG8 6JL
e-mail: mail@the-bruce-hotel.com
web: www.the-bruce-hotel.com
dir: Off A75 Newton Stewart rdbt towards town. Hotel
800mtrs on right

Named after the Scottish patriot Robert the Bruce, this
welcoming hotel is just a short distance from the A75.
One of the well-appointed bedrooms features a four-
poster bed, and popular family suites contain separate
bedrooms for children. Public areas include a traditional
lounge, a formal restaurant and a lounge bar, both
offering a good choice of dishes.

Rooms 20 (3 fmly) **S** £45-£49; **D** £80-£90 (incl. bkfst)*
Facilities New Year Wi-fi **Conf** Class 50 Board 14
Thtr 100 Del from £75 to £95* **Parking** 14 **Notes** LB

Creebridge House

★★★ 🅰 SMALL HOTEL

☎ 01671 402121 📄 01671 403258
DG8 6NP
e-mail: info@creebridge.co.uk
web: www.creebridge.co.uk
dir: Off A75, at Newton Stewart sign continue approx
0.75m to hotel sign

Rooms 18 (3 fmly) **Facilities** Fishing ⤷ Xmas New Year
Wi-fi **Conf** Class 50 Board 50 Thtr 70 **Parking** 45
Notes Civ Wed 70

PORTPATRICK Map 20 NW95

INSPECTORS' CHOICE

Knockinaam Lodge

★★★ ◉◉◉ HOTEL

☎ 01776 810471 📄 01776 810435
DG9 9AD
e-mail: reservations@knockinaamlodge.com
web: www.knockinaamlodge.com
dir: from A77 or A75 follow signs to Portpatrick.
Through Lochans. After 2m left at signs for hotel

Any tour of Dumfries & Galloway would not be complete
without a night or two at this haven of tranquillity and
relaxation. Knockinaam Lodge is an extended Victorian
house, set in an idyllic cove with its own pebble beach
and sheltered by majestic cliffs and woodlands. A
warm welcome is assured from the proprietors and
their committed team, and much emphasis is placed
on providing a sophisticated but intimate home-from-
home experience. The cooking is a real treat and
showcases superb local produce. Dinner is a set meal,
but choices can be discussed in advance.

Rooms 10 (1 fmly) **S** £145-£285; **D** £180-£400 (incl.
bkfst & dinner)* **Facilities** FTV Fishing ⤷ Shooting
Walking Sea fishing Clay pigeon shooting Xmas New
Year Wi-fi Child facilities **Conf** Class 10 Board 16
Thtr 30 **Parking** 20 **Notes** Civ Wed 40

Fernhill

★★★ 79% HOTEL

☎ 01776 810220 📄 01776 810596
Heugh Rd DG9 8TD
e-mail: info@fernhillhotel.co.uk
web: www.fernhillhotel.co.uk
dir: from Stranraer A77 to Portpatrick, 100yds past
Portpatrick village sign, turn right before war memorial.
Hotel 1st on left

Set high above the village, this hotel looks out over the
harbour and Irish Sea; many of the bedrooms take
advantage of the views. A modern wing offers particularly
spacious and well-appointed rooms; some have
balconies. The smart conservatory restaurant offers
interesting, freshly prepared dishes.

Rooms 36 (9 annexe) (3 fmly) (8 GF) **S** £63-£83;
D fr £116 (incl. bkfst & dinner)* **Facilities** Leisure
facilities available at sister hotel in Stranraer Xmas New
Year Wi-fi **Conf** Class 12 Board 12 Thtr 24 **Parking** 45
Notes LB Closed mid Jan-mid Feb Civ Wed 45

POWFOOT Map 21 NY16

Powfoot Golf Hotel

★★★ 78% HOTEL

☎ 01461 700254 📄 01461 700288
Links Av DG12 5PN
e-mail: reception@thepowfootgolfhotel.co.uk
dir: A75 onto B721, through Annan. B724, approx 3m, left
onto unclassified road

This hotel has well presented and comfortable modern
bedrooms, many of which overlook the championship golf
course. Public areas have panoramic views onto the
Solway Firth and the Lakeland hills beyond. The service is
friendly and relaxed, and quality food is served in a
choice of locations.

Rooms 24 (9 fmly) (5 GF) (2 smoking) **S** fr £60; **D** fr £90
(incl. bkfst) **Facilities** STV FTV ⌀ 18 Putt green Xmas New
Year Wi-fi **Conf** Class 80 Board 80 Thtr 80 Del from £100
Parking 30 **Notes** LB ⊗ Civ Wed 100

SANQUHAR — Map 21 NS70

Blackaddie House Hotel

[U]

☎ 01659 50270
Blackaddie Rd DG4 6JJ
e-mail: ian@blackaddiehotel.co.uk
dir: Off A76 just N of Sanquhar at Burnside Service Station. Private road to hotel 300mtrs on right

Currently the rating for this establishment is not confirmed. This may be due to a change of ownership or because it has only recently joined the AA rating scheme. For further details please see the AA website: theAA.com

Rooms 14 (5 annexe) (2 fmly) (2 GF) **S** £50-£60;
D £80-£120 (incl. bkfst)* **Facilities** Xmas New Year Wi-fi
Conf Class 12 Board 16 Thtr 20 Del from £97 to £120*
Parking 20 **Notes** LB Civ Wed 24

See advert on page 570

STRANRAER — Map 20 NX06

North West Castle

★★★★ 74% HOTEL

☎ 01776 704413 📠 01776 702646
DG9 8EH
e-mail: info@northwestcastle.co.uk
web: www.northwestcastle.co.uk
dir: on seafront, close to Stena ferry terminal

This long-established hotel overlooks the bay and the ferry terminal. The public areas include a lounge with large leather armchairs and blazing fire in season and a classically styled dining room where a pianist plays in the evening. There is a shop, leisure centre, and a curling rink that becomes the focus in winter. Bedrooms are comfortable and spacious.

Rooms 72 (2 annexe) (22 fmly) **S** £59.50-£83;
D £99-£136 (incl. bkfst & dinner)* **Facilities** 🏊 Gym Curling (Oct-Apr) Games room Xmas New Year Wi-fi
Conf Class 60 Board 40 Thtr 150 Del from £75 to £90*
Services Lift **Parking** 100 **Notes** LB Civ Wed 130

Corsewall Lighthouse Hotel

★★★ 77% HOTEL

☎ 01776 853220 📠 01776 854231
Corsewall Point, Kirkcolm DG9 0QG
e-mail: lighthousehotel@btinternet.com
web: www.lighthousehotel.co.uk
dir: A718 from Stranraer to Kirkcolm (approx 8m). Follow hotel signs for 4m

Looking for something completely different? A unique hotel converted from buildings that adjoin a listed 19th-century lighthouse set on a rocky coastline. Bedrooms come in a variety of sizes, some reached by a spiral staircase, and like the public areas, are cosy and atmospheric. Cottage suites in the grounds offer greater space.

Rooms 10 (4 annexe) (4 fmly) (2 GF) (2 smoking)
S £130-£150; **D** £150-£250 (incl. bkfst & dinner)*
Facilities FTV Xmas New Year **Conf** Thtr 20 Del from £100 to £140* **Parking** 20 **Notes** LB Civ Wed 28

CITY OF DUNDEE

DUNDEE — Map 21 NO43

Apex City Quay Hotel & Spa

★★★★ 81% ⊛⊛ HOTEL

APEX HOTELS

☎ 0845 365 0000 📠 01382 201401
1 West Victoria Dock Rd DD1 3JP
e-mail: dundee.reservations@apexhotels.co.uk
web: www.apexhotels.co.uk
dir: A85/Riverside Drive to Discovery Quay. Exit rdbt for City Quay

This stylish, purpose-built hotel occupies an enviable position at the heart of Dundee's regenerated quayside area. Bedrooms, including a number of smart suites, feature the very latest in design. Warm hospitality and professional service are an integral part of the appeal. Open-plan public areas with panoramic windows and contemporary food options complete the package.

Rooms 152 (16 fmly) (32 smoking) **Facilities** Spa FTV 🏊 Gym Steam room Sauna Xmas New Year Wi-fi
Conf Class 180 Board 120 Thtr 400 **Services** Lift Air con
Parking 150 **Notes** LB ⊛ Civ Wed 300

Travelodge Dundee

BUDGET HOTEL

☎ 0871 984 6135 📠 01382 610488
A90 Kingsway DD2 4TD
web: www.travelodge.co.uk
dir: On A90

Travelodge offers good quality, good value, budget accommodation. All offer family rooms sleeping up to four (two adults, two children) with en suite bathroom/shower-room, remote-control TV, tea- and coffee-making facilities and comfortable beds. Food options vary. Breakfast is at the on-site Bar Café restaurant (if available) or to take away. See also Hotel Groups pages.

Rooms 32 **S** fr £29; **D** fr £29

Travelodge Dundee Central

BUDGET HOTEL

☎ 0871 984 6301
152-158 West Marketgait DD1 1NL
web: www.travelodge.co.uk
dir: From Airport right towards city centre. At 3rd rbt take 1st exit. At next rbt take 2nd exit

Rooms 48 **S** fr £29; **D** fr £29

EAST AYRSHIRE

KILMARNOCK — Map 20 NS43

Fenwick

★★★ 75% HOTEL

☎ 01560 600478 📠 01560 600334
Fenwick KA3 6AU
e-mail: fenwick@bestwestern.co.uk
web: www.thefenwickhotel.co.uk
dir: B7038 right signed Fenwick. Through 1st rdbt, left at next. Hotel 1st on left

Benefiting from a great location alongside the M77 and offering easy links to Ayr, Kilmarnock and Glasgow. The spacious bedrooms are thoughtfully equipped; complimentary Wi-fi is available throughout the hotel. The bright restaurant offers both formal and informal dining and there are two bars to choose from.

Rooms 30 (1 fmly) (9 GF) **Facilities** STV Xmas New Year Wi-fi **Conf** Class 70 Thtr 160 **Notes** LB Civ Wed 110

KILMARNOCK *continued*

Travelodge Kilmarnock

BUDGET HOTEL

☎ 0871 984 6149 📄 01563 573810
Bellfield Interchange KA1 5LQ
web: www.travelodge.co.uk
dir: On Bellfield Interchange, just off A77

Travelodge offers good quality, good value, budget accommodation. All offer family rooms sleeping up to four (two adults, two children) with en suite bathroom/ shower-room, remote-control TV, tea- and coffee-making facilities and comfortable beds. Food options vary. Breakfast is at the on-site Bar Café restaurant (if available) or to take away. See also Hotel Groups pages.

Rooms 40 **S** fr £29; **D** fr £29

SORN   Map 20 NS52

The Sorn Inn

◎◎ RESTAURANT WITH ROOMS

☎ 01290 551305 📄 01290 553470
35 Main St KA5 6HU
e-mail: craig@sorninn.com
dir: A70 from S or A76 from N onto B743 to Sorn

Centrally situated in this rural village, which is convenient for many of Ayrshire's attractions, this renovated inn is now a fine dining restaurant with a cosy lounge area. There is also a popular chop house with a pub-like environment. The freshly decorated bedrooms have comfortable beds and good facilities.

Rooms 4 (1 fmly)

EAST LOTHIAN

DIRLETON   Map 21 NT58

The Open Arms

★★★ 77% ◎ SMALL HOTEL

☎ 01620 850241 📄 01620 850570
EH39 5EG
e-mail: openarms@clara.co.uk
web: www.openarmshotel.com
dir: from A1, follow signs for North Berwick, through Gullane, 2m on left

Long-established, this hotel lies across from the picturesque village green and Dirleton Castle. Inviting public areas include a choice of lounges and a cosy bar. Four of the garden bedrooms and the lounge provide particularly high standards. A variety of carefully prepared meals can be enjoyed in both the informal setting of Deveau's brasserie or the more intimate Library Restaurant.

Rooms 10 (1 fmly) **Facilities** Xmas **Conf** Class 150 Board 100 Thtr 200 **Parking** 30 **Notes** Closed 4-15 Jan

NORTH BERWICK   Map 21 NT58

Macdonald Marine Hotel & Spa

★★★★ 82% ◎◎ HOTEL

☎ 0870 400 8129 📄 01620 894480
Cromwell Rd EH39 4LZ
e-mail: sales.marine@macdonald-hotels.co.uk
web: www.macdonaldhotels.co.uk
dir: from A198 turn into Hamilton Rd at lights then 2nd right

This imposing hotel commands stunning views across the local golf course to the Firth of Forth. Stylish public areas provide a relaxing atmosphere; creative dishes are served in the restaurant and lighter bites in the lounge/bar. Bedrooms come in a variety of sizes and styles, all are well equipped and some are impressively large. The hotel boasts extensive leisure and conference facilities.

Rooms 83 (4 fmly) (4 GF) **Facilities** Spa ⓢ supervised Putt green Gym Indoor & outdoor salt water hydro pool Xmas New Year Wi-fi **Conf** Class 120 Board 60 Thtr 300 **Services** Lift **Parking** 50 **Notes** LB Civ Wed 150

EAST RENFREWSHIRE

UPLAWMOOR   Map 20 NS45

Uplawmoor Hotel

★★★ 80% ◎◎ HOTEL

☎ 01505 850565 📄 01505 850689
Neilston Rd G78 4AF
e-mail: info@uplawmoor.co.uk
web: www.uplawmoor.co.uk
dir: M77 junct 2, A736 signed Barrhead & Irvine. Hotel 4m beyond Barrhead

Originally an old coaching inn, this friendly hotel is set in a village off the Glasgow to Irvine road. The comfortable restaurant (with cocktail lounge adjacent) features

imaginative dishes, whilst the separate lounge bar is popular for freshly prepared bar meals. The modern bedrooms are both comfortable and well equipped.

Rooms 14 (1 fmly) (3 smoking) **S** £55-£70; **D** £95 (incl. bkfst)* **Facilities** STV Wi-fi **Conf** Class 12 Board 20 Thtr 40 Del from £90 to £109* **Parking** 40 **Notes** LB ⊗ Closed 26 Dec & 1 Jan

See advert on page 589

CITY OF EDINBURGH

EDINBURGH   Map 21 NT27

INSPECTORS' CHOICE

Prestonfield

★★★★★ ◎◎ TOWN HOUSE HOTEL

☎ 0131 225 7800 📄 0131 220 4392
Priestfield Rd EH16 5UT
e-mail: reservations@prestonfield.com
web: www.prestonfield.com
dir: A7 towards Cameron Toll. 200mtrs beyond Royal Commonwealth Pool, into Priestfield Rd

This centuries-old landmark has been lovingly restored and enhanced to provide deeply comfortable and dramatically furnished bedrooms. The building demands to be explored: from the tapestry lounge and the whisky room to the restaurant, where the walls are adorned with pictures of former owners. Facilities and services are up-to-the-minute, and carefully prepared meals are served in the award-winning Rhubarb restaurant.

Rooms 23 (6 GF) **Facilities** STV FTV ⚓ 18 Putt green ⛳ Free bike hire Xmas New Year Wi-fi **Conf** Class 500 Board 40 Thtr 700 **Services** Lift **Parking** 250 **Notes** LB Civ Wed 350

Balmoral

★★★★★ 87% ◉◉◉ HOTEL

☎ 0131 556 2414 📠 0131 557 3747
1 Princes St EH2 2EQ
e-mail: reservations.balmoral@roccofortecollection.com
web: www.roccofortecollection.com
dir: follow city centre signs. Hotel at E end of Princes St, adjacent to Waverley Station

This elegant hotel enjoys a prestigious address at the top of Princes Street, with fine views over the city and the castle. Bedrooms and suites are stylishly furnished and decorated, all boasting a thoughtful range of extras and impressive marble bathrooms. Hotel amenities include a Roman-style health spa, extensive function facilities, a choice of bars and two very different dining options; Number One offers inspired fine dining whilst Hadrians is a bustling, informal brasserie.

Rooms 188 (22 fmly) (15 smoking) **S** £305-£2000; **D** £360-£2000* **Facilities** Spa STV 🅣 Gym 🎵 Xmas New Year Wi-fi **Conf** Class 180 Board 60 Thtr 350 Del from £245 to £430* **Services** Lift Air con **Parking** 100 **Notes** LB ⊗ Civ Wed 120

The Howard

★★★★★ 84% ◉ TOWN HOUSE HOTEL

☎ 0131 274 7402 & 557 3500 📠 0131 274 7405
34 Great King St EH3 6QH
e-mail: reserve@thehoward.com
web: www.thehoward.com
dir: E on Queen St, 2nd left, Dundas St. Through 3 lights, right, hotel on left

Quietly elegant and splendidly luxurious, The Howard provides an intimate and high quality experience for the discerning traveller. It comprises three linked Georgian houses and is situated just a short walk from Princes Street. The sumptuous bedrooms, in a variety of styles, include spacious suites, well-equipped bathrooms and a host of thoughtful touches. Ornate chandeliers and lavish drapes adorn the drawing room, while the Atholl Dining Room contains unique hand-painted murals dating from the 1800s.

Rooms 18 (1 fmly) (1 GF) **S** £90-£155; **D** £180-£415 (incl. bkfst)* **Facilities** FTV Xmas New Year Wi-fi **Conf** Class 15 Board 20 Thtr 30 Del from £240 to £340* **Services** Lift **Parking** 10 **Notes** LB ⊗ Civ Wed 40

The Scotsman

★★★★★ 78% ◉ TOWN HOUSE HOTEL

☎ 0131 556 5565 📠 0131 652 3652
20 North Bridge EH1 1YT
e-mail: reservations@thescotsmanhotelgroup.co.uk
web: www.thescotsmanhotel.co.uk
dir: A8 to city centre, left onto Charlotte St. Right into Queen St, right at rdbt onto Leith St. Straight on, left onto North Bridge, hotel on right

Formerly the headquarters of The Scotsman newspaper this is a stunning hotel conversion. The classical elegance of the public areas, complete with a marble staircase, blends seamlessly with the contemporary bedrooms and their state-of-the-art technology. The superbly equipped leisure club includes a stainless steel swimming pool and large gym. Dining arrangements can be made in the funky North Bridge Brasserie or in the opulent Vermilion restaurant.

Rooms 79 (4 GF) **Facilities** Spa STV 🅣 supervised Gym Beauty treatments New Year Wi-fi **Conf** Class 50 Board 40 Thtr 100 **Services** Lift **Notes** Civ Wed 70

Sheraton Grand Hotel & Spa

★★★★★ 78% HOTEL   Sheraton
HOTELS & RESORTS

☎ 0131 229 9131 📠 0131 228 4510
1 Festival Square EH3 9SR
e-mail: grandedinburgh.sheraton@sheraton.com
dir: follow City Centre signs (A8). Through Shandwick Place, right at lights into Lothian Rd. Right at next lights. Hotel on left at next lights

This modern hotel boasts one of the best spas in Scotland - the external top floor hydro pool is definitely worth a look whilst the thermal suite provides a unique venue for serious relaxation. The spacious bedrooms are available in a variety of styles, and the suites prove very popular. There is a wide range of eating options including The Terrace and Santini's - both have a loyal local following.

Rooms 260 (21 fmly) **S** £105-£210; **D** £120-£240* **Facilities** Spa STV 🅣 🔆 Gym Indoor/Outdoor Hydropool Kinesis studioThermal suite Fitness studio 🎵 Xmas New Year Wi-fi **Conf** Class 350 Board 120 Thtr 485 Del from £199 to £400* **Services** Lift Air con **Parking** 122 **Notes** LB ⊗ Civ Wed 485

Channings

★★★★ ◉ TOWN HOUSE HOTEL

☎ 0131 332 3232 & 315 2226 📠 0131 332 9631
15 South Learmonth Gardens EH4 1EZ
e-mail: reserve@channings.co.uk
web: www.channings.co.uk
dir: From A90 & Forth Road Bridge, follow signs for city centre

Just minutes from the city centre, this elegant town house occupies five Edwardian terraced houses. The public areas include sumptuous, inviting lounges and a choice of dining options. The Ochre Vita wine bar and Mediterranean restaurant offer the popular choice, but for a special-occasion dinner try the seven-course tasting menu with wines, in the intimate Channings Restaurant. The attractive and individually designed bedrooms have a hi-tech spec for business guests.

Rooms 41 (4 GF) **S** £85-£200; **D** £125-£250 (incl. bkfst)* **Facilities** STV FTV 🎵 Xmas New Year Wi-fi **Conf** Class 40 Board 28 Thtr 60 **Services** Lift **Notes** LB ⊗

EDINBURGH *continued*

Norton House

★★★★ 88% ◉◉◉ HOTEL

☎ 0131 333 1275 📄 0131 333 5305
Ingliston EH28 8LX
e-mail: nortonhouse@handpicked.co.uk
web: www.handpicked.co.uk
dir: off A8, 5m W of city centre

This extended Victorian mansion, set in 55 acres of parkland, is peacefully situated just outside the city and is convenient for the airport. Both the contemporary bedrooms and the very spacious traditional ones have an impressive range of accessories including plasma screen TVs with DVD recorders. Public areas take in a choice of lounges as well as dining options, with a popular brasserie and Ushers, the intimate award-winning restaurant.

Rooms 83 (10 fmly) (20 GF) **S** £99-£495; **D** £109-£505 (incl. bkfst) **Facilities** Spa ⏺ Gym Archery Laser Clay shooting Quad biking Xmas New Year Wi-fi **Conf** Class 100 Board 60 Thtr 300 Del from £135 to £205 **Services** Lift **Parking** 200 **Notes** LB ⊗ Civ Wed 140

Marriott Dalmahoy Hotel & Country Club

★★★★ 81% ◉◉ HOTEL

☎ 0131 333 1845 📄 0131 333 1433
Kirknewton EH27 8EB
e-mail: mhrs.edigs.frontdesk@marriotthotels.com
web: www.marriottdalmahoy.co.uk
dir: Edinburgh City Bypass (A720) turn onto A71 towards Livingston, hotel on left in 2m

The rolling Pentland Hills and beautifully kept parkland provide a stunning backdrop for this imposing Georgian mansion. With two championship golf courses and a health and beauty club, there is plenty here to occupy guests. Bedrooms are spacious and most have fine views, while public rooms offer a choice of formal and informal drinking and dining options.

Rooms 215 (172 annexe) (59 fmly) (6 smoking) **S** £95-£175; **D** £95-£175* **Facilities** Spa STV ⏺ ♨ 18 🏊 Putt green Gym Health & beauty treatments Steam room Dance studio Driving range Golf lessons Xmas New Year Wi-fi **Conf** Class 200 Board 120 Thtr 300 Del from £150 to £195* **Services** Lift Air con **Parking** 350 **Notes** LB ⊗ Civ Wed 250

Hotel du Vin Edinburgh

★★★★ 80% ◉ TOWN HOUSE HOTEL

☎ 0131 247 4900 📄 0131 247 4901
11 Bristo Place EH1 1EZ

Situated on the site of a former lunatic asylum, this hotel offers very stylish and comfortable accommodation; all bedrooms display the Hotel du Vin trademark facilities - air conditioning, free Wi-fi, plasma TVs, monsoon showers

and Egyptian cotton linen to name but a few. Public areas include a whisky snug, a mezzanine bar that overlooks the brasserie where modern Scottish cuisine is served. For the wine connoisseur there's La Roche tasting room where wines from around the world can be appreciated.

Rooms 47

George Hotel Edinburgh

★★★★ 80% HOTEL

☎ 0131 225 1251 📄 0131 226 5644
19-21 George St EH2 2PB
e-mail: david.welch@principal-hayley.com
web: www.principal-hayley.com/thegeorge
dir: In city centre

A long-established hotel, the George enjoys a city centre location. The splendid public areas have many original features such as intricate plasterwork, a marble-floored foyer and chandeliers. The Tempus Bar offers menus that feature a wide range of dishes to suit most tastes. The elegant, modern bedrooms come in a mix of sizes and styles; the upper ones having fine city views.

Rooms 249 (20 fmly) (4 GF) **S** £79-£229; **D** £79-£399* **Facilities** STV Xmas New Year Wi-fi **Conf** Class 120 Board 50 Thtr 300 Del from £129 to £299* **Services** Lift **Notes** LB ⊗ Civ Wed 300

Edinburgh Marriott Hotel

★★★★ 79% HOTEL

☎ 0131 334 9191 📄 0131 316 4507
111 Glasgow Rd EH12 8NF
e-mail: edinburgh@marriotthotels.com
web: www.EdinburghMarriott.co.uk
dir: M8 junct 1 for Gogar, at rdbt turn right for city centre, hotel on right

This smart, modern hotel is located on the city's western edge which is convenient for the bypass, airport, showground and business park. Public areas include an attractive marbled foyer, extensive conference facilities and a restaurant serving a range of international dishes. The air-conditioned bedrooms are spacious and equipped with a range of extras.

Rooms 245 (76 fmly) (64 GF) (6 smoking) **Facilities** Spa STV ⏺ Gym Steam room Sauna Massage & beauty treatment room Hairdresser Xmas New Year Wi-fi **Conf** Class 120 Board 50 Thtr 250 **Services** Lift Air con **Parking** 300 **Notes** LB ⊗ Civ Wed 80

Apex International

★★★★ 78% ◉◉ HOTEL

☎ 0845 365 0000 & 0131 300 3456 📄 0131 220 5345
31/35 Grassmarket EH1 2HS
e-mail: edinburgh.reservations@apexhotels.co.uk
web: www.apexhotels.co.uk
dir: Into Lothian Rd at west end of Princes St, then 1st left into King Stables Rd, leads into Grassmarket

A sister to the Apex City Hotel close by, the International lies in a historic yet trendy square in the shadow of Edinburgh Castle. It has a versatile business and conference centre, and also Yu Time leisure and fitness facility with a stainless steel ozone pool. Bedrooms are contemporary in style and very well equipped. The fifth-floor restaurant boasts stunning views of the castle.

Rooms 171 (99 fmly) (12 smoking) **Facilities** ⏺ Gym Tropicarium Xmas New Year Wi-fi **Conf** Class 80 Board 40 Thtr 200 **Services** Lift **Parking** 60 **Notes** LB ⊗ Civ Wed 200

Apex Waterloo Place Hotel

★★★★ 78% HOTEL

☎ 0131 523 1819
23 - 27 Waterloo Place EH1 3BH

This stunning, newly converted hotel provides a state-of-the-art experience with slick interior design. Bedrooms, many with city views, are well appointed for both the business and leisure guest; stunning duplex suites provide extra space, surround-sound TV systems and luxurious feature bathrooms. The restaurant provides an appealing menu both at dinner and breakfast. There is also a well-equipped fitness centre and indoor pool. The hotel has direct, pedestrian access to Edinburgh's Waverley Station.

Rooms 187

The Bonham

★★★★ 77% ◎◎ TOWN HOUSE HOTEL

☎ 0131 274 7400 📄 0131 274 7405
35 Drumsheugh Gardens EH3 7RN
e-mail: reserve@thebonham.com
web: www.thebonham.com
dir: Close to West End & Princes St

Overlooking tree-lined gardens, this Victorian town house combines classical elegance with a contemporary style. Inviting day rooms include a reception lounge and smart restaurant. Bedrooms, in a variety of sizes, have a contemporary design and include good internet access and an interactive TV system.

Rooms 48 (1 GF) **S** £110-£250; **D** £135-£280 (incl. bkfst)* **Facilities** STV FTV Xmas New Year Wi-fi **Conf** Board 26 Thtr 50 **Services** Lift **Parking** 20 **Notes** LB ⊗

The Royal Terrace

★★★★ 77% ◎ HOTEL

☎ 0131 557 3222 📄 0131 557 5334
18 Royal Ter EH7 5AQ
e-mail: sales@royalterracehotel.co.uk
web: www.royalterracehotel.co.uk
dir: A8 to city centre, follow one-way system, left into Charlotte Sq. At end right into Queens St. Left at rdbt. At next island right into London Rd, right into Blenheim Place leading to Royal Terrace

Forming part of a quiet Georgian terrace close to the city centre, this hotel offers bedrooms that successfully blend the historic architecture of the building with state-of-the-art facilities. Although most rooms afford lovely views, the top floor rooms provide excellent panoramas of the city, and two of the 13 Ambassador Suites have glass bathrooms.

Rooms 107 (13 fmly) (7 GF) **Facilities** ⓢ Gym Steam room Sauna Aromatherapy shower Xmas New Year Wi-fi **Conf** Class 40 Board 40 Thtr 100 **Services** Lift **Notes** ⊗ Civ Wed 80

Best Western Bruntsfield

★★★★ 77% HOTEL

☎ 0131 229 1393 📄 0131 229 5634
69 Bruntsfield Place EH10 4HH
e-mail: sales@thebruntsfield.co.uk
web: www.thebruntsfield.co.uk
dir: from S into Edinburgh on A702. Hotel 1m S of west end of Princes Street

Overlooking Bruntsfield Links and only minutes from the city centre, this smart hotel has stylish public rooms including a spacious lounge and a new contemporary bar and brasserie with an outside terrace. The individually styled bedrooms come in a variety of sizes but all are well appointed. Smart staff provide good levels of service and attention.

Rooms 67 (5 fmly) (10 GF) **Facilities** STV FTV New Year Wi-fi **Conf** Class 70 Board 45 Thtr 120 **Services** Lift **Parking** 25 **Notes** ⊗ Closed 25 Dec Civ Wed 100

Novotel Edinburgh Park

★★★★ 77% HOTEL

☎ 0131 446 5600 📄 0131 446 5610
15 Lochside Av EH12 9DJ
e-mail: h6515@accor.com
dir: Near Hermiston Gate shopping area

Located just off the city by-pass and within minutes of the airport, this new concept hotel brings a modern and fresh approach to the Novotel brand. Bedrooms are spacious and comfortable as is the open-plan lobby, bar and restaurant with some tables that boast their own TVs.

Rooms 170 (130 fmly) **S** £89-£160; **D** £89-£160* **Facilities** ⓢ Gym Wi-fi **Conf** Class 60 Board 40 Thtr 150 Del from £120 to £160 **Services** Lift **Parking** 96 **Notes** LB

Apex City

★★★★ 76% ◎ HOTEL

☎ 0845 365 0000 & 0131 243 3456 📄 0131 225 6346
61 Grassmarket EH1 2JF
e-mail: edinburgh.reservations@apexhotels.co.uk
web: www.apexhotels.co.uk
dir: into Lothian Rd at west end of Princes St, 1st left into King Stables Rd. Leads into Grassmarket

This modern, stylish hotel lies in a historic yet trendy square dominated by Edinburgh Castle above. The design-led bedrooms are fresh and contemporary and each has artwork by Richard Demarco. Agua Bar and Restaurant is a smart open-plan area in dark wood and chrome that serves a range of meals and cocktails. Residents can use the spa at sister hotel, the International, which is nearby.

Rooms 119 (10 smoking) **Facilities** Complimentary use of leisure facilities at nearby hotel Xmas New Year Wi-fi **Conf** Class 30 Board 34 Thtr 70 **Services** Lift Air con **Parking** 10 **Notes** LB ⊗ Civ Wed 60

Macdonald Holyrood

★★★★ 75% ◎ HOTEL

☎ 0870 1942106 📄 0131 550 4545
Holyrood Rd EH8 8AU
e-mail: general.holyrood@macdonald-hotels.co.uk
web: www.macdonaldhotels.co.uk/holyrood
dir: Parallel to Royal Mile, near Holyrood Palace & Dynamic Earth

Situated just a short walk from Holyrood Palace, this impressive hotel lies next to the Scottish Parliament building. Air-conditioned bedrooms are comfortably furnished, whilst the Club floor boasts a private lounge. Full business services complement the extensive conference suites.

Rooms 156 (16 fmly) (13 GF) **Facilities** Spa STV ⓢ Gym Beauty treatment rooms Sun bed ♫ Xmas New Year Wi-fi **Conf** Class 100 Board 80 Thtr 200 Del from £160 to £290 **Services** Lift Air con **Parking** 35 **Notes** ⊗ Civ Wed 100

EDINBURGH *continued*

The King James by Thistle

thistle

★★★★ 75% HOTEL

☎ 0871 376 9016 📄 0871 376 9116
107 Leith St EH1 3SW
e-mail: edinburgh@thistle.co.uk
web: www.thistlehotels.com/edinburgh
dir: M8/M9 onto A8 signed city centre. Hotel at end of Princes St adjacent to St James shopping centre

This purpose-built hotel adjoins one of Edinburgh's premier shopping malls at the east end of Princes Street. A friendly team of staff are keen to please whilst stylish, well-equipped bedrooms provide excellent levels of comfort and facilities. Public areas include a spacious restaurant, popular bar, and an elegant lobby lounge.

Rooms 143 (12 fmly) **S** £60–£180; **Facilities** STV FTV Xmas New Year Wi-fi **Conf** Class 160 Board 50 Thtr 250 Del from £140 to £300* **Services** Lift **Parking** 18 **Notes** LB ⊗ Civ Wed 250

The Roxburghe Hotel

 MACDONALD HOTELS & RESORTS

★★★★ 74% HOTEL

☎ 0844 879 9063 & 0131 240 5500 📄 0131 240 5555
38 Charlotte Square EH2 4HQ
e-mail: general.roxburghe@macdonaldhotels.co.uk
web: www.macdonaldhotels.co.uk/roxburghe
dir: on corner of Charlotte Sq & George St

This long-established hotel lies in the heart of the city overlooking Charlotte Square Gardens. Public areas are

inviting and include relaxing lounges, a choice of bars (in the evening) and an inner concourse that looks onto a small lawned area. Smart bedrooms come in both classic and contemporary styles. There is a secure underground car park.

The Roxburghe Hotel

Rooms 196 (3 fmly) **S** £85–£260; **D** £95–£270
Facilities Spa FTV ⊙ Gym Dance studio Sauna Steam room Xmas New Year Wi-fi **Conf** Class 160 Board 50 Thtr 300 Del from £150 to £260 **Services** Lift Air con **Parking** 20 **Notes** LB ⊗ Civ Wed 280

Barceló Carlton Hotel

Barceló HOTELS & RESORTS

★★★★ 72% HOTEL

☎ 0131 472 3000 📄 0131 556 2691
North Bridge EH1 1SD
e-mail: carlton@barcelo-hotels.co.uk
web: www.barcelo-hotels.co.uk
dir: On North Bridge which links Princes St to The Royal Mile

The Carlton occupies a city centre location just off the Royal Mile. Inside, it is modern and stylish in design, with an impressive open-plan reception/lobby, spacious first-floor lounge, bar and restaurant, plus a basement leisure club. Bedrooms, many air-conditioned, are generally spacious, with an excellent range of accessories.

Rooms 189 (20 fmly) **Facilities** STV ⊙ supervised Gym Squash Table tennis Dance studio Creche Exercise classes Treatment rooms ♫ Xmas New Year Wi-fi **Conf** Class 110 Board 60 Thtr 220 Del from £115* **Services** Lift **Notes** Civ Wed 160

Novotel Edinburgh Centre

 NOVOTEL

★★★★ 72% HOTEL

☎ 0131 656 3500 📄 0131 656 3510
Lauriston Place, Lady Lawson St EH3 9DE
e-mail: H3271@accor.com
web: www.novotel.com
dir: From Edinburgh Castle right onto George IV Bridge from Royal Mile. Follow to junct, then right onto Lauriston Place. Hotel 700mtrs on right

One of the new generations of Novotels, this modern hotel is located in the centre of the city, close to Edinburgh Castle. Smart and stylish public areas include a cosmopolitan bar, brasserie-style restaurant and indoor leisure facilities. The air-conditioned bedrooms feature a comprehensive range of extras and bathrooms with baths and separate shower cabinets.

Rooms 180 (146 fmly) (17 smoking) **Facilities** STV ⊙ Gym Sauna Steam room Xmas Wi-fi **Conf** Class 50 Board 32 Thtr 80 **Services** Lift Air con **Parking** 15

Holiday Inn Edinburgh

 Holiday Inn HOTELS · RESORTS

★★★★ 🅰 HOTEL

☎ 0870 400 9026 📄 0131 334 9237
Corstorphine Rd EH12 6UA
e-mail: edinburghhi@ihg.com
web: www.holidayinn.co.uk
dir: On A8, adjacent to Edinburgh Zoo

Rooms 303 (76 fmly) (41 smoking) **Facilities** Spa STV ⊙ supervised Gym New Year Wi-fi **Conf** Class 60 Board 45 Thtr 120 Del from £135 to £185* **Services** Lift Air con **Parking** 105 **Notes** ⊗

Malmaison Edinburgh

Malmaison

★★★ 86% ⚘⚘ HOTEL

☎ 0131 468 5000 📄 0131 468 5002
One Tower Place EH6 7DB
e-mail: edinburgh@malmaison.com
web: www.malmaison.com
dir: A900 from city centre towards Leith, at end of Leith Walk , & through 3 sets of lights, left into Tower St. Hotel on right at end of road

The trendy Port of Leith is home to this stylish Malmaison. Inside, bold contemporary designs make for a striking effect. Bedrooms are comprehensively equipped with CD players, mini-bars and loads of individual touches. Ask for one of the stunning superior room for a really memorable stay. The smart brasserie and a café bar are popular with the local clientele.

Rooms 100 (18 fmly) **Facilities** STV Gym Xmas New Year Wi-fi **Conf** Class 30 Board 40 Thtr 55 **Services** Lift **Parking** 50 **Notes** LB

Dalhousie Castle and Aqueous Spa

★★★ 81% ◉◉ HOTEL

☎ 01875 820153 🖹 01875 821936
Bonnyrigg EH19 3JB
e-mail: info@dalhousiecastle.co.uk
web: www.dalhousiecastle.co.uk
dir: A7 S from Edinburgh through Lasswade/
Newtongrange, right at Shell Garage (B704), hotel 0.5m
from junct

A popular wedding venue, this imposing medieval castle
sits amid lawns and parkland and even has a falconry.
Bedrooms offer a mix of styles and sizes, including richly
decorated themed rooms named after various historical
figures. The Dungeon restaurant provides an atmospheric
setting for dinner, and the less formal Orangery serves
food all day. The spa offers many relaxing and
therapeutic treatments and hydro facilities. Von Essen
Hotels - AA Hotel Group of the Year 2009-10.

Rooms 36 (7 annexe) (3 fmly) **S** £125-£245; **D** £140-£345
(incl. bkfst)* **Facilities** Spa FTV Fishing Falconry Clay
pigeon shooting Archery Laserday Xmas New Year Wi-fi
Conf Class 60 Board 45 Thtr 120 Del from £188 to £208*
Parking 110 **Notes** LB Civ Wed 100

Apex Haymarket

★★★ 81% HOTEL

☎ 0845 365 0000 & 0131 474 3456 🖹 0131 474 3400
90 Haymarket Ter EH12 5LQ
e-mail: edinburgh.reservations@apexhotels.co.uk
web: www.apexhotels.co.uk
dir: A8 to city centre

Lying just west of the city centre, close to Haymarket
Station and handy for the Conference Centre, this modern
hotel is popular with business travellers. Smart, stylish
bedrooms offer an excellent range of facilities and have
been designed with work requirements in mind. Public
areas include Metro, an informal bistro. Service is friendly
and pro-active.

Rooms 66 (3 GF) (8 smoking) **Facilities** FTV Xmas New
Year Wi-fi **Conf** Class 30 Board 36 Thtr 80 **Services** Lift
Parking 10 **Notes** LB ⊗ Closed 24-27 Dec

Best Western Braid Hills

★★★ 80% HOTEL

☎ 0131 447 8888 🖹 0131 452 8477
134 Braid Rd EH10 6JD
e-mail: bookings@braidhillshotel.co.uk
web: www.braidhillshotel.co.uk
dir: 2.5m S A702, opposite Braid Burn Park

From its elevated position on the south side, this long-
established hotel enjoys splendid panoramic views of the
city and castle. Bedrooms are smart, stylish and well
equipped. The public areas are comfortable and inviting,
and guests can dine in either the restaurant or popular
bistro/bar.

Rooms 67 (14 fmly) (14 GF) **S** £60-£140; **D** £80-£195
(incl. bkfst)* **Facilities** STV Xmas New Year Wi-fi
Conf Class 50 Board 30 Thtr 100 **Parking** 38 **Notes** LB ⊗
Civ Wed 100

Best Western Edinburgh Capital

★★★ 80% HOTEL

☎ 0131 535 9988 🖹 0131 334 9712
187 Clermiston Rd EH12 6UG
e-mail: manager@edinburghcapitalhotel.co.uk
dir: from A8 into Clermiston Rd at National Tyre Garage.
Hotel at top of hill

Attracting business, conference and leisure guests alike,
this purpose-built hotel lies on the west side of the city
and is convenient for the airport and the north. Modern in
style throughout, the hotel offers a wide range of well-
appointed bedrooms including family rooms. The West
View restaurant and lounge bar is the setting for a good
choice of dishes and snacks.

Rooms 111 (6 fmly) (14 GF) **Facilities** FTV Gym
Sunbed room New Year Wi-fi **Conf** Class 130 Board 80
Thtr 320 **Services** Lift **Parking** 106 **Notes** Civ Wed 200

Mercure Point Hotel Edinburgh

★★★ 79% HOTEL

☎ 0131 221 5555 & 221 5554 🖹 0131 221 9929
34 Bread St EH3 9AF
e-mail: H6989@accor.com
dir: A71 to Haymarket Station. Straight on at junct &
right on Torphichen St, left onto Morrison St, straight on
to Bread St, hotel on right

Built in 1892 as a Co-op which once employed Sean
Connery as a milkman, the hotel has won many awards
for its design and presentation. Bedrooms are spacious
and cater well for the needs of the modern guest. Open-
plan public areas are enhanced with coloured lighting
and an array of artwork. The Point Restaurant offers
imaginative dishes. The Glass Box Penthouse conference
room affords fantastic views of the city.

Rooms 139 **S** £75-£145; **D** £80-£175 (incl. bkfst)
Facilities FTV New Year Wi-fi **Conf** Class 60 Board 40
Thtr 120 Del from £135 to £160* **Services** Lift **Parking** 8
Notes LB ⊗ Civ Wed 80

Old Waverley

★★★ 79% HOTEL

☎ 0131 556 4648 🖹 0131 557 6316
43 Princes St EH2 2BY
e-mail: reservations@oldwaverley.co.uk
web: www.oldwaverley.co.uk
dir: in city centre, opposite Scott Monument, Waverley
Station & Jenners

Occupying a commanding position opposite Sir Walter
Scott's famous monument on Princes Street, this hotel
lies right in the heart of the city close to the station. The
comfortable public rooms are all on first-floor level and
along with front-facing bedrooms enjoy the fine views. All
bedrooms have now been refurbished.

Rooms 85 (5 fmly) **S** £60-£209; **D** £80-£299*
Facilities Leisure facilities at sister hotel Wi-fi
Services Lift **Notes** ⊗

Best Western Edinburgh City

★★★ 78% HOTEL

☎ 0131 622 7979 🖹 0131 622 7900
79 Laurieston Place EH3 9HZ
e-mail: reservations@bestwesternedinburghcity.co.uk
dir: follow signs for city centre A8. Onto A702, 3rd exit on
left, hotel on right

Occupying a site where there was once a memorial
hospital, this stylish conversion is located close to the
city centre. Spacious bedrooms are smartly modern and
well equipped. Meals can be enjoyed in the bright
contemporary restaurant and guests can relax in the
cosy, bar and reception lounge. Staff are friendly and
obliging.

Rooms 52 (12 fmly) (5 GF) **Facilities** FTV New Year Wi-fi
Services Lift **Parking** 4 **Notes** ⊗

EDINBURGH *continued*

Best Western Kings Manor

★★★ 78% HOTEL

☎ 0131 669 0444 & 468 8003 📠 0131 669 6650
100 Milton Road East EH15 2NP
e-mail: reservations@kingsmanor.com
web: www.kingsmanor.com
dir: A720 E to Old Craighall junct, left into city, right at A1/A199 junct, hotel 400mtrs on right

Lying on the eastern side of the city and convenient for the by-pass, this hotel is popular with business guests, tour groups and for conferences. It boasts a fine leisure complex and a bright modern bistro, which complements the quality, creative cooking in the main restaurant.

Rooms 95 (8 fmly) (13 GF) **S** £50-£95; **D** £60-£180* **Facilities** Spa STV FTV Gym Health & beauty salon Steam room Sauna Xmas New Year Wi-fi **Conf** Class 70 Board 50 Thtr 140 **Services** Lift **Parking** 120 **Notes** LB Civ Wed 100

Quality Hotel Edinburgh Airport

★★★ 77% HOTEL

☎ 0131 333 4331 📠 0131 333 4124
Ingliston EH28 8AU
e-mail: info@qualityhoteledinburgh.com
dir: From M8, M9 & Forth Road Bridge follow signs for airport then follow brown tourist signs to hotel

Just 20 minutes from the city centre, this modern hotel is convenient for Edinburgh International Airport, which is only two minutes away by courtesy minibus. The spacious executive bedrooms are the pick of the accommodation, and there is a bright restaurant offering a range of contemporary dishes.

Rooms 95 (15 fmly) (35 GF) **S** £60-£200; **D** £60-£200 **Facilities** STV FTV Wi-fi **Conf** Class 24 Board 24 Thtr 70 **Services** Lift **Parking** 100 **Notes** LB Civ Wed 80

Holiday Inn Edinburgh North

★★★ 74% HOTEL

☎ 0870 400 9025 📠 0131 332 3408
107 Queensferry Rd EH4 3HL
e-mail: reservations-edinburgh@ihg.com
web: www.holidayinn.co.uk
dir: on A90 approx 1m from city centre

Situated on the north-west side of the city, close to Murrayfield Stadium and just five miles from the airport, this purpose-built hotel has a bright contemporary look. The colourful, modern bedrooms are well equipped and three specifications are available - with two double beds; with a double bed and sofa; or with a double bed and separate lounge. Some have great views of the city too. There is limited free parking.

Rooms 101 (17 smoking) **Facilities** STV New Year Wi-fi **Conf** Class 60 Board 50 Thtr 140 **Services** Lift Air con **Parking** 80 **Notes** LB ® Civ Wed 120

Express by Holiday Inn Edinburgh Waterfront

BUDGET HOTEL

☎ 0131 555 4422 📠 0131 555 4646
Britannia Way, Ocean Dr, Leith EH6 6JJ
e-mail: info@hiex-edinburgh.com
web: www.hiexpress.com/exedinburghwat
dir: follow signs for Royal Yacht Britannia. Hotel just before Britannia on right

A modern hotel ideal for families and business travellers. Fresh and uncomplicated, the spacious rooms include Sky TV, power shower and tea and coffee-making facilities. Continental buffet breakfast is included in the room rate; other meals may be taken at the nearby family pub or restaurant. See also the Hotel Groups pages.

Rooms 145 (36 fmly) **Conf** Class 15 Board 18 Thtr 35

Holiday Inn Express Edinburgh City Centre

BUDGET HOTEL

☎ 0131 558 2300 📠 0131 558 2323
Picardy Place EH1 3JT
e-mail: info@hieedinburgh.co.uk
web: www.hiexpress.com/edinburghctyct
dir: Follow signs to city centre & Greenside NCP. Hotel near east end of Princes St off Picardy Place rdbt

A modern hotel ideal for families and business travellers. Fresh and uncomplicated, the spacious rooms include Sky TV, power shower and tea and coffee-making facilities. Continental buffet breakfast is included in the room rate; other meals may be taken at the nearby family pub or restaurant. See also the Hotel Groups pages.

Rooms 161 (53 fmly) (27 GF) (13 smoking) **S** £79-£229; **D** £79-£229 (incl. bkfst)* **Conf** Class 8 Board 18 Thtr 20 Del from £90 to £180*

Holiday Inn Express Edinburgh Royal Mile

BUDGET HOTEL

☎ 0131 524 8400 📠 0131 524 8401
South Grays Close, Cowgate EH1 1NA
e-mail: info@hiexpressedinburgh.co.uk
web: www.hiexpressedinburgh.co.uk

A modern hotel ideal for families and business travellers. Fresh and uncomplicated, the spacious rooms include Sky TV, power shower and tea and coffee-making facilities. Continental buffet breakfast is included in the room rate; other meals may be taken at the nearby family pub or restaurant. See also the Hotel Groups pages.

Rooms 78 (50 fmly) (10 GF) **S** £59-£229; **D** £59-£229 (incl. bkfst)* **Conf** Class 20 Board 20 Thtr 40

Ibis Edinburgh Centre

BUDGET HOTEL

☎ 0131 240 7000 📠 0131 240 7007
6 Hunter Square, (off The Royal Mile) EH1 1QW
e-mail: H2039@accor.com
web: www.ibishotel.com
dir: M8/M9/A1 over North Bridge (A7) & High St, take 1st right off South Bridge, into Hunter Sq

Modern, budget hotel offering comfortable accommodation in bright and practical bedrooms. Breakfast is self-service and dinner is available in the restaurant. See also the Hotel Groups pages.

Rooms 99 (2 GF) **S** £57-£135; **D** £57-£135*

Innkeeper's Lodge Edinburgh West

BUDGET HOTEL

☎ 0845 112 6002 📠 0845 112 6298
114-116 St John's Rd, Corstophine EH12 8AX
web: www.innkeeperslodge.com/edinburghwest
dir: M8 junct 1, N on A720. At Gogar rdbt, right onto A8 towards Edinburgh, straight over next rdbt, lodge on left just past church at St John's Rd

Innkeeper's Lodge represents an exciting, high value concept within the budget hotel market. Comfortable bedrooms provide excellent facilities that include satellite TV and modem points. Options include family rooms; and for the corporate guest, cutting edge IT which includes Wi-fi access. A popular Carvery provides all-day food, including an extensive, complimentary continental breakfast. See also the Hotel Groups pages.

Rooms 28 (4 fmly)

Travelodge Edinburgh Central

BUDGET HOTEL

☎ 0871 984 6137 ▤ 0131 557 3681
33 Saint Marys St EH1 1TA
web: www.travelodge.co.uk
dir: From A1 follow signs to city centre, after Meadow Bank Stadium left at lights, follow signs to Earth Museum. Lodge opposite

Travelodge offers good quality, good value, budget accommodation. All offer family rooms sleeping up to four (two adults, two children) with en suite bathroom/shower-room, remote-control TV, tea- and coffee-making facilities and comfortable beds. Food options vary. Breakfast is at the on-site Bar Café restaurant (if available) or to take away. See also Hotel Groups pages.

Rooms 193 **S** fr £29; **D** fr £29

Travelodge Edinburgh Dreghorn

BUDGET HOTEL

☎ 0871 984 6139 ▤ 0131 441 4296
46 Dreghorn Link EH13 9QR
web: www.travelodge.co.uk
dir: E on A720 (city bypass) at Dreghorn/Colinton exit. 1 exit W of A702 junct

Rooms 72 **S** fr £29; **D** fr £29

Travelodge Edinburgh Haymarket

BUDGET HOTEL

☎ 0871 984 6365 ▤ 0131 347 2808
24 Eglinton Crescent, Haymarket EH12 5BY
e-mail: edinburghhaymkt@travelodge.co.uk
dir: From W: enter city centre, pass zoo, 1st left into Coates Grdns. Eglinton Cres ahead. From all other directions: towards West End, Haymarket & airport. Pass Haymarket rail station, 2nd right

Rooms 73 **S** fr £29; **D** fr £29

Travelodge Edinburgh Learmonth

BUDGET HOTEL

☎ 0871 984 6415 ▤ 01844 358681
18-20 Learmonth Ter EH4 1PW
dir: Please phone for detailed directions

Rooms 64 **S** fr £29; **D** fr £29

Travelodge Edinburgh Mussleburgh

BUDGET HOTEL

☎ 0871 984 6138 ▤ 0131 653 6106
Moto Service Area, A1, Old Craighall EH21 8RE
web: www.travelodge.co.uk
dir: At Services just off rdbt of A1 & A720 city bypass

Rooms 45 **S** fr £29; **D** fr £29

Travelodge Edinburgh West End

BUDGET HOTEL

☎ 0871 984 6418 ▤ 0131 315 4632
69 Belford Rd EH4 3DG
web: www.travelodge.co.uk
dir: From city centre take A90 towards W, left at 2nd rdbt into Queensferry Terrace, straight ahead into Belford Rd. Lodge on right

Rooms 146 **S** fr £29; **D** fr £29 **Conf** Class 50 Board 45 Thtr 120

INSPECTORS' CHOICE

The Witchery by the Castle
◉ RESTAURANT WITH ROOMS

☎ 0131 225 5613 ▤ 0131 220 4392
352 Castlehill, The Royal Mile EH1 2NF
e-mail: mail@thewitchery.com
web: www.thewitchery.com
dir: Top of Royal Mile at gates of Edinburgh Castle

Originally built in 1595, the Witchery by the Castle is situated in a historic building at the gates of Edinburgh Castle. The two luxurious and theatrically decorated suites, known as the Inner Sanctum and the Old Rectory are located above the restaurant and are reached via a winding stone staircase. Filled with antiques, opulently draped beds, large roll-top baths and a plethora of memorabilia, this ancient and exciting establishment is often described as one of the country's most romantic destinations.

Rooms 7 (5 annexe)

SOUTH QUEENSFERRY   Map 21 NT17

Innkeeper's Lodge Edinburgh South Queensferry

BUDGET HOTEL

☎ 0845 112 6001 ▤ 0845 112 6299
7 Newhalls Rd EH30 9TA
web: www.innkeeperslodge.com/southqueensferry
dir: M8 junct 2 follow signs for Forth Road Bridge, onto M9/A8000. At rdbt take B907, to junct with B249. Turn right

Innkeeper's Lodge represents an exciting, high value concept within the budget hotel market. Comfortable bedrooms provide excellent facilities that include satellite TV and modem points. This carefully restored lodge is in a picturesque setting and has its own unique style and quirky character. Food is served all day, and an extensive, complimentary continental breakfast is offered. See also the Hotel Groups pages.

Rooms 14 (5 fmly) **Conf** Thtr 40

FALKIRK

BANKNOCK   Map 21 NS77

Glenskirlie House & Castle
★★★★ 86% ◉◉ HOTEL

☎ 01324 840201 ▤ 01324 841054
Kilsyth Rd FK4 1UF
e-mail: macaloneys@glenskirliehouse.com
dir: M80 junct 4 (East), at T-junct turn right. Hotel 1m on right

This establishment offers guests stylish boutique-style accommodation within the castle. Bedrooms are beautifully designed and boast sumptuous beds, iPod stations and many accessories. Equally eye-catching bathrooms with under floor heating are equipped with high quality bespoke amenities. Guests can dine in the long-established, fine dining Glenskirlie House restaurant, or the new more informal Castle Grill. Two adjacent venues for meetings and special events are also available.

Rooms 15 (3 fmly) **S** £185-£205; **D** £205-£255 (incl. bkfst)* **Facilities** STV FTV Wi-fi **Conf** Class 100 Board 60 Thtr 150 **Services** Lift **Parking** 80 **Notes** LB ⊗ Civ Wed 150

FALKIRK   Map 21 NS88

Travelodge Falkirk

BUDGET HOTEL

☎ 0871 984 6359 ▤ 01324 715742
West Beancross Farm, Junction 5 M9 FK2 0XS
dir: M9 junct 5, A9. 1st right. Lodge behind Beancross restaurant

Travelodge offers good quality, good value, budget accommodation. All offer family rooms sleeping up to four (two adults, two children) with en suite bathroom/shower-room, remote-control TV, tea- and coffee-making facilities and comfortable beds. Food options vary. Breakfast is at the on-site Bar Café restaurant (if available) or to take away. See also the Hotel Groups pages.

Rooms 52 **S** fr £29; **D** fr £29

GRANGEMOUTH — Map 21 NS98

The Grange Manor

★★★★ 78% HOTEL

☎ 01324 474836 📠 01324 665861
Glensburgh FK3 8XJ
e-mail: info@grangemanor.co.uk
web: www.grangemanor.co.uk
dir: E: off M9 junct 6, hotel 200mtrs to right. W: off M9 junct 5, A905 for 2m

Located south of town and close to the M9, this stylish hotel, popular with business and corporate clientele, benefits from hands-on family ownership. It offers spacious, high quality accommodation with superb bathrooms. Public areas include a comfortable foyer area, a lounge bar and a smart restaurant. Wallace's bar and restaurant is adjacent to the main house in the converted stables. Staff throughout are very friendly.

Rooms 36 (30 annexe) (6 fmly) (15 GF) **S** £80–£140; **D** £90–£160 (incl. bkfst) **Facilities** STV FTV Xmas New Year Wi-fi **Conf** Class 68 Board 40 Thtr 190 Del from £120 to £180 **Services** Lift **Parking** 154 **Notes** LB Civ Wed 160

POLMONT — Map 21 NS97

Macdonald Inchyra Grange

★★★★ 72% HOTEL

☎ 01324 711911 📠 01324 716134
Grange Rd FK2 0YB
e-mail: inchyra@macdonald-hotels.co.uk
web: www.macdonaldhotels.co.uk
dir: just beyond BP Social Club on Grange Rd

Ideally placed for the M9 and Grangemouth terminal, this former manor house has been tastefully extended. It provides extensive conference facilities and a choice of eating options: the relaxed atmosphere of the Café Crema or the Opus 504 Restaurant, which provides a more formal dining experience. Bedrooms are comfortable and mostly spacious.

Rooms 98 (6 annexe) (35 fmly) (33 GF) **Facilities** Spa STV ⊛ ☞ Gym Steam room Sauna New Year **Conf** Class 300 Board 80 Thtr 750 **Services** Lift **Parking** 500 **Notes** LB Civ Wed

FIFE

ABERDOUR — Map 21 NT18

Woodside

★★★ Ⓐ HOTEL

☎ 01383 860328 📠 01383 860920
High St KY3 0SW
e-mail: reception@thewoodsidehotel.co.uk
web: www.thewoodsidehotel.co.uk
dir: M90 junct 1, E on A291 for 5m, hotel on left on entering village

Rooms 20 (4 fmly) **S** £57–£80; **D** £87.50–£97.50 (incl. bkfst) **Facilities** FTV Wi-fi **Conf** Class 80 Board 10 Thtr 60 **Parking** 22 **Notes** LB ⊛ Civ Wed 80

See advert on this page

The Cedar Inn

★★ 67% HOTEL

☎ 01383 860310
20 Shore Rd KY3 0TR
e-mail: cedarinn@btinternet.com
web: www.cedarinn.co.uk
dir: in Aberdour turn right off A921 into High St then right into Shore Rd. Hotel 100yds on left

Lying between the village centre and the beach, this small hotel has three character bars, one dedicated to malt whiskies, and impressive bar and dinner menus. Bedrooms offer a mix of standards but all are well equipped.

Rooms 9 (2 fmly) **S** £45–£55; **D** £65–£85 (incl. bkfst)* **Facilities** ♫ Xmas New Year Wi-fi **Parking** 12 **Notes** LB ⊛

ANSTRUTHER — Map 21 NO50

The Waterfront

RESTAURANT WITH ROOMS

☎ 01333 312200 📠 01333 312288
18-20 Shore St KY10 3EA
e-mail: chris@anstruther-waterfront.co.uk
dir: Off A917 opposite marina

Situated overlooking the harbour, The Waterfront offers spacious, stylish, contemporary accommodation with bedrooms located in lovingly restored buildings in a courtyard behind the restaurant. There is a comfortable lounge with a smartly fitted kitchen and dining room, and laundry facilities are available in the granary. Dinner and breakfast are served in the attractive restaurant that offers a comprehensive menu featuring the best of local produce.

Rooms 8 (8 annexe) (3 fmly)

BURNTISLAND — Map 21 NT28

Kingswood

★★★ 75% HOTEL

☎ 01592 872329 🖹 01592 873123
Kinghorn Rd KY3 9LL
e-mail: rankin@kingswoodhotel.co.uk
web: www.kingswoodhotel.co.uk
dir: A921 (coast road) at Burntisland, right at rdbt, left at T-junct, at bottom of hill to Kinghorn road, hotel 0.5m on left

Lying east of the town, this hotel has views across the Firth of Forth to Edinburgh. Public rooms feature a range of cosy sitting areas, a spacious and attractive restaurant serving good value meals. There is also a good-size function room and multi-purpose conservatory. Bedrooms include two family suites and front-facing rooms with balconies.

Rooms 13 (3 fmly) (1 GF) **S** £59-£75; **D** £99-£120 (incl. bkfst) **Facilities** New Year Wi-fi **Conf** Class 20 Board 40 Thtr 150 Del from £90 to £110* **Parking** 50 **Notes** LB ⊗ Closed 26 Dec & 1 Jan Civ Wed 120

Inchview Hotel

★★★ 73% SMALL HOTEL

☎ 01592 872239
65-69 Kinghorn Rd KY3 9EB
e-mail: reception@inchview.co.uk
dir: M90 junct 1, follow Fife Coastal Route signed Burntisland

Looking out across the links to the Firth of Forth, this friendly hotel has been sympathetically restored. Bedrooms provide a variety of styles, with the superior rooms reflecting the Georgian character of the house; front-facing rooms have excellent views of the coastline. Both the restaurant and bar menus offer a wide and interesting choice.

Rooms 12 **Facilities** FTV Wi-fi **Conf** Class 64 Board 16 Thtr 64 **Parking** 12 **Notes** LB ⊗ No children 14yrs

CRAIL — Map 21 NO60

Balcomie Links

★★ 71% SMALL HOTEL

☎ 01333 450237 🖹 01333 450540
Balcomie Rd KY10 3TN
e-mail: mikekadir@balcomie.fsnet.co.uk
web: www.balcomie.co.uk
dir: Follow road to village shops, at junct of High St & Market Gate turn right. This road becomes Balcomie Rd, hotel on left

Especially popular with visiting golfers, this family-run hotel on the east side of the village represents good value for money and has a relaxing atmosphere. Bedrooms come in a variety of sizes and styles and offer all the expected amenities. Food is served from midday in the attractive lounge bar, and also in the bright cheerful dining room in the evening.

Rooms 14 (2 fmly) **Facilities** Games room Xmas New Year Wi-fi **Parking** 20 **Notes** Civ Wed 45

DUNFERMLINE — Map 21 NT08

Best Western Keavil House Hotel

★★★★ 74% ⊛ HOTEL

☎ 01383 736258 🖹 01383 621600
Crossford KY12 8QW
e-mail: reservations@keavilhouse.co.uk
web: www.keavilhouse.co.uk
dir: 2m W of Dunfermline on A994

Dating from the 16th century, this former manor house is set in gardens and parkland. With a modern health club and conference rooms it is suited to both business and leisure guests. Bedrooms come in a variety of sizes and occupy the original house and a modern wing. The award-winning conservatory restaurant, Cardoon, is the focal point of public rooms.

Rooms 73 (4 fmly) (29 GF) **S** £90-£120; **D** £110-£150 (incl. bkfst)* **Facilities** STV 🏊 supervised Gym Aerobics studio Beautician Xmas New Year Wi-fi **Conf** Class 80 Board 60 Thtr 300 Del from £135 to £155* **Parking** 250 **Notes** LB ⊗ Civ Wed 200

Pitbauchlie House

★★★ 77% HOTEL

☎ 01383 722282 🖹 01383 620738
Aberdour Rd KY11 4PB
e-mail: info@pitbauchlie.com
web: www.pitbauchlie.com
dir: M90 junct 2, onto A823, then B916. Hotel 0.5m on right

Situated in three acres of wooded grounds this hotel is just a mile south of the town and has a striking modern interior. The bedrooms are well equipped, and the deluxe rooms now have 32-inch LCD satellite TVs and CD micro systems; there is one bedroom designed for less able guests. The eating options include Harvey's Conservatory bistro and Restaurant 47 where Scottish and French influenced cuisine is offered.

Rooms 50 (3 fmly) (19 GF) **S** £63-£95; **D** £75-£110 (incl. bkfst)* **Facilities** STV FTV Gym Wi-fi **Conf** Class 80 Board 60 Thtr 150 **Parking** 80 **Notes** LB Civ Wed 150

King Malcolm

PEEL HOTELS PLC

★★★ 71% HOTEL

☎ 01383 722611 🖹 01383 730865
Queensferry Rd KY11 8DS
e-mail: info@kingmalcolm-hotel-dunfermline.com
web: www.peelhotel.com
dir: on A823, S of town

Located to the south of the city, this purpose-built hotel remains popular with business clientele and is convenient for access to both Edinburgh and Fife. Public

continued

DUNFERMLINE *continued*

rooms include a smart foyer lounge and a conservatory bar, as well as a restaurant. Bedrooms, although not large, are well laid out and well equipped.

Rooms 48 (2 fmly) (24 GF) **Facilities** ♬ Xmas New Year Wi-fi **Conf** Class 60 Board 50 Thtr 150 **Parking** 60 **Notes** LB Civ Wed 120

Express by Holiday Inn Dunfermline

BUDGET HOTEL

☎ 01383 748220 📄 01383 748221
Lauder College, Halbeath KY11 8DY
e-mail: info@hiexpressdunfermline.co.uk
web: www.hiexpress.com/dunfermline
dir: M9 junct 7 signed A994/A907, 3rd exit Lynebank rdbt or M90 junct 3, 2nd exit for A907, next rdbt 3rd exit, next rdbt 1st exit

A modern hotel ideal for families and business travellers. Fresh and uncomplicated, the spacious rooms include Sky TV, power shower and tea and coffee-making facilities. Continental buffet breakfast is included in the room rate; other meals may be taken at the nearby family pub or restaurant. See also the Hotel Groups pages.

Rooms 82 **Conf** Class 8 Board 16 Thtr 25 Del from £70 to £80

Travelodge Dunfermline

BUDGET HOTEL

☎ 0871 984 6287
Halbeath Junction KY11 8PG
web: www.travelodge.co.uk
dir: M90 junct 3, follow signs for Halbeath, 1st right. Lodge on right

Travelodge offers good quality, good value, budget accommodation. All offer family rooms sleeping up to four (two adults, two children) with en suite bathroom/shower-room, remote-control TV, tea- and coffee-making facilities and comfortable beds. Food options vary. Breakfast is at the on-site Bar Café restaurant (if available) or to take away. See also Hotel Groups pages.

Rooms 50 **S** fr £29; **D** fr £29

GLENROTHES Map 21 NO20

Express by Holiday Inn Glenrothes

BUDGET HOTEL

☎ 01592 745509 📄 01592 743377
Leslie Roundabout, Leslie Rd KY6 3EP
e-mail: ebhi-glenrothes@btconnect.com
web: www.hiexpress.com/glenrothes
dir: M90 junct 2A left onto A911 for Leslie. Through 4 rdbts, hotel on left

A modern hotel ideal for families and business travellers. Fresh and uncomplicated, the spacious rooms include Sky TV, power shower and tea and coffee-making facilities. Continental buffet breakfast is included in the room rate; other meals may be taken at the nearby family pub or restaurant. See also the Hotel Groups pages.

Rooms 49 (40 fmly) (21 GF) **S** £59.95-£69.95; **D** £59.95-£69.95 (incl. bkfst)* **Conf** Class 16 Board 16 Thtr 30

Travelodge Glenrothes

BUDGET HOTEL

☎ 0871 984 6278 📄 01476 577500
Bankhead Park KY7 6GH
web: www.travelodge.co.uk
dir: M90/A92 to junct with A910/B981(signed Glenrothes), follow to Redhouse rdbt take 2nd exit (signed Glenrothes, Tay Bridge) follow to Bankhead rdbt junct with B921

Travelodge offers good quality, good value, budget accommodation. All offer family rooms sleeping up to four (two adults, two children) with en suite bathroom/shower-room, remote-control TV, tea- and coffee-making facilities and comfortable beds. Food options vary. Breakfast is at the on-site Bar Café restaurant (if available) or to take away. See also Hotel Groups pages.

Rooms 50 **S** fr £29; **D** fr £29

KIRKCALDY Map 21 NT29

Dean Park

★★★ 78% HOTEL

☎ 01592 261635 📄 01592 261371
Chapel Level KY2 6QW
e-mail: reception@deanparkhotel.co.uk
dir: Signed from A92, Kirkcaldy West junct

Popular with both business and leisure guests, this hotel has extensive conference and meeting facilities. Executive bedrooms are spacious and comfortable, and all are well equipped with modern decor and amenities. Twelve direct access, chalet-style rooms are set in the grounds and equipped to the same specification as main bedrooms. Public areas include a choice of bars and a restaurant.

Rooms 46 (12 annexe) (2 fmly) (5 GF) **Facilities** STV FTV Wi-fi **Conf** Class 125 Board 54 Thtr 250 **Services** Lift **Parking** 250 **Notes** ⊗

MARKINCH Map 21 NO20

INSPECTORS' CHOICE

Balbirnie House

★★★★ ◎◎ COUNTRY HOUSE HOTEL

☎ 01592 610066 📄 01592 610529
Balbirnie Park KY7 6NE
e-mail: info@balbirnie.co.uk
web: www.balbirnie.co.uk
dir: off A92 onto B9130, entrance 0.5m on left

The perfect venue for a business trip, wedding or romantic break, this imposing Georgian mansion lies in formal gardens and grounds amidst scenic Balbirnie Park. Delightful public rooms include a choice of inviting lounges. Accommodation features some splendid well-proportioned bedrooms with the best overlooking the gardens. But even the smaller standard rooms include little touches such as sherry, shortbread, fudge and mineral water. There is a choice of eating options, the Orangery or the more informal Bistro.

Rooms 30 (9 fmly) (7 GF) **S** £85-£115; **D** £170-£210 (incl. bkfst)* **Facilities** ⚘ Woodland walks Jogging trails Xmas New Year Wi-fi **Conf** Class 100 Board 60 Thtr 220 **Parking** 120 **Notes** LB Civ Wed 150

Town House

RESTAURANT WITH ROOMS

☎ 01592 758459 🖹 01592 755039
1 High St KY7 6DQ
e-mail: townhousehotel@aol.com
web: www.townhousehotel-fife.co.uk
dir: In town centre opposite railway station

Well situated on the edge of town and close to the railway station, this friendly establishment offers well presented bedrooms with pleasant colour schemes, modern furnishings, and a good range of facilities and extras. The attractive bar-restaurant is popular with locals and serves a choice of good-value dishes.

Rooms 3 (1 fmly)

PEAT INN   Map 21 NO40

The Peat Inn

☺☺ RESTAURANT WITH ROOMS

☎ 01334 840206 🖹 01334 840530
KY15 5LH
e-mail: stay@thepeatinn.co.uk
dir: At junct of B940 & B941, 5m SW of St Andrews

This 300-year-old former coaching inn enjoys a rural location yet is close to St Andrews. The spacious accommodation is very well appointed and all rooms have lounge areas. The inn is steeped in history and is a real haven for food lovers. The three dining areas create a romantic setting. Expect open fires and a relaxed ambiance.

Rooms 8 (8 annexe) (2 fmly)

ST ANDREWS   Map 21 NO51

INSPECTORS' CHOICE

The Old Course Hotel, Golf Resort & Spa

★★★★★ ☺☺☺ HOTEL

☎ 01334 474371 🖹 01334 477668
KY16 9SP
e-mail: reservations@oldcoursehotel.co.uk
dir: M90 junct 8 then A91 to St Andrews

A haven for golfers, this internationally renowned hotel sits adjacent to the 17th hole of the championship course. Bedrooms vary in size and style but all provide decadent levels of luxury. Day rooms include intimate lounges, a bright conservatory, a spa and a range of pro golf shops. The fine dining 'Grill', the seafood bar 'Sands' and the informal Jigger pub are all popular eating venues. Staff throughout are friendly and services are impeccably delivered.

Rooms 144 (5 fmly) (1 GF) **Facilities** Spa STV FTV ☜ ♨
18 Putt green Gym Thermal suite Xmas New Year Wi-fi
Conf Class 473 Board 259 Thtr 950 **Services** Lift
Parking 125 **Notes** ⊗ Civ Wed 180

INSPECTORS' CHOICE

Rufflets Country House

★★★★ ☺☺ HOTEL

☎ 01334 472594 🖹 01334 478703
Strathkinness Low Rd KY16 9TX
e-mail: reservations@rufflets.co.uk
web: www.rufflets.co.uk
dir: 1.5m W on B939

This charming property is set in extensive gardens a few minutes' drive from the town centre. Stylish, spacious bedrooms are individually decorated. Public rooms include a well-stocked bar, a choice of inviting lounges and the delightful Garden Room Restaurant that serves imaginative, carefully prepared cuisine. Impressive conference and banqueting facilities are available in the adjacent Garden Suite.

Rooms 24 (5 annexe) (2 fmly) (3 GF) **S** £140-£155;
D £195-£245 (incl. bkfst)* **Facilities** STV Putt green ♨
Golf driving net Xmas New Year Wi-fi **Conf** Class 60
Board 60 Thtr 200 Del from £150 to £250* **Parking** 50
Notes LB ⊗ Civ Wed 130

ST ANDREWS *continued*

Macdonald Rusacks

★★★★ 73% ◎◎ HOTEL

☎ 0844 879 9136 & 01334 474321 🖥 01334 477896
Pilmour Links KY16 9JQ
e-mail: general.rusacks@macdonald-hotels.co.uk
web: www.macdonald-hotels.co.uk
dir: A91 W, straight over rdbt entering St Andrews. Hotel
220yds on left

This long-established hotel enjoys an almost unrivalled
location with superb views across the famous golf course.
Bedrooms, though varying in size, are comfortably
appointed and well equipped. Classically styled public
rooms include an elegant reception lounge and a smart
restaurant.

Rooms 68 **Facilities** STV FTV Xmas New Year Wi-fi
Conf Class 35 Board 20 Thtr 80 Del from £95 to £365*
Services Lift **Parking** 21 **Notes** Civ Wed 60

Best Western Scores

★★★ 79% HOTEL

☎ 01334 472451 🖥 01334 473947
76 The Scores KY16 9BB
e-mail: reception@scoreshotel.co.uk
web: www.scoreshotel.co.uk
dir: M90 junct 2A onto A92 E. Follow signs Glenrothes
then St Andrews. Straight over at 1st two rdbts then left
onto Golf Place & right onto The Scores

Enjoying views over St Andrews Bay, this well presented
hotel is situated only a short pitch from the first tee of the
famous Old Course. Bedrooms are impressively furnished
and come in various sizes; many are quite spacious.
Smart public areas include a restaurant offering food all
day in addition to dinner. Alexander's Restaurant &

Cocktail Bar opens during the summer months and on
Friday and Saturday nights in winter.

Rooms 30 (1 fmly) **S** £84.50-£180; **D** £120-£286 (incl.
bkfst)* **Facilities** FTV New Year Wi-fi **Conf** Class 60
Board 40 Thtr 180 Del from £135 to £187* **Services** Lift
Parking 8 **Notes** ⊗ Civ Wed 100

Russell Hotel

★★ 78% ◎ HOTEL

☎ 01334 473447 🖥 01334 478279
26 The Scores KY16 9AS
e-mail: russellhotel@talk21.com
dir: From A91 left at 2nd rdbt into Golf Place, right in
200yds into The Scores, hotel in 300yds on left

Lying on the east bay, this friendly, family-run hotel
provides well appointed bedrooms in varying sizes; some
enjoy fine sea views. Cosy public areas include a popular
bar and an intimate restaurant, both offering a good
range of freshly prepared dishes.

Rooms 10 (3 fmly) **Facilities** New Year **Notes** ⊗

St Andrews Golf

Ⓤ

☎ 01334 472611 🖥 01334 472188
40 The Scores KY16 9AS
e-mail: reception@standrews-golf.co.uk
web: www.standrews-golf.co.uk
dir: follow 'Golf Course' signs into Golf Place, 200yds turn
right into The Scores

Currently the rating for this establishment is not
confirmed. This may be due to a change of ownership or
because it has only recently joined the AA rating scheme.
For further details please see the AA website: theAA.com

Rooms 22 **Facilities** New Year Wi-fi **Conf** Class 80
Board 20 Thtr 200 **Services** Lift **Parking** 6 **Notes** LB
Closed 26-28 Dec Civ Wed 180

See also **Clydebank (West Dunbartonshire) &
Uplawmoor (East Renfrewshire)**

INSPECTORS' CHOICE

Hotel du Vin at One Devonshire Gardens

★★★★ ◎◎◎ TOWN HOUSE HOTEL

☎ 0141 339 2001 🖥 0141 337 1663
1 Devonshire Gardens G12 0UX
e-mail: reservations.odg@hotelduvin.com
web: www.hotelduvin.com
dir: M8 junct 17, follow signs for A82, 1.5m turn left into
Hyndland Rd, 1st right, right at mini rdbt, right at end

Situated in a tree lined Victorian terrace this luxury
'boutique' hotel has stunning, individually designed
bedrooms and suites that have the trademark Egyptian
linen and seriously good showers. The oak-panelled
Bistro offers a daily-changing menu of both classic
and modern dishes with a Scottish influence. Naturally,
wine is an important part of the equation here, and
knowledgeable staff can guide guests around the
impressive wine list.

Rooms 49 (7 GF) **Facilities** Gym Tennis & Squash
facilities at nearby club Xmas New Year Wi-fi
Conf Class 30 Board 30 Thtr 50 **Notes** Civ Wed 70

City Inn Glasgow

★★★★ 77% ◎ HOTEL

☎ 0141 227 1010 & 240 1002 🖥 0141 248 2754
Finnieston Quay G3 8HN
e-mail: glasgow.citycafe@cityinn.com
web: www.citycafe.com
dir: M8 junct 19 follow signs for SECC. Hotel on left
200yds before entrance to SECC

A contemporary hotel sitting alongside the River Clyde
and the 'Squinty Bridge'. Modern, well-equipped
bedrooms and bathrooms have many thoughtful extras
for guests. Alfresco dining and drinking are a possibility;
the restaurant has panoramic views of the Clyde. The
hotel is ideally located for the SECC & Science Centre.

Rooms 164 **S** £89-£195; **D** £89-£195* **Facilities** STV FTV
Gym Xmas New Year Wi-fi **Conf** Class 20 Board 24 Thtr 45
Del from £125 to £270* **Services** Lift Air con **Parking** 120
Notes ⊗ Civ Wed 50

Glasgow Marriott Hotel

Marriott HOTELS & RESORTS

★★★★ 77% HOTEL

☎ 0141 226 5577 ▤ 0141 221 9202
500 Argyle St, Anderston G3 8RR
e-mail: london.regional.reservations@marriott.com
web: www.glasgowmarriott.co.uk
dir: M8 junct 19, turn left at lights, then left into hotel

Conveniently located for all major transport links and the city centre, this hotel benefits from extensive conference and banqueting facilities and a spacious car park. Public areas include an open-plan lounge/bar and a Mediterranean style restaurant. High quality, well-equipped bedrooms benefit from air-conditioning and generously sized beds; the suites are particularly comfortable.

Rooms 300 (89 fmly) **Facilities** ☞ Gym Beautician Poolside steam room Sauna New Year Wi-fi **Conf** Class 300 Board 50 Thtr 800 **Services** Lift Air con **Parking** 180 **Notes** ⊗ Civ Wed 700

Abode Hotel Glasgow

aBode

★★★★ 75% ☺☺ HOTEL

☎ 0141 221 6789 & 572 6000 ▤ 0141 221 6777
129 Bath St G2 2SZ
e-mail: reservationsglasgow@abodehotels.co.uk
web: www.abodehotels.co.uk
dir: From S, M8 junct 19 onto Bothwell St, turn left at Hope St, left onto Bath St. Hotel 0.3m on left

Set in the heart of the city, this concept hotel offers super rooms in a choice of sizes; all are contemporary and well appointed, including internet access and CD players. Formerly the Department of Education offices, the hotel has been transformed, yet keeps most of the grander features. The public areas are now rather 'funky' with a

stylish café bar, and the more formal, fine-dining Michael Caines restaurant which proves popular.

Rooms 60 (11 fmly) (5 GF) **D** £130-£245* **Facilities** STV ♫ Xmas New Year **Conf** Class 40 Board 35 Thtr 70 **Services** Lift Air con **Notes** LB ⊗ Civ Wed 100

Thistle Glasgow

thistle

★★★★ 75% HOTEL

☎ 0871 376 9043 ▤ 0871 376 9143
36 Cambridge St G2 3HN
e-mail: glasgow@thistle.co.uk
web: www.thistle.com/glasgow
dir: In city centre, just off Sauchiehall St

Ideally located within the centre of Glasgow and with ample parking, this hotel is well presented with the lobby area that gives a great impression on arrival. It also benefits from having a well-presented leisure club along with the largest ballroom in Glasgow. Service is friendly and attentive.

Rooms 300 (38 fmly) (1 smoking) **S** £70-£200; **D** £70-£200* **Facilities** STV ☞ Gym Sauna Steam room New Year Wi-fi **Conf** Class 800 Board 15 Thtr 1000 Del from £125 to £170* **Services** Lift Air con **Parking** 216 **Notes** LB Civ Wed 720

Millennium Hotel Glasgow

MILLENNIUM

★★★★ 74% HOTEL

☎ 0141 332 6711 ▤ 0141 332 4264
George Square G2 1DS
e-mail: glasgow.reservations@millenniumhotels.co.uk
web: www.millenniumhotels.co.uk
dir: From M8 junct 15 through 4 sets of lights, at 5th turn left into Hanover St. George Sq directly ahead, hotel on right

Right in the heart of the city, this hotel has pride of place overlooking George Square. Inside, the property has a

contemporary air, with a spacious reception concourse and a glass veranda overlooking the square. There is a stylish brasserie and separate lounge bar, and bedrooms come in a variety of sizes.

Rooms 116 (17 fmly) **S** £70-£199; **D** £70-£199* **Facilities** STV Soul therapies Health & beauty New Year Wi-fi **Conf** Class 24 Board 32 Thtr 40 Del from £125 to £175* **Services** Lift **Notes** LB ⊗ Closed 24-26 Dec Civ Wed 120

Beardmore

★★★★ 73% ☺ HOTEL

☎ 0141 951 6000 ▤ 0141 951 6018
Beardmore St G81 4SA
e-mail: info@beardmore.scot.nhs.uk

(For full entry see Clydebank, West Dunbartonshire)

Menzies Glasgow

MenziesHotels

★★★★ 72% HOTEL

☎ 0141 222 2929 & 270 2323 ▤ 0141 270 2301
27 Washington St G3 8AZ
e-mail: glasgow@menzieshotels.co.uk
web: www.menzieshotels.co.uk
dir: M8 junct 19 for SECC & follow signs for Broomielaw. Turn left at lights

Centrally located, this modern hotel is a short drive from the airport and an even shorter walk from the centre of the city. Bedrooms are generally spacious and boast a range of facilities, including high-speed internet access. Facilities include a brasserie restaurant and an impressive indoor leisure facility.

Rooms 141 (16 fmly) (15 smoking) **S** £65-£170; **D** £65-£170* **Facilities** STV ☞ supervised Gym Sauna Steam room Hair & beauty salon Xmas New Year Wi-fi **Conf** Class 60 Board 70 Thtr 160 Del from £130 to £165* **Services** Lift Air con **Parking** 50 **Notes** Civ Wed 150

GLASGOW *continued*

Crowne Plaza Glasgow

★★★★ 🅐 HOTEL

☎ 0870 443 1691 📄 0141 221 2022
Congress Rd G3 8QT
e-mail: cpglasgow@qmh-hotels.com
web: www.crowneplaza.co.uk
dir: M8 junct 19, follow signs for SECC, hotel adjacent to centre

Rooms 283 (15 fmly) **Facilities** Spa STV 🄌 supervised Gym Beauty salon Xmas New Year Wi-fi **Conf** Class 482 Board 68 Thtr 800 **Services** Lift Air con **Parking** 300 **Notes** ⊗ Civ Wed 120

Malmaison Glasgow

★★★ 83% ⊛ HOTEL

☎ 0141 572 1000 📄 0141 572 1002
278 West George St G2 4LL
e-mail: glasgow@malmaison.com
web: www.malmaison.com
dir: from S & E - M8 junct 18 (Charing Cross), from W & N - M8 city centre

Built around a former church in the historic Charing Cross area, this hotel is a smart, contemporary establishment offering impressive levels of service and hospitality. Bedrooms are spacious and feature a host of modern facilities, such as CD players and mini bars. Dining is a treat here, with French brasserie-style cuisine, backed up by an excellent wine list, served in the original crypt.

Rooms 72 (4 fmly) (19 GF) **Facilities** STV Gym Cardiovascular equipment New Year Wi-fi **Conf** Board 22 Thtr 30 **Services** Lift **Notes** Civ Wed 80

Uplawmoor Hotel

THE CIRCLE

★★★ 80% ⊛⊛ HOTEL

☎ 01505 850565 📄 01505 850689
Neilston Rd G78 4AF
e-mail: info@uplawmoor.co.uk
web: www.uplawmoor.co.uk

(For full entry see Uplawmoor, East Renfrewshire)

Holiday Inn

★★★ 80% ⊛ HOTEL

☎ 0141 352 8300 📄 0141 332 7447
161 West Nile St G1 2RL
e-mail: reservations@higlasgow.com
web: www.holidayinn.co.uk
dir: M8 junct 16, follow signs for Royal Concert Hall, hotel opposite

Built on a corner site close to the Theatre Royal Concert Hall and the main shopping areas, this contemporary hotel features the popular La Bonne Auberge French restaurant, a bar area and conservatory. Bedrooms are

well equipped and comfortable; suites are available. Staff are friendly and attentive.

Rooms 113 (20 fmly) (28 smoking) **Facilities** STV FTV Wi-fi **Conf** Class 60 Board 60 Thtr 100 **Services** Lift Air con **Notes** LB ⊗

Novotel Glasgow Centre

★★★ 75% HOTEL

☎ 0141 222 2775 📄 0141 204 5438
181 Pitt St G2 4DT
e-mail: H3136@accor.com
web: www.novotel.com
dir: M8 junct 18 for Charing Cross. Follow to Sauchiehall St. Take 3rd street on right

Enjoying a convenient city centre location and with limited parking spaces, this hotel is ideal for both business and leisure travellers. Well-equipped bedrooms are brightly decorated and offer functional design. Modern public areas include a small fitness club and a brasserie serving a range of meals all day.

Rooms 139 (139 fmly) (12 smoking) **Facilities** Gym Pool table Playstation Sauna Steam room Xmas Wi-fi **Conf** Class 20 Board 20 Thtr 40 Del from £100 to £140* **Services** Lift Air con **Parking** 19 **Notes** LB

Best Western Glasgow City Hotel

★★★ 73% TOWN HOUSE HOTEL

☎ 0141 227 2772 & 419 1915 📄 0141 227 2774
27 Elmbank St G2 4PB
e-mail: glasgowcity@mckeverhotels.co.uk
dir: Adjacent to Kings Theatre

A new hotel in the heart of the city offers spacious and well-equipped accommodation suitable for both families and business guests. Staff are friendly and helpful, and are mindful of the needs of the modern traveller. There is a secure pay car park close to the hotel.

Rooms 53 (4 fmly) (12 GF) **S** £49-£89; **D** £59-£109* **Facilities** FTV Xmas Wi-fi **Notes** LB ⊗

Campanile Glasgow

Campanile

BUDGET HOTEL

☎ 0141 287 7700 📄 0141 287 7701
10 Tunnel St G3 8HL
e-mail: glasgow@campanile.com
dir: M8 junct 19, follow signs to SECC. Hotel next to SECC

This modern building offers accommodation in smart, well-equipped bedrooms, all with en suite bathrooms. Refreshments may be taken at the informal bistro. See also the Hotel Groups pages.

Rooms 106 (2 fmly) (21 GF) **Conf** Class 60 Board 90 Thtr 150 Del from £95 to £125

Express by Holiday Inn Glasgow City Centre

BUDGET HOTEL

☎ 0141 331 6800 📄 0141 331 6828
165 West Nile St G1 2RL
e-mail: express@higlasgow.com
web: www.hiexpress.com/glasgowctyct
dir: follow signs to Royal Concert Hall

A modern hotel ideal for families and business travellers. Fresh and uncomplicated, the spacious rooms include Sky TV, power shower and tea and coffee-making facilities. Continental buffet breakfast is included in the room rate; other meals may be taken at the nearby family pub or restaurant. See also the Hotel Groups pages.

Rooms 118 (34 fmly) **Conf** Board 12 Thtr 20

Express by Holiday Inn Glasgow City Riverside

BUDGET HOTEL

☎ 0141 548 5000 📄 0141 548 5048
122 Stockwell St G1 4LT
e-mail: glasgow@expressholidayinn.co.uk
web: www.hiexpress.com/glascowcityct
dir: M8 E & S junct 19 SECC, left at end of exit, follow river under Central Station bridge to Stockwell St

Rooms 128 (79 fmly) (13 smoking) **S** £59-£149; **D** £59-£149 (incl. bkfst)* **Conf** Class 16 Board 16 Thtr 30

Ibis Glasgow

BUDGET HOTEL

☎ 0141 225 6000   🖷 0141 225 6010
220 West Regent St G2 4DQ
e-mail: H3139@accor-hotels.com
web: www.ibishotel.com

Modern, budget hotel offering comfortable accommodation in bright and practical bedrooms. Breakfast is self-service and meals are also available in the café-bar 24 hours. See also the Hotel Groups pages.

Rooms 141

Innkeeper's Lodge Glasgow/ Cumbernauld

BUDGET HOTEL

☎ 0845 112 6003   🖷 0845 112 6297
1 Auchenkilns Park, Cumbernauld G68 9AT
web: www.innkeeperslodge.com/glasgowcumbernauld
dir: M80 junct 3 or M73 (N'bound), or M80 junct 4 (S'bound), take A80 towards Cumbernauld. At Auchenkilns rdbt take B8048 signed Kirkintilloch

Innkeeper's Lodge represents an exciting, high value concept within the budget hotel market. Comfortable bedrooms provide excellent facilities that include satellite TV and modem points. Options include family rooms; and for the corporate guest, cutting edge IT includes Wi-fi access. Food is served all day in the adjacent Country Pub. The extensive continental breakfast is complimentary. See also the Hotel Groups pages.

Rooms 57 **Conf** Thtr 28

Travelodge Glasgow Central

BUDGET HOTEL

☎ 0871 984 6141   🖷 0141 333 1221
9 Hill St G3 6PR
web: www.travelodge.co.uk
dir: M8 junct 17, at lights left into West Graham St. Right into Cowcaddens Rd. Right into Cambridge St. Right into Hill St

Travelodge offers good quality, good value, budget accommodation. All offer family rooms sleeping up to four (two adults, two children) with en suite bathroom/shower-room, remote-control TV, tea- and coffee-making facilities and comfortable beds. Food options vary. Breakfast is at the on-site Bar Café restaurant (if available) or to take away. See also Hotel Groups pages.

Rooms 95 **S** fr £29; **D** fr £29

Travelodge Glasgow Paisley Road

BUDGET HOTEL

☎ 0871 984 6142   🖷 0141 420 3884
251 Paisley Rd G5 8RA
web: www.travelodge.co.uk
dir: M8 westbound junct 20 , through lights, pass Saab garage. Left onto Morrison St leads onto Paisley Rd. Left directly after Harry Ramsden's

Rooms 75 **S** fr £29; **D** fr £29

HIGHLAND

ABRIACHAN   Map 23 NH53

INSPECTORS' CHOICE

Loch Ness Lodge
◉◉ RESTAURANT WITH ROOMS

☎ 01456 459469   🖷 01456 459439
Brachla, Loch Ness-Side IV3 8LA
e-mail: escape@lodgeatlochness.com
dir: From A9 Inverness onto A82 signed Fort William, after 9m after 30mph speed sign, Lodge on right immediately after Clansman Hotel

This purpose-built house enjoys a prominent position overlooking Loch Ness and each of the individually designed bedrooms enjoys views of the loch. The bedrooms are of the highest standard, and beautifully presented with a nice mix of traditional luxury and modern technology, including Wi-fi. There is a spa with a hot tub, sauna and a therapy room offering a variety of treatments. Evening meals are served in the award-winning restaurant, and guests have a choice of attractive lounges which feature real fires in the colder months. AA Guest Accommodation for Scotland 2009-10.

Rooms 7

AVIEMORE   Map 23 NH81

Macdonald Highlands

★★★★ 75% HOTEL

☎ 01479 815100   🖷 01479 815101
Aviemore Highland Resort PH22 1PN
e-mail: general@aviemorehighlandresort.com
web: www.aviemorehighlandresort.com
dir: From N: Exit A9 to Aviemore (B970). Right at T-junct, through village. Right (2nd exit) at 1st rdbt into Macdonald Aviemore Highland Resort, follow reception signs. From S: Exit A9 to Aviemore, left at T-junct. Immediately after Esso garage, turn left into Resort

This hotel is part of the Aviemore Highland Resort which boasts a wide range of activities including a championship golf course. The modern, well-equipped bedrooms suit business, leisure guests and families, and Aspects Restaurant is the fine dining option. In addition there is a state-of-the-art gym, spa treatments and a 25-metre pool with a wave machine and flume.

Rooms 151 (10 fmly) (44 GF) **Facilities** Spa STV FTV ⓒ supervised ⚓ 18 Putt green Gym Steam room Sauna Out & indoor childrens playground Xmas New Year Wi-fi **Conf** Class 610 Board 38 Thtr 1000 **Services** Lift **Parking** 500 **Notes** LB ⊗ Civ Wed 300

BEAULY   Map 23 NH54

Priory

★★★ 74% HOTEL

☎ 01463 782309   🖷 01463 782531
The Square IV4 7BX
e-mail: reservations@priory-hotel.com
web: www.priory-hotel.com
dir: Signed from A832, into Beauly, hotel in square on left

This popular hotel occupies a central location in the town square. Standard and executive rooms are on offer, both providing a good level of comfort and range of facilities. Food is served throughout the day in the open-plan public areas, with menus offering a first rate choice.

Rooms 37 (3 fmly) (1 GF) (10 smoking) **S** £49.50-£65; **D** £55-£100 (incl. bkfst) **Facilities** STV FTV Xmas New Year Wi-fi **Conf** Class 40 Board 30 Thtr 40 Del from £65 to £80 **Services** Lift **Parking** 20 **Notes** LB ⊗

BEAULY *continued*

Lovat Arms
★★★ 72% HOTEL

☎ 01463 782313 📄 01463 782862
IV4 7BS
e-mail: info@lovatarms.com
web: www.lovatarms.com
dir: From The Square past Royal Bank of Scotland, hotel on right

This fine family run hotel enjoys a prominent position in this charming town which is a short drive from Inverness. The bedrooms are comfortable and well appointed. The spacious foyer has a real fire and comfortable seating, while the Strubag lounge is ideal for informal dining.

Rooms 34 (12 annexe) (3 fmly) **S** £40-£80; **D** £55-£100 (incl. bkfst) **Facilities** Wi-fi **Conf** Class 18 Board 36 Thtr 60 **Parking** 15

BOAT OF GARTEN Map 23 NH91

Boat
★★★ 82% ◉◉ HOTEL

☎ 01479 831258 & 831696 📄 01479 831414
PH24 3BH
e-mail: info@boathotel.co.uk
dir: Off A9 N of Aviemore onto A95, follow signs to Boat of Garten

This well established hotel is situated in the heart of the pretty village of Boat of Garten. The public areas include a choice of comfortable lounges and the restaurant has a well deserved reputation for fine dining; in addition the bistro serves meals until late. Individually styled bedrooms reflect the unique character of the hotel; all are comfortable, well equipped and have a host of thoughtful extras.

Rooms 34 (2 fmly) **Facilities** Xmas New Year Wi-fi **Conf** Class 30 Board 25 Thtr 40 **Parking** 36 **Notes** Civ Wed 40

BRORA Map 23 NC90

Royal Marine
★★★★ 75% ◉ HOTEL

☎ 01408 621252 📄 01408 621181
Golf Rd KW9 6QS
e-mail: info@royalmarinebrora.com
web: www.royalmarinebrora.com
dir: Off A9 in village towards beach & golf course

A distinctive Edwardian residence sympathetically extended, the Royal Marine attracts a mixed market. Its leisure centre is popular, and the restaurant, Hunters Lounge and café bar offer three contrasting eating options. A modern bedroom wing complements the original bedrooms, which retain period style. There are also luxury apartments just a short walk away.

Rooms 21 (1 fmly) (2 GF) **S** £89; **D** £134-£194 (incl. bkfst)* **Facilities** FTV 🕐 🏊 Putt green Fishing 🏌 Gym Steam room Sauna Xmas New Year Wi-fi **Conf** Class 40 Board 40 Thtr 70 **Parking** 40 **Notes** LB Civ Wed 60

CARRBRIDGE Map 23 NH92

Dalrachney Lodge
★★★ 74% SMALL HOTEL

☎ 01479 841252 📄 01479 841383
PH23 3AT
e-mail: dalrachney@aol.com
web: www.dalrachney.co.uk
dir: follow Carrbridge signs off A9. In village on A938

A traditional Highland lodge, Dalrachney lies in grounds by the River Dulnain on the edge of the village. Spotlessly maintained public areas include a comfortable and relaxing sitting room and a cosy well-stocked bar, which has a popular menu providing an alternative to the dining room. Bedrooms are generally spacious and furnished in period style.

Rooms 11 (3 fmly) **S** £60-£90; **D** £90-£140 (incl. bkfst)* **Facilities** Fishing Xmas New Year Wi-fi **Parking** 40 **Notes** LB

CONTIN Map 23 NH45

Coul House
★★★ 79% ◉ COUNTRY HOUSE HOTEL

☎ 01997 421487 📄 01997 421945
IV14 9ES
e-mail: stay@coulhousehotel.com
dir: Exit A9 north onto A835. Hotel on right

This imposing mansion house is set back from the road in extensive grounds. A number of the generally spacious bedrooms have superb views of the distant mountains and all are thoughtfully equipped. The Octagonal Restaurant offers guests the chance to enjoy contemporary Scottish cuisine.

Rooms 20 (3 fmly) (4 GF) **S** £45-£95; **D** £85-£190 (incl. bkfst)* **Facilities** 9 hole pitch & putt New Year Wi-fi Child facilities **Conf** Class 30 Board 30 Thtr 80 **Parking** 60 **Notes** LB Closed 24-26 Dec Civ Wed 100

Achilty
★★★ 73% ◉ SMALL HOTEL

☎ 01997 421355 📄 01997 421923
IV14 9EG
e-mail: info@achiltyhotel.co.uk
web: www.achiltyhotel.co.uk
dir: A9 onto A835, hotel 6m on right

Friendly owners contribute to great hospitality and a relaxed atmosphere at this roadside hotel. Public areas are full of interest; the lounges have books and games and the dining room has a musical theme. The Steading bar features exposed stone walls and offers a good selection of tasty home-cooked meals. Bedrooms are smartly furnished and cheerfully decorated.

Rooms 11 (1 annexe) (3 GF) (1 smoking) **Facilities** New Year **Conf** Class 50 Board 20 Thtr 50 **Parking** 100 **Notes** ⊗ Closed 3-10 Jan

DINGWALL — Map 23 NH55

Tulloch Castle
★★★★ 74% HOTEL

OXFORD
HOTELS & INNS

☎ 01349 861325 ▤ 01349 863993
Tulloch Castle Dr IV15 9ND
e-mail: info@tullochcastle.co.uk
web: www.oxfordhotelsandinns.com
dir: A9 N, Tore rdbt 2nd left signed Dingwall, at Dingwall turn left at 4th lights, hotel signed

Overlooking the town of Dingwall this 12th-century castle is still the gathering place of the Clan Davidson and boasts its own ghost in the shape of the Green Lady. The friendly team are very helpful and love to tell you about the history of the castle; the ghost tour after dinner is a must. The hotel has a self contained suite and a number of bedrooms with four-posters.

Rooms 20 (2 fmly) **Facilities** FTV Xmas New Year Wi-fi
Conf Class 70 Board 70 Thtr 120 Del from £115 to £180*
Parking 50 **Notes** ⊗ Civ Wed 110

DORNOCH — Map 23 NH78

Dornoch Castle Hotel
★★★ 74% ⊛ HOTEL

☎ 01862 810216 ▤ 01862 810981
Castle St IV25 3SD
e-mail: enquiries@dornochcastlehotel.com
web: www.dornochcastlehotel.com
dir: 2m N of Dornoch Bridge on A9, turn right to Dornoch. Hotel in village centre

Set opposite the cathedral, this fully restored ancient castle has become a popular wedding venue. Within the original castle are some splendid themed bedrooms, and elsewhere the more modern bedrooms have all of the expected facilities. There is a character bar and a delightful conservatory restaurant overlooking the garden.

Rooms 21 (3 fmly) (4 GF) **Facilities** FTV New Year Wi-fi
Conf Class 30 Board 30 Thtr 60 **Parking** 16 **Notes** LB
Civ Wed 95

See advert on this page

2 Quail Restaurant and Rooms
⊛⊛ RESTAURANT WITH ROOMS

☎ 01862 811811
Castle St IV25 3SN
e-mail: theaa@2quail.com
dir: On main street, 200yds from cathedral

The saying 'small is beautiful' aptly applies to this restaurant with rooms. Set in the main street the careful renovation of its Victorian origins transports guests back in time. Cosy public rooms are ideal for conversation, but there are masses of books for those just wishing to relax. The stylish, individual bedrooms match the character of the house but are thoughtfully equipped to include DVD players. Food is the main feature however, with excellent breakfasts and set four-course dinners.

Rooms 3 (1 fmly)

DRUMNADROCHIT — Map 23 NH53

Loch Ness Lodge
★★★ ◪ HOTEL

☎ 01456 450342 ▤ 01456 450429
IV63 6TU
e-mail: info@lochness-hotel.com
dir: Off A82 onto A831 (Cannich road)

Rooms 50 (4 fmly) (10 GF) **Facilities** FTV Visitors centre
Shops Cinema Boat cruises Hairdresser ♫ Wi-fi
Conf Class 40 Board 40 Thtr 150 **Parking** 80 **Notes** ⊗
Closed Nov-Feb Civ Wed 50

FORT AUGUSTUS — Map 23 NH30

Lovat Arms
★★★ 86% ⊛ HOTEL

☎ 0845 450 1100 & 01456 459250 ▤ 01320 366677
Loch Ness Side PH32 4DU
e-mail: info@lovatarms-hotel.com
web: www.lovatarms-hotel.com
dir: In town centre on A82

This charming country-house hotel enjoys an elevated position in the pretty town of Fort Augustus. It has impressively styled bedrooms with a host of thoughtful extras. Inviting public areas include a comfortable lounge with a log fire, a stylish bar, and contemporary restaurant were food is cooked with skill and care. The hospitality and commitment to guest care will leave a lasting impression.

Rooms 29 (6 annexe) (4 fmly) (7 GF) **Facilities** FTV Xmas
New Year Wi-fi **Conf** Class 20 Board 20 Thtr 50
Services Lift **Parking** 30

FORT WILLIAM Map 22 NN17

INSPECTORS' CHOICE

Inverlochy Castle
★★★★★
COUNTRY HOUSE HOTEL

☎ 01397 702177 📠 01397 702953
Torlundy PH33 6SN
e-mail: info@inverlochy.co.uk
web: www.inverlochycastlehotel.com
dir: Accessible from either A82 (Glasgow-Fort William) or A9 (Edinburgh-Dalwhinnie). Hotel 3m N of Fort William on A82, in Torlundy

With a backdrop of Ben Nevis, this imposing and gracious castle sits amidst extensive gardens and grounds overlooking the hotel's own loch. Lavishly appointed in classic country-house style, spacious bedrooms are extremely comfortable and boast flat-screen TVs and laptops with internet access. The sumptuous main hall and lounge provide the perfect setting for afternoon tea or a pre-dinner cocktail, whilst imaginative cuisine is served in one of three dining rooms. A snooker room and a DVD library are also available.

Rooms 17 (6 fmly) **S** £245-£345; **D** £380-£640 (incl. bkfst)* **Facilities** STV 🎣 Fishing 🎣 Fishing on loch Massage Riding Hunting Stalking Clay pigeon shooting Archery 🎵 Xmas New Year Wi-fi **Conf** Class 20 Board 20 Thtr 50 **Parking** 17 **Notes** LB Civ Wed 80

Moorings
★★★ 80% ⊛ HOTEL

☎ 01397 772797 📠 01397 772441
Banavie PH33 7LY
e-mail: reservations@moorings-fortwilliam.co.uk
web: www.moorings-fortwilliam.co.uk
dir: take A380 (N from Fort William), cross Caledonian Canal, 1st right

Located on the Caledonian Canal next to a series of locks known as Neptune's Staircase and close to Thomas Telford's house, this hotel with its dedicated team offers friendly service. Accommodation comes in two distinct styles and the newer rooms are particularly appealing. Meals can be taken in the bars or the spacious dining room.

Rooms 27 (1 fmly) (1 GF) (1 smoking) **S** £43-£116; **D** £86-£142 (incl. bkfst)* **Facilities** STV New Year Wi-fi **Conf** Class 60 Board 40 Thtr 140 Del from £95 to £120* **Parking** 60 **Notes** LB RS 24-27 Dec Civ Wed 120

Lime Tree Hotel & Restaurant
★★★ 78% ⊛ SMALL HOTEL

☎ 01397 701806 📠 01397 701806
Lime Tree Studio, Achintore Rd PH33 6RQ
e-mail: info@limetreefortwilliam.co.uk
dir: On A82 at entrance to Fort William

The Lime Tree is a charming small hotel with a super art gallery on the ground floor, with lots of original artwork displayed throughout. Evening meals can be enjoyed in the restaurant which has a loyal following. The hotel's comfortable lounges with their real fires are ideal for pre or post dinner drinks or maybe just to relax in. Individually designed bedrooms are spacious with some nice little personal touches courtesy of the artist owner.

Rooms 9 (4 fmly) (4 GF) **S** £60-£75; **D** £80-£100 (incl. bkfst)* **Facilities** New Year Wi-fi **Conf** Class 40 Board 30 Thtr 60 **Parking** 9 **Notes** Closed Nov

Alexandra
★★★ 75% HOTEL

☎ 01397 702241 📠 01397 705554
The Parade PH33 6AZ
e-mail: salesalexandra@strathmorehotels.com
dir: Off A82. Hotel opposite railway station

This charming old hotel enjoys a prominent position in the town centre and is just a short walk from all the major attractions. Front-facing bedrooms have views over the town and the spectacular Nevis mountain range. There is a choice of restaurants, including a bistro serving meals until late, along with several stylish and very comfortable lounges.

Rooms 93 (5 fmly) **Facilities** Free use of nearby leisure club 🎵 Xmas Wi-fi **Conf** Class 100 Board 40 Thtr 120 **Services** Lift **Parking** 50

See advert on page 617

Ben Nevis Hotel & Leisure Club
★★ 72% HOTEL

☎ 01397 702331 📠 01397 700132
North Rd PH33 6TG
e-mail: bennevismanager@strathmorehotels.com
dir: Off A82

This popular hotel is ideally situated on the outskirts of Fort William. It provides comfortable, well equipped bedrooms; many with views of the impressive Nevis mountains. The hotel's leisure centre is a firm favourite with guests at the hotel.

Rooms 119 (3 fmly) (30 GF) **Facilities** 🏊 supervised Gym Beauty salon 🎵 Xmas New Year Wi-fi **Conf** Class 60 Board 40 Thtr 150 **Parking** 100 **Notes** Civ Wed 60

See advert on page 617

Croit Anna

Leisureplex

★★ 64% HOTEL

☎ 01397 702268 📠 01397 704099
Achintore Rd, Drimarben PH33 6RR
e-mail: croitanna.fortwilliam@alfatravel.co.uk
dir: from Glencoe on A82 into Fort William, hotel 1st on right

Located on the edge of Loch Linnhe, just two miles out of town, this hotel offers some spacious bedrooms, many with fine views over the loch. There is a choice of two comfortable lounges and a large airy restaurant. The hotel appeals to coach parties and independent travellers alike.

Rooms 92 (5 fmly) (13 GF) **Facilities** FTV Pool table 🎵
Xmas New Year **Parking** 25 **Notes** LB ⊗ Closed Dec-Jan
(ex Xmas) RS Nov, Feb, Mar

FOYERS

Craigdarroch House

◉◉ RESTAURANT WITH ROOMS

☎ 01456 486400 📠 01456 486444
IV2 6XU
e-mail: info@hotel-loch-ness.co.uk
dir: Take B862 from either end of loch, then B852 signed Foyers

Craigdarroch is located in an elevated position high above Loch Ness on the south side. Bedrooms vary in style and size but all are comfortable and well equipped; front-facing have wonderful views. Dinner should not be missed and breakfasts are also impressive.

Rooms 10

GLENFINNAN   Map 22 NM98

The Prince's House

★★★ 78% ◉◉ SMALL HOTEL

☎ 01397 722246 📠 01397 722323
PH37 4LT
e-mail: princeshouse@glenfinnan.co.uk
web: www.glenfinnan.co.uk
dir: on A830, 0.5m on right past Glenfinnan Monument. 200mtrs from railway station

This delightful hotel enjoys a well deserved reputation for fine food and excellent hospitality. The hotel has inspiring views and sits close to where 'Bonnie' Prince Charlie raised the Jacobite standard. Comfortably appointed bedrooms offer pleasing decor. Excellent local game and seafood can be enjoyed in the restaurant and the bar.

Rooms 9 (1 fmly) **S** £55-£65; **D** £95-£120 (incl. bkfst)*
Facilities Fishing New Year **Conf** Class 20 Thtr 40
Parking 18 **Notes** LB Closed Xmas & Jan-Feb (ex New Year) RS Nov-Dec & Mar

---

GRANTOWN-ON-SPEY   Map 23 NJ03

Grant Arms Hotel

★★★ 78% HOTEL

☎ 01479 872526 📠 01479 873589
25-27IThe Square PH26 3HF
e-mail: info@grantarmshotel.com
web: www.grantarmshotel.com
dir: Exit A9 N of Aviemore & follow A95

Conveniently located in the centre of the town this fine hotel has now been refurbished and upgraded to a high standard yet its still retains its traditional character. The spacious bedrooms are all stylishly presented and very well equipped. The Garden Restaurant is a popular venue for dinner, and lighter snacks can be enjoyed in the comfortable bar. Modern conference facilities are available and the hotel is very popular with birdwatchers and wildlife enthusiasts.

Rooms 48 (4 fmly) **S** £65-£90; **D** £130-£340 (incl. bkfst & dinner)* **Facilities** STV 🎵 Xmas New Year Wi-fi
Conf Class 30 Board 16 Thtr 70 **Services** Lift **Notes** LB ⊗

INVERGARRY   Map 22 NH30

Glengarry Castle

★★★ 82% ◉ COUNTRY HOUSE HOTEL

☎ 01809 501254 📠 01809 501207
PH35 4HW
e-mail: castle@glengarry.net
web: www.glengarry.net
dir: on A82 beside Loch Oich, 0.5m from A82/A87 junct

This charming country-house hotel is set in 50 acres of grounds on the shores of Loch Oich. The spacious day rooms include comfortable sitting rooms with lots to read and board games to play. The classical dining room boasts an innovative menu that showcases local Scottish

continued

INVERGARRY *continued*

produce. The smart bedrooms vary in size and style but all boast magnificent loch or woodland views.

Glengarry Castle

Rooms 26 (2 fmly) **S** £62-£72; **D** £88-£168 (incl. bkfst) **Facilities** FTV Fishing Wi-fi **Parking** 32 **Notes** Closed mid Nov-mid Mar

See advert on page 595

INVERGORDON Map 23 NH76

Kincraig House

★★★★ 78% COUNTRY HOUSE HOTEL

☎ 01349 852587 ▤ 01349 852193
IV18 0LF
e-mail: info@kincraig-house-hotel.co.uk
web: www.kincraig-house-hotel.co.uk
dir: off A9 past Alness towards Tain. Hotel on left 0.25m past Rosskeen Church

This mansion house is set in well-tended grounds in an elevated position with views over the Cromarty Firth. It offers smart well-equipped bedrooms and inviting public areas that retain the original features of the house. However it is the friendly service and commitment to guest care that will leave a lasting impression.

Rooms 15 (1 fmly) (1 GF) **Facilities** STV Xmas Wi-fi **Conf** Class 30 Board 24 Thtr 50 **Parking** 30 **Notes** LB Civ Wed 70

See advert on opposite page

INVERNESS Map 23 NH64

The New Drumossie

★★★★ 80% HOTEL

☎ 01463 236451 & 0870 194 2110 ▤ 01463 712858
Old Perth Rd IV2 5BE
e-mail: stay@drumossiehotel.co.uk
dir: From A9 follow signs for Culloden Battlefield, hotel on left after 1m

Set in nine acres of landscaped hillside grounds south of Inverness, this hotel has fine views of the Moray Firth towards Ben Wyvis. Art deco style decoration together with a country-house atmosphere are found throughout. Service is friendly and attentive, the food imaginative and enjoyable and the bedrooms spacious and well presented. The main function room is probably the largest in this area.

Rooms 44 (10 fmly) (6 GF) **Facilities** STV Fishing New Year Wi-fi **Conf** Class 200 Board 40 Thtr 500 **Services** Lift **Parking** 200 **Notes** ⊗ Civ Wed 400

Dunain Park

★★★★ 79% SMALL HOTEL

☎ 01463 230512 ▤ 01463 224532
IV3 8JN
e-mail: info@dunainparkhotel.co.uk
web: www.dunainparkhotel.co.uk
dir: On A82, 1m from Inverness town boundary

Built in the Georgian era, this fine house has undergone an extensive refurbishment and is perfectly situated within its own six acre private Highland estate. The hotel has fifteen luxurious bedrooms, four of which are in the garden suite cottages. The stylish restaurant serves the best of local produce and guests have a choice of cosy well-appointed lounges for after dinner drinks. The garden terrace is ideal for relaxing and has splendid views over the landscaped gardens towards Inverness.

Rooms 13 (2 annexe) (8 fmly) (3 GF) **Facilities** FTV Xmas New Year Wi-fi Child facilities **Conf** Class 30 Board 20 Thtr 50 Del from £165 to £185* **Parking** 50 **Notes** Civ Wed 120

Culloden House

★★★★ 78% HOTEL

☎ 01463 790461 ▤ 01463 792181
Culloden IV2 7BZ
e-mail: info@cullodenhouse.co.uk
web: www.cullodenhouse.co.uk
dir: from Inverness take A96, turn right for Culloden. After 1m after 2nd lights left at White Church

Dating from the late 1700s this impressive mansion is set in extensive grounds close to the famous Culloden battlefield. High ceilings and intricate cornices are particular features of the public rooms, including the elegant Adam dining room. Bedrooms come in a range of sizes and styles, with a number situated in a separate house.

Rooms 28 (5 annexe) (1 fmly) **S** £85-£175; **D** £120-£375 (incl. bkfst)* **Facilities** STV Putt green Boules Badminton Golf driving net Putting green New Year Wi-fi **Conf** Class 40 Board 30 Thtr 60 Del from £125 to £275* **Parking** 50 **Notes** LB No children 10yrs Closed 24-28 Dec Civ Wed 65

Kingsmills

★★★★ 74% HOTEL

☎ 01463 237166 & 257100 ▤ 01463 225208
Culcabock Rd IV2 3LP
e-mail: reservations@kingsmillshotel.com
web: www.kingsmillshotel.com
dir: From A9 S, exit Culduthel/Kingsmills 5th exit at rdbt, 0.5m, over mini-rdbt past golf club. Hotel on left after lights

This manor house hotel is located just a short drive from the city, and is set in four acres of landscaped grounds. There is a range of spacious, well-equipped modern bedrooms; the rooms in newer wing are especially impressive. There is a choice of restaurants, a comfortable lounge, a leisure club and conference facilities.

Rooms 77 (5 fmly) (34 GF) (6 smoking) **S** £93-£176; **D** £93-£206 (incl. bkfst)* **Facilities** Spa STV supervised Putt green Gym Hairdresser Sauna Steam room Pitch & putt Xmas New Year Wi-fi **Conf** Class 34 Board 40 Thtr 100 **Services** Lift **Parking** 102 **Notes** LB Civ Wed 80

Bunchrew House

★★★★ 73% ⑧⑧ COUNTRY HOUSE HOTEL

☎ 01463 234917 📠 01463 710620
Bunchrew IV3 8TA
e-mail: welcome@bunchrew-inverness.co.uk
web: www.bunchrew-inverness.co.uk
dir: W on A862. Hotel 2m after canal on right

Overlooking the Beauly Firth this impressive mansion house dates from the 17th century and retains much original character. Individually styled bedrooms are spacious and tastefully furnished. A wood-panelled restaurant is the setting for artfully constructed cooking and there is a choice of comfortable lounges complete with real fires.

Rooms 16 (4 fmly) (1 GF) **S** £102-£176; **D** £147-£254 (incl. bkfst)* **Facilities** FTV Fishing New Year Wi-fi **Conf** Class 30 Board 30 Thtr 80 Del from £99 to £149* **Parking** 40 **Notes** LB ⊗ Closed 24-27 Dec Civ Wed 92

Columba

★★★★ 73% HOTEL

OXFORD
HOTELS & INNS

☎ 01463 231391 📠 01463 715526
Ness Walk IV3 5NF
e-mail: reservations.columba@ohiml.com
web: www.oxfordhotelsandinns.com
dir: From A9/A96 follow signs to town centre, past Eastgate shopping centre onto Academy St, at bottom take left to Bank St, right over bridge, hotel 1st left

Originally built in 1881 and with many original features retained, the Columba Hotel lies in the heart of Inverness overlooking the fast flowing River Ness. The bedrooms are very stylish, and public areas include a first floor restaurant and lounge. A second dining option is the ever popular McNabs bar bistro, which is ideal for less formal meals.

Rooms 76 (4 fmly) **Facilities** FTV Complimentary use of leisure facilities 0.5m away 🎵 Xmas New Year Wi-fi **Conf** Class 50 Board 60 Thtr 200 **Services** Lift **Notes** ⊗ Civ Wed 80

Glenmoriston Town House Hotel

★★★ 85% ⑧⑧⑧ HOTEL

☎ 01463 223777 📠 01463 712378
20 Ness Bank IV2 4SF
e-mail: reception@glenmoristontownhouse.com
web: www.glenmoristontownhouse.com
dir: On riverside opposite theatre

Bold contemporary designs blend seamlessly with the classical architecture of this stylish hotel, situated on the banks of the River Ness. Delightful day rooms include a piano bar and two restaurants - Abstract and Contrast. The smart, modern bedrooms have many facilities, including free Wi-fi, DVD players and flat-screen TVs.

Rooms 30 (15 annexe) (1 fmly) (6 GF) **Facilities** STV 🎵 Xmas New Year Wi-fi **Conf** Class 10 Board 10 Thtr 15 **Parking** 40 **Notes** ⊗ Closed 26-28 Dec & 4-6 Jan Civ Wed 70

INVERNESS *continued*

Royal Highland

★★★ 77% HOTEL

☎ 01463 231926 & 251451 📠 01463 710705
Station Square, Academy St IV1 1LG
e-mail: info@royalhighlandhotel.co.uk
web: www.royalhighlandhotel.co.uk
dir: From A9 into town centre. Hotel next to rail station &
Eastgate Retail Centre

Built in 1858 adjacent to the railway station, this hotel
has the typically grand foyer of the Victorian era with
comfortable seating. The contemporary ASH Brasserie
and bar offers a refreshing style for both eating and
drinking throughout the day. The generally spacious
bedrooms are comfortably equipped especially for the
business traveller.

Rooms 85 (12 fmly) (2 GF) (25 smoking) **S** £60-£119;
D £80-£159 (incl. bkfst) **Facilities** FTV Gym Xmas New
Year Wi-fi **Conf** Class 80 Board 80 Thtr 200
Del from £88.50 to £115 **Services** Lift **Parking** 8
Notes LB Civ Wed 200

Best Western Palace Hotel & Spa

★★★ 75% HOTEL

☎ 01463 223243 📠 01463 236865
8 Ness Walk IV3 5NG
e-mail: palace@miltonhotels.com
web: www.bw-invernesspalace.co.uk
dir: A82 Glenurquhart Rd onto Ness Walk. Hotel 300yds
on right opposite Inverness Castle

Set on the north side of the River Ness close to the Eden
Court theatre and a short walk from the town, this hotel
now has a contemporary look. Bedrooms offer good levels
of comfort and equipment, and a smart leisure centre
attracts a mixed market.

Rooms 88 (48 annexe) (4 fmly) **Facilities** Spa FTV ⓢ
supervised Gym Beautician Steam room Xmas New Year
Wi-fi **Conf** Class 40 Board 30 Thtr 80 **Services** Lift
Parking 38

Thistle Inverness

thistle

★★★ 75% HOTEL

☎ 0871 376 9023 📠 0871 376 9123
Millburn Rd IV2 3TR
e-mail: inverness@thistle.co.uk
web: www.thistlehotels.com/inverness
dir: From A9 take Raigmore Interchange exit (towards
Aberdeen) then 3rd left towards centre. Hotel opposite

Well located within easy distance of the town centre. This
well presented hotel offers modern bedrooms including
three suites. There is a well equipped leisure centre along
with an informal brasserie and open-plan bar and lounge.
Ample parking is an added benefit.

Rooms 118 **Facilities** ⓢ supervised Gym Sauna Steam
room Xmas New Year Wi-fi **Conf** Class 70 Board 50
Thtr 120 Del from £125 to £150* **Services** Lift
Parking 80 **Notes** ⓧ Civ Wed 120

Glen Mhor

★★★ 70% HOTEL

☎ 01463 234308 📠 01463 218018
8-15 Ness Bank IV2 4SG
e-mail: enquires@glen-mhor.com
web: www.glen-mhor.com
dir: On east bank of River Ness, below Inverness Castle

This hotel is a short walk from the city centre and
overlooks the beautiful River Ness. This fine old property
offers bedrooms and several suites that are up-to-the-
minute in design. The public areas include a cosy bar and
a comfortable lounge with its log fire.

Rooms 52 (34 annexe) (1 fmly) (12 GF) **S** £45-£69;
D £60-£160 (incl. bkfst)* **Facilities** FTV ⛏ Xmas New
Year Wi-fi **Conf** Class 30 Board 35 Thtr 60 Del from £85
to £129* **Parking** 26 **Notes** LB ⓧ

Express by Holiday Inn Inverness

BUDGET HOTEL

☎ 01463 732700 📠 01463 732732
Stoneyfield IV2 7PA
e-mail: inverness@expressholidayinn.co.uk
web: www.hiexpress.com/inverness
dir: From A9 follow A96 & Inverness Airport signs, hotel
on right

A modern hotel ideal for families and business travellers.
Fresh and uncomplicated, the spacious rooms include Sky
TV, power shower and tea and coffee-making facilities.
Continental buffet breakfast is included in the room rate;
other meals may be taken at the nearby family pub or
restaurant. See also the Hotel Groups pages.

Rooms 94 (43 fmly) (24 GF) (10 smoking) **S** £39-£140;
D £39-£140 (incl. bkfst)* **Conf** Class 20 Board 15 Thtr 35
Del from £95 to £175*

Travelodge Inverness

BUDGET HOTEL

☎ 0871 984 6148 📠 01463 718152
Stoneyfield, A96 Inverness Rd IV2 7PA
web: www.travelodge.co.uk
dir: At junct of A9 & A96

Travelodge offers good quality, good value, budget
accommodation. All offer family rooms sleeping up to four
(two adults, two children) with en suite bathroom/
shower-room, remote-control TV, tea- and coffee-making
facilities and comfortable beds. Food options vary.
Breakfast is at the on-site Bar Café restaurant (if
available) or to take away. See also Hotel Groups pages.

Rooms 58 **S** fr £29; **D** fr £29

Travelodge Inverness Fairways

BUDGET HOTEL

☎ 0871 984 6285 📠 01463 250703
Castle Heather IV2 6AA
web: www.travelodge.co.uk
dir: From A9 follow Raigmore Hospital signs. At 1st rdbt
take 3rd exit, B8082 towards Hilton/Culduthel. 1.5m, 2nd
exit at rdbt, 3rd exit at next rdbt .At 4th rdbt take 1st exit.
Lodge on left

Rooms 80 **S** fr £29; **D** fr £29

KINGUSSIE Map 23 NH70

INSPECTORS' CHOICE

The Cross at Kingussie

◉◉◉ RESTAURANT WITH ROOMS

☎ 01540 661166 📠 01540 661080
Tweed Mill Brae, Ardbroilach Rd PH21 1LB
e-mail: relax@thecross.co.uk
dir: From lights in Kingussie centre along Ardbroilach
Rd, 300yds left onto Tweed Mill Brae

Situated in the valley near Kingussie, this former tweed
mill sits next to a river, with wild flower gardens and a
sunny terrace. Hospitality and food are clearly
highlights of any stay at this special restaurant with
rooms. Locally sourced produce is carefully prepared
with passion and skill. Bedrooms are spacious and
airy, and little touches such as fluffy towels and handmade toiletries provide extra luxury. AA Wine Award for
Scotland 2009-10.

Rooms 8 (1 fmly)

LETTERFINLAY LODGE HOTEL Map 22 NN29

Letterfinlay Lodge

★★★ 77% SMALL HOTEL

☎ 01397 712622 📠 01397 712687
PH34 4DZ
e-mail: info@letterfinlaylodgehotel.co.uk
web: www.letterfinlaylodgehotel.co.uk
dir: 7m N of Spean Bridge, on A82 beside Loch Lochy

This hotel sits on the banks of Loch Lochy and boasts
breathtaking views over the Great Glen. Many of the
bedrooms overlook the loch from where guests can watch
the glorious sunsets or see the ospreys swoop over the
water; two rooms feature splendid Victorian period
bathrooms. Evening meals showcase the best of local
produce including seafood caught locally. There are
enjoyable walks along the loch.

Rooms 14 (1 annexe) (2 fmly) **S** £60-£80; **D** £65-£120
(incl. bkfst)* **Facilities** FTV Fishing Clay pigeon shooting
Boat hire Speed boat trips Waterskiing Xmas New Year
Conf Class 50 Board 50 Thtr 30 Del from £110 to £140*
Parking 20 **Notes** LB Civ Wed 70

LOCHINVER — Map 22 NC02

Inver Lodge
★★★★ ◎◎ HOTEL

☎ 01571 844496 📠 01571 844395
IV27 4LU
e-mail: stay@inverlodge.com
web: www.inverlodge.com
dir: A835 to Lochinver, through village, left after village hall, follow private road for 0.5m

Genuine hospitality is a real feature at this delightful, purpose-built hotel. Set high on the hillside above the village all bedrooms and public rooms enjoy stunning views. There is a choice of lounges and a restaurant where chefs make use of the abundant local produce. Bedrooms are spacious, stylish and come with an impressive range of accessories. There is no night service between 11pm and 7am.

Rooms 20 (11 GF) **S** £110; **D** £200 (incl. bkfst)
Facilities FTV Fishing Sauna Wi-fi **Conf** Board 20 Thtr 30 Del from £125 to £150* **Parking** 30 **Notes** LB Closed Nov-Mar Civ Wed 50

MALLAIG — Map 22 NM69

West Highland
★★ 72% HOTEL

☎ 01687 462210 📠 01687 462130
PH41 4QZ
e-mail: westhighland.hotel@virgin.net
dir: From Fort William take A830 (The Road to the Isles) to Mallaig. At rdbt before Mallaig ferry terminal turn right, then 1st right up hill (B8008)

Once the town's station hotel the original building was destroyed by fire and the current property was built on the same site in the early 20th century. Fine views over to Skye are a real feature of the public rooms which include a bright airy conservatory, whilst the attractive bedrooms are thoughtfully equipped and generally spacious.

Rooms 34 (6 fmly) **Facilities** FTV ♫ Wi-fi **Conf** Class 80 Board 100 Thtr 100 **Parking** 40 **Notes** Closed 16 Oct-15 Mar RS 16 Mar-1 Apr

MUIR OF ORD — Map 23 NH55

Ord House
★★ 72% ◎ SMALL HOTEL

THE CIRCLE

☎ 01463 870492 📠 01463 870297
IV6 7UH
e-mail: admin@ord-house.co.uk
dir: Off A9 at Tore rdbt onto A832. 5m, through Muir of Ord. Left towards Ullapool (A832). Hotel 0.5m on left

Dating back to 1637, this country-house hotel is situated peacefully in wooded grounds and offers brightly furnished and well-proportioned accommodation. Comfortable day rooms reflect the character and charm of the house, with inviting lounges, a cosy snug bar and an elegant dining room where wide-ranging, creative menus are offered.

Rooms 12 (3 GF) **S** £55-£80; **D** £100-£140 (incl. bkfst)*
Facilities Putt green ⛳ Clay pigeon shooting Wi-fi **Parking** 30 **Notes** LB Closed Nov-Apr

NAIRN — Map 23 NH85

Golf View Hotel & Leisure Club
★★★★ 74% ◎ HOTEL

☎ 01667 452301 📠 01667 455267
The Seafront IV12 4HD
e-mail: golfview@crerarhotels.com
dir: Off A96 into Seabank Rd, follow road to end, hotel on right

This fine hotel has wonderful sea views and overlooks the Morey Firth and the Black Isle beyond. The championship golf course at Nairn is adjacent to the hotel and guests have direct access to the long sandy beaches. Bedrooms are all of a very high standard and the public areas are charming. A well-equipped leisure complex and swimming pool are also available.

Rooms 42 (6 fmly) **S** £85-£120; **D** £120-£220 (incl. bkfst)* **Facilities** FTV ◎ supervised ◎ Gym Xmas New Year Wi-fi **Conf** Class 40 Board 40 Thtr 100 Del from £149 to £169* **Services** Lift **Parking** 40 **Notes** LB Civ Wed 100

See advert on this page

NAIRN *continued*

Newton

★★★★ 73% @ HOTEL

OXFORD
HOTELS & INNS

☎ 01667 453144   ▤ 01667 454026
Inverness Rd IV12 4RX
e-mail: reservations.newton@ohiml.com
web: www.oxfordhotelsandinns.com
dir: A96 from Inverness to Nairn. In Nairn, hotel signed on left

This former mansion house, set in 21 acres of mature parkland and bordering Nairn's championship golf course, was a favourite with the actor Charlie Chaplin who often visited with his family. Originally built as a family home in 1872 the hotel has been extensively refurbished over the years, including the addition of the Highland Conference Centre. Bedrooms are of a high standard, and many of the front-facing rooms having splendid sea views.

Rooms 56 (2 fmly) **Facilities** Xmas New Year Wi-fi **Conf** Class 220 Board 90 Thtr 400 **Services** Lift **Parking** 100 **Notes** LB Civ Wed 250

Boath House

★★★ @@@@ HOTEL

☎ 01667 454896   ▤ 01667 455469
Auldearn IV12 5TE
e-mail: info@boath-house.com
web: www.boath-house.com
dir: 2m past Nairn on A96, E towards Forres, signed on main road

Standing in its own grounds, this splendid Georgian mansion has been lovingly restored. Hospitality is first class. The owners are passionate about what they do, and have an ability to establish a special relationship with their guests that will be particularly remembered. The food is also memorable here - the five-course dinners are a culinary adventure, matched only by the excellence of breakfasts. The house itself is delightful, with inviting lounges and a dining room overlooking a trout loch. Bedrooms are striking, comfortable, and include many fine antique pieces.

Rooms 8 (1 fmly) (1 GF) **S** £180-£250; **D** £220-£380 (incl. bkfst)* **Facilities** Spa FTV Fishing ⤴ Gym Beauty salon Xmas New Year Wi-fi **Conf** Board 10 **Parking** 20 **Notes** Civ Wed 30

Alton Burn

★★ 61% HOTEL

☎ 01667 452051 & 453325   ▤ 01667 456697
Alton Burn Rd IV12 5ND
e-mail: enquiries@altonburn.co.uk
dir: follow signs from A96 at western boundary of Nairn

This long-established, family-run hotel is located on the western edge of town and enjoys delightful views over the Moray Firth and adjacent golf course. Bedrooms, originally furnished in the 1950s, have been thoughtfully preserved to provide a reminder of that era whilst spacious day rooms include a well-stocked bar, several comfortable lounges and a popular restaurant.

Rooms 23 (7 GF) **Facilities** ⤴ ⚘ Putt green ⛳ Table tennis Pool table **Conf** Class 50 Board 40 Thtr 100 **Parking** 40 **Notes** Closed Nov-Mar

---

NETHY BRIDGE   Map 23 NJ02

Nethybridge

★★★ 70% HOTEL

☎ 01479 821203   ▤ 01479 821686
PH25 3DP
e-mail: salesnethybridge@strathmorehotels.com
dir: A9 onto A95, then onto B970 to Nethy Bridge

This popular tourist and coaching hotel enjoys a central location amidst the majestic Cairngorm Mountains. Bedrooms are stylishly furnished in bold tartans whilst traditionally styled day rooms include two bars and a popular snooker room. Staff are friendly and keen to please.

Rooms 69 (3 fmly) (7 GF) **Facilities** Putt green Bowling green ♬ Xmas New Year **Conf** Thtr 100 **Services** Lift **Parking** 80 **Notes** LB

See advert on page 617

The Mountview Hotel

★★ 78% @@ HOTEL

☎ 01479 821248   ▤ 01479 821515
Grantown Rd PH25 3EB
e-mail: info@mountviewhotel.co.uk
dir: from Aviemore follow signs through Boat of Garten to Nethy Bridge. On main road through village, hotel on right

Aptly named, this country-house hotel enjoys stunning panoramic views from its elevated position on the edge of the village. It specialises in guided holidays and is a favoured base for birdwatching and for walking groups. Public rooms include inviting lounges, while imaginative, well-prepared dinners are served in a bright and modern restaurant extension.

Rooms 12 (1 GF) **S** £50-£85; **D** £90-£120 (incl. bkfst)* **Parking** 20 **Notes** ⊗

ONICH   Map 22 NN06

Onich

★★★ 79% @ HOTEL

☎ 01855 821214   ▤ 01855 821484
PH33 6RY
e-mail: enquiries@onich-fortwilliam.co.uk
web: www.onich-fortwilliam.co.uk
dir: Beside A82, 2m N of Ballachulish Bridge

Genuine hospitality is part of the appeal of this hotel, which lies right beside Loch Linnhe with gardens extending to its shores. Nicely presented public areas include a choice of inviting lounges and contrasting bars, and views of the loch can be enjoyed from the attractive restaurant. Bedrooms, with pleasing colour schemes, are comfortably modern.

Rooms 26 (6 fmly) **S** £49.50-£69.50; **D** £70-£199 (incl. bkfst) **Facilities** STV Games room ♫ Xmas New Year Wi-fi **Conf** Board 40 Thtr 150 Del from £110 to £189.50 **Parking** 50 **Notes** LB Civ Wed 120

PLOCKTON Map 22 NG83

The Plockton

★★★ 75% SMALL HOTEL

☎ 01599 544274 📠 01599 544475
41 Harbour St IV52 8TN
e-mail: info@plocktonhotel.co.uk
dir: 6m from Kyle of Lochalsh. 6m from Balmacara

This very popular hotel occupies an idyllic position on the waterfront of Loch Carron. Stylish bedrooms offer individual, pleasing decor and many have spacious balconies or panoramic views. There is a choice of three dining areas and seafood is very much a speciality. The staff and owners provide a relaxed and informal style of attentive service. In addition to the hotel a self-contained cottage is available for group bookings.

Rooms 15 (4 annexe) (1 fmly) (1 GF) **S** £62.50-£90; **D** fr £125 (incl. bkfst) **Facilities** STV Pool table ♫ New Year Wi-fi **Notes** LB ✖ Closed 25 Dec Civ Wed 55

ROY BRIDGE Map 22 NN28

Best Western Glenspean Lodge Hotel

★★★ 78% HOTEL

☎ 01397 712223 📠 01397 712660
PH31 4AW
e-mail: reservations@glenspeanlodge.co.uk
web: www.glenspeanlodge.com
dir: 2m E of Roy Bridge, right off A82 at Spean Bridge onto A86

With origins as a hunting lodge dating back to the Victorian era, this hotel sits in gardens in an elevated position in the Spean Valley. Accommodation is provided in well laid out bedrooms, some suitable for families. Inviting public areas include a comfortable lounge bar and a restaurant that enjoys stunning views of the valley.

Rooms 17 (4 fmly) **Facilities** Gym Sauna Xmas New Year Wi-fi **Conf** Class 16 **Parking** 60 **Notes** Civ Wed 60

SCOURIE Map 22 NC14

Scourie

★★★ 73% SMALL HOTEL

☎ 01971 502396 📠 01971 502423
IV27 4SX
e-mail: patrick@scourie-hotel.co.uk
dir: N'bound on A894. Hotel in village on left

This well-established hotel is an angler's paradise with extensive fishing rights available on a 25,000-acre estate. Public areas include a choice of comfortable lounges, a cosy bar and a smart dining room offering wholesome fare. The bedrooms are comfortable and generally spacious. The resident proprietors and their staff create a relaxed and friendly atmosphere.

Rooms 20 (2 annexe) (2 fmly) (5 GF) **S** £62-£73; **D** £114-£134 (incl. bkfst & dinner)* **Facilities** Fishing Wi-fi **Parking** 30 **Notes** LB Closed mid Oct-end Mar RS winter evenings

---

SHIEL BRIDGE Map 22 NG91

Grants at Craigellachie

⊛ RESTAURANT WITH ROOMS

☎ 01599 511331
Craigellachie, Ratagan IV40 8HP
e-mail: info@housebytheloch.co.uk
dir: From A87 turn to Glenelg, 1st right to Ratagn, opp Youth Hostel sign

Sitting on the tranquil shores of Loch Duin and overlooked by the Five Sisters Mountains, Grants really does have a stunning location. The restaurant has a well deserved reputation for its fine cuisine, and the bedrooms are stylish and have all the creature comforts. Guests are guaranteed a warm welcome at this charming house.

Rooms 4 (2 annexe)

SHIELDAIG Map 22 NG85

INSPECTORS' CHOICE

Tigh an Eilean

★ ⊛⊛ SMALL HOTEL

☎ 01520 755251 📠 01520 755321
IV54 8XN
e-mail: tighaneilean@keme.co.uk
dir: off A896 onto village road signed Shieldaig, hotel in centre

A splendid location by the sea, with views over the bay, is the icing on the cake for this delightful small hotel. It can be a long drive to reach Sheildaig but guests remark that the journey is more than worth the effort. The brightly decorated bedrooms are comfortable though don't expect television, except in one of the lounges. For many, it's the food that attracts, with fish and seafood featuring strongly.

Rooms 11 (1 fmly) **Facilities** Birdwatching Kayaks Wi-fi **Parking** 15 **Notes** LB Closed late Oct-mid Mar Civ Wed 40

SOUTH BALLACHULISH

The Ballachulish Hotel

★★★ 77% HOTEL

☎ 0844 855 9133 📠 01855 811629
PH49 4JY
e-mail: reservations.ballachulish@foliohotels.com
web: www.foliohotels.com/ballachulish
dir: on A828, Fort William-Oban road, 3m N of Glencoe

On the shores of Loch Linnhe and at the foot of dramatic Glencoe, guests are assured of a warm welcome here. A selection of bar meals is available at lunchtime, and evening meals are served in the Bulas Bistro which overlooks the stunning mountain scenery. The tastefully decorated bedrooms include the six Chieftain Rooms which are particularly comfortable.

Rooms 53 (2 fmly) (7 GF) **Facilities** Xmas New Year Wi-fi **Conf** Board 20 **Parking** 60 **Notes** LB Civ Wed 65

SOUTH BALLACHULISH *continued*

The Isles of Glencoe Hotel & Leisure Centre

★★★ 71% HOTEL

☎ 0844 855 9134 📄 0871 222 3416
PH49 4HL
e-mail: reservations.glencoe@foliohotels.com
web: www.foliohotels.com/isleofglencoe
dir: A82 N, slip road on left into village, 1st right, hotel in 600yds.

This hotel enjoys a spectacular setting beside Loch Leven. This friendly modern establishment has spacious bedrooms and guests have a choice of Loch or Mountain View rooms. Public areas include a popular restaurant and a family friendly leisure centre.

Rooms 59 (21 fmly) (21 GF) **Facilities** STV 🕲 Gym Hydroseat Bio-sauna 🎵 Xmas New Year Wi-fi **Conf** Class 40 Board 20 Thtr 40 **Notes** LB Civ Wed 65

SPEAN BRIDGE   **Map 22 NN28**

The Smiddy House

◉◉ RESTAURANT WITH ROOMS

☎ 01397 712335 📄 01397 712043
Roy Bridge Rd PH34 4EU
e-mail: enquiry@smiddyhouse.co.uk
web: www.smiddyhouse.co.uk
dir: In village centre, A82 onto A86

Set in the 'Great Glen', which stretches from Fort William to Inverness, this was once the village smithy, and is now a friendly establishment. The attractive bedrooms which are named after Scottish places, are comfortably furnished and well equipped. A relaxing garden room is available for guest use. Delicious evening meals are served in Russell's restaurant.

Rooms 4 (1 fmly)

STRONTIAN   **Map 22 NM86**

INSPECTORS' CHOICE

Kilcamb Lodge

★★★ ◉◉ COUNTRY HOUSE HOTEL

☎ 01967 402257 📄 01967 402041
PH36 4HY
e-mail: enquiries@kilcamblodge.co.uk
web: www.kilcamblodge.co.uk
dir: Off A861, via Corran Ferry

This historic house on the shores of Loch Sunart was one of the first stone buildings in the area and was used as military barracks around the time of the Jacobite uprising. Accommodation is provided in tastefully decorated rooms with high quality fabrics. Accomplished cooking, utilising much local produce, can be enjoyed in the stylish dining room. Warm hospitality is assured.

Rooms 10 (2 fmly) **S** £130-£150; **D** £210-£335 (incl. bkfst & dinner)* **Facilities** FTV Fishing Boating Hiking Bird, Whale & Otter watching Island hopping Stalking Xmas New Year Wi-fi **Conf** Class 18 Board 18 Thtr 18 Del from £158 to £200* **Parking** 18 **Notes** LB No children 10yrs Closed 2 Jan-1 Feb RS Nov & Feb Civ Wed 60

TAIN   **Map 23 NH88**

INSPECTORS' CHOICE

Glenmorangie Highland Home at Cadboll

★★★ ◉◉ COUNTRY HOUSE HOTEL

☎ 01862 871671 📄 01862 871625
Cadboll, Fearn IV20 1XP
e-mail: relax@glenmorangieplc.co.uk
web: www.theglenmorangiehouse.com
dir: From A9 onto B9175 towards Nigg. Follow tourist signs

This establishment superbly balances top class service with the intimate customer care of an historic highland home. Evenings are dominated by the highly successful 'house party' where guests are introduced in the drawing room, sample whiskies then take dinner (a set six course meal) together around one long table. Conversation can extend well into the evening. Stylish bedrooms are divided between the traditional main house and some cosy cottages in the grounds. This is an ideal base from which to enjoy the world famous whisky tours.

Rooms 9 (3 annexe) (4 fmly) (3 GF) **Facilities** Putt green ⛳ Falconry Clay pigeon shooting Beauty treatments Archery Xmas New Year Wi-fi **Conf** Board 12 **Parking** 60 **Notes** ⊗ No children 14yrs Closed 3-31 Jan Civ Wed 60

Forss House

★★★★ 76% ⚫ SMALL HOTEL

☎ 01847 861201 📄 01847 861301
Forss KW14 7XY
e-mail: anne@forsshousehotel.co.uk
web: www.forsshousehotel.co.uk
dir: On A836 between Thurso & Reay

This delightful country house is set in its own 20 acres of woodland and was originally built in 1810. The hotel offers a choice of bedrooms from the traditional styled rooms in the main house to the more contemporary annexe rooms in the grounds. All rooms are very well equipped and well appointed. The beautiful River Forss runs through the grounds and is a firm favourite with fishermen.

Rooms 14 (6 annexe) (1 fmly) (1 GF) **S** £95-£110; **D** £125-£160 (incl. bkfst)* **Facilities** FTV Fishing Wi-fi **Conf** Class 12 Board 16 Thtr 20 Del from £145 to £160* **Parking** 14 **Notes** LB Closed 23 Dec-3 Jan Civ Wed 30

See advert on this page

Ben Loyal

★★★ 70% ⚫ SMALL HOTEL

☎ 01847 611216 📄 01847 611212
Main St IV27 4XE
e-mail: benloyalhotel@btinternet.com
web: www.benloyal.co.uk
dir: at junct of A838/A836. Hotel by Royal Bank of Scotland

Enjoying a super location close to Ben Loyal and with views of the Kyle of Tongue, this hotel more often that not marks the welcome completion of a stunning highland and coastal drive. Bedrooms are thoughtfully equipped

and brightly decorated whilst day rooms extend to a traditionally styled dining room and a cosy bar. Extensive menus ensure there's something for everyone. Staff are especially friendly and provide useful local information.

Rooms 11 **S** £40; **D** £70-£80 (incl. bkfst) **Facilities** FTV Fishing Fly fishing tuition and equipment **Parking** 20 **Notes** Closed 30 Nov-1 Mar

Borgie Lodge Hotel

★★ 76% ⚫ HOTEL

☎ 01641 521332 📄 01641 521889
Skerray KW14 7TH
e-mail: info@borgielodgehotel.co.uk
dir: A836 between Tongue & Bettyhill. 0.5m from Skerray junct

This small outdoor-sport orientated hotel lies in a glen close to the river of the same name. Whilst fishing parties predominate, those who are not anglers are made equally welcome, and indeed the friendliness and commitment to guest care is paramount. Cosy public rooms offer a choice of lounges and an anglers' bar; all have welcoming log fires. The dinner menu is short but well chosen.

Rooms 8 (1 GF) **Facilities** Fishing ⚓ Shooting Stalking Boating **Parking** 20

INSPECTORS' CHOICE

The Torridon

★★★★ ⚫⚫ COUNTRY HOUSE HOTEL

☎ 01445 791242 📄 01445 712253
By Achnasheen, Wester Ross IV22 2EY
e-mail: info@thetorridon.com
web: www.thetorridon.com
dir: from A832 at Kinlochewe, take A896 towards Torridon. (Do not turn into village) continue 1m, hotel on right

Delightfully set amidst inspiring loch and mountain scenery, this elegant Victorian shooting lodge has been beautifully restored to make the most of its many original features. The attractive bedrooms are all individually furnished and most enjoy stunning Highland views. Comfortable day rooms feature fine wood panelling and roaring fires in cooler months. The whisky bar is aptly named, boasting over 300 malts and in-depth tasting notes. Outdoor activities include shooting, cycling and walking.

Rooms 19 (2 GF) **S** £150-£185; **D** £285-£485 (incl. bkfst & dinner)* **Facilities** STV Fishing ⚓ Absailing Archery Climbing Falconry Kayaking Mountain biking Xmas New Year Wi-fi **Conf** Board 16 **Services** Lift **Parking** 20 **Notes** LB ⊗ Closed 3-27 Jan RS Nov-14 Mar Civ Wed 42

WHITEBRIDGE · Map 23 NH41

Whitebridge

★★ 68% HOTEL

☎ 01456 486226 🖷 01456 486413
IV2 6UN
e-mail: info@whitebridgehotel.co.uk
dir: Off A9 onto B851, follow signs to Fort Augustus. Off A82 onto B862 at Fort Augustus

Close to Loch Ness and set amid rugged mountain and moorland scenery this hotel is popular with tourists, fishermen and deerstalkers. Guests have a choice of more formal dining in the restaurant or lighter meals in the popular cosy bar. Bedrooms are thoughtfully equipped and brightly furnished.

Rooms 12 (3 fmly) **S** £38-£42; **D** £58-£62 (incl. bkfst)*
Facilities Fishing Wi-fi **Parking** 32 **Notes** Closed 11 Dec-9 Jan

WICK · Map 23 ND35

Mackay's

★★★ 75% HOTEL

☎ 01955 602323 🖷 01955 605930
Union St KW1 5ED
e-mail: info@mackayshotel.co.uk
dir: opposite Caithness General Hospital

This well-established hotel is situated just outside the town centre overlooking the River Wick. MacKay's provides well-equipped, attractive accommodation, suited to both the business and leisure traveller. There is a stylish bistro offering food throughout the day and a choice of bars that also offer food.

Rooms 30 (2 fmly) **Facilities** FTV ♪ Wi-fi **Conf** Class 100 Board 60 Thtr 100 **Services** Lift **Notes** ❷ Closed 25-26 Dec & 1-3 Jan

INVERCLYDE

GREENOCK · Map 20 NS27

Express by Holiday Inn Greenock

BUDGET HOTEL

☎ 01475 786666 🖷 01475 786777
Cartsburn PA15 1AE
e-mail: greenock@expressbyholidayinn.net
web: www.hiexpress.com/greenockscot
dir: M8 junct 31, A8 to Greenock, right at 4th rdbt, hotel on right

A modern hotel ideal for families and business travellers. Fresh and uncomplicated, the spacious rooms include Sky TV, power shower and tea and coffee-making facilities. Continental buffet breakfast is included in the room rate; other meals may be taken at the nearby family pub or restaurant. See also the Hotel Groups pages.

Rooms 71 (11 fmly) (6 GF) (20 smoking) **Conf** Class 48 Board 32 Thtr 70

MORAY

ARCHIESTOWN · Map 23 NJ24

Archiestown

★★★ 77% ⚫ SMALL HOTEL

☎ 01340 810218 🖷 01340 810239
AB38 7QL
e-mail: jah@archiestownhotel.co.uk
web: www.archiestownhotel.co.uk
dir: A95 Craigellachie, follow B9102 to Archiestown, 4m

Set in the heart of this Speyside village this small hotel is popular with anglers and locals alike. It is rightly noted for its great hospitality, attentive service and good food. Cosy and comfortable public rooms include a choice of lounges (there is no bar as such) and a bistro offering an inviting choice of dishes at both lunch and dinner.

Rooms 11 (1 fmly) **S** £60-£75; **D** £120-£150 (incl. bkfst)
Facilities ♨ New Year Wi-fi **Conf** Board 12 Thtr 20 Del from £117.50 to £145 **Parking** 20 **Notes** LB Closed 24-27 Dec & 3 Jan-9 Feb

CRAIGELLACHIE · Map 23 NJ24

Craigellachie

★★★ 81% ⚫ HOTEL

OXFORD
HOTELS & INNS

☎ 01340 881204 🖷 01340 881253
AB38 9SR
e-mail: info@craigellachie.com
web: www.oxfordhotelsandinns.com
dir: On A95 between Aberdeen & Inverness

This impressive and popular hotel is located in the heart of Speyside, so it is no surprise that malt whisky takes centre stage in the Quaich Bar with over 600 varieties featured. Bedrooms come in various sizes but all are tastefully decorated and bathrooms are of a high specification. Creative dinners showcase local ingredients in the traditionally styled dining room.

Rooms 26 (1 fmly) (6 GF) **S** £85-£105; **D** £95-£185 (incl. bkfst)* **Facilities** Gym Xmas New Year Wi-fi
Conf Class 35 Board 30 Thtr 60 Del from £100 to £250*
Parking 30 **Notes** Civ Wed 60

CULLEN · Map 23 NJ56

Cullen Bay Hotel

★★★ 75% ⚫ SMALL HOTEL

☎ 01542 840432 🖷 01542 840900
A98 AB56 4XA
e-mail: stay@cullenbayhotel.com
web: www.cullenbayhotel.com
dir: on A98, 1m west of Cullen

This family-run hotel sits on the hillside west of the town and gives lovely views of the golf course, beach and Moray Firth. The spacious restaurant, which offers a selection of fine dishes, makes the most of the view, as do many of the bedrooms. There is a comfortable modern bar, a quiet lounge and a second dining room where breakfasts are served.

Rooms 14 (3 fmly) **Facilities** New Year Wi-fi
Conf Class 80 Board 80 Thtr 200 **Parking** 100 **Notes** ❷ Civ Wed 200

The Seafield Arms Hotel

★★★ 68% HOTEL

☎ 01542 840791 ▤ 01542 840736
Seafield St AB56 4SG
e-mail: info@theseafieldarms.co.uk
dir: In village centre on A98

Centrally located and benefiting from off-road parking, this is a small but friendly hotel. Bedrooms differ in size and style but all are comfortable. The popular restaurant serves well cooked meals using the very best of Scottish produce including the famous Cullen Skink.

Rooms 23 (1 fmly) **S** £59-£63; **D** £84-£94 (incl. bkfst)* **Facilities** FTV Xmas New Year Wi-fi **Conf** Class 16 Board 16 Thtr 16 **Parking** 17 **Notes** LB Civ Wed 200

ELGIN Map 23 NJ26

Mansion House

★★★ 74% HOTEL

☎ 01343 548811 ▤ 01343 547916
The Haugh IV30 1AW
e-mail: reception@mhelgin.co.uk
web: www.mansionhousehotel.co.uk
dir: ExitA96 into Haugh Rd, then 1st left

Set in grounds by the River Lossie, this baronial mansion is popular with leisure and business guests as well as being a popular wedding venue. Bedrooms are spacious, many having views of the river. Extensive public areas include a choice of restaurants, with the bistro contrasting with the classical main restaurant. There is an indoor pool and a beauty and hair salon.

Rooms 23 (2 fmly) (5 GF) **S** £88.50-£93.50; **D** £149-£192 (incl. bkfst)* **Facilities** 🕲 supervised Fishing Gym Hair studio New Year Wi-fi **Conf** Thtr 180 Del from £128 to £144 **Parking** 50 **Notes** LB ⊗ Civ Wed 160

FORRES Map 23 NJ05

Ramnee

★★★ 75% HOTEL

☎ 01309 672410 ▤ 01309 673392
Victoria Rd IV36 3BN
e-mail: info@ramneehotel.com
dir: Off A96 at rdbt on E side of Forres, hotel 200yds on right

Genuinely friendly staff ensure this well-established hotel remains popular with business travellers. Bedrooms,

including a family suite, vary in size, although all are well presented. Hearty bar food provides a less formal dining option to the imaginative restaurant menu.

Rooms 19 (4 fmly) (2 smoking) **S** £80-£120; **D** £90-£150 (incl. bkfst)* **Facilities** STV Wi-fi **Conf** Class 30 Board 45 Thtr 100 Del from £135 to £150* **Parking** 50 **Notes** LB Closed 25 Dec & 1-3 Jan Civ Wed 100

NORTH AYRSHIRE

IRVINE Map 20 NS33

Menzies Irvine

MenziesHotels

★★★★ 74% HOTEL

☎ 01294 274272 ▤ 01294 277287
46 Annick Rd KA11 4LD
e-mail: irvine@menzieshotels.co.uk
web: www.menzieshotels.co.uk
dir: From A78 at Warrix Interchange follow Irvine Central signs. At rdbt 2nd exit (town centre). At next rdbt right onto A71/Kilmarnock. Hotel 100mtrs on left

Situated on the edge of Irvine with good transportation links, this is a well-presented hotel that has an extremely friendly team with good customer care awareness. The decor in the lobby and bar are reminiscent of Tangier. For the family there is a large tropical lagoon swimming pool along with a 9-hole, par 3 golf course.

Rooms 128 (14 fmly) (64 GF) **S** £59-£160; **D** £59-£160* **Facilities** STV 🕲 ♨ 9 Putt green Fishing Xmas New Year Wi-fi **Conf** Class 140 Board 100 Thtr 280 Del from £95 to £135* **Parking** 220 **Notes** Civ Wed 200

LARGS Map 20 NS25

Willowbank

★★★ 74% HOTEL

☎ 01475 672311 & 675435 ▤ 01475 689027
96 Greenock Rd KA30 8PG
e-mail: iaincsmith@btconnect.com
dir: On A78

A relaxed, friendly atmosphere prevails at this well maintained hotel where hanging baskets are a feature in summer months. The nicely decorated bedrooms are, in general, spacious and offer comfortable modern appointments. The public areas include a large, well-stocked bar, a lounge and a dining room.

Rooms 30 (4 fmly) **S** £60-£100; **D** £80-£140 (incl. bkfst)* **Facilities** ♫ Xmas **Conf** Class 100 Board 40 Thtr 200 Del from £90 to £120* **Parking** 40 **Notes** LB

NORTH LANARKSHIRE

CUMBERNAULD Map 21 NS77

The Westerwood Hotel & Golf Resort

★★★★ 80% HOTEL

☎ 01236 457171 ▤ 01236 738478
1 St Andrews Dr, Westerwood G68 0EW
e-mail: westerwood@qhotels.co.uk
web: www.qhotels.co.uk

This stylish, contemporary hotel enjoys an elevated position within 400 acres at the foot of the Campsie Hills. Accommodation is provided in spacious, bright bedrooms, many with super bathrooms, and day rooms include sumptuous lounges and an airy restaurant; extensive golf, fitness and conference facilities are available.

Rooms 148 (15 fmly) (49 GF) **S** £65-£125; **D** £75-£135 (incl. bkfst) **Facilities** Spa 🕲 ♨ 18 ♨ Putt green Gym Beauty salon Jacuzzi Relaxation room Sauna Steam room Xmas New Year Wi-fi **Conf** Class 120 Board 60 Thtr 400 Del from £120 to £180* **Services** Lift **Parking** 250 **Notes** LB Civ Wed 400

Castlecary House

★★★ 77% HOTEL

☎ 01324 840233 ▤ 01324 841608
Castlecary Rd, Castlecary G68 0HD
e-mail: enquiries@castlecaryhotel.com
web: www.castlecaryhotel.com
dir: off A80 onto B816 between Glasgow & Stirling. Hotel by Castlecary Arches

Close to the Forth Clyde Canal and convenient for the M80, this popular hotel provides a versatile range of accommodation, within purpose-built units in the grounds and also in an extension to the original house. The attractive and spacious restaurant offers a short fixed-price menu, and enjoyable meals are also served in the busy bars.

Rooms 60 (3 fmly) (20 GF) **S** £70-£90; **D** £70-£90 (incl. bkfst)* **Facilities** FTV Wi-fi **Conf** Class 120 Board 60 Thtr 140 **Services** Lift **Parking** 100 **Notes** RS 1 Jan Civ Wed 90

MOTHERWELL — Map 21 NS75

Alona

★★★★ 78% HOTEL

☎ 01698 333888 📠 01698 338720
Strathclyde Country Park ML1 3RT
e-mail: keithd@alonahotel.co.uk
web: www.alonahotel.co.uk
dir: M74 junct 5, hotel approx 250yds on left

Alona is a Celtic word meaning 'exquisitely beautiful'. This hotel is situated within the idyllic beauty of Strathclyde Country Park, with tranquil views over the picturesque loch and surrounding forests. There is a very contemporary feel, from the open-plan public areas to the spacious and well-appointed bedrooms. Wi-fi is available throughout. M&D's, Scotland's Family Theme Park, is just next door.

Rooms 51 (24 fmly) (17 GF) **Facilities** FTV 🎵 Xmas New Year Wi-fi **Conf** Class 100 Board 76 Thtr 140 Del from £99 to £150* **Services** Lift Air con **Parking** 100 **Notes** ✪ Civ Wed 100

Express by Holiday Inn Strathclyde Park

BUDGET HOTEL

☎ 01698 858585 📠 01698 852375
Hamilton Rd, Hamilton ML1 3RB
e-mail: isabella.little@ichotelsgroup.com
web: www.hiexpress.com/strathclyde
dir: M74 junct 5 follow signs for Strathclyde Country park

A modern hotel ideal for families and business travellers. Fresh and uncomplicated, the spacious rooms include Sky TV, power shower and tea and coffee-making facilities. Continental buffet breakfast is included in the room rate; other meals may be taken at the nearby family pub or restaurant. See also the Hotel Groups pages.

Rooms 120 (58 fmly) **Conf** Class 10 Board 18 Thtr 30

Innkeeper's Lodge Glasgow/ Strathclyde Park

BUDGET HOTEL

☎ 0845 112 6004 📠 0845 112 6296
Hamilton Rd ML1 3RB
web: www.innkeeperslodge.com/glasgowstrathclydepark
dir: M74 junct 5, take exit for Strathclyde Country Park. Lodge on right, after entering park

Innkeeper's Lodge represents an exciting, high value concept within the budget hotel market. Comfortable bedrooms provide excellent facilities that include satellite TV and modem points. Options include family rooms; and for the corporate guest, cutting edge IT which includes Wi-fi access. A popular Carvery provides all-day food, including an extensive, complimentary continental breakfast. See also the Hotel Groups pages.

Rooms 28 **Conf** Thtr 20

STEPPS — Map 20 NS66

Best Western Garfield House Hotel

★★★ 81% HOTEL

☎ 0141 779 2111 📠 0141 779 9799
Cumbernauld Rd G33 6HW
e-mail: rooms@garfieldhotel.co.uk
dir: M8 junct 11 exit at Stepps/Queenslie, follow Stepps/A80 signs

Situated close to the A80, this considerably extended business hotel is a popular venue for local conferences and functions. Public areas include a welcoming reception lounge and the popular Distillery Bar/Restaurant, an all-day eatery providing good value meals in an informal setting. Smart, well-presented bedrooms come in a range of sizes and styles. Staff are friendly and keen to please.

Rooms 45 (10 fmly) (13 GF) **S** £60-£98; **D** £72-£116 (incl. bkfst) **Facilities** FTV Wi-fi **Conf** Class 40 Board 36 Thtr 100 **Parking** 90 **Notes** Closed 1-2 Jan Civ Wed 80

PERTH & KINROSS

AUCHTERARDER — Map 21 NN91

HOTEL OF THE YEAR
INSPECTORS' CHOICE

The Gleneagles Hotel
★★★★★ 🌐🌐🌐🌐 HOTEL

☎ 01764 662231 📠 01764 662134
PH3 1NF
e-mail: resort.sales@gleneagles.com
web: www.gleneagles.com
dir: Off A9 at exit for A823 follow signs for Gleneagles Hotel

With its international reputation for high standards, this grand hotel provides something for everyone. Set in a delightful location, Gleneagles offers a peaceful retreat, as well as many sporting activities, including the famous championship golf courses. All bedrooms are appointed to a high standard and offer both traditional and contemporary styles. Stylish public areas include various dining options - The Strathearn, with two AA Rosettes, as well as some inspired cooking at Andrew Fairlie at Gleneagles, a restaurant with four AA Rosettes. Service is always professional, staff are friendly and nothing is too much trouble.
AA Hotel of the Year for Scotland 2009-10.

Rooms 232 (115 fmly) (11 GF) **D** £305-£560 (incl. bkfst)* **Facilities** Spa STV FTV 🏊 supervised 🎾 ⛳ 54 ⛳ Putt green Fishing 🚴 Gym Falconry Off-road driving Golf range Archery Clay target shooting Gundog School Xmas New Year Wi-fi Child facilities **Conf** Class 240 Board 60 Thtr 360 **Services** Lift **Parking** 277 **Notes** LB Civ Wed 360

BLAIR ATHOLL · Map 23 NN86

Atholl Arms

★★★ 74% HOTEL

☎ 01796 481205 📠 01796 481550
Old North Rd PH18 5SG
e-mail: hotel@athollarms.co.uk
web: www.athollarmshotel.co.uk
dir: off A9 to B8079, 1m into Blair Atholl, hotel near entrance to Blair Castle

Situated close to Blair Castle and conveniently adjacent to the railway station, this stylish hotel has historically styled public rooms that include a choice of bars, and a splendid baronial-style dining room. Bedrooms vary in size and style. Staff throughout are friendly and very caring.

Rooms 30 (3 fmly) **S** £45-£60; **D** £75-£90 (incl. bkfst)*
Facilities Fishing Rough shooting ♫ New Year
Conf Class 80 Board 60 Thtr 120 **Parking** 103
Notes Civ Wed 120

COMRIE · Map 21 NN72

Royal

★★★ 83% ◉ HOTEL

☎ 01764 679200 📠 01764 679219
Melville Square PH6 2DN
e-mail: reception@royalhotel.co.uk
web: www.royalhotel.co.uk
dir: off A9 on A822 to Crieff, then B827 to Comrie. Hotel in main square on A85

A traditional façade gives little indication of the style and elegance inside this long-established hotel located in the village centre. Public areas include a bar and library, a bright modern restaurant and a conservatory-style brasserie. Bedrooms are tastefully appointed and furnished with smart reproduction antiques.

Rooms 13 (2 annexe) **S** £85-£105; **D** £140-£180 (incl. bkfst) **Facilities** STV Fishing Shooting arranged New Year Wi-fi **Conf** Class 10 Board 20 Thtr 20 **Parking** 22
Notes LB Closed 25-26 Dec

DUNKELD · Map 21 NO04

INSPECTORS' CHOICE

Kinnaird

★★★★ ◉◉◉ HOTEL

☎ 01796 482440 📠 01796 482289
Kinnaird Estate PH8 0LB
e-mail: enquiry@kinnairdestate.com
web: www.kinnairdestate.com
dir: from Perth, A9 towards Inverness towards Dunkeld (but do not enter town), continue N for 2m then take B898 on left

An imposing Edwardian mansion set in 9,000 acres of beautiful countryside on the west bank of the River Tay. Sitting rooms are warm and inviting with deep-cushioned sofas and open fires. Bedrooms are furnished with rich, soft, luxurious fabrics, and have marble bathrooms. Food is creative and imaginative, with abundant local produce featuring on all menus. While jacket and tie are required at dinner, the atmosphere overall is tranquil and relaxed.

Rooms 9 (1 GF) **Facilities** STV ◔ Fishing ◔ Shooting Croquet Xmas New Year Wi-fi **Conf** Class 10 Board 15 Thtr 25 **Services** Lift **Parking** 22 **Notes** ⊗ No children 7 yrs Civ Wed 36

FORTINGALL · Map 20 NN74

Fortingall

★★★★ 78% ◉◉ SMALL HOTEL

☎ 01887 830367 & 830368 📠 01887 830367
PH15 2NQ
e-mail: hotel@fortingallhotel.com
dir: B846 from Aberfeldy for 6m, left signed Fortingall for 3m. Hotel in village centre

Appointed to a very high standard, this hotel has plenty of charm. It lies at the foot of wooded hills in the heart of Glen Lyon. All the bedrooms are very well equipped and

have an extensive range of thoughtful extras. The comfortable lounge, with its log fire, is ideal for pre-dinner drinks, and the small bar is full of character.

Rooms 10 (1 fmly) **S** £99-£119; **D** £148-£194 (incl. bkfst)* **Facilities** STV Fishing Stalking ♫ Xmas New Year Wi-fi **Conf** Board 16 Thtr 30 **Parking** 20 **Notes** LB Civ Wed 30

GLENEAGLES

See Auchterarder

GLENFARG · Map 21 NO11

Famous Bein Inn

★★ 76% ◉ SMALL HOTEL

☎ 01577 830216 📠 01577 830211
PH2 9PY
e-mail: enquiries@beininn.com
web: www.beininn.com
dir: On intersection of A912 & B996

This inn, in a peaceful rural setting, was originally built to accommodate travellers on a journey between Edinburgh and the Highlands. A friendly welcome is guaranteed and there is relaxed informal atmosphere with blazing log fires a feature on colder evenings. The restaurant has a well deserved reputation for the careful preparation of the finest local produce.

Rooms 11 (4 annexe) (4 fmly) (4 GF) **S** £55-£65; **D** £75-£110 (incl. bkfst) **Facilities** FTV New Year **Conf** Class 35 Board 30 Thtr 50 Del from £75 to £100 **Parking** 26 **Notes** LB ⊗ Closed 25 Dec RS 24 & 26 Dec

---

Dalmunzie Castle

★★★ 81% ◉◉ COUNTRY HOUSE HOTEL

☎ 01250 885224 🖷 01250 885225
PH10 7QG
e-mail: reservations@dalmunzie.com
web: www.dalmunzie.com
dir: on A93 at Spittal of Glenshee, follow signs to hotel

This turreted mansion house sits in a secluded glen in the heart of a glorious 6,500-acre estate, yet is within easy reach of the Glenshee ski slopes. The Edwardian style bedrooms, including spacious tower rooms and impressive four-poster rooms, are furnished with antique pieces. The drawing room enjoys panoramic views over the lawns, and the restaurant serves the finest Scottish produce.

Rooms 17 (2 fmly) **S** £65-£125; **D** £100-£210 (incl. bkfst)* **Facilities** STV ⚓ 9 ⚲ Fishing ⚑ Clay pigeon shooting Estate tours Grouse shooting Hiking Mountain bikes Stalking New Year Wi-fi **Conf** Class 20 Board 20 Thtr 20 Del from £155 to £175* **Services** Lift **Parking** 33 **Notes** LB ⊗ Closed 1-28 Dec Civ Wed 70

Kenmore Hotel

★★★ 74% ◉ HOTEL

☎ 01887 830205 🖷 01887 830262
The Square PH15 2NU
e-mail: reception@kenmorehotel.co.uk
web: www.kenmorehotel.com
dir: off A9 at Ballinluig onto A827, through Aberfeldy to Kenmore, hotel in village centre

Dating back to 1572, this riverside hotel is Scotland's oldest inn and has a rich and interesting history.

Bedrooms have tasteful decor, and meals can be enjoyed in the restaurant which has panoramic views of the River Tay. The choice of bars includes one with real fires.

Rooms 40 (13 annexe) (4 fmly) (7 GF) (11 smoking) **S** £64.50-£79.50; **D** £99-£129 (incl. bkfst)* **Facilities** STV Fishing Salmon fishing on River Tay Xmas New Year Wi-fi **Conf** Class 60 Board 50 Thtr 80 Del from £99 to £114* **Services** Lift **Parking** 30 **Notes** LB Civ Wed 150

Ballathie House

★★★★ 78% ◉◉ COUNTRY HOUSE HOTEL

☎ 01250 883268 🖷 01250 883396
PH1 4QN
e-mail: email@ballathiehousehotel.com
web: www.ballathiehousehotel.com
dir: From A9, 2m N of Perth, B9099 through Stanley & signed, or from A93 at Beech Hedge follow signs for Ballathie, 2.5m

Set in delightful grounds, this splendid Scottish mansion house combines classical grandeur with modern comfort. Bedrooms range from well-proportioned master rooms to modern standard rooms, and many boast antique furniture and art deco bathrooms. It might be worth requesting one of the Riverside Rooms, a purpose-built development right on the banks of the river, complete with balconies and terraces. The elegant restaurant has views over the River Tay.

Rooms 41 (16 annexe) (2 fmly) (10 GF) **S** £95-£130; **D** £190-£260 (incl. bkfst) **Facilities** FTV Putt green Fishing ⚑ Xmas New Year Wi-fi **Conf** Class 20 Board 30 Thtr 50 Del from £160 to £180 **Services** Lift **Parking** 50 **Notes** LB Civ Wed 90

Dunalastair

★★★ 77% ◉ HOTEL

☎ 01882 632323 & 632218 🖷 01882 632371
PH16 5PW
e-mail: robert@dunalastair.co.uk
web: www.dunalastair.co.uk
dir: A9 to Pitlochry, at northern end take B8019 to Tummel Bridge then A846 to Kinloch Rannoch

A traditional Highland hotel with inviting public rooms that are full of character - log fires, stags heads, wood panelling and an extensive selection of malt whiskies. Standard and superior bedrooms are on offer. However, it is the friendly attentive service by delightful staff, as well as first-class dinners that will leave lasting impressions.

Rooms 28 (4 fmly) (9 GF) **Facilities** Fishing 4x4 safaris Rafting Clay pigeon shooting Bike hire Archery Xmas New Year Child facilities **Conf** Class 40 Board 40 Thtr 60 **Parking** 33 **Notes** LB Civ Wed 70

Macdonald Loch Rannoch Hotel & Resort

 MACDONALD
HOTELS & RESORTS

★★★ 73% HOTEL

☎ 0844 879 9059 & 01882 632201 🖷 01882 632203
PH16 5PS
e-mail: loch_rannoch@macdonald-hotels.co.uk
web: www.macdonald-hotels.co.uk
dir: Off A9 onto B847 Calvine. Follow signs to Kinloch Rannoch, hotel 1m from village

Set deep in the countryside with elevated views across Loch Rannoch, this hotel is built around a 19th-century hunting lodge and provides a great base for exploring this beautiful area. The superior bedrooms have views over the loch. There is a choice of eating options - The Ptarmigan Restaurant and also the Schiehallan Bar for informal eating. The hotel provides both indoor and outdoor activities.

Rooms 44 (25 fmly) **Facilities** ⚲ Fishing Gym Xmas New Year Wi-fi **Conf** Class 80 Board 50 Thtr 160 **Services** Lift **Parking** 52 **Notes** Civ Wed 130

The Green Hotel

★★★★ 73% ◉ HOTEL

☎ 01577 863467 🖷 01577 863180
2 The Muirs KY13 8AS
e-mail: reservations@green-hotel.com
web: www.green-hotel.com
dir: M90 junct 6 follow Kinross signs, onto A922 for hotel

A long-established hotel offering a wide range of indoor and outdoor activities. Public areas include a classical restaurant, a choice of bars and a well-stocked gift shop. The comfortable, well-equipped bedrooms, most of which are generously proportioned, boast attractive colour schemes and smart modern furnishings.

Rooms 46 (3 fmly) (14 GF) **Facilities** STV ⚲ supervised ⚓ 36 ⚲ Putt green Fishing ⚑ Gym Squash Petanque Curling (Sep-Apr) New Year Wi-fi **Conf** Class 75 Board 60 Thtr 130 **Parking** 60 **Notes** LB Closed 23-24 & 26-28 Dec RS 25 Dec Civ Wed 100

The Windlestrae Hotel & Leisure Centre

★★★ Ⓐ HOTEL

☎ 01577 863217 ▤ 01577 864733
The Muirs KY13 8AS
e-mail: reservations@windlestraehotel.com
web: www.windlestraehotel.com
dir: M90 junct 6 into Kinross, left at 2nd mini rdbt. Hotel 400yds on right

Rooms 45 (13 GF) **S** £60–£100; **D** £80–£140 (incl. bkfst)*
Facilities STV Ⓢ supervised ⌁ 36 ☟ Gym Beautician Steam room Toning tables Xmas New Year Wi-fi
Conf Class 100 Board 80 Thtr 250 Del from £90 to £160*
Parking 80 **Notes** LB Civ Wed 100

Travelodge Kinross (M90)

BUDGET HOTEL

☎ 0871 984 6241 ▤ 01577 861641
Kincardine Rd, Moto Service Area, Turfhill Tourist Area KY13 0NQ
web: www.travelodge.co.uk
dir: Off M90 junct 6, on A977,Turthills Tourist Centre

Travelodge offers good quality, good value, budget accommodation. All offer family rooms sleeping up to four (two adults, two children) with en suite bathroom/shower-room, remote-control TV, tea- and coffee-making facilities and comfortable beds. Food options vary. Breakfast is at the on-site Bar Café restaurant (if available) or to take away. See also Hotel Groups pages.

Rooms 35 **S** fr £29; **D** fr £29

MUTHILL Map 21 NN81

Barley Bree Restaurant with Rooms

⊚ RESTAURANT WITH ROOMS

☎ 01764 681451 ▤ 01764 910055
6 Willoughby St PH5 2AB
e-mail: info@barleybree.com
dir: A9 onto A822 in centre of Muthill

Situated in the heart of the small village of Muthill, and is just a short drive from Crieff, genuine hospitality and quality food are obvious attractions at this charming restaurant with rooms. The property has been totally refurbished under its new owners, and the stylish bedrooms are appointed to a very high standard. The public areas include a cosy lounge with a log burning fire.

Rooms 6 (1 fmly)

PERTH Map 21 NO12

Murrayshall House Hotel & Golf Course

★★★★ 76% ◉◉ HOTEL

☎ 01738 551171 ▤ 01738 552595
New Scone PH2 7PH
e-mail: info@murrayshall.co.uk
dir: From Perth take A94 (Coupar Angus), 1m from Perth, right to Murrayshall just before New Scone

This imposing country house is set in 350 acres of grounds, including two golf courses, one of which is of championship standard. Bedrooms come in two distinct styles: modern suites in a purpose-built building contrast with more classic rooms in the main building. The Clubhouse bar serves a range of meals all day, whilst more accomplished cooking can be enjoyed in the Old Masters Restaurant.

Rooms 41 (14 annexe) (17 fmly) (4 GF) **S** £100–£210; **D** £150–£210 (incl. bkfst)* **Facilities** STV ⌁ 36 ☟ Putt green Driving range New Year Wi-fi **Conf** Class 60 Board 30 Thtr 150 **Parking** 120 **Notes** LB Civ Wed 130

Parklands Hotel

★★★★ 73% ◉◉ SMALL HOTEL

☎ 01738 622451 ▤ 01738 622046
2 St Leonards Bank PH2 8EB
e-mail: info@theparklandshotel.com
web: www.theparklandshotel.com
dir: M90 junct 10, in 1m left at lights at end of park area, hotel on left

Ideally located close to the centre of town with open views over the South Inch. The enthusiastic proprietors continue to invest heavily in the business and the bedrooms have a smart contemporary feel. Public areas include a choice of restaurants with a fine dining experience offered in Acanthus.

Rooms 15 (3 fmly) (4 GF) **S** £89–£159; **D** £109–£199 (incl. bkfst) **Facilities** STV Wi-fi **Conf** Class 18 Board 20 Thtr 24 Del from £129.50 to £145.50 **Parking** 30 **Notes** LB Closed 26 Dec-3 Jan Civ Wed 40

The New County Hotel

★★★ 75% ◉◉ HOTEL

☎ 01738 623355 ▤ 01738 628969
22-30 County Place PH2 8EE
e-mail: enquiries@newcountyhotel.com
web: www.newcountyhotel.com
dir: A9 junct 11 Perth. Follow signs for town centre. Hotel on right after library

This is a smart boutique hotel in the heart of the beautiful garden city of Perth. Upgraded bedrooms have a modern stylish appearance and public areas include a popular bar and contemporary lounge area. No stay here is complete without a visit to the award winning Opus

One Restaurant, which has a well deserved reputation for fine dining.

Rooms 23 (4 fmly) **S** fr £45; **Facilities** New Year Wi-fi **Conf** Class 80 Board 24 Thtr 120 Del from £90 to £125* **Parking** 10 **Notes** LB ⊗

Best Western Huntingtower

★★★ 75% ◉ HOTEL

☎ 01738 583771 ▤ 01738 583777
Crieff Rd PH1 3JT
e-mail: reservations@huntingtowerhotel.co.uk
web: www.huntingtowerhotel.co.uk
dir: 3m W off A85

Set in landscaped grounds in a rural setting, this Edwardian house has been extended to offer smart, comfortable public areas and a series of high quality bedrooms. It's worth asking for one of the executive bedrooms. Comfortable lounges lead to a conservatory popular at lunchtime, whilst the elegant panelled Oak Room restaurant offers skilfully prepared dinners.

Rooms 34 (3 annexe) (2 fmly) (8 GF) **D** £50–£140* **Facilities** STV FTV Xmas Wi-fi **Conf** Class 140 Board 30 Thtr 200 Del from £99 to £145* **Services** Lift **Parking** 150 **Notes** LB Civ Wed 200

Best Western Queens Hotel

★★★ 75% HOTEL

☎ 01738 442222 ▤ 01738 638496
Leonard St PH2 8HB
e-mail: enquiry@queensperth.co.uk
dir: From M90 follow to 2nd lights, turn left. Hotel on right, opposite railway station

This popular hotel benefits from a central location close to both the bus and rail stations. Bedrooms vary in size and style with top floor rooms offering extra space and excellent views of the town. Public rooms include a smart leisure centre and versatile conference space. A range of meals is served in both the bar and restaurant.

Rooms 50 (4 fmly) **S** £50–£110; **D** £70–£125 (incl. bkfst)* **Facilities** STV FTV Ⓢ Gym Steam room Xmas New Year Wi-fi **Conf** Class 70 Board 50 Thtr 200 **Services** Lift **Parking** 50 **Notes** LB ⊗ Civ Wed 220

PERTH *continued*

Lovat

★★★ 74% HOTEL

☎ 01738 636555 📠 01738 643123
90 Glasgow Rd PH2 0LT
e-mail: enquiry@lovat.co.uk
dir: from M90 follow Stirling signs to rdbt. Right into Glasgow Rd, hotel 1.5m on right

This popular and long established hotel offers good function facilities and largely attracts a business clientele. There is a bright contemporary brasserie serving a good range of meals through the day until late.

Rooms 30 (1 fmly) (9 GF) **Facilities** Use of facilities at nearby sister hotel Xmas **Conf** Class 60 Board 50 Thtr 200 **Parking** 40 **Notes** LB ⊗ Civ Wed 180

Salutation

★★★ 70% HOTEL

☎ 01738 630066 📠 01738 633598
South St PH2 8PH
e-mail: salessalutation@strathmorehotels.com
dir: At end of South St on right before River Tay

Situated in heart of Perth, the Salutation is reputed to be one of the oldest hotels in Scotland and has been welcoming guests through its doors since 1699. It offers traditional hospitality with all the modern comforts. Bedrooms vary in size and are thoughtfully equipped. An extensive menu is available in the Adam Restaurant with its impressive barrel vaulted ceiling and original features.

Rooms 84 (5 fmly) **S** £45-£100; **D** £76-£150 (incl. bkfst) **Facilities** 🎵 Xmas New Year Wi-fi **Conf** Class 180 Board 60 Thtr 300 **Services** Lift **Notes** LB Civ Wed 100

See advert on page 617

Express by Holiday Inn Perth

BUDGET HOTEL

☎ 01738 636666 📠 01738 633363
200 Dunkeld Rd, Inveralmond PH1 3AQ
e-mail: info@hiexpressperth.co.uk
web: www.hiexpress.com/perthscotland
dir: Off A9 (Inverness to Stirling road) at Inveralmond rdbt onto A912 signed Perth. Right at 1st rdbt, follow signs for hotel

A modern hotel ideal for families and business travellers. Fresh and uncomplicated, the spacious rooms include Sky TV, power shower and tea and coffee-making facilities. Continental buffet breakfast is included in the room rate; other meals may be taken at the nearby family pub or restaurant. See also the Hotel Groups pages.

Rooms 81 (43 fmly) (19 GF) (8 smoking) **S** £49-£99; **D** £49-£99 (incl. bkfst)* **Conf** Class 15 Board 16 Thtr 30

Innkeeper's Lodge Perth A9 (Huntingtower)

BUDGET HOTEL

☎ 0845 112 6007 📠 0845 112 6293
Crieff Road (A85), Huntingtower PH1 3JJ
web: www.innkeeperslodge.com/perthhuntingtower
dir: From M90 junct 1, signed Inverness over Broxden rdbt onto A9. Left signed Perth. At rdbt onto A85. Lodge on left (shared entrance with Dobbies Garden World)

Innkeeper's Lodge represents an exciting, high value concept within the budget hotel market. Comfortable bedrooms provide excellent facilities that include satellite TV and modem points. Options include family rooms; and for the corporate guest, cutting edge IT includes Wi-fi access. Food is served all day in the adjacent Country Pub. The extensive continental breakfast is complimentary. See also the Hotel Groups pages.

Rooms 53

Innkeeper's Lodge Perth City Centre

BUDGET HOTEL

☎ 0845 112 6008 📠 0845 112 6292
18 Dundee Rd PH2 7AB
web: www.innkeeperslodge.com/perth
dir: From M90 junct 11, A85 towards Perth. 2m, follow signs for Perth & Scone Palace. After lights at Queens Bridge (A93), turn right into Manse Rd. Lodge on left

Rooms 41 **Conf** Class 120 Board 120 Thtr 200

Travelodge Perth Broxden Junction

BUDGET HOTEL

☎ 0871 984 6168 📠 01738 444783
PH2 0PL
web: www.travelodge.co.uk
dir: At junct of A9 & M90 (Broxden rdbt). Follow signs for Broxden Services & Perth Park & Ride

Travelodge offers good quality, good value, budget accommodation. All offer family rooms sleeping up to four (two adults, two children) with en suite bathroom/shower-room, remote-control TV, tea- and coffee-making facilities and comfortable beds. Food options vary. Breakfast is at the on-site Bar Café restaurant (if available) or to take away. See also Hotel Groups pages.

Rooms 87 **S** fr £29; **D** fr £29

PITLOCHRY   Map 23 NN95

See also **Kinloch Rannoch**

Green Park

★★★ 87% ☺ COUNTRY HOUSE HOTEL

☎ 01796 473248 📠 01796 473520
Clunie Bridge Rd PH16 5JY
e-mail: bookings@thegreenpark.co.uk
web: www.thegreenpark.co.uk
dir: turn off A9 at Pitlochry, follow signs 0.25m through town

Guests return year after year to this lovely hotel that is situated in a stunning setting on the shores of Loch Faskally. Most of the thoughtfully designed bedrooms, including a splendid wing, the restaurant and the comfortable lounges enjoy these views. Dinner utilises fresh produce, much of it grown in the kitchen garden.

Rooms 51 (16 GF) **S** £65-£93; **D** £130-£186 (incl. bkfst & dinner)* **Facilities** Putt green New Year Wi-fi **Parking** 51 **Notes** LB

Dundarach

★★★ 75% HOTEL

☎ 01796 472862 📄 01796 473024
Perth Rd PH16 5DJ
e-mail: inbox@dundarach.co.uk
web: www.dundarach.co.uk
dir: S of town centre on main road

This welcoming, family-run hotel stands in mature grounds at the south end of town. Bedrooms offer a variety of styles, including a block of large purpose-built rooms that will appeal to business guests. Well-proportioned public areas feature inviting lounges and a conservatory restaurant giving fine views of the Tummel Valley.

Rooms 39 (19 annexe) (7 fmly) (12 GF) **S** £68; **D** £110 (incl. bkfst)* **Facilities** Wi-fi **Conf** Class 40 Board 40 Thtr 60 **Parking** 39 **Notes** LB ⊗ Closed Jan RS Dec-early Feb

Moulin Hotel

★★★ 73% SMALL HOTEL

☎ 01796 472196 📄 01796 474098
11-13 Kirkmichael Rd, Moulin PH16 5EW
e-mail: sales@moulinhotel.co.uk
web: www.moulinhotel.co.uk
dir: Off A9 take A924 signed Braemar into town centre. Moulin 0.75m from Pitlochry

Steeped in history, original parts of this friendly hotel date back to 1695. The Moulin bar serves an excellent choice of meals as well as real ales from the hotel's own microbrewery. Alternatively, the comfortable restaurant overlooks the Moulin Burn. Bedrooms are well equipped.

Rooms 15 (3 fmly) **S** £50-£75; **D** £65-£90 (incl. bkfst) **Facilities** New Year Wi-fi **Conf** Class 12 Board 10 Thtr 15 Del from £85 to £110 **Parking** 30 **Notes** LB ⊗

ST FILLANS Map 20 NN62

The Four Seasons Hotel

★★★ 83% ◉◉ HOTEL

☎ 01764 685333 📄 01764 685444
Loch Earn PH6 2NF
e-mail: info@thefourseasonshotel.co.uk
web: www.thefourseasonshotel.co.uk
dir: on A85, towards W of village

Set on the edge of Loch Earn, this welcoming hotel and many of its bedrooms benefit from fine views. There is a choice of lounges, including a library, warmed by log fires during winter. Local produce is used to good effect in both the Meall Reamhar restaurant and the more informal Tarken Room.

Rooms 18 (6 annexe) (7 fmly) **S** £55-£90; **D** £110-£130 (incl. bkfst)* **Facilities** Xmas New Year Wi-fi **Conf** Class 45 Board 38 Thtr 95 Del from £104 to £124 **Parking** 40 **Notes** LB Closed 2 Jan-Feb RS Nov, Dec, Mar Civ Wed 80

Achray House

★★★ 74% ◉ SMALL HOTEL

☎ 01764 685231 📄 01764 685320
PH6 2NF
e-mail: info@achray-house.co.uk
web: www.achray-house.co.uk
dir: follow A85 towards Crainlarich, from Stirling follow A9 then B822 at Braco, B827 to Comrie. Turn left onto A85 to St Fillans

A friendly holiday hotel set in gardens overlooking picturesque Loch Earn, Achray House offers smart, attractive and well-equipped bedrooms. An interesting range of freshly prepared dishes is served both in the conservatory and in the adjoining dining rooms.

Rooms 10 (2 annexe) (2 fmly) (3 GF) **S** £40-£95; **D** £80-£150 (incl. bkfst)* **Facilities** Xmas New Year Wi-fi **Conf** Class 20 Board 20 Del from £70 to £110* **Parking** 30 **Notes** Closed 3-24 Jan Civ Wed 40

RENFREWSHIRE

GLASGOW AIRPORT Map 20 NS46

Holiday Inn Glasgow Airport

★★★ 78% HOTEL

☎ 0870 400 9031 & 0141 887 1266 📄 0141 887 3738
Abbotsinch PA3 2TR
e-mail: operations-glasgow@ihg.com
web: www.holidayinn.co.uk
dir: From E: M8 junct 28, follow hotel signs. From W: M8 junct 29, airport slip road to hotel

Located within the airport grounds and within walking distance of the terminal. Bedrooms are well appointed and cater for the needs of the modern traveller. The open-plan public areas are relaxing as is the restaurant which offers a carvary and a restaurant. Wi-fi is available in the public areas with LAN in all bedrooms.

Rooms 300 (6 fmly) (54 smoking) **S** £49-£189; **D** £55-£199* **Facilities** STV Wi-fi **Conf** Class 150 Board 75 Thtr 300 Del from £89 to £199* **Services** Lift Air con **Parking** 56 **Notes** LB Civ Wed 250

Express by Holiday Inn Glasgow Airport

BUDGET HOTEL

☎ 0141 842 1100 📄 0141 842 1122
St Andrews Dr PA3 2TJ
e-mail: glasgowairport@expressholidayinn.co.uk
web: www.hiexpress.com/ex-glasgow
dir: M8 junct 28, at 1st rdbt turn right, hotel on right

A modern hotel ideal for families and business travellers. Fresh and uncomplicated, the spacious rooms include Sky TV, power shower and tea and coffee-making facilities. Continental buffet breakfast is included in the room rate; other meals may be taken at the nearby family pub or restaurant. See also the Hotel Groups pages.

Rooms 141 (63 fmly) **Conf** Class 20 Board 30 Thtr 70

Travelodge Glasgow Airport

BUDGET HOTEL

☎ 0871 984 6335 📄 0141 889 0583
Marchburn Dr, Glasgow Airport Business Park, Paisley PA3 2AR
web: www.travelodge.co.uk
dir: M8 junct 28, 0.5m from Glasgow Airport

Travelodge offers good quality, good value, budget accommodation. All offer family rooms sleeping up to four (two adults, two children) with en suite bathroom/shower-room, remote-control TV, tea- and coffee-making facilities and comfortable beds. Food options vary. Breakfast is at the on-site Bar Café restaurant (if available) or to take away. See also Hotel Groups pages.

Rooms 98 (40 fmly) **S** fr £29; **D** fr £29

GLASGOW AIRPORT *continued*

Travelodge Glasgow Braehead

BUDGET HOTEL

☎ 0871 984 6372 📄 0141 885 1862
150 Kings Inch Rd PA4 8XQ
dir: From W: M8 junct 26, (from E: junct 25a) follow
Braehead Arena & Xscape signs. Left at 1st lights, right
at 2nd lights follow Braehead Arena & Xscape signs.
Pass Sainsbury's on right. Straight ahead 1st rdbt. Lodge
200yds on right

Travelodge offers good quality, good value, budget
accommodation. All offer family rooms sleeping up to four
(two adults, two children) with en suite bathroom/
shower-room, remote-control TV, tea- and coffee-making
facilities and comfortable beds. Food options vary.
Breakfast is at the on-site Bar Café restaurant (if
available) or to take away. See also Hotel Groups pages.

Rooms 99 **S** fr £29; **D** fr £29

HOWWOOD   Map 20 NS36

Bowfield Hotel & Country Club

★★★ 81% ⊛ HOTEL

☎ 01505 705225 📄 01505 705230
PA9 1DZ
e-mail: enquiries@bowfieldhotel.co.uk
web: www.bowfieldhotel.co.uk
dir: M8 junct 28a/29, onto A737 for 6m, left onto B787,
right after 2m, follow for 1m to hotel

This former textile mill is now a popular hotel which has
become a convenient stopover for travellers using
Glasgow Airport. The leisure club has been considerably
expanded and offers very good facilities. Public areas
have beamed ceilings, brick and white painted walls, and
welcoming open fires. Bedrooms are housed in a separate
wing and offer good modern comforts and facilities.

Rooms 23 (3 fmly) (7 GF) **S** £40-£95; **D** £60-£130 (incl.
bkfst)* **Facilities** Spa FTV ⓣ supervised ♨ 18 Gym
Squash Children's soft play Aerobics studio Health &
beauty Xmas New Year Wi-fi **Conf** Class 60 Board 40
Thtr 100 Del from £95 to £120* **Parking** 120 **Notes** LB ⊗
Civ Wed 80

LANGBANK   Map 20 NS37

Best Western Gleddoch House

★★★ 79% HOTEL

Best Western

☎ 01475 540711 📄 01475 540201
PA14 6YE
e-mail: sales.gleddochhouse@ohiml.com
web: www.oxfordhotelsandinns.com
dir: M8 to Greenock, onto A8, left at rdbt onto A789,
follow for 0.5m, turn right, 2nd on left

This hotel is set in spacious, landscaped grounds high
above the River Clyde with fine views. The period house is
appointed to a very high standard. The modern extension
remains impressive and offers spacious and very
comfortable bedrooms. Warm hospitality and attentive
service are noteworthy along with the hotel's parkland
golf course and leisure club.

Rooms 70 (20 fmly) (8 GF) **Facilities** ☜ ♨ 18 Putt green
Xmas New Year **Conf** Class 70 Board 40 Thtr 150
Parking 150 **Notes** LB ⊗ Civ Wed 120

RENFREW

For hotels see Glasgow Airport

SCOTTISH BORDERS

EDDLESTON   Map 21 NT24

The Horseshoe Inn

⊛⊛⊛ RESTAURANT WITH ROOMS

☎ 01721 730225 📄 01721 730268
EH45 8QP
e-mail: reservations@horseshoeinn.co.uk
web: www.horseshoeinn.co.uk
dir: A703, 5m N of Peebles

This inn is five miles north of Peebles and only 18 miles
south of Edinburgh. Originally a blacksmith's shop, it

---

was significantly refurbished by Vivienne Steele and her
partner, chef-director Patrick Bardoulet. It is now a
restaurant with rooms with a very good reputation for its
delightful atmosphere and its excellent classical French
inspired cuisine. There are eight luxuriously appointed
and individually designed bedrooms.

Rooms 8 (1 fmly)

See advert on page 614

GALASHIELS   Map 21 NT43

Kingsknowes

★★★ 75% HOTEL

☎ 01896 758375 📄 01896 750377
Selkirk Rd TD1 3HY
e-mail: enq@kingsknowes.co.uk
web: www.kingsknowes.co.uk
dir: Off A7 at Galashiels/Selkirk rdbt

An imposing turreted mansion, this hotel lies in attractive
gardens on the outskirts of town close to the River Tweed.
It boasts elegant public areas and many spacious
bedrooms, some with excellent views. There is a choice of
bars, one with a popular menu to supplement the
restaurant.

Rooms 12 (2 fmly) **S** fr £69; **D** fr £99 (incl. bkfst)*
Facilities Wi-fi **Conf** Class 40 Board 30 Thtr 60
Parking 65 **Notes** LB Civ Wed 75

KELSO   Map 21 NT73

The Roxburghe Hotel & Golf Course

★★★ 85% ⊛ COUNTRY HOUSE HOTEL

☎ 01573 450331 📄 01573 450611
Heiton TD5 8JZ
e-mail: hotel@roxburghe.net
web: www.roxburghe.net
dir: From A68 Jedburgh take A698 to Heiton, 3m SW of
Kelso

Outdoor sporting pursuits are popular at this impressive
Jacobean mansion owned by the Duke of Roxburghe, and
set in 500 acres of woods and parkland bordering the
River Teviot. Gracious public areas are the perfect
settings for afternoon teas and carefully prepared meals.
The elegant bedrooms are individually designed, some by

the Duchess herself, and include superior rooms, some with four posters and log fires.

Rooms 22 (6 annexe) (3 fmly) (3 GF) **Facilities** Spa STV ♨ 18 Putt green Fishing 🐟 Clay shooting Health & beauty salon Mountain bike hire Falconry Archery Xmas New Year **Conf** Class 20 Board 20 Thtr 50 **Parking** 150 **Notes** ⊗ Civ Wed 60

Ednam House

★★★ 77% HOTEL

☎ 01573 224168 📄 01573 226319
Bridge St TD5 7HT
e-mail: contact@ednamhouse.com
web: www.ednamhouse.com
dir: 50mtrs from town square

Overlooking a wide expanse of the River Tweed, this fine Georgian mansion has been under the Brooks family ownership for over 75 years. Accommodation styles range from standard to grand, plus The Orangerie, situated in the grounds, that has been converted into a gracious two-bedroom apartment. Public areas include a choice of lounges and an elegant dining room that has views over the gardens.

Rooms 32 (2 annexe) (4 fmly) (3 GF) **S** £75-£84.50; **D** £111-£155 (incl. bkfst)* **Facilities** FTV 🐟 Free access to Abbey Fitness Centre Wi-fi **Conf** Board 200 Thtr 250 **Parking** 60 **Notes** Closed 24 Dec-6 Jan Civ Wed 100

Lauderdale

★★ 74% HOTEL

☎ 01578 722231 📄 01578 718642
1 Edinburgh Rd TD2 6TW
e-mail: enquiries@lauderdalehotel.co.uk
web: www.lauderdalehotel.co.uk
dir: on A68 from S, through Lauder centre, hotel on right. From Edinburgh, hotel on left at 1st bend after passing Lauder sign

Lying on the north side of the village with spacious gardens to the side and rear, this friendly hotel is ideally placed for those who don't want to stay in Edinburgh itself. The well-equipped bedrooms come in a variety of sizes, and a good range of meals is served in both the bar and the restaurant.

Rooms 10 (1 fmly) **S** £50; **D** £80 (incl. bkfst)* **Facilities** STV FTV 🎵 Xmas New Year Wi-fi Child facilities **Conf** Class 200 Board 100 Thtr 200 **Parking** 200 **Notes** Civ Wed 180

The Townhouse Hotel

★★★ 79% HOTEL

☎ 01896 822645 📄 01896 823474
3 Market Square TD6 9PQ
e-mail: info@thetownhousemelrose.co.uk
web: www.thetownhousemelrose.co.uk
dir: From A68 into Melrose. Hotel in town square

Situated on the square this smart hotel, as the name suggests, has the typical style of a Scottish town house. Bedrooms vary in size and some have views of the hills but all are well equipped and beautifully decorated - it's worth requesting one of two superior rooms. Guests can eat in either the brasserie or more traditional restaurant - both offer the same menu.

Rooms 11 (1 fmly) (1 GF) **S** £75-£116; **D** £116-£128 (incl. bkfst) **Facilities** FTV New Year Wi-fi **Conf** Class 30 Board 40 Thtr 70 Del from £100 to £150 **Notes** LB ⊗ Closed 26-27 Dec & 4-12 Jan

---

Burt's

★★★ 75% ◉◉ HOTEL

☎ 01896 822285 📄 01896 822870
Market Square TD6 9PN
e-mail: enquiries@burtshotel.co.uk
web: www.burtshotel.co.uk
dir: A6091, 2m from A68 3m S of Earlston

Recognised by its whitewashed façade and colourful window boxes in the heart of this small market town, this hotel has been under the same family ownership for over 30 years and the genuine warmth of hospitality is notable. Food is important at Burt's and the elegant restaurant is well complemented by the range of tasty meals in the bar.

Rooms 20 **S** £70; **D** £130 (incl. bkfst)* **Facilities** STV FTV Salmon fishing Shooting New Year Wi-fi **Conf** Class 20 Board 20 Thtr 38 Del from £110 to £130* **Parking** 40 **Notes** Closed 24-26 Dec & 2-3 Jan

---

INSPECTORS' CHOICE

Cringletie House

★★★★ ◉◉ COUNTRY HOUSE HOTEL

☎ 01721 725750 📄 01721 725751
Edinburgh Rd EH45 8PL
e-mail: enquiries@cringletie.com
web: www.cringletie.com
dir: 2m N on A703

This long-established hotel is a romantic baronial mansion set in 28 acres of gardens and woodland with stunning views from all rooms. Delightful public rooms include a cocktail lounge with adjoining conservatory, whilst the first-floor restaurant is graced by a magnificent hand-painted ceiling. Bedrooms, many particularly spacious, are attractively furnished.

Rooms 13 (2 GF) **Facilities** STV Putt green 🐟 Petanque Giant chess & draughts In-room spa Xmas New Year Wi-fi **Conf** Class 20 Board 24 Thtr 45 Del from £200* **Services** Lift **Parking** 30 **Notes** Civ Wed 65

Macdonald Cardrona Hotel Golf & Country Club

★★★★ 77% ◉ HOTEL

☎ 01896 833600 📄 01896 831166
Cardrona Mains EH45 6LZ
e-mail: general.cardrona@macdonald-hotels.co.uk
web: www.macdonald-hotels.co.uk/cardrona
dir: On A72 between Peebles & Innerleithen, 3m S of Peebles

The rolling hills of the Scottish Borders are a stunning backdrop for this modern, purpose-built hotel. Spacious bedrooms are traditional in style, equipped with a range of extras, and most enjoy fantastic countryside. The hotel features some impressive leisure facilities, including an

continued

PEEBLES *continued*

18-hole golf course, 18-metre indoor pool and state-of-the+art gym.

Rooms 99 (24 fmly) (16 GF) **S** £82-£169; **D** £92-£179 (incl. bkfst) **Facilities** Spa STV ⟨⟩ ♪ 18 Putt green Gym Sauna Steam room Xmas New Year Wi-fi **Conf** Class 120 Board 90 Thtr 250 Del from £130 to £160 **Services** Lift **Parking** 200 **Notes** LB Civ Wed 200

Peebles Hotel Hydro

★★★★ 75% HOTEL

☎ 01721 720602 📄 01721 722999
EH45 8LX
e-mail: info@peebleshydro.co.uk
dir: On A702, 0.3m from town

A majestic building, this resort hotel sits in grounds on the edge of the town, its elevated position giving striking views across the valley. The range of indoor and outdoor leisure activities is second to none and makes the hotel a favourite with both families and conference delegates. · Accommodation comes in a range of styles and includes a number of family rooms.

Rooms 132 (24 fmly) (15 GF) **S** £105-£115; **D** £210-£230 (incl. bkfst & dinner)* **Facilities** Spa STV ⟨⟩ supervised ⌣ Putt green ⌣ Gym Badminton Beautician Hairdressing Giant chess/draughts Pitch & putt ♪ Xmas New Year Wi-fi Child facilities **Conf** Class 200 Board 74 Thtr 450 Del from £140 to £150 **Services** Lift **Parking** 200 **Notes** LB ⊗ Civ Wed 200

Tontine

★★★ 81% HOTEL

☎ 01721 720892 📄 01721 729732
High St EH45 8AJ
e-mail: info@tontinehotel.com
web: www.tontinehotel.com
dir: in town centre

Conveniently situated in the main street, this long-established hotel offers comfortable public rooms including an elegant Adam restaurant, inviting lounge and 'clubby' bar. Bedrooms, contained in the original house and the river-facing wing, offer a smart, classical style of accommodation. The lasting impression is of the excellent level of hospitality and guest care.

Rooms 36 (3 fmly) **S** £45-£65; **D** £65-£95 (incl. bkfst)* **Facilities** STV FTV Xmas New Year Wi-fi Child facilities **Conf** Class 24 Board 24 Thtr 40 Del from £85 to £115* **Parking** 24

Park

★★★ 75% HOTEL

☎ 01721 720451 📄 01721 723510
Innerleithen Rd EH45 8BA
e-mail: reserve@parkpeebles.co.uk
dir: In town centre opposite filling station

This hotel offers pleasant, well-equipped bedrooms of various sizes - those in the original house are particularly spacious. Public areas enjoy views of the gardens and include a tartan-clad bar, a relaxing lounge and a spacious wood-panelled restaurant, open for lunch and early-bird suppers

Rooms 24 **Facilities** STV Putt green Use of facilities at Peebles Hotel Hydro Xmas New Year Wi-fi **Conf** Class 15 Board 18 Thtr 30 Del from £50 to £160* **Services** Lift **Parking** 50

ST BOSWELLS   Map 21 NT53

Dryburgh Abbey Hotel

★★★★ 73% ⊛ ⊛⊛ COUNTRY HOUSE HOTEL

☎ 01835 822261 📄 01835 823945
TD6 0RQ
e-mail: enquiries@dryburgh.co.uk
web: www.dryburgh.co.uk
dir: B6356 signed Scott's View & Earlston. Through Clintmains, 1.8m to hotel

Found in the heart of the Scottish Borders, and sitting beside to the ancient ruins of Dryburgh Abbey and the majestic River Tweed. This country house hotel, dating from the mid 19th century, offers comfortable public areas and an array of bedrooms and suites, each still displaying original features. The award-winning Tweed Restaurant, overlooking the river, has now been refurbished, and offers an 8-course dinner menu showcasing the chef's dedication to producing modern Scottish cuisine. The Abbey Bar offers food throughout the day.

Rooms 38 (31 fmly) (8 GF) **S** £63-£205; **D** £126-£350 (incl. bkfst & dinner)* **Facilities** FTV ⟨⟩ Putt green Fishing ⌣ Sauna Xmas New Year Wi-fi **Conf** Class 80 Board 60 Thtr 150 Del from £140 to £200* **Services** Lift **Parking** 70 **Notes** LB Civ Wed 120

SELKIRK Map 21 NT42

Philipburn Country House

★★★★ ⚏ COUNTRY HOUSE HOTEL

☎ 01750 20747 📄 01750 21690
Linglie Rd TD7 5LS
e-mail: info@philipburnhousehotel.co.uk
dir: From A7 follow signs for A72/A707 Peebles/Moffat.
Hotel 1m from town centre

Rooms 12 (2 fmly) **S** £105-£135; **D** £125-£175 (incl.
bkfst)* **Facilities** FTV 🏊 Xmas New Year Wi-fi
Conf Class 12 Board 24 Thtr 40 Del from £145 to £175*
Parking 25 **Notes** LB ⊗ Closed 11-25 Jan Civ Wed 85

SWINTON Map 21 NT84

Wheatsheaf at Swinton

⚎⚎ RESTAURANT WITH ROOMS

☎ 01890 860257 📄 01890 860688
TD11 3JJ
e-mail: reception@wheatsheaf-swinton.co.uk
dir: In village centre on A6112

Overlooking the village green, this restaurant with rooms
has built its reputation on excellent food. Bedrooms are
stylishly furnished, all with smart en suite facilities, the
largest ones featuring a bath and separate shower
cubicle. The executive bedrooms are of a very high
standard.

Rooms 10 (2 fmly)

SOUTH AYRSHIRE

AYR Map 20 NS32

The Western House Hotel

★★★★ 84% ⚎⚎ HOTEL

☎ 0870 055 5510 📄 0870 055 5515
2 Whitletts Rd KA8 0HA
e-mail: pdavies@westernhousehotel.co.uk
dir: From Glasgow M77 then A77 towards Ayr. At Whitletts
rdbt take A719 towards town centre

This impressive hotel is located in its own attractive
gardens on the edge of Ayr racecourse. Bedrooms in the
main house are superbly appointed, and the courtyard
rooms offer much comfort too. Nicely appointed day
rooms include the light and airy restaurant with views
across the course. The staff are attentive and welcoming.

Rooms 49 (39 annexe) (39 fmly) (16 GF) **Facilities** STV
Xmas New Year **Conf** Class 300 Board 36 Thtr 1200
Services Lift **Parking** 250 **Notes** ⊗ Civ Wed 200

Fairfield House

★★★★ 78% ⚎⚎ HOTEL

☎ 01292 267461 📄 01292 261456
12 Fairfield Rd KA7 2AR
e-mail: reservations@fairfieldhotel.co.uk
dir: from A77 towards Ayr South (A30). Follow town centre
signs, down Miller Rd, left, then right into Fairfield Rd

Situated in a leafy cul-de-sac close to the esplanade, this
hotel enjoys stunning seascapes towards to the Isle of
Arran. Bedrooms are in either modern or classical styles,
the latter featuring impressive bathrooms. Public areas
provide stylish, modern rooms in which to relax. Skilfully
prepared meals are served in the casual brasserie or
elegant restaurant.

Rooms 44 (4 annexe) (3 fmly) (9 GF) **S** £75-£105;
D £89-£169 (incl. bkfst)* **Facilities** STV FTV ⊛
supervised Gym Fitness room Sauna Steam room Xmas
New Year Wi-fi **Conf** Class 50 Board 40 Thtr 80
Del from £125 to £145 **Services** Lift **Parking** 50 **Notes** LB
⊗ Civ Wed 150

Enterkine Country House

★★★★ 77% ⚎⚎ COUNTRY HOUSE HOTEL

☎ 01292 520580 📄 01292 521582
Annbank KA6 5AL
e-mail: mail@enterkine.com
dir: 5m east of Ayr on B743

This luxurious art deco country mansion dates from the
1930s and retains many original features, notably some
splendid bathroom suites. The focus is very much on
dining, and in country house tradition there is no bar,
drinks being served in the elegant lounge and library. The
well-proportioned bedrooms are furnished and equipped
to high standards, many with lovely countryside views.

Rooms 13 (7 annexe) (6 fmly) (5 GF) **Facilities** FTV
Beauty treatments Clay pigeon shooting Quad biking
Archery 🎵 Xmas New Year Wi-fi **Conf** Class 140
Board 140 Thtr 200 **Parking** 40 **Notes** Civ Wed 70

Savoy Park

★★★ 79% HOTEL

☎ 01292 266112 📄 01292 611488
16 Racecourse Rd KA7 2UT
e-mail: mail@savoypark.com
dir: from A77 follow A70 for 2m, through Parkhouse Str,
left into Beresford Terr, 1st right into Bellevue Rd

This well-established hotel retains many of its traditional
values including friendly, attentive service. Public rooms
feature impressive panelled walls, ornate ceilings and
open fires. The restaurant is reminiscent of a Highland
shooting lodge and offers a wide ranging, good-value
menu to suit all tastes. The large superior bedrooms
retain a classical elegance while others are smart and
modern; all have well equipped modern bathrooms.

Rooms 15 (3 fmly) **S** £50-£80; **D** £60-£120 (incl. bkfst)*
Facilities FTV Xmas New Year Wi-fi Child facilities
Conf Class 40 Board 30 Thtr 50 Del from £80 to £120
Parking 60 **Notes** LB Civ Wed 100

Express by Holiday Inn Ayr

BUDGET HOTEL

☎ 0870 890 5100 📄 0870 890 5200
Wheatpark Place KA8 9RT
web: www.hiexpress.co.uk

A modern hotel ideal for families and business travellers.
Fresh and uncomplicated, the spacious rooms include Sky
TV, power shower and tea and coffee-making facilities.
Continental buffet breakfast is included in the room rate;
other meals may be taken at the nearby family pub or
restaurant. See also the Hotel Groups pages.

Rooms 84

Travelodge Ayr

BUDGET HOTEL

☎ 08719 846 321 📄 01292 880357
Highfield Dr KA8 9SH
web: www.travelodge.co.uk
dir: A719, next rdbt 3rd exit onto B743

Travelodge offers good quality, good value, budget
accommodation. All offer family rooms sleeping up to four
(two adults, two children) with en suite bathroom/
shower-room, remote-control TV, tea- and coffee-making
facilities and comfortable beds. Food options vary.
Breakfast is at the on-site Bar Café restaurant (if
available) or to take away. See also Hotel Groups pages.

Rooms 56 **S** fr £29; **D** fr £29

BALLANTRAE — Map 20 NX08

INSPECTORS' CHOICE

Glenapp Castle
★★★★★ ⚜⚜⚜ HOTEL

☎ 01465 831212 📠 01465 831000
KA26 0NZ
e-mail: enquiries@glenappcastle.com
web: www.glenappcastle.com
dir: 1m from A77 near Ballantrae

Friendly hospitality and attentive service prevail at this stunning Victorian castle, set in extensive private grounds to the south of the village. Impeccably furnished bedrooms are graced with antiques and period pieces. Breathtaking views of Arran and Ailsa Craig can be enjoyed from the delightful, sumptuous day rooms and from many of the bedrooms. Accomplished cooking, using quality local ingredients is a feature of all meals; dinner is offered on a well crafted and imaginative, no-choice, five-course menu. Guest should make a point of walking round the wonderful grounds, to include the azalea lake and walled vegetable gardens with their fine restored greenhouses.

Rooms 17 (2 fmly) (7 GF) **S** £255-£455; **D** £375-£575 (incl. bkfst & dinner)* **Facilities** STV FTV ⊃ ⊱ New Year Wi-fi **Conf** Class 12 Board 17 Thtr 17 Del from £295 to £495* **Services** Lift **Parking** 20 **Notes** LB Closed Jan-mid Mar Civ Wed 40

PRESTWICK — Map 20 NS32

Parkstone
★★★ 77% HOTEL

☎ 01292 477286 📠 01292 477671
Esplanade KA9 1QN
e-mail: info@parkstonehotel.co.uk
web: www.parkstonehotel.co.uk
dir: From Main St (A79) W to seafront, hotel 600yds

Situated on the seafront in a quiet residential area only one mile from Prestwick Airport, this family-run hotel caters for business visitors as well as golfers. Bedrooms come in a variety of sizes; all are furnished in a smart, contemporary style. The attractive, modern look of the bar and restaurant is matched by an equally up-to-date menu.

Parkstone

Rooms 30 (2 fmly) (7 GF) **S** £59-£79; **D** £98-£109 (incl. bkfst)* **Facilities** FTV Xmas New Year Wi-fi **Conf** Thtr 100 **Parking** 34 **Notes** LB ⊗ Civ Wed 100

TROON — Map 20 NS33

INSPECTORS' CHOICE

Lochgreen House Hotel
★★★★ ⚜⚜⚜ COUNTRY HOUSE HOTEL

☎ 01292 313343 📠 01292 318661
Monktonhill Rd, Southwood KA10 7EN
e-mail: lochgreen@costley-hotels.co.uk
web: www.costley-hotels.co.uk
dir: From A77 follow Prestwick Airport signs. 0.5m before airport take B749 to Troon. Hotel 1m on left

Set in immaculately maintained grounds, Lochgreen House is graced by tasteful extensions which have created stunning public rooms and spacious, comfortable and elegantly furnished bedrooms. Extra facilities include a coffee shop, gift shop and beauty treatments in The Retreat. The magnificent Tapestry Restaurant provides the ideal setting for dinners that are immaculately presented.

Rooms 38 (7 annexe) (17 GF) **Facilities** Beauty treatments Xmas **Conf** Class 50 Board 50 Thtr 70 **Services** Lift **Parking** 50 **Notes** ⊗ Civ Wed 100

Barceló Troon Marine Hotel
★★★★ 72% HOTEL — **Barceló** HOTELS & RESORTS

☎ 01292 314444 📠 01292 316922
Crosbie Rd KA10 6HE
e-mail: marine@barcelo-hotels.co.uk
web: www.barcelo-hotels.co.uk
dir: A77, A78, A79 onto B749. Hotel on left after golf course

A favourite with conference and leisure guests, this hotel overlooks Royal Troon's 18th fairway. The cocktail lounge and split-level restaurant enjoy panoramic views of the Firth of Clyde across to the Isle of Arran. Bedrooms and public areas are attractively appointed.

Rooms 89 **Facilities** Spa STV ⊗ supervised Gym Squash Steam room Beauty room Xmas New Year Wi-fi **Conf** Class 100 Board 40 Thtr 200 Del from £95* **Services** Lift **Parking** 200 **Notes** ⊗ Civ Wed 100

TURNBERRY — Map 20 NS20

INSPECTORS' CHOICE

Turnberry Resort, Scotland
★★★★★ ⚜⚜ HOTEL

☎ 01655 331000 📠 01655 331706
KA26 9LT
e-mail: turnberry@luxurycollection.com
web: www.luxurycollection.com/turnberry
dir: From Glasgow take A77/M77 S towards Stranraer, 2m past Kirkoswald, follow signs for A719/Turnberry. Hotel 500mtrs on right

This famous hotel enjoys magnificent views over to Arran, Ailsa Craig and the Mull of Kintyre. Facilities include a world-renowned golf course, the excellent Colin Montgomerie Golf Academy, a luxurious spa and a host of outdoor and country pursuits. Elegant bedrooms and suites are located in the main hotel, while adjacent lodges provide spacious, well-equipped accommodation. The Ailsa lounge is very welcoming, and in addition to the elegant main restaurant for dining, there is a Mediterranean Terrace Brasserie and the relaxed Clubhouse.

Rooms 207 (89 annexe) (2 fmly) (12 GF) **S** £377-£792; **D** £397-£812 (incl. bkfst)* **Facilities** Spa STV ⊗ supervised ♨ 36 Putt green Fishing Gym Leisure club Outdoor activity centre Colin Montgomerie Golf Academy New Year Wi-fi **Conf** Class 145 Board 80 Thtr 300 **Services** Lift **Parking** 200 **Notes** LB Closed 25 Dec Civ Wed 220

Malin Court

★★★ 82% ◉ HOTEL

☎ 01655 331457 📠 01655 331072
KA26 9PB
e-mail: info@malincourt.co.uk
web: www.malincourt.co.uk
dir: On A74 to Ayr then A719 to Turnberry & Maidens

Forming part of the Malin Court Residential and Nursing Home Complex, this friendly and comfortable hotel enjoys delightful views over the Firth of Clyde and Turnberry golf courses. Standard and executive rooms are available; all are well equipped. Public areas are plentiful, with the restaurant serving high teas, dinners and light lunches.

Rooms 18 (9 fmly) **S** £84-£94; **D** £128-£148 (incl. bkfst)
Facilities STV Putt green Wi-fi **Conf** Class 60 Board 30
Thtr 200 Del from £105 to £160 **Services** Lift
Parking 110 **Notes** LB ⊗ RS Oct-Mar Civ Wed 80

SOUTH LANARKSHIRE

ABINGTON MOTORWAY SERVICE AREA (M74) Map 21 NS92

Days Inn Abington

BUDGET HOTEL

☎ 01864 502782 📠 01864 502759
ML12 6RG
e-mail: abington.hotel@welcomebreak.co.uk
web: www.welcomebreak.co.uk
dir: M74 junct 13, accessible from N'bound and S'bound carriageways

This modern building offers accommodation in smart, spacious and well-equipped bedrooms, suitable for families and business travellers, and all with en suite bathrooms. Continental breakfast is available and other refreshments may be taken at the nearby family restaurant. See also the Hotel Groups pages.

Rooms 52 (50 fmly) **S** £29-£59; **D** £39-£79*
Conf Board 10 Del from £69 to £99*

BIGGAR Map 21 NT03

Shieldhill Castle

★★★★ 71% ◉◉ COUNTRY HOUSE HOTEL

☎ 01899 220035 📠 01899 221092
Quothquan ML12 6NA
e-mail: enquiries@shieldhill.co.uk
web: www.shieldhill.co.uk
dir: A702 onto B7016 (Biggar to Carnwath road), after 2m left into Shieldhill Rd. Hotel 1.5m on right

The focus on food and wine are important at this imposing fortified country mansion that dates back almost 800 years. Public room are atmospheric and include the classical Chancellors' Restaurant, oak-panelled lounge and the Gun Room bar that offers its own menu. Bedrooms, many with feature baths, are spacious

continued

BIGGAR *continued*

and comfortable. A friendly welcome is assured, even from the estate's own dogs!

Rooms 26 (10 annexe) (10 GF) **Facilities** FTV ⌁ Cycling Clay shoot Hot air ballooning Falconry Laser & game bird shooting Xmas New Year Wi-fi **Conf** Class 200 Board 250 Thtr 500 **Parking** 50 **Notes** Civ Wed 200

BOTHWELL   Map 20 NS75

Bothwell Bridge

★★★ 79% HOTEL

☎ 01698 852246 📠 01698 854686
89 Main St G71 8EU
e-mail: enquiries@bothwellbridge-hotel.com
web: www.bothwellbridge-hotel.com
dir: M74 junct 5 & follow signs to Uddingston, right at mini-rdbt. Hotel just past shops on left

This red-sandstone mansion house is a popular business, function and conference hotel conveniently placed for the motorway. Most bedrooms are spacious and all are well equipped. The conservatory is a bright and comfortable restaurant serving an interesting variety of Italian influenced dishes. The lounge bar offers a comfortable seating area that proves popular as a stop for coffee.

Rooms 90 (14 fmly) (26 GF) **S** £64-£90; **D** £75-£120 (incl. bkfst)* **Facilities** STV ♫ Xmas New Year Wi-fi **Conf** Class 80 Board 50 Thtr 200 Del from £90 to £103* **Services** Lift **Parking** 125 **Notes** ⊗ Civ Wed 180

EAST KILBRIDE   Map 20 NS65

Macdonald Crutherland House

★★★★ 75% ◉◉ HOTEL

☎ 0844 879 9039 📠 01355 577047
Strathaven Rd G75 0QZ
e-mail: crutherland@macdonald-hotels.co.uk
web: www.macdonaldhotels.co.uk
dir: Follow A726 signed Strathaven, straight over Torrance rdbt, hotel on left after 250yds

This mansion is set in 37 acres of landscaped grounds two miles from the town centre. Behind its Georgian façade is a very relaxing hotel with elegant public areas plus extensive banqueting and leisure facilities. The bedrooms are spacious and comfortable. Staff provide good levels of attention and enjoyable meals are served in the restaurant.

Rooms 75 (16 fmly) (16 GF) **D** £80-£175 (incl. bkfst)* **Facilities** Spa STV ♨ Gym Sauna Steam room Xmas New Year Wi-fi **Conf** Class 100 Board 50 Thtr 500 Del from £115 to £155* **Services** Lift **Parking** 200 **Notes** LB ⊗ Civ Wed 300

See advert on this page

Holiday Inn Glasgow-East Kilbride

★★★★ 71% HOTEL

☎ 01355 236300 📠 01355 233552
Stewartfield Way G74 5LA
e-mail: salesmg@hieastkilbride.com
web: www.hieastkilbride.com
dir: M74 junct 5, A725 then A726

A modern hotel located in East Kilbride but within easy striking distance of Glasgow. Bedrooms are nicely appointed and cater well for the needs of the modern traveller. Food is served in La Bonne Auberge with a

definite French and Mediterranean feel. Good leisure facilities are an added bonus.

Rooms 101 (4 fmly) (26 GF) (8 smoking) **Facilities** Spa STV ♨ Gym Aerobics studio Spin cycle studio Sauna Steam room Xmas New Year Wi-fi **Conf** Class 120 Board 60 Thtr 400 Del from £99 to £145 **Services** Lift Air con **Parking** 200 **Notes** Civ Wed 200

HAMILTON   Map 20 NS75

Express by Holiday Inn Hamilton

BUDGET HOTEL

☎ 0141 419 3500 📠 0141 419 3500
Keith St ML3 7BL
web: www.hiexpress.com/hamilton

A modern hotel ideal for families and business travellers. Fresh and uncomplicated, the spacious rooms include Sky TV, power shower and tea and coffee-making facilities. Continental buffet breakfast is included in the room rate; other meals may be taken at the nearby family pub or restaurant. See also the Hotel Groups pages.

Rooms 104

LANARK   Map 21 NS84

See also **Biggar**

Best Western Cartland Bridge

★★★ 75% COUNTRY HOUSE HOTEL

☎ 01555 664426 📠 01555 663773
Glasgow Rd ML11 9UF
e-mail: sales@cartlandbridge.co.uk
dir: Follow A73 through Lanark towards Carluke. Hotel in 1.25m

Situated in wooded grounds on the edge of the town, this Grade I listed mansion continues to be popular with both business and leisure guests. Public areas feature wood

panelling, a gallery staircase and a magnificent dining room. The well-equipped bedrooms vary in size.

Rooms 20 (2 fmly) **Facilities** FTV Xmas New Year Wi-fi **Conf** Class 180 Board 50 Thtr 250 Del from £108 to £140 **Parking** 120 **Notes** ⊗ Civ Wed 200

NEW LANARK — Map 21 NS84

New Lanark Mill Hotel
★★★ 79% HOTEL

☎ 01555 667200 📠 01555 667222
Mill One, New Lanark Mills ML11 9DB
e-mail: hotel@newlanark.org
web: www.newlanark.org
dir: Signed from all major roads, M74 junct 7 & M8

Originally built as a cotton mill in the 18th century, this hotel forms part of a fully restored village, now a UNESCO World Heritage Site. There's a bright modern style throughout which contrasts nicely with features from the original mill. There is a comfortable foyer-lounge with a galleried restaurant above. The hotel enjoys stunning views over the River Clyde.

Rooms 38 (5 fmly) (6 smoking) **S** £79.50; **D** £119–£144 (incl. bkfst)* **Facilities** STV ⊗ Gym Beauty room Steam room Sauna Aerobics studios Xmas New Year Wi-fi **Conf** Class 60 Board 40 Thtr 200 Del from £120 to £130* **Services** Lift **Parking** 75 **Notes** LB Civ Wed 120

STRATHAVEN — Map 20 NS74

Rissons at Springvale
◉ RESTAURANT WITH ROOMS

☎ 01357 521131 & 520234 📠 01357 521131
18 Lethame Rd ML10 6AD
e-mail: rissons@msn.com
dir: A71 into Strathaven, W of town centre off Townhead St

Guests are assured of a warm welcome at this charming establishment close to the town centre. The bedrooms and bathrooms are stylish and well equipped. However it the food that's the main feature, with a range of interesting, well-prepared dishes served in Rissons Restaurant.

Rooms 9 (1 fmly)

STIRLING

ABERFOYLE — Map 20 NN50

Macdonald Forest Hills Hotel & Resort
★★★★ 74% HOTEL

☎ 0844 879 9057 & 01877 389500 📠 01877 387307
Kinlochard FK8 3TL
e-mail: forest_hills@macdonald-hotels.co.uk
web: www.macdonald-hotels.co.uk/foresthills
dir: A84/A873/A81 to Aberfoyle onto B829 along lochside to hotel

Situated in the heart of The Trossachs with wonderful views of Loch Ard, this popular hotel forms part of a resort complex offering a range of indoor and outdoor facilities. The main hotel has relaxing lounges and a restaurant which overlook landscaped gardens. A separate building houses the leisure centre, lounge bar and bistro.

Rooms 49 (16 fmly) (12 GF) **S** £94–£196; **D** £104–£206 (incl. bkfst)* **Facilities** Spa STV FTV ⊗ ⅀ Gym Children's club Snooker Watersports Quad biking Archery Clay pigeon shooting ♫ Xmas New Year Wi-fi **Conf** Class 60 Board 45 Thtr 150 Del from £130 to £165* **Services** Lift **Parking** 100 **Notes** LB ⊗ Civ Wed 100

CALLANDER — Map 20 NN60

Roman Camp Country House
★★★ 86% ◉◉◉ COUNTRY HOUSE HOTEL

☎ 01877 330003 📠 01877 331533
FK17 8BG
e-mail: mail@romancamphotel.co.uk
web: www.romancamphotel.co.uk
dir: N on A84, left at east end of High Street. 300yds to hotel

Originally a shooting lodge, this charming country house has a rich history. Twenty acres of gardens and grounds lead down to the River Teith, and the town centre and its attractions are only a short walk away. Food is a highlight of any stay and menus are dominated by high-quality Scottish produce that is sensitively treated by the talented kitchen team. Real fires warm the atmospheric public areas and service is friendly yet professional.

Rooms 15 (4 fmly) (7 GF) **S** £85–£135; **D** £135–£185 (incl. bkfst) **Facilities** STV FTV Fishing Xmas New Year Wi-fi **Conf** Class 60 Board 30 Thtr 120 Del from £200 to £285* **Parking** 80 **Notes** LB Civ Wed 100

Callander Meadows
◉ RESTAURANT WITH ROOMS

☎ 01877 330181
24 Main St FK17 8BB
e-mail: mail@callandermeadows.co.uk
web: www.callandermeadows.co.uk
dir: M9 junct 10 onto A84 to Callander, on main street just past A81 junct

Located on the high street in Callander, this family-run business offers comfortable accommodation and a restaurant that has quickly become very popular with the locals. The bedrooms have been appointed to a high standard. Private parking is available to the rear.

Rooms 3

DRYMEN — Map 20 NS48

Best Western Winnock
★★★ 75% HOTEL

☎ 01360 660245 🖹 01360 660267
The Square G63 0BL
e-mail: info@winnockhotel.com
web: www.winnockhotel.com
dir: from S: M74 onto M8 junct 16b through Glasgow.
Follow A809 to Aberfoyle

Occupying a prominent position overlooking the village green, this popular hotel offers well-equipped bedrooms of various sizes and styles. The public rooms include a bar, a lounge and an attractive formal dining room that serves dishes of good, locally sourced food.

Rooms 73 (18 fmly) (19 GF) **S** £34-£96; **D** £49-£129 (incl. bkfst)* **Facilities** FTV Xmas New Year Wi-fi **Conf** Class 60 Board 70 Thtr 140 Del from £59 to £109* **Parking** 60 **Notes** LB ⊗ Civ Wed 100

FINTRY — Map 20 NS68

Culcreuch Castle
★★★ 70% HOTEL

☎ 01360 860555 & 860228 🖹 01360 860556
Kippen Rd G63 0LW
e-mail: info@culcreuch.com
web: www.culcreuch.com
dir: On B822, 17m W of Stirling

Peacefully located in 1,600 acres of parkland, this ancient castle dates back to 1296. Tastefully restored accommodation is in a mixture of individually themed castle rooms, some with four-poster beds, and more modern courtyard rooms which are suitable for families. Period style public rooms include a bar, serving light meals, a wood-panelled dining room and an elegant lounge.

Rooms 14 (4 annexe) (4 fmly) (4 GF) **S** £81-£115; **D** £102-£180 (incl. bkfst) **Facilities** FTV Fishing New Year Wi-fi **Conf** Class 70 Board 30 Thtr 140 Del from £119 to £129 **Parking** 100 **Notes** LB ⊗ Closed 25-26 Dec Civ Wed 110

STIRLING — Map 21 NS79

Barceló Stirling Highland Hotel
★★★★ 75% HOTEL

☎ 01786 272727 🖹 01786 272829
Spittal St FK8 1DU
e-mail: stirling@barcelo-hotels.co.uk
web: www.barcelo-hotels.co.uk
dir: A84 into Stirling. Follow Stirling Castle signs as far as Albert Hall. Left, left again, follow Castle signs

Enjoying a location close to the castle and historic old town, this atmospheric hotel was previously the town's high school. Public rooms have been converted from the original classrooms and retain many interesting features. Bedrooms are more modern in style and comfortably equipped. Scholars Restaurant serves traditional and international dishes, and the Headmaster's Study is the ideal venue for enjoying a drink.

Rooms 96 (4 fmly) **Facilities** Spa STV ③ supervised Gym Squash Steam room Dance studio Beauty therapist Xmas New Year Wi-fi **Conf** Class 80 Board 60 Thtr 100 Del from £125* **Services** Lift **Parking** 96 **Notes** Civ Wed 100

Express by Holiday Inn Stirling
BUDGET HOTEL

☎ 01786 449922 🖹 01786 449932
Springkerse Business Park FK7 7XH
e-mail: stirling@expressbyholidayinn.co.uk
web: www.hiexpress.com/stirling
dir: M9/M80 junct 9/A91, Stirling/St Andrews exit. 2.8m, at 4th rdbt, take 2nd exit to sports stadium, 3rd exit to hotel

A modern hotel ideal for families and business travellers. Fresh and uncomplicated, the spacious rooms include Sky TV, power shower and tea and coffee-making facilities. Continental buffet breakfast is included in the room rate; other meals may be taken at the nearby family pub or restaurant. See also the Hotel Groups pages.

Rooms 78 (36 fmly) **S** £69-£119; **D** £69-£119 (incl. bkfst)* **Conf** Class 14 Board 18 Thtr 30

Travelodge Stirling (M80)
BUDGET HOTEL

☎ 0871 984 6178 🖹 01786 817646
Pirnhall Roundabout, Snabhead FK7 8EU
web: www.travelodge.co.uk
dir: M9/M80 junct 9

Travelodge offers good quality, good value, budget accommodation. All offer family rooms sleeping up to four (two adults, two children) with en suite bathroom/shower-room, remote-control TV, tea- and coffee-making facilities and comfortable beds. Food options vary. Breakfast is at the on-site Bar Café restaurant (if available) or to take away. See also Hotel Groups pages.

Rooms 37 **S** fr £29; **D** fr £29

STRATHYRE — Map 20 NN51

INSPECTORS' CHOICE

Creagan House
◉◉ RESTAURANT WITH ROOMS

☎ 01877 384638 🖹 01877 384319
FK18 8ND
e-mail: eatandstay@creaganhouse.co.uk
web: www.creaganhouse.co.uk
dir: 0.25m N of Strathyre on A84

Originally a farmhouse dating from the 17th century, Creagan House has operated as a restaurant with rooms for many years. The baronial-style dining room provides a wonderful setting for sympathetic cooking. Warm hospitality and attentive service are the highlights of any stay.

Rooms 5 (1 fmly)

Strathblane Country House

★★★ 74% COUNTRY HOUSE HOTEL

☎ 01360 770491 🖹 01360 770345
Milngavie Rd G63 9EH
e-mail: info@strathblanecountryhouse.co.uk
dir: From Glasgow city centre follow Bearsden road or
Maryhill road to Canniesburn toll, then A81 (Milneavie
road) to Strathblane. Hotel 0.75m past Mugdock Country
Park on righ

Set in 10 acres of grounds looking out on the beautiful
Campsie Fells, this majestic property, built in 1874,
offers a get-away-from-it-all experience, yet is just a 20
minute drive from Glasgow. Lunch and dinner are served
in the relaxed Brasserie Restaurant, and guests can visit
the falconry or just kick back and relax in front of the fire
with a book and a dram. Weddings are especially well
catered for.

Rooms 10 (3 fmly) **S** £55-£89; **D** £90-£150 (incl. bkfst)*
Facilities FTV Falconry ♫ Xmas New Year Wi-fi
Conf Class 60 Board 60 Thtr 180 Del from £110 to £150*
Parking 120 **Notes** LB ⊗ Civ Wed 180

WEST DUNBARTONSHIRE

Cameron House on Loch Lomond   DEVERE
collection

★★★★★ 84% ⊛ HOTEL

☎ 01389 755565 🖹 01389 759522
G83 8QZ
e-mail: reservations@cameronhouse.co.uk
web: www.devere.co.uk
dir: M8 (W) junct 30 for Erskine Bridge. A82 for
Crainlarich. 14m, at rdbt signed Luss, hotel on right

Enjoying an idyllic location on the banks of Loch Lomond
in over 100 acres of wooded parkland, this stylish hotel
offers an excellent range of leisure facilities. These
include two golf courses, a world-class spa and a host of
indoor and outdoor sporting activities. A choice of
restaurants and bars cater for all tastes and include the
Scottish-themed Cameron Grill and a fine dining
operation run by acclaimed chef, Martin Wishart.
Bedrooms are stylish, well equipped and many boast
wonderful loch views.

Rooms 96 (9 fmly) **Facilities** ⓢ ♨ 9 ♨ Fishing ⚑ Gym
Squash Outdoor sports Motor boat on Loch Lomond
Hairdresser Xmas **Conf** Class 80 Board 80 Thtr 300
Services Lift **Parking** 200 **Notes** LB ⊗ Civ Wed 200

Innkeeper's Lodge Loch Lomond

BUDGET HOTEL

☎ 0845 112 6006 🖹 0845 112 6294
Balloch Rd G83 8LQ
web: www.innkeeperslodge.com/lochlomond
dir: M8 junct 30 onto M898. Over Erskine Bridge onto A82
for Crainlarich towards Dumbarton/Loch Lomond. Follow
National Park signs, right onto A811, left into Davait Rd,
left into Balloch Rd. Lodge opposite

Innkeeper's Lodge represents an exciting, high value
concept within the budget hotel market. Comfortable
bedrooms provide excellent facilities that include satellite
TV and modem points. This carefully restored lodge is in a
picturesque setting and has its own unique style and
quirky character. Food is served all day, and an extensive,
complimentary continental breakfast is offered. See also
the Hotel Groups pages.

Rooms 12 (4 fmly)

Beardmore

★★★★ 73% ⊛ HOTEL

☎ 0141 951 6000 🖹 0141 951 6018
Beardmore St G81 4SA
e-mail: info@beardmore.scot.nhs.uk
dir: M8 junct 19, follow signs for Clydeside Expressway to
Glasgow road, then A814 (Dumbarton road), then follow
Clydebank Business Park signs. Hotel on left

Attracting much business and conference custom, this
stylish modern hotel lies beside the River Clyde and
shares an impressive site with a hospital (although the
latter does not intrude). Spacious and imposing public
areas include the stylish Arcoona Restaurant providing

innovative contemporary cooking. The café bar offers a
more extensive choice of informal lighter dishes.

Rooms 166 **Facilities** STV ⓢ supervised Gym Sauna
Steam room Whirlpool Xmas New Year Wi-fi **Conf** Class 84
Board 27 Thtr 240 Del from £115 to £165* **Services** Lift
Air con **Parking** 300 **Notes** ⊗ Civ Wed 170

Travelodge Dumbarton

BUDGET HOTEL

☎ 0871 984 6133 🖹 01389 765202
Milton G82 2TZ
web: www.travelodge.co.uk
dir: 2m E of Dumbarton, on A82 W'bound

Travelodge offers good quality, good value, budget
accommodation. All offer family rooms sleeping up to four
(two adults, two children) with en suite bathroom/
shower-room, remote-control TV, tea- and coffee-making
facilities and comfortable beds. Food options vary.
Breakfast is at the on-site Bar Café restaurant (if
available) or to take away. See also Hotel Groups pages.

Rooms 32 **S** fr £29; **D** fr £29

WEST LOTHIAN

Travelodge Livingston

BUDGET HOTEL

☎ 0871 984 6288 🖹 0121 521 6026
Almondvale Cresent EH54 6QX
web: www.travelodge.co.uk
dir: M8 junct 3 onto A899 towards Livingston. At 2nd rdbt
right onto A779. At 2nd rdbt left. Lodge on left

Travelodge offers good quality, good value, budget
accommodation. All offer family rooms sleeping up to four
(two adults, two children) with en suite bathroom/
shower-room, remote-control TV, tea- and coffee-making
facilities and comfortable beds. Food options vary.
Breakfast is at the on-site Bar Café restaurant (if
available) or to take away. See also Hotel Groups pages.

Rooms 60 **S** fr £29; **D** fr £29

UPHALL — Map 21 NT07

Macdonald Houstoun House

★★★★ 78% ❀ HOTEL

☎ 0844 879 9043 🖹 01506 854220
EH52 6JS
e-mail: houstoun@macdonald-hotels.co.uk
web: www.macdonaldhotels.co.uk
dir: M8 junct 3 follow Broxburn signs, straight over rdbt then at mini-rdbt turn right towards Uphall, hotel 1m on right

This historic 17th-century tower house lies in beautifully landscaped grounds and gardens and features a modern leisure club and spa, a choice of dining options, a vaulted cocktail bar and extensive conference and meeting facilities. Stylish bedrooms, some located around a courtyard, are comfortably furnished and well equipped.

Rooms 71 (47 annexe) (12 fmly) (10 GF) **Facilities** Spa STV 🕭 ♨ Gym Health & beauty salon Xmas New Year Wi-fi **Conf** Class 80 Board 80 Thtr 400 **Parking** 250 **Notes** ⊗ Civ Wed 200

WHITBURN — Map 21 NS96

Best Western Hilcroft

★★★ 78% HOTEL

☎ 01501 740818 & 743372 🖹 01501 744013
East Main St EH47 0JU
e-mail: hilcroft@bestwestern.co.uk
dir: M8 junct 4 follow signs for Whitburn, hotel 0.5m on left

This purpose-built, well-established hotel is popular with business travellers and easily accessible from all major transport routes. Smart contemporary public areas feature a spacious and inviting lounge bar and restaurant. Well-equipped bedrooms come in a variety of sizes.

Rooms 32 (7 fmly) (5 GF) **Facilities** STV FTV New Year Wi-fi **Conf** Class 50 Board 30 Thtr 200 **Parking** 80 **Notes** ⊗ Civ Wed 180

SCOTTISH ISLANDS
ISLE OF ARRAN

BLACKWATERFOOT — Map 20 NR92

Best Western Kinloch

★★★ 81% HOTEL

☎ 01770 860444 🖹 01770 860447
KA27 8ET
e-mail: reservations@kinlochhotel.eclipse.co.uk
web: www.bw-kinlochhotel.co.uk
dir: Ferry from Ardrossan to Brodick, follow signs for Blackwaterfoot, hotel in village centre

Well known for providing an authentic island experience, this long established stylish hotel is in an idyllic location. Smart public areas include a choice of lounges, popular bars and well-presented leisure facilities. Bedrooms vary in size and style but most enjoy panoramic sea views and several family suites offer excellent value. The spacious restaurant provides a wide ranging menu, and in winter when the restaurant is closed, the bar serves a choice of creative dishes.

Rooms 37 (7 fmly) (7 GF) **S** £40-£65; **D** £80-£130 (incl. bkfst) **Facilities** STV 🕭 Gym Squash Beauty therapy ♫ New Year Wi-fi **Conf** Class 20 Board 40 Thtr 120 **Del** from £80 to £110* **Services** Lift **Parking** 2 **Notes** LB Civ Wed 60

BRODICK — Map 20 NS03

INSPECTORS' CHOICE

Kilmichael Country House
★★★ ❀❀ COUNTRY HOUSE HOTEL

☎ 01770 302219 🖹 01770 302068
Glen Cloy KA27 8BY
e-mail: enquiries@kilmichael.com
web: www.kilmichael.com
dir: from Brodick ferry terminal towards Lochranza for 1m. Left at golf course, inland between sports field & church, follow signs

Reputed to be the oldest on the island, this lovely house lies in attractive gardens in a quiet glen less than five minutes' drive from the ferry terminal. It has been lovingly restored to create a stylish, elegant country house, adorned with ornaments from around the world. There are two inviting drawing rooms and a bright dining room, serving award-winning contemporary cuisine. The delightful bedrooms are furnished in classical style; some are contained in a pretty courtyard conversion.

Rooms 8 (3 annexe) (7 GF) **S** £76-£95; **D** £128-£199 (incl. bkfst)* **Facilities** Wi-fi **Parking** 14 **Notes** LB No children 12yrs Closed Nov-Feb (ex for prior bookings)

ISLE OF HARRIS

SCARISTA — Map 22 NG09

Scarista House

❀❀ RESTAURANT WITH ROOMS

☎ 01859 550238 🖹 01859 550277
HS3 3HX
e-mail: timandpatricia@scaristahouse.com
dir: On A859, 15m S of Tarbert

A former manse, Scarista House is a haven for food lovers who seek to explore this magnificent island. It enjoys breathtaking views of the Atlantic and is just a short stroll from miles of golden sandy beaches. The house is run in a relaxed country-house manner by the friendly hosts. Expect wellies in the hall and masses of books and CDs in one of two lounges. Bedrooms are cosy, and delicious set dinners and memorable breakfasts are provided.

Rooms 5 (2 annexe)

ISLE OF ISLAY

BOWMORE   Map 20 NR35

The Harbour Inn and Restaurant

◉ RESTAURANT WITH ROOMS

☎ 01496 810330   🖹 01496 810990
PA43 7JR
e-mail: info@harbour.inn.com
dir: Next to harbour

No trip to Islay would be complete without experiencing a night or two at the Harbour Inn. The humble whitewashed exterior conceals the sophisticated, quality environment that draws discerning travellers from all over the world. Spacious bedrooms are appointed to a high standard and the conservatory-lounge has stunning views over Loch Indaal to the peaks of Jura. The cosy bar is popular with locals, and the smart dining room showcases some of the best seafood. Welcoming peat fires burn in cooler months.

Rooms 7

PORT ASKAIG   Map 20 NR46

Port Askaig

★★ 60% SMALL HOTEL

☎ 01496 840245   🖹 01496 840295
PA46 7RD
e-mail: hotel@portaskaig.co.uk
web: www.portaskaig.co.uk
dir: at ferry terminal

The building of this endearing family-run hotel dates back to the 18th-century. The lounge provides fine views over the Sound of Islay to Jura, and there is a choice of bars that are popular with locals. Traditional dinners are served in the bright restaurant and a full range of bar snacks and meals is also available. The bedrooms are smart and comfortable.

Rooms 8 (1 fmly) (8 GF) **Parking** 21 **Notes** LB

ISLE OF MULL

TOBERMORY   Map 22 NM55

INSPECTORS' CHOICE

Highland Cottage
★★★ ◉◉ SMALL HOTEL

☎ 01688 302030
Breadalbane St PA75 6PD
e-mail: davidandjo@highlandcottage.co.uk
web: www.highlandcottage.co.uk
dir: A848 Craignure/Fishnish ferry terminal, pass Tobermory signs, straight on at mini rdbt across narrow bridge, turn right. Hotel on right opposite fire station

Providing the highest level of natural and unassuming hospitality, this delightful little gem lies high above the island's capital. Don't be fooled by its side street location, a stunning view over the bay is just a few metres away. 'A country house hotel in town' it is an Aladdin's Cave of collectables and treasures, as well as masses of books and magazines. There are two inviting lounges, one with an honesty bar. The cosy dining room offers memorable dinners and splendid breakfasts. Bedrooms are individual; some have four-posters and all are comprehensively equipped to include TVs and music centres.

Rooms 6 (1 GF) **S** £120-£135; **D** £150-£185 (incl. bkfst) **Facilities** Wi-fi **Parking** 6 **Notes** LB No children 10yrs Closed Nov-Feb

Western Isles Hotel
★★★ 75% HOTEL

☎ 01688 302012   🖹 01688 302297
PA75 6PR
e-mail: wihotel@aol.com
web: www.mullhotel.com
dir: fFom ferry follow signs to Tobermory. Over 1st mini-rdbt in Tobermory, over small bridge, immediate right, to T-junct. Right, keep left, 1st left. Hotel at top of hill on right

Sitting on top of the cliffs looking over Tobermory with amazing views, this well-established hotel has benefited from a refurbishment by the new owners. Many of the spacious bedrooms and the public areas enjoy the lovely views. Dining is in the relaxed atmosphere of the conservatory or in the traditional restaurant; menus offer fine quality food using locally sourced produce.

Rooms 26 (1 fmly) **S** £40-£60; **D** £70-£135 (incl. bkfst)* **Facilities** Xmas New Year **Conf** Class 60 Board 30 Thtr 70 **Parking** 15 **Notes** LB Civ Wed 70

Tobermory
★★ 76% ◉ HOTEL

☎ 01688 302091   🖹 01688 302254
53 Main St PA75 6NT
e-mail: tobhotel@tinyworld.co.uk
web: www.thetobermoryhotel.com
dir: On waterfront

This friendly hotel, with its pretty pink frontage, sits on the seafront amid other brightly coloured, picture-postcard buildings. There is a comfortable and relaxing lounge where drinks are served prior to dining in the stylish restaurant (there is no bar). Bedrooms come in a variety of sizes; all are bright and vibrant.

Rooms 16 (3 fmly) (2 GF) **S** £38-£98; **D** £76-£122 (incl. bkfst)* **Facilities** supervised New Year Wi-fi **Notes** Closed Xmas

SHETLAND

LERWICK   Map 24 HU44

Shetland

★★★ 71% HOTEL

☎ 01595 695515   🖶 01595 695828
Holmsgarth Rd ZE1 0PW
e-mail: reception@shetlandhotel.co.uk
dir: Opposite ferry terminal, on main road N from town centre

This purpose-built hotel, situated opposite the main ferry terminal, offers spacious and comfortable bedrooms on three floors. Two dining options are available, including the informal Oasis bistro and Ninians Restaurant. Service is prompt and friendly.

Rooms 64 (4 fmly) **S** £83; **D** £110 (incl. bkfst)*
Facilities FTV Wi-fi **Conf** Class 75 Board 50 Thtr 300
Services Lift **Parking** 150 **Notes** LB ⊗

ISLE OF SKYE

ARDVASAR   Map 22 NG60

Ardvasar Hotel

★★ 70% HOTEL

☎ 01471 844223   🖶 01471 844495
Sleat IV45 8RS
e-mail: richard@ardvasar-hotel.demon.co.uk
web: www.ardvasarhotel.com
dir: From ferry, 500mtrs & turn left

The Isle of Skye is dotted with cosy, welcoming hotels that make touring the island easy and convenient. This hotel ranks highly amongst its peers thanks to great hospitality and a preservation of community spirit. The hotel sits less than five minutes' drive from the Mallaig ferry and provides comfortable bedrooms and a cosy bar lounge for residents. Seafood is prominent on menus, and meals can be enjoyed in either the popular bar or the attractive dining room.

Rooms 10 (4 fmly) **S** £75-£110; **D** £95-£135 (incl. bkfst)
Facilities FTV ♫ Xmas New Year Wi-fi Child facilities
Conf Board 24 Thtr 50 Del from £105 to £160 **Parking** 30
Notes LB

See advert on opposite page

BROADFORD   Map 22 NG62

Broadford

★★★★ 73% SMALL HOTEL

☎ 01471 822204   🖶 01471 822414
IV49 9AB
e-mail: broadford@macleodhotels.co.uk
dir: From Skye Bridge take A87 towards Portree. Hotel at end of village on left

A stylish modern hotel located in centre of the charming town of Broadford. The hotel has been refurbished to a high standard and offers all the creature comforts. Many of the spacious bedrooms have wonderful sea views and all are attractively presented and very well equipped. Meals can be enjoyed in the fine-dining restaurant or more informal meals are served in traditional bar.

Rooms 11 (1 fmly) **S** £75-£115; **D** £88-£170 (incl. bkfst)
Facilities STV Fishing ♫ Xmas New Year Wi-fi
Conf Class 80 Board 50 Thtr 150 Del from £120 to £200
Parking 20 **Notes** LB Civ Wed 100

COLBOST   Map 22 NG24

INSPECTORS' CHOICE

The Three Chimneys and House Over-By

◉◉◉ RESTAURANT WITH ROOMS

☎ 01470 511258   🖶 01470 511358
IV55 8ZT
e-mail: eatandstay@threechimneys.co.uk
dir: 4m W of Dunvegan village on B884 signed Glendale

A visit to this delightful property will make a trip to Skye even more memorable. The stunning food is the result of a deft approach using quality local ingredients. Breakfast is an impressive array of local fish, meats and cheeses, served with fresh home baking and home-made preserves. The new stylish lounge-breakfast area has the real wow factor. Bedrooms, in the House Over-By, are creative and thoughtfully equipped – all have spacious en suites and wonderful views across Loch Dunvegan.

Rooms 6 (1 fmly) (6 GF)

ISLEORNSAY   Map 22 NG71

Duisdale House

★★★★ 74% ◉ SMALL HOTEL

☎ 01471 833202   🖶 01471 833404
IV43 8QW
e-mail: info@duisdale.com
web: www.duisdale.com
dir: 7m S of Bradford on A851 towards Armadale. 7m N of Armadale ferry

This grand Victorian house stands in its own landscaped gardens overlooking the Sound of Sleat. The hotel has a contemporary chic style which complements the original features of the house. Each bedroom is individually designed and the superior rooms have four-poster beds. The elegant lounge has sumptuous sofas, original artwork and blazing log fires in the colder months.

Rooms 18 (1 fmly) (1 GF) **S** £65-£150; **D** £65-£115 (incl. bkfst)* **Facilities** STV Sailing on hotel's private yacht Outdoor hydropool Xmas New Year Wi-fi **Conf** Board 28 Thtr 50 Del from £90 to £125 **Parking** 30 **Notes** LB ⊗ No children 5yrs Civ Wed 58

See advert on opposite page

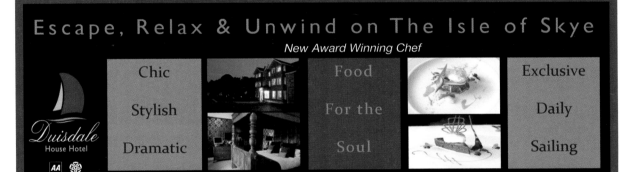

ISLEORNSAY *continued*

Kinloch Lodge

★★★ ◉◉◉ HOTEL

☎ 01471 833214 & 833333 📠 01471 833277
IV43 8QY
e-mail: reservations@kinloch-lodge.co.uk
web: www.kinloch-lodge.co.uk
dir: 6m S of Broadford on A851, 10m N of Armadale on A851

Owned and ran in a hands-on fashion by Lord and Lady MacDonald and their family, this hotel enjoys a picture postcard location surrounded by hills and a sea loch. Bedrooms and bathrooms are well appointed and comfortable, and public areas boast numerous open fires and relaxing areas to sit. There is a cookery school ran by Claire MacDonald and a shop selling her famous cookery books and produce.

Rooms 14 (1 GF) **S** £130-£250; **D** £260-£360 (incl. bkfst & dinner)* **Facilities** STV FTV Fishing New Year Wi-fi **Parking** 40 **Notes** LB

Toravaig House Hotel

★★★ 80% ◉◉ SMALL HOTEL

☎ 0845 055 1117 & 01471 833231 📠 01471 833231
Knock Bay IV44 8RE
e-mail: info@skyehotel.co.uk
web: www.skyehotel.co.uk
dir: From Skye Bridge, left at Broadford onto A851, hotel 11m on left. Or from ferry at Armadale take A851, hotel 4m on right

Set in two acres and enjoying panoramic views to the Knoydart Hills, this hotel is a haven of peace, with stylish, well-equipped and beautifully decorated bedrooms. Here is an inviting lounge complete with deep sofas and an elegant dining room where delicious meals are the order of the day. The hotel provides a sea-going yacht for guests' exclusive use.

Rooms 9 **D** £100-£190 (incl. bkfst) **Facilities** STV Daily excursions (Apr-Sep) for residents on hotel yacht Xmas New Year Wi-fi **Conf** Board 10 Thtr 25 Del from £150 to £300 **Parking** 15 **Notes** LB ⊗ No children 12yrs Civ Wed 25

See advert on page 625

Hotel Eilean Iarmain

★★★ 75% ◉◉ SMALL HOTEL

THE CIRCLE
Selected Individual Hotels

☎ 01471 833332 📠 01471 833275
IV43 8QR
e-mail: hotel@eileaniarmain.co.uk
web: www.eileaniarmain.co.uk
dir: A851, A852, right to Isleornsay harbour

A hotel of charm and character, this 19th-century former inn lies by the pier and enjoys fine views across the sea loch. Bedrooms are individual and retain a traditional style, and a stable block has been converted into four delightful suites. Public rooms are cosy and inviting, and the restaurant offers award-winning menus showcasing the island's best produce, especially seafood and game.

Rooms 16 (6 fmly) (4 GF) **Facilities** Fishing Shooting Exhibitions Whisky tasting ♫ Xmas **Conf** Class 30 Board 25 Thtr 50 **Parking** 35 **Notes** LB Civ Wed 80

See advert on opposite page

PORTREE Map 22 NG44

Cuillin Hills

★★★★ 73% ◉◉ HOTEL

☎ 01478 612003 📠 01478 613092
IV51 9QU
e-mail: info@cuillinhills-hotel-skye.co.uk
web: www.cuillinhills-hotel-skye.co.uk
dir: Turn right 0.25m N of Portree off A855. Follow hotel signs

This imposing building enjoys a superb location overlooking Portree Bay and the Cuillin Hills. Accommodation is provided in smart, well-equipped rooms that are generally spacious. Some bedrooms are found in an adjacent building. Public areas include a split-level restaurant that takes advantage of the views. Service is particularly attentive.

Rooms 26 (7 annexe) (3 fmly) (8 GF) **S** £170-£200; **D** £200-£300 (incl. bkfst)* **Facilities** STV Xmas New Year Wi-fi **Conf** Class 60 Board 40 Thtr 100 **Parking** 56 **Notes** LB ⊗ Civ Wed 45

See advert on opposite page

PORTREE *continued*

Bosville

★★★ 81% ⚙⚙ HOTEL

☎ 01478 612846 📠 01478 613434
Bosville Ter IV51 9DG
e-mail: bosville@macleodhotels.co.uk
web: www.macleodhotels.com
dir: A87 signed Portree, then A855 into town. After zebra crossing follow road to left

This stylish, popular hotel enjoys fine views over the harbour. Bedrooms are furnished to a high specification and have a fresh, contemporary feel. Public areas include a smart bar, bistro and the Chandlery restaurant where fantastic local produce is treated with respect and refreshing restraint.

Rooms 19 (2 fmly) **S** £69-£130; **D** £88-£240 (incl. bkfst)*
Facilities STV Use of nearby leisure club payable Xmas New Year Wi-fi **Conf** Class 20 Board 20 Thtr 20
Del from £120 to £160* **Parking** 10 **Notes** Civ Wed 80

See advert on opposite page

Rosedale

★★★ 73% ⚙ HOTEL

☎ 01478 613131 📠 01478 612531
Beaumont Crescent IV51 9DB
e-mail: rosedalehotelsky@aol.com
web: www.rosedalehotelskye.co.uk
dir: Follow directions to village centre & harbour

The atmosphere is wonderfully warm at this delightful family-run waterfront hotel. A labyrinth of stairs and corridors connects the comfortable lounges, bar and charming restaurant, which are set on different levels. The restaurant offers fine views of the bay. Modern bedrooms offer a good range of amenities.

Rooms 18 (1 fmly) (3 GF) **S** £30-£65; **D** £60-£150 (incl. bkfst)* **Facilities** Wi-fi **Parking** 2 **Notes** LB Closed Nov-mid Mar

---

SKEABOST BRIDGE	Map 22 NG44

Skeabost Country House

OXFORD
HOTELS & INNS

★★★ 75% ⚙
COUNTRY HOUSE HOTEL

☎ 01470 532202 📠 01470 532761
IV51 9NP
e-mail: reservations.skeabost@ohiml.com
web: www.oxfordhotelsandinns.com

This delightful property stands in mature, landscaped grounds at the edge of Loch Snizort. Originally built as a hunting lodge by the MacDonalds and steeped in history, Skeabost offers a welcoming environment from the caring and helpful staff. The hotel provides award-winning food, charming day rooms and well appointed accommodation. The pretty grounds include a challenging 9-hole golf course.

Rooms 14 (5 GF) **Facilities** STV FTV ♨ 9 Fishing Xmas New Year Wi-fi Child facilities **Conf** Class 20 Board 20 Thtr 40 **Parking** 40 **Notes** Civ Wed 80

STAFFIN	Map 22 NG46

Flodigarry Country House

★★★ 78% ⚙ COUNTRY HOUSE HOTEL

☎ 01470 552203 📠 01470 552301
IV51 9HZ
e-mail: info@flodigarry.co.uk
web: www.flodigarry.co.uk
dir: Take A855 from Portree, approx 20m, through Staffin. N to Flodigarry, signed on right

This hotel is located in woodlands on The Quiraing in north-east Skye overlooking the sea towards the Torridon Mountains. The dramatic scenery is a real inspiration here, and this charming house was once the home of the Scotland's heroine, Flora MacDonald. Guests are assured of real Highland hospitality and there is an easy going atmosphere throughout. A full range of activities is offered, with mountain walks, fishing and boat trips proving to be the most popular.

Rooms 18 (7 annexe) (3 fmly) (4 GF) **S** £80-£130; **D** £80-£200 (incl. bkfst) **Facilities** FTV Xmas New Year Wi-fi **Parking** 40 **Notes** LB Closed Nov-15 Dec & Jan Civ Wed 80

The Glenview

⚙ RESTAURANT WITH ROOMS

☎ 01470 562248
Culnacnoc IV51 9JH
e-mail: enquiries@glenviewskye.co.uk
web: www.glenviewskye.co.uk
dir: 12m N of Portree on A855

The Glenview is located in one of the most beautiful parts of Skye with stunning seas views; it is close to the famous Old Man of Storr rock outcrop. The individually styled bedrooms are very comfortable and front-facing rooms enjoy the dramatic views. Evening meals should not to be missed as the restaurant has a well deserved reputation for its locally sourced produce.

Rooms 5 (1 fmly)

STRUAN	Map 22 NG33

INSPECTORS' CHOICE

Ullinish Country Lodge

⚙⚙⚙ RESTAURANT WITH ROOMS

☎ 01470 572214 📠 01470 572341
IV56 8FD
e-mail: ullinish@theisleofskye.co.uk
dir: N on A863

Set in some of Scotland's most dramatic landscape, with views of the Black Cuillin and MacLeod's Tables, this lodge has lochs on three sides. Samuel Johnson and James Boswell stayed here in 1773 and were impressed with the hospitality even then! Hosts Brian and Pam hope to extend the same welcome to their guests today. As you would expect, all bedrooms have amazing views, and come with half-tester beds. The cuisine in the restaurant is impressive and uses the best of Skye's produce including locally sourced seafood and game.

Rooms 6

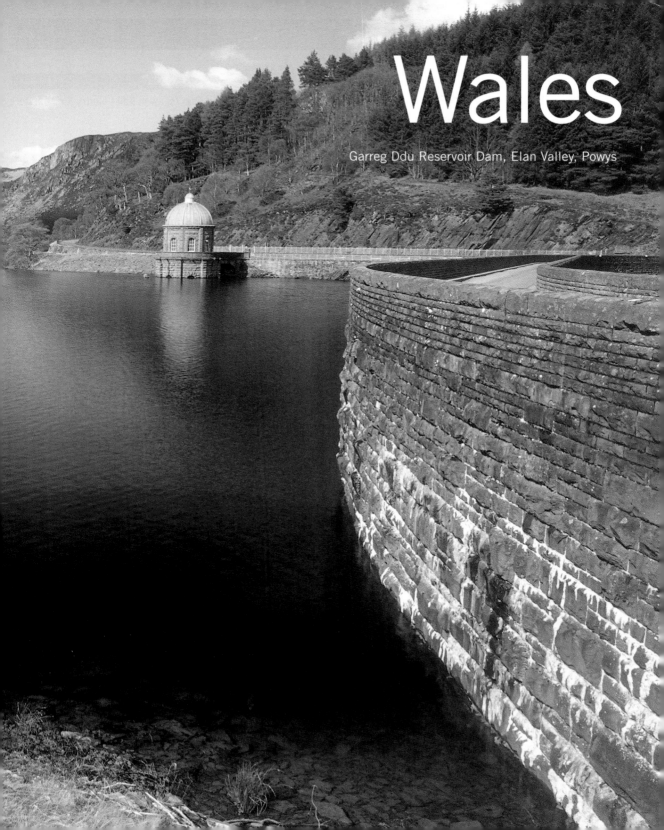

Wales

Garreg Ddu Reservoir Dam, Elan Valley, Powys

BEAUMARIS — Map 14 SH67

Best Western Bulkeley Hotel

★★★ 77% HOTEL

☎ 01248 810415 🖷 01248 810146
Castle St LL58 8AW
e-mail: reception@bulkeleyhotel.co.uk
web: www.bulkeleyhotel.co.uk
dir: From A55 junct 8a to Beaumaris. Hotel in town centre

A Grade I listed hotel built in 1832, the Bulkeley is just 100 yards from the 13th-century Beaumaris Castle in the centre of town; the friendly staff create a relaxed atmosphere. Many rooms, including 18 of the bedrooms, have fine panoramic views across the Menai Straits to the Snowdonian Mountains. The well-equipped bedrooms and suites, some with four-posters, are generally spacious, and have pretty furnishings. There is a choice of bars, a coffee shop, a restaurant and bistro.

Rooms 43 (5 fmly) **S** £60-£80; **D** £90-£140 (incl. bkfst)* **Facilities** New Year Wi-fi **Conf** Class 40 Board 25 Thtr 180 Del from £96 to £101* **Services** Lift **Parking** 25 **Notes** LB Civ Wed 140

Bishopsgate House

★★ 85% ◉ SMALL HOTEL

☎ 01248 810302 🖷 01248 810166
54 Castle St LL58 8BB
e-mail: hazel@bishopsgatehotel.co.uk
dir: From Menai Bridge onto A545 to Beaumaris. Hotel on left in main street

This immaculately maintained, privately owned and personally run small hotel dates back to 1760. It features fine examples of wood panelling and a Chinese Chippendale staircase. Thoughtfully furnished bedrooms are attractively decorated and two have four-poster beds. Quality cooking is served in the elegant restaurant and guests have a comfortable lounge and cosy bar to relax in.

Rooms 9 **S** £56; **D** £90 (incl. bkfst) **Parking** 8 **Notes** LB

HOLYHEAD — Map 14 SH28

Travelodge Holyhead

BUDGET HOTEL

☎ 0871 984 6342
Kingsland Rd LL65 2LB
web: www.travelodge.co.uk
dir: B4545 onto Kingsland Rd, hotel on left

Travelodge offers good quality, good value, budget accommodation. All offer family rooms sleeping up to four (two adults, two children) with en suite bathroom/shower-room, remote-control TV, tea- and coffee-making facilities and comfortable beds. Food options vary. Breakfast is at the on-site Bar Café restaurant (if available) or to take away. See also Hotel Groups pages.

Rooms 54 **S** fr £29; **D** fr £29

LLANGEFNI — Map 14 SH47

Tre-Ysgawen Hall Country House Hotel & Spa

★★★★ 74% ◉ COUNTRY HOUSE HOTEL

☎ 01248 750750 🖷 01248 750035
Capel Coch LL77 7UR
e-mail: enquiries@treysgawen-hall.co.uk
web: www.treysgawen-hall.co.uk
dir: From North Wales Expressway junct 6, take B5111 from Llangefni for Amlwch/Llanerchymedd. After Rhosmeirch right to Capel Coch. Hotel 1m on left at end of long drive

Quietly located in extensive wooded grounds, this charming mansion was built in 1882 and has been extended over time. It offers a range of delightful bedrooms with many personal touches. Public areas are elegant, spacious and comfortable. The restaurant offers an interesting choice of dishes. There is a bar/bistro, a coffee shop and extensive leisure facilities.

Rooms 29 (2 fmly) (8 GF) **S** £124; **D** £195 (incl. bkfst) **Facilities** Spa FTV ◈ ⤸ Gym Sauna Steam room Beauty suite Wi-fi **Conf** Class 75 Board 55 Thtr 200 Del from £140 to £162* **Parking** 100 **Notes** LB ⊗ Closed 24 Dec-3 Jan Civ Wed 200

See advert on this page

TREARDDUR BAY — Map 14 SH27

Trearddur Bay

★★★ 80% HOTEL

☎ 01407 860301 📠 01407 861181
LL65 2UN
e-mail: enquiries@trearddurbayhotel.co.uk
dir: From A55 junct 2 turn left, over 1st rdbt, left at 2nd rdbt, left after approx 2m

Facilities at this fine modern hotel include extensive function and conference rooms, an indoor swimming pool and a games room. Many of the well-equipped bedrooms have sea views; suites are also available. An all-day bar serves a wide range of snacks and lighter meals, supplemented by a cocktail bar and a more formal restaurant.

Rooms 40 (6 annexe) (7 fmly) **S** £60-£150; **D** £70-£200 (incl. bkfst)* **Facilities** STV 🐦 Sailing Shooting Horse riding Fishing Diving Golf packages 🎵 New Year Wi-fi **Conf** Class 100 Board 78 Thtr 190 Del from £100 to £160* **Parking** 200 **Notes** LB ⊗ Civ Wed 150

BRIDGEND

BRIDGEND — Map 9 SS97

Coed-Y-Mwstwr

★★★★ 76% COUNTRY HOUSE HOTEL

☎ 01656 860621 📠 01656 863122
Coychurch CF35 6AF
e-mail: hotel@coed-y-mwstwr.com
web: www.coed-y-mwstwr.com
dir: exit A473 at Coychurch, right at petrol station. Follow signs at top of hill

This Victorian mansion, set in 17 acres of grounds, is an inviting retreat. Public areas are full of character featuring an impressive, contemporary restaurant. Bedrooms have individual styles with a good range of extras, and two full suites are available. Facilities include a large and attractive function suite with syndicate rooms, a gym and an outdoor swimming pool.

Rooms 28 (2 fmly) **Facilities** STV 🐦 🏊 Gym Xmas New Year Wi-fi **Conf** Class 120 Board 50 Thtr 180 **Services** Lift **Parking** 100 **Notes** LB ⊗ Civ Wed 200

The Great House & Restaurant

WELSH RAREBITS

★★★ 81% ◉◉ HOTEL

☎ 01656 657644 📠 01656 668892
High St, Laleston CF32 0HP
e-mail: enquiries@great-house-laleston.co.uk
web: www.great-house-laleston.co.uk
dir: On A473, 400yds from junct with A48

A delightful Grade II listed building, dating back to 1550 with traditional features throughout that add plenty of character. The stylish, well-equipped bedrooms are located in the original building, and there are also separate garden suites; all are comfortable and provide a very good range of extras. Leicester's restaurant offers a wide choice of freshly prepared dishes at both lunch and dinner. The health suite has a jacuzzi, sauna and multi gym.

Rooms 12 (4 annexe) (4 GF) **S** £75-£110; **D** £85-£200 (incl. bkfst)* **Facilities** FTV Gym Sauna New Year Wi-fi **Conf** Class 28 Board 20 Thtr 35 **Parking** 35 **Notes** LB ⊗ Civ Wed 50

Best Western Heronston

Best Western

★★★ 73% HOTEL

☎ 01656 668811 & 666085 📠 01656 767391
Ewenny Rd CF35 5AW
e-mail: reservations@bestwesternheronstonhotel.co.uk
web: www.bw-heronstonhotel.co.uk
dir: M4 junct 35, follow signs for Porthcawl, at 5th rdbt turn left towards Ogmore-by-Sea (B4265), hotel 200yds on left

Situated within easy reach of the town centre and the M4, this large modern hotel offers spacious well-equipped accommodation, including ground floor rooms. Public areas include an open-plan lounge/bar, attractive restaurant and a smart leisure and fitness club. The hotel also has a choice of function/conference rooms and ample parking is available.

Rooms 75 (4 fmly) (37 GF) (8 smoking) **S** £65-£105; **D** £70-£125 (incl. bkfst)* **Facilities** STV 🐦 Gym Steam room Sauna Solarium Xmas New Year Wi-fi **Conf** Class 80 Board 60 Thtr 250 Del from £99.50 to £129* **Services** Lift **Parking** 160 **Notes** LB Civ Wed 200

PENCOED — Map 9 SS98

St Mary's Hotel & Country Club

★★★ 73% HOTEL

☎ 01656 861100 📠 01656 863400
St Marys Golf Club CF35 5EA
e-mail: stmarysgolfhotel@btinternet.com
dir: M4 junct 35, on A473

This charming 16th-century farmhouse has been converted and extended into a modern and restful hotel, surrounded by its own two golf courses. The well equipped bedrooms are generously appointed and most feature whirlpool baths. Guests have a choice of bars which prove popular with club members too, plus there's a good range of dining options.

Rooms 24 (19 fmly) (10 GF) **Facilities** STV ⌦ 30 Putt green Floodlit driving range New Year Wi-fi **Conf** Class 60 Board 40 Thtr 120 Del from £105 to £150* **Parking** 140 **Notes** ⊗ Civ Wed 120

Travelodge Bridgend Pencoed

BUDGET HOTEL

☎ 0871 984 6049 📠 01656 864404
Old Mill, Felindre Rd CF3 5HU
web: www.travelodge.co.uk
dir: on A473

Travelodge offers good quality, good value, budget accommodation. All offer family rooms sleeping up to four (two adults, two children) with en suite bathroom/shower-room, remote-control TV, tea- and coffee-making facilities and comfortable beds. Food options vary. Breakfast is at the on-site Bar Café restaurant (if available) or to take away. See also Hotel Groups pages.

Rooms 40 **S** fr £29; **D** fr £29

PORTHCAWL — Map 9 SS87

Seabank

★★★ 66% HOTEL

☎ 01656 782261 📠 01656 785363
The Promenade CF36 3LU
e-mail: info@seabankhotel.co.uk
dir: M4 junct 37, follow A4229 to seafront

This large, privately owned hotel stands on the promenade. The majority of the well-equipped bedrooms enjoy panoramic sea views and several have four-poster beds. There is a spacious restaurant, a lounge bar and a choice of lounges. The hotel is a popular venue for coach-tour parties, as well as weddings and conferences. There is ample parking.

Rooms 67 (2 fmly) (5 smoking) **S** £32-£65; **D** £64-£85 (incl. bkfst) **Facilities** STV Gym 🎵 Xmas New Year **Conf** Class 150 Board 70 Thtr 250 Del from £70 to £90 **Services** Lift **Parking** 127 **Notes** LB ⊗ Civ Wed 100

SARN PARK MOTORWAY SERVICE AREA (M4) — Map 9 SS98

Days Inn Cardiff West

BUDGET HOTEL

☎ 01656 659218 📠 01656 768665
Sarn Park Services CF32 9RW
e-mail: sarn.hotel@welcomebreak.co.uk
web: www.welcomebreak.co.uk
dir: M4 junct 36

This modern building offers accommodation in smart, spacious and well-equipped bedrooms, suitable for families and business travellers, and all with en suite bathrooms. Continental breakfast is available and other refreshments may be taken at the nearby family restaurant. See also the Hotel Groups pages.

Rooms 40 (39 fmly) (20 GF) **S** £29-£59; **D** £39-£69*

CAERPHILLY

BLACKWOOD — Map 9 ST19

Maes Manor

★★★ 72% COUNTRY HOUSE HOTEL

☎ 01495 220011 📠 01495 228217
NP12 0AG
e-mail: info@maesmanor.com
dir: A4048 to Tredega. At Pontllanfraith left at rdbt, along Blackwood High St. In 1.25m left at Rock Inn. Hotel 400yds on left

Standing high above the town, this 19th-century manor house is set in nine acres of gardens and woodland. Bedrooms are located either in the main house or an adjacent coach house, and are attractively decorated with co-ordinated furnishings. As well as the popular restaurant, public rooms include a choice of bars, a lounge/lobby area and a large function room.

Maes Manor

Rooms 28 (14 annexe) (6 fmly) (8 GF) **S** £30-£76; **D** £40-£140 (incl. bkfst)* **Facilities** STV FTV Xmas New Year Wi-fi **Conf** Class 200 Board 50 Thtr 200 **Parking** 175 **Notes** LB ⊗ Closed 24-25 Dec Civ Wed 200

See advert on this page

CAERPHILLY — Map 9 ST18

Travelodge Caerphilly

BUDGET HOTEL

☎ 0871 984 6364 📠 029 2086 2583
Castlegate, Nantgarw CF83 2BB
dir: M4 junct 32, A470 towards Merthyr Tydfil. At next rdbt 3rd exit onto A468 to Caerphilly. At next rdbt 3rd exit onto B4600. 1st exit at next rdbt. Lodge opposite Lidl

Travelodge offers good quality, good value, budget accommodation. All offer family rooms sleeping up to four (two adults, two children) with en suite bathroom/shower-room, remote-control TV, tea- and coffee-making facilities and comfortable beds. Food options vary. Breakfast is at the on-site Bar Café restaurant (if available) or to take away. See also the Hotel Groups pages.

MAESYCWMMER — Map 9 ST19

Bryn Meadows Golf, Hotel & Spa

★★★★ 79% HOTEL

☎ 01495 225590 📠 01495 228272
Maesycwmmer, Ystrad Mynach CF82 7SN
e-mail: reception@brynmeadows.co.uk
web: www.brynmeadows.co.uk
dir: A472 signed Ystrad Mynach. 1m before Ystrad Mynach off Crown rdbt signed for golf course

Surrounded by its own mature parkland and 18-hole golf course, this impressive hotel, golf, leisure and function complex provides a range of high quality, well-equipped bedrooms; several have their own balconies or patio areas. Public areas are attractively appointed and include a pleasant restaurant, which like many of the bedrooms, enjoys impressive views of the golf course and beyond. The hotel has impressive function facilities and is a popular venue for weddings.

Rooms 43 (1 annexe) (4 fmly) (21 GF) **S** £95-£130; **D** £115-£160 (incl. bkfst)* **Facilities** Spa FTV ⊙ supervised ♨ 18 Putt green Gym Sauna Steam room Aromatherapy suite New Year Wi-fi **Conf** Class 70 Board 60 Thtr 120 Del from £140* **Services** Air con **Parking** 120 **Notes** ⊗ Civ Wed 250

CARDIFF Map 9 ST17

See also **Barry (Vale of Glamorgan)**

St David's Hotel & Spa

★★★★★ 81% HOTEL

☎ 029 2045 4045 📠 029 2031 3075
Havannah St CF10 5SD
e-mail: st.davids.reservations@principal-hotels.com
web: www.thestdavidshotel.com
dir: M4 junct 33/A4232 for 9m, for Techniquest, at top exit slip road, 1st left at rdbt, 1st right

This imposing contemporary building sits in a prime position on Cardiff Bay and has a seven-storey atrium creating a dramatic impression. Leading from the atrium are the practically designed and comfortable bedrooms. Tides Restaurant, adjacent to the stylish cocktail bar, has views across the water to Penarth, and there is a quiet first-floor lounge for guests seeking peace and quiet. A well-equipped spa and extensive business areas complete the package.

Rooms 132 (6 fmly) (24 smoking) **S** £99-£260; **D** £99-£260 (incl. bkfst)* **Facilities** Spa FTV Gym Fitness studio Hydrotherapy pool Xmas New Year Wi-fi **Conf** Class 110 Board 76 Thtr 270 **Services** Lift Air con **Parking** 80 **Notes** LB Civ Wed 230

Parc Hotel by Thistle

thistle

★★★★ 85% HOTEL

☎ 0871 376 9011 📠 0871 376 9111
Park Place CF10 3UD
e-mail: theparkhotel@thistle.co.uk
web: www.thistle.com/cardiff
dir: M4 junct 29, A48, take 4th exit signed City Centre/A470. At rdbt take 2nd exit signed City Centre/A470

Ideally located in the very centre of Cardiff, this bustling hotel has been totally refurbished. The Victorian splendour of the external façade remains while the interior offers a contemporary and comfortable style. Bedrooms are spacious, modern and well equipped. A range of dining options is available including the Harlech Lounge and Bar, and Harmon's Restaurant which also includes a Champagne Bar.

Rooms 140 (5 fmly) **S** £79-£350; **D** £89-£350 (incl. bkfst)* **Facilities** STV Xmas New Year Wi-fi **Conf** Class 100 Board 50 Thtr 225 Del from £129 to £205* **Services** Lift Air con **Parking** 60 **Notes** Civ Wed 225

Cardiff Marriott Hotel

Marriott HOTELS & RESORTS

★★★★ 80% HOTEL

☎ 029 2039 9944 📠 029 2039 5578
Mill Ln CF10 1EZ
web: www.cardiffmarriott.co.uk
dir: M4 junct 29/A48M E follow signs city centre & Cardiff Bay. Continue on Newport Rd for 3m then turn right onto Mill Lane

Centrally located in the Café Quarter of the city, this modern hotel has spacious public areas and a good range of services to suit both business and leisure guests. The eating options include the informal Chats Café Bar, and the contemporary Brasserie Centrale for award-winning contemporary French cuisine that uses locally sourced ingredients. The well-equipped bedrooms are comfortable and air conditioned. The leisure suite includes a multi gym and a good sized swimming pool.

Rooms 184 (68 fmly) (4 smoking) **S** fr £125; **D** fr £125* **Facilities** STV Gym Steam room Sauna Xmas New Year Wi-fi **Conf** Class 200 Board 100 Thtr 400 Del from £135 to £165* **Services** Lift Air con **Parking** 146 **Notes** LB Civ Wed 200

CARDIFF *continued*

Park Plaza Cardiff

★★★★ 80% ◎ HOTEL

☎ 029 2011 1111 & 2011 1101 📄 029 2011 1112
Greyfriars Rd CF10 3AL
e-mail: ppcres@parkplazahotels.co.uk
web: www.parkplazacardiff.com
dir: From M4 follow city centre (A470) signs. Left into
Boulevard de Nantes then immediately left into Greyfriars
Rd. Hotel on left by New Theatre

A smart hotel located in the city centre that features eye-
catching, contemporary decor, a state-of-the-art indoor
leisure facility, extensive conference and banqueting
facilities and the spacious Laguna Kitchen and Bar.
Bedrooms are also up-to-the-minute in style and feature
a host of extras including a private bar, a safe and
modem points.

Rooms 129 (20 fmly) **S** £90-£230; **D** £100-£250 (incl.
bkfst)* **Facilities** Spa FTV ③ Gym Dance studio Steam
room Xmas New Year Wi-fi **Conf** Class 80 Board 60
Thtr 150 **Services** Lift Air con **Notes** ⊗ Civ Wed 120

Mercure Holland House Hotel & Spa

★★★★ 78% ◎◎ HOTEL

☎ 029 2043 5000 📄 029 2048 8894
24/26 Newport Rd CF24 0DD
e-mail: h6622@accor.com
web: www.mercure-uk.com
dir: M4 junct 33/A4232 to city centre, turn right at lights
facing prison, straight through next lights, hotel car park
end of lane facing Magistrates Court

Conveniently located just a few minutes' walk from the
city centre, this exciting hotel combines contemporary
styling with a genuinely friendly welcome. Bedrooms,
including five luxurious suites, are spacious and include
many welcome extras. A state-of-the-art leisure club and
spa is available in addition to a large function room. An
eclectic menu provides a varied range of freshly prepared,
quality dishes.

Rooms 165 (80 fmly) (8 smoking) **S** £80-£250;
D £90-£300 (incl. bkfst) **Facilities** Spa STV ③ supervised
Gym Wi-fi **Conf** Class 140 Board 42 Thtr 700
Del from £130 to £170 **Services** Lift Air con **Parking** 90
Notes LB Civ Wed 500

Novotel Cardiff Central

★★★★ 77% HOTEL

☎ 029 2047 5000 📄 029 2048 1491
Schooner Way, Atlantic Wharf CF10 4RT
e-mail: h5982@accor.com
web: www.novotel.com
dir: M4 junct 33/A4232 follow Cardiff Bay signs to
Atlantic Wharf

Situated in the heart of the city's development area, this
hotel is equally convenient for the centre and Cardiff Bay.
Bedrooms vary between standard rooms in the modern
extension and executive rooms in the original wing. The
hotel offers good seating space in public rooms, a
popular leisure club and the innovative 'Elements' dining
concept.

Rooms 138 (100 fmly) **Facilities** ③ supervised Gym Wi-fi
Conf Class 90 Board 65 Thtr 250 **Services** Lift Air con
Parking 120 **Notes** ⊗ Civ Wed 250

Copthorne Hotel Cardiff-Caerdydd

★★★★ 72% ◎◎ HOTEL

☎ 029 2059 9100 📄 029 2059 9080
Copthorne Way, Culverhouse Cross CF5 6DA
e-mail: reservations.cardiff@millenniumhotels.co.uk
web: www.millenniumhotels.co.uk
dir: M4 junct 33, A4232 for 2.5m towards Cardiff West.
Then A48 W to Cowbridge

A comfortable, popular and modern hotel, conveniently
located for the airport and city. Bedrooms are a good size
and some have a private lounge. Public areas are smartly
presented and include a gym, pool, meeting rooms and a
comfortable restaurant with views of the adjacent lake.

Rooms 135 (7 fmly) (27 GF) **S** £49-£159; **D** £49-£159*
Facilities STV ③ Gym Sauna Steam room ♫ New Year
Wi-fi **Conf** Class 140 Board 80 Thtr 300 **Services** Lift
Parking 225 **Notes** Civ Wed 200

Barceló Cardiff Angel Hotel

★★★★ 70% HOTEL

☎ 029 2064 9200 📄 029 2039 6212
Castle St CF10 1SZ
e-mail: angel@barcelo-hotels-co.uk
web: www.barcelo-hotels.co.uk/hotels/wales/barcelo-
cardiff-angel-hotel
dir: Opposite Cardiff Castle

This well-established hotel is in the heart of the city
overlooking the famous castle and almost opposite the
Millennium Stadium. All bedrooms offer air conditioning
and are appointed to a good standard. Public areas
include an impressive lobby, a modern restaurant and a
selection of conference rooms. There is limited parking at
the rear of the hotel.

Rooms 102 (3 fmly) **Facilities** STV Xmas New Year Wi-fi
Conf Class 120 Board 50 Thtr 300 Del from £110*
Services Lift Air con **Parking** 60 **Notes** Civ Wed 200

Holiday Inn Cardiff City

★★★ 74% HOTEL

☎ 0870 400 8140 📄 029 2023 1482
Castle St CF10 1XD
e-mail: cardiffcity@ihg.com
web: www.holidayinn.co.uk
dir: M4 junct 29 E/A48(M), follow city centre signs, onto
A470. Turn left to hotel

This hotel has a fantastic location in the heart of the city
and is just a short walk from the Millennium Stadium,
Cardiff Castle and Cardiff Bay. There are state-of-the-art
conference and meeting facilities available as well as
banqueting. The air-conditioned accommodation is
modern with many guest extras provided. The restaurant
offers a good menu choice or guests can take a snack in
the lounge/bar area.

Rooms 157 (20 fmly) (10 smoking) **Facilities** ♫ New
Year Wi-fi **Conf** Class 60 Board 50 Thtr 180 **Services** Lift
Air con **Parking** 80 **Notes** LB ⊗

Manor Parc Country Hotel & Restaurant

★★★ 73% ◎ HOTEL

☎ 029 2069 3723 📄 029 2061 4624
Thornhill Rd, Thornhill CF14 9UA
e-mail: enquiry@manorparc.com
dir: M4 junct 32. Turn left at lights, pass Den Inn. Take
next left, left at lights on A469

Set in open countryside on the outskirts of Cardiff, this
delightful hotel retains traditional values of hospitality
and service. Bedrooms, including a suite, are spacious
and attractive, whilst public areas comprise a
comfortable lounge and a restaurant, with a magnificent
lantern ceiling, that overlooks the well-tended grounds.

Rooms 21 (4 fmly) (1 GF) **Facilities** ☄ **Conf** Class 80
Board 50 Thtr 120 **Parking** 100 **Notes** ⊗ Closed 26
Dec-2 Jan Civ Wed 100

Best Western St Mellons Hotel & Country Club

★★★ 72% HOTEL

☎ 01633 680355 📠 01633 680399
Castleton CF3 2XR
e-mail: reservations.stmellons@ohiml.com
web: www.oxfordhotelsandinns.com
dir: M4 junct 28 follow A48 Castleton/St Mellons. Hotel on left past garage

This former Regency mansion has been tastefully converted into an elegant hotel with an adjoining leisure complex that attracts a strong local following. Bedrooms, some in purpose-built wings, are spacious and smart. The public areas retain their pleasing architectural proportions and include relaxing lounges and a restaurant serving a varied choice of carefully prepared and enjoyable dishes.

Rooms 41 (20 annexe) (9 fmly) (5 GF) **S** £50-£140; **D** £70-£190 (incl. bkfst)* **Facilities** Spa ⊗ Gym Squash Beauty salon Xmas **Conf** Class 185 Board 179 Thtr 480 Del from £130 to £170* **Parking** 100 **Notes** LB Civ Wed 160

Sandringham

★★ 69% HOTEL

☎ 029 2023 2161 📠 029 2038 3998
21 St Mary St CF10 1PL
e-mail: mm@sandringham-hotel.com
dir: M4 junct 29 follow 'city centre' signs. Opposite castle turn left into High St; leads to St Mary St. Hotel on left

This friendly, privately owned and personally run hotel is near the Millennium Stadium and offers a convenient base for access to the city centre. Bedrooms are well equipped, and diners can relax in Café Jazz, the hotel's adjoining restaurant, where live music is provided most week nights. There is also a separate lounge/bar for residents, and an airy breakfast room.

Rooms 28 (1 fmly) **S** £35-£100; **D** £45-£145 (incl. bkfst) **Facilities** FTV ♫ Wi-fi **Conf** Class 70 Board 60 Thtr 100 Del from £60 to £145 **Notes** LB ⊗ Closed 24-26 Dec(pm) & 1 Jan(pm)

Mercure The Lodge Cardiff

Ⓤ

☎ 029 2089 4000 📠 029 2049 3695
Wharf Road East, Tyndall St CF10 4BB
e-mail: h6623@accor.com
web: www.mercure-uk.com
dir: M4 junct 29/33 follow city centre signs

Currently the rating for this establishment is not confirmed. This may be due to a change of ownership or because it has only recently joined the AA rating scheme. For further details please see the AA website: theAA.com

Rooms 100 (48 fmly) (27 GF) (5 smoking) **S** £60-£150; **D** £60-£150 **Facilities** STV Wi-fi **Services** Lift Air con **Parking** 90

Campanile Cardiff

Campanile

BUDGET HOTEL

☎ 029 2054 9044 📠 029 2054 9900
Caxton Place, Pentwyn CF23 8HA
e-mail: cardiff@campanile.com
dir: Take Pentwyn exit from A489(M), follow signs for hotel

This modern building offers accommodation in smart, well-equipped bedrooms, all with en suite bathrooms. Refreshments may be taken at the informal bistro. See also the Hotel Groups pages.

Rooms 47 (47 annexe) **S** £41-£110; **D** £41-£110* **Conf** Class 18 Board 16 Thtr 35

Days Inn Cardiff

BUDGET HOTEL

☎ 01446 710787 📠 01446 719318
Port Rd, Rhoose, Barry CF62 3BT
e-mail: daysinncardiff@tiscali.co.uk
web: www.daysinn.com
dir: 0.25m on right before Cardiff Airport

This modern building offers accommodation in smart, spacious and well-equipped bedrooms, suitable for families and business travellers, and with en suite bathrooms. Continental breakfast is available and other refreshments may be taken at the nearby family restaurant. See also the Hotel Groups pages.

Rooms 50 (8 fmly) (20 GF) (7 smoking) **S** £38-£50; **D** £45-£70 (incl. bkfst)* **Conf** Class 10 Board 12 Thtr 15

Express by Holiday Inn Cardiff Airport

BUDGET HOTEL

☎ 01446 711117 📠 01446 713290
Port Rd, Rhoose CF62 3BT
e-mail: sales@exhicardiffairport.co.uk
web: www.hiexpress.com/cardiffairport

A modern hotel ideal for families and business travellers. Fresh and uncomplicated, the spacious rooms include Sky TV, power shower and tea and coffee-making facilities. Continental buffet breakfast is included in the room rate; other meals may be taken at the nearby family pub or restaurant. See also the Hotel Groups pages.

Rooms 111 **Conf** Board 20 Thtr 40

Express by Holiday Inn Cardiff Bay

BUDGET HOTEL

☎ 029 2044 9000 📠 029 2048 8922
Atlantic Wharf CF10 4EE
e-mail: info@exhicardiff.co.uk
web: www.hiexpress.com/cardiffbay
dir: M4 junct 33, A4232, follow road to end. Left at 1st rdbt, left (Country Hall on right). 1st right, hotel on right

Rooms 87 (48 fmly) (15 GF) **Conf** Class 12 Board 20 Thtr 30

Ibis Cardiff

BUDGET HOTEL

☎ 029 2064 9250 📠 029 2920 9260
Churchill Way CF10 2HA
e-mail: H2969@accor.com
web: www.ibishotel.com
dir: M4, then A48 2nd exit A4232. Follow signs to City Centre on Newport Rd, left after railway bridge, left after Queen St station

Modern, budget hotel offering comfortable accommodation in bright and practical bedrooms. Breakfast is self-service and dinner is available in the restaurant. See also the Hotel Groups pages.

Rooms 102 (19 GF) (7 smoking)

Ibis Cardiff Gate

BUDGET HOTEL

☎ 029 2073 3222 📠 029 2073 4222
Malthouse Av, Cardiff Gate Business Park, Pontprennau CF23 8RA
e-mail: H3159@accor.com
web: www.ibishotel.com
dir: M4 junct 30, follow Cardiff Service Station signs. Hotel on left

Rooms 78 (19 fmly) (22 GF) (7 smoking) **S** fr £49; **D** fr £49* **Conf** Class 24 Thtr 25

CARDIFF *continued*

Innkeeper's Lodge Cardiff

BUDGET HOTEL

☎ 0845 112 6080 📄 0845 112 6223
Tyn-y-Parc Rd, Whitchurch CF14 6BG
web: www.innkeeperslodge.com/cardiff
dir: M4 junct 32 southbound. 0.5m. Lodge on corner of
Tyn-y-Parc Rd

Innkeeper's Lodge represents an exciting, high value
concept within the budget hotel market. Comfortable
bedrooms provide excellent facilities that include satellite
TV and modem points. Options include family rooms; and
for the corporate guest, cutting edge IT which includes
Wi-fi access. A popular Carvery provides all-day food,
including an extensive, complimentary continental
breakfast. See also the Hotel Groups pages.

Rooms 52 (22 fmly) **Conf** Thtr 60

Travelodge Cardiff Atlantic Wharf

BUDGET HOTEL

☎ 0871 984 6424
Atlantic Wharf Leisure Park, Cardiff Bay CF10 4JY
dir: M4 junct 29, follow signs A48/City Centre signs. At
T-junct left onto A4119. At rdbt 2nd exit onto A4232. 3m
to Atlantic Wharf

Travelodge offers good quality, good value, budget
accommodation. All offer family rooms sleeping up to
four (two adults, two children) with en suite bathroom/
shower-room, remote-control TV, tea- and coffee-making
facilities and comfortable beds. Food options vary.
Breakfast is at the on-site Bar Café restaurant (if
available) or to take away. See also the Hotel Groups
pages.

Rooms 112 **S** fr £29; **D** fr £29

Travelodge Cardiff Central

BUDGET HOTEL

☎ 0871 984 6224 📄 029 2039 8737
Imperial Gate, Saint Marys St CF10 1FA
web: www.travelodge.co.uk
dir: M4 junct 32, A470 to city centre

Rooms 112 **S** fr £29; **D** fr £29

Travelodge Cardiff Llanedeyrn

BUDGET HOTEL

☎ 0871 984 6225 📄 029 2054 9564
Circle Way East, Llanedeyrn CF23 9PD
web: www.travelodge.co.uk
dir: M4 junct 30, A4232 to North Pentwyn junct. A48 &
follow Cardiff East & Docks signs. 3rd exit at Llanedeyrn
junct, follow Circle Way East signs

Rooms 100 **S** fr £29; **D** fr £29

Travelodge Cardiff (M4)

BUDGET HOTEL

☎ 0871 984 6226 📄 029 2089 9412
Moto Service Area, Pontyclun CF72 8SA
web: www.travelodge.co.uk
dir: M4, junct 33, A4232

Rooms 32 **S** fr £29; **D** fr £29 **Conf** Board 34 Thtr 45

The Old Post Office

 RESTAURANT WITH ROOMS

☎ 029 2056 5400 📄 029 2056 3400
Greenwood Ln, St Fagans CF5 6EL
e-mail: info@theoldpostofficerestaurant.co.uk
dir: 4m W of city centre. M4 junct 33 onto A4232, onto
A48 for Cardiff & 1st left for St Fagans

Located just five miles from Cardiff in the historic village
of St Fagans, this establishment offers contemporary
style based on New England design. Bedrooms, like the
dining room, feature striking white walls with spotlights
offering a fresh, clean feel. Delicious meals include a
carefully prepared selection of local produce.

Rooms 6 (2 fmly)

CARMARTHENSHIRE

CARMARTHEN Map 8 SN42

Ivy Bush Royal

★★★ 75% HOTEL

☎ 01267 235111 📄 01267 234914
Spilman St SA31 1LG
e-mail: reception@ivybushroyal.co.uk
web: www.ivybushroyal.co.uk
dir: M4 onto A48 W, over 1st rdbt, 2nd rdbt turn right.
Straight over next 2 rdbts. Left at lights. Hotel on right at
top of hill

This hotel offers guests spacious, well equipped
bedrooms and bathrooms, a relaxing lounge with outdoor
patio seating and a comfortable restaurant serving a
varied selection of carefully prepared meals. Weddings,
meetings and conferences are all well catered for at this
friendly, family run establishment.

Rooms 70 (4 fmly) **S** £55-£95; **D** £75-£140 (incl. bkfst)*
Facilities STV FTV Gym Xmas New Year Wi-fi
Conf Class 50 Board 40 Thtr 200 Del from £99 to £150*
Services Lift **Parking** 83 **Notes** LB ⊗ Civ Wed 150

Falcon

★★ 76% HOTEL

☎ 01267 234959 & 237152 📄 01267 221277
Lammas St SA31 3AP
e-mail: reception@falconcarmarthen.co.uk
web: www.falconcarmarthen.co.uk
dir: in town centre pass bus station turn left, hotel
200yds on left

This friendly hotel has been owned by the Exton family for
over 45 years. Personally run, it is well placed in the
centre of the town. Bedrooms, some with four-poster
beds, are tastefully decorated with good facilities. There
is a comfortable lounge with adjacent bar, and the
restaurant offers a varied selection of enjoyable dishes at
both lunch and dinner.

Rooms 16 (1 fmly) **Conf** Class 50 Board 40 Thtr 80
Parking 36 **Notes** Closed 26 Dec RS Sun

CROSS HANDS Map 8 SN51

Travelodge Llanelli Cross Hands

BUDGET HOTEL

☎ 0871 984 6230 📄 0870 191 1729
SA14 6NW
web: www.travelodge.co.uk
dir: on A48, westbound

Travelodge offers good quality, good value, budget
accommodation. All offer family rooms sleeping up to four
(two adults, two children) with en suite bathroom/
shower-room, remote-control TV, tea- and coffee-making
facilities and comfortable beds. Food options vary.
Breakfast is at the on-site Bar Café restaurant (if
available) or to take away. See also Hotel Groups pages.

Rooms 51 **S** fr £29; **D** fr £29

LLANDEILO Map 8 SN62

The Plough Inn

★★★ 83% @ HOTEL

☎ 01558 823431 📠 01558 823969
Rhosmaen SA19 6NP
e-mail: info@ploughrhosmaen.com
web: www.ploughrhosmaen.com
dir: 0.5m N of Llandeilo on A40

This privately owned hotel has memorable views over the Towy Valley and the Black Mountains. Bedrooms, situated in a separate wing, are tastefully furnished, spacious and comfortable. The public lounge bar is popular with locals, as is the spacious restaurant where freshly prepared food can be enjoyed. There are also conference facilities, a gym and a sauna.

Rooms 14 (8 fmly) (5 GF) **S** £70; **D** £100-£120 (incl. bkfst) **Facilities** FTV Gym Sauna Xmas New Year Wi-fi **Conf** Class 60 Board 30 Thtr 100 **Services** Air con **Parking** 70 **Notes** LB Civ Wed 120

White Hart Inn

★★ 71% HOTEL

☎ 01558 823419 📠 01558 823089
36 Carmarthen Rd SA19 6RS
e-mail: info@thewhitehartinnwales.co.uk
web: www.whitehartinnwales.co.uk
dir: Off A40 onto A483, hotel 200yds on left

This privately owned, 19th-century roadside hostelry is on the outskirts of town. The modern bedrooms are well equipped and tastefully furnished, and family rooms are available. Public areas include a choice of bars where a wide range of grilled dishes is available. There are several function rooms, including a large self-contained suite.

Rooms 11 (6 fmly) **S** £40-£45; **D** £60-£70 (incl. bkfst)* **Facilities** STV New Year Wi-fi **Conf** Class 80 Board 40 Thtr 100 Del from £70* **Parking** 50 **Notes** ⊗ Civ Wed 70

LLANELLI Map 8 SN50

Best Western Diplomat Hotel

★★★ 77% HOTEL

☎ 01554 756156 📠 01554 751649
Felinfoel SA15 3PJ
e-mail: reservations@diplomat-hotel-wales.com
web: www.diplomat-hotel-wales.com
dir: M4 junct 48 onto A4138 then B4303, hotel 0.75m on right

This Victorian mansion, set in mature grounds, has been extended over the years to provide a comfortable and relaxing hotel. The well-appointed bedrooms are located in the main house and there is also a wing of comfortable modern bedrooms. Public areas include Trubshaw's Restaurant, a large function suite and a modern leisure centre.

Rooms 50 (8 annexe) (2 fmly) (4 GF) **S** £55-£80; **D** £70-£100 (incl. bkfst)* **Facilities** FTV ⊙ supervised Gym Sauna Steam room Sun beds Hairdresser ♫ Xmas New Year Wi-fi **Conf** Class 150 Board 100 Thtr 450 Del from £70 to £110 **Services** Lift **Parking** 250 **Notes** LB Civ Wed 300

Ashburnham

★★ 74% HOTEL

☎ 01554 834343 & 834455 📠 01554 834483
Ashburnham Rd, Pembrey SA16 0TH
e-mail: info@ashburnham-hotel.co.uk
web: www.ashburnham-hotel.co.uk
dir: M4 junct 48, A4138 to Llanelli, A484 West to Pembrey. Follow brown information signs

Amelia Earhart stayed at this friendly hotel after finishing her historic trans-Atlantic flight in 1928. Public areas include the Brasserie Restaurant and the Conservatory Lounge Bar that serves an extensive range of bar meals. Bedrooms, varying from standard to superior, have modern furnishings and facilities. The hotel is licensed for civil ceremonies, and function and conference facilities are also available.

Rooms 13 (2 fmly) **Facilities** Wi-fi **Conf** Class 150 Board 80 Thtr 150 **Parking** 100 **Notes** ⊗ RS 24-26 Dec Civ Wed 130

ST CLEARS Map 8 SN21

Travelodge St Clears Carmarthen

BUDGET HOTEL

☎ 0871 984 6053 📠 01994 231227
Tenby Rd SA33 4JN
web: www.travelodge.co.uk
dir: A40 westbound, before rdbt junct of A477 & A4066

Travelodge offers good quality, good value, budget accommodation. All offer family rooms sleeping up to four (two adults, two children) with en suite bathroom/ shower-room, remote-control TV, tea- and coffee-making facilities and comfortable beds. Food options vary. Breakfast is at the on-site Bar Café restaurant (if available) or to take away. See also Hotel Groups pages.

Rooms 51 **S** fr £29; **D** fr £29

CEREDIGION

ABERAERON Map 8 SN46

Feathers Royal

★★★ 80% SMALL HOTEL

☎ 01545 571750 📠 01545 571760
Alban Square SA46 0AQ
e-mail: enquiries@feathersroyal.co.uk
dir: A482 Lampeter Rd, hotel opposite recreation grounds

This is a family run hotel ideally located in the picturesque Georgian town of Aberaeron. This charming, Grade II listed property, built in 1815 as a coaching house, underwent a transformation to coincide with the town's bicentenary celebrations. Accommodation is very comfortable with modern fittings and accessories provided, and the public areas are well appointed. A friendly welcome can be expected.

Rooms 13 (2 fmly) **Facilities** Xmas New Year Wi-fi **Conf** Class 120 Board 60 Thtr 200 **Parking** 20 **Notes** LB ⊗

ABERAERON *continued*

Ty Mawr Mansion

RESTAURANT WITH ROOMS

☎ 01570 470033
Cilcennin SA48 8DB
e-mail: info@tymawrmansion.co.uk
web: www.tymawrmansion.co.uk
dir: On A482 (Lampeter to Aberaeron road), 4m from Aberaeron

Surrounded by rolling countryside in its own naturally beautiful gardens, this fine country mansion house is a haven of perfect peace and tranquillity. Careful renovation has restored it to its former glory and, combined with lush fabrics, top quality beds and sumptuous furnishings, the accommodation is spacious, superbly equipped and very comfortable. Award-winning chefs create mouth-watering dishes from local and seasonal produce. There is also a 27-seat cinema with all the authenticity of the real thing. Martin and Cath McAlpine offer the sort of welcome which makes every visit to Ty Mawr a memorable one.

Rooms 9 (1 annexe) (1 fmly)

| **ABERYSTWYTH** | **Map 8 SN58** |

Conrah

★★★ 83% COUNTRY HOUSE HOTEL

☎ 01970 617941 🖹 01970 624546
Ffosrhydygaled, Chancery SY23 4DF
e-mail: enquiries@conrah.co.uk
dir: on A487, 3.5m S of Aberystwyth

This privately owned and personally run country-house hotel stands in 22 acres of mature grounds. The elegant public rooms include a choice of comfortable lounges with welcoming open fires. Bedrooms are located in the main house, a wing and converted outbuildings. The cuisine, which is modern with international influences, achieves high standards. Conference facilities are available.

Rooms 17 (6 annexe) (1 fmly) (3 GF) **S** £55-£85; **D** £80-£160 (incl. bkfst)* **Facilities** 🛥 New Year Wi-fi **Conf** Class 40 Board 40 Thtr 60 Del from £120 to £140* **Services** Lift **Parking** 100 **Notes** LB ⊗ Closed 24-26 Dec Civ Wed 80

Belle Vue Royal

★★★ 75% HOTEL

☎ 01970 617558 & 639240 🖹 01970 612190
Marine Ter SY23 2BA
e-mail: reception@bellevueroyalhotel.co.uk
dir: on promenade, 200yds from pier

This large privately owned seafront hotel dates back more than 170 years and is a short walk from the shops and visitor attractions. All bedrooms are well equipped and include both family and sea-view rooms. Public areas feature extensive function rooms and a choice of bars, and dining options include meals in the bar and more formal restaurant.

Rooms 34 (6 fmly) (1 GF) **Facilities** Xmas New Year Wi-fi **Conf** Class 30 Board 30 Thtr 100 **Parking** 14 **Notes** LB ⊗ Civ Wed 100

Marine Hotel & Leisure Suite

★★★ 74% HOTEL

☎ 01970 612444 🖹 01970 617435
The Promenade SY23 2BX
e-mail: marinehotel1@btconnect.com
web: www.marinehotelaberystwyth.co.uk
dir: From W on A44. From N or S Wales on A487. On seafront, west of pier

Located on the central promenade overlooking Cardigan Bay, this long established privately owned hotel has been sympathetically renovated to provide a range of well-equipped bedrooms with modern bathrooms. Spacious public areas include a choice of lounges and an elegant dining room. A fitness suite is also available.

Rooms 48 (9 fmly) **S** £38-£65; **D** £60-£130 (incl. bkfst) **Facilities** FTV Gym Steam room Xmas New Year Wi-fi **Conf** Class 150 Board 60 Thtr 220 **Services** Lift **Parking** 27 **Notes** LB Civ Wed 200

Richmond

★★★ 74% SMALL HOTEL

☎ 01970 612201 🖹 01970 626706
44-45 Marine Ter SY23 2BX
e-mail: reservations@richmondhotel.uk.com
web: www.richmondhotel.uk.com
dir: On entering town follow signs for Promenade

This privately owned and personally run, friendly hotel offers good sea views from its day rooms and many of the bedrooms. Major investment in recent years has resulted in good standards of comfort and facilities including refurbished bedrooms with smart modern bathrooms. An attractive dining room is the setting for imaginative dinners and comprehensive breakfasts.

Rooms 15 (2 fmly) **S** £55-£65; **D** £85-£95 (incl. bkfst)* **Facilities** FTV Wi-fi **Conf** Class 22 Board 28 Thtr 60 **Parking** 22 **Notes** LB ⊗ Closed 20 Dec-3 Jan

Queensbridge

★★ 64% METRO HOTEL

☎ 01970 612343 🖹 01970 617452
Promenade, Victoria Ter SY23 2DH
dir: 500yds N of town centre near Constitution Hill

The friendly Queensbridge is on the promenade at the north end of the town. The bedrooms, some suitable for families, have modern facilities and many have fine sea views. Public areas include a comfortable lounge with bar and a spacious lower ground floor dining room, where buffet breakfast are served. A small passenger lift serves all floors.

Rooms 15 (2 fmly) (2 smoking) **Services** Lift **Parking** 6 **Notes** LB

DEVIL'S BRIDGE — Map 9 SN77

The Hafod Hotel

★★★ 72% ⊛ HOTEL

☎ 01970 890232 📄 01970 890394
SY23 3JL
e-mail: hafodhotel@btconnect.com
dir: Exit A44 in Ponterwyd signed Devil's Bridge/
Pontarfynach onto A4120 for 3m, over bridge. Hotel facing

This former hunting lodge dates back to the 17th century and is situated in six acres of grounds. Now a family-owned and run hotel, it provides accommodation suitable for both business people and tourists. Family rooms and a four-poster room are available. In addition to the dining area and lounge, there are tea rooms.

Rooms 17 (2 fmly) **S** £49.50; **D** £75 (incl. bkfst)*
Facilities Xmas New Year Wi-fi **Conf** Class 70 Board 40
Thtr 100 **Parking** 200 **Notes** Civ Wed 40

EGLWYS FACH — Map 14 SN69

INSPECTORS' CHOICE

Ynyshir Hall

★★★ ⊛⊛⊛
COUNTRY HOUSE HOTEL

☎ 01654 781209 & 781268 📄 01654 781366
SY20 8TA
e-mail: ynyshir@relaischateaux.com
web: www.ynyshir-hall.co.uk
dir: off A487, 5.5m S of Machynlleth, signed from main road

Set in beautifully landscaped grounds and surrounded by a RSBP reserve, Ynyshir Hall is a haven of calm. Lavishly styled bedrooms, each individually themed around a great painter, provide high standards of luxury and comfort. The lounge and bar have different moods, and both feature abundant fresh flowers. The dining room offers outstanding cooking using best ingredients with modern flair. Von Essen Hotels - AA Hotel Group of the Year 2009-10.

Rooms 9 (2 annexe) **D** £275-£405 (incl. bkfst)*
Facilities 🧖 Xmas New Year **Conf** Class 20 Board 18
Thtr 25 Del from £245 to £350* **Parking** 20 **Notes** LB
No children 9yrs Civ Wed 40

GWBERT-ON-SEA — Map 14 SN69

The Cliff

★★★ 77% HOTEL

☎ 01239 613241 📄 01239 615391
SA43 1PP
e-mail: reservations@cliffhotel.com
dir: off A487 into Cardigan, follow signs to Gwbert, 3m to hotel

Set in 30 acres of grounds with a 9-hole golf course, this hotel commands superb sea views from its cliff-top location overlooking Cardigan Bay. Bedrooms in the main building offer excellent views and there is also a wing of 22 modern rooms. Public areas are spacious and comprise a choice of bars, lounges and a fine dining restaurant. The spa offers a wide range of up-to-the-minute leisure facilities.

Rooms 70 (6 fmly) (5 GF) **S** £59-£85; **D** £75-£135 (incl. bkfst) **Facilities** Spa FTV 🎱 🏹 ⚓ 9 Fishing Gym Xmas New Year **Conf** Class 150 Board 140 Thtr 250
Del from £85 to £120 **Services** Lift **Parking** 150 **Notes** LB
Civ Wed 200

LAMPETER — Map 8 SN54

Best Western Falcondale Mansion

★★★ 86% ⊛⊛ COUNTRY HOUSE HOTEL

☎ 01570 422910 📄 01570 423559
SA48 7RX
e-mail: info@falcondalehotel.com
web: www.falcondalehotel.com
dir: 800yds W of High St (A475) or 1.5m NW of Lampeter (A482)

Built in the Italianate style, this charming Victorian property is set in extensive grounds and beautiful parkland. The individually-styled bedrooms are generally spacious, well equipped and tastefully decorated. Bars and lounges are similarly well appointed with additional facilities including a conservatory and function room. Guests have a choice of either the Valley Restaurant for fine dining or the less formal Peterwells Brasserie.

Rooms 19 (2 fmly) **S** £100-£160; **D** £140-£180 (incl. bkfst)* **Facilities** FTV 🧖 Xmas New Year Wi-fi
Conf Class 30 Board 25 Thtr 60 Del from £132 to £164*
Services Lift **Parking** 60 **Notes** LB Civ Wed 60

CONWY

ABERGELE   Map 14 SH97

Kinmel Manor

★★★ 73% HOTEL

☎ 01745 832014   📠 01745 832014
St George's Rd LL22 9AS
e-mail: reception@kinmelmanorhotel.co.uk
dir: Exit A55 at junct 24, hotel entrance on rdbt

Parts of this family-run hotel complex date back to the 16th century and some original features are still in evidence. Set in spacious grounds, it provides a variety of well-equipped bedrooms and extensive leisure facilities. The Manor Restaurant, in the original house, has high ceilings and a log fire on cooler evenings; menus rely heavily on locally sourced ingredients.

Rooms 51 (3 fmly) (22 GF) **S** £75-£100; **D** £90-£130 (incl. bkfst)* **Facilities** FTV ③ Gym Steam room Sauna Spa bath Xmas New Year Wi-fi **Conf** Class 100 Board 100 Thtr 250 Del from £97.50 to £127.50* **Services** Lift **Parking** 120 **Notes** LB Civ Wed 250

The Kinmel Arms

◉ RESTAURANT WITH ROOMS

☎ 01745 832207   📠 01745 822044
The Village, St George LL22 9BP
e-mail: info@thekinmelarms.co.uk
dir: From A55 junct 24a to St George. E on A55, junct 25. 1st left to Rhuddlan, then 1st right into St George. Take 2nd right

This converted 17th-century coaching inn stands close to the church in the village of St George in the beautiful Elwy Valley. The popular restaurant specialises in produce from Wales and North West England, and the friendly and helpful staff ensures an enjoyable stay. The accommodation consists of four attractive, well-equipped suites; substantial continental breakfasts are served in the rooms.

Rooms 4

BETWS-Y-COED   Map 14 SH75

See also **Llanrwst**

Royal Oak

★★★ 83% ◉ HOTEL

☎ 01690 710219   📠 01690 710603
Holyhead Rd LL24 0AY
e-mail: royaloakmail@btopenworld.com
web: www.royaloakhotel.net
dir: On A5 in town centre, next to St Mary's church

Centrally situated in the village, this elegant, privately owned hotel started life as a coaching inn and now provides very comfortable bedrooms with smart modern en suite bathrooms. The extensive public areas retain original charm and character. The choice of eating options includes the Grill Bistro, the Stables Bar which is much frequented by locals, and the more formal Llugwy Restaurant.

Rooms 27 (1 fmly) **S** £75-£95; **D** £100-£170 (incl. bkfst)* **Facilities** STV ♫ New Year Wi-fi **Conf** Class 40 Board 20 Thtr 80 Del from £90 to £140* **Parking** 90 **Notes** LB ⊗ Closed 25-26 Dec Civ Wed 35

See advert on this page

Craig-y-Dderwen Riverside Hotel

★★★ 79% ◉ COUNTRY HOUSE HOTEL

☎ 01690 710293   📠 01690 710362
LL24 0AS
e-mail: info@snowdoniahotel.com
web: www.snowdoniahotel.com
dir: A5 to town, cross Waterloo Bridge, take 1st left

This Victorian country-house hotel is set in well-maintained grounds alongside the River Conwy, at the end of a tree-lined drive. Very pleasant views can be enjoyed from many rooms, and two of the bedrooms have four-poster beds. There are comfortable lounges and the atmosphere throughout is tranquil and relaxing.

Rooms 16 (2 fmly) (1 GF) (3 smoking) **S** £75-£95; **D** £90-£170 (incl. bkfst)* **Facilities** STV FTV ⑤ Badminton Volleyball New Year Wi-fi **Conf** Class 25 Board 20 Thtr 50 Del from £110 to £205* **Parking** 50 **Notes** Closed 23-26 Dec & 2 Jan-1 Feb Civ Wed 50

Best Western Waterloo

★★★ 78% HOTEL

☎ 01690 710411 🖷 01690 710986
LL24 0AR
e-mail: reservations@waterloo-hotel.info
web: www.waterloo-hotel.info
dir: A5, near Waterloo Bridge

This long-established hotel, named after the nearby Waterloo Bridge, is ideally located for visiting Snowdonia. Stylish accommodation is split between rooms in the main hotel and modern, cottage-style rooms located in buildings to the rear. The attractive Garden Room Restaurant serves traditional Welsh specialities, and the vibrant refurbished Bridge Inn provides a wide range of food and drink throughout the day and evening.

Rooms 39 (30 annexe) (2 fmly) (30 GF) **Facilities** ⊙ Gym Steam room Sauna New Year Wi-fi **Conf** Class 18 Board 12 Thtr 40 **Parking** 100 **Notes** LB ⊗ Closed 25-26 Dec

Fairy Glen

★★ 74% SMALL HOTEL

☎ 01690 710269
LL24 0SH
e-mail: fairyglenho@sky.com
web: www.fairyglenhotel.co.uk
dir: A5 onto A470 S'bound (Dolwyddelan road). Hotel 0.5m on left by Beaver Bridge

This privately owned and personally run former coaching inn is over 300 years old. It is located near the Fairy Glen beauty spot, south of Betws-y-Coed. The modern accommodation is well equipped and service is willing, friendly and attentive. Facilities include a cosy bar and a separate comfortable lounge.

Rooms 8 (1 fmly) **S** £30-£33; **D** £60-£66 (incl. bkfst)*
Parking 10 **Notes** ⊗ Closed Nov-Jan RS Feb

CAPEL CURIG	Map 14 SH75

Cobdens

★★ 65% SMALL HOTEL

☎ 01690 720243 🖷 01690 720354
LL24 0EE
e-mail: info@cobdens.co.uk
dir: on A5, 4m N of Betws-y-Coed

Situated in the heart of Snowdonia, this hotel has been a centre for mountaineering and other outdoor pursuits for many years. The bedrooms are modern and well equipped, and many enjoy lovely views. A wide range of meals using local produce is served in the restaurant or bar. A sauna room is also available.

Rooms 17 (4 fmly) **Facilities** Fishing Pool table **Conf** Class 25 Board 30 Thtr 50 **Parking** 40 **Notes** Closed Jan RS 24-25 & 31 Dec

---

COLWYN BAY	Map 14 SH87

Lyndale

THE INDEPENDENTS
HOTEL ASSOCIATION

★★ 74% HOTEL

☎ 01492 515429 🖷 01492 518805
410 Abergele Rd, Old Colwyn LL29 9AB
e-mail: lyndale@tinyworld.co.uk
dir: A55 junct 22 Old Colwyn, turn left. At rdbt through village, then 1m on A547

A range of accommodation is available at this friendly hotel, including suites that are suitable for family use and a four-poster bedroom. Public areas include a comfortable foyer lounge, separate well stocked bar and The Tamarind Thai Restaurant is the setting for imaginative dinners with a large choice and clear descriptions of dishes offered.

Rooms 14 (1 fmly) **S** £39-£49; **D** £59-£69 (incl. bkfst)*
Facilities STV Wi-fi **Conf** Class 20 Board 20 Thtr 30 Del from £50 to £70* **Parking** 20 **Notes** LB

CONWY	Map 14 SH77

Castle Hotel Conwy

WELSH RAREBITS

★★★★ 81% ⊛⊛ TOWN HOUSE HOTEL

☎ 01492 582800 🖷 01492 582300
High St LL32 8DB
e-mail: mail@castlewales.co.uk
web: www.castlewales.co.uk
dir: A55 junct 18, follow town centre signs, cross estuary (castle on left). Right then left at mini-rdbts onto one-way system. Right at Town Wall Gate, right onto Berry St then High St

This family-run, 16th-century hotel is one of Conwy's most distinguished buildings and offers a relaxed and friendly atmosphere. Bedrooms are appointed to an impressive standard and include a stunning suite. Public areas include a popular modern bar and the award-winning Shakespeare's restaurant.

Castle Hotel Conwy

Rooms 28 (2 fmly) **S** £70-£90; **D** £120-£265 (incl. bkfst) **Facilities** New Year Wi-fi **Conf** Class 20 Board 20 Thtr 30 Del from £95 to £120 **Parking** 34 **Notes** LB

DEGANWY	Map 14 SH77

Quay Hotel & Spa

★★★★ 82% ⊛⊛ HOTEL

☎ 01492 564100 🖷 01492 464115
Deganwy Quay LL31 9DJ
e-mail: info@quayhotel.com
dir: M56, A494, A55 junct 18, straight across 2 rdbts. At lights bear left into The Quay. Hotel on right

This boutique hotel occupies a stunning position beside the estuary on Deganwy's Quay. What was once an area for railway storage is now a statement of modern architectural design offering hotel-keeping of the highest standard. Spacious bedrooms, many with balconies and wonderful views, are decorated in neutral colours and boast a host of thoughtful extras, including state-of-the-art communication systems. The friendly staff provide a fluent service in a charmingly informal manner.

Rooms 74 (15 fmly) (30 GF) **Facilities** Spa ⊙ supervised Gym Steam & sauna room Xmas New Year Wi-fi **Conf** Class 40 Board 40 Thtr 100 Del from £135 to £150* **Services** Lift **Parking** 96 **Notes** ⊗ Civ Wed 100

INSPECTORS' CHOICE

Bodysgallen Hall and Spa
★★★★ ◉◉◉ COUNTRY HOUSE HOTEL

☎ 01492 584466   🖹 01492 582519
LL30 1RS
e-mail: info@bodysgallen.com
web: www.bodysgallen.com
dir: A55 junct 19, A470 towards Llandudno. Hotel 2m on right

Situated in idyllic surroundings of its own parkland and formal gardens, this 17th-century house is in an elevated position, with views towards Snowdonia and across to Conwy Castle. The lounges and dining room have fine antiques and great character.
Accommodation is provided in the house, but also in delightfully converted cottages, together with a superb spa. Friendly and attentive service is discreetly offered, whilst the restaurant features fine local produce prepared with great skill.

Rooms 31 (16 annexe) (4 fmly) (4 GF) **S** £115-£300; **D** £165-£395 (incl. bkfst)* **Facilities** Spa STV 🕤 ⛲ Gym Beauty treatments Steam room Relaxation room Sauna Xmas New Year Wi-fi **Conf** Class 30 Board 22 Thtr 50 **Parking** 50 **Notes** LB ⊗ No children 6yrs Civ Wed 50

INSPECTORS' CHOICE

Osborne House
★★★★ ◉ TOWN HOUSE HOTEL

☎ 01492 860330   🖹 01492 860791
17 North Parade LL30 2LP
e-mail: sales@osbornehouse.com
web: www.osbornehouse.com
dir: exit A55 junct 19. Follow signs for Llandudno then Promenade. Continue to junct, turn right. Hotel on left opposite pier entrance

Built in 1832, this Victorian house was restored and converted into a luxurious townhouse by the Maddocks family. Spacious suites offer unrivalled comfort and luxury, combining antique furnishings with state-of-the-art technology and facilities. Each suite provides super views over the pier and bay. Osborne's café grill is open throughout the day and offers high quality food, whilst the bar blends elegance with plasma screens, dazzling chandeliers and guilt-edged mirrors.

Rooms 6 (6 smoking) **S** £145-£200; **D** £145-£200 (incl. bkfst)* **Facilities** STV FTV Use of swimming pool & sauna at Empire Hotel (100 yds) New Year Wi-fi **Services** Air con **Parking** 6 **Notes** ⊗ No children 11yrs Closed 20-30 Dec

See advert on this page

St George's
★★★★ 79% ◉ HOTEL

☎ 01492 877544   & 862184   🖹 01492 877788
The Promenade LL30 2LG
e-mail: sales@stgeorgeswales.co.uk
dir: A55-A470, follow to promenade, 0.25m, hotel on corner

This large and impressive seafront property was the first hotel to be built in the town. Restored it to its former glory, the accommodation is of very high quality. Its many Victorian features include the splendid, ornate Wedgwood Room restaurant. The terrace restaurant and main lounges overlook the bay; hot and cold snacks are available all day. Many of the thoughtfully equipped bedrooms enjoy sea views.

Rooms 75 **S** £70-£120; **D** £95-£180 (incl. bkfst)* **Facilities** STV FTV Xmas New Year Wi-fi **Conf** Class 200 Board 45 Thtr 250 Del from £130 to £145* **Services** Lift Air con **Parking** 36 **Notes** LB ⊗ Civ Wed 200

See advert on opposite page

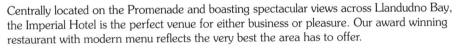

LLANDUDNO *continued*

Imperial

★★★★ 76% HOTEL

☎ 01492 877466 📠 01492 878043
The Promenade LL30 1AP
e-mail: reception@theimperial.co.uk
web: www.theimperial.co.uk
dir: A470 to Llandudno

The Imperial is a large and impressive hotel, situated on the promenade, and within easy reach of the town centre and other amenities. Many of the bedrooms have views over the bay and there are also several suites available. The elegant Chantrey Restaurant offers a fixed-price, monthly-changing menu that utilises local produce.

Rooms 98 (10 fmly) **Facilities** FTV ⓢ Gym Beauty therapist Hairdressing 🎵 Xmas New Year Wi-fi **Conf** Class 50 Board 50 Thtr 150 **Services** Lift **Parking** 25 **Notes** ⊗ Civ Wed 150

See advert on page 645

Empire

★★★★ 73% HOTEL

☎ 01492 860555 📠 01492 860791
Church Walks LL30 2HE
e-mail: reservations@empirehotel.co.uk
web: www.empirehotel.co.uk
dir: From Chester, A55 junct 19 for Llandudno. Follow signs to Promenade, turn right at war memorial & left at rdbt. Hotel 100yds on right

Run by the same family for over almost 60 years, the Empire offers luxuriously appointed bedrooms with every modern facility. The 'Number 72' rooms in an adjacent house are particularly sumptuous. The indoor pool is overlooked by a lounge area where snacks are served all day, and in summer an outdoor pool and roof garden are available. The Watkins restaurant offers an interesting fixed-price menu.

Rooms 54 (8 annexe) (1 fmly) (2 GF) (54 smoking) **S** £65-£85; **D** £95-£120 (incl. bkfst)* **Facilities** STV FTV ⓢ ⅂ Gym Beauty treatments Sauna Steam room Fitness suite New Year Wi-fi **Conf** Class 20 Board 20 Thtr 24 Del from £97.50 to £107.50* **Services** Lift Air con **Parking** 40 **Notes** LB ⊗ Closed 20-30 Dec

See advert on page 645

INSPECTORS' CHOICE

St Tudno Hotel and Restaurant

WELSH RAREBITS

★★★ ⓢⓢ HOTEL

☎ 01492 874411 📠 01492 860407
The Promenade LL30 2LP
e-mail: sttudnohotel@btinternet.com
web: www.st-tudno.co.uk
dir: On Promenade towards pier, hotel opposite pier entrance

A high quality family-owned hotel with friendly, attentive staff, and enjoying fine sea views. The stylish bedrooms are well equipped with mini-bars, robes, satellite TVs and many other thoughtful extras. Public rooms include a lounge, a welcoming bar and a small indoor pool. The Terrace Restaurant, where seasonal and daily-changing menus are offered, has a delightful Mediterranean atmosphere. Afternoon tea is a real highlight.

Rooms 18 (4 fmly) **S** fr £75; **D** £100-£230 (incl. bkfst) **Facilities** FTV ⓢ ⅂ Xmas New Year Wi-fi **Conf** Class 25 Board 20 Thtr 40 Del from £145 **Services** Lift **Parking** 12 **Notes** LB Civ Wed 70

Dunoon

★★★ 81% HOTEL

☎ 01492 860787 📠 01492 860031
Gloddaeth St LL30 2DW
e-mail: reservations@dunoonhotel.co.uk
web: www.dunoonhotel.co.uk
dir: Exit Promenade at war memorial by pier onto wide avenue. 200yds on right

This impressive privately owned hotel is centrally located and offers a variety of styles and sizes of attractive, newly refurbished, well-equipped bedrooms. Elegant public areas include a tastefully appointed restaurant, where competently prepared dishes are served together with a good choice of notable wines that are reasonably priced. The caring and attentive service is noteworthy.

Rooms 49 (7 fmly) **S** £59-£118; **D** £90-£140 (incl. bkfst)* **Facilities** FTV Pool table 🎵 **Services** Lift **Parking** 24 **Notes** LB Closed 22 Dec-early Mar Civ Wed 70

Tynedale

★★★ 77% HOTEL

☎ 01492 877426 📄 01492 871213
Central Promenade LL30 2XS
e-mail: enquiries@tynedalehotel.co.uk
web: www.tynedalehotel.co.uk
dir: on promenade opposite bandstand

Tour groups are well catered for at this privately owned and personally run hotel, and regular live entertainment is a feature. Vibrant modern public areas create a unique and comfortable setting, and an attractive seafront patio garden is an additional asset. Newly refurbished bedrooms provide good comfort levels. The staff provide friendly and efficient service.

Tynedale

Rooms 54 (1 fmly) **S** £37-£50; **D** £74-£118 (incl. bkfst)*
Facilities FTV 🎵 Xmas New Year Wi-fi **Services** Lift
Parking 20 **Notes** LB ⊗

Cae Mor Hotel

★★★ 75% HOTEL

☎ 01442 878101 📄 01492 876545
5-6 Penrhyn Crescent, N LL30 1BA
e-mail: info@caemorhotel.co.uk

Located in a stunning seafront position adjacent to Venue Cwmru, this tastefully renovated Victorian hotel provides a range of thoughtfully furnished bedrooms in minimalist style with smart modern bathrooms. Public areas include a choice of lounges and a stylish restaurant, the setting for imaginative dinners featuring the best of local seasonal produce.

Rooms 25 **Conf** Class 35 Board 28 Thtr 45

Merrion

★★★ 73% HOTEL

☎ 01492 860022 📄 01492 860378
Promenade, South Pde LL30 2LN
e-mail: enquiries@merrion-hotel.co.uk
dir: A55 follow Llandudno signs onto Llandudno Promenade then towards Pier. Hotel close to war memorial

Located on the seafront opposite The Victorian Pier and close to the town centre, this constantly improving owner-managed hotel offers comfortable, well-equipped accommodation; many rooms have sea views. Stylish air-conditioned public areas provide high standards of comfort and regular evening entertainment is a feature.

Rooms 65 (6 fmly) (3 GF) **S** £57-£67; **D** £114-£152 (incl. bkfst)* **Facilities** STV FTV 🎵 Xmas Wi-fi **Conf** Class 40 Board 20 Thtr 30 Del from £90 to £120* **Services** Lift **Parking** 24 **Notes** LB ⊗ Closed Jan

See advert on this page

LLANDUDNO *continued*

Epperstone

★★ 80% SMALL HOTEL

☎ 01492 878746 🖹 01492 871223
15 Abbey Rd LL30 2EE
e-mail: epperstonehotel@btconnect.com
dir: A55-A470 to Mostyn St. Left at rdbt, 4th right into
York Rd. Hotel on junct of York Rd & Abbey Rd

This delightful hotel is located in wonderful gardens in a
residential part of town, within easy walking distance of
the seafront and shopping area. Bedrooms are
attractively decorated and thoughtfully equipped. Two
lounges and a Victorian-style conservatory are available.
A daily changing menu is offered in the bright dining
room.

Rooms 8 (5 fmly) (1 GF) **S** £35-£45; **D** £70-£90 (incl.
bkfst) **Facilities** FTV Xmas Wi-fi **Parking** 8 **Notes** LB No
children 5yrs

Tan Lan Hotel

★★ 80% HOTEL

☎ 01492 860221 🖹 01492 870219
Great Orme's Rd, West Shore LL30 2AR
e-mail: info@tanlanhotel.co.uk
web: www.tanlanhotel.co.uk
dir: Off A55 junct 18 onto A546 signed Deganwy. Approx
3m, straight over mini-rdbt, hotel 50mtrs on left

Located on the quieter West Shore but in easy walking
distance of the pier and central attractions, this owner-
managed hotel provides a range of thoughtfully furnished
bedrooms with smart modern bathrooms. Public areas
include a choice of comfortable lounges and a warm
welcome is assured.

Rooms 17 (1 fmly) (6 GF) **S** £43-£50; **D** £65-£80 (incl.
bkfst)* **Facilities** FTV Xmas Wi-fi **Parking** 13 **Notes** LB ⊗
Closed Nov-mid Mar

Hydro Hotel

★★ 71% HOTEL   *Leisureplex*

☎ 01492 870101 🖹 01492 870992
Neville Crescent LL30 1AT
e-mail: hydro.llandudno@alfatravel.co.uk
dir: Follow signs for theatre to seafront, towards pier.
Hotel near theatre

This large hotel is situated on the promenade overlooking
the sea, and offers good, value-for-money, modern
accommodation. Public areas are quite extensive and
include a choice of lounges, a games/snooker room and a
ballroom where entertainment is provided every night.
The hotel is a popular venue for coach tour parties.

Rooms 120 (4 fmly) (9 GF) **S** £34-£44; **D** £70-£82 (incl.
bkfst)* **Facilities** Table tennis Snooker ♫ Xmas New Year
Conf Class 100 Board 60 Thtr 200 **Services** Lift
Parking 10 **Notes** LB ⊗ Closed Jan-mid Feb RS Nov-Dec
(ex Xmas) & mid Feb-Mar

Esplanade

★★ 68% HOTEL

☎ 0800 318688 & 01492 860300 🖹 01492 860418
Glan-y-Mor Pde, Promenade LL30 2LL
e-mail: info@esplanadehotel.co.uk
web: www.esplanadehotel.co.uk
dir: A55 junct 19 onto A470, follow signs to promenade.
Left towards Great Orme. Hotel 0.5m left

This family owned and run hotel stands on the
promenade, conveniently close to the town centre and
with views of the bay. Bedrooms vary in size and style,
but all have modern equipment and facilities. Public
areas are bright and attractively appointed, and include
a room for functions and conferences. The hotel is
popular with golfers.

Rooms 59 (17 fmly) **S** £20-£50; **D** £40-£100 (incl. bkfst)
Facilities ♫ Xmas New Year Wi-fi **Conf** Class 40
Board 40 Thtr 80 Del from £69 to £99* **Services** Lift
Parking 30 **Notes** LB ⊗ Closed 2-29 Jan

LLANRWST   Map 14 SH86
See also **Betws-y-Coed**

Maenan Abbey

★★★ 78% HOTEL

☎ 01492 660247 🖹 01492 660734
Maenan LL26 0UL
e-mail: reservations@manab.co.uk
dir: 3m N on A470

Set in its own spacious grounds, this privately owned
hotel was built as an abbey in 1850 on the site of a 13th-
century monastery. It is now a popular venue for
weddings as the grounds and magnificent galleried
staircase make an ideal setting for photographs.
Bedrooms include a large suite and are equipped with
modern facilities. Meals are served in the bar and
restaurant.

Rooms 14 (3 fmly) (4 smoking) **Facilities** Fishing Guided
mountain walks Xmas New Year Wi-fi **Conf** Class 30
Board 30 Thtr 50 **Parking** 60 **Notes** LB Civ Wed 55

DENBIGHSHIRE

LLANDEGLA   Map 15 SJ15

Bodidris Hall

★★★ 73% ⊛ COUNTRY HOUSE HOTEL

☎ 01978 790434 🖹 01978 790335
LL11 3AL
e-mail: reception@bodidrishall.com
dir: In village take A5104 towards Chester. Hotel 2m on
left, signed

This impressive manor house is in a quiet location
surrounded by ornamental gardens and mature
woodlands. It has an interesting history and a wealth of
original features including gallery ceilinged bedrooms
and inglenook fireplaces. Quality decor and furnishing
schemes include some fine antique pieces which add to
the intrinsic character of this notable property. Service is
friendly and attentive.

Rooms 9 (1 fmly) **S** £49-£149; **D** £49-£199 (incl. bkfst)*
Facilities Fishing Xmas New Year Wi-fi **Conf** Class 30
Board 30 Thtr 60 Del from £99 to £169 **Parking** 50
Notes LB No children 10yrs Civ Wed 90

RHYL   Map 14 SJ08

Barratt's at Ty'n Rhyl

⊛⊛ RESTAURANT WITH ROOMS

☎ 01745 344138 & 0773 095 4994 🖹 01745 344138
Ty'n Rhyl, 167 Vale Rd LL18 2PH
e-mail: ebarratt5@aol.com
dir: A55 onto A525 to Rhyl, pass Sainsburys & B&Q,
garden centre on left, Barratt's 400yds on right

This delightful 16th-century house lies in a secluded
location surrounded by attractive gardens. The quality of
the food reflects the skill of the owner-chef. Public areas
are smartly furnished and include a panelled lounge and
separate bar with attractive conservatory. Bedrooms are
comfortable and equipped with lots of thoughtful extras.

Rooms 3

RUTHIN — Map 15 SJ15

Ruthin Castle

★★★ 85% ◉◉ HOTEL

☎ 01824 702664 & 703435 📠 01824 705978
LL15 2NU
e-mail: reservations@ruthincastle.co.uk
web: www.ruthincastle.co.uk
dir: A550 to Mold, A494 to Ruthin, hotel at end of Castle St

The main part of this impressive castle was built in the early 19th century, but many ruins in the impressive grounds date back much further. The elegantly panelled public areas include Bertie's Restaurant, furnished in a sumptuous Victorian style and an elegant bar. Many of the refurbished bedrooms are spacious, designed with individual flair and include fine period pieces and superb modern bathrooms. The medieval banqueting hall is a popular venue for special events. Future plans include a new spa.

Rooms 61 (6 fmly) (14 GF) **S** £60-£95; **D** £60-£290 (incl. bkfst)* **Facilities** FTV Fishing Gym Beauty therapy Snooker table ♬ Xmas New Year Wi-fi **Conf** Class 108 Board 48 Thtr 130 Del from £129.50 to £142 **Services** Lift **Parking** 200 **Notes** LB ⊗ Civ Wed 130

The Wynnstay Arms

◉◉ RESTAURANT WITH ROOMS

☎ 01824 703147 📠 01824 705428
Well St LL15 1AN
e-mail: resevations@wynnstayarms.com
web: www.wynnstayarms.com
dir: In town centre

This former town centre period inn has been sympathetically renovated to provide good quality accommodation and a smart café-bar. Imaginative food is served in Fusions Brasserie, where the contemporary decor highlights the many retained period features.

Rooms 7 (1 fmly)

ST ASAPH — Map 15 SJ07

The Oriel

★★★ 81% ◉ HOTEL

☎ 01745 582716 📠 01745 585208
Upper Denbigh Rd LL17 0LW
e-mail: mail@theorielhotel.com
web: www.theorielhotel.com
dir: A55 onto A525, left at cathedral, 1m on right

Set in several acres of mature grounds south of St Asaph, Oriel House offers generally spacious, well-equipped bedrooms and has a friendly and hospitable staff. The Terrace restaurant serves imaginative food with an emphasis on local produce. Extensive function facilities cater for business meetings and weddings, and the leisure club is available to guests.

Rooms 33 (3 fmly) (13 GF) **S** £60-£105; **D** £70-£155 (incl. bkfst) **Facilities** Spa STV FTV ☜ Gym Steam room Sauna Xmas New Year Wi-fi **Conf** Class 100 Board 50 Thtr 220 **Parking** 200 **Notes** LB ⊗ Civ Wed 200

Plas Elwy Hotel & Restaurant

★★ 74% SMALL HOTEL

☎ 01745 582263 & 582089 📠 01745 583864
The Roe LL17 0LT
e-mail: enquiries@plaselwy.co.uk
dir: off A55 junct 27, A525 signed Rhyl/St Asaph. On left opposite Total petrol station

This hotel, which dates back to 1850, has retained much of its original character. Bedrooms in the purpose-built extension are spacious, and one has a four-poster bed; those in the main building are equally well equipped. Public rooms are smart and comfortably furnished and a range of food options is provided in the attractive restaurant.

Rooms 13 (6 annexe) (3 fmly) (2 GF) **Parking** 25 **Notes** LB ⊗ Closed 25 Dec-1 Jan

FLINTSHIRE

HALKYN — Map 15 SJ27

Travelodge Halkyn

BUDGET HOTEL

☎ 0871 984 6078 📠 01352 781966
CH8 8RF
web: www.travelodge.co.uk
dir: on A55, westbound

Travelodge offers good quality, good value, budget accommodation. All offer family rooms sleeping up to four (two adults, two children) with en suite bathroom/shower-room, remote-control TV, tea- and coffee-making facilities and comfortable beds. Food options vary. Breakfast is at the on-site Bar Café restaurant (if available) or to take away. See also Hotel Groups pages.

Rooms 31 **S** fr £29; **D** fr £29

MOLD — Map 15 SJ26

Beaufort Park Hotel

★★★ 74% HOTEL

☎ 01352 758646 📠 01352 757132
Alltami Rd, New Brighton CH7 6RQ
e-mail: info@beaufortparkhotel.co.uk
web: www.beaufortparkhotel.co.uk
dir: A55/A494. Through Alltami lights, over mini rdbt by petrol station towards Mold, A5119. Hotel 100yds on right

This large, modern hotel is conveniently located a short drive from the North Wales Expressway and offers various styles of spacious accommodation. There are extensive public areas, and several meeting and function rooms are available. There is a wide choice of meals in the formal restaurant and in the popular Arches bar.

Rooms 106 (8 fmly) (32 GF) **S** £95; **D** £110 (incl. bkfst) **Facilities** FTV Squash ♬ Xmas New Year Wi-fi **Conf** Class 120 Board 120 Thtr 250 **Parking** 200 **Notes** LB Civ Wed 250

NORTHOP HALL — Map 15 SJ26

Northop Hall Country House

★★★ 77% HOTEL

WELSH RAREBITS

☎ 01244 816181 📠 01244 814661
Chester Rd CH7 6HJ
e-mail: northop@hotel-chester.com
web: www.hotel-chester.com
dir: From Buckley/St David's Park 3rd exit at rdbt, 1st right to Northop Hall 2m. Left at mini-rdbt, 200yds on left

Located in large grounds and woodland, this sympathetically renovated and extended period house retains many original features in the public areas, and is a popular conference and wedding venue. Bedrooms provide both practical and thoughtful extras and a warm welcome is assured.

Rooms 39 (15 fmly) **S** £69-£85; **D** £85-£120 (incl. bkfst) **Facilities** STV FTV Beauty therapy ♬ Xmas New Year Wi-fi **Conf** Class 40 Board 50 Thtr 80 **Parking** 70 **Notes** LB Civ Wed 80

NORTHOP HALL *continued*

Holiday Inn A55 Chester West

★★★ 70% HOTEL

☎ 01244 550011 🖷 01244 550763
Gateway Services, Westbound A55 CH7 6HB
e-mail: bookings@holidayinnchesterwest.co.uk
web: www.holidayinn.co.uk
dir: M6 junct 20, M56 to Queensferry, follow signs for A55/Conwy. Hotel 500yds past A494 slip road

Conveniently located on the A55 close to Chester and North Wales, this hotel has a wide choice of bedrooms; all are equipped with modern amenities including Wi-fi. The master suite is sumptuously decorated with a feature bathroom and mezzanine. There is a mini gym, an attractive conservatory restaurant and a banqueting suite.

Rooms 81 (19 fmly) (31 GF) **S** £39-£99; **D** £39-£99
Facilities STV Gym New Year Wi-fi **Conf** Class 130 Board 60 Thtr 220 Del from £102.50 to £109 **Services** Lift Air con **Parking** 152 **Notes** LB ⊗ Closed 24-25 Dec Civ Wed 220

Travelodge Chester Northop Hall

BUDGET HOTEL

☎ 0871 984 6091 🖷 01244 816473
CH7 6HB
web: www.travelodge.co.uk
dir: on A55, eastbound

Travelodge offers good quality, good value, budget accommodation. All offer family rooms sleeping up to four (two adults, two children) with en suite bathroom/shower-room, remote-control TV, tea- and coffee-making facilities and comfortable beds. Food options vary. Breakfast is at the on-site Bar Café restaurant (if available) or to take away. See also Hotel Groups pages.

Rooms 40 **S** fr £29; **D** fr £29

GWYNEDD

ABERSOCH
Map 14 SH32

Porth Tocyn

★★★ 80% ⑯⑯ COUNTRY HOUSE HOTEL

☎ 01758 713303 & 07789 994942 🖷 01758 713538
Bwlch Tocyn LL53 7BU
e-mail: bookings@porthtocyn.fsnet.co.uk
web: www.porth-tocyn-hotel.co.uk
dir: 2.5m S follow Porth Tocyn signs after Sarnbach

Located above Cardigan Bay with fine views over the area, Porth Tocyn is set in attractive gardens. Several elegantly furnished sitting rooms are provided and bedrooms are comfortably furnished. Children are especially welcome and have a playroom. Award-winning food is served in the restaurant.

Rooms 17 (1 fmly) (3 GF) **S** £65-£80; **D** £90-£170 (incl. bkfst)* **Facilities** ⌇ ⌇ Table tennis Wi-fi Child facilities **Parking** 50 **Notes** LB Closed mid Nov-wk before Etr RS some off season nights

See advert on this page

Neigwl

★★ 81% ⑯ HOTEL

☎ 01758 712363 🖷 01758 712544
Lon Sarn Bach LL53 7DY
e-mail: relax@neigwl.com
web: www.neigwl.com
dir: on A499, through Abersoch, hotel on left

This delightful, small hotel is privately owned and personally run. It is conveniently located for access to the town, harbour and beach. It has a deservedly high reputation for its food and warm hospitality. Both the attractive restaurant and the pleasant lounge bar overlook the sea, as do several of the tastefully appointed bedrooms.

Rooms 9 (2 fmly) (2 GF) **Parking** 20 **Notes** LB ⊗ Closed Jan

BANGOR
Map 14 SH57

Travelodge Bangor

BUDGET HOTEL

☎ 0871 984 6061 🖷 0870 1911561
Llys-y-Gwynt LL57 4BG
web: www.travelodge.co.uk
dir: at junct of A5 & A55

Travelodge offers good quality, good value, budget accommodation. All offer family rooms sleeping up to four (two adults, two children) with en suite bathroom/shower-room, remote-control TV, tea- and coffee-making facilities and comfortable beds. Food options vary. Breakfast is at the on-site Bar Café restaurant (if available) or to take away. See also Hotel Groups pages.

Rooms 82 **S** fr £29; **D** fr £29

BARMOUTH — Map 14 SH61

Bae Abermaw
WELSH RAREBITS

★★★ 82% ◉ HOTEL

☎ 01341 280550 📄 01341 280346
Panorama Hill LL42 1DQ
e-mail: enquiries@baeabermaw.com
web: www.baeabermaw.com
dir: Off A496 above Barmouth Bridge

Situated on attractive landscaped grounds in an elevated position overlooking the sea, this impressive Victorian house has been sympathetically renovated to provide high standards of comfort and facilities. The interior is furnished and decorated in minimalist style and many bedrooms have stunning views.

Rooms 14 (4 fmly) **Facilities** Xmas New Year Wi-fi **Conf** Class 75 Board 20 Thtr 100 **Parking** 35 **Notes** ⊗ Civ Wed 100

BEDDGELERT — Map 14 SH54

The Royal Goat
THE CIRCLE

★★★ 77% HOTEL

☎ 01766 890224 📄 01766 890422
LL55 4YE
e-mail: info@royalgoathotel.co.uk
web: www.royalgoathotel.co.uk
dir: On A498 at Beddgelert

An impressive building steeped in history, the Royal Goat provides well-equipped accommodation, and carries out an annual programme of refurbishment that has included the smart, modern bathrooms. Attractively appointed, comfortable public areas include a choice of bars and restaurants, a residents' lounge and function rooms.

Rooms 32 (4 fmly) **S** £45-£60; **D** £75-£98 (incl. bkfst)* **Facilities** FTV Fishing Xmas New Year **Conf** Class 70 Board 30 Thtr 70 **Services** Lift **Parking** 100 **Notes** LB Closed Jan-1 Mar RS Nov-1 Jan

CAERNARFON — Map 14 SH46

INSPECTORS' CHOICE

Seiont Manor
HandPICKED

★★★ ◉◉ COUNTRY HOUSE HOTEL

☎ 01286 673366 📄 01286 672840
Llanrug LL55 2AQ
e-mail: seiontmanor@handpicked.co.uk
web: www.handpicked.co.uk
dir: E on A4086, 2.5m from Caernarfon

A splendid hotel created from authentic rural buildings, set in the tranquil countryside near Snowdonia. Bedrooms are individually decorated and well equipped, with luxurious extra touches. Public rooms are cosy and comfortable and furnished in country-house style. The kitchen team use the best of local produce to provide exciting takes on traditional dishes.

Rooms 28 (2 fmly) (14 GF) **S** £70-£135; **D** £80-£155 (incl. bkfst)* **Facilities** STV ⊙ Fishing Gym Xmas New Year Wi-fi **Conf** Class 40 Board 40 Thtr 100 Del from £125 to £145* **Parking** 60 **Notes** LB ⊗ Civ Wed 90

Celtic Royal Hotel

★★★ 79% HOTEL

☎ 01286 674477 📄 01286 674139
Bangor St LL55 1AY
e-mail: admin@celtic-royal.co.uk
web: www.celtic-royal.co.uk
dir: Exit A55 at Bangor. Follow A487 towards Caernarfon

This large, impressive, privately owned hotel is situated in the town centre. It provides attractively appointed accommodation, which includes bedrooms for less able guests and also family rooms. The spacious public areas include a bar, a choice of lounges and a pleasant split-level restaurant. Guests also have the use of the impressive health club.

Rooms 110 (12 fmly) **Facilities** ⊙ Gym Sun shower Steam room Sauna ♬ Xmas New Year **Conf** Class 120 Board 120 Thtr 300 Del from £109 to £115* **Services** Lift **Parking** 180 **Notes** ⊗ Civ Wed 200

Travelodge Caernarfon

Travelodge

BUDGET HOTEL

☎ 0871 984 6426 📄 01286 675228
Balaclava Rd LL55 1SR
dir: From A487 at main rdbt, near Morrisons superstore, follow Parking for Town Centre sign & brown tourist sign for Doc Victoria. At mini rdbt 1st exit into Balaclafa Rd. Lodge on right

Travelodge offers good quality, good value, budget accommodation. All offer family rooms sleeping up to four (two adults, two children) with en suite bathroom/shower-room, remote-control TV, tea- and coffee-making facilities and comfortable beds. Food options vary. Breakfast is at the on-site Bar Café restaurant (if available) or to take away. See also the Hotel Groups pages.

Rooms 59 **S** fr £29; **D** fr £29

CAERNARFON *continued*

Rhiwafallen Restaurant with Rooms

◉◉ RESTAURANT WITH ROOMS

☎ 01286 830172
Rhiwafallen, LLandwrog LL54 5SW
e-mail: ktandrobjohn@aol.com

Located south of Caernarfon on the Llyn Peninsula link, this former farmhouse has been tastefully renovated to provide high levels of comfort and facilities. Quality bedrooms are furnished in minimalist style with a wealth of thoughtful extras. The original modern art in public areas adds vibrancy to the interior. Warm hospitality and imaginative cooking ensure a memorable stay at this owner-managed establishment.

Rooms 5

| CRICCIETH | Map 14 SH43 |

Bron Eifion Country House

★★★ 86% ◉ COUNTRY HOUSE HOTEL

☎ 01766 522385 ▤ 01766 523796
LL52 0SA
e-mail: enquiries@broneifion.co.uk
dir: A497 between Porthmadog & Pwllheli, 0.5m from Criccieth, on right towards Pwhelli

This delightful country house built in 1883, is set in extensive grounds to the west of Criccieth. Now a privately owned and personally run hotel, it provides warm and very friendly hospitality as well as attentive service. The interior style highlights the many retained period features; there is a choice of lounges and the very impressive central hall features a minstrels' gallery.

Rooms 19 (1 fmly) (1 GF) **S** £95–£120; **D** £130–£180 (incl. bkfst)* **Facilities** FTV Xmas New Year Wi-fi **Conf** Class 40 Board 40 Thtr 50 Del from £140 to £170* **Parking** 50 **Notes** ⊗ Civ Wed 50

George IV

★★ 62% HOTEL

 Leisureplex

☎ 01766 522168 ▤ 01766 523340
23-25 High St LL52 0BS
e-mail: georgiv.criccieth@alfatravel.co.uk
dir: On A497 in town centre

This hotel which stands back from the A497 in the town centre. Generally spacious bedrooms are attractively furnished and equipped to meet the needs of both business guests and holidaymakers. George's Brasserie serves a menu based on locally sourced ingredients.

Rooms 47 (11 fmly) **Facilities** FTV ♪ Xmas New Year **Services** Lift **Parking** 16 **Notes** LB ⊗ Closed Jan RS Nov & Feb-Mar

| DOLGELLAU | Map 14 SH71 |

Penmaenuchaf Hall

 WELSH RAREBITS

★★★ ◉◉ COUNTRY HOUSE HOTEL

☎ 01341 422129 ▤ 01341 422787
Penmaenpool LL40 1YB
e-mail: relax@penhall.co.uk
web: www.penhall.co.uk
dir: Off A470 onto A493 to Tywyn. Hotel approx 1m

Built in 1860, this impressive hall stands in 20 acres of formal gardens, grounds and woodland, and enjoys magnificent views across the River Mawddach. Sympathetic restoration has created a comfortable and welcoming hotel with spacious day rooms and thoughtfully furnished bedrooms, some with private balconies. Fresh produce cooked in modern British style is served in an elegant conservatory restaurant, overlooking the countryside.
AA Hotel of the Year for Wales 2009-10.

Rooms 14 (2 fmly) **S** £95–£145; **D** £150–£230 (incl. bkfst)* **Facilities** STV FTV Fishing ⚐ Complimentary salmon & trout fishing Xmas New Year **Conf** Class 30 Board 22 Thtr 50 **Parking** 30 **Notes** LB No children 6yrs Civ Wed 50

Dolserau Hall

★★★ 81% ◉ HOTEL

☎ 01341 422522 ▤ 01341 422400
LL40 2AG
e-mail: welcome@dolserau.co.uk
web: www.dolserau.co.uk
dir: 1.5m outside Dolgellau between A494 to Bala & A470 to Dinas Mawddy

This privately owned, friendly hotel lies in attractive grounds that extend to the river and are surrounded by green fields. Several comfortable lounges are provided and welcoming log fires are lit during cold weather. The smart bedrooms are spacious, well equipped and comfortable. A varied menu offers very competently prepared dishes.

Rooms 20 (5 annexe) (1 fmly) (3 GF) **S** £70–£88; **D** £140–£210 (incl. bkfst & dinner)* **Facilities** Fishing Xmas New Year **Services** Lift **Parking** 40 **Notes** No children 10yrs Closed Dec-Jan (ex Xmas & New Year)

Royal Ship

★★ 74% HOTEL

☎ 01341 422209 ▤ 01341 424693
Queens Square LL40 1AR
e-mail: royal.ship.hotel@btconnect.com
dir: In town centre

This establishment dates from 1813 when it was a coaching inn. There are three bars and several lounges, all comfortably furnished and attractively appointed. It is very much the centre of local activities and a wide range of food is served. Well equipped bedrooms include family rooms. A secure car park is also available.

Rooms 24 (4 fmly) **S** £35–£60; **D** £70–£97.50 (incl. bkfst)* **Facilities** Fishing arranged Xmas New Year **Conf** Class 60 Board 60 Thtr 80 Del from £70 to £90* **Parking** 12 **Notes** LB ⊗

| LLANBEDR | Map 14 SH52 |

Ty Mawr

★★ 71% SMALL HOTEL

☎ 01341 241440 ▤ 01341 241440
LL45 2NH
e-mail: tymawrhotel@onetel.com
web: www.tymawrhotel.org.uk
dir: from Barmouth A496 (Harlech road). In Llanbedr turn right after bridge, hotel 50yds on left, brown tourist signs on junct

Located in a picturesque village, this family-run hotel has a relaxed, friendly atmosphere. The attractive grounds opposite the River Artro provide a popular beer garden during fine weather. The attractive, rustically furnished bar offers a blackboard selection of food and a good choice of real ales. A more formal menu is available in the restaurant. Bedrooms are smart and brightly decorated.

Rooms 10 (2 fmly) **S** £35–£50; **D** £70–£80 (incl. bkfst)* **Facilities** STV **Conf** Class 25 **Parking** 30 **Notes** Closed 24-26 Dec

LLANBERIS
Map 14 SH56

Legacy Royal Victoria

★★★ 70% HOTEL

☎ 0870 832 9903 📠 0870 832 9904
LL55 4TY
e-mail: res-royalvictoria@legacy-hotels.co.uk
web: www.legacy-hotels.co.uk
dir: on A4086 (Caernarfon to Llanberis road), directly opposite Snowdon Mountain Railway

This well-established hotel sits near the foot of Snowdon, between the Peris and Padarn lakes. Pretty gardens and grounds make an attractive setting for the many weddings held here. Bedrooms are well equipped. There are spacious lounges and bars, and a large dining room with a conservatory looking out over the lakes.

Rooms 106 (7 fmly) Facilities STV Mountaineering Cycling Walking ♬ Xmas New Year Conf Class 60 Board 50 Thtr 100 Services Lift Parking 100 Notes LB Civ Wed 100

PORTHMADOG
Map 14 SH53

Royal Sportsman

★★★ 75% HOTEL

☎ 01766 512015 📠 01766 512490
131 High St LL49 9HB
e-mail: enquiries@royalsportsman.co.uk
dir: By rdbt, at A497 & A487 junct

Ideally located in the centre of Porthmadog, this former coaching inn dates from the Victorian era and has been restored into a friendly, privately owned and personally run hotel. Rooms are tastefully decorated and well equipped, and some are in an annexe close to the hotel. There is a large comfortable lounge and a wide range of meals is served in the bar or restaurant.

Rooms 28 (9 annexe) (7 fmly) (9 GF) S £55-£80; D £84-£95 (incl. bkfst)* Facilities STV FTV Xmas New Year Wi-fi Conf Class 50 Board 30 Thtr 50 Parking 17 Notes LB

Travelodge Porthmadog

BUDGET HOTEL

☎ 0871 984 6421 📠 01766 514 049
Ffordd Penamswer LL49 9NY
dir: From A487 onto A498 for approx 0.5m. At road end turn left onto A497. Lodge on left in 1m

Travelodge offers good quality, good value, budget accommodation. All offer family rooms sleeping up to four (two adults, two children) with en suite bathroom/shower-room, remote-control TV, tea- and coffee-making facilities and comfortable beds. Food options vary. Breakfast is at the on-site Bar Café restaurant (if available) or to take away. See also the Hotel Groups pages.

Rooms 51 S fr £29; D fr £29

PORTMEIRION
Map 14 SH53

The Hotel Portmeirion
WELSH RAREBITS

★★★★ 77% ⊛⊛ HOTEL

☎ 01766 770000 📠 01766 770300
LL48 6ET
e-mail: hotel@portmeirion-village.com
web: www.portmeirion-village.com
dir: 2m W, Portmeirion village is S off A487

Saved from dereliction in the 1920s by Clough Williams-Ellis, the elegant Hotel Portmeirion enjoys one of the finest settings in Wales, located beneath the wooded slopes of the village, overlooking the sandy estuary towards Snowdonia. Many rooms have private sitting rooms and balconies with spectacular views. The mostly Welsh-speaking staff provide a good mix of warm hospitality and efficient service.

Rooms 42 (28 annexe) (4 fmly) Facilities STV ⚲ ⚲ Xmas New Year Wi-fi Conf Class 40 Board 30 Thtr 100 Parking 40 Notes ⊗ Civ Wed 130

Castell Deudraeth
WELSH RAREBITS

★★★★ 76% ⊛ HOTEL

☎ 01766 770000 📠 01766 771771
LL48 6EN
e-mail: castell@portmeirion-village.com
web: www.portmeirion-village.com
dir: A4212 for Trawsfynydd/Porthmadog. 1.5m beyond Penrhyndeudraeth, hotel on right

A castellated mansion that overlooks Snowdonia and the famous Italianate village featured in the 1960's cult series The Prisoner. An original concept, Castell Deudraeth combines traditional materials, such as oak and slate, with state-of-the-art technology and design. Dynamically styled bedrooms boast underfloor heating, real-flame gas fires, wide-screen TVs with DVDs and cinema surround-sound. The brasserie-themed dining room provides an informal option at dinner.

Rooms 11 (5 fmly) Facilities ⚲ ⚲ ♬ Xmas New Year Wi-fi Conf Class 18 Board 25 Thtr 30 Services Lift Air con Parking 30 Notes ⊗ Civ Wed 30

MERTHYR TYDFIL

MERTHYR TYDFIL
Map 9 SO00

Tregenna

★★ 🅰

☎ 01685 723627 & 382055 📠 01685 721951
Park Ter CF47 8RF
e-mail: reception@tregennahotel.co.uk
dir: M4 junct 32, onto A465 follow signs for Merthyr Tydfil signed from town centre

Rooms 21 (6 fmly) (7 GF) S £50-£55; D £60-£65 (incl. bkfst)* Facilities Wi-fi Parking 12 Notes LB

Travelodge Merthyr Tydfil

BUDGET HOTEL

☎ 0871 984 6371
Merthyr Tydfil Leisure Village CF48 1UT
dir: M4, junct 32, A470. Lodge off 3rd rdbt. Or from N on A470 pass retail park on left. Lodge off next rdbt

Travelodge offers good quality, good value, budget accommodation. All offer family rooms sleeping up to four (two adults, two children) with en suite bathroom/shower-room, remote-control TV, tea- and coffee-making facilities and comfortable beds. Food options vary. Breakfast is at the on-site Bar Café restaurant (if available) or to take away. See also the Hotel Groups pages.

Rooms 58 S fr £29; D fr £29

MONMOUTHSHIRE

ABERGAVENNY
Map 9 SO21

Llansantffraed Court
WELSH RAREBITS

★★★ 80% ⊛⊛ COUNTRY HOUSE HOTEL

☎ 01873 840678 📠 01873 840674
Llanvihangel Gobion, Clytha NP7 9BA
e-mail: reception@llch.co.uk
web: www.llch.co.uk
dir: At A465/A40 Abergavenny junct take B4598 signed Usk (do not join A40). Continue towards Raglan, hotel on left in 4.5m

In a commanding position and in its own extensive grounds, this very impressive property, now a privately owned country-house hotel, has enviable views of the Brecon Beacons. Extensive public areas include a relaxing lounge and a spacious restaurant offering imaginative and enjoyable dishes. Bedrooms are comfortably furnished and have modern facilities.

Rooms 21 (1 fmly) S £85-£97; D £115-£175 (incl. bkfst) Facilities STV FTV ⚲ Putt green Fishing ⚲ Clay pigeon shooting school Wi-fi Conf Class 120 Board 100 Thtr 220 Del from £140 to £190 Services Lift Parking 250 Notes LB Civ Wed 150

ABERGAVENNY *continued*

Angel

★★★ 77% ⊛ HOTEL

☎ 01873 857121 📄 01873 858059
15 Cross St NP7 5EN
e-mail: mail@angelhotelabergavenny.com
web: www.angelhotelabergavenny.com
dir: Follow town centre signs from rdbt, S of Abergavenny, past rail & bus stations. Turn left along side of hotel

Once a coaching inn this has long been a popular venue for both local people and visitors; the two traditional function rooms and a ballroom are in regular use. In addition there is a comfortable lounge, a relaxed bar and a smart, award-winning restaurant. In warmer weather there is a central courtyard that is ideal for alfresco eating. The bedrooms include a four-poster room and some that are suitable for families.

Rooms 32 (3 annexe) (2 fmly) **S** £65-£100; **D** £85-£130 (incl. bkfst)* **Facilities** ♫ Xmas New Year Wi-fi **Conf** Class 120 Board 60 Thtr 200 **Parking** 30 **Notes** LB Closed 25 Dec RS 24, 26 & 27 Dec Civ Wed 200

Llanwenarth Hotel & Riverside Restaurant

WELSH RAREBITS

★★ 79% HOTEL

☎ 01873 810550 📄 01873 811880
Brecon Rd NP8 1EP
e-mail: info@llanwenarthhotel.com
web: www.llanwenarthhotel.com
dir: A40 from Abergavenny towards Brecon. Hotel 3m past hospital on left

Dating from the 16th century and set in magnificent scenery, this delightful hotel offers guests the chance to relax and unwind in style. Bedrooms, in a detached wing, offer plenty of quality and comfort plus pleasant river views; many have a private balcony. The airy conservatory lounge and restaurant offer a varied selection of carefully prepared dishes.

Rooms 17 (3 fmly) (7 GF) **Facilities** Fishing **Parking** 30 **Notes** ⊗

CHEPSTOW	Map 4 ST59

Marriott St Pierre Hotel & Country Club

Marriott HOTELS & RESORTS

★★★★ 80% HOTEL

☎ 01291 625261 📄 01291 629975
St Pierre Park NP16 6YA
e-mail: mhrs.cwlgs.frontdesk@marriotthotels.com
web: www.marriottstpierre.co.uk
dir: M48 junct 2. At rdbt on slip road take A466 Chepstow. At next rdbt take 1st exit Caerwent A48. Hotel approx 2m on left

This 14th-century property offers an extensive range of leisure and conference facilities. Bedrooms are well equipped, comfortable and located in adjacent wings or in a lakeside cottage complex. The main bar, popular with golfers, overlooks the 18th green, whilst diners can choose between an elegant and traditional restaurant and a modern brasserie.

Rooms 148 (16 fmly) (75 GF) (4 smoking) **S** £89-£209; **D** £99-£219 (incl. bkfst)* **Facilities** Spa STV 🏊 ⚓ 36 🏌 Putt green Fishing 🛶 Gym Chipping green Floodlit driving range Health spa Sauna Steam room Xmas New Year Wi-fi Child facilities **Conf** Class 120 Board 90 Thtr 240 Del from £120 to £185 **Parking** 440 **Notes** LB ⊗ Civ Wed 220

Castle View

★★★ 64% HOTEL

☎ 01291 620349 📄 01291 627397
16 Bridge St NP16 5EZ
e-mail: castleviewhotel@btconnect.com
dir: M48 junct 2, A466 for Wye Valley, at 1st rdbt right onto A48 towards Gloucester. Follow 2nd sign to town centre, then to Chepstow Castle, hotel directly opposite

This hotel was built around 300 years ago and offers unrivalled views of Chepstow Castle. Accommodation is comfortable - there are family rooms, double-bedded rooms, and some bedrooms that are situated in a separate building; a good range of extras for guest comfort are provided. There is a cosy bar area and a small restaurant where home-cooked food using fresh, local ingredients is offered.

Rooms 13 (4 annexe) (7 fmly) **S** £45-£60; **D** £70-£85 (incl. bkfst) **Facilities** Xmas New Year Wi-fi **Notes** LB

See advert on this page

MAGOR SERVICE AREA (M4)   Map 9 ST48

Travelodge Newport Magor
BUDGET HOTEL

☎ 0871 984 6336   ⌁ 01633 881896
Magor Service Area NP26 3YL
web: www.travelodge.co.uk
dir: At M4 junct 23a

Travelodge offers good quality, good value, budget accommodation. All offer family rooms sleeping up to four (two adults, two children) with en suite bathroom/shower-room, remote-control TV, tea- and coffee-making facilities and comfortable beds. Food options vary. Breakfast is at the on-site Bar Café restaurant (if available) or to take away. See also Hotel Groups pages.

Rooms 43 **S** fr £29; **D** fr £29

RAGLAN   Map 9 SO40

The Beaufort Arms Coaching Inn & Restaurant
WELSH RAREBITS
★★★ 75% ◉ HOTEL

☎ 01291 690412   ⌁ 01291 690935
High St NP15 2DY
e-mail: enquiries@beaufortraglan.co.uk
web: www.beaufortraglan.co.uk
dir: M4 junct 24, A449/A40 junct Monmouth/Abergavenny, 0.5m into village opposite church

This friendly, family-run village inn dating back to the 15th century has historic links with nearby Raglan Castle. The bright, stylish and beautifully appointed bedrooms in the main house are suitably equipped for both tourists and business guests. Food is served in either the Brasserie restaurant or traditional lounge, and both offer a relaxed service with an enjoyable selection of carefully prepared dishes.

Rooms 15 (5 annexe) (1 fmly) (5 GF) **S** fr £60; **D** £75-£105 (incl. bkfst)* **Facilities** Use of facilities at Golf club in village Wi-fi **Conf** Class 60 Board 30 Thtr 120 Del from £85 to £110* **Parking** 30 **Notes** LB ⊗ RS 25-26 Dec

Travelodge Monmouth
BUDGET HOTEL

☎ 0871 984 6232   ⌁ 01600 740329
Moto Service Area, A40 Northbound NP25 4BG
web: www.travelodge.co.uk
dir: On A40 near junct with A449

Travelodge offers good quality, good value, budget accommodation. All offer family rooms sleeping up to four (two adults, two children) with en suite bathroom/shower-room, remote-control TV, tea- and coffee-making facilities and comfortable beds. Food options vary. Breakfast is at the on-site Bar Café restaurant (if available) or to take away. See also Hotel Groups pages.

Rooms 43 **S** fr £29; **D** fr £29

ROCKFIELD   Map 9 SO41

The Stonemill & Steppes Farm Cottages
◉◉ RESTAURANT WITH ROOMS

☎ 01600 775424
NP25 5SW
e-mail: michelle@thestonemill.co.uk
dir: A48 to Monmouth, B4233 to Rockfield. 2.6m from Monmouth town centre

Located in a small hamlet just west of Monmouth, close to the Forest of Dean and the Wye Valley, this operation offers accommodation comprising six very well-appointed cottages. The comfortable rooms (for self-catering or on a B&B basis) are architect designed and lovingly restored with many of the original features remaining. This location is also handy for golfers with a choice of many courses in the area. In a separate, converted 16th-century barn is the Stonemill Restaurant with oak beams, vaulted ceilings and an old cider press. Breakfast is served in the cottages on request.

Rooms 6 (6 fmly)

SKENFRITH   Map 9 SO42

INSPECTORS' CHOICE

The Bell at Skenfrith
◉◉ RESTAURANT WITH ROOMS

☎ 01600 750235   ⌁ 01600 750525
NP7 8UH
e-mail: enquiries@skenfrith.co.uk
web: www.skenfrith.co.uk
dir: On B4521 in Skenfrith, opposite castle

The Bell is a beautifully restored, 17th-century former coaching inn which still retains much of its original charm and character. It is peacefully situated on the banks of the Monnow, a tributary of the River Wye, and is ideally placed for exploring the numerous delights of the area. Natural materials have been used to create a relaxing atmosphere, while the bedrooms, which include full suites and rooms with four-poster beds, are stylish, luxurious and equipped with DVD players. AA Wine Award for Wales 2009-10.

Rooms 11 (2 fmly)

TINTERN PARVA   Map 4 SO50

Best Western Royal George
★★★ 73% HOTEL

☎ 01291 689205   ⌁ 01291 689448
Wye Valley Rd NP16 6SF
e-mail: royalgeorgetintern@hotmail.com
web: www.bw-royalgeorgehotel.co.uk
dir: off M48/A466, 4m to Tintern, 2nd on left

This privately owned and personally run hotel provides comfortable, spacious accommodation, including

bedrooms with balconies overlooking the well-tended garden and there are a number of ground-floor bedrooms. The public areas include a lounge bar and a large function room. A varied and popular menu choice is available in either the bar or restaurant. An ideal place to stay for exploring the counties of Monmouthshire and Herefordshire.

Rooms 15 (14 annexe) (6 fmly) (10 GF) **S** £55-£95; **D** £65-£105 (incl. bkfst)* **Facilities** STV Xmas New Year Wi-fi **Conf** Class 40 Board 30 Thtr 100 Del from £95 to £135* **Parking** 50 **Notes** LB Civ Wed 70

USK   Map 9 SO30

Glen-yr-Afon House
★★★ 79% HOTEL

☎ 01291 672302 & 673202   ⌁ 01291 672597
Pontypool Rd NP15 1SY
e-mail: enquiries@glen-yr-afon.co.uk
web: www.glen-yr-afon.co.uk
dir: A472 through High St, over river bridge, follow to right. Hotel 200yds on left

On the edge of this delightful old market town, Glen-yr-Afon, a unique Victorian villa, offers all the facilities expected of a modern hotel combined with the warm atmosphere of a family home. Bedrooms are furnished to a high standard and several overlook the well-tended gardens. There is a choice of comfortable sitting areas and a stylish and spacious banqueting suite.

Rooms 27 (2 fmly) **S** £94-£118; **D** £136-£159 (incl. bkfst)* **Facilities** STV FTV ⌁ Complimentary access to Usk Tennis Club New Year Wi-fi **Conf** Class 200 Board 30 Thtr 100 Del from £110 to £130* **Services** Lift **Parking** 101 **Notes** LB Civ Wed 200

USK *continued*

The Newbridge

⊛ RESTAURANT WITH ROOMS

☎ 01633 451000 🖹 01633 451001
Tredunnock NP15 1LY
e-mail: newbridge@evanspubs.co.uk

This 200-year-old inn stands alongside a flowing river and provides a peaceful escape to the country. The main inn and restaurant offer tables and seating on two levels as well as some outdoor seating for warmer months. Bedrooms are located in an adjacent building and have a well furnished, contemporary style. A good selection of dishes utilising fresh local produce is served in the main restaurant at both lunch and dinner.

Rooms 6

WHITEBROOK	Map 4 SO50

INSPECTORS' CHOICE

The Crown at Whitebrook
⊛⊛ RESTAURANT WITH ROOMS

☎ 01600 860254 🖹 01600 860607
NP25 4TX
e-mail: info@crownatwhitebrook.co.uk
dir: 4m from Monmouth on B4293, left at sign to Whitebrook, 2m on unmarked road, Crown on right

In a secluded spot in the wooded valley of the River Wye, this former drover's cottage dates back to the 17th century. Refurbished individually decorated bedrooms boast a contemporary feel with smart modern facilities. The restaurant and lounge combine many original features with a bright fresh look. Memorable cuisine features locally sourced ingredients skilfully prepared.

Rooms 8

NEATH PORT TALBOT

NEATH	Map 9 SS79

Castle Hotel

★★★ 70% HOTEL

☎ 01639 641119 🖹 01639 641624
The Parade SA11 1RB
e-mail: info@castlehotelneath.co.uk
web: www.castlehotelneath.co.uk
dir: M4 junct 43, follow signs for Neath, 500yds past rail station, hotel on right. Car park on left in 50yds

Situated in the town centre, this Georgian property, once a coaching inn, has a wealth of history and character. Lord Nelson and Lady Hamilton are reputed to have stayed here, and it is where the Welsh Rugby Union was founded in 1881. The hotel provides well-equipped accommodation and pleasant public areas. Bedrooms include family bedded rooms and one with a four-poster bed. Function and meeting rooms are available.

Rooms 29 (3 fmly) (14 smoking) **S** £45-£60; **D** £60-£80 (incl. bkfst) **Facilities** STV New Year Wi-fi **Conf** Class 75 Board 50 Thtr 160 Del from £64 to £95 **Parking** 26 **Notes** LB ⊗ Civ Wed 120

PORT TALBOT	Map 9 SS78

Best Western Aberavon Beach

★★★ 75% HOTEL

☎ 01639 884949 🖹 01639 897885
Neath SA12 6QP
e-mail: sales@aberavonbeach.com
web: www.aberavonbeach.com
dir: M4 junct 41/A48 & follow signs for Aberavon Beach & Hollywood Park

This friendly, purpose-built hotel enjoys a prominent position on the seafront overlooking Swansea Bay. Bedrooms, many with sea views, are comfortably appointed and thoughtfully equipped. Public areas include a leisure suite with swimming pool, open-plan bar and restaurant plus a choice of function rooms.

Rooms 52 (6 fmly) **S** £50-£120; **D** £60-£130 (incl. bkfst) **Facilities** FTV ⓢ All weather leisure centre Sauna ♬ Xmas New Year Wi-fi **Conf** Class 200 Board 100 Thtr 300 **Services** Lift **Parking** 150 **Notes** LB Civ Wed 300

See advert on page 665

NEWPORT

NEWPORT	Map 9 ST38

See also **Cwmbran (Torfaen)**

The Celtic Manor Resort

★★★★★ 85% ⊛⊛⊛ HOTEL

☎ 01633 413000 🖹 01633 412910
Coldra Woods NP18 1HQ
e-mail: postbox@celtic-manor.com
web: www.celtic-manor.com
dir: M4 junct 24, take B4237 towards Newport. Hotel 1st on right

This hotel is in the outstanding Celtic Manor Resort (home to the 2010 Ryder Cup). Here there are three challenging golf courses, a huge convention centre, superb leisure clubs and two hotels (see also entry below). This hotel has excellent bedrooms, including suites and two Presidential Suites, offering good space and comfort; stylish and extensive public areas are set around a spectacular atrium lobby that includes several eating options. The Crown at Celtic Manor resort is the award-winning, fine dining restaurant.

Rooms 400 (34 fmly) **S** £240-£1500; **D** £240-£1500 **Facilities** Spa STV FTV ⓢ ♨ 54 ♨ Putt green Gym Golf Academy Clay pigeon shooting Mountain bike trails Art gallery Table tennis ♬ Xmas New Year Wi-fi Child facilities **Conf** Class 150 Board 60 Thtr 1200 **Services** Lift Air con **Parking** 1300 **Notes** LB ⊗ Civ Wed 100

Manor House

★★★★ 73% HOTEL

☎ 01633 413000 🖹 01633 410236
The Celtic Manor Resort, Coldra Woods NP18 1HQ
e-mail: bookings@celtic-manor.com

Part of the complex of the Celtic Manor Resort (see entry above), this hotel offers country house charm combined with modern comforts. The current owner purchased this property some 30 years ago - he was born in the house when it was a maternity home. Today the house sits in beautiful landscaped gardens and offers traditionally styled bedrooms, three with four-poster beds. Several eating options are available at the Manor House, and also at the Celtic Manor Resort, where guests can also can advantage of all the leisure facilities.

Rooms 69 **Conf** Class 80 Thtr 200

Holiday Inn Newport

★★★ 70% HOTEL

☎ 01633 412777 🖹 01633 413087
The Coldra NP6 2YG
web: www.holidayinn.co.uk
dir: M4 junct 24, follow signs for B4237 towards Newport.
Hotel 200yds on left

A purpose-built and modern hotel, in a very convenient
location near to the M4, that caters equally well for both
leisure and business guests. There is Harpers, the
informal restaurant, a small leisure complex and a
business centre.

Rooms 119

Express by Holiday Inn Newport

BUDGET HOTEL

☎ 0870 990 4083 🖹 0870 990 4084
Lakeside Dr, Coedkernew NP10 8BB
e-mail: gm.newport@expressholidayinn.co.uk
web: www.hiexpress.com/exnewport
dir: M4 junct 28 at rdbt take St Mellons/Castleton exit .
Remain in right lane, at lights turn right. Hotel on left

A modern hotel ideal for families and business travellers.
Fresh and uncomplicated, the spacious rooms include Sky
TV, power shower and tea and coffee-making facilities.
Continental buffet breakfast is included in the room rate;
other meals may be taken at the nearby family pub or
restaurant. See also the Hotel Groups pages.

Rooms 125 (70 fmly) (34 GF) **S** £50-£150; **D** £50-£150
(incl. bkfst)* **Conf** Class 15 Board 15 Thtr 50
Del from £90*

Travelodge Newport Central

BUDGET HOTEL

☎ 0871 984 6411
66 Bridge St NP20 4AP
dir: M4 junct 25a, A4042 towards town centre. 0.2m left
into Shaftesbury St, straight ahead at rdbt. 0.6m at rdbt
3rd exit onto B4591/Old Green Interchange. 0.1m rdbt 1st
exit into Bridge St. Lodge 200yds on left

Travelodge offers good quality, good value, budget
accommodation. All offer family rooms sleeping up to
four (two adults, two children) with en suite bathroom/
shower-room, remote-control TV, tea- and coffee-making
facilities and comfortable beds. Food options vary.
Breakfast is at the on-site Bar Café restaurant (if
available) or to take away. See also the Hotel Groups
pages.

Rooms 62 **S** fr £29; **D** fr £29

BURTON   Map 8 SM90

Beggars Reach

★★★ 80% HOTEL

☎ 01646 600700 🖹 01646 600560
SA73 1PD
e-mail: stay@beggars-reach.com
web: www.beggars-reach.com
dir: 8m S of Haverfordwest, 6m N of Pembroke, off A477

This privately owned and personally run hotel was once a
Georgian rectory; it stands in eight acres of grounds
peacefully located close to the village of Burton. It
provides modern, well-equipped bedrooms, two of which
are located in former stables which date back to the 14th
century. Milford Haven and the ferry terminal at Pembroke
Dock are both within easy reach.

Rooms 30 (16 annexe) (4 fmly) (8 GF) (2 smoking)
S £79.50-£95; **D** £100-£130 (incl. bkfst)* **Facilities** STV
FTV Wi-fi **Conf** Class 60 Board 60 Thtr 100 Del from £110
to £120* **Parking** 80 **Notes** LB ⊗ Civ Wed 130

See advert on page 658

FISHGUARD   Map 8 SM93

Cartref

★★ 63% HOTEL

☎ 01348 872430 & 0781 330 5235 🖹 01348 873664
15-19 High St SA65 9AW
e-mail: cartrefhotel@btconnect.com
web: www.cartrefhotel.co.uk
dir: On A40 in town centre

Personally run by the proprietor, this friendly hotel offers
convenient access to the town centre and ferry terminal.
Bedrooms are well maintained and include some family
bedded rooms. There is also a cosy lounge bar and a
welcoming restaurant that looks out onto the high street.

Rooms 10 (2 fmly) **S** £35-£41; **D** £60-£68 (incl. bkfst)*
Facilities FTV **Parking** 4

HAVERFORDWEST   Map 8 SM91

Hotel Mariners

THE INDEPENDENTS
HOTEL ASSOCIATION

★★ 71% HOTEL

☎ 01437 763353 🖹 01437 764258
Mariners Square SA61 2DU
e-mail: hotelmariners@aol.com
dir: Follow town centre signs, over bridge, up High St, 1st
right down Dark St, hotel at end in Mariners Square

Located a few minutes walk from the town centre, this
privately owned and friendly hotel is said to date back to
1625. The bedrooms are equipped with modern facilities
and are soundly maintained. A good range of food is
offered in the popular bar, which is a focus for the local
community. Facilities include a choice of meeting rooms.

Rooms 28 (5 fmly) **S** £62.50-£72; **D** £83.50-£91 (incl.
bkfst)* **Facilities** STV Wi-fi **Conf** Class 20 Board 20
Thtr 50 **Parking** 50 **Notes** LB Closed 25-Dec-2 Jan

MANORBIER   Map 8 SS09

Castle Mead

THE CIRCLE
a search for individual hotels

★★ 72% HOTEL

☎ 01834 871358 🖹 01834 871358
SA70 7TA
e-mail: castlemeadhotel@aol.com
web: www.castlemeadhotel.com
dir: A4139 towards Pembroke, onto B4585 into village &
follow signs to beach & castle. Hotel on left above beach

Benefiting from a superb location with spectacular views
of the bay, the Norman church and Manorbier Castle, this
family-run hotel is friendly and welcoming. Bedrooms
which include some in a converted former coach house,
are generally quite spacious and have modern facilities.
Public areas include a sea-view restaurant, bar and
residents' lounge, as well as an extensive garden.

Rooms 8 (3 annexe) (2 fmly) (3 GF) **S** fr £45; **D** fr £86
(incl. bkfst) **Facilities** FTV Wi-fi **Parking** 20 **Notes** LB
Closed Dec-Feb RS Nov

NEWPORT

Llysmeddyg

◉◉ RESTAURANT WITH ROOMS

☎ 01239 820008
East St SA42 0SY
e-mail: contact@llysmeddyg.com
dir: On A487 in centre of town on Main St

Llysmeddyg is a Georgian townhouse with a blend of old
and new, elegant furnishings, deep sofas and a welcoming
fire. The owners of this property have used local craftsmen
to create a lovely interior that reflects an eclectic style
throughout. The focus of the restaurant menu is on quality
food through use of fresh seasonal ingredients sourced
locally. The spacious bedrooms are comfortable and
contemporary in design - the bathrooms vary in style.

Rooms 8 (3 annexe) (3 fmly)

PEMBROKE
Map 8 SM90

Best Western Lamphey Court
★★★ 80% HOTEL

☎ 01646 672273 🖨 01646 672480
Lamphey SA71 5NT
e-mail: info@lampheycourt.co.uk
web: www.lampheycourt.co.uk
dir: A477 to Pembroke. Turn left at Milton Village for
Lamphey, hotel on right

This former Georgian mansion is set in attractive
countryside and is well situated for exploring the
stunning Pembrokeshire coast and beaches. Well-
appointed bedrooms and family suites are situated in a
converted coach house in the grounds. The elegant public
areas include formal and informal dining rooms that both
feature dishes inspired by the local produce. Leisure
facilities include a tennis court, swimming pool, sauna,
jaccuzi and multi-gym.

Rooms 38 (12 annexe) (7 fmly) (6 GF) **S** £82-£105;
D £110-£160 (incl. bkfst)* **Facilities** FTV 🕉 ♨ Gym
Yacht charter Xmas New Year Wi-fi **Conf** Class 40
Board 30 Thtr 60 Del from £125 to £150* **Parking** 50
Notes LB ⊗ Civ Wed 80

Lamphey Hall
★★★ 77% HOTEL

☎ 01646 672394 🖨 01646 672369
Lamphey SA71 5NR
e-mail: andrewjones1990@aol.com
dir: From M4 follow signs for A48 towards Carmarthen,
then A40 to St Clears. Follow signs for A477, left at Milton
Village

Set in a delightful village, this very friendly, privately
owned and efficiently run hotel offers an ideal base from
which to explore the surrounding countryside. Bedrooms
are well equipped, comfortably furnished and include
family rooms and ground floor rooms. Diners have a
choice of three restaurants offering an extensive range of
dishes. There is also a small lounge, a bar and attractive
gardens.

Rooms 10 (1 fmly) (2 GF) **Parking** 32 **Notes** ⊗

PEMBROKE DOCK
Map 8 SM90

Cleddau Bridge
★★★ 75% HOTEL

☎ 01646 685961 🖨 01646 685746
Essex Rd SA72 6EG
e-mail: information@cleddauhotel.co.uk
dir: M4/A40 to St Clears. A477 to Pembroke Dock. At rdbt
2nd exit for Haverfordwest via toll bridge, left before toll
bridge

A modern, purpose-built hotel that is situated adjacent to
the Cleddau Bridge and with excellent views overlooking
the river. The well-equipped bedrooms are all on the
ground floor, while the comfortable public areas comprise
an attractive bar and restaurant, both taking advantage
of the impressive views.

Rooms 40 (2 fmly) (32 GF) **S** £50-£88; **D** £50-£97.50
(incl. bkfst)* **Facilities** Xmas Wi-fi **Conf** Class 100
Board 60 Thtr 300 Del from £90 to £120* **Parking** 140
Notes ⊗ Civ Wed 250

Travelodge Pembroke Dock

BUDGET HOTEL

☎ 0871 984 6207 📄 01646 684758
Pier Rd SA72 6DY
web: www.travelodge.co.uk
dir: A4139, right at 1st rdbt. Lodge opposite Lidl

Travelodge offers good quality, good value, budget
accommodation. All offer family rooms sleeping up to four
(two adults, two children) with en suite bathroom/
shower-room, remote-control TV, tea- and coffee-making
facilities and comfortable beds. Food options vary.
Breakfast is at the on-site Bar Café restaurant (if
available) or to take away. See also Hotel Groups pages.

Rooms 51 **S** fr £29; **D** fr £29

ST DAVID'S · Map 8 SM72

Warpool Court

WELSH RAREBITS

★★★ 79% ◉◉ COUNTRY HOUSE HOTEL

☎ 01437 720300 📄 01437 720676
SA62 6BN
e-mail: info@warpoolcourthotel.com
web: www.warpoolcourthotel.com
dir: At Cross Square left by The Bishops Restaurant (Goat
St). Pass Farmers Arms pub, after 400mtrs left, follow
hotel signs, entrance on right

Originally the cathedral choir school, this hotel is set in
landscaped gardens looking out to sea and is within easy
walking distance of the Pembrokeshire Coastal Path. The
lounges are spacious and comfortable, and the bedrooms
are well furnished and equipped with modern facilities.
The restaurant offers delightful cuisine.

Rooms 24 (3 fmly) **S** £95; **D** £130–£240 (incl. bkfst)*
Facilities 🐾 ⛳ 🏖 Table tennis Pool table Xmas New
Year Wi-fi **Conf** Class 25 Board 25 Thtr 40 **Parking** 100
Notes LB Closed Jan Civ Wed 120

TENBY · Map 8 SN10

Penally Abbey Country House

WELSH RAREBITS

★★★ 78% ◉ COUNTRY HOUSE HOTEL

☎ 01834 843033 📄 01834 844714
Penally SA70 7PY
e-mail: penally.abbey@btinternet.com
web: www.penally-abbey.com
dir: 1.5m from Tenby, off A4139, near village green

With monastic origins, this delightful country house
stands in five acres of grounds with views over
Carmarthen Bay. The drawing room, bar and restaurant
are tastefully decorated and attractively furnished and
set the scene for a relaxing stay. An impressive range of
comfortable accommodation is offered. In the main hotel
there are country-house style rooms or cottage-style
rooms with four posters, and the lodge has rooms that
combine both classic and contemporary style.

Rooms 12 (4 annexe) (3 fmly) **Facilities** 🐾 Xmas
Conf Board 14 **Parking** 17 **Notes** 🚫 Civ Wed 45

TENBY *continued*

Atlantic

★★★ 78% HOTEL

☎ 01834 842881 ▤ 01834 840911
The Esplanade SA70 7DU
e-mail: enquiries@atlantic-hotel.uk.com
web: www.atlantic-hotel.uk.com
dir: A478 into Tenby & follow town centre signs, keep town walls on left then turn right at Esplanade, hotel on right

This privately owned and personally run, friendly hotel has an enviable position looking out over South Beach towards Caldy Island. Bedrooms vary in size and style, and are well equipped and tastefully appointed. The comfortable public areas include a choice of restaurants and, in fine weather guests can also enjoy the cliff-top gardens.

Rooms 42 (11 fmly) (4 GF) **S** £79-£91; **D** £106-£190 (incl. bkfst) **Facilities** FTV ⓣ Steam room Spa bath **Conf** Board 6 **Services** Lift **Parking** 25 **Notes** LB Closed mid Dec-late Jan

Fourcroft

★★★ 75% HOTEL

☎ 01834 842886 ▤ 01834 842888
North Beach SA70 8AP
e-mail: staying@fourcroft-hotel.co.uk
web: www.fourcroft-hotel.co.uk
dir: A478, after 'Welcome to Tenby' sign left towards North Beach & Walled Town. At seafront turn sharp left. Hotel on left

This friendly hotel has been owned and run by the same family for over 50 years. It offers a beach-front location, together with a number of extra facilities that make it particularly suitable for families with children. Guests have direct access to Tenby's North Beach through the hotel's cliff top gardens. Bedrooms are of a good size and have modern facilities.

Rooms 40 (12 fmly) **S** £50-£80; **D** £100-£160 (incl. bkfst)* **Facilities** FTV ⚘ Table tennis Giant chess Human gyroscope Snooker Pool Xmas New Year Wi-fi **Conf** Class 40 Board 50 Thtr 90 Del from £125 to £150* **Services** Lift **Parking** 12 **Notes** LB Civ Wed 90

Clarence House

★★ 62% HOTEL

☎ 01834 844371 ▤ 01834 844372
Esplanade SA70 7DU
e-mail: clarencehotel@freeuk.com
dir: Off South Parade by town walls onto St Florance Parade & Esplanade

Owned by the same family for over 50 years, this hotel has superb views from its elevated position. Many of the bedrooms have sea views and all are comfortably furnished. The bar leads to a sheltered rose garden or a number of lounges. Entertainment is provided in high season, and this establishment is particularly popular with coach tour parties.

Rooms 76 (6 fmly) **S** £27-£37; **D** £27-£37 (incl. bkfst)* **Facilities** ♫ **Services** Lift **Notes** Closed 18-28 Dec

See advert on page 659

WOLF'S CASTLE   Map 8 SM92

Wolfscastle Country Hotel WELSH RAREBITS

★★★ 78% ⚛ COUNTRY HOUSE HOTEL

☎ 01437 741688 & 741225 ▤ 01437 741383
SA62 5LZ
e-mail: enquiries@wolfscastle.com
web: www.wolfscastle.com
dir: On A40 in village at top of hill. 6m N of Haverfordwest

This large stone house, a former vicarage, dates back to the mid-19th century and is now a friendly, privately owned and personally run hotel. It provides stylish, modern, well-maintained and well-equipped bedrooms.

There is a pleasant bar and an attractive restaurant, which has a well deserved reputation for its food.

Rooms 22 (2 annexe) (2 fmly) **Facilities** FTV New Year Wi-fi **Conf** Class 100 Board 30 Thtr 100 Del from £125 to £210* **Parking** 60 **Notes** Closed 24-26 Dec Civ Wed 70

POWYS

BRECON   Map 9 SO02

Peterstone Court

⚛⚛ RESTAURANT WITH ROOMS

☎ 01874 665387
Llanhamlach LD3 7YB
e-mail: info@peterstone-court.com
dir: 3m from Brecon on A40 towards Abergavenny

Situated on the edge of the Brecons Beacons this establishment affords stunning views and overlooks the River Usk. The style is friendly and informal, without any unnecessary fuss. No two bedrooms are alike, but all share comparable levels of comfort, quality and elegance. Public areas reflect similar standards, eclectically styled with a blend of the contemporary and the traditional. Quality produce is cooked with care in a range of enjoyable dishes.

Rooms 12 (4 annexe) (2 fmly)

BUILTH WELLS   Map 9 SO05

Caer Beris Manor   THE INDEPENDENTS
HOTEL ASSOCIATION

★★★ 75% COUNTRY HOUSE HOTEL

☎ 01982 552601 ▤ 01982 552586
LD2 3NP
e-mail: caerberis@btconnect.com
web: www.caerberis.com
dir: From town centre follow A483/Llandovery signs. Hotel on left

Guests can expect a relaxing stay at this friendly and privately owned hotel that has extensive landscaped grounds. Bedrooms are individually decorated and furnished to retain an atmosphere of a bygone era. The spacious and comfortable lounge and a lounge bar continue this theme, and there's an elegant restaurant, complete with 16th-century panelling.

Rooms 23 (1 fmly) (3 GF) **S** fr £69.95; **D** fr £119.95 **Facilities** FTV Fishing ⚓ Clay pigeon shooting Xmas New Year Wi-fi **Conf** Class 75 Board 50 Thtr 100 Del from £79.95 to £115.95 **Parking** 100 **Notes** LB Civ Wed 200

CAERSWS   Map 15 SO09

The Talkhouse

@@ RESTAURANT WITH ROOMS

☎ 01686 688919   🖹 01686 689134
Pontdolgoch SY17 5JE
e-mail: info@talkhouse.co.uk
dir: 1.5m NW of Caersws on A470

A highlight of this delightful 19th-century inn is the food, home-made dishes making good use of local produce. Bedrooms offer luxury in every area and the cosy lounge, filled with sofas, is the place to while away some time with a glass of wine or a pot of tea. The bar is very welcoming with its log fire.

Rooms 3

CRICKHOWELL   Map 9 SO21

Gliffaes Country House Hotel

★★★ 81% @ COUNTRY HOUSE HOTEL

☎ 01874 730371   🖹 01874 730463
NP8 1RH
e-mail: calls@gliffaeshotel.com
web: www.gliffaeshotel.com
dir: 1m off A40, 2.5m W of Crickhowell

This impressive Victorian mansion, standing in 33-acre gardens and wooded grounds by the River Usk, is a privately owned and personally run hotel. Public rooms retain elegance and generous proportions and include a balcony and conservatory from which to enjoy the views. Bedrooms are very well decorated and furnished and offer high levels of comfort.

Rooms 23 (4 annexe) (2 fmly) (1 GF) **S** £85-£106; **D** £94-£227 (incl. bkfst)* **Facilities** FTV 🏊 Fishing 🎣 Cycling Xmas New Year Wi-fi **Conf** Class 16 Board 16 Thtr 40 **Parking** 34 **Notes** LB ✖ Closed 2-26 Jan Civ Wed 50

Bear   WELSH RAREBITS

★★★ 77% @ HOTEL

☎ 01873 810408   🖹 01873 811696
NP8 1BW
e-mail: bearhotel@aol.com
dir: On A40 between Abergavenny & Brecon

A favourite with locals as well as visitors, the character and friendliness of this 15th-century coaching inn are renowned. The bedrooms come in a variety of sizes and standards including some with four-posters. The bar and restaurant are furnished in keeping with the style of the building and provide comfortable areas in which to enjoy some of the very popular dishes that use the finest locally-sourced ingredients.

Rooms 34 (13 annexe) (6 fmly) (6 GF) **S** £70-£117; **D** £86-£153 (incl. bkfst) **Facilities** STV FTV Wi-fi **Conf** Class 20 Board 20 Thtr 40 Del from £137 to £143 **Parking** 45 **Notes** LB No children 6yrs RS 25 Dec

Manor

★★★ 74% @ HOTEL

☎ 01873 810212   🖹 01873 811938
Brecon Rd NP8 1SE
e-mail: info@manorhotel.co.uk
web: www.manorhotel.co.uk
dir: On A40, Crickhowell/Brecon, 0.5m from Crickhowell

This impressive manor house, set in a stunning location, was the birthplace of Sir George Everest. The bedrooms and public areas are elegant, and there are extensive leisure facilities. The restaurant, with panoramic views, is the setting for exciting modern cooking.

Rooms 22 (1 fmly) **Facilities** STV FTV 🏊 Gym Fitness assessment Sunbed Xmas New Year Wi-fi **Conf** Class 250 Board 150 Thtr 300 Del from £125 to £145 **Parking** 200 **Notes** Civ Wed 150

KNIGHTON   Map 9 SO27

Milebrook House   WELSH RAREBITS

★★★ 79% @@ COUNTRY HOUSE HOTEL

☎ 01547 528632   🖹 01547 520509
Milebrook LD7 1LT
e-mail: hotel@milebrook.kc3ltd.co.uk
web: www.milebrookhouse.co.uk
dir: 2m E of Knighton, on A4113

Set in three acres of grounds and gardens in the Teme Valley, this charming house dates back to 1760. Over the years since its conversion into a hotel, it has acquired a well-deserved reputation for its warm hospitality, comfortable accommodation and the quality of its cuisine, that uses local produce and home-grown vegetables.

Rooms 10 (2 fmly) (2 GF) **S** £69-£74; **D** £108-£118 (incl. bkfst)* **Facilities** Fishing 🎣 Table tennis Trout fly fishing Xmas New Year Wi-fi **Conf** Class 30 **Parking** 21 **Notes** LB ✖ No children 8yrs RS Mon lunch

LLANDRINDOD WELLS   Map 9 SO06

The Metropole   CLASSIC BRITISH HOTELS

★★★ 82% @ HOTEL

☎ 01597 823700   🖹 01597 824828
Temple St LD1 5DY
e-mail: info@metropole.co.uk
web: www.metropole.co.uk
dir: On A483 in town centre

The centre of this famous spa town is dominated by this large Victorian hotel, which has been personally run by the same family for well over 100 years. The lobby leads to Spencers Bar and Brasserie and to the comfortable and elegantly styled lounge. Bedrooms vary in style, but all are quite spacious and well equipped. Facilities include an extensive range of conference and function rooms, as well as a leisure centre.

Rooms 120 (11 fmly) **S** £94-£96; **D** £120-£150 (incl. bkfst) **Facilities** Spa 🏊 Gym Beauty & holistic treatments Sauna Steam room Xmas New Year Wi-fi **Conf** Class 200 Board 80 Thtr 300 Del from £120 to £125 **Services** Lift **Parking** 150 **Notes** LB Civ Wed 300

See advert on page 662

LLANFYLLIN — Map 15 SJ11

Cain Valley
★★ 78% HOTEL

☎ 01691 648366 📄 01691 648307
High St SY22 5AQ
e-mail: info@cainvalleyhotel.co.uk
dir: At end of A490. Hotel in town centre, car park at rear

This Grade II listed coaching inn has a lot of charm and character including features such as exposed beams and a Jacobean staircase. The comfortable accommodation includes family rooms and a wide range of food is available in a choice of bars, or in the restaurant, which has a well-deserved reputation for its locally sourced steaks.

Rooms 13 (2 fmly) (13 smoking) **Parking** 10

LLANGAMMARCH WELLS — Map 9 SN94

INSPECTORS' CHOICE

The Lake Country House & Spa
★★★ ⬢⬢ COUNTRY HOUSE HOTEL

☎ 01591 620202 & 620474 📄 01591 620457
LD4 4BS
e-mail: info@lakecountryhouse.co.uk
web: www.lakecountryhouse.co.uk
dir: W from Builth Wells on A483 to Garth (approx 6m). Left for Llangammarch Wells, follow hotel signs

Expect good old-fashioned values and hospitality at this Victorian country house hotel. In fact, the service is so traditionally English, guests may believe they have a butler! The establishment offers a 9-hole, par 3 golf course, 50 acres of wooded grounds and a spa where the hot tub overlooks the lake. Bedrooms, some located in an annexe, and some at ground-floor level, are individually styled and have many extra comforts. Traditional afternoon teas are served in the lounge and award-winning cuisine is provided in the spacious and elegant restaurant.

Rooms 30 (7 GF) **Facilities** Spa FTV ⬢ ⬢ 9 ⬢ Putt green Fishing ⬢ Gym Archery Horse riding Mountain biking Quad biking Xmas Wi-fi **Conf** Class 30 Board 25 Thtr 80 **Parking** 72 **Notes** Civ Wed 100

LLANWDDYN — Map 15 SJ01

Lake Vyrnwy

★★★★ 76% ⬢
COUNTRY HOUSE HOTEL

☎ 01691 870692 📄 01691 870259
Lake Vyrnwy SY10 0LY
e-mail: info@lakevyrnwyhotel.co.uk
web: www.lakevyrnwyhotel.co.uk
dir: on A4393, 200yds past dam turn sharp right into drive

This elegant Victorian country-house hotel lies in 26,000 acres of woodland above Lake Vyrnwy. Sympathetically refurbished during the past few years, it provides a wide range of bedrooms, most with superb views and many with four-poster beds and balconies. Extensive public rooms retain many period features and more informal dining is available in the popular Tower Tavern. Relaxing and rejuvenating treatments are a feature of the stylish health spa.

Rooms 52 (4 fmly) **Facilities** Spa STV FTV ⬢ Fishing Gym Archery Birdwatching Canoeing Kayaking Clay shooting Sailing Fly fishing Cycling Xmas New Year Wi-fi **Conf** Class 80 Board 60 Thtr 200 Del from £145 to £165 **Services** Lift **Parking** 70 **Notes** Civ Wed 200

LLANWRTYD WELLS — Map 9 SN84

Carlton Riverside

RESTAURANT WITH ROOMS

☎ 01591 610248
Irfon Crescent LD5 4ST
e-mail: info@carltonriverside.com
dir: In town centre beside bridge

Guests become part of the family at this character property, set beside the river in Wales's smallest town. Carlton Riverside offers award-winning cuisine for which Mary Ann Gilchrist relies on the very best of local ingredients. The set menu is complemented by a well-chosen wine list and dinner is served in the delightfully stylish restaurant which offers a memorable blend of traditional comfort, modern design and river views. Four comfortable bedrooms have tasteful combinations of antique and contemporary furniture, along with welcome personal touches.

Rooms 4

Lasswade Country House

RESTAURANT WITH ROOMS

☎ 01591 610515   📠 01591 610611
Station Rd LD5 4RW
e-mail: info@lasswadehotel.co.uk
dir: Off A483 into Irfon Terrace, right into Station Rd, 350yds on right

This friendly establishment on the edge of the town has impressive views over the countryside. Bedrooms are comfortably furnished and well equipped, while the public areas consist of a tastefully decorated lounge, an elegant restaurant with a bar, and an airy conservatory which looks out on to the neighbouring hills. The kitchen utilises fresh, local produce to provide an enjoyable dining experience.

Rooms 8

MACHYNLLETH

See Eglwysfach (Ceredigion)

MONTGOMERY — Map 15 SO29

Dragon

★★ 79% ⊛ HOTEL

☎ 01686 668359   📠 0870 011 8227
SY15 6PA
e-mail: reception@dragonhotel.com
web: www.dragonhotel.com
dir: Behind town hall

This fine 17th-century coaching inn stands in the centre of Montgomery. Beams and timbers from the nearby castle, which was destroyed by Cromwell, are visible in the lounge and bar. A wide choice of soundly prepared, wholesome food is available in both the restaurant and bar. Bedrooms are well equipped and family rooms are available.

Rooms 20 (6 fmly) (2 smoking) **S** £56-£66; **D** £94.50-£104.50 (incl. bkfst)* **Facilities** ☺ 🎵 Xmas New Year Wi-fi **Conf** Class 30 Board 25 Thtr 40 Del from £86 to £125* **Parking** 21 **Notes** LB

WELSHPOOL — Map 15 SJ20

Royal Oak

★★★ 78% @ HOTEL — WELSH RAREBITS

☎ 01938 552217 ▤ 01938 556652
The Cross SY21 7DG
e-mail: relax@royaloakhotel.info
web: www.royaloakhotel.info
dir: By lights at junct of A483/A458

This traditional market town hotel dates back over 350 years. The public areas are furnished in a minimalist style that highlight the many retained period features, including exposed beams and open fires. Three different bedroom styles provide good comfort levels and imaginative food is served in the elegant Red Room or adjacent all day café/bar.

Rooms 25 (3 fmly) **Facilities** FTV Xmas New Year Wi-fi **Conf** Class 60 Board 60 Thtr 150 **Parking** 30 **Notes** ⊗ Civ Wed

RHONDDA CYNON TAFF

MISKIN — Map 9 ST08

Miskin Manor Country Hotel

★★★★ 75% @@ COUNTRY HOUSE HOTEL

☎ 01443 224204 ▤ 01443 237606
Pendoylan Rd CF72 8ND
e-mail: reservations@miskin-manor.co.uk
web: www.miskin-manor.co.uk
dir: M4 junct 34, exit onto A4119, signed Llantrisant, hotel 300yds on left

This historic manor house is peacefully located in 20-acre grounds yet only minutes away from the M4. Bedrooms are furnished to a high standard and include some located in converted stables and cottages. Public areas are spacious and comfortable and include a variety of function rooms. The relaxed atmosphere and the surroundings ensure this hotel remains popular for wedding functions as well as with business guests.

Rooms 43 (9 annexe) (2 fmly) (7 GF) **Facilities** ⊛ supervised ⊰ Gym Squash Xmas New Year Wi-fi **Conf** Class 80 Board 65 Thtr 160 **Parking** 200 **Notes** Civ Wed 120

See advert on page 663

PONTYPRIDD — Map 9 ST08

Llechwen Hall

★★★ 75% @ COUNTRY HOUSE HOTEL

☎ 01443 742050 & 743020 ▤ 01443 742189
Llanfabon CF37 4HP
e-mail: steph@llechwen.co.uk
dir: A470 N towards Merthyr Tydfil. At large rdbt take 3rd exit. At mini rdbt take 3rd exit, hotel signed 0.5m on left

Set on top of a hill with a stunning approach, this country house hotel has served many purposes in its 200-year-old history including a private school and a magistrates' court. The spacious, individually decorated bedrooms are well equipped; some are situated in the separate coach house nearby. There are ground-floor, twin, double and family bedrooms on offer. The Victorian-style public areas are attractively appointed and the hotel is a popular venue for weddings.

Rooms 20 (8 annexe) (6 fmly) (4 GF) **Facilities** FTV New Year Wi-fi **Conf** Class 40 Board 40 Thtr 80 **Parking** 150 **Notes** Closed 24-30 Dec Civ Wed 80

SWANSEA

BISHOPSTON — Map 8 SS58

Winston

★★ 68% @ HOTEL

☎ 01792 232074
11 Church Ln SA3 3JT
e-mail: enquiries@winstonhotel.com
dir: B4436 follow for 2.7m, left & immediately right down Church Lane, hotel 300yds on left

This family-run hotel is situated on the Gower Peninsular in an Area of Outstanding Natural Beauty with miles of sandy beaches and spectacular walks. The bedrooms are comfortable and some are ground-floor, courtyard rooms suitable for families and for pets. The food is locally sourced and creatively prepared. There is a small, heated indoor pool plus a spa with sauna, hot tub and steam room.

Rooms 17 (6 annexe) (3 fmly) (5 GF) **S** £50-£65; **D** £65-£105 (incl. bkfst)* **Facilities** New Year Wi-fi **Conf** Class 50 Board 50 Thtr 50 Del from £65 to £120* **Parking** 35 **Notes** LB ⊗ Civ Wed 120

REYNOLDSTON — Map 8 SS48

INSPECTORS' CHOICE

Fairyhill

@@ RESTAURANT WITH ROOMS

☎ 01792 390139 ▤ 01792 391358
SA3 1BS
e-mail: postbox@fairyhill.net
web: www.fairyhill.net
dir: M4 junct 47 onto A483, at next rdbt turn right onto A484. At Gowerton take B4295 10m

Peace and tranquillity are never far away at this charming Georgian mansion set in the heart of the beautiful Gower peninsula. Bedrooms are furnished with care and are filled with many thoughtful extras. There is also a range of comfortable seating areas with crackling log fires to choose from, and the smart restaurant offers menus based on local produce and complemented by an excellent wine list.

Rooms 8

SWANSEA — Map 9 SS69

See also **Port Talbot (Neath Port Talbot)**

Swansea Marriott Hotel — Marriott HOTELS & RESORTS

★★★★ 78% HOTEL

☎ 0870 400 7282 ▤ 0870 400 7382
The Maritime Quarter SA1 3SS
web: www.swanseamarriott.co.uk
dir: M4 junct 42, A483 to city centre past Leisure Centre, then follow signs to Maritime Quarter

Just opposite City Hall, this busy hotel enjoys fantastic views over the bay and marina. Bedrooms are spacious and equipped with a range of extras. Public rooms include a popular leisure club and Abernethy's restaurant which overlooks the marina. It is worth noting, however, that lounge seating is limited.

Rooms 122 (50 fmly) (11 GF) **Facilities** STV ⊛ Gym New Year Wi-fi **Conf** Class 120 Board 30 Thtr 250 **Services** Lift Air con **Parking** 122 **Notes** LB ⊗ Civ Wed 200

Dragon

★★★★ 76% ❀ HOTEL

☎ 01792 657100 & 0870 4299 848 📠 01792 456044
The Kingsway Circle SA1 5LS
e-mail: info@dragon-hotel.co.uk
web: www.dragon-hotel.co.uk
dir: A483 follow signs for city centre. After lights at Sainsbury's right onto Strand then left. Hotel straight ahead

This privately owned hotel is located in the city centre and offers spacious modern accommodation with well-equipped, comfortable bedrooms. There is a bar and lounge facility on the first floor along with the dining room for breakfast. On the ground floor, the Dragons Brasserie provides award-winning food from a vibrant continental menu for both residents and non-residents. The health and fitness club offers an excellent choice of facilities and there are a good range of conference rooms.

Rooms 106 (5 fmly) **Facilities** STV ☼ supervised Gym Beauty therapist Xmas New Year Wi-fi **Conf** Class 120 Board 60 Thtr 230 Del from £115 to £140* **Services** Lift Air con **Parking** 50 **Notes** ❀ Civ Wed 200

Ramada Swansea

® RAMADA

★★★ 77% HOTEL

☎ 01792 310330 📠 01792 797535
Phoenix Way, Swansea Enterprise Park SA7 9EG
e-mail: sales.swansea@ramadajarvis.co.uk
web: www.ramadajarvis.co.uk
dir: M4 junct 44, A48 (Llansamlet), left at 3rd lights, right at 1st mini rdbt, left into Phoenix Way at 2nd rdbt. Hotel 800mtrs on right

This large, modern hotel is conveniently situated on the outskirts of the city with easy access to the M4. Bedrooms are comfortably appointed for both business and leisure guests. Public areas include the Arts Restaurant, Arts Bar and elegant lounges. 24-hour room service is also available.

Rooms 119 (12 fmly) (50 GF) (10 smoking) **S** £49-£140; **D** £59-£160 (incl. bkfst)* **Facilities** STV FTV ☼ supervised Gym Sauna New Year Wi-fi **Conf** Class 80 Board 60 Thtr 200 Del from £99 to £149 **Parking** 180 **Notes** LB Civ Wed 120

Express by Holiday Inn Swansea - West

BUDGET HOTEL

☎ 0870 442 5560 & 01792 818700 📠 0870 442 5561
Neath Rd, Llandarcy SA10 6JQ
e-mail: gm.swansea@expressholidayinn.co.uk
web: www.hiexpress.com/swanseam4j43
dir: Off M4 junct 43

A modern hotel ideal for families and business travellers. Fresh and uncomplicated, the spacious rooms include Sky TV, power shower and tea and coffee-making facilities. Continental buffet breakfast is included in the room rate; other meals may be taken at the nearby family pub or restaurant. See also the Hotel Groups pages.

Rooms 91 (60 fmly) (18 GF) **Conf** Class 20 Board 16 Thtr 25

Travelodge Swansea Central

BUDGET HOTEL

☎ 0871 984 6326
Princess Way SA1 3LW
web: www.travelodge.co.uk
dir: A4067, right onto slip road, right onto Wind St, left after 3m then left onto St Mary St. Hotel on Princess Way

Travelodge offers good quality, good value, budget accommodation. All offer family rooms sleeping up to four (two adults, two children) with en suite bathroom/shower-room, remote-control TV, tea- and coffee-making facilities and comfortable beds. Food options vary. Breakfast is at the on-site Bar Café restaurant (if available) or to take away. See also Hotel Groups pages.

Rooms 70 **S** fr £29; **D** fr £29

Travelodge Swansea (M4)

BUDGET HOTEL

☎ 0871 984 6055 📠 01792 898972
Penllergaer SA4 9GT
web: www.travelodge.co.uk
dir: At M4 junct 47

Rooms 51 **S** fr £29; **D** fr £29 **Conf** Class 32 Board 20 Thtr 25

TORFAEN

CWMBRAN   Map 9 ST29

Best Western Parkway

★★★★ 78% HOTEL

☎ 01633 871199 📠 01633 869160
Cwmbran Dr NP44 3UW
e-mail: enquiries@parkwayhotel.co.uk
web: www.bw-parkwayhotel.co.uk
dir: M4 junct 25A/26, A4051 follow Cwmbran-Llantarnam Park signs. Turn right at rdbt then right for hotel

This hotel is purpose-built and offers comfortable bedrooms and public areas suitable for a wide range of guests. There is a sports centre and a range of conference and meeting facilities. The coffee shop offers an informal eating option during the day and there is fine dining in Ravello's Restaurant.

Rooms 70 (4 fmly) (34 GF) **S** £60-£100; **D** £70-£160 (incl. bkfst)* **Facilities** STV 🕲 Gym Steam room Solaria 🎵 Xmas New Year Wi-fi **Conf** Class 240 Board 100 Thtr 500 Del from £99 to £153* **Parking** 350 **Notes** LB ⊗ Closed 27-30 Dec Civ Wed 250

PONTYPOOL   Map 9 SO20

Travelodge Pontypool

BUDGET HOTEL

☎ 0871 984 6413 📠 01844 358 681
Lower Mill Field NP4 0XB
dir: M4 junct 25a, A4042. At Grove Park rdbt take 2nd exit. At Croes-y-mwyalch rdbt take 2nd exit. Through 3 more rdbts, at 4th, take 3rd exit. Left into Pont-y-felin Rd. Right into New Road Hangerberry

Travelodge offers good quality, good value, budget accommodation. All offer family rooms sleeping up to four (two adults, two children) with en suite bathroom/shower-room, remote-control TV, tea- and coffee-making facilities and comfortable beds. Food options vary. Breakfast is at the on-site Bar Café restaurant (if available) or to take away. See also the Hotel Groups pages.

Rooms 53 **S** fr £29; **D** fr £29

VALE OF GLAMORGAN

BARRY   Map 9 ST16

Egerton Grey Country House

★★★★ 81% ⊛ COUNTRY HOUSE HOTEL

☎ 01446 711666 📠 01446 711690
Porthkerry CF62 3BZ
e-mail: info@egertongrey.co.uk
web: www.egertongrey.co.uk
dir: M4 junct 33 follow airport signs, left at rdbt for Porthkerry, 500yds left down lane between thatched cottages

This former rectory enjoys a peaceful setting and views over delightful countryside with distant glimpses of the sea. The bedrooms are spacious and individually furnished. Public areas offer charm and elegance, and include an airy lounge and restaurant, which has been sympathetically converted from the billiards room.

Rooms 10 (4 fmly) **S** £100-£150; **D** £140-£180 (incl. bkfst)* **Facilities** FTV Putt green 🐾 Xmas New Year Wi-fi **Conf** Class 30 Board 22 Thtr 30 Del from £170 to £190* **Parking** 40 **Notes** LB Civ Wed 40

Best Western Mount Sorrel

★★★ 74% HOTEL

☎ 01446 740069 📠 01446 746600
Porthkerry Rd CF62 7XY
e-mail: reservations@mountsorrel.co.uk
dir: M4 junct 33 onto A4232. Follow signs for A4050 through Barry. At mini-rdbt (with church opposite) turn left, hotel 300mtrs on left

Situated in an elevated position above the town centre, this extended Victorian property is ideally placed for exploring Cardiff and the nearby coast. The public areas include a choice of conference rooms, a restaurant with a bar called Strings, and smart leisure facilities with an indoor swimming pool and multi-gym. There is a comfortable bar and separate, cosy lounge.

Rooms 42 (3 fmly) (5 GF) **Facilities** STV 🕲 Gym Xmas **Conf** Class 100 Board 50 Thtr 150 Del from £110 to £140* **Services** Lift **Parking** 17 **Notes** ⊗ Civ Wed 150

Innkeeper's Lodge Cardiff Airport

BUDGET HOTEL

☎ 0845 112 6081 📠 0845 112 6222
Port Road West CF62 3BA
web: www.innkeeperslodge.com/cardiffairport
dir: M4 junct 33, A4232 towards Cardiff. At rdbt with A4050 follow Barry signs. At rdbt with A4226 follow Cardiff Airport signs. Pass rdbt towards Cardiff Airport. Lodge on left

Innkeeper's Lodge represents an exciting, high value concept within the budget hotel market. Comfortable bedrooms provide excellent facilities that include satellite TV and modem points. Options include family rooms; and for the corporate guest, cutting edge IT which includes Wi-fi high speed internet access. A popular Carvery provides all-day food, including an extensive, complimentary continental breakfast. See also the Hotel Groups pages.

Rooms 28

HENSOL   Map 9 ST07

Vale Hotel Golf & Spa Resort

★★★★ 82% ⊛ HOTEL

☎ 01443 667800 📠 01443 667801
Hensol Park CF72 8JY
e-mail: reservations@vale-hotel.com
web: www.vale-hotel.com
dir: M4 junct 34 towards Pendoylan, hotel signed from junct

A wealth of leisure facilities are offered at this large and modern, purpose-built complex, including two golf courses and a driving range plus an extensive health spa with a gym, swimming pool, squash courts, orthopaedic clinic and a range of treatments. Public areas are spacious and attractive, whilst bedrooms, many with balconies, are well appointed. Meeting and conference facilities are available. Guests can dine in the traditional Vale Grill, a brasserie-style restaurant serving quality fresh ingredients.

Rooms 143 (114 annexe) (15 fmly) (36 GF) **Facilities** Spa STV 🕲 🎿 36 ⛳ Putt green Fishing Gym Squash Xmas New Year Wi-fi **Conf** Class 280 Board 60 Thtr 700 Del from £125 to £200* **Services** Lift Air con **Parking** 450 **Notes** ⊗ Civ Wed 700

See advert on page 635

LLANTWIT MAJOR   Map 9 SS96

West House Country Hotel

★★★ Ⓐ COUNTRY HOUSE HOTEL

☎ 01446 792406 📠 01446 796147
West St CF61 1SP
e-mail: enq@westhouse-hotel.co.uk
dir: From Bridgend take A48. At Llantwit Major sign left onto B4268, at rdbt straight over, under bridge, 1st right into West St

Rooms 21 (1 fmly) (2 GF) **S** £58.50-£62.50; **D** £75-£100 (incl. bkfst)* **Facilities** FTV New Year Wi-fi **Conf** Class 40 Board 26 Thtr 80 Del from £110 to £160 **Parking** 50 **Notes** LB Civ Wed 80

WREXHAM

CHIRK   Map 15 SJ23

Moreton Park Lodge

★★★ 75% HOTEL

☎ 01691 776666 📠 01691 776655
Moreton Park, Gledrid LL14 5DG
e-mail: reservations@moretonpark.com
web: www.moretonpark.com
dir: 200yds from the rdbt of the A5 and B5070

Located on the town's outskirts and convenient for the A5, this very well maintained property provides a range of spacious, well-equipped bedrooms ideal for both business and leisure guests. Breakfast, and a comprehensive choice at lunch and dinner is available in the adjacent Lord Moreton Bar & Restaurant. Service is friendly and attentive.

Rooms 46 (20 fmly) (7 smoking) **S** £35-£65; **D** £40-£80 **Facilities** STV Free use of facilities at sister hotel 0.5m away Wi-fi **Conf** Class 50 Board 20 Thtr 60 **Parking** 200 **Notes** LB ⊗

GLYN CEIRIOG   Map 15 SJ23

Golden Pheasant Country Hotel & Inn

★★★ 75% HOTEL

☎ 01691 718281 📠 01691 718479
Llwynmawr LL20 7BB
e-mail: info@goldenpheasanthotel.co.uk
web: www.goldenpheasanthotel.co.uk
dir: A5/B4500 at Chirk, then 5m to Pontfadog, follow hotel signs, 1st left after Cheshire Home. Left after bend to Llywnmawr in Dolywern. Hotel at top of small hill

Located in the heart of the unspoilt Ceriog Valley, this period hotel enjoys stunning views of the countryside. Popular with shooting and walking parties, the public areas retain many original features including a fine taxidermy collection of game birds, and a roaring fire burns in the character bars during the cooler months.

Rooms 20 (1 fmly) (1 GF) **S** £50-£100; **D** £95-£130 (incl. bkfst)* **Facilities** Fishing Various activities by arrangement Xmas New Year Wi-fi **Conf** Class 24 Board 20 Thtr 24 Del from £55 to £130* **Parking** 24 **Notes** LB

ROSSETT   Map 15 SJ35

Best Western Llyndir Hall

★★★ 79% HOTEL

☎ 01244 571648 📠 01244 571258
Llyndir Ln LL12 0AY
e-mail: llyndirhallhotel@feathers.uk.com
dir: 5m S of Chester on B5445 follow Pulford signs

Located on the English/Welsh border within easy reach of Chester and Wrexham, this elegant manor house lies in several acres of mature grounds. The hotel is popular with both business and leisure guests, and facilities include conference rooms, The Business Training Centre, an impressive leisure centre, a choice of comfortable lounges and a brasserie-style restaurant.

Rooms 48 (3 fmly) (20 GF) **Facilities** Ⓢ supervised Gym Steam room, Beauty salon. Xmas **Conf** Class 60 Board 40 Thtr 120 **Parking** 80 **Notes** LB ⊗ Civ Wed 120

WREXHAM   Map 15 SJ35

Best Western Cross Lanes Hotel & Restaurant

★★★ 75% ⊛ HOTEL

☎ 01978 780555 📠 01978 780568
Cross Lanes, Bangor Rd, Marchwiel LL13 0TF
e-mail: guestservices@crosslanes.co.uk
dir: 3m SE of Wrexham, on A525, between Marchwiel & Bangor-on-Dee

This hotel was built as a private house in 1890 and stands in over six acres of beautiful grounds. Bedrooms are well equipped and meet the needs of today's traveller; two rooms have four-poster beds. A fine selection of well prepared food is available in Kagan's Brasserie.

Rooms 16 (1 fmly) **Facilities** FTV Putt green ⅊ Wi-fi **Conf** Class 60 Board 40 Thtr 120 **Parking** 80 **Notes** ⊗ Closed 25 Dec (night) & 26 Dec Civ Wed 120

Travelodge Wrexham

BUDGET HOTEL

☎ 0871 984 6116 📠 01978 365705
Wrexham By Pass, Rhostyllen LL14 4EJ
web: www.travelodge.co.uk
dir: From A483 (Wrexham bypass) take B5605, then A5152 for access to Lodge. Lodge 2m S of Wrexham

Travelodge offers good quality, good value, budget accommodation. All offer family rooms sleeping up to four (two adults, two children) with en suite bathroom/shower-room, remote-control TV, tea- and coffee-making facilities and comfortable beds. Food options vary. Breakfast is at the on-site Bar Café restaurant (if available) or to take away. See also Hotel Groups pages.

Rooms 32 **S** fr £29; **D** fr £29

Ireland

Antra mhoir, Ballyconneely, Co Galway

Additional Information for Northern Ireland & the Republic of Ireland

Licensing Regulations

Northern Ireland: Public houses open Mon-Sat 11.30-23.00. Sun 12.30-22.00. Hotels can serve residents without restriction. Non-residents can be served 12.30-22.00 on Christmas Day. Children under 18 are not allowed in the bar area and may neither buy nor consume liquor in hotels.

Republic of Ireland: General licensing hours are Mon-Thu 10.30-23.30, Fri & Sat 10.30-00.30. Sun 12.30-23.00 (or 00.30 if the following day is a Bank Holiday). There is no service (except for hotel residents) on Christmas Day or Good Friday.

The Fire Services (NI) Order 1984

This covers establishments accommodating more than six people, which must have a certificate from the Northern Ireland Fire Authority. Places accommodating fewer than six people need adequate exits. AA inspectors check emergency notices, fire fighting equipment and fire exits here.

The Republic of Ireland safety regulations are a matter for local authority regulations. For your own and others' safety, read the emergency notices and be sure you understand them.

Telephone numbers

Area codes for numbers in the Republic of Ireland apply only within the Republic. If dialling from outside check the telephone directory (from the UK the international dialling code is 00 353). Area codes for numbers in Britain and Northern Ireland cannot be used directly from the Republic.

For the latest information on the Republic of Ireland visit the AA Ireland's website: www.AAireland.ie

---

NORTHERN IRELAND
CO ANTRIM

ANTRIM   Map 1 D5

Express by Holiday Inn
Antrim M2 Jct 1

BUDGET HOTEL

☎ 0870 890 9977 📄 0870 890 9977
Ballymena Rd BT4 1LL
e-mail: reception.antrim@expressbyholidayinn.net
web: www.hiexpress.com/antrim
dir: At Junction One Shopping Outlet

A modern hotel ideal for families and business travellers. Fresh and uncomplicated, the spacious rooms include Sky TV, power shower and tea and coffee-making facilities. Continental buffet breakfast is included in the room rate; other meals may be taken at the nearby family pub or restaurant. See also the Hotel Groups pages.

Rooms 90 (52 fmly) (10 GF) **S** £59.95-£69.95;
D £59.95-£69.95 (incl. bkfst)* **Conf** Class 20 Board 20 Thtr 40

BALLYMENA   Map 1 D5

Galgorm Resort & Spa

★★★★ 82% ⑳⑳ HOTEL

☎ 028 2588 1001 📄 028 2588 0080
BT42 1EA
e-mail: mail@galgorm.com
dir: 1m from Ballymena on A42, between Galgorm & Cullybackey

Standing in 85 acres of private woodland and sweeping lawns beside the River Maine, this 19th-century mansion offers spacious comfortable bedrooms. Public areas include a welcoming cocktail bar and elegant restaurant, as well as Gillies, a lively and atmospheric locals' bar. Also on the estate is an equestrian centre and a conference hall.

Rooms 75 (14 fmly) (25 GF) **Facilities** Spa STV FTV ⓣ Fishing Gym Clay pigeon shooting Archery Horseriding 🎵 Xmas New Year Wi-fi **Conf** Class 170 Board 30 Thtr 500 Del from £130 to £175* **Services** Lift **Parking** 300 **Notes** ⊗ Civ Wed 500

CARNLOUGH   Map 1 D6

Londonderry Arms

★★★ 73% ⑳ HOTEL

IRISH COUNTRY HOTELS

☎ 028 2888 5255 📄 028 2888 5263
20 Harbour Rd BT44 0EU
e-mail: lda@glensofantrim.com
dir: 14m N from Larne on A2 (coast road)

This delightful hotel was built in the mid-19th century by Lady Londonderry, whose grandson, Winston Churchill, also owned it at one time. Today the hotel's Georgian architecture and rooms are still evident, and spacious bedrooms can be found in the modern extension. The hotel enjoys a prime location in this pretty fishing village overlooking the Antrim coast.

Rooms 35 (15 fmly) **S** £60-£75; **D** £80-£115 (incl. bkfst)* **Facilities** Fishing New Year Wi-fi **Conf** Class 60 Board 40 Thtr 120 Del from £105 to £130* **Services** Lift **Parking** 50 **Notes** LB ⊗ Closed 24-25 Dec Civ Wed 60

CARRICKFERGUS — Map 1 D5

Dobbins Inn

★★ 65% HOTEL

☎ 028 9335 1905 📠 028 9335 1905
6-8 High St BT38 7AP
e-mail: bookingdobbins@btconnect.com
dir: M2 from Belfast, right at rdbt onto A2 to
Carrickfergus. Left opposite castle

Colourful window boxes adorn the front of this popular
inn near the ancient castle and seafront. Public areas are
furnished to a modern standard without compromising
the inn's interesting, historical character. Bedrooms vary
in size and style, all provide modern comforts. Staff
throughout are very friendly and attentive to guests
needs.

Rooms 15 (2 fmly) (3 smoking) **S** £50-£54; **D** £68-£78
(incl. bkfst)* **Facilities** STV 🎵 New Year **Notes** LB Closed
25-26 Dec & 1 Jan RS Good Fri

CO ARMAGH

ARMAGH — Map 1 C5

Charlemont Arms Hotel

★★★ 70% HOTEL

☎ 028 3752 2028 📠 028 3752 6979
57/65 English St BT61 7LB
e-mail: info@charlemontarmshotel.com
web: www.charlemontarmshotel.com
dir: A3 from Portadown or A28 from Newry, into Armagh.
Follow signs to Tourist Information. Hotel 100yds on right

Centrally located for all of this historic city's principal
attractions, this hotel has been under the same family
ownership for almost 70 years and offers a choice of
dining styles and bars. The mostly spacious bedrooms
have all been appointed in a contemporary style and
provide all the expected facilities.

Rooms 30 (2 fmly) **Facilities** 🎵 Xmas **Conf** Class 100
Board 80 Thtr 150 **Services** Lift **Parking** 30 **Notes** LB ⊗
Closed 25-26 Dec

BELFAST

BELFAST — Map 1 D5

Merchant

★★★★★ 81% ⊛ HOTEL

☎ 028 9023 4888 📠 028 9024 7775
35-39 Waring St BT1 2DY
e-mail: info@themerchanthotel.com
dir: In city centre, 2nd left at Albert clock onto Waring St.
Hotel on left

A magnificent hotel situated in the historic Cathedral
Quarter of the city centre. This Grade I listed building has
been lovingly and sensitively restored to reveal its original
architectural grandeur and interior opulence. All the
bedrooms, including five suites, have air-conditioning,
hi-speed internet access, flat-screen TVs and luxury
bathrooms. There are several eating options including the
grand and beautifully decorated Great Room Restaurant.

Rooms 26 (5 fmly) **D** £220-£450 (incl. bkfst)*
Facilities FTV 🎵 Xmas New Year Wi-fi **Conf** Class 24
Board 20 Thtr 40 **Services** Lift Air con **Parking** 26
Notes LB ⊗ Civ Wed 50

Malone Lodge

★★★★ 73% ⊛ HOTEL

☎ 028 9038 8000 📠 028 9038 8088
60 Eglantine Av BT9 6DY
e-mail: info@malonelodgehotel.com
web: www.malonelodgehotel.com
dir: At hospital rdbt exit towards Bouchar Rd, left at 1st
rdbt, right at lights at top, then 1st left

Situated in the leafy suburbs of the university area of
south Belfast, this stylish hotel forms the centrepiece of
an attractive row of Victorian terraced properties. The
unassuming exterior belies an attractive and spacious
interior with a smart lounge, popular bar and stylish
Green Door restaurant. The hotel also has a small, well-
equipped fitness room.

Rooms 46 (5 fmly) (1 GF) **Facilities** Gym Wi-fi
Conf Class 90 Board 40 Thtr 150 **Services** Lift
Parking 35 **Notes** ⊗ Civ Wed 120

Malmaison Belfast

★★★ 81% ⊛ HOTEL

☎ 028 9022 0200 📠 028 9022 0220
34 - 38 Victoria St BT1 3GH
e-mail: hcaters@malmaison.com
web: www.malmaison.com
dir: M1 along Westlink to Grosvenor Rd. Follow city centre
signs. Pass City Hall on right, turn left onto Victoria St.
Hotel on right

Situated in a former seed warehouse, this smart,
contemporary hotel is ideally located for the city centre.
Comfortable bedrooms offer a host of modern facilities,
whilst the stylish public areas include a popular bar and
a brasserie producing carefully prepared meals. The
warm hospitality is notable.

Rooms 64 **Facilities** STV Gym Wi-fi **Conf** Board 22
Services Lift **Notes** LB

Holiday Inn Belfast

★★★ 80% HOTEL

☎ 0870 400 9005 📠 028 9062 6546
22 Ormeau Av BT2 8HS
e-mail: belfast@ihg.com
web: www.holidayinn.co.uk
dir: M1/M2 onto West Link at Grosvenor Rd rdbt, follow
city centre signs. 1st right then 2nd left into Hope St, at
2nd lights turn left into Bedford St, at next lights turn
right into Ormeau Ave, hotel on right

This contemporary hotel is located in the heart of the city
centre's 'golden mile' which makes it ideal for business,
shopping and exploring the city's tourist attractions. The
air-conditioned bedrooms are modern in style and offer a
comprehensive range of facilities. Public rooms include a
staffed business centre and state-of-the-art health club.

Rooms 170 **D** £69-£169* **Facilities** Spa 🏊 Gym 🎵 Wi-fi
Services Lift Air con

Days Hotel Belfast

★★★ 68% HOTEL

☎ 028 9024 2494 📠 028 9024 2495
40 Hope St BT12 5EE
e-mail: reservations@dayshotelbelfast.co.uk
web: www.daysinn.com
dir: From end of M1 take exit off Grosvenor rdbt, at 1st
lights turn right. Over bridge, next left into Hope St

This large modern hotel is a short walk from the city
centre. Bedrooms are comfortable and well equipped,
while the smartly appointed public areas include a
spacious bistro-style restaurant and an open-plan bar/
lounge. The hotel is also ideally located for all transport
links as it is beside the Great Victoria Street bus and
train station. Central Station is just two minutes away,
and the City Airport and ferry terminals are within ten
minutes' drive.

Rooms 250 **Services** Lift **Parking** 300 **Notes** ⊗

BELFAST *continued*

Travelodge Belfast Central

BUDGET HOTEL

☎ 0871 984 6188 📄 028 9023 2999
15 Brunswick St BT2 7GE
web: www.travelodge.co.uk
dir: from M2 follow city centre signs to Oxford St. Right into May St, take 4th left

Travelodge offers good quality, good value, budget accommodation. All offer family rooms sleeping up to four (two adults, two children) with en suite bathroom/shower-room, remote-control TV, tea- and coffee-making facilities and comfortable beds. Food options vary. Breakfast is at the on-site Bar Café restaurant (if available) or to take away. See also Hotel Groups pages.

Rooms 90 **S** fr £29; **D** fr £29 **Conf** Class 50 Board 34 Thtr 65

CO DOWN

BANGOR   Map 1 D5

Clandeboye Lodge

★★★★ 78% ® HOTEL

☎ 028 9185 2500 📄 028 9185 2772
10 Estate Rd, Clandeboye BT19 1UR
e-mail: info@clandeboyelodge.co.uk
web: www.clandeboyelodge.com
dir: A2 from Belfast right at Blackwood Golf Centre & Hotel sign. 500yds into Ballysallagh Rd turn left into Crawfordsburn Rd. Hotel 200yds on left

The hotel is located three miles west of Bangor, and sits in delightful landscaped grounds adjacent to the Clandeboye Estate. The bedrooms have a contemporary design and all have Wi-fi, and flat-screen, satellite TVs. The hotel has extensive conference, banqueting and wedding facilities that are separate from the main hotel. Public areas also include a bright open-plan foyer bar and attractive lounge area.

Rooms 43 (2 fmly) (13 GF) **Facilities** FTV Xmas New Year Wi-fi **Conf** Class 150 Board 50 Thtr 450 **Services** Lift **Parking** 250 **Notes** LB ⊗ Closed 24-26 Dec Civ Wed 400

The Old Inn

★★★★ 74% ®® ⊚⊚ HOTEL

☎ 028 9185 3255 📄 028 9185 2775
15 Main St, Crawfordsburn BT19 1JH
e-mail: info@theoldinn.com
dir: A2, pass Belfast Airport & Holywood, 3m past Holywood sign for The Old Inn, 100yds left at lights, into Crawfordsburn, hotel on left

This delightful hotel enjoys a peaceful rural setting just a short drive from Belfast. Dating from 1614, many of the day rooms exude charm and character. Individually styled bedrooms, some with feature beds, offer comfort and modern facilities. The popular bar and intimate restaurant both offer creative menus, and staff throughout are keen to please.

Rooms 31 (1 annexe) (7 fmly) (6 GF) **Facilities** ♫ Xmas New Year Wi-fi **Conf** Class 27 Board 40 Thtr 120 **Parking** 84 **Notes** ⊗ Civ Wed 100

Marine Court

★★★ 75% HOTEL

☎ 028 9145 1100 📄 028 9145 1200
The Marina BT20 5ED
e-mail: marinecourt@btconnect.com
web: www.marinecourthotel.net
dir: Pass Belfast city airport, follow A2 through Holywood to Bangor, down main street follow to seafront

Enjoying a delightful location overlooking the marina, this hotel offers a good range of conference and leisure facilities suited to both the business and leisure guest. Extensive public areas include the informal first-floor Nelson's Restaurant with views over Belfast Lough, the lively Bar Mocha and the DJ Bar.

Rooms 51 (11 fmly) **Facilities** STV FTV 🏊 supervised Gym Steam room Whirlpool ♫ New Year Wi-fi **Conf** Class 150 Board 60 Thtr 350 Del from £110 to £135* **Services** Lift **Parking** 30 **Notes** ⊗ Closed 25 Dec Civ Wed 250

Royal

★★★ 61% HOTEL

☎ 028 9127 1866 📄 028 9146 7810
Seafront BT20 5ED
e-mail: royalhotelbangor@aol.com
web: www.royalhotelbangor.com
dir: A2 from Belfast. Through town centre to seafront. Turn right, hotel 300yds

This substantial Victorian hotel enjoys a prime seafront location and overlooks the marina. Bedrooms are comfortable and practical in style. Public areas include a choice of contrasting bars whilst traditional Irish cooking can be sampled in a popular brasserie venue.

Rooms 49 (5 fmly) **Facilities** ♫ Wi-fi **Conf** Class 90 Board 80 Thtr 120 **Services** Lift **Notes** LB ⊗ Closed 25-26 Dec

---

NEWCASTLE   Map 1 D5

Burrendale Hotel & Country Club

★★★ 77% HOTEL

☎ 028 4372 2599 📄 028 4372 2328
51 Castlewellan Rd BT33 0JY
e-mail: reservations@burrendale.com
web: www.burrendale.com
dir: On A24 from Belfast. From Newcastle towards Castlewellan, hotel 0.5m on right

Set in its own grounds this hotel is ideal for both business and leisure visitors. Bedrooms are comfortable and many having wonderful views of the Slieve Donard mountain. Guests can choose to dine in the stylish restaurant or enjoy lighter meals in the cosy bar. There are impressive leisure facilities, and the hotel is a firm favourite with walkers and golfers visiting the nearby championship course at Royal County Down.

Rooms 68 (13 fmly) (19 GF) **S** £80-£100; **D** £120-£140 (incl. bkfst) **Facilities** Spa STV 🏊 supervised Putt green Gym Spin bike room Sauna Solarium Hairdressers ♫ Xmas New Year **Conf** Class 80 Board 80 Thtr 300 Del from £99 to £130 **Services** Lift **Parking** 250 **Notes** LB ⊗ Civ Wed 200

CO FERMANAGH

ENNISKILLEN
Map 1 C5

Lough Erne Golf Resort

★★★★★ 86% ◉◉ HOTEL

☎ 028 6632 3230 🖥 028 6634 5758
Belleek Rd BT93 7ED
e-mail: info@loughernegolfresort.com
web: www.loughernegolfresort.com
dir: A46 from Enniskillen towards Donegal, hotel in 3m

This delightful resort enjoys a peaceful and idyllic setting and boasts championship golf courses, a wonderful Thai Spa and a host of outdoor and leisure pursuits. Bedrooms and en suites are spacious, particularly well appointed and include a number of luxury suites. Day rooms are spacious, luxurious and include lounges, bars and restaurants with splendid views. Service is friendly and extremely attentive.

Rooms 120 (61 annexe) **Facilities** Spa STV ☜ ⌔ 18 Fishing Gym ♫ Xmas New Year Wi-fi **Conf** Class 100 Board 40 Thtr 120 **Services** Lift **Parking** 240 **Notes** ⊗ Civ Wed 300

See advert on this page

Killyhevlin

 IRISH COUNTRY HOTELS

★★★★ 77% HOTEL

☎ 028 6632 3481 🖥 028 6632 4726
BT74 6RW
e-mail: info@killyhevlin.com
web: www.killyhevlin.com
dir: 2m S, off A4

This modern, stylish hotel is situated on the shores of Lough Erne, south of the town. The well-equipped bedrooms are particularly spacious and enjoy fine views of the gardens and lake. The restaurant, informal bar and comfortable lounges all share the views. Staff are friendly and helpful. There are extensive leisure facilities and a spa.

Rooms 70 (42 fmly) (22 GF) **S** £97.50-£107.50; **D** £135-£145 (incl. bkfst) **Facilities** Spa STV ☜ supervised Fishing Gym Aerobic studio Steam room Sauna Hydrotherapy area ♫ Xmas New Year Wi-fi **Conf** Class 160 Board 100 Thtr 500 **Services** Lift **Parking** 500 **Notes** LB Closed 25 Dec RS 24 & 26 Dec Civ Wed 250

IRVINESTOWN
Map 1 C5

Mahons

★★★ 70% HOTEL

☎ 028 6862 1656 & 6862 1657 🖥 028 6862 8344
Mill St BT94 1GS
e-mail: info@mahonshotel.co.uk
dir: on A32 midway between Enniskillen & Omagh

This lively hotel has been in the same family for over 137 years. The bar retains a wealth of charm and character, whilst other public rooms reflect a more modern style. In the spacious restaurant the menu offers a wide range of popular dishes. The bedrooms are spacious, very comfortable and well equipped.

Rooms 24 (10 fmly) (1 GF) (3 smoking) **Facilities** STV ☺ ♫ New Year Wi-fi **Conf** Class 250 Board 100 Thtr 400 **Services** Air con **Parking** 50 **Notes** LB Closed 25 Dec Civ Wed 130

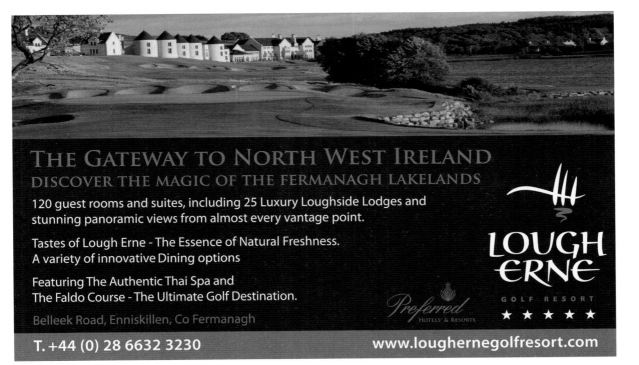

CO LONDONDERRY

AGHADOWEY — Map 1 C6

Brown Trout Golf & Country Inn

IRISH COUNTRY HOTELS

★★ 76% HOTEL

☎ 028 7086 8209 ▤ 028 7086 8878
209 Agivey Rd BT51 4AD
e-mail: jane@browntroutinn.com
dir: At junct of A54 & B66 junct on road to Coleraine

Set alongside the Agivey River and featuring its own 9-hole golf course, this welcoming inn offers a choice of spacious accommodation. Comfortably furnished bedrooms are situated around a courtyard area whilst the cottage suites also have lounge areas. Home-cooked meals are served in the restaurant and lighter fare is available in the charming lounge bar which has entertainment at weekends.

Rooms 15 (11 fmly) **S** £60-£75; **D** £70-£110 (incl. bkfst)* **Facilities** STV FTV ⚓ 9 Putt green Fishing Gym Game fishing ♫ Xmas New Year Wi-fi **Conf** Class 24 Board 28 Thtr 40 **Parking** 80 **Notes** LB

LIMAVADY — Map 1 C6

Radisson Blu Roe Park Resort

Radisson

★★★★ 76% ◉ HOTEL

☎ 028 7772 2222 ▤ 028 7772 2313
BT49 9LB
e-mail: reservations@radissonroepark.com
web: www.radissonblu.co.uk/resort-limavady
dir: on A2 (Londonderry-Limavady road), 1m from Limavady

This impressive, popular hotel is part of its own modern golf resort. The spacious, contemporary bedrooms are well equipped and many have excellent views of the fairways and surrounding estate. The Greens Restaurant provides a refreshing dining experience and the Coach House brasserie offers a lighter menu. The leisure options are extensive.

Rooms 118 (15 fmly) (37 GF) **Facilities** Spa STV ⚓ supervised ⚓ 18 Putt green Fishing ⚓ Gym Driving range Indoor golf academy ♫ Xmas New Year Wi-fi Child facilities **Conf** Class 190 Board 140 Thtr 450 **Services** Lift **Parking** 350 **Notes** LB ⊗ Civ Wed 300

LONDONDERRY — Map 1 C5

City Hotel

★★★★ 73% HOTEL

☎ 028 7136 5800 ▤ 028 7136 5801
Queens Quay BT48 7AS
e-mail: reservations@cityhotelderry.com
dir: Follow city centre signs. Hotel on waterfront

In a central position overlooking the River Foyle, this stylish, contemporary hotel will appeal to business and leisure guests alike. All bedrooms have excellent facilities including internet access; executive rooms make a particularly good working environment. Meeting and function facilities are extensive and there are good leisure facilities.

Rooms 146 (16 fmly) (11 smoking) **Facilities** ◉ supervised Gym Steam room ♫ Xmas Wi-fi **Conf** Class 150 Board 80 Thtr 350 **Services** Lift Air con **Parking** 48 **Notes** ⊗ Closed 25 Dec Civ Wed 350

Travelodge Derry

Travelodge

BUDGET HOTEL

☎ 0871 984 6234 ▤ 028 7127 1277
22-24 Strand Rd BT47 2AB
web: www.travelodge.co.uk
dir: Follow City Centre signs, then signs to Tourist Information Centre. Left at next rdbt. At lights with public car park on right (Travelodge car park on Level 3

Travelodge offers good quality, good value, budget accommodation. All offer family rooms sleeping up to four (two adults, two children) with en suite bathroom/shower-room, remote-control TV, tea- and coffee-making facilities and comfortable beds. Food options vary. Breakfast is at the on-site Bar Café restaurant (if available) or to take away. See also Hotel Groups pages.

Rooms 39 **S** fr £29; **D** fr £29 **Conf** Class 30 Board 25 Thtr 70

MAGHERA — Map 1 C5

Ardtara Country House

IRELAND'S BLUE BOOK

★★★ 85% ◉◉
COUNTRY HOUSE HOTEL

☎ 028 7964 4490 ▤ 028 7964 5080
8 Gorteade Rd, Upperlands BT46 5SA
e-mail: valerie_ferson@ardtara.com
web: www.ardtara.com
dir: From Maghera take A29 towards Coleraine, in 2m take B75 for Kilrea through Upperlands, pass sign Wm Clark & Sons then next left

Ardtara is a delightful, high quality Victorian country house set in eight acres of mature gardens and woodland. The stylish public rooms include a choice of lounges and a sunroom, whilst the elegant period dining room is the perfect venue for enjoying the skilfully prepared cuisine. Bedrooms vary in style and size; all are richly furnished with fine antiques, and have open fires and well equipped bathrooms.

Rooms 9 (1 fmly) (1 GF) **Facilities** FTV New Year Wi-fi **Conf** Board 20 Thtr 45 **Parking** 40 **Notes** ⊗ Civ Wed 150

CO TYRONE

CLOGHER — Map 1 C5

Corick House Hotel

★★★ 77% COUNTRY HOUSE HOTEL

☎ 028 8554 8216 ▤ 028 8554 9531
20 Corick Rd BT76 0BZ
e-mail: reservations@corickcountryhouse.com
dir: Off A4 (Augher & Clogher road)

A warm welcome is guaranteed at Corick House, a charming 17th-century William and Mary house set amid meandering streams and winding country roads in the heart of the beautiful Clogher Valley. The bedrooms are very spacious and many have breathtaking views of the valley and mountains. Public areas reflect much period charm and include a large dining room, a sun lounge and a cosy bar.

Rooms 19 (9 fmly) (3 GF) **Facilities** STV ⚓ **Conf** Class 150 Board 60 Thtr 250 **Notes** Civ Wed

DUNGANNON — Map 1 C5

Cohannon Inn & Autolodge

★★ 69% HOTEL

☎ 028 8772 4488 📠 028 8775 2217
212 Ballynakilly Rd BT71 6HJ
e-mail: enquiries@cohannon-inn.com
dir: 400yds from M1 junct 14

Handy for the M1 and the nearby towns of Dungannon and Portadown, The Cohannon Inn offers competitive prices and well-maintained bedrooms, located behind the inn complex in a smart purpose-built wing. Public areas are smartly furnished and wide-ranging menus are served throughout the day.

Rooms 42 (20 fmly) (21 GF) (5 smoking) **S** £49.95;
D £49.95-£99.90* **Facilities** New Year Wi-fi
Conf Class 100 Board 40 Thtr 160 **Parking** 160
Notes RS 25 Dec

FIVEMILETOWN — Map 1 C5

Valley Hotel

★★★ 72% HOTEL

☎ 028 8952 1505 📠 028 8952 1688
60 Main St BT75 0PW
e-mail: info@thevalleyhotel.com
web: www.thevalleyhotel.com

This family-run hotel offers smartly presented bedrooms that are appointed to a very high standard. Comfortable public areas include a cosy residents' lounge and the popular bar where an excellent range of bar meals is served. More formal dining can be enjoyed in the Bordeaux Restaurant. The hotel has extensive conferencing facilities.

Rooms 22 (1 fmly) (4 smoking) **S** £50-£70; **D** £80-£100
(incl. bkfst)* **Facilities** Fishing ♫ Xmas New Year Wi-fi
Conf Class 30 Board 30 Thtr 50 **Services** Lift **Parking** 150
Notes ⊗ Closed 25 Dec RS 26 Dec Civ Wed 200

REPUBLIC OF IRELAND
CO CARLOW

CARLOW — Map 1 C3

Seven Oaks

IRISH COUNTRY HOTELS

★★★ 78% HOTEL

☎ 059 9131308 📠 059 9132155
Athy Rd
e-mail: info@sevenoakshotel.com

This smart hotel is conveniently situated within walking distance of the town centre. Public areas include comfortable lounges, a traditional style bar and restaurant where food is available all day. Bedrooms are spacious and very well appointed. There are extensive leisure and banqueting facilities and a secure car park.

Rooms 89 (5 fmly) (7 GF) **S** €70-€100; **D** €100-€200
(incl. bkfst) **Facilities** STV ⊗ supervised Gym Aerobic studio Steam room ♫ Wi-fi **Conf** Class 150 Board 80
Thtr 400 Del from €130 to €150* **Services** Lift Air con
Parking 200 **Notes** LB ⊗ Closed 25-26 Dec RS Good Fri

TULLOW — Map 1 D3

Mount Wolseley Hotel, Spa & Country Club

★★★★ 80% ⊚ HOTEL

☎ 059 9180100 📠 059 9152123
e-mail: sales@mountwolseley.ie
dir: Take N7 from Dublin. In Naas take N9 towards Carlow. In Castledermot turn left for Tullow

Located on a vast estate associated with the Wolseley family of motoring fame, this hotel has much to offer. Public areas are very spacious and there are a range of comfortable bedrooms and suites. Leisure pursuits include golf, together with a health centre and spa facilities. The hotel offers a number of dining options.

Rooms 143 (10 fmly) (5 smoking) **S** €95-€140;
D €125-€220 (incl. bkfst) **Facilities** Spa STV ⊗
supervised ⚑ 18 ⚐ Putt green Gym ♫ Xmas New Year
Wi-fi **Conf** Class 288 Board 70 Thtr 750 **Services** Lift
Air con **Parking** 160 **Notes** LB ⊗ Closed 25-26 Dec
Civ Wed 400

CO CAVAN

CAVAN — Map 1 C4

Cavan Crystal

★★★★ 79% ⊚⊚ HOTEL

☎ 049 4360600 📠 049 4360699
Dublin Rd
e-mail: info@cavancrystalhotel.com
web: www.cavancrystalhotel.com
dir: N3 towards Cavan, at 1st rdbt take N55 signed Athlone

Contemporary design, matched with the use of native timber, handcrafted brick, and crystal chandeliers make this a particularly distinctive hotel. Expect excellent hospitality from all the highly trained staff. Located on the southern edge of the town, the hotel also features a well-equipped health plus beauty clinic, and extensive banquet and conference facilities.

Rooms 85 (2 fmly) (9 GF) **Facilities** ⊗ supervised Gym
Beauty & massage treatment Salon Gym ♫ New Year
Wi-fi **Conf** Class 300 Board 100 Thtr 500 **Services** Lift
Parking 216 **Notes** LB ⊗ Closed 24 & 25 Dec

Kilmore

★★★ 79% HOTEL

☎ 049 4332288 📠 049 4332458
Dublin Rd
e-mail: sales@hotelkilmore.ie
dir: approx 3km from Cavan on N3

Located near Cavan and easily accessible from the N3, this comfortable hotel features spacious and welcoming public areas. Good food is served in the Annalee Restaurant, which is always appreciated by guests returning from nearby fishing or golf.

Rooms 38 (16 fmly) (19 GF) **Facilities** Free use of facilities at Slieve Russell Golf & Country Club ♫ Xmas
Wi-fi **Conf** Class 200 Board 60 Thtr 500 **Services** Air con
Parking 450 **Notes** ⊗ Closed 25 Dec

COOTEHILL — Map 1 C4

Errigal Country House

★★★ 71% HOTEL

 IRISH COUNTRY HOTELS

☎ 049 5556901 📄 049 5556902
Cavan Rd
e-mail: info@errigalhotel.com
web: www.errigalhotel.com
dir: 1km from town centre on Cavan Rd (R188)

This modern hotel is located in landscaped gardens and within walking distance of Cootehill. Bedrooms are appointed to a high standard and public areas are very comfortable and attractively decorated. Reynards Restaurant serves dinner each evening, and a more informal fare is available in The Brewery Bar. The Eden Health & Wellness suite offers a range of treatments.

Rooms 22 (2 fmly) **Facilities** Spa New Year Wi-fi
Conf Class 215 Board 130 Thtr 420 **Services** Lift Air con
Parking 250 **Notes** LB ⊗

KINGSCOURT — Map 1 C4

Cabra Castle Hotel

★★★★ 77% ⊛ HOTEL

MANOR HOUSE HOTELS

☎ 042 9667030 📄 042 9667039
e-mail: sales@cabracastle.com
dir: R165 between Kingscourt & Carrickmacross

Rebuilt in 1808, Cabra Castle stands on 100 acres of parkland which is surrounded by Dun a Ri Forrest Park. There is a 9-hole golf course, tennis courts and helicopter pad. In addition to bedrooms in the castle, there are spacious courtyard rooms and family cottages in the grounds. The elegant reception rooms, cosy bar, Courtyard Restaurant and the extensive banqueting facilities all offer luxurious comfort.

Rooms 99 (79 annexe) (17 fmly) (30 GF) (20 smoking)
Facilities FTV ↨ 9 ♨ Wi-fi **Conf** Class 100 Board 50
Thtr 300 **Parking** 200 **Notes** ⊗ Closed 25-27 Dec
Civ Wed 200

MOUNTNUGENT — Map 1 C4

Crover House Hotel & Golf Club

★★★ 68% HOTEL

☎ 049 8540206 & 8540364 📄 049 8540365
Lough Sheelin
e-mail: crover@iol.ie
dir: On R154 (Oldcastle)

This hotel is located on the shores of Lough Sheelin close to Cavan and surrounded by a 9-hole golf course. Public areas include a comfortable lounge and bar where food is available throughout the day; dinner is served in the restaurant that overlooks the golf course. Bedrooms are spacious and well appointed. The banqueting facilities are impressive.

Rooms 37 (3 fmly) (12 GF) **S** €85-€95; **D** €150-€160
(incl. bkfst)* **Facilities** STV ↨ 9 **Conf** Thtr 300
Parking 300 **Notes** LB ⊗ Closed 24-26 Dec

VIRGINIA — Map 1 C4

The Park Hotel

★★★ 71% ⊛ HOTEL

☎ 049 8546100 📄 049 8547203
Virginia Park
e-mail: info@parkhotelvirginia.com
web: www.parkhotelvirginia.com
dir: Exit N3 in Virginia onto R194. Hotel 500yds on left

A charming hotel, built in 1750 as the summer retreat of the Marquis of Headford. Situated overlooking Lake Ramor on a 100-acre estate, it has a 9-hole golf course, lovely mature gardens and woodland. This hotel brings together generous hospitality and a relaxed leisurely way of life. The Marquis Dining room is renowned for good food that utilises fruit, herbs and vegetables grown in the estate's organic gardens.

Rooms 26 (1 fmly) (8 GF) **Facilities** ↨ 9 Fishing ♫ Xmas
New Year Wi-fi **Conf** Class 40 Board 40 Thtr 100
Parking 150 **Notes** ⊗ Closed 25 Dec Civ Wed 100

CO CLARE

BALLYVAUGHAN — Map 1 B3

INSPECTORS' CHOICE

Gregans Castle

★★★ ⊛⊛
COUNTRY HOUSE HOTEL

 IRELAND'S BLUE BOOK

☎ 065 7077005 📄 065 7077111
e-mail: stay@gregans.ie
dir: 3.5m S of Ballyvaughan on N67

The Haden family, together with their welcoming staff, offer a high level of personal service. Situated in the heart of The Burren, the hotel enjoys splendid views towards Galway Bay. The area is rich in archaeological, geological and botanical interest. Food focuses on top quality local and organic produce. Bedrooms are individually decorated; superior rooms and suites are particularly comfortable, and some of these are on the ground floor.

Rooms 21 (3 fmly) (7 GF) **Facilities** ⅃ ♫ Wi-fi
Conf Class 25 Board 14 Thtr 25 **Parking** 25 **Notes** LB
⊗ Closed Jan-12 Feb & 30 Nov-Dec

Hylands Burren

★★★ 72% HOTEL

 IRISH COUNTRY HOTELS

☎ 065 7077037 📄 065 7077131
e-mail: info@hylandsburren.com

This charming village hotel, dating from the 18th century, is set in the picturesque village of Ballyvaughan. In the heart of the unique Burren landscape, it is ideally located for touring County Clare. Traditional music is played nightly in the bar and lounges in the high season and local seafood is a speciality in the restaurant all year round. Bedrooms are comfortable and well appointed.

Rooms 29 (2 fmly) (6 GF) (10 smoking) **S** €55-€75;
D €75-€110 (incl. bkfst) **Facilities** STV FTV ♫ New Year
Wi-fi **Conf** Class 10 Board 12 Thtr 30 Del from €65 to
€95* **Parking** 30 **Notes** LB ⊗ Closed 22-25 Dec & 3-31
Jan

BUNRATTY — Map 1 B3

Bunratty Shannon Shamrock

★★★ 66% HOTEL

☎ 061 361177 ▤ 061 471252
e-mail: reservations@dunnehotels.com
dir: take Bunratty by-pass, exit off Limerick/Shannon dual carriageway

Situated in the shadow of Bunratty's famous medieval castle in a pretty village, this hotel is surrounded by well-maintained lawns and mature trees. Bedrooms and public areas are spacious and comfortable. There is a leisure centre plus impressive conference and banqueting facilities.

Rooms 115 (12 fmly) (91 GF) **Facilities** ☜ Gym Hair & beauty salon ♬ **Conf** Class 650 Board 300 Thtr 1200 **Parking** 300 **Notes** ⊗ Closed 24-26 Dec

ENNIS — Map 1 B3

Temple Gate

★★★ 78% HOTEL

☎ 065 6823300 ▤ 065 6823322
The Square
e-mail: info@templegatehotel.com
dir: Exit N18 onto Tulla Rd for 0.25m, hotel on left

This smart hotel is located in the centre of the town, accessed from the public car park at the rear. Incorporating an 19th-century Gothic-style building used for events, the public areas are well planned and include a comfortable lounge, popular pub and JM's Bistro restaurant. Bedrooms, including executive rooms, are attractive and well equipped.

Rooms 70 (3 fmly) (11 GF) (20 smoking) **Facilities** STV FTV ♬ New Year Wi-fi **Conf** Class 100 Board 80 Thtr 250 **Services** Lift **Parking** 52 **Notes** ⊗ Closed 25-26 Dec RS 24 Dec

LISDOONVARNA — Map 1 B3

Sheedys Country House

★★★ 75% ◉◉ HOTEL

☎ 065 7074026 ▤ 065 7074555
e-mail: info@sheedys.com
dir: 200mtrs from The Square in town centre

Dating in part from the 17th century and set in an unrivalled location on the edge of The Burren, this house is full of character and has an intimate atmosphere. Fine cuisine can be enjoyed in the contemporary restaurant. Bedrooms are spacious and well appointed. This makes an ideal base for touring as it is close to Doolin, Lahinch Golf Course, and the Cliffs of Moher.

Rooms 11 (1 fmly) (5 GF) **S** €90-€120; **D** €130-€200 (incl. bkfst)* **Facilities** STV Wi-fi **Parking** 40 **Notes** LB ⊗ Closed mid Oct-Apr

NEWMARKET-ON-FERGUS — Map 1 B3

INSPECTORS' CHOICE

Dromoland Castle

★★★★★ ◉◉ HOTEL

☎ 061 368144 ▤ 061 363355
e-mail: sales@dromoland.ie
dir: N18 to Ennis/Galway from Shannon for 8km to 'Dromoland Interchange' signed Quin. Take slip road left, 4th exit at 1st rdbt, 2nd exit at 2nd rdbt. Hotel 500mtrs on left

Dromoland Castle, dating from the early 18th century, stands on a 375-acre estate and offers extensive indoor leisure activities and outdoor pursuits. The team are wholly committed to caring for guests. The thoughtfully equipped bedrooms and suites vary in style but all provide excellent levels of comfort, and the magnificent public rooms, warmed by log fires, are no less impressive. The hotel has two restaurants, the elegant fine-dining Earl of Thomond, and less formal Fig Tree in the golf clubhouse.

Rooms 99 (20 fmly) **S** €238-€607; **D** €238-€607* **Facilities** Spa STV ☜ supervised ♨ 18 ⅃ Putt green Fishing Gym Beauty clinic Archery Clay shooting Mountain bikes Driven shoots Falconry ♬ New Year Wi-fi **Conf** Class 220 Board 80 Thtr 450 Del from €345 to €445* **Services** Lift **Parking** 120 **Notes** LB ⊗ Closed 25-26 Dec Civ Wed 70

Carrygerry Country House

◉ RESTAURANT WITH ROOMS

☎ 061 360500 ▤ 061 360700
Carrygerry
e-mail: info@carrygerryhouse.com

This charming country house was built around 1793 and has fine views over the Shannon Estuary. It has been refurbished by chef/proprietor Naill and Gillian Ennis. Bedrooms in the main house feature four-poster beds and there are family rooms in the courtyard. The drawing room and cosy bar are very comfortable; the Conservatory Restaurant has the perfect ambience for a romantic dinner. Shannon Airport and Bunratty Castle are just minutes away.

Rooms 11

SPANISH POINT — Map 1 B3

Armada

★★★ 78% HOTEL

IRISH COUNTRY HOTELS

☎ 065 7084110 ▤ 065 7084632
e-mail: info@burkesarmadahotel.com
dir: N18 from Ennis take N85 Inagh, then R460 to Miltown Malbay. Follow signs for Spanish Point

Situated on the coast overlooking breaking waves and golden sands, this hotel is in a natural, unspoiled location. Bedrooms, including superior Tranquillity Suites, offer good comfort and many have sea views. The Pearl Restaurant serves good food, and the Ocean Bar, with its splendid views, serves a carvery lunch and bar food all day. There are excellent water sports and golf courses nearby.

Rooms 61 (53 fmly) **Facilities** Gym ♬ Xmas **Conf** Class 400 Board 60 Thtr 600 **Services** Lift **Parking** 175 **Notes** LB ⊗

CO CORK

BALLYCOTTON — Map 1 C2

INSPECTORS' CHOICE

Bayview

★★★ ◉◉ HOTEL

MANOR HOUSE HOTELS

☎ 021 4646746 ▤ 021 4646075
e-mail: res@thebayviewhotel.com
dir: N25 Castlemartyr, turn right through Ladysbridge & Garryvoe, to Ballycotton

The gardens of the hotel hang on the cliffs overlooking the fishing port and Ballycotton Bay. All the comfortable public rooms and bedrooms with balconies take in the breathtaking coastal views. It is the warm and friendly team that impresses most, with dinner in the Capricho Room proving to be a special delight, with locally landed fish among the highlights.

Rooms 35 (5 GF) (10 smoking) **Facilities** STV ⅃ Pitch and putt Sea angling **Conf** Class 30 Board 24 Thtr 60 **Services** Lift Air con **Parking** 40 **Notes** LB ⊗ Closed Nov-Apr Civ Wed 100

BALLYLICKEY — Map 1 B2

INSPECTORS' CHOICE

Sea View House Hotel
★★★ ⊛⊛ HOTEL

☎ 027 50073 & 50462 📠 027 51555
e-mail: info@seaviewhousehotel.com
web: www.seaviewhousehotel.com
dir: 5km from Bantry, 11km from Glengarriff on N71

Colourful gardens and glimpses of Bantry Bay through the mature trees frame this delightful country house. Owner Kathleen O'Sullivan's team of staff are exceptionally pleasant and there is a relaxed atmosphere. Guest comfort and good cuisine are the top priorities. Bedrooms are spacious and individually styled; some on the ground floor are appointed to suit less able guests.

Rooms 25 (3 fmly) (5 GF) **Parking** 32 **Notes** Closed mid Nov-mid Mar

BALTIMORE — Map 1 B1

Casey's of Baltimore
★★★ 72% ⊛ HOTEL

IRISH COUNTRY HOTELS

☎ 028 20197 📠 028 20509
e-mail: info@caseysofbaltimore.com
web: www.caseysofbaltimore.com
dir: from Cork take N71 to Skibbereen, then take R595

This relaxed family run hotel is situated in the sailing and fishing village of Baltimore. Bedrooms are situated within the hotel and there are also six suites in another building just a few minutes' walk away. Traditional music is played in the cosy bar and lounge at weekends. The Casey's ensure that a variety of the freshest seafood, from Michael's fishing trawler and mussel farm is served

in the restaurant. They are happy to organise trips to the many nearby islands.

Rooms 14 (1 fmly) (4 GF) **S** €90-€110; **D** €150-€180 (incl. bkfst)* **Facilities** STV FTV ♬ New Year **Conf** Class 30 Board 25 Thtr 45 **Parking** 50 **Notes** LB ⊗ Closed 21-27 Dec

BANTRY — Map 1 B2

Westlodge
★★★ 71% HOTEL

☎ 027 50360 📠 027 50438
e-mail: reservations@westlodgehotel.ie
web: www.westlodgehotel.ie
dir: N71 to West Cork

A superb leisure centre and good children's facilities makes this hotel very popular with families. Its location on the outskirts of the town also makes it an ideal base for touring west Cork and south Kerry. All the staff are friendly and hospitable. There are extensive banqueting facilities and lovely walks in the grounds.

Rooms 90 (20 fmly) (20 GF) **Facilities** ⊕ supervised ⅜ Putt green Gym Squash ♬ New Year Wi-fi **Conf** Class 200 Board 24 Thtr 400 Del from €99 to €120* **Services** Lift Air con **Parking** 400 **Notes** ⊗ Closed 23-27 Dec Civ Wed 300

Maritime
Ⓤ

☎ 027 54700 & 54716 📠 027 54701
The Quay
e-mail: info@themaritime.ie
dir: On N71 towards Bantry hotel on right

Currently the rating for this establishment is not confirmed. This may be due to a change of ownership or because it has only recently joined the AA rating scheme. For further details please see the AA website: theAA.com

Rooms 114 (30 fmly) **Facilities** STV ⊕ supervised Gym Sauna Steam room ♬ New Year Wi-fi **Conf** Class 180 Board 120 Thtr 550 **Services** Lift **Parking** 85 **Notes** LB ⊗ Closed 24-28 Dec

BLARNEY — Map 1 B2

Blarney Golf Resort
★★★★ 76% ⊛ HOTEL

☎ 021 4384477 📠 021 4516453
Tower
e-mail: reservations@blarneygolfresort.com
dir: Exit N20 for Blarney, 4km to Tower, right onto Old Kerry Rd. Hotel 2km on right

Set amid a John Daly designed golf course on the outskirts of the village of Tower, this hotel offers a range of well-equipped comfortable bedrooms. Excellent standards of cuisine are on offer in the Inniscarra Restaurant, with more casual eating available throughout the afternoon in Cormac's bar. The hotel also features a Sentosa Spa.

Rooms 117 (56 annexe) (56 fmly) (30 GF) **Facilities** Spa FTV ⊕ supervised ⅃ 18 Putt green Gym Steam room Sauna ♬ Xmas New Year Wi-fi **Conf** Class 150 Board 40 Thtr 300 **Services** Lift Air con **Parking** 250 **Notes** LB ⊗

Blarney Castle

★★★ 73% HOTEL

☎ 021 4385116 🖹 021 4385542
The Village Green
e-mail: info@blarneycastlehotel.com
dir: N20 (Cork-Limerick road) onto R617 for Blarney. Hotel on village green

Situated in the centre of the town within walking distance of the renowned Blarney Stone, this friendly hotel has been in the same family since 1873. Many of the bedrooms are spacious, but all are appointed to a very comfortable standard. The popular bar serves good food throughout most of the day.

Rooms 13 (4 fmly) **S** €75-€95; **D** €100-€130 (incl. bkfst) **Facilities** STV ♫ Wi-fi **Services** Air con **Parking** 5 **Notes** ⊗ Closed 24-25 Dec

---

CARRIGALINE   Map 1 B2

Carrigaline Court Hotel

★★★★ 77% HOTEL

☎ 021 4852100 🖹 021 4371103
e-mail: reception@carrigcourt.com
web: www.carrigcourt.com
dir: From South Link road (E from airport or W from Dublin/Lee Tunnel) take exit for Carrigaline, stay in right lane

This smart, town centre modern hotel is situated only minutes' drive from Cork City Airport and the Ringaskiddy Port. Bedrooms are spacious and very well appointed. Public areas include Collins, the traditional Irish pub, The Bistro and extensive conference, leisure and beauty facilities. Golf, sailing, angling and horse riding are available locally.

Rooms 91 (2 fmly) **S** €103-€165; **D** €170-€220 (incl. bkfst) **Facilities** Spa STV ® supervised Gym Beauty salon Massage treatment rooms New Year Wi-fi **Conf** Class 200 Board 35 Thtr 350 Del from €176 to €200* **Services** Lift **Parking** 150 **Notes** LB ⊗ Closed 25 Dec Civ Wed 70

CASTLEMARTYR   Map 1 C2

Castlemartyr Resort

Ⓤ

☎ 021 4644050 🖹 021 4219002
e-mail: reception@castlemartyrresort.ie
dir: N25, 3rd exit signed Rosslare. Continue past Carrigtwohill & Midleton exits. At rdbt take 2nd exit into Castlemartyr

Currently the rating for this establishment is not confirmed. This may be due to a change of ownership or because it has only recently joined the AA rating scheme. For further details please see the AA website: theAA.com

Rooms 103 (6 fmly) (30 GF) (10 smoking) **Facilities** Spa STV ® ♨ 18 ⛳ Gym Fitness studio Steam room Sauna Xmas New Year Wi-fi **Conf** Class 32 Board 32 Thtr 80 **Services** Lift Air con **Parking** 200 **Notes** LB Civ Wed 80

CLONAKILTY   Map 1 B2

Inchydoney Island Lodge & Spa

★★★★ 83% ◉◉ HOTEL

☎ 023 33143 🖹 023 35229
e-mail: reservations@inchydoneyisland.com
dir: Follow N71 (West Cork road) to Clonakilty. At rdbt in Clonakilty take 2nd exit, follow signs to hotel

This modern hotel, with a striking interior, has a stunning location on the coast with steps down to two long sandy beaches. Bedrooms are decorated in warm colours and are well appointed. Diners have a choice of the third-floor Gulfstream Restaurant or the more casual Dunes Bar and Bistro. The Island Spa offers many treatments including seawater therapies.

Rooms 67 (24 fmly) (18 GF) **Facilities** Spa ® supervised Fishing Gym Sauna Steam room Snooker room Surfing Ocean safari ♫ Wi-fi **Conf** Board 50 Thtr 300 **Services** Lift **Parking** 200 **Notes** ⊗ Closed 24-26 Dec Civ Wed 300

Quality Hotel Clonakilty

★★★ 72% HOTEL

☎ 023 883 6400 🖹 023 883 5404
Skibbereen Rd
e-mail: info.clonakilty@qualityhotels.ie
web: www.qualityhotelclonakilty.com
dir: In Clonakilty take 2nd exit off small rdbt onto Skibbereen Bypass Rd. Hotel on left after approx 1m

A short distance from the town, in the heart of West Cork, this is good base for exploring the rich history and landscapes of the area. Families are particularly well catered for with a choice of bedroom styles and sizes. Oscars is a lively bar with entertainment at weekends. Use of the facilities of Club Vitae is complimentary to guests.

Rooms 96 (63 fmly) (41 GF) (10 smoking) **S** €65-€134; **D** €78-€218 (incl. bkfst) **Facilities** Spa ® supervised Gym 3-screen cinema Sauna Steam room ♫ New Year Wi-fi Child facilities **Conf** Class 75 Board 40 Thtr 140 Del from €99 to €130* **Services** Lift **Parking** 200 **Notes** LB ⊗ Closed 24-26 Dec

---

CORK   Map 1 B2

The Kingsley Hotel

★★★★ 85% HOTEL

☎ 021 4800500 🖹 021 4800527
Victoria Cross
e-mail: resv@kingsleyhotel.com
dir: off N22 opposite County Hall

Situated on the banks of the River Lee, this luxurious hotel has excellent facilities. The bedrooms are spacious and feature thoughtful additional touches. The contemporary bar and restaurant have an informal atmosphere, and both the lounge and library are elegant and relaxing.

Rooms 69 (4 fmly) **Facilities** ® supervised Fishing Gym Treatment rooms Xmas **Conf** Class 50 Board 32 Thtr 95 **Services** Lift Air con **Parking** 150 **Notes** ⊗

CORK *continued*

Maryborough Hotel & Spa

★★★★ 79% HOTEL

☎ 021 4365555 🖹 021 4365662
Maryborough Hill
e-mail: info@maryborough.com
dir: From Jack Lynch Tunnel take 2nd exit signed Douglas.
Right at 1st rdbt, follow Rochestown road to fingerpost
rdbt. Left, hotel on left 0.5m up hill

Dating from 1715, this house was renovated and
extended to become a fine hotel set in beautifully
landscaped grounds. The suites in the main house and
the bedrooms in the wing are well appointed and
comfortable. The extensive lounge is very popular for the
range of food served throughout the day.

Rooms 93 (6 fmly) **S** €95-€195; **D** €130-€350 (incl.
bkfst)* **Facilities** Spa STV 🕲 supervised Gym Sauna
Steam room 🎵 New Year Wi-fi **Conf** Class 250 Board 60
Thtr 500 Del from €140 to €190* **Services** Lift
Parking 300 **Notes** LB ⊗ Closed 24-26 Dec Civ Wed 100

Rochestown Park Hotel

★★★★ 78% HOTEL

☎ 021 4890800 🖹 021 4892178
Rochestown Rd, Douglas
e-mail: info@rochestownpark.com
dir: from Lee Tunnel, 2nd exit left off dual carriageway.
400mtrs then 1st left and right at small rdbt. Hotel
600mtrs on right

This modern hotel is situated in mature gardens on the
south side of the city. Various bedroom styles, including
suites, are available, most rooms are air-conditioned and
overlook Mahon Golf Club. Public areas include a
traditional bar and Gallery Restaurant. There are
extensive leisure, conference and exhibition facilities.
Convenient for both the airport and the ferries.

Rooms 160 (17 fmly) (23 GF) **Facilities** Spa 🕲
supervised Gym Thalassotherapy & beauty centre Xmas
Wi-fi **Conf** Class 360 Board 100 Thtr 700 **Services** Lift
Parking 300 **Notes** ⊗ Closed 25-26 Dec

Silver Springs Moran

★★★★ 78% HOTEL

☎ 021 4507533 🖹 021 4507641
Tivoli
e-mail: silverspringsres@moranhotels.com
web: www.silverspringshotel.ie
dir: N8 south, Silver Springs exit. Right across overpass
then right, hotel on left

Located on the main approach to the city, the public
areas of this hotel create a smart, contemporary
atmosphere. Bedrooms are comfortable, many offering
good views over the River Lee. Guests have use of a
nearby leisure centre. The lobby lounge is very popular for
all day dining, with more formal meals served in the
Watermarq Restaurant. Excellent conference facilities are
available in a separate building.

Rooms 109 (29 fmly) (12 smoking) **S** €115-€185;
D €140-€250 (incl. bkfst) **Facilities** 🕲 supervised 🏌
Gym Squash Aerobics classes 🎵 Xmas New Year Wi-fi
Conf Class 400 Board 30 Thtr 800 Del from €146
Services Lift **Parking** 325 **Notes** LB ⊗ Closed 24-27 Dec
Civ Wed 800

GARRYVOE

Map 1 C2

Garryvoe

IRISH COUNTRY HOTELS

★★★ 82% HOTEL

☎ 021 4646718 🖹 021 4646824
Ballycotton Bay, Castlemartyr
e-mail: res@garryvoehotel.com
dir: Off N25 onto L72 at Castlemartyr (between Midleton
& Youghal) then 6km

A comfortable, family-run hotel with caring staff, the
Garryvoe offers bedrooms that are appointed to a very
high standard. It stands in a delightful position
overlooking a sandy beach and Ballycotton Bay. A popular
bar serves light meals throughout the day, with a more
formal menu for dinner in the spacious dining room.

Rooms 65 (6 fmly) (10 smoking) **S** €69-€145;
D €69-€145 **Facilities** STV 🕲 supervised 🏌 Putt green
Gym Sauna Steam room 🎵 Wi-fi **Conf** Class 150 Board 12
Thtr 300 **Services** Lift **Parking** 100 **Notes** LB ⊗ Closed
24-25 Dec Civ Wed 150

GLANMIRE

Map 1 B2

Fitzgeralds Vienna Woods

IRISH COUNTRY HOTELS

★★★ 74% HOTEL

☎ 021 4556800 & 4821146 🖹 021 4821120
e-mail: reservations@viennawoodshotel.com
dir: 3.5m from Cork city centre

This long established hotel is located in the leafy suburb
of Glanmire amid 20 acres of woodland. Bedrooms in the
newer wing are comfortably furnished with those in the
original house individually decorated. This hotel
specialises in family celebrations for which their spacious
banqueting room makes an ideal venue.

Rooms 80 (32 annexe) (2 fmly) (20 smoking)
S €69-€159; **D** €79-€169 (incl. bkfst)* **Facilities** STV
🎵 New Year Wi-fi **Conf** Class 300 Board 70 Thtr 700
Del from €119 to €169* **Services** Lift **Parking** 250
Notes LB ⊗ Closed 24-26 Dec Civ Wed 400

GOUGANE BARRA — Map 1 B2

Gougane Barra

★★★ 72% ◉ HOTEL

IRISH COUNTRY HOTELS

☎ 026 47069 🖹 026 47226
e-mail: gouganebarrahotel@eircom.net
dir: On L4643, off R584 between N22 at Macroom & N71 at Bantry

Picturesquely situated on the shore of Gougane Barra Lake and at the entrance to the National Park this family run hotel offers tranquillity and very good cooking. Bedrooms and public areas are comfortable and enjoy lovely views. Guests can experience the unique theatre during high season and bikes and boats are available for exploring the area.

Rooms 26 (12 GF) Facilities STV FTV Fishing Boating Cycling ♫ Wi-fi Parking 26 Notes LB ⊗ Closed 10 Oct-18 Apr

KINSALE — Map 1 B2

Carlton Hotel Kinsale

★★★★ 76% HOTEL

☎ 021 4706000 🖹 021 4706001
Rathmore Rd
e-mail: info@carlton.ie
dir: Before Kinsale turn left signed Charles Fort. 2kms, hotel on left

This hotel is set on an elevated position overlooking Oysterhaven Bay in 90 acres of mature parkland, approximately five kilometres from the town centre. All of the bedrooms are spacious and well appointed; two-bedroom holiday options are available in the grounds. The contemporary public rooms are on the first floor, so making the most of the spectacular views.

Rooms 90 (20 annexe) (20 fmly) (24 GF) (24 smoking) Facilities Spa STV FTV ◌ supervised Gym Sauna Steam room Wi-fi Conf Class 140 Board 60 Thtr 200 Services Lift Air con Parking 200 Notes LB ⊗ Closed 23-26 Dec

Trident

★★★★ 73% ◉ HOTEL

☎ 021 4779300 🖹 021 4774173
Worlds End
e-mail: info@tridenthotel.com
dir: R600 from Cork to Kinsale, along Kinsale waterfront, hotel beyond pier

Located at the harbour's edge, this hotel has its own marina with boats for hire. Many of the bedrooms have superb views and two have balconies. The restaurant and lounge both overlook the harbour, and pleasant staff provide hospitable service.

Rooms 75 (2 fmly) S €70-€205; D €80-€260 (incl. bkfst)* Facilities Deep sea angling Yacht charter New Year Wi-fi Conf Class 130 Board 40 Thtr 200 Del from €185* Services Lift Parking 60 Notes LB ⊗ Closed 24-26 Dec Civ Wed 50

Blue Haven

★★★ 73% HOTEL

☎ 021 4772209 🖹 021 4774268
3 Pearse St
e-mail: info@bluehavenkinsale.com
dir: In town centre

At the heart of this historic town, the Blue Haven offers a welcoming lobby lounge, a popular and stylish bar with an airy bistro attached and an elegant restaurant. Live music is a feature seven days a week in the summer months. Bedrooms vary in size and are furnished to a high standard.

Rooms 17 S €65-€100; D €80-€195 (incl. bkfst)* Facilities ♫ Xmas New Year Wi-fi Conf Class 35 Board 25 Thtr 70 Del from €125 to €207.50* Notes LB ⊗ Closed 25 Dec

The White House

◉ RESTAURANT WITH ROOMS

☎ 021 4772125 🖹 021 4772045
Pearse St, The Glen
e-mail: whitehse@indigo.ie
dir: In town centre

Centrally located among the narrow, twisting streets of the charming town of Kinsale, this restaurant with rooms dates from 1850, and is a welcoming hostelry with modern smart, comfortable bedrooms. The bar and bistro are open for lunch and dinner; the varied menu especially features local fish and beef. The courtyard makes a perfect summer setting and there is traditional music in the bar most nights.

Rooms 10 (2 fmly)

MACROOM — Map 1 B2

Castle

★★★ 78% ◉ HOTEL

IRISH COUNTRY HOTELS

☎ 026 41074 🖹 026 41505
Main St
e-mail: castlehotel@eircom.net
dir: on N22 midway between Cork & Killarney

This town centre property offers excellent service provided by the Buckley Family and their team. Bedrooms are very comfortable, as are the extensive public areas. Secure parking is available to the rear.

Rooms 58 (6 fmly) (15 smoking) Facilities STV ◌ supervised Gym Steam room ♫ New Year Wi-fi Conf Class 80 Board 60 Thtr 200 Services Lift Air con Parking 30 Notes LB ⊗ Closed 24-28 Dec Civ Wed

MALLOW — Map 1 B2

Springfort Hall Country House Hotel

★★★ 72% HOTEL

☎ 022 21278 🖹 022 21557
e-mail: stay@springfort-hall.com
web: www.springfort-hall.com
dir: on Mallow/Limerick road N20, right at Two Pot House R581, hotel 500mtrs on right

This 18th-century country manor is tucked away amid tranquil woodlands located just 6km from Mallow. There is an attractive oval dining room, drawing room and lounge bar. The comfortable bedrooms are in a wing, and are spacious, well-appointed and command superb country views. There are extensive banqueting and conference facilities.

Rooms 49 (5 fmly) Facilities STV FTV ♫ Conf Class 200 Board 50 Thtr 300 Parking 200 Notes LB ⊗ Closed 23 Dec-2 Jan

ROSSCARBERY
Map 1 B2

Celtic Ross
★★★ 73% HOTEL

☎ 023 48722 🖹 023 48723
e-mail: info@celticross.com
dir: take N71 from Cork, through Bandon towards
Clonakilty. Follow signs for Skibbereen

This hotel is situated on the edge of the village
overlooking Rosscarbery Bay. Richly textured fabrics add
warmth to the polished-wood public areas that includes a
5000-year-old Bog Yew Tree sculpture. There is a library
plus a bar and a bistro that provides a second dining
option. The spacious bedrooms are comfortable and well
appointed.

Rooms 66 (30 fmly) **Facilities** ⓧ supervised Gym Steam
room Bubble pool ♫ Xmas **Conf** Class 150 Board 60
Thtr 300 **Services** Lift Air con **Parking** 200 **Notes** ⊗
Closed 24-26 Dec & mid Jan-mid Feb

CO DONEGAL

BALLYSHANNON
Map 1 B5

Heron's Cove
RESTAURANT WITH ROOMS

☎ 071 9822070 🖹 071 9822075
Creevy, Rossnowlagh Rd
e-mail: info@heronscove.ie
dir: From N side of Ballyshannon at rdbt take R231
towards Rossnowlagh 2m. Just after Creevy National
School on left

Heron's Cove is situated between Ballyshannon and
Creevy Pier and is close to the sandy beach at
Rossnowlagh. Bedrooms are comfortable, and there is a
cosy lounge bar and charming restaurant where locally
caught seafood features along with other imaginative
dishes. Friendly staff and attentive service ensure a loyal
local following.

Rooms 10 (1 fmly)

DONEGAL
Map 1 B5

Harvey's Point Country Hotel
★★★★ 85% ⊛⊛ HOTEL

☎ 074 9722208 🖹 074 9722352
Lough Eske
e-mail: sales@harveyspoint.com
web: www.harveyspoint.com
dir: N56 from Donegal, then 1st right (Loch Eske/Harvey's
Point)

Situated by the lakeshore, this hotel is an oasis of
relaxation. Comfort and attentive guest care are the norm
here. A range of particularly spacious suites are
available; they all make the best use of the views. The
kitchen brigade maintains consistently high standards in
the dining room, with a very popular Sunday buffet lunch
served each week.

Rooms 71 (16 GF) **S** €129-€420; **D** €158-€640 (incl.
bkfst) **Facilities** Treatment rooms Pitch 'n' putt Bicycle
hire Walking tours ♫ Xmas New Year Wi-fi
Conf Class 200 Board 50 Thtr 200 Del from €179 to
€250 **Services** Lift **Parking** 300 **Notes** LB Closed Mon &
Tue Nov-Mar Civ Wed

Mill Park

★★★ 75% HOTEL

☎ 074 9722880 🖹 074 9722640
The Mullins
e-mail: millparkhotel@eircom.net
dir: Take N15 signed Lifford. 2nd exit at rdbt to N56
signed Killybegs. Hotel on right

The gentle flow of the millstream and open fires create a
welcoming atmosphere at this hotel that is within
walking distance of the town centre. Wood and stone are
incorporated with flair in the design of the public areas,
as in the first-floor Granary restaurant and the less
formal café bar where food is served all day. Bedrooms
are spacious and well appointed. There are extensive
leisure and banqueting facilities.

Rooms 114 (15 fmly) (44 GF) **Facilities** ⓧ supervised
Gym Wellness centre ♫ New Year Wi-fi **Conf** Class 250
Board 80 Thtr 500 **Services** Lift **Parking** 250 **Notes** LB ⊗
Closed 24-26 Dec Civ Wed 200

DUNFANAGHY
Map 1 C6

Arnold's
★★★ 73% HOTEL

☎ 074 9136208 🖹 074 9136352
e-mail: enquiries@arnoldshotel.com
dir: on N56 from Letterkenny, hotel on left entering the
village

This family-run hotel is noted for its warm welcome and
good food. It is situated in a coastal village with sandy
beaches, links golf courses and beautiful scenery. Public
areas and bedrooms are comfortable; there is a
traditional bar with food served throughout the day, and
a popular bistro-style restaurant. A delightful garden and
riding stables are available.

Rooms 30 (10 fmly) **Facilities** Putt green Fishing ♫
Parking 60 **Notes** LB ⊗ Closed Nov-mid Mar

DUNGLOW (AN CLOCHÁN LIATH)
Map 1 B5

Ostan Na Rosann
★★★ 70% HOTEL

☎ 074 9522444 🖹 074 9522400
Mill Rd
e-mail: info@ostannarosann.com
dir: N56, at edge of town

Overlooking the spectacular Dungloe Bay within walking
distance of the town, this warm family-run hotel is known
for its informal and friendly atmosphere. Bedrooms are
comfortable. Local ingredients are prepared with care
and served in the restaurant, which makes the most of
the great views.

Rooms 48 (6 fmly) (24 GF) **Facilities** ⓧ supervised Gym
Beautician Steam room Sauna ♫ Xmas New Year Wi-fi
Conf Class 200 Board 50 Thtr 300 **Parking** 100 **Notes** LB
⊗

DUNKINEELY
Map 1 B5

Castle Murray House and Restaurant
⊛ RESTAURANT WITH ROOMS

☎ 074 9737022 🖹 074 9737330
St Johns Point
e-mail: info@castlemurray.com
dir: From Donegal take N56 towards Killybegs. Left to
Dunkineely

Situated on the coast road of St Johns Point, this
charming family-run house and restaurant overlooks
McSwynes Bay and the castle. The bedrooms are
individually decorated with guest comfort very much in
mind, as is the cosy bar and sun lounge. There is a strong
French influence in the cooking; locally landed fish, and
prime lamb and beef are featured on the menus.

Rooms 10 (2 fmly)

LETTERKENNY   Map 1 C5

Downings Bay

★★★ 70% HOTEL

☎ 074 9155586 & 9155770   📠 074 9154716
Downings
e-mail: info@downingsbayhotel.com
dir: In village centre

This hotel is situated on Sheephaven Bay in the picturesque village of Downings, north of Letterkenny. There is a cosy lounge, traditional style bar and a restaurant where food is available all day. The bedrooms are comfortable and well appointed. Guests have complimentary use of the local leisure centre, and the night club is open at weekends.

Rooms 40 (8 fmly) (4 smoking) **S** €40-€80;
D €80-€160 (incl. bkfst) **Facilities** ⓢ supervised Gym
Sauna Steam room Indoor adventure play area ♫ New
Year Wi-fi **Conf** Class 175 Board 50 Thtr 350
Del from €80 to €110 **Services** Lift Air con **Parking** 110
Notes LB ⊗ Closed 25-26 Dec

MALIN   Map 1 C6

Malin

★★ 67% HOTEL

☎ 074 9370606   📠 074 9370770
Malin Town
e-mail: info@malinhotel.ie
dir: From Derry on Molville Rd, turn left at Quigleys Point to Cardonagh, then follow to Malin

Overlooking the village green in the most northerly village in Ireland, the hotel has a friendly, welcoming atmosphere and is an ideal centre for exploring the rugged coastline and sandy beaches. Public areas include an attractive restaurant where dinner is served Wed/Sun and food is available daily in the cosy bar.

Rooms 18 (1 fmly) **Facilities** STV ⓢ Fishing Gym ♫
Xmas New Year Wi-fi Child facilities **Conf** Class 100
Board 60 Thtr 200 **Services** Lift **Parking** 40 **Notes** LB ⊗
Civ Wed 200

RATHMULLAN   Map 1 C6

Rathmullan House

★★★★ 79% ⊛⊛ COUNTRY HOUSE HOTEL

☎ 074 9158188   📠 074 9158200
e-mail: info@rathmullanhouse.com
dir: From Letterkenny, then Ramelton then Rathmullan
R243. Left at Mace shop, through village, hotel gates on right

Dating from the 18th-century, this fine property has been operating as a country-house hotel for the last 40 years under the stewardship of the Wheeler family. Guests are welcome to wander around the well-planted grounds and the walled garden, from where much of the ingredients

for the Weeping Elm Restaurant are grown. The numerous lounges are relaxing and comfortable, while many of the bedrooms benefit from balconies and patio areas.

Rooms 34 (4 fmly) (9 GF) **S** €80-€155; **D** €160-€240
(incl. bkfst)* **Facilities** Spa ⓢ ⓢ ⓢ New Year Wi-fi
Conf Class 90 Board 40 Thtr 135 Del from €150 to €195
Parking 80 **Notes** LB Closed 11 Jan-5 Feb RS 15 Nov-12
Mar Civ Wed 135

Fort Royal Hotel

★★★ 80% ⊛ HOTEL

☎ 074 9158100   📠 074 9158103
Fort Royal
e-mail: fortroyal@eircom.net
dir: R245 from Letterkenny, through Rathmullan, hotel signed

This family-run period house stands in 18 acres of well-maintained grounds that include a 9-hole golf and tennis court. Situated on the shores of Lough Swilly where private access is available to the secluded sandy beach. The restful lounges and inviting bar have open log fires, the fine dining restaurant overlooks the gardens and comfortable bedrooms enjoy the spectacular views.

Rooms 15 (4 annexe) (1 fmly) **Facilities** ⓢ 9 ⓢ ⓢ
Parking 30 **Notes** LB Closed Nov-Mar

ROSSNOWLAGH   Map 1 B5

INSPECTORS' CHOICE

Sandhouse

★★★ ⊛ HOTEL

☎ 071 9851777   📠 071 9852100
e-mail: info@sandhouse-hotel.ie
dir: from Donegal on coast road towards Ballyshannon

The Sandhouse is perched over Rossnowlagh's sandy beach which is a haven for surfers. It offers very comfortable lounges with open fires, a restaurant, a cocktail bar and the Surfers bar. The spacious bedrooms are well appointed and most enjoy the splendid sea views. This relaxing hotel is well known for its hospitality, good food and friendly service.

Rooms 55 (6 fmly) (10 smoking) **Facilities** Spa STV ⓢ
Mini-golf Surfing Canoeing Sailing Whale & bird
watching ♫ Wi-fi **Conf** Class 40 Board 30 Thtr 60
Services Lift **Parking** 42 **Notes** LB Closed Dec & Jan

DUBLIN

DUBLIN   Map 1 D4

INSPECTORS' CHOICE

The Merrion Hotel

★★★★★ ⊛⊛⊛⊛ HOTEL

☎ 01 6030600   📠 01 6030700
Upper Merrion St
e-mail: info@merrionhotel.com
dir: At top of Upper Merrion St on left, beyond
Government buildings on right

This terrace of gracious Georgian buildings, reputed to have been the birthplace of the Duke of Wellington, embraces the character of many changes of use over 200 years. Bedrooms and suites are spacious, offering comfort and a wide range of extra facilities. The lounges retain the charm and opulence of days gone by, while the Cellar bar area is a popular meeting point. Dining options include The Cellar Restaurant specialising in prime local ingredients and, for that very special occasion, award-winning Restaurant Patrick Guilbaud is Dublin's finest.

Rooms 142 (65 smoking) **S** €460-€3000;
D €480-€3000* **Facilities** Spa STV FTV ⓢ supervised
Gym Steam room Wi-fi **Conf** Class 25 Board 25 Thtr 60
Services Lift Air con **Parking** 60 **Notes** ⊗ Civ Wed 50

DUBLIN *continued*

The Shelbourne

★★★★★ 86% HOTEL

☎ 01 6634500 📠 01 6616006
27 St Stephen's Green
e-mail: aisling.mcdermott@renaissancehotels.com
web: www.theshelbourne.ie
dir: M1 to city centre, along Parnell St to O'Connell St towards Trinity College, take 3rd right into Kildare St, hotel on left

With over 185 years of offering hospitality, this Dublin landmark exudes elegance and a real sense of history. Following the completion of a renovation programme, the public areas are spacious and offer a range of dining and bar options. There is a selection of bedroom styles and suites available, many commanding views over St Stephen's Green. Leisure facilities and a spa are currently under construction.

Rooms 265 (20 smoking) **Facilities** STV FTV Xmas Wi-fi
Conf Class 180 Board 60 Thtr 500 **Services** Lift Air con
Notes Civ Wed 350

Westbury

★★★★★ 83% HOTEL

☎ 01 6791122 📠 01 6797078
Grafton St
e-mail: westbury@doylecollection.com

Located just off Grafton Street, Dublin's premier shopping district, this is an oasis of calm where all guests are well cared for amid smart contemporary surroundings. Public areas include the relaxing lounge, the Sandbank Bistro and more formal Russell Room. A range of suites and bedrooms is available, many overlooking the roofscape of the city. Valet parking is available.

Rooms 205 **Facilities** Gym 🎵 Wi-fi **Conf** Class 100
Board 46 Thtr 220 **Services** Lift Air con **Parking** 100
Notes ⊗

The Clarence

★★★★ ◎◎ HOTEL

☎ 01 4070800 📠 01 4070820
6-8 Wellington Quay
e-mail: reservations@theclarence.ie
web: www.theclarence.ie
dir: From O'Connell Bridge, W along Quays, through 1st lights (at Ha'penny Bridge) hotel 500mtrs

Located on the banks of the River Liffey in the city centre, The Clarence is within walking distance of the shops and visitor attractions. This is a very distinctive property; the character of the 1850 building has been successfully combined with contemporary design in the bedrooms and suites. The friendly staff provide unobtrusive professional service.

Rooms 49 (3 fmly) (7 smoking) **S** €135-€440;
D €135-€440* **Facilities** STV Gym Treatment & massage room New Year Wi-fi **Conf** Class 24 Board 35
Thtr 50 Del from €260 to €345* **Services** Lift
Parking 15 **Notes** LB ⊗ Closed 24-26 Dec Civ Wed 50

Dylan

★★★★ ◎ HOTEL

☎ 01 6603000 📠 01 6603005
Eastmoreland Ln
e-mail: justask@dylan.ie
dir: From St Stephen's Green into Baggot St, over canal bridge, 2nd left. Hotel on left

Public areas of this stylish boutique hotel are centred around a red bricked Victorian building, with a modern bedroom block to the side. The decor is all very contemporary, and although newly opened the hotel is proving to be a very trendy and popular meeting place. The individually designed bedrooms are superbly appointed and include plasma TVs, iPod docking stations and marble bathrooms with under floor heating; some bathrooms have their own TVs. Free Wi-fi is available throughout the hotel. The restaurant offers award-winning cuisine in smart surroundings, plus, when the weather's fine, alfresco eating is possible on the terrace.

Rooms 44 **Facilities** Massage and treatments
Conf Board 12 **Services** Lift Air con **Parking** 40
Notes ⊗ Closed 25-26 Dec RS 24 Dec

The Fitzwilliam

★★★★ 84% HOTEL

☎ 01 4787000 📠 01 4787878
St Stephen's Green
e-mail: enq@fitzwilliamhotel.com
dir: in city centre, adjacent to top of Grafton Street

In a central position on St Stephen's Green, this friendly hotel is a pleasant blend of contemporary style with all the traditions of good hotel keeping. Bedrooms, many overlooking an internal roof top garden, have been equipped with a wide range of thoughtful extras. There is plenty to tempt the palate - Citron offers an informal eating option while Thornton's provides a fine dining alternative.

Rooms 140 **Facilities** Gym Xmas **Conf** Class 50 Board 35
Thtr 80 **Services** Lift Air con **Parking** 85 **Notes** ⊗

Castleknock Hotel & Country Club

★★★★ 79% ⊛ HOTEL

☎ 01 6406300 📠 01 6406303
Porterstown Rd, Castleknock
e-mail: info@chcc.ie
web: www.castleknockhotel.com

This hotel has been finished to a very high standard. It has an airy feel to the open-plan public areas, with excellent conference and banqueting facilities. Bedrooms are particularly comfortable and well appointed. There is a choice of two bars, together with a brasserie and more formal Park Restaurant.

Rooms 143 (6 fmly) (25 smoking) **S** €89-€300; **D** €99-€340 (incl. bkfst) **Facilities** Spa ⊛ supervised ♨ 18 Gym Wi-fi **Conf** Class 200 Board 80 Thtr 500 Del from €199 to €235* **Services** Lift **Parking** 200 **Notes** LB ⊗ Closed 24-25 Dec Civ Wed 200

The Beacon Hotel

★★★★ 77% HOTEL

☎ 01 2915000 📠 01 2915005
Beacon Court, Sandyford Business Region
e-mail: sales@thebeacon.com
dir: from M50 follow Sandyford signs. Hotel on right in approx 2m

Chandeliers on the floor and a four-poster bed in the lobby greet you on arrival at this ultra modern hotel in south Dublin. While bedrooms are equally design-led, guest comfort is to the fore. The restaurant has a strong Thai theme, yet the friendly team are happy to suggest simpler fare if required.

Rooms 88 (14 smoking) **Facilities** STV FTV ♫ New Year Wi-fi **Conf** Class 20 Board 22 Thtr 40 **Services** Lift **Parking** 54 **Notes** LB ⊗ Closed 24-26 Dec

Clontarf Castle

★★★★ 77% HOTEL

☎ 01 8332321 & 8534336 📠 01 8330418
Castle Av, Clontarf
e-mail: pfurlong@clontarfcastle.ie
dir: M1 towards town centre, Dublin Airport take left at Whitehall Church, left at T-junct, straight on at lights, next lights take right turn onto Castle Ave, hotel entrance on right at rdbt

Dating back to the 12th century, this castle retains many historic architectural features which have been combined with contemporary styling in the well-equipped bedrooms. Public areas offer relaxing lounges, and modern cuisine is served in Fahrenheit Grill, Indigo Lounge and Knights Bar. The Great Hall is a versatile venue for banqueting and conferences.

Rooms 111 (7 fmly) (11 GF) (23 smoking) **Facilities** STV Gym New Year Wi-fi **Services** Lift Air con **Parking** 134 **Notes** LB ⊗ Closed 25 Dec

Gresham

GRESHAM HOTELS

★★★★ 77% HOTEL

☎ 01 8746881 📠 01 8787175
O'Connell St
e-mail: info@thegresham.com
dir: Just off M1, near GPO

This elegant hotel enjoys a prime location right in the centre of the city, close to theatres, restaurants and plenty of shopping opportunities. The wide range of bedrooms and suites are all comfortably appointed. Public areas are spacious, and include excellent conference facilities. Afternoon Tea is a feature of the Writers Bar amid contemporary artworks and sculpture. The hotel has multi-storey car parking at the rear at special rates for resident guests.

Rooms 288 (1 fmly) (50 smoking) **S** €89-€600; **D** €89-€600* **Facilities** STV FTV Gym Fitness room Wi-fi **Conf** Class 150 Board 80 Thtr 350 Del from €160 to €270* **Services** Lift Air con **Parking** 150 **Notes** ⊗

Stillorgan Park

★★★★ 76% ⊛ HOTEL

☎ 01 2001800 📠 01 2831610
Stillorgan Rd, Stillorgan
e-mail: sales@stillorganpark.com
web: www.stillorganpark.com
dir: on N11 follow signs for Wexford, pass RTE studios on left, through next 5 sets of lights. Hotel on left

This modern hotel is attractively decorated and is situated on the southern outskirts of the city. Comfortable public areas include a spacious lobby, a contemporary restaurant, an inviting bar and an air-conditioned

banqueting and conference centre. There is a bedroom wing, plus a gym, a spa and treatment rooms.

Rooms 150 (10 fmly) **Facilities** Spa Gym Beauty treatment room ♫ Xmas New Year Wi-fi **Conf** Class 220 Board 130 Thtr 500 **Services** Lift Air con **Parking** 350 **Notes** ⊗ RS 25 Dec Civ Wed 300

The Croke Park Hotel

★★★★ 76% HOTEL

☎ 01 8714444 📠 01 8714400
Jones's Rd
e-mail: crokepark@doylecollection.com

This newly built property is located directly opposite Croke Park, Ireland's largest stadium. It offers a range of comfortable rooms, some on an executive floor with complimentary snacks and meeting lounge. Sideline Bar and Bistro offers a contemporary menu that is served throughout the day. There are dedicated meeting rooms and a business centre, a gym and secure underground parking.

Rooms 232 (38 fmly) (4 GF) (47 smoking) **S** €87.50-€450; **D** €96-€450 (incl. bkfst) **Facilities** STV Gym New Year Wi-fi **Conf** Class 20 Board 24 Thtr 50 Del from €112.50 to €475 **Services** Lift Air con **Parking** 175 **Notes** LB ⊗

Red Cow Moran

Bewleys Hotels.com

★★★★ 75% HOTEL

☎ 01 4593650 📠 01 4591588
Red Cow Complex, Naas Rd
e-mail: redcowres@moranhotels.com
web: www.redcowhotel.com
dir: At junct of M50 & N7 (Naas road) on city side of motorway

Located just off the M50, this hotel is 20 minutes from the airport and only minutes away from the city centre via the Luas light rail system. The dedicated team of staff show a genuine willingness to make your stay memorable. Bedrooms are well equipped and comfortable, and the public areas and conference rooms are spacious. Ample free parking is available.

Rooms 123 (21 fmly) (48 smoking) **S** €89-€380; **D** €89-€380 (incl. bkfst) **Facilities** FTV Night club on complex ♫ Xmas New Year Wi-fi **Conf** Class 350 Board 150 Thtr 750 Del from €112.80 **Services** Lift Air con **Parking** 700 **Notes** LB ⊗ Closed 24-26 Dec Civ Wed 200

DUBLIN *continued*

Camden Court

★★★ 74% HOTEL

☎ 01 4759666 📠 01 4759677
Lower Camden St
e-mail: reservations@camdencourthotel.ie
dir: off Camden St close to St Stephen's Green & Grafton St adjacent to Luas Line

This hotel has a number of fine features in addition to its convenient location. These include spacious public areas, a leisure centre, well-equipped bedrooms, and the bonus of having a car park. Conference facilities are also available.

Rooms 246 (33 fmly) **Facilities** Spa 🕙 supervised Gym Sauna Steam room Wi-fi **Conf** Class 90 Board 30 Thtr 250 **Services** Lift **Parking** 125 **Notes** ⊗ RS 23-28 Dec

Grand Canal Hotel

★★★ 74% HOTEL

☎ 01 6461000 📠 01 6461001
Upper Grand Canal St, Ballsbridge
e-mail: reservations@grandcanalhotel.com
web: www.grandcanalhotel.com

This hotel is situated on the banks of the Grand Canal in Ballsbridge, close to Lansdowne Road Stadium, RDS and the city centre. Bedrooms are well appointed. The contemporary public areas are spacious and include a comfortable lounge, restaurant, Kitty O'Shea's pub and extensive conference rooms. Secure underground parking is available.

Rooms 142 (20 fmly) (36 smoking) **S** €89-€230; **D** €89-€230* **Facilities** 🎵 New Year Wi-fi **Conf** Class 64 Board 60 Thtr 140 **Del** from €189* **Services** Lift **Parking** 65 **Notes** LB ⊗ Closed 23-28 Dec

Montrose

★★★ 74% HOTEL

☎ 01 2693311 📠 01 2693376
Stillorgan Rd
e-mail: info@montrose.ie
web: www.montrosehotel.ie
dir: From city centre follow signs for N11

Opposite the university campus at Belfield, this hotel offers comfortable bedrooms and smart lounges with a choice of bars and dedicated meeting rooms. Casual dining is available throughout the day, with a more formal service in the restaurant at both lunch and dinner.

Rooms 180 **S** €59-€99; **D** €59-€99* **Facilities** Wi-fi **Conf** Class 30 Board 30 Thtr 80 **Services** Lift **Parking** 100 **Notes** LB ⊗

Mount Herbert Hotel

★★★ 74% HOTEL

☎ 01 6142000 📠 01 6607077
Herbert Rd, Sandymount
e-mail: info@mountherberthotel.ie
dir: Close to Lansdowne Road Rugby Stadium, 200mtrs from Dart Rail Station

Located in the leafy suburb of Ballsbridge, by Lansdowne Stadium and the RDS, this family-run hotel is an oasis of calm, offering true hospitality. Bedrooms are comfortable, as are the lounge areas. The bistro restaurant and bar overlook the lovely garden. There are conference facilities and ample free parking is available.

Rooms 168 (3 fmly) (56 GF) **S** €59-€270; **D** €59-€270 **Facilities** STV Free use of local gym Wi-fi **Conf** Class 45 Board 38 Thtr 100 **Services** Lift **Parking** 90 **Notes** LB ⊗ Closed 22-27 Dec

Bewleys Hotel Ballsbridge

★★★ 73% HOTEL

☎ 01 6681111 📠 01 6681999
Merrion Rd, Ballsbridge
e-mail: ballsbridge@bewleyshotels.com
dir: On corner of Merrion Rd & Simmonscourt Rd

This stylish hotel is conveniently situated near the RDS Showground and is close to city centre. It offers comfortable, good value accommodation, and bedrooms are well appointed. The Brasserie and café provide food throughout the day and offer interesting menus; the spacious lounge is a popular meeting place. There is secure underground parking.

Rooms 304 (64 fmly) (45 GF) (45 smoking) **S** €50-€299; **D** €50-€299 **Facilities** Wi-fi **Conf** Class 150 Board 80 Thtr 250 **Del** from €129 to €314 **Services** Lift **Parking** 220 **Notes** ⊗ Closed 24-26 Dec

Cassidys

★★★ 73% HOTEL

☎ 01 8780555 📠 01 8780687
6-8 Cavendish Row, Upper O'Connell St
e-mail: stay@cassidyshotel.com
dir: In city centre at north end of O'Connell St. Opposite Gate Theatre

This family-run hotel is located at the top of O'Connell Street, in a terrace of red-brick Georgian townhouses. The warm and welcoming atmosphere of Grooms Bar and Bistro creates a traditional atmosphere. The modern bedrooms are well appointed. Conference facilities and limited parking are available.

Rooms 113 (26 annexe) (3 fmly) (12 GF) (30 smoking) **S** €75-€250; **D** €85-€290 **Facilities** STV Gym Fitness suite Wi-fi **Conf** Class 45 Board 45 Thtr 80 **Del** from €125 to €235* **Services** Lift **Parking** 15 **Notes** ⊗ Closed 24-26 Dec

Bewleys Hotel Leopardstown

★★★ 72% HOTEL

☎ 01 2935000 & 2935001 📠 01 2935099
Central Park, Leopardstown
e-mail: leop@bewleyshotels.com
dir: M50 junct 13/14, follow signs for Leopardstown.
Hotel on right

This hotel is conveniently situated close to the Central
Business Park and Leopardstown racecourse, and
serviced by the Luas light rail system and Aircoach.
Contemporary in style, the open-plan public areas include
a spacious lounge bar, brasserie and a selection of
conference rooms. Bedrooms are well appointed.
Underground parking is available.

Rooms 352 (70 fmly) (50 smoking) **S** €50-€199;
D €50-€199 **Facilities** STV FTV Affiliation with local gym
Wi-fi **Conf** Board 16 Del from €119.50 to €309
Services Lift **Parking** 228 **Notes** ✖ Closed 23-25 Dec

Bewleys Hotel Newlands Cross

★★★ 71% HOTEL

☎ 01 4640140 & 4123301 📠 01 4640900
Newlands Cross, Naas Rd
e-mail: newlands@bewleyshotels.com
web: www.bewleyshotels.com
dir: M50 junct 9 take N7 (Naas road). Hotel near N7/
Belgard Rd junct

This modern hotel is situated on the outskirts of Dublin
off the N7 and close to M50 and the Luas rail system. The
pricing structure makes it popular for families. Bedrooms
are well furnished and the Brasserie restaurant is open
for casual dining all day and serves more formal meals in

the evening. There is a comfortable lounge bar,
conference facilities and ample parking.

Rooms 299 (176 fmly) (63 GF) **S** €50-€199;
D €50-€199 **Facilities** Wi-fi **Conf** Class 18 Board 12
Del from €98.50 to €299* **Services** Lift **Parking** 200
Notes ✖ Closed 24-26 Dec

Temple Bar

★★★ 71% HOTEL

☎ 01 6773333 📠 01 6773088
Fleet St, Temple Bar
e-mail: reservations@tbh.ie
web: www.templebarhotel.com
dir: from Trinity College towards O'Connell Bridge. 1st left
onto Fleet St. Hotel on right

This hotel is situated in the heart of Dublin's Temple Bar,
and is close to the shops, restaurants and cultural life of
the city. Bedrooms are comfortable and well equipped.
Food is served throughout the day in Buskers theme bar.
There is a multi-storey car park nearby.

Rooms 129 (6 fmly) (34 smoking) **Facilities** Wi-fi
Conf Class 40 Board 40 Thtr 70 **Services** Lift **Notes** ✖
Closed 23-25 Dec RS Good Fri

Abberley Court Hotel & Apartments

★★★ 68% HOTEL

☎ 01 4596000 📠 01 4621000
Belgard Rd, Tallaght
e-mail: abberley@iol.ie
dir: Opposite The Square at junct of Belgard Rd &
Tallaght by-pass (N81)

Located just off the M50 beside The Square Shopping
Centre and hospital, this hotel offers comfortable well-
appointed bedrooms, the choice of two bars, a carvery
and Kennedy's restaurant. There are sports and cinema
facilities available nearby.

Rooms 40 (34 fmly) **Facilities** ♫ Wi-fi **Conf** Class 25
Board 20 Thtr 40 **Services** Lift **Parking** 450 **Notes** LB ✖
Closed 25 Dec-2 Jan

The Mercer Hotel

★★★ 68% HOTEL

☎ 01 4782179 & 4744120 📠 01 4780328
Lower Mercer St
e-mail: stay@mercerhotel.ie
dir: St Stephen's Green before shopping centre turn left
into York St, right at end of road, hotel on right

This modern hotel is situated in the city centre close to
Grafton Street. Bedrooms are attractively decorated and
well equipped with fridges and CD players, as well as the
usual facilities. Public areas include an open-plan lounge
with cocktail bar and a restaurant. Parking is available
next door.

Rooms 41 **Conf** Class 80 Board 60 Thtr 100
Services Air con **Parking** 41 **Notes** ✖ Closed 24-26 Dec

West County Hotel

★★ 71% HOTEL

☎ 01 6264011 📠 01 6231378
Chapelizod
e-mail: info@westcountyhotel.ie
dir: From city centre follow signs for N4(W), 4m from city
centre between Palmerstown & Ballyfermot on N4

This family run hotel is situated just off the N4 and within
walking distance of Chapelizod. Bedrooms are well
appointed. Public areas include a comfortable lobby
lounge and bar where a carvery lunch is served daily, and
also the Pine Restaurant where dinner is served.

Rooms 48 (10 fmly) **S** €45-€70; **D** €85-€140 (incl.
bkfst) **Facilities** ♫ Xmas New Year Wi-fi **Conf** Class 100
Board 60 Thtr 200 Del from €95 to €150* **Services** Lift
Parking 200 **Notes** LB ✖ Closed 24-26 Dec

Travelodge Dublin Castleknock

BUDGET HOTEL

☎ 01 8202626
Auburn Avenue Roundabout, Navan Rd, Castleknock
web: www.travelodge.co.uk
dir: Just off M50 (Dublin ring road) at junct with Navan
Rd, N3 junct 6

Travelodge offers good quality, good value, budget
accommodation. All offer family rooms sleeping up to four
(two adults, two children) with en suite bathroom/
shower-room, remote-control TV, tea- and coffee-making
facilities and comfortable beds. Food options vary.
Breakfast is at the on-site Bar Café restaurant (if
available) or to take away. See also Hotel Groups pages.

Rooms 100 **S** fr €40; **D** fr €40

DUBLIN AIRPORT   Map 1 D4

See also **Portmarnock**

Carlton Hotel Dublin Airport

★★★★ 76% HOTEL

☎ 01 8667500 📠 01 8623114
Old Airport Rd, Cloughran
e-mail: info@carltondublinairport.com
dir: From city centre take M1 to airport rdbt then 1st exit
S towards Santry. Hotel 800mtrs on right.

Conveniently located for the airport and the M1, this
modern hotel offers courtesy coaches and parking for its
guests. Many of the comfortable and smartly appointed
bedrooms and suites are air conditioned. Food is served
throughout the day in the Kittihawk's Bar & Bistro, with a
more formal dinner served in the atmospheric rooftop
Clouds restaurant.

Rooms 100 (10 fmly) (14 GF) (14 smoking) **S** €89-€169;
D €99-€199 **Facilities** STV FTV Gym ♫ New Year Wi-fi
Conf Class 200 Board 100 Thtr 450 Del from €215 to
€245 **Services** Lift Air con **Parking** 260 **Notes** LB ✖
Closed 24-26 Dec Civ Wed 100

DUBLIN AIRPORT *continued*

Bewleys Hotel Dublin Airport

★★★ 73% HOTEL

☎ 01 8711000 🖹 01 8711001
Baskin Ln, Swords
e-mail: dublinairport@bewleyshotels.com
dir: At end of M50 N'bound, 2nd exit at rdbt (N32), left at next rdbt

In a convenient location for Dublin Airport on the M1/M50 interchange, this hotel has the added advantage of secure underground parking and a shuttle bus to the airport. Bedrooms are comfortable, and there is a spacious lounge bar and brasserie with a wide selection of dishes on offer. High quality meeting rooms are available.

Rooms 466 (232 fmly) (36 smoking) **S** €50-€199; **D** €50-€199 **Facilities** Wi-fi **Conf** Class 150 Board 12 Thtr 300 Del from €119.50 to €309 **Services** Lift **Parking** 900 **Notes** ⊗ Closed 24-25 Dec

CO DUBLIN

DONABATE
Map 1 D4

Waterside House

★★★ 71% HOTEL

☎ 01 8436153 🖹 01 8436111
e-mail: info@watersidehousehotel.ie
web: www.watersidehousehotel.ie
dir: Exit M1 at Swords rdbt, 1st left to Donabate

This family owned hotel is situated in an enviable position overlooking the beach at Donabate and close to Dublin Airport. The public areas and bedrooms are appointed in a contemporary style, with the comfortable lounge bar and restaurant taking advantage of the breathtaking views.

Rooms 35 (8 fmly) (8 GF) **Facilities** STV FTV Spa treatments ♫ Xmas New Year Wi-fi Child facilities **Conf** Class 150 Board 100 Thtr 350 **Services** Lift Air con **Parking** 100 **Notes** ⊗ Civ Wed 250

HOWTH
Map 1 D4

Deer Park Hotel, Golf & Spa

  IRISH COUNTRY HOTELS

★★★ 74% HOTEL

☎ 01 8322624 🖹 01 8392405
e-mail: sales@deerpark.iol.ie
dir: Follow coast road from Dublin via Clontarf. Through Sutton Cross pass Offington Park. Hotel 0.5m after lights on right

This modern hotel is situated on its own parkland golf courses and overlooking Dublin Bay and Ireland's Eye. The spacious well-equipped bedrooms have spectacular views. Public areas include Four Earls Restaurant, a lively bar and bistro, a spa, gym and swimming pool. Convenient to Dublin Airport, ferry ports and the DART service to the city centre.

Rooms 75 (4 fmly) (36 GF) **Facilities** Spa ☜ supervised ♨ 36 ⛳ Putt green Gym Wi-fi **Conf** Class 60 Board 25 Thtr 95 **Parking** 200 **Notes** LB ⊗ Closed 23-26 Dec

KILLINEY
Map 1 D4

Fitzpatrick Castle

★★★★ 80% ◉ HOTEL

☎ 01 2305400 🖹 01 2305430
e-mail: reservations@fitzpatricks.com
web: www.fitzpatrickcastle.com
dir: From Dun Laoghaire port turn left, on coast road right at lights, left at next lights. Follow to Dalkey, right at Ivory pub, immediate left, up hill, hotel at top

This family-owned, 18th-century castle is situated in lovely gardens with mature trees and spectacular views over Dublin Bay. The original castle rooms are appointed to a high standard and have four-poster beds, while the rooms in the modern wing are spacious and some have balconies. Lounges are comfortably furnished and PJ's restaurant serves dinner on certain days of the week; more casual fare is available each night in the trendy

Dungeon bar and grill. There are extensive leisure and conference facilities.

Rooms 113 (36 fmly) (12 smoking) **S** €120-€230; **D** €140-€300* **Facilities** STV ☜ supervised Gym Beauty/hairdressing salon Sauna Steam room Fitness centre ♫ New Year Wi-fi **Conf** Class 250 Board 80 Thtr 500 **Services** Lift **Parking** 300 **Notes** LB ⊗ RS 25-Dec Civ Wed 400

LUCAN
Map 1 D4

Finnstown Country House Hotel

★★★ 77% ◉ HOTEL

☎ 01 6010700 🖹 01 6281088
Newcastle Rd
e-mail: manager@finnstown-hotel.ie
dir: From M1 take 1st exit onto M50 s'bound then 1st exit for N4. Take slip road Newcastle/Adamstown. Straight at rdbt, through lights, hotel on right, signed

Set in 45 acres of wooded grounds, Finnstown is a calm and peaceful country house in an urban setting. High standard renovation has taken place in the public areas. The elegant bar and drawing room is where informal meals are served throughout the day, with more formal dining at lunch and dinner in the restaurant. There is a wide choice of bedroom styles, situated both in the main house and in the annexes. Staff members are all very guest focussed.

Rooms 81 (54 annexe) (6 fmly) (9 GF) (17 smoking) **S** €89-€145; **D** €89-€200 (incl. bkfst) **Facilities** ☜ ♨ ♨ Gym Turkish bath Massage ♫ Xmas New Year Wi-fi **Conf** Class 150 Board 50 Thtr 300 Del from €160 to €200* **Services** Lift Air con **Parking** 300 **Notes** LB ⊗ Closed 23-26 Dec Civ Wed 100

Lucan Spa

★★★ 67% HOTEL

☎ 01 6280494 📠 01 6280841
e-mail: info@lucanspahotel.ie
dir: On N4, approx 11km from city centre

Set in its own grounds and 20 minutes from Dublin Airport close to the M50, the Lucan Spa is a fine Georgian house with a modern extension. Bedrooms vary in size and are well equipped. There are two dining options; dinner is served in Honora D restaurant and The Earl Bistro for more casual dining. A conference centre is also available.

Rooms 71 (15 fmly) (9 GF) **Facilities** ♪ Wi-fi
Conf Class 250 Board 80 Thtr 600 Del from €95 to €150* **Services** Lift Air con **Parking** 200 **Notes** ⊗ Closed 25-Dec

PORTMARNOCK   Map 1 D4

INSPECTORS' CHOICE

Portmarnock Hotel & Golf Links

★★★★ ◉◉ HOTEL

☎ 01 8460611 📠 01 8462442
Strand Rd
e-mail: sales@portmarnock.com
web: www.portmarnock.com
dir: From Dublin Airport, N1, rdbt 1st exit, 2nd rdbt 2nd exit, next rdbt 3rd exit, left at T-junct, over x-rds. Hotel on left past Strand

This 19th-century former home of the Jameson whiskey family is now a well run and smartly presented hotel, enjoys a superb location overlooking the sea and the PGA Championship Golf Links. Bedrooms are modern and equipped to high standard, public areas are spacious and very comfortable. The Osborne Restaurant comes highly recommended and a team of friendly staff go out of their way to welcome guests.

Rooms 138 (13 fmly) (44 GF) (30 smoking)
S €89-€189; **D** €99-€199 **Facilities** Spa STV FTV ↕ 18 Putt green Gym Beauty clinic & massages with Ballinotherapy baths ♪ Xmas Wi-fi **Conf** Class 110 Board 80 Thtr 300 Del from €149 to €220 **Services** Lift **Parking** 200 **Notes** LB ⊗ RS 24 Dec (eve), 25 Dec Civ Wed 200

SKERRIES   Map 1 D4

Redbank House & Restaurant

◉ RESTAURANT WITH ROOMS

☎ 01 8491005 📠 01 8491598
5-7 Church St
e-mail: sales@redbank.ie
dir: N1 north past airport & bypass Swords. 3m N at end of dual carriageway at Esso station right towards Rush, Lusk & Skerries

Adjacent to the well-known restaurant of the same name, this comfortable double fronted period town house has two reception rooms, en suite bedrooms and a secluded garden. The restaurant is the setting for quality local produce used with an emphasis on fresh fish in imaginative cooking, served by friendly and attentive staff. Convenient for Dublin Airport and the ferry port.

Rooms 18 (2 fmly)

SWORDS   Map 1 D4

Carnegie Court Hotel

★★★ 73% HOTEL

☎ 01 8404384 📠 01 8404505
North St
e-mail: info@carnegiecourt.com
web: www.carnegiecourt.com
dir: From Dublin Airport take N1 towards Belfast. At 5th rdbt take 1st exit for Swords, then sharp left for hotel

This modern hotel has been tastefully built and is conveniently located close to Dublin Airport just off the N1 in Swords. The air-conditioned bedrooms are well appointed, and many are particularly spacious. Public areas include a residents' lounge, contemporary Courtyard Restaurant, a dramatically designed Harp Bar and modern conference and banqueting facilities. Extensive underground parking is available.

Rooms 36 (4 fmly) (1 GF) (28 smoking) **Facilities** ♪ Wi-fi **Conf** Class 50 Board 40 Thtr 280 **Services** Lift Air con **Parking** 150 **Notes** ⊗ Closed 25-26 Dec Civ Wed 250

CO GALWAY

CARNA (CARNA)   Map 1 A4

Carna Bay Hotel

★★★ 70% HOTEL

IRISH COUNTRY HOTELS

☎ 095 32255 📠 095 32530
e-mail: carnabay@iol.ie
dir: from Galway take N59 to Recess, then left onto R340 for approx 10m

This family owned and run hotel is in the little village of Carna on the Connemara coastline and has a very friendly and relaxed atmosphere. Public areas are bright and spacious with casual meals served in the bar at lunch and in the evenings. More formal dinner is available in the restaurant where there is an emphasis on good quality local ingredients.

Rooms 26 (1 fmly) (11 GF) **Facilities** New Year **Parking** 60 **Notes** Closed 23-26 Dec

CASHEL — Map 1 A4

INSPECTORS' CHOICE

Cashel House
★★★ ◉◉ COUNTRY HOUSE HOTEL

☎ 095 31001 ▤ 095 31077
e-mail: info@cashel-house-hotel.com
web: www.cashel-house-hotel.com
dir: S off N59, 1.5km W of Recess, well signed

Cashel House is a mid-19th century property, standing at the head of Cashel Bay, in the heart of Connemara. Quietly secluded in award-winning gardens with woodland walks. Attentive service comes with the perfect balance of friendliness and professionalism from McEvilly family and their staff. The comfortable lounges have turf fires and antique furnishings. The restaurant offers local produce such as the famous Connemara lamb, and fish from the nearby coast.

Rooms 29 (4 fmly) (6 GF) (4 smoking) Facilities STV ◡ Garden school Xmas New Year Wi-fi Child facilities Parking 40 Notes Civ Wed 80

Zetland Country House
★★★ 78% HOTEL

☎ 095 31111 ▤ 095 31117
Cashel Bay
e-mail: info@zetland.com
dir: N59 from Galway towards Clifden, right after Recess onto R340, left after 4m (R341), hotel 1m on right

Standing on the edge of Cashel Bay, this former sporting lodge dating from the early 1800s is a cosy and relaxing hotel that exudes charm. Many of the comfortable rooms have sea views, as has the restaurant where seafood is a particular feature. An atmospheric bar has now been added which makes a popular meeting place for locals and residents.

Rooms 19 (10 fmly) (3 GF) S €80-€120; D €100-€200 (incl. bkfst)* Facilities STV FTV ◡ Fishing ◡ Shooting Cycling Xmas New Year Wi-fi Conf Class 40 Board 20 Thtr 80 Parking 32 Notes LB

CLIFDEN — Map 1 A4

Abbeyglen Castle
★★★★ 80% ◉ HOTEL

☎ 095 21201 ▤ 095 21797
Sky Rd
e-mail: info@abbeyglen.ie
dir: N59 from Galway towards Clifden. Hotel 1km from Clifden on Sky Rd

The tranquil setting overlooking Clifden, matched with the dedication of the Hughes's father and son team and their attentive staff, combine to create a magical atmosphere. Well-appointed rooms and very comfortable suites are available, together with a range of relaxing lounge areas.

Rooms 45 (9 GF) S €130-€275; D €198-€326 (incl. bkfst)* Facilities STV ◡ Putt green Beauty treatment & relaxation centre ♫ Xmas New Year Wi-fi Conf Class 50 Board 40 Thtr 100 Del from €215 to €235* Services Lift Parking 50 Notes LB ⊗ No children Closed 10 Jan-4 Feb

Ardagh Hotel & Restaurant
★★★ 77% ◉◉ HOTEL

☎ 095 21384 ▤ 095 21314
Ballyconneely Rd
e-mail: ardaghhotel@eircom.net
dir: N59 (Galway to Clifden), signed to Ballyconneely

Situated at the head of Ardbear Bay, this family-run hotel takes full advantage of the spectacular scenery. The restaurant is renowned for its cuisine, which is complemented by friendly and knowledgeable service. Many of the spacious and well-appointed bedrooms have large picture windows and plenty of comfort.

Rooms 19 (2 fmly) Facilities Pool room ♫ Wi-fi Parking 35 Notes LB Closed Nov-Mar

Rock Glen Country House Hotel
★★★ 75% HOTEL

☎ 095 21035 ▤ 095 21737
e-mail: enquiry@rockglenhotel.com
web: www.rockglenhotel.com
dir: N6 from Dublin to Galway. N57 from Galway to Clifden. Hotel 1.5m from Clifden

The attractive clematis and creeper-framed façade of this former hunting lodge is an introduction to the comfort found inside. The hospitality of the staff makes a visit to this hotel a relaxing and very pleasant experience. Well-appointed bedrooms and comfortable lounges here have lovely views of the gardens and the bay.

Rooms 26 (2 fmly) (18 GF) Facilities ◡ Putt green ◡ ♫ Parking 50 Notes LB Closed mid Nov-mid Feb (ex New Year)

GALWAY — Map 1 B3

INSPECTORS' CHOICE

Glenlo Abbey
★★★★ ◉ COUNTRY HOUSE HOTEL

☎ 091 526666 ▤ 091 527800
Bushypark
e-mail: info@glenloabbey.ie
dir: 4km from city centre on N59

This lovingly restored, cut stone abbey was built in 1740 and features sculpted cornices and fine antique furniture. There is an elegant drawing room, a cocktail bar, a library, the delightful River Room restaurant and a cellar bar. The unique Orient Express Pullman Restaurant provides a second dining option. Bedrooms, in the modern wing, are spacious and well appointed.

Rooms 46 (16 GF) Facilities ◡ 18 Putt green Fishing Boating Clay pigeon shooting Archery Driving range ♫ New Year Wi-fi Conf Class 100 Board 50 Thtr 180 Services Lift Parking 150 Notes LB ⊗ Closed 24-27 Dec

Ardilaun Hotel & Leisure Club

★★★★ 79% ® HOTEL

☎ 091 521433 ▤ 091 521546
Taylor's Hill
e-mail: info@theardilaunhotel.ie
web: www.theardilaunhotel.ie
dir: N6 to Galway City West, then follow signs for N59
Clifden, then N6 towards Salthill

The Ardilaun is located on five acres of landscaped
gardens. Bedrooms have been thoughtfully equipped and
furnished and the new wing of executive rooms and
suites are particularly spacious. Public areas include
Camilaun Restaurant overlooking the garden, comfortable
lounges and Blazers bar. There are extensive banqueting
and leisure facilities.

Rooms 125 (17 fmly) (8 GF) (16 smoking) **S** €80-€280;
D €110-€320 (incl. bkfst)* **Facilities** Spa STV ⊙
supervised Gym Treatment & analysis rooms Beauty salon
Spinning room ♫ New Year Wi-fi **Conf** Class 300
Board 100 Thtr 650 Del from €175 to €275*
Services Lift **Parking** 380 **Notes** LB Closed 24-26 Dec
RS Closed pm 23 Dec Civ Wed 650

Radisson Blu Hotel & Spa Radisson

★★★★ 79% HOTEL

☎ 091 538300 ▤ 091 538380
Lough Atalia Rd
e-mail: reservations.galway@radissonblu.com
web: www.radissonblu.ie/hotel-galway
dir: Take N6 into city. At French rdbt 1st left. At next
lights left. 0.5m, hotel at next right junct at lights

This modern hotel is situated in a prime position on
Lough Atalia's waterfront and overlooks Galway Bay. The
striking interior design and levels of comfort are
impressive in the public areas. Bedrooms are well
equipped and there is an impressive penthouse suite,
plus an executive floor where privacy and personal service
are guaranteed. There are excellent corporate, leisure and
spa facilities. Underground parking is available.

Rooms 282 (21 annexe) (4 fmly) **Facilities** Spa ⊙
supervised Putt green Gym Outdoor Canadian hot-tub
Sauna Steam room ♫ Xmas New Year Wi-fi
Conf Class 650 Board 70 Thtr 1000 **Services** Lift Air con
Parking 260 **Notes** LB ⊗

Galway Bay Hotel Conference & Leisure Centre

★★★★ 78% ® HOTEL

☎ 091 520520 ▤ 091 520530
The Promenade, Salthill
e-mail: info@galwaybayhotel.com
dir: follow signs to Salthill from all major roads. Hotel on
promenade on coast road to Connemara

This modern hotel enjoys a really spectacular location
overlooking Galway Bay. The spacious bedrooms are well
appointed, and the public areas include comfortable
lounges, a sun patio and a bar - all enjoy the lovely views.
There are two dining options - fine dining in the Lobster
Pot, or in the Bistro featuring a less formal menu. The
conference and banqueting facilities are impressive.

Rooms 153 (10 fmly) (8 GF) **Facilities** ⊙ supervised Gym
Steam room Sauna Treatment rooms ♫ Xmas New Year
Wi-fi Child facilities **Conf** Class 325 Thtr 1100
Services Lift Air con **Parking** 300 **Notes** LB ⊗

Park House Hotel & Park Room Restaurant

★★★★ 77% ® HOTEL

☎ 091 564924 ▤ 091 569219
Forster St, Eyre Square
e-mail: parkhousehotel@eircom.net
web: www.parkhousehotel.ie
dir: city centre

This city centre property offers well decorated and
comfortable bedrooms that vary in size. The spacious
restaurant has been a popular spot for the people of
Galway for many years; a range of bar food is also
available in Boss Doyle's bar throughout the day.

Rooms 84 (13 smoking) **Facilities** STV FTV ♫ Wi-fi
Services Lift Air con **Parking** 48 **Notes** ⊗ Closed
24-26 Dec

Claregalway

★★★ 79% HOTEL

IRISH COUNTRY HOTELS

☎ 091 738300 & 738302 ▤ 091 738311
Claregalway Village
e-mail: stay@claregalwayhotel.ie
dir: At junct of N17 (Galway/Sligo) & N18 (Dublin/
Limerick)

Within easy reach of the city, this hotel offers comfortable
bedrooms and spacious public areas. Owner run by the
Gill family, food is served throughout the day in the
popular bar, with the River Room opening in the evenings.
Leisure facilities are complimentary to residents.

Rooms 48 (8 fmly) (15 smoking) **S** €50-€300;
D €50-€300 **Facilities** Spa ⊙ supervised Gym Sauna
Steam room Sunbeds ♫ New Year Wi-fi **Conf** Class 250
Board 100 Thtr 400 **Services** Lift Air con **Parking** 160
Notes ⊗ Closed 23-26 Dec

RECESS (SRAITH SALACH) — Map 1 A4

Ballynahinch Castle

★★★★ 84% ◎◎
COUNTRY HOUSE HOTEL

☎ 095 31006 📠 095 31086
Recess, Connemara
e-mail: bhinch@iol.ie
dir: W from Galway on N59 towards Clifden. After Recess turn left for Roundstone

Open log fires and friendly professional service are just some of the delights of staying at this castle originating from the 16th century. Set in 350 acres of woodland, rivers and lakes, this hotel has many suites and rooms with stunning views, as does the award-winning Owenmore restaurant where the linen is crisp and the silver gleams.

Rooms 40 (8 fmly) (3 GF) **S** €90-€250; **D** €120-€300 (incl. bkfst) **Facilities** STV FTV ♨ Fishing ⬧ Bicycles for hire River & lakeside walks ♫ New Year Wi-fi
Conf Class 20 Board 20 Thtr 30 Del from €260 to €380 **Parking** 55 **Notes** LB ⊗ Closed 1-26 Feb & 20-27 Dec RS Good Fri Civ Wed 40

INSPECTORS' CHOICE

Lough Inagh Lodge

★★★ ◎ COUNTRY HOUSE HOTEL

☎ 095 34706 & 34694 📠 095 34708
Inagh Valley
e-mail: inagh@iol.ie
dir: from Recess take R344 towards Kylemore

This 19th-century, former fishing lodge is akin to a family home where guests are encouraged to relax and enjoy the peace. It is situated between the Connemara Mountains and fronted by a good fishing lake. Bedrooms are smartly decorated and comfortable, there is a choice of lounges with turf fires and a cosy traditional bar. The delightful restaurant specialises in dishes of the local lamb and lake caught fish.

Rooms 13 (1 fmly) (4 GF) **Facilities** Fishing Hill walking Fly fishing Cycling **Conf** Class 20 Board 20 Thtr 20 **Services** Air con **Parking** 16 **Notes** LB Closed mid Dec-mid Mar

---

ROUNDSTONE — Map 1 A4

Roundstone House Hotel

★★ 71% ◎ HOTEL

☎ 095 35864 📠 095 35944
e-mail: vaughanshotel@eircom.net
dir: From Galway take N59. After Recess take 2nd left. Hotel in 9km

This delightful hotel has been in operation since 1894 and owned by the Vaughan family for many years. The comfortable bedrooms enjoy the magnificent sea views and the rugged Connemara landscape. There is a relaxing residents' lounge, cosy bar and Vaughan's Restaurant that is renowned for its extensive range of seafood.

Rooms 12 (1 fmly) **Notes** ⊗ Closed Oct-Etr Civ Wed

SALTHILL

See Galway

CO KERRY

BALLYHEIGE — Map 1 A2

The White Sands

★★★ 72% HOTEL

☎ 066 7133102 📠 066 7133357
e-mail: whitesands@eircom.net
dir: 18km from Tralee on coast road. Hotel in main street

Situated in the seaside town of Ballyheige this family run hotel has friendly staff. Attractively decorated throughout, facilities include a choice of lounges, a traditional pub where there is entertainment most nights, a restaurant and comfortable bedrooms. Guests can enjoy the sandy beaches and golf clubs close by.

Rooms 81 (2 fmly) **Facilities** ♫ Child facilities
Conf Class 40 Board 40 **Services** Lift Air con **Parking** 40 **Notes** ⊗ Closed Nov-Feb RS Mar-Apr & Oct

---

CAHERDANIEL (CATHAIR DÓNALL) — Map 1 A2

Derrynane

★★★ 73% ◎ HOTEL

☎ 066 9475136 📠 066 9475160
e-mail: info@derrynane.com
dir: just off main road, (N70)

A super clifftop location overlooking Derrynane Bay with spectacular views add a stunning dimension to this well run hotel where pleasant, efficient staff contribute to the very relaxed atmosphere. Public areas include spacious lounges, a bar and restaurant. Bedrooms are well appointed and most benefit from the views.

Rooms 70 (30 fmly) (32 GF) **Facilities** ⬧ supervised ♨ Gym Steam room Seaweed therapy room ♫ Xmas **Parking** 60 **Notes** LB ⊗ Closed 4 Oct-15 Apr

---

CAHERSIVEEN — Map 1 A2

Ring of Kerry Hotel

★★★ 71% HOTEL

☎ 066 9472543 📠 066 9472893
Valentia Rd
e-mail: ringhotel@eircom.net
web: www.ringofkerryhotel.ie
dir: on Ring of Kerry road

This hotel, situated in the town of Cahersiveen, is ideal for touring the Ring of Kerry and the nearby islands. Bedrooms are spacious and attractively decorated. There are two dining options - dinner is served nightly in the cosy restaurant and less formal fare is available in the inviting John D's bar.

Rooms 24 (4 fmly) **Facilities** ♫ New Year Wi-fi
Conf Class 150 Board 80 Thtr 450 **Parking** 24 **Notes** LB ⊗

DINGLE (AN DAINGEAN)   Map 1 A2

Dingle Skellig Hotel & Peninsula Spa

★★★★ 78% HOTEL

☎ 066 9150200 📠 066 9151501
e-mail: reservations@dingleskellig.com
dir: Enter Dingle from N86, hotel on harbour

This modern hotel, close to the town, overlooks Dingle Bay and has spectacular views from many of the comfortably furnished bedrooms and suites. Public areas offer a spacious bar and lounge and a bright, airy restaurant. There are extensive health and leisure facilities, and many family activities are organised in the Fungi Kids Club.

Rooms 113 (10 fmly) (31 GF) **S** €84-€160; **D** €118-€270 (incl. bkfst)* **Facilities** Spa STV FTV ⓩ supervised Gym ♫ New Year Wi-fi **Conf** Class 120 Board 100 Thtr 250 **Services** Lift **Parking** 110 **Notes** LB ⊗ Civ Wed 230

Dingle Benners

★★★ 67% HOTEL

☎ 066 9151638 📠 066 9151412
Main St
e-mail: info@dinglebenners.com
dir: In town centre

Located in the centre of the town with parking to the rear, this long-established property has a relaxed, traditional character. Bedrooms are well equipped and come in two styles - in the original house and in a newer block. Food is available in the popular bar.

Rooms 52 (2 fmly) (9 GF) **Services** Lift **Parking** 32

GLENBEIGH   Map 1 A2

Towers Hotel

★★★ 64% HOTEL

IRISH COUNTRY HOTELS

☎ 066 9768212 📠 066 9768260
e-mail: towershotel@eircom.net

Located on the northern side of the Ring of Kerry, this family run, long established hotel is full of character and charm. The traditional pub is very much the social centre of the village, and the restaurant has a reputation for the quality of its seafood.

Rooms 34

KENMARE   Map 1 B2

INSPECTORS' CHOICE

Sheen Falls Lodge

★★★★★ ⑧⑧ COUNTRY HOUSE HOTEL

☎ 06466 41600 📠 06466 41386
e-mail: info@sheenfallslodge.ie
dir: From Kenmare take N71 to Glengarriff over suspension bridge, take 1st left

This former fishing lodge has been developed into a beautiful hotel with a friendly team of professional staff. The cascading Sheen Falls are floodlit at night, forming a romantic backdrop to the enjoyment of award-winning cuisine in La Cascade restaurant. Less formal dining is available in Oscar's Restaurant. Bedrooms are very comfortably appointed; many of the suites are particularly spacious. The leisure centre and beauty therapy facilities offer a number of exclusive treatments.

Rooms 66 (14 fmly) (14 GF) **S** €220-€1310; **D** €240-€1330 (incl. bkfst)* **Facilities** Spa STV ⓩ supervised ⌇ Fishing ⌇ Gym Table tennis Steam room Clay pigeon shooting Cycling Vintage car rides Library ♫ Xmas New Year Wi-fi **Conf** Class 65 Board 50 Thtr 120 **Services** Lift **Parking** 76 **Notes** LB ⊗ Closed 2 Jan-1 Feb Civ Wed 100

KILLARNEY   Map 1 B2

Randles Court

★★★★ 81% HOTEL

☎ 064 6635333 📠 064 6639301
Muckross Rd
e-mail: info@randlescourt.com
dir: N22 towards Muckross, right at T-junct. From N72 take 3rd exit on 1st rdbt into town & follow signs for Muckross, hotel on left

Close to all the town's attractions, this is a friendly family-run hotel with an emphasis on customer care. Bedrooms are particularly comfortable. Guests can enjoy a relaxing drink in the cosy bar then dine in the chic Checkers bistro restaurant where good food is served in the evenings. A swimming pool and other leisure facilities are available.

Rooms 78 (4 fmly) **S** €60-€150; **D** €85-€170 (incl. bkfst) **Facilities** STV ⓩ supervised Sauna Steam room Hydrotherapy suite New Year Wi-fi **Conf** Class 50 Board 40 Thtr 90 **Services** Lift **Parking** 110 **Notes** LB Closed 22-27 Dec Civ Wed 140

The Brehon

★★★★ 80% ⑧ HOTEL

☎ 064 6630700 📠 064 6630701
The Brehon Hotel, Muckross Rd
e-mail: info@thebrehon.com
dir: 1m from Killarney on N71

This is a spectacular hotel close to Killarney National Park and the town. Public areas are particularly spacious with comfortable lounges, bars and a restaurant. Bedrooms are well equipped and there is a range of suites. The hotel offers a Thai spa and extensive conference facilities. Other leisure facilities are on offer at their nearby sister hotel.

Rooms 123 (3 fmly) **S** €110-€195; **D** €150-€300 (incl. bkfst)* **Facilities** Spa STV ⓩ supervised ⌇ Putt green Gym ♫ Xmas New Year Wi-fi **Conf** Class 120 Board 60 Thtr 250 **Services** Lift Air con **Parking** 126 **Notes** LB ⊗ Civ Wed 200

KILLARNEY *continued*

Cahernane House

★★★★ 79% ◉◉ HOTEL

☎ 064 6631895 📠 064 6634340
Muckross Rd
e-mail: info@cahernane.net
web: www.cahernane.com
dir: On N22 to Killarney, take 1st exit off rdbt then left at church, 1st exit at next rdbt to Muckross Rd

This fine country mansion, former home of the Earls of Pembroke, has a magnificent mountain backdrop and panoramic views from its lakeside setting. Elegant period furniture is complemented by more modern pieces to create a comfortable hotel offering a warm atmosphere with a particularly friendly team dedicated to guest care.

Rooms 38 (26 annexe) **S** €110-€145; **D** €150-€250 (incl. bkfst)* **Facilities** ⌇ Fishing ◄ Wi-fi **Conf** Class 10 Board 10 Thtr 15 **Services** Lift Air con **Parking** 50 **Notes** LB ⊗ Closed 21 Dec-Jan Civ Wed 60

Lake

★★★★ 76% HOTEL

☎ 064 6631035 📠 064 6631902
Muckross Rd
e-mail: info@lakehotel.com
dir: N22 to Killarney. Hotel 2km from town on Muckross road

Enjoying a delightful location on the shores of Killarney's lake shore, this hotel is operated by the second generation of the Huggard family together with a dedicated and friendly team. There is a relaxed atmosphere with log fires and stunning views from the lounges and the restaurant; guest may see a herd of Red Deer pass by. The smartly furnished bedrooms have both lake and woodland views;some have balconies and four-poster beds. The spa offers good facilities plus tennis, croquet and lovely walks and cycle paths.

Rooms 130 (6 fmly) (23 GF) **Facilities** Spa ⌇ Fishing ◄ Gym Sauna Steam room ♫ Wi-fi **Conf** Class 60 Board 40 Thtr 80 **Services** Lift **Parking** 140 **Notes** ⊗ Closed 2 Dec-15 Jan Civ Wed 60

Castlerosse Hotel & Golf Resort

★★★ 79% HOTEL

☎ 064 6631144 📠 064 6631031
e-mail: res@castlerosse.ie
web: www.castlerossehotel.com
dir: From Killarney take R562 for Killorglin & The Ring of Kerry. Hotel 1.5km from town on left

This hotel is situated on 6,000 acres overlooking Lough Leane. Bedrooms and junior suites are well appointed and comfortable. There are spectacular views of the lakes and mountains and at times guests will be able to spot deer from the restaurant and bar windows. Golf is available on site, together with a leisure centre and treatment rooms.

Rooms 120 (27 fmly) **S** €65-€100; **D** €95-€180 (incl. bkfst) **Facilities** Spa STV FTV ⊗ supervised ⌇ 9 ⌇ Putt green Gym Golfing & riding arranged ♫ **Conf** Class 100 Board 40 Thtr 200 **Services** Lift **Parking** 100 **Notes** LB ⊗ Closed Dec-Feb Civ Wed 80

Killeen House

★★★ 75% ◉ HOTEL

☎ 064 6631711 & 6631773 📠 064 6631811
Aghadoe, Lakes of Killarney
e-mail: charming@indigo.ie
dir: In Aghadoe, just outside Killarney, off Dingle road

Dating back to 1838 this charming Victorian country house is situated close to Killarney Park and Lakes. Stylishly decorated public areas include a cosy sitting room and bar where 'golf is spoken'. Good cuisine is served in the restaurant which overlooks the beautifully manicured garden. Bedrooms are well appointed and comfortable. The Rosney family and their staff take particular pride in extending a warm welcome to their guests.

Rooms 23 (10 GF) (10 smoking) **Facilities** STV FTV Wi-fi **Parking** 30 **Notes** LB Closed 21 Oct-19 Apr

Scotts Hotel

★★★ 75% HOTEL

☎ 064 6631060 📠 064 6636656
College St
e-mail: info@scottshotelkillarney.com
dir: N20, N22 to town, at Friary turn left. 500mtrs on East Avenue Rd to car park entrance

Enjoying a prominent town centre location, this modern hotel has comfortable public areas, a selection of bars and courtyard with nightly live entertainment during the high season and at weekends during the year. Bedrooms are spacious and furnished with guest comfort in mind. The suites have fitted kitchens and splendid views of the mountains. Secure underground parking is available.

Rooms 120 (10 fmly) **S** €75-€150; **D** €110-€240 (incl. bkfst) **Facilities** STV ♫ Xmas New Year Child facilities **Conf** Class 20 Del from €125 to €205 **Services** Lift **Parking** 200 **Notes** ⊗ Closed 24-25 Dec

Gleneagle

★★★ 74% HOTEL

☎ 064 6636000 📠 064 6632646
Muckross Rd
e-mail: info@gleneaglehotel.com
web: www.gleneaglehotel.com
dir: 1m outside Killarney on N71 (Kenmare road)

The facilities at this large hotel are excellent and numerous. Family entertainment is a strong element of the Gleneagle experience, popular with the Irish market for over 50 years. Comfortable rooms are matched with a range of lounges, restaurants, a leisure centre and INEC, one of Ireland's largest events' centres.

Rooms 245 (57 fmly) (35 GF) **S** €85-€130; **D** €100-€180 (incl. bkfst)* **Facilities** FTV ⊗ supervised ⌇ Gym Squash Pitch & putt Steam room Games room ♫ Xmas New Year Wi-fi Child facilities **Conf** Class 1000 Board 50 Thtr 2500 **Services** Lift **Parking** 500 **Notes** ⊗

Victoria House Hotel

★★★ 72% HOTEL

☎ 064 6635430 ▤ 064 6635439
Muckross Rd
e-mail: info@victoriahousehotel.com
dir: On N71, 1.5km from Killarney overlooking Killarney National Park

This family owned and managed hotel is just one kilometre from the town, and overlooks the National Park and mountains. Friendliness is the key word to the style of service, with good food served in both the restaurant and throughout the day in the bar. Bedrooms are comfortable, well equipped and attractively decorated.

Rooms 35 (2 fmly) (10 GF) **Facilities** STV Bicycle hire ♫ Wi-fi **Parking** 60 **Notes** LB ⊗ Closed 4 Dec-2 Feb

White Gates

IRISH COUNTRY HOTELS

★★★ 66% HOTEL

☎ 064 6631164 ▤ 064 6634850
Muckross Rd
e-mail: whitegates@iol.ie
dir: 1km from Killarney on Muckross road on left

The eye is definitely drawn to this hotel with its ochre and blue painted frontage. The same flair for colour is in evidence throughout the interior where bedrooms of mixed sizes are well decorated and very comfortable. There is also a light-filled restaurant, with casual dining in the bar, which has a popular local trade.

Rooms 27 (4 fmly) (4 GF) **Facilities** ♫ **Conf** Class 50 **Parking** 50 **Notes** ⊗ Closed 25-26 Dec

Muckross Park Hotel & Cloisters Spa

Ⓤ

☎ 064 6623400 ▤ 064 6631965
Lakes of Killarney
e-mail: johnkeating@muckrosspark.com
dir: From Killarney take N71 towards Kenmare

Currently the rating for this establishment is not confirmed. This may be due to a change of ownership or because it has only recently joined the AA rating scheme. For further details please see the AA website: theAA.com

Rooms 68 (3 fmly) **Facilities** Spa Fishing ⬐ Gym Archery Cycling Yoga ♫ Wi-fi **Conf** Class 280 Board 30 Thtr 350 **Services** Lift Air con **Notes** LB ⊗

| TRALEE | Map 1 A2 |

Manor West

★★★★ 78% ◉ HOTEL

☎ 066 7194500 ▤ 066 7194545
Killarney Rd
e-mail: info@manorwesthotel.ie
web: www.manorwesthotel.ie

Just five minutes from the centre of town this hotel is part of a large retail park with many shopping opportunities. Spacious well-equipped bedrooms are matched by smart public areas, including a high spec leisure facility. There is a spa with pools, steam room, sauna and jacuzzi, and a variety of treatments are offered in the Harmony Wellness suites. The popular Mercantile bar serves food throughout the day, with fine dining available in The Walnut Room in the evening.

Rooms 75 **S** €79-€135; **D** €120-€198 (incl. bkfst) **Facilities** Spa STV FTV ☜ supervised Gym Sauna Steam room Theray pools ♫ New Year Wi-fi **Conf** Class 150 Board 60 Thtr 200 Del from €90 to €145* **Services** Lift Air con **Parking** 200 **Notes** LB ⊗ Closed 24-26 Dec

Ballygarry House Hotel and Spa

★★★★ 78% HOTEL

☎ 066 7123322 ▤ 066 7127630
Killarney Rd
e-mail: info@ballygarryhouse.com
web: www.ballygarryhouse.com
dir: 1.5km from Tralee, on N22

Set in six acres of well-tended gardens, this fine hotel has been family run for the last 50 years and is appointed to a very high standard. The elegant and stylishly decorated bedrooms are spacious and relaxing. Good cuisine is served in the split-level restaurant. The staff are friendly and professional.

Ballygarry House Hotel and Spa

Rooms 64 (10 fmly) (16 GF) **S** €110-€170; **D** €150-€220 (incl. bkfst) **Facilities** Spa STV Steam room Sauna ♫ New Year Wi-fi **Conf** Class 100 Board 50 Thtr 200 Del from €155 to €210 **Services** Lift **Parking** 200 **Notes** LB ⊗ Closed 20-26 Dec Civ Wed 350

Fels Point

★★★★ 75% HOTEL

☎ 066 7119986 & 7199100 ▤ 066 7119987
Fels Point, Dan Spring Rd
e-mail: tvogels@felspointhotel.ie

This contemporary hotel is situated on the ring road and is within walking distance of the town centre. Public areas include a stylish lobby lounge where the grand piano is played at weekends. Bistro food is served in Clarets Bar all day, with finer dining available in Morels Restaurant at night. The smart bedrooms are air conditioned and have LCD TVs and high-speed internet connections. There are extensive conference/banqueting and leisure facilities.

Rooms 166 (29 smoking) **Facilities** STV FTV ⬐ Gym ♫ New Year Wi-fi **Conf** Class 250 Board 50 Thtr 350 **Services** Lift Air con **Parking** 227 **Notes** LB ⊗ Closed 24-26 Dec Civ Wed 100

Meadowlands Hotel

★★★★ 73% HOTEL

☎ 066 7180444 ▤ 066 7180964
Oakpark
e-mail: info@meadowlandshotel.com
dir: 1km from Tralee town centre on N69

This smart hotel is within walking distance of the town centre. Bedrooms are tastefully decorated and comfortable. Johnny Frank's is the very popular pub where a wide range of food is offered throughout the day, with more formal dining available in An Pota Stor which specialises in seafood.

Rooms 57 (1 fmly) (4 GF) (4 smoking) **Facilities** STV ♫ Wi-fi **Conf** Class 110 Board 30 Thtr 250 **Services** Lift Air con **Parking** 200 **Notes** LB ⊗ Closed 24-26 Dec

TRALEE *continued*

Ballyseede Castle

★★★ 79% HOTEL

☎ 066 7125799 📄 066 7125287
e-mail: info@ballyseedecastle.com
dir: Just outside Tralee on N21

Ballyseede Castle is steeped in history - it has been fought over, lived in and is now lovingly cared for by the Corscadden family. The spacious bedrooms are elegantly and individually furnished. There are gracious reception rooms with ornamental cornice and marble fireplaces, a carved oak library bar, a splendid banqueting hall and 30 acres of mature gardens and woodland.

Rooms 23 (5 fmly) **Facilities** STV FTV **Conf** Class 180 Board 50 Thtr 250 Del from €105 to €180 **Parking** 40 **Notes** ⊗ Closed 24-26 Dec & 6 Jan-28 Feb Civ Wed 220

WATERVILLE (AN COIREÁN)   Map 1 A2

Butler Arms

★★★ 80% ⊛ HOTEL

☎ 066 9474144 📄 066 9474520
e-mail: reservations@butlerarms.com
dir: Village centre on seafront. N70 (Ring of Kerry)

This smartly presented hotel on the Ring of Kerry, has been in the Huggard family for four generations. A range of comfortable lounges creates a relaxing atmosphere, and excellent bar food is served in the Fisherman's bar through the day. More formal evening dining is available in the restaurant, which has commanding views of the sea and town.

Rooms 40 (1 fmly) (10 GF) **S** €60-€250; **D** €70-€250 (incl. bkfst) **Facilities** STV 🏊 Fishing Billiards room Wi-fi **Services** Lift **Parking** 50 **Notes** LB ⊗ Closed Nov-Apr

CO KILDARE

ATHY   Map 1 C3

Clanard Court

★★★★ 73% HOTEL

☎ 059 8640666 📄 059 8640888
Dublin Rd
e-mail: sales@clanardcourt.ie
web: www.clanardcourt.ie
dir: Take N7 at Red Cow rdbt, take M7 signed Limerick & Cork. At junct 9 onto M9, exit signed Athy. Right onto N78

Located just one kilometre from Athy on the Dublin road, this family owned hotel enjoys a well earned reputation for hosting weddings and family celebrations. Concerts and events are also a regular feature here. Bedrooms are spacious and attractively decorated. Bailey's is a popular bar serving food throughout the day.

Rooms 38 (2 fmly) (17 GF) **S** €79-€135; **D** €89-€230 (incl. bkfst) **Facilities** STV FTV ⚡ 18 Putt green 🎵 New Year Wi-fi Child facilities **Conf** Class 300 Board 20 Thtr 400 **Services** Lift **Parking** 250 **Notes** LB ⊗ Closed 25 Dec Civ Wed 250

CASTLEDERMOT   Map 1 C3

Kilkea Castle Hotel

★★★★ 75% HOTEL

☎ 059 9145156 & 9145100 📄 059 9145187
e-mail: kilkeas@iol.ie
dir: From Dublin take M9 S, take exit for High Cross Inn. Left after pub, hotel 3m on right

Dating from 1180, this is reputed to be Ireland's oldest inhabited castle. Surrounded by an 18-hole golf course, it offers a comfortable bar and lounge, and D'Lacy's, a fine dining restaurant on the first floor. Bedrooms vary in both size and style, but are all well equipped. Popular banqueting and conference facilities are situated in the converted stables.

Rooms 35 (24 annexe) (2 fmly) (5 GF) (25 smoking) **Facilities** STV 🏊 supervised ⚡ 18 🏊 Putt green Fishing Gym Sauna Steam room Wi-fi **Conf** Class 30 Board 50 Thtr 300 **Services** Lift **Parking** 100 **Notes** LB ⊗ Closed 23-26 Dec

CLANE   Map 1 C4

Westgrove

[U]

☎ 045 989900 📄 045 989911
Abbeylands
e-mail: info@westgrovehotel.com
dir: From M4 (W of Dublin) follow Naas, Maynooth signs. At rdbt 2nd exit signed Naas, Straffan. At rdbt 3rd exit signed Clane (R403). At next rdbt (before Clane) 1st exit. At next rdbt 2nd exit, hotel on right

At the time of going to press the rating for this establishment was not confirmed. This may be due to a change of ownership or because it has only recently joined the AA rating scheme. For further details please see the AA website: theAA.com

Rooms 99 (14 fmly) (30 smoking) **Facilities** Spa STV 🦶 supervised Gym New Year Wi-fi **Conf** Class 220 Board 100 Thtr 500 **Services** Lift **Parking** 550 **Notes** LB ⊗ Closed 24-25 Dec Civ Wed 300

LEIXLIP   Map 1 D4

Courtyard

★★★★ 74% HOTEL

☎ 01 6295100 📄 01 6295111
Main St
e-mail: info@courtyard.ie
dir: From M4 follow R148 to town centre, then follow Main Street Car Park signs

Situated on the site of the brewery where the Guinness family first started their business, this hotel has stylish contemporary design that blends seamlessly with the original stonework. The bedrooms have been tastefully appointed with all guest needs catered for. The public areas include a choice of restaurants and bars, and a large open courtyard that often hosts music events during summer months.

Rooms 40 (16 GF) (16 smoking) **S** €55-€200; **D** €79-€400 (incl. bkfst)* **Facilities** 🎵 Xmas New Year Wi-fi **Conf** Class 80 Board 80 Thtr 120 Del from €135 to €165* **Services** Lift Air con **Parking** 100 **Notes** LB ⊗ Civ Wed 60

Leixlip House

★★★ 79% ⊛ HOTEL

☎ 01 6242268 📠 01 6244177
Captains Hill
e-mail: info@leixliphouse.com
dir: From Leixlip motorway junct to village. Turn right at lights, up hill

This Georgian house dates back to 1772 and retains many original features. Overlooking Leixlip, the hotel is just eight miles from Dublin city centre. Bedrooms and public areas are furnished and decorated to a high standard. The Bradaun Restaurant offers a wide range of interesting dishes at dinner, with a popular bar menu served throughout the day.

Rooms 19 (2 fmly) **Facilities** STV Wi-fi **Conf** Class 60 Board 40 Thtr 130 **Parking** 64 **Notes** LB ⊛ RS 24-27 Dec Civ Wed 60

NAAS   Map 1 D3

Killashee House Hotel and Villa Spa

★★★★ 80% ⊛ HOTEL

☎ 045 879277 📠 045 879266
e-mail: reservations@killasheehouse.com
dir: N7, then straight through town on Old Kilcullen Rd (R448), hotel on left, 1.5m from centre of Naas

This Victorian manor house, set among parkland and well-landscaped gardens, has been successfully converted to a large hotel with spacious public areas and very comfortable bedrooms. Two dining options are available - fine dining in Turners Restaurant and more casual fare in the Nuns Kitchen Bar on the lower level. There are extensive banqueting and conference facilities. The Villa Spa and a popular leisure centre are located in the grounds.

Rooms 141 (10 fmly) (48 GF) **Facilities** Spa ⓢ supervised ⬥ Gym Archery Biking Clay pigeon shooting Air Rifle shooting Falconry ♬ Xmas New Year Wi-fi **Conf** Class 144 Board 84 Thtr 1600 **Services** Lift **Parking** 600 **Notes** ⊛ Closed 25-26 Dec

---

Maudlins House

★★★ 79% ⊛⊛ HOTEL

☎ 045 896999 📠 045 906411
Dublin Rd
e-mail: info@maudlinshousehotel.ie
dir: Exit N7 approaching large globe, straight through 2 rdbts. Hotel on right

Located on the outskirts of Naas, this is a modern property incorporating an original country house. Bedrooms are well appointed with the coach rooms making ideal accommodation for long stay guests. The Virginia Restaurant, a series of comfortable rooms to the front of the house, offers good food at dinner; less formal dining is available in the bar throughout the day.

Rooms 25 (5 annexe) (5 GF) **S** €89-€129; **D** €130-€250 (incl. bkfst)* **Facilities** STV FTV Hair & beauty salon Use of nearby health & fitness club ♬ New Year Wi-fi **Conf** Class 50 Board 50 Thtr 100 **Services** Lift Air con **Parking** 70 **Notes** LB ⊛ Closed 24-25 Dec

---

NEWBRIDGE   Map 1 C3

Keadeen

★★★★ 81% ⊛⊛ HOTEL

☎ 045 431666 📠 045 434402
e-mail: info@keadeenhotel.ie
web: www.keadeenhotel.ie
dir: M7 junct 12, (Newbridge, Curragh) at rdbt follow signs to Newbridge, hotel on left in 1km

This family operated hotel is set in eight acres of award-winning gardens on the outskirts of the town. Comfortable public areas include spacious drawing rooms, an excellent leisure centre, fine dining in the Derby Restaurant and more casual fare in the Club Bar. Ideally located for the nearby Curragh racecourse.

Rooms 75 (4 fmly) (58 GF) **Facilities** STV ⓢ supervised Gym Aerobics studio Massage Treatment room ♬ Wi-fi **Conf** Class 300 Board 40 Thtr 800 **Services** Lift **Parking** 200 **Notes** LB ⊛ Closed 24 Dec-2 Jan

---

INSPECTORS' CHOICE

The K Club

★★★★★ ⊛⊛ COUNTRY HOUSE HOTEL

☎ 01 6017200 📠 01 6017298
e-mail: resortsales@kclub.ie
dir: from Dublin take N4, exit for R406, hotel on right in Straffan

The K Club, which has been host to the Ryder Cup, is set in 700 acres of rolling woodland. There are two magnificent championship golf courses and a spa facility that complements the truly luxurious hotel that is the centrepiece of the resort. Public areas and bedrooms are opulently furnished, and have views of the formal gardens. Fine dining is offered in the elegant Byerly Turk restaurant, with more informal dining provided in Legends and Monza restaurants in the golf pavilions.

Rooms 79 (10 annexe) (10 fmly) **Facilities** Spa ⓢ supervised ⬥ 36 Putt green Fishing ⬥ Gym Beauty salon Fishing tuition Clay pigeon shooting ♬ Xmas New Year Wi-fi **Conf** Class 300 Board 160 Thtr 300 **Services** Lift **Parking** 205 **Notes** LB ⊛

Barberstown Castle

★★★★ 80% ⊛⊛ HOTEL

☎ 01 6288157 📠 01 6277027
e-mail: info@barberstowncastle.ie
web: www.barberstowncastle.ie
dir: R406, follow signs for Barberstown

With parts dating from the 13th century, the castle is now a hotel providing the very best in standards of comfort. The inviting public areas range from the original keep, which is one of the restaurants, to the warmth of the drawing room. Bedrooms, some in a wing, are elegantly appointed. An airy tea room serves light meals throughout the day.

Rooms 58 (21 GF) **S** €150-€200; **D** €230-€300 (incl. bkfst) **Facilities** STV ♬ New Year Wi-fi **Conf** Class 120 Board 30 Thtr 150 Del from €229.90 to €251.90 **Services** Lift **Parking** 200 **Notes** LB ⊛ Closed 24-26 Dec & Jan Civ Wed 300

CO KILKENNY

KILKENNY
Map 1 C3

Kilkenny River Court Hotel

★★★★ 78% ⊛ HOTEL

☎ 056 7723388 📄 056 7723389
The Bridge, John St
e-mail: reservations@rivercourthotel.com
dir: At bridge in town centre, opposite castle

Hidden behind archways on John Street, this is a very comfortable and welcoming establishment. The restaurant, bar and many of the well-equipped bedrooms command great views of Kilkenny Castle and the River Nore. Attentive, friendly staff ensure good service in all areas. Excellent corporate and leisure facilities are provided.

Rooms 90 (4 fmly) (45 smoking) **S** €85-€190; **D** €90-€400 (incl. bkfst) **Facilities** Spa ⊛ supervised Gym Beauty salon Treatment rooms 🎵 Wi-fi **Conf** Class 110 Board 45 Thtr 260 Del from €145 to €290* **Services** Lift **Parking** 84 **Notes** LB ⊗ Closed 23-26 Dec Civ Wed 250

Newpark

★★★★ 78% HOTEL

☎ 056 7760500 📄 056 7760555
e-mail: info@newparkhotel.com
dir: On N77 (Castlecomer to Durrow road)

A short drive from the city centre, set in 40 acres of parkland, this hotel offers a range of well-appointed rooms and suites. There is a range of comfortable lounges, and a leisure club and health spa. Renowned for the friendliness of the staff, a choice of two dining areas is on offer, The Scott Dove Bistro and Gulliver's, a more formal option.

Rooms 129 (20 fmly) (52 GF) **Facilities** Spa ⊛ supervised Gym Plunge pool 🎵 Xmas New Year Wi-fi **Conf** Class 250 Board 50 Thtr 600 **Services** Lift **Parking** 350 **Notes** LB ⊗

Langton House Hotel

★★★ 73% HOTEL

☎ 056 7765133 & 5521728 📄 056 7763693
69 John St
e-mail: reservations@langtons.ie
dir: Take N9 & N10 from Dublin follow city centre signs at outskirts of Kilkenny, turn left to Langtons. 500mtrs on left after lights

This hotel has a long and well-founded reputation as an entertainment venue, nightclub and bar. There is a range of bedroom accommodation, many in the garden annexe; all are very comfortable, tastefully decorated and well appointed. The busy restaurant is popular with visitors and locals alike.

Rooms 34 (16 annexe) (4 fmly) (8 GF) (22 smoking) **S** €55-€150; **D** €89-€180 (incl. bkfst) **Facilities** STV 🎵 Xmas New Year Wi-fi **Conf** Class 250 Board 30 Thtr 400 Del from €95 to €150 **Services** Air con **Parking** 60 **Notes** LB Closed 24-25 Dec Civ Wed 100

The Kilkenny Inn Hotel

★★★ 71% HOTEL

☎ 056 7772828 & 7722821 📄 056 7761902
15/16 Vicar St
e-mail: info@kilkennyinn.com
web: www.kilkennyinn.com
dir: N7/N10 from Dublin. N25 from Rosslare to Waterford, N9 to Kilkenny

This family run hotel is within walking distance of the heart of Kilkenny medieval city, located close to St Canice's Cathedral in a quite area with the added advantage of complimentary parking. Designed to incorporate traditional features with modern comforts, the public areas include JB's bar and Grill Room Restaurant. Bedrooms are comfortable and stylishly appointed.

Rooms 30 (7 fmly) (10 smoking) **Facilities** Xmas New Year **Conf** Class 18 Board 25 Thtr 45 **Services** Lift **Parking** 25 **Notes** LB ⊗ Closed 24-26 Dec

THOMASTOWN
Map 1 C3

INSPECTORS' CHOICE

Mount Juliet Conrad

★★★★ ⊛⊛ COUNTRY HOUSE HOTEL

☎ 056 7773000 📄 056 7773019
e-mail: info@mountjuliet.ie
dir: M7 from Dublin, N9 towards Waterford then to Mount Juliet via Paulstown & Gowran

Mount Juliet Conrad is set in 1,500 acres of parkland with a Jack Nicklaus designed golf course and an equestrian centre. The elegant and spacious public areas retain much of the original architectural features including ornate plasterwork and Adam fireplaces. Bedrooms, in both the main house and the Hunters Yard annexe, are comfortable and well appointed. Fine dining is on offer at Lady Helen, overlooking the river, and more casual dining is available in Kendels in the Hunters Yard, which also has a spa and health club.

Rooms 57 (26 annexe) (14 GF) **S** €145-€365; **D** €175-€395 (incl. bkfst) **Facilities** Spa STV ⊛ supervised ⅃ 18 ⅊ Putt green Fishing ⅏ Gym Archery Cycling Clay pigeon shooting Equestrian Xmas Wi-fi **Conf** Class 40 Board 20 Thtr 75 Del from €225 to €350 **Parking** 200 **Notes** LB ⊗ Civ Wed 60

CO LAOIS

PORTLAOISE
Map 1 C3

Portlaoise Heritage Hotel

★★★★ 78% HOTEL

☎ 057 8678588 📄 057 8678577
Jessop St
e-mail: info@theheritagehotel.com
dir: Off N7 in town centre

This hotel is situated in the town just off the N7. Public areas include a spacious lobby lounge, two bars and dining options, The Fitzmaurice where breakfast and dinner are served and Spago, an Italian Bistro. Bedrooms are well appointed and there are extensive leisure and conference facilities.

Rooms 110 (6 fmly) (14 smoking) **Facilities** Spa ⊛ supervised Gym Health & fitness club Beauty spa 🎵 New Year Wi-fi **Conf** Class 300 Board 50 Thtr 500 Del from €129 to €199 **Services** Lift **Parking** 280 **Notes** ⊗ Closed 23-27 Dec RS Good Fri Civ Wed 160

Killeshin

★★★★ 74% HOTEL

☎ 057 8681870 ▤ 057 8681871
Dublin Rd
e-mail: info@thekilleshin.com
web: www.thekilleshin.com

The long established this hotel has now reopened following a complete rebuilding programme. It is a smart well-appointed property with contemporary decor schemes throughout. Cedarooms is the hotel's bar and restaurant facility where a range of dining options is on offer through the day. Secure underground parking and use of the Zest Health Club are complimentary to residents.

Rooms 91 **Facilities** 🕭 Gym Steam room 🎵 New Year Wi-fi **Conf** Class 100 Board 50 Thtr 200 **Services** Lift **Parking** 174 **Notes** ⊗ Closed 23-27 Dec

CO LEITRIM

CARRICK-ON-SHANNON   Map 1 C4

The Landmark

★★★★ 72% ⊛ HOTEL

☎ 071 9622222 ▤ 071 9622233
e-mail: reservations@thelandmarkhotel.com
dir: From Dublin on N4 approaching Carrick-on-Shannon, take 1st exit at rdbt, hotel on right

Overlooking the River Shannon, close to the Marina, this hotel offers smartly presented and comfortable public areas and well-equipped bedrooms and suites. The Boardwalk Café is a lively, stylish bar and restaurant that opens throughout the day, with a variety of pastries and light meals available in the Aroma Conservatory. The pleasant team are happy to arrange river cruises, horse riding, golf or angling.

Rooms 50 (4 fmly) (4 smoking) **Facilities** STV 🎵 Xmas Wi-fi **Conf** Class 210 Thtr 550 Del from €165 to €175 **Services** Lift **Parking** 100 **Notes** ⊗ Closed 24-25 Dec RS 26-Dec Civ Wed

Bush Hotel

 IRISH COUNTRY HOTELS

★★★ 73% HOTEL

☎ 071 9671000 ▤ 071 9621180
e-mail: info@bushhotel.com
dir: In town centre (accessed from N4 town bypass, follow signs

With a history dating as far back as the 13th century, this mid-Georgian house has been renovated and expanded into a fine hotel, with a number of bars and dining options. Bedrooms and suites are contemporary in style; there is a choice of lounges including a formal drawing room and an atmospheric bar in the original cellar.

Rooms 49 (3 fmly) (20 smoking) **Facilities** Wi-fi **Conf** Board 60 Thtr 300 **Services** Lift **Parking** 150 **Notes** ⊗ Closed 24 Dec-2 Jan

MOHILL   Map 1 C4

Lough Rynn Castle

MANOR HOUSE HOTELS

★★★★ 77% ⊛ HOTEL

☎ 071 9632700 & 9632714 ▤ 071 9632710
e-mail: enquiries@loughrynn.ie

Once to ancestral home of Lord Leitrim, set in 300 acres of parkland, the castle offers a range of luxurious rooms and suites. The many lounges are individually decorated; some feature antique furniture pieces. Additional rooms, a spa and leisure facilities are currently in development. A Nick Faldo designed golf course is due to be completed in 2010.

Rooms 43 (16 annexe) (5 fmly) (6 GF) **S** €70-€260; **D** €70-€260 (incl. bkfst) **Facilities** STV FTV 🎵 Xmas New Year Wi-fi **Conf** Class 200 Board 30 Thtr 450 Del from €145 to €310 **Notes** LB ⊗ Civ Wed 300

CO LIMERICK

ADARE   Map 1 B3

Dunraven Arms

MANOR HOUSE HOTELS

★★★★ 80% ⊛⊛ HOTEL

☎ 061 396633 ▤ 061 396541
e-mail: reservations@dunravenhotel.com

This charming hotel was established in 1792 in the heart of one of Ireland's prettiest villages. A traditional country inn both in style and atmosphere that has comfortable lounges, spacious bedrooms and junior suites, attractive gardens, leisure and beauty facilities and good cuisine, which all add up to an enjoyable visit. Golf, horse racing and equestrian sports are available nearby.

Rooms 86 (2 fmly) (40 GF) **Facilities** STV FTV 🕭 supervised Fishing Gym Beauty salon 🎵 Xmas Wi-fi **Conf** Class 60 Board 12 Thtr 180 **Services** Lift **Parking** 90

Fitzgeralds Woodlands House Hotel

 IRISH COUNTRY HOTELS

★★★ 74% HOTEL

☎ 061 605100 ▤ 061 396073
Knockanes
e-mail: reception@woodlands-hotel.ie
dir: On N21 S of Limerick at Lantern Lodge rdbt turn left. Hotel 0.5m on right

Located close to the picturesque village of Adare, this family-run hotel is friendly and welcoming. Bedrooms are well appointed. The comfortable public areas include, Woodcock bar, Timmy Mac's traditional bar and bistro and The Brennan Restaurant. There are extensive leisure and beauty facilities. Close to Limerick Racecourse, Adare Manor and many other golf courses.

Rooms 92 (36 fmly) (31 GF) (20 smoking) **S** €50-€165; **D** €50-€175 (incl. bkfst) **Facilities** Spa STV 🕭 supervised Gym Health & beauty salon Thermal spa 🎵 Xmas Wi-fi **Conf** Class 200 Board 50 Thtr 400 Del from €100 to €195 **Services** Air con **Parking** 290 **Notes** LB ⊗ Closed 24-25 Dec Civ Wed

LIMERICK   Map 1 B3

No 1 Pery Square Hotel & Spa

★★★★ 78% TOWN HOUSE HOTEL

☎ 061 402402 ▤ 061 313060
Pery Square
e-mail: info@oneperysquare.com

This period 19th-century townhouse is a haven in the heart of Limerick's Georgian quarter close to the city centre. The Roberts family have lovingly refurbished the property to its former glory; there is an elegant drawing room, cosy bar and delightful brasserie restaurant. Bedrooms have been given a modern twist to incorporate comfort and relaxation. A wonderful spa and treatment rooms are tucked away in the former coal bunkers! There is a lock-up car park nearby.

Rooms 20 (1 GF) (20 smoking) **S** €165; **D** €165 (incl. bkfst)* **Facilities** STV New Year Wi-fi **Conf** Class 40 Board 14 Thtr 40 Del from €190 to €235* **Services** Lift **Parking** 20 **Notes** ⊗ Closed 24-28 Dec

LIMERICK *continued*

Woodfield House

★★★ 66% HOTEL

☎ 061 453022 🖺 061 326755
Ennis Rd
e-mail: woodfieldhousehotel@eircom.net
dir: on outskirts of city on main Shannon road

This family-run hotel is situated on the N18 a short distance from the city centre, within easy reach of Shannon Airport and close to Thomand Park Stadium. There is a relaxing atmosphere in the cosy traditional bar and patio beer garden. Bedrooms are comfortable. Food is available in the bar all day and dinner is served in the restaurant.

Rooms 26 (3 fmly) (5 GF) **Facilities** FTV 🛝 Wi-fi
Conf Class 60 Board 60 Thtr 130 **Services** Air con
Parking 80 **Notes** ⊗ Closed 24-25 Dec Civ Wed 120

Limerick Marriott

Marriott
HOTELS & RESORTS

Ⓤ

☎ 061 448700 🖺 061 448701
Henry St
e-mail: reservations@limerickmarriott.ie
dir: From N7 follow signs for city centre

At the time of going to press the rating for this establishment was not confirmed. This may be due to a change of ownership or because it has only recently joined the AA rating scheme. For further details please see the AA website: theAA.com

Rooms 94 (3 fmly) (14 smoking) **Facilities** Spa STV FTV 🕲 Gym Steam room Sauna Treatment rooms 🎵 New Year Wi-fi **Conf** Class 140 Board 80 Thtr 220 **Services** Lift Air con **Parking** 100 **Notes** LB ⊗

DUNDALK Map 1 D4

Ballymascanlon House

★★★★ 77% HOTEL

☎ 042 9358200 🖺 042 9371598
e-mail: info@ballymascanlon.com
dir: R173 Carlingford. Take N52 exit off Faughart rdbt. Next rdbt 1st left. Hotel in approx 1km on left

This Victorian mansion is set in 130 acres of woodland at the foot of the Cooley Mountains. The elegant original house and the modern extension make this a very comfortable hotel with some really stylish bedrooms. Public areas include a restaurant and spacious lounge and bar, and a well-equipped leisure centre. A banqueting facility has now been added.

Rooms 90 (11 fmly) (5 GF) (34 smoking) **S** €100-€115; **D** €150-€185 (incl. bkfst)* **Facilities** STV FTV 🕲 supervised ♨ 18 🏌 Putt green Gym Steam room Plunge pool 🎵 Xmas New Year Wi-fi **Conf** Class 220 Board 100 Thtr 400 Del from €120 to €175 **Services** Lift **Parking** 250 **Notes** LB Civ Wed 200

CO MAYO

BALLINA Map 1 B4

HOTEL OF THE YEAR

Mount Falcon Country House

★★★★ 81% ⊛⊛ HOTEL

MANOR HOUSE HOTELS

☎ 096 74472 🖺 096 74473
Mount Falcon Estate
e-mail: info@mountfalcon.com
dir: On N26, 6m from Foxford & 3m from Ballina. Hotel on left

Dating from 1876, this house has been lovingly restored to its former glory, and has a bedroom extension that is totally in keeping with the original design. Relaxing lounges look out on the 100-acre estate, which has excellent salmon fishing on The Moy plus well-stocked trout lakes. Dinner is served in the original kitchen with choices from a varied and interesting menu; for lunch there is also the Boathole Bar. A state-of-the-art, air-conditioned gym is available.
AA Hotel of the Year for the Republic of Ireland 2009-10.

Rooms 32 (3 fmly) **Facilities** Spa STV 🕲 supervised Fishing Gym Sauna Steam room New Year Wi-fi **Conf** Class 120 Board 80 Thtr 200 **Services** Lift **Parking** 260 **Notes** LB ⊗ Closed 6 Jan-5 Feb

Ice House

★★★★ 75% HOTEL

☎ 096 23500 🖺 096 23598
The Quay
e-mail: chill@theicehouse.ie
dir: From Sligo on N59 to Ballina. Turn right at Judge's garage into Riverside Estate. Right at T-junct into Quay Rd. Hotel on left

With a fascinating history, this newly opened property, a mile or so from the town centre, is a stunning mix of old and new. The contemporary decor features lots of wood, steel and glass creating a very light and airy interior. The stylish bedrooms include suites that have river views from their balconies. An interesting menu is offered at dinner in the vaulted Pier Restaurant, once an ice store, with lighter fare offered during the day in the bright riverside bar.

Rooms 32 (7 fmly) (10 GF) **S** €135-€195; **D** €135-€250 (incl. bkfst)* **Facilities** Spa STV Laconium Steam room New Year Wi-fi Child facilities **Conf** Class 35 Board 30 Thtr 70 **Services** Lift **Parking** 32 **Notes** LB Closed 25-26 Dec Civ Wed 130

CASTLEBAR Map 1 B4

Days Hotel Castlebar

★★★ 77% HOTEL

☎ 094 9286200 🖺 094 9286201
Lannagh Rd
e-mail: res@dayshotelcastlebar.com
dir: Lannagh Rd off N5 towards Westport. Multi-storey car park with direct access to hotel

This smart hotel is appointed to a high standard and is located in the town centre with the added bonus of a multi-storey car park. Bedrooms and bathrooms are spacious and stylishly furnished with guest comfort in mind. There's comfortable seating in the open-plan public areas and an attractively decorated café bar and restaurant. Extensive, fully-equipped conference rooms are available, and the TF Royal Theatre venue is now open.

Rooms 90 (4 GF) (15 smoking) **Facilities** STV Wi-fi
Conf Class 40 Board 40 Thtr 140 **Services** Lift
Parking 120 **Notes** ⊗ Closed 23-26 Dec

CLAREMORRIS — Map 1 B4

McWilliam Park Hotel

★★★★ 76% HOTEL

☎ 094 9378000 📠 094 9378001
N
e-mail: info@mcwilliamparkhotel.ie
dir: Castlebar/Claremorris exit off N17, straight over rdbt. Hotel on right

This hotel is newly built and situated off the N17 on the outskirts of Castlebar, close to Knock Shrine and the airport. Public areas have comfortable lounges plus extensive conference, leisure and health facilities. Bedrooms are spacious and well appointed. Food is served all day in Kavanaghs bar, and dinner in J.G's restaurant. Traditional music and dance evenings are held regularly in the McWilliam Suite.

Rooms 103 (19 fmly) (15 GF) (44 smoking) **S** €75-€135; **D** €110-€180 (incl. bkfst)* **Facilities** Spa STV ⊙ supervised Gym ♫ Xmas New Year Wi-fi Child facilities **Conf** Class 250 Board 80 Thtr 600 Del from €135 to €149 **Services** Lift **Notes** LB ⊗

CONG — Map 1 B4

Ashford Castle

★★★★★ 88% HOTEL

☎ 094 9546003 📠 094 9546260
e-mail: ashford@ashford.ie
web: www.ashford.ie
dir: In Cross left at church onto R345 signed Cong. Left at Ashford Castle sign, through castle gates

Set in over 300 acres of beautifully grounds, this magnificent castle, dating from 1228, occupies a stunning position on the edge of Lough Corrib. Bedrooms vary in style but all benefit from a pleasing combination of character, charm and modern comforts. The hotel offers an extensive range of both indoor and outdoor leisure pursuits including falconry, golf, shooting, fishing and an equestrian centre.

Rooms 83 (6 fmly) (22 GF) **S** €195-€395; **D** €225-€425* **Facilities** STV ♪ 9 ⚘ Putt green Fishing Gym Archery Clay pigeon shooting Falconry Lake cruises Treatment rooms ♫ Xmas New Year Wi-fi **Conf** Class 65 Thtr 110 Del from €295 to €495 **Services** Lift **Parking** 200 **Notes** LB ⊗ Civ Wed 150

Lisloughrey Lodge

★★★★ 78% ⊛⊛ HOTEL

☎ 094 9545400 📠 094 9545424
The Quay
e-mail: lodge@lisloughrey.ie
dir: Take N84 from Galway to Cross. Left at Cong sign. Left at sign for hotel

Situated in an elevated position overlooking the quay and Lough Corrib, this property combines contemporary luxury with a traditional country house setting. The individually-styled bedrooms and suites are in a quiet courtyard linked to the main house; each is named after a wine region of the world. The rooms have flat-screen TVs, goose down duvets and bathrooms with under floor heating. Cuisine is important here, with dinner in the award-winning Salt Restaurant proving the highlight of a visit.

Rooms 50 (44 annexe) (5 fmly) (21 GF) **Facilities** Spa STV FTV Fishing Gym Outdoor sauna Beauty salon Screening room New Year Wi-fi Child facilities **Conf** Class 70 Board 40 Thtr 180 **Services** Lift **Parking** 100 **Notes** ⊗ Civ Wed 150

KILTIMAGH — Map 1 B4

Park Hotel

★★★ 75% HOTEL

IRISH COUNTRY HOTELS

☎ 094 9374922 📠 094 9374924
e-mail: info@parkhotelmayo.com

This smart hotel overlooks the Wetlands Wildlife Park and is within walking distance from Kiltimagh and just ten minutes from Ireland West Knock Airport. The spacious bedrooms are furnished for guest comfort. Public areas are attractively decorated and include comfortable lounges, café bar and restaurant. There are treatment rooms and outside hot tubs on the sun veranda.

Rooms 45

Cill Aodain Court Hotel

★★★ 70% HOTEL

IRISH COUNTRY HOTELS

☎ 094 9381761 📠 094 9381838
Main St
e-mail: info@cillaodain.ie
dir: In town centre opposite Market Square

Situated in the heart of historic Kiltimagh and close to Marian Shrine at Knock and also the airport, this smart, contemporary hotel offers comfortable well-appointed bedrooms. Public areas include The Gallery Restaurant, Court Bar & Bistro. There is off-street parking opposite the hotel.

Rooms 17 (4 fmly) (7 smoking) **S** €45-€85; **D** €70-€140 (incl. bkfst) **Facilities** STV ♫ New Year Wi-fi **Conf** Class 30 Board 25 Thtr 50 Del from €80 to €100 **Notes** ⊗ Closed 24-25 Dec

KNOCK — Map 1 B4

Knock House

★★★ 70% HOTEL

☎ 094 9388088 📠 094 9388044
Ballyhaunis Rd
e-mail: info@knockhousehotel.ie
dir: 0.5km from Knock

Adjacent to the Marian Shrine and Basilica at Knock, this creatively designed limestone-clad building is surrounded by landscaped gardens. There is a relaxing lounge bar, conference rooms and lunch and dinner are served in the Four Seasons Restaurant daily. Bedrooms are spacious and well appointed, and some rooms are adapted to facilitate wheelchair users.

Rooms 68 (12 fmly) (40 GF) **Facilities** FTV Xmas New Year Wi-fi **Conf** Class 90 Board 45 Thtr 150 **Services** Lift **Parking** 150 **Notes** ⊗

MULRANY — Map 1 B4

Park Inn

★★★★ 78% ⊛⊛ HOTEL

☎ 098 36000 📠 098 36899
e-mail: info@parkinnmulranny.ie
dir: R311 from Castlebar to Newport onto N59. Hotel on right

Set on an elevated site, this property has commanding views over Clew Bay. Dating back to the late 1800s, it retains many original features. Bedrooms vary in size but are comfortable and decorated in a contemporary style. Dinner in the Nephin Restaurant is a highlight of any stay.

Rooms 61 (22 fmly) (36 GF) (4 smoking) **S** €75-€105; **D** €130-€210 (incl. bkfst)* **Facilities** ⊙ supervised Gym Steam room Health & Beauty Suites Hairdressing New Year Wi-fi Child facilities **Conf** Class 140 Board 50 Thtr 400 Del from €150 to €250* **Services** Lift **Parking** 200 **Notes** LB ⊗ Closed 4-30 Jan Civ Wed 150

NEWPORT — Map 1 B4

Hotel Newport

★★★ 68% HOTEL

☎ 098 41155 📄 098 42548
Main St
e-mail: info@hotelnewportmayo.com
dir: On N59 from Westport to Achill Island. Hotel at top of Main St

Situated in the centre of the picturesque town of Newport and close to Achill Island and Westport. This hotel has a modern contemporary style of decor with a traditional exterior appearance. Bedrooms are well appointed and there are comfortable public areas. Food is served all day in the Seven Arches bar and a more formal style is available in the Inish Kee restaurant at night.

Rooms 30 (2 fmly) **Facilities** Fishing ♫ New Year **Conf** Class 80 Board 40 Thtr 200 **Services** Lift Air con **Parking** 25 **Notes** ⊗ Closed 25 Dec

SWINFORD — Map 1 B4

Kelly's Gateway

★★★ 70% HOTEL

☎ 094 9252156 📄 094 9251328
Main St
e-mail: info@gatewayswinford.com
dir: On main street

This long established town centre hostelry has been converted to a cosy hotel. The friendly approach at this family run business makes for a very pleasant experience. Bedrooms are warm and inviting, as are the lounge areas. Tasty food is served throughout the day in the bistro and bar, which proves a popular choice with the locals.

Rooms 22 (3 fmly) (5 smoking) **Facilities** STV FTV ♫ Wi-fi **Conf** Class 60 Board 40 Thtr 100 **Services** Lift **Parking** 16 **Notes** LB ⊗ Closed 25 Dec

WESTPORT — Map 1 B3

Knockranny House Hotel

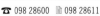

★★★★ 80% ⊛ HOTEL

☎ 098 28600 📄 098 28611
e-mail: info@khh.ie
web: www.khh.ie
dir: on N5 (Westport-Castlebar road)

Overlooking Westport with Clew Bay and Croagh Patrick in the distance, the reception rooms of this family-run hotel take full advantage of the lovely views. The luxurious furnishings create an inviting and relaxing atmosphere throughout the lounge, bar and restaurant. The spacious bedrooms are well appointed. There is a helicopter-landing pad in the well-maintained grounds, and also a luxury Spa Salveo.

Rooms 97 (4 fmly) **Facilities** Spa STV ⊙ supervised Gym ♫ Xmas New Year Wi-fi **Conf** Class 350 Board 40 Thtr 600 **Services** Lift **Parking** 150 **Notes** LB ⊗ Closed 24-26 Dec

Hotel Westport Leisure, Spa & Conference

★★★★ 77% HOTEL

☎ 098 25122 & 0870 876 5432 📄 098 25122
Newport Rd
e-mail: reservations@hotelwestport.ie
web: www.hotelwestport.ie
dir: N5 to Westport. Right at end of Castlebar St, 1st right before bridge, right at lights, left before church. Follow to end of street

Located in private woodlands and just a short river walk to the town, this hotel offers welcoming public areas, a spacious restaurant and comfortable bedrooms. Both leisure and business guests are well catered for by the enthusiastic and friendly team.

Rooms 129 (67 fmly) (42 GF) (12 smoking) **S** €70-€160; **D** €70-€270 (incl. bkfst) **Facilities** Spa STV ⊙ supervised Gym Children's pool Lounger pool Steam room Sauna Fitness suite ♫ Xmas New Year Wi-fi Child facilities **Conf** Class 150 Board 60 Thtr 500 Del from €115 to €185 **Services** Lift **Parking** 220 **Notes** LB ⊗ Civ Wed 300

Carlton Atlantic Coast

★★★★ 74% ⊛ HOTEL

☎ 098 29000 📄 098 29111
The Quay
e-mail: info@carltonatlanticcoasthotel.com
dir: From N5 follow signs into Westport then Louisburgh on R335. 1m from Westport

This distinctive hotel is in a former mill and has been renovated to a good contemporary standard with modern facilities. Many of the rooms have sea views, as has the award-winning restaurant on the fourth floor. The ground floor has comfortable lounge areas and a lively bar. A spa and treatment rooms have been added to the leisure centre.

Rooms 85 (6 fmly) **S** €69-€135; **D** €110-€270 (incl. bkfst) **Facilities** Spa ⊙ supervised Gym Treatment rooms Sauna Steam room Fitness suite ♫ Xmas New Year Wi-fi Child facilities **Conf** Class 100 Board 70 Thtr 180 Del from €128 to €184 **Services** Lift **Parking** 140 **Notes** LB ⊗ Closed 23-27 Dec

Clew Bay Hotel

IRISH COUNTRY HOTELS

★★★ 73% HOTEL

☎ 098 28088 📄 098 25783
e-mail: info@clewbayhotel.com
dir: at bottom of James St (parallel to main street)

This long established, family-run hotel offers a range of comfortable well-appointed bedrooms together with some very smart public areas. Guest can dine in the Riverside Restaurant or in the very popular Madden's Bistro. Arrangements can be made for residents to use the nearby leisure centre.

Rooms 35 (3 fmly) **Facilities** ⊙ supervised Gym Free use of nearby leisure club ♫ Child facilities **Conf** Class 12 Board 10 Thtr 20 **Services** Lift **Notes** ⊗ Closed Xmas & New Year

Mill Times Hotel

★★★ 70% HOTEL

☎ 098 29200 & 29130 📄 098 29250
Mill St
e-mail: info@milltimeshotel.ie
dir: N59 signed town centre, on Bridge St keep in left lane, left at top of Bridge St onto Mill St, hotel on left

Situated in the centre of Westport close to the shops and many pubs, and ideal for visiting the leisure centre, beaches and many golf courses nearby. Bedrooms are traditional in style and public areas are comfortable. There is a lively bar with entertainment at weekends.

Rooms 34 (6 fmly) **S** €49-€150; **D** €69-€240 (incl. bkfst)* **Facilities** ♫ New Year Wi-fi **Conf** Class 60 Board 60 Thtr 200 Del from €99 to €149 **Services** Lift **Parking** 15 **Notes** LB ⊗ Closed 24-25 Dec

The Wyatt

★★★ 70% HOTEL

☎ 098 25027 📄 098 26316
The Octagon
e-mail: info@wyatthotel.com
dir: Follow one-way system in town. Hotel by tall monument

This stylish, welcoming hotel is situated in the famous town centre Octagon. Bedrooms are attractively decorated and well equipped. Public areas are very comfortable with open fires and include a lively, contemporary bar. There are two dining options, JW for bar food and The Wyatt Restaurant offering more formal eating.

Rooms 51 (2 GF) (5 smoking) **S** €55-€85; **D** €110-€180 (incl. bkfst)* **Facilities** STV Complimentary use of nearby leisure park ♫ New Year Wi-fi **Conf** Class 200 Board 80 Thtr 300 Del from €109 to €129* **Services** Lift **Parking** 20 **Notes** LB ⊗ Closed 25-26 Dec Civ Wed 150

CO MEATH

ASHBOURNE — Map 1 D4

Ashbourne Marriott

★★★★ 75% HOTEL

☎ 01 8350800 📠 01 8010301
The Rath
e-mail: info@marriottashbourne.com
dir: On rdbt at end of N2

Located on the outskirts of Ashbourne and just off the N2 this hotel has been built to a high standard. Contemporary in style the public areas include the upbeat Red Bar and Grill Twenty One. There are extensive leisure, fitness, treatments rooms plus banqueting facilities. Bedrooms are spacious and comfortably furnished. The express coach to Dublin Airport is available to guests.

Rooms 148 (13 smoking) **S** €89-€199; **D** €100-€199* **Facilities** Spa 🅢 supervised Gym 🎵 New Year Wi-fi **Conf** Class 280 Board 30 Thtr 540 Del from €155 to €205 **Services** Lift Air con **Parking** 200 **Notes** LB ⊗ Closed 25 Dec

DUNBOYNE — Map 1 D4

Dunboyne Castle Hotel & Spa

★★★★ 78% HOTEL

☎ 01 8013500 📠 01 4366801
e-mail: info@dunboynecastlehotel.com
web: www.dunboynecastlehotel.com
dir: In Dunboyne take R157 towards Maynooth. Hotel on left

With a history dating back to the 13th century, this mid-Georgian house has been renovated and expanded into a fine hotel, with a number of bars and dining options. Bedrooms and suites are contemporary in style, with a choice of lounges, a formal drawing room and an atmospheric bar in the original cellar.

Rooms 145 (36 GF) (36 smoking) **S** €99-€280; **D** €120-€340 (incl. bkfst) **Facilities** Spa STV Gym 🎵 Xmas New Year Wi-fi **Conf** Class 200 Board 40 Thtr 350 **Services** Lift Air con **Parking** 300 **Notes** LB ⊗

DUNSANY — Map 1 C4

The Dunsany Lodge

RESTAURANT WITH ROOMS

☎ 046 9026339 📠 046 9026342
Kiltale
e-mail: info@dunsanylodge.ie

Dunsany Lodge is a contemporary building located less than 30 minutes from Dublin at the gateway to the historic and picturesque Boyne Valley. The bedrooms are smart and comfortably appointed, and the Bia Restaurant offers a wide range of international dishes cooked with care; less formal fare is served in the bistro bar.

Rooms 10

ENFIELD — Map 1 C4

The Hamlet Court Hotel

★★★ 73% HOTEL

☎ 046 9541200 📠 046 9541704
Johnstownbridge
e-mail: info@thehamlet.ie
web: www.thehamlet.ie
dir: After toll bridge take 1st exit at Kilcock on M4. Left then right at rdbt, hotel in 0.5km on left

This hotel has been developed behind the long established Hamlet bar and lounge. It features very comfortable bedrooms, a relaxing lounge and the Sabayon Restaurant where food standards are good. This is an ideal location for those with an interest in horseracing and golf. It is also a popular wedding venue.

Rooms 30 (2 fmly) (19 GF) **S** €65-€140; **D** €75-€250 (incl. bkfst) **Facilities** Fishing 🎵 Xmas New Year Wi-fi **Conf** Class 240 Board 80 Thtr 350 Del from €99 to €150 **Services** Lift **Parking** 320 **Notes** ⊗ Civ Wed 320

KELLS — Map 1 C4

Headfort Arms

★★★ 74% HOTEL

IRISH COUNTRY HOTELS

☎ 046 9240063 📠 046 9240587
Headfort Place
e-mail: info@headfortarms.ie
web: www.headfortarms.ie
dir: On N3 between Dublin & Donegal

Situated in the famous heritage town of Kells, the Duff family run a very smart hotel. Appointed to a high standard, there are comfortable lounges with open log fires, a café carvery, Vanilla Pod Brasserie, traditional pub, banqueting facilities and treatment rooms. The bedrooms, in both the newer block and the original building are impressively decorated and furnished.

Rooms 45 (5 fmly) **S** €75-€105; **D** €99-€285 (incl. bkfst) **Facilities** Spa 🎵 Xmas New Year Wi-fi **Conf** Class 200 Board 30 Thtr 400 **Services** Lift **Parking** 45 **Notes** LB ⊗ Civ Wed 300

KILMESSAN — Map 1 C/D4

The Station House Hotel

★★★ 72% ⚘ HOTEL

☎ 046 9025239 📠 046 9025588
e-mail: info@thestationhousehotel.com
web: www.thestationhousehotel.com
dir: M50, N3 towards Navan. At Dunshaughlin turn left at end of village, follow signs

The Station House saw its last train in 1963, and is now a comfortable, family-run hotel with a popular restaurant. The Carriage House has nicely appointed bedrooms, and the Signal Box houses a suite. There is a sun terrace and conference/banqueting suite.

Rooms 20 (14 annexe) (3 fmly) (5 GF) **Facilities** 🎵 Xmas Wi-fi **Conf** Class 300 Board 100 Thtr 400 **Parking** 200 **Notes** ⊗

NAVAN   Map 1 C4

Bellinter House

U

☎ 046 9030900   📄 046 9031367
e-mail: info@bellinterhouse.com
dir: N3 towards Navan, left at Tara Na Ri pub. Hotel on right

At the time of going to press the rating for this establishment was not confirmed. This may be due to a change of ownership or because it has only recently joined the AA rating scheme. For further details please see the AA website: theAA.com

Rooms 34 (5 fmly) (12 GF) **D** €140–€300 (incl. bkfst)*
Facilities Spa STV FTV 🐾 Fishing Steam room Sauna
New Year Wi-fi **Conf** Class 30 Board 24 Thtr 50
Del from €200 to €250* **Parking** 80 **Notes** LB ⊗ Closed 25-27 Dec Civ Wed 80

TRIM   Map 1 C4

Knightsbrook Hotel Spa & Golf Resort

★★★★ 77% HOTEL

☎ 046 9482100   📄 046 9482055
Dublin Rd
e-mail: info@knightsbrook.com

Overlooking 180 acres of rolling parkland and a golf course, a short distance from historical Trim, this hotel offers excellent facilities. Bedrooms are particularly well appointed with great attention to detail. The popular bars have their own styles and their own menus, and more formal dining is available in Rococo Restaurant.

Rooms 131 (3 fmly) (40 smoking) **Facilities** Spa STV FTV
🐾 supervised ♨ 18 Putt green Gym 🎵 New Year Wi-fi
Child facilities **Conf** Class 300 Board 50 Thtr 1100
Services Lift **Parking** 200 **Notes** LB ⊗ Closed 24-25 Dec Civ Wed 600

CO MONAGHAN

CARRICKMACROSS   Map 1 C4

Nuremore

★★★★ 79% ⊛⊛⊛ HOTEL

☎ 042 9661438   📄 042 9661853
e-mail: info@nuremore.com
web: www.nuremore.com
dir: M1 exit 14, N2 hotel 3km S of Carrickmacross

Overlooking its own golf course and lakes, the Nuremore is a quiet retreat with excellent facilities. Public areas are spacious and include an indoor pool and bar. Ray McArdle's award-winning cuisine continues to impress, with an imaginative range of dishes on offer.

Rooms 72 (6 fmly) (42 smoking) **S** €120–€200;
D €220–€350 (incl. bkfst) **Facilities** Spa STV FTV 🐾
supervised ♨ 18 🏌 Putt green Fishing Gym Beauty
treatments Aromatherapy Massage 🎵 Xmas New Year
Wi-fi **Conf** Class 300 Board 50 Thtr 600 Del from €180 to €250 **Services** Lift **Parking** 200 **Notes** LB ⊗
Civ Wed 200

Shirley Arms Hotel

U

☎ 042 9673100   📄 042 9673177
Main St
e-mail: reception@shirleyarmshotel.ie

At the time of going to press the rating for this establishment was not confirmed. This may be due to a change of ownership or because it has only recently joined the AA rating scheme. For further details please see the AA website: theAA.com

Rooms 25 (2 fmly) **S** €85-€105; **D** €140-€180 (incl.
bkfst) **Facilities** STV 🎵 New Year Wi-fi **Conf** Class 150
Board 200 Thtr 200 **Services** Lift **Parking** 80 **Notes** LB ⊗
Closed 24-26 Dec Civ Wed 150

MONAGHAN   Map 1 C5

Hillgrove Hotel, Leisure & Spa

★★★★ 74% HOTEL

☎ 047 81288   📄 047 84951
Old Armagh Rd
e-mail: info@hillgrovehotel.com
dir: Exit N2 at Cathedral, 400mtrs, hotel on left

This modern hotel on the outskirts of the town offers spacious bedrooms that are well equipped and comfortable. The public areas include a split-level dining room where good food is served, and a popular local bar, serving snacks throughout the day. Spectacular banqueting facilities and a well equipped leisure centre are available.

Rooms 87 (9 fmly) (9 GF) (40 smoking) **Facilities** Spa
STV 🐾 supervised Gym New Year Wi-fi **Conf** Class 500
Board 90 Thtr 1500 **Services** Lift Air con **Parking** 300
Notes ⊗ Closed 25 Dec Civ Wed

CO ROSCOMMON

ROSCOMMON   Map 1 B4

Kilronan Castle Estate and Spa

★★★★ 77% HOTEL

☎ 071 9618000   📄 071 9618001
e-mail: enquiries@kilronancastle.com

Set in over forty acres of forest and pasture overlooking Lough Meelagh, this castle hotel features elegant public rooms including an atmospheric bar and library. Bedrooms and suites are in the original house and also in the stylish modern extension. Dinner in the Douglas Hyde Room is the highlight of a visit. Leisure facilities include a gym, pool and spa treatment rooms.

Rooms 84 (66 annexe) (4 fmly) (3 smoking)
Facilities Spa STV 🐾 supervised Gym Xmas New Year
Wi-fi **Conf** Class 320 Board 15 Thtr 450 **Services** Lift
Air con **Parking** 100 **Notes** ⊗ Civ Wed 340

Abbey

IRISH COUNTRY HOTELS

★★★★ 73% HOTEL

☎ 090 6626240   📄 090 6626021
Galway Rd
e-mail: info@abbeyhotel.ie
web: www.abbeyhotel.ie
dir: On Galway road

The Grealy family have tastefully restored this fine manor house. The spacious bedrooms are tastefully furnished and overlook the magnificent gardens. The smart lounge, bar and Terrace Restaurant have views of the 12th-century Dominican Abbey, and the carvery is very popular at lunchtime. There are extensive leisure and conference facilities.

Rooms 50 (5 fmly) (10 GF) **S** €85-€180; **D** €99-€300 (incl. bkfst) **Facilities** ⓒ supervised Gym Sauna Steam room Therapy room Children's pool Wi-fi **Conf** Class 140 Board 50 Thtr 250 Del from €125 to €225 **Services** Lift **Parking** 100 **Notes** LB ⊗ Closed 24-26 Dec

CO SLIGO

COLLOONEY
Map 1 B5

Markree Castle

★★★ 75% HOTEL

☎ 071 9167800 🖷 071 9167840
e-mail: markree@iol.ie
dir: Off N4 at Collooney rdbt, take R290 towards Dromahaire. Just N of junct with N17, 11km S of Sligo, hotel gates on right after 1km

The castle, which has been in the Cooper family for over 370 years, is a gem of Irish Victorian architecture. The bedrooms vary in size and style, and all in keeping with the character of the building. Dinner is served in the spectacular Louis XIV-styled dining room. Horse riding, archery and clay-pigeon shooting can be arranged on the estate.

Rooms 30 (1 fmly) (3 GF) (15 smoking) **S** €99-€130; **D** €175-€195 (incl. bkfst) **Facilities** STV FTV Fishing Hiking Archery Clay pigeon shooting Wi-fi Child facilities **Conf** Class 50 Board 40 Thtr 75 **Services** Lift **Parking** 120 **Notes** LB Civ Wed 120

SLIGO
Map 1 B5

Radisson Blu Hotel & Spa Sligo

Radisson BLU

★★★★ 75% HOTEL

☎ 071 9140008 🖷 071 9140005
Rosses Point Rd, Ballincar
e-mail: info.sligo@radissonblu.com
dir: From N4 into Sligo to main bridge. Take R291 on left. Hotel 1.5m on right

Located two miles north of the town overlooking Sligo Bay, this hotel offers a range of bedroom suites and a very well-equipped leisure centre. The spacious lounges and restaurant make the most of the bay views as do some of the extensive meeting and banqueting facilities.

Rooms 132 (13 fmly) (32 GF) (19 smoking) **S** €85-€250; **D** €99-€400 (incl. bkfst) **Facilities** Spa STV ⓒ Gym Steam room Treatment rooms Thermal suite Xmas New Year Wi-fi **Conf** Class 420 Board 40 Thtr 750 Del from €172 to €247* **Services** Lift Air con **Parking** 395 **Notes** LB ⊗ Civ Wed 750

Glasshouse

★★★★ 74% ⊛ HOTEL

☎ 071 9194300 🖷 071 9194301
Swan Point
e-mail: info@theglasshouse.ie
dir: N4 Relief Road. Right at 2nd junct. Left at Post Office on Wine St. Hotel on right

This landmark building in the centre of town makes a bold statement with its cutting edge design and contemporary decor. Cheerful colours are used throughout the hotel; the bedrooms have excellent facilities including LCD TVs, workspace and internet access. There is a first floor café bar, a ground floor bar and a Mediterranean-style restaurant with great river views. Secure underground parking is complimentary to residents.

Rooms 116 **Facilities** STV FTV New Year Wi-fi **Conf** Class 100 Board 60 Thtr 120 **Services** Lift **Parking** 250 **Notes** ⊗ Closed 24-25 Dec Civ Wed 120

Sligo Park

★★★ 79% HOTEL

☎ 071 9190400 🖷 071 9169556
Pearse Rd
e-mail: sligo@leehotels.com
dir: On N4 to Sligo take Carrowroe/R287 exit. Follow signs for Sligo R287. Hotel 1m on right

Set in seven acres on the southern side of town, this hotel is well positioned for visiting the many attractions of the North West and Yeats' Country. Bedrooms are spacious and appointed to a high standard. There are two dining options, plus good leisure and banqueting facilities.

Rooms 137 (10 fmly) (52 GF) (23 smoking) **S** €79-€172; **D** €105-€185 (incl. bkfst) **Facilities** ⓒ supervised ⓢ Gym Holistic treatment suite Plunge pool Steam room ♫ Xmas New Year Wi-fi **Conf** Class 290 Board 80 Thtr 520 **Services** Lift **Parking** 200 **Notes** LB ⊗ RS 24-26 Dec

Castle Dargan Golf Hotel Wellness

Ⓤ

☎ 071 9118080 🖷 071 9118090
e-mail: info@castledargan.com
dir: Off N4 (Dublin-Sligo road) to Collooney rdbt, 3rd exit to Ballygawley

At the time of going to press the rating for this establishment was not confirmed. This may be due to a change of ownership or because it has only recently joined the AA rating scheme. For further details please see the AA website. www.theAA.com

Rooms 22 (11 GF) (6 smoking) **Facilities** Spa FTV ♿ 18 Putt green Wi-fi **Conf** Class 200 Board 70 Thtr 400 **Services** Lift **Parking** 200 **Notes** ⊗ Closed 24-26 Dec

CO TIPPERARY

CASHEL
Map 1 C3

Cashel Palace Hotel

★★★★ 80% ⊛ HOTEL

☎ 062 62707 🖷 062 61521
e-mail: reception@cashel-palace.ie
dir: On N8 through town centre, hotel on main street near lights

The Rock of Cashel, floodlit at night, forms the dramatic backdrop to this fine 18th-century house. Once an archbishop's palace, it is elegantly furnished with antiques and fine art. The drawing room has garden access, and luxurious bedrooms in the main house are very comfortable; those in the adjacent mews are ideal for families.

Rooms 23 (10 annexe) (8 fmly) **Facilities** Fishing Private path to Rock of Cashel ♫ Wi-fi **Conf** Class 45 Board 40 Thtr 80 **Services** Lift **Parking** 35 **Notes** LB ⊗ Closed 24-26 Dec Civ Wed 130

CLONMEL — Map 1 C2

Hotel Minella

★★★★ 73% HOTEL

IRISH COUNTRY HOTELS

☎ 052 22388 📠 052 24381
e-mail: frontdesk@hotelminella.ie
web: www.hotelminella.ie
dir: S of River Suir

This family-run hotel is set in nine acres of well-tended gardens on the banks of the Suir River. Originating from the 1860s, the public areas include a cocktail bar and a range of lounges; some of the bedrooms are particularly spacious. The leisure centre in the grounds is noteworthy. Two-bedroom holiday homes are also available.

Rooms 70 (8 fmly) (14 GF) Facilities ⊕ ⊕ Fishing ⊕ Gym Aerobics room Conf Class 300 Board 20 Thtr 500 Services Lift Parking 100 Notes ⊗ Closed 24-28 Dec

DUNDRUM — Map 1 C3

Dundrum House Hotel, Golf & Leisure Resort

★★★ 77% HOTEL

MANOR HOUSE HOTELS

☎ 062 71116 📠 062 71366
e-mail: reservations@dundrumhouse.ie
dir: R505 follow for 7m. Far side of Knockaville, hotel approx 0.5m on left

This Georgian mansion dates from 1730 and was tastefully restored by the Crowe family. Bedrooms vary in style and are comfortably furnished; rooms in the original house have antique pieces and the newer rooms follow a modern theme. There are relaxing lounges with open fires and a fine dining room, with more informal food available in the golf club. The extensive facilities include a leisure centre and an 18-hole championship golf course.

Rooms 68 (12 fmly) S €65-€130; D €100-€200 (incl. bkfst)* Facilities STV ⊕ ⊕ 18 Putt green Fishing Gym Wellness suites ♫ New Year Conf Class 100 Board 70 Thtr 400 Del from €135* Services Lift Parking 300 Notes LB ⊗ Closed 21-26 Dec Civ Wed 120

THURLES — Map 1 C3

Horse & Jockey Hotel

Ⓤ

☎ 0504 44192 📠 0504 44747
Horse & Jockey
e-mail: info@horseandjockeyhotel.com
dir: M8 junct 6, 800mtrs from junct in centre of village

At the time of going to press the rating for this establishment was not confirmed. This may be due to a change of ownership or because it has only recently joined the AA rating scheme. For further details please see the AA website: theAA.com

Rooms 67 (4 fmly) (15 GF) (7 smoking) S €70-€95; D €130-€170 (incl. bkfst)* Facilities Spa STV FTV ⊕ supervised Gym Sauna Steam room Hydro therapy area Wi-fi Child facilities Conf Class 24 Board 25 Thtr 200 Services Lift Parking 450 Notes LB ⊗ Closed 25 Dec RS 24 & 26 Dec

CO WATERFORD

ARDMORE — Map 1 C2

Cliff House

Ⓤ

☎ 024 87800 📠 024 87820
e-mail: info@thecliffhousehotel.com
dir: N25 to Ardmore. Hotel at end of village via The Middle Road

Currently the rating for this establishment is not confirmed. This may be due to a change of ownership or because it has only recently joined the AA rating scheme. For further details please see the AA website: theAA.com

Rooms 39 (8 fmly) (7 GF) D €170-€200 (incl. bkfst)* Facilities Spa STV FTV ⊕ Fishing Gym Sauna Steam room Relaxation room New Year Wi-fi Child facilities Conf Class 30 Board 20 Thtr 50 Del from €150 to €350* Services Lift Air con Parking 52 Notes LB ⊗ Closed Jan-14 Feb

DUNGARVAN — Map 1 C2

Lawlors

★★★ 68% HOTEL

☎ 058 41122 & 41056 📠 058 41000
e-mail: info@lawlorshotel.com
dir: off N25

This town centre hotel enjoys a busy local trade especially in the bar where food is served throughout the day. The Davitts Restaurant offers a wide choice of Italian, Mexican and seafood dishes. The bedrooms are of varying sizes; some are particularly spacious. Conference and meeting rooms are available. Public parking is nearby.

Rooms 89 (8 fmly) Facilities ♫ New Year Wi-fi Conf Class 215 Board 420 Thtr 420 Services Lift Notes Closed 25 Dec

TRAMORE — Map 1 C2

Majestic

★★★ 74% HOTEL

☎ 051 381761 📠 051 381766
e-mail: info@majestic-hotel.ie
dir: Exit N25 through Waterford onto R675 to Tramore. Hotel on right, opposite lake

A warm welcome awaits visitors to this long established, family friendly hotel in the holiday resort of Tramore. Many of the comfortable and well-equipped bedrooms have sea views. Public areas offer a selection of lounges, a traditional bar and spacious restaurant. The facilities at 'Splashworld' across from the hotel are available to residents.

Rooms 60 (4 fmly) S €70-€90; D €99-€140 (incl. bkfst)* Facilities STV FTV Free access to Splashworld swimming pool & leisure club ♫ New Year Wi-fi Conf Class 25 Board 25 Thtr 50 Del from €100 to €130* Services Lift Parking 10 Notes LB ⊗ Civ Wed 250

WATERFORD — Map 1 C2

Waterford Castle
★★★★ ◉◉ HOTEL

☎ 051 878203 📠 051 879316
The Island
e-mail: info@waterfordcastle.com
dir: From city centre turn onto Dunmore East Rd, 1.5m, pass hospital, 0.5m left after lights, ferry at bottom of road

This enchanting and picturesque castle dates back to Norman times and is located on a 320-acre island just a five minute journey from the mainland by chain-link ferry. Bedrooms vary in style and size, but all are individually decorated and offer high standards of comfort. Dinner is served in the oak-panelled Munster Room, with breakfast taken in the conservatory. The 18-hole golf course is set in beautiful parkland where deer can be seen.

Rooms 19 (2 fmly) (4 GF) **Facilities** ⚓ 18 ⛳ Putt green Boules Archery Clay pigeon shooting ♬ New Year Wi-fi **Conf** Board 15 Thtr 30 **Services** Lift **Parking** 50 **Notes** LB ⊗ RS 1st wk Jan-Feb Civ Wed 110

Faithlegg House

★★★★ 76% ◉ HOTEL

☎ 051 382000 📠 051 382010
Faithlegg
e-mail: reservations@fhh.ie
web: www.faithlegg.com
dir: From Waterford follow Dunmore East Rd then Cheerpoint Rd

This hotel is surrounded by a championship golf course and overlooks the estuary of the River Suir. The house has 14 original bedrooms, and the rest are in an adjacent modern block. There is a range of comfortable lounges together with comprehensive meeting facilities. The leisure and treatment rooms are the perfect way to work off the excesses of the food offered in the Roseville Restaurant.

Rooms 82 (6 fmly) (30 GF) (16 smoking) **Facilities** STV 🏊 supervised ⚓ 18 ⛳ Putt green Gym ♬ New Year Wi-fi **Conf** Class 90 Board 44 Thtr 180 **Services** Lift **Parking** 100 **Notes** LB ⊗ Closed 20-27 Dec

Athenaeum House
★★★ 80% ◉ HOTEL

☎ 051 833999 📠 051 833977
Christendon, Ferrybank
e-mail: info@athenaeumhousehotel.com
web: www.athenaeumhousehotel.com
dir: N25 to Wexford, through 1st lights, right, right again into Abbey Rd. 1st right after bridge, hotel on right

Set in parkland overlooking the banks of the River Suir and the City of Waterford, this hotel was originally built in the 18th century. The public rooms have been sympathetically restored in keeping with the age of the building, yet with a contemporary twist. Bedrooms are spacious and comfortably furnished. Zak's is the bright airy restaurant where innovative food is served.

Rooms 29 (5 GF) **S** €89-€170; **D** €80-€250 (incl. bkfst)* **Facilities** FTV ♬ New Year Wi-fi Child facilities **Conf** Class 35 Board 25 Thtr 50 Del from €120 to €180* **Services** Lift **Parking** 35 **Notes** LB ⊗ Closed 24-26 Dec Civ Wed 130

Granville
★★★ 79% HOTEL

☎ 051 305555 📠 051 305566
The Quay
e-mail: stay@granville-hotel.ie
web: www.granville-hotel.ie
dir: take N25 to waterfront, city centre, opposite Clock Tower

Centrally located on the quayside, this long established hotel is appointed to a very high standard, while still keeping its true character. The bedrooms come in a choice of standard or executive, and are all well equipped and very comfortable. Friendliness and hospitality are hallmarks of a stay here.

Rooms 100 (5 fmly) (10 smoking) **Facilities** STV ♬ New Year **Conf** Class 150 Board 30 Thtr 200 Del from €100 to €150 **Services** Lift **Parking** 300 **Notes** ⊗ Closed 25-26 Dec

See advert on this page

WATERFORD *continued*

Dooley's

★★★ 75% HOTEL

☎ 051 873531 📠 051 870262
30 The Quay
e-mail: hotel@dooleys-hotel.ie
dir: on N25, adjacent to Discover Ireland Centre

Situated on the quay in Waterford overlooking the River Suir at the harbour mouth, this hotel has been run by the same family for three generations and offers friendly and relaxed atmosphere. The contemporary public areas include the New Ship Restaurant, and also the Dry Dock Bar for more casual dining. Bedrooms are attractively decorated and offer a good standard of comfort. There is a car park opposite the hotel.

Rooms 113 (3 fmly) (40 smoking) **S** €70–€130; **D** €120–€198 (incl. bkfst)* **Facilities** STV ♫ New Year Wi-fi **Conf** Class 150 Board 100 Thtr 240 Del from €105 to €135 **Services** Lift **Notes** ⊗ Closed 25-27 Dec

Tower

★★★ 75% HOTEL

☎ 051 875801 & 862300 📠 051 870129
The Mall
e-mail: info@thw.ie
web: www.towerhotelgroup.ie
dir: opp Reginald's Tower in town centre. Hotel at end of quay

This long established hotel includes two smart restaurants, a riverside bar and smart bedrooms together with three river view suites. Parking is provided at the rear.

Rooms 139 (6 fmly) **Facilities** ⊙ supervised Gym ♫ Xmas Child facilities **Conf** Class 250 Board 80 Thtr 500 **Services** Lift **Parking** 100 **Notes** LB ⊗ Closed 24-28 Dec

Waterford Manor

★★★ 70% HOTEL

☎ 051 377814 📠 051 354545
Killotteran, Butlerstown
e-mail: sales@waterfordmanorhotel.ie
dir: N25 from Waterford to Cork, right 2m after Waterford Crystal, left at end of road, hotel on right

Dating back to 1730 this manor house is set in delightful landscaped and wooded grounds. It provides high quality accommodation as well as extensive conference and banqueting facilities. Public areas include a charming drawing room and restaurant for intimate dining, plus a brasserie with its own bar that serves a carvery lunch daily.

Rooms 21 (3 fmly) **Facilities** ⌣ **Conf** Class 300 Board 40 Thtr 600 **Parking** 400 **Notes** LB ⊗ RS 25 Dec

---

CO WESTMEATH

ATHLONE
Map 1 C4

Hodson Bay

★★★★ 78% ⊚ HOTEL

☎ 090 6442000 📠 090 6442020
Hodson Bay
e-mail: info@hodsonbayhotel.com
dir: from N6 take N61 to Roscommon. Turn right. Hotel 1km on Lough Ree

On the shores of Lough Ree, four kilometres from Athlone, this hotel has its own marina and is surrounded by the golf course. Spacious public areas are comfortable, with a carvery bar, an attractive restaurant and excellent conference and banqueting facilities. The spacious bedrooms have been designed to take in the magnificent lake views. The hotel has a leisure centre and treatment rooms.

Rooms 182 (32 fmly) (11 GF) **Facilities** ⊙ supervised ⌣ 18 Fishing Gym Steam room Sauna Thermal suite ♫ Xmas New Year Wi-fi Child facilities **Conf** Class 250 Board 200 Thtr 700 **Services** Lift **Parking** 300 **Notes** LB ⊗

Wineport Lodge

⊚ RESTAURANT WITH ROOMS

☎ 090 6439010
Glasson
e-mail: lodge@wineport.ie
web: www.wineport.ie
dir: From Athlone take N55 to Ballykeeran village. Fork left at Dog & Duck pub, 1m on left

Set in a wonderful location right on the shores of the inner lakes of Lough Rea on the Shannon and three miles north of Athlone. Guests can arrive by road or water, dine on the deck or in the attractive dining room. Cuisine is modern with innovative use of the best of local produce. Most of the luxurious bedrooms and suites have balconies - the perfect setting for breakfast. There is a Canadian hot tub on the roof terrace.

Rooms 29 (3 fmly)

MULLINGAR
Map 1 C4

Mullingar Park

★★★★ 79% HOTEL

☎ 044 9344446 & 9337500 📠 044 9335937
Dublin Rd
e-mail: info@mullingarparkhotel.com
web: www.mullingarparkhotel.com
dir: N4 junct 9, take exit for Mullingar

Situated off the N4 close to Mullingar this imposing modern hotel is contemporary in design and has much to offer, including spacious public areas, flexible banqueting suites and extensive meeting rooms with a business area, complemented by a well-equipped leisure centre. Bedrooms are well appointed. The Terrace Restaurant is particularly popular for its lunch buffet and fine dining at night.

Rooms 95 (12 fmly) (39 smoking) **S** €150–€180; **D** €160–€230 (incl. bkfst) **Facilities** Spa STV ⊙ supervised Gym Aerobic studio Childrens' pool Hydrotherapy pool New Year Wi-fi **Conf** Class 750 Board 60 Thtr 1200 Del from €220 to €260 **Services** Lift **Parking** 500 **Notes** LB ⊗ Closed 24-26 Dec Civ Wed 500

CO WEXFORD

ENNISCORTHY
Map 1 D3

Treacy's

★★★ 75% HOTEL

☎ 053 9237798 📠 053 9237851
Templeshannon
e-mail: info@treacyshotel.com
dir: N11 into Enniscorthy, over bridge in left lane. Hotel on right, car park on left

This modern hotel is family run and conveniently located near the town centre. There is a choice of dining options in the Chang Thai and Begenal Harvey restaurants, with Benedict's super-pub open at weekends. Guests have complimentary use of the nearby car park and a discount at the Waterfront Leisure Centre.

Rooms 57 (3 fmly) (20 smoking) **S** €60–€90; **D** €80–€160 (incl. bkfst)* **Facilities** STV FTV ⊙ supervised Gym Complimentary use of Waterfront Leisure Centre ♫ New Year Wi-fi **Services** Lift Air con **Parking** 70 **Notes** LB ⊗ Closed 23-25 Dec

Riverside Park Hotel & Leisure Club

★★★ 72% HOTEL

☎ 053 9237800 📄 053 9237900
The Promenade
e-mail: info@riversideparkhotel.com
dir: 0.5km from New Bridge, centre of Enniscorthy town, N11 (Dublin to Rosslare road)

This modern hotel is situated on the banks of the River Slaney, and has a dramatically designed foyer; the public areas, including the Promenade Bar, all take full advantage of the riverside views. There are two dining options - casual dining is available every night in the Alamo, with more formal dining in The Moorings at peak periods. Bedrooms, some with balconies, have every modern comfort. Guests have full use of the leisure centre.

Rooms 62 (15 fmly) **S** €115-€135; **D** €180-€21 (incl. bkfst) **Facilities** STV ⓢ supervised Gym ♫ New Year Wi-fi **Conf** Class 250 Board 100 Thtr 750 Del from €120 to €150 **Services** Lift **Parking** 150 **Notes** LB ⊗ Closed 24-25 Dec RS Good Fri Civ Wed 350

GOREY   Map 1 D3

Amber Springs

★★★★ 78% HOTEL

☎ 053 9484000 📄 053 9484494
Wexford Rd
e-mail: info@ambersprings.ie
dir: 500mtrs from Gorey by-pass at junct 23

This hotel on the Wexford road is within walking distance of the town. Bedrooms are spacious and very comfortable, and guests have full use of the leisure facilities. Dining in Kelby's Bistro is a highlight of a visit, with its combination of interesting food and really friendly service.

Rooms 80 (18 fmly) **S** €115-€140; **D** €180-€230 (incl. bkfst)* **Facilities** Spa ⓢ supervised Gym Supervised children's play area ♫ Xmas New Year Wi-fi Child facilities **Conf** Class 450 Board 30 Thtr 700 **Services** Lift Air con **Parking** 178 **Notes** LB ⊗ Civ Wed 700

Ashdown Park Hotel

★★★★ 75% ⊛ HOTEL

☎ 053 9480500 📄 053 9480777
The Coach Rd
e-mail: info@ashdownparkhotel.com
web: www.ashdownparkhotel.com
dir: N11 exit 22, on approaching Gorey, 1st left before railway bridge, hotel on left

Situated on an elevated position overlooking the town, this modern hotel has excellent health, leisure and banqueting facilities. There are comfortable lounges and two dining options - the popular carvery bar and first-floor, fine dining restaurant. Bedrooms are spacious and well equipped. Close to golf, beaches and hill walking.

Rooms 79 (12 fmly) (20 GF) **Facilities** ⓢ supervised Gym Leisure centre Gym Beauty salon Spa treatments ♫ New Year Wi-fi **Conf** Class 315 Board 100 Thtr 800 **Services** Lift **Parking** 150 **Notes** LB ⊗ Closed 25 Dec Civ Wed 200

COURTESY & CARE AWARD
INSPECTORS' CHOICE

Marlfield House Hotel

★ ★ ★ ⊛⊛ COUNTRY HOUSE HOTEL

☎ 053 9421124 📄 053 9421572
e-mail: info@marlfieldhouse.ie
web: www.marlfieldhouse.com
dir: Exit N11 junct 23, follow signs for Courtown. At Courtown Rd rdbt left for Gorey. Hotel 1m on left

This Regency-style building has been sympathetically extended and developed into an excellent hotel. An atmosphere of elegance and luxury permeates every corner of the house, underpinned by truly friendly and professional service led by the Bowe family who are always in evidence. The bedrooms are decorated in keeping with the style of the house, with some really spacious rooms and suites on the ground floor. Dinner in the restaurant is always a highlight of a stay at Marlfield. AA Ireland has awarded this hotel their Courtesy & Care Award for the Republic of Ireland 2009-10.

Rooms 19 (3 fmly) (6 GF) **S** €90-€145; **D** €180-€550 (incl. bkfst)* **Facilities** ♒ ♖ Xmas **Conf** Board 20 Thtr 60 Del from €190 to €380* **Parking** 100 **Notes** LB Closed 2 Jan-28 Feb Civ Wed 100

NEW ROSS   Map 1 C3

Brandon House Hotel & Solas Croi Eco Spa

★★★ 77% HOTEL

☎ 051 421703 📄 051 421567
e-mail: reception@brandonhousehotel.ie
dir: In New Ross over O' Honrahan bridge, turn right along quay, hotel on left, on N25

Located on the N25 on the eastern approach to New Ross, this well established property offers a range of comfortable bedroom styles together with good conference rooms, public areas and a choice of dining options. Excellent leisure facilities including spectacular Solas Croi Eco Spa are available to guests.

Rooms 79 (18 fmly) (39 GF) **Facilities** ⓢ supervised Gym Hydrotherapy Grotto ♫ New Year Wi-fi **Conf** Class 306 Board 96 Thtr 416 **Parking** 160 **Notes** LB ⊗ Closed 24-26 Dec

Cedar Lodge

IRISH COUNTRY HOTELS

★★★ 75% HOTEL

☎ 051 428386 & 428436 📄 051 428222
Carrigbyrne, Newbawn
e-mail: cedarlodge@eircom.net
web: www.prideofeirehotels.com
dir: On N25 between Wexford & New Ross

Cedar Lodge sits in a tranquil setting beneath the slopes of Carrigbyrne Forest, just a 30-minute drive from Rosslare Port. The Martin family extend warm hospitality and provide good food in the charming conservatory restaurant with its central log fire. Many of the spacious, thoughtfully appointed bedrooms overlook the attractively landscaped gardens.

Rooms 28 (2 fmly) (10 GF) **Conf** Class 60 Board 60 Thtr 100 **Parking** 60 **Notes** LB ⊗ Closed 21 Dec-Jan

NEW ROSS *continued*

ROSSLARE Map 1 D2

INSPECTORS' CHOICE

Kelly's Resort Hotel & Spa
★★★★ HOTEL

☎ 053 9132114   ᐧ 053 9132222
e-mail: info@kellys.ie
dir: Exit N25 onto Rosslare to Wexford road, signed Rosslare Strand

The Kelly Family have been offering hospitality here since 1895, where together with a dedicated team, they provide a very professional and friendly service. The resort overlooks the sandy beach and is within minutes of the ferry port at Rosslare. Bedrooms are thoughtfully equipped and comfortably furnished. The extensive leisure facilities include a smart spa, swimming pools, a crèche, young adults' programme and spacious well-tended gardens. The bistro, La Marine, serves food to AA Rosette standard.

Rooms 118 (15 fmly) (20 GF) **Facilities** Spa ☜ supervised ☺ ⛳ Gym Bowls Plunge pool Badminton Crazy golf ♫ Wi-fi Child facilities **Conf** Class 30 Board 20 Thtr 30 **Services** Lift **Parking** 120 **Notes** ☒ Closed mid Dec-late Feb

WEXFORD Map 1 D3

Whites of Wexford
★★★★ 77% HOTEL

☎ 053 9122311   ᐧ 053 9145000
Abbey St
e-mail: info@whitesofwexford.ie
dir: On Abbey St, Wexford Town

This long established hotel in the centre of the town has undergone major development in recent years. It now offers a fine range of bedroom styles all in smart contemporary schemes. Public areas are bright and airy and include a number of dining options. Excellent conference and leisure facilities are available, as is an underground car park.

Rooms 157 (50 annexe) (74 fmly) **Facilities** Spa STV ☜ supervised Gym Cryotherapy clinic High performance centre ♫ Xmas New Year Wi-fi **Conf** Class 532 Board 126 Thtr 1110 **Services** Lift Air con **Parking** 250 **Notes** ☒ Closed 24-26 Dec Civ Wed 200

Talbot Hotel Conference & Leisure Centre
★★★★ 74% HOTEL

☎ 053 9122566 & 9155559   ᐧ 053 9123377
The Quay
e-mail: sales@talbothotel.ie
dir: N11 from Dublin, follow Wexford signs, hotel at end of quay on right

Centrally situated on the quayside, this hotel offers well-equipped bedrooms that have custom-made oak furniture and attractive decor; many have sea views. Public areas include a spacious foyer, comfortable lounges and the Ballast Quay bar, serving food all day. The attractive Oyster Lane Restaurant serves interesting dishes. Good leisure facilities are complimentary to residents.

Rooms 109 (8 fmly) **Facilities** Spa ☜ supervised Gym Talbot Tigers Club ♫ Xmas New Year Wi-fi Child facilities **Conf** Class 250 Board 110 Thtr 450 **Services** Lift Air con **Parking** 160 **Notes** ☒ Closed 24-25 Dec Civ Wed 300

Whitford House Hotel Health & Leisure Club
★★★ 75% ◉ HOTEL

☎ 053 9143444   ᐧ 053 9146399
New Line Rd
e-mail: info@whitford.ie
web: www.whitford.ie
dir: Just off N25 (Duncannon rdbt) take exit for R733 (Wexford), hotel immediately left

This is a friendly family-run hotel just two kilometres from the town centre and within easy reach of the Rosslare Ferry. Comfortable bedrooms range from standard to the spacious and luxuriously decorated deluxe. Public areas include a choice of lounges and the popular Forthside Bar Bistro where a carvery is served. More formal meals are on offer in the award-winning Seasons Restaurant.

Rooms 36 (28 fmly) (18 GF) **S** €68-€124; **D** €110-€198 (incl. bkfst) **Facilities** Spa FTV ☜ supervised Gym Children's playground Football area Hairdresser ♫ Xmas New Year Wi-fi **Conf** Class 12 Board 25 Thtr 50 **Parking** 200 **Notes** LB ☒ RS 24-27 Dec Civ Wed 100

Newbay Country House & Restaurant
◉ RESTAURANT WITH ROOMS

☎ 053 42779   ᐧ 053 46318
Newbay, Carrick
e-mail: newbay@newbayhouse.com
dir: A11 from Wexford Bridge and turn right towards N25. Turn left before Quality Hotel and next right

Built in the 1820s, but only offering accommodation for some ten years, Newbay offers a choice of two dining areas, the casual Cellar Bistro on the lower floor, or the more formal restaurant in the original house. Unsurprisingly, seafood is a passion here; the freshest catch only has to travel a few hundred yards. The very comfortable bedrooms are situated in both the house and a wing; some have four-posters and all have lovely views.

Rooms 11 (1 fmly)

CO WICKLOW

AUGHRIM Map 1 D3

Lawless
Ⓤ

☎ 0402 36146   ᐧ 0402 36384
e-mail: info@lawlesshotel.com
dir: N11 to Rathnew, R752 to Rathdrum, R753 to Aughrim. Hotel between bridges on outskirts of village

At the time of going to press the rating for this establishment was not confirmed. This may be due to a change of ownership or because it has only recently joined the AA rating scheme. For further details please see the AA website:theAA.com

Rooms 14 (2 fmly) **Facilities** ☺ ♫ Wi-fi **Conf** Class 60 Board 40 Thtr 100 **Parking** 40 **Notes** ☒ Closed 23-26 Dec

BRAY Map 1 D4

Royal Hotel & Leisure Centre
★★★ 73% HOTEL

☎ 01 2862935 & 2724900   ᐧ 01 2867373
Main St
e-mail: royal@regencyhotels.com
dir: from N11, 1st exit for Bray, 2nd exit from rdbt, through 2 sets of lights, across bridge, hotel on left

Located in the town centre and walking distance from the seafront at Bray and close to Dun Laoighaire ferry port. Public areas offer comfortable lounges, traditional bar and The Heritage Restaurant. Bedrooms vary in size and are well appointed. There is a well-equipped leisure centre and a supervised car park is available.

Rooms 130 (10 fmly) **Facilities** ☜ supervised Gym Massage & beauty clinic Therapy room Whirlpool spa Creche ♫ Xmas Wi-fi **Conf** Class 300 Board 200 Thtr 500 **Services** Lift **Parking** 60 **Notes** LB ☒ Civ Wed 300

Glenview

★★★★ 75% HOTEL

☎ 01 2873399 📄 01 2877511
Glen O' the Downs
e-mail: sales@glenviewhotel.com
dir: from Dublin city centre follow signs for N11, past Bray on N11 southbound

Set in a lovely hillside location, overlooking terraced gardens, this hotel boasts an excellent range of leisure and conference facilities. Impressive public areas include a conservatory bar, lounge and choice of dining options. The bedrooms are spacious and many enjoy great views over the valley. A championship golf course, horse riding and many tourist amenities are available nearby.

Rooms 70 (11 fmly) (16 GF) **Facilities** ⚲ supervised 🏊
Gym Aerobics studio Massage Beauty treatment room ♫
Xmas Child facilities **Conf** Class 120 Board 50 Thtr 220
Services Lift **Parking** 200 **Notes** ⊗

The Glendalough

★★★ 69% HOTEL

☎ 0404 45135 📄 0404 45142
e-mail: info@glendaloughhotel.ie
dir: N11 to Kilmacongue, right onto R755, straight on at Laragh then right onto R756

Mountains and forest provide the setting for this long-established hotel at the edge of the famed monastic site. Many of the well-appointed bedrooms have superb views. Food is served daily in the very popular bar while relaxing dinners are served in the charming restaurant that overlooks the river and forest.

Rooms 44 (3 fmly) **Facilities** STV Fishing ♫ Wi-fi
Conf Class 150 Board 50 Thtr 200 **Services** Lift
Parking 100 **Notes** ⊗ RS Dec-Jan, Mon-Fri

Brooklodge Hotel & Wells Spa

★★★★ 86% ◎◎ HOTEL

☎ 0402 36444 📄 0402 36580
e-mail: info@brooklodge.com
web: www.brooklodge.com
dir: N11 to Rathnew, R752 to Rathdrum, R753 to Aughrim follow signs to Macreddin Village

A luxury country-house hotel complex, in a village setting, which includes Acton's pub, Orchard Café and retail outlets. Bedrooms in the original house are very comfortable, and mezzanine suites are situated in the landscaped grounds. Brook Hall with ground-floor and first floor bedrooms overlooking the 18th green of the golf course. The award-winning Strawberry Tree Restaurant is a truly romantic setting, specialising in organic and wild foods. The Wells Spa Centre offers extensive treatments and leisure facilities.

Rooms 90 (32 annexe) (27 fmly) (4 GF) **Facilities** Spa STV
FTV ⚲ ⚘ 🏌 18 Putt green Gym Archery Clay pigeon
shooting Falconry Off road driving Xmas New Year Wi-fi
Conf Class 120 Board 40 Thtr 300 **Services** Lift
Parking 200 **Notes** Civ Wed 180

Hunter's

★★★ 75% ◎ HOTEL

☎ 0404 40106 📄 0404 40338
e-mail: reception@hunters.ie
dir: 1.5km from village off N11

One of Ireland's oldest coaching inns, this charming country house was built in 1720 and is full of character and atmosphere. The comfortable bedrooms have wonderful views over prize-winning gardens that border the River Vartry. The restaurant has a good reputation for carefully prepared dishes which make the best use of high quality local produce, including fruit and vegetables from the hotel's own garden.

Rooms 16 (2 fmly) (2 GF) **Conf** Class 40 Board 16 Thtr 40
Parking 50 **Notes** ⊗ Closed 24-26 Dec

Woodenbridge

★★★ 70% ◎ HOTEL

☎ 0402 35146 📄 0402 35573
e-mail: reservations@woodenbridgehotel.com
dir: Between Avoca & Arklow, off N11.

Situated in the beautiful Vale of Avoca and owner-managed by the hospitable O'Brien family this smart hotel is beside the Woodenbridge Golf Club. Public areas are comfortable with open fires and good food is assured in the Italian restaurant. The lodge bedrooms are well equipped, spacious and enjoy a peaceful riverside setting.

Rooms 23 (13 fmly) **S** €60-€90; **D** €80-€140 (incl.
bkfst)* **Facilities** Pool table ♫ Xmas **Conf** Class 200
Board 200 Thtr 200 **Parking** 100 **Notes** LB ⊗ Civ Wed 70

Gibraltar

Caleta

★★★★ 78% ◎◎ HOTEL

☎ 00 350 20076501 📠 00 350 20042143
Sir Herbert Miles Rd, PO Box 73
e-mail: sales@caletahotel.gi
web: www.caletahotel.com
dir: Enter Gibraltar via Spanish border & cross runway. At
1st rdbt turn left, hotel in 2kms

For travellers arriving to Gibraltar by air the Caleta is an
eye catching coastal landmark that can be spotted by
planes arriving from the east. This imposing and stylish
hotel sits on a cliff top and all sea-facing rooms enjoy
panoramic views across the straights to Morocco.
Bedrooms vary in size and style with some boasting
spacious balconies, flat-screen TVs and mini bars.
Several dining venues are available but Nunos provides
the award-winning fine dining Italian experience. Staff
are friendly, service is professional.

Rooms 161 (89 annexe) (13 fmly) **S** £89-£189;
D £89-£189* **Facilities** Spa STV ↸ supervised Gym
Health & beauty club Xmas New Year **Conf** Class 172
Board 85 Thtr 200 **Services** Lift **Parking** 32 **Notes** LB ⊗
Civ Wed 300

Rock

★★★★ 78% ◎◎ HOTEL

☎ 00 350 200 73000 📠 00 350 200 73513
Europa Rd
e-mail: rockhotel@gibtelecom.net
web: www.rockhotelgibraltar.com
dir: From airport follow tourist board signs. Hotel on left
half way up Europa Rd

Enjoying a prime elevated location directly below the
Rock, this long established art deco styled hotel has been
the destination of celebrities and royalty since it was
built in 1932. Bedrooms are spacious and well equipped
and many boast stunning coastal views that stretch
across the Mediterranean to Morocco. Staff are friendly
and service is delivered with flair and enthusiasm.
Creative dinners and hearty breakfasts can be enjoyed in
the stylish restaurant.

Rooms 104 (25 smoking) **Facilities** STV ↸ supervised ♫
Xmas New Year Wi-fi **Conf** Class 24 Board 30 Thtr 70
Services Lift Air con **Parking** 40 **Notes** RS 5 Oct-1 Apr
Civ Wed 40

O'Callaghan Eliott

★★★★ 75% HOTEL

☎ 00 350 200 70500 & 200 75905
📠 00 350 200 70243
2 Governor's Pde
e-mail: eliott@ocallaghanhotels.com
web: www.ocallaghanhotels.com

Located in the heart of the old town, this hotel provides a
convenient central base for exploring the duty free
shopping district and other key attractions on foot. The
bedrooms are stylish, spacious and well equipped. The
roof top restaurant provides stunning bay views whilst
guests can also take a swim in the roof top pool.

Rooms 120 **Facilities** STV ↸ Gym ♫ Xmas New Year
Wi-fi **Conf** Class 80 Board 70 Thtr 180 **Services** Lift
Air con **Parking** 17 **Notes** LB ⊗ Civ Wed 120

Index of Hotels

ASHWATER	
Blagdon Manor Hotel & Restaurant	139
ASKRIGG	
White Rose	506
ASPLEY GUISE	
Best Western Moore Place	42
ASTON CLINTON	
Innkeeper's Lodge Aylesbury East	57
ATHERSTONE	
Chapel House Restaurant With Rooms	464
ATHLONE	
Hodson Bay	708
Wineport Lodge	708
ATHY	
Clanard Court	696
ATTLEBOROUGH	
Sherbourne House	358
AUCHENCAIRN	
Balcary Bay	570
AUCHTERARDER	
Gleneagles Hotel, The	606
AUGHRIM	
Lawless	710
AUSTWICK	
Austwick Traddock, The	506
AVIEMORE	
Macdonald Highlands	591
AXMINSTER	
Fairwater Head Hotel	139
AYLESBURY	
Hartwell House Hotel, Restaurant & Spa	57
Holiday Inn Aylesbury	57
Holiday Inn Garden Court Aylesbury	58
Innkeeper's Lodge Aylesbury South	58
AYNHO	
Cartwright Hotel	370
AYR	
Enterkine Country House	615
Express by Holiday Inn Ayr	615
Fairfield House	615
Savoy Park	615
Travelodge Ayr	615
Western House Hotel, The	615
AYSGARTH	
George & Dragon	506
BAGSHOT	
Pennyhill Park Hotel & The Spa	432
BAINBRIDGE	
Rose & Crown	506
BAKEWELL	
Monsal Head Hotel	131
Rutland Arms	131
BALDOCK	
Travelodge Baldock Hinxworth	248
BALLANTRAE	
Glenapp Castle	616
BALLATER	
Auld Kirk, The	563
Cambus O'May	563
Darroch Learg	563
Green Inn, The	563
Loch Kinord	563
BALLINA	
Ice House	700
Mount Falcon Country House	700
BALLOCH	
Cameron House on Loch Lomond	621
Innkeeper's Lodge Loch Lomond	621
BALLYCOTTON	
Bayview	677
BALLYHEIGE	
White Sands, The	692
BALLYLICKEY	
Sea View House Hotel	678
BALLYMENA	
Galgorm Resort & Spa	670
BALLYSHANNON	
Heron's Cove	682
BALLYVAUGHAN	
Gregans Castle	676
Hylands Burren	676
BALSALL COMMON	
Haigs	473
Nailcote Hall	473
BALTIMORE	
Casey's of Baltimore	678
BAMBURGH	
Lord Crewe, The	375
Victoria	375
Waren House	375
BANBURY	
Best Western Wroxton House	384
Cromwell Lodge Hotel	384
Express by Holiday Inn Banbury M40, Jct 11	384
Mercure Whately Hall	384
BANCHORY	
Banchory Lodge	564
Best Western Burnett Arms	564
BANGOR	
Clandeboye Lodge	672
Marine Court	672
Old Inn, The	672
Royal	672
BANGOR	
Travelodge Bangor	650
BANKNOCK	
Glenskirlie House & Castle	583
BANTRY	
Maritime	678
Westlodge	678
BARFORD	
Glebe at Barford, The	464
BARKING	
Ibis London Barking	342
Travelodge London Barking	342
BARLBOROUGH	
Ibis Sheffield South	131
BARMOUTH	
Bae Abermaw	651
BARNARD CASTLE	
Jersey Farm Country Hotel	187
Morritt, The	187
BARNBY MOOR	
Ye Olde Bell Hotel & Restaurant	378
BARNET	
Savoro Restaurant with Rooms	342
BARNHAM BROOM	
Barnham Broom Hotel, Golf & Restaurant	358
BARNSLEY	
Best Western Ardsley House Hotel	529
Brooklands Hotel	529
Tankersley Manor	529
Travelodge Barnsley	529
BARNSTAPLE	
Barnstaple Hotel	139
Cedars Lodge	140
Imperial, The	139
Park	140
Royal & Fortescue	140
Travelodge Barnstaple	140
BARROW-IN-FURNESS	
Abbey House	106
Clarke's Hotel	106
Lisdoonie	107
Travelodge Barrow-in-Furness	107
BARRY	
Best Western Mount Sorrel	666
Egerton Grey Country House	666
Innkeeper's Lodge Cardiff Airport	666
BARTON	
Barton Grange	268
BARTON MILLS	
Travelodge Barton Mills	422
BARTON STACEY	
Travelodge Barton Stacey	226
BARTON-ON-SEA	
Pebble Beach	226
BARTON-UNDER-NEEDWOOD	
Travelodge Burton (A38 Northbound)	416
Travelodge Burton (A38 Southbound)	416
BASILDON	
Campanile Basildon	192
Chichester	192
Holiday Inn Basildon	192
Travelodge Basildon	192
BASINGSTOKE	
Apollo	227
Audleys Wood	226
Barceló Basingstoke Country Hotel	227
Hampshire Court Hotel, The	226
Holiday Inn Basingstoke	227
Travelodge Basingstoke	227
Tylney Hall	226
BASLOW	
Cavendish	131
Fischer's Baslow Hall	131
BASSENTHWAITE	
Armathwaite Hall	107
Best Western Castle Inn	107
Pheasant, The	107
Ravenstone	107
BATH	
Bailbrook House Hotel	405
Barceló Combe Grove Manor	404
Bath Priory Hotel, Restaurant & Spa, The	403
Best Western Abbey Hotel	405
Best Western The Cliffe	404
Carfax	405
Dukes	405
Express by Holiday Inn Bath	406
Haringtons	405
Macdonald Bath Spa	402
Mercure Francis	405
Old Malt House	406
Pratt's	405
Queensberry	404
Royal Crescent, The	403
Travelodge Bath Central	406
Travelodge Bath Waterside	406
Wentworth House Hotel	406
BATTLE	
Brickwall Hotel	439

Travelodge Birmingham Oldbury	481
OLDHAM	
Best Western Hotel Smokies Park	223
Innkeeper's Lodge Oldham	223
Travelodge Oldham	223
Travelodge Oldham Manchester Street	223
OLDMELDRUM	
Meldrum House Hotel Golf & Country Estate	565
ONICH	
Onich	600
ORFORD	
Crown & Castle, The	429
ORMSKIRK	
West Tower Country House	275
OSWESTRY	
Lion Quays Waterside Resort	398
Pen-y-Dyffryn Country Hotel	398
Sebastian's Hotel & Restaurant	398
Travelodge Oswestry	398
Wynnstay	397
OTLEY	
Chevin Country Park Hotel & Spa	542
OTTERBURN	
Otterburn Tower Hotel, The	377
Percy Arms	377
OTTERSHAW	
Foxhills Resort & Spa	436
OTTERY ST MARY	
Tumbling Weir Hotel	153
OXFORD	
Balkan Lodge Hotel, The	391
Barceló Oxford Hotel	388
Bath Place	391
Best Western Linton Lodge	391
Cotswold Lodge	389
Express by Holiday Inn Oxford-Kassam Stadium	391
Hawkwell House	391
Holiday Inn Oxford	390
Le Manoir Aux Quat' Saisons	388
Macdonald Randolph	388
Malmaison Oxford	390
Manor House	391
Mercure Eastgate	390
Old Bank Hotel, The	388
Old Parsonage	389
Oxford Spires Four Pillars Hotel	390
Oxford Thames Four Pillars Hotel	390

Travelodge Oxford Peartree	391
Travelodge Oxford Wheatley	391
Victoria	391
Weston Manor	390
Westwood Country Hotel	390
OXFORD MOTORWAY SERVICE AREA (M40)	
Days Inn Oxford	392
PADSTOW	
Metropole, The	95
Old Ship Hotel, The	95
Seafood Restaurant, The	95
St Petroc's Hotel and Bistro	95
Treglos	95
PADWORTH	
Holiday Inn Reading West	48
PAIGNTON	
Redcliffe	153
Redcliffe Lodge Hotel	154
Summerhill	154
PANGBOURNE	
Elephant at Pangbourne	48
PATTERDALE	
Patterdale	121
PATTINGHAM	
Patshull Park Hotel Golf & Country Club	418
PEASMARSH	
Best Western Flackley Ash	447
PEAT INN	
Peat Inn, The	587
PECKFORTON	
Peckforton Castle	77
PEEBLES	
Cringletie House	613
Macdonald Cardrona Hotel Golf & Country Club	613
Park	614
Peebles Hotel Hydro	614
Tontine	614
PEMBROKE	
Best Western Lamphey Court	658
Lamphey Hall	658
PEMBROKE DOCK	
Cleddau Bridge	658
Travelodge Pembroke Dock	659
PENCOED	
St Mary's Hotel & Country Club	633
Travelodge Bridgend Pencoed	633
PENRITH	
Edenhall Country Hotel	122
George	122
North Lakes Hotel & Spa	121
Temple Sowerby House Hotel & Restaurant	122

Travelodge Penrith	122
Westmorland Hotel	122
PENZANCE	
Hotel Penzance	95
Queens	95
PERTH	
Best Western Huntingtower	609
Best Western Queens Hotel	609
Express by Holiday Inn Perth	610
Innkeeper's Lodge Perth A9 (Huntingtower)	610
Innkeeper's Lodge Perth City Centre	610
Lovat	610
Murrayshall House Hotel & Golf Course	609
New County Hotel, The	609
Parklands Hotel	609
Salutation	610
Travelodge Perth Broxden Junction	610
PETERBOROUGH	
Bell Inn	67
Best Western Orton Hall	67
Bull	67
Holiday Inn Peterborough West	68
Peterborough Marriott	67
Queensgate Hotel	68
Travelodge Peterborough Alwalton	68
Travelodge Peterborough Central	68
Travelodge Peterborough Eye Green	68
PETERHEAD	
Buchan Braes Hotel	565
Palace	565
PETERSFIELD	
Langrish House	238
PICKERING	
Best Western Forest & Vale	514
Fox & Hounds Country Inn	514
Old Manse	515
White Swan Inn, The	514
PICKHILL	
Nags Head Country Inn	515
PINNER	
Tudor Lodge	350
PITLOCHRY	
Dundarach	611
Green Park	610
Moulin Hotel	611
PLOCKTON	
Plockton, The	601

PLYMOUTH	
Best Western Duke of Cornwall	154
Copthorne Hotel Plymouth	155
Elfordleigh Hotel Golf Leisure	155
Holiday Inn Plymouth	154
Ibis Hotel Plymouth	155
Innkeeper's Lodge Plymouth	156
Innkeeper's Lodge Plymouth (Derriford)	156
Invicta	155
Langdon Court Hotel & Restaurant	155
New Continental	155
Novotel Plymouth	155
Travelodge Plymouth	156
POCKLINGTON	
Feathers	505
PODIMORE	
Travelodge Yeovil Podimore	411
POLMONT	
Macdonald Inchyra Grange	584
POLPERRO	
Talland Bay	96
PONTEFRACT	
Best Western Rogerthorpe Manor	543
Wentbridge House	542
PONTYPOOL	
Travelodge Pontypool	666
PONTYPRIDD	
Llechwen Hall	664
POOLE	
Antelope Inn	182
Arndale Court	182
Express by Holiday Inn Poole	182
Harbour Heights	181
Haven	182
Hotel du Vin Poole	181
Quarterdeck	182
Salterns Harbourside	182
Sandbanks	182
Thistle Poole	182
PORLOCK	
Oaks, The	411
PORT APPIN	
Airds	568
Pierhouse	568
PORT ASKAIG	
Port Askaig	623
PORT ERIN	
Falcon's Nest	557
PORT GAVERNE	
Port Gaverne	96
PORT TALBOT	
Best Western Aberavon Beach	656

SOUTH CERNEY
Cotswold Water Park Four
  Pillars Hotel — 211
SOUTH MIMMS SERVICE AREA
(M25)
Days Inn South Mimms — 255
SOUTH MOLTON
George Hotel, The — 161
Stumbles — 161
SOUTH NORMANTON
Derbyshire — 138
SOUTH QUEENSFERRY
Innkeeper's Lodge Edinburgh
  South Queensferry — 583
SOUTH RUISLIP
Days Hotel London South
  Ruislip — 352
SOUTH SHIELDS
Best Western Sea — 461
SOUTH WITHAM
Travelodge Grantham South
  Witham — 290
SOUTH WOODHAM FERRERS
Oakland Hotel, The — 199
SOUTHAMPTON
Chilworth Manor — 241
De Vere Grand Harbour — 241
Elizabeth House — 242
Highfield House Hotel — 242
Holiday Inn Express
  Southampton - M27, Jct 7 — 241
Holiday Inn Southampton — 242
Ibis Southampton Centre — 242
Legacy Botleigh Grange — 241
Novotel Southampton — 241
Southampton Park — 242
Travelodge Southampton — 242
SOUTHEND-ON-SEA
Balmoral Hotel — 198
Camelia — 198
Roslin Beach Hotel — 198
Travelodge Southend on Sea — 199
Westcliff — 198
SOUTHPORT
Balmoral Lodge — 357
Best Western Royal Clifton
  Hotel & Spa — 356
Cambridge House — 357
Scarisbrick — 356
Vincent — 356
SOUTHWAITE MOTORWAY SERVICE
AREA (M6)
Travelodge Carlisle (M6) — 123
SOUTHWELL
Saracens Head — 383

SOUTHWOLD
Blyth — 430
Crown, The — 430
Sutherland House — 430
Swan — 429
SPALDING
Travelodge Spalding — 290
SPANISH POINT
Armada — 677
SPEAN BRIDGE
Smiddy House, The — 602
SPENNYMOOR
Best Western Whitworth Hall
  Hotel — 191
STAFFIN
Flodigarry Country House — 629
Glenview, The — 629
STAFFORD
Abbey — 419
Moat House, The — 419
Swan, The — 419
Travelodge Stafford Central — 419
STAFFORD MOTORWAY SERVICE
AREA (M6)
Travelodge Stafford (M6) — 419
STAINES
Mercure Thames Lodge — 437
Travelodge Staines — 437
STALLINGBOROUGH
Stallingborough Grange Hotel — 290
STAMFORD
Candlesticks — 291
Crown — 290
Garden House Hotel — 290
George of Stamford, The — 290
STANLEY
Beamish Hall Country House
  Hotel — 192
STANSTED AIRPORT
Best Western Stansted Manor — 199
Express by Holiday Inn
  - Stansted Airport — 199
Radisson Blu Hotel Stansted
  Airport — 199
STANTON ST QUINTIN
Stanton Manor Hotel — 493
STAPLEFORD
Crab & Lobster, The — 456
STEEPLE ASTON
Holt Hotel, The — 392
STEPPS
Best Western Garfield House
  Hotel — 606
STEVENAGE
Best Western Roebuck Inn — 255

Holiday Inn Stevenage — 255
Ibis Stevenage Centre — 255
Novotel Stevenage — 255
STEYNING
Best Western Old Tollgate
  Restaurant & Hotel — 456
STILTON
Bell Inn — 69
STIRLING
Barceló Stirling Highland Hotel — 620
Express by Holiday Inn Stirling — 620
Travelodge Stirling (M80) — 620
STOCK
Greenwoods Hotel Spa &
  Retreat — 199
STOCKBRIDGE
Grosvenor Hotel — 242
STOCKPORT
Alma Lodge Hotel — 224
Bredbury Hall Hotel & Country
  Club — 224
Innkeeper's Lodge Stockport — 225
Wycliffe — 224
STOCKTON-ON-TEES
Best Western Parkmore Hotel
  & Leisure Club — 192
STOKE D'ABERNON
Woodlands Park — 437
STOKE POGES
Stoke Park — 62
STOKE-BY-NAYLAND
Crown — 430
STOKE-ON-TRENT
Best Western Manor House — 420
Best Western Stoke-on-Trent
  Moat House — 420
Express by Holiday Inn
  Stoke-on-Trent — 420
Haydon House — 420
Innkeeper's Lodge
  Stoke-on-Trent — 420
Manor at Hanchurch — 420
Quality Hotel Stoke — 420
Weathervane — 421
STON EASTON
Ston Easton Park — 412
STONE
Crown — 421
Stone House — 421
STONEHOUSE
Stonehouse Court — 211
Travelodge Stonehouse — 211
STOURPORT-ON-SEVERN
Menzies Stourport Manor — 501

STOW-ON-THE-WOLD
Fosse Manor — 211
Old Stocks — 212
Royalist, The — 212
Stow Lodge — 212
STOWMARKET
Cedars — 430
Travelodge Ipswich
  Stowmarket — 430
STRACHUR
Creggans Inn — 569
STRAFFAN
Barberstown Castle — 697
K Club, The — 697
STRANRAER
Corsewall Lighthouse Hotel — 575
North West Castle — 575
STRATFORD-UPON-AVON
Barceló Billesley Manor Hotel — 469
Best Western Grosvenor House — 470
Best Western Salford Hall — 470
Charlecote Pheasant Hotel — 470
Ettington Park — 468
Holiday Inn
  Stratford-upon-Avon — 469
Legacy Falcon — 469
Macdonald Alveston Manor — 468
Macdonald Swan's Nest — 470
Menzies Welcombe Hotel Spa
  & Golf Club — 468
Mercure Shakespeare — 469
New Inn Hotel &
  Restaurant, The — 470
Stratford Manor — 469
Stratford, The — 469
Thistle Stratford-upon-Avon — 470
Travelodge
  Stratford-upon-Avon — 470
STRATHAVEN
Rissons at Springvale — 619
STRATHBLANE
Strathblane Country House — 621
STRATHYRE
Creagan House — 620
STREATLEY
Swan at Streatley, The — 51
STREET
Wessex — 412
STRONTIAN
Kilcamb Lodge — 602
STROUD
Bear of Rodborough, The — 212
Burleigh Court — 212
STRUAN
Ullinish Country Lodge — 629

AA Media Limited would like to thank the following photographers and companies for their assistance in the preparation of this book.

Abbreviations for the picture credits are as follows: (t) top; (b) bottom; (l) left; (r) right; (c) centre (AA) AA World Travel Library.

1 Bibury Court; 2 Swinton Park; 3 Victoria at Holkham; 7 The Royal Crescent Hotel, Bath; 8l Feversham Arms Hotel & Verbena Spa; 8r The Connaught Hotel; 9l The Gleneagles Hotel; 9c Penmaenuchaf Hall; 9r Mount Falcon Country House Hotel; 10t The Greenway; 10r The Ickworth Hotel & Apartments; 10b Buckland Manor; 11t Pennyhill Park Hotel & Spa; 11c Manor House Hotel and Golf Club; 11b Lainston House Hotel; 12 Kinloch Lodge; 13 St Tudno Hotel & Restaurant; 14l Suzanne Mitchell; 14r, 15t Fitzpatrick Castle; 15r Royal Glen Hotel; 16, 17 Goring Hotel; 18, 19, 20, 21 Malmaison Hotels; 23 AA/J Freeman; 24l Black Swan, Helmsley; 24c AA/J Freeman; 24r The Ritz London; 26l Ye Olde Bell Hotel; 26c Twenty Nevern Square; 26r Bath Spa Hotel; 27t Randolph Hotel, Oxford; 27bc Corbin Head Hotel, Torquay; 27br Crouchers Country Hotel & Restaurant; 28 Kinloch Lodge; 29 The Shelbourne; 38 AA/N Hicks; 40/1 AA/ J Miller; 292 AA/J Tims; 558 AA/S L Day; 630 AA/N Jenkins; 668 AA/C Jones; 712/713 AA/J Tims; AA/P Wilson.

Every effort has been made to trace the copyright holders, and we apologise in advance for any accidental errors. We would be happy to apply the corrections in the following edition of this publication.

County Maps

England

1 Bedfordshire
2 Berkshire
3 Bristol
4 Buckinghamshire
5 Cambridgeshire
6 Greater Manchester
7 Herefordshire
8 Hertfordshire
9 Leicestershire
10 Northamptonshire
11 Nottinghamshire
12 Rutland
13 Staffordshire
14 Warwickshire
15 West Midlands
16 Worcestershire

Scotland

17 City of Glasgow
18 Clackmannanshire
19 East Ayrshire
20 East Dunbartonshire
21 East Renfrewshire
22 Perth & Kinross
23 Renfrewshire
24 South Lanarkshire
25 West Dunbartonshire

Wales

26 Blaenau Gwent
27 Bridgend
28 Caerphilly
29 Denbighshire
30 Flintshire
31 Merthyr Tydfil
32 Monmouthshire
33 Neath Port Talbot
34 Newport
35 Rhondda Cynon Taff
36 Torfaen
37 Vale of Glamorgan
38 Wrexham

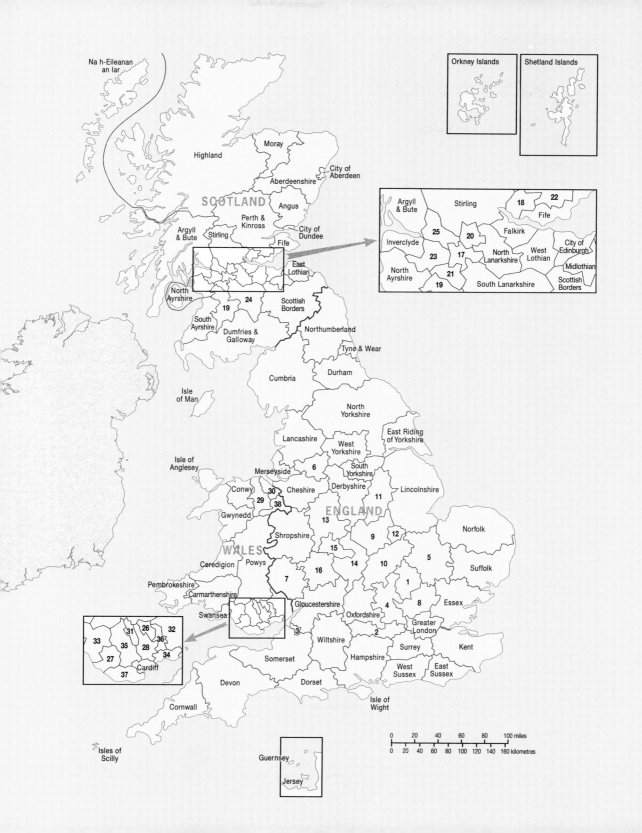

Orkney Islands

Shetland Islands

Na h-Eileanan an Iar

SCOTLAND

Highland

Moray

Aberdeenshire

City of Aberdeen

Angus

Perth & Kinross

City of Dundee

Argyll & Bute

Stirling

Fife

East Lothian

North Ayrshire

19

24

Scottish Borders

South Ayrshire

Dumfries & Galloway

Northumberland

Argyll & Bute

Stirling

18

22

Fife

Inverclyde

25

20

Falkirk

City of Edinburgh

23

17

North Lanarkshire

West Lothian

Midlothian

North Ayrshire

21

Scottish Borders

19

South Lanarkshire

Tyne & Wear

Durham

Cumbria

Isle of Man

North Yorkshire

Lancashire

East Riding of Yorkshire

West Yorkshire

Isle of Anglesey

Merseyside

6

South Yorkshire

Conwy

30

Cheshire

Derbyshire

Lincolnshire

29

38

11

Gwynedd

ENGLAND

13

Shropshire

9

12

WALES

15

Norfolk

Ceredigion

Powys

14

10

5

Pembrokeshire

16

1

Suffolk

Carmarthenshire

7

Swansea

Gloucestershire

4

8

Essex

Oxfordshire

Greater London

3

2

Kent

Wiltshire

Surrey

31

26

32

Somerset

Hampshire

33

36

West Sussex

East Sussex

35

28

34

27

Cardiff

Devon

Dorset

37

Isle of Wight

Cornwall

Isles of Scilly

Guernsey

Jersey

0   20   40   60   80   100 miles

0 20 40 60 80 100 120 140 160 kilometres

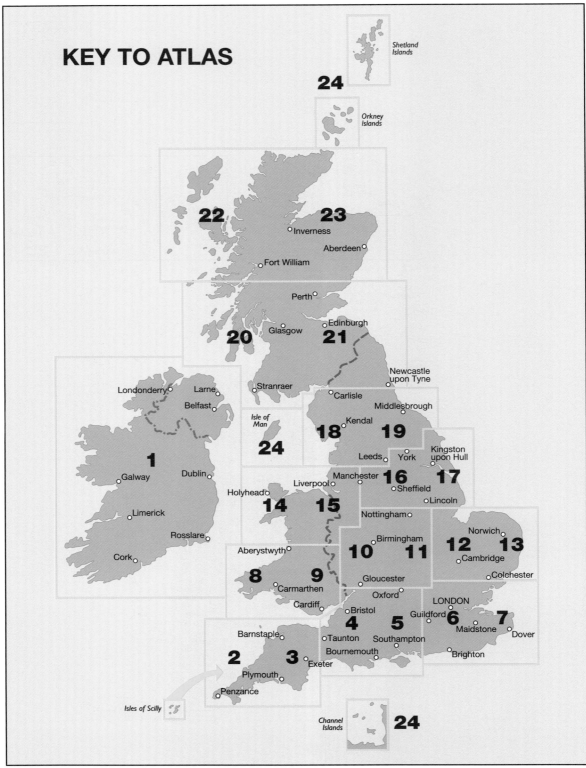

KEY TO ATLAS

Shetland Islands

24

Orkney Islands

22
Inverness

23
Aberdeen

Fort William

Perth

Edinburgh

Glasgow

20

21

Newcastle upon Tyne

Londonderry
Larne
Belfast

Stranraer

Carlisle

Middlesbrough

Isle of Man

Kendal

24

18

19

Leeds
York

Kingston upon Hull

1

Galway
Dublin

Liverpool
Manchester

16

17

Holyhead
Sheffield

Limerick

14

15

Lincoln

Rosslare
Nottingham

Cork

Birmingham

Norwich

Aberystwyth

10

11

12

13

Cambridge

8

9

Gloucester

Colchester

Carmarthen

Oxford

Cardiff

LONDON

Bristol

4

5

Guildford

6

7

Barnstaple

Taunton

Southampton

Maidstone

Dover

Bournemouth

Brighton

2

3

Exeter

Plymouth

Penzance

Isles of Scilly

Channel Islands

24

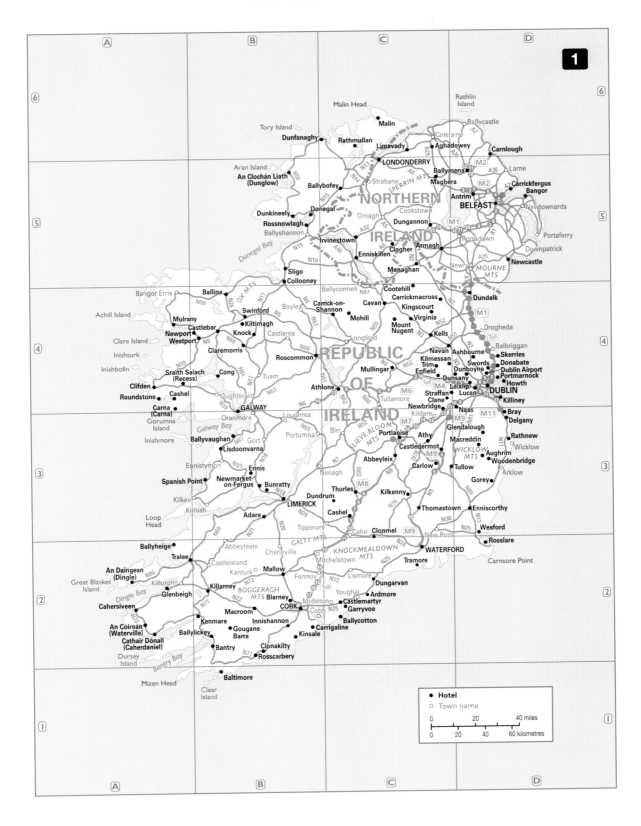

2

For continuation pages refer to numbered arrows

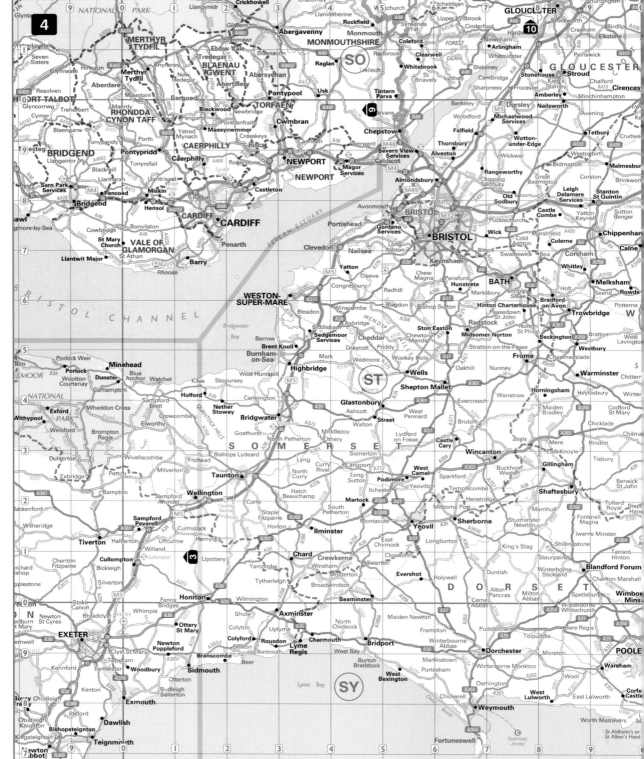

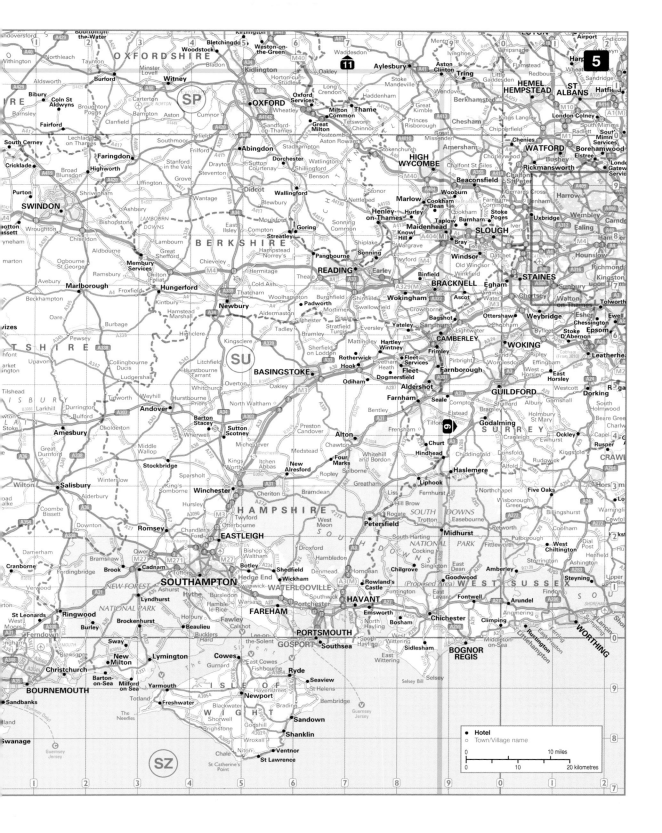

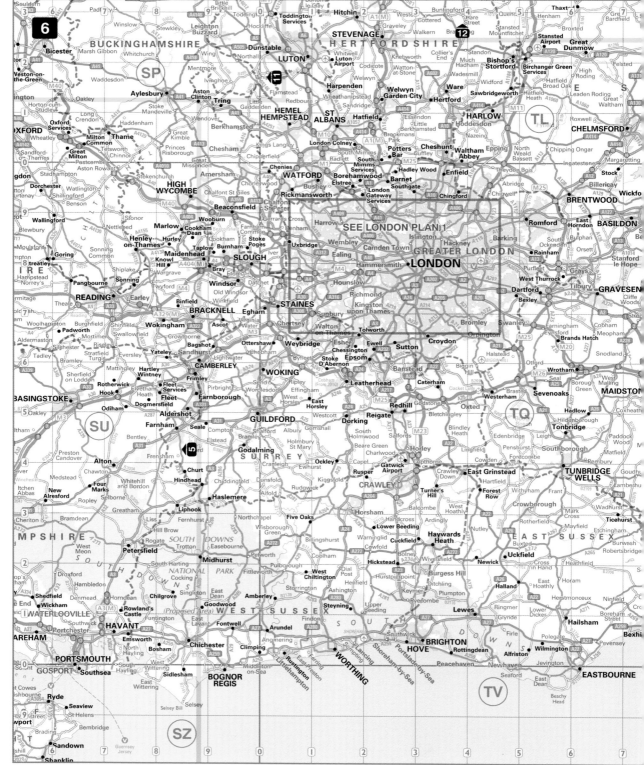

8

Hotel

Town/Village name

0 10 miles
0 10 20 kilometres

For continuation pages refer to numbered arrows

POWYS

Caersws · Newtown · Abermule · Churchstoke · Church Stretton · Long Mynd in the Dale · Bourton · Morville · Bridgnorth · Worcombe

Kerry · Lydham · Little Stretton · Hope Bowdler · Ditton Priors · Alveley · Highley · Stourton · STOURBRIDGE

Llandinam · Bishop's Castle · Lydbury North · Aston on Clun · Craven Arms · Munslow · Cleobury North · Bewdley · KIDD

Llanidloes · Beguildy · Clun · Bromfield · Cleobury Mortimer · Stourport-on-Severn · Abberley

Pant-y-dwr · Llanfair Waterdine · Leintwardine · Ludlow · Clows Top · Great Witley

Cwmystwyth · Llanbister · Knighton · Richards Castle · Woofferton · Newnham · Tenbury Wells · Ompersley

Rhayader · Bleddfa · Whitton · Presteigne · Kingsland · Holt Heath · WORCESTER

Elan Village · Penybont · New Radnor · Leominster · Bredenbury · Knightwick · Leigh Sinton

Llandrindod Wells · Walton · Pembridge · Lyonshall · Dilwyn · Hope under Dinmore · Weobley · Bishop's Frome · West Malvern · Great Malvern

Newbridge on Wye · Kington · Eardisley · HEREFORDSHIRE · Stoke Lacy · Malvern Wells · Upton upon Severn

Builth Wells · Garth · Clyro · Bredwardine · Credenhill · Withington · Newtown · Ledbury

Llanwrtyd Wells · Llangammarch Wells · Erwood · Hay-on-Wye · Dorstone · Hereford · Mordiford · Much Marcle · Dymock · Tewkesbury

MYNYDD EPPYNT · Llyswen · Bronllys · Three Cocks · Peterchurch · Kingstone · Allensmore · Fownhope · Much Birch · Newent

Llandovery · Talgarth · Glasbury · BLACK · Llanthony · Ewyas Harold · Pontrilas · Harewood End · Ross-on-Wye · Hartpury · Longford

Llangorse · SO · St Owens Cross · Pencraig · Huntley · GLOUCESTER

Brecon · Llanhamlach · MOUNTAINS · Pandy · Grosmont · Skenfrith · Whitchurch · Mitcheldean · Upper Lydbrook

Trecastle · Sennybridge · Bwlch · Llangynidr · Crickhowell · Llanvihangel Crucorney · Llanvetherine · Rockfield · Monmouth · Coleford · Cinderford · Hardwicke

BRECON BEACONS NATIONAL PARK · Gilwern · Abergavenny · MONMOUTHSHIRE · FOREST OF DEAN · Clearwell · Whitebrook · Arlingham

BLACK MOUNTAIN · Glyntawe · Brynmawr · Brynmawr · Blaenavon · Raglan · Redbrook · Whitebrook · Cambridge · Stonehouse

MERTHYR TYDFIL · Ebbw Vale · Tredegar · BLAENAU GWENT · Treilech · St Briavels · Sharpness · Frocester · Amberley

Seven Sisters · Rhymney · New Tredegar · Abersychan · Usk · Tintern Parva · Berkeley · Michaelwood Services · Nailsworth

Glynneath · Hirwaun · Merthyr Tydfil · Aberdare · Abertillery · Pontypool · Woodford · Dursley · M5

Ystradgynlais · Mountain Ash · Bargoed · Blackwood · Newbridge · Pontypool · Cwmbran · St Ar · Wotton-under-Edge

NEATH PORT TALBOT · Treherbert · RHONDDA CYNON TAFF · Pengam · Pontllanfraith · Caerleon · Chepstow · Falfield · Thornbury · Alveston · Wickwar

Neath · Cymer · Maerdy · Ystrad Mynach · Maesycwmmer · Crosskeys · Risca · Caerwent · Severn View Services · Rangeworthy · Chipping Sodbury

Baglan · Blaengarw · Tonypandy · Porth · CAERPHILLY · Rogerstone · NEWPORT · Magor Services · Almondsbury · Old Sodbury

SWANSEA · Maesteg · BRIDGEND · Pontypridd · Caerphilly · Caerleon · NEWPORT · Avonmouth · M49 · Pucklechurch · Castle Combe

Port Talbot · Llangeinor · Tonyrefail · Llantrisant · Castleton · Portishead · Gordano Services · BRISTOL · M32 · Wick · Marshfield · Colerne

Porthcawl · Sarn Park Services · Pencoed · Miskin · Radyr · Clevedon · Nailsea · BRISTOL · Bitton · Swainswick · Box

Bridgend · Hensol · CARDIFF · Long Ashton · Keynsham · Whit

VALE OF GLAMORGAN · St Mary Church · Bonvilston · CARDIFF · Penarth · Chew Magna · Pensford · BATH

Llantwit Major · Cowbridge · St Athan · Barry · SEVERN ESTUARY · ST · Yatton · Cleeve · Congresbury · Marksbury · Bradford-on-Avon

Ogmore-by-Sea · Rhoose · WESTON-SUPER-MARE · Bleadon · Winscombe · Blagdon · Bishop Sutton · Radstock · Midsomer Norton · Beckington

BRISTOL CHANNEL · Bridgwater Bay · Berrow · Brent Knoll · Axbridge · Cheddar · Chewton Mendip · Ston Easton · Norton St Philip · Frome

Lynton · Lynmouth · Porlock Weir · Minehead · Sedgemoor Services · Burnham-on-Sea · Mark · Wedmore · Wookey Hole · Oakhill · Nunney · Chapman

Woody Bay · Brendon · Porlock · Dunster · Blue Anchor · Watchet · Highbridge · West Huntspill · Wells

EXMOOR · A39 · Wootton

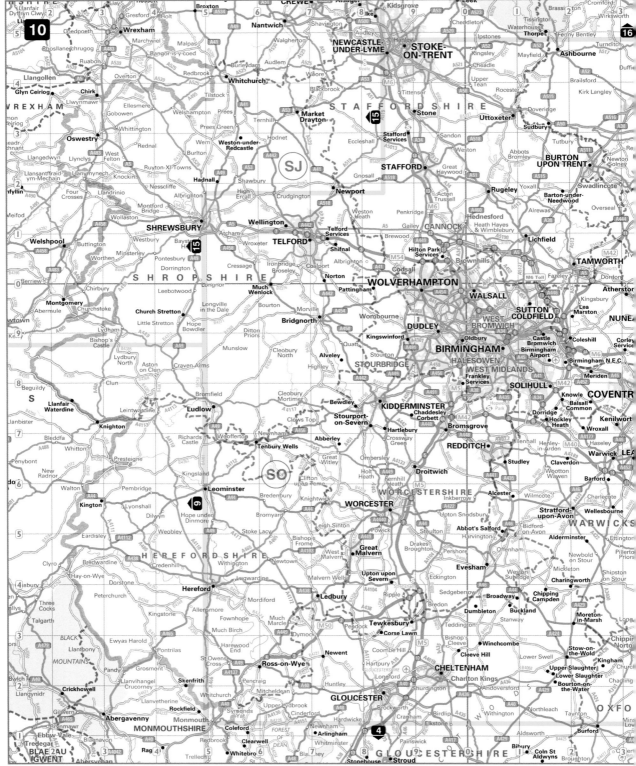

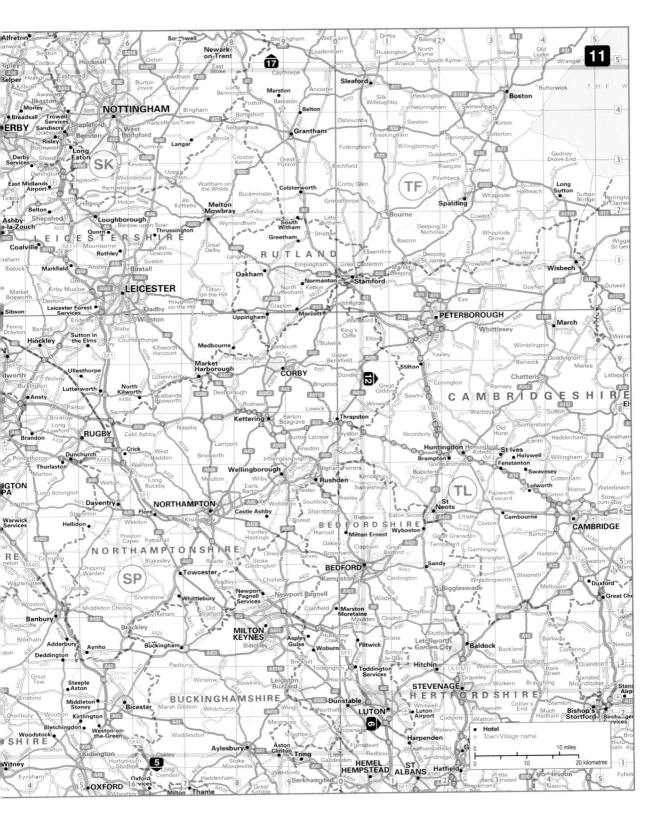

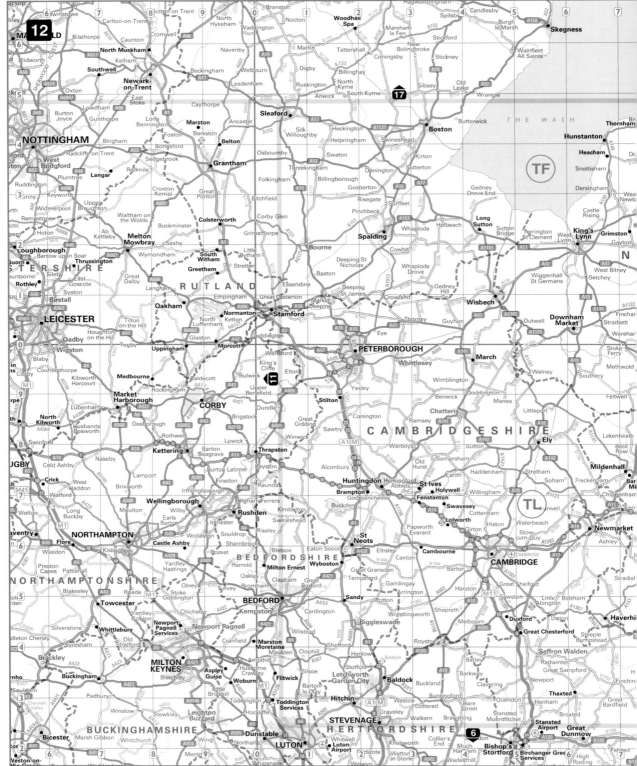

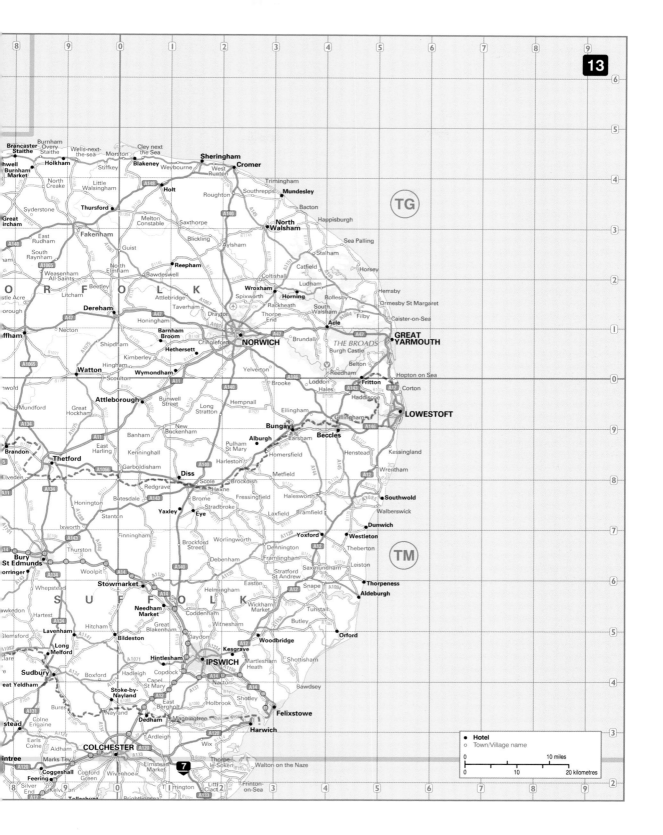

For continuation pages refer to numbered arrows

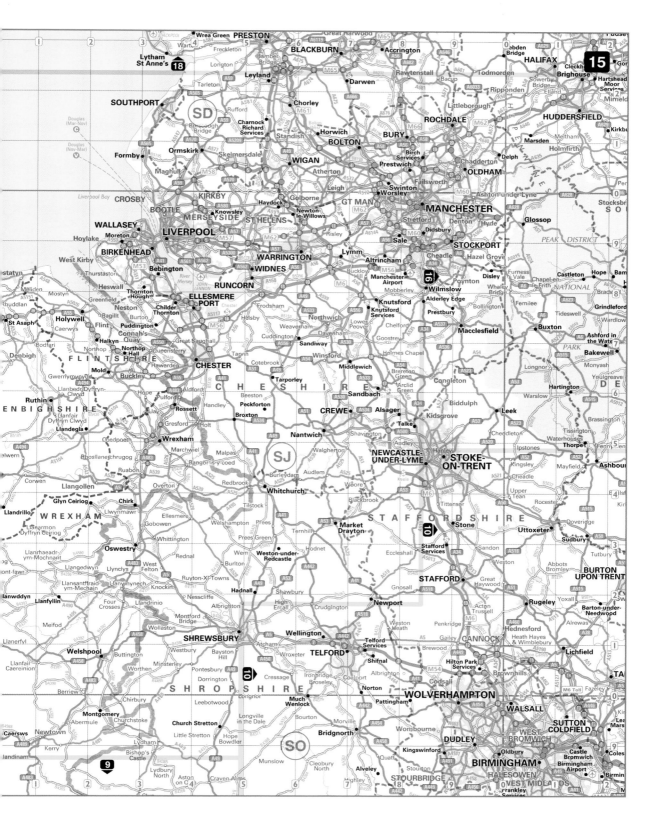

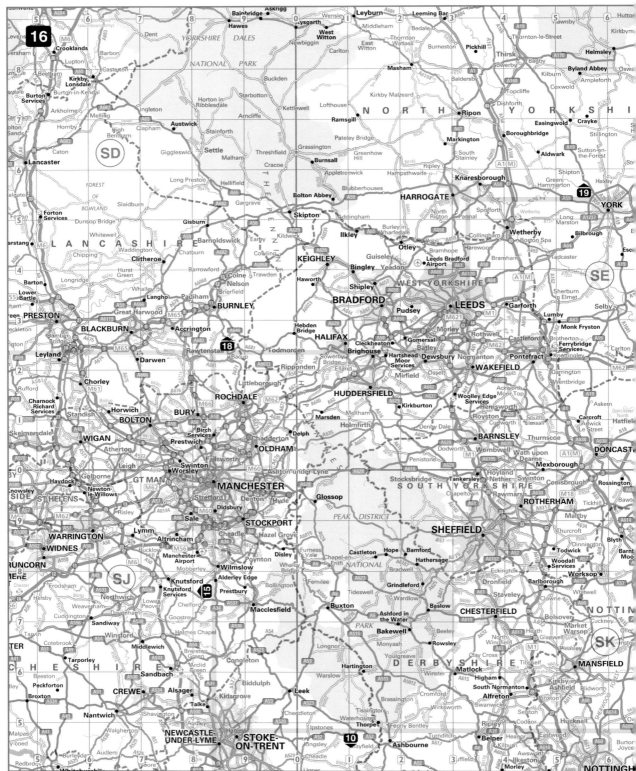

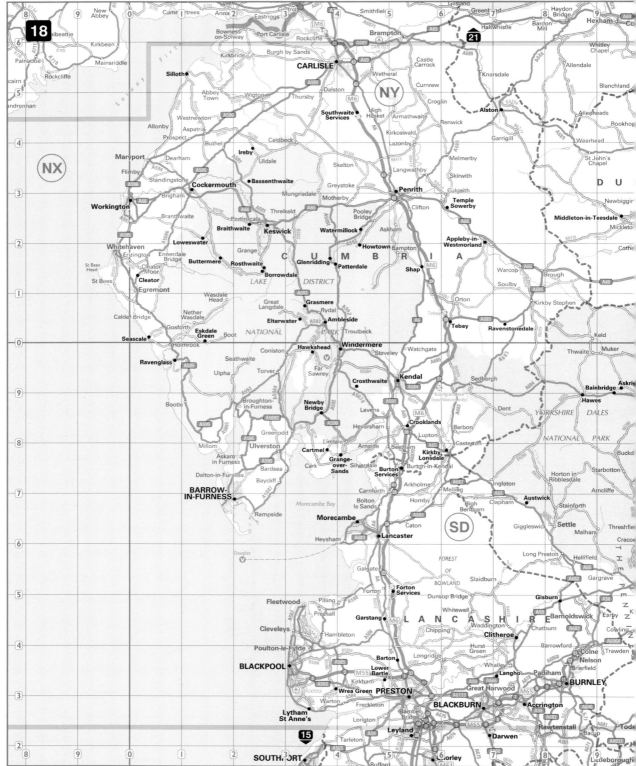

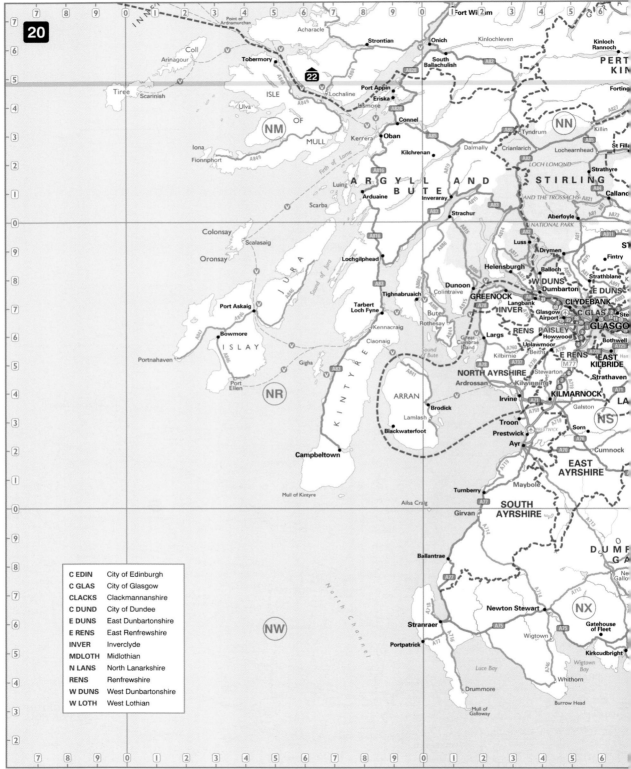

22

C EDIN   City of Edinburgh
C GLAS   City of Glasgow
CLACKS   Clackmannanshire
C DUND   City of Dundee
E DUNS   East Dunbartonshire
E RENS   East Renfrewshire
INVER   Inverclyde
MDLOTH   Midlothian
N LANS   North Lanarkshire
RENS   Renfrewshire
W DUNS   West Dunbartonshire
W LOTH   West Lothian

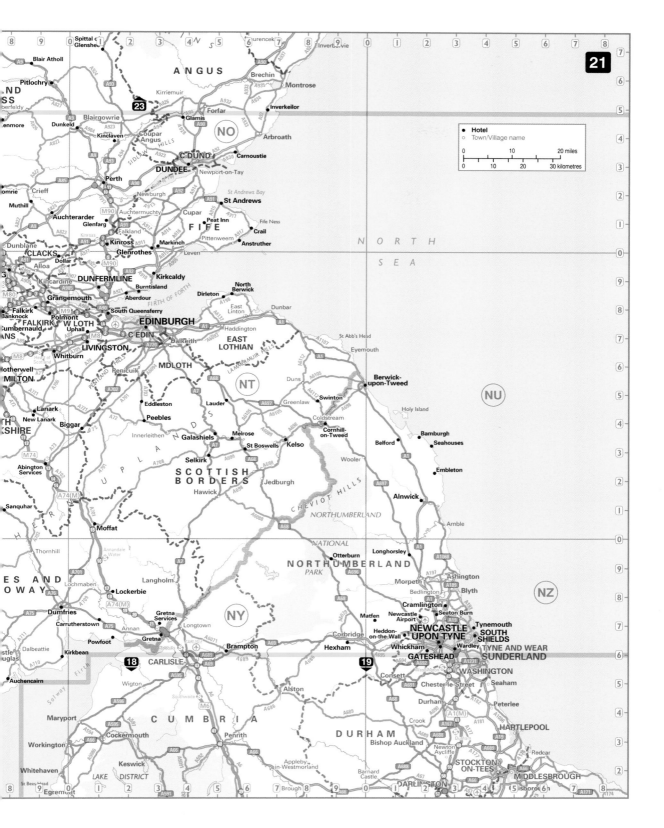

For continuation pages refer to numbered arrows

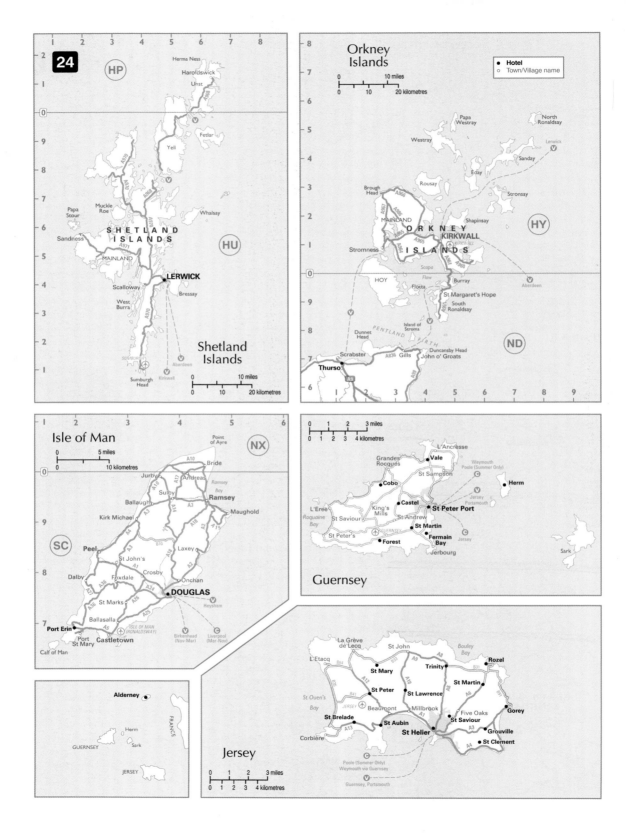